THE NEW BIOGRAPHICAL DICTIONARY OF FILM

David Thomson

LITTLE, BROWN

A *Little, Brown* Book

First published in Great Britain in 2002
by Little, Brown

First published in the United States in 2002
by Alfred A. Knopf

This edition published in 2003
by Little, Brown

Previously published in Great Britain in 1975 and 1980 by Martin, Secker &
Warburg Limited, London, as *A Biographical Dictionary of the Cinema*.
Published in the United States in 1976 and 1981 by William Morrow and
Company, Inc., New York, as *A Biographical Dictionary of Film*. The third
edition published in 1994 in Great Britain by Andre Deutsch, Ltd., London, and
in the United States by Alfred A. Knopf, a division of Random House, Inc.

A CIP catalogue record for this book
is available from the British Library.

Hardback ISBN 0 316 85905 2
Paperback ISBN 0 316 72660 5

Printed and bound in Poland

Little, Brown
An imprint of
Time Warner Books UK
Brettenham House
Lancaster Place
London WC2E 7EN

www.TimeWarnerBooks.co.uk

INTRODUCTION

This book is called *The New Biographical Dictionary of Film* because so much is fresh and different. But don't be alarmed that the insane scheme or attempt of the original book has been given up: This is the old book (the one first published in 1975), or the old book, revised, re-examined and with three hundred new entries (many on newcomers, but some on ancient figures who might have been included earlier). So if it is no longer simply the "old" book, why it is surely the work of an older—even an old—author.

In the introduction to the last edition, the third (in 1994), I described how the writer had shifted from being English to being American (but why not be both?). I should add that the reckless kid who once knew the dates of many films by heart, and their trivia, now needs to look such things up—and to remember not to use his own book for that task. It is up to the reader to decide whether that blurring of memory has been made up for by insight or wisdom.

The hardest matter to assess in that passage of time is the passion. This was a book conceived and first written in the early 1970s, when it was easy to be in love with cinema. So many exciting things were going on. Time and again, as I wrote, I was lifted by the exhilaration of a new film seen the night before. That soaring is harder to manage now, so I am left wondering whether I am heavier, or less "passionate"—or are the movies less? I'd far rather blame myself, but I know, from talk, that I am not alone in finding those transforming experiences less often.

Well, maybe transformation is for the young? Perhaps the movies (like playing sports) belong to the young. The risk of such a conclusion for me is that of feeling less in love with movies (or even with youth) than at other times in my life. I am so much more conscious of the things films can't do now—or of things they don't try to do. When a thing called *A Beautiful Mind* is so well received, I wonder why so few observe that film (or *that* film, anyway) doesn't know how to get into the mind.

My conclusion is that maybe this kind of book needs young authors to take up the challenge. In that spirit, I confess one pang I feel over the new title: it was always heretofore "a" biographical dictionary, not "the" one. The desperate but idealistic attempt was and is open to everyone else to do his or her own book. Indeed, the stance taken here as your needling, provocative, argumentative companion at the movies takes it for granted that in the reading you will begin to compose your own response.

So, to state the obvious: this is a book, and I think I have learned that I love books more than films. As in the past, there are people omitted who have a fine case for being included. I apologize to them and to their fans, and would only add that the book is by now so much bigger than it was in 1975.

Finally, this 2003 publication contains updating and some corrections of previous errors.

for Kate and Kieran

"But where's Bela Tarr and Barbara La Marr and . . ."
—from life, from readers of this book

WHEELER: A game-legged old man and a drunk—that's
all you've got?
CHANCE: That's *what* I've got.

—from *Rio Bravo*

ACKNOWLEDGMENTS

In the last few years, nothing has helped me more with this book, or so compelled me to think about the place of film in our culture, than having two young children in the house—Nicholas (whose tastes have moved naturally from those of infant prodigy to depraved early teenager: his favorite films are *Vanilla Sky, American Pie,* and *Dazed and Confused*) and Zachary (who was born shortly after the last edition was published—his tops are *Jimmy Neutron: Boy Genius, Big Fat Liar,* and *Big Momma's House*). I thank them for their existence, and for letting me have some time with the television set. And, of course, I thank their mother, Lucy, for refereeing and inspiring us all (she votes for *The Blue Angel, Lola Montes,* and *His Girl Friday*).

Many old friends have remained among my best companions at the movies: Richard (*The General, The Lady Eve,* and Nick Park's *The Wrong Trousers*) and Mary Corliss (*Dodsworth, Once Upon a Time in the West,* and *Grand Illusion*); Tom Luddy (*Sunrise, Sansho the Bailiff,* and *The Searchers*); Steven Bach (*Funny Face, Citizen Kane,* and *On the Waterfront*); Virginia Campbell (*My Man Godfrey, Shadow of a Doubt,* and *Chinatown*); Jim Toback (*Get Shorty, F for Fake,* and *The Leopard*); and Mark Feeney, who is a great friend and a fine editor. He read all the new material with his customary care and thoughtfulness (and he has soft spots for *Wings of Desire, His Girl Friday,* and *The Lady Eve*).

New friends who have had a big influence on the book are Jenny Turner, met through the *Independent on Sunday* in London (she selects *Red River, Working Girl,* and *The Eclipse*); Ann Kolson at the *New York Times* (*The Red Shoes, All About Eve,* and *Apocalypse Now Redux*); Leon Wieseltier at *The New Republic* (*Mouchette, Amarcord,* and *The Godfather*); and Max Palevsky (who treasures *Lady with a Dog, Vertigo,* and *The Rules of the Game*).

I have also benefited from talk with and encouragement from Godfrey Cheshire; Richard Jameson, and Kathleen Murphy; Gilbert Adair; David Thompson; Pat McGilligan; Andy Olstein; Peter Bogdanovich; Geoff Dyer; Greil Marcus; and Lorraine Latorraca, who did so much of the typing (her choices, the day I asked, were *Cinema Paradiso, Breaking Away,* and the Katharine Hepburn *Little Women*).

In the area of book publishing itself, Laura Morris has shifted over from being editor to friend and then agent (she will serve her time on the desert island with *The Discreet Charm of the Bourgeoisie, Nashville,* and *Mr. Hulot's Holiday*). She was instrumental in sorting out a difficult contractual situation, the upshot of which was getting Alan Samson as my editor at Little, Brown (the Errol Flynn *The Adventures of Robin Hood, The Bandwagon,* and *Now, Voyager*). At Knopf, the book—as before—has had no greater friend than Kathy Hourigan (*Red River, Force of Evil, On the Waterfront*), but it has also benefited from the high skills and patience of Kevin Bourke (*Women on the Verge of a Nervous Breakdown, The Birds,* and *Holiday*), Virginia Tan (*The African Queen, Quatermass and the Pit,* and *Blade Runner*), Carol Carson (*The Thirty-nine Steps, Watch on the Rhine,* and *Sweet Smell of Success*), Patrick Dillon (*Children of Paradise,* Cocteau's *Beauty and the Beast,* and *Juliet of the Spirits*), Roméo Enriquez (*Casablanca, Women on the Verge of a Nervous Breakdown, Moonstruck*), Kathy Zuckerman (*Holiday, Two for the Road,* and *The Great Escape*), and Sonny Mehta.

(In passing, I should note how far the Knopf office seems beset by thoughts of women close to breakdown and the thought of holiday. Enough said.)

Which leaves young Bob Gottlieb, the book's editor and friend for the second time. Bob has been brilliant, kind, funny, learned, decisive, and loyal—and all at the right time. He made the long haul of the book a pleasure; he put up with moods, handwriting, and delays, and never lost his good humor with show business or his passion for the art. (His choices are *Tokyo Story,* Lillian Gish in *The Wind,* and *The Lady Eve.*)

These choices began as a game posed to our sons at dinner one night. But the game grew into a way of personalizing the list of acknowledgments. In addition, it must be said that my circle (not the only one, of course) seems fixed on movies made some time ago. Whether or not that is to be regretted, I can't disavow a poll (no matter how informal) in which *The Lady Eve* and *His Girl Friday* are locked in victory.

—David Thomson (*His Girl Friday, Céline and Julie Go Boating, That Obscure Object of Desire*)

A

Abbott and Costello:
Bud (William A.) **Abbott** (1895–74),
b. Asbury Park, New Jersey; and
Lou Costello (Louis Francis Cristillo)
(1906–59), b. Paterson, New Jersey

The marital chemistry (or the weird mix of blunt instrument and black hole) in coupling is one of the most persistent themes in tragedy and comedy. At their best, you can't have one without the other. More than fifty years after they first tried it, Abbott and Costello's "Who's On First?" sketch is about the best remedy I know for raising laughter in a mixed bag of nuts—or for making the collection of forlorn individuals a merry mob.

Many people know the routine (written, like most of their stuff, by John Grant) by heart. Amateurs can get a good laugh out of it. But Bud and Lou achieve something lyrical, hysterical, and mythic. Watch them do the sketch and you feel the energy and hope of not just every comedian there ever was. You feel Beckett, Freud, and Wittgenstein (try it!). You see every marriage there ever was. You rejoice and despair at the impossibility of language. You wonder whether God believed in harmony, or in meetings that eternally proved our loneliness.

Lou is the one who has blood pressure, and Bud hasn't. So they are together in the world, yet together alone, doomed to explain things to each other. They are companions, halves of a whole, chums, lovers if you like. But they are a raw display of hatred, opposition, and implacable difference. They are also far better than all the amateurs. And if Lou is the performer, the valiant seeker of order, while Bud is the dumb square peg, the one who seems oblivious of audience, still, nobody did it better. If I were asked to assemble a collection of things to manifest America for the stranger, "Who's On First?" would be there—and it might be the first piece of film I'd use.

At the same time, they are not very good, rather silly, not really that far above the ocean of comedians. It isn't even that one can separate their good work from the poor. Nor is it that "Who's On First?" is simply and mysteriously superior to all the rest of their stuff. No, it's only that that routine feels an inner circle of dismay within all the others, the suffocating mantle next to Lou's heart. It isn't good, or superior; it's divine. Which is why no amount of repetition dulls it at all. I think I could watch it every day and feel the thrills and the dread as if for the first time.

They bumped into each other. Bud was a theatre cashier where Lou was playing (around 1930), and he grudgingly took the job when Lou's partner was sick. They were doing vaudeville and radio for ten years before they got their movie break at Universal: *One Night in the Tropics* (40, A. Edward Sutherland) was their first film, but *Buck Privates* (41, Arthur Lubin) was the picture that made them. There were twenty-three more films in the forties, a period for which they were steadily in the top five box-office attractions. *Buck Privates,* and their whole appeal, reflected the unexpected intimacies of army life.

They broke up in 1957, long since outmoded by the likes of Martin and Lewis. But there again, Abbott and Costello are the all-talking model (as opposed to the semi-silence of Laurel and Hardy) of two guys trapped in one tent.

Costello made one film on his own—for he had great creative yearnings—*The 30-Foot Bride of Candy Rock* (59, Sidney Miller). He died of a heart attack, which had always seemed about to happen. Bud lived on, doing next to nothing.

Ken (Klaus) Adam, b. Berlin, Germany, 1921

At the age of thirteen, Adam came to Britain, and stayed: he would be educated as an architect at London University and the Bartlett School of Architecture, and he served in the RAF during the war. It was in 1947 that he entered the British picture business, doing set drawings for *This Was a Woman* (48, Tim Whelan). Thereafter, he rose steadily as an assistant art director on *The Queen of Spades* (48, Thorold Dickinson); *The Hidden Room* (49, Edward Dmytryk); *Your Witness* (50, Robert Montgomery); *Captain Horatio Hornblower* (51, Raoul Walsh); *The Crimson Pirate* (52, Robert Siodmak); *Helen of Troy* (56, Robert Wise); he did uncredited work on *Around the World in 80 Days* (56, Michael Anderson), and assistant work on *Ben-Hur* (59, William Wyler).

Clearly, he was adept at getting hired by American directors, or on Hollywood productions, yet he did not seem overly interested in going to Hollywood. Indeed, he built a career as art director and then production designer in Britain, and he would be vitally associated with the design look and the huge, hi-tech interiors of the James Bond films: *Soho Incident* (56, Vernon Sewell); *Night of the Demon* (57, Jacques Tourneur); *The Angry Hills* (59, Robert Aldrich); *The Rough and the Smooth* (59, Siodmak); *The Trials of Oscar Wilde* (60, Ken Hughes); *Dr. No* (62, Terence Young); *Sodom and Gomorrah* (62, Aldrich); *Dr. Strangelove* (64, Stanley Kubrick); *Woman of Straw* (64, Basil Dearden); *Goldfinger* (64, Guy

Hamilton); *The Ipcress File* (65, Sidney J. Furie); *Thunderball* (65, Young); *Funeral in Berlin* (66, Hamilton); *You Only Live Twice* (67, Lewis Gilbert); *Chitty Chitty Bang Bang* (68, Hughes); *Goodbye, Mr. Chips* (69, Herbert Ross); to America for *The Owl and the Pussycat* (70, Ross).

An international figure now, he worked increasingly in America, while keeping his British attachment to Bond and Kubrick: *Diamonds Are Forever* (71, Hamilton); *Sleuth* (72, Joseph L. Mankiewicz); *The Last of Sheila* (73, Ross); winning an Oscar for *Barry Lyndon* (75, Kubrick); *Madam Kitty* (76, Tinto Brass); *The Seven-Per-Cent Solution* (76, Ross); *The Spy Who Loved Me* (77, Gilbert); *Moonraker* (79, Gilbert).

Illness caused a significant gap in his work in the early eighties, at which time his only credit was as design consultant on *Pennies from Heaven* (81, Ross). Since his return, he has been based in America and Bond-less. He also seems to work on more modest projects, while staying loyal to Herb Ross: *King David* (85, Bruce Beresford); *Crimes of the Heart* (86, Beresford); *The Deceivers* (88, Nicholas Meyer); *Dead Bang* (89, John Frankenheimer); *The Freshman* (90, Andrew Bergman); *The Doctor* (91, Randa Haines); *Undercover Blues* (93, Ross); *Addams Family Values* (93, Barry Sonnenfeld); then back to Britain, with another Oscar, on *The Madness of King George* (94, Nicholas Hytner); *Boys on the Side* (95, Ross); *Bogus* (96, Norman Jewison); *In & Out* (97, Frank Oz); *The Out-of-Towners* (99, Sam Weisman).

Isabelle Adjani, b. Paris, 1955

There is something so frank, so modern in her feelings, yet so classical in her aura, so passionate and so wounded, that Isabelle Adjani seems made to play Sarah Bernhardt one day. Why not? She is a natural wearer of costume capable of making us believe that the "period" world we are watching is happening *now*. She is bold, a mistress of her career, and has been a fiercely equal partner in her romantic relationships with Bruno Nuytten, Warren Beatty, and Daniel Day-Lewis.

Her mother was German, and her father Algerian and Turkish. When only a teenager, she was invited to join the Comédie Française, playing to great praise in Lorca and Molière. She has been making movies since the age of fourteen: *Le Petit Bougnat* (69, Bernard T. Michel); *Faustine ou le Bel Été* (71, Nina Companeez); *La Gifle* (74, Claude Pinoteau); and made an international impact as the love-crazed girl in *L'Histoire d'Adèle H.* (75, François Truffaut), for which she won an Oscar nomination.

She was on the brink again in *The Tenant* (76, Roman Polanski); *Barocco* (76, André Téchiné); *Violette et François* (76, Jacques Rouffio); made an uneasy American debut in *The Driver* (78, Walter Hill); as a woman infatuated with the vampire

in *Nosferatu, Phantom der Nacht* (79, Werner Herzog); as Emily in *The Brontë Sisters* (79, Téchiné); *Possession* (80, Andrzej Zulawski); and *Clara et les Chics Types* (80, Jacques Monnet).

She played the central victim, a version of Jean Rhys, in *Quartet* (81, James Ivory); *L'Année Prochaine si tout va bien* (81, Jean-Loup Hubert); *Tout Feu, Toute Flamme* (82, Jean-Paul Rappeneau); *Mortelle Randonnée* (82, Claude Miller); *Doktor Faustus* (82, Frank Seitz); as Antonieta Rivas Mercadi, a melodramatic arts patron, in *Antonieta* (82, Carlos Saura); was stark naked for much of *L'Été Meurtrier* (82, Jean Becker), something between an erotic force of nature and a village idiot; *Subway* (85, Luc Besson); entirely wasted in *Ishtar* (87, Elaine May).

She was the producer as well as the star of *Camille Claudel* (88, Bruno Nuytten), her most overwhelming and characteristic performance, as a woman in love with art, exhilaration, and danger. Once more, she was nominated for the Oscar. If only Warren Beatty could have given her a role as strong. After four years, she made *La Reine Margot* (94, Patrice Chéreau). Granted that she does films so seldom, why do *Diabolique* (96, Jeremiah S. Chechik), with Sharon Stone, or *La Repentie* (02, Laetitia Masson)? She has also made *Adolphe* (02, Benoit Jacquot) and was excellent again in *Bon Voyage* (03, Rappeneau).

Percy Adlon, b. Munich, Germany, 1935

1978: *The Guardian and His Poet* (d). 1981: *Céleste*. 1982: *Letze Fünf Tage/The Last Five Days*. 1983: *Die Schaukel/The Swing*. 1985: *Zückerbaby/Sugarbaby*. 1987: *Bagdad Cafe*. 1989: *Rosalie Goes Shopping*. 1991: *Salmonberries*. 1993: *Younger & Younger*. 1996: *Hotel Adlon*. 1999: *Die Strausskiste*. 2000: *Hawaiian Gardens*.

After years working in theatre, in radio, and doing television documentaries, Adlon made his debut with a fascinating, full-length documentary on the relationship between writer Robert Walser and publisher Carl Seelig which is far from conventional—the film's deepest intent is to undermine any set idea of the facts in the case. *Céleste* explored the way a maid viewed her employer, Marcel Proust. In both cases, there was a refreshingly practical and explorative sense of how creative people lead (and transform) their lives.

Since then, Adlon has moved toward a whimsical view of comedy that has won some international art-house following. *Sugarbaby* told the love story between a subway driver and a large woman who works in a funeral home. The woman was played by Marianne Sagebrecht, who went on to star in *Bagdad Cafe* and *Rosalie Goes Shopping*. These films are entertaining and serene screwball comedies, if not as challenging as *Céleste* or *The Guardian and His Poet*.

Ben (Benjamin Geza) **Affleck**,
b. Berkeley, California, 1972

Here is a test of critical responsibility. On the one hand, I have a soft spot for Mr. Affleck in that he is the only actor who has played, or is ever likely to play, the man who founded the school I attended. I refer to Edward (or Ned) Alleyne, the Shakespearian actor-manager and founder of Dulwich College, as offered in *Shakespeare in Love* (98, John Madden). I daresay I would be joined in this sentiment by other Old Alleynians—Michael Powell, Clive Brook, Leslie Howard, Raymond Chandler, P. G. Wodehouse, Michael Ondaatje, and Paul Mayersberg, among others. But I have heard not one word from any of them, or from anyone, come to that, to dispute my other view that Mr. Affleck is boring, complacent, and criminally lucky to have got away with everything so far. If there was any doubt in my mind it was settled by the mere presence—and it wasn't anything more than mere—of Affleck in the travesty called *Pearl Harbor* (01, Michael Bay).

Yet look what he has gotten away with: *The Dark End of the Street* (81, Jan Egleson); playing basketball in *Buffy the Vampire Slayer* (92, Fran Rubel Kuzui); *School Ties* (92, Robert Mandel); *Dazed and Confused* (93, Richard Linklater); *Mallrats* (95, Kevin Smith); the lead in *Chasing Amy* (97, Smith); *Going All the Way* (97, Mark Pellington); sharing in the script, and an Oscar, for *Good Will Hunting* (97, Gus Van Sant); *Phantoms* (98, Joe Chappelle); *Armageddon* (98, Michael Bay); *200 Cigarettes* (99, Risa Bramon Garcia); *Forces of Nature* (99, Bronwen Hughes); *Dogma* (99, Smith); *Boiler Room* (00, Ben Younger); *Reindeer Games* (00, John Frankenheimer); *Bounce* (00, Don Roos); *Jay and Silent Bob Strike Back* (00, Smith); *Changing Lanes* (02, Roger Michell); taking over as Jack Ryan in *The Sum of All Fears* (02, Phil Alden Robinson).

I note that, into his early thirties, he is still playing one of the lads, just as in *Pearl Harbor* he was too old to be the boyhood pal of Josh Hartnett. He then made *The Third Wheel* (02, Jordan Brady), *Daredevil* (03, Mark Steven Johnson) and *Gigli* (03, Martin Brest).

James Agee (1909–55),
b. Knoxville, Tennessee

James Agee looked a lot like a young Robert Ryan; he behaved as self-destructively as Nicholas Ray; but he was only himself as a writer on film. As one of his biographers, Laurence Bergreen, has written, "To Agee movies were not primarily a form of entertainment . . . they were . . . the indigenous art form. Good or bad, vulgar or exquisite, they were, more than any literary form, the mirror of American life. They were cheap, rude, hypocritical, democratic, occasionally inspired, usually humdrum—in short, they were American. For

this reason he longed to find his way, however roundabout, into them."

I take that last remark at face value: I think it was Agee's wish, not just to be involved with film people, in the making of the work, but—literally—to be in movies. That doesn't refer to some masked urge to act. It's something far more extensive: Agee wished to be perceived like a character from the best movies—intensely romantic, darkly handsome, and desirable, yet aloof, tough, moody, and doomed. Plainly, even if you know, intellectually, that some films are foolish, still, it follows that anyone wanting to live on the screen has to have faith in the grandeur and gravity of film. And so it follows that Agee's adult life coincides with the great age of self-belief in American cinema. Indeed, in 1945, he could write, in candor, "I can think of very few contemporary books that are worth the jackets they are wrapped in; I can think of very few movies, contemporary or otherwise, which fail to show that somebody who has worked on them . . . has real life or energy or intensity or intelligence or talent."

Happy days—even if from this moment in time it is easier to have more respect for books.

Agee went to Harvard, edited the *Advocate*, and took up booze and poetry in quantity. He was always a womanizer, and a mess personally, but he found a journalistic voice that lasted for about twenty years. It extended to the text for *Let Us Now Praise Famous Men* (1941), that classic of the rural Depression and hard lives, where Agee's text went with the photographs of Walker Evans—and in which Evans's photography shines with a sensuality that Agee delivered personally to some of the poor women. It also equipped him to be a film critic at *Time* and *The Nation* for much of the forties.

He was far from reliable—he could write off *Kane* as a reservoir of hackneyed tricks, and he was of the opinion that Chaplin and Huston were without equal in America. But he wrote like someone who had not just viewed the movie but been in it—out with it, as if it were a girl; drinking with it; driving in the night with it. That direct physical response was new, it was done with terrific dash and insight, and it surely intuited the way people responded to movies in the forties. It was also, it seems to me, a powerful influence on Pauline Kael—I have a fond dream of the two of them snarling at each other, like the characters in *The African Queen*.

Which brings us to the vexed matter of Agee's scripts. From the mid forties on, Agee made a set at Huston—it was authentic admiration, or hero worship, but it was also a pioneering case of the movie critic lusting to sit at the all-night dinner with the big guys and walk away with a writing job. Agee worked on the script and commentary of *The Quiet One* (49, Sidney Meyers); he did a script for *The African Queen* (51, Huston), which was substantially redone by others; he did the "Bride Comes to Yellow Sky" episode from *Face to Face* (52, John Brahm and Bretaigne Windust), and he wrote the first screenplay for *The Night of the Hunter* (55, Charles Laughton).

The last was undoubtedly his most valuable work, and even if it is true that Agee's script was painfully long and literary, and not even quite finished, I suspect that Agee's vision and his Tennessee roots meant a lot to Laughton as he rewrote the script and made the picture. So it comes to this: that good writing about film should be very wary of trying to get inside the business, let alone inside the screen. But how are we poor devils to be prevented once we've sniffed that wild air?

As if to show what might have been, three years after his death he won a Pulitzer for his novel *A Death in the Family*.

Danny (Daniel Louis) Aiello,
b. Brooklyn, New York, 1936

In *Once Upon a Time in America* (84, Sergio Leone), Danny Aiello plays a bullying police chief liked and trusted by no one. He has just had a baby son, but the gangsters play a trick on him by removing identifying tags and putting the baby in a room full of look-alike infants. Primogeniture gone with the wind, and all the puff and bulk of Aiello the actor seething and weeping. The name of the chief is Aiello. Draw your own conclusion.

Some students have marveled that Aiello, credited with over seventy movies in the years from 1973 till now, did nothing until the ripe old age of thirty-seven. In fact, he was for years an official in the Teamsters Union who talked his way into acting jobs. He is a natural comic, a rather good singer, and a big soft show-off who likes to be the heavy. When well cast he is a treat—but trusted with too much he can inspire that practical jokester in all film units.

I won't give a complete list, but here are the highlights: *Bang the Drum Slowly* (73, John Hancock); Tony Rosato in *The Godfather, Part II* (74, Francis Ford Coppola); *The Front* (76, Martin Ritt); *Fingers* (78, James Toback); *Bloodbrothers* (78, Robert Mulligan); *Hide in Plain Sight* (80, James Caan); *Fort Apache, the Bronx* (81, Daniel Petrie); *Broadway Danny Rose* (84, Woody Allen); a bigger part in *The Purple Rose of Cairo* (85, Allen); *Radio Days* (87, Allen); *Man on Fire* (87, Elie Chouraqui).

His own frequent suggestion that he was worthy of bigger things was matched with larger roles: *The Pick-Up Artist* (87, Toback); the betrothed in *Moonstruck* (87, Norman Jewison); *The January Man* (89, Pat O'Connor); Sal in *Do the Right Thing* (89, Spike Lee)—for which he got a supporting-actor nomination; *Harlem Nights* (89, Eddie Murphy); *Jacob's Ladder* (90, Adrian Lyne); *Hudson Hawk* (91, Michael Lehmann); *Mistress* (92, Barry Primus).

He had his great chance being cast—beautifully—as *Ruby* (92, John Mackenzie). He was very good, but nobody wanted to know. He had another lead in *Me and the Kid* (93, Dan Curtis). But then he tripped up completely, being cast in the lead of the sour *The Pickle* (93, Mazursky). Nothing has been quite the same since that.

But he was very good in *City Hall* (96, Harold Becker); *Two Much* (96, Fernando Trueba); *2 Days in the Valley* (96, John Herzfeld); on TV in the lead in the dreadful *The Last Don* (97–98, Graeme Clifford); *Dinner Rush* (01, Bob Giraldi); *Prince of Central Park* (00, John Leekley; a singer in *Off Key* (01, Manuel Gomez Pereira); *The Last Request* (02, John DeBellis); *Mail Order Bride* (03, Robert Capelli Jr and Jeffrey Wolf).

Anouk Aimée (Françoise Sorya Dreyfus),
b. Paris, 1932

Anouk—as she was originally known—is a princess of the French cinema, but a princess whose heart has been touched by Grimm cold. Those wide eyes and the grave face appeared to see a tragic destiny that could not be avoided, and that at times even held enchantment for her. She began in her teens in *La Maison sous la Mer* (47, Henri Calef); in Carné's unfinished *La Fleur de l'Age* (47); as a young lover on the outskirts of moviemaking in *Les Amants de Vérone* (48, André Cayatte); to England for *The Golden Salamander* (49, Ronald Neame). The part that best captured her fragile pessimism was in a short, *The Crimson Curtain* (52, Alexandre Astruc), as the girl who has a weak heart but submits nevertheless to her lover and dies. That soulful contemplation of self-destruction was borne out in *Les Mauvaises Rencontres* (55, Astruc); as one of Modigliani's suffering women in *Montparnasse 19* (57, Jacques Becker); and as the helpless girlfriend in *La Tête Contre les Murs* (58, Georges Franju). At this time, she moved vaguely between the new French cinema—*Les Dragueurs* (59, Jean-Pierre Mocky); *Le Farceur* (60, Philippe de Broca)—"international" parts, like the nymphomaniac in *La Dolce Vita* (60, Federico Fellini); and small parts in the Resistance in *Carve Her Name With Pride* (58, Lewis Gilbert) and *The Journey* (58, Anatole Litvak).

Lola (60, Jacques Demy) came as a surprise and a relief: at last she was allowed to giggle, flutter, to be animated, and to breathe a cryptic song into the camera—"C'est moi. C'est Lola." The most magical of the New Wave films, *Lola* freed Princess Anouk and allowed her the flighty, romantic self-absorption of a chambermaid. However, Anouk's newfound freedom did not result in an organized career, although she may not have cared too much, then or now. It must be said that serious roles have sometimes found her wanting. Perhaps so handsome and commanding a woman is really frivolous; certainly *Lola* has that effortless beauty that comes from relaxation.

After that, Anouk worked rather haphazardly: *L'Imprevisto* (61, Alberto Lattuada); *Il Giudizio Universale* (61, Vittorio de Sica); as one of Aldrich's first lesbians in *Sodom and Gomorrah* (62); *Les Grands Chemins* (63, Christian Marquand); looking severe in spectacles in *8½* (63, Fellini); *Il Terrorista* (63, Gianfranco De Bosio); *A Man and a Woman* (66, Claude Lelouch), which harked back to her capacity for being hurt; *Un Soir un Train* (69, André Delvaux); *The Appointment* (69, Sidney Lumet); as Lola again, stranded in America, in *Model Shop* (69, Demy)—a resigned woman now who sells herself to the fantasies of amateur photographers.

She was curiously indifferent to *Justine* (69, George Cukor). That normally most generous of directors called her "the great disaster . . . the only time I've ever had anything to do with somebody who didn't try . . . indomitably refined."

Well past forty, married to and divorced from Albert Finney, she appeared for Lelouch again in the forlorn *Second Chance* (76). Since then, she has been in *Salto Nel Vuoto* (80, Marco Bellocchio); as the wife in *Tragedy of a Ridiculous Man* (81, Bernardo Bertolucci); *Qu'est-ce qui fait courir David?* (82, Elie Chouraqui); *Le Général de l'Armée Morte* (83, Luciano Tovoli); briefly in *Success Is the Best Revenge* (84, Jerzy Skolimowski); and increasingly as a touchstone for Lelouch—*A Man and a Woman 20 Years Later* (86) and *Il y a des Jours . . . et des Lunes* (90).

Beyond age, locked into beauty, she kept going: *Bethune: The Making of a Hero* (90, Phillip Borsos); *Voices in the Garden* (92, Pierre Boutron); *Rupture(s)* (93, Christina Citti); *Les Marmottes* (93, Chouraqui); *Ready to Wear* (94, Robert Altman); *Dis-moi Oui* (95, Alexandre Arcady); with Daniel Gélin in *Hommes, Femmes, Mode d'Emploi* (96, Lelouch); at sixty-five, as Bathsheba in a TV *Solomon* (97, Hans Hulscher); *Riches, Belles etc.* (98, Bunny Schpoliansky); *L.A. Without a Map* (98, Mika Kaurismaki); *Une pour Toutes* (99, Lelouch); *1999 Madeleine* (99, Laurent Bouhnik); *Victoire, ou la Douleur des Femmes* (00, Nadine Trintignant); *2000 Eve* (00, Bouhnik); *L'Île Bleue* (01, Trintignant); *Napoléon* (02, Yves Simoneau); *Festival in Cannes* (02, Henry Jaglom); *The Birch Tree Meadow* (03, Marceline Loridan Ivens).

Robert Aldrich (1918–83),
b. Cranston, Rhode Island
1953: *The Big Leaguer.* 1954: *World for Ransom; Apache; Vera Cruz.* 1955: *Kiss Me Deadly; The Big Knife.* 1956: *Autumn Leaves; Attack!.* 1957: *The Garment Center* (completed by and credited

to Vincent Sherman). 1959: *The Angry Hills; Ten Seconds to Hell.* 1961: *The Last Sunset.* 1962: *Sodom and Gomorrah; What Ever Happened to Baby Jane?.* 1963: *4 for Texas.* 1964: *Hush . . . Hush, Sweet Charlotte.* 1965: *The Flight of the Phoenix.* 1967: *The Dirty Dozen.* 1968: *The Legend of Lylah Clare; The Killing of Sister George.* 1970: *Too Late the Hero.* 1971: *The Grissom Gang.* 1972: *Ulzana's Raid.* 1973: *The Emperor of the North Pole/Emperor of the North.* 1974: *The Longest Yard/The Mean Machine.* 1975: *Hustle.* 1977: *Twilight's Last Gleaming; The Choirboys.* 1979: *The Frisco Kid.* 1981: *All the Marbles.*

The decline in Aldrich, in the sixties especially, was a sad thing to behold. Distinct talent is no sure defense against the pressures of vulgarization and commerce, to say nothing of the talent's urge toward sensationalism. In other words, the *politique des auteurs*—of which Aldrich was once a test case—is an uncertain basis for assessing careers, more revealing of the movie-mad, would-be auteurs who invented it than of real battlers like Aldrich. Aldrich had great hits in the sixties: *Baby Jane, The Dirty Dozen,* and *Sister George* were box-office payoffs for a man who had striven early to be his own producer. It was in exactly that period that a talent like Nicholas Ray vanished, unable to string projects together. But the contrast between, say, *Kiss Me Deadly* and *The Grissom Gang,* or *Attack!* and *The Dirty Dozen,* shows the woeful sacrifices that can come from keeping in work.

Kiss Me Deadly is still one of the best, and most surprising, American films of the 1950s, a lucid transformation of pulp Spillane into a vicious, insolent allegory of violence, corruption, and forbidding futures in America. Did overbearing producers and more restrictive censorship push Aldrich into a disciplined and even ironic evocation of brutality? Did the cheerfulness of the fifties allow such glittering darkness to slip through? The greater freedom on *The Dirty Dozen* only exposed the lack of self-control in the director, and the ease with which opportunist cynicism filled in the bold outrage of the Eisenhower era in *Attack!* Yet no one could say *Dozen* is more realistic—it is nothing but a pretext for violent fantasies and a model for too many later films.

Then there was the visual slovenliness that had overtaken the feverish, trapped imagery of the fifties. Melodrama and hysteria were always there in Aldrich, but *Baby Jane, Sweet Charlotte,* and *Sister George* are horribly calculated, smirking exploitations of sub-Gothic emotional horror. They are humorless, overheated films, harsh to their actresses, and only rarely achieve a kind of hysterical poetry—the close of *Baby Jane* is an eerie moment that caught the madness in American emotionalism. But *The Dirty Dozen* succumbed to the complacent strength Lee Marvin was prone to. Compare Marvin in that and *Emperor of the North Pole* with the ravaged sensitivity of Jack Palance in *The Big Knife* and *Attack!*, and the subtle disowning of Ralph Meeker's Hammer in *Kiss Me Deadly*. (Compare Aldrich's Marvin with *The Killers* or *Point Blank*.)

It seems odd now to recollect the distinguished apprenticeship Aldrich served as assistant director: *The Southerner* (45, Jean Renoir); *The Story of G.I. Joe* (45, William Wellman); *The Private Affairs of Bel-Ami* (47, Albert Lewin); *Body and Soul* (47, Robert Rossen); *Arch of Triumph* (48, Lewis Milestone); *Force of Evil* (48, Abraham Polonsky); *The White Tower* (50, Ted Tetzlaff); *The Prowler* (51, Joseph Losey); *M* (51, Losey); *Limelight* (52, Charles Chaplin). Did Aldrich's first vitality grow out of the noir paranoia in Polonsky and Losey?

He tried to be his own man: the Associates and Aldrich was set up in 1955, and he had his own studio for a few years on the booty of *The Dirty Dozen*. But he had to sell it after a series of flops, and found himself back in the jungle again, suffering cuts from the interesting *Twilight's Last Gleaming*, and ending his life on a run of coarse, disagreeable movies. *Hustle*, though, was closer to the old style and his feeling for pain, a bleak cop/prostitute picture that paired Burt Reynolds's masochism with the lofty glamour of Catherine Deneuve.

Then there is *Ulzana's Raid*—a sequel to *Apache*, one of the best films of the seventies, and a somber adjustment of the Western to the age of Vietnam. Burt Lancaster has become the weary scout helping the cavalry track down a rogue Apache in a movie that uses terrain and loyalty as interactive metaphors. From a fine Alan Sharp script, *Ulzana's Raid* is austere and fatalistic. It is the one film in which Aldrich seems old, wise, and afraid. Suppose he had made only that and *Kiss Me Deadly*—he would loom as a master, magnificent in his sparing work. But he had to keep busy, and so his energy often went astray.

Marc Allégret (1900–73),
b. Basel, Switzerland
1927: *Voyage au Congo* (d). 1929: *Papoul*. 1930: *La Meilleure Bobonne; J'ai Quelque Chose a Vous Dire; Le Blanc et le Noir* (codirected with Robert Florey). 1931: *Les Amants de Minuit* (codirected with Augusto Genina); *Mam'zelle Nitouche; Attaque Nocturne*. 1932: *Fanny; La Petite Chocolatière*. 1934: *Le Lac-aux-Dames; L'Hôtel du Libre-Echange; Sans Famille; Zou-Zou*. 1935: *Les Beaux Jours*. 1936: *Sous les Yeux d'Occident; Aventure à Paris; Les Amants Terribles*. 1937: *Gribouille*. 1938: *La Dame de Malacca; Entrée des Artistes; Orage*. 1939: *Le Corsaire*. 1941: *Parade en Sept Nuits*. 1942: *L'Arlésienne; Félicie Nanteuil*. 1943: *Les Petites du Quai aux Fleurs*. 1944: *Lunégarde; La Belle Aventure*. 1946: *Pétrus*. 1947: *Blanche Fury*. 1949: *The Naked Heart/Maria Chapdelaine*. 1951: *Blackmailed; Avec André Gide; La Demoiselle et son Revenant*. 1952: *Jean Coton*. 1953: *Julietta*. 1954: *L'Amante di Paridi; Femmina*. 1955: *Futures Vedettes; L'Amant de Lady Chatterley*. 1956: *En Effeuillant la Marguerite/Mamzelle Striptease*. 1957: *L'Amour est en Jeu*. 1958: *Sois Belle et Tais-Toi*. 1959: *Un Drôle de Dimanche; Les Affreux*. 1961: "Sophie," an episode from *Les Parisiennes*. 1962: *Le Démon de Minuit*. 1963: *L'Abominable Homme des Douanes*. 1970: *Le Bal du Comte d'Orgel*.

The older brother of Yves Allégret and adopted nephew of André Gide, Marc Allégret had a long, pedestrian record, illustrating the way French cinema has sustained mediocre talents through warfare, the New Wave, and the pinched conditions of commercial cinema. Allégret's first film was made in his capacity as secretary to Gide on a trip to Africa in 1925. According to Gide, on their return Allégret languished, ". . . or at least has not really worked; I fear that, for greater facility, he may give up the best in him." A cryptic, poignant remark, followed by the confession that it was "for him, to win his attention, his esteem, that I wrote *Les Faux-Monnayeurs*." No Allégret film is anywhere near as good as the novel he inspired. When Allégret's appetite for work revived, he became assistant to Robert Florey, whose *Le Blanc et le Noir* he took over when Florey returned to Hollywood.

In 1947, Allégret went to England and directed three films there, including *Blackmailed*, with Dirk Bogarde and Mai Zetterling. *L'Amante di Paridi* was a Helen of Troy extravaganza with Hedy Lamarr as the lady. A more convincing beauty was shown by Brigitte Bardot in *Mamzelle Striptease*. It is a mark of Allégret's own staidness that he cultivated Roger Vadim as an assistant for ten years without ever dreaming of the lewd freshness with which Vadim would film Bardot—a meeting first accomplished through Allégret's own projects.

Yves Allégret (1907–87), b. Paris
1936: *Vous n'avez Rien à Déclarer?* (codirected with Leo Joannon). 1941: *Jeunes Timides; Tobie est un Ange* (not released). 1942: *La Roue Tourne* (uncompleted). 1943: *La Boîte aux Rêves*. 1945: *Les Démons de l'Aube*. 1948: *Dédée d'Anvers; Une Si Jolie Petite Plage*. 1949: *Manèges*. 1950: *Les Miracles n'ont Lieu qu'une Fois*. 1951: *Nez de Cuir*; "La Luxure," an episode from *Les Sept Péchés Capitaux*. 1952: *La Jeune Folle*. 1953: *Mam'zelle Nitouche; Les Orgueilleux*. 1954: *Oasis*. 1955: *La Meilleure Part*. 1957: *Méfiez-Vous Fillettes; Quand la Femme s'en Mêle*. 1958: *La Fille de Hambourg; L'Ambitieuse*. 1960: *Le Chien de*

Pique. 1962: *Konga Yo.* 1963: *Germinal.* 1967: *Johnny Banco.* 1970: *L'Invasion.* 1975: *Orzowei.* 1976: *Mords Pas On t'Aime.*

The younger brother of Marc Allégret, Yves worked his way into directing quite slowly. He assisted his brother on *Mam'zelle Nitouche* (31) (which he remade in 1953 with Fernandel in the Raimu part) and *Le Lac-aux-Dames* (34). Yves also worked with Renoir on *La Chienne* (32) but spent most of the 1930s directing shorts or working as an art director. It was during the war that he began directing features, quickly establishing a Carné-like blend of naturalism and black poetry. The films were mannered, good looking, and well acted, especially those starring his wife, Simone Signoret—*La Boîte aux Rêves, Dédée d'Anvers,* and *Manèges*—but nothing prepares one for the achievement of *Une Si Jolie Petite Plage,* an indelible image of hell on earth, set in a wretched seaside town in winter, marvelously photographed by Henri Alekan and arguably Gérard Philipe's finest study of romantic despair. The last scenes of that film are more chilling than any of Carné's effects and immeasurably graver than the rest of Allégret.

Joan Allen, b. Rochelle, Illinois, 1956
In person, Joan Allen is taller and prettier than you expect. On stage—especially in *Burn This* and *The Heidi Chronicles*—she has been a more expansive and compelling actress than film has admitted. And on the big screen, she is already one of our great supporting actresses, nearly automatically among the nominations, and a universal type whenever onlooking and long-suffering wives are involved. And, if you haven't noticed, those are often the kind of wives that our movies seem to know best. Is this a modern reflection of the private lives of Hollywood executives, or a profound comment on American marriage? Whatever, it's a limit that could be unfair to Ms. Allen—as witness the fact that Annette Bening got the "Joan Allen part" in *American Beauty.*

She had been closely associated with Chicago's Steppenwolf Company, and her movies amount to a textbook for acting classes: *Compromising Positions* (85, Frank Perry); the blind woman, superb in the scene with the tiger, in *Manhunter* (86, Michael Mann); *Peggy Sue Got Married* (86, Francis Coppola); *Tucker* (88, Coppola); *In Country* (89, Norman Jewison); a classic supportive wife, with Beau Bridges, in *Without Warning: The James Brady Story* (91, Michael Toshiyuki Uno); *Ethan Frome* (93, John Madden); *Searching for Bobby Fischer* (93, Steven Zaillian); *Mad Love* (95, Antonia Bird); so good as Pat in *Nixon* (95, Oliver Stone) that she effortlessly revived our sense of those years and the emotion of newsreel, but thereby left Anthony Hopkins seeming all the more of an imposter; outstanding again in *The Crucible* (96, Nicholas Hytner); *Face/Off* (97,

John Woo); *The Ice Storm* (97, Ang Lee); *Pleasantville* (98, Gary Ross); *All the Rage* (99, James D. Stein); Irish in *When the Sky Falls* (99, John Mackenzie).

She had a big part, and a nomination, in *The Contender* (00, Rod Lurie), but that horribly rigged film left her whiny, prim, overly "nice" and archaic. She was Morgause, the femme fatale, in TV's *The Mists of Avalon* (01, Uli Edel)—and she began to seem past prime; *Off the Map* (03, Campbell Scott).

Woody Allen (Allen Stewart Konigsberg), b. New York, 1935
1969: *Take the Money and Run.* 1971: *Bananas.* 1972: *Everything You Always Wanted to Know About Sex But Were Afraid to Ask.* 1973: *Sleeper.* 1975: *Love and Death.* 1977: *Annie Hall.* 1978: *Interiors.* 1979: *Manhattan.* 1980: *Stardust Memories.* 1982: *A Midsummer Night's Sex Comedy.* 1983: *Zelig.* 1984: *Broadway Danny Rose.* 1985: *The Purple Rose of Cairo.* 1986: *Hannah and Her Sisters.* 1987: *Radio Days; September.* 1988: *Another Woman.* 1989: *Crimes and Misdemeanors;* "Oedipus Wrecks," an episode from *New York Stories.* 1990: *Alice.* 1991: *Shadows and Fog.* 1992: *Husbands and Wives.* 1993: *Manhattan Murder Mystery.* 1994: *Bullets over Broadway; Don't Drink the Water* (TV). 1995: *Mighty Aphrodite.* 1996: *Everyone Says I Love You.* 1997: *Deconstructing Harry.* 1998: *Celebrity.* 1999: *Sweet and Lowdown.* 2000: *Small Time Crooks.* 2001: *The Curse of the Jade Scorpion.* 2002: *Hollywood Ending.* 2003: *Anything Else.*

"Woody" is by now the most famous film director in America, a reluctant household name as his famed soul-searching took a banana-skin skid into public scandal. Can he maintain his way of working? Is there funding for films whose budgets have steadily risen, and whose audience has never been large? Can he be merely amusing when he has drawn so melodramatic a trail through the courts and the public prints? More important, can he develop as an artist? Has he ever shown that unmistakable promise?

I am skeptical. In his films he seems so averse to acting yet so skittish about real confession that he risks dealing in self-glorification by neurosis. As an actor he stills momentum and betrays his films' reach for reality. Moreover, some of his films are so small and inconsequential, so much a matter of habit, that they make his productivity seem artificial.

But his sense of movie theatre and narrative intricacy soared in the eighties (along with the budgets and the photographic quality), and there are two films that even this sour spectator adores—*The Purple Rose of Cairo* and *Radio Days.* In neither does Allen figure as an actor (he *is* the narrator of *Radio Days*). The first is a wonderfully clever, blithely light comedy about movies and dogged real life, while the latter is a new kind of film, a sort of imagined documentary montage, or a notebook of memories and scenes, utterly consistent in tone, a true portrait of a time. Yet *Radio Days* has not been a seed. Instead, it looks like a random brainwave in the night.

Can he break out of the claustrophobic self-regard that has always threatened to make yet more "Woody Allen" films? Can he hold his small but influential following, when they are the group most quickly (or automatically?) offended by reports of "incorrectness" in an idol? Part of Allen's problem was only sharpened by the very messy battle with Mia Farrow and his own undeniable humiliation. For he always insisted on making movies about his own angst as a cunning diversion from true self-examination. For years, there had been an air of dissociation in his work that now seems fulfilled by some of his remarks during the year of public scandal. Has this authority on sensitivity ever trusted his own feelings or been their authentic victim?

Despite the fun of *Sleeper* and *Bananas,* Allen has never made a film free from his own panic. He has been a Chaplin hero for the chattering classes, yet he is trapped by something like Chaplin's neurotic vanity. No director works so hard to appear at a loss. The thought of his making a Bergman movie (and the thought runs from *Interiors* to *Shadows and Fog*) is grotesque. He is so near to Bergman already, yet so timid about the Swede's strength of commitment.

Allen is beset by certain death, elusive sex, the farfetched theory of romance, the immorality of pleasure, and the fracturing of cultural and personal ties that are replaced with chains. It sounds like respectable angst, but perhaps the ideals and the dismay were always precious and adolescent. The note of complaint in Allen's work is shrill and even frivolous because it prefers the quick flash of one-liners and mocked stereotypes. Woody is so jumpy he has no patience with developed humor. Though his films have gained in polish and visual depth, the humor remains in the words and the meetings. There is very little sense of purpose, principle, or character in Allen's way of looking at the worlds he creates. Thus we cannot escape the feeling of being trapped in an elevator with people who talk too much. (The idea of a blind director—treated in *Hollywood Ending*—was there years earlier.)

Human failure is Allen's faith, and we all seem to know about his awkward childhood (though *Radio Days* glows with humdrum happiness). He was a dropout from New York University and City College. Since then, most ventures have prospered except marriage and family—his second wife, Louise Lasser, acted in some of his early films and went on to be *Mary Hartman* after their split. (It is as a parent, and as an influence on the young, that the real Allen has most alarmed his loyalist supporters—and surely that could be a pressing future subject for him.)

Allen wrote jokes to order and was hired by Sid Caesar for his TV show. A great admirer of Mort Sahl, Allen moved into live routines in nightclubs, and by the late sixties he was a dramatist and a screenwriter: *What's New Pussycat?* (65, Clive Donner); *Casino Royale* (67, Ken Hughes et al.); and *Play It Again, Sam* (72, Herbert Ross), taken from an Allen play. His club routines were brilliant: his verbal dexterity had a higher energy level than we know from his films. He could assume, if briefly, the aggressiveness of a Groucho. But as he began a movie career, so his persona receded, and he acquired the security systems of being a victim. It took a long time—in life and on the screen—for the possibility to emerge that the "victim" might be tough, tyrannical company.

On Oscars night 1978, Allen was studiously playing Dixieland clarinet in a New York pub. Three thousand miles away Hollywood conceded the year to him: he won three Oscars (for script, direction, best picture) and Diane Keaton—his Isolde and his Nancy Drew then, as well as his girl—picked up the best actress prize. He avoided the awards night for reasons that could make an Allen movie—he might lose? he might win? it might look as if he expected to win? he preferred privacy to the cultivation of personality? or he preferred to nurture his persona in private? He claimed shyness, and nobody remarked on how oddly that sat with a film that revolves around its maker's insecurities and uses its actress's real name in the title—*Annie Hall.*

The film that followed, *Interiors,* seemed sculpted in Bergman's cold elegant bone. Yet it was only porcelain or plastic, a model from medical school, not a piece of a body. *Manhattan* was a love song to New York—and by now we can see that Allen's richest interest may be his city, for it is too vast and diverse to permit his glibness. *Manhattan* had a fine performance from Mariel Hemingway that was maybe the first piece of pure acting in Allen's work, as well as the debut of a tenderness toward dangerously young women. But the cuteness in *Manhattan*—in lines, compositions, and in its escapes from scenes that needed more—showed the embarrassment Allen felt about his own assigned challenge: "serious" pictures.

Allen's development in the eighties, his rate of work, and the sophistication of narrative were all seemingly devoted to ideas and attitudes against the grain of that decade. Yet Allen's audience relied on urban yuppies, and his films only fostered that group's self-satisfaction. He has tried darker views—in *Stardust Memories* and *Crimes and Misdemeanors*—and he has become very skilled with extensive, seething social contexts in which one piece of behavior is made more complex by the doings of others. He has fascinating ideas and ambitions as a screenwriter. Yet which Allen film challenges or threatens us, or burns into our memories? The films may run together—are we certain where that joke or this meeting occurred? Sometimes the context is so large as to be blurred; escape and slipperiness become more facile. There is something in Allen that always makes fun of ego, privacy, and obsession, and so with all his proclaimed inwardness he seems fearful of letting characters possess large inner lives. He makes many cameos of loneliness, but these are too often cute snapshots rather than tributes to an intractable condition.

But who else in American film provokes such arguments? And if Allen now faces a crisis because of his own behavior, we should recollect how smart and resourceful he is. Perhaps his indefatigable unconscious mind knew he needed trouble and disruption. That does not seek to excuse any damage he has done. But suppose real damage could become his subject—as opposed to wisecracks about it? If Allen could be persuaded to quit his own films as actor and to work more sparingly, with unmistakable lead actors (as opposed to a stock company of guest shots), then there is still a chance that he could create something close to gravity. For he is the most inquiring dramatist at work in American film. He could yet be the kind of writer desperately needed by Coppola, Scorsese, and so many others.

By the end of the twentieth century, it was clear that Allen's fecundity was chronic—though economics and his break with producer Jean Doumanian were further threats to the automatic one-film-a-year routine. Or was it that the routine, the momentum, kept Allen from proper examination of his work? Had habit overwhelmed the chance of art? It seemed to me that there was a wave of restored excellence—*Everyone, Harry,* and *Celebrity*—which came close to a really novel and brave scrutiny of modern reputation. But then Woody darted away into his own cuteness.

So there's too much—or too little reflection. Still, there are *Annie Hall, The Purple Rose of Cairo, Radio Days, Deconstructing Harry.* That's four brilliant films that no one else could have dreamed of. And that's what it's about.

June Allyson (Ella Geisman),
b. Bronx, New York, 1917
Trained as a dancer, she was a chorus girl while still at school, and went on to play in Broadway musicals. Her film debut was in *Best Foot Forward* (43, Edward Buzzell), which repeated a stage role. She was put under contract by MGM—as the sort of girl men overseas might like to come home to—for *Girl Crazy* (43, Norman Taurog); *Thousands*

Cheer (43, George Sidney); *Two Girls and a Sailor* (44, Richard Thorpe); and *Music for Millions* (44, Henry Koster). Her petite, sore-throated charm was perfected in *Till the Clouds Roll By* (46, Richard Whorf); *Good News* (47, Charles Walters); *Words and Music* (48, Taurog); as Jo in *Little Women* (49, Mervyn Le Roy); with her husband, Dick Powell, in *The Reformer and the Redhead* (50, Melvin Frank and Norman Panama); and *Too Young to Know* (51, Robert Z. Leonard). Her image of cheerful wholesomeness found its apotheosis in the wife and, supremely, the widow in *The Glenn Miller Story* (53, Anthony Mann). With that experience of tears, she took on more dramatic roles, with little success: *Battle Circus* (53, Richard Brooks), incredibly as the object of Bogart's affections; *Executive Suite* (54, Robert Wise); was surprisingly good (and nasty) in *The Shrike* (55, José Ferrer) and *Strategic Air Command* (55, Mann), in which she was forever looking for James Stewart in the sky. Thereafter she dwindled into romances and tame comedies: *You Can't Run Away From It* (56), produced and directed by Dick Powell and allegedly a remake of *It Happened One Night; The Opposite Sex* (56, David Miller), legally a remake of *The Women; My Man Godfrey* (57, Koster), so removed in tone and effect that it made the term "remake" null; *Interlude* (57, Douglas Sirk); and *A Stranger in My Arms* (58, Helmut Kautner). She moved briefly into TV, but retired when Powell died in 1963. More recently, she was the murderess in *They Only Kill Their Masters* (72, James Goldstone).

Nestor Almendros (Nestor Almendros Cuyas) (1930–92), b. Barcelona, Spain
Almendros was a beloved citizen of world film, a tender gentleman, a man of several languages, and an invaluable aid to many diverse directors. His book, *A Man with a Camera,* is as worthwhile as the movies he worked on, and so is the documentary *Mauvaise Conduite* (83), about gay life in Cuba that he photographed, cowrote, and codirected with Orlando Jimenez Leal. Yet Almendros is in this book because he was a very good director of photography, self-effacing yet inventive, and happiest if he could serve good directors.

Few cinematographers have demonstrated what I would call a singular creative character—John Alton comes to mind, Gregg Toland, Raoul Coutard perhaps. These are cameramen without whom certain careers and even genres might not have been the same. Yet photography is not that difficult, and not even that influential or decisive—I suspect that music and even editing have more effect on what we feel about a film than photography. The image is so fundamental and so wonderful in and of itself, but it *is* a given: every day, all over the world, millions of people take wonderful or useful pictures. Is it so remarkable that a few hundred people do it for movies?

In other words, I do not want to exaggerate Almendros as cameraman. He served several directors very well—Truffaut, Rohmer, Barbet Schroeder, Robert Benton. But do we *know* by their look or feel that, say, *Mississippi Mermaid, The Aviator's Wife, Reversal of Fortune,* or *Nadine* are *not* by Almendros? I trust not, for he *did* shoot *Nadine* (87). Equally, I find it hard to make claims for a consistent photographic personality in films as varied as *Places in the Heart, My Night at Maud's,* and *Two English Girls.* I am moved by the look of those films, but not convinced that Almendros brought more than appropriate skill and understanding to them.

There are two films where the photography is more forceful: *Sophie's Choice* (82, Alan J. Pakula), with the sickly-saintly paleness of Meryl Streep's face as she recollects; and *Days of Heaven* (78, Terrence Malick), with many miracles of natural light on the prairie, a movie in which—to my mind—photography has seeped into areas abandoned by the director. *Days of Heaven* is photographed to death. It is to the great credit of Almendros that he so seldom earned that rebuke.

He went to Cuba in 1948 and became an active cineaste there, photographing and directing many short films in what was a time of creative ferment. He studied at the University of Havana, at New York's City College, and at Centro Sperimentale in Rome, all in the 1950s. From the early sixties on, he worked as a cameraman in Europe and in America.

He did these for Truffaut: *The Wild Child* (69); *Bed and Board* (70); *Two English Girls* (71); *The Story of Adèle H.* (75)—with a good sense of the Caribbean; *The Man Who Loved Women* (77); *The Green Room* (78); *The Last Metro* (80); and *Confidentially Yours* (82).

Then for Rohmer: an episode for *Paris Vu Par . . .* (64); *La Collectioneuse* (66); *My Night at Maud's* (69); *Claire's Knee* (70); *Love in the Afternoon* (72); *The Marquise of O* (76); *Perceval le Gallois* (78); and *Pauline at the Beach* (82).

And for Benton: *Kramer vs. Kramer* (79); *Still of the Night* (82); *Places in the Heart* (84); *Nadine* (87); and *Billy Bathgate* (91).

Beyond those, Almendros worked on *The Wild Racers* (68, Daniel Haller and Roger Corman); *The Valley* (72, Schroeder); *La Gueule Ouverte* (74, Maurice Pialat); *General Amin* (74, Schroeder); *Cockfighter* (74, Monte Hellman); *Mes Petites Amoureuses* (75, Jean Eustache); *Maîtresse* (76, Schroeder); *Des Journées Entières dans les Arbres* (76, Marguerite Duras); *Madame Rosa* (77, Moshe Mizrahi); *Goin' South* (78, Jack Nicholson); *The Blue Lagoon* (80, Randal Kleiser); *Heartburn* (86, Mike Nichols); *Nobody Listened* (87, which he cowrote and codirected with Jorge Ulla); and the "Life

Lessons" episode for *New York Stories* (89, Martin Scorsese).

Pedro Almodóvar,

b. Calzada de Calatrava, Spain, 1951

1974: *La Caída de Sódoma* (s); *Dos Putas, o Historia de Amor que Termina en Boda* (s). 1975: *Homenaje* (s); *El Sueño* (s). 1976: *El Estrella* (s). 1977: *Complementos* (s); *Sexo Va* (s). 1978: *Folle, Folle, Fólleme, Tim; Salomé* (s). 1980: *Pepi, Luci, Bom y Otras Chicas del Montón/Pepi, Luci, Bom and Other Girls Like Mom.* 1982: *Laberinto de Pasiones/Labyrinth of Passion.* 1983: *Entre Tinieblas/Dark Habits.* 1984: *Qué He Hecho Yo Para Merecer Esto?/What Have I Done to Deserve This?.* 1985: *Trayler para Amantes de lo Prohibido* (s). 1986: *Mátador.* 1987: *La Ley del Deseo/Law of Desire.* 1988: *Mujeres al Borde de un Ataque de Nervios/Women on the Verge of a Nervous Breakdown.* 1990: *Tie Me Up, Tie Me Down!.* 1991: *High Heels.* 1993: *Kika.* 1995: *La Flor de Mi Secreto/The Flower of My Secret.* 1997: *Carne Trémula/Live Flesh.* 1999: *Todo Sobre Mi Madre/All About My Mother.* 2002: *Hable con Ella/Talk to Her.*

Almodóvar was one of the most welcome explosions of the eighties and a sign of the new Spain. Whereas Carlos Saura (nearly twenty years older than Almodóvar) made intensely measured and psychologically reflective films, with the innate secrecy of someone raised under the Franco regime, Almodóvar is excessive, garish, outlandishly inventive, and irrepressible. He is openly gay, devoted to sexual confusion, and eternally committed to the chance of love. His mode is satiric yet generous and free from moralizing. He has remarked on his debt not just to Hitchcock, Wilder, and Buñuel, but to Frank Tashlin. Indeed, there is a cartoonlike abandon and delirium in his best films and a complete faith in the torrential subconscious. But his generous, affectionate nature is all his own.

A frustrated provincial (he came from the area of La Mancha), he moved to Madrid in 1967 and worked for the telephone company. He joined an experimental theatre group, he wrote comic strips, and he was active in rock music. He began making short films on Super-8 at the time of Franco's death.

Almodóvar must mean more in Spain than anywhere else, yet his generation has been insistent on throwing out the country's past. Still, he has preferred to work in Spain, with a striking band of actors—notably Carmen Maura and Antonio Banderas. *Women on the Verge* is his most successful film, the one in which gaiety, violence, and tragedy jostle together most dangerously. *Tie Me Up, Tie Me Down!* was a relative disappointment. An energy like Almodóvar's needs to keep expanding or risk becoming mannered. So he may need to take on fresh, dangerous territory. America could prove a very fruitful inspiration, for he knows American culture, and he is ideally placed to smash our old, fixed dreams about what it is to be Hispanic. But *All About My Mother* was his largest and warmest film—a sweeping tribute to women, and one of those films to make you wonder if God didn't mean the movies to be gay.

Robert Altman,

b. Kansas City, Missouri, 1925

1955: *The Delinquents*. 1957: *The James Dean Story*. 1964: *Nightmare in Chicago*. 1967: *Countdown*. 1969: *That Cold Day in the Park*. 1970: *M°A°S°H; Brewster McCloud*. 1971: *McCabe and Mrs. Miller*. 1972: *Images; The Long Goodbye*. 1974: *Thieves Like Us; California Split*. 1975: *Nashville*. 1976: *Buffalo Bill and the Indians, or Sitting Bull's History Lesson*. 1977: *3 Women*. 1978: *A Wedding*. 1979: *Quintet; A Perfect Couple*. 1980: *Health; Popeye*. 1982: *Come Back to the 5 & Dime, Jimmy Dean, Jimmy Dean*. 1983: *Streamers*. 1984: *Secret Honor*. 1985: *Fool for Love*. 1987: "*Les Boreades,*" an episode from *Aria; Beyond Therapy; O.C. and Stiggs*. 1988: *Tanner '88* (TV). 1990: *Vincent and Theo*. 1992: *The Player*. 1993: *Short Cuts*. 1994: *Ready to Wear/Prêt-à-Porter*. 1996: *Kansas City; Jazz '34* (s). 1998: *The Gingerbread Man*. 1999: *Cookie's Fortune*. 2000: *Dr. T & The Women*. 2001: *Gosford Park*. 2003: *The Company*.

In 1975, before I had seen *Nashville*, I wrote, "Altman seems less interested in structure than in atmosphere; scheme and character recede as chronic, garrulous discontinuity holds sway." The tone was critical, and when I fell asleep in *Nashville* and then faced the unquestionable disaster of *Buffalo Bill*, I felt confirmed in my opinion of a director who could not tell stories but allowed us to assume or hope that he was interested in something else. As this is written, I remain uncertain about everything except the absence of a flawless film in Altman's work. But going back to *Nashville*, some of the earlier films, and the first half of *3 Women* made me reflect. Whether from confusion or density, Altman is that rarity in American cinema: a problem director, a true object of controversy, and a man whose films alter or shift at different viewings like shot silk.

M°A°S°H is still Altman's only substantial hit, and one of his most overrated films. The willful looking away from war's slaughter in favor of the preoccupations of camp life is original and arresting, but the movie is callous and flippant (so often, Altman wearies of his own experiments). The treatment of the Sally Kellerman and Robert Duvall characters is brutal, while the final football game is a feeble retreat to unenlightened conventions. That a cozy TV series could spin off from the movie reveals its compromises. Still, *M°A°S°H* began to develop the crucial Altman style of overlapping, blurred sound and images so slippery with zoom that there was no sense of composition.

That is what makes *Nashville* so absorbing—once you're awake. The notion of twenty-six roughly equal characters moving in random turmoil and coincidence is the ideal material for his style: he aspires to film not just eccentric groups but seething masses. It remains enigmatic how organized or purposeful *Nashville* is, but there is an attitude to individuals and society in it—of helpless, amused affection, only occasionally spoiled by Altman's weakness for cheap shots and druggy attitudinizing. The feeling of real time and space stretching to contain the actions of so many people, without moralizing, is both beautiful and demanding. The ending is a trite concession to the way commercial movies must end with some sort of resolution, but along the way there are countless moments of felt but uncaptioned human interaction that few American films have been wayward enough to notice. The mosaic, or the mix, permits a freedom and a human idiosyncrasy that Renoir might have admired.

In hindsight, I think *California Split, The Long Goodbye*, and *McCabe and Mrs. Miller* benefit from this style and lead it toward *Nashville*. But as soon as he concentrated on a few people, Altman looked an evasive fumbler, unable to focus character or to shape his films. As alternatives, he pursued improvisation and a sort of decorative dismay. *The Long Goodbye* is an ingenious variation on a known genre, yet it has an empty soul: so great is the attention to pretty reflections and the crazed fragmentation of the theme song. All its playfulness leaves one frustrated, for Altman backs away from tragedy or real comedy: a sort of alert, floating drift is his essence, and it works best when people are involved for whom depth can be avoided.

Images is a forbiddingly half-baked showing off and horrid warning of what Altman may believe he's striving for. *Thieves Like Us* has an authentic period flavor and a touchingly offhand treatment of the love story, but it is ruined by grotesque overemphasis and is far less an achievement than its model, Nicholas Ray's *They Live by Night*. *3 Women* starts off like a breakthrough, but then succumbs to florid illusions of poetry, dream, and the mystical sisterhood of glum women. *Buffalo Bill* is a mess, too cute or too feckless to give the supportive irony that Paul Newman's rather brave performance requires.

One of the fallacies attached to Altman is how good he is for actors. Evidently he inspires and captures the mood of a group, especially their vague sense of affinity. But individuals can suffer at his hands: Geraldine Chaplin is an actress for

Carlos Saura, while Altman makes fun of her; Harvey Keitel has been wasted, just as Keith Carradine has been damagingly indulged; Lily Tomlin offered a poignancy in *Nashville* that Altman was not prepared to explore; Janice Rule postures dreadfully in *3 Women;* and Sterling Hayden is allowed to substitute ham for pathos in *The Long Goodbye;* nonentities are mixed in with talented players. But no one else has made as much of Elliott Gould: the reappraisal of Chandler in *The Long Goodbye* emerges from Gould's restless, spacey humor; Warren Beatty achieves nobility in *McCabe and Mrs. Miller;* while Shelley Duvall in *3 Women* is a conception and a performance that take one's breath away as we forget Hollywood figureheads and face a daft, pretty girl whose personality is as unstable and grating as a marble on a hard floor, rolling this way and that.

Perhaps Altman himself hardly knows how far he rejects the well-made movie (in a spirit of innovation) or cannot reconcile himself to its discipline. He is no more articulate in print than he is coherent on-screen. Like it or not, his method and his nirvana lie beyond meaning. Like Renoir, Warhol, and Rivette, he is a filmmaker clumsily or acutely loyal to the camera's power of observation, and is bent on a new way of seeing. Drama—as Hollywood understood it—may have no place in the spectacle; the people may degenerate into shadows, reflections, and a hubbub of noise. It could be so aimless as to be antihuman; or it might embody a sense of people being like atoms whirling around to laws no one knows and thus part of a kind of play or hopeful gambling—as in *California Split,* among the most passionate of Altman's pictures, and one that sees a kind of philosophy in gentle futility.

In the eighties, Altman ran into hard times, obscure pictures, and a reliance on theatrical restagings for the camera that seemed pedestrian after the real movies of the previous decade. *Health* was pretty bad, and *Popeye* was too much the comic book for a large audience. *Come Back . . .* is worthy and well acted, yet Altman never finds a way of transcending the mediocre, sentimental play. Likewise, *Streamers* and *Secret Honor* meekly and rather leadenly live up to their originals. *Fool for Love* was as bad as Altman has been—how could Sam Shepard act in the film without realizing that Altman was unsuited to the play's intense, enclosed, and mounting explosiveness? (And Shepard had directed *Fool for Love* on stage.)

Thereafter, Altman's films found little or no release. But *Vincent and Theo* was a return to power and quality, even if it didn't seem Altmanesque. *The Player* was widely hailed as his comeback, and it is a pleasure—droll and sinuously explorative in its camera style. But that Wellesian opening gave the game away: no one else could have controlled or conceived it; yet the movements were also showy and needless—Altman was copying himself. *The Player* was a return to Altman's America as a place of frauds and dreamers. But the satire was inoffensive. No one was hurt. There was no damage done in the film: *The Player* came from a game, not life.

Short Cuts came from a number of Raymond Carver stories—though several Carver enthusiasts disputed the fidelity of the film. It *was* Altman, for good and ill. The movie caught the hazy, slippery looseness of L.A., its casual violence, and its childishness with a precision seldom attempted by mainstream Hollywood. Most of the people were both awkward and interesting, and in many of the transitions there was an inspired sense of incidents interacting, reflecting, and making a kind of helpless, numb philosophy. As in *Nashville,* the cuts, the pans, and the looking sideways overcame the director's innate cynicism. But there was also a squeamishness about people (except for pretty, undressed women) that curdled the film. The scale of *Short Cuts* made this bitterness obtrusive and as disconcerting as Altman's irritable superiority. He has so much facility, so little faith. Few people in L.A. liked *Short Cuts*—which suggests how good it is.

The years after *Short Cuts* showed a slackening: *Ready to Wear* and *Dr. T* were terrible. But *Kansas City*—Altman's hometown, of course—was fascinating, not least in the way it was backed up by a very lively jam-session movie. *The Gingerbread Man* was silly, but very atmospheric. And then *Gosford Park* appeared—a trip to Britain—and the old magic was back. No one else alive is as capable of a dud, or a masterpiece.

John Alton (Janos or Jacob Altman) (1901–96), b. Sopron, Hungary

In the early 1990s, nothing had been reported to say that John Alton was dead, but no one seemed to know where he was. And so his strange and often unaccountable career became the more mysterious and romantic. How easy it was to suppose that one of the great creators of shadow had simply opted for some rare obscurity. It was nearly thirty years since Alton had worked: he was the initial cinematographer on *Birdman of Alcatraz* (62), but he and director Charles Crichton were replaced by John Frankenheimer and Burnett Guffey. After that . . . ?

Was Alton disgusted or disappointed? Did he feel there was no more point in wasting his time on Hollywood? Or did he reckon that being sixty was enough? Did he resume some Hungarian name or identity—for surely he was not born "John Alton"? If this was hard enough to explain, there was a greater enigma. For years, Alton worked on the lowliest of movies, B pictures and quickies. Then in the space of a few years he helped create the look of film noir. And then . . . he went under contract to MGM, where he photographed a mixed bag of pictures but never really went back to noir.

Then movie buffs "rediscovered" Alton. Of course, *he* had known where he was all along—and he had been in Los Angeles much of the time, the most obvious place and for that very reason, perhaps, the best hiding place. And so the legend gave way to some verifiable facts.

Alton had come to America from Hungary in 1919–20. He had worked in the labs for MGM and then he had become an assistant to Clyde De Vinna and Woody Van Dyke. As such, he worked on *Spoilers of the West* (28, Van Dyke) and *Wyoming* (28, Van Dyke), David Selznick's first efforts at Metro. Alton was also traveling, and he did some location shooting in Germany for *The Student Prince* (27, Ernst Lubitsch). He did some shooting in Paris on *Song of the Flame* (30, Alan Crosland), *Better to Laugh* (31, E. W. Erno), and in Constantinople for *Der Mann, der Den Mord Beging* (31, Curtis Bernhardt).

At that point, Alton chose to go to Argentina to help develop that country's film industry. He shot over twenty films, and even directed: *El Hijo de Papa* (32, Alton); *Los Tres Berretines* (32, Enrique T. Susini); *La Vida Bohemia* (38, Joseph Berne); and *Puerta Cerrada* (39, Luis Saslavsky).

His American credits begin in 1940 on films that are hard to see, and which in some cases are likely lost: *The Courageous Dr. Christian* (40, Bernhard Vorhaus); *The Refugee* (40, Vorhaus); *Three Faces West* (40, Vorhaus); *Forced Landing* (41, Gordon Wiles); *The Devil Pays Off* (41, John H. Auer); *Mr. District Attorney in the Carter Case* (42, Vorhaus); *Moonlight Masquerade* (42, Auer); *The Sultan's Daughter* (43, Arthur Dreifuss); *Atlantic City* (44, Ray McCarey); *Lake Placid Serenade* (44, Steve Sekely); *Girls of the Big House* (45, George Archainbaud); *A Guy Could Change* (45, William K. Howard); *Affairs of Geraldine* (46, George Blair); *The Madonna's Secret* (46, William Thiel); and *The Ghost Goes Wild* (47, Blair).

Driftwood (47, Allan Dwan) was a step up, and it has some fine, atmospheric coverage of the young Natalie Wood. But the films Alton would be known for lay just ahead (and they were all small films in their day): *He Walked by Night* (48, Alfred L. Werker—and with some uncredited work by Anthony Mann); *Raw Deal* (48, Mann); *Hollow Triumph* (48, Sekely); *T-Men* (48, Mann); *Reign of Terror* (49, Mann); *Border Incident* (49, Mann); and *Devil's Doorway* (49, Mann).

Alton's vision was ideally suited to low-budget work: he used few lamps, and he abandoned standard setups; he was also ready to anger union electricians by bypassing their preferred procedures. He was as much at ease in the French Revolution setting of *Reign of Terror* as in the modern, urban

noir of *T-Men*. This was very arty lighting, despite its harsh mood: in 1945, Alton published a book called *Painting With Light*, which helped draw attention to his very mannered photography and to the influence of Rembrandt.

By 1950, he had been signed up by Metro, and he was at work on *Father of the Bride* (Vincente Minnelli)! A year later he shared an Oscar for color cinematography on *An American in Paris* (51, Minnelli)—his first ever color film. This was more prestigious work, and it paid better. For ten years, Alton was a studio cameraman, though Allan Dwan observed that he fought the unions with increasing zeal: *Grounds for Marriage* (50, Robert Z. Leonard); *Mystery Street* (50, John Sturges); *Father's Little Dividend* (51, Minnelli); *The People Against O'Hara* (52, Don Siegel); *Battle Circus* (52, Richard Brooks); *Count the Hours* (52, Don Siegel); *I, the Jury* (53, Henry Essex); *Take the High Ground* (53, Brooks); *Cattle Queen of Montana* (54, Dwan); *Passion* (54, Dwan); *Silver Lode* (54, Dwan); *The Big Combo* (55, Joseph H. Lewis)—perhaps the best noir he worked on; *Escape to Burma* (55, Dwan); *Pearl of the South Pacific* (55, Dwan); *Tennessee's Partner* (55, Dwan); *The Catered Affair* (56, Brooks); *Slightly Scarlet* (56, Dwan)—magnificent late Technicolor; *Tea and Sympathy* (56, Minnelli)—dismal early Metrocolor; *The Teahouse of the August Moon* (56, Daniel Mann); *Designing Woman* (57, Minnelli); *The Brothers Karamazov* (58, Brooks); *Lonelyhearts* (58, Vincent J. Donahue); *Twelve to the Moon* (60, David Bradley); and *Elmer Gantry* (60, Brooks).

Don Ameche (Dominic Felix Amici) (1908–1993), b. Kenosha, Wisconsin

Born in the birthplace of Orson Welles, but seven years ahead of George Orson, Ameche had two distinct movie careers. For something over ten years, he was a Fox stalwart, refusing to notice the secret rhyme of his mustache and the bowtie he wore so often in romances and musicals. Then he faded away in his forties, came back for a while in his fifties, but waited until he was past seventy for an unequivocal return that brought him a supporting actor Oscar and public affection.

He was in *Ladies in Love* (36, Edward Griffith); *One in a Million* (36, Sidney Lanfield); with Loretta Young in *Ramona* (36, Henry King); *Love Is News* (37, Tay Garnett); *Fifty Roads to Town* (37, Norman Taurog); with Alice Faye, a frequent screen partner, in *You Can't Have Everything* (37, Taurog); *Love Under Fire* (37, George Marshall); *In Old Chicago* (38, King); *Happy Landing* (38, Roy del Ruth); *Josette* (38, Allan Dwan); *Alexander's Ragtime Band* (38, King); as D'Artagnan in *The Three Musketeers* (39, Dwan); excellent in *Midnight* (39, Mitchell Leisen) as a Hungarian count and cabbie; inventing like crazy in *The*

Story of Alexander Graham Bell (39, Irving Cummings) and forever associated with the telephone; as Stephen Foster in *Swanee River* (39, Lanfield); *Lillian Russell* (40, Cummings); *Four Sons* (40, Archie Mayo); as an Argentinian with Betty Grable in *Down Argentine Way* (40, Cummings); *That Night in Rio* (41, Cummings); *Moon Over Miami* (41, Walter Lang); *Kiss the Boys Goodbye* (41, Victor Schertzinger); *The Feminine Touch* (41, W. S. Van Dyke II); *Confirm or Deny* (41, Mayo); *The Magnificent Dope* (42, Lang); *Girl Trouble* (42, Harold Schuster); *Heaven Can Wait* (43, Ernst Lubitsch); *Happy Land* (43, Irving Pichel); *Something to Shout About* (43, Gregory Ratoff); in the war film *Wing and a Prayer* (44, Henry Hathaway); *Greenwich Village* (44, Lang); *It's in the Bag* (45, Richard Wallace); *Guest Wife* (45, Sam Wood); *So Goes My Love* (46, Frank Ryan); as the villainous husband in *Sleep My Love* (48, Douglas Sirk); and *Slightly French* (49, Sirk).

In the 1950s, Ameche did a good deal of television, with just a few movie roles after 1960: *A Fever in the Blood* (61, Vincent Sherman); *Picture Mommy Dead* (66, Bert I. Gordon); *Suppose They Gave a War and Nobody Came?* (70, Hy Averback); *Ginger Gets Married* (72, E. W. Swackhamer); and *Won Ton Ton, the Dog Who Saved Hollywood* (76, Michael Winner).

But the real comeback waited for the eighties: *Trading Places* (83, John Landis); winning his Oscar in *Cocoon* (85, Ron Howard); *A Masterpiece of Murder* (86, Charles S. Dubin) and *Pals* (87, Lou Antonio), both for TV; *Harry and the Hendersons* (87, William Dear); *Cocoon: The Return* (88, Daniel Petrie); *Things Change* (88, David Mamet); *Oscar* (91, Landis); and *Folks!* (92, Ted Kotcheff).

Jon Amiel, b. London, 1948
1986: *The Singing Detective* (TV). 1989: *Queen of Hearts*. 1990: *Tune in Tomorrow. . . .* 1993: *Sommersby*. 1995: *Copycat*. 1997: *The Man Who Knew Too Little*. 1999: *Entrapment*. 2002: *The Core*.

Jon Amiel has gone from studying the wrecked skin of "Philip Marlowe" to ogling the up-thrust haunches of Catherine Zeta-Jones. Well, yes, there's room for both in this book, but here is a warning case about the risks in going to Hollywood. A seasoned television director in London, Amiel got his great chance with Dennis Potter's six-part serial. He may have complained at low budgets and tight schedules; still, there is nothing like material, and Ron Bass (the screenwriter on *Entrapment*) has a smoothness of personality that keeps him years away from understanding such characters as Potter's Marlowe.

The transition is sadder still when one recalls that *Queen of Hearts*—about Italians running a café in England—was full of charm, vitality and originality. *Tune in Tomorrow . . . ,* from the Vargas Llosa novel *Aunt Julia and the Scriptwriter,* was offbeat. But *Sommersby* is a numb remake of *The Return of Martin Guerre; Copycat* was contrived and nasty; and *Entrapment* is all concept and no material, and enough to strand its two likable star personalities.

Gillian Anderson, b. Chicago, 1968
Having given one of the best performances of its year, as Lily Bart in *The House of Mirth* (00, Terence Davies), and seeing it largely ignored, what is Gillian Anderson to think? That her Dana Scully on TV's *The X-Files* passes as real drama or more serious work? In fact, of course, all Lily Bart did was persuade the discerning that those hints of uncommon character and intelligence as Scully were not accidental. (In that strange series, many minimal things can seem larger than is really the case—let no one be fooled, high-class tosh has frequently wasted two of the smartest actors on any screen.)

As a child, Anderson was taken to live in London for over ten years. But she finished her school at the Goodman Theatre School in Chicago. After a small role in *The Turning* (92, L.A. Puopolo), she went into *The X-Files* in 1993. Her ventures beyond that hit show were odd to say the least: she narrated a documentary, *Why Planes Go Down* (97), presumably because Scully's deadpan encouraged the thought of unnatural reasons. She was "Southside Girl" in *Chicago Cab* (98, Mary Cybulski and John Tintori); *The Mighty* (98, Peter Chelsom); in the movie of *The X-Files* (98, Rob Bowman); *Playing by Heart* (98, Willard Carroll). And then Lily Bart, with an exceptional command of class, passion, bad luck, and despair. In fact, the reception given *The House of Mirth* seemed to prove one principle behind *The X Files*—there are a lot of dead heads out there.

Lindsay Anderson, (1923–94),
b. Bangalore, India
1948: *Meet the Pioneers* (d). 1949: *Idlers That Work* (d). 1951: *Three Installations* (d). 1952: *Wakefield Express* (d). 1953: *Thursday's Child* (codirected with Guy Brenton) (d); *O Dreamland* (d). 1954: *Trunk Conveyor* (d). 1955: *Foot and Mouth* (d); *A Hundred Thousand Children* (d); *The Children Upstairs* (d); *Green and Pleasant Land* (d); *Henry* (d); *£20 a Ton* (d); *Energy First* (d). 1957: *Every Day Except Christmas* (d). 1959: *March to Aldermaston* (codirected) (d). 1962: *This Sporting Life*. 1966: *The White Bus* (s). 1967: *Raz, Dwa, Trzy/The Singing Lesson*. 1968: *If. . . .* 1972: *O Lucky Man!*. 1974: *In Celebration*. 1979: *The Old Crowd* (TV); *Red White and Zero*. 1982: *Britannia Hospital*. 1987: *The Whales of August*. 1989: *Glory! Glory!* (TV).

The contradictoriness in Anderson's personality was vigorous enough to prevent him from a film-making career that had any continuity. And yet since the war he had been one of the more active and idiosyncratic figures in the British arts. Anderson had been so fiercely engaged with the problem of why it is so difficult to make good films in England, but his energies were unresolved and his rather prickly talent had never been fully expressed. England's fault or Anderson's? The question is crucial because Anderson was involved in some of the most thorough scrutiny of the British cinema. And just as there was never much doubt that he was more talented than his contemporaries—Tony Richardson and Karel Reisz—so he never allowed his solution to the questions to become tied to any noncinematic dogma. Briefly, in the mid-1950s, his sense of commitment fastened on that left-wing emotion that marched to Aldermaston. But Anderson was too good an artist to swallow politics whole. His need to be committed was itself the chief impulse of his career, and the catalogue of his causes is, by implication, the story of dissipation. His productions of David Storey's stage plays have an earnestness and need for significance that might alarm an author and certainly expose the texts. In retrospect, he seems a lesser figure than, say, Robert Hamer or Seth Holt—if only because he made so few features.

Anderson was the son of an officer in the Indian army. He came back to England to go to Cheltenham and Oxford: which underlines the biographical elements of Kipling and public school in *If. . . .* His period at university was interrupted by war service. But, still at Oxford, in 1947, he was one of the founders of the magazine *Sequence* (Karel Reisz was the other). He edited it for five years, by which time he was involved in documentary filmmaking. The simultaneous criticism and creativity was vital to *Sequence* but sadly peripheral to filmmaking and appreciation in Britain. Anderson's documentaries are no advance on the films of the 1930s and 1940s, while *Sequence* is an uneasy and inconsistent proponent of a director's cinema. Anderson's own taste was for what he called "poetic" cinema; but that led him to liking John Ford as much as Vigo. The beginnings of a proper appreciation of American cinema in *Sequence* were always evaded, perhaps through ultimate critical shortcomings, perhaps through distaste for America. In any event, Anderson missed the chance that *Cahiers du Cinéma* gobbled up, of a new movie aesthetic that took American sound films as its models.

But, even in 1958, Anderson seemed torn between irritation with *Cahiers* and the recognition that it had taken a rewarding path, above all in the way it led to actual, and marvelous, films: "Here you have a magazine like *Cahiers du Cinéma*, terribly erratic and over-personal in its criticism, which has been enraging us all for the last five years. But the great compensation is that its writers make films, that three or four of its critics are now making films independently. And this means that they have a kind of vitality which is perhaps finally more important than critical balance." That comes from a *Sight and Sound* discussion with Paul Rotha, Basil Wright, and Penelope Houston in which Anderson alone seems disturbed by English inertia. Those films he saw coming made Free Cinema—the hopeful blanket description of British documentary in the mid-1950s—look dreadfully insipid.

In fact, Anderson worked in TV and began to direct for the theatre. His first feature, *This Sporting Life*, was from a novel by David Storey and still smacked of Free Cinema in its flashy use of tenements, pubs, and rugby league. But the dogged boorishness of its subject, epitomized in the inescapable presence of Richard Harris, gave it a sad, plodding feeling in place of the sheer working-class tragedy to which it aspired.

In the 1960s, Anderson was more heavily involved in the theatre than in films. *The White Bus* was broken by production problems, and *The Singing Lesson* showed Anderson's rather forlorn resort to East Europe as an artistic influence. Indeed, Milos Forman owns up to a large debt to Anderson's encouragement. *If . . .* , in 1968, and for Paramount, was a real film, rooted in a world and feelings that Anderson knew, but alight with ideas and passions that would not have shamed Vigo. Its ending is bleakly and helplessly destructive (as if Anderson now was disenchanted with politics), but *If . . .* makes other English school films look halfhearted. It is pungent, sexy, socially accurate, funny, and exciting—what a film for a young man to have made. *O Lucky Man!*, though, is something an older man hopes to forget.

Anderson remained his own man: despite the geriatric delicacies of *The Whales of August* (nothing else had ever shown him as such a softy), *Britannia Hospital* was a rowdy satire on bureaucracy, while *Glory! Glory!* tore TV evangelism limb from limb with astonishing zest and Swiftian vengeance.

His death prompted revelations—of gay urgings, his own difficulty and frustration—all wonderfully covered in Gavin Lambert's biography, *Mainly About Lindsay Anderson.*

Paul Thomas Anderson,
b. Los Angeles, 1970
1997: *Hard Eight*. 1998: *Boogie Nights*. 1999: *Magnolia*. 2002: *Punch-Drunk Love*.

There were stories when *Magnolia* opened that Paul Thomas Anderson was upset at the way New Line were advertising his picture. The press ads for the picture were scarcely legible, let alone enticing—so Anderson had a point. Equally, New Line seemed to be so much in awe of their young director that they were ready to accept his suggestions. Yet, truly, how would you do a poster for *Magnolia*? How would you begin to convey the feeling and form of the picture? Would you bother to ask the question why it is called *Magnolia*? Would you let yourself ask, are posters the proper way to offer great movies?

Such awkward questions could accumulate in Hollywood marketing offices, which have so little time or practice with the crosscutting ironies and countervailing doubts that obsess Anderson and are the energy in his films. He was, before reaching thirty, a cult figure, profiled in the *New York Times Magazine*, and hardly bothered to muffle his youthful arrogance. He knows it all, you can hear some saying, except how to get a hit. And among the things he knows is the serpentine idea of a road that binds a city, and the necessary affront of a surreal accident like the frogs in *Magnolia*. (At least Robert Altman—one of Anderson's models—used a plausible earthquake as his device in *Short Cuts*.)

I like nearly everything about Anderson except the stances he seems bound to take up as self-defense, and the wilful arbitrariness of his work. For wilfulness in Hollywood is sooner or later interpreted as a challenge—no matter that no one his age can create such complex scenes, or build them into such ravishing patterns. I stress the latter because Anderson seems one of the relatively few new directors driven and inspired by ideas in editing.

It is also the case that anyone as good and smart as Anderson should be more perceptibly self-critical. In fact, *Magnolia* is his most youthful and indulgent film—and *Hard Eight*, his best and most austere. But there are poetic mysteries in the first film that come closer to pretension in *Magnolia*. In other words, Anderson is not handling himself well. He is drawing fire upon his own vulnerabilities. But is there any other way?

No other American director working today has such sad, tender, and smart ways of looking into the depths of society, or for feeling out their poignant juxtapositions. He writes great, ragged speeches, and he is like a fond parent with his family of actors. All his three films so far have used John Reilly, Philip Seymour Hoffman, and Philip Baker Hall. In addition, he has done remarkable things with such diverse figures as Tom Cruise, Julianne Moore, and Burt Reynolds. His way of blessing actors is so very close to his wish to rescue people from their drabness. Sooner or later, it will be perceived how desperately concerned he is about the society called America.

Of course, *Magnolia* is like *Short Cuts* in that both films are symphonies attempting to take in everything. They have the ambition of an Ives, say,

who could hardly get his work played, let alone make it popular. Altman has learned cunning ways of making that ambition into a career. But he is older, and far less kind. Anderson's energy and aspirations are destined to collide with Hollywood thinking, and he may be too young and too good to learn subterfuge. If he is as good as he thinks he is (and I think he is), there are bloody battles to come. But no one has a better chance of offering us new narrative forms for our movies.

Wes Anderson, b. Houston, Texas, 1970
1994: *Bottle Rocket* (s). 1996: *Bottle Rocket*. 1998: *Rushmore*. 2001: *The Royal Tenenbaums*.

Watch this space. What does that mean? That he might be something one day.

Bibi Andersson (Birgitta Andersson),
b. Stockholm, Sweden, 1935
Although Bibi Andersson was married to one director, Kjell Grede—for whom she has never filmed—our impressions of Bibi Andersson have been radically affected by another, to whom she seems to be spiritually committed: Ingmar Bergman. They first worked together when she was only seventeen and appeared in a television commercial for soap directed by Bergman. That effect of scrubbed, cheerful cleanliness took some time to wear off. She trained at the Royal Theatre, Stockholm, from 1954–56, and was already making small appearances in films: *Dum-Bom* (53, Nils Poppe); *En Natt pa Glimmingehus* (54, Torgny Wickman); *Herr Arnes Penngar* (54, Gustaf Molander); a bit part in *Smiles of a Summer Night* (55, Bergman); *Sista Paret Ut* (56, Alf Sjoberg); *Egen Ingang* (56, Hasse Ekman); and *Sommarnoje Sokes* (57, Ekman). She then played the wife in the pair of fairground innocents (the husband being Nils Poppe) who survive the apocalypse in *The Seventh Seal* (57, Bergman).

She offered at this time little more than the vague, childish prettiness that symbolized hope in Bergman's most pretentious and hollow period. Similarly, in *Wild Strawberries* (57, Bergman), she was one of the young hikers who brings comfort to the dying Isak Borg. In that film, Andersson seemed a lightweight beside the anguished Ingrid Thulin. She was more seriously tested as the prospective mother of an illegitimate child in *So Close to Life* (58, Bergman), but had only a small, repertory part in *The Face* (58, Bergman).

At about this time, she went back to the theatre and made only one film in 1959: *Den Kara Leken* (Kenne Fant). She was the virgin who irritates Satan in *The Devil's Eye* (60, and one of Bergman's more playful films). Over the next five years she waited to mature—or so it seems in hindsight: to Yugoslavia for *Nasilje Na Trgu* (61, Alf Kjellin); into a new sexual frankness with *The*

Mistress (62, Vilgot Sjoman); *Kort ar Sommaren* (62, Bjarne Henning-Jensen); *On* (64, Sjoberg, not released until 66); one of Bergman's women in *Now About These Women* (64); *Juninatt* (65, Lars-Erik Liedholm); uselessly to America for *Duel at Diablo* (65, Ralph Nelson).

She needed such a holiday to prepare for one of the most harrowing female roles the screen has presented: Nurse Alma in *Persona* (66, Bergman). That this masterpiece owed so much to Bibi Andersson was acknowledgment of her greater emotional experience. She was thirty now, and in that astonishing scene where Liv Ullmann and she look into the camera as if it were a mirror, and Ullmann arranges Andersson's hair, it is as if Bergman were saying, "Look what time has done. Look what a creature this is." Alma talks throughout *Persona* but is never answered, so that her own insecurity and instability grow. Technically the part calls for domination of timing, speech, and movement that exposes the chasms in the soul. And it was in showing that breakdown, in reliving Alma's experience of the orgy on the beach years before, in deliberately leaving glass on the gravel, and in realizing with awe and panic that she is only another character for the supposedly sick actress, that Andersson herself seemed one of the most tormented women in cinema.

She was in support, spiky and ill at ease in *A Passion* (69, Bergman), the center of regeneration in *The Touch* (71, Bergman), and in one episode from *Scenes from a Marriage* (73, Bergman). *The Touch* shows that she is the warmest, most free-spirited of Bergman's women, more broadly compassionate than Thulin or Ullmann. Being more robust, her distress is more moving, and her doggedness more encouraging.

Necessarily, that seems the core of her life as an actress. But in addition, she has played *Miss Julie* on Swedish TV, *After the Fall* and *Who's Afraid of Virginia Woolf?* on the stage, and these other films: *My Sister My Love* (66, Sjoman); *Le Viol* (67, Jacques Doniol-Valcroze); *Svarta Palmkronor* (68, Lars Magnus Lindgren); *The Girls* (68, Mai Zetterling); *Taenk pa et Tal* (69, Palle Kjaerulff-Schmidt); *Storia di una Donna* (69, Leonardo Bercovici); *The Kremlin Letter* (70, John Huston); *Afskedens Time* (73, Per Holst); *Blondy* (75, Sergio Gobbi); *I Never Promised You a Rose Garden* (77, Anthony Page); *An Enemy of the People* (78, George Schaefer); *Quintet* (79, Robert Altman); *L'Amour en Question* (79, André Cayatte); *The Concorde—Airport '79* (79, David Lowell Rich); *Twee Vrouen* (79, George Sluizer); *Barnforbjudet* (80, Johan Bergenstrahle); *Blomstrande Tider* (80, John Olsson); *Marmeedupprovet* (80, Erland Josephson and Sven Nykvist); *Jag Rodnar* (81, Sjoman); *Svarte Fugler* (83, Lasse Glom); as Nastassja Kinski's mother in *Exposed* (83, James Toback); *A Hill on the Dark Side of the Moon* (83,

Lennart Hjulstrom); *Sista Laken* (84, Jan Lindstrom); *Huomenna* (86, Julia Rosna); *Babette's Feast* (87, Gabriel Axel); *Los Dueños de la Silencia* (87, Carlos Lemos); *Zernando al Viento* (88, Gonzalo Suarez); and, for TV, *Wallenberg: A Hero's Story* (88, Lamont Johnson).

She works less often now, occasionally for Swedish TV: *Till Julia* (91, Margarete Garpe); *Una Estación de Paso* (92, Gracia Querejeta); *Blank Päls och Starka Tassar* (92, Arne Hedlund); *Drømspel* (94, Unni Straume); *Il Sogno della Farfalla* (94, Marco Bellocchio); *Det Blir Adrig Som Man Tänkt Sig* (00, Mans Herngren and Hannes Holm); *Anna* (00, Erik Wedersoe); *Elina—Som om jag inte fanns* (02, Klaus Haro); as Queen Alexandra in *The Last Prince* (03, Stephen Poliakoff).

Harriet Andersson,
b. Stockholm, Sweden, 1932

By the standards we have come to expect of Swedish actresses, Harriet Andersson is something of an outsider: a little coarse, sensual, dark, and slatternly, a creature of more homespun sensibility: thus, her fame was based originally on the arbitrary, sexy working girl, Monika, in *Summer with Monika* (52, Ingmar Bergman). Her own background was in revue and the chorus line, rather than the straight theatre. She began filming in her late teens: *Medan Staden Sover* (50, Lars-Eric Kjellgren); *Anderssonskans Kalle* (50, Rolf Husberg); *Biffen och Bananen* (51, Husberg); *Puck Heter Jag* (51, Schamyl Bauman); *Sabotage* (52, Eric Jonsson); *Ubat 39* (52, Erik Faustman); and *Trots* (52, Gustaf Molander). After *Summer with Monika*, she made several films for Bergman, invariably representing the sensual "lower" woman: first as the circus girl in *Sawdust and Tinsel* (53); *A Lesson in Love* (54); *Journey into Autumn* (55); and *Smiles of a Summer Night* (55). After that, she made three more films with Bergman: superb as the schizophrenic in *Through a Glass Darkly* (61); in *Now About These Women* (64); and as the dying sister in *Cries and Whispers* (72). If she did not work for him much more it may be because of her marriage to director Jorn Donner, a man more disposed to drawing out her vitality. Her other films include: *Hoppsan!* (55, Stig Olin); *Sista Paret Ut* (56, Alf Sjoberg); *Nattbarn* (56, Gunnar Hellstrom); *Kvinna i Leopard* (58, Jan Molander); *Flottans Overman* (58, Olin); *Brott i Paradlset* (59, Kjellgren); to Germany for *Barbara* (61, Frank Wisbar); *Siska* (62, Alf Kjellin); *Lyckodrommen* (63, Hans Abramson); *A Sunday in September* (63, Donner); *To Love* (64, Donner); *Loving Couples* (64, Mai Zetterling); *For Vanskaps Skull* (65, Abramson); *Lianbron* (65, Sven Nykvist); *Har Borjar Aventyret* (65, Donner); to Britain for *The Deadly Affair* (66, Sidney Lumet); *Ormen* (66, Abramson); in an episode from *Stimulantia* (67, Donner); *Rooftree* (67, Donner); *Mennesker Modes og Sod Musik Upstar in Hjertet* (67, Henning Carlsen); *Jag Alskar du Alskar* (68, Stig Bjorkman); *The Girls* (68, Zetterling); *Anna* (70, Donner); *Den Vita Vaggen* (75, Bjorkman); *Monismanien 1955* (75, Kenne Fant); *La Sabina* (79, José Luis Borau); as the kitchen maid in *Fanny and Alexander* (82, Bergman); *Rakenstram* (83, Hellstrom); *Summer Nights* (87, Gunnel Lindblom).

In recent years, she has done *Himmel og Helvede* (88, Morten Arnfred); *Blankt Vapen* (90, Carl-Gustav Nykvist); *Høyere enn Himmelen* (93, Berit Nesheim); *Majken* (95, Kjell-Ake Andersson); *Selma & Johanna* (97, Ingela Magner); *Pip-Larssons* (98, Eva Dahlman and Clas Lindberg); *Det Sjunde Skottet* (98, Ulf Alderinge); *Happy End* (99, Christina Olofson); *Judith* (00, Alexander Moberg); *Gossip* (00, Colin Nutley); *Kaspar i Nudadalen* (01, Asa Kalmer and Maria Weisby); *Stora Teatern* (02, Richard Looft); *Dogville* (03, Lars von Trier).

Dana Andrews (Carver Dana Andrews) (1909–92), b. Collins, Mississippi

By the time he died (only months after his best costar, Gene Tierney), Andrews was not sufficiently remembered as a movie actor. He had been unwell for years—which meant perhaps that he was an alcoholic. His final films were unworthy of him. So there's a need to stress how clever and subtle an actor he was, always at his best playing "ordinary," albeit fallen, guys.

He came to movies rather late, because he was already a qualified accountant and trained singer when he was seen by Goldwyn at the Pasadena Playhouse. Andrews kept as quiet as possible about his singing, and no one would boast in Hollywood about being an accountant. He had ten very good years with Fox (while Goldwyn wasted him), especially as an apparent hero with something to hide. Andrews could suggest unease, shiftiness, and rancor barely concealed by good looks. He did not quite trust or like himself, and so a faraway bitterness haunted him.

He made his screen debut in *Lucky Cisco Kid* (38, Bruce Humberstone), but had his first worthwhile part in *The Westerner* (39, William Wyler). The next few years he worked hard at Fox with occasional pictures for Goldwyn: *Sailor's Lady* (40, Allan Dwan); good in *Swamp Water* (41, Jean Renoir); *Belle Starr* (41, Irving Cummings); *Tobacco Road* (41, John Ford); not quite comfortable as hoodlum Joe Lilac in *Ball of Fire* (42, Howard Hawks)—it was more a Dan Duryea role, and Duryea played his sidekick; *Berlin Correspondent* (42, Eugene Forde); *The North Star* (43, Lewis Milestone); impressively resolute as a doomed man in *The Ox-Bow Incident* (43, William Wellman); *The Purple Heart* (43, Milestone); and *Up in Arms* (44, Elliott Nugent).

Then in 1944 he was exactly cast as the insecure, love-stricken police detective in *Laura* (44, Otto Preminger). Now a leading actor, he was in *State Fair* (45, Walter Lang); *A Walk in the Sun* (46, Milestone); not even nominated for his fine work in *The Best Years of Our Lives* (46, Wyler); *Canyon Passage* (46, Jacques Tourneur); *Boomerang* (47, Elia Kazan); *Night Song* (47, John Cromwell), playing a blind pianist; *The Iron Curtain* (48, Wellman); *No Minor Vices* (48, Milestone); in the J. D. Salinger adaptation *My Foolish Heart* (49, Mark Robson); *Britannia Mews* (49, Jean Negulesco); a priest in *Edge of Doom* (50, Robson); and *I Want You* (50, Robson), the end of his Goldwyn contract.

Preminger alone mined the strain of moral ambiguity in his bearing, the automatic smile and the slur in his voice: as the indecisive con man in *Fallen Angel* (45), the big shot who calls everyone "honeybunch" in *Daisy Kenyon* (47), and the crooked detective in *Where the Sidewalk Ends* (50).

He began to decline, and he was forced farther afield to find small pictures that would have him: *Sealed Cargo* (51, Alfred Werker); *Assignment Paris* (52, Robert Parrish); *Elephant Walk* (53, William Dieterle); *Duel in the Jungle* (54, George Marshall); *Strange Lady in Town* (55, Mervyn Le Roy); *While the City Sleeps* (56, Fritz Lang); ideal again as the lying hero in *Beyond a Reasonable Doubt* (56, Lang); *Night of the Demon* (57, Tourneur); *Zero Hour* (57, Hall Bartlett); and *Enchanted Island* (58, Dwan). He was briefly memorable in *In Harm's Way* (61, Preminger) and as the broken Red Ridingwood in *The Last Tycoon* (76, Kazan). His last films were *Good Guys Wear Black* (77, Ted Post); *The Pilot* (79, Cliff Robertson); and *Prince Jack* (84, Bert Lovitt).

Julie Andrews (Julia Elizabeth Wells), b. Walton-on-Thames, England, 1935

If you can't say something good, don't say nuthin' at all—so Thumper is taught in *Bambi*. (But maybe he turned into a killer rabbit under the stress.) Still, let me declare this: that Julie Andrews is a miracle, an English rose that never withers or pales, and the singing figurehead in two of the most successful films ever made: *The Sound of Music* (64, Robert Wise) and *Mary Poppins* (64, Robert Stevenson). That she makes wholesomeness seem like a terminal condition, that she valiantly resists being interesting, should teach me that many people find enormous pleasure at the movies for reasons that baffle me. Despite those hits, she has never had lasting support—indeed, her stirring (but somehow unstirred) brightness and rectitude resemble Christmas as an occasion all the family can enjoy, qualities that never seem to age.

Of course, she created the role of Eliza on-stage in New York and London for *My Fair Lady*, but was then denied the role in the film because Jack Warner reckoned she was not box office. So Audrey Hepburn got the part, but was not allowed to sing, and a year later, Andrews took the best actress Oscar for *Mary Poppins*. It may be worth adding that the bounty and reassurance of her two films came just as the social order and political optimism were cracking up, like ice floes in the spring.

The rest is very odd: *The Americanization of Emily* (64, Arthur Hiller) was beyond her; *Hawaii* (66, George Roy Hill) was an epic flop; while in *Torn Curtain* (66, Alfred Hitchcock), she simply declined to be sexy, fearful, or excited. *Thoroughly Modern Millie* (67, Hill) put her in the 1920s—she had done *The Boy Friend* on the London and New York stages—and was her last real hit. She played Gertrude Lawrence in *Star!* (68, Wise) and lost, for three hours.

She entered a second marriage, with director Blake Edwards, and began to work only for him. His customary tartness had no evident effect; indeed, it is more likely that she began to lead him to pictures made for Thumper's mother: the large failure of *Darling Lili* (70); *The Tamarind Seed* (74); *10* (79), in which she had to rise above Bo Derek, who sold the picture. She was in *Little Miss Marker* (79, Walter Bernstein); she made a famous baring of her breasts in the caustic but wayward *S.O.B.* (81, Edwards); she gave a good, smart performance in *Victor/Victoria* (82, Edwards); but she could do nothing to save *The Man Who Loved Women* (83, Edwards) or the glorified home movie, *That's Life* (86, Edwards). She worked pluckily as the violinist with multiple sclerosis in *Duet for One* (86, Andrei Konchalovsky), while overlooking the absence of talent or interest. She made *Our Sons* (91, John Erman) for TV.

She looked splendid at sixty-plus, but she had lost her voice and didn't seem unduly interested in working. After all, she's smart enough to know that she's not really an actress—so she did pictures the way the Queen tours, smiling and waving to a lucky public, refusing to notice its shrinkage: with Marcello Mastroianni in *Cin Cin* (91, Gene Saks); with James Garner in *One Special Night* (99, Roger Young); *Relative Values* (00, Eric Styles); reunited with Christopher Plummer in the TV *On Golden Pond* (01, Ernest Thompson); the queen of somewhere or other in the startling hit *The Princess Diaries* (01, Garry Marshall); as Nanny in *Eloise at the Plaza* (03, Kevin Lima).

Pier Angeli (Anna Maria Pierangeli)
(1932–71), b. Cagliari, Sardinia
Pier Angeli was one of the great beauties of the early fifties, but there was a tragic potential in her

melancholy gaze. She was the (or a) beloved of James Dean, but her family disapproved of him. So she married the singer Vic Damone in 1954, but that only lasted a few years. She returned to Europe in the 1960s and was declared a suicide when she was not yet forty, the victim of a drug overdose. She was a great deal more demure and accepting than, say, Jean Seberg, but it's a wonder that her small story hasn't yet been turned into a movie.

The twin sister of Marisa Pavan, she was discovered as a teenager by Léonide Moguy and starred in *Domani È Troppo Tardi* (49, Moguy) and *Domani È un Altro Giorno* (50, Moguy). "Utterly charming and fragile," she was hired by Fred Zinnemann for *Teresa* (50), and that led to an MGM contract. In America, she also made *The Light Touch* (51, Richard Brooks); *The Devil Makes Three* (52, Andrew Marton); *The Story of Three Loves* (53, Gottfried Reinhardt), in which she is a suicidal girl rescued by Kirk Douglas; *Sombrero* (53, Norman Foster); *The Flame and the Flesh* (54, Brooks); *The Silver Chalice* (54, Victor Saville); pretty good as the wife to Rocky Graziano in *Somebody Up There Likes Me* (56, Robert Wise); *Port Afrique* (56, Rudolph Maté); to France for *The Vintage* (57, Jeffrey Hayden); with Danny Kaye in *Merry Andrew* (58, Michael Kidd).

That's when she went back to Europe, and to more halting work: *S.O.S. Pacific* (60, Guy Green); the unlikely wife in *The Angry Silence* (60, Green); *Sodom and Gomorrah* (61, Robert Aldrich); *White Slave Ship* (62, Silvio Amadio), with Edmund Purdom; *Shadow of Evil* (64, André Hunebelle); *Spy in Your Eye* (65, Vittorio Sala); *Battle of the Bulge* (65, Ken Annakin); *One Step to Hell* (68, Sandy Howard); *Every Bastard a King* (70, Uri Zohar), made in Israel; *Octaman* (71, Harry Essex).

Theo Angelopoulos,
b. Athens, Greece, 1936
1968: *I Ekpombi/The Broadcast* (s). 1970: *Anaparastasis/Reconstruction*. 1972: *I Meres tou 36/Days of 36*. 1975: *O Thiassos/The Travelling Players*. 1977: *I Kinighi/The Hunters*. 1980: *O Megalexandros/Alexander the Great*. 1984: *Taxidi stin Kythera/Voyage to Cythera*. 1986: *O Melissokomos/The Beekeeper*. 1989: *Topio stin Omichli/Landscape in the Mist*. 1991: *To Meteoro Vina Tou Pelargou/The Suspended Step of the Stork*. 1995: *To Vlemma ton Odyssea/Ulysses' Gaze;* an episode of *Lumière et Compagnie*. 1998: *Mai Aiwniothta kai mia Mere/Eternity and a Day*.

The movies, or cinema, are nearly one hundred years old. How many of the medium's greatest practitioners are alive and/or still functioning? Bresson, Kurosawa, and Wilder are all gone. Antonioni is in ruined health. Rivette and Godard are working. There are a few others, a little younger, who might claim a place in the pantheon—Bertolucci, Scorsese, Chris Marker, Zhang Yimou, Marcel Ophuls even . . . ? But already, I think, this list has reached below the very top rank. It may be more helpful to be *more* stringent in making the list, in which case let it hold at Antonioni, Rivette . . . and Theo Angelopoulos, who is sixty-six and at work, no matter that he is the least-known director named in this paragraph.

Angelopoulos studied law at the University of Athens, and then film at I.D.H.E.C. in Paris. He was film critic for the Athens paper *Allagi* in the mid-sixties, when he worked on an unfinished feature project known as *Formix Story*.

In the seventies, he made three movies—all lengthy and not slow so much as preoccupied with duration—that addressed the history of modern Greece. *Days of 36* concerns a prisoner who makes a hostage out of a politician who visits his jail. *The Travelling Players* uses a band of actors to uncover Greek history in the years 1936 to 1952. In *The Hunter*, the years from 1949 to 1976 are dealt with through the fablelike incident of a hunting party that discovers a young man's body frozen in the snow.

Preeminently, those films showed the elaboration of one of the cinema's most sophisticated and beautiful "sequence shot" styles, with moving camera. In other words, Angelopoulos's camera tracks almost as constantly and naturally as photography employs light. Early critics said he was like Jancso, but Angelopoulos himself declared that Murnau, Mizoguchi, and Welles were stronger influences. By now, it has become clear that his style is deeply personal and poetic—and, of course, it has to be experienced, for the work is not just plastic but temporal. When Angelopoulos *moves*, he is sailing in time as well as space, and the shifts, the progress, the traveling make a metaphor for history and understanding. (*The Travelling Players* has just eighty shots in four hours.)

This is engrossing cinema, not fast or fluent, yet compelling once its rhythm has been yielded to. Not that Angelopoulos is determined on naturalism. His movies are theatrical, and nearly Brechtian: they are lessons in which "real life" is imposed upon by schema, clearly labeled points of view, and the nearly abstract emphasis on wintry space, desolation, and time spent waiting.

The Travelling Players is a masterpiece that owed a good deal to the political repressiveness of Greece in much of the director's lifetime. As the country has been liberated, so Angelopoulos has moved on to loftier, and more general, themes—to a kind of contemporary mythology.

Voyage to Cythera concerns a filmmaker who wants to make a movie about an elderly political refugee. And so he begins to watch him, and fol-low him, until the old man's life takes on the elements of story. The beauty of the film has seldom been equaled, and the balance of liquid movement and rocklike human interpretation is both tragic and exhilarating.

In *Landscape in the Mist*—the only one of these films to have had any commercial release in the United States—two children travel to a legendary "Germany" searching for their father. This is a story of mythic needs transcending borders, and it may prove an uncanny intuition about the real political/geographical future of Europe. Indeed, there are hints of recent Balkan chaos in *The Suspended Step of the Stork* that make the film more intriguing as time passes. This is a story of a journalist who believes he has discovered a former leading politician who is now living as a humble refugee.

It is hard for anyone to study Angelopoulos properly. The films deserve large screens—but one would settle for wretched video versions. Film culture has come a long way since the days when it was impossible to see "old" films in any form. Nevertheless, it is the case that many people who take the medium seriously have scarcely heard of, let alone encountered, the work of a master. And there are so few masters left now.

Ann-Margret (Ann-Margaret Olsson), b. Valsjöbyn, Sweden, 1941

People everywhere are fondly inclined to Ann-Margret. There does not seem to be an excess of personality in the sixty-year-old. But they remember the very exciting dancer, with such avid eyes, and they rejoice in her survival. Having come to America as a child, she attended Northwestern University and was working in nightclubs as a singer-dancer when George Burns discovered her. (Did this add thirty years to his life?) Most of her early films were wretched, but she was one of the best and most provocative partners Elvis ever had, and she surprised most people with her vulnerability as a sexpot yearning for domesticity in *Carnal Knowledge* (71, Mike Nichols).

Her movies were *Pocketful of Miracles* (61, Frank Capra); *State Fair* (62, José Ferrer); *Bye Bye Birdie* (63, George Sidney); very exciting and commanding in *Viva Las Vegas* (64, Sidney); *Kitten With a Whip* (64, Douglas Heyes); *The Pleasure Seekers* (65, Jean Negulesco); *Bus Riley's Back in Town* (65, Harvey Hart); *Once a Thief* (65, Ralph Nelson); *The Cincinnati Kid* (65, Norman Jewison); *Made in Paris* (66, Boris Sagal); *Stagecoach* (66, Gordon Douglas); *The Swinger* (66, Sidney); *Il Tigre* (67, Dino Risi); *Il Profeta* (68, Risi); *Sette Uomini e un Cervello* (70, Edward Ross); *C.C. and Company* (70, Seymour Robbie); *R.P.M.* (70, Stanley Kramer); *The Train Robbers* (73, Burt Kennedy); *Tommy* (75, Ken Russell); as Lady Booby in *Joseph Andrews* (76, Tony Richardson); *The Last Remake of Beau Geste* (77, Marty Feldman); *Magic* (78, Richard Attenborough).

She had a famous fall from a Las Vegas stage, and came back. She looked after her manager and husband, Roger Smith, when he was ill. And as she approached the age of forty, she was an increasingly impressive beauty. In movies, she might seldom be much more than decoration: *The Cheap Detective* (78, Robert Moore); *The Villain* (79, Hal Needham); *Middle Age Crazy* (80, John Trent); *The Return of the Soldier* (81, Alan Bridges); *I Ought to Be in Pictures* (82, Herbert Ross); *Lookin' to Get Out* (82, Hal Ashby); *Twice in a Lifetime* (85, Bud Yorkin); *52 Pick-Up* (86, John Frankenheimer); *A Tiger's Tale* (87, Peter Douglas); and *A New Life* (88, Alan Alda).

But she has been more eminent on TV, where her castled beauty and the intriguingly shy details of her acting were well suited to the medium, even if she hardly altered from soap opera to Tennessee Williams—she massages disparate scripts into the medium of one magnificently sated look. She has done some big TV productions, all with John Erman as director: as the dying mother in *Who Will Love My Children?* (83); as a soft-focus Blanche in *A Streetcar Named Desire* (84); *The Two Mrs. Grenvilles* (87); and *Our Sons* (91). She was the sweet filling in the sandwich of *Grumpy Old Men* (93, Donald Petrie) and *Grumpier Old Men* (95, Howard Deutsch) and a lush in *Any Given Sunday* (99, Oliver Stone). She also played a woman looking to adopt a Romanian child in *Nobody's Children* (96, David Wheatley).

She was in *Perfect Murder: Perfect Town* (00, Lawrence Schiller); Queen Cinderella in *The 10th Kingdom* (00, David Carson and Herbert Wise); *The Last Producer* (00, Burt Reynolds); *Blonde* (01, Joyce Chopra); *A Woman's a Helluva Thing* (01, Karen Leigh Hopkins); *Interstate 60* (02, Bob Gale).

Jean-Jacques Annaud,
b. Draveil, France, 1943
1977: *Noirs et Blancs en Couleur/Black and White in Color.* 1979: *Coup de Tête.* 1982: *La Guerre du Feu/Quest for Fire.* 1986: *The Name of the Rose.* 1988: *L'Ours/The Bear.* 1992: *L'Amant/The Lover.* 1997: *Seven Years in Tibet.* 2001: *Enemy at the Gates.*

Black and White in Color won the Oscar for best foreign film and was a talking-point movie for people who did not regularly go to the cinema. To this day, Annaud retains a little of that flavor—not so much "international" as coffee table. The fact is that I can hardly recall a thing about *Black and White*, and no more about *Quest for Fire* than the novelty of a movie about Stone Age people. These are ostensibly adventurous choices that soon languish into self-regard. There is a prettiness to the

style that attempts to make up for the absence of real stylistic choices. *The Name of the Rose* is an attempt to assert modish cleverness over atmosphere, and a disaster. The best of the films, I think, is *The Lover*, which holds the tricky, narcissistic emotion of the Marguerite Duras novel and allows literary prestige to be a veil to soft-core sex. *Enemy at the Gates* was a laborious, hollow recreation of war-torn Stalingrad to support a trite, old-fashioned story.

Michelangelo Antonioni,
b. Ferrara, Italy, 1912
1943–47: *Gente del Po* (d). 1948: *N.U. (Nettezza Urbana)* (d). 1949: *L'Amorosa Menzogna* (d); *Superstizione* (d); *Sette Canne un Vestito* (d). 1950: *La Funivia del Faloria* (d); *La Villa dei Mostri* (d); *Cronaca di un Amore.* 1953: *I Vinti; La Signora Senza Camelie;* "Tentato Suicidio," an episode in the film *L'Amore in Citta.* 1955: *Uomini in Piu* (d); *Le Amiche.* 1957: *Il Grido/The Cry.* 1958: *Nel Segno di Roma* (codirected with Riccardo Freda). 1960: *L'Avventura.* 1961: *La Notte.* 1962: *L'Eclisse/The Eclipse.* 1964: *Il Deserto Rosso/The Red Desert.* 1965: "Prefazione," an episode from the film *I Tre Volti.* 1966: *Blow-Up.* 1969: *Zabriskie Point.* 1972: *Chung Kuo* (d). 1975: *The Passenger.* 1980: *Ill Mistero di Oberwald/The Oberwald Mystery.* 1982: *Identificazione di una Donna/Identification of a Woman.* 1995: *Al di là Delle Nuvole/Beyond the Clouds* (codirected with Wim Wenders); "Rome", episode from *12 Registi 12 Citta.*

Antonioni's world of sentimental and metaphysical dismay ought to include just such a figure as himself: a man of vast intellectual sensibility and artistic aspiration; a film director capable of stripping people down to fragile skins that can hardly brush against one another without pain; but a visionary of emotional alienation, so morbidly convinced of the apartness of people that he sometimes ends by photographing figures in a landscape. In short, within a brief time span he veered from psychological exactness to abstraction. For if his suspicions of human dissolution are sound, then films are only an absurd response to the fretful human instinct for self-expression. Even if one cannot always share Antonioni's torment, it has been an engrossing, if humorless, prospect to see him gradually immolate himself with doubts. He is his own character, turned away from us, speechless at what has been lost. As Monica Vitti sighs near the end of *La Notte:* "Each time I have tried to communicate with someone, love has disappeared."

He graduated from the University of Bologna— in economics and business, because a girlfriend was studying those subjects. Writing stories and working in the theatre, he became film critic for *Il*

Corriere Padano and made his first amateur films. He edited *Cinema*, but was fired because he was too leftist for the Fascists. After a short period at Centro Sperimentale, he worked on the scripts of *Un Pilota Ritorna* (42, Roberto Rossellini) and *I Due Foscari* (42, Enrico Fulchignoni). The same year, he went to France to assist Marcel Carné on *Les Visiteurs du Soir.* In the years after the Liberation, he continued as a critic and worked intermittently on *Gente del Po,* a realist documentary on an area of Italy that he would return to for *Il Grido.*

It also inaugurated the feeling for social breakdown that has permeated his work, and that gave a subtly becalmed quality to the realism of his early documentaries. Despite left-wing sympathies, Antonioni's rural and urban documentaries tend to bypass the immediate problems of their subjects to identify a more profound unease. Thus, *N.U.*— about garbagemen—states facts and makes claims that pale beside the listless effect of gray streets. Whatever the verbal message, the visuals had the melancholy of Carné and of German cinema. However, even as this urban alienation grew into a disillusion with all communicative processes, Antonioni has never lost an interest in precise social events. The films with Monica Vitti do constitute a critique of modern Italy; *Blow-Up* is interested in the trite ethics of swinging London, and *Zabriskie Point* springs out of Californian student discontent. It is important to see that in all cases Antonioni's social awareness is based on a cliché view that is easily absorbed into his private lament for breakdown and that is easily diverted into extraneous visual grace. Like Thomas in *Blow-Up,* his later films tastefully ignore the complexities of situations and prefer to photograph the unreliable charm of their surroundings. Thus the eerie park in *Blow-Up* and the desert of *Zabriskie* loom over the human stories.

But the period from *Cronaca di un Amore* to *Il Grido* is triumphant. In those years he managed to discover a fluid, cinematic language to demonstrate the wounding aftermath of love affairs that was more in line with Renoir than Carné and that, incidentally, was the first new demonstration of Astruc's *la caméra-stylo* theory. These films are kept from being morbid by the tender rigor with which the camera traces feelings through actions. They combine a spontaneity of behavior and precision in observation that in *Le Amiche* is masterly. Here is Antonioni's account of how his style evolved out of the creative realization of behavior:

My habit of shooting rather long scenes was born spontaneously on the first day of filming *Cronaca di un Amore.* Having the camera fixed to its stand immediately caused me real discomfort. I felt paralysed, as if I were being prevented from following closely the one thing in the film that interested me: I mean, the charac-

ters. The next day, I called for a dolly, and I began to follow my characters till I felt the need to move on to another exercise. For me, this was the best way to be real, to be true.... I have never succeeded in composing a scene without having the camera with me, nor have I ever been able to make my characters talk in accordance with a pre-established script.... I needed to see the characters, to see even their simplest gestures.

That vitality of gesture ebbed away in the next period, constrained by the tragic posture of love. As Antonioni generalized the failure of love, so he idealized the forlorn woman—embodied in four films by Monica Vitti—and made her increasingly static and abstract. *L'Avventura, La Notte, L'Eclisse,* and *Il Deserto Rosso* become less moving the more urgently Antonioni himself cries out at their plight. They are dispirited films in which the urge for expression is distorted into pictorialism and lethargic compositions of entropy and in which an overall feeling of regret is oddly spiked by a type of visual lust. In *La Notte,* for instance, Jeanne Moreau walks aimlessly through Milan, witnessing the proof of social, emotional, and intellectual disarray. Yet that walk is erotic in the way it restricts her to the status of object. In all those films, but in *La Notte* especially, there is a relentless but hopeless advance on sexual intercourse as the last human action that can be taken. They are brilliant but despondent films, as if Antonioni had extended Renoir's "everyone has their own reason" to "everyone is their own justification." There is a constant, but unacknowledged, conflict between the senselessness of physical things, the elaborate, moribund beauty of the camera movements, and the radiance of Vitti.

But Antonioni was in the process of escaping "mere" melodrama. There is nothing more challenging in *L'Avventura* than the notion that a mystery does not need solving, that the young woman has gone away. A hole has formed in "story" so that life's formless air may seep in. Equally, in *La Notte* and *L'Eclisse,* we feel that there is some gentle force in the city and the world ready to wash over the characters, freeing us from the arid preoccupations of small, private stories. It isn't faith— Antonioni is an anxious unbeliever. Call it light, or continuity. The conclusion of *L'Eclisse*—with the meeting missed and the urban intersection carrying on regardless—is one of the seminal passages in modern cinema. Alas, it makes so much else seem old-fashioned.

There is a suicidal element in these films happily dispelled in *Blow-Up,* the nearest Antonioni has come to humor and a film that shifted his view of human separateness to photography itself— something hinted at in *La Signora Senza Camelie.* *Blow-Up* remains a cold, academic film, but it is lucid and very gripping in the central "dark-room" sequence. It had a bizarre commercial success that enabled Antonioni to make *Zabriskie Point,* his most beautiful inspection of emptiness. Whereas Renoir's films throb with brief understanding and misunderstanding between people, *Zabriskie Point* is a quietist contemplation of figures in a landscape, superbly filmed but as if by one of Don Siegel's body-snatchers. Its people are objects, either relics of a doomed humanist culture or the prelude to a new society in which people regress to the primitive energy of desert creatures. If only because *Zabriskie* is so cool, it demands attention. Indeed, there is a sly comparison between the "blow-ups" in *Blow-Up* and *Zabriskie Point*. In the first, the enlarged photographs illustrate the way human beings impose their instinct for meaning on external reality. While in the latter, the repeated explosions of the desert home—deprived of the violence by silence—speak for the helpless sterility of material things: not just of material goods, but the irrelevant accumulation of things that have no interior significance.

The desert is a philosophy in *The Passenger,* one of the great films of the seventies. Melodrama and regret are replaced by the serene faith in a world of light, space, and providence. The steady attempt of the camera to move away from people seems a truly mystical claim. *The Passenger* leaves no doubt about Antonioni's mastery, and radically advances on the earlier disquiet. The final sequence at the Hotel de la Gloria is the affirmation toward which Antonioni was always traveling. It inhales a warm, idle universe beyond intrigue, as if the movie were about space travel.

The Oberwald Mystery was shot on video, allowing for many experiments with color; it was both an adaptation of Cocteau's *L'Aigle à Deux Têtes* and a vehicle for Monica Vitti. *Identification of a Woman* deals with a movie director in search of both a wife and a new female character: it has elements of psychological thriller, and it is also an extension of his series of films that question identity in the modern world and that seem to hover on the brink of some ultimate memory loss. Few directors have been more affected by the nature and capacity of the camera. *Identification* has moments of oversolemnity, but it is the work of a great director, and seemingly his last—for Antonioni's future projects came to nothing, and now he was beset by the effects of a stroke. Yet again, the predicament of the world's greatest living filmmaker unable to work is a fit subject for one of his meditations. Only Bertolucci or Angelopoulos could attempt it.

The enigmas in Antonioni's work are as subject to time as monuments are to erosion, and the achievements of some films can offset or explain the apparent, or early, limits of others. For example, *The Passenger* helped us see the longing for escape and space in *L'Avventura,* and illumined the persistence of life at the end of *L'Eclisse.* I suspect that Antonioni's best films will continue to grow and shift, like dunes in the centuries of desert. In that process, if there are eyes left to look, he will become a standard for beauty.

He was the victim of a stroke in the early nineties, but still inclined to work. *Beyond the Clouds*—done with Wim Wenders at his shoulder—indicated a real decline. *Destinazione Verna* (based on material by Jack Finney, who wrote the novel *The Body Snatchers*) has hardly been seen.

Michael Apted,

b. Aylesbury, England, 1941

1963: *7 Up* (as assistant director) (d). 1968: *Number 10* (TV). 1972: *Another Sunday and Sweet F.A.* (TV). 1973: *Triple Echo/Soldier in Skirts.* 1974: *Kisses at Fifty* (TV); *Stardust.* 1976: *The Collection* (TV); *The Squeeze* (TV); *21* (TV) (d). 1977: *Stronger Than the Sun* (TV). 1979: *Agatha.* 1980: *Coal Miner's Daughter.* 1981: *Continental Divide.* 1982: *Kipperbang* (TV). 1983: *Gorky Park.* 1985: *28 Up* (d); *Firstborn; Bring on the Night* (d). 1987: *Critical Condition.* 1988: *Gorillas in the Mist.* 1989: *The Long Way Home* (TV). 1991: *Class Action; 35 Up* (d); *Incident at Oglala* (d). 1992: *Thunderheart.* 1994: *Blink.* 1996: *Extreme Measures.* 1997: *Inspirations* (d); 1998: *Always Outnumbered* (TV); *42 Up* (d), 1999: *Me & Isaac Newton* (d); *The World Is Not Enough; Nathan Dixon* (TV). 2001: *Enigma.* 2002: *Enough.* 2002: *Married in America* (TV).

Educated at City of London School and Cambridge, Apted trained with Granada TV and went on to work on *World of Action* and *Coronation Street.* He directed many films/plays for British TV before he broke into features in 1973. Yet he has never given up on television or documentaries. He has done commercials and he has produced several projects for cable in America.

Apted is not just an Englishman who has made an unusual commitment to American regionalism. He was born eight days before I was, and only fifty miles away—so I try to keep up with him. But since Apted's interests are so varied, and his personality so fleeting, this is no easy task. We have only to note that, in 1998, he put together the latest installment in his survey of a group of English lives *and* the latest James Bond movie with equal fairness, never letting one part of his mind judge the other.

That is barely the beginning. In successive years, Apted did what he could to handle that odd English mystery about the brief disappearance of Agatha Christie, *and* directed *Coal Miner's Daughter* without being glaringly un-American.

Throw in a very bad Richard Pryor film, *Critical Condition,* that fetching mix of documentary and career-woman melodrama, *Gorillas in the Mist,* and you can see how hard it is to account for Apted.

In truth, I do not detect more than proficient execution in his feature films. Apted's most lasting work is the series of English documentaries, begun when he was an assistant on the program *World In Action* and continued with *21, 28, 35,* and *42 Up.* I'm not sure how many more of the series I want to see: many lives, but English lives especially, gather sadness as they grow older, and Apted is stuck with the people he found at the outset. How many are ready to die on-screen? How far could Apted's rather removed, polite scrutiny stand up to all that demise? Still, the series was a great idea, and anyone hoping to understand England should watch the films. *28 Up* is the best of the bunch, probably because the people have energies and hopes still to burn.

I have to wonder whether Apted can yet find a way to deliver himself on-screen with something like the desperate or exuberant force that drives some of the people in that series. Or is he really just a calm, faithful watcher?

By the end of the nineties, he was was widening his documentary interests, keeping faith with his original English kids (and they were turning out pretty well), being prepared to make a Walter Mosley novel for television, and then getting the prize of a Bond film. *The World Is Not Enough* was no better or worse than the others, but it was clearer than ever that the *7 Up* series was a labor of love and enlightenment for all.

Roscoe (Fatty) **Arbuckle** (1887–1933),
b. Smith Center, Kansas

On Labor Day, 1921, in San Francisco, Roscoe Arbuckle, actor Lowell Sherman, and Freddy Fishback gave a party. Hollywood parties of that era were often uninhibited, and the movie colony either deserved or aped its own reputation for wild living. This party drifted on for a couple of days and no one has ever accused it of being good clean fun. But a model, Virginia Rappe, died and, after initial accusations of rape and murder, Arbuckle was charged with manslaughter. The case against him was always thin, but he was a juicy suspect and two juries failed to reach a verdict before the third acquitted him, in March 1922, and went out of its way to remark, "We feel that a great injustice has been done to him. . . . Roscoe Arbuckle is entirely innocent and free from all blame." But you had only to look at Arbuckle to know that, in many ways, he was far from innocent; the combined forces of scandal-mongery and puritanism would not be dissuaded. Arbuckle was made a scapegoat, as though after calling a man "Fatty" for years and rejoicing at his

humiliation on film the public could only move in on him with trained hostility. The Hearst press led the campaign against him, ensuring that many moviehouses boycotted his films. Will Hays then put pressure on Arbuckle's immediate employers, Joseph Schenck and Adolph Zukor, and he was barred from acting in movies again.

Thus the fat owl of the silent screen was removed, and this early spasm of rejection showed how fickle the public's faith in its stars could be. The moral realities of Hollywood life were something the public hardly dreamed of; even so, one hint was enough to furnish it with nightmares that demanded cleansing action. Arbuckle's own exaggerated ugliness drew upon him all the public's hypocritical loathing of depravity. For some seven years he had been one of the leading figures in comedy. From vaudeville, he had gone to Keystone in 1909. By 1913, Sennett was giving him leading parts so that he was the featured player at the studio when Chaplin arrived from Britain. By 1914 he was directing his own films—one- or two-reelers, often in the company of Mabel Normand: *Fatty and the Heiress; Fatty's Finish; An Incompetent Hero; Fatty's Wine Party; Leading Lizzie Astray; Fatty's Magic Pants;* and *Fatty and Minnie-He-Haw.* He also appeared in some of the Chaplin films at Keystone: *A Film Johnnie; The Knock-Out; The Masquerader;* and *The Rounders* (14). Fatty stayed at Keystone for two years after Chaplin's departure: *Mabel and Fatty's Wash Day; Fatty and Mabel's Simple Life; Mabel, Fatty and the Law; Mabel and Fatty's and Married Life; Fatty's Reckless Fling; Mabel and Fatty Viewing the World's Fair at San Francisco, Cal.;* and *Fickle Fatty's Fall* (15); *Fatty and Mabel Adrift; He Did and He Didn't; His Wife's Mistake; His Alibi;* and *A Cream Puff Romance* (16). In 1917, Arbuckle and Schenck formed the Comique Film Corporation with Fatty continuing to direct his own films. Mabel Normand did not go with him, but Fatty recruited the young Buster Keaton who appeared in a run of Arbuckle comedies: *The Butcher Boy; Rough House; His Wedding Night; Fatty at Coney Island; Oh Doctor!; Out West* (17); *The Bell Boy; Goodnight Nurse; Moonshine; The Cook* (18); *A Desert Hero; Backstage;* and *The Garage* (19). In 1920, Fatty made *A Country Hero* and in 1921 he played in *The Dollar-a-Year Man* (James Cruze) before disaster befell him.

Legend has it that Keaton cushioned some of the fall for Fatty—just as he often had in slapstick—by keeping him in funds and suggesting that he direct, under the name of "Will B. Goode." In 1927—as William Goodrich—he directed Marion Davies in *The Red Mill* for Cosmopolitan (Hearst's company—such is the stamina of scandal) and Eddie Cantor in *Special Delivery* for Paramount. Apart from that, he made educational films until 1931, when he directed some comedy shorts for Warners: *Smart Work; Windy Riley Goes to Hollywood* (31); *Keep Laughing; Moonlight and Cactus; Anybody's Goat; Bridge Wives; Hollywood Luck; Mother's Holiday;* and *It's a Cinch* (32). He died in New York in 1933 still fat, but Fatty forgotten.

Fanny Ardant, b. Monte Carlo, 1949

François Truffaut fell in love with Fanny Ardant in 1979, on television, when he saw her play the lead in the miniseries *Les Dames de la Côte*. She was the daughter of a soldier, who was advising the royal family of Monaco at the time of her birth. A study of political science led her astray—to the theatre—and in the seventies she became a notable figure on the Parisian stage in works by Racine, Claudel, and Montherlant. She appeared first on TV in 1978 in *Les Memoires de Deux Jeunes Mariées*, adapted from Balzac.

Truffaut's love was real, even if the small screen had prompted it. He liked "her large mouth, her deep voice and its unusual intonations, her big black eyes and her triangular face," and she became not just the muse of his final years, but his lover and companion, and the mother of his last daughter.

She made her movie debut in *Les Chiens* (79, Alain Jessua) and then in *Les Uns et les Autres* (81, Claude Lelouch), before doing her first film for Truffaut, *La Femme d'à Côté* (81), with Gerard Depardieu. Then she did *La Vie est un Roman* (83, Alain Resnais); the fond secretary in *Vivement Dimanche!* (83, Truffaut); *Benvenuta* (83, André Delvaux); *Swann in Love* (84, Volker Schlondorff); *L'Amour à Mort* (84, Resnais); *Les Enragés* (85, Pierre-William Glenn); *L'Été Prochain* (85, Nadine Trintignant); the wife in *Family Business* (86, Costa-Gavras); *Le Paltoquet* (86, Michel Deville); *Mélo* (86, Resnais); *The Family* (87, Ettore Scola); *Paura e Amore* (88, Margarethe von Trotta); *Pleure Pas My Love* (88, Tony Gatlif); *Australia* (89, Jean-Jacques Andrien); *Afraid of the Dark* (92, Mark Peploe); *The Deserter's Wife* (93, Michel Bat-Adam); *Amok* (93, Joel Farges); *Colonel Chabert* (94, Yves Angelou); *Sabrina* (95, Sydney Pollack); *Beyond the Clouds* (95, Michelangelo Antonioni and Wim Wenders); very handsome still in *Ridicule* (96, Patrice Leconte); *Pédale Douce* (97, Gabriel Aghion); *Elizabeth* (98, Shekhar Kapur); *La Cena* (98, Scola); the mistress to *Balzac* (99, Josée Dayan); *La Débandade* (99, Claude Berri); *Le Fils du Français* (99, Gérard Lauzier); *Le Libertin* (00, Aghion); *Change-Moi Ma Vie* (01, Liria Begeja); *Callas Forever* (01, Franco Zeffirelli); *8 Femmes* (02, François Ozon); *Sin Noticias de Dios* (02, Agustín Díaz Yanes); *Nathalie X* (03, Anne Fontaine).

Eve Arden (Eunice Quedens) (1912–90), b. Mill Valley, California

"Where's Eve Arden?" a couple of very good friends wondered about earlier editions. And I can't stand to leave the question unanswered, no matter that more pressing claims might be mounted for the merits of Binnie Barnes or Gladys Cooper. . . . Eve Arden *is* here, essential, one of the great deliverers of sour lines, capable of decking Katharine Hepburn or Groucho, a model of disbelieving yet enduring intelligence.

At sixteen she was in traveling theatre in northern California, and by the age of twenty she was in the Ziegfeld Follies. She made a couple of pictures under her real name—*The Song of Love* (29, Earle C. Kenton) and *Dancing Lady* (33, Robert Z. Leonard)—before she came up with her new name (Joan Crawford, briefly, had been Joan Arden). She was several years on Broadway, doing *Very Warm for May* and *Two for the Show*, but by the late thirties her movie identity was established—knowing eyes, sarcastic voice, in roles slightly off to the side which enlivened any picture: *Oh, Doctor* (37, Ray McCarey); handling Hepburn's loftiness in *Stage Door* (37, Gregory La Cava); *Cocoanut Grove* (38, Alfred Santell); *Letter of Introduction* (38, John M. Stahl); *Having Wonderful Time* (38, Santell); *Woman in the Wind* (39, John Farmer); *Big Town Czar* (39, Arthur Lubin); *The Forgotten Woman* (39, Harold Young); *Eternally Yours* (39, Tay Garnett); *At the Circus* (39, Edward L. Buzzell); *A Child Is Born* (40, Lloyd Bacon); *Slightly Honorable* (40, Garnett); *Comrade X* (40, King Vidor); *No, No Nanette* (40, Herbert Wilcox); *Ziegfeld Girl* (41, Leonard); *That Uncertain Feeling* (41, Ernst Lubitsch); *She Knew All the Answers* (41, Richard Wallace); *San Antonio Rose* (41, Charles Lamont); *Manpower* (41, Raoul Walsh); and *Bedtime Story* (41, Alexander Hall).

She was in *Cover Girl* (44, Charles Vidor); she got a supporting actress nomination as Ida in *Mildred Pierce* (45, Michael Curtiz); *My Reputation* (46, Curtis Bernhardt); *The Kid from Brooklyn* (46, Norman Z. McLeod); *Night and Day* (46, Curtiz); *Song of Scheherazade* (47, Walter Reisch); *The Arnelo Affair* (47, Arch Oboler); *The Unfaithful* (47, Vincent Sherman); *The Voice of the Turtle* (47, Irving Rapper); *One Touch of Venus* (48, William A. Seiter); *My Dream Is Yours* (49, Curtiz); *The Lady Takes a Sailor* (49, Curtiz); *Paid in Full* (50, William Dieterle); *Tea for Two* (50, David Butler); *Goodbye My Fancy* (51, Sherman); and *We're Not Married* (52, Edmund Goulding).

Branching out, in 1948, she had created the character of the wisecracking teacher, Connie Brooks, on radio in *Our Miss Brooks*. It ran on CBS until 1956, and in 1952 a TV series began—a big hit—that lasted until 1956 and won Arden an

Emmy. Finally, there was a movie, *Our Miss Brooks* (56, Al Lewis).

That was her peak, but she was a very droll secretary in *Anatomy of a Murder* (59, Otto Preminger); *The Dark at the Top of the Stairs* (60, Delbert Mann); *Sergeant Deadhead* (65, Norman Taurog); nicely cast as the school principal in *Grease* (78, Randal Kleiser) and *Grease II* (82, Patricia Birch).

Alan Arkin, b. New York, 1934

In the early sixties, Arkin seemed a hugely promising newcomer—a comic, yet a serious actor, who had been part of Chicago's Second City group and a great success on Broadway in *Enter Laughing*. Then he got an Oscar nomination in his first film as the Russian submariner ashore in the U.S. in *The Russians Are Coming! The Russians Are Coming!* (66, Norman Jewison). Next he was truly scary as the villain in *Wait Until Dark* (67, Terence Young). But he was maybe too clever, or too easily diverted from being one strong self. As he worked on, his reputation clouded: *Woman Times Seven* (67, Vittorio de Sica); nominated again as the deaf-mute in *The Heart Is a Lonely Hunter* (68, Robert Ellis Miller); trying to replace Peter Sellers in *Inspector Clouseau* (68, Bud Yorkin); with Second City in *The Monitors* (69, Jack Shea); and *Popi* (69, Arthur Hiller).

He was Yossarian in *Catch-22* (70, Mike Nichols), which might have made him if enough of Heller's humor had been captured. Decline began early, despite the somber *Little Murders* (71), which he also directed; *Last of the Red Hot Lovers* (72, Gene Saks), a disaster; with James Caan in *Freebie and the Bean* (74, Richard Rush); adrift in *Rafferty and the Gold Dust Twins* (75, Dick Richards); very funny as the movie director in *Hearts of the West* (75, Howard Zieff), but clearly now a supporting player.

He played Freud in *The Seven Per-Cent Solution* (76, Herbert Ross); he acted in and directed *Fire Sale* (77), a serious failure; to Canada for *Improper Channels* (79, Eric Till); good with Peter Falk in *The In-Laws* (79, Hiller); *The Magician of Lublin* (79, Menahem Golan); good in the black comedy *Simon* (80, Marshall Brickman); *Chu Chu and the Philly Flash* (81, David Lowell Rich); with his son Adam in *Full Moon High* (81, Larry Cohen).

In general, Arkin has been in too many minor films: *Deadhead Miles* (72, Vernon Zimmerman); *The Return of Captain Invincible* (83, Philippe Mora); *Bad Medicine* (85, Harvey Miller); *Big Trouble* (85, John Cassavetes), with Falk again; as the father in *Joshua Then and Now* (85, Ted Kotcheff), his best film in years; *Coupe de Ville* (90, Joe Roth); *Edward Scissorhands* (90, Tim Burton); *Havana* (90, Sydney Pollack); *The Rocketeer* (91, Joe Johnston); and brilliant in one cross-talk scene with Ed Harris in *Glengarry Glen Ross* (92, James Foley).

He was in the baseball story *Cooperstown* (93, Charles Haid); *Taking the Heat* (93, Tom Mankiewicz); *So I Married an Axe Murderer* (93, Thomas Schlamme); he directed a short, *Samuel Beckett Is Coming Soon* (93); *Indian Summer* (93, Mike Binder); *North* (94, Rob Reiner); on TV in *Doomsday Gun* (94, Robert Young); *The Jerky Boys* (95, James Melkonian); *Steal Big, Steal Little* (95, Andrew Davis); *Mother Night* (96, Keith Gordon); *Heck's Way Home* (96, Michael J. F. Scott); *Grosse Pointe Blank* (97, George Armitage); very good in *Four Days in September* (97, Bruno Barretto); *Gattaca* (97, Andrew Niccol); *Slums of Beverly Hills* (98, Tamara Jenkins); *Jakob the Liar* (99, Peter Kassovitz); on TV in *Blood Money* (99, Aaaron Lipstadt) and *Varian's War* (00, Lionel Chetwynd) and directing *Arigo* (00).

He appeared on TV in *100 Centre Street* (01, Jerry London and Sidney Lumet); *America's Sweethearts* (01, Joe Roth); *Thirteen Conversations About One Thing* (01, Jill Sprecher); *Forest Hills Bob* (01, Robert Downey Sr); *Counting Sheep* (01, Neal Miller); *The Pentagon Papers* (03, Rod Holcomb).

Samuel Z. (Zachary) Arkoff, (1918–2001), b. Fort Dodge, Iowa

The death of Samuel Arkoff was greeted with genuine regret and fondness. In so many respects—not least his choice of extra-long cigars and scornful talk about the artsy-fartsies—he was a caricature of the movie mogul. Yet few were as consistently modest in their aim, or as successful in their results. Indeed, Arkoff cast shame on those many better-known executives who have sought to make a fortune and great art in pictures. The fortune was all he wanted, or said he wanted. But beneath the cigar haze and the mocking manner, there was a huge love of movies—so long as they stayed vulgar, sensational, and silly.

It should be remembered that for Arkoff, going into the business was a life-or-death matter. He was the son of Russian immigrants who owned a clothing store. But he was a very bright kid who fell in love with pictures. He had nearly graduated from the University of Iowa when Pearl Harbor happened. He entered the services (cheating his way in, for he was overweight already), and he became a cryptographer. After the war, he read law at Loyola and had formed an entertainment law company when he was struck down by a cerebral hemorrhage that put him in a coma for seven days.

When he woke up, he didn't blame excessive eating or smoking; he reckoned it was the result of denying his great dream—to make movies. Thus, in 1954, with James H. Nicholson, he founded the American Releasing Corporation (it soon became

American International Pictures). Their trick was to see that after the anti-monopoly laws of the early fifties there was room for new distributors, as well as a need for B pictures, or the bottom halves of double bills, as the big studios retreated from that form. AIP rode the wave of youth culture and the drive-in theatre, and it pursued several lines: cheap horror and sci-fi; epics purchased from Italy or Spain and dubbed into English; beaches and bikinis; and eventually bikers and drugs. They loved hair-raising titles, kids who would act for next to nothing and ditto directors. AIP would become not just the factory for *I Was a Teenage Werewolf* (57, Gene Fowler Jr.); *Hot Rod Girl* (56, Leslie H. Martinson); *How to Stuff a Wild Bikini* (65, William H. Asher); and *Beach Blanket Bingo* (65, Asher), but a training ground for Roger Corman, Francis Coppola, Peter Bogdanovich, Martin Scorsese, John Milius, Robert Towne, Jack Nicholson, Woody Allen (*What's Up, Tiger Lily?*), and so many others of that rich and irreverent generation.

At the time, of course, there were those who said that AIP warped young minds—but it also trained some great young talents, and it trusted that in certain hackneyed and fatuous genres there was room for personality and fresh ideas. The story goes that Arkoff always regretted haggling with Peter Fonda and Dennis Hopper so much that they went off on their own road in *Easy Rider.* But if it had stayed an Arkoff picture it might have been better, and a good deal less pretentious.

It is true that Arkoff reckoned the movie was just a thing to make money on and have fun with—and he may have been right. The mind should be formed by other things—like family, education, and experience. The real warping of movie minds came when some people looked at *Easy Rider* and reckoned it was art, as well as a pile of money. You can have Goldwyn, Selznick, and Zanuck; no one kept to their mission more single-mindedly than Arkoff and Nicholson.

Arletty (Léonie Bathiat) (1898–1992),
b. Courbevoie, France
Long before movies, Arletty had worked in a munitions factory and as a fashion model. She posed for Braque and Matisse; she became a pacifist when her lover was killed in the First World War; and she played a wide range of roles on the stage.

She never made a lot of films, and she had a droll, distant air in many of them. Even her most famous parts, as in *Le Jour se Lève* (39, Marcel Carné), are actually very slight. And the fact that she is the most sane, least depressed character in *Le Jour se Lève* sets her farther apart. She is redundant to the plot, there only to explain how wicked Jules Berry is and to afford Gabin some

passing solace. She is admirably dry, without ever sacrificing amusement or tenderness. Her enigmatic, fatalistic warmth was better employed as Garance—the spirit of popular theatre—in *Les Enfants du Paradis* (44, Carné). Even there, Arletty was ready to be like a leaf blown on the winds of romance. At forty-five, she seemed like a very wise girl still.

She did not make films until 1930: *Un Chien qui Rapporte* (Jean Choux). It was a few years before Carné and Sacha Guitry promoted her to leading parts: very good in *Pension Mimosas* (35, Jacques Feyder); *Faisons un Rêve* (36, Guitry); *Les Perles de la Couronne* (37, Guitry); *Désiré* (38, Guitry); *Hôtel du Nord* (38, Carné); *Fric-Frac* (39, Claude Autant-Lara); *Madame Sans-Gêne* (41, Roger Richebé); and *Les Visiteurs du Soir* (42, Carné).

During the Second World War, she had a love affair with a Luftwaffe officer, and thus she was jailed as a collaborator when *Les Enfants du Paradis* opened—life competing with Jacques Prévert's taste for irony.

She was in Carné's uncompleted *La Fleur de l'Age* in 1947, and she had triumphs on the stage in *A Streetcar Named Desire* and *Huis-Clos.* But she made fewer films: *L'Amour Madame* (52, Gilles Grangier); *Le Grand Jeu* (53, Robert Siodmak); *Huis-Clos* (54, Jacqueline Audry); with Gabin again in *L'Air de Paris* (54, Carné); and *La Gamberge* (62, Norbert Carbonnaux).

In 1966, she was stricken with blindness—cruel fate for those very wary eyes. But in 1971, she wrote a book of memoirs, *La Défense,* and lived to be ninety-four.

George Arliss (1868–1946),
b. London, England
The two most unlikely stars of the early thirties—and both of them won Oscars—were George Arliss and Marie Dressler. (Imagine them together!) Maybe he was the odder: an old-fashioned British character actor who was sixty-one when he released the first of a series of Hollywood hits. It was *Disraeli* (1929), a role he had played on stage across America for five years. (This was the part for which he won the third Oscar for an actor—the award was for *The Green Goddess,* too.) Other impersonations of famous historical characters were to follow: *Alexander Hamilton* (1931), *Voltaire* (1933), Wellington in *The Iron Duke* (1934), *Cardinal Richelieu* (1935). There's no point naming the directors of these movies, because everything about them centers on Arliss, and he was in control of every aspect of their filming—that's clear from his second autobiography, *My Ten Years in the Studio,* which is short on detail but long on good-natured atmosphere. Bette Davis confirms his authority in her own autobiography: not only did Arliss personally

choose her for his film *The Man Who Played God* (1932)—at the close of their interview he says, " 'The part is yours. Go to the casting office right away'—but Mr. Arliss personally augmented my direction, supervised my makeup and wardrobe, and showed me every conceivable consideration. It may have been a Warner Bros. Film, but Mr. Arliss (as he was always called) was in charge.' "

You can tell his Disraeli from his Voltaire because the former has a spit curl on his forehead and the latter wears a mobcap, and it's in the scrupulous deployment of makeup and costume that Arliss shines. Not that he stints as an actor—he gives it all he's got, and though that's often far too much, it's honest work; he believes in these creations, and he has great charm if you don't mind its calculated quality. Actually, what you're seeing here is the last traces of English stage acting from the turn of the century—Arliss grew up the hard way in the British theatre, in rep companies for many years before cracking the West End and going on to stardom, a story that's charmingly told in volume 1 of his memoirs, *Up the Years from Bloomsbury*. He came to America early in the century in a company led by Mrs. Patrick Campbell and stayed on—neither the first nor the last English actor to make a bigger career in America. During the twenties, he starred in half a dozen silent films, several of which were based on his stage successes and which he then remade in sound: a *Disraeli* in 1921; *The Man Who Played God* in 1922; and his huge hit by William Archer, *The Green Goddess*, in 1923. The sound version, released in 1930 but actually filmed before the sound version of *Disraeli*, has him in dark skin, jeweled turban, and sinister smile as a crafty rajah—it's so stage-ridden you want to shout out "Curtain!" at key scene-ending lines.

The historical films alternate with jovial-old-man comedies (the best of them *Old English* in 1930), in which Arliss is all-knowing and twinkling with benevolence, usually toward a young couple in romantic difficulties. (Disraeli, Voltaire, and Richelieu also find time to play Cupid to young romance.) Well, you couldn't really have the supremely unsexy elderly Arliss in love stories, though there's an aborted marriage to Bette Davis in *The Man Who Played God*. He's a concert pianist deafened by a bomb explosion, she's a noble young thing who pretends to love him, but he discovers (by reading her lips through binoculars, of course) that she's sacrificing herself, and he frees her. In fact, Arliss's greatest contribution to the movies may have been his championing of Davis at a crucial moment in her young and failing career—he also demanded her presence in *The Working Man* (1932). The young, appealing Davis slashes through these minor, stagy movies like a glittering creature from an alien planet; the screen shimmers with real movie allure whenever she turns up.

In 1934, Darryl Zanuck brought Arliss to the new Twentieth Century for his best film, *The House of Rothschild*. This is a real *movie*, with energy and sweep, that happens to star Arliss (in a double role), not just a filmed vehicle; it's got an intelligent script by Nunnally Johnson, with Alfred Werker directing, and a strong supporting cast—Loretta Young and Robert Young as the obligatory young lovers, Helen Westley as the Rothschild matriarch, C. Aubrey Smith as Wellington, and an extraordinary Boris Karloff as the anti-Semitic Prussian Count Ledrantz. Probably the film most ardently sympathetic to Jews to come out of Hollywood in the thirties, *The House of Rothschild* was made by Gentiles—Arliss, Zanuck, Johnson.

The other Zanuck production featuring Arliss, *Cardinal Richelieu* (35, Rowland V. Lee), is another big historical drama, with the star in perfect Richelieu drag. These two movies show the studio launched on its path to epics like *The Rains Came*, while Warners went on to develop its own kind of inspirational biopics, like *The Story of Louis Pasteur* and *Dr. Ehrlich's Magic Bullet*. But then Paul Muni and Edward G. Robinson were echt Warners actors; Arliss represented English Class in a manner highly unsymptomatic of this grittiest of studios.

The Arliss phenomenon—and it was real—had about six good years, then petered out back in England with *Doctor Syn* (Roy William Neill) in 1937. By then he had been acting for more than fifty years and had had enough.

Gillian Armstrong,
b. Melbourne, Australia, 1950
1973: *Gretel* (d); *One Hundred a Day* (s); *Satdee Night* (s). 1975: *Smokes and Lillies* (s). 1976: *The Singer and the Dancer*. 1979: *My Brilliant Career*. 1980: *A Busy Kind of Bloke* (s); *Fourteen's Good, Eighteen's Better* (s). 1982: *Starstruck*. 1984: *Mrs. Soffel*. 1987: *High Tide*. 1988: *Bingo, Bridesmaids and Braces* (s). 1991: *Fires Within*. 1992: *The Last Days of Chez Nous*. 1994: *Little Women*. 1997: *Oscar and Lucinda*. 2001: *Charlotte Gray*.

This is one of the more entertaining careers around today, lit up by a series of documentary shorts on Australian girls growing up that is derived from Michael Apted's pictures about Britain. Armstrong has lived through being regarded as "Australian" and a woman; as someone especially intrigued by period and modern stories, comedy or drama. In truth, she has all those sides to her, and more. She has shown steady development, and it may be that she only needs the right conjunction of star and material to become recognized as a major director. In fact, she's already done one major film—*Mrs. Soffel*—one of those mercies in the grim eighties that went largely unnoticed by audiences. It's a great, strange love story, and the best work by Diane Keaton and Mel Gibson.

Actors invariably do well for Armstrong—Judy Davis (despite her scorn for *My Brilliant Career*), Lisa Harrow, Winona Ryder, and Cate Blanchett. Her *Little Women* seemed like the work of a feminist who had "settled down," but *Charlotte Gray* proved a big disappointment: despite valiant work by Blanchett and Michael Gambon, it never made me feel the violent shifts said to be occurring in its heroine.

Edward Arnold (Günther Edward Arnold Schneider) (1890–1956), b. New York

Around the age of forty-five, Edward Arnold became one of the most intriguing of supporting actors. He was large and seemingly good-natured. But a few films took him to a more sinister point, as a domineering boss figure, very rich, very powerful, very corrupt—just see how he moves in *Mr. Smith Goes to Washington* (39, Frank Capra) or *Meet John Doe* (41, Capra). That is a man who expects to be obeyed, and who has the arrogance that reckons it deserves power. He had charm and authority, and even as more simply jovial characters Arnold was a man to watch: for example, Louis XIII in *Cardinal Richelieu* (35, Rowland V. Lee); the policeman going after Peter Lorre in *Crime and Punishment* (35, Josef von Sternberg); *Diamond Jim* (35, Edward Sutherland); excellent and touching as the timber tycoon in *Come and Get It* (36, Howard Hawks and William Wyler); the millionaire in *Easy Living* (37, Mitchell Leisen); *Idiot's Delight* (39, Clarence Brown); as Diamond Jim Brady again to Alice Faye's *Lillian Russell* (40, Irving Cummings); and Daniel Webster in *The Devil and Daniel Webster* (41, William Dieterle).

It sounds unlikely, but Arnold had been a cowboy star in the years 1915–19. He turned to theatre and only really took up movies again in the early thirties: *Okay America* (32, Tay Garnett); *Rasputin and the Empress* (32, Richard Boleslavsky); *The Barbarian* (33, Sam Wood); *I'm No Angel* (33, Wesley Ruggles); *Jennie Gerhardt* (33, Marion Gering); *Roman Scandals* (33, Frank Tuttle); *The White Sister* (33, Victor Fleming); *Biography of a Bachelor Girl* (34, Edward Griffith); *The President Vanishes* (34, William Wellman); *Sadie McKee* (34, Brown); *Thirty Day Princess* (34, Gering); *The Glass Key* (35, Tuttle); *Remember Last Night?* (35, James Whale); as the detective in *Meet Nero Wolfe* (36, Herbert Biberman); *Sutter's Gold* (36, James Cruze); *John Meade's Woman* (37, Richard Wallace); *The Toast of New York* (37, Rowland V. Lee);

The Crowd Roars (38, Richard Thorpe); *You Can't Take It With You* (38, Capra); *Let Freedom Ring* (39, Jack Conway); *Man About Town* (39, Mark Sandrich); *The Earl of Chicago* (40, Richard Thorpe); and *Johnny Apollo* (40, Henry Hathaway).

By, say, 1946, Walter Brennan had won the supporting actor Oscar three times, while Claude Rains had had four nominations. I cherish both of them—but Arnold had earned nothing. And, sadly, from the early forties onward he went into hardworking decline—he ran out of good parts, and suffered badly from being based at MGM: *Design for Scandal* (41, Norman Taurog); *Johnny Eager* (41, Mervyn Le Roy); with Bob Hope in *Nothing But the Truth* (41, Elliott Nugent); *The Penalty* (41, Harold S. Bucquet); *Unholy Partners* (41, Le Roy); as a blind detective in *Eyes in the Night* (42, Fred Zinnemann) and *The Hidden Eye* (45, Richard Whorf); *The Youngest Profession* (43, Edward Buzzell); *Jamie* (44, Michael Curtiz); *Kismet* (44, Dieterle); *Mrs. Parkington* (44, Garnett); *Weekend at the Waldorf* (45, Robert Z. Leonard); *My Brother Talks to Horses* (46, Buzzell); *Ziegfeld Follies* (46, Vincente Minnelli); *Dear Ruth* (47, William D. Russell); *The Hucksters* (47, Jack Conway); and *Big City* (48, Taurog).

These are the years of film noir, when surely Arnold could have served as authoritative villains. But he was misplaced, and the list is horribly short of interest: *Command Decision* (48, Wood); *Three Daring Daughters* (48, Fred M. Wilcox); *John Loves Mary* (49, David Butler); *Take Me Out to the Ball Game* (49, Busby Berkeley); *Annie Get Your Gun* (50, George Sidney); *Dear Wife* (50, Richard Haydn); *Belles on Their Toes* (52, Henry Levin); *City That Never Sleeps* (53, John H. Auer); with Martin and Lewis in *Living It Up* (54, Taurog); *The Ambassador's Daughter* (56, Norman Krasna); and *Miami Expose* (56, Fred F. Sears).

Jack Arnold (1916–92), b. New Haven, Connecticut

1950: *With These Hands* (d). 1953: *Girls in the Night; It Came from Outer Space; The Glass Web.* 1954: *Creature from the Black Lagoon.* 1955: *Revenge of the Creature; The Man from Bitter Ridge; Tarantula.* 1956: *Red Sundown; Outside the Law.* 1957: *The Incredible Shrinking Man; The Tattered Dress.* 1958: *Man in the Shadow; The Lady Takes a Flyer; High School Confidential; The Space Children; Monster on the Campus.* 1959: *No Name on the Bullet; The Mouse That Roared.* 1961: *Bachelor in Paradise.* 1964: *A Global Affair; The Lively Set.* 1969: *Hello Down There.* 1974: *Black Eye.* 1975: *Boss Nigger; Games Girls Play.* 1977: *The Swiss Conspiracy.*

Jack Arnold seemed to go cheerfully with whatever flow came along—*Bachelor in Paradise* is minor Bob Hope; *Boss Nigger* is better than its awful title, but it's Fred Williamson in a piece of blaxploitation; *The Mouse That Roared* is a funny Peter Sellers movie (in which the Duchy of Fenwick declares war on the U.S.); *Man in the Shadow* is a melodrama in which Orson Welles and Jeff Chandler growl at each other; *No Name on the Bullet* is one of the better Audie Murphy Westerns; and *High School Confidential* (with marijuana threatening the young) has to be seen for a cast that includes Russ Tamblyn, John Drew Barrymore, Mamie Van Doren, and Jerry Lee Lewis.

But Arnold is really treasured for still another genre: the fifties sci-fi warning story in which something in nature has gone awry. So *Creature from the Black Lagoon* is famous as the film Marilyn Monroe has been stirred by in *The Seven Year Itch*. But *The Incredible Shrinking Man* (from a Richard Matheson novel) is a genuine classic in homemade special effects that seem to me more frightening than smooth stuff done forty years later. The connoisseur should also note *Tarantula* (what it says is what you get), the very clever *It Came from Outer Space,* and the unusual *The Space Children.*

Françoise Arnoul (F. Annette Gautsch), b. Constantine, Algeria, 1931

An infrequent appearer in French films, Arnoul in her prime was exceptionally pretty. Two films show how little her range from gaiety to somberness was ever exploited: as the young dancer in *French Can Can* (55, Jean Renoir) and as the brooding female object in the Venetian intrigue of *When the Devil Drives* (57, Roger Vadim). For Renoir she shows how the laundry girl matures in the process of becoming a performer; for Vadim she is one of the first modern girls, pleased when Christian Marquand notices there is no bra under her sweater.

Her other films include *L'Epave* (49, Willy Rozier); *Quai de Grenelle* (50, E. Reinert); *Les Amants de Tolède* (52, Henri Decoin); *Fruit Défendu* (52, Henri Verneuil); *La Rage au Corps* (53, Ralph Habib); *Napoléon* (54, Sacha Guitry); *Le Mouton à Cinq Pattes* (54, Verneuil); *Si Paris Nous Était Conté* (56, Guitry); *Le Pays d'ou Je Viens* (56, Marcel Carné); *La Chatte* (58, Decoin); *La Morte-Saison des Amours* (61, Pierre Kast); *Vacances Portugaises* (62, Kast); *Le Diable et les Dix Commandements* (63, Julien Duvivier); *Le Dimanche de la Vie* (66, Jean Herman); happily reunited with Renoir in the "Roi d'Yvetot" episode from *Le Petit Théâtre de Jean Renoir* (71).

In recent years, she has made *Les Années Campagne* (92, Philippe Leriche); *Billard à l'Etage* (96, Jean Marboeuf); *Temps de Chien* (96, Marboeuf); *Post-Coïtum, Animal Triste* (97, Brigitte Rouan); *Une Patronne de Charme* (97, Bernard Uzan); *Merci pour le Geste* (00, Claude Faraldo); *Duval: Un Mort de Trop* (01, Daniel Losset).

Jean Arthur (Gladys Georgianna Greene) (1900–91), b. New York

While enjoying great success as *Peter Pan* on the New York stage in 1950 (she was fifty, for 1900 has been proved as her birth date), Jean Arthur told an interviewer, "If I can get over the message that we should all try to be ourselves, to be free individuals, then I'm sure I'll have accomplished what [J. M.] Barrie wanted."

Such freedom was hardly what Ms. Arthur was known for. She had a turmoil of feelings about Hollywood—she hated all kinds of publicity and the loss of privacy. She had difficulty making up her mind about projects, and she was often indecisive about how to play scenes. None of that shows onscreen, except that she could bring earnest, furious thought to comedy and romance. What her character elected to do was often in the balance because of the actress's innate, heartfelt fluctuations. From 1935 to 1945 this gave her a rare, querulous charm, ranging from dreamy to inquisitive, always bent on discovering fresh inner truths. Yet her quality might have passed us by but for the way it served the soul-searching whimsy of Capra's films.

She was the daughter of a photographer, and she was raised in Manhattan. As a teenager, she did modeling work that brought her to the attention of Fox and a leading part in *Cameo Kirby* (23, John Ford). She made over twenty silent films without looking like more than a conventional, timid ingenue. But in 1927, she was taken up by Paramount where she became the protégée (and love interest) of David O. Selznick. (Yet in 1928, she married a photographer, Julian Anker—it lasted one day.) Her films improved: *Warming Up* (28, Fred Newmeyer); *Sins of the Fathers* (28, Ludwig Berger); *The Canary Murder Case* (29, Malcolm St. Clair); *The Greene Murder Case* (29, Frank Tuttle); *The Mysterious Dr. Fu Manchu* (29, Rowland V. Lee); *The Saturday Night Kid* (29, Edward Sutherland); *Street of Chance* (30, John Cromwell); and *Young Eagles* (30, William Wellman).

By 1931, Paramount had dropped her (Selznick married Irene Mayer), and Arthur went back to the New York stage and summer stock for two years. When she returned, she was married to producer Frank Ross, who may have been her best advisor. She made *Whirlpool* (34, Roy William Neill) and then signed with Columbia. Her first success at the studio was in *The Whole Town's Talking* (34, Ford), establishing the character of an ordinary but very decent young woman. She did a weepy, *Most Precious Thing in Life* (34, Lambert Hillyer); and *If You Could Only Cook* (35, William Seiter), a lively comedy that Harry Cohn tried to sell overseas as a Frank Capra film (enough to make Capra notice her).

After *The Ex-Mrs. Bradford* (35, Stephen Roberts) and two roles in *Diamond Jim* (35, Sutherland), she was cast by Capra as the newspaper writer in *Mr. Deeds Goes to Town* (36). That film made her the honest girlfriend and helper to a troubled good guy—Arthur needed nobility in a man for the screen romance to take. She was with Cooper again, as Calamity Jane, in unexpectedly rich scenes in De Mille's *The Plainsman* (37). Then she was "Mary Smith" whose life is changed when a fur coat falls on her head in *Easy Living* (37, Mitchell Leisen)—"Golly!" she gasps, on seeing what money can buy. She played opposite Boyer in *History Is Made at Night* (37, Frank Borzage) and then did two more for Capra—in *You Can't Take It With You* (38) and as the tough pro who is softened by James Stewart's Perot-like idealism in *Mr. Smith Goes to Washington* (39).

In the Capra films, Jean Arthur was the figure who related the strange philosophy of the parables to the audience: she was "one of us," yet susceptible to the director's overemotional high-mindedness. (By comparison, in *Meet John Doe* Barbara Stanwyck couldn't quite give up her natural incredulity. Arthur was gullible, but she could make that weakness seem like mere sincerity.) Arthur was also the stranded entertainer bullied and wooed by Cary Grant in *Only Angels Have Wings* (39, Howard Hawks), where she comes perilously close to tomboy twoshoes and hardly seems tricky enough to interest Grant, or Hawks. (Hawks complained that Arthur wouldn't try things on the spur of the moment.)

She was in *Arizona* (40, Wesley Ruggles); *Too Many Husbands* (40, Ruggles); *The Devil and Miss Jones* (41, Sam Wood); *Talk of the Town* (42, George Stevens); *A Lady Takes a Chance* (43, Seiter); and earned a best actress nomination in *The More the Merrier* (43, Stevens), where she has a stealthy, quite sexy conversation scene with the flawlessly honorable Joel McCrea.

She left Hollywood once more after *The Impatient Years* (44, Irving Cummings) and went back to the stage and a second education. *Born Yesterday* was written for her by Garson Kanin, but she dropped out before the play came to Broadway and was replaced by the young Judy Holliday. She made only two more films: *A Foreign Affair* (48, Billy Wilder) and, reunited with George Stevens, as the wife and mother in *Shane* (53)—was she fifty-three then? was she Brandon De Wilde's grandmother even? Her subsequent retirement included work in the drama department at Vassar, and then residence in Carmel, California, preferring not to talk about the old days.

Dorothy Arzner (1900–79),
b. San Francisco
1927: *Fashions for Women; Ten Modern Com-*

mandments; Get Your Man. 1928: *Manhattan Cocktail.* 1929: *The Wild Party.* 1930: *Sarah and Son; Anybody's Woman; Behind the Makeup* (codirected with Robert Milton); an episode from *Paramount on Parade.* 1931: *Honor Among Lovers; Working Girls.* 1932: *Merrily We Go to Hell.* 1933: *Christopher Strong.* 1934: *Nana.* 1936: *Craig's Wife.* 1937: *The Bride Wore Red.* 1940: *Dance, Girl, Dance.* 1943: *First Comes Courage.*

Dorothy Arzner was a professional director of American movies who worked regularly for over a decade, and was a woman. (Only Lois Weber could have made the same claim.) She was not a great filmmaker, and her pioneering should not inflate her reputation. But she turned out some fascinating pictures and clearly was able to pursue a personal if undoctrinaire interest in the issue of women's identity. That said, one has to confess that she generally played according to the Hollywood concept of "a woman's picture." She did not stretch or threaten the system, as Barbara Loden did with *Wanda;* but that is also a sign of how far the 1930s romance was susceptible to a feminist sensibility. And Dorothy Arzner made more films than ever came from Barbara Loden. Arzner got into pictures through hard work and paying her dues, and she stayed near the top long enough for her retirement to be an act of choice. All of which says very little about why she was unique.

The daughter of a Hollywood restaurateur, she dropped out of the University of Southern California and worked her way up at Paramount from typist to cutter to editor to director's assistant. As an editor, she worked on *Blood and Sand* (22, Fred Niblo), *The Wild Party* (23, Herbert Blache), *The Covered Wagon* (23, James Cruze), and *Inez from Hollywood* (24, Alfred E. Green). She was writing scripts, for Paramount and Columbia, and when she was on the point of going over to the small studio to direct her own work, Paramount promoted her, first as Esther Ralston's director.

Her early films were conventional, saucy comedies about love and marriage: *Get Your Man* is Clara Bow angling for an aristocrat husband, and in *The Wild Party* Bow forms a "hard-boiled maidens" group at a college to plague Professor Fredric March. *Sarah and Son* is a Ruth Chatterton weepie about a mother struggling to be with her son. *Honor Among Lovers* features the indispensable secretary (Claudette Colbert) who will not marry the boss (March), and *Working Girls* is another tribute to independent women. *Merrily We Go to Hell* is a comedy, with March and Sylvia Sidney, in which humor barely conceals the desperation of the brittle rich.

She left Paramount and free-lanced: *Christopher Strong* is Katharine Hepburn as an aviatrix, with hints of a superwoman persona emerging as the woman kills herself rather than have an illegitimate child—more romantic agony than feminist self-determination. *Nana* was a turgid Goldwyn spectacular built around Anna Sten. But *Craig's Wife* is a remarkably severe picture in which Rosalind Russell plays a monstrous housewife: the subject could have provided the basis for scathing criticism of a woman's demented domestic energy, but instead she is regarded as a misfit. *The Bride Wore Red* was a Joan Crawford vehicle, about a former prostitute who is on the point of respectability. *Dance, Girl, Dance*, at RKO, is Arzner's best film: a study of working girls and feminine career strategies, with Lucille Ball and Maureen O'Hara exemplifying the robust and the demure approaches.

Her long retirement saw her doing some teaching at UCLA, and making TV commercials for Pepsi-Cola for her old friend Joan Crawford.

Hal Ashby (1936–88), b. Ogden, Utah
1970: *The Landlord*. 1971: *Harold and Maude*. 1973: *The Last Detail*. 1975: *Shampoo*. 1976: *Bound for Glory*. 1978: *Coming Home*. 1979: *Being There*. 1981: *Second-Hand Hearts*. 1982: *Lookin' to Get Out; Let's Spend the Night Together* (d). 1985: *The Slugger's Wife*. 1986: *Eight Million Ways to Die*.

Ashby hitchhiked to California in his teens, and he worked on any and every job in pictures, rising to be an assistant editor on several William Wyler and George Stevens films: *Friendly Persuasion*, *The Big Country*, *The Diary of Anne Frank*, and *The Greatest Story Ever Told*. The influence of such pious liberalism should not be forgotten: despite his sixties aura, Ashby digested attitudes in the Eisenhower years when circumspect conservatives could get away with pledging themselves to tame causes. Ashby became a full editor on *The Loved One* (64, Tony Richardson), and worked for Norman Jewison with whom he won an editing Oscar for *In the Heat of the Night* (67), another example of rightmindedness allied with old-fashioned melodramatic corn.

Jewison gave Ashby his first chance to direct: a film about a rich kid touched by the plight and authenticity of his Harlem tenants. Soft-centered, *The Landlord* is still an offbeat picture with unusual characters. *Harold and Maude* inspired the hope that Ashby might be a genuine eccentric, instead of a cute, marketable oddball. But its dark humor never visited him again, and writer Colin Higgins seems responsible for its going as far as it did to abuse our settled ideas of taste. The love story is prettified and sanitary: there's no real sex between Bud Cort and Ruth Gordon. It slips away into another feeble endorsement of "do your own thing," the politics of the weary soul-searcher, too selfish and superficial to deal with public causes. Still, it has a few moments of bitter glee, and a very pleasing, distant contempt for the middle class that

explains its subsequent cult status: it allows establishment kids to scorn their affluence and status without risking either.

The Last Detail is Ashby's best film, but with what debt to writer Robert Towne and Jack Nicholson? Ashby executes a concept that is more bleak and analytical than he is used to: that living is a set of prisons. *The Last Detail* was as mutedly somber as *Shampoo* was boastfully risqué. But *Shampoo* was writers Towne and Warren Beatty, as the actor moved into the stage of his career that aspired to directing. It was a modish, bawdy film, but without any directorial personality. In the end, its restrained view of the hairdresser libertine colludes with his self-pity and the sensual pathos of Warren Beatty's sighing mouth. *Bound for Glory* was a blatant use of Depression picturesque to obscure human and social ugliness, an insipid piece of hero worship that glossed over the intransigence of Woody Guthrie while settling for the inflated pomp with which Hollywood biopics have always guided untidy history.

Yet that was nothing compared with *Coming Home*, a movie that looked like a TV commercial, patronized paraplegics, Vietnam, the military, and love with its maudlin nobility and the thought that soap-opera histrionics could enclose political subject matter. It was Jane Fonda's pet project this time, and in the process it threw away Nancy Dowd's very tough script and asked us to believe that Fonda could represent a lowly, unaware army wife, that Bruce Dern was an average soldier, and that the paraplegic screw is an ultimate panacea—the sex again as obscure and profound as in *Harold and Maude*. (If only prostrate Jon Voight had been given a merciful job by lusty Ruth Gordon.) *Coming Home* was adolescent and decadent. Its most ruinous failing is the self-satisfaction that confuses a vacuous cult of emotion with intelligence and responsibility. *Coming Home*, more than Ashby dreamed of, is a film about self-excuse and the isolation that learns to forget mistakes and problems.

Ashby's work in the eighties was fitful, and suffered from his difficulties with drugs. At least *Let's Spend the Night Together*—a Rolling Stones concert film—shows his skill as an editor. *Lookin' to Get Out* was on the shelf two years before it got a release. *Eight Million Ways to Die* was a thriller steeped in alcohol and drugs, as well as a project that had several helping hands. In hindsight, *The Last Detail* and *Shampoo* look like absorbing models of touch and control—and Ashby seems like a sad casualty who depended on strong collaborators.

Anthony Asquith (1902–68), b. London
1927: *Shooting Stars* (codirected with A. V. Bramble). 1928: *Underground*. 1929: *The Runaway Princess*. 1930: *A Cottage on Dartmoor*. 1931: *Tell*

England. 1932: *Dance, Pretty Lady; Marry Me; The Window Cleaner.* 1933: *The Lucky Number.* 1934: *Unfinished Symphony* (codirected). 1935: *Forever England; Moscow Nights.* 1938: *Pygmalion* (codirected with Leslie Howard). 1939: *French Without Tears.* 1940: *Freedom Radio; Channel Incident* (d); *Quiet Wedding.* 1941: *Cottage to Let/Bombsight Stolen; Rush Hour* (d). 1942: *Uncensored.* 1943: *We Dive at Dawn; The Demi-Paradise; Welcome to Britain* (codirected with Burgess Meredith). 1944: *Fanny by Gaslight; Man of Evil; Two Fathers* (d). 1945: *The Way to the Stars/Johnny in the Clouds.* 1947: *While the Sun Shines.* 1948: *The Winslow Boy.* 1950: *The Woman in Question.* 1951: *The Browning Version.* 1952: *The Importance of Being Earnest.* 1953: *The Net; The Final Test.* 1954: *The Young Lovers/Chance Meeting.* 1955: *On Such a Night.* 1956: *Carrington V.C.* 1958: *Orders to Kill.* 1959: *The Doctor's Dilemma; Libel.* 1960: *The Millionairess.* 1962: *Guns of Darkness.* 1963: *The V.I.P.s.* 1964: *The Yellow Rolls-Royce.*

Asquith was the son of the Liberal prime minister, a man apparently torn between social opposites. On the set, he affected a boilersuit and yet he was happiest with material that had built-in social distinctions. In the dark days of the British cinema—in the 1950s—he had a high and quite unmerited reputation. In fact, he was a dull, journeyman supervisor of the transfer to the screen of proven theatrical properties. The myth that his first film exploited sound audaciously survived only as long as its gimmicky claptrap remained unseen. For the rest, *Dance, Pretty Lady* is charming and *The Importance of Being Earnest* a decent reading of the play. *Pygmalion* is more than decent: it is a fine record of the play, and even if Leslie Howard is an odd Higgins, Wendy Hiller and Wilfred Lawson are matchless. But it is symptomatic of Asquith that he managed to make the Shaw of *The Doctor's Dilemma* no better a dramatist than the Rattigan of *The Browning Version* and *The Winslow Boy.* Venturing beyond such stagy subjects, he quickly floundered: *Orders to Kill* is a complete failure and *Libel* is lurid melodrama. In his last years he subsided into atrocious all-star vehicles, addled movies that accepted a 1920s notion of the intrinsic appeal of wealthy and successful people.

Olivier Assayas, b. Paris, 1955

1986: *Désordre.* 1989: *L'Enfant de l'Hiver.* 1991: *Paris S'Éveille/Paris at Dawn.* 1993: *Une Nouvelle Vie.* 1994: *L'Eau Froide.* 1996: *Irma Vep.* 1997: *Cinéma de Notre Temps: Hou Hsiao Hsien/HHH: A Portrait of Hou Hsiao-Hsien* (d). 1998: *Fin Août, Début Septembre.* 2000: *Les Destinées Sentimentales.* 2002: *Demonlover.*

It's a mark of changing times that Assayas—a one-time editor of *Cahiers du Cinéma,* and then a director himself—works in an age when the screening of his films outside France depends largely on film festivals and art museums. *Irma Vep* was released in America—with little response. And so we are back to an isolation in which foreign films, and foreign filmmakers of distinction, risk going unknown to all but a few in the English-speaking world. The risk in this affects French funding, of course. But it falls most heavily on American audiences. For there has never been an age in film history when America needed more external input—not least the works of a director who regards Hou Hsiao-Hsien as a master and a model. Of course, Assayas has his own world: that of young people, often Parisians, troubled about virtually everything in their lives—it is like *Paris Nous Appartient* for a later time when the huge threat may have dissipated, but only after pioneering the way for smaller, more intimate dreads. *Une Nouvelle Vie* is about half-sisters who only meet at the age of twenty. And Assayas is especially acute at showing us young people whose elders are in the same lost condition. In *Paris at Dawn,* Jean-Pierre Léaud is living with the dangerously young Judith Godreche, until his mixed-up son arrives and goes off with her.

Assayas benefits from the camerawork of Denis Lenoir, and he is adept at making noir situations seem everyday. He is already a master at overlap, betrayal, and stray coincidence, and he seems to be improving as time passes. Moreover, *Irma Vep* gave a welcome sign of humor in its awareness of the many poseurs and paranoids one meets in film production.

Fred Astaire (Frederick Austerlitz)
(1899–1987), b. Omaha, Nebraska

There is something very suggestive of Americana in the way a Napoleonic battle is turned into a name without roots or etymology. Yet how evocative that name is: run the parts together and the result is as rhythmic as Frenesi; separate them and it could be Fred a Star or Fred on a staircase, astride the stair—thus Astaire, *l'esprit d'escalier.*

It is proper to respond in this way because so much of Astaire is a matter of stylish carriage, and I do not think it accidental that the name evokes some specially serene agility. This leads to the questions, is Astaire a movie actor? and what makes for great acting in the cinema? There is a good case for arguing that, in the event of a visit by creatures from a far universe, ignorant of the cinema, one would do best to show them some steps by Astaire as the clinching evidence of the medium's potential. Better that than the noble actors—Olivier, Jannings, Brando, Barrymore, et al. Astaire is the most refined human expression of the musical, which is in turn the extreme manifestation of pure cinema: the lifelike presentation of human beings in magical, dreamlike, and imaginary situations. That might be thought to imply that Astaire's dancing depends on illusion. Not so. He was always the most technically exacting and ambitious of screen dancers, the most eager to perform in uninterrupted setups. In the 1920s, it would have been possible to see him dancing virtuoso routines on stage. The spatial and temporal continuity of theatre would have made clear how difficult the feat was. Cinema wipes away the sense of difficulty and substitutes the ease that permits every transformation needed by the chronic dreamer. Astaire is not a great dancer so much as a great filmed dancer. Nureyev on film is less than in the flesh, because he is himself most stimulated by an actual audience and a real leap. Astaire, like all dreamers, is a perfectionist who loved to work in the feverish secrecy of a studio toward the flawless image of his own grace. He lends himself to the detachment of cinema because he is a rather cold, even indistinct personality who celebrates the spirit of elegance as channeled through elaborate, rapid, photographed motion.

Such a notion was underlined by Astaire's latter-day appearance in "straight" parts. After *Silk Stockings,* in 1957, he largely gave himself up to television spectaculars and to acting. The first sour fruit of this was *On the Beach* (59, Stanley Kramer). If anyone had ever doubted Kramer's crassness, here was final proof. For he cast Astaire as a motor-racing driver, a man essentially hidden in the shell of a car. Surely nuclear holocaust could have been as glibly dramatized by Astaire's playing a golfer? Then at least we might have enjoyed his dainty prowling round the greens.

Yet once Astaire was asked to partake of earnest melodrama, it was a strain to watch him at all. In play-acting, he is downright shifty: like a philosopher at a bingo session, there is the embarrassing and depleting sense of a man having been caught on the blind side, but gamely trying to be polite. Furthermore, drama blurred his appearance. In *On the Beach*, he is sometimes disheveled, which is heresy against the perpetual grooming of his characteristic work. This applied as much to *Finian's Rainbow* (68, Francis Ford Coppola), a respectful and nostalgic tribute to his greatness, as to his other totally mediocre films of the 1960s: *The Pleasure of His Company* (61, George Seaton); *The Notorious Landlady* (62, Richard Quine); *The Midas Run* (69, Alf Kjellin); and *The Towering Inferno* (74, John Guillermin).

In musicals, too, Astaire is the man without character; sometimes not so far from the man without humanity. But in the musicals, this is not so much a shortcoming as an audacious emphasis on style. Astaire is preeminently the saint of 1930s sophistication, the butterfly in motion till he dies, whose enchanting light voice kids the sentimentality of his songs. (He is a great singer—no won-

der all the songwriters wanted him—who treats the song with reverence.) He is the man about town, empty of personality, opinions, and warmth, but a man who carries himself matchlessly. There is something of the eighteenth-century dandy in his preference for taking nothing seriously, save for the articulation of his superb movement. Compare him with Nick Charles, the Hammett private eye as played by William Powell. Both are more polish than substance, but Powell's Charles has an inkling of his own frivolousness and is cynical to conceal it. Astaire is utterly tranquil, hence the inane playboy figures he embodies, men who exist only to walk sweetly across lounges, to preserve rigorous trouser creases and that high, carefree tone of voice. Astaire is the supreme ideal of that gang of 1930s American misanthropes: Herman Mankiewicz, Robert Benchley, Dorothy Parker, Cole Porter, Ben Hecht. Seeing that life was at best absurd, at worst horrifying, they opted for shining grace in tiny things and some vivid, "useless" excellence, such as Astaire's dancing. Elsewhere, I have suggested that he could have been Jekyll to Cagney's Hyde. Astaire was also very near to Jay Gatsby, an insignificant man, bent on easing public occasions.

I was struck by this when taking some students through an extract from *Silk Stockings* (57, Rouben Mamoulian). The excerpt we were approaching was the sequence in which Astaire and Cyd Charisse dance across several deserted film sets. It is one of the greatest of movie-dance sequences: a compendium of moving camera, wide screen, counterpointed rhythms, and the intriguing contrast of masterful Astaire and frigid Charisse. But before the dancing begins, there is a prelude. Charisse arrives by car at the studio gates and Astaire, muttering "Hallo, hallo . . . ," hobbles over to meet her. That movement kept us from the dance, because it was exquisite, original, and Astaire. The emotion of the moment—of lovers reunited—hardly seems to strike him. But ask him to move from A to B and he is aroused.

This touches on a vital principle: that it is often preferable to have a movie actor who moves well than one who "understands" the part. A director ought to be able to explain a part, but very few men or women can move well in front of a camera. In *The Big Sleep*, there are numerous shots of Bogart simply walking across rooms: they draw us to the resilient alertness of his screen personality as surely as the acid dialogue. Bogart's lounging freedom captures our hopes. With Astaire this effect is far more concentrated, because it is his single asset.

His career is the story of a search for partners who could endure his glorious limitation. At first, he danced onstage with his sister, Adele: they were sensations in London and New York. But when she married (into the English aristocracy) in

1932, he dodged into films. Selznick was convinced of Astaire's charm "in spite of his enormous ears and bad chin line." His debut, at age thirty-four, was *Dancing Lady* (33, Robert Z. Leonard) at MGM, with Joan Crawford. But he was signed up by RKO and partnered with Ginger Rogers for nine films that are the least alloyed expression of self-sufficient movement. Above all, Ginger joined him in those intimate, but accelerating, conversational dances, where hard heels and glossy floors speak of bliss: *Flying Down to Rio* (33, Thornton Freeland); *The Gay Divorcee* (34, Mark Sandrich); *Roberta* (35, William A. Seiter); *Top Hat* (35, Sandrich); *Follow the Fleet* (36, Sandrich); *Swing Time* (36, George Stevens); *Shall We Dance?* (37, Sandrich); *Carefree* (38, Sandrich); and *The Story of Vernon and Irene Castle* (39, H. C. Potter). In 1937, he had played opposite Joan Fontaine in *A Damsel in Distress* (37, Stevens) with less happy results. And it is true that in some later films he seems too refined for the company he is keeping. But he is splendid with that other virtuoso, Eleanor Powell, in *Broadway Melody of 1940* (40, Norman Taurog) and with Paulette Goddard in *Second Chorus* (40, Potter). He worked well with the lofty glamour of Rita Hayworth in *You'll Never Get Rich* (41, Sidney Lanfield) and *You Were Never Lovelier* (42, Seiter), but had to settle for Bing Crosby as stimulus in *Holiday Inn* (42, Sandrich), and went back to RKO for *The Sky's the Limit* (43, Edward H. Griffith), which has a marvelous late-night solo passage.

Vincente Minnelli's sheer, visual extravagance was well suited to Astaire, and he excelled with another rather heartless dancer, Lucille Bremer, in *Ziegfeld Follies* (46) and *Yolanda and the Thief* (45). The high theatricality of the latter suits him exactly. The idea of an angel masquerading as a man is itself an insight into Astaire's personality. After *Blue Skies* (46, Stuart Heisler), with Crosby again, he replaced the injured Gene Kelly in *Easter Parade* (48, Charles Walters) and seemed a very cold mentor to Judy Garland. He and Ginger Rogers were flatly reunited in *The Barkleys of Broadway* (49, Walters) and the next four were unimpressive: evidently shrinking from Red Skelton as a songwriting team in *Three Little Words* (50, Richard Thorpe); with Betty Hutton in *Let's Dance* (50, Norman Z. McLeod); brilliant but showy in *Royal Wedding* (51, Stanley Donen); and *The Belle of New York* (52, Walters).

The Band Wagon (53) is one of Minnelli's fragmented films, but it introduced Astaire to Cyd Charisse and gave them the witty Spillane pastiche routine. *Daddy Long Legs* (55, Jean Negulesco) with Leslie Caron is dull, but Astaire ended with two of his finest films: *Funny Face* (57, Donen) and *Silk Stockings*. The first is his most successful romance, for it looks as though he was intrigued by the challenge of "musicalizing" the supposedly straight Audrey Hepburn. He choreographed *Funny Face* personally, but the ultimate authorship is due to Donen, if only for making the routines so enchantingly lyrical. Mamoulian is clear in every frame of *Silk Stockings,* but it is also the vindication of two rather frozen personalities obsessed by dance and its route to whirling rapture.

Mary Astor (Lucille Langhanke) (1906–87), b. Quincy, Illinois

Mary Astor's autobiography, *My Story,* published in 1951, is better written than most similar exercises and much more frank. Dotted through her more than one hundred movies, there are many signs of an intelligent woman. That those views are too rare was only one of her problems: originally, an ambitious German father had thrust her into the movies; after her affair with John Barrymore, her first husband, Kenneth Hawks, was killed in an air crash; three more marriages ended in divorce, and the second saw the scurrilous publication, in 1936, of alleged and lurid extracts from her diary, including a graphic love affair with playwright George Kaufman. She never stayed a star for more than one year at a time, and she slipped from supporting parts into alcoholism and sessions with an analyst that eventually led to the autobiography. Despite her long career, she disliked Hollywood—though whether for itself or for the way it thwarted her is an open question. Fairly early, she won a reputation for being independent, and later something stuck from the diary incident; as a result, she had her best chances playing polite bitches or demure snakes in the grass—above all Hammett's Brigid O'Shaughnessy in *The Maltese Falcon* (41, John Huston). That picture of chronic lying did not hinder her genuine warmth as the mother in *Meet Me in St. Louis* (44, Vincente Minnelli) and *Little Women* (49, Mervyn Le Roy).

She made her debut in 1921 with *Sentimental Tommy* (John S. Robertson), and worked nomadically without ever being more than a promising newcomer: *Bought and Paid For* (22, William C. De Mille); *Second Fiddle* (22, Frank Tuttle); *Puritan Passion* (23, Tuttle); *Success* (23, Ralph Ince); *The Fighting Coward* (24, James Cruze); *Beau Brummel* (24, Harry Beaumont); *Unguarded Woman* (24, Alan Crosland); *Inez from Hollywood* (24, Alfred E. Green); *Don Q, Son of Zorro* (24, Donald Crisp); *The Scarlet Saint* (25, George Archainbaud); *The Wise Guy* (26, Frank Lloyd); and *Don Juan* (26, Crosland). That innovatory sound film (opposite a Barrymore who would have preferred Dolores Costello to his discarded mistress) boosted her, but she rarely got good parts: *The Rough Riders* (27, Victor Fleming); *Two Arabian Knights* (27, Lewis Milestone); *No Place to Go* (27, Le Roy); *Dressed to Kill* (28, Irving Cum-

mings); and *Dry Martini* (28, Harry d'Arrast).
Despite her subsequent prowess with good dia-
logue, she failed a test for talkies and was briefly
put out of work before *Ladies Love Brutes* (30,
Rowland V. Lee); *The Runaway Bride* (30, Crisp);
Holiday (30, Edward H. Griffith); *Other Men's
Women* (31, William Wellman); *The Sin Ship* (31,
Louis Wolheim); *The Royal Bed* (31, Lowell Sher-
man); *Smart Woman* (31, Gregory La Cava); *Red
Dust* (32, Fleming); *The World Changes* (33, Le
Roy); *The Kennel Murder Case* (33, Michael Cur-
tiz); *Easy to Love* (34, William Keighley); *I Am a
Thief* (35, Robert Florey); and *Page Miss Glory*
(35, Le Roy). Her career seems to have been
enhanced by the diary scandal, for 1936–42 was
the period of her best parts: *Dodsworth* (36,
William Wyler); never more beautiful than in *The
Prisoner of Zenda* (37, John Cromwell); *Hurricane* (37, John Ford); *Listen Darling* (38, Edward
L. Marin); *There's Always a Woman* (38, Alexander Hall); pregnant and hilarious during the making of *Midnight* (39, Mitchell Leisen); *Brigham
Young* (40, Henry Hathaway); winning a best supporting actress Oscar opposite Bette Davis in *The
Great Lie* (41, Edmund Goulding); looking too
old in *Across the Pacific* (42, Huston); and *Palm
Beach Story* (42, Preston Sturges).

MGM put her under contract, but only for poor
leads or good supporting parts: *Young Ideas* (43,
Jules Dassin); *Thousands Cheer* (43, George Sidney); *Fiesta* (47, Richard Thorpe); *Desert Fury*
(48, Lewis Allen); fine as the hooker in *Act of Violence* (49, Fred Zinnemann); and *Any Number
Can Play* (49, Le Roy). Her crack-up meant that
she played only small parts thereafter: *So This Is
Love* (53, Gordon Douglas); *A Kiss Before Dying*
(56, Gerd Oswald); *The Devil's Hairpin* (57, Cornel Wilde); *This Happy Feeling* (58, Blake
Edwards); *A Stranger in My Arms* (58, Helmut
Kautner); *Return to Peyton Place* (61, José Ferrer); *Youngblood Hawke* (64, Delmer Daves); and
Hush . . . Hush, Sweet Charlotte (64, Robert
Aldrich). After her autobiography, she was
encouraged to go on to novels.

Alexandre Astruc, b. Paris, 1923

1948: *Aller-Retour* (s); *Ulysse et les Mauvaises
Rencontres* (s). 1952: *Le Rideau Cramoisi/The
Crimson Curtain* (s). 1955: *Les Mauvaises Rencontres.* 1958: *Une Vie.* 1960: *La Proie pour l'Ombre.* 1961: *L'Education Sentimentale 61.* 1963: *Le
Puits et le Pendule* (s). 1964: *Evariste Gallois* (s).
1966: *La Longue Marche.* 1968: *Flammes sur
l'Adriatique.* 1976: *Sartre par Lui-même* (d).

Astruc is a fascinating example of a man from literary culture identifying his true allegiance to the
movies. He holds a special place in the still small
library of worthwhile cinema theory, even if his
own films rarely live up to all his admirable principles. *Une Vie*, though, is a perfect collaboration of

Maupassant's novel, Astruc's treatment, the photography of Claude Renoir, Roman Vlad's music,
and the presence of Maria Schell, Christian Marquand, Ivan Desny, Pascale Petit, and Antonella
Lualdi. Rather out of fashion today, not even the
considerably inferior quality of Astruc's other
work can prevent it from some future rediscovery.
It justifies the man as surely as *Night of the
Hunter* does Charles Laughton. *Une Vie* is the
demonstration of a view of cinema—*la caméra-
stylo*—that is a most fruitful critical bond between
classical and modern cinema.

Astruc was a critic, a novelist—*Les Vacances*
(45)—and assistant to Marc Allégret on *Blanche
Fury* (47). In 1948, in *Écran Français*, he wrote a
short article, "The Birth of a New Avant-Garde:
La Caméra-Stylo." It argued for a new appreciation of the language of film:

> . . . the cinema will gradually break free from
> the tyranny of what is visual, from the image for
> its own sake, from the immediate and concrete
> demands of the narrative, to become a means of
> writing just as flexible and subtle as written lan-
> guage. . . . We have come to realise that the
> meaning which the silent cinema tried to give
> birth to through symbolic association exists
> within the image itself, in the development of
> the narrative, in every gesture of the characters,
> in every line of dialogue, in those camera move-
> ments which relate objects to objects and char-
> acters to objects. All thought, like all feeling, is
> a relationship between one human being and
> another human being. . . .

That can still claim to be the most important critical theory the cinema has yet produced. It led
Astruc to the identification of a pantheon that was
shared by most of the *Cahiers* group and that
enriched the films they made: Eisenstein, Welles,
Renoir, Bresson, von Stroheim, Murnau, Hawks,
Mizoguchi, Hitchcock, Lang, and Rossellini.

At the same time, it was not difficult to detect
the young novelist at work, who looked forward to
the cinema's achieving the autonomy of, say,
Sartre, Camus, or Faulkner. Astruc's own films
showed that in *la caméra-stylo* he remained very
conscious of the pen. His movies relied not only
on literary models, but what was often an academic demonstration of his theories. For example,
Le Rideau Cramoisi is a very cold film, more
engaged by the abstract realization of human connection than actually involved in it. Astruc is capable of passages of extraordinary beauty and utter
clarity, but the heart is often left behind. No surprise that he once listed Anthony Mann's *Men in
War* as a favorite film, for in that film Mann
achieves an eerie detachment through cinematic
grace. *Une Vie* works because of Maria Schell's
insistent emotionalism—a quality that has marred
other films, but brings a touching plaintiveness to

Une Vie. Elsewhere, Astruc's films have the distinction of blueprints; by contrast, Renoir's are untidy houses. It is a serious limitation, but Astruc's theory is still correct and vital. No student of the movies should neglect it or leave *Une Vie* unseen.

Lord Richard Attenborough,
b. Cambridge, England, 1923
1969: *Oh! What a Lovely War.* 1972: *Young Winston.* 1977: *A Bridge Too Far.* 1978: *Magic.* 1982: *Gandhi.* 1985: *A Chorus Line.* 1987: *Cry Freedom.* 1992: *Chaplin.* 1993: *Shadowlands.* 1996: *In Love and War.* 1999: *Grey Owl.*

Attenborough has blithely mapped out the way to success in the British film industry. He began at RADA, and in 1942 he won the Bancroft Medal there and made his debut as a seaman in *In Which We Serve* (42, Noel Coward and David Lean). The next year, he had a big success as Pinkie in the stage version of Graham Greene's *Brighton Rock* and was in the film *Schweik's New Adventures* (Karel Lamac). After war service with the RAF film unit, he appeared in *The Man Within* (46, Bernard Knowles), *A Matter of Life and Death* (46, Michael Powell), the film of *Brighton Rock* (47, John Boulting), and *London Belongs to Me* (48, Sidney Gilliat). Although his role as Pinkie was truly frightening it had not detracted from a grubby, baby-faced vulnerability. This youthful appeal was grotesquely exploited in *The Guinea Pig* (49, Roy Boulting) when, at age twenty-six, he played a lower-middle-class boy at Winchester half his age—and played it straight. Attenborough was swallowed by the British public as smoothly as margarine and for ten years he took whatever cheerful or heroic nonsense the industry spread him on: *Morning Departure* (50, Roy Baker); *Boys in Brown* (50, Montgomery Tully); *The Gift Horse* (52, Compton Bennett); *Private's Progress* (55, J. Boulting); *Brothers in Law* (57, J. Boulting); *The Man Upstairs* (58, Don Chaffey); and *Dunkirk* (58, Leslie Norman).

That was the turning point. In 1959, he produced (with Bryan Forbes) and acted in *The Angry Silence* (59, Guy Green), a portentous attempt to introduce realism to British features. In fact, the film is vulgar and sentimental. Only the subject matter had changed, but Attenborough has always believed more in content than style, in sincerity rather than intelligence. That film marked a new resolution to take himself seriously. As an actor Attenborough went in for some studied character parts and even ventured into American movies: *The League of Gentlemen* (60, Basil Dearden), which he also produced; *Only Two Can Play* (61, Sidney Gilliat); *The Great Escape* (63, John Sturges); *Seance on a Wet Afternoon* (64, Forbes), which he produced; *The Flight of the Phoenix* (65, Robert Aldrich); *The Sand*

Pebbles (66, Robert Wise); *Dr. Dolittle* (67, Richard Fleischer); *David Copperfield* (69, Delbert Mann); *Loot* (70, Silvio Narizzano); *A Severed Head* (70, Dick Clement); and very good as Christie the murderer in *10 Rillington Place* (70, Fleischer).

In addition to *League of Gentlemen* and *Seance on a Wet Afternoon*, Attenborough produced two other movies directed by Bryan Forbes—*Whistle Down the Wind* (62) and *The L-Shaped Room* (64). Such ventures stimulated him and in 1969 he directed and coproduced *Oh! What a Lovely War*—a gallant failure, helped by the initial ingenuity of using Brighton pier, but without any interest in how to photograph people. It was a commercial success, proving how far his preference for content was a national failing. After that, he delved deeper into patriotism with *Young Winston* (72), a movie more influenced by that seasoned middlebrow Carl Foreman.

At fifty-five, Attenborough still looked and behaved like head prefect for British films and was rewarded with a knighthood. He acted regularly: *Rosebud* (74, Otto Preminger); *And Then There Were None* (74, Peter Collinson); in lopsided harness with John Wayne in *Brannigan* (75, Douglas Hickox); *Conduct Unbecoming* (75, Michael Anderson); and a manipulating administrator in *The Chess Players* (77, Satyajit Ray). He also directed Joseph Levine's Arnhem epic, scattering $26 million like toy parachutes, and handling combat with a cheerful gusto that belied his first film's indignant horror.

At seventy, Attenborough was a lord, as if some parties in or around Buckingham Palace had been impressed by *Gandhi*, a soporific, nonthreatening tribute to nonviolence that allegedly moved millions to tears and to mending their ways. It won best picture and now looms over the real world like an abandoned space station—*eternal*, expensive, and forsaken. *A Chorus Line* set no toes tapping, and *Cry Freedom* failed to unleash the forces of political liberalism and safe correctness. But then came *Chaplin*, a disaster of concept and construction such as few people could deny or avoid. Not that Robert Downey Jr. was its flaw: he impersonated Charlie with skill and courage. The blame had to rest with Lord Attenborough, whose proud but unseeing eyes failed to notice what a remarkable little madman Chaplin was. And in all these drab years of making respectable epics, Attenborough the actor has been denied to us—except for *The Human Factor* (80, Preminger) and *Jurassic Park* (93, Steven Spielberg).

After *Chaplin*, *Shadowlands* was a pleasant relief, a well-crafted weepie for book people, energized by Debra Winger and Anthony Hopkins (for long a favorite of Attenborough's). It was Hopkins who gave such a hyperactive performance as the haunted ventriloquist in *Magic*,

Attenborough's best film. *Magic* also reminds us of the director as an actor: drawn to the creepy, as witness *10 Rillington Place, Seance on a Wet Afternoon,* and *Brighton Rock.*

After the 1994 edition, I felt that maybe I had been hard on milord—after all, he had once been a director at Chelsea Football Club. So I resolved to be kinder—and he made *In Love and War* and *Grey Owl!* As an actor, he played Kriss Kringle in *Miracle on 34th Street* (94, Les Mayfield)—why has no one thought to cast Attenborough in The Edmund Gwenn Story?; as the English ambassador, visible only in the long version of *Hamlet* (96, Kenneth Branagh); *E=mc2* (96, Benjamin Fry); as Cecil in *Elizabeth* (98, Shekhar Kapur); *The Railway Children* (00, Catherine Moorhead); as Magog in *Jack and the Beanstalk: The Real Story* (01, Brian Henson); *Puckoon* (02, Terence Ryan).

Stéphane Audran (Colette Suzanne
Jeannine Dacheville), b. Versailles, France, 1932
It is characteristic of Chabrol's enigmatic work that one might not deduce from it that Stéphane Audran was his wife. Counting the black comedy of the episode from *Paris Vu Par . . .* (64), she has made twenty-one films with her husband. At first her parts were small, but after a brief appearance in *Les Cousins* (59), she was one of *Les Bonnes Femmes* (59), in *Les Godelureaux* (61), and one of *Landru*'s victims (63). *L'Oeil du Malin* (62) was her first starred part. In *Paris Vu Par . . .* she was the quarrelsome mother whose son puts cotton wool in his ears so that he never hears her cry for help in an emergency. That seemed a sardonic, marital joke from Chabrol, and even in *La Ligne de Démarcation* (66) and *The Champagne Murders* (67), there was no hint that he regarded her as anything more than a conventionally beautiful fashion plate. It was *Les Biches* (68) that properly discovered her as an actress. In one sense, her acutely made-up beauty needed very little heightening to suggest lesbianism, but the eventual sexual reversal of the film allowed her a new poignancy that was an advance for both actress and director. From that point, the note of thoughtfulness beneath such mannequin elegance has become central to Chabrol's work. It is difficult not to attribute the tenderness and growing human commitment of *La Femme Infidèle* (69), *La Rupture* (70), and *Le Boucher* (70) to her presence, even if he continued to photograph her in a strangely detached manner. Or is it that there is a glossy coldness in the woman herself that makes her attractive to Chabrol? One thinks of the way her Dordogne teacher in *Le Boucher* wears false eyelashes throughout, and of her remote calm in the yoga sequence. She is herself exquisitely uncommitted, although it is her playing of the woods sequence in *Le Boucher* on which the inse-

cure humanity of the film is based. It remains impossible to see her as a major actress, as if Chabrol's ultimate reticence had affected her too.

She made a few films for other directors—*Le Signe du Lion* (59, Eric Rohmer); *La Peau de Torpedo* (70, Jean Delannoy); and she fitted admirably into *The Discreet Charm of the Bourgeoisie* (72, Luis Buñuel), smiling through every disaster as if it were glass and urgently hauling her husband into the rhododendrons for a quick one before lunch.

Her vapid glossiness suited comedy of manners and may have lured Chabrol away from character studies to the absurd games of people as much corrupted by pretense as their situations are by B pictures. She is so much an image, so little a person: *Juste Avant la Nuit* (71); *Les Noces Rouges* (72); *Folies Bourgeoises* (76); and *Blood Relatives* (78). At the same time, she worked outside France, but with no more warmth: *B. Must Die* (73, José Luis Borau); *And Then There Were None* (74, Peter Collinson); *The Black Bird* (75, David Giler); *Silver Bears* (77, Ivan Passer); and *Eagle's Wing* (78, Anthony Harvey). But she was revealed as a bitter middle-aged woman, dowdy beside Isabelle Huppert in *Violette Nozière* (78).

Since then, generally as a supporting actress, she has made *Le Gagnant* (79, Christian Gion); *Le Soleil en Face* (79, Pierre Kast); *The Big Red One* (80, Samuel Fuller); *Il Etait une Fois des Gens Heureux . . . les Plouffe* (80, Gilles Carle); *Coup de Torchon* (81, Bertrand Tavernier); *Brideshead Revisited* (81, Charles Sturridge); *Le Beau Monde* (81, Michel Polac); *Le Marteau Pique* (81, Charles Bitsch); *Le Choc* (82, Robin Davis); *Boulevard des Assassins* (82, Boramy Tioulong); *Les Affinités Electives* (82, Chabrol); *Le Paradis pour Tous* (82, Alain Jessua); *Mortelle Randonnée* (83, Claude Miller); *La Scaralyine* (83, Gabriel Aghion); *Thieves After Dark* (83, Fuller); *Le Sang des Autres* (84, Chabrol); *El Viajero de las Quatro Estaciones* (84, Miguel Littin); *Mistral's Daughter* (84, Douglas Hickox and Kevin Connor); *The Sun Also Rises* (84, James Goldstone); *Poulet au Vinaigre* (85, Chabrol); *Night Magic* (85, Lewis Furey); *La Cage aux Folles III* (85, Georges Lautner); *Le Gitane* (85, Philippe de Broca); *Suivez Mon Regard* (86, Jean Curtelin); *Un'isola* (86, Carlo Lizzani); as Babette in *Babette's Feast* (87, Gabriel Axel); *Les Saisons du Plaisir* (87, Jean-Pierre Mocky); *Poor Little Rich Girl: The Barbara Hutton Story* (87, Charles Jarrott); *Sons* (89, Alexandre Rockwell); and *Betty* (93, Chabrol).

She was in *The Turn of the Screw* (92, Rusty Lemorande); *Le Fils de Gascogne* (95, Pascal Aubier); *Au Petit Marguery* (95, Laurent Benegui); *Maximum Risk* (96, Ringo Lam); *Petit* (96, Patrick Volson); *Arlette* (97, Claude Zidi); as Lady Covington (née Cucuface) in *Madeline* (98, Daisy von Scherler Mayer); *Belle Maman* (99,

Aghion); *Le Pique-nique de Lulu Kreutz* (00, Didier Martiny); *La Bicyclette Bleue* (00, Thierry Binisti); *J'ai Faim!!!* (01, Florence Quentin); *Ma Femme . . . S'Appelle Maurice* (02, Jean-Marie Poire).

Bille August, b. Copenhagen, 1948

1978: *Honning Måne*. 1983: *Zappa*. 1985: *Tro, Håb og Kaerlighed/Twist and Shout*. 1987: *Pelle Erobreren/Pelle the Conqueror*. 1992: *Den Goda Viljan/Best Intentions;* an episode for the series *Young Indiana Jones* (TV). 1993: *The House of the Spirits*. 1996: *Jerusalem*. 1997: *Smilla's Sense of Snow*. 1998: *Les Misérables*. 2002: *A Song for Martin*.

August was trained as a still photographer in Stockholm, and at the Danish Film Institute. He worked as cinematographer for several years and worked on—among others—*Men Can't Be Raped* (78, Jorn Donner) and *The Grass Is Singing* (81, Michael Raeburn). As a director, he has gone from strength to weakness; *Zappa* is a very fresh, energetic film about children; *Twist and Shout* showed the kids in their teens; *Pelle the Conqueror* was a nineteenth-century epic about a widower and his son, Swedish immigrants in Denmark—its warmth won the Oscar for best foreign film. *Best Intentions* was from Ingmar Bergman's script about his own parents, and it was a triumph. But his attempt at Isabel Allende's *The House of the Spirits* had too many stars, too little mood or magic. *Jerusalem*, adapted from Selma Lagerlöf's novel, was made for Swedish TV. *Smilla* had a striking first half, followed by chaos. And his version of *Les Misérables* seemed restrained or half-hearted.

Claude Autant-Lara (1903–2000),
b. Luzarches, France

1923: *Fait Divers* (s). 1926: *Vittel* (d). 1927: *Construire un Feu* (s). 1930: *Buster se Marie*. 1932: *Le Plombier Amoureux; L'Athlète Incomplet; Le Gendarme est sans Pitié* (s); *Un Client Serieux* (s); *Monsieur le Duc* (s); *La Peur des Coups* (s); *Invite Monsieur à Diner* (s). 1933: *Ciboulette*. 1936: *My Partner Mr. Davis*. 1937: *L'Affaire du Courier de Lyon*. 1938: *Le Ruisseau*. 1939: *Fric-Frac*. 1942: *Le Mariage de Chiffon; Lettres d'Amour*. 1943: *Douce*. 1945: *Sylvie et le Fantôme*. 1947: *Le Diable au Corps/The Devil in the Flesh*. 1949: *Occupe-Toi d'Amélie*. 1951: *L'Auberge Rouge*. 1952: "L'Orgueil," an episode in *Les Sept Péchés Capitaux*. 1953: *Le Bon Dieu Sans Confession*. 1954: *Le Blé en Herbe; Le Rouge et le Noir*. 1955: *Marguérite de la Nuit*. 1956: *La Traversée de Paris*. 1958: *En Cas de Malheur/Love Is My Profession; Le Joueur*. 1959: *Les Régates de San Francisco; La Jument Verte*. 1960: *Le Bois des Amants*. 1961: *Non Uccidere; Tu ne Tueras Point; Vive*

Henri IV . . . Vive L'Amour!; *Le Comte de Monte Cristo*. 1962: *Le Meurtrier*. 1963: *Le Magot de Joséfa*. 1965: *Journal d'une Femme en Blanc*. 1966: *Une Femme en Blanc Se Révolte*. 1967: "Aujourd'hui," episode in *Le Plus Vieux Métier du Monde*. 1968: *Le Franciscain de Bourges*. 1970: *Les Patates*. 1971: *Le Rouge et le Blanc*. 1977: *Gloria*.

Autant-Lara is representative of the placid urbanity of French cinema of the 1950s so despised by the New Wave. He served a long and dutiful apprenticeship from 1919 onward; eventually graduated to features; gathered together a band of accomplished collaborators and adopted respectable literary subjects. There was a surface daring in his work—he was anticlerical and a proponent of sexual frankness—but it did not prevent a romantic and bourgeois realism from settling on him, evident in the most conventional use of structure and a style that surrenders to literary prestige, glamorous acting, and claustrophobically atmospheric settings.

He began as an art director and costume designer and worked in that capacity on *Le Carnaval des Vérités* (19, Marcel L'Herbier); *L'Homme du Large* (20, L'Herbier); *Don Juan et Faust* (22, L'Herbier); *L'Inhumaine* (23, L'Herbier); *Paris qui Dort* (23, René Clair); *Le Voyage Imaginaire* (25, Clair); and *Nana* (26, Jean Renoir). He made an experimental short, *Fait Divers* (23), and a few silent documentaries, and in the early 1930s he worked in America on French-language versions of Hollywood movies: *Buster se Marie*, for instance, is Keaton's *Spite Marriage*, and *Plombier Amoureux, The Passionate Plumber*. On his return to France he took up direction, but only became properly established during the war.

Douce was a meticulous study in female psychology, *Sylvie et le Fantôme* a pleasant comedy, but *Le Diable au Corps* was the film that really made him: a clever adaptation of the Raymond Radiguet novel by his all-but-constant writers, Jean Aurenche and Pierre Bost, that brought considerable psychological authenticity to a doomed love affair between a married woman and a teenager. Despite fine playing from Micheline Presle and Gérard Philipe, the film remains a bourgeois gesture toward *l'amour fou*, made from a stance that readily invokes fate as a disguise for its own reserve; it is an academic and decorative reference to a theme rather than an embodiment of it. That is Autant-Lara's besetting defect, and his periodic pursuit of lofty subjects—Colette's *Le Blé en Herbe*, Stendhal's *Le Rouge et le Noir*, the Faustian *Marguérite de la Nuit*, or the long-nurtured *Tu ne Tueras Point*—is never reinforced by anything more than narrative directness and production values. He was not abashed by the New Wave, but his palatable, academic seriousness is out of fashion. *En Cas de Malheur* is the best of the later films: a collision of generations and attitudes when Jean Gabin meets Bardot. He is the sort of director to film classic novels for educational television, adept at glossing meaning and arranging furniture.

Daniel Auteuil, b. Alger, Algeria, 1950

At first sight, Auteuil lacks the looks or the command to be a leading actor. Still, it's clear that he is second only to Gérard Depardieu now in France. He is very versatile: he could manage the hunchback Ugolin in *Jean de Florette* and *Manon of the Spring;* he can play comedy or drama with equal ease; and as his several affairs with beautiful actresses suggest, he has sex appeal.

He was the child of two singers, members of the Opéra chorus, so it was natural that he was drawn into theatre—and he continues to perform on the Paris stage. He began appearing on French TV in 1974 and he made his movie debut in *L'Agression* (75, Gérard Pirès). Since then, these are some of his more important jobs: *Attention les Yeux* (75, Pirès); *La Nuit de Saint-Germain-des-Prés* (76, Bob Swaim); *L'Amour Violé* (76, Yannick Bellon); *A Nous Deux* (79, Claude Lelouch); *La Banquière* (80, Francis Girod); *Les Fauves* (83, Jean-Louis Daniel); *Petit Con* (84, Gérard Lauzier); *Jean de Florette* (86, Claude Berri); *Manon of the Spring* (87, Berri).

That pair established him at a new level: *A Few Days with Me* (88, Claude Sautet); *Romuald et Juliette* (89, Coline Serreau); *Lacenaire* (90, Girod); *A Heart in Winter* (92, Sautet); with Catherine Deneuve in *My Favorite Season* (93, André Téchiné); Henri of Navarre in *La Reine Margot* (94, Patrice Chéreau); *Une Femme Française* (95, Regis Warnier); *Le Huitième Jour* (96, Jaco Van Dormael); *Les Voleurs* (96, Téchiné); *Passage à l'Acte* (96, Girod); *Lucie Aubrac* (97, Berri); *Le Bossu* (97, Philippe de Broca); *The Girl on the Bridge* (99, Patrice Leconte); working in English, though not with ease, in *The Lost Son* (99, Chris Menges); *The Widow of Saint-Pierre* (00, Leconte); as *Sade* (00, Benoît Jacquot); *The Closet* (00, Francis Veber); *Vajout—La Diga del Disonore* (01, Martinelli); *L'Adversaire* (02, Nicole Garcia); *Petites Coupures* (03, Pascal Bonitzer).

Gene Autry (Orvon Gene Autry)
(1907–98), b. near Tioga, Texas; and
Roy Rogers (Leonard Franklin Slye)
(1911–98), b. Cincinnati, Ohio

If you (or I) can't quite muster enough interest in Autry or Rogers on their own, is it any better if we put them together? Well, yes, I think so. This will never be a rivalry or a pairing to match that of Louella Parsons and Hedda Hopper, but there is a story. Consider, it's Gene Autry vs. Lennie Slye;

it's rural Texas against Cincinnati; it's two men less handsome than their horses but rated as singers on the principle that that whining sound sometimes keeps restless cattle calm. They were singing cowboys who went from next-to-nothing to fortunes in excess of $100 million. More than that, they are the link between people like Will Rogers, William S. Hart, and Tom Mix, and those guys in false teeth, ten-gallon hats, and swishy buckskins who can be found selling real estate subdivisions all over the modern West. They are— if you recall—the models for Curly Bonner, the Joe Don Baker character in Sam Peckinpah's *Junior Bonner.*

Autry worked as a railroad telegrapher in Oklahoma, and he sang a bit. That led to some radio work, being noticed and recommended by Will Rogers. By 1934, Autry had a brief appearance, singing in *In Old Santa Fe*, a Ken Maynard film. A year later, he starred in *Tumbling Tumbleweeds*, and by 1937 he figured high in the box-office charts. His character was impeccable. He neither smoked nor drank; he was meticulous with the ladies—if you discount the singing; and he was white hat through and through. He had a horse named Champion and a sidekick, Smiley Burnette. He also had a home studio that loved him— Republic—where he was a money machine until 1942, when he went into Air Transport Command.

Len Slye had come to California in 1930 to pick fruit. He reflected that his name was not a plus, became "Dick Weston" and joined a singing group called Sons of the Pioneers. He entered radio and made a number of films in the late thirties, sometimes in support of Autry. So when Autry went patriotic, Roy jumped in behind him. At this distance in time, it's unclear why he didn't serve his country—maybe his feet were as flat as his singing vowels. But Rogers was an Autry duplicate. His sidekick was Gabby Hayes. His horse was Trigger. He had only one innovation—a girl, Dale Evans, who became his second wife in 1947.

Roy held strong at Republic, but Gene found room after the war at Columbia, and they both kept going until the early 1950s. Roy even had a TV show that ran from 1951 to 1957. It's not really to the point to list any—let alone all—of their titles, though Roy occasionally appeared in bigger films—with Bob Hope and Jane Russell, for instance, in *Son of Paleface* (52, Frank Tashlin). That's the one where Bob goes to bed with Trigger!

Autry was a very good businessman, who made far more money in local radio and television stations than he had done in movies. Indeed, it was enough to support his ownership of the California Angels baseball team. Roy's métier was ranching, rodeo shows, thoroughbreds, and real estate.

They are without intrinsic screen interest now, I fear, but as examples of how a certain benign image of the cowboy became translated into Western lifestyles and politics (think of Barry Goldwater), they are fascinating. You can see them both blushing at that very notion.

John G. Avildsen, b. Chicago, 1936

1968: *Okay Bill* (s). 1969: *Turn on to Love* (s); *Sweet Dreams* (s). 1970: *Guess What We Learned in School Today?; Joe.* 1971: *Cry Uncle.* 1972: *The Stoolie.* 1973: *Save the Tiger.* 1975: *W.W. and the Dixie Dancekings; Foreplay.* 1976: *Rocky.* 1978: *Slow Dancing in the Big City.* 1980: *The Formula.* 1981: *Neighbors.* 1983: *A Night in Heaven.* 1984: *The Karate Kid.* 1986: *The Karate Kid II.* 1987: *Happy New Year.* 1988: *For Keeps; Guardian Angels; Lean on Me.* 1989: *The Karate Kid III.* 1990: *Rocky V: The Final Bell.* 1992: *The Power of One.* 1994: *8 Seconds.* 1998: *A Fine and Private Place.* 1999: *Coyote Moon.*

Avildsen worked as an assistant director and as a cameraman, and he had credits on *Mickey One* (65, Arthur Penn), *Hurry Sundown* (67, Otto Preminger), and *Out of It* (69, Paul Williams), before he made his own breakthrough with *Joe,* in which Peter Boyle played a blue-collar bigot. Since then, Avildsen has handled a best picture Oscar-winner (*Rocky*) and brought a trio of *Karate Kids* to fruition without demonstrating an atom of character. Far more interesting are the truly scabrous *Save the Tiger* and *Neighbors,* which was a decent shot at the delirious narrative spiral of Thomas Berger's novel.

George Axelrod (1922–2003)

b. New York

It is more entertaining to hear Axelrod talking about his work than to see it. As a raconteur, his glimpses of show business are smart, indiscreet, and funnier than the rather cautious smartness of his films. But Axelrod was a very good representative of the continuing influence on Hollywood of Broadway's fast repartee, decorative snideness, and skillful construction. His humor is too knowing, cold, and too much based on the lewd sneer to rival the work of Garson Kanin. Axelrod is indelibly associated with Marilyn Monroe, on account of his writing on *Bus Stop* (56, Joshua Logan) and *The Seven Year Itch* (55, Billy Wilder) and because of his reminiscences of her since her death. In both films she is a sexual object, unaware of the effect she has on other people. The innocence was never really convincing or wholesome, but was set up to enable us all to smirk at the dumb broad. Although Axelrod did not write *Let's Make Love,* Monroe has a line in it that might have been a reference to his style: "I got tired of being ignorant. I never knew what people were referring to."

Axelrod was a stage manager and actor before he began writing for TV. That led to the Broadway success of his play *The Seven Year Itch,* and Hollywood invitations. *Phffft* (54, Mark Robson) was his first film, from his own story. As well as the two Monroe films, he has scripted *Breakfast at Tiffany's* (61, Blake Edwards), a cool bowdlerization of Capote's story; *The Manchurian Candidate* (62, John Frankenheimer), from a book written so that an idiot could film it; *Paris When It Sizzles* (63, Richard Quine); *How to Murder Your Wife* (64, Quine), an amusing use of the profession of cartoonist; he also wrote the play of *Goodbye Charlie* (64, Vincente Minnelli). In the mid-sixties, he started directing his own material: two sex-oriented comedies, *Lord Love a Duck* (66) and *The Secret Life of an American Wife* (68). The latter is a soulless thing made for Walter Matthau's virtuosity. But *Lord Love a Duck* is his best script, helped by the inventive presence of Tuesday Weld as a blonde more sensitive than the script's conception of her.

After several years of obscurity, he got another credit as writer on *The Lady Vanishes* (79, Anthony Page). He also cowrote *The Holcroft Covenant* (85, Frankenheimer) and got a story-adaptation credit on *The Fourth Protocol* (87, John Mackenzie).

Lew Ayres (Lewis Ayer), (1908–96)

b. Minneapolis, Minnesota

The moment in *Advise and Consent* (62, Otto Preminger) when Vice President Lew Ayres (still youthful-looking, honest, and likeable) is elevated by the death of Franchot Tone to the biggest opportunity is both touching and ironic—one of those barely visible barbs that Preminger liked to leave in his films. For Ayres's career is sweet with youthful salad days, but bitter with public fickleness. Twice, he rose and fell; and still he remained decent and reasonable. It is not clear what special drive or ruthlessness he lacked or what led him from stardom into dreadful B pictures. But there went with it a calm that apparently enabled him to live through so much disappointment.

Although later events might make it seem implausible, he studied medicine at the University of Arizona. A versatile musician, he was spotted by Paul Bern—then at Pathé—and given a small part in *The Sophomore* (29, Leo McCarey). Bern moved to MGM and hired Ayres to play opposite Garbo in *The Kiss* (29, Jacques Feyder). On the strength of this, he was signed up by Universal to play the young soldier sickened by war in *All Quiet on the Western Front* (30, Lewis Milestone). For a few years Ayres remained at the top, only gradually undermined by his sheer boyishness: *Doorway to Hell* (30, Archie Mayo); *Common Clay* (30, Victor Fleming); *East Is West* (30, Tod Browning); *The Iron Man* (31, Browning); *The Impatient Maiden* (32, James Whale); *Night World* (32, W. S. Van Dyke); *Okay America* (32,

Tay Garnett); and *State Fair* (33, Henry King). Soon after this, Universal let him go to Fox, and he found himself in B pictures. One of them, *Hearts in Bondage* (36) at Republic, he even directed himself. He worked with hectic energy, but hardly anything memorable survived until in 1938 he was put with Cukor, Grant, and Hepburn in *Holiday,* and produced a beautiful performance. MGM retrieved him and gave him some vacuously jolly parts before launching him as Dr. Kildare. With Lionel Barrymore as Dr. Gillespie and Laraine Day as his sweetheart, Ayres made nine Kildare pictures in three years and became the idol of national hypochondria. But then he chose to display in life some of the humane feelings he was most admired for on-screen: he became a conscientious objector—and suffered a fierce boycott. He did not work again until Robert Siodmak's *The Dark Mirror* (46). He was good in *The Unfaithful* (47, Vincent Sherman) and a doctor again for *Johnny Belinda* (48, Jean Negulesco). But after *The Capture* (49, John Sturges), *New Mexico* (50, Irving Reis), and *No Escape* (53, Charles Bennett), he retired to make a personal, religious documentary, *Altars of the East.* There was another interval before Preminger recalled him to the highest office, after which he made only *The Carpetbaggers* (64, Edward Dmytryk); *Battlestar: Galactica* (79, Richard A. Colla); *Letters from Frank* (79, Edward Parone); *Salem's Lot* (79, Tobe Hooper); *Of Mice and Men* (81, Reza Badiyi); *Under Siege* (86, Roger Young); and *Cast the First Stone* (89, John Korty).

B

Hector Babenco,
b. Buenos Aires, Argentina, 1946
1975: *King of the Night.* 1978: *Lucio Flavio.* 1981: *Pixote.* 1985: *Kiss of the Spider Woman.* 1987: *Ironweed.* 1991: *At Play in the Fields of the Lord.* 1998: *Corazón Iluminado/Foolish Heart.* 2003: *Carandiru.*

Babenco is an idealist, possessed of a vivid documentary eye. As such, he was an important cultural figure in Brazil in the seventies—*Lucio Flavio* was the story of a real man, a criminal, who promised to tell stories about death squads run by the police. The film was hugely controversial, and Babenco's life was threatened. *Pixote* was a gruesome study of the homeless children in Brazil, much of it improvised from research Babenco had done with authentic street children. *Pixote* is like de Sica cut with Céline, and it is all the tougher to watch in that there seems so little scope for optimism left.

This achievement led Babenco beyond his natural range—I suggest. *Kiss of the Spider Woman* won great acclaim. It played on the international art-house circuit, and William Hurt's faded-flower performance won an Oscar. But *Spider Woman* is not really true to Manuel Puig, and it introduces a fatal strain of melodrama. For, in truth, Babenco is not a sophisticated storyteller. Similarly, given William Kennedy's *Ironweed,* he went for exactly the wrong starry cast and blurred the implacable firmness in Kennedy's book. The reality was gone, replaced by so much fussy, earnest attempt. *At Play in the Fields of the Lord* was all the more misguided, ponderously long, and placid in its human story.

So where does an Argentinian director go? Babenco's parents were Russian and Polish Jews. He traveled for much of the sixties, and went to Brazil originally as a visitor. Clearly, he was never "at home" doing American films, and he is not likely to get more offers from there. Can he go back to Brazil? Can he be Brazilian? Or is he at risk of being a wandering, universal poet of the outcast?

Lauren Bacall (Betty Joan Perske),
b. New York, 1924
Her parents divorced when she was six years old and she was raised by her German-Rumanian mother. She was educated at the Julia Richman High School and studied dancing for thirteen years. While still at school, she modeled and played truant to watch Bette Davis films. She was briefly at the American Academy of Dramatic Arts, and in 1942 made her Broadway debut in *January 2 × 4.* That and her next play were flops, and it was only when she appeared on the cover of *Harper's Bazaar* in March 1943 that Howard Hawks's wife recommended her to Hawks. He put her under a seven-year contract, perhaps showed her Ann Sheridan in *Torrid Zone,* and cast her opposite Humphrey Bogart in *To Have and Have Not* (44). Her Slim in that picture (named after Mrs. Hawks) was an outrageous reversal of the meek ingenue, instructing the master in whistling and watching everyone as if she had been up all night writing the script. Only nineteen years old, she stole that film, turned it from an adventure to a love story and captivated Bogart. Warners called her "The Look" and she was a publicity phenomenon for a season. Warners worked her hard: *Confidential Agent* (45, Herman Shumlin); magnificent again in set pieces with her new husband, Bogart, in *The Big Sleep* (46, Hawks); *Dark Passage* (47, Delmer Daves); *Key Largo* (48, John Huston); *Young Man With a Horn* (50, Michael Curtiz); and *Bright Leaf* (50, Curtiz). Hawks had sold his interest in her to Warners, and she was constantly in trouble, being suspended twelve times for refusing parts. But she made *How to Marry a Millionaire* (53, Jean Negulesco) and *Blood Alley* (55,

William Wellman). At last she bought her freedom and enjoyed better parts in Minnelli's *The Cobweb* (56), Sirk's *Written on the Wind* (56), and Minnelli's *Designing Woman* (57) without ever rekindling her earlier uniqueness. Indeed, the Sirk movie gave the straight role to her and the flashy one to Dorothy Malone, a cute sideshow only in *The Big Sleep*. After Bogart died, she seemed disenchanted with Hollywood. In 1961, she married Jason Robards Jr. (divorced in 1969) and made *Shock Treatment* (64, Denis Sanders), *Sex and the Single Girl* (64, Richard Quine), and *Harper* (66, Jack Smight). Meanwhile, in 1959 she returned to Broadway in *Goodbye Charlie* and achieved great success in 1965 in *Cactus Flower* and then, in 1970, in *Applause* (a musical version of *All About Eve,* in which she took the Bette Davis part). *Murder on the Orient Express* (74, Sidney Lumet) was her first film in eight years.

Perhaps she needed Bogart and Hawks and the remarkable combination of youth and dryness she shows in her two films with them. If so, two films are enough. She did make an honest landlady in *The Shootist* (76, Don Siegel), grim and proper but understanding the pains of heroic men.

After that, her career proceeded without evident explanation: on TV in *Perfect Gentleman* (78, Jackie Cooper); *Health* (79, Robert Altman); as a Broadway star pursued by an admirer in the lackluster *The Fan* (81, Edward Bianchi); playing *Sweet Bird of Youth* in London onstage—directed by Harold Pinter; *Appointment with Death* (88, Michael Winner); *Mr. North* (88, Danny Huston); in a version of the Marie Dressler role in the TV *Dinner at Eight* (90, Ron Lagomarsino); as James Caan's agent in *Misery* (90, Rob Reiner); *All I Want for Christmas* (91, Robert Lieberman); and *The Portrait* (93, Arthur Penn) for TV.

The saddest aspect of her longevity is her haughtiness, her rather hollow grandeur—it is just the pomp that her Slim would have deflated. She has been in *A Foreign Field* (93, Charles Sturridge); *The Parallax Garden* (93, David Trainer); *Ready to Wear* (94, Altman); *From the Mixed-Up Files of Mrs. Basil E. Frankweiler* (95, Marian Cole). She got a real movie and the mother's role in *The Mirror Has Two Faces* (96, Barbra Streisand). She was not good in it, but she was nominated, and she proved she couldn't act in the moment when she tried to pretend she didn't care about losing. *Le Jour et la Nuit* (97, Bernard-Henri Levy); the old lady in *Too Rich: The Secret Life of Doris Duke* (99, John Erman); *Diamonds* (99, John Mallory Asher); *The Venice Project* (99, Robert Dornhelm); *Presence of Mind* (99, Antonio Aloy).

Enough? No. How about Ma Ginger in *Dogville* (03, Lars von Trier)?

Kevin Bacon, b. Philadelphia, 1958

While there was never any malice in the media

game "Six Degrees of Kevin Bacon," it did have a quiet hint that his ubiquity in film was not exactly significant or valuable. Wasn't it more the case that everyone "knew" him, even if they couldn't quite place him? That mood has passed. In the last few years, Kevin Bacon has been too good too often to be taken for granted. He may become just a fine supporting actor, but he's more than just the emblem of faceless team play. He has also directed one film—*Losing Chase* (1996)—about the relationship between a disturbed woman and the younger woman who looks after her children, which starred Helen Mirren and Bacon's wife, Kyra Sedgwick.

He began on stage and won a place in movies as one of the gang: *National Lampoon's Animal House* (78, John Landis); *Starting Over* (79, Alan J. Pakula); *Hero at Large* (80, Martin Davidson); *Friday the 13th* (80, Sean Cunningham); *Only When I Laugh* (81, Glenn Jordan). Like everyone else, he benefited from the chance offered in *Diner* (82, Barry Levinson), and after *Forty Deuce* (82, Paul Morrissey), he got the lead in a hot movie—*Footloose* (84, Herbert Ross)—in which he led the young ensemble cast and danced well enough.

After that, he was in *Enormous Changes at the Last Minute* (83, Mirra Bank); *Quicksilver* (86, Tom Donnelly), about bike messengers; *White Water Summer* (87, Jeff Bleckner); *End of the Line* (87, Jay Russell); *Planes, Trains & Automobiles* (87, John Hughes); as the young filmmaker in *The Big Picture* (89, Christopher Guest); a psychopath in *Criminal Law* (89, Martin Campbell); *Tremors* (90, Ron Underwood); a student still in *Flatliners* (90, Joel Schumacher); the lead in *Queens Logic* (91, Steve Rash); with Kyra Sedgwick in *Pyrates* (91, Noah Stern); *He Said, She Said* (91, Ken Kwapis); excellent as a gay pickup in *JFK* (91, Oliver Stone); *A Few Good Men* (92, Rob Reiner); *The Air Up There* (94, Paul M. Glaser); an effective villain in *The River Wild* (94, Curtis Hanson); an astronaut in *Apollo 13* (95, Ron Howard). He was very good as the deranged convict in *Murder in the First* (95, Marc Rocco); creepy as the child abuser in *Sleepers* (96, Levinson); with Jennifer Aniston in *Picture Perfect* (97, Glenn Gordon Caron); wonderful in *Telling Lies in America* (97, Guy Ferland); nicely cool in *Wild Things* (98, John McNaughton); and the lead in *Stir of Echoes* (99, David Koepp). He was good in *My Dog Skip* (00, Jay Russell), and rather nasty in *Hollow Man* (00, Paul Verhoeven). He was uncredited in *Novocaine* (01, David Atkins); *Trapped* (02, Luis Mandoki); *In the Cut* (03, Jane Campion); *Mystic River* (03, Clint Eastwood).

Lloyd Bacon (1890–1955),
b. San Jose, California
1926: *Finger Prints; Private Izzy Murphy; Broken*

Hearts of Hollywood. 1927: *The Heart of Mary-
land; White Flannels; A Sailor's Sweetheart;
Brass Knuckles.* 1928: *Pay As You Enter; The
Lion and the Mouse; Women They Talk About;
The Singing Fool.* 1929: *Stark Mad; No Defense;
Honky Tonk; Say It With Songs; So Long, Letty.*
1930: *She Couldn't Say No; The Other Tomor-
row; A Notorious Affair; Moby Dick; Office Wife.*
1931: *Sit Tight; Kept Husbands; Fifty Million
Frenchmen; Gold Dust Gertie; Honor of the Fam-
ily.* 1932: *Fireman, Save My Child; Manhattan
Parade; Famous Ferguson Case; Miss Pinkerton;
You Said a Mouthful; Crooner; Alias the Doctor.*
1933: *Picture Snatcher; Mary Stevens M.D.; 42nd
Street; Footlight Parade; Son of a Sailor.* 1934:
*Wonder Bar; A Very Honorable Guy; Six-
Day Bike Rider; He Was Her Man; Here Comes
the Navy.* 1935: *Devil Dogs of the Air; In
Caliente; Frisco Kid; The Irish in Us; Broadway
Gondolier.* 1936: *Cain and Mabel; Gold Diggers
of 1937; Sons o'Guns.* 1937: *San Quentin; Marked
Woman; Submarine D-1; Ever Since Eve.* 1938: *A
Slight Case of Murder; Cowboy from Brooklyn;
Boy Meets Girl; Racket Busters.* 1939: *Wings of
the Navy; Indianapolis Speedway; Espionage
Agent; Invisible Stripes; The Oklahoma Kid; A
Child Is Born.* 1940: *Three Cheers for the Irish;
Brother Orchid; Knute Rockne—All American.*
1941: *Honeymoon for Three; Footsteps in the
Dark; Affectionately Yours; Navy Blues.* 1942:
Larceny Inc.; Wings for the Eagle; Silver Queen.
1943: *Action in the North Atlantic.* 1944: *Sunday
Dinner for a Soldier; The Sullivans.* 1945: *Cap-
tain Eddie.* 1946: *Wake Up and Dream; Home
Sweet Homicide.* 1947: *I Wonder Who's Kissing
Her Now.* 1948: *You Were Meant for Me; Give My
Regards to Broadway; An Innocent Affair/Don't
Trust Your Husband.* 1949: *Mother Is a Fresh-
man; It Happens Every Spring; Miss Grant Takes
Richmond.* 1950: *The Good Humor Man; The
Fuller Brush Girl/Affairs of Sally; Kill the
Umpire.* 1951: *Call Me Mister; The Frogmen;
Golden Girl.* 1953: *She Had to Say Yes; Walking
My Baby Back Home; The French Line; The I
Don't Care Girl.* 1954: *She Couldn't Say No.*

Bacon was a stage actor who worked with Chaplin
and became a director of shorts with Sennett in
1921. That led him into a seventeen-year spell as
director at Warners before, in 1944, he moved on
to Fox. It is not a career of special character, but
through his long period at Warners he was associated with several notable musicals: Jolson in *The
Singing Fool;* the classic backstage setting of *42nd
Street* and *Footlight Parade,* which have a special
tough sentiment and a clutch of good performances; and *Gold Diggers of 1937,* which has
some of Busby Berkeley's most floral dance patterns. *Marked Woman* is a good story of attempts
to break prostitution racketeering, with Bette

Davis as the informer and Bogart as the prosecutor. He also handled that unlikely Western, *The
Oklahoma Kid,* in which Bogart and Cagney make
very implausible hoods in ten-gallon hats, and two
of Edward G. Robinson's comedy thrillers: *A
Slight Case of Murder* and *Brother Orchid.* His
Fox years are much duller, but his last three films
were made at RKO, and *The French Line* has Jane
Russell in her bath and in some startlingly explicit
songs.

Carroll Baker,
b. Johnstown, Pennsylvania, 1931

A splendidly vulgar creature, capable of a specially daft sexiness. She was a nightclub dancer
and a pupil at the Actors' Studio—a mixture that
has never deserted her. She had a tiny part in
Easy to Love (53, Charles Walters) but came to
real notice brilliantly served by Tennessee
Williams, Elia Kazan, Karl Malden, and Eli Wallach so that she seemed genuinely overripe and
heedlessly erotic, in *Baby Doll* (56)—sucking her
thumb as if vaguely mindful of the sucked toe in
Buñuel's *L'Age d'Or.* In the same year, she was
reassessed by George Stevens as a dull little
blonde in *Giant. The Big Country* (58, William
Wyler) had her pouting throughout, while *The
Miracle* (59, Irving Rapper) was fatuous. She
strove in the next few years to dignify her blonde
voluptuousness, sometimes taking it to a point of
exaggeration. She is terribly serious in *Something
Wild* (62, directed by her then husband Jack Garfein); but perfectly exploited by Seth Holt as the
disruptive element at *Station Six Sahara* (63).
Her finest hour came for Joseph Levine in a
prurient series that caught her flamboyant
earnestness: *The Carpetbaggers* (64, Edward
Dmytryk); *Harlow* (65, Gordon Douglas); and
Sylvia (65, Douglas). Since then, she has been
unobtrusive in *Cheyenne Autumn* (64, John
Ford), as Veronica in *The Greatest Story Ever
Told* (65, Stevens), in *Mister Moses* (65, Ronald
Neame); and otherwise given up to lurid concoc-
tions, two of which claim to be called *The Sweet
Body of Deborah* (68, Romolo Guerrieri) and
Orgasmo (68, Umberto Lenzi). She was also in
Captain Apache (71, Alexander Singer); a witch
in *Baba Yaga* (73, Corrado Farina); *The Virgin
Wife* (76, Franco Martinelli); *Andy Warhol's Bad*
(76, Jed Johnson); *Confessions of a Frustrated
Housewife* (76, Andrea Bianchi); *Zerschossene
Traume* (77, Peter Petzak); *The Watcher in the
Woods* (81, John Hough); *Red Monarch* (83, Jack
Gold); the mama to Bud Cort's Freud in *The
Secret Diary of Sigmund Freud* (83, Danford B.
Greene); the mom to Dorothy Stratten in *Star 80*
(83, Bob Fosse); *Hitler's S.S.: Portrait in Evil*
(85, Jim Goddard); *Native Son* (86, Jerrold
Freedman); *On Fire* (87, Robert Greenwald); as
Jack Nicholson's wife in *Ironweed* (87, Hector

Babenco); *Kindergarten Cop* (90, Ivan Reitman); and *Blonde Fist* (91, Frank Clarke).

Most of her work nowadays is obscure, or for television, but she has been in *Judgment Day: The John List Story* (93, Bobby Roth); *Men Don't Tell* (93, Harry Winer); *A Kiss to Die For* (93, Leon Ichaso); *Gipsy Angel* (94, Al Fata); *Im Sog des Bözen* (95, Nikolai Mullerschon); *Dalva* (96, Ken Cameron); *North Shore Fish* (96, Steve Zuckerman); *Just Your Luck* (96, Gary Auerbach); *Skeletons* (96, David DeCoteau); *The Game* (97, David Fincher); *Heart Full of Rain* (97, Roger Young); *Rag and Bone* (97, Robert Lieberman); *Nowhere to Go* (98, John Caire); *Another Woman's Husband* (00, Noel Nosseck).

Rick (Richard A.) **Baker**,
b. Binghamton, New York, 1950

Once upon a time in the movies, makeup was apparently the province of the Westmore family: how George Westmore, a British barber and wig-maker, came to America, began doing makeup at Metro in 1917, and passed on the secrets of the trade to six sons—Monte, Perc, Ern, Wally, Bud, and Frank. Makeup in that era could go to wild extremes: it took Jekyll into Hyde, and so on; it was the treasury of an actor like Lon Chaney, supposedly collected together in one small case; and it was the application of cosmetics that made anyone and everyone look better (God save us, there is still in most of our minds a simple but unshakeable equation of smooth, handsome looks with virtue).

Rick Baker is the master craftsman of a following generation, yet even now stands like a primitive, his brushes and masks redundant as electronics simply adds a scar, a dimple, or a third eye to this face. Frequently in his very busy career, Baker has been credited as doing not just makeup, but "special effects." Equally, he has often enjoyed dressing up in monkey suits and acting in films—an activity that must be near its last days.

He was in pictures by the early seventies, working as an assistant to makeup artist Dick Smith. But then he went free-lance and began to accumulate fascinating credits: aging Cicely Tyson in *The Autobiography of Miss Jane Pittman* (74, John Korty); *It's Alive* (74, Larry Cohen); *King Kong* (76, John Guillermin), where he also played himself in some scenes, inserting himself in the ape suit he had made; *Star Wars* (77, George Lucas), where he played a couple of characters; *The Incredible Melting Man* (78, William Sachs); *The Fury* (78, Brian De Palma), with alarming skin eruptions; *The Howling* (80, Joe Dante); *The Incredible Shrinking Woman* (81, Joel Schumacher).

It was for his work on *An American Werewolf in London* (81, John Landis) that Baker won the first-ever Oscar for makeup (though honorary Oscars had gone to William Tuttle for *7 Faces of Dr. Lao*, in 1964, and John Chambers for *Planet of the Apes*, in 1968). Baker carried on with *Videodrome* (83, David Cronenberg); work on the Michael Jackson music video "Thriller" (83), where he also played a zombie; *Greystoke: The Legend of Tarzan, Lord of the Apes* (84, Hugh Hudson); *Ratboy* (86, Sondra Locke); *Harry and the Hendersons* (87, William Dear); *Coming to America* (88, Landis); *Gorillas in the Mist* (88, Michael Apted); *The Rocketeer* (91, Joe Johnston); *Ed Wood* (94, Tim Burton), where he did the Bela Lugosi makeup; *Wolf* (94, Mike Nichols); *Batman Forever* (95, Schumacher); *The Nutty Professor* (96, Tom Shadyac)—where extraordinary electronic enlarging effects set in.

He did *The Frighteners* (96, Peter Jackson); *Escape from L.A.* (96, John Carpenter); *Men in Black* (97, Barry Sonnenfeld); *Critical Care* (97, Sidney Lumet); *Mighty Joe Young* (98, Ron Underwood); *Life* (99, Ted Demme); *The Nutty Professor II: The Klumps* (00, Peter Segal); *How the Grinch Stole Christmas* (00, Ron Howard), on which he shared in a second Oscar; *Planet of the Apes* (01, Burton); *Men in Black II* (02, Sonnenfeld); *The Ring* (02, Gore Verbinski); *The Hulk* (03, Ang Lee); *The Cat in the Hat* (03, Bo Welch).

Sir Stanley Baker (1927–76),
b. Rhondda, Wales

Until the early 1960s, Baker was the only male lead in the British cinema who managed to suggest contemptuousness, aggression, and the working class. He is the first hint of proletarian male vigor against the grain of Leslie Howard, James Mason, Stewart Granger, John Mills, Dirk Bogarde, and the theatrical knights. Which is not to disparage these players, but to say that Baker was a welcome novelty, that he is one of Britain's most important screen actors, and that he has not yet been equaled—not even by Michael Caine. Baker was for years typed as ugly, boorish, indelicate: *Undercover* (43, Sergei Nolbandov); *All Over the Town* (48, Derek Twist); *Captain Horatio Hornblower* (51, Raoul Walsh); *Whispering Smith Hits London* (52, Francis Searle); *The Cruel Sea* (53, Charles Frend); *The Red Beret* (53, Terence Young); *Hell Below Zero* (54, Mark Robson); *Knights of the Round Table* (54, Richard Thorpe); and *The Good Die Young* (54, Lewis Gilbert). It was notable that his glowering hostility won him parts in American films—*Beautiful Stranger* (53, David Miller); *Alexander the Great* (55, Robert Rossen); and *Helen of Troy* (55, Robert Wise)—but in Britain he remained a heavy: as the upstart Welshman Henry Tudor in *Richard III* (55, Laurence Olivier) and in *Campbell's Kingdom* (57, Ralph Thomas). The turning point came through Cy Endfield who directed Baker in three surprisingly American films set in moderately plausible British settings: *Child in the Home* (56); *Hell Drivers* (57)—about lorry drivers;

and *Sea Fury* (58). Baker appeared as a credible Gestapo man in *The Angry Hills* (59, Robert Aldrich) and then fell in with Joseph Losey who capitalized on his growing power: first as the police inspector with a cold in *Blind Date* (59); next as Bannion, the doomed hero in *The Criminal* (60); and then as Tyvian, the fraud besotted with *Eve* (62). His Bannion captured all the rough strength of his early work and is one of Losey's subtlest heroes. As for Tyvian—a Welshman—Baker lost nothing of the man's maudlin self-loathing and showed that a utility-style actor was quite capable of the baroque.

As soon as he was established, Baker branched into production. Acting now seemed a secondary interest and he did not take enough time choosing his parts: *The Guns of Navarone* (61, J. Lee Thompson); *Sodom and Gomorrah* (62, Aldrich); *A Prize of Arms* (62, Cliff Owen); *In the French Style* (63, Robert Parrish); *Accident* (66, Losey); *La Ragazza con la Pistola* (67, Mario Monicelli); *Where's Jack?* (68, James Clavell); *The Games* (69, Michael Winner); and *The Last Grenade* (69, Gordon Flemyng).

He had produced, with great success: *Zulu* (64, Endfield), about Welsh soldiers in South Africa; *Sands of the Kalahari* (65, Endfield); *Robbery* (67, Peter Yates)—a rather coy version of the Great Train Robbery; and *Perfect Friday* (70, Peter Hall). Acting in all four, his thoughts had seemed fixed on the papers in his office.

Sir Michael Balcon (1896–1977),
b. Birmingham, England

Against the spectacular setting of Alexander Korda's attempt to make the British film industry a dashing, lightweight Hollywood, Michael Balcon cultivated a "little-England" production unit. He extolled aspects of Englishness that the English themselves would enjoy recognizing: both the Hitchcock thrillers and the Ealing comedies derive from a fantasy England of village seclusion, benign eccentrics, cockney spunk, official pomposity, pretty girls, and brisk young men. Although the feeling for cruelty in *The Man Who Knew Too Much* (34, Hitchcock) and for the macabre in *The Ladykillers* (55, Alexander Mackendrick) clearly derive from their directors, Balcon's cheerful endorsement of a conservative but independent England—just as capable of nurturing lurid antistate plots as schemes to preserve railway engines—is as consistent and entertaining as it is erroneous. His provincialism—*Passport to Pimlico* (49), *Whisky Galore* (49)—is idyllic and escapist. His England is the one that liberals liked to concentrate on during the 1930s until the Depression seeped away. Engaging silliness is the abiding theme and ideal of these films, but all credit goes to Balcon for picking directors who were able and free to lead his own good nature

into rather harsher territory. In the best sense, Balcon was a general manager of modest, thriving companies, a man who took pleasure in blending prickly talents, and the chief sponsor of Robert Hamer and Harry Watt.

He had had a spell in the rubber industry as a manager before he set up Victory, a film distribution company, with Victor Saville. They soon went into production and, with Graham Cutts, Balcon formed Gainsborough Pictures. He had charge there through the 1930s, furnishing films for Gaumont British. But from 1938, allowing for the making of war-service documentaries, he was head of Ealing Studios, producing films for Rank. He stayed there until 1959 and then formed his own company, which led to his unproductive chairmanship of Bryanston and British Lion. By 1960, his England was almost faded away and often the target for recrimination. In addition, his paternal notions of small, efficient studios had been undermined by the decay of the industry.

His long career included the producer's role on the following: *Woman to Woman* (22, Graham Cutts), with script and art direction by Hitchcock; *The White Shadow* (23, Cutts), Hitchcock doing art direction and editing; *The Passionate Adventure* (24, Cutts); *The Blackguard* (25, Cutts); *The Prude's Fall* (25, Cutts); *The Pleasure Garden* (25, Hitchcock); *The Mountain Eagle* (26, Hitchcock); *The Lodger* (26, Hitchcock)—subtitled "A Story of the London Fog"; *Downhill* (27, Hitchcock); *Easy Virtue* (27, Hitchcock); *The Good Companions* (33, Saville); *I Was a Spy* (33, Saville); *Man of Aran* (34, Robert Flaherty), which he persuaded Gaumont British to finance; *Little Friend* (34, Berthold Viertel); *The Thirty-nine Steps* (35, Hitchcock); *The Secret Agent* (36, Hitchcock); *Sabotage* (36, Hitchcock); *Tudor Rose* (36, Robert Stevenson); *A Yank at Oxford* (38, Jack Conway), made during a short spell at MGM; *The Ware Case* (39, Stevenson); *The Big Blockade* (41, Charles Frend); *Went the Day Well?* (42, Alberto Cavalcanti); *Next of Kin* (42, Thorold Dickinson); *Nine Men* (43, Harry Watt); *San Demetrio, London* (43, Frend); *The Bells Go Down* (43, Basil Dearden's first film); *Champagne Charlie* (44, Cavalcanti); *Painted Boats* (45, Charles Crichton); the ambitious *Dead of Night* (45, Cavalcanti, Crichton, Dearden, Robert Hamer); *Pink String and Sealing Wax* (45, Hamer); *The Captive Heart* (46, Dearden), based on an idea from Balcon's wife; *The Overlanders* (46, Watt); *Nicholas Nickleby* (47, Cavalcanti); *Frieda* (47, Dearden); *It Always Rains on Sunday* (48, Hamer); *Against the Wind* (48, Crichton); *Scott of the Antarctic* (48, Frend); *Kind Hearts and Coronets* (49, Hamer); *Passport to Pimlico* (49, Henry Cornelius); *Whisky Galore* (49, Mackendrick); *Eureka Stockade* (49, Watt); *The Blue Lamp* (50, Dearden); *The Man in the White Suit*

(51, Mackendrick); *The Lavender Hill Mob* (51, Crichton); *Where No Vultures Fly* (51, Watt); *Secret People* (52, Dickinson); *Mandy* (52, Mackendrick); *The Cruel Sea* (53, Frend); *The Long Arm* (56, Frend); *Man in the Sky* (56, Crichton); *Nowhere to Go* (58, Seth Holt); and *The Scapegoat* (59, Hamer).

Alec Baldwin, b. Amityville, New York, 1958
Year after year, American movies act as if Alec Baldwin were a proper lead player. To these eyes he's rarely convincing, or even comfortable. Think of the name—Alec Baldwin! It doesn't even sound American! It ought to go with a sturdy soccer center forward from the 1950s. But the movies insist that he's romantic and adventurous. . . . Is it all a cunning game to drive me mad?

Consider his Doc McCoy in the pallid remake of *The Getaway* (94, Roger Donaldson), less nasty than the Peckinpah version, which was already a tame account of the Jim Thompson novel. Baldwin is so much less resonant than Steve McQueen, no matter that his real wife, Kim Basinger, makes a splendid tramp (much better than the slumming model, Ali MacGraw). Baldwin never really seems jealous, in danger, or tired—qualities that grooved in McQueen's mean blue eyes. (In McQueen's version, Baldwin would have been cast as the guy who steals the bag—or would have been, if Richard Bright hadn't done it so well.)

Yet Baldwin is evidently smart—I wonder if he isn't better suited to comedy? Being tough all the time can be so stultifying. He was Joshua Rush for a season on *Knot's Landing* (84–85). He did some good theatre, including the role Gary Oldman originated in *Serious Money*, and *Prelude to a Kiss*. However, he managed to be no more than a party boy as Stanley Kowalski in the 1992 revival of *A Streetcar Named Desire*.

He made *Sweet Revenge* (84, David Greene); and *Love on the Run* (85, Gus Trikonis) for TV; and played Colonel Travis in the TV miniseries *The Alamo: 13 Days to Glory* (87, Burt Kennedy); *Forever, Lulu* (87, Amos Kollek); *Beetlejuice* (88, Tim Burton); very funny in *Married to the Mob* (88, Jonathan Demme) as the offed husband; *She's Having a Baby* (88, John Hughes); as the boyfriend in *Working Girl* (88, Mike Nichols); *Talk Radio* (88, Oliver Stone); *Great Balls of Fire!* (89, Jim McBride); and *Alice* (90, Woody Allen).

He got a lead role in *The Hunt for Red October* (90, John McTiernan), and he was frightening and comic as the psychopath in *Miami Blues* (90, George Armitage)—he seemed so much more alert when wicked. *The Marrying Man* (91, Jerry Rees) was his first pairing with Basinger, and the chemistry was palpable *and* funny. Since then, he was with Meg Ryan in the movie of *Prelude to a Kiss* (92, Norman René), briefly nasty in *Glen-garry Glen Ross* (92, James Foley), devilishly superior in *Malice* (93, Harold Becker); and as *The Shadow* (94, Russell Mulcahy).

An intriguing desperation has seemed to overtake Baldwin in recent years. His marriage to Kim Basinger ended; the quality of his films slipped. Yet he made more noise—in semi-political statements, in "appearances" and in something like effrontery. Is it that he can't quite believe, or accept, that we haven't heard of all the movies? He was in *A Streetcar Named Desire* opposite Jessica Lange (95, Glenn Jordan); *The Juror* (96, Brian Gibson); *Heaven's Prisoners* (96, Phil Joanou); *Looking for Richard* (96, Al Pacino); *Ghosts of Mississippi* (96, Rob Reiner); *The Edge* (97, Lee Tamahori); *Mercury Rising* (98, Becker); *The Confession* (99, David Hugh Jones); *Thick as Thieves* (99, Scott Sanders); uncredited as the movie-star boyfriend (hiss!) in *Notting Hill* (99, Roger Michell); *Scout's Honor* (99, Neil Leifer); *Outside Providence* (99, Michael Corrente).

He was Justice Robert Jackson in the TV miniseries *Nuremberg* (00, Yves Simoneau); *State and Main* (00, David Mamet); *Speak Truth to Power* (00, Marc Levin); *The Acting Class* (00, Jill Hennessy and Elizabeth Holder); as Jimmy Doolittle in *Pearl Harbor* (01, Michael Bay); *The Royal Tenenbaums* (01, Wes Anderson).

He acted in and directed a version of *The Devil and Daniel Webster* (02); as Robert McNamara in *Path to War* (02, John Frankenheimer); *Second Nature* (02, Ben Bolt); *The Cooler* (03, Wayne Kramer); *The Cat in the Hat* (03, Bo Welch).

Lucille Ball (1911–89),
b. Jamestown, New York
Even a half-thorough life of Lucille Ball would hold an important place in the history of the cinema. No one so completely outflanked the industry; certainly no woman has been as successful. For two decades, it is likely that most of us saw more of Lucille Ball than of any other actor or actress. Time well spent, it should be said, for she was a brilliant comedienne, endlessly resourceful and appealing in situation comedy, unsurpassed in the timing of visual disaster jokes, the best impersonator of Charlie Chaplin, and one of the few to maintain the hectic ballet of 1930s screwball comedy.

In her teens, she toured in *Rio Rita* and became a model. She was a Goldwyn Girl in her first film, *Roman Scandals* (33, Frank Tuttle), and she had a number of small parts at Columbia before RKO put her in *Roberta* (35, William A. Seiter) and gave her a contract. She was rather in the shadow of Ginger Rogers, even if events proved her to be the more versatile performer. But she gradually worked up to lead status with *I Dream Too Much* (35, John Cromwell); *Follow the Fleet* (36, Mark Sandrich); *Stage Door* (37,

Gregory La Cava); *The Joy of Living* (38, Tay Garnett); *Having Wonderful Time* (38, Alfred Santell); *Room Service* (38, Seiter); *Next Time I Marry* (38, Garson Kanin); *Five Came Back* (39, John Farrow); and *That's Right, You're Wrong* (40, David Butler). At about this time, Orson Welles considered using her in his first movie project but was overruled by RKO. Instead they wanted her in a series of comedies and cheap musicals—*Dance, Girl, Dance* (40, Dorothy Arzner); *Look Who's Laughing* (41, Allan Dwan); and *Seven Days' Leave* (42, Tim Whelan)—so that she made only one other worthwhile film at the studio: *The Big Street* (42, Irving Reis), with Henry Fonda. Her performance in that film, as a selfish cripple, only makes one regret the few real dramatic opportunities she was given. MGM signed her and starred her in *Du Barry Was a Lady* (43, Roy del Ruth). They talked about making her a major star, but she never managed that transition on the large screen and her relations with MGM were bad: *Best Foot Forward* (43, Edward Buzzell); *Thousands Cheer* (43, George Sidney); *Meet the People* (44); *Without Love* (45, Harold S. Bucquet); *Ziegfeld Follies* (46, Vincente Minnelli); *Easy to Wed* (46, Buzzell); and *Two Smart People* (46, Jules Dassin). She was free-lance now: *The Dark Corner* (46, Henry Hathaway); *Lured* (47, Douglas Sirk); *Her Husband's Affairs* (47, S. Sylvan Simon); *Sorrowful Jones* (49, Sidney Lanfield), her first film with Bob Hope; and *Easy Living* (49, Jacques Tourneur). She signed a three-picture deal with Columbia and made *Miss Grant Takes Richmond* (49, Lloyd Bacon) and *The Fuller Brush Girl* (50, Bacon). After *Fancy Pants* (50, George Marshall), with Hope again, she had to make *The Magic Carpet* (51) to complete her obligation to Columbia. Then pregnancy forced her out of *The Greatest Show on Earth* in favor of Gloria Grahame.

This was the turning point. In 1951, she had started the TV show *I Love Lucy* with her husband, Desi Arnaz. A few years later, their company, Desilu, purchased RKO and turned it over to TV work. Remarkably, after divorce, Lucille Ball bought out Arnaz and continued as a star of the medium with *The Lucy Show* and *Here's Lucy*. As well as an energetic performer, she was the majority shareholder of Desilu and executive president, selling only in 1968 to Gulf and Western for $17 million. Films took the second place that they persistently applied to her: *The Long, Long Trailer* (54, Minnelli); *Forever Darling* (56, Alexander Hall); *The Facts of Life* (60, Melvin Frank)—with Hope, as was *Critic's Choice* (63, Don Weis); and *Yours, Mine and Ours* (68, Melville Shavelson). In 1974, she made *Mame* (Gene Saks), and then in 1985, her last film, *Stone Pillow* (George Schaefer), trying to be a homeless person.

Anne Bancroft (Anna Maria Luisa Italiano), b. Bronx, New York, 1931

The daughter of Italian immigrants and educated at the American Academy of Dramatic Arts and the Actors' Studio, she worked in TV before going to Hollywood in 1952. Although she was not happy with this first film career, her early work is quirky and eye-catching: *Don't Bother to Knock* (52, Roy Baker); *Treasure of the Golden Condor* (53) and *Demetrius and the Gladiators* (54), both for Delmer Daves; *Gorilla at Large* (54, Harmon Jones); Fregonese's *The Raid* (54); Russell Rouse's *New York Confidential* (55); blonde in *The Last Frontier* (55), one of the few striking female performances in Anthony Mann's work; *Nightfall* (56, Jacques Tourneur); *Walk the Proud Land* (56); *The Girl in Black Stockings* (57, Howard W. Koch); and Allan Dwan's *The Restless Breed* (57). She went back to New York and made her stage debut, creating the leading parts in *Two For the Seesaw* and *The Miracle Worker*. It was Arthur Penn's film of the latter (1962) that brought her back to movies and to a working of raw emotion, torn between independence and her bond with Helen Keller, great enough to justify the dissatisfaction with her early films. The Oscar for that part was irrelevant to its frightening complexity. As well as nursing the performance of Patty Duke, she so dramatized the struggle between liberty and discipline that she probably helped reveal Penn's own talent to himself. She was again excellent as the agonized wife in Jack Clayton's *The Pumpkin Eater* (64); reminiscent of Robert Mitchum as the realist in Ford's *Seven Women* (66); as the attempted suicide in Pollack's *The Slender Thread* (66); and so wearily curt as Mrs. Robinson in *The Graduate* (68, Mike Nichols) as to throw the film off balance. She plainly needed large parts and demanding directors, for as the mother of *Young Winston* (72, Richard Attenborough) she got away with dutiful gestures, but she may think more highly of the theatre, where she played Golda Meir in an earnest tribute. She was out of place on *The Hindenburg* (75, Robert Wise), but delightful tangoing with her husband, Mel Brooks, in his *Silent Movie* (76). She seemed to go along with the silliness of *The Turning Point* (77, Herbert Ross), though her dedicated attempts to take up a ballet position—always forestalled by the cutting—hinted at a camp comic potential. A mad Bette Davis movie was lurking within Ross's dull tidiness, and Bancroft was the actress who might have rescued it.

In 1980, she acted in and also directed the uncertain *Fatso*. She made a fine cameo as the actress Madge Kendal in *The Elephant Man* (80, David Lynch—a Brooks film); she played with her husband in the misguided *To Be or Not to Be* (83, Alan Johnson); was very funny as the mother in *Garbo Talks* (84, Sidney Lumet); *Agnes of God*

49 **Tallulah Bankhead**

(85, Norman Jewison); was badly overdone as the mother in *'Night, Mother* (86, Tom Moore); as Helen Hanff in *84 Charing Cross Road* (87, David Jones); *Torch Song Trilogy* (88, Paul Bogart); *Bert Rigby, You're a Fool* (89, Carl Reiner); *Broadway Bound* (91, Bogart); and *Malice* (93, Harold Becker).

She is close to automatic casting in grand-old-lady roles (plus women in high office), which is fine, yet a loss—for she has the gusto for high comedy still: *Point of No Return* (93, John Badham); *Mr. Jones* (93, Mike Figgis); *The Oldest Living Confederate Widow Tells All* (94, Ken Cameron); doing Paddy Chayefsky in *The Mother* (94, Simon Curtis); *How to Make an American Quilt* (95, Jocelyn Moorhouse); *Home for the Holidays* (95, Jodie Foster); *Dracula: Dead and Loving It* (95, Brooks); *The Sunchaser* (96, Michael Cimino); *Homecoming* (96, Mark Jean); *G.I. Jane* (97, Ridley Scott); *Critical Care* (97, Lumet); *Great Expectations* (98, Alfonso Cuaron); *Deep in My Heart* (99, Anita W. Addison); *Keeping the Faith* (00, Edward Norton); *Up at the Villa* (00, Philip Haas); *In Search of Peace* (00, Richard Trank); *Haven* (01, John Gray); *Heartbreakers* (01, David Mirkin); the Contessa, on TV, in *The Roman Spring of Mrs Stone* (03, Robert Allan Ackerman).

Antonio Banderas (Jose Antonio Dominguez Banderas), b. Malaga, Spain, 1960

Only a little over forty, Banderas the actor has around fifty films to his credit—and that training shows. He is a very competent actor, handsome, yet happy to make fun of himself—which may speak to his upbringing as part of the Pedro Almodóvar circle. Come to that, being married to Melanie Griffith may bring its own ironies. Still, they seem wild about each other, and Banderas did a good job directing her in the entertaining *Crazy in Alabama* (99). He was also the producer of *The White River Kid* (99), so it won't be a surprise if he branches out as he becomes our best replacement for Cesar Romero. America is newly conscious of its growing Hispanic audience, and Banderas—a real Spaniard—might be the man to take advantage of it. He could play Desi Arnaz a treat.

He worked very hard in Spain for ten years: *Labyrinth of Passion* (82, Almodóvar); *El Señor Galíndez* (83, Rodolfo Kuhn); *Los Zancos* (84, Carlos Saura); *La Corte de Faraón* (85, José Luis García Sánchez); *Matador* (86, Almodóvar); *27 Horas* (86, Montxo Armendáriz); *Delirios de Amor* (86, Cristina Andreu and Luis Eduardo Aute); *Law of Desire* (87, Almodóvar); *El Placer de Matar* (87, Félix Rotaeta); *El Acto* (87, Héctor Faver); *Women on the Verge of a Nervous Breakdown* (88, Almodóvar); *Bâton Rouge* (88, Rafael Moleón); *Bajarse al Moro* (88, Fernando

Colomo); *La Blanca Paloma* (89, Juan Miñón); *Tie Me Up! Tie Me Down!* (90, Almodóvar); *Contra el Viento* (90, Francisco Periñán); *Madonna: Truth or Dare* (91, Alek Keshishian); *Terra Nova* (91, Calogero Salvo); *Cuentos de Borges I* (91, Héctor Olivera and Gerardo Vera).

His breakthrough in America came in *The Mambo Kings* (92, Arne Glimcher), and since then he has worked far more in the U.S. than in Europe: *¡Dispara!* (93, Saura); *The House of the Spirits* (93, Bille August); *Philadelphia* (93, Jonathan Demme); as Mussolini in *Il Giovane Mussolini* (93, Gianluigi Calderone); *Of Love and Shadows* (95, Betty Kaplan); Armand in *Interview with the Vampire* (94, Neil Jordan); *Miami Rhapsody* (95, David Frankel); *Four Rooms* (95, Robert Rodriguez); with Stallone in *Assassins* (95, Richard Donner); *Never Talk to Strangers* (95, Peter Hall); *Desperado* (95, Rodriguez); with Melanie in *Two Much* (96, Fernando Trueba); as Ché Guevara in *Evita* (96, Alan Parker); a big hit in *The Mask of Zorro* (98, Martin Campbell); *The 13th Warrior* (99, John McTiernan); boxing in *Play It to the Bone* (99, Ron Shelton); *The Body* (00, Jonas McCord); *Spy Kids* (01, Rodriguez); with Angelina Jolie in *Original Sin* (01, Michael Cristofer); as Siqueiros in *Frida* (02, Julie Taymor); *Femme Fatale* (02, Brian De Palma).

He was in *Spy Kids 2* (02, Rodriguez); *Ballistic: Ecks vs. Sever* (02, Wych Kaosayananda); *Imagining Argentina* (03, Christopher Hampton); *Once Upon a Time in Mexico* (03, Rodriguez).

Tallulah Bankhead (1903–68), b. Huntsville, Alabama

My admiration for Alfred Hitchcock cannot prevent the admission that *Lifeboat* (44) is a silly film from a crazy idea. But it has a lunatic justness in the way it uses Tallulah Bankhead, one of those very famous players who never adapted to the movies. By 1944, she and the movies had given one another up. Thus there is some of Hitch's malicious irony in asking her to dominate a lifeboat adrift in the Twentieth Century–Fox studio tanks. Such fatuous eminence is plainly a challenge to the actress's affected languor. To her credit, Tallulah remains damp but unaltered, allowing her bracelet to be used as pretty bait for nourishing fish. She ends by stealing the picture, underlining the film's limitations and serenely steering it into camp. It shows the sort of self-mocking grandiloquence at which she might have excelled had Hollywood not chosen to cast her as the sultry man-eater she pretended to be. Very early in her career, she had been in a movie—*When Men Betray* (18, Ivan Abramson)—but she opted for the London stage during the 1920s and was called to Paramount only when sound seemed to beg for her famous drawl. The films she made there were banal and dogged, instead of nutty and irreverent: *The Cheat* (31, George Abbott); *Tarnished Lady* (31, George Cukor); *My Sin* (31, Abbott); *Devil and the Deep* (32, Marion Gering); and *Thunder Below* (32, Richard Wallace). In all these, she was required to be the stirred point of action in romantic triangles. Unconvinced, she did not stay in place. Paramount let her go to MGM for *Faithless* (32, Harry Beaumont), whereupon she bounced back to the theatre. (Her best part was Regina Giddens in *The Little Foxes*. Bette Davis—who did the film—said she never got over seeing Tallulah on stage.) After *Lifeboat*, Fox cast her in *A Royal Scandal* (45, Otto Preminger and Ernst Lubitsch). But she dropped away again and appeared briefly in *Main Street to Broadway* (52, Tay Garnett) and more extensively in a dreadful British horror film, *Fanatic* (65, Silvio Narizzano), a last gesture toward neglected extravagance.

Theda Bara (Theodosia Goodman)
(1890–1955), b. Cincinnati, Ohio
The anagrammatic connection between Theda Bara and Arab Death so often evoked in awed tones is today like an archaeological find, proving only that we live in a different culture. But if Theda Bara is no longer perceived as sexy, there is at least an historical significance attached to her as securely as the flower-bloom bra she wore as *Cleopatra* (17, Gordon Edwards): she was the first woman offered commercially, in movies, as an object of sexual fantasy. In addition, the Fox Film Company was built on her dithery sultriness. For in 1914, William Fox bought the stage play *A Fool There Was*, and its director, Frank Powell, discovered Theodosia to play the vamp— "the woman who did not care." The success of the film encouraged Fox to form his company. He launched the first major publicity promotion for Bara and worked her hard for a few years in "Theda Bara Superproductions." She made over thirty-five films, most of them directed by Edwards, before rivals overtook her: among others, *Lady Audley's Secret* (15); *Carmen* (15); *The Serpent* (16); *The Eternal Sappho* (16); *East Lynne* (16); *Under Two Flags* (16); *Romeo and Juliet* (16); *The Vixen* (16); *The Tiger Woman* (17); *Camille* (17); *Madame Dubarry* (18); *The Soul of Buddha* (18); *When a Woman Sins* (18); *Salome* (18); *The She Devil* (18); *When Men Desire* (19); *The Siren's Song* (19); and *A Woman There Was* (19). A new director, Charles Brabin, could not save her from a disastrous Boucicault adaptation, *Kathleen Mavourneen* (19), and after *The Lure of Ambition* (19), Fox dropped her. She married Brabin and waited for a comeback. When it came, it was a brief pastiche of her former allure: *Unchastened Woman* (25, James Young) and *Madame Mystery* (26, Richard Wallace and Stan Laurel).

Juan Antonio Bardem (1922–2002),
b. Madrid, Spain
1949: *Paseo Sobre una Guerra Antigua* (codirected with Luis Garcia Berlanga). 1950: *Barajas, Aeropuerto Internacional*. 1953: *Ena Pareja Feliz* (codirected with Berlanga); *Novio a la Vista* (codirected with Berlanga). 1954: *Cómicos; Felices Pascuas*. 1955: *Muerte de un Ciclista/Death of a Cyclist*. 1956: *Calle Mayor*. 1957: *La Muerte de Pio Baroja* (unreleased). 1958: *La Venganza*. 1959: *Sonatas*. 1960: *A las Cinco de la Tarde*. 1962: *Los Inocentes*. 1963: *Nunca Pasa Nada*. 1965: *Los Pianos Mecánicos*. 1969: *El Último Día de la Guerra*. 1972: *La Corrupción de Chris Miller*. 1973: *L'Isola Misteriosa e il Capitano Nemo*. 1976: *El Puente*. 1978: *Seven Days in January 1977*. 1987: *Lorca, la Muerte de un Poeta*. 1993: *El Joven Picasso* (d). 1998: *Resultado Final*.

Death of a Cyclist attracted some attention in the mid-1950s; its melodramatic accomplishment was too readily identified as a new vitality in Spanish cinema. The fact is that Spanish cinema had been no more than an assortment of oddities that had managed to slip past the Spanish authorities. Buñuel's absence hung over Spain: *Las Hurdes, Viridiana*, and *Tristana* make a trio of night raids on sleeping territory. Bardem worked by daylight and seems callow in comparison. He was an actor, drawn into filmmaking through his contact with Berlanga. *Death of a Cyclist* was fatalistic, socially observant, and as terse as Lucia Bose's central performance. But Spain cries out for insane images: peasants eating poison; the depraved last supper; the sensuality of Tristana's artificial limb. It is a European country on the edge of the Third World—like Ireland—and the contrast is surreal. Bardem, at best, was a realist, helplessly copying American shock cuts. The distance that a pedestrian may lag behind is shown by the fact that *Calle Mayor*—made in 1956—was a version of the stolid naturalism of Sinclair Lewis's *Main Street*.

Brigitte Bardot (Camille Javal),
b. Paris, 1934
There is no clearer sign of the critical quality of Godard's art than *Contempt* (63), a film that, among other things, gave her most significant place in cinema history to Brigitte Bardot. *Contempt* is not just a commentary on the Godardian consciousness married to an actress, but a prediction of the eventual rupture between Godard and his own wife, Anna Karina. It is part of Godard's skill that he chose to make this personal statement—what Raoul Coutard called "a letter to his wife"—out of his most orthodox and expensive film. But it was appropriate that this story of an attempt to make a Cinecittá *Odyssey* should itself be a Carlo Ponti/Joseph Levine production, based with some fidelity on a novel by Alberto Moravia.

While Bardot was a commercial imposition, her presence may have enabled Godard to be more open in admitting his fears and in revealing that element of misogyny that recurs in his films. His first film in CinemaScope, *Contempt* opens with a magnificent reclining nude Bardot, shocking and scathing in terms of the sexual reticence of his other work. That scene, in which Bardot and Michel Piccoli describe Bardot's opulent but worthless nakedness, is a reference to the way Roger Vadim's camera had once stripped her bare. But it is also a pointer to the fact that Godard hardly removed a garment from Karina. Paradoxically, the admiring CinemaScope lavishness of all that creamy shoulder, back, bottom, and thigh is contemptuous. And Godard's taste for cryptic clues shows in the way the Bardot character in *Contempt* is named Camille Javal.

All of which is to say that the worldwide reputation of Bardot is the creation of those French magazines, of Vadim's lubricity, of the sociology of Simone de Beauvoir, and of Bardot's original epitome of the youthful sexuality that tanned itself on the Côte d'Azur once the austerity of war had worn off. Her actual screen appeal was as a brunette, pouting but smiling, and with a perfect body that she was casually willing to display. The attempt of her first husband Roger Vadim to advertise his own advantages through her seemed to exhaust her. She quickly turned blond and her eyes grew heavy fake lashes. Her face and smile seemed pumped up and only exposed the weird lack of personality or intelligence. There is an awful sadness in her return to Vadim for *Don Juan or if Don Juan Were a Woman* (73).

From modeling, she broke into films in the mid-1950s: *Le Trou Normand* (52, Jean Boyer); *Futures Vedettes* (54, Marc Allégret); very appealing in *Summer Manoeuvres* (55, René Clair); to England for *Doctor at Sea* (55, Ralph Thomas); *La Lumière d'en Face* (55, Georges Lacombe); *Cette Sacrée Gamine* (55, Michel Boisrond); *Helen of Troy* (55, Robert Wise); *Mio Figlio Nerone* (56, Steno); *Mamzelle Striptease* (56, Allégret); *And God Created Woman* (56, Vadim)—the film that made her an international sensation; *Heaven Fell That Night* (57, Vadim); *Une Parisienne* (57, Boisrond); *Love Is My Profession* (58, Claude Autant-Laura); *La Femme et le Pantin* (58, Julien Duvivier); *Babette S'en Va-t-en Guerre* (59, Christian-Jaque); *La Bride sur le Cou* (59, Jean Aurel and Vadim); monotonous in the "serious" acting role of *La Vérité* (60, Henri-Georges Clouzot); and then in the curiously self-pitying *Vie Privée* (62, Louis Malle), which was a polite and inane picture of some of her own anguish at being a sex object; *Warrior's Rest* (62, Vadim), which was the most baroque celebration of her as a sex object; *Une Ravissante Idiote* (63, Edouard Molinaro); jerky and nervous in *Viva María!* (65, Malle); *Dear*

Brigitte (65, Henry Koster); seen briefly on the Metro in *Masculin-Feminin* (66, Godard); *A Coeur Joie* (67, Serge Bourguignon); in the "William Wilson" episode from *Histoires Extraordinaires* (67, Malle); *Shalako* (68, Edward Dmytryk); *Les Femmes* (69, Aurel); *L'Ours et La Poupée* (69, Michel Deville); *Les Novices* (70, Guy Casaril); *Boulevard de Rhum* (71, Robert Enrico); *Les Pétroleuses* (71, Christian-Jaque). *Il Somiso del Grande Tentatore* (75, Damiano Damiani).

Bruno Barreto, b. Rio de Janeiro, Brazil, 1955
1973: *Tati, a Garoto.* 1976: *Dona Flor e Seus Dois Maridos/Dona Flor and Her Two Husbands.* 1978: *Amor Bandido.* 1981: *Lucia.* 1983: *Gabriela.* 1984: *Felizes para Sempre.* 1990: *A Show of Force.* 1992: *The Story of Fausta.* 1995: *Carried Away.* 1997: *O Que E Isso, Companheiro?/Four Days in September.* 1998: *One Tough Cop.* 1999: *Bossa Nova.* 2002: *View from the Top.*

Bruno Barreto was born into the business in Brazil: he was the son of two movie producers, who actually produced his breakthrough picture, *Dona Flor*, a clever, sexy fantasy about a woman torn between her dead husband (a rogue but a great lover) and the dull new guy. In truth, the film was pretty awkward, but it was helped to international success by Sonia Braga's central performance.

After that, Barreto struggled, though he did work on the screenplay for the worse-than-awkward American remake of *Dona Flor*, *Kiss Me Goodbye* (82, Robert Mulligan). Then, at the end of the eighties, as he became romantically involved with Amy Irving, Barreto moved to America. Two of his pictures there have been stories about South American political intrigue—Alan Arkin is good as the kidnapped American ambassador in Brazil in *Four Days in September*. But nothing prepared one for *Carried Away*, a rural story, based on a novel by Jim Harrison, about a teacher who has been engaged too long and who is then seduced by a teenager. Dennis Hopper was the teacher, Amy Irving the fiancée, and Amy Locane the kid. The result was sexy, anguished, and remarkable—one of the best American films of the nineties, and easily Barreto's finest work. After that, *One Tough Cop* seemed all the more sadly routine, but *View from the Top* was unforgivable.

Drew Barrymore, b. Los Angeles, 1975
I can't help finding it shocking, as well as startling, that Drew Barrymore was born so recently, and yet seems to have been here, and a problem, so long. For she is a part of show-biz family history, not just in her surname, and our wish that some part of the Barrymore line might be reasonably stable, happy, and productive. She is close

enough to our own family to make us all aware of the vicissitudes of show biz as an environment. She is the daughter of John Barrymore Jr.—the young man in Joe Losey's *The Big Night*. She is thus the grandchild of the unique John Barrymore (dead in 1942, more than thirty years before Drew was born) and Dolores Costello (the mother in *Ambersons*), who died when Drew was four.

Drew drank early, which means she drank too much. She has admitted to drugs, and more, in her book *Little Girl Lost*. And yet, she is maybe the most cheerful, resilient, and sensible of the Barrymores—there is a hint at least that she could grow up to be an Ethel, a wise old woman. It may take more than a hint; there may be urges toward naked revelation and self-destruction that are too much to resist. But Drew Barrymore has also been the child and the girlfriend we might like to have. She is not a great actress, yet she promises good company and genuine humor. God save her.

However, somehow, when she was only five, God let her get involved in *Altered States* (80, Ken Russell), and there has been no looking back: immortally naughty in *E.T.* (82, Steven Spielberg); inflammable in *Firestarter* (84, Mark L. Lester); very good in *Irreconcilable Differences* (84, Charles Shyer); *Cat's Eye* (85, Lewis Teague); being stalked in *Far from Home* (89, Meiert Avis); *See You in the Morning* (89, Alan J. Pakula); *Doppelganger: The Evil Within* (92, Avi Nesler), in which she played with her mother, Jaid Barrymore; pretty good in *Guncrazy* (92, Tamra Davis), if never burning in the cold way that Peggy Cummins managed in the 1949 film; as another bad and dangerous girl in *Poison Ivy* (92, Katt Shea Ruben); *Sketch Artist* (92, Phedon Papamichael); *Wayne's World 2* (93, Stephen Surjik); *The Amy Fisher Story* (93, Andy Tennant), for TV; *Bad Girls* (94, Jonathan Kaplan); rather neglected in *Batman Forever* (95, Joel Schumacher); excellent in *Boys on the Side* (95, Herbert Ross); a little crazy in *Mad Love* (95, Antonia Bird); *Scream* (96, Wes Craven); actually dubbed in her singing in *Everyone Says I Love You* (96, Woody Allen); *Wishful Thinking* (97, Adam Park); *Best Man* (97, Davis); delectable in *The Wedding Singer* (98, Frank Coraci); very lively in *Ever After: A Cinderella Story* (98, Tennant); *Home Fries* (98, Dean Parisot); pretending to be seventeen in, but coproducer of, *Never Been Kissed* (99, Raja Gosnell).

She was the fantasy girl in *Skipped Parts* (00, Davis); a voice on *Titan A.E.* (00, Don Bluth and Gary Goldman); a producer as well as actress on *Charlie's Angels* (00, McG); *Donnie Darko* (01, Richard Kelly); and getting her periodic redemption in *Riding in Cars with Boys* (01, Penny Marshall). She was in *Confessions of a Dangerous*

Mind (02, George Clooney); *So Love Returns* (03, Robert Nathan); *Duplex* (03, Danny De Vito); and in *Charlie's Angels: Full Throttle* (03, McG).

John Barrymore (John Blythe) (1882–1942), b. Philadelphia

The young brother of Ethel and Lionel, John was the son of English actor Maurice Barrymore and American actress Georgina Drew. There have been many attempts to take John Barrymore seriously: in these scenarios he was a genius actor dreadfully sapped by Hollywood's malicious willingness to pay for all his booze and by his efforts to justify the tag of the screen's great lover. His Hamlet, Richard III, and Mercutio are talked of in hushed voices as creations near to the sublime. The latter-day decline into B pictures and grotesque parodies of himself is offered as a tragedy from which we must stand back so that the echoes of Kean-like grandeur may have proper room. But who knows how great an actor Kean was? And Barrymore's Hamlet is now lost among opinions. Barrymore survives less as a Kean than as the Kean concocted by Sartre, Pierre Brasseur, Vittorio Gassman, and Alan Badel—note, the Barrymore of, say, 1926, "the great profile," astonishingly resembles Badel. That is to say, he is an actor who cannot believe in acting in the way that his romantic audience did. None of his own weapons—handsomeness, rhetoric, or flamboyance—actually convinces him. Acting becomes a trap and "John Barrymore" an onerous part that he alternately mocks and falls short of. The truth therefore is black comedy, and at that level alone is Barrymore important or serious. Luckily one masterpiece illustrates the helpless pursuit of himself: *Twentieth Century* (34, Howard Hawks), which has Barrymore as Oscar Jaffe, ham extraordinaire, an actor-manager engaged in a merciless upstaging affair with Carole Lombard: the limelit union of two rabid frauds. Like Badel in *Kean*, so Barrymore in *Twentieth Century* simultaneously glorifies and ridicules acting. He is a ham, but a skeptic, incredulous of romance yet hopelessly enthralled by it as the only alternative to chaos. In this light, Barrymore becomes the more engaging as his material deteriorates, and the drunken decline is the inevitable tragi-comedy that he brought upon himself. After all, is it likely that a handsome, charming American in 1925 would take Hamlet more seriously than Dolores Costello and a bottle of bourbon?

He made his film debut in 1913 in *An American Citizen* and worked for Famous Players–Lasky for the next few years, largely in comedies. It was after the First World War that he began to make his mark in featured roles: *Raffles the Amateur Cracksman* (17); *Here Comes the Bride* (18); *Test of Honor* (19); *Dr. Jekyll and Mr. Hyde* (20, John S.

Robertson); *The Lotus Eater* (21, Marshall Neilan); and *Sherlock Holmes* (22, Albert Parker). He made *Beau Brummel* (24, Harry Beaumont) for Warners and stayed with them for *The Sea Beast* (26, Michael Webb) and *Don Juan* (26, Alan Crosland). The first was a version of *Moby Dick* that contrived to add Dolores Costello to the crew, while the second was the first feature to have a musical soundtrack. It is more interesting for the way Barrymore tried in vain to have a former mistress, Mary Astor, replaced by the new one, Costello. He was with her again in *When a Man Loves* (27, Crosland) and he then played François Villon in *The Beloved Rogue* (27, Crosland), followed by *The Tempest* (28, Sam Taylor) and *Eternal Love* (29, Ernst Lubitsch). Sound was no obstacle to Barrymore: he kept alcohol for that. He made *General Crack* (29, Crosland), *The Man From Blankley's* (30, Alfred E. Green), *Moby Dick* (30, Lloyd Bacon)—this time with Joan Bennett—and two versions of the Svengali theme—*Svengali* (31, Archie Mayo) and *The Mad Genius* (31, Michael Curtiz)—before joining MGM. His looks were going and drink was doing all it is supposed to do, but Barrymore remained a leading star in *Arsene Lupin* (32, Jack Conway); hardly impressed by Garbo in *Grand Hotel* (32, Edmund Goulding); in *State's Attorney* (32, George Archainbaud); as Katharine Hepburn's father in *A Bill of Divorcement* (32, George Cukor); with his brother and sister in the notorious *Rasputin and the Empress* (32, Richard Boleslavsky); opposite Diana Wynyard in *Reunion in Vienna* (33, Sidney Franklin); in two all-star productions, *Dinner at Eight* (33, Cukor) and *Night Flight* (33, Clarence Brown); as the schoolteacher in *Topaze* (33, Harry d'Arrast); and *Counsellor-at-Law* (33, William Wyler).

Twentieth Century marked a break in his career. After abandoning a project to film Hamlet, he played a plump Mercutio in Cukor's *Romeo and Juliet* (36) and then slipped into supporting parts and B pictures: *Maytime* (37, Robert Z. Leonard); *True Confession* (37, Wesley Ruggles); three Bulldog Drummonds; *Spawn of the North* (38, Henry Hathaway); and Louis XV in the Norma Shearer *Marie Antoinette* (38, W. S. Van Dyke). His last years saw a succession of fascinating movies in which a dying Barrymore sardonically reveals his own fraudulence: *Hold that Co-Ed* (38, George Marshall); *The Great Man Votes* (39, Garson Kanin); a very funny observer of intrigue in *Midnight* (39, Mitchell Leisen); *The Great Profile* (40, Walter Lang); *The Invisible Woman* (41, Edward Sutherland); *World Premiere* (41, Ted Tetzlaff); and *Playmates* (41, David Butler). He died, of course.

Lionel Barrymore (Lionel Blythe)

(1878–1954), b. Philadelphia

The older brother of Ethel and John, Lionel was unlike John in all important ways: professional, hardworking, ambitious, humorless, and dull. He began in the theatre but in the years before the First World War he joined D. W. Griffith's company and acted in a great many two-reelers, occasionally contributing scripts. He became a leading player only in the mid-1920s when he established himself at MGM: *The Face in the Fog* (22, Alan Crosland); *The Eternal City* (23, George Fitzmaurice); *America* (24, Griffith); *The Splendid Road* (25, Frank Lloyd); *The Bells* (26, James Young); *The Barrier* (26, George Hill); *The Lucky Lady* (26, Raoul Walsh); *The Temptress* (26, Fred Niblo); *The Show* (27, Tod Browning); *Women Love Diamonds* (27, Edmund Goulding); *Drums of Love* (28, Griffith); as Atkinson in *Sadie Thompson* (28, Walsh); *West of Zanzibar* (28, Browning); *Alias Jimmy Valentine* (29, Jack Conway); and *The Mysterious Island* (29, Lucien Hubbard, Maurice Tourneur, and Benjamin Christensen). But it was in the years after the coming of sound that he was most active. As well as acting—in *A Free Soul* (30, Clarence Brown), for which he won the best actor Oscar; *The Yellow Ticket* (31, Walsh); *Arsene Lupin* (32, Conway); *Grand Hotel* (32, Goulding); *Mata Hari* (32, Fitzmaurice); *Rasputin and the Empress* (32, Richard Boleslavsky); *Dinner at Eight* (33, George Cukor); *Night Flight* (33, Brown); and *Carolina* (34, Henry King)—he worked as a director at MGM. His output is little seen today and surrounded with mystery. *Madame X* (29) is reputed to be one of the first films to use a moveable microphone, while *His Glorious Night* (29) is sometimes alleged to have been mounted in order to discredit John Gilbert. He directed only three other films, *The Rogue Song* (29), *The Unholy Night* (29), and *Ten Cents a Dance* (31). After his department store mogul in *Sweepings* (33, John Cromwell), he settled for extravagant character parts: *Treasure Island* (34, Victor Fleming); *David Copperfield* (34, Cukor); *Mark of the Vampire* (34, Browning); *Ah, Wilderness!* (35, Brown); *The Devil Doll* (36, Browning); *The Gorgeous Hussy* (36, Brown); *Camille* (36, Cukor); and *Captains Courageous* (37, Fleming). He played Judge Hardy in the first Andy Hardy movie, *A Family Affair* (37, George Seitz), and after *Saratoga* (37, Conway), *A Yank at Oxford* (38, Conway), *Test Pilot* (38, Fleming), and *You Can't Take It With You* (38, Frank Capra), arthritis forced him into a wheelchair. The most suitable role for this handicap was Dr. Gillespie to Lew Ayres's Kildare. In fact, Barrymore slogged on after Ayres had been struck off, and played the veteran doctor fourteen times—infirmity prospering at medicine's expense. As he grew older, the crust on his performances hardened until sometimes it could be lifted off to show a little old man asleep underneath: *The Man on America's*

Conscience (41, William Dieterle); *A Guy Named Joe* (43, Fleming); *Since You Went Away* (44, Cromwell); *Valley of Decision* (45, Tay Garnett); the rancher in *Duel in the Sun* (46, King Vidor); *The Secret Heart* (46, Robert Z. Leonard); the gloomy city boss, Potter, in *It's a Wonderful Life* (46, Capra); *Key Largo* (48, John Huston); *Down to the Sea in Ships* (49, Henry Hathaway); *Right Cross* (50, John Sturges); *Bannerline* (51, Don Weis); *Lone Star* (52, Vincent Sherman); and *Main Street Broadway* (53, Garnett).

Richard Barthelmess (1895–1963),
b. New York

The partnership of Lillian Gish and Barthelmess in *Way Down East* (20, D. W. Griffith) is arguably the most elevated acting in the American silent cinema. Actor and actress alike had a Victorian handsomeness that Griffith and Billy Bitzer suspended between the glowing images of Pre-Raphaelitism and the true animation of cinematography. It follows that Barthelmess was the ideal hero of romantic melodrama. *Tol'able David* (21, Henry King)—the first film made by his own company, Inspiration—is the model of his best work: in which he plays a young man, suspected of cowardice, who comes up trumps by carrying the U.S. Mail, thrashing the rascals, and winning the girl. The situation is corn but, like Griffith and Gish, Barthelmess invested it with a shining seriousness.

Barthelmess graduated from Trinity College in Hartford, Connecticut, and went into the theatre. By 1916, he made a film debut in *Gloria's Romance* (George King) and he followed it with *Camille* (17, J. Gordon Edwards); *The Moral Code* (17, Ashley Miller); *The Eternal Sin* (17, Herbert Brenon); *Rich Man, Poor Man* (18, J. Searle Dawley); and *The Hope Chest* (19, Elmer Clifton). He worked for Griffith for the first time in *The Girl Who Stayed at Home* (19) and was put under contract: *Boots* (19, Clifton); *Three Men and a Girl* (19, Marshall Neilan); *Peppy Polly* (19, Clifton); and *I'll Get Him Yet* (19, Clifton). In most of these he played opposite Dorothy Gish, but he starred with Lillian in *Broken Blossoms* (19, Griffith), in which he plays the Yellow Man. It is a marvelous performance, riveting because of how little Barthelmess emotes. He did four more with Griffith: *Scarlet Days* (19); *The Idol Dancer* (20); *The Love Flower* (20); and *Way Down East*, in which he plays the country boy who rescues Lillian Gish from death and dishonor.

After *Experience* (21, George Fitzmaurice), Barthelmess and Charles H. Duell formed the Inspiration Company, designed to produce films presenting the actor in idealistic material. By 1926, he had appeared in eighteen films for the company, mostly directed by Henry King— *Tol'able David* (21); *The Bond Boy* (22); *The Sev-* enth *Day* (22); *Sonny* (22); *Fury* (23); *The Fighting Blade* (23); *Twenty-One* (23); *Classmates* (24); *The Enchanted Cottage* (24); *New Toys* (25); *Shore Leave* (25); and *Soul-Fire* (25).

The company collapsed and Barthelmess joined First National for *The Patent Leather Kid* (27, Alfred Santell). That was a success, but his career was threatened, less by sound than by the fact that he was a little too old for the youthful parts with which he was associated. He made *The Noose* (28, John Francis Dillon); played twins in *Wheel of Chance* (28, Santell); he sang in *Weary River* (29, Frank Lloyd); played a man who thought he was Chinese in *Son of the Gods* (30, Lloyd). His days were numbered but he made several excellent films: *The Dawn Patrol* (30, Howard Hawks); *The Last Flight* (31, William Dieterle); *The Cabin in the Cotton* (32, Michael Curtiz); *Central Airport* (33, William Wellman); and *Heroes for Sale* (33, Wellman), the latter as a bitter war veteran. He played a Sioux in *Massacre* (34, Alan Crosland), and after *A Modern Hero* (34, G. W. Pabst), *Midnight Alibi* (34, Crosland), and *Four Hours to Kill* (35, Mitchell Leisen), he made *A Spy of Napoleon* (36, Maurice Elvey) in England. He retired for a few years and came back in an affectionate summation of his screen character, as the coward who makes good, in *Only Angels Have Wings* (39, Hawks). Amid the excellence of that cast, he more than holds his own and it is a loss that after supporting parts in *The Man Who Talked Too Much* (40, Vincent Sherman), *The Mayor of 44th Street* (42, Alfred E. Green), and *The Spoilers* (42, Lloyd), he retired for good.

Freddie Bartholomew (Frederick Llewellyn) (1924–92), b. London

Just as Hollywood kept a cricket team of English actors, to add tone or to be mocked, so among child actors Freddie was the little gent, wickedly exposed by Mickey Rooney. But before then he had played *David Copperfield* (34, George Cukor), contriving to coordinate such varied players as W. C. Fields, Elsa Lanchester, Lionel Barrymore, Basil Rathbone, and Edna May Oliver—and capturing producer David O. Selznick's dream of the perfect child. Next he was Garbo's son in *Anna Karenina* (35, Clarence Brown), with Victor McLaglen in *Professional Soldier* (36, Tay Garnett), and *Little Lord Fauntleroy* (36, John Cromwell). Rooney had a part in that film, and in *The Devil Is a Sissy* (36, W. S. Van Dyke), Bartholomew was put between Rooney and Jackie Cooper. He was Tyrone Power as a boy—unnecessary duplication—in *Lloyds of London* (36, Henry King) and a brat in *Captains Courageous* (37, Victor Fleming). Various members of his family were fighting in the courts over his earnings as his career declined: *Kidnapped* (38, Alfred Werker); *Lord Jeff* (38, Sam Wood);

Listen Darling (38, Edwin L. Marin); *The Spirit of Culver* (39, Joseph Santley); *The Swiss Family Robinson* (40, Edward Ludwig); *Tom Brown's Schooldays* (40, Robert Stevenson); *Naval Academy* (41); and *A Yank at Eton* (42, Norman Taurog). After *Junior Army* (43) and *The Town Went Wild* (44), he joined the American Air Force, and appeared in only two more films—*Sepia Cinderella* (47, Arthur Leonard) and *St. Benny the Dip* (51, Edgar G. Ulmer)—before drifting into TV, where work on commercials took him to a career in advertising.

Kim Basinger, b. Athens, Georgia, 1953

I don't always "get" Kim Basinger. I mean, why did she ever buy that small town in Georgia, and why is she virtually the only actress who's ever been sued successfully for getting out of a movie (*Boxing Helena*)? Why marry Alec Baldwin? Is she even, really, that beautiful?

Well, the paper didn't catch fire, so I'll press on. She was a singer and a model before she got into acting. Her effective debut was picking up the Donna Reed role (and making the prostitution far more obvious than Ms. Reed was ever allowed to do) in the TV *From Here to Eternity* (80). That meant that she was already leaning on thirty, and it may be that her great achievement is looking so much like a movie star (and a young sexy blonde) at a relatively mature age. After all, doesn't she say she could do Veronica Lake without surgery?

Her first movie was *Hard Country* (81, David Greene), and she followed that with *Mother Lode* (82, Charlton Heston—he said, "There was, even then, a special presence the camera turns to"); a Bond girl in *Never Say Never Again* (83, Irvin Kershner); *The Man Who Loved Women* (83, Blake Edwards); *The Natural* (84, Barry Levinson); a little out of her depth in *Fool for Love* (85, Robert Altman); recovering her iconic status as a sexual creature in the inane *9½ Weeks* (86, Adrian Lyne), with eyes that have that way of dilating or narrowing in perfect synchronicity with secret male desires; quite nicely Cajun in *No Mercy* (86, Richard Pearce); *Blind Date* (87, Blake Edwards)—with Bruce Willis in his first starring part; funny in *Nadine* (87, Robert Benton); *My Stepmother Is an Alien* (88, Richard Benjamin); *Batman* (89, Tim Burton); as Bugsy Siegel's squeeze, but falling for Alec Baldwin, in *The Marrying Man* (91, Jerry Rees); *Final Analysis* (92, Phil Joanou); in *Cool World* (92, Ralph Bakshi)—a fine idea gone wildly astray; *The Real McCoy* (93, Russell Mulcahy); *Wayne's World 2* (93, Stephen Sirjik); with Baldwin in the remake of *The Getaway* (94, Roger Donaldson), but not dislodging any memories of Ali MacGraw; *Ready to Wear* (94, Altman); and then, after an absence, *L.A. Confidential* (97, Curtis Hanson), for which she

won the supporting actress Oscar. That meant beating out Julianne Moore in *Boogie Nights*. Which brings me back to the stuff I don't get.

Well, the marriage ended, and the actress has wandered into stranger ventures: *I Dreamed of Africa* (00, Hugh Hudson), a mix of vanity production and animal rights special; *Bless the Child* (00, Chuck Russell), a spiritual thriller; *People I Know* (01, Daniel Algrant); *8 Mile* (02, Hanson).

Saul Bass (1920–96), b. New York

How rare it is nowadays to see credit sequences that try to convey the spirit, or even the formal concerns, of a film. Yet there was a moment, in the fifties and the early sixties, when Saul Bass made the handmade credit sequence nearly the prerequisite of a smart film. Nor was he simply an ambitious graphic artist who seized an opening. In Saul Bass's best work, there is the beginning of a fine critical appreciation of the films being treated. He was a filmmaker, eager to be asked further into a picture. In hindsight, his credits, trailers, and ads seem like part of a golden age. And so, today, when we have to read a couple of miles of meticulous credit-gathering, all in a tasteful white on black, it's one of the stray pleasures of watching movies on TV to see this grave pride being whisked past, too fast and too small to be read.

After training at Brooklyn College and work as a free-lance designer, Bass formed Saul Bass & Associates in 1946 (his wife, Elaine, was a significant contributor to the firm). He got into film, apparently, at the invitation of Otto Preminger—further proof of both his eye and his commercial acumen. Later, he would form a valuable partnership with Hitchcock, and it is clear that he did work—of a schematic, planning nature—on the shower scene in *Psycho*.

His best work can be seen in *Carmen Jones* (55, Preminger); *The Big Knife* (55, Robert Aldrich); *The Seven Year Itch* (55, Billy Wilder); *Saint Joan* (56, Preminger); the brilliant, desperate reaching hand for *The Man with the Golden Arm* (56, Preminger); *Johnny Concho* (56, Don McGuire); *Around the World in 80 Days* (56, Michael Anderson); *The Pride and the Passion* (57, Stanley Kramer); *Cowboy* (58, Delmer Daves); pendant tears in *Bonjour Tristesse* (58, Preminger); *Vertigo* (58, Hitchcock); *The Big Country* (58, William Wyler), using the stagecoach wheels and blending with the great score by Jerome Moross; superb on *Anatomy of a Murder* (59, Preminger); ditto on *North by Northwest* (59, Hitchcock); *Psycho* (60, Hitchcock); *Ocean's 11* (60, Lewis Milestone); *Exodus* (60, Preminger); *Spartacus* (60, Stanley Kubrick); *West Side Story* (61, Robert Wise); coaxing that slow-mo black cat for *Walk on the Wild Side* (62, Edward Dmytryk); *Advise and Consent* (62, Preminger); *Nine Hours to Rama*

(63, Mark Robson); *The Cardinal* (63, Preminger); *It's a Mad Mad Mad Mad World* (63, Kramer); *Bunny Lake Is Missing* (65, Preminger); *Seconds* (65, John Frankenheimer); *Grand Prix* (65, Frankenheimer).

In the seventies he gave up features, working on his own experimental short films. But he came back for *Broadcast News* (87, James L. Brooks); *Big* (88, Penny Marshall); *The War of the Roses* (89, Danny DeVito); *GoodFellas* (90, Martin Scorsese); *Cape Fear* (91, Scorsese), with fine use of watery reflections; *The Age of Innocence* (93, Scorsese).

Angela Bassett, b. New York 1958

In the early nineties, after a start in *City of Hope* (91, John Sayles), *Boyz N the Hood* (91, John Singleton), and *Passion Fish* (92, Sayles), Angela Bassett impressed nearly everyone with two very different, strong women. As the wife to *Malcolm X* (92, Spike Lee), she was uncommonly serene as well as long-suffering and enduring. But as Tina Turner in *What's Love Got to Do with It* (93, Brian Gibson), she took on one of the world's powerhouse performers and enriched our understanding of the great Tina. If, finally, Bassett and the movie needed footage of the real Turner, it was no reflection on Bassett—just a mark of the dead end in such biopics. Since then, Bassett has been a lot more conventional: *Innocent Blood* (92, John Landis); *Strange Days* (95, Kathryn Bigelow); *Vampire in Brooklyn* (95, Wes Craven); *Waiting to Exhale* (95, Forest Whitaker); as Betty Shabazz again in *Panther* (95, Mario Van Peebles); *Contact* (97, Robert Zemeckis); *How Stella Got Her Groove Back* (98, Kevin Rodney Sullivan); with Meryl Streep in *Music of the Heart* (99, Craven); *Supernova* (00, Thomas Lee); as Lena in *Boesman and Lena* (00, John Berry); with nothing to do in *The Score* (01, Frank Oz); on TV in *Ruby's Bucket of Blood* (01, Peter Werner). She then appeared in *Sunshine State* (02, Sayles), on TV as *Rosa Parks* (02, Julie Dash) and in *Masked & Anonymous* (03, Larry Charles).

Alan Bates, b. Allestree, England, 1934

Did Alan Bates ever hope to make it as a universal male comforter? In *An Unmarried Woman* (77, Paul Mazursky), he's a bearded English abstract expressionist, whimsical but reliable, who eats eggs out of the frying pan, lives in Vermont, and gives Jill Clayburgh a healing screw on the floor and the freedom to decline further risk. He's about as believable as daytime TV, but much drier and far more charming. Looking less than forty-three, Bates suddenly emerged as an old-fashioned romantic: brooding and touchy, but full of inner calm, unneurotic talent, and well-done orgasms. He was something like a cultivated Gable who'd been a Rhodes scholar, or a Dirk Bogarde with

more meat on him. An unexpectedly casual stardom lay around the set, like clothes ardently discarded.

But for most of the seventies, Bates had looked less than ever interested in films. There were long gaps between jobs, and several parts that proved greater allegiance to the theatre. Indeed, onstage, in *Butley,* he showed a self-destructive humor and gentlemanly malice that no movie has thought to uncover. He seems determined not to be glamorous, or to lose sight of the better, more rewarding work he can find onstage. Perhaps *An Unmarried Woman* was a fling?

Still, in the sixties, especially, he managed to get his self-effacing presence into several successful pictures, none of which ever depended on him: *The Entertainer* (60, Tony Richardson); *Whistle Down the Wind* (61, Bryan Forbes); *A Kind of Loving* (62, John Schlesinger); the suburban straight breaking out of his rut in *The Running Man* (63, Carol Reed); *The Caretaker* (63, Clive Donner); another cautious witness of the exotic in *Zorba the Greek* (64, Michael Cacoyannis); *Georgy Girl* (66, Silvio Narizzano); *King of Hearts* (66, Philippe de Broca); *Far from the Madding Crowd* (67, Schlesinger); *The Fixer* (68, John Frankenheimer); *Women in Love* (69, Ken Russell); *The Three Sisters* (70, Laurence Olivier); *The Go-Between* (71, Joseph Losey); *A Day in the Death of Joe Egg* (71, Peter Medak); *Impossible Object* (73, John Frankenheimer); *Butley* (73, Harold Pinter); *In Celebration* (74, Lindsay Anderson); *Royal Flash* (75, Richard Lester); *The Shout* (78, Jerzy Skolimowski); and *The Rose* (79, Mark Rydell).

As he grew older, Bates found some fascinating eccentric roles, yet he remains an actor whose outbursts never quite lose control: as Diaghilev in *Nijinsky* (80, Herbert Ross); as the Ford Madox Ford figure in *Quartet* (81, James Ivory); *The Return of the Soldier* (81, Alan Bridges); *Britannia Hospital* (82, Anderson); as the John Mortimer figure in *A Voyage Round My Father* (82, Alvin Rakoff), for TV; in the old James Mason role in *The Wicked Lady* (83, Michael Winner); brilliant as Guy Burgess in *An Englishman Abroad* (83, Schlesinger); *Dr. Fischer of Geneva* (83, Michael Lindsay-Hogg); *Separate Tables* (84, Schlesinger), for TV; the husband in *Duet for One* (86, Andrei Konchalovsky); *A Prayer for the Dying* (87, Mike Hodges); as the man from MI5 in *Pack of Lies* (87, Anthony Page); *Force Majeure* (88, Pierre Jolivet); *We Think the World of You* (88, Colin Gregg); *Docteur M* (89, Claude Chabrol); *Mister Frost* (90, Philip Setbon); as Claudius in *Hamlet* (90, Franco Zeffirelli); as Proust in *102 Boulevard Haussmann* (90, Udayan Prasad); and *Secret Friends* (91, Dennis Potter).

He is a character actor nowadays, at his best for the BBC, but drawn into airier international ventures: *Silent Tongue* (93, Sam Shepard); as Bounderby in *Hard Times* (94, Peter Barnes); *The Grotesque* (95, John-Paul Davidson); *Oliver's Travels* (95, Giles Foster); *Nicholas' Gift* (98, Robert Markowitz); as Gayev in *Varya* (99, Cacoyannis); *St. Patrick: The Irish Legend* (00, Robert Hughes and Robert C. Hughes); the Storyteller in *Arabian Nights* (00, Steve Barron); *In the Beginning* (00, Kevin Connor); Henry VIII in *The Prince and the Pauper* (00, Foster); *Love in a Cold Climate* (01, Tom Hooper); *Gosford Park* (01, Robert Altman); *Salem Witch Trials* (01, Joseph Sargent); *The Sum of All Fears* (02, Phil Alden Robinson); *Evelyn* (02, Bruce Beresford); *Hollywood North* (03, Peter O'Brian).

Kathy (Kathleen) Bates,
b. Memphis, Tennessee, 1948

It says something important about Kathy Bates, and actresses like her, that while she won awards for her lead role on stage in *Frankie and Johnny at the Clair de Lune,* when that play came to be filmed Michelle Pfeiffer was offered as the retiring waitress. In other words, to look and be as millions are is no way to get yourself into pictures. Yet Kathy Bates has won one Oscar and been nominated for another, and she has been the framework for several other pictures. She has insisted on herself, without being strident or monotonous. And we are all better off because of her. Even so, an actress like this needs the extraordinary opportunity of a *Misery* (90, Rob Reiner) to prove herself, and parts like that are not commonplace.

She attended Southern Methodist University, she was a singing waitress in the Catskills, and a regular on stage for many years—her work includes the daughter in *'night, Mother* (a role that went to Sissy Spacek in the movie).

After a tiny part in *Taking Off* (71, Milos Forman), her film work began properly with *Straight Time* (78, Ulu Grosbard); *Come Back to the Five and Dime, Jimmy Dean, Jimmy Dean* (82, Robert Altman); *Johnny Bull* (86, Claudia Weill); *Summer Heat* (87, Michie Gleason); *Arthur 2: On the Rocks* (88, Bud Yorkin); on TV in *Roe v. Wade* (89, Gregory Hoblit); *Signs of Life* (89, John David Coles); *Men Don't Leave* (90, Paul Brickman); *Dick Tracy* (90, Warren Beatty); *White Palace* (90, Luis Mandoki).

In truth, those parts had been small, but the role of the avid reader who gets her own *auteur* in *Misery* was served up on a plate. (Her rivals for the Oscar that year included Meryl Streep, Anjelica Huston, and Julia Roberts.) And now her roles grew larger and richer: *At Play in the Fields of the Lord* (91, Hector Babenco); *Fried Green Tomatoes* (91, Jon Avnet); *Shadows and Fog* (92, Woody Allen); *Prelude to a Kiss* (92, Norman René); *Used People* (92, Beeban Kidron); *Hostages* (93, David Wheatley), for TV; a single mother with six kids in

A Home of Our Own (93, Tony Bill); *North* (94, Reiner); *Curse of the Starving Class* (95, J. Michael McClary); excellent as the mother in *Dolores Claiborne* (95, Taylor Hackford), like *Misery* from a Stephen King novel; a bag lady in *The West Side Waltz* (95, Ernest Thompson); *Angus* (95, Patrick Read Johnson); the cop in *Diabolique* (96, Jeremiah Chechik); outstanding in *The War at Home* (96, Emilio Estevez); as Molly Brown in *Titanic* (97, James Cameron); followed by *Swept from the Sea* (98, Kidron); very funny as the agent (and nominated) in *Primary Colors* (98, Mike Nichols); *The Waterboy* (98, Frank Coraci); unbilled in *A Civil Action* (98, Steven Zaillian); on TV as Miss Hannigan in *Annie* (99, Rob Marshall).

She played a mother superior in *Bruno* (00, Shirley MacLaine) and Ma James in *American Outlaws* (01, Les Mayfield). *About Schmidt* (02, Alexander Payne).

In addition to some TV directing (*Homicide, Oz,* and *Six Feet Under*), she directed *Dash and Lily* in 1999. Then she was in *Dragonfly* (02, Tom Shadyac); *Unconditional Love* (02, P. J. Hogan); *The Tulse Luper Suitcases: The Moab Story* (03, Peter Greenaway); and played Queen Victoria in *Around the World in 80 Days* (03, Coraci).

Harry Baur (1880–1943),
b. Montrouge, France

One-volume histories of world film must omit so many important figures. (I know how many deserving cases are left out of this book.) Read any history and you will find that French film in the 1930s is treated as Renoir, Clair, Carné, Vigo, and Pagnol. But that survey is bound never to encounter Harry Baur—a great, noble actor—for he never worked with any of the "saved."

Baur was at least as good and as central to France in the thirties as Michel Simon or Louis Jouvet. Moreover, Baur's story is the more memorable because of his tragic end. His wife was Jewish, and when Baur went to Germany to make his last film, *Symphonie eines Lebens* (41, Hans Bertram), he was arrested and tortured. He was released, but shortly thereafter he was found dead.

He made some silent pictures, and he was always a force on the stage. But for ten years, he was a dominating figure in French movies, larger than life yet naturalistic: *David Golden* (30, Julien Duvivier); *Les Cinq Gentlemen Maudits* (32, Duvivier); *Poil de Carotte* (32, Duvivier); *La Tête d'un Homme* (33, Duvivier); as Jean Valjean in *Les Misérables* (34, Raymond Bernard); *Golgotha* (35, Duvivier); *Moscow Nights* (35, Anthony Asquith); *Les Hommes Nouveaux* (35, Marcel L'Herbier); *Crime and Punishment* (35, Pierre Chenal); *Le Golem* (36, Duvivier); *Samson* (36, Maurice Tourneur); as the composer in *Un Grand Amour de Beethoven* (36, Abel Gance); *Nitchevo* (37,

Jacques de Baroncelli); *Un Carnet de Bal* (37, Duvivier); as Rasputin in *La Tragédie Imperiale* (38, L'Herbier); *Mollenard* (38, Robert Siodmak); *La Patriote* (38, Tourneur); *L'Homme de Niger* (40, de Baroncelli); with Jouvet in *Volpone* (40, Tourneur); and *L'Assassinat de Père Noel* (41, Christian-Jaque).

Anne Baxter (1923–85),
b. Michigan City, Indiana
The granddaughter of Frank Lloyd Wright, she made her stage debut at age twelve in *Seen But Not Heard*, and her movie debut in *Twenty Mule Team* (40, Richard Thorpe). After testing unsuccessfully for *Rebecca* (at age sixteen!), she had her first hit in *The Great Profile* (40, Walter Lang) and was contracted by Fox. Without ever establishing a dominant screen persona, she made a string of good films and seldom appeared other than intelligent and attractive: capable at the age of nineteen of playing the "Goodbye, George" scene in *The Magnificent Ambersons* (42, Orson Welles); she won an Oscar as supporting actress in *The Razor's Edge* (46, Edmund Goulding); and was credibly a match for Bette Davis as the sweetly conniving Eve Harrington in *All About Eve* (50, Joseph L. Mankiewicz).

Her other films include *Charley's Aunt* (41, Archie Mayo); *Swamp Water* (41, Jean Renoir); *The Pied Piper* (42, Irving Pichel); *Five Graves to Cairo* (43, Billy Wilder); *The North Star* (43, Lewis Milestone); *Sunday Dinner for a Soldier* (44, Lloyd Bacon); *The Sullivans* (44, Bacon); *Guest in the House* (44, John Brahm); *The Eve of St. Mark* (44, John M. Stahl); *A Royal Scandal* (45, Otto Preminger and Ernst Lubitsch); *Angel on My Shoulder* (46, Mayo); *Blaze of Noon* (47, John Farrow); *The Walls of Jericho* (48, Stahl); *Yellow Sky* (48, William Wellman); *Homecoming* (48, Mervyn Le Roy); *You're My Everything* (49, Lang); as golfer Ben Hogan's wife in *Follow the Sun* (51, Sidney Lanfield); *The Outcasts of Poker Flats* (52, Joseph Newman); the "Last Leaf" episode of *O. Henry's Full House* (52, Jean Negulesco); *I Confess* (52, Alfred Hitchcock); *The Blue Gardenia* (52, Fritz Lang); *Carnival Story* (54, Kurt Neumann); *Bedevilled* (55, Mitchell Leisen); *The Ten Commandments* (56, Cecil B. De Mille); *Three Violent People* (57, Rudolph Maté); *Chase a Crooked Shadow* (58, Michael Anderson); *Summer of the Seventeenth Doll* (60, Leslie Norman); *Cimarron* (61, Anthony Mann); and *Walk on the Wild Side* (62, Edward Dmytryk).

After that, she made fewer films and too many wasteful TV appearances: *The Busy Body* (66, William Castle), and *Dynamite Man from Glory Jail* (71, Andrew V. McLaglen). But when Lauren Bacall left the American production of *Applause*, it was the original Eve who took her part as Margo Channing—one of life's braver attempts to match art.

Her 1976 autobiography, *Intermission*, was far better and funnier than most books of its kind, partly because it makes clear how important it was to her to be married to an American who ranched in Australia.

She played in *Jane Austen in Manhattan* (80, James Ivory); she was in the TV production of *East of Eden* (81, Harvey Hart); she narrated a documentary about Frank Lloyd Wright (Murray Grigor); and just before her death she appeared in *Sherlock Holmes and the Masks of Death* (84, Roy Ward Baker).

Warner Baxter (1891–1951),
b. Columbus, Ohio
By the early 1940s, Baxter's popularity was slipping away. All through the 1930s, he had seemed the "mature" man, looking rather older than was the case. Illness and public neglect added gravity to his face and he soldiered on for his last ten years, intent perhaps on making one hundred movies. He died two short, and is now hardly known because only a handful of his films are ever seen: *42nd Street* (33, Lloyd Bacon), in which he played the harassed director; *The Prisoner of Shark Island* (36, John Ford), his most agonized role, as the doctor imprisoned for setting John Wilkes Booth's broken leg; and *The Road to Glory* (36, Howard Hawks), where he fitted admirably into the fatalistic picture of the First World War. In all three, he is a man under pressure, his character hardened by stress. But only a few years before, Baxter had won fame as a carefree, Fairbanksian bandit.

Baxter was a traveling salesman before he went into the theatre; and after a debut in *All Woman* (18, Hobart Henley), he played on Broadway in *Lombardi Ltd.* But he soon concentrated on movies and had a variety of supporting parts at different studios: *Her Own Money* (22, Joseph Henabery); *If I Were Queen* (22, Wesley Ruggles); *Blow Your Own Horn* (23, James W. Horne); and *Christine of the Hungry Heart* (24, George Archainbaud). Then Paramount signed him and he played in *The Female* (24, Sam Wood); *The Garden of Weeds* (24, James Cruze); and *The Golden Bed* (25, Cecil B. De Mille). He worked steadily without ever making stardom: *Welcome Home* (25, Cruze); *A Son of His Father* (25, Victor Fleming); *Mannequin* (26, Cruze); *Miss Brewster's Millions* (26, Clarence Badger); *The Runaway* (26, William C. De Mille); *Aloma of the South Seas* (26, Maurice Tourneur); the title part in *The Great Gatsby* (26, Herbert Brenon); *Drums of the Desert* (27, John Waters); *The Tragedy of Youth* (28, Archainbaud); and *Three Sinners* (28, Rowland V. Lee). *Ramona* (28, Edwin Carewe) lifted him enormously and, after *Craig's*

Wife (28, W. C. De Mille), *Danger Street* (28, Ralph Ince), and *West of Zanzibar* (29, Tod Browning), he went to Fox to take over for the injured Raoul Walsh as the Cisco Kid in *In Old Arizona* (29, Irving Cummings). The loss of an eye settled Walsh as a director, and the Cisco Kid won Baxter the best actor Oscar.

Fox now treated him as a star, but few of his 1930s movies have lasted well: there was something subdued in Baxter, so that he often looked best in support of some other star—with Janet Gaynor in *Daddy Longlegs* (31, Alfred Santell), for instance. He also made *Behind that Curtain* (29, Cummings); *Romance of the Rio Grande* (29, Santell); *The Arizona Kid* (30, Santell); *Renegades* (30, Fleming); *Doctors' Wives* (31, Frank Borzage); *The Squaw Man* (31, C. B. De Mille); *Surrender* (31, William K. Howard); *Six Hours to Live* (32, William Dieterle); *Dangerously Yours* (33, Frank Tuttle); *Penthouse* (33, W. S. Van Dyke); *Broadway Bill* (35, Frank Capra); *One More Spring* (35, Henry King); *Under the Pampas Moon* (35, James Tinling); *Robin Hood of El Dorado* (36, William Wellman); *To Mary—with Love* (36, John Cromwell); *White Hunter* (36, Cummings); *Slave Ship* (37, Tay Garnett); as Alan Breck Stewart in *Kidnapped* (38, Alfred Werker).

As his ratings slumped, he had supporting parts in *Adam Had Four Sons* (41, Gregory Ratoff) and *Lady in the Dark* (44, Mitchell Leisen), but otherwise slipped into B pictures, including the dull Crime Doctor series.

Michael Bay, b. 1965, Los Angeles

1995: *Bad Boys*. 1996: *The Rock*. 1998: *Armageddon*. 2001: *Pearl Harbor*. 2003: *Bad Boys II*.

In the summer of 2001, there was a story going around Hollywood that Michael Bay was seriously depressed. No one wishes to be callous, but this could be the start of something useful. For in sharing a common, sad state of mind, is it possible that Mr. Bay will eventually come to recognize the natural materials of a narrative art—the lives of ordinary people? Or is it more likely that he will overcome passing melancholy and get on with a far more depleting mindscape—Hollywood thinking?

Still, it's worth explaining the reason for Bay being at bay: he was dismayed at the nearly universal load of critical bombs that had been dropped on *Pearl Harbor*. In other words, something in his innocence had coincided with the provincialism of Los Angeles to persuade him that having finished that vast film, and set off all its explosions, why, surely he had made a thing called art. So, in the event that Mr. Bay is ever looking for help, I'll spell it out here—he makes noisy garbage; it is his calling, his being and soul. There is no cure. We may respect his suffering, but we know this: ours is greater. And he has millions as medicine.

Nathalie Baye (Judith Mesnil),
b. Mainnerville, France, 1948

Baye didn't make a film until she was twenty-five. She had trained and worked as a dancer first. But the delay helped, making her a bit more mature than most debut actresses. Which began to explain why she was not the prettiest you've ever seen. A character began to emerge, if only because she played a version of Truffaut's maternal script girl, Helen Scott, in an early film, *Day for Night* (73).

She then made *La Gueule Ouverte* (74, Maurice Pialat); *La Gifle* (74, Claude Pinoteau); *Mado* (76, Claude Sautet); *The Man Who Loved Women* (77, Truffaut); *Monsieur Papa* (77, Philippe Monnier); *The Green Room* (78, Truffaut); *Mon Premier Amour* (78, Elie Chouraqui); *La Mémoire Courte* (79, Eduardo de Gregorio); *Every Man for Himself* (80, Jean-Luc Godard); *Je Vais Craquer!!!* (80, François Leterrier); *The Girl from Lorraine* (80, Claude Goretta); *A Week's Vacation* (80, Bertrand Tavernier); *Beau-Père* (81, Bertrand Blier); *L'Ombre Rouge* (81, Jean-Louis Comolli); *La Balance* (82, Bob Swaim); *The Return of Martin Guerre* (82, Daniel Vigne); *J'ai Epousé une Ombre* (82, Robin Davis), a remake of *No Man of Her Own; Détective* (84, Godard); *Notre Histoire* (84, Blier); *Rive Droite, Rive Gauche* (84, Philippe Labro); *Beethoven's Nephew* (85, Paul Morrissey); *Lune de Miel* (85, Patrick Jamain); *De Guerre Lasse* (87, Robert Enrico); *En Toute Innocence* (88, Alain Jessua); *La Baule-les-Pins* (90, Diane Kurys); *Un Weekend sur Deux* (90, Nicole Garcia); *The Man Inside* (90, Bobby Roth).

This extraordinary work rate has declined only a little, but she has worked more often for women directors: *La Voix* (92, Pierre Granier-Deferre); *And the Band Played On* (93, Roger Spottiswoode); *La Machine* (94, François Dupeyron); a voice on *Arabian Knights* (95, Richard Williams); *Enfants de Salaud* (96, Tonie Marshall); *Food of Love* (97, Stephen Poliakoff); *Paparazzi* (98, Alain Berberian); *Si Je T'Aime, Prends Garde à Toi* (99, Jeanne Labrunne); *Venus Beauty Salon* (99, Marshall); *A Pornographic Affair* (99, Frédéric Fonteyne); *Selon Matthieu* (00, Xavier Beauvais); *Ça Ira Mieux Demain* (00, Labrunne); *Absolument Fabuleux* (01, Gabriel Aghion).

She did *L'Enfant des Lumières* (02, Vigne) for French TV; came to Hollywood as the mother in *Catch Me If You Can* (02, Steven Spielberg); then did *La Fleur de Mal* (03, Claude Chabrol); *Les Sentiments* (03, Noemie Lvovsky); *France Boutique* (03, Marshall).

André Bazin (1918–58), b. Angers, France

Bazin would be exceptional if only because he is one of the few important writers on film for whom no one had an angry, or pained, word. He was so widely esteemed as a man. Jacques Rivette has called him "saintly." Jean Renoir said that his work would outlast cinema itself. Robert Bresson observed how he "had a curious way of taking off from what was false to arrive ultimately at what was true." And for François Truffaut, of course, Bazin was nothing less than a surrogate father, a friend and teacher bringing the wild child into being, and dying the day after shooting on *The 400 Blows* had begun (that film is dedicated to Bazin's memory).

As a child, Bazin was moved from Angers to La Rochelle. He studied there and at Versailles, and in 1938 he entered the Ecole Normale Superieure at St. Cloud. His academic record was exceptional, but he was denied teaching credentials because of his stammer. So, in the war years, he joined the Maison de Lettres, a form of schooling for the working classes and for those whose education had been disrupted by war. He also founded a film club and showed many films banned by the Nazis. After 1944, he was made film critic on *Le Parisien Liberé;* he wrote for several other papers and magazines; he was made a teacher at IDHEC (Institut des Hautes Etudes Cinématographiques); and he founded, with Jacques Doniol-Valcroze, *Les Cahiers du Cinéma.* He wrote books about Orson Welles and Vittorio de Sica, and at his death (from leukemia) he was at work on a large book about Renoir. But he was also the author of a variety of essays and reviews that make a coherent definition of cinema.

Bazin was a Catholic leftist, and a precise arguer and writer in the school of Sartre, but as a film theoretician everything for him was founded in the notion of film as a record of reality. As such, he loved documentary and any style that tended toward the use of real light, deep space, and long, extended takes. Naturally, therefore, he loved Renoir, Rossellini, and Welles, just as he aspired towards a kind of cinema that closely imitated real experience. He was also a humanist, devoted to the idea of performance and a lover of Chaplin and all kinds of natural acting. Though he was not overly fond of montage, or fragmented points of view, he was one of the first to grasp the importance of Bresson.

Cahiers was initially based on his work and example, and on an historic view that saw the best of American, European, and Japanese film working together (he was a great admirer of Mizoguchi). He also inspired and assisted the young directors who would become the New Wave, and made the essential assumption that critical writing and real filming need not be separate. Though seldom in good health, he worked very hard and he cared for animals as much as he did for movies and moviemakers.

It happens that I am writing this piece on the same day as writing about David Begelman. And it occurs to me that whereas Begelman would have found Bazin irrelevant, Bazin would have been fascinated by Begelman. We need to recall that in an age when the Begelmans have become so powerful.

Warren Beatty (Henry Warren Beaty),
b. Richmond, Virginia, 1937
1978: *Heaven Can Wait* (codirected with Buck Henry). 1981: *Reds.* 1990: *Dick Tracy.* 1998: *Bulworth.*

The prized son of well-to-do parents—professionals with strong creative instincts—Beatty is also the younger brother of Shirley MacLaine. (If he seems in some ways very different from her, that may only prove the strength of her influence—for Beatty has taken great pains to look like his own master.) Having grown up near Washington, Beatty did a year at Northwestern before opting for New York and show business. He did some TV drama (he would play Milton Armitage in *The Many Loves of Dobie Gillis* in 1959–60), and he had a lead role onstage in William Inge's *A Loss of Roses* in 1959. He has never again acted onstage.

Then, as a discovery of Elia Kazan's, he was running in the steps of Brando and Dean for his full-starring movie debut, *Splendor in the Grass.* He was sexual, cerebral, troubled, a little withdrawn. He had unquestioned beauty and the early legend of being the enchanter of costars and any other lady he met. But as an actor, Beatty was not open or generous. He seemed reluctant to yield himself up, and so early on he had more fame and critical attention than public love. But from the outset, he was regarded as either very intelligent or very difficult: sometimes his own puzzled look has seemed beset by the same question.

He was very good as the gigolo to Vivien Leigh in *The Roman Spring of Mrs. Stone* (61, Jose Quintero). But he seemed torn between playing aloof, unwholesome young men, or lending himself to lightweight packages. He was the phony hero and the unlikable older brother in *All Fall Down* (62, John Frankenheimer), and he was excellent as the nurse who risks his own breakdown in falling in love with *Lilith* (63, Robert Rossen). *Mickey One* (65, Arthur Penn) is a truly pretentious picture, but it still seems remarkable that the young actor got it made, and Beatty is brilliant as the paranoid nightclub entertainer. On the other hand, he was in *Promise Her Anything* (66, Arthur Hiller) and *Kaleidoscope* (66, Jack Smight), projects with no claim upon 1966, let alone eternity.

Beatty was a figure on the screen, yet he was not popular. Then, in 1967, he took responsibility and control and came of age, by starring in and producing *Bonnie and Clyde* (67, Penn). His performance was so remarkable in its mixture of good looks and stricken limp, of assertion and shyness, and of that convincingly youthful fatalism that says "Ain't life grand?" as he recounts how he shot off his toes the day before learning that he was to be released from prison. Moreover, he won an audience and drove a film to be a hit through his performance. Yet his contribution was greater still as a producer, for he had bought the script, hired Penn, done the casting, ordered the rewrites, and then *insisted* on the very startling film as a key expression of late-sixties sensibility. Few films have been better produced. It helped one see why Beatty was not always fully committed to mere acting or looking pretty.

But he did not advance decisively—as if some lassitude or disquiet flinched from a life in production, or that of running a studio. So his acting became odder and more distracted: *The Only Game in Town* (69, George Stevens) and *$* (71, Richard Brooks). But the right project could capture his interest: he has never been better as actor than in the moody, self-deluding, talking-himself-into-a-corner frontier producer in *McCabe and Mrs. Miller* (71, Robert Altman). He was good again as a spookily dark investigative journalist in *The Parallax View* (74, Alan J. Pakula), too frightening a film for public comfort.

Then he produced again: *Shampoo* (75, Hal Ashby), a tough comedy about love and sex, hairdressing and politics, set in Los Angeles. Beatty wrote the script with his friend Robert Towne, and he dominated a movie in which he was also seen as playing a side of himself—the Don Juan (Beatty had by then been linked with many women, including Joan Collins, Natalie Wood, Leslie Caron, and Julie Christie—some said he helped their careers, others believed he was always competitive).

There was then a three-year gap before *Heaven Can Wait* (78), which he wrote with Elaine May and directed with Buck Henry—how could so flimsy a hit bear up under so many talents? *Heaven Can Wait* now looks like the least interesting large project of a man determined to be significant. After another interval of three years, Beatty delivered *Reds* (81), a life of John Reed, with scenes of the International Revolution. He directed himself, as well as playing Reed, and got a terrific performance from his love of the time, Diane Keaton, playing Louise Bryant. In the first half of *Reds* there was a stirring balance of love story and mankind story—a balance that slipped in the second half. The film never did well enough, but Beatty got the directing Oscar and, in his use of real witnesses, made a very intriguing mix of melodrama and history. *Reds* is still a fascinating picture with passages of greatness—but it never seems the work of a Marxist.

Beatty may have been tired; yet he has a deserved reputation for tirelessness. Whatever the reasons, he waited six years to make . . . *Ishtar* (87, Elaine May), a folly and now a legend of extravagance. It is something of a mystery as to just what Beatty was doing in the mid-eighties. Was it weariness or the readiness to turn to politics? (He was much involved with Gary Hart, just as he had worked for McGovern in 1972.) Was it a life of women and the telephone? He did function as executive producer (even if he took no credit) on *The Pick-Up Artist* (87), which brought together unlikely protégés—actress Molly Ringwald and writer-director James Toback.

Dick Tracy (90) may have been one of the best-promoted films ever made. Beyond that, not a lot can be said except in praise of the comic-book design. Tracy figured the latest woman in Beatty's life, Madonna, and her documentary, *Truth or Dare* (91, Alek Keshishian), has exquisite glimpses of a Beatty who seems like a man trying to escape from a Borges story.

He found liberty, and a wife (at last) in *Bugsy* (91, Barry Levinson), an old-fashioned piece of gangster nostalgia, written by Toback, and costarring Annette Bening, who became Mrs. Beatty and the mother of their children. *Bugsy* is smart, at its best when funny, yet helplessly pledged to the fantasy that being (or acting like) a gangster ought to be fun and glamorous. Despite valiant efforts, Beatty the actor never persuaded me that he knew how to lose control, let alone become psychotic. Control *is* his thing—and maybe his curse. And now he has a daughter, the ultimate enchantress, perhaps, for the great seducer. He will be a veteran by the time she comes of age.

In 1994, having taken a long time over it, he produced and acted in *Love Story* (Glenn Gordon Caron). Annette Bening was his co-star again— and they were pregnant again.

The film was not, and suggested that there was no need for true love to translate to the screen. Beatty was a busy father now, a vague figure still in Democratic Party circles and a rather surprising Irving Thalberg Award recipient. His next film was *Bulworth*, a very lively and enterprising political satire (until around halftime), and then a sadder sign of Beatty's receding energy. Still, in the arid nineties, *Bulworth* was a real achievement. Whereas *Town & Country* was an evident travesty.

Harold Becker, b. New York, 1950

1972: *The Ragman's Daughter.* 1979: *The Onion Field.* 1980: *The Black Marble.* 1981: *Taps.* 1985: *Vision Quest.* 1988: *The Boost.* 1989: *Sea of Love.* 1993: *Malice.* 1995: *City Hall.* 1998: *Mercury Rising.* 1999: *Solo.* 2001: *Domestic Disturbance.*

Twelve films in thirty years hardly amounts to character or consistency. But there are plenty of virtues here. Becker can tell a complicated story, even if complexity is all you get. He can handle actors and let big stars have their set pieces. In *The Boost,* he delivered one of the rare films about ordinary people and money. Elsewhere, he has seemed just as happy in competently dealing with the everyday melodrama that exists only in the movies. He helped bring Al Pacino back to the scene with *Sea of Love,* and made that a wry, grubby glamorization of the police, no matter that *The Onion Field* had seemed concerned to reproduce the impossible realities of the job. And James Woods was way out of the ordinary in that picture. *Malice* is silly trickery, but *City Hall* is nearly an authentic study in local politics. I'd guess that Becker would be an entertaining raconteur on his own ups and downs and his gallery of tough-minded, ambivalent heroes.

Jacques Becker (1906–60), b. Paris
1934: *Le Commissaire est Bon Enfant* (s) (codirected with Pierre Prévert). 1935: *Tête de Turc* (s); *La Vie est à Nous* (codirected with Jean Renoir, Jean-Paul le Chanois, André Zwoboda, Pierre Unik, and Henri Cartier-Bresson). 1939: *L'Or du Cristobal* (codirected with and credited to Jean Stelli). 1942: *Dernier Atout.* 1943: *Goupi Mains-Rouges.* 1945: *Falbalas.* 1946: *Antoine et Antoinette.* 1949: *Rendez-Vous de Juillet.* 1951: *Edouard et Caroline.* 1952: *Casque d'Or.* 1953: *Rue de l'Estrapade.* 1954: *Touchez Pas au Grisbi.* 1955: *Ali-Baba et les Quarante Voleurs.* 1956: *Les Aventures d'Arsène Lupin.* 1957: *Montparnasse 19.* 1960: *Le Trou.*

Becker was a humane, observant, and inventive director who seemed willed into films by his apprenticeship to Jean Renoir on *Boudu, Chotard et Compagnie, Madame Bovary, La Vie est à Nous, Partie de Campagne, Les Bas-Fonds, La Grande Illusion,* and *La Marseillaise.* He lacked the master's innate passion for cinema, and he never properly discovered either a style or a subject matter in which he could immerse himself. His work is therefore very variable, more often exploring and searching than actually discovering truths. As if aware of the gap between himself and Renoir, he never entirely shrugged off modesty and worked as a sort of tribute: "I believe in the possibility of entertaining friendship and in the difficulty of maintaining love. I believe in the value of effort. And I believe above all in Paris. In my work I do not want to prove anything except that life is stronger than everything else." It might be from a devotional article on Renoir by a willing disciple who had observed and understood greatness but could never find it in himself. It was a kind gesture of Renoir's to revive the trio from *Casque d'Or* in *French Can Can.*

He was assistant to Renoir from 1932 onward, often playing small parts in the master's films: the poet who meets *Boudu* (32) in the park, or an English officer in *La Grande Illusion* (37). He withdrew from *L'Or du Cristobal,* his first feature, as war began, but managed to work during the war and came to notice with the rural film, *Goupi Mains-Rouges.* After the war, he veered from the deliberate social study of *Rendez-Vous de Juillet* to the Paramount-like airiness and inconsequentiality of *Edouard et Caroline* to the full-blooded romance of *Casque d'Or.* That is his richest film, a fated love story in the Paris of the 1890s, looking like Auguste Renoir, but with a summery sensuousness that is Becker's most personal achievement. Simone Signoret's blonde in bloom in it is one of the most convincing women in French cinema.

Thereafter, Becker seemed to lose his way. Jean Gabin was excellent in the carefully authentic *Touchez Pas au Grisbi,* but *Ali-Baba* was Fernandel fodder. He took over the subject of the life of Modigliani when Max Ophuls died, but despite Gérard Philipe, Lilli Palmer, and Anouk Aimée, *Montparnasse 19* was more decorative than affecting. His last film was his greatest departure: *Le Trou* is a story of prisoners attempting to escape— intense, claustrophobic, realistic but with all the unassertive faith in decency and feelings that distinguishes Becker's best work.

Wallace Beery (1886–1949),
b. Kansas City, Missouri
The movie world has always required go-betweeners to reassure audiences—who are essentially plain, insignificant, and anxious—that they need not be overawed by the flawless beauty of people in films. The movie comedians were envoys of the pathetic dream nursed by every man that he might be as athletic as Fairbanks, as conquering as Valentino, or as ardent as John Gilbert. But the comics are clearly isolated figures, benign inmates from an asylum who have been allowed out and who commune with themselves. Wallace Beery is the most notable example of the ugly, stupid, boorish man who was as successful in films as heroes or lovers. Although for most of the 1920s he played villains, that did not detract from the idea of homespun genuineness beneath such fearsomely ordinary features. In a world of unmitigated glamour, it is tacitly acknowledged that Quasimodo is an honest man. It is reality that shows in his face and promises a kindly sense of human woes.

Beery was the older half-brother of Noah Beery. As a youth, he joined the Ringling Circus and went into vaudeville and summer stock where he specialized in playing old ladies. From about 1912 he had small parts in movies, and in 1914 he made a series of one-reel comedies at Essanay in the role of a Swedish housemaid. He moved on, in the same skirts, to Universal, where he also worked as a director. At this time, he eloped with Gloria Swanson, who was a teenage ingenue in some of the Sweedie films, and they were briefly married. Divorce came in 1919, proving that two separate layers from the Dream could not coexist. It persuaded Beery to stay in trousers and he settled into a run of colorful villains and blundering oafs: *The Little American* (17, Cecil B. De Mille); *The Love Burglar* (19, James Cruze); *Soldiers of Fortune* (19, Allan Dwan); *Victory* (19, Maurice Tourneur); *The Virgin of Stamboul* (20, Tod Browning); *The Mollycoddle* (20, Victor Fleming); as Magua in *The Last of the Mohicans* (20, Tourneur); *A Tale of Two Worlds* (21, Frank Lloyd); *Wild Horsey* (22, Wesley Ruggles); *I Am the Law* (22, Edwin Carewe); *The Man from Hell's River* (22, Irving Cummings); as Richard the Lion-Hearted in *Robin Hood* (22, Dwan); *The Flame of Life* (23, Hobart Henley); *Bavu* (23, Stuart Paton); *Drifting* (23, Browning); *Ashes of Vengeance* (23, Lloyd); as the villain in *The Three Ages* (23, Buster Keaton and Eddie Cline); *The Spanish Dancer* (23, Herbert Brenon); *The White Tiger* (23, Browning); *The Signal Tower* (24, Clarence Brown); *The Sea Hawk* (24, Lloyd); *The Red Lily* (24, Fred Niblo); as Professor Challenger in *The Lost World* (25, Harry O. Hoyt); and *The Devil's Cargo* (25, Fleming).

His stock had risen steadily and he was signed up by Paramount: *Coming Through* (25, Edward Sutherland); *Adventure* (25, Fleming); *The Wanderer* (25, Raoul Walsh); *The Pony Express* (25, Cruze); on loan to play with Colleen Moore in *So Big* (25, Charles Brabin). Then Paramount teamed him with Raymond Hatton in a series of comedies: *Behind the Front* (26, Sutherland); *We're in the Navy Now* (26, Sutherland); *Fireman, Save My Child* (27, Sutherland); *Now We're in the Air* (27, Frank Strayer); *Wife Savers* (28, Ralph Cedar); *Partners in Crime* (28, Strayer); and *The Big Killing* (28, F. Richard Jones). The series did well, until *The Big Killing*. Paramount doubted Beery's staying power now that he needed to talk, and they let him go after *Beggars of Life* (28, William Wellman); *Chinatown Nights* (29, Wellman); *The Stairs of Sand* (29, Otto Brower); and *River of Romance* (29, Richard Wallace).

It was a notable mistake. MGM picked up Beery and made him a leading star of the early 1930s: as a convict in *The Big House* (30, George Hill); as Barnum in *A Lady's Morals* (30, Sidney Franklin); as Pat Garrett in *Billy the Kid* (30, King Vidor); with Marie Dressler in *Min and Bill* (30, Hill); with John Gilbert in *Way for a Sailor* (30, Sam Wood). With Fredric March he shared the best actor Oscar for his work in *The Champ* (31, Vidor), and for the next few years was at his peak: *Grand Hotel* (32, Edmund Goulding); as a wrestler in *Flesh* (32, John Ford); with Dressler again in *Tugboat Annie* (33, Mervyn Le Roy); the

husband of Jean Harlow in *Dinner at Eight* (33, George Cukor); *The Bowery* (33, Walsh); in the title part of *Viva Villa!* (34, Howard Hawks and Jack Conway); as Long John Silver in *Treasure Island* (34, Fleming); and as *The Mighty Barnum* (34, Walter Lang).

He slipped gradually into supporting parts, always looking for a replacement for Marie Dressler, who died in 1934: *China Seas* (35, Tay Garnett); *O'Shaughnessy's Boy* (35, Richard Boleslavsky); *Ah, Wilderness!* (35, Brown); *A Message to Garcia* (36, George Marshall); *Slave Ship* (37, Garnett); *Port of Seven Seas* (38, James Whale); *Stablemates* (38, Wood); *Stand Up and Fight* (39, W. S. Van Dyke); *Sergeant Madden* (39, Josef von Sternberg); and *Thunder Afloat* (39, George Seitz). Marjorie Main was Beery's partner in his last years in films of decreasing importance: *Twenty Mule Team* (40, Richard Thorpe); *Wyoming* (40, Thorpe); *The Bad Man* (41, Thorpe); *Barnacle Bill* (41, Thorpe); *Jackass Mail* (42, Norman Z. McLeod); *Barbary Coast Gent* (44, Roy del Ruth); *This Man's Navy* (45, Wellman); *A Date with Judy* (48, Thorpe); and *Big Jack* (49, Thorpe).

David Begelman (1921–95), b. New York

It's easy to assume that David Begelman—who was seventy-four when he died—had been in the picture business all his life, and that he therefore stands as one of its creations. That is not the case. The son of a tailor, he was raised in the Bronx, and he served in the Air Force during the war on a technical training program. Afterwards he drifted, and went into insurance. It wasn't until around 1950 that he met Freddie Fields, two years his junior and an agent at MCA. That contact allowed Begelman to get work at the agency in the mid-fifties. He rose swiftly, and he and Fields created the Creative Management Association.

That's when the Begelman persona developed. Though less than handsome, he dressed well and became very attractive to women. He was charming, funny, reckless, and unafraid. He lied, he gambled, and it is fairly obvious now that from an early stage he cheated whenever he felt the need. He was a limousine confessor, a man who picked up tabs and then charged them to other enterprises. He was also a very effective agent who would win the loyalty, the admiration, and the affection of such stars as Judy Garland, Paul Newman, Steve McQueen, Robert Redford, and Barbra Streisand. He also fucked Garland, and screwed her financially—but she was a mess, and she depended on him, and also had some of her best later years (as a concert performer) in his hands. The other careers he helped build involved a less intrusive relationship, but they didn't need it. By the late sixties, Begelman was one of the key power brokers in the business, an immense character, with a proven record of success, widely popular—and just as widely esteemed as a prince of a companion who'd steal your balls if you weren't alert, but do it with charm, and when he brought them back they'd have stories to tell. He was, as they said, "Hollywood."

And, as if to prove that such worldly assets were what made the business work, he was invited to be president of the ailing Columbia Pictures in 1973. Since the death of Harry Cohn (in 1957), Columbia had had mixed fortunes, led by Abe Schneider, Leo Jaffe, Mike Frankovich, and Stanley Schneider. With Alan Hirschfield, Begelman gave Columbia a far better ride—for which he deserved nearly as much credit as he took. It was a time of films as diverse as *Shampoo, Funny Lady, Taxi Driver, The Deep*, and *Close Encounters of the Third Kind*. At the same time, almost out of habit, Begelman had been committing check fraud. These were for small amounts, but they involved people like actor Cliff Robertson and director Martin Ritt. Was the money needed (to meet gambling debts)? Or was the theft a form of personality disorder—a version of low self-esteem—as Begelman's defense and doctors would claim?

All of this is the material of David McClintick's book *Indecent Exposure*. The fascination of that remorseless inquiry is that so many people in, and around, Columbia were disposed to let Begelman off—because he was liked, and because the behavior was decreed normal. In the end, much against the advice of Begelman's fierce ally Ray Stark, Alan Hirschfield insisted on Begelman being fired. But the board decision was far from united. In fact, Hirschfield's end was close, and Begelman came back. By 1980, he was the head of MGM. It didn't last. He slipped into independent production and he made some dire films—*The Sicilian* (87, Michael Cimino), *Mannequin* (87, Michael Gottlieb), *Weekend at Bernie's* (89, Ted Kotcheff). Nothing could stop his fall, and he was by now an older man.

In the end, he checked into the Century Plaza Hotel, took a good room, and shot himself. For years, it was said, he had carried a gun, just in case.

Harry (Harold George) **Belafonte**,
b. Harlem, 1927

When the splashy *Introducing Dorothy Dandridge* opened on TV in 1999, with Halle Berry as the nearly forgotten actress, no one asked out loud, "So where's the Belafonte biopic?" For the fact is that Belafonte and Dandridge became significant screen performers in the same film, as the lovers in *Carmen Jones* (55, Otto Preminger). That was only Belafonte's second film, for he was four years younger than Dandridge, as well as far less experienced in movie work.

Still, Belafonte is really a more exemplary show-business figure—and one with every bit as blighted a career as Dandridge's. From an early life of real poverty in New York and Jamaica, he became a very popular singer of folk music and especially calypso. It was Belafonte who made "Banana Boat" so popular, and who seemed a very "nice" light-skinned, handsome, polite black in the fifties. However, he was a radical and an activist, and a man with a great deal of justified anger—not least at the way he was used in pictures: *Bright Road* (53, Gerald Mayer), in which he played with Dandridge; *Island in the Sun* (57, Robert Rossen), in which he was allowed to kiss Joan Fontaine; as a survivor of nuclear disaster, with Inger Stevens, in *The World, the Flesh and the Devil* (59, Ranald MacDougall).

His own production company was the driving force behind the exceptionally tough and bleak *Odds Against Tomorrow* (59, Robert Wise), after which some kind of blackballing seems to have set in. It broke his promising career, and it was ten years before Belafonte began doing films again: *The Angel Levine* (70, Jan Kadar), with Zero Mostel; *Buck and the Preacher* (72, Sidney Poitier); very funny in *Uptown Saturday Night* (74, Poitier); he then coproduced *Beat Street* (84, Stan Latham); and then after bits in *The Player* (92, Robert Altman) and *Ready to Wear* (94, Altman), he did his best film work, as the sardonic gangster in *Kansas City* (96, Altman). He also appeared in *White Man's Burden* (95, Desmond Nakano) and *Swing Vote* (99, David Anspaugh).

Marco Bellocchio, b. Piacenza, Italy, 1939
1961: *La Colpa e le Pena* (s); *Abasso lo Zio* (s). 1962: *Ginepro Fatto Uomo* (s). 1965: *I Pugni in Tasca/Fists in the Pocket*. 1967: *La Cina è Vicina/China Is Near;* "Discutiamo, Discutiamo," episode from *Amore e Rabbia*. 1971: *Nel Nome del Padre/In the Name of the Father*. 1973: *Slap the Monster on Page One*. 1977: *Il Gabbiano/The Seagull*. 1978: *La Macchina Cinema* (codirected). 1980: *Salto Nel Vuoto; Vacanze in Val Trebbia*. 1982: *Gli Occhi, la Bocca/The Eyes, the Mouth*. 1984: *Enrico IV/Henry IV*. 1986: *Il Diavolo in Corpo/The Devil in the Flesh*. 1987: *La Visione del Sabba/The Visions of Sabbah*. 1992: *Autour du Désir*. 1994: *Il Sogno della Farfala*. 1995: *Sogni Infranti*. 1997: *Il Principe di Homburg*. 1998: *La Religione della Storia*. 1999: *La Balia*. 2002: *Ora de Religione/My Mother's Smile*.

Fists in the Pocket was one of the most striking debuts of the 1960s: a study of the incestuous mesh of a family of epileptics—passionate, neurotic, barbed, and destructive. Epilepsy served Bellocchio, as it had Dostoyevsky, as a sign of social decadence and family claustrophobia, and as the symptom of a distorted psychological nature. The central figure—played brilliantly by Lou Castel—is victim, hero, and destroyer, the life force running riot. How autobiographical is *Fists in the Pocket*? Bellocchio has confessed that the film was made to resolve many doubts about himself and his future. Furthermore, its intensity may have grown out of its necessary economy:

If I hadn't had such a tight budget, *Fists in the Pocket* would have been a naturalistic film, with a more accurate sociological—that is, social—background. . . .

It would maybe have been after the style of a Renoir or a Becker film, in other words close to the French novelistic tradition which has always fascinated me. They say that hunger sharpens the mind. Since I had to work in a family context, the family became my dramatic space; I found myself probing the relationship between the members of a nuclear cell.

There is no question but that the mood of pathology justified and sustained the trembling, surrealist pitch of the imagery and forced Bellocchio to obtain wounded performances from his cast. The difficulties of a first feature seemed to merge creatively with the pain of a young person.

Bellocchio had studied at the Centro Sperimentale and at the Slade School in London, and made a few shorts before *Fists in the Pocket*. Unfortunately, his subsequent films have hardly emerged from Italy. Reports of them suggest that they lack the quivering intensity of his first feature. *China Is Near* was made at a time when Bellocchio had joined the Italian Communist party. *In the Name of the Father* has a more comic edge to its study of a cheap Italian boarding school—such as the director himself once attended—that has aroused comparisons with Vigo. *Slap the Monster on Page One* fell to Bellocchio when Sergio Donati was overtaken by illness: a newspaper exposé, about victimized hippies, set at a time of election.

The Eyes, the Mouth (one of the finest films of the eighties), is an enlargement on *Fists in the Pocket*, with some scenes from the earlier film, with Lou Castel again as well as a terrific performance from Angela Molina. *Henry IV* is Marcello Mastroianni in a version of Pirandello. And in *The Devil in the Flesh* there was an explicit sexuality involving a blow job administered by Maruschka Detmers.

Jean-Paul Belmondo,
b. Neuilly-sur-Seine, France, 1933
The first period of Godard's work is marked off by the presence of Belmondo in *Breathless* (59) and *Pierrot le Fou* (65). Apart from these two films, Belmondo had been in Godard's short, *Charlotte et Son Jules* (59), and was to appear as one of the

two men in *Une Femme est une Femme* (61). But in *Breathless* and *Pierrot le Fou,* Godard used Belmondo to give dramatic form to his own shy fantasy involvement with cinema, life, and art. The paradoxical brusqueness and sensitivity in Godard's early films, the juxtaposition of desperate bouts of action and long, philosophical discussions, the desire to provide a constant commentary on action, all found a proper exponent in Belmondo. The connotations of the name "Pierrot le Fou" may all be found in the actor: he does embody the haphazard, arbitrary, antisocial behavior of the madman; but that rather beaten-up face does not conceal eyes hurt from seeing so much pain and settled in sad resignation at the inadequacy of his own pose as an abrasive primitive. Thus, in *Breathless* Belmondo plausibly connects the potentially dangerous and heartless layabout with the romantic moved by the memory of Humphrey Bogart. And in *Pierrot le Fou* he as easily carries off the role of novelist making a story of his own tragedy, as that of the instinctual, native man who moves helplessly through the action and paints himself like a savage clown before self-destruction. And just as Belmondo is the screen incarnation of Godard's pained conception of the artist exposed to life, so his ability to suggest a high romantic sensibility and the scorpionlike hostility of alienated and degraded man is reminiscent of Gaston Modot's man in *L'Age d'Or* who kicks dogs and knocks blind men on their backs but pursues his love forever. The other vivid instance of the balance of sensibility and instinct is Michel Simon—as *Boudu* for Renoir and as the bargeman Caliban in *L'Atalante*. At one moment in *Pierrot,* Belmondo does a tender impersonation of Simon's grotesque speech, and it is easy to see him playing a latter-day Boudu or revealing a hand preserved in a jar to a credulous girl. Belmondo was vital to Godard for the way he brought to life the director's view of "the poor, base, forked animal" within the prickly, pale-faced, and dark-shaded habitué of cinemas.

Although Belmondo has been hailed as an archetypal new French actor, he has too often been conventional and listless. The whole man revealed by Godard has appeared elsewhere only as the priest, disturbed by Emmanuelle Riva's emotionalism in *Leon Morin, Prêtre* (61, Jean-Pierre Melville); as the mordant, chronic thief in *Le Voleur* (67, Louis Malle); and as the man in *Mississippi Mermaid* (69, François Truffaut). There again, Truffaut seemed driven to insight by reclaiming Buñuel's view of the willing self-destruction of the man of passion.

Elsewhere, Belmondo has sometimes been rather lazily insolent in poor films, or content to ape the Bogart hero. For instance, his work for Melville as a raincoated betrayer amid the underworld of *Le Doulos* (62) has rather less mythological resonance than Alain Delon in *Le Samourai*. He made his debut in 1958 in *Sois Belle et Tais-Toi* (58, Marc Allégret) and *Les Tricheurs* (58, Marcel Carné). His other films since then have included *Web of Passion* (59, Claude Chabrol), excellent again as the disrupter of a bourgeois household; *Classe Tous Risques* (59, Claude Sautet); a little bemused by the sparse action of *Moderato Cantabile* (60, Peter Brook); *Un Nommé la Rocca* (61, Jean Becker); *La Viaccia* (61, Mauro Bolognini); *Two Women* (61, Vittorio de Sica); *Un Singe en Hiver* (62, Henri Verneuil); *Cartouche* (62, Philippe de Broca); as a boxer in *L'Ame des Ferchaux* (63, Melville); *Dragées au Poivre* (63, Jacques Baratier); *Peau de Banane* (63, Marcel Ophuls); *That Man from Rio* (63, de Broca); *Week-end à Zuydcoote* (64, Verneuil); *La Chasse à l'Homme* (64, Edouard Molinaro); *Par un Beau Matin d'Eté* (64, Jacques Deray); *Les Tribulations d'un Chinois en Chine* (65, de Broca); *Is Paris Burning?* (66, René Clément); *Tendre Voyou* (67, Becker); *Ho!* (68, Robert Enrico); *Le Cerveau* (68, Gérard Oury); *Un Homme Qui Me Plaît* (69, Claude Lelouch); *Borsalino* (70, Deray); *Les Mariés de l'An Deux* (71, Jean-Paul Rappeneau); *Le Casse* (71, Verneuil); *L'Héritier* (72, Philippe Labro); *La Scoumoune* (72, José Giovanni); *Docteur Popaul* (72, Chabrol); *How to Destroy the Reputation of the Greatest Secret Agent* (73, de Broca); *Stavisky* (74, Alain Resnais); *Peur sur la Ville* (75, Verneuil); *L'Incorrigible* (75, de Broca); and *L'Animal* (77, Claude Zidi).

More recently, Belmondo has become a middle-aged player in very middle-class films: brisk, urbane, successful, but cynical. He was the kind of actor (at sixty) who might be called upon once more to deliver a great performance—but which of his great directors could need him now? He has made *Flic ou Voyou* (79, Georges Lautner); *Le Guignolo* (80, Lautner); *Le Professionel* (81, Lautner); *Ace of Aces* (82, Gerard Oury); *Le Marginal* (83, Deray); *Les Morfalous* (83, Verneuil); *Joyeuses Paques* (84, Lautner); *Hold-Up* (85, Alexander Arcady); and *L'Itineraire d'un Enfant Gaté* (88, Lelouch).

After several years away, he came back as a charismatic Valjean in an ambitious, modernized and very successful version of *Les Misérables* (95, Lelouch); the Sacha Guitry play *Désiré* (96, Bernard Murat); with Alain Delon in *Une Chance sur Deux* (98, Patrice Leconte); *Peut-être* (99, Cedric Klapisch); *Amazone* (00, de Broca); *L'Aîné des Ferchaux* (00, Bernard Stora).

Laslo Benedek (1907–92),
b. Budapest, Hungary
1948: *The Kissing Bandit*. 1949: *Port of New York*. 1951: *Death of a Salesman*. 1953: *The Wild One*. 1954: *Bengal Brigade*. 1955: *Kinder, Mutter und ein General*. 1957: *Affair in Havana*. 1959: *Moment of Danger*. 1960: *Recours en Grâce*. 1966: *Namu the Killer Whale* (d). 1971: *The Night Visitor*. 1975: *Assault on Agathon*.

Benedek never settled, and he seemed as uneasy with the solemn allegory of *Death of a Salesman* as with the rampant motor-bike horniness of *The Wild One*. How that last film ever came to be banned in some tender quarters, or regarded highly anywhere, is a puzzle. It is too willing to be a motorized Western; too preoccupied with surly youth to catch the real urban baroque of shining motor-bikes and leather. And if, unlike Michael Curtiz, Benedek has never managed to adapt Hungarianness to Hollywood, he has not been much happier elsewhere. The French and German films are dull, and he later divided his time between American TV, a documentary study of whales and the hardly released *Night Visitor*. Benedek was a writer and photographer who worked as cameraman and editor in Germany in the 1930s: *Der Mann der den Mord Beging* (31, Kurt Bernhardt). He was one of several odd talents who gathered round Joe Pasternak and Universal in Berlin. Moving from Paris to London, he scripted *Secret of Stamboul* (36, Andrew Marton). In 1937 he went to Hollywood and to MGM's montage department. Thereafter, he became a production assistant to Pasternak who produced his first film, a musical starring Sinatra and Ann Miller.

Roberto Benigni, b. Misericordia, Italy, 1952
1983: *Tu Mi Turbi/You Upset Me*. 1984: *Addio a Enrico Berlinguer; Non Ci Resta Che Piangere/Nothing Left to Do But Cry; Il Piccolo Diavolo/The Little Devil*. 1991: *Johnny Stecchino*. 1994: *Il Mostro/The Monster*. 1997: *La Vita è Bella/Life Is Beautiful*. 2002: *Pinocchio*.

Despite the enormous effect Bambi had on me as a child, I have had difficulty digesting Thumperism—I mean, the philosophy that if you can't say anything nice, don't say nothing at all. I see the point, or the kindness, even if I am inclined on principle to suspect any nostrum offered by the Disney Corporation. And who, honestly, would want to spend much time with Thumper and his sealed lips? There are candidates for honest bad-mouthing, reaching from one's relatives to the alleged leaders of your world. And there is Roberto Benigni.

Now, I have credentials in this matter: I loathed his simpering and his weird mix of knockabout and sentimentality in such things as *Johnny Stecchino* (a massive hit in Italy), *The Monster*, and *Son of the Pink Panther* (93, Blake Edwards). I thought he was a time-wasting aberration in a few films by Jim Jarmusch—*Down by Law* (86),

Coffee and Cigarettes (86), and *Night on Earth* (91). But with that record, I would simply have omitted Benigni from this book and saluted Thumper. I might have thought to myself that *You Upset Me* and *Nothing Left to Do But Cry* were sufficient as titles.

Then came the thing called *La Vita È Bella*. As a matter of fact, I often echo that sentiment myself, but if there is anything likely to mar the *bella*-ness it is not so much Hitlerism (I am against it), which is fairly obvious, as Benigni-ism, which walks away with high praise, box office, and Oscars. I despise *Life Is Beautiful*, especially its warmth, sincerity, and feeling, all of which I believe grow out of stupidity. Few events so surely signaled the decline of the motion picture as the glory piled on that odious and misguided fable.

I am sure Mr. Benigni is kind to children and animals. I am prepared to accept that he is a model citizen and a good companion. Still, *Life Is Beautiful* is a disgrace.

Benigni has been an actor for well over twenty years: *Clair de Femme* (79, Costa-Gavras); *Chiedo Asilo* (79, Marco Ferreri); *La Luna* (79, Bernardo Bertolucci); *Letti Selvaggi* (79, Luigi Zampa); *Il Pap'occhio* (81, Renzo Arbore); *Il Minestrone* (81, Sergio Citti); *Effetti Personali* (83, Giuseppe Bertolucci); *La Voce della Luna* (89, Federico Fellini); *Asterix et Obelix Contre César* (99, Claude Zidi).

Annette Bening, b. Topeka, Kansas, 1958

Yesterday's paper announced that Annette Bening and Warren Beatty were expecting their fourth child. That campaign has been carried on with such diligence and love that her enterprising screen career deserves all the more respect. At the same time, I don't feel that she has securely won the public's affection, or their sense of exactly who she is. So she covers a range—and that's one of the things acting is supposed to be—but she seems too guarded and intelligent to settle on a definite or passionate inner being. This may be one of the several things she has in common with her husband.

Raised in San Diego, she did some theatre there and then moved north to San Francisco State University and the American Conservatory Theatre in San Francisco. Her stage work includes Tina Howe's *Coastal Disturbances*, for which she won a Tony nomination. Her first film was *The Great Outdoors* (88, Howard Deutsch), but she soon surpassed that with her stunning Madame Merteuil in *Valmont* (89, Milos Forman), a role ideally suited to her intelligence and its capacity for putting a chill on feelings. But then she was far more relaxed, very naughty, sexy and funny in *The Grifters* (90, Stephen Frears). At that point, her prospects seemed more than exciting.

After *Postcards from the Edge* (90, Mike

Nichols), she won the role of Virginia Hill and so met Warren Beatty in *Bugsy* (91, Barry Levinson). She was good enough in the film nearly to mask a flaw in its script—we never know whether or not Virginia is robbing Ben Siegel. Then, in the next few years, unaccountably, she made several poor films in a row: *Guilty By Suspicion* (91, Irwin Winkler); *Regarding Henry* (91, Nichols); and the really woeful *Love Affair* (94, Glenn Gordon Caron), with Warren. Somehow one had the impression that the happy couple would not work together again. And maybe she had learned to reject some of his advice.

She was lively and touching in the pleasant *The American President* (95, Rob Reiner), but again there were signs of drift with *Richard III* (95, Richard Loncraine); *Mars Attacks!* (96, Tim Burton); *The Siege* (98, Edward Zwick); and the unhappy *In Dreams* (98, Neil Jordan). But in *American Beauty* (99, Sam Mendes), she was restored to the high comedy of manners to very good effect, so that she went from being hilarious to wretched on a phrase. That rare skill was gone again in *What Planet Are You From?* (00, Nichols).

There was another gap before she did *Open Range* (03, Kevin Costner) and *Being Julia* (03, Istvan Szabo).

Alan Bennett, b. Leeds, England, 1934

In 1960, when *Beyond the Fringe* opened at the Edinburgh Festival, and in its glory years thereafter, Alan Bennett was the least known and spectacular of the team. By now, a case could be made that his work and his influence have risen far above that of the others. But as to being known . . . Bennett is the very image of privacy, and that alone could qualify him for a notable place in this survey of the most glaring and overpublicized of media.

In the early 1960s, there was brashness, youth, and energy in Peter Cook, Dudley Moore, and Jonathan Miller. Miller was so plainly electric; Moore was giddy with overthrown shyness, his piano, and the limping devil of teasing; and Cook was somewhere not too far from a Don Juan ready to be a thug. In their company—and Bennett was only in their company then—the sandy-haired Yorkshireman seemed like someone who had never known youth. He was guarded, cautious, a deft character actor. Yet he never seemed to risk the others' flights of improvisation. So he never stumbled, as they did, and never soared. He was word perfect, a fusspot, a writer more than a performer.

Bennett has become a major figure in the English landscape despite versatility and his steadfast wish to remain hidden. He has worked very little in what he might call "the cinema." Yet he commands a place, and a large one. For he is one of those people who have kept England's role in movies significant even as its picture business has withered. Principally, he has worked in television. But Bennett's influence is climatic: he is an astringent dampener that seeps in everywhere—in theatre, prose, and journalism, almost in the way of sniffing the air suspiciously. Bennett is a model for the notion that wintry wariness may be the surest way to memorialize the passage of feelings in this headlong world. Just as Noel Coward's collected talents, works, words, and pauses once delivered a kind of moral briskness that represented an age, so Bennett now is characteristic. He may be Britain's best and most stubborn surviving miniaturist.

To keep up with Alan Bennett, one needs to be in England all the time, for he is always popping up in some shape or manner, on television or in a literary weekly. (His other works include the stage play *The Madness of George III.*) Nothing is to be treated lightly: he is a gatherer of his own small things, a genius of the quotidian, a master of one-line roles or glances off in mid-interview. I can only list some things that bear broadly on film:

1. Bennett has done film scripts for hire: *The Insurance Man* (85, Richard Eyre); *A Private Function* (85, Malcolm Mowbray), on the treasuring of a pig in postwar provincial England; *Prick Up Your Ears* (87, Stephen Frears), his least adroit work in that it chose to dramatize writer John Lahr's inquiry into the life of playwright Joe Orton, and thus missed too much of the life.

2. Then he has done scripts, as it were, from the heart. In particular, there are two works that have saved the reputation of John Schlesinger in the last twenty years: *An Englishman Abroad* (84), which is derived from actress Coral Browne's meeting with the exiled spy Guy Burgess in Moscow; and *A Question of Attribution* (91), taken from Bennett's own play about Sir Anthony Blunt, scholarly guardian of the Queen's paintings—which included a delicious, dreamlike, and very subversive conversation between Blunt and HRH (James Fox and Prunella Scales; though it was Bennett himself and Ms. Scales on the London stage).

Ostensibly, Bennett the Yorkshireman, son of a butcher and then scholarship boy at Oxford, someone uneasy far away from London NW1 or Yorkshire, is a patriot as well as a determined, gloomy loner. Yet beneath the comedy of the two plays/films, there is so much rueful passion for the urge to remake England and such wistfulness about irregular sexual conduct. Bennett is only interested in writing about failure. Is there anything else? he might ask querulously. And so the passing triumph of Burgess and Blunt—in living well and in knowing the grace of Tiepolo—is all the more tender because they are losing point in Bennett's England. These are very sly works, as befits stories about spies.

3. Then there are "plays" written for television, especially a series of five done in 1978–79: *Me, I'm Afraid of Virginia Woolf* (Stephen Frears), narrated by Bennett, a study in health, happiness, and indefatigable unease; *All Day in the Sands* (Giles Foster; produced by Frears), on the desolation of seaside getaways; *One Fine Day* (Frears); *The Old Crowd* (Lindsay Anderson, produced by Frears); *Afternoon Off* (Frears).

These are Bennett's great works, plays about a society and its slow sighing way toward demise. It is no coincidence that the plays precede the violence of Mrs. Thatcher and seem to feel the last ebbing of the old England that cherished its humdrum decency. The stories are slight; the acting is communal. And these plays are also the best work Stephen Frears has ever done—a nagging question to him about why he ever went to America.

4. *Talking Heads*, six dramatic monologues—no, adramatic—done for BBC TV in 1988. These are shattered lives, no matter that the broken pieces are held politely together in the way a humble soldier on the Somme might have held his privates in place waiting for his turn with the surgeon. They are all from thirty to fifty minutes long, and they are one character chatting or sighing to the camera—they catch the woeful intimacy in which in the TV age lonely people talk to themselves as if in interview. The form is as poignant as the words or the performances. To see the six in a row is to cry out for some explosive energy that would destroy gentility once and for all. There is a passivity here that must count as Bennett's most profound limitation. But the six are beautiful black portraits:

> Maggie Smith in *Bed Among the Lentils* (Bennett);
> Patricia Routledge in *A Lady of Letters* (Foster);
> Stephanie Cole in *Soldiering On* (Tristram Powell);
> Thora Hird in *A Cream Cracker Under the Settee* (Stuart Burge);
> Julie Walters in *Her Big Chance* (Foster);
> Bennett himself in *A Chip in the Sugar* (Burge).

Bennett remains an important figure in British culture, a writer, a performer, and a presence far more trusted and beloved than the barbed work really merits. He adapted his own play to make the film, *The Madness of King George* (94, Nicholas Hytner), and in 1996 a second series of *Talking Heads* played on the BBC. This series was as exquisite as the first, but the darkness and the shift towards crime and suicide was far more marked.

Constance Bennett (1905–65),
b. New York
She was the older sister of actresses Joan and Bar-

bara Bennett, and the daughter of Richard Bennett (1873–1944—matinee idol onstage and Major Amberson on-screen). Now little known, in the early 1930s, Constance Bennett was one of the classiest and highest-paid stars, despite a rather fitful allegiance to Hollywood. She was not as good an actress as Joan, but she was a social figure in Hollywood, an expert gambler, much inclined to money and men, a fashion plate, and an arbiter of style. Very cunningly, she placed herself as someone who did not really need pictures—this allowed her to be bored, disdainful, and not even that good. She stressed the pose of an amused outsider, and she was so pretty, as well as heartless, that her humor was the more striking. High 1930s romantic comedy had few cleverer exponents, even if *Topper* is as much as most people know today. A good life of the Bennett sisters might help redress the balance.

She had a tiny part in her father's *The Valley of Decision* (16), and then small roles in *Reckless Youth* (22, Ralph Ince); *Evidence* (22, George Archainbaud); *What's Wrong with Women?* (22, R. William Neill)—before Goldwyn put her in *Cytherea* (24, George Fitzmaurice). In the next few years, she quickly built up her reputation: *Married?* (24, George Terwilliger); *The Goose Hangs High* (25, James Cruze); *Code of the West* (25, William K. Howard); *My Son* (25, Edwin Carewe); *My Wife and I* (25, Millard Webb); *The Goose Woman* (25, Clarence Brown); *Sally, Irene and Mary* (25, Edmund Goulding); and *The Pinch Hitter* (26, Joseph Henabery). But at this point, Bennett eloped with a millionaire, Philip Bland, and dropped out of films. She returned three years later, divorced, but ready to marry again, to the Marquis de la Falaise. Her agent, Myron Selznick, successfully negotiated the break in her career and, thanks to her fetching voice, got her huge salaries over the next few years: *This Thing Called Love* (29, Paul L. Stein); *Son of the Gods* (30, Frank Lloyd); *Rich People* (30, Edward H. Griffith); *Common Clay* (30, Victor Fleming); *Three Faces East* (30, Roy del Ruth); *Sin Takes a Holiday* (30, Stein); *The Easiest Way* (31, Jack Conway); *Born to Love* (31, Stein); *Bought* (31, Archie Mayo); *Lady With a Past* (32, Griffith); *What Price Hollywood?* (32, George Cukor), in which she is well cast as the Brown Derby waitress who becomes (inexplicably) a star; *Two Against the World* (32, Mayo); *Rockabye* (32, Cukor); *Our Betters* (33, Cukor); *Bed of Roses* (33, Gregory La Cava); *After Tonight* (33, Archainbaud); *Moulin Rouge* (34, Sidney Lanfield); *The Affairs of Cellini* (34, La Cava); *Outcast Lady* (34, Robert Z. Leonard); *After Office Hours* (35, Leonard); *Ladies in Love* (36, Griffith); *Topper* (37, Norman Z. McLeod); *Merrily We Live* (38, McLeod); *Service De Luxe* (38, Rowland V. Lee); *Topper Takes a Trip* (39, McLeod); and *Tailspin* (39, del Ruth).

By then, her box-office stock had slumped, she married (briefly) Gilbert Roland, but she worked on through the 1940s: *Escape to Glory* (40, John Brahm); *Law of the Tropics* (41, Ray Enright); *Two-Faced Woman* (41, Cukor); *Wild Bill Hickock Rides* (42, Enright); *Madame Spy* (42, Neill); *Paris Underground* (46, Gregory Ratoff), produced by Bennett herself with Gracie Fields as an unlikely costar; *Centennial Summer* (46, Otto Preminger); *The Unsuspected* (47, Michael Curtiz); *Smart Woman* (48, Edward A. Blatt); *As Young as You Feel* (51, Harmon Jones); *It Should Happen to You* (54, Cukor); and *Madame X* (65, David Lowell Rich), in which she is arguably younger looking than her "daughter-in-law" Lana Turner.

Joan Bennett (1910–90),
b. Palisades, New Jersey
The daughter of actor Richard Bennett and younger sister of actress Constance Bennett, Joan Bennett was educated in Connecticut and Paris. At sixteen she ran away with a millionaire and had a child—at much the same time that Constance eloped with a millionaire. After a rapid marriage and divorce she worked as an extra in *The Divine Lady* (29, Frank Lloyd). Her father then helped her into a larger part in *Bulldog Drummond* (29, E. Richard Jones) and she quickly became a blonde romantic lead. In fact, she made some forty movies before coming to the parts for which she is justly remembered. The blonde, pre–Walter Wanger years saw her in the George Arliss *Disraeli* (29, Alfred E. Green); in Lloyd Bacon's *Moby Dick* (30); Wellman's *Maybe It's Love* (30); Borzage's *Doctors' Wives* (31); *She Wanted a Millionaire* (32, John Blystone); *Wild Girl* (32) and *Me and My Gal* (32), both for Raoul Walsh; a demure Amy in Cukor's *Little Women* (33). At this stage she met Wanger and signed a contract with him. Her talent for comedy improved in *The Pursuit of Happiness* (34, Alexander Hall); *Mississippi* (35, Edward Sutherland); *She Couldn't Take It* (35, Tay Garnett); and *The Man Who Broke the Bank at Monte Carlo* (35, Stephen Roberts). In 1936 she made *Thirteen Hours by Air* for Mitchell Leisen and *Big Brown Eyes* for Walsh, and in 1937 Wanger showcased her in *Vogues of 1938* (Irving Cummings).

It was only in 1938, in a Tay Garnett romantic thriller, *Trade Winds*, that she changed from blonde to brunette. It is worth noting that Constance was blonde and that Joan flourished only when her sister was in decline. After *Artists and Models Abroad* (38) with Jack Benny for Leisen, she had a bustle of costume movies with Louis Hayward, including *The Man in the Iron Mask* (39, James Whale) and *Son of Monte Cristo* (40, Rowland V. Lee). But after *Housekeeper's Daughter* (39, Hal Roach) and *Green Hell* (40, Whale), she divorced her second husband and made *The*

House Across the Bay (40, Archie L. Mayo) for Wanger. She married him the next year and entered her most rewarding period as an actress: first in Pichel's *The Man I Married* (41) and then crucially in Lang's *Man Hunt* (41). Playing a London tart in that film, she revealed a special, sentimental coarseness that had never emerged before. She then made *Wild Geese Calling* (41, John Brahm); *Confirm or Deny* (41), a Lang project taken over by Mayo; and *Margin for Error* (43), one of the films Otto Preminger chose to disown. In 1944, she was Fritz Lang's *The Woman in the Window*, trapping Edward G. Robinson into dream, and then in 1946 she was brilliant as Lazy-Legs, who again brought disaster to Robinson in *Scarlet Street* (Lang). Whereas in *Woman in the Window* she is alluring, in *Scarlet Street* she is casually corrupt and endearingly vulgar. Not surprisingly, it is a continental performance in a film that seems to have very little to do with America, and its honest portrait of sensuality only makes some of the official love goddesses of 1946 look reserved.

She was the girl from *Nob Hill* (45) slumming with George Raft for Hathaway; in *Colonel Effingham's Raid* (46) for Pichel; and Hemingway's two-timing wife in Zoltan Korda's *The Macomber Affair* (47) before an astonishing trio of "European" films in America such as the blonde girlie of the 1930s might never have dreamed of: *The Woman on the Beach* (47, Jean Renoir); *The Secret Beyond the Door* (48, Lang); and *The Reckless Moment* (49, Max Ophuls)—the last two produced by her husband. Next, she had a great popular success as an ideal mother and grandmother in Minnelli's *Father of the Bride* (50) and *Father's Little Dividend* (51). But such domestic bliss was belied when Wanger felt compelled to shoot his wife's agent, Jennings Lang. He went briefly to prison and was reunited with Joan in 1953.

She never again starred in a good film and, as well as touring in several plays, she made: *The Guy Who Came Back* (51, Joseph M. Newman); *Highway Dragnet* (54, Nathan Juran); *We're No Angels* (55, Michael Curtiz); Sirk's *There's Always Tomorrow* (56); and then *Desire in the Dust* (60, William Claxton). In the mid-1960s she appeared to have retired, but when Wanger died in 1968 she took on a TV series, *Dark Shadows*, which in 1970 turned into an unnecessary film. In 1976, she played the head teacher in *Suspiria* (Dario Argento), and she appeared in a couple of TV movies: *This House Possessed* (81, William Wiard) and *Divorce Wars: A Love Story* (82, Donald Wrye).

Jack Benny (Benny Kubelsky) (1894–1974), b. Waukegan, Illinois

In his last twenty years, Jack Benny had appeared briefly, and often without credit, in a number of movies: *Somebody Loves Me* (53, Irving S.

Brecher); *Susan Slept Here* (54, Frank Tashlin); *The Seven Little Foys* (55, Melville Shavelson); *Beau James* (57, Shavelson); *Gypsy* (62, Mervyn Le Roy); *It's a Mad Mad Mad Mad World* (63, Stanley Kramer); and *A Guide for the Married Man* (67, Gene Kelly). That so many of those spots were unannounced is an acknowledgment that everyone knew Jack Benny and that, chances are, he was tricked into appearing and would not be paid. The long-running celebration of his meanness was one of the most creative forms of invalidism in the entertainment world. Additional symptoms were his steady assertion that he was only thirty-nine, and that he could play the violin beautifully.

Those movie walk-ons ground away at his reserves a little more painfully because cinema was the one medium in which he had not been entirely successful. In vaudeville, onstage, on radio, and on television, Benny had become an American institution and a huge star, the urbane, complacent man at ease with himself save for two fatal dreams: he loves art and money. His violin, despite his skill with it, becomes an instrument of self-laceration; his reluctance to hide a devotion to the dollar ridicules him in the eyes of a brazenly capitalist public. Easy to say that his meanness was an act, like Bob Hope's cowardice, from which the comedian was able to stand back. But Benny approached money with mystical reverence. Hope snaps and snarls at cowardice like a dog, but Benny is a romantic about money; it heals every hurt for him. His act grew slower, more meditative, less filled with gags, but given over to the beautiful absurdity of man worshiping money, and being scourged for his faith. Benny and money is a classic confrontation, like Don Quixote and the windmills. And over the years, he came to expect that he would be laughed at—this is truly graceful in a comedian—and schooled himself so that, though hurt, he would not be diminished. I have seen Benny set an audience going with his miserliness, then reduce them to helplessness with affront that he should be mocked. He walked with the slow-motion splendor of the ghost of Rockefeller, amazed that so many people can abuse their own church. That was Benny's real genius, that he briefly freed us from our greatest compulsion. It follows that he needed a live audience, for his reaction to laughter was not just his subtlest technique but his deepest thrust at us. In vaudeville, or with a studio audience on radio and TV, Benny was a major comedian. On film, he was deprived of half his act. Thus most of his films are poor, and deserved their failure. One is exceptional, not least in the way it uses Benny as a stage performer wounded by his audience. But Benny came from the vaudeville that produced most of America's screen comics and it is worth asking whether his loneliness on film did not afflict many others—including the Marx Brothers and Keaton—and crystallize a forlorn, tragic posture that vaudeville had spared them.

Benny's vaudeville career was interrupted but not broken by the First World War. MGM signed him when sound arrived, and he had a sketch in *The Hollywood Revue of 1929* (29, Charles Reisner) and a leading part in *Chasing Rainbows* (30, Reisner). But he did not grip the cinema public, and in 1932 he began his long radio career. He made a few movie shorts, and after two more features—*Mr. Broadway* (33, John Walker) and *Transatlantic Merry-Go-Round* (35, Ben Stoloff)—MGM put him in two more: *Broadway Melody of 1936* (35, Roy del Ruth) and *It's in the Air* (35, Charles Reisner). But they then let him go to Paramount where, for a few years, he was rated as a star, even if the films were not too special: *The Big Broadcast of 1937* (36, Mitchell Leisen); *College Holiday* (36, Frank Tuttle); *Artists and Models* (37, Raoul Walsh); *Artists and Models Abroad* (38, Leisen); *Man About Town* (39, Mark Sandrich); *Buck Benny Rides Again* (40, Sandrich); and *Love Thy Neighbor* (40, Sandrich). He went to Fox for *Charley's Aunt* (41, Archie Mayo) and then to United Artists for *To Be or Not to Be* (42, Ernst Lubitsch). Far beyond his ordinary range, this allowed Benny to play a ham Hamlet in Warsaw under the Nazis. It showed how much greater Benny's talent had been than most of his films required.

But he was already slipping. After *George Washington Slept Here* (42, William Keighley), and a short, *The Meanest Man in the World* (43, Sidney Lanfield), the disaster of *The Horn Blows at Midnight* (45, Walsh) warned him off the movies. A guest part in *It's in the Bag* (45, Richard Wallace) was the first of many woeful returns to the scene of loss—like a man who lost a dollar bill twenty-five years ago, but is still searching.

Robert Benton, b. Waxahachie, Texas, 1932

1972: *Bad Company.* 1977: *The Late Show.* 1979: *Kramer vs. Kramer.* 1982: *Still of the Night.* 1984: *Places in the Heart.* 1987: *Nadine.* 1991: *Billy Bathgate.* 1994: *Nobody's Fool.* 1998: *Twilight.* 2003: *The Human Stain.*

Benton was the Texan on *Bonnie and Clyde* (67, Arthur Penn), the man who knew the area and the landscape where those outlaws had driven. He studied painting at the University of Texas at Austin, and then went on to Columbia after the army. As art director at *Esquire* magazine, he met the writer David Newman. They collaborated on articles and scripts and conceived *Bonnie and Clyde* for Truffaut or Godard before it found Warren Beatty and Arthur Penn.

Benton has other coscreenplay credits—*There Was a Crooked Man* (70, Joseph L. Mankiewicz); *What's Up, Doc?* (72, Peter Bogdanovich); and *Superman* (78, Richard Donner).

As a director, his first two movies were unexpected and highly original, and they were marked by a sour regard for heroics. Subsequent pictures have become more conventional and sentimental. *Places in the Heart* and *Nadine* are good on Texas, but they are tepid works. *Still of the Night* was a shot at Hitchcock, but it seemed forced. *Kramer vs. Kramer* was a hit family story, well written and emphatically acted. *Billy Bathgate* was a famous flop, but it is a clever film with a script (by Tom Stoppard) that sharpens the E. L. Doctorow novel. The record suggests that Benton's undoubted decency needs inspiring (or even bad) company if his work is to be out-of-the-ordinary.

All of Benton's warmth and experience were on display in *Nobody's Fool,* which is that rare thing—a model of American humanism. Taken from a Richard Russo novel, it dealt with modest, common lives, was beautifully shaped and played by a cast in which people like Bruce Willis and Melanie Griffith seemed happy to have the chance to be character actors. *Twilight* was a touch too cute—benefit night for old-timers—but very enjoyable just the same. These were also films in which Benton managed to unlock something generally withheld in Paul Newman.

Bruce Beresford, b. Sydney, Australia, 1940

1972: *The Adventures of Barry McKenzie.* 1974: *Barry McKenzie Holds His Own.* 1976: *Don's Party.* 1977: *The Getting of Wisdom.* 1978: *Money Movers.* 1979: *Breaker Morant.* 1980: *The Club.* 1981: *Puberty Blues.* 1983: *Tender Mercies.* 1985: *King David; Crimes of the Heart; The Fringe Dwellers.* 1988: "Die Totestadt," an episode from *Aria.* 1989: *Her Alibi; Driving Miss Daisy.* 1991: *Mister Johnson; Black Robe.* 1993: *Rich in Love.* 1994: *A Good Man in Africa; Silent Fall.* 1996: *Last Dance.* 1997: *Paradise Road.* 1999: *Sydney: A Story of a City* (d); *Double Jeopardy.* 2002: *Evelyn.*

From Sydney University, Beresford went into advertising and thence to London. He spent two years in the mid-sixties in Nigeria working as a film editor, and in 1966 he got a post at the British Film Institute Production Board, where he administered funds. He began to direct features himself only on returning to Australia in 1971.

He shows what a fine line there can be today between struggling to stay in work and getting the laurel. Thus, in 1989 he was in charge of the stolid Tom Selleck–Paulina Porizkova comedy *Her Alibi,* and he helped get the best picture Oscar for *Driving Miss Daisy.* Of course, in the latter he was helped by Alfred Uhry's cute play, by Jessica Tandy and Morgan Freeman, by Zanuck's force

and determination, and by Hollywood's suscepti-
bility to feel-good liberalism. The picture did a
cozy, unthreatening bundle, and next year the
essentially nomadic, if not lost, Beresford turned
in a Joyce Cary adaptation, *Mister Johnson* (surely
helped by his time in Africa) and the startlingly
severe *Black Robe*, as if to prove he was no one's
stooge.

Beresford has often had strong company: Barry
Humphries and Nicholas Garland on the Barry
McKenzie films; playwright David Williamson on
Don's Party and *The Club;* Robert Duvall and
Horton Foote on *Tender Mercies.* But he is usually most interesting in Australia, or in out-of-the-
way places and periods: *Breaker Morant* was that
rare thing, a Boer War story, even if it ended up as
an attack on British imperialism; *The Fringe
Dwellers* was a return to aboriginal Australia; and
Black Robe was a journey into savagery such as
few people would have dared in the political correctness that hails American Indians as shame-
making heroes.

Black Robe may be Beresford's most original
picture. *Tender Mercies,* for me, is too commonplace to be interesting, despite its faith in ordinary
lives as redeemed by towering acting. Beth Henley's *Crimes of the Heart* claimed to be the
authentic South, yet it felt as secure and fake as a
poor play. *King David* is a genuine eccentricity,
the sort of implausible project that seems likely to
recur in Beresford's zigzagging progress.

Beresford's career is hard to predict: *Last
Dance* had Sharon Stone on death row; *Double
Jeopardy* had a story so weird I can't even recall it,
let alone repeat it. But *Paradise Road* was a wor-
thy ensemble piece about women prisoners of the
Japanese, with terrific performances from Glenn
Close, Frances McDormand and Cate Blanchett
(among others).

Candice Bergen,
b. Beverly Hills, California, 1946

Candice Bergen has been in movies, and very
social on the Hollywood scene, for over thirty
years. She is smart, funny, and she has show business in the blood (or the grain—one of her childhood companions was Charlie McCarthy, for she
was the daughter of ventriloquist Edgar Bergen).
For a while, she was the companion to innovative
producer Bert Schneider. She was in a few classy
pictures, like *Carnal Knowledge* (71, Mike
Nichols) and *The Group* (66, Sidney Lumet). But
she was taken for granted as a pretty piece of
female furnishing. No one noticed she could play
comedy. Not even marriage to Louis Malle, in
1980, promised salvation.

She was the lesbian in *The Group;* with Steve
McQueen in *The Sand Pebbles* (66, Robert Wise);
as a pretentious fashion model in *Vivre pour Vivre*
(67, Claude Lelouch); *The Magus* (68, Guy

Green); *Getting Straight* (70, Richard Rush); *Soldier Blue* (70, Ralph Nelson); *Carnal Knowledge;
The Hunting Party* (71, Don Medford); *T.R.
Baskin* (71, Herbert Ross); *11 Harrowhouse* (74,
Aram Avakian); and *Bite the Bullet* (75, Richard
Brooks). There was a flare of humor in her entertaining duel with Sean Connery in *The Wind and
the Lion* (75, John Milius). But there was nothing
to be done with *The Domino Principle* (77, Stanley Kramer); *A Night Full of Rain* (78, Lina Wertmuller); or *Oliver's Story* (78, John Korty).

But suddenly, in *Starting Over* (79, Alan J.
Pakula), she was hilarious, not least when bursting
into song. She got a supporting actress nomination
for *Rich and Famous* (81, George Cukor)—but
few noticed or saw the continuity of humor. By
then, Bergen was one of the few American
actresses fit for 1930s comedy.

In the eighties, as she neared the ominous age
of forty, Bergen's career declined. She was redundant as photojournalist Margaret Bourke-White
(Bergen is herself a photographer) in *Gandhi* (82,
Richard Attenborough), and she was stranded in
Stick (85, Burt Reynolds). By then, she had
nowhere to go but television: Guinevere in the
awful *Arthur the King* (85, Clive Donner); quite
believable in *Murder: By Reason of Insanity* (85,
Anthony Page); and driven to play Sydney Biddle
Barrows in *Mayflower Madam* (87, Lou Antonio).

Whereupon, magic happened. It's not that
Murphy Brown (88–onwards) was so great a show.
But it was a showcase for Bergen's wit and character. As Republican politicians blundered into challenging the show's mild liberalism, so Murphy
Brown became a figurehead. Bergen won Emmies
in 1989 and 1990, and the show played its small
part in the 1992 election. It would be a good deal
more useful if someone now cast Bergen in a fine
movie comedy of manners, something bigger than
Miss Congeniality (00, Donald Petrie).

Ingmar Bergman,
b. Uppsala, Sweden, 1918

1945: *Kris/Crisis.* 1946: *Det Regnar pa var Kär-
lek/It Rains on Our Love.* 1947: *Skepp till India-
land/A Ship to India; Musik i Mörker/Night Is My
Future.* 1948: *Hamnstad/Port of Call.* 1949: *Fän-
gelse/Prison; Törst/Thirst; Till Glädje/To Joy.*
1950: *Sant Händer Inte Här/This Can't Happen
Here; Sommarlek/Summer Interlude/Illicit Interlude.* 1952: *Kvinnors Väntan/Waiting Women;
Sommaren med Monika/Summer with Monika.*
1953: *Gycklarnas Afton/Sawdust and Tinsel.*
1954: *En Lektion i Karlek/A Lesson in Love.*
1955: *Kvinnodröm/Journey into Autumn; Som-
marnattens Leende/Smiles of a Summer Night.*
1957: *Det Sjunde Inseglet/The Seventh Seal;
Smultronstället/Wild Strawberries.* 1958: *Nära
Livet/So Close to Life; Ansiktet/The Face.* 1959:
Jungfrukällan/The Virgin Spring. 1960: *Djavu-*

lens Oga/The Devil's Eye. 1961: *Sasom i en Spegel/Through a Glass Darkly*. 1963: *Nattvardsgästerna/Winter Light; Tystnaden/The Silence*. 1964: *För Att Inte Tala Om Alla Dessa Kvinnor/Now About These Women*. 1966: *Persona*. 1967: "Daniel," an episode from *Stimulantia*. 1968: *Vargtimmen/Hour of the Wolf; Skammen/Shame*. 1969: *Riten/The Rite*. 1970: *En Pasion/A Passion*. 1971: *Beröringen/The Touch*. 1972: *Viskingar och Rop/Cries and Whispers*. 1973: *Scener ur ett Aktenskap/Scenes from a Marriage* (for TV). 1974: *Trollflojten/The Magic Flute*. 1975: *Ansikte mot Ansikte/Face to Face*. 1978: *The Serpent's Egg; Hostsonatem/Autumn Sonata*. 1979: *Farö-Dokument 79* (d). 1980: *Aus dem Leben der Marionetten/From the Life of the Marionettes*. 1982: *Fanny och Alexander/Fanny and Alexander*. 1983: *After the Rehearsal* (TV). 1986: *Dokument Fanny och Alexander* (d). 1992: *Markisinnan de Sade* (TV). 1995: *Sista Skriket* (TV). 1997: *Larmar och gör sig Till* (TV).

Bergman has never set out to be less than demanding; and as an artist his greatest achievement is in digesting such unrelenting seriousness until he sees no need to bludgeon us with it. The early Bergman worked with the split personality of someone who believed in his own genius. Even his comedies—*Waiting Women* and *Smiles of a Summer Night*—were philosophical disquisitions on the nature of love and identity. The latter, especially, was an Ophuls subject denied the warmth and sadness that keeps irony from being cynical and schematic. But looking out at the world from Sweden, Bergman has seen no reason to abandon his faith in a select audience, prepared and trained for a diligent intellectual and emotional involvement with cinema. In many of these early films there is the regrettable flavor of "this is good for you" about what are determinedly bleak neorealist studies of failed love affairs. Admittedly Bergman never neglected that central topic for such Italian themes as cried out from the streets. He was always fixed on the heart and the soul, but with a bristling neatness that was heartless and depressing. *The Seventh Seal* is the ultimate step in this rather academic way of recording human torment. Its medieval-ism and the wholesale allegory now seem frivolous and theatrical diversions from true seriousness.

But *The Seventh Seal*, like *Elvira Madigan* (67, Bo Widerberg) some ten years later, was the film swallowed by the most people. In England and America it made Bergman the central figure in the growth of art-house cinema. Many people of my generation may have joined the National Film Theatre in London to see a retrospective survey of Bergman's early films after *The Seventh Seal* and *Wild Strawberries* had come to represent "artistic" cinema. The first critical articles that I struggled with—as reader and writer—were on Bergman. Inevitably he suffered from being so suddenly revealed to a volatile world. Looking back, it seems no coincidence that those two films are his most pretentious and calculating. Within a few years he was being mocked and parodied for his earnestness and symbolism. The young cineastes led to the art houses were rediscovering the virtues of the American films that had delighted them as children. The new French cinema endorsed that love of development and replaced Bergman's concentration with improvisation, humor, offhand tenderness, and a non-Northern feeling for the beauty of camera movements as opposed to the force of composition.

By about 1961 Bergman held the unenviable position of a discredited innovator in a fashion-conscious world. That reputation was, I think, deserved. *So Close to Life, The Face, The Virgin Spring,* and *The Silence* suffer because the artistic virtuosity seems complacent beside the professed anguish of the work. Far from being moving and engrossing, these films verge on a dreadfully clear-eyed and articulated morbidity. The gap between preoccupation and art was amounting to decadence.

It is worth stressing the dilemma Bergman found himself in at this time because of his response to it. He was not the first figure from Swedish cinema to be invited to more lavish production setups. His international success had made him possibly the best known of living Swedish artists, a spokesman for the rather precious political neutrality and social enlightenment that Sweden embraced, and the prophet of its overriding sense of guilt. What has made Bergman a great director, it seems to me, is the recognition that he was (or had become) his own subject, that the anguish in his films could become central. For that to work, he had to decline attractive invitations and stay in Sweden.

Like Fellini, Ozu, and Warhol, he became the center of "family" cinema. In many ways, the Swedish environment had always fostered that feeling. Bergman had for many years been encouraged by the head of Svensk Filmindustri, Carl Anders Dymling, who undoubtedly saw the prospect of Swedish cinema being a substantial export item as well as a discreet source of propaganda and prestige. It was possible in Sweden to make films regularly and cheaply; thus, Bergman's productivity has had fewer obstacles than most other great directors must face. Cheapness did not mean tattiness: Bergman has worked with two fine cameramen, Gunnar Fischer and Sven Nykvist. Most important of all, the Royal Dramatic Theatre in Stockholm, which Bergman headed from 1963–66, was the source of a company of actors and actresses who became fixtures in his work.

At first, that was commented on as evidence of the detail and authenticity of his films. But Bergman made that company into a family and saw that the basic human predicament had a marvelous metaphor in the way that an artist treated his subject and his collaborators. It arose naturally from his convictions of the harrowing separateness of people, the intractable privacy of men and women even in love, that everyone was not a solid identity but an actor trying to play the self. Once those realizations were made, Bergman's style underwent a magisterial simplification. Allegory and symbolism were abandoned for the total unity of action and significance in, first, *Persona.* That was the beginning of a sequence of masterpieces in which the pessimism Bergman had always held to became unaffected, personal, and deeply moving.

In terms of style, these more recent films are strenuous close-up investigations of actresses and artists playing actresses and artists. One cannot approach these films without keeping careful check of the names of characters and of the interchange of such players as Max von Sydow, Ingrid Thulin, Liv Ullmann, Bibi Andersson, and Gunnar Björnstrand. Bergman himself has been married six times, he has had a child by Liv Ullmann, and there seems no reason to be disconcerted by the completeness of his involvement with his "family." It is essential to the autobiographical resonance that his films now give off. In that context, the artist/actor is his everyman figure, and a more fruitful one than the morality-play knight in *The Seventh Seal. Persona* is about an actress who has a breakdown. She dries up on the stage and becomes speechless in life. Alone on an island with a talkative nurse, she listens and gradually absorbs the nurse—part actress taking up a new role, part emotional vampire. *Hour of the Wolf* is about a painter living on an island, reviled by outsiders, insecure in his marriage, and about his descent into insanity. *Shame* is about a musician and his wife living on a Baltic island at a time of unexplained war. Their brittle love cracks apart when war intrudes on them, and the film concludes with feeble refugees adrift on the Baltic. *The Rite* deals with a trio of players, incestuously involved, whose performance is being investigated by a provincial magistrate. *A Passion* is an intricate circular story of one broken marriage being cyclically reenacted. And *The Touch,* the first of Bergman's films to use American money, is a subtle commentary on modern Jewry and on Sweden's relation to the world, told through an intimate triangle love story.

It is this sense of intimacy that most distinguishes Bergman. Artistically, it involves quite as much frankness as do Warhol's films. Bergman insists on the truths of how people feel toward others they need to love—in his TV play, *The Lie,*

as much as in his films. Neither will he ignore the increasing moral paralysis and mental breakdown that follow from that truthfulness. Thus his films are intimate and extreme at the same time. The close-up examination of the family, in rites or games that mirror the family's own situation, was wonderfully sustained from *Persona* to *Cries and Whispers.*

Bergman claims he is retired from directing films: *The Best Intentions* (92), was filmed by Bille August. In which case, *Fanny and Alexander* and his autobiographical books, *The Magic Lantern* and *Images,* must stand as his final gifts. *Fanny and Alexander* may be the gentlest of his great films, and the most intricate restaging of his own past. Bergman has survived his own fashion. His stature is secure, and the films are there for the ages. The very early films are now in need of rediscovery—but that will only prepare fresh generations for the journey through his career. For so many people, Bergman has been the man who showed the way to a cinema of the inner life.

Retirement still left the loophole of television, where Bergman has written and directed three "plays." I haven't seen them, but I would add that his script for *Faithless* (00, Liv Ullmann) shows a genius undiminished, just as *Faithless* is a vital work in Bergman's harrowed observation of himself.

Ingrid Bergman (1915–82),
b. Stockholm, Sweden

Ingrid Bergman is something of an enigma, even if she is a great "role." Yet who could play Bergman? She was crucially unique and her own chosen self: tall, "natural" looking, fluent in English yet unmistakably Swedish in her voice, a chronic actress who always strove to be a "true" woman. There was a time in the early and mid-1940s when Bergman commanded a kind of love in America that has been hardly ever matched. In turn, it was the strength of that affection that animated the "scandal" when she behaved like an impetuous and ambitious actress instead of a saint. Is she an example of the liberated woman, exercising her freedom even to the brink of self-destruction? Or is she a curiously empty life force dependent on the changing personalities of the several men in her life? Was she one of the film world's martyrs to publicity, or did she nurse a special aptitude for suffering?

The child of a German mother, she was an orphan by the age of twelve. She studied briefly at the Royal Dramatic Theatre in Stockholm and made her film debut in *Munkbrogreven* (34, Sigurd Wallen and Edvin Adolphson). She quickly became the darling of Swedish cinema, guided by director Gustaf Molander and her husband, Petter Lindstrom. She made *Swedenhielms* (35, Molander), *Dollar* (37, Molander), and *Pa Solsidan* (36, Molander) before the crucial appearance in *Intermezzo* (36, Molander).

That film was seen by employees of David Selznick, and then by Selznick himself: remake rights were purchased by Selznick International, and Bergman was brought along as part of the deal. Before going to Hollywood, however, she made *En Enda Natt* (38, Molander) and *En Kvinnas Ansikte* (38, Molander) and visited Germany for *Die Vier Gesellen* (37, Carl Froelich). Indeed, she had to decide between Selznick and a serious German career—something Selznick had to hush up. And so Bergman went to America, leaving her infant daughter, Pia, with Petter Lindstrom.

She starred with Leslie Howard in Selznick's *Intermezzo: A Love Story* (39, Gregory Ratoff). This was the start of an astonishing impact on Hollywood and America in which the alleged lack of makeup contributed to an air of nobility. Selznick appreciated her, and his wife, Irene, became an important friend and ally. But Selznick loaned Ingrid out more than he ever used her—thus he profited from her contract in ways not lost on Bergman or her husband. Her only Selznick films were *Intermezzo* and *Spellbound* (45, Alfred Hitchcock). At the same time, Selznick built her up and indulged her whims by loaning her out for *Adam Had Four Sons* (41, Ratoff) and the dreadful *Rage in Heaven* (41, W. S. Van Dyke). Then she persuaded MGM and Victor Fleming to let her switch parts with Lana Turner in *Dr. Jekyll and Mr. Hyde* (41, Fleming). Thus, for the first time she played a "bad" girl and reveled in it, especially the sultry lipstick.

The films that made her followed. When Hal Wallis elected to make the woman in *Casablanca* (43, Michael Curtiz) European, he soon abandoned thoughts of Hedy Lamarr for Bergman. That film shows how naturally she played romance in a mood of torment, indecision, and incipient suffering. When Vera Zorina proved inadequate, Selznick's steady boosting won her the part of Maria, with cropped hair, in *For Whom the Bell Tolls* (43, Sam Wood). Far better was *Gaslight* (44), in which George Cukor helped her to be very moving as the wife edged close to madness by Charles Boyer. Again, she excelled in an ordeal, and her beauty seemed more vivid in masochistic situations. The Oscar for *Gaslight* was the peak of her Hollywood glory. Asked to be a flamboyant Creole in *Saratoga Trunk* (46, Wood), she was coy and unconvincing. But she was adorable again (if hardly professional) as the psychiatrist in *Spellbound*, a very successful picture that was topped by *The Bells of St. Mary's* (45, Leo McCarey) in which she played a nun opposite Bing Crosby's priest. Then Hitchcock put her in *Notorious* (46), her best performance yet, as an espionage agent driven to drink and despair. Hitchcock had seen the melancholy within her, and its closeness to guilt. With her suf-

fering from Cary Grant's hard exterior, *Notorious* proved a major film.

Selznick wanted to renew Bergman's contract, but she insisted on going free-lance: first as a prostitute in *Arch of Triumph* (48, Lewis Milestone) and then as *Joan of Arc* (48, Fleming), based on the Maxwell Anderson stage play *Joan of Lorraine*, which she had played on Broadway. At this point, she went to London to make *Under Capricorn* (49, Hitchcock)—as an Irish aristocrat in Australia, married to an ex-convict who went to jail for a crime she committed. It is a searching study of deterioration through guilt and again dependent on drink. The film was a flop on release but now looks like a Hitchcock masterpiece, owing a good deal to Bergman's long confessional speech (in one torturous take, of course).

But Bergman had reached a crisis and she now proceeded to go to the stake in public. In fact, this icon of public love had had many affairs—with photographer Robert Capa, with Victor Fleming, and with harmonica-player Larry Adler. She approached Roberto Rossellini full of admiration. The result was her refugee wife wretched on *Stromboli* (50), and the birth of a child. The scandal in America was as contrived as her reception ten years before had been absurd. After a divorce from her husband, she married Rossellini and they went on to make *Europa '51*, an episode from *Siamo Donne*, *Viaggio in Italia* (53), *Giovanna d'Arco al Rogo* (54)—based on Claudel's play with music by Honegger—and *Angst* (54). Her performances in these films are, in fact, rather distant, if only because Rossellini does not make intense demands on actors. But the films are commentaries on Bergman and Rossellini as befits the cinema's most unhistrionic documentarist. The first two, at least, are masterpieces—but did Bergman understand them? In any event, the films were largely unshown in America and—as the films themselves describe—the marriage came to an end. But Bergman was rescued by another master, Jean Renoir, who made *Eléna et les Hommes* (56), the only genuinely lyrical film that this "girl of nature" ever appeared in.

The rest is turgid. Hollywood reclaimed the prodigal grotesquely in *Anastasia* (56, Anatole Litvak) and gave her a second Oscar to go with the one for *Gaslight* (it is to be hoped they were kept in different rooms). After that, she married again and became distinctly staid. Her films were a sad aftermath of turbulent youth: *Indiscreet* (57, Stanley Donen); *The Inn of the Sixth Happiness* (58, Mark Robson); *Goodbye Again* (61, Litvak); *The Visit* (64, Bernard Wicki); *The Yellow Rolls-Royce* (64, Anthony Asquith); in an episode from *Stimulantia* (67, reunited with Molander); *Cactus Flower* (69, Gene Saks); *A Walk in the Spring Rain* (69, Guy Green); *Murder on the Orient Express* (74, Sidney Lumet); and *A Matter of*

Time (76, Vincente Minnelli). She played a concert pianist in *Autumn Sonata* (78, Ingmar Bergman)—a long-awaited union with her namesake, a brilliant but chill performance in a calculated picture that drew directly upon her own struggle between career and family.

Her final performance came on television as the Israeli Prime Minister in *A Woman Called Golda* (82, Alan Gibson).

Bergman's children include Pia Lindstrom, the show business writer, and Isabella Rossellini, actress and model.

Busby Berkeley (William Berkeley Enos) (1895–1976), b. Los Angeles
1933: *She Had to Say Yes*. 1935: *Gold Diggers of 1935; Bright Lights; I live for Love*. 1936: *Stage Struck*. 1937: *The Go-Getter; Hollywood Hotel*. 1938: *Men Are Such Fools; Garden of the Moon; Comet Over Broadway*. 1939: *They Made Me a Criminal; Babes in Arms; Fast and Furious*. 1940: *Forty Little Mothers; Strike Up the Band*. 1941: *Blonde Inspiration; Babes on Broadway*. 1942: *For Me and My Gal*. 1943: *The Gang's All Here*. 1946: *Cinderella Jones*. 1949: *Take Me Out to the Ball Game*.

It is a delicious irony that as the cinema institutionalized its own morality—in the early 1930s—it promoted a visionary who made films (or directed sequences) that revealed once and for all, despite every reference to the moon in June/boy meets girl/love and marriage, that the cinema had a ready, lascivious disposition toward orgy. Sexual daydream had found its medium, and Busby Berkeley's was the cool gaze that made an endlessly flowering **O** in those Warner Brothers dance routines. As Jean Comolli argued, Berkeley

is not a choreographer: people do not dance in his films, they evolve, they move about, they make a circle, the circle tightens or is released, bursts forward and forms again. The syntactical unit of this ballet of images is not the pas de deux but the pas de mille, the dance of a thousand. And one can suspect Busby Berkeley of having given himself the ballet as an alibi for his mad frenzy— . . . to show in all possible fashions, in all situations and playing all parts, the largest possible number of uniformly dressed blonde girls, in the splendor of an impeccable alignment of their legs, making love in all the fan of poses with a shameless camera that forces the imagination to the point of passing, dollying in, under the arch of their thighs stretched out infinitely, forming a tunnel of dreams where it was desirable, once at least, that the cinema be engulfed.

The point is well made: Berkeley was more a

dance director than a director—for all that *They Made Me a Criminal* is a solid John Garfield vehicle. Berkeley was a lyricist of eroticism, the high-angle shot, and the moving camera; he made it explicit that when the camera moves it has the thrust of the sexual act with it. It is only remarkable that some viewers smile on what they consider the "period charm" of such libertinage. We betray Berkeley by patronizing him, for he was daring enough to give us unalloyed cinematic sensation, as in the imperceptible plot of *The Gang's All Here*, which contains in its opening sequence one of cinema's most breathtaking traveling shots and, at its conclusion, the endlessly erectile banana routine—lewdness has never been as merry. And where else, in 1934, was surrealism purveyed to so many as in the ostrich feather dance of *Fashions of 1934* that ends in the orgasmic fronds of a sea anemone and a swan-galley of slave girls on a heaving canvas ocean?

As an official dance director, he worked on *Whoopee* (30, Thornton Freeland); *Kiki* (31, Sam Taylor); *Palmy Days* (31, Edward Sutherland); *Flying High* (31, Charles Reisner); *Night World* (32, Hobart Henley); *Bird of Paradise* (32, King Vidor); *The Kid from Spain* (32, Leo McCarey); *42nd Street* (33, Lloyd Bacon); *Gold Diggers of 1933* (33, Mervyn Le Roy); *Footlight Parade* (33, Bacon); *Roman Scandals* (33, Frank Tuttle); *Wonder Bar* (34, Bacon); *Fashions of 1934* (34, William Dieterle); *Twenty Million Sweethearts* (34, Ray Enright); *Dames* (34, Enright); *Go Into Your Dance* (35, Archie Mayo); *In Caliente* (35, Bacon); *Stars Over Broadway* (35, William Keighley); *Gold Diggers of 1937* (36, Bacon); *Singing Marine* (37, Enright); *Varsity Show* (37, Keighley); *Gold Diggers in Paris* (38, Enright); *Broadway Serenade* (39, Robert Z. Leonard); *Ziegfeld Girl* (41, Norman Z. McLeod); *Lady Be Good* (41, McLeod); *Born to Sing* (41, Edward Ludwig); *Girl Crazy* (43, Norman Taurog); *Two Weeks—With Love* (50, Roy Rowland); *Call Me Mister* (51, Bacon); *Two Tickets to Broadway* (51, James V. Kern); *Billion Dollar Mermaid* (52, Le Roy); *Small Town Girl* (53, Leslie Kardos); *Easy to Love* (53, Charles Walters); *Rose Marie* (54, Le Roy); and *Billy Rose's Jumbo* (62, Walters).

It is notable that his Warners films are more downright suggestive than most of the films made after his move to MGM in 1939. *The Gang's All Here* is a surrealist escape, but at Warners he kept a lofty survey over lagoons of water-lily vaginas opening and closing with delirious facility. At MGM, he had to abide by the unambiguous view of teenagers impersonated by Mickey Rooney and Judy Garland: Innuendo and the **O** were beaten out of doors by Mr. Mayer and his prim lion.

Paul Bern (Levy) (1889–1932), b. Wandsbek, Germany

Nothing will ever alter the fact that Paul Bern is known for a scandal—though his tragedy was much eclipsed by the fame of his widow. In the summer of 1932, very soon after their marriage, Paul Bern was shot dead in the Hollywood Hills home he was hoping to share with Jean Harlow. Suffice it to say that MGM studio people (Louis B. Mayer and Howard Strickling) were on the site before the police or a coroner. Still, the rumors were unbeatable, and they were fueled by a note found in the house, in Bern's hand: "Dearest dear. Unfortunately this is the only way to make good the frightful wrong I have done you and to wipe out my abject humiliation. Paul. You understand that last night was only a comedy."

There were stories told that Harlow had shot Bern, after he had beaten her. Another said he was a suicide, driven to it by his inability to make love to his wife. Some argued that the note was written by, or improved by, Mayer. We will never know for sure, but the best and latest research (by Sam Marx and David Stenn) suggests that Bern was shot by a prior wife (Dorothy Millette), who later killed herself.

What's really far more interesting is how and why Harlow, twenty-one, ravishing and a sexpot, married Bern, who was twice her age, balding, a little tubby, and very shy. It's worth taking in the testimony of Irene Mayer Selznick, who knew both of them well: she said that Bern was "probably the single most beloved figure in Hollywood. . . . He was the only person I ever knew who cherished people he loved as much for their frailties as for their virtues. He had compassion, erudition, and great generosity. . . . He was a writer who became a director, then a producer, but he was more concerned with nurturing the talent of others."

He did have credits, though they are not overpowering. I suspect that he was a fine advisor to filmmakers more than the possessor of real talent. As such, he became a right-hand man to Irving Thalberg. But Bern was tender towards talent, and smart enough to be genuinely sympathetic and useful. Amid all the very uneasy egos of Hollywood, that kind of personality has always had a place. Bern may have risen beyond his level—he seemed so kind and helpful to the raw Harlow that she thought marriage was necessary. It wasn't, and it may have exposed Bern's sexual voyeurism—a man more pleasured by being with stars than by making love to them. I doubt that he was gay so much as a chronic onlooker (with dark secrets to his own life).

So just as his story may never die, his type goes on. He is to be remembered whenever you see, and puzzle over, the clearly intelligent, endlessly patient, and oddly deferential men who are to be found in the retinues of our great and appalling young stars.

Trained at the American Academy of Dramatic Arts, Bern had worked in the theatre before entering movies. He did scripts for *Women Men Forget* (20, John M. Stahl); *Suspicious Wives* (22, Stahl); *The Christian* (23, Maurice Tourneur); *Lost and Found on a South Sea Island* (23, Raoul Walsh); *The Wanters* (23, Stahl); *Name the Man* (24, Victor Sjöström); *The Marriage Circle* (24, Ernst Lubitsch); *The Great Deception* (26, Howard Higgin); *The Beloved Rogue* (27, Alan Crosland); *The Dove* (28, Roland West).

Curtis (Kurt) **Bernhardt** (1899–1981),
b. Worms, Germany
1926: *Qualen der Nacht; Die Waise von Lowood*. 1927: *Kinderseelen Klagen Au Das Mädchen mit den Fünf Nullen; Schinderhannes*. 1928: *Die Letzte Fort*. 1929: *Die Frau Nach der Man Sich Sehnt*. 1930: *Die Letzte Kompanie; L'Homme qui Assassina*. 1931: *Der Mann der den Mord Beging*. 1932: *Der Rebell* (codirected with Luis Trenker). 1933: *Der Tunnel; L'Or dans la Rue*. 1936: *The Beloved Vagabond*. 1938: *Carrefour; The Girl in the Taxi*. 1939: *Nuit de Decembre*. 1940: *My Love Came Back; The Lady With Red Hair*. 1941: *Million Dollar Baby*. 1942: *Juke Girl*. 1943: *Happy Go Lucky*. 1945: *Conflict*. 1946: *Devotion; My Reputation; A Stolen Life*. 1947: *Possessed*. 1948: *The High Wall*. 1949: *The Doctor and the Girl*. 1951: *Payment on Demand; Sirocco; The Blue Veil*. 1952: *The Merry Widow*. 1953: *Miss Sadie Thompson*. 1954: *Beau Brummel*. 1955: *Interrupted Melody*. 1956: *Gaby*. 1960: *Stephanie in Rio*. 1961: *Damon and Pythias*. 1964: *Kisses for My President*.

An actor first, and then a director of plays in Berlin, Bernhardt went into films casually but soon established himself sufficiently to be given one of the first German sound films: *Die Letzte Kompanie*. After being arrested by the Gestapo, in 1934 he went to France and in 1935 to England where he also produced *The Dictator* (35, Alfred Santell and Victor Saville). He returned to France, but in early 1940 he reached America under contract to Warners. By 1950, he was free-lancing and his work went into a steady decline—to the dull from the odd. Bernhardt is a slight talent, best at what he called "a certain romantic, brooding mood." Some of his German silents touch on that: *Die Waise von Lowood* is a version of *Jane Eyre; Der Mann der den Mord Beging* is a thriller set in Constantinople, starring Conrad Veidt, "with eternal danger behind it, and beautiful women, and elegance."

His Warners films are a mixed bag of assignments, inconsistent but with the occasional sparkle. *The Lady With Red Hair* is a flamboyant theatrical biopic with Miriam Hopkins as Mrs. Leslie Carter and Claude Rains as David Belasco. *Conflict* is an implausible psychological thriller with a tame ending, but lustrous to look at and with an atmospheric studio ravine down which Bogart, in fedora and trench coat, hobbles to discover his nemesis. *Devotion* is a portrait of the Brontë family, absurdly romantic, but interesting for de Havilland as Charlotte, Ida Lupino as Emily, and Arthur Kennedy as Branwell. *Possessed* is a Joan Crawford picture with an unexpectedly smart idea of mental illness. Best of all is *A Stolen Life*, a Bette Davis melodrama with the gimmick that she plays twin sisters. The trick photography is delightfully cunning and the whole mood close to hysteria. *Payment on Demand,* again with Davis, was a thriller done with clever flashbacks and some ingenious lighting that relied on transparent sets—an innovation that Bernhardt claims as his own. In the 1950s he managed to make Rita Hayworth tedious as *Miss Sadie Thompson,* and moved from one colored costume romance to another.

Claude Berri (Claude Langmann),
b. Paris, 1934

1963: *Les Baisers*. 1964: *Le Poulet* (s). 1968: *Mazel Tov ou le Mariage*. 1972: *Le Sex Shop*. 1975: *Le Male du Siècle*. 1976: *La Première Fois*. 1977: *Un Moment d'Egarement*. 1980: *Je Vous Aime*. 1983: *Tchao Pantin*. 1986: *Jean de Florette; Manon des Sources*. 1990: *Uranus*. 1993: *Germinal*. 1997: *Lucie Aubrac*. 1999: *La Débandade*. 2002: *Une Femme de Ménage*. 2003: *Le Bison; Les Sentiments*.

Berri has done nearly everything, from scratching around as an actor in small roles to being one of the most powerful entrepreneurs in European film today. There is something Selznick-like in this child of Jewish immigrants, who worked as a furrier before he was an actor. And there is something akin to *Gone With the Wind* in the astonishing success of *Jean de Florette* and *Manon des Sources*. These adaptations of Pagnol are richer than *GWTW* as human dramas, yet the sweep of the two pictures, the production values, the marvel that the whole thing has been done with such command of energy, detail, and taste has more to do with old-fashioned showmanship than with art. And Berri's empire is securely based on the two hits, whereas Selznick let the bounty of *GWTW* fall into other hands.

Nothing else directed by Berri is anywhere near as compelling as the two films from Pagnol. Nowhere else is his eye so fixed on nature, the quality of Gérard Depardieu, Yves Montand, and Daniel Auteuil, or a beauty like Emmanuelle Béart.

As an actor, Berri had appeared in *Les Bonnes Femmes* (60, Claude Chabrol)—he is Bernadette Lafont's fiancé; *Behold a Pale Horse* (64, Fred Zinnemann); *Stan the Slasher* (90, Serge Gains-

bourg); and in many of his own films. But as a producer, he has been vital to the careers of several directors: *Taking Off* (71, Milos Forman); *Tess* (79, Roman Polanski); *L'Homme Blessé* (83, Patrice Chéreau); *The Bear* (89, Jean-Jacques Annaud); *Trois Places pour le 26* (88, Jacques Demy); *Valmont* (89, Forman); as well as many films by Bertrand Blier and Maurice Pialat. More recently he was in *Va Savoir* (01, Jacques Rivette) and *Asterix & Obelix: Mission Cleopatre* (02, Alain Chabat).

Germinal felt like a battleship of cultural prestige—which accounts for its dire pacing. He then produced *La Reine Margot* (94) for Patrice Chéreau and Isabelle Adjani; *Arlette* (97, Claude Zidi); *Astérix et Obélix contre César* (99, Zidi); *Mauvaise Passe* (99, Michel Blanc); *Ma Femme est une Actrice* (01, Yvan Attal); *Les Rois Mages* (01, Didier Bourdon and Bernard Campan); *Asterix & Obelix: Mission Cleopatre* (02, Chabat); *Amen* (02, Costa-Gavras; *Le Bison* (02, Isabelle Nanty); *Les Sentiments* (03, Noemie Lvovsky).

Halle Berry, b. Cleveland, Ohio, 1968

Halle Berry's Leticia in *Monster's Ball* (01, Marc Forster) was so good a performance that, for many people, it masked the gaping implausibilities in that picture. No matter, there is an honorable tradition of great acting in rubbish, and it was surely time for a black to win the best actress Oscar. (Actually Halle Berry had a black father and a white mother.) I suspect, too, that the Oscar was deeply assisted by the way that poor, helpless Leticia, adrift in rural Georgia, was also, mysteriously, one of the most beautiful women in the world. But I mentioned the implausibilities already. The award was deserved, and Ms. Berry knew that she spoke for a legion of sisters—for all of us, even. It was about time.

And so a former Miss Teen All-American, named after a Cleveland department store, had made it all the way. It will be fascinating to see what happens now. Halle Berry is an easy knockout (and she was already lined up to play Jinx in the Bond film, *Die Another Day*, directed by Lee Tamahori, a man of color), and she could turn awfully cute. But she really can act, and there's not much doubt about the rough and difficult life that has made her.

She was in *Knots Landing* and *Living Dolls* on TV, but her movie chance came as a crack addict in *Jungle Fever* (91, Spike Lee). After that, she did *Strictly Business* (91, Kevin Hooks); *The Last Boy Scout* (91, Tony Scott); with Eddie Murphy in *Boomerang* (92, Reginald Hudlin); *Father Hood* (93, James Roodt); *The Program* (93, David S. Ward); as "Sharon Stone" in *The Flintstones* (94, Brian Levant); good in *Losing Isaiah* (95, Stephen Gyllenhaal); as Sheba, with Jimmy Smits on TV in *Solomon and Sheba* (95, Robert M. Young); *Exec-*

utive Decision (96, Stuart Baird); Hawaiian in *Race the Sun* (96, Charles T. Kanganis); *The Rich Man's Wife* (96, Amy Holden Jones); *B°A°P°S* (97, Robert Townsend).

In truth, she hadn't offered much yet, but she was very sharp in *Bulworth* (98, Warren Beatty), and then after *Why Do Fools Fall in Love* (98, Gregory Nava), she had a big personal success in *Introducing Dorothy Dandridge* (99, Martha Coolidge), a superior biopic that had the effect of putting Ms. Berry forward as a test case. She was Storm in *X-Men* (00, Bryan Singer) and then did *Swordfish* (01, Dominic Sena) before *Monster's Ball*.

It remains to be seen how she and the business will determine her career: *X2* (03, Singer); *Gothika* (03, Mathieu Kassovitz); *The Set-Up* (03, Sidney Lumet).

John Berry (Jak Szold) (1917–99), b. New York
1946: *Miss Susie Slagle's; From This Day Forward.* 1947: *Cross My Heart.* 1948: *Casbah.* 1949: *Tension.* 1951: *He Ran All the Way; Dix de Hollywood* (d). 1952: *C'est Arrivé à Paris.* 1954: *Ça Va Barder.* 1955: *Je Suis un Sentimental; Don Juan.* 1957: *Tamango.* 1959: *Oh! Que Mambo!.* 1964: *Maya.* 1967: *A Tout Casser.* 1974: *Claudine.* 1976: *Thieves.* 1978: *The Bad News Bears Go To Japan.* 1980: *Angel on My Shoulder* (TV). 1982: *Honeyboy* (TV); *Sister, Sister* (TV); *Le Voyage à Paimpol.* 1987: *Bad Deal.* 1990: *A Captive in the Land.* 2000: *Boesman and Lena.*

Berry was a victim and antagonist of the blacklist who never managed to find stability or to vindicate his early promise outside America. He was an actor and assistant with the Mercury Theater in the late 1930s and was assistant director on Welles's lost movie, *Too Much Johnson* (38). It was his Broadway production of *Cry Havoc* that won him a contract with Paramount. His first film there was a Veronica Lake movie. But by far his most interesting work was *From This Day Forward*, an RKO comedy with Joan Fontaine and Mark Stevens as a couple attempting to settle after the war. Thereafter, Berry was replaced on *Caught* by Max Ophuls, made *Tension* at MGM, and directed John Garfield's excellent last picture, *He Ran All the Way*. He settled in Paris but proved unable to string satisfactory pictures together.

He returned to America in the early 1970s for a very mixed bag: *Claudine* and *Sister, Sister* were groundbreaking treatments of black life; *Angel on My Shoulder* was a remake of the old Paul Muni movie; and *Honeyboy* was a cliché boxing picture with Erik Estrada. *A Captive in the Land* is a heartfelt but rather hokey story about political enemies who need each other's help, set in Siberia.

Jules Berry (Paufichet) (1889–1951), b. Paris
In a 1951 letter (the year Berry died), written while trying to cast the role of the Viceroy in *The Golden Coach,* Jean Renoir said, "We've begun, naturally, to envisage Pierre Brasseur in the role, for he is the only French actor who isn't too old, is capable of playing with words, ideas and who can wear a costume with truculence. I saw him in a play by Sartre. He parodied Jules Berry, but it was probably a natural parody due to the fact that his professional development has brought him to the same point that Jules Berry had reached."

Renoir doesn't explain the point, but I think it implies a kind of bored mastery that had begun to turn into decoration or posing. But the very idea of wearing a costume with truculence unfailingly brings back memories of Berry's magnificent scoundrel Batala, in *Le Crime de Monsieur Lange* (36, Renoir), masquerading as a priest, yet struck down—and calling, with his dying breath, for professional religious comfort. It is one of the great moments in film's dandy tradition of the self-regarding show-off—the very full-time actor. And, of course, in a few years' time, Berry would enlarge the role a good deal in his films for Marcel Carné. He was a worthy brother for George Sanders.

He was a stage actor who did a few silent films, but real fame waited for his voice—he had a throat that had all the tiny creaks and innuendos of fraud: *Cromwell* (11, Henri Desfautaines); *L'Argent* (29, Marcel L'Herbier); *Quick* (32, Robert Siodmak); *Arsène Lupin, Détective* (37, Henri Diamant-Berger); *Le Voleur de Femmes* (37, Abel Gance); *Carrefour* (39, Curtis Bernhardt); *Accord Final* (39, Ignacy Rosenkranz); *Le Jour Se Lève* (39, Carné); *La Symphonie Fantastique* (42, Christian-Jaque); the devil in *Les Visiteurs du Soir* (42, Carné); *Le Voyageur de la Toussaint* (42, Louis Daquin); *Etoile sans Lumière* (46, Marcel Blistène); *Rêves d'Amour* (47, Christian Stengel); *Portrait d'un Assassin* (49, Bernard Roland); *Les Maîtres-Nageurs* (51, Henri Lepage).

Bernardo Bertolucci, b. Parma, Italy, 1940
1962: *La Commare Secca.* 1964: *Prima Della Rivoluzione/Before the Revolution.* 1966: *La Via del Petrolio* (d). 1967: "'Agonia," episode from *Amore e Rabbia.* 1968: *Partner.* 1970: *Il Conformista/The Conformist; Strategia del Ragno/The Spider's Strategy.* 1972: *Last Tango in Paris.* 1975: *1900.* 1979: *La Luna.* 1981: *La Tragedia di un Uomo Ridicolo/Tragedy of a Ridiculous Man.* 1987: *The Last Emperor.* 1990: *The Sheltering Sky.* 1994: *Little Buddha.* 1996: *Stealing Beauty.* 1998: *Besieged;* "Bologna", episode from *12 Registi per 12 Citta* (d). 2002: "Histoire d'Eaux", episode from *Ten Minutes Older: The Cello.* 2003: *The Dreamers.*

Bertolucci has made a substantial journey, from the romantic disenchantment of *Before the Revolution,* through the canceling of feelings in *The Conformist,* to the misanthropic howl of *Last Tango in Paris,* to the internationalism of *The Last Emperor. Last Tango* was an international cause célèbre, reflecting on different countries according to how many seconds they cut from it, and enticing into cinemas people who hover round notoriety and who must have been baffled by most of *Last Tango.* What could he do next?

The breathtaking control of imagery at the end of *The Conformist* was near to being a disguise of the action: in which the hero watches a man being assassinated and then consents to the very bloody slaughter of a woman he loves. The filming of that sequence, with the view of Trintignant hunched in his shadowy car and the desperate hand-held tracking shots of Dominique Sanda fleeing through the woods, was a perfect climax to the physical contrast between cramped stealth and graceful, unwinding movement. It imprinted the tragedy, but not without a saving gloss of romantic melodrama. The finale is passionate, whereas the logic of the film is to show that the man without passion is symptomatic of the modern world. In part, this may be because Bertolucci's sympathy for the coldhearted, isolated fascist hero was too great to deny his crucial action the elements of performance. The killing was, therefore, the crab's dance, in response to the serpentine feminine dance earlier in the film that obliquely humiliates him. The idea of *The Conformist,* of this natural, unevil, but detached man, was graver and more penetrating than Bertolucci's pleasure at cinematic expression. Perhaps the images only struck him later, revealing the silent gap between substance and style. For that reason alone, one thinks of *The Conformist* initially as a very stylish movie.

If one can look at *Last Tango* unhindered by its own reputation, the impression is of antistyle. *The Conformist* is a pursuit thriller, as witness the sinister recurring musical motifs and the several motor-car sequences—memories, perhaps, of the opening car journey in Rossellini's *Viaggio in Italia.* But *Last Tango* constantly undercuts fluency: the characters live in the present tense, kept there by Brando's neurotic insistence on no names, explanations, or stories. The two plots—Brando and Léaud—interact only finally and at cross-purposes. (Few people can be expected to enjoy the "hidden" meaning of the clash of classical American cinema and Godard's doctrinaire frenzy.) And even the sexual progress of the film is brutal, separating, and uncommunicative. Indeed, that is the very essence of it. The first animal-like coupling is the only one that is at all human or touching, and it ends with two monsters rolling apart across a vast, empty floor. It shows Bertolucci's feeling for the image that this spatial dislocation is so telling throughout the film: in the crosscutting between Brando and Schneider, the desert spaces of this gaunt flat where their paths have crossed, and the intrusion of doors, furniture, and screens. But this has been signaled by the two Francis Bacon paintings in the credits—of imprisoned sexual meat—and is not taken any deeper.

In part this is because the Léaud subplot is lightweight by comparison, and because the girl is never a very sentient or interesting character. Brando seems like the old man of the fuck, always on the point of breathing life into the confrontation. But the girl is trite, a little stupid, and nothing like the probing company that Dominique Sanda was for Trintignant. Against her pettiness, Brando inevitably seems to be playing a poet, madman, or brute. A more compelling companion could have illuminated him much more testingly. As it is, the film is thoroughly ambivalent: is Brando a tragic hero, or is he meant to represent the perversion of self-centered and self-disgusted sexuality? Brando himself is plainly ready for the former. But if the film seeks the latter course, then I think its sex is too coy.

Warhol's cinema has shown how implacably sexuality on film is noncommunicative the more comprehensively it is expressed. *Last Tango* has given up the nuances of sexual antagonism in *The Conformist*—still a greater achievement, I think—and replaced it with an uneasy anthropological withdrawal. The more totally animal the sex, the less expressive it becomes: instead, it is like looking at ants and being told, "Now, they are in ecstasy . . . now misery." The states of mind are almost captioned, which is itself an ingredient of Bertolucci's vision—that emotions are not mutual and have to be signaled—but the approach seems a dead end.

Much of *Last Tango* is intriguingly abstract. Few Parisian films have less sense of the actual city. Bertolucci's one recognizable location, the Bir-Hakim Bridge, is itself an oddity, made to express Brando's vulnerability to pain, more emblematic than actual. Which leads one to ask how many references there are in *Last Tango* to other films: a legitimate question, if only because of the way *Before the Revolution* contains a discussion on cinema with the teasing promise of quotes. *Last Tango* has Jean-Pierre Léaud as a near hysterical, Godardian cinema verité director making another reference to Vigo's *L'Atalante.* That may be more than a passing joke. Vigo was a surrealist and *L'Atalante* has Parisian scenes that have more to do with the subconscious than with urban reality. More than that, the ill-fitting contrast between Léaud/marriage and Brando/mysteriously depraved sexuality is matched in

L'Atalante by the way that Dita Parlo responds to her young husband, Jean Daste, and to the aging, but infinitely more experienced, Michel Simon. And is it too fanciful to hear Buñuel in the tango sequence, when human sexual communion is scathingly mocked? Remember that the first tango in Paris could be the music Buñuel chose to be played with *Un Chien Andalou*.

Bertolucci has not been surefooted in the years since. *Luna* and *Tragedy of a Ridiculous Man* were failures in most respects; and though *The Sheltering Sky* was well cast and had desert scenes as good as Antonioni, still the final result was so much softer than the Paul Bowles novel. That book had fascinated so many filmmakers over the years, it was something of a tragedy to see Bertolucci subtly betray it. But *The Last Emperor* was a masterpiece about a reticent man pushed in so many directions beyond his simple needs. The use of color and space, of Peking and history, of John Lone and Peter O'Toole were all masterly. *The Last Emperor* is a true epic but with an alertness to feelings as small and humble as a grasshopper. Still, it is hard to escape the feeling that Bertolucci has relaxed after the danger of *The Conformist* and *Last Tango*. Thus, he hardly seemed to notice the terrible darkness waiting beyond Paul Bowles's bright sky.

For Bertolucci, *Stealing Beauty* was a trifle, but *Besieged* is a glorious meditation on perversity and order. These could be so much more—like a promised *Heaven and Hell*.

Luc Besson, b. Paris, 1959

1981: *L'Avant-Dernier* (s). 1984: *Le Dernier Combat*. 1985: *Subway*. 1988: *Le Grand Bleu/The Big Blue*. 1990: *Nikita/La Femme Nikita*. 1991: *Atlantis*. 1994: *Léon/The Professional*. 1997: *The Fifth Element/La Cinquième Elément*. 1999: *Jeanne d'Arc/The Messenger: Joan of Arc*.

From time to time, Besson has nursed a small following outside France—and he certainly shows every sign of wanting to go "international." *The Professional* was shot in New York City, and it had Jean Reno trying to pretend he was Robert De Niro. But, despite his considerable humor, Besson cannot see a way past very arty visuals that seem unaware of how much they derive from fashion photography and comic books. Indeed, he is what a very intelligent French approach can sometimes persuade itself is "American." There's that attitudinizing in plot and heroics that works in Godard only because the structure of the stories is in constant upheaval and revision. Structure for Besson is like statuary—portentous and pedestrian. It's notable that *The Big Blue* was huge in France, and negligible elsewhere. *Subway* is probably his most interesting film, with the stunning visuals and the bored stare of Isabelle Adjani alike in leading nowhere.

The Fifth Element was a fair entertainment, and it did well in America, which was no preparation for the unmitigated disaster and polished-armor look of *Joan of Arc*—after Besson had seemed ready to produce Kathryn Bigelow's version of the same subject. And Besson has served as producer for others: *Point of No Return* (93, John Badham), drawn from *Nikita; Les Truffes* (94, Bernaud Nauer); *Tonka* (97, Jean-Hugues Anglade); *Nil by Mouth* (97, Gary Oldman)—a mercifully far cry from Besson's own style; *Taxi* (98, Gérard Pirès).

Charles Bickford (1891–1967),
b. Cambridge, Massachusetts

Bickford usually had the taciturn ruggedness of an open-air man, drawn grudgingly into a film studio. He played a few villains, but it is a tribute to the feelings he conveyed of decency and reliability that for over thirty years he personified men ill at ease in the dramatic cockpit of a film: in one of his first films, *Anna Christie* (30, Clarence Brown), he was an uncomplicated seaman who eventually asks the prostitute Garbo to marry him. In terms of self-sufficiency, stern moral conventions, and the flavor of a tough life, Bickford carried a breath of the outside world. He was not glamorous, and that itself was the basis of his Hollywood appeal, so skillfully offered that it became a beautiful portrait in diffident straightforwardness—being polite to shams.

Bickford was an engineer by training who had fought in the First World War. But throughout the 1920s, he had a successful stage career that carried him to Hollywood when sound arrived. His movie debut was in *Dynamite* (29, Cecil B. De Mille). In his first years in films he was a lead actor, young enough to be a rough, romantic star: in *Hell's Heroes* (29, William Wyler); as a sea captain with a new young bride, Leonore Ulric, in *South Sea Rose* (29, Allan Dwan); *Passion Flower* (30, William De Mille); *River's End* (30, Michael Curtiz); *The Sea Bat* (30, Wesley Ruggles); *The Squaw Man* (31, C. B. De Mille); fighting with Paul Lukas for Tallulah Bankhead in *Thunder Below* (32, Richard Wallace); *No Other Woman* (32, J. Walter Ruben); *Vanity Street* (32, Nicholas Grinde); *This Day and Age* (33, C. B. De Mille); *Under Pressure* (35, Raoul Walsh); as the gunrunner Latigo in *The Plainsman* (37, C. B. De Mille); and *High, Wide and Handsome* (37, Rouben Mamoulian).

By now he was securely playing supporting parts, as he did for another twenty-five years, without real alteration: *Daughter of Shanghai* (37, Robert Florey); *Gangs of New York* (38, James Cruze); *Stand Up and Fight* (39, W. S. Van Dyke); *Mutiny in the Big House* (39, William Nigh); as the friendly foreman in *Of Mice and Men* (39, Lewis Milestone); *Reap the Wild Wind* (42, C. B.

De Mille); the priest in *The Song of Bernadette* (43, Henry King); *Mr. Lucky* (43, H. C. Potter); *Wing and a Prayer* (44, Henry Hathaway); *Fallen Angel* (45, Otto Preminger); *Captain Eddie* (45, Lloyd Bacon); excellent as the shy suitor to Jennifer Jones in *Duel in the Sun* (46, King Vidor); *The Farmer's Daughter* (47, Potter); as the blind painter in *The Woman on the Beach* (47, Jean Renoir); as the priest in *Brute Force* (47, Jules Dassin); *Johnny Belinda* (48, Jean Negulesco); *Four Faces West* (48, Alfred E. Green); *Command Decision* (49, Sam Wood); *Roseanna McCoy* (49, Irving Reis); *Whirlpool* (49, Preminger); *Riding High* (50, Frank Capra); *Branded* (51, Rudolph Maté); *Man of Bronze* (52, Curtiz); so sensitive as the studio boss in *A Star is Born* (54, George Cukor) it is hard to know why anyone ever had trouble; *The Prince of Players* (55, Philip Dunne); *Not as a Stranger* (55, Stanley Kramer); *The Court Martial of Billy Mitchell* (55, Preminger); *You Can't Run Away From It* (56, Dick Powell); *Mister Cory* (57, Blake Edwards); *The Big Country* (58, Wyler); *The Unforgiven* (59, John Huston); very touching as the uncomprehending father in *Days of Wine and Roses* (63, Edwards); and *A Big Hand for the Little Lady* (66, Fielder Cook).

As if to prove Bickford's actual appeal, when his death was announced, Jennifer Jones attempted suicide with sleeping pills.

Kathryn Bigelow,
b. San Carlos, California, 1951
1984: *The Loveless* (codirected with Monty Montgomery). 1987: *Near Dark*. 1990: *Blue Steel*. 1991: *Point Break*. 1995: *Strange Days*. 2000: *The Weight of Water*. 2002: *K-19: The Widowmaker*.

There was a moment around 1990 when, married to director James Cameron and honored by the Museum of Modern Art in New York, Kathryn Bigelow was cool, chic, and in. You didn't really need to know she'd been a painter before the movie bug hit; that past screamed tastefully out of movies like *The Loveless* (like lost love for Edward Hopper) and *Near Dark,* which is a pretty cute vampire film. But *Blue Steel* was a very bad story with terrible dialogue such that Jamie Lee Curtis and Ron Silver seemed trapped in its cold ambience. That was nothing compared with *Strange Days,* which is one of the loudest bad films ever made, and which acted like the panic brake on several careers.

Bigelow has been quoted as saying that "action cinema is pure cinema." To which one must add that it may only expose the dangers of trying to do without character or good sense. Why does the cinema need to be so pure? Has anyone ever observed that state in its manufacture? Since *Strange Days,* she has made two more films that struggled to get a proper release.

Juliette Binoche, b. Paris, 1964
Watching *Blue* (93, Krzysztof Kieslowski), you begin to wonder if there has ever been a more beautiful woman in movies than Binoche. You fancy that Kieslowski has succumbed to this thought, too. How many ways are there of watching her grave face? Are the cheeks carved by love's gaze? Did that hair fall on her head like night? And the eyes . . . are they part of her life, or their own living creatures? And yet . . . if only this magnificent, melancholy, and nearly stunned woman had just a touch of . . . Debbie Reynolds?

Perhaps she *is* too solemn, though Phil Kaufman got a great smile and a better blush from her in *The Unbearable Lightness of Being* (88). Moreover, she was a startling and often naked sexual explorer in *Rendez-Vous* (85, André Téchiné). She was also to be seen to great advantage in *Hail Mary* (85, Jean-Luc Godard) and *Bad Blood* (86, Leos Carax). But the nearly complete resignation of *Blue* did seem like the next stage of an illness that fell on her in the grisly *Damage* (92, Louis Malle), where her passion was inseparable from anomie.

She is outstanding and especially pathetic in *Les Amants du Pont Neuf* (92, Carax). She has also done a *Wuthering Heights* (93, Peter Kosminsky), with Ralph Fiennes as her Heathcliff.

That was written just before Binoche became the art-house actress for a generation—the smiling face that ought to be on the Euro coin with which film business is done. Her performance in *Les Amants du Pont Neuf* proved typical: a woman going blind for art, and being pushed to extremes for love. I had asked for Debbie Reynolds in my coarse way, but in truth there was something of Garbo and Donna Reed already. I soon had the chance to see Binoche onstage in London—in Pirandello's *Naked*. She was awesomely beautiful, but not quite there as an actress (a little like her Anna in *Damage*). I realized how uniquely the camera loved her.

Since then, she has done *The Horseman on the Roof* (95, Jean-Paul Rappeneau); *A Couch in New York* (96, Chantal Akerman); won the supporting actress Oscar as Hana in *The English Patient* (96, Anthony Minghella); *Alice and Martin* (98, Téchiné); played George Sand in *Les Enfants du Siècle* (99, Diane Kurys); *The Widow of Saint-Pierre* (00, Patrice Leconte); *Code Inconnu* (00, Michael Haneke); the mistress of *Chocolat* (00, Lasse Hallstrom); *Decalage Horaire* (02, Daniele Thompson); *Country of My Skull* (03, John Boorman).

Jacqueline Bisset,
b. Weybridge, England, 1944
Bisset scholars treasure an early quickie exploitation picture in which the lady appeared nude. Miss Bisset scorns to discuss the item, and follows her trade of lolling around in a wet T-shirt or mas-

querading as Jackie O. The scale of exploitation shifts, and as it grows greedier so shame and discretion fall away, leaving naked professionalism. Bisset is beautiful; no one has yet denied it. But she retains the clammed-up haughtiness of the South Kensington bitch-deb that Roman Polanski teased in *Cul-de-Sac* (66). She has not managed to look less than grimly anxious, as if the nicely brought up girl never got over the horror of stripping to the buff. One longs to drug her or slow her jittery pulse; but how could you soften that humorless frown?

But she has worked hard: *The Knack* (65, Richard Lester); *Drop Dead, Darling* (66, Ken Hughes); *Two for the Road* (67, Stanley Donen); *Casino Royale* (67); *The Cape Town Affair* (67, Robert D. Webb); *The Sweet Ride* (67, Harvey Hart); *The Detective* (68, Gordon Douglas); her first chance, as relief to motor-car assault courses, in *Bullitt* (68, Peter Yates); *La Promesse* (68, Paul Feyder); *The First Time* (69, James Neilson); *Airport* (69, George Seaton); *The Grasshopper* (69, Jerry Paris); *The Mephisto Waltz* (70, Paul Wendkos); *Believe in Me* (71, Stuart Hagman); *Stand Up and Be Counted* (71, Jackie Cooper); *Secrets* (71, Philip Saville); *The Life and Times of Judge Roy Bean* (72, John Huston); and *The Thief Who Came to Dinner* (72, Bud Yorkin).

Her part as the insecure actress in *Day for Night* (73, François Truffaut) used her kindly, and was far above the run of junk she had been used to. It probably helped to promote her to international stardom, but no one yet had trusted her with a complex part or much more than the duty of being photographed: *How to Destroy the Reputation of the Greatest Secret Agent* (73, Philippe de Broca); *Murder on the Orient Express* (74, Sidney Lumet); *The Spiral Staircase* (75, Peter Collinson); *St. Ives* (76, J. Lee Thompson); *The Deep* (77, Yates) as a species of dripping poster; *The Greek Tycoon* (78, Thompson); and *Who Is Killing the Great Chefs of Europe?* (78, Ted Kotcheff).

Since then, she has made *Inchon* (80, Terence Young); *When Time Ran Out* (80, James Goldstone); *Rich and Famous* (81, George Cukor), which she coproduced; *I Love You, I Love You Not* (82, Armenia Balducci); *Class* (83, Lewis John Carlino); as the wife in *Under the Volcano* (84, John Huston); *Forbidden* (85, Anthony Page), for TV; as *Anna Karenina* (85, Simon Langton), also on TV; *Choices* (86, David Lowell Rich); *High Season* (87, Clare Peploe); *Scenes from the Class Struggle in Beverly Hills* (89, Paul Bartel); *Wild Orchid* (90, Zalman King); and *The Maid* (90, Ian Toyton).

In some quarters, there has been a move to elevate Ms. Bisset to the level of Charlotte Rampling, or even Jeanne Moreau. Alas, the work points steadily in a different direction: *Rossini! Rossini!*

(91, Mario Monicelli); *Les Marmottes* (93, Elie Choraqui); *Hoffman's Hunger* (93, Leon de Winter); *Crimebroker* (93, Ian Barry); on TV in *Leave of Absence* (94, Tom McLoughlin); *La Cérémonie* (95, Claude Chabrol); *September* (96, Colin Bucksey); *Once You Meet a Stranger* (96, Tommy Lee Wallace); *End of Summer* (96, Linda Yellen); *Dangerous Beauty* (98, Marshall Herskovitz); *Joan of Arc* (99, Christian Duguay); as Mary in *Jesus* (99, Roger Young) for TV; *Les Gens Qui s'Aiment* (99, Jean Charles Tacchella); *Britannic* (00, Brian Trenchard-Smith); *Sex & Mrs. X* (00, Arthur Allan Seidelman); as Sarah in *In the Beginning* (00, Kevin Connor); *New Year's Day* (00, Suri Krishnamma); *Joan of Arc: The Virgin Warrior* (00, Ronald F. Maxwell); *The Sleepy Time Gal* (01, Christopher Munch).

Approaching sixty, and still a looker, she romanced kids in *Dancing at the Harvest Moon* (02, Bobby Roth); *Fascination* (02, Klaus Menzel); again played Jackie Kennedy in *American Prince: The John F. Kennedy Jr Story* (03, Eric Laneuville); *Swing* (03, Martin Guigui).

Anita Björk, b. Tällberg, Sweden, 1923
You have only to see *Miss Julie* (51, Alf Sjöberg), to understand that Anita Björk was one of the great screen actresses. Yet it seems like a part of Björk's bad luck that that very intelligent rendering of Strindberg, with different time periods in the same frame, has fallen into neglect. Another famous piece of her bad luck was that after Hitchcock had seen her in *Miss Julie* and wanted her for *I Confess* (opposite Montgomery Clift), Warners decreed that she was insufficient box office—so use Anne Baxter instead. (They were also anxious because Björk arrived with a lover and an illegitimate child, so that they feared another Ingrid Bergman–like scandal.) Slip Björk's pensive face into its images and *I Confess* becomes a subtler, more painful picture.

Still, the greatest mystery may be why Björk worked only once with Ingmar Bergman, in *Secrets of Women* (52). She was only one actress in a great generation, but one wonders if she had done something to offend the big man.

She made her debut in *The Road to Heaven* (42, Sjöberg), and she soon became a player with Stockholm's Royal Dramatic Theatre. Her other films include *Kvinna utan Ansikte* (47, Gustaf Molander); *Kvartetten Som Sprängdes* (50, Molander); to Germany for the American film *Night People* (54, Nunnally Johnson), where she plays the traitor; *Sången om den Eldröda Blomman* (56, Molander); *Damen i Svart* (58, Arne Mattsson); *Körkarlen* (58, Mattsson); *Mannekäng i Rött* (58, Mattsson); *Square of Violence* (61, Leonardo Bercovici); *Loving Couples* (64, Mai Zetterling); *Adalen 31* (69, Bo Widerberg).

Robert Blake (Michael Vijencio Gubitosi),
b. Nutley, New Jersey, 1933
How many people are there here? He was a kid in
Western serials—notably the Red Ryder pictures.
He was one of the most lustrous children of the
1940s, a kid with a nitrate smile. And he would
become a kind of great actor—half Method, half
himself—as well as a TV fixture, whether he was
being a real little toughie or a rather self-pitying
fellow mooning to Johnny Carson. He doesn't
work much now, but never forget that he was the
best thing in David Lynch's *Lost Highway* (97), a
haunted face gazing out of the darkness.

As Mickey Gubitosi, then as Bobby Blake, the
wide-eyed boy, he was in *I Love You Again* (40, W.
S. Van Dyke II); *Andy Hardy's Double Life* (42,
George B. Seitz); *Slightly Dangerous* (43, Wesley
Ruggles); *The Big Noise* (44, Malcolm St. Clair);
The Woman in the Window (44, Fritz Lang);
Dakota (45, Joseph Kane); *Pillow to Post* (45, Vin-
cent Sherman); *The Horn Blows at Midnight* (45,
Raoul Walsh); as the young John Garfield in
Humoresque (47, Jean Negulesco); *The Return of
Rin Tin Tin* (47, Max Nosseck); a Mexican kid in
The Treasure of the Sierra Madre (47, John Hus-
ton); *The Black Rose* (50, Henry Hathaway);
Apache War Smoke (52, Harold F. Kress); *Trea-
sure of the Golden Condor* (53, Delmer Daves);
The Rack (56, Arnold Laven).

But then, in his early twenties, he shifted his
name to "Robert" and gradually forged an adult
career that climaxed in the TV series *Baretta*
(75–78), for which he won an Emmy: *Rumble on
the Docks* (56, Fred F. Sears); *The Tijuana Story*
(57, Leslie Kardos); *The Beast of Budapest* (58,
Harmon Jones); *Revolt in the Big House* (58, R. G.
Springsteen); *Battle Flame* (59, Springsteen); *The
Purple Gang* (60, Frank McDonald); *Town Without Pity* (61, Gottfried Reinhardt); *The Connection* (61, Shirley Clarke); *PT 109* (63, Leslie
Martinson); *The Greatest Story Ever Told* (65,
George Stevens); *This Property Is Condemned*
(66, Sydney Pollack); outstanding, with Scott Wilson, in *In Cold Blood* (67, Richard Brooks); *Tell
Them Willie Boy Is Here* (69, Abraham Polonsky);
a boxer in *Ripped Off* (71, Franco Prosperi); a
stock-car racer in *Cooky* (72, Leonard Horn); the
smart cop in *Electra Glide in Blue* (73, James
William Guercio); *Busting* (74, Peter Hyams); a
trucker who takes on Dyan Cannon in *Coast to
Coast* (80, Joseph Sargent); *Second-Hand Hearts*
(81, Hal Ashby); acting in and producing a TV version of *Of Mice and Men* (81, Reza Badiyi); as
Jimmy Hoffa on TV in *Blood Feud* (83, Mike
Newell); *Money Train* (95, Joseph Ruben).

And then, in 2001, bizarre melodrama: a
wife—yet hardly a wife?—a restaurant, a car,
shots in the night. And they say that David Lynch
is fanciful.

Cate (Catherine Elise) **Blanchett**,
b. Melbourne, Australia, 1969
Whether or not director Anthony Minghella will
be proved right—that Cate Blanchett can do "anything"—remains to be seen. But it will be fun
finding out, I think, just because of what
Minghella discovered with her in *The Talented
Mr. Ripley* (99): that she has a comic imp inside
that can make a character out of something very
slight. Her Meredith Logue is enlarged from the
Highsmith novel for plot purposes, but Blanchett
found the special restlessness of a woman not
quite beautiful or rich enough, yet ill at ease if she
isn't dealing with people who do have money.

A student at Australia's National Institute of
Dramatic Art, Blanchett has done Miranda,
Ophelia, and *The Seagull*'s Nina in Australia, as
well as David Hare's *Plenty* in London. Her
screen debut was in *Police Rescue* (94, Michael
Carson); *Parklands* (96, Kathryn Millard); *Paradise Road* (97, Bruce Beresford); *Thank God He
Met Lizzie* (97, Cherie Nowlan); *Oscar and
Lucinda* (97, Gillian Armstrong); *Elizabeth* (98,
Shekhar Kapur), a big, fine performance, Oscar-
nominated, yet a little monotonous; the best thing
in *Pushing Tin* (99, Mike Newell); *An Ideal Husband* (99, Oliver Parker).

Yes, she had looked and felt like the Tudor Elizabeth, but she'd also been so sly, horny, and sad as
Connie Falzone in *Pushing Tin*, when she was surrounded with vaunted young Americans projecting "attitude." The world caught on, so that no one
has been busier in the last few years: *The Man
Who Cried* (00, Sally Potter); a psychic in *The Gift*
(00, Sam Raimi); showing up the posturing of Billy
Bob Thornton and Bruce Willis in *Bandits* (01,
Barry Levinson); and then, all in one December,
luminous as Galadriel in *The Lord of the Rings:
The Fellowship of the Ring* (01, Peter Jackson);
slutty in *The Shipping News* (01, Lasse Hallström); and let down by just about everything in
Charlotte Gray (01, Armstrong).

She was in *Heaven* (Tom Tykwer); *Lord of the
Rings: The Two Towers* (02, Jackson); and was
Irish in *Veronica Guerin* (03, Joel Schumacher).

Brenda Blethyn (Bottle),
b. Ramsgate, England, 1946
These days, Brenda Blethyn is thought of in the
picture business as a mother, if not a matron
(though she's not to be confused with Brenda
Fricker, the mother in *My Left Foot*). So it's
appealing to recall that in the early 1980s, when
the BBC was working its way through all of Shakespeare, she was Cordelia in *King Lear* and Joan in
Henry VI, Part One. In those days, she was at the
National Theatre. There was a good deal more TV
throughout the eighties, before her movie debut
in *The Witches* (90, Nicolas Roeg) and then *A
River Runs Through It* (92, Robert Redford). But

her real breakthrough was as the mother who meets her long-lost daughter in *Secrets and Lies* (96, Mike Leigh), for which she got an Oscar nomination. You can think of it as a raw slice of life or an overjuiced piece of shtick—it all depends on your response to Leigh.

Since then, she has been in *Remember Me?* (97, Nick Hurran); *Girls' Night* (97, Hurran); *Night Train* (98, John Lynch); to Australia for *In the Winter Dark* (98, James Bogle); *Little Voice* (98, Mark Herman); as Louella Parsons in *RKO 281* (99, Benjamin Ross); *Saving Grace* (00, Nigel Cole); on TV in *Anne Frank* (01, Robert Dornhelm); *Daddy and Them* (01, Billy Bob Thornton); *Lovely and Amazing* (01, Nicole Holofcener); *On the Nose* (01, David Caffrey); *The Sleeping Dictionary* (01, Guy Jenkin); *Pumpkin* (02, Adam Larson Broder and Tony Abrams); *Sonny* (02, Nicolas Cage); a voice on *The Wild Thornberries Movie* (02, Cathy Malkasian and Jeff McGrath); *Blizzard* (02, LeVar Burton).

Bertrand Blier, b. Paris, 1939
1962: *Hitler? . . . Connais Pas!* (d). 1967: *Si J'Etais un Espion*. 1974: *Les Valseuses/Going Places*. 1975: *Calmos/Femmes Fatales*. 1977: *Preparez Vos Mouchoirs/Get Out Your Handkerchiefs*. 1979: *Buffet Froid*. 1981: *Beau-Père*. 1983: *La Femme de Mon Pote/My Best Friend's Girl*. 1984: *Nôtre Histoire*. 1986: *Tenue de Soirée/Ménage*. 1989: *Trop Belle pour Toi/Too Beautiful for You*. 1991: *Merci la Vie*. 1993: *Un, Deux, Trois, Soleil*. 1996: *Mon Homme*. 2000: *Les Acteurs*. 2003: *Les Cotelettes*.

When Bertrand Blier was born, his father, the actor Bernard Blier (1916–89), was making *Le Jour se Lève* for Carné and Prevert. This may help to explain why Bertrand Blier, who came of age as the films of the New Wave were spilling on the shore, remains attached to prior tradition. Blier the son is a provocateur. His dialogue is not as good as Prevert's, but his ideas are lovely, cute reversals of order that tickle the bourgeois fancy. His commercial appeal rests in his exactly judged subversiveness, his titillating danger, and his use of successful actors in well-made scenarios. And we should note that Blier came into his own at the French box office just as the generation of the New Wave began to seem tired. It is not too great a stretch to see that Blier can be reckoned alongside not just Carné, but Lubitsch and Wilder. There is much to be said for movies that get under the skin, the nerves, and the safe thinking of the middle class. There are even moments when the cunning, opportunistic Blier seems a comrade to Buñuel.

He worked as an assistant to several directors notably not affiliated with the New Wave (including Christian-Jaque and Jean Delannoy). He made documentaries and wrote novels before the breakthrough of *Les Valseuses*—which came from

one of his own books. That was a movie that encouraged, or permitted, audiences to be thrilled by the very forces of outrage that most alarmed them. Gérard Depardieu's fame rose with the film's success, for Depardieu was exactly the Caliban Blier needed to bring into the salon.

Calmos was a sardonic attack on feminism—and even on women, for Blier has several strains of the classic reactionary in him. *Get Out Your Handkerchiefs* was an ostensible shocker—it involved sexual swapping and Carole Laure giving herself to a teenage boy—yet it won the Oscar for best foreign film. *Buffet Froid* was a satirical thriller, with Depardieu as a dumb innocent caught up in a murder story. *Beau-Père* was a version of *Lolita*. *My Best Friend's Girl* was another story about sexual restlessness. *Nôtre Histoire* was an odd mixture of Buñuel and Harold Pinter's *The Lover*. *Ménage* took the old pattern of sexual exchange into gay relationships, and *Too Beautiful for You* is a mockery of the whole notion of loveliness.

The piquant attitude in so many Blier films is invariably colored with cynicism. He is tender, but the air of the films is helpless, wry, or bemused. With just a touch of wonder, the films would be immeasurably better. But Blier is too aware of pulling off a cruel practical joke.

Joan Blondell (1909–79), b. New York
Having been called West by Warners along with James Cagney in 1930—they were young successes in the same Broadway play—Joan Blondell may have been struck by the way Cagney prospered while she stayed a supporting actress. In fact, she was a mainstay at that studio for men, able to sing and dance as well as swop sour dialogue with gangsters, cops, or hustling stage managers. A pretty girl, she was given a cutting edge by so much dull work. When, at last, she broke away from Warners—some ten years later—it was to discover that her talent was already out of date. From 1930–39, she made fifty-three movies, mostly at Warners; but in the next ten years she made only thirteen. Hardly any of her pictures were big or important for their time, but look back over the Warners product and see how her slightly blowsy blonde, as round and shiny as cultured pearls, has lasted. Time and again she brings life, fun, and worldliness to her scenes: *Sinner's Holiday* (30, John Adolfi), the screen version of the play she and Cagney had starred in; *Office Wife* (30, Lloyd Bacon); *Other Men's Women* (30, William Wellman); *Illicit* (31, Archie Mayo); *My Past* (31, Roy del Ruth); *Night Nurse* (31, Wellman); *Public Enemy* (31, Wellman); *Blonde Crazy* (31, del Ruth); *The Crowd Roars* (32, Howard Hawks); *Famous Ferguson Case* (32, Bacon); *Miss Pinkerton* (32, Bacon); *Big City Blues* (32, Mervyn Le Roy); *The Greeks Had a Word for Them* (32,

Lowell Sherman); *Three on a Match* (32, Le Roy); *Lawyer Man* (33, William Dieterle); *Blondie Johnson* (33, Ray Enright); *Gold Diggers of 1933* (33, Le Roy); *Goodbye Again* (33, Michael Curtiz); *Footlight Parade* (33, Bacon); *Havana Widows* (33, Enright); *Convention City* (33, Mayo); *The Kansas City Princess* (34, William Keighley); *Smarty* (34, Robert Florey); *I've Got Your Number* (34, Enright); *He Was Her Man* (34, Bacon); *Dames* (34, Enright); *The Traveling Saleslady* (35, Enright); *Broadway Gondolier* (35, Bacon); *We're in the Money* (35, Enright); *Miss Pacific Fleet* (35, Enright); *Colleen* (36, Alfred E. Green); *Bullets or Ballots* (36, Keighley); *Stage Struck* (36, Busby Berkeley); *Three Men on a Horse* (36, Le Roy and Mayo); *Gold Diggers of 1937* (36, Bacon); *The King and the Chorus Girl* (37, Le Roy); *The Perfect Specimen* (37, Curtiz); *Back in Circulation* (37, Enright); *Stand In* (37, Tay Garnett); *There's Always a Woman* (38, Alexander Hall); and *East Side of Heaven* (39, David Butler). After that, she went back to the theatre and married her third husband, Mike Todd; the first two had been cinematographer George Barnes and actor Dick Powell. She worked a lot on TV as well as on the stage, and managed to tickle our sense of nostalgia in a number of character parts: *A Tree Grows in Brooklyn* (45, Elia Kazan); *Adventure* (46, Victor Fleming); *Nightmare Alley* (47, Edmund Goulding); *For Heaven's Sake* (50, George Seaton); *The Blue Veil* (51, Curtis Bernhardt); *The Opposite Sex* (56, David Miller); *This Could Be the Night* (57, Robert Wise); *The Desk Set* (58, Walter Lang); *Will Success Spoil Rock Hunter?* (58, Frank Tashlin); *Angel Baby* (61, Paul Wendkos); *The Cincinnati Kid* (65, Norman Jewison); *Waterhole 3* (67, William Graham); and *Support Your Local Gunfighter* (71, Burt Kennedy).

She had a striking comeback a few years later with *Opening Night* (77, John Cassavetes); *Grease* (78, Randal Kleiser); *The Glove* (78, Ross Hagen); *The Champ* (79, Franco Zeffirelli); and *The Woman Inside* (80, Joseph Van Winkle).

Claire Bloom, b. London, 1931
Educated at Badminton, the Guildhall School, and the Central School of Speech and Drama, she made her London debut in 1947 and appeared at Stratford-upon-Avon the following year. In fact, her first film was *The Blind Goddess* (48, Harold French), but she was effectively "discovered" by Chaplin to play the ballerina in *Limelight* (52). A leading player at the Old Vic, she also appeared in *Innocents in Paris* (52, Gordon Parry) and *The Man Between* (53, Carol Reed). By 1955, she mixed a notable Juliet at the Old Vic with playing opposite Olivier in *Richard III* and with Burton in Robert Rossen's *Alexander the Great*. She then made films in England and America that seldom seemed worthy of her. She was simultaneously austere and passionate as the most Russian character in *The Brothers Karamazov* (57, Richard Brooks), while in *The Chapman Report* (62, George Cukor)—despite the invading discretion of the censor—she portrayed sexual appetite with an un-English clarity and masochism. As Cukor said, "she did all those ignoble things with a beautiful, sober face." But such hints of Camille have been ignored and too many movies have seemed content to keep her ladylike: *Look Back in Anger* (59, Tony Richardson); *Three Moves to Freedom* (60, Gerd Oswald); *The Haunting* (63, Robert Wise); to Italy for *Il Maestro di Vigevano* (63, Elio Petri) and the "Peccato nel Pomeriggio" episode from *Alta Infidelta* (64, Petri); *The Outrage* (64, Martin Ritt); *The Spy Who Came In from the Cold* (66, Ritt); *Charly* (68, Ralph Nelson); with her then husband Rod Steiger in *Three Into Two Won't Go* (69, Peter Hall); an amusing Honor Klein in *A Severed Head* (70, Dick Clement); *The Illustrated Man* (69, Jack Smight); and *A Doll's House* (72, Patrick Garland), produced by her second husband, Hillard Elkins. She also had a great personal success on the London stage as Blanche Du Bois in *A Streetcar Named Desire*, and she appeared in *Islands in the Stream* (76, Franklin Schaffner).

Married again (to author Philip Roth), she was in *Clash of the Titans* (81, Desmond Davis); a fabulously controlling Lady Marchmain in *Brideshead Revisited* (81, Charles Sturridge); *Déjà Vu* (84, Anthony Richmond); *Florence Nightingale* (85, Daryl Duke); *Promises to Keep* (85, Noel Black); *Shadowlands* (85, Norman Stone); *Sammy and Rosie Get Laid* (87, Stephen Frears); *Queenie* (87, Larry Pearce); *Shadow on the Sun* (88, Richardson); and *Crimes and Misdemeanors* (89, Woody Allen), in which she had so little to do it was disconcerting to have her doing it.

She works regularly, and she did two years in the nineties on the daytime soap *As the World Turns*. But her opportunities have been few: on TV in *The Mirror Crack'd* (92, Stone); *The Camomile Lawn* (92, Peter Hall); *It's Nothing Personal* (93, Bradford May); *Remember* (93, John Herzfeld); uncredited in *The Age of Innocence* (93, Martin Scorsese); *A Village Affair* (94, Moira Armstrong); *Mad Dogs and Englishmen* (95, Henry Cole); *Mighty Aphrodite* (95, Allen); *Daylight* (96, Rob Cohen); *Family Money* (97, Renny Rye); *Imogen's Face* (98, David Wheatley); the lead in *The Lady in Question* (99, Joyce Chopra); *Love and Murder* (00, George Bloomfield); *Yesterday's Children* (00, Marus Cole); *The Birth of Eve* (02, Claude Fournier); *Imagining Argentina* (03, Christopher Hampton).

Budd Boetticher (Oscar Boetticher Jr.)
(1916–2001), b. Chicago
1944: *One Mysterious Night.* 1945: *The Missing*

Juror; A Guy, A Gal and a Pal; Escape in the Fog; Youth on Trial. 1946: *The Fleet That Came to Stay.* 1948: *Assigned to Danger; Behind Locked Doors.* 1949: *Wolf Hunter; Black Midnight.* 1950: *Killer Shark.* 1951: *The Bullfighter and the Lady; The Sword of D'Artagnan; The Cimarron Kid.* 1952: *Red Ball Express; Bronco Buster; Horizons West.* 1953: *City Beneath the Sea; Seminole; The Man from the Alamo; Wings of the Hawk; East of Sumatra.* 1955: *The Magnificent Matador.* 1956: *The Killer Is Loose; Seven Men from Now.* 1957: *The Tall T; Decision at Sundown.* 1958: *Buchanan Rides Alone.* 1959: *Ride Lonesome; Westbound.* 1960: *The Rise and Fall of Legs Diamond; Comanche Station.* 1968: *Arruza.* 1969: *A Time for Dying.* 1985: *My Kingdom for . . .* (d)

The career of Boetticher is one of the most interesting ever confined to B pictures. After periods at Culver Military Academy and Ohio State University, he became a notable football and basketball player. A trip to Mexico introduced him to bullfighting and a career in the ring led to his being hired as advisor by Fox for *Blood and Sand* (41, Rouben Mamoulian). He stayed in films, served in the Marines, and after the war, began directing low-budget second features. Neither his first bullfighting film, *The Bullfighter and the Lady,* nor his films up to 1953 suggested that he was more or less than a competent director of adventure films, an excellent storyteller with a very simple style. But *The Bullfighter* was Robert Stack as an American trying to become a matador, resulting in awkwardness and tragedy. With hindsight, one can see how far that was autobiographical. *The Magnificent Matador* was a failure, but it showed that Boetticher was intent on greater significance. In fact, Anthony Quinn's grandiloquence was at odds with Boetticher's own restraint. *The Killer Is Loose* was his first important modern-dress film, a very tense thriller about a psychotic, played by Wendell Corey, threatening the staked-out Rhonda Fleming.

At this stage, Boetticher fell in with Randolph Scott. After *Seven Men From Now,* they were joined by producer Harry Joe Brown for a remarkable series of Westerns, all made cheaply and quickly in desert or barren locations. They have a consistent and bleak preoccupation with life and death, sun and shade, and encompass treachery, cruelty, courage, and bluff with barely a trace of sentimentality or portentousness. The series added the austere image of a veteran Randolph Scott to the essential iconography of the Western and proved that Boetticher was a masterly observer of primitive man. His style remained without any flourish or easy touch and the series brought him some critical attention. Two films at least—*The Tall T* and *Ride Lonesome*—must be in contention for the most impressive and least

handicapped B films ever made. Above all, Boetticher had stressed the character and mythic value in visual narrative, and he has a more secure place in the history of the Western than several more self-conscious narrators of its breakdown.

In 1960, Boetticher added a fine gangster film to his oeuvre, *The Rise and Fall of Legs Diamond,* which only proved the range of his talent. He then returned to Mexico and labored eight years over *Arruza,* his third bullfighting film. But probably he is better tested by an eight-day schedule, compelled into vigorous, long action setups.

After a long absence, he appeared very nicely as a rich oilman in *Tequila Sunrise* (88, Robert Towne).

Sir Dirk Bogarde (Derek Niven van den Bogaerde) (1921–99), b. London
He began as a commercial artist before going on the stage. After war service, he continued in the theatre and then made his film debut in *Esther Waters* (48, Ian Dalrymple). Next year, he had a big success as the killer in Basil Dearden's *The Blue Lamp.* Thereafter, he quickly became one of the leading men of British cinema: the worst fate that could have befallen him and which marked him for life, no matter how much he strove to overcome it. Suffice it to say that from 1950 until *The Servant* (63), Bogarde made some thirty British films, a smooth, urbane hero in comedy and adventure alike. Often a war hero—*Appointment in London* (52, Philip Leacock); *They Who Dare* (54, Lewis Milestone); *The Sea Shall Not Have Them* (54, Lewis Gilbert); the rather better *Ill Met by Moonlight* (57, Michael Powell)—he was also Simon Sparrow in four "Doctor" films as well as Dubedat in Asquith's *The Doctor's Dilemma* (59). But his real performances were very few and never without defects: in Charles Crichton's *Hunted* (52); as a brittle hoodlum in Losey's *The Sleeping Tiger* (54); as Liszt in the Charles Vidor/Cukor *Song Without End* (60)—a silly film, but a genuinely romantic performance compared with the English *Tale of Two Cities* (58, Ralph Thomas); and as the homosexual in *Victim* (61, Dearden).

In 1962, he was very funny in Andrew Stone's unexpected *The Password Is Courage* and in 1963 he gave a tactful performance in support of Judy Garland in *I Could Go On Singing* (Ronald Neame). Then, in 1963, he played *The Servant* for Losey: a portrait of malice more psychologically complex than Bogarde or the British cinema had ever attempted. It seemed to convince Bogarde that he was not just handsome but intelligent and talented, and that he had missed out on his real vocation. After that, he chose much more worthwhile parts: *King and Country* (64) for Losey; *Darling* (66) for Schlesinger; a delicious camp villain in *Modesty Blaise* (66) for Losey;

Accident (67) for Losey; *Our Mother's House* (67, Jack Clayton); *Sebastian* (67, David Greene); *The Fixer* (68, John Frankenheimer); *Justine* (69, Cukor); *The Damned* (69, Luchino Visconti); *Death in Venice* (71, Visconti); *Le Serpent* (73, Henri Verneuil); and *The Night Porter* (73, Liliana Cavani). He became an international star, living in France, the more praiseworthy because he was best in nonassertive, observing, and rather *piano* roles. To that extent, *The Servant* was outstanding, and *Accident, Darling,* and *The Fixer* speak out for his basic personality, just as *Modesty Blaise* and *Sebastian* show his skill at comedy. *Death in Venice* is a tour de force, but one imposed upon the actor by the arty narrowness of the film. While proving just how inventive and controlled a camera actor Bogarde is, it also shows the extent to which his very reserved character hovers at the point of mannerism. And in *The Night Porter,* Bogarde's own gentility did help to evade the sentimental cruelty of the picture.

His work grew less frequent, as if middle age and a wish to be discriminating had stranded an unusual personality: *Permission to Kill* (75, Cyril Frankel); caustic and quivering with affronted etiquette as the bitchy lawyer in *Providence* (77, Alain Resnais); harking back to blithe war heroes in *A Bridge Too Far* (77, Richard Attenborough); and *Despair* (78, Rainer Werner Fassbinder).

In the eighties, he was semiretired, giving most of his time to writing novels, but he appeared on TV as Roald Dahl in *The Patricia Neal Story* (81, Anthony Harvey and Anthony Page); in *The Vision* (87, Norman Stone); and in *Daddy Nostalgie* (90, Bertrand Tavernier).

Two years after his death, Arena did a wonderful, pained documentary that showed how repressed and denying he had been until the end. It made his achievement feel greater, even if Bogarde the man was harder to like.

Humphrey Bogart (1899–1957),
b. New York

"Bogie," sighs Belmondo at the beginning of *Breathless,* and the link was made between the Bogart of the 1940s and the anarchist, behaviorist hero of the 1960s. It was the start of a cult, especially among those too young to have seen Bogart's best movies when they were first released. A generation coming of age at a time of presidential assassination, cold war, international conspiracy, man-made pollution, the remorseless spread of corruption, and the ever darker threat of man's aptitude for self-destruction, claimed for itself the sardonic pessimism, the neutrality, and the unfailing honor of the Bogart character. Trotskyists adorned their walls with portraits of Bogart in *In a Lonely Place* and young rakes muttered all the acidities of *The Big Sleep,* unaware that they came

from Raymond Chandler's original. Underlying everything was the idea that Bogart had been honest, truthful, and that he looked chaos in the eye, that he knew the odds and was the only reliable companion in the night. Which is nonsense and probably only possible if Bogart took something like the same view of his work in the cinema. It is time for a reappraisal, and while Bogart is often very close to the illusory heart of movies, by the highest standards—Grant, Stewart, Mitchum—he is a limited actor, not quite honest enough with himself.

"How can a man so ugly be so handsome?" asks Marta Toren of Bogart in *Sirocco.* Perhaps only if that man has a high enough regard for himself. That means several things: the sort of insistence Hemingway made that a man be true to himself; the implication that there is no other criterion; disenchantment with most of the world's white lies; a certain blindness to some of the larger deceptions; a sense of intellectual isolation such as displayed and sheltered the private eyes of the 1930s and 1940s; a belief in another Hemingway ideal, of grace under pressure; and, with this last, the constant necessity to observe oneself, to take care that weakness never shows, and that the line of behavior retains style and elegance. Give such a man the best material—Hammett and Chandler, for instance—and allow him to act it out in movies, and it is no wonder that the detachment of the character begins to clash with self-regard. If millions go to the movies to persuade themselves that they are Humphrey Bogart, why should Bogart himself not share in the illusion?

This last trap is the greatest test of stars in the cinema and Bogart falls heavily into it. In that respect, it is worth noticing that he had had a rougher passage to success than many latter-day admirers might think. After navy service in the First World War, Bogart took to stage acting, playing handsome romantic leads. Louise Brooks met him in 1924, and said he was a "Humphrey" then—"a slim boy with charming manners." He was from the upper classes, and he usually played young men who asked girls for tennis.

In 1930 he was contracted by Fox and made *A Devil With Women* (Irving Cummings). He stayed at Fox two years and was in John Ford's *Up the River* (30) and Raoul Walsh's *Women of All Nations* (31) before the studio let him go. For the next few years he alternated between Broadway and Hollywood, appearing in two Joan Blondell/Mervyn Le Roy films at Warners—*Big City Blues* (32) and *Three on a Match* (32)—and playing Duke Mantee in the New York production of Robert Sherwood's *The Petrified Forest.* When that ossified play was filmed, in 1936, its star, Leslie Howard, insisted that Bogart play Mantee. It is often known as Bogart's breakthrough; but it is an appalling film and Bogart is dreadful in it.

For, although it may have persuaded Warners to use him further as a ruthless, cruel hoodlum, Bogart was incapable of bringing character or conviction to such a part. By contrast, Cagney and Robinson made the gangster vivid and credible. The classic instance of Bogart's failure is in Raoul Walsh's *The Roaring Twenties* (39) in which a supposedly malicious Bogart is called upon to cringe and howl for his life to be spared. But he cannot admit cowardice and his writhing is embarrassingly inept. In part, this is sheer technical limitation, such as mars his Irish groom in the Bette Davis/Edmund Goulding *Dark Victory* (39). But, more seriously, Bogart could not bring himself to portray loathsomeness with any imaginative honesty. Thus, the string of parts in the late 1930s as a convict or gangster are generally unconvincing, and for all Bogart's complaint at the way Warners made him play second fiddle to Cagney, Robinson, and Raft, he does not appear to have identified his own problem: *Bullets or Ballots* (36, William Keighley); *The Great O'Malley* (37, William Dieterle); *San Quentin* (37, Lloyd Bacon); as a district attorney in *Marked Woman* (37, Bacon); *Kid Galahad* (37, Michael Curtiz); *Dead End* (37, William Wyler); *The Amazing Dr. Clitterhouse* (38, Anatole Litvak); *The Oklahoma Kid* (39, Bacon); *Angels With Dirty Faces* (39, Curtiz); *Invisible Stripes* (39, Bacon); *It All Came True* (40, Lewis Seiler); *Brother Orchid* (40, Bacon); and *They Drive By Night* (40, Raoul Walsh).

Perhaps Raoul Walsh had detected the barrier in Bogart's work. For in 1941, they made the film that is the turning point in the actor's career, *High Sierra*, about an ex-convict driven toward inevitable destruction. Bogart was immediately at ease, sympathetic, and affecting as the lonely, self-sufficient, middle-aged man, aware of the fate that awaits him. He managed to suggest that this outsider was confronted with all the hostile and inhumane forces of the world; crime was offered as an existential gesture. He was detached from everything except his own standards and his reluctant feelings for Ida Lupino. In part, he expressed the stoicism with which a frightened man might equip himself for war. But, most richly, the part pushed Bogart back on his own resources and brought out wit, a greater gentleness, and a grudging humanity—it was as if the world had at last recognized the person he always believed himself to be. This character was nudged on with his rather hurried Sam Spade in *The Maltese Falcon* (41), a film that owes very little to its director, John Huston, and more to Hammett's original conception and to the background cast of Sydney Greenstreet, Mary Astor, Peter Lorre, and Elisha Cook. In 1943, the bittersweet romanticism was perfectly embodied in Michael Curtiz's *Casablanca*, a woman's picture

for men and the sort of unblinking tosh, set deep in never-never land, that is the essence of Hollywood. The most surprising thing today about *Casablanca* is its scene of drunken self-pity, proof of how far Bogart needed a great artist to help him rise above the level of maudlin resentment. Curtiz handles *Casablanca* with great aplomb, but he never tries to disturb the attitudinizing characters.

Then in 1944 Bogart met Howard Hawks and Lauren Bacall: together they made *To Have and Have Not* (44) and *The Big Sleep* (46). These are masterpieces, belonging to Hawks rather than to Bogart. Even so, the company warmed Bogart and if the scenes with Bacall are improved by the real feeling between them, that is only to ask what makes feelings real. For the idea of Bogart was later greatly enhanced by the way he had met his true (and fourth) love on a soundstage. These two films are mature, where *Casablanca* is a wet dream, because of the way Hawks turns thrillers into comedies. It is to Bogart's credit that he seems not only aware of this trick but a prime agent in it. Thus, they work on two levels: as beautiful fantasies and as commentaries by the participants on their very absurdity.

It was the high point of his career. Indeed, conventional thrillers—like *Conflict* (45, Curtis Bernhardt); *The Two Mrs. Carrolls* (47, Peter Godfrey); *Dead Reckoning* (47, John Cromwell); *Dark Passage* (47, Delmer Daves); *Key Largo* (48, Huston)—could hardly have the same urgency after *The Big Sleep* (by definition, the fullest immersion in the dream). *Dead Reckoning* is actually the first parody of the Bogart manner, with him muttering "Geronimo" at every crisis to the patently fake Lizabeth Scott. But in his last ten years Bogart played three parts that were clearly difficult and that involved a deliberate inspection of his own divided personality. Two of these are in glib films: *The Treasure of the Sierra Madre* (48, Huston) and *The Caine Mutiny* (54, Edward Dmytryk), but the other is in Nicholas Ray's marvelous *In a Lonely Place* (50). This last penetrates the toughness that Bogart so often assumed and reaches an intractable malevolence that is more frightening than any of his gangsters. In *Treasure* and *Caine* he plays suspicious, paranoid men whose characters are torn apart by working at different levels. His Queeg especially, made when he was already ill with cancer, is very moving. *In a Lonely Place* was made by Bogart's own production company, Santana, for whom he made three other movies: Ray's more conventional *Knock on Any Door* (49), *Tokyo Joe* (49, Stuart Heisler), and *Sirocco* (51, Curtis Bernhardt). Instead of for *Lonely Place*, he received his Oscar for Huston's *The African Queen* (51), a sentimental gesture to an offbeat role. *The Enforcer* (51, Bretaigne Windust and Walsh) was a clever throwback to Warners' films of the 1930s. *Beat the Devil* (54, Huston) was an insouciant parody in which Bogart (the coproducer) has little idea of what is going on. He was poor in two Richard Brooks films, *Deadline U.S.A.* (52) and *Battle Circus* (53), and not very funny in the comedy of *Sabrina* (54, Billy Wilder). But he was back to the sourness of *Casablanca* in Mankiewicz's *Barefoot Contessa* (54), a shameless reworking of earlier moods. His final films were sadly unworthy of him: *We're No Angels* (55, Curtiz); *The Desperate Hours* (55, Wyler); *The Left Hand of God* (55, Dmytryk); and *The Harder They Fall* (56, Mark Robson).

Bogart's work is complex and central to the issue of identification in the cinema. He made few wholly satisfactory films—*High Sierra, To Have and Have Not, The Big Sleep, In a Lonely Place*— and failed in a variety of parts outside the narrow range he saw fit for himself. But within that range he had the impact of Garbo or James Dean. Like them, he was a great Romantic. It is harder to see him as such because of the efforts he made to appear anti-Romantic. The implications of his work—as a comment on self-dramatization—are rather more daunting and disturbing than he ever realized.

Peter Bogdanovich,

b. Kingston, New York, 1939

1968: *Targets.* 1971: *The Last Picture Show.* 1972: *What's Up, Doc?.* 1973: *Paper Moon.* 1974: *Daisy Miller.* 1975: *At Long Last Love.* 1976: *Nickelodeon.* 1979: *Saint Jack.* 1983: *They All Laughed.* 1985: *Mask.* 1988: *Illegally Yours.* 1990: *Texasville.* 1992: *Noises Off.* 1993: *The Thing Called Love; Fallen Angels* (TV). 1996: *To Sir With Love 2* (TV). 1997: *The Price of Heaven* (TV); *Rescuers: Stories of Courage: Two Women* (TV). 1998: *Naked City: A Killer Christmas* (TV). 1999: *A Saintly Switch* (TV). 2002: *The Cat's Meow.*

It is a French pattern—if a relatively recent one— for critics to badger their way into making films of their own. Godard, Truffaut, Rohmer, Chabrol, and Rivette all took that course. But in the American cinema it is barely known. Only Susan Sontag springs to mind as a companion to Bogdanovich, and her films have been made under very different conditions, just as her writing on films was more obscure than his. The rigid barriers between criticism and direction are worth pointing out. In the early 1970s battle over who did what on *Citizen Kane*, it was the literary bias of critic Pauline Kael that put her in Herman Mankiewicz's corner, while Bogdanovich knew that Welles colored everything in all his films, if only because *Kane* is based on Welles himself. In that sense, Bogdanovich was a valuable, French-inspired critic who insisted on the director as auteur, so much so that many Americans began to take directors

more seriously because of what he wrote. In particular, he threw attention onto Hawks, Lang, and Allan Dwan with long, respectful interviews. As a director, Bogdanovich made four lovely picture shows, revealing marvelous accomplishment, wit, and sense of place. But, ironically, they are less an auteur's films than the extension of criticism. *Targets*—made under Roger Corman's aegis, after Bogdanovich had fueled the bikes for *Wild Angels*—is a tribute to AIP horror pictures, to Boris Karloff, and to Hawks, and also a stylistic nod in the direction of Hitchcock and Lang. That it works so well in mixing a story of a veteran horror actor with a survey of an all-American bourgeois killer is because of vigorous conception and first-class mise-en-scène at the drive-in cinema.

His second picture is, as everyone says, a tribute to 1950s America, to the plains of North Texas, to late 1940s black-and-white photography, to Ben Johnson, to Hawks again, and to the nostalgia of *Ambersons*. But the real flavor of *The Last Picture Show* is French. Few American films take so many clearly defined characters and manage to like them all. It is something we know from Renoir, and in Bogdanovich it seems to be the first profound sign of character, the most fruitful area for development. Which is not to be ungrateful for the wonderful screwball comedy of *What's Up, Doc?* But that again is in the Hawks style, though minus the sense of the dark in *Bringing Up Baby*. Nevertheless, to handle such set pieces as the car chase, to indulge oneself on top of a hotel with Streisand singing "As Time Goes By," and, simply, to make Streisand so appealing were major achievements pulled off without strain.

Paper Moon was perilously slight and charming, but sustained by its re-creation of 1930s John Ford and by its affectionate recollection of rural America. Above all, it shows Bogdanovich's boyish love for cinema, as witness that scene where the two O'Neals are in a diner while, across the street, *Steamboat Round the Bend* is playing at the Dream movie house.

Daisy Miller, At Long Last Love, and *Nickelodeon* were all ingenious ventures but miscasting, lack of personal or stylistic conviction, and dwindling commercial confidence brought Bogdanovich to a crisis. Saddest of all was *Nickelodeon*, where even the historian's loving sense of pioneering days yielded to a brittle smartness.

Bogdanovich is a friend; he made generous comments on the earlier editions of this book. And he has known difficult times of late. *They All Laughed* was a showcase for Dorothy Stratten, a *Playboy* model, and Bogdanovich's beloved. When she was murdered, the director wrote a lovelorn book about her sad story (these are, approximately, the events of *Star 80*), and then dated and married Dorothy's half-sister, Louise Hoogstraten, who had been a minor when Bogdanovich first met her. There was a storm of gossip surrounding these events, and not even a friend could argue that Bogdanovich emerged unsullied.

More to the point, *They All Laughed* had been a failure in which Ms. Stratten nowhere near eclipsed anyone's memories of Cybill Shepherd, an actress whose fortunes would rise, gradually, after she and Bogdanovich broke up. *Mask* was not recognizable; *Illegally Yours* was another flop; and *Texasville* was badly recut by others. Around this time, there were some who hailed Bogdanovich's finest, if inadvertent, contribution to modern movies in having provided the inspiration for *Irreconcilable Differences* (84, Charles Shyer), in which a Hollywood couple are sued for divorce by their ten-year-old daughter. Accordingly, some wondered if Bogdanovich's decline had not dated from his loss of the advice and guidance of Polly Platt, his first wife.

Noises Off had no commercial life, but it was a real comeback in that Bogdanovich mastered the wonderful Michael Frayn play and regained the speed, precision, and emotional vitality that had made *What's Up, Doc?* one of the great farces of the modern era. There is hope.

In the nineties he fell upon harder times—there were bankruptcies, and he moved back to New York from Hollywood. But he responded well: he went back to writing, and published a long interview book with Orson Welles and a very lively and popular book of interviews with film people; he did more acting—there was a shrink's shrink role on *The Sopranos* that cried out for more—and it was a reminder that he had begun as an actor. He also directed a good deal for television, and then made a theatrical comeback with a pleasant, if somewhat Christie-like mystery out of the Thomas Ince death. Whether his confidence is what it was is one question. But it was overconfidence that got him into a lot of trouble. He remains one of the best directors in America—if he can find the proper material and budgets—and a man persistently devoted to films and their world.

Richard Boleslavsky

(Ryszard Srzednicki Boleslavsky) (1889–1937), b. Warsaw, Poland
1918: *Khleb* (codirected with Boris Sushkevich). 1919: *Bohaterstwo Polskiego Skavto.* 1921: *Cud Nad Wisla.* 1930: *Treasure Girl; The Last of the Lone Wolf.* 1931: *The Gay Diplomat; Women Pursued.* 1933: *Rasputin and the Empress; Storm at Daybreak; Beauty for Sale.* 1934: *Men in White; Fugitive Lovers; Operator 13; The Painted Veil; Hollywood Party* (codirected with Allan Dwan and Roy Rowland). 1935: *Clive of India; Les Misérables; Metropolitan; O'Shaughnessy's Boy.* 1936: *The Garden of Allah; Theodora Goes Wild; Three Godfathers.* 1937:

The Last of Mrs. Cheyney (codirected with George Fitzmaurice).

For ten years before the First World War, Boleslavsky was an actor at the Moscow Arts Theatre; indeed, he was later to write books on Stanislavsky's teachings. He had acted in Russian films before he began to direct. During the Civil War he fought for the Poles and made a film about the war for them. He went to Germany and acted in *Die Gezeichneten* (22, Carl Dreyer) before going to America to direct, on Broadway. His first work in the American cinema was directing the musical numbers in *The Grand Parade* (30, Fred Newmeyer). He directed a few films for Columbia and RKO and was then called to MGM to conduct all three Barrymores in *Rasputin and the Empress,* the source of a major court case involving Prince Yusupov. Stanislavsky's method is hardly evident in Boleslavsky's most characteristic work, in which melodramas, romance, and costume pieces predominate: *The Painted Veil* is Somerset Maugham's novel with Garbo and Herbert Marshall; *Clive of India* was Ronald Colman; *Les Misérables* is the best version of Hugo's novel, with Fredric March and Charles Laughton confronting each other; but most memorable is the folly de Selznick of *The Garden of Allah,* with Dietrich and Charles Boyer, and the comedy of *Theodora Goes Wild,* which probably owes a lot to writer Sidney Buchman and to Mary McCarthy's original story.

Ward Bond (1903–60), b. Denver, Colorado

Ward Bond was only fifty-seven when he died, yet he had apparently worked in something like two hundred films, to say nothing of the TV series *Wagon Train,* which he starred in from 1957 until his death, playing Seth Adams, the wagon master, father figure, and general dispenser of Western wisdom. Now, some unkind people will say that he sometimes gave the impression of being stuffed and strapped into the saddle some time before his official death. But that begins to take us into his strange career as boaster, bully, boozer, and member of the unwholesome John Ford gang. As such, there are many stories about Bond's stupidity, his uncouthness, and his being the butt of jokes—and sadly these are more entertaining than many of the films he made. Which is not to say that Bond was a hopeless case: in *The Searchers* (56, John Ford), he notices the way Ethan's sister-in-law handles his coat; and in *Gentleman Jim* (42, Raoul Walsh)—as John L. Sullivan—he brings a tear to the eye. All too often, however, the tears are in his own eyes first.

He was a footballer out of USC, recruited by Ford, and always ready for Papa's call. But he worked all over the place, with or without mustache, gruff, grumpy, and someone who was likely far worse off camera: *Salute* (29, Ford); *The Big Trail* (30, Walsh); *Heroes for Sale* (33, William A. Wellman); *It Happened One Night* (34, Frank Capra); *Broadway Bill* (34, Capra); *Devil Dogs of the Air* (35, Lloyd Bacon); *Black Fury* (35, Michael Curtiz); *The Man Who Lived Twice* (36, Harry Lachman); *You Only Live Once* (37, Fritz Lang); *Dead End* (37, William Wyler); *Submarine Patrol* (38, Ford); *Made for Each Other* (39, John Cromwell); *Dodge City* (39, Curtis); *Young Mr. Lincoln* (39, Ford); *Drums Along the Mohawk* (39, Ford); *The Oklahoma Kid* (39, Bacon); a Yankee captain in *Gone With the Wind* (39, Victor Fleming).

He was a cop in *The Grapes of Wrath* (40, Ford); a seaman in *The Long Voyage Home* (40, Ford); *The Mortal Storm* (40, Frank Borzage); *Virginia City* (40, Curtiz); *Kit Carson* (40, George B. Seitz); *Santa Fe Trail* (40, Curtiz); *Tobacco Road* (41, Ford); *Sergeant York* (41, Howard Hawks); *Manpower* (41, Walsh); *The Shepherd of the Hills* (41, Henry Hathaway); *The Maltese Falcon* (41, John Huston); *Swamp Water* (41, Jean Renoir); *Ten Gentlemen from West Point* (42, Hathaway); *A Guy Named Joe* (43, Fleming); the lead in *Hitler—Dead or Alive* (43, Nick Grinde); *They Came to Blow Up America* (43, Edward Ludwig); *Tall in the Saddle* (44, Edwin L. Marin); *The Fighting Sullivans* (44, Bacon), about brothers in the war: Bond did not enlist; *Home in Indiana* (44, Hathaway); *Boats Mulcahey* in *They Were Expendable* (45, Ford); *Canyon Passage* (46, Jacques Tourneur).

He was Bert, the cop, in *It's a Wonderful Life* (46, Capra); Morgan Earp in *My Darling Clementine* (46, Ford); El Gringo in *The Fugitive* (47, Ford); *Unconquered* (47, Cecil B. DeMille); O'Rourke in *Fort Apache* (47, Ford); *Tap Roots* (48, George Marshall); *Joan of Arc* (48, Fleming); Perley "Buck" Sweet in *3 Godfathers* (48, Ford); *Riding High* (50, Capra); *Kiss Tomorrow Goodbye* (50, Gordon Douglas); Elder Wiggs in *Wagonmaster* (50, Ford); *Operation Pacific* (51, George Waggner); *The Great Missouri Road* (50, Douglas); *Only the Valiant* (51, Douglas); Father Peter Lonergan in *The Quiet Man* (52, Ford); *On Dangerous Ground* (52, Nicholas Ray); *Blowing Wild* (53, Hugo Fregonese); *Hondo* (54, John Farrow); *Johnny Guitar* (54, Ray); *The Long Gray Line* (55, Ford); *Mister Roberts* (55, Ford and Mervyn LeRoy); *The Halliday Brand* (57, Joseph H. Lewis); as John Dodge, a Ford-like movie director, in *The Wings of Eagles* (57, Ford); and leading the wagon train in *Rio Bravo* (59, Hawks).

Sandrine Bonnaire,
b. Clermont-Ferrand, France, 1967

Has any actress made a debut of such force—and such youth—as Sandrine Bonnaire managed in *À Nos Amours* (83, Maurice Pialat), made when she

was fifteen? The part was in many ways a slice of life: a teenage girl, tossed about in the storms of growing life, experimenting with love, in turmoil over her family. It sounds like James Dean in *East of Eden*, but Dean was twenty-four when he played the teenager, Cal Trask. If you wonder about other actresses who were fifteen, think of Elizabeth Taylor in *A Date with Judy*, Shirley Temple in *Since You Went Away*, Judy Garland in *Love Finds Andy Hardy*, Tuesday Weld in *Rally Round the Flag Boys!*, and Sue Lyon in *Lolita*.

When Kubrick made *Lolita*, of course, censorship would not permit what the book ordained—reason, in some eyes, for not making the film. Bonnaire's character in *À Nos Amours* was no Lolita but truly a young woman, excited, afraid, daring, sensual, and innocent. Everything was there, without coyness or boasting. From shot to shot, nearly, she seemed to be shifting in mood and age, and what was most uncanny of all—she had already one of the great watching, waiting, listening, attending faces. Here was a phenomenon of acting.

There were times when even the deliberately tough, worldly Pialat seemed enchanted by her, and was persuaded to do little but observe her—or attend her. And he was playing her father in the film, caressing her performance with direct attention. The father seemed daunted by the beauty of his daughter—and the director/actor became resigned to his mortality in her presence. They have a late-night conversation scene that may be the best father–teenage daughter scene in movies.

In other movies, too, directors seemed drawn into the simple and sufficient photography of her existence. In her bearing, her gestures, her resentful passivity, and especially in her movement, she dominates the excellent *Vagabond* (85, Agnes Varda) as well as the rather fatuous *La Captive du Désert* (89, Raymond Depardon), and she is the woman across the way in that exceptional voyeuristic movie, *Monsieur Hire* (89, Patrice Leconte).

Her other work includes: *Le Meilleur de la Vie* (84, Renaud Victor); *Tir à Vue* (84, Marc Angello); *Blanche et Marie* (84, Jacques Renard); *Police* (85, Pialat); *Jaune Revolver* (87, Oliver Langlois); *Sous le Soleil du Satan* (87, Pialat); *Peaux de Vachés* (88, Patricia Mazuy); *A Few Days with Me* (88, Claude Sautet); *La Révolution Française* (89, Robert Enrico and Richard Heffron); *Verso Sera* (90, Francesca Archibugi); *La Peste* (92, Luis Puenzo); and *Jeanne la Pucelle* (94, Jacques Rivette), worthy of comparison with Falconetti.

She played with William Hurt in *Secrets Shared with a Stranger* (94, Georges Bardawil); with Isabelle Huppert in *La Cérémonie* (95, Claude Chabrol); *Never Ever* (96, Charles Finch); *Die Schuld der Liebe* (96, Andreas Gruber); for French TV, doing Bette Davis in *La Let-*

tre (97, Bertrand Tavernier); as a surgeon in *Une Femme en Blanc* (97, Aline Issermann); *Secret Défense* (98, Rivette); *Voleur de Vie* (98, Yves Angelo); *Au Coeur de Mensonge* (99, Chabrol); *Est-Ouest* (99, Regis Wargnier); *Mademoiselle* (00, Philippe Lioret); *C'est la Vie* (01, Jean-Pierre Améris); *La Maison des Enfants* (03, Issermann); *Confidences Trop Intimes* (03, Patrice Leconte).

John Boorman,
b. Shepperton, England, 1933

1965: *Catch Us If You Can.* 1967: *Point Blank.* 1968: *Hell in the Pacific.* 1970: *Leo the Last.* 1972: *Deliverance.* 1973: *Zardoz.* 1977: *Exorcist II: The Heretic.* 1981: *Excalibur.* 1985: *The Emerald Forest.* 1987: *Hope and Glory.* 1990: *Where the Heart Is.* 1991: *I Dreamt I Woke Up.* 1995: *Beyond Rangoon.* 1998: *The General.* 2001: *The Tailor of Panama.* 2003: *Country of My Skull.*

The embattled mentality of anyone who has tried to make films in Britain shows through in most of John Boorman's work. Thus, *Point Blank* is the most authentic film made by an Englishman in America, almost as a challenge to the cramping attitudes of the British industry. Yet Boorman never *became* American, or settled into fixed genres. He is as commercially unreliable as he is artistically unpredictable.

The commercial success of *Point Blank* and *Deliverance* brought him to a position of eminence. That both films were intensely American shows how far the cinematic instincts of a young British filmmaker could fit into American subjects and idioms. The brilliant atmospheric eye that distinguished Boorman from most of his British contemporaries was itself an attribute of the American emphasis on violent action growing out of environment. And the fact that *Point Blank* was so urban and *Deliverance* such a unique portrait of wilderness showed, once again, Boorman's will to stretch the range of his own talent. The serious box-office failures in his list—*Hell in the Pacific, Leo the Last, Zardoz,* and *The Heretic*—bear witness to the strain of guessing where the next film is coming from. For there is a tension in his work between full-blooded entertainment and allegorical significance. *Hell in the Pacific* may have incurred the interference of distributors because it fell uneasily between a war film and a sort of *Robinson Crusoe/Territorial Imperative* in which Lee Marvin and Toshiro Mifune could not dispense with the enmity thrust upon them by war. Boorman tends to see subdivisions within the species of man. *Leo the Last* is a Brechtian parable of the rich man and his relations with the poor. Made in Britain, it is the most commercially fanciful of Boorman's films, the one most directed at the art houses.

In the same way, the superb physical realization of *Deliverance* is marred by the underdeveloped stereotypes of the characters and the way its message is hammered home without variation or subtlety. The wishful return to nature of four city men canoeing down an Appalachian river relates Thoreau and the world of ecological Cassandras. The visual account of the journey and the irrational hostility of the hill people are stunning. But the idea of the movie—that modern man is already so far from the wilderness that he is unsuited to its rigors—is so clear as to seem shallow as the film progresses. The characters of the four men are almost irrelevant to the visual grandeur—indeed, Boorman has not yet shown in any of his films the ability to develop complex character studies.

But that is to amass his failings. Though limited, *Deliverance* is a frightening and beautiful film. If mildly pretentious, *Leo the Last* does create its own spatial and social world. And if *Hell in the Pacific* was broken by timid handlers, its scenes of animal against animal on a desert island show off Boorman's eye for terrain. Beyond that, *Point Blank* is a masterpiece. Given the firm iconographic basis of the urban thriller, Boorman's view of man in his own jungles becomes much more compelling. It is a crucial film in the development of the cinema's portrait of America as a complex of organized crime. It uses the city as a structural model for society so that all the sites of the city—the prison, the sewers, the apartment block, the used-car lot—take on a natural metaphysical significance. The actual and the imaginary are perfectly joined in *Point Blank*. For it is not only an account of Lee Marvin's remorseless and romantic hacking away at the syndicate, but his dream in the instant that he dies. Because the thriller is so strong and vivid a genre, Boorman was able to exploit its potential for fantasy and make the Marvin character a spectator of his own story. His expressive somnambulism is not just a search for vengeance and satisfaction, but the signs of sleep and inertia in a man actually slipping away from the world, defeated by it but inventing a story in which he triumphs as he dies.

Point Blank's two levels showed the artistic ambition of Boorman. And even if the time cuts and the cuts from one body to another in the bed sequence are obviously derivative, they were nonetheless right for the fusion of action and fantasy. The total effect is the justification. For in addition to the incisive portrait of violence and businesslike crime, of lives harrowed by anxiety—especially the women—*Point Blank* ends on a note of mystery. When Marvin does not come forward to claim his money, he has both abandoned violence and finally died. The implication is marvelously sinister and the expression of modern man's dilemma in dealing with all organizations is set in terms of myth.

Boorman's talent may never be resolved. The genre basis of *Point Blank* is harder to come by now that the commercial rules are dissolving. *Zardoz* plunges into myth without creating a satisfactory context for it, no matter that it was shot amid the wild beauty of Wicklow, in Ireland, where Boorman now lives. It is too earnestly trying to be intelligent. Boorman must take on the mass audience or let his real aspirations lead him toward more deliberately intellectual cinema. His sequel to *The Exorcist* only proved the dilemma. Very long in the making, and apparently beset with occult hazards (including a strange illness that nearly killed Boorman), it was laughed at by audiences, recut, and withdrawn. Neither Warners nor the box office wanted it, and it is scarcely coherent, but it has extraordinary moments of a metaphysical scope that reminded us of the director's lasting wish to film *Lord of the Rings* and the Arthurian legends.

That wish was satisfied with *Excalibur*, which had a true sense of legendary past and pagan vitality, but which suffered from Boorman's difficulties in sustaining line and momentum. Equally, *The Emerald Forest* was a wondrous, original concept, full of breathtaking imagery, yet finally weak as a story. *Hope and Glory* was a great success: it explored the director's own childhood in suburban London, and it captured the child's innocent delight at the beautiful disruption of the Blitz. The reality of the situation seemed to give Boorman confidence. He is a unique, visionary filmmaker, but his yearning for new types of material does not quite hide a record more at ease with reliable genres. His most conventional pictures, the most accessible in their situation, have been the best.

If this suggests that Boorman is not at his best as a writer, or in dealing with writers, he has begun to publish diary materials on his working life—on the making of *The Emerald Forest* and on the period of 1991 (as projects came and vanished) that are lucid and compelling. He is also the founding editor of the annual magazine *Projections*, the first issue of which included a fascinating, candid account of his own difficulties in getting a film to make.

Projections is by now at a dozen volumes (Tom Luddy and I helped with one of them), and I am happy to have John Boorman as a friend who can at least tolerate my awe at the ups and downs of his own career: the disappointment of both *Beyond Rangoon* and *The Tailor of Panama*, with that peak of splendor, *The General* (one of the greatest Irish films), between them.

Ernest Borgnine (Ermes Effron Borgnine), b. Hamden, Connecticut, 1917

There have been three stages in Borgnine's career—from a bulging-eyed villain, to a ponderous hero of Hollywood's brief immersion in naturalism, to a dull and increasingly anxious-looking supporting actor. He made his debut in *The Whistle at Eaton Falls* (51, Robert Siodmak) and *The Mob* (51, Robert Parrish) and quickly fell into villainy: most notably as the stockade sergeant in *From Here to Eternity* (53, Fred Zinnemann) and in *Johnny Guitar* (54, Nicholas Ray); *Vera Cruz* (54, Robert Aldrich); *Bad Day at Black Rock* (54, John Sturges); *Run for Cover* (55, Ray); and *Violent Saturday* (55, Richard Fleischer). Then, as TV and Paddy Chayefsky became fashionable, Borgnine's ugliness was made sentimentally decent as *Marty* (55, Delbert Mann). He won the best actor Oscar, but remained a leading player for only a few more years: *Jubal* (56, Delmer Daves); *The Catered Affair* (56, Richard Brooks); *The Best Things in Life Are Free* (56, Michael Curtiz); and *Three Brave Men* (57, Philip Dunne). He slipped back, although never into such brutality as had once been his style: *The Vikings* (58, Fleischer); *The Rabbit Trap* (59, Philip Leacock); victimized by the Mafia in *Pay or Die* (60, Richard Wilson); *Summer of the 17th Doll* (60, Leslie Norman); *Go Naked in the World* (61, Ranald MacDougall); *Barabbas* (62, Fleischer); *The Flight of the Phoenix* (65, Aldrich); *The Dirty Dozen* (66, Aldrich); *Chuka* (67, Gordon Douglas); *The Legend of Lylah Clare* (68, Aldrich); *The Split* (68, Gordon Flemyng); *Ice Station Zebra* (68, John Sturges); a good deal better in *The Wild Bunch* (69, Sam Peckinpah); *The Adventurers* (69, Lewis Gilbert); *Bunny O'Hare* (70, Gerd Oswald); *Hannie Caulder* (71, Burt Kennedy); *Willard* (71, Daniel Mann); *The Revengers* (72, Mann); *The Poseidon Adventure* (72, Ronald Neame); as the train guard in *The Emperor of the North Pole* (73, Aldrich); *Sunday in the Country* (74, John Trent); *Law and Disorder* (74, Ivan Passer); *Hustle* (75, Aldrich); *The Devil's Rain* (75, Robert Fuest); *The Prince and the Pauper* (77, Fleischer); as Angelo Dundee in *The Greatest* (77, Tom Gries); and *Convoy* (78, Peckinpah).

He soldiered on, often in TV, not too far from a grotesque sometimes: *The Cops and Robin* (78, Allen Reisner); *Ravagers* (79, Richard Compton); *The Double McGuffin* (79, Joe Camp); *The Black Hole* (79, Gary Nelson); reunited with Delbert Mann for a TV version of *All Quiet on the Western Front* (79); *When Time Ran Out* (80, James Goldstone); *Super Fuzz* (81, Sergio Corbucci); *Deadly Blessing* (81, Wes Craven); *Escape from New York* (81, John Carpenter); *High Risk* (81, Stewart Raffill); *Young Warriors* (83, Lawrence D. Foldes); for TV, *Blood Feud* (83, Mike Newell); *Love Leads the Way* (84, Mann); *The Dirty Dozen: The Next Mission* (85, Andrew V. McLaglen); *Code Name: Wildgeese* (86, Anthony M. Dawson); two more TV "Deadly Dozens": *The Deadly Mission* (87) and *The Fatal Mission* (both for Lee H. Katzin); *Spike of Bensonhurst* (88, Paul Morrissey); *Any*

Man's Death (90, Tom Clegg); and *Appearances* (90, Win Phelps).

In 1964, he entered into a short-lived marriage with Ethel Merman, which somehow helped his transition from actor to inexplicable celebrity.

Borgnine passed eighty still doing obscure action films, or films for younger viewers in which he was a grandfather figure: *Tides of War* (90, Neil Rossati); as Professor Braun in *Laser Mission* (90, B. J. Davis); *Mountain of Diamonds* (91, Jeannot Szwarc); *Tierärztin Christine* (93, Otto Retzer); *Der Blaue Diamant* (93, Retzer); *Merlin's Shop of Mystical Wonders* (96, Kenneth J. Berton); as Cobra in *McHale's Navy* (97, Bryan Spicer); *Gattaca* (97, Andrew Niccol); and then a bizarre but fascinating-sounding one-man show in which he played *Hoover* (97, Rick Pamplin); *Abilene* (99, Joe Camp III); *Mel* (99, Joey Travolta); *The Last Great Ride* (99, Ralph Portillo); *The Long Ride Home* (01, Robert Marcarelli); *Crimebusters* (03, Pamplin).

Walerian Borowczyk,
b. Kwilcz, Poland, 1923
1953: *Glowa* (s). 1954: *Photographies Vivantes* (s); *Atelier de Fernand Léger* (s). 1956: *Jesien* (s). 1957: *Byl Sobie Raz/Os* (codirected with Jan Lenica) (s); *Striptease* (codirected with Lenica) (s). 1958: *Dom* (codirected with Lenica) (s); *Szkola* (s). 1959: *Terra Incognita* (s); *Le Magicien* (s); *Les Astronautes* (codirected with Chris Marker) (s). 1960: *Le Dernier Voyage de Gulliver* (uncompleted). 1961: *Boîte à Musique* (codirected with Lenica) (s); *Solitude* (codirected with Lenica) (s). 1962: *Le Concert de Monsieur et Madame Kabal* (s). 1963: *L'Encyclopédie de Grand-maman en 13 Volumes* (s); *Holy Smoke* (s); *Renaissance* (s). 1964: *Les Jeux des Anges* (s). 1965: *Le Dictionnaire de Joachim* (s). 1966: *Rosalie* (s). 1967: *Gavotte* (s); *Le Théâtre de Monsieur et Madame Kabal*; *Diptyque* (s). 1968: *Goto, L'Ile d'Amour.* 1969: *Le Phonographe* (s). 1971: *Blanche.* 1974: *Contes Immoraux/Immoral Tales.* 1975: *Dzieje Grzechu/ The Story of Sin; La Bête/The Beast.* 1976: *La Marge/The Streetwalker.* 1977: *L'Interno di un Convento/Behind Convent Walls.* 1979: *Collections Privées; Les Héroïnes du Mal.* 1980: *Lulu; Docteur Jekyll et les Femmes/The Bloodbath of Doctor Jekyll.* 1981: *Docteur.* 1983: *Ars Amandi.* 1986: *Emmanuelle 5.* 1988: *Cérémonie d'Amour.*

I have not dealt much with animation in this volume—for various reasons. It would have enlarged the book impossibly, and animation is too often conscious of its own playfulness. Only very recently, and in Eastern Europe, has animated cinema escaped the role of an amusing novelty for children. In this respect, Disney's innovation was crushingly banal. Not only did he invent Mickey, the skeletons, and the first jerking anthropo-

morphs, but he set them rigidly in a scheme of entertainment that has been one of the most influential factors in shaping modern America. Disneyland was once a marvelous grotto to visit; but today it looks increasingly like a prediction of America to come. The schizoid nature of animation—a childish form shuddering with adult preoccupation—may be seen in one of its finest flowerings, *Tom and Jerry*, the most concentrated cinematic violence, endlessly reinventing its tortured cat so that he will be pierced, shattered, and burned again. Is there a continuing work of art that so ably prepares children for our educated indifference to suffering?

The point that has to be realized about animation is that it is not essentially different from the form that is considered its opposite—live action. All films are a succession of still images, animated by the action of the projector—and by the anticipation and feelings of the audience. By that standard, *Dom,* say, is an animate film, brought to life by imaginative collaboration, and all those worthless live-action films you can think of remain inert and inanimate, despite the flickering effect of actual locomotion.

Borowczyk is included here because there is no crucial gap between his animated and live-action films. *Renaissance,* for instance, is like an essay on animation, in which a series of destroyed objects remake themselves through reversal of their filmed destruction, until a reassembled hand grenade pulls its own pin and reestablishes ruin.

His work is an extreme proof of the hypothesis that film suffers to the extent that it is realistic, and flourishes in accordance with its capacity for fantasy, poetry, and the surreal. What distinguishes it is the succession of images (motion) that prompts emotion. It is of secondary importance, which is to say, none at all, whether these images are records of reality or records of invention. The camera cannot lie, but such literalness makes it dull and helpless unless liberated by an artist. Borowczyk is one of the major artists of modern cinema, arguably the finest talent that East Europe has provided. He is the poet of destructive passions who never tolerates the glib pathos of extinction. The objects and people who suffer in his films are broken down and remade into new versions of themselves, sometimes identical, sometimes unrecognizable. This is innately cinematic: the explosion that kills produces gorgeous smoke and a rearrangement of limbs; execution is as Dada as any nude descending a staircase; wounds allow blood to escape; hair consumes plaster heads; and in *Rosalie,* the very items of evidence that involved us with the beautiful Ligia Branice are finally smoothed away to demonstrate the means of our emotion. *Rosalie* is a study of suffering on its first level; but beneath that, and more important, it is an elegy on our way of responding to suffering. Equally, *Goto,* a barbarous, lyrical fairy story, reduces the world to love and cruelty in the way of *L'Age d'Or* and, like Buñuel's film, ends with a touch—the heroine brought back to life—that is a commentary on our watching selves as critical and tender as the last tracking shot of *Lola Montes.*

Borowczyk has always mingled forms, "animating" real objects and still photographs as much as drawings, so that it was no surprise when he entered into full-length live action with *Goto* and *Blanche.* His partnership with Lenica was close, while that with Marker seems to have been the swapping of very different personalities. Borowczyk's feeling for suffering, and for the mysterious affirmation of reality in pain, destruction, and regeneration, places him with the great poets. Less a Pole perhaps—so much graver than Wajda—than a refugee with Buñuel.

As far as can be ascertained, the more recent Borowczyk has settled for sex and exploitation—yet it is hard to believe he could ever suppress his genius. And why not sex?

Frank Borzage (1893–1962),
b. Salt Lake City, Utah

1916: *Life's Harmony; Land o' Lizards; The Silken Spider; The Code of Honor; Nell Dale's Men Folks; That Gal of Burke's; The Forgotten Prayer; The Courtin' of Calliope Clew; Nugget Jim's Pardner; The Demon of Fear.* 1918: *Flying Colors; Until They Get Me; The Gun Woman; Shoes That Danced; Innocents' Progress; Society for Sale; An Honest Man; Who Is to Blame?; The Ghost Flower; The Curse of Iku.* 1919: *Toton; Prudence of Broadway; Whom the Gods Destroy.* 1920: *Humoresque.* 1921: *The Duke of Chimney Butte; Get-Rich-Quick Wallingford.* 1922: *Back Pay; Billy Jim; Silent Shelby* (reissue of *Land o'Lizards*); *The Good Provider; Hair Trigger Casey; The Pride of Palomar; The Valley of Silent Men.* 1923: *The Age of Desire; Children of Dust; The Nth Commandment.* 1924: *Secrets.* 1925: *The Circle; Daddy's Gone a'Hunting; The Lady; Lazybones; Wages for Wives.* 1926: *The Dixie Merchant; Early to Wed; The First Year; Marriage License?.* 1927: *Seventh Heaven.* 1928: *The River; Street Angel.* 1929: *Lucky Star; They Had to See Paris.* 1930: *Song o' My Heart; Liliom.* 1931: *Doctors' Wives; Bad Girl; Young as You Feel.* 1932: *Young America; After Tomorrow.* 1933: *A Farewell to Arms; Secrets; Man's Castle.* 1934: *No Greater Glory; Little Man, What Now?; Flirtation Walk.* 1935: *Living on Velvet; Stranded; Shipmates Forever.* 1936: *Desire; Hearts Divided.* 1937: *Green Light; History Is Made at Night; Big City.* 1938: *Mannequin; Three Comrades; The Shining Hour.* 1939: *Disputed Passage.* 1940: *Strange Cargo; The Mortal Storm; Flight Command.* 1941: *Smilin' Through.* 1942: *The Vanishing Virginian; Seven Sweethearts.* 1943: *Stage Door Canteen; His Butler's Sister.* 1944: *Till We Meet Again.* 1945: *The Spanish Main.* 1946: *I've Always Loved You; Magnificent Doll.* 1947: *That's My Man.* 1948: *Moonrise.* 1958: *China Doll; The Big Fisherman.* 1961: *Antinea, l'Amante della Citta Sepolta* (codirected with Edgar G. Ulmer and Giuseppe Masini).

Borzage was the son of Swedish parents. As a teenager he went on the stage and he began his movie career as an actor. Thomas Ince gave him his chance as a director and, by the mid-1920s, Borzage was one of the most successful Hollywood directors—as witness the fact that he won the newly created Oscar for direction twice in its first five years—for *Seventh Heaven* and *Bad Girl.* War, and the consequent taste for realism, destroyed the world he had created and after *The Mortal Storm,* only one other film—*Moonrise*—properly revealed his talent. As a result, he is now badly neglected.

The loss of romance during the war is all the more ironic in that Borzage's most poignant films of the 1930s involve lovers under the shadow of Hitler, fascism, or the slump. There is a dreamy preoccupation in those films, based on what Andrew Sarris called "a genuine concern with the wondrous inner life of lovers in the midst of adversity." Above all, this faith in the enchanted complicity of sentiment is borne out in three films starring Margaret Sullavan—*Little Man, What Now?, Three Comrades,* and *The Mortal Storm.* Just as Borzage ended the decade with Sullavan, so he had begun with Janet Gaynor—in *Seventh Heaven, Street Angel,* and *Lucky Star.* Among the rest, he emphasized the romantic undertones of Hemingway's *A Farewell to Arms* (with Gary Cooper and Helen Hayes); directed Mary Pickford's last movie, *Secrets;* made *Man's Castle* as true a picture of hope amid the Depression as *You Only Live Once* (37, Fritz Lang) is of fatalism; directed Dietrich in her best non-Sternberg film, *Desire;* and teamed Jean Arthur and Charles Boyer in the uncanny *History Is Made at Night.* That film, beginning as a romantic comedy but turning to tragedy once love has been proved, is typical of Borzage's serene confidence in the imagination when faced by material destruction.

The delicate pathos of *Three Comrades* should not conceal the chance that it might have been better still. Its central scenarist was Scott Fitzgerald, harrowed by the way MGM and his producer, Joseph Mankiewicz, handled the script: "Oh, Joe, can't producers ever be wrong? I'm a good writer—honest. I thought you were going to play fair." Fitzgerald's letters show some of the things lost between script and film, and certainly *Three Comrades* is the bones of a marvelous, Nicholas

Ray–like movie.

Borzage's political intuition is reliable, even if he treats it in conventional romantic terms. *The Mortal Storm* is a more perceptive and frightening study of fascism than, say, *The Great Dictator* (40, Charles Chaplin) or the Capra films. The shot of James Stewart and Margaret Sullavan, emotionally and philosophically hemmed in by a forest of saluting arms, is typical of Borzage's faith that love is a manifestation of political nature.

In recent years, at festivals, he has been recognized as a master.

The Boulting Brothers:
John (1913–85), b. Bray, England, and
Roy (1913–2001), b. Bray, England
Roy—1938: *The Landlady* (s); *Ripe Earth* (s); *Seeing Stars* (s); *Consider Your Verdict* (s). 1939: *Trunk Crime* (s). 1940: *Inquest; Pastor Hall; Dawn Guard* (s). 1942: *Thunder Rock; They Serve Abroad.* 1943: *Desert Victory* (d). 1944: *Tunisian Victory* (codirected with Frank Capra) (d). 1945: *Burma Victory* (d). 1947: *Fame Is the Spur.* 1948: *The Guinea Pig.* 1951: *Singlehanded.* 1954: *Seagulls Over Sorrento.* 1955: *Josephine and Men.* 1956: *Run for the Sun.* 1957: *Happy Is the Bride; Brothers in Law.* 1959: *I'm All Right, Jack; Carlton-Browne of the F.O.* 1960: *Suspect; A French Mistress.* 1966: *The Family Way.* 1968: *Twisted Nerve.* 1970: *There's a Girl in My Soup.* 1973: *Soft Beds, Hard Battles.* 1979: *The Last Word.* 1985: *The Moving Finger* (TV); *Brothers-in-Law* (TV).

John—1945: *Journey Together.* 1947: *Brighton Rock.* 1950: *Seven Days to Noon.* 1951: *The Magic Box.* 1956: *Private's Progress.* 1957: *Lucky Jim.* 1963: *Heavens Above!.* 1965: *Rotten to the Core.* 1979: *The Number.*

Twin brothers, the Boultings worked in harness whenever possible, and their work—good and bad alike—is interchangeable. They formed Charter Productions in 1938, with John producing for Roy, and after the war took turns swapping the roles of director and producer and often collaborating on the scripts. Their wartime documentaries are distinguished and, between them, they have mustered a clutch of economical, tightly plotted films, strong on local atmosphere and full of good acting: *Thunder Rock*, from Robert Ardrey's play, uses the lighthouse setting very well; *Singlehanded* exploits the potential of C. S. Forester's *Brown on Resolution; Run for the Sun* is an energetic and violent reworking of *The Hounds of Zaroff*, well played by Richard Widmark, Jane Greer, and Trevor Howard; *Brighton Rock* has the tang of fish and chips and captures British gang society with unusual accuracy; while *Seven Days to Noon* is a brilliant idea that exerts every extra half screw of tension. But, on the debit side, they both make limp, contrived comedies, bare of wit and true character, that encourage insecure comedians to overact. The later work of Roy is especially disappointing and the comedy series of *Private's Progress, Brothers in Law, I'm All Right, Jack,* and *Carlton-Browne of the F.O.* plays up to the most slapdash, fuddled views that the British like to hold of themselves. Since then, he has shown an unwelcome taste for brazen nastiness in *Twisted Nerve*, and established which twin he is by marrying its star, Hayley Mills—though the union did not last.

Clara Bow (1905–65),
b. Brooklyn, New York
Silent cinema pushed emotional character to extremes that could become prisons. Mary Pickford was sentimental, Gloria Swanson adventurous, Lillian Gish noble, and Pola Negri brooding. Clara Bow's identity was chiefly that of sexual advertisement. Her appeal may no longer operate urgently, but she is the first actress intent on arousing sexual excitement who is not ridiculous. She still looks pretty and her fevered agitation—the fluttering eyes, the restless fingering of men, and teasing angled glances—does seem to speak for the liberated lascivious energies of the new American girl of the twenties. She has a speed that is sensual. She is very funny. And she knows, and likes, more than her movies can admit.

For Bow herself and the women she played, the 1920s was an age of brutal but enticing opportunism: a girl with bounce, or energy, could make it, provided she had that much-talked-about but still hidden ingredient—"it"—a willingness. "It" was the promise of sex; and it was a ploy of advertising. Thus Bow's career demonstrates the busy collaboration of movies and publicity. She was the first mass-market sex symbol, and she complained that it was "a heavy load to carry, especially when one is very tired, hurt, and bewildered." Her hurt was a dry run for that awaiting Marilyn Monroe, whose mother came of sexual age in Bow's brief glory. Bow's mother and Marilyn's had something else in common: mental illness.

Clara Bow won a beauty contest and by 1922 she was in pictures: a tiny part in *Beyond the Rainbow* (22, W. Christy Cabanne); and a better one in *Down to the Sea in Ships* (23, Elmer Clifton). She was then signed up by B. P. Schulberg who worked her very hard in a succession of cheap films and loan-outs. B.P.'s son, Budd, has said that Bow was none too bright—"an irresistible . . . little know-nothing." But on-screen, she had a very knowing eye; if nothing else, she understood being photographed. The best films of this time are *Grit* (24, Frank Tuttle); *Black Oxen* (24, Frank Lloyd); *Wine* (24, Louis Gasnier); *Helen's Babies* (25, William A. Seiter); *Eve's Lover* (25, Roy del

Ruth); *Kiss Me Again* (25, Ernst Lubitsch); *The Plastic Age* (25, Wesley Ruggles); and *My Lady of Whims* (26, Dallas M. Fitzgerald).

Then, in 1926, Schulberg and Bow moved together to Paramount and her status improved: *Dancing Mothers* (26, Herbert Brenon); *Mantrap* (26, Victor Fleming); and *Kid Boots* (26, Tuttle). Next year, she was Betty Lou, the shop girl, who wows her boss, Antonio Moreno, in *It* (27, Clarence Badger). The film had the sixty-year-old Elinor Glyn appearing to explain what "It" was. But Bow carried the weight of education like a lipstick butterfly veering between old adages and fresh opportunities.

For the next three years, Clara Bow was a top star: *Children of Divorce* (27, Lloyd); *Rough House Rosie* (27, Frank Strayer); as an ambulance driver in *Wings* (27, William Wellman); *Hula* (27, Fleming); *Get Your Man* (27, Dorothy Arzner); *Red Hair* (28, Badger), with a color sequence to show off Bow's own red curls; *Ladies of the Mob* (28, Wellman); *The Fleet's In!* (28, Malcolm St. Clair); *Three Weekends* (28, Badger), another Glyn script; *The Wild Party* (29, Arzner); *Dangerous Curves* (29, Lothar Mendes); and *The Saturday Night Kid* (29, Edward Sutherland).

Her career faltered in 1930. She was only twenty-five, but she had made forty-eight films. Sound exposed her rough Brooklyn accent, and curtailed her reckless energy, for the unwieldy apparatus meant she could not move about the set so freely. Most damaging was the backlash of bourgeois hypocrisy. She had to buy off an aggrieved wife, she was dogged by gambling debts, and in 1931 she sued her former secretary, Daisy DeVoe, for selling stories about Bow fucking movie stars and most of the USC football team. DeVoe was trying blackmail on Bow, and it is possible that the secretary was jealous of Bow's romance with cowboy actor Rex Bell. The court hearings were sensational, and lurid accounts of Bow's private life became common currency.

Her last good year was 1930: *True to the Navy*, *Love Among the Millionaires*, and *Her Wedding Night*—all directed by Frank Tuttle. *No Limit* (31, Tuttle) and *Kick In* (31, Richard Wallace) were neglected by a prudish public and her last two films were made for Fox: *Call Her Savage* (32, John F. Dillon) and *Hoopla* (33, Lloyd). Comeback attempts failed and she grew only in weight, reclusiveness, and melancholy, married to Bell, residing in Nevada, and suffering breakdowns. All so sad, and unlikely, if one looks again at her astonishing vibrance. It was people like Clara Bow who taught cameras how lucky they were.

Charles Boyer (1897–1978), b. Figeac, France
Although his screen image was often frivolous and lightweight, Boyer's career speaks for the durability of a dedicated professional. But he did more

than survive: he kept intact that very "continental," flirtatious waywardness that made him a Hollywood exotic. It is no small accomplishment to have maintained his rather vacant intimations of Gallic romance in the face of constant parody and imitation. Even at the height of his comic notoriety in America as *the* French lover, sighing with thoughts of "the Casbah," he was a terrific and generous actor.

It is not the easiest career to record, simply because of Boyer's ingenious pursuit of work in all quarters. He studied at the Sorbonne and the Paris Conservatoire and, in his twenties, was a star of the French stage and screen: *L'Homme du Large* (20, Marcel L'Herbier); *L'Esclave* (22, Georges Monca); *Le Grillon du Foyer* (25, Jean Manoussi); *Le Capitaine Fracasse* (27, Alberto Cavalcanti); and *La Ronde Infernale* (28, Luitz Morat). He then joined UFA to make French versions of German movies, only to be lured away by MGM to play in French versions of *The Trial of Mary Dugan* and *The Big House*. When these duplications were stopped, Paramount used Boyer in his first American film, *The Magnificent Lie* (31, Berthold Viertel). He went back to UFA but was at Paramount again in 1932 for *The Man From Yesterday* (Viertel) and at MGM for a small part in *Red-Headed Woman* (32, Jack Conway). A little bemused, he went back to UFA and thence to Paris where, at least, he was a lover in his own language: *L'Epervier* (33, L'Herbier); *Le Bonheur* (33, L'Herbier); *La Bataille* (33, Nicolas Farkas); and *Liliom* (33, Fritz Lang). Twentieth Century now called Boyer back to the United States for *Caravan* (34, Erik Charrell), another American flop. At this point, he put himself in Walter Wanger's hands and gradually built up his reputation for sultry romance: *Private Worlds* (35, Gregory La Cava); *Break of Hearts* (35, Philip Moeller); *Shanghai* (35, James Flood); in Paris, *Mayerling* (36, Anatole Litvak); opposite Dietrich in *The Garden of Allah* (36, Richard Boleslavsky); *History Is Made at Night* (37, Frank Borzage); *Tovarich* (37, Litvak); as Napoleon opposite Garbo in *Conquest* (37, Clarence Brown); back in France with Michele Morgan for *Orage* (37, Marc Allégret); with Hedy Lamarr in *Algiers* (38, John Cromwell). Wanger dropped Boyer, but the actor flourished, with Irene Dunne, in *Love Affair* (39, Leo McCarey) and *When Tomorrow Comes* (39, John Stahl).

Boyer was working in France when the war began and was sent back to the United States by the French authorities for his value as a propagandist. He then made *All This and Heaven Too* (40, Litvak); *Back Street* (41, Robert Stevenson); *Hold Back the Dawn* (41, Mitchell Leisen); *Appointment with Love* (41, William A. Seiter); *Tales of Manhattan* (42) and *Flesh and Fantasy* (43), both for Julien Duvivier; *The Constant Nymph* (43,

Edmund Goulding); one of his best roles, as the husband of Ingrid Bergman in *Gaslight* (44, George Cukor); *Together Again* (44, Charles Vidor); *The Confidential Agent* (45, Herman Shumlin); with Jennifer Jones in *Cluny Brown* (46, Ernst Lubitsch); *A Woman's Vengeance* (47, Zoltan Korda); with Bergman again in *Arch of Triumph* (48, Lewis Milestone). He went on to the New York stage and returned in 1951 as a clearly older man: *The Thirteenth Letter* (51, Otto Preminger); *The First Legion* (51, Douglas Sirk); and *The Happy Time* (52, Richard Fleischer).

After that, versatility was his watchword. In the early 1950s he began returning to France—for the magnificent *Madame de . . .* (53, Max Ophuls); *Nana* (55, Christian-Jaque); and *La Parisienne* (57, Michel Boisrond). For American TV, he was one of the founders of Four Star Playhouse and of a series, *The Rogues*. In the cinema, he kept up a stream of character parts: *The Cobweb* (55, Vincente Minnelli); *The Buccaneer* (57, Anthony Quinn); *Fanny* (60, Joshua Logan); *The Four Horsemen of the Apocalypse* (61, Minnelli); *Love Is a Ball* (62, David Swift); *A Very Special Favor* (65, Michael Gordon); *How to Steal a Million* (65, William Wyler); *Barefoot in the Park* (67, Gene Saks); *The Madwoman of Chaillot* (69, Bryan Forbes); *The April Fools* (69, Stuart Rosenberg); as the sage of sages in *Lost Horizon* (72, Charles Jarrott); *Stavisky* (74, Alain Resnais); and *A Matter of Time* (76, Minnelli).

Boyer killed himself just two days after his wife died. They had been married forty-four years. Their only child, a son, had killed himself in 1965. It was a mark of the integrity and lasting feeling in a man famous as a "continental" seducer.

Danny Boyle, b. Manchester, England, 1956
1994: *Shallow Grave*. 1996: *Trainspotting*. 1997: *A Life Less Ordinary*. 2000: *The Beach*. 2001: *Vacuuming Completely Nude in Paradise; Strumpet; Alien Love Triangle*. 2003: *28 Days Later*.

In *Shallow Grave* and *Trainspotting*, writer John Hodge and director Danny Boyle seemed to have achieved a wonderfully nasty edge—as cold as Edinburgh in winter, but as startling to the taste as your first sip of Laphroaig whisky. *Shallow Grave* was a kind of screwball *Repulsion*, much affected by its bleak (yet pretty) flat, with spiffy performances from Kerry Fox, Christopher Eccleston, and Ewan McGregor. *Trainspotting* (adapted from Irvine Welsh's novel) was an hilarious surreal fantasia on hard drugs—overrated at the time, perhaps, but a very striking movie.

So much for promise. *A Life Less Ordinary* was a title that seemed upside down: the setup was very weird but nowhere near life. And Ewan McGregor and Cameron Diaz together were not quite chemistry. Still, that was a minor misstep

compared with the lamentable *The Beach*, an attempt to exploit Leonardo DiCaprio that proved all the wrong ways to go with a movie career.

So, in effect, Boyle has to start again—and my guess is that his most likely ground is still Edinburgh. *Vacuuming* and *Strumpet* were headed in the right direction: rigorously cheap, scathing social satire, and a thousand miles from Hollywood.

John Brahm (Hans Brahm) (1898–1982),
b. Hamburg, Germany
1935: *Scrooge* (codirected with Henry Edwards). 1936: *The Last Journey* (codirected with Bernard Vorhaus); *Broken Blossoms*. 1937: *Counsel for Crime*. 1938: *Penitentiary; Girls' School*. 1939: *Let Us Live; Rio*. 1940: *Escape to Glory*. 1941: *Wild Geese Calling*. 1942: *The Undying Monster*. 1943: *Tonight We Raid Calais; Wintertime*. 1944: *The Lodger; Guest in the House*. 1945: *Hangover Square*. 1946: *The Locket*. 1947: *The Brasher Doubloon/The High Window; Singapore*. 1951: *The Thief of Venice*. 1952: *The Miracle of Fatima;* "The Secret Sharer," episode from *Face to Face*. 1953: *The Diamond Queen*. 1954: *The Mad Magician; Die Goldene Pest*. 1955: *Special Delivery/Von Himmel Gefallen; Bengazi*. 1957: *Hot Rods to Hell*.

Brahm was the son of German stage director Otto Brahm, and he worked in the Vienna and Berlin theatres until 1934. He then went to England where he made his first three films. In 1937 he left for Hollywood and for the next ten years he worked in America as an accomplished and careful director of nonsense. His modest but entertaining peak was with Laird Cregar in *The Lodger* and *Hangover Square*, sumptuous Fox soundstage evocations of the London of Mrs. Belloc Lowndes and Patrick Hamilton. The latter is especially worthwhile. Marvelously photographed by Joseph La Shelle and with a thunderously romantic score from Bernard Herrmann, it has Cregar as a composer driven to murder at the sound of discord. Inevitably, Linda Darnell is one of his victims, but not before her beauty has been made clear. Brahm's flamboyance comes fully into play when Cregar dumps her body on a huge Guy Fawkes bonfire. Later he dies himself, playing his terrible concerto, surrounded by fire. That special mood did not last long, and Brahm went into TV after a poor Ava Gardner romance, *Singapore*, and *The High Window*, a very Germanic Chandler adaptation, suffering from George Montgomery's Marlowe, but blessed by two untrustworthy women, Florence Bates and Nancy Guild.

Kenneth Branagh,
b. Belfast, Northern Ireland, 1960
1989: *Henry V.* 1991: *Dead Again*. 1992: *Swan*

Song (s); Peter's Friends. 1993: Much Ado About Nothing. 1994: Mary Shelley's Frankenstein. 1995: In the Bleak Midwinter. 1996: Hamlet. 1999: The Betty Schimmel Story. 2000: Love's Labour's Lost. 2003: Listening (s).

By the age of thirty, Branagh was being talked of in Britain as the new Olivier. (And Olivier was thirty in 1937, the moment of Fire Over England.) Branagh had rather more to offer: he had directed, acted in, and generally assembled his stock company for Henry V; he had been a whirling triumph on the English stage, not just as Shakespearean actor but in a variety of contemporary plays; and was the leader of the Renaissance Theatre Company, a roving operation that took on the classics with modern attack, and that asked established actors to do the directing. More than that, Branagh had the glorious and very droll Emma Thompson on his arm—rather more interesting, and challenging, support than Vivien Leigh offered Olivier.

Nevertheless, caution reigned. Branagh's Henry V is spectacular, youthful, brutal, and listless, next to the exquisite interplay of Globe, rolling Irish countryside, and the Beautiful Hours of the Duc de Berri in Olivier's film. Of course, in 1944–45, Henry V meant so much more—it could be romantic, timeless, and mercurial.

Beyond that, Dead Again was a stupidity in which Branagh demonstrated little more than lofty superiority to the genre. Peter's Friends was another film that seemed hardly worth the effort. Has Branagh begun to think hard enough about what the screen requires, or might sustain? Has his fabled daring come into focus? Even as actor, he has not yet managed the qualities he showed in High Season (87, Clare Peploe); A Month in the Country (87, Pat O'Connor); in the TV series adapted from Olivia Manning, Fortunes of War (87, James Cellan Jones)—or, in the most impressive work I have seen from him, his Oswald in a made-for-TV Ghosts (86, Elijah Moshinsky). Branagh also made an inexplicable cameo appearance as a Nazi in Swing Time (93, Thomas Carter).

His Much Ado was sunny, alfresco, robust, and nearly as popular as Olivier's Henry V. Whereupon, Branagh elected to direct Frankenstein with himself as the doctor and Robert De Niro as the monster.

It was one of the worst films of the decade, and nothing suggests that Branagh is either competent or interesting when detached from Shakespeare. His Hamlet was much praised, but is it really good value at nearly one hundred minutes longer than the Olivier version? Olivier, it seems to me, had a true sense of the movies, and that's what makes his Henry V and Hamlet more lasting, mercurial and atmospheric.

In other fields: Branagh's marriage to Emma Thompson ended. He had become involved with Helena Bonham Carter (who was in his Frankenstein film). So Branagh tried to extend his range and appeal, with not much success. He has been in so many failures, that it was truly startling to see his superb Heydrich in Conspiracy (01, Frank Pierson), proof that ability has survived.

His recent acting credits are: Iago opposite Larry Fishburne's Othello (95, Oliver Parker); Looking for Richard (96, Al Pacino); southern in The Gingerbread Man (98, Robert Altman); a priest in The Proposition (98, Lesli Linka Glatter); so harassed you wanted to rescue him from Celebrity (98, Woody Allen); with Bonham Carter in the risible The Theory of Flight (98, Paul Greengrass); The Dance of Shiva (98, Jamie Payne); Wild Wild West (99, Barry Sonnenfeld); How to Kill Your Neighbor's Dog (00, Michael Kalesniko); Rabbit-Proof Fence (01, Phillip Noyce).

But he was good again as Shackleton (01, Charles Sturridge)—playing the hero. That and his Heydrich, in Conspiracy (01, Frank Pierson), leave room for hope. He was in Rabbit-Proof Fence (02, Phillip Noyce), and Harry Potter and the Chamber of Secrets (02, Chris Columbus).

Marlon Brando, b. Omaha, Nebraska, 1924

Educated at Shattuck Military Academy and the drama workshop of the New School for Social Research in New York, Brando came to movies from an uncertain Broadway career that culminated in his astonishing Stanley Kowalski in A Streetcar Named Desire (1947). There had never been such a display of dangerous, brutal male beauty on an American stage—its influence can still be felt, in fashion photography and sport as well as acting. More than that, Brando was used by director Elia Kazan to steal a part of the play from Tennessee Williams's vision. In its debut, Streetcar was more about Stanley and less about Blanche than it would ever be again.

Brando was established for a generation of Americans as a great actor. A career like Olivier's seemed in prospect. Yet Brando has never returned to the stage, and even allowing for his disillusion with movies, we have to feel a kind of laziness, or a decisive lack of ambition, compared, say, with Olivier. Or is there something in Brando that found so much pretending unwholesome or dishonorable? In his withdrawal, as much as in his best work, he has altered the way we think of acting.

Although an introspective person, Brando was at first cast as inarticulate, morose, and often violent men: his debut as a paraplegic in The Men (50, Fred Zinnemann); the film of Streetcar (51, Elia Kazan); Viva Zapata! (52, Kazan); the hero of that strangely dated hymn to motor-bikes, The Wild One (53, Laslo Benedek); again for Kazan, as the ex-fighter in *On the Waterfront* (54), for which he won an Oscar. In all these roles, Brando seemed intent on immersion in the shambling and muttering details of butchered simplicity. It was the Method at work, and few actors have so conscientiously applied a theory to their films. In popular terms, Brando became synonymous with mumbling rebellion, and he clearly reacted against such a stereotype. There followed a calculated attempt to widen and lighten his range. A respectable Antony in Mankiewicz's *Julius Caesar* (53) was followed by a richly conceived but imperfectly conveyed Napoleon in *Desirée* (54, Henry Koster); by an enjoyable Sky Masterson in *Guys and Dolls* (55, Mankiewicz), singing nasally and dancing like a boxer; the Okinawan in *Teahouse of the August Moon* (56, Daniel Mann); and a blond German in *The Young Lions* (58, Edward Dmytryk).

Even then, Brando seemed more possessed of power than actually in control of it. Too often, he impersonated characters he had thought out, rather than discover them in himself. Today, for instance, it is hardly possible to be moved by him in *On the Waterfront* for noticing the vast technical trick he is performing. There was a major attempt to uncover the real Brando in the only film he has ever directed—*One-Eyed Jacks* (61), a slow, confused story of revenge, always threatening significance, which only seemed to bemuse its maker the more. Publicly troubled by the world and involved in politics, Brando made only four more worthwhile films in the next decade: *The Fugitive Kind* (59, Sidney Lumet)—and the best screen adaptation of Tennessee Williams, in which Brando is the fallen angel hero; as the sheriff, beaten by the townsmen, in Penn's *The Chase* (66); loftily original as the homosexual in *Reflections in a Golden Eye* (67, John Huston); and as the gradually disconcerted English aristocrat in Pontecorvo's *Queimada!* (68).

On the other hand, he was involved in a great deal of nonsense: *Bedtime Story* (64, Ralph Levy); *The Saboteur* (65, Bernhard Wicki); *The Appaloosa* (66, Sidney J. Furie); *Candy* (68, Christian Marquand); *The Night of the Following Day* (68, Hubert Cornfield); *The Nightcomers* (71, Michael Winner); enduring every longueur in *A Countess from Hong Kong* (67, Charles Chaplin); and hopelessly reinventing an English version of Clark Gable in *Mutiny on the Bounty* (62, Lewis Milestone).

Despite so many failed or wrongheaded films, Brando still commanded total respect and attention. Even if his own uncertainty had never allowed him to dominate a whole film, he was capable of moments—like that in *The Chase* when he watches the wild horses pass by in the night— that excused everything. Then in the space of a year he reaffirmed his great talent, and took the disarray of his own career into the heart of a film. *The Godfather* (71, Francis Ford Coppola) permitted him an exercise in grand impersonation, as Don Corleone, the aging Mafia leader. Brando reveled in the careful assembly of an old man, even if he despised the limits of the film and of a Hollywood that could reward him for it with the best actor Oscar. *The Godfather* was always a resoundingly safe film, even if it may have restored Brando's confidence. There was, on the other hand, great risk in *Last Tango in Paris* (72, Bernardo Bertolucci), an uncompromising portrait of lost middle age, a film that deliberately drew on Brando's self and that insisted on a unique sexual participation from its actors. It is a tribute to Brando's unceasing dignity that he has striven to seem a true person on film, not gilded by attractiveness or reputation. *Last Tango* succeeds on many levels, but not least as an accurate and disturbing presentation of the cinema's most preoccupied actor.

He was less eager to work by now, but he had lost nothing of that power to transform a film and carry a project that needs creative daring. Could *The Missouri Breaks* (76, Penn) have been so rich and strange a movie, so open to whim and digression, so Shandyan, without Brando? His Robert E. Lee Clayton is a man of many parts, voices, and hats—the notebook of an actor, even—but truly frightening in that we believe he could do anything at any moment. Only Brando could have made the shameless pansy so lethal. But scores of other actors could have brought as much solemn, misguided presence to *Superman* (78, Richard Donner), and *Apocalypse Now* (79, Coppola) needed Klaus Kinski or Robert Duvall.

Our loss of Brando has become commonplace by now: he has suffered personal tragedy and family scandal; there was an absurd, yet half-gloating interview with Connie Chung; there is his monstrous size, and the fitful urge to be absent, a memory, an idea only. Yet now and again, whim or money brings him back, and our loss is underlined. He was wasted in *The Formula* (80, John G. Avildsen); he was eccentric in *A Dry White Season* (89, Euzhan Palcy). But all of a sudden he was enchanting and professional in *The Freshman* (90, Andrew Bergman), kidding his Corleone past and as dainty as Dumbo on the ice rink.

If Brando's status declined even further in the nineties, it had a lot to do with his mean-spirited and shortsighted autobiography, *Songs My Mother Taught Me*, published in 1994, full of his petty stories of stolen advantage. It exposed a small mind in hideous contrast with the overlarge body. There were a few movies, but they were so bizarre and so casual they only underlined the tragedy: as Torquemada in *Christopher Columbus: The Discovery* (92, John Glen); *Don Juan DeMarco* (95, Jeremy Leven), which had moments of charm and fun; *The Island of Dr. Moreau* (96, John Frankenheimer); and then two films that found no theatrical release—*The Brave* (97, Johnny Depp) and *Free Money* (98, Yves Simoneau). In *The Score* (01, Frank Oz)—with De Niro and Edward Norton—he had to stay seated most of the time, sighing between phrases. We know the feeling.

Pierre Brasseur (Pierre Espinasse) (1905–72), b. Paris

The son of an actress, the father of an actor, Brasseur's heyday was celebrated by his performance as Frederick Lemaître in *Les Enfants du Paradis* (44, Marcel Carné). In part one of that film, when a feud disrupts the stage performance, Brasseur/Lemaître is into the lion's skin in a trice, a replacement before the need for one is appreciated, with the droll warning, "Once you get me on the stage, you'll never get me off." The early Brasseur is generally inspired by that extrovert panache: a handsome Mr. Punch, always mocking the actor's need for sham. (*Kean* was written by Sartre for Brasseur.) It was a long career—onstage and screen, as playwright as well as actor—with more than his fair share of worthwhile films: *Madame Sans-Gêne* (25, Leonce Perret); *La Fille de l'Eau* (25, Jean Renoir, sadly, the only time they worked together); *Les Deux Timides* (25, René Clair); *Claudine à l'École* (28); *Quick* (32, Robert Siodmak); *Café de Paris* (33); *Le Sexe Faible* (34, Siodmak); *Vous n'avez Rien à Déclarer?* (36, Leo Joannon and Yves Allégret); *Pattes de Mouches* (36, Jean Gremillon); *Quai des Brumes* (38, Carné); *Jeunes Timides* (41, Allégret); *Lumière d'Été* (42, Gremillon); *Adieu Léonard* (43, Pierre Prévert); *Le Pays sans Étoiles* (44, Georges Lacombe); *Les Portes de la Nuit* (46, Carné); *Pétrus* (46, Marc Allégret); *Les Amants de Vérone* (48, André Cayatte); *Portraît d'un Assassin* (49, Bernard Roland); *Maître Après Dieu* (50, Louis Daquin); *Les Mains Sales* (51, Fernard Rivers); *Barbe-Bleue* (51, Christian-Jaque); *Le Plaisir* (52, Max Ophuls); *La Tour de Nèsle* (54, Abel Gance); *Oasis* (54, Y. Allégret); *Napoléon* (55, Sacha Guitry); *Porte des Lilas* (57, Clair); then startlingly somber and repressed as the conventional doctor in *La Tête Contre les Murs* (58, Georges Franju); *La Loi* (58, Jules Dassin); as the father/surgeon in *Eyes Without a Face* (59, Franju); *Candide* (60, Norbert Carbonnaux); *I Bell'-Antonio* (60, Mauro Bolognini); *Dialogue des Carmelites* (60, Philippe Agostini); *L'Affaire Nina B.* (61, Siodmak); *Pleins Feux sur l'Assassin* (61, Franju); *Vive Henri IV, Vive l'Amour* (61, Claude Autant-Lara); *Les Bonnes Causes* (63, Christian-Jaque); *Le Magot de Josefa* (63, Autant-Lara); *La Vie de Château* (65, Jean-Paul Rappeneau); *Un Mondo Nuovo* (65, Vittorio de Sica); *King of Hearts* (66, Philippe de Broca); *Les Oiseaux Vont Mourir au Pérou* (68,

Romain Gary); *Goto, l'Ile d'Amour* (68, Walerian Borowczyk); and *Les Mariés de l'An II* (71, Rappeneau).

Walter Brennan (1894–1974), b. Swampscott, Massachusetts

Brennan had been Hollywood's preeminent "oldtimer" for so long that his real age hardly seemed relevant. But now he has gone the unsentimental way of all Hawks heroes. When he approaches any pearly gates, he may wonder if St. Peter is a cantankerous old man with a shotgun who insists on the password. Three times Brennan won the supporting actor Oscar—for *Come and Get It* (36, Wyler and Hawks), *Kentucky* (38, David Butler), and *The Westerner* (41, Wyler). What, then, should he have won for *To Have and Have Not* (44, Hawks), *My Darling Clementine* (46, John Ford), *Red River* (48, Hawks), *The Far Country* (55, Anthony Mann), and *Rio Bravo* (59, Hawks)? His Stumpy in *Rio Bravo* is the culmination of the loyal, crabby old man he had played for twenty years, the veteran who must improvise a way of sharing in the heroics that occupy the younger members of the circle. It is a performance that has very little to do with old age. Indeed, it is intensely artificial, an Arcadian dream of romance saving man from decline and debility.

He began in films in 1923 after service in the First World War and after having made and lost a fortune in real estate. The decisive impact on his career was an accident in 1932 that knocked out his teeth. Ever afterwards, he had a great asset for any comic support—false teeth—that he removed or restored from part to part. In his last dozen or so years he reclined in children's films, but from 1930 to 1960 he was constantly in films of high quality. As well as those already mentioned, the list includes: *King of Jazz* (30, J. Anderson); *Man on the Flying Trapeze* (35, Clyde Bruckman); *Wedding Night* (35, King Vidor); *The Bride of Frankenstein* (35, James Whale); *Barbary Coast* (35, Hawks); *Three Godfathers* (36, Richard Boleslavsky); *These Three* (36, Wyler); *Fury* (36, Fritz Lang); *Banjo on My Knee* (37, John Cromwell); *The Buccaneer* (38, Cecil B. De Mille); *The Adventures of Tom Sawyer* (38, H. C. Potter and Norman Taurog); *Stanley and Livingstone* (39, Henry King); *The Story of Vernon and Irene Castle* (39, Potter); *Northwest Passage* (40, Vidor); *Sergeant York* (41, Hawks); *Meet John Doe* (41, Frank Capra); *Swamp Water* (41, Jean Renoir); *Pride of the Yankees* (42, Sam Wood); *The North Star* (43, Lewis Milestone); *Hangmen Also Die* (43, Lang); *Home in Indiana* (44, Henry Hathaway); *The Princess and the Pirate* (44, Butler); *A Stolen Life* (46, Curtis Bernhardt); *Centennial Summer* (46, Otto Preminger); *Driftwood* (47, Allan Dwan); *Task Force* (49, Delmer Daves); *Surrender* (50, Dwan); tormenting Kirk Douglas with a song in *Along the Great Divide* (51, Raoul Walsh); and *Bad Day at Black Rock* (54, John Sturges).

George Brent (George Brendan Nolan) (1904–79), b. Shannonsbridge, Ireland

Warners in the thirties had the market cornered on tough guys and adventurers: Cagney, Bogart, Edward G. Robinson, Errol Flynn, George Raft. And they had Muni for prestige. But the best first or second lead they could come up with for their female stars was George Brent. (Gene Raymond and Ricardo Cortez were runners-up.) In less than a dozen years he appeared in eleven movies with Bette Davis (she said he had "an excitement he rarely was in the mood to transfer to the screen"): *The Rich Are Always With Us* (32, Alfred E. Green); *So Big* (32, William A. Wellman); *Housewife* (34, Green); *Front Page Woman* (35, Michael Curtiz); *Special Agent* (35, William Keighley); *The Golden Arrow* (36, Green); *Jezebel* (38, William Wyler); *Dark Victory* (39, Edmund Goulding); *The Old Maid* (39, Goulding); *The Great Lie* (41, Goulding); and *In This Our Life* (42, John Huston); six movies with Kay Francis: *The Keyhole* (33, Curtiz); *Living on Velvet* (35, Frank Borzage); *Stranded* (35, Borzage); *The Goose and the Gander* (35, Green); *Give Me Your Heart* (36, Archie Mayo); and *Secrets of an Actress* (38, Keighley); four movies with Barbara Stanwyck: *So Big*—he was her boyish young protégé, although offscreen he was three years older than she was; *The Purchase Price* (32, Wellman); *Baby Face* (33, Green); and *The Gay Sisters* (42, Irving Rapper); and four movies with Ruth Chatterton: *The Crash* (32, William Dieterle), *The Rich Are Always With Us* (32, Green), *Lilly Turner* (33, Wellman), and *Female* (33, Dieterle). He married Chatterton, too, although she was considerably older and a far bigger star—one of a series of romantic conquests that seems inexplicable today. He later married Ann Sheridan. In his mid-forties he was still making a big impression—on the very young Jane Powell, who played his daughter in the 1948 *Luxury Liner* (Richard Whorf).

Brent was typed as a romantic lead despite his somewhat porcine face and his sticklike acting—his performances divide neatly between those in which he's wearing a mustache and those in which he isn't; not much else distinguishes them. That he was borrowed by other studios for *their* female stars—most bizarrely by MGM for Garbo in *The Painted Veil* (34, Richard Boleslavsky) and Myrna Loy in *Stamboul Quest* (34, Sam Wood)—would seem impenetrably mysterious if we didn't know that Garbo, too, had responded to that off-screen "excitement" noted by Bette Davis.

Born in Ireland in 1904, the young Brent got mixed up with the Abbey Theatre and The Troubles, from the latter of which he soon fled to

America and Broadway (once arrested by the Black and Tans, he hid documents in his hair). In 1931, he went to Hollywood and made six insignificant films—one, a serial (*The Lightning Warrior*); four for Fox: *Under Suspicion* (A. F. Erickson); *Once a Sinner* (Guthrie McClintic); *Fair Warning* (Alfred L. Werker); and *Charlie Chan Carries On* (Hamilton McFadden); and two for Universal: *Ex-Bad Boy* (Vin Moore) and *Homicide Squad* (George Melford), before moving on to Warners. There—when he wasn't playing first or second fiddle to important ladies—he was expected to carry minor films with the help of equally minor actresses, such as Margaret Lindsay—*From Headquarters* (34, Dieterle); Jean Muir—*Desirable* (34, Mayo); Josephine Hutchinson—*The Right to Live* (35, Keighley) and *Mountain Justice* (37, Curtiz); Beverly Roberts—*God's Country and the Woman* (37, Keighley); Anita Louise—*The Go-Getter* (37, Busby Berkeley, his first nonmusical); Doris Weston—*Submarine D-1* (37, Lloyd Bacon); Virginia Bruce—*The Man Who Talked Too Much* (40, Vincent Sherman); Brenda Marshall—*South of Suez* (40, Lewis Seiler) and *You Can't Escape Forever* (42, Jo Graham). During this period he played in several highly respectable films—*42nd Street* (33, Bacon), *The Rains Came* (39, Clarence Brown), and, with Merle Oberon in the roles originally taken by William Powell and Kay Francis, in *'Til We Meet Again*, Edmund Goulding's effective 1940 remake of his memorable tearjerker, *One Way Passage*. He also appeared in *They Call it Sin* (32, Thornton Freeland); *Miss Pinkerton* (32, Bacon); *Weekend Marriage* (32, Freeland); *Luxury Liner* (33, Lothar Mendes—not the one with Jane Powell); *Private Detective 62* (33, Curtiz); *In Person* (35, William Seiter); *Snowed Under* (36, Ray Enright); *The Case Against Mrs. Ames* (36, Seiter); *More Than a Secretary* (36, Green) *Gold Is Where You Find It* (38, Curtiz); *Racket Busters* (38, Bacon); *Wings of the Navy* (39, Bacon); *The Fighting 69th* (40, Keighley); *Adventures with Diamonds* (40, George Fitzmaurice); *Honeymoon for Three* (41, Bacon); *They Dare Not Live* (41, James Whale); *International Lady* (41, Tim Whelan); *Twin Beds* (42, Whelan); and *Silver Queen* (42, Bacon).

After a short break during the war, he came back for a few major pictures: with Hedy Lamarr in *Experiment Perilous* (44, Jacques Tourneur); with Joan Fontaine in *The Affairs of Susan* (45, Seiter); with Stanwyck in *My Reputation* (46, Curtis Bernhardt); a mad killer, for once, threatening Dorothy McGuire in *The Spiral Staircase* (46, Robert Siodmak); with Claudette Colbert and Orson Welles in *Tomorrow Is Forever* (46, Irving Pichel).

Then the slide began. In 1946, *Lover Come Back* (Seiter) and *Temptation* (Pichel). In 1947, *Slave Girl*, with Yvonne de Carlo and a talking camel named Lumpy (Charles Lamont); *The Corpse Came C.O.D.* (Henry Levin); *Out of the Blue* (Leigh Jason); and *Christmas Eve/Sinners' Holiday* (Edwin L. Marin). In 1948, the Jane Powell *Luxury Liner* and *Angel on the Amazon* (John H. Auer). In 1949, *Red Canyon* (George Sherman); *Illegal Entry* (Frederick de Cordova); *The Kid from Cleveland* (Herbert Kline); and *Bride for Sale* (William D. Russell). Nothing in 1950. In 1951, he was second-billed to Cesar Romero in *F.B.I. Girl* (William Berke). In 1952, *Man Bait* (Terence Fisher) and *Montana Belle* (Allan Dwan). In 1953, *Tangier Incident* (Lex Landers) and *Mexican Manhunt* (Rex Bailey). Three years later, a cameo in *Death of a Scoundrel* (56, Charles Martin). The rest was silence, except, amazingly, a brief appearance twenty-two years later as Judge Gesell in a Watergate recap, *Born Again* (78, Irving Rapper).

Eighty-eight films—the wonders of withheld interest!

Robert Bresson, (1907–99),
b. Bromont-Lamothe, France
1934: *Les Affaires Publiques.* 1943: *Les Anges du Péché.* 1945: *Les Dames du Bois de Boulogne.* 1950: *Le Journal d'un Curé de Campagne/Diary of a Country Priest.* 1956: *Un Condamné à Mort S'est Échappé/A Man Escaped.* 1959: *Pickpocket.* 1961: *Le Procès de Jeanne d'Arc.* 1966: *Au Hasard, Balthazar.* 1967: *Mouchette.* 1969: *Une Femme Douce/A Gentle Creature.* 1971: *Quatre Nuits d'un Rêveur.* 1974: *Lancelot du Lac.* 1977: *Le Diable Probablement/The Devil, Probably.* 1982: *L'Argent.*

Probably Bresson's gravity is so natural, his austerity so tranquil, that it is improper to attribute his slow productivity to the commercial shyness of such difficulty. The films themselves seem unaware of economy or complexity. They transcend any possible circumstances within which they might have been made, just as they are indifferent to contemporaneity. Bresson's world is one of faces, hands, detached views of human activity. They surpass beauty, in both intention and effect, and stress necessity. As if to prove the spiritual expressiveness of the blank face, Bresson has generally avoided professional actors and restrained "acting." The faces in his films are like those of spectators, stilled by contemplation. The director has also disliked the complicity of his actors; he often directs them minutely, insisting on a curiously placid intensity, but seldom informing them of the context or significance of a shot. Such a method stresses the privacy of minds, and Bresson has a unique gallery of proud, intractable, inaccessible creatures—some monsters of evil, some saints, one a donkey. And yet, his films unmistakably impress upon the viewer the universality that

overwhelms privacy. Bresson is a Catholic filmmaker, so much so that no one could easily think of Hitchcock as a spiritual director in comparison. Hitchcock's films do not readily warm to people. Bresson possesses a charity so great that liking is made to seem unnecessary. He is an example of pure cinema in the sense that he photographs reserved faces to evoke all the wildest emotions of the spirit. To see his films is to marvel that other directors have had the ingenuity to evolve such elaborate styles and yet restrict them to superficial messages. It might be said that watching Bresson is to risk conversion away from the cinema. His meaning is so clearly inspirational, and his treatment so remorselessly interior, that he seems to shame the extrinsic glamour and extravagance of movies. For that reason alone, he is not an easy director to digest. To go beyond admiration might be too near surrender. Although there is a matter-of-fact quality to his work, concentrated viewing brings out an extraordinary sense of passion. It is as if his characters are straight-faced for fear of exploding. Their human feelings are in turmoil with spiritual imperatives, and the struggle is as great as that in Dostoyevsky—one of Bresson's models.

As a young man, Bresson studied philosophy and painting. But in the mid-1930s, he worked as a scriptwriter and made *Les Affaires Publiques*, a comedy, for which he wrote the screenplay. He had writer credits also on *C'Etait un Musicien* (33, Frederic Zelnick), *Les Jumeaux de Brighton* (36, Claude Heymann), and *Courier Sud* (37, Pierre Billon), and was assistant to René Clair on the uncompleted *Air Pur* in 1939. After a year in a prisoner-of-war camp, he began his work as a director. *Les Anges du Péché*, set within a nunnery, had dialogue by Jean Giraudoux. Its radiance—photographed by Philippe Agostini—and its intramural concern with the worldly regrets of the nun may have seemed a part of wartime escapism. But there was no doubt about *Les Dames du Bois de Boulogne* being a landmark in cinema history. Taken from Diderot's *Jacques le Fataliste*, with dialogue by Jean Cocteau and a dreamy modern setting, the literary transposition was less important to Bresson than the first, triumphant use of abstraction in photographing people. Here, plainly, outward appearance was a formal shell for emotional and intellectual identity. The setting, though factual, was unreal; the emotional drama was not a symbol for deeper meanings, but an abstraction of them. *Les Dames* is still a modern film, and its influence on subsequent French cinema is far from exhausted.

Le Journal d'un Curé de Campagne, scripted by Bresson from the Bernanos novel, was made after a five-year interval. Ostensibly more religious in its following of the life and death of a young priest, it was Bresson's first serious use of "unknown"

actors and the first sign of the emotional undertones in his work. Few films so well suggest the
balance of self-determination and omniscience;
the pity and splendor of selfishness and sacrifice.
In that film, too, Bresson used a far more particu-
larized sense of the French countryside, even if
images and sounds were never merely naturalistic.
Thus, the raking of leaves—one of Bresson's finest
sound effects—is also a scathing of the soul. *Un
Condamné* is his most jubilant film, the successful
escape of a Frenchman from a Nazi prison, amazingly concentrated on the face in the cell and the
growth of faith there. The ritual of prison life
fades subtly into religious ceremony, while the use
of Mozart's C Minor Mass shows the extra spiritual power of the escape, fulfilling the earlier
litany of spoons scraping at woodwork and of distant firing squads.

Pickpocket was the first obvious resort to Dostoyevsky. It is near to the situation of *Crime and
Punishment,* using crime as a metaphor for pride,
and prison as a model of the soul. In all these
films, it was Bresson's ability to make his own
world that was most impressive. The Joan of Arc
film seemed something of a recession in that its
familiarity dissipated the searching attention that
Bresson demands.

Balthazar and *Mouchette* were great advances,
returning to a rural or provincial world, strangely
invaded by fragments of modernity, but really the
settings for elegies to resignation. The destruction
of the donkey, Balthazar, and the eventual suicide
of Mouchette are among the most distilled and
moving events in cinema. For the first time, Bresson seemed to have gone beyond Catholic dogma.
It is from this period that it becomes possible to
see an Eastern, mystical calm in his work. In their
account of suffering and of human reaction to it,
Balthazar and *Mouchette* appear now as his greatest works.

After that, Bresson used color, something that
once would have been unimaginable. He made
two films from Dostoyevsky and both show a special interest in femininity—Dominique Sanda's in
Une Femme Douce is arguably the first performance in Bresson's work, and none the worse for
that. Once again the subject for analysis is the way
distress and anguish in life have been clarified and
betrayed by suicide.

His work never slackened: *Lancelot* and *L'Argent* are magnificent studies of two human codes,
honor and greed, centuries apart, yet fraternal.

A short commentary on Bresson is a hopeless
task. He is a great director, even if no other great
director seems less intrigued by cinema itself. The
simplicity of his work, the sense in which he is cinema, comes in this runic motto—"there is only
one way of shooting people: from near and in
front of them, when you want to know what is
happening inside." Is that a true description of his

method? Or is Bresson perhaps rigorously divided
on what happens inside and on how much of it
interests him? His films are less predesigned than
ordered in advance: the conflict of faces in his
films is the montage of a parable in which every
measured item is part of the formal organization.
Bresson's is a cinema of demonstration, so broad
in its consequences that its worldly narrowness is
made irrelevant. The method is luminous and
utterly methodical—a perfect example of interior
meaning and exterior behavior.

Martin Brest, b. New York, 1951
1978: *Hot Tomorrow.* 1979: *Going in Style.* 1984:
Beverly Hills Cop. 1988: *Midnight Run.* 1992:
Scent of a Woman. 1998: *Meet Joe Black.* 2003:
Gigli.

Martin Brest has now lapsed into Bressonian
intervals between pictures—and creeping running time in the films themselves. *Scent of a
Woman,* for instance, was 157 minutes long,
which only drew attention to its many implausibilities. God knows how the project evolved out
of the 1974 Italian film, with script by the
admirable Bo Goldman. But the suggestion that
any army on earth would ever have made Al
Pacino a colonel still seems to me the greatest
comic coup in the picture. Maybe that's one reason why he won the Oscar. The film is not without
fun—and Brest can handle set pieces quite well,
as witness the amiable *Midnight Run* (a mere 122
minutes). Of course, *Beverly Hills Cop* was his
breakthrough, and the keystone of Brest's taste
for warped buddy pictures—a couple of guys who
have to learn to get on. He's certainly a Hollywood figure by now, and—in the present climate
for length—he may be planning on three, or four,
pictures. One harks back to the old-man panache
of *Going in Style* (96 minutes) fondly, for in truth
Brest makes modest entertainments that should
stay modest. Let's just note that *Meet Joe Black*
was 178 minutes—not that many people waited
that long.

Jeff Bridges, b. Los Angeles, 1949
Jeff Bridges is as close as the modern era has
come to Robert Mitchum. Which is to say that
Bridges works steadily, without any show of self-
importance or dedication, his natural sourness or
skepticism picking up weariness with the years.
He was never as handsome as Mitchum, nor does
he seem quite as ready to admit aging. Admit it,
he is not in Mitchum's class: he does not seem
capable of *The Night of the Hunter, Track of the
Cat,* or *Cape Fear.* Still, Bridges's reliability, his
skill and his hangdog, wounded grace are very
appealing in an era of self-glorying superstars.

As the son of actor Lloyd Bridges (and the
younger brother of Beau), he did the odd *Sea*

Hunt as a child. After military academy and the Coast Guard, he became a regular actor. He has paid his dues: *Halls of Anger* (70, Paul Bogart); *The Last American Hero* (73, Lamont Johnson); *Lolly Madonna XXX* (73, Richard C. Sarafian); *Thunderbolt and Lightfoot* (74, Michael Cimino); *Stay Hungry* (76, Bob Rafelson); *King Kong* (76, John Guillermin); *Somebody Killed Her Husband* (78, Johnson); two William Richert films—*Winter Kills* (79) and *The American Success Company* (79); as "Nick Ray" in *Heaven's Gate* (80, Cimino); *Kiss Me Goodbye* (82, Robert Mulligan); *Tron* (82, Steven Lisberger); actually filling a Mitchum role in *Against All Odds* (84, Taylor Hackford); *8 Million Ways to Die* (86, Hal Ashby); *The Morning After* (86, Sidney Lumet); nicely comic and foolish in *Nadine* (87, Robert Benton); *See You in the Morning* (89, Alan Pakula); *Texasville* (90, Peter Bogdanovich); and *The Fisher King* (91, Terry Gilliam).

On the other hand, he has always been ready for better material. He was wonderfully brash as Duane in the original *The Last Picture Show* (71, Bogdanovich)—it has often been his choice to play someone none too bright, and to do it easily and openly, without coyness or pathos. He was brilliant as the punk fighter in *Fat City* (72, John Huston); indeed, he brought Brando to mind at moments. *Bad Company* (72, Benton) was excellent. He rose to the challenge of Frankenheimer's TV *The Iceman Cometh* (73). He was very good in *Rancho Deluxe* (75, Frank Perry) and *Hearts of the West* (75, Howard Zieff).

But in the eighties, he turned in a number of performances that had a unique character: in *Cutter's Way* (81, Ivan Passer) he was utterly candid as the wastrel who longs to be better, heartbreaking in a great film; *Starman* (84, John Carpenter) was a brave venture; in *Jagged Edge* (85, Richard Marquand) he was truly deceptive; in *Tucker* (88, Francis Coppola), he had a manic exuberance that could have been learned from his director; and in *The Fabulous Baker Boys* (89, Steve Kloves) he was, at last, at Mitchum level—adult, pained, resigned, and angelic.

It would be pretty to think that in the next few years, as Bridges passes fifty, Hollywood will understand his true potential. He took big risks as the villain in *The Vanishing* (92, George Sluizer), and in *American Heart* (93, Martin Bell). He was at his very best as the stunned survivor in *Fearless* (93, Peter Weir) but just stunned in *Blown Away* (94, Stephen Hopkins).

The pretty hope turned to ash. Yet I find myself falling more in love with Bridges with each new bout of box-office chagrin. He grows deeper, stronger and more ironic as an actor. He is a model of stoicism, and a guarantee of the forlorn. I should add the discovery that he is also the taker of some of the best on-set still photographs I have

ever seen. As for the list, find a quiet corner and weep: a lovely performance in *Wild Bill* (95, Walter Hill); *White Squall* (96, Ridley Scott)—a very touching film; *The Mirror Has Two Faces* (96, Barbra Streisand)—a lesson in taking yourself too seriously; the rare, fragrant "Dude" in *The Big Lebowski* (98, Joel Coen); uncredited in *A Soldier's Daughter Never Cries* (98, James Ivory); in the truly spooky *Arlington Road* (99, Mark Pellington); *The Muse* (99, Albert Brooks); the inexplicable *Simpatico* (99, Matthew Warchus); a droll, snacking president—and nominated—in *The Contender* (00, Rod Lurie); and—could this be the hit?—with Kevin Spacey in *K-PAX* (01, Iain Softley). No.

He did *Masked & Anonymous* (03, Larry Charles), which had no chance but here at last, was this his hit, riding *Seabiscuit* (03, Garry Ross) to victory?

Albert R. Broccoli (1909–96), b. New York "Cubby" Broccoli won his Thalberg Award (1982), and holds his reputation, because of the extraordinary worldwide success, and longevity, of the James Bond films that he made in partnership with Harry Saltzman. What is worth stressing now, all those years after *Dr. No* (1962), is that Ian Fleming's Bond novels had been out and about for several years before they clicked on screen. In turn, the films are more comic, more gadget-prone, and less morose than the books. Where did that rescuing insight come from? There are several candidates: Broccoli-Saltzman, Sean Connery, the writer Richard Maibaum, and even Kevin McClory, an Irish writer and producer, trained by Mike Todd and John Huston, who has never quite given up his claim on the movie Bond.

Broccoli had worked in Hollywood without making much impact. But in the early fifties he went to England and made a partnership with Irving Allen (Warwick Pictures) that made adventure films with fading Hollywood stars: Alan Ladd in *The Red Beret* (53, Terence Young); *Hell Below Zero* (54, Mark Robson); *The Black Knight* (54, Tay Garnett); *A Prize of Gold* (55, Robson); *Cockleshell Heroes* (55, José Ferrer); *Safari* (56, Young); *Zarak* (57, Young); *Odongo* (57, John Gilling); *The Gamma People* (57, Gilling); *Fire Down Below* (57, Robert Parrish); *The Man Inside* (58, Gilling); *Killers of Kilimanjaro* (59, Richard Thorpe); and their class acts—*The Trials of Oscar Wilde* (60, Ken Hughes); *Johnny Nobody* (61, Nigel Patrick); *The Hellions* (62, Ken Annakin).

It was then that the Bond industry took over, moving from Connery to George Lazenby to Roger Moore to Timothy Dalton to Pierce Brosnan. On several occasions, one had reason for thinking that the series was over. But it keeps coming back, and Broccoli's daughter, Barbara, remains a vital part of the company, Eon Productions. On the other hand, you may take the view that the Bond pictures are essentially as banal as the films Broccoli helped produce in the 1950s.

The list is as follows: *Dr. No* (62, Young); *From Russia with Love* (63, Young); *Goldfinger* (64, Guy Hamilton); *Thunderball* (65, Young); *You Only Live Twice* (67, Lewis Gilbert); *On Her Majesty's Secret Service* (69, Peter R. Hunt); *Diamonds Are Forever* (71, Hamilton); *Live and Let Die* (73, Hamilton); *The Man with the Golden Gun* (74, Hamilton); *The Spy Who Loved Me* (77, Gilbert); *Moonraker* (79, Gilbert); *For Your Eyes Only* (81, John Glen); *Octopussy* (83, Glen); *A View to a Kill* (85, Glen); *The Living Daylights* (87, Glen); *Licence to Kill* (89, Glen); *GoldenEye* (95, Martin Campbell); and *The World Is Not Enough* (99, Michael Apted).

Matthew Broderick, b New York, 1962
Despite instinctive whimsy (that Matthew Broderick might be an offshoot of Broderick Crawford), he is actually the son of actor James Broderick and writer Patricia Broderick. At forty, he is still the epitome of all well-intentioned, nice-looking kids—though in fact he is securely married to Sarah Jessica Parker and has been an enormous hit on Broadway in the musical version of *The Producers* (where he had the Gene Wilder role). Still, it was some relief to find him in *Election* (98, Alexander Payne) as someone on the down curve of disillusion, getting puffy and overweight and generally being shafted. Can his looks ever really give the impression of being lived in? Or must he be elderly and baby-faced at the same time? It's a pressure that might suddenly set free the limitless banks of anger in a Broderick Crawford, say. In other words, good old whimsy somehow wants to see Matthew running amok.

He had earlier stage successes: for Neil Simon in *Brighton Beach Memoirs* and *Biloxi Blues,* and later in *How to Succeed in Business Without Really Trying.* He made his movie debut in *Max Dugan Returns* (83, Herbert Ross), but it was *WarGames* (83, John Badham) that made him, where he was a school kid hacking into Pentagon computers.

Then he did *Ladyhawke* (85, Richard Donner); *On Valentine's Day* (86, Ken Harrison); a big hit in *Ferris Bueller's Day Off* (86, John Hughes), still playing teenage at twenty-four; *Project X* (87, Jonathan Kaplan); *Biloxi Blues* (88, Mike Nichols); *Torch Song Trilogy* (88, Paul Bogart); *Family Business* (89, Sidney Lumet); as the commanding officer in *Glory* (89, Edward Zwick); *The Freshman* (90, Andrew Bergman); *Out on a Limb* (92, Francis Veber); *The Night We Never Met* (93, Warren Light); with Jack Lemmon in *A Life in the Theater* (93, Gregory Mosher); as Charles MacArthur in *Mrs. Parker and the Vicious Circle*

(94, Alan Rudolph); a voice on *The Lion King* (94, Roger Allers and Rob Minkoff).

He was in *The Road to Wellville* (94, Alan Parker); a voice on *Arabian Knight* (95, Richard Williams); rather good with Jim Carrey in *The Cable Guy* (96, Ben Stiller). In 1996, with his mother as cowriter, he wrote and directed *Infinity,* a pleasant film about the life of physicist Richard Feynman (*WarGames* indeed!). He was a little out of his element in *Addicted to Love* (97, Griffin Dunne); stranded in *Godzilla* (98, Roland Emmerich); and belittled as *Inspector Gadget* (99, David Kellogg); *Walking to the Waterline* (99, Matt Mulhern); *You Can Count on Me* (00, Kenneth Lonergan); as Professor Harold Hill in a TV *The Music Man* (01).

Charles Bronson (Charles Buchinsky), b. Ehrenfield, Pennsylvania, 1921
That face did not become an image until the age of fifty. It took that long for lines, sleepy eyes, and a drooping mustache to soften the sculptured Lithuanian rock often cast as an Indian. But, by 1970, the weathering process had confused shyness and menace, and there followed a brief glory as the dispenser of monumental violence, always with an expression of geological impassivity. Nevertheless, his four films for Michael Winner—*Chato's Land* (71), *The Mechanic* (72), *The Stone Killer* (73), and *Death Wish* (74)—had audiences cheering at the celebration of "justified" homicide. In the history of American film, they represent the legalized separation of violent energy and offended honor. They were cold-blooded pictures that relied on Bronson's impregnability—he might claim to be hurt, but he was immune to damage or doubt.

He was Buchinsky until 1954, a miner, in the navy, and then doing anything to pay for acting lessons. His debut was in *You're in the Navy Now* (51, Henry Hathaway) and he was also in *The Mob* (51, Robert Parrish); *Red Skies of Montana* (52, Joseph M. Newman); *My Six Convicts* (52, Hugo Fregonese); being beaten up by Katharine Hepburn in *Pat and Mike* (52, George Cukor); *House of Wax* (53, André de Toth); *Miss Sadie Thompson* (53, Curtis Bernhardt); *Crime Wave* (54, de Toth); *Tennessee Champ* (54, Fred M. Wilcox); *Apache* (54, Robert Aldrich); *Drum Beat* (54, Delmer Daves); *Vera Cruz* (54, Aldrich); *Big House, U.S.A.* (55, Howard W. Koch); *Jubal* (56, Daves); as Blue Buffalo in *Run of the Arrow* (57, Samuel Fuller); his first starring part in a poverty B picture, *Machine Gun Kelly* (58, Roger Corman), where his comic-book strength of feature suits the man's inner flaws; *Never So Few* (59, John Sturges); *The Magnificent Seven* (60, Sturges); *A Thunder of Drums* (61, Newman); *Kid Galahad* (62, Phil Karlson); *The Great Escape* (62, Sturges); *4 for Texas* (63, Aldrich); as the painter in *The Sandpiper* (65, Vincente Minnelli); *This Property Is Condemned* (66, Sydney Pollack); and *The Dirty Dozen* (67, Aldrich).

Short of stardom, he only got leading parts in several films made in Europe: *Guns for San Sebastian* (67, Henri Verneuil); *Farewell, Friend* (68, Jean Herman); *Villa Rides* (68, Buzz Kulik); *Once Upon a Time in the West* (68, Sergio Leone); *Twinky* (69, Richard Donner); *Le Passager de la Pluie* (69, René Clément); *You Can't Win 'Em All* (70, Peter Collinson); *Cold Sweat* (70, Terence Young); *Red Sun* (71, Young); *Someone Behind the Door* (71, Nicolas Gessner); and *The Valachi Papers* (72, Young).

He was a star now, but not young, not expressive, and so reticent a personality that his later films have not done very well. They were humdrum affairs, not much brightened by the regular presence of his wife, Jill Ireland: *Valdez the Halfbreed/Chino* (73, Sturges); *Mr. Majestyk* (74, Richard Fleischer); *Breakout* (75, Tom Gries); *Hard Times* (75, Walter Hill); *Breakheart Pass* (75, Gries); the more adventurous *From Noon Til Three* (75, Frank D. Gilroy); *St. Ives* (76, J. Lee Thompson); as General Shomron in *Raid on Entebbe* (76, Irvin Kershner); *The White Buffalo* (77, Thompson); and *Telefon* (77, Don Siegel).

He made *Love and Bullets* (79, Stuart Rosenberg); *Caboblanco* (80, Thompson); *Borderline* (80, Jerrold Freeman); *Death Hunt* (81, Peter Hunt); *Death Wish II* (82, Winner); *Ten to Midnight* (83, Thompson); *The Evil That Men Do* (84, Thompson); *Death Wish 3* (85, Winner); *Act of Vengeance* (86, John Mackenzie) for TV; *Murphy's Law* (86, Thompson); *Assassination* (87, Hunt); *Death Wish 4: The Crackdown* (87, Thompson); *Messenger of Death* (88, Thompson); and *Kinjite: Forbidden Subjects* (89, Thompson).

Jill Ireland died, of cancer, in 1990.

Since then, Bronson has done *The Indian Runner* (91, Sean Penn), *The Sea Wolf* (93, Michael Anderson) and the nasty *Death Wish V: The Face of Death* (94, Allan A. Goldstein). For TV, he did *Family of Cops* (95, Ted Kotcheff), with sequels.

Clive Brook (Clifford Brook) (1887–1974), b. London

The son of an opera singer, Brook was educated at Dulwich College. After working as a writer and violinist, he served with distinction in the First World War: that effortless reference to military service in *Shanghai Express* was based on Vimy Ridge. After the war, he became an actor, onstage, but principally in the British cinema: *Trent's Last Case* (20, Richard Garrick); *The Loudwater Mystery* (21, Norman MacDonald); *Daniel Deronda* (21, Walter Rowden); *Sonia* (21, Denison Clift); *Shirley* (22, A. V. Bramble); *Married to a Woman* (22, H. B. Parkinson); *Debt of Honor* (22, Maurice Elvey); *Through Fire and Water* (23, Thomas Bentley); *Royal Oak* (23, Elvey); *Woman to Woman* (23, Graham Cutts); *The White Shadow* (24, Cutts); and *The Passionate Adventure* (24, Cutts). He then went to America under contract to Thomas Ince: *Christine of the Hungry Heart* (24, George Archainbaud); *The Mirage* (24, Archainbaud); *Compromise* (25, Alan Crosland); *Enticement* (25, Archainbaud); *Seven Sinners* (25, Lewis Milestone); and *For Alimony Only* (26, William De Mille). Thereafter he worked generally for Paramount: *You Never Know Women* (26, William Wellman); *Barbed Wire* (27, Rowland V. Lee); *The Devil Dancer* (27, Fred Niblo); *French Dressing* (27, Allan Dwan); opposite Clara Bow in *Hula* (27, Victor Fleming); as "Rolls Royce" in *Underworld* (27, Josef von Sternberg); *The Perfect Crime* (28, Bert Glennon); *The Yellow Lily* (28, Alexander Korda); *A Dangerous Woman* (29, Lee); *The Four Feathers* (29, Merian Cooper and Ernest Schoedsack); *Anybody's Woman* (30, Dorothy Arzner), with Ruth Chatterton; *Slightly Scarlet* (30, Louis Gasnier); *Sweethearts and Wives* (30, Clarence Badger); *East Lynne* (31, Frank Lloyd); and *Tarnished Lady* (31, George Cukor). It was then that Brook played "Doc," or Captain Harvey, in *Shanghai Express* (32, von Sternberg). Repeated viewings of that masterpiece impress upon one the mock heroic stylization in Brook's underplaying. His restraint was oddly sexy, his disdain alluring. Few actors have ever engaged so musically in cross talk with Dietrich; their conversations in that film are not just one of the achievements of early sound, but immensely influential of the Hawks pictures and *Johnny Guitar,* for instance. After a wintry *Sherlock Holmes* (32, William K. Howard) and *Cavalcade* (33, Lloyd), Brook returned to England to make *The Dictator* (35, Victor Saville); *Love in Exile* (36, Alfred Werker); *Action for Slander* (37, Saville); *The Lonely Road* (37, James Flood); *The Ware Case* (39, Robert Stevenson); *Return to Yesterday* (39, Stevenson); *Convoy* (40, Penrose Tennyson); *Freedom Radio* (40, Anthony Asquith); *Breach of Promise* (42, Harold Huth); *The Flemish Farm* (43, Jeffrey Dell); and *Shipbuilders* (44, John Baxter). In 1945, he directed himself and Bea Lillie in the delightful *On Approval,* and then opted for the theatre. He made an engagingly tetchy reappearance in *The List of Adrian Messenger* (63, John Huston).

Sir Peter Brook, b. London, 1925

1953: *The Beggar's Opera.* 1960: *Moderato Cantabile.* 1962: *Lord of the Flies.* 1966: *The Persecution and Assassination of Jean-Paul Marat, as performed by the inmates of the Asylum of Charenton, under the direction of the Marquis de Sade.* 1967: "Red, White and Zero," an episode from *The Ride of the Valkyries* (unreleased). 1968: *Tell Me Lies.* 1969: *King Lear.* 1978: *Meetings With*

Remarkable Men. 1983: *La Tragédie de Carmen.* 1989: *The Mahabharata.*

Very few men who have worked as directors in British cinema have spoken so penetratingly on the experience of making and watching films as Peter Brook. It is a misfortune for the cinema that it has never overcome his primary commitment to theatre. Yet one obvious reason for that is the way Brook's persistent interest in the potential of the relationship between performance and audience has found more creative room in the theatre than it could in the British cinema. Only *The Beggar's Opera* was really made from within the industry, and that hedged by the resort to theatrical heritage and by the prestigious but distracting presence of Olivier as Macheath. *Moderato Cantabile* is a French film, made partly out of a faith in the "denser impression of reality" possible in the new French cinema. *Lord of the Flies* was once intended as a Sam Spiegel production. But big money grew fearful of the project and it was eventually filmed as a low-cost, independent, collaborative venture. Since then, apart from a very short episode in the abortive *Ride of the Valkyries*, Brook's films have been transpositions of notable theatrical productions. His *King Lear*, with Paul Scofield, is in the dismal tradition of film records of great moments of the theatre—clumsy, rather grubby looking, and serving to expose stage actors as vulnerable show-offs. Not as garish as the film of Olivier's *Othello*, it is still a sad throw-off from a man who took as much care with the cameras as Brook did on *Moderato Cantabile*. As for the films of *Marat-Sade* and *Tell Me Lies* (from the stage production *US*), they are striking despite the inevitable diminution of an essentially theatrical tension in which the spectator is addressed or threatened from the stage.

In both cases, the films seem inspired by a vigorous intellectual and political concern with the material, rather than an initial conception of it in film terms. *Marat-Sade* has a dazzling lightness in its images, but only as a simpleminded contrast to the community of the insane. Brook's career still seems like that of an intelligent, creative man interested in cinema but not possessed by it. He responds to exciting material, but appears unable to generate it from within himself or find a way of expressing it in which the form and the content are inseparable. Just as, while at university, he made a film of Sterne's *Sentimental Journey* that is really an admiration and interpretation of that great work, so his *Lord of the Flies* springs from the wish to bring to the screen a "great modern novel," whereas the screen reveals it as a pretentious and unconvincing allegory.

That seems like a traditionally British intellectual approach to the cinema, preoccupied by theme and seeing the moving image as simply transport for it. But Brook plainly does appreciate many of the basic qualities of film as a language. In 1963 he gave an interview in which he flatly identified Godard as the most important contemporary director, and recognized the way that improvisation and an easier system of working supported Godard. For instance, he picked on two great British failings: "British films are financed and planned and controlled in such a way that everything goes into this crippling concept of screenplay. And a breakthrough can only come about thoroughly and satisfactorily if the working conditions can be freed, so that smaller crews and lower budgets give people the opportunity to take more time, and to go back on their tracks if necessary, without anyone worrying them"; and "We've been prisoners for years of a naive simplification of what realism means hence the British cinema view that it is all a matter of art direction, something to be achieved by being more honest than the Americans in the amount of rain that beats upon a heroine."

The concern with interior truth, with Godard's layers of realism, and a sense of the moving image's creation of it are the qualities so often lacking in British films. *Moderato Cantabile* was a deliberate attempt to escape academicism, and to make a film of a subject that no British money would have supported. Sadly, it is a dull film, despite the sensitive wide-screen exploration of a French provincial town and despite the presence of Jeanne Moreau. It is a story about passion, and although Brook, as director of the actress, may have grasped that, his camera remains polite and staid. The film, in consequence, is ladylike and reticent when it should have been painful.

Albert Brooks (Einstein),
b. Los Angeles, 1947
1979: *Real Life.* 1981: *Modern Romance.* 1985: *Lost in America.* 1991: *Defending Your Life.* 1996: *Mother.* 1999: *The Muse.*

It's a subject for Woody Allen: you have this very smart, anxiety-ridden comedian—the son of a comic, too—who takes the prudent early step of changing his name. Because how can anyone else get away with being Albert Einstein? So he becomes Albert Brooks—as in Brooks Brothers, mainstream. He does stand-up, and he makes a series of funny short films for *Saturday Night Live.* Gradually he gets to make his own features—writing, acting, and directing—which are about a smart, jittery guy who isn't Albert Einstein. They're about the way reality turns into living theatre; about failures in love, and anything else; failures in general; guilt; your mother; and whether you deserve a muse. And everyone says, "Oh, kinda like Woody Allen?" So Albert never gets hits or awards and never quite makes his unequivocal knockout film. And the anxiety only grows. Maybe he should have stuck with "Einstein"?

He also turns in nice acting jobs: as the bumptious campaign worker in *Taxi Driver* (76, Martin Scorsese); *Private Benjamin* (80, Howard Zieff); *Unfaithfully Yours* (84, Zieff); *Broadcast News* (87, James L. Brooks); *I'll Do Anything* (94, Brooks)— in which he's very funny working for a director named Brooks. It gives you the shakes if you think about it too much. He was good again, with Leelee Sobieski, in *My First Mister* (01, Christine Lahti); *The In-Laws* (03, Andrew Fleming).

James L. Brooks,
b. North Bergen, New Jersey, 1940
1983: *Terms of Endearment.* 1987: *Broadcast News.* 1994: *I'll Do Anything.* 1997: *As Good As It Gets.*

Jim Brooks is living proof that American television, week after week, can deliver smart, well-written, beautifully played comedy series that are devoted to being decent and humane without seeming smug or idiotic. This is an extraordinary achievement, and one to be borne in mind whenever the mood takes us to think the worst of TV. With Allan Burns, three seasons in a row (74–75, 75–76, 76–77—years of turmoil), Brooks won the Emmy for best comedy series as executive producer of *The Mary Tyler Moore Show.* Then, with other collaborators, he did the same thing another three years in a row (78–79, 79–80, 80–81—more years of the same) with *Taxi.* And that's not all.

He graduated from NYU and joined CBS as a newswriter before becoming a documentary-maker. But by 1969 he was creating the TV series *Room 222* (about a big-city high school) which ran until 1974, and which won more awards for its responsible treatment of problems than it did big ratings. But with the *MTM Show* and *Taxi*, Brooks had the whole package—brilliant entertainment, credible people and situations, a steady source of social responsibility, and very large audiences.

When he moved sideways, into feature films, he took Larry McMurtry's novel and made a smart hit for which he won the Oscars for script, direction, and best picture. A few years later, *Broadcast News* was only a little less successful while being a tender portrait of the confusion and hypocrisy in doing TV. *I'll Do Anything* is the least of his movies, but it was a musical once. When test screenings showed that it was failing with audiences, Brooks had the skills (and the freedom) to reedit it. Nevertheless, it is his single large venture to result in disappointment.

In the meantime, for the small screen, he had also helped create *The Associates* (79–80, about the law), *The Tracey Ullman Show* (87–90), *The Simpsons* (89–), and *The Critic* (94–95). Of those, *The Simpsons* was by far the most innovative and adventurous, for it shows the grimy underside to that optimistic world preferred in Brooks's live-action series.

Brooks has spoken about trying to chart the urge toward decency, a mainstream subject one might suppose, yet one ignored by so much of Hollywood. There is a case to be made, I think, that Brooks remains unknown as a personality— he is a manager of good material, a producer who likes to make things work. He lacks the edge of, say, a Lubitsch or a Buñuel. But, of course, you say—whoever thought that American TV was open to such people? True enough, but then we have to face the fact that mass media may always move in search of a kind of anonymous, benevolent proficiency more suited to politicians than to artists.

He helped produce *Jerry Maguire* (96, Cameron Crowe), and then delivered another very effective social comedy for the big screen, *As Good As It Gets,* which actually embodied TV ethics (be nicer to one another) and paired a movie star (Jack Nicholson) with a TV star (Helen Hunt). It was a picture like soap in your hands—but, afterwards, you felt cleaner and better.

Louise Brooks (Mary Louise Brooks)
(1906–85), b. Cherryvale, Kansas

In her last years, Louise Brooks did all that an often bedridden old woman could manage to secure her enigmatic reputation. She had been a recluse in Rochester, New York, it was said. Her passions were arthritis and emphysema. But she had ended up there largely because of the admiration of James Card, curator of films at Eastman House. And she could still draw men to upstate New York: Kenneth Tynan went there to write an affectionate and very influential essay for *The New Yorker;* Richard Leacock went to film her. And there were others. Before she died, *Lulu in Hollywood* was published (with a William Shawn introduction). That gathering of essays was intelligent, fascinating, cryptic, chilly, and certainly more than most movie stars would think of trying. But reliable, complete, honest? She had once written an autobiography, it was claimed—*Naked On My Goat*—but only bits survived after the book had been thrown into an incinerator—by its author, of course.

After her death, Barry Paris wrote a careful, very useful biography in which lacunae were wonderfully bridged by breathtaking stills. (Brooks made stills that were thirty years ahead of their time.) But Paris was attempting to net a very elusive butterfly, as well as a woman who had brilliant instincts about modern publicity and cult obsession. Actress? Fleetingly. Playactor? Totally. She was also one of the first stars whose creativity was morbid, or self-destructive: she had a hunch that might last better than simple success.

In *The Parade's Gone By,* Kevin Brownlow told a delicious story of how Louise Brooks regretted the way Lotte Eisner had clarified an early description of her. In the first edition of *Écran Demoniaque,* Eisner had written: "Was Louise Brooks a great artist or only a dazzling creature whose beauty leads the spectator to endow her with complexities of which she herself was unaware?" Years later, Eisner had altered that passage to: "Today we know that Louise Brooks is an astonishing actress endowed with an intelligence beyond compare and not only a dazzling creature." Yet Brooks had rather preferred the earlier mystery.

She was by then in Rochester, quoting Proust to eager interviewers, still seductive, still difficult, a snob and a gossip, and a connoisseur of her own mystique. She exists in fragments that do not make a tidy whole. Just as she made few films, most of which are seldom seen, so she turned her life into a basis for speculation and conjuring. For example, for years Brooks alleged that she was concealing William Paley as her ex-lover and later patron—yet the cheerfully vain Paley was bursting to be named as one of her conquests. The very rich man was magically the servant to the lost lady.

At the age of fifteen she became a dancer, first with Ruth St. Denis, then in *George White's Scandals* and the *Ziegfeld Follies.* Paramount saw her and gave her a tiny part in *The Street of Forgotten Men* (25, Herbert Brenon). She made a flurry of comedies in which she was a capricious femme fatale playing with a reserve that unfailingly monopolized attention amid so much mugging: *The American Venus* (26, Frank Tuttle); *A Social Celebrity* (26, Malcolm St. Clair); *It's the Old Army Game* (26), a W. C. Fields film directed by Edward Sutherland, to whom she was briefly married; *The Show-Off* (26, St. Clair); *Just Another Blonde* (26, Alfred Santell); *Love 'Em and Leave 'Em* (26, Tuttle); *Evening Clothes* (27, Luther Reed); *Rolled Stockings* (27, Richard Rossen); *The City Gone Wild* (27, James Cruze); *Now We're in the Air* (27, Frank Strayer); *A Girl in Every Port* (28, Howard Hawks); and *Beggars of Life* (28, William Wellman).

There then occurred one of the few instances of an American going to Europe to discover herself. G. W. Pabst saw *A Girl in Every Port* and fixed on Brooks as the actress to play Wedekind's Lulu in *Pandora's Box* (29). Paramount objected but, undaunted, Brooks abandoned her contract and went to Germany. She has described the way Pabst protected her from xenophobia and obtained so animated a performance from her. His hunch that this American girl (only twenty-three) might understand the psychological truths of sexual alertness was fulfilled—even if it would be twenty-five years before the performance was fully appreciated. Today, Brooks in close-up gives a sense of vivacious, fatal intimacy that enormously enriches Lulu's tragedy. *Pandora's Box* is

still among the most erotic films ever made—and it was more than Pabst would ever dare again. Immediately, she played in Pabst's *Diary of a Lost Girl* (29) and then returned to America.

She had offended Paramount, but the excursion had had much more serious effects on her. The studio asked her to dub *The Canary Murder Case* (29, Tuttle and St. Clair), which had been made before her departure. She declined and went to France to make *Prix de Beauté* (30, Augusto Genina). Back in Hollywood, her position had so deteriorated that she played in a two-reeler, *Windy Riley Goes to Hollywood,* directed by Fatty Arbuckle. It is by no means clear how she had fallen from grace, but in 1931 she managed only supporting parts in *It Pays to Advertise* (Tuttle) and *God's Gift to Women* (Michael Curtiz).

She resumed her dancing career, only to make a blighted comeback in the late 1930s in which she was wasted in small parts: *Empty Saddles* (36, Lesley Selander); *When You're in Love* (37, Robert Riskin); *King of Gamblers* (37, Robert Florey); and *Overland Stage Riders* (38, George Sherman).

She made no more films and went gradually into a retreat from which she was recovered two decades later, by movie enthusiasts, her own articles in film journals, and the tribute to her made by Godard and Anna Karina in *Vivre Sa Vie* (62). Why is it that she exerts such influence still? In part, it is a cult superbly handled by the lady herself—so much more ingenious than the attempt Norma Desmond makes in *Sunset Boulevard.* But more than that, she was one of the first performers to penetrate to the heart of screen acting. That original doubt of Lotte Eisner's applies not only to Louise Brooks but to all the great movie players. Quite simply, she appreciated that the power of the screen actress lay not in impersonation or performance, in the carefully worked-out personal narrative of stage acting, "but in the movements of thought and soul transmitted in a kind of intense isolation." An actress had fully to imagine the feelings of a character. And perhaps it was in imagining the self-consuming rapture of Lulu that Louise Brooks laid in store her own subsequent isolation.

Mel Brooks (Melvin Kaminsky),
b. Brooklyn, 1926
1968: *The Producers.* 1970: *The Twelve Chairs.* 1974: *Blazing Saddles; Young Frankenstein.* 1976: *Silent Movie.* 1977: *High Anxiety.* 1981: *History of the World—Part I.* 1987: *Spaceballs.* 1991: *Life Stinks!.* 1993: *Robin Hood: Men in Tights.* 1995: *Dracula: Dead and LovingIt.*

A besetting handicap of modern comedy is its belief that media conventions and genre takeoffs are funnier than human predicaments. The noblest comedians created a character who might have lived and suffered anywhere, without self-consciousness. The events of their comedies are everyday and ordinary. But for Woody Allen and Mel Brooks, humor grows in the hothouse of burlesque. Their own comic attitudes are less subtle and appealing because their clenched personalities are preoccupied with the clichés of entertainment and the task of rip-off parody. With Allen, this may be a substantial loss. But in the case of Brooks, everything suggests a brash, superficial personality dependent on the role of stage schmuck. Nothing shows Brooks's vulgarity more than the reckless idea that Hitchcock merited pastiche. A serious comic would respect fat Alfred for being an inimitable black humorist, far more dainty and piercing than the clumsy efforts of *High Anxiety*.

Brooks is the product of live-audience TV, hired to write gags for Sid Caesar's *Your Show of Shows* in 1950. For over a decade, he was a script doctor for TV, radio, and stage musicals. In 1964, he did the voice on Ernest Pintoff's cartoon, *The Critic*. His first two features are his most personal and dangerous works. *The Producers* has moments of rich bad taste, and its Jewish show-biz angle is all the sharper for having Hitlerism as an opponent and Zero Mostel as its spokesman.

But those early works were too prickly for popular acceptance, and *Blazing Saddles* was a concession to the masses, devoid of wit or a feeling for Westerns. There is a facetious, mindless desperation grabbing laughs anywhere, anyhow, regardless of the intrinsic amusement of men in cowboy hats always appreciated by the directors of good Westerns. *Young Frankenstein* has more sense of the horror genre's dignity, and *Silent Movie* is an unashamed revue, including fine sketches with Burt Reynolds and Brooks's wife, Anne Bancroft. *High Anxiety* is a disaster: coarse and repetitive and without the shocking malice that Hitchcock employs to make us smile. How could the overdone Cloris Leachman role be funny, nearly forty years after the delicate ambiguity of Mrs. Danvers? It has only one unflawed sequence, when Brooks himself sings a love song and discloses a forlorn, pompous ham. That character is both funny and touching, and might be the basis of something much more worthwhile. But can Brooks risk abandoning his frantic cover?

There is little more to be said for Brooks the director. He has acted occasionally—in *To Be or Not to Be* (83, Alan Johnson) and as a voice in *Look Who's Talking, Too!* (91, Amy Heckerling). But it is as an executive producer that he has been most adventurous and useful: *The Elephant Man* (80, David Lynch); *Frances* (82, Graeme Clifford); *The Doctor and the Devils* (85, Freddie Francis); *84 Charing Cross Road* (86, David Jones); *The Fly* (86, David Cronenberg); and *Solarbabies* (86, Johnson)—a remarkable attention to deformity and the grotesque.

Anything else? Yes, of course—the prodigious Broadway success of *The Producers*, and its final proof that setting out to fail is as sure a way as any.

Richard Brooks (1912–92), b. Philadelphia
1950: *Crisis*. 1951: *The Light Touch*. 1952: *Deadline, U.S.A.* 1953: *Battle Circus; Take the High Ground*. 1954: *The Flame and the Flesh; The Last Time I Saw Paris*. 1955: *Blackboard Jungle*. 1956: *The Last Hunt; The Catered Affair/Wedding Breakfast*. 1957: *Something of Value; The Brothers Karamazov*. 1958: *Cat on a Hot Tin Roof*. 1960: *Elmer Gantry*. 1962: *Sweet Bird of Youth*. 1964: *Lord Jim*. 1966: *The Professionals*. 1967: *In Cold Blood*. 1969: *The Happy Ending*. 1971: *$/The Heist*. 1975: *Bite the Bullet*. 1977: *Looking for Mr. Goodbar*. 1982: *Wrong Is Right*. 1985: *Fever Pitch*.

A sports reporter and radio commentator, Brooks had screenwriting credits on *Sin Town* (42, Ray Enright), *White Savage* (43, Arthur Lubin), *My Best Gal* (44, Anthony Mann), and *Cobra Woman* (45, Robert Siodmak) before war service in the Marines. He emerged with his first novel, *The Brick Foxhole*, which became the movie *Crossfire* (47, Edward Dmytryk). He then scripted *Swell Guy* (47, Frank Tuttle), *Brute Force* (47, Jules Dassin), *To the Victor* (48, Delmer Daves), *Key Largo* (48, John Huston), *Mystery Street* (50, John Sturges), *Storm Warning* (50, Stuart Heisler), and *Any Number Can Play* (50, Mervyn LeRoy) before Cary Grant's good offices enabled him to direct the script he had written for *Crisis*.

In interviews, Brooks often gave pungent and hilarious accounts of his early life in the film world. But his own films are solemnly respectable, exactly what one might expect from "the writer" figure as presented in American films. Attempts to see great pictorial or thematic virtues in his work are an ingenious diversion from his characteristic preference for literary properties and unambiguous messages. His early films are at best neat—*Crisis*—and at worst corn—*Take the High Ground* and *The Last Time I Saw Paris*. One has only to compare him with Kazan, especially in the matter of Tennessee Williams adaptations, to see how far emotional intensity eludes him. And whenever he has taken on larger subjects—Dostoyevsky, Conrad, and *In Cold Blood*—he has settled for a rendering of the plot that is elementary and cautious. Nor did John Alton's arty color photography supply the proper complexity to *Brothers Karamazov*. *The Last Hunt* is an unusual Western and *Elmer Gantry* has a good period flavor. But Sinclair Lewis is not the most stimulating of models and *Gantry* is too obvious a vehicle for Burt Lancaster.

He took great risks personally to make *Goodbar,* and made large demands on Diane Keaton. But it is a coarse, brutal film, unaware that its own sensationalism stops any chance of a serious commentary on sexuality.

Pierce Brosnan,
b. Navan, County Meath, Ireland, 1951

Some people regard Pierce Brosnan as touched by Irish luck. He got the lead role in the TV series *Remington Steele* by just happening to be in the right place at the right time. It made his name when he had few other claims on fame. Then the role of James Bond was offered to him—as that strange franchise languished—and he had to turn it down because of the *Steele* commitment. But then Bond waited for him and was available again in the mid-nineties. Since when, he has undoubtedly helped pump life back into the ailing beast.

On the TV show (1982–87), Brosnan was said to be "debonair." As Bond, he is sometimes called "authoritative." So be it. But in *The Thomas Crown Affair* (99, John McTiernan), which he helped produce, Brosnan was eaten alive and raw by the sheer warmth and presence of Rene Russo. Indeed, he looked like a stick being toyed with by a lush cat.

He made his feature movie debut in *The Long Good Friday* (80, John Mackenzie); and then in *The Mirror Crack'd* (80, Guy Hamilton) he had the right period look for an Agatha Christie man; *Nomads* (86, McTiernan); *The Fourth Protocol* (87, Mackenzie), in which he was Russian; the inexplicable *Taffin* (88, Francis Megahy); *The Deceivers* (88, Nicholas Meyer), a disaster made in India; *Mister Johnson* (90, Bruce Beresford); *Live Wire* (92, Christian Duguay); *Mrs. Doubtfire* (93, Chris Columbus); *Love Affair* (94, Glenn Gordon Caron); his Bond debut, *GoldenEye* (95, Martin Campbell); *Dante's Peak* (97, Roger Donaldson), with no box office carry-over from Bond; *The Mirror Has Two Faces* (96, Barbra Streisand); *Mars Attacks!* (96, Tim Burton); *Tomorrow Never Dies* (97, Roger Spottiswoode); *The World Is Not Enough* (99, Michael Apted); *The Tailor of Panama* (01, John Boorman); very Irish and good in *Evelyn* (02, Beresford), and Bond again in *Die Another Day* (02, Lee Tamahori).

Clarence Brown (1890–1987),
b. Clinton, Massachusetts

1920: *The Last of the Mohicans* (codirected with Maurice Tourneur); *The Great Redeemer*. 1921: *The Foolish Matrons* (codirected with Tourneur). 1922: *The Light in the Dark*. 1923: *Don't Marry for Money; The Acquittal*. 1924: *The Signal Tower; Butterfly*. 1925: *Smouldering Fires; The Eagle; The Goose Woman*. 1926: *Kiki; Flesh and the Devil*. 1928: *The Cossacks* (codirected with and credited to George Hill); *A Woman of Affairs*. 1929: *The Trail of '98; Wonder of Women; Navy Blues*. 1930: *Anna Christie; Romance*. 1931: *Inspiration; A Free Soul; Possessed*. 1932: *Emma; Letty Lynton; The Son-Daughter*. 1933: *Looking Forward; Night Flight*. 1934: *Sadie McKee; Chained*. 1935: *Anna Karenina; Ah, Wilderness!*. 1936: *Wife vs. Secretary; The Gorgeous Hussy*. 1938: *Conquest/Marie Walewska; Of Human Hearts*. 1939: *Idiot's Delight; The Rains Came*. 1940: *Edison, the Man*. 1941: *Come Live With Me; They Met in Bombay*. 1943: *The Human Comedy*. 1944: *The White Cliffs of Dover; National Velvet*. 1946: *The Yearling*. 1947: *Song of Love*. 1949: *Intruder in the Dust*. 1950: *To Please a Lady; It's a Big Country* (codirected). 1951: *Angels in the Outfield*. 1952: *When in Rome; Plymouth Adventure*.

Brown studied at the University of Tennessee and was an engineer before getting a job as assistant to Maurice Tourneur. He acknowledged a great debt to Tourneur, with whom he worked for seven years. Brown's first solo film was scripted with John Gilbert and by the mid-1920s he was with Universal. Subsequently he joined MGM and stayed there until the 1940s. He was one of their leading directors of female stars. Five times he worked with Joan Crawford: *Possessed, Letty Lynton, Sadie McKee, Chained,* and *The Gorgeous Hussy*. More important, he had the reputation of being Garbo's director: *Flesh and the Devil, A Woman of Affairs, Anna Christie, Anna Karenina,* and *Conquest*. But these are not Garbo's best films—just as the Crawford movies are more reserved than those she made with, say, Michael Curtiz or Robert Aldrich. Brown had a gentle, reflective taste, inclined to persist with lush visual effects learned in the silent cinema. He was at his best with atmosphere, and least assured with dialogue. *Idiot's Delight,* for instance, is a garrulous muddle, but *The Yearling* and *Intruder in the Dust* are touching works, even if old-fashioned and very slow. Attempts to elevate Brown's status are stopped in their tracks by a comparison with George Cukor. It is more useful to see him as a pictorialist who managed to negotiate sound without effectively altering his style. Like so many directors of that generation in America he was conventional, placid, and humorless. He never outgrew novelettish material, and *The Goose Woman, Anna Karenina,* and *National Velvet* have the same soothing plush of absorbency. Essentially, Brown treated Louise Dresser, Garbo, the young Elizabeth Taylor, and animals in *The Yearling* and *National Velvet* with the same considerate but uncritical awe.

Tod Browning (Charles Albert Browning)
(1882–1962), b. Louisville, Kentucky

1917: *Jim Bludso; Peggy, the Will o' the Wisp; The Jury of Fate*. 1918: *Which Woman; The Eyes of Mystery; The Legion of Death; Revenge; The Deciding Kiss; The Brazen Beauty; Set Free*. 1919: *The Wicked Darling; The Exquisite Thief; The*

Unpainted Woman; A Petal in the Current. 1920: *Bonnie, Bonnie Lassie; The Virgin of Stamboul.* 1921: *Outside the Law; No Woman Knows.* 1922: *The Wise Kid; The Man Under Cover; Under Two Flags.* 1923: *Drifting; The White Tiger; The Day of Faith.* 1924: *The Dangerous Flirt; Silk Stocking Sal.* 1925: *The Unholy Three; The Mystic; Dollar Down.* 1926: *The Blackbird; The Road to Mandalay.* 1927: *The Show; The Unknown; London After Midnight.* 1928: *West of Zanzibar; The Big City.* 1929: *Where East Is East; The Thirteenth Chair.* 1930: *Outside the Law.* 1931: *Dracula; The Iron Man.* 1932: *Freaks.* 1933: *Fast Workers.* 1935: *Mark of the Vampire.* 1936: *The Devil Doll.* 1939: *Miracles for Sale.*

Browning ran away from school to join a circus, and in the next few years he roamed all over the world with traveling acts—this in the last years of the nineteenth century. It is Boys' Own romance and Browning emerged from it an actor. From 1913 he was with Biograph and he went on to work for D. W. Griffith on *Intolerance.* Thus inspired, he began directing, generally for Universal. In 1919, he made *The Wicked Darling,* in which Lon Chaney had a small part. They worked together again on *Outside the Law,* a Priscilla Dean vehicle in which Chaney filled two roles. For a few years, Browning made romantic melodramas: Dean again as Cigarette in *Under Two Flags,* and in *Drifting* and *White Tiger;* Eleanor Boardman and Tyrone Power Sr. in *The Day of Faith;* and two Evelyn Brent pictures—*The Dangerous Flirt* and *Silk Stocking Sal.* Then, in 1925, Chaney persuaded MGM to hire Browning. Reunited, they made *The Unholy Three, The Blackbird, The Road to Mandalay, The Unknown, London After Midnight, West of Zanzibar, The Big City,* and *Where East Is East.* It was a fruitful collaboration. Browning wrote many of the original stories, stimulating Chaney's extraordinary inventiveness at distorting makeup. The result often came close to that poignant conception of deformed creatures that makes *Freaks* so influential a film and that has constantly colored the best films in the horror genre. In *The Unknown,* for instance, Chaney plays a man who has had his arms amputated because Joan Crawford cannot bear to be touched. While in *London After Midnight,* Chaney was a hideous vampire so deformed that the makeup could be worn only for short periods. He also played the detective pursuing the vampire—an interesting reflection on the way horror films engage the two fantasy aspects of ourselves.

Briefly, Browning returned to Universal to make *Outside the Law,* an Edward G. Robinson thriller, and *Dracula.* Chaney was now dead and the title part was taken by Bela Lugosi. Although one of the original sound horror films, *Dracula* owes more to Lugosi than to Browning. James Whale was able to exploit the basic nineteenth-century plots rather better than Browning, and seemed to be more in tune with the two levels on which such films work. The contortions of Chaney had impressed Browning and he returned to MGM to make his masterpiece, *Freaks,* an allegory on the antagonism between the beautiful and the damned, and an inexplicably harrowing insight from the studio of so much glamour. A commercial flop, and widely banned, *Freaks* now seems less a horror picture than an indictment of the cult of attractiveness. Before his retirement, Browning made two more worthwhile pictures: *Mark of the Vampire,* a remake of *London After Midnight,* with Lionel Barrymore and Lugosi splitting Chaney's original roles; and *The Devil Doll,* scripted with Erich von Stroheim, with Barrymore as an escaped convict selling dolls that are miniaturized humans. But neither of these is as interesting as the Whale films or as suggestive as the silent pictures made with Chaney.

Yul Brynner (Youl Bryner) (1915–1985), b. Sakhalin, Russia

The only bald, ex–trapeze artist, philosophy graduate of the Sorbonne to star in films, Yul Brynner had so much originality, so little interest. The son of Swiss and Mongolian parents, Brynner always carried himself with an air of enjoyable implausibility. But all too often the film world accepted him as a true exotic rather than an amused sham. Briefly, in *Once More With Feeling* (59, Stanley Donen), he was permitted to make fun of his own mysterious glamour; and in *Le Testament d'Orphée* (60, Jean Cocteau) he had a moment of studied inscrutability. But set down in any of the naturalistic environs of American genres he looked like a man from nowhere, relying on the dubious notion that bald men appeal to women. The record of his career suggests that the novelty soon wore off, but that baldness was an extreme gesture that could not be abandoned. Imagine the humiliation of a Brynner in hair; picture the ordeal of forever shaving his head for increasingly mediocre films.

He went to America in 1941 and entered the theatre. It was the part of the king in *The King and I* that brought him fame and, incredibly, the Oscar for best actor in the film made of it in 1956, directed by Walter Lang. That was his second film. In 1949 he had appeared in *Port of New York* (Laslo Benedek), amid a career in TV as performer and producer. His King of Siam was an inconsequential performance, full of brooding stares that already suggested a sense of the ridiculous.

But domed sex was not to be denied, and for a few years Brynner tried to live up to a public relations picture of domineering, sensual cruelty: as Pharaoh in *The Ten Commandments* (56, Cecil B. De Mille); *Anastasia* (56, Anatole Litvak); helplessly trying to be passionate as Dmitri in *The Brothers Karamazov* (57, Richard Brooks); *The Journey* (58, Litvak); escaping into hair as Jason in *The Sound and the Fury* (59, Martin Ritt) and in *The Buccaneer* (58, Anthony Quinn); stepping into Tyrone Power's sandals and armor for *Solomon and Sheba* (59, King Vidor); and then playing the lead in *The Magnificent Seven* (60, John Sturges). That film was a great success, but it was the beginning of Brynner's decline into European-based thrillers and Spanish Westerns, with the occasional return to an Oriental period piece: *Taras Bulba* (62, J. Lee Thompson); *Escape to Zahrain* (62, Ronald Neame); *Kings of the Sun* (63, Thompson); *Invitation to a Gunfighter* (64, Richard Wilson); *Flight from Ashiya* (64, Michael Anderson); *The Saboteur* (65, Bernhard Wicki); *The Return of the Seven* (66, Burt Kennedy); *Triple Cross* (66, Terence Young); *The Double Man* (67, Franklin Schaffner); *The Long Duel* (67, Ken Annakin); *Villa Rides!* (68, Buzz Kulik); *The Madwoman of Chaillot* (69, Bryan Forbes); *The File of the Golden Goose* (69, Sam Wanamaker); *Catlow* (71, Wanamaker); *The Light at the Edge of the World* (71, Kevin Billington); *Romance of a Horse Thief* (71, Abraham Polonsky); and *Le Serpent* (73, Henri Verneuil). He regressed to a short-lived TV series based on *The King and I*, in which he looked no older than in 1956—the first, eerie vindication of baldness. But then, in *Westworld* (73, Michael Crichton), he confirmed suspicions of hollowness: baldness seemed a simple disguise when the face itself unscrewed, leaving the dour smirk intact.

He was in *The Ultimate Warrior* (75, Robert Clouse); *Death Rage* (76, Anthony M. Dawson); and *Futureworld* (76, Richard T. Heffron). But in his last years, as long as he was strong enough, he was back onstage, touring *The King and I*.

Geneviève Bujold,
b. Montreal, Canada, 1942

Coma (78, Michael Crichton) is only a thriller with an unusually real setting and a crazy plot. It is made decently, without ulterior ambition. But Geneviève Bujold is so remarkable in it that she makes one conscious of how a steady career has neglected her real virtues. She is past that hard sexual radiance so arresting in *La Guerre est Finie* (66, Alain Resnais). But her face is as sharp and watchful as ever, more drawn than ripe now. She ignored the silliness of *Coma* and went about her job like a young mother with too much to do. A gritty actuality lies within her dramatic vulnerability, and in *Coma* it amounts to heroic courage and persistence.

Legend has it that she played a small part in *French Can Can* (55, Jean Renoir). But she grew up in French Canada and studied at the Montreal Conservatory of Acting before making *Amanita*

Pestilens (63, Rene Bonniere); *La Terre à Boire* (64, Jean-Paul Bernier); and an episode from *La Fleur de l'Age, ou Les Adolescentes* (64, Michel Brault). As well as working for Resnais in France, she appeared in *Le Voleur* (66, Louis Malle) and played the porcelain waif in *King of Hearts* (66, Philippe de Broca).

Back in Canada, she was very active in TV and the theatre. She met and married the director Paul Almond: *Isabel* (67, Almond); *Entre la Mer et l'Eau Douce* (67, Brault); an unhappy venture into big pictures, as *Anne of the Thousand Days* (69, Charles Jarrott); *Act of the Heart* (70, Almond); a short, *Marie-Christine* (70, Claude Jutra); *The Trojan Women* (71, Michael Cacoyannis); *Journey* (72, Almond); *Kamouraska* (73, Jutra); another Hollywood dud, *Earthquake* (74, Mark Robson); *Alex and the Gypsy* (76, John Korty); *Swashbuckler* (76, James Goldstone); *Obsession* (76, Brian De Palma), which with a more humane director would seem an outstanding performance in which woman and child merge in the way of Geraldine Chaplin and Ana Torrent in *Cria*; *Another Man, Another Chance* (77, Claude Lelouch); and *Coma*.

She was in *Murder by Decree* (79, Bob Clark); *The Last Flight of Noah's Ark* (79, Jarrott); *Final Assignment* (80, Almond); on TV fighting voodoo in *Mistress of Paradise* (81, Peter Medak); *Monsignor* (82, Frank Perry); in *Choose Me* (84, Alan Rudolph); with Clint Eastwood in *Tightrope* (84, Richard Tuggle); *Trouble in Mind* (85, Rudolph); wonderful in a very tough role in *Dead Ringers* (88, David Cronenberg); funny as the art dealer in *The Moderns* (88, Rudolph); *Red Earth, White Earth* (89, David Greene); and *A Paper Wedding* (90, Brault).

In Canada frequently, and for TV often, she worked on: *Rue du Bac* (90, Gabriel Aghion); *False Identity* (90, James Keach); *The Dance Goes On* (91, Almond); *Oh, What a Night* (92, Eric Till); *An Ambush of Ghosts* (93, Everett Lewis); *Mon Amie Max* (94, Brault); *The Adventures of Pinocchio* (96, Steve Barron); *Dead Innocent* (96, Sara Botsford); *The House of Yes* (97, Mark S. Waters); *Last Night* (98, Don McKellar); *You Can Thank Me Later* (98, Shimon Dotan); *Eye of the Beholder* (99, Stephan Elliott); *The Bookfair Murders* (00, Wolfgang Panzer); *Finding Home* (02, Laurence D. Foldes); *La Turbulence des Fluides* (02, Marion Briand); *Downtown: A Street Take* (02, Rafal Zielinski); *Jericho Mansion* (03, Alberto Sciamma).

Sandra Bullock, b. Arlington, Virginia, 1964

From *Speed* (94, Jan De Bont) to *Speed 2: Cruise Control* (97, De Bont), Sandra Bullock went from $500,000 a picture to $12.5 million. All this, of course, in a society where, famously, you are worth whatever you get. Though possibly some relic remains of an earlier culture which—while liking Ms. Bullock well enough—could reckon that $500,000 was generous for her Annie Porter in that first *Speed*. Would it amaze you to hear the proposal that 500,000 young women in America could have done as well in the part? Or am I missing the point?

As I said, I like Ms. Bullock: she is fun, tomboyish, gutsy, observant, and pretty. But she has become a business, her own production company, and what is called a national favorite. So be it—but, as I go through the list, I defy you to be quite sure which film was which.

She is the daughter of a German opera singer, Helga Bullock, and as a child the family traveled widely, following the mother's career. Sandra can sing, too. She was educated at Washington-Lee High School, and then briefly at East Carolina University before she went into acting. She did some TV and she had the lead role (the Melanie Griffith part) in a short-lived TV series, *Working Girl* (90). Her first significant movie was *When the Party's Over* (92, Matthew Irmas), followed by *Demolition Man* (93, Marco Brambilla); *Wrestling Ernest Hemingway* (93, Randa Haines); *The Vanishing* (93, George Sluizer); *The Thing Called Love* (93, Peter Bogdanovich), and then *Speed*.

That was followed with *While You Were Sleeping* (95, Jon Turteltaub), her first vehicle; *The Net* (95, Irwin Winkler); *Two if by Sea* (96, Bill Bennett); *A Time to Kill* (96, Joel Schumacher); seriously out of her depth as Hemingway's girl in *In Love and War* (96, Richard Attenborough); and then *Speed 2*.

For *Hope Floats* (98, Forest Whitaker), she was co–executive producer; with Nicole Kidman in *Practical Magic* (98, Griffin Dunne); the voice of Miriam on *The Prince of Egypt* (98); *Forces of Nature* (99, Bronwen Hughes); *Gun Shy* (00, Eric Blakeney), which she produced; *28 Days* (00, Betty Thomas); a comeback in *Miss Congeniality* (00, Donald Petrie); *Murder by Numbers* (02, Barbet Schroeder); *Divine Secrets of the Ya-Ya Sisterhood* (02, Callie Khouri); *Two Weeks Notice* (02, Marc Lawrence).

And so the girl next door edges up on forty, a household name, but not yet in a single vital movie.

Luis Buñuel (1900–83), b. Calanda, Spain
1928: *Un Chien Andalou* (codirected with Salvador Dalí). 1930: *L'Age d'Or.* 1932: *Las Hurdes/Land Without Bread.* 1947: *Gran Casino.* 1949: *El Gran Calavera.* 1950: *Los Olvidados/ The Young and the Damned.* 1951: *Susana/Demonio y Carne; La Hija del Engaño; Una Mujer Sín Amor; Subida Al Cielo.* 1952: *El Bruto; Robinson Crusoe; El.* 1953: *Cumbres Borrascosas/Abismos de Pasión; La Ilusión Viaja en Tranvia.* 1954: *El Río y la Muerte.* 1955: *Ensayo de un Crimen/ The Criminal Life of Archibaldo de la Cruz; Cela S'Appèlle l'Aurore.* 1956: *La Mort en ce Jardin/ Evil Eden.* 1958: *Nazarin.* 1959: *La Fièvre Monte à El Pao.* 1960: *The Young One/La Joven.* 1961: *Viridiana.* 1962: *El Angel Exterminador/The Exterminating Angel.* 1964: *Le Journal d'une Femme de Chambre/Diary of a Chambermaid.* 1965: *Simón del Desierto.* 1967: *Belle de Jour.* 1968: *La Voie Lactée/The Milky Way.* 1970: *Tristana.* 1972: *Le Charme Discret de la Bourgeoisie/ The Discreet Charm of the Bourgeoisie.* 1974: *Le Fantôme de la Liberté.* 1977: *Cet Obscur Objet du Désir/That Obscure Object of Desire.*

There has always been a temptation to view Buñuel as one of the few towering artists who have condescended to adopt film as their means of expression. According to that approach, we may assess him as a Spaniard, as a surrealist, and as a lifelong antagonist of the bourgeoisie. All those strains persisted in Buñuel's films and they repay close attention. But it seems to me an error to think that Buñuel—often working quickly—was casual about the medium. On the contrary, I believe that he is one of the greatest of directors simply because of the expressive mastery of his films.

There is an approach that sees no "beauty" in Buñuel, as if so fierce a social critic could have no business with the bourgeois taste for cinematic grace. But this is to confuse prettiness with beauty, Lelouch with Renoir. The detachment of Buñuel's camera, the apparent emphasis on the inner potency of an image as distinct from its form, Raymond Durgnat's point about the amount of three-quarter-length shots, do not detract from the constant elegance of Buñuel's films. Color and the presence of Catherine Deneuve have helped some people to discern a growing interest in style on Buñuel's part. But where are the ugly shots in earlier films, where are there moments when the image is not essential in all its items? Beauty in cinema is the integrity of meaning and means—not the matching of the two, but a unified conception. Thus *Un Chien Andalou*—and every film after it—is made with the calm and simplicity that only come when an artist has understood his or her medium. That is why *Un Chien Andalou* is able to make fun of continuity—a bourgeois fetish; why the exact angle and texture of its images haunt the mind long after analyses of them have been digested. The eye opened to be cut in half is the prompting mirror of our response: nothing is more sensual than the breasts that dissolve into buttocks; more energetic than the pluck of the girl defending herself with a tennis racket; more tender than the hermaphrodite oblivious of traffic; more atmospheric than the funeral cortege. And long before Warhol's cinema, the lovers in *L'Age d'Or* engage us in the epic awkwardness that afflicts love. Could a film have been banned so long if its power was not in the explosive mixture of style and sense? Could Buñuel have kept himself from directing for so long if he did not view the medium serenely? Could assigned projects make so little difference to the art of a director if that art was not within his images? Could anyone so sustain an inquiry into imaginative life and an unaffected account of externals if he was not a great filmmaker?

There is some use in trying to correct the impressions that Buñuel's social criticism is deeply hostile to people, that he is antagonistic to popular cinema, that he worked in a vacuum unaffected by other films. To take the last point, he delights in the presence of Fernando Rey as a "connection" in *Discreet Charm*, just as his use of Delphine Seyrig, Stéphane Audran, and Jean-Pierre Cassel cannot be evaded as a wicked if gentle reproof of the modishness in the work of Resnais and Chabrol. Again, when a disembodied hand advances on one of the marooned guests in *The Exterminating Angel*, that is not just a "Buñuel hand"—the means of touch and emblem of sexuality—but a recollection of *The Beast with Five Fingers* (47, Robert Florey) a Warners film made at the time when Buñuel was in charge of dubbing their films into Spanish. Earlier, in 1935, he had worked for Warners and may have been so impressed by the melting waxworks in *The Mystery of the Wax Museum* (33, Michael Curtiz), that something remained for *Archibaldo de la Cruz*. Those are some small, ill-buried links. What is more worthy of research is the way, over the years, Renoir and Buñuel exchanged ideas, actors, and images.

The sooner one allows that the interruption of bourgeois ceremonies and affairs in *L'Age d'Or*, *Exterminating Angel*, and *Discreet Charm* is of a kind with that in *La Règle du Jeu*, the sooner one sees that Buñuel is a comic director and that his reputed savagery is only a consistent view of the neurotic frailty with which we lead our lives. It is too easy to call *El*, *Archibaldo*, or *Belle de Jour* black comedies. How much more useful to see that, as with Renoir, Buñuel allows himself no villains, no unflawed heroes, but claims that everyone is on a level—as witness the austere distance that his camera keeps—similarly engaged to address fantasy and reality. Even the more overtly harsh pictures—*Los Olvidados*, *Nazarin*, and *Viridiana*—in which Spanish anticlericalism asserts itself as Buñuel's one artistic overemphasis, the social criticism does not disparage one person more than another. Rather, it shows that we live imaginary lives in which we hold varying symbolic reference for different people. In Buñuel's films, all men are facets of the libido, all women resemblances of love: remember that in *Un Chien Andalou* several parts were played by the same actor and actress.

The "realism" of his films—whether the squalor of *Los Olvidados*, the table settings of *Discreet Charm*, Crusoe's island, or that reluctance to use a subjective camera should not mislead us into thinking that Buñuel believed in reality. That way lies the trap of claiming him as an anarchist, communist, anti-Catholic director. On the contrary, he is ideally suited to popular cinema and the emphasis it puts on dreams, identification, and the manifestation of fantasy. Surrealist manifestos could not have had a better arena than commercial cinema. The stylist Buñuel never forgets us sitting in the dark, hanging on the brightness. How could the power of the "cut" be better demonstrated than in *Un Chien Andalou*'s opening? See how clearly *L'Age d'Or* describes the essential overlap of documentary and fantasy as scorpions and man illuminate one another. Recollect how far *Archibaldo de la Cruz* is a fantasist, trying to convert plastic imagination into flesh. What better demonstration is there of the comparison of watching film and dreaming than the sequence, some twenty-five minutes into *Exterminating Angel*, when the anxious guests settle down to sleep, perchance to dream? Its sheer photographic feeling of slumber is one of the most sensuous moments in cinema. And what is *Belle de Jour* but a bourgeoise who indulges her daydreams and thereby reveals the way our open eyes are clouded by feelings?

To conclude, I think Buñuel emerged from his refugee career fascinated by cinema. *Belle de Jour*, *Discreet Charm*, and the supreme *Obscure Object of Desire* are in love with the medium, still surrealist, still Spanish, but tolerant of human weakness. Is there a film with such sly charm as *Discreet Charm*? Or an occupation more bourgeois and contradictory than that of a film director? Buñuel does not savage us. He says that we are like scorpions and like sheep, fluctuating, desperate creatures, as likely to build a maze round our hearts as to obey them, but dreadfully funny. He is as intent on comedy as Kafka was, as little intent on showing off style, and as much a victim of the joke he tells.

George Burns (Nathan Birnbaum)
(1896–1996), b. New York City, and
Gracie (Grace) **Allen** (1902–64),
b. San Francisco

What an extraordinary story this is—and one that reaches far beyond the movies, of course—but who can resist the tender trap, or the liberating confinement, that marriage meant for George and Gracie? Who can ever quite forget the look on the ninety-year-old George's face, the serenity with which he knew that Gracie was still listening in, and the flawless admiration he gave her? He was a man who always knew he had met his superior, been able to hold on to her, and then re-create a semblance of their harmony. Is there a happier pairing in American folklore—or one so happy that doesn't act as a sedative?

They seem very different—New York meets San Francisco, at a time when those were very distant worlds. But in truth they were both raised in show business. And both performed as children. They met and formed the comedy team Burns and Allen, and in 1926 they married. As such, they excelled in vaudeville, on radio (there was a wondrous contrast of gruff and plaintive in their voices), and then moved on to movies, where they were maybe a degree too placid or happy to be really commanding. So they were often supporting figures for Bing Crosby: *The Big Broadcast* (32, Frank Tuttle); *College Humor* (33, Wesley Ruggles); *International House* (33, A. Edward Sutherland); *Six of a Kind* (34, Leo McCarey); *We're Not Dressing* (34, Norman Taurog); *Many Happy Returns* (34, Norman McLeod), where they are the leads; *Love in Bloom* (35, Elliott Nugent); *College Holiday* (36, Tuttle), with their friend Jack Benny; *The Big Broadcast of 1937* (36, Mitchell Leisen); *A Damsel in Distress* (37, George Stevens), an Astaire film, where they sing "Stiff Upper Lip"; *College Swing* (38, Raoul Walsh); *Honolulu* (39, Edward Buzzell).

Then a gap. *Honolulu* would be their last film together. Yet surely they could have continued during the war. In fact they went back to radio, and to family life, though Gracie did make *Mr. and Mrs. North* (41, Robert B. Sinclair) and *Two Girls and a Sailor* (44, Richard Thorpe). And they did not really come back until the fall of 1950, when CBS television began *The George Burns and Gracie Allen Show,* a classic hit that ran until 1958. That is still the format in which they are best known, and even if the TV show sometimes yielded to old vaudeville patter routines, still, it was the foundation of their marital image: George, smart, rational, businesslike, and a success; Gracie, sweet, daffy, instinctive, and right. What made it work was not the exasperation and frustration that bonds so many married people (in life and on the screen), but the eternally forgiving way in which George perceived this scatterbrain who had the answers.

It's worth noting that *The Burns and Allen Show* began a year before *I Love Lucy*—at the same network. In other words, Desi and Lucy (who had other ingredients, to be sure) were pushed by CBS to repeat a proven model.

Then, in 1958, Gracie decided to retire. George mounted another TV show, *The George Burns Show,* with some of the old cast, and a hole in the middle. It lasted four months. At which point he stopped too, and then was nursing Gracie.

He did nothing until 1975, when he made a comeback of slowly mounting glory, in the course

of which he became a team (he and his huge cigar) on TV talk shows, where he quietly alluded to his sexual potency (see the cigar?) and ridiculed death. He became a phenomenon of survival, but he remained unfailingly decent (so it was OK with all faiths that he should be God), and he was always smiling at a place just off camera. He was looking at Gracie in the way, on the TV show, he had pioneered stepping out of character and talking to the camera, the audience, and the possibility of common sense.

The later films are *The Sunshine Boys*—for which he won an Oscar (75, Herbert Ross); *Oh, God!* (77, Carl Reiner), with John Denver; *Movie Movie* (78, Stanley Donen); *Just You and Me Kid* (79, Leonard Stern), with Brooke Shields; *Going in Style* (79, Martin Brest), with Art Carney and Lee Strasberg; *Oh, God! Book II* (80, Gilbert Cates); *Oh, God! You Devil* (84, Paul Bogart); *18 Again!* (88, Paul Flaherty); *Radioland Murders* (94, Mel Smith).

He died aged one hundred plus six weeks. Goodnight, George.

Ken Burns (Kenneth Lauren Burns),
b. Brooklyn, New York, 1953
1981: *Brooklyn Bridge* (d). 1984: *The Shakers* (d). 1985: *Huey Long* (d); *The Statue of Liberty* (d). 1988: *Thomas Hart Benton* (d); *The Congress* (d). 1990: *The Civil War* (d). 1991: *Empire of the Air* (d). 1994: *Baseball* (d). 1997: *Lewis & Clark: The Journey of the Corps of Discovery* (d); *Thomas Jefferson* (d). 1998: *Frank Lloyd Wright* (d). 1999: *Not For Ourselves Alone: The Story of Elizabeth Cady Stanton & Susan B. Anthony* (d). 2001: *Jazz* (d). 2002: *Mark Twain*(d).

America is self-consciously loaded up with information systems, and it has the worst education in the developed world. It has developed one of the supreme storytelling media in the history of stories, and yet that medium has neglected the real history of America, to the point of nearly doctrinal insistence. America has more televisions than any country in the world, but the multiplicity of channels remains fearful of documentaries made with any sort of vision or aesthetic structure. There has been nothing in America in the age of television to match Dziga Vertov, Humphrey Jennings, Resnais, Marcel Ophuls, or Claude Lanzmann. Nothing? Certainly not Frederick Wiseman, whose movies have made an increasing cult of passivity. Only Ken Burns has shown what might be.

Moreover, Burns has both the energy and the educational zeal of one of the great nineteenth-century historians. His films are old-fashioned, romantic, made in the spirit of the time they are describing—essentially, the America of the nineteenth and early twentieth centuries. He believes in still pictures (paintings, prints, or photographs), new live footage that evokes place and atmosphere, and words. Burns makes composed, written films, in which the interplay of narrative, interview, and original document is intricate and moving.

A graduate of Hampshire College, he spent ten years working for PBS, developing his own unit and his powers as a fund-raiser. This was like a campaign for *The Civil War*, five years in the making, eleven hours on the screen, one of the great American films and the redemption of national history for a large audience. Above all, it was the emotional undertaking that was so powerful. Burns knew that we needed to rediscover the feeling of the war before we could have a chance of understanding it. The achievement was such that one could feel the series entering the mind and nervous system of the country.

Burns did the history of baseball and the history of jazz next. He asserts that he has no interest in doing features—and one believes him, for he shows no *need* for fiction. But can he easily take on smaller subjects after the Civil War?

Burns's quilt of American history grows. For me, his series on ideas (like baseball and jazz) are richer than those on heroes (Jefferson or Twain). But the study of race is both earnest and committed—and it makes the mindset of feature film seem frivolous. On the other hand, there is by now a Burns tone that has earned parody, and some critical disquiet. For it is lofty, so high-minded, that it is sometimes hard to see how America has ever gone astray. One would like to see Burns face ordinary iniquity, or shortcoming. That omission was a serious flaw in *Jazz*, a series that could not account for—and therefore ignored—the decline in the music.

Raymond Burr (1917–93),
b. New Westminster, Canada

Educated at the universities of Stanford, California, and Columbia, he was director of the Pasadena Community Playhouse and an experienced stage actor before making his screen debut in *San Quentin* (46, Gordon Douglas). How can one avoid calling him the archetypal heavy? His bulk was invested with every degree of villainy, from the robust to the perverted. To add to his size, his sad features were always ready to sink into grave jowls and puffy malice. Burr worked hard and this list mentions only his best-remembered parts: *Desperate* (47, Anthony Mann); *Pitfall* (48, André de Toth); *Ruthless* (48, Edgar G. Ulmer); *Sleep, My Love* (48, Douglas Sirk); *Raw Deal* (48, Mann); *Walk a Crooked Mile* (48, Douglas); *Bride of Vengeance* (49, Mitchell Leisen); *Abandoned* (49, Joseph M. Newman); *The Adventures of Don Juan* (49, Vincent Sherman); *Fort Algiers* (50, Lesley Selander); *Key to the City* (50, George Sidney); *His Kind of Woman*

(51, John Farrow); *New Mexico* (51, Irving Reis); *M* (51, Joseph Losey); *Meet Danny Wilson* (51, Joseph Pevney); as the hostile, limping district attorney in *A Place in the Sun* (51, George Stevens); *Horizons West* (52, Budd Boetticher); *The Blue Gardenia* (53, Fritz Lang); *Passion* (54, Allan Dwan); *Gorilla at Large* (54, Harmon Jones); *Godzilla* (55, Inoshiro Honda); *Count Three and Pray* (55, George Sherman); *A Man Alone* (55, Ray Milland); *Great Day in the Morning* (56, Jacques Tourneur); *The Brass Legend* (56, Gerd Oswald); *A Cry in the Night* (56, Frank Tuttle); *Crime of Passion* (57, Oswald); and *Affair in Havana* (57, Laslo Benedek). Having incurred so much audience hostility, how Hitchcockian it is that in *Rear Window* (54)—as the killer across the courtyard—he should finally confront us, so troubled that he wins our sympathy. In the cinema, Burr's mold had been cast and, no matter how many times he might fill it, it could not be remade. Astutely, he moved into TV, and two great successes: first as *Perry Mason,* an attorney triumphant from 1957 to 1966 and then, as if all that pacing round witnesses had tired him, as *Ironside,* a wheelchair detective. Perhaps that posture gave him pleasant memories of James Stewart in *Rear Window.*

He had no need to make films and only appeared twice in a decade: *New Face in Hell* (67, John Guillermin) and *Tomorrow Never Comes* (77, Peter Collinson). But in the eighties, he was back on TV as Perry Mason again, and he did a few more movies: *Out of the Blue* (80, Dennis Hopper); *The Return* (81, Greydon Clark); *Airplane II: The Sequel* (82, Ken Finkleman); and *Godzilla 1985* (85, Kohji Hashimoto and R. J. Kizer).

Ellen Burstyn (Edna Rae Gillooly),
b. Detroit, Michigan, 1932

In all of Ellen Burstyn's best work (though there is not too much of it), a desperate cheerfulness struggles with grim prospects and her battered good nature comes near to breaking down. She has a round face, a little swollen, like a doll soaked in tears or straining to hold back crying. Her finest moment is as the aging girlfriend in *The King of Marvin Gardens* (72, Bob Rafelson), trying not to notice that her own stepdaughter is appropriating her man. Her good spirits are listless, as if she kept going back to that dread worry. And when it is too much for her, she turns first to self-abuse, hacking off her hair, before the helpless yielding to violence in what is one of the cinema's most understandable and distressing killings.

That part is a woman whose life has been filled with struggle and compromise, and who is defiantly aware that she is nothing more magical than a pretty forty-year-old. And Edna Rae Gillooly came up the hard way too. She worked as a waitress, a store clerk, a model, and many other things, trying to get into show business. All through the fifties, she worked under the name of Ellen McRae: on TV as a chorus girl on the Jackie Gleason show and in *The Doctors;* in the theatre, in *Fair Game,* a Broadway comedy; and with tiny parts in several films, including *Goodbye Charlie* (64, Vincente Minnelli).

She played a bigger part in *Tropic of Cancer* (69, Joseph Strick), but it was the talent display of *The Last Picture Show* (71, Peter Bogdanovich) that established her. Her frustrated wife in that movie is probably a cleverer performance than Cloris Leachman's (who got the supporting actress Oscar). Burstyn frets, sighs, lusts, and lies, but there is a kindness in her understanding of, and brief temptation by, the young, and a wholesome delight in her memories of "the Lion." She was the wife in *Alex in Wonderland* (71, Paul Mazursky); the mother in *The Exorcist* (73, William Friedkin)—a part not really accessible to humane acting; *Harry and Tonto* (74, Mazursky); winning her own Oscar in *Alice Doesn't Live Here Anymore* (74, Martin Scorsese), a good performance in a flawed film, but far from her best work; helplessly out of her element being asked to model clothes and esoteric time schemes in *Providence* (77, Alain Resnais); and more removed from her roots still in *A Dream of Passion* (78, Jules Dassin). *Same Time, Next Year* (78, Robert Mulligan) was as close as she had ever come to a standard American entertainment.

In the eighties, she did what she could and what she had to do. She was closely associated with the Actors Studio (as spokesperson and leader), and sometimes in her movies she seemed to be too much an advocate of "acting": very good in *Resurrection* (80, Daniel Petrie); *The Silence of the North* (81, Allan Winton King); as the convicted killer on TV in *The People vs. Jean Harris* (81, George Schaefer), catching Harris's self-destructive loftiness; *The Ambassador* (84, J. Lee Thompson); *Surviving* (85, Waris Hussein); *Into Thin Air* (85, Roger Young); *Twice in a Lifetime* (85, Bud Yorkin); *Act of Vengeance* (86, John Mackenzie); *Something in Common* (86, Glenn Jordan); beautifully suburban-net-curtained as the unwitting neighbor to spies in *Pack of Lies* (87, Anthony Page); *Hanna's War* (88, Menahem Golan); *When You Remember Me* (90, Harry Winer); *Dying Young* (91, Joel Schumacher); and excellent in *The Cemetery Club* (93, Bill Duke).

Burstyn is by now our most daring old lady—it is hard to think of anyone who could so lower her defenses as she did in the harrowing *Requiem for a Dream* (00, Darren Aronofsky). But such commitment isn't often rewarded, and Burstyn has more than her share of TV sentimentality: *Getting Out* (94, John Korty); *Getting Gotti* (94, Young); *Trick of the Eye* (94, Ed Kaplan); *When a Man Loves a Woman* (94, Luis Mandoki); *The Color of*

Evening (94, Stephan Stafford); *Roommates* (95, Peter Yates); *The Baby-Sitters Club* (95, Melanie Mayron); *How to Make an American Quilt* (95, Jocelyn Moorhouse); *My Brother's Keeper* (95, Jordan); *Follow the River* (95, Martin Davidson); *The Spitfire Grill* (96, Lee David Zlotoff); *Deceiver* (97, Jonas and Joshua Pate); *The Patron Saint of Liars* (98, Stephen Gyllenhaal); *Playing by Heart* (98, Willard Carroll); *Flash* (98, Simon Wincer); *Night Ride Home* (99, Jordan); *The Yards* (00, James Gray); *Mermaid* (00, Peter Masterson); *Walking Across Egypt* (00, Arthur Allan Seidelman); *Dodson's Journey* (01, Gregg Champion); *Within These Walls* (01, Mike Robe); *Divine Secrets of the Ya-Ya Sisterhood* (02, Callie Khouri); *Cross the Line* (02, Jamal Joseph); *Red Dragon* (02, Brett Ratner); *Brush With Fate* (03, Brent Shields).

Richard Burton (Richard Walter Jenkins Jr.) (1925–84), b. Pontrhdyfen, Wales
Educated at Port Talbot and Oxford, and in the RAF from 1944 to 1947, he made his stage debut in 1943 and by the mid-1950s had established himself as one of the more exciting young actors on the British stage. His film career had begun in 1948 with *The Last Days of Dolwyn* (Emlyn Williams), and he made *Now Barabbas Was a Robber* (49, Gordon Parry), *Waterfront* (50, Michael Anderson), *The Woman With No Name* (51, Ladislas Vajda), and *Green Grow the Rushes* (51, Derek Twist) before Fox called him to Hollywood. Thus after the ponderously romantic *My Cousin Rachel* (52), Burton starred in the first CinemaScope picture, *The Robe* (53)—both films directed by Henry Koster. Arguably, Burton was never able to shake off the image of a latter-day Barrymore, and he gradually succumbed to the quantity of costume drama he was asked to play in. That is to say nothing of his meeting with Elizabeth Taylor while campaigning on *Cleopatra* (63, Joseph L. Mankiewicz), their marriage, and the lugubrious pairing of them in so many films. A man beset by obstacles and probably always a little contemptuous of the cinema, Burton had the equipment, in voice and face, demanded by the screen. But only once, and then in one of his least noted films, did his talent really show itself: as the fatalistic officer in Nicholas Ray's *Bitter Victory* (58).

Otherwise, there is not much to choose between his early costume romances—*The Prince of Players* (54, Philip Dunne), *Rains of Ranchipur* (55, Jean Negulesco), and Rossen's *Alexander the Great* (55)—and the international prestige packages: *The Taming of the Shrew* (67, Franco Zeffirelli); *Dr. Faustus* (67), directed by Burton and Neville Coghill; and *Anne of the Thousand Days* (70, Charles Jarrott). As these films show, Burton was all too willing to dress up and indulge in a rather hollow, grand manner of acting. He was just as evasive in those films with his wife that were marketed as a vicarious peep into one of the notorious romances of the 1960s: *The V.I.P.s* (63, Anthony Asquith); Minnelli's *The Sandpiper* (65); Mike Nichols's *Who's Afraid of Virginia Woolf?* (66); *The Comedians* (67, Peter Glenville); even the Losey/Tennessee Williams *Boom!* (68).

From his earliest days in Hollywood, Burton preserved the illusion of independence, working when he wanted in the theatre, returning to England for a few films, and finding time to watch rugby matches. But the films seldom proved worthwhile: *Seawife* (57, Bob McNaught); *Look Back in Anger* (59, Tony Richardson); *Dr. Faustus;* and Donen's *Staircase* (69). Just as Burton seemed to shrink from conventional roles, so he never established a firm screen character. There are only glimpses of what it might be in such as *The Desert Rats* (53, Robert Wise); *Bitter Victory; The Bramble Bush* (60, Daniel Petrie); Huston's *The Night of the Iguana* (64), Martin Ritt's *The Spy Who Came in from the Cold* (65); and *The Assassination of Trotsky* (72, Joseph Losey). In the seventies, he gave himself up to a run of uniquely unsatisfying films: *Villain* (71, Michael Tuchner); *Raid on Rommel* (71, Henry Hathaway); *Hammersmith Is Out* (72, Peter Ustinov); *Bluebeard* (72, Edward Dmytryk); for TV, the ridiculous *Divorce His, Divorce Hers* (72, Waris Hussein), shown only weeks before he and Taylor drifted into noisy separation; *The Journey* (74, Vittorio de Sica); *Rappresaglia* (74, Georges Pan Cosmatos); *The Klansman* (74, Terence Young); *The Medusa Touch* (78, Jack Gold); *The Wild Geese* (78, Andrew V. McLaglen); and *Breakthrough* (79, McLaglen).

Notoriety, fatigue, and alcohol kept him off the screen for a few years and he returned with a new, uncomfortable brand of haggard, aghast tension in *Exorcist II: The Heretic* (77, John Boorman) and *Equus* (77, Sidney Lumet), which brought him close enough to a sentimental Oscar for the public humiliation of ". . . and the winner is Richard . . . Dreyfuss," whereupon he gave his most reserved rendering of pain in years.

Little was left in the last years but the eyes— still lovely, but horrified—and the voice, which had turned into the rasp of mortification: *Lovespell* (79, Tom Donovan); *Circle of Two* (80, Jules Dassin); *Absolution* (81, Anthony Page); for TV, *Wagner* (83, Tony Palmer) and *Ellis Island* (84, Jerry London); and the interrogator in *1984* (84, Michael Radford).

Tim Burton, b. Burbank, California, 1960

1982: *Vincent* (s). 1983: *Hansel and Gretel* (s). 1984: *Frankenweenie* (s); "Aladdin," an episode in *Faerie Tale Theatre*. 1985: *Pee-Wee's Big Adventure*. 1988: *Beetlejuice*. 1989: *Batman*. 1990: *Edward Scissorhands*. 1992: *Batman Returns*. 1994: *Ed Wood*. 1996: *Mars Attacks!*. 1999: *Sleepy Hollow*. 2001: *Planet of the Apes*. 2003: *Big Fish*.

There is a way in which Tim Burton's life so far has been the opposite of the kind of story he wants to tell. For he keeps returning to the theme of a displaced or misshapen child who must try to make a way in a hostile world. *Vincent*, his first short (done when he was an animator at Disney, with narration by Vincent Price), set out to show the nightmarish inner life of an outwardly ordinary child; *Pee-Wee* is a classic dysfunctional child who goes around looking like an adult; *Beetlejuice* is a rogue sprite, a kind of Peter Pan whose shadow took a course in special effects; *Edward Scissorhands* is a classic inventor's mistake; and then there is *Batman*, which in Burton's two pictures has become a comic-book world for foundlings and repressed personalities, with the Penguin as a babe so hideous he is put in a closed basket and sent to the sewers—Moses in Harry Lime Land.

Meanwhile, Burton, still only in his forties, has gone from working-class Burbank and a childhood spent watching Vincent Price in Roger Corman movies, to teenage years on Super 8, to Disney and the California Institute of Arts . . . to amazing stories, untold fame, and residuals enough to fill the banks of Gotham. How can he stand such happiness?

Burton is the most clear-cut example of the movie brat made by an age of horror, fantasy, animation, and effects. There is not really a hint of the straight world in his films, and those who miss such things should face the possibility that Burton (and his contemporaries) have never noticed such a thing. In other words, photography for him is only a way of making effects. He does not understand that it was ever reckoned as a way of recording nature. Everything in a Burton film expresses the distorted feelings of a resolute, inescapable loneliness—his world is constitutionally warped and explosive.

The picture business has elected to regard Burton as a genius who brings children and teenagers into the movie theatres. Yet his two biggest pictures, the *Batman* pair, are strangely dark and slyly adult. They are not content with the comic books or the TV *Batman* of the 1960s. They can be read as very disturbing films—or might be, if they were better organized. For Burton's unquestioned visual genius has not yet mastered or found a way of doing without narrative. *Batman Returns*, especially, is an unlikely chaos of fascinating characters jostling and trying to make themselves heard in an incoherent story.

Not many futures are as eagerly awaited. The tragedy of *Edward Scissorhands* seems to me not just Burton's best work so far, but the film most suited to his inclinations. However, can he insist on furthering that search when so many people in Hollywood tell him he is gold? Can he last as a lost, hurt child? Or does he become a woeful, burnt-out boy wonder, like Orson Welles?

Not too many Burton fans can be happy with

recent developments. He did produce the very elegant *Nightmare Before Christmas* (93, Henry Selick), while *Ed Wood* was a rare and charmingly kind treatment of Hollywood lowlife. But the mix of visual extremism and deadpan attitude has not thrived—as witness the calamity of *Mars Attacks!*, the cliché prettiness of *Sleepy Hollow*, and the violent confusion of *Planet of the Apes*, which was so much less witty than the original series.

Steve Buscemi, b. Brooklyn, New York, 1957
1992: *What Happened to Pete* (s). 1996: *Trees Lounge*. 2000: *Animal Factory*.

There is now in America a group of excellent character actors who also direct—it includes Tom Noonan, Kevin Spacey, Sean Penn, and Steve Buscemi, who has also made himself one of the best-known faces in modern movies. As an actor, Buscemi is easily cast as hood, low-life, baby-faced thug, sleazeball, scumbag—or as a kind of Brooklyn Peter Lorre (there is a poetic resemblance). But just as his acting is invariably spot on, so he has adjusted to directing without any sense of being intimidated or needing to show off. *Animal Factory* is a very tough look at prison life, while *Trees Lounge* had Buscemi as the lead in scenes from a Long Island bar (in a way, both are about being confined). In addition, he has done excellent work directing episodes from *Oz*, *Homicide*, and *The Sopranos* (he did the great lost-in-the-woods story).

The directing could yet become his big thing. Still, for the moment he is our best sickly psychopath: he had been doing bit parts for several years already before he began to attract notice in *Parting Glances* (86, Bill Sherwood); *Mystery Train* (89, Jim Jarmusch); *Slaves of New York* (89, James Ivory); *King of New York* (90, Abel Ferrara); Mink in *Miller's Crossing* (90, Joel and Ethan Coen); the hood who tries to shoot Nicole Kidman in *Billy Bathgate* (91, Robert Benton); *Barton Fink* (91, Coen); *In the Soup* (92, Alexander Rockwell); Mr. Pink in *Reservoir Dogs* (92, Quentin Tarantino); *CrissCross* (92, Chris Menges); *Rising Sun* (93, Philip Kaufman).

He was in *The Hudsucker Proxy* (94, Coen); *Somebody to Love* (94, Rockwell); *Pulp Fiction* (94, Tarantino); the harassed filmmaker in *Living in Oblivion* (95, Tom DiCillo); *Dead Man* (95, Jarmusch); *Things to Do in Denver When You're Dead* (95, Gary Fleder); *Desperado* (95, Robert Rodriguez); not willing to debate the matter in *Fargo* (96, Coen); *The Search for One-Eyed Jimmy* (96, Sam Henry Kass); *Escape from L.A.* (96, John Carpenter); *Kansas City* (96, Robert Altman); the Marietta Mangler in *Con Air* (97, Simon West); *The Real Blonde* (98, DiCillo); *The Wedding Singer* (98, Frank Coraci); Donny in *The Big Lebowski* (98, Coen).

Armageddon (98, Michael Bay) was one of his few mainstream films, but he reestablished his below-ground credentials with *The Impostors* (98, Stanley Tucci); a homeless guy in *Big Daddy* (99, Dennis Dugan); *28 Days* (00, Betty Thomas); and Seymour in *Ghost World* (01, Terry Zwigoff).

He is now established as a favourite character actor: *Double Whammy* (02, DiCillo); *The Grey Zone* (01, Tim Blake Nelson); *Domestic Disturbance* (01, Harold Becker); *Forest Hills Bob* (01, Robert Downey Sr); *The Laramie Project* (02, Moises Kaufman); *Love in the Time of Money* (02, Peter Mattei); *13 Moons* (02, Rockwell); *Mr Deeds* (02, Steve Brill); *Spy Kids 2* (02, Rodriguez); *Deadrockstar* (02, Mark Boon Jr).

David Butler (1894–1979),
b. San Francisco, California
1927: *High School Hero*; *Win That Girl*; *Masked Emotions* (codirected with Kenneth Hawks). 1928: *The News Parade*; *Prep and Pep*. 1929: *William Fox Movietone Follies of 1929*; *Chasing Through Europe* (codirected with Alfred Werker); *Sunny Side Up*. 1930: *Just Imagine*; *High Society Blues*. 1931: *Delicious*; *A Connecticut Yankee*; *Down to Earth*; *Handle With Care*; *Hold Me Tight*. 1932: *Business and Pleasure*. 1933: *My Weakness*. 1934: *Bottoms Up*; *Handy Andy*; *Have a Heart*; *Bright Eyes*. 1935: *The Little Colonel*; *The Littlest Rebel*; *Doubting Thomas*. 1936: *Captain January*; *White Fang*; *Pigskin Parade*. 1937: *You're a Sweetheart*; *Ali Baba Goes to Town*. 1938: *Kentucky*; *Three Men and a Girl*; *They're Off*. 1939: *East Side of Heaven*; *That's Right, You're Wrong*. 1940: *If I Had My Way*; *You'll Find Out*. 1941: *Caught in the Draft*; *Playmates*. 1942: *Road to Morocco*; *They Got Me Covered*. 1943: *Thank Your Lucky Stars*. 1944: *Shine on Harvest Moon*; *The Princess and the Pirate*. 1946: *San Antonio* (codirected with Raoul Walsh); *The Time, the Place and the Girl*; *Two Guys from Milwaukee*. 1947: *My Wild Irish Rose*. 1948: *Two Guys from Texas*. 1949: *Look for the Silver Lining*; *It's a Great Feeling*; *John Loves Mary*; *The Story of Seabiscuit*. 1950: *Tea for Two*; *The Daughter of Rosie O'Grady*. 1951: *Painting the Clouds with Sunshine*; *Lullaby of Broadway*. 1952: *Where's Charley?*; *April in Paris*. 1953: *By the Light of the Silvery Moon*; *Calamity Jane*. 1954: *The Command*; *King Richard and the Crusaders*. 1955: *Jump Into Hell*; *Glory*; *The Right Approach*. 1956: *The Girl He Left Behind*. 1967: *C'mon, Let's Live a Little*.

Having worked as a stage actor, Butler joined Thomas Ince in 1913 and moved on to D. W. Griffith and acted in *The Greatest Thing in Life* (18) and *The Girl Who Stayed at Home* (19). He continued acting until 1927: *The Sky Pilot* (21, King Vidor); *According to Hoyle* (22, W. S. Van Dyke), made for his own production company; *The Wise*

Kid (22, Tod Browning); *Desire* (23, Rowland V. Lee); *The Narrow Street* (24, William Beaudine); *Code of the West* (25, William K. Howard); *Havoc* (25, Lee); *Wages for Wives* (25, Frank Borzage); *The Blue Eagle* (26, John Ford); and *Seventh Heaven* (27, Borzage).

As a director, Butler served long in the cause of wholesomeness, usually in the form of second-class musicals. At Fox, Paramount, and Warners, he handled the bland energies of Shirley Temple, Bing Crosby, and Doris Day without any aside other than the good-natured digs at Jack Carson in *It's a Great Feeling,* in which Butler himself appears, declining to direct that resident Warners ham. It spoke for durability that in the mid-1950s Butler even moved into wide-screen action films.

Gabriel Byrne, b. Dublin, Ireland, 1950
Somehow, I always have the urge to reach out and tickle Gabriel Byrne. I think it's because his uncommon aura of gloom and sadness seems so complete it likely masks a teaser or a practical joker. But looking the way he does, how is he ever going to get cast in comedy—especially when films incline so naturally towards ruined priests, morose gangsters, and depressed terrorists? And, truth to tell, he did the poker-faced, life-is-short routine so superbly in *Miller's Crossing* (90, Joel and Ethan Coen) that he might as well laugh sometimes. That's not just his best film, it's one of the best performances in American film—the whole melancholy routine. And too much sadness will weaken you. I am also tempted by the legend that his sour, stoic gaze set firm after *The Usual Suspects,* in which he had been led to believe that his character was Keyser Soze.

There are reference books that say, before acting, he taught Spanish to girls—so don't tell me he doesn't see a joke. He played at the Abbey Theatre, and is constitutionally Irish still, no matter that he seems to reside in Southern California and was once married to Ellen Barkin. Surely she made him smile.

He was in *The Outsider* (79, Tony Luraschi); *Excalibur* (81, John Boorman); *The Keep* (83, Michael Mann); *Wagner* (83, Tony Palmer); *Hanna K.* (83, Costa-Gavras); *Defence of the Realm* (85, David Drury); as Byron in *Gothic* (86, Ken Russell); *Lionheart* (87, Franklin J. Schaffner); with Ellen Barkin in *Siesta* (87, Mary Lambert); the husband in *Julia and Julia* (87, Peter Del Monte); *Hello Again* (87, Frank Perry); *A Soldier's Tale* (88, Larry Parr); *Diamond Skulls* (89, Nicholas Broomfield); *Shipwrecked* (90, Nils Gaup), made in Norway; *Cool World* (92, Ralph Bakshi); *Point of No Return* (93, John Badham); associate producer on *Into the West* (93, Mike Newell); *Little Women* (94, Gillian Armstrong); *A Simple Twist of Fate* (94, Gillies MacKinnon); *Trial by Jury* (94, Heywood Gould); *Frankie Starlight*

(95, Michael Lindsay-Hogg); as Dean Keaton in *The Usual Suspects* (95, Bryan Singer)—his first hit; *Dead Man* (96, Jim Jarmusch); *Mad Dog Time* (96, Larry Bishop); *The Last of the High Kings* (96, David Keating), which he also cowrote; *The Brylcream Boys* (96, Terence Ryan); *The End of Violence* (97, Wim Wenders); *Smilla's Sense of Snow* (97, Bille August); as Lionel Powers, tycoon plus, in TV's *Weapons of Mass Destruction* (97, Steve Surjik); *Polish Wedding* (98, Theresa Connelly); *Enemy of the State* (98, Tony Scott); as d'Artagnan in *The Man in the Iron Mask* (98, Randall Wallace); *Stigmata* (99, Rupert Wainwright); as Satan himself, dry and amusing, in the woefully disappointing *End of Days* (99, Peter Hyams); *When Brendan Met Trudy* (00, Kieron J. Walsh).

As well as being very hard-working, he has clear ambitions as writer, producer, and director. He was executive producer on *In the Name of the Father* (93, Jim Sheridan), and there is a film mentioned in references sources—*The Lark in the Clear Air* (96)—which he wrote, produced, and directed. But I've never seen it.

He was on TV in the series *Madigan Men* (00); *Virginia's Room* (02, Peter Markle); *Spider* (02, David Cronenberg); *Emmett's Mark* (02, Keith Snyder); *Shade* (03, Damian Nieman).

C

James Caan, b. Queens, New York, 1939
Sonny Corleone dies too soon—don't we all feel that, as he is shot to tatters at the tollbooth on Long Island? Not that he could survive, not with his intemperate preference for instinct over strategy. Still, with Sonny's going, Michael's overcast has no rival, or alternative. We want more of James Caan's silly, flaky, hair-on-the-chest Sonny, because he stands up for life. If *you* were going to get eliminated, you'd rather Sonny did it than Michael.

The Godfather (72, Francis Coppola) was the end to Caan's youth. He was more reserved thereafter, and likely took himself too seriously. But in the decade or so before Sonny, Caan had tried anything: a tiny piece in *Irma La Douce* (63, Billy Wilder); *Lady in a Cage* (64, Walter Grauman); *The Glory Guys* (65, Arnold Laven); *Red Line 7000* (65, Howard Hawks); *El Dorado* (67, Hawks); *Games* (67, Curtis Harrington); *Countdown* (68, Robert Altman); *Journey to Shiloh* (68, William Hale); as the feebleminded footballer in *The Rain People* (69, Coppola); and as Rabbit Angstrom in *Rabbit, Run* (70, Jack Smight)—if only the movies had persisted with those Updike novels. But the role that made Caan, before Sonny, was that of dying footballer Brian Piccolo for TV in *Brian's Song* (70, Buzz Kulik).

He had a supporting part in *T. R. Baskin* (71, Herbert Ross), and after a supporting actor nomination for *The Godfather,* he did *Cinderella Liberty* (73, Mark Rydell); *Slither* (73, Howard Zieff); and *Freebie and the Bean* (74, Richard Rush)—wayward choices. He was far better in *The Gambler* (74, Karel Reisz), where his energy was channeled into the story's Dostoyevskyan depths. He was briefly reprised in *The Godfather, Part II* (74, Coppola), and he played Billy Rose in *Funny Lady* (75, Ross). Then came *The Killer Elite* (75, Sam Peckinpah); *Rollerball* (75, Norman Jewison); *Harry and Walter Go to New York* (76, Rydell); *Another Man, Another Chance* (77, Claude Lelouch); *A Bridge Too Far* (77, Richard Attenborough); *Comes a Horseman* (78, Alan J. Pakula); and *Little Moon & Jud McGraw* (79, Bernard Girard).

So many of these pictures were duds, and still Caan had not carried a successful movie. In *Chapter Two* (79, Robert Moore), he seemed remote from both the part and the film. In truth, he was embarked on a crisis involving marriage, drugs, and finances, to say nothing of his attempts to direct and complete *Hide in Plain Sight* (80), a touching movie about a father who risks losing his child when the stepfather disappears into the witness relocation program.

Thief (81, Michael Mann) was a throwback to the earlier Caan, and a fine, stoic, but desperate movie—it may be the actor's best work. *Les Uns et les Autres* (81, Lelouch) was a disaster, and *Kiss Me Goodbye* (82, Robert Mulligan) might have been taken as a verdict on Caan's career.

He was away five years and came back markedly heavier, grayer, and sadder: but *Gardens of Stone* (87, Coppola) was affecting. Then came *Alien Nation* (88, Graham Baker), a cameo in *Dick Tracy* (90, Warren Beatty), and a fine performance of beleaguered authorial machismo in *Misery* (90, Rob Reiner). He missed warmth or plausibility as another gangster in *Honeymoon in Vegas* (91, Andrew Bergman), and found himself in one more major flop, *For the Boys* (91, Rydell). He was in *The Program* (93, David S. Ward); *Flesh and Bone* (93, Steve Kloves).

The idea persists—not least in his mind—that Caan might have been a big star. So he is cast, and sometimes indulged, a lot. Still, he begins to gather a few nice world-weary hitters, and it is good to see him holding himself together: *Tashunga* (95, Nils Gaup); *A Boy Called Hate* (95, Mitch Mason); *Bottle Rocket* (96, Wes Anderson); *Eraser* (96, Chuck Russell); *Bulletproof* (96, Ernest Dickerson); *This Is My Father* (98, Paul Quinn); as Philip Marlowe in *Poodle Springs* (98, Bob Rafelson) for TV; awful in *Mickey Blue Eyes* (99, Kelly Makin); *The Yards* (00, James Gray); *Luckytown Blues* (00, Paul Nicholas); good in *The Way of the Gun* (00, Christopher McQuarrie);

Viva Las Nowhere (00, Jason Bloom); *In the Boom Boom Room* (00, Barbara Kopple); *Warden of Red Rock* (01, Stephen Gyllenhaal); *A Glimpse of Hell* (01, Mikael Salomon); *In the Shadows* (01, Ric Roman Waugh); *Night at the Golden Eagle* (01, Adam Rifkin); *City of Ghosts* (02, Matt Dillon); *The Lathe of Heaven* (02, Philip Haas).

We begin to wonder why he isn't in *The Sopranos,* he seems to be in nearly everything else: *Blood Crime* (02, William A. Graham); *Dogville* (03, Lars von Trier); *This Thing of Ours* (03, Danny Provenzano); *Jericho Mansion* (03, Alberto Sciamma); *The Incredible Mrs Ritchie* (03, Paul Johansson); *Elf* (03, Jon Favreau).

Michael Cacoyannis, b. Cyprus, 1922
1953: *Kyriakatiko Xypnima/Windfall in Athens.* 1955: *Stella; To Koritsi Me Ta Mara/The Girl in Black.* 1957: *To Telefteo Psemma/A Matter of Dignity.* 1960: *Eroica/Our Last Spring; Il Relitto/The Wastrel.* 1961: *Elektra.* 1965: *Zorba the Greek.* 1967: *The Day the Fish Came Out.* 1971: *The Trojan Women.* 1975: *Attilas '74* (d). 1977: *Iphigenia.* 1987: *Sweet Country.* 1993: *Pano Kato ke Plagios/Up, Down, and Sideways.* 1999: *Varya/ The Cherry Orchard.*

When the Second World War began, Cacoyannis was studying law in England. He stayed, worked for the BBC, and eventually joined the Old Vic as an actor. When he returned to Greece he began to direct films and quickly became the luminary of Greek cinema. His first films were impressive by any standards: intense emotional melodramas, set in Athens and the provinces, often graced by the photography of Walter Lassally. *Stella* introduced Melina Mercouri, while *The Girl in Black* and *A Matter of Dignity* centered on the melancholy beauty of Elli Lambetti. But the strain of sustaining a native and modern Greek cinema proved too much, and in the 1960s he fell back on classical adaptations, with Irene Papas as *Electra* and a spectacular international cast in *The Trojan Women.* Worst of all, and most successful, was *Zorba the Greek,* a film that reeked of tourist ouzo and encouraged Anthony Quinn to see himself as a noble savage. His work was evidently inhibited by the political situation in Greece. *Attila* was a partisan account of the Turkish invasion of his home island, but *Iphigenia* was a return to Euripides and Irene Papas's blatant declaiming. Like the earlier attempts, it came off as an inducement to high-culture tourists.

Nicolas Cage (Nicholas Kim Coppola), b. Long Beach, California, 1964
Around the time of *Leaving Las Vegas* (95, Mike Figgis)—a stunning performance and deserved Oscar winner—Nicolas Cage let it be known that he had a policy of mixing dangerous, offbeat roles with mainstream entertainment pictures. Even at

the time, it sounded like an attempt at self-persuasion, and now it has to be said that the Cage of the last few years has been distressingly fixed on money-making movies of questionable worth. This is the more disappointing in that he was always a lead actor riven with intriguing flaws, whereas lately he has seemed entranced with being cast as surly badasses, too full of attitude to leave room for the human complexity of *Leaving Las Vegas.*

Still, he is a determined maverick, a natural outsider, with Coppola blood that insists on doing things the unlikely way. David Lynch once called him "the jazz musician of actors," and even if he has seemed to be coasting lately, Cage could develop into a very rare middle-aged figure. If he doesn't have enough money yet to settle for risk, then what is the point of money?

He is the son of dancer Joy Vogelsong and literature professor August Coppola (the older brother to Francis), and he has always shown the large, if sometimes incoherent, artistic aspirations of his father. He left Beverly Hills High School at seventeen and has been acting ever since: *Fast Times at Ridgemont High* (82, Amy Heckerling); *Valley Girl* (83, Martha Coolidge); *Rumble Fish* (83, Coppola); *Racing with the Moon* (84, Richard Benjamin); *The Cotton Club* (84, Coppola); a big challenge in *Birdy* (84, Alan Parker); rowing in *The Boy in Blue* (86, Charles Jarrott).

Then a run of romantic roles helped establish him (and he sounded like Jimmy Stewart)—*Peggy Sue Got Married* (86, Coppola); wooing Cher with great feeling in *Moonstruck* (87, Norman Jewison); *Raising Arizona* (87, Joel Coen). As if to warn people, he ate a live roach in *Vampire's Kiss* (89, Robert Bierman), and gave off a wonderful comic-book sheen in *Wild at Heart* (90, Lynch). He followed with *Fire Birds* (90, David Green); *Zandalee* (91, Sam Pillsbury); *Honeymoon in Vegas* (92, Andrew Bergman); *Red Rock West* (92, John Dahl); *Amos & Andrew* (93, E. Max Frye); *Deadfall* (93, Christopher Coppola, his brother); *Trapped in Paradise* (94, George Gallo); *It Could Happen to You* (94, Bergman); *Guarding Tess* (94, Hugh Wilson); very villainous in *Kiss of Death* (95, Barbet Schroeder).

Then came *Leaving Las Vegas* and the maximization of opportunity: *The Rock* (96, Michael Bay); *Con Air* (97, Simon West); *Face/Off* (97, John Woo), a further study in nastiness; *City of Angels* (98, Brad Silberling); *Snake Eyes* (98, Brian De Palma); *8MM* (99, Joel Schumacher); working very hard in *Bringing Out the Dead* (99, Martin Scorsese), which costarred Patricia Arquette, his wife from 1995 to 2000; close to shameful in the absurd *Gone in 60 Seconds* (00, Dominic Sena); *The Family Man* (00, Brett Ratner); *Captain Corelli's Mandolin* (01, John Madden); *Windtalkers*, (02, Woo).

Unpredictability is now his only constant: he acted in and directed *Sonny* (02); he was close to brilliant as twins in *Adaptation* (02, Spike Jonze); and the *Matchstick Men* (03, Ridley Scott); *Land of Destiny* (03, Woo).

James Cagney (1899–1986), b. New York
Cagney never lent himself to a cult. Just as in the 1930s he complained of having to make too many undistinguished pictures, so he was in fixed retirement for many years, after a last working decade in which he was beset by unworthy material. Nevertheless, he had become such a household figure that every nightclub entertainer thought himself obliged to carry an impersonation of Cagney. Such imitations do not conceal the fact that Cagney is one of the most original and compelling performers in American cinema. Although endlessly associated with the supposedly "brutal" and "realistic" qualities of the gangster film, Cagney is one of the most stylized of actors. Look past that familiar belligerence and you will find a compressed gaiety and a delight in outrageous, inventive movement. His reputation for slugging women on the screen needs to be compared with Dietrich's man-eating act: in both cases, there is an innate tenderness and a real sexual inquisitiveness that makes the action ambiguous. Cagney is charged with restlessness, and yet he always contrives to discharge the agitation daintily or with conscious style. Watch him listen to other players and you will realize how often other actors cruised. If he is frightening it is because of that attentiveness and the feeling that what is being said or done to him may provoke extraordinary and unexpected reactions. No one could move so arbitrarily from tranquillity to dementia, because Cagney was a dancer responding to a melody that he alone heard. Like a sprite or goblin he seemed to be in touch with an occult source of vitality. What a Bilbo Baggins he would have made; or imagine his Hyde to Fred Astaire's Jekyll.

Cagney began in vaudeville and was a song-and-dance man with Joan Blondell in *Penny Arcade* when Warners bought the show as a package and turned it into *Sinner's Holiday* (30, John Adolfi). He was signed up by Warners and, after appearing in *Doorway to Hell* (30, Archie Mayo) and William Wellman's *Other Men's Women* (31), he made his first great impact in *Public Enemy* (31, Wellman), one of the original gangster films, in which Cagney smacked Mae Clarke in the face with a cut grapefruit and ended a ballet of hysterical expiration dead on his mother's doorstep. It was the gleeful smartness in Cagney's playing that made *Public Enemy* so influential and that induced the public's ambivalent feelings toward the criminal classes. There was no doubt about the violence within Cagney, but he managed to relate the bootlegger's swagger to the boldly extended death throes of the finale in a way that made the character exotic and magical. He quickly became a star, cast largely as gangsters or tough, cynical men, notably harsh to women. After two films for Roy del Ruth—*Blonde Crazy* (31) and *Taxi!* (32)—he played a race-car driver in Hawks's *The Crowd Roars* (32) and a boxer in del Ruth's *Winner Take All* (32). Always snappy and aggressive, he was the dynamo at Warners: in Le Roy's *Hard to Handle* (33); Lloyd Bacon's *Picture Snatcher* (33); Mayo's *Mayor of Hell* (33); and then brilliant as the producer in Bacon's backstage musical, *Footlight Parade* (33). In del Ruth's *Lady Killer* (34) he again roughed up Mae Clarke, and in Michael Curtiz's *Jimmy the Gent* (34) he turned to comedy as rapid as automatic fire. It was at this time that Warners teamed him with the more stolid Pat O'Brien, perhaps because there was hardly an actress who could stand up to him—typical of this association was Lloyd Bacon's *The Irish in Us* (35). He was one of William Keighley's *G Men* (35) and then a redneck Bottom in Reinhardt's *A Midsummer Night's Dream* (35), a hint of Cagney's neglected comic impulse. Not that he wasted any of the black jokes in Hawks's *Ceiling Zero* (36), one of the most breathtaking analyses of the hard man in the American cinema. Cagney was on bad terms with Warners and made two poor pictures at Grand National—*Something to Sing About* (37, Victor Schertzinger) and *Boy Meets Girl* (38, Bacon)—before acting the coward to impress the kids in Curtiz's *Angels With Dirty Faces* (38), with O'Brien again and Ann Sheridan; *Boy Meets Girl*; the pleasantly silly *The Oklahoma Kid* (39, Bacon); and two more crime movies: Keighley's *Each Dawn I Die* (39) and Raoul Walsh's *The Roaring Twenties* (39). It is worth noting that these two films show how much more at ease he was in the genre than either of his costars, George Raft and Humphrey Bogart.

Cagney's Warners contract expired. He was anxious to form his own company, but was persuaded to stay at the studio for Wellman's *The Fighting 69th* (40); Keighley's *Torrid Zone* (40); Litvak's *City for Conquest* (40); Walsh's *Strawberry Blonde* (41); Keighley's *The Bride Came C.O.D.* (41); and Curtiz's *Captain of the Clouds* (42). Charges of Communist associations had been made against Cagney, and with his brother William he persuaded Warners to put him in *Yankee Doodle Dandy* (42), the biography of the superpatriotic showman, George M. Cohan, directed by Michael Curtiz. It won Cagney an Oscar, even if it did not fully reinstate him. It survives as his masterpiece, a manic Punchinello Uncle Sam, arse out, head forward, strutting his way through routines as if he had reinvented dance. Only this ferocious animation could have tamed the jingoism of the film; as Cohan, above

all, Cagney seems to be driven by nonhuman forces, like a toy running wild.

He was at the point now of having either to search for a mellower character or reprise his earlier roles. He was less successful as sentimental heroes in *Johnny Come Lately* (43, William K. Howard); Hathaway's *13 rue Madeleine* (46); and H. C. Potter's Saroyan adaptation, *The Time of Your Life* (48). He was happier in the rough stuff of Frank Lloyd's *Blood on the Sun* (46) and Warners invited him back to play Cody Jarrett in Walsh's *White Heat* (49), a delirious, psychopathic farewell to gangsterdom in which he was able to kick Virginia Mayo off a chair, cuddle in his mother Margaret Wycherly's lap, and perish in a lurid explosion. But most fascinating of all was the way Cagney "choreographed" Jarrett when suffering from one of his "headaches": he staggered endlessly, moaning and shrieking until some half a dozen prison guards were needed to restrain the rapt, seething doll. All the naïveté of Cagney's character was brought out in these crises and *White Heat* is one of his finest films.

Sadly, his career then declined: del Ruth's *West Point Story* (50); two films for Gordon Douglas—*Kiss Tomorrow Goodbye* (50) and *Come Fill the Cup* (51); John Ford's failure, *What Price Glory?* (52); as a demagogue in Walsh's *A Lion Is in the Streets* (53); good as a veteran gunfighter in Nicholas Ray's *Run for Cover* (55); in Charles Vidor's *Love Me or Leave Me* (55), not nearly as rough on Doris Day as he might once have been. He was in Robert Wise's *Tribute to a Bad Man* (56) and then rediscovered all his old interest as Lon Chaney in Joseph Pevney's *Man of a Thousand Faces* (57)—being called upon to portray a master of the grotesque revived Cagney's strange mime and the film carries great conviction. He then directed his only film, *Short Cut to Hell* (58); played Admiral Halsey in Robert Montgomery's *The Gallant Hours* (60); and roared off on the overdrive acceleration of Billy Wilder's *One, Two, Three* (61). Happily, the conniving Pepsi-Cola executive of that Berlin farce is one of his best parts and proof of how near Cagney's devil was to comedy.

He came back again, as police chief Rheinlander Waldo, in *Ragtime* (81, Milos Forman), sitting very still, but issuing his lines with whispered force, and on TV in *Terrible Joe Moran* (84, Joseph Sargent), as an ex-boxer in a wheelchair.

Dead and undimmed, he is proverbial now, a force of life and one of those stars who grow more lovely and mysterious as the years pass.

Sir Michael Caine (Maurice Micklewhite), b. London, 1933

The movie business once monopolized surreal success stories: lumberjacks who conveyed the proper thrill in Paramount boudoirs; failed nuns who found themselves in low-key close-ups.

Today, such unlikely metamorphoses are reserved for politics and commerce. But Michael Caine is an ex-porter at Smithfield meat market, quite securely in the movies, and seemingly perplexed that he has not yet turned into a swan. Perhaps the public is heartened by his ordinariness, yet it seldom enables Caine to relax. He tends to be as cold and barricaded as his spectacles; he may need to be rescued by a Pygmalion who will take away the horn-rims and discover something more than a cockney made nervous by awesome circumstances. He made one film in 1956—*A Hill in Korea* (Julian Amyes)—but it was in the early 1960s that he became what swinging Britain took for a star, principally as Len Deighton's sour hero, Harry Palmer: *Zulu* (64, Cy Endfield); *The Ipcress File* (65, Sidney J. Furie); *Alfie* (66, Lewis Gilbert)—his big hit; *The Wrong Box* (66, Bryan Forbes); *Gambit* (66, Ronald Neame); *Funeral in Berlin* (66, Guy Hamilton); *Hurry Sundown* (67, Otto Preminger); *Woman Times Seven* (67, Vittorio de Sica); *Billion Dollar Brain* (67, Ken Russell); *Play Dirty* (68, André de Toth); *Deadfall* (68, Forbes); *The Magus* (68, Guy Green); *The Italian Job* (69, Peter Collinson); *The Battle of Britain* (69, Hamilton); *Too Late the Hero* (70, Robert Aldrich); *Get Carter* (71, Mike Hodges); *The Last Valley* (71, James Clavell); *Kidnapped* (71, Delbert Mann); *Pulp* (72, Hodges); *Sleuth* (72, Joseph L. Mankiewicz), in which the trite two-hander makes him look sentimental; *The Black Windmill* (74, Don Siegel); *The Marseille Contract* (74, Robert Parrish); *The Wilby Conspiracy* (74, Ralph Nelson); *Peeper* (75, Peter Hyams); as the novelist in *The Romantic Englishwoman* (75, Joseph Losey); at last interesting and engaged in *The Man Who Would Be King* (75, John Huston); *Harry and Walter Go to New York* (76, Mark Rydell); *The Eagle Has Landed* (76, John Sturges); *A Bridge Too Far* (77, Richard Attenborough); *Silver Bears* (77, Ivan Passer); *Swarm* (78, Irwin Allen); *California Suite* (78, Herbert Ross); and *Ashanti* (79, Richard Fleischer).

Caine has risen to the state of beloved veteran, widely acclaimed as a resourceful actor who will try anything (he has done a clever, if rather obvious, book and video onscreen acting). By the time he published his autobiography, in 1992, he seemed like an institution. This writer remains unconvinced: Caine's work is indiscriminate, and he is still more at ease in supporting roles. I do not see or feel the evidence of character or depth in the mass of parts: *Beyond the Poseidon Adventure* (79, Allen); *The Island* (80, Michael Ritchie); as the killer in *Dressed to Kill* (80, Brian De Palma); *The Hand* (81, Oliver Stone); *Victory* (81, Huston); *Deathtrap* (82, Sidney Lumet); the professor in *Educating Rita* (83, Gilbert); *The Honorary Consul* (83, John Mackenzie); *Blame It On Rio* (84, Stanley Donen); *The Jigsaw Man* (84, Ter-

ence Young); *Water* (85, Dick Clement); and *The Holcroft Covenant* (85, John Frankenheimer).

He won the supporting actor Oscar in *Hannah and Her Sisters* (86, Woody Allen)—Berenger and Dafoe in *Platoon* were among the losers. He also played in *Sweet Liberty* (86, Alan Alda); *Mona Lisa* (86, Neil Jordan); *Half Moon Street* (86, Bob Swaim); *The Whistle Blower* (86, Simon Langton); *Jaws—The Revenge* (87, Joseph Sargent); *The Final Protocol* (87, Mackenzie); *Surrender* (87, Jerry Belson); *Without a Clue* (88, Thom Eberhardt); *Dirty Rotten Scoundrels* (88, Frank Oz); as the police inspector in *Jack the Ripper* (88, David Wickes), for TV; *A Shock to the System* (90, Jan Egelson); *Mr. Destiny* (90, James Orr); out of his depth in *Jekyll & Hyde* (90, Wickes); *Bullseye* (90, Michael Winner); very adroit in *Noises Off* (92, Peter Bogdanovich); as Scrooge in *The Muppet Christmas Carol* (92, Brian Henson); and *Blue Ice* (93, Russell Mulcahy).

Well, the Queen obviously reckons him as an actor; she knighted him in 2000. He's certainly worked for it, and stayed very cheerful, but I can only think of all the films HRH must have missed: like *On Deadly Ground* (94, Steven Seagal); a very silly and inscrutable Stalin in *World War II: When Lions Roared* (94, Sargent)—see Robert Duvall instead; doing Harry Palmer again in *Midnight in St. Petersburg* (95, Douglas Jackson) and *Bullet to Beijing* (95, George Mihalka); *Blood and Wine* (97, Bob Rafelson); again vacuous in *Mandela and de Klerk* (97, Sargent); Nemo in *20,000 Leagues Under the Sea* (97, Michael Anderson); *Shadow Run* (98, Geoffrey Reeve).

But I suspect the Queen saw *Little Voice* (98, Mark Herman) and *The Cider House Rules* (99, Lasse Hallstrom), where his Wilbur Larch won a second supporting-actor Oscar. After that, Sir Michael went back to habit with *The Debtors* (99, Evi Quaid); *Curtain Call* (99, Peter Yates); *Quills* (00, Philip Kaufman), where he is a little monotonous; *Shiner* (00, John Irvin); *Get Carter* (00, Stephen T. Kay); *Miss Congeniality* (00, Donald Petrie); *Last Orders* (01, Fred Schepisi).

He worked hard on *The Quiet American* (02, Phillip Noyce)—especially in saving it from the shelf—and he got an Oscar nomination. But truly he lacked the English class the role needed—the sourness of Graham Greene himself. After that he did *The Actors* (03, Conor McPherson); *Secondhand Lions* (03, Tim McCanlies).

James Cameron,
b. Kapuskasing, Canada, 1954
1982: *Piranha II: The Spawning*. 1984: *The Terminator*. 1986: *Aliens*. 1989: *The Abyss*. 1991: *Terminator 2: Judgment Day*. 1994: *True Lies*. 1997: *Titanic*. 2002: "Fresh Nation", episode from *Dark Angel* (TV); *Expedition Bismarck* (d). 2003: *Ghosts of the Abyss* (d).

It could be said of Cameron that no one did so much to redeem the eighties genre of high-tech threat through the overlay of genuine human interest stories. But that description smacks of the formulaic. Perhaps it would be more to the point to ask who smothered so many promising stories with effects and apparatus? All is likely to be made clear soon, for Cameron has a uniquely bounteous production deal. But he has been so successful already, what awaits him now except some personal abyss?

After a degree in physics from California State University, Fullerton, Cameron found work with Roger Corman building miniature sets. He went on to do process work and to be an art director on *Escape From New York* (81, John Carpenter); *Galaxy of Terror* (81, B. D. Clark); *Forbidden World* (82, Allan Holzman); and *Battle Beyond the Stars* (80, Jimmy T. Murakami).

Of his directorial films, *The Terminator* has an echoing mythic story, a raw, gutsy Linda Hamilton, Schwarzenegger cast with flair and humor, and a relaxed, economical air. *T2*, seven years later, was then the most expensive film ever made, desperate to show it, and minus the original poetry.

Along the way, *Aliens* was the most human of that trio, while *The Abyss* had the start of a rich, troubled marriage between Ed Harris and Mary Elizabeth Mastrantonio, before some stunning but lugubrious effects took over. Marriage might be Cameron's real subject: he has had and ended four marriages already—to a civilian, to his producer Gale Ann Hurd, to director Kathryn Bigelow, whose *Point Break* (91) he produced; and to actress Linda Hamilton.

He also made *Titanic*, which . . . well, made him "king of the world," if he thought so. Beyond its taking in more money than any other movie (so far), there's little to be said for it—except that it is the least interesting of his films. Anyway, he has been living like a king, I suppose. He is married again—to actress Suzy Amis—and he brought a strange and silly TV series into being, *Dark Angel*.

He was doodling a bit in his fondness for dead ships, and he contented himself with doing just the script (and the producer job) on *Terminator 3* (03, Jonathan Mostow).

Donald Seton Cammell (1934–96),
b. Edinburgh
1970: *Performance* (codirected with Nicolas Roeg). 1977: *Demon Seed.* 1987: *White of the Eye.* 1996: *Wild Side.*

As the sultry age of the late sixties and early seventies recedes, so Donald Cammell may seem most plausible as an invented or literary figure—the brilliant, handsome boy with roots in fine art, the occult, and drugs, who has only a few, threatened, credits for films that may be more intriguing in description than actually witnessed on screen. But Cammell was a real person—and in a future age of electronic amateurism, where countless characters and geniuses have fragmentary career outlines, he may even seem like a prototype. On a more mundane and tragic level, it is clear that, at the age of sixty-two, as a longtime and failed resident of Los Angeles, Cammell killed himself because he could not get enough opportunity to work.

He was the son of Charles Richard Cammell, who wrote about Byron and Aleister Crowley. As a youth, Donald attended the Royal College of Art and became a noted portrait painter (and an expert on portrait society) in London. He did illustrations for Alice Mary Hatfield's *King Arthur and the Round Table* when he was only nineteen. As such, he was very well placed as an artistic figure in what became "swinging London." That's how he got to be a screenwriter—on *The Touchables* (68, Robert Freeman), in which some groupies try to kidnap a pop singer, and *Duffy* (68, Robert Parrish), about half-brothers, played by James Coburn and James Fox.

One may see these ingredients feeding into the spectacularly outrageous yet enigmatic *Performance.* How did Roeg and Cammell collaborate? Maybe, like the Mick Jagger and James Fox characters, trying to resist osmosis. We know that Roeg shot the film, and that Cammell edited it— and legend has it that the larger aura of perverse experiment was more to Cammell's taste than Roeg's. Somehow, I have the feeling that not many people have ever watched *Performance* all the way through too many times. On the other hand, moments from it are as unforgettable as they are influential. Seldom has there been a vaguer, but more idyllic, stew of poisoned drugs and wicked sex—it may well be revealed one day as an ideal diversion for very self-consciously naughty children. And it could be a rare case where being there as it was done remained more interesting than any viewing of the finished film.

Demon Seed is awful, yet the idea of a computer mating with Julie Christie moved many people at the time. By now, Cammell was living largely in America, married to China Kong, and attracting the long-winded and ultimately misty overtures of such figures as Marlon Brando—who allegedly wanted Cammell to do a pirate film with him. Nothing developed until *White of the Eye,* which may be Cammell's most coherent film—and not to be damned on that account. Taking advantage of the tortured landscape around Globe, Arizona, it is a story of sex and serial killing that builds towards real fear. It also has good performances from David Keith and Cathy Moriarty.

What else is there to say? Cammell died in possession of a screenplay for *Pale Fire,* and a collaboration with Kenneth Tynan on a Jack the Ripper film. There was also a script set in Istanbul in

1933—called just '33—about the heroin trade, for which Cammell wanted Stanley Kubrick as director. Aren't such dreams more potent than the actual release of a bizarre sexual story—*Wild Side*—from which there dangles the eventual hope that we may one day get "the director's cut." As it was, New Image removed it from Cammell, and he asked for his name to be dropped.

There is a good, atmospheric documentary film (by Chris Rodley), and surely one day there must be a biography—for which Christopher Walken (he's in *Wild Side*) is the providential casting.

Jane Campion,
b. Waikanae, New Zealand, 1954

1982: *Peel* (s). 1983: *A Girl's Own Story* (s). 1984: *Passionless Moments* (s). 1985: *Two Friends*. 1989: *Sweetie*. 1990: *An Angel at My Table*. 1993: *The Piano*. 1996:*The Portrait of a Lady*. 1999: *Holy Smoke*. 2003: *In the Cut*.

From Europe or America, New Zealand looks like an offshore island of Australia, and films from New Zealand are easily misread as Australian products. But Cook Strait—the narrows between the two islands of New Zealand—is at least one thousand miles from the nearest Australian coast. That's about the distance between Paris and Moscow, or Dallas and Detroit. So New Zealand is a place unto itself, with thoughts of its own secret landscapes, the neighborliness of Australia, and the oceanic desert of the southwest Pacific. New Zealand has a cinema that should not be confused with Australia's, and in Jane Campion it has one of the more daring directors anywhere in the world.

After studying film in Australia, she made a number of shorts that won great acclaim at Cannes in 1986. *Two Friends* was a TV movie—made for Australian television—about two teenage girls. They were so real and particular, so unglamorous, so fresh in word and deed that one could feel a movie sensibility that easily seemed "literary"—in other words, the film had the feeling of novelistic texture and privacy, as well as a remarkable naturalness in the acting.

Campion remained most interested in awkward, shy, or marginal young women, people close to being outcasts or rejects, but in whom there is a great strength of private vision and tranquillity. Thus in *An Angel at My Table*—the autobiography of writer Janet Frame—the years in a mental hospital, the mistaken diagnosis, the pain and the humiliation, are all reduced by the talent that we know exists in this unprepossessing, chronically timid, and unactressy heroine. Such unworldliness has a way of looking after itself, Campion seems to suggest, and the film is not too far from a religious serenity amid all the travails.

This confidence owes a lot to Campion's style. She leaves things out; sometimes the viewer is frustrated by the lack of basic information. Some-

times this oddity of emphasis seems like a mirroring of the near-insanity, or the lack of ordinariness, in the central figures (this is true of *Sweetie*, too). Campion may still be wary of or uneasy with old-fashioned narrative. But her films exert their power through the mysterious or the cryptic collisions of their structure. The slightly fractured air leaves the films to heal in our minds, knitted together by the appetite for life and the invisible guidance of performance from actresses (notably Kerry Fox as Janet Frame) who come from so far away they are like people we are meeting.

The Piano was an astonishing step forward, yet it helped reveal Campion's earlier talent. This is a film about that commonplace genius, the human will, set in the semitropical frontier of New Zealand, with muddy oceans and wild shores. The sense of place, of spirit, and of silence is Wordsworthian. The love story needs so little charm or romance. And in the very severe look of Holly Hunter as her heroine, Campion found the rare poetry of *The Piano*. No one has better caught the mix of sensitivity and ferocity in the human imagination. *The Piano* is a great film in an age that has nearly forgotten such things.

As well as acting Oscars, *The Piano* won a screenplay Oscar for Campion. The international success of the film may make it harder for Campion to remain simply a New Zealander.

The Portrait of a Lady had major mistakes (as I thought): the several dream raptures damaged the tone; Malkovich was allowed to be too sinister—and if you can't stop him, then why cast him; and even Kidman seemed more valiant than natural. That said, and despite its complete commercial failure, it had passages of intense beauty and passionate cinema. *Holy Smoke* passed over me too easily, but *In the Cut* is one of the more promising things in sight, granted Ms. Campion's dedication to danger.

Milena Canonero, b. Turin, Italy
These days, the costume designer in movies personifies the way the industry has gone free-lance. Edith Head reigned at one studio (in her case, Paramount) for nearly four decades, rising from the rank of designer to creating the role of head of the design department, and thus mistress of a vast wardrobe. Head was as responsible for the Paramount "look" as any one person, and vital to the careers of many of that studio's stars. By contrast, there are now very few wardrobe departments. Instead, there are costume shops (open for parties, live events, and "ordinary" requirements as much as for show business) and there are great designers and their private workshops.

Costuming may seem a less secure job because of that, but costumiers are paid better, credited more lavishly, and they often have fruitful connections with the fashion industry—for the crossover of new clothing ideas from movie to street (and salon) is quicker now and more complicated. No respectable magazine can shoot a movie star without crediting designers, stylists, and the stores where the clothes can be bought. The screen is a ramp. From *Bonnie and Clyde* to *Moulin Rouge,* we live in an age where everyone has an urge to look like someone in a movie. Once upon a time, the arts may have taught us ethics; today they often settle for lifestyle accessories. Ward-robe consultancy has become an adjunct of psycho-therapy.

In that movement, Milena Canonero is a goddess—and she is generally accepted as one of the leading designers for movies (if they can afford her). Her work ranges from the modern exotic depraved (*A Clockwork Orange*), to the J. Peterman catalogue style (*Out of Africa*), to the authentic, everyday, and cool grungy (*Single White Female*). But she is at her best with a fusion of antique and modern that comes close to science fiction (*Titus*).

She began working in England with *A Clockwork Orange* (71, Stanley Kubrick), and she won her first Oscar for the fragrant, gossamer Gainsborough world of *Barry Lyndon* (75, Kubrick). But she was just as impressive with the prison range of *Midnight Express* (78, Alan Parker) and that tweed jacket Nicholson wears in *The Shining* (80, Kubrick). She won another Oscar for *Chariots of Fire* (81, Hugh Hudson), and has since worked on *The Hunger* (83, Tony Scott), where clothes blend into skin; *The Cotton Club* (84, Francis Ford Coppola); *Out of Africa* (85, Sydney Pollack); the skid-row chic of *Barfly* (87, Barbet Schroeder); *Tucker: The Man and His Dream* (88, Coppola); the comic-book primary of *Dick Tracy* (90, Warren Beatty), with Dick's heavy yellow coat nearly embossed on the screen; *The Godfather: Part III* (90, Coppola); *The Bachelor* (91, Roberto Faenza); *Single White Female* (92, Schroeder); *Damage* (93, Louis Malle), where the clothes are so right for those people it's creepy; *Only You* (94, Norman Jewison); *Love Affair* (94, Glenn Gordon Caron); *Death and the Maiden* (94, Roman Polanski); *Camilla* (95, Deepa Mehta); *Bulworth* (98, Beatty); *Tango* (98, Carlos Saura); *Titus* (99, Julie Taymor); *In the Boom Boom Room* (00, Barbara Kopple); *The Affair of the Necklace* (02, Charles Shyer); *Solaris* (02, Steven Soderbergh).

Eddie Cantor (Edward Israel Iskowitz) (1892–1964), b. New York

Al Jolson may have been America's biggest star in the early decades of the twentieth century, but Eddie Cantor wasn't far behind him—and in certain fields surpassed him. Orphaned early, he was brought up in poverty on New York's Lower East Side by his grandmother and by himself: as a young kid, he was already inventing the entertainer he was to become. By his mid-twenties, he was starring in successive editions of the Ziegfeld

Follies, alongside his great pals Will Rogers, W. C. Fields, and Fanny Brice. Throughout the twenties he triumphed on Broadway and in the recording studio—twenty top-ten hits in fifteen years (paltry compared to Jolson's eighty-plus, but including such standards as "Margie," "If You Knew Susie," and "Makin' Whoopee").

Then came his first Hollywood hit, the silent *Kid Boots* (26, Frank Tuttle), based on his big stage success. It's an oddity, because in the absence of his voice and his singing-dancing routines, his physical lightness and mournful face read more like Buster Keaton than the upbeat Cantor we get in sound. What's more, he's not only in pursuit of a girl—and the girl is Clara Bow!—but he gets her. (It's a golf story, by the way.) In his Goldwyn sound films, he's almost always desperately shy and trying to fend off determined young women. A second silent—*Special Delivery* (27, Roscoe Arbuckle)—flopped. And then, after a cameo in *Glorifying the American Girl* (29), came the first of the Goldwyns.

It was *Whoopee!* (30, Thornton Freeland), based on what was perhaps the biggest of his Broadway shows, and sold to Goldwyn by producer Ziegfeld in need of cash. Ziegfeld came along as coproducer, but it was a Goldwyn picture all the way, and since he kept it close to the original, it's a revelation today about twenties Broadway musical comedy: numbers that don't have a lot to do with anything, lots of glorious girls in over-the-top outfits, and too much of a silly plot (a politically incorrect story about a white girl and a supposed Indian who ends up acceptable because he isn't an Indian after all). Who cares? Cantor plays a weakling hypochondriac on the run from his determined nurse, Ethel Shutta, and when the action stops and he bursts forward to belt out "My Baby Don't Care for Clothes," it's heartstopping—the first time I watched *Whoopee!* on video, I ran this sequence seven times. Cantor is incandescent, strutting and hopping back and forth, spilling over with gaiety, demonstrating what the best of vaudeville and musical comedy had to offer: a tremendously generous personality, giving every ounce of itself to making you feel good. Jolson, like Garland, demands love from the audience; Cantor just wants you to be happy. The fact that he's in blackface for this number (and occasionally in his other Goldwyns) is irrelevant—neither politically correct nor incorrect—because this blackface is purely cosmetic: there's not the slightest suggestion of imitating or patronizing or colonizing blacks, not a touch of Jolsonish minstrelsy; this is just a Cantor trademark that works for him (and for us).

There were to be five more Goldwyn films, all to the same formula and most of them including routines Cantor had developed on the stage—like the orthopedic one in which he's tied up in knots.

First came *Palmy Days* (31, A. Edward Sutherland), about a criminal fake seer defeated by brave
little Eddie, who ends up with the strong-willed
Charlotte Greenwood; she literally wrestles him
to the ground (Oh, Miss Martin, you simply carry
me away!) There's *The Kid from Spain* (31, Leo
McCarey), with Eddie in the bullring; *Roman
Scandals* (33, Tuttle)—he dreams he's back in
ancient times; *Kid Millions* (34, Roy Del Ruth),
with a scheming Ethel Merman pretending to be
his mother; and *Strike Me Pink* (36, Norman Taurog), with Merman again. Cantor made extravagant claims for the box-office success of this run of
films, but *Variety* confirms that he was Hollywood's number-one attraction overseas, ahead of
Garbo, Dietrich, et al. By then Cantor was established as one of the biggest of all radio stars—his
show was in the top ten for at least a decade—and
he felt underappreciated by Goldwyn; they agreed
to disagree.

His later film career is relatively thin. Movies in
which he's the main attraction are the funny *Ali
Baba Goes to Town* (37, David Butler); *Forty Little Mothers* (40, Busby Berkeley, who had choreographed the first Goldwyns); *Show Business* (44,
Edward L. Marin); *If You Knew Susie* (48, Gordon
Douglas). And there are cameos in movies in
which he appears as himself, like the 1943 all-star
Thank Your Lucky Stars (43, Butler). Finally, just
as Jolson sang for Larry Parks in the hugely successful *Jolson Story* (46), Cantor provides the
voice for Keefe Brasselle in the far less successful
Eddie Cantor Story (53, Alfred E. Green). By
then he was a legend—for his tremendous career,
his almost obsessive philanthropizing (he invented
the March of Dimes), and his public devotion to
his wife, Ida, and their five daughters, a running
gag through his decades on radio and TV. Somehow, those big rolling banjo eyes, that good-
natured exuberance, that combination of delicacy
and boisterousness, of the naïve and the risqué,
gave him an endearing appeal that carried him
through a career of almost fifty years and is still
effective today.

Frank Capra (1897–1991),
b. Bisacquino, Sicily
1926: *The Strong Man.* 1927: *For the Love of
Mike; Long Pants.* 1928: *The Power of the Press;
Say It With Sables; So This Is Love; That Certain
Thing; The Way of the Strong; The Matinee Idol;
Submarine.* 1929: *The Donovan Affair; Flight;
The Younger Generation.* 1930: *Ladies of Leisure;
Rain or Shine.* 1931: *Dirigible; The Miracle
Woman; Platinum Blonde.* 1932: *Forbidden;
American Madness; The Bitter Tea of General Yen.*
1933: *Lady for a Day.* 1934: *It Happened One
Night; Broadway Bill.* 1935: *Opera Hat.* 1936: *Mr.
Deeds Goes to Town.* 1937: *Lost Horizon.* 1938:
You Can't Take It With You. 1939: *Mr. Smith Goes

to Washington.* 1941: *Meet John Doe.* 1942: *Prelude to War* (d); *The Nazis Strike* (codirected with
Anatole Litvak) (d). 1943: *The Battle of Britain*
(d); *Divide and Conquer* (codirected with Litvak)
(d); *The Battle of China* (codirected with Litvak)
(d). 1944: *Arsenic and Old Lace.* 1945: *Know Your
Enemy: Japan* (codirected with Joris Ivens) (d);
Tunisian Victory (codirected with Roy Boulting)
(d); *Two Down and One to Go* (d). 1947: *It's a
Wonderful Life.* 1948: *State of the Union.* 1950:
Riding High. 1951: *Here Comes the Groom.* 1959:
A Hole in the Head. 1961: *Pocketful of Miracles.*

When I wrote the first edition of this book, I did
not conceal my distaste for most of Capra's work.
The essay that resulted provoked surprise and dismay, the beginnings of some agreement, but a
feeling that I had been so "prosecutorial" that I
had refused to see Capra's enormous talent, or
facility. In 1975, Capra's reputation was seldom
assailed. The only suspicion came from his self-
glorifying but less-than-honest autobiography,
The Name Above the Title, published in 1972. And
I knew I was challenging orthodoxy (though I was
following in the excellent steps of Andrew Sarris)
by saying: "The most odious aspect of these films
[those of the late thirties and early forties] is the
way they bowdlerize politics by suggesting that
the tide of corruption can be turned by one hero.
Deeds and Smith admonish indolent or cynical
government assemblies with a soulful list of
clichés that Capra persuades himself is libertarian
poetry, rather than a call for unadventurous conformity."

Since then, there has been time and reason for
reconsideration, but I think I like Capra less than
ever, even if I have become more interested in his
emotional muddle. First of all, I have lived in
America, and Capra's attempts and failures are
more paining if one is, or is trying to be, American
(and Capra was himself an immigrant who longed
to be accepted).

In America I "discovered" the uneasy depths
of *It's a Wonderful Life.* I had seen the film in
England, but I had not grasped it and it had not
gripped me. But, in America, *Wonderful Life* was
an institution, all over the TV airwaves at Christmas, bringing good cheer without quite letting us
forget a vision of dread. For happiness here was
pursued by the hounds of living hell; the American dream was so close to the nightmare. The film
that failed in 1947 had become a token of uplifting
fellowship, yet it was a film noir full of regret, self-
pity, and the temptation of suicide. How could so
many people convince themselves that it was
cheery? I turned the film over in my mind and
wrote a kind of novel (*Suspects*) that was inspired
by my mixed feelings.

That would not have been possible without the
craft, the guile, the magic of *It's a Wonderful Life.*

Because that movie is so beautifully made, so rich in texture and nuance, it set me on a line of thought that wonders if some of the most central American films do not offer an uncanny conjuring of "genius" and the unwholesome—I would put *The Godfather, Citizen Kane, The Searchers,* and *Taxi Driver* (at least) in the same category: terrific movies with their own plunge into the abyss. Call them problem films, call them secret revelations of the medium. They remind me of *Triumph of the Will.*

Then there has been Joseph McBride's careful and horrified biography of Capra. I say "horrified" because McBride was once a leading fan of the director. Yet in the research he did on Capra's archive he found all kinds of flaws in the man: a hypocrite, a careerist and credit grabber, a rearranger of the facts, a liar, a reactionary, a bogus liberal, an anti-Semite, a self-serving fabulist, and an informer. And a big admirer of Mussolini.

Would these charges fit others in Hollywood? Perhaps. There is every likelihood that a Hollywood career leaves its owner exhausted, saddened, and profoundly compromised. There is no guarantee that bad, or compromised, people may not make good films. But in Capra's case, the human shortcomings are especially suggestive and important because he was so determined to seem righteous. Compromise is that wicked ploy loathed and condemned by Jefferson Smith—and thus his horrendous, hysterical reduction of the Senate to grotesque melodrama, game show, and a Ross Perot rally.

Capra came to America at the age of six from Sicily. The family lived quite well in Los Angeles (they had been able to pay for the boat to New York and the train West—six tickets). He went to Throop College of Technology (which would become Cal Tech) and graduated. By the early 1920s, Capra's inventive streak had led him to be a gagman with Hal Roach and Mack Sennett. Then he replaced Harry Edwards as Harry Langdon's director. *The Strong Man* is Langdon's funniest picture, and if *Long Pants* is less good it hardly explains the sudden rupture between the two men. Capra was fired, and he responded with a savage attack that seems to have made Langdon falter.

The turning point for Capra, and in the event for Columbia, came when Harry Cohn hired him. The early films at that studio are varied entertainments, full of life, speed, and cinematic flair. That their director was personally ambitious did not yet overwhelm the material. With Robert Riskin as his writer and Joseph MacDonald as his cameraman most of the time, he turned out *The Miracle Woman,* with Barbara Stanwyck as an evangelist—Stanwyck and Capra had an affair; *Ladies of Leisure,* with Stanwyck as a gold digger; *Platinum*

Blonde, one of Jean Harlow's best movies; *American Madness,* with Walter Huston as a bank president during the Crash; *The Bitter Tea of General Yen,* uncommonly erotic, with Stanwyck as a missionary and Nils Asther as a Chinese warlord; and *Lady for a Day,* from Damon Runyon, about an old apple seller (May Robson) who impersonates class.

At that point, Capra made *It Happened One Night,* a pioneering romantic comedy; it won Oscars for best picture, actor, actress, director, and adapted screenplay (Riskin); it also boosted Columbia in the corporate landscape of Hollywood. As for Capra, he was turned into a man who was set on something like the Nobel Prize for Cinema. He began to preach humanity in what was obviously a very troubled time.

What followed showed unflagging talent: Riskin and then Sidney Buchman (*Mr. Smith*) were superb at construction and dialogue—Capra films move like hunting dogs; the eye for oddballs and extras was unfailing, and Capra loved stray incidents; the playing was often daring and unexpected—he got a lot out of Jean Arthur, say, but he turned the noble Gary Cooper increasingly to self-doubt and morbidity. And the films, it seems to me, are a kind of fascistic inspirationalism in which the true daily, tedious difficulty of being American is exploded in the proposed rediscovery of simple goodness. Ross Perot may look and sound like Preston Sturges's Weeny King (in *The Palm Beach Story*), but he is a figure from and for Capra.

The films of this age are *Mr. Deeds,* the dopey *Lost Horizon, You Can't Take It With You, Mr. Smith, Meet John Doe,* and even the postwar *State of the Union.* These same years saw several war documentaries and the grating *Arsenic and Old Lace.* The "political films" get worse, generally; *State of the Union* is awkward and beyond middle age. *Meet John Doe* is probably the most dishonest. The best made is *Mr. Smith,* and for that very reason I find it the most disturbing. I despise the resort to patriotism, statuary, and quotation in defiance of gridlock, back-room deals, and compromise. Democracy in America is a noble hope that needs to be guarded against corruption, but compromise is the essential American way—without it we risk dictatorship. Jefferson Smith is a tyrant, a wicked folksy idiot, who commandeers James Stewart's alarming sweetness. He is the real threat in that film. Claude Rains's Senator Payne is the best-written, best-acted, and most interesting figure in the film, but he is locked in such ignominy that he can veer, crazily, from kindness to malice to suicide attempt to repentance in order that this fevered story can get off.

No one really argues about Capra's decline after 1947—even the facility goes then. No one need dispute the vitality of everything up to and including *It*

Happened One Night. In between fall the problem films, made in Capra's glory—he won the directing Oscar three times. Better by far that we argue over them than fall for their woeful messages.

Leos Carax (Alexandre Oscar Dupont), b. Paris, France, 1960

1980: *Strangulation Blues* (s). 1984: *Boy Meets Girl.* 1986: *Mauvais Sang/Bad Blood.* 1991: *Les Amants du Pont-Neuf/The Lovers on the Bridge.* 1999: *Pola X.*

First of all, Carax is a great self-fabulist, something like a mixture of Tarantino and Godard of the sixties, thoroughly caught up in the melodrama of being a Great Moviemaker. To say that this is tiresome and self-defeating only raises the possibility that Carax is looking for some fulminating disaster. As it is, his best work is burning with a feeling for tragedy and apocalypse. Even an admirer, Gavin Smith, speaking of *Pola X,* says that "his narrative and formal risk-taking are indistinguishable from failure."

If you think about it, that could fit a Godard who, after 1968, had simply continued with narrative films while growing increasingly besieged and enraged. But it also alerts one to the way in which the ostensible passion in Carax—his best or worst quality, depending on your point of view—is actually rather calculated, or intellectual. And it is in the degree to which he seems conscious and self-conscious of being a modern enfant terrible that Carax might yet do his best work. So far, it seems to me, he is both insufferable and extraordinary—and that's too rich a tradition among film directors for one to dismiss it.

His first two films are the most ordinary or accessible, and they are vivid and compelling. *Les Amants du Pont-Neuf* is unforgettable, a monstrosity and yet a work of real fascination. It is also very moving, and shows a terrific use of Juliette Binoche. *Pola X* (which came after a significant interval) is a bizarre updating of Herman Melville's *Pierre, or the Ambiguities* ("Pola" is actually an acronym on the French title—but, of course "Leos Carax" was an anagram of "Alex Oscar").

Jack Cardiff, b. Great Yarmouth, England, 1914

1958: *Intent to Kill.* 1959: *Beyond This Place.* 1960: *Sons and Lovers; Scent of Mystery; Holiday in Spain.* 1962: *My Geisha; The Lion.* 1964: *The Long Ships.* 1965: *Young Cassidy* (codirected with John Ford); *The Liquidator.* 1967: *The Mercenaries.* 1968: *Girl on a Motorcycle.* 1973: *Penny Gold; The Mutations.*

No wonder film students ask whether directors of photography are sometimes the authors of films when some reviewers still end unfavorable notices with "but beautifully photographed by . . ." It is a contradiction in terms for a bad film to be "beautifully photographed," just as it is nonsensical to expect a commercial movie not to be adequately photographed—i.e., with correct exposure, level framing, smooth movements, sharp focus, good color reproduction. A more reliable guide for newcomers is the legend that when directors lose their impulse or interest they degenerate into photographers. Photography is a moderately complex technology, accessible to many people; direction is an art, denied to most. A "correct" image is much easier than a creative and personal visual style. Some directors may choose never to use the viewfinder, but only if they have preconceived a shot and can trust an operator and lighting cameraman to achieve it. If more dramatic evidence is needed, we have only to ask how many photographers have proved themselves interesting directors. With a man like Jack Cardiff, the difference in potential between photography and direction is manifest. Cardiff's own films are characterless works, either flashy or drab. Yet as a photographer Cardiff was so famous for his bold color effects that that reputation promoted him to directing.

Cardiff became a camera operator in England in the mid-1930s and worked on *The Ghost Goes West* (35, René Clair) and *Knight Without Armour* (37, Jacques Feyder). He joined Technicolor and was operator on *Wings of the Morning* (37, Harold Schuster), the first full-color film made in Britain. He went on to photograph several travelogues for Technicolor—ironically, since his most characteristic work in later years was exaggerated, heavily dramatic color, rather than the cool clarity for which Technicolor is famous. He began working as a lighting cameraman in 1939 and, after the war, photographed some rather eccentric, gimmicky but very striking pictures: *The Four Feathers* (39, Zoltan Korda); *Western Approaches* (44, Pat Jackson); *Caesar and Cleopatra* (45, Gabriel Pascal); *A Matter of Life and Death* (46, Michael Powell); Kathleen Byron's red lipstick in *Black Narcissus* (47, Powell); *The Red Shoes* (48, Powell); the breathtakingly elaborate movements of *Under Capricorn* (49, Alfred Hitchcock); *The Black Rose* (50, Henry Hathaway); *Pandora and the Flying Dutchman* (51, Albert Lewin); *The African Queen* (51, John Huston); *The Barefoot Contessa* (54, Joseph L. Mankiewicz); *War and Peace* (56, King Vidor); *The Brave One* (56, Irving Rapper); *The Prince and the Showgirl* (57, Laurence Olivier); *Legend of the Lost* (57, Hathaway); *The Vikings* (58, Richard Fleischer); and *Fanny* (61, Joshua Logan).

By the mid-seventies, he was a cameraman again, often on location or in the service of poor action pictures: *Scalawag* (73, Kirk Douglas); *Death on the Nile* (78, John Guillermin); *The Fifth Musketeer* (79, Ken Annakin); *Avalanche*

Express (79, Mark Robson); *The Awakening* (80, Mike Newell); *The Dogs of War* (80, John Irvin); *Ghost Story* (81, Irvin); *The Wicked Lady* (83, Michael Winner); *Conan the Destroyer* (84, Fleischer); *Scandalous* (84, Rob Cohen); *Rambo: First Blood Part II* (85, George P. Cosmatos); *Cat's Eyes* (85, Lewis Teague); *Tai-Pan* (86, Daryl Duke); *Million Dollar Mystery* (87, Fleischer); *Call from Space* (89, Fleischer); *The Magic Balloon* (90, Ronald Neame); *The Dance of Shiva* (98, Jamie Payne).

These late films are without interest, and are well photographed. Cardiff no longer has the right projects or directors—and no one has Technicolor, now, a beauty that we all abandoned. Cardiff got an honorary Oscar in 2001, and was the hit of the show.

Claudia Cardinale, b. Tunis, Tunisia, 1938
From beauty queen to international movie star in seven years is a modern fairy story, and Cardinale is proof that if a woman has a luscious enough body, an attentive face, and some animation, then she can be the princess in that story. The fairy godfather in her case was producer Franco Cristaldi. After Claudia had been voted the most beautiful Italian girl in Tunis, and played a small part in *Goha* (57, Jacques Baratier), he saw that she was worthy of more comprehensive titles and that, where BB had prospered, CC might do as well. She played in *I Soliti Ignoti* (58, Mario Monicelli) and came to England for *Upstairs and Downstairs* (58, Ralph Thomas). Whereupon she had a string of parts in Italian films, often as a glamorous object but more thoughtfully used by Visconti, until she was taken up by Hollywood: *La Prima Notte* (59, Alberto Cavalcanti); *Un Maledetto Imbroglio* (59, Pietro Germi); *I Bell' Antonio* (59, Mauro Bolognini); *Austerlitz* (59, Abel Gance and Roger Richebé); *Il Delfini* (60, Francisco Maselli); *La Ragazza con la Valigia* (60, Valerio Zurlini); *Rocco and His Brothers* (60, Luchino Visconti); *La Viaccia* (61, Bolognini); *Cartouche* (61, Philippe de Broca); *Senilità* (62, Bolognini); *8½* (63, Federico Fellini); *The Leopard* (63, Visconti); *La Ragazza di Bube* (63, Luigi Comencini); *The Pink Panther* (63, Blake Edwards); *The Magnificent Showman* (64, Henry Hathaway); *Gli Indifferenti* (64, Maselli); *Blindfold* (65, Philip Dunne); *Of a Thousand Delights* (65, Visconti); *Lost Command* (66, Mark Robson); *The Professionals* (66, Richard Brooks); in the "Fata Armenia" episode from *Le Fate* (66, Monicelli); *Don't Make Waves* (67, Alexander Mackendrick); *Il Giorno della Civetta* (67, Damiano Damiani); *Once Upon a Time in the West* (69, Sergio Leone); *A Fine Pair* (69, Maselli); *The Adventures of Gerard* (70, Jerzy Skolimowski); with Bardot in *The Legend of Frenchie King* (71, Christian-Jaque); *The Red Tent* (71, Mikhail Kala-

tozov); *La Scoumoune* (72, Jose Giovanni); *Il Giorno del Furore* (73, Antonio Calenda); and *Libera, Amore Mio* (73, Bolognini).

The time may be at hand when she has to go to make the pasta, but she has had her day and has been married to Cristaldi and to Pasquale Squitieri. Her sumptuousness will never quite be forgotten, nor that raucous voice that seems to belong to another face. Meanwhile, she has been in *La Part du Feu* (77, Etienne Perrier); *Corleone* (77, Pasquale Squitieri); *L'Arma* (78, Squitieri); *La Petite Fille en Velours Bleu* (78, Alan Bridges); *Escape to Athens* (79, George Pan Cosmatos); *La Pelle* (81, Liliana Cavani); *The Salamander* (81, Peter Zinner); *Le Cadeau* (81, Michel Lang); *Fitzcarraldo* (82, Werner Herzog); *Le Ruffian* (83, Giovanni); *Princess Daisy* (83, Waris Hussein) for TV; with Mastroianni in *Enrico IV* (83, Marco Bellocchio); *L'Été Prochain* (85, Nadine Trintignant); *La Donna delle Meraviglie* (85, Alberto Bevilacque); *La Storia* (85, Luigi Comencini); *Un Homme Amoureux* (87, Diane Kurys); *Blu Eletricco* (88, Elfriede Gaeng); *Hiver 54, l'Abbé Pierre* (89, Denis Amar); *La Revolution Française* (89, Robert Enrico and Richard T. Heffron); *The Son of the Pink Panther* (93, Edwards); *Elles Ne Pensent qu'à ça . . .* (94, Charlotte Dubreuil); *Nostromo* (96, Alastair Reid); *Riches, Belles, Etc.* (98, Bunny Schpoliansky); *Brigands* (99, Squitieri); *Elisabeth* (99, Squitieri); *And Now . . . Ladies and Gentlemen* (02, Claude Lelouch).

Julien Carette (1897–1966), b. Paris
Jean Renoir always looked kindly on survivors, even if they were unashamed opportunists. In *La Règle du Jeu* (39), Carette embodied this vagrant figure as the poacher first seen taking a rabbit. He inveigles himself into the household, flirting with the gamekeeper's wife, and then conspires with the keeper in the final tragedy in error. But at the end, he shrugs his shoulders and packs, stops to offer a word and a smoke to the gamekeeper, and is off with a "good luck" to Renoir's Octave. A small, dark man, by turns sighing and spiteful, Carette brought a pagan unscrupulousness to the part, as when he sings to the keeper's wife: "People like me never show themselves twice. If their first shot's not a bull's-eye they're off in a trice." That scapegoat charm made Carette a delightful supporting figure in several of Renoir's films: *La Grande Illusion* (37); *La Marseillaise* (38); *La Bête Humaine* (38); and *Elena et les Hommes* (56).

As a student actor it was in Carette's character to fail his exams. Nevertheless, he found work and made his film debut in 1932 in *L'Affaire est dans le Sac* (Pierre Prévert), the first of over a hundred films. Seldom ranging far outside his sly spiv, these are his best movies: *Les Gaietés de l'Escadron* (32, Maurice Tourneur); *Gonzague ou l'Accordeur* (33,

Jean Grémillon); *Aventure à Paris* (36, Marc Allégret); *Gribouille* (37, Allégret); *Entrée des Artistes* (38, Allégret); *Menaces* (39, Edmond T. Greville); *Battements de Coeur* (39, Henri Decoin); *Parade en Sept Nuits* (41, Allégret); *Lettres d'Amour* (42, Claude Autant-Lara); *Adieu Léonard* (43, Prévert); *Sylvie et le Fantôme* (45, Autant-Lara); *Les Portes de la Nuit* (46, Marcel Carné); in Carné's unfinished *La Fleur de l'Age* (47); *Une Si Jolie Petite Plage* (48, Yves Allégret); *Occupe-toi d'Amélie* (49, Autant-Lara); *La Marie du Port* (50, Carné); *L'Auberge Rouge* (51, Autant-Lara); *La Fête à Henriette* (53, Julien Duvivier); *Le Bon Dieu Sans Confession* (53, Autant-Lara); *L'Amour d'une Femme* (53, Grémillon); *Si Paris Nous Était Conté* (56, Sacha Guitry); *Le Joueur* (58, Autant-Lara); *Pantalaskas* (59, Paul Pariot); *Archimède, le Clochard* (59, Gilles Grangier); *La Jument Verte* (61, Autant-Lara); *Vive Henri IV, Vive l'Amour* (61, Autant-Lara); and *Les Aventures de Salavin* (65, Pierre Granier-Deferre).

But the blithe gypsy's life ended tragically. He went to sleep one night, a cigarette in his lips, and burned himself to death.

Hoagy (Hoagland Howard) Carmichael

(1899–1981), b. Bloomington, Indiana

He sits at a piano that manages to be set aslant everything else in the world. He has white pants (they might be cream or ivory) with a dark stripe in them, and it could be crimson or dark blue against the cream (this is Martinique light). And in the shirt there is the same pattern of vertical dark striping on a pale ground, except that the stripes are twice as regular. He has a tie too, a rather full, floppy, silly thing, with big diamond patterns on it. And I'll be damned if he hasn't got a decorated band above his right elbow, of the kind card players or saloon pianists sometimes wear to keep their hands free.

He is called Cricket, and he has the sharpest face in the whole sharp film. And more or less we are at the heart of the whole matter, in a place where perfection and the absurd slide together in a way that is unbearably cool. This is 1944, at Warner Bros., *To Have and Have Not*—even the title knows what is happening, and appreciates that this is the mystery of cinema, the dream itself.

I don't know, but I suspect that Hoagland Carmichael dressed himself for the occasion, checking every now and then with the Howard Hawks he revered as both friend and style master. For Hawks was a dandy, and I suspect that both men could wax lyrical together as connoisseurs on what a hip piano player reckoned to look like in the 1920s if he had done Indiana U. (law) first and was knocking around with Bix and Trumbauer, and Eddie Condon was due in tonight.

That was how Carmichael had put his life in order, dropping the law for "Star Dust," which he wrote in 1927. And he had had songs in movies aplenty in the thirties, like Crosby doing "Moonburn" in *Anything Goes* (36, Lewis Milestone). And somehow Hoagland had got to be acquaintanced with Slim and Howard Hawks and Howard had asked him to hang around the *To Have and Have Not* set and be atmospheric.

And it worked out that the new girl, Bacall, had this little song to sing, so why shouldn't it be something Cricket was working up? It won't be hard work, said Howard, you can do the whole thing sitting down. And if maybe Hoagland said, "Howard, I haven't been on camera before," Hawks could have said, "It doesn't show. You can do this stuff yourself, if you try."

So Carmichael and Bacall play around with "How Little We Know," and the whole film is this strange new tango Bogart and Bacall do, with three guys—Marcel Dalio, Walter Brennan, and Carmichael—riding point. And you realize the weird luck that could fall on an Ernest Hemingway having such magic fall on his not-the-worst-book-in-the-world novel.

The story goes that whenever Carmichael was working, William Faulkner came to the set to watch. To be so lucky.

Sure, Hoagy Carmichael is there again and very good in *The Best Years of Our Lives* (46, William Wyler), in *Night Song* (47, John Cromwell), and in *Young Man with a Horn* (50, Michael Curtiz). And he has his songs in and out of pictures—he shared an Oscar for "In the Cool, Cool, Cool of the Evening" in *Here Comes the Groom* (51, Frank Capra). But the rest was relatively normal, and sensible, and what you might expect. Whereas Cricket was out of nowhere. Nowhere except the best and kindest mind that ever made an American picture. If you could get your clothes halfway decent.

Marcel Carné (Albert Cranche) (1909–96), b. Paris

1936: *Jenny*. 1937: *Drôle de Drame*. 1938: *Quai des Brumes; Hôtel du Nord*. 1939: *Le Jour se Lève*. 1942: *Les Visiteurs du Soir*. 1944: *Les Enfants du Paradis*. 1946: *Les Portes de la Nuit*. 1947: *La Fleur de l'Âge* (uncompleted). 1950: *La Marie du Port*. 1951: *Juliette ou la Clé des Songes*. 1953: *Thérèse Raquin*. 1954: *L'Air de Paris*. 1956: *Le Pays d'où Je Viens*. 1958: *Les Tricheurs*. 1960: *Terrain Vague*. 1963: *Du Mouron pour les Petits Oiseaux*. 1965: *Trois Chambres à Manhattan*. 1968: *Les Jeunes Loups*. 1971: *Les Assassins de l'Ordre*. 1974: *La Merveilleuse Visite*. 1984: *La Bible*.

Originally a photographer, Carné was camera assistant on *Les Nouveaux Messieurs* (28, Jacques Feyder) and *Cagliostro* (29, Richard Oswald). He turned to writing and in 1930 he codirected a documentary short, *Nogent, El Dorado du Dimanche,* with Michel Sanvoisin. Thereafter, he was assistant to Feyder on *Le Grand Jeu* (33), *Pension Mimosas* (34), and *La Kermesse Héroïque* (35) before, on his own, directing Feyder's wife, Françoise Rosay, in *Jenny*.

In the period 1936–46, Carné was probably the most highly regarded of French directors. The six films he made after *Jenny* earned him a great reputation as a tidy pessimist and adroit technician. Those films still have virtues: the scripts by Jacques Prévert are as witty as the cinema has ever been; amazing studio exteriors, designed often by Alexandre Trauner; and memorable performances from Rosay, Michel Simon, Louis Jouvet, Jean-Louis Barrault, Gabin, Michèle Morgan, Arletty, Jules Berry, and Pierre Brasseur. It was once claimed that films like *Quai des Brumes* and *Le Jour se Lève* spoke for prewar despair. But they are less harsh than Fritz Lang's films, and less poignant than Renoir's. Carné's forte was theatricality and it was the limelight of worldly melancholy that really inspired him. Thus, his films are less disenchanted than enchanted. He had an instinct for the tragic fairy story, evident in the near allegory of *Quai des Brumes* and spelled out in the medievalism of the wartime *Les Visiteurs du Soir*. There is no passion or anger in his work, but a rather meretricious resignation and an eye for the sad romance of fog-laden streets and squalid lodging houses. His most entertaining film, *Les Enfants du Paradis*, is a glorification of French theatre by a magnificent troupe of actors. It shows Carné's strength—his sympathy with actors, his taste for pretty sets, and his nostalgia—but his weakness, too, in that he does not appreciate the way theatre reflects back on life. *Les Enfants du Paradis* is a lesser film than *The Golden Coach*, which balances stage and reality.

After the war, Carné gradually lost his best collaborators and his own momentum. *Les Portes de la Nuit* was a pretentious fable so overlaid by false pessimism that that quality was read into his earlier work. It lost so much money that Carné was forced to be more cautious. *La Marie du Port* is a simple, realistic story, well acted by Gabin and Nicole Courcel. But *Juliette* was another extravagant attempt to rediscover fantasy: about a man in prison, Gérard Philipe, who dreams himself into Bluebeard's castle. *Thérèse Raquin* was conventional melodrama, spiked by the sensuality of Simone Signoret. After that, Carné deteriorated steadily. His attempt to cash in on youth with *Les Tricheurs* was woeful and he became restricted to antiquated, run-of-the-mill pictures. It seems clear that his world depended heavily on collaborators, and that it was at best bittersweet escapist; but the urban fatalism of *Quai des Brumes, Hôtel du Nord,* and *Le Jour se*

Lève is unique and *Les Enfants du Paradis* splendidly undiminished.

Martine Carol (Marie-Louise Mourer) (1922–67), b. Biarritz, France

In the still, if not turgid, waters of French cinema in the early 1950s, Martine Carol was the foremost ladylike voluptuary: a blonde, red-lipped courtesan, forever in and out of baths and peignoirs, seen to best effect with contented smile on crushed pillows. The epitome of these roles was *Caroline Chérie* (50, Richard Pottier) and its sequels, but she was also proudly exposed by her then husband Christian-Jaque in a series of undress costume films: *Adorables Créatures* (52), *Lucrezia Borgia* (52), and *Nana* (55). Her personality was at the same time florid and genteel and, despite their gloss of daringness, her films reaffirmed very old-fashioned attitudes to sex. It was with his characteristic irony and tenderness that Max Ophuls made her famous forever by casting her as *Lola Montès* (55), that archetype of the woman driven to offer herself as substance for men's dreams. Carol was no actress, but she was suitably picturesque and she seemed genuinely stirred by some of the implications in Ophuls's film. *Lola Montès* is a masterpiece and proof that a commonplace actress can be made resplendent by the greatest directors. Carol's career began in the war years and included a brief, unhappy excursion to America in the late 1950s. Significantly, and despite their love for Ophuls, she was ignored by the New Wave directors. Among her films were *Les Inconnus dans la Maison* (42, Henri Decoin); *Voyage Surprise* (46, Pierre Prévert); *Les Amants de Vérone* (48, André Cayatte); *Night Beauties* (52, René Clair); *La Spiaggia* (53, Alberto Lattuada); *Les Carnets de Major Thompson* (57, Preston Sturges); *Action of the Tiger* (57, Terence Young); *La Prima Notte* (58, Alberto Cavalcanti); *Ten Seconds to Hell* (59, Robert Aldrich); *Natalie, Agent Secret* (59, Decoin); *Le Cave se Rebiffe* (61, Gilles Grangier); good again in *Vanina Vanini* (61, Roberto Rossellini); and *Hell Is Empty* (66, John Ainsworth and Bernard Knowles).

Leslie Caron, b. Boulogne-Billancourt, France, 1931

When she first appeared, in *An American in Paris* (51, Vincente Minnelli), her ballet training was more impressive than her looks. She had the face of someone who had been doing exercises: tight, preoccupied, and dull. But with the years, she grew into beauty. From *Gigi* (58, Minnelli) onwards, she is truly handsome, even if nothing has suggested that she acts better than a thousand others. Nor, in truth, is she a dancer to set the screen alight. *Lili* (53, Charles Walters), a touching portrait of gaucheness, is her best film, even if it is too fey. Her marriage to Peter Hall had the effect of removing her from Hollywood to London, a move ill-advised for one so restrained: *Glory Alley* (52, Raoul Walsh); Farley Granger's governess in *The Story of Three Loves* (52, Minnelli); *The Glass Slipper* (54, Walters); *Daddy Long Legs* (55, Jean Negulesco); *Gaby* (56, Curtis Bernhardt); *The Doctor's Dilemma* (58, Anthony Asquith); *The Man Who Understood Women* (58, Nunnally Johnson); *The Subterraneans* (60, Ranald MacDougall); *Fanny* (61, Joshua Logan); *Guns of Darkness* (62, Asquith); *The L-Shaped Room* (62, Bryan Forbes); *Father Goose* (64, Ralph Nelson); *A Very Special Favor* (65, Michael Gordon); *Promise Her Anything* (66, Arthur Hiller); and *Is Paris Burning?* (66, René Clément). In 1955, she acted on the stage in Jean Renoir's play *Orvet*.

More recently, she has become active again: as the housekeeper in *Sérail* (76, Eduardo de Gregorio); Nazimova in *Valentino* (77, Ken Russell); *The Man Who Loved Women* (77, François Truffaut); *Goldengirl* (79, Joseph Sargent); *Tous Vedettes* (79, Michel Lang); *Kontrakt* (80, Krzysztof Zanussi); *Chanel Solitaire* (81, George Kaczender); *The Imperative* (82, Zanussi); *The Unapproachable* (82, Zanussi); *Dangerous Moves* (85, Richard Dembo); *Guerriers et Captives* (89, Edgardo Cozarinsky); *Courage Mountain* (89, Christopher Leitch); *Blue Notte* (90, Giorgio Serafini); as the mother in *Damage* (92, Louis Malle); *Funny Bones* (95, Peter Chelsom); *The Reef* (97, Robert Allan Ackerman); *The Last of the Blonde Bombshells* (00, Gillies MacKinnon); *Chocolat* (00, Lasse Hallstrom); *Le Divorce* (03, James Ivory).

John Carpenter,
b. Carthage, New York, 1948
1970: *The Resurrection of Bronco Billy* (s). 1974: *Dark Star.* 1976: *Assault on Precinct 13.* 1978: *Halloween.* 1980: *The Fog.* 1981: *Escape from New York.* 1982: *The Thing.* 1983: *Christine.* 1984: *Starman.* 1986: *Big Trouble in Little China.* 1987: *Prince of Darkness.* 1988: *They Live.* 1992: *Memoirs of an Invisible Man.* 1993: *Body Bags.* 1995: *Village of the Damned; In the Mouth of Madness.* 1996: *Escape from L.A.* 1998: *Vampires.* 2001: *Ghosts of Mars.*

At the outset, John Carpenter knew he was a throwback, but he had no guilt: "If I had three wishes, one of them would be 'Send me back to the '40s and the studio system and let me direct movies.' Because I would have been happiest there. I feel I am a little bit out of time. I have much more of a kinship for older-style films, and very few films that are made now interest me at all. I get up and walk out on them."

His early work was a fond and felicitous tribute to the aura of RKO in the forties: very low-budget pictures full of visceral excitement and rich cinematic texture that belie their cost. He adores and refers to the style of Hitchcock and the atmosphere of Hawks, and he made *Dark Star* as a rebuke to *2001* and an affirmation of the innocent wonder of *The Thing* or *Forbidden Planet.* With effect, for *Dark Star* is among the best space-travel film since the early fifties.

Carpenter was a movie-mad child who went to study film at the University of Southern California. But he is not a member of the coterie of young directors from that hothouse, and he is proud that *Dark Star* began as a student movie and cost only $60,000—so much less money and so many more ideas than *Star Wars* can claim. It is a very witty film about a crisis in deep space, the metaphysical dimension always restrained by the homemade special effects and the dry portrait of men and machines grumbling at one another in a shared mood of grievance.

Precinct 13 is a Hawksian set piece of a police station besieged by hoodlums—economical, tense, beautiful, and highly arousing. It fulfils all Carpenter's ambitions for gripping the audience emotionally and never letting go. But it has a natural taste that uses violence or sensation quickly and obliquely—so much more tender a play upon audiences than De Palma's ruthless grip.

Halloween showed that, despite remarkable facility with the medium, Carpenter remained loyal to his B-movie revivalism. It was likely that someone would insist that he work with a big budget—cheap films frighten financiers more than blockbusters. Big budgets mean commercial decisions and projects compromised by profit sharers and residual artists. Could he retain that precarious ground?

Carpenter also wrote scripts, to keep in practice and to make money for his own projects. He had no great esteem for such work, and probably regards *The Eyes of Laura Mars* (78, Irvin Kershner), which he wrote with David Zelag Goodman, with the scorn it deserves. However, suppose that Jon Peters, Kershner, and Dunaway had yielded to Carpenter and Lauren Hutton and you have a brilliantly contrived TV thriller called *High Rise* (78).

Carpenter did not advance. *The Fog* has some creepy moments; *Escape from New York* is not just a great title—it's a complete vision of New York's dread of where it is going; *The Thing* is retread Hawks; and *Starman* is that rarity, a love story that grows out of sci-fi, with a fine performance by Jeff Bridges. There's not a lot to be said for the rest—and the rest also includes the producer's job on some *Halloween* repeats. Since 1984, Carpenter has become terminally boyish in his pursuit of spooks, devils, and thrills. *Memoirs of an Invisible Man* has Chevy Chase as a comic special effect: that is a working definition of being at the end of one's tether.

Jim Carrey,
b. Newmarket, Ontario, Canada, 1962
In the space of two years, Jim Carrey went from a
$350,000 salary on *Ace Ventura, Pet Detective* (94,
Tom Shadyac) to being ranked at the $20 million
level per picture. No wonder he behaves as if it's a
wild and crazy world—no wonder his very face
and figure seem elastic, ready to stretch with
dreams and horrors. He is an authentic clown,
enormously energized, furiously "on," yet curiously reliant on others for his material. He has
been compared to Jerry Lewis, and Lewis apparently asked Carrey to consider a remake of *The
Patsy*. But Lewis was always the master of his own
material—maybe that's one reason why he gradually acquired the reputation and the atmosphere
of a monster, or of someone far from just plain
funny. Whereas it is vital to Carrey's character that
he seems decent, kind, far more relaxed, and
even—let's face it—attractive! Jim Carrey is sexy?
Or would hope to be?

Though he is often described as an overnight
success, the night was long and the preparation
hard. He worked in Canada as a kid, and only
slowly found his way into television: his 1984
show, *The Duck Factory*, flopped in three months,
though his character—Skip Tarkenton, an innocent, enthusiastic cartoonist—was a big influence
on his future. He had actually become James Carrey by the time of *In Living Color*, which debuted
in 1990 and in which he was one of the few white
performers. It was there that he began to attract
serious attention as a physically inventive comic
with an instinct for characters who mixed vulnerability and freakishness.

He had been doing movies: *Finders Keepers*
(84, Richard Lester), *Once Bitten* (85, Howard
Storm); *Peggy Sue Got Married* (86, Francis Coppola); *The Dead Pool* (88, Buddy Van Horn);
Earth Girls Are Easy (89, Julien Temple); *Pink
Cadillac* (89, Van Horn). But he was away from
the big screen for the years of *In Living Color*, and
only returned with the first *Ace Ventura* vehicle.

After that, the rise was very rapid: *The Mask*
(94, Charles Russell) relied a good deal on effects,
and it was rather more violent and disturbing than
was comfortable for its natural audience of kids,
but Carrey's spirit shone through, and the best
parts of the movie are a fascinating addition to the
Jekyll-and-Hyde principle. *Dumb and Dumber*
(94, Peter Farrelly) was a vast hit, and its appeal to
little boys had as much to do with gross-out jokes
as the play upon stupidity. (Note that while Jeff
Daniels made a good foil, that role nearly went to
Carrey's close friend Nicolas Cage. It says something instructive about both of them that they still
hope to act together.)

Then Carrey's Riddler was the star turn in *Batman Forever* (95, Joel Schumacher), dainty but
truly sinister, and with a masterful mockery of his

own camp risk-taking. Moreover, Carrey clearly
moved with something akin to grace. *Ace Ventura:
When Nature Calls* (95, Steve Oedekerk) was a
routine sequel, short on invention, and compen-
sating with bathroom jokes. But *The Cable Guy*
(96, Ben Stiller)—a flop—was his darkest work,
hinging on a quality of true danger or mania. *Liar
Liar* (97, Shadyac) was closer to the helplessness
of Jerry Lewis, propelled and ordered by some
trick of nature.

The film that clarified, and advanced, Carrey's
artistic ambition, of course, was *The Truman
Show* (98, Peter Weir), a Day-Glo noir scarcely
imaginable without Carrey, and ample proof of
the actor waiting behind the clown's costume.
Moreover, the not-quite-delivered tragedy in that
story owed a lot to Carrey's awareness of pain—
even his need for it? His next film role, as Andy
Kaufman in *Man on the Moon* (99, Milos Forman), was nowhere near as successful, but it
showed the courage with which Carrey was ready
to test his own fan base.

Where will it end? Or begin? Is Carrey himself
yet, or still growing? *Me, Myself and Irene* (00, the
Farrellys) was another brilliant small comedy
exposing the demon within niceness. *How the
Grinch Stole Christmas* (00, Ron Howard) was
apparently a little too nasty for some children. But
it was a huge hit and one more piece of ecstatic
pantomime disclosing fabulous depths of misanthropy. But then *The Majestic* (01, Frank
Darabont)—awful, misguided, and with Carrey
on TV promoting it, so gosh-darn nice he seemed
to need to explode. So maybe it hasn't begun yet.
Whatever, if you doubt the power of headlong,
natural, unguided genius in American film—just
look at Carrey. There was another disappointment
(but a box-office hit) with *Bruce Almighty* (03,
Shadyac), but again it seemed reasonable that
Carrey might move from mortal to god, and back,
with giddy speed.

Jean-Claude Carrière,
b. Colombière, France, 1931
In his autobiography, *My Last Sigh* (published in
France in 1982), Luis Buñuel made a generous
nod to Carrière: "I'm not a writer, but my friend
and colleague Jean-Claude Carrière is. An attentive listener and scrupulous recorder during our
many long conversations, he helped me write this
book." The debt may have been greater still.
Something magical happened to Buñuel as he
passed sixty. Some force, or angel, reinterpreted
his spirit of surrealism for a modern age and found
a way of making dreams possible with smooth
photography and big stars. Carrière wrote those
films, and I suspect that he was an angel of enable-
ment for Buñuel on some of the smartest, funniest, and flat-out best movies ever made: *Le
Journal d'une Femme de Chambre* (63); *Belle du*

Jour (67); *La Voie Lactée* (68); *The Discreet Charm of the Bourgeoisie* (72); *The Phantom of Liberty* (74); and *That Obscure Object of Desire* (77).

That would be achievement enough for our gratitude. But Carrière has served many other directors with tact and grace—even if there is nothing that matches the Buñuel films. Moreover, Carrière has his own directorial ambitions—he made a short, *La Pince à Ongles* (68), and a feature, *L'Unique* (85)—and thus his willingness to be a vital, yet necessarily rather secret, helper to others is all the more admirable.

He has many skills: he was a cartoonist who collaborated with Pierre Etaix; he wrote plays—*L'Aide-Mémoire* (68)—and novels—*Le Lézard* (57) and *L'Alliance* (63). He also acted occasionally. But he is too good at the furnishing of deft screenplays, especially adaptations, to be allowed much liberty for anything else: *Le Soupirant* (62, Etaix); *Nous n'Irons pas au Bois* (63, Etaix); *Insomnie* (63, Etaix); *La Reine Verte* (64, Robert Mazoyer); *Yoyo* (64, Etaix); *Viva Maria!* (65, Louis Malle); *Tant qu'on à la Sante* (65, Etaix); *Cartes sur Table* (65, Jesus Franco); *Le Voleur* (66, Malle); *Hotel Paradiso* (66, Peter Glenville); *La Piscine* (68, Jacques Deray); *Le Grand Amour* (68, Etaix); *L'Alliance* (70, Christian de Chalonge); *Borsalino* (70, Deray); *La Cagna* (70, Marco Ferreri); *Un Peu de Soleil dans l'Eau Froide* (71, Deray); *Taking Off* (71, Milos Forman); *Le Moine* (72, Ado Kyrou); *Un Homme est Morte* (72, Deray); *France S.A.* (73, Alain Corneau); *Dorothea Rache* (74, Peter Fleischmann); *Un Amour de Pluie* (74, Jean-Claude Brialy); *Le Clair et L'Orchidée* (74, Patrice Chereau); *Grande Nature* (74, Luis Berlanga); *La Femme aux Bottes Rouge* (74, Jean-Luis Buñuel); *Sérieux comme le Plaisir* (74, Robert Benayoun); *Le Gang* (77, Deray); *Julie Pot-de-Colle* (77, Philippe de Broca); *Photo Souvenir* (78, Edmond Sechan); *Un Papillon sur L'Epaule* (78, Deray); *The Tin Drum* (79, Volker Schlondorff); *Une Semaine de Vacances* (80, Bertrand Tavernier); *Every Man for Himself* (80, Jean-Luc Godard); *Circle of Deceit* (81, Schlondorff); *Danton* (82, Andrzej Wajda); *The Return of Martin Guerre* (82, Daniel Vigne); *La Tragédie de Carmen* (83, Peter Brook); *Swann in Love* (84, Schlondorff); *Max Mon Amour* (86, Nagisa Oshima); *Wolf at the Door* (87, Henning Carlsen); *The Possessed* (87, Andrzej Zulawski); *The Unbearable Lightness of Being* (88, Philip Kaufman); *The Mahabharata* (89, Brook); *Valmont* (89, Forman); *Cyrano de Bergerac* (90, Jean-Paul Rappeneau); and *May Fools* (90, Malle).

In the nineties, it was evident that Carrière was working more often on TV adaptations of classic novels. It might be added that, after Buñuel's death, Carrière was unable to reclaim the master's light lethal touch. He worked on *At Play in the Fields of the Lord* (91, Hector Babenco); *Le Retour de Casanova* (92, Edouard Niermans); *La Controverse de Valladolid* (92, Jean-Daniel Verhaeghe); *The Night and the Moment* (94, Anna Maria Tato); *La Duchesse de Langeais* (94, Verhaeghe); the very exuberant *The Horseman on the Roof* (95, Rappeneau); *Der Unhold* (96, Schlondorff); *The Associate* (96, Donald Petrie); *Une Femme Explosive* (96, Deray); *Chinese Box* (97, Wayne Wang); *Clarissa* (98, Deray); *Salsa* (00, Joyce Buñuel); *Madame de . . .* (01, Verhaeghe); *Lettre d'une Inconnue* (01, Deray); *La Bataille d'Hernani* (02, Verhaeghe); *Ruy Blas* (02, Jacques Weber); *Les Thibault* (03, Verhaege); and a co-writer on the intriguing *Birth* (04, Jonathan Glazer).

Madeleine Carroll (1906–87),
b. West Bromwich, England

The first English rose transplanted to America, Madeleine Carroll had all the regal beauty of the English leading lady and nothing that a dozen others did not share. But in the early 1930s she was so popular in England that her reception in Hollywood established a model to aim at for women in the English cinema. Twenty years after she left England, and ten years after her career had petered out, British cinema admired the fragrance and bloom of Virginia McKenna—the same bush in flower. Carroll made her debut in *The Guns of Loos* (28, Sinclair Hill) and quickly rose to British stardom: *Atlantic* (29, E. A. Dupont); *Young Woodley* (30, Thomas Bentley); *Lady Teazle* in *The School for Scandal* (30, Maurice Elvey); *Fascination* (31, Miles Mander); *I Was a Spy* (33, Victor Saville), the latter after a stately retirement to mark marriage—the first of four. Fox invited her to America for *The World Moves On* (34, John Ford), but it was her two films for Hitchcock that added a little spice to blondeness—even if no other director ever detected it. She was handcuffed to Robert Donat in *The Thirty-nine Steps* (35), and plainly frightened by Peter Lorre in *The Secret Agent* (36). America then took her up: *The General Died at Dawn* (36, Lewis Milestone); *Lloyds of London* (36, Henry King); *On the Avenue* (37, Roy del Ruth); *It's All Yours* (37, Elliott Nugent); *The Prisoner of Zenda* (37, John Cromwell); *Blockade* (38, William Dieterle); *Cafe Society* (39, Edward H. Griffith); *Honeymoon in Bali* (39, Griffith); *Virginia* (40, Griffith), with another husband, Sterling Hayden; *My Son, My Son!* (40, Charles Vidor); *Safari* (40, Griffith); *North West Mounted Police* (40, Cecil B. De Mille); *One Night in Lisbon* (41, Griffith); and *Bahama Passage* (41, Griffith). She worked for the Red Cross during the war and returned only for *White Cradle Inn* (46, Harold French), *Don't Trust Your Husband* (48, Lloyd Bacon), and a rather meek Mrs. Erlynne in *Lady Windermere's Fan* (49, Otto Preminger).

Nancy Carroll (Ann Veronica La Hiff) (1904–65), b. New York

The pretty, talented, and versatile Nancy Carroll is a textbook case of a mismanaged career. Her family had theatrical connections, but—according to her—her ambition was to become a teacher. She had to go to work, though (she was one of eleven children), and with her winning personality, vivid red hair, Cupid's-bow mouth, and bounce, she was soon a chorus girl on Broadway. One show led to another, and to marriage with reporter Jack Kirkland (he wrote the record-shattering dramatization of *Tobacco Road*). They moved to Los Angeles and soon she was on the stage there, and taking screen tests—more than a dozen of them, all of which failed: her face was too round.

She came in at the tail end of the silents—her first big role was the Irish Rose herself in the film of Anne Nichols's *Abie's Irish Rose* (28, Victor Fleming), opposite Buddy Rogers's Abie. They added some music and a song for her, proving that she could handle sound. Within two years she was Paramount's most popular star.

Her real breakthrough was the quintessential weeper *Shopworn Angel* (29, Richard Wallace), opposite Gary Cooper. But Carroll sang and danced—*Sweetie* (29, Frank Tuttle); *Honey* (30, Wesley Ruggles); *Follow Thru* (31, Lawrence Schwab and Lloyd Corrigan)—and did both romantic comedy and heavy drama. One of the problems was that no one seemed able to decide just what she was; another was that her behavior alienated colleagues and the studio—she was known as "the Firebrand of Hollywood." Apparently she had a violent temper and was suspicious of everyone. ("Because you think differently, you're considered disagreeable, and upstage, and difficult. An original thinker always has to fight.") By 1934 her career was on the rocks, with only a few films to come. But she went on to years of theater work, mostly on the road, in summer stock, etc., and often with her daughter, Patricia Kirkland. She also appeared in a TV series, *The Aldrich Family,* in the early fifties and went through another marriage or two. Long before her death, her real stardom had been forgotten.

Still, at least four movies deserve serious attention: *The Shopworn Angel; Laughter* (30, Harry d'Abbadie d'Arrast), opposite Fredric March in a romantic comedy that proves that love and laughter (cavorting under a couple of polar bear rugs) and the carefree Bohemian life count more than money and respectability and marriage to stuffy old Frank Morgan; *The Devil's Holiday* (30, Edmund Goulding), very convincing as a gold digger turned fine through love of Phillips

Holmes, and apparently a close second to Norma Shearer for that year's Oscar; and, best of all, the 1929 *The Dance of Life* (John Cromwell and A. Edward Sutherland), based on the Broadway play *Burlesque* (it had made a star out of Barbara Stanwyck) and starring the play's leading man, the extraordinary Hal Skelly. This may be the most moving version of that old chestnut, the burlesque/vaudeville couple who suffer ups and downs—she leaves him when he gives way to alcohol, comes back when he needs her, and there's a tear in every eye. But she was also involved in disasters like Goulding's *Night Angel* (31) and a mismatch with Lubitsch in *The Man I Killed.* The roles and the movies got worse and worse, and she was gone, her place at Paramount superseded by Claudette Colbert, who could also do everything, but who also knew how to control herself and her career. Of course, she was French, not Irish.

Her costar (twice) George Murphy tactfully put it, "Nancy herself wasn't too easy to work with. She was potentially one of the great stars, but she never quite made it—maybe because she used stage tricks instead of her God-given talents . . . She seemed to enjoy making others uncomfortable." Still photographer John Engstead was less tactful: "Nancy Carroll was a little bit of a bitch. She was a very talented woman . . . But she always went around with a chip on her shoulder like someone was going to do her in . . . she approached *everything* that way." Clearly, the person who did her in was herself. Among her more respectable films: *Manhattan Cocktail* (28, Dorothy Arzner)—romance/melodrama, opposite Richard Arlen; *Scarlet Dawn* (32, William Dieterle)—revolutionary Russia, opposite Douglas Fairbanks Jr.; *Hot Saturday* (31, William A. Seiter)—charming as a small-town girl choosing between the very young Cary Grant and Randolph Scott; *Child of Manhattan* (33, Eddie Buzzell)—dance-hall girl wins, gives up, rewins rich guy John Boles; *Springtime for Henry* (34, Tuttle)—an amusing farce, with Carroll second-billed behind Otto Kruger. Her final film was *That Certain Age* (38, Edward Ludwig), sixth-billed in a Deanna Durbin vehicle. It had come to that.

Jack (John Elmer) Carson (1910–63), b. Carman, Manitoba, Canada

Never nominated or celebrated, never given lead roles in front-rank pictures, Jack Carson could be stupid, vacant, coarse, vain, amiable, decent, touching, nasty, hateful . . . even ordinary. Somehow one doubts that he ever got, or needed, much direction. Instead he understood story and character. He was cast and he was relied on, and let us say that one in ten times he was indelible—as the soft-hearted sucker who kills himself for love and dignity in *The Hard Way* (42, Vincent Sherman);

as the scapegrace dreamer/schemer in *Roughly Speaking* (45, Michael Curtiz); as the hopeless lech and would-be smartie in *Mildred Pierce* (45, Curtiz); as Matt Libby, the odious studio publicity man, in *A Star Is Born* (54, George Cukor) and as the father to no-neck monsters in *Cat on a Hot Tin Roof* (58, Richard Brooks).

Apart from that, he was only perfect: *Stage Door* (37, Gregory La Cava); *You Only Live Once* (37, Fritz Lang); *Vivacious Lady* (38, George Stevens); a roustabout in *Bringing Up Baby* (38, Howard Hawks); *Carefree* (38, Mark Sandrich); *Mr. Smith Goes to Washington* (39, Frank Capra); *Destry Rides Again* (39, George Marshall); *I Take This Woman* (40, W. S. Van Dyke); *Lucky Partners* (40, Lewis Milestone); *Typhoon* (40, Louis King); *Mr. and Mrs. Smith* (41, Alfred Hitchcock); *The Strawberry Blonde* (41, Raoul Walsh); very funny in *Love Crazy* (41, Jack Conway); *The Bride Came C.O.D.* (41, William Keighley); *Navy Blues* (41, Lloyd Bacon); *The Male Animal* (42, Elliott Nugent); *Larceny Inc.* (42, Bacon); *Wings for the Eagle* (42, Bacon); *Gentleman Jim* (42, Walsh); *Princess O'Rourke* (43, Norman Krasna); newly wed to Jane Wyman in *The Doughgirls* (44, James V. Kern).

In *The Hard Way,* he and Dennis Morgan had played a show-biz double act, and they were teamed up in several more pictures, like *Shine On, Harvest Moon* (44, David Butler); he was a detective in *Make Your Own Bed* (44, Peter Godfrey); with Morgan in *One More Tomorrow* (46, Godfrey), *Two Guys from Milwaukee* (46, Butler), and *The Time, the Place and the Girl* (46, Butler); *Love and Learn* (47, Frederick De Cordova); with Ann Sothern in *April Showers* (48, Kern); *Romance on the High Seas* (48, Curtiz), his first Doris Day picture; with Morgan again in *Two Guys from Texas* (48, Butler); with Morgan and Day in *It's a Great Feeling* (49, Butler); with Day in *My Dream Is Yours* (49, Curtiz); with Ronald Reagan in *John Loves Mary* (49, Butler); *Bright Leaf* (50, Curtiz).

He was *The Good Humor Man* (50, Bacon), with Lola Albright, who became his fourth wife; a wrestling promoter in *Mr. Universe* (51, Joseph Lerner); *The Groom Wore Spurs* (51, Richard Whorf); *Dangerous When Wet* (53, Charles Walters); *Red Garters* (54, Marshall); *Phffft!* (54, Mark Robson); *Ain't Misbehavin'* (55, Edward Buzzell); *The Bottom of the Bottle* (56, Henry Hathaway); *The Tattered Dress* (57, Jack Arnold); *Rally 'Round the Flag, Boys!* (58, Leo McCarey); *The Bramble Bush* (60, Daniel Petrie); *King of the Roaring 20s* (61, Joseph M. Newman).

Johnny Carson, b. Corning, Iowa, 1925

Why Johnny Carson in a book about movies? The short answer goes like this:

1. Carson's *Tonight Show* ran thirty years. Make a generous allowance for reruns and days when Johnny was absent, and still, at the very least, he was there, on the screen for five thousand hours (or twenty-five hundred movies).

2. He came away from that scrutiny as both an American ideal and a mystery man: agreeable and withdrawn; good company and intensely alone; attractive yet cold, and in some ways defensive or grim; always there, never graspable.

I like Johnny Carson, though I feel he has stayed unknowable so as to be seductive, to stay *there*, on TV. It was a power play. I liked him long ago, in the late sixties, in England where I lived. Wimbledon tennis was on television, and the camera searched the crowd between games. There sat this upright, smart, CIA-ish fellow, more pepper than salt then, watching play. "And that," said the English commentator, "that, I am told, is Mr. Johnny Carson, who is a television personality in America."

The face was pinched, blank but impatient; the head seemed narrow, the dot eyes close together; the figure was like a pretzel or flute. He could snap—or make music; the balance seemed delicate. Yet he looked tough in spirit, raised in winter country, capable of meanness; and I know a movie director who once dreamed of casting Carson as a hard, cold power-monger. But his face wanted to be amused; and if that was impossible, then it would be amusing. Before I heard or knew Johnny, I guessed at his most endearing tic—the panicky, eager laugh, so yearning to be spontaneous. After thirty years, he remained curiously hopeful, and on the direst *Tonight*s that could lift the spirit.

He negotiated so many awkward hours for us: that hesitation between a bad night out, a quarrel, the fateful close to one more disappointing day, and going to bed, making up in the dark and discovering some scrap of hope again. It is an old joke that people went to bed with Johnny Carson, but do not forget the thirty years of forgiveness and farfetched romance made out of his sad smile. Do not overlook the children, or the saving in Valium. Marriage has always been his subtext, somber but wistful. He stirred the embers of its absurdity, yet he could not abandon the habit or the hope. He and Ed McMahon complained about the alimony they had to pay. But only the very plush are so rueful, and what else was a frost like Johnny going to do with his money?

How many titanium sets of slacks and sports coat could he sustain? Has there ever been such anonymous tailoring in a man? Such a mix of cloth and stealth? Or such reason to worry over his very severe grace? Carson was never relaxed. He may have exercised all his life, but fretting kept him lean. He shifted that mug endlessly. He drummed with the pencils and checked the knot of his tie as if it were his fly. He was all antennae, sweeping an audience for sullenness or the sweet mercy that liked him. "I don't know why, but I'm in a silly mood tonight," he'd claim, a thousand times, trying to believe it. Whereas Johnny Carson was about as silly as Jack Nicklaus putting for money.

There is nothing new in remarking on the enigma or chill of Carson, or in wondering what this affable chatster did when he went home, or when he was off. Kenneth Tynan found him happier on the air than at social gatherings. Truman Capote (close to the second Mrs. Carson) believed Johnny was "consumed by rage." Research will tell you that Johnny did tennis, traveled, and waited in Malibu to be on the air again. Little enough considering his bounty. Yet it's hard to picture Carson occupied or doing things away from his set. Out and about in America, what could he have done . . . except be president? By which, I mean, be the decoy running back for secret service blockers; grin his brittle way across the White House lawn; and do the whiplash monologue, the good news and the bad, a Carnak on the state of the nation. Johnny didn't just do a brilliant and understanding Reagan impersonation. He had laid down a public pose in which Reagan daydreamed. President Ronnie owed as much to Johnny's elusive authority as to Reagan's own past as an actor.

Of course, Johnny was always apolitical. That was how he felt able to make jokes about everyone—often sharp, sometimes damaging. No one questioned the fairness of his mockery, or charged him with allegiances. It was the implicit philosophy of *Tonight* that decent, wry, common-sense Americans knew to trust no one in office. There was never the faintest notion that politics ought to be part of the American soul.

Johnny had tough competition. His era saw the chaos of the sixties, the assassinations, Vietnam, the Americanness of racism, Watergate, and at last, the nullity of Washington. And now we know there are worse things, unrevealed, plots too hideous to be described. Without having to own up to it, Carson was close to the see-no-evil blitheness of Reagan: he was very rich; in the eighties, he earned more for doing less; and around sixty, he insisted on being smart, urbane, and prosperous, as if to say, "Look, it can be done! You can have the love of this country forever if you never take on an issue."

Johnny had Reagan's luck in getting away with it. That good fortune was akin to his drab perfect clothes, and the way clubhouse smartness eclipsed character. But near the end, Johnny got caught. The parade of big names for the last month, all coming to Burbank to honor him, was interrupted by fear and loathing in South-Central L.A. This was more than the monologue could stretch around. It wasn't deemed manageable for Johnny

to nod solemnly while such as Jesse Jackson, Spike Lee, or Bill Cosby orated. The show was simply canceled, which isn't exactly what we ask of the daily talk show that reaches most Americans.

At the very outset of Carson's term on the *Tonight* show, in October 1962, he did at least refer to a current problem. With riots at the University of Mississippi, Carson said, "I don't think we should get involved in that. We should just let that go. I feel, like I think most of you do, that we hope all of this works out in the right way." Is that Reagan, or what? And if things haven't worked out right yet, if the old problem has grown uglier, how far is that because so central a voice of conventional wisdom stayed mute?

Carson's mastery depended on his pinnacle of celebrity, not on the fruits of discussion. He did not court challenge or allow much talk without punch line. He would sooner be made a fool of by Joan Embery's animals or the licensed outrage of Don Rickles than risk being led into matters of structure and nature by his house wisemen— Gore Vidal, William Buckley, or Carl Sagan. (Unknown writers and academics never got on the Carson show—and these days it is unknowns who have the truth.) He never messed with eloquent guests; some caution kept him agreeing until the break, desperate not to be exposed in ignorance or personal opinion. There was no idea for Johnny as potent as a wisecrack.

Yes, he was brilliant. He was a stand-up comic who mastered the less common form of sit-down bemused reaction. So often in his opening monologues he was searching sideways, less for Ed than for his own poker-faced va-voom at the desk. Talking to himself. Johnny Carson could be as dead-on expert, fast, funny, smart, and tireless as a great drummer. A great white drummer who had settled for a safe, moneymaking band. Think of the overflow, the tumult, and the mania in a Buddy Rich and you can see how repressive Johnny's beat was. (Think of Jack Nicholson's axeman, "Here's Johnny!" in *The Shining* to feel some of the restrained energy.)

Carson had Ed, Doc, Tommy, Freddie de Cordova, and the stupefied musicians—not a threat in the bunch, no gesture toward independence that was more than a setup for Johnny's perfectly timed rebukes. And when he punished, one could see the depth of anger. How loyally they withstood his distance; how steadily they pretended to be a bunch of the boys. Just recently, the show reran a chat between Johnny and Doc Severinsen that ran close to revealing how little these buddies knew each other—and Doc was relishing it behind his sweet, pious grin, as if he'd relied on the deft fraud getting his comeuppance one day.

No woman could penetrate this five o'clock mob masquerading as late-nighters (for the show was taped early in front of a nocturnal photograph). Betty White was a regular on the Mighty Carson Art Players. Charo did her bit for Latin women, and did it over and over again, the person as catchphrase. Joan Rivers came, and went, as the miscast "heiress," so clearly scary to Johnny's sense of order, and so grindingly intimate. Otherwise, there was a parade of gorgeous bimbos who strolled on for the new sponsor spots, carnal but silent except for the simpering content of being next to Mr. Cool, never noticing his disdain, let alone his self-loathing. That was left to the wives, the ones who had to watch Johnny at home when he was not on.

Now, this may sound as if I don't really or entirely like Johnny. Not so. I can never resist a magnificent, triumphant performer whose appearance and aplomb are drawn tight to conceal loneliness, dismay, anger, and disgust. And if the *Tonight* show was usually cowardly and irrelevant, Carson could fairly ask, "Why blame me? It's only entertainment. It's only television. And if you're going to have television, you've got to expect fixtures like me." All true: the omissions of the *Tonight* show are no more Johnny's fault than the lapses of the Reagan years are the burden of their president. After all, it was only ever the *Tonight* show *with* Johnny Carson. He never recognized responsibility.

They say he kept NBC alive and well for years. But network entertainment has lost its hold. The rivals for his slot are discovering that the hallowed hour lost its allure with the monster's retreat. America is not honestly a late-night country. Prime time is beginning and ending earlier. The TV set is more at our mercy. There are no real talk shows now, only plugging sessions and celebrity roasts. Do you recall a time when Dick Cavett gave five nights in a row to a beguiling, forgotten scoundrel-genius named Jed Harris? That was when TV talked.

Johnny was a model of mainstream hopes and fears. He was what the middle of the country dreamed of being if it made it—a star, but a gray star, matte finish, with all the confusions that entailed. It was the battle between glory and folksiness that made Carson like Nixon, a little more worrying the cheerier he became. All Nixon wanted was to be presidential, and Johnny lasted so long because he didn't know what to do except be on TV. And as the decades passed, so the mainstream proved itself a narrow inch of iced water. Whereas we deserve floods and torrents.

Helena Bonham Carter, b. London, 1966

I must confess that, around the time of the ignominiously flashy *Mary Shelley's Frankenstein* (94, Kenneth Branagh), I did raise the notion of a fund, or a campaign, to urge Miss BC's retirement, before she got hurt or stepped on. Not that she really seemed susceptible to damage. I was proved wrong by the transformation of her Kate Croy in *The Wings of the Dove* (97, Iain Softley), so fully grown up, so beguiling in her varieties of blue, and so scaldingly beautiful in the somber nude scenes. She was nominated for an Oscar, and could easily have won. A real actress was delivered.

The great-granddaughter of Prime Minister Herbert Asquith, and the granddaughter of Lady Violet Bonham Carter, HBC's pedigree could hardly be sounder. But there was a time when it seemed at odds with her tininess and her immature attitudes—all of which suited such early roles as *Lady Jane* (86, Trevor Nunn); *A Room with a View* (86, James Ivory); *Maurice* (87, Ivory); *The Mask* (88, Fiorella Infascelli); *Francesco* (89, Liliana Cavani); *Getting It Right* (89, Randal Kleiser); Ophelia to Mel Gibson's *Hamlet* (90, Franco Zeffirelli); *Where Angels Fear to Tread* (91, Charles Sturridge); Helen Schlegel in *Howards End* (92, Ivory).

She was unexpectedly good on television as Marina Oswald in *Fatal Deception* (93, Robert Dornhelm); not too credible as Woody's wife in *Mighty Aphrodite* (95, Woody Allen); Olivia in *Twelfth Night* (96, Nunn); *Portraits Chinois* (96, Martine Dugowson); *Keep the Aspidistra Flying* (97, Robert Bierman). She was much improved in *Margaret's Museum* (97, Mort Ransen), and very good as Morgan Le Fay in *Merlin* (98, Steve Barron). She then played a brave but misguided role, as a sexually hungry cripple, with her real-life companion, Kenneth Branagh, in the awful *Theory of Flight* (98, Paul Greengrass). A year later she was very funny as a caricature of the hard slut in *Fight Club* (99, David Fincher); *Women Talking Dirty* (99, Coky Giedroyc); *Carnivale* (99, Deane Taylor); as the liberal voice in *Planet of the Apes* (01, Tim Burton); *Novocaine* (01, David Atkins).

She was in *Till Human Voices Wake Us* (01, Michael Petroni); as Mum in the short, *Football* (01, Gaby Dallal); *The Heart of Me* (02, Thaddeus O'Sullivan); good in *Live from Baghdad* (02, Mick Jackson); *Big Fish* (03, Burton).

John Cassavetes (1929–89), b. New York
1961: *Shadows*. 1962: *Too Late Blues; A Child Is Waiting*. 1968: *Faces*. 1970: *Husbands*. 1971: *Minnie and Moskowitz*. 1974: *A Woman Under the Influence*. 1976: *The Killing of a Chinese Bookie*. 1978: *Opening Night*. 1980: *Gloria*. 1983: *Love Streams*. 1985: *Big Trouble*.

Shadows was once hailed as the breakthrough of what was called American underground cinema. But the film jumped up above ground like a wired groundhog. Cassavetes was depicted as a frustrated genius obliged to act in passing Hollywood nonsense as a way of saving money for his own "sincere" films. *Shadows was* sincere, as student movies are. Cassavetes was really the first modern American independent. His half-swaggering, half-aggressive integrity was highly influential. Like booze, it seemed to exalt the man himself. He could rouse audiences against commercial pictures like Warren Beatty working himself up into socialist wrath playing John Reed. Except that, as an actor, Cassavetes had harsh metal in his soul.

Something of this cult had once embraced the far more agreeable, and more slippery, Orson Welles. Like Cassavetes, Welles could be an actor who delighted in the coarsest melodrama, and never resisted it. Whereupon, it was supposed, such hams walked through a transforming doorway, or aura, and became selfless artists. "American independent" can be a large contradiction in terms. Sooner or later, making movies is getting down in the dirt of money and crowds—and Cassavetes's shark's grin seemed to suggest he understood that.

He was earnest and obsessive; he had a grinding laugh when he acted, yet I'd guess he was humorless. He was an actor first and last, and someone belligerently alone and secret in his dogged pursuits. That which seemed independent was the helpless course of temperament. He was seldom a graceful filmmaker; whereas, Welles was maybe cursed with the knack of making everything seem oiled and easy—except writing. There's the rub with many American independents. The Cassavetes films are far more thoroughly written than was once believed; and they are badly written. What makes John Sayles more interesting than Cassavetes is his attitude as a writer. Sayles is no Welles. He may find the visual rather secondary, but his pictures benefit from material, ideas, and talk. They are constructed, and so Sayles gets better performances from actors than Cassavetes. He directs them; he knows what they should do. Cassavetes indulges them, he invites them in and waits to see what they will do. He treats them like adorable pets; and we sometimes feel as if they were his vacation snapshots.

When he is acting, he thrusts a snarling intensity at the camera. But as a director, he is like a guy who begs us to hang around because these people are fascinating—and not just drunks. What may be most interesting in his work is the sociology of his middle America. He chooses basic, unenlightened, and unhappily successful people. They are a rarity in American film, rigorously shunned by most directors: they are bores.

Cassavetes was the son of a Greek immigrant who made and lost a fortune. He went from drama school to stock to TV. His film debut was briefly in *Taxi* (53, Gregory Ratoff), but it was only two solid years as a TV juvenile delinquent that got him proper film work. Then his lean nervousness was well used in *The Night Holds Terror* (55, Andrew Stone); *Crime in the Streets* (57, Don Siegel);

Edge of the City (57, Martin Ritt); *Affair in Havana* (57, Laslo Benedek); and *Saddle the Wind* (58, Robert Parrish). After the innocent diversion of *Virgin Island* (58, Pat Jackson) and a TV series, *Johnny Staccato*, Cassavetes made *Shadows* in New York. It is a clumsy, callow film, struggling between the hope that improvisation will uncover truth and the imprint of Hollywood clichés. But worse than the film was the praise it received. *Shadows* was such a success that Paramount approached Cassavetes in 1961 to make cheap, quality pictures. It reveals his mixture of naïveté and cunning that he accepted the offer and made two films: the atrocious *Too Late Blues* and, for Stanley Kramer, the affecting but flawed *A Child Is Waiting*, in which Cassavetes seemed most pleased that he had gotten Hollywood to use actually handicapped children, along with that figurehead of worked-up emotion, Judy Garland.

Both films flopped and Cassavetes went back to acting. He may have intended just to gather funds, but *The Killers* (64, Siegel) was one of the best things he did. Hard cash was all that emerged from *The Dirty Dozen* (67, Robert Aldrich) and two Italian gangster films: *Machine Gun McCain* (68, Giuliano Montaldo) and *Roma come Chicago* (68, Alberto de Martino). He was excellent again as the husband in *Rosemary's Baby* (68, Roman Polanski). By now, however, he was in funds and made two more of his "own" films: *Faces* and *Husbands*. The first benefits from the acting of his own wife, Gena Rowlands, and is the best organized of all his films. The latter has all his faults, not least the bizarre congruence of companionable self-indulgence in the three characters and in their self-sacrificing actors: Cassavetes, Ben Gazzara, and Peter Falk. But *Minnie and Moskowitz*, played by Gena Rowlands and Seymour Cassel, is more naturally entertaining; its comparison with movie glamour is less a protestation of faith in genuineness than a well-managed middlebrow joke.

Gena Rowlands was a virtuoso in *Woman Under the Influence*, but the grueling domestic scenes of that movie showed how far a camera confused the director's adoration of pressurized performance. Rowlands is a test case of the Cassavetes approach. Was she a great actress, a prisoner in her husband's films, or the chief recipient of Cassavetes's assumption that performance was the heartfelt metaphor for life? He believed in an actor's burrowing into a role as almost a behavioral credential. Gena Rowlands is so moving and pathetic in *Woman Under the Influence*, yet I'm not sure that her part actually deserves a movie. Or is a movie. Doesn't it seem more like an endless actor's improvisation? Then consider that Cassavetes wrote and contrived such things. *Gloria* feels not like life but a deliberate remaking of an old movie in rehearsal. *Opening Night* is pretentious, then confused, and finally lost.

No one could deny that Cassavetes died tragically early, and an unyielding outcast still. But was that something he demanded, or unconsciously designed? He was courageous, unruly, an enemy to Hollywood for many good reasons. Yet he was a tyrant, too, a man who had to be right. Still, it is going a long way to claim that he was as good a filmmaker as he wanted to be. I have argued with myself and with Raymond Carney (his most eloquent defender), but I cannot find what Carney sees in the films. *Love Streams* seems a wounded beast, clumsy, sentimental, overdone, yet evasive, too. But I would love to read a thorough, honest biography of the man that balanced his own work, his family story, and his unique, Satanic anguish. If only he could have played Elia Kazan in a biopic.

He acted in other films, too: with Peter Falk (his longtime actor) in *Mikey and Nicky* (76, Elaine May), a film that is surely affected by its actors and their history, and which is great or obscure, depending on your point of view; a sinister villain in *The Fury* (78, Brian De Palma); *Brass Target* (78, John Hough); *Flesh and Blood* (79, Jud Taylor) for TV; *Incubus* (81, Hough); *Whose Life Is It, Anyway?* (81, John Badham); *Tempest* (82, Paul Mazursky); and *Marvin and Tige* (83, Eric Weston).

Alberto Cavalcanti (Alberto de Almeida Cavalcanti) (1897–1982), b. Rio de Janeiro, Brazil
1926: *Rien Que les Heures* (d). 1928: *En Rade; Yvette; Le Train sans Yeux.* 1929: *La P'tite Lilie; La Jalousie de Barbouille; Le Capitaine Fracasse; Le Petit Chaperon Rouge; Vous Verrez la Semaine Prochaine.* 1930: *Toute Sa Vie.* 1931: *Dans une Île Perdue; A mi-chemin du Ciel; Les Vacances du Diable.* 1932: *Tour de Chant* (d); *En Lisant le Journal; Le Jour du Frotteur; Revue Montmartroise; Nous ne Ferons Jamais du Cinéma* (d). 1933: *Le Mari Divorce.* 1934: *Coralie et Cie; Le Tour de Chant; Pett and Pott* (s); *New Rates.* 1935: *Coalface* (d); *SOS Radio Service* (d). 1936: *Message from Geneva* (d). 1937: *We Live in Two Worlds* (d); *The Line to Tschierva Hut* (d); *Who Writes to Switzerland?* (d). 1938: *Four Barriers* (d). 1939: *Men of the Alps* (d); *A Midsummer Day's Work* (d). 1941: *The Yellow Caesar* (d). 1942: *Film and Reality* (d); *Went the Day Well?; Alice in Switzerland* (s); *Greek Testament* (d). 1943: *Watertight.* 1944: *Champagne Charlie.* 1945: "The Ventriloquist's Dummy," episode from *Dead of Night.* 1947: *Nicholas Nickleby; They Made Me a Fugitive; The First Gentleman.* 1949: *For Them That Trespass.* 1952: *Simão, o Caolho; O Canto do Mar.* 1954: *Mulher de Verdade.* 1955: *Herr Puntila und Sein Knecht Matti.* 1956: *Die Vind Rose* (supervised, in collaboration with Joris Ivens). 1958: *La Prima Notte; Les Noces Veniti-*ennes. 1960: *The Monster of Highgate Ponds* (s). 1967: *The Story of Israel* (d); *Thus Spake Theodor Herzl* (d).

Was Cavalcanti a nomad or an idealist always being edged out of compromising establishments? The very scattering of his work makes him a difficult man to assess. But it seems clear that there is always something artificial about his naturalism, a taste for cinema that is more experimental than expressive. Grierson acclaimed Cavalcanti as one of the founders of realism, but it was Grierson who enthused over the "creative" treatment of actuality and who often dignified it with the attention of renowned and deliberate artists from other fields. The British documentary movement of the 1930s all too often treated realism as if it were dogma; to work in documentary was a vouchsafe of good faith. But within years of his work for the Crown Film Unit, Cavalcanti showed every sign of interest in the polished mysteries of *Dead of Night.* Even there, his invocation of the supernatural is more obtrusive but less disturbing than Robert Hamer's. *Dead of Night* is the best-known example of Cavalcanti's work and it suggests a proficient but shallow craftsman. To prove or disprove that theory requires a chance to see much more of his work than is generally available.

He was an architecture student, who went from interior design to set decoration for Marcel L'Herbier on *L'Inhumaine* (24) and *Feu Mathias Pascal* (24). By 1926, he was making *Rien Que les Heures*, a symphonic but rather nostalgic study of the Parisian poor. To call it realistic is only to expose the standards of 1926; but undoubtedly the film influenced Walter Ruttmann as well as the British. Cavalcanti worked in France until 1934, directing Renoir in two films and writing *Tire au Flanc* (28). In 1934, he came to Britain and worked for the GPO Film Unit. Sound recordist on *Night Mail* (36, Basil Wright and Harry Watt), he produced *Big Money* (36, Pat Jackson and Watt); *The Savings of Bill Blewett* (37, Watt); *The First Days* (39, Humphrey Jennings); *Speaking from America* (39, Jennings); *Squadron 992* (39, Watt); *Spare Time* (39, Jennings); and *Spring Offensive* (40, Jennings). He joined the Crown Film Unit and produced *The Big Blockade* (41, Charles Frend); *The Foreman Went to France* (42, Frend); and *Find, Fix and Strike* (42, Compton Bennett). He then went to Ealing and produced *Halfway House* (44, Basil Dearden). His own films at Ealing include Henry Kendall in *Champagne Charlie*, Michael Redgrave's highly strung ventriloquist in *Dead of Night*, and Trevor Howard in *They Made Me a Fugitive.* In 1949, he went to Brazil and to an executive position, only to be dismissed after American complaints that he was a Communist. He worked with Brecht on *Herr Puntila* and with

Joris Ivens on *Die Vind Rose,* before splitting his time between directing for the theatre, teaching in America, and working for French TV.

André Cayatte (1909–89),

b. Carcassonne, France

1942: *La Fausse Maîtresse.* 1943: *Au Bonheur des Dames.* 1944: *Pierre et Jean; Le Dernier Sou.* 1945: *Roger-la-Honte; Sérénade aux Nuages.* 1946: *Le Revanche de Roger-la-Honte; Le Chanteur Inconnu.* 1947: *Les Dessous des Cartes.* 1948: *Les Amants de Vérone.* 1949: "Tante Emma," episode from *Retour à la Vie.* 1950: *Justice est Faite.* 1952: *Nous Sommes Tous des Assassins.* 1954: *Avant le Déluge.* 1955: *Le Dossier Noir.* 1956: *Oeil pour Oeil.* 1958: *Le Miroir à Deux Faces.* 1960: *Le Passage du Rhin.* 1962: *Le Glaive et la Balance.* 1963: *La Vie Conjugale* (in two parts: "Jean-Marc" and "Françoise"). 1965: *Piège pour Cendrillon.* 1967: *Les Risques du Métier.* 1969: *Les Chemins de Khatmandou.* 1970: *Mourir d'Aimer.* 1974: *Verdict.* 1975: *Le Testament.* 1977: *A Chacun son Enfer.* 1978: *La Raison d'Etat.*

Throughout the 1930s, Cayatte was a novelist, journalist, and lawyer. His first involvement with films was as a scriptwriter: *Entrée des Artistes* (38, Marc Allégret); *Remorques* (41, Jean Grémillon); *Caprices* (41, Leo Joannon); and *Le Camion Blanc* (42, Joannon). Cayatte's own work returned with grim fervor to attacks on capital punishment, skeptical examinations of justice, and humane generalizations: *Justice est Faite; Nous Sommes Tous des Assassins; Oeil pour Oeil; Le Passage du Rhin;* and *Le Glaive et la Balance.* These five are not as trenchant or subtle as one reel from *Fury* or *Anatomy of a Murder,* but Cayatte was a reformer and his role as a voice of protest in France should not be underestimated. His films are mundane because their messages are unequivocal; it is the actual French context that gives them bite. More interesting are his tender, brooding accounts of young love: *Les Amants de Vérone,* written by Jacques Prévert, with Anouk and Serge Reggiani blighted by odious family repression and charmed by the romance of the movie world; and La *Vie Conjugale,* with Jacques Charrier and Marie-Jose Nat fretting at the bonds of society. Cayatte always seemed a man of the 1930s, and his love stories aspire to the awful resignation of *You Only Live Once* (37, Fritz Lang) but are kept short of Lang's vivid pessimism by the muddy constructivism of a lawyer turned filmmaker.

Claude Chabrol, b. Paris, 1930

1958: *Le Beau Serge.* 1959: *Les Cousins; A Double Tour/Web of Passion; Les Bonnes Femmes.* 1961: *Les Godelureaux.* 1962: "L'Avarice," episode in *Les Sept Péchés Capitaux; L'Oeil du Malin; Ophelia.* 1963: *Landru.* 1964: "L'Homme qui Vendit la Tour Eiffel," episode in *Les Plus Belles Escroqueries du Monde;* "La Muette," episode in *Paris Vu Par . . . ; Le Tigre Aime la Chair Fraîche.* 1965: *Marie-Chantal Contre le Docteur Kha; Le Tigre Se Parfume à la Dynamite.* 1966: *La Ligne de Démarcation; Le Scandale/The Champagne Murders.* 1967: *La Route de Corinthe.* 1968: *Les Biches; La F mme Infidèle.* 1969: *Que la Bête Meure.* 1970: *Le Boucher; La Rupture.* 1971: *Juste avant la Nuit; La Décade Prodigieuse/Ten Days' Wonder.* 1972: *Les Noces Rouges; Docteur Popaul.* 1974: *Nada; Une Partie de Plaisir/Love Match.* 1975: *Les Innocents aux Mains Sales/Innocents with Dirty Hands.* 1976: *Les Magiciens; Folies Bourgeoises/The Twist.* 1977: *Alice, ou la Dernière Fugue.* 1978: *Les Liens de Sang/Blood Relatives; Violette Nozière.* 1979: *Le Cheval d'Orgeuil.* 1982: *Les Fantômes du Chapelier.* 1984: an episode in *Paris Vu Par . . . 20 Ans Apres; The Blood of Others* (TV). 1985: *Poulet au Vinaigre.* 1986: *Inspector Lavardin.* 1987: *Le Cri de Hibou; Masques.* 1988: *Une Affaire des Femmes/Story of Women.* 1989: *Docteur M.* 1990: *Quiet Days in Clichy.* 1991: *Madame Bovary.* 1993: *Betty; The Eye of Vichy* [d]. 1994: *Enfer.* 1995: *La Cérémonie/ The Ceremony.* 1996: *Cyprien Katsaris* (TV). 1997: *Rien Ne Va Plus.* 1999: *Au Coeur du Mensonge/The Color of Lies.* 2000: *Merci pour le Chocolat.* 2001: *Les Redoutables* (TV). 2003: *La Fleur du Mal.*

Chabrol is one of the most enigmatic directors at work today. A fringe instigator of the original New Wave, he has managed to create a world for himself—some private Hollywood—in which it is possible to produce a stream of subtle studies of human motivation. He has never shared Godard's political preoccupations; never been willing to work as slowly as Rohmer or Rivette; and never faced the difficulties that haunted Truffaut in finding subjects. Above all, Chabrol has made commercially viable films, and come through as the most industrious of his generation. Andrew Sarris once claimed that Chabrol liked to keep his hand in, even when his heart wasn't in a film. But does that properly describe the way in which Chabrol has settled for reticence, rather than exploring the veiled thematic originality in his early work? Sometimes, it seems, the hand moves to obscure the troubled heart.

For there is a contradiction between the man who (with Rohmer) first drew attention to the moral complexity of guilt transference in Hitchcock and the rather aggressive denigrator of "big themes." In a famous article in *Cahiers* in 1959, Chabrol attacked the portentousness of Stanley Kramer's type of cinema, in which significance is belabored to the exclusion of precise human truth. There is no intrinsic difference, he said, between "the final hours of a hero of the Resistance or an enquiry into the murder of a prostitute." The true test is whether or not cinematic detail adds up to artistic size. It is a credo allied to Chabrol's delight in spontaneous, plastic cinema, comfortable in the Hollywood genres; it comes across in his pleasure at color, detachment, beautiful women, and narrative complexity. But it is also a sign of his resort to murder rather than life, melodrama rather than the everyday. Chabrol has repeatedly taken us to the brink of novel themes and developed them only obliquely, as if slightly shy of them.

Despite such surface distractions as Antonella Lualdi and Provence in *A Double Tour;* the tribute to the Dordogne in *Le Boucher;* the discovery of Nice in winter in *Les Biches;* and the parody of intrigue in *Marie-Chantal* and the *Tigre* movies— despite all those things, Chabrol's strength is a unique sense of the unspoken shifts of character in human relations. That may derive from his admiration for Hitchcock, and it is often connected with guilt, but it goes further—into sexual ambiguity and the idea of one person morally or emotionally overpowering another. Thus, the relationship between Brialy and Blain in *Les Cousins* hints at a deeper meaning than the distinction between irresponsibility and doggedness; *Les Godelureaux*—an adventurous movie—seems to endorse stylish intellectual dandyism; *Les Biches* is not just a study of a lesbian relationship, but of one personality consuming another; above all, *Le Boucher* studies human tenderness with an almost Oriental dispassion within a plot that involves horrifying murder.

There is also a beady-eyed cynicism in many of Chabrol's films that was evident in the eccentric performances he gave in such movies as *Le Coup de Berger* (56, Rivette); *L'Eau à la Bouche* (59, Jacques Doniol-Valcroze); and *Paris Nous Appartient* (60, Rivette). It was an assumed blackness that permitted lurid ill manners, as if to emphasize the paramount importance of cinema. And in his films, Chabrol has scourged bourgeois values: *Les Cousins* and *Les Godelureaux* are as offensive to middle-class propriety as *Les Bonnes Femmes* is destructive of the aspiring innocence of its working-class girls. "La Muette" is a scabrous anecdote about family incompatibility, while in later films the willingness to kill has been obscurely offered as the surest proof of love. In *A Double Tour,* Belmondo assaults conventional manners time and again, just as Bernadette Laffont scandalizes the ideal of gentle feminine sexuality. And in *Landru, Le Boucher, Violette Nozière,* and *Une Affaire des Femmes* the way Chabrol seemed to explain murder away is that society's crimes are far worse. Even in *Les Bonnes Femmes,* the shock of murder was as much lyrical as destructive. That film ended with murder, and Truffaut's point that it should have begun with it

seemed a telling criticism. In the same way, *Le Boucher* abruptly curtails the interest it has slowly aroused: the relationship between Stéphane Audran and the butcher is so subtly established that the melodramatic action seems evasive. Is the film urging that the woman is responsible in part for the man's murders, or that her type of sexual denial is at the roots of slaughter? Is it also saying that such crimes are peripheral to emotional revelation? That is hinted at in *La Femme Infidèle, Landru, Juste avant le Nuit,* and even in *Les Bonnes Femmes,* where the victim seems to attain ecstasy just before she is killed.

More lately, Chabrol films have had a harder time making their way outside France. He has done several thrillers, as well as the Sartre adaptation for American television. *Une Affaire des Femmes* is an excellent movie—feminist, yet wry and unexpected, and making fine use of Isabelle Huppert. But sad to say, with the same actress, Chabrol made an academic, passionless thing out of *Madame Bovary.* Despite such ups and downs, this is a career that cries out for retrospectives—is *Les Bonnes Femmes* still as great as it once seemed? Better. Is *Violette Nozière* disturbing? And some.

Lon Chaney (Alonso Chaney) (1883–1930), b. Colorado Springs, Colorado
Chaney has the sweet, slow stealth of a magician who lingers at the moment of revealing a transformation, to avoid any hint of trickery and to leave everything to poetic imagination. There is not a screen performer who so illustrates the fascination for audiences of the promise and threat of metamorphosis. Why do we go to the cinema, sit in the dark before overwhelming fantasies that appear real? To share in these plastic movements, to change our own lives, and to encourage the profound spiritual notion of our flexible identity. Hope breeds on the exercised fantasy. Cinema has always depended upon the moment when screen creation and spectator begin to partake of one another. Who embodies that potential for transformation better than the actor known as "the man of a thousand faces"? That description was not just the boast of a versatile makeup box, but one of the most alluring invitations to an audience. For the man in the cinema with the endlessly changing face is the spectator. Chaney's fluctuating appearance seethed with the audience's lust for vicariousness.

The facts of his own life are as stark as the events of a scenario: they seem factually unlikely but imaginatively inevitable. He was the child of deaf-and-mute parents. When Alonso was nine his mother was made an invalid by rheumatism. Inert, unhearing, and unable to reply, she was the first, tragic representative of the movie audience that Chaney had. The story goes that he mimed his own experiences to entertain her. Perhaps that seems closer to the retrospective sentiment of the publicity machine than to actual family life. It may also be a sign of Chaney's discovering the imaginative truth in his own life. The facts of his screen work make it clear that he was a supreme pantomimist. But did he subject his mother to mimes of suffering and horror? That, again, seems unlikely, even if her plight made him conscious of the suffering in life, just as it created a yearning for miraculous cure or transformation.

He became a traveling player and, by 1912, he drifted, broke, to Los Angeles and the Universal studio. Already, he carried a makeup box and liked to disguise himself, play jokes with false noses, and slip in and out of grotesque characters. Allan Dwan interpreted this as touting for work and began to use Chaney as an exotic heavy. His prowess with makeup often enabled him to play several parts within one film. From 1913 to 1917 he made over seventy films at Universal, from two- to five-reelers. The directors he worked with included Dwan—*Back to Life* (13); *Red Margaret—Moonshiner* (13); *The Lie* (13); *Discord and Harmony* (13); *The Embezzler* (13); *The Tragedy of Whispering Creek* (14); *The Forbidden Room* (14); more often Joseph de Grasse—*Her Bounty* (14); *Her Escape* (14); *The Threads of Fate* (15); *Maid of the Mist* (15); *The Stronger Mind* (15); *Bound on the Wheel* (15); *Quits* (15); *Grasp of Greed* (16); *The Mark of Cain* (16); *Place Beyond the Winds* (16); and occasionally, Chaney himself—*The Stool Pigeon* (15); *For Cash* (15); *The Oyster Dredger* (15); *The Violin Maker* (15); and *The Trust* (15).

He hauled himself into public recognition as a San Francisco gangster at the time of the earthquake in *Hell Morgan's Girl* (17, de Grasse), a melodrama in which Chaney was in love with a girl who loves someone else. His physical harshness often led to this theme of unrequited love, and it heralds a major theme of horror films whereby romantic and sexual frustration provoke misanthropic, demonic revenge. Chaney's ugliness is often interpreted as an effect of brutal society. In *Phantom of the Opera*, he says, "If I am a Phantom it is because man's hatred has made me so."

In the next few years, he moved nearer the center of his own films, asserting himself as a star rather than a heavy. That in itself was an innovation; the way in which Chaney's stardom was so allied to mutation was a further novelty. He made *A Doll's House* (17, de Grasse); and was von Tirpitz in *The Kaiser, the Beast of Berlin* (18, Rupert Julian); was encouraged by William S. Hart in *Riddle Gawne* (18, Lambert Hillyer); and then met Tod Browning who gave him a part in *The Wicked Darling* (19). Universal was hostile to his claims for more money and Chaney went to Paramount

for his first study in illusion: the sham cripple in *The Miracle Man* (19, George Loane Tucker). While there, he made two with Maurice Tourneur: *Victory* (19) and *Treasure Island* (20), in which he played George Merry and Blind Pew. He went back to Universal for *Outside the Law* (21, Browning) in which he took two parts—a gangster and a Chinaman—and in which the Chinaman finally shoots the gangster. Clearly, the Jekyll and Hyde potential within metamorphosis was becoming evident.

After *The Light in the Dark* (22, Clarence Brown); Fagin in *Oliver Twist* (22, Frank Lloyd); *All the Brothers Were Valiant* (23, Irvin S. Willat); *While Paris Sleeps* (23, but actually filmed in 1920, Tourneur); and *The Shock* (23, Hillyer); he played Quasimodo in *The Hunchback of Notre Dame* (23, Wallace Worsley), an extraordinary immersion in deformity and a great box-office success.

Chaney was now a major star, competed for by Universal and MGM. Irving Thalberg had admired him at Universal and eventually won him over to MGM. Chaney's work in the mid- and late-1920s is now seldom seen. Yet he is surely one of the greatest imaginative artists of silent cinema, undoubtedly most stimulated by Tod Browning, but compelling under all circumstances: *The Next Corner* (24, Sam Wood); *He Who Gets Slapped* (24, Victor Sjostrom), a more conventional drama, about a scientist who becomes a circus clown when his wife leaves him; *The Monster* (25, Roland West); the very frightening *The Unholy Three* (25, Browning) in which he is a crook who dresses up as an old woman; *The Phantom of the Opera* (25, Rupert Julian), a true classic containing one of the great horrific discovery scenes and in which Chaney moves with a stunning languor, as if he knew of Conrad Veidt in *Caligari;* another Sjostrom drama, *The Tower of Lies* (25); *The Blackbird* (26, Browning), about a man who poses as brothers; *The Road to Mandalay* (26, Browning), as a one-eyed crook; a "straight" role as the sergeant in *Tell It to the Marines* (27, George W. Hill); *Mr. Wu* (27, William Nigh); as Alonzo the Armless in *The Unknown* (27, Browning); *Mockery* (27, Benjamin Christensen), another disguise story; superb as the detective and the vampire in *London After Midnight* (27, Browning); *The Big City Sleeps* (28, Jack Conway); *West of Zanzibar* (28, Browning); *Laugh, Clown, Laugh* (28, Herbert Brenon); *Where East Is East* (29, Browning); *Thunder* (29, Nigh); and his last film and first talkie, a remake of *The Unholy Three* (30, Conway). His voice in that was as varied as his appearance, but he had cancer of the throat and died within a few months. Only forty-four, he had made over 140 films. He was to have played Dracula for Browning, a part that went to Bela Lugosi. It is perhaps the secret of his quality that Chaney could have played most of the parts taken by both Lugosi and Karloff. He had laid down the basis of horror. No one has surpassed his conviction.

Jackie Chan (Kong-sang Chan),
b. Hong Kong, 1954

When you go to any database to get information on Jackie Chan (not yet fifty), page after page is produced. Not just because so many of his projects go under different titles in all their outlets; not just because Chan is involved on them in so many capacities—actor, writer, director, producer, stunt creator, and engineer—but because the guy works like crazy. But how can that come as a surprise, granted the inordinate, good-humored energy that seems the essential characteristic of Jackie Chan?

I am not a fan or an enthusiast. This does not mean I don't like him. Rather, I see him as the lifelike embodiment of all those comic-book warriors in the video combat games that my twelve-year-old son loves. They are less virtuous or noble (in the way Gary Cooper was, say) than charged with elan, readiness, perfect athletic skill, resilience, and something like the capacity to withstand enormous violence (or degradation) that was the keynote of Tom in the Tom and Jerry cartoons, but which there seemed like a curse—for the wretched feline could not even die in peace, but was compelled to be inventive and hopeful anew so that he could be shattered. I suppose what I mean by this is to venture the suggestion that Jackie Chan seems to be alive, too. Or is he just *on*?

He is often called the modern Buster Keaton. Someone else I know compares him with Douglas Fairbanks Sr. And there's a point in both ideas. After all, Chan more than anyone else is responsible for introducing a self-deprecatory humor into the world of martial arts. He grins a lot. But, of course, that is untypical of Keaton, who inspired humor so often in the numb, aghast, or stoical ways in which he tried to ignore outrage and tumult. Doug grinned, and bounded and twisted, very much in the way of Chan, who has lasted in the business despite his pride in doing his own stunts and seemingly defying the laws of physics. The one law that does apply is that of box office. Chan comes from a notoriously piratical world where film and video are concerned (a big reason, perhaps, for getting a foothold in America), but he is not just big business. He is an industry. That he can never have time to enjoy his own wealth is just one factor underlining that condition of being alive, yet not obviously—or do I mean fatally?—human.

As a small boy, Chan was taken by his parents to Australia, and it was there that he did a Peking Opera training in acrobatics, mime, and the mar-

tial arts. In fact, he got his first credits as a child performer in Hong Kong films of the early and mid-1960s. A key step in his progress was working on *Fists of Fury* (73), which was Bruce Lee's acting debut. After Lee's death, Chan was one of several contending successors, and it was at that point that he elected (and the decision seems to have been his) to opt for comic action instead. *Half a Loaf of Kung Fu* (78) was the decisive film in that move.

Chan came to America in the early eighties and he appeared in *The Big Brawl* (80, Robert Clouse) and *The Cannonball Run* (81, Hal Needham). In hindsight, it is sad to think of him coiled yet unreleased as Burt and the aging Rat Pack did their desultory routines.

So the human spring went back to Hong Kong and embarked on what purists feel is his best work—no doubt being assisted by being in his physical prime: *Project A* (87), *Police Force* (89), *Operation Condor* (90), *Crime Story* (93).

Then, for *Rumble in the Bronx* (96), his character came back to the U.S. (looking like Vancouver), and the phenomenon took root in America. *No More Mr. Nice Guy* (98) was another Hong Kong picture, but then came *Rush Hour* (98, Brett Ratner) and the teaming with Chris Tucker. That was a colossal hit, yet not as big as *Rush Hour 2* (01, Ratner); *The Tuxedo* (02, Kevin Donovan); *Shanghai Knights* (03, David Dobkin).

Jackie Chan should be past his peak as an acrobat. But he is bigger than ever commercially. Putting those two realities together may make for some sad compromises. But nothing, I'd guess, will remove the smile from his face.

Stockard Channing (Susan Stockard),
b. New York, 1944

I am fond of actors and actresses who, while very idiosyncratic, serve a long time without quite making the shore of stardom. In a book that has to be selective, I feel bound to omit too many of them—and so there is no Anne Revere, no Ann Dvorak, no Madeline Kahn, no Blythe Danner, even. And there would have been no Stockard Channing until the extraordinary movie of *Six Degrees of Separation* (93, Fred Schepisi), a tour de force of humor, silliness, great intelligence, vulnerability, and abiding empty-headedness. Here was a big part in an important picture, with a deserved Oscar nomination. So at last I had to consider the byways of being Stockard Channing.

Was she too clever, too sharp, too comic? Was she separated from beauty by one or two degrees too many? Whatever, I am not alone in thinking at various times that major success was about to fall on her. Perhaps there has been an aversion in her, a sturdy perversity, that just refused to get wet.

She was educated at Radcliffe. She has worked regularly in the theatre: that's where she first did

Six Degrees. Her movie debut was a small role in *The Hospital* (71, Arthur Hiller) and then *Up the Sandbox* (72, Irvin Kershner). She really attracted attention in a TV movie, *The Girl Most Likely To . . .* (73, Lee Philips). Its script, by Joan Rivers, described a plain young woman, transformed by cosmetic surgery, but turned into an avenging angel seeking out the men who wronged her. Any Channing fan should hound the airwaves for this one, for it is rare black comedy—maybe it alarmed too many people.

Still, it won her the hotly contested role between Beatty and Nicholson in *The Fortune* (75, Mike Nichols), a flop that seems to have fallen only on her head. Thereafter, her roles were not nearly as encouraging: *The Big Bus* (76, James Frawley); *Dandy, the All-American Girl* (77, Jerry Schatzberg); *The Cheap Detective* (78, Robert Moore); very funny in *Grease* (78, Randal Kleiser); as a deaf stuntwoman in *Silent Victory: The Kitty O'Neal Story* (79, Lou Antonio) for TV.

Within the next year, two TV sitcoms were built around her—*Stockard Channing in Just Friends* and *The Stockard Channing Show*—that lasted about eight months. Increasingly, she concentrated on theatre, with these trips to film and TV: *The Fish that Saved Pittsburgh* (79, Gilbert Moses); *Safari 3000* (82, Henry Hurwitz); *Without a Trace* (83, Stanley R. Jaffe); *Not My Kid* (85, Michael Tuchman); *Heartburn* (86, Nichols); *The Men's Club* (86, Peter Medak); *The Room Upstairs* (87, Stuart Margolin); *Echoes in the Darkness* (87, Glenn Jordan); *A Time of Destiny* (88, Gregory Nava); *Staying Together* (89, Lee Grant); *Perfect Witness* (89, Robert Mandel); *Meet the Applegates* (91, Michael Lehman); *Married to It* (93, Hiller); and *Bitter Moon* (93, Roman Polanski).

She continues to work very hard, often on TV where she is the First Lady on *The West Wing.* She is sometimes cast in emotional family dramas, but her great urge is to be funny and wicked—long may it all last: *David's Mother* (94, Robert Allan Ackerman); *Smoke* (95, Wayne Wang); *To Wong Foo, Thanks for Everything, Julie Newmar* (95, Beeban Kidron); *The First Wives Club* (96, Hugh Wilson); *Up Close & Personal* (96, Jon Avnet); *Moll Flanders* (96, Pen Densham); *An Unexpected Family* (96, Larry Elikann); *Lily Dale* (96, Peter Masterson); *Edie & Pen* (97, Matthew Irmas); warming Paul Newman up in *Twilight* (97, Robert Benton); *The Baby Dance* (98, Jane Anderson); *Practical Magic* (98, Griffin Dunne); *Isn't She Great* (00, Andrew Bergman); *Where the Heart Is* (00, Matt Williams); *The Business of Strangers* (01, Patrick Stettner).

As she begins to gather awards, so her appetite for work extends: *A Girl Thing* (01, Lee Rose); *Confessions of an Ugly Step-sister* (02, Gavin Millar); *The Matthew Shepard Story* (02, Roger Spot-

tiswoode); *Life or Something Like It* (02, Stephen Herek); *Behind the Red Door* (02, Matia Karrell); *Le Divorce* (03, James Ivory); *Anything Else* (03, Woody Allen).

Sir Charles Chaplin (1889–1977),
b. London
1914: *Making a Living; Kid Auto Races at Venice; Mabel's Strange Predicament; Between Showers; A Film Johnnie; Tango Tangles; His Favourite Pastime; Cruel, Cruel Love; The Star Boarder; Mabel at the Wheel; Twenty Minutes of Love; Caught in a Cabaret; Caught in the Rain; A Busy Day; The Fatal Mallet; Her Friend the Bandit; The Knockout; Mabel's Busy Day; Mabel's Married Life; Laughing Gas; The Property Man; The Face on the Bar-Room Floor; Recreation; The Masquerader; His New Profession; The Rounders; The New Janitor; Those Love Pangs; Dough and Dynamite; Gentlemen of Nerve; His Musical Career; His Trysting Place; Tillie's Punctured Romance; Getting Acquainted; His Prehistoric Past.* 1915: *His New Job; A Night Out; The Champion; In the Park; The Jitney Elopement; The Tramp; By the Sea; Work; A Woman; The Bank; Shanghaied; A Night in the Show.* 1916: *The Burlesque on Carmen; Police; The Floorwalker; The Fireman; The Vagabond; One A.M.; The Count; The Pawnshop; Behind the Screen; The Rink.* 1917: *Easy Street; The Cure; The Immigrant; The Adventurer.* 1918: *Triple Trouble; A Dog's Life; The Bond; Shoulder Arms.* 1919: *Sunnyside; A Day's Pleasure.* 1920: *The Kid; The Idle Class.* 1922: *Pay Day.* 1923: *The Pilgrim; A Woman of Paris.* 1925: *The Gold Rush.* 1928: *The Circus.* 1931: *City Lights.* 1936: *Modern Times.* 1940: *The Great Dictator.* 1947: *Monsieur Verdoux.* 1952: *Limelight.* 1957: *A King in New York.* 1967: *A Countess from Hong Kong.*

The worldwide appeal of Chaplin, and his persistent handicap, have lain in the extent to which he always lived in a realm of his own—that of delirious egotism. Is there a more typical or revealing piece of classic Chaplin than *One A.M.* (or I AM), in which he exists in virtuoso isolation for fifteen minutes, executing every variation on the drunk-coming-home theme? It is like a dancer at the bar, confronting himself in a mirror.

The list above includes early films in which Chaplin was only an actor, and which were credited to directors like Mabel Normand and Mack Sennett. But to the world and to Chaplin himself any film in which he appeared has been his own. On *A Countess from Hong Kong* he demonstrated every piece of business for Marlon Brando and Sophia Loren to copy as best they could; and Chaplin the actor has an overbearingly winsome personality that cajoles his films into mawkishness. Chaplin was led to direct because it was a logical extension of the power to be obtained through acting. For there is a paradox between the tramp's woeful simpleton character and the clear-eyed inquisitiveness with which Chaplin the director and owner of the film is prompting our response. Here is a fascinating moment from his *Autobiography* telling how at the age of five he was forced onto the music-hall stage when his mother's failing voice was booed off by a callous audience. The child went on and sang a song:

Half-way through, a shower of money poured on to the stage. Immediately I stopped and announced that I would pick up the money first and sing afterwards. This caused much laughter. The stage manager came on with a handkerchief and helped me to gather it up. I thought he was going to keep it. This thought was conveyed to the audience and increased their laughter, especially when he walked off with it with me anxiously following him. Not until he handed it to Mother did I return and continue to sing. I was quite at home. I talked to the audience, danced, and did several imitations including one of Mother singing her Irish march song.

A number of inferences can be legitimately based on that passage that throw light on Chaplin's later career:

First, Chaplin's early life was a time of considerable emotional hardship. His father deserted the family when Charlie was an infant and later died of alcoholism. That strain affected the sanity of his mother, whose music-hall career was ruined. When she had to go into an asylum, Charlie was sent to an orphanage—this after being born into a home of enough gentility to keep a maid. He was not born deprived, but saw his family lose almost everything while still a child. "I was quite at home" on the stage is not just the narrative conclusion of the first section of *My Autobiography,* but the emotional escape from such real loss and pain.

Second, there is in Chaplin a strange mixture of coy charm and heartless cold, and it is not too far-fetched to see it as the response to suffering inflicted on a sensitive and lonely child. The pathos in Chaplin's work is always focused on himself. That recollection in tranquillity of his first stage appearance is colored by the drama of the child facing the mob, by the romance of championing his mother, and then by the unwitting revelation that he began to imitate her to win more applause.

Chaplin adored his mother, and his films worship women with an ingratiating but crippled awe. The beautiful women in his films are not just dream women that Charlie loves from afar, but emblems of grace that he aspires to. The delicacy of Chaplin's own features, the Italianate daintiness

of his gestures, and above all, the mooning after misty emotional contentment are feminine characteristics as conceived by an exquisite man. Indeed, Chaplin's persona is often very close to eighteenth-century sentimentality: a beautifully mannered dreamer who has trained himself into the emotional sensibility that will sometimes shame a woman with its refinement. The history of bisexuality in the movies begins with Chaplin, and the impression of sophistication that he gave in his earliest work is less a quality of the films than his own Cherubino-like refinement amid so much mugging.

But the cruelty in Chaplin is also feminine, impetuous, and instinctive. Chaplin was forever revenging himself on gross, ugly men. His slapstick is often violent and one of the abiding images of Chaplin is of the sharp-toed ballet dancer kicking some thug's ass. As a mime, too, he used impersonation as a weapon. The most famous instance of this is his Hitler caricature in *The Great Dictator.* But just as he was prepared and able at five to imitate his mother, so the tramp relates to the outside world through his ability to master it with mime.

Such egotism expresses Chaplin's hostility to the world, and suggests how his portrait of the little man pandered to the desire for recognition in anonymous audiences. Similarly, Chaplin's wistful admiration of women seems ultimately prettier and more rarefied than any woman is capable of— as witness the last, tremulous close-up of *City Lights.* Was Chaplin's common man so far from Hitler? He spoke to disappointment, brutalized feelings, and failure and saw that through movies he could concoct a daydream world in which the tramp thrives and in which his whole ethos of self-pity is vindicated.

Third, in his line, "This thought was conveyed to the audience," there is the early appreciation of the need to signal emotion and laughter to an audience. The tramp's famous glance into the camera, for all its simpering, is an acute grab for sympathy. Just as in *A Night in the Show*—the film of Chaplin's most successful music-hall act— as the drunken toff in the balcony about to destroy the stage show, he looks at the camera as if to say "Shall we? Let's . . . ," so Chaplin's private world is one that he could only reach out from through personal rhetoric. He does not make an artistic, comic statement on the world but channels it through himself and that demagogic moment when he knows that he has an audience's attention. The instinct for that attention is central to the workings of cinema, and I believe Chaplin understood years before anyone else the way in which audiences might identify with a star. It is no accident that he often employed dream sequences in his early films—for example, *The Bank* and *Shoulder Arms.* Intuitively, he sensed how ready the viewers were to have their fantasies indulged.

But that instinct usually lacked artistic intelligence, real human sympathy, and even humor. Chaplin's isolation barred him from working with anyone else. He needed to fulfil every creative function on a film, whether it is scripting, composing, or directing actors. He is isolated, too, in the sense that his later films seem as cut off from any known period or reality as the earlier ones. That eerie feeling one has in reading the later parts of *My Autobiography*—that Chaplin was still unable to appreciate the world on any other than his own terms—is borne out by the films that supposedly deal with the world's problems but in a social setting that seems increasingly implausible. Only a great egotist could have made films as unspecific as *Limelight, A King in New York,* and *A Countess from Hong Kong.* Of course, comedy should be its own world, but Chaplin seems innocent of realities of place, time, character, and situation. And in the end such numbness is disturbing, just as Chaplin's weird old age seemed unreal and deluded. More and more, with that thin, unlocalized voice forever talking the dictionary, and with silver-haired prettiness untouched, Chaplin looked like a great instinct narrowed by the absence of the other qualities that would mature an artist.

His later films are dreadful, and they are few and far between. The early work seems to me narrow when put beside the films of Keaton and the Marx Brothers. But the early shorts do have a strange sophistication that derives from Chaplin's intuitive skill at easing himself into an audience's mind. Their jokes are usually corny and repetitive, but Chaplin's attempt to charm the viewer is masterly. Those recurring conclusions that iris in on the figure of Chaplin walking away from us are ingenious fosterings of our own sense of loss and our hope that he will be back soon. And as an actor/performer who has impinged on the world's huddling round the idea of the oppressed little man, Chaplin may be the most famous image of the twentieth century. It is a marvelous and intriguing story, and one that needs major biographies to make up for the inconsequence of most of his own book.

The facts of Chaplin's career amply bear out the theory of overweening abstraction from the world. He toured America with Fred Karno twice before 1914 when he went to work for Sennett at Keystone. By 1915 he moved on to Essanay, by now the writer and director of all his films. His salary rose prodigiously as in 1916 he went to Mutual. From 1917 he was producing his films independently, to be handled by First National. Then in 1919 he was one of the founding members of United Artists, for whom *A Woman of Paris* was his first film. It was also his first full-length film.

After that, in fifty years he made only ten films. Increasingly, around the period 1935–50, his dissatisfaction with the world was voiced in films. Like many more learned men, he feared progress and the agony of choosing between capitalism and socialism. It was only petulance that made him resist sound until 1936, and then horribly misuse it. *The Great Dictator* is an extraordinary mixture of comic mime, halting construction, and an embarrassing sermon at the end.

The crisis in his life came after the war. *Monsieur Verdoux* is by far his most interesting film, the story of a Landru figure and the only undisguised expression of his distaste for women and the world. At this time he was mildly sympathetic to communism and, in 1952, he chose to leave America, hurt by official hostility. His political philosophy was actually threadbare and the move now looks like a final retreat into the cloud cuckoo land of Switzerland. As early as *Easy Street,* Chaplin's withdrawn sensitivity had depicted an intractable town, dominated by bullies, that the cop Charlie made safe for the bourgeois to walk about in. Chaplin's return to Europe was a sorrowful gesture that could only, eventually, prompt a guilty change of heart in America. Eventually, he was reclaimed and must have taken great satisfaction in the way so vast an audience came round. In truth, Chaplin is the looming mad politician of the century, the demon tramp. It is a character based on the belief that there are "little people." Whereas art should insist that people are all the same size.

Geraldine Chaplin,
b. Santa Monica, California, 1944

The father's place in film history is automatic, but there are those who found his personality hard to receive. Yet to criticize Charlie Chaplin amounts, in some quarters, to an unforgivable heresy that marks one down as the baleful, inhuman, and antilife anti-Charlie. I believe I would give up all of Charlie's work for *Cria Cuervos* (75, Carlos Saura), which contains a performance of the utmost emotional rigor and depth from his daughter Geraldine. Geraldine's eloquent features are like a territory helpless against invasion. In *Cria,* she is especially touching in that she seems to have been devastated by feelings that cannot be fobbed off or acted out. She has the natural face of vulnerability: the same resolute stare belonged to Lillian Gish, the young Anna Karina, and to Ana Torrent, her other self in the magnificent *Cria.*

This European actress is too little appreciated in America, thanks in part to the very different, garrulous cuckoo Robert Altman created in *Nashville* (75), where Chaplin gave herself to Opal from the BBC as generously as she aided Saura's film. Of course, Carlos Saura was her lover and may be expected to see and know an inner person. Whereas Altman's gallery pictures are more concerned with the oddities of first impression. But it is just as likely that the actress herself is creatively divided. Her own history of London, Beverly Hills, Geneva, and Madrid may be the surface turmoil of remarkable pedigree: the first child of Chaplin's happy, last marriage to Oona, daughter of that implacably tragic playwright Eugene O'Neill. It's easy to see Chaplin's dark romanticism in Geraldine's face; but listen as well for the echo of *Anna Christie* and *Long Day's Journey into Night*.

She was a ballet student as a child, and it is likely that her lessons inspired part of her father's *Limelight,* as well as the debut of Claire Bloom, a woman with O'Neill looks. Geraldine made her first film in 1964, and since then she has worked hard in a variety of countries and languages: *Par un Beau Matin d'Été* (64, Jacques Deray); an introduction to Madrid in *Doctor Zhivago* (65, David Lean); *Peppermint Frappé* (67, Saura); *Stranger in the House* (67, Pierre Rouve); *Stress es Tres, Tres* (68, Saura); *I Killed Rasputin* (68, Robert Hossein); *La Madriguera* (69, Saura); *The Hawaiians* (70, Tom Gries); *Zero Population Control* (71, Michael Campus); *Ana y los Lobos* (72, Saura); *Innocent Bystanders* (72, Peter Collinson); as Anne of Austria, overshadowed by Dunaway and Raquel Welch in *The Three Musketeers (The Queen's Diamonds)* (73, Richard Lester) and *The Four Musketeers (The Revenge of Milady)* (74, Lester); *Noroit* (75, Jacques Rivette); Annie Oakley in *Buffalo Bill and the Indians* (76, Altman); bemused and wandering in *Welcome to L.A.* (76, Alan Rudolph); a classic victim in *Roseland* (77, James Ivory); *Brief Letter, Long Farewell* (77, Herbert Vessely); *Un Page d'Amour* (77, Maurice Rabinowicz); *Elisa, Vida Mia* (77, Saura); the distraught mistress of ceremonies in *A Wedding* (78, Altman); brilliant as the woman out of prison in *Remember My Name* (78, Rudolph); and *L'Adoption* (78, Marc Grunebaum).

Older, gaunt sometimes, yet oddly childlike, she remained capable of indelible moments: *Mama Cumple 100 Anos* (79, Saura); *Le Voyage en Douce* (79, Michel Deville); *The Mirror Crack'd* (80, Guy Hamilton); *Les Uns et les Autres* (81, Claude Lelouch); *La Vie est un Roman* (83, Alain Resnais); *L'Amour par Terre* (84, Rivette); *The Corsican Brothers* (85, Ian Sharp); *White Mischief* (87, Michael Radford); superb as the vain collector in *The Moderns* (88, Rudolph); *Return of the Musketeers* (89, Lester); *Je Veux Rentre à la Maison* (89, Resnais); *The Children* (90, Tony Palmer); as her own deranged grandmother in *Chaplin* (92, Richard Attenborough), the one reason for seeing that picture; *The Age of Innocence* (93, Martin Scorsese); and *Words Upon the Window Pane* (94, Mary McGuckian).

By the mid-nineties, she was working a lot in Europe or in films of a religious nature: *Home for the Holidays* (95, Jodie Foster); *Para Recibir el Canto de los Pájaros* (95, Jorge Sanjiner); *Gulliver's Travels* (96, Charles Sturridge); *Jane Eyre* (96, Franco Zeffirelli); *Os Olhos da Asia* (96, João Mario Grilo); *Crimetime* (96, George Sluizer); *The Odyssey* (97, Andrei Konchalovsky); the lead in *Mother Teresa: In the Name of God's Poor* (97, Kevin Connor); *Cousin Bette* (98, Des McAnuff); *Finisterre, Donde Termina el Mundo* (98, Xavier Villaverde); *To Walk with Lions* (99, Carl Schultz); *Beresina* (99, Daniel Schmid); *Mary, Mother of Jesus* (99, Connor); *Tu Qué Harias por Amor* (99, Carlos Saura Medrano—the son of Carlos Saura); *In the Beginning* (00, Connor); *Hable con Ella* (02, Pedro Almodovar); *Dinotopia* (02, Marco Brambilla); *Winter Solstice* (03, Martyn Friend).

Cyd Charisse (Tula Ellice Finklea),
b. Amarillo, Texas, 1921

She was the daughter of a ballet enthusiast who made her take dancing lessons. She joined Colonel de Basil's Ballet Russe and married Nico Charisse, a ballet instructor, with whom she opened a dance school in Hollywood (she subsequently married singer Tony Martin). After small parts in *Something to Shout About* (43, Gregory Ratoff) and *Mission to Moscow* (43, Michael Curtiz), she had a brief spot as the ballerina in *Ziegfeld Follies* (46, Vincente Minnelli). Thereafter she played in a number of musicals, often in dance cameos: *The Harvey Girls* (45, George Sidney); *Till the Clouds Roll By* (46, Richard Whorf); *Fiesta* (47, Richard Thorpe); *Words and Music* (48, Norman Taurog); and *Singin' in the Rain* (52, Stanley Donen and Gene Kelly). By then, her dancing carried her as an actress in *Sombrero* (53, Norman Foster); *The Band Wagon* (53, Minnelli); *Brigadoon* (54, Minnelli); *It's Always Fair Weather* (55, Donen and Kelly); *Silk Stockings* (57, Rouben Mamoulian); *Party Girl* (58, Nicholas Ray). She appears at events still, but has done nothing worthwhile since the ex-wife in *Two Weeks in Another Town* (62, Minnelli).

Exceptionally tall, austere in features but elegant in the legs, she is perhaps the greatest female movie dancer. Her acting is like the songs in Marx Brothers films, though there were attempts to make the public accept her in straight parts: *The Unfinished Dance* (47, Henry Koster); *Tension* (49, John Berry); *East Side, West Side* (49, Mervyn Le Roy); *Mark of the Renegade* (51, Hugo Fregonese); *The Wild North* (52, Andrew Marton). But in the nightclub dance in *Party Girl* and all her dancing in *Silk Stockings* she is as sensual and moving as most actresses have managed to be with words. In *Silk Stockings,* her rapturous introduction to expensive lingerie conveys emotions denied to her as an actress; while in *Party Girl* her dancing discloses the scarlet woman invisible in the ostensibly dramatic moments.

In the last fifteen years, she has been in *Warlords of Atlantis* (78, Kevin Conner); *Portrait of an Escort* (80, Steven Hilliard Stern); and *Swimsuit* (89, Chris Thomson), while remaining an icon of old-fashioned glamour.

Ruth Chatterton (1893–1961), b. New York

"Miss Ruth Chatterton" was a stage actress of lofty reputation and pedigree. Even in her brief movie heyday at Paramount, she was likely to be asked to drop in on Clara Bow to give the "It" girl lessons in diction. Onstage, Chatterton had had her greatest success in *Daddy Long Legs.* But by the time she accompanied her first husband, Ralph Forbes (1902–51), to Hollywood, she was marked as a "mature" woman. And in Hollywood "maturity" is warning of the kiss of death. Emil Jannings got her a part in *Sins of the Fathers* (28, Ludwig Berger), and Paramount put her under contract as a worldly, often tragic figure in melodramas: *The Doctor's Secret* (29, William C. De Mille) and *The Dummy* (29, Robert Milton). Her first movie hit was at MGM as *Madame X* (29, Lionel Barrymore), where a teary courtroom scene led to an Oscar nomination.

Paramount then cast her in *Charming Sinners* (29, Milton); *The Laughing Lady* (29, Harry Beaumont); *Sarah and Son* (30, Dorothy Arzner), in which she is an impoverished, downbeaten housewife one minute and an international opera star the next—and for which she was nominated again for best actress; and *Anybody's Woman* (30, Arzner). For a moment, she was a movie star, and MGM borrowed her again for *Lady of Scandal* (30, Sidney Franklin). In *The Right to Love* (31, Richard Wallace), she excelled as both mother and daughter. She also made *Unfaithful* (31, John Cromwell); *The Magnificent Lie* (31, Berthold Viertel); *Once a Lady* (31, Guthrie McClintic); and *Tomorrow and Tomorrow* (32, Wallace).

The moment had passed. She was taken on at Warners, and she married again—to actor George Brent (1904–79), another younger man. They played together in some second-string pictures of unusual plot novelty: *The Crash* (32, William Dieterle) is only fifty-eight minutes, but Chatterton plays a tough, money-minded woman with a philandering husband; in *Frisco Jenny* (33, William Wellman), she survives the earthquake; *Lilly Turner* (33, Wellman); in *Female* (33, Michael Curtiz) she is the Don Juanish boss of an automobile company; and *Journal of a Crime* (34, William Keighley).

For two years she was out of work, and then Columbia put her in *Lady of Secrets* (36, Marion Gering) and Fox cast her in *Girls' Dormitory* (36, Irving Cummings). Her last great role was as the wife in *Dodsworth* (36, William Wyler): she and Wyler fought because Chatterton saw the woman as a bitch and had to be persuaded to Wyler's richer, gentler view. She was also aware that Mrs. Dodsworth—like Miss Chatterton—was someone trying hard to deny age.

Her screen career ended with two films in Britain: *The Rat* (37, Jack Raymond) and *The Royal Divorce* (38, Raymond). Subsequently, she returned to the theatre and wrote several novels.

Paddy Chayefsky

(Sidney Aaron Chayefsky) (1923–81),
b. Bronx, New York

At two distinct periods of a brief career, Chayefsky the writer put a personal stamp on groups of movies. They were well acted and well directed, but few could argue that the energy or tone of the films came from anyone but the writer. That is wonder enough in the history of American film. What is more astonishing, the two periods seem to belong to different men. Indeed, the careful and care-heavy realist dramas of the fifties are not that far from a stale, sitcom genre that might have been cheerfully scorned in *Network*. What is so bracing about Chayefsky in the seventies is his throwing aside the dull baggage of earlier attitudes. But was this a crucial change, or was Chayefsky a mix of rebellion and ambition that would have had to change again if he had lived longer? Whatever the answer (or attempt at answer), Chayefsky was a very skilled constructionist, brilliant in diatribe and dialogue, and a three-time winner of the best screenplay Oscar.

Wounded in the war, and convalescing in England, he turned to writing and became a novelist, a playwright, and a scenarist. He did the story for *As Young as You Feel* (51, Harmon Jones), and then, in the mid-fifties, he wrote a series of TV dramas that brought common lives and humble settings to the new medium. Many of the plays went on to make films (e.g., Rod Steiger played *Marty* on TV before Ernest Borgnine in the movie): *Marty* (55, Delbert Mann), which won Oscars for best picture, best director, best actor, and best screenplay; *The Catered Affair* (56, Richard Brooks); *The Bachelor Party* (57, Mann); *The Goddess* (58, John Cromwell); and *Middle of the Night* (59, Mann).

Then came a gap before Chayefsky wrote *The Americanization of Emily* (64, Arthur Hiller) and *Paint Your Wagon* (69, Joshua Logan)—Logan had produced *Middle of the Night* onstage, and he found Chayefsky to be close to a genius, but too close to stubborn.

The Hospital (71, Hiller) has the best of Chayefsky, a piece of institutional gallows humor, years ahead of its time, in which desperate eloquence (George C. Scott's doctor) tries to beat back the forces of entropy. Few films capture the disaster of

America's self-destructive idealism so well. The film did poorly, but Chayefsky got another Oscar. *Network* (76, Sidney Lumet) does for television what *The Hospital* did for medicine. It is superb entertainment, a fantasy set firmly in a knowledge of TV—daring, uninhibited, and prophetic. No one else would have dreamed of doing it.

All that remained was *Altered States* (79, Ken Russell), so botched a job that Chayefsky took his professional name off the picture and went as "Sidney Aaron"—no matter that the project came from his own novel.

Don Cheadle, b. Kansas City, Missouri, 1964

Don Cheadle has directed for the stage. He is a good musician—as witness his Sammy Davis Jr. And he is a mercurial actor—by turns comic, nasty, frightening, or pathetic. He can go from a growl to a lament as fast as Sidney Bechet, and his tone is just as stinging. More often than not, he's cast in support, but he has the capacity to take fire in lead roles. He graduated from Cal Arts in Valencia and went into television—he had recurring roles in both *The Fresh Prince of Bel-Air* and *Picket Fences.* He made his movie debut in *Moving Violations* (85, Neil Israel); *Hamburger Hill* (87, John Irvin); *Colors* (88, Dennis Hopper); *Roadside Prophets* (92, Abbe Wool); *The Meteor Man* (93, Robert Townsend); *Lush Life* (94, Michael Elias); Mouse in *Devil in a Blue Dress* (95, Carl Franklin); Rooster in *Things to Do in Denver When You're Dead* (95, Gary Fleder); *Rosewood* (97, John Singleton); *Volcano* (97, Mick Jackson); *Boogie Nights* (98, Paul Thomas Anderson); *Bulworth* (98, Warren Beatty); *Out of Sight* (98, Steven Soderbergh); winning awards as Sammy Davis Jr. in *The Rat Pack* (98, Rob Cohen); *Mission to Mars* (00, Brian De Palma); *Fail Safe* (00, Stephen Frears); *The Family Man* (00, Brett Ratner); *Traffic* (00, Soderbergh); *Swordfish* (01, Dominic Sena); Cockney in *Ocean's Eleven* (01, Soderbergh); *The Hire* (02, John Woo); *The United States of Leland* (03, Matthew Ryan Hoge).

Chen Kaige, b. Beijing, China, 1952

1984: *Huang Tu Di/Yellow Earth.* 1986: *Da Yue Bing/The Big Parade.* 1988: *Hai Zi Wang/King of the Children.* 1991: *Bian Zou Bian Chang.* 1993: *Ba Wang Bie Ji/Farewell My Concubine.* 1996: *Feng Yue/Temptress Moon.* 1999: *Jing Ke Ci Qin Wang/The Emperor and the Assassin.* 2002: *Han Ni Zai Yiki/Together.*

At the 1993 Cannes Film Festival, the Palme d'Or was shared between Jane Campion's *The Piano* and Chen Kaige's *Farewell My Concubine.* One understood the urge to pay attention to Chen. China in the time of his first films as a director had seen one more movement in the symphony of tur-

moil. Chen's movies had faced censorship and graver threats to the director's liberty. Further, he was a central figure in the very promising new wave of Chinese films, along with Zhang Yimou, who photographed *Yellow Earth* and *The Big Parade.* In addition, Chen Kaige had set out to make movies that address the periodic assaults on its own culture and hope, the convulsion of modern China. He has never lacked courage, and in *Farewell My Concubine* he had mounted an epic picture, a Chinese response to *The Last Emperor,* if you will. (Chen acted in that picture and he seems impressed not just by its scale, but by the theme of refined spirits who are battered by history or fate.)

That said, the Palme d'Or to *Farewell* seemed to me a gesture of generosity. It has a fine eye, a vivid way with actors (Leslie Cheung, Zhang Fengyi, and Gong Li), and that dramatic sense of color that is most striking now in China. But, for its length, the picture is monotonous and evasive. The characters are not truly revealed (compared with *The Piano*) and the pattern of history's unkindness is eventually simpleminded. We do not learn enough about the inner life—as if that vital territory was still unfamiliar in China.

Temptress Moon and *The Emperor and the Assassin* seem to me further assertions of the same talent—spectacular, genuinely energetic films, still full of excitement for the medium—yet overlong, unduly complicated (or even incoherent) and not really anxious to go beyond the limits of genre. *The Emperor and the Assassin* was said to be the most lavish film ever made in China, set in the fourth century B.C., with Gong Li again (no one's complaining) as the concubine who links the worlds of court and crime. *Temptress Moon,* set in Shanghai in the twenties, seemed better and more urgent just because it was an attempt to see the roots of China's modern history. Chen does the epic style too easily. He is better on character when taking on modern times. But, plainly, the epic is more comfortable and likely more profitable for the Chinese film authorities.

Cher (Cherilyn Sarkisian),

b. El Centro, California, 1946

First, *Moonstruck* (87, Norman Jewison): it is a pleasant, enjoyable sitcom movie that plays off a series of conventions and clichés. Examined closely, it is not just impossible but fatuous, that this Medusa-like Italian woman is leading a humdrum life with Danny Aiello as her only likely man. It would have been no sillier if the younger Sophia Loren had been cast in the part. For the woman is Cher, the nominal monosyllable, tattoo woman, Cher of Sonny-and-, "I've Got You, Babe," and I can do without you, perennial cover girl and outrageous clothes horse. Face it, Cher is a celebrity, and making her a wallflower is addled.

So she got the Oscar, as if playing a handicapped person.

Sonny and Cher were a great act: the horny little guy amazed that he had this languid statue. Their timing was drugged and dead on. When they sang together it was absurd and delicious. Sonny was over his head and under her chin, and Cher was plainly so tender that she had learned to act tough. Like most showbiz marriages, it was a contractual hell. But do not forget it. They were a lively piece of the sixties.

They were together in *Good Times* (67, William Friedkin) and Cher did her best in *Chastity* (69, Alesso de Paola), which Sonny wrote—in ketchup or lipstick.

The partnership broke apart, and Cher had wild times—a wild decade, nearly—singing, wearing very little, and adhering to fabricated men. She decided that she might act and Robert Altman cast her, on Broadway, in *Come Back to the 5 & Dime, Jimmy Dean, Jimmy Dean* in 1982. He put her in the movie and she was okay—no more. But in 1983, she got the role of the lesbian friend in *Silkwood* (Mike Nichols). Suddenly she was an actress—dowdy, louche, working class, bitter, and reckless. It is a performance that so far exceeds *Moonstruck* as to make Oscar melt with embarrassment.

She made a handsome, piratical hippie mother in *Mask* (85, Peter Bogdanovich), but it was evident that she was not easily cast. Anyone photographed so much for stills is surrounded by her armory of attitude and looks: this is what happened to Monroe. There was evidently a hoodlum in Cher, a capacity for wickedness and intrigue. Think of her as Mae Rose in *Prizzi's Honor* or as a Connie Corleone trying to take over the family.

In 1987, she had three films released: *The Witches of Eastwick* (87, George Miller), where she seemed the actress least comfortable with either the comedy or Jack Nicholson's Satanic charm; *Suspect* (87, Peter Yates), where she was said to be a lawyer; and *Moonstruck*. Showtime.

Three years passed, for reasons only Cher has a hope of understanding. What were we waiting for? Her *Hedda Gabler*? Her Elektra? Her Lady Macbeth? Her lady road warrior? No, it was *Mermaids* (90, Richard Benjamin), another nice little movie. Since then, she has spent more time singing and doing specials and fitness videos—*A New Attitude* and *Body Confidence*—than movies. But she was in *Ready to Wear* (94, Altman); *Faithful* (96, Mazursky); acting in and directing an episode of *If These Walls Could Talk* (96); and *Tea with Mussolini* (99, Franco Zeffirelli).

Maurice Chevalier (1888–1972), b. Paris

Despite longevity and the sort of reputation that passes off full-frontal charm as the very spirit of France, Chevalier did not make many films. Still, too many, as anyone who had to sit through his second American period will attest. That he brought to Paramount in the first adventure of sound a restrained lewdness is beyond question. But it seems equally clear that his act was artificial and limited. "I'll admit you're very funny," Jeanette MacDonald says to him in *The Merry Widow*, "but not terrific...not colossal." Smiling innuendo in youth lasted only a few years; it got rather more mileage in old age, perhaps because audiences were tickled by the Humbert Humbert–like double entendre of "Thank Heaven for Little Girls."

Chevalier was a café singer in the early years of this century and became partner and lover to Mistinguett at the Folies Bergère. All the more pity, therefore, that his experience of uninhibited, erotic entertainment was abandoned in favor of a grinning and not very convincing sexual knowingness. In his defense, it should be said that Chevalier was irked by the ineffable gay Parisian Paramount thrust upon him. But what he wanted to put in its place is not clear. He was a vast, popular success in Paris in the 1920s and went on to England and America. MGM tested but declined him; Paramount saw the test and signed him. His first film was *Innocents of Paris* (29, Richard Wallace). In his next, *The Love Parade* (29, Ernst Lubitsch), the presence of Jeanette MacDonald—a very smart lady—helped to emphasize his bawdiness, which was well suited to Lubitsch's coy humor. After that, he made *The Big Pond* (30, Hobart Henley), *The Playboy of Paris* (30, Ludwig Berger), *The Smiling Lieutenant* (31, Lubitsch), and with MacDonald once more, *One Hour with You* (32, George Cukor). He was most at home in that crazy concoction *Love Me Tonight* (32, Rouben Mamoulian), wooing MacDonald in rhyming dialogue and excelling in the "Poor Apache" routine. But after two dull Norman Taurog films—*A Bedtime Story* (33) and *The Way To Love* (33)—Paramount let him go to MGM. There he made *The Merry Widow* (34, Lubitsch), still an attendant to MacDonald, and *Folies Bergère* (35, Roy del Ruth).

Discarded again, he went back to France and made *L'Homme du Jour* (35, Julien Duvivier) and *Avec le Sourire* (36, Maurice Tourneur). In England, he was in *The Beloved Vagabond* (36, Curtis Bernhardt) and *Break the News* (37, René Clair). Just before the war, in France, he made *Pièges* (39, Robert Siodmak). He made no films during the war, and when there were suggestions that he had collaborated Chevalier appeared in a newsreel to clear himself. His next film was his best piece of acting, a rare hint of depth as the film director in *Le Silence est d'Or* (47, Clair). He made another three films in France over the next eight years, but was recalled to screen fame by

Hollywood as a sort of male duenna with a leer face-lifted into a smile: *Love in the Afternoon* (57, Billy Wilder); *Gigi* (58, Vincente Minnelli); *Count Your Blessings* (59, Jean Negulesco); *Pepe* (59, George Sidney); *Can-Can* (60, Walter Lang); *A Breath of Scandal* (60, Michael Curtiz); *Fanny* (61, Joshua Logan); *Jessica* (62, Negulesco); *In Search of the Castaways* (62, Robert Stevenson); *A New Kind of Love* (63, Melville Shavelson); *I'd Rather Be Rich* (64, Jack Smight); *Panic Button* (64, George Sherman); and *Monkeys Go Home* (66, Andrew V. McLaglen).

Christian-Jaque (Christian Maudet)
(1904–94), b. Paris
1933: *Adémar Lampiot* (codirected with Paul Mesnier); *Le Tendron d'Achille.* 1936: *François 1er.* 1937: *Les Perles de la Couronne* (codirected with Sacha Guitry). 1938: *Les Disparus de Saint-Agil.* 1941: *L'Assassinat du Père Noël.* 1942: *La Symphonie Fantastique; Carmen.* 1944: *Sortilèges; Voyage sans Espoir.* 1945: *Boule de Suif.* 1946: *Revenant.* 1947: *La Chartreuse de Parme.* 1948: *D'Homme à Hommes.* 1949: *Souvenirs Perdus.* 1951: *Fanfan la Tulipe.* 1952: *Adorables Créatures; Lucrezia Borgia.* 1954: *Madame Du Barry.* 1955: *Si Tous les Gars du Monde; Nana.* 1957: *La Loi c'est la Loi.* 1959: *Babette s'en Va-t-en Guerre.* 1960: "Le Divorce," episode from *La Française et l'Amour.* 1961: *Madame Sans-Gêne.* 1963: *Les Bonnes Causes; La Tulipe Noire.* 1964: *La Fabuleuse Aventure de Marco Polo* (codirected with Denys de la Patellière and Noel Haoward); *Le Repas des Fauves.* 1965: *La Guerra Segrèta/The Dirty Game* (codirected with Terence Young and Carlo Lizzani). 1968: *Lady Hamilton Zwischen Schmach und Liebe/Lady Hamilton.* 1969: *Qui Veut Tuer Carlos?.* 1971: *Les Pétroleuses/The Legend of Frenchie King.* 1977: *La Vie Parisienne.*

An unabashed exponent of ooh-la-la, Christian-Jaque is the sort of director of French films imagined by English audiences, who always thought Margaret Lockwood was rather racy. He makes costume romances, full of curtains, candlesticks, and cleavage. Martine Carol was one of the several actresses he married and sedately disrobed in films like *Adorables Créatures, Lucrezia Borgia,* and *Nana.* They were cheerfully prim sexy films, with the subtitles buzzing around the nipples. He seemed somewhat stranded, but from 1945 to 1955 he was very successful and remorselessly trite. He had studied architecture and music, and his films lacked little in production lushness. Before directing, he was assistant and art director to Julien Duvivier.

Julie Christie, b. Assam, India, 1941
Educated at the Central School of Drama, she first came to attention in the TV serial *A for Andromeda,* in 1962. After a bright debut in an otherwise crushing comedy, *The Fast Lady* (62, Ken Annakin), she was ostentatiously introduced as the spirit of swinging, libertarian youth in John Schlesinger's *Billy Liar* (63). The acclaim that greeted that performance is bewildering, for Christie lacks exactly the qualities of grace, spontaneity, and humor that the part required. She is, sadly, obvious in her efforts, lacking in either gaiety or insight and, most serious of all, gawky, self-conscious, and lantern-jawed. She grins rather than smiles, and her movements are either nervously darting or ponderous. Nonetheless, she has had a career of dramatically sudden success. After the mishmash of *Young Cassidy* (65, Jack Cardiff and John Ford), she won an Oscar for her callow work in Schlesinger's *Darling* (65) and then gazed plaintively out of David Lean's *Dr. Zhivago* (66). She is plainly numb in Truffaut's *Fahrenheit 451* and becalmed by Hardy's classic status in *Far From the Madding Crowd* (67, Schlesinger). Attempts to extend her range have confirmed her limitations: *Petulia* (68, Dick Lester); *In Search of Gregory* (69, Peter Wood). But she is tough, world weary, and a real actress with her then lover, Warren Beatty, in *McCabe and Mrs. Miller* (71, Robert Altman). She attempted the selfish aristocrat in Losey's *The Go-Between* (71) and still seemed gauche, limited, and overextended. After that she played the wife in a rapt, consuming love scene with Donald Sutherland in *Don't Look Now* (73, Nicolas Roeg); *Shampoo* (75, Hal Ashby); a walk-on as herself in *Nashville* (75, Robert Altman); very harassed in *Demon Seed* (77, Donald Cammell); and the token love interest in *Heaven Can Wait* (78, Warren Beatty and Buck Henry).

That was a kind of Hollywood farewell. In the years since, she has been unpredictable, giving herself to adventurous and politically radical ventures, yet still beautiful if the story needed it: she narrated *The Animals' Film* (81, Victor Schonfeld), an animal-rights documentary; she played in the Doris Lessing adaptation *Memoirs of a Survivor* (81, David Gladwell); *The Return of the Soldier* (81, Alan Bridges); *The Gold Diggers* (83, Sally Potter); *Heat and Dust* (83, James Ivory); *Separate Tables* (84, Schlesinger) for TV; *Power* (86, Sidney Lumet); *Miss Mary* (86, Maria Luisa Bemberg); *Fools of Fortune* (90, Pat O'Connor); and was reunited with Donald Sutherland in *The Railway Station Man* (91, Michael Whyte).

Since then, she has had a part in *Karaoke* (96, Renny Rye); she played Gertrude in *Hamlet* (96, Kenneth Branagh); she had a fond, generous role in *Afterglow* (97, Alan Rudolph); *Belphégor—Le Fantôme du Louvre* (01, Jean-Paul Salome); *No Such Thing* (01, Hal Hartley); *Snapshots* (02, Rudolf van den Berg); *I'm With Lucy* (02, Jon Sherman); as Thetis in *Troy* (04, Wolfgang Petersen).

Michael Cimino, b. New York, 1943
1974: *Thunderbolt and Lightfoot.* 1978: *The Deer Hunter.* 1980: *Heaven's Gate.* 1985: *The Year of the Dragon.* 1987: *The Sicilian.* 1990: *Desperate Hours.* 1996: *The Sunchaser.*

The flimsy nastiness of his last four pictures is no reason to suppose we have seen the last of Michael Cimino. We should recollect that when United Artists first sat down to consider projects with Cimino, his love script was a new *The Fountainhead.* The studio recalled King Vidor's earlier commercial failure with the Ayn Rand novel; they wondered if the "model" buildings Cimino talked about might not grow into real edifices. They might have settled there and then for a modest city in the San Gabriel mountains, a retreat for jobless studio folks to go to. And moviegoers should treasure the detail that, in *The Fountainhead*, the rogue genius Howard Roark, the uncompromiser, thinks little of a decade here or there in the wilderness. But these days it takes a visionary to tell wilderness from sainted city. Meanwhile, Cimino is proverbial—a warning, to be sure, but a sultry beacon, too. If he ever reemerges at full budgetary throttle, his own career should be his subject.

Cimino earned a bachelor's and then a master's degree in art from Yale in the early sixties. He studied acting and directing with Lee Strasberg, and then worked in New York on industrial films, documentaries, and TV commercials. As a screenwriter, he had a shared credit on *Silent Running* (71, Douglas Trumbull) and *Magnum Force* (73, Ted Post). The introduction to Clint Eastwood led to *Thunderbolt and Lightfoot*, which is expert, scary, and a rare example of character interplay in an Eastwood film. In the bracing 1970s, that kind of modest debut could set a guy up with a great challenge.

The Deer Hunter won best picture and best director; it made a lot of money at 183 minutes; it was the subject of bitter controversy, being deemed fascist, racist, historically inaccurate, and small-minded, despite its epic canvas. I can recall people in the first audience crying out with anguish, regret, and suspense. Few movies have ever stirred audiences so powerfully. And, upon consideration, I think it is a great picture, large enough to carry its flaws.

Consider these virtues: the working-class setting, managed without condescension; the symphonic shift of tone and pace as it moves from steel-town doldrums to the fearful jungle of Southeast Asia; the desperate tension of the first roulette sequence; the group playing of De Niro, Walken, Cazale, Savage, and Dzundza; the forlorn attempt at something like love or comfort between De Niro and Meryl Streep; the primeval air of the hunting sequence; and the overall notion of a blinded, battered American self-belief strug-gling to move forward. *The Deer Hunter* is not politically correct, but it is one of the few American movies that understand the state of outrage and mistake within American hope. It is a picture to put beside *Bonnie and Clyde*, *King Kong*, and *Birth of a Nation*, monuments worthy of some shame and much exhilaration.

Its success changed the movie world, and led to one of our best pieces of contemporary movie history, Steven Bach's *Final Cut*, a book one is ready to trust because it never denies the executives' blame or Cimino's creative urge on what became *Heaven's Gate*. Egomania destroyed budget; United Artists succumbed; the film was a disaster, at 205 or 149 minutes. It seemed like a Western, as opposed to some mixing of Charles Ives, Edward Hopper, and Willa Cather. In its making, it paraded all the ordinary madnesses of Hollywood, and it showed how disastrous the cult of the director had become: this was *la pathologie des auteurs*.

The full version survives on video, whereas it is very hard now to see the shorter form. *Heaven's Gate* was poorly cast and badly written, and Cimino was, for the first time, the sole credited writer. The Harvard sequence is a perverse folly of delay; the violence sickens us without ever bringing moral pain. Still, anyone should be able to see the scheme of immigrant and individual against the capitalist system; and even with its handicaps, one feels the gigantic tug of faith and dismay about America. But the famous "beauty" is fatally apparent just because we have so much time to study it and no sense of its dramatic place.

Heaven's Gate needed, let us suppose, the chance to start again (something painters and novelists take for granted). It needed Redford and De Niro, instead of Kristofferson and Walken; it needed to shed an hour—something only possible in a restart and a script by someone like Richard Brooks, an old-timer and a taut storyteller. Then Cimino needed to be bullied, oppressed, and treated wretchedly, until he felt for the poor immigrants. But perhaps he wanted to make an impossible film. We should not exclude that wanton urge.

What next? The four subsequent films are by someone in hiding, at rest, or gone away. Perhaps he cannot muster the guile, the nerve, or the need to become enormous again. Just as he seemed dormant, the monster stirred: there were rumors of sex change—but from what to what? He wrote a novel, in French. Was it man or ghost?

René Clair (René-Lucien Chomette) (1898–1981), b. Paris
1923: *Paris Qui Dort* (s). 1924: *Entr'acte* (s); *Le Fantôme du Moulin Rouge.* 1925: *Le Voyage Imaginaire.* 1926: *La Proie du Vent.* 1927: *Un Chapeau de Paille d'Italie/The Italian Straw Hat.*

1928: *La Tour* (s); *Les Deux Timides*. 1930: *Sous les Toits de Paris*. 1931: *Le Million; A Nous la Liberté*. 1932: *Quatorze Juillet*. 1934: *Le Dernier Milliardaire*. 1935: *The Ghost Goes West*. 1937: *Break the News*. 1939: *Air Pur* (uncompleted). 1941: *The Flame of New Orleans*. 1942: an episode from *Forever and a Day; I Married a Witch*. 1944: *It Happened Tomorrow*. 1945: *And Then There Were None/Ten Little Indians*. 1947: *Le Silence est d'Or*. 1950: *La Beauté du Diable*. 1952: *Les Belles de Nuit/Night Beauties*. 1955: *Les Grandes Manoeuvres/Summer Manoeuvres*. 1957: *Porte des Lilas*. 1960: "Le Mariage," episode from *La Française et l'Amour*. 1961: *Tout l'Or du Monde*. 1962: "Les Deux Pigeons," episode from *Les Quatre Vérités*. 1965: *Les Fêtes Galantes*.

Clair now looks something less than the major director he was known as in 1935. His work since that first venturing outside France has seldom lacked amusement or a sense of fantasy, but it does seem lightweight. Even his finest films—those made in the first experiment of sound—are rather precious and too vaguely opposed to "progress" when set beside *L'Age d'Or, L'Atalante, Boudu,* or *Toni.* Clair's world is brilliantly conceived and wrought, but it remains self-contained. Increasingly, the orchestration of sounds and the balletic view of activity feel as emotionally detached as his slightly fey preference for the idea of companionship to the complexity of emotional reality. The comedy is slow and mannered, and the films have shrunk into glowing, ingenious miniatures. The adventurous range of a Vigo or Renoir are the highest comparisons, but Clair does not match up to them. Perhaps it is the very "finished" gloss on his films, the tying into decorative bows of loose ends, that makes his work seem too neat and restricted.

Wounded in the First World War, he spent some time in a monastery but soon opted for journalism. As well as writing film criticism he worked as an actor: *Les Deux Gamines* (20, Louis Feuillade); *Parisette* (21, Feuillade); *L'Orpheline* (21, Feuillade); *Pour une Nuit d'Amour* (21, Jacob Protazanov); and *Le Sens de la Mort* (22, Protazanov). Clair was assistant to Jacques de Baroncelli before starting to direct himself.

From the beginning, Clair was intent on ways of gently exposing social absurdity through deliberately artificial farces and by various forms of stylization that sprang from the cinema's scope for movement and later its capacity for sound. Years later, in a book, *Reflexion Faite* (1951), Clair stated his faith in the autonomous reality of the concocted image; and it is this prettiness that now seems a crucial handicap. Thus, there was an academic, mechanical feeling to images that were merely illustrating a meticulous script—the preparation of which Clair has always regarded as the most creative stage in filmmaking. The whimsical and musical fabrication of *Le Million*, the satire on the machine in *A Nous la Liberté*, and the studio artifice of *Sous les Toits de Paris* are notional achievements that smother cinematic interest with the sheer cleverness of the conception and the technical mastery of the execution. The comparison between Renoir and Clair shows how much more fruitful open-air realism was in defining the potential of sound pictures. Too often, the human figures in Clair's tableaux seem to be straining to stand on eggshells in a breeze.

It always was Clair's practice to surround himself with master craftsmen, such as designer Lazare Meerson and photographer Georges Perinal. At times, he even left subsidiary scenes to be filmed by assistants, with something of Hitchcock's indifference to the moment in front of the lens. That was a later recourse. On the key films of the early 1930s—*Sous les Toits de Paris, Le Million, A Nous la Liberté, Quatorze Juillet,* and *Le Dernier Milliardaire*—Clair was fully engaged if greatly aided by Meerson and Perinal. These films show a kindly sympathy for the little man—a Chaplinesque figure—but always dissipate their social criticism through the Méliès-like taste for the fantastic and the elaborate portrait of a toy world.

Clair's silent films are surprisingly varied. *Entr'acte,* for instance, belongs to the most self-indulgent wing of the French avant-garde. Intended as a companion piece to an actual ballet, it was scripted by Francis Picabia and also involved Erik Satie, Duchamp, and Man Ray. Full of visual surrealism, it is almost entirely empty of purpose. More immediately elegant than, say, *Un Chien Andalou,* it grows stale as Buñuel's lurcher dog becomes ever randier. *Entr'acte* was a diversion for Clair, not really in character. *Paris Qui Dort* was a comedy involving a ray that suspends motion; while *Voyage Imaginaire* was about a young man who dreams that he travels to fairyland. *The Italian Straw Hat,* his greatest early success, was taken from a stage farce by Eugene Labiche and Marc Michel and shows his taste for contrived narrative consequences and a rather dandified mocking of the bourgeoisie.

In 1935, Clair went to England for Korda and directed Robert Donat in *The Ghost Goes West*. He stayed on for *Break the News,* with Jack Buchanan and Maurice Chevalier. After the abortive *Air Pur,* he went to Hollywood. His films there are modest but benign, far less vigorous than the American work of Renoir, Lang, or Ophuls. *The Flame of New Orleans* is a confection that allows Dietrich to be more than usually tender and is well photographed by Rudolph Maté, who had filmed *Le Dernier Milliardaire. I Married a Witch* was one of the films that established Veronica Lake, but it and *It Happened Tomorrow* have a relentlessly inventive infusion of fantasy that seems mannered. *And Then There Were None* is a version of Agatha Christie's *Ten Little Indians*, not frightening, not funny, seemingly content with the restraints of the material.

The postwar Clair is perhaps the most interesting. Playfulness slipped away. *Le Silence est d'Or* is an ironic comedy that has emotional depth; *Les Belles de Nuit* is a fantasy rooted in sex; while *Les Grandes Manoeuvres* is a tragi-comedy worthy of Ophuls. Michèle Morgan in that film, as a woman uncertain of her lover, Gérard Philipe, is the most mature and touching character creation in Clair's work. The film itself is warmed by color and a loving care for the detail of a 1914 barracks town. *Porte des Lilas* was again a more sombre film, with a fine performance from Pierre Brasseur. After that, Clair's work slipped back into shallow comedies and fragments.

Alan Clarke (1935–90),
b. Seacombe, England

1967: *Shelter* (TV, s); *A Man Inside* (TV, s); *George's Room* (TV, s); *Thief* (TV, s); *A Man of Our Times* (TV); *The Gentleman Caller* (TV, s); *Which of These Two Ladies Is He Married To?* (TV, s); an episode from *Sleeping Dogs Lie* (TV). 1968: *Goodnight Albert* (TV, s); *Stella* (TV, s); *Nothing's Ever Over* (TV, s); *The Fifty-Seventh Birthday* (TV, s); *Stand by Your Screens* (TV); *Gareth* (TV); *The Piano Tuner* (TV). 1969: an episode from *The Arrangement* (TV); *The Ladies: Doreen & Joan* (TV); *The Last Train Through the Harecastle Tunnel* (TV). 1970: *Sovereign's Company* (TV); *I Can't See My Little Willie* (TV); *Hallelujah Handshake* (TV). 1971: *Everybody Say Cheese* (TV). 1972: *Under the Age* (TV, s); *Horace* (TV); *To Encourage the Others* (TV); *Achilles Heel* (TV); *A Life Is Forever* (TV); *Horatio Bottomley* (TV). 1973: *Man Above Men* (TV); *The Love Girl and the Innocent* (TV). 1974: *Penda's Fen* (TV); *A Follower for Emily* (TV). 1975: *Funny Farm* (TV); *Diane* (TV). 1976: an episode from *Love for Lydia* (TV); *Fast Hands* (TV). 1977: *Scum* (TV, not shown). 1978: *Danton's Death* (TV); *Nina* (TV). 1980: *Scum*. 1981: *Beloved Enemy* (TV); *Psy-Warriors* (TV). 1982: *Baal* (TV). 1983: *Made in Britain* (TV). 1984: *Stars of the Roller State Disco* (TV). 1985: *Contact* (TV); *Billy the Kid & the Green Baize Vampire*. 1986: *Rita, Sue & Bob, Too*. 1987: *Christine* (TV); *Road* (TV). 1989: *Elephant* (TV); *The Firm* (TV).

Alan Clarke was a genius of TV—which means that he was better (or, to use Stephen Frears's phrase, "more formidable") than most regular theatrical filmmakers. He believed TV was an opportunity for looking beneath the rocks of the social order and giving voice to the anonymous, the wretched—the scum, even. One of his films was

actually called *Scum,* and for years it frightened its makers, the BBC. They banned it, because it was exaggerated, too dramatic, too documentary, too disturbing, or too true—take your pick. These are the flavors in Clarke's talent.

He was born near Liverpool, the son of a bricklayer. He worked as a laborer, and did his best as an insurance salesman before two years of National Service in Hong Kong. Then he emigrated to Canada, and while there he began to study acting and directing. In 1961, he returned to Britain and became a floor manager in television. From that, he worked his way into directing, and by 1969 he was at the BBC. In the rest of his life he made only three theatrical films: a second version of *Scum* (80), to evade the BBC ban; *Billy the Kid & the Green Baize Vampire* (85), an apparent disaster; and *Rita, Sue & Bob, Too* (86), a rowdy, randy sexual comedy about unglamorous people.

The rest is television in the British tradition of filming "plays"—i.e., worthwhile scripts commissioned from established writers and newcomers—that had something to say about life in Britain, something constructive maybe, but often something dangerous and angry. These plays were filmed modestly, on 16mm, yet with outstanding casts and crews. For example, Chris Menges photographed some of Clarke's plays, and they feature actors such as Gary Oldman and Tim Roth.

Clarke filmed some short stories in his early days, including work by Alun Owen, Edna O'Brien, and William Trevor; he made a biopic on Horatio Bottomley, a famous British swindler from the years 1900–30; he filmed a David Hare script, a story from Solzhenitsyn, a version of Buchner's *Danton's Death,* and an episode from *Love for Lydia.* David Rudkin's *Penda's Fen* was rural, Arthurian, and mythic; *To Encourage the Others* was a treatment of the Bentley-Craig case filmed again later by Peter Medak as *Let Him Have It* (91). Clarke even directed Bertolt Brecht's *Baal.* The director in British TV was dependent on what the writer provided—that may be the lesson of this last great example of the studio system.

Still, by the time of his maturity, Britain was in or close to the Thatcher era, and Clarke's best work is an unflinching but haunted view of a country savaged by that lady's revolution and of the hopelessness felt—and acted out—by those excluded from the revolution's benefits.

Scum (77), written by Roy Minton, is set in a juvenile prison, a prison for young offenders. Clarke sees a confinement for officers as well as youths, a rat-warren of power, intimidation, corruption, and violence. There is a protagonist, a new prisoner, who seems Cagney-like and heroic—until he takes charge and "becomes the

Daddy here." The language is foul, and, as so often in Clarke's work, it is lower class and regional, not easy for an American to decipher. But there is no missing the damage of the Borstal, or the implication that prisons serve as our forgetting places . . . until they are full.

Made in Britain (83), written by David Leland, is about a skinhead (Tim Roth) with a swastika tattoo on the bridge of his nose, who is headed for Borstal and seeks only violence, absurdity, and nihilism. The film never addresses why he is as he is, so "antisocial" and intransigent. But the kid, Trevor, is also so lively, so fuck-off eloquent, so much Tim Roth, that we are left to ponder whether such cases are hopeless or whether society needs to go back to zero.

Contact (85) is a war film that might have been made by Anthony Mann in its depiction of a platoon of English soldiers patrolling the border between Northern and southern Ireland. There are no real characters (though Sean Chapman is riveting as the demoralized officer), and very little talk. Instead, we see the implacable prowling in idyllic terrain, searching for guns, trouble, or mines. It is as if the "Irish problem" had been filmed by a shell-shocked bird in a blasted tree, equipped with infra-red night-sight vision.

Elephant (89, and written by Clarke) is Ireland again, taken to a terrible, surreal extreme: it is—no more, no less—the filming of eighteen murders. The people are actors and the deaths are arranged "action," filmed with something like beauty. But there is no talk, no hint of context or explanation, just the list, the monotony, and the wonder in so many deaths (the real Ireland has had over two thousand sectarian killings). Viewers can walk away, become connoisseurs of slaughter, go into outrage, or face their helplessness.

Road (89), from a play by Jim Cartwright, is set on a bleak housing estate in the North of England, a hellish existence, a prison without guards. The film is theatrical in that humble characters have long and even grand speeches; but the film is harsh and realistic, with momentous Steadicam tracking shots as these people walk the estate, lost in revery, anger, or the neurotic habit of marching.

The Firm (89), written by Al Hunter, is a band of soccer hooligans. But these gang members are not unemployed kids. The leader, Gary Oldman, is an estate agent, a family man, and someone who has to have "the buzz." *The Firm* is very funny and lethal (a mixture characteristic of Clarke), and only incidentally does it expose England as hardly fit for living in.

These are not easy or comforting films. Their power is cumulative, and Clarke is an amazing director, lucid, quick, pungent, very entertaining, unsentimental, a master with actors, and a poet for all those beasts who pace and measure the limits of their cages. No one has ever grasped the central metaphor of cramped existence in walking as well as Alan Clarke.

Jack Clayton (1921–95), b. Brighton

1958: *Room at the Top.* 1961: *The Innocents.* 1964: *The Pumpkin Eater.* 1967: *Our Mother's House.* 1973: *The Great Gatsby.* 1983: *Something Wicked This Way Comes.* 1987: *The Lonely Passion of Judith Hearne.* 1992: *Memento Mori* (TV).

The brief list tells its own story. Despite a lauded debut, curiously identified in some quarters as a revived British cinema, Clayton had difficulty sustaining projects. He was for many years an assistant producer—raucously called for throughout *Beat the Devil* (54, John Huston), and also involved on *Moulin Rouge* (53, Huston) and *I Am a Camera* (55, Henry Cornelius). He directed the short, *Bespoke Overcoat,* in 1955 and always pursued the same neatly wrapped up and faintly realized exercises in literary emotion. *Room at the Top* was as brutal, inauthentic, and complacent as its book; *The Innocents* is an Arts Council–like piece of Jamesiana. Only *The Pumpkin Eater* is touching, because of the forlorn, bitter gulfs between Anne Bancroft and James Mason, Peter Finch and Maggie Smith.

Clayton's six-year silence before *Gatsby* was warning of that disastrous film made with such erroneous and vulgar care. *Gatsby* is an unfilmable novel, if only because the last pages are so abstract and because Fitzgerald took great risks in leaving out things that a film must scrape together for fear of seeming bereft, arty, and enervated. If you wish to see the film of *Gatsby,* go to *The Magnificent Ambersons* (42, Orson Welles). Clayton's movie has one salutary peak, when Robert Redford's Gatsby laments, "It's all been a terrible mistake."

John Cleese,
b. Weston-Super-Mare, England, 1939

With ubiquity, and the great success of *A Fish Called Wanda* (88, Charles Crichton), it has seemed possible that John Cleese might pass as an amiable, middle-of-the-road, decent, jolly gent. He is in so many commercials; and, for actors, such ventures have a deafening common sense. He is known as the codirector of a company that makes comic training films. He has become relaxed on talk shows—garrulous, even—and at the time of *Wanda* he was even an appealingly gallant flirt with Jamie Lee Curtis. Altogether, there has been a concerted and by no means unimpressive effort to suggest that Cleese is a good, boring fellow.

I am unmoved. This is one of the authentic madmen that moving imagery has given us. This is desperation, the chronic urge to murder; this is the fury that has tried dealing with women; this is loftiness that goes in dread of pratfalls. This is the iron jaw of law and order that knows he will begin to speak in gibberish. There is hardly a screen presence that so instantly evokes the howls of laughter that are achieved by daily torture. And, of course, the greatness of Cleese is not in *Wanda*, or even in Monty Python; it is *Fawlty Towers*, an English defeat as dire as Hastings, a hotel of humiliation and mortification. If ever one is tempted to see humor in pathetic little men, Cleese is the corrective. There is nothing funnier than a huge man trying to inspire order in the world. Basil Fawlty is the tragedy of fascism, and Cleese is one of the screen's great explosive clowns.

Fawlty Towers was not long lived, nor did it air too often. It was blessed with a wife, Sybil (Prunella Scales), of such a sublime wisdom and stupidity that Basil had to know the gods were aiming at him. The hotel is all Spanish waiters, English colonels, colossal twenty-five-minute spirals of misunderstanding, with a severely deft half-landing where necks are meant to be broken. There is also the subtext of Polly (an American called Polly!), the maid, played by Cleese's cowriter and ex-wife, Connie Booth, so delectable that the maddened, neutered Basil cannot notice her. So her presence is further provocation to murder the eternal Sybil. These episodes are sometimes as lacerating as the reportage of natural horrors and disasters. Even Buñuel might be breathless to see Cleese, his head rigid but revolving, his eyes driven into the skull by the certainty of disaster's cunning.

Cleese met Booth, and Terry Gilliam, while touring in America in the early sixties with a comedy show put together by fellow students at Cambridge. He then wrote for TV before becoming the tent pole/minister/Frankenstein monster for the Monty Python assemblage. He has been in all of their films, of course, which are minor works compared with the TV shows. And he has acted in several non-Python films: *The Bliss of Mrs. Blossom* (68, Joe McGrath); *The Magic Christian* (70, McGrath); *The Statue* (71, Rod Amateau); *Time Bandits* (81, Gilliam); *Privates on Parade* (82, Michael Blakemore); *Yellowbeard* (83, Mel Damski); *Silverado* (85, Lawrence Kasdan); *Clockwise* (86, Christopher Morahan); and *Splitting Heirs* (93, Robert Young).

Most of these are so tedious and inconsequential that *Wanda* came as a special surprise. It was as if Cleese had realized there was a prospect in movies, and so he worked on the script and was executive producer, as well as a central actor. Still, it is hard to see him finding a role to match Basil Fawlty—although Prince Charles might be worth trying.

The Cleese of recent years has seemed lost. He has never really been an actor without the apparatus of *Fawlty Towers* or the Python zoo. He has turned very solemn sometimes in his self-help videos, and he has generally looked like a tall man with an unfunny stance wandering around: *Frankenstein* (94, Kenneth Branagh); *The Jungle Book* (94, Stephen Sommers); *Fierce Creatures* (97, Robert Young and Fred Schepisi), a sequel to *Wanda*, but a mess; *Parting Shots* (98, Michael Winner); *The Out-of-Towners* (99, Sam Weisman); as "R" in *The World Is Not Enough* (99, Michael Apted); *Isn't She Great?* (00, Andrew Bergman); *Quantum Project* (00, Eugenio Zanetti); *Rat Race* (01, Jerry Zucker); *Harry Potter and the Sorcerer's Stone* (01, Chris Columbus).

He works very hard nowadays, but the grim truth sinks deeper: this great man is no longer funny: in a short, *Taking the Wheel* (02, David Ackerman); *Scorched* (02, Gavin Grazer); *The Adventures of Pluto Nash* (02, Ron Underwood); *Harry Potter and the Chamber of Secrets* (02, Chris Columbus); Q in *Die Another Day* (02, Lee Tamahori); *Charlie's Angels: Full Throttle* (03, McG).

René Clément (1913–96), b. Bordeaux

1936: *Soigne ton Gauche* (s). 1937: *L'Arabie Interdite* (d). 1938: *La Grande Chartreuse* (d). 1939: *La Bièvre* (d). 1940: *Le Triage* (d). 1942: *Ceux du Rail* (d). 1943: *La Grande Pastorale* (d). 1944: *Chefs de Demain* (d). 1946: *La Bataille du Rail; Le Père Tranquille.* 1947: *Les Maudits.* 1948: *Au-delà des Grilles.* 1950: *Le Château de Verre.* 1952: *Jeux Interdits/Forbidden Games.* 1954: *Monsieur Ripois/Knave of Hearts.* 1955: *Gervaise.* 1958: *Barrage contre le Pacifique/The Sea Wall.* 1959: *Plein Soleil.* 1961: *Quelle Joie de Vivre.* 1962: *Le Jour et l'Heure.* 1964: *Les Félins/The Love Cage.* 1966: *Paris, Brûle-t-il?/Is Paris Burning?.* 1969: *Le Passager de la Pluie.* 1971: *La Maison sous les Arbres/The Deadly Trap.* 1975: *Baby Sitter—Un Maledetto Pasticcio/Wanted: Babysitter.* 1972: *La Course du Lièvre à Travers les Champs.*

Clément's first film was a short, *Soigne ton Gauche,* in which Jacques Tati acted. He made several more documentaries during the war before his first feature, *La Bataille du Rail,* a deliberate attempt to revive authenticity after so many allegorical films made under the Occupation. As a tribute to the Resistance it is moving if rather limited, and its stress on accurate reconstruction is more political than artistic. *Les Maudits,* however, was a conventional war melodrama, concerning a submarine of Nazis fleeing to South America. Clément's work on Cocteau's *La Belle et la Bête* (45) was in a technical rather than an artistic capacity and it was only in the 1950s that he began to show a personality of his own. *Jeux Interdits* is a sensitive study of the effects of war on children. But in *Knave of Hearts,* filmed in London, Clément suddenly revealed humor and romantic gaiety. The story, of a philandering

Gérard Philipe, is enriched by a use of real locations that was years ahead of its time and showed a London largely neglected by British filmmakers. *Gervaise* was transcribed Zola with the most careful period reconstruction and an early, agonized performance from Maria Schell. The veering from near improvisation to studio re-creation suggested Clément's indecisiveness. *The Sea Wall* was another unexpected enterprise, a version of a Marguerite Duras novel about the tensions within a family, using several American actors. *Plein Soleil* is a suntanned film noir redolent of the American thriller: indeed, its basis is a Patricia Highsmith novel. The ambiguity of Alain Delon's playing and Henri Decaë's vivid Mediterranean photography make this the most satisfying film of a director probably at his best when setting out to entertain. After that, Clément's work grew dull, and *Is Paris Burning?* has all the slow caution of an international epic as well as being a sad decline from the raw verity of *La Bataille du Rail*.

Montgomery Clift (1920–66),
b. Omaha, Nebraska

Clift is the sainted mess in that trio of American actors who loomed in the 1950s—Brando, Clift, and Dean (two of them born in Omaha). We know now how far Clift was destroyed by drink, drugs, and neurosis; and we recognize the neurosis being intensified by his gay yearnings that had to lurk within a heterosexual image. In *Red River*, Clift was a trail-hardened cowboy; in *A Place in the Sun,* he was in some of the screen's most clinging, infatuated, heterosexual embraces; while in *From Here to Eternity,* he was a model of rugged male integrity, but a boxer who wants to fight no more. And Clift was beautiful—which is the way movie stars are expected to be. Does his torture bear out that secret permission by which viewers can aspire to same-sex fantasies? Is it possible that Clift, too, had to look at his own pictures to see what he might be? Clift's career helps us see (or suspect) that sort of sexual double agentry in all films. After all, the dark is the greatest closet, and the most obliging.

He began in amateur theatricals in his teens and appeared in summer stock before making his Broadway debut in 1935 in *Fly Away Home,* subsequently appearing in *The Skin of Our Teeth, Our Town,* and *You Touched Me.* His first released film was Zinnemann's *The Search* (48) as a GI in Europe caring for a child refugee. But a year before, Hawks had cast him as Mathew Garth in *Red River* (the release of which was delayed): a memorable performance in one of Hawks's finest films, worthwhile not only for its picture of a lean, practical, and independent cowboy but for the way it seemed to compel John Wayne into thinking about his part. That film made Clift a star, and thereafter he worked sparingly in dramatic parts:

as the flawed lover in Wyler's *The Heiress* (49); in *The Big Lift* (50, George Seaton); as Dreiser's doomed hero in *A Place in the Sun* (51, George Stevens); as the conscience-torn priest in Hitchcock's *I Confess* (52); as Prewett, the rebellious soldier, in *From Here to Eternity* (53, Zinnemann).

His career faltered with the unhappy Selznick–Jennifer Jones–de Sica *Indiscretion of an American Wife* (54), and, in 1957, while making *Raintree County* (Edward Dmytryk), he was seriously injured in a car accident. His handsomeness was visibly undermined and the earlier concentration collapsed. In *The Young Lions* (58, Dmytryk), *Lonelyhearts* (59, Vincent J. Donehue), and *Judgment at Nuremberg* (61, Stanley Kramer), he was reduced from a tragic hero to a victim irretrievably damaged by suffering. He filled in less demanding roles for Mankiewicz in *Suddenly Last Summer* (59) and for Huston in *The Misfits* (60), but only Kazan's *Wild River* (60) fruitfully used his new, insecure character. In 1962, he delved further into neurosis for Huston in *Freud: The Secret Passion,* but made only one more film, *L'Espion* (66, Raoul Levy), in France, before his death.

George Clooney,
b. Maysville, Kentucky, 1961

George Clooney is a little reminiscent of William Holden in the early fifties—he seems able to sustain anything, from a live TV version of *Fail Safe* (00, Stephen Frears) to providing the chemical bonding with Jennifer Lopez in *Out of Sight* (98, Steven Soderbergh). But there's something flippant or facetious in his attitude—a touch of Mel Gibson—that stops him short of the anguish, or the commitment, that Holden commanded. After all, by the time Holden was forty, he had made *Sunset Boulevard, Stalag 17,* and *Picnic,* and it's easier to think of Clooney smirking in those roles than taking on the pain. He's likable and versatile, to be sure, but not for one minute in *The Perfect Storm* (00, Wolfgang Petersen) did he make me think of a Massachusetts fisherman.

He is the son of TV newscaster Nick Clooney and the nephew of singer Rosemary. He studied journalism at Northern Kentucky University and went to Los Angeles, where he eventually appeared on two different shows called *ER* (84–85 and 94–99). His movie debut seems to have been *Combat High* (86, Neil Israel), before *Return of the Killer Tomatoes* (88, John De Bello); *Red Surf* (90, H. Gordon Boos); *Without Warning* (91, Michael Toshiyuki Uno); *Unbecoming Age* (92, Deborah and Alfred Ringel); *The Harvest* (93, David Marconi); *From Dusk Till Dawn* (96, Robert Rodriguez).

His breakthrough began in being cast opposite Michelle Pfeiffer in the bland *One Fine Day* (96, Michael Hoffman). Then he was another forgettable Batman in *Batman & Robin* (97, Joel Schumacher); and with Nicole Kidman in *The Peacemaker* (97, Mimi Leder). But it was *Out of Sight* and then *Three Kings* (99, David O. Russell) that suggested a real following. He was briefly in *The Thin Red Line* (98, Terrence Malick), and his flair for humor brought a lot to *O Brother, Where Art Thou?* (00, Joel Coen).

He had a small part in *Spy Kids* (01, Rodriguez), did nothing to save *Ocean's 11* (01, Soderbergh) by exuding a bland self-satisfaction that made one all the more mournful for Sinatra's self-hating grandeur.

His performance in *Solaris* (02, Soderbergh) was yet another sign of indecision—of a kind of latter-day William Holden who couldn't locate or hold on to the absolute ease, the self-love, that made the young Holden. But then Clooney turned up trumps: his directorial debut, *Confessions of a Dangerous Mind* (02), is a terrific film, very smart, very ironic and truly mysterious.

Glenn Close,

b. Greenwich, Connecticut, 1947

Playing Gertrude to Mel Gibson's *Hamlet* (90, Franco Zeffirelli) may define Glenn Close's dilemma: men are permitted to play younger, so actresses have to move up a generation—and down a class, for Close is an experienced stage actress who has played in *Love for Love, The Real Thing,* and *Death and the Maiden.* She is only nine years older than Mel Gibson.

This is a strange movie career, full of English-like mums or brave girls (she does rather resemble Virginia McKenna): *The World According to Garp* (82, George Roy Hill); *The Big Chill* (83, Lawrence Kasdan); *The Stone Boy* (84, Chris Cain); and *The Natural* (84, Barry Levinson). She dubbed Andie McDowell in *Greystoke* (84, Hugh Hudson), failed at comedy in *Maxie* (85, Paul Aaron), and did a competent lawyer in love amid the hokum of *Jagged Edge* (85, Richard Marquand).

Then she won one of the plum roles of the eighties, Alex in *Fatal Attraction* (87, Adrian Lyne). Her hair went wild, she lost control, and she was better than the film or its final resolution deserved. Indeed, she transcended the box-office melodrama and showed us how deranging such a passion might be.

She was meticulous in *Dangerous Liaisons* (88, Stephen Frears), but could not find human depth in that very cold play and novel. She was routine again in *Immediate Family* (89, Jonathan Kaplan), and a voice-over as well as a would-be supine Sunny von Bulow in *Reversal of Fortune* (90, Barbet Schroeder). For TV, she made *Sarah, Plain and Tall* (91, Glenn Jordan). Dubbed herself this time (by Kiri Te Kanewa), she played the opera singer in *Meeting Venus* (91, Istvan Szabo). In

1993, she had a great success as Norma Desmond in the Los Angeles production of *Sunset Boulevard,* so much so that she beat out Patti Lupone for the same part on Broadway. She acted in *The House of the Spirits* (93, Bille August) and *The Paper* (94, Ron Howard).

She was a scabrous brothel-keeper in *Mary Reilly* (96, Frears), before she found a role to match that of Norma Desmond (and not so far from it)—Cruella de Vil in *101 Dalmatians* (96, Stephen Herek) and *102 Dalmatians* (00, Kevin Lima). That was her theatrical side. In a plainer mood, with little or no makeup, she did *Serving in Silence: The Margarethe Cammermeyer Story* (95, Jeff Bleckner) for television and *Paradise Road* (97, Bruce Beresford), as a prisoner of the Japanese. She has also been seen in *Mars Attacks!* (96, Tim Burton); as the vice president in *Air Force One* (97, Wolfgang Petersen); *In the Gloaming* (97, Christopher Reeve); *In & Out* (97, Frank Oz); *Cookie's Fortune* (99, Robert Altman); a voice on *Tarzan* (99, Lima); *Things You Can Tell Just by Looking at Her* (01, Rodrigo Garcia).

She remains very enterprising in her search for work: *The Ballad of Lucy Whipple* (01, Jeremy Paul Kagan); on TV in a revival of *South Pacific* (01, Richard Pearce); *The Safety of Objects* (01, Rose Troche); *Brush with Fate* (03, Bill Shields); in the old Hepburn part in a TV remake of *The Lion in Winter* (03, Andrei Konchalovsky); *Le Divorce* (03, James Ivory).

Henri-Georges Clouzot (1907–77),

b. Niort, France

1942: *L'Assassin Habité au 21.* 1943: *Le Corbeau.* 1947: *Quai des Orfèvres.* 1948: *Manon.* 1949: "Le Retour de Jean," episode in *Retour à la Vie.* 1950: *Miquette et Sa Mère.* 1953: *Le Salaire de la Peur/The Wages of Fear.* 1955: *Les Diaboliques/ The Fiends.* 1956: *Le Mystère Picasso* (d). 1958: *Les Espions.* 1960: *La Vérité.* 1968: *La Prisonnière.*

If Renoir is the *sud* of French cinema, then Clouzot is an exponent of the *nord.* The enormous commercial success of *Le Salaire de la Peur*—one of the first French films to obtain a wide showing in English-speaking countries—and the deliberate emphasis on "putting the audience through it" in *Les Diaboliques* have made Clouzot artistically suspect. But he has a consistent vision that is more jaundiced than any other in the French cinema. Where Renoir tends always toward the acceptance of failings, Clouzot's world disintegrates through mistrust, alienation, and a willful selfishness that is like an illness.

Clouzot began as an assistant director and it is worth noting that he worked in Berlin in the early 1930s, directing French versions of German films.

He was a scriptwriter for some ten years: *Un Soir de Rafle* (32, Carmine Gallone); *Le Duel* (39, Pierre Fresnay); and *Les Inconnus dans la Maison* (41, Henri Decoin). His first film was a romantic thriller, but *Le Corbeau* proved a sensation. Its baleful view of a French provincial town split by hatred and the intrigue of a poison-pen letter writer was interpreted as being blatantly anti-French and led to a virtual ban on Clouzot until 1947. The film was made by pro-Nazi interests; but the sense of destructive misanthropy now seems characteristic of Clouzot. Even *Quai des Orfèvres,* a more conventional police thriller, shows suspicion widening the cracks in a central love relationship. The comparison with Hitchcock was clear, but Clouzot's rather gloating concentration on weakness is also Balzacian. His updated *Manon* was utterly unromantic, with Cécile Aubry a slut and an opportunist.

Clouzot honeymooned in South America and after writing a book about Brazil—*Le Cheval des Dieux*—he made *Le Salaire de la Peur.* Again, he subjects characters to such strain that they break up. For all the attempt to endorse comradeship, the film is more a study of a rat race induced by spiritual boredom and capitalist greed. The style of the film so ably adds to the physical tension that there is never any doubt that Clouzot regards the destructive competition as unavoidable. Two years later he made *Les Diaboliques,* one of the most frightening of all films and starring his wife, Vera, as its victim. The character she plays is an invalid, eventually frightened to death. The shabby private school setting, with its swimming pool clogged by weed, offers some of the most disturbingly poisoned images in all Clouzot's work. The director was himself dogged by illness, and Vera Clouzot died young, in 1960. *Les Diaboliques* certainly looks like the product of a pathological imagination, and the implausibility of the story does not detract from the conviction that it brings to the idea of decay.

After that, Clouzot had to abandon two more projects because of illness; the four finished films he made are an odd collection. The Picasso study is a documentary, ingeniously photographed, and catching the painter's goblin playfulness. *Les Espions* was a failed attempt to keep his international audience, and *La Vérité* was a strident but unfeeling account of a girl's wretched life, based on her trial for murder. Again, the tone and accumulation of crushing detail are nineteenth century, and Brigitte Bardot's performance is melodramatic. *La Prisonnière* returned to the way one partner in a relationship may corrupt another. He occupied himself after that in filming orchestral concerts for TV. Clouzot is not easy to take; for all that his visual style is facile. Although *Le Salaire de la Peur* is crammed with exciting action, his real object for dissection is the personality and it is as difficult to warm to him as it is to shrug off the loathsome memories of *Les Diaboliques*. This is a cinema of total disenchantment.

Lee J. Cobb (Leo Jacob) (1911–76),
b. New York

He had worked extensively in the American theatre before making his screen debut in *North of the Rio Grande* (37, Norman Watt) followed by *Ali Baba Goes to Town* (37, David Butler). Having played in the stage production of Clifford Odets's *Golden Boy* (through his participation in the Group Theatre), Cobb also played in the movie, directed by Rouben Mamoulian in 1939. Cobb (in a supporting part) must have been intrigued by the story of a man torn between the violin and boxing, for as a child, only a broken wrist had prevented him from pursuing the violin. From the mid-1940s, he became a leading character actor, chiefly for Fox: *Men of Boy's Town* (41, Norman Taurog); *The Moon Is Down* (43, Irving Pichel); *Tonight We Raid Calais* (43, John Brahm); as the doctor in *The Song of Bernadette* (43, Henry King); *Winged Victory* (44, George Cukor); and *Anna and the King of Siam* (46, John Cromwell). Never abandoning the theatre, he created the role of Willy Loman in the Broadway production of *Death of a Salesman.* But his greatest screen impact was as a gangster villain, a character he returned to over twenty-five years with a loudmouth bravado that tends to become monotonous when dressed up in Actors' Studio realism. He was happiest if encouraged to be grandiose: *Johnny O'Clock* (47, Robert Rossen); *Boomerang!* (47, Elia Kazan); *The Dark Past* (48, Rudolph Maté); *Call Northside 777* (48, Henry Hathaway); *The Miracle of the Bells* (48, Pichel); *Thieves' Highway* (49, Jules Dassin); and *Sirocco* (51, Curtis Bernhardt). After some difficulties with Joe McCarthy, he came back strong as the hoodlum-in-chief in *On the Waterfront* (54, Kazan); *The Racers* (55, Hathaway); *The Left Hand of God* (55, Edward Dmytryk); as the last relenter in *12 Angry Men* (57, Sidney Lumet); *The Garment Center* (57, Vincent Sherman and Robert Aldrich); as the crazed outlaw chief in *Man of the West* (58, Anthony Mann); as the mobster fond of acid in *Party Girl* (58, Nicholas Ray). The snarl in these films is more credible than the occasional venture into fulsomeness: *The Brothers Karamazov* (57, Richard Brooks); *Exodus* (60, Otto Preminger); and *The Four Horsemen of the Apocalypse* (61, Vincente Minnelli). In the 1960s, he spent some time in the TV series, *The Virginian,* but still turned in some rather mellow performances: *Our Man Flint* (65, Daniel Mann); *Coogan's Bluff* (68, Don Siegel); *Mackenna's Gold* (69, J. Lee Thompson); *The Liberation of L. B. Jones* (70, William Wyler); *Macho Callahan* (70, Bernard Kowalski); *Lawman* (71, Michael

Winner); and *The Exorcist* (73, William Friedkin).

Charles Coburn (1877–1961),
b. Savannah, Georgia

Only at the age of fifty-eight did Coburn weary of the life of a traveling player and turn himself into a character actor for the movies. He had been on the stage since the 1890s and, with his wife, had formed a touring Shakespeare company. But he settled into movies like an old man relaxing in a comfortable armchair in the club library. He was, invariably, a benign, elderly spectator, bewildered by energetic comedy, with a favorite trick of having his monocle pop out when he was startled. There was never a trace of rhetoric, but a most subtle comic timing, brought to a fine pitch in *Monkey Business* (52, Howard Hawks) when his senile businessman scents monkey glands in the air and feels the primordial urge whenever Marilyn Monroe fluctuates past. "Look at that old chimp, Miss Laurel," says Coburn. "Eighty-four years old. Fourteen years older than I am! And just look at him!" In fact, Coburn was only nine years younger than the chimp, but still hopeful enough to make the laurels wobble.

Coburn worked especially hard during the 1940s and never let a film down: *The People's Enemy* (35, Crane Wilbur); *Of Human Hearts* (38, Clarence Brown); *Vivacious Lady* (38, George Stevens); *Lord Jeff* (38, Sam Wood); *Bachelor Mother* (39, Garson Kanin); *Idiot's Delight* (39, Brown); *Made for Each Other* (39, John Cromwell); *Stanley and Livingstone* (39, Henry King); *In Name Only* (39, Cromwell); *The Road to Singapore* (40, Victor Schertzinger); *Edison, the Man* (40, Brown); glorious at the card table in *The Lady Eve* (41, Preston Sturges); *The Devil and Miss Jones* (41, Wood); *Our Wife* (41, John M. Stahl); *H. M. Pulham Esq.* (41, King Vidor); *King's Row* (42, Wood); *In This Our Life* (42, John Huston); *George Washington Slept Here* (42, William Keighley); the supporting actor Oscar for *The More the Merrier* (43, Stevens) and very good at the physical comedy; *The Constant Nymph* (43, Edmund Goulding); *Heaven Can Wait* (43, Ernst Lubitsch); *Princess O'Rourke* (43, Norman Krasna); *My Kingdom for a Cook* (43, Richard Wallace); *Wilson* (44, King); *Knickerbocker Holiday* (44, Harry Brown); *The Impatient Years* (44, Irving Cummings); *A Royal Scandal* (45, Otto Preminger); *Rhapsody in Blue* (45, Irving Rapper); *Over 21* (45, Charles Vidor); *Colonel Effingham's Raid* (45, Irving Pichel); *The Green Years* (46, Victor Saville); *Lured* (47, Douglas Sirk); *The Paradine Case* (47, Alfred Hitchcock); *B.F.'s Daughter* (48, Robert Z. Leonard); *Everybody Does It* (49, Goulding); *Louisa* (50, Alexander Hall); *Mr. Music* (51, Richard Haydn); *The Highwayman* (52, Lesley Selander); *Has Anybody Seen My Gal?* (52, Sirk); still marveling at the prospect of Monroe in *Gentlemen Prefer Blondes* (53, Hawks); *Trouble Along the Way* (53, Michael Curtiz); *The Long Wait* (54, Saville); *How to be Very, Very Popular* (55, Nunnally Johnson); *The Power and the Prize* (56, Henry Koster); *Town on Trial* (57, John Guillermin), as a villain; as Benjamin Franklin in *John Paul Jones* (59, John Farrow); and *Pepe* (60, George Sidney).

In hindsight, a droll bonus comes to many Coburn films—did he only look like George Schultz, or was he father to that deft, impassive, and fatally humorless survivor?

James Coburn (1928–2002),
b. Laurel, Nebraska

Coburn is a modern rarity: an actor who projects lazy, humorous sexuality. It is the lack of neurosis, the impression of an amiable monkey, that makes him seem rather dated: a more perceptive Gable, perhaps, or even a loping Midwest Grant. He has made a variety of flawed, pleasurable films, the merits of which invariably depend on his laconic presence.

After work in TV he established himself as a supporting player in: *Ride Lonesome* (59, Budd Boetticher); *Face of the Fugitive* (59, Paul Wendkos); *The Magnificent Seven* (60, John Sturges); *Hell Is for Heroes* (62, Don Siegel); *Charade* (63, Stanley Donen); *The Great Escape* (63, Sturges); *The Americanization of Emily* (64, Arthur Hiller); *A High Wind in Jamaica* (65, Alexander Mackendrick); and *Major Dundee* (65, Sam Peckinpah). Increasingly, he was the best thing in his movies, smiling privately, seeming to suggest that he was in contact with some profound source of amusement.

He became a star only thanks to the most abstract of the post-Bond agents: *Our Man Flint* (65, Daniel Mann) and *In Like Flint* (67, Gordon Douglas). He then gave his eminence to a series of unusually adventurous movies, most of which drew their character from his playing: *What Did You Do in the War, Daddy?* (66, Blake Edwards); *Dead Heat on a Merry-go-round* (66, Bernard Girard); *Waterhole 3* (67, William Graham), in which he gracefully defines rape as "assault with a friendly weapon"; *The President's Analyst* (68, Theodore J. Flicker); *Hard Contract* (69, S. Lee Pogostin); *Blood Kin* (69, Sidney Lumet); *The Honkers* (71, Steve Ihnat); *The Carey Treatment* (72, Edwards); *Harry in Your Pocket* (73, Bruce Geller); and *The Last of Sheila* (73, Herbert Ross). *The Honkers*, an engagingly modest rodeo story, was a second feature, suggesting that Coburn's ease was unduly out of date. The more somber side of the aging man of action, not without the capacity for reflection, was shown in his fine performance as the reluctantly impelled sheriff in *Pat Garrett and Billy the Kid* (73, Peckinpah).

Since then he has fluctuated with the market's fitful taste for heroes: *Bite the Bullet* (75, Richard Brooks); the promoter in *Hard Times* (75, Walter Hill); *Sky Riders* (76, Douglas Hickox); seeking vengeance in *The Last Hard Men* (76, Andrew V. McLaglen), and grinning despite the title; *Midway* (76, Jack Smight); as the honest soldier in *Cross of Iron* (77, Peckinpah), enduring his own prowess, medals, and the iniquity of others—a sort of laid-back Errol Flynn; on TV, with more irony, the lean, laconic cowboy who asked for "Schlitz Light," in commercials; and a stylish operative in *The Dain Curse*. He then played in *Firepower* (78, Michael Winner) and *Golden Girl* (79, Joseph Sargent).

In the eighties, he was hampered somewhat by illness: *The Baltimore Bullet* (80, Robert Ellis Miller); *Mr. Patman* (80, John Guillermin); *Loving Couples* (80, Jack Smight); *Jacqueline Susann's Valley of the Dolls* (81, Walter Grauman) for TV; *High Risk* (81, Stewart Raffill); the mogul in *Looker* (81, Michael Crichton); *Malibu* (83, E. W. Swackhamer) for TV; *Martin's Day* (84, Alan Gibson); *Draw!* (84, Steven Hilliard Stern); *Sins of the Father* (85, Peter Werner); in Australia for *Death of a Soldier* (86, Philippe Mora); *Walking After Midnight* (88, Jonathon Kay), a documentary about near-death experiences; *Tag till Himlen* (89, Torgny Anderberg); *Young Guns II* (90, Geoff Murphy); *Hudson Hawk* (91, Michael Lehmann); *The Player* (92, Robert Altman); *Sister Act II* (93, Bill Duke); and *Maverick* (94, Richard Donner).

He has done a lot of voice work in recent years, and he is the grinning host in a series of videos on how to win at the tables in Las Vegas. Luckily, there have been worthier tasks: *Eraser* (96, Charles Russell); *The Nutty Professor* (96, Tom Shadyac); *Keys to Tulsa* (97, Leslie Greif); a supporting-actor Oscar for his fearsome father to Nick Nolte in *Affliction* (97, Paul Schrader) . . . he worked on, but let's close on that deserving note.

Jean Cocteau (1889–1963),
b. Maisons-Lafitte, France
1930: *Le Sang d'un Poète*. 1945: *La Belle et la Bête/Beauty and the Beast* (assisted by René Clément). 1947: *L'Aigle à Deux Têtes*. 1948: *Les Parents Terribles*. 1950: *Orphée*. 1960: *Le Testament d'Orphée*.

Cocteau's lyrical self-preoccupation makes it difficult to extract the films from his total poetic autobiography in art. But in retrospect, Cocteau seems to have been most engaged by cinema, despite the relatively brief period that he worked in it. And although its technical and financial web might have seemed too bothersome for his spidery dance, Cocteau responded as eagerly as a Victorian inventor. That self-poeticizing fancy sometimes looks slippery and insubstantial in the other arts. But with film, Cocteau was obliged to define and concentrate his own fey sprightliness, simply to avoid having it smothered by the medium. His egotism made him a solitary, maverick figure. But in stressing playfulness, amateurism, and the disposition to the dream experience of movies, Cocteau is a vital link between the avant-garde and the underground. The curious weightlessness in his work, although it might be thought to conform to his own ideals of lightness, bars him from greatness. Arguably, there are films based on his works by other men that are more searching than his own pictures. But Cocteau serves as a comet, passing over French cinema, throwing a vivid light on the landscape.

Above all, Cocteau found in the *cinématographe*—he liked to retain the pioneering terminology—a useful image of his lifelong dream of the poet's brave delaying of death, and of the refreshing discovery of the magical in the real. His poetic instinct could seem precious and overtechnical in words, but on film he was able to invest the everyday with fantastic resonance. In that, he was influenced by surrealism, and *Le Sang d'un Poète* was privately financed by the Vicomte de Noailles, who also sponsored Buñuel's *L'Age d'Or*. Buñuel's is a greater film, but *Le Sang d'un Poète* inaugurates Cocteau's overriding image of the poet's passing through the mirror of dream; and that is a very suggestive metaphor for the way a movie audience can pass into the celluloid domain. In *Le Sang d'un Poète*, *La Belle et la Bête*, *Orphée*, and *Le Testament d'Orphée*, the same situation recurs, with a constant emphasis on the poet's need to believe that he can pass through. For Cocteau, that faith was often a rather vaguely significant principle of the religion of the artist. But in the actual transformation of his films, especially the vat of mercury mirror in *Orphée*, the elision of real and fantasy is marvelously achieved. This passage from *Le Testament* shows how far Cocteau himself restricted that metamorphosis to a self-indulgent portrait of himself as the mischievous fracturer of mundane rules:

PRINCESS: Unless I am mistaken, you make a priesthood of disobedience?

POET: Without it, what would become of the children, the artists, the heroes?

HEURTEBISE: They would count their lucky stars.

PRINCESS: We are not here to listen to oratorical jousts. Put that flower on the table....Where did you obtain this flower?

POET: It was given me by Cégeste.

HEURTEBISE: Cégeste....If I'm not mistaken that is the name of a Sicilian temple?

POET: It's also the name of the young poet in my film *Orphée*. First of all it was the name of the angels in my poem *L'Ange Heurtebise*.

PRINCESS: What do you understand "film" to mean?

POET: A film is a petrifying source of thought. A film resuscitates dead actions. A film permits one to give the appearance of reality to the irreal.

PRINCESS: What do you call the irreal?

POET: That which projects beyond our poor limits.

HEURTEBISE: In sum, according to you, there would exist individuals like a sleeping invalid, with neither arms nor legs, who dreams that he runs and gestures.

POET: You have given there an excellent definition of the poet.

PRINCESS: What do you mean by "poet"?

POET: The poet, in composing poems, makes use of a language, neither living nor dead, which few people speak and few understand.

PRINCESS: And why do these persons speak this language?

POET: In order to meet their compatriots in a world where too often that exhibitionism which consists in displaying one's soul utterly naked is practiced only by blind men.

That is the worst and best of Cocteau. It has the shrill cheerfulness of his aestheticism, as well as the hollow elegance of glib definitions. It was Cocteau's shortcoming that, when he came to treat a subject to this poetic pressure, he fell back on either mythology or melodrama. His overwrought cult of the self, as well as the homosexual cluster that attended him, served to cut him off from mundane material. By comparison, Orson Welles—a man Cocteau admired—though as much an egotist, was able to direct his creative impulse into the invention of credible human situations that subtly dramatize his sense of self. Welles was a man of the theatre, Cocteau of theatricality. Thus even *Les Parents Terribles*, a play made into a film, is a piece of barnstorming melodrama, overplayed by unstable actors. Its use of a voyeuristic camera is intense and original, but not sufficient to make up for the bloated state of the play. Not unlike *The Magnificent Ambersons*, all its drama is in the words and facial expressions, whereas *Ambersons* can only be described in terms of the way it is filmed. The virtuoso claustrophobia of *Les Parents Terribles*—what Cocteau called the attempt "to catch my wild beasts unawares

with my tele-lens"—is heartless and artificial. It is worth noting that in four crucial cases, it needed other directors to bring human gravity to Cocteau's material: thus Jean-Pierre Melville directed the film of *Les Enfants Terribles*, Bresson his dialogue for *Les Dames du Bois de Boulogne*, Franju his novel *Thomas l'Imposteur*, while Rossellini directed Anna Magnani in the "La Voix Humaine" episode from *L'Amore*.

I would rather have those films than all of Cocteau's, if forced to choose by Maria Casares's Princess of Death. They all contain a poignant sense of the reality of death and of the wounding strength of passion. Whereas Cocteau's death and love are cold things, always pretty but seldom moving.

But his mythical films do have one great asset: despite his mannered literary style, Cocteau quickly grasped the nature of filmic expression. Far from welcoming visual mystification, sensuous fantasy, and expressive imagery, he preferred concrete, plain images, knowing that the medium itself was fantastic. On *La Belle et la Bête*, he tried to discourage his photographer, Alekan, from technical virtuosity. Thus the magic of the fairy story is charmingly literal, the more beautiful for being innocent and offhand. Even so, *La Belle et la Bête* does suffer from too deliberate and successful an attempt to make the farmhouse scenes look like Vermeers, a pointless attractiveness that happily does not distract from the factual wondrousness of the beast's home. And the beast himself is a tender monster, all the better for seeming kin to Kong and Karloff's Frankenstein. *La Belle et la Bête* has a postwar sunniness and a childlike pleasure in transformation that makes up for the barely characterized love story. But for Cocteau's poet, the notion of love always exceeds its realization.

Best of all is the physically exact myth in *Orphée*. The dusty French provincial town, the prop-box menace of the motorcyclists, the car radio that crackles with spirit poetry, and Heurtebise in a white shirt and slacks are immensely thrilling. Cocteau always worked *en famille*—as is clear from the book on the making of *La Belle et la Bête*—but *Orphée* is richly based in the amateur gathering of imaginative people. So splendidly free from the picturesque, it is a stepping-stone from Méliès and Feuillade to the Godard of *Les Carabiniers* and *Alphaville*. Indeed, *Orphée* may prove Cocteau's greatest achievement, in which the poet at last transcended himself.

The Coen Brothers:
Joel, b. St. Louis Park, Minnesota, 1955, and **Ethan**, b. St. Louis Park, Minnesota, 1958
1984: *Blood Simple*. 1987: *Raising Arizona*. 1990: *Miller's Crossing*. 1991: *Barton Fink*. 1994: *The Hudsucker Proxy*. 1996: *Fargo*. 1998: *The Big Lebowski*. 2000: *O Brother, Where Art Thou?*

2001: *The Man Who Wasn't There*. 2003: *Intolerable Cruelty*.

The Coen brothers grew up in Minneapolis, the sons of college professors. Joel studied film at N.Y.U., while Ethan did philosophy at Princeton. Joel is the director of the team, and he was an assistant editor on *The Evil Dead* (80, Sam Raimi) and *Fear No Evil* (81, Frank Laloggia). They write together, and Ethan operates as the producer. They helped write Raimi's *Crimewave* (85), and Ethan did some TV writing for *Cagney and Lacey*.

My mind is not made up. In the summer of 1984, I was one of the selection panel that voted *Blood Simple* into the New York Film Festival—yet I think I liked it least among the group, for its skill and noirish expertise seemed without destination or purpose. *Raising Arizona* was, for me, close to unwatchable: unfunny, technologically impelled, showy, and not just empty but condescending. *Barton Fink* was show-off time again, a dash of Nathanael West, a pinch of sophomore surrealism, numb satire, another kid's film—yet much more promising whenever John Goodman was on-screen, and fearsomely beautiful in the burning corridors, as if at last the Coens were on their way.

Still, not one of these films worked for me as a whole. Then there is *Miller's Crossing*, the film that dismayed their followers. It is derivative again, of Hammett. Yet it had an emotional core that seemed to burn through the serpentine plot: here was a film about the difficulty, and nearly the shame, in admitting feeling. In Gabriel Byrne, Albert Finney, and John Turturro, the Coens had at last found people to believe in and be moved by. Was that an aberration? If so, was it theirs, or only mine?

Hudsucker Proxy was a return to zero—or less. Sam Raimi helped in the writing, and Capra was a model for the story. But that left the plot ponderous *and* flimsy, and the people stooges to a dumb comic-book style. A travesty.

I am still unresolved. I liked *Fargo* nearly as much as its many fans, but then *Lebowski*—despite the camaraderie and Jeff Bridges's lazy "Dude"—felt too cute by half, like a film watching itself, more intent on being droll than life. Is it just my shortcoming, or is there something in fraternal support that means they need never feel alone? I can't shake the feeling of one dude showing the pictures to the other, and them chuckling together. *The Man Who Wasn't There* was so arty and mannered in its look—but, truly, there was so little there.

Harry Cohn (1891–1958), b. New York

You have to cut through the equatorial forest of outrageous stories concerning Harry Cohn to find a scoundrel helplessly in love with pictures. Of course, money, power, girls, and himself were all close rivals that had their day, during which the cause of art and the Bill of Rights took a battering. Hindsight makes it easy to romanticize the brutality of the man, and to regard it as the robust swagger of a pioneer so much more forthright and intuitive than a dozen David Begelmans. Cohn trampled on some people, habitually exploited his position, and took it for granted that a movie mogul had the right to use and humiliate because he owned people. But many dedicated professionals admired him, and few were not entertained by him.

Cohn's record is very good; he makes Louis Mayer look like a dreamer. What he took upon himself was effectively the life and soul of a company producing and distributing films. And the most vivid portraits of a megalomaniac tycoon appear in pictures his own company made. There is a story of his very well attended funeral and the acid comment: "Give the people what they want and they'll come to see it." Cohn would have liked the barb: he had no scruples when it came to that recurring test of all show business—can you hold the audience? He claimed his ass itched whenever a movie went on for too long—which is like a witch doctor making a cult out of hunches. Still, his best movies do not dawdle, and Cohn died before an infestation of sores might have overtaken his sensitive rear.

He was the son of a German tailor and a Polish mother. In his youth he was a trolley conductor, a singer in vaudeville, and a song plugger. His older brother, Jack, was working for Carl Laemmle, and in 1913 Jack produced a sleazy exploitation movie, *Traffic in Souls,* that proved to be a huge earner, thanks in part to Harry's efforts selling it. The Cohn brothers stayed with Laemmle, and met Joe Brandt. In 1920 the trio formed the CBC sales company, and in 1924 it assumed the name Columbia. The brothers were not friendly, and soon after the advent of sound there was a struggle for control. Brandt retired, Jack and Harry fought for mastery, and eventually—with a little help from his friends, it was alleged—Harry emerged as both president of the company and controller of West Coast production. Harry was the only mogul to have such sway, and he retained it until his death, confining Jack to the New York office and dealing with him through intermediaries. Part of Columbia's unusual enterprise came from the extent of Harry's power and the will and energy for acting on it that never deserted him.

For a long time, Columbia was regarded as the sordid underside of the business. Cohn made quickies, B pictures, and short subjects. His chief trade was program filling. But, gradually, in the mid-thirties, he felt drawn to better pictures. Frank Capra played a substantial part in this development. He started at Columbia on shorts, but nagged Cohn to let him try more ambitious pictures. Capra was the studio's top director until 1939: *The Bitter Tea of General Yen* (32); *It Happened One Night* (34); *Mr. Deeds Goes to Town* (36); *Lost Horizon* (37); *You Can't Take It With You* (38); and *Mr. Smith Goes to Washington* (39). In the same years, Columbia made *Crime and Punishment* (35) and *The King Steps Out* (36), for Josef von Sternberg; *Twentieth Century* (34), *Only Angels Have Wings* (39), and *His Girl Friday* (41), for Howard Hawks; Leo McCarey's *The Awful Truth* (37); and George Cukor's *Holiday* (38). Cohn's own taste must show in so much sophisticated comedy of manners.

He liked Rita Hayworth, too, and spent much of the forties promoting her and trying to deter her from ill-judged marriages. Cohn regarded her as his discovery and, as well as loaning her out, he put her in *Angels Over Broadway* (40, Ben Hecht and Lee Garmes); with Fred Astaire in *You'll Never Get Rich* (41, Sidney Lanfield) and *You Were Never Lovelier* (42, William Seiter); *Cover Girl* (44, Charles Vidor); the trashy but very suggestive *Gilda* (46, Vidor); *Down to Earth* (47, Alexander Hall); *The Loves of Carmen* (48, Vidor); *Salome* (53, William Dieterle); and—thankfully—*The Lady from Shanghai* (48, Orson Welles), in which Everett Sloane may stand for Cohn in the reptile-pit of actress/director/owner that is alluded to in that romantically despairing film. Hayworth was never more than a very pretty girl for Cohn; it was Welles who discovered or invented the monster as a going-away present. Her Columbia films are a montage of pinups, but they show the earnest erotic respect of an older boss.

Cohn by now was at the height of his tyranny and flamboyance, and it is likely that he is a model for Broderick Crawford in *All the King's Men* (49, Robert Rossen) and *Born Yesterday* (50, Cukor), and the basis of the tycoon in the play *The Big Knife*, written by his friend Clifford Odets. Around this time, Columbia produced Humphrey Bogart's Santana films: *Knock on Any Door* (49, Nicholas Ray) and *In a Lonely Place* (50, Ray)—as well as Douglas Sirk's *Shockproof* (48) and Joseph Losey's *M* (50).

It was in the fifties that Columbia bloomed, partly in contrast to the shrinking nerve of the major studios and partly because Cohn grew in confidence as he tried more prestigious pictures. There was an association with Stanley Kramer that produced *Death of a Salesman* (51, Laslo Benedek); *The Wild One* (53, Benedek); and *The Caine Mutiny* (54, Edward Dmytryk). In addition, Cohn contributed Kim Novak to history and blocked her wish to marry Sammy Davis Jr. He had a major success and many Oscars with *From Here to Eternity* (53, Fred Zinnemann); he distributed Sam Spiegel's films—*On the Waterfront* (54, Elia Kazan) and *The Bridge on the River Kwai* (57,

David Lean). He produced two Fritz Lang films: *The Big Heat* (53) and *Human Desire* (54); two by Anthony Mann—*The Man from Laramie* (55) and *The Last Frontier* (56). He also launched Judy Holliday and Jack Lemmon, and allowed Richard Quine to make his best pictures. There were *The Marrying Kind* (52, Cukor); *It Should Happen to You* (54, Cukor); *The Harder They Fall* (56, Mark Robson); *Picnic* (56, Joshua Logan); *3:10 to Yuma* (57, Delmer Daves); *Cowboy* (58, Daves); *Bitter Victory* (57, Ray); *Autumn Leaves* (57, Robert Aldrich); *Fire Down Below* (57, Robert Parrish); *Pal Joey* (57, George Sidney); *Pushover* (54, Quine); *Operation Mad Ball* (57, Quine); *Bell, Book and Candle* (58, Quine); *Verboten!* (58, Samuel Fuller); *The Crimson Kimono* (59, Fuller); *Bonjour Tristesse* (58, Otto Preminger); and *Anatomy of a Murder* (59, Preminger).

If one adds that Columbia was one of the first studios to recognize the opportunity of the TV market—Columbia Screen Gems—then Cohn deserves to be known as one of the few Hollywood moguls who understood his own business in the 1950s. We owe too many good films to him to be distracted by the legend of the foulmouthed slave-master.

Claudette Colbert (Claudette Lily Chauchoin) (1903–96), b. Paris

At her best, she was sophisticated gaiety personified, a tender yet spirited comedienne, most stimulated by the chance to be provocative. She was less convincing in sultry or tearjerker parts, and she could turn smug or superficial in dull roles. She was also fixed in her ways, preferring to give her left face to the camera, a stickler for regular hours, and so demanding before *State of the Union* ("By five in the afternoon I am tired and my face shows it") that Capra replaced her with Katharine Hepburn. Maybe Colbert knew a thankless part when she read it.

Her family came to New York when she was six, and after secretarial training she went on the stage, playing romantic leads by the late twenties. She made one silent picture, *For the Love of Mike* (27, Capra), but it was her facility with dialogue (she never seemed French—but English) that persuaded Paramount to sign her up in 1929. She began modestly but by 1930 was taking on a wide range of parts: *Manslaughter* (George Abbott); *Honor Among Lovers* (Dorothy Arzner); *His Woman* (31, Edward Sloman); and *The Smiling Lieutenant* (31, Ernst Lubitsch).

De Mille liked her enough to make her his leading lady: as Poppaea, bathing in asses' milk and the director's boyish lasciviousness in *The Sign of the Cross* (32); in *Four Frightened People* (34); as a delectable if silly *Cleopatra* (34). But if Roman dress (and undress) left no doubt about her beauty, the mock period language made her mischievous and impatient. Modern costume and smart talk suited her better and after two flat, serious roles—*I Cover the Waterfront* (33, James Cruze) and *Three-Cornered Moon* (33, Elliott Nugent)—she went rather reluctantly to Columbia for *It Happened One Night* (34, Capra). Her classiness made natural flirt with Gable's view of dames; her darting eyes indicated a lot of the comedy; and her upraised skirt has become part of the American dream of the road. The stars won Oscars, and Colbert's status at Paramount was strengthened.

For the next decade, she was a top star. She was a leading social figure in Hollywood with her second husband, Dr. Joel Pressman (before that, she had been the wife of director Norman Foster). She made *Imitation of Life* (34, John M. Stahl); *The Gilded Lily* (35, Wesley Ruggles); *Private Worlds* (35, Gregory La Cava), with Charles Boyer; *She Married Her Boss* (35, La Cava); as Cigarette in *Under Two Flags* (36, Frank Lloyd); with Boyer again, as Russians in *Tovarich* (37, Anatole Litvak); *Maid of Salem* (37, Lloyd); worthy of less censorship in *Bluebeard's Eighth Wife* (38, Lubitsch); delectable in *Zaza* (39, George Cukor) and *Midnight* (39, Mitchell Leisen); defeated by the Colonial wife in *Drums Along the Mohawk* (39, John Ford); *It's a Wonderful World* (40, W. S. Van Dyke); with Gable and Tracy in *Boom Town* (40, Jack Conway); *Arise My Love* (40, Leisen); *Skylark* (41, Mark Sandrich); and *Remember the Day* (41, Henry King).

The Palm Beach Story (42, Preston Sturges) only showed how seldom she came to full life. After *No Time for Love* (43, Leisen) and *So Proudly We Hail* (43, Sandrich), she was loaned to Selznick to play the home-front madonna in *Since You Went Away* (44, John Cromwell), in which she quietly outshone Jennifer Jones and proved very touching. This was her best noncomedic role. *Practically Yours* (44) was her fourth film with Leisen, who shared the actress's feeling that she should be allowed to play somewhat older women.

Her Paramount contract ended, and she could not negotiate the postwar years easily: she was married to George Brent and Orson Welles in *Tomorrow Is Forever* (45, Irving Pichel), but the comic possibilities were defiantly ignored; *Guest Wife* (45, Sam Wood); *Without Reservations* (46, Mervyn Le Roy); with Fred MacMurray in *The Egg and I* (47, Chester Erskine), her last big hit; *Sleep, My Love* (48, Douglas Sirk); *Three Came Home* (50, Jean Negulesco); *The Secret Fury* (50, Mel Ferrer); as a nun in *Thunder on the Hill* (51, Sirk).

Soon after this, she left America, first for Britain, where she made *The Planter's Wife* (52, Ken Annakin), and to France for *Destinées* (53) and *Si Versailles m'était Conté* (53, Sacha Guitry). *Texas* (55, Tim Whelan) was a forlorn Western.

After that, she was in *Parrish* (61, Delmer Daves), played occasionally onstage, lived in magazined splendor in Barbados, and still looked terrific on TV in *The Two Mrs. Grenvilles* (87, John Erman).

Ronald Colman (1891–1958),
b. Richmond, England

While working for the British Steamship Company, Colman took part in amateur dramatics; invalided out of the First World War, he went on the stage professionally. He was successful and made a few films in Britain before going to America in 1920. While working there in the theatre, he was seen by Henry King and chosen to play with Lillian Gish in *The White Sister* (23, King).

Goldwyn put him under contract and Colman quickly became a romantic star: *Romola* (24, King); *Tarnish* (24, George Fitzmaurice); *Her Night of Romance* (24, Sidney Franklin); *A Thief in Paradise* (25, Fitzmaurice); *His Supreme Moment* (25, Fitzmaurice); *The Sporting Venus* (25, Marshall Neilan); *Her Sister from Paris* (25, Franklin); *The Dark Angel* (25, Fitzmaurice); *Stella Dallas* (25, King); *Lady Windermere's Fan* (25, Ernst Lubitsch); *Kiki* (26, Clarence Brown); *Beau Geste* (26, Herbert Brenon); *The Winning of Barbara Worth* (26, King); *The Night of Love* (27, Fitzmaurice); *The Magic Flame* (27, King); *Two Lovers* (28, Fred Niblo); and *The Rescue* (29, Brenon).

As an actor, Colman was not troubled by the coming of sound—indeed, his aura of class gained from it. No more handsome than several silent rivals, when he spoke he revealed himself as urbane and sympathetic. Nearly forty, his mustache, his manners, and his Englishness cast him perfectly as the mature, amused romantic, and as such he won a huge following. He was not a searching actor, but he had learned how attractive consistent underplaying could be, and he took care to preserve his looks. His first great success with sound was *Bulldog Drummond* (29, F. Richard Jones) and he carried on with *Condemned* (29, Wesley Ruggles); *Raffles* (30, Harry d'Arrast and George Fitzmaurice); *The Unholy Garden* (31, Fitzmaurice); and *The Devil to Pay* (31, Fitzmaurice). Colman did not work as often as many other stars: he often pondered over accepting parts, but scarcity added to his gentlemanly distinction. Invariably, his parts were ideally suited to his talent: *Arrowsmith* (31, John Ford); *Cynara* (King Vidor); and *The Masquerader* (33, Richard Wallace).

At this stage, Colman left Goldwyn after his employer suggested that Colman acted better when he had been drinking. Colman now joined Twentieth and made *Bulldog Drummond Strikes Back* (34, Roy del Ruth), *Clive of India* (35, Richard Boleslawsky), and *The Man Who Broke the Bank at Monte Carlo* (35, Stephen Roberts). He was a very good, alcoholic Sidney Carton at MGM in *A Tale of Two Cities* (35, Jack Conway) and at the same studio in *Under Two Flags* (36, Frank Lloyd). In 1937, he made two of his best remembered movies: at Columbia, *Lost Horizon* (Frank Capra) and, for Selznick, *The Prisoner of Zenda* (John Cromwell). He played François Villon in *If I Were King* (38, Lloyd) and was unusually touching as the painter in *The Light That Failed* (39, William Wellman); *Lucky Partners* (40, Lewis Milestone); *My Life With Caroline* (41, Milestone); *The Talk of the Town* (42, George Stevens); the shrewdly calculated sentiment of *Random Harvest* (43, Mervyn Le Roy), in which Colman was opposite Greer Garson. After *Kismet* (44, William Dieterle) he worked less and less and was more clearly in middle age in *The Late George Apley* (47, Joseph L. Mankiewicz) and *A Double Life* (47, George Cukor), for which he won the best actor Oscar as an actor who gets too far inside "Othello." He was also very good in *Champagne for Caesar* (49, Richard Whorf) and thereafter retired, returning only for two guest roles: *Around the World in 80 Days* (56, Michael Anderson) and *The Story of Mankind* (57, Irwin Allen).

Sean Connery (Thomas Sean Connery),
b. Edinburgh, Scotland, 1930

In his first movie kingdom, Connery had an immaculate, but enclosing, image as 007. He was glossy, supercilious, rather cruel, close to absurdly attractive, and as hard and abstract as the wig he wore. He played James Bond six times—*Dr. No* (62, Terence Young); *From Russia With Love* (63, Young); *Goldfinger* (64, Guy Hamilton); *Thunderball* (65, Young); *You Only Live Twice* (67, Lewis Gilbert); and *Diamonds Are Forever* (71, Hamilton). But those films grew tamer with habit and excess special effects. Producers Saltzmann and Broccoli had no urge to explore Connery's potential. Bondism was more fully treated—to the point of sadism—in Connery's Mark Rutland in *Marnie* (64, Alfred Hitchcock). Still, the first edition of this book was rash in supposing that Connery would never escape, or transcend, Bond.

Connery had been around a while without getting anywhere—Sidney Lumet was the one director who saw promise, but Lumet did not really transplant Connery to an American setting: *No Road Back* (56, Montgomery Tully); *Action of the Tiger* (57, Young); *Hell Drivers* (57, Cy Endfield); *Time Lock* (57, Gerald Thomas); *Another Time, Another Place* (58, Lewis Allen); *Tarzan's Greatest Adventure* (59, John Guillermin); *Darby O'Gill and the Little People* (59, Robert Stevenson); *The Frightened City* (60, John Lemont); *On the Fiddle* (61, Cyril Frankel); *Woman of Straw* (63, Basil Dearden); *The Hill* (65, Sidney Lumet); *A Fine Madness* (66, Irvin Kershner); *Shalako* (68,

Edward Dmytryk); *The Molly Maguires* (68, Martin Ritt); *The Anderson Tapes* (71, Lumet); *The Offence* (72, Lumet); *Zardoz* (73, John Boorman); *Ransom* (74, Caspar Wrede); and *Murder on the Orient Express* (74, Lumet).

The turning point came in 1975 and 1976 with a trio of flamboyant, romantic roles that needed costume and epic perspectives. In the process, Connery picked up humor, flourish, and a depth of humanity not much evident before. He had come from lowly stock, and in England he may have been advised to mask his Scottishness. Now he let the accent roar, he showed how little hair he owned, and he grasped nobility: as a very Scots Arab in *The Wind and the Lion* (75, John Milius); with Michael Caine as Kipling opportunists in *The Man Who Would Be King* (75, John Huston); as the aging ex-outlaw in *Robin and Marian* (76, Richard Lester).

The magic wasn't complete; Connery makes strange choices still. But he has become a versatile movie star, an old-fashioned man who commands the love of the public. The closest comparison may be Gable, who had the same mix of mustache and twinkle and a similar hint of uncompromising force. Happily battered and world weary, he is past seventy and capable of becoming one of the great old men of movies.

The list is *The Next Man* (76, Richard Sarafian); *A Bridge Too Far* (77, Richard Attenborough); *The Great Train Robbery* (78, Michael Crichton); *Meteor* (79, Ronald Neame); *Cuba* (79, Lester); *Time Bandits* (81, Terry Gilliam); *Outland* (81, Peter Hyams); *Wrong Is Right* (82, Richard Brooks); the mountaineer in *Five Days One Summer* (82, Fred Zinnemann); *Never Say Never Again* (83, Kershner)—Bond again, after twelve years, suggesting the vulnerability to big offers; *Sword of the Valiant* (85, Stephen Weeks); *Highlander* (86, Russell Mulcahy); *The Name of the Rose* (86, Jean-Jacques Annaud); winning the supporting actor Oscar for his beat cop who dies a samurai death in *The Untouchables* (87, Brian De Palma); *The Presidio* (88, Hyams); as Indy's dad in *Indiana Jones and the Last Crusade* (89, Steven Spielberg); walking away with *Family Business* (89, Lumet); the Russian officer in *The Hunt for Red October* (90, John McTiernan); a credible man in love and a boozy, jazz-mad publisher in *The Russia House* (90, Fred Schepisi); briefly as Robin's father in *Robin Hood: Prince of Thieves* (90, Kevin Reynolds); *Highlander II—The Quickening* (91, Mulcahy); the awful *Medicine Man* (92, McTiernan) and a smart cop in *Rising Sun* (93, Philip Kaufman), on both of which he was also executive producer.

If one agrees that it's too long since Connery has made a decent film, one should add that he has helped produce many of them—*Just Cause* (95, Arne Glimcher); *The Rock* (96, Michael Bay);

Entrapment (99, Jon Amiel); *Finding Forrester* (00, Gus Van Sant). It's a waste, because he owns the screen still, even if he looks a little silly leering at Catherine Zeta-Jones. If only he'd do a serious film about an older man and a younger woman. But he seems locked into the mocking, mercenary mode: *A Good Man in Africa* (94, Bruce Beresford); as Arthur in *First Knight* (95, Jerry Zucker); *The Avengers* (98, Jeremiah S. Chechik); *Playing by Heart* (98, Willard Carroll).

Elisha Cook Jr. (1906–99), b. San Francisco
There are big stars in the movies who pass by, leaving us uninterested. And there are supporting actors whose faces will stop you dead as you flip through an album history. Who really wants to know more about Robert Taylor, say? But who wouldn't want to read a good biography of Elisha Cook Jr.? He was small, scrawny; he was losing his hair, and he had a high-pitched voice; he had eyes screwed into his head with all the desperate resolve of wanting to be taken seriously. He could be a loudmouth bullying the air around him, like Wilmer in *The Maltese Falcon* (41, John Huston), and he could be a quiet, gutsy squirt, like Henry Jones in *The Big Sleep* (46, Howard Hawks). It wasn't a big adjustment, going from one to the other; and maybe it wasn't a huge range. But Elisha Cook was guaranteed. Put him in a bad picture, and he made it watchable for ten minutes. Put him in something good and he was a metaphor for glue, or the medium itself. He could make you trust a film.

The list is longer than this, because he kept working: *Her Unborn Child* (29, Charles McGrath and Albert Ray); *Pigskin Parade* (36, David Butler), as a campus radical; *Two in a Crowd* (36, Alfred E. Green); *Love Is News* (37, Tay Garnett); *They Won't Forget* (37, Mervyn LeRoy); *Submarine Patrol* (38, John Ford); *The Stranger on the Third Floor* (40, Boris Ingster); *Tin Pan Alley* (40, Walter Lang); *Love Crazy* (41, Jack Conway); *I Wake Up Screaming* (41, H. Bruce Humberstone); with Laurel and Hardy in *A-Haunting We Will Go* (42, Alfred Werker); as the hopped-up drummer who notices Ella Raines in *Phantom Lady* (44, Robert Siodmak); *Up in Arms* (44, Elliott Nugent); *Dark Waters* (44, André de Toth); *Dillinger* (45, Max Nosseck).

He was in *Cinderella Jones* (46, Busby Berkeley); *Two Smart People* (46, Jules Dassin); *The Falcon's Alibi* (46, Ray McCarey); *Born to Kill* (47, Robert Wise); *The Long Night* (47, Anatole Litvak); *The Gangster* (47, Gordon Wiles); *Flaxy Martin* (49, Richard Bare); *The Great Gatsby* (49, Nugent); *Behave Yourself* (51, George Beck); *Don't Bother to Knock* (52, Roy Baker); lifted off his feet by Jack Palance's gunfire in *Shane* (53, George Stevens); *I, the Jury* (53, Harry Essex); *Thunder Over the Plains* (53, de Toth); *Drum Beat* (54, Delmer Daves); *The Indian Fighter* (55, de Toth); never better than as the henpecked teller, George Peatty, in *The Killing* (56, Stanley Kubrick).

He did *The Lonely Man* (57, Henry Levin); *Chicago Confidential* (57, Sidney Salkow); *Voodoo Island* (57, Reginald Le Borg); *Baby Face Nelson* (57, Don Siegel); *Plunder Road* (57, Hubert Cornfield); *House on Haunted Hill* (58, William Castle); *Day of the Outlaw* (59, de Toth); *Platinum High School* (60, Charles Haas); *College Confidential* (60, Albert Zugsmith); *One-Eyed Jacks* (61, Marlon Brando); *Black Zoo* (63, Robert Gordon), *The Haunted Palace* (63, Roger Corman); *Johnny Cool* (63, William Asher); *Blood on the Arrow* (64, Salkow); *Welcome to Hard Times* (67, Burt Kennedy); *Rosemary's Baby* (68, Roman Polanski); *The Great Bank Robbery* (69, Hy Averback); *El Condor* (70, John Guillermin); *The Great Northfield Minnesota Raid* (72, Philip Kaufman).

He is beaten senseless in *Pat Garrett and Billy the Kid* (73, Sam Peckinpah); *Emperor of the North* (73, Robert Aldrich); *Electra Glide in Blue* (73, James William Guercio); *The Outfit* (74, John Flynn); *Winterhawks* (76, Charles B. Pierce); after the falcon again in *The Black Bird* (76, David Giler); *St. Ives* (76, J. Lee Thompson); *The Champ* (79, Franco Zeffirelli); *1941* (79, Steven Spielberg); *Carny* (80, Robert Kaylor); *Tom Horn* (80, William Wiard); *Harry's War* (81, Keith Merrill); *Hammett* (82, Wim Wenders).

Gary Cooper (Frank James Cooper)
(1901–61), b. Helena, Montana
The young Cooper was a laconic, beautiful, solitary soul, saved from vanity by his preoccupation with some deeper mystery. Like so many of the great stars, he gave the impression of being caught unexpectedly in his own thoughts. His shyness enabled him to seem aloof from or abashed by stories. But as time went by, his beauty cracked and his face began to show the dreadful anxiety of his own thoughts.

It is only in retrospect that one recognizes the astonishing integrity of Cooper's work: he never played a malicious or dishonest man. That worry he had nursed for so many years, and that eventually grew into the cancer that made his face wretched, was wondering how the American hero could remain a good man in this world. The iconography of classical American virtues of simplicity and honor being racked by violence, corruption, and compromise is traced in the succession of images of Cooper, his sheriff's stride becoming ever more spindly and perilous with the years. It is especially notable how he appealed to such varied interpretations of the American dream: other actors marveled at the astonishingly uncluttered submission of himself to the cameras;

Hemingway always saw Cooper as the embodiment of his detached heroes; while Carl Sandburg called him "one of the most beloved illiterates this country has ever known." Cooper could have played most of the nineteenth-century Americans: he was Tom Sawyer grown up; he could have appreciated Ishmael or even the baleful obsession of Ahab; he was a Hawkeye and an Adam Verver. Look at Cooper and you will see the stoical knowledge of the world that stares out of late portraits of Lincoln. In cinematic terms, he proved amazingly flexible. Who else could have been a central character for Hawks, Capra, von Sternberg, De Mille, Lubitsch, Borzage, King Vidor, and Anthony Mann? As he told Niven Busch, one of his screenwriters, "Just make me the hero."

Ironically, Cooper's parents were both English, only lately come to America when he was born. And in the years from 1910 to 1917, Cooper himself lived in Britain. When he came back to Montana, he studied agriculture and worked on a ranch. A variety of jobs led him in 1924 to Los Angeles, where he took up working as an extra. The name "Gary" was given him by an agent, after the town in Indiana, and Henry King chose him for the second male lead in *The Winning of Barbara Worth* (26) when the original actor failed to turn up. That was a Goldwyn picture, but the producer let Cooper go to Paramount who gradually built him up into one of their most successful stars: briefly with Clara Bow (embarrassed by her directness) in *It* (27, Clarence Badger) and *Children of Divorce* (27, Frank Lloyd); *Arizona Bound* (27, John Waters); *Nevada* (27, Waters); *The Last Outlaw* (27, Arthur Rossen); *Beau Sabreur* (28, Waters); *Legion of the Condemned* (28, William Wellman); *Doomsday* (28, Rowland V. Lee); *Half a Bride* (28, Gregory La Cava); *Lilac Time* (28, George Fitzmaurice); *The First Kiss* (28, Lee); *The Shopworn Angel* (28, Richard Wallace); *Wolf Song* (29, Victor Fleming); *Wings* (29, Wellman); and *Betrayal* (29, Lewis Milestone). His first all-talking picture was as *The Virginian* (29, Fleming), which established him as a Western hero. After *Only the Brave* (30, Frank Tuttle), *The Texan* (30, John Cromwell), *Seven Days' Leave* (30, Wallace), *A Man from Wyoming* (30, Lee), and *The Spoilers* (30, Edwin Carewe), came the first of his great films: as Tom Brown, in *Morocco* (30, von Sternberg), a sardonic, independent soldier, too taciturn to spell out his love for Dietrich. After *Fighting Caravans* (31, Otto Brower), he excelled in the Dashiell Hammett adaptation, *City Streets* (31, Rouben Mamoulian). This is the period of Paramount salon flirtations and Cooper proved as attractive in a lounge suit as he had been in buckskins: with Carole Lombard in *I Take This Woman* (31, Marion Gering); Claudette Colbert in *His Woman* (31, Edward Sloman); and Tallulah Bankhead in *Devil and the Deep* (32, Gering). It

was remarkable how the haltingly eloquent Cooper overawed sophisticated women. His first Hemingway role was as Frederick Henry opposite Helen Hayes in *A Farewell to Arms* (33, Frank Borzage). He went to MGM for the Faulkner-scripted *Today We Live* (33, Howard Hawks) and for *Operator 13* (34, Richard Boleslavsky). But usually Paramount kept him to themselves: *Design for Living* (33, Ernst Lubitsch); as the White Knight in *Alice in Wonderland* (33, Norman Z. McLeod); *One Sunday Afternoon* (33, Stephen Roberts); and with Lombard and Shirley Temple in *Now and Forever* (34, Henry Hathaway). This was the period when all his films were exceptional, so that by the end of the 1930s he was America's top earner: *Wedding Night* (35, King Vidor); *The Lives of a Bengal Lancer* (35, Hathaway); with Ann Harding as the dream-crossed lovers in *Peter Ibbetson* (35, Hathaway); reunited with Dietrich in *Desire* (36, Borzage); and as *Mr. Deeds Goes to Town* (36, Frank Capra), an Everyman figure pushed close to self-pity by Capra, and the first note of Cooper's capacity for pain. After *The General Died at Dawn* (36, Lewis Milestone), he was very moving as the fatalist Wild Bill Hickok in *The Plainsman* (37, Cecil B. De Mille), driving Jean Arthur mad with his understatement; *Souls at Sea* (37, Hathaway); the one thumping failure—for Goldwyn—of *The Adventures of Marco Polo* (38, Archie Mayo); *Bluebeard's Eighth Wife* (38, Lubitsch); *The Cowboy and the Lady* (38, H. C. Potter); *Beau Geste* (39, Wellman); and *The Real Glory* (Hathaway).

The early 1940s saw him in *The Westerner* (40, William Wyler); *North West Mounted Police* (40, De Mille); opposite Barbara Stanwyck in *Meet John Doe* (41, Capra) and *Ball of Fire* (41, Hawks); and winning an Oscar for his portrayal of *Sergeant York* (41, Hawks), a pacifist rewarded for killing. He then played Lou Gehrig in *The Pride of the Yankees* (42, Sam Wood); Robert Jordan in *For Whom the Bell Tolls* (43, Wood); *The Story of Dr. Wassell* (44, De Mille); and *Along Came Jones* (45, Stuart Heisler).

His work was now more variable. The strain of action on moral conscience grew into one of the most affecting, troubled sights of postwar films: *Saratoga Trunk* (46, Wood) was a slow romance with Ingrid Bergman, but Fritz Lang's *Cloak and Dagger* (46) has all the subtle dilemma of the director's best work and makes Cooper credible as a nuclear scientist caught up in espionage, a decent man faced by the danger implicit in his own work; *Unconquered* (47) was the last of De Mille's epics. *Good Sam* (48, Leo McCarey) dragged. But *The Fountainhead* (49, Vidor) is a beautiful film, with Cooper as the "creative force" revealed in an architect. Ostensibly beyond his intellectual means, *The Fountainhead* thrives on Cooper's undaunted naturalism. He was now at

Warners and in the doldrums: briefly at a bar saying "Yup" in *It's a Great Feeling* (49, David Butler); *Task Force* (49, Delmer Daves); *Bright Leaf* (50, Michael Curtiz); in *Dallas* (50, Heisler); *You're in the Navy Now* (51, Hathaway); and Raoul Walsh's *Distant Drums* (51). Then came *High Noon* (52, Fred Zinnemann), an obvious, surface-deep suspense Western, with McCarthyist allegory, but dignified by Cooper's own identification with the lone sheriff. There are few clearer instances of an actor's taking over the personality of a primed but unintelligent movie. It won Cooper a second Oscar and defined his last years. *Springfield Rifle* (52, André de Toth) had him as the victim of treachery. *Return to Paradise* (53, Mark Robson) is the film seen in *Lola. Blowing Wild* (53, Hugo Fregonese) is an offbeat gem, with Stanwyck again. *Garden of Evil* (54, Hathaway) and *Vera Cruz* (54, Robert Aldrich) are standard Westerns. But in *The Court Martial of Billy Mitchell* (55, Otto Preminger) Cooper suffered again for his foresight. In *Friendly Persuasion* (56, Wyler) he was a Quaker drawn reluctantly into war, and in *Love in the Afternoon* (57, Billy Wilder) and *11 North Frederick* (58, Philip Dunne) he played men in love with much younger women.

Man of the West (58, Anthony Mann) is his final masterpiece, as an ex-outlaw forced to destroy his former colleagues through the violence he had hoped to expunge from himself. Now clearly old and ill, Cooper's personal agony brought emotional drama to Mann's immaculate direction. In his last years, Cooper made minor films: *The Hanging Tree* (59, Daves); *They Came to Cordura* (59, Robert Rossen); *The Wreck of the Mary Deare* (59, Michael Anderson); and *The Naked Edge* (61, Anderson).

Merian C. Cooper (1893–1973),
b. Jacksonville, Florida

There were two distinct phases in Cooper's idiosyncratic movie career, since his effective work as a producer was done with only two directors: Ernest B. Schoedsack and John Ford, primitives both, but one striving for the authentic, the other garrulously myth-making. Cooper graduated from Annapolis and worked on sailing ships before war service as a flier, latterly as part of the Western intervention against the Bolsheviks. It was while a roving journalist that he met Schoedsack and collaborated with him—as producer and director—on a series of actual-location films: *Grass* (26); *Chang* (27); and *Rango* (31). But Cooper seems always to have had a more entrepreneurial turn of mind, since he wedded Schoedsack's interest in ethnographic cinema with Lothar Mendes's story flair in *The Four Feathers* (29). After a spell as an aviation executive, Cooper joined RKO at the behest of David Selznick and produced *The Most Dangerous Game* (32, Schoedsack and Irving Pichel) and *King Kong* (33, codirected with Schoedsack). Not only was *Kong* Cooper's original idea, but he chose to film it in the studio, opting for the ingenious tricks of Willis M. O'Brien rather than the more natural wonder of Schoedsack.

When Selznick left RKO, Cooper was in charge of production for a while, but illness led to independence: *The Lost Patrol* (34, John Ford); *She* (35, Pichel); *The Last Days of Pompeii* (35, Schoedsack); and *The Toy Wife* (38, Richard Thorpe). During the war, he was in the U.S. Army Air Corps at high ranks serving in China. But afterwards, he formed a production company with John Ford that was to produce that director's best and most appalling films. On all of them, Cooper was coproducer with Ford: *The Fugitive* (47); *Fort Apache* (48); *Three Godfathers* (48); *She Wore a Yellow Ribbon* (49); *Wagonmaster* (50); *Rio Grande* (50); *The Quiet Man* (52); *The Sun Shines Bright* (53); and *The Searchers* (56). The cavalry trilogy, *Wagonmaster*, and, above all, the long, drawn-out pursuit of *The Searchers* are entertaining films, notable for the novel characters they offer Wayne. *The Fugitive, Three Godfathers,* and *The Sun Shines Bright* are among the most depleting movie experiences. While working with Ford, Cooper also produced *Mighty Joe Young* (49, Schoedsack) and *This Is Cinerama* (53, Ruth Rose and, uncredited, Schoedsack). Cooper died, coincidentally, on the weekend that saw the death of Robert Armstrong, who had played the "hero," Carl Denham, in *King Kong*. Of course, not many could put a face to Armstrong's name, whereas Kong's furious innocence stares into all our dreams, Cooper's most potent bequest.

Francis Ford Coppola,
b. Detroit, Michigan, 1939

1962: *Dementia 13*. 1967: *You're a Big Boy Now.* 1968: *Finian's Rainbow.* 1969: *The Rain People.* 1972: *The Godfather.* 1974: *The Conversation; The Godfather, Part II.* 1979: *Apocalypse Now.* 1982: *One from the Heart.* 1983: *The Outsiders; Rumble Fish.* 1984: *The Cotton Club.* 1985: *Rip Van Winkle* (TV). 1986: *Captain Eo* (s); *Peggy Sue Got Married.* 1987: *Gardens of Stone.* 1988: *Tucker: The Man and His Dream.* 1989: *"Life Without Zoe,"* an episode from *New York Stories.* 1990: *The Godfather, Part III.* 1992: *Bram Stoker's Dracula.* 1996: *Jack.* 1997: *The Rainmaker.* 2000: *Supernova* (uncredited). 2001: *Apocalypse Now Redux.*

He is multitudes: Coppola, Francis Ford Coppola, "Francis," a Don to would-be filmmakers, Renaissance man, winemaker, visionary of electronic cinema, and sometimes St. Francis of the Troubles. He tries to be everything for everyone; yet that furious effort may mask some inner emptiness. For he is very gregarious *and* very withdrawn, the life and soul of some parties, and a depressive. He is Sonny and Michael Corleone, for sure, but there are traces of Fredo, too—and he is at his best when secretly telling a part of his own story, or working out his fearful fantasies. His reputation has fallen a good deal as a filmmaker in the years since *Apocalypse Now* (a chaos of ideas and hopes, crippled by indecision and the urge to take flight in drop-dead scenes). But no American career has had such endless, entertaining turmoil, or says as much about making movies in America now. No one retains so many jubilant traits of the kid moviemaker, or has inspired darker comments. Robert Evans, his colleague on *The Godfather* and *The Cotton Club*, has recently said of Coppola: "He's an evil person...a direct descendant of Machiavelli's prince. He is so seductive, so brilliant [at] bringing people in[to] his web, he makes Elmer Gantry look like Don Knotts."

Coppola was the son of Toscanini's flute player, a very ambitious and often thwarted composer, whose music would be too fondly indulged in the son's movies. But family was always the richest base and the greatest pressure for Coppola. He grew up as the homely, less-than-brilliant younger son in the shadow of his brother, August; their sister was Talia, later Talia Shire and Connie Corleone. Francis had periods of illness and he became a drama major at Hofstra University. From there, he made his way as an apprentice into Roger Corman's exploitative factory, and he earned a solid reputation as a screenwriter. As a film student at UCLA, his screenplay *Pilma Pilma* won the Samuel Goldwyn Award for 1962.

The early films are not very good. Coppola was more highly esteemed as a writer: he made significant contributions to *Is Paris Burning?* (66, René Clément) and *This Property Is Condemned* (66, Sydney Pollack). He was highly praised for his contribution to *Patton* (70, Franklin Schaffner)—he and Edmund H. North shared the Oscar for adapted screenplay. That he could do nothing to save *The Great Gatsby* (73, Jack Clayton) was not his fault.

But by then, he had made *The Godfather*, his true debut as artist and family confessor. *The Godfather* deserved all its success because it had the nerve to take its 175 minutes slowly. For a young director without a hit, and with Paramount, Mario Puzo, Robert Evans, and Brando breathing down his neck—not to mention the attention of real-life Corleones—it was an achievement to coax that vulnerable dinosaur of a property into such supple, stealthy life. (There are still stories that Coppola needed help in organizing the footage he had shot; but *The Godfather* ended up so comprehensively organized that that was its greatest testament to criminal power and authority.)

The Godfather is a feast of a movie—you come out of it craving lasagna and meat sauce. It has a

calm faith in narrative control that had not been current in Hollywood for twenty years. It was like a film of the forties in its nostalgic decor; its command of great supporting actors; in Gordon Willis's bold exploration of a film noir in color; and in its fascination with evil. The plot is rooted in the sinister charm of action foreseen, spelled out, and finally delivered: Michael's use of arms against Sollozo and McCloskey is the perfect example of this, and it is a killing in which we are his accomplices.

In addition, *The Godfather* is deeply reassuring in its rejection of chaos and disorder, and its paranoid insistence on the family as that dark, mysterious home where all strangers are enemies. When family is so strong, so loving, then the Corleones seem to be standing up for an old fine order, no matter that slaughter and graft are their trades. There is a benevolent gravity in the way Brando's Vito Corleone warns against narcotics as too dangerous to be traded in. No American film in years had been so opposed to destruction, decay, entropy, or change—or so schizophrenically ecstatic about bloodletting and the beautifully timed and shot assassination. The mise-en-scène merged with the delicate finesse of the hit men.

When *The Godfather* measured its grand finale of murder against the liturgy of baptism, Coppola seemed mesmerized by the trick, and its nihilism. A Buñuel, by contrast, might have made that sequence ironic and hilarious. But Coppola is not long on those qualities and he could not extricate himself from the engineering of scenes. The identification with Michael was complete and stricken.

Coppola was suddenly a power. He talked of innovations in production, of a small studio as benevolent as family. He produced the delightful *American Graffiti* (73, George Lucas), doing a favor for one of his best kids, and thereby launching a career that would dwarf his own, and which would make a small, rich kingdom of film in San Francisco and Marin. Coppola himself had no clearer creative character than that of a versatile, adept, but rather soulless student.

He made *The Conversation* on the fruits of *The Godfather* as a more personal and expressive picture. It seems at first more difficult and searching; and it is so dense in its plotting and its layered sound track that it requires several viewings—Walter Murch was the sound designer and he ran postproduction when Coppola had to concentrate on *The Godfather, Part II*.

Wishful thinking can claim that *The Conversation* is a study of Nixonian America, that it is an intricate thriller. Yet it seems to me that the picture is rather more a glorification of what a movie can do with sound (as magic and trickery), and a helpless, collapsing view of solipsism, paranoia, and the self-pity of depression. Harry Caul is left alone, and solitude is a terrible grandeur in Coppola's mind—see how it takes over Michael Corleone, and Kurtz in *Apocalypse Now*. Is there a more morbid, anal figure in American film than Harry Caul? Or one who so dominates and represses his own film?

The Godfather, Part II was a natural cashing in that made Coppola an impresario (something that lay heavy on the next ten years of his life); it allowed Robert De Niro to imagine an early life for Vito Corleone; it exhibited a mastery of so many periods and locations as to be entrancing; and it sought some way to redeem the alleged glamorization of the Mafia in the original film. Certainly the Michael of *Part II* is unequivocally wicked: he turns on his own family. But still Coppola cannot disown the adolescent authority, the acting tough, of the gangsters; and he cannot detach himself from Michael. There is no horror in *Part II*, no moral outrage. There is instead the numb, passive acceptance that such things are done in the name of order.

I am being tough on Coppola for the very reason I have been hard on Capra and Ford. These are three men of remarkable talent and facility. They shoot riveting, ravishing film; they are very good with actors (though Coppola is shy of women in his films); they are storytellers capable of . . . well, "genius" is the word Hollywood would use. But that genius is not enough. There is a talent in American films that makes for adolescent attitudes, veiled fascism, and a work that leads one to recognize the proximity of talent and meretricious magic. In all three, the work eventually seeks to hide its profound muddle in hysterical gesture and demagogic assertion. There is something in the best of American films that is not good enough, and that is dangerous. The disorder so easily seems visionary. *Apocalypse Now* was meant as a great film and a big statement: it was destroyed on the size of its hope, by the vagaries of a difficult location, by an ultimate vagueness of intent, and by the megalomania of Brando and Coppola. Make no mistake, it is a mess—or a war, lit up by beautiful explosions that no one can forget.

I suspect that the experience of *Apocalypse Now* did dreadful things to Coppola's morale and his constitution. The risk of family crackup was very public in his wife Eleanor's book *Notes*. But just as glaring was his own chronic indecision over the film, a profound loss of confidence. By 1982, his company, Zoetrope, was a disaster: the very delicate *One from the Heart* was a massive failure, the Los Angeles studio dream was over, and Coppola faced personal as well as business bankruptcy. For most of the eighties, he worked on assignment to stave off ruin. If he did not collapse, that does not mean that depression and dismay did no damage. He and his wife lost a son, too, in an accident near the set of *Gardens of Stone*. Then, when he cast his daughter Sofia in *The Godfather, Part III*, he seemed caught in an awkward mix of generosity and recklessness. Family remains the endless riddle in his life and work.

A number of his recent films seem to me as short on interest, meaning, or heart as they are long on spectacle: *The Cotton Club*, *Tucker*, and especially *Dracula*. But *One from the Heart* is enchanting and touching—even if it cost too much. *Rumble Fish* is a rueful story of a father and brothers. And then there is *The Godfather, Part III*. When I saw that film in a theater I was terribly disappointed: Pacino seemed to have lost the role; the papal politics felt misguided; Sofia Coppola was striking, but she missed the classical resonance of her role; and the whole thing seemed aimless and uncertain. How could *The Godfather* work with a reformed Michael? If the director sought redemption, then didn't it have to come in other places—in Kay, earlier on in the story, or in Michael's children? I urge readers to screen the revised version of *Part III* that is now available in the video edition of all three parts of *The Godfather*. Walter Murch did that assembly, and he continued a policy of cutting on *Part III* that had been terminated by the pressure for a December release. This revised version is not as good as the first two parts, but it is far superior to the theatrical release. The new Michael is clearer and more touching. Connie becomes a dominant figure. I could still do without the Vatican: Michael's proper nemesis should be in Washington. Still, *Part III* is autumnal, sad, and full of confessions. It is more worthwhile than general opinion suggests, and one of Coppola's most candid films.

There is another Coppola, still—the impresario, the executive producer on projects as mixed as his own films. But surely there is credit in this astonishing variety: *The Black Stallion* (79, Carroll Ballard); *The Escape Artist* (82, Caleb Deschanel); *Hammett* (82, Wim Wenders); *The Black Stallion Returns* (83, Robert Dalva); *Mishima: A Life in Four Chapters* (85, Paul Schrader); *Tough Guys Don't Dance* (87, Norman Mailer); *Wind* (92, Ballard); and *The Secret Garden* (93, Agnieszka Holland).

In the course of the nineties, Coppola developed his winery in the Napa Valley, he founded a magazine, *Zoetrope*, for short stories, and also helped to produce his daughter Sofia's feature debut, *The Virgin Suicides* (00). He took a close interest in the struggling affairs of MGM-UA, which accounts for his editorial assistance on *Supernova* (00, Thomas Lee). He was also still at work on a project to be called *Megalopolis*, at least twenty years in the making. For his own films, *Jack* was one of the worst and *The Rainmaker* was thoroughly old-fashioned and entertaining. But the real movie event was like the reclaiming of a child—*Apocalypse Now Redux* was a fascinating reworking of old material, with fifty-three minutes of cut material restored. It seemed to me to alter the film enormously and to make it into a masterpiece that left the contemporary landscape of films in 2001 looking even more threadbare. Whether Coppola has another great film in him is to be seen. That he has been a great filmmaker, and the inspiration for the northern Californian idea, is beyond question.

Roger Corman, b. Los Angeles, 1926
1955: *Five Guns West; Apache Woman; The Day the World Ended; Swamp Women; The Oklahoma Woman.* 1956: *Gunslinger; It Conquered the World; Not of This Earth; The Undead; The She Gods of Shark Reef; Naked Paradise; Attack of the Crab Monsters; Rock All Night.* 1957: *Teenage Doll; Carnival Rock; Sorority Girl; The Viking Women and the Sea Serpent; War of the Satellites.* 1958: *Machine Gun Kelly; Teenage Caveman; I Mobster.* 1959: *A Bucket of Blood; The Wasp Woman.* 1960: *Ski Troop Attack; The House of Usher; The Little Shop of Horrors; The Last Woman on Earth; Creature from the Haunted Sea; Atlas.* 1961: *The Pit and the Pendulum; The Intruder; The Premature Burial; Tales of Terror.* 1962: *Tower of London; The Young Racers; The Raven; The Terror.* 1963: *The Man With the X-Ray Eyes; The Haunted Palace; The Secret Invasion.* 1964: *The Masque of the Red Death; The Tomb of Ligeia.* 1966: *The Wild Angels.* 1967: *The St. Valentine's Day Massacre; The Trip.* 1969: *De Sade* (codirected with Cy Endfield). 1970: *Bloody Mama; GAS, or It Became Necessary to Destroy the World in Order to Save It.* 1971: *The Red Baron.* 1990: *Roger Corman's Frankenstein Unbound.*

In 1970, the enterprising Edinburgh Festival ran a program of Corman films to crystallize the growing interest in his work among avant-garde critics. It was a proper gesture, since Corman was one of the most interesting and influential "operators" in the tortuous world of commercial cinema. "Operator" is chosen carefully: Corman had produced and directed more than forty films in seventeen years at a time when better known and larger talents were giving up the ghost—there is an obvious comparison with Nicholas Ray or Minnelli. In addition, Corman had an admirable record as a sponsor of new talent: in particular, Monte Hellman, Francis Ford Coppola, Peter Bogdanovich, and Martin Scorsese owed their debuts to him. But Corman's most characteristic achievement was to flourish with the B picture, made for very little money in ridiculously little time. Corman seized what was a dying form, reestablished its worth, and managed to introduce its crazy disciplines to the indulgent perceptions of underground cinema.

The Edinburgh tribute took Corman very solemnly: it exposed him to criticism that he had not courted; it camouflaged his mixture of vulgarity, humor, psychological insight, chronic lack of detail, and the ability to revive stale genres. Nothing weighs down *The St. Valentine's Day Massacre* or *Bloody Mama* more than to claim that they surpass *Bonnie and Clyde* (67, Arthur Penn). While the enterprise of *The Man With the X-Ray Eyes, Machine Gun Kelly,* and *The Last Woman on Earth* is dwarfed by the determination to see them as the work of an immense, despairing philosophy. No matter what authorities are wheeled out in defense of the apocalyptic undercurrent in Corman's work, his films never approach the emotional and intellectual resonance in the work of Penn, Nicholas Ray, or Welles. On the other hand, few B-picture directors have wrought so much under such harassed circumstances. *The Tomb of Ligeia*, at least, is worthy of a place in the history of screen horror and *Bloody Mama* is a scathing portrait of maternal smothering. And if Corman seems a gadfly, more inventive than creative, more interested in setting up audacious ventures than in pursuing serious themes, in diverting the cumbersome, inert quickie into unexpected ideas—there is room for a hundred such figures amid so much dullness.

Corman obtained an engineering degree in California and then went to England to read English. In the early 1950s he began writing screenplays and went into production before turning to direction. He was closely associated with American International Pictures and, in turn, has renovated the cheap Western, the cheap sci-fiction, the cheap horror flick—in this case Edgar Allan Poe adaptations—the gangster picture, and the drug movie. He worked at frantic speed with skimpy resources—often aided by photographer Floyd Crosby and art director Daniel Haller—but it is unhelpful to allege that those handicaps do not show. The visual art in his films is more meager than the ideas that flutter haphazardly through them.

As a producer or best friend, he has been responsible for, among others, *Highway Dragnet* (53, Nathan Juran); *Stake Out on Dope Street* (57, Irvin Kershner); *Crime and Punishment* (58, Denis Sanders); *The Beast from Haunted Cave* (59, Monte Hellman); *Night Tide* (60, Curtis Harrington); *Dementia 13* (62, Francis Ford Coppola); *Queen of Blood* (65, Harrington); *The Shooting* (66, Hellman); *Ride the Whirlwind* (66, Hellman); *The Wild Racers* (67, Daniel Haller); *Targets* (68, Peter Bogdanovich); *Boxcar Bertha* (72, Martin Scorsese); *Big Bad Mama* (74, Steve Carver); *Grand Theft Auto* (77, Ron Howard); *Piranha* (78, Joe Dante); *Rock 'n' Roll High School* (79, Allan Arkush); and *Saint Jack* (79, Bogdanovich). In the long term, Corman's creativity must be seen chiefly in terms of the opportunities he has given to young people.

Corman seldom directs nowadays. But he continues to produce, and to be a synonym for blithe exploitation. It will be fascinating to see whether a second generation of talents will emerge from his more recent output—note the willingness to use women directors (is this feminism? or economy?): *Smokey Bites the Dust* (81, Charles B. Griffith); *Forbidden World* (82, Allan Holzman); *Love Letters* (83, Amy Jones)—a good movie; *Space Raiders* (83, Howard R. Cohen); *Streetwalkin'* (85, Joan Freeman); *Hour of the Assassin* (87, Luis Llosa); *Slumber Party Massacre II* (87, Deborah Brock); *Big Bad Mama II* (88, Jim Wynorski); *The Drifter* (88, Larry Brand); *Nightfall* (88, Paul Mayersberg); *The Lawless Land* (89, Jon Hess); *Lords of the Deep* (89, Mary Ann Fisher); and *Transylvania Twist* (90, Wynorski).

Since the close of the last paragraph, Corman has not directed again, though he has been producer or coproducer on over 130 films. The great majority of these you have never heard of—because they went straight to video or played regionally in places where drive-in exploitation still thrives. What is sadly clear is that this stress on sex, violence and horror has become a self-sufficient enterprise. Not that the training ground for talent was ever Corman's intention. But the exploitation film is now a way of life—for audiences as well as filmmakers. The cynicism has become constitutional, and Corman is having too much fun to stop.

Axel Corti (1933–93), b. Paris
1972: *Der Verweigerung*. 1975: *Totstellen*. 1984: *A Woman's Pale Blue Handwriting*. 1985: *An uns Glaubt Gott Nicht Mehr/God Does Not Believe in Us Anymore; Santa Fe*. 1986: *Welcome in Vienna*. 1990: *The King's Whore*. 1994: *Radetzky March*(TV).

Corti had a wandering childhood, living and being educated in Italy, Switzerland, England, Germany, and Austria. He studied German and Romance literature at university, but, as befits a determined survivor in unstable times, he had also acquired training as a farmer. While still in school he began working for the Austrian Broadcasting Corporation as an actor and reporter. His career as a stage director began in 1958, and has included productions in Vienna, Berlin, Brussels, and Stuttgart, as well as work with Peter Brook in London.

At the same time, he has directed films, from such varied sources as Frank Wedekind, Alfred Doblin, and Truman Capote. He has won several important awards, notably the Grosser Osterreichischer Staatspreis für Filmkunst in 1976 (the only other recipient to date has been Billy Wilder), and the 1985 Prix Italia for *A Woman's Pale Blue Handwriting*, a two-part film for television, adapted from Franz Werfel. Since 1972, he has also been a professor of film directing at the University of Vienna.

His major work is a trilogy, made with the writer Georg Stefan Troller, under the general title, *Where To and Back*, describing the fate of Austria and Austrians in the 1940s. In the first film (made for Austrian television originally), *God Does Not Believe in Us Anymore*, the setting is Vienna in 1938, on the morning after "Crystal Night." A Jewish youth is trying to avoid deportation to the camps by escaping to America. As he makes his way first to Prague, and then through France to Marseille, living underground, hoping for a boat, he meets a German officer who rebelled against Nazism, and was sent to and escaped from Dachau, who helps enlarge the movie's sense of victimization.

The second film, *Santa Fe*, is set entirely in New York (though a twenty-minute harbor sequence was filmed in Trieste). The ship arrives from Europe, and the Austrians try to make new lives in the city. One of them is Freddy Wolff, who works in a sweatshop and a delicatessen and who longs to go to New Mexico. These immigrants are all impoverished and overwhelmed. They struggle with the English language and the astonishing, frightening liberty of America. We see an actor, a surgeon, a writer, and a photographer trying to adjust but recognizing that for the first generation of newcomers there is only the humor and tragedy of loss and dislocation, and the desperate assertion that, "We are good Americans."

In the climax, *Welcome in Vienna* (the one film made for theatrical release), Freddy is an American soldier sent back to Austria to interrogate prisoners. Now we are in the world of *The Third Man*—a time of survival at any cost, compromise, lying, and forgetting. Another Austrian-American soldier, Adler, thinks of going over to the Russians. But when he is rebuffed by them, he becomes as cynical as Harry Lime. Freddy falls in love with Claudia, a young actress, the daughter of a Nazi who is now set up in America because he had secrets to sell. Freddy wants a reason for remaining in Austria. But the country is ruined by its ordeal and the cheating required for survival, and Freddy is welcome in Vienna only so long as he wears the conqueror's uniform.

The overall story is absorbing, as we see Austria carried from the age of Schnitzler, Musil, and Freud toward that of Kurt Waldheim. But it is the manner of Axel Corti's work that is most remarkable. He is a realist whose appetite for life, gesture, and place is inseparable from his moving camera and his reluctance to repeat camera setups. Without hysteria or ostentation, he is always showing us new points of view in a human and social panorama in which there is so much ambiguity, caution, comparison, and irony that any naïve rush to judgment is drained of energy. We see people who have lied, cheated, and pretended in these films; but in the next instant we have to recognize that few resorts are more human or inevitable. Everyone is compromised. Not that Corti becomes cynical. He cherishes ideas and principles and the urge to be just. But he is faithful to the terrible struggle to stay alive, with dignity, in such times.

Axel Corti was the first in a great line of Viennese filmmakers who actually worked in Vienna. He was the true successor to von Stroheim, Lang, Wilder, and Preminger. Think of the five of them and you can begin to appreciate an "Austrian attitude"—amused, wary, hopeful, sad, but strong.

Bill (William H.) **Cosby**, b. Philadelphia, 1937
From Temple University, Cosby became a stand-up comedian in the early sixties who addressed political and social realities with lazy confidence and an edge of protest. That took him into TV and a costarring role with Robert Culp in the series *I Spy* (65–68), in which Cosby played a man who happened to be black. The series was very successful, and encouragingly influential in its natural, unstrained partnership of a black and a white. Three times in a row, Cosby won the Emmy for best actor in a drama series.

He followed that with the sitcom, *The Bill Cosby Show* (69–71), in which he played a high school gym teacher in Los Angeles. For the first time, Cosby surrounded himself with kids. At the same time, he went back to school, getting a doctorate in education at the University of Massachusetts.

He began to make movies, acting in and being executive producer on *Man and Boy* (72, E. W. Swackhamer); reunited with Culp in *Hickey & Boggs* (72, Culp); *Uptown Saturday Night* (74, Sidney Poitier); *Let's Do It Again* (75, Poitier); *Mother, Jugs & Speed* (76, Peter Yates); *A Piece of the Action* (77, Poitier); with Richard Pryor in *California Suite* (78, Herbert Ross).

These movies did well, but it was notable that Cosby was working now more often in a merely black context. And while he was funny in movies, his intimacy was far more interesting on the small screen. *The New Bill Cosby Show* (72–73) was a variety show that lasted only one season. But *Fat Albert and the Cosby Kids* was a cartoon series he narrated that ran from 1972–77. Equally, Cosby translated his rapport with kids into very successful ads for Jell-O Pudding and Coca-Cola.

He made *The Devil and Max Devlin* (81, Steven Hilliard Stern), a flop, at Disney. But then, in 1984, at NBC (after having been turned down originally) he launched *The Cosby Show*, one of TV's most prodigious successes. It was the ongoing story of the Huxtable family, living in New York (where it was filmed). Cliff was an obstetrician, with a lovely, sweet, reasonable wife (Phylicia Rashad) and a gang of kids to rival Shirley

Temple, Dickie Moore, and Freddy Bartholomew. Cosby ran the show, and it often seemed as if he had thrown out scripts in favor of freewheeling improv sessions. He was also billed as Dr. William Cosby, a sign of how far the show was meant to embody his views on child rearing.

The Cosby Show was the most popular show on television from 1985 to 1990. (There was a spin-off, *A Different World*.) It carried NBC, and it made a fortune for Cosby, especially as it went into syndication. The show was very cute: it had great warmth, conservative attitudes and liberal rhetoric, Cosby's adroit, wry leadership, and the kids. Some argued that its portrait of black family life was highly atypical (these were the years of Reagan and Bush, of deterioration of real black family life, and of growing anger in the work of Spike Lee and others). Cosby himself said that the show was a vital role model for black families.

There's no knowing the effect it had. There's every reason to regard it as show business: and clearly the show worked as well as it did because so many white households felt comfortable with it. In years to come, it may look embarrassing (even at the time it could be very sweet, very manipulative, and breathtakingly rosy). Surely the Cosby of *I Spy* could have done a more mixed and challenging show. Yet white America grew up on impossibly happy family shows. Doesn't black America deserve the same chance?

Cosby made two more poor films: *Leonard, Part 6* (87, Paul Weiland) and *Ghost Dad* (90, Poitier). Otherwise, he rested. But he was still only in his fifties, and he has proved himself full of ideas in the past. He may yet deliver a TV show to confront the toughest problems of race relations in America, and a show in which some black kids meet darker destinies than the Huxtables ever knew.

Alas, Cosby has seemed content to be an icon. He has appeared in two more films—*The Meteor Man* (93, Robert Townsend) and *Jack* (96, Francis Ford Coppola). He has also produced a picture, *Men of Honor* (00, George Tillman Jr), about a black military hero.

Costa-Gavras (Konstantinos Gavros),
b. Klivia, Greece, 1933
1965: *Compartiment Tueurs/The Sleeping Car Murders*. 1967: *Un Homme de Trop/Shock Troops*. 1969: *Z*. 1970: *L'Aveu/The Confession*. 1973: *Etat de Siège/State of Siege*. 1975: *Section Spéciale*. 1979: *Clair de Femme/Womanlight*. 1982: *Missing*. 1983: *Hannah K*. 1986: *Conseil de Famille*. 1988: *Betrayed*. 1989: *The Music Box*. 1991: *Contre l'Oubli*; 1993: *La Petite Apocalypse*; "Les Kankobals," an episode from *À propos de Nice, la Suite*. 1997: *Mad City*. 2002: *Amen/Eyewitness*.

Z was a sensation in its day, a political thriller that

seemed to combine authentic events, star players, and a restless way of presenting action journalistically that was a mix of early Frankenheimer and cinema verité. *Z* won the jury prize at Cannes and the Oscar for best foreign film at that historical moment when filmmakers believed they were not just politicized but capable of affecting the outcome of events.

Time has exposed Costa-Gavras as the maker of sketchy melodrama. Still his films of the late sixties and early seventies are better and more urgent than his recent, dismal association with the screenplays of Joe Eszterhas (*Betrayed* and *The Music Box,* the latter so conventional that its bald mechanics came as a relief after the idiocies of *Betrayed*). Before that, *Missing* and *Hannah K.* were steps in decline, movies in which political consciousness became more and more strident. It is as if Costa-Gavras had learned that real politics had a complexity not reachable in his work.

The son of a Russian father and a Greek mother, he went to France in his teens and studied at the Sorbonne and IDHEC. He got his start as an assistant: *Tout l'Or du Monde* (61, René Clair); *La Baie des Anges* (63, Jacques Demy); and *Jour et l'Heure* (63, René Clément). Two decades later, he took over the directorship of the Cinematème Française, where he had had so much of his education.

Mad City suddenly suggested that the director had lost touch with the realities of politics and the media.

Kevin Costner, b. Los Angeles, 1955

For a few years in the middle to late 1980s, it was possible for trend-hungry journalists to hail Costner as *our* Gary Cooper—as if we had lost the original, or lived in an age that could sustain such stars anew. With four films—*The Untouchables, No Way Out, Bull Durham,* and *Field of Dreams*—Costner had made himself, suddenly, the star that nearly every would-be bankable script was sent to. He was reasonably handsome, passably virile, unequivocally ordinary—and his pictures made money. In the years since, he had only scooped up Oscars with *Dances With Wolves* (90, Costner) and done his best to test the limits of his own reliability.

He had immense power. Who else could have had *JFK* (91, Oliver Stone) made on the same lavish scale? Still, his limits were all too apparent: he made not the least concession to period for *Robin Hood: Prince of Thieves* (91, Kevin Reynolds); his narrative in *Dances With Wolves* harped on the untrained flatness and modernity of his voice; *Revenge* (90, Tony Scott) was a disaster he could not avert; and in *The Bodyguard* (92, Mick Jackson) he seemed stranded between being a secret service fussbudget and doing homage to Steve McQueen. He can be very uninteresting, and in

The Bodyguard he showed an embarrassment with love (not to mention sex) that reminded me of *No Way Out* (87, Roger Donaldson), where he seemed alarmed by the reckless but very open Sean Young.

Costner had been around for years before he made it: he was nineteen for a few moments in *Sizzle Beach* (Richard Brander—made in 1974 and given a video release in 86); *Shadows Run Black* (81, Howard Heard); *Night Shift* (82, Ron Howard); *Chasing Dreams* (82, Sean Roche); a B picture lead in *Stacy's Knights* (83, Jim Wilson); and *Table for Five* (83, Robert Lieberman).

He was famously cut as the dead Alex from *The Big Chill* (83, Lawrence Kasdan); he had a small role in *Testament* (83, Lynne Littman); and the lead in *The Gunrunner* (84, Nardo Castillo), another film that went unseen until 1989 video salvation. *American Flyer* (85, John Badham) was actually the first film to identify his common decency, and *Fandango* (85, Reynolds) was another helpful step forward. Then Kasdan used him and kept him in *Silverado* (85). But his first unmistakable hit was playing backup to everyone else, as Eliot Ness in *The Untouchables* (87, Brian De Palma), and really understanding the clerical tenor of the role.

In *No Way Out,* there was no way of acting that inside-out trickster—plot shock was everything, or nothing. But he was very good in *Bull Durham* (88, Ron Shelton), and as good as he has ever been in *Field of Dreams* (89, Phil Alden Robinson).

Dances With Wolves can easily be attacked. Yet the movie works, and—to these eyes—it has all the intelligence of a David Lean epic. As for Costner's Jim Garrison in *JFK,* it is as specious and threadbare as the whole film, and exposed by our one glimpse of the real Garrison, who evidently was somewhere between Buster Keaton and one of America's great con men. Humor is not yet Costner's strength.

What a nice, ironic intro that remark makes for Kevin Costner's last decade. For what has emerged is the most blatant example in screen history of an actor following his own fantasies—at enormous cost sometimes, without any offsetting humor, but doggedly, like some lone scout mapping the far northwest. It is dazzling, alarming and a warning to all in the last gasp of the age of film. And if anyone could ever have been close enough to Costner, observing, surviving and staying cool, it might make a fabulous book. For he is not like others—he has resolved not to be.

In hindsight, there were clues in *A Perfect World* (93, Clint Eastwood)—it was so slow and lugubrious for a Clint picture, and there was this mystical thing between Kevin and the kid, a kind of frontier philosophy was evolving and Clint seemed too bewildered to interfere. Then, with Costner producing, he was *Wyatt Earp* (94, Kasdan)—probably the longest, slowest, dullest film about Earp ever (there is competition), and that vague air of the whole thing being a political program. *The War* (94, Jon Avnet) was another curiosity, with Kevin speaking wisely to children, and seeming to take over the project.

This was as nothing compared with *Waterworld* (95, Reynolds—though apparently with Costner doing his bit) in which the daft, reactionary loner creed emerged in one of the more ravishingly absurd films of the nineties (there was competition). Whereupon looking just like your favorite puppy, Kevin did *Tin Cup* (96, Shelton), a lovely, fatuous dream for every Sunday golfer, in which Kevin does his Zen of the game act.

We hadn't seen anything yet: *The Postman* (97), which he produced and directed, was his noble disaster in which the lone mail carrier may save the world from apocalypse. I have to admit that the film had a dire fascination—it was enough to make one get up, abandon one's miserable life and follow St. Kevin into the lands of the heathen, if you could discern them (there was competition).

Then, o my brothers, he was Billy Chapel, the great old pitcher with a dead arm and a lost love—could he throw *For Love of the Game* (99, Sam Raimi)? He was a ringside fan to the shameless pugilism of *Play It to the Bone* (99, Shelton). And then he was Kenny O'Donnell helping the Pres save the world in *Thirteen Days* (00, Donaldson).

But Kevin likes Elvis, too, so he did *3000 Miles to Graceland* (01, Demian Lichtenstein). And let's not forget *Dragonfly* (02, Tom Shadyac), tempting as that would be.

And here is what it comes to: a man like Costner would be killed by humor. The gravity stands high and bright, like an eagle on the peak (no contest). He then acted in and directed a Western, *Open Range* (03).

Joseph Cotten (1905–94),
b. Petersburg, Virginia

Cotten was already a star of the stage when drawn to Hollywood by Orson Welles. Since 1930, he had appeared on Broadway in *The Postman Always Rings Twice*, with Katharine Hepburn in *The Philadelphia Story*, and in *Accent on Youth*. His association with Welles began through the Mercury Theater and Federal Theater Productions. It was perhaps Welles's slyness to cast Cotten—whose first job in the theatre had been as a reviewer—as the dramatic critic of the *Inquirer* and the most skeptical admirer of *Citizen Kane* (41). Ever after, Cotten hardly seemed the master of his own career. In *The Magnificent Ambersons* (42) he was again utterly convincing as the turned away suitor, not quite up to the proud Ambersons. Cotten also appeared in *Lydia* (41, Julien

Duvivier) and both acted in and wrote that Mercury charade *Journey into Fear* (43, Norman Foster). From Welles's influence he passed into the not quite as embracing hands of David Selznick. Despite Cotten's disturbingly good performance as the murderous uncle in Hitchcock's *Shadow of a Doubt* (43), Selznick carelessly loaned him out or employed him as orthodox romantic leads for Jennifer Jones: thus, the policeman in *Gaslight* (44, George Cukor); *Since You Went Away* (44, John Cromwell); *I'll Be Seeing You* (44) and *Love Letters* (45) both for Dieterle; the pale, good brother in *Duel in the Sun* (46, King Vidor); *The Farmer's Daughter* (47, H. C. Potter); and the wistful, morbid painter in *Portrait of Jennie* (49, Dieterle). His talents were briefly revived as the truculent groom-husband in Hitchcock's *Under Capricorn* (49) and, again teased by Welles, as Holly Martins, the gullible American in Vienna, in Carol Reed's *The Third Man* (49). After *September Affair* (50, Dieterle), *Two Flags West* (50, Robert Wise), and *Peking Express* (52, Dieterle), he settled increasingly for portrayals of henpecked middle age, as Monroe's wizened husband in *Niagara* (53, Henry Hathaway), in *Beyond the Forest* (49, Vidor), and *The Steel Trap* (52, Andrew L. Stone). He was more vigorous in *Untamed Frontier* (52, Hugo Fregonese); *Blueprint for Murder* (53, Stone); *Special Delivery* (55, John Brahm); *The Bottom of the Bottle* (56, Hathaway); *The Killer Is Loose* (56, Budd Boetticher); and *The Halliday Brand* (57, Joseph H. Lewis). But he began to take smaller parts in big pictures, like *Hush, Hush...Sweet Charlotte* (64, Robert Aldrich) and *Petulia* (68, Dick Lester); as boozed Southern colonels in Italian Westerns; as a surgeon unbelievably pursued by Vincent Price in *The Abominable Dr. Phibes* (71, Robert Fuest); the victim in *Soylent Green* (73, Richard Fleischer) and in *A Delicate Balance* (75, Tony Richardson); *Airport '77* (77, Jerry Jameson); *Twilight's Last Gleaming* (77, Aldrich); *Caravans* (78, James Fargo); *L'Isola degli Uomini Pesce* (79, Sergio Martino); *Guyana: The Crime of the Century* (79, René Cardona Jr.); *The House Where Evil Dwells* (79, Kevin Connor); *The Concorde Affair* (79, Ruggero Deodato); *The Hearse* (80, George Bowen); "Reverend Doctor" at the Harvard graduation in *Heaven's Gate* (80, Michael Cimino); and *The Survivor* (81, David Hemmings).

Cotten was never quite the romantic star Selznick took him for. His grace and attentiveness were also detached and dreamy, and Hitchcock saw how easily the crinkled face might be made morose. His best performances are in parts outside Hollywood conventions. Cotten was known as a practical joker, and he probably enjoyed testing Welles's guess at his future in *Kane*, where Leland is seen as both a youthful idealist and an old man left plotting with his memories and scrounging cigars. But he answered Welles's call, in 1958, to appear uncredited as the drunken coroner in *Touch of Evil*.

Sir Noël Coward (1899–1973),
b. Teddington, England

There was a time, in the last fifteen years or so of his life, when you could believe—if you were inclined—that a vigorous, manly, and rough-spoken generation of actors were sweeping "Cowardy custard" off the English stage. And a good thing, too? For some people growing up then, Coward was a bit of a mystery: his later plays were not very good; his pose as a model of cool manners was regarded as effete or snobbish; and the well-intentioned determination to get down to the nitty-gritty left little room for Coward. He and the underspeak of *Brief Encounter* (45, David Lean) had become dated, and I daresay that hurt him, for a part of him was terribly anxious to be up-to-date (even if he once, à la Wilde, said that no pursuit left you looking more old-fashioned).

And yet, if you take a film like *North by Northwest* (1959), it's hard to think that Cary Grant or James Mason could have carried on as they do but for Coward's example and legacy. It may be argued that Grant and Mason—and others, not least Olivier—actually played the Coward type more intriguingly than the master ever managed. So he wasn't that good an actor—or not on stage, where the limits of the day first restricted and then bored him. But how can one eliminate Noël Coward—his tone, his attitude, his way of speaking, his model—from the amazing invasion of Hollywood by actors born in England, often keeping their English voice and perversely trained to hide the point of the drama?

For Coward, it may have had as much to do with the need to veil gay yearnings as with the wish to suppress vulgar emotionalism; still, Coward more than anyone created (as author as much as actor) the manner of speaking that left us to read between the lines. Grant was actually much better at it than Olivier. And it's possible that Grant himself hardly noticed the influence (that is not true for Olivier, who admitted it, and surely came very close to an affair with Coward when they did *Private Lives* together). I don't think that matters. The way of acting had entered Grant's mind. It affected his bearing and the meaning of his films. So there's no need to dispute influence.

And we haven't even got yet to *In Which We Serve* (42, Lean and Coward) and *This Happy Breed* (44, Lean) and Coward's tremendous impact on the age of English (or British) actors that included Jack Hawkins, John Mills, Dirk Bogarde, David Niven, Richard Todd, Trevor Howard (though he heard other voices), Eric Port-man, Dennis Price, Nigel Patrick, and even Rex Harrison.

There are many incidentals about Coward that can get in the way: the fact that he had played in *Hearts of the World* (18, D. W. Griffith); his acting in *The Scoundrel* (35, Ben Hecht and Charles MacArthur); the chance that he could have been Harry Lime in *The Third Man;* the actual, older man in pictures like *Our Man in Havana* (60, Carol Reed); *Bunny Lake Is Missing* (65, Otto Preminger), and *Boom!* (68, Joseph Losey)—all interesting and acute but beside the point because he was no longer beautiful; to say nothing of the filmed plays, like *Design for Living* (33, Ernst Lubitsch), where Gary Cooper plainly doesn't know what it's all about; or even that the film of *Cavalcade* (33, Frank Lloyd) won best picture.

No, the influence is intimate and actorly, and it affects ideas of what a man, or a gentleman, is. And it certainly goes on. Listen to Harold Pinter and you will find the rhythms of Noël Coward, as well as the same awkward fascination with gayness. And now that the lust for male authenticity that so spurred the Method seems quaint, it's much easier to see gender ambiguity in, say, Kevin Spacey, Johnny Depp, Ralph Fiennes, Rupert Everett, Jude Law, Matt Damon, Hugh Grant . . . and how about Anthony Hopkins in *Hannibal?*

Paul Cox (Paulus Henriqus Benedictus Cox),
b. Venlo, Netherlands, 1940

1975: *Illuminations*. 1977: *Inside Looking Out*. 1979: *Kostas*. 1981: *Lonely Hearts*. 1983: *Man of Flowers*. 1984: *My First Wife*. 1985: *Death and Destiny*. 1986: *Cactus*. 1987: *Vincent—The Life and Death of Vincent Van Gogh* (d). 1989: *Island*. 1990: *The Golden Braid*. 1991: *A Woman's Tale*. 1992: *The Nun and the Bandit*. 1993: *Touch Me* (s). 1994: *Exile*. 1996: *Lust and Revenge*. 1997: *The Hidden Dimension* (d). *Molokai: The Story of Father Damien*. 2000: *Innocence*. 2002: *Nijinsky*.

So many directors have left Australia, it is important to stress that Cox only reached that land in his early twenties, bringing with him the anguished, visionary sensibility of one of his countrymen—Van Gogh. (Cox is the only Dutchman to have taken the painter as a subject, in a heartfelt documentary in which John Hurt was the voice of Van Gogh.)

In truth, Cox has not really used Australia. Rather, he has made his best pictures as intimate studies of solitude, madness, and dreams in faded middle-class settings that are occasionally illumined by the radiance of some lonely person's vision. *Man of Flowers* is his best work, with Norman Kaye outstanding as the Magritte-like figure who loves beauty. The autobiographical *My First Wife* is one of the most unrelievedly tortured accounts of a marital breakdown. *Lonely Hearts,* the film that established Cox, is still his most accessible film, with touching performances from Kaye and Wendy Hughes.

More recently, Cox has explored the theme of mortality and undying beauty in the world in *Cactus* (where Isabelle Huppert plays a woman going blind) and *A Woman's Tale,* made with a dying actress, Sheila Florance, and filled with wonder at the ways in which flesh reaches its terminus.

There can be a depressive tone in Cox's work, an aching sincerity that comes close to solemnity. But when his eye is encouraged into showing us inner worlds, he can be intransigent, secure, and immensely valuable. He may yet need to go to some smaller, finally remote island. Cox remains a brave personal adventurer, variable, romantic but driven. *Touch Me* was erotic, and *Innocence* is one of his best films—a story of elderly but passionate love. *Molokai* is exactly what its title says, but it is like *Exile* in that it shares a fascination with remote location and moral isolation. I have seen some of the material for *Nijinsky,* and failed to understand it—but it seems the kind of vision of the great dancer that a man might have if he lived on a tropic isle with shadows as his dancers.

Jeanne Crain, b. Barstow, California, 1925

Miss Long Beach of 1941, then a model, Jeanne Crain was one of the prettiest adornments of Fox costume films during the 1940s: *Home in Indiana* (44, Henry Hathaway); *In the Meantime, Darling* (44, Otto Preminger); *Winged Victory* (44, George Cukor); *State Fair* (45, Walter Lang); *Leave Her to Heaven* (45, John Stahl); *Centennial Summer* (46, Preminger); playing mother and daughter in *Margie* (46, Henry King), and very funny in its falling knickers sequence; *A Letter to Three Wives* (48, Joseph L. Mankiewicz); *Lady Windermere's Fan* (49, Preminger); *Pinky* (49, Elia Kazan), purportedly as a black, photographed in lustrous low key to show the studio's liberal intentions—Kazan said he relied on her "submissive vacuity"; *Cheaper by the Dozen* (50, Lang); *Take Care of My Little Girl* (51, Jean Negulesco); *The Model and the Marriage Broker* (51, Cukor); *People Will Talk* (51, Mankiewicz); "The Gift of the Magi" episode from *O. Henry's Full House* (52, King); *Belles on Their Toes* (52, Henry Levin); *Dangerous Crossing* (53, Joseph Newman); and *Vicki* (53, Harry Horner).

Ironically, once away from Fox, her sweet prettiness was subtly altered to a more sophisticated glamour and hints of sexiness in King Vidor's *Man Without a Star* (55). But no one cared to exploit this properly and her career trailed tamely away: *Duel in the Jungle* (54, George Marshall); *Gentlemen Marry Brunettes* (55, Richard Sale); *The Fastest Gun Alive* (56, Russell Rouse); *The Joker Is Wild* (57, Charles Vidor); *Madison Avenue* (61, Bruce Humberstone); *Twenty Plus Two* (61, Newman); *Pontius Pilate* (61, Irving Rapper); *Queen of the Nile* (63, Fernando Cerchio); *Hot Rods to Hell* (67, John Brahm); *The Night God Screamed* (71, Lee Madden); and *Skyjacked* (72, John Guillermin).

Wes Craven, b. Cleveland, Ohio, 1939

1972: *Last House on the Left.* 1977: *The Hills Have Eyes.* 1981: *Deadly Blessing.* 1982: *Swamp Thing.* 1984: *A Nightmare on Elm Street.* 1985: *The Hills Have Eyes II.* 1986: *Deadly Friend.* 1987: *A Nightmare on Elm Street 3—Dream Warriors.* 1988: *The Serpent and the Rainbow.* 1990: *Shocker.* 1991: *The People Under the Stairs.* 1994: *Wes Craven's New Nightmare.* 1995: *Vampire in Brooklyn.* 1996: *Scream.* 1999: *Scream 2.* 1999: *Music of the Heart.* 2000: *Scream 3.*

Is it humorless to be angry at Wes Craven? Or is it simply long past anyone's caring that someone with an excellent education, and already started as a teacher, should leap over into the drivel he has perpetrated, which veers from being cruel and hideous to saying, well, who ever thought to take this stuff seriously? Are the people who would vote, vaguely and blindly, for better pay for teachers (a swinging 7 percent increase on a salary of $35,000, say) just as likely to chuckle at one dry-as-dust academic who chucked it all for gold and gore?

Of course, it is worth saying that horror can be as valuable as good teaching (they can come very close). There are horror films—from *The Night of the Hunter* to *Vampyr,* from *Blue Velvet* to *Alien*—that are remarkable works of beauty, the imperiled imagination and our hope for virtue. Horror need not be as blunt and cynical as a giggly rip-off and the dank knowingness of the *Scream* pictures. Horror can be a basis for taste, skill, and poetry—Mr. Craven has not yet troubled the scorer on any of those accounts. Yet he is intelligent enough to know how surely the darts of horror do penetrate the vulnerable mind. He would surely have a smooth, funny riposte for why that reproach is archaic and sentimental. He is very rich.

Still, having studied philosophy at Johns Hopkins, he started to teach and then entered into filmmaking with *Last House on the Left,* a modernization of Bergman's *The Virgin Spring,* with loathsome rape and murder scenes. Craven directed, wrote, and edited, but he has seldom shown a real interest in any of those things. His concern has been to shock, and to profit from it.

His commercial breakthrough came with Freddie Krueger and the *Elm Street* pictures, though I find Louis Jourdan in *Swamp Thing* more intriguing, largely because Jourdan is a grave, melancholy actor rarely fulfilled. But there have been times when Craven the academic has shown through in his ironic appreciation of family structure as an horrific thing in itself.

But over the years maybe the most odious thing

about him is the postmodern self-reflection of *Wes Craven's New Nightmare* and the *Scream* pictures, which amounts to a frenzied, disdainful redoubling of nastiness because no one really believes in it. That is a dreadful manipulation of his own audience, with a view to excusing him and letting him feel superior. He is not alone, of course: real academe has people who write learned treatises on the imagery in Wes Craven, people who might faint at a drop of blood, but who have learned to gaze through the revolting fury of his films and see tenure beckoning. And surely there are kids in the dark who have lost their sense of secure reality, too, who hardly know what to believe. They see the stabbings of *Scream* and struggle to reconcile them with the film's "cool" pose. They are expected to share Mr. Craven's contempt, but they have less funding to help ensure that it stops short of self-contempt.

Meanwhile, having seen some kind of light, Mr. Craven can claim to be a reformed character: and so he splits his time between more *Scream*ing and the prestige of Meryl Streep going to East Harlem to help deprived kids. Why not? She plays a teacher!

Broderick Crawford (1911–1986), b. Philadelphia

The son of actors Lester Crawford and Helen Broderick, Broderick Crawford was squat, burly, fast talking, and belligerent. He began playing gangsters and knockabout comedy: *Woman Chases Man* (37, John Blystone); Hathaway's *The Real Glory* (39); *Beau Geste* (39, William Wellman); Tay Garnett's *Eternally Yours* (39); *Slightly Honorable* (40, Garnett); George Marshall's *When the Daltons Rode* (40); *Seven Sinners* (40, Garnett); *Trail of the Vigilantes* (40, Allan Dwan); *The Black Cat* (41, Albert S. Rogell); *Larceny Inc.* (42, Lloyd Bacon); and *Broadway* (42, William A. Seiter). After war service, he returned to cheap Westerns, *Night Unto Night* (47, Don Siegel); *Slave Girl* (47, Charles Lamont); *The Time of Your Life* (48, H. C. Potter); *A Kiss in the Dark* (49, Delmer Daves); and Irving Rapper's white *Anna Lucasta* (49). Robert Rossen then cast him as the demagogue in *All the King's Men* (49), a part so suited to Crawford's loudmouth style that he won an Oscar. But the same character is more cleverly portrayed in Cukor's *Born Yesterday* (50)—a Columbia film in which Crawford gives a remarkable likeness of the studio boss, Harry Cohn. Crawford never capitalized on these successes, and after *Lone Star* (52, Vincent Sherman), *Last of the Comanches* (52, André de Toth), *Scandal Sheet* (52, Phil Karlson), *Night People* (54, Nunnally Johnson), and Fritz Lang's *Human Desire* (54), he cashed in as the central figure in the TV series *Highway Patrol* (55–59). As a relaxation he played one of the swindlers in

Fellini's *Il Bidone* (55); in *New York Confidential* (55, Russell Rouse); *Not as a Stranger* (55, Stanley Kramer); *Big House, USA* (55, Howard W. Koch); Rouse's *The Fastest Gun Alive* (58); and as the heavy in *The Decks Ran Red* (58, Andrew L. Stone). When his TV career faded out, he returned to movies in small parts but his own monotonous bluster and the TV familiarity had largely exhausted his appeal. He became a support in B Westerns, such as *Red Tomahawk* (66, R. G. Springsteen); in *Embassy* (72, Gordon Hessler); *Smashing the Crime Syndicate* (73, Al Adamson); and *Terror in the Wax Museum* (73, Georg Fenady). He was also the victim of a serious automobile accident, but came back full force as the nation's top cleaner in *The Private Files of J. Edgar Hoover* (77, Larry Cohen); and played "Brod" in *A Little Romance* (79, George Roy Hill); *There Goes the Bride* (79, Terence Marcel); *Harlequin* (80, Simon Wincer); *Den Tuchtigen Gehort Die Welt* (81, Peter Patzak); and *Liar's Moon* (81, David Fisher).

Joan Crawford (Lucille Fay Le Sueur) (1906–77), b. San Antonio, Texas

One year after Joan Crawford's death, her adopted daughter Christina published *Mommie Dearest;* in another three years, that book had been brought to the screen, without any effort to balance or challenge the injured daughter's point of view. In the movie, Faye Dunaway offered a brilliant but lynching impersonation in which startling resemblance overwhelmed tougher tests of character credibility. And so Joan Crawford has passed into myth as a demented martinet whose greatest need or belief concerned padded clothes hangers. *Mommie Dearest* is, arguably, the most influential Hollywood memoir ever published. It changed the way publishers, readers, stars, and ghosts approached such volumes; and it pushed home the growing awareness that "Hollywood" was only a bad movie where lives were played out in the chiaroscuro of "camp."

I am not questioning the gist of what Christina Crawford had to say—the history of child abuse in the movie world is all too rich (even if most of the abuse is in spoiling), and well worth telling as a corrective to the burnished advertising with which Hollywood has regularly marketed the ideas of home and family. Still, *Mommie Dearest* threatens to obscure the real story of Joan Crawford; in turning her into nothing but a witch, it loses the fascinating ordeal and tragedy of her career. Remember that in wanting to adopt and possess perfect children (and in *believing* in perfect children), she was doing her best to live up to the crackpot ideology she had done so much to illustrate.

If nothing else, Crawford was the living and movie example of how a woman from very lowly, if not shady, places could triumph in that version of the American class system known as Hollywood royalty. Crawford sought to be an egalitarian heroine, standing up for herself among nobs, snobs, foreigners, and allegedly classy, educated actresses. For she was a star at MGM to rival Garbo, Norma Shearer, Jeanette MacDonald, Katharine Hepburn, Myrna Loy, and Lassie. Crawford was from hot, Latino Texas; her name had changed—her parents were a touch mysterious—and there was no end to the nasty stories about the things she had done to get ahead. That same Joan Crawford sought class, respectability, *respect*, and her terrific struggle to get there is one of the great career stories in pictures. Maybe the effort unhinged her; surely she behaved badly; and clearly her work deteriorated. But her Hollywood lost confidence long before she did, and she had to become strident and exaggerated. In the best Crawford films, she has the eye of aspiration and of a sweet hope that clothes, makeup, and position will mask all compromises made on the way: she was as Texan as Lyndon Johnson, as insecure and as close to caricature. And in two films called *Possessed*, as well as *Grand Hotel, Sadie McKee, Mannequin, The Women, Mildred Pierce, Daisy Kenyon, Harriet Craig, Johnny Guitar,* and *What Ever Happened to Baby Jane?*, there is a career as interesting as politics.

Her parents were divorced before or soon after her birth and the mother remarried Harry Cassin, owner of a vaudeville theatre—for a time thereafter she was known as Billie Cassin. At the age of six, she spent a year in bed after an accident to her foot. Two years later her mother and stepfather separated. The family traveled and the daughter's education suffered. In her teens, she wanted to be a dancer and she worked as a shopgirl to take lessons and enter dance competitions. She got small nightclub jobs before J. J. Shubert hired her for the Broadway chorus of *Innocent Eyes* in 1924. Spotted by Harry Rapf, in 1925 she was put under contract by MGM and made her debut in *Pretty Ladies* (Monta Bell). MGM organized a magazine contest to find her a new name and "Joan Crawford" was the winner. Her first films involved her in small, dancing parts but she won more attention in *Sally, Irene and Mary* (25, Edmund Goulding), played opposite Harry Langdon in *Tramp, Tramp, Tramp* (26, Harry Edwards), and had her first big success in *Our Dancing Daughters* (28, Harry Beaumont). She was the epitome of the flapper, but already marked for unhappiness.

Strongly backed by Louis B. Mayer, she became one of MGM's leading ladies: *Paid* (30, Sam Wood); *Dance, Fools, Dance* (31, Beaumont), the first of several appearances with Clark Gable; *Possessed* (31, Clarence Brown); *Grand Hotel* (32, Goulding), from which she emerged more cred-

itably than Garbo, one of her chief rivals at MGM; and *Dancing Lady* (33, Robert Z. Leonard). Despite a failure as Sadie Thompson in Lewis Milestone's *Rain* (32), she made the transition to more sophisticated parts: Howard Hawks's *Today We Live* (33); *Sadie McKee* (34) and *Chained* (34), both for Clarence Brown; *No More Ladies* (35, Edward H. Griffith); *I Live My Life* (35, W. S. Van Dyke); and *The Last of Mrs. Cheyney* (37, Richard Boleslavsky and George Fitzmaurice). She still played women tainted by humble origins and blighted in love.

The similarity of parts led to a crisis, and by 1938 she was considered box-office poison. She was restored by two Frank Borzage films, *Mannequin* (38) and *The Shining Hour* (38), and by Cukor's *The Women* (39), a picture that emphasized her glamorous hardness, her social disqualification, and her eventual failure in romance. After *Strange Cargo* (40, Borzage), *Susan and God* (40, Cukor), and *A Woman's Face* (41, Cukor), her career again slumped and in 1943 she left MGM.

Despite signing with Warners, she made no film for almost two years and even took singing lessons with opera in mind. Jerry Wald asked her to return in *Mildred Pierce* (45, Michael Curtiz)—her first film as a mother, which was built around her capacity for suffering and won her an Oscar. Securing her image of a middle-aged career woman, she made *Humoresque* (47, Jean Negulesco), was very good having a breakdown in *Possessed* (47, Curtis Bernhardt), and *Daisy Kenyon* (47, Otto Preminger), the latter one of her most controlled and touching performances. But her suffering became more bizarre—in *Flamingo Road* (49, Curtiz) and *This Woman Is Dangerous* (52, Felix Feist) she ended up in jail. In *Harriet Craig* (50, Vincent Sherman), she was outstanding and prescient as a domestic perfectionist. David Miller's *Sudden Fear* (52) involved her in genuine menace, beset by the youthful Jack Palance, but in *Torch Song* (53, Charles Walters) she had only blind-pianist Michael Wilding as a feed.

As she grew fiercer, so her films and male stars seem to have become weaker. In 1954, she made *Johnny Guitar* for Nicholas Ray, and it was all Sterling Hayden could do to stand up to her in recriminating dialogues. And in 1957 she was the horrified guardian of a raped girl in *The Story of Esther Costello* (Miller). Only Robert Aldrich subsequently rescued her from dross—in *Autumn Leaves* (56) and *What Ever Happened to Baby Jane?* (62), which reflects more on her life in movies than on Bette Davis's. Not content with that ordeal, she went on to more grotesque horrors, chiefly in the hands of William Castle: *Strait Jacket* (64) and *I Saw What You Did* (65).

Much of her fictional agony was borne out in

reality. After a series of failed marriages—to Douglas Fairbanks Jr., Franchot Tone, and Philip Terry—and several miscarriages, she adopted four children and, in 1955, married Alfred Steele, the chairman of Pepsi-Cola. After his death, in 1959, she became the first female director of the company and its official hostess. Her career is that of a preeminent star, digesting poor material and impressing her own image on everything. Always rising to good directors and stories, she is most herself in pulp, staring out at us with savage mouth and rueful eyes. As such, she is an icon in a woman's magazine dreamworld—as one character refers to her in *Torch Song*, a "gypsy madonna." Scott Fitzgerald captured its monolithic fierceness: "She can't change her emotions in the middle of a scene without going through a sort of Jekyll and Hyde contortion of the face. . . . Also, you can never give her such a stage direction as 'telling a lie,' because if you did, she would practically give a representation of Benedict Arnold selling West Point to the British." In truth, she could do much more: she was a pioneer of tough, hurt feelings—until that cause made her too bitter.

Laird Cregar (Samuel Laird Cregar) (1916–45), b. Philadelphia
Cregar was an oddity who had a short hour at the feast. Younger than he looked and seriously overweight, he went in for fierce diets that contributed to fatal heart strain. He would not have been as interesting if lean, for he was the perfect example of shambling bulk harboring an etiolated spirit. It helps explain his high-strung menace and fastidious grossness to note that, at the beginning of his career, he had a great success playing Oscar Wilde onstage. Up to that point, he had had only small parts in movies: *Granny Get Your Gun* (40, George Amy). But after Oscar, he went to Fox and over the next five years put together some florid character studies. He could be contemporary and malicious—as in *This Gun for Hire* (42, Frank Tuttle)—but he is at his best as a cultivated man possessed by evil. He was in *Hudson's Bay* (40, Irving Pichel); *Blood and Sand* (41, Rouben Mamoulian); *Charley's Aunt* (41, Archie Mayo); *I Wake Up Screaming* (41, Bruce Humberstone); *Joan of Paris* (42, Robert Stevenson); *Rings On Her Fingers* (42, Mamoulian); *Ten Gentlemen from West Point* (42, Henry Hathaway); *The Black Swan* (42, Henry King); as a suave Devil in *Heaven Can Wait* (43, Ernst Lubitsch); and *Holy Matrimony* (43, John M. Stahl).

He finished with his best work, two enjoyably lurid accounts of mad genius for John Brahm: as Jack the Ripper in *The Lodger* (44), and the "composer," George Harvey Bone, in *Hangover Square*. However, the film of *Hangover Square* is also a wretched travesty of Patrick Hamilton's novel (in which Bone is not a composer). Cregar had urged the book on the studio; and he was mortified by the result. His friend George Sanders (who is in the film) believed that the shock hastened Cregar's death. *Hangover Square*—for all Brahm's style, and Bernard Herrmann's mad music—still waits to be filmed properly.

Donald Crisp (1880–1974),
b. Aberfeldy, Scotland
Donald Crisp was a grand old man of the cinema who became increasingly endearing the more he tried to be a stern Scot. Although retired for his last ten years—since the age of eighty-three—his span was remarkable.

After Eton and Oxford, he served in the Boer War. In 1906 he went to America as an actor. By 1910, he had joined D. W. Griffith at Biograph: *The Two Paths* (10); *Fate's Turning* (10); *The Battle* (11); *The Battle of the Sexes* (14); *The Escape* (14); *Home Sweet Home* (14); as Grant in *The Birth of a Nation* (15); *Intolerance* (16); and Battling Burrows in *Broken Blossoms* (19). As well as acting for the master, Crisp apparently worked for the British secret service during the First World War and began directing himself, for Reliance-Majestic and Mutual: *The Dawn* (14); *Ramona* (16); *The Countess Charming* (17); *Under the Top* (18); *It Pays to Advertise* (19); *Too Much Johnson* (19); and *The Six Best Cellars* (20). He worked steadily as a director throughout the 1920s, though no more than an enthusiastic recorder of such stars as Douglas Fairbanks and Keaton. Indeed, Keaton hired him for *The Navigator* (24) and found that Crisp's experience with drama so swiftly adapted to gags that the Scot had to be restrained—there is something very appealing in "old stoneface" having to tell the eager Crisp to calm down. In addition, Crisp directed *Appearances* (21); *The Barbarian* (21); *The Bonnie Brier Bush* (21), in which he acted; *The Princess of New York* (21); *Ponjola* (23); *Don Q, Son of Zorro* (25), in which he acted; *Man Bait* (26); *Sunny Side Up* (26); *Young April* (26); *Dress Parade* (27); *The Fighting Eagle* (27); *Nobody's Widow* (27); *Vanity* (27); *The Cop* (28); *Stand and Deliver* (28); and *The Runaway Bride* (30).

That was the last film he directed. With sound, perhaps he found direction too complex—he was almost fifty. Thereafter, he concentrated on acting: *The River Pirate* (28, William K. Howard); *The Pagan* (29, W. S. Van Dyke); as Sigsbee Manderson in *Trent's Last Case* (29, Howard Hawks); as Leif Ericsson in *The Viking* (29, Roy William Neill); *Scotland Yard* (30, Howard); *Svengali* (31, Archie Mayo); *A Passport to Hell* (32, Frank Lloyd); *Red Dust* (32, Victor Fleming); *What Every Woman Knows* (34, Gregory La Cava); *The Little Minister* (34, Richard Wallace); *Laddie* (35,

George Stevens); *Oil for the Lamps of China* (35, Mervyn Le Roy); *Mutiny on the Bounty* (35, Lloyd); *Mary of Scotland* (36, John Ford); *The Charge of the Light Brigade* (36, Michael Curtiz); *A Woman Rebels* (36, Mark Sandrich); *Parnell* (37, John M. Stahl); *The Life of Emile Zola* (37, William Dieterle); *Jezebel* (38, William Wyler); *The Amazing Dr. Clitterhouse* (38, Anatole Litvak); *Wuthering Heights* (39, Wyler); as Bacon in *The Private Lives of Elizabeth and Essex* (39, Curtiz); *Juarez* (39, Dieterle); *The Sea Hawk* (40, Curtiz); *Brother Orchid* (40, Lloyd Bacon); *Dr. Jekyll and Mr. Hyde* (41, Fleming); as the father in *How Green Was My Valley* (41, Ford), winning the supporting actor Oscar; *The Gay Sisters* (42, Irving Rapper); *Lassie Come Home* (43, Fred McLeod Wilcox); *National Velvet* (44, Clarence Brown); *The Uninvited* (44, Lewis Allen); *The Adventures of Mark Twain* (44, Rapper); *Son of Lassie* (45, Sylvan Simon); *Valley of Decision* (45, Tay Garnett); *Ramrod* (47, André de Toth); *Challenge to Lassie* (49, Richard Thorpe); *Bright Leaf* (50, Curtiz); *Prince Valiant* (54, Henry Hathaway); *The Long Gray Line* (55, Ford); in his best performance, as the Lear-like father in *The Man from Laramie* (55, Anthony Mann); *Drango* (57, Hall Bartlett); *Saddle the Wind* (58, Robert Parrish); *The Last Hurrah* (58, Ford); *Pollyanna* (60, David Swift); and *Spencer's Mountain* (63, Delmer Daves).

John Cromwell (Elwood Dagger Cromwell) (1888–1979), b. Toledo, Ohio

1929: *Close Harmony* (codirected with Edward Sutherland); *The Dance of Life* (codirected with Sutherland); *The Mighty*. 1930: *Street of Chance; The Texan; For the Defense; Tom Sawyer*. 1931: *Scandal Sheet; Unfaithful; The Vice Squad; Rich Man's Folly*. 1932: *The World and the Flesh*. 1933: *Sweepings; The Silver Cord; Double Harness; Ann Vickers*. 1934: *This Man Is Mine; Spitfire; Of Human Bondage; The Fountain*. 1935: *Village Tale; Jalna; I Dream Too Much*. 1936: *Little Lord Fauntleroy; To Mary—With Love; Banjo On My Knee*. 1937: *The Prisoner of Zenda*. 1938: *Algiers*. 1939: *Made for Each Other; In Name Only; Abe Lincoln in Illinois*. 1940: *Victory*. 1941: *So Ends Our Night; Son of Fury*. 1944: *Since You Went Away*. 1945: *The Enchanted Cottage*. 1946: *Anna and the King of Siam*. 1947: *Dead Reckoning; Night Song*. 1950: *Caged; The Company She Keeps*. 1951: *The Racket*. 1958: *The Goddess*. 1961: *De Sista Stegen/A Matter of Morals*. 1963: *The Scavengers*.

When sound hit the movies, Cromwell was nearly forty, and he had a fine career as actor and director onstage. But then, for over twenty years (until he came under suspicion for leftist sympathies), he had a successful Hollywood career as a deft, self-effacing director who was especially sensitive to women and respectful of novels and plays. Was there more than that? I find it hard to detect theme or personality, and nothing Cromwell ever offered in interviews encouraged such hopes. It was his intent to "realize" scripts and do the best job possible. It may be telling that he was one of the favorite directors of David O. Selznick, who appreciated men prepared to be the humble and tireless enablers of his dreams and second thoughts. Thus, Cromwell did Selznick International's first film, the Freddie Bartholomew *Little Lord Fauntleroy,* without a tremor of shame over the old-fashioned material and attitudes. He did a good job with the plot and the action of *The Prisoner of Zenda,* though Selznick was driven to bringing Cukor and Woody Van Dyke in for scenes that needed more than routine work. Above all, Cromwell directed Claudette Colbert, Jennifer Jones, and Shirley Temple in *Since You Went Away,* a picture that bled from Selznick's soft heart.

But there is much more that is interesting: Kim Stanley, otherwise a nonentity in the American cinema, is very striking in *The Goddess* and even occasionally persuades us that she is beautiful enough to be a great movie star; Bette Davis gloated over Mildred's acidity in *Of Human Bondage;* Laura Hope Crews is one of film's most disastrous, smothering mothers in *The Silver Cord;* Charles Boyer and Hedy Lamarr made a broody couple in *Algiers;* Irene Dunne and Rex Harrison did *Anna and the King of Siam* with all talk and no songs; *Sweepings* is a kind of weepie with Lionel Barrymore as the businessman head of the family; *The Fountain* is an exceptional rendering of a Charles Morgan novel, with a fine performance from Ann Harding; Raymond Massey is a very subtle Lincoln in *Abe Lincoln in Illinois; Caged* is a remorseless account of prison turning Eleanor Parker into a hardened criminal, and a shrewd estimate of fascism as personified by Hope Emerson's monstrous matron; while *Dead Reckoning* is an overly complex flashback thriller with Bogart being double-crossed by Lizabeth Scott. Years later, Bogart's "Geronimo" in *Dead Reckoning* is memorable for its self-pastiche, quivering but droll.

There are several failures—*The Enchanted Cottage* does not wear well; *The Racket* is listless, no matter that Nicholas Ray came in to direct some of it after an ailing Cromwell quit; *In Name Only* manages to waste Cary Grant and Carole Lombard in lengthy tearjerker passages.

The idiosyncratic casting eye of Robert Altman recalled Cromwell to the screen in a small part in *3 Women* (77), playing with his last wife, Ruth Nelson, and a classic scene-stealer as a fuddled bishop in *A Wedding* (78).

David Cronenberg,

b. Toronto, Canada, 1943

1966: *Transfer* (s). 1967: *From the Drain* (s). 1969: *Stereo* (s). 1970: *Crimes of the Future* (s). 1975: *The Parasite Murders/They Came from Within/ Shivers*. 1977: *Rabid*. 1979: *The Brood; Fast Company*. 1981: *Scanners*. 1983: *The Dead Zone; Videodrome*. 1986: *The Fly*. 1988: *Dead Ringers*. 1991: *Naked Lunch*. 1993: *M. Butterfly*. 1996: *Crash*. 1999: *eXistenZ*. 2000: *Camera* (s). 2002: *Spider*.

If one entertains suspicions that the post-*Psycho* vogue for horror pictures by new directors is far too much of a bad thing—slick, overeffectsy, heartless, spectacular, adolescent, exploitative— then Cronenberg is perhaps the most valuable item in the argument. Horror for Cronenberg is not a game or a meal ticket; it is, rather, the natural expression for one of the best directors working today. For Cronenberg's subject is the intensity of human frailty and decay: in short, the body and its many accelerated mutations, whether out of disease, anger, dread, or hope. These are not easy films to take. But how can horror be easy? Anyone born and reckoning on dying needs to confront Cronenberg.

His father was a pulp-fiction writer, his mother a musician. Cronenberg was an outstanding student, and at the University of Toronto he switched honors courses, from science to English language and literature—thus his fearsome poetics of machinery?

From experimental, art-school-like shorts at university, Cronenberg plunged into what looked like low-budget exploitation movies. *They Came from Within* (the most Cronenbergian title for his first feature) was a metaphor for syphilis, as if from the point of view of the disease. For usually in Cronenberg the malady or the great warping of life is itself a new life force, as innocent as King Kong. He has the mind-set that could make cancer a hero.

Rabid cast porn actress Marilyn Chambers as a vampire who grows a secret impaling prong in her armpit. Here was the debut of Cronenberg's urge to examine the body as a remarkable glory: in truth, his freaks are no stranger than our wholesome selves. *The Brood* used Oliver Reed and Samantha Eggar in its brilliant metaphor for the distortions of anger.

By the 1980s, Cronenberg had become a controversial artist, especially in Canada. Many viewers and critics were repulsed by the shocking bodily flowerings he showed us. And not enough people had the stomach to see either the beauty, or the dismayed respect for life in Cronenberg's films. *The Dead Zone* and *Videodrome* demonstrated not only his intelligence, but his response to all the controversy. They are films in which he seems ready to educate us in how to watch him.

The Dead Zone was not "his"; it came from a Stephen King story, and cast Christopher Walken as an archetypically pale, wasted Cronenberg hero, a man afflicted with being able to see the end of life in anyone he touches. There was less blood, less bodily malfunction, and every effort made to show the Walken character as a cursed intelligence. *Videodrome,* on the other hand, is a commentary on how films and television have altered our notions of reality and fantasy. It contains the superbly witty invention of an outlet in the human body where image may be plugged in.

Cronenberg's development was now momentous. *The Fly* was a genuine Hollywood film, a love story, rich in morbid humor, and a metaphor for genius and for any and every disease mankind has faced. As never before, in the relationship between Jeff Goldblum and Geena Davis, Cronenberg's compassion was revealed. Indeed, *The Fly* is only incidentally a horror film; it is primarily a screwball romance, one of the great movies about the kinship of freaks and . . . the rest of us.

As if that were not enough, *Dead Ringers* was a masterpiece—one of the few such achievements in the 1980s. It is about twins, about sadomasochism, surgery, dread of sexuality, the juxtaposition of warm flesh and bright steel, and it is about Jeremy Irons. For here, at last, Cronenberg was revealed as a director who cherished actors and could see their capacities. *Dead Ringers* is also a masterly exploration of decor, editing, and narrative structure; it has some of the austerity of Fritz Lang, or Ernst Lubitsch.

Naked Lunch seemed casual by comparison, and it may show some problem for Cronenberg in finding new material. The use of Burroughs was dry and inventive, and the film as a whole took drugs for granted in a way movies still find hard. But it had less kick than any other Cronenberg film. He seemed a little tamed, or perhaps to be marking time. The dilemma is a measure of where the medium stands. Cronenberg might be thought of as the proper director for a film about AIDS, except that he has done it several times already. He requires great challenges, and it may be that telepathic communication is the subject that really beckons him. *M. Butterfly* was a misguided choice and a difficult film to take seriously.

It seems to me that, in recent years, Cronenberg has come close to self-parody: *Crash* never seemed to realize how inadvertently comic it had become—and it missed the real shock of J. G. Ballard's literary original. As for *eXistenZ*, it seemed to indicate Cronenberg's increased difficulty in finding fruitful metaphors for his obsessions.

Bing Crosby (Harry Lillis Crosby) (1903–77),

b. Tacoma, Washington

Crosby excelled in that area where film meets

advertising. He was the proof that unexceptional, lazy pleasantry was more desirable than prickly, difficult originality. All of Crosby's assertions that he was plain-looking, sang casually, and acted hopefully only demonstrated his unerring nearness to American hearts. No one could argue that his contribution to cinema has been significant. Still, he has a good case as the most popular American to appear in movies. He was the most successful entertainer of the 1930s; he made movies as Elvis did thirty years later. His singing had all the charming naturalness that every amateur crooner believed lay within his grasp. He moved smoothly from college glee singer to the lead in light musicals to an unstuffy young priest and on to the relaxed veteran status. He existed, pipe in mouth, straw hat perched on his ears, beneath which the widow's peak toupee stood as firm as the faces on Mount Rushmore. It would be unjust to call him dull. More accurate to say that for forty years he skirted risk. His ease is that of the soft option. It is barely noticeable that he is interested in nothing, for interest dies away on his soft voice and drowsy smile.

He went from college to sing with Paul Whiteman and, after a series of shorts for Mack Sennett, he appeared with the band in *King of Jazz* (30, John Anderson). After *Reaching for the Moon* (31, Edmund Goulding) and a successful radio show, he was contracted by Paramount and began a long series of musicals: *The Big Broadcast* (32, Frank Tuttle); *Too Much Harmony* (33, Edward Sutherland); *Going Hollywood* (33, Raoul Walsh); *She Loves Me Not* (34, Elliott Nugent); with W. C. Fields in *Mississippi* (35, Sutherland); *Two for Tonight* (35, Tuttle); *The Big Broadcast of 1936* (36, Norman Taurog); *Anything Goes* (36, Lewis Milestone); *Pennies from Heaven* (36, Norman Z. McLeod); *Waikiki Wedding* (37, Tuttle); *Dr. Rhythm* (38, Tuttle); *Paris Honeymoon* (39, Tuttle); *East Side of Heaven* (39, David Butler); and *The Star Maker* (39, Roy del Ruth).

In 1940, he was teamed with Bob Hope and Dorothy Lamour in *The Road to Singapore* (40, Victor Schertzinger), still an alumnus, even if sometimes driven to trickery to confound the craven Hope. His easy tidiness bound the trio and his singing papered the tattered plots together. War only boosted his reassuring appeal: *If I Had My Way* (40, Butler); *Rhythm on the River* (40, Schertzinger); *The Road to Zanzibar* (41, Schertzinger); *Birth of the Blues* (41, Schertzinger); a good deal enlivened by Astaire in *Holiday Inn* (42, Mark Sandrich), where he sang "White Christmas"—another ingredient of the advertising dream; *The Road to Morocco* (42, Butler); and *Dixie* (43, Sutherland).

Then came the part of Father O'Malley, opposite Barry Fitzgerald, in *Going My Way* (44, Leo McCarey), a feast of righteous sentimentality that

won an Oscar for Crosby. The follow-up was *The Bells of St. Mary's* (45, McCarey), with Ingrid Bergman in the Barry Fitzgerald role. Crosby was unaltered in *Blue Skies* (46, Stuart Heisler) and *The Road to Utopia* (46, Hal Walker), but he was gradually made to look pale by the style of the MGM musicals and by the abrasiveness of Sinatra in the early 1950s. Crosby still seemed to belong to college: *Welcome Stranger* (47, Elliott Nugent); *The Road to Rio* (47, McLeod); *The Emperor Waltz* (48, Billy Wilder); *A Connecticut Yankee in King Arthur's Court* (49, Tay Garnett); *Top o' the Morning* (49, David Miller); *Riding High* (50, Frank Capra); *Here Comes the Groom* (51, Capra); *Just for You* (52, Nugent); and *The Road to Bali* (52, Walker).

He had a great success in *White Christmas* (54, Michael Curtiz) and then took on the role of a failed star in *The Country Girl* (54, George Seaton), opposite Grace Kelly. It was mournful rather than touching but as assured as everything he had ever done. In 1956 he rehashed *Anything Goes* (Robert Lewis) and had the luck to appear in *High Society* (56, Charles Walters), a measured application of gloss that exactly suited him. After that, his family life (with Kathryn Grant) and the pursuit of golf were interrupted only by *Man on Fire* (57, Ranald MacDougall); as a priest again in *Say One for Me* (59, Frank Tashlin); *High Time* (60, Blake Edwards); *The Road to Hong Kong* (62, Norman Panama); *Robin and the Seven Hoods* (64, Gordon Douglas); and *Stagecoach* (66, Douglas). He drifts on straight down the middle, goes fishing to where the blue of the night meets the gold of the day—it's all on the map for the treasure hunt on the back of the cereal box. That he was, in fact, a rather bitter man, a fierce parent, and a cold companion only adds to the marvel.

Cameron Crowe,

b. Palm Springs, California, 1957
1989: *Say Anything*. 1992: *Singles*. 1996: *Jerry Maguire*. 2000: *Almost Famous*. 2001: *Vanilla Sky*.

Cameron Crowe was writing for *Rolling Stone* as a child—well, technically, a young teenager—and he jumped over into movies when his novel *Fast Times at Ridgemont High* (82, Amy Herkerling) was made into a hit movie, with Crowe doing the screenplay. He then wrote and coproduced a flat follow-up, *The Wild Life* (84, Art Linson)—but maybe the fault there was Linson's. A few years later, Crowe was back on form writing and directing *Say Anything*, which had a lovely John Cusack and the intriguing theme of charm meeting brains. *Singles* was fine, but not as deep, and no preparation for *Jerry Maguire*—a fanciful story about being a top sports agent and being happy, so cunning a bit of humor, romance, and whimsy that it grabbed all of America and gave Tom Cruise an unmissible role. *Almost Famous* was his own start at *Rolling Stone,* and a lot of fun, yet maybe sanitized enough for Mom.

It's not quite clear where Crowe will go now. He is full of promise, but is he really in the Billy Wilder class? No matter the 1999 publication of his fond yet rather superficial book *Conversations with Billy Wilder. Vanilla Sky* should pass as an aberration, or as a debt of friendship to Tom Cruise. That horribly far-fetched fabrication does not seem like Crowe's kind of venture.

Russell (Ira) **Crowe,**
b. Wellington, New Zealand, 1964
In the late nineties, the thought stirred that perhaps a great new actor had come to the movies who was not French, Italian, American, or British. These are early days for Russell Crowe, but it really isn't outrageous to say that so far, he's delivered no less than three performances that surpass his Oscar-winning *Gladiator* (00, Ridley Scott). Not that I mean to minimize the skill, the determination, and the smarts that could play a Roman of honor at a time when that model is scorned, or who could insist on presence in a film so full of special effects.

Still, there's even more to be said for his brutish but brutalized cop, the working-class Bud, in *L.A. Confidential* (97, Curtis Hanson); for his bulky, insecure whistle-blower in *The Insider* (99, Michael Mann); and for the troubled genius in *A Beautiful Mind* (01, Ron Howard).

Just as remarkable as those four roles in four years is the way in which, until a moment before his breakthrough, Crowe was treated like a rugged action hero, another Mel Gibson (though without the cheek or charm). Today, his advantages in any comparison with Gibson are painfully apparent. The question arises as to whether there are things he can't do.

He was raised in Australia and he was acting on TV as a child. Later he worked in theatre and film, but then came to America with a run of little-known pictures: *The Crossing* (90, George Ogilvie); as a POW in *Prisoners of the Sun* (91, Stephen Wallace); *The Efficiency Expert* (92, Mark Joffe); *Proof* (92, Jocelyn Moorhouse); winning awards as the skinhead thug in *Romper Stomper* (92, Geoffrey Wright); *Hammers Over the Anvil* (93, Ann Turner); *Love in Limbo* (93, David Elfick); *The Silver Stallion* (93, John Tatoulis); *For the Moment* (94, Aaron Kim Johnston); as the gay son in *The Sum of Us* (94, Kevin Dowling).

Settling in America, he did *The Quick and the Dead* (95, Sam Raimi); *Virtuosity* (95, Brett Leonard); *Rough Magic* (95, Clare Peploe); *No Way Back* (97, Frank A. Cappello); *Breaking Up* (97, Robert Greenwald); *Heaven's Burning* (97,

Craig Lahiff); *Mystery, Alaska* (99, Jay Roach).

He also made *Proof of Life* (00, Taylor Hackford), where his man of honor turned subtly into a romantic figure. The effect this had on costar Meg Ryan was one more sign that Russell Crowe is a serious proposition. *A Beautiful Mind* was further evidence that Crowe was established as an actor of nearly infinite reach. Equally, it raised some doubts as to where his creative character could settle. Or would he have to be different with every film?

He can also be seen in *Master and Commander: The Far Side of the World* (03, Peter Weir).

Billy Crudup, b. Manhasset, New York, 1968
Did Billy Crudup go for doing *The Elephant Man* onstage to escape all the talk about how good-looking he is? Put it another way, how long before we pick up on what a very promising actor he is— a natural figure of youth, hope, and energy, yet smart enough to suggest so much more? He made his debut in *Sleepers* (96, Barry Levinson), and he had a small part in *Everyone Says I Love You* (96, Woody Allen). But he began to develop with *Inventing the Abbotts* (97, Pat O'Connor); *Grind* (97, Chris Kentis); *Snitch* (98, Ted Demme) and *Without Limits* (98, Robert Towne), where he was so appealing as Steve Prefontaine, and so impressive a runner, we really wanted him to win.

He had another lead role in *The Hi-Lo Country* (98, Stephen Frears); as the Denis Johnson druggie in *Jesus' Son* (98, Alison Maclean); excellent in *Waking the Dead* (00, Keith Gordon); very touching in *Almost Famous* (00, Cameron Crowe); *World Traveler* (01, Bart Freundlich); and credibly French in *Charlotte Gray* (01, Gillian Armstrong); *Big Fish* (03, Burton).

Tom Cruise (Thomas Cruise Mapother IV),
b. Syracuse, New York, 1962
There are those who like to jump on Tom Cruise as the representative of all that is most immature in America cinema today. They see the cockiness, the grin, the huge box-office success, and the sudden lapses. In that spirit, Cruise is the worst of the brats because he has gone the farthest.

But consider: when Clark Gable was thirty (in 1931), he had only just begun to make movies like *A Free Soul, Possessed,* and *Susan Lenox: Her Fall and Rise.* Now, in our collective recollection, Gable may seem older, worldlier, and more grown-up than Cruise was at thirty. But when did Gable ever risk playing the jerk to whom Cruise was totally committed in *The Color of Money* (86, Martin Scorsese)? When was Gable as uninhibitedly tender as Cruise managed in *Risky Business* (83, Paul Brickman)? And could Gable have survived the black-hole narcissism of Dustin Hoffman in *Rain Man* (88, Barry Levinson) and let us know we were watching a more complex and worthwhile character at the edges of the story, while Oscar was being won?

Cruise is very good. Consider that pack of novices in Francis Coppola's *The Outsiders* (83). Cruise was not much noticed then among Matt Dillon, Rob Lowe, Emilio Estevez, Patrick Swayze, Ralph Macchio, and C. Thomas Howell (this team is a great tribute to the foresight of Coppola and his casting wizard, Fred Roos). But he has gone on to so much richer and more coherent a career and so little wish to impose himself or his attitude upon his pictures. Cruise is one of the first young actors who seems unaffected by the impact of Brando or Clift, and much more inspired by the example of a Gable or a Grant. He wants to work.

Not that his early life was free from the bases for neuroses or unease. Cruise came from a broken home. His life was nomadic. He had a form of dyslexia. He had a very poor early relationship with his father. But a wrestling injury at school urged him into musicals, and after school he had a few roaming years, trying to learn, trying to stay alive. Very few.

He had a small role in *Endless Love* (81, Franco Zeffirelli) and he made a big impression as the belligerent cadet in *Taps* (81, Harold Becker). *Losin' It* (83, Curtis Hanson) was a disaster lost in the dazzle of *The Outsiders, Risky Business,* and *All the Right Moves* (83, Michael Chapman).

Since then, his career has taken some odd or mistaken directions, increasingly because he is so bankable—big stars can fall into the worst hands: *Legend* (85, Ridley Scott); *Top Gun* (86, Tony Scott), the picture that made him, and a piece of high-tech jingoism so remarkably depressing it is all the more admirable that he survived. *Cocktail* (88, Roger Donaldson) was the silliest vehicle, and *Days of Thunder* (90, Tony Scott) was all vehicles and crash helmets, apart from introducing him to his second wife, Nicole Kidman (he was previously married to Mimi Rogers). He and Kidman were teamed in *Far and Away* (92, Ron Howard), without much joy or chemistry.

Born on the Fourth of July (89, Oliver Stone) was a key step in the decline of its director, but Cruise was unrestrained and passionate as the hero. If Cruise had not yet been in an unmistakably good film, he had shown a range as an actor, and a willingness, that are impressive. By the time he was forty, Gable had done *Red Dust, It Happened One Night, Mutiny on the Bounty, China Seas, San Francisco, Idiot's Delight,* and Rhett Butler. Of course, careers do not know such ease now. Cruise is going to have to remake himself at every turn—and there may not be enough good people to trust. He is very professional—but is there now a profession? Thus he made himself the motor of *A Few Good Men* (92, Rob Reiner), and mounted a real challenge to Jack Nicholson in the climax. Similarly, he carried the long, complicated *The Firm* (93, Sidney Pollack) and let us see how his quick eyes were working out the story.

Following Cruise has not been easy going the last few years. *Interview with the Vampire* (94, Neil Jordan) was plainly a brave departure—and one that surely added to the legends about his sexual orientation. But it was a bad film, and he was hardly comfortable in it. Next he secured his treasury with those two horrible wastes of time, expertise and writing talent: *Mission: Impossible* (96, Brian De Palma) and *Mission: Impossible II* (00, John Woo).

Then there is *Eyes Wide Shut* (99, Stanley Kubrick) and the whole business of Tom and Nicole. That film, and its prolonged mission to England, were heavy commitments for the couple—and who knows how far their marriage and their psychic welfare were caught up in the picture? So again, the boldness was admirable—and the film was lousy. Worse than that, Cruise seemed more ill at ease and had less fruitful screen time than Kidman. So the marriage ended.

On the other hand, there was *Jerry Maguire* (96, Cameron Crowe)—not profound, but decent, touching and very entertaining, and probably a model for what Cruise wants to be. There was also *Magnolia* (99, Paul Thomas Anderson), his most searching and self-critical performance. So, after bad years, I remain hopeful, even if all the *Impossibles* put a greater load on things that might be. Still, *Vanilla Sky* (01, Crowe) was a large burden of absurdity to lay on fans and followers. It may have tweaked naive earnestness—but forty is too late for that.

He worked hard in *Minority Report* (02, Steven Spielberg), and gave it a new toughness, but then the film let him down. Can he be helped by *The Last Samurai* (03, Edward Zwick)? Does he have to do a third *Mission Impossible*?

James Cruze (Jens Cruz Bosen) (1884–1942), b. Five Points, Utah
1919: *Valley of the Giants; Roaring Road; The Dub; Alias Mike Moran; Too Many Millions; You're Fired; Love Burglar.* 1920: *Hawthorne of the U.S.A.; The Lottery Man; Mrs. Temple's Telegram; An Adventure in Hearts; Terror Island; What Happened to Jones.* 1921: *The Charm School; The Dollar-a-Year Man; Crazy to Marry; Gasoline Gus.* 1922: *One Glorious Day; Is Matrimony a Failure?; The Dictator; The Old Homestead; Thirty Days.* 1923: *The Covered Wagon; Hollywood; Ruggles of Red Gap; To the Ladies.* 1924: *The Fighting Coward; The Enemy Sex; The City That Never Sleeps; The Garden of Weeds; Merton of the Movies.* 1925: *The Goose Hangs High; Waking Up the Town; Welcome Home; Marry Me; Beggar on Horseback; The Pony Express.* 1926: *Mannequin; Old Ironsides.* 1927:

We're All Gamblers; The City Gone Wild. 1928: *On to Reno; The Mating Call; The Red Mark; Excess Baggage.* 1929: *The Duke Steps Out; A Man's Man; The Great Gabbo.* 1930: *Once a Gentleman; She Got What She Wanted.* 1931: *Salvation Nell.* 1932: *Washington Merry-Go-Round; If I Had a Million* (codirected). 1933: *Sailor Be Good; Racetrack; I Cover the Waterfront; Mr. Skitch.* 1934: *David Harum; Their Big Moment.* 1935: *Helldorado; Two Fisted.* 1936: *Sutter's Gold.* 1937: *The Wrong Road.* 1938: *Prison Nurse; Gangs of New York; Come On, Leathernecks.*

Cruze was of Danish parentage and married once to actress Betty Compson. He began as an actor and became a director in 1915—the above list is deficient for those first years. Very little of his work is known today. But as well as such ponderous Westerns as *The Covered Wagon,* which is of historical interest in the way it initiated the pioneering theme, he made some Fatty Arbuckle comedies. By the mid-1920s, James Cruze, Inc. or Productions was formed, and he mixed direction with the vague "supervision." *The Great Gabbo* starred von Stroheim, but Cruze still seems that sort of nonentity to contrast with the more vital figures of the 1920s. Few people can have seen enough of his films to be sure.

Billy Crystal, b. Long Beach, New York, 1947
The movie business likes Billy Crystal. He's naturally funny, and especially good at show-business jokes—as befits a kid who grew up in "entertainment." He's not threatening; he has charm; and he's a decent actor, even if he's never as relaxed then as when he's "on," doing stand-up. Above all, in recent times, he is acknowledged to be by far the best, and most ingratiating, host to the Academy Awards show on television. But Crystal is over fifty now, and he has never had a movie hit that stood to him alone. Does he try too hard (*Mr. Saturday Night,* which he directed, was emblematic enough to be pretentious)? Or is it that his ease sometimes simply cannot translate itself to real life? There's something in the cock of his head and the tightness of his eyes that cannot hide the knowledge that a laugh line is coming.

From his stand-up comedy, he went to play a gay character on *Soap* (77–81) on TV, and then doing *Saturday Night Live.* He made his movie debut in *Rabbit Test* (78, Joan Rivers); he had a bit in *This Is Spinal Tap* (84, Rob Reiner); with Gregory Hines in *Running Scared* (86, Peter Hyams); a cameo in *The Princess Bride* (87, Reiner); *Throw Momma from the Train* (87, Danny DeVito); helping to write and produce the maudlin *Memories of Me* (88, Henry Winkler); in his best movie, yet overshadowed by Meg Ryan, *When Harry Met Sally . . .* (89, Reiner); executive producer on *City Slickers* (91, Ron Underwood)—and superb support to Jack Palance at the

subsequent Oscars; *City Slickers 2: The Legend of Curly's Gold* (94, Paul Weisland), which he coproduced and cowrote; directing, cowriting, and acting in *Forget Paris* (95), where he simply seemed too feeble for Debra Winger; the gravedigger in *Hamlet* (96, Kenneth Branagh); with Robin Williams in *Father's Day* (97, Ivan Reitman); *Deconstructing Harry* (97, Woody Allen); with Gheorghe Muresan in *My Giant* (98, Michael Lehmann).

At last, in 1999, with Robert De Niro as his patient, he had a hit in *Analyze This* (Harold Ramis). That teaming promises sequels, and Crystal also appeared in *America's Sweethearts* (01, Joe Roth), which he helped write. Among his other chores, he did the voice of Mike in *Monsters, Inc.* (01, Peter Docter and David Silverman). But his best work, the warmest, the most likable, was directing *61°* (01) for HBO, a fond account of the home-run struggle between Roger Maris and Mickey Mantle. He also acted in *Analyze That* (02, Ramis).

George Cukor (1899–1983), b. New York
1930: *Grumpy* (codirected with Cyril Gardner); *The Virtuous Sin* (codirected with Louis Gasnier). 1931: *The Royal Family of Broadway* (codirected with Gardner); *Tarnished Lady; Girls About Town.* 1932: *One Hour With You* (directed by Cukor but planned by and credited to Ernst Lubitsch); *What Price Hollywood?; A Bill of Divorcement; Rockabye; Our Betters.* 1933: *Dinner at Eight; Little Women.* 1934: *David Copperfield.* 1935: *Sylvia Scarlett.* 1936: *Romeo and Juliet; Camille.* 1938: *Holiday; Zaza.* 1939: *Gone With the Wind* (uncredited, Cukor prepared the film and was its first director, replaced by Victor Fleming and Sam Wood); *The Women.* 1940: *Susan and God; The Philadelphia Story.* 1941: *A Woman's Face; Two-Faced Woman.* 1942: *Her Cardboard Lover; Keeper of the Flame.* 1943: *Resistance and Ohm's Law* (d). 1944: *Gaslight; Winged Victory.* 1947: *Desire Me* (codirected with Jack Conway). 1948: *A Double Life; Edward, My Son.* 1949: *Adam's Rib.* 1950: *A Life of Her Own; Born Yesterday.* 1951: *The Model and the Marriage Broker.* 1952: *The Marrying Kind; Pat and Mike.* 1953: *The Actress.* 1954: *It Should Happen to You; A Star Is Born.* 1956: *Bhowani Junction.* 1957: *Les Girls; Wild Is the Wind.* 1959: *Heller in Pink Tights; Song Without End* (completed by Cukor after the death of Charles Vidor). 1960: *Let's Make Love.* 1962: *The Chapman Report.* 1963: *Something's Got to Give* (uncompleted). 1964: *My Fair Lady.* 1969: *Justine.* 1972: *Travels With My Aunt.* 1975: *Love Among the Ruins* (TV). 1976: *The Blue Bird.* 1979: *The Corn Is Green* (TV). 1981: *Rich and Famous.*

George Cukor is now taken for granted as a test

case of the embattled homosexual in Hollywood. Patrick McGilligan's biography of him made a hinge in Cukor's life of the way the director was fired by his old friend David Selznick a few days into the shooting of *Gone With the Wind*. Hearsay evidence and crusty legend were invoked to claim that Cukor was victimized because he was gay, and because he troubled Clark Gable. There is better evidence to suggest that Cukor had grown tired of *Gone With the Wind*, overfamiliar with scenes he had screen-tested for years, and deadly slow in pacing on a project that desperately needed drive and energy if it was to avoid turning to stone.

Cukor and Selznick remained friends. Cukor was reassigned to *The Women* at MGM. He thrived, as did other gay directors such as Mitchell Leisen and Vincente Minnelli. Cukor was a fine director of women; he was also the director of some of the screen's most complex and mature heterosexual relationships—I'm thinking of the Tracy-Hepburn pictures. *GWTW* was a blow to Cukor, and I suspect that he was someone who went in dread of not being found pleasing (but that anxiety is known to heterosexuals, too). More than that, these Hollywood rules should be remembered: stars did not have the power attributed to Gable; people who did the job effectively were hired; gays no more dreamed of forcing their life-style on their movies than radicals thought to promote Red messages; and gay sensibility was, and is, so central to movies that there was never any need for promotion.

Throughout the 1920s, Cukor worked as a stage director in Rochester and New York, rising to prominence with productions of *The Great Gatsby*, *The Constant Wife*, and *Her Cardboard Lover*. In 1929, he did dialogue direction for Milestone's *All Quiet on the Western Front*, and that led him swiftly into direction, originally at Paramount, and then at RKO and MGM. These moves were made as the friend and most trusted director of David Selznick. It was a two-way exchange, for Cukor gave the producer his best films: the gentle satire of *What Price Hollywood?*; Hepburn's debut in *A Bill of Divorcement*; the knockout comedy ensembles of *Dinner at Eight*; and the magnificent *David Copperfield*, still a landmark in literary adaptation because of its fidelity to the spirit and the look of Dickens.

It is only proper that Cukor should be admired for his work with actresses, but that is not his sole or most vital asset. For what Cukor delights in with women, and especially groups of women, is the element of play or masquerade. His abiding preoccupation is theatricality and the various human postures between acting and lying. He made so many films dealing with theatre, movies, or show business: *The Royal Family of Broadway*; *What Price Hollywood?*; *Zaza*; *A Double Life*; *The Actress*; *A Star Is Born*; *Les Girls*; *Heller in Pink Tights*; and *Let's Make Love*. But many of the others turn on deception between man and woman, the attempt to alter personality or some whimsical make-believe. *Sylvia Scarlett* has Hepburn dressed as a boy. *Keeper of the Flame* is about an erroneous and manipulated public image. *Born Yesterday* and *My Fair Lady* are versions of the Pygmalion legend. *The Philadelphia Story*, *Adam's Rib*, and *A Double Life* involve role-playing in the theatre of life. *David Copperfield* might have emerged from the sort of dramatic company that Dickens loved. *Gaslight*—unusually somber in the body of Cukor's work—concerns a sinister plot to distort reality. While *Little Women*, *The Women*, and *Les Girls*—an unwitting trilogy—show the battling imaginations in a gathering of females beating down the chance of truth.

And what of Cukor's actresses? His great discovery was Katharine Hepburn, and she thoroughly repaid his trust and generosity, especially in *A Bill of Divorcement*, *Sylvia Scarlett*, *Holiday*, *Philadelphia Story*, *Keeper of the Flame*, and *Adam's Rib*, and she was denied Graham Greene's aunt only because of studio anxiety. But Cukor did as well by Constance Bennett in *What Price Hollywood?*; Garbo in *Camille*; Vivien Leigh in *Gone With the Wind* (he prepared her and his influence remained); Ingrid Bergman in *Gaslight*; Judy Holliday in *Adam's Rib*, *Born Yesterday*, and *It Should Happen to You*; Ava Gardner in *Bhowani Junction*; Sophia Loren in *Heller*; Claire Bloom in *The Chapman Report*; and Judy Garland in *A Star is Born*.

But don't forget Grant and Stewart in *Philadelphia Story*; Barrymore in *A Bill of Divorcement*; Lowell Sherman in *What Price Hollywood?*; Grant and Lew Ayres in *Holiday*; James Mason in *A Star is Born*; Fields as Micawber; Ronald Colman in *A Double Life*; an unusually restrained Anthony Quinn in *Heller*; and the grunting naturalism of Spencer Tracy in a handful of films.

Cukor's work was seldom assertive; he was never as sure of himself or as eager after about 1960. He seemed always comfortable within the scope of the industry and the glamour of the studios. But his kindliness and his unforced visual grace do not date, or simplify, stories. He hardly knew how to turn in an ugly frame; and he would work hard to maintain wit and originality, so long as the effort did not show. It is a body of work that will improve with age, surpassing that of many directors more highly prized at the time.

Peggy Cummins, b. Prestatyn, Wales, 1925

As a tiny, bright-blond super-shot—as Annie Laurie Starr—in *Gun Crazy* (49, Joseph H. Lewis), Peggy Cummins was making a farewell to America. She is brilliant, dangerous, and very sexy, with a wide-eyed love of adrenaline, but her patron in the U.S., Fox, had decided already that she was through. And *Gun Crazy* was a small picture—as well as a triumph.

She made her debut as a teenager in *Dr. O'Dowd* (40, Herbert Mason); *Salute John Citizen* (42, Maurice Elvey); *Old Mother Riley Detective* (43, Lance Comfort); *Welcome Mr. Washington* (45, Leslie Hiscott); *English Without Tears* (44, Harold French).

At that moment, with great fanfare, Cummins was recruited by Fox to play the world-famously sexy lead in *Forever Amber*. But she was as quickly abandoned and replaced with Linda Darnell. The studio tried to recover by casting her as Ronald Colman's daughter in *The Late George Apley* (47, Joseph L. Mankiewicz), but she was reckoned a failure again in *Moss Rose* (47, Gregory Ratoff). So she was put with horses in *Green Grass of Wyoming* (48, Louis King) and sent back to England to make *Escape* (49, Mankiewicz); *If This Be Sin* (49, Ratoff); and *Operation X* (50, Ratoff).

Back in Britain, she made *Who Goes There?* (52, Anthony Kimmins); *Street Corner* (53, Muriel Box); *Always a Bride* (53, Ralph Smart); *Love Lottery* (54, Charles Crichton); *To Dorothy a Son* (54, Box); *Carry On Admiral* (57, Val Guest); *Hell Drivers* (57, Cy Endfield), where she needs to be a good deal sexier; *Night of the Demon* (57, Jacques Tourneur); *The Captain's Table* (58, Jack Lee); *Your Money or Your Wife* (59, Anthony Simmons); *Dentist in the Chair* (60, Don Chaffey); *In the Doghouse* (61, D'Arcy Conyers).

Jamie Lee Curtis, b. Los Angeles, 1958

She is the second daughter of Tony Curtis and Janet Leigh, born soon after *Touch of Evil*. (She is also the godchild of Lew Wasserman.) Her father had left her mother by the time *Psycho* opened, and so Jamie Lee was raised by Janet Leigh and her next husband, Robert Brandt. She has said that while her home life was secure, it was still a lonely childhood. For years she hardly knew her father; then they became druggies together. A toughness has been left in her face, a hardness that is eerily at odds with her "perfect" and intelligently revealed body. *Blue Steel* (90, Kathryn Bigelow) was the first film that hinted at her androgynous quality, and it was a picture too conscious of its own style, too devoid of human exploration. But this ambiguity accounts for the Curtis cult, and makes her hard to cast well.

She did *Operation Petticoat* on TV before she got the role of the threatened and eventually angered girl in *Halloween* (78, John Carpenter), a film that drew on her iron-jawed air of integrity. Thereafter, she was in a run of scary rip-offs: *Prom Night* (80, Paul Lynch); *Terror Train* (80, Roger Spottiswoode); *The Fog* (80, Carpenter), with her mother; *Road Games* (81, Richard Franklin); and *Halloween II* (81, Rick Rosenthal).

For television, she was in a replicant *Private Benjamin—She's in the Army Now* (81, Hy Averback)—and she was impressive in *Death of a Centerfold: The Dorothy Stratten Story* (81, Gabrielle Beaumont). But *Love Letters* (83, Amy Jones) was the best part she has ever had, as a young woman who has an affair with an older man as she begins to realize the secret her recently dead mother kept from her. *Love Letters* is a small gem, and Curtis made herself achingly naked and vulnerable for it. At the same time, there was a hint of limits or guards in her that did not want to put feelings on show. In her best performance so far, she seemed to be letting us see her distrust of acting.

She had the female lead, as a hooker, in a big picture, *Trading Places* (83, John Landis); *Grandview U.S.A.* (84, Randal Kleiser); and *The Adventures of Buckaroo Banzai* (84, W. D. Richter). But *Perfect* (85, James Bridges) was a career-stopper, and a movie made to be mocked. Since then, she has never regained her place (or her need?) to dominate movies. The TV series *Anything But Love* (89–90) may have fulfilled her as much as *Dominick & Eugene* (88, Robert M. Young); *A Man in Love* (87, Diane Kurys); *Amazing Grace & Chuck* (87, Mike Newell); and *As Summer Dies* (86, Jean-Claude Tramont) on TV with Bette Davis. *A Fish Called Wanda* (88, Charles Crichton) was a hit and her best opportunity for comedy. But *Blue Steel* wiped the smile off everyone's face. Since then, she has been in *Queens Logic* (91, Steve Rash); *My Girl* (91, Howard Zieff); *Forever Young* (92, Steve Miner); *Mother's Boys* (94, Yves Simoneau); and *True Lies* (94, James Cameron).

She works steadily, usually in family comedies or the obligatory horror films (which also fit her increasingly haunted look—or is that just keeping in such tip-top condition so long?): *My Girl 2* (94, Zieff); *The Heidi Chronicles* (95, Paul Bogart); *House Arrest* (96, Harry Winer); *Fierce Creatures* (97, Fred Schepisi and Young); *Homegrown* (98, Stephen Gyllenhaal); *Nicholas' Gift* (98, Robert Markowitz); *Halloween H2O* (98, Miner); *Virus* (99, John Bruno); *Drowning Mona* (00, Nick Gomez); *The Tailor of Panama* (01, John Boorman); *Halloween: Resurrection* (02, Rick Rosenthal); *Freaky Friday* (03, Mark S. Waters).

Tony Curtis (Bernard Schwartz), b. Bronx, New York, 1925

Curtis was for years one of the test cases cited to illustrate the follies of the cinema. How, it was asked, could this Bronx kid with greasy hair dripping over his forehead be taken seriously? After the Navy and various drama schools, he made his debut in Siodmak's *Criss Cross* (48) and was soon signed up by Universal slave market of young talent.

Two came through: Rock Hudson and Curtis. One benefit of the system was that it enabled Curtis to make a lot of movies in a short time—mostly enjoyable hokum: *City Across the River* (49, Maxwell Shane); Enright's *Kansas Raiders* (50); a bit part as a cavalryman in Anthony Mann's *Winchester 73* (50); and then a succession of leads in quickie adventure spectaculars—a rapid historical wind-up for Bernie Schwartz: *Sierra* (50, Alfred E. Green); Rudolph Maté's *The Prince Who Was a Thief* (51); a first clear success in George Marshall's *Houdini* (53), costarring with his wife, Janet Leigh; *Son of Ali Baba* (53, Kurt Neumann); *The All-American* (53, Jesse Hibbs); *Forbidden* (53) and *The Black Shield of Falworth* (54), both for Maté; *Beachhead* (54, Stuart Heisler); *The Purple Mask* (55, Bruce Humberstone); *Six Bridges to Cross* (55, Joseph Pevney); *The Square Jungle* (56, Jerry Hopper); and *The Rawhide Years* (56, Maté).

Perhaps it was a test of endurance, but Curtis wore tights and uniforms honorably and never took himself as solemnly as some of his scolds chose to. In 1956, he began earnestly to improve himself with Carol Reed's *Trapeze,* a film that carefully blended the athletic and the sentimental. But he came into his own when readmitted to a modern urban world, and in *Mister Cory* (57, Blake Edwards) and as Sidney Falco in Mackendrick's *Sweet Smell of Success* (57) he was able to show some of the things a Bronx Ali Baba had learned about life. In the latter, he gave one of the first portrayals of unprincipled American ambition and of the collapsible personality that goes with it. He was man on all fours some years before America really noticed the posture. The script has many cutting things to say about Falco that are like cigarettes put out in Tony's "ice-cream face." In response, Curtis was hurt, brave, and bitter—a terrific performance.

Curtis did not escape flabby costume films: *The Vikings* (58, Richard Fleischer); *Spartacus* (60, Stanley Kubrick); and *Taras Bulba* (62, J. Lee Thompson). But he next adventured into comedy, thrust there first by Billy Wilder in *Some Like It Hot* (59). He is the subtlest thing in that outrageous film: more cunningly feminine than Lemmon and throwing in a superb impersonation of Cary Grant as a bonus. Blake Edwards immediately cast him with Grant in *Operation Petticoat* (59) and Curtis was now a comic Falco, still convincing but several shades rosier. After *Who Was That Lady?* (60) for George Sidney, he gave one of his best performances as the chronically flexible *Great Imposter* (60, Robert Mulligan), an underrated film that owes a lot to Curtis's fallible grasp of himself. He was now cast in the comedian's mold in Jewison's *Forty Pounds of Trouble* (62); Quine's *Paris When It Sizzles* (64); and *Sex and the Single Girl* (64); Minnelli's *Goodbye Charlie* (64); and Edwards's *The Great Race* (65) before the zest began to trickle away. The come-

dies became more contrived and further from Curtis's territory: *Boeing Boeing* (65, John Rich); *Drop Dead, Darling* (66, Ken Hughes); Mackendrick's wretched *Don't Make Waves* (67); *The Chastity Belt* (68, Pasquale Festa Campanile) in Italy; and *Monte Carlo or Bust* (69, Ken Annakin), God knows where. Working his way through marriages and psychiatrists, Curtis toppled into the gravity that had always lain in wait: it led him to make *The Boston Strangler* (68, Fleischer), which he no doubt thought was a significant movie. He worked in England on a TV series, *The Persuaders,* and was disappointing as *Lepke* (74, Menahem Golan); a rogue in *The Count of Monte-Cristo* (74, David Greene); an insecure actor in *The Last Tycoon* (76, Elia Kazan); a stooge in *The Bad News Bears Go to Japan* (78, John Berry); *The Manitou* (78, William Girdler); *Sextette* (78, Ken Hughes); *Casanova and Company* (78, François Legrand); *It Rained All Night the Day I Left* (79, Nicolas Gessner); *Little Miss Marker* (80, Walter Bernstein); as David O. Selznick in *Moviola: The Scarlett O'Hara War* (80, John Erman); *The Mirror Crack'd* (80, Guy Hamilton); *Inmates* (81, Guy Green); *The Million Dollar Face* (81, Michael O'Herlihy); *Portrait of a Showgirl* (82, Steven Hilliard Stern); *Brainwaves* (82, Ulli Lomel); as Joe McCarthy in *Insignificance* (85, Nicolas Roeg); *Mafia Princess* (86, Robert Collins); *Der Passagier* (88, Thomas Brasch); *Tarzan in Manhattan* (89, Michael Schultz); *Lobster Man from Mars* (89, Stanley Sheff), as a movie executive looking to make a tax-loss picture—some of these are movies such as Sidney Falco might seek out, clinging to the dark, waiting for the heat to pass.

There are more films, strictly from hunger, as Sidney would say: *Midnight* (89, Norman Thaddeus Vane); *Prime Target* (91, David Heavener and Phillip J. Roth); *Center of the Web* (92, David A. Prior); *The Mummy Lives* (93, Gerry O'Hara); *Naked in New York* (94, Daniel Algrant); *The Immortals* (95, Brian Grant); *Hardball* (97, George Erschbamer); *Louis & Frank* (98, Alexandre Rockwell); *Stargames* (98, Greydon Clarke).

Michael Curtiz (Mihaly Kertesz) (1888–1962), b. Budapest, Hungary
1919: *Die Dame mit dem Schwarzen Handschuhen; Der Stern von Damaskus; Göttesgeissel; Die Dame mit Sonnenblumen.* 1920: *Herzogin Satanella; Miss Dorothy's Bekenntnis; Labyrinth des Grauens.* 1921: *Miss Tutti Frutti; Wege des Schrecken.* 1922: *Sodom und Gomorrha.* 1923: *Samson und Dalila.* 1924: *Die Sklavenkönigin.* 1925: *Der Junge Medardus; Der Spielzeng von Paris.* 1926: *Fiaker N13; Der Goldene Schmetterling; The Third Degree; Red Heels; The Road to Happiness.* 1927: *The Desired Woman; Good Time Charley; A Million Bid.* 1928: *Noah's Ark;*

Tenderloin. 1929: *The Gamblers; The Glad Rag Doll; Hearts in Exile; The Madonna of Avenue A*. 1930: *Bright Lights; Under a Texas Moon; Mammy; The Matrimonial Bed; River's End; A Soldier's Plaything*. 1931: *God's Gift to Women; The Mad Genius*. 1932: *Alias the Doctor; The Woman from Monte Carlo; The Strange Love of Molly Louvain; Doctor X; The Cabin in the Cotton; 20,000 Years in Sing Sing*. 1933: *The Mystery of the Wax Museum; The Keyhole; Private Detective 62; Goodbye Again; The Kennel Murder Case; Female*. 1934: *Mandalay; Jimmy the Gent; The Key; British Agent*. 1935: *The Case of the Curious Bride; Black Fury; Front Page Woman; Little Big Shot; Captain Blood*. 1936: *The Walking Dead; The Charge of the Light Brigade*. 1937: *Stolen Holiday; Kid Galahad; Mountain Justice; The Perfect Specimen*. 1938: *Gold Is Where You Find It; The Adventures of Robin Hood* (codirected with William Keighley); *Four Daughters; Four's a Crowd; Angels with Dirty Faces*. 1939: *Dodge City; Daughters Courageous; The Private Lives of Elizabeth and Essex; Four Wives*. 1940: *Virginia City; The Sea Hawk; Santa Fe Trail*. 1941: *The Sea Wolf; Dive Bomber*. 1942: *Captains of the Clouds; Yankee Doodle Dandy*. 1943: *Casablanca; Mission to Moscow; This Is the Army*. 1944: *Passage to Marseilles; Janie*. 1945: *Roughly Speaking; Mildred Pierce*. 1946: *Night and Day*. 1947: *Life with Father; The Unsuspected*. 1948: *Romance on the High Seas*. 1949: *My Dream Is Yours; Flamingo Road; The Lady Takes a Sailor*. 1950: *Young Man with a Horn; Bright Leaf; The Breaking Point*. 1951: *Jim Thorpe—All-American; Force of Arms; I'll See You in My Dreams*. 1952: *The Will Rogers Story; The Jazz Singer*. 1953: *Trouble Along the Way*. 1954: *The Boy from Oklahoma; The Egyptian; White Christmas*. 1955: *We're No Angels*. 1956: *The Scarlet Hour; The Vagabond King; The Best Things in Life Are Free*. 1957: *The Helen Morgan Story*. 1958: *King Creole; The Proud Rebel*. 1959: *The Man in the Net; The Hangman*. 1960: *A Breath of Scandal; The Adventures of Huckleberry Finn*. 1961: *Francis of Assisi; The Comancheros*.

The long career of Michael Curtiz began in the Budapest theatre in the last decade of the Austro-Hungarian Empire. He was an actor and a producer before beginning to work for the cinema in Sweden, Hungary, and Germany. He served in the First World War and then directed in Germany before being invited to Hollywood by Harry Warner. He remained Warners' loyalest director until 1953. His thrillers are slacker than Raoul Walsh's, but the Errol Flynn picture was really more Curtiz's invention than the actor's, and Curtiz's status improved notably after *Captain Blood*. Thus he began to act and talk like a Hungarian star. There were more Curtiz jokes than films, and

David Niven named a book after one of them—*Bring on the Empty Horses*.

Eventually, durability betrayed him, and by the 1950s his adventure films and biopics were uninspired throwbacks. But until about 1945 he was an admirable exponent of American genres and an enthusiastic orchestrator of actors and technicians. *The Adventures of Robin Hood* is a classic swashbuckler; *Yankee Doodle Dandy* is one of the most enjoyable of biopics; *Casablanca* is the best of wartime espionage movies; and *Mildred Pierce* is the most throbbing of Joan Crawford melodramas. None of those films survives as art, but Curtiz seems to have been intoxicated by Americana in those war years. Granted that the players make special contributions to all those films, still one must allow Curtiz the credit for making melodrama and sentimentality so searingly effective and such glowing causes for nostalgia for the 1940s. To adopt a musical term, in the early 1940s Curtiz achieved an outstanding vibrato, as if Hollywood's swan song sensed its climax. *Yankee Doodle Dandy*, *Casablanca*, and *Mildred Pierce* are an unrivaled trinity of inventiveness transforming soppiness to such an extent that reason and taste begin to waver at the conviction of genre in full flow. One has only to compare *Yankee Doodle Dandy* with Curtiz's later biopics, or *Casablanca* with *White Christmas*, to gauge the real distinction of the earlier films. Nor is there any reason to scorn the craft of the wartime films, not even the flashback within a flashback within a flashback of the nutty *Passage to Marseilles*. It would be a happier cinema today if complex stories could be told as swiftly and clearly as *Casablanca*. Perhaps the shooting of *Casablanca* was only days ahead of the script; in which case, what clearer proof could there be of instinct?

John Cusack, b. Evanston, Illinois, 1966

It seems as if John Cusack has been adorably promising for close to twelve years now, without quite establishing himself or seeming indispensable. But he is only in his midthirties and he has acquired enough experience along the way to make a stand sometime soon. After all, by now there's a whole new generation of fresh-faced young men, as sharp and smart as he was. So when is he going to be emphatically grown up? He is the younger brother of actress Joan Cusack, and he was with her in the Pivan Theatre Workshop. His films are *Class* (83, Lewis John Carlino); *Sixteen Candles* (84, John Hughes); *Grandview, U.S.A.* (84, Randal Kleiser); *The Sure Thing* (85, Rob Reiner); *Better Off Dead* (85, Savage Steve Holland); *The Journey of Natty Gann* (85, Jeremy Kagan); *Stand by Me* (86, Reiner); *One Crazy Summer* (86, Holland); *Hot Pursuit* (87, Steven Lisberger); very good in *Eight Men Out* (88, John Sayles); *Tapeheads* (88, Bill Fishman); delivering true charm, with Ione Skye, in *Say Anything* (89, Cameron Crowe); good again in *Fat Man and Little Boy* (89, Roland Joffe); lacking a little depth in *The Grifters* (90, Stephen Frears), and seeming a little too young; *True Colors* (91, Herbert Ross); *Shadows and Fog* (91, Woody Allen); *Roadside Prophets* (92, Abbe Wool); *The Player* (92, Robert Altman); *Map of the Human Heart* (92, Vincent Ward); *Bob Roberts* (92, Tim Robbins); *Money for Nothing* (93, Ramón Menéndez); funny in *Bullets Over Broadway* (94, Woody Allen); *Floundering* (94, Peter McCarthy); *The Road to Wellville* (94, Alan Parker); Pacino's assistant in *City Hall* (96, Harold Becker); cowriter and coproducer on *Grosse Pointe Blank* (97, George Armitage); pretty much an outsider in *Con Air* (97, Simon West); kicking his heels in *Midnight in the Garden of Good and Evil* (97, Clint Eastwood); doing a voice in *Anastasia* (97, Don Bluth); *The Thin Red Line* (98, Terence Malick); *This Is My Father* (99, Paul Quinn); too busy in *Pushing Tin* (99, Mike Newell); the puppeteer in *Being John Malkovich* (99, Spike Jonze); Nelson Rockefeller in *The Cradle Will Rock* (99, Tim Robbins); clever, but still only on the edge of breakthrough in *High Fidelity* (00, Frears); *America's Sweethearts* (01, Joe Roth); and *Serendipity* (01, Peter Chelsom) where he's no more or less boyish and impetuous than he was in *Say Anything*. He was Hitler's art dealer in *Max* (02, Menno Meyjes); *Identity* (03, James Mangold); *The Runaway Jury* (03, Gary Fleder).

Can he look forty?

D

Willem (William) Dafoe,
b. Appleton, Wisconsin, 1955

Dafoe has not been the easiest actor to place or cast. Yet he has appealed to directors as figures of both extreme good and extreme evil. His ideal man, Sergeant Elias, in *Platoon* (86, Oliver Stone) must have been very hard to establish within the context of that film's thorough horror, but Dafoe seemed to be possessed by a necessary spiritual force. Indeed, the tenderness in Elias, the openness to pleasure, was actually more impressive than the lead role in *The Last Temptation of Christ* (88, Martin Scorsese), where he seemed uneasy with the flawed interpretation of the picture. On the other hand, he has often been cast as lurid villains, and increasingly nowadays he seems to be a supporting player. But Dafoe has the resources to come back at us with a huge surprise still.

He has remained loyal to the theatre and to the Wooster Group, of which he is a longtime member. He made his movie debut in *The Loveless* (83, Kathryn Bigelow); *The Hunger* (83, Tony Scott); the gang leader in *Streets of Fire* (84, Walter Hill);

Roadhouse 66 (84, John Mark Robinson); another nasty in *To Live and Die in L.A.* (85, William Friedkin); *Off Limits* (88, Christopher Crowe); one of the investigators in *Mississippi Burning* (88, Alan Parker); *Born on the Fourth of July* (89, Stone); a boxer in Auschwitz in *Triumph of the Spirit* (89, Robert M. Young); a spot in *Cry-Baby* (90, John Waters); wonderfully exaggerated as Bobby Peru in *Wild at Heart* (90, David Lynch); *Flight of the Intruder* (91, John Milius).

He was the local cop in *White Sands* (92, Roger Donaldson); very good as the connection who has dreams, John LeTour, in *Light Sleeper* (92, Paul Schrader); keeping a straight face and a hard bod with Madonna in *Body of Evidence* (93, Uli Edel); a kind of Elias again in *Clear and Present Danger* (94, Phillip Noyce); as T. S. Eliot, terribly rattled and wasted, in *Tom & Viv* (94, Brian Gilbert); as Axel Heyst in *Victory* (95, Mark Peploe); *Basquiat* (96, Julian Schnabel).

He was Caravaggio, the least felt character in *The English Patient* (96, Anthony Minghella); his worst villain yet in *Speed 2: Cruise Control* (97, Jan de Bont); *Lulu on the Bridge* (98, Paul Auster); *Affliction* (98, Schrader); *eXistenZ* (99, David Cronenberg); *New Rose Hotel* (99, Abel Ferrara); *The Boondock Saints* (99, Troy Duffy); *American Psycho* (00, Mary Harron); the prison boss in *Animal Factory* (00, Steve Buscemi).

Then he found his perfect role, part wronged saint, part repressed monster, that of Max Schreck, playing the vampire from the heart, funny, pathetic, and fearsome, in *Shadow of the Vampire* (00, E. Elias Merhige); *Pavilion of Woman* (01, Yim Ho), as a priest struggling with a lot of sex; the Green Goblin in *Spider-Man* (02, Sam Raimi); superbly ingratiating in *Autofocus* (02, Schrader).

John Dahl, b. Billings, Montana, 1956
1989: *Kill Me Again*. 1993: *Red Rock West*. 1994: *The Last Seduction*. 1996: *Unforgettable*. 1998: *Rounders*. 2001: *Joy Ride*.

The transition from *The Last Seduction* to *Unforgettable* was one of the most embarrassed gulps in modern film. Despite the presence of Linda Fiorentino, *Unforgettable* was in title denial from its first few minutes. Again, despite the radiant gloom of Ms. Fiorentino in *Last Seduction*, the film was more than just her—it had a bunch of nicely weak men, a terrific feeling for money, and real guile in the filming. It could have been better: the woman might have been more steadily aggressive, instead of content to be in hiding. But *The Last Seduction* is one of the movies of the nineties, and it makes everything else by Dahl look limp.

Dahl was at the AFI and then he worked as an assistant director and storyboard artist on *The Dungeonmaster* (85, too many directors to name);

Something Wild (86, Jonathan Demme); and *Married to the Mob* (88, Demme), and made his debut on *Kill Me Again*, which he also wrote, with Val Kilmer and his then-wife, Joanne Whalley-Kilmer. He wrote *Red Rock West*, too, which won high praise, though it seemed to me predictable and very derivative. Still, it had a humor that bloomed in *Last Seduction* (which was written by Steve Barancik). The later films, however, are those of a talent that has lost its way, and its momentum. *Rounders* was especially regrettable in that it seemed so promising in its lineup.

Dan Dailey (1915–78), b. New York
Dan Dailey began with dancing school, then was in a minstrel show as a boy, in vaudeville in his teens, and then Minsky's, Broadway, and his first film, *The Mortal Storm* (40, Frank Borzage). Even before he went into the army in 1942, he had smiled his way into a place as an honest hoofer: *Susan and God* (40, George Cukor); *Ziegfeld Girl* (41, Robert Z. Leonard); *Moon Over Her Shoulder* (41, Alfred Werker); *Lady Be Good* (41, Norman Z. McLeod); *Panama Hattie* (42, McLeod); *Give Out, Sisters* (42, Eddie Cline); and *Sunday Punch* (42, David Miller). After the war, he became a mainstay of dull Fox musicals: *Mother Wore Tights* (47, Walter Lang); *You Were Meant for Me* (48, Lloyd Bacon); *Give My Regards to Broadway* (48, Bacon); *When My Baby Smiles at Me* (48, Lang); *Chicken Every Sunday* (49, George Seaton); and *My Blue Heaven* (50, Henry Koster). Not even such cheerfulness could wipe the grin off his face. He tried to branch out into straight acting and made three films for John Ford: *When Willie Comes Marching Home* (50), *What Price Glory?* (52), and *The Wings of Eagles* (57). Though musicals were his homeground, he had a few dramatic roles: *I Can Get It for You Wholesale* (51, Michael Gordon); *Call Me Mister* (51, Bacon); as baseball pitcher Dizzy Dean in *The Pride of St. Louis* (52, Harmon Jones); *Meet Me at the Fair* (52, Douglas Sirk); *Taxi* (53, Gregory Ratoff); *There's No Business Like Show Business* (54, Lang); *It's Always Fair Weather* (55, Stanley Donen and Gene Kelly); *Meet Me in Las Vegas* (56, Roy Rowland); and *The Best Things in Life Are Free* (56, Michael Curtiz). His decline was swift, albeit cushioned by TV: *Oh, Men! Oh, Women!* (57, Nunnally Johnson); *The Wayward Bus* (57, Victor Vicas); *Underwater Warrior* (58, Andrew Marton); *Hemingway's Adventures of a Young Man* (62, Martin Ritt); and as Clyde Tolson in *The Private Files of J. Edgar Hoover* (77, Larry Cohen).

Marcel Dalio (Israel Mosche Blauschild) (1900–83), b. Paris
"Gentlemen, tomorrow we shall leave the château weeping for this wonderful friend, this excellent companion who knew so well how to make us forget that he was a famous man. . . . And now, my dear friends . . . it is cold, you are running the risk of catching a chill and I suggest that you go inside." It is night, on the steps outside a French country house, and a slight, dark man in evening dress is speaking to his guests after one of them has been shot. The year, 1939, when the danger of chill was a metaphor for a much greater threat coming from Germany. For both the character—a French aristocrat of Jewish descent—and the Jewish actor, Marcel Dalio, that speech was to prove a farewell to France. Within two years Dalio was in America playing small parts with the same aptitude for the skills of a butler that underlies his delicately insecure Marquis de la Chesnaye in *La Règle du Jeu* (39, Jean Renoir).

Dalio had been in revue and music hall since the end of the First World War: a bright, dapper, and knowing Parisian. From the early 1930s he worked in French films, chiefly as a pokerfaced crook, a harbinger of Melville's fatalistic world: *Mon Chapeau* (33); *Un Grand Amour de Beethoven* (36, Abel Gance); *Pépé le Moko* (37, Julien Duvivier); *Cargaisons Blanches* (37, Robert Siodmak); *Les Perles de la Couronne* (37, Sacha Guitry and Christian-Jaque); *Marthe Richard* (37, Raymond Bernard); *Mollenard* (38, Siodmak); *Entrée des Artistes* (38, Marc Allégret); and *La Maison du Maltais* (38, Pierre Chenal).

In 1937, he played Rosenthal, one of the escaping prisoners of war in Renoir's *La Grande Illusion*, and two years later Renoir asked Dalio to play la Chesnaye. Why? asked Dalio, "when I had always played burlesque parts or traitors?" First, said Renoir, to break the cliché, to create an aristocrat by casting against type. Second, because real aristocrats are sometimes as unconvincing as Dalio, whereas only stage nobility feel no discomfort. "There is another thing, too," said Renoir. "It is that I believe that you were the only actor who could express a certain feeling of insecurity which is the basis of the character." Thus, Dalio's marquis is invaded by doubts: that he is not a satisfactory aristocrat, that his wife is unfaithful, that the assembly may not applaud his new fairground organ. Brisk, incisive, and commanding, he can quickly grow as fussy as a stage magician uncertain whether a trick will work. Wandering round his own estate, he frets about rabbits but refuses to tolerate fences. In the equally unsegregated house, he murmurs about the pain that comes from hurting people. And although Renoir's own presence in the film obscures the fact, Dalio's la Chesnaye is one of Renoir's first "producers" of life. Nothing will reassure him better than that life's show—the house party—goes with a bang. He loves organized human activity as much as the precise performance of the figures in the organ. When he announces the sudden conclusion of affairs he is like an actor-manager who has hurried onto the stage with news that the star has really died, blanks replaced by bullets. The show must be put away. La Chesnaye was a lead part, but still a character part. It was clear that Dalio would never be a star. When he fled to America he was cast in supporting roles, as café owners or servants, just as real European nobility were forced to imitate their own valets when the great German pressure forced them westward (some of Dalio's family died in concentration camps). Nothing to be depressed by, however, in his marvelous cameos in the American cinema: exactly the same impulsive courage and dandyish shyness that la Chesnaye had lived by. The massive alteration of circumstances did not affect artistic continuity: a croupier in *The Shanghai Gesture* (41, Josef von Sternberg); *Unholy Partners* (41, Mervyn Le Roy); *The Constant Nymph* (43, Edmund Goulding); as another croupier, with the happy knack of bringing up 22 on the roulette wheel, in *Casablanca* (43, Michael Curtiz); as the perplexed gendarme in *The Song of Bernadette* (43, Henry King); *Wilson* (44, King); *A Bell for Adano* (45, King); as Gerard, worthy companion of Bogart in another neutral cockpit, in *To Have and Have Not* (44, Howard Hawks).

After the war, Dalio did make more films in France, but he seems to have been emotionally based in America. He never quite matched the panache of his wartime films, but he often enlivened otherwise dull projects: *Les Maudits* (47, René Clément); *Temptation Harbour* (47, Lance Comfort); *Dédée d'Anvers* (48, Yves Allégret); *Les Amants de Vérone* (48, André Cayatte); *Black Jack* (49, Duvivier); *On the Riviera* (51, Walter Lang); *The Snows of Kilimanjaro* (52, King); *The Happy Time* (52, Richard Fleischer); *Flight to Tangier* (53, Charles Marquis Warren); as the judge in *Gentlemen Prefer Blondes* (53, Hawks); *Razzia sur la Chnouf* (54, Henri Decoin); *Sabrina* (54, Billy Wilder); *Lucky Me* (55, Jack Donohue); *Les Amants du Tage* (55, Henri Verneuil); *Miracle in the Rain* (56, Rudolph Maté); *The Sun Also Rises* (57, King); *China Gate* (57, Samuel Fuller); *Pillow Talk* (59, Michael Gordon); *Lafayette Escadrille* (59, William Wellman); *Classe Tous Risques* (59, Claude Sautet); *The Man Who Understood Women* (59, Nunnally Johnson); *Can-Can* (60, Lang); *Cartouche* (62, Philippe de Broca); *Wild and Wonderful* (63, Michael Anderson); *Donovan's Reef* (63, John Ford); *Le Monocle Rit Jaune* (64, Georges Lautner); *Un Monsieur de Compagnie* (64, de Broca); *Lady L* (65, Peter Ustinov); *La Vingt-Cinquième Heure* (66, Verneuil); *Made in Paris* (66, Boris Sagal); *How to Steal a Million* (66, William Wyler); in the "Aujourd'hui" episode from *Le Plus Vieux Métier*

du Monde (67, Claude Autant-Lara); *Justine* (69, George Cukor); *Catch-22* (70, Mike Nichols); *The Great White Hope* (70, Martin Ritt); *Aussi Loin que l'Amour* (71, Frederic Rossif); *The Mad Adventures of Rabbi Jacob* (73, Gérard Oury); *The Beast* (75, Walerian Borowczyk); *Un Page d'Amour* (77, Maurice Rabinowicz); *Chausette Surprise* (78, Jean-François Davy); and *L'Honorable Société* (78, Anielle Weinberger).

Matt (Matthew Paige) **Damon**,
b. Cambridge, Massachusetts, 1970
One has to hope that Matt Damon isn't too deterred by the response to his work in *The Talented Mr. Ripley* (99, Anthony Minghella). He got neither a nomination nor much thanks for his furtive, underclassed guy on the rise—and perhaps, in hindsight, the film could have given more scope to his appetite for daring and impersonation. Still, it was a great performance, streets ahead of the unruly-puppy stuff that got recognized in the altogether deplorable *Good Will Hunting* (97, Gus Van Sant), for which Damon the actor was nominated, and Damon and his pal Ben Affleck walked off with the original screenplay Oscar—they should have been given an Oscar à la Frisbee.

What's most interesting about Damon is the very lack of Affleckian good looks, the feel of a squashed and rebuilt face, the uneasiness. *Ripley*, I'm sure, is the best forecast of his future and some promise of an intelligent sourness not seen on screens since the days of Holden and Mitchum.

He dropped out of Harvard to pursue acting, and he built his career with *The Good Mother* (88, Leonard Nimoy); *Mystic Pizza* (88, Donald Petrie); *Rising Son* (90, John David Coles); *School Ties* (92, Robert Mandel); *Geronimo: An American Legend* (93, Walter Hill); *The Good Old Boys* (95, Tommy Lee Jones); very good as a jittery soldier in *Courage Under Fire* (96, Edward Zwick); carrying the load in *The Rainmaker* (97, Francis Coppola); *Chasing Amy* (97, Kevin Smith); *Saving Private Ryan* (98, Steven Spielberg); *Rounders* (98, John Dahl); *Dogma* (99, Smith); a voice in *Titan A.E.* (00, Don Bluth and Gary Goldman).

A few years later, I think, one has to ask where he's going. He could make little out of *The Legend of Bagger Vance* (00, Robert Redford) or *All the Pretty Horses* (00, Billy Bob Thornton). He had a bit part as himself in *Jay and Silent Bob Strike Back* (01, Smith); *The Third Wheel* (01, Jordan Brady) seemed like a lark. The TV series *Project Greenlight* (01) seemed more personal and far more rewarding than being lost in the crowd of *Ocean's Eleven* (01, Steven Soderbergh) or *The Bourne Identity* (02, Doug Liman). He and Affleck also wrote *Gerry* (02, Van Sant).

Dorothy Dandridge (1923–65),
b. Cleveland, Ohio

In 1999, Halle Berry—also from Cleveland—brought *Introducing Dorothy Dandridge* (Martha Coolidge) to the television screen. The biopic was closer to the facts than is usual in these things: the failed marriage to Harold Nicholas, and the retarded daughter; the affair with Otto Preminger; and the awful second marriage to a restaurateur—all were there. Moreover, Halle Berry looked a lot like Dandridge, though she was prettier, newer, fresher, less abused. There was the point. I looked at *Carmen Jones* (54, Preminger) a day later and all that Dandridge had on her side was that shadow of all the pain and oppression. That is not to say that Ms. Berry has gone through life free, but the thing about Dandridge is when she did it, and how warm, real, wicked, and hurt she seemed. It's the same difference as exists between Lena Horne and Whitney Houston.

Dandridge had been in show business since childhood, for she was the daughter of an actress. She had a double act with her sister, Vivian, and by, say, 1939, she was a sixteen-year-old sexpot who could sing and dance—in the age of Butterfly McQueen and Hattie McDaniel. And so her real youth was wasted away in black nightclubs and in movies like *A Day at the Races* (37, Sam Wood); *Going Places* (38, Ray Enright); *Lady from Louisiana* (41, Bernard Vorhaus); *Sundown* (41, Henry Hathaway); with the Nicholas Brothers, doing "Chattanooga Choo-Choo" in *Sun Valley Serenade* (41, H. Bruce Humberstone); *Bahama Passage* (41, Edward Griffith); *Lucky Jordan* (42, Frank Tuttle); *Hit Parade of 1943* (43, Albert S. Rogell); *Since You Went Away* (44, John Cromwell); *Atlantic City* (44, Ray McCarey); *Tarzan's Peril* (51, Byron Haskin); *The Harlem Globetrotters* (51, Phil Brown).

Then she got a real part, opposite Harry Belafonte, in *Bright Road* (53, Gerald Mayer), and after *Remains to Be Seen* (53, Don Weis) she got *Carmen Jones*. She was nominated for that: the first time a black player had been proposed for the Oscar in a lead role—her rivals were Judy Garland in *A Star Is Born*, Audrey Hepburn in *Sabrina*, Jane Wyman in *Magnificent Obsession*, and, the winner, Grace Kelly in *The Country Girl*.

Of course, life only got harder after that breakthrough. Preminger liked to keep their affair secret (what a subject for a Preminger movie). No one could find a lead role for her. So she could not even kiss John Justin three years later in *Island in the Sun* (57, Robert Rossen). She is very good in *The Decks Ran Red* (58, Andrew L. Stone), and then Preminger cast her again, opposite Sidney Poitier, in *Porgy and Bess* (59). In fact, her best role was as Curt Jurgens's mistress (a part she played in life, too) in *Tamango* (57,

John Berry). Her last film was *Malaga* (60, Laslo Benedek).

Then she lost her money in a swindle and went back to minor nightclub work. It is likely that she took her own life.

Bebe Daniels (Virginia Daniels) (1901–71),
b. Dallas, Texas

As a child, she acted with her parents on the stage and in 1914 she signed with Hal Roach at Pathé. In the next few years, she was the ingenue in many shorts, principally as the dewy-eyed girlfriend of Harold Lloyd. She then joined Cecil B. De Mille and was thrust into his gossip's world of would-be sexual sophistication: *Male and Female* (19) and the other woman in *Why Change Your Wife?* (20)—Gloria Swanson was the wife. It indicates public gullibility and De Mille's shortsighted prurience that a wholesome teenager could fill such roles. Although playing "Satan Synne" in *The Affairs of Anatol* (21, De Mille), Bebe Daniels was far more comfortable as a Paramount comedienne—light, girlish, and genuinely vivacious: *The Dancin' Fool* (20, Sam Wood); *Ducks and Drakes* (21, Maurice Campbell); *One Wild Week* (21, Campbell); *The Speed Girl* (21, Campbell), a reference to Bebe's brief spell in prison for reckless driving; *Nancy from Nowhere* (22, Chester M. Franklin); *Nice People* (22, William De Mille); *The World's Applause* (23, W. De Mille); *The Glimpses of the Moon* (23, Allan Dwan); *Daring Youth* (24, William Beaudine); with Valentino in *Monsieur Beaucaire* (24, Sidney Olcott); *Dangerous Money* (24, Frank Tuttle); *Argentine Love* (24, Dwan); *Miss Bluebeard* (25, Tuttle); *The Manicure Girl* (25, Tuttle); *Wild, Wild Susan* (25, Edward Sutherland); *Lovers in Quarantine* (25, Tuttle); *The Palm Beach Girl* (26, Erle Kenton); *Stranded in Paris* (26, Arthur Rossen); *Feel My Pulse* (28, Gregory La Cava); *Take Me Home* (28, Marshall Neilan); and *What a Night!* (28, Sutherland). She was at her best in a string of carefree comedies directed by Clarence Badger: *Miss Brewster's Millions* (26); *The Campus Flirt* (26); *A Kiss in a Taxi* (27); *Senorita* (27); *Swim, Girl, Swim* (27); *She's a Sheik* (27), in which Bebe, in Arab costume, abducts a European husband for herself; *The Fifty-Fifty Girl* (28); and *Hot News* (28).

When sound arrived, Paramount neglected her and she went eventually to RKO for a great personal success in *Rio Rita* (29, Luther Reed), in which she sang. She stayed there for *Love Comes Along* (30, Rupert Julian) and *Alias French Gertie* (30, George Archainbaud). Her costar in that film was Ben Lyon, and in the same year they married. After *Dixiana* (30, Reed) and *Lawful Larceny* (30, Lowell Sherman), she went to United Artists for *Reaching for the Moon* (31, Edmund Goulding) and to Warners for *My Past* (31, Roy del Ruth). She remained there for a few years, but her reputation was declining: *The Maltese Falcon* (31, del Ruth); *Silver Dollar* (32, Alfred E. Green); the temperamental star in *42nd Street* (33, Lloyd Bacon) who loses the part to Ruby Keeler; and *Registered Nurse* (34, Robert Florey). She went to Columbia for *Cocktail Hour* (33, Victor Schertzinger), to Universal for *Counsellor at Law* (33, William Wyler); and then to Britain to make *The Song You Gave Me* (33, Paul L. Stein) and *A Southern Maid* (33, Harry Hughes)—two disasters.

She returned to America for *Music Is Magic* (35, George Marshall), and in 1936 she and Lyon went to London, first to play at the Palladium, but eventually to settle. She made two awful pictures there—*Not Wanted on Voyage* (36, Emil E. Reinert) and *The Return of Carol Deane* (38, Arthur Woods)—but had an enormous wartime success, with Lyon and Vic Oliver, in the radio show *Hi Gang!* A film was made of the show in 1941, directed by Marcel Varnel. After the war they went back to America and Bebe made *The Fabulous Joe* (48) for Hal Roach.

But they were soon back in London with their children, doing more radio shows, which led to the inevitable movie exploitation: *Life with the Lyons* (53, Val Guest) and *The Lyons in Paris* (55, Guest). She retired and spent her last ten years seriously ill.

Jeff Daniels, b. Chelsea, Michigan, 1955
Was he *Dumb or Dumber* (94, Peter Farrelly)? And was that really appropriate preparation for playing George Washington on TV in *The Crossing* (00, Robert Harmon)? By then, aged forty-five or so, the long-suffering Jeff Daniels was smart enough to burn no boats so, as William McDonald noted, "his expression generally remains as impenetrable as the one on the dollar bill." Daniels seems a decent man and a likable, subtle actor, with at least one terrific picture built around his easygoing normalcy: *Something Wild* (86, Jonathan Demme), where he is blown inside out into his real nature by the pure force of Melanie Griffith.

In short, he has been the guy next door, often weak, yet the reliable carer for *101 Dalmatians* (96, Stephen Herek) and a valiant Colonel Joshua Chamberlain in *Gettysburg* (93, Ronald Maxwell). One has the hunch that he might yet deliver a fine performance as some kind of hesitating Everyman. Meanwhile, count on his survival.

He made his debut in *Ragtime* (81, Milos Forman) and followed it with the husband in *Terms of Endearment* (83, James L. Brooks); *The Purple Rose of Cairo* (85, Woody Allen); *Marie* (85, Roger Donaldson); *Heartburn* (86, Mike Nichols); *Radio Days* (87, Allen); *The House on Carroll Street* (88, Peter Yates); *Sweet Hearts Dance* (88, Robert Greenwald); *Checking Out* (89, David

Leland); *Love Hurts* (90, Bud Yorkin); *Welcome Home, Roxy Carmichael* (90, Jim Abraham); *The Butcher's Wife* (91, Terry Hughes); *There Goes the Neighborhood* (92, Bill Phillips); *Speed* (94, Jan de Bont); *2 Days in the Valley* (96, John Herzfeld); *Fly Away Home* (96, Carroll Ballard); *Trial and Error* (97, Jonathan Lynn); *Pleasantville* (98, Garry Ross); *My Favorite Martian* (99, Donald Petrie); *All the Rage* (99, James D. Stern); *Cheaters* (00, John Stockwell); *Chasing Sleep* (00, Michael Walker).

Another person beats within, as witness two attempts to write and direct—both greeted with derision: *Escanaba in da Moonlight* (01) and *Super Sucker* (02). But he returned to regular acting in *Blood Work* (02, Clint Eastwood); *The Hours* (02, Stephen Daldry); as Chamberlain again in *Gods and Generals* (03, Maxwell); *I Witness* (03, Rowdy Herrington).

Frank Darabont,
b. Montebeliard, France, 1959
1994: *The Shawshank Redemption.* 1999: *The Green Mile.* 2001: *The Majestic.*

Twice now, Frank Darabont has drawn upon the writing of Stephen King to make circuitous parables about the mystery of fate in stories set in antiquated prison systems. It's a kind of genre, I fear—frisson turned with prison—and I don't want to have to face one more sentence behind these bars. It's not that Darabont lacks skill or warmth, or even a sense of human vagary. *The Shawshank Redemption* established its own world and rhythm, not to mention charm. Equally, I think there's a chance that the very expansiveness of its parable could quickly become vacant and hollow. So let this director go. Ask him to deal with liberty.

Darabont began as an assistant on *Hell Night* (81, Tom DeSimone), and he did set decoration on *Crimes of Passion* (84, Ken Russell). But by then he was writing scripts: *A Nightmare on Elm Street 3: Dream Warriors* (87, Chuck Russell); *The Blob* (88, Russell); *The Fly II* (89, Chris Wales); and the dreadful *Mary Shelley's Frankenstein* (94, Kenneth Branagh), which seemingly persuaded some people that he was ready for higher things.

Of course, *Shawshank* won many awards and nominations, and among the young it often passes for a piece of profound humanism. Times are hard. But Darabont seems impressed by his following—as witness a kind of portentous gradualism that was awaiting him. At a full three hours *The Green Mile* was all limitless—even to the point where one wondered whether the title referred to the Tom Hanks character's vexed urinary tract. Again, some were certain *The Green Mile* was profound. But when *The Majestic* came along, nothing could be discerned but the fragments of very soulful intentions.

Linda Darnell (Monetta Eloyse Darnell) (1921–65), b. Dallas, Texas

A dark-eyed, sultry actress, Darnell was one of the sirens of the 1940s whose rose-at-twilight looks seemed to stimulate every Fox cameraman—indeed, one of her husbands was photographer Peverell Marley. Her best work was done for Preminger, and she exists imaginatively as the loose-living sister of Gene Tierney, a girl bruised by experience but still making up her lips till they bulge with prospects. After working as a model, she made her debut in Gregory Ratoff's *Hotel for Women* (39), then *Day-Time Wife* (39, Ratoff), and she is a splendid female object in Hathaway's *Brigham Young* (40); as Lolita in Mamoulian's *The Mark of Zorro* (40); King's *Chad Hanna* (40); and Mamoulian's *Blood and Sand* (41)—all made while still in her teens. She was still not quite a star and played supporting parts: *Rise and Shine* (41, Allan Dwan); as the Virgin Mary (uncredited) in *The Song of Bernadette* (43, Henry King); as an Indian girl, Dawn Starlight, in *Buffalo Bill* (44, William Wellman); René Clair's *It Happened Tomorrow* (44); Sirk's *Summer Storm* (44); and Archie Mayo's *Sweet and Lowdown* (44). Upon encountering Otto Preminger, she made four films: *Fallen Angel* (45); *Centennial Summer* (46); blonde in *Forever Amber* (47); and *The 13th Letter* (51). This counts as her best work, but she is also good in John Brahm's *Hangover Square* (45); *The Great John L.* (45, Frank Tuttle); "I'm Chihuahua" in Ford's *My Darling Clementine* (46); as Algeria Wedge in John Stahl's *The Walls of Jericho* (48); as the wife in Preston Sturges's *Unfaithfully Yours* (48), subtly different in Rex Harrison's several daydreams for disposing of her; in *Slattery's Hurricane* (49, André de Toth); and in two Joseph Mankiewicz films, *A Letter to Three Wives* (48) and *No Way Out* (50). Her success did not carry over into the 1950s and, after Robert Wise's *Two Flags West* (50); Stuart Heisler's *Saturday Island* (51); Raoul Walsh's *Blackbeard the Pirate* (52); Rudolph Maté's *Second Chance* (53); *This Is My Love* (54, Heisler); and *Zero Hour* (57, Hall Bartlett), she worked only intermittently.

She died in a fire that started while she was watching one of her own movies on TV.

Harry d'Abbadie d'Arrast (1893–1968), b. Argentina

1927: *Service for Ladies; A Gentleman of Paris; Serenade.* 1928: *The Magnificent Flirt; Dry Martini.* 1930: *Raffles* (codirected with George Fitzmaurice); *Laughter.* 1933: *Topaze.* 1935: *The Three-Cornered Hat.*

From French aristocratic origins, d'Arrast came to Hollywood to assist Chaplin on *A Woman of Paris* (23) and *The Gold Rush* (25). A shadowy figure now, he had a reputation for smart comedy and highly strung fractiousness. He crossed cocktail sticks with Goldwyn on *Raffles*, with Selznick on *Topaze*, and eventually quit Hollywood for lack of work. He began at Paramount with three society romances starring Adolphe Menjou as, in order, head waiter, marquis, and famous composer. *The Magnificent Flirt* was a farce he wrote with Jean de Limur and Herman Mankiewicz that starred Albert Conti and Florence Vidor. *Dry Martini*, made at Fox with Mary Astor and Matt Moore, is the epitome of romantic cynicism undaunted by the Depression. After *Raffles*, he returned to his true home, Paramount, for Nancy Carroll and Fredric March in *Laughter*, written by himself and Donald Ogden Stewart and produced by Mankiewicz—a barrage of acerbity. *Topaze* came from the Pagnol play and starred John Barrymore. His last film had in its cast d'Arrast's wife, Eleanor Boardman. Those huge Paramount salons, slim girls in satin, and waspish dark men may have been presented as clearly by d'Arrast as anyone. Paramount condescended to its audience, and he seemed to fit that tone.

Danielle Darrieux, b. Bordeaux, France, 1917

For fifty years a leading French actress, she has made the occasional venture into American cinema and specialized in sophisticated, tender women. It was Max Ophuls who truly kindled her warmth: in *La Ronde* (50), she is the young woman in bed with Daniel Gélin. He has been thinking of it all day, but when the moment comes he cannot. She tells him not to worry. Gélin wonders if she has read Stendhal's account of cavalry officers who talk all their sex away. There is a large close-up of Darrieux, with this direction in the script: "The young woman must not appear to be mocking. She should be very sympathetic, but not really convinced." That instruction is close to the nerve of Ophuls's sad smile, and Darrieux realizes it beautifully. She worked twice again for him: in the Maison Tellier episode of *Le Plaisir* (51) and as the heartrending wife in *Madame de . . .* (53). She was never as good elsewhere, but never less than beautiful, and always in good humor: *Le Bal* (31, William Thiele); *L'Or dans la Rue* (33, Kurt Bernhardt); *Mauvaise Graine* (34, Billy Wilder and Alexandre Esway); *Mayerling* (36, Anatole Litvak); *Abus de Confiance* (37, Henri Decoin, her then husband); *Katia* (38, Maurice Tourneur); *The Rage of Paris* (38, Henry Koster); *Battements de Coeur* (39, Decoin); *Premier Rendezvous* (41, Decoin); *La Fausse Maîtresse* (42, André Cayatte); *Ruy Blas* (47, Pierre Billon); *Occupe-toi d'Amélie* (49, Claude Autant-Lara); scheming with James Mason in *Five Fingers* (52, Joseph L. Mankiewicz); *Rich, Young and Pretty* (51, Norman Taurog); *La Vérité sur le Bébé Donge* (51, Decoin); *Adorables Créatures* (52, Christian-

Jaque); *Le Bon Dieu Sans Confession* (53, Autant-Lara); as Madame de Renal in *Le Rouge et le Noir* (54, Autant-Lara); *Napoléon* (54, Sacha Guitry); *L'Amant de Lady Chatterley* (55, Marc Allégret); *Alexander the Great* (55, Robert Rossen); *Le Salaire du Péché* (56, Denys de la Patellière); *Pot-Bouille* (57, Julien Duvivier); *Marie-Octobre* (59, Duvivier); *The Greengage Summer* (61, Lewis Gilbert); as a victim of *Landru* (62, Claude Chabrol); *Patate* (64, Robert Thomas); *Le Dimanche de la Vie* (65, Jean Herman); *Le Coup de Grâce* (65, Jean Cayrol); *L'Homme à la Buick* (66, Gilles Grangier); *The Young Girls of Rochefort* (67, Jacques Demy), reluctant to marry a man named Monsieur Dame; as the madame in *Les Oiseaux vont Mourir au Pérou* (68, Romain Gary); *24 Heures de la Vie d'une Femme* (68, Dominique Delouche); *La Maison de Campagne* (69, Jean Girault); *La Divine* (75, Delouche); *L'Année Sainte* (76, Girault); *Le Cavaleur* (78, Philippe de Broca); *Une Chambre à Ville* (82, Demy); *En Haut des Marches* (83, Paul Vecchiali); *Scene of the Crime* (86, André Téchiné); and *Quelques Jours Avec Moi* (88, Claude Sautet).

She can still be seen, often on French TV, and elegant as always: *La Tête dans les Nuages* (88, Vecchiali); *Bille en Tête* (89, Carlo Cotti); *Le Jour des Rois* (91, Marie-Claude Treilhon); *Les Mamies* (92, Annick Lanoe); *La Vérité en Face* (93, Etienne Perier); *Jalna* (94, Philippe Monnier); *Ça Ira Mieux Demain* (00, Jeanne Labrune); *Que Reste-t-il . . .* (00, Perier); *8 Femmes* (02, François Ozon).

Jane Darwell (Patti Woodward) (1880–1967), b. Palmyra, Missouri

A bar parlor Mother Courage, or a Senate House Ma Kettle, Jane Darwell illustrates that intemperate cross between universality and hodgepodge in John Ford's work. Her supporting actress Oscar was won for Ma Joad in *The Grapes of Wrath* (40, John Ford)—a performance and a film that I find as touching as a politician's apology. And Darwell's "great speech" about the Joads being the sort of people who go on forever is a slur upon actual stoicism, a piece of Ford's bigoted optimism, based on a cliché view of working people offered to them like a meal on polling day. There is something nightmarish about all the Darwell jowls over which must run tears she has just failed to bite back. It is traditional to describe her success in "warmhearted motherly roles," but this is devouring motherhood, complacent, sanctimonious, and self-conscious.

Darwell was a stage actress who went to Hollywood in 1914 and played a few parts, among them *The Capture of Aguinaldo* (14) and *Rose of the Rancho* (14, Cecil B. De Mille). But she returned to the stage and only really entered on a movie career in 1930, when she was fifty: *Tom Sawyer* (30, John Cromwell); *Huckleberry Finn* (31, Norman Taurog); *Back Street* (32, John M. Stahl); *Bondage* (33, Alfred Santell); *Before Dawn* (33, Irving Pichel); *Only Yesterday* (33, Stahl); *Roman Scandals* (33, Frank Tuttle); *The Firebird* (34, William Dieterle); *Heat Lightning* (34, Mervyn Le Roy); *The Scarlet Empress* (34, Josef von Sternberg); *One Night of Love* (34, Victor Schertzinger); *Journal of a Crime* (34, William Keighley); *One More Spring* (35, Henry King); *Navy Wife* (35, Allan Dwan); *Paddy O'Day* (35, Lewis Seiler); *Life Begins at Forty* (35, George Marshall); *The Country Doctor* (36, King); *Captain January* (36, David Butler); *White Fang* (36, Butler); *Ramona* (36, King); *Nancy Steele Is Missing* (37, Marshall); *Slave Ship* (37, Tay Garnett); *Love Is News* (37, Garnett); *Dangerously Yours* (37, Malcolm St. Clair); *Jesse James* (39, King); *The Rains Came* (39, Clarence Brown); *Gone With the Wind* (39, Victor Fleming); *Chad Hanna* (40, King); *Brigham Young* (40, Henry Hathaway); *All That Money Can Buy* (41, Dieterle); *All Through the Night* (42, Vincent Sherman); *The Ox-Bow Incident* (43, William Wellman); *Government Girl* (43, Dudley Nichols); *Tender Comrade* (43, Edward Dmytryk); *The Impatient Years* (44, Irving Cummings); *Sunday Dinner for a Soldier* (44, Lloyd Bacon); *My Darling Clementine* (46, Ford); *Keeper of the Bees* (47, John Sturges); *Three Godfathers* (48, Ford); *Wagonmaster* (50, Ford); *Caged* (50, John Cromwell); *The Daughter of Rosie O'Grady* (50, Butler); *Surrender* (50, Dwan); *The Lemon Drop Kid* (51, Sidney Lanfield); *Fourteen Hours* (51, Hathaway); *Journey into Light* (51, Stuart Heisler); *We're Not Married* (52, Edmund Goulding); *The Sun Shines Bright* (53, Ford); *Affair with a Stranger* (53, Roy Rowland); *Hit the Deck* (55, Rowland); *There's Always Tomorrow* (56, Douglas Sirk); *The Last Hurrah* (58, Ford); and *Mary Poppins* (64, Robert Stevenson).

Jules Dassin,
b. Middletown, Connecticut, 1911
1942: *Nazi Agent; The Affairs of Martha; Reunion in France.* 1943: *Young Ideas.* 1944: *The Canterville Ghost.* 1945: *A Letter for Evie.* 1946: *Two Smart People.* 1947: *Brute Force.* 1948: *The Naked City.* 1949: *Thieves' Highway.* 1950: *Night and the City.* 1956: *Rififi.* 1958: *Celui qui doit Mourir/He Who Must Die; La Loi.* 1960: *Never on Sunday.* 1962: *Phaedra.* 1964: *Topkapi.* 1966: *10:30 p.m. Summer.* 1968: *Survival!; Up Tight.* 1970: *Promise at Dawn.* 1978: *A Dream of Passion.* 1980: *Circle of Two.*

The gap in Dassin's career during the early 1950s followed his departure from America for political reasons. But in Europe he found Melina Mercouri instead. Together, they made some of the most entertainingly bad films of the sixties and seventies: pictures that outstrip their own deficiencies and end up being riotously enjoyable as one waits to see how far pretentiousness will stretch. In good company, and a little drunk, *He Who Must Die, Phaedra,* and *10:30 p.m. Summer* might cure would-be suicides. There are those who found *Never on Sunday* charming, and *Topkapi* exciting. They may have been very drunk. *Topkapi* is incoherent, while Mercouri is about as inviting as Medusa. Dassin is an unashamed gimmick director—thus his implausible European films and the irrelevant exercise in silence in *Rififi*.

It follows that the "realism" of his postwar films in America was equally peripheral. Certainly one could not think it characteristic of the maker of *Reunion in France,* an espionage story of blithe absurdity. But *Brute Force* is striking; *Naked City* still looks an innovation in its use of location and the sly glamorizing of a policeman's day; *Thieves' Highway* is a robust, conventional thriller; while *Night and the City*—Dassin's best film—does show a London neglected by British directors. In those years, at least, Dassin made movies that were enjoyable because of modest, fulfilled intentions. The pleasure later came only from the grand distortion implicit in the scheme.

Factual account does not really seem appropriate, but in the mid-1930s Dassin studied drama in Europe, and in 1936 he was acting with the Yiddish Theatre and then the Group Theater (he appears, rather helplessly, as an actor in *Thieves' Highway, Rififi,* and *Never on Sunday*). He wrote for radio and directed for the stage before serving a director's apprenticeship making shorts on famous people (Rubinstein, Casals, etc.) at MGM. He was also an assistant on *They Knew What They Wanted* (40, Garson Kanin) and *Mr. and Mrs. Smith* (41, Alfred Hitchcock). *Survival!* was a tribute to Zionism, and *Promise at Dawn* an adaptation of Romain Gary's memoir of his mother, with Mercouri as Mom.

Delmer Daves (1904–77), b. San Francisco

1943: *Destination Tokyo.* 1944: *The Very Thought of You.* 1945: *Hollywood Canteen; Pride of the Marines.* 1947: *The Red House; Dark Passage.* 1948: *To the Victor.* 1949: *A Kiss in the Dark; Task Force.* 1950: *Broken Arrow.* 1951: *Bird of Paradise.* 1952: *Return of the Texan.* 1953: *Treasure of the Golden Condor; Never Let Me Go.* 1954: *Demetrius and the Gladiators; Drum Beat.* 1956: *Jubal; The Last Wagon.* 1957: *3:10 to Yuma.* 1958: *Cowboy; Kings Go Forth; The Badlanders.* 1959: *The Hanging Tree.* 1960: *A Summer Place.* 1961: *Parrish; Susan Slade.* 1962: *Lovers Must Learn.* 1963: *Spencer's Mountain.* 1964: *Youngblood Hawke.* 1965: *The Battle of the Villa Fiorita.*

Having studied at Stanford University, Daves began as an assistant to James Cruze in 1927 and worked at MGM as a technical advisor on college movies and as an actor: *The Duke Steps Out* (29, Cruze); *The Bishop Murder Case* (30, Nick Grinde); and *Good News* (30, Grinde). It is most suitable to regard him as a grown-up boy and a purveyor of nonreflective action movies. He spent most of the 1930s as a scriptwriter: *So This Is College* (29, Sam Wood); *Shipmates* (31, Harry Pollard); *Flirtation Walk* (34, Frank Borzage); *Page Miss Glory* (35, Mervyn Le Roy); *The Go-Getter* (37, Busby Berkeley); *The Singing Marine* (37, Ray Enright); *The Petrified Forest* (36, Archie Mayo); *Love Affair* (39, Leo McCarey); and *You Were Never Lovelier* (42, William A. Seiter). Writing many of his own scripts, he made his debut with a war movie.

There have been two purple passages in his career—1947, with *The Red House,* an Edward G. Robinson melodrama, and *Dark Passage,* a Bogart thriller; and then in the mid-1950s with several well-characterized Westerns that made full use of Daves's eye for dramatic landscape and crane shots: *Drum Beat; Jubal; The Last Wagon; Cowboy. 3:10 to Yuma* does not deserve its high reputation, largely because of its contrived situation and Glenn Ford's inability to be nasty. Daves's long association with Warners had an unhappy climax in the 1960s with a series of romances that he made with the studio's hopeful young talent (notably Sandra Dee and Troy Donahue—doll-kids). But Daves always seemed to enjoy his own films and it would take a severe viewer to hold out entirely.

Marion Davies (Marion Cecilia Douras) (1897–1961), b. New York

Marion Davies was *not* Susan Alexander Kane. Yet, as time goes by, it may be that only the second Mrs. Kane keeps Davies alive. Susan Alexander could not sing; she did not want to make the attempt in anything larger than the parlor; she had her disasters onstage; and she deserted the Kane who had sought to invent her. Marion Davies, on the other hand, was a genuinely funny actress who did good work. She then stayed loyal to her lover and patron, William Randolph Hearst, no matter that he had foolishly insisted on putting her in grand and serious roles.

The story of Marion Davies and William Randolph Hearst is sadder and funnier than Herman Mankiewicz and Orson Welles allowed; it's as intricate as the picture in Peter Bogdanovich's *The Cat's Meow* (02). Hearst was a lumbering, softhearted fool, devoted to his young mistress and deeply hurt by the picture of her in *Kane*. Susan Alexander, Kane's second wife, is forced into the unlikely career of opera singer, has a rowdy New York accent, and mopes in the desolate caverns of Xanadu over huge jigsaw puzzles.

That last point was typical of the gratuitous cruelty in the film: Marion Davies, too, occupied herself with jigsaws at Hearst's San Simeon mansion. It is a wonder that *Kane* did not mimic Davies's stammer as well. (And Gore Vidal has reported that "Rosebud" was Mr. Hearst's pet name for Marion's clitoris. How can fact compete with such Velcro stories?)

But whereas Susan Alexander is a forlorn soprano, Marion Davies had more screen potential than Hearst's heavy care noticed. The saddest stroke of all is not that Hearst imposed his mistress on the film public, but that the industry exploited his fondness for the girl. And when a man is caught up in the heroic gesture of founding a production company to showcase his mistress, no wonder that he likes to see her looking her best in romantic parts, even if her real talent is for knockabout comedy. King Vidor tells a story about his attempts to persuade Hearst to let Marion play comedy, to be met by this woolly dignity: "King's right. But I'm right, too—because I'm not going to let Marion be hit in the face with a pie."

Davies was in the Ziegfeld Follies when she met Hearst. She became his mistress and remained so until the great man died in 1951. Hearst was determined to make her a star and he founded Cosmopolitan Pictures to produce her films. By 1919, her movies were being distributed by Paramount: *Getting Mary Married* (19, Allan Dwan); *The Dark Star* (19, Dwan); *April Folly* (19, Robert Z. Leonard); *The Restless Sex* (20, Leonard); *Buried Treasure* (21, George D. Baker); *Enchantment* (21, Robert Vignola); *The Bride's Play* (22, George W. Terwilliger); *Beauty's Worth* (22, Vignola); *The Young Diana* (22, Albert Capellani and Vignola); *When Knighthood Was in Flower* (22, Vignola); and *Adam and Eva* (23, Vignola).

Adolph Zukor was content for Cosmopolitan to move over to Goldwyn: few of the Davies films had failed to make a loss. But through Goldwyn, Marion Davies became a bargaining counter in MGM's search for glory. Louis Mayer lavished attention and money on Davies and allowed her a magnificent bungalow on the lot. These rewards exceeded her worth, but not the value of constant MGM publicity in the Hearst papers. MGM carried Davies through eight of their headiest years, relying on a favorable press from Hearst. The economics of the deal would need careful research, but the Hearst boycott on *Kane* shows how potent his favor could be. With MGM, Davies was seldom allowed to laugh as much as her limited abilities encouraged: *Yolanda* (24, Vignola); *Janice Meredith* (24, E. Mason Hopper); *Zander the Great* (25, George Hill); *Lights of Old Broadway* (25, Monta Bell); *Beverley of Graustark* (26, Sidney Franklin); *The Red Mill* (27, Roscoe Arbuckle); *Tillie the Toiler* (27, Hobart Henley);

The Fair Co-Ed (27, Sam Wood); *Quality Street* (27, Franklin); *The Patsy* (28, King Vidor); *The Cardboard Lover* (28, Leonard); *Show People* (28, Vidor); *Not So Dumb* (30, Vidor); *The Florodora Girl* (30, Harry Beaumont); *The Bachelor Father* (31, Leonard); *It's a Wise Child* (31, Leonard); *Five and Ten* (31, Leonard); *Polly of the Circus* (32, Alfred Santell); *Blondie of the Follies* (32, Edmund Goulding); *Peg o' My Heart* (33, Leonard); *Going Hollywood* (33, Raoul Walsh); and *Operator 13* (34, Richard Boleslavsky).

Mayer was then caught between two ladies anxious to play Elizabeth Barrett Browning: Davies, supported by Hearst, and Norma Shearer, backed by her husband, Irving Thalberg. Shearer won and Davies, Cosmopolitan, and her bungalow went to Warners for four films before she retired: *Page Miss Glory* (35, Mervyn Le Roy); *Hearts Divided* (36, Frank Borzage); *Cain and Mabel* (36, Lloyd Bacon); and *Ever Since Eve* (37, Bacon).

When her career was over, and after Hearst was broke and sick, Davies again escaped the legend. She behaved with common decency, offering back the jewels Hearst had given her, and standing by him. This final story, all the way to Hearst's death in 1951, is worthy of a movie—something far better than the 1985 TV job that hired Robert Mitchum and Virginia Madsen, but gave them nothing to do. What a reunion the story could be for Beatty and Dunaway—*Twilight at San Simeon*? Or at Wyntoon, Hearst's smaller estate, in northern California, where one of the "cottages" has murals in which the fairytale character, Rose Red, was based on the young and undyingly lovely Marion Davies.

Terence Davies,
b. Liverpool, England, 1945
1983: *The Terence Davies Trilogy*. 1988: *Distant Voices, Still Lives*. 1992: *The Long Day Closes*. 1995: *The Neon Bible*. 2000: *The House of Mirth*.

Davies is an utterly personal lyric filmmaker who moves as swiftly as music from the lacerating to the ecstatic. The *Trilogy* was three short films made over a period of years for small budgets, about a Roman Catholic and homosexual who lives in Liverpool: "Children" was made in 1974–76 on a British Film Institute grant; "Madonna and Child" was released in 1980 as a graduation project at the National Film School in England; and "Death and Transfiguration" was made with funds from the BFI and the Greater London Arts Association.

All these pictures were shot in black and white, which in Davies's eyes, "has the ability to strip bare, to rid the image of all superfluity and to create a beauty that is all the more powerful because of its very starkness." Moving backward and forward in time, torn between the similar appeals of real mothers and icons of the madonna, filled with situations of dread and pain, revelation and consolation, the trilogy makes us think of Bresson and Graham Greene, and it comes close to the thrilled remorse of Gerard Manley Hopkins.

Distant Voices, Still Lives was in color, it was 35mm as opposed to 16mm, and it was an epic of abused childhood, offset by the comfort in popular songs. It is less a narrative than a musical progress, and to these eyes it was marred by self-pity. But no one else had ever dreamed of such a film, and as if mindful of criticism about morbidity, Davies next produced *The Long Day Closes,* a poem to ordinary bliss as seen through the eyes of a child growing up in a dark, impoverished world in which sometimes nothing more momentous occurs than a change in the light. But Davies knows that that *is* momentous.

The Long Day Closes is about a state of being, a kind of paradise, despite the rain, the harsh circumstances, and the cramped tenement house. Memory has graced all the elements with imagery that is part Flemish, part Bill Brandt, and part a tribute to the lost glory of three-strip Technicolor. Songs mingle with passages of classic movie sound tracks. The camera moves with extraordinary elegance. Nothing happens, yet lives and a time have been opened up and gently restored, as in a tender anatomy lesson.

It must be a large question where Davies goes beyond autobiography. But *The Long Day Closes* is a triumph of common experience. *The Neon Bible* seemed to me an enterprising failure, based on a novel by John Kennedy Toole, but *The House of Mirth* was a great film (dreadfully missed by public and critics alike) in which a thorough sense of literary values was driven home by Davies's rare capacity for naked feelings. If he can keep working freely—or as he elects—he has great things ahead.

Andrew Davis, b. Chicago, 1947

1978: *Stony Island.* 1981: *The Final Terror.* 1985: *Code of Silence.* 1988: *Above the Law.* 1989: *The Package.* 1992: *Under Siege.* 1993: *The Fugitive.* 1995: *Steal Big Steal Little.* 1996: *Chain Reaction.* 1998: *A Perfect Murder.* 2002: *Collateral Damage.* 2003: *Holes.*

Andrew Davis has made an unusual journey. After studying journalism at the University of Illinois, he was a camera assistant to Haskell Wexler on *Medium Cool* (69). From that, he became the cinematographer on a number of low-budget action pictures: *Cool Breeze* (72, Barry Pollack); *Private Parts* (72, Paul Bartel); *Hit Man* (72, George Armitage); *The Slams* (73, Jonathan Kaplan); *Lepke* (75, Menahem Golan). That led to *Stony Island,* an independent feature, done in the

Chicago area, about a racially integrated musical group.

But after photographing *Over the Edge* (79, Kaplan), he directed a cheap horror film, *The Final Terror,* which helped him get the Chuck Norris picture *Code of Silence.* Three years later, he was handling Steven Seagal in *Above the Law.* *The Package* was that rarity, a poor Gene Hackman film—with Tommy Lee Jones in support. *Under Siege* marked the commercial triumph of Seagalism, and from that Davis jumped to the blockbuster *The Fugitive* (with Jones in pursuit of Harrison Ford). That picture raised a rabble, and won Jones an Oscar, but in truth it's devoid of the long-running suspense of the TV original, to say nothing of the depressive foreboding David Janssen brought to it.

Nothing since has been as big. But *A Perfect Murder* was a singularly inept "opening up" of *Dial M for Murder,* which seemed blind to the contained theatrical charm of the original. *Collateral Damage* was set back six months because of its inadvertent overlap with the events of September 11. When will they realize that so much of American film has nothing to do with life, death, damage, or duty?

Bette Davis (Ruth Elizabeth Davis) (1908–89), b. Lowell, Massachusetts

Bette Davis trailed the subject of acting across the audience's path with all the preemptive originality of Queen Elizabeth spreading ermine on the ground before Raleigh.

Davis's unexpectedness began with the implausibility of a far-from-pretty girl becoming a movie star. At once hysterically mortified and daring us to admit that she was not attractive, how could the lady with pulsing eyes succeed unless she was a serious actress? This implied that she alone in Hollywood was a real professional; those others, more beautiful and calm, must also be lazier and emptier. Davis always stressed how hard she worked and left us to gather the rarity of such diligence. She went to war with her studio for better scripts and directors, even if in circumstances that were straight from the overheated script conferences that produced the movies she was fleeing. But the smoke of that battle had still not cleared when she took her greatest part, Margo Channing in *All About Eve,* the grandest cinematic expression of high theatre. In that film Davis is a curdled cocktail, her lips ashine with greasepaint and her hair youthfully long, seeming to merge with her fur coat. But what sort of actress is Margo Channing? Not just ham, but ham baked in honey, and studded with cloves.

Margo brags that she "detests cheap sentiment," but her self-projection depends upon it. And Davis was a vulgar, bullying actress, who made mannerism a virtue by showing us how it expresses the emotion of the self. When Davis's autobiography, *A Lonely Life,* was published in 1962, Brigid Brophy compared the actress to St. Teresa and remarked on the nature of a great actress's being rooted in an hysterical personality:

> The essence is not belief (which is merely and involuntarily mad) but make-belief in the fantasy—to the extent of giving a great performance or of having, as a deliberately cultivated act of will, a mystical experience. Miss Davis needed her bad scripts as sorely as they needed her; they were what she needed to wrestle through in pursuit of that "truth" and "realism" . . . which to her are "more than natural." For in Miss Davis' control is always chasing after the fantasy, insight after melodrama; the chase creates, in her autobiography as in St. Teresa's, a wonderful spiral of intensity.

Bette Davis—the name was an allusion to Balzac's Cousin Bette—made her stage debut in 1928. Universal hired her and put her in her first film, *Bad Sister* (31, Hobart Henley). She had small parts in *Seed* (31, John Stahl), *Waterloo Bridge* (31, James Whale), and *The Menace* (32, Roy William Neill) before Warners took her up to play with George Arliss in *The Man Who Played God* (32, John Adolfi). This began her long period under contract to Warners, a studio run on a team of male stars. She took supporting roles in *So Big* (32, William Wellman) and *The Rich Are Always With Us* (32, Alfred E. Green) and worked her way up singing "Willie the Weeper" in *Cabin in the Cotton* (32, Michael Curtiz); in *Three on a Match* (32, Mervyn Le Roy); *20,000 Years in Sing Sing* (32, Curtiz); *Ex-Lady* (33, Robert Florey); *Bureau of Missing Persons* (33, Roy del Ruth); *Fashions of 1934* (34, William Dieterle); *Jimmy the Gent* (34, Curtiz); and *Fog Over Frisco* (34, Dieterle). But Warners only began to take notice after RKO borrowed her to play Mildred in *Of Human Bondage* (34, John Cromwell), an important role and the first to show her as a woman living ruthlessly by her wits. Warners then gave her a real chance in *Bordertown* (35, Archie Mayo); *Front Page Woman* (35, Curtiz); and *Dangerous* (35, Green), in which she played a Warners "Persona" actress and won the Oscar. In 1936 she was in *The Petrified Forest* (Mayo), *The Golden Arrow* (Green), and *Satan Met a Lady* (Dieterle).

The last, a bad adaptation of *The Maltese Falcon,* summed up her dissatisfaction with the material Warners gave her. She refused her next film and, while on suspension, sailed to Britain to make a movie outside her contract. Warners sued and a hectic court case in London went against her. She was apparently humiliated and penniless, but the case had publicized her flamboyant independence. Never averse to the role of proud martyr, she returned to more consideration: *Marked Woman* (37, Lloyd Bacon); *Kid Galahad* (37, Curtiz); *That Certain Woman* (37, Edmund Goulding); and *It's Love I'm After* (37, Mayo). This last was one of the first concessions the studio made to romantic melodrama on her behalf. They went further with *Jezebel* (38, William Wyler), a lurid Deep South women's picture that allows Davis first to scheme then repent: it is lit up by her little girl's conviction—a trash heap glowing with fire at twilight. It won her a second Oscar, though it killed any chance at Scarlett O'Hara. Now, at last, she was in her tortured element: *The Sisters* (38, Anatole Litvak); as a rich girl who goes blind in *Dark Victory* (39, Goulding)—making death the great performance; as the demented Carlotta in *Juarez* (39, Dieterle); *The Old Maid* (39, Goulding); as the fidgety Virgin Queen in *The Private Lives of Elizabeth and Essex* (39, Curtiz).

The part of Elizabeth drew on the emotions of a woman fearful of romantic neglect who makes a cult of highly strung capriciousness. Within a few years, Davis had given up modern, masculine films for costume melodrama. She excelled in the tearjerker *All This and Heaven Too* (40, Litvak), and she was at her best in *The Letter* (40, Wyler) and *The Great Lie* (41, Goulding) before *The Little Foxes* (41, Wyler), which made explicit her command of the emotional woman, thwarted or spurned, who becomes a malicious tyrant. The good scripts she had called for needed only to be red-blooded and to turn upon her passionate ugliness. After *The Man Who Came to Dinner* (42, William Keighley) and *In This Our Life* (42, John Huston), she played Charlotte Vale in *Now, Voyager* (42, Irving Rapper), a classic exaltation of the women's picture. Much quieter in *Watch on the Rhine* (43, Herman Shumlin), she was then in *Old Acquaintance* (43) and a very nasty wife to Claude Rains in *Mr. Skeffington* (44), both by Vincent Sherman.

At about this time, her material withered away: *The Corn Is Green* (45, Rapper), when movie corn should be aflame with ripeness; *A Stolen Life* (46, Curtis Bernhardt) as twins, one with icing and one without; and then three duds in a row—*Deception* (46, Rapper); *Winter Meeting* (48, Bretaigne Windust); and *June Bride* (48, Windust). Her last film at Warners, *Beyond the Forest* (49, King Vidor), was one she disliked, and yet Vidor was a director made for her, and the film has some exotic moments.

As a free-lancer, she made *All About Eve* (50, Joseph L. Mankiewicz). But if that looked like the dawn of a new pop-eyed opulence, it deceived. She faltered throughout the 1950s in efforts to revive earlier successes: *Payment on Demand* (51, Bernhardt); *Another Man's Poison* (52, Rapper); *Phone Call from a Stranger* (52, Jean Negulesco); *The Star* (53, Stuart Heisler); *The Virgin Queen* (55, Henry Koster); *Storm Center* (56, Daniel

Taradash); *The Catered Affair* (56, Richard Brooks); *The Scapegoat* (58, Robert Hamer); *John Paul Jones* (59, John Farrow); and *Pocketful of Miracles* (61, Frank Capra).

Her career, like that of Joan Crawford, was given a new lease on life by Robert Aldrich's *What Ever Happened to Baby Jane?* (62), an extraordinary extension of the sadomasochistic strains in their film work. It made Davis henceforward the star of a number of subhorror films. She was not unsuited to these, but she was alien to their camp knowingness. Her classic period had dealt with silly, overblown material, but she had always compelled audiences into sharing her belief in it. That faith was being modishly exploited in the sad spectacle of an actress submitting to a carpetbagger perversion of what was a rich and neurotic personality: *Dead Ringer* (64, Paul Henreid); *Where Love Has Gone* (64, Edward Dmytryk); *Hush . . . Hush, Sweet Charlotte* (64, Aldrich), much better than the rest, if just as calculated; nicely starched as *The Nanny* (65, Seth Holt); *The Anniversary* (67, Roy Ward Baker); *Connecting Rooms* (70, Franklin Gollings); and *Bunny O'Hare* (70, Gerd Oswald).

In 1977, the American Film Institute chose her as the first woman to receive its Life Achievement Award—a deserved prize, sadly offset by the death of Joan Crawford a few weeks later.

She made only a few more films—*Return from Witch Mountain* (77, John Hough); *Death on the Nile* (78, John Guillermin); *The Watcher in the Woods* (81, Hough); *The Whales of August* (87, Lindsay Anderson); and *The Wicked Stepmother* (90, Larry Cohen). She became frighteningly thin and bizarre in her public appearances. She had a feud with her daughter, B. D. Hyman. And her best late work was on television: *Strangers: The Story of a Mother and Daughter* (79, Milton Katselas), in which she was paired with Gena Rowlands and for which she won an Emmy; *White Mama* (80, Jackie Cooper); *Skyward* (80, Ron Howard); *Family Reunion* (81, Fielder Cook); *A Piano for Mrs. Cimino* (82, George Schaefer); *Little Gloria . . . Happy at Last* (82, Waris Hussein); with James Stewart in *Right of Way* (82, Schaefer); and *As Summers Die* (86, Jean-Claude Tramont).

Geena Davis (Virginia Davis),
b. Wareham, Massachusetts, 1957

Geena Davis is so smart, funny, gorgeous, full-mouthed, and knowing that it's just a little too much to believe, in *Thelma and Louise* (91, Ridley Scott), that she has been stewing in that marriage and that part of the humdrum Southwest without ever getting her rocks off or being hired into the movies. There *is* a look that slips past the best acting: it says this one is hot, and anyone can see it. But if we are going to have a good time at the movies, we have to know when voyeurism needs to turn a blind eye.

Many, many actresses have depended on it, for we have not yet found a way of having movies in which waifs, strays, wallflowers, and slowpoke earth girls look less than a hot fudge sundae.

Geena Davis went from theatre studies at Boston University to the Zoli modeling agency, and from there into a small, eye-catching role in *Tootsie* (82, Sydney Pollack). She was in *Fletch* (85, Michael Ritchie), and a vampire in *Transylvania 6-5000* (85, Rudy DeLuca), where she met her future husband, Jeff Goldblum. They were together, and very touching, in *The Fly* (86, David Cronenberg), before—somewhat unexpectedly—she won the supporting actress Oscar as Muriel, the dog trainer, in *The Accidental Tourist* (88, Lawrence Kasdan). Since then she has done *Beetlejuice* (88, Tim Burton); *Earth Girls Are Easy* (89, Julien Temple)—with Goldblum again, just before their breakup; *Quick Change* (90, Bill Murray and Howard Franklin); and *A League of Their Own* (92, Penny Marshall).

She also played in the TV series *Buffalo Bill* (1983–84), and wrote one episode of it. Her future may well depend on her ability to shape (or write) her own material—she had the promise of a new Carole Lombard or Jean Arthur. But hot comes in great supply, and *Hero* (92, Stephen Frears) did not make enough use of her. In 1993, she married director Renny Harlin and acted in *Angie* (94, Martha Coolidge).

More mysterious careers have lasted longer. But few pretty bubbles burst as suddenly as hers. Her new marriage led to *Cutthroat Island* (95, Harlin), a major disaster, and then *The Long Kiss Goodnight* (96, Harlin), a role too muddled and gloomy to suit her. Since then, she has done only *Stuart Little* (99, Rob Minkoff); a TV sitcom, *The Geena Davis Show*, to which too many people said, "Who?"; and *Stuart Little 2* (02, Minkoff).

Judy Davis, b. Perth, Australia, 1956

Not many actresses these days have such a rich line of gruffness, intelligence, and superiority; none can give such rapid hints of the perverse or the eccentric; and no one has ever been so unabashedly freckled and scrawny, without losing an atom of appeal. It will take brave ventures to cast Judy Davis. She does not seem interested in having the love of the people. But there is a cult following her, and it thrills to stories from Australia that she is an outstanding stage actress. Imagine her Miss Julie, Hedda Gabler, Lady Macbeth, Mother Courage, and Tracy Lord (she does have a Hepburnish brusqueness).

She attended the National Institute of Dramatic Art in Sydney and, apparently, left a convent school to sing rock and roll: liturgy and abandon have shaped her. It is a career of moments and scenes and of films that killed her off or hardly had the nerve to run with her: *High Rolling* (77, Igor

Auzins); *My Brilliant Career* (79, Gillian Armstrong); *Heatwave* (81, Phillip Noyce); *The Winter of Our Dreams* (81, John Duigan); *The Final Option* (82, Ian Sharp); rather neglected as Miss Quested in *A Passage to India* (84, David Lean), but nominated for best actress; *Kangaroo* (86, Tim Burstall), with her husband, Colin Friels, playing versions of D. H. Lawrence and Frieda; *High Tide* (87, Armstrong); *Alice* (90, Woody Allen); as George Sand in *Impromptu* (91, James Lapine); *Where Angels Fear to Tread* (91, Charles Sturridge); as a Southern ghostwriter in *Barton Fink* (91, Joel and Ethan Coen); fighting the Nazis on TV in *One Against the Wind* (91, Larry Elikann), where she resembles Vivien Leigh; *Naked Lunch* (92, David Cronenberg); *Shadows and Fog* (92, Allen); nominated for supporting actress in *Husbands and Wives* (92, Allen), in which she has some spot-on Bette Davis scenes; *The Ref* (94, Ted Demme).

The difficulty in casting, or exercising her fully, began to show: she had small roles and wayward films, and more and more TV. Yet she continues to triumph, one of the few unmissable actresses of our time: *The New Age* (94, Michael Tolkin); very good in *Serving in Silence: The Margarethe Cammermeyer Story* (95, Jeff Bleckner); brilliant in *Children of the Revolution* (96, Peter Duncan); horribly abused in *Blood & Wine* (96, Bob Rafelson); *Deconstructing Harry* (97, Allen); regarded as a bitch in *Absolute Power* (97, Clint Eastwood); *Celebrity* (98, Allen); as Ms. Hellman, opposite Sam Shepard, in *Dash and Lilly* (99, Kathy Bates); *Gaudi Afternoon* (01, Susan Seidelman). But her difficulties were compensated for by her inspired *Life with Judy Garland: Me and My Shadows* (01, Robert Allan Ackerman); *The Man Who Sued God* (01, Mark Joffe); *Swimming Upstream* (03, Russell Mulcahy).

Doris Day (Doris von Kappelhoff),
b. Cincinnati, Ohio, 1924

Doris Day is redolent of the early 1950s, a pop-art blonde who lived on to an age when her simplicity was reinterpreted by instant nostalgia. She hoped to suggest that the world was okay, that wholesome blonde girls with cheerful voices and big tits were destined to meet nice guys who would woo them chastely and tunefully *On Moonlight Bay* (51, Roy del Ruth) or in some such Californian paradise. She was the home fire that refused to admit the cold war. She was, too, a grand confidence trick, boasting in *Young at Heart* (54, Gordon Douglas) that she was "Ready, Willing and Able" but demonstrating throughout her career the very opposite. Above all, she was optimistic, just as the years of her first success were defiantly hopeful and religiously preoccupied with dating, 78s, and banana splits. She is easy to deride. But her fans were devoted and her energy was authentic. She was not sophisticated, but in the early 1950s that in itself was cool. What is most impressive about her professionalism is the way she survived into the 1960s, riding new fashions without actually changing her nature.

She was a famous band singer seen by Michael Curtiz, who gave her a starring debut in *Romance on the High Seas* (48). She had a few straight roles—in *Young Man With a Horn* (50, Curtiz) and *Storm Warning* (50, Stuart Heisler)—but it was in Warners musicals that she found fame: as the studio waitress in *It's a Great Feeling* (49, David Butler); *My Dream Is Yours* (49, Curtiz); *Tea for Two* (50, Butler); *The West Point Story* (50, del Ruth); *Lullaby of Broadway* (51, Butler); *I'll See You in My Dreams* (51, Curtiz); *April in Paris* (52, Butler); *By the Light of the Silvery Moon* (52, Butler); *Calamity Jane* (53, Butler); and *Lucky Me* (54, Jack Donohue). Nor should it be forgotten that she was one of the first singers whose records were bought as "pop" by teenagers. I can remember girls who worked to look like Doris, and boys who responded warmly to those efforts.

We should not underestimate the quality of her voice. Not only was she a fine singer, technically, but her singing voice had a natural dramatic force that carried her beyond her acting ability. Thus, in many cases, her songs deepen the movie she is in—I am thinking especially of "Secret Love" in *Calamity Jane* and most of *Love Me or Leave Me* (57, Charles Vidor), where she had a triumph playing singer Ruth Etting and proved her readiness for musicals of more developed content. (If only she and Sondheim could have worked together.) Listening to her sound tracks makes you believe her films were richer or more moving than was really the case.

In addition to *Love Me or Leave Me*, in the midfifties she broadened her range, emoting enormously and slipping a ludicrous song ("Che Sera Sera") into *The Man Who Knew Too Much* (55, Alfred Hitchcock); somehow managing to land an aeroplane in *Julie* (56, Andrew L. Stone); and her best film, *The Pajama Game* (57, Stanley Donen and George Abbott), which harnessed her bounce to the role of factory shop steward. Her work turned to romantic comedy in *The Tunnel of Love* (58, Gene Kelly) and *Teacher's Pet* (58, George Seaton), and she contrived to become the untainted subject of Ross Hunter's sexual innuendo (and a top box-office attraction) in *Pillow Talk* (59, Michael Gordon); *Lover Come Back* (61, Delbert Mann); and *That Touch of Mink* (62, Mann). She was wide-eyed with fright in *Midnight Lace* (60, David Miller); funny in *Please Don't Eat the Daisies* (60, Charles Walters); and returned to music in *Billy Rose's Jumbo* (62, Walters), but pillow talk held sway: *The Thrill of It All* (63, Norman Jewison); *Move Over, Darling* (63, Gordon);

Send Me No Flowers (64, Jewison); and *Do Not Disturb* (64, Ralph Levy). But since two Frank Tashlin films—the amusing *The Glass Bottom Boat* (66) and the woeful *Caprice* (67)—she has made nothing of interest and now seems to have retired to the world of margarine commercials and looking after animals.

This may also have been influenced by the death in 1968 of Martin Melcher, her husband and frequent producer—and also the exploiter of her money.

Daniel Day-Lewis (Michael Blake Day-Lewis), b. London, 1958

The son of actress Jill Balcon (daughter of Michael Balcon) and writer C. Day-Lewis, Daniel was trained at the Bristol Old Vic, and he has already done impressive work in the theatre—in Christopher Bond's *Dracula,* Julian Mitchell's *Another Country,* as Mayakovsky in *Futurists,* and in several Shakespeare plays, including a London *Hamlet* that he gave up because of exhaustion. There is an electric volatility to Day-Lewis, as well as a rare poetic feeling, that makes him seem like the Olivier of his talented generation. At present, Day-Lewis is seriously stretching his own range in ways that promise a career of uncommon power.

He had small roles in *Gandhi* (82, Richard Attenborough), and *The Bounty* (84, Roger Donaldson), and he played Mr. Kafka in *The Insurance Man* (85, Richard Eyre), written by Alan Bennett. His breakthrough was in *My Beautiful Laundrette* (85, Stephen Frears), playing a mysterious drifter who develops a serious gay relationship. He was very funny in *A Room with a View* (86, James Ivory), and then at a loss in *Nanou* (87, Conny Templeman) and *Stars and Bars* (88, Pat O'Connor).

Philip Kaufman cast him in the lead role, Tomas, in Milan Kundera's *The Unbearable Lightness of Being* (88), but Day-Lewis seemed too young and thus too deliberately cynical in the part—it needed more age and a more hard-earned sourness. But he seized on the role of Christy Brown in *My Left Foot* (89, Jim Sheridan), as hungrily as Jimmy Greaves with a loose ball in the goal area. Day-Lewis had strong Irish sympathies, and he felt no inhibition about delivering Brown's anger and sexuality to the screen. Actors playing cripples have won Oscars before, but Day-Lewis let us see and feel how true and human a warped spirit can be. The part begged for bravura playing, but Day-Lewis took the performance into real areas of danger. He made Christy fearsome and uncontainable. He was better than the modest context of the film.

For no clear reason, he played a spokesman for dental consciousness in *Eversmile, New Jersey* (89, Carlos Sorin), filmed in Argentina. Whereupon, Day-Lewis took a great challenge: as Hawkeye in *The Last of the Mohicans* (92, Michael Mann), the kind of role that even Olivier would have declined. He seemed physically changed—larger, more muscular, and completely in his element, hurtling silently through the primal forest. He then returned to fine clothes and complicated manners as Newland Archer in *The Age of Innocence* (93, Martin Scorsese). But he seemed lost, and even effete, and he could not bring the necessary tragedy to bear.

He fell on the role of Gerry Conlon in *In the Name of the Father* (93, Sheridan) like a freed prisoner. Day-Lewis was bold enough to show Conlon as a martyr scarcely deserving of a film—feckless, immature, lazy—until prison made him a man worthy of his own father. The performance brought substance to an overly simple film.

Day-Lewis continues to be hard to please: in the last ten years he has made five pictures—De Niro, with whom he is sometimes compared, did twenty-three. I'd argue that both numbers are excessive, and hope that Day-Lewis finds a happier medium. He played John Proctor in *The Crucible* (96, Nicholas Hytner) and married Arthur Miller's daughter, Rebecca. He was *The Boxer* (97, Jim Sheridan), which had little more than Irishness to recommend it—but he is an Irish citizen. Then years of absence turned into his gangleader in *Gangs of New York* (02, Scorsese).

James Dean (1931–55), b. Fairmount, Indiana

It is sad for any moviegoer to have no great star burning during his or her most impressionable years. Many stars, no matter how well they survive passing time, are only eminent because of the way they first mark consciousness. Once penetrated, we never forget the scar. And knowing what Dean meant in 1955 and 1956 makes it possible to understand how Valentino once moved viewers to the quick. It is reasonable to say that Dean and I came in together. Eight years earlier, Montgomery Clift in *Red River* had seemed a possible older brother; but Dean was oneself and, at first, one marveled in the way a savage might be awed by a mirror.

I first saw Dean in *Rebel Without a Cause* (55, Nicholas Ray) at the Granada, Tooting. That is relevant because it was a huge and fabulously decorated cinema, the most beautiful I have ever known, modeled on a Venetian palace. It had mirrored corridors, the softest of carpets, and an interior so spacious that it was possible to evade the usherettes. Especially in the dark. I arrived early, some ten minutes before the end of the previous showing. As I stepped into the auditorium, my feet pushing through the pile, so, on the screen, Dean edged into the planetarium, doing what he could to talk Sal Mineo into surrendering to the police. Even then, it was apparent how far the moment drew upon Ray's use of color and composition. But so much also depended on Dean. He made it clear that he wanted Mineo's safety, but guessed already that the cause was perilous. Dean's cry of anguish when Mineo is shot down was the very antithesis of the film's inadequate title.

No matter that it was seized on at the time, Dean's potency was not that of a rebel without a cause. Although he was vulnerable and sensitive, he never suggested youthfulness or callowness. On the contrary, he seemed older, sadder, and more experienced than the adults in his films. More than that, he seemed to sense his own extra intuition and to see that it was of no use. His resignation and fatalism showed up the restricted personality of the world he inhabited. Occasionally driven to anger or violence, Dean was not a rebel, but a disenchanted romantic, as brooding and knowing as the darkest Bogart—the Bogart of *In a Lonely Place*. Dean's isolation is that of profound understanding; and his dislike of the world, far from being causeless, was based on the extent to which the world had fallen away from its proper nobility, into vulgarity, materialism, and self-deception. America today is broken apart. But in 1955 it seemed whole, tight, and solid, except when Dean's tragic eyes surveyed it.

He appealed to the young because he understood that youth knew some truths about the world that adults had looked away from: about the unfriendly cities, the instinct for violence, and forsaken emotional sensibility. The parents in *Rebel* are trite, hollow people: Ray signaled that by casting Jim Backus (Mr. Magoo) as the father. And in *East of Eden* (55, Elia Kazan), it is Dean alone who is prepared to make the trip from Salinas to Monterey, who bridges the worlds of his arrogant, puritan father and his resentful, unprincipled mother. It was through Dean's eyes and Kazan's dramatic skill that we saw no need to condemn either and no prospect of their ever living together. Thus he had a kind of bastard robustness, horribly caricatured in his Jet Rink in *Giant* (56, George Stevens), too plain a film to sense Dean's depth. Nevertheless Dean was lucky with directors. Kazan gave him a charge, confidence, patience, and Julie Harris. But only Nicholas Ray could have given him a part that guessed at the looming alienation in America.

Dean died in a car crash as *Giant* finished shooting. He was set next to play in *Somebody Up There Likes Me*, proof that he could not always have expected parts or directors as good as *Rebel* and Ray. He might have faltered, as often as Brando has done. Equally, he might have become the man in *Last Tango*.

Before fame, he won prizes playing an Arab boy in a Broadway version of Gide's *The Immoralist*, and then went to Hollywood and three small parts: *Sailor Beware* (51, Jack Arnold); *Fixed Bayonets* (51, Samuel Fuller); and *Has Anybody Seen My Gal?* (52, Douglas Sirk).

When Dean died, Valentino had been gone just thirty years. Now, Dean is nearly forty years dead. But Dean is not dated yet. New kids, without great movie theatres to find him in, still fall under his sway. It's easier now to see Dean's intelligence, his dismay, and his sexual ambiguity. But he changed so much, in such a short time.

Basil Dearden (1911–71),
b. Westcliffe-on-Sea, England
1941: *The Black Sheep of Whitehall* (codirected with Will Hay). 1942: *The Goose Steps Out* (codirected with Hay). 1943: *My Learned Friend* (codirected with Hay); *The Bells Go Down*. 1944: *Halfway House; They Came to a City*. 1945: "The Hearse Driver," episode from *Dead of Night*. 1946: *The Captive Heart*. 1947: *Frieda*. 1948: *Saraband for Dead Lovers* (codirected with Michael Relph). 1949: *Train of Events* (codirected with Sidney Cole and Charles Crichton); *The Blue Lamp*. 1950: *Cage of Gold*. 1951: *Pool of London; I Believe in You* (codirected with Relph). 1952: *The Gentle Gunman*. 1953: *The Square Ring* (codirected with Relph). 1954: *The Rainbow Jacket*. 1955: *Out of the Clouds* (codirected with Relph); *The Ship that Died of Shame; Who Done It?* (codirected with Relph). 1957: *The Smallest Show on Earth*. 1958: *Violent Playground*. 1959: *Sapphire*. 1960: *The League of Gentlemen; Man in the Moon* (codirected with Relph). 1961: *The Secret Partner; Victim*. 1962: *All Night Long* (codirected with Relph); *Life for Ruth*. 1963: *The Mindbenders; A Place to Go; Woman of Straw*. 1964: *Masquerade*. 1966: *Khartoum*. 1968: *Only When I Larf; The Assassination Bureau*. 1970: *The Man Who Haunted Himself* (codirected with Relph).

When Dearden died, in a road accident, *The Guardian* called him "a proficient technician who could tell a good story well and get a film completed on schedule and without over-budgeting." Such a breathless epitaph was capped by this brief absurdity from *The Times:* "a versatile British film director."

Kindness and tact in obituaries are civilized things, but Dearden's versatility was with essentially inert subjects and his proficiency was at the expense of inventiveness or artistic personality. Filmmaking is not a matter of telling a good story well when the end product is the spurious social alertness of *The Blue Lamp*, *Sapphire*, and *Victim*. Nor is there any virtue—for the audience—in that a film was completed at 5:30 on the proper day with the due number of tea breaks. Dearden's coming in on time is replete with the obedient, leaden dullness of British studios. His films are decent, empty, and plodding and his association with Michael Relph is a fair representative of the British preference for bureaucratic cinema. It stands for the underlining of obvious meanings, for the showy resort to "realism," for the middle-brow ticking off of "serious" subjects, for the lack of cinematic sensibility, for the acceptance of all the technical shortcomings of British productions, for the complacent description of problems and the resolute refusal to adopt critical intelligence for dealing with them.

Dearden worked for Basil Dean at Ealing in the early 1930s and was involved on several George Formby films. From being the executive producer on Will Hay films, he moved without demur from the postwar refugee in *Frieda* to the tosh of *Saraband for Dead Lovers*. And in later years, the string of problem films was unalloyed by the coziness of *The Smallest Show on Earth* and *The League of Gentlemen*. The posting to *Khartoum* was outside his normal range, and if the film was better than one feared—especially in Heston's Gordon—still it was blind to the agonizing dilemma that, say, Nicholas Ray might have discerned in it.

Jan de Bont, b. Eindhoven, Holland, 1943
1994: *Speed.* 1996: *Twister.* 1997: *Speed 2: Cruise Control.* 1999: *The Haunting.*

To say that de Bont's four directing jobs have shown a steady decline in interest is to be generous to *Speed,* which was riveting, and absolutely of its time, but proof, too, that excruciating tension could be a test of patience. De Bont is likely to get several more effects shows yet, for two out of four have been hits, and he has an eye for sensation as well as enthusiasm for that mad hurry that threatens to take over modern films. Also, in his odd way, he prefers "real" marvels to the entirely fabricated—it may be all that is left of his Dutch tradition.

He won his chance as a director by being an expert director of photography on action films, in Holland and Los Angeles: *Turkish Delight* (73, Paul Verhoeven); *Cathy Tippel* (75, Verhoeven); *Max Havelaar* (76, Fons Rademakers); *Soldier of Orange* (79, Verhoeven); *Private Lessons* (81, Alan Myerson); *I'm Dancing As Fast As I Can* (82, Jack Hofsiss); the mad-dog *Cujo* (83, Lewis Teague); *All the Right Moves* (83, Michael Chapman); the eroticism of *The Fourth Man* (83, Verhoeven); *The Jewel of the Nile* (85, Teague); *Flesh & Blood* (85, Verhoeven); *Ruthless People* (86, Jim Abrahams, David Zucker and Jerry Zucker); *Die Hard* (88, John McTiernan); *Black Rain* (89, Ridley Scott); *The Hunt for Red October* (90, McTiernan); *Flatliners* (90, Joel Schumacher); *Shining Through* (92, David Seltzer); *Basic Instinct* (92, Verhoeven); *Lethal Weapon 3* (92, Richard Donner).

Philippe de Broca, b. Paris, 1933
1959: *Les Jeux de l'Amour/Playing at Love.* 1960: *Le Farceur/The Joker.* 1961: *L'Amant de Cinq Jours/Infidelity;* "La Gourmandise," episode from *Les Sept Péchés Capitaux.* 1962: *Cartouche;* "La Vedette," episode from *Les Veinards.* 1963: *L'Homme de Rio/That Man from Rio.* 1964: *Un Monsieur de Compagnie.* 1965: *Les Tribulations d'un Chinois en Chine.* 1966: *Le Roi de Coeur/King of Hearts.* 1967: "Mademoiselle Mimi," episode from *Le Plus Vieux Métier du Monde.* 1968: *Le Diable par le Queue.* 1969: *Les Figurants de Nouveau Monde.* 1971: *La Poudre d'Escampette.* 1972: *Chère Louise.* 1973: *Le Magnifique/How to Destroy the Reputation of the Greatest Secret Agent.* 1975: *L'Incorrigible.* 1977: *Julie Pot de Colle; Tendre Poulet/Dear Inspector.* 1978: *Le Cavaleur.* 1979: *On a Volé Le Cuisse de Jupiter.* 1981: *Psy.* 1983: *L'Africain.* 1984: *Louisiane* (TV). 1985: *La Gitane.* 1988: *Chouans!.* 1990: *Sheherezade.* 1991: *Les Clés du Paradis.* 1993: *Regarde-moi Quand Je Te Quitte* (TV); 1995: *Le Jardin des Plantes* (TV); 1996: *Le Veilleur de Nuit* (TV). 1997: *Les Hommes et les Femmes Sont Faits pour Vivre Heureux . . . mais Pas Ensemble* (TV); *Le Bossu.* 2000: *Amazone.* 2002: *On Guard.*

In his first three films, de Broca kept us breathless with a furiously gay comic tenderness that never allowed bedroom frolics or adulterous intrigue to lose sight of emotional reality. His tone was that of a sprinting Ophuls, and the great pleasure of the films lay in their elaborate frothiness. The lighthearted view of playacting sexuality that so occupied the New Wave was never more imaginatively done than in *Les Jeux de l'Amour* or *L'Amant de Cinq Jours.* Sheer exuberance, agility, and an eye for pretty, surrendering women—the character of his actor, Jean-Pierre Cassel—flowed out of de Broca's movies. But the accelerator was plainly full on. There were fears, even then, that when he drew breath de Broca might stumble and begin to imitate his own gaiety. So it has turned out, and been exacerbated by the international success of films like *That Man from Rio* and *King of Hearts.* The latter film had a prodigious reputation in America, and a marvelous idea—a lunatic institution becoming an image of sanity amid war. But that is a facile vision with the increasing ponderousness of de Broca's actual execution. In slowing, he has shown that his talent was all a matter of pace. Those early films, I suspect, are still darting and touching. But Belmondo in *That Man from Rio* is too impressed by the idea of being an amateur, joky James Bond; while *King of Hearts* is struck solemn by the greater significance implicit in it. A dissipated talent is sad to see, but the early achievement may last because of its very modesty and the engaging exhibitionism of Cassel. When the cinema of charm is assessed, de Broca must always be remembered.

Olivia de Havilland, b. Tokyo, 1916

The older sister of Joan Fontaine, de Havilland has had a career with a turning point. It came in 1943 when her seven-year contract with Warners lapsed. She wanted to be free, but the studio claimed that, in having refused a part and being suspended, she had incurred a six-month penalty. For two years, she and Warners were engaged in litigation, from which the actress emerged victorious. A major test case (advancing the earlier case between Warners and Bette Davis), the decision radically altered the pattern of de Havilland's own career.

She was the child of British parents who separated when she was five. The mother took Olivia and Joan to California, and while still at college Olivia was chosen by Max Reinhardt to play Hermia in *A Midsummer Night's Dream* (35). Warners signed her and worked her hard for seven years as the romantic interest in costume adventure pictures, most notably as Errol Flynn's damsel in *Captain Blood* (35); *The Charge of the Light Brigade* (36); *The Adventures of Robin Hood* (38); *Four's a Crowd* (38); *Dodge City* (39); *Santa Fe Trail* (40)—all directed by Michael Curtiz—and in Raoul Walsh's *They Died With Their Boots On* (41).

In addition, she played opposite Cagney in *The Irish in Us* (35, Lloyd Bacon); Fredric March in *Anthony Adverse* (36, Mervyn Le Roy); and Brian Aherne in *The Great Garrick* (37, James Whale). She provided decorative support in *Call It a Day* (37, Archie Mayo); *It's Love I'm After* (37, Mayo); *Gold Is Where You Find It* (38, Curtiz); *Wings of the Navy* (39, Bacon); and *Raffles* (40, Sam Wood).

She worked hard behind the scenes to secure the part of Melanie in *Gone With the Wind* (39, Victor Fleming), and she got a supporting actress nomination. Then, gradually, she made more impact at Warners, especially in Walsh's *Strawberry Blonde* (41), Huston's *In This Our Life,* and Elliott Nugent's *The Male Animal.* Loaned to Paramount, she was excellent in Mitchell Leisen's *Hold Back the Dawn* (41); while at RKO she was in *Government Girl* (43, Dudley Nichols). She finished at Warners with Norman Krasna's *Princess O'Rourke* (43) and as Charlotte Brontë in Curtis Bernhardt's *Devotion* (46).

Once free from Warners and the courts, she made *The Well-Groomed Bride* (45, Sidney Lanfield) and Robert Siodmak's *The Dark Mirror* (46)—playing twins—before coming to her best film, Mitchell Leisen's *To Each His Own* (46). Not only did she appear more beautiful than ever before, but the change to a world centered on the

female disclosed a warmth and gentleness that Warners had never bothered about. She won the best actress Oscar and went on to major dramatic roles in Litvak's *The Snake Pit* (48)—a lurid but innovatory examination of madness—and as Catherine Sloper in Wyler's *The Heiress* (49), for which she won her second Oscar.

Independence could have hardly anticipated better rewards, but in the event she seemed to lose her appetite for films. In 1955, having married the editor of *Paris Match* (her second husband), she moved to Europe and her films became strangely assorted: Henry Koster's *My Cousin Rachel* (52); Terence Young's *That Lady* (55); miscast in Kramer's *Not as a Stranger* (55); delightful in Krasna's *The Ambassador's Daughter* (56); reunited with Curtiz for *The Proud Rebel* (58); opposite Dirk Bogarde in Asquith's *Libel* (59); very good in Guy Green's *Light in the Piazza* (62); horribly harrowed in *Lady in a Cage* (64, Walter Grauman); enjoying herself in *Hush . . . Hush, Sweet Charlotte* (64, Robert Aldrich); inexplicably present in *The Adventurers* (69, Lewis Gilbert); as the Mother Superior in *Pope Joan* (72, Michael Anderson); and *The Swarm* (78, Irwin Allen).

She was in *The Fifth Musketeer* (79, Ken Annakin), and then she settled for roles in royal TV: *Murder Is Easy* (82, Claude Whatham); playing the Queen Mother in *The Royal Romance of Charles and Diana* (82, Peter Levin); in the Helen Hayes role, opposite Amy Irving, in *Anastasia: The Mystery of Anna* (86, Marvin J. Chomsky); and *The Woman He Loved* (88, Charles Jarrott) as Wallis Simpson's aunt.

Dino de Laurentiis,

b. Torre Annunziata, Italy, 1918

Since the end of the Second World War, de Laurentiis has striven to be the most "international" of Italian film producers. But despite an assiduous pursuit of major directors and subjects, both mythological and modern, he has seldom coincided with the significant moments or movements within Italian cinema.

He worked in a variety of minor capacities before becoming a producer during the German Occupation. In the immediate postwar years he produced several successful films featuring Silvana Mangano, whom he married in 1949. In the early 1950s, he formed a partnership with Carlo Ponti that involved their using both Rossellini and Fellini. But *Ulisse* marked his serious venturing out into the world market for epics: *Il Bandito* (46, Alberto Lattuada); *La Figlia del Capitano* (47, Mario Camerini); *Bitter Rice* (49, Giuseppe de Santis); *Il Brigante Musolino* (50, Camerini); *Napoli Milionaria* (50, Eduardo de Filippo); *Anna* (51, Lattuada); *Guardie e Ladri* (51, Steno and Mario Monicelli); *Europa '51* (52, Rossellini); *Dov'e la Liberta?* (53, Rossellini); *La Lupa* (53,

Lattuada); *Mambo* (54, Robert Rossen); *La Strada* (54, Fellini); *La Romana* (54, Luigi Zampa); *Gold of Naples* (54, Vittorio de Sica); *Ulisse* (55, Camerini); *La Donna del Fiume* (55, Mario Soldati); *War and Peace* (56, King Vidor); *Nights of Cabiria* (57, Fellini); *The Sea Wall* (58, René Clément); *Tempest* (58, Lattuada); *Fortunella* (58, de Filippo); *Five Branded Women* (60, Martin Ritt); *La Grande Guerra* (60, Monicelli); *Il Gobbo* (60, Carlo Lizzani); *Il Giudizio Universale* (61, de Sica); *The Best of Enemies* (62, Guy Hamilton); *Barabbas* (62, Richard Fleischer); *Il Mafioso* (62, Lattuada); *Il Boom* (63, de Sica); *The Bible* (66, John Huston); *Lo Straniero* (67, Luchino Visconti); *Barbarella* (68, Roger Vadim); *Bandits in Rome* (68, Alberto de Martino); *A Brief Season* (69, Renato Castellani); *Waterloo* (70, Sergei Bondarchuk); *The Deserter* (71, Burt Kennedy); *The Valachi Papers* (72, Terence Young); *Serpico* (73, Sidney Lumet); and *Death Wish* (74, Michael Winner).

It was around this time that Laurentiis advanced on America in the hope of being the last authentic tycoon. He has certainly been active, and he has had no qualms about balancing exploitation, middle-of-the-idiot entertainment, and arty "risks": *Mandingo* (75, Fleischer); big-business Southern melo-miscegenation; *Three Days of the Condor* (75, Sydney Pollack); *Face to Face* (75, Ingmar Bergman); *Lipstick* (76, Lamont Johnson); *Buffalo Bill and the Indians* (76, Robert Altman), after which he fired Altman from the projected *Ragtime; Drum* (76, Steve Carver), a sequel to *Mandingo* from which the new snob Dino removed his name, but not his lifeline; *The Shootist* (76, Don Siegel); the amusing remake of *King Kong* (76, John Guillermin), which he produced personally; *Orca . . . Killer Whale* (77, Michael Anderson); *The White Buffalo* (77, J. Lee Thompson); *King of the Gypsies* (78, Frank Pierson); *Hurricane* (79, Jan Troell); and *Flash Gordon* (80, Mike Hodges).

He produced *Ragtime* (81, Milos Forman), *Conan the Barbarian* (82, John Milius), *The Dead Zone* (83, David Cronenberg), and *The Bounty* (84, Roger Donaldson), and then he moved to America, set up studios in North Carolina, and founded DEG (De Laurentiis Entertainment Group). The venture was short-lived, but it produced *Dune* (84, David Lynch); *Year of the Dragon* (85, Michael Cimino); *Tai-Pan* (86, Daryl Duke); and *Blue Velvet* (86, Lynch), which was actually set in North Carolina and testified to either the generosity or the sleepiness of Dino. He has since produced *Desperate Hours* (90, Cimino); and *Body of Evidence* (93, Uli Edel)—thus, from Mangano to Madonna.

Age has not diminished him, or his enthusiasm for movie sensation. He has produced *Army of Darkness* (93, Sam Raimi); *Assassins* (95, Richard Donner); *Slave of Dreams* (95, Robert M. Young) and *Solomon & Sheba* (95, Young), both for TV; *Unforgettable* (96, John Dahl); the enterprising *Breakdown* (97, Jonathan Mostow); *U-571* (00, Mostow); and the delectable *Hannibal* (01, Ridley Scott), which was doing big business at the time he was given the Thalberg Award.

Georges Delerue (1925–92),
b. Roubaix, France

I would far rather listen to Delerue's scores for his French films than to the American music. Nevertheless, in his final years Delerue was nominated five times for best score: for *Anne of the Thousand Days* (69, Charles Jarrott), for *The Day of the Dolphin* (73, Mike Nichols), for *Julia* (77, Fred Zinnemann), for *Agnes of God* (85, Norman Jewison), and—his one winner—for *A Little Romance* (79, George Roy Hill). His music was naturally quiet, wistful, and atmospheric, and he had a knack for small chanson-like themes that grew over the course of a film. Those base motifs were especially vital to his work for François Truffaut. But in his early years, it is remarkable how many fine films Delerue worked on.

He studied with Darius Milhaud, and worked for theatre and TV (including the Comédie Française and the Théâtre Nationale Populaire) as well as films: *Un Amour de Poche* (57, Pierre Kast); a short film, *Les Marines* (57, François Reichenbach); *La Premiere Nuit* (58, Georges Franju); *L'Opéra-Mouffe* (58, Agnès Varda); just the waltz for *Hiroshima Mon Amour* (59, Alain Resnais); *Le Farceur* (60, Philippe de Broca); getting the style immediately for *Shoot the Piano Player* (60, Truffaut); *L'Amant de Cinq Jours* (61, de Broca); *Une Aussi Longue Absence* (61, Henri Colpi); *Jules et Jim* (62, Truffaut); *Cartouche* (62, de Broca); *Le Mépris* (63, Jean-Luc Godard); *La Peau Douce* (64, Truffaut); *The Pumpkin Eater* (64, Jack Clayton); *That Man from Rio* (64, de Broca); *Viva Maria* (65, Louis Malle); *King of Hearts* (66, de Broca); *A Man for All Seasons* (66, Zinnemann).

He was international by now: *Our Mother's House* (67, Clayton); *Le Diable par la Queue* (69, de Broca); *Women in Love* (69, Ken Russell); *A Walk with Love and Death* (69, John Huston); perhaps his greatest score for *The Conformist* (71, Bernardo Bertolucci); *Two English Girls* (71, Truffaut); *The Day of the Jackal* (73, Zinnemann); *Day for Night* (73, Truffaut); *Calmos* (76, Bertrand Blier); *Get Out Your Handkerchiefs* (78, Blier); *Love on the Run* (79, Truffaut); *The Woman Next Door* (81, Truffaut).

He wrote scores for *True Confessions* (81, Ulu Grosbard); *Rich and Famous* (81, George Cukor); *A Little Sex* (82, Bruce Paltrow); *Man, Woman and Child* (83, Dick Richards); *Confidentially Yours* (83, Truffaut); *Silkwood* (83, Nichols); *Sal-*

vador (86, Oliver Stone); *Platoon* (86, Stone); *Crimes of the Heart* (86, Bruce Beresford); *A Man in Love* (87, Diane Kurys); *The Lonely Passion of Judith Hearne* (87, Clayton); *Biloxi Blues* (88, Nichols); *A Summer Story* (88, Piers Haggard); *Memories of Me* (88, Henry Winkler); *Beaches* (88, Garry Marshall); *Heartbreak Hotel* (88, Chris Columbus); *Steel Magnolias* (90, Herbert Ross); *Joe Versus the Volcano* (90, John Patrick Shanley); *Black Rose* (91, Beresford); *Rich in Love* (92, Beresford); *Man Trouble* (92, Bob Rafelson).

Alain Delon, b. Sceaux, France, 1935
At forty, the face that made Delon one of the most beautiful leading men in international cinema began to blur. It was that saintly grace, allied to the unmistakable aura of a modern young man, that had made Delon's best films so interesting. This intrinsic contradiction was only heightened by the growing awareness that in real life he had something more than a nodding acquaintance with the French underworld. Inevitably, the shifting mixture of scandal and canonization was exploited in some bad gangster films—*Le Clan des Siciliens* (69, Henri Verneuil) and *Borsalino* (70, Jacques Deray), which he also produced, but Delon had appeared in two of Jean-Pierre Melville's authentic reworkings of criminal mythology: as the schizophrenic in *Le Samourai* (67) and *Le Cercle Rouge* (70), in which he is a mysteriously lethal angel in trench coat and fedora. The mixture is a fascinating one. It draws on the dissolute Riviera opportunist in *Plein Soleil* (59, René Clément), which catches the chill perversity in Patricia Highsmith's work rather more clearly than does *Strangers on a Train* (51, Alfred Hitchcock) and, in part, on the callow, leather-jacketed archetype—a café kid fed on *The Wild One*, Kenneth Anger, and Harley-Davidson brochures—in *Mélodie en Sous-Sol* (62, Verneuil) and *Girl on a Motorcycle* (68, Jack Cardiff). But there was always a note of Alyosha-like serenity in Delon that gave some substance to the operatic *Rocco and His Brothers* (60, Luchino Visconti).

Perhaps it is just a matter of physical presence with the sense to remain enigmatic, but time and again Delon holds pictures together and stares into the camera like a sleek cat. Nor should one forget his energetic tyro of the Rome stock exchange in *The Eclipse* (62, Michelangelo Antonioni), one of the most vigorous male characters in Antonioni's work. Of course, he has made other, duller films: *Quand la Femme s'en Mêle* (57, Yves Allégret); *Sois Belle et Tais-Toi* (58, Marc Allégret); *Quelle Joie de Vivre* (61, Clément); *Le Diable et les Dix Commandements* (62, Julien Duvivier); *The Leopard* (63, Visconti); *La Tulipe Noire* (63, Christian-Jaque); *Les Felins* (63, Clément); and *L'Insoumis* (64, Alain Cavalier). There followed an unimpressive venture into English-speaking cinema: *The Yellow Rolls-Royce* (64, Anthony Asquith); *Once a Thief* (65, Ralph Nelson); *Lost Command* (66, Mark Robson); and *Texas Across the River* (66, Michael Gordon).

After that, he was torn between silly commercial ventures and more enterprising films: as Jacques Chaban-Delmas in *Is Paris Burning?* (66, Clément); *Les Aventuriers* (66, Robert Enrico); the "William Wilson" episode in *Histoires Extraordinaires* (68, Louis Malle); *Diaboliquement Vôtre* (67, Duvivier); *Adieu l'Ami* (68, Jean Herman); *La Piscine* (68, Jacques Deray); *Jeff* (69, Herman); *Madly* (71, Roger Kahane); *Red Sun* (71, Terence Young); *The Assassination of Trotsky* (72, Joseph Losey); *Scorpio* (72, Michael Winner); *Dirty Money* (72, Melville); and *The Doctor in the Nude* (72, Alain Jessua).

The success of *Borsalino* encouraged the businessman in Delon, and in the seventies he remained a major actor and a varied producer, his poker face less serene, but still suited to underworld tensions. He had a major achievement in *Mr. Klein* (76, Joseph Losey), in which his glamour was glassy with creeping anxiety and fragile identity. In addition, he produced and acted in *Deux Hommes dans la Ville* (73, Jose Giovanni); *Big Guns* (73, Duccio Tessari); *Borsalino & Co.* (74, Deray); *Flic Story* (75, Deray); *Le Gitan* (75, Giovanni); and *Le Gang* (76, Deray). He has also acted in *Les Granges Brûlées* (73, Jean Chapot); *La Race des "Seigneurs"* (74, Pierre Granier-Deferre); *Zorro* (75, Tessari); and *Attention! Les Enfants Regardent* (78, Serge Leroy).

Since then, he has been a French institution (as actor and a recurring figure in underworld gossip), often the producer of his films and on two occasions—*Pour le Peau d'un Flic* (81) and *Le Battant* (83)—the director. He has also appeared in *The Concorde—Airport '79* (79, David Lowell Rich); *Trois Hommes a Abbattre* (80, Deray); *Teheran 1943* (81, Alexander Alov and Vladimir Naumov); *Le Choc* (82, Robin Davis); very beautiful as Charlus in *Swann in Love* (84, Volker Schlondorff); *Notre Histoire* (84, Bertrand Blier); *Parole de Flic* (85 Jose Pinheiro); *Le Passage* (86, René Manzor); *Dancing Machine* (90, Gilles Behat); and *Nouvelle Vague* (90, Jean-Luc Godard).

His work rate declined, but he was a presence still: *Dancing Machine* (90, Gilles Behat) the lead in *Le Retour de Casanova* (92, Edouard Niermans); *Un Crime* (93, Jacques Deray), which he wrote himself; *Le Jour et la Nuit* (97, Bernard-Henri Levy); with Belmondo in *Une Chance sur Deux* (98, Patrice Leconte); and in the TV series *Fabio Montale* (01, Jose Pinheiro).

Dolores del Rio (Lolita Dolores Asunsolo de Martinez) (1905–83), b. Durango, Mexico
If it can find nothing else, the cinema can always turn to florid human beauty—as David Selznick

realized: "I want del Rio and McCrea in a South Sea romance," he said. "Just give me three wonderful love scenes like you had in *The Big Parade* and *Bardelys the Magnificent*. I don't care what story you use so long as we call it *Bird of Paradise* and del Rio jumps into a flaming volcano at the finish."

And so King Vidor set sail for the Pacific to make the purest visual tribute to del Rio's burning loveliness. This Lolita had been the child of wealthy parents, married at sixteen, when her Humbert appeared: the American film director Edwin Carewe. He whisked her away to Hollywood and directed her in *Joanna* (25), *High Steppes* (26), and *Pals First* (26). In time, she was better appreciated by other directors, principally Raoul Walsh who cast her as Charmaine, beguiling Victor McLaglen and Edmund Lowe in *What Price Glory?* (26), and then as the Spanish girl in *The Loves of Carmen* (27). Carewe directed her as the peasant girl in *Resurrection* (27) and she went on to make *The Gateway of the Moon* (28, John Griffith Wray); *The Trail of '98* (28, Clarence Brown); *No Other Woman* (28, Lou Tellegen); and *The Red Dunce* (28, Walsh). With Carewe again, she made *Ramona* (28), *Revenge* (28), and *Evangeline* (29). Mrs. Carewe divorced her husband around this time and del Rio's Mexican husband died. But the Carewes were reunited and Dolores married the MGM art director, Cedric Gibbons.

She remained a leading player for another four years: *The Bad One* (30, George Fitzmaurice); *Bird of Paradise* (32); *Flying Down to Rio* (33, Thornton Freeland); *Wonder Bar* (34, Lloyd Bacon); *Madame Du Barry* (34, William Dieterle); *In Caliente* (35, Bacon); and *I Live for Love* (35, Busby Berkeley). She went to Britain to make *Accused* (36, Freeland) and made only second features—*Lancer Spy* (37, Gregory Ratoff); *International Settlement* (38, Eugene Forde); and *The Man from Dakota* (40, Leslie Fenton). After appearing in *Journey into Fear* (42, Norman Foster)—she was beloved of Orson at the time—she went back to Mexico and flourished there. In 1947, she was the Magdalene figure in John Ford's *The Fugitive* (47) and in the 1960s she had two notable supporting parts in American films: *Flaming Star* (60, Don Siegel) and *Cheyenne Autumn* (64, Ford). Those films, as well as her appearances in Mexican, Spanish, and Italian movies, show her beauty unabated, as in *Cinderella, Italian Style* (67, Francesco Rosi).

Benicio Del Toro,
b. Santurce, Puerto Rico, 1967

The supporting actor Oscar that went to Del Toro for his Mexican cop in *Traffic* (00, Steven Soderbergh) was generally hailed as a reward for authenticity. So what does it reveal to discover that the actor is Puerto Rican? In a way, of course, it shows that the old Anthony Quinn code of the supporting actor (that to be foreign is sufficient, and universal) is still in operation. Or was it that Benicio Del Toro simply did the actorly thing and spent long enough observing the frustration of honest cops along the border? The question is likely to receive more focus now: with an Oscar, Del Toro will find it less easy to bury himself in accent, obscure behavior, and mannerism (he is a champion where such things are concerned) and may have to find out whether he is the Robert Mitchum for a new America. It will be worth watching.

He was raised in Pennsylvania, and he then studied at the University of California, San Diego, and at the Stella Adler Conservatory in New York. He began in movies with *Big Top Pee-wee* (88, Randall Kleiser) and *Licence to Kill* (89, John Glen), and he did his time as regulation Hispanic scum on TV in *Miami Vice*. But it wasn't long before he attracted attention for his lazy grace, his deadpan humor, and his very bendable voice: *The Indian Runner* (91, Sean Penn); *Christopher Columbus: The Discovery* (92, Glen); *Fearless* (93, Peter Weir); *Money for Nothing* (93, Ramón Menéndez); the sidekick cop in *China Moon* (94, John Bailey); *Swimming with Sharks* (94, George Huang); as Fenster in *The Usual Suspects* (95, Bryan Singer); *Basquiat* (96, Julian Schnabel); *The Fan* (96, Tony Scott); *The Funeral* (96, Abel Ferrara); *Excess Baggage* (97, Marco Brambilla); as the Samoan attorney, Dr. Gonzo, in *Fear and Loathing in Las Vegas* (98, Terry Gilliam); *The Way of the Gun* (00, Christopher McQuarrie); *Snatch* (00, Guy Ritchie); *The Pledge* (00, Penn); *The Hunted* (03, William Friedkin).

Cecil Blount De Mille (1881–1959),
b. Ashfield, Massachusetts

1913: *The Squaw Man* (codirected with Oscar Apfel). 1914: *The Call of the North; The Virginian; What's His Name?; The Man from Home; Rose of the Rancho*. 1915: *The Girl of the Golden West; The Warrens of Virginia; The Unafraid; The Captive; The Wild Goose Chase; The Arab; Chimmie Fadden; Kindling; Carmen; Chimmie Fadden Out West; The Cheat; The Golden Chance*. 1916: *Temptation; The Trail of the Lonesome Pine; The Heart of Nora Flynn; Maria Rosa; The Dream Girl*. 1917: *Joan the Woman; Romance of the Redwoods; The Little American; The Woman God Forgot; The Devil Stone*. 1918: *The Whispering Chorus; Old Wives for New; We Can't Have Everything; Till I Come Back to You; The Squaw Man*. 1919: *Don't Change Your Husband; For Better, For Worse; Male and Female*. 1920: *Why Change Your Wife?; Something to Think About*. 1921: *Forbidden Fruit; The Affairs of Anatol; Fool's Paradise*. 1922: *Saturday Night; Manslaughter*. 1923: *Adam's Rib; The Ten Command-*

ments. 1924: *Triumph; Feet of Clay.* 1925: *The Golden Bed; The Road to Yesterday.* 1926: *The Volga Boatman.* 1927: *The King of Kings.* 1929: *The Godless Girl; Dynamite.* 1930: *Madame Satan.* 1931: *The Squaw Man.* 1932: *The Sign of the Cross.* 1933: *This Day and Age.* 1934: *Four Frightened People; Cleopatra.* 1935: *The Crusades.* 1937: *The Plainsman.* 1938: *The Buccaneer.* 1939: *Union Pacific.* 1940: *North West Mounted Police.* 1942: *Reap the Wild Wind.* 1944: *The Story of Dr. Wassell.* 1947: *Unconquered.* 1949: *Samson and Delilah.* 1952: *The Greatest Show on Earth.* 1956: *The Ten Commandments.*

De Mille was the son of a man torn between being a minister and a David Belasco–like playwright—which is a proof of genetics as emphatic as the primitive confidence in American righteousness in De Mille's own films. Many of the best Hollywood anecdotes feature De Mille's extravagance; directors like Hawks and von Sternberg are on record as finding his tasteless exuberance as bewildering as his enormous popular success. There is a photograph in *Fun in a Chinese Laundry* of von Sternberg and Lubitsch chuckling together as they watch De Mille directing *Cleopatra.* And it is ironic that De Mille should have flourished with his unique ·independent unit within Paramount, the studio pledged to sophistication. But De Mille predated both Lubitsch and Sternberg and he still thrived at Paramount after Lubitsch was dead and Sternberg retired.

He attended Pennsylvania Military College and the American Academy of Dramatic Arts before he began acting and writing plays. In 1913, he, Jesse Lasky, and Samuel Goldfish (Goldwyn) formed the Lasky Feature Play Company, for which he made *The Squaw Man* in the frontier village of Hollywood. When, in 1916, Lasky merged with Adolph Zukor's Famous Plays, that allowed Paramount to gain an early foothold in Hollywood. De Mille stayed at Paramount until after *The Golden Bed* (25), when he formed Producers Distributing Corporation. It was short-lived: *Dynamite, Madame Satan,* and *The Squaw Man* (for the third time) were made at MGM, whereupon he returned to Paramount and stayed there for the rest of his life—briefly interrupted by the visit Norma Desmond/Gloria Swanson makes in *Sunset Boulevard* (50, Billy Wilder).

A case can be made that, from about 1918 to 1950, De Mille did more than anyone—including Griffith—to make the American public appreciate directors (especially through the Lux Radio Theater movie adaptations, begun in 1936). He was personally flamboyant; he made hit films that introduced what some regarded as "new ideas"—as Benjamin Hampton put it, "De Mille decided that the majority of theatre patrons were fundamentally curious about only money and sex." But

we need to be finessed on that, and De Mille did the trick. That he became a figure of fun, a synonym for blind arrogance ("Ready when you are, C.B.!") disturbed him not a bit. Forget auteurism—he knew the show needed a ringmaster (and he did turn to the circus in *The Greatest Show on Earth,* which won him best picture and the Thalberg award). Gloria Swanson was his star turn and his discovery, and she persuaded him to give up theatre greats for new faces.

De Mille's movies are barnstormers, rooted in Victorian theatre, shamelessly stereotyped and sentimental, but eagerly courting twentieth-century permissiveness, if only solemnly to condemn it. The movies are simple, raw, pious, and jingoistic; but though De Mille was commercially cynical, his conviction in the human relevance of his rubbish is undisturbed, and the energy of his imagination seldom flags. He is silliest in his biblical and Roman films—peeping lewdly at Claudette Colbert's Poppaea in a bath of milk, seemingly oblivious of Laughton's reckless overacting in *Sign of the Cross,* hampered by the huge, rigid sets and unconscious of his dreadful dialogue. But in the 1930s, De Mille made a series of "American" films, not as good as King Vidor's, but worth comparing with them. They are twopence-colored historical Westerns, celebrating the pioneering spirit, racial purity, tomboy heroines, and the American flag. *The Plainsman, Union Pacific, North West Mounted Police,* and *Unconquered* stand up amazingly well.

Gary Cooper was the De Mille hero—naïve as Hawkeye—Barbara Stanwyck, Jean Arthur, and Paulette Goddard were his hoydens. In fact, the four films all reflect one another: they share the military, an independent hero, his gutsy girl, and rogues selling guns and hooch to the savages. They share, too, the second-unit direction of Arthur Rossen who provided most of their action set pieces. But they still have a boyish gusto and an enthusiastic relish at forests being carved into pulp by noble enterprise. They are not historically authentic, but they are dead in line with American idealism. In that sense, De Mille had a purity that survived every compromise.

His final films lose nothing in their own grand claims. *The Ten Commandments* is burdened by sound, and some very amateurish effects, but in 1956 Heston as Moses still seemed to carry the weight of law. Heston believed what he was doing, and the film was a solemn hit in the moment before millions got their egalitarian hands on "sin." Finally, a word for *Samson and Delilah*—one of the great trash epics, superbly cast, and made without one drop of irony or shame, and with momentous sexual daydreams in every scene.

Jonathan Demme,
b. Baldwin, New York, 1944

1974: *Caged Heat.* 1975: *Crazy Mama.* 1976: *Fighting Mad.* 1977: *Handle With Care/Citizens Band.* 1978: *Murder in Aspic* for *Columbo* (TV). 1979: *The Last Embrace.* 1980: *Melvin and Howard.* 1982: *Who Am I This Time?* (TV). 1984: *Swing Shift; Stop Making Sense* (d). 1986: *Something Wild.* 1987: *Swimming to Cambodia* (d). 1988: *Haiti Dreams of Democracy* (d); *Married to the Mob.* 1991: *The Silence of the Lambs.* 1992: *Cousin Bobby* (d). 1993: *Philadelphia.* 1994: *The Complex Sessions* (s). 1997: "Subway Car from Hell," episode in *Subway Stories* (TV). 1998: *Storefront Hitchcock* (d); *Beloved.* 2002: *The Truth About Charlie.*

Around 1990, Demme seemed the most versatile director in America. He was interested in more odd things and people; he noticed and heard more. He loved the provinces, music of all kinds, character actors, the fusion of comedy and high drama. He had a way of guarding his rather capricious integrity in every testing commercial setup. He had not yet stopped surprising us. And he had already given us many lengthy passages of sheer *movie* that would grace the careers of Minnelli, Cukor, or the other Demy, Jacques. He was a natural in an age when so many people made moviemaking feel like a duty or a scam.

He moved as a kid from Long Island to Miami, where his father worked (let us hope that very soon Demme has a shot at doing Miami on-screen—its fusion of races, its music, its smeary tropical air—beyond just producing George Armitage's *Miami Blues* in 1990). He was a bit of a film critic, a salesman, and a maker of commercials before he found himself with Roger Corman. He did much more than survive that training: *Crazy Mama* is a rich movie, full of music, back country, and wild women—all later trademarks.

Handle With Care, written by Paul Brickman, was an adventurous comedy in which a gang of loonies and mavericks were held in story by CB radio. *The Last Embrace* was an expert thriller. *Melvin and Howard,* written by Bo Goldman, made a lovely comedy of a piece of American apocrypha. It took a very special, very romantic comedian to envisage the film and to harness the desert, the infirmity of Howard Hughes, and the mundanity of Melvin Dummar without having the film veer off the road. *Who Am I This Time?* was a Kurt Vonnegut story done for *American Playhouse* with Christopher Walken and Susan Sarandon. *Swing Shift* was a major study of war and the home front until producer Goldie Hawn regulated it (Demme's cut can sometimes be seen, and it is to be hoped that one day it may emerge as the best version of that film). *Stop Making Sense* is one of the best concert movies, as light, mercurial, and wicked as David Byrne's stage presence.

It may be said that Demme has not yet made a great film. Maybe, but *Something Wild* is close to it, a miraculously zigzagging movie where screwball goes into sexpot, romance, and menace (several times) before the wildness settles. This may be Demme's surest tribute to wayward vitality, and it works so well because he enjoys all the characters with the same uncritical wariness. By 2000, I'll guess, *Something Wild* will be a great film—a fate that the very enjoyable *Married to the Mob* does not risk.

And so . . . *The Silence of the Lambs?* This has been Demme's greatest hit, and some have seen in it the director's concession to box office. But, remember, Demme was raised in exploitation films; and he seems to have suffered no damage. Hannibal Lecter is an unruly demon. Hopkins does make a hero of him. The sly hints of love story between Lecter and Clarice are disconcerting, and the close, with Lecter going off to dinner with all our good wishes is nothing to be proud of. Moreover, Demme is now so quick and assured he can't hide his amusement at the plot mechanics. It *is* a problem picture, funnier and more lovelorn than we had any reason to expect. And surely Jodie Foster owes a great deal to Demme.

Philadelphia—alas. Hollywood now congratulates itself on the courage of the project, and its success—after many had been terrified of the film. I think it's feeble, devoid of the things Demme is best at: character, the unexpected, mischief. The plot is full of holes; the mindset is out-of-date. The Hanks lawyer is a blank beneath the grim make-up. Yet large audiences watched in awe: *Philadelphia* is not quite about AIDS, but it may be the first Hollywood film that says, it's OK, hug a gay. Which is something, I suppose—but no reason for anyone as hip as Demme being involved.

Demme's latest years have not been very satisfactory. He has done a lot of work on small films and helped produce *Devil in a Blue Dress* (95, Carl Franklin); *That Thing You Do!* (96, Tom Hanks) and the TV documentary *Mandela* (96, Jo Menell and Angus Gibson), for which he deserves thanks. But Demme is at his prime, and *Beloved* is not much to show for that. Indeed, *Beloved* is very boring—which is something no one would, or should, expect from this director.

Rebecca De Mornay,
b. Los Angeles, 1961

At this point, I feel some obligation to offer pen and page to *The New Republic*'s Stanley Kauffmann: no actress in recent times has enjoyed more gallant, persevering, or intelligent support than Ms. De Mornay has had from Mr. Kauffmann. If only he could reliably get her into a string of more worthwhile pictures—except that then the by-no-means young Mr. K might burst (here would be a subject fit for von Sternberg, Michael Powell or . . . so many).

At any rate, Mr. Kauffmann's raptures are understandable; I hope he can understand they are not his alone. Ms. De Mornay is a sumptuous, pale-eyed blonde whose intelligence gives her a decided edge of coolness, or of thinking about something else. Of course, in great roles—as Hedda Gabler, Elektra, or Blanche DuBois—her looks and her mind might close together with a very satisfying click. But the possibility remains that her intelligence may be a little bewildered or daunted by her beauty—indeed, it may be provoked by it. As a unified woman, she could prove a little less mysterious—not that Hollywood is likely to challenge her in the roles listed above.

So *The Hand That Rocks the Cradle* (92, Curtis Hanson) may be as good as it gets: an unashamed, expert potboiler, yet founded in unusual psychological interest, with the barbs on Hanson's script depending on the authenticity and precision of the actress. (Hanson may have been expressly cunning in setting up De Mornay and Anabella Sciorra as mother and nanny—thus De Mornay has a serenity and Sciorra a breathless ineptness that seem wrong, but very revealing.) Of course, De Mornay can only hint at poignant derangement in the nanny, and only make a bit more of many moments than they deserve. The project does not begin to grasp unity or development, and so the actress's very epiphanies ensure our final disappointment, just as they surely give energy to the character's climactic malice. Good actresses do deserve better people to play.

De Mornay had a European upbringing (another subtle undercurrent against the mainstream) as well as an education at the Lee Strasberg Institute. She was a sharp, funny, and utterly memorable customer in *One From the Heart* (82, Francis Coppola) and then a kid's dream whore in *Risky Business* (83, Paul Brickman). That first smash hit was just as unreal and acute as *Cradle*, and it employed the same faintly dreamy or distracted distance in the actress's performance. In the process, she reduced maybe 90 percent of the male audience to the level of Tom Cruise's dreams.

She was in *Testament* (85, Lynne Littman); hardly recognizable but valiant and fierce in *Runaway Train* (85, Andrei Konchalovsky); she was the utility infielder actress in *The Slugger's Wife* (85, Hal Ashby); she was allowed to be an actress in *The Trip to Bountiful* (85, Peter Masterson)—can you remember? She faced up to "necessary career choices" in *And God Created Woman* (87, Roger Vadim); and has to take responsibility for *Feds* (88, Dan Goldberg) and *Dealers* (89, Colin Bucksey). She was also in *Backdraft* (91, Ron Howard); *Blind Side* (93, Geoff Murphy); *Guilty as Sin* (93, Sidney Lumet); and *The Three Muske-*

teers (93, Stephen Herek).

Most of her later work has been for TV only, and it's not very distinguished: *Getting Out* (94, John Korty); *Never Talk to Strangers* (95, Peter Hall); *The Winner* (96, Alex Cox); Wendy in the TV version of *The Shining* (97, Mick Garris); *The Con* (98, Steven Schachter); *Thick as Thieves* (99, Scott Sanders); *Night Ride Home* (99, Glenn Jordan); *A Table for One* (99, Ron Senkowski); *Range of Motion* (00, Donald Wrye); *The Right Temptation* (00, Lyndon Chubbuck); *Salem Witch Trials* (01, Joseph Sargent); *Identity* (03, James Mangold)—"Didn't you used to be an actress?" someone asks her.

Jacques Demy (1931–90),
b. Pont-Château, France
1960: *Lola.* 1961: "La Luxure," episode in *Les Sept Péchés Capitaux.* 1962: *La Baie des Anges.* 1964: *Les Parapluies de Cherbourg/The Umbrellas of Cherbourg.* 1967: *Les Demoiselles de Rochefort/The Young Girls of Rochefort.* 1969: *Model Shop.* 1970: *Peau d'Âne/The Magic Donkey.* 1972: *The Pied Piper.* 1973: *L'Événement le Plus Important depuis que l'Homme a Marché sur la Lune/The Slightly Pregnant Man.* 1979: *Lady Oscar.* 1980: *La Naissance du Jour* (TV). 1982: *Une Chambre à Ville.* 1985: *Parking.* 1988: *La Table Tournante; Trois Places pour le 26.*

Of all the New Wave directors who once professed their joy in cinema, Demy remained most faithful to the delights of sight and sound and to the romance of movie iconography. With loving attention to those Atlantic coast towns—Nantes, Rochefort, and Cherbourg—where he grew up, Demy invented a world of benign and enchanting imagination. It is constantly on the verge of fairy story, but never yields to the foreboding of the Grimm brothers. Instead, Demy has his own domain of chivalry and love, born out of Perrault and schoolgirls' novelettes, the rural sentiment of Rouquier, and the Hollywood scheme of coincidence and happily-ever-after, but as distinguished and ennobling as, say, *The Beautiful Hours of the Duc de Berry.*

La Baie des Anges is the test: if you feel that it evades such issues as the moral deterioration and familial breakdown that come from gambling, then Demy is a frivolous dabbler; but if you respond to the plunging music of Michel Legrand, the luminous black-and-white Côte d'Azur, the doting over Jeanne Moreau's performance, and the saintly insistence on love conquering all, then Demy is a spellbinder who brings a religious awe to rose-colored hokum. And it is not sufficient to concede that *La Baie des Anges* is delightful entertainment. It is a description of paradise that is entirely consistent and inviting. Consider who else in the cinema deals in paradise, and you begin to recognize Demy's rare achievement. This is the frivolity that only von Sternberg and Ophuls had risked to ameliorate sadness.

After studying at ENPC, Demy assisted the animator Paul Grimault and then Georges Rouquier on *Lourdes et Ses Miracles* (54), *Honegger* (55), and *SOS Noronha* (57). Through the late fifties, he made shorts for himself: *Le Sabotier du Val-de-Loire* (55); *Le Bel Indifférent* (57), from Cocteau; *Musée Grévin* (58, with Jean Masson); *Ars* (59); and *La Mère et l'Enfant* (59, with Masson). Then, in 1960, after the dedication—to Max Ophuls—and accompanied by Beethoven's Seventh Symphony, a white Cadillac fills the CinemaScope frame and a tall, blond man all in white, even his Stetson, stares out at the sea. Immediately, a unique vision was established: the reverent rediscovery of hackneyed images, and the bold coupling of classical and romantic culture. *Lola* was a plan for a career: it not only contained a handful of variants on the themes of chance meeting and long-lost love, but set up signposts leading to other films. Later, Demy pursued some of those paths, reveling in his own nostalgia. Lola reappeared (much sadder) in *Model Shop;* the young man in *Lola* marries Catherine Deneuve in *Les Parapluies;* the sailor who visits Lola at the cabaret is revived in *Les Demoiselles*—as both the central sailors and a Gene Kelly who has not quite forgotten the steps of *On the Town.* As for Lola herself, she is not just a curtsy to *Lola Montès* and *The Blue Angel,* not only the tenderest direction that Anouk Aimée has ever had, but the archetype of Demy's heroine—beautiful, sentimental, hopeful, resigned, gay, nervy, trembling between tears and laughter. The epigraph for *Lola* says it all (from a Chinese proverb): "Pleure qui peut . . . Rit qui veut . . ."

Demy adored his players: Aimée, Elina Labourdette, Annie Dupeyroux, and the marvelously serious Marc Michel in *Lola;* Moreau and Claude Mann in *La Baie des Anges,* the former forever dithering like the ball in a slowing roulette wheel, the latter still and watchful as a croupier; Catherine Deneuve and Anne Vernon in *Cherbourg;* Deneuve, Dorléac, and Darrieux in *Rochefort.* He was, too, a constructor of intricate screenplays in which every episode reflects on others: *Lola* is as shapely a drama as *The Marriage of Figaro* or *Pale Fire.* These are great virtues, but they would be literary ones without the luxurious richness of his imagery and his unrivaled sense of music. Who else could have made *Baie des Anges* so radiant in black and white? Who else could have proved *Cherbourg* so pretty? Demy had taken over Ophuls's fluid camera, but restrained its most lavish movements. He delighted rather more in tableaux—sudden lyrical effects like the slow-motion roundabout in *Lola,* the vivid scarlet bar in *Parapluies,* the churchlike shadow of the casino in *La Baie des Anges.* Notice, too, his persistent use of white in *Lola* and the contrast of black lace and fur boa in the cabaret.

As for music, *Les Parapluies* is a notional folly made utterly reasonable by Demy's conviction and Legrand's melodies. But music had already been used in *Lola* and *La Baie des Anges* with exhilarating force—the roulette tune in the latter is one of the finest uses of music to accentuate drama in all cinema, while Lola's song is a delightful piece of offhand recitative. The whimsical use of song in René Clair's early films is gloriously enlarged in Demy's movies.

It should be said that Demy's first three films are his best. *Rochefort* seems more hampered by the stress on song. *Model Shop* shows some signs of unease with American conditions. *Peau d'Âne* is his clearest acceptance of fairy story (it is from Perrault), chilly in its modernity of character, but minus the fruitful correlative of some mundane French provincial town as its setting (something Demy may have noticed first in Cocteau's *Orphée*). However, *The Pied Piper* fatally lacks the intense control that Demy had previously exercised over such light material.

His later work was not as convincing as the early films, though *Une Chambre à Ville* is a fascinating application of the operatic technique to an unusually dark story. *Trois Places* had Yves Montand, playing himself, returning to Marseilles and searching for a lost love—the lyricism seemed a touch strained.

Demy was married to Agnes Varda. After his death she made a film that recounted his life, *Jacquot de Nantes*—on which he had script credit.

Twenty-plus years after Demy's astonishing productivity in the sixties and early seventies, he does not seem quite possible. Did he really live? Have those wistful, gentle, and melodic films been made? Or is he only an ideal director one has dreamed? Already, young film-goers do not know his name. It is more plausible as legend than as film fact that someone made movies in which all the dialogue was sung (years before *Pennies from Heaven*). It is already more forlorn hope than likelihood that anyone would make pictures as graceful and humane as those of Max Ophuls, as poised between speech and music as Stephen Sondheim. It may be more comfortable in this age of dread-ridden movies to believe Demy never existed.

Dame Judi (Judith Olivia) Dench,
b. York, England, 1934

In Britain, universally, and in America now, Judi Dench is recognized as not just a great actress, but as a model for acting. She has authority and experience. That's what the "Dame" is supposed to signify. It's inherent in television documentaries that observe her developing a role—on stage, say, for *A Little Night Music.* It's there in the sinecure called "M" in the Bond films—and the subsequent enlargement of that role for her sake. Over the years, she has been known on stage for *Amy's View, Absolute Hell, The Cherry Orchard, Antony and Cleopatra* (opposite Antony Hopkins), *Mother Courage, Pack of Lies,* a sexy Lady Bracknell, *Macbeth* (opposite Ian McKellen)— and we're still only as far back as 1976. Working reliably within the rich range of the English theatre and its institutions, she had taken on the classical tradition and several modern parts. She had abided and built a citadel, starting with her Old Vic work in the late fifties and her 1960 Zeffirelli *Romeo and Juliet,* with John Stride.

That Juliet was not admired by everyone. Her cracking voice was not exactly in the tradition of fine verse-speaking; but she could seem intense, raw, needy—like an actual teenager. Some said she was not as pretty as Juliet ought to be. Add to this a line of actresses more or less the contemporaries of Judi Dench who were certainly pretty— Claire Bloom, Mary Ure, Susannah York—and who grew far ahead of Dench as movie actresses, yet have not quite lasted, or had the depth of character to insist on sexual attractiveness as well as vapid "prettiness."

I wouldn't stress this but for what is now largely forgotten: that as a young actress, in difficult material, Judi Dench took a big shot at the screen and then—after it had seemingly failed—she gave up. Her looks and her raw feeling did not suit that time, and so few people saw her films, or were seduced by her: *The Third Secret* (64, Charles Crichton); *He Who Rides a Tiger* (65, Crichton); *A Study in Terror* (65, James Hill); the most important, a genuine attempt at a new kind of film, *Four in the Morning* (65, Anthony Simmons); and *A Midsummer Night's Dream* (68, Peter Hall). One would have to add to that list her most searing screen performance, for TV, in the four-part *Talking to a Stranger* (66, Christopher Morahan), written by John Hopkins, who had liked her in one of his episodes for *Z Cars.*

She concluded that the camera didn't like her, and did only a little TV and the movie *Dead Cert* (73, Tony Richardson), before returning in the early eighties, often in supporting parts. On TV again, opposite Frederic Forrest, in the excellent *Saigon: Year of the Cat* (82, Stephen Frears); *Wetherby* (84, David Hare); *A Room with a View* (85, James Ivory); *84 Charing Cross Road* (86, David Jones); *A Handful of Dust* (87, Charles Sturridge); Mistress Quickly in *Henry V* (88, Kenneth Branagh); *Jack and Sarah* (94, Tim Sullivan); her first M in *GoldenEye* (95, Martin Campbell); Hecuba in *Hamlet* (95, Branagh); as Queen Victoria, Oscar-nominated in *Mrs. Brown* (96, John Madden); *Tomorrow Never Dies* (97, Roger Spottiswoode); winning the supporting actress Oscar for a few words as Elizabeth in *Shakespeare in Love* (98, Madden); *Tea with Mussolini* (99,

Franco Zeffirelli); very much a capital M in *The World Is Not Enough* (99, Michael Apted); *Chocolat* (00, Lasse Hallstrom).

And now, she contrives to show us another Dench—a movie star, in her sixties: haunting as the failing *Iris* (01, Richard Eyre) and the only authentic human being in *The Shipping News* (01, Hallstrom). She repeated her stage Lady Bracknell for *The Importance of Being Earnest* (02, Oliver Parker), and she was back as M in *Die Another Day* (02, Lee Tamahori).

Catherine Deneuve (Catherine Dorléac), b. Paris, 1943

She is the younger sister of Françoise Dorléac (1942–67). I was watching a TV program on Buñuel with a friend when it showed a clip of Buñuel directing a scene from *Belle de Jour* (67). It was the beach scene in which Catherine Deneuve stands tethered to a post in a long white gown that leaves her arms bare. Buñuel was supervising the way mud would be thrown at Deneuve and, as the ordurelike filth splattered over her, he and she joked together. "How can a woman do that sort of thing for a living?" asked my friend. To which I replied, "Exactly in the way that a bourgeoise in her tasteful home one fine day might dream herself a whore."

Acting and cinema free the fantasies and Deneuve is a fantastic actress, her beauty a receptacle for any imagination, perhaps the greatest cool blonde, forever hinting at intimations of depravity. In her best work, she deserves a place with the most enchanting women of cinema, childlike, reserved, a novice on the way to a brothel. Of course, Buñuel is the master at uncovering the imaginative potency of bourgeois fashion plates; still photographer David Bailey may have married Deneuve, but it was Buñuel who revealed her. Thus, the sensual visibility of *Belle de Jour* and *Tristana* (70) is suffused with blondeness. And it was Buñuel, in two films, who showed that Deneuve was one of those few actresses who could be transformed by a touch or a thought. In *Belle de Jour* she moves within seconds from the threatened virgin to the voluptuary. And in *Tristana,* it is the height of her art to be the ingenue in pigtails and beret and the scarlet woman on the balcony who condescendingly shows herself to the boy.

She began in her teens and has worked hard ever since: *Les Portes Claquent* (60, Jacques Poitrenaud/Michel Sermaud); in the "Sophie" episode from *Les Parisiennes* (61, Marc Allégret), on which she met Roger Vadim. She had a child by Vadim, but never married him and proved a rather deeper woman than he was used to: *Et Satan Conduit le Bal* (62, Grisha M. Dabat); *Le Vice et la Vertu* (62, Vadim), based on de Sade's Justine; *Vacances Portugaises* (63, Pierre Kast); in the "L'Homme qui Vendit la Tour Eiffel" episode from

Les Plus Belles Escroqueries du Monde (63, Claude Chabrol); *La Chasse à l'Homme* (64, Edouard Molinaro); *Un Monsieur de Compagnie* (64, Philippe de Broca); *The Umbrellas of Cherbourg* (64, Jacques Demy); as the girl who goes mad in a Kensington flat in *Repulsion* (65, Roman Polanski); *Das Liebenskarussel* (65, Rolf Thiele); *La Vie de Château* (65, Jean-Paul Rappeneau); *Le Chant du Monde* (65, Marcel Camus); *Les Créatures* (66, Agnes Varda); with her sister in *The Young Girls of Rochefort* (66, Demy); *Le Dimanche de la Vie* (66, Jean Herman); *Benjamin* (67, Michel Deville); *Manon 70* (68, Jean Aurel); *La Chamade* (68, Alain Cavalier); to America, to play opposite Jack Lemmon in *The April Fools* (69, Stuart Rosenberg); *Mayerling* (69, Terence Young); as the femme fatale in *The Mississippi Mermaid* (69, François Truffaut); *Peau d'Âne* (70, Demy); *Ça n'Arrive qu'aux Autres* (71, Nadine Trintignant); *Dirty Money* (72, Jean-Pierre Melville); and *The Slightly Pregnant Man* (73, Demy).

In America, by advertising perfume and expensive cars she became an epitome of classy beauty and marketable romance. That aura of moneyed glamour was vital to her call girl in *Hustle* (75, Robert Aldrich). She has also made *L'Agression* (75, Gerard Pires); *Les Sauvages* (75, Rappeneau); *Anima Persa* (76, Dino Risi); *La Grande Bourgeoise* (77, Mauro Bolognini); *March or Die* (77, Dick Richards); *Coup de Foudre* (77, Robert Enrico); *L'Argent des Autres* (78, Christian de Chalonge); *Ecoute Voir . . .* (78, Hugo Santiago); and *Ils Sont Grands Ces Petits* (79, Joel Santoni).

By the age of forty, Deneuve was better known outside France in cosmetics advertisements than in films. She was only rarely international, but in France, and at Cannes, especially, she was an empress, heavier perhaps as the years passed, but impassive and exquisite still: *À Nous Deux* (79, Claude Lelouch); *Courage, Fuyons* (80, Yves Robert); having a big hit, with Depardieu, in *The Last Metro* (80, Truffaut); *Je Vous Aime* (80, Claude Berri); *Le Choix des Armes* (81, Alain Corneau); *Reporters* (81, Raymond Depardon); *Hôtel des Ameriques* (81, André Téchiné); *Le Choc* (82, Robin Davis); *L'Africain* (82, Philippe de Broca); *The Hunger* (83, Tony Scott); *Le Bon Plaisir* (83, Francis Girod); *Fort Saganne* (84, Corneau); *Love Songs* (84, Elie Chouraqui); *Let's Hope It's a Girl* (85, Mario Monicelli); *Scene of the Crime* (86, Téchiné); *A Strange Place to Meet* (88, François Dupeyron); *Fréquence Meurtre* (88, Elizabeth Rappeneau); *Terres Jaunes* (89, Regis Wargnier); *La Reine Blanche* (91, Jean-Loup Hubert); and in a stirring comeback, nominated as best actress, in *Indochine* (92, Wargnier); *Ma Saison Préférée* (93, Téchiné), which also starred her daughter (by Marcello Mastroianni), Chiara Deneuve.

She is still a leading player, very beautiful, but a touch dilute. It's the loss of youth, of course. She seems a fine lady now, one who has smoothed away the fascinating contrasts that once made her a phenomenon: *La Partie d'Echecs* (94, Yves Hanchar); *The Convent* (95, Manoel de Oliveira); *Les Voleurs* (96, Téchiné); *L'Inconnu* (96, Pierre Montazel); *Généalogies d'un Crime* (97, Raul Ruiz); *Place Vendôme* (98, Nicole Garcia); *Le Vent de la Nuit* (99, Philippe Garrel); *Belle Maman* (99, Gabriel Aghion); *Pola X* (99, Leos Carax); *Le Temps Retrouvé* (99, Ruiz); *Est-Ouest* (99, Wargnier); *Dancer in the Dark* (00, Lars von Trier); *The Musketeer* (01, Peter Hyams); *Le Petit Poucet* (01, Olivier Dahan); *Je Rentre à la Maison* (01, Oliveira); *8 Femmes* (02, Francois Ozon); *Au Plus Près du Paradis* (02, Tonie Marshall; as Mme de Merteuil in a TV *Les Liaisons Dangereuses* (03, Josee Dayan).

Robert De Niro, b. New York, 1943

De Niro is the kind of actor who reminds you how genteel American movies are. They may say "fuck" and "damn," and leave their victims in the gutter, but the blood is always Carmine Interlude, and the mad-dog killers are household pets. The people in films are models hired at ridiculous expense, people who can hold a pose for seven hours with minds just as set. Most of them. They neither smell nor lie; they get their lines right—all their mistakes are thrown away. Their fraud and their sordidness are clever charades for the comfortable classes. Nothing gives us the coarse, monotonous, and unpredictable undergrowth existence of life. The movies are fake, and De Niro is hanging on by broken fingertips, for he seems as averse to charm as a lurcher dog. As a screen presence, he's as threatening and ungraspable as a sweet-faced madman who pours a torrent of talk over you on the subway, trapped in the tunnel between Bellevue and Groucho.

De Niro seems no cozier offscreen than on it. He is reported to be immersed in his character preparation, and he resists most public relations. Yet American stars, eventually, live by finding ways of being likeable and digestible. If he's got sense, he makes no more trouble than a president. But De Niro likes awkward, unmanageable people: it is hard to think of one dutifully sentimental scene in which he has figured. Has he ever kissed a girl on screen without eating her? But it is easy to conjure up his frosty, recessive victims of solitude, in all of whom there is a harsh flame of inspiration. *New York, New York* (77, Martin Scorsese) is so painful a film because De Niro's drive prefers private, sinister ecstasies to the wholesome bliss of the 1940s musical. He makes the musical noir. In the long opening sequence, he "wins" Liza Minnelli not out of sentiment, but because she is the available target that his fierce boredom selects. His Jimmy

Doyle overpowers people or ignores them; he cannot deal with them. Thus, the abrupt humor, the compulsive routines just like sax solos (he never makes it to sex)—and that steel-trap grin. Communication systems, but not the natural gestures of feeling. How astute it was in *Taxi Driver* to have him talk to himself.

That is the impulse behind Travis Bickle in *Taxi Driver* (76, Scorsese), and why the film is so disturbing in its portrait of a man of good intent and weirdly fine nature driven to slaughter. Travis cannot express his anguish or perplexity, except in coffin-solitary monologue and ritual violence. This leaves him more unable to comprehend his own tangled sense of right and wrong. The street kid struts to prove he is significant. Killing for Travis is the only creative alternative to breakdown or a kind of reflection that would undermine his dynamic. Still, the goodness of his own ideal of himself shows in the ravishing razor-blade smile, the chilling kindness, and the naïveté that understands Betsy's freeze-dried personality. Travis wants to save others, unable to help himself. The lean body he straps with guns and knives is like a saint's in a flagellation. Its livid whiteness shows spiritual stress. He needs a child whore or a presidential stooge to absorb his yearning for nobility. De Niro's presence substantiates the allusions to Bresson better than Paul Schrader's screenplay.

The genius of the acting consists of De Niro's refusal to simplify. He never opts for sacred monster or shaman. The long, lone sequences establish an hallucinatory confessional with the audience who know how severe this Travis could be from the way he goads his own dread of being watched: "Are you talking to me? You must be, 'cause I'm the only one here."

Travis and Jimmy Doyle are his great parts, but *Mean Streets* (73, Scorsese) was training for them both, and an assertion of how out of conventional control he was. For all his special affinity with Scorsese, *Mean Streets* is shaped by the actor's willful privacy. In that and Roger Corman's *Bloody Mama* (69) he gave us a character so unpredictable and so locked in his own urgings as to be incoherent, a mess of spasm behavior sustained only by his rapture. That may be the perilous vein of reality the movies now need. Better that than the woefully respectable, dead-eyed civility of *The Last Tycoon* (76, Elia Kazan). Johnny in *Mean Streets* is self-destructive, if you want to moralize; crazy if you see it as a movie about purpose or ambition. But when it was first shown, and we were less familiar with the actor, it looked as if a rogue had come in off the streets.

By comparison, his Vito Corleone in *The Godfather, Part II* (74, Francis Ford Coppola) looks professional but overawed as if he felt unusual duty in having to furnish Brando's youth for so expensive and prestigious a film. It is an intricate performance—sly, diffident, and deeply in period—but it is actorly. It shows the difference between working for Coppola compared with the charged huddle he shares with Scorsese.

De Niro once had a similar bond with Brian De Palma: *Greetings* (68), *The Wedding Party* (69), *Hi, Mom!* (70)—signs of a poker-faced anarchy. He also made *Jennifer On My Mind* (71, Noel Black); *Born to Win* (71, Ivan Passer); *The Gang That Couldn't Shoot Straight* (71, James Goldstone); and played the catcher in *Bang the Drum Slowly* (73, John Hancock), a tearful waste of his willingness to become a stupid, dying athlete. His largest failure is *1900* (75, Bernardo Bertolucci), in which he seems miscast and cut adrift from his improvisational language. But he is still the most beguiling person in that distended movie. *The Deer Hunter* (78, Michael Cimino) would not have existed without De Niro's fierce generation of pain and honor, and the curiosity of an emotional movie with a restrained center who is preoccupied with unutterable things.

The surge in De Niro's audacity as an actor reached its peak (and perhaps toppled over) in his Jake La Motta in *Raging Bull* (80, Scorsese), for which he won the best actor Oscar. He put on not just weight, but the burden of degradation. While in the ring, he was a terrifying spectacle, as credible as any movie boxer has ever been, despite Scorsese's cheerful ignorance of how fights work. In his scenes with Cathy Moriarty, and with the "guys," there were remarkable insights into sexual insecurity or ambivalence. This bull was in terror of steers, and the film sometimes leaned toward being a nightmare for the stud who dreads gayness. But the power of the performance and the extremity of the film have been hard to follow, for director and actor both.

De Niro's priest in *True Confessions* (81, Ulu Grosbard) was all the better for being repressed. His Rupert Pupkin in *The King of Comedy* (83, Scorsese) had a frantic comic exuberance that we have hardly seen since. His Noodles in *Once Upon a Time in America* (84, Sergio Leone) seemed a little routine. But then De Niro fell on a stretch of odd choices and uncertain performances. The films were often unworthy of him, and there were signs that he was cashing in—no matter that he has never been a popular favorite: trying romance in *Falling in Love* (84, Grosbard); briefly in *Brazil* (85, Terry Gilliam); *The Mission* (86, Roland Joffe); Satanic in *Angel Heart* (86, Alan Parker); as Al Capone in *The Untouchables* (87, De Palma); with Charles Grodin in the amusing *Midnight Run* (88, Martin Brest); *Jacknife* (89, David Jones); *We're No Angels* (89, Neil Jordan); and *Stanley and Iris* (90, Martin Ritt).

GoodFellas (90, Scorsese) was a return to home ground for everyone, and De Niro was appropriately chilling, even if Joe Pesci overshadowed him.

At the opposite extreme, he gave a virtuoso performance in *Awakenings* (90, Penny Marshall), but still seemed like a Bickle trying to kid the hospital. *Guilty by Suspicion* (91, Irwin Winkler) was another poor choice. *Backdraft* (91, Ron Howard) was standard. But his Max Cady in *Cape Fear* (91, Scorsese) was so intricately nasty, so repellent, and so clever, that one wondered if the actor hadn't developed too much devil worship. *Night and the City* (92, Winkler) was so much less interesting than Widmark had been in the original. While in *Mad Dog and Glory* (92, John McNaughton) De Niro was outdone by Bill Murray.

At fifty, he began to seem increasingly difficult to cast, or satisfy. He played the father in *This Boy's Life* (93, Michael Caton-Jones). And in 1993 he directed for the first time: *A Bronx Tale*.

In the years since that was written, De Niro has done twenty-three pictures (Warren Beatty has done one less in a lifetime). And since several of those films have been made for De Niro's own production company, this is not just an actor taking assignments. It's a business, not necessarily more compelling to the boss or useful to the public than his restaurant operation. To be blunt, De Niro has gone a long way to squander his own high reputation by the remorseless greed for minor or trashy projects. Of the twenty-three, I'd argue that less than a quarter are worthy of him, while many are grim chores that only draw attention to his glum attitude and ungenerous presence: the monster in *Frankenstein* (94, Kenneth Branagh); *Casino* (95, Scorsese); very good in *Heat* (95, Michael Mann); *The Fan* (96, Tony Scott); *Sleepers* (96, Barry Levinson); *Marvin's Room* (96, Jerry Zaks); *Cop Land* (97, James Mangold); *Wag the Dog* (97, Levinson); *Jackie Brown* (97, Quentin Tarantino); *Great Expectations* (98, Alfonso Cuadron); *Ronin* (98, John Frankenheimer); *Analyze This* (99, Harold Ramis); *Flawless* (99, Joel Schumacher); *The Adventures of Rocky and Bullwinkle* (00, Des McAnuff); *Men of Honor* (00, George Tillman Jr); *Meet the Parents* (00, Jay Roach); *15 Minutes* (01, John Herzfeld); *The Score* (01, Frank Oz); *City by the Sea* (02, Caton-Jones); *Showtime* (02, Tom Dey); *Analyze That* (02, Ramis); *Godsend* (03, Nick Hamm).

Claire Denis, b. Paris, 1948

1988: *Chocolat*. 1989: *Man No Run*. 1990: *S'en Fout la Mort/No Fear, No Die; Jacques Rivette, le Veilleur* (d). 1991: *Keep It for Yourself*; "Pour Ushari Ahmed Mahmoud," an episode from *Contre l'Oubli*. 1994: *J'Ai Pas Sommeil/I Can't Sleep; US Go Home* (d); *Boom-Boom* (d). 1995: "Nice, Very Nice," an episode from *À Propos de Nice, la Suite* (d). 1996: *Nénette et Boni*. 1999: *Beau Travail/Good Work*. 2001: *Trouble Every Day*. 2002: *Vendredi Soir/Friday Night*.

Despite the enthusiastic support of *Film Comment*, *Beau Travail* didn't really "take" with American audiences—so much the worse for them. For plainly, this beautiful reverie on the culture of men in a regiment, set in the Djibouti where Denis had spent some of her childhood, and managing to take in allusions to Herman Melville, and Benjamin Britten as well as Godard's *Le Petit Soldat* (63), is a movie that makes *Full Metal Jacket* (87, Kubrick), say, look adolescent and sheltered (as well as clumsy and underlined). Denis was doing *Billy Budd* in the context of the Foreign Legion, yet she was also making a kind of poem to the corps—both the body and the regiment. It's a stunning, beautiful film that marked an important career.

Denis paid her dues as an assistant director—on *Sweet Movie* (74, Dusan Makavejev); *Serail* (76, Eduardo de Gregorio); *Hanna K.* (83, Costa-Gavras); *Paris, Texas* (84, Wim Wenders); *Down by Law* (86, Jim Jarmusch)—but I noticed her first in the tender, probing documentary on the very shy Jacques Rivette (indeed, I think that film nearly deserves to be included in Rivette's own filmography, for it is so sensitive to his work).

In addition, Denis did the excellent *I Can't Sleep*, which bears comparison with the unease of *Paris Nous Appartient* (60, Rivette); the comedy of *Nénette et Boni*; and *No Fear, No Die*, a daring and graceful contemplation of male bonding that is less homoerotic than fascinated by all the fresh gender associations in modern society and film—Kent Jones has talked about this mood being due to the revolutionary impact of Jean Eustache's *The Mother and the Whore* (73). So it's clear, I think, how far certain running ideas in French cinema—evident in the thirties and hurried forward in the New Wave—are still being pursued. Claire Denis reminds one not just of the wonder of French film, but of its sense of history.

Brian De Palma,
b. Newark, New Jersey, 1940
1964: *The Wedding Party* (not released till 1969). 1966: *Murder à la Mod*. 1968: *Greetings*. 1970: *Hi, Mom!; Dionysus in '69* (d). 1972: *Get to Know Your Rabbit; Sisters/Blood Sisters*. 1974: *Phantom of the Paradise*. 1976: *Obsession; Carrie*. 1978: *The Fury*. 1979: *Home Movies*. 1980: *Dressed to Kill*. 1981: *Blow Out*. 1982: *The First Time*. 1983: *Scarface*. 1984: *Body Double*. 1986: *Wise Guys*. 1987: *The Untouchables*. 1989: *Casualties of War*. 1990: *The Bonfire of the Vanities*. 1992: *Raising Cain*. 1993: *Carlito's Way*. 1996: *Mission: Impossible*. 1998: *Snake Eyes*. 2000: *Mission to Mars*. 2002: *Femme Fatale*.

There is a self-conscious cunning in De Palma's work, ready to control everything except his own cruelty and indifference. He is the epitome of mindless style and excitement swamping taste or character. Of course, he was a brilliant kid. But his usefulness in an historical survey is to point out the dangers of movies falling into the hands of such narrow movie-mania, such cold-blooded prettification. I daresay there are no "ugly" shots in De Palma's films—if you feel able to measure "beauty" merely in terms of graceful or hypnotic movement, vivid angles, lyrical color, and hysterical situation. But that is the set of criteria that makes Leni Riefenstahl a "great" director, rather than the victim of conflicting inspiration and decadence. De Palma's eye is cut off from conscience or compassion. He has contempt for his characters and his audience alike, and I suspect that he despises even his own immaculate skill. Our cultural weakness admires and rewards technique and impact bereft of moral sense. If the thing works, it has validity—the means justify the lack of an end. De Palma is a cynic, and not a feeble one; there are depths of misanthropy there.

De Palma was the son of a surgeon, and he has been heard to joke that that may account for his high tolerance of blood: the movie director as glib interviewee. He studied at Columbia and Sarah Lawrence, switching from sciences to film and carrying into his professional career the hustling ways and the reference-book style of a domineering student. His films of the sixties were nearly underground: cheap, inventive works of cinema verité, pulp satire, and comic-book essay form. They showed the mark of Godard, and they had the vigor of a rock album: a collage of pieces that got a pungent mood across. Their originality is worth underlining because the films were and are still very little seen, and because their humor and their interest in the world has been replaced by a sardonic imitation of Hitchcock's engineering movies.

De Palma wanted to make more popular pictures—a very American trait, but a good illustration of the choice between independence and commercialism that faces the film student. The turning point was *Sisters,* an artful homage to Hitchcock. It is a psychological suspense film, drawing upon *Psycho* but still raw with the background naturalism of student films. That has long since faded and been replaced with studied picture compilation. In *The Fury,* even, one sequence relies on back projection. De Palma absorbed Hitchcock's storyboard preparation, and his films are easily the closest screen approximation to the master's grid system for anguished characters. The elegance of the pictures is in churlish opposition to the pain the people suffer.

Phantom of the Paradise may be De Palma's best film yet in that it needs florid artificiality and brimstone imagery. Its reworking of an old movie legend (Opera becomes Rock) is striking and witty, and there is a gusto to the picture that carries the elements of grand guignol lightly. *Obses-*

sion was *Vertigo* at sleepwalking pace as De Palma stepped in Hitchcock's footprints: it was not helped by the numbed performances of Cliff Robertson and Geneviève Bujold.

Carrie is anything but turgid, but crazy with startling presence and sensational event. It was De Palma's greatest hit, and his most showy film. To its credit, the uncomfortable feverishness of teenage menstruation is captured, thanks in part to Sissy Spacek's arrested-development Medusa. But the cruelty of the plot, the poisoned sundae of humiliation, revivalist hysteria, and telekinetic effects are grotesque. It is a parody of a well-made film, as it keeps on battering you with its own style. Can a holocaust be tidy too? At times, the color does rise above the director's knowing glee. The ending is without rival and undeniably cathartic. But *Carrie* is the work of a glittering, callous surgeon who left his knife in the body.

The Fury is incoherent, silly, and just as removed from real feelings and pain. It is a Frank Yablans production, and De Palma may not have been as free as he was on *Carrie.* That high-school cockpit at least afforded him a concentrated piece of action, and a plot that was a single, vicious spiral. *The Fury* shows only his inability to negotiate a complex story: he lacks faith in the depth or mystery of people; he cannot even sustain an anecdote. *The Fury,* like *Carrie,* ends in an outburst of destruction that would be appalling (rather than trite) if there were any real people in the film.

De Palma has lost many of his old allies in the last decades—and he hasn't won me. Even his more noted films dismay me: *Dressed to Kill* is loony, despite some good sequences; *Body Double* is close to insane, despite a few hysterical sequences; *The Untouchables* is no more than the sum of good things in its actors—plus Sean Connery's death scene; *Casualties of War* struck me as exploitation. And there is not one good scene in *Bonfire of the Vanities.*

But *Scarface* is something else: an authentic black comedy, with red for blood, white for cocaine, and that overall smeared look so true to Miami. Give Oliver Stone credit for the script. The film was also the real debut of Michelle Pfeiffer, and it had a Mary Elizabeth Mastrantonio still as fresh as jalapeño. There are fine performances from F. Murray Abraham, Harris Yulin, Steven Bauer, and Robert Loggia. Pacino is delirious with accent, coke, and the sinuousness of his own genius. The richness of the film begins in his having such a ball. But I give De Palma credit, too, and hereby admit that I prefer it to the Hawks version.

On the other hand, *Carlito's Way* had little except the director's nostalgia for the danger and riot of *Scarface,* and set-piece sequences that exemplify the nullity of "movie genius" when it has no ideas.

I'd be surprised if De Palma still has followers enough to argue against the proposition that his three most recent pictures have to be included with his worst.

Gérard Depardieu,

b. Chateauroux, France, 1948

Depardieu has the air of a rugby player (after a game played in heavy mud) crossed with a great violinist—he is Charles Laughton, yet he has eyes worthy of Montgomery Clift. Thus, he has managed on several occasions to be a thug, a lout, a brute even, who has an inner reticence that belies his appearance. The fascination has easily traveled beyond his native France. Depardieu is an "international" actor, yet he shows no sign of being able to improve his English enough to play a lead role in an English-speaking film. Still, no actor is more industrious—and Depardieu has never given up his allegiance to theatre. A little over fifty, he is not far from one hundred films, many of which have only been made bankable by his willingness to take a chance.

He came from humble origins, and he was a street kid who led a rough, unsavory life. But he has an authentic, self-trained identification with literature and drama that may not be far from Olivier's love of the classics. Depardieu has done plenty of "modern roles," but he seems more inspired by period and costume. It could be no undue stretch of the imagination to see Depardieu playing Tamburlaine, Shylock, and Stanley Kowalski—or Hamlet, Romeo, and Charles Bovary. He has an appetite, or capacity, that could take on anyone—he has called himself less a star than a storyteller, a balladeer.

As far as I can tell, his debut was in a short film, *Le Beatnik et le Minet* (65, Roger Leenhardt). But by the early seventies, he had begun the hardworking career that he has never abandoned: *Le Cri du Cormoran le Soir Au-Dessus des Jonques* (70, Michel Audiard); *Un Peu de Soleil dans l'Eau Froide* (71, Jacques Deray); *Le Tueur* (71, Denys de la Patelliere); *L'Affaire Dominici* (71, Claude Bernard-Aubert); *Nathalie Granger* (72, Marguerite Duras); *Au Rendez-Vous de la Mort Joyeuse* (72, Juan Buñuel); *La Scoumoune* (72, José Giovanni); *Le Viager* (72, Pierre Tcherina); *Deux Hommes dans la Ville* (73, Giovanni); *Les Gaspards* (73, Tcherina); and *Rude Journée pour la Reine* (73, Rene Alio).

It was his role as the free-ranging, existential terrorist roadie in *Going Places* (74, Bertrand Blier) that established Depardieu. But he was just as good as the briefly seen shy inventor of the metroscope in *Stavisky* (74, Alain Resnais). He then did *La Femme du Gange* (74, Duras); *Vincent, François, Paul et les Autres* (74, Claude Sautet); *Pas si Méchant que Ça* (74, Claude Goretta); *Maîtresse* (74, Barbet Schroeder); *7 Morts sur*

Ordonnance (75, Jacques Rouffio); *Je t'Aime, Moi Non Plus* (75, Serge Gainsbourg); *Calmos* (75, Blier); the peasant in *1900* (76, Bernardo Bertolucci); as the helpless male who mutilates himself in *L'Ultima Donna* (76, Marco Ferreri); and *Barocco* (76, André Téchiné).

He was in two more Marguerite Duras films—*Baxter, Vera Baxter* (76) and *Le Camion* (77)—and he was in *The Left-Handed Woman* (77, Peter Handke); *Dites-Lui que J'Aime* (77, Claude Miller); *Get Out Your Handkerchiefs* (77, Blier); *Les Chiens* (78, Alain Jessua); *Rêve de Singe* (78, Ferreri); *Le Sucre* (78, Rouffio); a kind of idiotic murderer in *Buffet Froid* (79, Blier); *Mon Oncle d'Amérique* (79, Resnais); as the "wild thing" lover in *Loulou* (80, Maurice Pialat); *The Last Metro* (80, François Truffaut); and *Inspecteur la Bavure* (80, Claude Zidi).

By the early eighties, he was able to work a little less often, but with no lack of daring: *Le Choix des Armes* (81, Alain Corneau); *The Woman Next Door* (81, Truffaut); *Danton* (82, Andrzej Wajda); *The Return of Martin Guerre* (82, Daniel Vigne); *The Moon in the Gutter* (83, Jean-Jacques Beneix); *Fort Saganne* (84, Corneau); a movie version of a stage production of *Le Tartuffe* (84), which he directed himself; *Les Compères* (84, Francis Veber); *Une Femme ou Deux* (85, Vigne); *Police* (85, Pialat); *Les Fugitifs* (86, Veber); *Jean de Florette* (86, Claude Berri); as a homosexual in *Ménage* (86, Blier); *Sous le Soleil de Satan* (87, Pialat); as Rodin in *Camille Claudel* (87, Bruno Nuytten); and *A Strange Place to Meet* (88, François Dupeyron).

He had a great international success in *Cyrano de Bergerac* (89, Jean-Paul Rappeneau); *Je Veux Rentre à la Maison* (89, Resnais); *Too Beautiful for You* (89, Blier); trying to stay in the United States in *Green Card* (90, Peter Weir); *Uranus* (91, Berri); *Merci la Vie* (91, Blier); as Columbus in *1492: Conquest of Paradise* (92, Ridley Scott), one of his few unequivocal failures; playing with his son, Guillaume, as Marin Marais in *Tous les Matins du Monde* (92, Corneau); *Germinal* (93, Berri); *My Father, The Hero* (93, Steve Miner); *Hélas pour Moi* (93, Jean-Luc Godard).

Depardieu has often played men in history or fiction hounded and obsessed: Balzac, Jean Valjean, the Count of Monte Cristo. It seems clear that he sees himself in that light, for no one works harder—not even Robert De Niro. Not that Depardieu's choice of roles is often cynical. It seems as if every role entails upheaval; he is so seldom casual. And I fear he's paying the price of being so committed and demanding. Am I alone in feeling that I've seen his every mood and urge, over and over again? Does he not begin to be tedious?

As you consider that, here is the record: *Una Pura Formalità* (94, Giuseppe Tornatore); *Le*

Colonel Chabert (94, Yves Angelo); *La Machine* (94, Francois Dupeyron); *Elisa* (95, Jean Becker); *The Horseman on the Roof* (95, Rappeneau); *Les Anges Gardiens* (95, Jean-Marie Poire); *Le Garçu* (95, Pialat); *Unhook the Stars* (96, Nick Cassavetes); *Bogus* (96, Norman Jewison); *The Secret Agent* (96, Christopher Hampton); *Le Plus Beau Métier du Monde* (96, Gerard Lauzier); *Hamlet* (96, Kenneth Branagh); *XXL* (97, Ariel Zeitoun); Porthos in *The Man in the Iron Mask* (98, Randall Wallace); *La Parola Amore Esiste* (98, Mimmo Calopresti); to TV for *Le Comte de Monte Cristo* (98, Josee Dayan); *Bimboland* (98, Zeitoun); *Astérix et Obélix contre César* (99, Zidi); *The Bridge* (99, Depardieu and Frederic Auburtin)— and one of his poorest; *Balzac* (99, Dayan)—one of his best.

Breathe—*Mirka* (99, Rachid Benhaj); *Tutto l'Amore che C'è* (00, Sergio Rubini); *Vatel* (00, Roland Joffe); Valjean in *Les Misérables* (00, Dayan); *Bérénice* (00, Jean-Daniel Verhaeghe); *Zavist Bogov* (00, Vladimir Menshov); *102 Dalmatians* (00, Kevin Lima); *The Closet* (00, Veber); *Concorrenza Sleale* (01, Ettore Scola); *C.Q.* (01, Roman Coppola); *Vidocq* (01, Pitof); *City of Ghosts* (01, Matt Dillon); *Astérix & Obélix: Mission Cléopâtre* (01, Alain Chabat).

He still works as hard as Cagney at Warners (yet not as amusingly): *I Am Dina* (02, Ole Boredal); *Aime Ton Père* (02, Jacob Berger); *Between Strangers* (02, Edoardo Ponti); as D'Artagnan in *Blanche* (02, Bernie Bonvoisin); as Fouche in the TV mini-series, *Napoleon* (02, David Grubin); *Ruy Blas* (02, Jacques Weber); *Le Pacte du Silence* (03, Graham Guit); *Wanted* (03, Brad Mirman); *Bon Voyage* (03, Rappeneau); *Volpone* (03, Auburtin).

Johnny (John Christopher) **Depp**,
b. Owensboro, Kentucky, 1963

Depp has had the press of someone following in Sean Penn's image—damage to hotels, lurid tattoos, troubled love affairs with actresses, and an overall moody aloofness. But his screen character is very different. There, he is gentle, benign, nearly mystical, and entirely enterprising. For an actor with a huge following, and many mainstream offers (like *Speed*), Depp has studiously avoided blockbusters and cast his lot with more adventurous projects. It's hard to think of another actor of his generation who would have done *Ed Wood* (94, Tim Burton) or been so happy exploring the man's bland enthusiasms amid a supporting cast with stronger or more obvious roles to play. He is already a legend of dedication.

As a child, Depp moved with his family to Florida. He played a lot of music as a kid, and was part of a band. He made his debut in *A Nightmare on Elm Street* (84, Wes Craven), and then appeared in the trashy *Private Resort* (85, George

Bowers). He was a soldier in *Platoon* (86, Oliver Stone), and then 1987–90 he was an undercover cop in the TV series *21 Jump Street*.

He was a biker stud in *Cry-Baby* (90, John Waters), but it was as *Edward Scissorhands* (90, Burton) that he revealed himself and his sense of outcast pathos. He had a cameo in *Freddy's Dead: The Final Nightmare* (91, Rachel Talalay). In *Benny & Joon* (93, Jeremiah S. Chechik) he once more sought the offbeat. He also excelled in the scenes where he aspired to be Buster Keaton. In *What's Eating Gilbert Grape* (93, Lasse Hallström), he was the strong center in a troubled family, aiding the more showy performance of Leonardo DiCaprio.

Since then, as well as *Ed Wood*, he has made *Arizona Dream* (93, Emir Kusturica), *Nick of Time* (95, John Badham); with Brando in *Don Juan DeMarco* (95, Jeremy Levin); and *Dead Man* (96, Jim Jarmusch)—there's not a conventional choice in the list. And who could put together a rarer quintet than *Donnie Brasco* (97, Mike Newell), *Fear and Loathing in Las Vegas* (98, Terry Gilliam), *The Astronaut's Wife* (99, Rand Ravich), *The Ninth Gate* (99, Roman Polanski), and *Sleepy Hollow* (99, Tim Burton)?

It was around this time that he discovered that a film he had directed, *The Brave* (97)—with Brando in it—could hardly get released. But as an actor he admits no barriers: *The Man Who Cried* (00, Sally Potter); *Before Night Falls* (00, Julian Schnabel); *Chocolat* (00, Hallström); *Blow* (01, Ted Demme); the London copper in *From Hell* (01, Albert and Allen Hughes); *Nailed Right In* (03, Griffin Dunne); *Pirates of the Caribbean: The Curse of the Black Pearl* (03, Gore Verbinski).

Bruce Dern, b. Winnetka, Illinois, 1936

Sometimes a movie ad reveals the secret being of a star. In the American promotion of *Coming Home* (78, Hal Ashby), a rapturous embrace between Jane Fonda and Jon Voight was being watched by a wistful, suspicious Bruce Dern, his eyes lime pits of paranoia and resentment. Fonda and Voight were not only the upholders of enlightenment in that soft-centered liberal movie . . . in Dern's eyes, they were established stars. Fonda had one Oscar already, and Voight would win the best actor Oscar for *Coming Home*.

Dern was then one of the most striking actors on the screen, but a professional haunted by failures, and a man whose own unease flowed into his querulous screen persona. No one was as plausible and frightening as the slightly unbalanced man who believes he has been wronged.

He is not glamorous, or made for triumph. His voice has a high, midwestern twang, inclined to sneer or whine. His face is narrow, nearly gaunt; his curly hair goes wild with his thoughts. And the looming eyes monopolize our feelings toward him. He can be fearsome, loathsome, or pitiful, but he is neither calm nor commanding.

It may grind the more on Dern that he is from the Illinois aristocracy. One grandfather was Roosevelt's secretary of war, the other was chairman of a leading Chicago department store. Bruce was educated at New Trier High School, but he dropped out of the University of Pennsylvania and joined the Actors' Studio.

Elia Kazan gave Dern his movie debut, in *Wild River* (60), as one of the country hoodlums who beat up Montgomery Clift. He had his hands chopped off in *Hush . . . Hush, Sweet Charlotte* (64, Robert Aldrich); he was the sailor poker-pulped in *Marnie* (64, Alfred Hitchcock). Dern's friendship with Jack Nicholson drew him into the Roger Corman circle and ensured him work for the next few years as a desperado or druggy: Loser in *The Wild Angels* (66, Corman); *St. Valentine's Day Massacre* (66, Corman); *The Trip* (67, Corman); killed by John Wayne in *The War Wagon* (67, Burt Kennedy); *Will Penny* (67, Tom Gries); *Waterhole 3* (67, William Graham); *Psych-Out* (68, Richard Rush); *Castle Keep* (68, Sydney Pollack); *Hang 'Em High* (68, Ted Post); *Support Your Local Sheriff* (69, Kennedy); stoned on exhaustion in *They Shoot Horses, Don't They?* (69, Pollack); *Bloody Mama* (70, Corman); *The Incredible Two-Headed Transplant* (70, Anthony M. Lanza); brilliant as the demented basketball coach in *Drive, He Said* (70, Jack Nicholson); and, notoriously, as the dirty, rotten longhair who kills John Wayne in *The Cowboys* (71, Mark Rydell).

Dern felt trapped and depressed by parts in which he was a gross heavy who never lived to see The End or get a girl. As a result, he tried to find better or more respectable parts and is very touching and forlorn as the lonely spaceman in *Silent Running* (71, Douglas Trumbull); his best performance yet as the brother high on dreams of Hawaii in *The King of Marvin Gardens* (72, Bob Rafelson); a nervy sidekick in *The Laughing Policeman* (73, Stuart Rosenberg); palpably dangerous as Tom Buchanan in *The Great Gatsby* (74, Jack Clayton); funny in *Smile* (74, Michael Ritchie)—comedy could be his best vein; *Posse* (75, Kirk Douglas); *Family Plot* (75, Hitchcock); a dog's best friend in *Won Ton Ton, The Dog Who Saved Hollywood* (75, Michael Winner); *The Twist* (76, Claude Chabrol); the Vietnam veteran terrorist riding the blimp in *Black Sunday* (77, John Frankenheimer); and *The Driver* (78, Walter Hill).

But then the plot took hold—the plot that Dern's eyes had always believed—the plot to shaft him. His career began to decline, and the line has not stopped: *Middle Age Crazy* (80, John Trent); *Tattoo* (81, Bob Brooks)—which tries to make a sexual creature of Dern; *Harry Tracy, Desperado* (82, William A. Graham); *That Cham-*

pionship Season (82, Jason Miller); running, running, running in *On the Edge* (85, Rob Nilsson); *Toughlove* (85, Glenn Jordan) for TV; *Uncle Tom's Cabin* (87, Stan Latham) for TV; *The Big Town* (87, Ben Bolt); *Roses Are for the Rich* (87, Michael Miller); *World Gone Wild* (88, Lee H. Katzin); *1969* (88, Ernest Thompson); *The 'burbs* (89, Joe Dante); *Trenchcoat in Paradise* (89, Martha Coolidge) for TV; *The Court Martial of Jackie Robinson* (90, Larry Peerce); *After Dark, My Sweet* (90, James Foley); *Diggstown* (93, Ritchie); on TV in *It's Nothing Personal* (93, Bradford May).

He is the father of Laura Dern (b. 1966).

By now, Dern has become an old-timer, a veteran and a sly know-all—and he's just as watchable: *Dead Man's Revenge* (94, Alan J. Levi); as the husband in *Amelia Earhart: The Final Flight* (94, Yves Simoneau); *Mrs. Munck* (95, Diane Ladd—the mother of Laura Dern); *Wild Bill* (95, Hill); *A Mother's Prayer* (95, Larry Elikann); *Down Periscope* (96, David S. Ward); very good as the chief in *Mulholland Falls* (96, Lee Tamahori); *Last Man Standing* (96, Hill); *Comfort, Texas* (97, Ritchie); *Perfect Prey* (98, Howard McCain); *Hard Time: The Premonition* (99, David S. Carr); *The Haunting* (99, Jan De Bont); *If . . . Dog . . . Rabbit* (99, Matthew Modine); *All the Pretty Horses* (00, Billy Bob Thornton); *Madison* (00, William Bindley); *The Glass House* (01, Daniel Sackheim); *Milwaukee, Minnesota* (02, Allan Mindel); *Masked & Anonymous* (03, Larry Charles); *The Monster* (03, Patty Jenkins).

Laura Dern, b. Los Angeles, 1966

Laura Dern is in her thirties now, heading steadily away from the mode in which she has been most effective—by which I mean not simply youth, but a kind of readiness for teen fable as demonstrated in two poles-apart roles for David Lynch (her one-time partner), the virginal girl in *Blue Velvet* (86) and the lipstick hotshot, Lula, in *Wild at Heart* (90). Her acting in those two films is much more imaginative than naturalistic. It suggests how far she is suited to a kind of fairy-tale approach—not mainstream, but based in her nearly childlike sincerity.

She is the daughter of Bruce Dern and Diane Ladd, and she could be seen in bits in her parents' films before she settled into her own career: *White Lightning* (73, Joseph Sargent); *Alice Doesn't Live Here Anymore* (74, Martin Scorsese); *Foxes* (80, Adrian Lyne); *Ladies and Gentlemen, the Fabulous Stains* (82, Lou Adler); *Teachers* (84, Arthur Hiller); *Mask* (85, Peter Bogdanovich); winning praise as the young girl seduced in *Smooth Talk* (85, Joyce Chopra); *Sister, Sister* (87, Bill Condon); *Haunted Summer* (88, Ivan Passer); *Fat Man and Little Boy* (89, Roland Joffé); nominated for an Oscar in *Ram-*

bling Rose (91, Martha Coolidge); *Afterburn* (92, Robert Markowitz); *Jurassic Park* (93, Steven Spielberg); *A Perfect World* (93, Clint Eastwood); *Down Came a Blackbird* (95, Jonathan Sanger); an extremist in *Ruby Ridge: An American Tragedy* (96, Roger Young); narrator on *Bastard Out of Carolina* (96, Anjelica Huston); *Citizen Ruth* (96, Alexander Payne); *The Baby Dance* (98, Jane Anderson); *October Sky* (99, Joe Johnston); *Dr. T & the Women* (00, Robert Altman); *Daddy and Them* (01, Billy Bob Thornton); *Jurassic Park III* (01, Johnston); *Within These Walls* (01, Mike Robe); *Novocaine* (01, David Atkins); *Focus* (01, Neil Slavin); *I Am Sam* (01, Jessie Nelson); *Damaged Care* (02, Harry Winer).

Vittorio de Sica (1902–74), b. Sora, Italy
1940: *Rose Scarlatte; Maddalena Zero in Condotta.* 1941: *Teresa Venerdi.* 1942: *Un Garibaldino al Convento.* 1943: *I Bambini ci Guardano/ The Children Are Watching Us.* 1945: *La Porta del Cielo.* 1946: *Sciuscia/Shoeshine.* 1948: *Ladri di Biciclette/Bicycle Thieves.* 1951: *Miracolo a Milano/Miracle in Milan.* 1952: *Umberto D.* 1953: *Stazione Termini/Indiscretion of an American Wife.* 1954: *L'Oro di Napoli/Gold of Naples.* 1956: *Il Tetto.* 1961: *La Ciociara/Two Women; Il Giudizio Universale.* 1962: "La Riffa," episode from *Boccaccio 70; I Sequestrati di Altona/The Condemned of Altona.* 1963: *Il Boom.* 1964: *Ieri, Oggi, Domani/Yesterday, Today and Tomorrow; Matrimonio all'Italiana/Marriage, Italian Style.* 1965: *Un Mondo Nuovo.* 1966: *Caccia alla Volpe/After the Fox;* "Una Sera Come le Altre," episode from *Le Streghe.* 1967: *Sept Fois Femme/Woman Times Seven.* 1968: *Gli Amanti/A Place for Lovers.* 1969: *I Girasoli/Sunflower.* 1970: *Il Giardino dei Finzi-Contini/The Garden of the Finzi-Contini.* 1971: "Il Leone," episode from *Le Coppie.* 1973: *Una Breva Vacanza.* 1974: *The Journey.*

It is not always remembered that de Sica—pioneer sponsor of the nonprofessional actor—was originally a young romantic lead actor on the stage and in the movies. Thus, the slightly fake gallantry, the silver hair that might be tin, which Hollywood made use of and which Rossellini observed so tactfully in *Il Generale della Rovere* (59), were the remains of an early emphasis on charm and brightness. In the 1930s, he played in *Gli Uomini . . . che Mascalzoni* (32, Mario Camerini); *Daro un Milione* (35, Camerini); *Ma Non e Una Cosa Serza!* (36, Camerini); *Il Signor Max* (37, Luigi Comencini); *Castelli in Aria* (39, Augusto Genina); and *I Grandi Magazzini* (39, Camerini).

He also acted in the earliest films that he directed, and *The Children Are Watching Us* is his first serious resort to realism. It was scripted by Cesare Zavattini, whom de Sica had known since 1932. There is no doubt about the social and political involvement de Sica felt with war-torn Italy. He spoke of his films being a struggle "against the absence of human solidarity, against the indifference of society towards suffering. They are a word in favor of the poor and the unhappy." It could be argued that that strength of feeling requires more than a word. Time soon caught up with neo-realism and left it looking like an idealistic stance, not fully participated in by its practitioners. This is not to say that *The Children Are Watching Us, Shoeshine, Bicycle Thieves (The Bicycle Thief* in America), and *Umberto D* are not moving films, or that they are inaccurate or misleading portraits of Italy in the years after Mussolini.

The difficulty is that they are schematically contrived: *Bicycle Thieves,* for instance, is either too long a telling of a fragment from urban problems, or too sketchy an examination of the pressurized mind of a man on the brink of unemployment. Not all the real locations and "real" people disguise the way that the story has been set up—that the man has a son to create the necessary sentimental commentary on his dilemma, that once his bicycle is stolen, other cycles crowd the screen and the trilling of bells runs through the music. In the same way, the enlargement of the subject, to show how the victim himself becomes a thief, and the implication that all the city is caught in the same spiral, is trite compared with, say, the dynamic analysis Losey makes in *M* and *The Criminal.* The more one sees *Bicycle Thieves,* the duller the man becomes and the more poetic and accomplished de Sica's urban photography seems. The disappearing perspective of a sunny, dusty Rome, briefly puddled by a thunderstorm, but with streets and squares receding into hopelessly empty expanses, is not only very beautiful but a clear heralding of the elegant alienation in Antonioni's work.

Perhaps *Bicycle Thieves* would work best in thirty minutes, one episode among several—a form de Sica used in *L'Oro di Napoli.* As it is, it functions like a plan; it is emotional only to the extent that the plan is relevant to a real human plight. Like many would-be documentarists, de Sica is actually uneasy about feeling. When it arises, he shuts it off brusquely, as if he mistrusted an oversentimental reaction from his innate coldness. I do not mean that he was callous, but that his films skirt round feelings and prefer not to investigate character. Thus, it is the idea of the man in *Bicycle Thieves* that moves us, and always the cinematic realization in a Renoir film that affects our response. Neo-realism was a naïve regime, far less rewarding than the cinema verité movement that came some twelve years later. Because de Sica and Zavattini were most attached to it, they have been the most misunderstood.

Far better to accept the shortcomings of the cursory gestures to working-class solidarity and see that *Miracolo a Milano* has that curiously Italian fusion of fantasy and the everyday that Fellini has thrived on, that *Umberto D* takes objectivity toward abstraction in a way that can be usefully related to the work of Renoir. In other words, de Sica is a less emotional but more reflective director than is sometimes alleged.

It was the overreliance on the heart on his sleeve that led to charges of betrayal when the impetus went out of neo-realism. *Stazione Termini* was not a sellout to David Selznick, but an underachieved emotional melodrama; a subject close to Italian tradition, given the advantages of Jennifer Jones and Montgomery Clift, but let down by de Sica's reticence (with such material, Ophuls could have made a masterpiece). *Il Tetto* was an ostensibly working-class subject undermined by compromise. At this stage, de Sica resumed the acting career that he had never entirely abandoned: *I Nostri Sogni* (43, Vittorio Cottafavi); *Nessuno Torna Indietro* (44, Alessandro Blasetti); *Roma, Citta Libera* (46, Marcello Pagliero); *Lo Sconosciuto di San Marino* (48, Cottafavi and M. Waszinsky); *Altri Tempi* (52, Blasetti); the faithless lover in *Madame de . . .* (53, Max Ophuls); and an increasing emphasis on a twinkling-eyed father figure—*Pane, Amore e Gelosia* (54, Comencini); *Il Segno di Venere* (55, Dino Risi); *Pane, Amore e . . .* (55, Risi); *Padri e Figli* (57, Mario Monicelli); *It Happened in Rome* (57, Antonio Pietrangeli); *Amore e Chiacchiere* (57, Blasetti); Rinaldi in *A Farewell to Arms* (57, Charles Vidor); *Kanonenserenade* (58, Wolfgang Staudte); *La Prima Notte* (58, Alberto Cavalcanti); and *Les Noces Vénitiennes* (58, Cavalcanti).

His playing of the swindler trapped into heroism in *Il Generale della Rovere* was an affectionate glimpse of the two halves of de Sica's nature. Far from the betrayer of an early vision, he was a once interesting director in decline. The emotion that had once been denied by a sort of shyness was swamped by cliché and overemphasis: *Two Women* supposedly rehabilitated him commercially, just as it brought Sophia Loren an Oscar. But his work in the 1960s was slick and tasteless. The pictorial grace and the emotional severity were both abandoned in a series of concocted comedies about sexual hypocrisy. *The Garden of the Finzi-Contini* was a regeneration only in that it was a serious, literary subject that de Sica transcribed with rather hollow rectitude. He stands now as a minor director. But the films from 1943–52, and *L'Oro di Napoli*, are still worth seeing.

André de Toth (Sasvrai Farkasfawi Tothfalusi: Toth Endre Antai Mihaly), (1913–2002)
b. Mako, Hungary
1938: *Toprini Nasz; Ot Ora 40; Ket Lany Az Utcan; Hat Het Boldogsag; Semmelweiss.* 1943: *Passport to Suez; None Shall Escape.* 1944: *Dark Waters.* 1947: *Ramrod; The Other Love.* 1948: *Pitfall.* 1949: *Slattery's Hurricane.* 1951: *Man in the Saddle.* 1952: *Carson City; Springfield Rifle; Last of the Comanches/Sabre and the Arrow.* 1953: *House of Wax; The Stranger Wore a Gun; Thunder Over the Plains.* 1954: *Riding Shotgun; The City Is Dark/Crime Wave; The Bounty Hunter; Tanganyika.* 1955: *The Indian Fighter.* 1957: *Monkey On My Back; Hidden Fear.* 1959: *The Two-Headed Spy; Day of the Outlaw.* 1960: *Confessions of a Counterspy; Morgan Il Pirata/Morgan the Pirate* (codirected with Primo Zeglio). 1961: *I Mongoli* (codirected with Riccardo Freda). 1962: *Oro Per I Cesari/Gold for the Caesars* (codirected with Freda). 1968: *Play Dirty.*

De Toth's early career is far from clear. He was apparently an actor and scriptwriter in Hungary and Germany during the 1930s. He was a frequent visitor to England and America, and helped Alexander Korda on *Elephant Boy* (37, Zoltan Korda and Robert Flaherty). Report says that after a handful of Hungarian features, he was involved filming the Nazi invasion of Poland, but that he slipped away to England, where he worked for Korda as an editor and assistant director on *The Four Feathers* (39, Z. Korda), *Thief of Bagdad* (40, Michael Powell, Ludwig Berger, and Tim Whelan), and *The Jungle Book* (42, Z. Korda). By 1943, however, he was a director in Hollywood, where he had fifteen years as a maker of adventures, and half that as the husband of Veronica Lake.

A skiing accident restricted his work, but he reemerged to take over the interesting *Play Dirty* from René Clément and as a producer: *Billion Dollar Brain* (67, Ken Russell); and *El Condor* (70, John Guillermin).

De Toth is an entertaining director, especially when dealing with violence, treachery, and the psychological cruelty beneath them. His films are economical and sardonic. The main body of his work is Westerns: several Randolph Scott movies—*Man in the Saddle, Carson City, The Stranger Wore a Gun,* and *The Bounty Hunter*—which prefigure the Boetticher films, and three other creditable Westerns—*Springfield Rifle, Ramrod,* and *The Indian Fighter.* But *Crime Wave* is an excellent thriller; *House of Wax*—despite 3D gimmicks—is an ingenious horror; and *Monkey on My Back* is a startling, early treatment of drug addiction.

Michel Deville,
b. Boulogne-sur-Seine, France, 1931
1958: *Une Belle dans le Canon* (codirected with Charles Gérard). 1960: *Ce Soir ou Jamais.* 1961: *Adorable Menteuse.* 1962: *A Cause, À Cause d'une Femme.* 1963: *L'Appartement des Filles.* 1964: *Lucky Jo.* 1965: *On a Volé la Joconde.* 1966: *Martin Soldat.* 1967: *Benjamin.* 1968: *Bye Bye,*

Barbara. 1970: *L'Ours et la Poupée.* 1971: *Raphael, ou le Débauché.* 1972: *La Femme en Bleu.* 1974: *Le Mouton Enragé/The French Way/Love at the Top.* 1976: *L'Apprenti Salaud.* 1977: *Dossier 51.* 1979: *Le Voyage en Douce/Sentimental Journey.* 1981: *Eaux Profondes.* 1983: *La Petite Bande.* 1984: *Péril en la Demeure/Death in a French Garden.* 1986: *Le Paltoquet.* 1988: *La Lectrice.* 1990: *Nuit d'Été en Ville.* 1991: *Contre l'Oubli.* 1992: *Toutes Peines Confondues.* 1996: *Aux Petits Bonheurs.* 1997: *La Divine Poursuite.* 1999: *La Maladie de Sachs.* 2002: *Un Monde Presque Paisible.*

Very little of Deville's work has traveled far outside France. *Benjamin* is not the happiest representative of a director who, at his best, is a complex and tender comedian of the emotions. Nothing seems to have equaled the musical interplay of *Ce Soir ou Jamais* and *Adorable Menteuse,* films about the resort to deception and masquerade among young lovers. With witty scripts by Deville himself and Nina Companeez, the use of such actresses as Anna Karina, Marina Vlady, Macha Meril, and Françoise Dorléac, and a camera style that delighted in filming social groups so that individuals or couples were never cut off from their context, Deville seemed a very promising director. It was mannered, literary comedy, harking back to the intrigue of *Twelfth Night* and classical French theatre. In fact, after working for several years as assistant to Henri Decoin, Deville had collaborated with Jean Meyer on the filming of two Comédie Française productions: *Le Bourgeois Gentilhomme* (58) and *Le Mariage de Figaro* (59). In the early 1960s, at least, he looked capable of taking up Renoir's pursuit of winged cupid in something like the house-party atmosphere of *La Règle du Jeu.* But neglect may have forced him to coarsen his style and broaden his material.

Péril and *La Lectrice* were successes beyond France:the latter had Miou-Miou as a professional reader who enters into her stories and her readers' lives—a pretty idea, scripted by Deville and his wife.

Danny DeVito,
b. Neptune, New Jersey, 1944

1987: *Throw Momma from the Train.* 1989: *The War of the Roses.* 1992: *Hoffa.* 1996: *Matilda.* 2001: *How to Lose a Guy in 10 Days.* 2002: *Death to Smoochy.* 2003: *Duplex.*

There is a goblin of anger in DeVito the actor (and maybe not much else) that seemed to inspire him as a director. *Throw Momma* was demonically cruel, as if DeVito had understood both Hitchcock and slapstick and had a Rumpelstiltskin magic for drawing them together. *The War of the Roses* was a mess (nowhere more clearly than in DeVito's own acting role), but it grasped the demented malice of married partners, and had an air of Buñuel in some scenes. As a result, *Hoffa* seemed very promising, for here was an authentic little beast who grabbed America by the balls.

This is not far from that lovable demon, DeVito the actor and husband to Rhea Perlman (she of *Cheers* and he from *Taxi*). But as an actor, DeVito is either ingratiating or apoplectic, and he so dominates any role in which he is cast that he is always a DeVito type: *Lady Liberty* (72, Mario Monicelli); *Hurry Up, or I'll Be 30* (73, Joseph Jacoby); *Scalawag* (73, Kirk Douglas); very sweet in *One Flew Over the Cuckoo's Nest* (75, Milos Forman); *The Van* (76, Sam Grossman); *Goin' South* (78, Jack Nicholson); *Terms of Endearment* (83, James L. Brooks); *Johnny Dangerously* (84, Amy Heckerling); *Romancing the Stone* (84, Robert Zemeckis); *The Jewel of the Nile* (85, Lewis Teague); *Head Office* (86, Ken Finkleman); delirious in *Ruthless People* (86, Jim Abrahams, David Zucker, and Jerry Zucker); doing his best in *Wise Guys* (86, Brian De Palma); *Tin Men* (87, Barry Levinson); with Arnold Schwarzenegger in *Twins* (88, Ivan Reitman). His Penguin in *Batman Returns* (92, Tim Burton) is only frightening *before* he appears: the black cradle in the sewer is a great, macabre image. But DeVito's complete Penguin is just a ranting, rubber demon. Val Lewton knew the wisdom of never showing the worst things. As it is, the Penguin becomes a shrew.

Hoffa was a box-office failure, widely attacked for its departures from the facts. These are important failures, for we live in a time when biopics carry a great burden in preserving a popular grasp of history. But *Hoffa* is an epic film, enormously daring in its crowd scenes, and just as dynamic in its portrayal of a flawed charismatic. DeVito handled the raging vitality of Jack Nicholson, the delicate symbolism of two scenes involving Karen Young, and the eventual truth of Hoffa's life. It was like a movie from the seventies.

He has acted in *Other People's Money* (91, Norman Jewison); *Jack the Bear* (93, Marshall Herskovitz); *Renaissance Man* (94, Penny Marshall); *Get Shorty* (95, Barry Sonnenfeld); *Mars Attacks!* (96, Burton); *L.A. Confidential* (97, Curtis Hanson); *The Rainmaker* (97, Francis Coppola); *Living Out Loud* (98, Richard LaGravenese); *The Virgin Suicides* (99, Sofia Coppola); *The Big Kahuna* (99, John Swanbeck); *Man on the Moon* (99, Forman); *Drowning Mona* (00, Nick Gomez); *Screwed* (00, Scott Alexander and Larry Karaszewski); *What's the Worst That Could Happen?* (01, Sam Weisman); *Heist* (01, David Mamet).

His company, Jersey Films, has been an important producer: *Pulp Fiction* (94, Quentin Tarantino); *Reality Bites* (94, Ben Stiller); *Get Shorty;*

Gattaca (97, Andrew Niccol); *Out of Sight* (98, Steven Soderbergh); *Erin Brockovich* (00, Soderbergh).

Cameron Diaz, b. San Diego, California, 1972
There was a moment at least when Cameron Diaz meant the sight of her blond forelock stiff with semen in *There's Something About Mary* (98, Bobby and Peter Farrelly). A great start—or an impossible obstacle? She's a terrific looker with an exceptionally fresh, vivid face—she was doing a lot of commercials between Long Beach Polytechnic High and getting the girl's part opposite Jim Carrey in *The Mask* (94, Charles Russell). She showed a good comic touch in *My Best Friend's Wedding* (97, P. J. Hogan) and held her own with the far mightier Julia Roberts. But just as Roberts has credibly grown into being a woman in her thirties, so Diaz has to show us that she's more than a knockout; there are so many knockout women around: *Feeling Minnesota* (96, Steven Baigelman); *The Last Supper* (96, Stacy Tittle); *She's the One* (96, Edward Burns); not very convincing as Harvey Keitel's wife in *Head Above Water* (96, Jim Wilson); *A Life Less Ordinary* (97, Danny Boyle); *Very Bad Things* (98, Peter Berg); looking quite different in *Being John Malkovich* (99, Spike Jonze), and tougher than usual as the young team owner in *Any Given Sunday* (99, Oliver Stone).

It's hard for people like Diaz, and *Charlie's Angels* (00, McG) was no help. She was good in *The Invisible Circus* (01, Adam Brooks), but so few saw it. Then came *Things You Can Tell Just by Looking at Her* (01, Rodrigo García); the heroine's voice in *Shrek* (01, Andrew Adamson and Vicky Jensen); *Vanilla Sky* (01, Cameron Crowe), where she was battling to survive the nonsense; *The Sweetest Thing* (02, Roger Kumble); *Gangs of New York* (02, Martin Scorsese); *Charlie's Angels: Full Throttle* (03, McG).

Leonardo (Wilhelm) **DiCaprio**,
b. Los Angeles, 1974
DiCaprio earned at least $20 million to make *The Beach* (00, Danny Boyle), his drab follow-up to *Titanic* (97, James Cameron). And the picture's box office dropped by over 70 percent after its second week. No one has ever quite been able to explain the success of *Titanic* (something that leaves the business the more jittery). But many believed it was because teenage girls went back to see "Leonardo" and his Caravaggio teen carnality over and over again. In which case, don't knock the reality that those kids were different creatures, three years later, when *The Beach* reached their screens.

In the meantime, some gloom has overtaken the extraordinary actor. In two films—*What's Eating Gilbert Grape* (93, Lasse Hallström) and *This Boy's Life* (93, Michael Caton-Jones)—DiCaprio had seemed brushed by genius. In *Gilbert Grape*, especially, where he said he had improvised much of the picture, there was a wild, poetic streak that seemed to promise so much. Add the fact that those two films were unusually interesting properties, well directed—in *Grape*, there is a rare spirit in the cast that included Johnny Depp and Juliette Lewis.

But now that he is past twenty-five, and beginning to look a touch puffy, there are those ready to dismiss DiCaprio. We'll see how much creative stamina he possesses, but I fear a kind of fey magic has slipped from his face. The world does not seem to please him—whereas the kid in *Gilbert Grape* was intoxicated and enchanting. He made his debut in *Critters 3* (92, Kristine Peterson); *Poison Ivy* (92, Katt Shea Ruben), with Drew Barrymore; and then, after the breakthrough films—with a supporting actor nomination for *Gilbert Grape*—he started veering from the pretentious to the obvious: replacing River Phoenix in *The Basketball Diaries* (95, Scott Kalvert); and looking very unathletic; *The Quick and the Dead* (95, Sam Raimi); as Rimbaud in *Total Eclipse* (95, Agnieszka Holland); *Marvin's Room* (96, Jerry Zaks); *Romeo + Juliet* (96, Baz Luhrmann), the hit that set up *Titanic*; *The Man in the Iron Mask* (98, Randall Wallace), a significant failure; *Celebrity* (98, Woody Allen), a rather nasty revelation of some inner nature; and the virtually unreleased *Don's Plum* (98, R. D. Robb and John Schindler).

So there was a serious interval, such as any young person deserves, until he appeared in *Gangs of New York* (02, Martin Scorsese) and was seriously lacking. But he was funny, smart and young again in *Catch Me If You Can* (02, Steven Spielberg).

Ernest R. Dickerson,
b. Newark, New Jersey, 1952
1992: *Juice*. 1994: *Surviving the Game*. 1995: *Tales from the Crypt Presents Demon Knight*. 1996: *Bulletproof*. 1998: *Blind Faith; Ambushed; Futuresport* (TV). 1999: *Strange Justice* (TV). 2001: *Bones*. 2002: *Monday Night Mayhem* (TV). 2002: *Our America; Big Shot: Confessions of a Campus Bookie* (TV); *Good Fences* (TV). 2003: *Never Die Alone*.

Ernest Dickerson has made the shift from cameraman to director, but it has not been easy. In the last decade he has had to take jobs that became available—*Juice* was a striking, violent debut, but *Bulletproof* showed the same kind of material being jacked up for the box office to the point of absurdity. *Bones* was a good film, but it found no audience, so Dickerson had to go along with a conventional movie about Monday-night football. It is especially difficult for any black director to escape the bad habits and assumptions of black genre films—or to find fresh subjects. So Dickerson's struggle serves to underline the special insistence of a man like Carl Franklin.

As a film student at New York University, Dickerson became the house cameraman for a generation of independent movies: *Joe's Bed-Stuy Barbershop: We Cut Heads* (83, Spike Lee); *The Brother from Another Planet* (84, John Sayles); *Krush Groove* (85, Michael Schultz); *She's Gotta Have It* (86, Lee); *Enemy Territory* (87, Peter Manoogian); *Eddie Murphy Raw* (87, Robert Townsend); *School Daze* (88, Lee); *Do the Right Thing* (89, Lee), which is unique in its sense of the colors of urban heat; *Def by Temptation* (90, James Bond III); *Mo' Better Blues* (90, Lee); *Sex, Drugs, Rock & Roll* (91, John McNaughton); *Jungle Fever* (91, Lee); *Malcolm X* (92, Lee); *Cousin Bobby* (92, Jonathan Demme).

Angie Dickinson (Angeline Brown),
b. Kulm, North Dakota, 1931

The author is torn between his duty to everyone from Thorold Dickinson to Zinnemann and the plain fact that Angie is his favorite actress. Not that one thousand words of analysis would carry more weight than a well-chosen still. Many people think of her as TV's *Police Woman* rather than as an actress. Her career never gathered proper momentum; and nor has she seemed too distressed by having to make dull movies. Her virtues are probably not those of a leading actress, and it is significant that in her best film, *Rio Bravo* (59), she appeared very happy with Hawks's masculine code and ensemble playing. But equally, her Feathers in that film could be defended as a portrait of an intelligent, nervous, attractive woman that perfectly embodies the director's philosophy. For all that the role seems restricted to genre, Feathers is one of the truest female characters in modern cinema. And it characterized Angie's ability to inhabit a man's world without asking for concessions and without needing to rock the conventions.

She began in very small parts: *Lucky Me* (55, Jack Donohue); *Man With the Gun* (55, Richard Wilson); *Tennessee's Partner* (55, Allan Dwan); *Gun the Man Down* (56, Andrew McLaglen); and *Tension at Table Rock* (56, Charles Marquis Warren). But she came to life in Samuel Fuller's *China Gate* (57) as the half-caste girl, and as Steiger's girlfriend in *Cry Terror* (58, Andrew L. Stone). That led to *Rio Bravo*, which in turn was the prelude to a career in which she has often seemed much more assured than her films. But, given reason and good company, she is totally compelling: *The Bramble Bush* (60, Daniel Petrie); *Ocean's 11* (60, Lewis Milestone); *A Fever in the Blood* (61, Vincent Sherman); *Rachel Cade* (61, Gordon Douglas); *Lovers Must Learn* (62, Delmer Daves); *Jessica* (62, Jean Negulesco); *Captain Newman, M.D.* (63, David Miller);

treacherous, but still endearing, in *The Killers* (64, Don Siegel); *The Art of Love* (65, Norman Jewison); as Brando's wife in *The Chase* (66, Arthur Penn); *Cast a Giant Shadow* (66, Melville Shavelson); *The Pistolero of Red River* (67, Richard Thorpe); rising to her dangerous decoy mission in *Point Blank* (67, John Boorman); *Sam Whiskey* (69, Arnold Laven); *Young Billy Young* (69, Burt Kennedy); *Pretty Maids All in a Row* (71, Roger Vadim); *Un Homme est Mort* (72, Jacques Deray); and *Big Bad Mama* (74, Steve Carver).

Not even my adoration has kept Angie's career from some slippage. I notice, too, that she is a little older—thank God I have not suffered in the same way. Still, readers not sure whether to believe what they are reading should immediately get themselves in a position to see *Rio Bravo, China Gate, The Killers, Point Blank,* and *The Chase*. Meanwhile, Dickinson has been in *L'Homme en Colore* (79, Claude Pinoteau); *Jack London's Klondike Fever* (79, Peter Carter); *The Suicide's Wife* (79, John Newland); *Dressed to Kill* (80, Brian De Palma), using a body double; *Death Hunt* (81, Peter R. Hunt); *Charlie Chan and the Curse of the Dragon Queen* (81, Clive Donner); and *Big Bad Mama II* (87, Jim Wynorski).

She has also done a lot of television: in the Grace Kelly part in *Dial M for Murder* (81, Boris Sagal); *One Shoe Makes It Murder* (82, William Hale); *Jealousy* (83, Jeffrey Bloom); *A Touch of Scandal* (84, Ivan Nagy); *Stillwatch* (87, Rod Holcomb); *Police Story: The Freeway Killings* (87, William A. Graham); *Once Upon a Texas Train* (88, Kennedy); *Prime Target* (89, Robert Collins); *Fire and Rain* (89, Jerry Jameson); in *Wild Palms* (93, Phil Joannu and Kathryn Bigelow); and *Even Cowgirls Get the Blues* (94, Gus Van Sant).

In recent years, she has been seen in *Sabrina* (95, Sydney Pollack); *The Maddening* (96, Danny Huston); *Remembrance* (96, Bethany Rooney); *The Sun, the Moon and the Stars* (96, Geraldine Creed); *The Don's Analyst* (97, David Jablin); *Deep Family Search* (97, Arthur Allan Seidelman); *Sealed with a Kiss* (99, Ron Lagomarsino); *The Last Producer* (00, Burt Reynolds); *Duets* (00, Bruce Paltrow); *Pay It Forward* (00, Mimi Leder); *Big Bad Love* (01, Arliss Howard).

Thorold Dickinson (1903–84),
b. Bristol, England

1937: *The High Command.* 1938: *Spanish ABC* (d). 1939: *The Arsenal Stadium Mystery.* 1940: *Gaslight.* 1942: *The Prime Minister; Next of Kin.* 1946: *Men of Two Worlds* (d). 1948: *The Queen of Spades.* 1952: *Secret People.* 1954: *Hill 24 Doesn't Answer* (d).

Dickinson was a refugee from moviemaking. In 1956 he was appointed chief of film services for the UN Department of Public Information, after which he became head of London University film studies at the Slade School. It was a loss, hardly made up for by the results of his teaching or by the publication of *A Discovery of Cinema* in 1971. As more young people study film with the old-fashioned zeal that once marked potential poets, do they notice that they are often taught by older men who gave up the hope of making films?

Dickinson had begun as assistant on *Mr. Preedy and the Countess* (22, George Pearson). He wrote *The Little People* (36, Pearson), edited *Perfect Understanding* (33, Cyril Gardner), and was production manager on *Midshipman Easy* (35, Carol Reed). That rather spasmodic involvement was borne out by his work as director: *High Command* was a conventional and stagy thriller, while *Spanish ABC* was a Civil War documentary. But *Gaslight* has a great reputation for stylish melodrama, and *The Queen of Spades* is both very frightening and a brilliant evocation of Pushkin and Eisensteinian pictorialism.

Wilhelm/William Dieterle (1893–1972), b. Ludwigshafen, Germany

1923: *Menschen am Wege.* 1927: *Der Mann, der Nicht Lieben Darf.* 1928: *Geshlecht in Fesseln.* 1929: *Die Heilige und ihr Nahrr; Frühlingsrauschen; Ich Lebe für Dich; Konig von Bayern; Das Schweigen im Walde; Eine Stunde Glueche.* 1930: *Der Tanz Geht Weiter; Die Maske Fallt.* 1931: *The Last Flight; Her Majesty, Love.* 1932: *Man Wanted; Jewel Robbery; The Crash; Six Hours to Live; Scarlet Dawn; Lawyer Man.* 1933: *Grand Slam; Adorable; The Devil's in Love; From Headquarters.* 1934: *Fashions of 1934; Fog Over Frisco; Madame Du Barry; The Firebird; The Secret Bride.* 1935: *Dr. Socrates; A Midsummer Night's Dream* (codirected with Max Reinhardt); *The Story of Louis Pasteur; Concealment; Men on Her Mind.* 1936: *The White Angel; Satan Met a Lady.* 1937: *The Great O'Malley; Another Dawn; The Life of Emile Zola.* 1938: *Blockade.* 1939: *Juarez; The Hunchback of Notre Dame.* 1940: *The Story of Dr. Ehrlich's Magic Bullet; A Dispatch from Reuter's/This Man Reuter.* 1941: *All That Money Can Buy.* 1942: *Syncopation; Tennessee Johnson.* 1944: *Kismet; I'll Be Seeing You.* 1945: *Love Letters; This Love of Ours.* 1946: *The Searching Wind.* 1948: *Portrait of Jennie.* 1949: *Accused; Rope of Sand.* 1950: *Paid in Full; Volcano; Dark City.* 1951: *September Affair; Peking Express; Red Mountain.* 1952: *Boots Malone; The Turning Point.* 1953: *Salome.* 1954: *Elephant Walk.* 1956: *Magic Fire.* 1957: *Omar Khayyam.* 1959: *Il Vendicatore/Dubrowsky.* 1960: *Die Fastnachtsbeichte; Herrin der Welt.* 1964: *Quick, Let's Get Married.*

Dieterle was an actor by training. Having worked with Max Reinhardt in Berlin, he made his movie acting debut in *Fiesco* (1913). He worked steadily as an actor throughout the silent era in, among others, *Der Rattenfanger von Hameln* (16, Rochus Gliese); *Die Geierwally* (21, E. A. Dupont); *Hintertreppe* (21, Paul Leni and Leopold Jessner); *Lukrezia Borgia* (22, Richard Oswald); *Carlos und Elisabeth* (24, Oswald); *Waxworks* (24, Leni); *Faust* (26, F. W. Murnau); and *Qualen der Nacht* (26, Kurt Bernhardt).

In the late 1920s he worked more as a director, and by 1930 he had moved to Hollywood, originally to make German-language versions of American films. *Der Tanz Geht Weiter* was *Those Who Dance* (William Beaudine) and *Die Maske Fallt, The Way of All Men* (Frank Lloyd). Dieterle proved a prolific workhorse, serving Paramount, Warners, and David Selznick. His earliest American films are rarities today, although *The Last Flight* has a high reputation, and he is best known for *A Midsummer Night's Dream,* the biopics he made at Warners, and for the Laughton *Hunchback* which has an uninhibited grotesque romance. It is hard to see the *Dream* as anything other than Reinhardt gleefully making use of such camera technicians as Hal Mohr and Byron Haskin. Absurd but delightful, the *Dream* is lighter and funnier than most things Dieterle touched, though *Fog Over Frisco* is a fast-talking and faster-progressing Bette Davis movie.

The biopics are ponderous, Germanic works, suffering from staginess and the unrestrained histrionics of Paul Muni who, presumably, was to Dieterle's taste. *Pasteur* and *Zola* are sententious films, pap history disguising cliché, but *Juarez* is more enjoyable because it goes further into exaggeration and because Bette Davis gives a truly hysterical performance that relieves Muni's Aztec impassivity in the title role. Better than the Muni celebration of impossible heroes are Edward G. Robinson's thorough immersion in the character of Reuter and Ehrlich, the man who found a cure for syphilis.

By the mid-1940s Dieterle was under Selznick's wing and his sense of almost supernatural atmosphere was not unsuited to the producer's dreamy-mystical conception of Jennifer Jones in *Portrait of Jennie*—indication of how often the women's picture encourages moderate talent into abandoning caution. He also directed Jones at Paramount in *Love Letters,* an intriguing story of amnesia—and one of Jones's best films. It should be added that Dieterle directed the flamboyant saloon opening to *Duel in the Sun* (46, King Vidor). *Rope of Sand, September Affair, Peking Express,* and *The Turning Point* all suggest if not a late flowering, a realization that his talent was for the lavish romantic. All the sadder then that *Salome* is a restrained movie and Rita Hayworth a rather inhibited voluptuary.

He returned to Germany in the late 1950s, but soon retired.

Marlene Dietrich (Maria Magdalena
Dietrich von Losch) (1901–92),
b. Schöneberg, Germany

Dietrich is an extreme case—not just because she
simultaneously emphasized the erotic and the
ridiculous in sexuality, but because it is unclear
how far this was her projection. Although she
seemed self-possessed, tantalizing the feelings she
aroused with her very indifference, it is possible
that, more than any other great star, she was a cinematic invention—a message understood by viewers but not by herself. Was that knowingness the
product of her mind, the vision of an audience, or
the light laid on her skin by Josef von Sternberg?

Chapter 9 of *Fun in a Chinese Laundry*, von
Sternberg's elliptical, deadpan, but outrageous
memoir, is like a short story describing the intense
relationship between actress and director. Just
like the films they made together, the tone of the
chapter is contradictory: scathing and adoring; at
one moment regarding the affair as history, the
next attempting to show how it lived on. By his
own claim, Sternberg alone recognized the qualities in Dietrich when he cast her in *The Blue
Angel* (30). Of course, Dietrich was no longer
truly young, and a collection of serious directors
had used her already without properly "discovering" her: *Der Kleine Napoleon* (23, Georg Jacoby);
Tragodie der Liebe (23, Joe May); *Menschen am
Wege* (23, Wilhelm Dieterle); *Die Glucklicke Mutter* (24, Rudolf Sieber, her husband); *Die Freudlose Gasse* (25, G. W. Pabst); *Eine DuBarry von
Heute* (28, Alexander Korda); *Die Frau, Nach der
Man Sich Sehnt* (29, Kurt Bernhardt); and *Das
Schiff der Verlorenen Menschen* (29, Maurice
Tourneur). Sternberg's minions thought that Dietrich was a commonplace German girl. Even after
a screen test they saw none of the extra radiance
that Sternberg intended. Dietrich herself is portrayed by Sternberg as hardly aware of her talent.
But the chapter is written in retrospect and begins
with one of those exercises in paranoid hostility so
characteristic of the book: "Her constant praise
[of von Sternberg] is rated as one of her admirable
virtues—by others, not by me. She has never
ceased to proclaim that I taught her everything.
Among the many things I did not teach her was to
be garrulous about me." Certainly, after their
parting Dietrich acknowledged von Sternberg,
but often with the unconsidered Teutonic sentimentality that her career as a chanteuse indulged.
It was not the way of Amy Jolly or Shanghai Lily to
flatter anyone.

Garrulousness is the antithesis of the von Sternberg Dietrich, so that praise in an alien style might
be the most distressing. At other times, Dietrich
turned into a sober haus-frau, eager to dismiss
those first years at Paramount and to explain that
von Sternberg created a woman that had nothing
to do with her. One cannot escape the feeling

that Dietrich never fully understood those years.
Thus there is an artistic truth in von Sternberg's
grotesquely cruel reporting of rumor: "I was told
that during the many films made after my 'fiasco'
with her she would often go through a scene and
finish it by whispering through the microphone,
'Where are you, Jo?' Well, I'm right here, and
should she be angry once more, when she reads
this, she might recall that she was often angry with
me, and for no good reason."

It is those later films that underline the crucial
role of von Sternberg. With him, Dietrich made
seven masterpieces, films that are still breathtakingly modern, which have no superior for their
sense of artificiality suffused with emotion and
which visually combine decadence and austerity,
tenderness and cruelty, gaiety and despair. After
1935, however, Dietrich appeared in another
twenty-four films, some only in small parts, like
the dark-haired fortune-teller, maker of hot chili,
who watches fatalistically over Welles's destruction in *Touch of Evil* (58). In how many of those is
she even presentable as a serious actress? In
Desire (36, Frank Borzage); in *Angel* (37, Ernst
Lubitsch); in *The Flame of New Orleans* (41, René
Clair); in *Rancho Notorious* (52, Fritz Lang). Otherwise she is anything from dull, tense, tight-
lipped, and inhibited to a ghostly imitation of her
earlier self, florid where once she had bloomed,
extravagant where she was implicit, more a female
impersonation than the essence of the sado-
masochist female that von Sternberg made her.

That may seem hard or exaggerated. After all,
Dietrich survived for thirty years as a great enter-
tainer, a singer, a mistress of hesitation, a wearer
of clothes, a nightclub figure. But see those other
films and realize how far reputation carried
her. See *Judgment at Nuremberg* (61, Stanley
Kramer); *Witness for the Prosecution* (57, Billy
Wilder); *Stage Fright* (50, Alfred Hitchcock); *A
Foreign Affair* (48, Wilder); *Golden Earrings* (47,
Mitchell Leisen); *Kismet* (44, William Dieterle);
The Spoilers (42, Ray Enright); *The Lady Is Will-
ing* (42, Leisen); *Manpower* (41, Raoul Walsh);
Seven Sinners (40, Tay Garnett); *Destry Rides
Again* (39, George Marshall); *Knight Without
Armour* (37, Jacques Feyder); *The Garden of
Allah* (36, Richard Boleslavsky), and you will see a
haughty, mannered woman striving to relax.
Selznick believed that she was not an emotional
actress, that she could not make audiences cry.
She had tricks, to be sure: she could be girlish
momentarily; she had the seductive ploys of a
street singer; and she could always wear exotic
costume with intimations of depravity. But in how
many of these other films does she look strained,
vacant, inept, unsure of herself? In how many of
those films, either through makeup or her famous
efforts to control the way in which she is photographed, is she trying to re-create von Stern-

berg's image of her? If anyone doubts my comments on her other work, see *The Blue Angel* and then, in order, preferably, those six films she made for him at Paramount: *Morocco* (30), *Dishonored* (31), *Shanghai Express* (32), *Blonde Venus* (32), *The Scarlet Empress* (34), and *The Devil Is a Woman* (35). They are totally manufactured films: locations built at Paramount; foreign countries conjured up with light; the plots are literary farragos in which the visual poetry is everything. It would only be in keeping if the Dietrich in these films was not authentic but man-made. One might say made by love, except that so clear a confession offended Sternberg's horror of excess. Thus, there is a feeling of tormented passion in these films, of exquisite physical beauty not delaying temporal decay. Invariably, they are love stories in which the lovers conspire by their own independence to avoid the frankest admissions to one another. For Cooper in *Morocco* and Clive Brook in *Shanghai Express,* expressions of love are extracted only under torture. Both men mistrust women and fear the dependence that comes with love. At the same time, they are moved immeasurably by the beloved. Dietrich is the perfect icon in this ecstasy of frustration, and she survives as the central figure in superb tableaux: as Amy Jolly the entertainer in *Morocco,* shyly wondering whether to kiss a woman in her audience; as X27 in *Dishonored,* a spy shot in immaculate black leather; most enchanting of all, sitting on the observation platform at the end of the *Shanghai Express,* a feather boa like a halo round her head; her legs open like shark's teeth in *Blonde Venus;* as the depraved virginal *Scarlet Empress,* as hard as a jewel; and finally as a nun turned voluptuary in a Spain of the mind that involved Paramount in a lunatic quarrel with a country claiming to be the real Spain.

She was never again that woman, and she may have resented the loss just as much as she failed to comprehend it. One can hardly explore her career chronologically. Those few years at Paramount grow in history just as the subsequent decades shrink. She stands as an ambiguous demonstration of how people are transformed and glorified by cinema. No matter how many words one expends, the moving image says everything about Dietrich. Perhaps she was a plain German girl, forever intrigued by the glimpses of herself that von Sternberg had given her. When they made *Rancho Notorious,* in 1952—in which Dietrich is at least good—she constantly told Fritz Lang how Sternberg would have filmed it. She was not a great popular star; indeed, her persona was always too barbed and the insights of the Sternberg films too disturbing for coziness. But great men aspired to her, and she was the darling of the intellectuals. Though she never divorced her husband, she had many affairs—as if real sex could ever keep up with the dream. Let Sternberg have the last word: "Here was no enthusiast, but a cold-eyed mechanic critical of every movement. If there was any flattery, it was concentrated in a 'That's fine, it will do.' More often she listened to 'Turn your shoulders away from me and straighten out . . . Drop your voice an octave and don't lisp . . . Count to six and look at that lamp as if you could no longer live without it . . . Stand where you are and don't move; the lights are being adjusted.'"

Having been away from movies for nearly two decades, she returned as the Baroness in *Just a Gigolo* (78, David Hemmings), in great pain, but in greater need of the money. She lived in Paris, reclusive yet eternally on the phone. There was the sketch of an autobiography, and she kept several biographers on strings. She gave her voice to a remarkable documentary, *Marlene* (84, Maximilian Schell), which is a magisterial maintaining of the legend, to such an extent that she managed not to appear. She was radio, and in charge.

She died, and there was a flurry of books, including an expert, fond, and witty biography by Steven Bach, and a fascinating memoir by her daughter, Maria Riva, that quoted from Marlene's diaries and letters. The death helped one see that a certain creature had been left to us all—in stills, as a wearer of clothes, as a mask on which a smile is drawn. Was she always a ghost? Isn't it incidental that some actual woman had to be Marlene Dietrich, for surely the idea of her and its mystery were only waiting to be freed?

Matt Dillon, b. New Rochelle, New York, 1964

There was a moment when the world seemed ready—it was the late eighties—to say that Matt Dillon hadn't really made the transition from a teen to a young man. Then came *Drugstore Cowboy* (89, Gus Van Sant). A few years later, opinion had shifted: now the pretty-boy adult was never going to take on a fully adult edge. Next came *Wild Things* (98, John McNaughton), and his amazing restraint in the face of a witty, sexy movie all set up for him. At this rate, he could outlive the medium.

He began when he was still in junior high school: *Over the Edge* (79, Jonathan Kaplan); *Little Darlings* (80, Ronald F. Maxwell); *My Bodyguard* (80, Tony Bill); *Liar's Moon* (81, David Foster); attracting real attention in the S. E. Hinton adaptation *Tex* (82, Tim Hunter), and then in two more films from Hinton—*The Outsiders* (83, Francis Ford Coppola) and *Rumble Fish* (83, Coppola); excellent in *The Flamingo Kid* (84, Garry Marshall); Gene Hackman's son in *Target* (85, Arthur Penn); to Australia to make *Rebel* (85, Michael Jenkins); *Native Son* (86, Jerrold Freedman); disappointing in *The Big Town* (87, Ben Bolt); *Kansas* (88, David Stevens);

The Bloodhounds of Broadway (89, Howard Brookman).

After his electric junkie for Gus Van Sant, he did the manipulative lead in *A Kiss Before Dying* (91, James Dearden); *Singles* (92, Cameron Crowe); *Mr. Wonderful* (93, Anthony Minghella); *The Saint of Fort Washington* (93, Hunter); *Golden Gate* (93, John Madden); *Frankie Starlight* (95, Michael Lindsay-Hogg); the dumb husband in *To Die For* (95, Van Sant); *Albino Alligator* (96, Kevin Spacey); *Beautiful Girls* (96, Ted Demme); *Grace of My Heart* (96, Allison Anders); *In & Out* (97, Frank Oz); *There's Something About Mary* (98, Bobby and Peter Farrelly).

He has branched out further still. He started directing, for the HBO series *Oz*, and in 2001 he directed a movie, *Beneath the Banyan Tree*, a noir story set in Cambodia, and coscripted with Barry Gifford. It all suggests how much the "kid" has learned. He was in *One Night at McCool's* (01, Harold Zwart); *Deuces Wild* (02, Scott Kalvert).

Walt Disney (Walter Elias Disney) (1901–66), b. Chicago

There have been plenty of books on Disney and the world he made, and there will be more. He is one of the great American subjects: the unholy mix of artist and businessman; the slender soul who exerts enormous influence; a giant of movies, yet one of its betrayers; and the pied piper to fifty years of American children whose extraordinary insistence on fantasy has come to change the look of the land and the jungle of suburbia. In the career of Walt Disney one may see the passage from a culture of comic books to that of computer-generated imagery. He makes God seem a little slow and old-fashioned.

An article like this can only scratch the surface. We should say first that Walter Elias was educated at the Kansas City Art Institute, which he gave up (still only sixteen) to be a volunteer ambulance driver on the Western Front. On his return to Kansas City, he teamed up with commercial artist Ub Iwerks (1901–71) and they began to work on cartoons and short animated films—the filming of progressive drawings. They formed a company, Laugh-O-Gram, but they went bust, and so, in 1923, allegedly with $40, Walt, his brother Roy, and Iwerks went to Hollywood.

Animation was very competitive in the 1920s, and it was not until the end of the decade that Disney gained supremacy. Mickey Mouse was created in 1928, and with his third film, *Steamboat Willie* (28), he gained sound. Iwerks was doing the drawing, Roy Disney was the manager, and Walt was boss—no one disputed his authority, or his role as ideas man. The Silly Symphony cartoons began in 1929, and Disney started to build a team of young animators. By the early thirties, he was working with two-strip Technicolor and building his zoo with Minnie, Donald Duck, Goofy, and Pluto. By 1935, he was using three-strip color and the new multiplane cameras.

It was Walt's drive never to settle for what he had. This was a relentlessly ambitious man, driven more by technology than ideas or ideology. His next goal was a full-length animated feature—*Snow White and the Seven Dwarfs* (37), which grossed about $8 million in its first release. (Two years later, *The Wizard of Oz* pulled in $2 million.)

Yet the Disney organization was still hanging on by Mickey's whiskers. The costs of development kept it in debt until that run of animation features made during the war—note, Disney was always reassuring in his message. *Snow White* was a popular sensation, *and* a travesty of the original story. From the outset, Disney was digesting great stories and complex material to produce pretty pabulum. Not even the fantastic skills in animation disguised this. Disney's drawing was never more intricate or lovely than in the forties, but the prettiness had no core or heart. It was the start of technological beauty: *Pinocchio* (40); the very ambitious *Fantasia* (40); *The Reluctant Dragon* (41); *Dumbo* (41); *Bambi* (42), which—in the death of Bambi's mother—was maybe the most daring film he ever made, as well as the grossest example of anthropomorphic garbage; *The Three Caballeros* (44); *Make Mine Music!* (46); and *Song of the South* (46), which mixed animation and live action.

The next step was a series of live-action features and natural-history documentaries: *Treasure Island* (50, Robert Stevenson) was a very good version of the old classic, while *The Living Desert* (53, James Algar) was a grotesque alliance of documentary coverage and the "moods" established by films like *Bambi*.

In 1954, *Walt Disney* began on television (on ABC)—it ran, in one form or another, until 1990. Moreover, in 1954, this was the first attempt by a movie major to get into TV production. ABC paid Disney $500,000 for the deal, plus $50,000 per show. Everyone profited: ABC had their first big hit show, while Disney used the money to fund the Disneyland park at Anaheim (it opened in 1955). The TV show was an anthology, but it introduced such live-action characters as Davy Crockett, many Westerns, and new animated characters.

Movies continued: *Cinderella* (49); *Alice in Wonderland* (51); *The Story of Robin Hood* (52, Ken Annakin)—live action, filmed in England, with Richard Todd as Robin; *Peter Pan* (53); *20,000 Leagues Under the Sea* (54, Richard Fleischer); *The Vanishing Prairie* (54, Algar); *Lady and the Tramp* (55); *Sleeping Beauty* (58); *Kidnapped* (60, Stevenson); *Pollyanna* (60, David Swift); *101 Dalmations* (61); *Mary Poppins* (65, Stevenson)—in which Julie Andrews became the first player in a Disney film to win an Oscar; and *The Jungle Book* (67), which had maybe one percent of the power of Kipling's story.

Walt supervised *The Jungle Book,* but he died in December 1966. There is no question but that the drive was gone by then in anything but a marketing sense. The quality of animation was in decline. The live-action films are—it seems to me—less valuable as entertainment for children than, say, *The Secret Garden; Winchester 73;* Renoir's *The River; Scaramouche; Shane; Singin' in the Rain;* or *The Glenn Miller Story* (to take just the early fifties). In other words, Disney had sold the notion that there should be special films for children, backed up by merchandise advertised on the TV show. From cradle to college, Disney had possession of kids. There were protests, but we are reaping the rewards in so many ways, as "adult" films become more childish.

For most of the late sixties and seventies, Disney was a passive force, except in the steady accumulation of profit from TV, at Disneyland and Disney World, which opened in Orlando, Florida, in 1971. Nothing of note happened until 1984 when the company was effectively taken over by two young executives from Paramount, Michael Eisner and Jeffrey Katzenberg. They were worthy heirs to Walt, and demons of energy and efficiency. They set up Touchstone and Hollywood Pictures to develop live-action projects, many of which were tougher than Disney was used to. They built up the parks and they even returned to the tradition of feature-length animated films: *Return to Oz* (85, Walter Murch); *Down and Out in Beverly Hills* (86, Paul Mazursky); *Ruthless People* (86, Jim Abraham, David Zucker, and Jerry Zucker); *The Color of Money* (86, Martin Scorsese); *Stakeout* (87, John Badham); *Outrageous Fortune* (87, Arthur Hiller); *Adventures in Babysitting* (87, Chris Columbus); *Three Men and a Baby* (87, Leonard Nimoy); *Good Morning, Vietnam* (87, Barry Levinson); *Who Framed Roger Rabbit* (88, Robert Zemeckis)—maybe the best movie Disney ever made; *Cocktail* (88, Roger Donaldson); *Honey, I Shrunk the Kids* (89, Joe Johnston); *Dead Poets Society* (89, Peter Weir); *Three Fugitives* (89, Francis Veber); *The Little Mermaid* (89, John Musker and Ron Clements); *Pretty Woman* (90, Garry Marshall); *Dick Tracy* (90, Warren Beatty); *Stella* (90, John Erman); *Beauty and the Beast* (91, Gary Trousdale and Kirk Wise); *Father of the Bride* (91, Charles Shyer); *The Hand that Rocks the Cradle* (92, Curtis Hanson); *3 Ninjas* (92, Jon Turtletaub); *Aladdin* (92, Musker and Clements); *Sister Act* (92, Emile Ardolino); and *Mighty Ducks* (92, Stephen Herek).

There are failures to report: Eurodisney, the attempt to establish a Disney World in France, which incurred huge early losses; and, then,

towards the millennium, a faltering in the whole business that not even Eisner (alone now in control) could prevent or disguise.

Disney is *the* test case. We may regret the limits the empire of the mouse has set on children's reading and all our imagination. Yet "Disney" has delighted and consoled millions of children. There is no blunter example of the debate between the force of a mass medium and the depth of more elite work. For many people, movies held the promise of being both a great art and a pleasure for the people. But it is not quite enough now to say, "Trust the crowd." For Disney would twist that trust to monopolize choice.

I once argued with an Ivy League dean about whether nuclear weapons or television had most seriously affected the world since 1945. The weapons, said the dean, because of the Damocles danger in the air. Television, I said, an attack that has been carried on "safely," day after day.

So here is the question: can film stay a mass medium—or should it? Do we face a time when movies resemble theatre or the novel? Must we give up the hope of films that reach "everyone"? Can great filmmakers still redeem the hope? Or was it, simply, an historical curiosity that for a few decades (or a few movies) the hope was alive?

Richard Dix (Ernest Brimmer) (1894–1949), b. St. Paul, Minnesota

Although Dix's greatest popular success was a sound film, *Cimarron* (31, Wesley Ruggles), he is a striking example of a major star of silents who clung to more than fifteen years of sound B pictures, unable or unwilling to retire. He was big and gruff and very masculine, even if sometimes he seemed too heavy. A medical student, he gave up that career for the theatre and, by 1921, was in movies: *Not Guilty* (21, Sidney Franklin); *Poverty of Riches* (21, Reginald Barker); *The Sin Flood* (22, Frank Lloyd); *Yellow Men and Gold* (22, Irvin V. Willat); *Fools First* (22, Marshall Neilan); and *The Bonded Woman* (22, Phil Rosen). After going to England to make *The Christian* (23, Maurice Tourneur), he was put under contract by Paramount as a replacement for Wallace Reid. He stayed with that studio until 1929, very successful if seldom in their most notable films: *Racing Hearts* (23, Paul Powell); *The Woman with Four Faces* (23, Herbert Brenon); *To the Last Man* (23, Victor Fleming); *The Call of the Canyon* (23, Fleming); in the modern section of *The Ten Commandments* (23, Cecil B. De Mille); *The Stranger* (24, Joseph Henabery); *Sinners in Heaven* (24, Alan Crosland); *Unguarded Women* (24, Crosland); *Too Many Kisses* (25, Paul Sloane); *Men and Women* (25, William De Mille); *Lucky Devil* (25, Frank Tuttle); and *The Vanishing American* (25, George B. Seitz). He was in a handful of Gregory La Cava's films: *Womanhandled* (25); *Let's Get*

Richard Dix   240

Married (26); *Say It Again* (26); *Paradise for Two*
(27); and *The Gay Defender* (27). But by the late
1920s, Dix and Paramount were already on bad
terms, partly because he preferred to work in New
York: *Knockout Reilly* (27, Malcolm St. Clair); *Man
Power* (27, Clarence Badger); *Sporting Goods* (28,
St. Clair); *Easy Come, Easy Go* (28, Tuttle); *Red-
skin* (29, Victor Schertzinger); and *Nothing But the
Truth* (29, Schertzinger). He moved on to RKO
and thrived briefly: *Seven Keys to Baldpate* (29,
Barker); *Lovin' the Ladies* (30, Melville Brown);
Shooting Straight (30, George Archainbaud);
Edna Ferber's adventurer in *Cimarron; Young
Donovan's Kid* (31, Fred Niblo); *The Lost
Squadron* (32, Archainbaud); *The Roar of the
Dragon* (32, Ruggles); *Hell's Highway* (32, Row-
land Brown); and *The Conquerors* (32, William
Wellman). Only rarely thereafter did he have lead
parts or big films: *The Great Jasper* (33, J. Walter
Ruben); *Stingaree* (34, Wellman); *The Arizonian*
(35, Charles Vidor); *The Tunnel* (35, Maurice
Elvey) in Britain; *Blind Alley* (38, Vidor); *Here I
Am a Stranger* (39, Roy del Ruth); *Reno* (39, John
Farrow); *Badlands of Dakota* (41, Alfred E.
Green); *American Empire* (42, William McGann);
and *The Ghost Ship* (43, Mark Robson).

At the end of his career, he played the title role
in a series of cheap thrillers, made by William
Castle, and based on the radio character: *The
Whistler* (44); *The Mark of the Whistler* (44); then
the *Power* (45), *Voice* (45); and *Secret of the
Whistler* (46). His last film was *The Thirteenth
Hour* (47, William Clemens).

Edward Dmytryk, (1908–99)
b. Grand Forks, Canada
1935: *The Hawk.* 1939: *Television Spy.* 1940:
*Emergency Squad; Mystery Sea Raider; Golden
Gloves; Her First Romance.* 1941: *The Devil Com-
mands; Under Age; Sweetheart of the Campus;
The Blonde from Singapore; Confessions of
Boston Blackie; Secrets of the Lone Wolf.* 1942:
Seven Miles from Alcatraz; Counter Espionage.
1943: *The Falcon Strikes Back; Hitler's Children;
Captive Wild Woman; Behind the Rising Sun;
Tender Comrade.* 1945: *Murder My Sweet/
Farewell My Lovely; Back to Bataan; Cornered.*
1946: *Till the End of Time.* 1947: *Crossfire; So
Well Remembered.* 1949: *Give Us This Day.* 1950:
Obsession/The Hidden Room. 1952: *Mutiny; The
Sniper; Eight Iron Men.* 1953: *The Juggler.* 1954:
*The Caine Mutiny; Broken Lance; The End of the
Affair.* 1955: *Soldier of Fortune; The Left Hand of
God.* 1956: *The Mountain.* 1957: *Raintree County.*
1958: *The Young Lions.* 1959: *Warlock; The Blue
Angel.* 1962: *Walk on the Wild Side; The Reluctant
Saint.* 1964: *The Carpetbaggers; Where Love Has
Gone.* 1965: *Mirage.* 1966: *Alvarez Kelly.* 1968:
The Battle for Anzio; Shalako. 1972: *Bluebeard.*
1975: *The "Human" Factor.*

The son of Ukrainian parents, Dmytryk entered
the film industry at the age of fifteen. He rose from
assistant to full editor and worked in that capacity
throughout the 1930s: *Only Saps Work* (30, Cyril
Gardner and Edwin Knopf); *Million Dollar Legs*
(32, Edward Cline); *Belle of the Nineties* (34, Leo
McCarey); *Ruggles of Red Gap* (35, McCarey); and
Zaza (39, George Cukor). As a director he served
a long apprenticeship in B pictures at Columbia
and RKO—including two good horror movies,
The Devil Commands and *Captive Wild Woman.*
Farewell My Lovely was his turning point—as it
was for actor Dick Powell—and it established
Dmytryk as a director of low-key thrillers: *Till the
End of Time* and *Crossfire,* although less striking
than some reports suggest, are still his best work.
In the first postwar year, he was reckoned as one of
the most promising young directors.

Then, in 1947, Dmytryk was one of the ten
called before the House Un-American Activities
Committee. He went to England for three pictures but returned to a fine, six months' imprisonment, and an eventual recantation for the
Committee. By 1951 he was cleared, and he
worked on some of Stanley Kramer's low-budget
pictures at Columbia. *The Sniper* is one of the
best of a bad bunch, but commercially Dmytryk
was lucky enough to land the last and best
financed of the series, its single success: *The
Caine Mutiny.* That proved him as a director
of expensive, dramatic material. Sadly, it also
showed his characteristic waste of meaty stories
and leading actors. For the next ten years
Dmytryk made one dud after another, mostly at
Fox, polishing meanings until they were blunt
and usually passing on his own solemnity to his
players. Brando, Clift, Gable, Tracy, Widmark,
and Bogart all passed through his wringer, but
worst of all was the misuse of Stanwyck, Anne
Baxter, Capucine, and Jane Fonda in such potentially enjoyable nonsense as *Walk on the Wild
Side.* Against all reason, Dmytryk seemed more
interested in the film's putative male star, Laurence Harvey, and allowed Saul Bass and a cat to
walk away with the picture. After that he worked
less often but no more imaginatively. Indeed,
there might be a case for a committee to investigate filmmakers capable of rendering the Bluebeard story dull.

In the eighties, Dmytryk taught at USC and
wrote several books on filmmaking, most notably
On Directing.

Robert Donat (1905–58),
b. Manchester, England
The son of a Pole, in twenty-five years as a film
actor, Donat made only nineteen pictures. Illustrious as his record is, the list of parts he had to
decline—either because of his chronic asthma, or
because of a more profound tentativeness, itself at

the root of his stammer and nervous breathlessness—is even more striking: it includes Peter
Ibbetson, Chopin, Lawrence of Arabia, Romeo,
Mr. Darcy, the Chorus in *Henry V,* and the James
Stewart part in *No Highway.* By the end of the
war, illness had seriously restricted Donat; but in
the late 1930s he might have become a major
international star, more masculine than Leslie
Howard, more restrained than Olivier. He acted
then with a sense of contained riches that is rare in
English stage-trained actors. Donat had a great
quality: that he could draw us further into himself
by his very modesty.

Elocution lessons to conquer his stammer led
Donat toward the stage and in his late teens he
joined Sir Frank Benson's company. By the early
1930s he was earning a name in London and in
1932 he made his screen debut for Korda in *Men
of Tomorrow* (Leontine Sagan). Korda gave him a
few more parts—*That Night in London* (32, Rowland V. Lee) and *Cash* (33, Zoltan Korda)—before
he won special attention as Culpeper in *The Private Life of Henry VIII* (33, A. Korda). At this,
Hollywood redoubled earlier efforts to hire him
and Donat went to America to play *The Count of
Monte Cristo* (34, Lee). Back in England, he was a
very cool Richard Hannay in Hitchcock's *The
Thirty-nine Steps* (35), and in the dual role in *The
Ghost Goes West* (36, René Clair). At this stage,
there was a special romantic aura about Donat,
enhanced by the diffident way he moved from one
prestige project to another. He followed with a
silly but amusing Russian revolution confrontation
with Marlene Dietrich in *Knight Without Armour*
(37, Jacques Feyder), a good performance as the
young doctor in *The Citadel* (38, King Vidor), and
an Oscar in the prewar weepie, *Goodbye, Mr.
Chips* (39, Sam Wood).

Rather than stay in America during the war,
Donat returned to London to work on the stage
and in 1942 made *The Young Mr. Pitt* (Carol
Reed). Next year he was in *The Adventures of
Tartu* (Harold S. Bucquet), and in 1945 he was
with Deborah Kerr in *Perfect Strangers* (A.
Korda). His career now was invaded by doubts
and obstacles, and his asthma was a perpetual
handicap. In 1947 he appeared briefly as Parnell
in *Captain Boycott* (Frank Launder), and he fol-
lowed this with his last serious bout of film work:
The Winslow Boy (48, Anthony Asquith); *The
Cure for Love* (49, which he directed himself); as
Friese-Greene in the Festival of Britain project,
The Magic Box (51, John Boulting).

He was a harrowed man, his face drawn and the
superb voice gruff. When, in 1955, he appeared in
the play *Murder in the Cathedral,* oxygen cylin-
ders were maintained off-stage. Only two more
films were to come: *Lease of Life* (54, Charles
Frend) and, in 1958, the mandarin in *The Inn of
the Sixth Happiness* (Mark Robson). That part is
startlingly raw amid so much sentiment: a dying
man as he acted, his presence seems to awe the
rest of the film into respect.

Stanley Donen,

b. Columbia, South Carolina, 1924
1949: *On the Town* (codirected with Gene Kelly).
1951: *Royal Wedding/Wedding Bells; Love Is Bet-
ter Than Ever.* 1952: *Singin' in the Rain* (codi-
rected with Kelly); *Fearless Fagan.* 1953: *Give a
Girl a Break.* 1954: *Seven Brides for Seven
Brothers; Deep in My Heart.* 1955: *It's Always Fair
Weather* (codirected with Kelly). 1957: *Funny
Face; The Pajama Game* (codirected with George
Abbott); *Kiss Them for Me.* 1958: *Indiscreet;
Damn Yankees/ What Lola Wants* (codirected with
Abbott). 1959: *Once More, With Feeling.* 1960:
Surprise Package; The Grass Is Greener. 1963:
Charade. 1966: *Arabesque.* 1967: *Two for the
Road.* 1968: *Bedazzled.* 1969: *Staircase.* 1974: *The
Little Prince.* 1975: *Lucky Lady.* 1978: *Movie
Movie.* 1980: *Saturn 3.* 1984: *Blame It On Rio.*

Donen began as a dancer in the New York produc-
tions of *Pal Joey* and *Best Foot Forward* and then
joined MGM as a choreographer. He appeared in
the film of *Best Foot Forward* (43, Edward
Buzzell) and did the dance direction for *Hey,
Rookie; Cover Girl* (44, Charles Vidor); *Anchors
Aweigh* (45, George Sidney); *Holiday in Mexico*
(46, Sidney); *Living in a Big Way* (47, Gregory La
Cava); *A Date with Judy* (48, Richard Thorpe);
The Kissing Bandit (48, Laslo Benedek); *Take Me
Out to the Ball Game* (49, Busby Berkeley).

His friendship with Gene Kelly led Donen into
directing *On the Town,* and to the problem in
assessing his career: who did what in their collabo-
rations? And what is Donen's real standing as a
director? Since 1960, perhaps because of the virtual disappearance of the modest-size musical,
Donen has drifted into comedy, the attempt to
transpose Peter Cook and Dudley Moore to
movies and the hopelessly unsuitable *Staircase.* At
best, *The Grass Is Greener* is a pleasant, unnecessary comedy; *Charade* is a modest bow to Hitchcock; and *Two for the Road* a sign of lasting
affection for Audrey Hepburn. But the cinema
would be not one jot the poorer without the lot of
them. Whereas, no enthusiast in his right mind
would give up a foot of *On the Town, Singin' in the
Rain, Seven Brides for Seven Brothers, It's Always
Fair Weather, Funny Face, The Pajama Game,* or
Damn Yankees.

Donen is obviously a central figure in the story
of the MGM musical and unarguably the author
of two of the greatest musicals—*Singin' in the
Rain* and *Funny Face.* Nothing in his career suggests that Gene Kelly could have filmed himself
singing in the rain with the exhilaration of Donen's
retreating crane shot, while no one has made

gravure color so intrinsic a part of smart romance as in *Funny Face*. More than that, Donen led the musical in a triumphant and personal direction: out of doors. The garbage-can dances in *It's Always Fair Weather* and the mock snowscapes of *Seven Brides* are preludes to "Bonjour Paris" and the enchanting lakeside dance in *Funny Face,* or the magnificent "Once-a-year Day" picnic in *The Pajama Game.* Not only did Donen dare to stage elaborate routines in real locations, but he threw his camera about with the freedom of the studio. Not even Minnelli can rival the fresh-air excitement of such sequences. And very few can equal his integration of song, dance, and story in *Funny Face,* which is a love story put to music. Add to that "Good Morning," the satire on Hollywood faced with sound, and Cyd Charisse in the "Broadway Ballet" in *Singin';* the randy ensembles of *Seven Brides;* Charisse in the boxing ring in *It's Always Fair Weather;* the darkroom sequence in *Funny Face;* and Carol Haney doing "Steam Heat" in *Pajama Game,* and Donen has a secure place forever.

Vincent D'Onofrio,
b. Brooklyn, New York, 1959

It's hard to think of another contemporary actor who has so fully taken on the challenge that was once Robert De Niro's—to play extraordinary characters (because of nature or situation) on the fringes of our society, in ways that may leave the actor scarcely recognizable, let alone a fit subject for adulation or big money. D'Onofrio thrives on difficulty, the rare and the remote. As such, it is hardly surprising that he is not widely known or even established. But his prickly integrity shows through a dry survey of what he has attempted.

He had done some TV work before he first drew attention, bleached blond, in *Adventures in Babysitting* (87, Chris Columbus). He then put on a mass of flab to play the victimized Private Pyle in *Full Metal Jacket* (87, Stanley Kubrick). After that he was in *Mystic Pizza* (88, Donald Petrie); to Australia for *The Blood of Heroes* (90, David Peoples); *Signs of Life* (89, John David Coles); in the very strange *Naked Tango* (91, Leonard Schrader); with one speech as a spectator in Dealey Plaza in *JFK* (91, Oliver Stone); in *Fires Within* (91, Gillian Armstrong), with Greta Scacchi, to whom he was briefly married; *Dying Young* (91, Joel Schumacher); *Crooked Hearts* (91, Michael Bortman); as the wretched writer in *The Player* (92, Robert Altman).

In *Malcolm X* (92, Spike Lee), he again played the man in Dealey Plaza. He was Judith Malina's son in *Household Saints* (93, Nancy Savoca); *Mr. Wonderful* (93, Anthony Minghella); *Being Human* (94, Bill Forsyth); astonishingly good as Orson Welles in *Ed Wood* (94, Tim Burton); *Imaginary Crimes* (94, Anthony Drazan); *Stuart*

Saves His Family (95, Harold Ramis); *Strange Days* (95, Kathryn Bigelow).

Then came *The Whole Wide World* (96, Dan Ireland), coproduced by D'Onofrio, in which he played the pulp novelist, Robert E. Howard, and achieved a remarkable love story with Renée Zellweger. That was followed by the Las Vegas story *The Winner* (97, Alex Cox); *Feeling Minnesota* (96, Steven Baigelman). Then he played the victim of a bizarre subway accident on maybe the most arresting episode of *Homicide* (97). He was a paraplegic in *Good Luck* (97, Richard LaBrie); a bug in *Men in Black* (97, Barry Sonnenfeld); *The Newton Boys* (98, Richard Linklater); *Claire Dolan* (98, Lodge Kerrigan); *The Thirteenth Floor* (99, Josef Rusnak); as Abbie Hoffman in *Steal This Movie* (00, Robert Greenwald), which he also helped produce; *The Cell* (00, Tarsem Singh), playing the serial killer; *Impostor* (02, Gary Fleder); *The Salton Sea* (02, D. J. Caruso); *Last Word on Paradise* (aka *Chelsea Walls*) (01, Ethan Hawke); *The Dangerous Lives of Altar Boys* (01, Peter Care); *Happy Accidents* (01, Brad Anderson).

Since 2001 he's had a lead role in *Law & Order.* He has also acted in *Bark* (02, Kasia Adamik); *The Red Sneakers* (02, Gregory Minor); and as Moriarty in *Case of Evil* (02, Graham Theakston).

Brian Donlevy (1899–1972),
b. Portadown, Ireland

Donlevy was invariably cast as a villain, against every hunch that he was an amiable rough diamond. When he tried to be menacing—narrowing his eyes and bristling his mustache—he only managed to look like a grumpy toy lion. But as an innocent, well-intentioned roughneck he had a unique and appealing vitality. Despite King Vidor's regret that Spencer Tracy did not play the part, Donlevy is excellent as the Polish immigrant who becomes a tycoon in *An American Romance* (44)—with all the vigorous simplicity of Dos Passos's chronicles. It was this naïve honesty that Preston Sturges used for the hobo who becomes governor in *The Great McGinty* (40), which also shows up well in *Hangmen Also Die!* (43, Fritz Lang) and *The Glass Key* (42, Stuart Heisler). But much more often, Donlevy merely glowered. After a debut in 1928, he had a string of parts, including: *Barbary Coast* (35, Howard Hawks); *Human Cargo* (36, Allan Dwan); *High Tension* (36, Dwan); *This Is My Affair* (37, William A. Seiter); *In Old Chicago* (38, Henry King); *Jesse James* (39, King); *Beau Geste* (39, William Wellman); *Destry Rides Again* (39, George Marshall); *Brigham Young* (40, Henry Hathaway); *Birth of the Blues* (41, Victor Schertzinger); *Billy the Kid* (41, David Miller); *The Great Man's Lady* (42, Wellman); *Wake Island* (42, John Farrow); *Nightmare* (42, Tim Whelan); *The Remarkable Andrew* (42, Heisler); *Two Years Before the Mast* (46, Farrow); *Song of*

Scheherazade (46, Walter Reisch); and *Kiss of Death* (47, Hathaway). He slipped into B pictures, and sometimes worked abroad, but there was still a gruff distinction: *Kansas Raiders* (51, Ray Enright); *Slaughter Trail* (51, Irving Allen); *The Woman They Almost Lynched* (53, Dwan); *The Big Combo* (55, Joseph H. Lewis); *The Quartermass Experiment* (55, Val Guest); *A Cry in the Night* (56, Frank Tuttle); *Cowboy* (58, Delmer Daves); *Never So Few* (59, John Sturges); *The Errand Boy* (61, Jerry Lewis); *Curse of the Fly* (65, Don Sharp); *Waco* (66, R. G. Springsteen); *Hostile Guns* (67, Springsteen); and *Rogue's Gallery* (67, Leonard Horn).

Clive Donner, b. London, 1926
1956: *The Secret Place.* 1958: *Heart of a Child.* 1959: *Marriage of Convenience.* 1960: *The Sinister Man.* 1962: *Some People.* 1963: *The Caretaker.* 1964: *Nothing But the Best.* 1965: *What's New, Pussycat?.* 1967: *Luv.* 1968: *Here We Go Round the Mulberry Bush.* 1969: *Alfred the Great.* 1974: *Vampira.* 1978: *The Thief of Baghdad.* 1980: *The Nude Bomb.* 1981: *Charlie Chan and the Curse of the Dragon Queen.* 1982: *Oliver Twist* (TV); *The Scarlet Pimpernel* (TV). 1983: *Arthur the King* (TV). 1984: *A Christmas Carol* (TV); *To Catch a King* (TV). 1986: *Agatha Christie's Dead Man's Folly* (TV); *Babes in Toyland* (TV). 1989: *Stealing Heaven.* 1990: *Not a Penny More, Not a Penny Less* (TV); *Arrivederci Roma.* 1992: *Terror Stalks the Class Reunion* (TV). 1994: *Charlemagne, le Prince à Cheval* (TV).

Donner looks a sad instance of a modest talent out of work in an increasingly nervous industry. *Alfred the Great* was not only his worst film, but an expensive flop. No matter that he may have been compelled to take it on, and then hampered, its lack of success could be enough to damn him. It seems to show that only artistic personalities capable of transcending the industry can stay in work. Donner's inventiveness is essentially sensible and effacing, so that *The Caretaker* was made with a self-advertised, experimental low budget. It proved a faithful reading of a play already well established. His best films—*Some People* and *Nothing But the Best*—are skillful efforts to expand British conventions. The first was a refreshingly authentic picture of young people, diffident about true improvisation and restrained if compared with TV, but a modest success. The second, from a good Frederic Raphael script, is a much more finely wrought and sardonic comment on British hypocrisy, a film in the vein of *Kind Hearts and Coronets*. *What's New, Pussycat?* now looks dated and unfunny; it has always seemed a waste of Paula Prentiss, Capucine, and Romy Schneider on Sellers and O'Toole. *Here We Go Round the Mulberry Bush* was lively, but some-

how desperate that it could be no more.

In fact, Donner flowered rather late after a dutiful preparation as an editor: *The Way Ahead* (44, Carol Reed); *On Approval* (45, Clive Brook); *The Passionate Friends* (48, David Lean); *Madeleine* (49, Lean); *Pandora and the Flying Dutchman* (51, Albert Lewin); *Scrooge* (51, Brian Desmond Hurst); *The Card* (52, Ronald Neame); *Genevieve* (54, Henry Cornelius); *The Million Pound Note* (53, Neame); *The Purple Plain* (54, Robert Parrish); and *I Am a Camera* (55, Cornelius).

Donner has now become essentially a TV director: he has had the chance to work with George C. Scott as Fagin and Scrooge, Ian McKellan as Chauvelin, Malcolm McDowell and Candice Bergen in *Arthur the King*, and Drew Barrymore in *Babes in Toyland*.

Richard Donner (Richard Donald Schwartzberg), b. New York, 1939
1961: *X-15.* 1968: *Salt and Pepper.* 1969: *Twinky.* 1976: *The Omen.* 1978: *Superman.* 1980: *Inside Moves.* 1982: *The Toy.* 1985: *The Goonies; Ladyhawke.* 1987: *Lethal Weapon.* 1988: *Scrooged.* 1989: *Lethal Weapon 2.* 1992: *Radio Flyer; Lethal Weapon 3.* 1994: *Maverick.* 1995: *Assassins.* 1997: *Conspiracy Theory.* 1998: *Lethal Weapon 4.* 2003: *Timeline.*

Mr. Donner has made several of the most successful and least interesting films of his age. And one doubts it's over yet.

Mark Donskoi (1890–1980), b. Odessa, Russia
1927: *V Bolshom Gorodye* (codirected with Mikhail Averback). 1928: *Tsena Cheloveka* (codirected with Averback). 1929: *Pizhon.* 1930: *Chuzhoi Berez; Ogon.* 1934: *Pesnya o Schastye* (codirected with Vladimir Legoshin). 1938: *Detstvo Gorkovo/The Childhood of Gorky.* 1939: *V Lyudyakh/My Apprenticeship.* 1940: *Moi Universiteti/My Universities.* 1941: *Romantiki.* 1942: *Kak Zakalyalas Stal.* 1944: *Raduga/The Rainbow.* 1945: *Nepokorenniye Semia Tarassa.* 1947: *Selskaya Uchitelnitsa.* 1949: *Alitet Ukhodit v Gori.* 1950: *Nachi Chempiony.* 1956: *Mat.* 1958: *Dorogoi Tsenoi.* 1959: *Foma Gordeyev.* 1962: *Zdravstvuitye Detil.* 1967: *Serdtsye Materi/Heart of a Mother; Vernost Materi/A Mother's Devotion.* 1978: *Suprugi Orlovy/The Orlovs.*

The "Gorky trilogy" has been one of the better influences on Western liberal attitudes to the Soviet Union. It was not as rigorously geared to propaganda as many other Russian films; indeed, when the films were made, Donskoi himself was not a member of the Communist party. The Gorky films have had rather the same appeal as the Pagnol movies: they are based on rich, authentic emotional treatment; they deal with human beings in terms of the family and traditional aspirations. In that sense, Gorky is a Copperfield-like hero, and the charm of the films, backed up by Donskoi's skill at period re-creation, is partly one of nostalgia for social solidity and the unflawed hopes of nineteenth-century youth. The sentiment, the sense of family, and the dense texture of everyday reality in those films will have won more friends than the montages of Eisenstein or Dziga Vertov's cameraman protagonist.

Donskoi fought in the Civil War and was taken prisoner by the Whites before he entered films in 1925, first as an assistant to Eisenstein. He did a variety of jobs, including acting and writing. His early films showed an interest in homely, emotional stories, but it was clearly his own friendship with Gorky that gave an extra imaginative intensity to the trilogy. During the war, Donskoi made patriotic films, including *The Rainbow,* a melodramatic, inspirational story of partisans resisting the Nazis. After the war, he was persuaded to repeat his Gorky success: both *Mat* and *Foma Gordeyev* were based on the writer's work. Nothing equaled the trilogy until *Serdtsye Materi* and *Vernost Materi,* two films about the early life of Lenin, but concentrating on the character of the mother. Again, potential hagiography stimulated Donskoi's feeling for the turn of the century and allowed his sympathy for matriarchal actresses to come through: Elena Fadeyeva was as moving in these films as Varvara Massalitinova had been as Gorky's grandmother.

Diana Dors (Fluck) (1931–84), b. Swindon, England

Tall, curvaceous, with pillows of silver-blond hair, bumper-pad hips, and self-consciously naughty eyes, Diana Dors cried out for some Frank Tashlin or Luis Buñuel who knew how to use her. But all she got was the J. Arthur Rank charm school, endless pinups in the *News of the World,* a succession of disastrous, controlling men, and the British picture business of the forties and fifties. She did get to Hollywood, but it was too late. Of course, those who knew her report that she was "a bit of a prude," but so was the audience in her day. She could act a little bit; enough, probably, given the right material and sympathetic collaboration. But she was too bold for British timidity, too repressively channeled into still photography and moments of everlasting innuendo. That said, let us not forget the considerable part played in a forlorn career by her fatal choices and gruesome timing. Nevertheless, the Arena documentary on Dors—*Swinging Dors* was the cute title to a book of 3-D nudie shots she did—is a lovely tribute to getting it all wrong.

She began when better parents would have kept her in school: *The Shop at Sly Corner* (46,

George King); *Holiday Camp* (47, Ken Annakin); *Good Time Girl* (48, David MacDonald); as Charlotte in *Oliver Twist* (48, David Lean, who made a pass at her); *Here Come the Huggets* (48, Annakin), wowing Jack Warner; *Diamond City* (49, MacDonald); *Dance Hall* (50, Charles Crichton); *Lady Godiva Rides Again* (51, Frank Launder); *The Last Page* (52, Terence Fisher); *My Wife's Lodger* (52, Maurice Elvey); *The Great Game* (53, Elvey); *Is Your Honeymoon Really Necessary?* (53, Elvey); *The Weak and the Wicked* (53, J. Lee Thompson); *It's a Grand Life* (54, John Blakely); *As Long As They're Happy* (54, Thompson); *A Kid for Two Farthings* (55, Carol Reed); *Value for Money* (55, Annakin); *An Alligator Named Daisy* (55, Thompson); in prison in *Yield to the Night* (56, Thompson), her best part; *The Long Haul* (57, Ken Hughes).

She got to Hollywood at last for *The Unholy Wife* (57, John Farrow), costarring with Rod Steiger—an immediate affair; *I Married a Woman* (58, Hal Kanter); but it was back to England for *Tread Softly Stranger* (58, Gordon Parry); *Passport to Shame* (59, Alvin Rakoff). Then to America for *Scent of Mystery* (60, Jack Cardiff); *On the Double* (61, Melville Shavelson), with Danny Kaye; *King of the Roaring Twenties* (61, Joseph M. Newman); *The Counterfeit Constable* (64, Robert Dhéry), which was made in France.

The Sandwich Man (66, Robert Hartford-Davis) was made back in England, as were *Berserk* (67, Jim O'Connelly); *Danger Route* (67, Seth Holt); *Hammerhead* (68, David Miller); *Baby Love* (69, Alistair Reid); *There's a Girl in My Soup* (70, Roy Boulting); *Deep End* (70, Jerzy Skolimowski), the best film she was ever in; *Hannie Caulder* (71, Burt Kennedy); *The Pied Piper* (62, Jacques Demy); *The Amazing Mr. Blunden* (72, Lionel Jeffries); *Nothing But the Night* (72, Peter Sasdy); *Theatre of Blood* (73, Douglas Hickox); *From Beyond the Grave* (73, Kevin Connor); *Praise* (74, Freddie Francis); *Swedish Wildcats* (74, Joseph W. Sarno); *Adventures of a Taxi Driver* (75, Stanley Long); "Mrs. Horne" in *Adventures of a Private Eye* (77, Long); *Confessions from the David Galaxy Affair* (79, Willy Roe); *Steaming* (84, Joseph Losey).

Gordon Douglas (1909–93), b. New York

1936: *General Spanky* (codirected with Fred Newmeyer); *Pay as You Exit; Spooky Hooky; Reunion in Rhythm; Glove Taps.* 1937: *Three Smart Boys; Hearts Are Thumps; Rushin' Ballet; Bored of Education; Roamin' Holiday; Night 'n' Gales; Fishy Tales; Our Gang/Follies of 1938; Framing Youth; The Pigskin Palooka; Mail and Female.* 1938: *Bear Facts; Canned Fishing; Came the Brawn; Feed 'em and Weep; Hide and Shriek; The Little Ranger; Aladdin's Lantern.* 1939: *Zenobia.* 1940: *Saps at Sea.* 1941: *Road Show; Broad-*

way Limited; Niagara Falls. 1942: *The Devil with Hitler; The Great Gildersleeve.* 1943: *Gildersleeve's Big Day; Gildersleeve on Broadway.* 1944: *A Night of Adventure; Gildersleeve's Ghost; Girl Rush; The Falcon in Hollywood.* 1945: *Zombies on Broadway.* 1946: *First Yank into Tokyo; San Quentin; Dick Tracy vs. Cueball.* 1948: *The Black Arrow; If You Knew Susie; Walk a Crooked Mile.* 1949: *The Doolins of Oklahoma; Mr. Soft Touch* (codirected with Henry Levin). 1950: *The Nevadan; Fortunes of Captain Blood; Rogues of Sherwood Forest; Kiss Tomorrow Good-Bye; Between Midnight and Dawn; The Great Missouri Raid.* 1951: *Only the Valiant; I Was a Communist for the FBI; Come Fill the Cup.* 1952: *Mara Maru; The Iron Mistress.* 1953: *She's Back on Broadway; The Charge at Feather River; So This Is Love.* 1954: *Them.* 1955: *Young at Heart; The McConnell Story; Sincerely Yours.* 1956: *Santiago.* 1957: *The Big Land; Bombers B52/No Sleep Till Dawn.* 1958: *Fort Dobbs; The Fiend Who Walked the West; Up Periscope.* 1959: *Yellowstone Kelly.* 1961: *Rachel Cade/The Sins of Rachel Cade; Gold of the Seven Saints; Claudelle Inglish/Young and Eager.* 1962: *Follow That Dream.* 1963: *Call Me Bwana.* 1964: *Robin and the Seven Hoods; Rio Conchos.* 1965: *Sylvia; Harlow.* 1966: *Stagecoach; Way . . . Way Out.* 1967: *Chuka; In Like Flint; Tony Rome.* 1968: *The Detective; Lady in Cement.* 1969: *Skullduggery.* 1970: *Barquero; They Call Me Mister Tibbs!.* 1973: *Slaughter's Big Rip-Off.* 1977: *Viva Knievel!.*

When so many American directors were retiring or missing out, it says a lot for Douglas's zest and flexibility that he made eighteen movies during the 1960s. As throughout the rest of his career, he moved arbitrarily from competence to rubbish and from tedium to a genuinely fresh and engaging film. The productivity befits a man who was trained by Hal Roach and who made some thirty shorts in the *Our Gang* series before graduating to features. Douglas was initially a comedy director: *Zenobia* had Oliver Hardy with Harry Langdon, while *Saps at Sea* is classic Laurel and Hardy.

For ten years, Douglas was working on one cheap series or another and only in the 1950s did he advance to substantial movies. Variety and variability have always characterized him more than anything else, but he is the director of several entertaining movies: *Come Fill the Cup,* with James Cagney as an alcoholic; *The Charge at Feather River,* an exciting Western that carries its 3D lightly; *Them,* an excellent science-fiction film about giant ants, with some atmospheric desert scenes; and *Young at Heart,* a Doris Day musical made sour by a disenchanted Sinatra. Thereafter he declined under Liberace and some dull Clint Walker Westerns. *Call Me Bwana,* with Bob Hope, had little of his early talent, but *Sylvia* and

Harlow saw him turn Joseph Levine and Carroll Baker to unexpected advantage. That early skill at handling Sinatra suddenly bore fruit with the delicious *Tony Rome; Lady in Cement* was not its equal but *The Detective* is a striking early picture of the policeman losing faith in his job. Douglas remained one of the few directors who could hold Sinatra's interest.

Kirk Douglas (Issur Danielovich Demsky), b. Amsterdam, New York, 1916

Demsky still grins through, for surely Douglas was made for Dostoyevsky. He is the manic-depressive among Hollywood stars, one minute bearing down on plot, dialogue, and actresses with the gleeful appetite of a man just freed from Siberia, at others writhing not just in agony but mutilation and a convincingly horrible death. Thus, he left a finger in Hawks's *The Big Sky* (52), an ear in *Lust for Life* (56, Vincente Minnelli), and an eye in *The Vikings* (58, Richard Fleischer), was beaten up in *Champion* (49, Mark Robson), stuck in the belly with scissors in Billy Wilder's *Ace in the Hole* (51), rolled in barbed wire in King Vidor's *Man Without a Star* (55), crucified in *Spartacus* (60), whipped by his own servant (at his own order) in *The Way West* (67, Andrew V. McLaglen), and generally harassed in several other films.

This is not to say that Douglas cannot make such agony credible and moving. On the contrary, in Wyler's *Detective Story* (51), Raoul Walsh's *Along the Great Divide* (51), Kubrick's *Paths of Glory* (57), and above all as Van Gogh in *Lust for Life,* his sometimes facile intensity is marvelously harnessed to the subject of the film and the sense of tragedy is perfectly judged. The balance of passionate creativity and crippling personal inadequacy in *Lust for Life* is all the more praiseworthy in that it is outside Minnelli's usual territory. At other times, however, Douglas seems on the verge of ridiculing his own outrageousness: thus *The Vikings, The Devil's Disciple* (59, Guy Hamilton), much of *Spartacus,* and most of his later films are the crude obverse of what can be a highly individual line in flamboyant comic villains. This is probably Douglas most at ease, and again it has a Russian original: Rasputin. Thus, his first screen success was as the laughing gangster in Tourneur's *Out of the Past* (47); and the same scheming relish was to be seen as the reporter in *Ace in the Hole;* as Jonathan Shields, the movie producer, in Minnelli's *The Bad and the Beautiful* (52); as Doc Holliday in *Gunfight at the OK Corral* (57, John Sturges); as the outlaw in Burt Kennedy's *The War Wagon* (67); and as the robber in Mankiewicz's *There Was a Crooked Man* (70).

Douglas's career began properly after the war, although he had worked on the stage before war service in the navy. In 1946, Hal Wallis signed him and Douglas made his debut in Milestone's *The*

Strange Love of Martha Ivers (46). He made his way in *I Walk Alone* (47, Byron Haskin), John Stahl's *The Walls of Jericho* (48), and Mankiewicz's *A Letter to Three Wives* (49) before reaching stardom as the boxer in *Champion*. After that, he has never lost his popularity, nor the ability to enjoy himself. He is endearing in that he has so seldom been involved in solemnity or pretension. These vices seem to have been worked out of the system early with *Mourning Becomes Electra* (47, Dudley Nichols) and *The Glass Menagerie* (50, Irving Rapper) and have only reappeared in Anatole Litvak's *Act of Love* (53), Reinhardt's awful *Town Without Pity* (61), in *Seven Days in May* (64, John Frankenheimer) and, sadly, in Kazan's *The Arrangement* (69).

Douglas more usually goes to the extreme of playfulness—as in the very enjoyable *20,000 Leagues Under the Sea* (54, Fleischer) and de Toth's *The Indian Fighter* (55). In addition, he has made a few out-of-the-way movies well worth recording: Richard Quine's excellent *Strangers When We Meet* (60)—in which Kim Novak explores the cleft in his chin, as if wondering in which film he got that wound; David Miller's *Lonely Are the Brave* (62); and recovering from breakdown and the shakes in Minnelli's *Two Weeks in Another Town* (62), a fond companion piece to *The Bad and the Beautiful*.

By the late sixties Douglas had slipped into lazy action films and weak comedies and such guest spots as Patton in *Is Paris Burning?* (66, René Clément). He often made films through his own production company, Bryna, and in 1968 he produced Martin Ritt's *The Brotherhood* in which he played an old-fashioned Mafioso upset by a new generation of grey-suit executives. He was in *A Gunfight* (71, Lamont Johnson); tortured by Yul Brynner in *The Light at the Edge of the World* (71, Kevin Billington); cast against type as a mousey biology teacher in *Cat and Mouse* (74, Daniel Petrie).

In 1973, he directed his first film, *Scalawag*, sadly without the Shields touch. But *Posse*, in 1975, was an accomplished Western in which Kirk had Bruce Dern as worthy opposition. He seems less interested in acting alone to judge by Jacqueline Susann's *Once Is Not Enough* (74, Guy Green)—in which he claims that his balls have been cut off; *Victory at Entebbe* (76, Marvin J. Chomsky); and *Holocaust 2000* (77, Alberto de Martino). But he was his old urgent self, as a father searching for a lost son, in *The Fury* (78, Brian De Palma), horribly betrayed by the film.

Douglas has probably given more care in the eighties to writing his autobiography and a novel—to say nothing of eyeing his son Michael's new power competitively. But he has acted a good deal, keeping his most intense work for television: *The Villain* (79, Hal Needham); *Home Movies* (79, De

Palma); *Saturn 3* (80, Stanley Donen); *The Final Countdown* (80, Don Taylor); *The Man from Snowy River* (82, George Miller); *Remembrance of Love* (82, Jack Smight) for TV; *Eddie Macon's Run* (83, Jeff Kanew); *Draw!* (84, Steven Hilliard Stern); as a man in a nursing home in *Amos* (85, Michael Tuchner), which resembled *One Flew Over the Cuckoo's Nest;* with Burt Lancaster in *Tough Guys* (86, Kanew); *Queenie* (87, Larry Peerce) for TV, playing the Alexander Korda figure; as William Jennings Bryan in TV's *Inherit the Wind* (88, David Greene); *Oscar* (91, John Landis); and *Greedy* (94, Jonathan Lynn).

He survived a serious stroke, strove in his special way for rehabilitation, and returned in the obvious, but rousing, *Diamonds* (99, John Asher). He is a Jonathan Shields still—someone we can't hang up on though *It Runs in the Family* (03, Fred Schepisi) was strictly on hold.

Melvyn Douglas (Melvyn Edouard Hesselberg) (1901–81), b. Macon, Georgia

In his films, Douglas was an escort, husband, lover, or good friend to every love queen of the 1930s and 1940s. A sampling of titles shows how invariably attention was on the lady—*There's Always a Woman* (38, Alexander Hall); *I'll Take Romance* (37, Edward H. Griffith); *Women of Romance* (37); *There's That Woman Again* (39); *Good Girls Go to Paris* (39, Hall); *Too Many Husbands* (40, Wesley Ruggles); *He Stayed for Breakfast* (40, Hall); and *They All Kissed the Bride* (42, Hall).

The son of a concert pianist, Douglas was a stage actor. In 1931, he was in a play, *Tonight Or Never;* Gloria Swanson asked for him to play opposite her in the movie, produced by Goldwyn and directed by Mervyn Le Roy. An auspicious debut, followed by the male lead to Garbo in *As You Desire Me* (32, George Fitzmaurice). But Douglas was too pale a copy of William Powell to prosper. He was released from his contract to Goldwyn and dwindled for several years until Columbia put him opposite Claudette Colbert in *She Married Her Boss* (35, Gregory La Cava). Comedy suited him better and he cemented a new status with Irene Dunne in *Theodora Goes Wild* (36, Richard Boleslavsky). He now moved to MGM, initially to support Joan Crawford in *The Gorgeous Hussy* (36, Clarence Brown). Over the next few years, he remained dependent on the lady star of his films, but he managed several notable pairings: with Dietrich in *Angel* (37, Ernst Lubitsch); Crawford again in *The Shining Hour* (38, Frank Borzage); with Garbo in *Ninotchka* (39, Lubitsch); Loretta Young in *He Stayed for Breakfast* (40); with Merle Oberon in *That Uncertain Feeling* (41, Lubitsch); as the surgeon restoring Joan Crawford's beauty in *A Woman's Face* (41, George Cukor); squire to Garbo in her last film, *Two-Faced Woman* (42, Cukor).

Douglas had a distinguished war record and returned to less romantic parts. Although not especially successful, greater demands seemed to encourage him: *Sea of Grass* (47, Elia Kazan); *The Guilt of Janet Ames* (47, Henry Levin); *Mr. Blandings Builds His Dream House* (48, H. C. Potter); *A Woman's Secret* (48, Nicholas Ray); *The Great Sinner* (49, Robert Siodmak); and *My Forbidden Past* (51, Robert Stevenson).

He spent the next ten years on the stage and in TV and returned to films as a character actor, apparently much more seasoned than his former self: as the Dansker in *Billy Budd* (62, Peter Ustinov); a supporting actor Oscar in *Hud* (62, Martin Ritt); *Advance to the Rear* (63, George Marshall); *The Americanization of Emily* (64, Arthur Hiller); *Rapture* (65, John Guillermin); *Hotel* (67, Richard Quine); *I Never Sang For My Father* (70, Gilbert Cates); *The Candidate* (72, Michael Ritchie); *The Tenant* (76, Roman Polanski); *Twilight's Last Gleaming* (77, Robert Aldrich); *The Seduction of Joe Tynan* (79, Jerry Schatzberg); *The Changeling* (79, Peter Medak); *Being There* (79, Hal Ashby), for which he won another best supporting actor Oscar; *Ghost Story* (81, John Irvin); and *Tell Me a Riddle* (81, Lee Grant).

Michael Douglas,
b. New Brunswick, New Jersey, 1944
By June 1992, after thirteen weeks in release, *Basic Instinct* (Paul Verhoeven) reported $105.7 million in U.S. domestic film rentals. Anything near $100 million feels comfortable. But *Instinct* had been a very early bloomer. There was so much advance word (on the expensive script; on the writer's second thoughts; on gay/lesbian protest; on the X or R rating; on Sharon Stone's insolent looks), and such a canny TV promo, that there were lines around the block that first week. The sensation passed. *Instinct* did not really reach as far down into the hopeful dreams of middle America as *Fatal Attraction* (87, Adrian Lyne). From week seven onward, *Basic Instinct* was doing modest business. Even at $105 million, profit was some nominal way away: and profit in Hollywood is subject to Heisenbergian uncertainty—one may determine mass or momentum but seldom the two together, and never the day when it will come. Profit had to be set beside such things as Michael Douglas's $14 million salary.

I doubt Sharon Stone earned a tenth of Douglas's pay. Yet she was the talking point of the movie and the leg-crossing come-on in the promos. She could have been bitter; she should have felt blessed that, after an untidy, hardly managed career, she had gotten that part. Douglas's name was above the title, but hers was the face that gazed out balefully over his shoulder in the poster image. Her nails were sinking into the flesh of his shoulder. So the instinct in the title seemed to promise her aggression and his masochism. Just another movie about women having the power . . .

That is not to disparage Douglas. In Hollywood, one is worth whatever the system will give out, and that is only prompted by clout. Clout comprises past record and present demeanor. Michael Douglas has sold movies, and he has possessed a rare ability to be strong and weak at the same time. There is in his eyes, his jaw, his hairline, and his voice the memory of his father. But there is also something like his horror at being so like Kirk. What fuel for an actor! It has allowed Michael Douglas to play a man who is weak, culpable, morally indolent, compromised, and greedy for illicit sensation without losing that basic probity or potential for ethical character that we require of a hero.

Thus, in *Fatal Attraction*, the trap of the movie worked because Douglas could commit adultery and enjoy it on our behalf (it has wild, comic, clumsy couplings that owe a lot to Douglas's grasp of comedy in passion) and still be a properly threatened family man. One may argue that this was humbug and hypocrisy, but it worked. That's why and how the family survived at the end of the film, while truer, dramatic resolutions were discarded. Like any hit movie, *Fatal Attraction* had to be an advertisement for American dreaming—share the fantasy.

When *Basic Instinct* came along, it drew upon the spineless spine in Douglas and used the selling line: "A brutal murder. A brilliant killer. A cop who can't resist the danger." There would be very few American movies if we did not feel drawn toward the vicarious experience of wondering whether *we* could resist the danger. Douglas is perfect meat for the experiment, prime USDA but just a little aged, on the marbled brink of decay.

All of which leads us back to Kirk Douglas, the model and mentor over whom Michael is most confused. Few grant that Kirk Douglas on-screen was both stronger and weaker than Michael has a taste for (this is more melodrama than modesty). Still, the senior Douglas was a pioneer of good intention yielding to temptation, and of resolve coming apart. He resonated with his own fall in *Champion, Ace in the Hole, Detective Story, The Bad and the Beautiful,* and *Lust for Life*—in most of the most Kirkian films, the ones where he is fit to be a Karamazov.

We must remember that Michael Douglas is the son of the son of a Russian Jewish immigrant—and of a Wasp mother. The parents were divorced when Michael was only a kid, and there was a stepfather, gentler and more able to talk to the boy. But in Michael Douglas's extraordinary success—in Hollywood, in America—in his seeming smoothness, we may begin to understand Kirk's sense of failure and roughness. For it isn't only sons who have a cross to bear.

Michael Douglas was raised in the East and sent to prep schools. But he rejected Yale for the University of California at Santa Barbara, not as good or tough a school, but a pretty place. Douglas still has a house in Santa Barbara, the place he prefers, and an important friend he found there, Danny DeVito.

By the late sixties, he had decided to be an actor, and he was the second lead to Karl Malden in the TV series *Streets of San Francisco*. That led to movies: *Hail, Hero!* (69, David Miller); *Adam at 6 A.M.* (70, Robert Scheerer); *Summertree* (71, Anthony Newley); and for Disney, *Napoleon and Samantha* (72, Bernard McEveety).

There was little hint then of a lasting actor. But at that point, Michael persuaded Kirk to give up hopes of playing in a movie of *One Flew Over the Cuckoo's Nest*, for which the father had the rights. Instead, Michael would try to get the picture made. It worked: with Saul Zaentz, Milos Forman, and Jack Nicholson, the son produced the picture and brought it in to great acclaim and box-office success. He collected the Oscar for best picture. Kirk made a lot of money, and was surely proud. He was also mortified. Which is not to say Michael's feelings were unalloyed. For Douglases, triumph may need to be ambivalent.

Michael was established as a producer, and it may still be the case that that job moves him more than acting. His next few films as an actor were not much more than keep-fit workouts in which he let the actresses take the center of energy: *Coma* (78, Michael Crichton) and *It's My Turn* (80, Claudia Weill). He was certainly energetic in *Running* (79, Steven Howard Stern), but without the intensity of, say, Bruce Dern. Nor was he better than a bystander in *The China Syndrome* (79, James Bridges), but again he had produced that film, which opened shortly before Three Mile Island. There is no rule against luck for a producer, and no need to ponder whether the luck is good or bad.

In the 1980s, Douglas had two more big successes as a producer. He acted in these films— *Romancing the Stone* (84, Robert Zemeckis) and *Jewel of the Nile* (85, Lewis Teague)—and enjoyed himself as the adventurer. But he was preoccupied with two difficult locations and readily conceded the pictures to Kathleen Turner and Danny DeVito.

As if there had been a campaign, he moved toward better roles and more responsibility, even if he never quite dominated a film. He is the motor of *Fatal Attraction,* but the film concerns a crazy driver (Glenn Close). And though he won the Oscar for best actor as Gordon Gekko in *Wall Street* (87, Oliver Stone), that is actually a film about the Charlie Sheen character. It was just that

Gekko's power felt greater, and his ambiguity came across as more intriguing than Sheen's dollar-book dilemma. Douglas's view of Gekko is a fascinating sign of how a producer-actor thinks: "I don't think Gekko's a villain. Doesn't beat his wife or his kid. He's just taking care of business. And he gives a lot of people chances."

Douglas has not finished his journey. He produced *Starman* (84, John Carpenter) and *Black Rain* (89, Ridley Scott) in which he also acted, making a lot of the role of a shabby, corrupt cop. He also acted in and encouraged the bold, unruly *The War of the Roses* (89, DeVito), and he acted in *Shining Through* (92, David Seltzer).

Douglas has his own production company, Stonebridge, which has made *Flatliners* (90, Joel Schumacher) and *Radio Flyer* (92, Richard Donner). But Douglas split from his partner, Rick Bieber, and scaled down the new company after several failures.

In 1993, he played the ordinary man who goes over the edge in *Falling Down* (Schumacher). This could have been another exploitation of urban resentment in the mass psyche—but only if Douglas's character had been other than crazy— or more comic?

If this length begins to seem excessive, I would say two things: Michael Douglas is very characteristic of modern Hollywood; and I like him. For those of us in that boat, the nineties were hard times. Douglas's often uncertain marriage ended. There was talk—from him, not just others—that he was addicted to sex. It made him Clintonian— but don't we all feel we're addicted to sex? Well, not many of us can expect rescue in the form of Catherine Zeta-Jones—his new bride and mother of his child. They seem happy—and Douglas, like Kirk, enjoys happiness.

He made some poor films, and some that were just silly, but he never lost his following: *Disclosure* (94, Barry Levinson), where he was the man of the moment to be sexually harassed—he does know pulse issues; *The American President* (95, Rob Reiner)—a daft picture, but close to the "Look, I can fly" surprise of Bill Clinton; *The Ghost and the Darkness* (96, Stephen Hopkins)— which was nearly good. *The Game* (97, David Fincher), too, was halfway fascinating. Only *A Perfect Murder* (98, Andrew Davis) was unforgivable.

And then he rewarded all those who like him with the beautiful shabbiness of *Wonder Boys* (00, Curtis Hanson). In truth, he was pretty perfunctory in *Traffic* (00, Steven Soderbergh)—but our modern problem czars are like that. On *Don't Say a Word* (01, Gary Fleder), I won't. Then came *One Night at McCool's* (01, Harold Zwart); *It Runs in the Family* (03, Fred Schepisi); *The In-Laws* (03, Andrew Fleming).

Paul Douglas (1907–59), b. Philadelphia

If he ever had doubts, Douglas settled on being grouchy and bad-tempered when, having played Harry Brock in over one thousand performances of *Born Yesterday* on Broadway, he turned down the movie and let Broderick Crawford make a meal of it. A few years later, Douglas and Judy Holliday were brought together in that obvious but appealing imitation, *The Solid Gold Cadillac* (56, Richard Quine). But the stage Harry Brock had carried Douglas to Fox where he made his debut in *A Letter to Three Wives* (49, Joseph L. Mankiewicz). That first part showed some vulnerability beneath the bluster, but Douglas quickly became typed as a bulldozer, either a comic butt or a cantankerous figure of authority: *It Happens Every Spring* (49, Lloyd Bacon); *Everybody Does It* (49, Edmund Goulding); *Panic in the Streets* (50, Elia Kazan); *Love that Brute* (50, Alexander Hall); *Fourteen Hours* (51, Henry Hathaway); *The Guy Who Came Back* (51, Joseph Newman); *Angels in the Outfield* (51, Clarence Brown); *When in Rome* (52, Brown). He was much more touching as the naïve fisherman husband of Barbara Stanwyck in *Clash by Night* (52, Fritz Lang), a sign that once his energies were modified he became more interesting. Too often he got away with a slightly nerve-racking performance of boorishness: *We're Not Married* (52, Goulding); *Forever Female* (53, Irving Rapper); and *Executive Suite* (54, Robert Wise). Because his huffing and puffing was so automatic, it was amusingly deflated in *The Maggie* (54, Alexander Mackendrick), in which he played an American tycoon remorselessly sapped by Scots prevarication. In the years before he finally wore himself out he was in *Green Fire* (54, Andrew Marton); *Joe Macbeth* (56, Ken Hughes); *The Leather Saint* (56, Alvin Ganzer); *This Could Be the Night* (57, Wise); *Beau James* (57, Melville Shavelson); *Fortunella* (58, Eduardo de Filippo); and *The Mating Game* (59, George Marshall), in which he played an Americanized version of H. E. Bates's Pa Larkin.

Alexander Dovzhenko (1894–1956), b. Sosnitsa, Ukraine

1926: *Vasya Reformator* (codirected with F. Lokatinsky and Iosif Rona); *Yagodka Lyubvi*. 1927: *Sumka Dipkurera*. 1928: *Zvenigora*. 1929: *Arsenal*. 1930: *Zemlya/Earth*. 1932: *Ivan*. 1935: *Aerograd*. 1939: *Shchors* (codirected with Yulia Solntseva). 1940: *Osvobozhdenie* (codirected with Solntseva). 1945: *Pobeda na Pravoberezhnoi Ukrainye i Izgnanie Nemetsikh Zakhvatchikov za Predeli Ukrainskikh Sovetskikh Zemel* (codirected with Solntseva). 1948: *Michurin*.

Of all the first generation of Russian directors—Pudovkin, Dziga Vertov, and Eisenstein—Dovzhenko needs the least allowance and the least explanation of political context. Whereas other directors seem aggressively theoretical or populist, Dovzhenko is the first intensely personal artist in the Russian cinema. Although his career was subject to the problems that faced any filmmaker in Soviet Russia, the films themselves are free from them. *Earth* is a stirring symphony of pastoral life and the calm acceptance of death, deriving from the clash between peasants and kulaks, but essentially indifferent to local origins.

Dovzhenko's cinema is poetic, lyrical, possessed of a Blake-like somber innocence and a burning passion for existence. It is important to note that *Earth* has the barest of stories, and that its real subject is the moving image of a Ukrainian village. In feeling and purpose it is far away from the busy self-conscious city of *Man With a Movie Camera* (28, Vertov), where the workers are encouraged by the technological ardor of the cameraman; from the editing table blueprints that Pudovkin carried over to celluloid; and from Eisenstein's eventually self-destructive attempt to sympathize with the Revolution. Dovzhenko loves his subject, making the camera the means of transmitting his emotion. The natural vitality of faces, sunlight on hay, animals in a meadow—these are Dovzhenko's bases for hope. Today they look subtler and more credible than all of Eisenstein's violent juxtapositions of the crowd and outrage, or Vertov's exultant comparison of machines and happiness. Dovzhenko emerges as a filmmaker who might have grown up on Tolstoy's estate.

In reality, he was from a farm in the Ukraine. He studied to be a teacher and moved inquisitively from economics to biology to physics. But after the war, he worked for the education service and then went to Poland and Germany as a clerk in the diplomatic service. On his return, he studied painting and he contributed to magazines. But in 1926 he went to Odessa for his first films. *Sumka Dipkurera* was a naïve spy story; but *Zvenigora* initiated the vein of peasant stories in which Dovzhenko was to excel and that—in his own words—amounted to "a catalogue of all my creative possibilities."

The four years that followed saw his greatest work—*Arsenal*, *Earth*, and *Ivan*. *Arsenal* was a tribute to the Ukraine, moving from the last year of the war to the suppression of a workers' revolt in Kiev. But it lacks the strident, doctrinaire dialectic of *Strike* (24, Eisenstein), and the hysterical images of slaughter. Instead, it subordinates its revolutionary conviction to the poignant poetry of failure. *Earth* was so great a success that Dovzhenko visited Berlin and Paris with the film. When he returned, it was to make *Ivan*, his first and still little-known sound film. Again it is richly beautiful, and turning on the relations between the individual and nature. But almost alone among the Russians, Dovzhenko the provincial and rural director grasped the freedom of sound and made *Ivan* an intriguing mixture of moods.

He left the Ukraine to make *Aerograd* and was then commissioned by Stalin to make *Shchors*— "a Ukrainian Chapayev." It was a fine film, but one hampered by bureaucracy, and also markedly more propagandist. As a result, Dovzhenko was made head of the Kiev studios. During the war, he served at the front and wrote a great deal. His film work was confined to newsreels, especially the portentously titled account of the war in the Ukraine. His last film, *Michurin*, was based on one of the plays he wrote during the war.

In his last years, he prepared a Ukrainian trilogy and, when he died, on the point of filming, his wife, Yulia Solntseva, directed them—*Poema o Morye* (58); *Povest Plamennykh Let* (61); and *Zacharovanaya Desna* (65).

Robert Downey Jr., b. New York, 1965

Not long ago, Robert Downey Jr. was in the California prison system on drug-related convictions. The events leading up to that disaster had revealed his chronic need for drugs, and the failure of so much good advice and hopeful therapy. At the same time, he is one of the most fascinating, mercurial actors around—if one cherishes the notion of the actor as jazz improviser: sudden, lyrical, absurd, tragic, comic, and ready to destroy himself for truth. Of course, some people—especially those who have to love, care for, and rescue such a person—are wearied and appalled by any romance applied to his sociopathy. The horrible feeling dawns that a stable, calm, "well" Downey might be a lot less compelling as an actor. Perhaps that is the fear that prompts his use of drugs.

He is the son of Robert Downey (b. 1936), the experimental filmmaker, and he made his first appearances in his father's films: *Pound* (70); *Greaser's Palace* (72); *Up the Academy* (80). Then came *Baby It's You* (83, John Sayles); *Firstborn* (84, Michael Apted); *Tuff Turf* (85, Fritz Kiersch); *Weird Science* (85, John Hughes); *To Live and Die in L.A.* (85, William Friedkin).

By 1985, he was a regular on *Saturday Night Live* as well as making *Back to School* (86, Alan Metter) and *America* (86, Downey). He had the lead role in *The Pick-Up Artist* (87, James Toback); a junkie in *Less Than Zero* (87, Marek Kanievska); *Johnny Be Good* (88, Bud Smith); *Rented Lips* (88, Downey); *1969* (88, Ernest Thompson); law clerk to James Woods in *True Believer* (89, Joseph Ruben); *Chances Are* (89, Emile Ardolino); with Mel Gibson in *Air America* (90, Roger Spottiswoode); *Too Much Sun* (91, Downey); *Soapdish* (91, Michael Hoffman).

In 1992, he was nominated as best actor for *Chaplin* (Richard Attenborough)—it was an inge-

nious performance, if very uneasy with the older man. But Downey was not easily cast in mainstream films: *Heart and Souls* (93, Ron Underwood); *Short Cuts* (93, Robert Altman); *Hail Caesar* (94, Anthony Michael Hall); *Natural Born Killers* (94, Oliver Stone); *Only You* (94, Norman Jewison); *Home for the Holidays* (95, Jodie Foster); *Restoration* (95, Hoffman); *Richard III* (95, Richard Loncraine); *Danger Zone* (96, Allan Eastman); *One Night Stand* (97, Mike Figgis); *Hugo Pool* (97, Downey); *U.S. Marshals* (98, Stuart Baird).

He gave his most brilliant (and pained) performance as the chronic liar in *Two Girls and a Guy* (98, Toback); *The Gingerbread Man* (98, Altman); *In Dreams* (99, Neil Jordan); *Friends & Lovers* (99, George Haas); *Bowfinger* (99, Frank Oz); very funny in *Wonder Boys* (00, Curtis Hanson); flirting with Mike Tyson in *Black and White* (00, Toback). He showed great calm in a recurring role on *Ally McBeal* (00–01). The future is his to make or break, but he will have to prove that the big money can trust him.

A new beginning started with *Lethargy* (02, David Gelb and Joshua Safdie); in the Michael Gambon role in *The Singing Detective* (03, Keith Gordon); *Whatever We Do* (03, Kevin Connolly); *Gothika* (03, Mathieu Kassovitz).

Marie Dressler (Leila Marie Koerber) (1869–1934), b. Coburg, Canada

Dressler was as close to a Mother Courage as Hollywood could run. She was a large, ugly woman who had generally been imposed on as the ungainly object of comedy for more agile and appealing spirits. *Tillie's Punctured Romance* (14, Mack Sennett), her film debut, and an adaptation of one of her most successful stage roles, was the original of this character: a harridan, armed only with money, trying to divert the gigolo Chaplin from the lovely Mabel Normand. Suffering had not been limited to the screen for Dressler. In the 1920s, she slumped drastically from fame and only generous offers from the movies had rescued her. David Shipman has argued that her popularity in the first years of sound was based not only on her talent as a comedienne but because she was, visibly, a fustian woman who had survived depression, her resilience intact. In fact, she proved a worldly and engagingly cynical old lady. It is Dressler who, in *Dinner at Eight* (33, George Cukor), listens skeptically to Jean Harlow's anxiety that machinery will take the place of every profession and murmurs, "Oh my dear, that is something you need never worry about."

Marie Dressler began in opera, moved on to straight theatre—where she played Mrs. Malaprop—but was most successful in vaudeville from about 1900 onward. That led to *Tillie's Punctured Romance*, as important an innovation in comedy films as *Judith of Bethulia* had been in dramas. She made four more films for Sennett and Goldwyn, but none was successful and by 1919 she was in decline.

Her part in the chorus-girl strike of 1917 seems to have made it hard for her to find work, either onstage or in the movies, and she was driven to France where she made some comedy shorts. She was in real need when she got a small part in *The Joy Girl* (27, Allan Dwan); Dwan saw her in a hotel one day, sent her a note, and Dressler almost fainted from relief. Dwan claimed that she told him she was about to kill herself. In fact, Dressler had the cancer that would kill her seven years later, and in her famous films she often looks ill. But the meeting changed her fortunes. Frances Marion, a writer at MGM, insisted that she play in *The Callahans and the Murpheys* (27, George Hill), with Polly Moran. Slowly she regained popularity: *Breakfast at Sunrise* (27, Malcolm St. Clair); *Bringing Up Father* (28, Jack Conway), with Moran; and with Marion Davies in *The Patsy* (28, King Vidor). Talkies really underlined her weather-beaten dryness: *The Divine Lady* (29, Frank Lloyd); *The Vagabond Lover* (29, Marshall Neilan); *Chasing Rainbows* (29, Charles Reisner); with Garbo in *Anna Christie* (30, Clarence Brown); with Lillian Gish in *One Romantic Night* (30, Paul Stein); *The Girl Said No* (30, Sam Wood); *Caught Short* (30, Reisner); and *Let Us Be Gay* (30, Robert Z. Leonard). Then in *Min and Bill* (30, Hill), she was cast with Wallace Beery, and won the best actress Oscar. With Polly Moran, she made *Reducing* (31, Reisner) and in 1932, she was with Jean Hersholt in *Emma* (Clarence Brown). The year before her death, she and Beery played together in *Tugboat Annie* (33, Mervyn Le Roy) and she was in *Dinner at Eight* and *The Late Christopher Bean* (Wood).

In those last few years, she was an enormous box-office star and a grand old lady. Louis B. Mayer reckoned that he had only ever had three great actors (apart from himself): Garbo, Tracy, and Dressler.

Carl Theodor Dreyer (1889–1968),
b. Copenhagen, Denmark
1919: *Praesidenten/The President; Blade af Satans Bog/Leaves from Satan's Book.* 1920: *Prastankan/The Parson's Widow.* 1922: *Die Gezeichneten/Love One Another; Der Var Engang/Once Upon a Time.* 1924: *Mikael.* 1925: *Du Skal Aere Din Hustru/Thou Shalt Honour Thy Wife/Master of the House; Glomsdalsbruden/The Bride of Glomdal.* 1928: *La Passion de Jeanne d'Arc.* 1932: *Vampyr/The Strange Adventure of David Gray.* 1943: *Vredens Dag/Day of Wrath.* 1945: *Tva Maniskor/Two People.* 1954: *Ordet/The Word.* 1964: *Gertrud.*

It is easy, because of his Danishness, Lutheran upbringing, and the outward attention to spiritual ordeal in his films, to regard Dreyer as an austere, Scandinavian examiner of psychological guilt and metaphysical concentration. But the Danishness is of limited relevance; Dreyer made some of his finest films in Norway, France, and Germany. Nor is it wise to accept the traditional interpretation of him as a foreboding and transcendental religious artist.

Dreyer's work is always based on the beauty of the image, which in turn is a record of the luminous conviction and independence of human beings. His films are devoted principally to human emotions, and if they seem relatively subdued, then that may be a proper reason for calling in Danishness. But simplicity and purity of style do not argue against intensity. Dreyer's greatness is in the way that he makes a tranquil picture of overwhelming feelings. His art, and his intelligence, make passion orderly without ever cheating on it. Passion is the word—so often included in the title of the Joan of Arc film without proper consideration. Dreyer films human passion and it is only as a secondary function that that passion takes on a universal spiritual significance. The sanctity of emotions is his faith and the cinematic ability to make an aesthetic and ordered narrative work is his aim. All his works are passions—in the sense of being like musical celebrations of feelings, and in the sense that they are devoted to specific human responses to situations defined by stories. To say that Dreyer is concerned simply with the life of the emotions is to rescue him from that northern recess where he still, sadly, remains and put him where he belongs—in the company of Mizoguchi, Vigo, Ophuls, Renoir, Rossellini, Bergman, and Godard.

That last name recalls the most moving attempt to place Dreyer in the mainstream of cinema. When, in *Vivre Sa Vie* (62), Anna Karina goes to a cinema and is moved to tears by the sight of Falconetti in *La Passion de Jeanne d'Arc*, Godard was bowing in respect to Dreyer, referring to Karina's Danishness (her mother worked for Dreyer), and comparing Karina with Falconetti—both beautiful women made grave by contemplation of themselves through acting. He was also asserting a vital cinematic continuity through the potency of the close-up that evokes the inner life, and thereby seeing that there may be an emotional saintliness in the mind of a Parisian tart. It is a bitter footnote to this that, after so eloquent a French tribute, when *Gertrud* opened in Paris it was greeted with such brutal incomprehension that it had to be withdrawn within days. Yet *Gertrud* is the last masterpiece of one of the greatest of directors.

Thirty when he first directed, Dreyer had been a journalist before he joined Nordisk to write titles for their films and then to work on scripts. As a journalist, he had reviewed plays and films and also served as a court reporter. The early stress on accuracy of records, the resort to legal confrontation, and the discipline of distilling narrative into cogent titles are all influences that one may detect in his work. His first films were confessedly made under the influence of Sjostrom and Griffith, especially *Intolerance. Praesidenten* is an uninhibited melodrama about illegitimate children, while *Leaves from Satan's Book* is an imitation of *Intolerance,* even to the extent of being in four episodes.

The Parson's Widow, shot in the Norwegian countryside, is the first masterpiece. Its story shows Dreyer's growing feeling for emotional surprise: a young clergyman comes to a new living, but has to marry the late incumbent's elderly widow. He has a girl he loves who comes to the household as his sister. The young couple plan to kill the widow, only for it to be revealed that she is not an ogress but a wise and kind woman who understands their feelings and looks warmly on them. By the time she dies, the young people's conception of love has been enriched by her example and by her description of her own happiness when young. Another melodrama has been elevated, without strain, into a celebration of happiness and spiritual intelligence. It is worth noting that the woman who played the widow was herself very old and died shortly after the shooting. This is an extreme example, perhaps, but typical of the importance Dreyer placed on the "emotional resemblance" between actor and character.

His next three films were made in Germany, and it is clear that Dreyer responded to the Expressionist taste for revealing emotion through decor and lighting. On *Mikael,* for instance, he had Karl Freund and Rudolph Maté as his cameramen. Another major film, *Mikael* is an important item in the collection of works that have an artist as a central figure. It deals with the triangular relationship between an elderly painter, his young male model, and the girl he loves. The casting is extraordinary: the director Benjamin Christensen as the artist, Walter Slezak as the young man, and Norah Gregor (Renoir's Christine in *La Règle du Jeu*) as the girl. It is a tragic but resigned film, showing vitality slipping away from the artist as the love affair grows. Dreyer's sense of precision was greatly developed and the emotional concentration is accentuated by the fin-de-siècle clutter of the sets. Back in Denmark, *Master of the House* showed how far Dreyer was abandoning narrative eventfulness for emotional action. With special care for the actuality of a small house in which man and wife live, Dreyer made a film out of the emotional interplay in a failing marriage. Again, reconciliation is achieved—as in *The Parson's Widow*—and *Master of the House,* made in 1925, now looks like a superb piece of emotional

realism. It foreshadows *Gertrud* in its study of a woman who feels herself oppressed by her husband and yet accomplishes emotional reawakening without melodrama.

Then to France for his best-known film, *La Passion de Jeanne d'Arc,* based rigorously on the records of the trial, demonstrating triumphantly that the close-up was not just a means but an end. It may be that Griffith first regularly employed the close-up for illustrative emphasis, but who can argue that *La Passion* is not built upon its variety and profundity? Dreyer's method is illustrated by his own account of how he coaxed Falconetti through these close-ups to "give" the emotional charge that is still so moving:

> With Falconetti, it often happened that, after having worked all afternoon, we hadn't succeeded in getting exactly what was required. We said to ourselves then: tomorrow we will begin again. And the next day, we would have the bad take from the day before projected, we would examine it, we would search and we always ended by finding, in that bad take, some little fragments, some little light, that rendered the exact expression, the tonality we had been looking for. It is from there that we would set out again, taking the best and abandoning the remainder. It is from there that we took off, in order to begin again . . . and succeed.

Maté photographed *La Passion* and Dreyer's next film, *Vampyr,* made in France from private money. It is a story by Sheridan le Fanu, played largely by amateurs, and one of the greatest of horror films. Its quality is not supernatural but inevitable. All talk of emotional or psychological content in the horror genre begins with *Nosferatu* and *Vampyr.* Filmed in real settings, it is invaded by a misty light, achieved by reflecting a light off a gauze back into the lens. Without ever discarding the Gothic elements of vampirism, it sees in its subject a universal emotional encounter. Thus the happenings of horror become heightened expressions of an inner life. Its intensity reflects back on all Dreyer's other films, showing how entirely they are creations of light, shade, and camera position.

There followed an eleven-year gap between *Vampyr* and *Day of Wrath,* not fully explained. As he returned to features in 1943, so at the same time he began to make documentaries: on art and architecture and, with special impact, on road safety. *Day of Wrath* and *Ordet* are both religious subjects conditioned by the puritan harshness of Scandinavia. *Day of Wrath* is about the trial of a witch in which a dying witch curses the pastor. The pastor's wife loves a younger man, the discovery of which kills the pastor so that the wife is now regarded as a witch. The passion here is malign and destructive and it is hard not to see the film as being influenced by war. At the same time, it concentrates on the human loneliness that in the past Dreyer had usually managed to redeem. *Ordet* is an allegory, from a play by Kaj Munk, filmed in the village where Munk had been the pastor. The film reaffirms Dreyer's vision of human and religious love as being inseparable.

Another ten years passed before *Gertrud*, the story of a forty-year-old woman, unhappy with her husband, who loves a younger man but is loved insufficiently in return, and who decides to go to Paris and live alone. The conclusion of insistent independence is kept within a frame of calm beauty. And yet beneath the order of the film there is, stronger than ever, the exultant sense of passion. When it was made, the reserve and slowness of *Gertrud* were so out of fashion that its emotion was missed. But it awaits the world's discovery as Dreyer's finest film and vindication of his method:

What interests me—and this comes before technique—is reproducing the feelings of the characters in my films . . . The important thing . . . is not only to catch hold of the words they say, but also the thoughts behind the words. What I seek in my films, what I want to obtain, is a penetration to my actors' profound thoughts by means of their most subtle expressions. For these are the expressions . . . that lie in the depths of his soul. This is what interests me above all, not the technique of the cinema. *Gertrud* is a film that I made with my heart.

Richard Dreyfuss,
b. Brooklyn, New York, 1947

By the late 1970s, Richard Dreyfuss had reason to feel cock of the new walk. He had won the Oscar for his showy performance as a flashy, failed actor in *The Goodbye Girl* (77, Herbert Ross). He had been the central figure in the parade of *American Graffiti* (73, George Lucas), and the most appealing hero in *Jaws* (75, Steven Spielberg). He had given his best performance as a Muncie man who refuses to deny that he has seen wonders in *Close Encounters of the Third Kind* (77, Spielberg). Then something happened, something made of vanity, drug involvement, overassertiveness, fickle public taste . . . and maybe the fact that Dreyfuss is happier as a character actor than as a great star.

When he was a child, his family moved to Los Angeles and Dreyfuss was educated at San Fernando Valley State College. He had tiny parts in *The Graduate* (67, Mike Nichols) and *Valley of the Dolls* (67, Mark Robson), but he showed a first sign of spirited arrogance in *The Young Runaways* (68, Arthur Dreifuss). After *Hello Down There* (69, Jack Arnold), he played Baby Face Nelson in *Dillinger* (73, John Milius).

In his rich years, he also appeared in *The Apprenticeship of Duddy Kravitz* (74, Ted Kotcheff); *Inserts* (76, John Byrum); *Victory at Entebbe* (76, Marvin J. Chomsky) for TV; *The Big Fix* (78, Jeremy Paul Kagan), which he also produced; *The Competition* (80, Joel Oliansky); and paralyzed from the neck down, but hyperactive above, in *Whose Life Is It Anyway?* (81, John Badham).

He was away for a few years and when he returned he seemed older and more drawn: *The Buddy System* (84, Glenn Jordan) and *Down and Out in Beverly Hills* (86, Paul Mazursky). He was the narrator in *Stand By Me* (86, Rob Reiner) and at his best in the desperate comedy of *Tin Men* (87, Barry Levinson) and *Stakeout* (87, Badham), which also drew upon his exceptional speed and precision. He was Streisand's lawyer in *Nuts* (87, Martin Ritt) and a very broad actor-cum-dictator in *Moon Over Parador* (88, Mazursky).

He was a gambler in *Let It Ride* (89, Joe Pytka) and a rather cheerless version of Spencer Tracy in *Always* (89, Spielberg). Then he did *Postcards From the Edge* (90, Nichols); *Once Around* (91, Lasse Hallstrom); the Player King in *Rosencrantz and Guildenstern Are Dead* (91, Tom Stoppard); *What About Bob?* (91, Frank Oz); and the officer who supported Alfred Dreyfuss (a distant relative) in *Prisoner of Honor* (91, Ken Russell) for cable TV. He also appeared in *Lost in Yonkers* (93, Martha Coolidge).

He keeps his status: *Another Stakeout* (93, Badham); *Silent Fall* (94, Bruce Beresford); *The Last Word* (94, Tony Spiridakis); the bad guy in *The American President* (95, Reiner); as the teacher in *Mr. Holland's Opus* (95, Stephen Herek); the voice of the centipede in *James and the Giant Peach* (96, Henry Selick); *Mad Dog Time* (96, Larry Bishop); *Night Falls on Manhattan* (97, Sidney Lumet); as Fagin in a TV *Oliver Twist* (97, Tony Bill); *Krippendorf's Tribe* (98, Todd Holland); as *Lansky* (99, John McNaughton) for TV; the president in *Fail Safe* (00, Stephen Frears); *The Crew* (00, Michael Dinner); *The Old Man Who Read Love Stories* (00, Rolf de Heer); *Who Is Cletis Tout?* (01, Chris Ver Wiel); in the TV series *The Education of Max Bickford* (01, Rod Holcomb); as Alexander Haig in *The Day Reagan Was Shot* (01, Ken Welsh Baker and Cyrus Nowrasteh); on TV in *The Education of Max Bickford* (01).

Joanne Dru (Joanne Letitia La Cock)
(1923–96), b. Logan, West Virginia

It is a sign of the times that this wholesome, very pretty, and assured actress saw fit to change her name. Twenty years later, anyone called Letitia La Cock would have been welcomed rapturously at the Warhol factory and could hardly fail to have been lit up with the Day-Glo camp of the name.

Her invented name sounded much more plausible, especially as the dark-eyed tomboy to be found in various wagon trains heading West. She had been a model and—to add spice to the Warhol stew—a "Samba Siren" before she made her movie debut in *Abie's Irish Rose* (46, Edward Sutherland). But it was as Tess Millay in *Red River* (48, Howard Hawks), barely fazed by the arrow that pins her to a wagon and still able to take pleasure in smacking Montgomery Clift's face, that she established herself. John Ford then took her up—in uniform in *She Wore a Yellow Ribbon* (49) and as "Denver" in *Wagonmaster* (50). She was more serious and less striking in *All the King's Men* (49, Robert Rossen). That was the extent of her real prominence. She slipped into more modest adventure films in less carefully elaborated parts: *711 Ocean Drive* (50, Joseph M. Newman); *Vengeance Valley* (51, Richard Thorpe); *Mr. Belvedere Rings the Bell* (51, Henry Koster); *Return of the Texan* (52, Delmer Daves); *The Pride of St Louis* (52, Harmon Jones); *My Pal Gus* (52, Robert Parrish); *Thunder Bay* (53, Anthony Mann); *Hannah Lee* (53, Lee Garmes and John Ireland—her then husband), a lost 3D movie; *Forbidden* (53, Rudolph Maté); *The Siege at Red River* (54, Maté); *Day of Triumph* (54, Irving Pichel); *Hell on Frisco Bay* (55, Frank Tuttle); *Dark Avenger* (55, Henry Levin); *Sincerely Yours* (55, Gordon Douglas); *Three Ring Circus* (55, Joseph Pevney)—this last as Dean's girlfriend in a Martin and Lewis comedy, a sure sign of distress. Perhaps that first freshness had gone. Since then, she has worked only rarely: *September Storm* (60, Byron Haskin); *Sylvia* (65, Douglas); and *Super Fuzz* (81, Sergio Corbucci).

Margaret Dumont (1889–1965),
b. Brooklyn, New York

A Night at the Opera (35, Sam Wood), on an ocean liner, in the dining room, together at last, Groucho's Otis B. Driftwood and Margaret Dumont's Mrs. Claypool, a sweet, stately, stupid lady, pearls dipping into décolletage, the face simpering at the silliness of films:

MRS. CLAYPOOL: Mr. Driftwood, three months ago you promised to put me into society. In all that time you've done nothing but draw a very handsome salary.

DRIFTWOOD: You think that's nothing, huh? How many men do you suppose are drawing a handsome salary nowadays? Why, you can count them on the fingers of one hand, my good woman.

MRS. CLAYPOOL: I'm not your good woman.

DRIFTWOOD: Don't say that, Mrs. Claypool. I don't care what your past has been. To me,

you'll always be my good woman, because I love you. There, I didn't mean to tell you, but you, you dragged it out of me. I love you.

MRS. CLAYPOOL: It's rather difficult to believe that when I find you dining with another woman.

DRIFTWOOD: That woman? Do you know why I sat with her?

MRS. CLAYPOOL: No.

DRIFTWOOD: Because she reminded me of you.

MRS. CLAYPOOL: Really?

DRIFTWOOD: Of course! That's why I'm sitting here with you, because you remind me of you. Your eyes, your throat, your lips, everything about you reminds me of you, except you.

That is the secret of the lady. She was a collection of external signs, prepared to tolerate every extravagance from Groucho, as flexible and lofty in her love as a mother and as drained of independence. Her tidy hairstyle, her jewelry, her round hips were like the attributes of any bridge-playing lady asked to sit in on a film set. She is especially touching in the Marx Brothers' films because she looks amateur and domestic; and, of course, the uncontrived often appears hollow in films. She had played a small part in *A Tale of Two Cities* (17, Frank Lloyd), but chiefly worked on the stage. She was Groucho's punchbag in the stage versions of *The Cocoanuts* and *Animal Crackers* and transferred to films when Paramount signed the brothers. She worked with them seven times: *The Cocoanuts* (29, Robert Florey and Joseph Santley); *Animal Crackers* (30, Victor Heerman); *Duck Soup* (33, Leo McCarey); *A Night at the Opera; A Day at the Races* (37, Sam Wood); *At The Circus* (39, Edward Buzzell); and *The Big Store* (41, Charles Reisner). The wonder is that she made other films: deprived of Groucho's insults, she would seem like a tent without ropes. But they are, in the main, films that slipped under the door: *Kentucky Kernels* (34, George Stevens); *Rendezvous* (35, William K. Howard); *Anything Goes* (36, Lewis Milestone); *The Song and Dance Man* (36, Allan Dwan); *Never Give a Sucker an Even Break* (41, Edward Cline); *Sing Your Worries Away* (42, Edward Sutherland); in the W. C. Fields episode cut from *Tales of Manhattan* (42, Julien Duvivier); with Laurel and Hardy in *The Dancing Masters* (43, Malcolm St. Clair); *Up in Arms* (44, Elliott Nugent); *Bathing Beauty* (44, George Sidney); *The Horn Blows at Midnight* (45, Raoul Walsh); *Susie Steps Out* (46, Reginald le Borg); *Stop, You're Killing Me* (52, Roy del Ruth); *Shake, Rattle and Rock* (56, Edward L. Cahn); *Auntie Mame* (58, Morton Da Costa); and *What a Way to Go!* (63, J. Lee Thompson).

She died only weeks after playing in a TV sketch with Groucho.

Faye Dunaway, b. Bascom, Florida, 1941

Educated at the University of Florida and Boston University, she worked on the New York stage and was three years with the Lincoln Center Repertory Company before bursting on the screen in 1967 as Bonnie for Arthur Penn, in Preminger's *Hurry Sundown,* and in Elliot Silverstein's *The Happening.* Her Bonnie was a touching confusion of sensuality and innocence, fundamental to Penn's faith in vitality but a great personal achievement, as quick and vivid as a flame.

However, she soon revealed that she was prepared to make herself a dutiful, middlebrow fashion plate—as in Norman Jewison's *The Thomas Crown Affair* (68) and de Sica's *A Place for Lovers* (68). Subsequently, she gave a very mixed performance in *The Arrangement* (69, Elia Kazan), a competent comedy cameo in *Little Big Man* (70, Penn), and a modish study of breakdown in *Puzzle of a Downfall Child* (70, Jerry Schatzberg). Her Katie Elder in Frank Perry's *Doc* (71) showed that she had yet to come to terms with her early fame, and *The Deadly Trap* (71, René Clément) suggested a misplaced respect for continental gravity. She enjoyed herself in *Oklahoma Crude* (73, Stanley Kramer) and as Milady de Winter in *The Three Musketeers* (73, Richard Lester), but looked tense and hot in *The Towering Inferno* (74, John Guillermin).

Then in *Chinatown* (74, Roman Polanski), she was the shifty heart of a film, far more so than Jack Nicholson. It is Dunaway who most effectively relates the worlds of the elegant Mrs. Evelyn Mulwray (a woman from a Lubitsch film, condescending to appear in a George Raft picture) and the glowing, mango-colored China doll who sleeps with Nicholson's detective and has an ingrowing family tree. She looks like a cross between Joan Crawford and Sylvia Sidney until she turns her head to the light and her arched brows show the flawed iris nemesis of Chinatown.

She was not very necessary to *Three Days of the Condor* (75, Sydney Pollack), and only star cargo in *Voyage of the Damned* (76, Stuart Rosenberg). But in *Network* (76, Sidney Lumet), she was the nerve center of the film—agitated, sensation seeking, and as cold as TV itself. At the same time, she was a believable neurotic career woman and a comic-book video creature—the medium and a massage—and she won the best actress Oscar for it. With that status, she slowed down and found herself a lush vehicle, *The Eyes of Laura Mars* (78, Irvin Kershner), and looked very faded in the remake of *The Champ* (79, Franco Zeffirelli).

In the eighties, Dunaway slipped out of leading actress parts, though not before her magnificent impersonation of Joan Crawford in *Mommie Dearest* (81, Perry), a performance that deserved a more humane approach. As it was, Dunaway was herself touched by the grotesqueness of Crawford (she might have been more at ease in the 1930s) and the film may have made her unpopular in Hollywood—or added to her own reputation for being difficult. Elsewhere, she was the bedridden wife in *The First Deadly Sin* (80, Brian G. Hutton); for TV she was *Evita Peron* (81, Marvin Chomsky); to England for *The Wicked Lady* (83, Michael Winner); *Ordeal by Innocence* (84, Desmond Davis); *Supergirl* (84, Jeannot Szwarc); on TV in *Ellis Island* (84, Jerry London), *Thirteen at Dinner* (85, Lou Antonio), and *Beverly Hills Madam* (86, Harvey Hart); bravely bedraggled in *Barfly* (87, Barbet Schroeder); *Casanova* (87, Simon Langton) for TV; *Burning Secret* (88, Andrew Birkin); *Midnight Crossing* (88, Roger Holzberg); on TV for *Cold Sassy Tree* (89, Joan Tewksbury) and *Silhouette* (90, Carl Schenkel); *Wait Until Spring, Bandini* (89, Dominique Deruddere); *The Handmaid's Tale* (90, Volker Schlondorff); *Scorchers* (91, David Beaird); a TV series, *It Had to Be You* (93); and *The Temp* (93, Tom Holland).

She works wherever she can, but she is one more helpless example of what happens to star actresses as they grow older: *A Family Divided* (95, Donald Wrye); *Don Juan DeMarco* (95, Jeremy Leven); *Drunks* (95, Peter Cohn); *Dunston Checks In* (96, Ken Kwapis); *The Chamber* (96, James Foley); *Albino Alligator* (96, Kevin Spacey); *The People Next Door* (96, Tim Hunter); *En Brazos de la Mujer Madura* (96, Manuel Lombardero); *The Twilight of the Golds* (97, Ross Kagan Marks); Mrs. Van Hopper in *Rebecca* (97, Jim O'Brien); *Gia* (98, Michael Cristofer); as Margaret Sanger in *A Will of Their Own* (98, Karen Arthur) on TV; *Love Lies Bleeding* (99, William Tannen); as the shrink in *The Thomas Crown Affair* (99, John McTiernan); *The Messenger: The Story of Joan of Arc* (99, Luc Besson); *The Yards* (00, James Gray); *Stanley's Gig* (00, Marc Lazard); *Running Mates* (00, Ron Lagomarsino); a short film, *Yellow Bird* (01), which she directed herself; Mae West in *The Calling* (01, Richard Caesar); *The Rules of Attraction* (02, Roger Avary); *Mid-Century* (02, Scott Billups); *El Padrino* (03, Damian Chapa).

Irene Dunne (1898–1990),
b. Louisville, Kentucky

What is it about Irene Dunne? She was not a great beauty, or a commanding actress. I'm not even sure she was innately funny. There are times in her work when respectability shows: she was staunch as both Republican and Catholic, and she favored what she regarded as serious roles—drama and weepies—as opposed to the comedies for which she is treasured. Stanley Cavell once wrote of *The Awful Truth* that "if one is not willing to yield to Irene Dunne's temperament, her talents, her reactions, following their detail almost to the loss of one's own identity, one will not know, and will not care, what the film is about." Richard Schickel's obituary tribute noted, "She always knew how to put a man in his place, but at the same time leave him room to maneuver out of it." I would add that, in two very different films with Cary Grant—*The Awful Truth* and *Penny Serenade*—she seems smarter or more knowing than Grant, yet graceful enough to watch him catch up, without letting him feel it. And Grant was testing company (he, too, revered her timing).

Then there is her age. For some time, it was believed that Dunne had been born in 1904, but 1898 is now taken as the true date. Which means that she was over thirty when she made her screen debut. Very few actresses cast in romance simply missed their twenties. (Jean Harlow never met her thirties.) Dunne had a happy family life until her father died when she was eleven. Harder years followed: she sang in church choirs for money (her mother was a musician), she taught music herself, and studied at Chicago Musical College. In 1920, she failed an audition for the Metropolitan Opera in New York.

So she went into musical comedy, rising slowly to the role of Magnolia in the touring production of *Show Boat*. By 1930, she was under contract to RKO, initially as a singer. But her first film, *Leathernecking* (30, Edward Cline), was stripped of its songs. Then Richard Dix chose her to play Sabra Cravat opposite him in *Cimarron* (31, Wesley Ruggles). That proved a huge success, and Sabra is really the heart of what is a soggy Western. So Dunne was set up as an actress.

She worked hard at RKO, but not always in good material: *Bachelor Apartment* (31, Lowell Sherman); *Consolation Marriage* (31, Paul Sloane); as the crippled teacher in *Symphony of Six Million* (32, Gregory La Cava); and *Thirteen Women* (32, George Archainbaud). She had a great success at Universal as the secret mistress in *Back Street* (32, John M. Stahl), and suffering and sacrifice seemed to appeal to her—Dunne herself approved of the character's unself-pitying acceptance of her life. This sort of role was repeated in *The Secret of Madame Blanche* (33, Charles Brabin); *If I Were Free* (33, Elliott Nugent); *The Silver Cord* (33, John Cromwell), where Joel McCrea nearly gives her up for his mother; very good in *Ann Vickers* (33, Cromwell), where she plays Walter Huston's mistress with unusual intelligence; and *This Man Is Mine* (34, Cromwell). The series was topped off by her blind woman in *Magnificent Obsession* (35, Stahl).

That Dunne is worthy, but not overly interesting. She sang at last in *Stingaree* (34, William Wellman), and got into a series of musicals: *Sweet*

Adeline (35, Mervyn Le Roy); with Astaire and Rogers in *Roberta* (35, William A. Seiter), singing Jerome Kern's "Yesterdays" and "Smoke Gets in Your Eyes"; and repeated her stage role in *Show Boat* (36, James Whale).

She did not want to do *Theodora Goes Wild* (36, Richard Boleslavsky), in a Sidney Buchman script from a Mary McCarthy story. But she did it, and a great comic talent was revealed in the story of a woman who writes a best-selling book and falls in love with her New York illustrator (Melvyn Douglas).

At Paramount, she did *High, Wide and Handsome* (37, Rouben Mamoulian), singing "The Folks Who Live on the Hill" (Kern again). But Columbia and Leo McCarey grabbed her for *The Awful Truth* (37), for which she got her third Oscar nomination (*Theodora* and *Cimarron* had preceded it).

So she was established in musicals, melodrama, and high comedy—that versatility had few rivals. Still, she was forty and the decade was ending uneasily. She had more success, but nothing as bracing as *The Awful Truth: Joy of Living* (38, Tay Garnett); *Invitation to Happiness* (39, Ruggles); nominated again for the wonderful *Love Affair* (39, McCarey—with Charles Boyer), one of the most influential of romances; *When Tomorrow Comes* (39, Stahl); with Grant again in *My Favorite Wife* (40, Garson Kanin), which has the first feel of retread; very touching in the weepy *Penny Serenade* (41, George Stevens); *Unfinished Business* (41, La Cava); *Lady in a Jam* (42, La Cava); rather awkward with Spencer Tracy in *A Guy Named Joe* (43, Victor Fleming); *The White Cliffs of Dover* (44, Clarence Brown)—in Greer Garson territory; *Together Again* (44, Charles Vidor); and *Over 21* (45, Vidor).

She was with Rex Harrison in *Anna and the King of Siam* (46, Cromwell), and she had considerable success sentimentally in *Life With Father* (47, Michael Curtiz) and *I Remember Mama* (48, Stevens), and a fifth nomination. But staidness was in sight: *Never a Dull Moment* (50, George Marshall) did not live up to its title; and then in *The Mudlark* (50, Jean Negulesco), she put on makeup, years, and dignity to play Queen Victoria. She was unrecognizable and the film was a folly—perhaps it had snob appeal for her. After *It Grows on Trees* (52, Arthur Lubin), she retired and turned to political volunteer work, with special interest in the United Nations.

Kirsten Dunst,
b. Point Pleasant, New Jersey, 1982

Made when she was still short of twenty, *The Cat's Meow* (02, Peter Bogdanovich) gave clinching proof that Kirsten Dunst the child actress had graduated. Playing Marion Davies (when she was actually twenty-seven), Dunst did a terrific job at showing that actress's flair for comedy as well as her deep, if mixed, feelings for William Randolph Hearst. All she needs are good parts that keep her working in that range of laughter and dismay.

She did a great deal of work as a child, starting with *Bonfire of the Vanities* (90, Brian De Palma); a very grown-up performance in *Interview with the Vampire* (94, Neil Jordan); Amy in *Little Women* (94, Gillian Armstrong); *Greedy* (94, Jonathan Lynn); *Jumanji* (95, Joe Johnston); good in *Mother Night* (96, Keith Gordon); *Ruby Ridge: An American Tragedy* (96, Roger Young); the voice of the young girl in *Anastasia* (97, Don Bluth); *Wag the Dog* (97, Barry Levinson); on TV in *Fifteen and Pregnant* (98, Sam Pillsbury); *Small Soldiers* (98, Joe Dante); *All I Wanna Do* (98, Sarah Kernochan); *The Virgin Suicides* (99, Sofia Coppola); *Drop Dead Gorgeous* (99, Michael Patrick Jann); *Dick* (99, Andrew Fleming); *Bring It On* (00, Peyton Reed); *Get Over It* (01, Tommy O'Haver); *Crazy/Beautiful* (01, John Stockwell); *Spider-Man* (02, Sam Raimi); *Levity* (03, Ed Solomon); *Kaena: The Prophecy* (03, Chris Delaporte and Pascal Pinon).

E. A. Dupont (Ewald André Dupont),
(1891–1956), b. Leitz, Germany
Before 1918: *Die Buchhalterin; Durchlaucht Hypochonder; Der Ewige Zweifel; Mitternacht; Nur am Tausend Dollars; Der Onyxkopf; Das Perlenhalsband; Der Saratogakafer; Die Sterbenden Perlen; Die Japanerin.* 1918: *Das Geheimnis der Amerika-Docks; Der Mann aus Neapel; Die Schwarze Schachdame; Der Lebende Schatten; Der Teufel.* 1919: *Die Apachen; Das Grand Hotel Babylon.* 1920: *Mord ohne Tater; Der Weisse Pfau.* 1921: *Die Geierwally; Kinder der Finsternis.* 1922: *Sie und die Drei.* 1923: *Das Alte Gesetz; Die Grune Manuela; Ein Film aus dem Sueden.* 1925: *Der Demutige und die Sangerin; Variété.* 1927: *Love Me and the World Is Mine.* 1928: *Moulin-Rouge; Piccadilly.* 1929: *Atlantic.* 1930: *Cape Forlorn; Two Worlds.* 1931: *Salto Mortale.* 1932: *Peter Voss, der Millionendieb.* 1933: *Der Laufer von Marathon; Ladies Must Love.* 1935: *The Bishop Misbehaves.* 1936: *A Son Comes Home; Forgotten Faces; A Night of Mystery.* 1937: *On Such a Night; Love on Toast.* 1939: *Hell's Kitchen* (codirected with Lewis Seiler). 1951: *The Scarf.* 1953: *Problem Girls; The Neanderthal Man; The Steel Lady.* 1954: *Return to Treasure Island.*

A film critic, Dupont began writing scripts: *Renn Fieber* (16, Richard Oswald); *Es Werde Licht* (18, Oswald). As a director, *Variété* is his best work, a story of sexual exchange among a troupe of trapeze artists. It is the film in which Emil Jannings resolutely turned his back on the camera, the sort of schematic device favored by Dupont. He excelled, in Lotte Eisner's words, at "capturing and fixing fluctuating forms which vary incessantly under the effect of light and movement. His objective is always and everywhere the ebb and flow of light." This is especially so in the shots of illuminated white trapeze performers above the crowd.

Dupont went to America to make *Love Me and the World Is Mine* for Universal and then to Britain for five films. In *Moulin-Rouge* and *Piccadilly,* especially, his use of lighting is very successful. But *Atlantic,* the first complete sound film to be made in Europe, was very slow and too preoccupied with the novelty of sound. In 1933, Dupont opted for America, but was rarely more than a director of second features. In 1939, he went back to journalism and started an agency for actors. He returned, twelve years later, with *The Scarf,* an oddity starring John Ireland, but slipped back to B pictures. Before his death he wrote the script for *Magic Fire* (56, William Dieterle).

Marguerite Duras (Marguerite
Donnadieu) (1914–96), b. Giodinh, Indochina
1966: *La Musica* (codirected with Paul Sebau). 1969: *Détruire, Dit-Elle.* 1971: *Jaune le Soleil.* 1972: *Nathalie Granger.* 1975: *India Song.* 1976: *Des Journées Entières dans les Arbres/Entire Days in the Trees; Son Nom de Venise dans Calcutta Desert.* 1977: *Baxter, Vera Baxter; Le Camion/The Truck.* 1979: *Le Navire Night.* 1984: *Les Enfants/The Children.*

Although Marguerite Duras came to moviemaking rather late, and despite her participation in the development of that strictly literary form—*le nouveau roman*—she seems to be as movie-mad as another experimentalist with words, Alain Robbe-Grillet. For by now, with *The Lover* (92, Jean-Jacques Annaud), and with the Duras novel that inspired the film *and* her response to Annaud's film, *The North China Lover,* Duras is a character in film, not just a creative force. And as with Lillian Hellman in some of her suspect nonfiction writing, Duras's passion has blurred boundaries of truth and fiction. Duras the adult is decidedly more homely than Jane March in the Annaud film. But Duras has aged rather as Simone Signoret did— and we know that Duras regarded herself as a part to be played. Indeed, the formal exchanges of *Hiroshima, Mon Amour* (59, Alain Resnais) took on the fire of obsession once one realized the sheer perseverance of Duras with the situation of Oriental man and French woman. Thus, Marguerite Duras has been a little like a Bette Davis hiding within a Gertrude Stein or a Virginia Woolf.

We see Duras now as someone equally at ease in the novel, the stage play, or the movie, and someone accustomed to rewriting material in different media. Her themes are memory, loss, and the interplay of reality and fictional perception.

Her own films make a rarefied yet absorbing body of work. Yet her influence goes much further—into scripts she has written for others, in her ability to crystallize their talents, and in her poised balancing of intellect and melodrama. Her scripts include: *Moderato Cantabile* (60, Peter Brook); *Une Aussi Longue Absence* (61, Henri Colpi); and *10:30 P.M. Summer* (66, Jules Dassin). But, in addition, her novels have led to *The Sea Wall* (57, René Clément) and *The Sailor from Gibraltar* (67, Tony Richardson).

Her own films make great play with words, and with words that are more than normally separated from their images. *India Song,* for example, has most of its talk "off" camera; and then *Son Nom de Venise . . .* takes the track from the first film and plays it over exploring shots of the house where the movie was made. *Le Camion* has Mme. Duras reading the film's script to actor Gérard Depardieu, gradually broken in on by the images of the film. In *Nathalie Granger,* Jeanne Moreau and Lucia Bosé do little more than exist in a house and garden talking and in juxtaposition with radio commentaries.

If much of this sounds like radio, there is no denying Duras's love of words and incantation (the music of the dialogue was striking in *Hiroshima Mon Amour*). But the films show an equal fascination with movement, faces, and even decor. Duras is one of those people quite happy to be stunned by moving imagery.

Deanna Durbin (Edna Mae Durbin),
b. Winnipeg, Canada, 1921
When still only fourteen years old, her singing caught the ear of MGM. But they used her only in one short, *Every Sunday* (36, Felix Feist). Instead, she was taken to Universal by producer Joe Pasternak as a way of saving that studio from financial disaster. Pasternak appears to have grasped that Durbin was a rarity: a true teenage star, pretty, cheerful, clean, and tuneful. He used her as a beaming social worker to unhappy adults, and such balm proved very efficacious just before and in the early years of the war. Usually, Pasternak entrusted his protégée to director Henry Koster: *Three Smart Girls* (36, Koster); *One Hundred Men and a Girl* (37, Koster), in which she acts as matchmaker for Leopold Stokowski and some unemployed musicians; *Mad About Music* (38, Norman Taurog); *Three Smart Girls Grow Up* (39, Koster); *First Love* (39, Koster); *It's a Date* (40, William A. Seiter); *Spring Parade* (40, Koster); *Nice Girl* (41, Seiter); and *It Started with Eve* (41, Koster).

At this point Pasternak left for MGM and Durbin foundered without his guidance. Already married, she tried to take on fully adult parts but hardly had the talent required. Jean Renoir quit *The Amazing Mrs. Holliday* (43, Bruce Manning) either because of her inability or because of producer Manning's pressure, and although she was mostly successful in *His Butler's Sister* (43, Frank Borzage), she was hopelessly adrift playing a shady nightclub chanteuse in *Christmas Holiday* (44, Robert Siodmak). She stayed on for several years but in quicker and cheaper films: *Can't Help Singing* (44, Frank Ryan); *Because of Him* (46, Richard Wallace); *I'll Be Yours* (47, Seiter); and *Up in Central Park* (48, Seiter). She retired in 1949 and went to live in France.

She had been the un-Judy, a good girl, talented, but the perfect example to all those foolish people ready to sacrifice everything for talent.

Dan Duryea (1907–68),
b. White Plains, New York
In striped suit, bow tie, and straw hat, the Duryea of *Scarlet Street* (45, Fritz Lang) is a delicious villain. A sly man, he creeps up on malice as if it were a cat to catch, and is unable to prevent a giggle cracking his high-pitched voice: a door-to-door salesman just waiting for bored wives. Duryea's three films for Lang, his gunman in *Winchester 73* (50, Anthony Mann), and his debut as cousin Leo in *The Little Foxes* (41, William Wyler) are his best work, but he was never dull, even when called on to be friendly: *Ball of Fire* (41, Howard Hawks); *The Pride of the Yankees* (42, Sam Wood); *Sahara* (43, Zoltan Korda); *Man from Frisco* (44, Robert Florey); *None but the Lonely Heart* (44, Clifford Odets); *Mrs. Parkington* (44, Tay Garnett); flexing a pair of scissors in *Ministry of Fear* (44, Lang); *The Woman in the Window* (44, Lang); *The Great Flamarion* (45, Mann); *Valley of Decision* (45, Garnett); *Along Came Jones* (45, Stuart Heisler); *Black Angel* (47, Roy William Neill); *Another Part of the Forest* (48, Michael Gordon); *Criss Cross* (48, Robert Siodmak); *Too Late for Tears* (49, Byron Haskin); *One Way Street* (50, Hugo Fregonese); *Underworld Story* (50, Cy Endfield); *Thunder Bay* (53, Mann); *World for Ransom* (54, Robert Aldrich); *This Is My Love* (54, Heisler); *Silver Lode* (54, Allan Dwan); *Foxfire* (55, Joseph Pevney); *Storm Fear* (56, Cornel Wilde); *Battle Hymn* (57, Douglas Sirk); *The Burglar* (57, Paul Wendkos); *Walk a Tightrope* (63, Frank Nesbitt); *Taggart* (64, R. G. Springsteen); *The Flight of the Phoenix* (65, Aldrich); and *Stranger on the Run* (67, Don Siegel).

Robert Duvall,
b. San Diego, California, 1931
Was ever a role better designed for its actor than that of Tom Hagen in both parts of *The Godfather*? Robert Duvall the actor relates to high stardom like an Irishman among Italians. He is not beautiful or forceful enough to carry a big film—his starring parts reveal both his limitations and his lack of clout. But stars and Italians alike

depend on his efficiency, his tidying up around their grand gestures, his being perfect shortstop on a team of personality sluggers. His Tom Hagen is a detailed study of a self-effacing man, a time server, someone fulfilled by being discreet and helpful. A hero worshiper, perhaps, all the more vulnerable at the end of *Part II* when Michael Corleone deliberately humiliates him: a trusted servant is always a slave to such tyranny. Duvall has worked harder than any of his star contemporaries. He seems likely to remain a treasured support, but on occasions his prominent forehead and his possessed gaze have conveyed an anguish or obsession that might be more worthwhile than moody glamour.

He was the son of a rear-admiral, and he was educated at Principia College before entering the army. He studied at the Neighborhood Playhouse in New York and was praised in a 1955 off-Broadway production of *A View from the Bridge*. Duvall has remained attached to the stage, as witness his villain in *Wait Until Dark* and his championing of David Mamet's *American Buffalo*.

His first movie role was as the recluse in *To Kill a Mockingbird* (62, Robert Mulligan). His early parts were mostly in a vein of troubled loneliness that testifies to the staring severity of his face: a catatonic in *Captain Newman M.D.* (63, David Miller); the forlorn husband of Janice Rule in *The Chase* (66, Arthur Penn); *Countdown* (68, Robert Altman); *The Detective* (68, Gordon Douglas); *Bullitt* (68, Peter Yates); *True Grit* (69, Henry Hathaway); very good in *The Rain People* (69, Francis Ford Coppola); an outsider driven mad by the gang in *M*°*A*°*S*°*H* (70, Altman); *The Revolutionary* (70, Paul Williams); *THX 1138* (70, George Lucas); *Lawman* (71, Michael Winner); *Tomorrow* (71, Joseph Anthony), from a Faulkner story in a part he had created onstage; Jesse James in *The Great Northfield Minnesota Raid* (71, Philip Kaufman); *The Godfather* (71, Coppola); *Joe Kidd* (72, John Sturges); *Lady Ice* (73, Tom Gries); *Badge 373* (73, Howard W. Koch); as a loner taking on the mob in *The Outfit* (73, John Flynn); *The Godfather, Part II* (74, Coppola); as the mogul in *The Conversation* (74, Coppola), as impressive and as remote as his Doberman; *Breakout* (75, Gries); *The Killer Elite* (75, Sam Peckinpah); the domineering boss in *Network* (76, Sidney Lumet); a German in *The Eagle Has Landed* (76, Sturges); as Dr. Watson in *The Seven-Percent Solution* (76, Herbert Ross); and *The Greatest* (77, Gries).

In 1977, he directed a documentary, *We're Not the Jet Set*, about Nebraska farm people he had met during the making of *The Rain People*. He was the son hating his stronger father in *The Betsy* (78, Daniel Petrie); a dynamic Kilgore in *Apocalypse Now* (79, Coppola); and *The Great Santini* (79, Lewis Carlino).

Just before doing Kilgore, he had played the lead on TV in *Ike: The War Years* (78, Melville Shavelson). He was the cop in *True Confessions* (81, Ulu Grosbard); *The Pursuit of D. B. Cooper* (81, Roger Spottiswoode). He directed *Angelo, My Love* (83), and in the same year won the best actor Oscar for *Tender Mercies* (83, Bruce Beresford).

He may have felt that that would lead to star roles, but Duvall is by nature a supporting actor: on TV in *The Terry Fox Story* (83, Ralph Thomas); *The Stone Boy* (84, Chris Cain); *The Natural* (84, Barry Levinson); brilliant in *The Lightship* (86, Jerzy Skolimowski) as a very swishy Southern gent; *Hotel Colonial* (87, Cinzia Torrini); *Let's Get Harry* (87, Stuart Rosenberg); *Colors* (88, Dennis Hopper); outstanding on TV in *Lonesome Dove* (89, Simon Wincer); *The Handmaid's Tale* (90, Volker Schlondorff); *Days of Thunder* (90, Tony Scott); *A Show of Force* (90, Bruno Barretto); excellent as the father in *Rambling Rose* (91, Martha Coolidge); on TV doing *Stalin* (92, Ivan Passer); *Falling Down* (93, Joel Schumacher); *The Plague* (93, Luis Puenzo); *Geronimo* (93, Walter Hill); *Wrestling Ernest Hemingway* (93, Randa Haines); and *The Paper* (94, Ron Howard).

Duvall's good-natured persistence is one of the more comforting things in contemporary film. He does not resist every offer to be hammy. He walks through some parts. But he retains the passions for such things as his film *The Apostle* (97), one of the events of the decade. Over seventy now, he plans a new film about one of his passions—*Assassination Tango* (it's the dance he loves). The recent credits are: *Something to Talk About* (95, Lasse Hallstrom); *The Stars Fell on Henrietta* (95, James Keach); *The Scarlet Letter* (95, Roland Joffe); *A Family Thing* (96, Richard Pearce); *Phenomenon* (96, Jon Turteltaub); *Sling Blade* (96, Billy Bob Thornton); as Eichmann on TV in *The Man Who Captured Eichmann* (96, William A. Graham); *The Gingerbread Man* (98, Altman); *Deep Impact* (98, Mimi Leder); a crusty lawyer in *A Civil Action* (98, Steven Zaillian); *Gone in Sixty Seconds* (00, Dominic Sena); *A Shot at Glory* (00, Michael Corrente); *The 6th Day* (00, Spottiswoode); *John Q* (02, Nick Cassavetes); as Robert E. Lee in *Gods and Generals* (02, Ronald F. Maxwell).

He danced in and directed *Assassination Tango* (02), and he acted in *Open Range* (03, Kevin Costner).

Shelley Duvall, b. Houston, Texas, 1950

Only once has Shelley Duvall played a large part for anyone except Robert Altman—and that is her wife in *The Shining* (80, Stanley Kubrick) where, arguably, she is meant as a parody of helplessness, and felt as the casting coup of misogyny. (Like Jack Torrance, Kubrick seemed to regard women as children, hags, or silent beauties—no character allowed.)

It's as if most other directors didn't know what to do with Duvall—was she too odd, too Texan, too much an Olive Oyl in waiting? Yet in *3 Women* (77, Altman), she is endlessly intriguing—was that acting, casting, or Altman's eye? Elsewhere, Altman used her (often briefly) in *Brewster McCloud* (70); *McCabe and Mrs. Miller* (71); in the lead in *Thieves Like Us* (74); as the kooky L.A. Joan in *Nashville* (75); *Buffalo Bill and the Indians* (76), as President Cleveland's wife; and at last as Olive Oyl in *Popeye* (80).

In addition, she had a scene in *Annie Hall* (77, Woody Allen) for her strangeness; and she appeared in *Time Bandits* (81, Terry Gilliam); *Roxanne* (87, Fred Schepisi); and *Suburban Commando* (91, Burt Kennedy).

But in the 1980s the unaccountable woman became a very successful producer for cable TV, notably with *Faerie Tale Theatre*, a variable series, but one of the few on American TV that sought to reach children in their gentler imaginations. It also gave interesting opportunities to directors and actors.

She plays small roles now, or bigger parts in films about children (or sometimes horror): *Underneath* (95, Steven Soderbergh); *The Portrait of a Lady* (96, Jane Campion); *Twilight of the Ice Nymphs* (97, Guy Maddin); *Shadow Zone: My Teacher Ate My Homework* (97, Stephen Williams); *Alone* (97, Michael Lindsay-Hogg); *Tale of the Mummy* (98, Russell Mulcahy); *Casper Meets Wendy* (98, Sean McNamara); *Home Fries* (98, Dean Parisot); *Big Monster on Campus* (98, Mitch Marcus); *The 4th Floor* (Josh Klausner); *Dreams in the Attic* (00, Bob Willems); *Manna from Heaven* (01, Gabrielle Burton).

Julien Duvivier (1896–1967),
b. Lille, France

1919: *Haceldama*. 1920: *La Réincarnation de Serge Renaudier*. 1921: *L'Agonie des Aigles* (codirected with Bernard Deschamps). 1922: *Les Roquevillard; L'Ouragan sur la Montagne; Der Unheimliche Gast*. 1923: *Le Reflet de Claude Mercoeur; Credo; L'Oeuvre Immortelle*. 1924: *La Nuit de la Revanche; Coeurs Farouches; La Machine à Refaire la Vie* (codirected with H. Lepage) (d). 1925: *L'Abbé Constantin; Poil de Carotte*. 1926: *Le Mariage de Mlle. Beulemans*. 1927: *L'Agonie de Jérusalem; Le Mystère de la Tour Eiffel; L'Homme à l'Hispano*. 1928: *Le Tourbillon de Paris; La Divine Croisière*. 1929: *La Vie Miraculeuse de Thérèse Martin; Maman Colibri; Au Bonheur des Dames*. 1930: *David Golder*. 1931: *Cinq Gentilshommes Maudits*. 1932: *Allo Berlin! Ici Paris!; Poil de Carotte; La Vénus du Collège*. 1933: *La Tête d'un Homme; La Machine à Refaire la Vie* (d); *Le Petit Roi*. 1934: *Le Paquebot*

Tenacity; Maria Chapdelaine. 1935: *Golgotha; L'Homme du Jour*. 1936: *La Bandera; La Belle Équipe; Le Golem*. 1937: *Pépé le Moko; Un Carnet de Bal*. 1938: *The Great Waltz*. 1939: *La Fin du Jour; La Charrette Fantôme*. 1940: *Untel Père et Fils*. 1941: *Lydia*. 1942: *Tales of Manhattan*. 1943: *Flesh and Fantasy*. 1944: *The Imposter*. 1946: *Panique*. 1948: *Anna Karenina*. 1949: *Au Royaume des Cieux; Black Jack*. 1950: *Sous le Ciel de Paris Coule la Seine*. 1951: *Le Petit Monde de Don Camillo*. 1953: *La Fête à Henriette; Le Retour de Don Camillo*. 1954: *L'Affaire Maurizius; Marianne de Ma Jeunesse*. 1956: *Voici le Temps des Assassins*. 1957: *L'Homme à l'Imperméable; Pot-Bouille*. 1958: *Marie-Octobre; La Femme et le Pantin*. 1960: *Boulevard; La Grande Vie*. 1961: *La Chambre Ardente*. 1963: *Le Diable et les Dix Commandements*. 1964: *Chair de Poule*. 1967: *Diaboliquement Votre*.

Duvivier was a professional survivor in troubled times: a man who managed always to look spruce but seldom original or interesting. He never lost composure in a long, industrious career, but he never found much else. Beginning as an actor, he was assistant to Louis Feuillade and Marcel L'Herbier. As a director, he displayed a cyclical complacency, remaking several of his own films, including *La Machine à Refaire la Vie*, a documentary on the movie process. During the 1930s he was very successful commercially: *Poil de Carotte*, *Pépé le Moko*, and *Un Carnet de Bal* are all blandly proficient works. As war came nearer, Duvivier went to MGM to direct Luise Rainer in the inane *Great Waltz*. By 1941, he was in Britain for Korda making *Lydia*—a virtual remake of *Carnet de Bal*; and he returned to Hollywood to make the episodic *Tales of Manhattan* and *Flesh and Fantasy*. *The Imposter*, starring Jean Gabin, was made in Algeria—the setting for his melancholy thriller, *Pépé le Moko*—while *Anna Karenina*, again for Korda, starred an uneasy Vivien Leigh. These excursions into a rather lusher romance than France offered did not encourage Duvivier's fancy. It was in his character to be discreet with luxury— a less cautious man would have made Leigh relax. Duvivier returned to France and found a national hero in Fernandel's Don Camillo. He went on, shy of the beauty of Danielle Darrieux in *Marie-Octobre*, of Françoise Arnoul, Micheline Presle, and Darrieux in *Le Diable et les Dix Commandements*. It is hard to feel warmly toward a director reluctant to celebrate beautiful women.

Allan Dwan (Joseph Aloysius Dwan)
(1885–1981), b. Toronto, Canada

1914: *Richelieu; Wildflower; The Country Chairman; The Straight Road; The Conspiracy; The Unwelcome Mrs. Hatch*. 1915: *The Dancing Girl; David Harum; The Love Route; The Commanding*

Officer; May Blossom; The Pretty Sister of Jose; A Girl of Yesterday; The Foundling; Jordan Is a Hard Road. 1916: Betty of Greystone; The Habit of Happiness; The Good Bad Man; An Innocent Magdalene; The Half-Breed; Manhattan Madness; Fifty-Fifty. 1917: Panthea; The Fighting Odds; A Modern Musketeer. 1918: Mr. Fix-It; Bound in Morocco; He Comes Up Smiling. 1919: Cheating Cheaters; Getting Mary Married; The Dark Star; Soldiers of Fortune. 1920: The Luck of the Irish; The Forbidden Thing. 1921: A Perfect Crime; A Broken Doll; The Scoffer; The Sin of Martha Queed; In the Heart of a Fool. 1922: The Hidden Woman; Superstition; Robin Hood. 1923: The Glimpses of the Moon; Lawful Larceny; Zaza; Big Brother. 1924: A Society Scandal; Manhandled; Her Love Story; Wages of Virtue; Argentine Love. 1925: Night Life of New York; The Coast of Folly; Stage Struck. 1926: Sea Horses; Padlocked; Tin Gods; Summer Bachelors. 1927: The Music Master; The Joy Girl; East Side, West Side; French Dressing. 1928: The Big Noise. 1929: The Iron Mask; Tide of Empire; The Far Call; Frozen Justice; South Sea Rose. 1930: What a Widow!; Man to Man. 1931: Chances; Wicked. 1932: While Paris Sleeps. 1933: Her First Affair; Counsel's Opinion. 1934: The Morning After; Hollywood Party (codirected with Richard Boleslavsky and Roy Rowland). 1935: Black Sheep; Navy Wife. 1936: The Song and Dance Man; Human Cargo; High Tension; 15 Maiden Lane. 1937: Woman-Wise; That I May Live; One Mile from Heaven; Heidi. 1938: Rebecca of Sunnybrook Farm; Josette; Suez. 1939: The Three Musketeers; The Gorilla; Frontier Marshall. 1940: Sailor's Lady; Young People; Trail of the Vigilantes. 1941: Look Who's Laughing; Rise and Shine. 1942: Friendly Enemies; Here We Go Again. 1943: Around the World. 1944: Up in Mabel's Room; Abroad With Two Yanks. 1945: Brewster's Millions; Getting Gertie's Garter. 1946: Rendezvous with Annie. 1947: Calendar Girl; Northwest Outpost; Driftwood. 1948: The Inside Story; Angel in Exile. 1949: Sands of Iwo Jima. 1950: Surrender. 1951: Belle le Grand; The Wild Blue Yonder. 1952: I Dream of Jeanie; Montana Belle. 1953: The Woman They Almost Lynched; Sweethearts on Parade. 1954: Flight Nurse; Silver Lode; Passion; Cattle Queen of Montana. 1955: Escape to Burma; Pearl of the South Pacific; Tennessee's Partner. 1956: Slightly Scarlet; Hold Back the Night. 1957: The River's Edge; The Restless Breed. 1958: Enchanted Island. 1961: The Most Dangerous Man Alive.

Dwan's filmography ought to be sufficient tribute—except that it is limited to films of four reels or more. In the years 1911–14, he made at least another two hundred one- or two-reelers. These were churned out at the American Film Company after he had begun as a lighting man at Essanay in 1909. In 1913, he moved to Universal, in 1914 to Famous Players, and in 1915 to Griffith's Triangle Company. Within the next few years he worked for Douglas Fairbanks and Mary Pickford and, after Robin Hood, he went to Famous Players–Lasky where he made several of Gloria Swanson's best films. But in 1926 he joined Fox and remained there with occasional distractions—like his trip to England, 1933–34—until 1941. While there, he usually directed second features, but returned to prominence with two of the better Shirley Temple films and the spectacular Suez. He moved to RKO and worked for Edward Small before joining Republic in 1945. His movies there were haunted by the interference of Herbert Yates, the icy presence of Vera Ralston, and the penury of the studio. But he produced films of constant invention, charm, and action. Sands of Iwo Jima has the surge of unaccustomed resources. In 1954, he went back to RKO and the producer Benedict Bogeaus. The films they made together are oddly assured products of working circumstances worthy of Catch-22. Only in 1961 did Dwan retire from a long and honorable battle against every handicap the industry could invent.

Inevitably, Dwan is best known for his more recent pictures, the fragmentary splendor of his travails with Yates and Bogeaus: the very funny situation in Rendezvous with Annie; Natalie Wood signaling her talent in Driftwood; Sands of Iwo Jima; the B-29 in The Wild Blue Yonder; Jane Russell in Montana Belle; the lunatic transposition of sexual roles in The Woman They Almost Lynched; the happy acceptance of the Western genre in Silver Lode and Tennessee's Partner; the florid erotic rivalry of Rhonda Fleming and Arlene Dahl in Slightly Scarlet; the violence of The River's Edge; the hysterical eavesdropping of The Restless Breed.

In almost every case, these are distinct if small-scale treasures brought home against great odds. Dwan himself preferred silent pictures and remembers Robin Hood, Manhandled, and Big Brother fondly. Who can argue, or present a coherent view of Dwan's career? Few have seen or can remember more than a fraction of his output. Only two obvious conclusions remain. Dwan was a natural, unpretentious storyteller, capable of real invention on the grand and the intimate scale; but with such competence and determined survival, how did he come to make so many forlorn films when men of far less talent were given better projects? Dwan told Peter Bogdanovich that he signed too many stupid contracts, but that he had no regrets. That sunniness speaks for his real nature and his origins in the days when one made two films a week. He is the Jack Crabb of the movie world, capable of endorsing both the boyish pleasure of all Fairbanks's vaulting and the delicious Ritz Brothers parody of musketeering made in

1939. Dwan's liking for visual narrative proved stronger than all the foolish corners he was forced to occupy. His flexibility was proof of imaginative cheerfulness.

E

Clint Eastwood (Clinton Eastwood Jr.),
b. San Francisco, 1930
1971: *Play Misty for Me.* 1973: *High Plains Drifter; Breezy.* 1975: *The Eiger Sanction.* 1976: *The Outlaw Josey Wales.* 1977: *The Gauntlet.* 1980: *Bronco Billy.* 1982: *Firefox; Honkytonk Man.* 1983: *Sudden Impact.* 1985: *Pale Rider.* 1986: *Heartbreak Ridge.* 1988: *Bird.* 1989: *Pink Cadillac.* 1990: *White Hunter, Black Heart; The Rookie.* 1992: *Unforgiven.* 1993: *A Perfect World.* 1995: *The Bridges of Madison County.* 1997: *Absolute Power; Midnight in the Garden of Good and Evil.* 1999: *True Crime.* 2000: *Space Cowboys.* 2002: *Blood Work.* 2003: *Mystic River.*

In September 1993, at London's National Film Theatre, H.R.H. Prince Charles presented Clint Eastwood with the fellowship of the British Film Institute. Their briefly shared stage was a fascinating study in celebrity and fame's divinity. A visitor from another planet, advised on how to recognize modern royalty—its natural eminence, its grace and authority, its sense of divine right made agnostic in simple glamour—would have had no doubt which man was the prince. In a tuxedo, with close-cut salt and silver hair, a gaunt head, and a tranquil boy's smile, Clint may be as good as sixty-three has ever looked. About a month before the date in London, he had had a child by the actress Frances Fisher (from *Unforgiven*). There had been no scandal or mockery. Nearly everything that comes to Eastwood now is rendered fitting by his majesty. Whereas, Charles Windsor (he sounds like a spiv who sells secondhand cars off the South Circular Road) can hardly pick up the phone without making himself a laughingstock, and he could not stand beside Clint without looking uneasy, a sad fidget, a tailor's dummy denied life or glory.

Has it occurred to you that, by 1994, Clint Eastwood was among the very few Americans admired and respected at home and abroad, without qualification or irony? When the onetime mayor of Carmel insists that he is not running for anything else, we feel regret. We have had such shifty actors looking after us—don't we deserve Clint? For he has become an authentically heroic image, a man cast in Gary Cooper's rock, even if his eyes are still rather more self-satisfied than Cooper's. He is a magnificent businessman, the boss at Malpaso Productions, and golden goose for the studios lucky enough to have his films, a model of managerial economy and fruitful independence. Has there ever been so unneurotic, so steadfast, or so steadily improving a moviemaker? As a director, he matches his own work as an actor: acutely aware of his limitations, he knows how to look good, how to serve and broadcast himself, while doing interesting, honest work in the mainstream. There is nothing coy, boastful, or unstable, nothing out of balance or true. As he said at the National Film Theatre, he felt himself lucky—and he leaves us feeling fortunate to be in his presence (a true attribute of stardom). There is no one else in Hollywood today who can bear up under such success without the savage, twisted grin of plunder, vengeance, or absurdity. He is our knight—somehow—and he shames the astrologers, the alchemists, the courtesans, and the robber barons who otherwise run the court.

By the late seventies, Eastwood had already proved himself in three distinct areas: on TV, in Italian Westerns, and as a Don Siegel hero. His own company, Malpaso (named after a creek in Carmel, his primary residence), had allowed him to direct his first film, *Play Misty for Me*, a generous nod in Siegel's direction and an intriguing study of masculine assurance whittled away by feminine paranoia. Even then, Eastwood had wit and humor enough to undermine the very male supremacy that had made him famous. It is in the area of self-education that Eastwood is most liberal.

His parents were not well off. Clint had worked as a lumberjack and served in the army before being signed up as a tall, pretty athlete by Universal. He played tiny parts in *Francis in the Navy* (51, Arthur Lubin); *Lady Godiva* (55, Lubin); *Never Say Goodbye* (56, Jerry Hopper); *The First Traveling Saleslady* (56, Lubin); *Ambush at Cimarron Pass* (58, Jodie Copeland); and *Lafayette Escadrille* (58, William Wellman). Wider fame came with a seven-year spell (1959–66) playing Rowdy Yates in the TV series *Rawhide* (where he started to take a hand in script and direction).

That status helped him go to Italy to play the taciturn "man with no name" in Sergio Leone's trilogy of mercenary violence and Spanish deserts: *A Fistful of Dollars* (64); *For a Few Dollars More* (66); *The Good, the Bad and the Ugly* (67); and in an episode from *Le Streghe* (66, Vittorio de Sica). Wildly successful and influential, those films had a camp attitude that Eastwood gradually disowned. But he came back to America to set up Malpaso and to make the first American Italian Western, *Hang 'em High* (68, Ted Post). Two lavish attempts to extend his appeal into war film and the musical were less than totally successful: *Where Eagles Dare* (68, Brian G. Hutton); *Paint Your Wagon* (69, Joshua Logan); and *Kelly's Heroes* (70, Hutton). He could still look stiff and anxious as an actor, as if persuaded by Leone that it was enough to be an icon.

Eastwood was luckier to find himself, his humor, and some ease in the increasingly beleaguered heroes of Don Siegel. Their relationship proved mutually beneficial. Siegel got a new lease of life while Eastwood found an education—"if there is one thing I learned from Don Siegel, it's to know what you want to shoot and to know what you're seeing when you see it." Their films together are *Coogan's Bluff* (68); *Two Mules for Sister Sara* (69); *The Beguiled* (70); *Dirty Harry* (71); *Play Misty for Me* (with Siegel playing a small role); and *Escape from Alcatraz* (79).

As an actor, Eastwood flowered under Siegel, exchanging arbitrary brutality for an impressive gallery of brutalized loners. His work in *Dirty Harry*, for instance, is more complex and enticing than Gene Hackman's extravagantly commended mugging in *The French Connection*. While Hackman turns the subway sequence into situation slapstick, in *Dirty Harry* Eastwood gives a very moving account of the infuriated lawman driven to abandon his badge by the intractable growth of disorder and liberal bureaucracy. *Harry* was called fascist in some quarters, but by now it is clearer that Eastwood was offering a tortured vision of conservative ideals at breaking point.

Eastwood was still torn in different directions—to make easy hits, or to insist on new territory and attitudes. *Joe Kidd* (72, John Sturges) showed that he might revert to enigmatic violence. His second direction, *High Plains Drifter*, owed more to the Leone films than to Siegel. In *Magnum Force* (73, Post) and *The Enforcer* (76, James Fargo) one saw how Detective Harry Callahan could become a cynical institution, complete with vicious one-liners and total destruction. *The Eiger Sanction* was his silliest film. But *Josey Wales* (taken away from its writer, Philip Kaufman) was an unusual, picaresque Western, exposing its resolute hero in search of vengeance to the wintry humor of an old Indian and a disorderly group of eccentrics.

It was remarkable how, in the eighties, more "distinguished" careers—Beatty, Hoffman, Redford, say—dwindled or stalled, while the ostensibly "lower-class" Eastwood had learned, improved, developed, and become one of the most respected and loved figures in American film. The rather dangerous Clint of *Dirty Harry* yielded to a grizzled veteran, allegedly older, wiser, and gentler.

There is argument still over Eastwood the director—though no one can dispute the benefits of having done ten films in the years 1980–90 (so few match that figure, let alone anyone who acted in nine of the ten!). Moreover, Eastwood's refinement as an icon has affected his directing: there is a larger air of wisdom, irony, and regret that now coexists with his very practical, professional pre-

cision. I don't yet feel eloquence, let alone poetry or beauty, and I have to underline the failure of *Bird*, his most ambitious film. The music was cleaned up, and Parker was sanitized in the casting of the sweet Forest Whitaker. The real Parker, I suspect, was rougher and more aggressive. Indeed, *Bird* left the feeling that Eastwood was closer in temperament to Benny Goodman or Stan Kenton.

Bronco Billy and *Honkytonk Man* were welcome departures from male supremacy: *Tightrope* (84, Richard Tuggle) was a startling treatment of sexual dysfunction in the hard cop, and an altogether impressive, if disconcerting, picture. Against that, *City Heat* (84, Richard Benjamin) with Clint and Burt Reynolds, *Firefox, Sudden Impact,* and *Pale Rider* were risk-free and mind-dulling meal tickets.

White Hunter, Black Heart was another honorable failure, and one that showed Eastwood's definite limits as an actor. *Unforgiven* was his best performance, and certainly his best script (from David Webb Peoples). But the film was overpraised: Why or how can this man leave his children on the prairie? And how does his understandable ineptness as a gunfighter suddenly and conveniently fall aside to reveal the old Leone-esque angel of death?

But this may be a touch too grudging. Eastwood has become a surprising, enterprising man: he produced the documentary *Thelonious Monk: Straight, No Chaser* (88, Charlotte Zwerin); he was a friend to *'Round Midnight* (86, Bertrand Tavernier); and he sponsored the directorial debut of a girlfriend in *Ratboy* (86, Sondra Locke). In addition, he keeps rare company: not just an orangutan in *Every Which Way But Loose* (78, Fargo) and *Any Which Way You Can* (80, Buddy Van Horn), but a string of interesting, odd (and economical) actresses: Sondra Locke, Marsha Mason, Diane Venora, Bernadette Peters, and Geneviève Bujold.

When *Unforgiven* won best picture and best director (with the supporting actor Oscar going to Gene Hackman), the enshrinement of Eastwood was manifest. His next film—*In the Line of Fire* (93, Wolfgang Petersen)—was its perfect proof: this was mainstream entertainment, beautifully cast and played, suspenseful—and ridiculous. It gave Clint his best screen romance yet (with Rene Russo) and a superb opponent in John Malkovich (all the better that they did not quite play scenes together, thus masking the radical clash in acting styles). The picture had everything—except one hint or glimmer that Eastwood wants to be more than the best and smoothest running engine on the road. He *is* a Cadillac, yet he prefers a Ford superstructure. He is earnestly middlebrow, and dedicated to efficiency. Yet Gary Cooper—the obvious comparison—became a tragic figure. The test that awaits Eastwood is whether he can find himself in neurosis and failure.

Not yet. In years of mounting glory and respect, Eastwood directed six more films (from *Madison County* to *Blood Work*). Let's be candid: if the last was mild, geriatric fun, *Absolute Power* was silly, *True Crime* was lazy, *Madison County* was in awe of Meryl Streep, and *Garden* was atrocious. Not one was interesting, memorable or the work of an individual—as opposed to a placid production system. As time passes, I suspect, Clint will seem merely a success, a classic producer, a pragmatist who could never muster enough interest in his own work.

Thomas Alva Edison (1847–1931),
b. Milan, Ohio

Just because a man gets credit for inventing the incandescent filament doesn't keep him from being dull. For all his outpouring of patents, innovations, and conveniences, Edison the man always seemed grim, suspicious, and costive. There's an eerie contradiction between his own humorlessness and the way so many of his inventions made more fun for more people more of the time. Yet Edison probably reckoned he'd discovered the light bulb so that people could work longer hours. He's a grinch, and only his investors warmed to him.

The funniest thing he ever said—"Everyone steals in industry and commerce. I've stolen a lot myself. The thing is to know how to steal"—was actually meant to be helpful. It also alerts us to his most significant pioneering in terms of movie history: it was Edison, the chronic thief, who got lawyers in to protect his rights. And today there are more lawyers than bulbs.

Edison employed people, and his involvement with film is really all to do with W.K.L. Dickson (1860–1935), an inventor who used Edison's money and resources to develop a camera, a system of film stock, and a means to mount the show. In 1891, they put in a patent for a Kinetoscope camera and the subsequent peepshow apparatus: Edison's invention was to have a system by which a viewer put his or her eyes to a hole and saw whatever was on the filmstrip. It was movie, but it was Walkman movie as opposed to theatrical show.

By 1892, Dickson had established the "Black Maria" in West Orange, New Jersey—a crude film studio where he recorded scenes on film from Eastman. In 1894, Kinetoscope parlors were opening up, and doing very well. Dickson urged Edison to pursue some kind of projector—a light show for the masses. But Edison was unimpressed. He said that in all of America there would be no call for more than ten projectors. And then, the Lumières put on the first film show in Paris in 1895.

Of course, once he had been beaten, Edison caught up and tried to rewrite the rules. He began a lengthy campaign to take credit for the invention, and this would lead him into a key role in the Motion Picture Patents Company. Court judgments made clear his meagre achievement, but Edison wanted everything, and he had the means to nail it down. He became the first great imperialist of the picture business, the harbinger of American TV series playing in huts in Third World countries.

Years later, MGM sought to celebrate the inventor with two films, *Young Tom Edison* (40, Norman Taurog) and *Edison the Man* (40, Clarence Brown), in which Mickey Rooney and Spencer Tracy played the thankless part. If only Edison had had one atom of the great Mick's fun!

Blake Edwards, b. Tulsa, Oklahoma, 1922
1955: *Bring Your Smile Along.* 1956: *He Laughed Last.* 1957: *Mister Cory.* 1958: *This Happy Feeling; The Perfect Furlough.* 1959: *Operation Petticoat; High Time.* 1961: *Breakfast at Tiffany's.* 1962: *Experiment in Terror/The Grip of Fear.* 1963: *Days of Wine and Roses.* 1964: *The Pink Panther; A Shot in the Dark.* 1965: *The Great Race.* 1966: *What Did You Do in the War, Daddy?.* 1967: *Gunn.* 1968: *The Party.* 1969: *Darling Lili.* 1971: *Wild Rovers.* 1972: *The Carey Treatment.* 1974: *The Tamarind Seed; The Return of the Pink Panther.* 1976: *The Pink Panther Strikes Again.* 1978: *The Revenge of the Pink Panther.* 1979: *10.* 1981: *S.O.B..* 1982: *Victor/Victoria; Trail of the Pink Panther.* 1983: *Curse of the Pink Panther; The Man Who Loved Women.* 1984: *Micki and Maude.* 1986: *A Fine Mess; That's Life.* 1987: *Blind Date.* 1988: *Sunset; Justin Case* (TV). 1989: *Skin Deep; Peter Gunn* (TV). 1991: *Switch.* 1993: *Son of the Pink Panther.*

Edwards was originally a writer and actor. As an actor, he appeared in *Ten Gentlemen from West Point* (42, Henry Hathaway); *Strangler of the Swamp* (45, Frank Wisbar); *Leather Gloves* (48, Richard Quine); *Panhandle* (48, Lesley Selander); and *Stampede* (49, Selander). He wrote the scripts for the two latter films, and for six Richard Quine films: *Rainbow 'Round My Shoulder* (52); *All Ashore* (53); *Cruisin' Down the River* (53); *Drive a Crooked Road* (54); *My Sister Eileen* (55); and the effervescent *Operation Madball* (57).

Like so many of his generation, Edwards has not lived up to the promise of his first few movies. In his case, the loss is sharper because he seemed wittier and more perceptive than most. Above all, he had a good writer's sense of character, dialogue, and construction, allied to an original, black-lacquer comedy. *Mister Cory* was an exceptional film and *Operation Petticoat* and *High Time* were tart comedies, with some of the extravagant fun of *Operation Madball.* But *Breakfast at Tiffany's*, despite being Edwards's best-looking film, was nervous of Capote's original and now looks like one of the series of American films made of bitter chocolate but with soft centers. *Experiment in Terror* was frightening, but no more than an exercise. *Days of Wine and Roses* went much deeper; indeed, its pessimism got out of artistic control and showed a dark side that Edwards has otherwise concealed. Inevitably, one compares it with *The Lost Weekend:* Edwards's is a more somber film, but it shares Wilder's fatal inability to see his characters as much more than lines in a script. The tidy sense of character, as so often in American cinema, tends to make neat drama out of tragic material.

Since then, Edwards has gradually lost his way. *The Pink Panther* shows all his wit, but *A Shot in the Dark* and *The Party* only illustrate the undisciplined talents of Peter Sellers. *Gunn* was the cinema version of a TV series launched by Edwards; *The Great Race* is high farce, much longer than it should be, but full of good jokes that build gradually; *What Did You Do in the War, Daddy?* is an entertaining exposure of military stereotypes. Most distressing, however, is *Darling Lili,* starring Edwards's second wife, Julie Andrews, and his most disastrous failure. *Wild Rovers* has a certain fatalistic charm, but the resort to a Western hinted at the way Edwards was running out of steam. *The Carey Treatment* lacked even the hopeless ambition of *Darling Lili* and seemed the work of a tired man.

He has worked occasionally as a writer on other people's films: *The Notorious Land-lady* (62, Quine); *Soldier in the Rain* (63, Ralph Nelson); and *Inspector Clouseau* (68, Bud Yorkin). Three more Panthers kept him working. What next— *The Pink Panther Born Free?*

In fact, not even the death of Peter Sellers (in 1980) deterred Edwards: he pushed on with three more ghostly Panthers, the one from old Sellers footage, the next with young comedian Ted Wass as a replacement, and finally with Roberto Benigni as Clouseau Jr.

For the rest, Edwards has gone from the crazy satire of *S.O.B.* and the gender confusion of *Victor/Victoria* into the flat doldrums of modern comedy. *The Man Who Loved Women* has Burt Reynolds in a reworking of Truffaut's film; several movies had star pairings that refused to get chemical—Dudley Moore and Amy Irving in *Micki and Maude;* Ted Danson and Howie Mandel in *A Fine Mess;* Kim Basinger and Bruce Willis in *Blind Date;* Willis and James Garner in *Sunset.* Worst of all, though, is Julie Andrews and Jack Lemmon in the insufferable *That's Life.* Life should have sued.

In 1993, the combined decision of the Directors' and the Writers' Guilds gave the Preston Sturges Award to Edwards. There was something so macabre, inappropriate, and inevitable in that decision—somehow the decline of Hollywood had been encapsulated.

Atom Egoyan, b. Cairo, Egypt, 1960
1984: *Next of Kin.* 1987: *Family Viewing.* 1989: *Speaking Parts.* 1991: *The Adjuster;* "En Passant," a segment from *Montréal Vu Par. . . .* 1993: *Calendar.* 1994: *Exotica.* 1997: *The Sweet Hereafter.* 1999: *Felicia's Journey.* 2000: *The Line.* 2001: *Diaspora* (s). 2002: *Ararat.*

Egoyan is a remarkable and admirable figure. Of Armenian descent, he was born in Egypt, where he lived for a few years as a child before moving to western Canada. To be a Canadian filmmaker is, in the words of a movie on which Egoyan assisted, to exist "in the shadow of Hollywood." And there is no country of which the ordinary American is more dismissive than Canada. But Egoyan has not simply made a fruitful career there, he has impressed the outside world—*The Sweet Hereafter,* his best-known film but not necessarily his best, won an Oscar nomination for directing (it succumbed to James Cameron and *Titanic*). Yet he does not seem to have been swayed away from his own course, which is quiet, introspective, rather wistful, and very fond of that delicate area where the imagination becomes the spirit.

After the University of Toronto, and having had painters for parents, he was drawn into filmmaking. He has also done a good deal of work for Canadian television, especially documentaries with musical subjects. Family is very important to him, and he regularly works with his wife, the actress Arsinée Khanjian.

Exotica drew a lot of attention in that it was a story of meetings at a strip club, and a model of his tender observation. Equally, *The Sweet Hereafter*—taken from a Russell Banks novel—in which an insurance man (Ian Holm) comes to a community devastated by a bus accident, explored so many subtle feelings beyond the evident tragedy. By those standards, *Felicia's Journey* (based on a William Trevor novel) seemed heavy-handed—but that may be a measure of Ian Holm being more inward an actor than Bob Hoskins. A masterpiece from Egoyan would come as no surprise.

Sergei Mikhailovitch Eisenstein
(1898–1948), b. Riga, Russia
1923: *Kinodnevik Glumova* (s). 1924: *Stachka/ Strike.* 1925: *Bronenosets Potyomkin/Battleship Potemkin.* 1927: *Oktyabre/October* (codirected with Grigori Alexandrov). 1928: *Staroie i Novoie/ The General Line* (codirected with Alexandrov). 1931–32: *Que Viva Mexico* (unfinished; material later edited by Marie Seton and released as *Time in the Sun,* 1939). 1936: *Bezhin Lug/Bezhin Meadow* (unfinished). 1938: *Alexander Nevsky* (codirected with Dmitri Vasiliev). 1942: *Ivan the Terrible, part 1* (released in 1945). 1945: *Ivan the Terrible, part 2* (not released until 1958).

The son of a Jewish architect, Eisenstein was deserted as a child by his mother and lived in Riga and St. Petersburg. He studied to be an architect but, after service in the Red Army, he went into the theatre as a painter and designer. In the early 1920s, he worked in experimental theatre before making his debut as a director in 1923 on a film used in a stage production by Alexander Ostrovsky. His next four films are the basis of his contested reputation and key works in the uneasy relationship between art and propaganda. Inside Russia, they made Eisenstein one of the most honored of Soviet artists; while abroad, he was hailed by radical intellectuals as the model creative director to shame the prostituted talents who had supposedly sold out to the stereotypes of commercial cinema.

That now seems a very unsatisfactory interpretation. Compared with the abiding influence on cinema of Renoir, Murnau, or Fritz Lang, it is no longer possible to view Eisenstein as the man who laid down the theoretical basis of the medium— the British Film Institute once had that as part of a trilogy, with Griffith supplying the alphabet and Chaplin the humanity.

It is true that early Eisenstein is a stirring propagandist: in those first four films, the identification with Soviet ideals and myths is based on concrete realization—the outraged faces and vivid human gestures of *Strike* and *Potemkin,* and the agricultural processes of *General Line.* But the argument of those films is often foolish and, ultimately, inhumane. Indeed, actual political machines never live up to the purity of their own early propaganda. The propagandist purpose in Eisenstein's films diminishes the human beings dressed up as authority just as uncompromisingly as the authorities are supposed to oppress the workers.

In short, the Soviet attitude to art was as narrow and totalitarian as its political history proved. One is less moved by the Odessa massacre in *Potemkin* than excited by it: the frenzied pictorial dynamism and the pulsing montage refute the message that cruelty is destructive. As montage always suggested, the sequence is cumulative, taking emphasis to the point of hysteria. Prejudice, bias, and emotional coldness are secondary to Eisenstein's eye for the physical expression of power. It is the titles that carry the message, the images that overwhelm it. If you wish to find pathos in Russian cinema it is in Dovzhenko; as for a view of the people that embodies naïve Bolshevik idealism, look to Dziga Vertov. With Eisenstein, you confront a demonic, baroque visual theatricality, helplessly adhering to the confused theories of his writing on film. And he was quickly in decline: *Strike* is the finest of his films, the one in which the images show an inflamed imagination and a director as much obsessed by Freud as by Marx—for

instance, Eisenstein's treatment of violence is always participatory and masochistic. The images alone suggest how well he might have acquitted himself in the horror genre.

Few of his admirers wondered why, in 1930, Eisenstein went to America. From childhood, he had spoken English, French, and German, and been familiar with European culture; but he was also an immense, ambitious egotist, inhibited by the growing retrenchment in Russia. If his actions can be judged, he went to America to relax—to find new company and new subjects. And this idol of the kino-clubs signed with Paramount: after several aborted projects, he settled for Theodore Dreiser's *An American Tragedy.* In the event, incompatibility was recognized before shooting began; the project was eventually taken up by von Sternberg, who made it into something immeasurably subtler than Eisenstein could have dreamed of.

In bizarre anticipation of Orson Welles some ten years later, Eisenstein went south, to Mexico, to make an epic documentary. The venture was sponsored by novelist Upton Sinclair. Over 100,000 feet of film were shot before Sinclair turned cold over the Russian's extravagance, tales of his lurid life in Mexico, and pressure from Stalin. The surviving footage reveals Eisenstein as a blazing decadent—increasingly preoccupied by the exotic yet striving for an iconography of Mexican morbidity. It is like dreadful Church baroque beside Buñuel's pungent theses nailed on a door.

Eisenstein went slowly home, too famous to be abandoned, but often too ill to trouble the authorities. He was clearly persecuted by the bureaucracy: Paul Robeson as Toussaint L'Ouverture fell through; and *Bezhin Meadow,* based on a Turgenev sketch, was abandoned and Eisenstein made to admit to its failings. He escaped into the historical setting of *Alexander Nevsky,* his most spectacular film and his most plainly American in style. The allegory in *Nevsky* attacked Germany and the film was played down after the Soviet-Nazi pact; Eisenstein was also made to broadcast to Germany, welcoming the unexpected alliance.

Ivan the Terrible was made under stress of war, but it suffers least from economy. Indeed, it is his most ornate film, with the actors reduced to gesturing gargoyles, their bodies subordinated to his all-important visual shapes, themselves an unhealthy mixture of iconography and melodrama. What does *Ivan* mean, setting aside the suffocating tedium that comes from its remorseless pictorial richness? It seems to me that it endorses the harsh stress on authority that Ivan pursues: again, the style of the film is like that of the tyrant. Some said that the movie was a disapproving comment on Stalin; and part 2 (including its garish color) was banned by the state and the director once more instructed to recant. The explanation is not clear, and one must allow something for the inane contortions of Soviet bureaucracy. A plan for part 3 was shelved and Eisenstein's heart condition steadily deteriorated. There are those who still acclaim him, but his influence is now hard to detect.

So I became someone who hardly watched Eisenstein films any longer. If they came my way, my eyes were already clenched in regret. I could not help but blame Eisenstein for all the nonsense written about him, and for the fanciful position thrust upon him of montage pioneer.

My antagonism relaxed, gradually, on the morning of November 2, 1988, as I explored an art exhibit, "Eisenstein at Ninety," at London's Hayward Gallery (the show had originated at the Museum of Modern Art in Oxford). There were television monitors playing scenes from the films, to be sure, but there was so much else: the crowded life of Eisenstein, the range of things he read, saw, and was intrigued by; his psychology, emotional and jazzy with Freudian prospects; the astonishing graphic work that seemed to spill out on paper like ink, or blood; and the delight in dance, gesture, and theatrical moments. The movies were but a part of the whole, and not necessarily the most lively. Eisenstein was more compelling to me as a painter, and as a life lived out with a self-mocking, cartoony exuberance. For he had a brilliance that elected to play the buffoon. He was a shooting star whose course helped us see the desperate but inescapable adjacency of the old Russia, Bolshevism, Amerika, and Mexico. His life was like a journal with drawings, and when one sees the whole strip form, then montage yields to mosaic. There is a gaiety, a frenzy, and a cruelty in the drawings that are missing in the movies. Suppose that—like Griffith—Eisenstein was one of the last geniuses of raw theatre who found himself trapped in movies . . .

Michael Eisner,

b. Mount Kisco, New York, 1942

On Sunday, September 16, 2001, the ABC network on American television premiered an alleged biography of Walt Disney—an atrociously rose-colored picture about the man in this book and in the culture of the world who has probably had the most influence. This broadcast took place five days after the demolition of the World Trade Center towers in New York City. It played with commercials—whereas in the days after the disaster in New York, ABC, like other networks, had forsaken them (presumably on grounds of "taste").

It goes without saying—and it did go without saying—that ABC is now part of the business empire that includes Disney. It was taken for granted that the American public no longer cared about such conflicts of interest and had no real conception of historical objectivity—so why

bother? But the program was introduced and concluded (this is called bookending—as if books any longer had anything to do with the state of things) by film of Michael Eisner, head of the Disney Company, telling us how much everyone at Disney felt for the dead and those left behind—but isn't entertainment useful at such times?

It is not Mr. Eisner's fault that he looks like a thug and speaks in a way that makes you want to get out of the room. It is certainly not his fault that he may remind us of Shrek. But it was, presumably, his decision to make and run the show and to think that a few cans of syrup would ease away any obstruction to our taking in the feeble ad for Disney.

Mr. Eisner is one of the most richly rewarded executives in the U.S. He began in television, and then moved to Paramount, where he was chief operating officer from 1976 to 1984. After that, he joined Disney, revived it after years of faltering, led it into the making of regular movies—from *Pretty Woman* to *Pearl Harbor*—as well as reviving the animated feature, and carrying the pleasure-dome principle into Europe with Euro Disney. Though, of late, the Disney and ABC numbers have faltered, I am certain that he works ferociously and that he is a brilliant businessman, whose immense salary and bonus schedules can be justified. He has had to have heart operations, and he has survived such things as the death of his second-in-command, Frank Wells, the defection of his onetime lieutenant Jeffrey Katzenberg (the mind behind *Shrek*), as well as his own misguided hiring of Michael Ovitz. He masterminded the merger of Disney with ABC and Cap Cities. He is a giant figure, breathlessly positive and chronically shallow. And—as Kane once said of Walter Thatcher—he represents everything I hate.

Denholm Elliott (1922–92),

b. London, England

In 1968, in his *Guide to British Cinema*, Denis Gifford said of Denholm Elliott that he was a "gentlemanly lead now skillfully adding a touch of mannered decay to character parts." Well, indeed. The graduate from Malvern College had been a fine young lieutenant in *The Cruel Sea* (53, Charles Frend) and a hero with distinct hints of class. Elliott had been a prisoner of war of the Germans for three years, and he was married to Virginia McKenna in the mid-fifties. If he let down some of those hopes, and if the "decay" became a little florid at times, still Elliott (who died of AIDS) was for years a cherished character actor in whom the flickering light of decency never went out—no matter the temptation or the opportunity. He was the kind of actor adored by other actors, which is a way of saying that his combined resources of technique, observation, and kindness could get away with nearly anything. The list is long, but one must always remember that an actor at Elliott's level lived from one phone call to the next. That surely helps account for his confused look of desperation and absurdity.

He made his debut in *Dear Mr. Prohack* (49, Thornton Freeland) and then got a break in *The Sound Barrier* (52, David Lean). After that he was in *The Holly and the Ivy* (52, George More O'Ferrall); *The Ringer* (52, Guy Hamilton); *The Heart of the Matter* (53, O'Ferrall); *They Who Dare* (53, Lewis Milestone); *Lease of Life* (54, Frend); *The Man Who Loved Redheads* (54, Harold French); *The Night My Number Came Up* (55, Leslie Norman); *Pacific Destiny* (56, Wolf Rilla).

There was then a notable gap in his work, coinciding with the failure of his marriage to McKenna. He picked up again with *Scent of Mystery* (60, Jack Cardiff); *Station Six Sahara* (63, Seth Holt); *Nothing but the Best* (63, Clive Donner); *The High Bright Sun* (64, Ralph Thomas); *You Must Be Joking* (65, Michael Winner); *King Rat* (65, Bryan Forbes); *Alfie* (66, Lewis Gilbert)—surely a signal moment in that Elliott was still in support, but to a very novel kind of English actor, Michael Caine; *The Spy with a Cold Nose* (67, Daniel Petrie); *Maroc 7* (67, Gerald O'Hara); *Here We Go Round the Mulberry Bush* (67, Donner).

By now, Elliott had a new international reputation as a reliable support, as evident in occasional trips to Hollywood: *The Night They Raided Minsky's* (68, William Friedkin); *The Sea Gull* (68, Sidney Lumet); *Too Late the Hero* (70, Robert Aldrich), with Caine again; *The Rise and Rise of Michael Rimmer* (70, Kevin Billington); *Percy* (71, Thomas); *Quest for Love* (71, Thomas); *A Doll's House* (73, Patrick Garland); *Madame Sin* (73, David Greene); *The Apprenticeship of Duddy Kravitz* (74, Ted Kotcheff); *Russian Roulette* (75, Lou Lombardo); *Robin and Marian* (76, Richard Lester), as Will Scarlett; *To the Devil a Daughter* (76, Peter Sykes); a weatherman in *A Bridge Too Far* (77, Richard Attenborough); *The Boys from Brazil* (78, Franklin J. Schaffner); brilliant and fully appreciated in *Saint Jack* (79, Peter Bogdanovich).

His work may have seemed both stranger and loftier in his last decade or so, but he gathered one Oscar nomination (*A Room with a View*) and two British Film Awards (*A Private Function* and *Defence of the Realm*). He was in *Cuba* (79, Lester); the husband in *Bad Timing* (80, Nicolas Roeg); *Sunday Lovers* (80, Bryan Forbes); *Raiders of the Lost Ark* (81, Steven Spielberg); *The Missionary* (82, Richard Loncraine); *Brimstone and Treacle* (82, Loncraine); *The Wicked Lady* (83, Winner); *The Hound of the Baskervilles* (83, Douglas Hickox); *Trading Places* (83, John Landis); *The Razor's Edge* (84, John Byrum); *A Private Function* (85, Malcolm Mowbray); *A Room with a View* (86, James Ivory); superb as the aging journalist in *Defence of the Realm* (86, David Drury); *Maurice* (87, Ivory); *September* (87, Woody Allen); *The Bourne Identity* (88, Roger Young); in the twelfth century in *Stealing Heaven* (88, Donner); *Indiana Jones and the Last Crusade* (89, Spielberg); *Toy Soldiers* (91, Daniel Petrie Jr.); *Noises Off* (92, Bogdanovich)—with Caine once more, and brilliant.

Roland Emmerich,

b. Stuttgart, Germany, 1955
1979: *Franzmann.* 1984: *Das Arche Noah Prinzip.* 1985: *Joey.* 1987: *Hollywood Monster.* 1990: *Moon 44.* 1992: *Universal Soldier.* 1994: *Stargate.* 1996: *Independence Day.* 1998: *Godzilla.* 2000: *The Patriot.* 2004: *The Day After Tomorrow.*

Despite the horrendously stupid (and dull) *Godzilla,* the word in Hollywood is that Emmerich (with his producer partner, Don Devlin) is a ready-made handler for big sci-fi and special-effects franchises. This is because of the surprise hit of *Stargate* and the box-office sensation of *Independence Day.* The latter was spectacular, zany, and touched up with wild humor—things strikingly absent from *Godzilla,* or the brutal, history-less *The Patriot.* Emmerich was raised in Germany and trained at the Munich Film School. He made some awful cheap pictures in Germany—and then carried on in America. It has to be said that no other German director has known his commercial success in the U.S. But in the globalization of film history, why are we obliged to swallow the preposterous and coarse Emmerich when once we had Murnau and Lubitsch? If the latter had "touch," then Emmerich may become famous for "crunch."

Cy Endfield (Cyril Raker Endfield) (1914–95),

b. Scranton, Pennsylvania
1946: *Gentleman Joe Palooka.* 1947: *Stork Bites Man.* 1948: *The Argyle Secrets.* 1949: *Joe Palooka in the Big Fight.* 1950: *The Underworld Story; The Sound of Fury.* 1952: *Tarzan's Savage Fury.* 1953: *Limping Man* (codirected with Charles de Latour). 1954: *The Master Plan.* 1955: *Impulse* (codirected with de Latour); *The Secret.* 1956: *Child in the House* (codirected with de Latour). 1957: *Hell Drivers.* 1958: *Sea Fury.* 1959: *Secret Storm.* 1961: *Mysterious Island.* 1964: *Hide and Seek; Zulu.* 1965: *Sands of the Kalahari.* 1969: *De Sade* (codirected with Roger Corman). 1971: *Universal Soldier.*

From Joe Palooka to the Marquis de Sade is an eventful journey, especially with Tarzan and Welsh soldiers fighting Zulus along the way. Endfield had a very respectable grounding in the American theatre. From Yale and the New Theatre School he became a producer and a drama teacher. After the war, he went into movies as a writer and then took up direction. He was compelled to leave America during the McCarthy period and worked in England uncredited or under a pseudonym.

Hell Drivers was an unexpectedly raw look into the lives of English lorry drivers with much of the flavor and violence of an American thriller. It is an obvious, sensational film, but still Endfield's best and worth seeing for its pitching together of Stanley Baker and Patrick McGoohan. The meeting with Baker proved very profitable for Endfield; it led to a joint production company that made *Zulu* and *Sands of the Kalahari*. The first is a well-told, old-fashioned war story that includes some exciting footage of tribesmen.

Endfield has been rediscovered, or factually amended. Most reference books—this one included—said he had been born in South Africa. One went so far as to say he had died in 1983. I met him in the summer of 1992, in his cottage not far from Oxford, England, and there established that he had been a magician who had caught the attention of, and worked with, Orson Welles around the time of *The Magnificent Ambersons*.

He helped with the scripts of most of his own films and contributed to *Sleep My Love* (48, Douglas Sirk); *Crashout* (55, Lewis R. Foster); *Night of the Demon* (58, Jacques Tourneur); and *Zulu Dawn* (79, Douglas Hickox).

Of his own films, *The Underworld Story* is revealed as an unusually somber mood piece, much helped by Dan Duryea. *Impulse*, made in England, has Arthur Kennedy in a rut as an estate agent and drawn into romance and intrigue while his wife's away. The plot grows far-fetched, but the first half hour is very sharp and Losey-like. But many of Endfield's films are still very hard to find.

Ray Enright (1896–1965),
b. Anderson, Indiana

1927: *Girl from Chicago; Jaws of Steel; Tracked by the Police*. 1928: *Domestic Troubles; Land of the Silver Fox; Little Wildcat*. 1929: *Stolen Kisses; Skin Deep; Kid Gloves*. 1930: *Dancing Sweeties; Scarlet Pages; Golden Dawn; Song of the West*. 1932: *Play Girl; The Tenderfoot*. 1933: *Blondie Johnson; Silk Express; Tomorrow at Seven; Havana Widows*. 1934: *I've Got Your Number; Twenty Million Sweethearts; Circus Clown; Dames; St. Louis Kid*. 1935: *Travelling Saleslady; While the Patient Slept; Alibi Ike; We're in the Money; Miss Pacific Fleet*. 1936: *Snowed Under; Earthworm Tractors; China Clipper; Sing Me a Love Song*. 1937: *Ready, Willing and Able; Slim; Back in Circulation; The Singing Marine; Swing Your Lady; Gold Diggers in Paris*. 1938: *Hard to Get; Going Places*. 1939: *Naughty But Nice; On Your Toes; Angels Wash Their Faces*. 1940: *An Angel from Texas; Brother Rat and a Baby; River's End*. 1941: *The Wagons Roll at Night; Thieves Fall Out; Bad Men of Missouri; Law of the Tropics; Wild Bill Hickok Rides*. 1942: *The Spoilers; Men of Texas; Sin Town*. 1943: *The Iron Major; Gung Ho!; Good Luck, Mr. Yates*. 1945: *China Sky; Man Alive; One Way to Love*. 1947: *Trail Street; Albuquerque*. 1948: *Return of the Bad Men; Coroner Creek*. 1949: *South of St. Louis*. 1950: *Montana* (codirected with Raoul Walsh); *Kansas Raiders*. 1951: *Flaming Feather*. 1953: *The Man from Cairo*.

The coloring of an unassuming artisan's career could alter radically if he switched companies. For Ray Enright, the change came in 1941 when he left Warners for Universal. Trained as an editor and supplier of comic material by Mack Sennett, he had served Warners for a dozen years, handling its cheerful musicals. *Dames* is Dick Powell, Ruby Keeler, and Joan Blondell, with choreography by Busby Berkeley. The title is expressive of Warners' attitude to musicals and women, just as Berkeley's presence speaks for their most creative aspect. But *Twenty Million Sweethearts* (Powell and Ginger Rogers); *Ready, Willing and Able; Gold Diggers in Paris;* and *Naughty But Nice* are robust, run-of-the-mill products. By 1940, Warners had shifted Enright into action pictures, and when he left the studio it meant his abandonment of the musical for good. Instead, he directed Universal adventures and Westerns, several of them B pictures. They proved no better and no worse than the musicals, routine products, sure of their own limits, too knowing to waste stars or mishandle set pieces. *The Spoilers* has Dietrich, John Wayne, and Randolph Scott; *Gung Ho!* is Scott again; while *Trail Street*, at RKO, is an excellent Western with Scott and Robert Ryan. *South of St. Louis*, back at Warners in 1949, is a Western made with some skill, still looking better than later, more ambitious works in the genre. In short, Enright is usually worth seeing, so long as certain limits are recognized in advance.

Nora Ephron, b. New York, 1941

1992: *This Is My Life*. 1993: *Sleepless in Seattle*. 1994: *Mixed Nuts*. 1996: *Michael*. 1998: *You've Got Mail*. 2000: *Lucky Numbers*.

Up until about the early nineties, it seemed that Nora Ephron had done, and succeeded at, everything. She had gone from being the child of a screenwriting partnership (Henry Ephron and Phoebe Wolkind), to a juvenile character in their play *Take Her, She's Mine* (played on screen by Sandra Dee), to a Wellesley student, a writer, a wit, a cook, a novelist, a screenwriter, and even a director, and the director of a smash hit, *Sleepless in Seattle*.

She makes films on just the kind of ideas that might appeal to a newspaper columnist—and with a superficiality that even the public now seems to have caught on to. Though blessed with the amiable couple from *Sleepless,* Tom Hanks and Meg Ryan, *You've Got Mail* did less well. Never forget (or forgive) that it also sought to improve and smarten up *The Shop Around the Corner,* many lines from which could adorn Ms. Ephron's grave—make that the grave around the corner.

Her first screenplay—for *Silkwood,* written with Alice Arlen (83, Mike Nichols)—was not just her best, but the one that shows the most interest in real people. *Heartburn* (85, Nichols), from her "novel" (based on her marriage to Carl Bernstein—her second—and its failure) was an embarrassment. But *When Harry Met Sally . . .* (89, Rob Reiner) showed a grave case of "cutes," and its deli orgasm scene pushed Ms. Ephron into the realm of shtick for which there are no maps home. It's a sign that she may like actors more than people. She also wrote *My Blue Heaven* (90, Herbert Ross).

Just because she rates as a successful woman in Hollywood is no reason to omit the feeling that she is the director of at least five supine pictures.

Joe Eszterhas,
b. Gaskanydoroszlo, Hungary, 1944

Mr. Eszterhas is one of those professionals who read an earlier edition of this book and felt disgruntled. He complained to a magazine that had asked me to write about him that I viewed the writing of Ben Hecht as essentially subordinate to the achievement of von Sternberg, Preminger, and others. "I can't believe he's serious," wrote Eszterhas. "Sternberg? *Preminger?*" He was aggrieved—with justice—that I had omitted such screenwriters as Paddy Chayefsky, Ernest Lehman, Robert Riskin, and William Goldman.

Well, I have filled some of those holes, and so I ought to say a few words about Mr. Eszterhas. We did have lunch together, and I found him enormously entertaining. He is large, hirsute, florid, reflective, anecdotal, self-deprecating (he admitted that he had done script doctoring for as little as $600,000 a week), and someone to make the Korda family young again.

If only his work was as much fun. After coming to this country as a child, and graduating from Ohio State, he became a journalist at the Cleveland *Plain Dealer.* He was bold and controversial: on one story he interviewed children without their parents' permission so that the paper lost an invasion-of-privacy suit. He went on to *Rolling Stone* and wrote two books: *Thirteen Seconds: Confrontation at Kent State* (1970) and *Charley Simpson's Apocalypse* (1974), which won the National Book Award.

By the late seventies, he was doing screenplays: *F.I.S.T.* (78, Norman Jewison) was his debut, and it shows a valiant attempt to handle difficult material. But as time went by and Eszterhas

became more successful, so his "working class" awareness became bowdlerized—especially in *Flashdance* (83, Adrian Lyne)—and he fell into a pattern of implausibility, self-repetition, and an almost unconscious interest in forms of betrayal: *Jagged Edge* (85, Richard Marquand), an effective thriller; *Hearts of Fire* (87, Marquand); *Pals* (87, Lou Antonio); *Big Shots* (87, Robert Mandel); the singularly unbelievable *Betrayed* (88, Costa-Gavras); *Checking Out* (89, David Leland); and the touching if predictable *Music Box* (89, Costa-Gavras).

Eszterhas is a useful combination of old-fashioned technique and modern shock value, as witness *Basic Instinct* (92, Paul Verhoeven). Nothing in that film is as shocking as the writer's $3 million fee, but *Basic Instinct,* in title, marketing, and spurious sensation is a very characteristic American film of its moment, at the same time nasty and irrelevant. As the film was shot, Eszterhas made something of a spectacle of himself by discovering that his script might be hostile to the gay community. He asked the producers to be allowed to do rewrites, and they couldn't believe he was serious.

I do. Eszterhas has a dangerous rhinolike sincerity allied to the guile of a fox. All of this was evident in his most enjoyable paperwork: the widely distributed fax copies of letters between himself and Michael Ovitz when Eszterhas elected to leave CAA. Joe's account of how Ovitz had responded is as concise a portrait of idealism and betrayal in Hollywood as one will find—but the reader has to decide which is which.

He also wrote the script for *Sliver* (93, Phillip Noyce); *Showgirls* (95, Verhoeven); *Jade* (95, William Friedkin); *Telling Lies in America* (97, Guy Ferland); *An Alan Smithee Film: Burn Hollywood Burn* (99, Arthur Hiller). And you can't make five films so bad without hearing the air go out of your balloon—and worrying whether it smells. In addition, Joe divorced one wife and married another on the way to stagnation. It was enough to encourage the thought that his brief notoriety had been just a spasm in midlife crisis. It also urged him toward Art, and his first, defining novel, *American Rhapsody* (00).

Jean Eustache (1938–81),
b. Pessac, France
1967: *Les Mauvaises Fréquentations/Bad Company.* 1973: *La Maman et la Putain/The Mother and the Whore.* 1975: *Mes Petites Amoureuses.*

I have seen only one Eustache film, *The Mother and the Whore,* but it is enough to put him in any film book. There are so many films that reckon they are dealing with love and sex that we take the steam for granted. Just every now and then, a film rises up as abrupt, elemental, and wounding as rocks. *The Mother and the Whore* is 219 minutes; it relies on naked performances—Jean-Pierre

Léaud, Bernadette Lafont, Françoise Lebrun, and Isabelle Weingarten; and it is more shocking than *Last Tango,* or nearly any other "sexy" film you can think of. On seeing Eustache's masterpiece, one feels like someone trapped into confrontation with a pit of wild creatures. It is a film that deserves to be in perpetual repertory—yet, I'm not sure I wouldn't rather hold it back, in secrecy and threat, and then show it occasionally, without warning, when another film has failed to arrive. *The Mother and the Whore* should be rumored rather than known. It is a dark, vaguely perceived beast on the edge of polite society. Beware.

Robert Evans (Robert Shapera),
b. New York, 1930

For a moment, Evans was bathed in the media wash of being the perfect new producer. His smile had the unshy self-love of a man seeing his own dazzle in the mirror. But moments pass. After seven years in charge of production at Paramount (1967–73), he moved into the independence he reckoned he deserved. His first venture was *Chinatown* (74, Roman Polanski), a producer's coup in terms of holding together warring elements long enough for high rentals and good reviews.

After that, the magic touch deserted him and left two box-office toads: *Marathon Man* (76, John Schlesinger) and *Black Sunday* (77, John Frankenheimer). They were no worse nor more foolish than pictures that had flourished a few years before. But producers live by the invisible and scarcely predictable rule of what the public will swallow. All the hard work, faith, and ruthlessness his survivors attribute to a producer are empty air if his horse medicine does not sell. Evans has charm and no fear of exhausting schedules: four marriages and four divorces have not deterred him from the company of pretty women, and he has the boyish love of pictures still that has guarded all long-lived producers.

He has a youthful face, as if being starstruck came out in his ardent expression. As a child in New York, he worked as a radio actor by night. The strain caught up with him: a lung collapsed, leaving the febrile intensity of a restored invalid. He convalesced for a year and then bounced back to be sales director of a sportswear firm his brother had helped found.

Selling sneakers and jock straps taught him trade and made him wealthy. Then, in 1956, in Beverly Hills he met Norma Shearer, and she was so taken with him that she got him the cameo part of her husband, Irving Thalberg, in *Man of a Thousand Faces* (57, Joseph Pevney). He was pretty, but not an actor. Still, he had several other parts: the matador in *The Sun Also Rises* (57, Henry King); the odious killer in *The Fiend Who Walked the West* (58, Gordon Douglas); and *The*

Best of Everything (59, Jean Negulesco).

He never made it as a star, and he went back to peddling sportswear. When the company sold out to Revlon, Evans's cut left him a millionaire. He then went back to Hollywood with the wish to produce and the means to buy in. Fox took him on and he set up one picture there—*The Detective* (68, Douglas)—before accepting Paramount's invitation.

It speaks for Evans's glamour and the shortage of distinguished production executives that Paramount gave him power with so little track record. His time at Paramount started uncertainly, but he soon reached a plateau of success that helped to revitalize the company. *The Godfather* may look cast-iron now, but it was hedged with early doubts, against which Evans gave the director's job to the still problematic Coppola. Other films he produced include: *The Molly Maguires* (68, Martin Ritt); *Rosemary's Baby* (68, Polanski); *Romeo and Juliet* (68, Franco Zeffirelli); *Paint Your Wagon* (69, Joshua Logan); *Goodbye, Columbus* (69, Larry Pierce); *Darling Lily* (70, Blake Edwards); *Catch-22* (70, Mike Nichols); and *Love Story* (70, Arthur Hiller). This last and *Goodbye, Columbus* had starred Ali MacGraw, Evans's third wife (others have been Sharon Huegeny, Camilla Sparv, and Phyllis George). *Love Story* was a major hit, unexpected to all the people who doubted a cynical, permissive society's readiness for sappy romance. Evans guessed that hidden softness and also backed the far greater harshness of *The Godfather*. Such versatility promised that he would be back with other things we could not resist.

I wish—he wishes. After *Marathon Man* and *Black Sunday* Evans has had disaster, under the influence of drugs and also under suspicion in various scandals as well as being linked to one notable murder case. He was a producer on *Players* (79, Anthony Harvey), *Popeye* (80, Robert Altman), and *The Cotton Club* (84, Coppola), and his own disarray cannot have helped that disappointing picture. He was intended not just as producer on *The Two Jakes,* but as the actor playing Jake Berman. His insecurities stopped Robert Towne's first attempt to film his script in 1985, and Evans was a producer in name only when the film was finally done, in 1990, under Jack Nicholson's direction.

So Evans is a very notable casualty. But in all his stages of chaos and distress, he has remained a would-be actor, putting on a grand show. For example, as late as 1982, Robert Towne wrote of him: "Bob Evans remains, in memory and in life, a standard for every kind of human generosity, and one I have yet to see matched in this town."

Of course, that was said before Evans took producer's credit and backed one old pal against another on *The Two Jakes* (90, Jack Nicholson).

Since then, Evans has had his name attached to a few more films—*Sliver* (93, Phillip Noyce); *Jade* (95, William Friedkin); *The Phantom* (96, Simon Wincer); *The Saint* (97, Noyce); *The Out-of-Towners* (99, Sam Weisman). That all have been bad is just a signal of Evans's general relaxation—which is good for him. As is amply borne out in his all-too-short memoir, *The Kid Stays in the Picture.* So long as he stays a kid!

Rupert Everett, b. Norfolk, England, 1959
In another age, Rupert Everett might have been mistaken for Flashman, the cruel bully in *Tom Brown's Schooldays,* or regarded as a scion of that wonderfully languid English character actor James Villiers. Everett exudes class, even if he is more plausible as the black sheep of some lofty family. He is an authentic beauty, and one of the few leading actors who has admitted to and relished his gayness. It has been a remarkably brave and enterprising career, and I think it's possible that Everett could take on great roles in an age that might begin to admit gender confusion—and enjoy it.

He dropped out of school (Ampleforth) to go to the Central School of Speech and Drama, and he made a splashy debut in the London stage production of *Another Country.* In turn, that led to his start in movies: on TV in *Princess Daisy* (83, Waris Hussein); *Another Country* (84, Marek Kanievska); as Lancelot in *Arthur the King* (85, Clive Donner); excellent as the sports-car cad in *Dance with a Stranger* (85, Mike Newell); *Duet for One* (86, Andrei Konchalovsky); to Australia for *The Right Hand Man* (87, Di Drew); *Chronicle of a Death Foretold* (87, Francesco Rosi); *Gli Occhiali d'Oro* (87, Giuliano Montaldo); *Hearts of Fire* (87, Richard Marquand); *Tolerance* (89, Pierre-Henry Salfati).

He was perfect as the effete Englishman overwhelmed by Christopher Walken in *The Comfort of Strangers* (91, Paul Schrader); *Inside Monkey Zetterland* (92, Jefery Levy); *Cemetery Man* (93, Michele Soavi); as the Prince of Wales in *The Madness of George III* (94, Nicholas Hytner); *Ready to Wear* (94, Robert Altman); *Dunston Checks In* (96, Ken Kwapis); clearly helpful to Julia Roberts in *My Best Friend's Wedding* (97, P. J. Hogan); *B. Monkey* (98, Michael Radford); as Kit Marlowe, uncredited, in *Shakespeare in Love* (98, John Madden); *An Ideal Husband* (99, Oliver Parker); as Oberon in *A Midsummer Night's Dream* (99, Michael Hoffman); narrating the documentary on Nazi treatment of gays, *Paragraph 175* (99, Robert Epstein and Jeffrey Friedman); *Inspector Gadget* (99, David Kellogg); *The Next Best Thing* (00, John Schlesinger); as Algernon in *The Importance of Being Earnest* (02, Parker).

He made *South Kensington* (01, Carlo Vanzina); *Unconditional Love* (02, Hogan); a voice in *The Wild Thornberrys Movie* (02, Cathy Malkasian and Jeff McGrath); as Charles I in *To Kill a King* (03, Mike Barker); as Valmont, in French, in *Les Liaisons Dangereuses* (03, Josee Dayan); *A Different Loyalty* (03, Kanievska).

F

Douglas Fairbanks (Douglas Elton Ulman) (1883–1939), b. Denver, Colorado
There is a rare combination in Fairbanks of abilities required by the film world: he was a transforming movie actor whose presence so embodied the spirit of naïve adventure that, unwittingly, he made swashbuckling like verse; in addition, he was a man of sure commercial instinct, great organizing effort, and an innovator in film production and distribution. In the making and selling of adventure films, there is not another actor who has significantly improved on the noble Doug's contribution. Yet his greatest legacy was in identifying modern celebrity. He was *so* famous; no one had been known in this way before Doug, Mary, and Charlie stumbled on stardom. And Doug was the most casual about it.

After a comfortable upbringing, it seems proper that Fairbanks enjoyed a playboy youth before going on the stage. By 1915 he was a star, and Triangle signed him up. His debut was in *The Lamb* (15, Christy Cabanne). D. W. Griffith, the seer at Triangle, rather scorned Fairbanks's boyish high spirits, and most of his films were directed by John Emerson and Allan Dwan: *The Habit of Happiness* (16, Dwan); *The Good Bad Man* (16, Dwan); *The Half-Breed* (16, Dwan); *Manhattan Madness* (16, Dwan); and *The Americano* (16, Emerson). In 1917, Fairbanks left Triangle, with the two directors, and formed his own production company: *In Again, Out Again* (17, Emerson); *The Man from Painted Post* (17, Joseph Henabery); *A Modern Musketeer* (17, Dwan); *Mr. Fix-It* (18, Dwan); *Bound in Morocco* (18, Dwan); *He Comes Up Smiling* (18, Dwan); *Arizona* (18, Albert Parker); and *The Knickerbocker Buckaroo* (19, Parker).

In 1919, Fairbanks was the moving spirit in the formation of United Artists with Chaplin, Griffith, and Mary Pickford. Henceforward, his own productions were distributed by UA: *His Majesty the American* (19, Henabery) and *The Mollycoddle* (19). In 1920, he married his partner Mary Pickford (his second wife) and settled down to the adventure epics with which he is associated. As well as acting in them, he took the role of producer very seriously and was responsible for the insistence on authentic spectacle: he liked to do his own stunts and was wise enough to invest in proper historical research. The films he made in the 1920s were invariably handled by first-class action directors, and they still move dazzlingly well. Allan Dwan explained the nature of Fairbanks's appeal:

. . . he was very athletic and active, liked movement and space, so he enjoyed every minute. Pictures were made for him. The theatre was too little. . . . He worked with speed and, basically, with grace. . . . The only thing that could possibly interest either one of us was a swift, graceful move—the thing a kid visualizes in his hero. . . . If he was to leap on a table to fight a duel, we'd cut the legs of that table so it would be just the leap he ought to make. He never had to reach an extra inch for anything. Otherwise, it wouldn't be graceful—it wouldn't be him and it wouldn't be right. He was a good, strong athlete but he never strained.

He took time and trouble over these films and rationed them to one a year: *The Mark of Zorro* (20, Fred Niblo); *The Nut* (21, Theodore Reed), the only modern piece; *The Three Musketeers* (21, Niblo); *Robin Hood* (22, Dwan), twice as expensive as *Intolerance; The Thief of Bagdad* (24, Raoul Walsh); *Don Q, Son of Zorro* (25, Donald Crisp); *The Black Pirate* (26, Parker); *The Gaucho* (27, F. Richard Jones); and *The Iron Mask* (29, Dwan).

For his first talking picture, he played Petruchio, opposite Mary Pickford in *The Taming of the Shrew* (29, Sam Taylor). His voice was not good and he was now forty-seven. He made three more films in America—*Reaching for the Moon* (31, Edmund Goulding), *Around the World in 80 Minutes* (31, Victor Fleming), and *Mr. Robinson Crusoe* (32, Edward Sutherland)—before going to England to make *The Private Life of Don Juan* (34, Alexander Korda). In 1935 the marriage with Pickford ended and Fairbanks retired. He married Lady Sylvia Ashley and spent his last years relaxed, despite the strain of a weak heart.

A revival of his films in 1973 showed the scapegrace vitality unabated, the fondness for make-believe still enchanting.

Douglas Fairbanks Jr. (Douglas Elton Ulman Jr.) (1909–2000), b. New York

The son of Doug senior and Rhode Island heiress Anna Beth Sully, Doug junior was more voguishly handsome than his father. Doug Sr. always had rather narrow eyes, a hooked nose, and a tendency to double chins. The son was, and remains, the epitome of glossy charm, even if nothing he has done has ever suggested a man aspiring beyond the attempt to live up to his father. The parents separated when Doug was nine and he lived with his mother until, at age fourteen, he was coaxed into movies by Jesse Lasky. Lasky only wanted the pull of the great man's name, and Doug Sr. was,

not surprisingly, hostile to his son's career for many years. The irony is that Jr. tried all the harder to swashbuckle honorably whereas the screen evidence suggests that he might have been more telling as a gigolo, weakling, or black sheep of the family.

His career dragged on until he and Britain took to each other during the war. By 1951, he retired as an actor, went into production, and became a prominent figure in London society. (He was a figure in the great Duchess of Argyll scandal of 1963.) Most of his films are easily forgotten, but here are some that have lasted better or that had some local significance in his overshadowed career: *Stephen Steps Out* (23, Joseph Henabery); *Wild Horse Mesa* (25, George B. Seitz); *Stella Dallas* (25, Henry King); *Padlocked* (26, Allan Dwan); *Man Bait* (27, Donald Crisp); *Women Love Diamonds* (27, Edmund Goulding); *The Power of the Press* (28, Frank Capra); *The Barker* (28, George Fitzmaurice); *A Woman of Affairs* (29, Clarence Brown); *Our Modern Maidens* (29, Jack Crawford), with Joan Crawford, his wife at that time; *Loose Ankles* (29, Ted Wilde); *The Dawn Patrol* (30, Howard Hawks); *The Way of All Men* (30, Frank Lloyd); *Little Caesar* (30, Mervyn Le Roy); *Chances* (31, Dwan); *Union Depot* (32, Alfred E. Green); *Love Is a Racket* (32, William Wellman); *Scarlet Dawn* (32, William Dieterle); *Morning Glory* (33, Lowell Sherman); *The Life of Jimmy Dolan* (33, Archie Mayo); and *Captured!* (33, Roy del Ruth).

He went to Britain to play the tsar opposite Elizabeth Bergner's *Catherine the Great* (34, Paul Czinner) and stayed for *Mimi* (35, Paul L. Stein); *Man of the Moment* (35, Monty Banks); *The Amateur Gentleman* (36, Thornton Freeland); *Accused* (36, Freeland); and *When Thief Meets Thief* (37, Raoul Walsh). He went back to America to be a very merry black-satin Rupert of Hentzau in *The Prisoner of Zenda* (37, John Cromwell); *Joy of Living* (38, Tay Garnett); *The Rage of Paris* (38, Henry Koster); *Young in Heart* (38, Richard Wallace); *Gunga Din* (39, George Stevens); *Rulers of the Sea* (39, Lloyd); *Green Hell* (40, James Whale); and *Angels Over Broadway* (41, Ben Hecht and Lee Garmes). Then, having played twins in *The Corsican Brothers* (41, Gregory Ratoff), he went into the U.S. navy and was in Britain for much of the war. He had one last fling in the peace as *Sinbad the Sailor* (47, Richard Wallace); as the escapee Charles II in *The Exile* (48, Max Ophuls); *That Lady in Ermine* (48, Otto Preminger and Ernst Lubitsch); then to Britain for *State Secret* (50, Sidney Gilliat) and *Mr. Drake's Duck* (51, Val Guest).

He did a little producing thereafter—*Another Man's Poison* (52, Irving Rapper), a Bette Davis film, unavailable for many years later on, and *Chase a Crooked Shadow* (58, Michael Anderson). He acted only rarely: *The Crooked Hearts* (72, Jay Sandrich), with Rosalind Russell; *The Hostage Tower* (80, Claudio Guzman); *Ghost Story* (81, John Irvin); and *Strong Medicine* (86, Guy Green).

Frances Farmer (1914–70),
b. Seattle, Washington, and
Sharon Stone,
b. Meadville, Pennsylvania, 1958

Why put these two together? They never met, and there is only the faintest possibility that they could have been mother and daughter. Nor am I proposing that Stone play Farmer. There have already been three Frances Farmer biopics, so that the actress who had her moment of wonder in the late 1930s is now chiefly known as a Jessica Lange role. No, the pairing owes itself to some caprice of untidiness. The desk, the floor, the rooms that have made this book are a sea of untidiness on which the author makes a Columbus-like assertion of knowing where everything is. Of course, he does not. Notes, reports, articles, and pictures ebb and flow, and one morning in that flux it happened that pictures of Frances Farmer and Sharon Stone were briefly side by side. Anyone could have seen the sisterhood of blondeness, wide intelligent brows, and a gaze so frank and unshakable that it left one wondering where looker and self-destruction met.

Then, on reflection, I thought I saw some useful pattern that concerns the muddle and peril of wanting to be a beautiful blonde in pictures.

Farmer's life is "known" now—or understood; but there is a special mystery that clings to established history, the paranoia that knows we may be wrong. So Frances Farmer is celebrated as a victim: she was too intelligent, supposedly, too radical, too difficult, too determined to be an artist, an actress, a woman, a free spirit. You can hardly have a Jessica Lange play a Frances Farmer without that sense of victimization and lost greatness. And there has never been a problem in rounding up a crowd that wants to think badly of Hollywood and the show business system.

So Frances Farmer went from the University of Washington on a trip to Soviet Russia, to the Group Theater and Hollywood, to an affair with Clifford Odets, and got the female role in the stage debut of *Golden Boy*, the cast of which included Elia Kazan, who saw "a special glow, a skin without flaw, lustrous eyes—a blonde you'd dream about. She also had a wry and, at times, rather disappointed manner, a twist of the mouth, which suited the part."

That was 1937. The year before, Farmer had been in Hollywood. She had made *Too Many Parents* (36, Robert McGowan) and *Border Flight* (36, Otho Lovering). Then she met Howard Hawks, who cast her in the challenging dual role of mother and daughter in *Come and Get It* (36,

Hawks and William Wyler, after Hawks was fired). Hawks believed she was the best actress he ever worked with. He recalled her playing a scene with the experienced Edward Arnold, and giving the pro some quiet help on timing. "Hey, look," said Arnold to Hawks, "she's pretty good."

"She's so good," Hawks replied, "that you'd better get right to work or she's going to take it and walk off with it."

She is so good in *Come and Get It,* you marvel that that's the only good film she ever made. What happened? She was difficult, some say—though not Hawks. She was marked as a leftist, she would talk back, she intimidated too many people, and she reckoned that the film work she was offered was lousy: *Rhythm on the Range* (36, Norman Taurog); *The Toast of New York* (37, Rowland V. Lee); *Ebb Tide* (37, James P. Hogan); *Exclusive* (37, Alexander Hall); *Ride a Crooked Mile* (38, Alfred E. Green); *South of Pago Pago* (40, Green); *Flowing Gold* (40, Green); *World Premiere* (41, Ted Tetzlaff); *Badlands of Dakota* (41, Green); *Among the Living* (41, Stuart Heisler); and *Son of Fury* (41, John Cromwell).

Hawks said "she went to pieces." There was trouble with the law, with alcohol, with . . . too many men as strong, alluring, and careerist as Odets, Hawks, Kazan, and her husband, actor Leif Erickson (they were married from 1934 to 1942). And perhaps it was too much for her to seem that lovely or poised on the brink of fame and greatness. Perhaps she was disturbed, or self-destructive—perhaps she was out of control. One of the screen's great lies is the way it sanctifies control and seems to make a unified image of passion and intelligence. Whatever, she was treated as if she were crazy. She was institutionalized and she had operations, a lobotomy. She was years in the state hospital at Steilacoom, Washington. She came to the surface again in the late fifties, on television, and she made a couple of TV movies, including *The Party Crashers* (58, Bernard Girard). Admirers regretted that she was not the same person—but on the screen forty-four is never the same as twenty-two. This is barely a career, yet it is one of the most poignant Hollywood lives, heavy with meanings.

Sharon Stone does have Farmer's looks. She enjoys the chance to be dangerous on screen, and she is one of the best interviews Hollywood has ever had. Talking smart, tough, and funny for an interview isn't necessarily intelligence, yet it makes a threat out of the actress's loveliness.

Not that Stone is anyone's victim. She only came to success at an age when Farmer was finished. While waiting to click, Stone had been a model, an actress in wretched films, and possibly several things that are still beyond even her candor. Just as people wonder where Frances Farmer went after 1936–37, so we can ask now why the world didn't seize on Sharon Stone before *Basic Instinct* (92, Paul Verhoeven).

She had been around most of a decade, and she actually had better scenes to show than Frances Farmer: the dream girl in *Stardust Memories* (80, Woody Allen), kissing the window; *Deadly Blessing* (81, Wes Craven); a role in the short-lived TV series *Bay City Blues* (83); very funny in *Irreconcilable Differences* (84, Charles Shyer); *The Vegas Strip Wars* (84, George Englund); *King Solomon's Mines* (85, J. Lee Thompson); a role in the miniseries *War and Remembrance* (85); *Allan Quatermain and the Lost City of Gold* (87, Gary Nelson); *Police Academy 4* (87, Jim Drake); *Action Jackson* (88, Craig R. Baxley); *Above the Law* (88, Andrew Davis); *Tears in the Rain* (88, Don Sharp); *Personal Choice* (89, David Saperstein); *Blood and Sand* (89, Javier Elorrieta); *Total Recall* (90, Verhoeven); *He Said, She Said* (91, Ken Kwapis and Marisa Silver); *Scissors* (91, Frank De Felitta); and *Year of the Gun* (91, John Frankenheimer).

No one is funnier about this journey than Ms. Stone herself—as if she was determined to trump the bad jokes preemptively. And being in bad movies has by now become not just a personal disaster, but a camp routine. The once-upon-a-time victim has to learn rueful humor, and hope that her own ridiculous urge to be creative has not been darkened.

Basic Instinct is a dreadful film, but Stone is triumphant in it. She runs through the gamut of fantasy role-playing, as if she were doing a series of ads. She dominates the film and the several men (Verhoeven, Joe Eszterhas, and Michael Douglas) who were paid so much more than she could get. And she is so funny, so smart, and so quick that one laments the lack of Howard Hawks today. I suspect that Sharon Stone could have been a comedienne in the class of Carole Lombard, as well as a romantic, a sexpot, and a destroyer of feeble men.

She cashed in, and she knew she had only a few years. She is obliged to stay camp and ruthless, so she has to chuckle that the fruits of glory come as stupid as *Sliver* (93, Phillip Noyce) or as plain as *Intersection* (94, Mark Rydell). No one as smart as Sharon Stone could survey her own and Frances Farmer's career and do anything other than marry well and form a business. Which only helps reveal some likelihood that Sharon Stone is crazy, too.

Stone did marry—Phil Bronstein, a leading San Francisco newspaper executive. And she has turned herself into a business, reckoning to realize her accumulated value swiftly, before it ran out: *The Quick and the Dead* (95, Sam Raimi); her finest work, as Ginger in *Casino* (95, Martin Scorsese), for which she received an Oscar nomination; *Diabolique* (96, Jeremiah S. Chechik); *Last Dance* (96, Bruce Beresford); *Sphere* (98, Barry Levinson); *The Mighty* (98, Peter Chelsom): the voice of Princess Bala in *Antz* (98, Eric Darnell and Tim Johnson); *Gloria* (99, Sidney Lumet); *The Muse* (99, Albert Brooks); *Simpatico* (99, Matthew Warchus); *If These Walls Could Talk 2* (00, Anne Heche); *Picking Up the Pieces* (00, Alfonso Arau); *Beautiful Joe* (00, Stephen Metcalfe); *Cold Creek Manor* (03, Mike Figgis).

Richard Farnsworth (1920–2000),
b. Los Angeles

One saw Richard Farnsworth at the Academy Awards in March 2000. He wore an old-fashioned white scarf, like a cowboy come to town from Lincoln, New Mexico, and he grinned sourly when Kevin Spacey won the Oscar for *American Beauty*. It was an obvious reward for a film that had been a hit, whereas no one knew how to see *The Straight Story* (99, David Lynch) without seeming sentimental. Hollywood has so little experience with seventy-nine-year-olds.

I had talked to Farnsworth a few weeks earlier, on the phone, and he was sweetly polite about having a chance at Oscar, and he said, oh yes, he would surely be in Los Angeles for the night. Which meant a two-day drive, because he was spooked by flying. He might have ridden, but he wasn't riding anymore—not until he got a new hip.

But it turned out that he had cancer, too, had had it a couple of years. The pain was so bad he talked about it to his young fiancée, Jewel—they were on his ranch, ninety acres, outside Lincoln, on Bonita Creek. In October he shot himself. I'd say maybe it could have been an accident, but Farnsworth was no more of a fool with guns than he was with horses.

The Straight Story was so simple and clear, about an old man in Iowa who fears he could die anytime, so maybe he ought to visit his brother in Wisconsin. But Alvin Straight (a real person) had no horse—just a John Deere tractor. So he makes his journey that way, a few hundred miles by back roads, and it's the story of people he meets, plus Alvin and his daughter, who is a little simple (Sissy Spacek), and the brother, who turns out to be Harry Dean Stanton.

Once upon a time, the Academy would have given the Oscar to Richard Farnsworth out of respect for kindness, and feeling a whole life spread out like a picnic on the grass. He was born in Los Angeles, but his father died when he was young, and Richard got a job at a local polo stable. It was a place where stars kept their horses. He cleaned out and groomed the animals, so that's where he learned to ride. Within a few years he was offered stunt roles in pictures. He was never credited, but he'd ride in galloping chases, where actors might fall off and get hurt. From that he got promoted to stand-in work and stunting for fights.

He was a soldier in *Gone With the Wind* (39, Victor Fleming); he was in *Gunga Din* (39, George Stevens) and *Fort Apache* (48, John Ford). But the best time he ever had was on *Red River* (48, Howard Hawks), when Hawks cast Montgomery Clift as the young cowboy. Well, Clift was a hell of an actor, but he didn't know the West from Central Park West. When they told him to put on a pair of six-guns, Clift sagged and could hardly cross the street. Put him on a horse and he was a very insecure young actor.

So Hawks asked Farnsworth to hang out with Clift. Help him pick out a hat, teach him to walk, make sure he could stay on a horse and read lines, and roll a cigarette for himself. It worked; Farnsworth liked Clift and had no envy of him. At ten dollars a day, Farnsworth was getting more than he could from anything else, and the anything else would have been work.

There was a community of stunt riders, rodeo people, and wranglers from movies, and Farnsworth was one of them. He kept his own horses and hired them out to the movies, too. It was fun for a while, until the world lost the habit for Westerns. So he ranched a little. But then in 1968, on a picture called *The Stalking Moon* (Robert Mulligan), they decided they needed an extra to read a line or two. The producer, Alan J. Pakula, asked him, and Farnsworth did it for him. Then a whole ten years later, on *Comes a Horseman*, with Pakula directing, there was this real part—the old-timer who helps Jane Fonda work her ranch. They had no one for it, and Pakula saw Richard, and remembered him, and said, "Maybe you'd like to do that?" The cowboy asked his wife, and she promised she'd help him.

He got a best supporting actor nomination for that—lost to Christopher Walken in *The Deer Hunter*. No complaining about that. Then, for a decade or so, Farnsworth really acted. He had one lead role, as Bill Miner, the gentleman train robber, in a Canadian picture called *The Grey Fox* (82, Phillip Borsos). It's the best thing he ever did. See what a soft-spoken, tender, wry man he could be, and ask yourself whether it was acting or whether he just had a way about him that the camera liked.

He's in a number of other pictures—like *The Natural* (84, Barry Levinson), *The Two Jakes* (90, Jack Nicholson), *Misery* (90, Rob Reiner), and the remake of *The Getaway* (94, Roger Donaldson)—where he does fine work. Probably everyone on those pictures knew the story of how he'd been a rodeo man and a stunt rider and just been noticed. And it charmed them. But what happened in New Mexico tells you how strong he was. He'd been classified 4-F at the time of World War II—he had spots on his lung—but I don't think he'd been in a hospital a night in his life,

and he didn't plan on it. So, long before he became an embarrassment, or less than a hard rider, he took the decision his way.

John Farrow (1904–63), b. Sydney, Australia
1937: *Men in Exile; West of Shanghai; War Lord*. 1938: *The Invisible Menace; She Loved a Fireman; Little Miss Thoroughbred; My Bill; Broadway Musketeers*. 1939: *The Saint Strikes Back; Women in the Wind; Sorority House; Five Came Back; Reno; Full Confession*. 1940: *Married and in Love; A Bill of Divorcement*. 1942: *Wake Island; Commandos Strike at Dawn*. 1943: *China*. 1944: *The Hitler Gang*. 1945: *You Came Along*. 1946: *Two Years Before the Mast*. 1947: *California; Easy Come, Easy Go; Blaze of Noon; Calcutta*. 1948: *The Big Clock; Beyond Glory; The Night Has a Thousand Eyes*. 1949: *Alias Nick Beal; Red Hot and Blue*. 1950: *Where Danger Lives; Copper Canyon*. 1951: *His Kind of Woman; Submarine Command*. 1953: *Ride, Vaquero!; Plunder in the Sun; Hondo; Botany Bay*. 1954: *A Bullet Is Waiting*. 1955: *The Sea Chase*. 1956: *Back from Eternity*. 1957: *The Unholy Wife*. 1959: *John Paul Jones*.

Farrow was educated in Australia and at Winchester. He was originally a writer: of stage plays and, from 1927, of movie scripts, including *Ladies of the Mob* (28, William Wellman); *Wolf Song* (29, Victor Fleming); *A Dangerous Woman* (29, Rowland V. Lee); *Seven Days' Leave* (30, Richard Wallace); *Woman of Experience* (31, Harry Joe Brown); and, years later, with S. J. Perelman and James Poe, for *Around the World in 80 Days* (56, Michael Anderson).

In addition, Farrow was a Roman Catholic convert who wrote books about Thomas More and the papacy as well as some novels. Indeed, his daughter Mia Farrow (by his marriage to actress Maureen O'Sullivan) has said that "He was very friendly with the Jesuits, and the house was always filled with priests; to some extent he looked down on Hollywood."

Such condescension hardly shows in Farrow's movies, and whatever the indignity of writing *Tarzan Escapes* (36, Richard Thorpe), it was then that Farrow met his wife, Johnny Weissmuller's Jane. Indeed, he seems one of the more engaging, enterprising, and critically neglected of entertainment directors. (There are enough tales of famous temper and eccentricity to help one understand later Farrows.)

It may have been the writer in him, or the Australian Wykhamist, but his films invariably pick on novel settings or plots, managing to lift routine products through ingenuity and freshness. The lack of authenticity or thrill in *Botany Bay* ill befits an Australian. But *Two Years Before Mast, Blaze of Noon, The Big Clock, Alias Nick Beal, Where Danger Lives, His Kind of Woman, Ride,*

Vaquero!, *Hondo*, and *Back from Eternity* are films that do not fit readily into any genre, and that are worth staying up late for. Farrow never scorned adventure movies, or missed a chance to add an extra imaginative character to them. *The Big Clock* and *Alias Nick Beal* are thrillers with a serious interest in evil. *Hondo* is a Western with rare emphasis on psychology and atmosphere. While *His Kind of Woman* is a comedy thriller that admirably exploits Mitchum, Jane Russell, Vincent Price, and Raymond Burr.

Farrow generally showed special interest in his players and in turn won better-than-usual performances. In his early days he used Boris Karloff well in *West of Shanghai* and *Invisible Menace*, and Ann Sheridan in *She Loved a Fireman* and *Broadway Musketeers*. As well as directing Veronica Lake in her debut (*Sorority House*), he worked often with Alan Ladd and Ray Milland—the latter in *California, The Big Clock, Alias Nick Beal,* and *Copper Canyon*. Above all, he tickled Charles Laughton's wandering fancy for *The Big Clock*, and subjugated John Wayne in *Hondo*.

Mia Farrow (Maria de Lourdes Villiers Farrow), b. Los Angeles, 1945

It's tempting to regard Mia Farrow as the waif overshadowed by the potent men in her life: she was married briefly and uneasily to Frank Sinatra (66–68), more fruitfully to André Previn (70–79), and then there was Woody Allen. But after her prolonged battle in court revealed a Farrow who fought like a lioness, and who leads her own life. The thought remains that her father—John Farrow, director, Catholic, and something of a wild man—may still be the dominant male influence in her life. He or her children, for Ms. Farrow takes on cubs, by birth or adoption, out of some primitive need.

She is the daughter of Farrow and actress Maureen O'Sullivan, and she was raised at Catholic schools, but in the Hollywood community. As a child she had polio, and that surely added to her vulnerability as a young woman—an effect deepened by her cropped hair and pale face.

When she was very young, she had a small role in her father's *John Paul Jones* (59), and she played onstage in *The Importance of Being Earnest*. At nineteen, she began two seasons as Allison Mackenzie in the TV *Peyton Place* (64–66), and she made her real movie debut in *Guns at Batasi* (64, John Guillermin).

She became a phenomenon when cast as the young mother-to-be in *Rosemary's Baby* (68, Roman Polanski). That very visceral, erotic, and frightening film owes so much to her: not just because of her gauntness and the sense of her life being sucked away from her as it grows inside her, but in her exceptional interest in what it is like to be pregnant. She was good again in *Secret Cere-*

mony (68, Joseph Losey), but she quickly became conventional in *A Dandy in Aspic* (68, Anthony Mann) and the forgettable *John and Mary* (69, Peter Yates).

It was as if she needed Polanski's black magic. She was no more than competent in *Blind Terror* (71, Richard Fleischer) and *Follow Me!* (71, Carol Reed), and she made *Docteur Popaul* (72) for Claude Chabrol. Then she was cast as Daisy in *The Great Gatsby* (73, Jack Clayton), probably because Robert Evans had lost Ali McGraw. She was eerily close to the vapid, hard nonentities Fitzgerald was so good at describing, but she brought no pathos or irony to the shimmering soft focus. And she was not sexy or alluring—why was Gatsby crazy about her?

Her career was in decline and she was away for a few years being a mother. Then came *Full Circle* (76, Richard Loncraine); *Death on the Nile* (78, Guillermin); *Avalanche* (78, Corey Allen); virtually silent but very carnal in *A Wedding* (78, Robert Altman)—she looked healthy at last; *Hurricane* (79, Jan Troell); and then along came Woody.

By now, it is a subject for intense argument and legal dispute as to whether Woody did her good or ill. Their living arrangement led to grotesque melodrama, with children—biological and adopted—as front-line soldiers. Farrow was in most of the films Allen made in the eighties, often as his apparently available female, but just as often in fresh roles. She rose to every acting challenge, though she has not recaptured the piercingly tragic figure she had been for Polanski. Her look of childhood had lasted eerily long. Still, looking like a woman, she has been more ordinary.

She has been in *A Midsummer Night's Sex Comedy* (82); *Zelig* (83); excellent as the gangster's moll in *Broadway Danny Rose* (84); just as good as the usherette in *The Purple Rose of Cairo* (85); the center of the family, yet actually hard to grasp, in *Hannah and Her Sisters* (86); funny and clever in *Radio Days* (87).

Is it just hindsight, and our enforced knowledge of love running out, or was she indeed less interesting, to us and to Allen, in *September* (87), *Another Woman* (88), "Oepidus Wrecks" from *New York Stories* (89), *Crimes and Misdemeanors* (89), *Alice* (90), and *Shadows and Fog* (91)? As for *Husbands and Wives* (92), was the interest there only a matter of gossip?

She went to Ireland to make *Widow's Peak* (94, John Irvin); *Miami Rhapsody* (95, David Frankel); *Reckless* (95, Norman Rene); *Angela Mooney* (96, Tommy McArdle); *Private Parts* (97, Betty Thomas); *Redux Riding Hood* (97, Steve Moore); *Miracle at Midnight* (98, Ken Cameron); *Coming Soon* (99, Colette Burson); *Forget Me Never* (99, Robert Allan Ackerman); *A Girl Thing* (01, Lee

Rose); *Purpose* (01, Alan Ari Lazar); *The Secret Life of Zoey* (02, Robert Mandel).

Rainer Werner Fassbinder (1946–82),
b. Bad Wörrishofen, Germany

1965: *Der Stadtstreicher* (s). 1966: *Das Kleine Chaos* (s). 1969: *Liebe ist Kälter als der Tod/Love Is Colder than Death; Katzelmacher.* 1970: *Götter der Pest; Warum Laüft Herr R. Amok?/Why Does Herr R. Run Amok?; Der Amerikanische Soldat/The American Soldier; Die Niklashauser Fahrt.* 1971: *Rio das Mortes; Pioniere in Ingolstadt; Whity; Warnung vor einer Heiligen Nutte/Beware of a Holy Whore.* 1972: *Handler der Vier Jahreszeiten/The Merchant of Four Seasons; Die Bitteren Tränen der Petra Von Kant/The Bitter Tears of Petra Von Kant; Acht Stunden Sind Kein Tag/Eight Hours Don't Make a Day.* 1973: *Wildwechsel; Welt am Draht.* 1974: *Angst Essen Seele Auf/Fear Eats the Soul/Ali; Martha; Effi Briest.* 1975: *Faustrecht der Freiheit; Mütter Kusters Farht zum Himmel/Mother Kuster's Trip to Heaven; Angst vor der Angst/Fear of Fear; Faustrecht der Freiheit/Fox.* 1976: *Satansbraten/Satan's Brew; Chinesisches Roulette/Chinese Roulette.* 1977: *Bolwieser;* episode from *Deutschland im Herbst/Germany in Autumn; Eine Reise im Licht/Despair.* 1978: *Die Ehe der Maria Braun/The Marriage of Maria Braun; In einem Jahr mit 13 Monden.* 1979: *Die Dritte Generation/The Third Generation.* 1980: *Berlin Alexanderplatz; Lili Marleen.* 1981: *Lola; Theater in Trance; Veronika Voss.* 1982: *Querelle.*

There can be no doubt about the opportunities German cinema offered in the 1970s to politically committed but formally experimental films: Fassbinder had made nearly thirty feature films by his early thirties, and was working at a pace that must have helped kill him.

He came from fringe theatre in Munich. Originally an actor, he set up an antitheatre company, drastically adapted several classics, and wrote plays himself. Strongly influenced by Godard and Straub, he seemed possessed of ample creative vigor to become a leading cinematic figure in the next ten years. Like Straub, he was an exponent of pure film, minus vibrato or expressiveness, so uncompromisingly plain that we rediscover social realism beneath all the petty guises of life's performance. And like Godard, Fassbinder was in love with cinema, throwing off references and becoming increasingly preoccupied with the process of being in and watching film as his subject. His style was antistyle, and his material invoked the classical imagery of the thriller only to dispel its hardened familiarity. Composed memories of the gangster thriller prove illusory havens for would-be criminals hopelessly alienated from the style of their consumer world. Fassbinder punctures traditional romance, but mocks

the new urban dreariness with lavishly romantic accomplishments. His actors straightfacedly intone platitudes as if they were verse; grubby private disasters are underlined by the Sirk-like, Hollywood captioning that no longer has any relevance.

Above all, Fassbinder attacked the materially contented life of the new Germany, insisting on the unresolved anxieties and dreams that lurk behind it. Thus, *Herr R.* is an apparently successful man who kills his family, goes to the office, and commits suicide. *Katzelmacher* concerns the way a newly arrived immigrant, played by Fassbinder himself, reveals the moribund human and social responses of the inhabitants of a block of flats. *Der Handler der Vier Jahreszeiten* is about a barrowboy, so oppressed by the mundane details of his life that he kills himself. *Beware of a Holy Whore* is about a film crew that runs out of money and sits around idly until animosity slowly gathers into an extraordinary unordered but theatrical process of self-destruction.

Time and again, Fassbinder's characters sit around a table, apparently exchanging commonplaces. They are filmed as flatly as possible, denied facial expressiveness, and ordered to stylize flaccid dialogue with crazy rhythm. This is both an alienation effect and a dramatization of Fassbinder's view of our demoralized lives. It is not popular cinema: the manner is stark, and the implications are outrageously hostile to the bourgeois. Indeed, *Eight Hours Don't Make a Day,* for TV, is the offensive reworking of a typical family soap opera, dismantled until its innate fractures are horrifying.

It was not possible to keep up with Fassbinder, and there was much in the man that was determined to be unliked. But the rapidity and the cheapness were vital. *Despair* was his most lavish picture and the expense only showed a mind far more trite than that of Nabokov. *Despair* is one of the most dreadful spectacles of bull filmmaking being humiliated by literature's droll veronicas.

I would guess that the world of film commentary is still somewhat exhausted by Fassbinder—for he was prolific until the end: *Berlin Alexanderplatz,* from the Alfred Doblin novel, was a fourteen-part TV series that ran 931 minutes; *Veronika Voss* was among his most succinct films; and *Querelle* (from Genet) was unrestrainedly gay and rather foolishly gorgeous. Indeed, like Godard, Fassbinder hurled himself at us with such fury that we have retreated. But this astonishing body of work waits to be rediscovered. The bare fact is enough: Fassbinder died well short of forty, the maker of at least half a dozen extraordinary pictures: *The Bitter Tears of Petra von Kant* still has no equal in its simultaneous delight in "style" while pouring acid over the image; *Beware of a Holy Whore, Fear Eats the*

Soul, The Marriage of Maria Braun, and *Lola* (at least) are outstanding examples of how contemporary history can be focused on the screen in short, tough tales.

Alice Faye (Alice Fay Leppert) (1912–98), b. New York

Plump and wholesome as a Mable Lucy Atwell illustration grown up, Alice Faye was a friendly, sentimental star of musicals from 1935–45 and a big star with a warm singing voice. She was discovered as a chorus girl with *George White's Scandals* and featured in the film of the show for her debut in 1934. Fox put her under contract, gave her conventional parts—*Now I'll Tell* (34, Edwin Burke) and *She Learned About Sailors* (34, George Marshall)—and loaned her to Paramount for *Every Night at Eight* (35, Raoul Walsh). She attracted more attention in *Music Is Magic* (35, Marshall), and *King of Burlesque* (36) and *Sing, Baby, Sing* (36), both for Sidney Lanfield, but really came to the fore in *On the Avenue* (37, Roy del Ruth); *Wake Up and Live* (37, Lanfield); and *You Can't Have Everything* (37, Norman Taurog). Fox now eagerly starred her opposite Tyrone Power in *In Old Chicago* (38, Henry King) and *Alexander's Ragtime Band* (38, King). She had a few more straight parts: *Tail Spin* (39, del Ruth); *Barricade* (39, Gregory Ratoff); *Little Old New York* (40, King); and *Lillian Russell* (40, Irving Cummings), but was more successful in frivolous wartime musicals, often with John Payne and Jack Oakie: *Sally, Irene and Mary* (38, William A. Seiter); as the Fanny Brice figure in *Rose of Washington Square* (39, Ratoff); *Tin Pan Alley* (40, Walter Lang); *The Great American Broadcast* (41, Archie Mayo); *That Night in Rio* (41, Cummings); *Weekend in Havana* (41, Lang); *Hello, Frisco, Hello* (43, Bruce Humberstone); and *The Gang's All Here* (43, Busby Berkeley).

Already thinking of retirement (with her second husband, bandleader Phil Harris), she was suddenly very touching as the wife in Preminger's *Fallen Angel* (45). Still, she left the movies and returned only for the tame remake of *State Fair* (62, José Ferrer) and *The Magic of Lassie* (78, Don Chaffey).

Paul Fejos (Pál Fejös) (1897–1963), b. Budapest, Hungary

1920: *Pán; Hallucination; The Resurrected.* 1921: *A Fekete Kapitány/The Black Captain; Arsène Lupin Utalsá Kalandia/Arsene Lupin's Last Adventure.* 1922: *Szenzáció/Sensation/Pique Dame/ The Queen of Spades.* 1927: *The Last Moment.* 1928: *Lonesome.* 1929: *Broadway; The Last Performance/Erik the Great.* 1930: *Captain of the Guard* (credited to John S. Robertson); *Révolte dans la Prison/The Big House* (French version of the George Hill film). 1932: *Fantômas.* 1932: *Tavaszi Zápor; Ítél a Balaton.* 1933: *Sonnenstrahl; Fruhlingstimmen.* 1934: *Flugten fra Millionerne/Millions in Flight.* 1935: *Fange nr. 1/ Prisoner No. 1; Det Gyldne Smil/The Golden Smile.* 1936: *Black Horizons* (d). 1939: *Man och Kvinna/A Handful of Rice* (d). 1941: *Yagua* (d).

In just over twenty years (as indicated above), Paul Fejos made films in Hungary, Hollywood, France, Austria, Denmark, Madagascar, Thailand, and Peru—the last three represent the documentaries that closed his career. Yet he lived until 1963, most of the time in New York, where he was research director for the Viking Fund. Surely it is the subject for a biography, or a novel. Yet, the warning legend goes, nobody has heard of Paul Fejos.

His early Hungarian films are all, apparently, lost. Even for those who do know Fejos, a great deal of his reputation depends on *Lonesome,* a romance shot through with urban realism and that profound modern solitude the title addressed. *Broadway,* with Evelyn Brent, furthered his interest in moving camerawork. *The Last Performance* is Conrad Veidt as a crazed illusionist. *Tavaszi Zápor* (back in Hungary) is the dark story of a woman's fall, with Annabella supposedly at her best.

One day, perhaps, archival and videotape resources might come together, so that a reasonably full account can be offered of Fejos's career. For the moment, we know just that *Lonesome* is a great achievement, enough to convince anyone that Fejos could hardly use a camera without being eloquent. Scott Eyman has called *Lonesome* a small classic—and so it is. As for Fejos as a whole—one suspects a major neurotic.

María Félix (María de los Angeles Félix Guereña) (1914–2002), b. Alamos, Sonora, Mexico

You can call her a terrible actress, you can call her a diva of divas, but you can't deny that she was Mexico's greatest woman film star, and probably the biggest of all Spanish-language stars. Beginning in the early 1940s and on through three decades, she not only dominated the Mexican film industry but became a national idol—or at least a gigantic celebrity. Every artist from Orozco to Diego Rivera (who adored her: "He threw himself on me, like misery throws itself on the poor," she said) drew or painted her, and when she went to Europe in the fifties, Cocteau, Carrington, Leonor Fini, et al did the same. She knew the Peróns, King Farouk—you get the picture: the drive and ambition of a Callas but without the talent.

There are dozens of her Mexican films, and the few I've seen all give us the same Maria—the vamp, the resolute woman, and (later) the revolutionary. What made Mexicans mad about her was her male pride, and her refusal to be submissive. Her acting involves flashing eyes and tossed hair, and an absolute conviction that she is the most seductive woman alive. Five husbands agreed, including the songwriter Agustín Lara and one of Mexico's greatest male stars, Jorge Negrete, who died young, but not until the happy couple had appeared on the screen together. The Félix movies often echo Hollywood dramas of the period, except that in plot, acting, and production values it's strictly B features they resemble. In fact, Félix is something of a B-level Joan Crawford, combining Joan's torrid early style with her late steely one. She's at her best for director Emilio Fernández in *Río Escondido* (46) and *Enamorada* (47).

Félix made a number of films in Europe: in Spain, *Mare Nostrum* (48), costarring Fernando Rey and directed by Rafael Gil; it's a remake of the Blasco Ibáñez novel memorably filmed by Rex Ingram in 1926. There's a second-rate Buñuel film, *La Fièvre Monte à El Pao* (59). She went to Italy to be *Messalina* (51, Carmine Gallone). And then there's her real claim to fame, her role as La Belle Abbesse in Jean Renoir's beautiful *French Can Can* (1954). Here her Crawford look shades into an Ava Gardner look—she's really striking. She holds her own opposite Jean Gabin, she performs her belly dances like a real trouper, and she dominates the screen with that Matisse look Renoir deliberately developed for her. Renoir believed that she had Indian blood and ate raw meat. She also nearly killed Françoise Arnoul in a screen fight.

Her memoirs, by the way, are called *Todos Mis Guerras—All My Wars*. That reflects her prolonged feud with Carlos Fuentes, who had depicted her in a novel and a play as a national myth. In addition, Octavio Paz said she was "free like the wind, she disperses the clouds, or illuminates them with the lightning flash of her gaze."

Federico Fellini (1920–93), b. Rimini, Italy
1950: *Luci del Varieta/Lights of Variety* (codirected with Alberto Lattuada). 1952: *Lo Sciecco Bianco/The White Sheik*. 1953: *I Vitelloni*; "Una Agenzia Matrimoniale," episode from *Amore in Citta*. 1954: *La Strada*. 1955: *Il Bidone*. 1956: *Le Notti di Cabiria/Nights of Cabiria*. 1959: *La Dolce Vita*. 1962: "Le Tentazioni del Dottor Antonio," episode from *Boccaccio '70*. 1963: *8½*. 1965: *Giulietta degli Spiriti/Juliet of the Spirits*. 1967: "Toby Dammit," episode from *Histoires Extraordinaires*. 1969: *Fellini: A Director's Notebook; Fellini's Satyricon*. 1970: *I Clowns*. 1972: *Fellini's Roma*. 1973: *Amarcord*. 1976: *Fellini's Casanova*. 1978: *Prova d'Orchestra/Orchestra Rehearsal*. 1980: *La Citta delle Donne/City of Women*. 1983: *E la Nave Va/And the Ship Sails On*. 1985: *Ginger e Fred/Ginger and Fred*. 1987: *Intervista/The Interview*. 1990: *La Voce della Luna/The Voice of the Moon*.

Although the confessional element in Fellini's work was only unmistakable from 8½ onward, we can now see that no other Italian so absorbed himself in the act of being an international film director. No other director—apart from Orson Welles—so insisted on the personal derivation of all his work, nor managed to make even fragments of film or biographical incidents seem like parts of a total oeuvre. Fellini often takes the pose of the innocent fascinated but bewildered by the picaresque variety of life. Yet the question must be asked whether his films have made a sham of vitality in the process of smothering life with affectionate but self-indulgent egotism? There is a special aptness in that Welles—a provincial who persistently gathered accomplishment and urbanity to himself—should be the source of this comment on Fellini: "His films are a small-town boy's dream of the big city. His sophistication works because it's the creation of someone who doesn't have it. But he shows dangerous signs of being a superlative artist with little to say."

From the Adriatic coast—packed in summer, desolate in winter, and the source of so many crucial beach scenes—Fellini developed several talents: as a cartoonist, a gagman for comedians, and a radio writer. There is a famous photograph of him newly arrived in Rome in 1940, a *vitellone* already, sharp-faced but soft-skinned, in a pose of indolent self-preoccupation, yet slyly alert to the camera. It is a very intelligent, responsive face that waits for some attitude to inhabit. Sitting at a café, he looks on the point of devouring a big opportunity; it is the face of one of Stendhal's young men ready to take Holy Orders, a military commission, or a friend's wife if it will allow him a pretext for escaping inertia.

He took up writing for the movies, as well as radio. In 1943, he married the actress Giulietta Masina, and with the liberation he began to gain credits: *Avanti c'e Posto* (42, Mario Bonnard); *Apparizione* (43, Jean de Limur); and *Tutta la Citta Canta* (45, Riccardo Freda). His real sponsor was Roberto Rossellini: Fellini worked on the scripts of *Open City* (45), *Paisan* (46), and the "Il Miracolo" episode of *L'Amore* (48), in which he also played the part of the vagrant who seduces Anna Magnani. He also worked on the scripts of *Il Delitto di Giovanni Episcopo* (47, Alberto Lattuada); *Senza Pieta* (48, Lattuada); *In Nome della Legge* (49, Pietro Germi); *Il Mulino del Po* (49, Lattuada); and *Francesco, Giullare di Dio* (50, Rossellini).

Fellini's first independent direction, *The White Sheik,* was a comic but baleful work, scourging the world of hack writing that had bred Fellini himself. Pierre Leprohon has compared its saving revelation of Masina (as a prostitute) at the end of the film with the way the prostitute character changes Chaplin's Monsieur Verdoux. In retrospect, therefore, *The White Sheik* seems a clear promise of autobiography. But Fellini moved on to the most conventional and least interesting phase of his life. *I Vitelloni* is good social observation, a rather old-fashioned story about the layabout character close to Fellini's heart. *La Strada* is a desperately portentous film, laboriously drawing a trite humanist message out of a picture of a circus brute that encouraged Anthony Quinn to think there was splendor in overacting. *Il Bidone* was another Maupassant-like *conte* in which Broderick Crawford and Richard Basehart masqueraded as priests to enhance their career as confidence tricksters. *Cabiria* is a woefully sincere story about a tart with a heart that seems oblivious of its own coarseness or the risibility of the pluck with which Masina bites back her tears. This quartet needs to be put firmly in its place. They are slick, mechanical stories, feeding on superficial feelings and uncritical of sentimentality or grand effects. As to style or creative intelligence, they do not begin to intrude upon the achievement of *La Signora Senza Camelie, Le Amiche,* much less the films Rossellini was making at the same time.

In its day, *La Dolce Vita* was hailed as a brilliant satire on the new self-conscious permissiveness of European high society. Only a facile spectator could be more anguished by its sluggish dismay at corruption than by the metaphysical alienation of *L'Avventura.* And it is a glib intelligence that can find any gravity in the soulful beach ending with the central observer—Marcello Mastroianni—solacing his lazy spirit with the enigmatic tolerance of a smiling child. But the film was a scandalous success and made Fellini into the self-sufficient star name that he playfully grappled with ever after.

Besieged by interviewers and critical attention, the provincial boy grew worldly wise. His actual intellectual shallowness was passed off as the dilemma of a warmhearted man in a disintegrating world. With great skill, Fellini persuaded many viewers that his dwelling on freaks, underworld degenerates, and the chattering infantile crowd was both satirical and charitable. In 8½ he invented a director who was the representation of himself and called the man's empty talent the mark of philosophy. It is at about this time that he introduced the metaphor of the circus as a way of papering over the artistic cracks:

> The cinema is very much like the circus; and in fact, if it didn't exist, I might well have become a circus director. The circus, too, is an exact mixture of technique, precision and improvisation. While the rehearsed spectacle is on, you

are still taking risks: that is, simultaneously, you live. I love this way of creating and living at the same time, without the limits set to a writer or a painter, through being plunged into action.

That is an intriguing definition or apologia, but Godard or Warhol are more searching demonstrations of it than Fellini. The deliberate confusion of documentary and fantasy is wearisome in Fellini, largely because he has never proved himself in the way all directors must—through style and the use of film as a language. In fact, Fellini's style is very sparse and undeveloped. He has seldom done more than arrange elaborate grotesque tableaux for the camera or listen to idle chatter from his characters. The precise point of view that is essential to the movies is too demanding for his theatre-in-the-round generalizations. Fascinated by ugliness and grotesques, he expresses himself on film without grace.

I mistrust the rather smarmy wrapping up of *Fellini: A Director's Notebook* when the director says, "Yes, I know it must seem sinful, cruel, but no, I am very fond of all those characters who are always chasing after me, following me from one film to another. They are all a little mad, I know that. They say they need me, but the truth is that I need them more. Their human qualities are rich, comic, and sometimes very moving." The defense is disarming; but there are no characters in Fellini's work, only caricatures. And for all the autobiography we know nothing more about Fellini than that he was an obsessional, vacuous poseur. It is not an artistic response to breakdown to be charmed by the parades of unhappiness and to call it "rich, comic, and sometimes very moving." Fellini appears to me a half-baked, playacting pessimist, with no capacity for tragedy. He makes Welles seem a giant and a romantic marvelously able to create tragedy without being depressing. Welles holds to order while Fellini is doodling in chaos.

The Fellini of the last fifteen years did nothing to change my mind. *And the Ship Sails On* and *Ginger and Fred* were especially fussy and disappointing. In recent years, *La Dolce Vita* has been rereleased, and it seemed very dated. Fellini had his fashion, to be sure, and he was a key figure in the bringing of foreign films to Britain and America. But I wonder how many fervent admirers he has today?

Emilio Fernández (Romo) (1904–86),
b. El Seco, Mexico
1941: *La Isla de la Pasión/Passion Island.* 1942: *Soy Puro Mexicano.* 1943: *Flor Sylvestre; María Candelaria.* 1944: *Las Abandonadas; Bugambilia.* 1945: *Pepita Jiménez.* 1946: *La Perla/The Pearl; Enamorada.* 1947: *Río Escondido/Hidden River.* 1948: *Malcovia; Salón México.* 1949: *Pueblerina;*

La Malquerida; Duelo en las Montañas. 1950: *The Torch; Un Día de Vida; Víctimas del Pecado.* 1951: *La Bienamada; Acapulco; Islas Marías; Soave Patria; Siempre Tuya.* 1952: *Tu y el Mar; Cuando Levanta la Niebla.* 1953: *La Red/The Net; El Reportaje; El Rapto.* 1954: *La Rosa Blanca; La Rebelión de los Colgados; Nostros Dos.* 1955: *La Tierra del Fuego Se Apaga.* 1956: *Una Cita de Amor.* 1957: *El Impostor.* 1962: *Pueblito.* 1966: *Un Dorado de Pancho Villa/A Loyal Soldier of Pancho Villa.* 1968: *El Crepúscolo de un Dios.* 1973: *La Choca.* 1976: *Zona Roja.*

"El Indio," as he was named (because of an Indian mother), was the supreme figure in Mexican film, and one of the most flamboyant of directors. (He was ready to take a gun to an ungenerous critic.) He fought in the Mexican revolutionary wars and was actually sentenced to a twenty-year jail term (murder was at issue), from which he escaped to California.

When he returned, he took up acting, and then directing. He specialized in romantic melodramas, vividly photographed by Gabriel Figueroa and featuring María Félix (*Río Escondido, Enamorada*), Dolores del Rio (*Flor Sylvestre, María Candelaria, Bugambilia*), and his wife, Columba Domínguez.

In later years, he turned to acting, and he is superb as Mapache, struggling to cling on to a rampant machine gun (and all our worst notions of Mexico) in *The Wild Bunch* (69, Sam Peckinpah), and as Paco in *Pat Garrett and Billy the Kid* (73, Peckinpah).

Abel Ferrara, b. Bronx, New York, 1952
1979: *The Driller Killer.* 1981: *Ms. 45/Angel of Vengeance.* 1984: *Fear City.* 1987: *China Girl.* 1989: *King of New York.* 1990: *Cat Chaser.* 1992: *Bad Lieutenant.* 1993: *Dangerous Game.* 1994: *Body Snatchers; Snake Eyes.* 1995: *The Addiction.* 1996: *The Funeral.* 1997: *The Blackout.* "Love on the Train," an episode from *Subway Stories: Tales from the Underground* (TV). 1998: *New Rose Hotel.* 2001: *R-Xmas.*

Ferrara seems determined to remain a fringe figure—and I'd guess he knows himself best. His closest to a hit, the very violent, very sexual *Bad Lieutenant,* did not lure him into anything like a mainstream career. (The recent *New Rose Hotel*—taken from a William Gibson story—is his fullest collapse into the ludicrous extreme that has always beckoned.) But the terminal self-abuse of *Bad Lieutenant,* plus the dedication of that mode's master, Harvey Keitel, was certainly disturbing (as well as very clever—witness the inspired but invented baseball series in the background). It seems to me a little too self-aware, a little too desperate to be true. Whereas in other films Ferrara

has been more fully immersed, so that one feels less urge to question the gloomy religiousness or the seething depression. *Ms. 45,* done for peanuts, is a deserved classic. *King of New York* is a genuine cult favorite, and an early sign of the mad grace in Christopher Walken. *The Addiction* is brilliant, with a great performance by Lili Taylor. But *The Funeral* is his best work—full of the comic, tragic reach of family, a *Sopranos* for the madhouse.

José Ferrer (José Vicente Ferrer De Otero y Cintron) (1912–92), b. Santurce, Puerto Rico
Educated at Princeton, Ferrer intended to be an architect, but went into summer stock as a stage manager and actor. In New York, in 1944–45, he played Iago to Paul Robeson's Othello. His first movie part was the Dauphin to Ingrid Bergman's *Joan of Arc* (48, Victor Fleming). Thereafter, he was cast in flamboyant or foreign parts: the hypnotist, Korvo, in *Whirlpool* (49, Otto Preminger); the Peronist dictator in *Crisis* (50, Richard Brooks); and then as *Cyrano de Bergerac* (50, Michael Gordon), for which he received an Oscar. After *Anything Can Happen* (52, George Seaton), John Huston cut him down to size for Toulouse-Lautrec in *Moulin Rouge* (53), and he followed this with *Miss Sadie Thompson* (54, Curtis Bernhardt); as the defending officer in *The Caine Mutiny* (54, Edward Dmytryk); and as an assured Sigmund Romberg in *Deep in My Heart* (54, Stanley Donen). At this point, he became an actor-director: *The Shrike* (55); *Cockleshell Heroes* (56); *The Great Man* (56); *I Accuse* (57)—as Dreyfus; and *The High Cost of Loving* (58). Unusual films, they never manage to be personal, but *The Shrike* is uncomfortable, and *The Great Man* knows just how wicked media life can be (but how it talks!).

After the colorless *Return to Peyton Place* (61) and a remade *State Fair* (62), Ferrer settled for acting, generally as a saturnine Hollywood wog: the Turkish officer in *Lawrence of Arabia* (62, David Lean); *Nine Hours to Rama* (62, Mark Robson); *Stop Train 349* (64, Rolf Haedrich); Herod Antipas in *The Greatest Story Ever Told* (65, George Stevens); the anti-Semite in *Ship of Fools* (65, Stanley Kramer); *Enter Laughing* (67, Carl Reiner); as Hassan Bey in *Cervantes* (67, Vincent Sherman); *Order to Kill* (73, José Moresso); a priest in *e' Lollipop* (75, Ashley Lazarus); *The Sentinel* (76, Michael Winner); *Voyage of the Damned* (76, Stuart Rosenberg); *Zoltan . . . Hound of Dracula* (77, Albert Band); *The Private Files of J. Edgar Hoover* (77, Larry Cohen); *The Amazing Captain Nemo* (78, Alex March); *The Swarm* (78, Irwin Allen); *Fedora* (78, Billy Wilder); and *The 5th Musketeer* (79, Ken Annakin).

His last years made a very mixed bag: *The Big Brawl* (80, Robert Clouse), a Jackie Chan martial arts movie; *The Being* (80, Jackie Kong); *Berlin Tunnel 21* (81, Richard Michaels); *A Midsummer Night's Sex Comedy* (82, Woody Allen); *To Be or Not to Be* (82, Alan Johnson); *Blood Feud* (83, Mike Newell); *Dune* (84, David Lynch); *The Evil That Men Do* (84, J. Lee Thompson); *Samson and Delilah* (84, Lee Philips) for TV; *Hitler's SS: Portrait in Evil* (85, Jim Goddard); *Seduced* (85, Jerrold Freedman); and *The Sun and the Moon* (87, Kevin Conway).

He had been married to Uta Hagen, and then later to singer Rosemary Clooney.

Mel Ferrer (Melchior Gaston Ferrer),
b. Elberon, New Jersey, 1917
Technically, Ferrer has five pictures to his credit as a director, even if one of them is the multiflavored *Vendetta*. But, like José Ferrer, he is an actor who has striven to direct, only to make films that seem not just without purpose, but unattended. It is an odd, dilettante involvement in films by a man who has promised more soulful intelligence than he has ever delivered.

Ferrer went to Princeton and worked in publishing while he was cultivating himself as a rep actor. His Broadway debut was as a dancer. After working as an actor and director for radio, he entered films in 1947—as an actor—in *Lost Boundaries* (Alfred Werker); and as the director of *The Girl of the Limberlost*. When *Vendetta* was eventually released in 1950, Ferrer was given the credit for the stew of himself, Howard Hughes, Max Ophuls, Preston Sturges, and Stuart Heisler—presumably on the principle of passing it off on the least vigorous. By then, Ferrer was shooting out in all directions: under contract to Selznick as actor and director; as a founder member of the La Jolla Playhouse; as a Broadway director; and as assistant to John Ford on *The Fugitive* (47). In 1950, at RKO, he directed Claudette Colbert and Robert Ryan in *The Secret Fury* and then settled for a period of acting: *Born to Be Bad* (50, Nicholas Ray); *The Brave Bulls* (51, Robert Rossen); *Scaramouche* (52, George Sidney); *Rancho Notorious* (52, Fritz Lang); *Lili* (53, Charles Walters); *Saadia* (53, Albert Lewin); *Knights of the Round Table* (54, Richard Thorpe); *Oh, Rosalinda!!* (55, Michael Powell); as Andrei in *War and Peace* (56, King Vidor); to France for *Elena et les Hommes* (56, Jean Renoir); as Robert Cohn in *The Sun Also Rises* (57, Henry King); *The Vintage* (57, Jeffrey Hayden); and *Mayerling* (57, Anatole Litvak).

In 1954, Ferrer had married Audrey Hepburn and in 1959 he directed her as Rima in *Green Mansions*, full of plastic studio jungle, Villa-Lobos music, and Katherine Dunham dancers, but implacably dull and managing to make Hepburn look less than exquisite. He and his wife moved to Europe in the 1960s and Ferrer continued his

somewhat ineffectual flowering. As an actor, he gathered some eccentric parts: *Fraulein* (57, Henry Koster); *The World, the Flesh and the Devil* (59, Ranald MacDougall); *Et Mourir de Plaisir* (60, Roger Vadim); *The Hands of Orlac* (61, Edmond Greville); and *The Fall of the Roman Empire* (63, Anthony Mann). He went to Spain to produce and play the lead in *El Greco* (64, Luciano Salce); and in the same year he acted in *Sex and the Single Girl* (Richard Quine). In 1967 he produced, wrote, and directed *Cabriola*, and then produced his wife in *Wait Until Dark* (67, Terence Young).

Next year they were divorced, and Ferrer later suffered a heart attack. But in 1971, he produced and acted in *Time for Loving* (Christopher Miles); in 1972 he produced *Embassy* (Gordon Hessler); in 1974 he produced *W* (Richard Quine); *The Antichrist* (74, Alberto de Martino); *Brannigan* (75, Douglas Hickox); *Death Trap* (76, Tobe Hooper); *Zwischengleis* (78, Wolfgang Staudte); *The Amazing Captain Nemo* (78, Alex March); and *The Norsemen* (78, Charles B. Pierce).

Since then, he has had an "international" career, in films few people have seen: as an extraterrestrial in *The Visitor* (79, Michael J. Paradise); *Top of the Hill* (80, Walter Grauman) for TV; *The Fifth Floor* (80, Howard Avedis); *The Memory of Eva Ryker* (80, Grauman); a Spanish-Italian coproduction, *City of the Walking Dead* (80, Umberto Lenzi); *Fugitive Family* (80, Paul Krasny); *Lili Marleen* (81, Rainer Werner Fassbinder), as a man who helps Jews escape the Nazis; *One Shoe Makes It Murder* (82, William Hale); *Seduced* (85, Jerrold Freedman); *Outrage!* (86, Grauman); and *Peter the Great* (86, Marvin Chomsky and Lawrence Schiller). He had also played in TV's *Falcon Crest* for a few years in the early eighties.

Marco Ferreri (1928–97), b. Milan, Italy
1957: *El Pisito*. 1959: *Los Chicos*. 1960: *El Cochecito*. 1961: "L'Indelta Conjugale," episode from *Le Italiene e l'Amore*. 1963: *Una Storia Moderna; L'Ape Regina*. 1964: "Il Professore," episode from *Controsesso; La Donna Scimmia*; "L'Uomo dai Cinque Palloni," episode from *Oggi, Domani e Dopo-Domani*. 1965: *Marcia Nuziale*. 1967: *L'Harem*. 1968: *L'Uomo dai Palloncini*. 1969: *Dillinger e Morto; Il Seme dell' Uomo*. 1970: *L'Udienza*. 1972: *La Grande Bouffe/Blow-Out*. 1976: *L'Ultima Donna/The Last Woman*. 1978: *Ciao Maschio/Bye Bye Monkey*. 1979: *Chiedo Asilo*. 1981: *Storie di Ordinaria Follia/Tales of Ordinary Madness*. 1982: *Storia di Piera/The Story of Piera*. 1984: *Il Futuro e Donna*. 1986: *Te Amo/I Love You*. 1988: *Y'a bon les Blancs/Um Good, de White Folks*. 1990: *La Casa del Sorriso*. 1991: *La Carne*. 1993: *Diario di un Vizio*. 1996: *Nitrato d'Argento*.

Non-Italian audiences were hardly prepared for the beauty of *Dillinger e Morto*. Amid the abstraction of Antonioni's films and Fellini's gloating advertising of his own fantasies, here, without much announcement, was a superb account of the universal alienation of materialism and dream. *Dillinger* is a domestic Odyssey that so thoroughly explores the spiritual distances between people and the dazzling objects of their lives that it can merely refer to the actual journey that its central character will make to Tahiti when he has shot his wife. Quite simply, the film deals with an evening at home in the house of a designer of industrial masks, played by Michel Piccoli, and with his nearly lyrical resort to disruption to overcome the oppressive weight of household objects and the dead emotions caught between their cold, plastic surfaces. *Dillinger* is a major film made with tranquil clarity so that its fierce sense of humanity seems almost apologetic. Its content is totally cinematic: in color, composition, form, spatial relationship, and in small movements within so many fixed tableaux.

And yet, we know too little about Ferreri before *Dillinger*. He was a journalist who, in 1951, helped to found a regular celluloid magazine consisting of fictional episodes, newsreels, documentaries, and cinema verité exercises. "Documenti Mensile" was something like the sort of cinematic venture Dziga Vertov had intended in the 1920s. Although it failed, it still seems an interesting venture, albeit an attempt to imitate the variety offered by TV and to give it a structural awareness denied by the small box. It was during this period that Ferreri collaborated with Cesare Zavattini on the episode-film, *L'Amore in Citta* (53).

Then, with something of the blithe arbitrariness of *Dillinger*, he went to Spain to sell anamorphic lenses. That led him into his first three films, of which only *El Cochecito* is well known: a black comedy about a healthy, wealthy man determined against all social opposition to have a wheelchair of his own. At the time, it seemed like a deliberate miming of Buñuel's black comedy, but *Dillinger* suggests that Ferreri is a companion surrealist and anarchist, worthy of attention and opportunity. *La Grande Bouffe* is an assault on the grossness and hypocrisy of human appetites, a shocking, tumultuous, but oddly self-contained film; whereas *Dillinger's* initial blandness allows meanings to stream out of it.

Later Ferreri grew increasingly eccentric, but *Tales of Ordinary Madness* was an adaptation of stories by Charles Bukowski that starred Ben Gazzara and Ornella Muti, while *The Story of Piera* had Hanna Schygulla and Isabelle Huppert as mother and daughter.

Louis Feuillade (1873–1925),
b. Lunel, France

Incomplete list: 1906: *C'est Papa qui Prend le Plunge; Le Billet de Banque*. 1907: *Un Facteur trop Ferré; Vive le Sabotage; La Course des Belles-Mères; L'Homme Aimante*. 1908: *Le Roman de Soeur Louise; Un Tic*. 1909: *Les Heures*. 1910–13: *Bébé* (series in sixty-three parts). 1911: *Aux Lions des Chrétiens*. 1911–13: *La Vie Telle qu'Elle est* (series in fifteen parts). 1912: *Le Proscrit*. 1912–16: *Bout-de-Zan* (series in forty-five parts). 1913: *L'Intruse; Erreur Tragique; Une Drame au Pays Basque; Fantômas* (serial in five episodes); *Juve Contre Fantômas* (serial in four episodes); *La Mort qui Tuer* (serial in six episodes). 1914: *Fantômas Contre Fantômas* (serial in four parts); *Le Faux Magistrat*. 1915–16: *Les Vampires* (serial in ten episodes). 1916: *Judex* (serial in twelve episodes). 1917: *La Nouvelle Mission de Judex* (serial in twelve episodes). 1918: *Vendémiaire* (in four parts); *Tih Minh* (serial in twelve episodes). 1919: *Le Nocturne; L'Homme sans Visage; Énigme; Barabas* (serial in twelve episodes); *Les Deux Gamines* (serial in twelve episodes). 1921: *L'Orpheline* (serial in twelve episodes); *Parisette* (serial in twelve episodes); *Saturnin ou le Bon Allumeur*. 1922: *Le Fils du Filibustier* (serial in twelve episodes). 1923: *Vindicta* (in five parts); *Le Gamin de Paris*. 1924: *La Fille bien Gardée; Lucette; Le Stigmate* (serial in six episodes).

The fact that *Fantômas* antedates *Birth of a Nation* by two years is immaterial, so great is the gap between them in cinematic and theatrical reality. *Fantômas* is the first great movie experience, Feuillade the first director for whom no historical allowances need to be made. See him today and you still wonder what will happen next. With Griffith, we are forever urging him to come to a point we have foreseen.

Whereas Griffith's world harks back to a Victorian, bourgeois morality and was tinged by nostalgia for the gentility of Gish-like ladies, Feuillade predicts a twentieth-century world yet to come. Even in the years of the First World War, he looked past the horrific clash of machine guns and cavalry, of mud and dress uniform, to an atmosphere of urban anxiety. The city scenes in his serials have all the ghostly anonymity of the street sets in Lang's work, of the grey depths of *Paris Nous Appartient* and *Bande à Part*, or of the fantastic melodrama of Dealey Plaza in Dallas, 1963.

Feuillade's genius is simply measured: he saw that it was possible to achieve intense photographic naturalism and yet convey an imaginative experience of the world. Thus his films still involve audiences. They respond to the startling contrast of the mundane and the unexpected; and they are intrigued by the relentless criminal organizations in *Fantômas* and *Vampires*. All the roots of the thriller and suspense genres are in Feuillade's sense that evil, anarchy, and destructiveness speak to the frustrations banked up in modern society. Even the originality of Lang and Hitchcock fall into place when one has seen Feuillade: Mabuse is the disciple of Fantômas; while Hitchcock's persistent faith in the nun who wears high heels, in the crop-spraying plane that will swoop down to kill, and in a world mined for the complacent is inherited from Feuillade. As Alain Resnais has said, ". . . Feuillade's cinema is very close to dreams—therefore it's perhaps the most realistic." Not only has Feuillade's pregnant view of grey streets become an accepted normality; his expectation of conspiracy, violence, and disaster spring at us every day.

Feuillade managed this alertness despite all the impediments of the age: he was the son of a civil servant; educated at a Catholic seminary; four years in the cavalry. He worked as a journalist and ran a magazine before he began to submit scripts to Gaumont. His energy was prodigious and when Alice Guy left Gaumont for New York he took her place as artistic director. He plunged into his serials and in a directing life of less than twenty years produced more than seven hundred films, despite service in the French army in 1915 and a wound sufficient for his discharge.

Fantômas and the Vampires were criminal gangs intent on gaining material and psychological power over a decadent bourgeoisie. Their names show how far they are destructive angels, dreaded and craved by their victims. And Feuillade's inventiveness—of plot, action, and visual revelation—has exactly the same inspiration as the gang's plans: a cheerful contempt for society that gains as much from Anarchism as it looks forward to Dada and Surrealism. Mabuse expresses the same compulsion in a narrower German setting in which anarchy fades into fascism. For that reason alone, Mabuse is ugly and frightening whereas Feuillade's criminals—especially Musidora's Irma Vep in *Vampires*—are glowing black humorists with all the ambiguous charm of Dracula. That is the importance of Feuillade as a cultural bridge: he transferred perhaps the most psychologically potent of Victorian fantasies to the new medium. It is worth emphasizing that, at the time, *Vampires* alarmed the authorities. The serial was briefly banned and *Judex* was Feuillade's attempt to reassure the trembling bourgeois. *Tih Minh,* however, returns to organized malice, with the remnants of the Vampires in Nice planning world destruction, with England as first target.

The films themselves are still hard to see; only good anarchists have preserved Feuillade. The serials run for between four and six hours, and they are dreamlike if only because of the endlessly regenerating plots. The action is hallucinatory, but the images are astonishingly concrete.

By comparison with Feuillade's relaxed, subtle camera, Griffith's is pompous and prettifying. Tom Milne has acclaimed the moment in *Fantômas* when a character in a box at the theatre is shown conceiving an idea—to use the actor masquerading on stage as Fantômas to replace the real one in jail—in the same shot as we see the stage behind her. It is this immediate appetite for the real world and the stirring up of fantastic events that make Feuillade the most serious of the pioneers. He foresaw that people who went into the dark to participate in stories, no matter how sophisticated their world, were still primitive creatures.

Jacques Feyder (Jacques Frédérix) (1885–1948), b. Ixelles, Belgium
All films are shorts up to 1919.
1915: *M. Pinson, Policier* (codirected with Gaston Ravel). 1916: *Têtes de Femmes, Femmes de Tête; L'Homme de Compagnie; Tiens, Vous Êtes à Poitiers?; L'Instinct est Maître; Le Pied qui Étreint; Le Bluff; Un Conseil d'Ami; Le Frère de Lait; Le Billard Cassé; Abrégons les Formalités; Le Trouvaille de Bouchu.* 1917: *Le Pardessus de Demi-Saison; Les Vieilles Dames de l'Hospice; Le Ravin sans Fond* (codirected with Raymond Bernard). 1919: *Le Faute d'Orthographie.* 1921: *L'Atlantide.* 1923: *Crainquebille; Visages d'Enfants* (codirected with Françoise Rosay). 1925: *L'Image; Gribiche.* 1926: *Carmen* (codirected with Rosay). 1927: *Au Pays du Roi Lépreux.* 1928: *Thérèse Raquin.* 1929: *The Kiss; Les Nouveaux Messieurs.* 1930: German version of *Anna Christie;* French version of *The Unholy Night; Si l'Empereur Savait Ça.* 1931: *Son of India; Daybreak.* 1934: *Le Grand Jeu.* 1935: *Pension Mimosas; La Kermesse Héroïque.* 1937: *Knight Without Armor; Fahrendes Volk.* 1939: *La Loi du Nord.* 1942: *Une Femme Disparaît.*

There was a time when Feyder was claimed as a great realist director, when *Kermesse Héroïque* was thought of as an important French film. It looks now like an intolerably pretty Dutch interior, proof that as fine a photographer as Harry Stradling can be reduced to inertia if asked simply to produce exquisite shots. Feyder is more interesting as a sympathetic director of women in fanciful material—his wife Françoise Rosay in several films, Garbo in *The Kiss* and the German *Anna Christie,* Dietrich in the dotty *Knight Without Armor*—Tom Milne has noted Feyder's thematic pursuit of the woman who means different things to different men. And if overshadowed by such as *Vertigo, Lola Montès,* and *Elena et les Hommes,* Feyder may be unfairly neglected today just as once he was injudiciously acclaimed.

An actor originally, he worked for Louis Feuillade. Wounded in the First World War, he roamed around France, Switzerland, and Austria; wrote *Poil de Carotte* (25, Julien Duvivier); and in 1929 went to Hollywood. He did not last long there, and after some work on foreign language versions and two Ramon Novarro films—*Son of India* and *Daybreak*—he worked in France, England, and Germany before the outbreak of war. He went to Switzerland and made *Une Femme Disparaît*, and in 1946 he collaborated on *Macadam* (Marcel Blistène).

Sally Field, b. Pasadena, California, 1946

Such a stubborn, anxious face, with three expressions: pert, sulky, and the rapture that knows we love her. Yet how swiftly glory passes on for an actress. The two-time Oscar winner of the early eighties is now hard-pressed to find worthwhile roles, and she must wonder whether anyone remembers.

She is the daughter of actress Margaret Field, and the stepdaughter of actor Jock Mahoney. By the time she was twenty-two, she was a veteran of TV series: *Gidget* and *The Flying Nun*, successes that she battled hard to live down. But on the big screen, she has often been a redneck girl, aligned with the South and reliant on such things as her friendship with Burt Reynolds and the kindness of Martin Ritt: *The Way West* (67, Andrew V. McLaglen); *Stay Hungry* (76, Bob Rafelson); an Emmy on TV as *Sybil* (76, Daniel Petrie), a case of multiple personalities; *Smokey and the Bandit* and *II* (77, 80, Hal Needham); *Heroes* (77, Jeremy Paul Kagan); *Hooper* (78, Needham); *The End* (78, Reynolds); *Beyond the Poseidon Adventure* (79, Irwin Allen); an Oscar for *Norma Rae* (79, Ritt); *Absence of Malice* (81, Sydney Pollack); *Back Roads* (81, Ritt); *Kiss Me Goodbye* (82, Robert Mulligan); another Oscar in *Places in the Heart* (84, Robert Benton); *Murphy's Romance* (85, Ritt); *Surrender* (87, Jerry Belson); *Punchline* (88, David Seltzer); *Steel Magnolias* (89, Herbert Ross); *Not Without My Daughter* (91, Brian Gilbert); *Soapdish* (91, Michael Hoffman); *Mrs. Doubtfire* (93, Chris Columbus); and mother to *Forrest Gump* (94, Robert Zemeckis).

These days, a lot of her work is for TV: *A Woman of Independent Means* (95, Robert Greenwald); *Eye for an Eye* (96, John Schlesinger); as George's mother and the narrator in *Merry Christmas, George Bailey* (97, Matthew Diamond and Rae Kraus); as codirector and Trudy Cooper in *From the Earth to the Moon* (98, David Carson); *A Cooler Climate* (99, Susan Seidelman); *Where the Heart Is* (00, Matt Williams); as Betsey Trotwood in *David Copperfield* (00, Peter Medak)—did Edna Mae Oliver growl in her grave?; *Time of Our Lives* (00, Mary Agnes Donoghue); *Say It Isn't So* (01, James B. Rogers). Plus her schizy mother on *ER* and a Supreme Court justice on *The Court*.

She was in *Legally Blonde 2: Red, White and Blonde* (03, Charles Herman-Wurmfeld).

W. C. Fields (William Claude Dukinfield) (1879–1946), b. Philadelphia

My Dear Wilkie,

Fields died yesterday. Poor Bill Fields, you will say, until it strikes you that the scoundrel contrived to juggle his passing on to Christmas Day, that day he despised above all and which, he believed, needed some small alternative to the celebrations that have been attached to its other anniversary. It occurs to me that we might work up a bright little piece on misanthropes all over the world, roused from the Christmas stupor of dandling children on their knees and having to share hard drink with nephews by word that Fields had put a permanent stain on the day. No man who has ever passed Christmas Day on his own trying to avoid the sounds of others' happiness could resist a nod to old Bill. Of course, he was wrecked by the end and thus, as ever, unwarmed by his own joke.

As you know, I had been acquainted fleetingly with Fields for many years, and I am by no means within the film-making fraternity— though I might have written a great deal more but for the distractions of their offerings. Nevertheless, I always found it remarkable that so many shrewd, not to say incredulous, men took Fields for a comedian. As though our laughing at a creature made him a clown! I have hardly comprehended the fearful wretchedness of his life, but the mottling of his sad face, and the horrid knowledge that those plum blotches were blood ready to force a way through papery skin, were enough to shame anyone who has sat in the lamplight and tried to invent a plausible illness for some literary character. Nor could even your own ingenuity for narrative, my dear Collins—and you know what honest admiration I have for it—begin to trace the anxiety with which Fields hid away his money in some several hundred separate bank accounts; nor invent the strange names in which those accounts were lodged. There was no reasoning with him in this, and no kind comfort that convinced him of any other fate than a brutal alcoholic death.

There was nothing amusing in the complete absence of pathos in his view of himself. Have you not noticed among the Hollywood folk that faces attempt constantly to make themselves more attractive? Not Fields. He had the expression of a man sunk in despair and yet untouched by self-pity. The world is very bad, Fields' face seemed to say, which is exactly what anyone would expect. When his Micawber assured us that he was for ever expecting something to turn up, who was left in any doubt but that he foresaw some fresh disaster, as prickly and unpredictable as those strange names he invented for himself: Mahatma Kane Jeeves, Egbert Souse, Cuthbert J. Twillie? Although their characters were opposite, I was always reminded of Sterne's Toby, a figure all the more tragically comic for his ignorance of the humour that floats off him. Fields became funnier, the more desperately he resorted to that baleful view of treacherous, cowardly and disgusting humankind. He made it clear that any man who does not do away with himself once he is old enough to measure the poison is a public laughing stock.

"Mr. Dickens," he once said to me, "what oversight permitted you to omit from the good Micawber's ploys to captivate Father Time some elementary juggling? Were there no carving knives idle?" It was that drawling politeness that drew me to him, with its suggestion that Fields was either a fraudulent manservant or a drunk uncertain of his articulation. You will remember how the earnest Selznick would have no juggling: take care to remember that that exclusion was not of my doing. As it was, Fields made me breathless and I could not escape the thought of my own irresponsibility in concocting Micawber when such broken men trudged on. I could not advise him; I would have trusted him with every invention. As long as he was not encouraged to be amusing he was particularly comic. If he realised he was in motley, it made him vague and fussy. It was his mode to stand amid chaos, bereft of any comfort save sourness. No comedian, no actor, but an ordinary failure who would not be coaxed into the last face-saving.

Only to think of him is to splutter with laughter and tears. I have appended a few facts so that you may print a proper notice in *Household Words*—not that it can convey the man.

Yours ever,

Charles Dickens

A leading vaudeville performer by 1900, Fields became a star of the Ziegfeld Follies: *Pool Shark* (15) is a short film of his stage act. But his films show a great extension of his character in that he does not have to act, but reacts to the world. After a small part in *Janice Meredith* (24, E. Mason Hopper), a stage success, *Poppy*, was filmed by Paramount as *Sally of the Sawdust* (25, D. W. Griffith). There followed *That Royale Girl* (26, Griffith); *It's the Old Army Game* (26, Edward Sutherland); *So's Your Old Man* (26, Gregory La Cava); *The Potters* (27, Fred Newmeyer); *Running Wild* (27, La Cava); *Two Flaming Youths* (27, John Waters); *Tillie's Punctured Romance* (28,

Sutherland); *Fools for Luck* (29, Charles Reisner); *The Golf Specialist* (30, Monte Brice); *Her Majesty Love* (31, William Dieterle); *The Dentist* (32, Leslie Pierce); an episode from *If I Had a Million* (32, Edward Cline); *Million Dollar Legs* (32, Cline); *International House* (33, Sutherland); *The Barber Shop* (33, Arthur Ripley); *The Fatal Glass of Beer* (33, Ripley); *The Pharmacist* (33, Ripley); Humpty Dumpty in *Alice in Wonderland* (33, Norman Z. McLeod); *Tillie and Gus* (33, Francis Martin); *Six of a Kind* (34, Leo McCarey); *You're Telling Me* (34, Erle Kenton); *Mrs. Wiggs of the Cabbage Patch* (34, Norman Taurog); *It's a Gift* (34, Taurog); *The Old-Fashioned Way* (34, William Beaudine); *The Man on the Flying Trapeze* (34, Clyde Bruckman); *David Copperfield* (34, George Cukor); *Mississippi* (35, Sutherland); *Poppy* (36, Sutherland); *The Big Broadcast of 1938* (38, Mitchell Leisen); *You Can't Cheat an Honest Man* (39, George Marshall); *The Bank Dick* (40, Cline); *My Little Chickadee* (40, Cline); *Never Give a Sucker an Even Break* (41, Cline); in an episode cut from *Tales of Manhattan* (42, Julien Duvivier); *Follow the Boys* (44, Sutherland), reprising his poolroom act; a cameo in *Song of the Open Road* (44, S. Sylvan Simon); and *Sensations of 1945* (45, Andrew L. Stone).

Ralph (Nathaniel) **Fiennes**,
b. Suffolk, England, 1962

With RADA and many leading stage roles behind him, Ralph Fiennes looms as the latest in the line of Great English Actors. There are those who find him beautiful, inherently imbued with class, and with forces of intellect burning deep. Some see all three. Others remark on the extraordinary opportunities he has had, coupled with the strange reticence—call it a lack of stamina, a kind of metaphysical disinterest, or a reluctance to expose himself. (I mean his spirit—he takes his clothes off regularly.) He sometimes acts as if he would rather be off-screen. The large public surely feels this, and has learned a similar detachment or distance. For some people, his mere presence is a warning of a kind of self-lacerating intelligence or hidden malice. It all suggests how well cast he was in *Schindler's List* (93, Steven Spielberg), still his best film work by far.

He was Heathcliff opposite Juliette Binoche in a TV version of *Wuthering Heights* (92, Peter Kosminsky); *The Baby of Macon* (93, Peter Greenaway); adroit and subtle, and very evasive, in *Quiz Show* (94, Robert Redford); horribly miscast in *Strange Days* (95, Kathryn Bigelow); suitably remote in *The English Patient* (96, Anthony Minghella); with Cate Blanchett in *Oscar and Lucinda* (97, Gillian Armstrong); the voice of Rameses in *The Prince of Egypt* (98, Brenda Chapman, Steve Hickner, and Simon Wells); *One-*

gin (99, Martha Fiennes, his sister); anemic and unlikable in *The End of the Affair* (99, Neil Jordan); *Sunshine* (00, István Szabó); for British TV as Proust in *How Proust Can Change Your Life* (00, Peter Bevan); the voice of Jesus in the animated *The Miracle Maker* (00, Derek W. Hayes and Stanislav Sokolov).

He was villainous in *Red Dragon* (02, Brett Ratner); desperately schizophrenic in *Spider* (02, David Cronenberg); and a very unlikely mate for JLo in *Maid in Manhattan* (02, Wayne Wang)).

Mike Figgis, b. Carlisle, England, 1949
1988: *Stormy Monday.* 1990: *Internal Affairs.* 1991: *Liebestraum.* 1993: *Mr. Jones.* 1994: *The Browning Version.* 1995: *Leaving Las Vegas.* 1997: *One Night Stand.* 1998: *The End of Sexual Innocence.* 1999: *Miss Julie.* 2000: *Timecode.* 2001: *Hotel; The Battle of Orgreave* (d). 2003: *Cold Creek Manor.*

Though Mike Figgis had never made a dull or worthless film before *Leaving Las Vegas,* still nothing prepared us for the intensity of that work. Did it prosper because a low budget and a short schedule allowed Figgis to work undisturbed? Because John O'Brien's autobiographical (and suicidal) novel released a kind of emotional directness hitherto veiled? Or was it because two players—Nicolas Cage and Elisabeth Shue—seized on the opportunity of profound roles securely set in a tragic love story? Let's assume that all those things played their part. Does that mean Figgis can manage to reproduce such favorable circumstances? Can he build on the most revolutionary (and classical) American film of the nineties? It is a revolution now to make a film so simple, so naked, so modest in means and yet so large in impact.

As a boy, Figgis was raised in colonial Kenya. On returning to England, and the Newcastle area, he gravitated towards jazz and a theatre group called the People Show. It was with them that he developed as writer, director, actor, musician, and sound engineer—and note that Figgis is one of those people who like to serve a lot of roles in a close-knit group. He was rejected by the National Film School and so found himself as a self-avowed maverick. This has had the valuable result of making him unusually open to non-British material.

Stormy Monday was a self-consciously noir and bluesy view of Newcastle, with a lot of jazz and a distinct assurance at handling genre violence. But the human story never sought depth. *Internal Affairs,* on the other hand, was an L.A. police story that included brilliant character studies—Richard Gere and Andy Garcia have never been better—and the handling of Gere showed a rare talent in Figgis for seeing hitherto untried resources. It also felt as if Figgis was excited by L.A., by the place and its unstable society.

After that, *Liebestraum* seemed unduly cultish and confused, a failure despite the welcome (if gloomy) resurrection of Kim Novak. *Mr. Jones* had major studio battles and enforced changes, all of which left the central subject, that of a schizophrenic, intriguing, novel, and maybe a bit beyond Richard Gere. A remake of *The Browning Version* was the first sign that Figgis might face difficulties just staying in work.

Then *Leaving Las Vegas*—made on Super 16mm for $3.5 million—revealed nothing less than a major director in charge of story, atmosphere, and courageous performances. There may be small errors—a little too much music, perhaps—but the beauty and the severity of the film are things seen, felt, and measured by the director. American film in the nineties has had few triumphs, but *Leaving Las Vegas* was one that shone a baleful light on more costly disasters. It also reveals a true romantic in Figgis, a trait he is bound to trust and pursue. For this movie, nearly too grim to take, was an unrivaled love story, too.

The encouragement of a hit and nominations only made Figgis more independent, and a more deliberate explorer of sexual dreams. *One Night Stand* (inherited from a Joe Eszterhas script, but redone) was an unusual study of interracial romance. But *The End of Sexual Innocence* was a radical departure into fable and therapy-like approach. His low-budget *Miss Julie* showed little more than an obsession with his actress, Saffron Burrows. In addition, Figgis edited *Projection 10,* maybe the most coherent volume in that series. It is, somehow, in his nature to be tidy and untidy against all expectations. *Timecode* got a lot of attention for its split-screen simultaneities. But Figgis's best preoccupation is people, not machinery.

Gabriel Figueroa (1907–97), b. Mexico City
Figueroa was a small, macho man with terrific personality and a great reputation. He was "artistic," a man who had been trained in painting and still photography, and who then went to Hollywood to be Gregg Toland's student. He had pronounced ideas of beauty and the rather glamorous portrayal of poverty: "His work was full of filtered clouds and peasant madonnas, their heads covered with *rebozos.* There was sure to be a scene in each of his films where fifty of those creatures would be standing in a clump, holding burning candles." That is Elia Kazan, who was introduced to Figueroa by John Steinbeck prior to working on *Viva Zapata!* and quickly reached the conclusion that he didn't want the prestigious "Gaby" or his way of sentimentalizing the working class. It's a fair point, and one notes that Luis Buñuel (who used Figueroa often) had to curb the photographer's pictorialism—having to prove that he knew as much as Figueroa about classical painting

before he could get Gaby to do a decent job of recording images or trust the implicit dream for, say, *Los Olvidados* (50), *El* (52), and *The Exterminating Angel* (62). The florid Figueroa was also too evident in *The Pearl* (48, Emilio Fernández), taken from Steinbeck's story, and the quite ghastly *The Fugitive* (47, John Ford), for which Ford seems to have been a complacent onlooker.

He began in the late thirties, but became celebrated with *Flor Silvestre* (43, Fernández); the exquisite use of Dolores del Rio in *María Candelaria* (43, Fernández); *Las Abandonadas* (44, Fernández); glorifying María Félix in *Enamorada* (46, Fernández) and *Rio Escondido* (47, Fernández); *Tarzan and the Mermaids* (48, Robert Florey); *Malcovia* (48, Fernández); *Salón México* (48, Fernández); *La Malquerida* (49, Fernández); *Duelo en las Montañas* (49, Fernández); the English-language film *The Torch* (50, Fernández); *Víctimas del Pecado* (50, Fernández); *Nazarin* (59, Buñuel); *La Fièvre Monte à El Pao* (59, Buñuel); *The Young One* (61, Buñuel); *The Night of the Iguana* (64, John Huston); *Simon of the Desert* (65, Buñuel); *The Big Cube* (69, Tito Davison); *Two Mules for Sister Sara* (70, Don Siegel); *Kelly's Heroes* (70, Brian G. Hutton); *Interval* (73, Daniel Mann); *Under the Volcano* (86, Huston). Sad to say, the American films he shot look very ordinary. As others have observed, the light alters south of the border—but more than the light.

Peter Finch (William Mitchell) (1916–77), b. London

The son of an Australian father, Finch went to Sydney at the age of ten and spent his youth in Australia. Among a variety of jobs he made one film there, *Mr. Chedworth Steps Out* (38, Ken G. Hall), before war service. After that he was acting in the Australian theatre and cinema—*Rats of Tobruk* (44, Charles Chaurel) and *Eureka Stockade* (47, Harry Watt)—before Laurence Olivier, on tour, recommended that he go to England, and in time Finch had a melodramatic affair with Vivien Leigh. He appeared on the London stage (Iago once to Welles's *Othello*), but soon settled for films, at first in small parts, then with a mixture of heavies and romantic leads, with an early involvement in American films: *Train of Events* (49, Charles Crichton and Basil Dearden); *The Miniver Story* (50, H. C. Potter); *The Wooden Horse* (50, Jack Lee); *The Story of Robin Hood* (52, Ken Annakin); *The Heart of the Matter* (53, George More O'Ferrall); *The Story of Gilbert and Sullivan* (54, Sidney Gilliat); *Elephant Walk* (54, William Dieterle); *Father Brown* (54, Robert Hamer); *Make Me an Offer* (54, Cyril Frankel); *Dark Avenger* (55, Henry Levin); *Josephine and Men* (55, Roy Boulting); *Passage Home* (55, Roy Baker); and *Simon and Laura* (55, Muriel Box).

He was nearly forty now, and with a breath of accent and a face weathered by sun he was more masculine than most men in the British cinema. As his parts improved, so he showed himself increasingly subtle and capable. Unlike many other British actors, he seemed to leave reserves untapped that implied a full character of which we were seeing only a part. In essence it comes from the ability to discover a part of yourself in whatever character you are playing. Because no effort seems to have been made, the effect of authority is all the more compelling: as the German commander in *The Battle of the River Plate* (56, Michael Powell); as an Australian soldier in *A Town Like Alice* (56, Lee); *Robbery Under Arms* (57, Lee); *Windom's Way* (58, Ronald Neame); *The Nun's Story* (59, Fred Zinnemann); *Operation Amsterdam* (59, Michael McCarthy); stylish and touching in *The Trials of Oscar Wilde* (60, Ken Hughes); *Kidnapped* (60, Robert Stevenson); *Rachel Cade* (60, Gordon Douglas); *No Love for Johnnie* (61, Ralph Thomas); *I Thank a Fool* (62, Robert Stevens); *In the Cool of the Day* (63, Stevens); *The Girl With Green Eyes* (64, Desmond Davis); as the husband in *The Pumpkin Eater* (64, Jack Clayton); *Judith* (65, Daniel Mann); *The Flight of the Phoenix* (65, Robert Aldrich); *10:30 P.M. Summer* (66, Jules Dassin); *Far From the Madding Crowd* (67, John Schlesinger); as the von Sternberg figure in *The Legend of Lylah Clare* (68, Aldrich); *The Red Tent* (71, Mikhail Kalatazov); as the only truly believable character, the homosexual doctor, in *Sunday, Bloody Sunday* (71, Schlesinger); *Something to Hide* (71, Alastair Reid); as Nelson in *Bequest to the Nation* (72, James Cellan Jones); *England Made Me* (72, Peter Duffell); bearing up manfully in the Ronald Colman part in the musical *Lost Horizon* (72, Charles Jarrott); and *The Abdication* (74, Anthony Harvey).

He played Yitzhak Rabin in *Raid on Entebbe* (76, Irvin Kershner). But he will be treasured for his last part, as Howard Beale in *Network* (76, Sidney Lumet), because it won him the best actor Oscar, posthumously, and because it seemed, with hindsight, a prediction of his own dropping dead. Beale is less a role than a balloon inflated by Chayefsky's sermon, but Finch gave the ranting warnings a bloodshot desperation, and he made one line famous—"I'm mad as hell and I'm not going to take it anymore."

David Fincher, b. Denver, Colorado, 1962
1992: *Alien³*. 1995: *Se7en*. 1997: *The Game*. 1999: *The Fight Club*. 2002: *Panic Room*.

It's to David Fincher's credit that his films take place somewhere beyond our edge—yet in a recognizable extension of our nightmares. As such, he has an interest in film noir, science fiction, and a kind of sardonic speculation, plus the ability to cross over from one to another. Grant, too, that he has not yet made a film that is either dull or less than the work of a fevered filmmaker. Still, neither is there a picture in which the self-satisfied horrifics avoid some sense of pretension and absurdity. Thus, so far, Fincher's pessimism is too decorative, too much worn on his flounced sleeve. This is especially the case with his most impressive film—*Se7en*—where the macabre exhilaration of the enterprise (the malignant delight in cleverness) comes close to worshiping Kevin Spacey's scholar killer. Yes, there are heroes in *Se7en*, and Morgan Freeman finds a real nobility, but the film cannot separate itself from the meticulous madness. It cannot spare us anything—yet it cannot grasp real pain.

Fincher was raised in Ashland, Oregon, and Marin, California. He worked for a while for John Korty and then joined the Lucas organization and got credits for matte and effects photography on *Return of the Jedi* (83, Richard Marquand) and *Indiana Jones and the Temple of Doom* (84, Steven Spielberg). Since then, along the way, he has become a very proficient director of commercials and music videos. Few young directors have such command of streamlined imagery. And it is his assurance that leaves his aim more questionable.

Alien³ was, in some ways, the most thematically interesting of the series, yet it was also the film that tried to kill its own franchise. *The Game* has astonishing initial bravura before it turns playfulness into a grind. And *The Fight Club* made the fatal mistake of settling for its own split-identity scheme. The failures are real—and everywhere so far—and it's all too easy to see Fincher as a key instance of technical proficiency succumbing to morbid mannerism. He does not much like or trust the world, but there's no evidence yet to suggest that the dismay has been earned. He is capable of great work, but he could become an ordeal.

Panic Room was brilliant, very suspenseful, very smart in how to use Jodie Foster, yet incapable of finding depth or meaning.

Albert Finney, b. Salford, England, 1936

After RADA, he worked at Birmingham Rep. and the Old Vic. On the stage, he created the roles of *Billy Liar, Luther*, and *Armstrong's Last Goodnight*, without ever fulfilling promise. His screen career is equally incomplete. At first, he was barely noticed in *The Entertainer* (60, Tony Richardson); merely naturalistic in Reisz's *Saturday Night and Sunday Morning* (60); helpless amid the technical riot of *Tom Jones* (63, Richardson); and at best an interesting failure in Reisz's *Night Must Fall* (64). Unhappily, he was next cast in a purely personality role—in Donen's *Two for the Road* (67)—for which he had little instinct. Then came *Charlie Bubbles* (67), which he directed for his own company, Memorial Enterprises, and in which he acted. His playing was as

plain as always, but the film abounded in fresh, humorous views of an England rarely seen in the movies—one of the most auspicious of British directorial debuts. Not that it has been capitalized on. Instead, Finney appeared in the unreleased *Picasso Summer* (69, Robert Sallin) and in Ronald Neame's *Scrooge* (70), in which he managed to look more misanthropic as his young self than as Dickens's miser. But in *Gumshoe* (71, Stephen Frears), as the bingo-caller swept into Hammett intrigue, he at last found a part that seemed to strike into his own imagination. The result was a very funny performance and the revelation of an actor with a real love of movies. But he hesitated again before dressing up as a much more dilute detective, Hercule Poirot, in *Murder on the Orient Express* (74, Sidney Lumet). He had a small part in *The Duellists* (77, Ridley Scott).

He put on weight with the years, he married and was divorced from Anouk Aimée and made a specialty of large, boozy, blustery men. Is he ready to play Victor McLaglen? Still, Finney is an actor of great charge and courage, and one never knows when he is coasting or when he will strike a vein of lovely savagery. It leaves him always worth watching: *Loophole* (80, John Quested); the plastic surgeon in *Looker* (81, Michael Crichton); the detective in *Wolfen* (81, Mike Wadleigh); the husband in *Shoot the Moon* (82, Alan Parker), a performance of discomforting pain; as Daddy Warbucks in *Annie* (82, John Huston); as theatrical as Donald Wolfit in *The Dresser* (83, Peter Yates); gruelingly drunk and despairing, but wonderful, as the consul in *Under the Volcano* (84, Huston), despite the hapless state of the rest of the film; very good in *Orphans* (87, Alan J. Pakula); a TV anchorman in *The Image* (90, Peter Werner); *The Endless Game* (90, Bryan Forbes); the gangster chief in *Miller's Crossing* (90, Joel Coen), a formidable man; on television in Britain, alcoholic and hallucinating, in *The Green Man* (90, Elijah Moshinsky); convincingly tragic as the policeman in *The Playboys* (92, Gillies MacKinnon); *Rich in Love* (93, Bruce Beresford); and *The Browning Version* (94, Mike Figgis).

At and past sixty, Finney was sailing along. He looked battered sometimes, but he had gusto and energy: very good as the romantic bus conductor in *A Man of No Importance* (94, Suri Krishnamma); *The Run of the Country* (95, Yates); doing Dennis Potter in *Karaoke* (96, Renny Rye) and *Cold Lazarus* (96, Rye); as Dr. Monygham in *Nostromo* (96, Alaistair Reid); as Dr. Sloper in *Washington Square* (97, Agnieszka Holland); with Tom Courteney in *A Rather English Marriage* (98, Paul Seed); as Kilgore Trout in *Breakfast of Champions* (99, Alan Rudolph); *Simpatico* (99, Matthew Warchus); terrific support in *Erin Brockovich* (00, Steven Soderbergh); *Traffic* (00, Soderbergh); *Joan of Arc: The Virgin Warrior* (00,

Ronald F. Maxwell); *Delivering Milo* (00, Nick Castle); *My Uncle Silas* (00, Philip Saville); and rather bored as Churchill in *The Gathering Storm* (02, Richard Loncraine).

Linda (Clorinda) **Fiorentino**,
b. Philadelphia, 1960

Fiorentino made a startling debut as the sexy, unpredictable cabaret performer in *After Hours* (85, Martin Scorsese)—she was a nymph who might have just got off the Buñuel bus. Thereafter, for a full decade, she seemed in decline or meandering, or too hard to cast: *Gotcha!* (85, Jeff Kanew); *Vision Quest* (85, Harold Becker); oddly gloomy until the end of *The Moderns* (88, Alan Rudolph); *Queens Logic* (91, Steven Rash); *Shout* (91, Jeffrey Hornaday); *Beyond the Law* (92, Larry Ferguson); *Chain of Desire* (92, Temistocles Lopez); *Acting on Impulse* (93, Sam Irvin); *Charlie's Ghost Story* (94, Anthony Edwards); *The Desperate Trail* (94, P. J. Pesce).

Then, out of the blue, she was a ravishing and comic angel of death (and money) in *The Last Seduction* (94, John Dahl)—a film that, in hindsight, seems beyond her and her director. Once again, she had carried American noir idioms into a fascinating brush with surrealism.

But she then sank back into dismal films and a rather listless attitude—but the latter may have been prompted by the ridiculous *Jade* (95, William Friedkin); *Larger Than Life* (96, Howard Franklin); *Unforgettable* (96, Dahl)—in which she plays a professor!; *Men in Black* (97, Barry Sonnenfeld)—the story goes that she won the part playing poker with the director; *Kicked in the Head* (97, Matthew Harrison); *Body Count* (98, Robert Patton-Spruill); *Dogma* (99, Kevin Smith); *What Planet Are You From?* (00, Mike Nichols); rather nice with that other great sourpuss, Paul Newman, in *Where the Money Is* (00, Marek Kanievska); *Liberty Stands Still* (02, Kari Skogland).

Laurence/Larry **Fishburne**,
b. Georgia, 1961

The erstwhile "Larry" recently elected to become "Laurence"—no matter, there is hardly an actor of his age around who exhibits more flash, energy, and intelligence. Fishburne has had to play a lot of regulation black hoodlums and threats, but he is an actor who might get cast despite his color, and might carry a big film. His Ike Turner in *What's Love Got to Do With It* (93, Brian Gibson) was a tour de force founded on Fishburne's own reworking of a role that had been flattened in concept by Tina Turner's angry stomping. As it was, the finished film left Angela Bassett's Tina seeming just too good to be true, while Ike was the self-destructive force of his own charisma, and riveting. His Oscar nomination was a pleasant surprise.

Fishburne began very early. At age nine, he did several seasons on the TV soap opera *One Life to Live*. He was in the movie *Cornbread, Earl and Me* (75, Joe Manduke), and then, at fourteen, he went on location to the Philippines to play the young soldier in *Apocalypse Now* (79, Francis Coppola)—one of the best performances in that film. He was in *Willie & Phil* (80, Paul Mazursky); *Death Wish II* (82, Michael Winner); *Rumble Fish* (83, Coppola); *For Us the Living* (83, Michael Schultz); *The Cotton Club* (84, Coppola); *The Color Purple* (85, Steven Spielberg); *Band of the Hand* (86, Paul Michael Glaser); *Quicksilver* (86, Tom Donnelly); *Gardens of Stone* (87, Coppola); *A Nightmare on Elm Street 3* (87, Chuck Russell); *Red Heat* (88, Walter Hill); *School Daze* (88, Spike Lee); *King of New York* (90, Abel Ferrara); *Class Action* (91, Michael Apted); the father in *Boyz N the Hood* (91, John Singleton); *Deep Cover* (92, Bill Duke); *Searching for Bobby Fischer* (93, Steven Zaillian); and *The Tool Shed* (94, Damian Harris).

It was not easy to lay hands on real stardom: *Higher Learning* (95, Singleton); *Bad Company* (95, Damian Harris); *Just Cause* (95, Arne Glimcher); *The Tuskegee Airmen* (95, Robert Markowitz); as *Othello* (95, Oliver Parker); *Fled* (96, Kevin Hooks); *Miss Evers' Boys* (97, Joseph Sargent); *Event Horizon* (97, Paul Anderson III); *Hoodlum* (97, Duke); *Always Outnumbered* (98, Apted); in the hit *The Matrix* (99, Andy and Larry Wachowski); writing and directing *Once in the Life* (00); *Osmosis Jones* (01, Bobby and Peter Farrelly).

He was in *Biker Boys* (03, Reggie Rock Blythewood); back again in *The Matrix Reloaded* (03, Wachowski brothers); *Mystic River* (03, Clint Eastwood).

Carrie Fisher, b. Los Angeles, 1956

It's nearly an insult to call Carrie Fisher a survivor. Yet she's a mercurial gadfly, and so witty an observer, that there is a certain lack of center or self—as if only as a protective device. Say only that her parents were Debbie Reynolds and Eddie Fisher and it's hard to resist shuddering attacks of doom prediction. Fisher became a wreck, and then came through to write the witty novels (especially *Postcards from the Edge*) that tell a scary story while asserting her Teflon coating. And she is young enough, and surely smart enough, yet to write a book as good as *Haywire,* in which she might find the literary ease and peace that no longer needs to be hilarious.

Of course, no small part of her comic routine is that she also starred—with Emily Dickinson hairstyle and some of the strangest costumes—in three of the most successful films ever made, in the far distant past when Harrison Ford could still be fun. But so did Mark Hamill, and try finding him now.

In her teens, she was part of her mother's Las Vegas act, and that led her into pictures: in tennis clothes, maneuvering Warren Beatty in *Shampoo* (75, Hal Ashby). Two years later, a grave-faced nineteen, she was Princess Leia in *Star Wars* (77, George Lucas). After that, the list is chaotic: *Mr. Mike's Mondo Video* (79, Michael O'Donoghue); *The Empire Strikes Back* (80, Irvin Kershner); *The Blues Brothers* (80, John Landis); *Under the Rainbow* (81, Steve Rash); *Return of the Jedi* (83, Richard Marquand); *Garbo Talks* (84, Sidney Lumet); *The Man with One Red Shoe* (85, Stan Dragoti); *Hannah and Her Sisters* (86, Woody Allen); *Hollywood Vice Squad* (86, Penelope Spheeris); *Amazon Women on the Moon* (87, Joe Dante); *Appointment with Death* (88, Michael Winner); *The 'burbs* (89, Dante); *Loverboy* (89, Joan Micklin Silver); *When Harry Met Sally . . .* (89, Rob Reiner).

When *Postcards from the Edge* (90, Mike Nichols) came to be filmed, Shirley MacLaine and Meryl Streep were given Debbie and Carrie, but Fisher kept her hand on the script. That the roles were not entrusted to the originals is clinching proof of the fatal weakness for taste in Mike Nichols. Since then, she has appeared in *Sibling Rivalry* (90, Carl Reiner); *Sweet Revenge* (90, Charlotte Brandstrom); *Drop Dead Fred* (91, Ate de Jong); *Soapdish* (91, Michael Hoffman); *This Is My Life* (92, Nora Ephron); and doing a writing polish on *Sister Act* (92, Emile Ardolino).

More recently, she was in *Scream 3* (00, Wes Craven) and *Jay and Silent Bob Strike Back* (01, Kevin Smith), and she apparently did some uncredited writing on *Star Wars: Episode I—The Phantom Menace* (99, Lucas); credited writing, and uncredited acting, on the TV movie *These Old Broads* (01, Matthew Diamond)—her idea— which gathered together Elizabeth Taylor, Debbie Reynolds, Joan Collins, and Shirley MacLaine. That's surviving.

Terence Fisher (1904–80), b. London
1948: *Colonel Bogey; To the Public Danger; Portrait from Life; Song for Tomorrow.* 1949: *Marry Me.* 1950: *The Astonished Heart* (codirected with Anthony Darnborough); *So Long at the Fair* (codirected with Darnborough). 1951: *Home to Danger.* 1952: *The Last Page; Stolen Face; Wings of Danger.* 1953: *Four-Sided Triangle; Mantrap; Spaceways; Blood Orange.* 1954: *Final Appointment; Mask of Dust; Face the Music; Children Galore; The Stranger Came Home.* 1955: *Murder by Proxy; Stolen Assignment; The Flaw.* 1956: *The Last Man to Hang.* 1957: *The Curse of Frankenstein; Kill Me Tomorrow.* 1958: *Dracula; The Revenge of Frankenstein.* 1959: *The Mummy; The Hound of the Baskervilles; The Stranglers of Bombay; The Man Who Could Cheat Death.* 1960: *The Brides of Dracula; Sword of Sherwood Forest; The Two Faces of Dr. Jekyll.* 1961: *The Curse of the Werewolf.* 1962: *The Phantom of the Opera.* 1963: *Sherlock Holmes.* 1964: *The Earth Dies Screaming; The Horror of It All; The Gorgon.* 1965: *Dracula, Prince of Darkness.* 1966: *Island of Terror; Frankenstein Created Woman.* 1967: *Night of the Big Heat.* 1968: *The Devil Rides Out.* 1969: *Frankenstein Must Be Destroyed.* 1973: *Frankenstein and the Monster from Hell.*

The English are proud of Hammer Films: it appeals to their need for the ridiculous made respectable that the company devoted to horror films should have won a Queen's Award for Industry and commendations for their export record. But Hammer's prosperity only supports the theory that, artistically, horror requires conviction. No matter how assiduously a company concocts Gothic atmosphere, still commercial bias withers the proper sense of awe. Hammer horrors have always seemed the work of decent men who tended the garden on weekends. This is sadly true of Terence Fisher, the man responsible for most of them. Middle-aged before he began to direct, he was in his fifties when Hammer committed itself to *Dracula* and *Frankenstein*. A merchant seaman first, he worked as an editor before and after the war: *Tudor Rose* (36, Robert Stevenson); *On the Night of the Fire* (39, Brian Desmond Hurst); *The Wicked Lady* (45, Leslie Arliss); and *Master of Bankdam* (47, Walter Forde). His first features were light and romantic, including Noel Coward in *The Astonished Heart*. But in *So Long at the Fair* he made no mistake over the first frisson that greets the discovery that the hotel has disclaimed one of its guests and lost a room.

Fisher worked for Hammer as early as 1953 on its two modest science fiction ventures, *Four-Sided Triangle* and *Spaceways*. From 1957 onward, he was effectively incarcerated in the neo-Gothic product. There are some who rate his achievement there very highly. Paul Willemen has referred to Fisher's films as "a major example of what a truly creative artist can achieve within the limits of an ostensibly sensational and popular genre." My own feeling is that anyone with a studio's resources and some twenty films ought to have established his talent more clearly. We celebrate Val Lewton for less, Tod Browning on much less evidence. Fisher's films are rich in color and setting, but not as vividly imaginative as Roger Corman's pictures. Too often one has to wait for odd, piercing moments, like the ending of *Brides of Dracula*, a dull film suddenly brilliant as Dracula dies in the cruciform shadow of a windmill's sails. Again, the conception of *Two Faces of Dr. Jekyll*—that Hyde is a sexual charmer—is bereft of any proper development. Overall, the invention in the films seems fitful, desperate, and cynically detached from the genre. Revealingly, Hammer tamely remade earlier films and resurrected hardly any of the worthwhile subjects in English Gothic literature. The studio's originality may rest more on the English aristocracy of Christopher Lee's Dracula than on Fisher's invention.

Barry Fitzgerald (William Shields)
(1888–1961), b. Dublin, Ireland

Years before Hollywood was challenged for not allowing black actors to play anything other than "Negro" characters, Irishness had been forced into a similar straitjacket. Thus Barry Fitzgerald's accent could only become a more extreme version of itself. When we laugh at him or warm to his cozy sentimentality, it is to as serious a distortion of ethnic character as ever the Negro suffered. And, appropriately, it was the Irish-inclined John Ford who first called Fitzgerald before the cameras to play the tourist's Irishman.

Previously, Fitzgerald had been a stage actor at the Abbey Theatre. But he could hardly be blamed for abandoning that in favor of the rewards lavished on his movie Irishman: *The Plough and the Stars* (36, Ford); *Ebb Tide* (37, Arthur Rossen); gloriously double-taking at the drunken realization that he is sitting beside a leopard in *Bringing Up Baby* (38, Howard Hawks); *Four Men and a Prayer* (38, Ford); *The Long Voyage Home* (40, Ford); *The Sea Wolf* (41, Michael Curtiz); *How Green Was My Valley* (41, Ford); *The Amazing Mrs. Holiday* (43, Bruce Manning); *None But the Lonely Heart* (44, Clifford Odets); winning a supporting actor Oscar as the senior priest in *Going My Way* (44, Leo McCarey); *Incendiary Blonde* (45, George Marshall); *And Then There Were None* (45, René Clair); *Two Years Before the Mast* (46, John Farrow); *Welcome Stranger* (46, Elliott Nugent); *California* (47, Farrow); *Easy Come, Easy Go* (47, Farrow); *Miss Tatlock's Millions* (48, Richard Haydn); as Lieutenant Muldoon, the goblin cop in *The Naked City* (48, Jules Dassin); *Top o' the Morning* (49, David Miller); *The Story of Seabiscuit* (49, David Butler); *Union Station* (50, Rudolph Maté); *Silver City* (51, Byron Haskin); *The Quiet Man* (52, Ford); *Happy Ever After* (54, Mario Zampi); *The Catered Affair* (56, Richard Brooks); *Rooney* (57, George Pollock); and *Broth of a Boy* (58, Pollock).

Robert J. Flaherty (1884–1951),
b. Iron Mountain, Michigan

1922: *Nanook of the North* (d). 1925: *Story of a Potter* (d). 1926: *Moana* (d); *The 24 Dollar Island* (uncompleted) (d). 1928: *White Shadows in the South Seas* (completed by and credited to W. S. Van Dyke); *Acoma, the Sky City* (unreleased) (d). 1931: *Tabu* (codirected with F. W. Murnau); *Industrial Britain* (d). 1934: *Man of Aran* (d).

1936: *Elephant Boy* (codirected with Zoltan Korda). 1942: *The Land* (d). 1948: *Louisiana Story* (d).

Flaherty's troubled career is perversely worthier of study than the films themselves. Because he pioneered the documentary form, and drew up lines of battle between conviction and commercialism, so Flaherty remains relevant in any study of nonfiction filmmaking. While he was alive, his warmth and visionary purity loaded opinion about him with emotion. Now that he has been dead more than forty years, it is easier to look at the films with objectivity and to put Flaherty in perspective. But that solves very little. The films are turbulent with self-contradiction and with all the doctrinal issues that still confront documentarists. Flaherty moved sometimes with the witheringly obdurate confidence of a Victorian explorer. He had the defects of a romantic faith in the noble savage and an eye for the picturesque—in both respects he was nearer to the nineteenth century than to this, possessed of that curious liberalism that enabled Ruskin to advocate Communism and support the South in the Civil War. But Flaherty's films ask all the intriguing questions about documentary. Is it enough to film actuality? Or is actuality modified by the filming process? If so, can the camera become secret, unseen, or do events have to be reconceived to convey their original essence? The question that remains unsolved is whether Flaherty himself appreciated those mysteries.

The life of the man is vital. The son of a miner, he went with his father on expeditions in northern Canada before 1900. Here are the roots of Flaherty's authenticity and of his insistence on living with his subject. It should also be said that he was trained in a spirit of Victorian commercial zeal; his fondness for natives grew out of an initial, full-blooded imperialism. From mining, he took to exploring and map-making on behalf of the Canadian Northern Railway. As he moved farther north, he had more to do with Eskimos and made a private film of a trip to Baffin Island. The Revillon Fur Company then financed *Nanook,* a film eventually distributed by Pathé.

It is not hard to feel the impact *Nanook* made. Until then, relatively little had been done to reveal the corners of the earth on film. The actuality of the filming and the terrible rigor of the Eskimo life still strike home. The imperative of hunger, the extent of snow and ice, and the pitted faces of Nanook and his family were the first widely received images of peasant life on the screen. *Nanook* is moving for several reasons: Flaherty shot it virtually alone, and was thus compelled to be simple—the seal-catching episode is in one long setup because of this tension. It also utilizes depth in the way we see help coming to Nanook from the distance. In addition, the Eskimo life was so stark as to be almost stylized. In the obvious sense black and white, the search for food over-rode all other considerations. Thus, if Flaherty himself was a naïve man, this subject exposed none of his limits. Indeed, the most charming thing about it is the sympathy between Nanook and Flaherty, the way in which the Eskimo smiles cheerfully at the Great White Father and draws the camera effortlessly into his life.

Jesse Lasky thereupon hired Flaherty to make *Moana*. Flaherty lived in Samoa for a year before filming and pioneered panchromatic stock to capture the skin tones of the islanders. The film centered on initiation rites, and was exotically beautiful in a way *Nanook* had never hinted at. But the more complex social system in Samoa was simplified by Flaherty's view of a paradise existence. The South Sea of Captain Cook's discovery, or of *Typee*, is hardly imagined by Flaherty. For the first time, his private mythology of native life obtruded.

The legend says that in essence Flaherty diverged from Hollywood story-manufacturing. But, in truth, he was disposed to a heroic view of his materials; it was his painstaking preparation and reluctance to collaborate that led to most of his troubles. And those troubles were, to some extent, courted as a proof of nobility. *Story of a Potter* was made for the Metropolitan Museum; *The Twenty-Four Dollar Island* was a fanciful project inevitably abandoned. The first serious clash was over *White Shadows in the South Seas*, the story of a white man, Monte Blue, in the Marquesas Islands, and of eventual exploitation of the natives. An MGM project, it was shot on location and with studio pressure to hurry and to glamorize. Flaherty quit and was replaced by W. S. Van Dyke. He went to Fox to make *Acoma*, about Pueblo Indians, but the film was destroyed by fire.

Then came the most notorious incident of his career. He joined with F. W. Murnau to make *Tabu*, again shot in the South Seas. They were no match, even if the film was made without studio finance. Flaherty was an original, a pathfinder, and a seer, but Murnau was a profound artist. He bewildered Flaherty by making a film that could as easily have been shot in the studio. *Tabu* is nearer to *The Saga of Anatahan* than to anthropological cinema. The incompatibility is sad, but it shows Flaherty's limits.

Disappointed over *White Shadows* and *Tabu*, he went to Britain and joined Grierson for *Industrial Britain* and *Man of Aran*, which was financed by Gaumont British. The latter is an extraordinary work, epic in its visual style, like a parody in its treatment of the remoteness of Aran. If nothing else, Flaherty was restored to a world of primitive people and himself—and no one else. The film is splendidly silly, rather like the extremist life on Aran itself. Here, at last, Flaherty was exposed as a man who explored to escape. Even Grierson was forced to qualify this lonely eminence: "A succeeding documentary exponent is in no way obliged to chase off to the ends of the earth in search of old-time simplicity, and the ancient dignities of man against the sky. Indeed, if I may for the moment represent the opposition, I hope the Neo-Rousseauism implicit in Flaherty's work dies with his own exceptional self. Theory of naturals apart, it represents an escapism, a wan and distant eye, which tends in lesser hands to sentimentalism."

In fifteen more years, Flaherty had three finished projects. On *Elephant Boy* he was engaged as a talisman to guarantee Sabu and the Hungarian Kordas against the spurious. *The Land* was made in America for the U.S. Film Unit, while *Louisiana Story* was sponsored by Standard Oil. Uselessly beautiful, it seems blind to the conflict between oil-company prestige and Flaherty's unreasoned preference for raw nature. It was shot in Louisiana but is really sited in a dream world. It has banal symbols—the comparison of the boy's bare feet and the metalwork of the derricks. But it also has the final version of a vigorous image that runs through Flaherty's work—of a man hauling some object from the water: in *Nanook*, it is the walrus; in *Man of Aran*, the nets; in *Louisiana Story*, an alligator. Such repetition, and the poetic rapture that goes with it, speaks for the instinctive wildness embedded in Flaherty's romantic style.

Richard Fleischer,

b. Brooklyn, New York, 1916

1946: *Child of Divorce*. 1947: *Banjo*. 1948: *So This Is New York; Bodyguard*. 1949: *Make Mine Laughs; The Clay Pigeon; Follow Me Quietly; Trapped*. 1950: *Armored Car Robbery*. 1952: *The Narrow Margin; The Happy Time*. 1953: *Arena*. 1954: *20,000 Leagues Under the Sea*. 1955: *Violent Saturday; The Girl in the Red Velvet Swing*. 1956: *Bandido; Between Heaven and Hell*. 1958: *The Vikings; These Thousand Hills*. 1959: *Compulsion*. 1960: *Crack in the Mirror*. 1961: *The Big Gamble*. 1962: *Barabbas*. 1966: *Fantastic Voyage*. 1967: *Dr. Dolittle*. 1968: *The Boston Strangler*. 1969: *Che!*. 1970: *Tora! Tora! Tora!; 10 Rillington Place*. 1971: *Blind Terror; The Last Run*. 1972: *The New Centurions/Precinct 45—Los Angeles Police*. 1973: *Soylent Green; The Don Is Dead*. 1974: *Mr. Majestyk; The Spikes Gang*. 1975: *Mandingo*. 1976: *The Incredible Sarah*. 1977: *The Prince and the Pauper/Crossed Swords*. 1979: *Ashanti*. 1980: *The Jazz Singer*. 1982: *Tough Enough*. 1983: *Amityville 3D*. 1984: *Conan the Destroyer*. 1985: *Red Sonja*. 1987: *Million Dollar Mystery*. 1989: *Call from Space*.

Fleischer is the son of Max Fleischer the cartoonist. He studied medicine and drama and in 1940 joined RKO to work on documentaries. While there, he made several pictures in the *This Is America* series and directed *Flickers Flashback,* an anthology of silent films.

Once upon a time, Richard Fleischer was a competent director of action pictures—*The Narrow Margin, Violent Saturday;* inclined to settle for schoolboy rough-and-tumble—*20,000 Leagues Under the Sea, Bandido,* and *The Vikings;* the director of one excellent study of turn-of-the-century New York high society—*The Girl in the Red Velvet Swing.* But there were alarming signs of pretentiousness: not only *Compulsion* and *Crack in the Mirror* (which look like an insubstantial talent being buffeted by Darryl Zanuck and Orson Welles), but *Barabbas,* which is religiose and slow. There was a gap in his career in the midsixties after which Fleischer redoubled his efforts, veering from hokum (*Fantastic Voyage* and *Tora! Tora! Tora!*) to projects notable for their implausibility—*Dr. Dolittle, Che!,* and *10 Rillington Place.* Most remarkable of all is the way Fleischer has trudged from one famous murder case to another—*The Girl in the Red Velvet Swing; Compulsion; The Boston Strangler; 10 Rillington Place*—without suggesting more than a Sunday newspaper's interest in the theme. It is an odd seriousness that can investigate such cases and still produce *The New Centurions,* a routine endorsement of the police, illuminated only by the brooding sequence in which George C. Scott kills himself. In the late sixties and early seventies, Fleischer aimed at being the most prolific and least identifiable director in America: twelve films in eight years is eccentric energy now. Yet he recognized no limitations and came unscathed through Charles Bronson and Glenda Jackson, and some British over-appreciation of the deft melodramatics of *Mandingo.*

Since then, Fleischer has become a director who will do anything—and thus he seems to have no character. His work in the eighties was dire, but evidently he was obliged to do whatever was offered. As one who never thought much of *Mandingo,* I feel it necessary to stress that *The Narrow Margin* is still excellent, while many other Fleischer films are genuine entertainments.

Victor Fleming (1883–1949),
b. Pasadena, California
1920: *When the Clouds Roll By* (codirected with Ted Reed); *The Mollycoddle.* 1921: *Mama's Affair.* 1922: *Woman's Place; Red Hot Romance; The Lane That Had No Turning; Anna Ascends.* 1923: *Dark Secrets; Law of the Lawless; To the Last Man; Call of the Canyon.* 1924: *Empty Hands; The Code of the Sea.* 1925: *A Son of His Father; Adventure; The Devil's Cargo; Lord Jim.* 1926: *Blind Goddess; Mantrap.* 1927: *Rough Riders; The Way of All Flesh; Hula.* 1928: *Abie's Irish Rose; The Awakening.* 1929: *Wolf Song; The Vir-*

ginian. 1930: *Common Clay; Renegades.* 1931: *Around the World in 80 Minutes.* 1932: *The Wet Parade; Red Dust.* 1933: *The White Sister; Bombshell.* 1934: *Treasure Island.* 1935: *Reckless; The Farmer Takes a Wife.* 1937: *Captains Courageous.* 1938: *Test Pilot.* 1939: *The Wizard of Oz; Gone With the Wind* (codirected with George Cukor and Sam Wood). 1941: *Dr. Jekyll and Mr. Hyde.* 1942: *Tortilla Flat.* 1943: *A Guy Named Joe.* 1946: *Adventure.* 1948: *Joan of Arc.*

Originally a cameraman with Griffith and Douglas Fairbanks, Fleming was known as a director of masculine adventure pictures. But ironically, he obtained some excellent performances from leading actresses, if often ones that resembled those portraits of erotic splendor seen through the smoke above the bar in Westerns. Above all, Clara Bow in *Mantrap* and *Hula,* and Jean Harlow in *Red Dust* and *Bombshell.* In the 1920s, Fleming was a Paramount director, but by 1932 he had moved to MGM. Chances are that he would have been happier at Warners. But his career is sprinkled with interest: *Red Hot Romance* was an Anita Loos satire; *Adventure* came from Jack London, and *Lord Jim* from Conrad, with Percy Marmont in the title part; *Wolf Song* and *The Virginian* were big roles for the young Gary Cooper. At MGM, both *Treasure Island* and *Captains Courageous* were big successes, but as nothing compared with the extraordinary one-two of *The Wizard of Oz* and *Gone With the Wind* in 1939. It is easy to say that those fascinating perennials appear undirected, or that they owe their life to Mervyn Le Roy and David Selznick. The first was far outside Fleming's territory, but it is by turns a moving and dark fantasy, beautifully played by an adventurous cast. Fleming was the second director on *Gone With the Wind,* Gable's defender after Cukor had become enchanted by Vivien Leigh and slowed by years of screen tests. That *Wind* got completed, with energy on the screen, surely owes a lot to Fleming's bad-tempered urge to get the damn thing done. After that, Fleming declined. His *Jekyll and Hyde* is a plain version of the story, apart from the blatant eroticism in the frenzy of transformation, while *Joan of Arc* is the director at the stake for an Ingrid Bergman who claims to hear voices.

Robert Florey (1900–79), b. Paris
1923: *50–50.* 1927: *One Hour of Love; The Romantic Age; Face Value.* 1928: *The Life and Death of 9413—A Hollywood Extra* (s); *The Loves of Zero* (s); *Johann the Coffinmaker* (s); *Skyscraper Symphony* (s); *Night Club* (s). 1929: *Pusher-in-the-Face* (s); *The Hole in the Wall; The Cocoanuts* (codirected with Joseph Santley); *The Battle of Paris.* 1930: *La Route est Belle; L'Amour Chante; Le Blanc et le Noir* (codirected with Marc Allé-

gret). 1932: *Murders in the Rue Morgue; Man Called Back; Those We Love.* 1933: *Girl Missing; Ex-Lady; House on 56th Street.* 1934: *Bedside; Smarty; Registered Nurse; I Sell Anything.* 1935: *I Am a Thief; The Woman in Red; The Florentine Dagger; Going Highbrow; Don't Bet on Blondes; The Pay-Off; Ship Cafe.* 1936: *The Preview Murder Mystery; 'Til We Meet Again; Hollywood Boulevard.* 1937: *Outcast; King of Gamblers; Mountain Music; This Way Please; Daughter of Shanghai.* 1938: *Dangerous to Know; King of Alcatraz.* 1939: *Disbarred; Hotel Imperial; The Magnificent Fraud; Death of a Champion.* 1940: *Women Without Names; Parole Fixer.* 1941: *The Face Behind the Mask; Meet Boston Blackie; Two in a Taxi.* 1942: *Dangerously They Live; Lady Gangster.* 1943: *The Desert Song.* 1944: *Roger Touhy, Gangster; Man From Frisco.* 1945: *God Is My Co-Pilot; Danger Signal.* 1947: *The Beast with Five Fingers.* 1948: *Tarzan and the Mermaids; Rogue's Regiment.* 1949: *Outpost in Morocco; The Crooked Way.* 1950: *Johnny One-Eye; The Vicious Years.*

Florey is an idiosyncrat seen fleetingly at the ends of film-world corridors. He is usually presented as a charming dilettante, rather overwhelmed by the few large projects that came his way, but flourishing as an intellectual fed on crazy B pictures. If nothing else, he is an early instance of full-blooded French enthusiasm for American movies; so much so that it is strange that his twilight work at Warners and Paramount should not have been more fully endorsed. In truth, his films are fragments, skillfully arranged to imply disappointed greatness. The films themselves offer little to suggest that Florey had any real idea about how to stick the fragments together. Disarray is the style that expresses him best, despite his various publications on cinema.

He sounds like the sort of man who gathered in experiences with future interviewers in prospect. As a child, he met and observed Méliès at work. As an adolescent, he acted in Swiss movies—he was schooled privately near Geneva. He went to France and acted in and assisted Feuillade on *L'Orpheline* (21). Then he went to Hollywood, as a journalist and as publicity man for Douglas Fairbanks. He toured with Valentino handling publicity, from which he retreated to the probably less demanding task of making films. MGM hired him for second-unit and tests work and he assisted King Vidor and John Stahl. Eventually he attained actual credits as assistant director: *The Masked Bride* (25, Christy Cabanne); *Parisian Nights* (25, Alfred Santell); *The Exquisite Sinner* (26, Phil Rosen, after von Sternberg had been fired); *The Magic Flame* (27, Henry King); and *Seventh Heaven* (27, Frank Borzage).

He rose to full director and in 1928 made several aggressively "experimental" shorts—espe-

cially *The Life and Death of 9413*—and was in charge of Paramount's sound studios at Long Island. Perhaps to remove such temptations, Paramount put him to direct. He began more auspiciously than his later credits might suggest: Gertrude Lawrence and Charles Ruggles in *The Battle of Paris;* Claudette Colbert and Edward G. Robinson in *The Hole in the Wall;* the Marx Brothers in *Cocoanuts.* In 1930 Florey went to Britain to direct French films and collaborated on the script of *Frankenstein* (31, James Whale). Universal liked that enough to give Florey Bela Lugosi in *Murders in the Rue Morgue,* a stylish horror film. From 1933–35, Florey worked for Warners and First National and made enough bad films to dash his quirky reputation: notably Bette Davis in *Ex-Lady* and Stanwyck in *Woman in Red.* Then he went back to Paramount and made B pictures there until 1940. He proved the director for Akim Tamiroff and directed the little Russian in *King of Gamblers, Dangerous to Know,* and *The Magnificent Fraud.* After that, he free-lanced, edging farther out into smaller companies and more lurid rubbish. Even so, he dealt blithely with the tender madness of Peter Lorre in *The Face Behind the Mask* and *The Beast with Five Fingers.* In 1947, he assisted Chaplin on *Monsieur Verdoux* and then, after a jolly Foreign Legion backlot picture, *Outpost in Morocco,* again with Tamiroff, he retired from movies and worked for TV.

Errol Flynn (Errol Leslie Thomson Flynn) (1909–59), b. Hobart, Tasmania

In 1992, with a three-year-old son, I had occasion to see *The Adventures of Robin Hood* (38, Michael Curtiz and William Keighley) some twenty times or so. That the movie stands up to such regular inspection is not just because of rippling action, the stained-glass Technicolor, or the fabulous Korngold score. It is because of Errol Flynn, an actor previously so confined to my bad books that I had stopped seeing him. Flynn does not deal in depth, but he has a freshness, a galvanizing energy, a cheerful gaiety (in the old sense) made to inspire boys. Chaucer knew Flynn: he is "a verray parfit gentle knight" and "as fresh as is the month of May." Of course, the zest faded: scandal, booze, nymphets, and the rapid mottling of age made for undeniable sadness. He became a bad joke, and he looked ten or fifteen years more than his real age. But we should not forget the vivacity of the late thirties and early forties, when his sword flashed and he was the true heir to Douglas Fairbanks.

He had had a variety of jobs around the Pacific before appearing as Fletcher Christian in the documentarylike *In the Wake of the Bounty* (32). This encouraged him to go to England, to repertory theatre and a British film, *Murder at Monte Carlo* (34, Ralph Ince). Warners shipped him to the

United States and, after *The Case of the Curious Bride* (35, Michael Curtiz) and *Don't Bet on Blondes* (35, Robert Florey), they elected to make him a swashbuckler. The trick worked, but it is of interest to note how. Of his next thirty-one movies (until 1948), nineteen were directed by Curtiz or Raoul Walsh. Having quarreled with Curtiz (his most compatible director), Flynn was more than lucky to find Walsh at Warners, though Walsh had a more searching view of heroism than Curtiz, who adored surface action. Still, these are very graceful adventures—travesties of history, but lovely, expert routines that needed speed, music, and such regulars as Olivia de Havilland (his partner seven times, wide-eyed and won over), such adversaries as Claude Rains, Basil Rathbone, sundry Spaniards, savages, and Japanese, *and* his mustache—he could look naked and a little wolfish without it.

Here is the list of films. With Curtiz: *Captain Blood* (35); *The Charge of the Light Brigade* (36)—Flynn was a Remington bronze on horseback, though he often fell off and broke brittle bones; *The Perfect Specimen* (37); *Robin Hood* (38); *Four's a Crowd* (38)—a modern comedy; the Australian twang insouciant at court in *The Private Lives of Elizabeth and Essex* (39)—he and Bette Davis were under consideration for Rhett and Scarlett; *Dodge City* (39); *Virginia City* (40); *The Sea Hawk* (40); as cavalry genius Jeb Stuart in *Santa Fe Trail* (40); and *Dive Bomber* (41). And for Walsh: a longhair Custer in *They Died With Their Boots On* (41); *Desperate Journey* (42); wonderful as both pugilist and man of honor playing James J. Corbett in *Gentleman Jim* (42), probably his best acting; *Northern Pursuit* (43); *Uncertain Glory* (44); *Objective Burma* (45), a war picture that aroused British and Australian anger for seeming to make victory an American trick; and *Silver River* (48).

Along the way, Flynn had become notorious. In 1942, he was charged with raping two eighteen-year-old girls. The grand jury cleared him, but the authorities decided to prosecute anyway. Flynn was eventually acquitted, but only after the extent of his sexual appetite had been made clear. "In like Flynn" became a battle cry for hopeful ladykillers. Today, I doubt if a star (like Tom Cruise) could suffer such charges and keep his career going.

Flynn had made films without costume, swords, and carefree action, and he had looked ordinary: *Green Light* (37, Frank Borzage); *Another Dawn* (37, William Dieterle); *The Sisters* (38, Anatole Litvak); *The Dawn Patrol* (38, Edmund Goulding); *Footsteps in the Dark* (41, Lloyd Bacon); *Edge of Darkness* (43, Lewis Milestone)—a somber story of the Norwegian resistance; and *Cry Wolf* (47, Peter Godfrey).

Close to forty, he was going out of fashion—and

he had neither the grin nor the leaping power of the new Burt Lancaster. He was awful as a composer in *Escape Me Never* (47, Godfrey); *The Adventures of Don Juan* (48, Vincent Sherman) tried to exploit his reputation, but the picture had no flourish, and Flynn seemed sadder and slower. He was Soames in *That Forsyte Woman* (49, Compton Bennett), but he was better in *Kim* (50, Victor Saville).

His tide went out fast: *Montana* (50, Ray Enright); *Adventures of Captain Fabian* (51, William Marshall); *Against All Flags* (52, George Sherman); *Mara Maru* (52, Gordon Douglas); in a lamentable *The Master of Ballantrae* (53, William Keighley); and the dreadful *William Tell* (54). Near bankruptcy, he squired Anna Neagle in two Herbert Wilcox films—*Lilacs in Spring* (54) and *King's Rhapsody* (55). His drinking was so bad that he ended up having to play drunks. Thus, after *The Warriors* (55, Henry Levin) and *The Big Boodle* (57, Richard Wilson), he finished with *The Sun Also Rises* (57, Henry King); as John Barrymore in *Too Much, Too Soon* (58, Art Napoleon); *The Roots of Heaven* (58, John Huston); and *Cuban Rebel Girls* (59, Barry Mahon), in which he played with his last girlfriend, the sixteen-year-old Beverly Aadland. After his death, a mild autobiography, *My Wicked, Wicked Ways*, was published.

James Foley, b. New York

1984: *Reckless*. 1985: *At Close Range*. 1987: *Who's That Girl?* 1990: *After Dark, My Sweet*. 1992: *Glengarry Glen Ross*. 1995: *Two Bits*. 1996: *Fear; The Chamber*. 1999: *The Corruptor*. 2003: *Confidence*.

Is there a dull Foley film? No, though *Who's That Girl?* keeps one going out of a wish to see just what inanity will fulfill Madonna next. The same sort of glee keeps one attuned to Al Pacino's old man in *Two Bits*. Then there's *Glengarry Glen Ross*, which I found riveting yet absolutely without resonance or reason or interest. How can that be? Put it down to Mamet's intimidation of attention at the expense of all other responses. But then you have to allow that *After Dark, My Sweet* is well worthwhile, just as the confrontations between Sean Penn and Christopher Walken in *At Close Range* are impossible to forget. What does it all mean? Well, in part, that it's possible to possess quite an intense notion of movie without any capacity to make a coherent film. But you could put together a montage of scenes by Foley that might convince anyone that he was—and is—a very hot director.

Henry Fonda (1905–82),
b. Grand Island, Nebraska
Educated at the University of Minnesota, he joined the Omaha Community Players and Joshua Logan's University Players. He edged his way on

to the Broadway stage, was briefly married to Margaret Sullavan, and in 1934 he signed a contract with Walter Wanger.

Having done *The Farmer Takes a Wife* (35, Victor Fleming) on the stage, Fonda was put in the movie opposite Janet Gaynor. Tall (if gangling), handsome (in a boyish way), and gentle spoken (with only a hint of whine), Fonda was first used as a romantic lead to bend fondly over star actresses. But after the remake of *Way Down East* (35, Henry King) and *I Dream Too Much* (35, John Cromwell), he made his first venture into American epic in *The Trail of the Lonesome Pine* (36, Henry Hathaway).

It is difficult now not to see a ponderous relevance in the title: for there is something of assumed solitariness about the soulful way Fonda became the repository of honesty and decency. Even in his late sixties, voice, looks, and bearing sustained this image. Only the glimpses of a much harsher man in private (a difficult husband and tempestuous father to Peter and Jane) detract from the feeling of typicality and dreamy vision.

He made *Spendthrift* (36, Raoul Walsh) before his first major role as the doomed but undiminished fugitive in *You Only Live Once* (37, Fritz Lang). He alternated romances and adventure pictures: *That Certain Woman* (37, Edmund Goulding), solacing Bette Davis; *I Met My Love Again* (38, Joshua Logan and Arthur Ripley); with Davis again in *Jezebel* (38, William Wyler), just avoiding priggishness; *Blockade* (38, William Dieterle), a muffled Spanish Civil War story cherished by Wanger; *Spawn of the North* (38, Hathaway); and brother Frank in *Jesse James* (39, King).

After playing support in *The Story of Alexander Graham Bell* (39, Irving Cummings), Fonda found his most suitable director, John Ford. Fonda's statuesque gentleness, with politeness only reluctantly giving way to anger, was very close to Ford's conception of a prairie Galahad. They made three films in a row that established Fonda's nobility: *Young Mr. Lincoln* (39); *Drums Along the Mohawk* (39); Tom Joad in *Grapes of Wrath* (40), a part that admirably identified the rural twang and lope that Fonda never lost. As Lincoln, especially, he captured a dreamy political calm, torn between peach and apple pie, but drawn to justice unfailingly.

But Fonda's time with Wanger had now elapsed and he signed a seven-year contract with Fox that was not always to his liking. In fact, the next few years did not live up to his early success: opposite Alice Faye in *Lillian Russell* (40, Cummings); *The Return of Frank James* (40, Lang); and *Chad Hanna* (40, King). Paramount borrowed him to be a marvelous learned stooge for Stanwyck in *The Lady Eve* (41, Preston Sturges), virtually the only good comedy that Fonda ever made, tribute to

Stanwyck's wit, to Sturges's grace, and to Fonda's own solemnity. He continued in a run of dull or modest films: *Wild Geese Calling* (41, John Brahm); *The Male Animal* (42, Elliott Nugent); *The Big Street* (42, Irving Reis); *Rings on Her Fingers* (42, Rouben Mamoulian); *Tales of Manhattan* (42, Julien Duvivier), with Ginger Rogers; and *The Magnificent Dope* (42, Walter Lang). Then two films restored Fonda as the emblem of liberal conscience: *The Immortal Sergeant* (42, John M. Stahl) and *The Ox-Bow Incident* (43, William Wellman). At which point he joined the navy and saw active service in the Pacific.

Back from the war, Fonda edged deeper into the American myth as Wyatt Earp, sat precariously on a veranda, his feet propped up on a post, in *My Darling Clementine* (46, Ford). He followed this with the husband in *Daisy Kenyon* (47, Otto Preminger), an underrated film that uses the stubbornness in Fonda cleverly. He played the Jean Gabin part in Anatole Litvak's awful *The Long Night* (47) and then had his one failure with Ford, the priest in an attempt at Graham Greene's *The Power and the Glory* called *The Fugitive* (47). He was in an episode of *On Our Merry Way* and then rather eclipsed by John Wayne in *Fort Apache* (48, Ford) in which he played a stiff-backed disciplinarian.

He returned to the theatre and had great success in *Mister Roberts, Point of No Return*, and *The Caine Mutiny Court Martial*. Hollywood lured him back only in 1955 for the film of *Mister Roberts*. Ford began the project, but he and Fonda quarreled and Mervyn Le Roy took over when Ford fell ill. Once back, Fonda carried on as if he had never been away, falling into new idioms remarkably well. After playing Pierre in *War and Peace* (56, King Vidor), he was at his very best, harrowed into resignation, as the bass player wrongly charged with robbery in Hitchcock's *The Wrong Man* (57)—it is a performance of simplicity and intensity from a man instinctively aware of the camera. But it was his next film that really brought Fonda back into public attention: as the white-coated voice of reason amid *Twelve Angry Men* (57, Sidney Lumet). The technical skill and glib liberalism of that film were built around Fonda and he was once more revealed as Hollywood's statue of liberty. He was lordly in *Stage Struck* (58, Lumet) and a less than robust bounty hunter in *The Tin Star* (57, Anthony Mann). What was most remarkable was the way his persona was used in political subjects: a presidential candidate in *Advise and Consent* (61, Preminger) and *The Best Man* (64, Franklin Schaffner), eventually too pure for the hurly-burly; and the president himself, tortured by imminent holocaust in *Fail-Safe* (63, Lumet).

After Kennedy, so honorable a figure went out of fashion. Vietnam and Watergate made *The Best*

Man seem rather virginal. Is it possible, too, that as Peter and Jane Fonda became personalities in their own right, so Henry was spoken of as something less than the nicest guy in town? Whatever the answer, stodginess set in during his last years. A turgid TV series, *The Deputy*, showed the stolid father figure, as did *Madigan* (68, Don Siegel) and *The Boston Strangler* (68, Richard Fleischer). Fonda tried to discover a more mischievous, warped character, especially in subcomic Westerns—but with mixed success: *A Big Hand for the Little Lady* (66, Fielder Cook); *Welcome to Hard Times* (67, Burt Kennedy); *Firecreek* (67, Vincent McEveety); very good as the villain in *Once Upon a Time in the West* (69, Sergio Leone); *The Cheyenne Social Club* (70, Gene Kelly); *There Was a Crooked Man* (70, Joseph Mankiewicz); *Sometimes a Great Notion* (71, Paul Newman); *Le Serpent* (73, Henri Verneuil); *Ash Wednesday* (73, Larry Pierce); *My Name Is Nobody* (73, Tonino Valerii); *The Red Pony* (73, Robert Totten); as Admiral Nimitz in *Midway* (76, Jack Smight); *Tentacles* (76, Oliver Hellman); *Rollercoaster* (77, James Goldstone); and *The Swarm* (78, Irwin Allen).

He had not made a good film in ten years. One hoped that someone might give him a chance as, say, a bogus-priest, rapist confidence trickster who picks his nose. That wicked prospect never dawned. Fonda was in poor health near the end, grim-looking and slow, but capable of being very touching: as a man recovering from a stroke in *Home to Stay* (78, Delbert Mann) for TV; briefly in *Fedora* (78, Billy Wilder); *Wanda Nevada* (79, Peter Fonda); *City on Fire* (79, Alvin Rakoff); *Meteor* (79, Ronald Neame); *Gideon's Trumpet* (80, Robert Collins); *The Oldest Living Graduate* (80, Jack Hofsiss); with Myrna Loy in *Summer Solstice* (81, Ralph Rosenblum) for TV; and finally winning the best actor Oscar, with Katharine Hepburn and his daughter, in the entirely autumnal *On Golden Pond* (81, Mark Rydell).

Jane Fonda, b. New York, 1937

Jane Fonda assures us that she is retired. But she has a history of firm stands that come to be rewritten. Her emphatic quality as an actress is the secret entrance to her insecurity: that's what made her Bree Daniels in *Klute* so compelling. The retired businesswoman has given up Ted Turner and fitness tapes. But what is she thinking about? Worrying about?

Otherwise, her final screen appearances were limited to glimpses of her and her new husband, Ted Turner, dozing at Atlanta Braves games. And so, maybe, the fiercest opinionist in American show business has revealed yet another aspect of herself in terms of the men in her life—that severe father, Henry, with a temper never disclosed on-screen; director Roger Vadim, the sophisticated voyeur who made Jane sexy; the politician and liberal activist, Tom Hayden, with whom she recognized issues; and then Turner, mogul, macho, conservative, and old-fashioned.

Jane Fonda was the child of her father's second marriage, to Frances Seymour Brokaw (it was her second marriage, too). Peter Fonda was the younger child of this marriage. Frances Fonda suffered from poor health and anxiety. Henry was away on war service. Then, in 1950, as Henry sought a divorce so that he might marry a younger woman, Frances cut her throat. Henry told Jane that her mother had died from a heart attack. Jane only learned the truth in a movie magazine.

Educated at Vassar and the Actors' Studio, she modeled and worked in the theatre in the late 1950s. She made her film debut in Joshua Logan's charming *Tall Story* (60) and then played supporting parts in Dmytryk's *Walk on the Wild Side* (62), Cukor's *The Chapman Report* (62), and in George Roy Hill's *Period of Adjustment* (62). In addition to the promise of *Tall Story* and her hints of blooming with Cukor, the Drew-Leacock essay *Jane* (63) was perhaps the clearest glimpse of her talent. After *Sunday in New York* (63) for Peter Tewksbury, she went to France, made *Les Félins* (64, René Clément), married Roger Vadim, and necessarily revealed all in *La Ronde* (64) and *La Curée* (66).

It remained an uncoordinated career, torn between the personalities of her father and her husband. She was wasted in *Cat Ballou* (65, Elliot Silverstein) but, at last, in Penn's *The Chase* (66) she showed a real maturity. Toward the end of the 1960s she became articulate and insistent about many political issues, about the difficulty of living with Henry Fonda and Vadim, and these films added to her range: Preminger's *Hurry Sundown* (66); *Barefoot in the Park* (67, Gene Saks); with her brother in the "Metzengerstein" episode of *Histoires Extraordinaires* (68, Vadim); and *Barbarella* (68), in which she is as vacantly sexy as Vadim's listless prurience.

Seemingly independent (and remarried to Tom Hayden), she became much more resolute and aggressive; it helped make her one of the best young actresses anywhere. *They Shoot Horses, Don't They?* (69, Sydney Pollack) is an ordinary film made riveting by her unblinkingly fierce nihilism. While Alan Pakula's *Klute* (71) is a fascinating exploration of the art and life of acting. Far from a nostalgic thriller, or a Kafkaesque study, it is as much an investigation of Jane Fonda as the Drew-Leacock film. It is a frightening movie because of the feeling of self-destruction at its heart. The role won her the Oscar and it remains her most complex work.

After that, she seemed intent on drawing together her public and professional performances. An energetic opponent of America in

Vietnam and of woman in bondage, she made two films intent on their propaganda value: *Tout Va Bien* (72, Jean-Luc Godard) and *A Doll's House* (73, Joseph Losey). In addition, she has been the subject of two further documentary essays: *Letter to Jane: Investigation of a Still* (72, Godard and Jean-Pierre Gorin); and a second *Jane* (73, Midge Mackenzie), made for TV. However, she was refreshingly funny in *Steelyard Blues* (72, Alan Myerson).

In 1974, with Hayden and Haskell Wexler, she directed a documentary, *Vietnam Journey*. One grew used to seeing her in battle dress; then, suddenly, she was helping give out the 1977 Oscars in gown and created hair. She also reverted to middle-class comedy in *Fun With Dick and Jane* (76, Ted Kotcheff). In *Julia* (77, Fred Zinnemann) she pretended to be Lillian Hellman and was a firm, anxious center for a flimsy film. *Coming Home* (78, Hal Ashby) was a testament of a kind, all but produced by the actress. Yet its political awareness is half-baked, and the movie wraps national hurt in romance. The look in Fonda's eyes was always too determined and convinced for the very conventional, unenlightened wife she was trying to play.

Nevertheless, she won a second Oscar for *Coming Home*, appeared in *Comes a Horseman* (78, Pakula), and rode the box-office swarm of Three Mile Island with the wretched, lucky, and ultimately frivolous *The China Syndrome* (79, James Bridges).

She became a complete American heroine in the eighties, not just as actress and producer, but as the starring body in her own series of workout books and videotapes. Like so many of her films, the tapes were ardent, solemn, and modestly erotic—she was true to herself. Her body went to whiplash (which supposedly was the intent), yet some concerned observers noted that aging went on nevertheless.

Her last films were *9 to 5* (80, Colin Higgins); *On Golden Pond* (81, Mark Rydell), her gift to her father, and a suitably showy unification of their starry temperaments; *Rollover* (81, Pakula); on TV with *The Dollmaker* (84, Daniel Petrie), for which she won an Emmy; *Agnes of God* (85, Norman Jewison); a return to albeit fading glamour in *The Morning After* (86, Sidney Lumet), for which she got a best actress nomination; *Old Gringo* (89, Luis Penzo); and *Stanley and Iris* (90, Martin Ritt).

Her marriage to Tom Hayden ended in divorce—and so she became the friend of and then the wife to Ted Turner. There were stories that she had lost parts—*The Music Box*, for instance—because she looked too old. But she has seldom been irreversible; she is a good and maybe helpless actress; and she may have the basis of a great old lady.

Peter Fonda, b. New York, 1939

The son of Henry, younger brother of Jane, and father of Bridget, Peter still walks and moves like Henry: shoulders drooping, flat-footed, seeming to be propelled from the knee joints. And, like his father, Peter has that coltish, humorless idealism of a young Mr. Lincoln or Tom Joad. Jane alone seems anxious about life; Henry and Peter address it, as if it were a jury or a political meeting. Thus, even the supposed modernity of *Easy Rider* (69, Dennis Hopper) fits into the American legend of its own idealism that Henry had done so much to incarnate. It is as elaborate and artificial a piece of "realism" as all those films Henry made for John Ford, and as simplistic as *Twelve Angry Men*. *Easy Rider* was also part produced by Fonda, with great profit. That is another subtle compromise, for its apparent underground movie was as glossy and expensive as the streamlined motorbikes, and nearly as roadworthy. Nevertheless, Fonda is an interesting figure—an actor of handsome nobility, and a director of muddled plainness, for instance, *The Hired Hand* (71). His record as an actor is already very varied: *Tammy and the Doctor* (63, Harry Keller); *The Victors* (63, Carl Foreman); especially good as the neurotic admirer of *Lilith* (63, Robert Rossen); *The Young Lovers* (64, Samuel Goldwyn Jr.); *The Rounders* (65, Burt Kennedy); *The Wild Angels* (66, Roger Corman); *The Trip* (67, Corman); in the "Metzengerstein" episode from *Histoires Extraordinaires* (68, Roger Vadim); *The Last Movie* (71, Hopper); *Dirty Mary, Crazy Larry* (74, John Hough); *Race with the Devil* (75, Jack Starrett); *The Diamond Mercenaries* (75, Val Guest); *92 in the Shade* (75, Thomas McGuane); *Fighting Mad* (76, Jonathan Demme); *Futureworld* (76, Richard T. Heffron); and *Outlaw Blues* (77, Heffron).

He directed and acted in *Wanda Nevada* (78); and acted in *The Hostage Tower* (80, Claudio Guzman); *The Cannonball Run* (81, Hal Needham); as a cult leader in *Split Image* (82, Ted Kotcheff); *Dance of the Dwarfs* (82, Gus Trikonis); *Spasms* (83, William Fruet); *Peppermint Frieden* (84, Marianne Rosenbaum); *A Reason to Live* (84, Peter Levin); *Certain Fury* (85, Stephen Gyllenhaal); *Hawken's Breed* (89, Charles B. Pierce); and *The Rose Garden* (89, Fons Rademakers).

The easygoing indifference of Fonda's acting went on for a few more years—with *Fatal Mission* (90, George Rowe), which he cowrote; *South Beach* (92, Fred Williamson); *Deadfall* (93, Christopher Coppola); *Molly & Gina* (93, Paul Leder); *Nadja* (94, Michael Almereyda); *Love and a .45* (94, C. M. Talkington); *Escape from L.A.* (96, John Carpenter). Most of those got and deserved a limited release. But then Fonda delivered a very good (if overrated) performance in *Ulee's Gold* (97, Victor Nunez), which got a nomination. Since then, he was good as the smooth heel in *The Limey* (99, Steven Soderbergh); *The Passion of Ayn Rand* (99, Christopher Menaul); *South of Heaven, West of Hell* (00, Dwight Yoakam); *Second Skin* (00, Darrell Roodt); *Wooly Boys* (01, Leszek Burzynski); *The Laramie Project* (02, Moises Kaufman).

Joan Fontaine (Joan Fontaine
de Havilland), b. Tokyo, 1917

The younger sister of Olivia de Havilland, Fontaine was the daughter of English parents. The father, an eccentric, had elected to live in Japan where he maintained the role of a gentleman who had a Cambridge blue for rowing as well as an M.A., and who rejoiced in tales of aristocratic Norman ancestors on the island of Guernsey. So there is irony in Fontaine's having her greatest success as an interloper at a swank English household. This lady is very conscious of her own classiness. She may be a natural Rebecca, which makes her acting all the more praiseworthy.

Rebecca (40, Alfred Hitchcock) is an instance of film exploiting an audience's kindness toward an anxious performer. Fontaine won the nameless central role against tough opposition: Vivien Leigh, Margaret Sullavan, Anne Baxter, and Loretta Young. Several advisors to producer David Selznick were against Fontaine. Hitchcock was uncertain. But Selznick knew Fontaine; he had been smitten with her. He backed his hunch. And Hitchcock saw that the long-drawn-out casting procedure meant that she came to the part in the spirit that the character in Daphne du Maurier's novel comes to Manderley—stricken with doubts, dowdy, hunch-shouldered, a willing victim for the oppressive psychological forces that Mrs. Danvers had preserved in the house. Fontaine's ability to show that ordeal working on her is central to the film and a fine example of the concealed sadism Hitchcock brings to bear. It should also be said that *Rebecca* is a disguised horror film, with Fontaine at peril in an "old dark house." That peril seriously threatens her sanity, and the way she is drawn so near to suicide in the window scene was a major, psychological intensification in Hitchcock's work.

Suspicion (41, Hitchcock) makes fewer demands on her, but of essentially the same sort. And if she won her Oscar for that, rather than for *Rebecca*, it may have been because Hollywood realized belatedly that a new female character had been introduced to the screen.

It is necessary to stress this early excellence to show how disappointing her career as a whole has been. She made her debut in *No More Ladies* (35, Edward H. Griffith), had a small part in *Quality Street* (37, George Stevens), and played opposite Astaire in *A Damsel in Distress* (37, Stevens). After *Gunga Din* (39, Stevens), she was in *Man of*

Conquest (39, George Nicholls), and the sheep in *The Women* (39, George Cukor) before *Rebecca*. But with her Oscar, she went after stately, romantic parts, lacking the real emotional sophistication of a Lombard or a Loy, and entered into weepies without the conviction of a Joan Crawford: *This Above All* (42, Anatole Litvak); *The Constant Nymph* (43, Edmund Goulding); effective in *Jane Eyre* (44, Robert Stevenson); *Frenchman's Creek* (44, Mitchell Leisen); *The Affairs of Susan* (45, William A. Seiter); *From This Day Forward* (46, John Berry); as a poisoner in *Ivy* (47, Sam Wood); and *The Emperor Waltz* (48, Billy Wilder).

The romantic vulnerability that Hitchcock had touched on was revealed again by Max Ophuls in the beautiful *Letter From an Unknown Woman* (48) where she is exceptional in getting the youth, the vulnerability, and the romanticism of the character. Thus, twice, Fontaine was so good as to leave us baffled by her general indifference. She was at least presentable in *Born to Be Bad* (50, Nicholas Ray) and *Beyond a Reasonable Doubt* (56, Fritz Lang). Otherwise, her list of films is sadly undistinguished: *You Gotta Stay Happy* (48, H. C. Potter); *September Affair* (50, William Dieterle); nicely anxious in *Darling, How Could You!* (51, Leisen); *Something to Live For* (52, Stevens); *Ivanhoe* (52, Richard Thorpe); *Decameron Nights* (53, Hugo Fregonese); *The Bigamist* (53, Ida Lupino); *Casanova's Big Night* (54, Norman Z. McLeod); *Serenade* (56, Anthony Mann); *Island in the Sun* (57, Robert Rossen); *Until They Sail* (57, Robert Wise); *A Certain Smile* (58, Jean Negulesco); *Tender Is the Night* (61, Henry King); and *The Witches* (66, Cyril Frankel). Since then, she has appeared on television in *The Users* (78, Joseph Hardy) and *Dark Mansions* (86, Jerry London).

Bryan Forbes (John Theobald Clarke),
b. London, 1926

1961: *Whistle Down the Wind*. 1962: *The L-Shaped Room*. 1964: *Seance on a Wet Afternoon*. 1966: *King Rat; The Wrong Box*. 1967: *The Whisperers*. 1968: *Deadfall*. 1969: *The Madwoman of Chaillot*. 1971: *The Raging Moon*. 1975: *The Stepford Wives*. 1976: *The Slipper and the Rose*. 1978: *International Velvet*. 1981: an episode from *Sunday Lovers*. 1982: *Better Late Than Never*. 1983: *A King in Yellow* (TV). 1985: *The Naked Force*. 1990: *The Endless Game*.

Here is a career to illustrate the misleading storybook road to success in the British film industry. In March 1971, still only forty-five years old, Forbes resigned from one of the rare executive positions in charge of British production. For two years he had headed the EMI setup, pledged to distinguished, modest-priced movies. To its credit was the bonanza of *The Railway Children*, the eccentricity of *The Tales of Beatrix Potter,* and a string of mediocre, bloodless ventures: *Hoffmann, The Breaking of Bumbo,* and his own *The Raging Moon.* As a group, the films seemed to retract from opportunity, rather than grasp it. The fact is that as actor, writer, director, and executive he has often lacked creative confidence and character.

In his enforced rest he wrote a novel. This was a true reversal since, while still a drama student, he had begun by writing fiction. After military service he went into films as a supporting actor, as bright and callow as a midshipman: *The Small Back Room* (48, Michael Powell); *All Over the Town* (48, Derek Twist); *Dear Mr. Prohack* (49, Thornton Freeland); *The Wooden Horse* (50, Jack Lee); *Green Grow the Rushes* (51, Twist); *The World in His Arms* (52, Raoul Walsh); *Appointment in London* (52, Philip Leacock); *Sea Devils* (53, Walsh); *The Million Pound Note* (53, Ronald Neame); *An Inspector Calls* (54, Guy Hamilton); *The Colditz Story* (54, Hamilton); *Passage Home* (55, Roy Baker); *Now and Forever* (55, Mario Zampi); *The Last Man to Hang* (56, Terence Fisher); *It's Great to Be Young* (56, Cyril Frankel); *The Key* (58, Carol Reed); *I Was Monty's Double* (58, John Guillermin); and *Yesterday's Enemy* (59, Val Guest).

But earnest effort got him nowhere as an actor. It was as a writer that he promoted himself, partly on the wings of the spurious realism that regenerated British cinema: *Cockleshell Heroes* (56, José Ferrer); *House of Secrets* (56, Guy Green); *I Was Monty's Double; The Captain's Table* (59, Lee); and *The Angry Silence* (60, Green), which he also coproduced with Richard Attenborough. The mixture of emotional melodrama and industrial setting was well intentioned but fixedly middle-brow. No doubt Forbes worked out of a sense of dissatisfaction with the complacency of British films, but instead of vigor he brought neatness, stridency, and eventually pretentiousness to them. *The League of Gentlemen* (60, Basil Dearden), in which he also acted, was polished entertainment and *Only Two Can Play* (61, Sidney Gilliat) was amusing. But his script of *Station Six Sahara* (64, Seth Holt) depended on Holt's unstable vitality. His work on *Of Human Bondage* (64, Ken Hughes and Henry Hathaway) was simply routine.

But *The Angry Silence* had led Forbes toward direction and a recurring compromise between anodyne seriousness and popular taste. His films tend to run together, without dominant themes or personal style. All too easily they surrender to plot novelty and obvious, slick effect. The best that can be said for them is that they have won some good performances from Hayley Mills, Richard Attenborough, and Edith Evans. But their range seems insecure and the gulf between the women's magazine romanticism of *The L-Shaped Room* and the cynicism of *King Rat* is that of a bureaucrat too harassed by his financiers to find a personality. *Seance on a Wet Afternoon* is a good subject, but taken out of Forbes's hands by Kim Stanley's over-acting.

His last credit was on the screenplay of *Chaplin* (92, Attenborough).

Glenn Ford (Gwyllyn Samuel Newton), b. Quebec, Canada, 1916

After a few years on the stage, Ford made his movie debut in *Heaven With a Barbed Wire Fence* (40, Ricardo Cortez). Before service in the marines, he had also appeared in John Cromwell's *So Ends Our Night* (41), George Marshall's *Texas* (41), and in two Charles Vidor movies, *The Lady in Question* (40) and *The Desperadoes* (43). After the war, he returned as a decent, pipe-smoking idealist, dealing with the two Bette Davises in Curtis Bernhardt's *A Stolen Life* (46). But he achieved real stardom at Columbia with Rita Hayworth in Vidor's *Gilda* (46), playing an uncommonly nasty and twisted hero, a misogynist with fond eyes on George Macready's sword-stick.

Ford is generally likable on-screen and has managed to make genial, relaxed sincerity interesting. Such ease has often directed him toward Westerns, to comedies, and to romantic dramas. To all these genres he has brought care, authenticity, and intelligence. Thus, among a score of Westerns, he is good in Levin's *The Man from Colorado* (48), Boetticher's *The Man from the Alamo* (53), Russell Rouse's *The Fastest Gun Alive* (56), and Burt Kennedy's *The Rounders* (65), but was ill at ease as the outlaw in *3:10 to Yuma* (57, Delmer Daves), erroneously the most famous of the five. He showed a hardness beneath the calm as *Jubal* (56, Daves), as the foreman in *Cowboy* (58, Daves), and in Jerry Thorpe's *Day of the Evil Gun* (68).

He hardly touched on comedy until Daniel Mann's *The Teahouse of the August Moon* (56), but quickly achieved exceptional timing with jokes and an instinct for character and emotion within humor: this was made clear in George Marshall's excellent spoof, *The Sheepman* (58), in Capra's *Pocketful of Miracles* (61), and above all in Minnelli's *The Courtship of Eddie's Father* (63), a film that depends upon Ford's thoughtful portrait of a widower.

Such sympathetic good looks also made Ford ideal casting for weepies and romances, and in this category Charles Vidor's *The Loves of Carmen* (48), Bernhardt's *Interrupted Melody* (55), Anthony Mann's *Cimarron* (60), Minnelli's *Four Horsemen of the Apocalypse* (61), and Delbert Mann's *Dear Heart* (64) should all be mentioned.

In a hardworking career, Ford has also appeared in several adventure films: *Framed* (47, Richard Wallace); *The White Tower* (50, Ted Tetzlaff);

Joseph H. Lewis's *Undercover Man* (49); *The Green Glove* (52) and *Forbidden* (53), both for Rudolph Maté; *Terror on a Train* (53, Tetzlaff); *Plunder in the Sun* (53, John Farrow); Tourneur's *Appointment in Honduras* (53); Maté's *The Violent Men* (55); Blake Edwards's *Experiment in Terror* (62); and *Fate Is the Hunter* (64, Ralph Nelson).

It is because Ford has proved so durable, and because he is so close to the mainstream of entertainment movies, that in the late 1960s his career began to decline into dull Westerns: *Rage* (66, Gilberto Gazcon), made in Mexico; *The Pistoleros of Red River* (67); Karlson's *A Time for Killing* (67) and *Heaven with a Gun* (69, Lee H. Katzin). It was a sign of the times that he turned to a TV series, *Cade's County,* but *Santee* (72, Gary Nelson) was as good as his best. He was one of the rear admirals in *Midway* (76, Jack Smight); and he had a superb death scene in *Superman* (78, Richard Donner).

The professional thoroughness of Ford's work is distinguished by three films: he was the teacher-hero in Richard Brooks's *Blackboard Jungle* (55), the lover in Fritz Lang's *Human Desire* (54), and most memorably, the detective in Lang's *The Big Heat* (53)—one of the most intense and characteristic expressions of righteous vengeance in all of Lang's work and one of Ford's best studies in widower nobility.

As a veteran, he has done sadly forgettable work, much of it for television: *Evening in Byzantium* (78, Jerry London); *The Sacketts* (79, Robert Totten); *Beggarman, Thief* (79, Lawrence Doheny); *The Gift* (79, Don Taylor), playing an old Irish seaman with great feeling; *Virus* (80, Kinji Fukasaku); *Happy Birthday to Me* (81, J. Lee Thompson); *Border Shootout* (90, C. J. McIntyre); *Final Verdict* (91, Jack Fisk); *Raw Nerve* (91, David A. Prior).

Harrison Ford, b. Chicago, 1942

Is there an actor in the history of movies whose films have grossed more money? Harrison Ford has starred in three Indiana Jones pictures; he played Han Solo three times; he was part of *American Graffiti;* and a lead in such clear-cut hits as *Witness, Working Girl,* and *The Fugitive.* He has been a staple of the last twenty-five years, on film and video, an unquestioned hero to millions of kids all over the world. On the other hand, I have never had the feeling that Ford has won—or much wants to win—the love of the masses. There is a distance about him, a restrained, chilling patience that seems wary of going beyond his own known limits. On the few occasions of adventurousness in Ford's career, he has revealed himself as a limited, anxious actor. If *The Mosquito Coast* (86, Peter Weir) and *Regarding Henry* (91, Mike Nichols) have been his greatest tests, then Ford has hardly dared compete. In *Mosquito Coast,* he

never approached the insane, fascist charm of the character; while as *Henry,* he settled for a woefully shallow pathos.

He attended Ripon College in Wisconsin, and went straight to Hollywood and contracts at Columbia and Universal. He was a full decade in development, on TV and in small movie parts: *Dead Heat on a Merry-Go-Round* (66, Bernard Girard); *Luv* (67, Clive Donner); *A Time for Killing* (67, Phil Karlson); *Journey to Shiloh* (68, William Hale); *The Intruders* (70, William Graham); *Getting Straight* (70, Richard Rush); *American Graffiti* (73, George Lucas), in which he was one of the least notable new faces; memorable as the gray-suit aide in *The Conversation* (74, Francis Ford Coppola).

Star Wars (77, Lucas) changed his status, yet Ford seldom seems susceptible to confidence. He continued to make forgettable films as his power grew: *Heroes* (77, Jeremy Paul Kagan); *The Possessed* (77, Jerry Thorpe) for TV; *Force 10 from Navarone* (78, Guy Hamilton); *Hanover Street* (79, Peter Hyams), where he showed no instinct for romance; small roles in *Apocalypse Now* (79, Coppola) and *More American Graffiti* (79, B. L. W. Norton); and *The Frisco Kid* (79, Robert Aldrich).

It was in the early eighties that he became a passive phenomenon, though he clearly enjoyed the role of Indiana Jones and gave a nice self-deprecating humor to those films: *The Empire Strikes Back* (80, Irvin Kershner); *Raiders of the Lost Ark* (81, Steven Spielberg); *Blade Runner* (82, Ridley Scott), his best film to date, and one helped by Ford's willingness to be harsh and shabby; *Return of the Jedi* (83, Richard Marquand); and *Indiana Jones and the Temple of Doom* (84, Spielberg).

The straightforward needs of *Witness* (85, Peter Weir) suited him very well, and the love scenes with Kelly McGillis were touching. In *Frantic* (88, Roman Polanski), he ran around getting nowhere—and it was clear that he was growing an anxious gaze, like that of Gary Cooper. *Working Girl* (88, Mike Nichols) had him as the least active corner of a triangle, but his comedy was deft. In *Indiana Jones and the Last Crusade* (89, Spielberg) he benefited from the presence of Sean Connery.

In *Presumed Innocent* (90, Alan J. Pakula), he enhanced the overall mood of joylessness. In *Regarding Henry,* he seemed to pass. *Patriot Games* (92, Phillip Noyce) was further evidence of the look of ordeal on his face. He did Indiana Jones again in an episode of the TV series *Young Indiana Jones* (93, Carl Schultz). As for *The Fugitive* (93, Andrew Davis), he did his usual solid work, but the picture and its implausibility owed so much to the storming energy of Tommy Lee Jones. Ford may be a superstar—but had he ever carried a picture? In general, he slipped in the nineties—especially in *Sabrina* (95, Sydney Pollack), *The Devil's Own* (97, Pakula), *Six Days, Seven Nights* (98, Ivan Reitman); *Random Hearts* (99, Pollack) and *What Lies Beneath* (00, Robert Zemeckis)—which is a lot of especially. But in *Air Force One* (97, Wolfgang Petersen) he did carry the entire daft venture—indeed, he seemed to be carrying the aircraft itself. He is Russian in *K-19: The Widowmaker* (02, Kathryn Bigelow)—for $25 million. Then he did *Hollywood Homicide* (03, Ron Shelton).

John Ford (Sean Aloysius O'Feeney) (1895–1973), b. Cape Elizabeth, Maine
1917: *The Tornado; The Trail of Hate; The Scrapper; The Soul Herder; Cheyenne's Pal; Straight Shooting; The Secret Man; A Marked Man; Bucking Broadway*. 1918: *Phantom Riders; Wild Women; Thieves' Gold; The Scarlet Drop; Hell Bent; Delirium; A Woman's Fool; Three Mounted Men*. 1919: *Roped; A Fight for Love; The Fighting Brothers; Bare Fists; The Gun Packer; Riders of Vengeance; The Last Outlaw; The Outcasts of Poker Flat; Ace of the Saddle; Rider of the Law; A Gun Fightin' Gentleman; Marked Men*. 1920: *The Prince of Avenue A; The Girl in Number 29; Hitchin' Posts; Just Pals*. 1921: *The Big Punch; The Freeze-Out; The Wallop; Desperate Trails; Action; Sure Fire; Jackie*. 1922: *Little Miss Smiles; Silver Wings* (codirected with Edwin Carewe); *The Village Blacksmith*. 1923: *The Face on the Bar-Room Floor; Three Jumps Ahead; Cameo Kirby*. 1924: *Hoodman Blind; North of Hudson Bay; The Iron Horse; Hearts of Oak*. 1925: *Lightnin'; Kentucky Pride; The Fighting Heart; Thank You*. 1926: *The Blue Eagle; The Shamrock Handicap; Three Bad Men*. 1927: *Upstream*. 1928: *Four Sons; Mother Machree; Napoleon's Barber; Riley the Cop; Hangman's House*. 1929: *Strong Boy; The Black Watch* (codirected with Lumsden Hare); *Salute*. 1930: *Men Without Women; Born Reckless* (codirected with Andrew Bennison); *Up the River*. 1931: *Seas Beneath; The Brat; Arrowsmith*. 1932: *Air Mail; Flesh*. 1933: *Pilgrimage; Doctor Bull*. 1934: *The Lost Patrol; The World Moves On; Judge Priest*. 1935: *The Whole Town's Talking; The Informer; Steamboat Round the Bend*. 1936: *The Prisoner of Shark Island; Mary of Scotland*. 1937: *The Plough and the Stars; Wee Willie Winkie*. 1938: *The Hurricane; Four Men and a Prayer; Submarine Patrol*. 1939: *Stagecoach; Young Mr. Lincoln; Drums Along the Mohawk*. 1940: *The Grapes of Wrath; The Long Voyage Home*. 1941: *Tobacco Road; Sex Hygiene* (d); *How Green Was My Valley*. 1942: *The Battle of Midway* (d). 1943: *December 7th* (d); *We Sail at Midnight* (d). 1945: *They Were Expendable*. 1946: *My Darling Clementine*. 1947: *The Fugitive*. 1948: *Fort Apache; Three Godfathers*. 1949: *She Wore a Yellow Ribbon*. 1950: *When Willie Comes Marching Home; Wagonmaster; Rio Grande*. 1951: *This Is Korea* (d). 1952: *What Price Glory?; The Quiet Man*. 1953: *Mogambo; The Sun Shines Bright*. 1955: *The Long Gray Line; Mister Roberts* (codirected with Mervyn Le Roy). 1956: *The Searchers*. 1957: *The Wings of Eagles; The Rising of the Moon*. 1958: *The Last Hurrah; Gideon's Day*. 1959: *Korea* (d); *The Horse Soldiers*. 1960: *Sergeant Rutledge*. 1961: *Two Rode Together*. 1962: *The Man Who Shot Liberty Valance*. 1963: *How the West Was Won* (Civil War episode); *Donovan's Reef*. 1964: *Cheyenne Autumn*. 1965: *Young Cassidy* (a Ford project, taken over by and credited to Jack Cardiff). 1966: *Seven Women*. 1968: *Vietnam, Vietnam* (d).

Sheer longevity made Ford a major director. If that suggests no personal enthusiasm, I must confess to being daunted by the booze mythology of complacency and sentimentality in Ford's films. No one has done so much to invalidate the Western as a form. Apart from *The Searchers*—which is a very moving and mysterious film that does not cheat on a serious subject, and that beautifully relates the landscape to its theme—I find his Westerns pictorial, tediously rowdy, and based on cavalier treatment of American history. With *Liberty Valance* and *Cheyenne Autumn*, Ford had seemed slightly guilty about the travesty of Tombstone in *My Darling Clementine* and the offhand dismissal of Indians in the cavalry films. But it is notable that *Cheyenne Autumn* was disorganized, deprived of Ford's ball-and-socket military simplicity.

It might be argued that Hawks's West is equally romantic. But in *Red River* and *Rio Bravo* it is only a background for character studies that are profound, humane, and touched by sadness. Ford was so often bigoted, grandiloquent, and maudlin. It cannot be escaped that his curious Irish/American romance celebrated the tyrannical hero without any great qualification or demur. The rank emotionalism of the Victor McLaglen character in *The Informer* is the obverse of the vaunted resolution of the John Wayne character in *She Wore a Yellow Ribbon, Rio Grande, The Quiet Man, The Searchers, The Horse Soldiers,* and *Donovan's Reef*. Ford's male chauvinism believes in uniforms, drunken candor, fresh-faced little women (though never sexuality), a gallery of supporting players bristling with tedious eccentricity and the elevation of these random prejudices into a near-political attitude—thus Ford's pioneers talk of enterprise but show narrowness and reaction. Above all, his characters are accepted on their own terms—the hope of every drunk—and never viewed critically. In *Red River,* Wayne's brutality is revealed as odious, and in *Rio Bravo* he is made to respond to other characters. But *The Quiet Man* is an entertainment for an IRA club night, the cavalry films as much endorsements of the military as the wartime documentaries, and *My Darling Clementine* nostalgia for a world and code that never existed.

The Ford philosophy is a rambling apologia for unthinking violence later disguised by the sham legends of old men fuddled by drink and glory. The visual poetry so often attributed to Ford seems to me claptrap in that it amounts to the prettification of a lie—Fonda in the chair in *Clementine*, the lines of cavalry in so many films, the lone figure in Monument Valley, the homestead interior, as airy and vulgar as gravure advertisements for kitchenware. It is worth emphasizing how far Penn, Anthony Mann, Fuller, Nicholas Ray, and Peckinpah have disproved those rosy, statuesque images. Could Ford match the harrowing historical perspective of *Little Big Man*, the moral ambiguity of *The Far Country*, the painful violence of *Run of the Arrow*, the passion of *Johnny Guitar*, or the unsentimental veterans of *The Wild Bunch*?

But if the Westerns are fraudulent, what of Ford's other movies? When diverted to literature or socioreligious gravity he is as bad a director as Kramer. *The Grapes of Wrath* is an appallingly hollow posture of stoicism; *The Informer* risible; *How Green Was My Valley* a monstrous slurry of tears and coal dust; *Tobacco Road* meandering nonsense; *Three Godfathers* shameless; and *The Fugitive* inane. *Mister Roberts* is pious; *Gideon* boring; *The Long Gray Line* monotonous. *Stagecoach* is sometimes cited for its masterly construction. But it stresses narrative sequence and visual prettiness to the disadvantage of character, action, and the out-of-doors. The assembly of stock caricatures, the ritual images of Monument Valley—of Wayne firing into the back projection and of Indians tumbling in the dust—are as mechanical as the supposedly more reflective "human" touches: Mitchell's alcoholic doctor being regenerated, for instance. As for the very striking interior compositions—at the prairie way station—next year, in *The Long Voyage Home*, Ford innocuously indulged Gregg Toland's deep-focus studio photography in as senseless a display of beauty as Hollywood ever achieved. Ford's visual grace, it seems to me, needs the flush of drink in the viewer before it is sufficiently lulling to disguise the lack of intellectual integrity. It is a tipsy, self-regarding director that could repeat the abstract elegance of shadows on the ground before the house is destroyed in *The Grapes of Wrath*. Ford is walled up in a tradition of helpless, rosy lament, the cinema of distracting pipe dream.

I should add that Andrew Sarris has compared Ford with Orson Welles, as two poets of nostalgia. But that seems to me only to reveal Ford's weakness. Welles recalls a lost order, but sees all its flaws; whereas Ford dumbly regrets the passing of

a make-believe stability that has served as an obstacle to any necessary critical sensibility.

It is sometimes claimed that Ford is a superb visual storyteller; that he unerringly places his camera and edits his footage. But the same could be said for Leni Riefenstahl. The glorification of Ford's simplicity as an artist should not conceal the fact that his message is trite, callous, and evasive. Sadly, it comes as no surprise to discover that Ford was most attached to the reckless, barnstorming bigotry of *Steamboat Round the Bend* and *The Sun Shines Bright*. His message is the stupid, beaming farewell from *Stagecoach*, as Wayne and Claire Trevor go off together— "They're safe from the blessings of civilization."

The above was written for the 1975 edition, when Ford was already dead. It was also written before the author had spent any time in the American West, and before he had begun to consider the tangle that has been made between Hollywood movies and what Americans take for their history. I say that to deter the hopes of those who like Ford *and* this book, and who anticipated some greater kindness toward the director. My dismay is deeper now; my case, it seems to me, is more damning.

Still, I erred if my earlier blast suggested that Ford was without talent or interest. He was a natural storyteller; he made lovely scenes—he understood his own effects; he had an eye. Though, with the latter, I would point to the odd artistic link between Ford's Monument Valley Westerns and the current wave of automobile and fashion advertising that has seized on the Valley as a backdrop. In both cases, there is a lust for epic, clichéd panoramas, which forgets or forsakes the real meaning of that location—as geology, for its natives, and for the rest of America living on the edges of the empty quarter. In other words, the West deserves real journey, witness, walking, riding, living, and being there, patient enough to see through the first spectacle. It also requires a study of its culture: what it has meant to, say, the Navajo, the Hopi, Willa Cather, Edward Abbey, and Edward Curtis. Ford's eye refused to contemplate history or responsibility.

That leads on to Ford's notorious belief—spanning the years from *Fort Apache* to *The Man Who Shot Liberty Valance*—that "No sir! This is the West, sir. When the legend becomes fact, print the legend." There have been defenders of Ford—notably Joseph McBride and Michael Wilmington—who have tried to claim irony and historical sophistication in this. But they fail to recall that Ford's art was always that of a mythmaker, a wishful thinker, a man without stamina for reality—a moviemaker? In an age of diminishing historical sense in America, but of regular crises that dramatize our need to ask what happened (with Watergate, Vietnam, Iran-Contra, etc.), I marvel that Ford's heady obscurantism has such defenders. But to take Ford properly to task may be to begin to be dissatisfied with cinema.

Adherence to legend at the expense of facts will ruin America—the work is well under way. And lovers of the movies should consider how far film has helped the undermining. Ford is not the only culprit: Clint Eastwood's overpraised return to the West, *Unforgiven,* begins as an attempt to see things fresh, but at last its rigor collapses and it becomes not the West but just another Western. Still, Ford is the pioneer of this vision, and that is what I railed against in 1975.

The Searchers is still a riveting, tragic, and complex experience, a movie in which Ford gives up many of his false certainties, and a story filled with disturbing, half-buried thoughts of race and failure. In recent years, valuable books by Scott Eyman and Joseph McBride have shown how troubled and troubling a man he was, just as they have allowed the chance that we can't like (or stomach) all of his films.

Carl Foreman (1914–84), b. Chicago

There is no reason why the House Committee on Un-American Activities should be regarded as a more reliable test of talent than any other. To be sure, it righteously excluded or impeded some of the most interesting writers, directors, and actors in America during the McCarthy era. But it was not always so discriminating; it also blacklisted Carl Foreman. Thus, in retrospect, the "talking clock" Western, *High Noon* (52, Fred Zinnemann), that Foreman had written, was reassessed as a trenchant critique of American social spirit—this in the year that *The Lusty Men* and *Bend of the River* (true American pictures) were neglected. Foreman glowed like a martyr, went to England, worked under pseudonyms, and gradually revealed himself as a plodding middlebrow, possessed of dull ideas and rigidly conventional means of expressing them. *High Noon* remains the product of pretension, commonplace mentality, and an inability to relate the Western genre to credible or intriguing people.

Foreman was on the edges of the film industry until the war, but then worked on military documentaries. In the peace, he joined Stanley Kramer and George Glass in what some took for the breakthrough of "tough, journalistic, socially orientated works." These were problem pictures for complacent audiences, films that voiced commitment but offered easy answers. Foreman wrote many of them: *So This Is New York* (48, Richard Fleischer); *The Clay Pigeon* (49, Fleischer); *Home of the Brave* (49, Mark Robson); *Champion* (49, Robson); more at home with the Bix Beiderbecke biopic, *Young Man With a Horn* (50, Michael Curtiz); *The Men* (50, Fred Zinnemann); and *Cyrano de Bergerac* (50, Michael Gordon). As late as 1968, a National Film Theatre program thought that such films had helped "establish the concept that good movies require good scripts." Whereas, they are bad, underlined scripts, vastly inferior to such contemporaries as: *I Was a Male War Bride, The Fountainhead, Adam's Rib, They Live by Night, Whirlpool, Winchester 73, In a Lonely Place, All About Eve, Sunset Boulevard,* or *Strangers on a Train.*

In England, Foreman worked in pseudonymous collaboration on *The Sleeping Tiger* (54, Joseph Losey) and without credit on *The Bridge on the River Kwai* (57, David Lean). But soon after that, he set up as a writer/producer and moved toward his real home—mundane, commercial cinema: *The Key* (58, Carol Reed), a pretentious love story against a war background; *The Guns of Navarone* (61, J. Lee Thompson); *The Victors* (63, which he also directed); *Born Free* (65, James Hill), a film that not even McCarthy could have disapproved of; *The Virgin Soldiers* (69, John Dexter), which he only produced; *MacKenna's Gold* (69, Thompson), as writer and producer; *Living Free* (72, Jack Couffer); that inane piece of conservative hagiography, *Young Winston* (72, Richard Attenborough); *Force 10 from Navarone* (78, Guy Hamilton), a sad return to past glory; and *When Time Ran Out* (80, James Goldstone).

Milos Forman,

b. Káslov, Czechoslovakia, 1932

1963: *Konkurs/Talent Competition* (s); *Kdyby Ty Muziky Nebyly/If There Was No Music* (s). 1964: *Cerny Petr/Peter and Pavla.* 1965: *Lásky Jedné Plavovlásky/A Blonde in Love.* 1967: *Horí má Penenko/The Firemen's Ball.* 1971: *Taking Off.* 1973: "The Decathlon," episode from *Visions of Eight* (d). 1975: *One Flew Over the Cuckoo's Nest.* 1979: *Hair.* 1981: *Ragtime.* 1984: *Amadeus.* 1989: *Valmont.* 1996: *The People vs. Larry Flynt.* 1999: *Man on the Moon.*

It indicates Forman's preference for the everyday rather than the melodramatic that the modest *Taking Off* was derived from a newspaper story in which an apparently diligent teenager was one day found murdered. The idea that intrigued Forman was that daughter and parents could be leading intense private lives out of sight of the common family ground. Perhaps it is because a Czech coming to America has known more brutal disruptions of life that *Taking Off* is so charmingly unemphatic: the girl in Forman's film wanders off only briefly and comes back, at an inopportune moment, to find her parents driven by perplexity to strip poker. Most American directors would have scathed the parents with rhetoric, adored the young, and spared nothing from the eventual tragedy.

Forman's own parents were taken to die in concentration camps when he was a child—as were Polanski's, a director unable to look on people as warmly as Forman. (But, years later, Forman learned that the man he called father was not his real father.) He went to the Prague Film Faculty of the Academy of Dramatic Arts and graduated from there in 1957. His first work was as scriptwriter on *Dedecek Automobil* (56, Alfred Radok), and he was with Radok for several years in magic lantern theatre.

His Czech films showed a new vitality and relaxation for that country, and a very interesting set of influences. The Italian neo-realists, Karel Reisz, and Lindsay Anderson may have affected his liking for casual, ordinary stories and his affection for nonprofessional players. Equally, Forman was intrigued by the possibilities of candid camera, telephoto filming of amateurs in some formal situation that made them try to be professional. But Forman was not a grainy realist so much as a man able to fit spontaneity into a disguised and rather artful, old-fashioned narrative. He has confessed a liking for silent American comedy, and *A Blonde in Love* and *Firemen's Ball* could be the sort of romantic/ironic short story beloved of Maupassant and D. W. Griffith. Certainly, they are more frank, more inventive, and charged by the generally withdrawn recording of party scenes where Forman shows a sharp skill at catching people in the moment of revelation. And although his stories endeavor to like all the characters, he does not go too deep into the characters or the environment.

Without in any way dispelling or questioning the genuineness of Forman's sympathy for people, *Taking Off* showed the mannered comedian more clearly and raised serious questions about his style. That moment when Buck Henry almost swallows his wineglass on hearing that his daughter has fallen into the company, not of a layabout but of a pop music composer who made $290,000 last year, before taxes, is as predictable and accomplished a double take as anything in 1930s comedy. The central pose of baffled parents abandoning their own inhibitions is a mild version of Feiffer cartoons. Above all, the exhilarating editing of the audition—especially when Forman has a song sung by dozens of girls, phrase cut into phrase—is no more than playful. The skill of execution and the wit of the motion only emphasize his withdrawal from the central characters.

Cuckoo's Nest, by contrast, was full of risk, pain, and inventive courage. Whatever the project owed to Ken Kesey's novel and the cohesive presence of Jack Nicholson, Forman deserves great credit for the sudden but controlled movements from hilarity to tragedy. The metaphor of the insane institution works in terms of challenging entertainment, largely because of Forman's very balanced awareness that oddity, madness,

and acting are overlapping conditions. The asylum may be the more sinister because of Kafka and 1968.

Forman made three films in the eighties, all literary adaptations and all period pictures. One may wish, or hope, that his very shrewd observation of the world around him will return to the America he lives in. But that is not to scorn the adaptations. *Ragtime* was an underrated film, true to Doctorow, complex and challenging, a movie about a time and its ideas—just as the title supposes. *Amadeus* repeated the *Cuckoo's Nest* triumph, winning Oscars for best picture and best director. It is a rich, smart entertainment, lustrous yet eccentric in its period re-creation, luminous and satanic in its Salieri, and so entirely assured that its final impersonality comes as a surprise. In *Valmont,* Forman was scooped. Stephen Frears's *Dangerous Liaisons* (88) came out first, with a starrier cast, and took all the praise. Yet *Valmont* is the better film, the one that grasps tragedy as well as irony in the Laclos story.

Forman is seventy now, committed to America and New York (he chaired the film program at Columbia for a while), an engaging storyteller—surely he should have acted: imagine him as the man in *The Unbearable Lightness of Being.* Yet he works too sparingly—and with too much smart, worldly distance, finally—to be a major artist. But he is searching for material, and he is good enough to find it yet. *The People vs. Larry Flynt* was an intriguing view of American rights as seen from outside, and *Man on the Moon* was a study of comedian Andy Kaufman. Neither film worked well (especially with audiences), but they reaffirmed how far Forman is an outsider, devoted to Americana.

Bill Forsyth (William David Forsyth), b. Glasgow, Scotland, 1946
1969: *Language* (d). 1970: *Waterloo* (d); *Still Life with Honesty* (d). 1972: *Islands of the West* (d). 1973: *Shapes in the Water* (d). 1974: *Tree Country* (d). 1976: *Connection* (d). 1977: *The Legend of Los Tayos* (d). 1979: *That Sinking Feeling.* 1980: *Gregory's Girl.* 1981: *Andrina* (s). 1982: *Local Hero.* 1984: *Comfort and Joy.* 1987: *Housekeeping.* 1989: *Breaking In.* 1994: *Being Human.* 1999: *Gregory's Two Girls.*

Forsyth has nothing to do with the very positive thoughts of the average moviemaker who loves the medium and what he or she is doing with it. Indeed, he was candid about his own loss of belief after 1989: "And so the passion ultimately fizzles out because of the limitations of the goal; because movies are really not that important. At the very end of the day you're sitting with an audience of four or five hundred people and all they want is to be entertained. . . . You see we're dealing with a medium which really only wants to involve itself in the superficial manipulation of emotions."

That dispassionate estimate is by no means inconsistent with the dry, droll mood of Forsyth's world. He is a Scot, evidently, yet he is French in many of his instincts. He likes slight, unsettling situations that do not solve the lives of his characters. He is funny, yet his world is steeped in melancholy. He dislikes the compromise of production and big budgets—he is, maybe, a classic BBC TV–type of director. Not that Forsyth ever did any TV fiction until *Andrina.*

From *That Sinking Feeling* to *Breaking In,* Forsyth told a series of wry, moral tales with feeling and skill. If *Housekeeping* is his most profound film that may be because of Marilynne Robinson's novel, Christine Lahti's performance, and the vast perspectives of the Pacific Northwest, epic yet endlessly sad. It may simply be that Forsyth is a melancholy man who has gone as far as he can, like Bartleby the Scrivener.

Bob Fosse (1927–87), b. Chicago

1968: *Sweet Charity.* 1972: *Cabaret.* 1974: *Lenny.* 1979: *All That Jazz.* 1983: *Star 80.*

Fosse was a dancer on the Broadway stage before appearing in and choreographing *Kiss Me Kate* (53, George Sidney). He also danced in *The Affairs of Dobie Gillis* (53, Don Weis), *Give a Girl a Break* (53, Stanley Donen), *My Sister Eileen* (55, Richard Quine), *Damn Yankees* (58, Donen and George Abbott), and later, *The Little Prince* (75, Donen). As a choreographer, he worked on *My Sister Eileen, The Pajama Game* (57, Donen), *Damn Yankees,* and *How to Succeed in Business Without Really Trying* (66, David Swift).

Remembering the spontaneity of the bandstand dance in *My Sister Eileen* and the exhilarating "Once a Year Day" picnic sequence from *The Pajama Game,* it is no wonder that as a director Fosse is at his best with dance. But did he ever really do a "new" musical—a musical work with story, like Sondheim? *Sweet Charity* had a soft, romantic bittersweet center—it was taken from Fellini's *Nights of Cabiria*—that permitted Shirley MacLaine to be lovable. In the same way, *Cabaret* built up the women's-pic story to suit Liza Minnelli's mannered gaucheness. In both cases, there was a maudlin overemphasis on trite stories that seriously slowed the films. This tendency is the sadder because in musical numbers Fosse had a clear-eyed and witty grasp of the exploitation in both films: "Hey, Big Spender" in *Sweet Charity* and "Money, Money, Money" in *Cabaret* are brilliant routines, revealing a major talent. But *Cabaret* is slack and shabby in the long narrative sections: in the club, it is as precise, acid, and lewd as Joel Grey's emcee. "Money," "If You Could See Her Through My Eyes," and

"Mein Herr" are numbers not equaled since *Pajama Game,* even if they owe a lot to the iconography of Dietrich and George Grosz. One has only to imagine all of *Cabaret* within the club, and seen through Grey's eyes, to recognize how it compromises.

Another version of Grey's master of ceremonies is the American poet of desperate humor, Lenny Bruce, impersonated for Fosse by Dustin Hoffman. *Lenny* has no real songs or dance, but Bruce "sang" to his audience, acidulous blues that dared interruption; arguably only a director of musicals could have handled the subject.

Star 80 proved one of show business's bleakest self-portraits. Mariel Hemingway made a blank, siliconized heroine, while Eric Roberts was a frenzied lover/killer. *All That Jazz* had been a delirious, romanticizing account of Fosse's own flirtation with death—but at least the danger there was offset by the excitement of dance and work. Glamour was *Star 80*'s equivalent, and few American filmmakers have looked on that ghost with such loathing. There is a mood of Nathanael West in the film. With more humor and less helpless despair, it could have been a black masterpiece.

Jodie Foster (Alicia Christian Foster), b. Los Angeles, 1962

Little Man Tate (91), Jodie Foster's first directing job, is a decent, thoughtful TV-like movie about the dilemma of having and being a brilliant kid. It shows skill, care, and an absolute liberal regularity that is the more welcome and endearing from someone who has led Jodie Foster's life. Consider what she has been through: she has been a young American in tumultuous times; her mother and father separated before she was born; she was very smart—at least as difficult as its opposite; she was a child actress, in commercials, TV, and movies; at the age of thirteen, she had to understand and present the character of Iris in *Taxi Driver* (76, Martin Scorsese); she then became the helpless goal of John Hinckley's insanity—and of all the press attention that followed; she became an adult actress, though without any conventional glamour; and now she has won the best actress Oscar twice before the age of thirty.

Of course, such lives teach us the fallacies of conventional causation and the virtues of unique character. Jodie Foster is her own person, able to benefit from the Lycée Français and Yale, ready for the challenge of directing, resolutely articulate, and generous enough to make *Little Man Tate* a bow to mothers like her own.

Her movie career began with *Napoleon and Samantha* (72, Bernard McEveety); *Kansas City Bomber* (72, Jerrold Freedman); *Tom Sawyer* (73, Don Taylor); *One Little Indian* (73, McEveety); *Alice Doesn't Live Here Anymore* (74, Scorsese); and *Echoes of a Summer* (76, Taylor).

Taxi Driver required her to say things and be in actions that were shocking on-screen—and which are unthinkable (if everyday) for a child in real life. Her performance seemed unconscious of its shock value; indeed, Foster made Iris amazingly mundane and petty. Obviously she had help— from Scorsese, Schrader, De Niro, and Keitel— but no screen child had ever been so stark or so resistant to our need for sentimentality.

Bugsy Malone (76, Alan Parker) was a bizarre return to real childhood acting grown-up. Then she did *Freaky Friday* (77, Gary Nelson); *Moi, Fleure Bleue* (77, Eric Le Hung); *Il Casotto* (77, Sergio Citti); *The Little Girl Who Lives Down the Lane* (77, Nicolas Gessner); *Candleshoe* (78, Norman Tokar); *Carny* (80, Robert Kaylor); *Foxes* (80, Adrian Lyne); *O'Hara's Wife* (82, William S. Bartman); and Trilby to Peter O'Toole's *Svengali* (83, Anthony Harvey) for TV.

She was clearly a young adult in *The Hotel New Hampshire* (84, Tony Richards), and in France she was in *Le Sang des Autres* (84, Claude Chabrol). She coproduced and acted in *Mesmerized* (86, Michael Laughlin). Then came *Siesta* (87, Mary Lambert); *Five Corners* (88, Tony Bill); *Stealing Home* (88, Steven Kampmann); and *The Accused* (88, Jonathan Kaplan), for which she won the Oscar as the raped woman who goes to court. Again, she was startlingly coarse and tough—so few actresses can put the ladylike aside as thoroughly.

Then after a flirtation with sexiness in *Backtrack* (90, Dennis Hopper), she played Clarice Starling in *The Silence of the Lambs* (91, Jonathan Demme)—another Oscar. The surprise here was her gentleness and naïveté, the slowness of a country girl, and the very subtle receptivity to the scent of romance, or allure, between her and Hannibal Lecter.

She was the wife in *Sommersby* (93, Jon Amiel), given her first real screen romance, with Richard Gere. It didn't work, which means that Foster may never be easy casting. It is hard to know why she agreed to be in the futile *Maverick* (94, Richard Donner).

The encouraging thing about Foster in recent years is her wise opting for life. Why not, when you have had a "career" so long, and come so close to several forms of celebrity disaster? So it's more positive, I think, that she has had two children, and made it clear that the means of birth are her business, and hers alone. I'm sure she means to be a real mother, and I think she has succeeded at most things she takes on. That is the best explanation for the new mildness in her film work—directing the undisturbing *Home for the Holidays* (95) and acting in *Contact* (97, Robert Zemeckis), *Anna and the King* (99, Andy Tennant) and *The Dangerous Lives of Altar Boys* (02, Peter Care). She is young and strong enough to be back one day with something remarkable. She was at her best again— under threat—in *Panic Room* (02, David Fincher).

James Fox, b. London, 1939

Could Tony in *The Servant* (63, Joseph Losey) be a son of Lord Darlington in *The Remains of the Day* (93, James Ivory)? The question is prompted by the unusual way in which the actor James Fox has mined the uneasy ground on the fringes of the English upper class. He's so good as someone who doesn't quite understand quickly enough what's happening, and as guilty (rather gloomy) privilege that sees its own ghost in the mirror.

He got his start as a child actor, under the name William Fox, in *The Magnet* (50, Charles Frend)—he was the son of an agent, Robin Fox. Then he came back as a young adult: *The Loneliness of the Long Distance Runner* (62, Tony Richardson); very good in the cockpit of *The Servant* (he was amorously involved with Sarah Miles at the time); *Tamahine* (63, Philip Leacock); *King Rat* (65, Bryan Forbes); *Those Magnificent Men in Their Flying Machines* (65, Ken Annakin); playing an American comfortably in *The Chase* (66, Arthur Penn)—but a Texan with the English disease of feeling inadequate; *Arabella* (67, Adriano Barocco); *Thoroughly Modern Millie* (67, George Roy Hill); *Duffy* (68, Robert Parrish); as Edward Gordon Craig in *Isadora* (68, Karel Reisz); and trying his best to be a gangster, with Mick Jagger, in *Performance* (70, Donald Cammell and Nicolas Roeg).

Did that scabrous movie shock Fox himself? He gave up acting and joined a religious sect for nearly ten years, working only once, in a film made by the Billy Graham organization: *No Longer Alone* (78, Nicholas Webster). In that time, it was his older brother, Edward, who seemed likely to be the best-remembered actor in the family—it is a great pity that no one has ever cast them together.

James did come back: *Country* (81, Richard Eyre); *Pavlova* (83, Emil Lotianou); touching as the father of a runaway daughter in *Runners* (83, Charles Sturridge); *Greystoke* (84, Hugh Hudson); Fielding in *A Passage to India* (84, David Lean); *Absolute Beginners* (86, Julien Temple); *The Whistle Blower* (86, Simon Langton); *High Season* (87, Clare Peploe); *Farewell to the King* (89, John Milius); *She's Been Away* (90, Peter Hall); *The Russia House* (90, Fred Schepisi); magnificently fastidious and evasive as Sir Anthony Blunt in *A Question of Attribution* (92, John Schlesinger); and *Heart of Darkness* (94, Roeg).

He remains a stalwart of British TV and of any effort to depict Britishness: *Fall from Grace* (94 Waris Hussein); *Doomsday Gun* (94, Robert Young); *The Old Curiosity Shop* (94, Kevin Connor); *The Dwelling Place* (94, Gavin Millar); *The*

Choir (95, Ferdinand Fairfax); *Gulliver's Travels* (96, Sturridge); *Never Ever* (96, Charles Finch); as Karenin in *Anna Karenina* (97, Bernard Rose); *Kings in Grass Castles* (97, John Woods); *Shadow Run* (98, Geoffrey Reeve); as Mountbatten in *Jinnah* (98, Jamil Dehlavi); *Mickey Blue Eyes* (99, Kelly Makin); *Metropolis* (00, Peter Morgan); *Up at the Villa* (00, Franco Zeffirelli); *The Golden Bowl* (00, James Ivory); *Sexy Beast* (00, Jonathan Glazer); *Armadillo* (01, Howard Davies); *The Mystic Masseur* (01, Ismail Merchant).

He was Professor Summerlee in *The Lost World* (01, Stuart Orme); *Shaka Zulu: The Citadel* (01, Joshua Sinclair); *Hans Christian Andersen: My Life as a Fairy Tale* (01, Philip Saville); as Lord Carrington in *The Falklands Play* (02, Michael Samuels); *Trial & Retribution VI* (02, Ferdinand Fairfax).

Kay Francis (Katherine Edwina Gibbs) (1903–68), b. Oklahoma City, Oklahoma

Kay Francis was a short-lived bloom, as far-fetched as the sophisticated romances of the early thirties where clothes *were* identity. But in *A Woman's View* (1993), Jeanine Basinger makes a good case for remembering the intensity of Kay Francis's brief impact, and the curiosity of her special reliance on the glamour (or religion) of clothes and jewels. She was a strange couture goddess who lived with the rumor that she had some black blood, as well as coded diaries that alluded to boozing and sleeping around. She soldiered on, despite a lisp that let her "r"s sound like "w"s; and despite a huge salary engineered by agent Myron Selznick who got her away from Paramount and over to Warner Brothers. In truth, that was a tough shift, for Paramount was a studio that loved clothes and those ladies who treasured them.

The daughter of actress Katherine Clinton, she went into the theatre and played opposite Walter Huston in *Elmer the Great*. He engineered her movie debut in *Gentlemen of the Press* (29, Millard Webb) and Paramount put her under contract. Several small parts, largely as dark seductresses, led to *Street of Chance* (30, John Cromwell), opposite William Powell. She was usually best in sympathetic, melting, and sacrificial parts—thus *The Virtuous Sin* (30, George Cukor and Louis Gasnier); *Scandal Sheet* (31, Cromwell); *The Vice Squad* (31, Cromwell); *Guilty Hands* (31, W. S. Van Dyke); and *Girls About Town* (31, Cukor).

She moved to Warners and they put her in *Man Wanted* (32) and *Jewel Robbery* (32), both directed by William Dieterle, before several great successes: the first again with William Powell, *One Way Passage* (32, Tay Garnett), in which she played a lover fatally ill; Ernst Lubitsch's *Trouble in Paradise* (32), a witty and elegant return to Paramount; and *Cynara* (32, King Vidor). She continued with *The Keyhole* (33, Michael Curtiz); *Storm at Daybreak* (33, Richard Boleslavsky); *Mary Stevens M.D.* (33, Lloyd Bacon); *I Loved a Woman* (33, Alfred E. Green); *House on 56th Street* (33, Robert Florey); *Mandalay* (34, Curtiz); *Wonder Bar* (34, Bacon); *Dr. Monica* (34, William Keighley); as Lenin's perfectly groomed secretary in *British Agent* (34, Curtiz); *Living on Velvet* (35, Frank Borzage); *Stranded* (35, Borzage); and *I Found Stella Parrish* (35, Mervyn Le Roy).

But her stock was declining and a Florence Nightingale biopic, *The White Angel* (36, Dieterle), proved disastrous. Warners persevered for a few years: *Give Me Your Heart* (36, Archie Mayo); *Stolen Holiday* (37, Curtiz); *Confession* (37, Joe May); and *Another Dawn* (37, Dieterle). Then in 1938 the studio demoted her to B pictures. She worked on for several years, but never survived the humiliation: *My Bill* (38, John Farrow); *Comet Over Broadway* (38, Busby Berkeley); *King of the Underworld* (39, Lewis Seiler); cruelly put down in *In Name Only* (39, Cromwell), where a child takes her for Cary Grant's mother.

She left Warners and free-lanced, taking mother roles, for instance in *It's a Date* (40, William A. Seiter). There was a brief revival in the war years with the Jack Benny *Charley's Aunt* (41, Mayo), *The Feminine Touch* (41, Van Dyke), and *Playgirl* (41, Frank Woodruff), while her war work was celebrated in *Four Jills in a Jeep* (44, Seiter). But she ended in Monogram cheapies, the last of which were *Divorce* (45, William Nigh) and *Wife Wanted* (46, Phil Karlson).

Georges Franju (1912–87), b. Fougères, France

1934: *Le Métro* (codirected with Henri Langlois) (d). 1949: *Le Sang des Bêtes* (d). 1950: *En Passant par la Lorraine* (d). 1952: *Hôtel des Invalides* (d); *Le Grand Méliès* (d). 1953: *Monsieur et Madame Curie* (d). 1954: *Les Poussières* (d); *Navigation Marchande* (d). 1955: *A Propos d'une Rivière* (d). 1956: *Mon Chien* (d); *Le Théâtre Nationale Populaire* (d); *Sur le Pont d'Avignon* (d). 1957: *Nôtre-Dame, Cathédrale de Paris* (d). 1958: *La Première Nuit* (d); *La Tête Contre les Murs*. 1959: *Les Yeux Sans Visage/Eyes Without a Face*. 1961: *Pleins Feux sur l'Assassin*. 1962: *Thérèse Desqueyroux*. 1963: *Judex*. 1965: *Thomas l'Imposteur*. 1966: *Les Rideaux Blancs; Marcel Allain*. 1970: *La Faute de l'Abbé Mouret*. 1973: *Nuits Rouges/Shadowman*. 1978: *Le Dernier Mélodrame/The Last Melodrama*.

Franju's films are fragile, fierce elegies against inhumanity. He has achieved single images that are among the most disturbing in the cinema: the slaughterhouse in *Le Sang des Bêtes;* the escape across burning stubble fields in *La Tête Contre les*

Murs; the deathly oppressiveness of the woods in *Thérèse Desqueyroux;* quivering veterans in *Hôtel des Invalides;* Edith Scob's precarious purity in *Eyes Without a Face.* Franju insists on the throb of surrealism within the matter-of-fact, and at his best the two modes interchange without strain. But there is often a feeling of contrivance as he attempts to coax lyricism out of horror, as in *Les Yeux Sans Visage,* or to assert universal madness, as in *La Tête Contre les Murs* and *Thomas l'Imposteur.*

More than with most directors, it is necessary to see his features—taken up only in middle age—as a continuation of work in documentary. In fact, there is something of a contrast between the intense, muddled anarchy of the features, and twenty years spent in documentary and the general service of the cinema. As early as 1934, Franju made a short, *Le Métro,* with Henri Langlois. Three years later, the two men founded the Cinémathèque Française. All through the war, Franju served as secretary of the International Federation of Film Archives. The personality of his films is not really that of an archivist or administrator, but the interest in early cinema is clear all through Franju's own work: one of his most tender documentaries is *Le Grand Méliès,* a tribute to a forgotten innovator, who shared Franju's own sense of fantasy; while *Judex* is a re-creation of the vision of Louis Feuillade, a very entertaining movie, but more offhand and discursive than the Franju of *La Tête*—and *Les Yeux*—ever seemed capable of. More basically, Franju concentrates on the poetic resonance of pure visual narrative; he is often indifferent to plot or dialogue, but takes great pains over superb grey-and-white photography, invariably directed by Marcel Fradetal or Eugen Schufftan. Indeed, the presence of Schufftan, and the morbid view of a deranged, cruel world organized by misguided doctors, indicates Franju's debt to classical German cinema.

His great documentaries show the alarming company that civilized society keeps with nightmare; this effect is achieved by photography that is beautiful but stark. Above all, in *Hôtel des Invalides,* the dry cataloguing of a national institution is penetrated by an anguish that is rare in strident antiwar films.

The features are all flawed to some extent by mistaken conception or unrealization, so that passages from Franju's work seem more impressive than any single film. It is to the credit of Buñuel—a figure to whom Franju seems akin—that the Spaniard has so often found a form that expresses his calm fury. Franju, by contrast, is possessed by a furious but fluctuating grace. There are passages in *La Tête Contre les Murs*—the asylum gardens, the roulette scene, even the opening wasteland—that are as factual and as fantastic as *Sang des Bêtes* and *Hôtel des Invalides.* But Franju's equa-

tion of helpless beasts and human creatures is facile and disproportionate because of his inability to sustain the vision against melodrama, a specious faith in innocent madness and whimsy. *Les Yeux sans Visage* is fearsome when content to be a horror picture, but shallow when it emerges from the genre. *Thomas l'Imposteur* is too preoccupied by the blithe chaos of the First World War for the stray moments of agony to be more than decoration. *Judex* is probably his most balanced film in that it successfully inhabits the old serial form and invests it with melancholy.

John Frankenheimer (1930–2002)

b. Malba, New York

1959: *The Young Stranger.* 1961: *The Young Savages.* 1962: *All Fall Down; Birdman of Alcatraz; The Manchurian Candidate.* 1964: *Seven Days in May.* 1965: *The Train.* 1966: *Seconds; Grand Prix.* 1968: *The Fixer.* 1969: *The Extraordinary Seaman; The Gypsy Moths.* 1970: *I Walk the Line; The Horsemen.* 1973: *The Iceman Cometh* (for TV). 1974: *99 and 44/100% Dead; Impossible Object.* 1975: *French Connection II.* 1977: *Black Sunday.* 1979: *Prophecy.* 1982: *The Challenge.* 1985: *The Holcroft Convenant.* 1986: *52 Pick-Up.* 1989: *Dead-Bang.* 1990: *The Fourth War.* 1991: *Year of the Gun.* 1994:*Against the Wall* (TV). *The Burning Season* (TV). 1996: *Andersonville* (TV); *The Island of Dr. Moreau.* 1997: *George Wallace* (TV). 1998: *Ronin.* 2000: *Reindeer Games.* 2001: *Ambush* (s). 2002: *Path to War* (TV).

In his first few years as a director there was a modish aura about Frankenheimer. He came from television and seemed sensitive to the problems of the young. *The Young Stranger* was a good debut, with a troubled puppy performance from James MacArthur and excellent small-town atmosphere. But Frankenheimer gradually abandoned intimacy for glossy production values, a speculative eye on subject matter, and a flashy, insecure style. *All Fall Down* was his most accomplished film, with good performances from Warren Beatty, Eva Marie Saint, and Angela Lansbury, and some deliberate Wellesian deep-focus interiors. *The Manchurian Candidate*'s stunning set pieces (mostly coming from Richard Condon) do not disguise its real neglect of Americana. And the performances now seem good despite Frankenheimer's busy interest in visual hysteria. At about this time, Frankenheimer became a little overshadowed by Burt Lancaster. That actor had been good in *The Young Savages* and *Birdman of Alcatraz,* even if the latter is too solemn a vehicle for his icy domination. But *Seven Days in May* only furthered Frankenheimer's craze for TV screens within his frame, while *The Train* was a silliness from which Arthur Penn was lucky to escape. The division in Frankenheimer's identity was clearly shown in 1966 with the arty pretentiousness of *Seconds* and the schoolboy thrills of *Grand Prix*. After that, he became hopelessly lost in adaptations of novels—*The Fixer* and *The Horsemen*—and twice attempted to recapture his sense of provincial America: *The Gypsy Moths* and *I Walk the Line*.

Frankenheimer's films of the eighties were not an improvement, even if they were always quick and accomplished. He no longer had good material, and so it was hard to recollect his startling debut in the early sixties. However, when *The Manchurian Candidate* was rereleased, it had hardly dated. Also, I would say on re-viewing *Seven Days in May* and *I Walk the Line* that these two films are a lot better than originally indicated—the first is a clockwork plot such as brings out Frankenheimer's precision, yet it has time for several fine studies in loyalty and betrayal. As for *I Walk the Line*, it is a gradual rural tragedy, founded in hopeless infatuation, and inspired by one of Tuesday Weld's best performances.

By 1994, Frankenheimer was back in TV with a story about the Attica riots. He was also frank about how far alcoholism had set him back in the late seventies and eighties.

Frankenheimer was emphatically back in the nineties, on the big and the small screens. But it's instructive that *The Island of Dr. Moreau*, *Ronin* and *Reindeer Games* were worth so much less than his brilliant *George Wallace*, well written by Paul Monash, and starring Gary Sinise, Mare Winningham and Angelina Jolie. Anyone with Frankenheimer's experience and talent will be better received nowadays by TV than by big-picture making.

Carl Franklin, b. Richmond, California, 1949
1986: *Punk*. 1989: *Nowhere to Run*; *Eye of the Eagle II: Inside the Enemy*. 1990: *Full Fathom Five*. 1991: *One False Move*. 1993: *Laurel Avenue* (TV). 1995: *Devil in a Blue Dress*. 1998: *One True Thing*. 2002: *High Crimes*. 2003: *Out of Time*.

One False Move is, quite simply, one of the best American movies of the nineties, in which the trappings of violent crime fall way to reveal a subtle story about family ties, rural feeling, and the varieties of love. There are also not many films that handle black and white characters without feeling intimidated by all the prospects. Put that film beside the period flavor and narrative intricacy of *Devil in a Blue Dress* and the intense family atmosphere of *One True Thing*, and you may begin to fathom exactly how hard it is for a black director to be employed as one of the best directors in America. One might slip out of the dilemma by saying that Franklin is "promising," but he is in his early fifties already. It's not just that he's a lot better than Spike Lee, it's more that he makes a Sydney Pollack look pale.

An actor and a writer as well as a director, Franklin was educated at the University of California, Berkeley, and the American Film Institute, as well as the school of Roger Corman. He has cheerfully worked in exploitation junk, and don't let anyone tell you that he's anything less than ready and good enough for actresses as diverse as Cynda Williams, Renée Zellweger, and Meryl Streep.

Even so, *High Crimes* is an awful setback, and a quite unnecessary film.

Sidney A. Franklin (1893–1972),
b. San Francisco
1918: *Six Shooter Andy*; *Confession*; *Bride of Fear*; *The Safety Curtain*; *The Forbidden City*; *Her Only Way*; *Heart of Wetona*. 1919: *Probation Wife*; *Heart o' the Hills*; *The Hoodlum*. 1920: *Two Weeks*. 1921: *Not Guilty*; *Unseen Forces*; *Courage*. 1922: *Smilin' Through*; *The Primitive Lover*; *East Is West*. 1923: *Brass*; *Dulcy*; *Tiger Rose*. 1924: *Her Night of Romance*. 1925: *Learning to Love*; *Her Sister from Paris*. 1926: *The Duchess of Buffalo*; *Beverly of Graustark*. 1927: *Quality Street*. 1928: *The Actress*. 1929: *Wild Orchids*; *The Last of Mrs. Cheyney*; *Devil-May-Care*. 1930: *The Lady of Scandal*; *A Lady's Morals*. 1931: *The Guardsman*; *Private Lives*. 1932: *Smilin' Through*. 1933: *Reunion in Vienna*. 1934: *The Barretts of Wimpole Street*. 1935: *The Dark Angel*. 1937: *The Good Earth* (codirected with Sam Wood, George Hill, Fred Niblo, and Andrew Marton). 1957: *The Barretts of Wimpole Street*.

From 1914, Franklin and his brother, Chester, codirected comedy shorts, films for children, and several Norma Talmadge pictures. In his twenty-year career as a solo director, Franklin worked with most of the leading actresses of the period in placid romances: Mary Pickford in *Heart o' the Hills* and *The Hoodlum*; Norma Talmadge in *Smilin' Through*; Constance Talmadge in *East Is West*, *The Primitive Lover*, *Dulcy*, *Her Night of Romance*, *Learning to Love*, *Her Sister from Paris*, *The Duchess of Buffalo*, *Beverly of Graustark*, and *Quality Street*. His polite and meretricious handling of the ladies brought him to Irving Thalberg's attention and in 1928 he joined MGM to direct Norma Shearer in *The Actress* (based on Pinero's *Trelawney of the Wells*). He worked with her again on *The Last of Mrs. Cheyney*, and directed Garbo in *Wild Orchids* and Ruth Chatterton in *The Lady of Scandal*. As so often with Thalberg's choices, Franklin was a colorless director. This comment from Clarence Brown may suggest the source of Franklin's reputation: "Too good; he overemphasized goodness. He was beyond perfection in his work." Such a paragon spent several years as a producer nursing *The Yearling* (46)—directed by Brown and fastidiously overbred.

Nevertheless, Franklin did duty on several major MGM films, directing Shearer in *Private Lives* and the inane *Barretts of Wimpole Street,* and struggling to make Paul Muni, Luise Rainer, and a million coffee-ground locusts interesting in *The Good Earth.* That was beyond his customary territory, and the necessary assistance of four others, as well as the death of his patron, Thalberg, may have persuaded him to abandon direction. He came back only in 1957—by some nostalgic quirk—to try again with Elizabeth Barrett Browning. Whereas he had made it earlier with a mogul's lady, so the remake had Jennifer Jones on the sofa and Selznick in attendance.

As if to show his respect for Thalberg, Franklin became a producer of respectable dullness: respectful of conventional stars, tidy stories, and production values. His films glow with comforting assurances and cheerfully evade harshness. The war in *Mrs. Miniver,* for instance, is merely a threat to a bland American household; Greer Garson was the epitome of Franklin's polite lady. He produced *On Borrowed Time* (39, Harold S. Bucquet); *Waterloo Bridge* (40, Mervyn Le Roy); *Mrs. Miniver* (42, William Wyler); *Random Harvest* (42, Le Roy); *Madame Curie* (43, Le Roy); *The White Cliffs of Dover* (44, Brown); *Homecoming* (48, Le Roy); *Command Decision* (49, Wood); *The Miniver Story* (50, H. C. Potter); *The Story of Three Loves* (53, Gottfried Reinhardt and Vincente Minnelli); and *Young Bess* (53, George Sidney).

In addition, he gets a solo credit on *Bambi* (42, David Hand), thanking him for his "inspired collaboration."

Brendan Fraser,
b. Indianapolis, Indiana, 1968

In so many happy ways, Brendan Fraser is a throwback—to the days of such expert idiot comedy as Ralph Bellamy practiced, or even to the silent era. He has a face that registers hurt hopes and innocent optimism as easily as a child's, and without a tremor of Method neurosis. In a cleverly arranged series of films, he has played a large, handsome, manly goof thrust out of his own time or against the grain of modern cynicism, and handling the tension with sweet good humor. He is a comedian of such confident understatement that, on *Gods and Monsters* (98, Bill Condon), Ian McKellen said that he was as occupied as he could be learning from Fraser's rapport with the camera. It's easy to see Fraser in gorgeous romance—less easy to see him in darkness, much less gloom. But he begins to show signs of tragic ambition.

His parents are Canadian, and the boy traveled widely in early life. He studied theatre at Cornish College in Seattle and made his debut in *Dogfight* (91, Nancy Savoca). In *Encino Man* (92, Les Mayfield), he was the Cro-Magnon who has to cope with modern suburban L.A. He was very good as the Jewish boy at the prep school in *School Ties* (92, Robert Mandel); *Younger and Younger* (93, Percy Adlon); *Twenty Bucks* (93, Keva Rosenfeld); *Airheads* (93, Michael Lehmann); a Harvard man in *With Honors* (94, Alek Keshishian); *The Scout* (94, Michael Ritchie); *Mrs. Winterbourne* (96, Richard Benjamin); *George of the Jungle* (97, Sam Weisman); gay in *Twilight of the Golds* (97, Ross Marks); as a young man in L.A. kept in a fallout shelter for thirty-five years in *Blast from the Past* (99, Hugh Wilson)—his funniest work yet.

His biggest hit came in *The Mummy* (99, Stephen Sommers), yet in truth he was rather wasted having to make worried faces at special effects. For Fraser is good enough to see the peril in real people. *Dudley Do-Right* (99, Wilson) cashed in on his stupid decency and cast him as the Mountie. He was the chump who deals with the devil (Elizabeth Hurley) in the remake of *Bedazzled* (00, Harold Ramis); *Monkeybone* (01, Henry Selick) was another good idea not worked out. *The Mummy Returns* (01, Sommers) didn't even bother to disguise its being too much of a good thing.

It's now that the beast awakes. In London, he played Brick on stage in a revival of *Cat on a Hot Tin Roof,* and in movies he attempted the Audie Murphy role (no joke) in *The Quiet American* (02, Phillip Noyce)—"God save us," said the Michael Caine character, referring to him, "from the innocent and the good." Well, generally, yes—but in Fraser's case, I think not.

Stephen Frears,
b. Leicester, England, 1941

1967: *The Burning* (s). 1971: *Gumshoe.* 1972: *A Day Out* (TV). 1973: *England Their England* (TV); *Match of the Day* (TV). 1974: *The Sisters* (TV). 1975: *Sunset Across the Bay* (TV); *Three Men in a Boat* (TV); *Daft as a Brush* (TV). 1976: *Play Things* (TV); *Early Struggles* (TV). 1977: *Eighteen Months to Balcombe Street* (TV); *Last Summer* (TV); *Able's Will* (TV); *Black Christmas* (TV); *A Visit from Miss Protheroe* (TV). 1978: *Cold Harbour* (TV); *Me! I'm Afraid of Virginia Woolf* (TV); *Doris and Doreen* (TV); *Afternoon Off* (TV); *One Fine Day* (TV). 1979: *Bloody Kids* (TV); *Long Distance Information* (TV). 1981: *Going Gently* (TV). 1982: *Walter* (TV). 1983: *Walter and June* (TV); *Saigon—Year of the Cat* (TV). 1984: *The Hit.* 1985: *My Beautiful Laundrette.* 1986: *Song of Experience.* 1987: *Prick Up Your Ears; Sammy and Rosie Get Laid.* 1988: *Dangerous Liaisons.* 1990: *The Grifters.* 1992: *Hero.* 1993: *The Snapper.* 1994: *A Personal History of British Cinema by Stephen Frears* (TV). 1996: *Mary Reilly; The Van.* 1998: *The Hi-Lo Country.* 2000: *High Fidelity; Fail Safe* (TV). 2001: *Liam.* 2002: *Dirty Pretty Things.*

The above list is as full as I can discover, but it includes only nine films released as theatrical movies—or ten if one includes *Bloody Kids,* which did play theatrically a few years after its debut on television. The rest is TV—and it is a great deal.

Late in the 1970s, writing in the admirable reference magazine *Film Dope,* Bob Baker said, "To put it plainly, 'Cold Harbour' was the best (i.e., the clearest, most moving, most resonant) film I saw in 1978. The same will very probably apply to 'One Fine Day' in 1979. I suppose one should wish for Frears to return to the big screen. Unfortunately there's no guarantee—indeed, there's the contrary—that he would find anything like the opportunities and relative freedom of expression that he has with television."

Well, the opportunities have come. Almost casually, in 1985, *My Beautiful Laundrette* (made for TV) was promoted to the status of a festival movie with theatrical openings. Its ironic view of mixed races and mixed sex in a London under Mrs. Thatcher made for a hit. Then, after the Joe Orton biopic and the modern agitprop of *Sammy and Rosie,* Frears became an "A" list director in Hollywood. However, the results have been odd: to these eyes, the smart, brisk, sexy *Dangerous Liaisons* is a lot less interesting than Forman's *Valmont.* Despite its fine acting, *The Grifters* seemed to derive from memories of film noir more than it grasped a real America or the Jim Thompson novel. *Hero* was, quite simply, a failure.

Thus, there is still a case to be made for the quality and character of Frears's TV work done in England. Moreover, after Baker's observation, Frears was still to do *Bloody Kids,* the two *Walter* films, and *Saigon—Year of the Cat.* The TV work points to the director's virtues, and needs: he surely understands the English class system, the varieties of place in Britain, and the various subterfuges that block candor (this is true even for *Saigon,* which has important English characters). In Britain, Frears established valuable creative ties with a few writers—notably Peter Prince, Alan Bennett, David Hare, and Hanif Kureishi. Also, the modesty of those ventures—in terms of budget and schedule—is close to Frears's own personality: he is one of the least self-important of directors.

By now, it is clear that Frears does need to understand the world of his stories, and that he is frankly dependent on writers. Of course, his problem is that the British cinema does not often enough mount ventures worthy of him. But he does not want to commit to America, and he has said that he is not really happy in America when working. In so many ways he is a throwback to those classic studio directors who pretend to be assigned. In which case, British TV was his studio. As years pass, I suspect that things like *A Day Out, Sunset Across the Bay, One Fine Day,* and *Walter* will look like models of "small" cinema—rich, honest, and touching—whereas *The Grifters* and *Dangerous Liaisons* will be seen as rather empty entertainment.

Frears's talents—his love of people, his sense of humor and pain sitting side by side, his skill with actors, and his deftness as a storyteller—are deserving of some large subject. I have a hunch it will be European rather than American. And it might be that his best chance is to provoke Alan Bennett into some final, convulsive tale. They both need that sort of danger. Until then, let him do more things like *The Snapper*—from a Roddy Doyle novel—small, quick, cheap, funny, raucous, and overflowing with life, a film that might have been made in the space (and on the budget) of one Dustin Hoffman tantrum.

Frears is still open to just about anything: a droll, rather lazy essay on British cinema; a return to live TV drama with *Fail Safe;* a couple more Irish films—*The Van* and *Liam.* He even had a modest American hit, with *High Fidelity,* based on a Nick Hornby book. But please don't forget *Mary Reilly,* a famous failure but a remarkably frightening film, very well acted by Julia Roberts and John Malkovich. It all goes to prove his characteristic deflection of high praise (which he deserves) that, after all, he's likely to do anything.

Arthur Freed (Arthur Grossman)
(1894–1973), b. Charleston, South Carolina

There is not a producer who can be so identified with a single genre and studio as Arthur Freed. Yet it remains very difficult to say how far his influence over the MGM musical was creative, conceptual, coincidental, or that of a Renoir-like organizer—Danglars in *French Can Can*—blending and cajoling a company of brilliant talents.

A few essential pointers can be mentioned: Freed is a lyricist, not in the class of Cole Porter or Johnny Mercer, perhaps, but good enough to make us remember that when Gene Kelly does the title number in *Singin' in the Rain* (52, Gene Kelly and Stanley Donen) he is singing Freed's words, which, in rhythm and mood, are integral to the sequence; second, the MGM musical shifts gear with his arrival at the studio, principally in the way that he drafted in a number of Broadway-trained artists; and, perhaps most important, the Freed musical addresses itself more directly and wittily to the elements of fantasy, dream, and Chinese-box convolution in the backstage musical: *The Wizard of Oz, Meet Me in St. Louis, The Pirate, An American in Paris,* and *Singin' in the Rain* are full of piquant moments when the artifice of the musical form is penetrated to reveal a quality of human truth scarcely touched on in the 1930s musical.

The Wizard of Oz and *Meet Me in St. Louis* deserve an honorable place in the roll of movies about child psychology; *St. Louis* is a chamber musical, with an enchanting nostalgia; *The Pirate* is an emotionally dry and visually garish portrait of forced feelings and ham acting; *An American in Paris* is one of the cinema's most complete ventures into dream; while *Singin' in the Rain* is not just a witty history of the arrival of sound but a parody of the musical. Remember that moment when Kelly's buildup dissolves into the "Broadway Ballet" sequence—a good ten-minute exercise—only for the producer, Millard Mitchell, to say "I can't quite visualize it."

In other words, the tone in Freed musicals is self-aware and amused, and the form is not a celebration of homeliness, energy, or innuendo—the 1930s themes—but of sophistication. *Silk Stockings,* that late Freed masterpiece, honestly prefers the culture of America and Paris to that of Russia, and supports the seduction of commissar Charisse by Astaire's dancing. The "All of You" sequence in that film, where Astaire coaxes Charisse into dance—as an end in itself—might be the emblem of Freed's achievement: a self-sufficient beauty based on excellence and splendid frivolousness.

In the 1920s, Freed was a performer in vaudeville. But once sound arrived, he went into films as a lyricist for MGM, often with Nacio Herb Brown. Many of their songs—"You Were Meant for Me," "Hold Your Man," and "You Are My Lucky Star"—were used several times in different Metro films: *The Broadway Melody* (29, Harry Beaumont); *Hollywood Revue* (29, Charles Reisner); *Blondie of the Follies* (32, Edmund Goulding); *Dancing Lady* (33, Robert Z. Leonard); *Broadway Melody of 1936* (35, Roy del Ruth); *Broadway Melody of 1938* (37, del Ruth); and *Thoroughbreds Don't Cry* (37, Alfred E. Green).

In 1939, MGM made him a producer and he became effectively for the next twenty years in charge of their musicals. As well as the most obvious talent he gathered at the studio—Busby Berkeley, Minnelli, Donen, Charles Walters—he encouraged such people as choreographer Michael Kidd, writers Adolph Comden and Betty Green, orchestrator André Previn, and art directors like Randall Duell, Cedric Gibbons, and Preston Ames. From the very beginning, with *The Wizard of Oz* project and his determination that Judy Garland should play in it, Freed revealed himself as a sure judge of talent. He lasted as long as the musical, its godfather, even if he failed to prolong its life beyond the 1950s: *Babes in Arms* (39, Busby Berkeley, taken away from Warners as one of Freed's first actions); *The Wizard of Oz* (39, Victor Fleming; coproduced with Mervyn Le Roy); *Strike Up the Band* (40, Berkeley); *Little Nellie Kelley* (40, Norman Taurog); *Babes on Broadway* (41, Berkeley); *Lady Be Good* (41, Norman Z. McLeod); *Cabin in the Sky* (42, Vincente Minnelli); *For Me and My Gal* (42, Berke-

ley); *Du Barry Was a Lady* (43, del Ruth); *Girl Crazy* (43, Taurog); *Best Foot Forward* (43, Edward Buzzell); *Meet Me in St. Louis* (44, Minnelli); *Yolanda and the Thief* (45, Minnelli); *The Harvey Girls* (45, George Sidney); *Ziegfeld Follies* (46, Minnelli); *Till the Clouds Roll By* (46, Richard Whorf); *Summer Holiday* (47, Rouben Mamoulian); *The Pirate* (47, Minnelli); *Easter Parade* (48, Charles Walters); *Words and Music* (48, Taurog); *Take Me Out to the Ball Game* (49, Berkeley); *On the Town* (49, Donen and Kelly); *The Barkleys of Broadway* (49, Walters); *Annie Get Your Gun* (50, Sidney), and uniquely vulgar in Freed's output; *An American in Paris* (51, Minnelli); *Show Boat* (51, Sidney); *Royal Wedding* (51, Donen); *The Belle of New York* (52, Walters); *Lovely to Look At* (52, Le Roy); *Singin' in the Rain* (52, Donen and Kelly); *The Band Wagon* (53, Minnelli); *It's Always Fair Weather* (55, Donen); *Silk Stockings* (57, Mamoulian); *Gigi* (58, Minnelli); and *Bells Are Ringing* (60, Minnelli).

It seems like a fine record, but as the musical withered, Freed tried to branch out into drama, with dismal results: *The Subterraneans* (60, Ranald MacDougall) and *Light in the Piazza* (62, Guy Green).

Morgan Freeman,
b. Memphis, Tennessee, 1937

When Morgan Freeman was cast and did such fine work in *Unforgiven* (92, Clint Eastwood), the choice seemed to be a way of saying, here is one of our great supporting actors, a man of honor and unflinching competence, an actor to set beside the most reliable, stalwart friends in the great Westerns, an actor worthy of the company of Ward Bond, Walter Brennan, Arthur Kennedy. At the same time, Eastwood's resolute decision to ignore Freeman's blackness set up one more deep implausibility in *Unforgiven*. Would blackness have gone unremarked in that time and place? Somehow Woody Strode in the Ford films seemed a more honest casting decision.

Still, in several films Freeman has absolutely transcended color: as the pimp in *Street Smart* (87, Jerry Schatzberg), where he was nominated for a supporting actor Oscar; *Clean and Sober* (88, Glenn Gordon Caron); and *Johnny Handsome* (90, Walter Hill).

In other words, Freeman could play Iago as easily as Othello. But can he expect that offer? And, at sixty plus, how much of his effort must go, quite simply, into keeping in work?

He had acted a good deal in television and the theatre before he became a familiar movie presence: *Who Says I Can't Ride a Rainbow?* (71, Edward Mann); *Brubaker* (80, Stuart Rosenberg); *Eyewitness* (81, Peter Yates); *Harry & Son* (84, Paul Newman); *Teachers* (84, Arthur Hiller); *Marie* (85, Roger Donaldson); *That Was Then,*

This Is Now (85, Christopher Cain); as the chauffeur in *Driving Miss Daisy* (89, Bruce Beresford), nominated for best actor; excellent and nineteenth-century in *Glory* (89, Edward Zwick); *Lean on Me* (89, John G. Avildsen); an all-round concession as the judge in *Bonfire of the Vanities* (90, Brian De Palma); *Robin Hood: Prince of Thieves* (91, Kevin Reynolds); and *The Power of One* (92, Avildsen).

In 1993, Freeman directed *Bopha!*, set in South Africa in 1980, with Danny Glover and Alfre Woodard as parents whose son is an anti-apartheid activist—and Glover is a cop.

Freeman then took on a series of films that established him not just as a great American actor, but as a rare authority figure above reproach or irony: *The Shawshank Redemption* (94, Frank Darabont); *Outbreak* (95, Wolfgang Petersen); as William Somerset, the world-weary detective in *Se7en* (95, David Fincher); *Moll Flanders* (96, Pen Densham); *Chain Reaction* (96, Andrew Davis); *Kiss the Girls* (97, Gary Fleder); *Amistad* (97, Steven Spielberg); *Hard Rain* (98, Mikael Salomon); *Deep Impact* (98, Mimi Leder). He produced and played a small role in *Mutiny* (99, Kevin Hooks), a TV dramatization of the Port Chicago mutiny. He also helped produce *Under Suspicion* (00, Stephen Hopkins); *Along Came a Spider* (01, Lee Tamahori) and *The Sum of All Fears* (02, Phil Alden Robinson). Other films are *Nurse Betty* (00, Neil LaBute) and *High Crimes* (02, Carl Franklin).

He produced and acted in *Levity* (01, Ed Solomon); acted in *Dreamcatcher* (02, Lawrence Kasdan); and as God (about time) in *Bruce Almighty* (03, Tom Shadyac).

Hugo Fregonese (1908–87),
b. Buenos Aires, Argentina
1943: *Pampa Barbara*. 1946: *Donde Mueren las Palabras*. 1947: *Apenas un Delincuente*. 1950: *Saddle Tramp; One Way Street*. 1951: *Apache Drums; Mark of the Renegade*. 1952: *My Six Convicts; Untamed Frontier*. 1953: *Blowing Wild; Decameron Nights; Man in the Attic*. 1954: *The Raid; Black Tuesday*. 1956: *I Girovaghi*. 1957: *Seven Thunders*. 1958: *Live in Fear; Harry Black*. 1961: *Marco Polo*. 1964: *Apache's Last Battle/Old Shatterhand*. 1966: *Savage Pampas*. 1975: *Mas Alla del Sol*.

In the days when European art houses were welcoming the rather sweaty films of Leopoldo Torre Nilsson, Hugo Fregonese was hard put to find work. He may not be worthy of Borges, but he was an exponent of American violence: economical, abrupt, a visual narrator able to inflict ordeal on his characters within moments of a film's start. *Black Tuesday* and *The Raid*—both from Sidney Boehm scripts—are intricately organized, the first

a true gangster movie, the second about a Confederate attack on a Vermont town. *Harry Black* and *Blowing Wild* are triangle stories set in exotic parts—the first in India, the second in South America—pressurized in one case by a rogue tiger and in the other by an unruly oil well. *Blowing Wild* has Fregonese's laconic bleakness at its best: Gary Cooper is visited one night by an old flame, Barbara Stanwyck; in a darkened room, he puts on a desk lamp, directs it first at her face, and then at her legs.

It is a dislocated career, begun in Argentina, the bulk in Hollywood, disappointed by the death of Val Lewton (who produced *Apache Drums*) and by the failure of Stanley Kramer at Columbia, for whom he made *My Six Convicts*, and then driven out into Europe. There are dull films—*Untamed Frontier* is one—but at his best, Fregonese has that smoldering, grudging beauty that is characteristic of Boetticher and Ulmer—men who clung to Hollywood's underbelly. Given an opening—such as Jack Palance as Jack the Ripper in *Man in the Attic*—Fregonese shows all his instinct for sharpness. On second thought, who better to handle those Borges stories about gauchos, machismo, and the communion of knife fights?

Karl Freund (1890–1969),
b. Königinhof, Czechoslovakia
He entered the German industry in 1906 as a newsreel cameraman and became one of the greatest lighting cameramen, a master of shadow and movement, and the favorite photographer of F. W. Murnau, for whom he shot *Setanas* (19), *Der Bucklige und die Tanzerin* (20), *Der Januskopf* (20), *Marizza, genannt die Schmugglermadonna* (21), *Der Brennende Acker* (22), *The Last Laugh* (24), and *Tartuff* (25). In addition, Freund worked on *Venetianische Nacht* (14, Max Reinhardt); *Der Golem* (20, Paul Wegener/Carl Boese); *Die Spinnen, part 2* (20, Fritz Lang); *Der Verlorene Schatten* (21, Rochus Gliese/Wegener); *Lukrezia Borgia* (22, Richard Oswald); *Mikael* (24, Carl Dreyer); *Variété* (25, E. A. Dupont); *Metropolis* (27, Lang); and *Donna Juana* (27, Paul Czinner). Freund also helped to write the script of Ruttmann's *Berlin, die Symphonie der Grosstadt* (27).

In 1930 he went to America, thus forming one of the most interesting links between German expressionism and the American horror film. For he photographed two of the best early sound horror films at Universal: *Dracula* (31, Tod Browning) and *Murders in the Rue Morgue* (32, Robert Florey) as well as the women's picture harrowed soft focus of *Back Street* (32, John M. Stahl). The studio even promoted him to director and he made *The Mummy* (32), *Moonlight and Pretzels* (33), *Madame Spy* (33), *The Countess of Monte Cristo* (34), *Uncertain Lady* (34), *Gift of Gab* (34),

I Give My Love (34), and *Mad Love* (35). The first is a subtle picture of the occult, while the last is one of the enigmas of film history: starring Peter Lorre, and with Gregg Toland as one of its photographers, it clearly influenced Welles in some details of Kane.

Freund then went back to photography, and his output included *Camille* (36, George Cukor); *The Good Earth* (37, Sidney Franklin et al.); *Manproof* (37, Richard Thorpe); *Parnell* (37, Stahl); *Conquest* (38, Clarence Brown); *Letter of Introduction* (38, Stahl); *Rose of Washington Square* (39, Gregory Ratoff); *Golden Boy* (39, Rouben Mamoulian); *Pride and Prejudice* (40, Robert Z. Leonard); *A Yank at Eton* (42, Norman Taurog); *Du Barry Was a Lady* (43, Roy del Ruth); *The Seventh Cross* (44, Fred Zinnemann); *Key Largo* (48, John Huston); and *South of St. Louis* (49, Ray Enright). Notice the range here: from the dark opulence of *Camille*, to MGM's Jane Austen lightness, to the fog-bound images of *Key Largo;* from the ingenious tricks of *The Good Earth*, to the heartfelt romance of the Stahl films. His last years were spent working in TV, especially for Lucille Ball.

William Friedkin, b. Chicago, 1939

1967: *Good Times.* 1968: *The Night They Raided Minsky's; The Birthday Party.* 1970: *The Boys in the Band.* 1971: *The French Connection.* 1973: *The Exorcist.* 1977: *Sorcerer/The Wages of Fear.* 1978: *The Brink's Job.* 1980: *Cruising.* 1983: *Deal of the Century.* 1985: *To Live and Die in L.A.* 1986: *Stalking Danger* (TV). 1987: *Rampage.* 1990: *The Guardian.* 1994: *Blue Chips; Jailbreakers* (TV). 1995: *Jade.* 1997: *12 Angry Men* (TV). 2000: *Rules of Engagement.* 2003: *The Hunted.*

Out of television and into movies, William Friedkin has impressed mainly with his energy for hustling up projects, several that would have been better left to rest, but two of which—*The French Connection* and *The Exorcist*—put him, temporarily at least, on top of the creaking, swaying pile.

Friedkin looks like a jumped-up TV director, glib enough to make a credo out of price-cutting and convinced that the zoom and the insistent violence of unexpected images need only a raw feeling for sensation to outflank traditional requirements of construction and meaning. *The French Connection* is an inept film that shoves its impact in our face and employs the most deliberately mechanical sort of editing. Time and again it becomes incoherent or impossible to follow—*The Godfather* is a paragon of exposition and dramatic pace beside it, while *Dirty Harry* presents a far more somber view of the predicament of the policeman. As with *Naked City* twenty years before, *French Connection* is made in the blind hope that authenticity will disguise insight. Its one

touch of originality—that the crook is well mannered and the cop boorish—seems unnoticed by Friedkin.

The success, commercially, of *The French Connection* followed two faithful translations of very different stage works, neither of which had any compelling reason for being made. The compulsion of *The Exorcist* is sadly short-lived and exploitative. The movie is an efficient Val Lewtonesque horror story, reveling in dirty language, swiveling heads, blood and bile, shock cuts, and Mercedes McCambridge's voice coming out of the wizened Linda Blair. The effects are frightening, but not as fearful as the simpleminded conception of evil. To see *The Exorcist* is to renew one's respect for those glimpses of grim malignance in Bresson's films.

There was a significant rest, during which he entered into a brief marriage with Jeanne Moreau, before the hugely expensive and obscure *Sorcerer.* Chastened by its failure, he went back to being the modest, conventional Friedkin and made a nice period comedy out of the story of Boston's biggest heist ever.

In the eighties, Friedkin looked increasingly stranded. He tried comedy in *Deal of the Century* and his old car-chase skills in *To Live and Die in L.A.*, but the results were conventional at best. *Rampage* is the interesting exception, a film made in 1987 but not properly released for several years and then much changed. It is a murder story, the first version of which was opposed to capital punishment. But by the time of the second version, Friedkin had shifted his ground and become a spokesman for the victims.

Friedkin's recent years have had one highlight—the revival of *The French Connection* and *The Exorcist.* But who can then fail to wonder what has happened to the guy that he should make *Jade* or *Rules of Engagement?* The TV *12 Angry Men* supplies the answer: this is a chronic sensationalist driven to sobriety to stay in work.

Samuel Fuller (1911–97),
b. Worcester, Massachusetts
1948: *I Shot Jesse James.* 1950: *The Baron of Arizona; The Steel Helmet.* 1951: *Fixed Bayonets.* 1952: *Park Row.* 1953: *Pickup on South Street.* 1954: *Hell and High Water.* 1955: *House of Bamboo.* 1957: *Run of the Arrow; China Gate; Forty Guns.* 1958: *Verboten!.* 1959: *The Crimson Kimono.* 1961: *Underworld USA; Merrill's Marauders.* 1963: *Shock Corridor.* 1964: *The Naked Kiss.* 1968: *Caine/Shark.* 1972: *Dead Pigeon on Beethoven Street.* 1980: *The Big Red One.* 1982: *White Dog.* 1983: *Thieves After Dark/Les Voleurs de la Nuit.* 1988: *Sans Espoir de Retour.*

Fuller is one of the most harsh artistic presences

in the cinema. Like that preoccupied, cigar-smoking greyhead in dark glasses at the party in *Pierrot le Fou,* he concedes only that film is a battleground of alienated human energies all pursuing their private obsessions to the point of exhaustion. His films are like scenarios made from communities of rats, the camera itself a king rat, scarred and hurt, but still swooping in and out of every scuffle, commanding the spectacle and jumping in for gross close-ups like a thumb on a bug. Fuller's meaning is expressed by this supremely active style: that every man must be his own protagonist, and that this free-for-all morality is exactly mirrored in the larger political arena. In turn, he had been involved in crime journalism and war and his great originality was in seeing the constant criminal element in life—whether in the American city, on the range, or in every theatre of war. The community is interchangeable with the criminal underworld. In *Pickup on South Street, House of Bamboo,* and *Underworld USA,* the police and the crooks are observed as identical instruments without even the saving gloss of cynicism. His central characters are invariably psychotics, chronically hostile to organization, thriving on double-cross, and resolving doubts through brutality. Their fate is usually absurd; the means contradictory. *Merrill's Marauders* survive uselessly. O'Meara in *Run of the Arrow* returns to his own people without any hope. In *House of Bamboo* it is Robert Ryan's single humane action that destroys him—and though we appreciate that fact, Fuller himself does not endorse it. The relentless grilling of his camera almost compels the gesture and then drives on victorious.

Fuller's career passed from the obscurity of B pictures to intense critical controversy. But he made no concessions to interpreters. Many of his films were made at desperate speed and with little money, and yet they boast some of the most complex and successful traveling camera shots ever put on film. Although his material is at one level gutter plots, Fuller is the complete author—"written, produced, and directed by . . ." His opponents call him barbarous and even fascist, and his supporters have quoted Hobbes to elucidate him. In truth he is barbarous and that is why he is unique. No other American director has described American experience with such unremitting and participatory relish for its competitive corruption. Nicholas Garnham's monograph on Fuller constantly relates the films to the works of Norman Mailer. In many ways the men are different, but Fuller is familiar with the creeping madness that Mailer warns against.

Is he a good director? becomes a meaningless question. His films are staggering visual achievements. But there is no assurance of the director's being aware of what he is doing. It is a good thing that he is not, for there is a vulgarity in Fuller that

would move swiftly from the impulsive to the ponderous if he once listened to his best critics. Fuller may be a tabloid director, as witness the sense of identity and commitment in *Park Row,* a newspaper story. That sort of outrageous vulgarity has always to resist respectability and seriousness; self-consciousness is the greatest enemy. If the director does not need to comprehend his own art, then it is not art—but raw cinema. In that case, the real meaning of Fuller's films is in the minds of the mass audience from whom he has never been distracted. But one thing is clear: from the Civil War to the Vietnam War, Fuller has dealt with every major phase of American experience and returned with the conclusion that the world is a madhouse where ferocity alone survives.

In 1977, he was honored by Wim Wenders by being cast as the ultimate cigar-chewing gangster in *The American Friend,* and by being given a magnificent death roll down a flight of steps. At the same time, he had the go-ahead to make a long-cherished project, *The Big Red One,* which proved to be an immaculate study of frailties and courage in the infantry, a film made as if the Second World War had ended ten minutes ago.

White Dog was banned for a while, and consequently defended and overpraised—in fact, it shows some decline in Fuller. His subsequent films had a very limited release. But Fuller kept active, his cigar erect, acting in a few films: *Scotch Myths* (82, Murray Grigor); *Red Dawn* (84, John Milius); *Slapstick of Another Kind* (84, Steven Paul); and *La Vie de Bohème* (92, Aki Kaurismaki). He also supplied the story for *Let's Get Harry* (86, Alan Smithee).

Jules Furthman (1888–1960), b. Chicago

Here is a character to dream over. Jules Furthman was often regarded as a sharp-tongued, nasty son-of-a-bitch—and this from friends, like Howard Hawks, who depended upon him. It was only a modest exaggeration from Pauline Kael when she opined that Furthman had his name on about half of the most entertaining films Hollywood ever produced. At the same time, he is clearly the secret sharer with both von Sternberg and Howard Hawks, and even the connection that allowed Hawks to pick up so much of Sternberg's sophistication. The claim is clear, I think, that going from Dietrich to Angie Dickinson, by way of Frances Farmer and Lauren Bacall, Furthman created the paper outline of the most challenging woman in American pictures.

Yet Furthman was a recluse. He lived in Culver City, did not socialize, looking after a retarded son and growing prize orchids. He did not give interviews, and he was sufficiently well off to endure scandalous unemployment at a time when his unsociability had deterred so many people. What a tragedy, when pious dullards in their self-importance have laid down miles and years of flat-ulent interview. I have the feeling that an hour with Furthman could have amounted to a lifetime of education.

He was the son of a judge, educated at North-western and then a journalist. But he was in movies, as a writer, by 1915, working those first few years as "Stephen Fox," because his real name might seem Germanic—there's a first hint of his endearing sarcasm.

The list is long, but there's a lot worth mention-ing: from 1915–18, he contributed just stories, but thereafter he was a screenwriter: *A Camouflage Kiss* (18, Harry Millarde); *A Japanese Nightingale* (18, George Fitzmaurice); *All the World to Noth-ing* (18, Henry King); *When a Man Rides Alone* (18, King). There were several other pictures for King in 1919 before a work one longs to see—or done ten years later by von Sternberg: Conrad's *Victory* (19, Maurice Tourneur).

The Valley of Tomorrow (20, Emmett J. Flynn); *Treasure Island* (20, Tourneur), with Lon Chaney as Silver; *The Great Redeemer* (20, Clarence Brown), which Furthman apparently wrote with John Gilbert; *Land of Jazz* (20), which he directed himself; *The Big Punch* (21, John Ford); *The Blushing Bride* (21, Furthman); *Colorado Pluck* (21, Furthman); *The Last Trail* (21, Flynn); *Ara-bian Love* (22, Jerome Storm); *Pawn Ticket 210* (22, Scott Dunlap); *Lovebound* (23, Henry Otto); *North of the Hudson Bay* (23, Ford), a Tom Mix film; *The Aquittal* (23, Brown); *Call of the Mate* (24, Alvin J. Neitz).

He was back with Henry King for *Sackcloth and Scarlet* (25) and *Any Woman* (25), both Alice Terry films; *Before Midnight* (25, John Adolfi); *The Wise Guy* (26, Frank Lloyd). He did *Hotel Imperial* (27, Mauritz Stiller); the crucial *Underworld* (27, von Sternberg); *Fashions for Women* (27, Dorothy Arzner); *Barbed Wire* (27, Rowland V. Lee); *The Way of All Flesh* (27, Victor Fleming); *The Drag-net* (28, von Sternberg); *The Docks of New York* (28, von Sternberg); *Abie's Irish Rose* (28, Flem-ing); *The Case of Lena Smith* (29, von Sternberg); *Thunderbolt* (29, von Sternberg); *New York Nights* (29, Lewis Milestone); *Common Clay* (30, Flem-ing); *Renegades* (30, Fleming); *Morocco* (30, von Sternberg) on which he did the script and the dia-logue and helped shift the Sternbergian "glance" into laconic talk. A masterpiece, on the one hand, *Morocco* is also a landmark influence on a grown-up way of looking at men and women so needy for one another they are shy of admitting it.

It's striking now to see how Furthman's output diminished with him at a peak: *Body and Soul* (31, Alfred Santell); *Merely Mary Ann* (31, King); *The Yellow Ticket* (31, Raoul Walsh); *Over the Hill* (31, King); *Shanghai Express* (32, von Sternberg)—is there a better-written movie in the early years of sound?; *Bombshell* (33, Fleming); *China Seas* (35,

Tay Garnett); one of several hands on *Mutiny on the Bounty* (35, Lloyd); *Come and Get It!* (36, Hawks and William Wyler), where his chief responsibility was the Frances Farmer character; *Spawn of the North* (38, Henry Hathaway); *Only Angels Have Wings* (39, Hawks); *The Shanghai Gesture* (41, von Sternberg); *The Outlaw* (43, Howard Hughes).

Then, with William Faulkner in the first instance and with Faulkner and Leigh Brackett in the second, he wrote *To Have and Have Not* (44, Hawks) and *The Big Sleep* (46, Hawks), which are not just masterworks and the creation of Bacall, but a new genre—the screwball noir; *Moss Rose* (47, Gregory Ratoff); *Nightmare Alley* (47, Edmund Goulding), one of the most misanthropic Hollywood pictures ever made; *Pretty Baby* (50, Bretaigne Windust); *Peking Express* (51, William Dieterle), a remake of *Shanghai Express; Jet Pilot* (51, von Sternberg); *Rio Bravo* (59, Hawks), where the Angie Dickinson girl has the same name as the Evelyn Brent figure in *Underworld*— "Feathers."

G

Jean Gabin (Jean-Alexis Gabin Moncorgé) (1904–76), b. Paris

No other French screen actor seemed to the French to embody so many of their admirable characteristics. Like the best American actors, Gabin was subdued out of strength, a knowing lis-tener more than a speaker, anticipatory rather than active. Although in his last years he repre-sented the enduring appeal of a rather stolid bour-geois, in the late 1930s Gabin was the perfect expression of a working-class figure, hating his squalid environment—in factory or lodgings—but drawn toward a dangerously innocent woman and consequent fatal violence as the only means to dignity.

It is a theme returned to in *Pierrot le Fou*, and that is what André Bazin saw in Gabin's alleged insistence on a death scene in his films: "So Gabin was quite right in demanding of his scriptwriters a crisis scene of homicidal fury. It constitutes the significant moment in a rigid destiny where the spectator recognizes the same hero in film after film—a hero of the sprawling metropolis, a subur-ban, working-class Thebes where the gods take the form of the blind but equally transcendent imperatives of society." The best exponents of this mood are his deserter in *Quai des Brumes* (38, Marcel Carné) and François in *Le Jour se Lève* (39, Carné), a becapped factory worker, unlucky but romantically undaunted: "You know when you're waiting for a tram and it's pouring with rain—the tram doesn't stop . . . Ding! Full up. So you wait for the next one . . . Ding, ding! Full up, full up. The trams all go by . . . Ding! And you stay there, you wait . . . But now you're with me, everything's going to be different . . ." That dream muffled by fog and shabbiness is the essence of the Carné/Prévert poetry, but it is a restricted achievement compared with Gabin's work for Renoir: the doomed hero in *Les Bas-Fonds* (36), the homicidal engine-driver in *La Bête Humaine*, and above all, the common-man escapee in *La Grande Illusion* (37), a man of uncontrived kindness and unconscious nobility.

Gabin was in music hall before his movie debut: *Paris Béguin* (31, Augusto Gerina) and *Les Gaietés de l'Escadron* (32, Maurice Tourneur). By the mid-1930s he was well established: *Maria Chapdelaine* (34, Julien Duvivier); *Zouzou* (34, Marc Allégret), with Josephine Baker; *Variétés* (35, Nikolas Farkas); *Golgotha* (35, Duvivier); *La Bandéra* (36, Duvivier); *La Belle Équipe* (36, Duvivier); *Pépé le Moko* (37, Duvivier); outstanding with Mireille Balin in *Gueule d'Amour* (37, Jean Grémillon); the tugboat skipper in *Remorques* (41, Grémillon).

He went to America during the war—he was having a passionate affair with Marlene Dietrich—and appeared in *Moontide* (42, Archie Mayo) and *The Imposter* (44, Duvivier), but he returned to join the Free French and never again ventured on an international career: *Martin Roumagnac* (46, Georges Lacombe), with Dietrich; *Au-Delà des Grilles* (48, René Clément); excellent as a Normandy restaurateur enmeshed by a waitress in *La Marie de Port* (50, Carné); *La Vérité sur Bébé Donge* (51, Henri Decoin); *Le Plaisir* (52, Max Ophuls); *La Minute de Vérité* (52, Jean Delannoy); *Touchez-pas au Grisbi* (54, Jacques Becker); *L'Air du Paris* (54, Carné); and as the impresario Danglars in *French Can Can* (55, Renoir) sat backstage in a huge chair as his cancan erupts, too nervous to watch, but unable to stop his foot stamping to the rhythm.

After that, Gabin worked with dull directors and with decreasing zest. He and the New Wave were not on good terms and it is especially regrettable that he never worked for Melville: *Razzia sur la Chnouf* (54, Decoin); *La Traversée de Paris* (56, Claude Autant-Lara); *Crime et Châtiment* (56, Georges Lampin); *Voici le Temps des Assassins* (56, Duvivier); *Maigret Tend un Piège* (57, Delannoy); *Les Misérables* (57, Jean-Paul le Chanois); amusedly contemplating the bare Bardot in *Love Is My Profession* (58, Autant-Lara); *Archimède le Clochard* (58, Gilles Grangier), from an idea by Gabin; *Le Baron de l'Ecluse* (59, Delannoy); *Le Président* (61, Henri Verneuil); *Un Singe en Hiver* (62, Verneuil); *Monsieur* (64, le Chanois); *L'Age Ingrat* (64, Grangier); *Du Rififi à Paname* (65, de la Patellière); *Le Tonnerre de Dieu* (65, de la Patellière); *Le Pacha* (67, Georges Lautner); *Le Clan des Siciliens* (69, Verneuil); *Le*

Chat (71, Pierre Granier-Deferre); as the farmer in *L'Affaire Dominici* (73, Claude Bernard-Aubert); and *Verdict* (74, André Cayatte).

Clark Gable (William Clark Gable) (1901–60), b. Cadiz, Ohio

Gable succeeded on-screen because of the promise of force behind the smile—that's what made the smile knowing. As a young man, especially without the "wink" of his mustache, he had a hard, menacing quality. He was like Jack Dempsey in a tuxedo. He was sexy for his time (the only time for that trick), and Joan Crawford was just one of those who fell for his confidence. She said that being near him gave her "twinges of a sexual urge beyond belief." It *is* believable: you can feel their desire on-screen (it is the getting together of two lower-class animals in Metro's grand hotel) and her wide-eyed lust for him. They helped each other to stardom and their affair flew in the face of real marriages (Gable was married to Josephine Dillon and Ria Langhan, older, wealthy women who had helped his career). Gable and Crawford were greedy for each other, and Louis B. Mayer was such a sanctimonious enemy to (and profiteer from) their affair, it's a wonder more hasn't been made of it.

Gable had a variety of jobs, including laborer, movie extra, and stage actor (in *The Last Mile*) before Lionel Barrymore got him a screen test at MGM. It failed, but when Gable made a debut as a Western villain in *The Painted Desert* (31, Howard Higgins), MGM changed their mind. He would be under contract to them for twenty-three years, a major earner most of the time, but a hireling who felt exploited and underpaid.

He was a star within a year, and in 1931 he made more movies than in any other year: *The Easiest Way* (Jack Conway); a gangster in *A Free Soul* (Clarence Brown); *The Secret Six* (George Hill); very good in *Night Nurse* (William Wellman); *Sporting Blood* (Charles Brabin); *Dance, Fools, Dance* (Harry Beaumont), with Crawford; a Salvation Army preacher with Crawford again in *Laughing Sinners* (Beaumont), in a reshoot after Johnny Mack Brown had done the part; in his best Crawford teaming, *Possessed* (Brown); with Garbo in *Susan Lenox: Her Fall and Rise* (Robert Z. Leonard); and *Hell Drivers* (32, Hill).

There was a refreshing comic edge in *Red Dust* (32, Victor Fleming, a Gable buddy). He played with Jean Harlow there for the first time and he was her most natural screen partner (as well as her lover at the Château Marmont). In *No Man of Her Own* (32, Wesley Ruggles), he played with Carole Lombard, who would become his third wife in 1939. He was opposite Norma Shearer in the Eugene O'Neill adaptation *Strange Interlude* (32, Leonard). He was also in *The White Sister* (33, Fleming); *Night Flight* (33, Brown), a notable failure; and with Crawford in *Dancing Lady* (33, Leonard).

He was fighting Metro for better roles. But he was having to defend a disordered private life. Then he killed a woman in a drunk driving accident. While a Metro executive took the blame and went to jail, Gable was loaned out to Columbia for what became *It Happened One Night* (34, Frank Capra). He was unhappy about the deal, but the comedy warmed him up, he changed the nation's ideas about undershirts, and he got an Oscar. So somehow Metro had to reappraise their wild boy.

These were the years of his greatest fame and ease: he seemed to love making movies, and his smile became an institution: a doctor in *Men in White* (34, Richard Boleslavsky); sparring with William Powell in *Manhattan Melodrama* (34, W. S. Van Dyke)—the last film seen by Dillinger; with Crawford once more in *Chained* (34, Brown) and *Forsaking All Others* (34, Van Dyke); *After Office Hours* (35, Leonard); doing Jack London with Loretta Young in *Call of the Wild* (35, Wellman); as Fletcher Christian (nominated for an Oscar) in *Mutiny on the Bounty* (35, Frank Lloyd); *China Seas* (35, Tay Garnett); *Wife vs. Secretary* (36, Brown); with Spencer Tracy in *San Francisco* (36, Van Dyke); with Crawford in *Love On the Run* (36, Van Dyke); with Marion Davies in *Cain and Mabel* (36, Lloyd Bacon); in the flop *Parnell* (37, John M. Stahl); with Harlow—who died in the middle of filming—in *Saratoga* (37, Conway); with Tracy and Loy in *Test Pilot* (38, Fleming); *Too Hot to Handle* (38, Conway); and *Idiot's Delight* (39, Brown).

Gable was no keener to make *Gone With the Wind* (39, Fleming) than he had been to do *It Happened One Night*. But Selznick was prepared to trade away distribution rights for Gable and some cash, and in years to come that became the controlling rights in the film. Gable would not do a Southern accent for Rhett Butler, and he turned up late so that George Cukor had begun to cultivate and favor the bloom of Vivien Leigh's Scarlett. Gable was not happy with Cukor, and he let that be known. But Cukor was fired because the film was going badly, and slowly. His replacement was Vic Fleming, and that helped accelerate and rebalance the film. Rhett was always secondary to Scarlett, but Gable made him the best-liked character in the film. His last words, "Frankly, my dear, I don't give a damn," made men proud and women agitated. Yet he was one of the few people on *Wind* who missed an Oscar.

Back at MGM, he made *Strange Cargo* (40, Frank Borzage), escaping from a penal colony, with Crawford; *Boom Town* (40, Conway), with Colbert and Tracy; *Comrade X* (40, King Vidor), with Hedy Lamarr; *They Met in Bombay* (41, Brown); *Honky Tonk* (41, Conway), with Lana Turner—the next generation of actresses; *Some-*

where I'll Find You (42, Ruggles), in which he and Turner play war correspondents. This run of films after *Gone With the Wind* hardly befitted a national idol, and they began Gable's decline. The death of Carole Lombard in a plane crash, in 1942, was an extra burden: Gable seemed sadder all of a sudden and once merriment left his smile, age set in. He joined the Army Air Corps and though there were stories about his war being all for show, he did do work for Army Intelligence.

But he was never the same again. The pictures that followed the war were lackluster, and Gable hardly seemed to realize that for the public he was still a great star. It may help explain what happened to see that as Gable sank so Bogart came into his own. Gable was with Greer Garson in *Adventure* (45, Fleming); trying to preserve his integrity in *The Hucksters* (47, Conway)—once upon a time Gable's integrity had been natural and as quick as the grin; *Homecoming* (48, Mervyn Le Roy); *Command Decision* (49, Sam Wood); *Any Number Can Play* (49, Le Roy); *Key to the City* (50, George Sidney); *To Please a Lady* (50, Brown); *Across the Wide Missouri* (51, Wellman); *Lone Star* (51, Vincent Sherman); *Never Let Me Go* (53, Delmer Daves); *Mogambo* (53, John Ford), an enjoyable remake of *Red Dust*; and *Betrayed* (54, Gottfried Reinhardt), his last picture at MGM.

He moved to Fox, first for *Soldier of Fortune* (55, Edward Dmytryk) and then for one of his best pictures, *The Tall Men* (55, Raoul Walsh)—he hadn't looked so relaxed for years. Two more with Walsh followed, contented reminiscences of Gable's own past—*The King and Four Queens* (56) and *Band of Angels* (57). But after a conventional war picture, *Run Silent, Run Deep* (58, Robert Wise), he became trapped in flat comedies—*Teacher's Pet* (58, George Seaton) and *It Started in Naples* (60, Melville Shavelson)—with yet another generation of female stars, Doris Day and Sophia Loren.

His last film, *The Misfits* (60, John Huston), with Marilyn Monroe, gave him the chance for a tender, veteran cowboy. He was brave and patient in the heat of Nevada, waiting for Monroe and doing tough scenes with horses. He had a fatal heart attack shortly thereafter, just before the birth of his only son by a fifth wife. Thus he never saw *The Misfits* or the look on Monroe's face, radiant at being with so huge a star.

Abel Gance (1889–1981), b. Paris

1911: *La Digue*; *Le Nègre Blanc* (codirected with Jean Joulout); *Il y a des Pieds au Plafond*. 1912: *Le Masque d'Horreur*; *Un Drame au Château d'Acre*; *L'Enigme de Dix Heures*; *Les Morts Reviennent-Ils?*. 1915: *La Folie du Docteur Tube*; *Fioritures*; *Le Fou de la Falaise*; *Le Périscope*; *Ce que les Flots*

Racontent. 1916: *Barbereuse; L'Héroïsme de Paddy; Strass et Compagnie; Les Gaz Mortels; La Fleur des Ruines; Le Droit à la Vie; La Zone de la Mort.* 1917: *Mater Dolorosa.* 1918: *La Dixième Symphonie; J'Accuse!.* 1922: *La Roue.* 1923: *Au Secours!.* 1926: *Napoléon Vu par Abel Gance.* 1928: *Marines et Cristaux.* 1931: *La Fin du Monde.* 1933: *Mater Dolorosa; Le Maître des Forges.* 1934: *Poliche; La Dame aux Camélias; Napoléon Bonaparte.* 1935: *Le Roman d'un Jeune Homme Pauvre; Lucréce Borgia.* 1936: *Le Voleur de Femmes; Un Grand Amour de Beethoven; Jerome Perreau, Héros des Barricades.* 1937: *J'Accuse!.* 1939: *Louise; Paradis Perdu.* 1940: *La Vénus Aveugle.* 1941: *Une Femme dans la Nuit* (codirected with Edmond Greville). 1942: *Le Capitaine Fracasse.* 1944: *Manolete* (unfinished). 1953: *Quatorze Juillet.* 1954: *La Tour de Nèsle.* 1956: *Magirama.* 1960: *Austerlitz* (codirected with Roger Richebé). 1963: *Cyrano et d'Artagnan.* 1971: *Bonaparte et la Révolution.*

Gance is the hero of those who regret the loss of purity when the cinema gained sound. In *The Parade's Gone By*—a book dedicated to Gance and culminating in a breathless tribute to him—Kevin Brownlow says of Gance that "with his silent productions, *J'Accuse, La Roue,* and *Napoléon,* he made a fuller use of the medium than anyone before or since."

Such extravagance could prejudice the actual claims Gance has on our attention. Much silent cinema now looks primitive, melodramatic, and naïve—Gance's especially. To claim that it is superior, artistically, to the intelligence and emotional depths of, say, *La Règle du Jeu, Citizen Kane, Ugetsu Monogatari,* or *Viva l'Italia* is to prefer Dumas to Proust. Most foolish of all is the self-imposed need to sacrifice one for another. As with Griffith, it is more than ever necessary to assess the importance of Gance within the historical perspective. Epic heroism, technical ingenuity, a sense of visual spontaneity, and raw melodrama are too easily made the stuff of martyrdom. Thus it is preposterous of Brownlow to paint this vivid picture of Gance's fate—"The motion-picture industry, in France or elsewhere, was alarmed by Gance's monumental talents, and frightened by his revolutionary ideas. They determined to control him, and to limit the length of his artistic leash. Unfortunately for all of us, they succeeded"—and not realize that the wit, poetry, and farsightedness of Louis Feuillade exceed the merits of Gance's films.

Just as Griffith's lament, "give us back our beauty," when sound came in revealed a limited view of cinematic beauty, so Gance tied himself to a stake—the triptych Polyvision—that was irrelevant to real cinema, even if it epitomized the grandiose, individualistic venture that obsessed Gance. Allow that he was a director inspired by superficial feelings, undiscriminatingly inventive, and it becomes possible to see him as an immensely appealing pioneer, as the source of many important enlargements of cinematic perception, and as one of the first apostles of the medium. Gance loved cinema, and that is why the New Wave reclaimed him.

Gance grew up at the turn of the century. He described his youth as if it came from a Victorian novel: the young man constrained to work for a solicitor, but preferring to sit in the Bibliothèque Nationale reading Racine, Rimbaud, Omar Khayyam, Edgar Allan Poe—it is the romantic notion of art held by the young man in *Lola.* He loved to act, and in 1907 he wrote a screenplay, the first of many that he sold to the infant French film industry. Watching others direct inspired him to do better. His first films are characteristic of the period, if already inquisitive and exploratory. *La Folie du Docteur Tube* employed distorting lenses to convey a psychological impression of fantasy. The sheer novelty enthralled Gance and he thrived on the opportunities of newness. *Barbereuse* and *Les Gaz Mortels* were filmed concurrently with the same actors on the same location after Gance had been instructed by Film d'Art to take actors and crew on a train and come back with two features.

But as Griffith rose above such frenzy on the wings of the Gish sisters to enshrine them in throbbing emotional dramas, so war crystallized Gance's grandiloquent view of human history. *J'Accuse!* was his turning point, an emotional onslaught on the folly of war, strangely allied to martial visual imagination. The film's idea of the dead returning to ask whether their loss was justified is an instance of emotional self-inducement on Gance's part, as moving but as contradictory as the shots of crowds in *Triumph of the Will.* In other words, there is a naïve passion in the conception that has more to do with melodramatic pageant than with true disenchantment. His inventiveness makes the film cheerful, and there is an awful irony in the way Gance enlisted troops on leave to play the dead, days before they themselves were to be killed at Verdun.

It is true of all his career that Gance's technical developments, his stress on the novelty of the image, are seldom related to the meaning of his films. *J'Accuse!* is vibrant with the energy that a few years later made *Napoléon*—Gance's great hero, the model of superhuman energy and enterprise. What is marvelous about *Napoléon* and *La Roue* is the narrative enthusiasm, the sweeping exposition of events, and the way images reveal interior feelings through dynamic editing. But the attitude to Napoleon was a banal and thorough endorsement, so much so that Charles de Gaulle was among the film's greatest admirers. It is a remarkable film, but recollect that 1926–28 was the period of *A Girl in Every Port, The General, Metropolis, Sunrise, Underworld, Seventh Heaven, Queen Kelly,* and *The Crowd.*

The least important thing about *Napoléon* is the most talked about: Polyvision, or the simultaneous projection of three images. The famous example is of a central close-up of Bonaparte, flanked by two screens showing his armies marching in long shots. In practice, few have seen that effect: Gance was always hampered by the technical obstacles to such projection. But the device abandons the thread of cinema: the need to select one image at a time, and to relate one to another in a sequence. The effect of three images simultaneously may be spectacular, but it dissipates the viewer's concentration. Especially as Gance uses it—as a crude addition of image in preference to choice—it is downright silly. *Chelsea Girls* arguably uses the idea more creatively, by projecting unrelated images. That very openness may regenerate an audience's sensibilities, compelling them to find connections. But three images of the same action speak for lavish indecision.

Far more satisfying are Gance's "intimate" emotional melodramas. He was an unabashed wallower in trite feelings and he overcame silliness only when his images made nonsense credible and moving. In this area, *La Roue, Un Grand Amour de Beethoven,* and *La Vénus Aveugle* are truly impressive. They deal with emotional triangles, thwarted love, overweening selfishness, and the recurring theme of blindness. These ingredients of pulp fiction are invested with Gance's emotional imagery, his rapid cutting, and the communion with his players. Thus Severin-Mars in *La Roue,* as the engine driver who loves the girl he has adopted, is a forerunner of the man destroyed by passion. And the train is used as a marvelous commentary on that destructive but exciting force. Seen today, *La Roue* is one of the most unashamed of silent movies. Make the effort to imagine it in 1921 and Gance's importance becomes clear: *La Roue* trembles with feeling, like a building shuddering as a train passes by.

His strength and limitations are revealed in this comment from Gabriel de Gravase, an actress in *La Roue:*

> What actor wouldn't want to make pictures with this innovator, this marvelous director, this perfectionist, who obtains the most impressive lighting one can get in photography and does it all with simple means, which are available to every director. Indicating, thinking, playing, living each role with each player. He is not merely the author of the scenario, the cutter, the chief mechanic, the electrician, the cameraman—he is everything: the heart and soul of the film. During the shooting of the

scenes, he invariably repeats the same words: "Human, simple, great intensity." Everything is contained in those words.

Bruno Ganz, b. Zurich, Switzerland, 1941

For twenty-five years, Bruno Ganz has been the ideal melancholy angel, watching over sad times even if there's little he can do to improve them. Though Swiss, he seems to link hands with the ages of Harry Lime and George Smiley. He is the kind of actor who might have been trained by Trevor Howard or Gérard Philipe—which is a reminder that both of those actors could ignite a love story and knock women off their feet. Ganz can be battered, hangdog, at the end of his tether, but he has charm and humor just beneath the surface. He has been a wandering actor, with much work done for German television (including a Faust as recently as 2000). He is modest and restrained in most of what he does, as if touched by a Graham Greene–like realization that we are too far gone now for tragic heroes. He has a way of watching more showy actors that rivets attention.

This list cannot be complete, but its range is still awesome: he began acting in about 1960, but it was only in the 1970s that he came into his own: *Lumière* (76, Jeanne Moreau); the Count in *The Marquise of O* (76, Eric Rohmer); *The Wild Duck* (76, Hans W. Geisendorfer), with Jean Seberg; as Jonathan in *The American Friend* (77, Wim Wenders); *The Left-Handed Woman* (77, Peter Handke); obsessed by chess in *Black and White Like Day and Night* (78, Wolfgang Petersen); breaking up in *Knife in the Head* (78, Reinhard Hauff); *The Boys from Brazil* (78, Franklin M. Schaffner); as Harker in *Nosferatu* (79, Werner Herzog); *The Girl from Lorraine* (80, Claude Goretta); *Lady of the Camelias* (81, Mauro Bolognini); *Circle of Deceit* (81, Volker Schlöndorff); *Hands Up!* (83, Jerzy Skolimowski); never better than as the man increasingly lost in Lisbon in *In the White City* (83, Alain Tanner); an angel in *Wings of Desire* (87, Wenders); brilliantly irresponsible in *Strapless* (89, David Hare); *Especially on Sunday* (91, Giuseppe Tornatore); *The Last Days of Chez Nous* (92, Gillian Armstrong); *Faraway, So Close* (93, Wenders); as Saint-Exupéry in *Saint-Ex* (97, Anand Tucker); *Bread and Tulips* (00, Tornatore).

He played the lead in a film of a stage performance, *Faust* (01, Thomas Grimm and Peter Schonhofer); *Epsteins Nacht* (01, Urs Egger); *La Forza del Passato* (02, Piergiorgio Gay); as *Luther* (03, Eric Till); as *Hitler in Der Untergang* (04, Oliver Hirschbiegel).

Greta Garbo (Greta Lovisa Gustafsson) (1905–90), b. Stockholm, Sweden

The only way men can respond to a star is to gaze at it from their remote planet. And even when a star passes out of our sight in the sequence of orbits, we believe that it exists still and feel the gravitational pull it exerts. Garbo is the extreme definition of stardom in the cinema: not only because she is the star most people would name first, but because her life and work were made into contingent expressions of the domination that a star treats us to; and because within that inscrutability, what drew audiences was the impression of its antithesis—anxiety, vulnerability, distraction. The energy needed to burn bright hurt Garbo, and that pain permeated her appeal. That is why retirement never altered her career but extended it. Her films frequently show her on the verge of withdrawal, and fifty years of inactivity did not deprive us of her. The logic of the gloomy woman made radiant by artificial light was inevitably to retreat. Those magazine photographs over the years kept her in contact and the curious dying words before death—"I want to be alone"—are not resented, but accepted as the clinching proof that Garbo was natural, homely, like us, in wanting privacy. For in the cinema, the audience is alone, sheltered by the dark. Coming into our hearts and minds, Garbo aspired to that shelter; in making the journey away from fame into privacy she established herself forever as a magical figure, a true goddess, remote and austere, but intimate and touching.

In his chapter on Garbo in *The Celluloid Sacrifice*, Alexander Walker begins with a wrong direction that he quickly abandons: "The only way of trying to penetrate the mystery that has gathered round Greta Garbo is to assume that it does not exist; to think oneself back to her screen beginnings; to refuse to be decoyed by the legends put out about her; to acknowledge the metaphysics of personality, but also to look for the less abstract ways in which she employed her talent to gain her effects; in short, to see Garbo plain."

But it is a fallacy to believe in a plain Garbo, or to expect legend to peel away, disclosing truth. Her essence is a matter of myth and the conjunction of natural performance with legendary and supernatural personality. She speaks and appears on behalf of the millions of plain people who require a lofty "She who must be obeyed," but who can secretly possess the goddess and see in her the elevated traces of their own inadequacy and diffidence. The goddess must be indifferent to her worshipers, not quite able to concentrate on them. That feeling of distraction draws them to her so much more securely and confirms their secret belief that she too has worries and moments of defeat.

Just as Christ simultaneously asserted godliness and humanity by going off—into the wilderness, into a secluded part of the garden, simply to be alone—so Garbo is forever held back from that peace by films, and ineluctably seeing her way through the action to eventual solitude. Her actual aloneness—retired; cut off from MGM; never married; away from her own country—was predicted in so many of her major parts. Time and again, her screen love affairs are fated to dissolve, impossible to realize: Queen Christina goes into abdication; twice Garbo played Anna Karenina—in 1935 and in *Love*—discarded by Vronsky; in *Flesh and the Devil* she falls to a death where lovers are reunited; in *A Woman of Affairs* she dies in a car crash; in *Mata Hari* she perishes; in *Grand Hotel* she chooses ballet rather than love; in *Conquest* she gives up Bonaparte for the greater good of the world; in *Camille* she relinquishes Robert Taylor to accord with the consumptive consciences of Dumas fils, MGM, and the bourgeois everywhere.

And it is the most curious manifestation of stardom that decent men and women all over the world would have been outraged by *Camille*'s dying happy—in the lewd way described by Jean-Pierre Léaud in *Masculin-Féminin*—but were moved to complacent pity by her self-inflicted solitariness.

Garbo's films keep her for the audiences. They allow us to leave the cinema with the thought that she escaped the plot, the settings, and the other characters to perform endlessly in our dreams. Of course, that effect was not casual. Scriptwriters produced material that was in key with the "private" image of Garbo, itself promoted by the publicity department of MGM. There is no campaign to sell unattainability so enduring as that involving Garbo, and few cases where the "public" and "private" images are so threaded together in artifice. Thus, even Alexander Walker wonders whether the scene in *Queen Christina*, where Garbo roams around the room after a night of love to memorize it—"In future, in my mind, I shall live a great deal in this world"—is not founded upon a moment from her life when she came to the room of the recently dead Mauritz Stiller (her discoverer) and walked about touching things.

Did such an incident occur in life? If not, it should have. Could a living legend fail to behave in life as she would in art? The comparison of incidents is hardly useful biographically, for it only shows the way in which legend has overwhelmed history in Garbo's case. But it does point to the technique of the goddess: she was supremely good at being observed, as if unawares. The Stiller incident comes from the words of a bystander, lulled into thinking that Garbo's preoccupation was affording him a private insight. That is exactly the means by which Garbo wins us in her films, by seeming so enrapt in her own feelings that she encourages us into the breathless expectancy of voyeurs.

That technique should not be passed off as cynical or instinctive. We believe in stars only when a natural reticence is perfectly allied to the discipline of performance. Garbo graciously allowed herself to be photographed and gently made it clear that she was turning a blind eye to the intrusion. Any actress in intimate close-up does the same thing by looking discreetly away from the lens. Garbo did it more enchantingly than most. And there are valuable comments from some of her most experienced midwives (or altar boys) to illustrate this. MGM took care of her and persisted with men who understood her or in whose company she felt at ease.

Clarence Brown was an insipid depictor of glamour, but he directed Garbo six times, partly because he recognized the command she held over the camera: "Garbo had something behind the eyes that you couldn't see until you photographed it in close-up. You could see thought. If she had to look at one person with jealousy, and another with love, she didn't have to change her expression. You could see it in her eyes as she looked from one to the other."

Nobody photographed Garbo so often in close-up as William Daniels, who worked on twelve of her fourteen sound pictures. He has mentioned a method, evident in any of her films: "She was always taken in close-ups or long shots, hardly ever intermediate or full figure. The latter do not come out well." The fact was that in full-length shot—the glory of, say, Bette Davis, Katharine Hepburn, or Carole Lombard—Garbo was gawky, louche, embarrassed, and clumsy. She needed to be seen from afar, in full shot or in glowingly soft close-up: how well that style responds to the voyeur impulse, and how clearly it derives from silent cinema. Garbo had her origins in that, of course, but she always spoke cautiously, because she never made English as subservient to her mouth and manner as did Dietrich.

The facts of her career show that her desire to escape was begun almost as soon as she entered films. Her childhood had not been happy, but stage training and short films led to her being chosen by Mauritz Stiller for *Gösta Berling's Saga* (24). Stiller seems to have known what he had found and to have impressed upon her the response to being filmed that she always employed. They went to Istanbul to make a second film together, but funds ran out and Garbo was seconded to *Joyless Street* (25, G. W. Pabst).

She was then hired by MGM's Louis B. Mayer, with Stiller taken along in tow. She made ten silent films at the studio and quickly established herself as the new woman, passionate but restless and insecure: *The Torrent* (26, Monta Bell); *The Temptress* (26, Fred Niblo); *Flesh and the Devil* (26, Brown); *Love* (27, Edmund Goulding); *The Divine Woman* (28, Victor Sjostrom); *The Mysterious Lady* (28, Niblo); *A Woman of Affairs* (29, Brown); *Wild Orchids* (29, Sidney Franklin); *The Single Standard* (29, John Robertson); *The Kiss* (29, Jacques Feyder).

She talked, eventually, in *Anna Christie* (30, Brown), and thereafter dominated MGM in the 1930s with a diminishing trickle of films: *Romance* (30, Brown); *Inspiration* (31, Brown); *Susan Lenox: Her Fall and Rise* (31, Robert Z. Leonard); *Mata Hari* (32, George Fitzmaurice); *Grand Hotel* (32, Goulding), the only time on record that she asked to be alone; *As You Desire Me* (32, Fitzmaurice); *Queen Christina* (33, Rouben Mamoulian); *The Painted Veil* (34, Richard Boleslavsky); *Anna Karenina* (35, Brown); *Camille* (36, George Cukor); *Conquest* (38, Brown); *Ninotchka* (39, Ernst Lubitsch)—by now, her best-known and most-loved performance; and *Two-Faced Woman* (41, Cukor).

The war had cut her off from vast European popularity, whereas in America her foreignness always offended in some quarters. In addition, the wartime mood was against the romantically lovelorn. She seized the moment herself and generously released MGM from a very demanding contract. In later years, there were repeated efforts to lure her back, many of which are captivating in prospect: as Bernhardt for Selznick; as George Sand for Cukor; as Dorian Gray for Albert Lewin; as the Duchesse de Langeais for Max Ophuls; in Proust for Visconti. But why should such authority risk appearance, especially if Garbo was as insecure as we liked to think?

When she died, there was plentiful evidence of how ordinary and how dull the real woman had been. And she had never managed to escape that legendary figure—or see the joke. Books appeared and her Sutton Place apartment was photographed—like a liberated shrine. For a few years arguments may persist on whether she was wise or dumb, androgynous or uninterested. But sooner or later such trivia will evaporate and a mysterious truth will be left—she was photographed. She was all in the silver.

Andy Garcia (Andrés Arturo García-Menéndez), b. Havana, Cuba, 1956

Just as Al Pacino played Cuban refugee Tony Montana in *Scarface* (83, Brian De Palma), so Andy Garcia brought fresh Cuban blood to the flagging Corleones for *The Godfather, Part III* (90, Francis Ford Coppola). Garcia's Vincent was a ready whip looking for a masterful hand, and the most urgent force of ambition in that autumnal and resigned picture. And Garcia is surely the actor best poised to inherit the force and position of "the Italian generation."

He came to Miami as a kid and was trained in theatre. For the screen, he has done *Blue Skies Again* (83, Richard Michaels); *The Mean Season* (85, Phillip Borsos); a snakelike villain in *Eight Million Ways to Die* (86, Hal Ashby); *The*

Untouchables (87, De Palma); *American Roulette* (88, Maurice Hatton); *Stand and Deliver* (87, Ramon Menendez); *Black Rain* (89, Ridley Scott); *Internal Affairs* (90, Mike Figgis); *A Show of Force* (90, Bruno Barreto); *Dead Again* (91, Kenneth Branagh); *Hero* (92, Stephen Frears); *Jennifer 8* (92, Bruce Robinson); and *When a Man Loves a Woman* (94, Luis Mandoki).

In 1993, Garcia directed a feature-length documentary, *Cachao*, a tribute to the Cuban musician Israel López. In addition, he has been working with fellow Cuban Guillermo Cabrera Infante on a feature script.

That collaboration has not borne fruit yet, but in the meantime Garcia has moved away from the mainstream and towards increasingly Hispanic material: *Steal Big, Steal Little* (95, Andrew Davis); *Things to Do in Denver When You're Dead* (95, Gary Fleder); *Somos un Solo Pueblo* (95, Marcos Zurinaga); *Night Falls on Manhattan* (97, Sidney Lumet); *The Disappearance of Garcia Lorca* (97, Zurinaga); as Lucky Luciano in *Hoodlum* (97, Bill Duke); *Desperate Measures* (98, Barbet Schroeder); *Just the Ticket* (99, David Anspaugh); executive producer and playing Arturo Sandoval in *For Love or Country* (00, Joseph Sargent); *Lakeboat* (00, Joe Mantegna); *The Unsaid* (01, Tom McLoughlin); *The Man from Elysian Fields* (01, George Hickenlooper); *Ocean's Eleven* (01, Steven Soderburgh); *Confidence* (03, James Foley); *Just Like Mona* (03, Joe Pantoliano); *The Blackout Murders* (03, Philip Kaufman).

Ava Gardner (Lucy Johnson) (1922–90), b. Grabton, North Carolina

Gardner's exceptional Spanish beauty was carried proudly for many years, with head thrown back, half dutifully for so many artistic still photographers and half to compensate for short sight. No doubt about her vivid looks, but rather more concerning the character and intelligence behind them. Apart from being glamorous, she was good as a man's woman, a sort of gypsy Jean Harlow—indeed, she took the Harlow role in *Mogambo* (53), John Ford's remake of *Red Dust*.

She made her debut, in 1942, in Robert Z. Leonard's *We Were Dancing* and had a mixed career for the next few years, playing in the first American films by Fred Zinnemann and Douglas Sirk—*Kid Glove Killer* (42) and *Hitler's Madman* (43)—in *Young Ideas* (43, Jules Dassin), and adorning Dr. Kildare movies. It was after the war that she broke through to stardom, first as a gangster's moll in *Whistle Stop* (46, Leonide Moguy) and then in Siodmak's *The Killers* (46). MGM pushed her hard, in Jack Conway's *The Hucksters* (47), John Brahm's *Singapore* (47), and *One Touch of Venus* (48, William A. Seiter), but she was more suited to exotic romance: thus, she never looked

better than as the gambling beauty in Siodmak's *The Great Sinner* (49), in *The Bribe* (49, Leonard), modestly touching in George Sidney's *Show Boat* (51), and dottily mythic in Albert Lewin's *Pandora and the Flying Dutchman* (51).

She made more conventional films—such as Mervyn Le Roy's *East Side, West Side* (50)—but was generally put out of doors and/or in costume. Her own busy romantic life (including marriage to Mickey Rooney, Artie Shaw, and Frank Sinatra), her looks, and her taste for sporting activities led to her being cast as a Hemingway woman, first in *The Snows of Kilimanjaro* (52) and then, incredibly, as Brett Ashley in *The Sun Also Rises* (57), both films by Henry King. Otherwise, she made *Lone Star* (52, Vincent Sherman), *Ride, Vaquero!* (53, John Farrow), and *Knights of the Round Table* (54, Richard Thorpe) before playing the title part in Mankiewicz's *The Barefoot Contessa* (54), perfect casting and clever use of her narrow range. Cukor's *Bhowani Junction* (56) was much more demanding and the Anglo-Indian in that film is her most touching performance. She then played in Robson's *The Little Hut* (57) and was an overdressed *Naked Maja* (59, Henry Koster).

She worked sparingly in later years, without distinction in *On the Beach* (59, Stanley Kramer) and Nunnally Johnson's *The Angel Wore Red* (60), but gloriously good-looking and worldly wise in Ray's *55 Days at Peking* (63), Frankenheimer's *Seven Days in May* (64), and Huston's *Night of the Iguana* (64)—in the last of which she almost manages to be an earth mother. She gave herself up to lavish gesture—as Sarah in *The Bible* (66, Huston) and as an overblown Hapsburg in *Mayerling* (68, Terence Young)—but played a Queen of the Fairies in the fascinating *The Devil's Widow* (71, Roddy McDowall); was still very beautiful as Lily Langtry in *The Life and Times of Judge Roy Bean* (72, Huston); *Earthquake* (74, Robson); *Permission to Kill* (75, Cyril Frankel); *The Sentinel* (76, Michael Winner); *The Cassandra Crossing* (76, George Pan Cosmatos); and *Blue Bird* (76, Cukor).

She was in *City on Fire* (79, Alvin Rakoff); *The Kidnapping of the President* (80, George Menduluk); Mabel Dodge Luhan in *Priest of Love* (80, Christopher Miles); on TV in *The Long Hot Summer* (85, Stuart Cooper); in the miniseries *A.D.* (85, Cooper); and in *Harem* (86, Billy Hale).

John Garfield (Jacob Julius Garfinkle) (1913–52), b. New York

With the Group Theater in the late 1930s, he played in Clifford Odets's *Golden Boy*. Warners signed him and launched him as male interest in a Michael Curtiz sentimental series: *Four Daughters* (38), *Daughters Courageous* (39), *Four Wives* (39) (in flashback), and in *Juarez* (39, William Dieterle). But by Hollywood standards, Garfield was rugged, half-ugly, and belligerent; indeed, as a kid, he had been in and out of Bronx street gangs. He soon became typed as a social outsider, so intransigent that he often went wrong: *They Made Me a Criminal* (39, Busby Berkeley) and *Dust Be My Destiny* (39, Lewis Seiler). He was a prisoner in Litvak's *Castle on the Hudson* (40) and an ex-prisoner in *East of the River* (40, Alfred E. Green). There followed Curtiz's *The Sea Wolf* (41), Litvak's *Out of the Fog* (41), Robert Florey's *Dangerously They Live* (42), and Victor Fleming's *Tortilla Flat* (42), on loan to MGM. War brought him parts as one of the crew with a chip on his shoulder: in Hawks's *Air Force* (43) and Daves's *Destination Tokyo* (43) and *Pride of the Marines* (45), where he is terrific and raw as the blinded hero.

He broadened his range after the war, at MGM, shaded by Lana Turner in Tay Garnett's *The Postman Always Rings Twice* (46) and in two Negulesco women's pix: *Nobody Lives Forever* (46) and, with Joan Crawford in *Humoresque* (47) where Isaac Stern's hands and a clever suit allowed him to "play" the violin.

His contract with Warners ended, Garfield set up independently, and through his own company, Enterprise Productions, he starred in Rossen's *Body and Soul* (47), as a boxer, and Polonsky's *Force of Evil* (48). *Body and Soul* was tough but orthodox. But *Force of Evil* allows Garfield to show what a stylish little Caesar he could be. In truth, his crooked organizer is mesmerizing. He also played the Jew in Kazan's *Gentleman's Agreement* (47) and was a Cuban revolutionary in Huston's *We Were Strangers* (49).

The tone of his later work, plus the novelty of his breakaway and the list of his associates, brought him under suspicion as a possible Communist. Uncooperative with the House Committee on Un-American Activities, he found it hard to get movie work, played the actor in Odets's *The Big Knife* on stage, but was forced back to earlier modes: *Under My Skin* (50, Negulesco) and *The Breaking Point* (50, Curtiz), a remake of *To Have and Have Not* with Garfield too short on Bogart's panache, but nearer to Hemingway's mid-1930s radicalism. He died of a heart attack having reacted badly to neglect, and after a last interesting movie, John Berry's *He Ran All the Way* (51). As Polonsky has said, "He defended his street-boy's honor and they killed him for it."

Judy Garland (Frances Ethel Gumm) (1922–69), b. Grand Rapids, Minnesota

Garland left deep impressions on many viewers, but ruinous ones in herself. Long before her actual death, it was clear how far her career had been given over to disasters, breakdown, and a general messiness that sprang from her emotional intensity. Her greatest admirers were able to interpret the chaos as almost a proof of her integrity. And as if to torment herself, she never completely lost her talent. Not only was she capable of the deepest sentimental immersion in her material, but her own technical flaws and professional shortcomings were made to seem touching proof of her survival. She was always much more than a film actress. She was a great *dramatic* singer, and she thrived on personal appearances when, at her best, she could dominate the Palladium or Carnegie Hall.

If not born in a trunk, she was the daughter of vaudeville parents who introduced her to the stage at the age of three. With her sister she survived billing as "The Gumm Sisters," and at the age of thirteen she was taken on by MGM for her screen debut in 1936 in a short, *Every Sunday* (Felix Feist), and *Pigskin Parade* (David Butler), on loan to Fox. She was never more successful than as a teenage star, often with Mickey Rooney: *Thoroughbreds Don't Cry* (38, Alfred E. Green); *Everybody Sing* (38, Edwin L. Marin); *Listen Darling* (38, Marin); *Love Finds Andy Hardy* (38, George Seitz); entering folklore as Dorothy in Victor Fleming's *Wizard of Oz* (39), where she first sang "Over the Rainbow"; in four Busby Berkeley musicals: *Babes in Arms* (39); *Strike Up the Band* (40); *Babes on Broadway* (41); and *For Me and My Gal* (42). In these hectic late teenage years, she also made *Little Nellie Kelly* (40, Norman Taurog); *Andy Hardy Meets Debutante* (40, Seitz); *Ziegfeld Girl* (41, Robert Z. Leonard); *Life Begins for Andy Hardy* (41, Seitz); *Presenting Lily Mars* (43, Taurog); *Girl Crazy* (43, Taurog); and *Thousands Cheer* (43, George Sidney).

But she was several degrees more beautiful and touching in four films made by her then husband Vincente Minnelli: at her very best in *Meet Me in St. Louis* (44); *The Clock* (45); *Ziegfeld Follies* (46); and *The Pirate* (47). Already marked down as temperamental, her career at Metro petered out—despite *The Harvey Girls* (45, Sidney) and Charles Walters's *Easter Parade* (48) with Fred Astaire—and ended in 1950 with *Summer Stock* (Walters) after she had broken down during the making of *Annie Get Your Gun*. In *Summer Stock* she is evidently plump—the more so for her farm-girl's dungarees—in everything except the beautifully smart and streamlined "Get Happy" (the result of crash dieting and a bizarre farewell to the hungry lion).

Having worked hectically for fourteen years, she made only four more films before her death. In one, *Judgment at Nuremberg* (61, Stanley Kramer), she was very bad. In another, Cassavetes's *A Child Is Waiting* (62), she was miscast. A third, *I Could Go On Singing* (63, Ronald Neame), with the generous support of Dirk Bogarde, has fine moments despite a grotesque note of autobiography. The fourth, Cukor's *A Star Is Born*

(54), is one of the greatest flawed movies ever made and shows Garland as the actress with the surest intuition of the drama in musicals. Warners took evident fright at the notion of a puffy Garland playing an ingenue who finds fame in the movies. But every physical handicap could not prevent Garland from catching the scent of her own horrible greasepaint life. Because it is the man who suffers—the James Mason part—Garland was enabled to see showbiz's glib tragedy from a distance. She sang and yearned for someone else and the scenes with Mason, wonderfully assisted by Cukor, are as moving as "Have Yourself a Merry Little Christmas" in *Meet Me in St. Louis* where she comforts Margaret O'Brien. Perhaps she yearned to care for people; is that the vibrato always trembling in her voice? Her voice is alive still, and Judy Davis—on TV—helped show why people keep writing and reading books about Garland.

James Garner (James Scott Baumgarner),
b. Norman, Oklahoma, 1928

This book has always believed that its target was careers made in film—the movies. Yet even in the mid-seventies it was evident that many movie stars had moved over to the smaller screen to keep in business. There was still an active snobbery at work that believed movies were more prestigious than television. To this day, there are a few stars who don't do television. But there are careers like that of Lucille Ball that say, Wake up. For decades now, more people have watched TV than have gone to the movies. In the last twenty years, there have been undoubted star careers made on the small screen (and not included in this book): for instance, Mary Tyler Moore, Ed Asner, Carroll O'Connor, Henry Winkler, Larry Hagman, Joan Collins . . . Shelley Long, Ted Danson, and Roseanne Arnold.

With apologies to all of those people, and with a profound sense that television has been neglected, let us consider the case of James Garner. Garner has made a lot of movies; he has been nominated as best actor. Yet he is known for his presence on television—in the living room. I stress that domestic intimacy because it is one of Garner's strengths. Thus, his "series" have included the droll ads for Polaroid with Mariette Hartley, as well as *Maverick* (which ran from 1957–62) and *The Rockford Files* (which ran from 1974 to 1980). Approximately, for Garner, that was an hour a week for twenty-six weeks a year for ten years. That is the equivalent of well over one hundred movies—and if any actor could claim one hundred movies made with the wit, narrative speed, and good-natured ease of *Maverick* and *Rockford Files* he would be . . . Cary Grant?

So let us at least list the mere movies that Garner made, no matter that he could seldom muster the intensity to match the great screen actors: *The Girl He Left Behind* (56, David Butler); *Toward the Unknown* (56, Mervyn Le Roy); *Sayonara* (57, Joshua Logan); *Shoot Out at Medicine Bow* (57, Richard L. Bare); *Darby's Rangers* (58, William Wellman)—his first lead role; *Cash McCall* (59, Joseph Pevney); *Up Periscope* (59, Gordon Douglas); the male stooge in *The Children's Hour* (61, William Wyler); *Boys' Night Out* (62, Michael Gordon); *The Great Escape* (63, John Sturges); with Doris Day in *Move Over, Darling* (63, Gordon), which had been intended as the Monroe–Dean Martin *Something's Got to Give; The Thrill of It All* (63, Norman Jewison), with Doris Day again; and *The Wheeler Dealers* (63, Arthur Hiller).

The closest he came to true movie stardom was in the clever *36 Hours* (64, George Seaton); *The Americanization of Emily* (64, Hiller); *The Art of Love* (65, Jewison); *Mister Buddwing* (66, Delbert Mann); *Duel at Diablo* (66, Ralph Nelson); *Grand Prix* (66, John Frankenheimer); *A Man Could Get Killed* (66, Ronald Neame); as Wyatt Earp in *Hour of the Gun* (67, Sturges); *How Sweet It Is!* (68, Jerry Paris); *The Pink Jungle* (68, Mann); doing Raymond Chandler in *Marlowe* (69, Paul Bogart)—actually a model for Rockford; very funny in *Support Your Local Sheriff!* (69, Burt Kennedy); rather nasty in *A Man Called Sledge* (70, Vic Morrow); very good in *Skin Game* (71, Bogart); *Support Your Local Gunfighter* (71, Kennedy); *They Only Kill Their Masters* (72, James Goldstone); *One Little Indian* (73, Bernard McEveety); and *The Castaway Cowboy* (74, Vincent McEveety).

Too many of these films were like bad TV movies, so Garner settled for the very demanding *Rockford,* which eventually took its physical toll on him. But he won an Emmy in it in 1977 and became a beloved figure.

He has made only a few theatrical movies since then: *H.E.A.L.T.H.* (80, Robert Altman); *The Fan* (81, Edward Bianchi); very funny in *Victor/Victoria* (82, Blake Edwards); the very silly *Tank* (84, Marvin Chomsky); getting his nomination as the pharmacist in *Murphy's Romance* (85, Martin Ritt); as Wyatt Earp again in *Sunset* (88, Edwards); *Fire in the Sky* (93, Robert Lieberman); with Mel Gibson, in *Maverick* (94, Richard Donner).

But that is not all. He has become the actor and producer of prestigious TV movies: with Mary Tyler Moore in *Heartsounds* (84, Glenn Jordan); *Promise* (86, Jordan), in which he looks after a schizophrenic brother (James Woods); *My Name Is Bill W.* (89, Daniel Petrie), in which he and Woods form Alcoholics Anonymous; most spectacularly, in the satiric *Barbarians at the Gate* (92, Jordan), a project that made *Wall Street* seem slow and cautious; and *Breathing Lessons* (94, John Erman).

Garner's popularity is undimmed: with Jack

Lemmon as ex-presidents in *My Fellow Americans* (96, Peter Segal); *Dead Silence* (97, Petrie); *Twilight* (98, Robert Benton); *Legalese* (98, Jordan); *One Special Night* (99, Roger Young); as God in *God, the Devil and Bob* (00, Jeff DeGrandis and Dan Fausett); *Space Cowboys* (00, Clint Eastwood); *The Last Debate* (00, John Badham); *Roughing It* (01, Charles Martin Smith); on TV in *First Monday* (02, *Divine Secrets of the Ya-Ya Sisterhood* (02, Callie Khouri).

Tay Garnett (William Taylor Garnett) (1898–1977), b. Los Angeles
1928: *Celebrity; The Spieler.* 1929: *The Flying Fool; Oh Yeah!.* 1930: *Officer O'Brien; Her Man.* 1931: *Bad Company.* 1932: *One Way Passage; Okay America; Prestige.* 1933: *Destination Unknown; S.O.S. Iceberg* (codirected with Arnold Fanck). 1935: *China Seas; She Couldn't Take It; Professional Soldier.* 1937: *Slave Ship; Love Is News; Stand-In.* 1938: *Joy of Living; Trade Winds.* 1939: *Eternally Yours.* 1940: *Slightly Honorable; Seven Sinners.* 1941: *Cheers for Miss Bishop.* 1942: *My Favorite Spy.* 1943: *Bataan; The Cross of Lorraine.* 1944: *Mrs. Parkington.* 1945: *Valley of Decision.* 1946: *The Postman Always Rings Twice.* 1947: *Wild Harvest.* 1948: *A Connecticut Yankee in King Arthur's Court.* 1950: *The Fireball.* 1951: *Soldiers Three; Cause for Alarm.* 1952: *One Minute to Zero.* 1953: *Main Street to Broadway.* 1954: *The Black Knight.* 1956: *Seven Wonders of the World* (codirected). 1960: *A Terrible Beauty.* 1963: *Cattle King/Guns of Wyoming.* 1970: *The Delta Factor.*

A writer first, Garnett spent several years scripting and adapting: *Who's Your Friend* (25, Forrest K. Sheldon); *The Cruise of the Jasper B* (26, James W. Horne); *No Control* (27, Scott Sidney and E. J. Babille); *Rubber Tires* (27, Alan Hale); *Turkish Delight* (27, Paul Sloane); *White Gold* (27, William K. Howard); *The Wise Wife* (27, E. Mason Hopper); *The Cop* (28, Donald Crisp); *Power* (28, Howard Higgins); and *Skyscraper* (28, Higgins).

Garnett's early movies are his best: *Her Man* is a lost film with a great reputation, a version of "Frankie and Johnny" set in Havana; *One Way Passage* is a classic women's picture, with Kay Francis and William Powell deliriously sophisticated in forlorn romance, while *China Seas* benefits from a Jules Furthman script tossed back and forth by Gable and Harlow. But within two years, Garnett was landed instead with Tyrone Power and Loretta Young in *Love Is News. Stand-In* is a wordy comedy about Hollywood, and *Trade Winds* and *Eternally Yours* are far behind the earlier films. *Seven Sinners* has Dietrich and John Wayne uneasy with each other, and by the end of the war Garnett was producing routine, patriotic fodder, *Bataan,* and two Greer Garson pictures:

Mrs. Parkington and *Valley of Decision.* But *The Postman Always Rings Twice* begins as a sultry and moody melodrama with John Garfield and Lana Turner, and *Wild Harvest* is a good Alan Ladd adventure. After that, Garnett made an assortment of poor films and worked as a director in TV.

Greer Garson (1903–96), b. County Down, Northern Ireland
Having worked with some success in the English theatre, she was spotted by Louis B. Mayer, signed up, and given an impressive cameo debut in Sam Wood's *Goodbye, Mr. Chips* (39). After a poor comedy, *Remember* (40, Norman Z. McLeod), she embarked on a sequence of films in which she embodied qualities of ladylike appeal, uxorial and maternal loyalty, and above all (blowing back her stray curls) dutiful sacrifice that made her almost an Allied totem of the war years: badly miscast as Elizabeth Bennett in *Pride and Prejudice* (40, Robert Z. Leonard); *Blossoms in the Dust* (41, Mervyn Le Roy); *When Ladies Meet* (41, Leonard); phenomenally popular opposite Walter Pidgeon as *Mrs. Miniver* (42, William Wyler), a film that won her the best actress Oscar and conditioned American public opinion to the sentimental explanation for a necessary war; opposite Ronald Colman in *Random Harvest* (42, Le Roy); again with Pidgeon in one of the last old-fashioned biopics, *Madame Curie* (43, Le Roy); and in *Mrs. Parkington* (44, Tay Garnett). *Mrs. Miniver, Random Harvest,* and *Madame Curie*—her most characteristic work—were all produced by Sidney Franklin. She was a major star, nominated for the Oscar every year from 1941 to 1945.

Two more films sustained her, *The Valley of Decision* (45, Garnett) and *Adventure* (46, Victor Fleming), which was billed, "Gable's back, and Garson's got him." But with peace her popularity faded as suddenly as it had materialized. She had little innate talent other than the ability to gather a rather sedate gaiety to her bosom: she could easily seem like a duke's wife talking to peasants. After the war, she made several blighted attempts to broaden her range: *Desire Me* (47, Jack Conway and George Cukor); *Julia Misbehaves* (48, Conway); was more convincing as Irene in *That Forsyte Woman* (49, Compton Bennett); was mistakenly persuaded to reprise past successes in *The Miniver Story* (50, H. C. Potter). Her career at MGM petered away with *The Law and the Lady* (51, Edwin H. Knopf); *Scandal at Scourie* (53, Jean Negulesco); Calpurnia in Mankiewicz's *Julius Caesar* (53); and *Her Twelve Men* (54, Leonard). At that point she asked for her release, made *Strange Lady in Town* (55, Le Roy) at Warners, and then went back to the theatre. She made only three more films: as Eleanor Roosevelt in the disastrous *Sunrise at Campobello* (60, Vincent J.

Donohue); as a benign Mother Prioress in Henry Koster's *The Singing Nun* (65); and as Fred Mac-Murray's wife in the Disney *Happiest Millionaire* (67, Norman Tokar).

Vittorio Gassman (1922–2000),
b. Genoa, Italy

In the early 1950s, Gassman's conceited beauty brought him a Hollywood contract and marriage to Shelley Winters. Neither association lasted long. Indeed, any director might have shied away from pairing those two, anticipating the juicy smack of colliding hams. For Gassman has always been an outrageous monopolizer of films. To call him an overactor is to suggest a willful stepping on the gas. Whereas the swamping effusion seems quite natural and innocent. In drama, or in parts that exploited his posturing handsomeness, he was persistently overpowering. But in 1957, he acted in and directed with Francesco Rosi *Kean*, based on Sartre's study of the great English actor. The dissection in that play of histrionic manipulation may have taught Gassman to see the humor in acting, for afterwards he concentrated on comedy as well as his own stage company, the Teatro Popolare Italiano.

Although originally a stage actor, Gassman has worked regularly in films since the end of the war: *Preludio d'Amore* (46); *La Figlia del Capitano* (47, Mario Camerini); *Daniele Cortis* (47, Mario Soldati); *Bitter Rice* (49, Giuseppe De Santis); *Anna* (51, Alberto Lattuada); *Cry of the Hunted* (53, Joseph H. Lewis); *Sombrero* (53, Norman Foster); *Mambo* (54, Robert Rossen); *Rhapsody* (54, Charles Vidor); *La Donna Piu Bella del Mondo* (55, Robert Z. Leonard); *War and Peace* (56, King Vidor); *Tempest* (57, Lattuada); *I Soliti Ignoti* (57, Mario Monicelli); *Audace Colpi dei Soliti Ignoti* (59, Nanni Loy); *Il Mattatore* (59, Dino Risi); *La Grande Guerra* (60, Monicelli); *Il Giudizio Universale* (61, Vittorio de Sica); *La Marcia su Roma* (62, Risi); *Barabbas* (62, Richard Fleischer); *Il Sorpasso* (62, Risi); *Frenesia dell'Estate* (63, Luigi Zampa); *I Mostri* (63, Risi); *Il Gaucho* (64, Risi); *L'Armata Brancaleone* (65, Monicelli); *Questi Fantasmi* (67, Renato Castellani); *Il Tigre* (67, Risi); *Il Profeta* (67, Risi); *Woman Times Seven* (67, de Sica); *Contestazione Generale* (70, Zampa); *In Nome del Popolo Italiano* (71, Risi); *Brancaleone alle Croziate* (71, Monicelli); *Che c'Entriamo noi con la Rivoluzione?* (73, Sergio Corbucci); *Tosca* (73, Luigi Magni); *Profumo di Donna* (74, Risi); *Riva Italia* (78, Risi); excellent as the waiter in high places in *A Wedding* (78, Robert Altman); and *Quintet* (79, Altman).

Gassman remained very active in fields not easy to observe: *The Immortal Bachelor* (79, Marcello Fondato); *The Nude Bomb* (79, Clive Donner); *Sono Fotogenico* (80, Risi); *La Terrazza* (80, Ettore Scola); *Sharky's Machine* (81, Burt Reynolds); *Camera D'Albergo* (81, Monicelli); *Tempest* (82, Paul Mazursky); *De Padre in Figlio* (82, which he directed with his son Alessandro); *Il Conte Tacchia* (81, Corbucci); *La Vie est un Roman* (83, Alain Resnais); *Benvenuta* (83, André Delvaux); *Le Pouvoir du Mal* (85, Kryzstof Zanussi); *I Solitia Ignoti—20 Anni Doppo* (86, Amanzio Todini); *La Famiglia* (87, Scola); *I Picari* (87, Monicelli); *Di Menticare Palermo* (90, Francesco Rosi); and *Sheherezade* (90, Philippe de Broca).

Any Italian will tell you that to appreciate Gassman you had to behold him on stage. But, till the end, he gave his presence to the movies, too: *I Divertimenti della Vita Privata* (90, Cristina Comencini); *Rossini! Rossini!* (91, Monicelli); *El Largo Invierno* (91, Jaime Camino); *Tolgo il Disturbo* (92, Risi); *Quando Eravamo Repressi* (92, Dino Quartullo); *Abraham* (94, Joseph Sargent); *Tutti gli Anni una Volta l'Anno* (94, Gianfrancesco Lazotti); splendid and saturnine in *Sleepers* (96, Barry Levinson); *Deserto di Fuoco* (97, Enzo G. Castellari); *La Cena* (98, Scola); *La Bomba* (99, Giulio Base).

Janet Gaynor (Laura Gainor) (1906–84),
b. Philadelphia

Having worked four years as an extra, she won parts in two-reel Westerns. Fox put her in her first full-length movie, *The Johnstown Flood* (26, Irving Cummings), and signed her up. She had an impressive wide-eyed appeal in *The Blue Eagle* (26, John Ford), *The Midnight Kiss* (26, Cummings), *The Shamrock Handicap* (26, Ford), and *The Return of Peter Grimm* (26, Victor Schertzinger); and she rose to eminence in three films that won her the first best actress Oscar: *Seventh Heaven* (27, Frank Borzage), as a tart brought to pure love by Charles Farrell; *Street Angel* (28, Borzage), again with Farrell; F. W. Murnau's *Sunrise* (27)—a glorious performance of humility and sacrifice in one of the silent cinema's masterpieces.

For a moment, she was a huge star, the nation's waif. Fox, in the person of Winfield Sheehan, adored her—as did cinema audiences, especially when she was teamed with Farrell. In 1929 she made *Christina* (William K. Howard); *Four Devils* (Murnau); *Lucky Star* (Borzage), with Farrell; her first sound picture, *Sunny Side Up* (David Butler). She was by now established as an innocent victim —a character enhanced by her wholesome beauty and saucer eyes. But after *High Society Blues* (30, Butler), she quarreled with Fox, was suspended, and returned, humiliated, as a drug addict in *The Man Who Came Back* (31, Raoul Walsh). Contrite, she settled back into "sweetheart" roles: *Daddy Long Legs* (31, Alfred Santell); *Merely Mary Ann* (31, Henry King); *Delicious* (31, Butler); *Tess of the Storm Country* (32, Santell); and

The First Year (32, Howard). Fox put her in *State Fair* (33, King) with Will Rogers. She then made *Adorable* (33, William Dieterle); *Carolina* (34, King); *Change of Heart* (34, John Blystone); *Servant's Entrance* (34, Frank Lloyd); *One More Spring* (35, King); and *The Farmer Takes a Wife* (35, Victor Fleming), opposite Henry Fonda.

The studio now had little time for her, and she made *Small Town Girl* (36, William Wellman) at MGM before joining Selznick for *A Star Is Born* (37, Wellman), where she felt too old for the ingenue. She is the emotional engine of that film, but time has been kinder to Fredric March's elegant despair. She was also in *The Young in Heart* (38, Richard Wallace). After *Three Loves Has Nancy* (38, Richard Thorpe) at MGM, she retired. Perhaps she had waited for a flourish, sensing that she was more happily a silent screen actress, too demure and loyal for the 1930s. The retirement was broken, for no clear reason, in 1957, when she appeared as Pat Boone's mother in *Bernardine* (Henry Levin).

In 1939, she married the clothes designer Adrian—but stories abound now about her feelings for Mary Martin.

Ben Gazzara (Biago Anthony Gazzara), b. New York, 1930

The son of Sicilian immigrants, he spoke Italian as his first language. In 1948 he was awarded a drama scholarship and in 1951 he joined the Actors' Studio, where he stayed three years, attracting special attention as Jocko de Paris in the Studio production of *End as a Man,* a role he repeated for his film debut in 1957. On the stage, he also starred in *A Hatful of Rain* and *Cat on a Hot Tin Roof.* His movies have not fulfilled the promise of stored-up hostility so casually implied in *End as a Man* (57, Jack Garfein). It remains an open question as to whether he is a remarkable actor or simply a glowering ham. Characteristically, Preminger emphasized this very ambiguity in *Anatomy of a Murder* (59). After that, amid much work for TV, he has made only a few, insignificant films: *The Young Doctors* (61, Phil Karlson); *La Citta Prigioniera* (62, Joseph Anthony); *Reprieve* (62, Millard Kaufman); *A Rage to Live* (65, Walter Grauman); *The Bridge at Remagen* (69, John Guillermin); as one of the central trio in John Cassavetes's *Husbands* (70); and *The Neptune Factor* (73, Daniel Petrie). The question at the end of *Anatomy* remains attached to Gazzara. Nor is it settled by the florid *Capone* (75, Steve Carver), tamer than de Paris. He was the strip-club operator in *The Killing of a Chinese Bookie* (76, Cassavetes); in *Opening Night* (77, Cassavetes); secondhand Rick in *Saint Jack* (79, Peter Bogdanovich); and in *Bloodline* (79, Terence Young).

Since then, he has become an actor who moves easily between Italy and America: *Inchon* (81, Young); *They All Laughed* (81, Bogdanovich); *Tales of Ordinary Madness* (81, Marco Ferreri); as the cop in the Budd Schulberg–scripted *A Question of Honor* (82, Jud Taylor) for TV; *La Ragazza di Trieste* (82, Pasquale Festa Campanile); *Uno Scandalo Perbene* (84, Campanile); *La Donna delle Meraviglie* (85, Alberto Bevilacqua); *Figlio Mio Infinitamente Caro* (85, Valentino Orsini); *A Letter to Three Wives* (85, Larry Elikann); *Il Comorrista* (86, Giuseppe Tornatore); as the father in *An Early Frost* (86, John Erman) on TV; *Downpayment on Murder* (87, Waris Hussein); *Police Story: The Freeway Killings* (87, William A. Graham); *Quicker than the Eye* (88, Nicolas Gessner); and *Road House* (89, Rowdy Herrington). In 1990, he acted in and directed *Oltre l'Oceano.*

In the nineties, Gazzara made a movie called *Too Tired to Die* (98, Wonsuk Chin)—one of those titles that reflects on a career. Gazzara was nearly a star once, a figure of promise on stage and screen. Yet he has been reduced to working constantly in small roles in pictures hardly seen or heard of by the people he meets. The glamour of acting: *Blindsided* (93, Thomas Michael Donnelly); as Joe Bonanno in *Love, Honor & Obey* (93, John Patterson); *Fatal Vows: The Alexander O'Hara Story* (94, John Power); *Hirondelles ne Meurent pas à Jerusalem* (94, Ridha Behi); *The Zone* (95, Barry Zetlin); *Banditi* (95, Stefano Mignucci); *Shadow Conspiracy* (97, George P. Cosmatos); *The Spanish Prisoner* (97, David Mamet); *Vicious Circles* (97, Alexander Whitelaw); *Buffalo '66* (98, Vincent Gallo); *The Big Lebowski* (98, Joel Coen); *Happiness* (98, Todd Solondz); *Illuminata* (98, John Turturro); *Summer of Sam* (99, Spike Lee); *The Thomas Crown Affair* (99, John McTiernan); *Very Mean Men* (00, Tony Vitale); *The List* (00, Sylvain Guy); *Home Sweet Hoboken* (00, Yoshifumi Hosoya).

He was in *Believe* (00, Robert Tinnell); *Brian's Song* (01, John Gray); *Hysterical Blindness* (02, Mira Nair); *Dogville* (03, Lars von Trier); *The Shore* (03, Denis Adam Zervos).

Daniel Gélin (1921–2002), b. Angers, France

Gélin has invariably appeared as a sophisticated, literate, and sensitive man, especially suited to articulate inquirers into their own emotions. Born a little later, he might easily have played one of the men in Eric Rohmer's *contes moraux.* But doubtless his young man in *La Ronde* (50, Max Ophuls), who goes to bed with Danielle Darrieux but cannot quite, and recollects Stendhal's *De l'Amour,* was a moment from cinema that influenced Rohmer. Gélin has published poetry and directed one film himself, *Les Dents Longues* (53).

He played small parts during the war and only took on large roles in the late 1940s: *Premier Rendez-Vous* (41, Henri Decoin); *Martin Rouma-*

gnac (46, Georges Lacombe); *Rendez-Vous de Juillet* (49, Jacques Becker); *Edouard et Caroline* (51, Becker); *Les Mains Sales* (51, Fernand Rivers); as the painter in the "Modèle" episode from *Le Plaisir* (52, Ophuls); *La Minute de Vérité* (52, Jean Delannoy); *Rue de l'Estrapade* (53, Becker); *Sang et Lumières* (53, Georges Rouquier); *Si Versailles M'Était Conté* (53, Sacha Guitry); *L'Affaire Maurizius* (54, Julien Duvivier); *La Romana* (54, Luigi Zampa); *Napoléon* (55, Guitry); *Les Amants du Tage* (55, Henri Verneuil); as the dying man whose whispers ensure that James Stewart is *The Man Who Knew Too Much* (55, Alfred Hitchcock); *Mamzelle Striptease* (56, Marc Allégret); *Mort en Fraude* (57, Marcel Camus); *Retour de Mainivelle* (57, Denys de la Patellière); *La Fille de Hambourg* (58, Yves Allégret); *Charmants Garçons* (58, Decoin); *Cartagine in Fiamme* (59, Carmine Gallone); *Le Testament d'Orphée* (60, Jean Cocteau); *La Proie pour l'Ombre* (60, Alexandre Astruc); *Austerlitz* (60, Abel Gance and Roger Richebé); *La Morte-Saison des Amours* (61, Pierre Kast); *Climats* (62, Stellio Lorenzi); *Les Vacances Portugaises* (63, Kast); *La Bonne Soupé* (64, Robert Thomas); *The Sleeping Car Murders* (65, Costa-Gavras); *Is Paris Burning?* (66, René Clément); *Soleil Noir* (66, de la Patellière); *La Ligne de Demarcation* (66, Claude Chabrol); *La Trêve* (68, Claude Guillemot); *Détruire, Dit-Elle* (69, Marguerite Duras); *Dearest Love* (71, Louis Malle); and *Pardon Mon Affaire, Too* (77, Yves Robert).

More recently, he has been in *Nous Irons Tous au Paradis* (77, Robert); *L'Honorable Société* (78, Anielle Weinberger); *La Nuit de Varennes* (82, Ettore Scola); *Les Enfants* (85, Duras); and *Mister Frost* (90, Philip Setbon).

He is the father of actress Maria Schneider, by his own marriage to actress Danielle Delorme.

In his seventies, Gélin still worked very hard: *Mauvaise Fille* (90, Regis Franc); as the Shah in *L'Amérique en Otage* (91, Kevin Connor); *Un Type Bien* (91, Laurent Benegui); *Crimes et Jardins* (91, Jean-Paul Salome); *Les Marmottes* (93, Elie Chouraqui); *Roulez Jeunesse!* (93, Jacques Fansten); *Warrior Spirit* (94, Rene Manzor); *Maigret et la Vente à la Bougie* (94, Pierre Granier-Deferre); with Daniel Delorme in the TV series *Madame le Proviseur* (94, Sebastien Grall and Alice Vandelen); *Fugueuses* (95, Nadine Trintignant); *Fantôme avec Chauffeur* (96, Gerard Oury); *Hommes, Femmes, Mode d'Emploi* (96, Claude Lelouch); *Obsession* (97, Peter Sehr); *Une Femme d'Action* (97, Didier Albert); *Les Marmottes* (98, Jean-Denis Robert and Daniel Vigne).

Sergei Gerasimov (1906–85),
b. Zlatoust, Russia
1930: *Dvadtsat Dva Neschastya/Twenty-two Misfortunes* (codirected with C. Bartenev). 1932: *Serdtsye Solomona/The Heart of Solomon* (codi-

rected with M. Kressin). 1934: *Lyubliyu li Tebya/Do I Love You?*. 1936: *Semero Smelykh/Seven Brave Men*. 1938: *Komsomolsk*. 1939: *Uchitel/The Teacher*. 1941: *Maskarad/Masquerade*. 1943: *Nepobedimye/The Invincibles* (codirected with Mikhail Kalatozov). 1944: *Bolshaya Zemlya/The Big Land*. 1948: *Molodaya Gvardiya/The Young Guard* (in two parts). 1952: *Osvobozhdennyi Kitai/China Liberated; Selskii Vrach/The Country Doctor*. 1955: *Nadezhda*. 1956: an episode from *Die Vind Rose*. 1958: *Tikhii Don/Quiet Flows the Don* (in two parts). 1962: *Lyudi i Zveri/Men and Beasts* (in two parts). 1967: *Zhurnalist/The Journalist*. 1970: *U Ozera/By the Lake*. 1984: *Leo Tolstoy*.

Gerasimov was one of those sleepy animals in the Soviet zoo—Wild once? Who knows? But inured to captivity and regarding it as a natural state. In 1969, he was interviewed for *Film* and gave this unprincipled statement of the necessary alertness in the artist/bureaucrat in Russia:

> Being a convinced dialectician, I believe that life is developing towards a synthesis. It is inevitable that the old will die out and be replaced by the new. I am convinced we can influence people's consciousness by creative activity such as films but only by the dialectic. . . . We should affirm the need to fight the old and welcome the new . . . but this doesn't mean that within a year I wouldn't criticize what I've just said, because the world is always changing.

The potential for sudden change inflicted on society from above had for years overawed the creative spirit in Russia. How essential it was for a Gerasimov to be ready to jump in newly perceived directions. In 1947, for instance, while he was directing the first part of it, *The Young Guard* was revealed to be based on unviable notions. But dialectic found a way, and Gerasimov went back on his tracks, expunging the unworthy.

He had the credentials that admit a Soviet artist to high office. Originally an actor with the Factory for Eccentric Actors, he only began directing in the 1930s, attempting whenever possible "to show a piece of life"—"I'm sure no artist should close his eyes to life because he'll miss the most important things and because any self-appraising, withdrawing into oneself is the beginning of the end in art, the end of communication. The force of the artist is his ability to express his opinion about life which is common to everybody and therefore understandable to everybody."

Anybody, I think, could see that *Quiet Flows the Don* is flatulent melodrama dressed up as if it were Tolstoy and filmed without taste, talent, or a sense of the moment. One had only to recollect that Russian art was also represented by Nabokov to realize that the leaden handicaps to Russian cinema had kept it as yet from the main event. Gerasimov was also in charge of acting and directing at the Soviet Institute of Cinematography and a member of the State Committee for Film.

Richard Gere,
b. Philadelphia, 1949

There are times when Richard Gere has the warm affect of a wind tunnel at dawn, waiting for work, all sheen, inner curve, and posed emptiness. And those are not his worst times. Indeed, the rather grimly passive beauty of Gere is his greatest asset; it is what made his confrontation with the folded designer shirts in *American Gigolo* (80, Paul Schrader) one of the great movie moments of a man looking in a mirror. Even in *Pretty Woman* (90, Garry Marshall), it was Gere's subtlest trick (he can be a nearly motionless thief of scenes) to seem, in spirit, prettier than even Julia Roberts, more dedicated to the hope of some unruffled aestheticism. Only Alain Delon has been this way before, and it makes one realize that Gere was born to play Patricia Highsmith's Ripley.

He has been in enough bad films to make one think his career was drawing to a close, to reveal the limits of his self-love, and to warn us that his most active, spontaneous outbursts of behavior are sometimes as calculated as dance. He *is* generally more interesting when doing less. But there have been sufficient occasions in which he has been unique to hold the attention. He is matured now; he is a good learner and capable of surprise, especially when encouraged to be sinister. He cannot relax; he seems afraid to let humor mar a superior sense of wit; but he has a whim of ineffable, albeit ridiculous grace.

He was raised in upstate New York, from which he went to the University of Massachusetts (in 1967) to study philosophy and film. Then he wandered, as an actor, from Provincetown, to Seattle, to New York, and to London. He would play Danny Zuko on Broadway in *Grease,* and a few years later he was very impressive in Sam Shepard's *Killer's Head* and in Martin Sherman's *Bent.*

He had small roles in *Report to the Commissioner* (75, Milton Katselas); on TV in *Strike Force* (75, Barry Shear); and in *Baby Blue Marine* (76, John Hancock). But he grabbed attention as Diane Keaton's most flamboyant and seemingly dangerous pickup in *Looking for Mr. Goodbar* (77, Richard Brooks). Gere's "Tony" was really an extended audition piece—riveting but rootless—and it promised a Brando-like physicality that was actually anathema to Gere's removed watchfulness.

For a few years, he was a hot actor: good in *Bloodbrothers* (78, Robert Mulligan); one of the photographed surfaces in *Days of Heaven* (78, Terrence Malick), not so much an actor as a model; passably ordinary in *Yanks* (79, John Schlesinger); and so vital to *American Gigolo* that it is easy to forget he was a late replacement for John Travolta. Travolta may have seen how easily he could be exposed in a precarious balance between modishness and pretension. Gere seems to have known Julian Kaye, and felt the acid poetry in the film's view of Los Angeles. It is Schrader's vision (and an important film), but Gere made it recognizable for a large audience, and introduced moral enervation as a theme in our movies. Seen again, *Gigolo* is oddly quietist, stoic, and resigned; there was already a hint of Oriental mind-set.

An Officer and a Gentleman (82, Taylor Hackford) was a much bigger hit, a mainstream film about a man eager to explain himself and find resolution. It was not Gere's territory, and if the love scenes with Debra Winger had some heat, still the actress let it be known that Gere was off in his own head. He has never been an easy interacter in love scenes.

As soon as he was made, the luck ran out. *Breathless* (83, Jim McBride) was a flop. Yet it is Gere's most adventurous work, his funniest and least guarded. Of course, the project was a remake of a pastiche, so no one could make claims on human nature. Still, Gere was startlingly kinetic, and he really goosed his staid leading lady.

Decline followed: *Beyond the Limit* (83, John Mackenzie), a shot at Graham Greene's *The Honorary Consul;* the chaotic *Cotton Club* (84, Francis Ford Coppola), in which Gere played some trumpet and did some music while trying to hold the picture together; *King David* (85, Bruce Beresford); trying to be like Eastwood in *No Mercy* (86, Richard Pearce); *Power* (86, Sidney Lumet); and *Miles from Home* (88, Gary Sinise).

All of a sudden, in *Internal Affairs* (90, Mike Figgis) he delivered a smiling reptile, a cop who treated the LAPD as a talent agency. He was brilliant in a modest film, just as he did a great deal to steer *Pretty Woman* past its most lunatic and offensive holes.

He was by then a man of the world, somehow a fashion plate of meditation, with the Dalai Lama on one arm and Cindy Crawford on the other. He appeared in *Rhapsody in August* (90, Akira Kurosawa), and was then reunited with pulp romance and Kim Basinger in the loony *Final Analysis* (91, Phil Joanou). He was the man returned from war in *Sommersby* (93, Jon Amiel), even if he had no idea how to live in the nineteenth century. He had a small role that helped to launch *And the Band Played On* (93, Roger Spottiswoode), and he worked for Figgis again in *Mr. Jones* (93); he made *Intersection* (94, Mark Rydell).

Gere eased up somewhat in the nineties. His marriage to model Cindy Crawford ended, but he was a valiant defender of the Dalai Lama and other causes. He was Lancelot in *First Knight* (95, Jerry Zucker); in *Primal Fear* (96, Gregory Hoblit), where newcomer Edward Norton ran rings around him; *Red Corner* (97, Jon Avnet)—certainly not pro-Chinese; "Irish" in *The Jackal* (97, Michael Caton-Jones); reunited with Julia in *Runaway Bride* (99, Garry Marshall); *Autumn in New York* (00, Joan Chen), where he and Winona Ryder hardly connected; at his glossy worst in *Dr. T & the Women* (00, Robert Altman).

Then he bounced back with *The Mothman Prophecies* (02, Mark Pellington), as the husband in *Unfaithful* (02, Adrian Lyne) and the lawyer in *Chicago* (02, Rob Marshall).

Mel (not Melvin) Gibson,
b. Peekskill, New York, 1956

One of eleven children, Gibson was the son of a railroad brakeman and an Australian opera singer. But on both sides of the family the roots were Irish Catholic (St. Mel was an Irish saint). The actor, however, has excelled as a roughhouser with an irreverent sense of humor. Gibson does look as if he came from the wrong side of the tracks, a quality that few American actors now hope to muster. They look like the product of health insurance, good diets, and tender loving care, no matter the stories of broken homes and hard times. There is a wildness in Gibson's eyes—a feeling of dangerous farce. Maybe it is Peekskill, or the Australian upbringing, for Gibson's family went to that country when he was twelve. Maybe it is just Mel. Whatever the answer, it would be pretty to think that some role could capture the demon better than a bagful of *Lethal Weapons* and *Hamlet*. Mel could end up rich and depressed. He's better than cop capers, but he was woefully lost as the Dane. If only there were screwball comedies in anyone's mind—imagine Gibson trying *It Happened One Night* or *The Miracle of Morgan's Creek*.

In Sydney, he attended the National Institute of Dramatic Art and as a lad he even played Romeo to Judy Davis's Juliet—imagine them together in *It Happened One Night!* He made his debut in *Summer City* (76, Christopher Fraser), as the shy one in a surfing gang. But George Miller cast him as the altogether rugged Max Rockatansky in the best material Gibson ever had: *Mad Max* (79), *The Road Warrior* (81), and *Mad Max Beyond Thunderdome* (85). He did well as a retarded man in *Tim* (79, Michael Pate), and he was in *Attack Force Z* (81, Tim Burstall). But it was Peter Weir's *Gallipoli* (81) that drew him to Hollywood's attention as a romantic hero.

He worked for Weir again in *The Year of Living Dangerously* (83) and he brushed against the legend of Gable playing Fletcher Christian in the staid *The Bounty* (84, Roger Donaldson). His best work yet as an actor is in *Mrs. Soffel* (84, Gillian Armstrong), a role that used his recklessness and

in which he wooed and warmed Diane Keaton beyond mannerism. *The River* (84, Mark Rydell) was dull and *Tequila Sunrise* (88, Robert Towne), a major disappointment.

By then, Gibson was into *Lethal Weapon* and its sequels (87, 89, 92) with Danny Glover and Richard Donner—the movie equivalent of college football on January 1. He did his *Hamlet* (90, Franco Zeffirelli), but otherwise he has wandered into such dingbat fare as Goldie Hawn's male equivalent in *Bird on a Wire* (90, John Badham), an alleged pirate of disenchantment in the very corny *Air America* (90, Roger Spottiswoode), and *Forever Young* (92, Steve Miner). It might have been better if Goldie had done Ophelia (with Judy Davis as Gertrude) in a *Hamlet* directed by John Cleese.

In 1993, he acted in and directed *The Man Without a Face*, a respectable, diligent weepie about kids and parents. He also played *Maverick* (94, Donner).

But he was preparing for a grand venture, and it turned out to be *Braveheart* (95, Gibson), the tale of Scots rebel, William Wallace. The film won more Oscars than was decent (including best picture and best director—a sign that the definition of directing had shifted ground towards producing). It didn't deserve Oscars, but it is a rousing old-fashioned adventure film with a lovely princess and a wicked king (Sophie Marceau and Patrick McGoohan) and a great deal of blood and lost limbs. It is also a pretty accurate portrait of Gibson's ultra-naïve politics.

He was the voice of John Smith in *Pocahontas* (95, Mike Gabriel and Eric Goldberg); *Ransom* (96, Ron Howard); rather bad in *Conspiracy Theory* (97, Donner); *Lethal Weapon 4* (98, Donner); trying to do Lee Marvin in *Payback* (99, Brian Helgeland); very odd in *The Million Dollar Hotel* (00, Wim Wenders); a voice in *Chicken Run* (00, Peter Lord and Nick Park); taking on the English as enemy again in *The Patriot* (00, Roland Emmerich): funny, if too self-congratulatory in *What Women Want* (00, Nancy Meyers); and very pro–U.S. army in *We Were Soldiers* (02, Randall Wallace); *Signs* (02, M. Night Shyamalan).

He has produced and acted in *The Singing Detective* (03, Keith Gordon), and he will direct and produce *The Passion* (04)—the big one, alas.

Sir John Gielgud (1904–2000), b. London

For decades, Gielgud regarded the movies with airy, tolerant amusement. He was not interested, or reached: pictures could not compete with theatre in catering to his divinely permitted talent. In a film, he was like a bishop at the seaside, rolling up his trousers and giggling but certain that the whole thing was frivolous. He made movies if asked, perplexed at the art's fragmentation, the peculiar way of working, and the vulgarity of the money. There were often years between his movies: *Who Is the Man?* (24, Walter Summers); *The Clue of the New Pin* (29, Arthur Maude); *Insult* (32, Harry Lachman); very good as Inigo Jollifant in *The Good Companions* (33, Victor Saville); intriguingly matched with Peter Lorre in *The Secret Agent* (36, Alfred Hitchcock); Disraeli in *The Prime Minister* (42, Thorold Dickinson).

Then nothing for over ten years until his seething, lean, and hungry Cassius in *Julius Caesar* (53, Joseph L. Mankiewicz)—on which he mailed in speech tracks for looping that exactly fitted his camera performance; Clarence in *Richard III* (55, Laurence Olivier); a choleric Barrett in *The Barretts of Wimpole Street* (57, Sidney Franklin)—but with Jennifer Jones as his daughter?

By 1960, therefore, Gielgud had just this mixed bag of slightly absentminded performances. Whereas, his contemporaries had been *in* films, immersed, finding themselves: Olivier had his Shakespeares and *Rebecca;* Richardson had done *The Fallen Idol* and *The Heiress;* Redgrave could claim *Dead of Night* and *The Browning Version;* Alec Guinness was a shy genius in movies.

So Gielgud carried on regardless: he was properly cold and urbane as Warwick in *Saint Joan* (57, Otto Preminger); *Becket* (64, Peter Glenville); *The Loved One* (65, Tony Richardson); a lonely Henry IV in *Chimes at Midnight* (66, Orson Welles); the Head of Intelligence in *Sebastian* (67, David Greene); Lord Raglan in *The Charge of the Light Brigade* (68, Richardson); *Assignment to Kill* (68, Sheldon Reynolds); as the Pope who dies in *The Shoes of the Fisherman* (68, Michael Anderson); as Count Berchtold in *Oh! What a Lovely War* (69, Richard Attenborough); as *Julius Caesar* himself (70, Stuart Burge); the mandarin in *Lost Horizon* (72, Charles Jarrott); *Galileo* (74, Joseph Losey); *Aces High* (76, Jack Gold); the preacher in *A Portrait of the Artist as a Young Man* (77, Joseph Strick).

Then came the miracle: in 1977, he came upon David Mercer's script and played the radiant, racked novelist in *Providence* (77, Alain Resnais). Mortal pain and helpless creation worked together like the instruments in a double concerto—and Gielgud looked like a man in a trap, not just an actor on holiday.

Did he then appreciate that real work could be done in film? Did that confidence foster his urge for senior-citizen security? Whatever, he plunged into film with magnificent, indiscriminate zest. Like notorious starlets, he will do anything now to get in a picture: *Les Misérables* (78, Glenn Jordan) on TV; *The Human Factor* (79, Preminger); *The Conductor* (79, Andrzej Wajda); *Caligula* (80, Tinto Brass); the surgeon, Carr Gomm, in *The Elephant Man* (80, David Lynch); *The Formula* (80, John G. Avildsen); *Lion of the Desert* (80, Moustapha Akkad); as Charles Ryder's dry father

in *Brideshead Revisited* (81, Charles Sturridge); *Sphinx* (81, Franklin J. Schaffner); winning the supporting actor Oscar as the butler in *Arthur* (81, Steve Gordon); *Chariots of Fire* (81, Hugh Hudson); on TV in *The Hunchback of Notre Dame* (82, Michael Tuchner); *Inside the Third Reich* (82, Marvin J. Chomsky); Lord Irwin in *Gandhi* (82, Attenborough); *The Scarlet and the Black* (83, Jerry London) on TV; *Wagner* (83, Tony Palmer); *Invitation to the Wedding* (83, Joseph Brooks); *The Wicked Lady* (83, Michael Winner); *The Master of Ballantrae* (84, Douglas Hickox); *Scandalous* (84, Rob Cohen); *Camille* (84, Desmond Davis); *The Shooting Party* (84, Alan Bridges); *Leave All Fair* (85, John Raid); as the ambassador with a little knowledge of Ingmar Bergman in *Plenty* (85, Fred Schepisi); *Time After Time* (85, Bill Hays); *Romance on the Orient Express* (85, Lawrence Gordon Clark); *The Whistle Blower* (86, Simon Langton); *Appointment with Death* (88, Michael Winner); *A Man for All Seasons* (88, Charlton Heston) as Wolsey; *Arthur 2: On the Rocks* (88, Bud Yorkin); *Getting It Right* (89, Randal Kleiser); *Strike It Rich* (90, James Scott); realizing a dream in doing *The Tempest* on film in *Prospero's Books* (91, Peter Greenaway), and then realizing he hadn't seen enough Greenaway films; and *Shining Through* (91, David Seltzer).

He exited as only he could, in a flurry of work, all fun, some of it distinguished: *The Power of One* (92, Avildsen); as Sydney Cockerell in *The Best of Friends* (94, Alvin Rakoff); *First Knight* (95, Jerry Zucker); *Haunted* (95, Lewis Gilbert); as the Professor of Sunlight in *Gulliver's Travels* (96, Sturridge); *Looking for Richard* (96, Al Pacino); as the teacher in *Shine* (96, Scott Hicks); as Priam in *Hamlet* (96, Kenneth Branagh); as Touchett, superb in death, in *The Portrait of a Lady* (96, Jane Campion); *A Dance to the Music of Time* (97, Rakoff and Christopher Morahan); King Constant in *Merlin* (98, Steve Barron); the voice of Merlin for *Quest for Camelot* (98, Frederik Du Chau); as the pope in *Elizabeth* (98, Shekhar Kapur); *The Tichborne Claimant* (98, David Yates); *Catastrophe* (00, David Mamet).

John Gilbert (John Pringle) (1895–1936), b. Logan, Utah

Gilbert is one of the notorious instances of Hollywood stars destroyed or rejected by the system. But it is hard to view him with much sympathy. He seems more like a dinosaur in film history, an extravagant creature hobbled by evolution.

In Gilbert's case, sound was his ostensible crisis. And yet the details of why he declined from a great star to a has-been within a few years are still not clear. The general version is that his voice was inappropriate to his handsomeness. But he did make sound films. Perhaps it is more to the point to ask whether he was really handsome. Or were his looks not too staring and brooding, too carried away by the *thought* of handsomeness? Others say that MGM planned his downfall, driven beyond endurance by his posturing, the endless problems of handling him, and the vast salaries he demanded ($250,000 a picture).

Probably both factors played their part. His voice was prim, and the studio made little effort to avert or cushion his humiliation. But Gilbert's central difficulty had less to do with voice production or bad relations with the studio than with the conception of himself as an actor that he had acquired. For he was committed to emotional grandeur and to the conviction that he needed to lose himself in his part. King Vidor has recalled the way Gilbert liked romantic music played while he acted, and preferred never to read a script. He carried his parts home with him and attempted to bathe his private life in their warmth. As Vidor puts it: "John Gilbert was an impressionable fellow, not too well established in a role of his own in life. The paths he followed in his daily life were greatly influenced by the parts that some scriptwriter had written for him. When he began to read the publicity emanating from his studio which dubbed him the 'Great Lover,' his behavior in real life began to change accordingly."

Vidor directed five of Gilbert's most successful silent pictures, and knew him socially. He made this comment on why the actor failed to survive sound: "Jack's speaking voice on the sound track was a problem, but I don't think it was a question of tone or quality. The literal content of his scenes, which in silent films had been imagined, was too intense to be put into spoken words." That is a charitable way of saying that Gilbert had always been a coarse actor. The wonder is that he flourished in the silent era, for it is hard to see how his playing can ever have been thought other than it seems now—blatant, monotonous, and unappealing. Gilbert defines ham by seeming oblivious of his own excessiveness. Sound may have exposed that ignorance, but it always marred Gilbert as an actor.

When Garbo came to Metro, Gilbert was designated as her screen lover. The two actors then fell in love—or in that heady sex that is infected by endless takes—and the studio played up the romance to help the pictures. This was not a kindness. Garbo was capricious, and Gilbert was insecure. There was a famous "wedding" in 1926 when Garbo left Gilbert at the altar. The facts are now buried in legend, but some say Louis B. Mayer nudged the actor and said, why worry, you can always fuck her. Gilbert went berserk. He attacked Mayer and turned dislike into enmity. At the heart of it all, he had been laughed at in public, the great lover humiliated.

Gilbert was educated at military academies and had a variety of jobs before he joined Thomas Ince

to play bit parts. He struggled for several years, and was sacked by Ince. It was Maurice Tourneur who rediscovered him in 1919 and engaged him as writer and assistant as well as actor. Gilbert was in *The White Heather* (19, Tourneur), *The Great Redeemer* (20, Clarence Brown), *The White Circle* (20, Tourneur), and *Deep Waters* (21, Tourneur), and he was put under contract by Fox. Still less than a star, he made a number of dull films, directed by Jack Dillon and Jerome Storm. He won more acclaim for *Monte Cristo* (22, Emmett J. Flynn), *Cameo Kirby* (23, John Ford), *While Paris Sleeps*, a Tourneur film shot years before but only released in 1923, and *The Wolf Man* (24, Edmund Mortimer).

But it was only at MGM that Gilbert reached his brief eminence: *He Who Gets Slapped* (24, Victor Sjostrom); *His Hour* (24, Vidor); *The Snob* (24, Monta Bell); *Wife of the Centaur* (24, Vidor); a big hit in *The Big Parade* (25, Vidor); *The Merry Widow* (25, Erich von Stroheim); *La Bohème* (26, Vidor); and *Bardelys the Magnificent* (26, Vidor). This was his triumphant period, perhaps because he was best displayed by the romantic exuberance of Vidor.

His second period at MGM was still successful, but he was increasingly shown up by the detailed reticence of his costar, Greta Garbo, in *Flesh and the Devil* (26, Clarence Brown); *Love* (27, Edmund Goulding); and *A Woman of Affairs* (28, Brown). She dominated their very potent love scenes—she was the center of attention. In addition, he made *Man, Woman and Sin* (27, Bell), with Jeanne Eagels; *The Show* (27, Tod Browning) and *The Cossacks* (28, George Hill and Brown), with Renée Adorée; two films with Joan Crawford: *Twelve Miles Out* (27, Jack Conway) and *Four Walls* (28, William Nigh).

By 1929, he was compelled to speak on film. His debut was disastrous—as Romeo to Norma Shearer's Juliet in the balcony scene cameo from *Hollywood Revue of 1929* (29, Charles Reisner). He then made two features: *His Glorious Night* (29, Lionel Barrymore)—allegedly a deliberate studio sabotage—and *Redemption* (30, Fred Niblo). The drop in his following was immediate, and after *Way for a Sailor* (30, Sam Wood), *A Gentleman's Fate* (31, Mervyn Le Roy), *The Phantom of Paris* (31, John S. Robertson), *West of Broadway* (32, Harry Beaumont), and *Downstairs* (32, Bell), he placed the famous notice in *Variety* to the effect that MGM would neither release him nor give him parts.

In fact the studio put him in *Fast Workers* (33, Browning) and agreed to Garbo's request that he play with her in *Queen Christina* (33, Rouben Mamoulian). His last film was made at Columbia, *The Captain Hates the Sea* (35, Lewis Milestone), and within a year Gilbert had drunk himself to death. Dietrich bought his bed sheets at auction;

Garbo was widely reported as his mistress; and he had been married to actresses Olivia Burwell, Leatrice Joy, Ina Claire, and Virginia Bruce.

Lewis Gilbert, b. London, 1920

1947: *The Little Ballerina*. 1950: *Once a Summer; There Is Another Sun*. 1951: *The Scarlet Thread*. 1952: *Emergency Call; Time, Gentlemen, Please; Cosh Boy*. 1953: *Johnny on the Run; Albert R.N.; The Good Die Young*. 1954: *The Sea Shall Not Have Them*. 1955: *Cast a Dark Shadow*. 1956: *Reach for the Sky*. 1957: *The Admirable Crichton*. 1958: *Carve Her Name With Pride; A Cry from the Streets*. 1959: *Ferry to Hong Kong*. 1960: *Sink the Bismarck!; Light Up the Sky*. 1961: *The Greengage Summer/Loss of Innocence*. 1962: *H.M.S. Defiant*. 1964: *The Seventh Dawn*. 1966: *Alfie*. 1967: *You Only Live Twice*. 1969: *The Adventurers*. 1971: *Friends*. 1974: *Paul and Michelle*. 1975: *Operation Daybreak*. 1976: *Seven Nights in Japan*. 1977: *The Spy Who Loved Me*. 1979: *Moonraker*. 1983: *Educating Rita*. 1986: *Not Quite Paradise*. 1989: *Shirley Valentine*. 1991: *Stepping Out*. 1995: *Haunted*. 2002: *Before You Go*.

Gilbert was a child actor. His first feature was for children, and his most appealing movie, *The Greengage Summer,* is a whimsy on adolescence that makes good use of Susannah York and Jane Asher, while *Friends* and *Paul and Michelle* are further sticky studies of young love.

In the war, he was attached to the American Air Corps film unit and immediately afterwards he made documentaries. But there is precious little authenticity in his jingoistic war films: *Reach for the Sky,* the Douglas Bader story for audiences with wooden heads; *Carve Her Name With Pride,* with Virginia McKenna insisting on Englishness in the French Resistance; and *Sink the Bismarck,* with an exclamation mark. *The Seventh Dawn* harked back to the Malaya troubles, but *H.M.S. Defiant* went much further, to faded memories of *Mutiny on the Bounty*. Gilbert abandoned all in two tame James Bond films, the shameful *Adventurers,* and a coy romance about a navy Prince and a pretty Japanese.

But he made a comeback with the crowd-pleasing *Educating Rita* and *Shirley Valentine,* clever variations on the idea that a middle-aged woman can still make a lot out of life—and both taken from plays by Willy Russell.

Terry Gilliam,
b. Minneapolis, Minnesota, 1940

1974: *Monty Python and the Holy Grail* (codirected with Terry Jones). 1976: *Jabberwocky*. 1981: *Time Bandits*. 1985: *Brazil*. 1988: *The Adventures of Baron Munchausen*. 1991: *The Fisher King*. 1995: *Twelve Monkeys*. 1998: *Fear and Loathing in Las Vegas*.

With two very costly box-office failures to his credit (*Brazil* and *Munchausen*), it remains to be seen how much license will be given to Gilliam's unquestioned visual imagination. Those last two words might seem essential to moviemaking, yet there are times when this viewer would sooner settle for the visual simplicity of, say, Joseph Mankiewicz, Billy Wilder, Ozu, or even Hawks, than suffer the visual battering of Abel Gance, David Lean, Stanley Kubrick, or Terry Gilliam. There are times when "visual imagination" is a diversion from failures of content or sensibility.

Brazil is Orwellian—yet, isn't it also art direction run amok at the expense of any scrutiny? *Munchausen* has far fewer defenders—it is a lavish, unholy bore of the spectacular. For, as Alexandre Astruc realized more than forty years ago, there is a tyranny in the visual if it is indulged for its own sake. Gilliam began as a contributor of effects, sequences, etc. for *Monty Python,* a TV show crammed with wordsmiths. This may have urged him deeper into visual excess. But, to these eyes, he has not yet appreciated the dramatic coherence necessary in film direction.

Gilliam was a cartoonist who met John Cleese (touring America) and became a part of the *Monty Python Flying Circus* team. He was also active on most of the Python films, as animator, writer, and sometimes as actor. He was nominated for the best screenplay Oscar on *Brazil,* a film that he defended vigorously against understandable studio disquiet.

It happens that Gilliam then took on two projects to which I am devoted, and I have to say that, with *Twelve Monkeys,* I would far rather address the runic calm of Chris Marker's *La Jetée* (62), instead; as for *Fear and Loathing in Las Vegas*—the original (by Hunter Thompson and Ralph Steadman) is scarier, more visual and so much more fun.

Dorothy Gish (1898–1968) b. Dayton, Ohio

From the start, Lillian Gish, the older of the sisters, insisted that it was Dorothy who had the real talent, because Dorothy could do comedy. ("I'm as funny as a barrel of dead babies," said Lillian.) And it's true that from the start they were cast that way: Lillian in tragedy, drama, melodrama; Dorothy as the cutup and charmer she was in real life. Of course, there were exceptions—Lillian played sophisticates (*Diane of the Follies,* 1916) and Dorothy could be Serious (as a nun, for instance, in the 1915 *Her Mother's Daughter*). But on the whole, their film personas matched their real-life temperaments.

Actually, it was Dorothy who first set foot on stage, as Little Willie in *East Lynne;* she was four years old. Both sisters were to barnstorm in melodrama throughout their childhoods, until in 1912 they went down to the Biograph studio to look up their old pal Gladys Smith, who turned out to be Mary Pickford. Griffith instantly put them in a one-reeler, *An Unseen Enemy,* described as the terrible experience of two young girls in a lonesome villa. Also in this suspense film was young Bobby Harron, with whom Dorothy would fall in love, and who would die young, probably a suicide, to the anguish of the Griffith family.

The two sisters appeared in countless Biograph movies—Dorothy was in more than thirty in 1914 alone—vying for roles with Blanche Sweet, Mae Marsh, and others, but not with each other. If there was rivalry or jealousy between them—which Lillian steadfastly denied—it was never apparent. Each had her territory, and it's hard to imagine Dorothy in *Enoch Arden* or Lillian in *Old Heidelberg,* both made in 1915 with Wallace Reid as leading man. Nor would Lillian have seemed at home in, say, *Atta Boy's Last Race* (1916) or *Out of Luck* (1918)—when you look at stills of Dorothy making faces and posturing in that one or in her Western satire *Nugget Nell* (1919), you can understand why Paramount offered her a million dollars for a series of five-reel comedies. (She turned them down, saying, "At my age all that money would ruin my character.")

By this time Dorothy was a real star: in 1919 in *I'll Get Him Yet* (Elmer Clifton), the him being Richard Barthelmess, whom she convinced Griffith to hire; and in *Remodeling Her Husband* (1920), the only film Lillian directed; and *Flying Pat* (F. Richard Jones), also in 1920, the latter two with James Rennie, whom she was to marry, to the bewilderment of Lillian and Mother Gish, who didn't believe in men. Although the sisters had appeared in many films together, including Griffith's World War I *Hearts of the World* (1918), their indelible joint appearance was as the sisters in the 1921 *Orphans of the Storm,* their final Griffith film. Dorothy is the blind Louise, separated from Lillian's Henriette in the turmoil of the French Revolution. In its most famous scene, when Lillian hears Dorothy's voice out in the street but can't get to her, it's easy to be overwhelmed by Lillian's extraordinary projection of emotion, but Dorothy actually is her match, her somewhat more stolid face transported with hope and despair. At the end, when all is harmony (and Louise's sight has been restored), there's a flicker of roguishness in Dorothy that is all hers.

She went on to a series of successful films: *The Bright Shawl* (23, John S. Robertson), in which she's a Cuban dancer who dies in the arms of Barthelmess (the supporting cast included William Powell, Mary Astor, Edward G. Robinson, and Jetta Goudal); with Lillian in *Romola* (24, Henry King); an Irish colleen in the 1925 *The Beautiful City* (Kenneth S. Webb), again with Barthelmess and Powell; a big hit in the 1926

British-made *Nell Gwynne,* followed by several other films made there by Herbert Wilcox, including *Tip Toes* with Will Rogers and *Madame Pompadour* with Antonio Moreno, both in 1927. Then, as sound came in, it was back to the theatre, first in a play called *Young Love* directed by George Cukor. For the rest of her life, she was on the stage, appearing in only four movies after 1930: *Our Hearts Were Young and Gay* (44, Lewis Allen); *Centennial Summer* (46, Otto Preminger); *The Whistle at Eaton Falls* (51, Robert Siodmak); and *The Cardinal* (63, Preminger). Her biggest stage hit was as Mrs. Oliver Wendell Holmes in *The Magnificent Yankee,* opposite Louis Calhern, who became another alcoholic man in her life; and like Lillian, she played Mother in *Life with Father* out of town for more than a year. The sisters' last performance together was in the touring company of *The Chalk Garden* in 1956.

Whether or not she had the talent of her more famous sister, it's clear that Dorothy had the happier nature, and the more normal life: she liked men, she liked a good drink, she liked a good party, she liked a good time. Her career was a satisfying one, but it wasn't everything.

Lillian Gish (1893–1993),
b. Springfield, Ohio

It was said, when she died in March 1993, that Lillian Gish was only months short of her 100th birthday. Yet it had been reported for decades that 1896 was the year of her birth. Her manager, James Frasher, simply asserted, "She was the same age as film. They both came into the world in 1893." And so legend begins where questions are begged. By surviving, Gish had become a great lady of the history of film. She promoted Griffith; she helped get him on a stamp. She told the old story, and who knew how true it was. Her Griffith was a strong, gentle visionary. But suppose that he was also a barnstormer, a hustler, a showman, and enough of a rogue—things she ignored. Gish had such great eyes, but did they see everything?

One thing was certain: when she died, it was as if our last mooring rope to the first moment of movies had fallen away. Miss Gish had become not just a means of grasping history; she was the muse of History itself, just as in *Intolerance* she tended the cradle of humanity. The young woman raised in Griffith's shameless melodrama had become an old lady for whom discrepancies of fact and vagaries of memory were just dust in the wind (it is hard not to fall into the inter-title language of her movies).

That there was something innately pure about Lillian Gish had been substantiated by her enduring spinsterhood; the reverence for Griffith in her touching book, *The Movies, Mr. Griffith and Me;*

and the fact that in her sixties she remained as serenely beautiful as ever, bringing the benign authority of a Wasp fairy godmother to *The Night of the Hunter* (55, Charles Laughton).

She has a secure place among the great actresses of the cinema, even if her emotional range was uncommonly narrow. Only great discretion and integrity prevented her from seeming coy or sententious; for instance, Susie (of *True Heart Susie*) is now a tedious creature, but Lillian Gish is, simply, true-hearted—a feeling intelligence, recognizable apart from the Victorian primness of the role. Indeed, there are moments when one feels that she may have possessed a subtler artistic personality than Griffith. Her best work, which was not done for Griffith, and her life as a whole seem to glow with the robust integrity of a great singer or dancer.

She was a rare mixture of the unbridled and the very restrained. Was that Gish herself, or simply the conflicting strains of late Victorian melodrama? King Vidor was very interesting on working with Gish on *La Bohème* (26). The actress then was a great power at MGM. She was highly paid and her contract gave her liberties with cast, director, and rehearsal. Gish prevailed upon Vidor and her costar John Gilbert to do a *Bohème* in which the lovers never touched. The two men were perplexed—wasn't this a love story? and movie love in 1926 was measured against Gilbert and Garbo and their open-mouthed kisses. But Gish had her contract and her profound, devout authority (that was there into her nineties). So they shot the lovers apart, looking, yearning, kissing from either side of a windowpane. It was lovely and precious, but Mayer and Thalberg looked at the cut and said, "Are you kidding? Do it again with flesh!"

And then, as the day for shooting Mimi's death drew near, Gish began to fast. She grew gaunt. She drank nothing. She used cotton pads to dry up her saliva. She seemed as ill as Mimi. And Vidor could have sworn that she stopped breathing as the cameras rolled. He was persuaded she might be dead—he believed that Gish would have given everything, not just physically but in the way of emotional commitment.

Gish was possessed by a phenomenal romantic intensity—she was like a nun with Christ when it came to meeting the camera. And so real men felt jilted or unnecessary. You can see in these stories why men as good as Vidor marveled at her, and why her career was doomed by 1926. And so the question remains: did she turn claptrap into art (like Verdi)? Or was she one of the last relics of the nineteenth century in movies? I'm still not sure, but I suspect she drew equally upon veins of hysteria and transcendence, abandon and purity, that leave her eternally fascinating.

When their father deserted them, the Gish children, Lillian and her younger sister Dorothy (1898–1968) went into traveling theatre. Visiting an old friend, Mary Pickford, at Biograph one day in 1912, they were both coaxed into movies by D. W. Griffith: *An Unseen Enemy*. Lillian made twenty two-reelers for Griffith in two years and then appeared in *Judith of Bethulia* (13), the first four-reeler. When Griffith left Biograph she worked with him on *The Battle of the Sexes* (14); *The Escape* (14); *Home Sweet Home* (14); and *The Birth of a Nation* (15), in which she played Elsie Stoneman. She made *The Lost House* (15), *Enoch Arden* (15, Christy Cabanne), *The Lily and the Rose* (15), *Daphne and the Pirate* (16), and *An Innocent Magdalene* (16), before Griffith cast her as the girl rocking the cradle of humanity in *Intolerance* (16)—it was entirely suitable that so frail a figure should be the driving force in Griffith's view of the world, and that Gish should make the conception memorable.

She made *Diane of the Follies* (16), *Pathways of Life* (16), *The House Built Upon Sand* (17), and *Souls Triumphant* (17), before going to France to make *Hearts of the World* (18, Griffith). There followed a run of films for Griffith that were the finest flowering of the director's view of a virginal, self-sacrificing heroine: *The Great Love* (18); *The Greatest Thing in Life* (19); *A Romance of Happy Valley* (19); amazing in *Broken Blossoms* (19), as a battered Limehouse waif; *True Heart Susie* (19); a wronged innocent driven onto the ice floes in the White River in *Way Down East* (20); and, with Dorothy, in *Orphans of the Storm* (21). Her thorough competence and overall imagination were demonstrated when she directed Dorothy in *Remodelling Her Husband* (20).

But she left Griffith in 1921, incredibly over a money dispute. She went to Inspiration and there made *The White Sister* (23, Henry King) and *Romola* (24, King). There followed one of the unprovoked "incidents" of her career. Charles Duell, the president of Inspiration, first manipulated her contract and then claimed that she had promised to marry him: she sued and won, and very few credited the scandal.

As a result, she signed with MGM for six films and a fee of $800,000. What happened next is one of the most interesting skirmishes in studio-star relations. Gish herself was more discreet about the story than fellow-actress Louise Brooks, who wrote a trenchant article in 1958 describing how MGM had set out to humiliate Gish. From MGM's point of view, she earned too much and was too sober beside the flappers and sexual generosity of the 1920s. Contrary to general practice, Gish seems to have taken pains to modify her actual attractiveness on screen. Stills and studio portraits reveal a warmer, softer woman than appeared on film. Gish was staggered when Irving Thalberg even offered to arrange a scandal for her so that she might be brought nearer to the level of public taste. *Photoplay* campaigned against her austerity, and Louis B. Mayer alternately bullied her and posted Garbo on her set as a sign of the "new woman."

Under her contract with MGM, Gish had script approval, and it was usually honored: thus she made *La Bohème;* was magnificent as Hester Prynne in *The Scarlet Letter* (26, Victor Sjöström), a mixture of New England sobriety and nineteenth-century melodrama close to her heart; *Annie Laurie* (27, John S. Robertson) was thrust upon her; *The Enemy* (28, Fred Niblo) was dull; but *The Wind* (28, Sjöström) is her greatest film, a prairie tragedy, filmed under very trying conditions, and still intensely moving.

MGM hardly released that film and Lillian Gish walked proudly away. She made *One Romantic Night* (30, Paul L. Stein) and *His Double Life* (33, Arthur Hopkins and William C. De Mille), and then retired to the theatre. She was out of her time, but that is not to say that great directors might not have melted her—George Cukor, for instance.

She slipped back into movies in character parts: *Commandos Strike at Dawn* (42, John Farrow); *Miss Susie Slagle's* (46, John Berry); *Duel in the Sun* (46, Vidor); *Portrait of Jennie* (48, William Dieterle); *The Cobweb* (55, Vincente Minnelli), in which her underlying severity is very clear; *Orders to Kill* (58, Anthony Asquith); *The Unforgiven* (60, John Huston); *Follow Me, Boys* (66, Norman Tokar); *Warning Shot* (66, Buzz Kulik); and *The Comedians* (67, Peter Glenville). She reappeared ten years later as the matriarch gracefully delivering the most unexpected nuptial gift in *A Wedding* (78, Robert Altman).

Well into her eighties, she was vivacious and a tireless advocate for movies. She made appearances in *Thin Ice* (81, Paul Aaron); *Hobson's Choice* (83, Gilbert Cates); *Hambone and Hill* (84, Roy Watts), searching for her lost dog; *The Adventures of Huckleberry Finn* (85, Peter H. Hunt); *Sweet Liberty* (86, Alan Alda); and *The Whales of August* (87, Lindsay Anderson).

Her will left money to The Museum of Modern Art so they could protect the work of Mr. Griffith.

Danny Glover,

b. San Francisco, California, 1947
Glover's reasonable, professional, and cautious cop in the *Lethal Weapon* series is vital to the chemistry of the films. Yet I wonder whether Glover commands the same salary as Mel Gibson. After all, it is Gibson who plays the outrageous and reckless member of the team. He *is* the more flamboyant; so maybe he gets the greater rewards.

Glover has worked steadily for over two decades now, balancing box-office action movies with some genuinely adventurous explorations of black experience. He is easily called solid, com-

manding, and reliable; yet his strength is in his gentleness. Though well established, he seems worthy of more demanding work than the system has called for, even if he is still short of the leaping imagination of James Earl Jones.

After training in San Francisco at the American Conservatory Theatre, Glover worked as follows: *Escape from Alcatraz* (79, Don Siegel); *Chu Chu and the Philly Flash* (81, David Lowell Rich); *Out* (82, Eli Hollander); *Iceman* (84, Fred Schepisi); *Places in the Heart* (84, Robert Benton); as the husband in *The Color Purple* (85, Steven Spielberg); *Silverado* (85, Lawrence Kasdan); a spiffy killer in *Witness* (85, Peter Weir); *Lethal Weapon* (87, Richard Donner); *Mandela* (87, Philip Saville) for TV; *A Raisin in the Sun* (88, Bill Duke); *Bat 21* (88, Peter Markle); *Lethal Weapon 2* (89, Donner); *Lonesome Dove* (89, Simon Wincer) for TV; *Predator 2* (90, Stephen Hopkins); *To Sleep With Anger* (90, Charles Burnett), on which he was also executive producer; *Flight of the Intruder* (91, John Milius); *A Rage in Harlem* (91, Duke); *Pure Luck* (91, Nadia Tass); *Grand Canyon* (91, Kasdan); *Lethal Weapon 3* (92, Donner); *Queen* (93, John Erman) for TV; and *Bopha!* (93, Morgan Freeman).

He was in *Angels in the Outfield* (94, William Dear); *Kidnapped* (94, Bruce Seth Green); *Operation Dumbo Drop* (95, Wincer); *America's Dream* (96, Duke and Paris Barclay); *Gone Fishin'* (97, Christopher Cain); *Switchback* (97, Jeb Stuart); the judge in *The Rainmaker* (97, Francis Coppola); *Buffalo Soldiers* (97, Charles Haid); *Lethal Weapon 4* (98, Donner); *Beloved* (98, Jonathan Demme); the voice of Jethro in *The Prince of Egypt* (98); *Wings Against the Wind* (99, Euzhan Palcy); *Freedom Song* (00, Phil Alden Robinson); *Bàttu* (00, Cheich Oumar Sissoko); *Boesman and Lena* (00, John Berry); *3 A.M.* (01, Lee Davis); *The Royal Tenenbaums* (01, Wes Anderson); *Good Fences* (03, Ernest R. Dickerson); *The Henry Lee Project* (03, Kevin Rodney Sullivan).

Jean-Luc Godard, b. Paris, 1930

1954: *Opération Béton* (s). 1955: *Une Femme Coquette* (s). 1957: *Tous les Garçons S'Appellent Patrick* (s). 1958: *Charlotte et Son Jules* (s); *Une Histoire d'Eau* (codirected with François Truffaut) (s). 1959: *A Bout de Souffle/Breathless*. 1960: *Le Petit Soldat/The Little Soldier*. 1961: *Une Femme est une Femme/A Woman Is a Woman;* "La Paresse," an episode from *Les Sept Péchés Capitaux*. 1962: *Vivre Sa Vie/It's My Life;* "Le Nouveau Monde," an episode from *RoGoPaG*. 1963: *Les Carabiniers/The Soldiers; Le Mépris/Contempt;* "Le Grand Escroc," an episode from *Les Plus Belles Escroqueries du Monde;* "Montparnasse-Levallois," an episode from *Paris Vu Par.* 1964: *Bande à Part/The Out-*

siders; *Une Femme Mariée/A Married Woman.* 1965: *Alphaville; Pierrot le Fou.* 1966: *Masculin-Féminin; Made in USA; Deux ou Trois Choses que Je Sais d'Elle/Two or Three Things I Know About Her.* 1967: *La Chinoise; Loin du Vietnam* (codirected with Joris Ivens, William Klein, Alain Resnais, and Claude Lelouch); *Week-end;* "Anticipation, ou l'An 2,000," an episode from *Le Plus Vieux Métier du Monde;* "L'Enfant Prodigue," an episode from *Vangelo '70.* 1968: *Le Gai Savoir; Un Film Comme les Autres* (codirected with Jean-Pierre Gorin); *One Plus One/Sympathy for the Devil; One American Movie* (uncompleted). 1969: *Communications* (uncompleted); *British Sounds* (codirected with Gorin); *Pravda* (codirected with Gorin); *Vent d'Est/Wind from the East* (codirected with Gorin); *Lotte in Italia/Struggle in Italy* (codirected with Gorin). 1970: *Jusqu'à la Victoire.* 1971: *Vladimir et Rosa* (codirected with Gorin). 1972: *Tout Va Bien* (codirected with Gorin); *Letter to Jane: Investigation of a Still* (codirected with Gorin). 1975: *Numéro Deux; Comme Ça Va.* 1980: *Sauve Qui Peut/Every Man for Himself.* 1982: *Passion.* 1983: *Prenom Carmen/First Name Carmen.* 1984: an episode from *Paris Vu Par . . . 20 Ans Après.* 1985: *Detective; Je Vous Salue, Marie/Hail, Mary.* 1986: *Grandeur et Décadence d'un Petit Commerce de Cinéma* (d). 1987: *King Lear;* "Armide," an episode from *Aria.* 1987: *Soigne Ta Droite* (d); *Meeting WA* (d); *Duras/Godard* (d). 1989: *Histoire (s) du Cinéma/History (ies) of the Cinema* (d). 1990: *Nouvelle Vague/New Wave.* 1991: *Allemagne Neuf-Zero.* 1993: *Hélas pour Moi; Les Enfants Jouent à la Russie.* 1995: *JLG / JLG—autoportraite de Décembre; Deux Fois Cinquante Ans de Cinéma Français* (d). 1996: *For Ever Mozart.* 1998: *The Old Place; Histoire(s) du Cinéma: Une Vague Nouvelle; Seul le Cinéma; Les Signes Parmi Nous; Le Contrôle de l'Univers; Le Monnaie de l'Absolu; Fatale Beauté* (d). 2000: *L'Origine du XXième Siècle.* 2001: *Elogie de l'Amour/In Praise of Love.* 2003: *Notre Musique.*

Impossible to avoid a Godardian treatment of Godard, here is an exposition in seven paragraphs (with a coda to update).

1. Godard is the first filmmaker to bristle with the effort of digesting all previous cinema and to make cinema itself his subject. He emerged from the darkness of the Cinémathèque rather than from any plausible biographical background. Thus, it is inadequate to accept the definition he prompted from Samuel Fuller in *Pierrot le Fou:* "The film is like a battlefield . . . Love . . . Hate . . . Action . . . Violence . . . Death . . . In one word Emotion." Emblems or slogans in Godard are chronic and palindromic. One might amend the definition in two ways: "Cinema is slogans" or "What is emotion? . . . It is cinema."

Godard's collected works are an Encyclopedia Cinematografica, the insistence that all things exist only to the extent that they can be expressed in cinema. Godard more than any other director taunts reality. It is not that life imitates art, but that it is all art, all fictional as much as documentary, and it is cinema once any lens—in camera or eye—notices it. Filmmaking for Godard is neither occupation nor vocation, it is existence itself. His inescapable dialectic is in terms of cinema and his politics have arisen—disastrously, I think—from cinema theory. It was only as Godard abandoned the *politique des auteurs*—as a child might throw out a once favorite toy—that he became a politicized author.

2. Like Welles, he is trapped in the role of Young Turk. Anger (or contempt), his most abiding mood, increases as he becomes aware of his inability to relinquish it. He was an extraordinary critic, hurling down one dogma after another in the pages of *Cahiers du Cinéma* and *Arts.* Richard Roud has said that he was "unkind, unfair, unreasonable," but that seems secondary to the schizoid mingling of incoherence and penetration in his writing. Already, he was the noble madman, *Pierrot le Fou,* in that truly useful insights were offered in writing that was appalling, trite, chaotic, and gratuitously unreadable. It came armed with frightful name-dropping from literature and painting. Hardly a film could be classified without reference to Faulkner, Proust, Auguste Renoir, or Velázquez. In part, this was his need for classification, the unappeasable urge to cross-refer rather than to describe a thing itself. And these references are meaningless. What is it to wonder whether eyes are Renoir grey or Velázquez grey, but to doodle with the coffee-table art expertise no different from the grotesque advertisement language parodied in *Pierrot?* Godard's criticism is so aggressive that one feels only its insecurity. The craving for a Pantheon and the inverted appeal to conspiracy that hopes for others whose tastes will support the same gods is like the atmosphere of Rivette's *Paris Nous Appartient.* It means that his articles are addressed to himself, rather than to readers. The tone is austere and forbidding, as if to exclude others from cinema in the very act of celebrating it.

3. The first young Godard adored Americana. In violence to French cinema of the 1950s and the history of art or intellectual cinema, he recognized the virtues of every director from Griffith to Fuller, with running and contradictory confusion as to whether Hawks, Nicholas Ray, Minnelli, or Anthony Mann was the greatest of directors. It was sufficient that the director he admired at any moment was the greatest; the urge to classify had a weak memory and a helpless index. The vital admiration of the beauty of American action cinema, and of the way it expressed character, emotion, and universal meanings within rigid genres

and unwholesome production systems took too little account of the commercial position of the American director, of genres, and of the inability of revered directors to understand his praise of them. But in terms of plot, image, and character, Godard's first films were a magnificent critical explanation of American movies. The tragic pitch of *Pierrot le Fou* lies partly in the sense of a dying American cinema.

4. As American cinema shrank into seriousness, and as more young people rediscovered its earlier glory, Godard moved violently to shun such company. He went first into his own invented sociology that allied the exploitation of film directors with a diffuse notion of prostitution throughout society. The idea had been expressed best in *Vivre Sa Vie* and *Le Mépris*, and recurs with decreasing precision in *Une Femme Mariée, Alphaville,* and *Deux ou Trois Choses.* That conception thrust Godard forward into a near-total abandonment of America for Marxist cinema. But the new political awareness was as shy of reality as his liking for American movies had been insecurely rooted. He could only make his revolutionary films in groups named after Dziga Vertov or Medvedkin. And from *Made in USA* onward, the political imperative accelerates his incoherence, replaces action with slogan and human meetings with the barren exchange of dialectic. *Deux ou Trois Choses* is the film in which his generalization of people works best, poised on the edge of a numbing obscurity that is a grotesque proof of the alienation Godard sees in the world. His protests, therefore, are pathological and humorless.

5. Godard's greatness rests in his grasping of the idea that films are made of moving images, of moments from films, of images projected in front of audiences. A critic once asked why there was so much blood in *Pierrot.* That is not blood, answered Godard, but red. Equally, his films are not stories photographed, but a record of actors playing parts. The focus of his films is the distance between camera and actors and between screen and audience. He involves viewers more thoroughly (and more politically) in a film like *Bande à Part* when he describes the action he is showing than in any of the direct didactic onslaughts. *Les Carabiniers* is still his most political film, largely because he is so stimulated by its specific location—the urban wasteland. He knows only cinema: on politics and real life he is childish and pretentious.

6. It follows that the very thing his films lack is emotion. They deal with moments of cinema and with his jungle of reference, but never with feelings. It is when he photographs Anna Karina, his first wife, that this gap is wistfully admitted. That is what makes *Pierrot* a real tragedy and moments from earlier films with Karina elegies for an unexperienced feeling. Godard's anger and intellect sit together guarding his cold, empty heart, mad-

dened by it. He is the first director, the first great director, who does not seem to be a human being. It was the discovery that he loved Karina more in moving images than in life that may have broken their marriage. And that rupture shocked his chaste heart even further, into vain protestations of caring for the world.

7. Thus Godard proves that cinema is no more or less than cinema, that art has scant need of reality, that it depends on imagination. He is the inaugurator of a new beauty that is the beginning of modern cinema—uncomposed, but snapped. Movements observed, transformed by being watched.

Godard has not stopped, or reached Fassbinder's terminus. Nor is his recent work negligible: *Nouvelle Vague* was very beautiful; *Detective* was a rather casual tribute to film noir; *King Lear* had the backhanded virtue of demonstrating how capriciously a film could be contracted, and executed; *Hail, Mary* was banned and berated—that, really, is its claim to fame. But admirers could not escape the pinched, cynical, and misogynist aura of Godard. If he had taught us the absurdity, and even the corrupt iniquity, of making more movies—why make them? There are dead ends that precede death, and show us a morbidity that was not previously apparent.

Whenever I have re-viewed early Godard (I mean films from the sixties), they have seemed fresh still, moving, and exciting. But for the moment, Godard has very little audience. It may be that moviemaking of his intensity—both cerebral and emotional—cannot maintain itself very long. There are so many careers for which the peak lasted ten or so years; and so few in which directors came back again, renewed—that is what makes Renoir so remarkable, and Fritz Lang. Godard does require a sense of urgency and occasion, a feeling for political and cultural pregnancy, that has gone now. Thus, the more enduring humanism of Ingmar Bergman begins to loom larger than Godard's furious essay-making. What's more, Godard was too brilliant, too rapid: he saw a new way of doing film that is still beyond the generality of directors, and audiences.

But Godard has a frenzied interest in TV and video. If the media changed enough, that could bring him back into our lives. As for the earlier films, they are one of the inescapable bodies of work. They deserve retrospectives—if film proves an art or a force that commands such backwards survey. Will there be a place for retrospective seasons? Or was it a matter of luck to be alive when Godard could not stop throwing out his amazing pictures?

Of course, it was natural that Godard would provide his own retrospective—and sweep up the entire medium. *Histoire(s) du Cinéma* is a great catalogue work, worthy of Robert Musil or Walter

Benjamin—or Chris Marker. But in its astonishing beauties, and the suggestiveness of its editing, one may still see and feel the Godard of the early sixties. Thus, the *Histoire(s)* reasserted, beyond doubt, that his is one of the great critical yet poetic minds in the medium.

Paulette Goddard (Marion Levy) (1911–90), b. Great Neck, New York

By 1932, Paulette Goddard was replete with alimony from a first broken marriage, barely blooded in movies, an ex-Goldwyn girl, and now with Hal Roach. She met Charlie Chaplin, contributed herself and her money to *Modern Times* (36), and was his wife from 1933 to 1942. Of all Chaplin's leading ladies she is the most lively and appealing, as well as the one who seems to have pushed him near a real warmth for women. At her prime she was delectably gay and vivacious—she had the nickname "Sugar"—with an underlying strength and stubbornness that was brought out in her De Mille films.

Her success in *Modern Times* almost won her the part of Scarlett O'Hara, but Selznick used her in *The Young in Heart* (38, Richard Wallace); she was also in *The Women* (39, Cukor)—before he sold her to Paramount. She duly became one of the leading ladies of that studio; opposite Bob Hope in *The Cat and the Canary* (39, Elliott Nugent) and *The Ghost Breakers* (40, George Marshall); her first hoyden, in De Mille's *North West Mounted Police* (40). She also appeared in Chaplin's *The Great Dictator* (40).

Throughout the war years, she flourished at Paramount yet she never quite carried a film or laid hands on unequivocal stardom: *Second Chorus* (41, H. C. Potter), with Fred Astaire and Burgess Meredith; *Hold Back the Dawn* (41, Mitchell Leisen); *Nothing But the Truth* (41, Nugent); *Reap the Wild Wind* (42, De Mille); *The Forest Rangers* (42, Marshall); *The Crystal Ball* (43, Nugent); *So Proudly We Hail* (43, Mark Sandrich); *Standing Room Only* (44, Sidney Lanfield); *I Love a Soldier* (44, Sandrich); *Kitty* (45, Leisen), a vehicle that didn't really own the road.

By now, she had married Burgess Meredith, and she appeared delightfully with him in Renoir's *The Diary of a Chambermaid* (46). Next, she was in *Suddenly It's Spring* (47, Leisen), a slave girl in De Mille's *Unconquered* (47), and then Mrs. Cheveley in Alexander Korda's *An Ideal Husband* (48). Not many actresses could have played those four films in a row so well, and even she couldn't quite manage the last, although she worked hard to "look like a woman with a past." Her career began to decline, but never forsook the adventurous: *Hazard* (48, Marshall); *On Our Merry Way* (48, King Vidor and Lesley Fenton); as Lucretia Borgia in *Bride of Vengeance* (49, Leisen); and in the all-white *Anna Lucasta* (49, Irving Rapper).

After *The Torch* (50, Emilio Fernandez) she made yet another curiosity, Edgar G. Ulmer's *Babes in Bagdad* (52). The rest is unworthy: *Vice Squad* (53, Arnold Laven); *The Sins of Jezebel* (53, Reginald Le Borg); *The Charge of the Lancers* (54, William Castle); and *The Stranger Came Home* (54, Terence Fisher). In 1958, she married Erich Maria Remarque and retired. But she made one more film, in Italy, *Gli Indifferenti* (64, Francesco Maselli), and she played a murdered movie star on TV in *The Snoop Sisters* (72, Leonard Stern).

Whoopi Goldberg (Caryn Johnson), b. New York, 1949

Whoopi Goldberg is a famous American. She has had careers as comedienne, actress, and TV talk show hostess. She seems emancipated, outspoken, a citizen. But when she won the best supporting actress for *Ghost* (90, Jerry Zucker)—a big hit that needed her vitality and force—I was reminded of Hattie McDaniel. Ms. McDaniel played Mammy in *Gone With the Wind*, and on the night of February 29, 1940, she was the first black ever to win an Oscar. When *Gone With the Wind* opened in Atlanta, ten weeks earlier, Georgian sensibilities had had her picture removed from the souvenir program. The actress was advised not to attend the premiere. David Selznick protested the exclusion, but went along with it. And on February 29, at the Cocoanut Grove, he did not have Hattie McDaniel sitting at the *Gone With the Wind* table. She and her husband were parked off in a corner at what seemed like the only table for two. The actress had a long walk to pick up the Oscar.

That was then. Whoopi Goldberg is not parkable, off to the side. Yet not many black women are in this book. Whitney Houston hardly makes it on the strength of *The Bodyguard*, where she certainly sings, too. But there is something to be said about that hokey film. Ms. Houston acts; she plays a character at least as credible as Kevin Costner's; she is plainly involved in the plot as a mature lead—by which, it follows, she is available for our fantasies; and the film never notices that she is black. This could be the first time a negotiably attractive black woman has played a romantic role that could as easily have gone to a white.

Am I forgetting someone? Do I have to go along with the notion that Jeanne Crain was colored in *Pinky*? Are we expected to overlook the rumor and even the visual hint that Kay Francis and Merle Oberon had "mixed" blood?

All of which is a way of saying that Whoopi Goldberg may have gotten this far because she is not patently available for romance in a movie. She is a clown, and a supporting actress. But there are those working now—Alfre Woodard or Angela Bassett—who could audition for "white" roles as easily as Olivier or Welles played *Othello*. Some day soon such "outrages" must occur. The movies are so hungry for things never seen before, and America will not prevent the logical destiny of interracial love affairs.

Meanwhile, Whoopi Goldberg has done the following: *The Color Purple* (85, Steven Spielberg); *Jumpin' Jack Flash* (86, Penny Marshall); *Burglar* (87, Hugh Wilson); *Fatal Beauty* (87, Tom Holland); *Clara's Heart* (88, Robert Mulligan); *The Telephone* (88, Rip Torn); *Homer & Eddie* (90, Andrei Konchalovsky); *The Long Walk Home* (90, Richard Pearce); *Soapdish* (91, Michael Hoffman); *Sarafina!* (92, Darrell James Roodt); *The Player* (92, Robert Altman); *Sister Act* (92, Emile Ardolino); *Made in America* (93, Richard Benjamin); and *Sister Act II* (93, Bill Duke). Several of these films are so bad, it is unlikely a white actress could have survived them.

In 1994, Whoopi hosted the Oscars—uneasily: she was often funny, but she didn't master that oddly old-fashioned crowd. So she challenged them all the more (which some found healthier than *Sister Act*).

Whoopi has done the Oscars again, in 1996, 1999, and 2002—but more recently she seems to have settled for *Hollywood Squares*. She does nearly anything, with a lot of voice work and very few good pictures: the voice of Shenzi in *The Lion King* (94, Roger Alters and Rob Minkoff); *Star Trek: Generations* (94, David Carson); a voice in *The Pagemaster* (94, Maurice Hunt); *The Little Rascals* (94, Penelope Spheeris); *Corrina, Corrina* (94, Jessie Nelson); *Boys on the Side* (95, Herbert Ross); *Moonlight and Valentino* (95, David Anspaugh); *Theodore Rex* (95, Jonathan R. Betuel); *The Sunshine Boys* (95, John Erman); *Eddie* (96, Steve Rash); *Bogus* (96, Norman Jewison); *The Associate* (96, Donald Petrie); Myrlie Evers in *Ghosts of Mississippi* (96, Rob Reiner); *In the Gloaming* (97, Christopher Reeve); *Cinderella* (97, Robert Iscove); *How Stella Got Her Groove Back* (98, Kevin Rodney Sullivan); *A Knight in Camelot* (98, Roger Young); *Alegría* (98, Franco Dragone); the Cheshire Cat in *Alice in Wonderland* (99, Nick Willing); *The Deep End of the Ocean* (99, Ulu Grosbard); *Girl, Interrupted* (99, James Mangold); *Monkeybone* (01, Henry Selick); *Rat Race* (01, Jerry Zucker); *Call Me Claus* (01, Peter Werner).

She was the voice of Miss Clavel in *Madeline: My Fair Madeline* (02, Scott Heming); a voice in *Blizzard* (02, LeVar Burton); *Good Fences* (03, Ernest R. Dickerson); *Bitter Jester* (03, Maija Di Giorgio); and in a TV series, *Whoopi*.

William Goldman,
b. Chicago, 1931

"Storyteller" is how Goldman would like to be remembered. And that is the sensible way of regarding him, whether as novelist, screenwriter, or the author of two enjoyably anecdotal books about Hollywood, *Adventures in the Screen Trade* (1983) and *Hype and Glory* (1990). He would prefer to be a novelist and, like most of the best movie writers, he has no illusions about the power or creative personality of writing for the screen: "If *all* you do is write screenplays, then it *becomes* denigrating to the soul." Goldman is caustic, unsentimental, and penetrating, so long as those qualities can be delivered briefly and instantaneously. In other words, he thinks in knockout lines and argues in brilliant segues. Like all the long-lived Hollywood writers (though Goldman opts for New York), it is Goldman's instinct to prefer speed and efficiency to commitment. He seems never to have shown any interest in directing, nor in having control over his films.

Nevertheless, *Butch Cassidy and the Sundance Kid* (69, George Roy Hill) was an original script, an acute mixing of Western formula and contemporary idiom, just sufficiently real, touching, funny, and disarming to gather up the world's pleasure. No one else let the film down, but Goldman made it. More intriguingly, one could claim that his adapted screenplay saved *All the President's Men* (76, Alan Pakula) from plot labyrinth, gave it the necessary melodrama, and enshrined the fallacy of indefatigable news hounds. The clarity of the movie was only made possible by Goldman—think of the book, think of the real events, and marvel at how the picture *works*. Deep Throat seems to have written it, and so screenwriting and the paranoia about conspiracy become interdependent.

Goldman's novels have made many of his films: *No Way to Treat a Lady* (book 64; film 68, Jack Smight); *The Princess Bride* (book 73; film 87, Rob Reiner); *Marathon Man* (book 74; film 76, John Schlesinger); and *Magic* (book 76; film 78, Richard Attenborough).

As a writer for hire, he has also done *Masquerade* (65, Basil Dearden); *Harper* (66, Smight); *The Hot Rock* (72, Peter Yates); *The Stepford Wives* (75, Bryan Forbes); *The Great Waldo Pepper* (75, Hill); *A Bridge Too Far* (77, Attenborough); *Butch and Sundance—The Early Days* (79, Richard Lester); *Mr. Horn* (79, Jack Starrett) for TV; the dismal *Heat* (87, R. M. Richards); and a very effective comeback, Stephen King's *Misery* (90, Reiner), beautifully plotted, even if it shirks some of the crazier ambiguities about writing freely or under duress. He also did the screenplay for *Year of the Comet* (92, Peter Yates); and *Maverick* (94, Richard Donner).

Few movies nowadays have the narrative intricacy or the speed of which Goldman is capable. He is one of the writers on Attenborough's *Chaplin*, but one doubts that he was present or conscious when the device of the publisher/interlocutor was conceived.

In truth, it's too long since Goldman worked on a good film. If he means to go on writing very smart books about his trade, he needs steadier credentials than *The Chamber* (96, James Foley); *The Ghost and the Darkness* (96, Stephen Hopkins)—which did have the signs of something good; *Fierce Creatures* (97, Robert Young and Fred Schepisi), where his work is uncredited; *Absolute Power* (97, Clint Eastwood) where you might want it to be uncredited; *The General's Daughter* (99, Simon West); and two adaptations from Stephen King—*Hearts in Atlantis* (01, Scott Hicks) and *Dreamcatcher* (02, Lawrence Kasdan).

Samuel Goldwyn (Schmuel Gelbfisz)
(1879–1974), b. Warsaw, Poland

Goldwyn withdrew in splendid, insufferable egotism from the two most significant mergers in the history of the American film industry. This led to his being known as the greatest "independent" film producer in a world of vast corporations. But all those corporations grew from a tiny band of entrepreneurs who knew and mistrusted one another. Now that the majors have perished or are living on transfusions from larger corporations, it is easier to look back eighty years and see the shabby way they came into being. In those terms, Goldwyn looks less an "independent" than an opinionated loser, edged out by marginally shrewder men. The structure of the film industry emerged from the squabbles of a gang of boys. Goldwyn was the kid who would play no game but his own, and thus he had to play alone. It is as generous to build him up as a creative or far-seeing man, as it would be wrong to disparage the achievement of an immigrant who became very rich indeed. The tragedy—if one is in that frame of mind—is that an untutored Polish glove merchant, within so short a period, should have achieved such eminence as a purveyor of mass-market fiction that he turned "respectable."

Bernard Shaw pierced Goldwyn's pretentious core when he said of the producer's attempts to buy the film rights of a play: "The trouble, Mr. Goldwyn, is that you are only interested in art and I am only interested in money." The history of the movie tycoons has a clear lesson: they neglected money, or were inept with it, but adored meaning and message in their films, despite every omission of taste or talent. Is it any wonder, battered by Wall Street and the critics, that they ended up as studied, bewildered eccentrics, desperately seeking distinction? Thus Goldwyn is likely to survive as the author of so many non sequiturs, a mogul's clangers. One of those—"Include me out"—could be the motto of his career.

Goldwyn left Poland at age eleven, worked in England for four years with a blacksmith, and arrived in America in 1899. Tired of hot irons and horses, he went in for smart gloves and smooth

hands. When the glove business faltered, he switched into movies. With his brother-in-law, Jesse Lasky, and Cecil B. De Mille he formed Lasky Feature Plays. When that outfit merged with Adolph Zukor's Famous Players, Zukor and Goldfish stared balefully at one another across a small, crowded empire. Goldfish left and in 1916 teamed up with the Selwyn brothers. He changed his name to that of the new company, thus making it seem his own. (This is the touch of business genius knowing that the brothers would hardly alter their names to Selfish. And Goldwyn was dottily famous for his "touch.") It was at this time that Goldwyn launched Will Rogers. But Goldwyn quarreled with the Selwyns and broke away from them in 1922. As a result, he was only a stockholder when the Goldwyn company was sold out to Metro. But from 1924 on, with his assumed name holding hyphens for the largest major, Goldwyn himself produced independently, through United Artists until 1940, and then usually with RKO.

Goldwyn liked movies, and he had a better-than-average record in choosing directors, even if he seldom let them do their best work. His eye for actors and actresses was much less reliable, while he had a positive craving for spending large amounts on serious writers and unpromising material. *Wuthering Heights* is typical of this ambition outreaching itself. Only Goldwyn would have applied Ben Hecht and Charles MacArthur to Emily Brontë, asked Gregg Toland to photograph Haworth in California, and given Olivier's Heathcliff Merle Oberon as Cathy.

There is no pattern to his product, save that of restless opportunism: *The Highest Bidder* (21, Wallace Worsley); *Doubling for Romeo* (21, Clarence Badger); *The Eternal Cry* (23, George Fitzmaurice); *Potash and Perlmutter* (23, Badger); *Cytherea* (24, Fitzmaurice); *In Hollywood with Potash and Perlmutter* (24, Alfred Green); *Tarnish* (24, Fitzmaurice), the first of many Goldwyn pictures starring Ronald Colman; *The Dark Angel* (25, Fitzmaurice); *A Thief in Paradise* (25, Fitzmaurice); *His Supreme Moment* (25, Fitzmaurice); *Stella Dallas* (25, Henry King); *Partners Again* (26, King); *The Winning of Barbara Worth* (26, King); *The Magic Flame* (27, King); *The Night of Love* (27, Fitzmaurice); *The Awakening* (28, Victor Fleming); *Bulldog Drummond* (29, F. Richard Jones); *Condemned* (29, Wesley Ruggles); *The Rescue* (29, Herbert Brenon); *This Is Heaven* (29, Alfred Santell); *Whoopee!* (30, Thornton Freeland), the first of several Eddie Cantor films; *Raffles* (30, Harry d'Arrast and Fitzmaurice), still with the suave Colman; *Street Scene* (31, King Vidor); *Arrowsmith* (31, John Ford); *Cynara* (32, Vidor); two more Cantor pictures, *The Kid from Spain* (33, Leo McCarey) and *Roman Scandals* (33, Frank Tuttle); *Nana* (34,

Dorothy Arzner), with Goldwyn's lamentable European importation, Anna Sten; *Kid Millions* (34, Roy del Ruth); *The Dark Angel* (35, Sidney Franklin); *Wedding Night* (35, Vidor), with Sten again; *Barbary Coast* (35, Howard Hawks); *Come and Get It* (36, Hawks and William Wyler); the excellent *Dodsworth* (36, Wyler); *Stella Dallas* (37, Vidor); *Beloved Enemy* (37, H. C. Potter); *Dead End* (37, Wyler); *The Adventures of Marco Polo* (38, Archie Mayo); *The Goldwyn Follies* (38, George Marshall); *The Cowboy and the Lady* (38, Potter); *The Hurricane* (38, Ford); *Wuthering Heights* (39, Wyler); *The Westerner* (40, Wyler); *The Little Foxes* (41, Wyler); *Ball of Fire* (41, Hawks); *The Pride of the Yankees* (42, Sam Wood); *The North Star* (43, Lewis Milestone); *The Princess and the Pirate* (44, David Butler); *Up in Arms* (44, Elliott Nugent); *Wonder Man* (45, Bruce Humberstone), both with Goldwyn's new star, Danny Kaye; *The Best Years of Our Lives* (46, Wyler); *The Kid from Brooklyn* (46, Norman Z. McLeod); *The Secret Life of Walter Mitty* (47, McLeod); *The Bishop's Wife* (47, Henry Koster); *A Song Is Born* (48, Hawks); *Enchantment* (48, Irving Reis); *My Foolish Heart* (49, Mark Robson); *Roseanna McCoy* (49, Reis); *Our Very Own* (50, David Miller); *Edge of Doom* (50, Robson); *I Want You* (51, Robson); *Hans Christian Andersen* (52, Charles Vidor); *Guys and Dolls* (55, Joseph L. Mankiewicz); and *Porgy and Bess* (59, Otto Preminger).

I have to confess that I would shed few tears if most of that cargo sank. How could anyone who has read Emily Brontë take the movie *Wuthering Heights* seriously? And why would anyone pleased with the film read the book? Danny Kaye and Eddie Cantor were discoveries reliant on Goldwyn's faith. There are good pictures—*Dodsworth, Stella Dallas, Ball of Fire, The Letter,* and some that are very entertaining (*Come and Get It, The Little Foxes, My Foolish Heart*), but anything great? *The Best Years of Our Lives* is undeniably honest and touching, and it's easy to see why it had such an impact in its tender time. It brought Goldwyn his best picture Oscar, and a lot of money. It is also one of those few movies that alludes to (and adores) an enormous, middle America scarcely seen in pictures. And—may I suggest—as seldom encountered in America itself. In other words, *Best Years* is a sweet, conservative dream, a longing to return to peaceful sleep after the war, very ably abetted by Wyler, the director who made a career out of reckoning himself "above" Goldwyn.

Michael Gordon (1909–93),

b. Baltimore, Maryland

1943: *Crime Doctor; One Dangerous Night.* 1947: *The Web.* 1948: *Another Part of the Forest; An Act of Murder.* 1949: *The Lady Gambles; Woman in Hiding.* 1950: *Cyrano de Bergerac.* 1951: *I Can Get It for You Wholesale; The Secret of Convict Lake.* 1953: *Wherever She Goes.* 1959: *Pillow Talk.* 1960: *Portrait in Black.* 1962: *Boys' Night Out.* 1963: *For Love or Money; Move Over, Darling.* 1965: *A Very Special Favor.* 1966: *Texas Across the River.* 1968: *The Impossible Years.* 1970: *How Do I Love Thee?.*

The gap in Gordon's career is the blacklist. Only two years after the prestigious *Cyrano,* and its Oscar for José Ferrer, he was forced to go to Australia to make *Wherever She Goes.* When he returned, it was as bedmaker in Ross Hunter's lush apartments. *Boys' Night Out* and *Texas Across the River* have pleasant moments, but the rest is dross. Gordon had, already, come to the cinema a little late, delayed by drama studies at Yale, before he joined Columbia as an editor. The best of his early films is a version of Lillian Hellman's *Another Part of the Forest,* with Fredric March, Edmond O'Brien, Ann Blyth, and Dan Duryea.

Ruth Gordon (Ruth Gordon Jones)

(1896–1985), b. Wollaston, Massachusetts

Even Garson Kanin trod warily with Ruth Gordon, and she was his wife. She was famous in the business for being . . . very difficult and rather horrible. If you feel tempted to regard her as a sweet old lady, or a sprightly "character," then beware the sudden swoop of witch or mystic. She is neither cozy nor sentimental; she has the authority of a woman who knows she has grown perversely sexy and commanding with age. The "secret" to Ruth Gordon is that her macabre confidante in *Rosemary's Baby* (68, Roman Polanski) and the fairy godmother hippie in *Harold and Maude* (71, Hal Ashby) are made of the same rare metal, and are just as serenely willful. Indeed, I wonder if the actress could not have taught Polanski to be more matter-of-fact and Ashby more outrageous, with advantage to both films. If Maude screwed, there would be no doubt about her being as awesome as the Manhattan harpy. It is an error to find Ruth Gordon quaint or eccentric. She is the Queen of Hearts, Electra, and Lilith all crammed into one small frame.

Her movie career was intermittent, as if there were often more compelling things on her mind. She spent rather more time acting on and writing for the stage. In the thirties, she was a very striking stage actress, drawn into a bizarre affair with producer Jed Harris, by whom she had a child. Two of her plays have been filmed: *Over 21* (45, Charles Vidor) and *The Actress* (53, George Cukor). Legend has it that she had a bit part in *Camille* (15, Albert Capellini), and only returned to the screen in 1940, a sharp-faced middle-aged woman: *Abe Lincoln in Illinois* (40, John Cromwell); *Dr. Ehrlich's Magic Bullet* (40, William Dieterle); *Two-Faced Woman* (41, Cukor); *Edge of Darkness*

(42, Lewis Milestone); and *Action in the North Atlantic* (42, Lloyd Bacon).

She married Kanin, her second husband, during this flurry of work, and they became a very successful comedy writing team, notably for Cukor, Spencer Tracy, and Katharine Hepburn: *A Double Life* (48); *Adam's Rib* (49), among the most urbane studies of belligerent marriage; *The Marrying Kind* (52); and *Pat and Mike* (53).

Whereupon, she disappeared from films for another dozen years and returned for a grand gallery of elderly nymphs: *Inside Daisy Clover* (66, Robert Mulligan); *Lord Love a Duck* (66, George Axelrod); a supporting actress Oscar for *Rosemary's Baby; What Ever Happened to Aunt Alice?* (69, Lee H. Katzin); *Where's Poppa?* (70, Carl Reiner); *The Big Bus* (76, James Frawley); *Every Which Way But Loose* (78, James Fargo); *Boardwalk* (79, Stephen Verona); *Any Which Way You Can* (80, Buddy Van Horn); *My Bodyguard* (80, Tony Bill); *Don't Go to Sleep* (82, Richard Lang); *Jimmy the Kid* (83, Gary Nelson); *Mugsy's Girl* (85, Kevin Brodie); and *Maxie* (85, Paul Aaron).

Heinosuke Gosho (1902–81), b. Tokyo

1925: *Nanto no Haru; Otoko Gokoro; Seishun; Sora wa Haretari; Tosei Tamatebako.* 1926: *Hatsukoi; Musume; Itoshino Wagako; Kanojo; Machi no Hitobito; Honryu; Haha-yo Koishi; Kaeranu Sasabue.* 1927: *Karakuri Musume; Shojo no Shi; Okame; Sabishii Ranbomono; Hazukashii Yume; Mura no Hanayome.* 1928: *Suki Nareba Koso; Doraku Goshinan; Kami Eno Michi; Hito no Yo no Sugata; Gaito no Kishi; Yoru no Meneko; Shin Joseikan.* 1929: *Jonetsu no Ichiya; Ukiyo Buro; Oyaji to Sonoko.* 1930: *Dokushin-sha Goyojin; Dai-Tokyo no Ikkaku; Hohoemo Jensei; Shojo Nyuyo; Onna-yo Kimi no Na o Kegasu Nakare; Dai Shinrin; Kinuyo Monogatari; Aiyuko no Yoru; Jokyu Aishi.* 1931: *Madamu to Byobo; Wakaki Hi no Kangeki; Shima no Ratai Jiken; Yoru Hiraku; Gutei Kenkei.* 1932: *Niisan no Baka; Ginza no Yanagi; Satsueijo Romansu-Renai Annai; Hototogisu; Koi no Tokyo.* 1933: *Hanayome no Negoto; Izu no Odoriko; Tengoku ni Musube Koi; Juku no Haru; Shojo-yo Sayonara; Aibu.* 1934: *Onna to Umareta Karanya; Sakuru Ondo; Ikitoshi Ikerumono; Hanamuko no Negoto.* 1935: *Hidari Uchiwa; Akogare; Fukeyo Koikaze; Jinsei no Onimotsu.* 1936: *Okusama Shakuyosha; Oboroyo no Onna; Shindo.* 1937: *Hana-kago no Uta.* 1940: *Mokuseki.* 1942: *Shinsetsu.* 1944: *Goju no To.* 1945: *Izu no Musumetachi.* 1947: *Ima Hitotabi no.* 1948: *Omokage.* 1951: *Wakare-Gumo.* 1952: *Asa no Hamon.* 1953: *Entotsu no Mieru Basho/Where Chimneys Are Seen.* 1954: *Ai to Shi No Tanima; Niwatori wa Futatabi Naku; Osaka no Yado.* 1955: *Takekurabe.* 1956: *Aru yo Futatabi.* 1957: *Kiiroi Karasu; Banka.* 1958: *Hotarubi; Yoku; Ari no Machi no Maria; Hibari no Takekurabe.* 1959: *Karatachi Nikki.* 1960: *Waga Ai; Shiroi Kiba.* 1961: *Ryoju; Kumo ga Chigierru Toki; Aijo no Keifu.* 1962: *Kaachan Kekkon Shiroyo.* 1963: *Hyakuman-nin no Musumetachi.* 1965: *Osorezan no Onna.* 1966: *Kaachan to Juichi-nin no Kodomo.* 1967: *Utage.* 1968: *Onna to Misoshiru; Meiji Haru Aki.*

The son of a rich father and a geisha, Gosho illustrates the possibility for breaking down the class barriers of Japanese society. Legitimized, he went to Keio University and became one of the most successful and hardworking directors in the Japanese film industry. In fact, *Madamu to Byobo* was the first full sound-on-film movie made in Japan. An immense, popular success, it launched Gosho on carefully acted film adaptations of plays and novels. Very little of his work is known in the West, and we must be content with the standard two- or three-line reference to a director in the school of, if rather less than, Mizoguchi. But Gosho made ninety-nine films, and he could be several degrees inferior to Mizoguchi yet still a thoroughly worthwhile director. The film enthusiast still lives in a vaguely charted world—Gosho is proof of the current reliance on "Here be dragons" terminology.

Elliott Gould (Elliott Goldstein),
b. Brooklyn, New York, 1938

If you lifted off the music in *The Long Goodbye* (73, Robert Altman), the endless attempts at the title tune, you might not realize that Elliott Gould's performance is like a brilliant, very cool, stoned musician—Art Pepper, say—doing "I Can't Get Started" in a Bogart mood. He's hunched over his instrument, very sad, very alone, yet chronically musical. It's a great performance, with a lovely, secret beat that everyone else in the movie feels but cannot quite get. Who knows if even Altman got it?

Clearly, that kind of acting wasn't going to start a trend, and Gould's career was slipping away by the mid-seventies. Not that he was the man to resist slippage. Still, his doomed cameo in *Bugsy* (91, Barry Levinson) was enough to remind us all of what we have missed over the years and of the rare gentleness in Gould.

The list is not cheerful: a deaf-mute in *Quick, Let's Get Married* (64, William Dieterle); *The Night They Raided Minsky's* (68, William Friedkin); a supporting actor nomination in *Bob & Carol & Ted & Alice* (69, Paul Mazursky); *Getting Straight* (70, Richard Rush); *I Love My . . . Wife* (70, Mel Stuart); *M*A*S*H.* (70, Altman); *Move* (70, Stuart Rosenberg); having and missing his big chance, in *The Touch* (71, Ingmar Bergman); *Little Murders* (71, Alan Arkin); *Busting* (74, Peter Hyams); *California Split* (74, Altman); *S.P.Y.S.*

(74, Irvin Kershner); *Who?* (74, Jack Gold); *I Will, I Will . . . For Now* (76, Norman Panama); briefly in *Nashville* (75, Altman); *Whiffs* (75, Ted Post); *Harry and Walter Go to New York* (76, Mark Rydell); *Mean Johnny Barrows* (76, Fred Williamson); *A Bridge Too Far* (77, Richard Attenborough); *Capricorn One* (78, Hyams); *Escape to Athena* (79, George Pan Cosmatos); *The Lady Vanishes* (79, Anthony Page); *The Muppet Movie* (79, James Frawley); *Falling in Love Again* (80, Steven Paul); *The Last Flight of Noah's Ark* (80, Charles Jarrott); *The Devil and Max Devlin* (81, Steven Hilliard Stern); *Dirty Tricks* (81, Alvin Rakoff); *Over the Brooklyn Bridge* (84, Menahem Golan); *The Naked Face* (85, Bryan Forbes); *Inside Out* (86, Robert Taicher); *Dangerous Love* (88, Marty Ollstein); *The Telephone* (88, Rip Torn); *The Lemon Sisters* (90, Joyce Chopra); and *Night Visitor* (90, Rupert Hitzig).

For years now, Gould has done little bits all over the place, apparently cheerful, and always ready to rise to good material. Is there another screen presence so innately appealing and so steadily wasted? *Wet and Wild Summer!* (92, Maurice Murphy); *Togo il Disturbo* (92, Dino Risi); *Amore!* (93, Lorenzo Doumani); *Bleeding Hearts* (94, Gregory Hines); *The Glass Shield* (94, Charles Burnett); *The Feminine Touch* (94, Conrad Janis); *Kicking and Screaming* (95, Noah Baumbach); *Let It Be Me* (95, Eleanor Bergstein); *Johns* (96, Scott Silver); *Busted* (96, Corey Feldman); *City of Industry* (97, John Irvin)—uncredited; the TV version of *The Shining* (97, Mick Garris); *The Big Hit* (98, Kirk Wong); *American History X* (98, Tony Kaye); *Picking Up the Pieces* (00, Alfonsau Arau); *Playing Mona Lisa* (00, Matthew Huffman); a recurring role as Ross and Monica's father in *Friends*; *Ocean's Eleven* (01, Steven Soderbergh); *The Experience Box* (01, Reid Green and Florian Sachsthal); *Baby Bob* (02, John Forternberry and Rob Schiller); *Puckoon* (02, Terence Ryan).

Edmund Goulding (1891–1959),
b. London

1925: *Sun-Up; Sally, Irene and Mary.* 1926: *Paris.* 1927: *Women Love Diamonds; Love.* 1929: *The Trespasser.* 1930: *Paramount on Parade* (codirected); *The Devil's Holiday.* 1931: *Reaching for the Moon; The Night Angel.* 1932: *Grand Hotel; Blondie of the Follies.* 1934: *Riptide.* 1935: *The Flame Within.* 1937: *That Certain Woman.* 1938: *White Banners; The Dawn Patrol.* 1939: *Dark Victory; We Are Not Alone; The Old Maid.* 1940: *'Til We Meet Again.* 1941: *The Great Lie.* 1943: *The Constant Nymph; Claudia; Forever and a Day* (codirected). 1946: *Of Human Bondage; The Razor's Edge.* 1947: *Nightmare Alley.* 1949: *Everybody Does It.* 1950: *Mister 880.* 1952: *We're*

Not Married; Down Among the Sheltering Palms. 1956: *Teenage Rebel.* 1958: *Mardi Gras.*

Goulding was a boy actor who appeared in *Alice in Wonderland* and *The Picture of Dorian Gray* (16, Fred Durrant). After war service, he went to America and, with Edgar Selwyn, wrote the play *Dancing Mothers.* That led him to write for the movies, with Inspiration, Tiffany, and Fox: *Dangerous Toys* (21, Samuel Bradley); *The Man of Stone* (21, George Archainbaud); *Tol'able David* (21, Henry King); *Broadway Rose* (22, Robert Z. Leonard); *Fascination* (22, Leonard); *The Seventh Day* (22, King); *Till We Meet Again* (22, Christy Cabanne), which Goulding later remade; *Dark Secrets* (23, Victor Fleming); *Fury* (23, King), which Goulding also turned into a book; *Tiger Rose* (23, Sidney Franklin); *Dante's Inferno* (24, Henry Otto); and *Havoc* (25, Rowland V. Lee). His writing credits also include *Broadway Melody* (29, Harry Beaumont) and many of his own early films. He acted again in *Three Live Ghosts* (22, George Fitzmaurice).

As a director, Goulding was an expert handler of actresses in expert romantic melodrama, a man rooted in 1930s cinema who was ill at ease after the Second World War. His best-known film, *Grand Hotel,* is not his best, and it seems likely that on so prestigious a movie his control was reduced by executives and the stars themselves. Contrary to legend, Joan Crawford is the best thing in that film, and it is worth noting that Goulding had directed her in one of her first important roles: *Sally, Irene and Mary.* Goulding was at his best in four extravagant Bette Davis films: *That Certain Woman, Dark Victory, The Old Maid,* and *The Great Lie.* The latter also contains an acid performance from Mary Astor. He made excellent, if conventional, use of Joan Fontaine and Charles Boyer in *The Constant Nymph;* of Tyrone Power, Gene Tierney, and Anne Baxter in *The Razor's Edge;* and of Dorothy McGuire in *Claudia.*

Despite a reputation that had been won with actresses, immediately after the war Goulding made two films around unbeguiling actors: *Mister 880,* a weird mixture of Fox's postwar realism and grass-root sentimentality, with Edmund Gwenn so benign one could wring his neck; and *Nightmare Alley,* a bleak study of breakdown that struggled to make Tyrone Power affecting.

Betty Grable (Elizabeth Ruth Grable) (1916–73), b. St. Louis, Missouri

There is something touching in *The Beautiful Blonde from Bashful Bend* (49, Preston Sturges) about the way supporting characters persist in remarking on Betty Grable's lovely shape and the remorseless ingenuity with which the plot uncovers her legs. Her huge wartime fame was all based on leggy virtuosity and her very good-natured, long-distance sexiness, and *Pin-Up Girl* (44, Bruce Humberstone) was a tribute to the taste of GIs everywhere. Did she really recur in the dreams of frightened men on Pacific atolls as the blonde looking over her shoulder at the boys supposedly ogling the backs of her knees? She was brassy, energetic, and amused, but her body was too pert to be disturbing, too thoroughly healthy to be interesting.

The importance of the moment in certain careers is perfectly demonstrated by Betty Grable. For ten years she had labored away at glamour without really rising above supporting parts. She began as a very young chorine, and after *Let's Go Places* (29, Frank Strayer) and *Whoopee!* (30, Thornton Freeland), Samuel Goldwyn signed her up and changed her name to Frances Dean. She had small parts in *Palmy Days* (31, Edward Sutherland) and *The Kid from Spain* (32, Leo McCarey), before RKO used her as an ingenue in musicals and comedies: *The Gay Divorcee* (34, Mark Sandrich); *The Nitwits* (35, George Stevens); *Follow the Fleet* (36, Sandrich); and *Pigskin Parade* (36, David Butler). RKO dropped her and she went briefly into variety with her new husband, Jackie Coogan. Paramount called her back to replace Shirley Ross in *This Way Please* (37, Robert Florey), and she stayed at the studio for *College Swing* (38, Raoul Walsh); *Give Me a Sailor* (38, Elliott Nugent); and *Man About Town* (39, Sandrich).

Yet again she was dropped. But after some stage work, Fox asked her to replace a sick Alice Faye in *Down Argentine Way* (40, Irving Cummings). At last she was the leggy centerpiece of boisterous, Technicolor musicals (and from 1943 on she was married to Harry James—there was some surreal import in her legs and his horn): *Tin Pan Alley* (40, Walter Lang); *Moon Over Miami* (41, Lang); *Song of the Islands* (42, Lang); *Springtime in the Rockies* (42, Cummings); *Coney Island* (43, Lang); *Sweet Rosie O'Grady* (43, Cummings); and *Billy Rose's Diamond Horseshoe* (45, George Seaton).

After the war, she kept a brave face against changed tastes: *The Dolly Sisters* (46, Cummings) and *Mother Wore Tights* (47, Lang). She flopped in a straight role—*That Lady in Ermine* (48, Otto Preminger and Ernst Lubitsch)—the first since *A Yank in the RAF* (41, Henry King) and *I Wake Up Screaming* (41, Humberstone). Her last few years at Fox were spent waiting for some new blonde goddess: *When My Baby Smiles at Me* (48, Lang); *My Blue Heaven* (50, Henry Koster); *Wabash Avenue* (50, Koster); *Call Me Mister* (51, Lloyd Bacon); and *The Farmer Takes a Wife* (53, Henry Levin). Marilyn Monroe settled her fate. They were together in *How to Marry a Millionaire* (53,

Jean Negulesco), after which Grable made only two films—*How to Be Very, Very Popular* (55, Nunnally Johnson) and *Three for the Show* (55, H. C. Potter).

Gloria Grahame (Gloria Grahame Hallward) (1925–81), b. Los Angeles

The excellent English critic Judith Williamson has said of Grahame (in *Human Desire*): ". . . she seems to represent a sort of acted-upon femininity, both unfathomable and ungraspable. She slips through the film like a drop of loose mercury. Neither we nor the other characters know whether to believe what she says; elusive as a cat, she is the focus of terrible actions, but unknowable herself."

How well those words apply to most of Grahame's films—and how surely they reach out for that strange life of hers, so easily mistaken for film noir. Just a few years before her death, there she was in England, doing theatre—Sadie Thompson in *Rain*, and a new play about a movie star, *A Tribute to Lili Lamont*. In an interview at the time, she kissed the writer on the lips, and said, "Well, I couldn't go home and write an article about *you*. Or maybe I could . . ." If that isn't a loaded hesitation from one of her pictures, how do we place her wretched death, not long afterwards, or its half-fictional, half-biographical treatment in her young lover Peter Turner's *Film Stars Don't Die in Liverpool*?

Ms. Williamson was right: Grahame was always mysterious, or less than reliable. Even in *In a Lonely Place*, where she is ostensibly the fixed character who must judge another, there are hints of turbulence ready to break out, and of a past that makes her absentminded. If she only ever really played supporting parts, that may be because that level of work allowed her to be most enigmatic. But things happened when she was around: any room became a place where coffee was coming to the boil.

Her Scottish mother had been a singer and an actress before she became drama coach at the Pasadena Playhouse. Her father, too, was British, and his father, Basil Hallward, was a painter referred to in Wilde's *The Picture of Dorian Gray*. Little Gloria was in the theatre as a kid, an understudy, when she made her movie debut as a waitress in *Blonde Fever* (44, Richard Whorf).

She married the actor Stanley Clements (1945–48), and appeared in *It Happened in Brooklyn* (46, Whorf); as flirty Violet in *It's a Wonderful Life* (47, Frank Capra), who becomes a hooker in the nightmare; and *Merton of the Movies* (47, Robert Alton). She was then riveting, and nominated for supporting actress, as a tart in *Crossfire* (47, Edward Dmytryk), perhaps the most decent woman she ever played.

In 1948, she appeared in Nicholas Ray's *A Woman's Secret,* and married the director. (They were divorced in 1952.) She was also in *Song of the Thin Man* (47, Edward Buzzell) and *Roughshod* (49, Mark Robson) but, despite her sultry, deadpan looks, she was not getting lead roles until *In a Lonely Place* (50), where she is the great and lost love that Bogart suffers—angel of rescue, or clinching failure? Who knows how far that great movie alludes to the Ray-Grahame marriage? They were at odds by 1950, and Ray made tortured statements about how little the marriage ever meant to him. But they had a son.

Grahame worked for Ray and Josef von Sternberg on *Macao* (52); she won the supporting actress Oscar for her Southern wife in *The Bad and the Beautiful* (52, Vincente Minnelli), a role as funny as it was close to danger—for that woman goes fatally too far, offscreen; she was stunning as Jack Palance's companion in menace in *Sudden Fear* (52, David Miller); and she was the blithe elephant girl in *The Greatest Show on Earth* (52, Cecil B. De Mille).

She was in *Man on a Tightrope* (53, Elia Kazan), and went to England for *The Good Die Young* (53, Lewis Gilbert). But she was at her best, half lovely, half scalded by coffee (preeminently two-faced) in *The Big Heat* (53, Fritz Lang), and unaffectedly sexual but distant in Lang's *Human Desire* (54). And in 1954, she married producer Cy Howard—it lasted until 1957.

Her movie fortunes slipped slowly: *Naked Alibi* (54, Jerry Hopper); Widmark's wife in *The Cobweb* (55, Minnelli); Ado Annie in *Oklahoma!* (55, Fred Zinnemann); neglected in *Not as a Stranger* (55, Stanley Kramer); *The Man Who Never Was* (56, Ronald Neame); and *Odds Against Tomorrow* (59, Robert Wise).

In 1961, she married her stepson, Anthony Ray, Nick Ray's child by his first marriage. As she grew older, the pout turned very sad, and her films matched that mood: *Ride Beyond Vengeance* (66, Bernard McEveety); *Blood and Lace* (70, Philip Gilbert); *The Loners* (72, Sutton Roley); *Mama's Dirty Girls* (74, John Hayes); *Mansion of the Doomed* (75, Michael Pataki); *Head Over Heels/Chilly Scenes of Winter* (79, Joan Micklin Silver); *A Nightingale Sang in Berkeley Square* (79, Ralph Thomas); *Melvin and Howard* (80, Jonathan Demme); and *The Nesting* (81, Armand Weston).

Farley Granger,
b. San Jose, California, 1925

Granger was a pretty-boy hero, shifting sands to trap a woman's hopes, and a mannequin athlete. Hitchcock remorselessly breaks down his tennis champion, Guy Barnes, in *Strangers on a Train* (51) to the well-dressed smoothie posing with rackets but not out of breath since he left dancing school; the stand-in for action shots is plainly unlike Granger; while those close-ups of Granger show him lashing at the fleeting ball. It is a matter of casting and assessment of actorly character that Granger so subtly suggests the culpable opting for the easy way out in Guy Barnes. Pretty but dull, innocent but fallible, wronged but petulant, Granger is the unappetizing hero to Robert Walker's absorbing villain. Granger was for years under contract to Goldwyn, but his brittleness was invariably discovered by others.

Curly-headed, fresh-faced softness stayed with Granger for a dozen years: for his debut as a young soldier in *The North Star* (43, Lewis Milestone) and *The Purple Heart* (44, Milestone); through notable war service; as the impulsive, doomed innocent in *They Live By Night* (48, Nicholas Ray); as the more highly strung of the two killers in *Rope* (48, Alfred Hitchcock); *Enchantment* (48, Irving Reis); *Roseanna McCoy* (49, Reis); *Side Street* (49, Anthony Mann); *Our Very Own* (50, David Miller); *Edge of Doom* (50, Mark Robson); *I Want You* (51, Robson); in "The Gift of the Magi" episode from *O. Henry's Full House* (52, Henry King); *Hans Christian Andersen* (52, Charles Vidor); saying "Suckertash" to Ricky Nelson's "Suffering" in *The Story of Three Loves* (53, Vincente Minnelli); and *Small Town Girl* (53, Leslie Kardos).

He went to Italy to play the fainthearted, swindling lover of Alida Valli in *Senso* (54, Luchino Visconti). But after *Naked Street* (55, Maxwell Shane) and a spiteful Harry Thaw in *The Girl in the Red Velvet Swing* (55, Richard Fleischer), he went into TV. Since then, he has been seen in *Rogue's Gallery* (67, Leonard Horn); *The Challengers* (68, Leslie H. Martinson); *Qualcosa Striscia nel Buio* (70, Mario Colucci); *Lo Chiamarano Trinita* (70, Enzo Barboni); *The Man Called Noon* (73, Peter Collinson); *Le Serpent* (73, Henri Verneuil); *Rivelazioni di un Maniaco Sessuale al Capo della Squadra Mobile* (73, Roberto Montero); *The Lives of Jenny Dolan* (75, Jerry Jameson); *Rosemary's Killer* (81, Joseph Zito); *Deathmask* (84, Richard Friedman); *The Imagemaker* (86, Hal Weiner); *The Next Best Thing* (01, P. J. Posner).

Stewart Granger (James Stewart)
(1913–1993), b. London

Granger always had a swashbuckling flair that might have excelled in silent pictures or won him a more permanent reputation in the hands of, say, Michael Curtiz. He might have been a real star if not for Errol Flynn.

After a few years in repertory theatre and some walk-on film work, he made his real debut in *So This Is London* (38, Thornton Freeland). During the war years he became a romantic star of the British cinema: *Secret Mission* (42, Harold

French); *The Man in Grey* (43, Leslie Arliss); *The Lamp Still Burns* (43, Maurice Elvey); *Fanny by Gaslight* (44, Anthony Asquith); *Waterloo Road* (44, Sidney Gilliat); *Love Story* (44, Arliss); *Madonna of the Seven Moons* (44, Arthur Crabtree); as Apollodorus in *Caesar and Cleopatra* (45, Gabriel Pascal); *Caravan* (46, Crabtree); *Captain Boycott* (47, Frank Launder); *Blanche Fury* (47, Marc Allégret); *Saraband for Dead Lovers* (48, Basil Dearden and Michael Relph); *Woman Hater* (48, Terence Young); and *Adam and Evelyne* (49, Harold French).

This last film was made with his second wife, Jean Simmons, and in 1950 they both went to Hollywood. But Granger's career hardly altered. Without ever becoming a big star he continued to be enjoyable in costume and adventure movies, initially at MGM: as Allan Quatermain in *King Solomon's Mines* (50, Compton Bennett and Andrew Marton); *Soldiers Three* (51, Tay Garnett); *The Light Touch* (51, Richard Brooks); at his best in *Scaramouche* (52, George Sidney); Rassendyll in *The Prisoner of Zenda* (52, Richard Thorpe); *Young Bess* (53, Sidney); *Salome* (53, William Dieterle); *All the Brothers Were Valiant* (53, Thorpe); as *Beau Brummel* (54, Curtis Bernhardt); *Green Fire* (55, Marton); *Footsteps in the Fog* (55, Arthur Lubin); *Moonfleet* (55, Fritz Lang); *Bhowani Junction* (56, George Cukor); *The Last Hunt* (56, Brooks); *Gun Glory* (57, Roy Rowland); beginning to age in *Harry Black* (58, Hugo Fregonese); and *North to Alaska* (60, Henry Hathaway).

His hair turned white but he had not lost his stone-cracking grin. Only *Sodom and Gomorrah* (62, Robert Aldrich), *The Secret Invasion* (64, Roger Corman), and *The Last Safari* (67, Hathaway) have been worth noting amid several European Westerns and an unhappy spell in *The Virginian* on TV.

But more than a decade later he played Prince Philip in *The Royal Romance of Charles and Diana* (82, Peter Levin); in *A Hazard of Hearts* (87, John Hough); and *Fine Gold* (88, Anthony J. Loma).

Cary Grant (Archibald Alexander Leach) (1904–86), b. Bristol, England

There is a major but very difficult realization that needs to be reached about Grant—difficult, that is, for many people who like to think they take the art of film seriously. As well as being a leading box-office draw for some thirty years, the epitome of the man-about-town, as well as being the ex-husband of Virginia Cherrell, Barbara Hutton, Betsy Drake, and Dyan Cannon, as well as being the retired actor, still handsome executive of a perfume company—as well as all these things, he was the best and most important actor in the history of the cinema.

The essence of his quality can be put quite simply: he can be attractive and unattractive simultaneously; there is a light and dark side to him but, whichever is dominant, the other creeps into view. It may be that this is Grant (or Archie Leach) himself transmitted by camera and screen thanks to a rare willingness to commit himself to the camera without fraud, disguise, or exaggeration, to take part in a fantasy without being deceived by it. But the effect he achieves is one of art; it shows malice, misogyny, selfishness, and solitariness beneath good manners and gaiety; and it reveals a sense of grace-in-humor buoying up a near-sadistic playing upon lesser people's nerves and good nature. For instance, consider the hint of a real madman beneath the playfulness in *Suspicion* (41, Alfred Hitchcock); the masterly portrait of moral fecklessness stopped in its tracks in *North by Northwest* (59, Hitchcock); hurt pride turning into a cold, calculating manipulation of Ingrid Bergman in *Notorious* (46, Hitchcock), only to relent finally. Consider again the masculine chauvinism that shows through the sombrero-wearing flyer in *Only Angels Have Wings* (39, Howard Hawks); the merciless delight in teasing in *His Girl Friday* (40, Hawks); the bringing to life of a sheltered, near-sighted bone specialist in *Bringing Up Baby* (38, Hawks); the demented sexual frustration in *I Was a Male War Bride* (49, Hawks); and the hilarious mixture of adult and schoolboy in *Monkey Business* (52, Hawks). If this list is confined to Hitchcock and Hawks, that only underlines how no one else has or could have done so well for two directors as radically opposed in attitude. The same disturbing and living ambiguity can be seen in many other films, along with an unrivaled sense of timing, encouragement of fellow actors, and the ability to cram words or expressions in gaps so small that most other actors would rest. Grant could not be the demanding portrait of man that he is but for a technical command that is so complete it is barely noticeable. It is a conclusive failing of the Oscar system that Grant won nothing for a specific performance. Thus, in shame and confusion, in 1969 the Academy gave him a general award "with the respect and affection of his colleagues."

His mother had a mental breakdown when he was twelve, and young Archie found his education at the Bristol Hippodrome with a troupe of acrobats. He went to America as a tumbler in 1920 (his physical aplomb owes much to this training), but returned to the English theatre and only went back to the United States in a musical, *Golden Dawn*. By 1932, he had earned a small contract with Paramount and made his debut in *This Is the Night* (32, Frank Tuttle). After a few more supporting parts, he played opposite Dietrich in *Blonde Venus* (32, Josef von Sternberg) and Sylvia Sidney in *Madame Butterfly* (33, Marion Gering). But it was Mae West who knew him for what he was, choosing Grant to swop taunts with her in *She Done Him Wrong* (33, Lowell Sherman) and *I'm No Angel* (33, Wesley Ruggles).

In the second half of the decade, he emerged from support to a fully fledged comedian. He was opposite Loretta Young in *Born to Be Bad* (34, Lowell Sherman). RKO borrowed him to play with Katharine Hepburn in *Sylvia Scarlett* (35, George Cukor), and next year he signed contracts with Columbia and RKO. On this basis, the films flowed: *The Awful Truth* (37, Leo McCarey) with Irene Dunne; *Topper* (37, Norman Z. McLeod) with Constance Bennett; *Bringing Up Baby*, with Hepburn, in a love story as poignant as it is crazy—in this writer's opinion, Grant got better things out of Hepburn than Tracy ever managed; with Hepburn again in *Holiday* (38, Cukor); as a Cockney soldier in *Gunga Din* (39, George Stevens); *Only Angels Have Wings*, making Jean Arthur yelp with anger; with Carole Lombard in *In Name Only* (39, John Cromwell); *My Favorite Wife* (40, Garson Kanin) with Irene Dunne; *His Girl Friday*, goading Rosalind Russell into being bearable; *The Philadelphia Story* (40, Cukor), with Hepburn and James Stewart (the wrong man got the Oscar); *Penny Serenade* (41, Stevens), with Dunne again; *Suspicion*, preying on Joan Fontaine; *The Talk of the Town* (42, Stevens), with Jean Arthur and Ronald Colman; *Once Upon a Honeymoon* (42, McCarey) with Ginger Rogers.

None But the Lonely Heart (44, Clifford Odets) was close to Grant's guarded heart: it described a mother-son relationship that reminded him of his own (Ethel Barrymore was very good as the mother); and Odets was a friend. But the film was received as a gloomy failure, something that betrayed or wasted the usual Grant, no matter that the Cockney drifter he played said a lot about Grant's uneasiness. But the failure frightened him away from further interest in production. His Cole Porter in *Night and Day* (46, Michael Curtiz), therefore, was a business-as-usual travesty biopic, no matter that Grant knew the real Porter quite well.

Notorious may be the darkest Grant ever offered for popular approval. He was urbanity at the end of its comic tether in *The Bachelor and the Bobby Soxer* (47, Irving Reis) and *Mr. Blandings Builds His Dream House* (48, H. C. Potter), with Myrna Loy as his partner in both. He made *Every Girl Should Be Married* (48, Don Hartman), with Betsy Drake—and soon they were married. In *I Was a Male War Bride*, Ann Sheridan seems sometimes helpless with laughter. On *Crisis* (50), it was Grant's say-so that gave Richard Brooks his directorial debut. *People Will Talk* (51, Joseph L. Mankiewicz) was well suited to his aloof, almost pained intelligence. *Dream Wife* (53, Sidney Sheldon) was a dud. In *To Catch a Thief* (55, Hitchcock), it was just conceivable that he

was a cat burglar, yet his fine moral discrimination hesitated when Grace Kelly offered him a leg or a breast. He had such a thing for Sophia Loren that he made two foolish pictures with her—*The Pride and the Passion* (57, Stanley Kramer) and *Houseboat* (58, Melville Shavelson). He was far better with Deborah Kerr in *An Affair to Remember* (57, Leo McCarey) and with Ingrid Bergman in *Indiscreet* (58, Stanley Donen).

Apart from *North by Northwest*, the final films were no more than modest exercise for Grant. Retirement recognized the real onset of age, but perhaps he was a little bored by *Kiss Them for Me* (57, Donen); *Operation Petticoat* (59, Blake Edwards); *The Grass Is Greener* (60, Donen); *That Touch of Mink* (62, Delbert Mann); *Charade* (65, Donen); and *Walk, Don't Run* (66, Charles Walters).

Grant made bad or dull films along the way, to be sure—*Born to Be Bad; Big Brown Eyes* (36, Raoul Walsh); *The Toast of New York* (37, Rowland V. Lee); *The Howards of Virginia* (40, Frank Lloyd); *Destination Tokyo* (43, Delmer Daves); *Mr. Lucky* (43, Potter); *Arsenic and Old Lace* (44, Frank Capra); *Dream Wife;* and *The Pride and the Passion*. He was rather cheap, and too suspicious—so he missed being in *The Third Man* and opposite Garland in *A Star Is Born*. He was, very likely, a hopeless fusspot as man, husband, and even father. How could anyone *be* "Cary Grant"? But how can anyone, ever after, not consider the attempt?

Hugh Grant, b. London, 1962
With his drooping chin and pouty lips, his quaff of hair and dithery manner, Hugh Grant seems like a refugee from 1930s theatre—or an incipient sneeze looking for a vacant nose. That he gets away with it—or has done so far—attests to the special American sentimentality for soft toffee in Brits. Of course, it is no small part of this that his successful romantic comedies all give up the ghost before they're over, as if succumbing to the itchy mannerisms that pass for acting in Grant.

He went to Oxford and worked on stage. His first movie—as Hughie Grant—was the Oxford-based *Privileged* (82, Michael Hoffman), as "Lord Adrian." He also played Apsley Cherry-Garrard in a TV version of *The Last Place on Earth* (85, Ferdinand Fairfax). His screen career began properly a few years later: *Maurice* (87, James Ivory); *White Mischief* (88, Michael Radford); *The Lair of the White Worm* (88, Ken Russell); as Byron in *Rowing with the Wind* (89, Gonzalo Suárez); as Chopin in *Impromptu* (90, James Lapine); *Crossing the Line* (91, David Leland); *Bitter Moon* (92, Roman Polanski); a breakthrough in *Four Weddings and a Funeral* (94, Mike Newell); *Night Train to Venice* (95, Carlo U. Quinterio); *Sirens* (94, John Duigan);

An Awfully Big Adventure (95, Newell); *The Eng-
lishman Who Went Up a Hill but Came Down a
Mountain* (95, Christopher Monger); *Nine
Months* (95, Chris Columbus); *Restoration* (95,
Hoffman); *Sense and Sensibility* (95, Ang Lee);
Extreme Measures (96, Michael Apted)—which
was produced by Elizabeth Hurley, his then-
companion (when he wasn't availing himself of
Hollywood prostitutes, and getting caught—the
homeless sneeze syndrome); allegedly breathing
the same air as Julia Roberts in *Notting Hill* (99,
Roger Michell); *Mickey Blue Eyes* (99, Kelly
Makin); *Small Time Crooks* (00, Woody Allen);
Bridget Jones's Diary (01, Sharon Maguire);
About a Boy (02, Paul Weitz and Chris Weitz);
Two Weeks Notice (02, Marc Lawrence).

Guy Green, b. Somerset, England, 1913
1953: *River Boat.* 1955: *Portrait of Allison; Lost.*
1956: *House of Secrets.* 1958: *The Snorkel; Sea of
Sand.* 1959: *S.O.S. Pacific.* 1960: *The Angry
Silence.* 1961: *The Mark.* 1962: *Light in the
Piazza; Diamond Head.* 1965: *A Patch of Blue.*
1967: *Pretty Polly.* 1968: *The Magus.* 1969: *A
Walk in the Spring Rain.* 1973: *Luther.* 1974:
Jacqueline Susann's Once Is Not Enough. 1977:
Der Teufels Advokat/The Devil's Advocate. 1979:
The Incredible Journey of Doctor Meg Laurel
(TV); *Jennifer: A Woman's Story* (TV). 1980:
Jimmy B. and Andre (TV). 1981: *Isabel's Choice*
(TV). 1987: *Strong Medicine.*

From the mid-1930s, Green was a camera opera-
tor: *One of Our Aircraft Is Missing* (42, Michael
Powell) and *In Which We Serve* (42, Noel Coward
and David Lean). He went on to be lighting cam-
eraman on *The Way Ahead* (44, Carol Reed);
Great Expectations (46, Lean); *Take My Life* (47,
Ronald Neame); *Oliver Twist* (48, Lean); *Captain
Horatio Hornblower* (51, Raoul Walsh); *The Beg-
gar's Opera* (53, Peter Brook); and *Rob Roy* (53,
Harold French). His early work as a director was
neat and promising: *House of Secrets* and *The
Snorkel* are ingenious and entertaining thrillers.
But *The Angry Silence,* supposedly a break-
through, encouraged his flashiness into the open.
As a director of larger projects he has only
exposed himself. *The Mark* was solemnly preten-
tious, *A Patch of Blue* strictly sentimental, and *The
Magus* completely bewildered.

Peter Greenaway, b. London, 1942
1966: *Train* (s); *Tree* (s). 1967: *Revolution* (s);
Five Postcards from Capital Cities (s). 1969:
Intervals (s). 1971: *Erosion* (s). 1973: *H Is for
House* (s). 1974: *Windows* (s); *Water* (s). 1975:
Water Wrackets (s). 1976: *Goole by Numbers* (s).
1977: *Dear Phone* (s). 1978: *1–1000* (s); *A Walk
Through H* (s); *Vertical Features Remake* (s).
1979: *Zandra Rhodes* (s). 1980: *The Falls.* 1981:

Act of God (s). 1982: *The Draughtsman's Contract.* 1983: *Four American Composers* (d). 1984:
Making a Splash (s); *A TV Dante—Canto 5* (s).
1985: *Inside Rooms—26 Bathrooms* (s); *A Zed
and Two Noughts.* 1986: *Belly of an Architect.*
1987: *Fear of Drowning* (s). 1988: *Drowning by
Numbers; A TV Dante—Cantos 1–8* (s). 1989:
*The Cook, the Thief, His Wife and Her Lover;
Death in the Seine* (s). 1991: *Prospero's Books.*
1993: *The Baby of Macon; Darwin* (TV). 1995:
Stairs 1 Geneva (d). 1996: *The Pillow Book.* 1999:
*8½ Women; The Death of a Composer: Rosa, a
Horse Drama.* 2001: *A Man in the Bath.* 2003:
The Tulse Luper Suitcases: the Moab Story.

Greenaway is not to everyone's taste—but he does
not claim to be. "I have often thought it was very
arrogant to suppose you could make a film for anybody but yourself." Which doesn't mean that the
lone, self-sufficient artist may not also be marked
by arrogance. Greenaway is a filmmaker as one
might be a modern painter or an experimental
novelist. Despite the considerable art-house success of both *The Draughtsman's Contract* and *The
Cook, the Thief . . .* , he is not just a confessed
intellectual, but someone fascinated by games,
number theory, structuralist principles, and
unmitigated aesthetics. ". . . I am arguing for cinema for its own sake, and for its ability to hold
thought and ideas without necessarily demanding
that an audience should be battered into suspend-
ing disbelief or that such a thing is cinema's sole
function."

As a young child, Greenaway and his family
moved to London where he would study at
Walthamstow College of Art. He failed to get into
the Royal College of Art film school, but as he
began painting so his obsession with film grew. He
found work with the British Film Institute, where
he was able to see many of the classic experimental films. He became an editor, at the Central
Office of Information. But he had purchased a
16mm Bolex and so—with his own money—he
began to make short films. In time, his formalism
would become a beneficiary of patronage from the
B.F.I. Production Fund, Channel 4, and European television. Yet, by now, *The Cook, the
Thief . . .* has earned close to $10 million in Amer-
ica, and Greenaway has grown warily into some
taste for actors and melodrama.

The Draughtsman's Contract had an air of
erotic thriller that was made more piquant by its
mixture of cinematic stringency and baroque lushness. But in *The Cook, the Thief . . .* the celebration of form only made the cruelty in the material
more excruciating, and vacant. John Boorman (by
no means a happy sailor in midstream) has gone
into print to speak of the cruelty, the coldness, and
the awesome, sterile certainty in Greenaway.
Those are valid criticisms of a man who admires

The Seventh Seal and *Blue Velvet* but who has rarely captured their humanity. Whereas *Belly of an Architect* was probably changed for the better by Brian Dennehy's bulky warmth, *Prospero's Books* is an unkindness not just to Shakespeare but to John Gielgud, too.

Greenaway is a test case in the question as to whether cinema can really be as solitary as art or literature. Or is there not an inevitable, maudlin, melodramatic sense of the crowd as soon as one throws light on a wall?

Greenaway *is* an authentic misanthrope. There is a barely veiled disdain for the pale weakness of human flesh amid the posed swagger of bunting, decor, and food in *The Cook, the Thief*. . . . And when Greenaway's camera makes its rapid, sidelong tracking movements from space to space it resembles a rat in the skirting boards, thrilled by human squalor.

Graham Greene (1904–91),
b. Berkhamstead, England

In his written fiction, Graham Greene kept a bleak wariness for what he called "cinemas," tawdry caves where pictures played. He did not trust their comfort or diversion, any more than he relied on consolation from their neighbors on gray streets, the churches. Both buildings smelled to him of guilt and embalming.

But in life, Greene ignored his own warnings; he loved to make himself available for the dark and its threats. His father, a schoolteacher, once took a group of boys to a Tarzan picture (this in the Elmo Lincoln era), believing the film had anthropological and educational value. When raw fantasy became apparent, the disappointed father left the cinema. But Graham and the boys stayed to see it through.

As a journalist in Nottingham, in the 1920s, Greene escaped afternoon light by seeing whatever the local theatres offered. He preferred to go on his own, because being alone (and hidden) among strangers gazing at the bright sensation was so stimulating: "Cinemas have a peculiar effect. . . . Is it the concentrated emotion of lots of people? Because it doesn't work if one's not alone, for then one's withdrawn from the general audience and can scoff at the ridiculousness of the picture. It's all very curious."

There's something critically Greene in that: the half-hypnotized, half-removed admission of a creepy solitude in which things pass solemnly when they would be fatuous in company. The mood is furtive but intellectual, a little prurient but dreamily aloof—it is like watching oneself watching, a mixture of rapt voyeurism and smiling distaste.

"When I describe a scene," he told Marie-Françoise Allain, "I capture it with the moving eye of the cine-camera rather than with the photographer's eye—which leaves it frozen. In this precise domain I think that the cinema has influenced me. Authors like Walter Scott and the Victorians were influenced by paintings and constructed their backgrounds as though they were static and came from the hands of a Constable. I work with the camera, following my characters and their movements. So the landscape moves. When I turn my head and look at the harbor, my head moves, the houses move, the boats move, don't they?"

You can call this cinematic or voyeuristic; the human itch existed before the machinery, but it gained nerve or insolence when film industrialized the shy glance:

> Mr. Tench went out to look for his ether cylinder, into the blazing Mexican sun and the bleaching dust. A few vultures looked down from the roof with shabby indifference: he wasn't carrion yet.
>
> —The opening of
> *The Power and the Glory*, 1940

Three clear shots—but, in a movie, how could the vultures be made the watchers, and how could their verdict then become Tench's point of view? The narrative is so much more slippery than the celluloid.

> "If somebody asked you what your deepest sexual experience had been what would you say?"
> I knew the answer to that, "Lying in bed early one morning and watching a woman in a red dressing-gown brush her hair."
>
> —Pyle and Fowler in
> *The Quiet American*, 1955

But if you film that, do you cut away to the woman recollected, making an epiphany of her, so that you have to find a right actress and a proper dressing gown? Or do you just hold on Fowler's fallen face speaking the line? Somehow the book eludes visibility just as it evokes it, for we envisage Fowler and the woman—who can be any woman—as we read, and even wonder if her preciousness is fabricated (to impress Pyle? to impress Fowler?).

> He looks out of the window of the swaying, rising car at the figures diminishing below them with what looks like genuine commiseration. Very slowly, on one side of them, the city sinks: very slowly on the other, the great cross girders of the wheel rise into sight. As the horizon slides away, the Danube becomes visible, and the piers of the Reichsbrucke lift above the houses.
>
> —From the screenplay
> for *The Third Man* (48)

This describes the Great Wheel sequence, just before Harry Lime speaks of dots and lives down below at £20,000 a dot, "free of income tax, old man." But the scene on screen cannot capture the airy lurch of the cabin—the true nausea of Lime's presence—because Carol Reed had to shoot the cabin in the studio in front of process work.

I watched him striding off on his overgrown legs after the girl. He caught her up and they walked side by side. I don't think he said a word to her: it was like the end of a story except that before they turned out of my sight her hand was through his arm—which is how a story usually begins.

—The close to the story
"The Third Man"

The story was written before the script but not published until 1950, and the ending is a mercy not permitted in the film, where Anna/Valli just walks away, ignoring Holly Martins and the camera. It was an ending over which Greene and Carol Reed argued. Reed felt the audience would find a yielding Anna cynical and opportunistic. Greene "held the view that an entertainment of this kind was too light an affair to carry the weight of an unhappy ending."

So Greene's standing as a "natural" or skilled screenwriter does not confine him as just a "cinematic novelist." Still, film let him insinuate himself into a level of intimacy, or secrecy, that is very modern. What helped was a knack of writing that producers and moguls grasped, his instinct for suspense, his own worldly charm, and his interest in danger—this was a bookworm who found friendship with Alexander Korda (and some other dictators).

It was possible to see Greene as a respectable Englishman. That's how François Truffaut used him, credited as Henry Graham, in *Day for Night*, as a London insurance man sent to advise a troubled project. Greene's father would rise to be headmaster of a minor public school. Graham himself went to Balliol College, Oxford, and worked for the *Times*, for British intelligence in Sierra Leone (the site of *The Heart of the Matter*) and in publishing. He also maintained a steady flow of writing—novels, nonfiction, essays, scripts, and three produced stage plays. He was a Companion of Honour and he held the Order of Merit.

All that fits with the Greene of photographs—tall, straight, eyes so pale they seemed nearly empty, a little withdrawn and wry, unsmiling yet not angry, and notably free from excess or passion. It was a tidy, wrapped face; and it changed little in sixty years. "I have no talent," he once said, like a bank manager (the young man's profession in *Travels with My Aunt*), "it's just a question of working, of being willing to put in the time." There was a quality of silence in the face, something evident, say, in the face of Ralph Richardson's Baines in *The Fallen Idol*. It's the hush of despairing hope, or desperate gambling.

He had tried several kinds of suicide and the spin of Russian roulette as a youth. He traveled in perilous places—Mexico in the thirties, Indochina in the fifties, Haiti from time to time, the hot spots of Africa and London in the Blitz. A friend to bosses, he had been a Communist and he could be fired by causes even as late as *J'Accuse*, in 1982, when he was more crank than Zola, blazing away at corruption on the Côte d'Azur. He tried opium and whores in matter-of-fact ways. He was sued by lawyers on behalf of Shirley Temple for calling her "a totsy." There was a recklessness to him; it was like a shy man doing something flagrant out of a need to be shocking, or exposed.

He had taken up film reviewing in 1935 for the *Spectator*. In retrospect, he claimed it was a drunken idea formed "after the dangerous third Martini." But he had real money problems in the thirties, and he needed a means of distancing himself from the dark. It was not until 1972, when his reviews were published as *The Pleasure Dome*, that Greene admitted the element of fun:

Four and a half years of watching films several times a week. . . . I can hardly believe in that life of the distant thirties now, a way of life which I adopted quite voluntarily from a sense of fun. More than four hundred films—and I suppose there would have been many more if I had not suffered during the same period from other obsessions—four novels had to be written, not to speak of a travel book which took me away for months to Mexico, far from the Pleasure-Dome—all those Empires and Odeons of a luxury and a bizarre taste we shall never see again."

The reviews are good reading still because of Greene's range and the bite of his observations. The films were a trigger for life, or for his novelizing alchemy. For instance, he fell with delight on Wesley Ruggles's comedy *True Confessions* just because it had pierced the screen's "life-like" armor and found that unruly vibrancy we call the ordinary. Whereupon he offered a thought worthy of one of his own characters, aghast at the way the world was wearing out:

I advise a quick visit [to *True Confessions*]: the public, I think, found it oddly shocking, for the middlebrow screen is more and more dictating how people ought to behave—even at a deathbed. I remember lying in bed a few years ago in a public ward listening with fascinated horror to a mother crying over her child who had died suddenly and unexpectedly after a minor operation. You couldn't question the appalling grief, but the words she used . . . they were the cheapest, the most improbable, the most untrue . . . one had heard them on a dozen British screens. Even the father felt embarrassed standing there beside her in the open ward, avoiding every eye.

That mix of horror and the hideous reminds one how regularly Greene held back from praising Alfred Hitchcock. To which one should add their having been born only five years and twenty-five miles apart, with the saving gap of having a greengrocer and a teacher for fathers.

Perhaps it takes one misanthropic voyeur to know (and cut) another. Even in 1972, after he might have seen the later, richer, Greener stages of Hitch's inner journey, Greene held to opinions based on the English films of the thirties. He had detected then "an inadequate sense of reality. . . . His films consist of a series of small, 'amusing' melodramatic situations: the murderer's button dropped on the baccarat board; the strangled organist's hands prolonging the notes in the empty church . . . very perfunctorily he builds up to those tricky situations (paying no attention on the way to inconsistencies) and then drops them: they mean nothing; they lead to nothing."

Greene's claim is warranted. Yet the trickiness in Hitchcock, the indifference to reality, and even the disdain, can be found in Greene, too. To say nothing of the vague outlines of Catholic consequences for noir setups. In both bodies of work, we can feel how dread, desire, and solitariness have separated the authors from reality. Both men had difficulty expressing their strong feelings naturally; in both cases that left a disconcerting edge of judgmental hostility, a way of sneering at treasured things. And in both artists we feel the outcast sadness of lifelong watchers. Their work could suddenly go taut with religious suspense: this happens as the wife declines in *The Wrong Man,* and in *The End of the Affair,* one of Greene's most harrowing novels, love is abandoned in return for a granted prayer.

Greene liked to sound lofty (perhaps it made God feel a better bet), but he was practical when he had to be. In 1937 he wrote a short piece, "Film Lunch," about being at an MGM press junket and having to listen to Louis B. Mayer. The writing is blurry—half tight on Metro liquor, half dozing through Mayer's windy speech—but the impressionistic scanning of the crowd picks out the writers who "lean back and dream of the hundred pounds a week—and all that's asked in return, the dried imagination and the dead pen."

Greene was estimating a career. His 101-page treatment "The Tenth Man" was bought and shelved by MGM. In 1936 he reviewed Carol Reed's *Laburnum Grove* favorably, but said, "Mr. Reed, when he gets the right scripts, will prove far more than efficient." But he was not just an opportunist; he wanted to be tested and scourged. So he weighed the drama of life in terms of betrayal. Sooner or later, we all fail there. In his novels, Greene is a vulture hovering above the stricken first-person narrative, or those numb third-person autopsies on the central souls. As *A Burnt-Out Case* begins: "The cabin-passenger wrote in his diary a parody of Descartes: 'I feel discomfort, therefore I am alive!' "

Film could not hold on to that nagging "I" voice. *The Third Man* does begin with a narrator—"I never knew the old Vienna before the war . . ."—and it is actually Carol Reed speaking the lines in the British version. But that voice and its vantage never return, and so we lose the chance of a cool, pitiless amusement that watches Holly and Harry do their brief dance to the zither. Whereas in the novella, or treatment, which Greene wrote first (and which sold the venture to Korda and Selznick), the whole thing is narrated in that mood by Calloway, the military policeman played by Trevor Howard.

He half imagines and half inherits from Holly the talk between Lime and Martins in the Wheel. The movie would be clumsy like that. Still, Calloway's fatalistic point of view is what pins down Lime's wickedness—the evil that is magicked away on screen. Maybe that ugliness would have stuck if Noël Coward had played the part—that was an early thought. But Orson Welles was so begging to be liked. The film does not quite cheat on Greene. But Lime's limelight charm joins with the stealthy allure of evil on the screen—when watched from the safety or the nullity of the dark. Voyeurs can't be judges.

Suppose Calloway was the grim, helpless core to *The Third Man.* That is not so hard, for Trevor Howard was an ideal Greene protagonist. Howard had a rueful harshness, tight with emotion, and some hint of not liking himself. He was the only man who could have played Bendrix in *The End of the Affair,* the only voice for this tortured reverie:

> I sat on my bed and said to God, You've taken her but You haven't got me yet. I know Your cunning. It's You who take us up to a high place and offer us the whole universe. You're a devil, God, tempting us to leap. But I don't want your Peace and I don't want Your love. I wanted something very simple and very easy: I wanted Sarah for a lifetime, and You took her away. With Your great schemes You ruin our happiness as a harvester ruins a mouse's nest. I hate You, God. I hate You as though You existed.

For over sixty years Greene had mixed feelings about the movies—the only legitimate ones. Yet I wish he had written a movie on Kim Philby—another role made for Howard—that consummate dishonest team-player who had to be so guarded an observer. Greene knew Philby and wrote about him in a strangled mix of compassion and confession: " 'He betrayed his country'—yes, perhaps he did, but who among us has not committed treason to something or someone more important than a country?"

Philby could have made Greene's most troubling watcher, leading the life of the club while slipping colleagues down the greased chute. The admiration for Philby is shocking when one recalls how that traitor's career killed off others. Dots? Greene once said he'd rather live in the Soviet Union than in the United States. Yet the persistent traveler knew little of those places. From bases in the elitist Albany, in London, and in Antibes, he only pictured himself as Philby's neighbor in Moscow.

That envisioning was Greene's highest flight of imagination, and it could be dishonest as well as creative. Sometimes it was both at once—that's why he's so important to the movies. But one cannot forget the tortured, secret witnessing granted his people: Harry Lime back as ghost and player in his own life; Baines in *The Fallen Idol*, watching the slow flight of a paper plane that may ruin him; the man in *The Tenth Man* who has purchased a coward's rescue and with it the humiliation of being saved; Fowler in *The Quiet American* looking back on the life and death of Pyle—"Everything had gone right with me since he had died, but how I wished there existed someone to whom I could say that I was sorry."

But in an age where all of us may watch and spy, omniscience and other godlike attributes are retired.

Sydney Greenstreet (1879–1954),
b. Sandwich, England

It has always been a convention of the film industry to "introduce" potent new players. But few introductions have been as dramatic as that of Greenstreet: monstrous, over sixty, hostile, and so clearly familiar with every wrinkle in the world's corruption. Where could such bulk have been hiding? (In fact, he was a seasoned stage actor, a regular with the Lunts.) How would audiences feel less than cheated that he had been withheld for so long? To redress the balance, Warners worked him hard over the next eight years—twenty-four pictures—forgetting perhaps that he was an old man who needed to sit down for as much of a film as possible. Indeed, there were several men trapped in his grossness: the conventional thin man; a young man; an aesthete; a romantic. He made a florid, sybaritic monster. His Gutman in *The Maltese Falcon* (41, John Huston) was very close to Hammett's conception, perpetually devious and yet tickled by such a complicated plot and by Spade's professionalism. It was a happy chance that his first film put him in the company of Peter Lorre, for they were inspired, tormenting company held together by some unspoken perversity.

He took what came thereafter: *They Died With Their Boots On* (41, Raoul Walsh); *Across the Pacific* (42, Huston); *Casablanca* (43, Michael Curtiz); *Danger* (43, Walsh); *Passage to Marseilles* (44, Curtiz) and the Eric Ambler adaptation, *The Mask of Dimitrios* (44, Jean Negulesco), both with Lorre. His long stage career was now subsumed by Warners' shadowy melodrama: tormenting Bogart in *Conflict* (45, Curtis Bernhardt); *Christmas in Connecticut* (45, Peter Godfrey); *Pillow to Post* (45, Vincent Sherman); with Lorre and Geraldine Fitzgerald as *Three Strangers* (46, Negulesco); as Thackeray in the Brontës' biopic *Devotion* (46, Bernhardt); as a Victorian London police inspector in *The Verdict* (46, Don Siegel), his last film with Lorre; *The Hucksters* (47, Jack Conway) at MGM; *Ruthless* (48, Edgar G. Ulmer); as Wilkie Collins's Count Fosco in *The Woman in White* (48, Godfrey); with Joan Crawford in *Flamingo Road* (49, Curtiz); and *Malaya* (49, Richard Thorpe). It is difficult not to believe that he is still in search of the falcon—"Ah yes, sir, the falcon!"

Joan Greenwood (1921–87), b. London

The British cinema allowed audiences to see and hear just enough of Joan Greenwood to let them know what they were missing. In another time or place—Cukor's Hollywood or Renoir's France of the 1950s—there might have been whole films devoted to her. Above all, she possessed the unerring voice of exaggeration and restraint, drawling forth in unison. What seemed at first like a mannerism proved within minutes entirely genuine: a rather dotty, genteel sexpot. She was what Lady Bracknell must have been like when young.

She was a stage actress who made her film debut in the early years of the war, and was at her peak in the period 1948–55: *John Smith Wakes Up* (41, Jiri Weiss); *My Wife's Family* (41, Walter Charles Mycroft); *He Found a Star* (41, John Paddy Carstairs); *The Gentle Sex* (43, Leslie Howard and Maurice Elvey); *They Knew Mr. Knight* (44, Norman Walker); *Latin Quarter* (45, Vernon Sewell); *Girl in a Million* (46, Francis Searle); *The Man Within* (47, Bernard Knowles); *The October Man* (47, Roy Baker); *The White Unicorn* (48, Knowles); *Saraband for Dead Lovers* (48, Basil Dearden and Michael Relph); as Lady Caroline Lamb in *Bad Lord Byron* (48, David Macdonald); *Whisky Galore* (49, Alexander Mackendrick); *Kind Hearts and Coronets* (49, Robert Hamer); *Flesh and Blood* (50, Anthony Kimmins); *The Man in the White Suit* (51, Mackendrick); *Young Wives' Tale* (51, Henry Cass); perfect in *The Importance of Being Earnest* (52, Anthony Asquith); *Father Brown* (54, Hamer); *Knave of Hearts* (54, René Clément); *Moonfleet* (55, Fritz Lang); *Stage Struck* (58, Sidney Lumet); *Mysterious Island* (61, Cy Endfield); *The Amorous Mr. Prawn* (62, Kimmins); *Tom Jones* (63, Tony Richardson); *The Moon-Spinners* (64, James Neilson); *Girl Stroke Boy* (71, Bob Kellett);

The Hound of the Baskervilles (77, Paul Morrissey); *The Uncanny* (77, Denis Heroux); *The Water Babies* (79, Lionel Jeffries); in a Barbara Cartland adaptation for TV, *The Flame Is Love* (79, Michael O'Herlihy); *Country* (81, Richard Eyre); *Ellis Island* (84, Jerry London); *Past Caring* (85, Eyre); and *Little Dorrit* (87, Christine Edzard).

Jane (Bettejane) **Greer** (1924–2001),
b. Washington, D.C.
"I go there sometimes," says Kathie Moffat, as an afterthought, to Jeff Bailey. They have met, as if by chance, in a cafe in Acapulco next to a small movie house. She has strolled in out of the day's last sunlight in a pale dress and a wide-brimmed straw hat. In fact, he's been sent to find her, and maybe she knew that or guessed it already. Knowing things seems to be her trade, or her personality. She tells Jeff about this other place, where they play American music, and the way she says it—"I go there sometimes"—makes for one of the more mysterious lines in American film. Somehow, you have the worst thoughts about the other things she does.

This is *Out of the Past* (47, Jacques Tourneur). Jeff is Robert Mitchum, and Kathie Moffat is Jane Greer—who didn't have much more going for her than dark hair that stirred like drapes in a breeze, the best mouth, eyes like blueberries in cream, and that threat of knowledge. That's what Howard Hughes noticed, and Rudy Vallee, when they saw pictures of her modeling uniforms for the Women's Army Corps. That's what a war can do for you: Hughes signed her up with a contract that forbade marriage; and then she married Vallee, who was twenty-three years older than she was, and wild! As for Jane Greer, did it mean she was naughty, or perverse? "Can't I be both?" she would have asked.

And maybe there was something in her that knew, after *Out of the Past*, that bothering or building her career seriously was hardly worthwhile, not with people like Hughes running the show. So she didn't take herself seriously. She did just a few movies in the late forties and the early fifties, and then, maybe, wandered in and out of rooms waiting for someone to say. "My God, aren't you Jane Greer?" And she'd say, "Sometimes"?

Well, yes and no. She also married again, had sons, and lived quite well. All of which should be remembered and nailed down—but hardly stands up to the possibility that in Acapulco, in 1947, having run away with forty thousand dollars of Kirk Douglas's money, she has rented a cottage where she listens to Charlie Parker records and works her way through *The Sheltering Sky*, cutting the uncut pages with this knife she has acquired.

These are some of her other films: *Two O'Clock Courage* (45, Anthony Mann); *Dick Tracy* (45,

William Berke); *The Falcon's Alibi* (46, Ray McCarey); *The Bamboo Blonde* (46, Mann); *Sinbad the Sailor* (47, Richard Wallace); *They Won't Believe Me* (47, Irving Pichel); *Station West* (48, Sidney Lanfield); with Mitchum again, and very funny, in *The Big Steal* (49, Don Siegel); *The Company She Keeps* (50, John Cromwell), a melo where she has the lead; *You're in the Navy Now* (51, Henry Hathaway); *You for Me* (52, Don Weis); in the old Mary Astor role in *The Prisoner of Zenda* (52, Richard Thorpe); *Desperate Search* (52, Joseph H. Lewis); *The Clown* (53, Robert Z. Leonard), with Red Skelton; *Down Among the Sheltering Palms* (53, Edmund Goulding); *Run for the Sun* (56, Roy Boulting), with Richard Widmark and Trevor Howard; and one of the wives in *Man of a Thousand Faces* (57, Joseph Pevney).

There were a few later films, but the only interesting one was the remake of *Out of the Past*— *Against All Odds* (84, Taylor Hackford)—where she plays the mother of the Kathie Moffat character. "I go there sometimes."

Jean Grémillon (1901–59),
b. Bayeux, France
1923–28: eighteen shorts. 1926: *Un Tour au Large.* 1927: *Maldone; Gratuites.* 1928: *Bobs.* 1929: *Gardiens de Phare.* 1930: *La Petite Lise.* 1931: *Dainah la Métisse; Pour un Sou d'Amour.* 1932: *Le Petit Babouin.* 1933: *Gonzague, ou l'Accordeur.* 1934: *La Dolorosa.* 1935: *Centinella! Alerta!.* 1936: *La Valse Royale; Pattes de Mouches.* 1937: *Gueule d'Amour.* 1938: *L'Étrange Monsieur Victor.* 1941: *Remorques.* 1943: *Lumière d'Été.* 1944: *Le Ciel est à Vous.* 1945: *Le Six Juin à l'Aube* (d). 1949: *Pattes Blanches.* 1950: *L'Apocalypse de Saint-Sevres; Les Charmes de l'Existence* (codirected with Pierre Kast) (d). 1951: *L'Etrange Madame X; Les Désastres de la Guerre* (codirected with Kast) (d). 1952: "Alchimie" and "Astrologie," episodes from *Encyclopédie Filmée* (d). 1953: *L'Amour d'une Femme.* 1954: *Au Coeur de l'Ile de France* (d). 1956: *La Maison aux Images* (d). 1957: *Haute Lisse* (d). 1958: *André Masson et les Quatre Eléments* (d).

Grémillon was trained as a musician; his first contact with cinema was as a violin accompanist to silent films. He made many industrial documentaries and began directing features in 1926. Because of scant success, he was forced to look for assignments in Germany and Spain: *Centinella! Alerta!* had Buñuel as its executive producer. Grémillon often composed the music for his own films. Only with war did he return to France and produce fully personal films, especially *Lumière d'Été*, a Jacques Prévert allegory about a group of failures living on the edge of the abyss, mordant and sad. Grémillon's essential bleakness was maintained in *Pattes Blanches*, an Anouilh script about sexual rivalry, and in his documentary on the

D-Day landings, which concentrates on the ravages left in the Normandy countryside—the director's own homeland. After the war, Grémillon was president of the Cinémathèque until his death, and largely preoccupied with documentaries. Thus, he made few features with real freedom. He may be a subject for reevaluation. Certainly his films are intensely felt, the work of a man sensitive to music, painterly composition, and the subtleties of Normandy and Brittany.

Gueule d'Amour leaves one in no doubt—Grémillon was a remarkable director. It has Gabin as a soldier with a reputation for having his way with women . . . until he meets a wealthy Parisian (played by Mireille Balin). This is a cinema of inner, emotional realism, with subtle, secretive performances and an eye that invests objects and places with poetic meaning. The film is unerringly modern and it makes one want to see anything by Grémillon.

Edmond T. Gréville (1906–66),
b. Nice, France

1931: *Le Train de Suicides*. 1932: *Plaisirs de Paris* (uncredited); *Le Triangle de Feu*. 1933: *Remous*. 1935: *Marchand d'Amour; Princesse Tam-Tam*. 1936: *Gypsy Melody*. 1937: *Brief Ecstasy; Mademoiselle Docteur*. 1938: *Secret Lives; What a Man!; Veetig Jaren/Forty Years* (d). 1939: *Menaces/Cinq Jours d'Angoisse*. 1941: *Une Femme dans la Nuit* (codirected with Abel Gance). 1946: *Dorothée Cherche l'Amour*. 1947: *Pour une Nuit d'Amour/Passionelle; Le Diable Souffle*. 1948: *Noose; Neit Tevergeefs/But Not in Vain*. 1949: *The Romantic Age*. 1950: *Im Banne der Madonna* (unreleased). 1953: *L'Envers du Paradis*. 1955: *Le Port du Désir/Sauveur d'Epaves/The House on the Waterfront; Tant Qu'il Y A Aura des Femmes*. 1956: *Je Plaide Non Coupable/Guilty?*. 1958: *L'Île du Bout du Monde/Temptation*. 1960: *Beat Girl/Wild for Kicks*. 1961: *Les Mains d'Orlac/The Hands of Orlac; Les Menteurs/The Liars*. 1963: *L'Accident*. 1967: *Peril au Paradis* (TV).

Edmond Gréville was French, but with British blood, and so for much of his career he made films in England as well as France—ranging from Mai Zetterling and Hugh Williams in *The Romantic Age* (truly a trifle) to the wistful teen exploitation of *Beat Girl*, or *Wild for Kicks*, to a remake of *The Hands of Orlac*. Also known as a novelist and playwright, Gréville has his supporters in France as a stylist director. But few people, so far, have seen enough of his pictures for a consensus to develop. *Mademoiselle Docteur* was an English version of the Pabst film, with von Stroheim and Dita Parlo. *Le Port du Désir* is a good, moody Jean Gabin film, and *L'Envers du Paradis* was Stroheim again.

John Grierson (1898–1972),
b. Deanstown, Scotland

Grierson was a harsh, restrictive enthusiast. Although he proclaimed a yearning to liberate and extend filmmaking, he evolved a narrow doctrine hostile to many other types of cinema, essentially bigoted and unintelligent and isolated by history. Yet he was a man of fierce organizing energy and the undoubted centerpiece of the British documentary movement. If that movement now looks either stolid or arty and oblivious of some of the subtler implications of documentary, is Grierson to blame?

Alan Lovell has suggested that Scottish Calvinism influenced this righteous isolation and quoted Grierson's underlying belief in a necessary severity: "Several of the young directors responsible for the success of the British documentary film have been Scots; and there may even be some odd relation between the Knoxist background and a theory of cinema which throws overboard the meretricious trappings of the studio."

Grierson was at Glasgow University and then spent three years in America. But in 1927 he began his involvement with British documentary when he joined the Empire Marketing Board Film Unit. In 1928 he headed the unit and directed his only film, *Drifters*, which is symptomatic of the academic, Russian-influenced beauty of much British documentary, but which has little flavor of fish or men. From then until 1937 he was the key executive in documentary by virtue of his position as head of the GPO Film Unit. He functioned as producer, as muscular scrum leader of assorted talents and as critic and theorist. He brought Robert Flaherty and Alberto Cavalcanti to Britain and produced, among others: *Industrial Britain* (31, Flaherty); *The Voice of the World* (32, Arthur Elton); *Aero-Engine* (33, Elton); *Pett and Pott* (34, Cavalcanti); *Song of Ceylon* (34, Basil Wright); *BBC: The Voice of Britain* (35, Stuart Legg); *Coal Face* (35, Cavalcanti); *Night Mail* (36, Wright and Harry Watt); and *We Live in Two Worlds* (37, Cavalcanti).

As a writer, he hacked out what he called a "minor manifesto" on the virtuousness of documentary. Its principles were that

the cinema's capacity for getting around, for observing and selecting from life itself can be exploited in a new and vital art form. The studio films largely ignore this possibility of opening up the screen on the real world. . . . We believe that the original (or native) actor, and the original (or native) scene, are better guides to a screen interpretation of the modern world. . . . They give it power of interpretation over more complex and astonishing happenings in the real world than the studio mind can conjure up or the studio mechanician recreate. . . . We believe that the materials and the stories thus taken from the raw can be finer (more real in the philosophical sense) than the acted article. . . . Add to this that documentary can achieve an intimacy of knowledge and effect impossible to the shimsham mechanics of the studio, and the lily-fingered interpretations of the metropolitan actor.

Grierson went on, without much conviction, to say that he didn't mean that studios could not produce works of art. But his fervor detected something unclean in their product and, like a pulpit orator, he warned: "I make this distinction to the point of asserting that the young director cannot, in nature, go documentary and go studio both." The limb he chose for himself now looks very naked. The films of the 1930s look monotonous and dreary beside the fusion of documentary and fiction in many of the Drew-Leacock films, in the work of Rouch and Marker, and in the films of Godard. What would Grierson have made of Godard, Resnais, or Warhol—three men who have seen much more variety and complexity in the "raw" than the confident Grierson ever identified?

After 1937, Grierson went through the mill of international bureaucracy. All through the war he was Film Commissioner for Canada and instrumental in setting up the National Film Board of Canada. He returned to Europe after the war under a cloud, worked briefly for UNESCO, and then, from 1948–54, was Controller of Film at the Central Office of Information, as unrewarding an experience as it is possible to imagine. His creative energy at this period was channeled into Group Three, an offshoot of the National Film Finance Corporation, for whom he produced *Judgment Deferred* (51, John Baxter); *Brandy for the Parson* (51, John Eldridge); *The Brave Don't Cry* (52, Philip Leacock); *Laxdale Hall* (52, Eldridge); *The Oracle* (52, C. M. Pennington-Richards); *Time, Gentlemen, Please* (52, Lewis Gilbert); *You're Only Young Twice* (52, Terry Bishop); and *Orders Are Orders* (54, David Paltenghi)—a drab collection.

He then returned to Scotland and from 1955–65 produced and presented for Scottish TV an anthology of international documentary, *This Wonderful World*. His breezy zest was undiminished and he seemed quite happy inside a studio.

D. W. Griffith (David Wark Griffith) (1875–1948), b. La Grange, Kentucky
1908: two-reel pictures made at Biograph (1908, 61; 1909, 141; 1910, 87; 1911, 70; 1912, 67; 1913, 30), itemized in Robert Henderson's *D. W. Griffith: The Years at Biograph*. 1913: *Judith of Bethulia*. 1914: *The Battle of the Sexes; The Escape; Home Sweet Home; The Avenging Conscience; The Mother and the Law*. 1915: *The Birth of a Nation*. 1916: *Intolerance*. 1918: *Hearts of the World; The Great Love; The Greatest Thing in Life*. 1919: *A Romance of Happy Valley; The Girl Who Stayed at Home; Broken Blossoms; True

Heart Susie; The Fall of Babylon; The Mother and the Law; Scarlet Days; The Greatest Question*. 1920: *The Idol Dancer; The Love Flower; Way Down East*. 1921: *Dream Street; Orphans of the Storm*. 1922: *One Exciting Night*. 1923: *The White Rose*. 1924: *America; Isn't Life Wonderful?*. 1925: *Sally of the Sawdust; That Royale Girl*. 1926: *The Sorrows of Satan*. 1928: *Drums of Love; The Battle of the Sexes*. 1929: *Lady of the Pavement*. 1930: *Abraham Lincoln*. 1931: *The Struggle*. 1940: *One Million B.C.* (produced by and credited to Hal Roach, some of this film was supervised by Griffith).

Griffith was the son of a Confederate officer who died from the effects of a war wound when the boy was ten. The family lived simply on a farm, reduced by the war, and then ran a boardinghouse in Louisville, Kentucky. At the age of twenty, Griffith was drawn into amateur theatricals and thence into the precarious life of an actor in small touring companies. He wrote for the stage and, in 1907, *The Fool and the Girl* was produced in Washington. Next year he approached the Edison company with some of his stories and, after initial success there, he moved to Biograph. That studio needed a director and was sufficiently impressed by Griffith's varied talents to offer the post to him. Innocently, and penuriously, he accepted.

At Biograph, he had the opportunity to release American cinema from the technical and artistic limitations of constant reference to the theatre. To distill the stylistic advances of over three hundred films, Griffith abandoned the fixed point of view of the audience in the stalls and made his camera selective. He saw that there might be a balance between long shot, medium shot, and close-up, and that action might be heightened by the insertion of faces reflecting on or moved by the actions. The effect of introducing a cinematic language should not conceal Griffith's preference for the standard sentimental melodrama of nineteenth-century theatre and cheap fiction, but he established the emotional impact of films by recognizing the value of sensitive acting. He stressed rehearsal, eliminated crude overacting, and saw that close-ups were more effective if restrained. The outstanding proponents of this novel cinema-acting style are Miriam Cooper in *Intolerance* and Lillian Gish, but Griffith organized a company of excellent players, just as he liked to use the same, loyal technicians—most notably the cameraman Billy Bitzer.

The longer films being made in Italy—particularly *Quo Vadis?*—urged Griffith into making the four-reel *Judith of Bethulia*. Biograph were unhappy at the expense of that film and Griffith moved on to Mutual, taking most of his chosen actors and technicians. But even at this stage, Griffith yearned for independence and the concentration of forces of the creative figures in cinema: thus he formed Triangle with Sennett and Thomas Ince, and produced those two flamboyant claims for the entertainment and artistic appeal of the cinema—*Birth of a Nation* and *Intolerance.* They made use of every innovation Griffith had begun at Biograph, and they are packed with brilliant fragments. But their overall effect is of portentousness: the size exceeds Griffith's sense of detail; the racism in *Birth* is embarrassing; the notion of four separate stories to illustrate *Intolerance,* united as the film progresses, is essentially silly despite the liveliness of the editing, the pathos of the women, and the spectacle of the Babylonian sequences. The most damaging exposure is of Griffith's adherence to a shallow, sentimental code of morality, at variance with the authenticity that he was able to obtain in performance and that he cultivated in art direction. For that reason, both the big films survive less as cinematic experiences than as works of historical interest.

This is not true of many of the films that followed. *Intolerance* had been financially disastrous and it forced Griffith back to simpler, intimate romances. *Hearts of the World* is a moving love story set against the background of the First World War. *Broken Blossoms* is a marvelous evocation of Limehouse and another tender love story, with Gish as good as ever, and with the bonus of a fine performance from Richard Barthelmess. (Griffith was better with women: perhaps he saw that their stoicism was made for the camera; certainly he adored his own leading ladies; but, in addition, he seems to have retained a Southern courtliness toward women.) *True Heart Susie* is a glorious piece of rural charm and Gish's best performance as the archetype of the self-sacrificing girl at the heart of the women's-pic genre. *Way Down East* subdues sentimentality with melodrama and visual excitement, and *Orphans of the Storm,* with the Gish sisters versus the French Revolution, is his most satisfying treatment of suspense.

In the years after the war, Griffith's insistence on conservative sentimentality marooned him. But, as he admitted, he was not amenable to the monopoly of the large studios. He could cope with neither the new morality nor the factory product. His participation in United Artists had been vague. Throughout the 1920s he lived uneasily, and *America*—a solemn and slow account of the War of Independence—put him in debt. In 1924, he made a deal with Adolph Zukor at Paramount and went to Germany to make *Isn't Life Wonderful?* When De Mille left Paramount, *Sorrows of Satan* was handed to Griffith. Long before sound, he was looked on as a throwback and, though the commercial hostility may have been malicious, artistically the pioneer had been bypassed. Griffith, after all, mourned the loss of silence and said,

"Give us back our beauty." His twopence-colored view of story content could not absorb the enormous extra realism that came with sound, no matter that his eye for an image was very sophisticated. *Abraham Lincoln,* his first talkie, is, even so, very good, with a fine performance from Walter Huston.

Why did Griffith hardly work in his last twenty years? It can only be half the answer that the studios mistrusted him; it was also a matter of his disdain for the cinema of the 1930s. He had always been a proud man, and bitterness may have been inevitable. Like Orson Welles in years to come, Griffith carved out his eventual solitude, perhaps a little attracted to its splendor. He died at the Knickerbocker Hotel in Hollywood, a drunken, womanizing spectator of the industry to which he had acted as frontier scout.

Melanie Griffith, b. New York, 1957

Does this actress have a better grasp on what she's doing than her admirers? She has married Don Johnson twice (the first time as a teenager); she has had recurring problems with drink and drugs—to say nothing of men and her own weight. Volatility here seems very close to disturbance. Maybe the little girl *was* traumatized when Alfred Hitchcock gave her a toy coffin with a doll of mother in it. Or maybe the joke was Melanie's idea.

She was the daughter of Hitchcock's actress Tippi Hedren (*The Birds* and *Marnie,* made when Melanie was five and six) and of a real estate agent, Peter Griffith. Hedren married again, to Noel Marshall, a keeper of wild animals: one result of that was *Roar* (81, Marshall), a disastrous picture that took many years to make and which featured the family and their man-eaters.

Griffith was riveting in her screen debut, *Night Moves* (75, Arthur Penn), as a full-bodied child keeping grown-up company, bewildered by the mismatch of her carnality, her shy manner, and her infant voice. That dilemma has never quite been settled.

She was in *Smile* (75, Michael Ritchie); *The Drowning Pool* (76, Stuart Rosenberg); *One on One* (77, Lamont Johnson); and *Joyride* (77, Joseph Ruben). There was a gap of four years before the onset of her "adult" career, first stunning and seeming stunned as Holly Body in *Body Double* (84, Brian De Palma), and in *Fear City* (84, Abel Ferrara).

Nothing suggested the depth of *Something Wild* (86, Jonathan Demme), where she goes from the Brooksian tempest of Lulu to the wounded, provincial Audrey with absolute ease: these two halves of one creature showed Griffith as an actress, but they also illustrated the talent of Demme. Nothing since has been in the same class: *Cherry 2000* (88, Steve DeJarnatt) had been on the shelf and was probably freed by *Something*

Wild; The Milagro Beanfield War (88, Robert Redford) was a party for guest spots; *Stormy Monday* (88, Mike Figgis) was too intent on making Newcastle look like Gotham; she was a solid worker in *Working Girl* (88, Mike Nichols), yet unaccountably Rubens-like in her underwear, leered at by the hitherto unarousable Nichols. *In the Spirit* (90, Sandra Seacat) was an oddity; in *Pacific Heights* (90, John Schlesinger) she did not always look like herself; and she was blithely perky in the archaic *Shining Through* (91, David Seltzer).

She played on TV in the Hemingway story "Hills Like White Elephants," in *Women and Men: Stories of Seduction* (90, Tony Richardson). She was the one leading figure in *Bonfire of the Vanities* (90, De Palma) who might have been retained in sensible recasting. With Don Johnson, she made the minor and harmless *Paradise* (91, Mary Agnes Donoghue). But *A Stranger Among Us* (92, Sidney Lumet) is such a folly it seems more like a camp dream than a project that survived a daily schedule of work. She was with Johnson again in a remake of *Born Yesterday* (93, Luis Mandoki), reliably a half-beat off Billie Dawn's dumb rhythms.

And yet . . . Despite the loss of Don Johnson, and perhaps because of gaining Antonio Banderas, Melanie keeps going. Who knows what reconstructions there may have been? On screen, she has become funnier without losing one drop of sexiness. She begins to become an institution (and one I would lean on): *Milk Money* (94, Richard Benjamin); given a sublime moment in *Nobody's Fool* (94, Robert Benton); on TV in *Buffalo Girls* (95, Rod Hardy); *Now and Then* (96, Lesli Linka Glatter); with Banderas in *Two Much* (96, Fernando Trueba); very touching in *Mulholland Falls* (96, Lee Tamahori); as Charlotte Haze in *Lolita* (97, Adrian Lyne); brilliant in *Another Day in Paradise* (98, Larry Clark); very sexy in *Celebrity* (98, Woody Allen); a lush Marion Davies in *RKO 281* (99, Benjamin Ross); eating up the fun in *Crazy in Alabama* (99, Banderas); *Cecil B. Demented* (00, John Waters).

She was *Forever Lulu* (00, John Kaye); *Tart* (01, Christine Wayne); *Tempo* (03, Eric Styles); as Frank Sinatra's last wife in *The Night We Called It a Day* (03, Paul Goldman).

John Guillermin, b. London, 1923
1949: *Torment*. 1951: *Smart Alec; Two on the Tiles; Four Days*. 1952: *Song of Paris; Miss Robin Hood*. 1953: *Operation Diplomat*. 1954: *Adventure in the Hopfields; The Crowded Day*. 1955: *Dust and Gold; Thunderstorm*. 1957: *Town on Trial*. 1958: *The Whole Truth; I Was Monty's Double*. 1959: *Tarzan's Greatest Adventure*. 1960: *The Day They Robbed the Bank of England; Never Let Go*. 1962: *Waltz of the Toreadors; Tarzan Goes to India*. 1964: *Guns at Batasi*. 1965:

Rapture. 1966: *The Blue Max*. 1967: *New Face in Hell*. 1968: *House of Cards*. 1969: *The Bridge at Remagen*. 1970: *El Condor*. 1972: *Skyjacked*. 1973: *Shaft in Africa*. 1974: *The Towering Inferno*. 1976: *King Kong*. 1978: *Death on the Nile*. 1980: *Mr. Patman*. 1984: *Sheena, Queen of the Jungle*. 1986: *Kong Lives*. 1988: *Dead or Alive; The Tracker* (TV).

Guillermin has come a long way from the modest charm of a children's film like *Adventure in the Hopfields* to the sham Apache Western, *El Condor*. Not that there is any feeling of progress. He has jumped as frantically as spit on a stove: thus in one year the bittersweet *Waltz of the Toreadors* and a Tarzan adventure. On the whole, however, Guillermin has a taste for violence and tension, and *House of Cards* is pastiche Hitchcock. He was trained in France and launched initially by John Grierson, but no trace of either shows. *Town on Trial* was a moderate thriller, but his larger action films are very impersonal. It speaks for the unease of modern cinema that so plain a director should handle *The Towering Inferno*. But the remake of *King Kong* was a delight: pretty, amused, touching, and very clever in seeing the love story within the famous horror.

Sir Alec Guinness (1914–2000), b. London
Of all the British "theatrical knights," Guinness had the most interesting career in films. Not that he ever forsook theatre. But Guinness had a remote, reflective personality that often worked well in movies. Perhaps film taught him a love of detail best noticed by the camera. It may also be that he enjoyed the challenge to stay hidden or secret when under intense scrutiny. His 1985 autobiography was called *Blessings in Disguise*, and it made clear his tranquil pleasure doing films, as well as the dreamy Catholic assurance that nothing in life is too important.

Despite his Oscar for *The Bridge on the River Kwai* (57, David Lean) and an honorary Oscar in 1979; despite his high reputation in America, where he was seen as the key actor in Ealing comedies—and he *was* nominated for best actor in *The Lavender Hill Mob* (51, Charles Crichton); despite all of that, he never went Hollywood. Instead, he sometimes pursued personal projects that must have seemed farfetched. Thus his superb, monstrous Gulley Jimson in *The Horse's Mouth* (59, Ronald Neame), which he scripted out of love for the Joyce Cary novel (and he got an Oscar nomination for the script—in the same year, Spencer Tracy was nominated for *The Old Man and the Sea*, but Guinness's Jimson was ignored—you see, nothing is too important); and the religious *The Prisoner* (55, Peter Glenville), from a Bridget Boland play.

He made his debut in *Evensong* (34, Victor Saville), but *Great Expectations* (46, Lean) was the true beginning, and it was his Fagin in *Oliver Twist* (48, Lean) that drew attention. The real man was unrecognizable within that wonderfully Dickensian performance. Then the multiplicity of roles in *Kind Hearts and Coronets* (49, Robert Hamer) established him as a master of makeup and artful disguise.

He worked steadily in the fifties, in English films: *A Run for Your Money* (49, Charles Frend); as the man who thinks he is dying in *Last Holiday* (50, Henry Cass); playing Disraeli in *The Mudlark* (50, Jean Negulesco); the inventor in *The Man in the White Suit* (51, Alexander Mackendrick); *The Card* (52, Neame); *The Captain's Paradise* (53, Anthony Kimmins); in a dismal war picture, *The Malta Story* (53, Brian Desmond Hurst); as *Father Brown* (54, Hamer); quite frightening in *The Ladykillers* (55, Mackendrick); *To Paris With Love* (55, Hamer); and to Hollywood to do *The Swan* (56, Charles Vidor), which began a great friendship with Grace Kelly.

After *Kwai* (which really is a thoughtful rendering of an English bureaucrat, even if the film yields to Lean's overemotionalism), Guinness had a new stature that did not quite suit him. He got bigger parts, but they were not always suitable: *Our Man in Havana* (59, Carol Reed); uneasy with Bette Davis in *The Scapegoat* (59, Hamer); over the top in *Tunes of Glory* (60, Neame)— without Dickens or Jimson as an inspiration, he was happier playing reticent men; *A Majority of One* (62, Mervyn Le Roy), which required him to be Japanese; the captain in *H.M.S. Defiant* (62, Lewis Gilbert); an Arab king, but rather empty in *Lawrence of Arabia* (62, Lean); Marcus Aurelius in *The Fall of the Roman Empire* (64, Anthony Mann); and *Doctor Zhivago* (65, Lean).

What followed was his least distinguished period, with many poor films and showy parts: *Situation Hopeless—But Not Serious* (65, Gottfried Reinhardt); *Hotel Paradiso* (66, Glenville); *The Quiller Memorandum* (66, Michael Anderson); *The Comedians* (67, Glenville); Charles I in *Cromwell* (70, Ken Hughes); *Scrooge* (70, Neame); a Pope in *Brother Sun, Sister Moon* (72, Franco Zeffirelli); Hitler in *The Last Ten Days* (73, Ennio de Concini); *Murder by Death* (76, Robert Moore); and magisterial as Obi-Wan Kenobi in *Star Wars* (77, George Lucas), on which he received 2¼ percent of the profits.

He created the role of John le Carré's George Smiley for TV in *Tinker, Tailor, Soldier, Spy* (79, John Irvin), and he was very good in it—yet there was something too cautious in Smiley for Guinness's alertness. One wanted more aberration, more poetry—it became all too clear, at such length, that Guinness could do Smiley standing on his head. He was also in *Raise the Titanic* (80, Jerry Jameson); on TV in *Little Lord Fauntleroy*

(80, Jack Gold); *Smiley's People* (82, Simon Langton); *Lovesick* (83, Marshall Brickman); sadly at odds with David Lean playing an Indian in *A Passage to India* (84); *Edwin* (84, Rodney Bennett); *Monsignor Quixote* (85, Bennett); *Little Dorrit* (85, Christine Edzard); as Mr. Todd in *A Handful of Dust* (88, Charles Sturridge), settling to listen to Dickens, like a dinosaur hatching an egg; as Heinrich Mann in a TV *Tales from Hollywood* (92, Howard Davies); *A Foreign Field* (93, Sturridge); *Mute Witness* (94, Anthony Waller); *Eskimo Day* (96, Piers Haggard).

Sacha Guitry (1885–1957),
b. St. Petersburg, Russia

1935: *Pasteur; Bonne Chance.* 1936: *Le Nouveau Testament* (codirected with Alexandre Ryder); *Le Roman d'un Tricheur; Mon Père Avait Raison; Faisons un Rêve; Le Mot de Cambronne.* 1937: *Les Perles de la Couronne* (codirected with Christian-Jaque); *Quadrille.* 1938: *Désirée; Remontons les Champs-Elysées.* 1939: *Ils Etaient Neuf Célibataires.* 1941: *Le Destin Fabuleux de Désirée Clary.* 1942: *La Nuit du Cinéma.* 1943: *Donne-Moi Tes Yeux; La Malibran.* 1947: *Le Comédien.* 1948: *Le Diable Boiteux.* 1949: *Aux Deux Colombes; Toa.* 1950: *Le Trésor de Cantenac; Tu M'as Sauvé la Vie; Deburau.* 1951: *Adhémar, ou le Jouet de la Fatalité* (codirected with Fernandel); *La Poison.* 1952: *La Vie d'un Honnête Homme; Je l'Ai Été Trois Fois.* 1953: *Si Versailles M'Était Conté.* 1955: *Napoléon.* 1956: *Si Paris Nous Était Conté; Assassins et Voleurs.* 1957: *Les Trois Font la Paire* (codirected with Clement Duhour).

The son of actor Lucien Guitry, and a prolific playwright, Sacha Guitry engagingly transferred many of his plays and his own self-indulgent acting to the screen. Unhappy unless author, director, and actor, Guitry is the example of unbridled theatricality that ought to make a fool of himself or cinema but whose films generally work very well. He is still a notable figure in French (or Parisian) culture: a playwright-performer, an example referred to—like Noël Coward.

Guitry had a tribute at the 1993 New York Film Festival that ranged from the romantic comedy *Bonne Chance* to the bedroom farce, *Faisons un Rêve.* As actor, or sheer presence, Guitry is an unashamedly charming tyrant, a Napoleon by way of Lubitsch. Robert Horton observed of *Le Roman d'un Tricheur's* narrative structure (a man trying to write his life story—the pages fluttering): "The movie trips along, nimble and sweet, and so quick that you barely notice the unconventional technique.... The freshest film of the festival." For years a legend, a rumor even, Guitry was *there,* on the screen, and audiences had to pick up their pace for him.

Yilmaz Güney (Pütün) (1937–84),
b. Adana, Turkey

1966: *The Horse, the Woman, and the Gun.* 1967: *Bullets Cannot Pierce Me; My Name Is Kerim.* 1968: *Nuri the Flea; Bride of the Earth.* 1969: *The Hungry Wolves; An Ugly Man.* 1970: *Osman the Wanderer* (codirected with Serif Gören); *The Seven Bastards* (codirected with Irfan Atasoy). 1971: *The Fugitives; The Wrongdoers; The Example* (codirected with Gören); *Umutsuzlar/The Hopeless Ones; The Father.* 1974: *Endise/Anxiety* (codirected with Gören). 1975: *Zavallilar/The Poor Ones* (codirected with Yilmaz Atif). 1978: *Sürü/The Herd* (directed by Zeki Okten). 1979: *Düsman/The Enemy* (directed by Okten). 1982: *Yol* (codirected with Gören). 1983: *Duvar/The Wall.*

When directors in and out of Hollywood despair of the hard time they are having, they should be reminded of the story of Yilmaz Güney. That process would bring several vital questions to life—not least, what are the movies for? Are they a career, an entertainment, a business, or may they even be the most effective way of enlightening a population and thus ensuring the victimization, and worse, of the filmmaker? There are young people in the comfort of southern California who tell you they would die if they could not make "their" movies. Yilmaz Güney made his, under the most impossible conditions. And he died, of cancer, in a foreign country, deprived of his own citizenship, at the age of forty-seven.

The child of poor Kurds, he managed to get to university, and he began writing. That soon got him into trouble with the Turkish authorities (this in the late 1950s), and he may have sought some shelter in working as an actor. He was good-looking, and appealing enough to win a place in Turkish cinema as an heroic figure. But he could hardly help himself from getting involved in political stories, which led to his arrest. While in prison in the early sixties he wrote a novel, *They Died With Their Heads Bowed.*

As time passed, he became more involved in writing and producing his films, but as the subject matter became more urgent and provocative, he was jailed again in the early seventies. Then in 1975 he was arrested again on false murder charges and given a very long sentence. Somehow he continued to function as the long-distance director of projects while still in jail: *The Herd* and *The Enemy.* Those prepared the way for *Yol,* written by Güney in jail and actually realized by Serif Gören according to Güney's instructions: as such, it is one of the most moving film protests against tyranny. He escaped from prison in 1981 and was able to finish the editing of *Yol.* He made one other film, *The Wall,* before his death.

For the general Western audience Turkey on film is Alan Parker's *Midnight Express.* No one doubts the worth of that film, or its power. But it says something bleak about our regard for Moslem countries that Güney's story, and his films, are relatively unknown. Had he been European, his story would have been told by now—he would be Al Pacino or Gérard Depardieu. He would be a legend.

Edmund Gwenn (1877–1959),
b. Glamorgan, Wales

My trouble with Gwenn was that the more cozy he grew in old age, the more resolutely my toes curled. Half a sentence of leisurely explanation from that gentle voice and a film was already dragging. Since Hitchcock showed some interest in Gwenn, it is a wonder that he never saw the pleasure in a situation that had Gwenn as a grindingly benevolent wealthy uncle, whose death is plotted at by nephews, but who uncannily survives every attempt and is forever garrulous about how he has come through. Imagine the mounting frustration: audiences stamping their feet for this senile chatterbox to be throttled.

Gwenn had been on the stage since 1900, a fact that glowed out of his Pickwick face. He made very few films before sound elicited that monotonous articulateness: *Unmarried* (20, Rex Wilson); as Hornblower, the part he had created onstage, in *The Skin Game* (20, Bernard Doxat-Pratt); *How He Lied to Her Husband* (31, Cecil Lewis); as Hornblower again in *The Skin Game* (31, Alfred Hitchcock); *Hindle Wakes* (31, Victor Saville); *Money for Nothing* (32, Monty Banks); *Frail Women* (32, Maurice Elvey); *Condemned to Death* (32, Walter Forde); *Love on Wheels* (32, Saville); *Tell Me Tonight* (32, Anatole Litvak); as Jess Oakroyd in *The Good Companions* (33, Saville); *Cash* (33, Zoltan Korda); *Early to Bed* (33, Ludwig Berger); *I Was a Spy* (33, Saville); *Channel Crossing* (33, Milton Rosmer); *Smithy* (33, George King); *Marooned* (33, Leslie Hiscott); *Friday the 13th* (33, Saville); as Johann Strauss in *Waltzes from Vienna* (33, Hitchcock); *The Admiral's Secret* (34, Guy Newald); *Java Head* (34, T. Walter Reuben); *Father and Son* (34, Banks); and *Spring in the Air* (34, W. Victor Hanbury).

He then went to America for his first film there, *The Bishop Misbehaves* (35, E. A. Dupont). For the next few years, he worked in both countries: *Sylvia Scarlett* (35, George Cukor); *Laburnum Grove* (36, Carol Reed); *Anthony Adverse* (36, Mervyn Le Roy); *The Walking Dead* (36, Michael Curtiz); *Parnell* (37, John M. Stahl); *South Riding* (38, Saville); *A Yank at Oxford* (38, Jack Conway); *Penny Paradise* (38, Reed); *Cheer Boys, Cheer* (39, Forde); *An Englishman's Home* (39, George Dewhurst).

Thereafter he settled in America and became a "lovable" character actor: as the butler in *The Earl of Chicago* (40, Richard Thorpe, but produced by

Victor Saville); indisputably an MGM Mr. Bennett in *Pride and Prejudice* (40, Robert Z. Leonard); *Foreign Correspondent* (40, Hitchcock); *The Devil and Miss Jones* (41, Sam Wood); *Cheers for Miss Bishop* (41, Tay Garnett); *Charley's Aunt* (41, Archie Mayo); *A Yank at Eton* (42, Norman Taurog); showing that a dog's best friend is someone who will talk to it in *Lassie Come Home* (43, Fred M. Wilcox); *Between Two Worlds* (44, Edward A. Blatt); *The Keys of the Kingdom* (44, Stahl); *Of Human Bondage* (46, Edmund Goulding); *Undercurrent* (46, Vincente Minnelli); an Oscar as Father Christmas in *Miracle on 34th Street* (47, George Seaton); *Life with Father* (47, Michael Curtiz); *Hills of Home* (48, Wilcox); a forger with a true heart in *Mister 880* (50, Goulding); *Peking Express* (51, William Dieterle); *Pretty*
Baby (52, Bretaigne Windust); *Something for the Birds* (52, Robert Wise); *Les Misérables* (52, Lewis Milestone); *The Bigamist* (53, Ida Lupino); as a professor who tries to talk to giant ants in *Them* (54, Gordon Douglas); as the Captain in *The Trouble with Harry* (55, Hitchcock); and *Calabuch* (56, Luis Garcia Berlanga).

H

Taylor Hackford,
b. Santa Barbara, California, 1945
1978: *Teenage Father* (s). 1980: *The Idolmaker.* 1982: *An Officer and a Gentleman.* 1984: *Against All Odds.* 1985: *White Nights.* 1987: *Chuck Berry: Hail! Hail! Rock 'n' Roll.* 1988: *Everybody's All-American.* 1993: *Bound by Honor.* 1995: *Dolores Claiborne.* 1997: *The Devil's Advocate.* 2000: *Proof of Life.* 2004: *Unchain My Heart: The Ray Charles Story.*

Taylor Hackford follows his own star, and over the years he has been good value. There isn't a great film in his list, but there's so much that is very entertaining. *The Idolmaker* revealed a young man with a rich, comic understanding of show-business fraud, and it sparkles with the best performance by the much lamented Ray Sharkey. *An Officer and a Gentleman* was a big hit in which Hackford managed to make disputing stars seem as if they were crazy about each other. *Against All Odds* is not as good as its basis, *Out of the Past*, but it has some torrid sex scenes in Mexico and a sure eye for Rachel Ward. *White Nights* is pretty silly, but it introduced Hackford to his longtime companion, and now wife, Helen Mirren. Jessica Lange is terrific in *Everybody's All-American*. *Bound by Honor* is a study of Chicago gang life; and *Dolores Claiborne* is really a study of heavily spiced acting. As for the delirious *The Devil's Advocate*, what can one say except that it is very

funny and might have been better still if Hackford had trusted the venom of satire.

More than that, Hackford is an enterprising, amiable man ready to try lots of things. He was in the Peace Corps. He did several early documentaries on figures like Charles Bukowski and Budd Boetticher. *Teenage Father* was an Oscar-winning short. And in the eighties, he became a producer: *La Bamba* (87, Luis Valdez); *The Long Walk Home* (90, Richard Pearce); *Sweet Talker* (90, Michael Jenkins); *Queens Logic* (91, Steve Rash); *When We Were Kings* (96, Leon Gast).

Gene Hackman,
b. San Bernardino, California, 1930
In the sixties and early seventies, Hackman forced himself forward by dint of persistent, rowdy work. Sadly, his most celebrated, Oscar-winning performance—as the cop in *The French Connection* (71, William Friedkin)—is a calculated impersonation of hardheadedness that, like the film, stares blindly through all the consequences. Popeye Doyle is vivid and all there: but he does not grow. Indeed, the pitch of Hackman's mugging goes straight back to Keystone policing. Up to that film, Hackman had established himself as an interesting character actor, capable of grainy authenticity. From the stage, he made a film debut as the grating small-town husband in *Lilith* (63, Robert Rossen) and, after *A Covenant with Death* (66, Lamont Johnson), *Hawaii* (66, George Roy Hill), *First to Fight* (67, Christian Nyby), and *Banning* (67, Ron Winston), he played Clyde's older but "junior" brother in *Bonnie and Clyde* (67, Arthur Penn). After that, he mixed tedious cantankerousness in shoddy movies with more thoughtful versions of an abrasive, not readily appealing American seldom offered in the cinema: *The Split* (68, Gordon Flemyng); *Riot!* (69, Buzz Kulik); *The Gypsy Moths* (69, John Frankenheimer); *Downhill Racer* (69, Michael Ritchie); *Marooned* (69, John Sturges); *I Never Sang for My Father* (70, Gilbert Cates); *Doctors' Wives* (70, George Schaefer); *The Hunting Party* (71, Don Medford); *Cisco Pike* (72, Bill L. Norton); *The Poseidon Adventure* (72, Ronald Neame); *Scarecrow* (73, Jerry Schatzberg); his best performance as the hollowed-out surveillance man, Harry Caul, in *The Conversation* (74, Francis Ford Coppola); *Young Frankenstein* (74, Mel Brooks); and as a private eye whose confidence is undone in *Night Moves* (75, Penn).

In *French Connection II* (75, John Frankenheimer) he made a harrowing portrait of a heroin addict going cold turkey; in *Bite the Bullet* (75, Richard Brooks) he was a routine cowboy; and in the dreadful *Lucky Lady* (75, Stanley Donen) his grin and his scowl seemed set in cement. His energy is most interesting when suppressed—*I Never Sang for My Father*, *The Conversation*, and

Night Moves, all studies in anxiety, were his best early films. He was a full eighteen months away from the screen before *March or Die* (77, Dick Richards); a Polish officer in *A Bridge Too Far* (77, Richard Attenborough); a wildly misconceived Lex Luthor in *Superman* (78, Richard Donner).

In the eighties, Hackman had few rivals as hardworking—he did eventually have to go a little slower because of heart problems. But too many of his pictures felt like chores, and too few made full use of his power and range. He stands for that small group of actors who are much better than the films offered to them. Well into his sixties, he struggled to be a hero in adventure films, or search for the few roles that required a mature man: *Superman II* (80, Richard Lester); with Barbra Streisand in *All Night Long* (81, Jean-Claude Tramont); *Reds* (81, Warren Beatty); as the prospector in *Eureka* (81, Nicolas Roeg); a voice-over in *Two of a Kind* (83, John Herzfeld); *Under Fire* (83, Roger Spottiswoode); *Uncommon Valor* (83, Ted Kotcheff); *Misunderstood* (84, Schatzberg); *Twice in a Lifetime* (85, Bud Yorkin); *Target* (85, Penn); *Power* (86, Sidney Lumet); as the basketball coach in *Hoosiers* (86, David Anspaugh); as the Secretary of Defense in *No Way Out* (87, Roger Donaldson); *Superman IV: The Quest for Peace* (87, Sidney J. Furie); with one fine scene in *Another Woman* (88, Woody Allen); *Bat 21* (88, Peter Markle); *Full Moon in Blue Water* (88, Peter Masterson); *Split Decisions* (88, David Drury); very good as the illusionless FBI agent in *Mississippi Burning* (88, Alan Parker), and nominated for best actor; *The Package* (89, Andrew Davis); *Loose Cannons* (90, Bob Clark); *The Narrow Margin* (90, Peter Hyams); as the figure of sanity in *Postcards from the Edge* (90, Mike Nichols); as the father and lawyer in *Class Action* (90, Michael Apted); superb as the sheriff in *Unforgiven* (92, Clint Eastwood), for which he won the supporting actor Oscar; as one of the lawyers in *The Firm* (93, Sydney Pollack); and *Geronimo* (93, Walter Hill).

Anyone now would agree that Hackman is reliable in a film—but so many of his roles take that for granted and do not think to test him. All too often he is asked to deliver little more than a standard version of gruff decency. So it's no surprise if he's more interesting when nasty: he was father to all the Earps in *Wyatt Earp* (94, Lawrence Kasdan); *The Quick and the Dead* (95, Sam Raimi); *Get Shorty* (95, Barry Sonnenfeld); *Crimson Tide* (95, Tony Scott); *The Chamber* (96, James Foley); *The Birdcage* (96, Mike Nichols), which gave him a chance to be funny; *Extreme Measures* (96, Apted); *Absolute Power* (97, Eastwood)—as a wicked president; *Twilight* (98, Robert Benton); the voice of General Mandible in *Antz* (98, Eric Darnell and Tim Johnson); *Enemy of the State*

(98, Scott); *Under Suspicion* (00, Stephen Hopkins); *The Replacements* (00, Howard Deutch); *The Mexican* (01, Gore Verbinski); *Heartbreakers* (01, David Mirkin); *Heist* (01, David Mamet); *The Royal Tenenbaums* (01, Wes Anderson); and then—with the man over seventy!—*Behind Enemy Lines* (01, John Moore), again!

Bat 21 or *Behind Enemy Lines*? *Under Suspicion* or *Extreme Measures*? Can you be sure which was which?

Philip Baker Hall, b. Toledo, Ohio, 1931

No one looking could muster the conviction to deny it—Philip Baker Hall is over seventy. His official record as an actor only begins around 1970—after a late graduation from the University of Toledo—so there may have been several other attempts on life along the way that could help account for the most squeezed, rueful, weary face in films. Which is to say that Philip Baker Hall is not what we are accustomed to beholding in the bright lights. He looks like a guy on the subway, at the end of the diner counter, a face that knows its place is in the crowd—and several rows back. On the other hand, around 1999 it began to be difficult to find a movie for which he hadn't been hired—if only to listen to the silly talk of others. Mr. Hall has a face that could reduce Bill Clinton to silence.

Of course, he first drew attention in 1984 playing Richard Nixon in *Secret Honor,* a one-man show written by Donald Freed and Arnold M. Stone as a stage play, but taken up by Robert Altman and turned into a film. It was a startling piece of work, and Mr. Hall was wild and wonderful, without ever seeming like Richard Nixon. It was an effective debut that had no apparent buyers. It was another decade before Paul Thomas Anderson rediscovered Hall and let him be Hall. You may be of the opinion, still, that Mr. Hall should not be in pictures (or as many). So be it. I find him a wonderfully sour presence, and exactly what we now deserve.

His record includes a great deal of television, most of it beyond recall, though he has been a judge on *The Practice* and a cop in the finale of *Seinfeld.* Similarly, there are many films or TV movies listed under his name, yet only a few that have been seen. This seems an ideal case for a week of Charlie Rose (just as Dick Cavett once explored Jed Harris) in which Mr. Hall could recount the wretched, hopeless, but alluring life of the player of small parts.

So, be alert to what is a much reduced list: *The Man with Bogart's Face* (80, Robert Day); *Ghostbusters II* (89, Ivan Reitman); *Say Anything* (89, Cameron Crowe); *An Innocent Man* (89, Peter Yates); *How I Got into College* (89, Savage Steve Holland); *Live Wire* (92, Christian Duguay); *Cigarettes and Coffee* (93, Anderson); *Roswell*

(94, Jeremy Kagan); *Kiss of Death* (95, Barbet Schroeder); *Eye for an Eye* (96, John Schlesinger).

His real breakthrough came in *Hard Eight* (96, Anderson), which was originally called "Sydney" after his character—a shabby casino resident, a lost father-figure, and a kind of exhausted angel; *The Rock* (96, Michael Bay); *Buddy* (97, Caroline Thompson); *Air Force One* (97, Wolfgang Petersen); *Boogie Nights* (97, Anderson); *Sour Grapes* (98, Larry David—the cocreator of *Seinfeld*); *The Truman Show* (98, Peter Weir); *Rush Hour* (98, Brett Ratner); *Enemy of the State* (98, Tony Scott); in the old John McIntire part in *Psycho* (98, Gus Van Sant); *The Cradle Will Rock* (99, Tim Robbins); as Don Hewitt in *The Insider* (99, Michael Mann); "Jimmy Gator," at his best, in *Magnolia* (99, Anderson); *The Talented Mr. Ripley* (99, Anthony Minghella); *The Contender* (00, Rod Lurie); as Aristotle Onassis in the TV miniseries *Jackie Bouvier Kennedy Onassis* (00, David Burton Morris); *The Sum of All Fears* (02, Alden Robinson); as Everett Dirksen in *Path to War* (02, John Frankenheimer); *Die, Mommie, Die* (03, Mark Rucker).

Robert Hamer (1911–63),
b. Kidderminster, England

1945: "The Haunted Mirror," episode from *Dead of Night; Pink String and Sealing Wax*. 1947: *It Always Rains on Sunday*. 1949: *Kind Hearts and Coronets; The Spider and the Fly*. 1951: *His Excellency*. 1952: *The Long Memory*. 1954: *Father Brown; To Paris with Love*. 1959: *The Scapegoat*. 1960: *School for Scoundrels*.

By far the best episode in *Dead of Night* is Hamer's, concerning a mirror in which Ralph Michael sees the reflection of a much older room where a murder was committed. Also starring the admirable Googie Withers, the episode exploits the magical possibilities of mirrors and interiors and is swift and frightening. For several years Hamer lived up to that debut, even if he made black comedies rather than suspenseful subjects. He started as an editor in 1935 and worked on *Vessel of Wrath* (38, Erich Pommer), *Jamaica Inn* (39, Alfred Hitchcock), and *Ships with Wings* (41, Sergei Nolbandov).

Of his earlier films four are exceptional: *It Always Rains on Sunday* has an ambitious structure and a true feeling for the East End underworld; *Pink String and Sealing Wax* is a fond recreation of Victoriana with Googie Withers, again, as a Brighton poisoner; *The Spider and the Fly* is a gripping study of complicity and duplicity set in France at the beginning of the First World War; *Kind Hearts and Coronets* is an English classic, with an elaborate but lightly borne scheme of flashbacks. Its comedy is at the expense of English eccentricity, tied to the alien, amoral, but appeal-

ing hero figure played by Dennis Price. It also introduced Hamer to Alec Guinness, a pairing that was restored for *Father Brown, To Paris With Love,* and *The Scapegoat.*

Those later films are all disappointing, and one has the feeling that Hamer needed more discipline to concentrate his style. It should be added that Hamer's career was blighted by alcoholism, and that he now looks like the most serious miscarriage of talent in the postwar British cinema. In the year he died, he was credited for additional dialogue on *Fifty-Five Days at Peking* (Nicholas Ray).

Guy Hamilton, b. Paris, 1922

1952: *The Ringer.* 1953: *The Intruder.* 1954: *An Inspector Calls; The Colditz Story.* 1956: *Charley Moon.* 1957: *Manuela.* 1959: *The Devil's Disciple; A Touch of Larceny.* 1962: *I Due Nemici/The Best of Enemies.* 1963: *The Party's Over* (uncredited; Hamilton had his credit removed). 1964: *Man in the Middle; Goldfinger.* 1966: *Funeral in Berlin.* 1969: *The Battle of Britain.* 1971: *Diamonds Are Forever.* 1973: *Live and Let Die.* 1974: *The Man with the Golden Gun.* 1978: *Force 10 from Navarone.* 1980: *The Mirror Crack'd.* 1982: *Evil Under the Sun.* 1985: *Remo Williams: The Adventure Begins.* 1989: *Sauf Votre Respect.*

He spent his youth in France and, after a period at the Victorine studio in Nice, he came to England in 1940, joining British Paramount News. He served in the navy and after the war became an assistant director: *They Made Me a Fugitive* (47, Alberto Cavalcanti); *Mine Own Executioner* (47, Anthony Kimmins); *Anna Karenina* (48, Julien Duvivier); *The Fallen Idol* (48, Carol Reed); *The Third Man* (49, Reed); *Outcast of the Islands* (51, Reed); and *The African Queen* (52, John Huston).

Briefly, it seemed that Hamilton might have an urbane talent. Although a failure, *Manuela* was a more penetrating view of sexual attraction than the British cinema usually allowed, and *A Touch of Larceny* was moderately funny. But events have revealed Hamilton as no more than a fluctuating technician, sometimes capable of anonymous economy and a shallow, cynical wit—*Goldfinger, Funeral in Berlin,* and *Diamonds Are Forever*—but elsewhere, barely competent: *The Battle of Britain* and *The Devil's Disciple,* which he took over at short notice from Alexander Mackendrick.

Christopher Hampton,
b. Fayal, Azores, 1946

1995: *Carrington.* 1996: *The Secret Agent.* 2003: *Imagining Argentina.*

As playwright, screenwriter, and director—and even as translator—Christopher Hampton has shown a steady interest in the nature and alchemy of the artistic process. Of course, to help support that judgment, one has to decide that in *Dangerous Liaisons,* Valmont and Mme. de Merteuil are artists of life, gamblers playing with living elements, not cold cards. It's a sardonic and academic approach in some ways, and it signifies a well-read man with a taste for existential dangers. He is often, in making a play, gathering together the kinds of knowledge we may have about an historical situation. This is palpably so in his play *Tales from Hollywood* (about European exiles in the movie town around 1940), which is an inspired mingling of research and speculation.

Lest this sounds only academic, let's say that *Carrington* is a very emotional film, far from the fusty air of Bloomsbury studies but made in the spirit of modern feminist vulnerability. It's the work of someone ready and poised to take on more difficult films.

Unfortunately, neither it nor *The Secret Agent* (from Conrad) had any commercial success.

As a screenwriter, Hampton has done *A Doll's House* (73, Patrick Garland); *Tales from the Vienna Woods* (81, Maximilian Schell); *Beyond the Limit* (83, John Mackenzie), adapted from Graham Greene's *The Honorary Consul;* Anita Brookner's *Hotel du Lac* (86, Giles Foster), adapted for British TV; *The Wolf at the Door* (87, Henning Carlsen), with Donald Sutherland as Gauguin; *The Good Father* (87, Mike Newell); *Dangerous Liaisons* (88, Stephen Frears); *Total Eclipse* (95, Agnieszka Holland), about Rimbaud and Verlaine; *Mary Reilly* (96, Frears), a brilliant reworking of Stevenson's *Dr. Jekyll and Mr. Hyde; The Quiet American* (02, Phillip Noyce).

Tom Hanks (Thomas J. Hanks),
b. Concord, California, 1956

People like Tom Hanks. They find him amiable, decent, and nonthreatening. They excuse him from the complete horror of *Bonfire of the Vanities* (90, Brian De Palma); they indulge him in the considerably empty, wishful whimsy of *Sleepless in Seattle* (93, Nora Ephron). And that's why he was cast, to disguise and carry, the "dangerous" subject of *Philadelphia* (93, Jonathan Demme). Why not admit that he is a good deal less than was required in all three pictures, and seemingly too deferential to impose himself on excessively cautious (or lacking) material. His lawyer in *Philadelphia* is a set of conceptual gestures, wrapped in harrowing makeup, and defiantly nongay. It is not Hanks's fault that the movie needs courage, convictions, or some resolution of what it is about. Nor is he unmoving. But he carries the automatic sentiment of a dog in a film about people. He is a given; he is the makeup.

Hanks dropped out of Cal State, Sacramento, to act—and no one can dispute the decision. If he still seems reticent as an actor, there is no question about his comedic skills. He made his screen debut

in the sitcom *Bosom Buddies* (80–82), and then broke into movies: *He Knows You're Alone* (81, Armand Mastroianni); playing "Dungeons and Dragons" to the max for TV in *Mazes and Monsters* (82, Steven H. Stern); *Bachelor Party* (84, Neal Israel); making his own splash with Daryl Hannah's mermaid in *Splash* (84, Ron Howard); *The Man With One Red Shoe* (85, Stan Dragoti); with his second wife, Rita Wilson, in *Volunteers* (85, Nicholas Meyer); *Every Time We Say Goodby* (86, Moshe Mizrahi); building a house with Shelley Long in *The Money Pit* (86, Richard Benjamin); *Nothing in Common* (86, Garry Marshall); and *Dragnet* (87, Tom Mankiewicz).

To this point, Hanks had survived getting on for ten worthless pictures of the sort that should be kept for crowded flights. Then, at least, he had a real chance, as the twelve-year-old who finds himself *Big* (88, Penny Marshall), for which he got a best actor nomination for sheer charm and skill.

But woe to those who got too excited. Hanks was set up as a bigger star, but the projects were no better: *Punchline* (88, David Seltzer); *The 'burbs* (89, Joe Dante); *Turner & Hooch* (89, Roger Spottiswoode); *Bonfire of the Vanities; Joe Versus the Volcano* (90, John Patrick Shanley); uncredited in *Radio Flyer* (92, Richard Donner); *A League of Their Own* (92, Penny Marshall); *Sleepless in Seattle; Philadelphia,* for which he won the Oscar; and *Forrest Gump* (94, Robert Zemeckis), for which he won the Oscar again, two in a row, with a performance that did nothing to sharpen or argue with the benign mindlessness of the picture.

Now, it is seven years later. I like Tom Hanks. I've met him and found him smart, funny, and interested in the larger world. But, truly—apart from his two voice-overs, as Sheriff Woody in *Toy Story* (95, John Lasseter) and *Toy Story 2* (99, Lasseter)—what challenges has he faced as an actor? Instead, he has become the American Actor, rather than someone actually involved in character and story—thus *Apollo 13* (95, Ron Howard), where he played a dull man to a T; *Saving Private Ryan* (98, Steven Spielberg), surely the film that gave him the sense of capital letters descending on him; the schtick of *You've Got Mail* (98, Ephron); the empty humanism of *The Green Mile* (99, Frank Darabont); the abominable, FedEx promo (and I like FedEx, too, but I don't go to them to be moved, just sent) *Cast Away* (00, Zemeckis).

It actually helps understand the numbness of those films, the aura around Hanks that protects him, to see that he is more than ever a producer, a figure who walks through his own films as if they were on parade for him. Hanks has become that person—supervising a vast TV series on space travel, and then *Band of Brothers* (01), a spin-off from *Saving Private Ryan.* What I'm saying is that he has become always Tom Hanks, without letting us into that persona.

He has directed one film, *That Thing You Do!* (96), and it was a promising debut, without ever revealing substantial character. He was the father in *Road to Perdition* (02, Sam Mendes) and the FBI man in *Catch Me If You Can* (02, Spielberg).

Curtis Hanson, b. Reno, Nevada, 1945
1987: *The Bedroom Window*. 1990: *Bad Influence; The Hand That Rocks the Cradle*. 1994: *The River Wild*. 1997: *L.A. Confidential*. 2000: *Wonder Boys*. 2002: *8 Mile*.

In the first four films he directed, Curtis Hanson had proved himself to be workmanlike, suspenseful, and blessed with a writer's strong sense of situation. *The Bedroom Window* begins with a very human attempt to escape an embarrassing situation; *Bad Influence* is a variation on the chance-meeting setup; *The Hand That Rocks the Cradle* is rooted in the reasonable notion that child minders can become overattached; and *The River Wild* has the novel idea of letting a woman be the hero. Equally, those films are really no more than their own smart proposals. *L.A. Confidential* is a different kind of picture: a period piece; a group portrait; and a multilevel study of corruption. It was fair to the James Ellroy original, to our nostalgia for forties and fifties noir. But it was more than that in making the Bud character into an unusual, unsmart hero.

Hanson edited *Cinema* magazine before he became a screenwriter: *The Silent Partner* (78, Daryl Duke), a bank-robbery film with unusual plot departures; *White Dog* (82, Samuel Fuller), derived from a Romain Gary novel; *Never Cry Wolf* (83, Carroll Ballard), adapted from Farley Mowat.

It is worth adding—in light of *L.A. Confidential*—that for a period Hanson was an assistant to Robert Towne, who served as executive producer on *The Bedroom Window*. You can feel that influence in *Confidential*, I think, and above all in *Wonder Boys* (adapted from Michael Chabon), one of the best recent American films and a terrific encouragement to the middle-aged.

Setsuko Hara, b. Yokohama, Japan, 1920
The two things said about Setsuko Hara are that she was Ozu's favorite actress, and the Garbo of Japan. Certainly she was Ozu's favorite—she appeared in six films for him between 1949 and 1961, and they were close offscreen as well. And, like Garbo, she retired at the height of her popularity: in 1962, she announced that she had never enjoyed making films and secluded herself in an elegant suburb of Tokyo. She is still there, spending time with family and school friends and remaining an object of curiosity and affection for the public. Like Garbo, Hara came to represent

an ideal of womanliness, nobility, and generosity.

She was discovered in 1935 and cast in a German-Japanese venture, *The New Earth* (37, Mansaku Itami and Arnold Fanck). By the time Japan entered the war, she was a star and the perfect war-movie heroine in such films as *The Suicide Troops of the Watchtower* (42, Tadashi Imai) and *Toward the Decisive Battle in the Sky* (43, Kunio Watanabe). When the war ended, she made two important movies: Kurosawa's *No Regrets for Our Youth* (46), in which she is a politically committed idealist who embraces the life of her peasant in-laws, clawing away implacably in the fields; and Kozaburo Yoshimura's *Ball at the House of Anjo* (47), a Chekhovian drama of an upper-class family down on its luck in the postwar world—and the critics' best picture of the year.

She made one movie with Kinoshita, *A Toast to the Young Miss* (49); and four with Naruse—his comeback film, about a failing marriage, *Repast* (51); *Sounds from the Mountains* (54), *Sudden Rain* (56), and *Daughters, Wives and Mothers* (60). And there was a second (misguided) film with Kurosawa, *The Idiot* (51), in which she was cast against type. But it was her work with Ozu that dominated.

Their best-known film in the West is *Tokyo Story* (53), in which she is the widowed daughter-in-law of the old couple who come to Tokyo to visit their children—the emblem of feminine duty and love, redeemed from sentimentality by her grave understanding and acceptance of the sadness life brings. In 1949, she had been the daughter in *Late Spring*, content to live on with her widower father until he realizes that she must marry—that life must go on—and gently tricks her into abandoning him. Remarkably, only eleven years later Ozu remade this film as *Late Autumn*, this time casting Hara as the sacrificing parent, a widow who maneuvers her daughter into marriage. Together, the films justify Ozu's belief in the continuities of life. Their other films together were *Early Summer* (51); the uncharacteristically melodramatic *Tokyo Twilight* (57); and *The End of Summer* (61).

Less versatile than Kinuyo Tanaka, less erotic than Machiko Kyo, less provocative than Hideko Takamine, Hara, with her long face, broad shoulders, and sorrowful eyes, her outward modesty and inner strength, stands as the epitome of Japanese womanhood. As Ozu said of her, "Every Japanese actor can play the role of a soldier and every Japanese actress can play the role of a prostitute to some extent. However, it is rare to find an actress who can play the role of a daughter from a good family."

Ann Harding (1901–81),
b. Fort Sam Houston, Texas
Elegant, refined, serene, classy, superior, noble,

aristocratic—perhaps "patrician" best suggests the quality Ann Harding conveyed at the height of her starring career, from 1929 through the mid-thirties. Even her hair was patrician—usually parted in the middle and pulled back in a simple yet starry bun, and pure ash blond rather than rowdy platinum blond or, even worse, sleazy bleached blond. She had been a successful Broadway leading lady in the twenties, and it's not by accident that three of her early vehicles were from Philip Barry plays: her first movie, *Paris Bound* (29, Edward H. Griffith), *The Animal Kingdom* (32, Griffith), and in between, the first version of *Holiday* (30, Griffith yet again). Harding's *Holiday* sticks closer to the Barry play than the later Hepburn version and has a different but considerable effect, Harding being more plaintive and vulnerable, less take-charge, than Hepburn. (It also has the advantage of Mary Astor as the sister, and the disadvantage of Robert Ames, rather than Cary Grant, as the leading man.)

Like other Broadway actresses imported to Hollywood to cope with sound (Ruth Chatterton, Helen Hayes, Hepburn herself), Harding started at the top—she is the star, and the essence of fineness, in every one of her thirties vehicles: *Her Private Affair* (29, Alexander Korda); *Condemned*, a penal colony movie with Ronald Colman (29, Wesley Ruggles); *The Girl of the Golden West*, Belasco rather than Barry (30, John Francis Dillon); *East Lynne* (30, Clive Brook); *Devotion*, with Leslie Howard (31, Robert Milton); *Prestige*, in a different penal colony, with Melvyn Douglas (32, Tay Garnett); *Westward Passage*, with the young Laurence Olivier (32, Milton); *The Conquerors*—imitation *Cimarron*, with Richard Dix (32, William A. Wellman); the first version of *When Ladies Meet*—the lady she meets is Myrna Loy, the man they share is Robert Montgomery (33, Harry Beaumont); *Double Harness*, with William Powell (33, John Cromwell); *The Right to Romance* (33, Alfred Santell); *Gallant Lady* (34, Gregory La Cava); *The Life of Vergie Winters* (34, Santell)—imitation *Back Street*; *The Fountain*, from a prestigious and pretentious best-seller by Charles Morgan (34, Cromwell); *Biography of a Bachelor Girl*, Sam Behrman in place of Barry (35, Griffith); *Enchanted April* (35, Beaumont), a flop, unlike the recent remake; *The Flame Within* (35, Edmund Goulding); in a time warp with Gary Cooper in George Du Maurier's *Peter Ibbetson* (35, Henry Hathaway); *The Lady Consents* (36, Stephen Roberts); *The Witness Chair* (36, George Nicholls, Jr.). By this time, bad scripts and changing tastes had undercut Harding's Hollywood career, and after escaping from Basil Rathbone's wife-killer in *Love from a Stranger*, a cheap British thriller (37, Rowland V. Lee), she retired from the screen. But she had been a unique icon of amused sophistication, throaty vulnerability,

and brave integrity—at her best when coolly composed and wryly humorous, at her worst when turned into fodder for weepies.

Five years after her retreat from Hollywood, she was back—for a series of appealing wife-and-mother roles. First came *Eyes in the Night* (42, Fred Zinnemann). Then she was Walter Huston's wife on their *Mission to Moscow* (43, Michael Curtiz); *North Star* (43, Lewis Milestone); Joyce Reynolds's mother in the teenage comedy *Janie* (44, Curtiz); *Nice Girls* (44, Leigh Jason); Laraine Day's mother in *Those Endearing Young Charms* (45, Lewis Allen); Janie's mother again but with a different Janie, Joan Leslie, in *Janie Gets Married* (46, Vincent Sherman); *It Happened on Fifth Avenue* (47, Roy Del Ruth); and performing the hat trick in *Christmas Eve* (47, Edward L. Marin), in which her three sons grow up to be George Brent, Randolph Scott, and George Raft. Then a gap of three years until she's Jane Powell's mother in *Two Weeks with Love* (50, Roy Rowland); Mrs. Oliver Wendell Holmes in *The Magnificent Yankee* (51, John Sturges); and *The Unknown Man* (51, Richard Thorpe). Finally, in 1956, three last ventures: Fredric March's wife in *The Man in the Gray Flannel Suit* (Nunnally Johnson) and two programmers: *I've Lived Before* (Richard Bartlett) and *Strange Intruder* (Irving Rapper). Only Mary Astor and Myrna Loy had managed the transition from leading lady to Mom so successfully.

Sir Cedric Hardwicke (1896–1964),
b. Stourbridge, England

By today's standards, it is a mystery that Hardwicke should have been knighted for his acting when only thirty-eight years old. By that date, 1934, he was successful, but hardly aristocratic. On the stage, he had played in Shaw, Eden Philpotts, and *The Barretts of Wimpole Street;* and on the screen he was in *Dreyfus* (31, Milton Rosmer); *Rome Express* (32, Walter Forde); *Orders Is Orders* (33, Forde); *The Ghoul* (33, T. Hayes Hunter); as Charles II opposite Anna Neagle's *Nell Gwynn* (34, Herbert Wilcox); as the Rabbi in *Jew Süss* (34, Lothar Mendes); and in *The Lady Is Willing* (34, Gilbert Miller). Less than a knight, Hardwicke was a poker-faced Malvolio—short, tending to baldness, and with a voice so deep it could have come from a ventriloquist.

Was there a mischievous anarchist behind that solemn face that made Hardwicke bear his title through a career of hapless disorder? Did he take special pleasure in the shabby? Here is Don Siegel explaining why he wanted Hardwicke for the crooked doctor in *Baby Face Nelson* (57), arguably his best film: "Hardwicke, particularly in those days, was a terrible villain. He drank a great deal and was a great deal of fun and he looked like a sleazy doctor. The picture everybody has is of someone very prim and proper, but he was not at all that way."

There is a note of lazy debauch in his Steyne in *Becky Sharp* (35, Rouben Mamoulian), and he appeared as David Garrick in *Peg of Old Drury* (35, Wilcox), as the Bishop in *Les Misérables* (35, Richard Boleslavsky) before making a last London stage appearance in *Tovarich*. After *Things to Come* (36, William Cameron Menzies), *Tudor Rose* (36, Robert Stevenson), *Laburnum Grove* (36, Carol Reed), and Allan Quatermain in *King Solomon's Mines* (37, Stevenson), Hardwicke crossed the Atlantic to become a Hollywood actor.

For a few years he played leads: *Green Light* (37, Frank Borzage); as the missionary in *Stanley and Livingstone* (39, Henry King); Dr. Arnold in *Tom Brown's Schooldays* (39, Stevenson); *On Borrowed Time* (39, Harold S. Bucquet); *The Hunchback of Notre Dame* (39, William Dieterle); and *Victory* (40, John Cromwell). But RKO, his studio, loaned him out at random and his career soon lost shape: *The Invisible Man Returns* (40, Joe May); *Suspicion* (41, Alfred Hitchcock); *Sundown* (41, Henry Hathaway); and *The Ghost of Frankenstein* (41, Erle C. Kenton). In 1943, Hardwicke played a leading if forlorn part in organizing a war-effort movie contributed to by British artists working in America: *Forever and a Day* (Frank Lloyd, Hardwicke, et al.). Fox then cast him as the Nazi in *The Moon Is Down* (43, Irving Pichel) and for a few years he had better parts at that studio: *The Lodger* (44, John Brahm); as Henry Cabot Lodge in *Wilson* (44, Henry King); *Wing and a Prayer* (44, Hathaway); *The Keys of the Kingdom* (44, John M. Stahl); and *Sentimental Journey* (46, Walter Lang).

But after the war his parts oscillated wildly: in Britain, *Beware of Pity* (46, Maurice Elvey); Ralph in *Nicholas Nickleby* (47, Alberto Cavalcanti); *The Winslow Boy* (48, Anthony Asquith); and *Now Barabbas . . .* (49, Gordon Parry). And in the United States, *Tycoon* (47, Richard Wallace); *A Woman's Vengeance* (48, Zoltan Korda); *I Remember Mama* (48, George Stevens); *Rope* (48, Hitchcock); *A Connecticut Yankee in King Arthur's Court* (49, Tay Garnett), in which he sang "Busy Doing Nothing" with Crosby and William Bendix; and *The Desert Fox* (51, Hathaway).

It must be said that Hardwicke was seldom less than absorbing in these films: in middle age he had acquired a sunken gravity like that of Rumpelstiltskin once his name has been discovered. But with the 1950s he made whatever was offered: *The White Tower* (50, Ted Tetzlaff); *The Green Glove* (52, Rudolph Maté); *Botany Bay* (53, John Farrow); *Salome* (53, Dieterle); *Bait* (54, Hugo Haas); *Helen of Troy* (55, Robert Wise); the fascinating insight of *Baby Face Nelson*, which came only two years after his Edward IV in *Richard III* (55, Laurence Olivier); and *The Vagabond King*

(56, Michael Curtiz). Thereafter he had tiny parts in epics and, in the year of his death, a fine cameo as the father in *The Pumpkin Eater* (64, Jack Clayton).

David Hare,
b. St. Leonard's-on-Sea, England, 1947
1977: *Licking Hitler* (TV). 1980: *Dreams of Leaving* (TV). 1985: *Wetherby*. 1988: *Paris by Night*. 1989: *Strapless*. 1991: *Heading Home* (TV). 1992: "Paris, May 1919," episode from *The Young Indiana Jones Chronicles* (TV). 1997: *The Designated Mourner.*

After an education at Lancing College and Cambridge, Hare grew into one of the best playwrights concerned with Britain's sense of decline in the seventies and eighties. His plays include *Fanshen* (75); *Plenty* (78); *Pravda* (85), written with his sometime collaborator, Howard Brenton; *The Secret Rapture* (88); and, most recently, a trilogy on the Church, the law, and politics. His movie career cannot be distinguished from his life in the theatre; both media have shared his projects and themes, and Hare began to direct some of his own plays, as if stimulated by the company of actors. He has been less than happy with the impact of his movies—whereas several of his plays had great critical and commercial success—but it is likely that Hare will move fluently from one medium to another so long as his concern, and Britain's troubles, persist.

This is especially welcome, for the three movies Hare made for theatrical release in the late eighties—*Wetherby, Paris by Night,* and *Strapless*—are unsurpassed in Britain in those years. In the world as a whole, it is hard to think of films so focused on real social and political dilemma, but which seem so expansive, so ready to be about anything and everything. Hare is far from stagy in his movies. His direction of actors works through the intimate observation of gesture, and even in those kinds of rest, passivity, or inner being that would be impossible on stage. In structure, he never employs anything as obvious as acts or scenes; instead, he assembles fragments, broken pieces of action, and likes to move back and forth in time. As early as *Plenty* on stage, he seemed influenced by editing and movie assembly. By now, his sense of structure appears as excited by film as by theatre.

If there is still a note of severity in his mise-en-scène that may be Hare's wariness over the sheer delight of filming. Even then, any threat of schematic composition is removed by his fascination with complicated women and the actresses who play them. There has been in Hare's films so far something of the intellectual tension of a fallible monk examining wonderful women.

Yet the woman who hovers above and beyond Hare's three movies is a monster, a black hole of liberty, Mrs. Thatcher. It was her regime and spirit, Hare believes, that undermined not just English institutions but the taste for tolerance, argument, diversity, and inner life in Britain. Thus, probably, his movies mean more to the British (and maybe the English) than they ever could to foreigners. What counters the particularity is the airy vastness of spiritual concern that pervades these entirely agnostic pictures. For it is not just the educational system, the National Health Service, or the language of Tory managers that are under scrutiny. Hare is touched by memory, bond, loss, and hope, in ways that link him to the novels of Hardy, George Eliot, and Henry James. He is the most Leavisite of moviemakers.

Wetherby, I think, is his best film, largely because its prompting suicide leads us into a consideration of when, how, and whether passion needs to be shifted or freed; and because Vanessa Redgrave has never done anything better. *Paris by Night* is his biggest failure (it was never released in America): it comes close to implausibility at times, and Charlotte Rampling is not required to be pleasant as its heroine. Still, the speed of consequence in its story is fascinating, and the movie develops Hare's faith in the rush of melodrama beneath English manners and propriety. (*Plenty* is filled with the same struggle.)

Strapless has Blair Brown as an American doctor in London, swept off her feet by a mysterious, faithless man, and troubled by her own, rootless sister. The title is too blunt, for the film's point is that life stands up on its own, despite our worries. There is hardly another modern film of which one can say that its subject is, simply, the force of life, the endurance that rolls over error, death, and disaster.

Hare's films are not easy—he works with the subtlety of a novelist. But they repay repeated viewing and I am confident they will survive as a landmark of work in the 1980s. As to the future, so much depends on what happens to Britain. He stands now as something like the documentarian Humphrey Jennings as the war ended. What *is* his subject?

As well as his own films, Hare has done the screenplays for *Saigon—Year of the Cat* (83, Stephen Frears), a brilliant invasion of American territory, and the best evidence that he could go beyond home; *Plenty* (85, Fred Schepisi); and *Damage* (92, Louis Malle), the first thing Hare has done that seemed like an opportunistic chore—for the people in *Damage* never convince us that they deserve a moral life. He also adapted his own play, *The Secret Rapture* (94, Howard Davies).

Hare's chief efforts are for the theatre—and why not?—but he has also scripted and appeared in *Via Dolorosa* (00, John Bailey), and he has adapted the Michael Cunningham novel for *The Hours* (02, Stephen Daldry). As a director, his most significant new work is *The Designated Mourner*, which was far better received by some others than by this writer.

Veit Harlan (1899–1964), b. Berlin
1935: *Die Pompadour* (codirected with Willy Schmidt-Gentner and Heinz Helbig); *Krach im Interhaus*. 1936: *Der Mude Theodor; Kater Lampe; Alles für Veronika; Maria der Magd*. 1937: *Mein Sohn, der Herr Minister; Die Kreutzersonate; Der Herrscher*. 1938: *Jugend; Verwehte Spuren*. 1939: *Die Reise nach Tilsit; Das Unsterbliche Herz*. 1940: *Jud Süss*. 1941: *Pedro Soll Hangen*. 1942: *Die Goldene Stadt; Der Grosse Konig*. 1943: *Immensee*. 1944: *Opfergang*. 1945: *Kolberg; Der Puppenspieler* (uncompleted). 1950: *Unsterbliche Geliebte*. 1951: *Hanna Amon*. 1953: *Die Blaue Stunde*. 1954: *Sterne uber Colombo; Die Gefangene des Maharadscha*. 1955: *Verrat an Deutschland*. 1957: *Anders als Du und Ich*. 1958: *Liebe Kann wie Gift Sein; Ich Werde Dich auf Handen Tragen*. 1962: *Die Blonde Frau des Maharadscha*.

There is still an unthinking orthodoxy that distinguishes those directors who quit Germany in the 1930s from those who stayed there. There are major figures whose choice of where to work was an expression of artistic personality—most obviously, Lang. But beneath Lang, there are several artisan directors who were content to flourish within one system or another. Michael Curtiz worked as enjoyably in Germany until 1926 as he did in Hollywood thereafter. And there is perhaps rather less than the barrier we have been taught to see between, on the one hand, Curtis Bernhardt and even Douglas Sirk, and on the other, Veit Harlan.

That is not to say that *Jud Süss* is not an uncompromising piece of anti-Semitism, made at a time when Harlan had no right to be ignorant of Germany's treatment of Jews. Nor can one deny the odious mixture of sentimentality and inspirational grandeur in many of Harlan's films as an expression of Nazi attitudes. But much American cinema has the same uneasy defects. Griffith inaugurated them. Many American war films are horribly bigoted. Do not forget the glee with which we applaud Conrad Veidt's death in *Casablanca*. The level of caricature in that film may be wittier than the way German films ridiculed the Allies, but the resort to caricature was common. Winning sides often condition our tolerance toward hokum. With a German victory, the Curtiz of *Casablanca* might have been just as trenchantly investigated as the Harlan of *Jud Süss* was blacklisted from 1945–50. Of course, that case can be overstated. The clearest corrective is the fact that Harlan survived to make more films, whereas Curtiz (and many others) could have had no such hopes. But the point needs making: we could safely advance beyond righteous condemnation of German cinema after that celebrated night when Lang fled.

Harlan did not begin directing until 1935, and it is clear that he was only favored by Goebbels because so many more incisive talents had departed. But *Jud Süss* is not really typical of his rather cloying, period-bedecked emotional heaviness. Most of his films are sentimental pieces or history films, strenuously trying to make an allegorical justification of the war. It is revealing that Germany reached backwards for support, whereas America cheerfully reconstructed the war and turned it into fiction. *Verwehte Spuren* was the original of *So Long at the Fair*, more sympathetic to Paris of 1868 than the later English version; *Die Reise nach Tilsit* was a remake of Murnau's *Sunrise* starring Harlan's third wife, the Swedish actress Kristina Soderbaum; *Der Grosse Konig* was a study of Frederick the Great; *Kolberg* was an elaborate vindication of German unification in the nineteenth century; but *Immensee* and *Opfergang* were ponderous, pastoral romances, as pledged to Soderbaum as Paul Czinner's movies were to Elizabeth Bergner; and *Die Goldene Stadt* was made in Prague extolling the improved qualities of Agfacolor.

After the war, Harlan was tried for his work on *Jud Süss* but acquitted—this in 1950 when some American artists were also suffering at the hands of inquisitors. He went back to work, still intent on romances and loyal to the matured Soderbaum.

Before directing, he had been an actor, first on stage, then in films: *Eins plus Eins Gleich Drei* (27, Felix Basch); *Das Mädchen mit den Fünf Nullen* (27, Kurt Bernhardt); *Der Meister von Nurnberg* (27, Ludwig Berger); *Somnambul* (29, Adolf Trotz); *Torck* (31, Gustav Ucicky); *Gefahren der Liebe* (31, Eugen Thiele); *Die Unsichtbare Front* (32, Richard Eichberg); *Fluchtlinge* (33, Ucicky); *Polizeiakte 909* (34, Robert Wiene); *Das Mädchen Johanna* (35, Ucicky); and *Stradivari* (35, Geza von Bolvary).

Jean Harlow (Harlean Carpenter) (1911–37), b. Kansas City, Missouri

David Stenn's invaluable life and death of Jean Harlow—can it be the last word on her short, chaotic career?—makes it clear that the child Harlean born in 1911 was already the daughter of "Jean Harlow"—Jean Harlow Carpenter, the star's mother, guide, chief audience, and effective jailer, who was looking for fulfillment and extension. She was the ensuring factor in her daughter's lurid glory.

It is still shocking to realize that the famous Harlow was only twenty-six when she died, for in few of her films does she look less than that age. Not only was her screen persona worldly, salty, and undisguisedly pleased with her own sexuality;

her looks seemed bruised by experience and by a forty-year-old's hard-earned knowledge. There was never the shine of youth or innocence. She had a young woman's body—for a moment—yet she offered it to the camera maternally, or like a seasoned whore. Her neglect of underwear seemed aggressive just because her breasts and the oceanic roll of her hips were so mature. The movie voyeur prefers an edge of youth that does not grasp how much is showing. That dissembling innocence was not Harlow's way. She was too candid. She winked, she liked her nipples to pout, as if to say, "Get a load of this." And the sheer load always fed into Harlow's nature as an actress—her comedy.

In that glorious moment from *Dinner at Eight* where Harlow and Marie Dressler are talking—

HARLOW: Do you know that the guy said that machinery is going to take the place of *every profession.*

DRESSLER: Oh, my dear, that's something *you* need never worry about—

Harlow is not just a glowing white sexpot. She is hardly less billowy and effulgent than Dressler—the voluptuous body, the clouds of hair, the apple cheeks, and the sheer ballooning *fun* of Harlow. She is as plump as one of Boucher's young women—and expanding before our eyes.

Yet she seldom looked well: her eyes gazed sadly from dark surrounds; her hair seemed to have been treated by a blowtorch or by poisonous alchemy—the platinum blonde was a great tag, but if you looked at the face you had to think of toxic associations; and Harlow's skin, from early on, seemed puffy and not quite fresh. When her death came, from acute nephritis, her body was terribly bloated from wastes she could not get rid of. She stank when she breathed—it is the ugliest end for a goddess, and it leaves her seeming like an eighty-year-old.

At the age of sixteen she eloped with a millionaire and after a quick divorce she began to work as an extra in films, including *The Love Parade* (29, Ernst Lubitsch) and *City Lights* (31, Charles Chaplin). She worked for Hal Roach in a few Laurel and Hardy pictures and then played her first substantial part at Paramount in Edward Sutherland's *The Saturday Night Kid* (29). But her real fame owed itself to the choice of Howard Hughes, who picked her out to replace Greta Nissen in *Hell's Angels* (1930). It may not have pleased Hughes, but Harlow's wise-cracking sexual adventuress rather eclipsed the aerial dynamics. An arbitrary master of his own inventions, Hughes loaned Harlow out indiscriminately: *The Secret Six* (31, George Hill); Tod Browning's *The Iron Man* (31); Wellman's *Public Enemy* (31); Benjamin Stoloff's *Goldie* (31); and most successful of all, Frank Capra's *Platinum Blonde* (31), for Columbia, a genuinely sexy comedy, in which Capra randily photographed Harlow's body. One shot, tracking with Harlow, is an unashamed sexual homage, a desert island shot.

At this stage, Harlow stood out for a one-studio contract and Hughes sold her to MGM. Her first film there, *The Beast of the City* (32, Charles Brabin), was not successful, but her next, Jack Conway's *Red-Headed Woman* (32), achieved the notoriety of prompting the Hays Office to issue sterner edicts against unpunished screen adultery. She married Paul Bern, Thalberg's right hand at MGM, and survived the scandal that followed his suicide only weeks later.

Bern's death knows no burying. But its mystery is a lot less than the mystery of why he and Harlow ever dreamed of marrying. Bern was an intellectual, a watcher, an insecure man. There may be no better example in Hollywood history of the longing for class and the dream of earthy vitality making for tragedy. Was Bern impotent? Could Harlow be as potent as on screen or in George Hurrell's great stills? Bern did have a common-law wife from the past, and she came to the house on the fateful night. David Stenn believes the two wives met, and that Harlow stormed off, telling Bern to sort it all out. So he shot himself, unable to stop behaving like someone in a Metro melodrama. I buy that version: in Hollywood, I'd always trust the plain messy answer rather than the sinister secret. A few days later, the common-law wife killed herself. Harlow soldiered on—she would have another marriage, of eight months, to cameraman Hal Rosson. She acted like an idiot offscreen—what better reason for staying onscreen as much as possible? But she *really* loved William Powell, or whomever. She was really the creation of her mother and her own foolishness. MGM tried a cover-up in the Bern death, but it was inept. They wanted Jean free from scandal—so *they* could exploit it.

Harlow's next film, Victor Fleming's *Red Dust* (32)—in which for the first time she played opposite Clark Gable—was her most uninhibited sexual encounter, and the clearest proof that she was a man's woman. It was as much Harlow's attitude as her deportment that achieved the effect of frankness.

She stayed with Gable for Sam Wood's *Hold Your Man* (33), Tay Garnett's enjoyable *China Seas* (35), Clarence Brown's *Wife vs. Secretary* (36), and her last film, *Saratoga* (37, Conway). In addition to these, before her death she made *Bombshell* (33, Fleming); *Dinner at Eight* (33, George Cukor); *The Girl from Missouri* (34, Conway); *Reckless* (35, Fleming), with William Powell, in which she marries wastrel Franchot Tone and, when he kills himself, suffers the sanctimonious disapproval of Tone's socialite friends;

Riffraff (36, Walter Ruben); *Suzy* (36, George Fitzmaurice); *Libeled Lady* (36, Conway); and *Personal Property* (37, W. S. Van Dyke).

Ed (Edward Allen) **Harris**,
b. Englewood, New Jersey, 1950

For the 1996 Oscars, Ed Harris was nominated as best supporting actor for his spiffy-vested Mission Control in *Apollo 13* (95, Ron Howard)—it was a terrific performance, terse, manly to the point of macho, utterly competent, and with a ghost of a smile in those sad, wise eyes that kidded the man's mix of decision, decorum, and stiff upper lip. (Harris has maybe the best eyes among contemporary American actors.) Yet Harris could easily have been one of the astronauts—chipper, laconic, modest, grim in a crisis and a pal at chow time, chasing the strands of orange juice like a kid bobbing for apples. He had done that role—twelve years earlier, he had been John Glenn in *The Right Stuff* (83, Philip Kaufman), when the real Glenn suffered on the campaign trail because he wasn't as dry, loose, or charismatic as Ed. Meanwhile, of course, for 1996, Harris might just as easily have been nominated for the true id to people like John Glenn, Howard Hunt in *Nixon* (95, Oliver Stone), a chronic agent who wore his vests and his soul inside out.

Harris has been a lead actor, and learned to live with his being a touch too short and several inches too hair-impaired—not that he has ever toupéed up. Indeed, he is more likely to go hairless, as for his FBI man in *The Firm* (93, Sydney Pollack). But he has become a faithful, unfailing supporting actor, increasingly respected, and loved.

What with a talent for football, he graduated college slowly, and it was 1975 before he settled for theater, an abiding pursuit: he won an Obie for creating the lead role in Sam Shepard's *Fool for Love* (83), and he played with his wife, Amy Madigan, in Murray Mednick's *Scar* (85).

His other films are as follows: as a doctor in *Coma* (78, Michael Crichton); *Borderline* (80, Jerrold Freedman); *Knightriders* (81, George A. Romero); *Creepshow* (82, Romero); *Under Fire* (83, Roger Spottiswoode); *Swing Shift* (84, Jonathan Demme); *Places in the Heart* (84, Robert Benton); the reporter in *A Flash of Green* (84, Victor Nuñez); *Alamo Bay* (85, Louis Malle); *Code Name: Emerald* (85, Jonathan Sanger); husband to Jessica Lange's Patsy Cline in *Sweet Dreams* (85, Karel Reisz); the soldier of fortune in *Walker* (88, Alex Cox); the policeman in *To Kill a Priest* (88, Agnieszka Holland); *Jackknife* (89, David Jones); in his biggest role, the husband in *The Abyss* (89, James Cameron); *State of Grace* (90, Phil Joanou), where he outplays Sean Penn and Gary Oldman; *Paris Trout* (91, Stephen Gyllenhaal); *China Moon* (92, John Bailey), as the cop who gets framed; *Glengarry Glen Ross* (92, James

Foley); *Needful Things* (93, Fraser Heston); with Melanie Griffith in *Milk Money* (94, Richard Benjamin); as a delirious madman in *Just Cause* (95, Arne Glimcher); the rogue general in *The Rock* (96, Michael Bay); on TV, with Madigan, in *Riders of the Purple Sage* (96, Charles Haid); *Eye for an Eye* (96, John Schlesinger); *Absolute Power* (97, Clint Eastwood); caught between Susan Sarandon and Julia Roberts in *Stepmom* (98, Chris Columbus); never better than as Christof, the director, in *The Truman Show* (98, Peter Weir); a priest in *The Third Miracle* (99, Holland).

In 2000, he played the lead in and directed *Pollock*, a heartfelt personal venture, with more feeling than depth, but a good picture. As an actor, he kept going with *Waking the Dead* (00, Keith Gordon); *The Prime Gig* (00, Gregory Mosher); a German marksman in *Enemy at the Gates* (01, Jean-Jacques Annaud); *Buffalo Soldiers* (01, Gregor Jordan); a rather seamy security man in *A Beautiful Mind* (01, Howard).

He got another Oscar nomination, while being the weakest link, in *The Hours* (02, Stephen Daldry); *Masked & Anonymous* (03, Larry Charles); *The Human Stain* (03, Robert Benton); *Radio* (03, Michael Tollin).

Richard Harris (1930–2002), b. Limerick, Ireland, 1930

Educated in Ireland and at LAMDA, Harris made his stage debut in 1956 in *The Quare Fellow* and subsequently worked for Joan Littlewood. He has made occasional returns to the theater—in *The Ginger Man* and a version of Gogol's *Diary of a Madman*—but he now works largely in the cinema or in the insecure world of "all-round personalities," giggling his way through intemperate TV interviews as stooges provoke him into disorderliness. His debut was in *Alive and Kicking* (58, Cyril Frankel), but he first attracted attention in Irish parts: *Shake Hands With the Devil* (59, Michael Anderson), *The Wreck of the Mary Deare* (59, Anderson), and Tay Garnett's *A Terrible Beauty* (60). He came to stardom with three studies in loudmouthed boorishness: *The Long and the Short and the Tall* (61, Leslie Norman); in Milestone's *Mutiny on the Bounty* (62); as the rugby player with a mind of leather in Lindsay Anderson's *This Sporting Life* (63). Despite seeming more lost than Monica Vitti in Antonioni's *The Red Desert* (64) and doing all an Irish Confederate ham could to slow down Peckinpah's *Major Dundee* (65), Harris became a star of international films: *The Heroes of Telemark* (65, Anthony Mann); *The Bible* (66, John Huston); and *Hawaii* (66, George Roy Hill). He was perhaps the least likely leading man for Frank Tashlin in *Caprice* (67); he discovered that he could sing in *Camelot* (67, Joshua Logan); and was used moderately well in *The Molly Maguires* (69, Martin Ritt). But he is

most at home in terrible films: *A Man Called Horse* (69, Elliot Silverstein), *Cromwell* (70, Ken Hughes), and *Man in the Wilderness* (71, Richard C. Sarafian). He gobbled up the role of the cripple in a tearstained TV version of Paul Gallico's *The Snow Goose* (75, Patrick Garland); acted in and directed *Bloomfield* (71), an Israeli film about a footballer; appeared in the brutal *The Deadly Trackers* (73, Barry Shear), after he had quarreled with the original director, Samuel Fuller; *Juggernaut* (74, Richard Lester); and 99 44/100% *Dead* (74, John Frankenheimer). He was in *Echoes of a Summer* (75, Don Taylor); King Richard in *Robin and Marian* (76, Lester); *The Return of a Man Called Horse* (76, Irvin Kershner); *Gulliver's Travels* (76, Peter Hunt); *The Cassandra Crossing* (76, George Pan Cosmatos); *Orca . . . Killer Whale* (77, Michael Anderson); *Golden Rendezvous* (77, Ashley Lazarus); and *The Wild Geese* (78, Andrew V. McLaglen).

His credits became increasingly bizarre: *Ravagers* (79, Richard Compton); *Game for Vultures* (79, James Fargo), set in Rhodesia, and costarring Joan Collins; *Your Ticket Is No Longer Valid* (79, George Kaczender); *Highpoint* (80, Peter Carter); as the explorer in the Bo Derek–laden *Tarzan, The Ape Man* (81, John Derek); *Triumph of a Man Called Horse* (83, John Hough); *Martin's Day* (84, Alan Gibson); as an inescapably Irish *Maigret* (88, Paul Lynch) for TV; *Mack the Knife* (89, Menahem Golan); *King of the Wind* (90, Peter Duffell); nominated for best actor in *The Field* (90, Jim Sheridan); unexpectedly lovely as the fraudulent gunslinger English Bob in *Unforgiven* (92, Clint Eastwood); *Patriot Games* (92, Phillip Noyce); *Silent Tongue* (92, Sam Shepard); *Wrestling Ernest Hemingway* (93, Randa Haines); on TV as *Abraham* (94, Joseph Sargent).

The charming point about turning seventy for Harris was that he became a public figure with his Albus Dumbledore in *Harry Potter and the Sorcerer's Stone* (01, Chris Columbus). Thus, all his Celtic rogues, epic seers, and Anthony Quinn leanings were swept up in one grand old ham: *Cry, the Beloved Country* (95, Darrel Roodt); *The Great Kandinsky* (95, Terry Winsor); *Savage Hearts* (95, Mark Ezra); *Trojan Eddie* (96, Gillies MacKinnon); *Smilla's Sense of Snow* (97, Bille August); *The Hunchback* (97, Peter Medak); *This Is the Sea* (98, Mary McGuckian); *The Barber of Siberia* (98, Nikita Mikhalkov); as George Adamson in *To Walk with Lions* (99, Carl Schultz); *Grizzly Falls* (99, Stewart Raffill); as Marcus Aurelius in *Gladiator* (00, Ridley Scott); *The Royal Way* (00, Andrei Konchalovsky); *The Pearl* (01, Alfredo Zacharias); as a kind of Lear in *My Kingdom* (01, Don Boyd).

Rex Harrison (Reginald Carey Harrison) (1908–90), b. Huyton, England

Harrison had never escaped lightweight inadequacy in films before he played Caesar in *Cleopatra* (63, Joseph L. Mankiewicz). The fact that he found it easy to be detached from that decorous extravagance, and his no more testing transfer of Henry Higgins from stage to screen in *My Fair Lady* (64, George Cukor), made him an international star. The point was hammered home by his shameless self-enjoyment in *Doctor Dolittle* (67, Richard Fleischer). Age had made him a little warmer and heavier in personality, but he was still able to look like an inane, high-pitched Aguecheek: *The Yellow Rolls-Royce* (64, Anthony Asquith); *The Agony and the Ecstasy* (65, Carol Reed); *The Honey Pot* (67, Mankiewicz); and *Staircase* (69, Stanley Donen).

Harrison went on the stage in 1924, and he always divided his time between theatre and movies. On the stage he played in *French Without Tears, The Cocktail Party, Bell, Book and Candle,* and *Platonov* as well as *My Fair Lady.* His first film was *The Great Game* (30, Jack Raymond), and he was in *Leave It to Blanche* (34, Harold Young); *All at Sea* (35, Anthony Kimmins); *Men Are Not Gods* (36, Walter Reisch); *Storm in a Teacup* (37, Victor Saville); *St. Martin's Lane* (38, Tim Whelan); *The Citadel* (38, King Vidor); *Over the Moon* (39, Thornton Freeland); *Ten Days in Paris* (39, Whelan); *Night Train to Munich* (40, Carol Reed); and *Major Barbara* (40, Gabriel Pascal). After naval service, he made *I Live in Grosvenor Square* (45, Herbert Wilcox), *Blithe Spirit* (45, David Lean), and *The Rake's Progress* (45, Sidney Gilliat).

Then he went to Hollywood to play opposite Irene Dunne in *Anna and the King of Siam* (46, John Cromwell). He stayed on for a ragbag of films: *The Ghost and Mrs. Muir* (47, Mankiewicz); *The Foxes of Harrow* (47, John M. Stahl); as the scheming conductor in *Unfaithfully Yours* (48, Preston Sturges)—one of the few films that made use of his grating charm; and *Escape* (48, Mankiewicz). In the 1950s he made whatever movies came along: *The Four Poster* (52, Irving Reis); *Main Street to Broadway* (53, Tay Garnett); as Saladin in *King Richard and the Crusaders* (54, David Butler); *The Constant Husband* (55, Gilliat); *The Reluctant Debutante* (58, Vincente Minnelli); rather good as the villain in *Midnight Lace* (60, David Miller); and *The Happy Thieves* (62, George Marshall).

In his last years, he appeared in *Crossed Swords* (77, Fleischer); in India, trying to steal a great ruby in *Shalimar* (78, Krishna Shah); *Ashanti* (79, Fleischer); *The Fifth Musketeer* (79, Ken Annakin); *Time to Die* (83, Matt Cimber); and *Anastasia: The Mystery of Anna* (86, Marvin J. Chomsky).

Harrison was married six times, four times to actresses: Lilli Palmer, Kay Kendall, Rachel Roberts, and Elizabeth Harris.

William S. Hart (1870–1946),
b. Newburgh, New York

Hart is one of those Americans who stepped from the actual West into the cinematic version of it. As a young man—in the late 1880s—he had worked on a cattle drive, and he subsequently opened a riding school. But from 1890 to 1910 he was a stage actor, achieving a notable success in the Broadway production of *Ben Hur.*

He would never have turned to movies but for a friendship with Thomas Ince. From a series of two-reel films, Hart became the first cowboy hero. He was already middle-aged, with an austere, horselike countenance and a fixed moral preoccupation. It is interesting that he often played an outlaw, reformed by the love of a good woman. From its beginnings, the Western was concerned to tranquilize the energies of the frontiersman. And, like Gary Cooper in later years, Hart was able to convey the burden of youthful wildness that lay on the shoulders of a pillar of society. He was also archaically chivalrous to women, and his solemn good manners did not always escape the impression of being downright elderly.

Hart is especially interesting because he wrote and directed many of his own films. Even with Ince and Triangle he had considerable independence, though *The Aryan* (16, Reginald Barker) and *Hell's Hinges* (16, Ince) were not credited to him. For the next two years, he directed most of his own films: *The Silent Man* (17); *The Narrow Trail* (17); *Blue Blazes Rawden* (18); *The Border Wireless* (18); *Wolves of the Rail* (18); and *Shark Monroe* (18). But from 1919, Ince's director, Lambert Hillyer, handled the Hart output: *Breed of Men* (19); *The Money Corral* (19); *Square Deal Sanderson* (19); *Wagon Tracks* (19); *Sand!* (19); *The Cradle of Courage* (20); *The Toll Gate* (20); *O'Malley of the Mounted* (21); *Three Word Brand* (21); *The Whistle* (21); *White Oak* (21); and *Travelin' On* (22). In 1923, Hart went to Famous Players for *Wild Bill Hickok* (Clifford S. Smith) and *Singer Jim McKee* (24, Smith). He retired in 1925 after *Tumbleweeds,* which he codirected with King Baggot.

Hal Hartley, b. Lindenhurst, New York, 1959
1984: *Kid* (s). 1987: *The Cartographer's Girlfriend* (s). 1988: *Dogs* (s). 1990: *The Unbelievable Truth.* 1991: *Trust; Theory of Achievement* (s); *Surviving Desire* (TV); *Ambition* (s). 1992: *Simple Men.* 1994: *Amateur; Opera No. 1* (s); *NYC 3/94* (s). 1995: *Flirt.* 1997: *Henry Fool.* 1998: *The Book of Life* (s). 2000: *New Math* (s); *Kimono* (s). 2001: *No Such Thing.*

Hal Hartley is offbeat enough to be one of his own characters—an odd, distracted independent filmmaker who comes to town (well, not quite town—rather more that quality of shabby suburbia he knows from Long Island), attracts some good-looking but disaffected people, and draws them into some modest fable of ironic reversal. And every few years comes out with a nice, tart, dead-pan comedy—like a midlist literary novel—that plays to subtly diminishing audiences.

Lest that sound dismissive, let me say I like Hartley and would like to encourage him (even if I'm not as fervent an admirer as Andrew Sarris). But what interests me especially here is the plight of the classic independent filmmaker, the distinct yet pale voice that has never really dreamed of going Hollywood and seeks only the kind of art-house audience that has never been as uncertain of itself in America as now.

Yes, of course there should be a place for such a thing—for Hartley, John Sayles, and Whit Stillman (and many others). Yet still the feeling lurks: that the movie in America has some duty to be large, embracing (and uniting)—that it requires some kind of sensational reach or vulgarity that wants everyone. That it is un-American to resist that.

So I at least understand the criticism that Hartley has created his own mannered forms and turned them into cliché in ten years: the unexpected meeting; the rather listless men; the beautiful but hushed women; the studied introduction of startling situations with every subsequent effort to downplay the surprise. *Sight and Sound* in 1999 could speak of his risk of becoming "vapid and obsolete," and I think it's true that in ten years Hartley has managed to make his new films seem unexciting. Is it that he is not seized by the medium? Is it that film in America is a beast that has to be lusted after, raped, and exploited? Can there be the kind of quiet, wry, but rather boring marriage that Hartley prefers? Or does such quiescence demand a far more evolved style (like Antonioni's, say) than he dreams of?

Laurence Harvey (Laruschka Mischa Skikne) (1928–73), b. Janiskis, Lithuania
Educated in Johannesburg, he served in the South African army before going to RADA and thence to work in the English theatre.

"I've never been able to like you," says Richard Boone's Sam Houston to Harvey's Colonel Travis in *The Alamo* (60, John Wayne) and moments later Wayne's Davy Crockett tells him to "Step down off your high horse." Not many actors lasted as long on cold starch, or endured such illness. Although not the man I would want to defend Texas with, Harvey was icily effective as the brainwashed Raymond Shaw in *The Manchurian Can-*

didate (62, John Frankenheimer) and as the double-agent Eberlin, a man instructed to liquidate himself, in *A Dandy in Aspic* (68, completed by Harvey after the death of Anthony Mann).

Elsewhere, he tended to bare his teeth and arch his cheekbones, whether trying to suggest nastiness—as in *Butterfield 8* (60, Daniel Mann), *The Outrage* (64, Martin Ritt), *Darling* (65, John Schlesinger)—or hoping to be appealing, as in *Two Loves* (61, Charles Walters), *Walk on the Wild Side* (62, Edward Dmytryk), *The Wonderful World of the Brothers Grimm* (62, Henry Levin), *The Running Man* (63, Carol Reed), or *Of Human Bondage* (64, Ken Hughes and Henry Hathaway).

Harvey made his debut in *House of Darkness* (48, Oswald Mitchell) and his reputation in the British cinema in *The Scarlet Thread* (51, Lewis Gilbert); *The Good Die Young* (53, Gilbert); as Romeo, opposite Susan Shentall, in *Romeo and Juliet* (54, Renato Castellani); in Henry Cornelius's *I Am a Camera* (55); as Joe Lampton in Jack Clayton's *Room at the Top* (59)—his breakthrough; in *Expresso Bongo* (59, Val Guest); and *The Long and the Short and the Tall* (61, Leslie Norman). He drifted to Hollywood out of no clear conviction or demand and often returned to work in England—as Lampton again in *Life at the Top* (65, William Kotcheff). What more can you say of a man only interesting as a zombie, except that in 1963 he directed and produced a film, *The Ceremony*, and in 1969 produced another, *L'Assoluto Naturale* (69, Mauro Bolognini)? After that, he played in *Der Kampf um Rom* (69, Robert Siodmak), *WUSA* (70, Stuart Rosenberg), and *Night Watch* (73, Brian G. Hutton) before succumbing to cancer. Among several wives, he included Margaret Leighton and Harry Cohn's widow, Joan.

Byron Haskin (1899–1984),
b. Portland, Oregon
1927: *Ginsberg the Great; Irish Hearts; Matinee Ladies; The Siren.* 1947: *I Walk Alone.* 1948: *Man-Eater of Kumaon.* 1949: *Too Late for Tears.* 1950: *Treasure Island.* 1951: *Tarzan's Peril; Warpath; Silver City.* 1952: *Denver & Rio Grande.* 1953: *The War of the Worlds; His Majesty O'Keefe.* 1954: *The Naked Jungle.* 1955: *Long John Silver; Conquest of Space.* 1956: *The First Texan; The Boss.* 1958: *From the Earth to the Moon.* 1959: *The Little Savage; Jet Over the Atlantic.* 1960: *September Storm.* 1961: *Armoured Command.* 1963: *Captain Sinbad.* 1964: *Robinson Crusoe on Mars.* 1968: *The Power* (codirected with George Pal).

Haskin (or Haskins, as he was often known) was a photographer from 1922, and *Bobbed Hair* (25, Alan Crosland), *On Thin Ice* (25, Malcolm St. Clair), and *Across the Pacific* (26, Roy del Ruth) led to his participation on the earliest exercise in

sound, *Don Juan* (26, Crosland). He is credited
with some of the detailed engineering that made
filming with sound less cumbersome and, after
When a Man Loves (27, Crosland) and *Wolf's
Clothing* (27, del Ruth), he worked briefly as a
director himself. But for the next twenty years he
concentrated on photography. Only in 1947 did he
resume as a director.

His films are cheerful adventures with a special
enthusiasm for space fiction, often in George Pal
productions. Invariably, they center on ingenious
special effects photography, and the roar of
Robert Newton's Long John Silver (in two films) is
one of Haskin's few human achievements. With
Pal, Haskin made several engaging movies: *The
War of the Worlds, The Conquest of Space, Robinson Crusoe on Mars*, and, not least, *The Naked
Jungle*, which has Charlton Heston troubled by a
mail-order marriage with Eleanor Parker and an
unexpected invasion of ants.

Henry Hathaway (Henri Leopold de
Fiennes) (1898–1985),
b. Sacramento, California

1932: *Wild Horse Mesa*. 1933: *Heritage of the
Desert; Under the Tonto Rim; Sunset Pass; Man of
the Forest; To the Last Man*. 1934: *Come On,
Marines!; The Last Round-Up; Thundering Herd;
The Witching Hour; Now and Forever*. 1935: *The
Lives of a Bengal Lancer; Peter Ibbetson*. 1936:
*The Trail of the Lonesome Pine; Go West, Young
Man; I Loved a Soldier* (uncompleted). 1937:
Souls at Sea. 1938: *Spawn of the North*. 1939: *The
Real Glory*. 1940: *Johnny Apollo; Brigham Young*.
1941: *The Shepherd of the Hills; Sundown*. 1942:
Ten Gentlemen from West Point; China Girl.
1944: *Home in Indiana; Wing and a Prayer*. 1945:
Nob Hill; The House on 92nd Street. 1946: *The
Dark Corner*. 1947: *13 rue Madeleine; Kiss of
Death*. 1948: *Call Northside 777*. 1949: *Down to
the Sea in Ships*. 1950: *The Black Rose*. 1951:
*You're in the Navy Now; Rawhide; Fourteen
Hours; The Desert Fox/Rommel, Desert Fox*.
1952: *Diplomatic Courier; "The Clarion Call,"*
episode from *O. Henry's Full House*. 1953: *Nia-
gara; White Witch Doctor*. 1954: *Prince Valiant;
Garden of Evil*. 1955: *The Racers/Such Men Are
Dangerous*. 1956: *The Bottom of the Bottle; 23
Paces to Baker Street*. 1957: *Legend of the Lost*.
1958: *From Hell to Texas/Manhunt*. 1959: *Woman
Obsessed*. 1960: *Seven Thieves; North to Alaska*.
1963: *How the West Was Won* (codirected). 1964:
*Circus World/The Magnificent Showman; Of
Human Bondage* (codirected with Ken Hughes).
1965: *The Sons of Katie Elder*. 1966: *Nevada
Smith*. 1967: *The Last Safari*. 1968: *Five Card
Stud*. 1969: *True Grit*. 1971: *Raid on Rommel;
Shoot Out*. 1973: *Hangup*.

After a debut as a ten-year-old actor, Hathaway

progressed from assistant to Frank Lloyd to director of two-reel Westerns for Paramount before
commencing a forty-year career as director. Durability cannot conceal great oscillations in his work.
And professionalism and the legend of his colorful
temper should not excuse frequent dullness.
Because a man has directed for so long does not
ensure that his character has matured. Close study
of Hathaway reveals, at best, an amiable enthusiasm for adventure, but at worst, the considerable
endurance test of, say, the overrated *Call Northside 777, Down to the Sea in Ships, The Black
Rose, The Desert Fox, White Witch Doctor, The
Racers, The Bottom of the Bottle, 23 Paces to
Baker Street*, and *Legend of the Lost*. Hathaway
has only to be compared with the genuinely inventive Don Siegel for all his lethargy and lost opportunities to fall into place.

He was always a workhorse, generally with
Paramount and Fox, competent at rough-house
action but otherwise likely to be influenced by his
compatriots on a film. Thus *Peter Ibbetson* is
unlike any of his other films in its sense of dream;
The Shepherd of the Hills is a charming rural
fable with a wonderful, shy Betty Field; *13 rue
Madeleine* is diverted by the energy of James
Cagney; *Kiss of Death* is made nasty by Richard
Widmark's hoodlum; *Fourteen Hours* is a bedlam
of talented supporting players; *Niagara* throbs
with the implausibility of Joseph Cotten and Monroe being married; *Garden of Evil* is built on the
niggling confrontation of Widmark and Gary
Cooper; and *True Grit* is an unashamed Oscar
vehicle for John Wayne.

Hathaway's sort of naïve enthusiasm is out of
fashion now, but is real nonetheless, as much in
Lives of a Bengal Lancer and *Spawn of the North*
as in the tightly organized *Seven Thieves*, the slapstick boisterousness of *North to Alaska*, or the
small-scale suspense of *Rawhide*. In search of pattern, one notices a zest for physical destruction
and a recurring use of the journey motif. But,
artistically, it is a career without consistency or
growth. Thus within one year, 1945, he moved
without demur from the turgid period reconstruction of *Nob Hill* to Fox's modish venture into
urban realism with *The House on 92nd Street*.

Jack Hawkins (1910–73), b. London

Hawkins's trembling stiff upper lip—a grotesque
struggle between emotionalism and rigor mortis—is redolent of those British war films of the
1950s. Pictures like *Angels One Five* (51, George
More O'Ferrall), *The Cruel Sea* (53, Charles
Frend), and *The Malta Story* (53, Brian Desmond
Hurst) established him as central to the British
myth of ossified pluck in the face of war. Hawkins
always struck me as a rather oppressive actor,
more interesting when resentful or truculent.
Indeed, he might have made a nasty heavy had

anyone encouraged him. There are, however, a few films in which his hostility is quite impressive and frightening: *State Secret* (50, Sidney Gilliat); *The Prisoner* (55, Peter Glenville); and *Rampage* (63, Phil Karlson).

As a juvenile, he appeared on the English stage and by 1930 he was into films: *Birds of Prey* (30, Basil Dean); *The Lodger* (32, Maurice Elvey); *The Good Companions* (33, Victor Saville); *The Lost Chord* (33, Elvey); *The Jewel* (33, Reginald Denham); *A Shot in the Dark* (33, George Pearson); *Autumn Crocus* (34, Dean); *Death at Broadcasting House* (34, Denham); *Peg of Old Drury* (35, Herbert Wilcox); *The Frog* (37, Jack Raymond); *Beauty and the Barge* (38, Henry Edwards); *A Royal Divorce* (38, Raymond); *Murder Will Out* (39, Roy William Neill); and *Next of Kin* (42, Thorold Dickinson).

During the war, he served in India and was then made colonel in command of ENSA. He returned to the screen in peace and gradually hauled himself to the top: *The Fallen Idol* (48, Carol Reed); *Bonnie Prince Charlie* (48, Anthony Kimmins); *The Small Back Room* (48, Michael Powell); the Prince of Wales in *The Elusive Pimpernel* (50, Powell); *The Adventurers* (50, David MacDonald); *Home at Seven* (50, Ralph Richardson); *No Highway* (50, Henry Koster); *The Black Rose* (50, Henry Hathaway); *Mandy* (52, Alexander Mackendrick); and *The Planter's Wife* (52, Ken Annakin). His employment in American films was not the least curious aspect of his success, and from 1955 onward he worked on both sides of the Atlantic: *The Intruder* (53, Guy Hamilton); *The Seekers* (54, Annakin); helplessly lost in *Land of the Pharaohs* (55, Howard Hawks); *The Long Arm* (56, Frend); *The Man in the Sky* (56, Charles Crichton); *Fortune Is a Woman* (57, Gilliat); *The Bridge on the River Kwai* (57, David Lean); *Gideon's Day* (58, John Ford); *The Two-Headed Spy* (58, André de Toth); *Ben-Hur* (59, William Wyler); *The League of Gentlemen* (60, Basil Dearden); *Two Loves* (61, Charles Walters); *Five Finger Exercise* (62, Daniel Mann); as Allenby in *Lawrence of Arabia* (62, Lean); *Guns at Batasi* (64, John Guillermin); *Zulu* (64, Cy Endfield); *Masquerade* (64, Dearden); *Lord Jim* (65, Richard Brooks); and *Judith* (65, Mann).

In 1966, he was operated on for cancer of the throat with the result that his vocal cords were affected. After that he was dubbed or spoke with the somber, rasping voice of Alpha 60, thereby adding to the effect of misanthropy: *Great Catherine* (67, Gordon Flemyng); *Shalako* (68, Edward Dmytryk); *Monte Carlo or Bust* (69, Annakin); *Oh! What a Lovely War* (69, Richard Attenborough); *Waterloo* (70, Sergei Bondarchuk); *The Adventures of Gerard* (70, Jerzy Skolimowski); *Jane Eyre* (71, Delbert Mann); *Nicholas and Alexandra* (71, Franklin J. Schaff-

ner); *Kidnapped* (71, Delbert Mann); and *Young Winston* (72, Attenborough).

Howard Hawks (1896–1977),
b. Goshen, Indiana
1926: *The Road to Glory; Fig Leaves.* 1927: *The Cradle Snatchers; Paid to Love.* 1928: *A Girl in Every Port; Fazil; The Air Circus.* 1929: *Trent's Last Case.* 1930: *The Dawn Patrol.* 1931: *The Criminal Code.* 1932: *The Crowd Roars; Scarface, Shame of the Nation; Tiger Shark.* 1933: *Today We Live.* 1934: *Viva Villa!* (credited to Jack Conway, but codirected with Hawks); *Twentieth Century.* 1935: *Barbary Coast.* 1936: *Ceiling Zero; The Road to Glory; Come and Get It* (codirected with William Wyler). 1938: *Bringing Up Baby.* 1939: *Only Angels Have Wings.* 1940: *His Girl Friday; The Outlaw* (codirected with Howard Hughes, not released until 1946). 1941: *Sergeant York; Ball of Fire.* 1943: *Air Force.* 1944: *To Have and Have Not.* 1946: *The Big Sleep.* 1948: *Red River; A Song is Born.* 1949: *I Was a Male War Bride/You Can't Sleep Here.* 1951: *The Thing* (credited to Christian Nyby, with Hawks as producer, but seeing is believing). 1952: *The Big Sky; "The Ransom of Red Chief,"* episode from *O. Henry's Full House; Monkey Business.* 1953: *Gentlemen Prefer Blondes.* 1955: *Land of the Pharaohs.* 1959: *Rio Bravo.* 1962: *Hatari!.* 1964: *Man's Favorite Sport.* 1965: *Red Line 7000.* 1967: *El Dorado.* 1970: *Rio Lobo.*

When critics play children's games—such as selecting the ten best films of all time—the majority behave like dutiful understudies for a Platonic circle, opting for milestone movies, turning points in the art of film. But imagine yourself a Crusoe, as the ship goes down: a ship transporting the movie resources of the world, the S. S. *Langlois.* Put aside thoughts of urgency; there is time in this sort of dream for one Lang, one Ophuls, one Mizoguchi, one Rossellini, one Hitchcock, one Sternberg, one Murnau, one Renoir, one Buñuel, one Ozu, and one Hawks to while away the days on that island.

But a Crusoe needs to be honest with himself, just as Defoe's hero foresaw that money would be out of place on the island but still could not bear to let it go down, knowing that rescue would vindicate his prudence. So, hold the raft while I lay my hands on *Twentieth Century, Bringing Up Baby, Only Angels Have Wings, His Girl Friday, To Have and Have Not, The Big Sleep, Red River, I Was a Male War Bride, Gentlemen Prefer Blondes,* and *Rio Bravo.*

Too easy, too superficial a response to the total archive, you protest? Quite right. All the way to the island, paddling my raft, I shall be regretting *Man's Favorite Sport* (full of useful aquatic hints) already underwater, quite broken up by the thought of *Monkey Business* left behind, and gnawed at by the loss of *Air Force, Ceiling Zero,* and *Scarface.*

Back in the civilized world there will be libraries crowded with works of cinema history that patronize Howard Hawks. The staffs of *Sight and Sound* may still wake in the night shuddering with the memory that they did not bother to review *Rio Bravo.* And those willing to compromise will concede that "Old Hawks certainly does make entertaining films . . ." with the hollow, wide-eyed charity of minds keen to search out the good in every man. But the reservations mount up: Hawks is old-fashioned, subject to the limitations of the entertainment film, prone to a romantic view of men in action; in short, a moviemaker for boys never quite grown up.

The implication is that Hawks was an obedient, placid artisan within a narrow and corrupting framework. Hawks did nothing to deny that interpretation himself. Even the amusing and revealing interview that Peter Bogdanovich did with Hawks did not coax the laconic veteran further than the admission that he always liked to put as much fun and business into his pictures as possible. He disparaged plot and content and barely referred to camera effects. There was no attempt to conceal the stress on masculine values in his films. And no interest in going beyond the understatement shared by most of his characters or in elaborating on the implications and undertones of the recurring, ritualistic situations that obsess him. Like Monet forever painting lilies or Bonnard always re-creating his wife in her bath, Hawks made only one artwork. It is the principle of that movie that men are more expressive rolling a cigarette than saving the world.

The point should be made that Hawks attends to such small things because he is the greatest optimist the cinema has produced. Try to think of the last optimistic film you saw and it may dawn on you that the achievement is not minor. Not that he fails to notice tragedy. The optimism comes out of a knowledge of failure and is based on the virtues and warmth in people that go hand-in-hand with their shortcomings. Death, rupture, and loss abound in Hawks's world, even if they are observed calmly. The unadvertised sense of destruction in *Ceiling Zero* and *The Road to Glory* is the most breathtakingly frank view of depression in the 1930s American film. *Bringing Up Baby*—not for nothing photographed by Russell Metty—is a screwball comedy surrounded by darkness, forever on the brink of madness. *Sergeant York* is a barely admitted story of outraged conscience. *The Big Sleep* contains not only the General, unwarmed in his sweltering hot house, but Elisha Cook swallowing poison. *Red River* is a story of youth usurping age. *I Was a Male War Bride* only comes so close to sexual frustration by making it ridiculous.

The clue to Hawks's greatness is that this somber lining is cut against the cloth of the genre in which he is operating. Far from the meek purveyor of Hollywood forms, he always chose to turn them upside down. *To Have and Have Not* and *The Big Sleep,* ostensibly an adventure and a thriller, are really love stories. *Rio Bravo,* apparently a Western—everyone wears a cowboy hat— is a comedy conversation piece. The ostensible comedies are shot through with exposed emotions, with the subtlest views of the sex war, and with a wry acknowledgment of the incompatibility of men and women. Men and women skirmish in Hawks's films on the understanding that an embrace is only a prelude to withdrawal and disillusion. The dazzling battles of word, innuendo, glance, and gesture—between Grant and Hepburn, Grant and Jean Arthur, Grant and Rosalind Russell, John Barrymore and Carole Lombard, Bogart and Bacall, Wayne and Angie Dickinson, Rock Hudson and Paula Prentiss—are Utopian procrastinations to avert the paraphernalia of released love that can only expend itself. In other words, Hawks is at his best in moments when nothing happens beyond people arguing about what might happen or has happened. Bogart and Bacall in *The Big Sleep* are not only characters tangled in a tortuous thriller but a constant audience to the film, commenting on its passage. The same is true of all those scenes in *Rio Bravo* when the tenuous basis of the plot is mulled over. That is why, at the end of *Red River,* Joanne Dru interrupts the fight between Wayne and Clift with, "Whoever thought either one of you would kill the other?"

The "style" of Hawks rests in this commenting astuteness; no other director so bridges the contrived plots of genre and the responses of a mature spectator. And because there is such emotional intelligence, such witty feeling, the camera is almost invisible. It is insufficient to say that Hawks put the camera in the most natural and least obtrusive place. The point is that his actors played to and with him, as he sat to one side of the camera that recorded them. His method involved the creation of a performance in rehearsal for which the script was merely an impetus. Whatever the script said, Hawks always twisted it into those abiding tableaux. It was a requirement of the method that he selected actors and actresses who responded to this sort of badgering companionship and whom the audience accepted as being grown up. No wonder then that Cary Grant is so central to Hawks's work. But notice how far *Rio Bravo* shows us a Wayne and Dean Martin hardly recognized by other directors. And do not forget the list of people either discovered or brought to new life by Hawks: Louise Brooks (chosen by Pabst for *Pandora's Box* after seeing *A Girl in Every Port*); Boris Karloff; Carole Lombard; Rita

Hayworth; Richard Barthelmess; Jane Russell; Lauren Bacall; Dorothy Malone; Montgomery Clift; George Winslow; Angie Dickinson; and James Caan.

The optimism derived from a delight in people expressed in the finding of new faces and the production of new expressions on old faces. In that sense Hawks blended classical narrative cinema and cinema verité. After all, *The Big Sleep* was like a home movie, made amid the dark interiors of a Warners studio; that view of intimacy has time and again shattered the supposedly imprisoning circumstances of entertainment movies. Hawks is the supreme figure of classical cinema. Because he is so unassuming an innovator, so natural an entertainer, his work has still not been surpassed.

Which leaves me on my island: with Lombard kicking Barrymore in the stomach in *Twentieth Century;* with Hepburn sinking that long putt in *Bringing Up Baby;* with Grant asking "Who's Joe?" in *Only Angels Have Wings;* with the flower pot coming through the window in *Rio Bravo;* with the slow dawn pan before the cattle drive begins in *Red River;* and with Bacall snapping "help yourself" in *The Big Sleep.*

There's a motto, if you want one: you need only relax old, dull muscles, flex those undiscovered by other movies, and help yourself.

Thirty years after writing the above, I don't want to change a word of it, or do without the Hawks pictures on my island. Nothing I have reviewed has dated or deteriorated—and I wish I could say as much for most American directors of the golden age. There's only one thing to add: that the mystery of Hawks builds.

The more one learns of his life, the clearer it is that he was a chronic liar and compartmentalizer, a secretive rogue, a stealthy dandy, and a ruinous womanizer. The Todd McCarthy biography began to set the mess of his life beside the heroic grace of the films. But Hawks was always a maker of comedy and play (even when the tone is tragic). There was an absurdist in Hawks, and a Nabokovian delight in the game for its own sake. Thus, in a very important way, this seeming American may have been against the grain of his time and place. That may help explain why the films grow in wonder.

Goldie Hawn, b. Washington, D.C., 1945

I don't think any film has ever captured the lyrical blonde naïveté that Goldie showed on TV's *Laugh-In.* She is usually pert and engaging: amiability perches on her high, child's voice and gurgles from her baby's mouth. The eyes are still eyes from Lolita's face. But she will soon be too old to play the gamine, and may suffer the problems of a middle-aged baby-face. As it is, in most of her pictures she has been no more than a pretty, available comedienne, whose pop-eyed surprise reminds us

of her sublime merriment on *Laugh-In.* That show had an extraordinary capacity for finding fresh comic personalities and presenting them in a familylike context, presided over by Uncles Dan and Dick. Goldie was hired for the show as a dancer, and she regularly undulated in a bikini and body paint. But she was given a few lines to read, and in fluffing them she uncovered a comic potential all the more delicious when the older men on the show became paternal in their efforts to help her see straight or to comfort her helpless giggles. She disrupted the stupid propriety of TV and was one of the few people who ever caught the amateurishness of the medium with style and nerve. She went bananas forgetting things, but she never lost her cool. She didn't worry, and that gave her a lovable dignity. She was a ding-a-ling, but never dumb, and she managed to bridge the gulf between daffy nymphet and tipsy lady.

Her pictures are an odd lot: a supporting actress Oscar for her none too remarkable debut in *Cactus Flower* (69, Gene Saks); with Peter Sellers in *There's a Girl in My Soup* (70, Roy Boulting); with Warren Beatty in *$* (71, Richard Brooks); *Butterflies Are Free* (72, Milton Katselas); helping to produce *The Girl from Petrovka* (74, Robert Ellis Miller), a major flop; easily her best performance as the muddle-headed wife, determined to rescue her husband in *The Sugarland Express* (74, Steven Spielberg); Beatty's girlfriend again in *Shampoo* (75, Hal Ashby); *The Duchess and the Dirtwater Fox* (76, Melvin Frank); *Foul Play* (78, Colin Higgins); and *Travels with Anita* (79, Mario Monicelli).

Her career peaked with *Private Benjamin* (80, Howard Zieff), which grossed over $100 million, and on which she was executive producer. But new power only exposed her as a repetitive comedienne, with questionable judgment of material: *Seems Like Old Times* (80, Jay Sandrich); *Best Friends* (82, Norman Jewison); *Swing Shift* (84, Jonathan Demme), which she produced, took away from Demme, and reworked to the film's detriment; *Protocol* (84, Herbert Ross); *Wildcats* (86, Michael Ritchie); *Overboard* (87, Garry Marshall), in which she played with Kurt Russell, her companion; *Bird on a Wire* (90, John Badham); and *Deceived* (91, Damien Harris). The films were getting more strained, yet she won a long-term production deal at Hollywood Pictures: *Crisscross* (92, Chris Menges); *Housesitter* (92, Frank Oz); and *Death Becomes Her* (92, Robert Zemeckis).

She has gracefully backed away from the camera while taking on more demanding roles. And so she directed for the first time—a TV melodrama, *Hope* (97)—and she produced *Something to Talk About* (95, Lasse Hallstrom) and the far more entertaining *When Billie Beat Bobby* (01, Jane Anderson), about the King-vs.-Riggs tennis match. As an actress, she has done the very successful *The First Wives Club* (96, Hugh Wilson); *Everyone Says I Love You* (96, Woody Allen); *The Out-of-Towners* (99, Sam Weisman); *Town & Country* (01, Peter Chelsom); *The Banger Sisters* (02, Bob Dolman). She also produced *The Matthew Shepard Story* (02, Roger Spottiswoode).

Sterling Hayden (Sterling Relyea Walter) (1916–86), b. Montclair, New Jersey

Hayden always looked shy of glossy stardom, more his own master than smile-flexing Flynns and Powers. At his best, Hayden was solid, weathered, and fatalistic: a taciturn, gangling John Hamilton, as calm as a Melville sailor who had seen great sights and was puzzled by the need to talk of them. Three times that placid strength was invoked: as the horse-loving perfectionist in *The Asphalt Jungle* (50, John Huston); as the stranger in *Johnny Guitar* (53, Nicholas Ray), deliberating over the operatic dialogue of that film; as the organizer in *The Killing* (56, Stanley Kubrick), finally dismayed by the dollar bills winnowed in aircraft slipstream. His seeming spiritually wearied by that debacle only added to the impression of stoicism that he conveyed.

He came to the movies as a sailor who married the English actress Madeleine Carroll. He appeared with her at Paramount in *Virginia* (41, Edward H. Griffith) and *Bahama Passage* (41, Griffith). Apart from *Manhandled* (44, Lewis R. Foster), he spent the war years in the marines. When he emerged, the marriage ended in divorce and Hayden found himself moving from studio to studio: *Blaze of Noon* (47, John Farrow); *Albuquerque* (47, Ray Enright); *Flaming Feather* (51, Enright); *Journey into Light* (51, Stuart Heisler); *So Big* (52, Robert Wise); *Denver & Rio Grande* (52, Byron Haskin); *The Star* (53, Heisler); *Take Me to Town* (53, Douglas Sirk); *Prince Valiant* (54, Henry Hathaway); *Crime Wave* (54, André de Toth); *Suddenly* (54, Lewis Allen); as Jim Bowie in *The Last Command* (55, Lloyd); *Naked Alibi* (55, Jerry Hopper); *Arrow in the Dust* (56, Lesley Selander); *Valerie* (57, Gerd Oswald); *Crime of Passion* (57, Oswald); and *Terror in a Texas Town* (58, Joseph H. Lewis).

He dropped out of circulation during the early 1960s, apart from his colonel in *Dr. Strangelove* (63, Kubrick). He sailed some more and published an autobiography, *Wanderer*. Only at the end of the decade did he return to movies: *Hard Contract* (69, S. Lee Pogostin); in the remarkable *Sweet Hunters* (69, Ruy Guerra); *Loving* (70, Irvin Kershner); *Le Saut de l'Ange* (71, Yves Boisset); as the corrupt policeman assassinated over the pasta in *The Godfather* (71, Francis Ford Coppola); the drunken writer in *The Long Goodbye* (72, Robert Altman); as Major Wrongway Lindbergh in *The Final Programme* (73, Robert Fuest).

His undoubted resonance as a Lord Jim–like flawed hero was aided by his tattered, maudlin self-contempt at the way he abandoned friends by turning state's evidence to the House Un-American Activities Committee. The willing self-portrait in *The Long Goodbye* testified to Hayden's real-life prowess as a novelist in *Voyage*. On screen, he was a newspaper editor called Pulitzer in *Cry Onion* (75, Enzo Castellari) and a peasant patriarch in *1900* (76, Bernardo Bertolucci). He refused to shave, but still played *King of the Gypsies* (78, Frank Pierson), and he was at ease in the madness of *Winter Kills* (79, William Richert). He went to Ireland for *The Outsider* (79, Tony Luraschi), and also appeared in *9 to 5* (80, Colin Higgins); *Gas* (81, Les Rose); and *Venom* (82, Piers Haggard).

Helen Hayes (Helen Brown) (1900–93), b. Washington, D.C.

When *Miss* Helen Hayes departed, at the age of ninety-two, obituaries observed how far she had been inspired by a moment in her greatest hit, the stage play *Victoria Regina*, when a citizen cries out to the queen on her ninetieth birthday, "Go it, old girl! You've done well!" Long before the end, the actress was as beloved as the queen, and esteemed as one of the great actresses, or one of the first ladies, of the American theatre.

There was no doubt about her Broadway reputation in the twenties and thirties, earned in *Dear Brutus, What Every Woman Knows, Coquette,* Maxwell Anderson's *Mary of Scotland,* and *Victoria Regina* (which she played for three years). Subsequently, she had successes as a rather older actress in *Harriet, Mrs. McThing, The Skin of Our Teeth,* and *Happy Birthday*. Her reputation was also boosted by her long, devoted marriage to the playwright Charles McArthur.

She had done a couple of short silent films, but her movie career began seriously with her Oscar for the grand weepie *The Sin of Madelon Claudet* (31, Edgar Selwyn). Yet she never found popularity in movies as a young woman. The business doubted her because she was reckoned unattractive. Did audiences find her too solemn, or was it simple bad luck that got her in a series of failures: *Arrowsmith* (31, John Ford); as Catherine Barkley with Gary Cooper in *A Farewell to Arms* (32, Frank Borzage); very poor in *The Son-Daughter* (32, Clarence Brown); with Gable in *The White Sister* (33, Victor Fleming); with Robert Montgomery in *Another Language* (33, Edward H. Griffith); *Night Flight* (33, Brown), a famous disaster; *What Every Woman Knows* (34, Gregory La Cava); and *Vanessa, Her Love Story* (35, William K. Howard), which closed her "young" career.

By the time she returned to pictures, she was a

mother or a little old lady—and now, at last, public affection came her way: *My Son John* (52, Leo McCarey); as the Grand Duchess in *Anastasia* (56, Anatole Litvak); winning the supporting actress Oscar in *Airport* (70, George Seaton); on TV with Mildred Natwick in the series *The Snoop Sisters* (73–74); *Herbie Rides Again* (74, Robert Stevenson); *One of Our Dinosaurs Is Missing* (76, Stevenson); *Victory at Entebbe* (76, Marvin J. Chomsky); *Candleshoe* (77, Norman Tokar); *A Family Upside Down* (78, David Lowell Rich); *Murder Is Easy* (82, Claude Whatham); as Miss Marple in *A Caribbean Mystery* (83, Robert Lewis) and *Murder with Mirrors* (85, Dick Lowry).

Todd Haynes, b. Los Angeles, 1961
1985: *Assassins: A Film Concerning Rimbaud* (s). 1987: *Superstar: The Karen Carpenter Story* (s). 1991: *Poison*. 1995: *Safe*. 1998: *Velvet Goldmine*. 2002: *Far from Heaven*.

For me, *Velvet Goldmine* was a serious disappointment after *Poison* and *Safe*—the latter one of the most arresting, original, and accomplished films of the nineties, in which abstraction and a very strange human situation were perfectly embodied in Julianne Moore's immense but tenuous presence.

At that point, the semiotics student from Brown had a fair claim as the most talented independent filmmaker in America—for consider the documentary-with-dolly reflection on Karen Carpenter; the tripartite study of warping in *Poison;* and the strange sci-fi hypothesis in *Safe*. *Velvet Goldmine*, on the other hand, was a clumsy gesture towards the mainstream—a mixture of glam-rock iconography with *Citizen Kane*, so much less than one had hoped for. Still, only a real mind could have produced *Velvet Goldmine*, and there are few careers that deserve more anticipation.

Far From Heaven was a breakthrough for Haynes, and a gorgeous recreation of Douglas Sirk. Beyond the detailed ditto of 1957, one had to ask, why? Might the film have been more urgent still set in 2002? So Haynes seemed more talented, yet more hidden, too.

Susan Hayward (Edythe Marrener)
(1918–75), b. Brooklyn, New York
Susan Hayward was a trouper who never saw any reason to do anything other than sock it to us. If, as I feel, she is largely devoid of appeal, it is a credit to her determination and uncompromising directness that she lasted so long. Indeed, her jaw had that firmness of a girl who came nearer than many to playing Scarlett O'Hara and who resolved to show everyone that she could have had the part.

After modeling, she made her debut in *Girls on Probation* (38) and for several years cultivated bright sweetness—as in Alfred Santell's *Our*

Leading Citizen (39); Wellman's *Beau Geste* (39); Ratoff's *Adam Had Four Sons* (41); Stuart Heisler's *Among the Living* (41); and De Mille's *Reap the Wild Wind* (42). She worked throughout the 1940s without really distinguishing herself: *The Forest Rangers* (42, George Marshall); *Young and Willing* (42, Edward H. Griffith); *I Married a Witch* (42, René Clair); *Jack London* (43, Santell); *And Now Tomorrow* (44, Irving Pichel); *The Hairy Ape* (44, Santell); *Canyon Passage* (46, Jacques Tourneur); *Deadline at Dawn* (46, Harold Clurman); a very good drunk and a disaster in *Smash-Up* (47, Heisler); uncommonly severe in *The Lost Moment* (47, Martin Gabel); *They Won't Believe Me* (47, Pichel); *The Saxon Charm* (48, Claude Binyon); *Tulsa* (49, Heisler); *My Foolish Heart* (49, Mark Robson); and *House of Strangers* (49, Joseph L. Mankiewicz).

But in the 1950s, she came gradually into her own kingdom. After a spell at Fox in costume and as an adventurer's woman—*I Can Get It For You Wholesale* (51, Michael Gordon); *Rawhide* (51, Henry Hathaway); *David and Bathsheba* (51, Henry King); *The Snows of Kilimanjaro* (52, King); *White Witch Doctor* (53, Hathaway); *Demetrius and the Gladiators* (54, Delmer Daves); *Garden of Evil* (54, Hathaway); *Untamed* (55, King); *The Conqueror* (55, Dick Powell)—she settled for being a woman's woman. Ironically, the first and best film in this new vein was Nicholas Ray's *The Lusty Men* (52), in which she is the brusque wife attempting to dissuade her husband from the rodeo life. Gradually, she gathered suffering to herself, first as Jane Froman in Walter Lang's *With a Song in My Heart* (52), and then nominated as the alcoholic Lillian Roth in *I'll Cry Tomorrow* (55, Daniel Mann). Suffering was again triumphant and Oscar-winning in Robert Wise's *I Want to Live!* (58), in which she played a woman on death row.

In the 1960s, sheer survival brought her major parts in women's pictures, the tears of which she stirred as vigorously as a strong-armed cook: *Ada* (61, Mann); *Back Street* (61, David Miller); *Stolen Hours* (63, Daniel Petrie); *I Thank a Fool* (63, Robert Stevens); Bette Davis's daughter in *Where Love Has Gone* (64, Edward Dmytryk). She was not very happy in Mankiewicz's *The Honey Pot* (67), but undiminished in Robson's *Valley of the Dolls* (67) and in *The Revengers* (71, Mann).

Rita Hayworth (Margarita Carmen Cansino)
(1918–87), b. Brooklyn, New York
The cousin of Ginger Rogers, her father a Spanish dancer, and her mother a Ziegfeld girl, no wonder Margarita joined her father's act and danced at Los Angeles clubs while still in her teens. Fox noticed her and put her in *Under the Pampas Moon* (35, James Tinling), *Dante's Inferno* (35, Harry Lachman), and *Human Cargo* (36, Allan

Dwan). Her contract at Fox was largely due to Winfield Sheehan, who planned to star her in *Ramona*, but when Fox became Twentieth Century–Fox, Sheehan was fired and Cansino replaced by Loretta Young. She was reduced to B pictures, one of which, *Meet Nero Wolfe* (36, Herbert Biberman), was her first job at Columbia. In 1937 she married Edward Judson; he engineered a contract for her at Columbia, who changed her name to Rita Hayworth and put her in *Girls Can Play* (37, Lambert Hillyer) and *Paid to Dance* (37, Charles Coleman). Judson also ordered the electrolysis that radically altered her hairline. Around 1938–39, her looks became classier. She had better parts in *There's Always a Woman* (38, Alexander Hall) and Peter Godfrey's *The Lone Wolf Spy Hunt* (39), but it was as Richard Barthelmess's wife in Howard Hawks's *Only Angels Have Wings* (39) that her glamour acquired luster and assurance.

The sudden revelation of a balanced but vulnerable woman in Hawks's banana republic was the origin of the Hayworth cult. Columbia now began to exploit her by loaning her out—to MGM for George Cukor's *Susan and God* (40); to Warners for Raoul Walsh's *Strawberry Blonde* (41) and Lloyd Bacon's *Affectionately Yours* (41); and to Fox for Rouben Mamoulian's *Blood and Sand* (41). Meanwhile, at her contract studio she appeared in Ben Hecht's *Angels Over Broadway* (40), replacing Jean Arthur, and in Charles Vidor's *The Lady in Question* (40).

Success did wonders for her looks, and it was this blooming that made Hayworth a forces favorite. Columbia teamed her with Fred Astaire in Sidney Lanfield's *You'll Never Get Rich* (41) and loaned her to Fox for *My Gal Sal* (42, Irving Cummings). Although always dubbed for singing, she was a good dancer (sensual and romantic), and Columbia concentrated on her as a star of musicals, with Astaire again in William Seiter's *You Were Never Lovelier* (42), with Gene Kelly in Charles Vidor's *Cover Girl* (44), and in *Tonight and Every Night* (45, Victor Saville). But she was more than just a dancer, and in Charles Vidor's *Gilda* (46) she played a sexy woman of the world, quite riveting in the casual eroticism of "Put the Blame on Mame," languorously discarding elbow-length black satin gloves. It is worth emphasizing how much of her best work was done for the less-than-profound Vidor.

In 1943 she had married Orson Welles and, as their marriage broke up, he exposed her in *The Lady from Shanghai* (48) as an insanely beautiful, mercilessly predatory woman. There was surely something of the rage of Welles's Kane-like disappointment in the notorious beauty he had taken for a wife. Intensely misogynist, that film somehow added to the Hayworth mystique. But her career was on the point of decline. After the failure of *Down to Earth* (47, Hall), in which she had to play the goddess Terpsichore, she was far from credible in Vidor's *The Loves of Carmen* (48). It was as if, when asked to play the scarlet woman, she appeared abashed; whereas in conventional material she felt able to introduce her own sexual frankness.

Reputation now conspired to ruin her. No matter how ardently Columbia had described her voluptuousness, it could not tolerate her elopement with Aly Khan in 1949. Scandal sheets hounded her and, when her third marriage had failed, she returned, visibly faded, to a fourth marriage, a disaster, with singer Dick Haymes, and to conventional movies about fallen women: *Affair in Trinidad* (52, Vincent Sherman), Dieterle's *Salome* (53), and Curtis Bernhardt's *Miss Sadie Thompson* (54). Fame, looks, and confidence deserted her all at once, but her unresolved character meant that even bad films might offer moments of interest: thus she is good in Parrish's *Fire Down Below* (57) and in George Sidney's *Pal Joey* (57). But *Separate Tables* (58, Delbert Mann), Rossen's *They Came to Cordura* (59), and Clifford Odets's *The Story on Page One* (59) all too clearly presented a middle-aged woman. Her later films dwindled toward obscurity: *The Happy Thieves* (61, George Marshall); *Circus World* (64, Henry Hathaway); *The Money Trap* (65, Burt Kennedy); *The Rover* (67, Terence Young); *Sons of Satan* (69, Duccio Tessari); and *The Wrath of God* (72, Ralph Nelson).

It is one of Hollywood's sadder stories, the more so because of the feeling that her talent was seldom used properly. She was, briefly, the emblem of vaguely decadent beauty—thus she is on the poster on which the father is working in *Bicycle Thieves* when his bike is stolen. Perhaps that is why so many retain memories of her—like the sheikh in John Huston's *Beat the Devil*. Fond feelings were shocked toward the end of 1976 when it became known that alcoholic breakdown had so disabled her that her business affairs had been taken in hand by the Orange County Public Guardian's Office. She had Alzheimer's disease, and for the last few years of her life she depended on the care of her daughter, Princess Yasmin, her child by Aly Khan.

Edith Head (1907–81), b. Los Angeles

Edith Head won eight Oscars for costuming, and she was nominated thirty-five times between 1948 and 1977—thus John Huston's wisecrack that the Academy Award was written into her contract. In fact, that load of nominations is not the record: that is forty-three (he won nine times) for Alfred Newman, whose brother, Lionel, was head of music at Twentieth Century–Fox. I don't mean to belittle Newman (no matter that his wins included many musicals, where the music belonged to other composers; *Love Is a Many Splendored Thing*, which somehow beat *Picnic;* and *Song of Bernadette*, where even God might have flinched). Newman put his name on most Fox films, while Edith Head genuinely approved the costumes on those films she hadn't worked on directly. You can make the case that she was the most influential woman in Hollywood—as witness the way, from 1945 onwards, she was a regular on Art Linkletter's radio show, giving advice on what to wear.

Her childhood was spent roaming around Western mining camps, but she picked up enough education to get into Stanford, where she got a degree in French. She was teaching French and art at Hollywood High School when she grew bored, walked into Paramount, and said she knew clothes. She got a job, and by the end of the thirties she was in charge of the department. That lasted until 1967, when she moved over to Universal. Far from glamorous herself, she kept a very tidy, severe style, with dark bangs and tinted spectacles.

Her Oscars were awarded for *The Heiress* (49, William Wyler); *All About Eve* (50, Joseph L. Mankiewicz)—she created Bette Davis's famous off-the-shoulder gown; *Samson and Delilah* (50, Cecil B. De Mille)—there were separate awards for color and black-and-white in those days; *A Place in the Sun* (51, George Stevens); *Roman Holiday* (53, Wyler); *Sabrina* (54, Billy Wilder); *The Facts of Life* (60, Melvin Frank); *The Sting* (73, George Roy Hill).

But just as we may recall clothes from those films, and see how much Head had to do with the image of Audrey Hepburn, still it's worth noting credits that did not get an Oscar: *She Done Him Wrong* (33, Lowell Sherman)—Head helped develop that feeling of Mae West being wrapped within an inch of her life in silk; *The Lady Eve* (41, Preston Sturges)—just think of Stanwyck's look in that picture; *Lady in the Dark* (44, Mitchell Leisen—a clothes expert, enjoying her work); *Double Indemnity* (44, Wilder)—did Head think of that anklet and the burning sexiness of Stanwyck's pale, tight sweater?; *Notorious* (46, Alfred Hitchcock); *Sunset Boulevard* (50, Wilder)—recall the clothes bought for Joe Gillis; *Shane* (53, Stevens)—Alan Ladd's buckskin suit, Jack Palance's black boots; *Rear Window* (54, Hitchcock)—which means Grace Kelly in coming attractions; as well as *Funny Face, Vertigo,* and *Breakfast at Tiffany's.* All of which, if I may remind you, did not win.

Edith Head was a marvel and a kind of genius. For example, on *Window,* when Grace Kelly is in the night dress, Hitchcock felt she needed a little more bosom. So Edith Head was called in. Head and Kelly retired to a dressing room. Kelly said she would not wear falsies. So Head took in a tuck

here and there and told Grace to stand tall. Hitch was delighted—and so were the rest of us, ever after.

Anne Heche, b. Aurora, Ohio, 1969

Yes, that Anne Heche: the most eventful private life in show business at the turn of the century. But no one else delivers what Anne Heche brings to the screen. She's tart, slender, pale, altogether lemony—and this in a culture where actresses are encouraged to be peaches, strawberries, or jelly doughnuts. Remember her acid, nearly forsaken wife in *Donnie Brasco* (97, Mike Newell), her wintry, murmured asides in *Wag the Dog* (97, Barry Levinson), and even her tremendous efforts to mask the daft fabrication of *Return to Paradise* (98, Joseph Ruben) and make its love story human.

Of course, this is a career that could easily succumb to the volatility of her life. With so much melodrama here, there, and along the highways of California, there needs to be no doubt about her acting. But it was only the stalwart loyalty of Harrison Ford that kept her in *Six Days, Seven Nights* (98, Ivan Reitman), after her romance with Ellen DeGeneres had gone public. And she and Ford did have chemistry. On the other hand, she has had far too much public disorder.

She began in theatre as a child, and she played twins in the TV soap opera *Another World*, so she knows strangeness. Her earlier movies are: *The Adventures of Huck Finn* (93, Stephen Sommers); *Against the Wall* (94, John Frankenheimer), for TV; *Milk Money* (94, Richard Benjamin); *Girls in Prison* (94, John McNaughton); *I'll Do Anything* (94, James L. Brooks); *The Investigator* (95, Matthew Tabak); *Kingfish: A Story of Huey P. Long* (95, Thomas Schlamme); *Wild Side* (95, Donald Cammell); *Pie in the Sky* (96, Bryan Gordon); very good with Catherine Keener in *Walking and Talking* (96, Nicole Holofcener); *The Juror* (96, Brian Gibson); *Volcano* (97, Mick Jackson); *I Know What You Did Last Summer* (97, Jim Gillespie).

The work ranged from the enterprising to the trashy, but who knows why she thought to be Janet Leigh in *Psycho* (98, Gus Van Sant)? She was far better in *The Third Miracle* (99, Agnieszka Holland), and she directed DeGeneres and Sharon Stone in *If These Walls Could Talk II* (00). Since then, with other calls (such as marriage and childbirth), she has done *One Kill* (00, Christopher Menaul); *Beyond Suspicion* (00, Tabak); *Prozac Nation* (02, Erik Skjoldbjaerg); *John Q* (02, Nick Cassavetes).

Ben Hecht (1893–1964), b. New York
1934: *Crime Without Passion.* 1935: *The Scoundrel; Once in a Blue Moon.* 1936: *Soak the Rich* (all codirected with Charles MacArthur). 1940:

Until I Die; Angels Over Broadway (codirected with Lee Garmes). 1946: *Specter of the Rose.* 1952: *Actors and Sin* (codirected with Garmes).

In the suspicious relations between the American intelligentsia and its national cinema, Ben Hecht plays a fascinating but ambivalent part. He had a quick-witted, plot-making skill that was as welcome and highly paid in Hollywood as its practitioners were despised or ignored. Hecht responded savagely: scorning the films on which he worked; deploring the effect of movies on theater, American cultural standards, and his own creative career; scathing but living off its follies de dollars; using Oscars as doorstops; and, most sadly, failing in an attempt to beat it at its own game.

It is easy to claim that *Citizen Kane* taught Americans that their own cinema could be dignified. But Pauline Kael's book on that film shows how far the bitter spirit of the New York wordsmith still curdles. Thus Kael quotes the telegram that Herman Mankiewicz sent to Hecht in 1926, still with a sense of needing to be superior to the film world's extravagance: "Will you accept 300 per week to work for Paramount Pictures? All expenses paid. 300 is peanuts. Millions are to be grabbed out here and your only competition is idiots. Don't let this get around." Mankiewicz, Hecht, and Kael never forgave the financial draw of those idiots, and never saw that there were great talents working in Hollywood unabashed by lurid salaries. All credit to Mankiewicz for the malicious original of *Kane*, but it is a finished work by Welles. And if Hecht deserves to be regarded as the most variedly successful of screenwriters, his best work is still subordinate to the cinematic achievement of Hawks, Hitchcock, and Preminger.

Hecht's first job was to write the story that Sternberg made into *Underworld* (27). He pocketed the $10,000 for a week's work and accepted the Oscar for the story, but reviled the system that could reward such hurried work so lavishly. His mistake was to lump Sternberg in with inflated salaries and pretentious awards. What hurt most was the realization that the writer in movies had everything but power. His bitterness overcame him and stopped him from seeing the vastly greater visual contribution that lay in Sternberg's control.

Hecht was raised in Chicago, with a career in journalism and as a novelist, as well as friendship with the young David Selznick before he answered Mankiewicz's cable. His first success with *Underworld* and his facility for turning out clever plots and dialogue kept him in demand: *The Big Noise* (28, Allan Dwan); *The Unholy Night* (29, Lionel Barrymore); *The Great Gabbo* (29, James Cruze); and *Roadhouse Nights* (30, Hobart Henley). In

1928, in collaboration with Charles MacArthur (1895–1956), he had written the play, *The Front Page*, which, in 1931, Lewis Milestone filmed. Hecht carried on as story- or scriptwriter on *Scarface* (32, Hawks), which he wrote in eleven days; *Topaze* (33, Harry d'Arrast); *Hallelujah, I'm a Bum* (33, Milestone); *Design for Living* (33, Ernst Lubitsch), from the Noel Coward play; and *Viva Villa!* (34, Jack Conway and Hawks).

In 1934, Hecht and MacArthur adapted their play for Hawks's *Twentieth Century*, and established their own New York production company that made *Crime Without Passion* and *The Scoundrel*, both photographed by Lee Garmes. The latter, starring Noel Coward, is a splendid black comedy, and Hecht's best direction. Otherwise, the films he made with MacArthur and Lee Garmes only illustrate the limits of a top writer and cameraman. *Twentieth Century* is a masterpiece of sexual antagonism made from a funny but limited play about a ham actor. Hecht was to direct four more pictures—two of them with Garmes—but the precision and confidence of his written material is absent from those films, whereas it flourishes in, say, *His Girl Friday*, *Notorious*, and *Whirlpool*.

He continued to supply scripts for the West Coast: the disappointing *Barbary Coast* (35, Hawks); *The Florentine Dagger* (35, Robert Florey), an adaptation of one of his own novels; the pungently funny *Nothing Sacred* (37, William Wellman), which pursued his favorite theme of hypocrisy in the media; *The Goldwyn Follies* (38, George Marshall); with MacArthur again on *Gunga Din* (39, George Stevens); with Herman Mankiewicz on *It's a Wonderful World* (39, W. S. Van Dyke); *Lady of the Tropics* (39, Conway); with MacArthur making Brontë bland for Goldwyn's *Wuthering Heights* (39, William Wyler); and *Comrade X* (40, King Vidor).

In the same year, Hawks made *His Girl Friday*, a variation on *Front Page*, scripted by Charles Lederer, turning it into a male-female confrontation. The viewers must judge for themselves, both the virtues of the Hecht/MacArthur original and the deepening (or not) of the Hawks movie.

From about this time, Hecht began to be involved on poorer and plainer pictures: *Lydia* (41, Julien Duvivier); *Tales of Manhattan* (42, Duvivier); *The Black Swan* (42, Henry King); and *China Girl* (42, Henry Hathaway). Then he scripted two Hitchcock films: *Spellbound* (45) and the magnificent *Notorious* (46), arguably his best screenplay. Next, *Ride the Pink Horse* (47, Robert Montgomery); *Kiss of Death* (47, Hathaway), more violent than any of Hecht's other films; *The Miracle of the Bells* (48, Irving Pichel); *Whirlpool* (49, Preminger); *Perfect Strangers* (50, Bretaigne Windust), from a play written with MacArthur; *Where the Sidewalk Ends* (50, Preminger); *Monkey Busi-*

ness (52, Hawks), which he wrote with Lederer and I. A. L. Diamond; as one of several dispirited writers on *Ulysses* (54, Mario Camerini); *The Indian Fighter* (55, André de Toth); *Miracle in the Rain* (56, Rudolph Maté); *The Iron Petticoat* (56, Ralph Thomas); *Legend of the Lost* (57, Hathaway); *A Farewell to Arms* (57, Charles Vidor)—the last of five movies for Selznick; Billy Rose's *Jumbo* (62, Charles Walters); and *Circus World* (64, Hathaway).

Tippi Hedren (Nathalie Hedren),
b. Lafayette, Minnesota, 1935
On the strength of her post-Hitchcock work—R. G. Springsteen's *Tiger by the Tail* (68), Chaplin's *A Countess from Hong Kong* (67), and *The Harrad Experiment* (73, Ted Post)—it would be easy to dismiss Tippi Hedren as just another pretty model who made the unnecessary and unrewarding move into films. But her first two films tell a different story, for she was discovered by Alfred Hitchcock for *The Birds* (63) and *Marnie* (64). Hitchcock (who lusted after her) drew out all the brittle insecurity in her Melanie Daniels in the first: that might simply be a performance nursed by a great director. But *Marnie* is an actress's triumph as well as a director's, and the way in which Tippi Hedren mutters "There . . . there now" when she shoots her horse is typical of the insight and pathos she brings to the sexually inhibited thief.

She appeared in the strange wild life/family picture *Roar* (81), directed by her husband Noel Marshall, and featuring their daughter, Melanie Griffith. She was briefly in *Deadly Spygames* (89, Jack M. Sell); as Melanie Griffith's mother in *Pacific Heights* (90, John Schlesinger); and in the old Patricia Collinge role in a TV remake of *Shadow of a Doubt* (91, Karen Arthur).

She worked more in the nineties, yet rarely in decent pictures: *Through the Eyes of a Killer* (92, Peter Markle); *The Birds II: Land's End* (94, Rick Rosenthal); *Treacherous Beauties* (94, Charles Jarrott); *Teresa's Tattoo* (94, Julie Cypher); *Inevitable Grace* (94, Alex Canawati); *Sense, Sixth* (95, Gregg Cannizzaro); *Citizen Ruth* (96, Alexander Payne); *Mulligans!* (97, Miles Hood Swarthout); *I Woke Up Early the Day I Died* (98, Aris Iliopulos); *Replacing Dad* (98, Joyce Chopra); *The Darklings* (99, Jeffrey Reiner); *The Storytellers* (99, James D. R. Hickox); the documentary *Life with Big Cats* (00, Deborah Rivel); *Ice Cream Sundae* (01, Desiree Nosbusch).

Van Heflin (Emmett Evan Heflin Jr.)
(1910–71), b. Walters, Oklahoma
Heflin never looked as smooth as a star, and he was not the sort of personality to contain the fantasizing pressure of mass audiences. Unlike many American movie stars, he looked recognizably American. This served him well in his best performances, interesting, unsentimental portraits of middle America: as the cop in *The Prowler* (51, Joseph Losey), an inventive study of a shallow, athletic materialist, a dissatisfied policeman who spends his time reading muscle magazines and who may be the very prowler that Evelyn Keyes first complains of. The density of Losey's film and its view of American opportunism owes a lot to Heflin's grasp of the character.

He was again good as the farmer in *Shane* (53, George Stevens), a blunt, honorable, not very perceptive man, as ignorant of violence as Alan Ladd is familiar with it—once more, the sense of family and of pioneering farming enterprise springs from Heflin's rugged plainness; and as the coward in *3:10 to Yuma* (57, Delmer Daves), the nerve-shattered reverse of the farmer, harrowed by the task of taking a relaxed Glenn Ford to jail.

There were other good character studies, but what began as a very promising career petered out in the 1960s, perhaps because Heflin was a little too authentic. He was a young stage actor recommended to the movies by Katharine Hepburn: *A Woman Rebels* (36, Mark Sandrich); *The Outcasts of Poker Flat* (37, Christy Cabanne); *Santa Fe Trail* (40, Michael Curtiz); *The Feminine Touch* (41, W. S. Van Dyke); *H. M. Pulham Esq.* (41, King Vidor); drunk, and the only good thing in *Johnny Eager* (41, Mervyn Le Roy), for which he won the supporting actor Oscar; *Kid Glove Killer* (42, Fred Zinnemann); *Seven Sweethearts* (42, Frank Borzage); *Tennessee Johnson* (42, William Dieterle); *Presenting Lily Mars* (42, Norman Taurog); *The Strange Love of Martha Ivers* (46, Lewis Milestone); *Green Dolphin Street* (47, Victor Saville); *Possessed* (47, Curtis Bernhardt); very good as the haunted coward in *Act of Violence* (48, Zinnemann); *Tap Roots* (48, George Marshall); *The Three Musketeers* (48, George Sidney); as the husband in *Madame Bovary* (49, Vincente Minnelli); *Weekend with Father* (51, Douglas Sirk); *My Son John* (51, Leo McCarey); *Wings of the Hawk* (53, Budd Boetticher); *Woman's World* (54, Jean Negulesco); *Black Widow* (54, Nunnally Johnson); *Tanganyika* (54, André de Toth); *The Raid* (54, Hugo Fregonese); *Count Three and Pray* (55, George Sherman); *Battle Cry* (55, Raoul Walsh); *Patterns* (56, Fielder Cook); *Gunman's Walk* (58, Phil Karlson); *Tempest* (57, Alberto Lattuada); *They Came to Cordura* (59, Robert Rossen); *Five Branded Women* (60, Martin Ritt); *To Be a Man* (63, Irving Lerner); *Once a Thief* (65, Ralph Nelson); *Stagecoach* (66, Gordon Douglas); *The Big Bounce* (68, Alex March); and *Airport* (70, George Seaton).

Stuart Heisler (1894–1979), b. Los Angeles
1936: *Straight from the Shoulder; Poppy.* 1937: *The Hurricane* (codirected with and credited to

John Ford). 1940: *The Biscuit Eater; God Gave Him a Dog.* 1941: *The Monster and the Girl; Among the Living.* 1942: *The Remarkable Andrew; The Glass Key.* 1944: *The Negro Soldier* (d). 1945: *Along Came Jones.* 1946: *Blue Skies; Vendetta* (codirected with Mel Ferrer, Howard Hughes, Max Ophuls, and Preston Sturges). 1947: *Smash-Up.* 1949: *Tulsa; Tokyo Joe.* 1950: *Chain Lightning; Dallas.* 1951: *Storm Warning; Journey into Light.* 1952: *Saturday Island/Island of Desire.* 1953: *The Star.* 1954: *Beach-Head; This Is My Love.* 1955: *I Died a Thousand Times.* 1956: *The Lone Ranger; The Burning Hills.* 1961: *Hitler.*

Heisler waited a long time before being allowed to direct. He had joined Famous Players in 1913, and later worked for Sennett, Fox, Mary Pickford, First National, and Goldwyn before becoming an editor in the 1930s: *Condemned* (29, Wesley Ruggles); *The Kid from Spain* (32, Leo McCarey); *Roman Scandals* (33, Frank Tuttle); *The Dark Angel* (35, Sidney Franklin); *Wedding Night* (35, King Vidor); *Peter Ibbetson* (35, Henry Hathaway); and *Klondike Annie* (36, Raoul Walsh). In 1937, he was second unit director on John Ford's *The Hurricane,* and by 1940 he was directing at Paramount.

For a man nearly fifty before he got into his stride, Heisler kept a youthful enthusiasm for visual excitement. Although willing to take on any project, he was at his best with thrillers and action films. *The Biscuit Eater* benefits from Georgia locations and fine acting from two kids, one black, one white. He made the best Ladd-Lake movie, *The Glass Key;* directed three enjoyable Susan Hayward pictures: *Among the Living, Smash-Up,* and *Tulsa;* directed Gary Cooper in the actor's own production of *Along Came Jones* and in a good Western, *Dallas;* somehow made Ginger Rogers and Doris Day interesting in *Storm Warning;* celebrated the delightful Linda Darnell in *Saturday Island* and *This Is My Love;* made one vivid war picture, *Beach-Head;* and an excellent thriller, *I Died a Thousand Times* (a remake of *High Sierra*), with Jack Palance and Shelley Winters. It should be said that there was rubbish amid the pleasures: *Blue Skies* is dull; *Tokyo Joe* is a waste of Bogart; and *Hitler* was dreadful.

Mark Hellinger (1903–47), b. New York
His short career as a producer earned Hellinger much respect from his writers and directors, especially Richard Brooks, whose novel, *The Producer,* is based on Hellinger. It is easy to see in his films a wish to bring authenticity to the crime picture. But his earlier films—more conventional studio works—are much more satisfactory than the attempt to make neo-realist police stories. In other words, Hellinger lived at a time when substantial cinema novelty in America was still dependent on genre. In the streets of New York, Hellinger only dissipated the studio-furnished darkness of the film noir. Where he is interesting is in treating criminals as real, vulnerable people, and not as monolithic archetypes or subverted heroes. Bogart in *High Sierra* (41, Raoul Walsh) is a turning point for the actor and the genre. While *The Killers* (46, Robert Siodmak) is a fascinating fusion of Germanic atmosphere, Hemingway's understatement, and the genre's emphasis on ritual double cross. Especially in its detailed account of a criminal operation, it inaugurated a trend.

Hellinger was a New York journalist of high reputation as wisecracker, drinker, buddy, and Runyon-like man-about-town. He wrote for the theater and had his play *Night Court* (32, W. S. Van Dyke) purchased by MGM. He went on to work as a writer on *Broadway Bill* (34, Frank Capra) and, with Jerry Wald, *The Roaring Twenties* (39, Walsh). In 1940 he joined Hal Wallis at Warners as an associate producer and was engaged on *Torrid Zone* (40, William Keighley); *Brother Orchid* (40, Lloyd Bacon); *It All Came True* (40, William A. Seiter); *They Drive by Night* (40, Walsh); *The Strawberry Blonde* (41, Walsh); *Manpower* (41, Walsh); and *High Sierra.* He went to Fox to produce *Rise and Shine* (41, Allan Dwan), and then returned to Warners for *Moontide* (42, Archie Mayo) and *Thank Your Lucky Stars* (43, David Butler).

He was a war correspondent in the Pacific from 1943–45, but, in his last two years, worked at Warners and Universal: *The Horn Blows at Midnight* (45, Walsh); *The Killers; Swell Guy* (46, Frank Tuttle); the prison exposé *Brute Force* (47, Jules Dassin); *The Two Mrs. Carrolls* (47, Peter Godfrey); and the film that was to launch so many TV series, *The Naked City* (48, Dassin), which Hellinger narrates with the loving wryness of cozy journalese.

When he died, of a massive heart attack, he was on the point of joining Selznick, with plans to film a lot of Hemingway.

Lillian Hellman (1905–84), b. New Orleans
In 1947, at the height of what she called "scoundrel time" (never trust good title people), Lillian Hellman wrote an editorial for the Screen Writers Guild magazine. She called it "The Judas Goats," and it's a stirring attack on the HUAC effort to find red streaks in the Hollywood picture. It includes this penetrating and undeniable truth: "There has never been a single line or word of Communism in any American picture at any time." To which I would only add, "And anyone searching for the participation in Hollywood of absolutely dedicated writers, armored in talent and integrity—and whatever else—is doomed to find disappointment."

But if you're talking about writers with a taste for expensive fur coats, the best hotel rooms, dining with celebrities and sometimes taking them home, to say nothing of astonishing, discreet per diem arrangements, Hollywood is still the place. And still full of appeal to many of those writers essentially pledged to the word and its forms but in great need of a check—before the banks open tomorrow.

This is how it went with Lillian Hellman. She was more than just a good title person. She could see dramatic arcs and she could write dialogue. She was also a tough (if not bullying) woman with radical attitudes and hot pants. And just as the hot pants could pick on any new guy any day, so the radical attitudes were similarly flexible. And if sometimes there was a surprising shift from one point of view to another, why, ferocity and a foul-mouthed, "kidding" intimidation was usually enough to blur the gap. You may feel I am mocking such a personality. Not so. It is one of the few halfway decent ways of getting through the whole mess. Further, I always have time for liars if they have hot pants: that is an imperative that will not stand for dissimulation.

In 1934, her first play, *The Children's Hour,* opened on Broadway. One of her lovers, Herman Shumlin, produced it, and it ran 691 performances. Katherine Emery and Anne Revere played the teachers who are lovers. This was enough to get a screenwriting contract out of Samuel Goldwyn for $2,500 a week. Goldwyn was buying Broadway celebrity and more—for Hellman also had Dashiell Hammett as a lover, and the young legend that Nick and Nora Charles in Hammett's *The Thin Man* (also published in 1934) were based on Dash and Lilly (to use the title of the 1999 TV movie where Sam Shepard and Judy Davis played the two writers).

Hellman's initial movie assignment was a piece of silliness called *The Dark Angel* (35, Sidney Franklin). But the deal was founded, naturally enough, on doing a movie of *The Children's Hour.* When Goldwyn heard that it involved lesbians, he said, "Never mind, we'll make them Americans." Whether that is genius or idiocy is still a profound question. But Goldwyn had credentials as an idiot, and Miss Lillian did not. In other words, at the very outset, the firebrand writer settled in her own mind to take the money while "they" bowdlerized her material. It became, said Ms. Hellman, a story about the dangers of slander. As *These Three* (36, William Wyler), with Miriam Hopkins and Merle Oberon and a screenplay credited to Hellman, it also became a muffled, wishy-washy picture that confirmed for any serious theatre person that Hollywood was for the birds.

Hellman persevered. She got into a long-term Goldwyn arrangement, and she was a picture person, selling her plays and doing adaptations of other writers' work, and even originals: *Dead End* (37, Wyler), from the Sidney Kingsley play; *The Little Foxes* (41, Wyler), from her own play; *The North Star* (43, Lewis Milestone); *The Searching Wind* (46, William Dieterle)—plus, scripted by others, but from Hellman plays, *Watch on the Rhine* (43, Shumlin); *Another Part of the Forest* (48, King Vidor).

Put all of those together and *The Little Foxes* is the only one that would hold an audience today—and that owes a good deal to Gregg Toland's camerawork, to a fine supporting cast, and to the chemistry between Wyler and Bette Davis. *Watch on the Rhine* is so ponderous and talky that it should serve as a warning on what governmental worries over morale can do to the entertainment picture. *Dead End* is schematic, horribly stagy, and dated. *Another Part of the Forest* was always camp material and is best known as a prequel to *The Little Foxes.*

But *The North Star* is the most absurd, and the best illustration of Hellman's 1947 admission that not a word of communism ever got into an American film. It was a very far-fetched venture, meant to celebrate the spirit of the ordinary Russian under Nazi threat. Hellman labored with the research, worked herself up into a stew of identification, and wrote in blood. Lewis Milestone took over as Wyler escaped to the real war, and—he was Russian—he tried to temper the appalling mix of ignorance and high-mindedness in a film that ended up with Anne Baxter and Farley Granger as peasants. Hellman was in tears when she saw the picture—but she let the script be published.

All I'm trying to say is that this was an author and screenwriter who wanted to have her cake and eat it. But what is cake for? And how in hell do you eat it without having it?

Of course, Hellman survived, marinaded in ugliness, booze, spite, and the question of what could you believe. *These Three* came back as *The Children's Hour* (62, Wyler) and still couldn't quite admit what it was about. A year later, her play *Toys in the Attic* (63, George Roy Hill) was filmed, scripted by James Poe, and costarring Wendy Hiller and Dean Martin.

Hellman's adaptation of a Horton Foote play became *The Chase* (66, Arthur Penn). She reviled the film and said Sam Spiegel had ruined it. But it looks pretty good still to me. By then, however, Lillian Hellman was on her way to grand-old-ladyhood, which included being a witness in *Reds,* being seen on Warren Beatty's arm, uttering the last word on Hammett, writing *Scoundrel Time* and *Pentimento,* watching herself turn into Jane Fonda in *Julia* (77, Fred Zinnemann), and then having to hear that its story was a fraud. For myself, I prefer the more chaotic, unreliable but heated Judy Davis.

Monte Hellman, b. New York, 1932

1959: *The Beast from Haunted Cave.* 1964: *Back Door to Hell; Flight to Fury.* 1966: *The Shooting; Ride in the Whirlwind.* 1970: *Two-Lane Blacktop.* 1974: *Cockfighter.* 1978: *China 9, Liberty 37.* 1988: *Iguana.* 1989: *Silent Night, Deadly Night III—Better Watch Out.*

Hellman was an operator in fringe cinema who in one film—*The Shooting*—turned the uncompromising bones of a quickie Western into a movie about mythic identity and violent fate, without too much strain or pretentiousness. *The Shooting,* within moments, makes clear deeper meanings beneath its legitimate Western observation of figures in a landscape. But it is only gradually that one realizes how far the pessimism of the film is expressed in an elementary and withdrawn camera style. Both the sound and the visuals are rough—the film does not conceal its limited funds—but the imaginative conception is pure, philosophical, and esoteric. Although its tone is existentialist, its images of Millie Perkins, Warren Oates, and Jack Nicholson, increasingly worn down by the desert, seem more authentically Western than, say, *The Wild Bunch.*

It is characteristic of Hellman's fringe career that *The Shooting* and *Ride in the Whirlwind* were made simultaneously, in the Utah desert, with a minimal crew, two cameras, and screenplays by Adrien Joyce and Jack Nicholson. Hellman has chosen to say of them that, "We thought they would be a couple more Roger Corman movies that would play on the second half of a double bill somewhere. So any thoughts about doing something different were for our own personal satisfaction. We never thought that anybody would ever notice." In fact, their stark originality prevented either film from having a wide release in America, and contributed to making Hellman a cult figure.

Hellman studied drama at Stanford University and then moved to film at UCLA. Like so many young cinema talents, he fell in with Roger Corman, who produced his first film. Thereafter, Hellman directed a lot of *The Terror* (62, Corman) and did some editing. His next two films were quickies made in the Philippines; the two Utah Westerns were again made at Corman's behest, costing $150,000 for the pair. After that he had many lost projects—including *MacBird*—edited *The Wild Angels* (66, Corman), and worked as dialogue director on *The St. Valentine's Day Massacre* (67, Corman).

Two-Lane Blacktop was by far his largest assignment, an $850,000 project for Universal. It starred Warren Oates, Dennis Wilson, James Taylor, and Laurie Bird, and was filmed nomadically in a tight unit, made uneasy by Hellman's sparse communications with his actors on the script.

Blacktop is another transformation of contemporary America into existential parable. The surface story of a wager auto race across America is casually denied narrative tension to emphasize the resonance of character and situation. Again, Hellman seems to have gone out of his way to neutralize the potential of his subject. *Blacktop* could have been made as gripping as *Duel,* or as atmospheric as *American Graffiti.* Instead, it is elliptical, oblique, and equivocal, marred by its own lofty intransigence toward audiences. It would seem that Hellman needs to be embattled, turning big projects into arbitrary, near-underground movies. Such fierceness may keep him out of work; he has been abandoned by several commercial projects. But no system could digest the willful arbitrariness of his best films. *Cockfighter* was once more dark, cryptic, and mythic—as well as hard to track down—but its use of Warren Oates as a silent pursuer of fate has few equals.

He worked as an editor on Peckinpah's *Killer Elite* (75). *China 9, Liberty 37* was an uneasy mixture of commercial anxiety and mythic stereotypes perched uncomfortably between satire and conviction. It has become increasingly difficult for Hellman to keep working as a director: *Iguana* had little or no release, and it was as obscure as it was violent in its story of power on a remote island. But it was more interesting than *Silent Night,* a chore of no resort or hope.

Hellman has worked as a kind of doctoring editor—he served on Mark Robson's *Avalanche Express* (79) after Robson died. He was also an executive producer on *Reservoir Dogs* (92, Quentin Tarantino).

Sonja Henie (1912–69), b. Oslo, Norway

On ice, she was all twirling blades, chubby cheeks, and dimply smiles. (There was a look of Mae West's kid sister.) Off ice, she was a bulldozer—no doubt you have to be, to become world champion at fifteen and a gold medalist in three successive Olympics (1928, 1932, and 1936). Her determination carried her to a phenomenal triple career as competitive skater, ice-show entrepreneur, and movie star: she not only bullied Darryl Zanuck into the contract she wanted from Fox (plus renegotiations), but catapulted herself into the American Film Exhibitors' list of top box-office attractions for three successive years—she was the number-four female star in 1937, number two in 1938, and number four again in 1939. Then it all began to melt.

According to her autobiography, *Wings on My Feet,* everything was sweetness, spunk, and hard work. According to her brother, Lars, in a book that could well have been called *Sister, Dearest,* she was egomaniacal, greedy, sexually voracious, and far too friendly with Hitler & Co. (One of her gold medals, of course, was won at the 1936 games in Garmisch.) She married several times, but failed to snag Tyrone Power, with whom she starred in two films—*Thin Ice* (37, Sidney Lanfield) and *Second Fiddle* (39, Lanfield)—and with whom, according to Lars, a considerable amount of athletic activity took place in their dressing rooms. Most of her pictures were harmless (and brainless) excuses for the big skating numbers: *One in a Million* (36, Lanfield); *Happy Landing* (38, Roy del Ruth); *My Lucky Star* (39, del Ruth); *Everything Happens at Night* (39, Irving Cummings)—and already fading; *Sun Valley Serenade*, which was a hit, despite Henie, due to Glenn Miller, Lena Horne, and "The Chattanooga Choo Choo" (41, H. Bruce Humberstone); *Iceland* (42, Humberstone); *Wintertime* (43, John Brahm). In 1945 there was *It's a Pleasure* (William A. Seiter). Three years later, *The Countess of Monte Cristo* (Frederick de Cordova). Finally, in 1958, *Hello London/London Calling* (Sidney Smith). There's a Sonja Henie museum in Norway, where you can visit her medals and trophies, her jewels and her skates.

Paul Henreid (Paul George Julius von Henreid) (1908–92), b. Trieste, Austria
1952: *For Men Only*. 1956: *A Woman's Devotion*. 1958: *Live Fast, Die Young; Girls on the Loose*. 1964: *Dead Ringer/Dead Image*. 1966: *Blues for Lovers*.

Ten years after Henreid's birth, Trieste became Italian. He made his early career on the Austrian stage, but was destined for wider fame as an archetypal refugee, such as Victor Laszlo, the Resistance hero, who sets the mechanism of *Casablanca* (43, Michael Curtiz) into motion. It is a nice thought that the benign endeavors of everyone in that film except Conrad Veidt save him for noble work in America. Whereas, the real-life Henreid stayed on in Hollywood to direct several pieces of shamelessly crass hokum. What a marvelous cockpit of movie history *Casablanca* is: looking back to *La Règle du Jeu* and *M*; but as capable of anticipating *Dead Ringer* and that eerie moment in *The Four Horsemen of the Apocalypse* (61, Vincente Minnelli), when Henreid is once more a Resistance agent whose wife has a neutralist lover.

Along with the Laszlos of Europe, Henreid came west in the late 1930s, first to England and then to America. He lasted throughout the 1940s as an insubstantial romantic support, and it was only when that appeal faded that he took to direction: *Victoria the Great* (37, Herbert Wilcox); *Goodbye, Mr. Chips* (39, Sam Wood); *Night Train to Munich* (40, Carol Reed); *Joan of Paris* (42, Robert Stevenson); very good with Bette Davis in *Now, Voyager* (42, Irving Rapper); *Between Two Worlds* (44, Edward A. Blatt); *The Conspirators*

(44, Jean Negulesco); *In Our Time* (44, Vincent Sherman); *The Spanish Main* (45, Frank Borzage); *Hollywood Canteen* (45, Delmer Daves); *Deception* (46, Rapper); *Of Human Bondage* (46, Edmund Goulding); *Devotion* (46, Curtis Bernhardt); as Schumann in *Song of Love* (47, Clarence Brown); *Rope of Sand* (49, William Dieterle); *Thief of Damascus* (52, Will Jason); *Siren of Bagdad* (53, Richard Quine); *Deep in My Heart* (54, Stanley Donen); *Meet Me in Las Vegas* (56, Roy Rowland); *Ten Thousand Bedrooms* (57, Richard Thorpe); *Never So Few* (59, John Sturges); *Operation Crossbow* (64, Michael Anderson); *The Madwoman of Chaillot* (69, Bryan Forbes); a cardinal in *Exorcist II: The Heretic* (77, John Boorman).

Of his own films, *Dead Ringer* is a juicy shocker with Henreid as referee between twin Bette Davises.

Jim Henson (1936–90),
b. Greenville, Massachusetts
I'm writing this entry late in 2001, and it happens that in the paper today there's talk of next year's new Oscar—the one for the best animated film—as well as steady marveling over the success of *Harry Potter and the Sorcerer's Stone*. Of course, that blockbuster movie was always an AOL Time Warner project—it was bound to be a hit, and it had to have that safe magic that would please children of all ages all over the world. Whereas, as kids know, some kids get it and some don't. And what I wonder is what has happened to the odd kids, the weird ones, the prickly, difficult, bright, awkward, shining kids—the real ones?

Jim Henson's early death was all the harder to take in that he worked with the odd, the personal, the wild, and the homemade, and flourished in the last age before the computer. It's therefore very important that Henson was not just the entrepreneur and the visionary, but often the hand in the glove, the voice, and the tall man bent double, putting on the show.

When only a senior in high school, Henson began to work as a puppeteer for a Washington, D.C., television show, *Sam and His Friends*. Thus, throughout the sixties, Henson made and characterized a series of puppets that were to become international figures: the Cookie Monster, Bert and Ernie, Kermit the Frog (Henson's chief alter ego), and, eventually, Miss Piggy. It was in 1969, when American public television launched *Sesame Street*, that Henson moved from being a local entertainer to a national figure.

He was playing to preschool children for the most part, and he created a style—slow, tender, repetitive—that was easily parodied, but which actually fits in with all our knowledge about how children learn, and was even more accentuated with *Teletubbies*. Inevitably, Henson and his band of Muppets were drawn into movies—and extraordinary success, which led to toys and other forms of merchandising.

Henson had mixed feelings about the success, and its exploitation. It is not easy to predict the way in which he would have moved. He had sought an offer to be bought out, by Disney, for $150 million. But before the contracts were complete, Henson died, suddenly, from a respiratory illness. Since when, his company has passed into the Disney machine, just as his special character has nearly vanished.

It's not easy nowadays to ensure that work made for children stays personal. Any sign of success is taken over, promoted, and deprived of strangeness. The several Muppet movies were not always natural or comfortable solutions. Miss Piggy could not quite resist the urge to be the last of the Gabors. And the guest stars came from a disturbingly different species.

At the same time, Henson's vision had already been of huge value to a few uncommon films: *Dreamchild* (85 Gavin Millar), where Henson provided characters to go with Dennis Potter's script and the live actors; *Labyrinth* (86, Henson), where Terry Jones's script incorporates David Bowie's King of the Goblins and Henson's imaginary landscape; and *The Witches* (90, Nicolas Roeg), a rare combination of child's story and horror.

Of course, it was always asking too much to expect Jim Henson to withstand Walt Disney. But he has left a valuable tradition or direction, and we are in urgent need of young artists taking it up all over the world.

Audrey Hepburn (Edda van Heemstra Hepburn-Ruston) (1929–1993), b. Brussels

Of Irish-Dutch parents, Hepburn was brought up in Holland, worked in England from 1948–51, and then moved to Hollywood, where she was a fairy queen for some fifteen years. She seemed English; she had a sense of manners and kindness that came close to grace; and she achieved a "look"— the knockout gamin who inspired a generation of thin, flat-chested, upper-class girls. *Funny Face* (57, Stanley Donen) was the movie that embraced her different atmospheres—from blue stocking to a *Vogue* Ondine. It also gave her an older man as company. She was a perfect princess for veteran knights: Astaire, Cooper, Bogart, Holden, Fonda, Grant. She was never as happy with men her own age; she made them seem older and crude. There was always an untouched glory in her: it was close enough to the quality of Lillian Gish for their meeting in *The Unforgiven* to seem blessed, like a discovery of lost links.

In England, she had small or barely detectable roles in *Laughter in Paradise* (51, Mario Zampi); *The Lavender Hill Mob* (51, Charles Crichton);

and *Secret People* (52, Thorold Dickinson), before being cast as the incognito princess in *Roman Holiday* (53, William Wyler)—released in the year of Queen Elizabeth II's coronation. Her Oscar for that was generous, but it showed how far Hollywood had been swept off its democratic feet by her outrageous purity. She was rather better in *Sabrina* (54, Billy Wilder) and beautifully presented as Natasha by King Vidor in *War and Peace* (56). *Love in the Afternoon* (57, Wilder) was touching, and she had the face for the white surround of *The Nun's Story* (59, Fred Zinnemann). But Rima in *Green Mansions* (59) was beyond her, past sense, and too much for her husband and director, Mel Ferrer.

Hepburn was a creature of the fifties: she was sustained by the real-life royalty of Princesses Margaret and Grace (neither of whom matched the actress's perfection). Hepburn's most testing performance came in a failure, as the Indian girl in *The Unforgiven* (60, John Huston), where she was a kind of cousin to Natalie Wood in *The Searchers* (both films came from novels by Alan Le May). Though *Breakfast at Tiffany's* (61, Blake Edwards) was a hit, Hepburn largely ignored and smoothed away the ironies and awkwardness in Capote's woman. She was uneasy in *The Children's Hour* (62, Wyler), but social realism and teary melodrama were not her strengths. So she was quickly restored to romantic comedy in *Paris When It Sizzles* (63, Richard Quine) and *Charade* (63, Donen). The last vindication of her box-office appeal came when Jack Warner preferred her to Julie Andrews for the film of *My Fair Lady* (64, George Cukor). But he would not let her sing, and could not keep her from seeming like a clothes horse.

After that, she made *How to Steal a Million* (66, Wyler) and had a hit in *Two for the Road* (67, Donen), playing the wife of Albert Finney—a match of very different styles. She was very well cast as the blind girl in *Wait Until Dark* (67, Terence Young). Her marriage to Mel Ferrer ended a year later and she went into semiretirement: lovely still, and nostalgic, in *Robin and Marian* (76, Richard Lester) and in the awful *Bloodline* (79, Young).

In middle age, Hepburn gave far more time to charitable work than to movies, though she took modest roles in *They All Laughed* (81, Peter Bogdanovich); *Love Among Thieves* (87, Roger Young) on TV; and in *Always* (89, Steven Spielberg). The feeling of public loss at her death spoke to how fondly her look and her benevolence were remembered. Retrospectives had standing room only, and Audrey—in eyes, voice, and purity—rang as true as a small silver bell. The great women of the fifties had a character that is in short supply now.

Katharine Hepburn, (1907–2003),
b. Hartford, Connecticut

Survival alone might have enshrined Hepburn as one of the cinema's greatest actresses, or characters. Add to that twelve Academy Award nominations and four Oscars, three of them when she was past sixty. She is so remarkable, she may have given the misleading impression that Hollywood is interested in old people. There was also the sentimental appeal of her long friendship offscreen (and the affectionate bantering on it) with Spencer Tracy.

She is no longer quite here (her health has been bad for several years), but it's no wonder she is regarded with reverence. She has become an institution, claiming to be mystified that so many millions of strangers adore her. But she has avoided scandal and those eccentric flights of folly that beset so many elderly stars. When she came to do her autobiography, she took it for granted that we would know who *Me* was. The book was as brisk as a swim before breakfast, full of omissions and commissions, blissfully egocentric, and glowingly proud of her tomboy fondness for "strong" men like Tracy, George Stevens, John Ford, Howard Hughes, John Huston, and Louis B. Mayer (who never had a better champion). The book was bought by just about anyone who had two hours to read it. But maybe it changed Hepburn a little in our eyes. The vanity was breathtaking—from another age.

Hepburn was long regarded by Hollywood as an outsider, partly because she could not conceal her disdain or her healthy superiority. She did not work that much: after seventeen films in her first ten years, she made only twenty-one in the next thirty years. That sounds like discrimination, yet she made plenty of clinkers. It is likely that in the 1940s and 1950s she was hurt and perplexed that her best work so often confirmed her reputation as box-office poison. She smacked of class; her very voice rose above the mainstream, like a lace hem being lifted above mud. But there is something else: she had character, wit, intelligence, and moral being, and those things can seem cold and sexless on camera. She was most romantic when busy, doing things; not for her the passionate stillness of close-ups, rapt kissing, or worse. There are many women who like her just because she refused such "nonsense." But the neglect had to do with her coldness, too. She is a true loner, someone who concentrates on herself.

The young Hepburn was a creature of enormous imaginative potency and showy breeding. It was said that she was not beautiful. Nonsense: she was ravishing despite thoroughbred features, a skinny body, and a deliberately, if not aggressively, emphasized Bryn Mawr accent. Her beauty grew out of her own belief in herself and from the viewer's sense that she was living dangerously, exposing her own nerves and vulnerability along with her intelligence and sensibility. Like Jane Austen's Emma Woodhouse, she was a moral being, sometimes at odds with herself, deluded or mistaken, but able to correct herself out of a grave and resilient honesty. Nobody on the screen could be so funny and so moving in making a fool of herself, or so touching in reclaiming her dignity. That is why screwball comedy seemed in her hands one of Hollywood's most civilized forms and it is why *Bringing Up Baby* is so serious a film—without ever losing the status of being one of the funniest.

Hepburn began in the theatre, without special success. But she attracted attention in 1932 in an updating of *Lysistrata* and went to RKO to play John Barrymore's daughter in *A Bill of Divorcement* (32, George Cukor). Cukor had urged the studio to use her and he was to prove her most sympathetic director. She had fine notices, and followed it with the silly *Christopher Strong* (33, Dorothy Arzner); with *Morning Glory* (33, Lowell Sherman), and her first Oscar; and with Jo in *Little Women* (33, Cukor). Two poor films came next: *Spitfire* (34, John Cromwell) and *The Little Minister* (34, Richard Wallace). But she was brilliant in *Alice Adams* (35, George Stevens) and in *Sylvia Scarlett* (35, Cukor) masqueraded as a boy—the androgyny of Hepburn is still only a hint, and it got short shrift in *Me*. She drooped again with *Break of Hearts* (35, Philip Moeller); *Mary of Scotland* (36, John Ford); and *A Woman Rebels* (36, Mark Sandrich). Then came four classics in a row: *Quality Street* (37, Stevens); *Stage Door* (37, Gregory La Cava); *Bringing Up Baby* (38, Howard Hawks); and *Holiday* (38, Cukor). It is worth noting that in two of these four her costar was Cary Grant, an actor who stimulated her on screen rather more fruitfully than Tracy.

Bringing Up Baby was her last film at RKO, chiefly because the studio was at a loss as to how to make her popular. Hepburn herself urged that the play *Holiday* (by Philip Barry), which she had understudied onstage, be sold, complete with Cukor, to Columbia. When Selznick made up his mind not to use her as Scarlett O'Hara (because she couldn't convey the sex, he said), Hepburn commissioned a new play from Barry (using money from Howard Hughes), played in it on Broadway, and then wrapped it up for MGM with herself and Cukor. The studio wisely added Grant and James Stewart and made *The Philadelphia Story* (40). For all the success of that film, MGM were unwilling to sign her up, and only in 1942, after *Woman of the Year* (42, Stevens), did they put her under contract. No wonder, for her edge, beauty, and intimacy in that film are still breathtaking.

That was her first film with Tracy. From the start, it was clear that despite the surface snap between them, they had a mellowing effect on one another. Whatever went on between them offscreen, on-screen they had an unspoken agreement about being grown-up, above and beyond it. She aged, perhaps to match him, and became a shade motherly where once she had been as emotionally aflame as Rosalind. Most of the comedies with Tracy are marvelous, tender, and warm, but those with Grant had been more penetrating and dangerous. In addition, she made fewer films: *Keeper of the Flame* (43, Cukor), with Tracy again; *Stage Door Canteen* (43, Frank Borzage); *Dragon Seed* (44, Jack Conway and Harold S. Bucquet), a piece of Oriental nonsense; *Without Love* (45, Bucquet), another Barry comedy with Tracy; *Undercurrent* (46, Vincente Minnelli), an odd, psychological drama with Robert Taylor and Robert Mitchum, striking but not convincing; *Song of Love* (47, Clarence Brown) as Clara Schumann; and *The Sea of Grass* (47, Elia Kazan) with Tracy.

It was now that her films came at longer intervals. She made *State of the Union* (48, Frank Capra) and *Adam's Rib* (49, Cukor), with Tracy, the latter written for them by Garson Kanin. She tried Rosalind (too late) in New York and came back to play in *The African Queen* (52, John Huston), essentially a character part, easy for her and unrevealing, but a great hit. Indeed, her films edged closer to soft, comfortable answers. *Pat and Mike* (52, Cukor) was good, but *Summertime* (55, David Lean) was a women's picture of a cautious sentimentality that would not have fooled the girl of the 1930s. Crazily, she was with Bob Hope in the awful *The Iron Petticoat* (56, Ralph Thomas) and played a caricature spinster in *The Rainmaker* (56, Joseph Anthony). *Desk Set* (57, Walter Lang), with Tracy, was very poor and suggested that Hepburn was more interested in the several classical theatrical roles she took on during the 1950s. She played the devouring mother in *Suddenly, Last Summer* (59, Joseph L. Mankiewicz), and it was clear that she now acted where once she had existed. In 1962 she played the mother in *Long Day's Journey into Night* (62, Sidney Lumet), the best of her late performances, histrionic and tragic but not as moving as many of the earlier ones.

For five years she was in virtual retirement, but in 1967 she made *Guess Who's Coming to Dinner?* (Stanley Kramer), a drab movie, Tracy's last, for which she received an Oscar—as if a maudlin computer had gone wrong. Another Oscar next year for *The Lion in Winter* (Anthony Harvey), an implausible piece of medievalism. Since then, as well as playing *Coco* on stage she has been in two more prestigious but irrelevant films: *The Madwoman of Chaillot* (69, Bryan Forbes) and *The Trojan Women* (71, Michael Cacoyannis). Sadly, in 1972, she stepped out of George Cukor's *Travels with My Aunt,* and was replaced by Maggie

Smith. Graham Greene's aunt might have been made for her, from the family that produced those late 1930s heroines who dragged appalled men through disaster. In 1975 she appeared in the film of Edward Albee's *A Delicate Balance* (Tony Richardson), and with John Wayne in *Rooster Cogburn.*

It was a pleasure to see her on TV with Laurence Olivier in *Love Among the Ruins* (75, Cukor); far less than pleasure to watch her in Cukor's TV version of *The Corn Is Green;* and bewildering that she could be tempted by *Olly, Olly, Oxen Free* (78, Richard A. Colla).

She rallied for *On Golden Pond* (81, Mark Rydell), winning her twelfth nomination and her fourth Oscar—both records. In the years since, her enormously vigorous constitution and her even more robust attitude have been somewhat reduced by illness. But she has worked from time to time—in the bizarre *The Ultimate Solution of Grace Quigley* (85, Harvey); in *Mrs. Delafield Wants to Marry* (86, George Schaefer); and in *Laura Lansing Slept Here.* Her best work has not dated a fraction of an inch: from 1932 to 1945, she had it in her to be the most interesting, difficult, challenging woman in American pictures. Why? I'd guess it has to do with her confusion, for she loved movies while disapproving of them.

Bernard Herrmann (1911–75),
b. New York

The author pleads guilty to any charge that "subsidiary" arts have been poorly treated in this book. I have yielded here and there to pressures from the best organized lobby, that of screenwriters, even if I know how bitter so many writers feel, not just at their treatment in movies, but at the medium as a whole. Yes, scripts and writers are hugely important—and yet, beyond that, writers are feeble bystanders (and many of them know it). I willingly agree that some photographers are masters. Yet I stand by the notion that photography itself is more the miracle than what individuals do with it. And the best cameramen know how many millions can take good pictures. So, as it happens, I feel rather guiltier about having omitted designers and composers—above all, composers.

It is in the nature of movies to be melodramatic. They need just you and the night and the music, and there was music long before there were sound tracks. There is an extraordinary skill or trick in writing snatches of music that enhance the mood and life of a film. And there is art in making music a raft on which the whole movie may sail away. If I begin to examine my memory of movies, I am amazed at how far sound is the key. And great movie music always harmonizes with the voices and the sound effects: was the sound of arrows at Agincourt in *Henry V* Olivier and/or William Walton, and when did feathers in the air become music?

Nearly every great composer is left out of this book. There is no Erich Wolfgang Korngold, with transcendent flourishes as men ride through the forest in *The Adventures of Robin Hood* (38, Michael Curtiz and William Keighley). I cannot detail the joy in following Max Steiner, and hearing chords of alarm carried over from *King Kong* (33, Merian C. Cooper and Ernest B. Schoedsack) to *The Big Sleep* (46, Howard Hawks). I would need pages to recount the mock grandeur of Dimitri Tiomkin in *Duel in the Sun* (47, King Vidor) and the true grandeur in *Red River* (48, Hawks)— both exactly right for the films in question. How could *Rebecca, Sunset Boulevard,* or *Rear Window* be what they are without Franz Waxman, or have that same level of secret menace? For years I have listened to Michel Legrand's score for *The Umbrellas of Cherbourg* (63, Jacques Demy), and I know that Demy would not be as great a director without Legrand. I could and should add Maurice Jaubert (for Vigo) and Miklos Rozsa (for *Spellbound* and *Lust for Life*).

One should add all those composers whose music comes by the yard and the mile, illustrious names with a hundred credits each, and so plain that they prove how nearly *any* music works in the dark with any film. I will not mention that army of the night by name, except to say that (apart from Walt Disney) the person who has won the most Oscars in the history of the Academy is composer Alfred Newman (1901–70). He won for these films: *Alexander's Ragtime Band; Tin Pan Alley; The Song of Bernadette; Mother Wore Tights; With a Song in My Heart; Call Me Madam; Love Is a Many Splendored Thing; The King and I;* and *Camelot.*

You may notice, on reflection, that music was written for *Camelot* by Alan Jay Lerner and Frederick Loewe. Equally, *The King and I* occupied Richard Rodgers and Oscar Hammerstein for many moons. *Call Me Madam* was from a show by Irving Berlin, who had much to do with *Alexander's Ragtime Band,* too. You go back to Mr. Newman's list and you recollect, gratefully, that lovely, soupy song, "Love Is a Many Splendored Thing"—written by Sammy Fain and Paul Francis Webster (they got an Oscar for the song).

So music is a funny business. The great and indispensable Bernard Herrmann won just once—for *All That Money Can Buy* (41, William Dieterle). That was the beginning of Herrmann's movie career (the Dieterle film beat out *Citizen Kane*). At its close, Herrmann's score for *Taxi Driver* (76, Martin Scorsese) lost out to Jerry Goldsmith's for *The Omen.*

Why choose Herrmann above all others? I believe he was the best. He had an overall theatrical sense: he had worked with Orson Welles in

radio, and he supplied the lazy, "live" and louche sounds of Ramón Raquello from the Meridian Room in the Park Plaza in *The War of the Worlds.* But, more than that, Herrmann gave himself to the art of Welles, Hitchcock, Truffaut, and Scorsese. He knew how to make music that came not just from the action we are seeing or the characters, not just from the heart of a film or the incoherent dream of its director, but from the unique marriage of a particular film and the large medium. Herrmann knew how lovely the dark should be, and he was at his best in rites of dismay, dark dreams, introspection, and the gloomy romance of loneliness. No one else would have dared or known to make the score for *Taxi Driver* such a lament for impossible love. Try that film without the music and the violence is nearly unbearable. Yet the score for *Taxi Driver* is universally cinematic: it speaks to sitting in the dark, full of dread and desire, watching.

The list: *Citizen Kane* (41, Orson Welles), including the "opera"; *The Magnificent Ambersons* (42, Welles); *Jane Eyre* (44, Robert Stevenson); the lurid, hammering piano for *Hangover Square* (45, John Brahm); *Anna and the King of Siam* (46, John Cromwell); *The Ghost and Mrs. Muir* (47, Joseph L. Mankiewicz); *The Day the Earth Stood Still* (51, Robert Wise); brilliant alarums and brooding excursions for *On Dangerous Ground* (51, Nicholas Ray); *Five Fingers* (52, Mankiewicz); *The Snows of Kilimanjaro* (52, Henry King); rich underwater effects in *Beneath the Twelve Mile Reef* (53, Robert Webb); *The Wages of Fear* (53, Henri-Georges Clouzot); *White Witch Doctor* (53, Henry Hathaway); *The Egyptian* (54, Michael Curtiz); a resonant stereo score for *Garden of Evil* (54, Hathaway); *King of the Khyber Rifles* (54, King); *The Kentuckian* (55, Burt Lancaster); *The Man in the Gray Flannel Suit* (56, Nunnally Johnson); and *Prince of Players* (55, Philip Dunne).

Herrmann worked with Hitchcock for the first time on *The Trouble with Harry* (56), and he actually played the Albert Hall conductor in *The Man Who Knew Too Much* (56). He also did the bass-broody score for the story of a wronged bassist, *The Wrong Man* (57, Hitchcock); *A Hatful of Rain* (57, Fred Zinnemann); *The 7th Voyage of Sinbad* (58, Nathan Juran); *The Fiend Who Walked the West* (58, Gordon Douglas); and *The Naked and the Dead* (58, Raoul Walsh).

Then came *Vertigo* (58, Hitchcock), music that pioneered a blending of fatal romance, mystery, and horror—it was a uniquely psychological score; *Blue Denim* (59, Dunne); *Journey to the Center of the Earth* (59, Henry Levin); *North by Northwest* (59, Hitchcock); *Psycho* (60, Hitchcock), with sly borrowings from Beethoven's *Eroica*—Norman's favorite music; *The Three Worlds of Gulliver* (60, Jack Sher); *Mysterious Island* (61, Cy Endfield);

Cape Fear (62, J. Lee Thompson); *Tender Is the Night* (62, King); *The Birds* (63, Hitchcock), where the music is indistinguishable from the overall sound design; *Jason and the Argonauts* (63, Don Chaffey); *Marnie* (64, Hitchcock); *Joy in the Morning* (65, Alex Segal); *Fahrenheit 451* (66, François Truffaut); *The Bride Wore Black* (68, Truffaut); *The Night Digger* (71, Alastair Reid); *Endless Night* (71, Sidney Gilliat); *Sisters* (73, Brian De Palma); *It's Alive!* (74, Larry Cohen); *Obsession* (76, De Palma); and *Taxi Driver* (76, Scorsese).

Werner Herzog (Werner Stipetic),
b. Sachrang, Germany, 1942

1962: *Herakles* (s). 1964: *Spiel im Sand* (s). 1966: *Die Beispiellose Verteidigung der Festung Deutschkreutz/The Unprecedented Defense of the Fortress "Deutschkreutz"* (s). 1967: *Letzte Worte/ Last Words* (s); *Lebenszeichen/Signs of Life.* 1968: *Massnahmen Gegen Fanatiker/Measures Against Fanatics* (s). 1969: *Die Fliegenden Arzte von Ostafrika/The Flying Doctors of East Africa* (d). 1970: *Auch Zwerge Haben Klein Angefangen/Even Dwarfs Started Small; Fata Morgana.* 1971: *Land des Schweigens und der Dunkelheit/Land of Silence and Darkness* (d). 1972: *Aguirre, der Zorn Gottes/Aguirre, the Wrath of God.* 1974: *Jeder Für Sich und Gott Gegen Alle/Each Man for Himself and God Against All/The Enigma of Kaspar Hauser.* 1975: *Die Grosse Ekstase des Bildschnitzers Steiner/The Great Ecstasy of Woodcarver Steiner* (s). 1976: *Herz aus Glas/Heart of Glass.* 1977: *La Soufrière* (d); *How Much Wood Would a Woodchuck Chuck* (d); *Stroszek.* 1979: *Nosferatu: Phantom der Nacht; Woyzeck.* 1980: *Huie's Sermon* (d); *Glaube und Wahrung/Faith and Fortitude* (d). 1982: *Fitzcarraldo.* 1983: *Wo die Grünen Ameisen Traumen/Where the Green Ants Dream.* 1984: *Ballade von Kleinen Soldaten/Ballad of the Little Soldier* (d). 1985: *Gasherbrum, Der Leuchtende Berg/Gasherbrum, The Little White Peak* (d). 1988: *Cobra Verde; Herdsmen of the Sun* (d). 1990: *Echos aus Einem Düsteren Reich* (d). 1991: *Schrei aus Stein/Scream of Stone.* 1992: *Lessons of Darkness* (d); *La Donna del Lago.* 1993: *Glocken aus der Tiefe* (d). 1994: *Die Verwandlung der Welt in Musik* (d). 1995: *Tod für Fünf Stimmen* (d). 1997: *Little Dieter Needs to Fly* (d). 1998: *Julianes Sturz in den Dschungel/Wings of Hope* (d). 1999: *Mein Liebster Feind—Klaus Kinski.* 2001: *Invincible.*

In 1965, it would not have been credited that West Germany might hold a leading place in radical filmmaking. Perhaps it was the specially clotted character of German movies, and the rigid industrial setup, that provoked the German outburst that followed. With Alexander Kluge and Volker Schlondorff as harbingers and very valuable support, West Germany became the base for exceptional directors: Rainer Werner Fassbinder, Jean-Marie Straub, Wim Wenders, and Werner Herzog.

A student of literature and theatre, Herzog was at the University of Pittsburgh and worked briefly in American TV. An enthusiastic traveler, he began with several shorts and documentaries before making his first feature in 1967. *Signs of Life* is a title and film that predicts Herzog's work. Ostensibly a Second World War picture, it is far more an allegory that deals with the hopeless and tragic struggle between social forms and the rebellious individual's self-assertion, between order and life. Its situation is that of a young German soldier on a Greek island whose self-destructive standing out against the army is less local than mythological.

It was immediately clear that Herzog possessed a quick sense of narrative; a withdrawn, mobile camera; and a dark, inquisitive humor. All these characteristics were concentrated in the apocalypse of *Even Dwarfs Started Small*, a pungent and brutal parable about an institution of dwarfs that turns against its governor. The grotesqueness of the dwarfs becomes as apt a comment on the warped nature of mankind as, say, the school authorities in *Zéro de Conduite* or the pillars of society in *L'Age d'Or.*

This was followed by the extraordinary *Fata Morgana*, filmed entirely in the Sahara and based on an Indian creation legend. Once again, desert is a model for mankind. The film is in three sections: the first showing an unpeopled, beautiful wasteland; the second introducing signs of human wreckage; and the third showing wretched vestiges of life. Totally imaginative, it is a legend of life at extremes that exposes the fatuity of *2001.* Whereas Kubrick glibly assumes some all-powerful, riddle-making consciousness behind the universe, Herzog's creator is as fallible, quirky, and uncertain as man himself. The camera style for Herzog is the steady source of reason, simultaneously describing the beauty and the madness of the desert.

Land of Silence and Darkness is a feature-length documentary about a middle-aged German woman, deaf and blind, who tries to help fellow-sufferers. Herzog avoids sentimentality and uses the handicapped people—as he does dwarfs and the desert—to bring out the primitive, incommunicable nature of people. The film catches that sense of dangerous, private freedom alluded to by Arthur Penn in *The Miracle Worker.* Most strikingly, the elements of documentary—the real German, actual sufferers—are subsumed by the larger idea of man's being his own handicap. In this film, Herzog established how far he stood apart from socialist cinema in Germany; he stressed the innately damaged quality of man as being natural, essential, and insuperable. That said, the liberated experience of the band of hand-icapped people is often very touching and excit-ing, but in the way that the dwarf community bristled with its own flawed nature.

Not to settle or become labeled, Herzog went to Peru to make *Aguirre*, about a band of con-quistadors in search of El Dorado. Herzog's reserved, observant style easily adapts to adven-ture and epic locales, and the film is paced with exciting action sequences. But its subject is turned to a Herzog extreme: Aguirre's band becomes increasingly wild, destructive, and pathological, as if the South American setting were reverting to desert and the animal humans destroying themselves. Again one recollects the Buñuel of *L'Age d'Or*, but Herzog has made a vivid identification with Aguirre, a psychotic opti-mist who ends cast adrift on a raft with dead men and living apes. The film was all the more power-ful (and conventional) because of Herzog's first real identification with an actor—the willful, manic Klaus Kinski.

As attention fell on Herzog, so his pursuit of extremism became a little more studied; it began to seem more zealous than natural. But *Kaspar Hauser* was one of his best works; *La Soufrière* was a magnificent deadpan (or deadcone) joke; and *Stroszek*, for all its failure, sees America as part of the kingdom of silence and darkness.

Herzog pictures were events in the seventies, but they have become very hard to see. *Fitzcar-raldo* was the last film to get wide screenings. Its story of opera in the jungle and a boat being car-ried over a mountain was effective, but it came close to being a parody of Herzog. And that was the close of the partnership Herzog had had with Klaus Kinski. So he lost the actor, yet he has never run out of mountains, remote locations, and epic trials of will. Perhaps the sameness has affected Herzog. Going too often to extremes can turn the remoteness into a habit. Herzog lives in California now, and he has great dreams—of a big feature film about Cortés and Montezuma. But he has to follow stricter economies, and a lot of his recent films have been personal documentaries. Several are haunted by music—bells in religion; opera—but always the subject of ecstatic/perilous experi-ence pulls at Herzog. He is not the ideal doc-umentarian. You feel he has his mind made up about so many things—and so you do not always want to trust what you are seeing. Grant, too, that one of these documentaries concerns Klaus Kin-ski—who would, certainly, have had things (and curses) to add. The saddest thing of all is *Invinci-ble*, a fable about magic under the Nazis, that falls like lead on the screen.

Charlton Heston (Charles Carter),
b. St. Helen, Missouri, 1924

Heston has sometimes been cited as the clearest instance of the "monolithic" actor: the man who contributes to a film through his presence and the innate splendor of honest muscle and strong-jawed virtue. He was *the* screen hero of the 1950s and early 1960s, a proven stayer in epics, and a pleasing combination of piercing blue eyes and tanned beefcake. A closer examination of his record suggests how far this characterization may have offended the man himself. Heston began with the classics, has gone out of his way to retain contact with them, and still mixes lofty projects with dull adventures. But just as he seems slightly musclebound the longer he talks, so as an athletic hero his greatest distinction was the suggestion that he had hankerings to be articulate. It seems likely that he has been overrated by all his follow-ers: by the intellectuals who were thrilled with his existence, and by the masses who loved such res-olute handsomeness. On both counts he falls a lit-tle short—not as reflective as Mitchum, but not as gaily agile as Burt Lancaster.

Heston attended Northwestern University and played Peer Gynt and Mark Antony in two enter-prising amateur 16mm films, both directed by David Bradley (42 and 49). He went on the pro-fessional stage, and by the late 1940s was playing Antony, Rochester, Heathcliffe, and Petruchio for CBS TV. This brought him to Hollywood's atten-tion, and in 1950 he made his professional debut in *Dark City* (William Dieterle). But it was Cecil B. De Mille who properly launched Heston as the tough circus owner in *The Greatest Show on Earth* (52). That part marked Heston down for ruggedness, and he played an Indian in *The Sav-age* (52, George Marshall) and Buffalo Bill in *Pony Express* (52, Jerry Hopper). It took King Vidor to draw out his sexual swagger in *Ruby Gen-try* (52). Generally, since then, Heston has kept closer to gentlemanly heroics, needing to be goaded into action. Principally he was a costumed Paramount hero: as Andrew Jackson in *The Presi-dent's Lady* (53, Henry Levin); *Bad for Each Other* (53, Irving Rapper); *The Naked Jungle* (54, Byron Haskin); *Secret of the Incas* (54, Hopper); *Lucy Gallant* (55, Robert Parrish); *The Far Hori-zons* (55, Rudolph Maté); and *The Private War of Major Benson* (55, Hopper).

De Mille raised him from this rut to be a rather Aryan Moses in *The Ten Commandments* (56). After playing with Anne Baxter and Tom Tryon in *Three Violent People* (57, Maté) and enabling Welles to direct *Touch of Evil* (58), in which Hes-ton went Mexican, he was used by William Wyler as the ranch foreman in *The Big Country* (58). He played Jackson again in *The Buccaneer* (58, Anthony Quinn), and then starred as *Ben-Hur* (59, Wyler), that thinking-man's epic. This was the peak of his popular success, even if *Ben-Hur* is a tame movie. Heston was far better used in his two

Samuel Bronston epics: *El Cid* (61, Anthony Mann) and *55 Days at Peking* (63, Nicholas Ray). The first is the finest expression of his Arthurian dignity, while the second coaxed out the most thoughtful acting he has yet shown, and, especially in the scene with the Chinese child, drew on a sense of human inadequacy beneath all Heston's muscle.

He made *Diamond Head* (62, Guy Green), and as well as playing John the Baptist in *The Greatest Story Ever Told* (65, George Stevens), he made the thwarted *Major Dundee* (65, Sam Peckinpah); was Michelangelo in *The Agony and the Ecstasy* (65, Carol Reed); essayed the medieval in *The War Lord* (65, Franklin Schaffner); outpointed Olivier in *Khartoum* (66, Basil Dearden)—he played Gordon; and descended to lesser films: *Counterpoint* (67, Ralph Nelson); *Will Penny* (67, Tom Gries); *Planet of the Apes* (67, Schaffner)—a big commercial success; *Pro* (68, Gries); Antony in *Julius Caesar* (70, Stuart Burge); *Master of the Islands* (70, Gries); and *The Omega Man* (71, Boris Sagal). The decline was maintained with yet another return to Mark Antony: playing in and directing *Antony and Cleopatra* (72), a film that suggests that he learned more from Wyler than from Mann, Ray, Vidor, or Maté. He then played in *The Call of the Wild* (72, Ken Annakin); the detective in *Soylent Green* (73, Richard Fleischer); Richelieu for a day in *The Three Musketeers* (73, Richard Lester); *Earthquake* (74, Mark Robson); and *Airport 1975* (74, Jack Smight).

It was to Heston's commercial credit that he still commanded leading roles in disaster pictures, just as he spearheaded the taste for epics fifteen years before. Nevertheless, after *Earthquake* he began to seem stranded by his films. It did not suit his dignity, or his duty as chairman of the trustees of the American Film Institute, to prolong this sort of work. He might one day reveal himself as a closet old man, but by then strength will be impacted: *The Last Hard Men* (76, Andrew V. McLaglen); *Midway* (76, Smight); *Two-Minute Warning* (76, Larry Peerce); Henry VIII in *The Prince and the Pauper* (77, Richard Fleischer); and *Gray Lady Down* (78, David Greene).

In his sixties, Heston has become a spokesman for conservative causes. He has not really aged (as if rock withered), but he has a harder time finding parts that need his commitment. He has been in *The Awakening* (80, Mike Newell), a Bram Stoker adaptation; a fur trapper in *The Mountain Men* (80, Richard Lang); he acted in and directed *Mother Lode* (82), playing twins—the film was written and produced by his son, Fraser; *The Nairobi Affair* (84, Marvin J. Chomsky); *Proud Men* (87, William A. Graham); playing More in and directing *A Man for All Seasons* (88); *Original Sin* (89, Ron Satlof); as Long John Silver in *Trea-*

sure Island (90, Fraser Heston); *The Little Kidnappers* (90, Donald Shebib); as God in *Almost an Angel* (90, John Cornell).

By 1990, one great characteristic was clear: he loved acting so much he would do small roles without being difficult. He also took a few leads in smaller pictures, and he gave his great voice as a narrator to many causes once espoused by his best films, such as the ownership of guns. Not far from eighty now, he is a classic survivor: he was Sherlock Holmes in *The Crucifer of Blood* (91, Heston); *Crash Landing: The Rescue of Flight 232* (92, Lamont Johnson); *Wayne's World 2* (93, Stephen Surjik); *Tombstone* (93, George Pan Cosmatos); *True Lies* (94, James Cameron); as Brigham Young in *The Avenging Angel* (95, Craig R. Baxley); *In the Mouth of Madness* (95, John Carpenter); *Alaska* (96, Heston); the narrator of *The Jungle Book* (96, Stephen Sommers); *Gideon* (99, Claudia Hoover); the commissioner of the NFL in *Any Given Sunday* (99, Brian De Palma); *Toscano* (99, Dan Gordon); *Town & Country* (01, Peter Chelsom); surveying the new fiasco in *Planet of the Apes* (01, Tim Burton); *The Order* (01, Sheldon Lettick); *The Last Man Club* (01, Heston).

In 2002, Heston announced that he might be a victim of Alzheimer's. But he appeared—as an interviewee—in *Bowling for Columbine* (02, Michael Moore). One might not share Heston's views of guns, but the last view of him in that documentary—walking away, bowed by arthritis—was maybe the most moving scene in all of his work.

Kieran Hickey (1936–93),
b. Dublin, Ireland

I met Kieran Hickey, as far as my records can ascertain, early in 1960. This was on the steps of the National Film Theatre in London. He was coming out of a film, and I was in line for the next screening. As I look at the list of films I saw then, I rather hope that the movie was a Renoir or a Bresson—*Les Dames du Bois de Bologne,* perhaps. We were introduced, I'm sure, by Ross Devenish. All three of us, it turned out, were attached to what was then called the London School of Film Technique in Brixton. I had just started a course there, Kieran had just finished. But he would come in in the evenings to edit a film he was making, a documentary on James Joyce's Dublin.

Immediately, on the steps of the NFT, we started talking. And I should say something about what words meant to Kieran. He took pains never to sound obviously (or only) Irish. But he was proud of the old adage that the best English was spoken in Dublin. He was a terrific, eloquent talker—gruff, tender, lyrical, sarcastic. You could feel yourself starting to think better and faster in his company. And if, like me, you were emerging slowly from a life of stammering, you had to learn to get on with talking, or use the stammer strategically to better his arguments. We got into the best talking relationship of my life.

Film was our chief topic. Kieran was a filmmaker, and a film-goer, too. In the early 1960s, as he worked at a large department store and I worked at a scientific publishing house, we would confer by telephone in the day about what to see that night. In those days, London was a collective of repertory theatres, and we were busy charting the past of the medium we loved (and longed to work in). I have the list of those years still, and here is one week for 1961:

Affair in Havana (Laslo Benedek)
Queen's, Bayswater
The Naked Dawn (Edgar G. Ulmer)
the Tolmer
Men in War (Anthony Mann) the Tolmer
Saint Tropez Blues (Marcel Moussy)
Cameo Royal
Blast of Silence (Allen Baron)
Cameo Royal
A Taste of Honey (Tony Richardson)
Leicester Square Theatre
Bonjour Tristesse (Otto Preminger)
Cameo, Victoria
La Coup de Berger (Jacques Rivette)
Everyman, Hampstead
Les 400 Coups (François Truffaut)
Everyman, Hampstead
Dark Victory (Edmund Goulding) N.F.T.
L'Avventura (Michelangelo Antonioni)
Classic, Tooting
Bellissima (Luchino Visconti) N.F.T.
Beyond the Forest (King Vidor) N.F.T.
Senso (Luchino Visconti) N.F.T.

Using the library of the British Film Institute, we compiled filmographies for directors: in 1961, no such things were available. We were less scholars than people trying to determine what we needed to see. Again, in 1961, there was no more than a handful of books on movie subjects, and none of those claimed to be a work of reference. So we were working rather against the grain, discovering from somewhere that Anthony Mann, King Vidor, and Otto Preminger were as interesting and worthy as Ingmar Bergman, Antonioni, or Truffaut.

As we saw the films, we talked about them. It was Kieran who taught me that not to talk about something was to risk losing it, or letting it escape. We knew what we liked, and had fairly conceited attitudes, but we were led toward the nature of good style. That pursuit depended on our own reaction in the dark, and reading *Cahiers du Cinéma*—the only magazine that admired the directors we loved, and that tried to address the glory of those films. However, as our school-boy French improved enough to keep up with *Cahiers*, we had to admit that acres of it were incoherent and pretentious. So our talk ruled.

Kieran went back to Dublin, having failed to find a way into the British picture business. But he was a family friend by then, an uncle to my children such as no actual family ties could provide, and a friend to both my wives. He began to make films, a couple of which I was lucky enough to write: *Faithful Departed*, a reverie on Dublin on Bloomsbury; a life of *Jonathan Swift;* a little short story, *A Child's Voice;* several documentaries, including one on Irish movies in the years 1945–58; and a series of exceptional short fictional films that explored such topics as sexuality and education in Ireland—*Exposure, Criminal Conversation, Attracta* (adapted by William Trevor from his own story, and starring Wendy Hiller), and *The Rockingham Shoot* (from a John McGahern story).

Our talk continued: in letters, over the phone, and in frequent visits. And the talk made this book. I do not mean to shift the responsibility. Kieran helped in the research on all editions of this book; he commented and improved it at every page. But his deepest contribution was to the years of talk, the climate of taking pictures seriously, that made me think the book possible. If you feel the need and the urge to talk back to the book, then know that Kieran paved the way.

I visited Dublin in the summer of 1993. He was to have open-heart surgery; I was in England for my father's funeral, and so I went over to Dublin for the weekend. He was a very hospitable man: there were visitors in and out of the house all the time, and he was busy making tea and cutting cake. We talked some more and watched a few things he had on tape—a documentary about Rossellini; *Bitter Victory* in a nicely letter-boxed format; and Stephen Frears's *The Snapper*, which had just played on television. We talked about this book, as it limped along.

The bypass was a success. He was doing beautifully, until an embolism took him off in an hour or so. The day after his death I got a postcard from him, saying his improvement was marked. He was the best friend I'll ever have, and in a way I feel the movies are over now that he's gone.

George Roy Hill, (1922–2002)

b. Minneapolis, Minnesota

1962: *Period of Adjustment*. 1963: *Toys in the Attic*. 1964: *The World of Henry Orient*. 1966: *Hawaii*. 1967: *Thoroughly Modern Millie*. 1969: *Butch Cassidy and the Sundance Kid*. 1972: *Slaughterhouse Five*. 1973: *The Sting*. 1975: *The Great Waldo Pepper*. 1977: *Slap Shot*. 1979: *A Little Romance*. 1982: *The World According to Garp*. 1984: *The Little Drummer Girl*. 1988: *Funny Farm*.

Forty before he directed, Hill has sometimes seemed to be trying to look less than his age. *Butch Cassidy* is relentlessly smart but rootless. Based on a very funny script, it is unable to decide whether to parody or join in the Western legend. Its final frozen frame is the perfect expression of fissured purpose, as is its rather gloating "best photograph of the year" imagery. Hill had been an actor, a soldier, a playwright, and a director for TV before he got into movies. He hurried through a variety of genres without ever finding anything in them to anchor him. It is hard, therefore, to see his interest in Vonnegut's *Slaughterhouse Five* as anything more than fashionable. With Tennessee Williams and Lillian Hellman, he proved incapable of making us forget the proscenium arch. But *The World of Henry Orient* was modestly charming and suggested the sense of humor that carried off the best jokes in *Butch Cassidy. The Sting*, too, was a shaggy dog story uneasily slowed by gangster realism and threadbare 1930s atmosphere. But it was a vast, easeful fantasy in the way that it let us believe an enterprising, attractive individualist could beat the system.

In the eighties, Hill made two literary adaptations—from John Irving and Le Carré—that fell flat: *The Little Drummer Girl* is scarcely coherent and way beyond Diane Keaton's range.

Walter Hill, b. Long Beach, California, 1942
1975: *Hard Times.* 1978: *The Driver.* 1979: *The Warriors.* 1980: *Southern Comfort.* 1982: *48 HRS.* 1984: *Streets of Fire.* 1985: *Brewster's Millions.* 1986: *Crossroads.* 1987: *Extreme Prejudice.* 1988: *Red Heat.* 1989: *Johnny Handsome.* 1990: *Another 48 HRS.* 1992: *Trespass.* 1993: *Geronimo.* 1995: *Wild Bill.* 1996: *Last Man Standing.* 1999: *Supernova* (credited as Thomas Lee). 2002: *Undisputed; The Prophecy.*

Here is contemporary success without mercy, comfort, or irony. Passing lightly over details from the young Hill's life—that he wanted to be a comic-book illustrator; that asthma kept him from the Vietnam War; that he felt "there is nothing more absurd than properly motivated characters"—one can survey the broken-down landscape of visual energy and commercial compromise, managed with a shrug that hopes to disguise irresponsibility as cool insolence.

There has always been something in movies to sustain Hill's fear of motivation—just as there has always been a lot in craven, lazy, and half-baked writers that flinched from it. There is something inherently reasonable in Hill's further description of his own movies: "I very purposely—more and more so every time I do a script—give characters no back story. The way you find out about these characters is by watching what they do, the way

they react to stress, the way they react to situations and confrontations. In that way, character is revealed through drama rather than being *explained* through dialogue."

That could be Fuller or Anthony Mann; it could be some exponent for painting or ballet; and it is a credo that comes alive from time to time in the delirious momentum of the entirely artificial *Streets of Fire,* a beautiful and entertaining fantasy. But the concentration on action in Fuller or Mann always led us into aspects of character or life that needed to be talked about, even if their characters were generally inarticulate. There is no drama without behavior, ideas, and experience—and sooner rather than later in Hill's work, cliché and violence had to take their place. Thus his undoubted talent for action—his eye—has rarely regained the lightness of *Streets of Fire.* Brutal comedy, violence, human indifference seep in. Big movies are too large for such sparse ambition. Eventually boredom or self-loathing are likely in the underoccupied filmmaker. It may be significant that Hill was part of the team that made *Alien* and *Aliens* (as coproducer and cowriter), yet not their director. Is that because Sigourney Weaver became too motivated, or too real, in those pictures?

Hill was an assistant on *The Thomas Crown Affair* (68, Norman Jewison) and *Take the Money and Run* (69, Woody Allen). He wrote *Hickey and Boggs* (72, Robert Culp) as a story for two white men; he had Jason Robards and Strother Martin in mind, and "Hickey" came from Robards's stage performance in *The Iceman Cometh.* Commerce made it the black-and-white pairing of Culp and Bill Cosby—a trick that Hill learned well enough for Nick Nolte and Eddie Murphy in *48 HRS.* He also did scripts for *The Getaway* (72, Sam Peckinpah), a singularly motivated action story; *The Thief Who Came to Dinner* (73, Bud Yorkin); and *The Mackintosh Man* (73, John Huston).

Hill admirers must look back on the nineties with regret. *Wild Bill* was a mess and a disaster, yet it had the makings of a fine interplay of fact and legend. It also had a hazy, umber-colored look that seemed to have soaked into the film stock for *Last Man Standing*—a remake of *Yojimbo,* set in rural and very dusty Texas that a two-year-old could have picked and predicted inside the first ten minutes (and then napped). Add to that the humiliation of *Supernova*—from which Hill removed his name—and you have a career coming to a standstill.

Arthur Hiller, b. Edmonton, Canada, 1923
1963: *The Flight of the White Stallions; The Wheeler Dealers/Separate Beds.* 1964: *The Americanization of Emily; This Rugged Land.* 1966: *Promise Her Anything; Penelope.* 1967: *Tobruk; The Tiger Makes Out.* 1969: *Popi.* 1970: *The Out-*

of-Towners; Love Story; Plaza Suite. 1971: The Hospital. 1972: Man of La Mancha. 1974: The Crazy World of Julius Vrooder. 1976: W. C. Fields and Me; Silver Streak. 1979: The In-Laws; Nightwing. 1982: Author! Author!; Making Love. 1983: Romantic Comedy. 1984: The Lonely Guy; Teachers. 1987: Outrageous Fortune. 1989: See No Evil, Hear No Evil. 1990: Taking Care of Business. 1991: Married to It. 1992: The Babe. 1996: Carpool. 1997: An Alan Smithee Film: Burn, Hollywood, Burn.

Long before 1971, the filmgoer might have safely given up Arthur Hiller. What is authorship if it is not the capacity to make a dozen consistently impersonal and unexciting movies? To which, in 1970, was added the irrelevant commercial success of Love Story, a film only justified by its deflation at the end of What's Up, Doc? But in 1971, there emerged, under Hiller's name, The Hospital, a most despairing comedy and a witheringly accurate portrait of the lunacy of attempting a benevolent act. It is easy to point out that The Hospital has a scurrilous script by Paddy Chayefsky, which flies like a vulture round the noble wreck of George C. Scott. Nothing in it smacks of direction, but not many films of its year were as entertaining or touching. Had it been a first film, we might have cherished high hopes. But a dull first dozen, and the immediate reversal to type with Man of La Mancha indicates only that even a trimmer has his day. Rod Steiger was his W. C. Fields: a brilliant impersonation in a film that studiously avoids the contrasts of the man and his surreal refusal to seem a comedian. Silver Streak is a heartless and uncommitted running of a great old locomotive—one of the first worthless train movies.

Among the later films, Teachers is the most engaging: it has a little of the institutional gallows humor remembered from The Hospital. Making Love was announced as a breakthrough—it had a married man character who found he was gay— but the picture was hushed and reverent about its own daring, and it lacked any bold or challenging actors. As one of his titles suggests, Hiller is the kind of director who gets pictures done on time, on budget, without troubling or threatening anyone.

Dame Wendy Hiller (1912–2003),
b. Bramshall, Cheshire, England

Acting in films over the space of six decades, Wendy Hiller was nominated for an Oscar three times. Still, she would no doubt reckon that her best work was on the stage she preferred. Perhaps the truth is rather that because she was never quite glamorous, a lot of shallow filmmakers missed the chance to work with a great actress: Lancashire Luck (37, Henry Carr); nomination for her Eliza opposite Leslie Howard in Pygmalion (38, Gabriel Pascal); as Major Barbara (41, Pascal); enchanting and brilliant in I Know Where I'm Going (45, Michael Powell); Outcast of the Islands (51, Carol Reed); Single Handed/Sailor of the King (53, Roy Boulting); Something of Value (57, Richard Brooks); How to Murder a Rich Uncle (57, Nigel Patrick); winning the supporting actress Oscar in Separate Tables (58, Delbert Mann); the mother in Sons and Lovers (60, Jack Cardiff); Toys in the Attic (63, George Roy Hill); nominated again for A Man for All Seasons (66, Fred Zinnemann), playing More's wife; Mrs. Micawber in David Copperfield (70, Mann); Murder on the Orient Express (74, Sidney Lumet); Voyage of the Damned (76, Stuart Rosenberg); The Cat and the Canary (78, Radley Metzger); The Elephant Man (80, David Lynch); Making Love (82, Arthur Hiller); in William Trevor's short story Attracta (83, Kieran Hickey); The Lonely Passion of Judith Hearne (87, Jack Clayton); The Countess Alice (92, Moira Armstrong).

Sir Alfred Hitchcock (1899–1980),
b. London

1922: Number Thirteen (uncompleted). 1925: The Pleasure Garden. 1926: The Mountain Eagle; The Lodger. 1927: Downhill; Easy Virtue; The Ring. 1928: The Farmer's Wife; Champagne; The Manxman. 1929: Blackmail. 1930: Elstree Calling (codirected); Juno and the Paycock; Murder. 1931: The Skin Game. 1932: Rich and Strange; Number Seventeen. 1933: Waltzes from Vienna. 1934: The Man Who Knew Too Much. 1935: The Thirty-nine Steps. 1936: The Secret Agent; Sabotage. 1937: Young and Innocent. 1938: The Lady Vanishes. 1939: Jamaica Inn. 1940: Rebecca; Foreign Correspondent. 1941: Mr. and Mrs. Smith; Suspicion. 1942: Saboteur. 1943: Shadow of a Doubt; Lifeboat. 1944: Bon Voyage (s); Adventure Malgache (s). 1945: Spellbound. 1946: Notorious. 1947: The Paradine Case. 1948: Rope. 1949: Under Capricorn. 1950: Stage Fright. 1951: Strangers on a Train. 1952: I Confess. 1954: Dial M for Murder; Rear Window. 1955: To Catch a Thief; The Man Who Knew Too Much. 1956: The Trouble with Harry. 1957: The Wrong Man. 1958: Vertigo. 1959: North by Northwest. 1960: Psycho. 1963: The Birds. 1964: Marnie. 1966: Torn Curtain. 1969: Topaz. 1971: Frenzy. 1976: Family Plot.

The critical dogfights over Hitchcock's status were fought at a crucial time, in the early 1960s, to assert the value of his greatest works—Rear Window, Vertigo, North by Northwest, Psycho, and The Birds. And these films are without equal for the way they adjust the cinematic image to our expectations. They are deeply expressive of the way we watch and respond to stories. Their greatness is often employed to explain the nature and workings of cinema. Thus Hitchcock became a way of defining film, a man exclusively intent on the moving image and the compulsive emotions of the spectator.

Hitchcock in England is a career unto itself, no matter that the American films take on a greater power and ease—like driving a Cadillac after a Morris Minor. The English films are playful, and sometimes facetious or silly. But they have dark moments and there are stirrings of sexual menace. The comic adventure of *The Lady Vanishes,* for instance, turns into a parable on appeasement, in which stock English fools get hurt. The first *Man Who Knew Too Much* is startlingly grim and cruel, and *Sabotage* is not unworthy of Conrad's novel *The Secret Agent.* But it was Hitch's storytelling flair—and visual storytelling—that got him to America, where his new boss, Selznick, saw the need to teach that Brit plausibility and character. Selznick was a pompous teacher, but he had a point. And the sardonic Hitchcock did study in those first years. Thus, immediately, *Rebecca* moves us.

The first point to make about Hitchcock, therefore, is the variability of his work. That is the more important in that Hitchcock's defenders frequently praise his technical and commercial knowingness. But no matter how many times the profit ratio of *Psycho* is repeated, it does not alter the fact that Hitchcock made several flops, several films in which the entire narrative structure—over which he spent such time and care—is grotesquely miscalculated. *Stage Fright, The Trouble with Harry, Lifeboat,* and *Torn Curtain* seem to me thumpingly bad films, helpless in the face of intransigent plots, true delicacy of humor, and uncooperative players. *Spellbound, The Paradine Case,* and *Rope* are flawed by unwieldy or wrongheaded situations. *Dial M for Murder* is unadventurous suspense, *Saboteur* a monotonous chase film. The rich emotional undertones of *North by Northwest* show how simple many of the other thrillers are. Furthermore, those defects often affect much better films. *Strangers on a Train* is one of Hitchcock's most fascinating films, but Farley Granger and Ruth Roman are coldly abandoned by their director. Even *Psycho,* made with a torturemaster's refinement, stumbles over the implausibility of the car-purchase scene. And while it is legitimate to defend and praise his use of back projection as proof of the preference for emotional to actual reality, it is equally clear that so celebrated a technician ought to be able to achieve such inner realism without jolting the audience from its identification with the film.

To see Hitchcock's films, in my opinion, is not to confront an author of supreme technical and narrative confidence, or a moral philosopher of great wisdom. I believe him when he said he was nervous about whether *Psycho* would prosper. After all, he swapped endings on *Topaz,* allowed

bizarre passages of inconsequential chatter in *Frenzy,* and watched stonily over drab performances from Paul Newman and Julie Andrews in *Torn Curtain.* And all this in the years when virtually every quarter of the film world was prepared to acknowledge the significance of his work. One might argue that age was catching him up, except that *Frenzy* is almost a parody Hitchcock film, packed with moments that spring from his best work, which are persistently ruined by the uneasy jokiness of the film and by its ignorance of the real world.

Ignorance and fear are the abiding impressions left by his films. Just as his suspense works through deliberately withheld knowledge—and withheld from the hypersensitive voyeurist curiosity that he has aroused—so he teaches us to share the fear of the world that he always owned up to. Why not face the implications of his two celebrated admissions: that he feared, above all, arrest; and that his aim in cinema was to put the audience through it? I would not deny that his films can lead to great insights of an intensely pessimistic vision. But I do not see how a man so fearful, and so chronically adept at conveying fear, can be judged as a profound artist. Suffering in his films invariably depends upon the victim's being unbalanced or demented. The pain felt by Perkins in *Psycho* or Stewart in *Vertigo* is savage, yet it is more limited than that in Renoir, Mizoguchi, or Welles because of Hitchcock's resort to mania and melodrama.

Hitchcock's most profound subject and achievement is the juxtaposition of sanity and insanity, of bourgeois ordinariness and criminal outrage. The crisscross motif, derived from thriller fiction, is itself a map of the way audiences willingly cross over from their seats to involve themselves in a film. James Stewart being drawn into Kim Novak in *Vertigo* is a model of the way we are sucked into films. Charming Robert Walker and boring Farley Granger make a trap for our need to identify. The method of *Rear Window*—a voyeur in the dark inspecting other lives—is the principle of cinematic spectacle. Hitchcock's best films all grow out of his instinctive employment of our impulses and fantasy life in the cinema. And his moral seriousness consists of showing us the violent, psychotic fruits of some of those impulses and shyly asking us to claim them as our own. I say "shyly" because Hitchcock did not properly own up to his seriousness. It is not enough to paint Hitchcock the interviewee as a sly legpuller who teased earnest questions. The truth may be that he did not fully grasp his own films. Truffaut's book amply reveals a man of very mundane, shallow moral and social attitudes, flip rather than witty, genuinely more interested in technique than in meaning. And, it must be said, there is a degree of spiritual coarseness and callousness in Hitchcock's work that chimes with the career-long taste for brutalizing our nerves.

So how does Hitchcock stand? There are astonishing achievements: *Rebecca* is a gorgeous Gothic women's picture; *Notorious* a tragic love story; *Under Capricorn,* a rich account of emotional self-sacrifice; *Strangers on a Train,* a key exposition of the madman hero; *Rear Window* and *Vertigo,* superb commentaries on watching films; *The Wrong Man,* an exemplary study of chance and routine in conflict; *North by Northwest,* a brilliant view of a frivolous Cary Grant being sobered by feelings; *Psycho,* a scream of horror at the idea of madness; *The Birds,* an audacious use of science-fiction apocalypse to dramatize intimate emotional insecurity. Here are ten films that are masterly and repay endless viewing. Gothic melodrama runs through his work, as does the cruel tenderness toward suffering of the women's picture. Hitchcock never forsook the dream-dotty England of the 1930s, just as he never really noticed anything in America beyond the equipment resources of the big studios and the tourist sites. Film is his world, and other filmmakers his sole points of reference, especially Fritz Lang and Val Lewton (*The Testament of Dr. Mabuse* was the source of many of the English thrillers, while Lewton's sense of undisclosed horror is an essential influence on Hitchcock's stimulated voyeurism).

His great films are only partly his; they also belong to the minds that interpret them. There is an artistic timidity in Hitchcock that, having put the audience through it, must allow them to come to terms with the experience. But his own personality is withdrawn, cold, insecure, and uncharitable. The method, despite its brilliance, is equally private and restrictive. To plan so much that the shooting becomes a chore is an abuse not just of actors and crew, but of cinema's predilection for the momentary. It is, in fact, the style of an immense, premeditative artist—a Bach, a Proust, or a Rembrandt. And beside those masters, Hitchcock seems an impoverished inventor of thumbscrews who shows us the human capacity for inflicting pain, but no more. Such precision can only avoid seeming overbearing and misanthropic if it is accompanied by creative untidiness. In the last resort, his realized blueprints affirm film's yearning for doubt and open endings.

Mike Hodges, b. London, 1932

1971: *Get Carter.* 1972: *Pulp.* 1974: *The Terminal Man.* 1979: *Damien: Omen II.* 1980: *Flash Gordon.* 1985: *Moron from Outer Space.* 1987: *A Prayer for the Dying.* 1990: *Black Rainbow.* 1999: *Croupier.*

This is not an easy career to explain. By the late nineties, for instance, *Get Carter* was a cult movie, famous for its abrupt violence and poker-faced comedy, and for its absolute logical fatalism. Not that *Get Carter* wasn't a hit in its day. Nearly thirty years later, with a good script by Paul Mayersberg, *Croupier* was one of the pleasant surprises of its season, and an assured handling of underworld material. What happened in between? Why, close to the age of seventy, is Hodges so little appreciated? The films made between *Carter* and *Croupier* are not as good, but they're not that terrible, either. Plenty of lesser talents have had steadier careers, but Hodges—who was experienced in TV directing in the late 1960s even—looks like a novice. Indeed, if *Croupier* had been a first film, its director would have been hailed and offered a portion of the world.

Dustin Hoffman, b. Los Angeles, 1937

Hoffman's screen character is reticent but stubborn. He is small and often timid, but a nucleus of hard identity never wavers, never seems fully threatened, and never floods us with animation. In an age of dynamic male stars who toss opposition aside, Hoffman has had the courage and the need to be inept. A wary and sometimes pious liberalism lurks in his anticipation of suffering at the world's rough hands. His hangdog charm resists radiant winners ideologically; indeed, there has often been a suspicion that he was more a character actor than a lead. Things have always happened to him, as witness his success as the least active person in *The Graduate.* He has chosen his parts carefully, avoiding the standard Hollywood product and often employing makeup or impersonation to vindicate the role of craftsmanlike acting.

Al Pacino has all the authority of self Hoffman avoids, and may well have taken some of Hoffman's better prospects because of it. Either of them could have played in *Dog Day Afternoon, Serpico,* or *Scarecrow,* but only Pacino could summon up the passion for power in Michael Corleone or the dispassionate self-regard that drives Bobby Deerfield. Hoffman is not a credible screen lover: he does not idealize himself enough to make a woman's awe natural. He's best as a muddler, or the forlorn creature swept back and forth by fate. However, such haplessness is rare in American film actors if not cushioned by the sentimental dismay of a clown. Early on, a helpless kindness hovered within Hoffman's nature, too shy or too sure of the world's harshness to venture into the open. But he has grown harder, and more controlling: in his very set looks, we may guess how difficult he is to direct.

He was the son of a props man at Columbia, and studied music at the Santa Monica City College before acting at the Pasadena Playhouse. But he soon transferred his base and all his cultural allegiances to New York. He soldiered on there for ten years, in TV and theatre, before his big opportunity. Interestingly, he was nearly thirty when he played *The Graduate* (67, Mike Nichols). It seemed brilliant casting, though, and Hoffman was very appropriate as the numb focus of comic disasters and sexual opportunity. It is not often noticed, but he is the only innocent in the picture; a more subtle or demanding treatment would be bound to see him as an insufferable prig. He was less plausible toward the end of the film, when a little boy's urgency is supposed to take him over. But the passivity that could not stop the tide of Mrs. Robinson, or hold on to its own moral reserve, was funny and absorbing.

His Ratso in *Midnight Cowboy* (69, John Schlesinger) was a dazzling assembly of technical devices, as emotionless as it was compelling to watch. The script, the direction, and the acting all settled for pathos as Ratso's due from an audience, and made him a sleazy exotic more than a failed street urchin and a chronic cheat. Schlesinger is too sloppy an artist to let Ratso emerge as less than adorable, but Hoffman was probably capable of nastiness had he been trusted. The actor was at a loss in the entirely unnecessary *John and Mary* (69, Peter Yates), one of his few concessions to the big-salary syndrome. He was near his best in *Little Big Man* (70, Arthur Penn), managing the old age easily and riding the picaresque adventures of a put-upon outcast all the better because of his own denial of starriness. Still, it was easier to accept Hoffman as Penn's spokesman than as someone actually living through the film.

Feeling established and unsatisfied by Hollywood ventures, he had a year of odd experiments: to Italy for *Alfredo, Alfredo* (71, Pietro Germi); to England to play the mathematics graduate in *Straw Dogs* (71, Sam Peckinpah); and, in America, *Who Is Harry Kellerman and Why Is He Saying Those Terrible Things About Me?* (71, Ulu Grosbard—Hoffman's longtime friend).

Straw Dogs was the only one of those three seen by the general public, and Hoffman is not the most memorable element in its deadly ritual. His adoption of violence at the climax is the more troubling because Peckinpah never seems to have explained its need to the gentle and perplexed actor. The gloating contrivance of *Straw Dogs* is accentuated by Hoffman's guardedness. He fights back like someone under orders; he never concedes the thrill of revenge or the trembling orgasm of blood. The one aspect of his character that works is the appeal of mathematics; but the actor's cerebral dimension never appeared to win Peckinpah over. Pacino might have shocked us with a sudden appetite for destruction—but Hoffman is as unlikely a killer as he is husband to the very ripe Susan George.

He was in *Papillon* (73, Franklin Schaffner), but as *Lenny* (74, Bob Fosse) he could not compete with films and records of the real Lenny Bruce. What may have seemed to him his most important film proved a tame, redundant work in which Hoffman was overawed by the mixture of show-off, paranoid, poet, and self-destructive in Bruce. It is his most sentimental performance. As Carl Bernstein in *All the President's Men* (76, Alan J. Pakula), he was a model of detail, precision, and deadpan humor; but, again, actual events absolved the actor from serious involvement and left Hoffman's skill overshadowed by Redford's dull but forceful presence. *Marathon Man* (76, Schlesinger) was a bad picture for all concerned, and something Hoffman should have been able to decline. He also appeared in *Agatha* (78, Michael Apted).

Straight Time (78) was originally a picture for Hoffman to direct as well as to star in. For the first thirty minutes, it is strikingly raw and unusual, and it allows Hoffman to be middle-aged and wearily resentful of a stupid, legalistic society. But overwork forced Hoffman to assign the direction to Ulu Grosbard, and the broken back of the movie was the result of their quarrel as it progressed. Hoffman sued the distributor, alleging interference, but it seems more likely that the abrupt change of tone and narrative after about thirty minutes was Hoffman's choice and mistake.

In the eighties, Hoffman became recognized as one of America's great actors. To these eyes, the films did not always support the claim. But Hoffman seemed convinced, and became a good deal harder to work with because of it. Thus, he has acquired the reputation of being a sometimes unmanageable actor, taking films out of a director's control, and into his own narcissistic doubts. In recent years, especially, the results do not suggest the process is very fruitful.

He won the best actor Oscar for *Kramer vs Kramer* (79, Robert Benton), and then was nominated for the very clever work in *Tootsie* (82, Sydney Pollack). He played Willy Loman in *Death of a Salesman* (85, Volker Schlondorff), with a lot more self-pity and whining than I liked. (That production was observed in a fascinating 1985 documentary, *Private Conversation*, directed by Christian Blackwood, which shows how much attention had to be paid to the lead actor.)

Ishtar (87, Elaine May) was a disaster for everyone, but Hoffman promptly recovered with another best actor Oscar in *Rain Man* (88, Barry Levinson) as Tom Cruise's idiot savant brother (some think Cruise did a better and less obtrusive job). Hoffman had a cameo in *Dick Tracy* (90, Beatty), but he has also done four films that failed at the box office and left the actor looking puzzled or peeved: *Family Business* (89, Sidney Lumet); *Billy Bathgate* (91, Benton); *Hook* (91, Steven Spielberg); and *Hero* (92, Stephen Frears).

You can see doubt and indifference setting in

already, but as the nineties went on it was sad to see the stagnation in a once dynamic actor: *Outbreak* (95, Wolfgang Petersen); as Teach in *American Buffalo* (96, Michael Corrente); *Sleepers* (96, Barry Levinson); *Mad City* (97, Costa-Gavras); very funny doing Robert Evans in *Wag the Dog* (97, Levinson), the liveliest he had been for years; *Sphere* (98, Levinson); and dotty as The Conscience in *Messenger: The Story of Joan of Arc* (99, Luc Besson).

He gets life achievement awards these days, but all he delivers in return are *Moonlight Mile* (02, Brad Silberling); an asinine "genius" in the dreadful *Confidence* (03, James Foley); *The Runaway Jury* (03, Gary Fleder).

Philip Seymour Hoffman,

b. Fairport, New York, 1967

Where do we begin, where will he end? Philip Seymour Hoffman does not—he must have been told this often enough—seem like a movie star. He's boyish but untidy, a little overweight, hopelessly immature. He's all of those things as Freddie, the prep-school thug in *The Talented Mr. Ripley* (99, Anthony Minghella). Yet I'm not sure there's been a better performance in recent years—so nasty yet so vulnerable, such a cross of Mussolini and Billy Bunter.

Freddie is on screen not much more than twenty minutes, and it's easy to foresee Hoffman as a brilliant supporting actor. But in the year after *Ripley,* he alternated lead roles in Sam Shepard's *True West* with John C. Reilly on Broadway; and he played the flamboyant drag queen in *Flawless* (00, Joel Schumacher), a film that had little purpose but to showcase a great actor.

That's further proof, if anyone still needs it, of the gap between working for a Minghella and a Schumacher. Hoffman could be turned into an institution—but never properly tested. He is so good that only the best material is going to help build our sense of him. Meanwhile, search him out, as you might Kevin Spacey. There is the same very dangerous talent at work—astounding, yet so pronounced it could help make its own prison.

He made his debut in *Triple Bogey on a Par Five Hole* (91, Amos Poe); *Scent of a Woman* (92, Martin Brest); *My New Gun* (92, Stacy Cochran); *Leap of Faith* (92, Richard Pearce); *My Boyfriend's Back* (93, Bob Balaban); *Nobody's Fool* (94, Robert Benton); *The Getaway* (94, Roger Donaldson); on TV in *The Yearling* (94, Rod Hardy); *When a Man Loves a Woman* (Luis Mandoki); *Hard Eight* (96, Paul Thomas Anderson); *Twister* (96, Jan de Bont); *Boogie Nights* (97, Anderson); *Happiness* (98, Todd Solondz); *The Big Lebowski* (98, Joel Coen); *Patch Adams* (98, Tom Shadyac); *Magnolia* (99, Anderson); *State and Main* (00, David Mamet); Lester Bangs in *Almost Famous* (00, Cameron Crowe).

He shows every sign of being determined to uncover the kinds of American seldom seen in Hollywood movies: *Forest Hills Bob* (01, Robert Downey Sr); *Love Liza* (02, Todd Louiso); *Punch-Drunk Love* (02, Anderson); *Red Dragon* (02, Brett Ratner); *25th Hour* (02, Spike Lee); magnificent as the depressed gambler (Canadian) in *Owning Mahowney* (03, Richard Kwietniowski); *Cold Mountain* (03, Minghella).

William Holden (William Franklin Beedle Jr.) (1918–81), b. O'Fallon, Illinois

When Holden died, he was sixty-three—Clint Eastwood's age in *In the Line of Fire*. That's a way of illustrating the variable effects of age on a face. For Holden, at the end, could look like the most "used" person in Hollywood. Alcohol must take a lot of the credit, for Holden had been so serious a victim of drink that he had killed a bystander in a car accident in Europe. He had had his day: in the late fifties, he was so powerful at the box office nearly every script went through his agent. But the suffering in his face found no solace in power. The look of pain sustained two fine films—*The Wild Bunch* and *Network*—so that we rubbed our eyes to recall the fresh-faced enthusiast from *Golden Boy*. You could pick a dozen or so maturing close-ups of Holden and the series would tell the horrible story of movies as a marinade called early embalming.

Educated at Pasadena Junior College, he was appearing at the Pasadena Playhouse in 1937 when Paramount put him under contract. But they offered him no films, and it was Columbia who gave him his start as the young man torn between boxing and the violin in Mamoulian's *Golden Boy* (39). Holden's easy charm was further exploited in *Invisible Stripes* (39, Lloyd Bacon); Sam Wood's *Our Town* (40); *Arizona* (40, Wesley Ruggles); *I Wanted Wings* (41, Mitchell Leisen); *Texas* (41, George Marshall); and *The Remarkable Andrew* (42, Stuart Heisler), before he joined the air force. He returned in 1947 for John Farrow's *Blaze of Noon; The Man from Colorado* (48, Henry Levin); *Apartment for Peggy* (48, George Seaton); and *Rachel and the Stranger* (48, Norman Foster). He was essentially nonassertive and could do no better than ordinary adventure stories and sketchy romantic leads: *The Dark Past* (49, Rudolph Maté); *Streets of Laredo* (48, Lesley Fenton); *Miss Grant Takes Richmond* (49, Bacon); and *Father Is a Bachelor* (50, Foster and Abby Berlin).

It was Billy Wilder who encouraged Holden's breakthrough by showing us the sleazy reverse of charm: first by casting him as Joe Gillis, the weak-willed, would-be writer who narrates *Sunset Boulevard* (50), face down in Norma Desmond's swimming pool; then by persuading him to play the stooge part for Judy Holliday in Cukor's *Born*

Yesterday (50), and as a reward, giving him the Oscar part of the cynical, racketeer sergeant in *Stalag 17* (53).

But Wilder's bitterness hardly rubbed off on Holden. He still figured in adventures: *Union Station* (50, Maté); Curtiz's *Force of Arms* (51); *Submarine Command* (51, Farrow); and *Escape from Fort Bravo* (53, John Sturges). And he remained an epitome of shallow handsomeness in Dieterle's *The Turning Point* (52); *The Moon Is Blue* (53, Otto Preminger); *Forever Female* (53, Irving Rapper); *Sabrina* (54, Wilder); *The Country Girl* (54, Seaton) and *The Bridges at Toko-Ri* (55, Mark Robson), both opposite Grace Kelly; as the European lover in Henry King's *Love is a Many Splendored Thing* (55). He was much more sympathetic as a has-been in Logan's *Picnic* (56), but made rigid by the gravity of *The Bridge on the River Kwai* (57, David Lean) and Carol Reed's *The Key* (58). He barely perked up for Ford's *The Horse Soldiers* (59) or McCarey's *Satan Never Sleeps* (62). Unadventurousness came close to inertia in *The World of Suzie Wong* (60) and *Paris When It Sizzles* (63), both for Richard Quine, and an atrophied solemnity set in for *Alvarez Kelly* (66, Edward Dmytryk).

All of a sudden, it disappeared and a real middle-aged anxiety colored the outlaw in Peckinpah's *The Wild Bunch* (69)—as outstanding in Holden's career as *Stalag 17*—but it gave way to relaxation in *The Christmas Tree* (69, Terence Young); Blake Edwards's muted *Wild Rovers* (71); the man caught up with *Breezy* (73, Clint Eastwood); the slack builder of *The Towering Inferno* (74, John Guillermin); a sentimental anchorman, the Marlboro man at menopause, beaten upon by Faye Dunaway's fitful waves in *Network* (76, Sidney Lumet); *21 Hours at Munich* (76, William A. Graham); fearing, and getting, the very worst in *Damien—Omen II* (78, Don Taylor); as another worried movie man in *Fedora* (78, Wilder); *Ashanti* (79, Richard Fleischer); *When Time Ran Out* (80, James Goldstone); and, finally, in one more aghast Hollywood story, *S.O.B.* (81, Blake Edwards).

Agnieszka Holland,
b. Warsaw, Poland, 1948
1977: *Zdjecia Probne/Screen Tests.* 1979: *Aktorzy Prowincjonalni/Provincial Actors.* 1980: *Goraczka.* 1981: *Kobieta Samotna/A Woman Alone.* 1985: *Bittere Ernte/Angry Harvest.* 1988: *Popielusko.* 1990: *Europa, Europa.* 1992: *Olivier Olivier.* 1993: *The Secret Garden; Fallen Angels* (TV). 1995: *Total Eclipse.* 1997: *Washington Square.* 1999: *The Third Miracle.* 2001: *Shot in the Heart* (TV), *Julie Walks Home; Golden Dreams* (d).

In several films over the years, Agnieszka Holland showed a remarkable talent for stories about dis-

placement—the farmer who protects a Jewish woman during the war in *Angry Harvest;* the Jewish youth whose escape leads him into the German army in *Europa, Europa;* the fairy tale of *Olivier Olivier,* in which a lost child seems to return. These were pictures in which a tough, unsentimental structure and attitude were allied to a magical eye. It was all the more disappointing then that Holland's *Secret Garden* felt staid and unadventurous, and much less than Fred Wilcox's 1949 version, which has maybe the best ensemble of child actors ever seen. Holland's version had many virtues, but it felt like a TV movie.

Holland was educated in Prague, studying with Milos Forman and Ivan Passer. In Poland, she encountered persecution such that eventually she moved to Paris. But her career began in Warsaw, and she was Andrzej Wajda's screenwriter on several films: *Without Anesthesia* (78); *Danton* (82); *A Love in Germany* (83); *The Possessed* (87); and *Korczak* (90). She also wrote the screenplay for another fascinating study in displacement, *Anna* (87, Yurek Bogayevicz), and helped on the script for *Blue* (93, Krzysztof Kieslowski).

Holland continues to be inconsistent. Despite a script by Christopher Hampton and the presence of DiCaprio and David Thewlis (or was it because of those threatening assets?), *Total Eclipse* proved to be Rimbaud and Verlaine for strict beginners. Whereas, *Washington Square* was an admirable translation that used Albert Finney and Jennifer Jason Leigh very well. *The Third Miracle* was another dud. But *Shot in the Heart,* for HBO, was a superb telling of the problems of the Gilmore family (as in Gary Gilmore) with thrilling performances from Elias Koteas and Giovanni Ribisi. So it's a very tricky career to read—an obviously talented, intelligent director, who seldom does what is exactly expected of her.

Judy Holliday (Judith Tuvim) (1922–65),
b. New York
The story goes that *Adam's Rib* (49, George Cukor) was a conspiracy between Cukor, Katharine Hepburn, and Garson Kanin to convince Harry Cohn, the boss of Columbia, that Judy Holliday should play the dumb blonde in the film of *Born Yesterday.* It is a pleasant memoir from one of the most talented cliques within the movie world. And it is probably based on truth, even if we would be naïve to put much trust in benign conspiracies.

The film itself looks set up, especially in that early scene when attorney Hepburn interviews client Holliday. The scene is long, elaborately written, but filmed in one blatantly convenient setup—convenient, that is, for the virtuoso playing from Holliday. She does not simply steal the scene, but plays with it like a cat with a mouse. The effect is the more startling and contradictory in that such technical mastery is emanating from a character ostensibly stupid, impetuous, and imperceptive. Even granted Hepburn's complicity, the upstaging is lurid. There are moments at which Hepburn seems to say to herself, "My, my, what a clever girl you are." Holliday seldom looks at Hepburn. Like a child, she stares away into emptiness, the better to concentrate on herself. Yet, without looking, she dominates, so that Hepburn ends up as edgy and hesitant as the client should be.

Cohn saw the point—or so it is said. But Holliday was a strange actress, uneasily bending her own intelligence to the dumbest of New York blondes so that the performance in *Born Yesterday* often appears studied, cute, and condescending. It is a part of this curious meticulousness that she never seemed sexy on the screen. Never the "open, honest, bland, funny, sexy girl" that Kanin intended, but a neurotic barrage of timing, expression, and gestures. Still, her Billie Dawn won the Oscar, beating out Davis and Baxter in *All About Eve* and Swanson in *Sunset Boulevard*.

Holliday started in cabaret: she formed a group, the Revuers, with Betty Comden and Adolph Green. As such, she was a Greenwich Village star, and Nicholas Ray was one of her lovers. She had had three small film parts in 1944: *Greenwich Village* (Walter Lang); *Something for the Boys* (Lewis Seiler); and *Winged Victory* (George Cukor). But she then concentrated on the stage and played in Kanin's *Born Yesterday* when Jean Arthur withdrew. *Adam's Rib* secured her the film of *Born Yesterday*, where she won the best actress Oscar as reliably as she did every game of rummy. She had a chance to show a more rounded character in *The Marrying Kind* (52, Cukor), but her comic business obscured that potential. Thereafter she made *It Should Happen to You* (54, Cukor); *Phffft!* (54, Mark Robson); *The Solid Gold Cadillac* (56, Richard Quine); *Full of Life* (57, Quine); and, last—after playing the role on Broadway—as the telephonist, and much more pleasingly subdued, in *Bells Are Ringing* (60, Vincente Minnelli).

Sir Ian Holm (Ian Holm Cuthbert),
b. Goodmayes, England, 1931

Around the early sixties, on stage and TV, Holm seemed like a leading actor of great potential. He was dark, thoughtful, and intense, and his Richard III at the Royal Shakespeare Company can be compared with those of Olivier and Ian McKellen. But Holm had handicaps: he liked to work regularly; he was versatile; and he was not tall. Thus he became what is known as a supporting actor, a prodigious worker, a shy comic, and a mark of reliability. The list is more even than these: *The Bofors Gun* (68, Jack Gold); *The Fixer* (68, John Frankenheimer); *Oh! What a Lovely War* (69, Richard Attenborough); as the Al Bowlly enthusiast in Dennis Potter's *Moonlight on the Highway* (69, James MacTaggart); *A Severed Head* (71, Dick Clement); *Nicholas and Alexandra* (71, Franklin Schaffner); *Mary, Queen of Scots* (71, Charles Jarrott); *Young Winston* (72, Attenborough); *The Homecoming* (73, Peter Hall); *Juggernaut* (74, Richard Lester); King John in *Robin and Marian* (76, Lester); *March or Die* (77, Dick Richards); *Alien* (79, Ridley Scott); the dour trainer in *Chariots of Fire* (81, Hugh Hudson); *The Return of the Soldier* (82, Alan Bridges); as F. R. Leavis in *The Last Romantics* (82, Jack Gold); as Napoleon in *Time Bandits* (81, Terry Gilliam); the Belgian explorer in *Greystoke* (84, Hudson); very touching as the cuckold in *Dance With a Stranger* (85, Mike Newell); *Wetherby* (85, David Hare); as Lewis Carroll in *Dreamchild* (85, Gavin Miller); *Brazil* (85, Gilliam); *Another Woman* (88, Woody Allen); *Henry V* (89, Kenneth Branagh); *Hamlet* (90, Franco Zeffirelli); *Kafka* (91, Steven Soderbergh); *Naked Lunch* (91, David Cronenberg); and *Blue Ice* (93, Russell Mulcahy).

Holm was well established: he won a supporting actor nomination for *Chariots of Fire*. Yet his growing range and volume was something to behold. Just consider the one year 1997, which offered Holm in five films—the adaptation of his National Theatre *King Lear* (Richard Eyre); *A Life Less Ordinary* (Danny Boyle); *The Fifth Element* (97, Luc Besson); and two phenomenal performances, as the insurance investigator in *The Sweet Hereafter* (97, Atom Egoyan), and as a New York cop who could have fooled Cagney in *Night Falls on Manhattan* (97, Sidney Lumet).

As well as all that, this great actor did *The Hour of the Pig* (93, Leslie Megahey); Pod in *The Borrowers* (93, John Henderson) and *The Return of the Borrowers* (93, Mary Norton); *Frankenstein* (94, Branagh); *The Madness of King George* (94, Nicholas Hytner); with his new wife, Penelope Wilton, on TV in *The Deep Blue Sea* (94); *Loch Ness* (95, Henderson); *Big Night* (96, Stanley Tucci); *eXistenZ* (99, Cronenberg); *Simon Magus* (99, Ben Hopkins); *The Match* (99, Mick Davis); *Shergar* (99, Dennis C. Lewiston); *Alice Through the Looking Glass* (99, Henderson); outstanding in *Joe Gould's Secret* (00, Tucci); the voice of Pilate in *The Miracle Maker* (00, Derek W. Hayes and Stanislav Sokolov); *Esther Kahn* (00, Arnaud Desplechin); *Beautiful Joe* (00, Stephen Metcalfe); *Bless the Child* (00, Chuck Russell); *The Last of the Blonde Bombshells* (00, Gillies MacKinnon); Napoleon in *The Emperor's New Clothes* (01, Alan Taylor); Gull in *From Hell* (01, Allen and Albert Hughes).

And then, Bilbo Baggins in *The Lord of the Rings* (01, Peter Jackson). In the first edition of this book, in 1975, I suggested—when it was too late already—what a Bilbo Cagney might have made. Now Holm has the part and it signifies the class he honors.

Seth Holt (James Holt) (1923–71), b. Palestine

1958: *Nowhere to Go.* 1961: *A Taste of Fear.* 1964: *Station Six Sahara.* 1965: *The Nanny.* 1967: *Danger Route.* 1971: *Blood from the Mummy's Tomb* (finished by Michael Carreras when Holt died).

An intimate biography of Seth Holt would make a pretty picture of the razor lining to the film industry. When he died he was engaged on his least interesting film, a merciless potboiler. He was a man of fascinating, unfulfilled projects and of a casual talent that never swallowed a film whole. It speaks for his frustration that *If. . . .* (69) was his project originally, only passed on to Lindsay Anderson when Holt began to decline. His death—from heart disease and exhaustion—was little noticed by the press. Similarly, few people remarked on the death of Holt's brother-in-law, Robert Hamer.

Despite the fact that Holt seemed unable to escape flawed, unfinished work, the creator of marvelous sequences within melodramas, he was the most gifted British director working in Britain. *Nowhere to Go* is an out-of-the-ordinary thriller (scripted by Holt and Kenneth Tynan); *A Taste of Fear* was genuinely frightening; and *Station Six Sahara* is a jittery account of sexual tension. *The Nanny* was subtle guignol and *Danger Route* an especially fragmented work. But even the cheapskate espionage of that film contains the enigmatic sequence in which Richard Johnson kills Carol Lynley.

The final disarray, complete with two abandoned films—*Diabolique* and *Monsieur LeCoq*—and a script about Bakunin (done with Al Alvarez), is the stranger because Holt served a dutiful apprenticeship. From acting, he joined Ealing in 1944 as an assistant editor. In that capacity he worked on *Return to the Vikings* (44, Charles Frend); *Champagne Charlie* (44, Alberto Cavalcanti); *Dead of Night* (45, Cavalcanti, et al.); *Hue and Cry* (46, Charles Crichton); *Scott of the Antarctic* (48, Frend); *Passport to Pimlico* (48, Henry Cornelius); *Kind Hearts and Coronets* (49, Robert Hamer); *The Lavender Hill Mob* (51, Crichton); *His Excellency* (51, Hamer); *Mandy* (52, Alexander Mackendrick); *The Titfield Thunderbolt* (52, Crichton); and *Saturday Night and Sunday Morning* (60, Karel Reisz). He was also an associate producer on Mackendrick's *The Ladykillers* (55) and Crichton's *The Man in the Sky* (56).

As a director he made many episodes for TV series and nurtured forlorn projects. His early career might have been textbook, but once he had made the grade he was antitraditional. His taste for visual excitement was more American than British, and not the least point in his favor was his skill at directing an oddly assorted range of actresses: Maggie Smith, Susan Strasberg, Carroll Baker, Bette Davis, and Carol Lynley.

Bob Hope (Leslie Townes Hope), b. Eltham, England, 1903

In 1970, Bob Hope was in London to rattle off jokes while the ladies changed costume in the Miss World competition. He was heckled by women's rights demonstrators and a bag of flour burst beside him on the stage. He looked old and anxious, both understandable. But it was a surprise that his act seized up, and the nice guy who for years had made comedy out of cowardice was transformed into a nervy reactionary shooting off inappropriate and sententious sneers at those trying to disrupt his act. "Brave men run in my family"—Painless Potter's admission in *The Paleface*—suddenly seemed relevant.

That awkward little performance confirmed Hope's shortcomings as a film comedian: the habitual reliance on prepared verbal gags; the monotony of the boaster who turns coward with the wind; and his inability to organize his films or his screen character into anything more profound than a mouthpiece for jokes written by an army of scriptwriters. Of course, at that purely mechanical level—of calculated asides, smart answers, and double takes—he can be very funny. But there is never the sense—as there is with Groucho, Fields, or even Jerry Lewis—that he sees comedy as a way of expressing or relieving anxieties, and that good lines are of secondary importance. There are no great comedians who do not occasionally admit to us what a sad business it is making people laugh.

Hope came to America at the age of four and moved from vaudeville to Broadway and, in 1934, to radio. He was such a hugely popular figure there that he was cast by Paramount in *The Big Broadcast of 1938* (38, Mitchell Leisen), singing "Thanks for the Memory" with Shirley Ross. That song became a film, directed by George Archainbaud, and after a few Martha Raye musicals—*College Swing* (38, Raoul Walsh); *Give Me a Sailor* (38, Elliott Nugent); and *Never Say Die* (39, Nugent)—he was put in *The Cat and the Canary* (39, Nugent), the first demonstration of his comedy of alarm; and *Caught in the Draft* (41, David Butler).

But it was the market for uncomplicated, companionable humor brought about by the war that really established Hope. The "Road" films are inventive without being imaginative, amusing but not penetrating, and Hope fitted perfectly with Crosby and Lamour in a bland trio: *Road to Singapore* (40, Victor Schertzinger); *Road to Zanzibar* (41, Schertzinger); *Road to Morocco* (42, Butler);

Road to Utopia (45, Hal Walker); *Road to Rio* (47, Norman Z. McLeod); and *Road to Bali* (52, Walker).

Apart from that series, Hope's career has been a largely fruitless search for material that would suit him: *Louisiana Purchase* (41, Irving Cummings); *My Favorite Blonde* (42, Sidney Lanfield); *The Princess and the Pirate* (44, Butler); *Monsieur Beaucaire* (46, George Marshall); the excellent *The Paleface* (48, McLeod), unexpectedly well matched by Jane Russell; *The Great Lover* (49, Alexander Hall); *Fancy Pants* (50, Marshall); *The Lemon Drop Kid* (51, Lanfield); *My Favorite Spy* (51, McLeod); *Son of Paleface* (52, Frank Tashlin); as Eddie Foy in *The Seven Little Foys* (55, Melville Shavelson); bemused by Katharine Hepburn in *The Iron Petticoat* (56, Ralph Thomas) and by Fernandel in *Paris Holiday* (58, Gerd Oswald); as Mayor Jimmy Walker of New York in *Beau James* (57, Shavelson); and in Paleface country again in *Alias Jesse James* (59, McLeod).

His last good partner was Lucille Ball in *The Facts of Life* (60, Melvin Frank) and *Critic's Choice* (63, Don Weis). After the ill-advised *The Road to Hong Kong* (62, Norman Panama), his films became an annual ordeal: *Call Me Bwana* (63, Gordon Douglas); *A Global Affair* (64, Jack Arnold); *I'll Take Sweden* (65, Frederick de Cordova); *Boy, Did I Get a Wrong Number!* (66, Marshall); *Eight on the Lam* (67, Marshall); *How to Commit Marriage* (69, Norman Panama); and *Cancel My Reservation* (72, Paul Bogart).

As a senior citizen, he has been devoted to golf, USO specials (still going overseas to entertain troops), and to the occasional TV special. He did cameos in *The Muppet Movie* (79, James Frawley) and *Spies Like Us* (85, John Landis), and he teamed up with Don Ameche in *A Masterpiece of Murder* (86, Charles S. Dublin), his first TV movie.

In May 2003, Hope passed his 100th birthday—the tributes were genuine and they showed what an amazing live act he had always been, live and wired.

Sir Anthony Hopkins,
b. Port Talbot, Wales, 1937

Though he grew up very consciously as a neighbor and disciple to Richard Burton, Hopkins has a range that reaches from Charles Laughton to Laurence Olivier. Belatedly, but with a sense of the obvious being made manifest at last, Hannibal Lecter in *The Silence of the Lambs* (91, Jonathan Demme) allowed the public, and the business, to see that Hopkins was that age's brilliant British actor. And, like Olivier, Hopkins's versatility, his sheer love of danger, amounts to a box-office charm never quite achieved by lovable personality. He is a loner, someone who prefers America, who works relentlessly, even if on poor projects sometimes.

He has been a momentous stage actor in England, often with the National Theatre (he auditioned before Olivier and did a scene from *Othello*): as Coriolanus and King Lear; in *M. Butterfly* and *Antony and Cleopatra;* and as Lambert Le Roux, the press tycoon, in David Hare's *Pravda.*

His movie debut was in *The Lion in Winter* (68, Anthony Harvey); he was Claudius to Nicol Williamson in *Hamlet* (69, Tony Richardson); *The Looking Glass War* (70, Frank R. Pierson); *When Eight Bells Toll* (71, Etienne Perier); Lloyd George in *Young Winston* (72, Richard Attenborough); Torvald to Claire Bloom in *A Doll's House* (73, Patrick Garland); *The Girl from Petrovka* (74, Robert Ellis Miller); *Juggernaut* (74, Richard Lester); *Audrey Rose* (77, Robert Wise); *A Bridge Too Far* (77, Attenborough); *International Velvet* (78, Bryan Forbes); and *Magic* (78, Attenborough).

He was like a boozer game for any drink, the classics or nonsense, to all of which he brought the same steadfast earnestness. In truth, when he was good it was largely because of technique and natural authority. He didn't want to be seen trying—another affinity with Olivier. But *Magic* was a real part, and a more disturbing psychopath than even Hannibal Lecter would prove. The film was a failure but the evidence showed that Hopkins had something like genius.

For a time, he lived in America, his life barely under control. As ever, his parts were unaccountable: *A Change of Seasons* (80, Richard Lang); the doctor in *The Elephant Man* (80, David Lynch); Bligh in *The Bounty* (84, Roger Donaldson); creepily pathetic in *The Good Father* (87, Mike Newell); *84 Charing Cross Road* (87, David Jones); *The Tenth Man* (88, Jack Gold); in the Alan Ayckbourn adaptation *A Chorus of Disapproval* (88, Michael Winner); and *Desperate Hours* (90, Michael Cimino).

Hopkins has admitted that Hannibal Lecter was not difficult to do, once he had found a look and a voice. Brian Cox's Lecter in *Manhunter* (86, Michael Mann) is arguably more intriguing and more frightening. Hopkins is playing to the camera, to the faint hints of a love story, to humor, and to Demme's indulgent last scene. There is something Wellesian in the ham. Still, it is as riveting and probably as influential as Anthony Perkins in *Psycho*. Hopkins took his best actor Oscar in gracious humor, knowing that when a plum falls nothing can stop it. He went on to a fine Wilcox in *Howards End* (91, James Ivory); the inane *Freejack* (91, Geoff Murphy); a cheery Van Elsing amid the *son et lumière* chaos of *Dracula* (92, Francis Coppola); and the butler in *Remains of the Day* (93, Ivory). The latter was fiendishly clever, emotional, and intricate, and it was only later that one remembered he was supposed to be playing a man who was limited, cold, and unable to express any feelings!

But this is not all. Hopkins has been a steady actor on TV, on both sides of the Atlantic, capable of winning a string of fascinating roles and acting with hushed bravura: as Pierre in the BBC *War and Peace* (72, John Davies); as the doctor in *Dark Victory*, with Elizabeth Montgomery as Bette Davis (76, Robert Butler); as Yitzhak Rabin in *Victory at Entebbe* (76, Marvin J. Chomsky); as Bruno Hauptmann in *The Lindbergh Kidnapping Case* (76, Buzz Kulik); as the great actor *Kean* (78, James Cellan Jones); as *Othello* (81, Jonathan Miller); as Hitler in *The Bunker* (81, George Schaefer); as St. Paul in *Peter and Paul* (81, Robert Day); as Quasimodo in *The Hunchback of Notre Dame* (82, Michael Tuchman); as Count Ciano in *Mussolini: The Decline and Fall of Il Duce* (85, Alberto Negrin); in *Hollywood Wives* (85, Day); *Guilty Conscience* (85, David Greene); redoing Boyer in *Arch of Triumph* (85, Waris Hussein); a superb Guy Burgess in *Blunt* (86, John Glenister); and as a persecuted Paraguayan in *One Man's War* (91, Sergio Toledo).

The Queen knighted him on January 1, 1993, while she still had the chance, before he played Queen Victoria—or, one guesses, before she'd seen the dire *Chaplin* (92, Attenborough) in which Hopkins plays the publisher with a few small narrative problems to sort out with the great man.

At the end of 1993, he did an artful job playing C. S. Lewis in *Shadowlands* (Attenborough)— though this was close to the butler from *Remains of the Day* promoted to a don. Hopkins must be wary of playing this character too often.

Indeed, his brilliance and ease may be his greatest threats, for he can be cast as nearly anything—especially if one is to feel far mountains and close-up sighs and tics in the character's mental landscape. There's not another actor around better equipped to take on large, eccentric characters, or with so little fuss. So it's important to stress his failures, as well as the projects hardly worth the trouble. In other words, Hopkins will be big in a picture, whatever you give him. Answer: make sure the part and the challenge are big.

He is whimsical, happy to move from small ventures, like playing writer Gwyn Thomas in *Selected Exits* (93, Tristram Powell) on BBC TV to the patriarch in *Legends of the Fall* (94, Edward Zwick), a movie that lacked the O'Neill-like horizons the actor saw. The same slippage hurt *The Road to Wellville* (94, Alan Parker), and then, more fatally, *Nixon* (96, Oliver Stone), where his inordinate resources could not dispel our collective history with that man. He directed and acted in *August* (96), which was a cosy Welsh version of *Uncle Vanya;* the awful *Surviving Picasso* (96, Ivory); the amusing *The Edge* (97, Lee Tamahori); a meticulous John Quincy Adams

in *Amistad* (97, Steven Spielberg); lazy and lovely in *The Mask of Zorro* (98, Mark Campbell); *Meet Joe Black* (98, Martin Brest); *Instinct* (99, Jon Turteltaub); very good in *Titus* (99, Julie Taymor); uncredited in *Mission: Impossible II* (00, John Woo).

And then, just as he was beginning to seem on automatic, or doing it for the check, along came *Hannibal* (01, Ridley Scott), where it is his exquisite performance that lets the film become a delicate tribute to lost love and rare expertise. But then there was *Hearts in Atlantis* (01, Scott Hicks); and there will soon be *The Devil and Daniel Webster* (02, Alec Baldwin); Lecter again in *Red Dragon* (02, Brett Ratner); *Bad Company* (02, Joel Schumacher); with Nicole Kidman in *The Human Stain* (03, Robert Benton).

Miriam Hopkins (1902–72),
b. Bainbridge, Georgia

The career of Miriam Hopkins is curiously curtailed, almost as if her reputation for being difficult to work with eventually caught up with her. But in the 1930s she was a leading actress, crackling in comedy, and capable of real ferocity. There was always a glittering, choleric intensity about her, a sense of pride and superiority that often seemed to be reflecting on the listless films she had to make.

Educated at Syracuse University, she was a dancer and then a stage actress before a movie debut in *Fast and Loose* (31, Fred Newmeyer). Paramount signed her up and she excelled in *The Smiling Lieutenant* (31, Ernst Lubitsch); *Two Kinds of Women* (32, William C. De Mille); glowingly carnal as the barmaid in *Dr. Jekyll and Mr. Hyde* (32, Rouben Mamoulian); in *The World and the Flesh* (32, John Cromwell); outstanding and razorlike in *Trouble in Paradise* (32, Lubitsch); on loan to MGM for *Stranger's Return* (33, King Vidor); in *Design for Living* (33, Lubitsch); and *All of Me* (34, James Flood).

Samuel Goldwyn put her under contract when her time at Paramount elapsed, but hardly used her profitably. He loaned her out for *The Richest Girl in the World* (35, William A. Seiter), and to Mamoulian to play *Becky Sharp* (35)—good, but a little eclipsed by the attention to the novel Technicolor process. Goldwyn then wasted her in *Barbary Coast* (35, Howard Hawks) and *Splendor* (35, Elliott Nugent), but did better by her in *These Three* (36, William Wyler), a bowdlerized version of Lillian Hellman's *The Children's Hour.* She was loaned to Alexander Korda for *Men Are Not Gods* (37, Walter Reisch); and to RKO for *Wise Girl* (37, Leigh Jason) and *The Woman I Love* (37, Anatole Litvak, to whom she was briefly married). For Goldwyn, she made *Woman Chases Man* (37, John Blystone), and then joined Warners for *The Old Maid* (39, Edmund Goulding), *Vir-*

ginia City (40, Michael Curtiz), *The Lady With Red Hair* (40, Curtis Bernhardt), and in lifelong rivalry with Bette Davis in *Old Acquaintance* (43, Vincent Sherman).

At this point, she returned to the theatre and made only a few more movies in character parts: as Aunt Penniman in *The Heiress* (49, Wyler); *The Mating Season* (51, Mitchell Leisen); *The Outcasts of Poker Flat* (52, Joseph H. Newman); the hateful wife in *Carrie* (52, Wyler); as the aunt in a remade *The Children's Hour* (62, Wyler); a German *Fanny Hill* (64, Russ Meyer); as Bubber's hysterical mother in *The Chase* (66, Arthur Penn); and *Comeback* (70, Donald Wolfe).

Dennis Hopper,
b. Dodge City, Kansas, 1936
1969: *Easy Rider* (codirected with Peter Fonda). 1971: *The Last Movie*. 1980: *Out of the Blue*. 1988: *Colors*. 1990: *Backtrack; The Hot Spot*. 1994: *Chasers*.

In the middle 1980s, Dennis Hopper underwent a much publicized "recovery." He admitted to years of drugs and drink—to say nothing of impossible ambitions as actor, artist, and spirit of the 1960s. He had a run of interesting parts that seemed to bear out this rehabilitation, by far the best of which was *Blue Velvet* (86, David Lynch), where his Frank Booth is both a roaring villain and, eventually, a psychosexual infant who is father to Kyle McLachlan's son. There was a nakedness in the performance, especially in his spied-upon scenes with Isabella Rossellini, in which Hopper's unquestioned daring was more under control than he had ever managed before. It was a terrific performance, and it seemed to signal a new maturity in the man, even if some people who supposedly knew looked at Frank, and said, "Yes, that's how Dennis Hopper is."

I treasure his work in *Blue Velvet;* I think that *Out of the Blue* is a painfully eloquent myth about incest, despite all its pretensions; I found Hopper credible and effective as the father in *Rumble Fish* (83, Francis Coppola) and as *Paris Trout* (91, Stephen Gyllenhaal) for TV. But there is so much else to endure.

In this writer's considered opinion, Dennis Hopper was an ardent young man fatally unlucky to cross the path of James Dean—in *Rebel Without a Cause* (55, Nicholas Ray) and *Giant* (56, George Stevens). He believed he was somehow the heir to something. He knew he wanted to act, and he believed rebellion was some proof of artistic integrity. Much of Hollywood—Henry Hathaway most famously—found Hopper a pain in the neck. Let spectators simply observe that the young actor was staring, strident, and monotonous. He was not capable of the intricacy or the intimacy that made Dean so remarkable: *I Died a*

Thousand Times (55, Stuart Heisler); *Gunfight at the O.K. Corral* (57, John Sturges); *Sayonara* (57, Joshua Logan); *The Story of Mankind* (57, Irwin Allen); *From Hell to Texas* (58, Hathaway); *The Young Land* (59, Ted Tetzlaff); *Key Witness* (60, Phil Karlson); *Night Tide* (63, Curtis Harrington); *The Sons of Katie Elder* (65, Hathaway); *Queen of Blood* (66, Harrington); *Cool Hand Luke* (67, Stuart Rosenberg); *The Trip* (67, Roger Corman); *The Glory Stompers* (67, Anthony M. Lanza); *Hang 'em High* (68, Ted Post); *Panic in the City* (68, Eddie Davis); and *True Grit* (69, Hathaway).

Then came *Easy Rider*, a disaster in the history of film to set beside the loss of Technicolor, the invention of gross participation, the early death of Murnau, and the longevity of Richard Attenborough. Millions would dispute all of this: they saw *Easy Rider* over and over, until the movie was scarcely distinguishable from the haze in the auditorium. In the process, "youth" was given the kingdom—not just as filmmakers, but as the controlling element in the audience; incoherence became sensitive; drugginess was for a time a mainstream mode; and every studio drove itself stupid trying to repeat the hit. Dennis Hopper became a genius, and very rich.

This did have the advantage of letting him do less. Indeed, he labored over *The Last Movie*, a title that flattered to deceive, but which remains a marker for pretentious nonsense. He acted in *Kid Blue* (73, James Frawley); *Mad Dog* (76, Philippe Mora); he was decent as the soldier in *Tracks* (76, Henry Jaglom); opaque in *The American Friend* (77, Wim Wenders); and stranglable in *Apocalypse Now* (79, Coppola).

Out of the Blue was a picture in which he had been hired only as an actor. He took over the direction at the last moment from coproducer and cowriter, Leonard Yakir. With a fine dead-eyed performance from Linda Manz, and an agonized one from Hopper, the symbolic associations are kept under restraint. The picture works.

Hopper acted in *Wild Times* (80, Richard Compton) on TV; *King of the Mountain* (81, Noel Nosseck); *Human Highway* (82, Bernard Shakey); *The Osterman Weekend* (85, Sam Peckinpah); *My Science Project* (85, Jonathan Beteul); *Riders of the Storm* (86, Maurice Phillips); as an alcoholic in *Hoosiers* (86, David Anspaugh), for which he got a supporting actor Oscar nomination; *The Texas Chainsaw Massacre Part 2* (86, Tobe Hooper); *Stark: Mirror Image* (86, Nosseck) for TV; the shortest-lived husband in *Black Widow* (87, Bob Rafelson); *River's Edge* (87, Tim Hunter); *O.C. & Stiggs* (87, Robert Altman); *Straight to Hell* (87, Alex Cox); and *The Pick-up Artist* (87, James Toback).

Colors was a routine cops versus gangs story set in L.A. *Backtrack* and *The Hot Spot* have been hack jobs, the one briefly illuminated by Jodie

Foster, the other exactly what a Don Johnson–Virginia Madsen pairing would lead one to expect. Hopper still acts—he is in *Backtrack*, as well as *Blood Red* (88, Peter Masterson); *Chattahoochee* (90, Mick Jackson); *Flashback* (90, Frank Amurri); *Doublecrossed* (91, Roger Young); *The Indian Runner* (91, Sean Penn—who acted in *Colors*); *Nails* (92, John Flynn); *The Heart of Justice* (93, Bruno Baretto); *Boiling Point* (93, James B. Harris); *True Romance* (93, Tony Scott); *Red Rock West* (93, John Dahl); and *Speed* (94, Jan De Bont).

Late in 1993, he did a series of commercials for Nike, playing a football freak, so precise, so funny, and so daring (and perverse—sniffing Bruce Smith's shoe), they may be his finest work.

Well, the legend of Hopper as a director seems to have been put away. As for his acting, it is a grim sequence in which, in his sixties, he has returned to a worse form of the stuff in which he spent the sixties. But here's the true rub: in one film—*Carried Away* (96, Barreto)—he was not just good, but marvelous (as well as quiet, shy, anxious, and simple). That makes this toll all the more nightmarish: *Witch Hunt* (94, Paul Schrader); *Search and Destroy* (95, David Sale); *Waterworld* (95, Kevin Reynolds); *Basquiat* (96, Julian Schnabel); *Samson and Delilah* (96, Nicolas Roeg); *The Blackout* (97, Abel Ferrara); *Road Ends* (97, Rick King); *Top of the World* (97, Sidney J. Furie); *Meet the Deedles* (98, Steve Boyum); *Michael Angel* (98, William Gove); as William S. Burroughs in *The Source* (99, Chuck Workman); *EdTV* (99, Ron Howard); *Straight Shooter* (99, Thomas Bohn); *Jesus' Son* (99, Alison Maclean); *The Venice Project* (99, Robert Dornhelm); *Bad City Blues* (99, Michael Stevens); *Lured Innocence* (99, Kikuo Kawasaki); *Luck of the Draw* (00, Luca Bercovici); *Held for Ransom* (00, Lee Stanley); *The Spreading Ground* (00, Derek Van Lint); *Ticker* (01, Albert Pyun); *Unspeakable* (01, Thomas J. Wright); *Leo* (02, Mehdi Norowzian); *The Piano Player* (02, Jean-Pierre Roux); as Frank Sinatra in *The Night We Called It a Day* (03, Paul Goldman).

Bob Hoskins,
b. Bury St. Edmunds, England, 1942

Twice at least, Bob Hoskins has commanded the perilous ground at the center of extraordinary ventures. In the one, *Pennies From Heaven* (81, Piers Haggard, for British TV), he was the essential bond between drama and song; and in the other, *Who Framed Roger Rabbit?* (88, Robert Zemeckis), he was the character who talked to humans and toons—and had a hard time with both. Perhaps the bursting energy of Hoskins needs some unusual challenge, some heightening of forms. Asked to do no more than act, he can seem too much of a good thing, especially when

trying to be sympathetic. In *Roger Rabbit*, it is particularly useful that the technological tensions required him to underplay. His energy is so great that it shines forth. But when the little man feels bound to generate, to mime, to signal—then some viewers need to back away.

He had small parts in *The National Health* (73, Jack Gold); in Dennis Potter's *Schmoedipus* (74, Barry Davis); *Royal Flash* (75, Richard Lester); *Inserts* (75, John Byrum); and *Zulu Dawn* (79, Douglas Hickox), before he made an explosive impact as the gangster in the overblown *The Long Good Friday* (80, John Mackenzie). He was then Iago to Anthony Hopkins's *Othello* (81, Jonathan Miller); *Pink Floyd—The Wall* (82, Alan Parker); *Beyond the Limit* (83, Mackenzie); very effective as Owney Madden in *The Cotton Club* (84, Francis Coppola); *Lassiter* (84, Roger Young); *Brazil* (85, Terry Gilliam); *The Dunera Boys* (85, Sam Lewin) for Australian TV; as Il Duce for TV in *Mussolini* (85, Alberto Negrin); verging too much on pathos in *Mona Lisa* (86, Neil Jordan); *Sweet Liberty* (86, Alan Alda); *The Lonely Passion of Judith Hearne* (87, Jack Clayton); rather painful as the priest in *A Prayer for the Dying* (87, Mike Hodges).

He acted in and directed the antiwar picture *The Raggedy Rawney* (88), and he has acted in *Major League* (89, David S. Ward); *Heart Condition* (90, James D. Perriott); *Mermaids* (90, Richard Benjamin); as Smee in *Hook* (91, Steven Spielberg); *Shattered* (91, Wolfgang Peterson); *The Favor, the Watch and the Very Big Fish* (92, Ben Levin); *Passed Away* (92, Charlie Peters); and *Super Mario Brothers* (93, Rocky Morton and Annabel Jankel).

Around this time one noted the stealthy way in which Hoskins was collecting the roles of leaders in modern history. He had done Mussolini already. He was Beria in *The Inner Circle* (92, Andrei Kochalovsky). Just ahead was his Churchill in the fatuous *World War II: When Lions Roared* (94, Joseph Sargent). Keep alert: *The Big Freeze* (93, Eric Sykes); *The Changeling* (94, Simon Curtis); J. Edgar Hoover in *Nixon* (95, Oliver Stone); *Rainbow* (95, which he directed); *The Secret Agent* (96, Christopher Hampton); *Michael* (96, Nora Ephron); *Twentyfour Seven* (97, Shane Meadows); *Cousin Bette* (98, Des McAnuff); *Parting Shots* (98, Michael Winner); *Captain Jack* (98, Robert Young); *A Room for Romeo Brass* (99, Meadows); *The White River Kid* (99, Arne Glimcher); Micawber in *David Copperfield* (99, Curtis); *Felicia's Journey* (99, Atom Egoyan); *American Virgin* (00, Jean-Pierre Marois); as Manuel Noriega in *Noriega: God's Favorite* (00, Roger Spottiswoode); as Sancho Panza in *Don Quixote* (00, Peter Yates); Nikita Khrushchev in *Enemy at the Gates* (01, Jean-Jacques Annaud); excellent in *Last Orders* (01, Fred Schepisi);

Where Eskimos Live (02, Tomasz Wiszniewski).

With six biggies already, he could easily make ten—The Harold Wilson Story? Gorbachev? Justice Scalia? A Pope Looks Back?

Hou Hsiao-Hsien, b. Meixian, China, 1947
1980: *Jiushi Liuliu De Ta/Cute Girl.* 1981: *Feng Er Ti Ta Cai/Cheerful Wind.* 1983: *Zai Na Hepan Quingcao Qing/The Green, Green Grass of Home; Fengkuei-lai-te Jen/All the Youthful Days; Erzi De Dawan'ou/The Sandwich Man.* 1984: *Dongdong De Jiaqi/A Summer at Grandpa's.* 1985: *Tong Nien Wang Shi/The Time to Live and the Time to Die.* 1986: *Lianlian Fengchen/Dust in the Wind.* 1987: *Niluohe Nuer/Daughter of the Nile.* 1989: *Beiqing Chengshi/City of Sadness.* 1993: *Hsimeng Jensheng/The Puppetmaster.* 1995: *Haonan Haonu/Good Men, Good Women.* 1996: *Nanguo Zaijan, Nanguo/Goodbye South, Goodbye.* 1998: *Hai Shang Hua/Flowers of Shanghai.* 2001: *Qianxi Manbo/Millennium Mambo.*

Ang Lee and Hou Hsiao-Hsien are just seven years apart in age. Ang Lee was actually born in Taiwan, whereas Hou arrived there only at the age of one, brought by parents escaping the Communist upheaval in China. Yet, by now, Ang Lee is one of the best-known directors in the world, the bold master of so many supposedly foreign idioms, while Hou is hardly known outside the narrow circuit of international film festivals. He is also a person who travels reluctantly, and who therefore finds his material in the experience of Taiwan. As Godfrey Cheshire put it, "Taiwan looks at itself in Hou's films and confronts indeterminacy: people, places, and eras caught always in the flux of becoming something else." Yet might not the very same words apply to the anguish or the uncertainty in the best works by Ang Lee?

What I'm trying to suggest is that, increasingly as the medium grows older, so great filmmaking is invariably an urge to resist the massive, stupid, melodramatic, and false certainties of the medium, and the wish to stay loyal to doubt, quandary, and indeterminacy. Yet that steady need to use the camera to see, or to discover, infinite question as opposed to reliable message is more than ever at odds with the terrible commercial overloading of filmmaking. So, is it braver of Ang Lee to travel or of Hou to stay home? Which strategy has the better chance of deeper self-awareness, for them and for us?

Yet if one has the feeling that the Hou of *The Time to Live and the Time to Die, City of Sadness,* and *The Puppetmaster* is that of the highest mastery, how easy is it for the ordinary reader (I mean the conventional filmgoer) to find those films (on video, let alone at a theatre)? Which only leads to the question of whether the best of film can remain a universal art, or must it become as confined and elitist as, say, poetry, modern music, and the experimental novel? Not the least reason for asking that is because I don't think film can actually compete with those narrow forms.

Hou is an extraordinary director—gentle, reflective, beautifully composed, inclined to hold his shots in space and duration. He exemplifies that natural, fluent style that unites so many of the most thoughtful directors. I urge any reader to seek out his work, in whatever form it can be found. I accept the criticism that he should have been in the previous edition of this book. And I regret all the ways in which the "internationalism" of the film world (and of your chance to see a picture) has actually been a loss of variety, richness, and difficulty. But I wonder, too, if the vitality of the medium is not always going to depend on those phenomena—from Chaplin to Spielberg—who can assert an astonishing sharing (and vulgarization) in human experience. In a real sense, it is a matter of whether cultures like those of Taiwan and Iran (and smaller places still—say, Bloomsbury, or Berkeley, California) can actually survive in our global village, as one gigantic screen dominates the world?

John Houseman (Jacques Haussmann) (1902–88), b. Bucharest, Rumania
The regrettable lack of personal memoirs from movie people that are literate, characteristic, and halfway frank was illustrated by the publication, in 1972, of Houseman's *Run-Through*. Perhaps its intelligence and enterprise are alien to the role of movie producer. Yet Houseman was in or around film production for some thirty years and contrived to nurse along an impressive list of works. *Run-Through* and its two sequels, *Front & Center* and *Final Dress*, comprise one of the best autobiographies in show business—honest, detailed, well written, generous without being sentimental, firm without sinking to cruelty.

Houseman's most significant part in film history may be the way he coaxed Herman Mankiewicz—on the wagon with a broken leg—into writing the screenplay of *Citizen Kane*. Houseman describes the scriptwriting modestly, but the scenario has the qualities of subtle structure, dialogue, and character that he is most likely to have learned in theatre and radio. Of course, the film is Welles's, just as the screenplay is Mankiewicz's. Producers may be no more than potentially destructive, interfering creatures. Houseman on *Kane* looks like a good example of how to skirt that odious potential, and, instead, ease the path of a volatile project. How he thought Welles or RKO might evade the wrath of Hearst is another matter. It is clear from his books that Houseman was so moved by Welles and his recklessness that sometimes he just wanted to see what the boy would do next.

Houseman was the son of an English mother

and a father from Alsace. After he went to school at Clifton, he traveled to Argentina before moving into the American theatre. His notable work as a stage producer led, in 1937, to his founding of the Mercury Theater with Welles. Houseman admired Welles's talent deeply and took to mollifying the tender ego of his young compatriot. Their years together were hectically rich and, even if they parted angrily, *Kane* seems to have implanted an interest in movies in Houseman.

In 1941, he became a vice-president to David Selznick and did packaging work on *Saboteur* (42, Alfred Hitchcock) and *Jane Eyre* (44, Robert Stevenson) before he moved on to *Voice of America*. After the war, however, he shared his time between the theatre, the cinema, and, latterly, TV. He was an independent producer with attachments to Paramount, RKO, and MGM: *The Unseen* (45, Lewis Allen); *Miss Susie Slagle's* (46, John Berry); *The Blue Dahlia* (46, George Marshall); *They Live By Night* (48, Nicholas Ray); *Letter From an Unknown Woman* (48, Max Ophuls); *The Company She Keeps* (50, John Cromwell); *On Dangerous Ground* (51, Ray); *The Bad and the Beautiful* (52, Vincente Minnelli); *Julius Caesar* (53, Joseph L. Mankiewicz); *Executive Suite* (54, Robert Wise); *Her Twelve Men* (54, Robert Z. Leonard); *Moonfleet* (55, Fritz Lang); *The Cobweb* (55, Minnelli); *Lust for Life* (56, Minnelli); *All Fall Down* (62, John Frankenheimer); *Two Weeks in Another Town* (62, Minnelli); and *In the Cool of the Day* (63, Robert Stevens).

Four of Minnelli's best, Nicholas Ray's debut, and Ophuls' finest American picture make a tremendous record. Yet another career opened up when Houseman played a Harvard Law School professor in *The Paper Chase* (73, James Bridges)—and won the supporting actor Oscar. This encouraged him to act again, in *Rollerball* (75, Norman Jewison); *Three Days of the Condor* (75, Sydney Pollack); and *St. Ives* (76, J. Lee Thompson). He had great success in the TV series of *Paper Chase* and then appeared in *The Cheap Detective* (78, Robert Moore) and *Old Boyfriends* (79, Joan Tewkesbury).

The TV series promoted Houseman to prominent TV commercials (notably for Smith, Barney: "They make money the old-fashioned way—they earn it."). Thus in his last decade, Houseman became a recognized figure, and a much-trusted man. He appeared in *A Christmas Without Snow* (80, John Korty); *Wholly Moses!* (80, Gary Weis); *My Bodyguard* (80, Tony Bill); *Murder by 'Phone* (80, Michael Anderson); *The Fog* (80, John Carpenter); he produced and acted in *Gideon's Trumpet* (80, Robert Collins); *Ghost Story* (81, John Irvin); *Scrooged* (88, Richard Donner); and *Another Woman* (89, Woody Allen).

Leslie Howard (Leslie Howard Stainer)
(1893–1943), b. London

He was the son of Hungarian immigrants. The great reputation that Howard enjoyed seems remote to a generation that knows him only through revivals of *Gone With the Wind*. His Ashley Wilkes in that film is such a nonentity, and the comparison with Gable so diminishing, that one wonders not only what people saw in Howard, but how Selznick's epic ever survived. No matter that central Europe haunted his features, Hollywood adopted him as its shyest English gentleman and as the epitome of class. Britain fell for this image a little later but devoured it wholesale after his patriotic wartime movies and his death, shot down in a plane from Lisbon to London. There has always been the scent of mystery about that death. Had Howard been used as a decoy—he was on a government mission—to divert attention from Churchill who was also flying that day? It is the sort of heroic sacrifice that a whey-faced exile from land-locked Hungary might have dreamed of.

Howard was educated at Dulwich College, and after working in a bank and suffering shell shock in the First World War he recalled that that school had been founded by an actor. He soon established himself as a leading player in London and New York, playing *Her Cardboard Lover* opposite Tallulah Bankhead and producing a play of his own, *Tell Me The Truth*. One of his stage successes had been in *Outward Bound*, a strange postwar blues production about a liner full of dead souls. Warners elected to film it in 1930 and invited Howard to take the lead, directed by Robert Milton. After that, MGM acquired him for *Never the Twain Shall Meet* (31, W. S. Van Dyke), *Five and Ten* (31, Robert Z. Leonard), and *A Free Soul* (31, Clarence Brown). For a few years he shifted between England—*Service for Ladies* (32, Alexander Korda) and *The Lady Is Willing* (34, Gilbert Miller)—and America—*Devotion* (31, Robert Milton); *Smilin' Through* (32, Sidney Franklin); *The Animal Kingdom* (32, Edward H. Griffith); *Secrets* (33, Frank Borzage); *Captured!* (33, Roy del Ruth); and *Berkeley Square* (33, Frank Lloyd).

In 1934, he signed for Warners and made *British Agent* (Michael Curtiz) before being loaned to RKO for *Of Human Bondage* (34, John Cromwell, with Bette Davis), and to Korda for Sir Percy Blakeney in *The Scarlet Pimpernel* (34, Harold Young)—a costume romance in keeping with Howard's fragility. He was well cast as the half-baked writer in *The Petrified Forest* (36, Archie Mayo), and partly responsible for Bogart's being in that film; but horribly exposed in MGM's *Romeo and Juliet* (36, George Cukor), a film that, remarkably, did not harm his reputation. Warners limited him to modern-day dress comedy: *It's*

Love I'm After (37, Tay Garnett) and, in 1938, Howard returned to Britain to act in and codirect (with Anthony Asquith) *Pygmalion*. His Higgins is cold, like so many of Shaw's intellectuals, but he carried the film's wit with great ease.

His last films in Hollywood were both for Selznick: *Gone With the Wind* (39, Victor Fleming) and *Intermezzo* opposite Ingrid Bergman (39, which he coproduced with Gregory Ratoff)—the latter as generous to Howard as the former was unflattering. At this point he returned to an England at war and became not only one of the most active of producer-directors, but something of an emotional figurehead: *Pimpernel Smith* (39, actor and director); *49th Parallel* (41, Michael Powell) in which he is a humanist in a wigwam, reading Thomas Mann and gloating over a Picasso; *The Lamp Still Burns* (41, producer); *The First of the Few* (42, director and actor—as R. J. Mitchell, the inventor of the Spitfire); and *The Gentle Sex* (43, codirector, with Maurice Elvey).

Ron Howard, b. Duncan, Oklahoma, 1954
1977: *Grand Theft Auto*. 1982: *Night Shift*. 1984: *Splash*. 1985: *Cocoon*. 1986: *Gung Ho*. 1988: *Willow*. 1989: *Parenthood*. 1991: *Backdraft*. 1992: *Far and Away*. 1994: *The Paper*. 1995: *Apollo 13*. 1996: *Ransom*. 1999: *Ed TV*. 2000: *How the Grinch Stole Christmas*. 2001: *A Beautiful Mind*.

Ron Howard is the exemplary child given over to the Society of Jesus called Hollywood. The son of actors, he was a regular in a hit TV series, *The Andy Griffith Show*, from the ages of six to fourteen. He played the ideal, freckled American boy—Tom Sawyer without the wit—safe, satisfying, and sedulous about every item of American faith that was being dismantled in the 1960s.

Then he was the central youth, already equipped with a girlfriend for life, in *American Graffiti* (73, George Lucas), the movie that inaugurated a culture, of which *Happy Days* is a key part. On TV, that show lasted a decade, from Nixon to Reagan, yet oblivious of all but the securely small and local concerns that advertisers would wish upon the young man growing up.

In the process, by the age of thirty, Ron Howard was folkloric. He had more hours of moving-image time to his name than anyone of his age. He was hugely popular in the business—and he seems flawlessly likeable and unthreatening. Why should anyone be threatening, you ask, or adventurous, or difficult? There's no good reason at all—unless such wayward thoughts take you.

He was a good child actor, and tolerable as a teenager; and he is a proficient director of mild entertainments that make people feel good about their fellows. It's just that I could scream.

As a movie actor, he was in *The Journey* (59, Anatole Litvak); *The Music Man* (62, Morton Da

Costa); very good in *The Courtship of Eddie's Father* (63, Vincente Minnelli); *Village of the Giants* (65, Bert I. Gordon); *The Wild Country* (71, Robert Totten); *Happy Mother's Day, Love George* (73, Darren McGavin); *The Spikes Gang* (74, Richard Fleischer); *The First Nudie Musical* (76, Mark Haggard); *Eat My Dust* (76, Charles Griffith); *The Shootist* (76, Don Siegel); and *More American Graffiti* (79, B. W. L. Norton).

As a director, there is fun and novelty in his early work: Daryl Hannah could not ask for better than *Splash*; *Cocoon* did raise the dread topic of old age; and no one has looked at flame with the awe of *Backdraft*. But such virtues pale in the larger blandness of the works. His record shows just how much of a market there is for what Howard does, but I can hardly watch such profit with pleasure.

It must be said that, through his company, Imagine, Howard has begun to lend his reputation as a producer or executive producer to far less viable projects: *No Man's Land* (87, Peter Werner); *Clean and Sober* (88, Glenn Gordon Caron); *The Burbs* (89, Joe Dante); and *Closet Land* (91, Radha Bharadway).

He directs big films now, even if most of them seem derived from prior works or topical situations. But *The Grinch* was very unusual, and a huge success, and *A Beautiful Mind* was an unusual exploration of inner worlds, even if it settled for a false kindliness. Just as it won best picture, so Howard is a Thalberg Award winner one day—and a deserved one: he makes Hollywood feel better about itself. And these days that is a tough trick. Of course, it might be better for the artist in Howard if he felt less settled or secure about things—about everything.

Trevor Howard (1913–87),
b. Cliftonville, England
Educated at Clifton and RADA. He worked on the stage from 1934–40, when he joined the army. In 1943, having been wounded, he returned to the theatre and to his film debut in Carol Reed's *The Way Ahead* (44). When one considers Howard the actor—a candid, scathing personality—it is remarkable to discover how very few good films he made. In part, this was the dilemma of an English actor reluctant to commit himself to Hollywood, but it must also owe something to persistently bad selection by Howard himself.

He is another rarity in that his first English films are better than anything he did later: Asquith's *The Way to the Stars* (45), David Lean's *Brief Encounter* (45), in which he and Celia Johnson stood for the love lives of the unglamorous, and Carol Reed's *The Third Man* (49), three quite distinct and interesting Howards; and he seems to have had a strong personal commitment to Reed's *Outcast of the Islands* (51), and especially to

George More O'Ferrall's adaptation of Graham Greene's *The Heart of the Matter* (53). In these years, he also made *I See a Dark Stranger* (46, Frank Launder); *Green for Danger* (46, Sidney Gilliat); *So Well Remembered* (47, Edward Dmytryk); *They Made Me a Fugitive* (47, Alberto Cavalcanti); *The Passionate Friends* (49, Lean); *Odette* (50, Herbert Wilcox); *The Golden Salamander* (50, Ronald Neame); and *The Clouded Yellow* (50, Ralph Thomas).

His choice of larger parts, however, sometimes seemed willfully inconsequential and the films were invariably blighted: José Ferrer's *Cockleshell Heroes* (56); Reed's *The Key* (58); Huston's *The Roots of Heaven* (58); as Bligh in Milestone's *Mutiny on the Bounty* (62). He was good in Guy Hamilton's *Manuela* (57) and as the father in Jack Cardiff's *Sons and Lovers* (60), but gradually he slipped into supporting or cameo parts, often playing morose, recalcitrant men: *The Lion* (62, Cardiff); Ralph Nelson's *Father Goose* (64); Mark Robson's *Von Ryan's Express* (65); Bernhard Wicki's *Morituri* (65); Ken Annakin's *The Long Duel* (66); Hamilton's *The Battle of Britain* (69); the dreadful *Twinky* (69, Richard Donner); and *The Night Visitor* (71, Laslo Benedek). Only three performances stand out in this waste: a willful and randy eccentric in *The Charge of the Light Brigade* (68, Tony Richardson); as the priest in David Lean's *Ryan's Daughter* (69); as Dr. Rank to Jane Fonda in *A Doll's House* (73, Joseph Losey). Otherwise, there was *The Count of Monte-Cristo* (74, David Greene); *Hennessy* (75, Don Sharp); Squire Western in *The Bawdy Adventures of Tom Jones* (75, Cliff Owen); *Death in the Sun* (75, Jurgen Goslar); *Conduct Unbecoming* (75, Michael Anderson); *Aces High* (76, Jack Gold); *The Last Remake of Beau Geste* (77, Marty Feldman); *Slavers* (77, Goslar); *Stevie* (78, Robert Enders); *Superman* (78, Richard Donner); and *Hurricane* (79, Jan Troell).

He was very good as a boozy aristocrat in *Sir Henry at Rawlinson End* (80, Steve Roberts); *The Sea Wolves* (80, Andrew V. McLaglen); as an Indian chief in *Windwalker* (80, Keith Merrill); *Light Years* (81, Alain Tanner); as a judge in *Gandhi* (82, Richard Attenborough); reunited with Celia Johnson in *Staying On* (82, Silvio Narizzano); *Inside the Third Reich* (82, Marvin J. Chomsky); *The Missionary* (82, Richard Loncraine); *Sword of the Valiant* (85, Stephen Weeks); very good in *Dust* (85, Marion Hansel); *Time After Time* (85, Bill Hays); *Christmas Eve* (86, Stuart Cooper); *Foreign Body* (86, Neame); *Peter the Great* (86, Chomsky and Lawrence Schiller); *White Mischief* (88, Michael Radford); and *The Dawning* (88, Robert Knights).

William K. Howard (1899–1954), b. St. Marys, Ohio

1921: *What Love Will Do; Get Your Man* (codirected with George W. Hill); *Play Square.* 1922: *Extra! Extra!; Deserted at the Altar* (codirected with Al Kelley); *Lucky Dan; The Crusader; Captain Fly-by-Night; Trooper O'Neil.* 1923: *Danger Ahead; The Fourth Musketeer; Let's Go.* 1924: *The Border Legion; East of Broadway.* 1925: *Code of the West; The Light of Western Stars; The Thundering Herd.* 1926: *Volcano; Red Dice; Bachelor Brides; Gigolo.* 1927: *White Gold; The Main Event.* 1928: *The River Pirate; A Ship Comes In.* 1929: *Christina; The Valiant; Love, Live and Laugh.* 1930: *Good Intentions; Scotland Yard.* 1931: *Don't Bet on Women; Transatlantic; Surrender.* 1932: *The Trial of Vivienne Ware; The First Year; Sherlock Holmes.* 1933: *The Power and the Glory.* 1934: *The Cat and the Fiddle; This Side of Heaven; Evelyn Prentice.* 1935: *Vanessa; Rendezvous; Mary Burns, Fugitive.* 1936: *The Princess Comes Across.* 1937: *Fire Over England; The Squeaker.* 1939: *Back Door to Heaven.* 1940: *Money and the Woman.* 1941: *Bullets for O'Hara.* 1942: *Klondike Fury.* 1943: *Johnny Come Lately.* 1944: *When the Lights Go On Again.* 1945: *A Guy Could Change.*

After war service, Howard worked on the sales side for Vitagraph and Universal, and then became an assistant director. During the 1920s, he was with Fox, Paramount, De Mille, and Fox again. But in 1934 he joined MGM for a year. After a brief spell at Paramount he went to England to make the patriotic Tudor epic, *Fire Over England,* and an Edgar Wallace adaptation, *The Squeaker.* On returning to America, he found it hard to get back into first features. He moved from one studio to another and only *Johnny Come Lately,* with Cagney, was as important as his earlier work.

In fact, Howard made several good pictures, so that the decline is all the stranger. As a director of silents, he was generally confined to the athletic adventures of Richard Talmadge and Rod La Rocque. But with sound he became much more polished. Clive Brook made an authoritative Sherlock Holmes, while *The First Year* was a successful Janet Gaynor/Charles Farrell film. *The Power and the Glory,* from a Preston Sturges script, was an ambitious study of a tycoon, sometimes regarded as a forerunner of *Kane. Evelyn Prentice* and *Mary Burns, Fugitive* were both glossy melodramas, but *The Princess Comes Across* is his best, set on a liner, with Carole Lombard as a fake princess. A more elevated, but just as contrived view of royalty made *Fire Over England* a very entertaining picture.

Rock Hudson (Roy Harold Scherer Jr.) (1925–85), b. Winnetka, Illinois
When he came out of the navy in 1946, Roy

Scherer was taken up by talent scout Henry Willson and offered to David Selznick. Selznick saw only a truck-driver hunk with the unlikely new name of "Rock Hudson." So Willson got the kid installed at Universal as prime potential movie meat, something like a sincere Victor Mature, a soft rock. We have to marvel now about who knew what when. Henry Willson was a known homosexual. And Hudson, for all his physique, was already possessed of comedic talent and more intelligence than his first films had time for.

Although he made his debut at Warners, in Raoul Walsh's *Fighter Squadron* (48), he was really the product of Universal. He began with bit parts and supports: *Undertow* (49, William Castle); an Indian in Mann's *Winchester 73* (50); *The Desert Hawk* (50, Frederick de Cordova); Fregonese's *One Way Street* (50); in 1951—*Air Cadet* and *Iron Man* for Joseph Pevney and *Bright Victory* for Mark Robson. He grew into longer parts in a series of adventure and B pictures. In the space of three years, he worked as often as possible in Hollywood's last great profusion of adventure excitement: 1952—*Bend of the River* (Mann); *Scarlet Angel* (Sidney Salkow); *Has Anybody Seen My Gal?* (Douglas Sirk); and *Horizons West* (Budd Boetticher); 1953—*Seminole* (Boetticher); *Sea Devils* (Walsh); *Back to God's Country* (Pevney); *Gun Fury* (Walsh); and *Bengal Brigade* (Laslo Benedek); 1954–55—four films for his perceptive patron, Douglas Sirk: *Taza, Son of Cochise; Captain Lightfoot; Magnificent Obsession;* and *All That Heaven Allows.*

Sirk had seen that, despite so many escapades, Hudson was innately gentle and sympathetic. Thus he began a new career as a sustaining figure in women's pictures. He surprised many people with his quiet authority in George Stevens's *Giant* (56) and worked three more times for Sirk: in *Battle Hymn* (57) conventionally, but in *Written on the Wind* (56) and *The Tarnished Angels* (57) exceptionally. In the latter, the drunken reporter is one of his better performances and a sign of depths that were never fully explored.

After Richard Brooks's worthy *Something of Value* (57) and a respectable Frederick Henry in the Selznick–Charles Vidor *A Farewell to Arms* (57), he became embroiled with Ross Hunter and usually Doris Day or Gina Lollobrigida in a number of comedies that bridged the gap between gaiety and permissiveness, largely through innuendo. They were uneasy films, but they were very successful, and at last Hudson was proved in comedy: *Pillow Talk* (59, Michael Gordon); *Come September* (61, Robert Mulligan); *Lover Come Back* (61, Delbert Mann); *Send Me No Flowers* (64, Norman Jewison); *Strange Bedfellows* (65, Panama/Frank); and *A Very Special Favor* (65, Gordon). Between times, he made a few offbeat failures: *The Last Sunset* (61) for Aldrich, *The Spiral Road*

(62) for Mulligan, and *A Gathering of Eagles* (63) for Delbert Mann. His best comedy by far is Hawks's *Man's Favorite Sport?* (64), as memorably beset by Paula Prentiss as ever Grant was by Hepburn, and admirably clutching at the flawed calm of the angling authority who has never caught a fish.

After that, Hudson made no worthwhile films: he was uneasy as the hero in Frankenheimer's pretentious *Seconds* (66); unable to do better than some slack war films and tame comedies: *Tobruk* (67, Arthur Hiller); John Sturges's *Ice Station Zebra* (68); *The Undefeated* (69, Andrew V. McLaglen) with mustache and John Wayne; the dreadful *Darling Lili* (69) with Blake Edwards and darling Julie; Phil Karlson's *Hornet's Nest* (69); mustachioed and portly in Vadim's *Pretty Maids All in a Row* (71), in which he seemed placidly amused at the chance of grappling with so many naked adolescents. In fact, Vadim neglected the comic potential of Hudson as a cool, campus Bluebeard.

At fifty-five (I felt in 1975), Hudson faced a crisis: without good comedies he might dwindle into such TV series as *MacMillan and Wife*. The crisis proved much greater. *MacMillan* was a hit on TV, and Hudson made few worthwhile films: *Showdown* (73, George Seaton); *Embryo* (76, Ralph Nelson); *Avalanche* (78, Corey Allen); *The Mirror Crack'd* (80, Guy Hamilton); as a movie director in *The Star Maker* (81, Lou Antonio) bedding all the starlets; as the President in *World War III* (82, David Greene); *The Ambassador* (84, J. Lee Thompson); and as a casino owner in *The Vegas Strip Wars* (84, George Englund).

Hudson was reluctant to admit that he had AIDS—who could blame him? Hollywood remains in conflict over any admission of homosexuality. But Hudson became the first famous victim of AIDS in movies, and everything he ever did became recast or reappraised in the light of the tragedy. Books said his marriage had been arranged to avert scandal. At the very least, the vaunted, rocklike masculinity of great male stars moved closer to the light. The rocks, sometimes, are cardboard shapes moved around by props people.

Howard Hughes (1905–76),
b. Houston, Texas

Picture people cannot get enough of Howard Hughes—no matter the nagging suggestion from factual accounts that there was not a lot there. But the little is so primed for legend, it leaves one feeling that the doleful, suspicious Hughes had some hygienic plan for missing life altogether and going straight into myth. So his associates wrote books about him—Robert Maheu and Noah Dietrich. There has been a life by Charles Higham, and the documented business history, *Empire,* by Donald

Barlett and James Steele—to say nothing of Hughes's viruslike recurrence in so much contemporary political history.

Then there is Jason Robards's shaggy vagrant story in the desert in *Melvin and Howard* (80, Jonathan Demme), Dean Stockwell's thoughtful cameo in *Tucker* (88, Francis Coppola), and the most complete screen portrait, brilliant and pathological, like an uncle for Gary Gilmore, by Tommy Lee Jones in *The Amazing Howard Hughes* (77, William A. Graham). Over all these has hung the chance that Warren Beatty will one day—when he is old enough?—play Howard Hughes. That prospect is itself legendary, or airborne, and it reminds us that Hughes came very close to contriving his own death in his favorite, infinite setting, the sky (Barlett and Steele establish that he was already a corpse when loaded on the plane at Acapulco). So he just missed Gregory Arkadin's sublime demise in *Confidential Report* (55, Orson Welles). But that reminds us that Hughes had surely affected movie romance since the time of *Citizen Kane*.

My favorite piece of Hughes mythology is Joan Didion's 1967 essay, a tribute to a haunted house forsaken by its ghost, "7000 Romaine, Los Angeles 38" (the title refers to the Hughes office in Los Angeles—still there, still closed). Didion could see even then that Hughes—in his wondrous, if not lyrical, absence—had become chiefly a subject for stories, a living fiction: "That we have made a hero of Howard Hughes tells us something interesting about ourselves, something dimly remembered, tells us that the secret point of money and power in America is neither the things that money can buy nor power for power's sake . . . but absolute personal freedom, mobility, privacy."

As a hopeless Hughes admirer (who once horrified a future father-in-law by waxing suggestive on hapless Howard), I can testify to the wings of Didion's soaring. And I think it's plain why Hughes excites movie people: the daft wealth, the amazing fame, *and* the yearning to be nothing; the obsession with flying; the taste for hotels, Las Vegas, and bloodless food delivered in plastic bags—this is the little boy's kingdom; the foolish resort to movies, to running studios, to brunettes, blondes, and breasts. He is the fan who walked in off the street, who made movies and bossed a studio, and who was crazy and hopeful enough to think of having Jean Harlow, Jane Russell, Katharine Hepburn, Ida Lupino, Jean Simmons, Janet Leigh, Faith Domergue, even Jean Peters (the one he married) and so on, into the night. Hughes did what every shy, lonely moviegoer dreams of doing. And he went as mad as a hatter, leaving the legend to Clifford Irving and the rest of us.

Some people mock his preoccupation with Jane Russell, as if sexual devotion were not a noble thing. Russell was a very amiable, amused woman; especially when young, she was extremely sexy in that same tongue-in-cheek manner, as if aware that there was only one way we were ever going to find out whether her breasts were real or not; the cinematography of breasts was thrust forward by *The Outlaw*, as was the medium's creative teasing of prudery and censorship; Hughes's record shows that he endorsed Russell's blatant and honest reckoning of sexual pleasure, and at the same time looked on it as a joke; in that respect, as in others, Hughes's intermittent association with Hawks shows in their style and attitudes; but, most interesting, it was the drollery of Russell as any boy's erection kit that looked forward to the lyrical gilding of the pinup by American pop artists of the 1950s; and that anticipates the philosophically amused bisexual emphasis of Warhol's films—which, in turn, reminds us that that mistreated vagrant, *The Outlaw*, was the first American film to suggest that homosexuality might be pleasant.

Hughes and cinema had two resounding confrontations. As a very young millionaire, he formed the Caddo Corporation and produced movies: *Two Arabian Knights* (27, Lewis Milestone); *The Mating Call* (28, James Cruze); *The Racket* (28, Milestone); and then spent two years over *Hell's Angels* (30), which he directed personally. *Hell's Angels* is dramatically commonplace, clumsily strung together, and without clear authorship, but the aerial photography is superb and the scenes with Jean Harlow are from another, much better picture. Hughes discovered Harlow when others had passed her by. She, too, had the slightly lazy sexual aggression that characterizes his discoveries. But, like a great romantic, he tired of her or found nothing that suited her. Instead he loaned her out to MGM at a colossal profit, and finally sold her altogether, reserving the right to produce one last picture with her, one of her very best, *Bombshell* (33, Victor Fleming). In the meantime, Hughes had produced the film of the Hecht-MacArthur play, *The Front Page* (31, Milestone), the fastest talking picture yet, and *Scarface* (32, Hawks), the most baroque of the early gangster pictures. After one more flying picture, *Sky Devils* (32, Edward Sutherland), he withdrew, intent on flying himself.

Several years before his second period, he discovered Jane Russell and put her in *The Outlaw*. Hawks began the film in 1940, but left when Hughes decided to shoot at night. Thus he had to finish the film himself, the first indoor Western. But he waited six years before releasing it, time to stir up a storm of puritan protest that duly clinched the film's success. By 1946, he had a fresh interest in film: Faith Domergue. He concocted a film called *Vendetta* for her, made that year with himself filling in as he fired Preston Sturges, Max Ophuls, and Stuart Heisler, and finally credited it (when it was released in 1950) to Mel Ferrer. In the same year, he produced Harold Lloyd in *The Sin of Harold Diddlebock* (46, Sturges). Neither film is a success, *Vendetta* is even bad, but stays in the memory for its bizarre manner of production.

In 1947, Hughes began to buy himself into RKO, that ailing outsider, which eventually he tired of and sold into the hands of TV in 1955. Head of the studio, he was often unavailable, occasionally intently involved on a film or actress that took his fancy. But he was good to such talents as Nicholas Ray, Robert Ryan, and Don Siegel. At the least, he retained RKO's aversion to dullness; at best, he threw out the broken pieces of some fascinating films. Research still needs to ascertain where his hand fell, but he seems to have known about at least these: *The Big Steal* (49), for which he hired Don Siegel; *The Woman on Pier 13* (49, Robert Stevenson), which voiced his rabid anti-Communism; *The Racket* (51, John Cromwell); *Jet Pilot* (51, Josef von Sternberg, with several impeding hands); *Flying Leathernecks* (51, Nicholas Ray); *Second Chance* (53, Rudolph Maté); seven films starring Jane Russell—the amusing *His Kind of Woman* (51, John Farrow); *Double Dynamite* (51, Irving Cummings); *The Las Vegas Story* (52, Stevenson); *Macao* (52, von Sternberg); *Montana Belle* (52, Allan Dwan); *The French Line* (53, Lloyd Bacon); *Underwater* (54, John Sturges); and *Son of Sinbad* (55, Ted Tetzlaff).

He also consigned Jean Simmons to *Angel Face* (52, Otto Preminger) when she would not talk to him, and advised Robert Ryan on how to play the paranoid, vicious tycoon in *Caught* (49, Max Ophuls). It would be depressing to think that any of this will ever be sorted out as either fact or hokum. Hughes is one of those pioneers who saw how little difference there was between the two.

John Hughes, b. Lansing, Michigan, 1950
1984: *Sixteen Candles.* 1985: *The Breakfast Club; Weird Science.* 1986: *Ferris Bueller's Day Off.* 1987: *Planes, Trains and Automobiles.* 1988: *She's Having a Baby.* 1989: *Uncle Buck.* 1991: *Curly Sue.*

John Hughes has made a very sweet business, and often a lovely entertainment, out of movies for high school kids that their parents would be happy to have them see. This is no common compromise, for many teenagers like to see pictures that their parents regard as unsuitable or alarming. Thus, in all of Hughes's young people there is a faint air of premature middle age that sometimes seems true to life, and sometimes blankly depressing. Hughes is a smart director and a good writer, but he does not really expose those traits as much as he relishes the larger role of entrepreneur or high school entertainment coordinator. Nothing he has done has been quite as successful, or as

gleeful and wicked, as the *Home Alone* pictures, which concern a far younger person and which were actually directed by Chris Columbus. In the original *Home Alone,* especially, Macaulay Culkin had a wild, pure narcissism such as, long ago, Mickey Rooney and Margaret O'Brien possessed. By contrast, Hughes's best girl—Molly Ringwald—seemed the child of Freddie Bartholomew.

In the Ringwald pictures, the fidelity of observation, the wit, and the tenderness for kids never quite transcend the general air of problem-solving and putting on a piously cheerful face. No one has yet dared in America to portray the boredom or hopelessness of many teenage lives—think of Mike Leigh's pictures to see what could be done.

Hughes dropped out of the University of Arizona and then tried to be an advertising copywriter, a novelist, and a joke writer. He joined *National Lampoon* magazine and that led him into pictures as a screenwriter: *National Lampoon's Class Reunion* (82, Michael Miller); *Mr. Mom* (83, Stan Dragoti); *Nate and Hayes* (83, Ferdinand Fairfax); and *National Lampoon's Vacation* (83, Harold Ramis).

On those films he directed, Hughes was always the screenwriter. But as he became successful, so he turned to writing and/or some producing role on others' pictures: *National Lampoon's European Vacation* (85, Amy Heckerling); *Pretty in Pink* (86, Howard Deutsch); *Some Kind of Wonderful* (87, Deutsch); *The Great Outdoors* (88, Deutsch); *National Lampoon's Christmas Vacation* (89, Jeremiah S. Chechik); *Home Alone* (90, Columbus); *Career Opportunities* (91, Bryan Gordon); *Only the Lonely* (91, Columbus); *Home Alone 2* (92, Columbus); and *Baby's Day Out* (94, Patrick Read Johnson).

In the last few years he has been an impresario writer-producer—and let's note that such work interests some minds most; and almost certainly draws down more revenue. So he has written and produced *Miracle on 34th Street* (94, Les Mayfield); *101 Dalmatians* (96, Stephen Herek); *Flubber* (97, Mayfield); *Home Alone 3* (97, Raja Gosnell); *Reach the Rock* (98, William Ryan).

Helen Hunt, b. Los Angeles, 1963
In hindsight, the Oscar awarded to Helen Hunt for her world-weary waitress and single mother in *As Good As It Gets* (97, James L. Brooks) looks generous. She was funny and touching, and she worked well with Jack Nicholson, but there she was beating out four Brits: Kate Winslet in *Titanic;* Judi Dench in *Mrs. Brown;* Julie Christie in *Afterglow;* and Helena Bonham Carter in *The Wings of the Dove.* OK, so you can see why she won: it was a thin year, and there she was, the nation's sweetheart from the TV series *Mad About You,* for which she had three Emmys and a salary of $1 million per episode.

However, would she do more in film? Did she really have the range? Or was another TV series more likely, and more comfortable? For the fact is, before *As Good As It Gets*, Hunt had been trying to break through in movies for nearly twenty years: *Rollercoaster* (77, James Goldstone); as a brain-damaged teenager in *The Miracle of Kathy Miller* (81, Robert Lewis), for TV; *Girls Just Want to Have Fun* (85, Alan Metter); the girlfriend in *Trancers* (85, Charles Band); *Peggy Sue Got Married* (86, Francis Coppola); *Project X* (87, Jonathan Kaplan); *Stealing Home* (88, Steven Kampmann); *Miles from Home* (88, Gary Sinise); *Next of Kin* (89, John Irvin); *Queens Logic* (91, Steve Rash); *Trancers 2* (91, Band); *Bob Roberts* (92, Tim Robbins); *Only You* (92, Betty Thomas); *Mr. Saturday Night* (92, Billy Crystal); *The Water Dance* (92, Neal Jimenez); *Trancers III* (92, Courtney Joyner); *Kiss of Death* (95, Barbet Schroeder); *Twister* (96, Jan de Bont).

She was Viola on stage and televised, in *Twelfth Night* (98, Nicholas Hytner); *Dr. T & the Women* (00, Robert Altman); doing her best with the shlock called *Pay It Forward* (00, Mimi Leder); marginal in *Cast Away* (00, Robert Zemeckis); funny in *What Women Want* (00, Nancy Meyers); *The Curse of the Jade Scorpion* (01, Woody Allen); *Timepiece* (02). A lot of work, but so little development.

Holly Hunter, b. Conyers, Georgia, 1958

No wonder Jane Campion had some reservations when Holly Hunter sought the central role in *The Piano* (93). Hunter had established herself as a tiny fireball of energy, Southern abrasiveness, and talk, talk, talk. She was pretty, yet she easily offered the look of a modern Southern shopping-mall belle. But Hunter created the severe, less-than-dainty look of a nineteenth-century woman repressed in nearly everything except silent pride. She delivered a stunning performance, and in doing so she expanded her own horizons and won the Oscar. Can American film provide equal opportunities?

She came from rural Georgia (not far from Tara) and studied at Carnegie Mellon. Her debut was in *The Burning* (81, Tony Maylam), after which she played on TV in *Svengali* (83, Anthony Harvey); *With Intent to Kill* (84, Mike Robe); *Swing Shift* (84, Jonathan Demme); *Raising Arizona* (87, Joel Coen); *A Gathering of Old Men* (87, Volker Schlöndorff); *End of the Line* (87, Jay Russell); getting her first best actress nomination in *Broadcast News* (87, James L. Brooks); repeating a stage success in Beth Henley's *Miss Firecracker* (89, Thomas Schlamme); *Animal Behavior* (89, H. Anne Roley); getting an Emmy as "Roe" in *Roe v. Wade* (89, Gregory Hoblit); *Always* (89, Steven Spielberg); *Once Around* (91, Lasse Hallstrom); *Crazy in Love* (92, Martha Coolidge); very funny

and Oscar-nominated as the secretary in *The Firm* (93, Sydney Pollack); and brilliant in *The Positively True Adventures of the Alleged Texas Cheerleader-Murdering Mom* (93, Michael Ritchie).

She continues to be adventurous, going from TV and provincial theatre to film—and even then few films in the mainstream. But she is one of several living examples that the American mainstream is now dysfunctional: the cop in *Copycat* (95, Jon Amiel); *Home for the Holidays* (95, Jodie Foster); *Crash* (96, David Cronenberg); from heaven in *A Life Less Ordinary* (97, Danny Boyle); excellent in *Living Out Loud* (98, Richard LaGravenese); *Jesus' Son* (99, Alison Maclean); at her best in *Woman Wanted* (99, Kiefer Sutherland); *Things You Can Tell Just by Looking at Her* (00, Rodrigo Garcia); *Timecode* (00, Mike Figgis); *O Brother, Where Art Thou?* (00, Coen); and then to TV for a pair of admirable real-life stories: *Harlan County War* (00, Tony Bill), and as Billie Jean King in *When Billie Beat Bobby* (01, Jane Anderson).

Ross Hunter (Martin Fuss) (1920–96), b. Cleveland, Ohio

It was Douglas Sirk who said Ross Hunter was "like iron." Take *Magnificent Obsession* (54). Hunter, an established producer but only just, came to Sirk and said that the studio, Universal, had some availability with Jane Wyman. Sirk was interested. And then Hunter gave him the Lloyd C. Douglas novel *Magnificent Obsession* to read. Sirk couldn't get anywhere with it. So Hunter gave him a short treatment of the movie John Stahl had made from the same book in 1935, with Irene Dunne. Now Sirk got it. He liked it. He could see what he wanted to do with it. That's fine, said Hunter, but he knew the way Sirk's mind began to go gloomy. So here was the iron. "Just keep the ending happy," said Hunter.

Hunter is famous for being the top producer at Universal, not just Sirk's best patron, but the driving force behind some of the best melodramas and romances of that decade. But he was more than that. He had an earlier career, in the mid forties, as an actor in B pictures—things like *Louisiana Hayride* (44, Charles Barton), *A Guy, a Gal and a Pal* (45, Budd Boetticher), *Hit the Hay* (46, Del Lord). When he flopped, he went away and taught school for a few years before returning to Universal as an associate producer.

Universal was the last walled city in old Hollywood, a place famous for dotty adventures and its stable of young talent. He learned his trade as the associate producer on a group of authentic entertainments: *Flame of Araby* (51, Charles Lamont), a really gorgeous desert adventure, with Jeff Chandler and Maureen O'Hara; *Steel Town* (52, George Sherman); *Untamed Frontier* (52, Hugo Fregonese); *Son of Ali Baba* (52, Kurt Neumann), with Tony Curtis and Piper Laurie; *The Duel at Silver Creek* (52, Don Siegel); *The Battle at Apache Pass* (52, Sherman).

He was promoted to producer and that's when he and Sirk really took off, but it was always mixed in with other directors: *All I Desire* (53, Sirk); *Tumbleweed* (53, Nathan Juran); *Take Me to Town* (53, Sirk); *Magnificent Obsession* (54); *The Yellow Mountain* (54, Jesse Hibbs); *Taza, Son of Cochise* (54, Sirk); *Naked Alibi* (54, Jerry Hopper); *Captain Lightfoot* (55, Sirk); *The Spoilers* (55, Hibbs); *All That Heaven Allows* (56, Sirk); *Battle Hymn* (57, Sirk); *Tammy and the Bachelor* (57, Joseph Pevney); *Interlude* (57, Sirk); *My Man Godfrey* (57, Henry Koster); *This Happy Feeling* (58, Blake Edwards); *The Restless Years* (58, Helmut Kautner); *A Stranger in My Arms* (59, Kautner); *Imitation of Life* (59, Sirk).

Sirk retired, and Helmut Kautner was no replacement, but Ross Hunter carried on, with Doris Day and Sandra Dee as his new motors: *Pillow Talk* (59, Michael Gordon); *Portrait in Black* (60, Gordon); *Midnight Lace* (60, David Miller); *Back Street* (61, Miller); *Flower Drum Song* (61, Koster); *Tammy Tell Me True* (61, Harry Keller); *If a Man Answers* (62, Henry Levin); *The Thrill of It All* (63, Norman Jewison); *Tammy and the Doctor* (63, Keller); *The Chalk Garden* (64, Ronald Neame); *I'd Rather Be Rich* (64, Jack Smight); *Madame X* (66, David Lowell Rich)—which really is the end of its genre's line.

There were a few more years left in movies: *Thoroughly Modern Millie* (67, George Roy Hill); *Airport* (70, George Seaton), a new kind of genre and a smash hit; *Lost Horizon* (73, Charles Jarrott), proof that you can go to the remake well too often. After that, there were a few years in TV: *The Lives of Jenny Dolan* (75, Jerry Jameson); *Arthur Hailey's The Moneychangers* (76, Boris Sagal); *A Family Upside Down* (78, Rich); *Suddenly, Love* (78, Stuart Margolin); *The Best Place to Be* (79, Miller).

Isabelle Huppert, b. Paris, 1955

The greatest surprise and failure in Huppert's career came when she was not very good as Emma in Claude Chabrol's lifeless *Madame Bovary* (91). In Chabrol's conception, she seemed doomed, and contemplating poison, from the outset. There was none of the laughter, the flights of gaiety, romance, and casual earthiness of which Isabelle Huppert is capable. Ironically, she had come closer to the range and tumult of Emma Bovary a few years earlier, for Chabrol, in the very moving *Une Affaire de Femmes* (87). Was Chabrol simply constrained by the big prestigious subject? Or is there something innately wistful or watchful in Huppert, a pale, numb quality that cannot dominate large stories?

She has been industrious and versatile for over thirty years, unusually comfortable in English for a French actress, and intriguing to a great variety of directors (though she never worked for Truffaut). Indeed, she has to rate as one of the most accomplished actresses in the world today, even if she seems short of the passion or agony of her contemporary, Isabelle Adjani. An Adjani Bovary would not have been as controlled—and viewers would not have left the theatre underexercised.

Huppert began as a teenager: *Faustine et le Bel Été* (71, Nina Companeez); *César et Rosalie* (72, Claude Sautet); *Le Bar de la Fourche* (72, Alain Levent); *L'Ampélopède* (73, Rachel Weinberg); *Glissements Progressifs du Plaisir* (74, Alain Robbe-Grillet); *Making It* (74, Bertrand Blier); *Dupont Lajoie* (74, Yves Boisset); *Sérieux Comme le Plaisir* (74, Robert Benayoun); *Rosebud* (74, Otto Preminger); *Le Grand Délire* (74, Dennis Berry); *Aloise* (74, Liliane de Kermadec); *Docteur Françoise Gailland* (75, Jean-Louis Bertucelli); *Le Juge et L'Assassin* (75, Bertrand Tavernier); *Je Suis Pierre Rivière* (75, Christine Lipinska); *Le Petit Marcel* (75, Jacques Fansten); *The Lacemaker* (76, Claude Goretta), the film that won attention outside France; *Des Enfants Gâtés* (77, Tavernier); *Les Indiens Sont Encore Loin* (77, Patricia Moraz); to great acclaim as the young murderess, fascinating just because of her intent passivity, in *Violette Nozière* (78, Chabrol); *Retour à la Bien-Aimée* (78, Jean-François Adam); as Anne in *The Brontë Sisters* (78, André Téchiné); excellent, sensual, and commonplace in *Heaven's Gate* (80, Michael Cimino), even if she seemed to sniff out a small, intimate picture about how frontier life was lived, instead of a fulminating epic; *Sauve Qui Peut* (80, Jean-Luc Godard), her placidity enduring or encouraging Godard's frenzy of lecture; excellent in *Loulou* (80, Maurice Pialat); *La Dame aux Camelias* (80, Mauro Bolognini)—she does have a consumptive glow; *Orokseg* (80, Marta Meszaros); *Les Ailes de la Colombe* (81, Benoit Jacquot); *Coup de Torchon* (81, Tavernier); *Eaux Profondes* (81, Michel Deville); *Passion* (82, Godard); *The Trout* (82, Joseph Losey); *Entre Nous* (83, Diane Kurys); *Storia di Piera* (83, Marco Ferreri); *My Best Friend's Girl* (83, Blier); *Signé, Charlotte* (84, Caroline Huppert, her sister); *La Garce* (84, Christine Pascal, her costar from *Enfants Gâtés*— Huppert has worked frequently with women directors); *Sac de Noeuds* (85, Josianne Balasko); losing her sight in *Cactus* (84, Paul Cox); doing Dostoyevsky in *Les Possédés* (87, Andrzej Wajda) and Bette Davis in *The Bedroom Window* (87, Curtis Hanson); *Milan Noir* (87, Ronald Chammah); *La Vengeance d'une Femme* (89, Jacques Doillon); *Malina* (90, Werner Schroeter); *Après l'Amour* (92, Kurys); and *L'Inondation* (93, Igor Minaev), from a novella by Yevgeny Zamyatin, which the actress had optioned personally.

She has remained a leading actress, versatile and ready for daring or unusual material: well paired with Sandrine Bonnaire in *La Cérémonie* (95, Chabrol); *Lumière et Compagnie* (95, Abbas Kiarostami); the voice of a horse in *Gulliver's Travels* (96, Charles Sturridge); the interviewer in *Poussières d'Amour* (96, Schroeter); *Elective Affinities* (96, the Taviani Brothers); Marie Curie in *Les Palmes de M. Schutz* (97, Claude Pinoteau); *Rien ne Va Plus* (97, Chabrol); *Pas de Scandale* (99, Jacquot); *La Vie Moderne* (99, Laurence Ferreira Barbosa); *La Fausse Suivante* (00, Jacquot); Mme de Maintenon in *Saint-Cyr* (00, Patricia Mazuy); *Les Destinées Sentimentales* (00, Olivier Asssayas); *Comédie de l'Innocence* (00, Raul Ruiz); *Merci pour le Chocolat* (00, Chabrol); Clara Schumann in *Clara* (00, Helma Sanders-Brahms); startlingly erotic in *La Pianiste* (01, Michael Haneke); *8 Femmes* (02, François Ozon); *La Vie Promesse* (02, Olivier Dahan); *Deux* (02, Schroeter); *Le Temps du Loup* (03, Haneke).

John Hurt,
b. Shirebrook, England, 1940
Hurt has not just the name but the haggard face for presiding over crazy films. Equally, he has a remarkably diverse record as a supporting, or even a lead, player. In short, he is rarely dull and often playful, inventively desperate, and someone to treasure.

He was an art student at St. Martin's School in London before going on to RADA. Among British actors, he is notable in that most of his work is in film and television, and not the theatre. He made his debut in *The Wild and the Willing* (62, Ralph Thomas), but drew serious attention as the betrayer in *A Man for All Seasons* (66, Fred Zinnemann). Zinnemann could not cast the part until he saw Hurt onstage in *Little Malcolm* and recognized his "explosive nervous energy."

A run of worthwhile films followed: *The Sailor from Gibraltar* (67, Tony Richardson); *Before Winter Comes* (68, J. Lee Thompson); the lead as the young rogue in *Sinful Davey* (69, John Huston); the wretched Timothy Evans in *10 Rillington Place* (70, Richard Fleischer); *In Search of Gregory* (70, Peter Wood); with Hayley Mills in *Mr. Forbush and the Penguins* (71, Al Viola); *The Pied Piper* (72, Jacques Demy); the film of *Little Malcolm* (74, Stuart Cooper); and *The Ghoul* (75, Freddie Francis).

But what made him famous in Britain was his rich Quentin Crisp for TV in *The Naked Civil Servant* (75, Jack Gold); and his Caligula in TV's *I, Claudius* (76, Herbert Wise). His best years now came in a rush: *East of Elephant Rock* (76, Don Boyd); *The Disappearance* (77, Cooper); a supporting actor nomination for *Midnight Express* (78, Alan Parker); *The Shout* (78, Jerzy Skolimowski); nursing the beast in *Alien* (79, Ridley

Scott); much put-upon by make-up, but getting a best actor nomination as *The Elephant Man* (80, David Lynch); and in the most cuttable role in *Heaven's Gate* (80, Michael Cimino)—he took the part in the spirit of "a lark," worked a day and a half in ten weeks and nearly lost *The Elephant Man* (which was shot later *and* released earlier—do you see why some actors look like Hurt?).

In the same period, he delivered excellent voice-over to several animated films: *The Lord of the Rings* (78, Ralph Bakshi); *Watership Down* (78, Martin Rosen); and *The Plague Dogs* (82, Rosen).

As a live presence on-screen, he has never again been what he was in 1980 or so: *History of the World, Part I* (81, Mel Brooks) as Jesus; getting out of East Berlin in a balloon in *Night Crossing* (81, Delbert Mann); a gay cop in *Partners* (82, James Burrows); a jockey in *Champions* (83, John Irvin); *The Osterman Weekend* (83, Sam Peckinpah); as Winston Smith in *1984* (84, Michael Radford); a killer in *The Hit* (84, Stephen Frears); and *Success Is the Best Revenge* (84, Skolimowski).

He did voice-over on *The Black Cauldron* (85, Ted Berman); was in *Jake Speed* (86, Andrew Lane); *From the Hip* (87, Bob Clark); *Spaceballs* (87, Brooks); the voice of Van Gogh for *Vincent* (87, Paul Cox); *White Mischief* (87, Radford); very good as Stephen Ward in *Scandal* (89, Michael Caton-Jones); *The Field* (90, Jim Sheridan); *Resident Alien* (90, Jonathan Nossiter), a documentary about Quentin Crisp; *Frankenstein Unbound* (90, Roger Corman); *King Ralph* (91, David S. Ward); and *A Lapse of Memory* (91, Patrick DeWolf).

Hurt is universally known, and admired. He does three or four projects a year, and very few of them are in the mainstream—he is as adventurous as the best strain of British acting, yet he is safe casting in a blockbuster like *Harry Potter. Six Characters in Search of an Author* (92, Bill Bryden); *L'Oeil Qui Ment* (92, Raul Ruiz); *Even Cowgirls Get the Blues* (93, Gus Van Sant); *Monolith* (93, John Eyres); *Great Moments in Aviation* (93, Beeban Kidron); *Second Best* (94, Chris Menges); an odious Montrose in *Rob Roy* (95, Michael Caton-Jones); *Dead Man* (95, Jim Jarmusch); *Wild Bill* (95, Walter Hill)—very like his *Heaven's Gate* part; *Two Nudes Bathing* (95, John Boorman); *Saigon Baby* (95, David Attwood); *Prisoners in Time* (95, Stephen Walker).

He was excellent as Giles De'Ath in *Love and Death on Long Island* (97, Richard Kwietniowski); *Contact* (97, Robert Zemeckis); *Bandyta* (97, Maciej Dejczer); *Tender Loving Care* (97, David Wheeler); *The Commissioner* (98, George Sluizer); *The Climb* (98, Bob Swaim); *Night Train* (98, John Lynch); *All the Little Animals* (98, Jeremy Thomas); *You're Dead* (98, Andy Hurst); on TV, *Krapp's Last Tape* (00, Atom Egoyan); *Lost Souls* (00, Janusz Kaminski); as

Porfiry in *Crime and Punishment* (00, Golan Menahem); *Captain Corelli's Mandolin* (01, John Madden); as Mr. Ollivander in *Harry Potter and the Sorcerer's Stone* (01, Chris Columbus).

He was in *Tabloid* (01, David Blair); *Miranda* (02, Marc Munden); *Bait* (02, Nicholas Renton); as the casino boss in *Owning Mahowny* (03, Kwietniowski); *Dogville* (03, Lars von Trier).

William Hurt, b. Washington, D.C., 1950
In the days when William Hurt was being hailed as the Leading Man of the Eighties, he was sometimes typed as a Wasp. It was fair up to a point. His father had been in the State Department, and the boy had lived in Africa and the Pacific on tours of duty. When the parents divorced, young Hurt had a stepfather, Henry Luce III. The boy was sent to prep school and to Tufts. He was tall, fair, and handsome. Still, there was more of the wasp than the Wasp. And while he was evidently smart—he graduated with honors—he was overly inclined to lecture others, and to rise on clouds of obscurity. He was not liked by the press, and he has never won the love of the public. He was not far away from being cast as a villain.

He strove with a problematic venture and the background of special effects in *Altered States* (80, Ken Russell). He was an oddball, voyeuristic janitor in *Eyewitness* (81, Peter Yates), not within arm's length of wholesome. And he was brilliant as the lazy lawyer, Ned Racine, in *Body Heat* (81, Lawrence Kasdan), so easily taken in by his own superiority.

This was his moment. He was narcissistic in *The Big Chill* (83, Kasdan), and already one felt that films were exploiting his overweening self-regard. He went grim as the Russian cop in *Gorky Park* (83, Michael Apted); he rose to the bravura opportunity of *Kiss of the Spider Woman* (85, Hector Babenco), in which the material gave him a welcome sense of contempt for himself. The role was so exotic, Hurt won the Oscar.

Next he helped Marlee Matlin to a similarly sentimental award in *Children of a Lesser God* (86, Randa Haines). But Hurt was making less impact, and in *Broadcast News* (87, James Brooks), as the anchorman light as a feather, he was an object of mockery. It was a clever performance, but Hurt was being shown up. *A Time of Destiny* (88, Gregory Nava), in which he played an odious villain, was a disaster; while in *The Accidental Tourist* (88, Kasdan) he seemed depressed and out of reach. He was a blind, proud husband in *Alice* (90, Woody Allen); in *I Love You to Death* (90, Kasdan); and then, in *The Doctor* (91, Haines), he had a great chance as a trapped misanthropist, only for the movie to lob batting-practice happy endings at his character and his problems. *The Doctor* was as bad as any film of tough ideas in panicked times, and Hurt

was stranded, an actor no longer credible as a leading or heroic figure. He appeared as a wanderer in *Until the End of the World* (91, Wim Wenders), once more leaning away from the mainstream and toward allegedly higher things. He was in *The Plague* (93, Luis Penzo) and *Mr. Wonderful* (93, Anthony Minghella).

In a way, his own status was more intriguing than most of his parts, but he didn't seem a jot less prickly: a shy Welsh postmaster in *Second Best* (94, Chris Menges); very strange as the enforcer in *Trial by Jury* (94, Heywood Gould); *Smoke* (95, Wayne Wang); *Secrets Shared with a Stranger* (95, Georges Bardawil); *A Couch in New York* (96, Chantal Akerman); a haunted Mr. Rochester in *Jane Eyre* (96, Franco Zeffirelli); *Michael* (96, Nora Ephron); *Loved* (97, Erin Dignam); *Dark City* (98, Alex Projas); bizarre in *Lost in Space* (98, Stephen Hopkins); *The Proposition* (98, Lesli Linka Glatter); very good as the writer-husband in *One True Thing* (98, Carl Franklin).

He had the thankless lead in *The Big Brass Ring* (99, George Hickenlooper); and then delivered one of his best performances in *Sunshine* (99, István Szabó). But he was soon restored to oddity: *Do Not Disturb* (99, Dick Maas); *The 4th Floor* (99, Josh Klausner); *The Simian Line* (00, Linda Yellen); in the TV *Dune* (00, John Harrison); very good as Varian Fry in *Varian's War* (00, Lionel Chetwynd); *The Contaminated Man* (00, Anthony Hickox); *The Flamingo Rising* (01, Martha Coolidge); *A.I.* (01, Steven Spielberg); *Rare Birds* (01, Sturla Gunnarsson).

Let this be said: he once starred in a picture from which Kevin Costner was dropped. And Costner now is a kind of star. But Hurt's range of choices makes him look stay-at-home.

He was in *Changing Lanes* (02, Roger Michell); *Au Plus Près du Paradis* (02, Tonie Marshall); *Tuck Everlasting* (02, Jay Russell); on TV as *Master Spy: The Robert Hansson Story* (02, Lawrence Schiller); *The Blue Butterfly* (02, Lea Pool); *The Tulse Luper Suitcases: The Moab Story* (03, Peter Greenaway).

Anjelica Huston, b. Los Angeles, 1951
1996: *Bastard out of Carolina* (TV). 1999: *Agnes Browne.*

In the early nineties, we looked upon Anjelica Huston as one of America's acting treasures—she was bold visually and emotionally; she seemed passionate yet truthful; and she has an air of pedigree in our minds. Yet in 1980, it was all she could do to find a decent part, let alone develop a career—and she was already thirty. In other words, there has been a sentimental view that sees her as having been nurtured by her father, John Huston, and by her former longtime lover, Jack Nicholson. Show business families are stranger than that. I do not mean to say the two men deliberately blocked her (though John had been discouraging). Perhaps their example simply intimidated her. Though admired for her great strength now, Anjelica Huston may have felt overwhelmed, an appendage. Whatever, she needed to move out of their shadow to become herself.

She was the daughter of Huston's third wife, Ricki Soma, a model. As such, she was raised largely in Galway, Ireland, and in London—a child who viewed her father as a romantic traveler who came home now and then with exotic gifts, and sometimes with other women.

She had a small part in her father's *Sinful Davey* (69), and the female lead in his medieval romance, *A Walk with Love and Death* (69). The latter was an unhappy experience that propelled Anjelica into modeling. She had a tiny role in *Hamlet* (70, Tony Richardson), and then a moment of mistaken identity in *The Last Tycoon* (76, Elia Kazan), so haunting that one marvels at the movie persisting with Ingrid Boulting as its lead. She had another moment in *Swashbuckler* (76, James Goldstone) and was seen briefly with Nicholson as the animal trainer in *The Postman Always Rings Twice* (81, Bob Rafelson). She was without a line as an asylum inmate, barely detectable, in *Frances* (82, Graeme Clifford). *The Ice Pirates* (84, Stewart Raffill) was a bigger role, but it was as Mae Rose in *Prizzi's Honor* (85, John Huston) that she seized attention. Her scenes brought the ponderous film to taut life and won her a supporting actress Oscar—if only it had been a film about Mae Rose.

In *Gardens of Stone* (87, Francis Coppola), she was a decent pal to pained men. She did all she could in *The Dead* (87, Huston), but that complex story was far beyond the film's attempt. She was an aviatrix in *A Handful of Dust* (88, Charles Sturridge), and she appeared in *Mr. North* (88, Danny Huston, her half-brother).

But in *Crimes and Misdemeanors* (89, Woody Allen), we could see a character actress emerging—rather plain, grating, unafraid of looking like a reject. She was better still in *Enemies, A Love Story* (89, Paul Mazursky). Still, she is not easily cast. Her looks tend easily such things as *The Witches* (90, Nicolas Roeg) and *The Addams Family* (91, Barry Sonnenfeld), neither of which made adequate demands on her.

The Grifters (90, Stephen Frears), though, led her into a bleak careerist who might think of killing her child. The look that the actress found was startling, and her toughness was a little too serious for the film. But just because the movie flinched a little, we can see how hard it may be for Anjelica Huston to persist with her most dangerous feelings. We should recall just how dark and fatalistic her father could be.

Like several others, she has found valuable opportunities in television: in *Lonesome Dove* (89, Simon Wincer) and *Family Pictures* (93, Philip Saville). She had a good supporting role in *Manhattan Murder Mystery* (93, Allen); a small part in *And the Band Played On* (93, Roger Spottiswoode); and Morticia again, alas, in *Addams Family Values* (93, Sonnenfeld).

In recent years, she has turned to directing—once harshly, once rather sentimentally. But there's no reason why she shouldn't yet find herself, and it's clear that she has other projects in mind, especially Irish ones. As an actress, her fortunes have been mixed, and really there hasn't been enough to sustain the talent seen in *Prizzi's Honor* and *The Grifters*. There's been *Buffalo Girls* (95, Rod Hardy); *The Perez Family* (95, Mira Nair); *The Crossing Guard* (95, Sean Penn); *Buffalo '66* (98, Vincent Gallo); *Phoenix* (98, Danny Cannon); *Ever After* (98, Andy Tennant); Mrs. Assingham in *The Golden Bowl* (00, James Ivory); *Time of Our Lives* (00, Mary Agnes Donoghue); *The Mists of Avalon* (01, Ulrich Edel); *The Man from Elysian Fields* (01, George Hickenlooper); *The Royal Tenenbaums* (01, Wes Anderson); *Blood Work* (02, Clint Eastwood).

John Huston (1906–87),
b. Nevada, Missouri

1941: *The Maltese Falcon*. 1942: *In This Our Life; Across the Pacific*. 1943: *Report from the Aleutians* (d). 1944: *The Battle of San Pietro* (d). 1947: *The Treasure of the Sierra Madre*. 1948: *Key Largo*. 1949: *We Were Strangers*. 1950: *The Asphalt Jungle*. 1951: *The Red Badge of Courage*. 1952: *The African Queen*. 1953: *Moulin Rouge*. 1954: *Beat the Devil*. 1956: *Moby Dick*. 1957: *Heaven Knows, Mr. Allison*. 1958: *The Barbarian and the Geisha; The Roots of Heaven*. 1960: *The Unforgiven; The Misfits*. 1962: *Freud: The Secret Passion*. 1963: *The List of Adrian Messenger*. 1964: *Night of the Iguana*. 1966: *The Bible*. 1967: *Casino Royale* (an episode); *Reflections in a Golden Eye*. 1969: *Sinful Davey; A Walk With Love and Death*. 1970: *The Kremlin Letter*. 1971: *Fat City*. 1972: *The Life and Times of Judge Roy Bean*. 1973: *The Mackintosh Man*. 1975: *The Man Who Would Be King*. 1979: *Wise Blood*. 1980: *Victory*. 1982: *Annie*. 1984: *Under the Volcano*. 1985: *Prizzi's Honor*. 1987: *The Dead*.

Huston was always ready to be presented as the movie director who told manly, energetic stories, and liked to end them on a wry chuckle. He was himself a writer, a painter, a boxer, a horseman, a wanderer, a gambler, an adventurer, and a womanizer. More than most, he relished the game of getting a movie set up and the gamble of out-daring and intimidating the studios. His best pictures reflect those tastes and that attitude and had an expansive, airy readiness for ironic endings, fatal bad luck, and the laughter that knows men are born to fail.

He was assisted in this broad, fetching act by his own rough-hewn face, his gambler's insolence, and his courtly eloquence. He was a character, at least as large as those in his films; there are also stories of a hard, mean streak that did not stop short of cruelty. Roaming all over the world, he could seem Hemingwayesque, though he possessed a serene confidence denied to the writer. And he was such a character that eventually people thought to use him in front of the camera. For he always had his act: that's what makes Peter Viertel's novel, *White Hunter, Black Heart*, so fascinating and so frightening. Viertel (who worked on several Huston ventures, including *The African Queen*) loved and admired the man; but he knew the malign devil who was dangerous to be with.

That's what makes Huston's Noah Cross in *Chinatown* (74, Roman Polanski) one of his greatest gifts to the screen: a man of the West, a pioneer and maker of cities, a realist, a killer, and a man of unflawed confidence and selfishness—a terrible, charismatic paradox, a bastard and an aristocrat.

The act and the legend keep getting in the way of the movies he made. His troubles with MGM over *The Red Badge of Courage* had been publicized by Lillian Ross in her book *Picture* and accepted as a fable of individual enterprise thwarted by the stupid system. But *Red Badge* remains as a series of gracious battle scenes, a noble aspiration, but a folly and a mess. Much later, Huston was reported as devoted to the point of his own extinction, surviving on oxygen, as he shot *The Dead* (in California). No doubt about the courage or the gambling perseverance. But that movie is muddled and a travesty of the Joyce story, for all the care and delicacy in art direction and the array of Dublin players.

Yes, Huston was always ambitious to exceed the set limits of American genres, and surely he loved distant and difficult locations (not only for the films, but for the chance of adventure they provided). Yes, he was a born storyteller, and someone who easily got bored with his own movies if the story proved slack or misbegotten. How often? Well, if Huston was a grand or good director, we have to reconcile ourselves to the banality and sheer boredom of, at least, *Across the Pacific; We Were Strangers; The Barbarian and the Geisha; Freud: The Secret Passion; The List of Adrian Messenger; The Bible; Sinful Davey; A Walk With Love and Death* (the first movie chance for his daughter, Anjelica, yet an ordeal for her, too—a warning even?); *The Kremlin Letter; The Life and Times of Judge Roy Bean; The Mackintosh Man; Victory; Phobia;* and *Annie.*

Then there are the famous or alleged successes that crack apart on investigation because of arty pretension (*Moulin Rouge* and *Under the Volcano,* for instance) or because of the star-struck kindness of critics. *The Maltese Falcon* was a striking debut, and it did put Lorre and Greenstreet together, as well as allowing Mary Astor to be Brigid O'Shaughnessy. But it's overrated, talky, slow, and often clumsy in its shooting. Bogart goes in and out of moods in uncertainty, and Mary Astor's Brigid cannot help but illustrate Huston's misogyny. *The African Queen* is a beloved film for many, yet is it about real people or the chutzpah of brave casting and actors' schtick? *Prizzi's Honor* has several droll passages, and in casting his daughter as Mae Rose, Huston pulled off a coup and helped heal old wounds. But the picture is so lugubriously slow, and Nicholson seems so unsure about the mood to play it in—just like Bogart years before (Huston was not known for directing actors—he cast them and watched how the cards played). Nor did Huston see that Richard Condon's novel might have translated better to the screen if Mae Rose had been at its center.

But Huston never quite trusted women as characters. He married a lot—Evelyn Keyes and the model/dancer Ricki Soma were two of his wives—and there were many affairs. But in the movies women are sometimes nowhere to be seen (*Red Badge, Treasure of the Sierra Madre, Moby Dick,* and most of *The Man Who Would be King*—and wouldn't Huston have preferred a *Misfits* without Monroe?). Elsewhere they are exotic adornments, prizes for the men, or emblems of treachery as witness Brigid O'Shaughnessy, Monroe in *The Asphalt Jungle* (an unwitting doll), and Lily Langtry in *Roy Bean.* There are so few films in which women matter. As for love stories, *The African Queen* is the best that Huston could do—and that, really, is just another version of *Heaven Knows, Mr. Allison,* the intriguing but truly safe (because impossible) mismatch, so that love and sex need not be explored. There is no real female challenge to the male smoke-room atmosphere of the films. But there is a list of female onlookers as wan and powerless as Jacqueline Bisset in *Under the Volcano,* Lauren Bacall in *Key Largo,* Elizabeth Taylor in *Reflections in a Golden Eye,* and Dominique Sanda in *The Mackintosh Man.*

Huston had begun in movies as a screenwriter: *A House Divided* (31, William Wyler); *Law and Order* (32, Edward L. Cahn); *Murders in the Rue Morgue* (32, Robert Florey); *Death Drives Through* (35, Cahn); *Rhodes of Africa* (36, Berthold Viertel); *Jezebel* (38, Wyler); *The Amazing Dr. Clitterhouse* (38, Anatole Litvak); *Juarez* (39, William Dieterle); *Dr. Ehrlich's Magic Bullet* (40, Dieterle); *High Sierra* (41, Raoul Walsh); and *Sergeant York* (41, Howard Hawks). Later on, he had a hand in the scripts for *The Killers* (46, Robert Siodmak); *The Stranger* (46, Orson

Welles); and *Three Strangers* (46, Jean Negulesco). And as a director, he was usually involved in reworking the scripts he shot.

But Huston showed his allegiance to the golden age in that he preferred to work from proven books and plays. Indeed, sometimes he showed a Selznick-like urge to cover the respectable literary waterfront: Melville, Tennessee Williams, Flannery O'Connor, Arthur Miller, Kipling, C. S. Forester, B. Traven . . . and so on (it's a surprise that Huston ducked out of the Selznick *A Farewell to Arms*). There is hardly an original in Huston's career. Yet the diverse materials are shaped to his vision, as well as to his shortcomings.

So I am not a big fan. Still, there are Huston films that are hard to deny: *The Treasure of the Sierra Madre* is so happy with its own story it has a chipper fatalism, Walter Huston and Bogart are fine, and you feel you're in Mexico; *The Asphalt Jungle* is a taut thriller, a model story of a brilliant plan and its certain disaster full of Huston's strengths—story atmosphere and lively supporting actors: Calhern, Hayden, and Sam Jaffe; *Beat the Devil* is startlingly loose and free, and very funny—it gets better as time passes—and who else would have dared do it?; *Fat City* is close to a great film, dark, sordid, despairing, and deeply provincial, free from Huston's besetting cynicism, and with fine performances from Stacy Keach and Jeff Bridges; and *The Man Who Would Be King* would have pleased Kipling himself. Then there is *Moby Dick*, a big failure in its day, forced into some awkward process shots, yet beautiful in its windblanched coloring, true to Melville and with Gregory Peck far better than one might have expected.

That's a rich handful to go with *Chinatown*, the links to father Walter and daughter Anjelica (very honest actors), the sheer dazzle of his own legend, and the wonder of just how he got away with being thought of for so long as a great director.

He also acted more: good in *The Cardinal* (63, Otto Preminger) and *The Wind and the Lion* (75, John Milius), but variously wasted, foolish, and shameless in *The Bible* (as Noah); *De Sade* (69, Cy Endfield and Roger Corman); *Man in the Wilderness* (71, Richard C. Sarafian); *Sherlock Holmes in New York* (76, Boris Sagal); *Angela* (77, Sagal); *The Great Battle* (78, Umberto Lenzi); *The Visitor* (79, Giuli Parasisi); *Jaguar Lives!* (79, Ernest Pintoff); *Winter Kills* (79, William Richert); *Head On* (80, Michael Grant); narrating *Cannery Row* (82, David S. Ward); and *Lovesick* (83, Marshall Brickman).

Walter Huston (Walter Houghston)
(1884–1950), b. Toronto, Canada
Huston lacked the raw material of a star: he was not beautiful; he was forty-six before he made his

first film; he never entirely gave up Broadway for Hollywood. Above all, he was never ingratiating: indeed, some of his earlier films—*The Criminal Code* (31, Howard Hawks), for instance—are startling for their unaffected understatement. Huston is one of those actors who seem to hide most of their feelings and thoughts. As a cinematic method it has no equal and Huston—although as years went by he succumbed more readily to overplaying—is a constantly interesting actor.

He trained as an engineer, but gave that up for vaudeville and then the legitimate theatre. When sound came, he was one of the many stage actors invited to Hollywood; in this case to Paramount for *Gentlemen of the Press* (29, Millard Webb) and *The Lady Lies* (29, Hobart Henley). He made a big impact as the villain in *The Virginian* (29, Victor Fleming) and then showed his versatility in the title role of *Abraham Lincoln* (30, D. W. Griffith); a romance, *The Virtuous Sin* (30, George Cukor and Louis Gasnier); the prison governor in *The Criminal Code*. At Warners, he made *Star Witness* (31, William Wellman); *The Ruling Voice* (31, Rowland V. Lee); and *The Woman from Monte Carlo* (32, Michael Curtiz). He also played in William Wyler's *A House Divided* (31), a reworking of *Desire Under the Elms*, which Huston had done on the stage.

This was his busiest period and he managed to dominate every film he made: as Wyatt Earp in *Law and Order* (32, Edward L. Cahn); a policeman in *Beast of the City* (32, Charles Brabin); a drunk in *The Wet Parade* (32, Fleming); the banker in Capra's *American Madness* (32); and Reverend Davidson, opposite Joan Crawford's Sadie Thompson, in *Rain* (32, Lewis Milestone). But he was not a star and the quality of his movies began to fluctuate: *Hell Below* (32, Jack Conway); the president in *Gabriel Over the White House* (33, Gregory La Cava); *The Prizefighter and the Lady* (33, W. S. Van Dyke); going to prison in *Ann Vickers* (33, John Cromwell); and *Storm at Daybreak* (33, Richard Boleslavsky).

He played Sinclair Lewis's *Dodsworth* (36, Wyler) on stage, and then on film, and gave a beautiful portrait of an ordinary, truthful man of wealth and power. He went to England to play *Rhodes of Africa* (36, Berthold Viertel) and *The Tunnel* (36, Maurice Elvey), but had few offers of further work and only made *Of Human Hearts* (38, Clarence Brown) and *The Light that Failed* (39, Wellman) in the next four years. With the war, he found more work, although almost exclusively in character parts: *All That Money Can Buy* (41, William Dieterle); staggering into Spade's room with the bundle and then expiring in *The Maltese Falcon* (41, the first film directed by his son, John); *Swamp Water* (41, Jean Renoir); *The Shanghai Gesture* (41, Josef von Sternberg); the father in *Yankee Doodle Dandy* (42, Curtiz);

the ambassador in *Mission to Moscow* (43, Curtiz); *The North Star* (43, Milestone); deliciously funny as Pat Garrett in *The Outlaw* (the Howard Hughes/Howard Hawks melange, shot in 1940, released in 1946, and better than most critics claim); *Dragonseed* (44, Conway); *And Then There Were None* (45, René Clair); *Dragonwyck* (46, Joseph Mankiewicz); the preacher in *Duel in the Sun* (46, King Vidor).

Huston's career ended with four shaggy parts: the rather callow old-timer in his son's *Treasure of the Sierra Madre* (47) for which he got the supporting actor Oscar; *Summer Holiday* (47, Rouben Mamoulian); the gambling-mad father in *The Great Sinner* (49, Robert Siodmak); and the patriarch in *The Furies* (50, Anthony Mann).

Betty Hutton (Betty June Thornburg),
b. 1921, Battle Creek, Michigan

1944: "Betty Hutton is almost beyond good and evil, so far as I am concerned . . ."

1945: "I may begin to tire of Betty Hutton's violence some day, but I haven't yet . . ."

1945: "Betty Hutton just about saves [*Incendiary Blonde*], but no more, for those who like her, and I do."

The uncharacteristically defensive note is James Agee's, and I feel defensive, too, about liking her—but I do. A lot of people couldn't (and can't) stand her, but for a decade she was a highly popular star, appearing in at least three central movies of the period. She belted, she hoofed, she grinned, she smirked, she goofed, she mugged—she was a bombshell, or at least a hand grenade. But the more you watch her, the more she appeals, with her naïve belief that she can blast you into appreciation. And as the years, and films, go by, she actually starts to act. In *The Perils of Pauline* (47, George Marshall) she softens after the classically rambunctious sewing-machine number, and her singing of the hit ballad "I Wish I Didn't Love You So" is simple and affecting. And how would *you* cope with having John Lund as your love interest? (Hutton is usually the girl pursuing rather than the girl pursued—in other words, she's cast in the girl-comic tradition, like a Martha Raye or Cass Daley; but she's pretty, too, so she can get the handsome guy at the end, even if he *is* a lox.)

It's the old story: vanished father, alcoholic mother, singing anywhere and everywhere to help the family survive (her sister became the successful band singer Marion Hutton, vocalist with the Vincent Lopez band. Then Broadway—*Two for the Show* and Cole Porter's *Panama Hattie*, from which she was plucked by Paramount and her first feature movie, *The Fleet's In* (1942, Victor Schertzinger). (Dorothy Lamour got William Holden, Hutton got comic Eddie Bracken—but she also got Johnny Mercer's "Arthur Murray Taught Me Dancing in a Hurry.")

She was to appear opposite Bracken in her finest movie by far, Preston Sturges's hilarious *The Miracle of Morgan's Creek* (44), as the ultimate ditzy blonde, Trudy Kockenlocker, who—apparently unmarried—gives birth to sextuplets. (This movie was considered too risqué for kids!) She and Bracken were also together as a kind of glue for the all-star *Star-Spangled Rhythm* (42, Marshall) and in *Happy Go Lucky* (43, Curtis Bernhardt), in which she steals the show—from Mary Martin and Dick Powell—with the Frank Loesser–Jimmy McHugh "Murder He Says." She played opposite Bob Hope in *Let's Face It* (43, Sidney Lanfield), Bing Crosby in *Here Come the Waves* (44, Mark Sandrich), even Fred Astaire in *Let's Dance* (50, Norman Z. McLeod)—less terrible than people claim. But her Big Two in terms of box office were *Annie Get Your Gun* (50, George Sidney), in which she replaced the ailing Judy Garland for MGM and did a frenzied but more than acceptable job, and De Mille's *The Greatest Show on Earth*, which won the Oscar as best picture of 1952. It's pretty ghastly, but she's okay as the trapeze artist, Holly. This movie earned more money than anything Paramount had released before.

You'd think Hutton was riding high, but there was only one more real vehicle, a biopic of Blossom Seeley, *Somebody Loves Me* (52, Irving Brecher). She had been getting more and more temperamental and confrontational, and walked out of Paramount in a contract dispute. There was to be a minor film in 1957, and then decades of trying to make it in theatre and TV, followed by breakdowns and recovery with the help of a Catholic priest. (She became a housekeeper in a Rhode Island rectory.) With the help of God and therapy, she's apparently found her way to self-acceptance and a decent life, appearing in 2001 in a sympathetic documentary about her career and her travails. The career lasted a decade, but while it lasted she was at the top. And as she said, "Some kinds of fun last longer than others."

Films: *The Fleet's In* (42, Victor Schertzinger/Hal Walker); *Star Spangled Rhythm* (42, George Marshall); *Happy Go Lucky* (43, Curtis Bernhardt); *Let's Face It* (43, Sidney Lanfield); *And the Angels Sing* (44, Marshall); *The Miracle of Morgan's Creek* (44, Sturges); *Here Come the Waves* (44, Mark Sandrich); *Incendiary Blonde* (45, Marshall), as Texas Guinan; *The Stork Club* (45, Marshall), a mess, but it gave her a number-one hit, "Doctor, Lawyer, Indian Chief"; *Duffy's Tavern* (45, Walker), in a cameo as herself; *Cross My Heart* (46, John Berry), a remake of Lombard's *True Confession* and a big mistake; *The Perils of Pauline* (47, Marshall), as Pearl White, the Serial Queen; *Dream Girl* (48, Mitchell Leisen); *Red, Hot and Blue* (49, Robert Fellows)—not, alas, the Cole Porter musical; *Annie Get Your Gun* (50,

George Sidney); *Let's Dance* (50, Norman Z. McLeod), Hutton first-billed over Astaire!; *The Greatest Show on Earth* (52, De Mille); *Somebody Loves Me* (52, Irving Brecher); *Spring Reunion* (57, Robert Pirosh).

Any remaining doubters should be aware that Betty Hutton was Ludwig Wittgenstein's favorite actress.

I

Kon Ichikawa, b. Ujiyamada, Japan, 1915
1946: *Musume Dojoji* (unreleased). 1947: *Toho Sen-Ichiya* (unfinished). 1948: *Hana Hiraku; Sanbyaku Rokujugo-ya* (two parts). 1949: *Ningen Moyo; Hateshinaki Jonetsu.* 1950: *Ginza Sanshiro; Netsudei-chi; Akatsuki no Tsuiseki.* 1951: *Ye-Rai-Shang; Koibito; Mukokuseki-Mono; Nusumareta Koi; Bungawan Solo; Kekkon Koshin-kyoku.* 1952: *Lucky San; Wakai Hito; Ashi ni Sawatta Onna; Ano te Kono te.* 1953: *Pusan; Aoiro Kakumei; Seishun Zenigata Heiji; Aijin.* 1954: *Watashi no Subete O; Okuman Choja/A Billionaire; Josei ni Kansuru Junisho.* 1955: *Seishun Kaidan; Kokoro/ The Heart.* 1956: *Biruma no Tategoto/The Burmese Harp; Shokei no Heya/Punishment Room; Nihonbashi.* 1957: *Manin Densha; Ana; Tohoku no Zunmutachi/The Men of Tohoku.* 1958: *Gennama to Bijo to San-Akunin; Enjo/Conflagration.* 1959: *Sayonara Konnichiwa; Kagi/The Key; Nobi/ Fires on the Plain; Keisatsukan to Boroyuku-dan.* 1960: *Ginza no Mosa; Bonchi; Jokyo; Ototo/Her Brother.* 1961: *Kuroi Junin no Onna.* 1962: *Hakai/The Sin; Watashi wa Nisai/Being Two Isn't Easy.* 1963: *Yukinojo Henge/An Actor's Revenge; Taiheiyo Hitoribotchi/Alone on the Pacific.* 1964: *Dokonji Monogatari.* 1965: *Tokyo Orinpukko/ Tokyo Olympiad* (d). 1966: *Genji Monogatari* (episodic film for TV). 1967: *Topo Gigio e i sei Ladri.* 1968: *Tournament/Kyoto.* 1971: *Ai Futatabi.* 1973: *Matatabi/The Wanderers.* 1975: *Wagahai wa Neko Dearu.* 1977: *Akuma no Temari-uta; Inugamike no Ichizoku.* 1978: *Gokumon-to; Hi no Tori; Joh-on Bachi.* 1980: *Koto* (d); *Hi no Tori.* 1982: *Kofuku.* 1983: *Sasame Yuki; Biruma no Tategoto; Ohan.* 1986: *Rokumeikan.* 1987: *Eiga Joyu; Taketori Monogatari.* 1988: *Tsuru.* 1991: *Tenkawa Densetsu Satsujin Jiken.* 1993: *Fusa.* 1994: *Shijushichinin no Shikaku.* 1996: *Yatsuhaka-mura.* 1999: *Dora-heita.* 2001: *Kah-Chan.*

Ichikawa is a director of contradictions, a haphazard obsessive, disconcertingly versatile for the Western spectator who expects concentration and integrity in Oriental cinema. With Mizoguchi, such anticipation seems justified. The greatest characteristic of his films is the elegiac, narrative camera style and the vindication of traditional material—although that appreciation may owe

something to our being familiar with only his late work. Ichikawa, in contrast, is restless, speculative, and unresolved; it is easy to call him flashy, unstable, and modish. Donald Richie has commented on the unpredictable talent of Ichikawa and quoted the director: "People are always surprised at my humor and then they are always surprised at the bleakness of whatever philosophy I have. To me they seem perfectly complementary."

At the same time, Ichikawa has frankly conceded that he sometimes makes films to order. And it is ultimately difficult to reconcile the technological preoccupation with muscle in *Tokyo Olympiad* and the gloating over flesh in *The Key*. The first was a film made in the spirit of the Japanese photographic industry—all ingenious lens effects, picking out spectacular detail, but oblivious of the overall effect, whether sport or public occasion. *The Key* is a study of sexual obsession within a family, compelling but lewd, perhaps reflective of Japanese society but mordantly unsympathetic to characters. Both films seemed inspired by a cold-eyed interest in the mechanics of the body. Against that, *Alone on the Pacific* is a charmingly homespun account of the mundane heroics of a singlehanded trans-Pacific sailor. While *The Burmese Harp* is sometimes hailed as a monument of humanist cinema. Which is to say nothing of the startling cross-fertilization of identities in *An Actor's Revenge;* the calm anguish of *The Sin;* the frenzy of *Conflagration,* based on a Yukio Mishima novel; or the remorseless ordeal of *Fires on the Plain.* When all is said and done, the variety is alarming, the inconsistency his most striking trait.

Ichikawa was a cartoonist when he left school, and he worked on animated films during the 1930s and the war years. This led to employment as an assistant director at Toho and his first project—*Musume Dojoji*—a puppet film banned by the occupying authorities. Animation has remained one of Ichikawa's interests: thus *Pusan, Topo Gigio e i sei Ladri,* and *Being Two Isn't Easy,* which uses cartoon to illustrate a child's view of the world. That playfulness may or may not be complementary to the anguish that dominates many of the films. The sudden sliding into humor may be creative, or evasive. Perhaps Ichikawa proves how many differences of understanding separate us from Japanese cinema. It may also be that his oscillation shows the distracted modern Japanese torn between his past and present.

Shohei Imamura, b. Tokyo, Japan, 1926
1958: *Nusumareta Yokujo/Stolen Desire; Nishi Ginza ekimae/Nishi Ginza Station.* 1959: *Nianchan/My Second Brother.* 1961: *Buta to Gunkan/ Pigs and Battleships.* 1963: *Nippon Konchuki/The*

Insect Woman. 1964: *Akai Satsui/Intentions of Murder*. 1966: *Jinruigaku Nyumon/The Pornographers—An Introduction to Anthropology*. 1967: *Ningen Johatsu/A Man Vanishes*. 1968: *Kamigami no Fukaki Yokubo/The Profound Desire of the Gods*. 1970: *Nippon Sengoshi—Madame Onboro no Seikatsu/History of Postwar Japan as Told by a Bar Hostess* (d). 1971: *In Search of Unreturned Soldiers* (d). 1972: *Pirates of Bubuan* (d). 1973: *Muhomatsu Returns Home* (d). 1974: *Karayuk-isan—The Making of a Prostitute* (d). 1975: *Still in Search of Unreturned Soldiers* (d); *Report on Two People Named Yoshinobu* (d). 1979: *Fukusho Suruwa Ware Ni Ari/Vengeance Is Mine*. 1981: *Eijanaika/Why Not?* 1983: *Narayama-bushiko/The Ballad of Narayama*. 1987: *Zegen*. 1989: *Kuroi Ame/Black Rain*. 1997: *Unagi/The Eel*. 1998: *Kanzo Sensei/Dr. Akagi*. 2001: *Akai Hashi no Shita no Nurui Mizu*.

Imamura has never been easy to pin down. Although he often seems to identify with the lower orders, he was a doctor's son. But when he failed to gain admission to agricultural school, he studied Western history at Waseda University and then made another sideways leap to a film studio job. As such, he became an assistant to Ozu—only to declare that he wanted to explore a kind of cinema opposed to that of his master. He wanted more real turbulence or untidiness, less literary resignation and acceptance, more actual greed and desire. "I am interested in the relationship of the lower part of the human body and the lower part of the social structure," he proclaimed.

Fair enough: Imamura came of age in a Japan of convulsions, and he has been fascinated by lowlife sexuality, prostitution, and television. He has exhibited a robust, sensual approach that is not unlike the style of Dennis Potter. In the seventies, he stepped aside from feature filmmaking to do a series of TV documentaries with a special interest in the lost soldiers of Japan and the prostitutes that the country had employed or dragooned. This period also crystallized his belligerent, ironic wariness with documentary—as evident in *A Man Vanishes*, an apparent documentary survey of missing persons in which the fiancée whose man has vanished begins to fall for the interviewer. Similarly, in *Intention of Murder*, the raped woman develops a strange fascination with the rapist. Whether he really believes in such forces, or whether emotionally he prefers them to more rational schemes, Imamura is a gourmet of the dark, irrational underside. If he had made *Kane*, Thompson might have become the tyrant.

There's no denying the energy of his best work, the unruly inventiveness, and the subversive attitudes. Thus, his Cannes prizewinner, *Ballad of Narayama*, is a brutally physical realization of a cherished Japanese legend. Still active, Imamura

stands up for the modern Japan, as if to point to the genteel ways of Mizoguchi and Ozu. But the exposé works both ways. And there is no doubt as to who are the greater artists.

Thomas Harper Ince (1882–1924),
b. Newport, Rhode Island

Should Ince be treated as a director, or as a producer? Or is his relevance simply a matter of the historical contrast he offers with D. W. Griffith? Ince is not a name that rings many bells today; yet, he had a very active career and, in the early 1920s, was thought of as one of the most important, and self-important, of men. It was Buster Keaton, in *The Playhouse* (21), who mocked Ince's overweening claim to story, production, and direction on films that were made by his company. Keaton's joke seems to have made ostentation retract, and research discovers few full-length films that Ince directed on his own.

Nevertheless, he was a pioneer in the way he insinuated himself into film production and set about organizing it. In addition, in 1916, he built new studios at Culver City that were to become the basis of the MGM complex (his second home—just down the street—would later be the home of David O. Selznick, and thus a famous logo image). "Thomas H. was my Ince-spiration," said Keaton of *The Playhouse*. But, in fact, Thomas H's shameless self-aggrandizement seems the original of a brand of ambition central to American films. In that sense, he was the first tycoon, more businesslike than Griffith and much more prosperous. Remember that he died in early middle age, and it is possible to surmise that he might have become one of the moguls of the 1930s.

His own origins were theatrical. He had been in stock and vaudeville for some ten years before he entered the infant film industry, probably through the agency of his wife, Eleanor Kershaw, who was an actress in Griffith's company. Ince was briefly at Biograph before moving on to Independent to direct. From 1911–14 he directed several hundred one- or two-reelers. But he seemed less interested in the product than in the marketing of it. He joined the New York Motion Picture Company and went to California to make Westerns, hiring a Wild West show for authenticity and buying up land for a celluloid range. The "Western" as a spectacle owes much to Ince's labor as did William S. Hart whose films Ince supervised. In 1914 he directed his first feature, *The Battle of Gettysburg*—and, probably, his last, for he plunged into production and supervision.

In 1915, with Griffith and Sennett, he formed Triangle, the clear forerunner of United Artists. Ince himself produced *The Coward* (15, Reginald Barker) and *Civilization* (16), which, reputedly, he codirected with Barker. *Civilization* was as much a success as *Intolerance* was a failure. It is set in a mythical country, deals portentously with the threat of war, and is dedicated to "the mothers of the dead." Nothing suggests that Ince thought or felt deeper than such blatantly rabble-rousing sentiments. Nor that he was shy about seeing himself as the benign patron of civilization.

In the last years of the war, he continued to produce William S. Hart movies, and his stable of directors included Barker, Irvin Willat, Frank Borzage, Arthur Rossen, Victor Schertzinger, and Jack Conway. He left Triangle in 1918 and produced films for Adolph Zukor to distribute. In 1919 he joined with Sennett, Maurice Tourneur, Allan Dwan, and Marshall Neilan in Associated Producers. Ince continued to be released through Zukor until late in 1921—producing such films as *Beau Revel* (21, John Griffith Wray); *The Bronze Bell* (21, James Horne); *The Cup of Life* (21, Rowland V. Lee); *Mother o' Mine* (21, Fred Niblo); and *Passing Thru* (21, William A. Seiter). When he broke with Zukor, Associated Producers went over to First National, and in his last years Ince maintained his "personal supervision" on *The Hottentot* (22, Horne); *Skin Deep* (22, Lambert Hillyer); *Anna Christie* (23, Wray); *Bell Boy 13* (23, Seiter); *Her Reputation* (23, Wray); *A Man of Action* (23, Horne); *Scars of Jealousy* (23, Hillyer); *Soul of the Beast* (23, Wray); *The Sunshine Trail* (23, Horne); *What a Wife Learned* (23, Wray); *Barbara Frietchie* (24, Hillyer); *Christine of the Hungry Heart* (24, George Archainbaud); *Idle Tongues* (24, Hillyer); *The Marriage Cheat* (24, Wray); and *Those Who Dance* (24, Hillyer).

Ince contributed something else to Hollywood legend—the mystery of his death—and it is probably the aspect of his career that is most interesting now. In November 1924, William Randolph Hearst threw a yachting party on his boat, the *Oneida*, sailing off the southern California coast. The passengers included Marion Davies, Chaplin, Ince, Elinor Glyn, and the young Louella Parsons. Ince was taken off the yacht at San Diego. He died two days later, and the official cause of death was given as heart failure following what had been severe indigestion. But rumors sprang up that there had been drinking on the boat, that shots had been fired, that Chaplin (and/or Ince) had made a pass at Marion Davies. It is one of the great Hollywood enigmas still, in that richly scandalous moment of the early 1920s. And surely it is beyond solution now.

Rex Ingram (Reginald Hitchcock)
(1893–1950), b. Dublin, Ireland

1916: *The Great Problem; Broken Fetters; Chalice of Sorrow.* 1917: *Black Orchids; The Reward of Life; The Flower of Doom; His Robe of Honour; Humdrum Brown.* 1919: *The Day She Paid.* 1920: *Shore Acres; Under Crimson Skies.* 1921: *The Four Horsemen of the Apocalypse; Hearts Are Trumps; The Conquering Power.* 1922: *The Prisoner of Zenda; Trifling Women; Turn to the Right.* 1923: *Scaramouche; Where the Pavement Ends.* 1924: *The Arab.* 1926: *The Magician; Mare Nostrum.* 1927: *The Garden of Allah.* 1929: *The Three Passions.* 1933: *Baroud.*

Few careers are as mysteriously romantic as Ingram's. He was obviously an independent and unusually imaginative man; those few of his films that survive suggest that he is an important director with a rapturous visual style.

He was the son of a clergyman who brought him to America in 1911. At the Yale School of Fine Arts, he studied sculpture. He worked for Edison, Vitagraph, Fox, and joined Universal in 1916, but he was "discovered" by June Mathis and assigned to direct Valentino in *Four Horsemen of the Apocalypse* and *The Conquering Power,* both of which also starred Ingram's wife, Alice Terry. He was known as a director of swashbuckling spectacles and of supernatural or horror movies. *Trifling Women,* based on one of Ingram's own stories, has Barbara La Marr as a femme fatale. That film, *Scaramouche, Where the Pavement Ends,* and *The Arab* all starred Ramon Novarro. Ingram had hoped to be allowed to direct *Ben-Hur;* when disappointed he threatened to retire, and von Stroheim and Dmitri Buchowetzki insisted on his return, calling him the world's greatest director. Von Stroheim and Ingram were friends—itself a sign of Ingram's imaginative reach—and when *Greed* was beset by problems, it was Ingram who cut it from twenty-four to eighteen reels.

In fact, Ingram and Alice Terry left America after *Ben-Hur,* complaining of studio ineptness, but allowed MGM to help them set up their own studio, Victorine, in Nice. There they made *The Magician,* from a Somerset Maugham novel, photographed by John Seitz, starring Paul Wegener as an Aleister Crowley–like evil genius. Stills suggest that it is, at the least, an ornate fantasy with erotic undertones. *Mare Nostrum* was made in the Mediterranean and for *Garden of Allah* Ingram took his company to North Africa. He made only one talking picture, *Baroud,* also in Morocco, in which he acted.

One of Ingram's apprentices in the south of France was Michael Powell, who has testified to Ingram's charisma, knowledge, taste, and capacity for being easily bored. Ingram became fascinated by Islam, but neither he nor Alice Terry enjoyed sound. *The Three Passions* and *Baroud* were failures, and Ingram and Terry went back to live in Los Angeles where he worked as painter, sculptor, and novelist, rarely tempted by the movie scene. Alice Terry, maybe, was never quite wild enough for his visions.

There is a useful biography of Ingram, by Liam

O'Leary, that stresses the Irishness and the unusual interest Ingram felt for so many things beyond film. But Powell's tribute, and that of David Lean, suggest that for the 1920s, in the English-speaking film world, Ingram personified artistic ambition and a visual style that made one think of painting. Of course, his life was also a bold gesture meant to show the hopeless vulgarity of Hollywood.

John Ireland (1914–92), b. Vancouver, Canada

Over the years, I know of two young women who caught one glimpse of John Ireland as Cherry Valance in *Red River* (48, Howard Hawks) and had to know more. I suggested that he might have been related in some way to Liberty Valance in John Ford's picture—and both of the young women knew just what I meant. In other words, that rangy, dangerous cowboy from Valverde way in *Red River* may stop a bullet, but he grows in your mind. More or less, as the years go by, I value most of all the actors and the characters who will not stay as they were made. So John Ireland is here now as someone I always want to know more about.

He spent his childhood years in New York, and then he was a carnival swimmer and a theatre actor before doing movies. By the standards of 1947, I daresay, he looked like a villain, what with that leer and the grating voice. But look at Ireland then with modern eyes and you've got a knockout—there are some whose looks are forty or fifty years ahead of public taste. Ireland nearly made it. He got a supporting actor nomination for *All the King's Men* (49, Robert Rossen), and he played the lead in B pictures. But he was now employable as a threat or a hood, and it's as if he took that opinion to heart and turned away from being the flawed hero that was within his reach.

Later on still, he went to Europe and did shlock, combing his hair forward. Those of us who noticed forgave him. And we feel the self-destructiveness as well as the glory in the fact that after *Red River,* it was not Howard Hawks or Montgomery Clift who went off with Joanne Dru, but John Ireland: another young woman who noticed the way he watched her.

It's a very long list, for a guy who seemed to have swallowed his cynic's pills very early in life: *A Walk in the Sun* (46, Lewis Milestone); Billy Clanton in *My Darling Clementine* (46, John Ford); a vicious gangster in *Railroaded* (47, Anthony Mann); *The Gangster* (47, Gordon Wiles); *Raw Deal* (48, Mann); *Joan of Arc* (48, Victor Fleming); *A Southern Yankee* (48, Edward Sedgwick); as Bob Ford in *I Shot Jesse James* (49, Samuel Fuller); *Roughshod* (49, Mark Robson); *Anna Lucasta* (49, Irving Rapper); *The Doolins of Oklahoma* (49, Gordon Douglas); *Cargo to Capetown* (50, Earl McEvoy); *Vengeance Valley* (51, Richard

Thorpe); trying to prove his innocence, with Mercedes McCambridge, in *The Scarf* (51, E. A. Dupont); *Little Big Horn* (51, Charles Marquis Warren); *The Bushwhackers* (52, Rod Amateau); as Quantrill in *Red Mountain* (51, William Dieterle); *Hurricane Smith* (52, Jerry Hopper); after A-bomb spies in *The 49th Man* (53, Fred F. Sears).

He then coproduced, codirected (with Lee Garmes), and acted with Joanne Dru in *Outlaw Territory* (53), and carried on as if nothing had happened: in Korea in *Combat Squad* (53, Cy Roth); *Security Risk* (54, Harold Schuster); with Dru again in *Southwest Passage* (54, Ray Nazarro); *The Fast and the Furious* (54, Edwards Sampson, with Ireland), a film written and produced by Roger Corman; *The Steel Cage* (54, Walter Doniger); *Queen Bee* (55, Ranald MacDougall); *Hell's Horizon* (55, Tom Gries); *Gunslinger* (56, Corman); and Ike Clanton in *Gunfight at the O.K. Corral* (57, John Sturges).

He was forty-three, and it was 1957 in Hollywood. All the lights were going out. The marriage to Joanne Dru had broken down. Ireland's B pictures were close to dead. One longs for a book that tells us what he felt then. *Party Girl* (58, Nicholas Ray); *Spartacus* (60, Stanley Kubrick); with Elvis and Tuesday Weld in *Wild in the Country* (61, Philip Dunne); *55 Days at Peking* (63, Ray); *The Ceremony* (63, Laurence Harvey); *The Fall of the Roman Empire* (64, Mann); *I Saw What You Did* (65, William Castle).

He did at least another thirty films, including *Guyana: Cult of the Damned* (80, Rene Cardona) and *Messenger of Death* (88, J. Lee Thompson), with a final bow called *Waxwork II: Lost in Time* (92, Anthony Hickox). But he never got to play Old Man Clanton.

Jeremy Irons, b. Cowes, England, 1948

For several years, Irons was best known as Charles Ryder in the universally admired TV adaptation of Evelyn Waugh's *Brideshead Revisited* (81, Charles Sturridge and Michael Lindsay-Hogg). He seemed so well cast as the gaunt, slightly out-of-his-element, and increasingly melancholy observer of grandeur's decline. His sad, subtle voice was made for the voice-over narrative. His soulful reticence was an unstressed sustenance to the larger sense of erratic but worthy aristocracy he beheld. His Charles Ryder was fit for Waugh, and for Graham Greene. If one looked ahead, it was to imagine Irons as, maybe, Richard II, Uncle Vanya, or any of Greene's mortified witnesses to their own lack of quality.

He had been educated at Sherborne and the Bristol Old Vic Theatre School, and he was one of those English actors who had seen and felt the upper reaches of the class system. Yet he seemed happier doing exotics than gents: he was Mikhail

Fokine in *Nijinsky* (80, Herbert Ross) and a very credible Pole in *Moonlighting* (82, Jerzy Skoli-mowski). Whereas he seemed conventional and staid in *The French Lieutenant's Woman* (81, Karel Reisz), in the D. H. Lawrence story, *The Captain's Doll* (82, Claude Whatham), and in the Pinter wrong-way-rounder, *Betrayal* (83, David Jones).

That he was looking for something different was evident from *The Wild Duck* (83, Henri Safran), and the very unsatisfying *Swann in Love* (84, Volker Schlöndorff), to say nothing of the woefully pretentious *The Mission* (86, Roland Joffé). Having wearied a little of lofty cinema, Irons turned to lower depths: hence his magnificent double performance as the twins in *Dead Ringers* (88, David Cronenberg), one of the greatest performances of the eighties. Moreover, Irons's capacity for gentleness and gallows humor surely enabled Cronenberg to enrich his own film. Thus, out of potentially exploitative material came a masterpiece, as well as the realization that Irons was adventurous, in love with disguise, play, and very bold strokes. In short, he was no Charles Ryder.

Whether that spirit can find the right parts remains in question. For the moment, Irons seems attached to Englishness and small subjects—*A Chorus of Disapproval* (89, Michael Winner), from Alan Ayckbourn; *Danny the Champion of the World* (89, Gavin Millar); and *Waterland* (92, Stephen Gyllenhaal), a curious and misguided adaptation of Graham Swift that seeks to transfer the Fenland to Pittsburgh, Pennsylvania. Still, *Waterland* did allow Irons to work with his wife, Sinead Cusack.

Meanwhile, Irons won his Oscar for a very skilled one-note impersonation as Claus von Bulow in *Reversal of Fortune* (90, Barbet Schroeder). The result is sketchy, and a fraction of *Dead Ringers*, but it does show that Irons's English gentlemen need to be bogus, and out of the dafter reaches of imagination, if they want to hold the actor's interest. He was wasted in *Kafka* (91, Steven Soderbergh) and he could not bring sympathy, belief, or the required monstrous, uncontrollable need to the M.P. in *Damage* (92, Louis Malle). He played one more aghast onlooker in *Tales from Hollywood* (92, Howard Davies) for TV. He was helplessly adrift in *M. Butterfly* (93, Cronenberg) and *The House of the Spirits* (93, Bille August), projects that began to suggest how easily Irons could become an outcast actor.

That 1994 prediction gets fair marks. Irons has wandered, he has done voices, and he has had some offbeat parts in films not widely seen: the voice of Scar in *The Lion King* (94, Roger Allers and Rob Minkoff); another awful villain in *Die Hard: With a Vengeance* (95, John McTiernan); taking a long, wordy time to expire in *Stealing*

Beauty (96, Bernardo Bertolucci); the voice of Siegfried Sassoon on TV's *The Great War* (96); *Chinese Box* (97, Wayne Wang); valiant as Humbert Humbert in *Lolita* (97, Adrian Lyne), but a touch too sinister compared with James Mason's healthy intellectual superiority; Aramis in *The Man in the Iron Mask* (98, Randall Wallace); voices in animated films—*Poseidon's Fury* (99) and *Faeries* (99); *Longitude* (00, Sturridge—his old discoverer); a voice on *Dungeons & Dragons* (00, Courtney Solomon); *Ohio Impromptu* (00, Sturridge); *The Fourth Angel* (01, John Irvin); *The Night of the Iguana* (01, Predrag Antonijevic); *Callas Forever* (02, Franco Zeffirelli); *The Time Machine* (02, Simon Wells); as F. Scott Fitzgerald in *Last Call* (02, Henry Bromell); *And Now . . . Ladies and Gentlemen* (02, Claude Lelouch).

Amy Irving, b. Palo Alto, California, 1953

From 1985–89, Amy Irving was Mrs. Steven Spielberg—and it wasn't easy. Mutual friend Matthew Robbins is quoted as saying in Joseph McBride's *Spielberg* biography, "It was no fun to go [to their home—or one of their four houses], because there was an electric tension in the air. It was competitive as to whose dining table this is, whose career we're gonna talk about, or whether he even approved of what she was interested in— her friends and her actor life. . . . The child in Spielberg believed so thoroughly in the possibility of perfect marriage. . . . And Amy was sort of a glittering prize, smart as hell, gifted, and beautiful, but definitely edgy and provocative and competitive. She would not provide him any ease."

Has it worked out better, even with the $100 million (more or less) in divorce settlement? Or is there always going to be something smart and aggrieved in Amy Irving? She is the daughter of theatre director Jules Irving and actress Priscilla Pointer—and she has been heard to say that she had that to get over first. Having been trained at ACT in San Francisco and RADA in London, she began early on as the witness in *Carrie* (76, Brian De Palma) and then the inane *The Fury* (78, De Palma), where she moved with exceptional grace.

But she was hard to cast—for she had a virginal look that did not exactly fit her mind: as a deaf woman in *Voices* (79, Robert Markovitz); *Honeysuckle Rose* (80, Jerry Schatzberg); as a pianist in *The Competition* (80, Joel Oliansky); nominated as supporting actress in *Yentl* (83, Barbra Streisand); *Micki + Maude* (84, Blake Edwards).

The most notable sign of Spielberg's influence was that she sang for Jessica Rabbit in *Who Framed Roger Rabbit* (88, Robert Zemeckis). And she did a voice for *An American Tail: Fievel Goes West* (91, Phil Nibbelink). But she was lovely and touching in *Crossing Delancey* (88, Joan Micklin Silver), albeit in another underlined Jewish role. And she played the reporter in *A Show of Force*

(90, Bruno Barreto).

She had a son with Spielberg and, after the divorce, she had a child with Barreto, whom she later married. Then, after *Benefit of the Doubt* (93, Jonathan Heape), she helped produce and acted in Barreto's outstanding *Carried Away* (96)—she played the neglected fiancée, and has never been better. After that, she played in *I'm Not Rappaport* (96, Herb Gardner); *Bossa Nova* (99, Barreto); *Traffic* (00, Steven Soderbergh); *13 Conversations About One Thing* (01, Jill Sprecher); *Tuck Everlasting* (02, Jay Russell).

Joris Ivens (Georg Henri Anton Ivens) (1898–1989), b. Nijmegen, Holland

All films are documentaries, except those marked (f):
1928: *De Brug; Etude de Mouvements; La Bar de Juffrouw Heyens; Branding* (codirected with Mannus Franken). 1929: *Regen* (codirected with Franken); *Schaatsenrijden; IK-Film* (codirected with Hans van Meerten). 1930: *Zuiderzee; Wij Bouwen* (in four parts); *Congres der Vak-vereenigingen; Timmerfabriek.* 1931: *Symphonie van den Arbeid; Creosoot.* 1932: *Komsomol.* 1933: *Borinage* (codirected with Henri Storck); *Hein.* 1934: *Nieuwe Gronden.* 1937: *Spanish Earth.* 1939: *The Four Hundred Million.* 1940: *Power and the Land.* 1941: *Our Russian Front* (codirected with Lewis Milestone); *New Frontiers* (uncompleted). 1942: *Action Stations; Alone.* 1945: *Know Your Enemy: Japan* (codirected with Frank Capra). 1946: *Indonesia Calling.* 1947: *Pierwsze Lata.* 1950: *Pokoj Zwyeciezy Swiata* (codirected with Jerzy Bossak). 1951: *My Za Mir* (codirected with Ivan Pyriev). 1952: *Wyscig Pokoju Warszawa-Berlina-Praga.* 1954: *Das Lied der Ströme.* 1956: *Die Vind Rose* (supervised with Alberto Cavalcanti) (f); *Les Aventures de Till L'Espiègle* (codirected with Gérard Philipe) (f). 1957: *La Seine a Recontré Paris; Lettres de Chine* (in three parts). 1958: *Six Cents Million avec Vous.* 1959: *L'Italia non e'un Paese Povero.* 1960: *Demain à Nanguila.* 1961: *Carnet de Viaje; Pueblo en Armas.* 1962: . . . *A Valparaiso; El Circo mas Pequeno del Mundo.* 1964: *Le Train de la Victoire.* 1965: *Viet-Nam!.* 1966: *Le Mistral; Le Ciel, la Terre; Rotterdam-Europoort.* 1967: *Loin du Viet-nam* (codirected with Jean-Luc Godard, William Klein, Alain Resnais, and Claude Lelouch). 1968: *Dix-septième Parallèle* (codirected with Marceline Loridan); *Le Peuple et Ses Fusils; La Guerre Pop-ulaire au Laos* (codirected); *Rencontre avec le Président Ho Chi Minh* (codirected with Loridan). 1976: *Comment Yukong Déplaces les Montagnes* (codirected with Loridan). 1988: *Une Histoire de Vent/A Story of the Wind* (codirected with Lori-dan).

Joris Ivens was like one of those long-serving suit-cases held together by the labels of a lifetime's travel. Having fought in the First World War and studied photography, he made scientific films for the University of Leyden, worked as a documen-tarist in Holland, and then went to Russia to make *Komsomol.* Thereafter, he pursued the vio-lent troubles of the world. First, he coordinated the many indignant talents involved on *Spanish Earth;* he went to China for *The Four Hundred Million;* and made *Power and the Land* for the U.S. government. During the war, he lectured at UCLA and worked for the American and Cana-dian governments. In 1945, he went to the East in an official capacity for the Dutch government, only to resign when Holland refused to recognize the independence of Indonesia. For the next ten years he worked in Eastern Europe. In 1956, he collaborated with Cavalcanti on *Die Vind Rose* and also produced and codirected with Gérard Philipe, *Les Aventures de Till l'Espiègle.* Nearing sixty, he traveled again—through China, South America, and Africa. Those seemed more tran-quil years, but he was steadied in the Far East and reinforced as a radical by the war in Vietnam. Ivens's work gradually shed formality. As a young Dutch documentary-maker, he was firmly in the "symphonic" tradition. But *Spanish Earth* was a crucial film in that it admitted the existence of sit-uations where one could only film what was possi-ble, put it together, and let the terrible urgency be known to the rest of the world. Ivens is thus the original international cameraman, intent on showing the recesses of current events and the horrors, triumphs, and injustices that occur. He was vastly traveled, but not dejected. And although he made films for Western and Eastern interests, it is the world that has fluctuated. The same humanitarianism drove him throughout. He reminds us of an age when there were no TV units or photojournalists to crowd out disasters with description.

James Ivory, b. Berkeley, California, 1928
1963: *The Householder.* 1965: *Shakespeare Wal-lah.* 1968: *The Guru.* 1970: *Bombay Talkie.* 1972: *Savages; Adventures of a Brown Man in Search of Civilization* (d). 1975: *The Autobiography of a Princess; The Wild Party.* 1977: *Roseland.* 1978: *Hullabaloo Over Georgie and Bonnie's Pictures.* 1979: *The Europeans.* 1981: *Quartet.* 1983: *Heat and Dust.* 1984: *The Bostonians.* 1986: *A Room With a View.* 1987: *Maurice.* 1989: *Slaves of New York.* 1990: *Mr. and Mrs. Bridge.* 1992: *Howards End.* 1993: *The Remains of the Day.* 1995: *Jeffer-son in Paris.* 1996: *Surviving Picasso.* 1998: *A Sol-dier's Daughter Never Cries.* 2001: *The Golden Bowl.* 2003: *Le Divorce.*

It was over forty years ago that Ivory and the pro-ducer Ismail Merchant began their remarkable partnership, notably with an adaptation of Ruth Prawer Jhabvala's novel *The Householder*. The trio has stayed together, and it may have reached its greatest triumph—and, it seems to me, its most characteristic work—in their collaboration on the film of the Kazuo Ishiguro novel *The Remains of the Day*. That film is all the more a vindication for them in that it was originally intended as a Mike Nichols film from a Harold Pinter script (Nichols remained one of the producers). Why did those two powerhouses cede the project? Presumably because they acknowledged the wisdom that no one did such things better than Ivory-Merchant (they are actually known as Merchant-Ivory—to avoid that odd note of the Indian market?).

And no one does it nicer. I saw the first public screening of *The Remains of the Day* in San Francisco, and emerged from the Presidio theatre into the roaring dazzle of Chestnut Street, at three or so in the afternoon, in a throng of elderly viewers congratulating each other on how nice, how lovely, how perfect it had all been, and how "they" didn't make many films as good as that. Nichols and Pinter must have imagined such scenes, and acted accordingly—after all, deference and self-denial are the heart and soul of *The Remains of the Day*.

Let me look on the bright side first. Anyone must admire the friendly partnership that has stayed intact, surviving growing success and carving out a very respectable place in the picture business—for Merchant-Ivory films now do quite nicely at the box office, and they have done so well with the Academy's statuettes that some cynics have wondered if those figures might not be called Maurice instead of Oscar. Ismail Merchant must be patient, an astute mix of the strong and the yielding, the diplomat and the magician. He must be likeable and seductive. Ruth Jhabvala has become a very adroit adapting screenwriter, even if she tranquilly overlooks all the things that such adaptation loses. And James Ivory, the director, seems decent, diffident, tasteful, and the least pronounced or necessary of the three. No one could accuse him of being seductive.

I suspect that Ivory would be gratified to hear that one finds little guile or direction in his films—not much directorial assertion. For wouldn't that mean that the literary originals have come through clearly, like the view through one of the burnished windows at Darlington Hall? Far more vital to the films is the shapeliness of the screenplays, the pavilionlike distinction of the casts, and the banquet, the very feast, that might be called decor—allowing that England's intimate countryside and a well-laid table are just kinds of art direction filling the screen.

The Remains of the Day seems crucial because it depends on repressed emotion, and a level of morality that is indistinguishable from etiquette or good service. The film is built around the astonishing performance of Anthony Hopkins, who is so very clever, so lyrically hidden, so minutely detailed and expressive in his rendering of a man who cannot show his feelings that I felt tortured. I do not blame Hopkins. Actors can do very little but be, or try to be, intelligent, brilliant, and revealing. Stevens, the butler, is unactable, in truth. The concept of the character breaks apart once we see an actor trying. The book allowed him to be unseen, and so the implausibility of the character slipped by. In the book he is also a constipated fusspot who for no good reason tells the story (such men don't tell anyone, not even themselves). Still, Stevens in the novel is closer to the smug, stupid fellow one must suppose from the facts of the story. There is no need to idealize servants. But Hopkins in the film is a kind of saint, a true and perfect knight no matter that the social order denies him.

The loveliness of Merchant-Ivory gives me the creeps. Their audience, I suspect, is that of people who have lost the habit of going to the movies—and why not?—but who have not read the books they adapt. Perhaps the team is a boon to book sales, to libraries and literacy, and to students who have too little time to read. Perhaps some people have read some of these books because of the films. In which case, why do they say "lovely" and pass by? Why do they not cry out that Henry James is much more? Even that there is distress, irony, doubt, and mystery in the voice of E. M. Forster that these films miss? Next to Merchant-Ivory, I still prefer the Cukor-Selznick *David Copperfield* because it is so alive, so passionate, and as close to crazy as Dickens.

Merchant-Ivory is *Masterpiece Theatre* moviemaking: prestigious, well furnished, accurate, prettily cast—and bland, anonymous, and stealthily interchangeable. Can you tell one Ivory-ized classic author from another? Is there virtue in the ultimate endorsement of buried hearts in *Remains of the Day*? Or may it just be the fallacy that those servants have hearts or are better than stuffed imitations of their idiotic and dangerous betters?

Ivory is American, and there is an American period, or wing, to his work, to go with the Indian and the English. But his "American" films—*Mr. and Mrs. Bridge*, *Slaves of New York*, *The Bostonians*, *Jane Austen in Manhattan*, *Roseland*, *The Wild Party*—are sometimes disasters, and seldom comfortable. And Ivory, I think, does like to be comfortable, which may be a way of saying he is uneasy if pushed into original thought or unhindered energy. He does not seem to ask large questions about his characters' options. Nor is he inclined to employ robust or dangerous American actors. The impregnably ungiving Paul Newman was his choice for *Mr. Bridge*.

Still, he pleases many people, and it is not easy

to dismiss their pleas for, say, *Howards End* and *The Remains of the Day* instead of *Look Who's Talking Too, Demolition Man,* or *True Romance*—wastelands of energy. What troubles me most is not that there is room and an audience for Merchant-Ivory: after all, British TV adaptations of the classics established that long ago. Rather, I regret that for so many people they have come to be the epitome of intelligent, sensitive film. That has only been possible because the business, and so many good filmmakers, have given up on winning what is difficult territory. The calamity is that *Howards End* is better, more sophisticated, and more understanding than Scorsese's *The Age of Innocence.*

More recently, he has had increasing trouble taking on real history, the life of Picasso, and maximum-depth Henry James. But he made a good movie out of the life of James Jones—*A Soldier's Daughter Never Cries.*

J

Glenda Jackson,
b. Birkenhead, England, 1936

Not even two Oscars ever softened the abrasive edge of Glenda Jackson's militant intelligence, or gave it more understanding. She is a good illustration of stage authority seeming aggressive to the camera. We have so few actresses brave enough to scorn charm, it seems rash to chide her rarity. But she bullied with seriousness, and her calculated comedies reveal no true lightness. I think that so many floridly worthy parts and her gruff Englishness have helped disguise her doctrinaire flatness as a screen presence. She looks tense and determined, and only the palpable sense of strain has accounted for the respect in which some people hold her.

She was the daughter of a contractor, and she bristles with a politicized social worker's antieloquence, biting at her listeners. Her manner is faintly aggrieved, as if to relax might involve forgiving essential resentments. She studied at the Royal Academy of Dramatic Arts and joined the Royal Shakespeare Company in 1963. On stage, she was Charlotte Corday in *Marat/Sade;* Masha in *Three Sisters;* the voice of haranguing rebuke in *US;* a sex-mad Joan of Arc in *Henry VI;* and an Ophelia so managing that one critic, Penelope Gilliatt, thought she was ready to play the Prince.

Her movie career began with a small part in *This Sporting Life* (63, Lindsay Anderson); Charlotte Corday again in the film of *Marat/Sade* (66, Peter Brook); *Negatives* (68, Peter Medak); an Oscar for *Women in Love* (70, Ken Russell); *Sunday, Bloody Sunday* (71, John Schlesinger), scripted by Penelope Gilliatt; *The Music Lovers* (71, Russell); *Mary, Queen of Scots* (71, Charles

Jarrott), as Queen Elizabeth, a part she played with great success on a BBC TV series, *Elizabeth R; The Triple Echo* (72, Michael Apted); another Oscar for *A Touch of Class* (72, Melvin Frank), her first comedy; as Emma Hamilton in *Bequest to the Nation* (73, James Cellan Jones); as a nun in *The Tempest* (74, Damiano Damiani); in a film of Genet's *The Maids* (74, Christopher Miles); *The Romantic Englishwoman* (75, Joseph Losey); *Hedda* (75, Trevor Nunn) from Ibsen's *Hedda Gabler;* halfway to Hamlet, playing Bernhardt in *The Incredible Sarah* (76, Richard Fleischer); as the Nixon nun in *Nasty Habits* (76, Michael Lindsay-Hogg); and trying acid romance again in *House Calls* (78, Howard Zieff). She played the eccentric English poet in *Stevie* (78, Robert Enders); the teacher in *The Class of Miss MacMichael* (78, Silvio Narizzano); and *Lost and Found* (79, Melvin Frank).

She played with Walter Matthau in *Hopscotch* (80, Ronald Neame); *H.E.A.L.T.H.* (80, Robert Altman); as the actress afflicted by a stroke in *The Patricia Neal Story* (81, Anthony Harvey and Anthony Page); *The Return of the Soldier* (82, Alan Bridges); as a documentary filmmaker in *Giro City* (82, Karl Francis); as Elena Bonner in *Sakharov* (84, Jack Gold); *Turtle Diary* (85, John Irvin); *Beyond Therapy* (86, Altman); *Business as Usual* (87, Lezli-An Barrett); *Salome's Last Dance* (88, Russell); as the mother to the character she played in *Women in Love* in *The Rainbow* (88, Russell); *Doombeach* (89, Colin Finbow); and *King of the Wind* (90, Peter Duffell).

In Britain's 1992 General Election, she was returned to the House of Commons as Labour M.P. for Hampstead.

Peter Jackson,
b. Pukerua Bay, New Zealand, 1961

1987: *Bad Taste.* 1989: *Meet the Feebles.* 1992: *Braindead.* 1994: *Heavenly Creatures.* 1996: *The Frighteners; Forgotten Silver* (s). 2001: *The Lord of the Rings: The Fellowship of the Ring.* 2002: *The Lord of the Rings: The Two Towers.*

When your children ask you where the screen story of *The Lord of the Rings* is going, you might remember to tell them Michael Atkinson's description of how Jackson's *Braindead* ends: "The hero's Mum transforms into a giant Moloch and swallows him up her uterine canal." Or perhaps not. Nevertheless, the visionary epic style of the Tolkien films (if you can trust the first part) was forged originally in the gleeful manufacture of low-budget gore movies. And nothing stands between the two extremes of anti-respectability and who knows how many Oscars but the astonishing *Heavenly Creatures,* the giddiest teenage murder spree in the movies and one of the most rapturous portraits of adolescent pathology.

It's enough to leave you wondering whether the

frighteners in the *Rings* might not get out of hand before the series ends. And it only leads one to marvel at what Jackson might do when he is rich, famous, and secure after Tolkien. Beware. But in the meantime, just realize that Jackson has rediscovered the serial epic and given it an energy and dread not known since Fritz Lang's *Nibelungen*. Maybe that's what he does next—*Meet the Nibelungen!*

Samuel L. Jackson,

b. Chattanooga, Tennessee, 1949

Samuel Jackson is his own man, but if you propose that he is also Morgan Freeman cut directly with Eddie Murphy, then I think you begin to understand his terrific popularity, his ease, and the way, in *Pulp Fiction* (94, Quentin Tarantino), say, one of his breakthrough films, he can go from the laid-back repartee of fast-food terminology to the laying on of spirits. He has handled mainline, sentimental roles very well, but anyone not letting his humor loose is missing the real point. If ever there was an actor ready to play some of the jazz greats—Miles, Mingus, or even Ellington—this is the guy.

He made his debut in *Ragtime* (81, Milos Forman); *Eddie Murphy Raw* (87, Robert Townsend); *School Daze* (88, Spike Lee); *Coming to America* (88, John Landis); *Sea of Love* (89, Harold Becker); *Do the Right Thing* (89, Lee); *A Shock to the System* (90, Jan Egleson); *The Return of Superfly* (90, Sig Shore); *Mo' Better Blues* (90, Lee); *Goodfellas* (90, Martin Scorsese); *The Exorcist III* (90, William Peter Blatty); *Def by Temptation* (90, James Bond III); *Betsy's Wedding* (90, Alan Alda); *Strictly Business* (91, Kevin Hooks).

A lot of people felt he stole *Jungle Fever* (91, Lee) as the junkie brother; *Johnny Suede* (91, Tom DiCillo); *Jumpin' at the Boneyard* (92, Jeff Stanzler); *Patriot Games* (92, Phillip Noyce); *Juice* (92, Ernest Dickerson); *White Sands* (92, Roger Donaldson); *National Lampoon's Loaded Weapon I* (93, Gene Quintano); *True Romance* (93, Tony Scott); *The Meteor Man* (93, Townsend); *Menace II Society* (93, Allen and Albert Hughes); *Jurassic Park* (93, Steven Spielberg); *Amos & Andrew* (93, E. Max Frye).

After *Pulp Fiction*, he did *The New Age* (94, Michael Tolkin); *Fresh* (94, Boaz Yakin); in Attica in *Against the Wall* (94, John Frankenheimer); *Kiss of Death* (95, Barbet Schroeder); *Losing Isaiah* (95, Stephen Gyllenhaal), where he played with LaTanya Richardson, his wife; *Die Hard with a Vengeance* (95, John McTiernan); the voice of the dog, *Fluke* (95, Carlo Carlei); a boxing promoter in *The Great White Hype* (96, Reginald Hudlin); the father driven to murder in *A Time to Kill* (96, Joel Schumacher); with Geena Davis in *The Long Kiss Goodnight* (96, Renny Harlin); *The Search for One-Eyed Jimmy* (96, Sam Henry

Kass); *Trees Lounge* (96, Steve Buscemi); *Hard Eight* (97, Paul Thomas Anderson); *187* (97, Kevin Reynolds); producing as well as acting in *Eve's Bayou* (97, Kasi Lemmons); outstanding in *Jackie Brown* (97, Tarantino); *Sphere* (98, Barry Levinson); with Kevin Spacey in *The Negotiator* (98, F. Gary Gray); *Out of Sight* (98, Steven Soderbergh); doing very little in *Star Wars: Episode I—The Phantom Menace* (99, George Lucas); a little fancy in *The Red Violin* (99, François Girard); *Deep Blue Sea* (99, Harlin); *Rules of Engagement* (00 William Friedkin); *Shaft* (00, John Singleton); *Unbreakable* (00, M. Night Shyamalan); *The Caveman's Valentine* (01, Lemmons); *The 51st State* (01, Ronny Yu); *Changing Lanes* (02, Roger Michell); wasted again in *Star Wars: Episode II, Attack of the Clones* (02, Lucas); *Formula 51* (02, Ronny Yu); *The House on Turk Street* (02, Bob Rafelson); *XXX* (02, Rob Cohen); *Basic* (03, John McTiernan); *The Blackout Murders* (03, Philip Kaufman); *Kill Bill* (03, Tarantino).

Henry Jaglom, b. London, 1939

1971: *A Safe Place*. 1976: *Tracks*. 1979: *Sitting Ducks*. 1981: *National Lampoon Goes to the Movies* (codirected with Bob Giraldi). 1983: *Can She Bake a Cherry Pie?*. 1985: *Always*. 1987: *Someone to Love*. 1989: *New Year's Day*. 1990: *Eating*. 1992: *Venice/Venice*. 1994: *Baby Fever*. 1995: *Last Summer in the Hamptons*. 1998: *Déjà Vu*. 2001: *Festival in Cannes*. 2003: *Shopping*.

How long can someone remain a maverick, if he is as busy and as natural a self-promoter as Henry Jaglom? On the one hand, Jaglom makes films that are chronically sui generis. On the other, he has become so industrious, and so regular a figure at international festivals, that their panorama seems incomplete unless his sun-hat head is there bobbing around, as Henry talks beneath it. This maverick is so anxious to be liked. Perhaps no one has made so many films out of the pure, naked need to be loved. And if Henry is a narcissist, he is far too smart and talented to let that role play solemn or merely self-concerned. Someone would have shot him years ago if it were not for his intelligent whimsy and ironic charm. Henry is a fictional character and it is somehow all the more wondrous that he traffics so much on the borders of cinema verité. He has become not just the figment of his own imagination, but its fixture and supreme hope. As he would be the first to admit, he deserves not just an entry, but a book of his own.

He was originally an actor. No, that won't do. Doesn't one know that, even within the womb, he must have been a player rehearsing improvisational riffs on how to secure attention when he made his entrance? Still, he studied at the University of Pennsylvania and the Actors' Studio, to be a performer, and he has appeared in a few films beyond his own: *Psych-Out* (68, Richard Rush); *Drive, He Said* (71, Jack Nicholson); and *The Last Movie* (71, Dennis Hopper). He was a part of the Hollywood avant-garde around 1970 that included Nicholson, Hopper, and Bob Rafelson, and Jaglom was credited as a consultant on *Easy Rider* (69, Hopper and Peter Fonda). His debut picture, *A Safe Place*, was part of the BBS deal with Columbia.

Acting has edged over into psychotherapy for Jaglom—in other words, the decisions an actor faces have become for the filmmaker a model for the search for happiness and for the infinite metaphysics of being. It is also a way of meeting women, and some might say that the value of Jaglom's films depends very much on the loveliness and personality of the women.

But these are films made resolutely outside the mainstream. Not that Henry is uninterested in money or naïve at business. He works from independent means, yet he has been very successful at making and marketing his economical pieces of pseudo-verité in the 1980s. Thus, he is an odd mixture of the therapist/pilgrim open to everything and the sweet-talking tyrant who does *everything* absolutely his way. Yet he is well aware of, and eloquent about, the spoiled child–ism of Henry Jaglom—and that *is* a great subject, and not only in America.

To my eyes, he is an awkward photographer of scenes, and a rather aimless editor. Moreover, he has sometimes found himself with women who do not quite stand up to the adoration of a whole film. There is no way of denying that Jaglom, at his best even, walks very close to the pit of absurd self-involvement and pretension.

But he has done remarkable things: *Always* (an account of the breakup in his marriage with Patrice Townsend) is a lovely, heartbreaking picture that adds to the list of great Hollywood bittersweet comedies on marriage and remarriage; *Can She Bake a Cherry Pie?* finds real pain in Karen Black's performance; *Someone to Love* is a loving farewell to Orson Welles (a friend to Jaglom and a profound influence). And even in the early films there are moments of wonder—Tuesday Weld in the epochally pretentious *A Safe Place* (which also stars Welles as a magician—now Jaglom's logo), and Dennis Hopper as the cracking soldier in *Tracks*.

Jaglom's most recent films have seemed increasingly forced: *Venice/Venice*, in which Jaglom is a movie director at the Venice Film Festival who meets a new lady . . . , is painfully et cetera—as well as a fatal reminder that Henry is not a good enough actor to play Henry Jaglom. That great role needs someone subtler. Jaglom also needs scripts, and a more structured way of shooting. Otherwise, his process might actually bring some-

one to lay hands on a weapon. He could be the first auteur to be silenced in the middle of one of his own films.

It has been said with wisdom that some great directors make the same film over and over again—Hawks, Ozu, Antonioni. But that great family-feeling sinks in slowly. Whereas, when the audience sees the ditto marks before they stick in the director's eye—then something is wrong. And, truly, Henry Jaglom is far too smart, far too creative, and far too insecure to repeat himself so much.

Miklós Jancsó, b. Vac, Hungary, 1921
1958: *A Herangok Rómabá Mentek/The Bells Have Gone to Rome.* 1960: *Három Csillag/Three Stars* (codirected with Karoly Wiedemann and Zoltan Varkonyi). 1963: *Oldás es Kötés/Cantata.* 1964: *Igy Jöttem/My Way Home.* 1965: *Szegénylegenyek/The Roundup.* 1967: *Csillagosok, Katonák/The Red and the White.* 1968: *Csend és Kiáltás/Silence and Cry.* 1969: *Fényes Szelek/The Confrontation; Sirrokó/ Winter Sirocco.* 1970: *Egi Bárány/Agnus Dei; La Pacifista/The Pacifist.* 1971: *La Tecnica e il Rito/Technique and Ritual; Meg Kér a Nép/Red Psalm.* 1973: *Roma Rivuole Cesare/Rome Wants Caesar Back.* 1975: *Szerelmem, Elektra/Elektreia.* 1976: *Vizi Privati, Pubbliche Virtu/Private Vices.* 1979: *Allegro Barbarao Magyar Rapszodia/Hungarian Rhapsody; Eletunket es Verunket.* 1981: *Zsarnok szive avagy Bocaccio Magyarorszagon.* 1982: *Omega, Omega.* 1984: *Faustus, Faustus, Faustus* (TV); *Budapest/Muzsika* (d). 1986: *L'Aube/Dawn.* 1987: *Szornyek Evadja.* 1988: *Jezus Krisztus Horoszopja.* 1992: *Kék Duna Keringö.*

It was in 1966 that Jancsó first made an impression outside Hungary with *The Roundup*. That much nearer the 1956 uprising, it was difficult not to see the film as growing out of specifically Hungarian circumstances and experiences. Writing in *Sight and Sound*, the Hungarian critic Robert Vas seemed to confirm this feeling: "With a burning intellectual charge, he invites his viewers to throw away the pleasant, comfortable dream of Hungary's romantic-heroic history and face up to reality: black as much as white, oppressor as much as oppressed. A challenge to self-analysis of a small and tragic country surrounded by so many different tensions in the middle of Europe."

It is significant that Jancsó was trained in law and ethnography—the two courses of study overlapping, just as dispassion and formalism mingle in his work. Indeed, he became a doctor of law before the end of the Second World War, but did ethnological research in Transylvania in the following years. It is unclear how he found his way into filmmaking, but in the early 1950s he made newsreels and over a dozen shorts on ethnological and artistic subjects.

Cantata is judged by Jancsó as the first feature of his own. Like *My Way Home*, it is a work of conventional poetic realism, dealing with precise, unique characters. The first is about a young doctor's spiritual crisis as he returns to his rural home. The second concerns a young Hungarian, taken prisoner by the Russians in 1945, and put to work with a Russian soldier tending cows. Observant, sensitive films, these two were compared with the work of Olmi, and taken as a sign of fresh authenticity and humane concern in the Hungarian cinema.

The Roundup really revealed Jancsó. Ostensibly, its basis is historical: the period after 1848 when Austrian soldiers trap, round up, interrogate, torture, and kill a band of Hungarian partisans. But the way of showing these things was so much more impressive than the non-Hungarian's sense of Hungarian history. First of all, Jancsó had defined the flat Hungarian *puzta* in the way that Ford mapped out Monument Valley for himself, or Antonioni the London park in *Blow-Up*. Robert Vas saw this as a "specifically *Hungarian* vision. The horizontal line was surely dictated by the landscape, the domineering plain that left so rich a mark on the national character and literature. Its hard blacks against white suggest the toughness, the contrasts of this character: the rich fertility of summer as much as the tragedy, secretly maturing under the blazing heat."

But was the tragedy merely Hungarian, and was the roundup tragic or a ritualistic exercise, a dance variation of the inevitable power struggle? *The Roundup* paid much less attention to individuals than had *Cantata* or *My Way Home*. The camera style became increasingly decorative, abstract, and domineering. Thus, a sense of mysterious fatalism muffled the plight of the partisans and the unhindered cruelty of their captors. That meant that the viewer did not actually experience plight or cruelty so much as share in the ethnologist observer's view of an unfamiliar culture. Visually, *The Roundup* is a matter of pattern and shape, like a visitor from Mars describing a firing squad. And when Richard Roud suggested that it was as if Bresson had filmed Kafka's *In the Penal Colony*, that served to remind one of Jancsó's origins. *The Roundup* did have something of Kafka's worried but meek attitude to divine law, and it did study human groupings with a semiscientific remoteness.

This situation—of irrational authorities and hopeful revolutionists confronting one another in the open—has run through *The Red and the White, The Confrontation, Agnus Dei,* and *Red Psalm*. The historical bases of these films seem very tenuous, less important than the chance to persist with the same visual ingredients—solemn girls, ominous riders, the sun on the plain, and the extraordinary, balletic, mathematical behavior of the camera. These films have very little speech, no character, and very opaque sequences of events. They do have an overwhelming camera sequence built on some of the most elaborate traveling shots in cinema. The shots are as beautiful and as blank as the slim, dark, half-naked girls in *Red Psalm*. But that is to talk of beauty in a way that reveals the gulf between prettiness and character. And when some critics came away from *Winter Sirocco* with the report that it has only thirteen shots, and from *Red Psalm* that it has but twenty-six, then I wonder whether fluid cinema has not become oppressively academic and premeditated.

The mechanical movements are the more disturbing in that Jancsó does have an eye for sudden revelations. There is no doubt about the poetic generalizations he can achieve with horses, sunshine, the river, riders, grass, and his herded victims. What makes him seem cold-blooded and frivolous is the need to decorate this vision with senseless movement. When the camera does not move with a character, an emotion, or an idea then I fear it is impelled by the director's vanity.

Emil Jannings (Theodor Friedrich Emil Janenz) (1884–1950), b. Rorschach, Switzerland

In *Fun in a Chinese Laundry*, Josef von Sternberg gives an artfully bewildered, matter-of-fact account of how he handled Emil Jannings that is as wickedly comic as his description of Dietrich is balefully enchanted. The book omits, though demonstrates, the fact that Sternberg was himself one of the most laconic and rebarbative of men. But it makes clear how far Jannings's screen persona—of swollen, emotional nobility that is humiliated by fate—was based in the way he behaved. Indeed, von Sternberg makes himself out as Hal to Jannings's Falstaff, and it is the case that after *The Blue Angel* (30, von Sternberg) the actor never regained the eminence he had enjoyed in the silent era.

Supreme among German actors, he had gone to America and won a best actor Oscar in *The Last Command* (28, von Sternberg) before sound grated on his impossible accent. The story of *The Last Command*—of an exiled Tsarist general forced into working as a Hollywood extra—was typical of the way Jannings fed masochistically on pathos. (The attempts to relate Caligari to German national character might do better to examine the vast appeal of Jannings's gloomy humiliation.) In *The Last Command*, William Powell plays a director who observes the posturing general; while in reality, only two years later, von Sternberg humbled Jannings by making Dietrich the center of power and attention in *The Blue Angel*. If only a fraction of Sternberg's account is accurate, then Jannings was a gross, overwhelming sentimentalist, the exaggeration of a great actor that so many critics were ready to admire. Seen today, he is cloyingly unsympathetic. He has only to be compared with Michel Simon, a dignified creator of larger-than-life characters, for his obtuse self-love to be made clear. He was perfectly adjusted to the scale of stylized tyranny or slow-motion self-abasement that fitted German expressionism.

After stage training at Zurich, he traveled in repertory and joined Max Reinhardt in Berlin. He made his film debut in 1914 in *Arme Eva* (Robert Wiene) and *Im Banne der Leidenschaften*. He also appeared in *Passionels Tagebuch* (14, Luis Ralph); *Stein unter Steinem* (15, Felix Basch); and *Nacht des Grauens* (16, Richard Oswald). Thereafter, his career amounts to a catalogue of German cinema of the period, with Fritz Lang the only notable absentee: *Wenn Vier Dasselbe Tun* (17, Ernst Lubitsch); *Brüder Karamazoff* (18, Dmitri Buchowetzki); *Der Stier von Oliviera* (Buchowetzki); Louis XV in *Madame Dubarry* (19, Lubitsch); *Rosa Bernd* (19, Alfred Halm); Henry VIII in *Anna Boleyn* (20, Lubitsch); *Köhlhiesel's Töchter* (20, Lubitsch); *Tragödie der Liebe* (21, Joe May); *Das Weib des Pharao* (21, Lubitsch); *Die Ratten* (21, Hans Kobe); *Die Grafin von Paris* (22, Buchowetzki); *Othello* (23, Buchowetzki); *Peter der Grosse* (23, Buchowetzki); *Alles für Geld* (23, Reinhold Schunzel); as Nero in *Quo Vadis?* (23, Georg Jacoby and Gabriellino d'Annunzio); *Nju* (24, Paul Czinner); the hotel doorman in *The Last Laugh* (24, F. W. Murnau); Haroun al Raschid in *Waxworks* (24, Paul Leni); *Tartuff* (25, Murnau); *Variété* (25, E. A. Dupont); Mephistopheles in *Faust* (26, Murnau).

He then signed with Paramount and went to America for *The Way of All Flesh* (27, Victor Fleming); *The Last Command* and *The Patriot* (28, Lubitsch); *Sins of the Fathers* (28, Ludwig Berger); *The Street of Sin* (28, Mauritz Stiller); and *Betrayal* (29, Lewis Milestone).

He returned to Germany and to the part of Professor Unrath, the sexual victim of Dietrich's Lola, in *The Blue Angel*. Thereafter, he made fewer films, though remaining a German cultural figurehead: *Liebling der Götter* (30, Hanns Schwarz); *Stürme der Leidenschaft* (32, Robert Siodmak); *Der Schwarze Walfisch* (34, Fritz Wendhausen); *Der Alte und der Junge König* (35, Hans Steinhoff); *Traumulus* (35, Carl Froelich); *Der Herrscher* (37, Veit Harlan); *Der Zerbrochene Krug* (37, Gustav Ucicky); and *Robert Koch* (39, Steinhoff). In 1940, he was made a director of UFA, and the same year he played the Boer leader in the propagandist *Ohm Krüger* (40, Steinhoff). In 1942, he made *Die Entlassung* (Wolfgang Liebeneiner) and *Alters Herz Wird Wieder Jung* (Erich Engel). But after 1945, his enthusiastic role in the war effort excluded him from further work and he died in Austria in retirement.

Derek Jarman (Michael Derek Jarman) (1942–94), b. Northwood, England

1976: *Sebastiane*. 1978: *Jubilee*. 1979: *The Tempest*. 1980: *In the Shadow of the Sun* (s). 1984: *Imagining October* (s). 1985: *The Angelic Conversation; The Dream Machine* (s). 1986: *Caravaggio;* "Louise," an episode from *Aria*. 1987: *The Last of England*. 1988: *War Requiem*. 1990: *The Garden*. 1991: *Edward II*. 1993: *Wittgenstein; Blue*. 1994: *Glitterbug*.

Jarman is like a prisoner whose relentless eye turns his bars into vines, barber poles, and beribboned serpents. His prisons are, variously, very low budget, aestheticism, the beleaguered position of gays, and the peril of having AIDS. These prisons are not just inescapable, they are essential. For Jarman's hysterical inventiveness, his camaraderie, his serene anger—all these things need the condition of confinement. The films may also need an audience of inmates. In other words, he has a habit of alienating and scorning those on the other side of the bars.

Nevertheless, he is a heroic figure whether he is battling commercial hostilities, the staid attitude of England (he is nearly unthinkable in another society), or his own illness. The filmography above is enlarged by a journal-like stream of home movies, by some music videos, and by three books—*Dancing Ledge*, an autobiography, *Modern Nature*, journals from the period 1989–90, and *At Your Own Risk*.

He is a true experimenter in forms—notably in *Angelic Conversation*, where he uses rephotographed home movies against Judi Dench's reading of Shakespearean sonnets. He is a furious scold to the deterioration of nature and social fabric in Britain—as witness *Jubilee, The Last of England*, and *War Requiem*. And he is an uninhibited celebrant of gay sex—as in *Sebastiane, Caravaggio*, and *Edward II*. *Blue* proved to be the work of blindness, with just a field of blue and seas of ecstatic talk.

Jim Jarmusch, b. Akron, Ohio, 1953

1982: *Permanent Vacation* (s). 1984: *Stranger Than Paradise*. 1986: *Coffee and Cigarettes* (s); *Down by Law*. 1988: *Coffee and Cigarettes, Part Two* (s). 1989: *Mystery Train*. 1991: *Night on Earth*. 1995: *Dead Man*. 1997: *Year of the Horse*. 1999: *Ghost Dog: The Way of the Samurai*. 2002: "Trailer Night", an episode from *Ten Minutes Older: The Trumpet*.

Jarmusch has a rare feeling for urban desolation, for loneliness, and the sweet, whimsical overlap of chance and companionship. It is gentle, offbeat, and poignant—but does it make whole films? And does it really make a marriage of Jarmusch's leaning toward raw pop culture and SoHo modishness? I'd guess that Jarmusch feels drawn to shorter film forms—videos or even deadpan, a-commercial commercials. There's plenty of evidence by now that he lacks the drive or the will to sustain narrative, or even character, over a long haul. In hindsight, *Stranger Than Paradise* (still his best film) seems to have the innocent energy of beginning. By now, he seems like a born maker of episodes.

He was educated at Columbia and NYU; he immersed himself in film study at the Cinémathèque Française; and he was an assistant to Nicholas Ray at the end of Ray's life. In addition to his own films, Jarmusch has often worked for others in New York's avant-garde: he was an assistant on *Lightning Over Water* (80, Wim Wenders and Ray); he did sound on *Burroughs* (83, Howard Brookner); he acted in *Straight to Hell* (87, Alex Cox), in *Leningrad Cowboys Go America* (89, Aki Kaurismaki), and in *In the Soup* (92, Alexandre Rockwell).

Even in *Stranger Than Paradise*, the value of the people was tenuous. Their lives were so much at the mercy of randomness, entropy, and dispersal. As time has passed, that melancholy hangs in Jarmusch's way sometimes (as in *Down By Law*) in oppressively pretty compositions. It is hard to see where he is going—and very likely that he would retort that the notion of "going" anywhere is a fallacy.

Dead Man had many enthusiasts, who saw an ironic deconstruction of the Western. I could see that tone, too, but I couldn't tell where it was going, or why Jarmusch might be interested in the Western. His strength originally was the empty duration in very plain lives (which is not a very commercial area). But giving it up for a certain genre glamour—see also *Ghost Dog* and its "samurai" shadowing—leaves a very private filmmaker wondering just how independent he can manage to be.

Humphrey Jennings (1907–50),
b. Walberswick, England
All films are documentaries:
1938: *Penny Journey*. 1939: *Spare Time; Speaking from America; S.S. Ionian (Her Last Trip); The First Days* (codirected with Harry Watt and Pat Jackson). 1940: *London Can Take It* (codirected with Watt); *Spring Offensive/An Unrecorded Victory; Welfare of the Workers* (codirected with Jackson). 1941: *Heart of Britain; Words for Battle*. 1942: *Listen to Britain* (codirected with Stewart McAllister). 1943: *Fires Were Started; The Silent Village*. 1944: *The Eighty Days; The True Story of Lilli Marlene*. 1945: *A Diary for Timothy*. 1946: *A Defeated People*. 1947: *The Cumberland Story*. 1949: *Dim Little Island*. 1950: *Family Portrait*.

Most of Jennings's work was commissioned by the guiding patrons of the British documentary movement—the GPO Film Unit, the Ministry of Information, and the Crown Film Unit. Nor is there much doubt that Jennings's rather hesitant initiation in film was confirmed by the experi-

ence of war, which was the vindication of the whole documentary movement. His films were made for patriotic purposes, and belong to the climactic period of British documentary as inspired by Grierson. It would seem to be difficult to function as Jennings did and not belong to the documentary brotherhood. Yet, the lasting distinction of his work emphasizes the ways in which he was a private if not solitary figure, an individual artist inspired by a nation at war and able to take advantage of the artistic opportunity it provided.

When Grierson spoke of the "creative treatment of actuality" he was aspiring to some fusion of filmmaking and social action. He wanted, at the least, to educate the public into a greater involvement in the ordering of its own affairs. By contrast, Jennings is much more fatalistic and aloof, even if he had deeper insights into the British. In retrospect, one can see how far his wartime films pursued a personal vision, rooted in English life but full of intellectual and poetic reference, so that he seems now to rise above war and the immediate circumstances of his films. In short, he looks like one of the few major English directors, a true war artist in the way that Henry Moore's drawings in the Underground and Evelyn Waugh's *Sword of Honour* trilogy transcend war and reassert the primacy of the human imagination.

It is important to stress the background that led Jennings to film. East Anglia offers one of the most self-contained and enduring of educations in English social history and art: it is the world of agricultural peasantry, of Constable, Benjamin Britten, and Akenfield. Jennings went to Perse School and Cambridge, where he won a starred first in English. He stayed on to do research into the Elizabethans and became a member of an exceptional intellectual and artistic circle that produced the magazine *Experiment*. It was as concerned with science and history as with the arts, and Jennings conceived the project of a vast anthology of readings in British history, to be called *Pandemonium*. The scholarly book speaks for his academic training and for a mystical involvement with the idea of England. It is not too much to call it Blakean: Jennings viewed industry and the machine with a mixture of wonder and mistrust. Like Blake, he measured the span of civilization in England and was wary of the future. This accounts for the pessimism that hardens in his work, especially after the war.

Jennings wrote poetry and painted. In 1936 he helped to organize an important surrealist art exhibition in London. His own work was not as extreme, but it used imagery with the same combined emotional and intellectual force. Jim Hillier has drawn attention to the way Jennings employs the images of Tarot cards and stressed how far the compositions in his films are reinforced by such a code, which is not apparent to many viewers. Or not immediately so. In fact, Jennings's image is not simply more elegant than most, but more contradictory and poignant. He has an eye for absurdity, for the beauty of violence, the oddity of the everyday, and the disruptive liberation that can come from pictures of a city—like London—suddenly made naked by war. His images of blitz are not only documentary but examinations of the potential for discovery in circumstances that dislodge us from fixed systems and responses. Houses torn open disclose inane domestic interiors: no doubt about the violence that has been done, but Jennings also seems to ponder over those once neat containers of soft civilization. War acted for Jennings like the high-pressure inspiration that carries the surrealist into the subconscious.

He joined the GPO unit in 1934 as designer, editor, and actor. After a period with Len Lye, at Shell, where he was in charge of the color work on *The Birth of a Robot* (36), he returned to the GPO and began directing. His early work is conventional, although it shows an unusual visual awareness. His most creative period was very brief: *Listen to Britain, Fires Were Started,* and *A Diary for Timothy.*

Perhaps it was Jennings's intuition of pandemonium that makes those three films the most vivid and accurate account of civilian Britain at war. But it is the artist's awareness of the threat of chaos that gives them a very moving feeling for all culture threatened by destruction. They are war films without an enemy. There is something anonymous and all-pervasive in the dangers that hover over London and from which "fires were started." Of course, London seldom saw its enemy face to face, and the films record that long-distance battle. But, philosophically, Jennings sees war as an inevitable ordeal that binds people together. In *Fires Were Started,* for instance, the Germans who drop fire bombs are barely referred to. The loss of one fireman is not harped on sentimentally, but treated with resignation. There is something almost quietist in the view of human figures battling the blazes, just as Jennings never quenches the wild beauty of fire. *A Diary for Timothy* ends with a dissolve from flames to the face of the baby Timothy and with a worried question about what peace will mean. Just as *Fires Were Started* was made after the blitz, but retained a sense of possible apocalypse, so *Diary* was made when victory was undoubted but as Jennings grew more fearful of the consequences of peace.

As an artist he faltered after the war, unable to escape the declining system of documentary patronage or to maintain the passion of his wartime films. It is difficult to imagine what feature films Jennings might have made. His view of people was fond but impersonal, like Japanese paintings. But, had he lived—he was killed in an accident in Greece—he could not have condoned the ugliness and lazy socialism of Free Cinema. In the subdued caution of postwar Britain, he might have found sufficient anger to become a Buñuel-like figure. His fires were, like Blake's, a condition of the soul and might even have burned down English good manners.

Norman Jewison, b. Toronto, Canada, 1926
1962: *Forty Pounds of Trouble.* 1963: *The Thrill of It All.* 1964: *Send Me No Flowers.* 1965: *The Art of Love; The Cincinnati Kid.* 1966: *The Russians Are Coming, The Russians Are Coming.* 1967: *In the Heat of the Night.* 1968: *The Thomas Crown Affair.* 1969: *Gaily, Gaily.* 1971: *Fiddler on the Roof.* 1973: *Jesus Christ Superstar.* 1975: *Rollerball.* 1978: *F°I°S°T.* 1979: *And Justice for All.* 1982: *Best Friends.* 1984: *A Soldier's Story.* 1985: *Agnes of God.* 1987: *Moonstruck.* 1989: *In Country.* 1991: *Other People's Money.* 1994: *Only You.* 1996: *Bogus.* 1999: *The Hurricane.* 2001: *Dinner with Friends* (TV).

After studying at the University of Toronto, Jewison worked in British TV as a writer and actor. He returned to Canada and in 1958 joined CBS to direct spectaculars. Jewison has long since dissipated the promise of *Forty Pounds of Trouble; The Thomas Crown Affair* has shown the depths of hollow prettiness of which he is capable. Yet, he remains unpredictable, a gadfly among directors, lavish with real locations, but indifferent to authenticity so that *In the Heat of the Night* could have been shot in the studios of the 1940s. With big projects, Jewison has seemed overawed—thus *The Cincinnati Kid* suffers from Steve McQueen's dullness and compares badly with *The Hustler; The Russians Are Coming,* however, an ostensible loser, is very funny. *Forty Pounds of Trouble* turned a potentially sentimental picture about a knowing child into a very funny study of Tony Curtis. Nor were the two Doris Day movies as bad as they threatened to be. *In the Heat of the Night* and *Fiddler on the Roof* are at least enjoyable hokum, too sophisticated to stress their spurious significance. While directing *Jesus Christ Superstar* in Israel, Jewison also contrived to produce a Western, *Billy Two Hats* (73, Ted Kotcheff), in which Gregory Peck plays an elderly Scottish outlaw—with such flexibility can movies perish?

Jewison has continued to produce for others: *The Dogs of War* (80, John Irvin); *Iceman* (84, Fred Schepisi); and *The January Man* (89, Pat O'Connor). His own films included the meritorious *Soldier's Story* (note that Jewison was intending to do a Malcolm X film until Spike Lee claimed the project for a black director). *Soldier's Story* got a best picture nomination, as did the charming *Moonstruck,* a lightweight work based in generous human observation and a lot of canny acting.

In 1999, Jewison picked up the Irving Thalberg

Award. If "picked up" sounds a little casual, I have to say that the movies have reached a strange point when a Jewison can get that lofty award—one that was kept for the top stream of filmmakers—whereas Jewison has never been better than, say, *In the Heat of the Night*, a carefully rigged melodrama, and *The Hurricane* (made in the year of his award), a hideously contrived selling of the facts in the Rubin Carter case. It is all very well to say that no one now remembers Thalberg. In which case, abandon his award. Don't cheapen it.

Roland Joffé, b. London, 1945

1984: *The Killing Fields*. 1986: *The Mission*. 1989: *Fat Man and Little Boy*. 1992: *The City of Joy*. 1995: *The Scarlet Letter*. 1999: *Goodbye Lover*. 2000: *Vatel*.

Initially a director for stage and television documentaries, Joffé's first film was the natural, gruesome subject of Cambodia. On that outing, and with *The Mission*, there were Oscar nominations for best director and best picture—no matter that *The Mission* was a silly, old-fashioned melodrama lit up with National Geographic scenery. On the strength of those two films, *Fat Man and Little Boy* could hardly have had a bigger (or more scenic) subject than Los Alamos. But its drama was muffled and made respectable. Still, nothing suggested the fatuous action of *City of Joy* or the inane big-star direction of Demi Moore as Hester Prynne. It's a strange career, not explained by Joffé's role as producer on *Super Mario Bros.* (93, Rocky Morton and Annabel Jankel).

Ben Johnson (1918–96),

b. Foraker, Oklahoma

Part Irish and part Cherokee, Johnson has always been a rider, a man acquainted with horses. He was a rodeo cowboy once, and a horse rancher in Arizona. Along the way, he kept company with the picture business, and plenty enough times acquitted himself as an absolutely natural actor. He acted from the saddle at first, but later on there was not a horse in sight, and there was Johnson (with Strasbergians for company), rising to a well-deserved Oscar.

He got into pictures first when he worked as a wrangler on *The Outlaw* (43, Howard Hughes). He doubled in dangerous sequences for John Wayne and Joel McCrea, and in a few years he was in real parts: *The Naughty Nineties* (45, Jean Yarbrough); *Badman's Territory* (46, Tim Whelan); *Wyoming* (47, Joseph Kane); *Fort Apache* (48, John Ford); *3 Godfathers* (48, Ford); as Sergeant Tyree in *She Wore a Yellow Ribbon* (49, Ford); *Mighty Joe Young* (49, Ernest B. Schoedsack); as Travis Blue in *Wagonmaster* (50, Ford); *Fort Defiance* (51, John Rawlins); *Wild Stallion* (52, Lewis D. Collins); and loyally letting a pint-size Alan Ladd beat him up in *Shane* (53, George Stevens).

He was in *Oklahoma!* (55, Fred Zinnemann); *Rebel in Town* (56, Alfred J. Werker); *War Drums* (57, Reginald Le Borg); *Fort Bowie* (57, Howard W. Koch); *Slim Carter* (57, Richard Bartlett); *Ten Who Dared* (60, William Beaudine); *Tomboy and the Champ* (61, Francis D. Lyon); *One-Eyed Jacks* (61, Marlon Brando); *Cheyenne Autumn* (64, Ford); *Major Dundee* (64, Sam Peckinpah); *The Rare Breed* (66, Andrew V. McLaglen); *Will Penny* (67, Tom Gries); and *Hang 'Em High* (67, Ted Post).

He played Tector Gorch, brother to Warren Oates's Lyle, in *The Wild Bunch* (69, Peckinpah); *The Undefeated* (69, McLaglen); *Ride a Northbound Horse* (69, Robert Totten); *Chisum* (70, McLaglen); weather-beaten, wistful, and restrained as Sam the Lion in *The Last Picture Show* (71, Peter Bogdanovich), and winning the supporting actor Oscar; *Something Big* (71, McLaglen); *Corky* (71, Leonard Horn); *Junior Bonner* (72, Peckinpah); as the villain in *The Getaway* (73, Peckinpah); as Melvin Purvis, every bit as set on celebrity as *Dillinger* (73, John Milius); *Kid Blue* (73, James Frawley); *Blood Sport* (73, Jerold Freedman); *Runaway!* (73, David Lowell Rich); *The Train Robbers* (73, Burt Kennedy); *The Red Pony* (73, Totten); *Locusts* (74, Richard T. Heffron); as the tolerant police chief in *The Sugarland Express* (74, Steven Spielberg); *Bite the Bullet* (75, Richard Brooks); *Hustle* (75, Robert Aldrich); *The Savage Bees* (76, Bruce Geller); *Breakheart Pass* (76, Gries); *The Town that Dreaded Sundown* (77, Charles B. Pierce); *The Greatest* (77, Gries); *Greyeagle* (77, Pierce); *The Swarm* (78, Irwin Allen); *The Sacketts* (79, Totten); *Wild Times* (79, Richard Compton); *Ruckus* (80, Max Kleven); *The Hunter* (80, Buzz Kulik); *Soggy Bottom U.S.A.* (80, Ted Flicker); *Terror Train* (80, Roger Spottiswoode); *Tex* (82, Tim Hunter); *The Shadow Riders* (82, McLaglen); *Champions* (83, John Irvin); *Red Dawn* (84, Milius); *Wild Horses* (85, Dick Lowry); *Cherry 2000* (86, Steve DeJarnatt); *Let's Get Harry* (86, Stuart Rosenberg); *Trespass* (86, Loren Bivens); *Dark Before Dawn* (88, Totten); *Stranger On My Land* (88, Larry Elikann); *My Heroes Have Always Been Cowboys* (90, Rosenberg); *The Chase* (91, Paul Wendkos); on TV in *Bonanza: The Return* (93, Jerry Jameson); *Angels in the Outfield* (94, William Dear); *The Evening Star* (96, Robert Harling); *Ruby Jean and Joe* (96, Geoffrey Sax).

Celia Johnson (1908–82),

b. Richmond, England

In the 1930s, Celia Johnson was one of the most promising young actresses on the London stage, someone ranked with Peggy Ashcroft and Diana Wynyard. But she did not play too many of the great roles; nor did she have the push or vanity to make herself great. She was, famously, more interested in domestic life, no matter that she was often brilliant on stage and usually less than competent at home. (She once insisted to the management on a certain actor for one of her plays because he lived near her, and could give her a lift home every night.)

There's the germ of a comic character there, and it may be regretted that Celia Johnson never got enough chances to be funny. Her Laura Jesson in *Brief Encounter* (45, David Lean)—far and away her best known film—is resigned to home life, and her romance may only flourish in the steadfast assurance that it can never be lived. Roger Manvell once wrote of that performance: "I do not remember any more moving performance . . . I do not remember a moment when [her] performance falters in a part where overplaying or false intonations would have turned the film from a study of life itself into another piece of cinematic fiction. . . . She looks quite ordinary until it is time for her to look like what she feels."

That last observation is acute, but it points to the ways in which Noel Coward's script and Lean's direction are forlornly sure about what must happen. Her alive look is a bird whose flight is so short-lived that a life of regret is guaranteed thereafter. So the love story is faintly masochistic and a little self-righteous.

Ms. Johnson's understatement did nothing to disturb that, or to suggest that Laura might end up crazy. If the film had let the love story be disruptive it would have been truer to the volatile England of 1945, and the film might seem less preciously jeweled and contained. But, for that, the bogus cover of the dull, decent husband would have had to be blown. *Brief Encounter* will not risk that: Coward's gayness was too tolerant of such hollow men. Thus, the brevity of the encounter is desperately necessary to the shaky upper lip.

Brief Encounter did not make her a film actress. After the war, she remained most notable theatrically, in Rattigan's *The Deep Blue Sea*, William Douglas Home's *The Reluctant Debutante*, and Robert Bolt's *Flowering Cherry*. She played in *The Three Sisters* and *The Cherry Orchard*, too, but made the latter seem a little too suburban.

Her other movies were *In Which We Serve* (42, Lean and Coward); *Dear Octopus* (42, Harold French); *This Happy Breed* (44, Lean); *The Astonished Heart* (50, Terence Fisher and Anthony Darnborough); *I Believe In You* (51, Basil Dearden); *The Captain's Paradise* (53, Anthony Kimmins); *The Holly and the Ivy* (54, George More O'Ferrall); *A Kid for Two Farthings* (55, Carol Reed); and *The Good Companions* (56, J. Lee Thompson). The modulated acid of her headmistress in *The Prime of Miss Jean Brodie*

(68, Ronald Neame) revealed her at last as a character actress.

She was not seen much more, but she was in *Les Misérables* (78, Glenn Jordan) for TV; *The Hostage Tower* (80, Claudio Guzman); and playing with Trevor Howard once more in *Staying On* (82, Silvio Narizzano).

Nunnally Johnson (1897–1977),
b. Columbus, Georgia
1954: *Night People; Black Widow*. 1955: *How to Be Very, Very Popular*. 1956: *The Man in the Gray Flannel Suit*. 1957: *The Three Faces of Eve; Oh, Men! Oh, Women!*. 1959: *The Man Who Understood Women*. 1960: *The Angel Wore Red*.

From scriptwriting, Johnson moved laboriously through producing to directing. But his long career is sadly short of creative character. (His published letters, though, are very witty and informative. So often, in the golden age, people were smarter than their movies indicated.) His scripts may be bland simplifications of novels, orderly in sequence and digestible in character, but they are too often the blueprints for routine films. His best writing credit—on *The Woman in the Window* (44, Fritz Lang)—is somewhat diminished by Lang's report that he had to battle with Johnson to use the dream structure that activates the black comedy of the film. But what sort of view of authorship is it that could rate the writer more seriously than the eye that foresaw Joan Bennett appearing out of the darkness beside an Edward G. Robinson musing over her portrait? I do not admire *The Grapes of Wrath* (40, John Ford), but the film has more to do with Ford's spurious feeling of family nobility than with Steinbeck's soulful pessimism or Johnson's script. And consider that moment in *O. Henry's Full House*, when we see the hapless kidnappers make off with J.B. in the same frame as his indifferent parents. Is that O. Henry's story, Johnson's script, or Hawks's decision to see both levels of action in one setup? Always, it is the visual element that indicates the author, because it is the sharp point that pricks our senses.

Johnson was a journalist and short-story writer who entered film as a writer in 1933, and became an associate producer two years later, usually for Fox: *Baby Face Harrington* (35, Raoul Walsh, w); *The Prisoner of Shark Island* (36, Ford w/as.p); *Slave Ship* (37, Tay Garnett, as.p); *Rose of Washington Square* (39, Gregory Ratoff, w/p); *Jesse James* (39, Henry King, w/as.p); *I Was an Adventuress* (40, Ratoff, as.p); *Tobacco Road* (41, Ford, w); *Roxie Hart* (42, William Wellman, w/p); *Holy Matrimony* (43, John M. Stahl, w/p); *The Pied Piper* (42, Irving Pichel, w/p); *Life Begins at Eight Thirty* (42, Pichel, w/p); *The Moon Is Down* (43, Pichel, w/p); *The Keys of the Kingdom* (44, Stahl, w); *Casanova Brown* (44, Sam Wood, w/p); *Along*

Came Jones (45, Stuart Heisler, w); *The Dark Mirror* (46, Robert Siodmak, w/p); *The Senator Was Indiscreet* (48, George Kaufman, p); *Three Came Home* (50, Jean Negulesco, w/p); *The Gunfighter* (50, King, p); *The Mudlark* (50, Negulesco, w/p); *Rommel, Desert Fox* (51, Henry Hathaway, w/p); the "Ransom of Red Chief" episode from *O. Henry's Full House* (52, Howard Hawks, w); *My Cousin Rachel* (52, Henry Koster, w/p); *Phone Call from a Stranger* (52, Negulesco, w/p); *We're Not Married* (52, Edmund Goulding, w/p); and *How to Marry a Millionaire* (53, Negulesco, w/p). Johnson produced most and wrote all of his own films. But in the 1960s, he went back to writing alone: *Mr. Hobbs Takes a Vacation* (62, Koster); *The World of Henry Orient* (64, George Roy Hill); and *The Dirty Dozen* (67, Robert Aldrich), written with Lukas Heller.

Van (Charles Van) **Johnson**,
b. Newport, Rhode Island, 1916

MGM spotted Johnson in the chorus of *Pal Joey* on Broadway. He was one of Mr. Mayer's projects— red-haired, freckled, naïve, and enthusiastic—a nice safe guy. So he joined the studio, and he had done a few small things—*Somewhere I'll Find You* (42, Wesley Ruggles), *The War Against Mrs. Hadley* (42, Harold S. Bucquet)—when he was assigned to attend the premiere of *Keeper of the Flame*. But his car crashed, and Johnson had to have a small metal plate put in his head. He was 4-F for keeps, but ready, willing, and able. And so his career bloomed as so many possible rivals went off to war.

Whatever he owed to luck, the young public was crazy for Johnson, and his following showed in the work he got: *Madame Curie* (43, Mervyn LeRoy); *A Guy Named Joe* (43, Victor Fleming); *Pilot #5* (43, George Sidney); *The Human Comedy* (43, Clarence Brown); *The White Cliffs of Dover* (44, Brown); with June Allyson and Gloria DeHaven in *Two Girls and a Sailor* (44, Richard Thorpe); *Thirty Seconds over Tokyo* (44, LeRoy); with Esther Williams in *Thrill of a Romance* (45, Thorpe); *Weekend at the Waldorf* (45, Robert Z. Leonard); *Till the Clouds Roll By* (46, Richard Whorf).

After the war, the studio tried to build him up with more adult pictures: *State of the Union* (48, Frank Capra); *Command Decision* (48, Sam Wood); and *Battleground* (49, William Wellman), where he was fine as one of the soldiers. But he seemed more relaxed in lighter stuff: *The Romance of Rosy Ridge* (47, Roy Rowland), with Janet Leigh; *The Bride Goes Wild* (48, Norman Taurog), with Allyson; *Mother Is a Freshman* (49, Lloyd Bacon), with Loretta Young; *In the Good Old Summertime* (49, Leonard), with Judy Garland. He also did *The Big Hangover* (50, Norman Krasna), where he played a guy with a drinking problem.

Gradually he began to fade in the fifties, though not before opportunities in big dramatic roles: *Plymouth Adventure* (52, Brown); Lieutenant Maryk in *The Caine Mutiny* (54, Edward Dmytryk); *The Last Time I Saw Paris* (54, Richard Brooks), with Elizabeth Taylor; and even Bendrix in *The End of the Affair* (55, Dmytryk). His best work was as a drunk in *The Bottom of the Bottle* (56, Henry Hathaway), taken from a Simenon novel.

He was forty, and he looked it, despite the baby face. He also started working out of England more: *Miracle in the Rain* (56, Rudolph Maté), with Jane Wyman; *Action of the Tiger* (57, Terence Young), with Martine Carol; *Beyond This Place* (59, Jack Cardiff); *Subway in the Sky* (59, Muriel Box). Then there were fewer films: *Wives and Lovers* (63, John Rich); *Divorce American Style* (67, Bud Yorkin); *Where Angels Go, Trouble Follows* (68, James Neilson).

Since then it's been mostly TV or foreign productions, with the occasional gem like *The Purple Rose of Cairo* (85, Woody Allen), where his high-voiced charm still worked.

Angelina Jolie (Voight),
b. Los Angeles, 1975

No one writing about Angelina Jolie's arrival on screen in the late 1990s was able to mask sheer wonder at the carnal embouchure that is her mouth. It is like a mouth made in braille on the flattest of screens, and it could blind anyone. She was the sexiest new thing, yet she was also a remarkable actress, full of daring (or its excess). There was a temptation (and it affected her films and her public posing) to play up the dangerous sensuality. Thus, she did her best work (and won an Oscar) as the lifer in *Girl, Interrupted* (99, James Mangold), whose friendship and instincts are the greatest threat to Winona Ryder's survival. Jolie didn't let that role turn into a she-devil, but it was a close call. Similarly, in the press she has not resisted the allure of behaving like an exotic tattoo on a private part of her husband, Billy Bob Thornton. But if they knit in the evenings, why not admit it?

She is also the daughter of Jon Voight and the actress Marcheline Bertrand, and thus the spectator to their divorce when she was still a child. For years, she was on poor terms with her father, but reportedly the rift has been mended. She studied with Lee Strasberg and made her actual debut, briefly, in *Lookin' to Get Out* (82, Hal Ashby), on which Voight was star, cowriter, and coproducer.

Her career began properly with *Cyborg 2* (93, Michael Schroeder); *Hackers* (95, Iain Softley); *Without Evidence* (95, Gill Dennis); *Mojave Moon* (96, Kevin Dowling); *Foxfire* (96, Annette Haywood-Carter); an Emmy nomination for the second wife in *George Wallace* (97, John Frankenheimer); *Playing God* (97, Andy Wilson); and another Emmy nomination for *Gia* (98, Michael Cristofer).

She met Thornton while acting in *Pushing Tin* (97, Mike Newell); *Playing by Heart* (98, Willard Carroll); *Hell's Kitchen* (98, Tony Cinciripini); making a big advance as the cop who acts for Denzel Washington in *The Bone Collector* (99, Phillip Noyce); just slutting around in *Gone in 60 Seconds* (00, Dominic Sena); a big hit for horny boys in *Lara Croft: Tomb Raider* (01, Simon West); with Antonio Banderas in *Original Sin* (01, Cristofer), based on Cornell Woolrich; *Life or Something Like It* (02, Stephen Herek); *Beyond Borders* (03, Martin Campbell).

Al Jolson (Asa Yoelson) (1886–1950),
b. Srednik, Lithuania

It is as if printing had been invented to fill labels on ketchup bottles: that sound on film—the innovation that led to Fred Astaire's heels on hard floors, to Bacall asking Bogart if he knew how to whistle, to Cherbourg being alive with song, to Tippi Hedren/Marnie saying, "There . . . there now" to the horse she had shot—should have been born on the lips of a Lithuanian Jew blackface minstrel encouraging his mother to love him.

The Jazz Singer (Alan Crosland) opened in New York in October 1927, and it contained, as well as songs, these witless threats: "You ain't heard nothing yet" and "Hey, Ma, listen to this!" The hero of *The Jazz Singer* is Jackie Rabinowitz, the son of a cantor, who opts for a career in vaudeville, changes his name to Jack Robin, and manages to be a Broadway star and to substitute for his ailing father at Yom Kippur. It seems implausible that the part would have been offered to anyone other than Jolson, but apparently both George Jessel and Eddie Cantor had turned it down.

As it happened, Jolson's father was a cantor, too. But when the family brought the child Asa to America he soon yearned for the limelight. In the years before the First World War, Jolson put on blackface, and by the early 1920s he was a phenomenal star of vaudeville, musical comedy, and records, firing off such a barrage of sentimental songs of such banality that they could be explained away only by "personality." There are people alive still who insist that Jolson was hugely compelling from the stage. So be it. But on film he seems like a caged beast, unaware how ably the medium conspires with the drama in songs. Jolson seems nineteenth century, while Judy Garland, say, is modern. But they had the same target—tearing your heart out.

Even before *The Jazz Singer* he had experimented with the movies. In 1923 he walked out on a D. W. Griffith project, and in 1926 he sang in a short film for Warners. *The Jazz Singer* increased Jolson's status, even if it alarmed many people about the vulgarity sound films portended. Jolson made more pictures, but was in no sense a film actor. He was content to use movies as vehicles for his songs. In time, fashion changed and the industry opted instead for reticence: *The Singing Fool* (28, Lloyd Bacon); *Sonny Boy* (29, Archie Mayo); *Say It With Songs* (29, Bacon); *Mammy* (30, Michael Curtiz); *Big Boy* (30, Crosland); *Hallelujah, I'm a Bum* (33, Lewis Milestone); *Wonder Bar* (34, Bacon); *Go Into Your Dance* (35, Mayo), with his then wife, Ruby Keeler; *The Singing Kid* (36, William Keighley); and *Rose of Washington Square* (39, Gregory Ratoff). The last called on Jolson to sing all his great hits and is less spectacular than the collision of such hams as Jolson and Ratoff promises. In 1940, he played minstreller E. P. Christy in *Swanee River* (Sidney Lanfield); after which he appeared briefly as himself in the Gershwin biopic, *Rhapsody in Blue* (45, Irving Rapper).

During the war, he sang to the forces (who presumably fought all the harder at the thought of their mothers). In 1946, Columbia did a biopic of Jolson, in which Larry Parks mimed to the master's voice: *The Jolson Story* (46, Alfred E. Green). It was a smash success and prompted a sequel in which Jolson congratulates Larry Parks: *Jolson Sings Again* (49, Henry Levin). He died after returning from a tour of Korea entertaining troops. Mothers everywhere remember him.

James Earl Jones,
b. Arkabutla, Mississippi, 1931

His is a voice that everyone recognizes, even if we cannot always name it. It is one of the great basses of our time, selling things on TV or emanating from behind the visor of Darth Vader in *Star Wars* (77, George Lucas), *The Empire Strikes Back* (80, Irvin Kershner), and *Return of the Jedi* (83, Richard Marquand).

He was educated at the University of Michigan, and from there he went on stage, coming to prominence as the Jack Johnson–like boxer in the play *The Great White Hope* in 1966. His movie career had begun in *Dr. Strangelove* (64, Stanley Kubrick), and he went on to do *The Comedians* (67, Peter Glenville); *The End of the Road* (70, Aram Avakian); the movie of *The Great White Hope* (70, Martin Ritt), for which he got a best actor Oscar nomination; as the president in *The Man* (72 Joseph Sargent); *Claudine* (74, John Berry); *The River Niger* (76, Krishna Shah); *The Bingo Long Traveling All-Stars and Motor Kings* (76, John Badham); *Deadly Hero* (76, Ivan Nagy); *Swashbuckler* (76, James Goldstone); *Exorcist II: The Heretic* (77, John Boorman); as Malcolm X in *The Greatest* (77, Tom Gries); *The Last Remake of Beau Geste* (77, Marty Feldman); *A Piece of the Action* (77, Sidney Poitier); as Alex Haley in *Roots:*

The Next Generation (79) on TV; *The Bushido Blade* (79, Tom Kotani); *Conan the Barbarian* (82, John Milius); *City Limits* (85, Aaron Lipstadt); *My Little Girl* (86, Connie Kaiserman); *Soul Man* (86, Steven Miner); *Allan Quatermain and the Lost City of Gold* (87, Gary Nelson); *Gardens of Stone* (87, Francis Ford Coppola); *Matewan* (87, John Sayles); *Coming to America* (88, John Landis); *Best of the Best* (89, Bob Radler); *Field of Dreams* (89, Phil Alden Robinson); *Three Fugitives* (89, Francis Veber); *The Hunt for Red October* (90, John McTiernan); *Scorchers* (91, David Beaird); *Patriot Games* (92, Phillip Noyce); *Sneakers* (92, Robinson); *Excessive Force* (93, Jon Hess); *The Sandlot* (93, David Mickey Evans); and *Meteorman* (93, Robert Townsend).

Mr. Jones works as hard as a man with a rambling old house that needs many repairs—if it is to contain his resonant voice: *Hallelujah* (93, Charles Lane); *The Vernon Johns Story* (94, Kenneth Fink); *Confessions: Two Faces of Evil* (94, Gilbert Cates); the voice of Mufasa in *The Lion King* (94, Roger Allers and Rob Minkoff); *Clear and Present Danger* (94, Phillip Noyce); *Clean Slate* (94, Mick Jackson); *Jefferson in Paris* (95, James Ivory); a voice in *Judge Dredd* (95, Danny Cannon); *Cry, the Beloved Country* (95, Darrell Roodt); *A Family Thing* (96, Richard Pearce); *Rebound* (96, Eriq La Salle); *Timepiece* (96, Marcus Cole); *What the Deaf Man Heard* (97, John Kent Harrison); *Alone* (97, Michael Lindsay-Hogg); a voice in *Primary Colors* (99, Mike Nichols); *Summer's End* (98, Helen Shaver); *The Annihilation of Fish* (98, Charles Burnett); *Santa and Pete* (99, Duwayne Dunham); *Undercover Angel* (99, Bryan Michael Stoller); *Quest for Atlantis* (00, Kenyon Zehner); *When Willows Touch* (00, Shonde Rhimes); *Finder's Fee* (00, Jeff Probst); *Recess Christmas: Miracle on Third Street* (01, Chuck Sheetz).

Jennifer Jones (Phylis Isley),
b. Tulsa, Oklahoma, 1919

Of all actresses loved and promoted by producers (as opposed to directors), the case of Jennifer Jones is the most intriguing. For a fair argument can be made that David Selznick both made and nearly destroyed her career. She was an ardent young actress before she met Selznick, but it is hard now to be sure whether we would know her if his great wind had not picked her up like a leaf. He treated her like his dream; he may have driven her to neurotic illness, and worse. But Jones survived. Indeed, she has buried three husbands, all of them strong and demanding personalities.

Her father was in dusty show business in Oklahoma: he owned a few theatres and ran a touring show. As Phylis Isley, she appeared in two B movies at Republic, *New Frontier* (39, George Sherman) and *Dick Tracy's G-Men* (39, William Whitney). In the same year, she married the young actor Robert Walker; they had two sons together. But in 1941, she auditioned at Selznick's New York office for the role of *Claudia* (eventually taken by Dorothy McGuire), Selznick saw her, called her out to Hollywood, and put her in a one-act play by William Saroyan, *Hello Out There*, in a brief theatre festival at Santa Barbara.

He put her under contract; he ordered and paid for many lessons; he found her a new name; and an affair began. Yet at that time, Selznick had Vivien Leigh, Joan Fontaine, and Ingrid Bergman under contract as well. Compared with those women, Jones was a novice, willing clay, obedient, adoring, and an unknown. Selznick got her the lead role at Fox in *The Song of Bernadette* (43, Henry King), for which she won the best actress Oscar. Her earnestness, her simplicity, and her wide, credulous eyes all worked for the young woman who sees visions. It was less acting than blessed casting—Jones had been educated at a Catholic school.

As their affair came to threaten his marriage, and help end hers, Selznick cast Jones as the elder daughter in *Since You Went Away* (44, John Cromwell) and loaned her to Hal Wallis for *Love Letters* (45, William Dieterle), in which she is very good as an amnesiac.

Selznick and his wife broke up in the summer of 1945, and not long thereafter he and Jennifer Jones began to be seen as a couple. His control of her, even on loan-out work, was so suffocating and detailed, and so dependent on eternal memos, that he began to earn her a bad reputation. This was increased by her own uncommon shyness and insecurity. In the years that followed, there was great love, but terrible guilt and anxiety as well as confusion and suicide attempts by Jones. She was overwhelmed by Selznick's care, and probably grew more helpless as he made more strenuous efforts to look after her and to promote her as the greatest actress in the world. He controlled her career decisions, but began to lose his own momentum and judgment in the process.

She did *Cluny Brown* (46, Ernst Lubitsch) at Fox with great charm. But the major screen event of that time was her Pearl Chavez in *Duel in the Sun* (46, King Vidor), a lurid Western in which the strain of being a wanton half-breed and the notoriety of the sex scenes laid the groundwork for the film's camp reputation. She was not well cast, but she tried so hard as Pearl, and she was granted the very best inflamed mood that Technicolor could manage. *Duel in the Sun* is foolish, yet moving— and it could not be so without the turmoil Selznick and Jones had made for themselves.

She had to play a child who becomes a woman in *Portrait of Jennie* (49, Dieterle), and she was loaned out for two duds—*We Were Strangers* (49, John Huston) and *Madame Bovary* (49, Vincente Minnelli). She was at her peak, commercially; she had many offers; yet those two films were the best that plenty of indecision and personal chaos could manage. Most notably, there was a gap of nearly two years in which she was off the screen.

As she and Selznick were married, in 1949, she gave one of her best performances as the Shropshire lass torn between squire and parson in the Selznick-Korda *Gone to Earth* (50, Michael Powell). It was in 1951 that Robert Walker died, a disturbed man badly served by doctors, and a further spur to Jones's guilt.

She was at her best, seemingly inspired and supported by Olivier, in *Carrie* (52, William Wyler), and she did a kind of remake of *Duel in the Sun*—*Ruby Gentry* (52, Vidor). She was funny, maybe without knowing why, in *Beat the Devil* (54, Huston) and helpless in *Indiscretion of an American Wife* (54, Vittorio De Sica). Selznick's dominance faltered, and it may not be coincidental that *Love Is a Many Splendored Thing* (55, King) proved her first box-office hit in years. She aged considerably in the feeble *Good Morning, Miss Dove* (55, Henry Koster), but she began to show her age in *The Man in the Gray Flannel Suit* (56, Nunnally Johnson), and she was a very vague Elizabeth Barrett Browning in *The Barretts of Wimpole Street* (57, Sidney Franklin).

She was plainly too mature and sedate for the Selznick production of *A Farewell to Arms* (57, Charles Vidor), the making of which was a succession of problems. The film flopped and effectively closed Selznick's career as a producer. He insisted on casting her as Nicole—much too young, far too disturbed—in *Tender Is the Night* (62, King), a project that he prepared but could take no direct credit on.

When Selznick died, in 1965, she was left with much debt, their young daughter, a broken career, and the emotional wreckage that a great wind leaves behind. It did not all go well. Their daughter, Mary Jennifer, killed herself. Jones's film career turned to *The Idol* (66, Daniel Petrie); *Angel, Angel, Down We Go* (69, Robert Thom); and *The Towering Inferno* (74, John Guillermin and Irwin Allen). But she married again—to the millionaire art collector Norton Simon—and she became not just his attendant in a paralyzing illness, but a surrogate in his business affairs.

Selznick's unquestioned adoration often meant that she was miscast: for her true range was narrow; her looks went quite early; and her own agonies, mixed with her husband's interference, lost her many good opportunities. But who else has survived such travails? Who knows how far she understood what was going on, or the effect she was having? She was an actress who caused a huge stir, on and off the screen. And she was such a creature of the 1940s, it seems odd in hindsight that her dark looks and her real experience as femme fatale and harassed woman never graced a

film noir—though *Laura* was one of the projects Selznick deemed unworthy of her.

Tommy Lee Jones,
b. San Saba, Texas, 1946

For twenty years, Jones had kicked around in bad movies, generally playing gloomy villains or taciturn friends. He never let rip, and so he seemed depressed. But in the same period, he had three remarkable TV movies in which he proved himself to everyone (except Hollywood): a very clever take on the unease within *The Amazing Howard Hughes* (77, William A. Graham); winning an Emmy for his disturbed but very insecure Gary Gilmore in *The Executioner's Song* (82, Lawrence Schiller), looking like a hood, but moving like a nerd; and as a classic cowboy in *Lonesome Dove* (89, Simon Wincer). Note that in all three, he was inhabiting the wild spaces of the West—Jones lives resolutely still, in Texas.

From a Dallas prep school he went to Harvard, where he studied English and played football and was part of a group of actors that included James Woods and Stockard Channing. He made his debut as Tom Lee Jones in *Love Story* (70, Arthur Hiller); and followed it with *Jackson County Jail* (76, Michael Miller); *Rolling Thunder* (77, John Flynn); *The Betsy* (78, Daniel Petrie); *The Eyes of Laura Mars* (78, Irvin Kershner); the husband in *Coal Miner's Daughter* (80, Michael Apted); with Sally Field in *Back Roads* (81, Martin Ritt); going piratical in *Nate and Hayes* (83, Ferdinand Fairfax); very good as the ex-con in scenes with a daughter (Martha Plimpton) in *The River Rat* (84, Tom Rickman, the writer of *Coal Miner's Daughter*); *Black Moon Rising* (86, Harley Cokliss); *The Big Town* (87, Ben Bolt); *Stormy Monday* (88, Mike Figgis); *The Package* (89, Andrew Davis); *Firebirds* (90, David Green).

Did *Lonesome Dove* remind people of what he might do? Suddenly, as Clay Shaw in *JFK* (91, Oliver Stone), Jones played rich, swish, and languid—and got a supporting actor nomination. Then he brought rascally panache to the mayhem of *Under Siege* (92, Davis). *House of Cards* (93, Michael Lessac) was a dud, but in *The Fugitive* (93, Davis), Jones was the motor that drove a film so implausible that it had to keep moving. He nearly eclipsed the nominal hero, and won the supporting actor Oscar and a lot of big offers for leading roles. Thus he made *Heaven and Earth* (93, Stone); *Blown Away* (94, Stephen Hopkins); and *The Client* (94, Joel Schumacher).

For a few years after his Oscar, Jones seemed encouraged. He found good parts and pictures in a range of moods: the very touching husband in *Blue Sky* (94, Tony Richardson); *Natural Born Killers* (94, Stone); the black frog croak of *Cobb* (94, Ron Shelton); the TV Western he directed and acted in, *The Good Old Boys* (95), and even his clever Two-Face in *Batman Forever* (95, Joel Schumacher). But that energy faded. He became coarse—or was it depressed?—and you felt he had lost faith in the business as his checks grew bigger: *Volcano* (97, Mick Jackson); *Men in Black* (97, Barry Sonnenfeld); *U.S. Marshals* (98, Stuart Baird); *Double Jeopardy* (99, Bruce Beresford); *Rules of Engagement* (00, William Friedkin); *Space Cowboys* (00, Clint Eastwood); *MIIB* (02, Sonnenfeld); *The Haunted* (03, William Friedkin).

Neil Jordan, b. Sligo, Ireland, 1950
1982: *Angel/Danny Boy*. 1985: *The Company of Wolves*. 1986: *Mona Lisa*. 1988: *High Spirits*. 1989: *We're No Angels*. 1991: *The Miracle*. 1992: *The Crying Game*. 1994: *Interview with the Vampire*. 1996: *Michael Collins*. 1997: *The Butcher Boy*. 1999: *In Dreams; The End of the Affair*. 2002: *The Good Thief*.

When that excellent critic, Donald Lyons, claimed that *The Crying Game* was the best film of 1992, his position was reasonable, if depressing. There might be arguments preferring *Raise the Red Lantern*. There would certainly be those who voted for *Howards End* and *Unforgiven*—worthy pictures, not bad films, yet flawed, cautious, and archaic. When James Ivory and Clint Eastwood vie for a year's best film, it may be that the movies can see their End.

And, similarly, *The Crying Game* is only a good, promising picture, leaped upon by hopeful critics in their longing to find something that might be a "best" film. Neil Jordan has distinct virtues: he is a writer, interested in fable and construction for their own sake, and a first-rate dialoguist (he won the original screenplay Oscar for *The Crying Game*); he has a world—the desolate, embittered wasteland of Ireland, and the shining city streets at night; he can present strong women and weak men, without having his own personality threatened; and he has a Maupassant-like taste for consequences that is torn between being unexpected and giving warning hints of destiny or fate. It may be to the point to see Jordan as a kid raised in movies, music, and Catholicism, struggling to apply the lessons to the woeful state of Anglo-Irish relations in our time.

Still, *The Crying Game* has problems of contrivance and plausibility, and of finding a way for Jordan's kindness to infiltrate brutal lives. This is a recurring issue in his work and we may note the one deliberate resort to fairy story as well as a larger reliance on movie genres that can sit awkwardly with the realism of the city, of race, and confused sexual tenderness in unlikely situations.

But what's an Irish moviemaker to do? *High Spirits* and *We're No Angels* showed how easily wrong roads may spring up after early success. Jordan remains a developing talent, most provoked by small towns and infinite cities. He is a master of both the shabby, neglected provinces and the dreamy cityscape. He has genuine promise, and already, in Cathy Tyson for *Mona Lisa* and Jaye Davidson in *The Crying Game*, he has given us a pair of native odalisques who are siblings in their tenuous existence and their sweet gloomy smiles. These are two remarkable characters, or presences, and they testify to the eagerness with which Jordan looks at novel sights.

Jordan is a novelist and short-story writer who got into movies as a script assistant to John Boorman on *Excalibur*. If he succumbs again to Hollywood offers, let us hope that someone orders him to come no farther west than Boston. Better still, Jordan is the director most qualified to do a movie about the IRA that could make North, South, England, and all other observers less angry and more respectful.

Instead, at David Geffen's urging, he went away and filmed Anne Rice, with results that only confirmed the intensity and the limits to that author's following. Jordan keeps going, and I found *The Butcher Boy* as good as his best. But *Michael Collins* was a pretty empty-headed biopic. *In Dreams* was daft. And *The End of the Affair* was one of the more regrettable films of the nineties—regrettable in that it would be very hard to botch that story, even without his cast. But in truth, the Edward Dmytryk film (with Deborah Kerr and Van Johnson) was more moving. So, after a dozen films, Neil Jordan seems as unsettled as a beginner.

Louis Jourdan (Gendre),
b. Marseilles, France, 1919
Louis Jourdan has been one of the best-looking men on screen. He is, in addition, an intelligent man and a sympathetic actor of real ability. No wonder David O. Selznick put him under contract soon after the war, when Jourdan had several French movies to his credit, as well as prolonged, courageous service in the Resistance. He had a long career: he was in one great hit (*Gigi*) and one indisputably great picture (*Letter from an Unknown Woman*). Yet it was a career that did not really take, no matter that Jourdan and his wife, Quique, were popular figures in Hollywood society. Was he too smart, too shy, too modest? Time and again, you have the feeling that he needed just one part, and the urging to play it to the full—a great villain, perhaps?

The son of a hotelier, he traveled widely as a boy, and was trained at the Ecole Dramatique in Paris. His French films are *Le Corsaire* (39, Marc Allegret); *Premier Rendez-Vous* (41, Henri Decoin); *L'Arlésienne* (42, Allegret); *Félicie Nanteuil* (42, Allegret); *La Vie de Bohème* (42, Marcel L'Herbier); *Untel Père et Fils* (43, Julien Duvivier); *La Belle Aventure* (45, Allegret).

In America, against his director's wishes, he was

the valet in *The Paradine Case* (48, Alfred Hitchcock); the man in *Letter from an Unknown Woman* (48, Max Ophuls); Rodolphe in *Madame Bovary* (49, Vincente Minnelli); *Bird of Paradise* (50, Delmer Daves); *Anne of the Indies* (51, Jacques Tourneur); *The Happy Time* (52, Richard Fleischer); back to France for *Rue de l'Estrapade* (53, Jacques Becker); *Decameron Nights* (52, Hugo Fregonese); *Three Coins in the Fountain* (54, Jean Negulesco); to France for *The Bride Is Much Too Beautiful* (56, Pierre Gaspard-Huit), with Brigitte Bardot; *The Swan* (56, Charles Vidor); *Julie* (56, Andrew L. Stone); *Gigi* (58, Minnelli); *Dangerous Exile* (58, Brian Desmond Hurst); *The Best of Everything* (59, Negulesco); *Can-Can* (60, Walter Lang).

Nothing was quite the same after that, but Jourdan seems never to have announced a retirement: *The Count of Monte Cristo* (61, Claude Autant-Lara); *Disorder* (62, Franco Brusati); *The VIPs* (63, Anthony Asquith); *Made in Paris* (66, Boris Sagal); *To Commit a Murder* (67, Edouard Molinaro); *Young Rebel* (67, Vincent Sherman); *A Flea in Her Ear* (68, Jacques Charon); *Silver Bears* (77, Ivan Passer); *The Man in the Iron Mask* (77, Mike Newell); very funny in *Swamp Thing* (82, Wes Craven); the villain to Bond in *Octopussy* (83, John Glen); *The Return of the Swamp Thing* (89, Jim Wynorski); *Year of the Comet* (92, Peter Yates).

Louis Jouvet (1887–1951),
b. Crozon, France

Jouvet was an immense movie presence in the late thirties, so plainly powerful and intelligent—and determined to have the world know that theatre was more important than movies. In 1913, he had joined Jacques Copeau's company; but in 1922 he set up his own company and combined acting and directing. He had an especially close relationship with Giraudoux, whose glossy wit suited Jouvet's style. One of his great stage successes was in Jules Romain's *Knock*, which he filmed twice—in 1933, directed by Roger Goupillières, and in 1951 (his last film), directed by Guy Lefranc. He had made a few silent pictures, but his film career began properly in 1933 with *Topaze* (Louis Gasnier) and was pursued seriously until the outbreak of war, even if it was usually out of step with the understated naturalism of the period: *La Kermesse Héroïque* (35, Jacques Feyder); *Mister Flow* (35, Robert Siodmak); as the Baron in *Les Bas-Fonds* (36, Jean Renoir); *Mademoiselle Docteur* (36, Edmond T. Greville); *Un Carnet de Bal* (37, Julien Duvivier); *Drôle de Drame* (37, Marcel Carné); *L'Alibi* (37, Pierre Chenal); *La Marseillaise* (38, Renoir); *Entrée des Artistes* (38, Marc Allégret); *Hotel du Nord* (38, Carné); and *La Fin du Jour* (39, Duvivier).

In the first year of war, Jouvet planned to film another of his stage hits, Moliere's *L'Ecole des*

Femmes, with Max Ophuls in Switzerland. It fell through and, instead, he played Mosca in *Volpone* (40, Maurice Tourneur) and *Untel Père et Fils* (40, Duvivier). He spent most of the war years in South America, but returned in 1946 and filmed steadily if without much distinction until his death: *Revenant* (46, Christian-Jaque); *Les Chouans* (46, Henri Calef); as the detective in *Quai des Orfèvres* (47, Henri-Georges Clouzot); *Entre Onze Heures et Minuit* (48, Henri Decoin); in the "Retour de Jean" episode from *Retour à la Vie* (49, Clouzot); *Lady Paname* (49, Henri Jeanson); and *Miquette et Sa Mère* (50, Clouzot).

Raul Julia (1940–94), b. San Juan, Puerto Rico

A clever and interesting stage actor, Julia made plenty of films (some of them from strange corners and circumstances), but not enough that did him justice. He was seldom a convincing villain—comedy was a much more fruitful way of using him. He had worked ten years on the stage before he ever got into movies: *The Panic in Needle Park* (71, Jerry Schatzberg); *Been Down So Long It Looks Like Up to Me* (71, Jeffrey Young); *The Organization* (71, Don Medford); very funny (and Italian) in *The Gumball Rally* (76, Chuck Bail); *Eyes of Laura Mars* (78, Irvin Kershner); *Strong Medicine* (79, Richard Foreman); *One from the Heart* (82, Francis Coppola); *The Escape Artist* (82, Caleb Deschanel); *Tempest* (82, Paul Mazursky); in his biggest role, opposite William Hurt, in *Kiss of the Spider Woman* (85, Hector Babenco); *Compromising Positions* (85, Frank Perry); *The Morning After* (86, Sidney Lumet); *Trading Hearts* (88, Neil Leifer); *La Gran Fiesta* (88, Marcos Zurinaga), set in San Juan in 1942; *Tango Bar* (88, Zurinaga); *The Penitent* (88, Cliff Osmond); *Moon Over Parador* (88, Mazursky); *Tequila Sunrise* (88, Robert Towne); as Archbishop Oscar Romero in *Romero* (89, John Duigan); playing Macheath, one of his stage successes, in *Mack the Knife* (89, Menahem Golan); *Presumed Innocent* (90, Alan J. Pakula); *Frankenstein Unbound* (90, Roger Corman); *The Rookie* (90, Clint Eastwood); without credit in *Havana* (90, Sydney Pollack).

After all this, his first unequivocal hit was as Gomez in *The Addams Family* (91, Barry Sonnenfeld); *The Plague* (91, Luis Puenzo); *Addams Family Values* (93, Sonnenfeld); *Street Fighter* (94, Steven E. de Souza). He was looking unwell, and in 1994 he died from a sudden stroke.

K

Pauline Kael (1919–2001),
b. Petaluma, California

Pauline Kael gave up writing about "our" movies in 1991. I suspect there were several reasons for that. Her health had declined—she had Parkinson's disease and heart problems—and there was every chance that it would worsen. The journey to New York screening rooms from her home in Great Barrington, Massachusetts, was an increasing burden. And Kael was never happy with videotapes. She was a sensationalist, and I suspect she grieved that so many screening rooms were on the small side. She was passionate about being overwhelmed—you can hear it in the happy, flagrant sexual innuendo of the titles to so many of her collections: *I Lost It at the Movies; Kiss Kiss Bang Bang; Reeling;* and so on. Being unsteady was her forte.

But there was another reason for retiring, and in a way it was the worst: the pictures weren't worth talking about. No, not all of them, but the defining majority. She relied on her own excitement, and for at least ten vital years so did we, and so did the elusive art of film in America. But never forget how long she had to wait, for that begins to explain her zest, her anger, and her impatience.

She was the child of Polish immigrants, and in particular of an intellectual chicken farmer, born and raised about an hour north of San Francisco, until the late 1920s, when the family had to sell up and move to the city. So she was San Franciscan all through the 1930s, at seventeen entering the University of California at Berkeley, majoring in philosophy. She was radical, petite but fierce, opinionated and Bohemian, and while she loved movies she was more deeply into sex and getting around. In the years between graduation and her beginnings as a film critic—the time from 1940 to about 1955 (from twenty to thirty-five—in so many people, the real age for falling for the movies), she shared her life between New York and the Bay Area. She married and divorced three times. She had a daughter. She was involved with several artistic men—like poet Robert Horan and experimental filmmaker James Broughton.

I don't know whether she thought she was waiting, or simply reckoned that she was living life to the full. She moved in arty circles, and it's likely that that sharpened her later disdain for highbrow or self-consciously artistic films. But she wasn't doing anything about it, not even in the forties she later adored. Maybe she just devoured the films the way people have to eat. Forever afterwards, despite her own powerful position, she was uneasy about film as an art: she called it a shallow art; she always poked wicked fun at solemnity; and she warned repeatedly of what might happen to film if it ever fell into the hands of academe.

In the mid–1950s, she stirred. She wrote for *City Lights,* a San Francisco literary magazine—it was there she called *Limelight* "Slimelight." She began to contribute essays to *Sight and Sound,* and then she got a radio column on KPFA and took over the Berkeley Cinema Guild Theatre, for

which she wrote pungent program notes. And people began collecting them. Again, it's worth stressing her businesslike position. She watched the films, but she watched audiences, too, and she loved what happens in the dark.

In 1964, she published a collection, *I Lost It at the Movies,* which served notice that no other voice was as serious or as funny about movies. It led to magazine commissions, and there may have been a real campaign—though I'm not sure she could bring herself to be that organized. But she moved to New York, and after she had offended *Redbook* by loathing *The Sound of Music,* she began to write for *The New Yorker.* The thing there that identified her early on was a rapturous rereview of *Bonnie and Clyde,* a paean that helped in the rescue act of that film, and which placed Kael in the camp of the new, the American, the sexy, and the violent. And, of course, she was right about a film that had bewildered many other critics.

Here was the wondrous serendipity: that she and a very bright age of film coincided. Thus Kael was there to greet not just Arthur Penn and Warren Beatty, but Coppola, Scorsese, De Palma, Altman, Peckinpah, and Bernardo Bertolucci. She wrote so well that she made herself central to *The New Yorker* (they resisted by having another film critic, too, Penelope Gilliatt) and to the surging culture of film as evident in the new rage for film classes in colleges and universities (note: she was a great impromptu lecturer, but she never took up a teaching post).

How good was she? Very, very good, because she was a terrific journalist who took immense pains to seem spontaneous, who believed that it ought to be possible to write about entertainments in ways that made them more stimulating for thousands of people. Her luck was in having such good films. But that worked both ways too, for she formed odd, dangerous ties with some filmmakers, where her early word (or tone) may have influenced the films they were making. That led, in 1979, to her accepting Warren Beatty's invitation to be a kind of producer—helping James Toback on *Love and Money*—at Paramount, in Hollywood itself. That experiment didn't work, and she was mocked for it as she withdrew to *The New Yorker* again. But it showed her urge; she might have been a Hollywood person.

Hers was a heady time—it was America in the seventies, as well!—and she was thrilled and aroused by her own power. There were problems with that. Her writing could turn bullying. And as she grew older, I think she yielded to a younger, tougher style. She let herself become the godmother and career broker for too many young critics (the Paulettes), and she did not always see her own vanity or sharp edges. But I'm hardly the one to criticize her too much for that. I loved her work, but did not like her much as a person—and I think many felt that way.

She was too fierce, sometimes: she rather neglected foreign films; she hurt De Palma and Walter Hill, at least, by making too much of them; she seemed to make a perverse case out of attacking Orson Welles and *Citizen Kane* (for the sake of being provocative) when both were so much her kind of thing (shallow masterpieces). She made a cult out of seeing a film just once, and so she tended to stifle reflection. She was obstinately anti-auteurist, because she fell into a stupid New York feud with Andrew Sarris (and because he'd made that key point first). And she didn't often enough let her intelligence explore more general or profound issues. I can see her sneering at that even now.

But she established for a while something that had not been true since the impact of television—that the movies were "ours," that they spoke to and for a society and were the most telling, deeply felt impression of who we were and might be. That may never come again. And I think she had foreseen that. For the movies needed an America like that of the thirties and the forties, where passion was respectable and being moved was an everyday thing. In which case, as time passes, so I suspect she will seem more remarkable, more useful as a measure of her time, and more sexy. I suspect she would have given it all up if she could have had one scene in one film—like Dorothy Malone with Bogart in *The Big Sleep*.

Garson Kanin (1912–99),

b. Rochester, New York
1938: *A Man to Remember; Next Time I Marry.*
1939: *The Great Man Votes; Bachelor Mother.*
1940: *My Favorite Wife; They Knew What They Wanted.* 1941: *Tom, Dick and Harry.* 1942: *Ring of Steel* (d); *Salut à la France* (codirected with Jean Renoir) (d). 1945: *The True Glory* (codirected with Carol Reed). 1969: *Where It's At; Some Kind of a Nut.*

Kanin passed through the film world in an unusual direction, from director to writer, enjoying the reputation of perverse smartness. At his best in sophisticated comedy based on thorough character studies and unashamed of staginess, Kanin never concealed his liking for a witty élite scheming against the grain of a fatuous industry. His record vindicated that approach and if this account of the making of *Adam's Rib* seems cozy, it should be remembered that comedies of sexual antagonism do not come much better:

The original script was bought by Metro for I think the highest price they had ever paid for an original: they paid $175,000. Then all sorts of things happened, like getting the supporting players together, and it was really us, as a little

unit, doing everything. We worked on the script with Dore Schary and Kate and Spence; we got Orry Kelley in on the clothes; Kate went out and got Cole Porter to write the song. Ruth [R. Gordon, Kanin's wife] and I went to work with the designer, Cedric Gibbons, and one day he looked up at us and said, "You know, this is an historic day. I've been at the studio twenty-five years, and this is the first time writers have ever been in my office. . . ."

It was because the work of the writer and director was so often at the mercy of insensitive front office scissors that Kanin lost heart for directing. But he could argue that, as a writer, he had a greater effect upon finished films because of his ability to slip a project past the blind side of men like Harry Cohn. He had begun in the theatre, working with George Abbott, and then joined Samuel Goldwyn in a vague but humiliating role—"he called me Thalberg all the time." He left and went to RKO, where he directed his prewar films. Although he never took any script credit, they show his growing skill at satirical, domestic comedy: *The Great Man Votes* was one of the more worthwhile pictures John Barrymore made as he sank into alcohol; *Bachelor Mother* is a good Norman Krasna script with David Niven and Ginger Rogers; while *My Favorite Wife*, with Cary Grant and Irene Dunne, was directed by Kanin after Leo McCarey had been involved in a road accident. Not as boisterous as McCarey or as dry as Hawks, it is still enjoyable and a touchstone for Kanin's own work.

During the war he went to Europe, worked with Carol Reed on *The True Glory*, and at the same time wrote the play *Born Yesterday*. Its Broadway success and *Adam's Rib* (49, George Cukor) capitalized on his first script (written with Ruth Gordon): *A Double Life* (48, Cukor). Perhaps the Broadway success, and his harmony with Tracy and Hepburn, explained the influence he had at this time. He and Gordon appear to have been instrumental in devising the Judy Holliday character, and in seeing that Holliday herself should bring it to life. They scripted Cukor's film of *Born Yesterday* (50), *The Marrying Kind* (52, Cukor), and *Pat and Mike* (52, Cukor). After that, and without Ruth Gordon, he scripted *It Should Happen to You* (54, Cukor); *The Girl Can't Help It* (56, Frank Tashlin); *High Time* (59, Blake Edwards); and *The Rat Race* (60, Robert Mulligan).

His 1969 return as a director suggested a man who had outlived his time. Indeed, his memoir, *Tracy and Hepburn*, published in 1971, is glazed with his own nostalgia for one vivid decade. At this distance, it is hard to see him as the most talented member of that group, but there are situations that call for go-betweens: if it was Adam and Eve that played the main parts, it still needed someone with the wit to see that shifting a rib would set them in motion.

His book *Moviola*, published in 1979, was turned into a television mini-series (80, John Erman). In the same year, he and Ruth Gordon cowrote a TV movie, *Hardhat and Legs* (Lee Philips).

Anna Karina (Hanne Karin Blarke Bayer), b. Copenhagen, Denmark, 1940

When Jean-Luc Godard and Anna Karina separated, it marked Godard's abandonment of the heritage of commercial, and especially American, cinema. Within that heritage, the idea of a relationship between a director and an actress that becomes virtually the subject of their films was often illustrated, but never as trenchantly worked out as it was between Godard and his wife. Griffith and Lillian Gish always spoke with Victorian respect for one another; parted, von Sternberg and Dietrich still shimmered in the ambiguous glow of their films at Paramount.

The closest ancestor to the mutual despair in *Pierrot le Fou* is Orson Welles's *The Lady from Shanghai*, made when he and Rita Hayworth were already separated, but with the couple held together by the revelation of incompatibility. The personal confession at the end of that film is mordant and harsh, but it is only a single film into which the entire sequence of meeting, enchantment, struggle, and alienation is compressed. With Godard and Karina, the story was drawn out over seven full-length films. And because Godard is so intellectual an artist—classifying his own responses but not always feeling them—his work with Karina is the peak of his art, where he attains a glimpse of emotion that illuminates its omission in the rest of his films. Throughout *Pierrot le Fou*, Belmondo represents Godard, forever discussing and writing about art and emotion, but Karina is the feminine movie sensibility, a photographed woman who turns the spectator's heart with the speed of the projector. Her silence withers the desperate words of Ferdinand/Pierrot; her staring into the camera transfixes Godard behind it. *Pierrot le Fou* is Karina's masterpiece as well as Godard's. It shows how far a former model had progressed in six years, and proves how intense an impression a girl can make if she knows how to be filmed, if she divines how far the camera exploits her and yet still consents to it without mannerism, irritation, or prudishness. There is not a fuller picture of a woman in movies: beautiful and ugly; spontaneous but brooding; tender but arbitrary; reflective and instinctive; turning capriciousness into an assertion of transience that astounds Ferdinand's fixed commentaries on her:

FERDINAND (off): What's the matter, Marianne?
MARIANNE: I'm fed up! I'm fed up with the sea, with the sun, with the sand, tinned food,

everything! . . . I'm fed up with wearing the same dress every day! . . . I want to get away from here! . . . I want to live!
FERDINAND (off): What do you want me to do?
MARIANNE: I don't know, I want just to go. Anyway, I've thrown away the money we had to keep us for the winter.
FERDINAND (off): Where did you throw it?
MARIANNE: Into the sea, you idiot!

The film is caught in an anguished mixture of rapture and incomprehension at the cinematic beauty of Karina in the south in the sun: standing on a balcony experimenting with scissors; weaving through the trees singing about her luck; Girl Friday to her melancholy lover Crusoe; tucking a rifle butt into her breast; lying on a beach at evening; or, finally, wreathed in red. There is a magnificent passage in which Ferdinand admits to the camera his inability to treat this nymph as real, even though he suffers from the effects she has on his imagination. This moment is like the last room in the Museum of Romantic Cinema:

FERDINAND: Perhaps I am dreaming even though I am awake. . . . Her face makes me think of music. We have entered the age of the Double-Man. One no longer needs a mirror to speak to oneself. When Marianne says "It is a fine day" what is she really thinking? I have only this image of her, saying "It is a fine day." Nothing else. What is gained by trying to explain this? We are made of dreams . . . and dreams are made of us. . . . It is a fine day, my love, in dreams, in words, and in death. It is a fine day, my love. . . . It is a fine day . . . in life.

Karina had come to Paris in 1958, having made one short in Denmark. She turned down the part in *Breathless* played by Jean Seberg, but appeared in Godard's second feature, *Le Petit Soldat* (60), and was immediately rhapsodized over by his camera but pushed into betrayal through the force of the film's suspicions. In the same year she was in Michel Deville's *Ce Soir ou Jamais*. In 1961 she went to England for *She'll Have to Go* (61, Robert Asher), appeared in *Une Femme est une Femme* (Godard), and married its director. They appeared together briefly in the film within *Cléo from 5 to 7* (62, Agnès Varda), and then they made *Vivre Sa Vie* (62).

As the hapless girl in Paris who turns to prostitution, but who is moved by Falconetti in Dreyer's *Passion de Jeanne d'Arc*, who is a home-movie Cyd Charisse round the billiard table, and who converses with the philosopher Brice Parain, she is the fragments of Godard's ideal but always an actual, diffident, self-sufficient girl. Close-ups of her in that film are made consciously in the tradition of Gish, Falconetti, and Louise Brooks, but there is also that long opening when she sits with her back to the camera and the "documentary" letter-writing sequence. In another episode, Karina and her man read over Edgar Allan Poe's *The Oval Portrait,* as if Godard already foresaw the dilemma of the artist who let his beloved perish as he refined her portrait.

Twice more for Godard, before *Pierrot,* she was a creature of intense black-and-white romance: as the timid girl in *Bande à Part* (64), and as Natasha von Braun, saint of the Capital of Tears, in *Alphaville* (65). Between these films she made one episode of *Les Quatres Vérités* (62); *Dragées au Poivre* (63, Jacques Baratier); *De l'amour* (64, Jean Aurel); *Le Voleur du Tibidabo* (64, Maurice Ronet); and *La Ronde* (64, Roger Vadim).

Immediately after *Pierrot* she played Diderot's novice, Suzanne Simonin, in *La Religieuse* (66, Jacques Rivette) and worked for Godard, but in a visibly more professional way, in *Made in USA* (66) and in the episode "Anticipation," from *Le Plus Vieux Métier du Monde* (67). She then ventured outside France, mostly in mediocre or over-ambitious films. In so many ways, she had fought to be free of Godard—yet, without him, she was ordinary. It isn't the camera that loves an actress, or makes her exceptional. It's the intent behind the camera, the awful hope: *Lo Straniero* (67, Luchino Visconti); *Lamiel* (67, Aurel); *Before Winter Comes* (68, J. Lee Thompson); *The Magus* (68, Guy Green); *Justine* (69, George Cukor); *Michael Kohlhaas* (69, Volker Schlöndorff); *Laughter in the Dark* (69, Tony Richardson); *L'Alliance* (70, Christian de Chalonge); excellent in the brooding *Rendezvous à Bray* (71, André Delvaux); *The Salzburg Connection* (72, Lee H. Katzin); and *Pane e Ciccolata* (73, Franco Brusati).

She acted in and directed *Vivre Ensemble* (74) and appeared in *Chinese Roulette* (76, Rainer Werner Fassbinder). Since then, she has appeared in *Historien om en Moder* (79, Claus Weeke); *L'Ami de Vincent* (83, Pierre Granier-Deferre); *Ave Maria* (84, Jacques Richard); *L'Ile au Trésor* (85, Raul Ruiz); *Cayenne-Palace* (87, Alain Maline); *L'Eté Dernier à Tanger* (87, Alexandre Arcady); *L'Oeuvre au Noir* (88, André Delvaux); and *Man, Der Ville Vaere Skyldig* (90, Ole Roos).

In recent years, she was in *Chloé* (94, Dennis Berry); *Up, Down, Fragile* (95, Rivette); *The Truth About Charlie* (02, Jonathan Demme). And a pop singer!

Boris Karloff (William Henry Pratt)
(1887–1969), b. Dulwich, England

It is a credit to Peter Bogdanovich's imaginative kindness that amid all the harassments of his first film, *Targets* (68), he managed to make it—among other things—an affectionate valediction to Karloff. In *Targets,* Karloff is barely disguised as

Byron Orlok, the mandarin of horror, eighty years old, leaning on a stick and a lovely Asiatic secretary, his skin a blend of Californian tan, jaundice, and the old parchments of Gothic castles. Orlok thinks of himself as an antique: so used to the conventions of the horror genre, he can no longer play a straight role. But he is appalled by the efficient, spiritless slaughter of the young rifleman who hides behind the screen at a drive-in theatre, waits for Orlok/Karloff in *The Terror* (62, Roger Corman) to be projected, and then begins to pick off the audience in their cars. The end is grand guignol with apologetic built-in significance, as Orlok in life and Orlok on the screen both stride vengefully toward the killer.

At that moment the rather glib director's conception is lent seriousness by the presence of Karloff: not just in the elderly dignity of his walk, but because he carried with him an honorable record of insisting on human values within one of the cinema's most exploited forms. Karloff had always shown us monsters and mad magicians who had been isolated by the unthinking cruelty of the "wholesome" world.

Karloff died two years later in the rural setting of a Sussex hospital. He had opted for England in 1955, visiting America only to work. That choice was to be expected: in Hollywood, Karloff had retained English citizenship, read *Wisden,* and never yielded his lugubrious articulation. He was the son of a diplomat in the Indian Civil Service—and there were always stories that he had Indian blood. At Uppingham and Merchant Taylor's he found his great passion: cricket. But something in the scheme of English duty must have rankled, for in 1909 he went to Canada and, after a variety of jobs, he took to acting with traveling companies. The roots of melodrama lay there, and, inevitably, by 1919 he wandered into the movies: a tall man, with striking, gaunt features and a natural slowness that could suggest menace.

For twelve years he worked in small parts, specializing in Oriental bogeymen, but hardly doing well enough to make up for missing English summers of Jack Hobbs and Maurice Tate. Between pictures, he often had to work as a laborer—one reason perhaps why he remained physically striking into old age: *The Last of the Mohicans* (20, Maurice Tourneur); *Cheated Hearts* (21, Hobart Henley); *The Infidel* (22, James Young); *The Altar Stairs* (22, Lambert Hillyer); *Omar the Tentmaker* (22, Young); *The Prisoner* (23, Jack Conway); *Dynamite Dan* (24, Bruce Mitchell); *Lady Robinhood* (25, Ralph Ince); *The Golden Web* (26, Walter Lang); with Lionel Barrymore in *The Bells* (26, Young); *Old Ironsides* (26, James Cruze); *Tarzan and the Golden Lion* (27, J. P. McGowan); *The Meddlin' Stranger* (27, Richard Thorpe); *Two Arabian Knights* (27, Lewis Milestone); *The Love Mart* (28, George Fitzmaurice); *Phantom of the*

North (29, Harry Webb); *The Unholy Night* (29, Barrymore); *Behind that Curtain* (29, Irving Cummings); and *The Sea Bat* (30, Wesley Ruggles).

In 1931, Hawks cast Karloff as the prisoner who works as the governor's butler in *The Criminal Code*. Karloff had already played the part on the stage, but the film established him. Hawks recognized the way violence in Karloff was related to gravity. His butler is aloof, disapproving, a man hurt by vulgarity, a noble savage scornful of civilization. But his moment comes when he is able to kill the stool pigeon in the prison. The butler's white coat then becomes the uniform of a vengeful angel, and the superb slow advance on the cowering victim is the first sign of the sleepy rhythm that Karloff was to bring to horror. In the same year, he had good parts in *Five Star Final* (31, Mervyn Le Roy), *The Mad Genius* (31, Michael Curtiz), and *The Yellow Ticket* (31, Raoul Walsh). But he became a household name when James Whale took over the Frankenstein project and preferred Karloff to Lugosi for the monster. That part was a crucial innovation: his makeup and interpretation have remained essential to the monster ever since; above all, Karloff presented a feeling creature, a vulnerable colossus, capable of destruction but touched by beauty. As such, Karloff's monster is an important forerunner of the madman hero, and the scene in which he and the little girl float flowers on a pond, before he kills her, has become more moving and suggestive with the years.

It is not easy to chart purpose in a career in horror: the genre is subject to fashion, the reckless cheapness of many productions, and the wild variation of directors. Karloff's work rises and falls in response to all these. He made trite, rushed movies that must have offended him. He had the obligatory encounters with *Abbott and Costello* and *The Ghost in the Invisible Bikini* (66). But most of the great horror directors appreciated him and the successive revivals of the genre renewed his enthusiasm. Say first that he made a few straight films—*Scarface* (32, Hawks); *The Lost Patrol* (34, John Ford); *The House of Rothschild* (34, Alfred Werker); *The Secret Life of Walter Mitty* (47, Norman Z. McLeod); *Unconquered* (47, Cecil B. De Mille)—and then remember his best films: *The Mummy* (32, Karl Freund); *The Mask of Fu Manchu* (32, Charles Vidor and Charles Brabin); *The Old Dark House* (32, Whale); *The Miracle Man* (32, McLeod); *The Ghoul* (33, T. Hayes Hunter); *The Black Cat* (34, Edgar G. Ulmer); *The Bride of Frankenstein* (35, Whale); *The Raven* (35, Lew Landers); *The Invisible Ray* (36, Hillyer); *The Walking Dead* (36, Curtiz); *The Man They Could Not Hang* (39, Nick Grinde); *Son of Frankenstein* (39, Rowland V. Lee); *The Tower of London* (39, Lee); *Before I Hang* (40, Grinde); *The Devil Commands* (41, Edward Dmytryk); *The House of Frankenstein* (45, Erle C. Kenton); *The Body Snatcher* (45, Robert Wise); *Isle of the Dead* (45, Mark Robson); *Bedlam* (46, Robson); *Tap Roots* (48, George Marshall); *The Strange Door* (51, Joseph Pevney); *The Raven* (62, Corman); *The Terror* (62, Corman); *Black Sabbath* (63, Mario Bava); *Comedy of Terrors* (64, Jacques Tourneur); and *Die, Monster, Die* (65, Daniel Haller).

Phil Karlson (Philip N. Karlstein) (1908–85), b. Chicago
1944: *A Wave, a Wac and a Marine*. 1945: *There Goes Kelly; G.I. Honeymoon; The Shanghai Cobra*. 1946: *Live Wires; Swing Parade of 1946; Dark Alibi; Behind the Mask; Bowery Bombshell; The Missing Lady; Wife Wanted*. 1947: *Black Gold; Louisiana; Kilroy Was Here*. 1948: *Rocky; Adventures in Silverado; Thunderhoof*. 1949: *The Big Cat; Ladies of the Chorus; Down Memory Lane*. 1950: *The Iroquois Trail*. 1951: *Lorna Doone; The Texas Rangers; Mask of the Avenger*. 1952: *Scandal Sheet; The Brigand; Kansas City Confidential*. 1953: *99 River Street*. 1954: *They Rode West*. 1955: *Hell's Island; Tight Spot; Five Against the House; The Phenix City Story*. 1957: *The Brothers Rico*. 1958: *Gunman's Walk*. 1959: *The Scarface Mob*. 1960: *Hell to Eternity; Key Witness*. 1961: *The Secret Ways; The Young Doctors*. 1962: *Kid Galahad*. 1963: *Rampage*. 1966: *The Silencers*. 1967: *A Time for Killing/The Long Ride Home*. 1968: *The Wrecking Crew*. 1970: *Hornets' Nest*. 1972: *Ben*. 1973: *Walking Tall*. 1974: *Framed*.

Karlson has a modest but secure place in the history of crime movies with *Scandal Sheet*, *The Phenix City Story*, *The Brothers Rico*, and *The Scarface Mob*. It took some fifteen years of odd jobs around the industry before he directed. Karlson had a long duty as assistant director: *The Countess of Monte Cristo* (34, Karl Freund); *Manhattan Moon* (35, Stuart Walker); *Rio* (39, John Brahm); and *Seven Sinners* (40, Tay Garnett). He soon showed himself a competent director of adventure pictures, but had an especially fertile period with violent, urban thrillers. The acute sense of corruption in *Phenix City Story* is several years ahead of a general acknowledgment of sordid city life in America. While in *Five Against the House* he made one of the most exciting planned-crime movies, aided by the sultry presence of a young Kim Novak. Also notable are the character studies in his Western, *Gunman's Walk*, and the uninhibited brutality of an early European espionage movie, *The Secret Ways*. His final work lacked the impact of the pictures made in the middle and late 1950s.

Lawrence Kasdan,
b. Miami Beach, Florida, 1949
1981: *Body Heat.* 1983: *The Big Chill.* 1985: *Silverado.* 1988: *The Accidental Tourist.* 1990: *I Love You to Death.* 1991: *Grand Canyon.* 1994: *Wyatt Earp.* 1995: *French Kiss.* 1999: *Mumford.* 2003: *Dreamcatcher.*

After receiving a B.A. and then an M.A. from the University of Michigan, Kasdan became an advertising copywriter in Detroit and then in Los Angeles. By the late seventies he was trying his hand as a screenwriter. This led to a cowriting credit on *The Empire Strikes Back* (80, Irvin Kershner), and then to the start of his own directing career.

Body Heat was a brilliant thriller: it captured place and weather as well as a real feeling for erotic moment. It used William Hurt cleverly; it made Kathleen Turner's career, so that several other less focused roles hardly shook her from her place. *Body Heat* was old-fashioned, and as simpleminded as it was complicated. But it works better than Kasdan's later efforts to give us people truer to ordinary life.

The Big Chill seems to me like a smart gloss rather than a real portrait; so much is going on nothing searching is expected. *Silverado* felt relentlessly wooden. *The Accidental Tourist* underlined the fact that Anne Tyler could be a TV dramatist as well as a novelist if she had lived in Britain, whereas in America she has no reason to go beyond the page. On *I Love You to Death*, Kasdan later believed he had erred in rejecting awkward, ugly elements in favor of smoothness.

Grand Canyon was something more. It has large faults—too much tidiness, an overly benevolent view of blacks, an inescapable but hollow ending, and the insistent unreality of Steve Martin in a cast striving for the mundane. But *Grand Canyon* caught the mood of L.A. in the age of Rodney King, and it is an unconscious record of Hollywood's pious liberalism. Very few American films outside Altman have had so interesting a sense of the crowded context in which we live. The film gave a hint of a Kasdan who was not happy with his own narrative choices, and had found a reason to put them aside. But if he developed and improved along that resolute line, could he be employed? His next picture proved to be not an advance into danger, but a throwback—*Wyatt Earp*, with Kevin Costner seeking to rekindle memories of *My Darling Clementine.*

What had happened to Kasdan? *Wyatt Earp* was 195 minutes, and not just the dullest Earp film but one exposed by *Tombstone,* made in the same year. Not that Kasdan's picture was bursting with new ambitions, or a fresh vision of the frontier. But *French Kiss* was the real disaster, far too

charming for its own good. As for *Mumford*, it was decent, observant, and benign, but somehow there seemed to be a pall of solemnity, drawn up above the head, by a talent that had begun to flinch from film's essential energy or force. It's a progress that leaves one more aware of the deep disquiet *Grand Canyon* represented.

Kasdan has also written or helped to write films for others: *Continental Divide* (81, Michael Apted); *Raiders of the Lost Ark* (81, Steven Spielberg); *The Return of the Jedi* (83, Richard Marquand)—it might be fascinating to see Kasdan try a movie about a figure like Steven Spielberg. Though it is more likely that Anne Tyler would do a better job in a novel.

His years-on-the-shelf script led to *The Bodyguard* (92, Mick Jackson), which Kasdan coproduced.

Philip Kaufman, b. Chicago, 1936
1965: *Goldstein.* 1969: *Fearless Frank.* 1972: *The Great Northfield Minnesota Raid.* 1974: *The White Dawn.* 1978: *Invasion of the Body Snatchers.* 1979: *The Wanderers.* 1983: *The Right Stuff.* 1988: *The Unbearable Lightness of Being.* 1990: *Henry & June.* 1993: *Rising Sun.* 2000: *Quills.* 2003: *The Blackout Murders.*

Phil Kaufman has sometimes been described as a "maverick" filmmaker, someone who has deliberately set himself apart from the Hollywood stream. He lives just a few blocks away from where I am writing, in San Francisco, and for going on ten years now, we have been friendly. Phil has striven to keep his base in the Bay Area, without ever becoming an identified part of the Lucas or Coppola groups. Wherever he has filmed, he brings his movies back here for postproduction. When he prepares, he works closely with his wife, Rose (cowriter on *The Wanderers* and *Henry & June*), and his son, Peter (who has produced *Rising Sun*). And while he has eschewed Los Angeles, he has built his allure as a top director in that city. That is more than steadfast northern Californian; it is downright adroit.

He does have to be an American filmmaker, and I'm sure he hopes for American success. The sharpest moment in that life of hope was *The Right Stuff,* his best film (I believe) and the most painful commercial failure. That adaptation of Tom Wolfe's book draws on two of Phil's great strengths, even if it discovered a conflict between them: he is romantic about American heroes, and thus he loved Sam Shepard's presence as a Gary Cooper–like Yeager, as phlegmatic and unaffected as chewing gum at Mach 1. But Kaufman has an ironic cast of mind and a wary, critical (if not satirical) view of American pomp, cant, and circumstance. And so in *The Right Stuff* he reveled in the hype and crazy self-deception of the Moon program. He made a movie that was classical and subversive at the same time.

It remains a model for anyone who cares to look at it, a bold, dangerous, and uncategorizable picture (maybe the last movie of the heroic 1970s). Kaufman's script was publishable—he had wanted to be a novelist once. His delight in gangs of good actors was proven in what is a monument to supporting players. The picture was comic and inspiring; it was as if someone had managed to make a mix of Preston Sturges, Capra, and Anthony Mann. *The Right Stuff* got flying, the sky, the desert, flimflam, team spirit, cartoon, and an Ivesian noise or tumult. Moreover, Phil managed to film great chunks of it in disguised and ingeniously reinvented parts of the Bay Area.

The film failed. Audiences, I think, didn't quite want it. The project's original writer, William Goldman, made an interesting case for commercial confusion in Kaufman's approach (Goldman dropped out after they attempted collaboration) as the Yeager spirit battled the NASA ale-and-quail club. This is possible, yet it may only be a way of defining Kaufman's originality. As time passes, only the achievement survives.

But the box-office failure urged Kaufman into trying to make American European films. He seemed to agree with the numbers: he must be too intelligent, too artistic, too much the outsider. So Paris became his setting for much of two films, the adaptation of Milan Kundera and Anaïs Nin.

The Unbearable Lightness did not, could not, convey Kundera's spiral of thought or expression. It also refashioned his hero and, in Daniel Day-Lewis, found an actor too young, too pretty. The weary fatalism of the book was sacrificed. But in its place Kaufman did justice to Prague of 1968, to the politics, and to the women. It was a far better study of sex, love, and jealousy than *Henry & June* would prove, and it drew a brilliant performance from Lena Olin and a great one from Juliette Binoche.

Henry & June had to live under the spurious clamor of being the first NC-17 film. In addition, it showed how hard it is for anyone to like Nin as much as she liked herself. And as she became a pain in the neck, so it was easier to see that Henry Miller was monotonous and self-centered. I found the film arty and showy, and too obviously the work of an American infatuated with bohemianism.

Commercially, the two films were failures, and Kaufman sought return to the mainstream with *Rising Sun*. In hindsight, I wish that his European films had had American characters. For while Kaufman is plainly open to Europe and the whole world in ways not common in Hollywood (his family lived in Europe in the early sixties), his strength may be in seeing the outside through American eyes. After all, in his early pictures,

Kaufman was often intent on Americana: the James gang; the frozen north as experienced by a variety of Americans; empty bodies in San Francisco.

Rising Sun was probably too deft, too wry, and quick, to be a big hit. In the end, it was just a police story shadowboxing with the question of Japanese character and intent. Sean Connery's hero was a little too independent to be true, and finally the picture lacked pain or shock.

Still, Kaufman is an outsider in several ways, friendly but a stubborn loner, too. He was fired from *The Outlaw Josey Wales* (76, Clint Eastwood)—which he wrote—because of an impasse with Eastwood. He remains, I think, attached to wry heroes: he did write the story for *Raiders of the Lost Ark* (81, Steven Spielberg). He is a director equipped to handle large American subjects—the life of Nixon, or LBJ, say. He has a better than ordinary grasp of America's need for rogue tricksters—and of their longing to be treated as good guys.

No one regretted the seven-year wait before *Quills* more than Kaufman. There had been many projects, but nothing to reach fruition. And *Quills* was a low-budget picture, set in France but shot in England, that left one marveling at Kaufman's wit and skill. This is a man who ought to be making a couple of pictures a year. But *Quills* had no paper to write on—its rare mixture of tenderness and cruelty, black comedy and the erotic, liberty and censorship, found few viewers because it seemed too hard for the mainstream to identify with Sade (despite Geoffrey Rush's passionate commitment to it).

Aki Kaurismäki, b. Orimattila, Finland, 1957
1981: *Saimaa-ilmiö*. 1983: *Rikos ja Rangaistus*. 1985: *Calamari Union*. 1986: *Varjoja Paratiisissa*. 1987: *Hamlet Liikemaailmassa/Hamlet Gets Business; Thru the Wire; Rich Little Bitch*. 1988: *Ariel*. 1989: *Leningrad Cowboys Go America; Tulitikkutehtaan Tyttö/The Match Factory Girl; Likaiset Kadet*. 1990: *I Hired a Contract Killer*. 1992: *La Vie de Bohème; Those Were the Days; These Boots*. 1993: *Leningrad Cowboys Meet Moses*. 1994: *Pida Huivista Kiinni, Tatjana; Total Balalaika Show*. 1996: *Kauas Pilvet Karkaavat/Drifting Clouds*. 1999: *Juha*. 2002: *Man Without a Past*.

In the late eighties and early nineties, the Kaurismäki brothers thrust Finnish movies onto the international festival scene. At first, Aki (a writer-director) worked closely with his older brother, Mika, but subsequently Aki established himself as the more productive. He has a refreshing passion for shorter films (often in the seventy-five-minute range), and he has the cool, dry, ironic affection for American culture that sometimes one sees in

Godard. Kaurismäki can be very funny—so long as no one laughs. His vein is not quite black humor, but a droll fatalism that marks the Finns as eternal spectators for the silliness of the world. He was most impressive with *Ariel, The Match Factory Girl,* and *Leningrad Cowboys Go America,* and he was fond of the road picture format. More recently he seems to have lost some edge, but in the early twenty-first century there is plenty of room available if his sardonic eye turned to politics.

Helmut Kautner (1908–80),
b. Düsseldorf, Germany

1939: *Kitty und die Weltkonferenz; Die Acht Entfesselten.* 1940: *Frau Nach Mass; Kleider Machen Leute.* 1941: *Auf Wiedersehn, Franziska.* 1942: *Anuschka; Wir Maken Musik.* 1943: *Romanze in Moll.* 1944: *Grosse Freiheit Nr 7.* 1945: *Unter den Brucken.* 1947: *In Jenen Tagen.* 1948: *Film ohne Fitel; Der Apfel ist ab.* 1949: *Konigskinder.* 1950: *Epilog.* 1951: *Weisse Schatten.* 1952: *Kapt'n Bay-Bay.* 1954: *Die Letzte Brucke; Bildnis einer Unbekannten.* 1955: *Des Teufels General; Ludwig II; Griff nach den Sternen; Himmel ohne Sterne; Ein Madchen aus Flandern.* 1956: *Der Hauptmann von Kopenick.* 1957: *Die Zurcher Verlobung; Monpti.* 1958: *The Wonderful Years; A Stranger in My Arms; Der Schinderhannes.* 1959: *Der Rest ist Schweigen; Die Gans von Sedan.* 1960: *Das Glas Wasser; Schwarzer Kies.* 1961: *Des Traum von Lieschen Muller.* 1962: *Die Rote.* 1964: *Das Haus in Montevideo; Lausbubengeschichten.* 1970: *Die Feuerzangenbowle.*

After studying art history, philology, and theatre at Munich University, Kautner wrote and directed cabaret and stage productions. He also worked as an actor—*Kreuzer Emden* (32, Louis Halph)—and appeared in many of his own early films. He came to prominence in the years after 1945 and was associated with several worthy, prestigious, and dull movies: *Des Teufels General,* with Curt Jurgens in the Zuckmayer play; O. W. Fischer as *Ludwig II;* an adaptation of his own play, *Himmel ohne Sterne; Der Hauptmann von Kopenick,* from a Zuckmayer script; and *Der Rest ist Schweigen,* a Hamlet in modern Germany with Hardy Kruger as the prince. Belatedly, he went to Hollywood in 1957, but only to direct two clotted weepies at Universal: *The Wonderful Years,* with Teresa Wright, and a June Allyson–Jeff Chandler picture, *A Stranger in My Arms.*

He played the lead in *Karl May* (74, Hans-Jurgen Syberberg).

Danny Kaye (David Daniel Kominski)
(1913–87), b. New York

Danny Kaye is one of those people who was a wonder once, but who looks frantic and alien now. He was called a genius. *The Secret Life of Walter Mitty* was an international event. When he appeared to do stand-up routines on stage, there were stories that he gave command performances after the official curtain fell—for royalty, celebrities, or sick children—that went on into the early hours, riots of improvisation. You had to be there. But to be a wow in pictures you only have to do it *now.* Later will sort itself out. Danny Kaye had his *now:* it is even said that Laurence Olivier got a crush on him. (Kaye was especially popular in England.) And even now one can pick up the feeling of nearly inhuman energy in Kaye on screen, somewhere between child, machine, and rogue cuckoo clock.

Kaye had a mixed career in entertainment before his screen debut. He was a vaudevillian, a dancer, a singer, and comedian, and a flop in all directions. He even appeared in some two-reel comedies that failed dismally. But he made a Broadway debut in 1940 and then had a success in *Lady in the Dark.* He also met and married lyricist Sylvia Fine, the "brains" behind his subsequent success. She wrote most of those tortuous songs and controlled his material. It was Samuel Goldwyn who brought Kaye to the screen in *Up in Arms* (44, Elliott Nugent). In the years immediately after the war Kaye was all the rage: twins in *Wonder Man* (45, H. Bruce Humberstone); *The Kid from Brooklyn* (46, Norman Z. McLeod); *The Secret Life of Walter Mitty* (47, McLeod), a beautiful subject vulgarized by Kaye; *A Song Is Born* (48, Howard Hawks); *The Inspector General* (49, Henry Koster); and *On the Riviera* (51, Walter Lang).

The woeful miscalculation of *Hans Christian Andersen* (52, Charles Vidor) marked the first slackening in his popularity. After *Knock on Wood* (54, Melvin Frank and Norman Panama) and *White Christmas* (54, Michael Curtiz), which he merely shared, he made *Assignment Children* (54) for UNICEF. Only seven films after that: *The Court Jester* (56, Frank and Panama); *Me and the Colonel* (57, Peter Glenville); the moderately lively *Merry Andrew* (58, Michael Kidd); as Red Nichols in *The Five Pennies* (59, Melville Shavelson); *On the Double* (62, Shavelson); *The Man from the Diner's Club* (63, Frank Tashlin); and *The Madwoman of Chaillot* (69, Bryan Forbes).

He did work all the time for UNICEF, and he became a cooking enthusiast. But he seemed a little bewildered by the change in his reputation—he may never have approved that much of what he had done; perhaps he was torn over playing the fool. His last work was on TV as a concentration camp survivor caught up in anti-neo-Nazi action in *Skokie* (81, Herbert Wise).

Elia Kazan (Elia Kazanjoglou),
b. Constantinople, Turkey, 1909

1945: *A Tree Grows in Brooklyn.* 1947: *The Sea of*

Elia Kazan

Grass; Boomerang; Gentleman's Agreement. 1949: *Pinky.* 1950: *Panic in the Streets.* 1951: *A Streetcar Named Desire.* 1952: *Viva Zapata!.* 1953: *Man on a Tightrope.* 1954: *On the Waterfront.* 1955: *East of Eden.* 1956: *Baby Doll.* 1957: *A Face in the Crowd.* 1960: *Wild River.* 1961: *Splendor in the Grass.* 1964: *America America/The Anatolian Smile.* 1969: *The Arrangement.* 1972: *The Visitors.* 1976: *The Last Tycoon.*

Kazan is a fascinating twentieth-century American. An immigrant, he was brought to America when he was only four. While he has never lost his Greek-Turkish roots—as witness *America America*—few native directors made films that so persistently dealt with American problems and subjects, or that were so absorbed in the American regard for sincere intensity of performance.

He is a superficial radical. From 1934–36, amid the Group Theater, Kazan was a member of the Communist party, and yet, in 1952, he reversed an earlier stand and declared the names of fellow Communists to the House Committee on Un-American Activities. Some may have consented to that admission, but others felt betrayed and noted that shortly after the hearing Kazan signed a contract (at reduced salary) in Hollywood. From this, the question arises: how committed are his films? Is he an exponent of radical concern, or just a master of naturalistic melodrama? Is Kazan an original author of films or a great director of actors who manages to disguise conventional material and commonplace attitudes?

He joined the Group Theater in 1932, originally as an actor: he appeared in *Waiting for Lefty* and *Golden Boy* by Clifford Odets and later acted in two films directed by Anatole Litvak—*City for Conquest* (40) and *Blues in the Night* (41). But direction was his real aim and by the mid-1940s he was the leading director of new plays on Broadway. This side to his work continued throughout most of his career: *Truckline Cafe* (46), *All My Sons* (47), *A Streetcar Named Desire* (47), *Death of a Salesman* (49), *Camino Real* (53), *Tea and Sympathy* (53), *Cat on a Hot Tin Roof* (55), *The Dark at the Top of the Stairs* (57), *JB* (58), *Sweet Bird of Youth* (59), and *After the Fall* (64).

Kazan's first six films—all but one made for Fox—are barely recognizable as his. Their realism is in the muted postwar fashion, they are muffled by players like Dorothy McGuire, Gregory Peck, and Jeanne Crain, they take on controversial issues in a literal or discreet manner, and they seem to reflect the character of Darryl F. Zanuck as much as Kazan himself. *Boomerang* and *Panic in the Streets* profit from being thrillers, enhanced by unfamiliar locations and making their social points indirectly. *Panic*, especially, has some effective deep-focus photography of New Orleans by Joe MacDonald that dramatizes the contrived

sense of community. But the crusading pictures—*Gentleman's Agreement* and *Pinky*—are naïve and clumsy, showing very little awareness of the medium, and smothering their issues with sentimentality.

Kazan's personal impact began only with *Streetcar*, a film taken from the stage, employing a method nurtured at the Actors Studio, founded by Kazan and Bobby Lewis in 1948. It was the new actor—originally Brando—that best expressed Kazan, although in this instance he was burdened by a traditionally florid actress, Vivien Leigh. Thus the film is more a conflict of acting styles than the poetic struggle Tennessee Williams described.

Of course, Kazan had directed *Streetcar* on Broadway. In that process, through the casting of Marlon Brando and the very physical promotion of Brando's Stanley Kowalski, Kazan actually countered some of the playwright's intentions. Kazan was *not* a homosexual. He invariably needed some kind of sexual investment in a show—imaginative and actual. So he made the Stanley-Stella bond more central and arousing than Williams had intended. He also shifted Blanche, from heroine to natural victim. And so the play worked in part, in 1947, because its poetry had been converted into a raw need Kazan could feel. That incident is a clue to his appetite for acting and actors. For Kazan backed the psychological thrust of Method acting most when he could himself identify with a character. In a real sense, he made the theatre as sexy as movies.

The next films are deeper explorations into emotional naturalism in acting: Brando as Zapata; Brando, Rod Steiger, Karl Malden, and Lee J. Cobb in *On the Waterfront;* James Dean, Raymond Massey, and Julie Harris in *East of Eden;* Carroll Baker, Eli Wallach, and Malden in *Baby Doll. Zapata* still looks an original movie, but *On the Waterfront* is glossy with skill and has less to do with the New York docks than with the mixture of grand guignol and neo-realism. It is certainly emotional, but the feelings are all planned in advance, and the possible comparison between the Brando who informs on the mob and Kazan's own readiness to talk is embarrassing.

East of Eden is Kazan's best film: partly because of Dean's prickly hesitation; partly because the absorbing clash of acting styles (Dean and Raymond Massey) suited Steinbeck's high-class weepie novel; and also because CinemaScope seemed to stimulate Kazan into treating his camera with some of the emphatic care he lavished on actors. *Baby Doll*, while always a minor chamber play, is atmospheric and catches the tender humor of Williams. *A Face in the Crowd* was the conscience-stricken radical, crudely manhandling the media and unable to deal with an intransigent chief actor. *Wild River* is the concerned American thinking and feeling in unison, a more speculative film than Kazan usually allowed himself, subtle in its situation, its coloring, and its acting. *Splendor in the Grass,* however, is intense to the point of hysteria, the most extreme instance of Kazan's emotional involvement with his characters, the source of all that is vital and most alarming in his work. As a result, it is a violent film, lurching between great beauty (especially in Natalie Wood's performance) and excess.

At this stage, Kazan grew reflective on his own life. *America America* was based on his novel, as was *The Arrangement,* a very obvious commentary on materialism in America. Sadly, the defects of that film seem to Kazan its greatest virtues. The novels he wrote in the sixties and seventies were solidly second-rate, overwritten, and underthought. They showed how banal the energy of a director could seem on the page. But in the woeful *Last Tycoon,* Kazan had lost his essential energy.

After 1980, he had appeared occasionally in documentaries about Greece or the Actors Studio. But his largest venture was the writing of his lengthy, controversial, and fascinating *A Life.* The autobiography is far and away his best book, destructively candid and boastful about his treatment of women, but a lasting work to be put beside his best films and his enormous glamorization of the American actor. For good and ill, this is one of the great lives in American theatre arts. But when the Academy gave him an honorary Oscar, in 1999, all the old enmities sprang up—and Kazan refused the chance of apologizing. He didn't feel it, and that's how he directed performances.

Buster Keaton (Joseph Francis Keaton)

(1895–1966), b. Pickway, Kansas

1920: *The High Sign; One Week; Convict 13; The Scarecrow; Neighbors.* 1921: *The Haunted House; Hard Luck* (all codirected with Eddie Cline); *The Goat* (codirected with Malcolm St. Clair); *The Playhouse; The Boat; The Paleface.* 1922: *Cops; My Wife's Relations* (all codirected with Cline); *The Blacksmith* (codirected with St. Clair); *The Frozen North; The Electric House; Daydreams; Balloonatics* (all codirected with Cline); *Our Hospitality* (codirected with John Blystone). 1924: *Sherlock Jr.; The Navigator* (codirected with Donald Crisp). 1925: *Seven Chances; Go West.* 1926: *Battling Butler; The General* (codirected with Clyde Bruckman).

Keaton strikes a chord with the world of post-1960 that was not heard when his greatest films were made. It has been argued, with justice, that his films are "beautiful," which means that their comedy is expressed in photography that is creative, witty, and excited by the appearance of things. That sounds obvious, but most comedy films of the silent era did little more than film the comedian's "act." Even Chaplin tended to plonk the camera in a good seat in the stalls. But in Keaton's

films there is an extraordinary use of space in the jokes that is faithfully and beautifully recorded: *Go West* is a masterpiece of the moving camera; in *The Navigator* the ship is a deserted, and nearly haunted, house. *The General* has the topographical vividness of an Anthony Mann film; and that dissolve in *Seven Chances* from a church empty but for Buster to one crowded out with hopeful women is typical of Keaton's instinct for interiors. It remains something of a puzzle as to how far that design was conscious. Nothing suggests such thoughtful talent among Keaton's various collaborators: but nothing significantly detracts from the visual consistency of the films from *The Three Ages* to *The General;* and yet descriptions of Keaton on set, and the story of his ruin, seem to indicate a haphazard working style that put great strains on those different codirectors.

Perhaps the explanation is Keaton's pleasure in authenticity and the way in which his own supercilious screen persona dominated the direction. Unlike Chaplin, who tended to reinvent the world of Victorian melodrama, and unlike those comics who merely dressed up vaudeville routines, Keaton conceived of films as specifically American. In this, he seems to have had the notion of parodying current American cinema and an awareness of American landscape more usual in the Western. *The General, Our Hospitality, Go West,* and *Steamboat Bill Jr.* are all fond evocations of period and place. Similarly, the railroad in *The General* is real and the train's maneuvers credible and dangerous. It is well known that Keaton performed personally in scenes that involved considerable risk. In *Our Hospitality* there is the waterfall sequence, while in *Sherlock Jr.* Keaton had a fall that, years later, it was discovered, had broken his neck. Such physical peril did not make him a slapstick artist. On the contrary, his reactions when threatened were untheatrical and near mystical in his haughty recognition of a malign fate and the deadpan that might honorably confront it.

That is what strikes us today as the most admirable thing about Keaton: the serene capacity for absorbing frustration and turning a blind eye to fear and failure. If Chaplin's films are always working toward self-centered pathos, Keaton never disguises the element of absurdity in a lone romantic's dealings with the world. Those repeated attempts by directors and producers to make Keaton smile on screen were contrary not just to the screen persona of a commercial property but to Keaton's knowledge that there never was or would be much to smile at.

Few people ever recognized that Keaton's impassivity was to save him from crying. In maudlin, self-reflective close-up, Chaplin wept in crises. Keaton is the more profound artist because he was not beguiled into comfort by his own self-pity. He saw that the conscientious, humorless hero he played must prove himself by facing frustrations and disasters without ever cracking.

The General is not only a comedy but a genuinely heroic film. Buster's troubles with trains in that film are based on Keaton's own inquisitive interest in machinery. It was a matter of art that his own handyman's fascination was translated on film into a Quixotic bewilderment with machinery. Thus I would swap all of *Modern Times* for that glorious moment in *The General* when Buster's meditation fails to notice the growing motion of the engine's drive shaft on which he is sitting. That illustrates the character of the dreamer so brilliantly revealed in his masterpiece, *Sherlock Jr.,* about a cinema projectionist who dreams his way into a movie. Only an artist aware of the complex appeal to fantasy in cinema could have conceived *Sherlock Jr.,* the most philosophically eloquent of silent comedies.

The best films antedate the tragedy of his life and thereby make irrelevant the question of whether his art and his terrible decline were connected. In his book on Keaton, Rudi Blesh chose to describe that ruin as a Keaton scenario that Buster accepted with calm, self-destructive passivity. The truth seems to me more confused. Keaton provoked his own disaster, partly because he was a sketchy businessman, partly because the screen character was far from his real personality. Offscreen he seems to have been brash, noisy, and impulsive. That may rule out the neatness of Blesh's interpretation, but it adds to our idea of Keaton as an artist capable of inventing a screen character.

Keaton was the son of a vaudeville partnership; he entered the family act at the age of three and stayed with it nearly twenty years. It was in 1917 that he joined Fatty Arbuckle at Comique and played a string of shorts directed by Fatty: *The Butcher Boy* (17); *Rough House* (17); *His Wedding Night* (17); *The Bell Boy* (18); *Goodnight Nurse* (18); *Moonshine* (18); *The Cook* (18); *A Desert Hero* (19); *Backstage* (19); *A Country Hero* (19); *The Garage* (19). He moved to Metro and made more shorts, as his own director, as well as one feature, *The Saphead* (20, Winchell Smith). In 1923, he made the first of his sequence of features, *The Three Ages,* and married Natalie Talmadge, the sister-in-law of Joseph Schenck.

Schenck managed Keaton. They produced films together for MGM to distribute, until in 1926 Schenck joined United Artists. Keaton had to tag along and *The General, College* (27, James Horne), and *Steamboat Bill Jr.* (28, Charles Reisner) were made for UA. Was the appearance of separate directors a foreshadowing of what was to happen? In 1928, Joseph Schenck calmly transferred Buster to his brother Nicholas Schenck at MGM. It seems that Keaton was arbitrarily cut off from the revenue of his earlier films and sold into the unsympathetic hands of a giant corporation.

With Joseph Schenck he had had his own unit, and his ideas had been allowed to flower by trial and error as films went along. MGM wanted complete, plot-heavy scripts in advance, proper schedules, and safe men to supervise Keaton. The arrangement foundered. If, as he said later, Keaton had predicted that, then he ought to have extricated himself when there was still time. MGM, equally, should have been more generous to his proven working methods, if only because he was a major money-spinner and one of the few silent comedians stimulated by sound.

Perhaps the studio disliked independence per se, perhaps they marked Keaton down as representative of a bygone age, but it is also true that Keaton cracked personally. He drank heavily and his marriage broke up. His films at MGM deteriorated steadily: *The Cameraman* (28, Edward Sedgwick); *Spite Marriage* (29, Sedgwick); *Free and Easy* (30, Sedgwick); *Doughboys* (30, Sedgwick); *Speak Easily* (31, Sedgwick); *Sidewalks of New York* (31, Jules White and Zion Myers); *Parlor, Bedroom and Bath* (32, Sedgwick); *The Passionate Plumber* (32, Sedgwick); and *What, No Beer?* (33, Sedgwick). In 1933, he was divorced and fired by MGM; he was also seriously injured in a fall incurred during an alcoholic stupor.

He never recovered. He went to Europe for two films—*Le Roi des Champs-Elysées* (34, Max Nosseck) and *An Old Spanish Custom* (35, Adrian Brunel), but needed frequent treatment and recuperation. From 1934–47 he made some comedy shorts for Educational; and between 1939–41 he did the same at Columbia. But he worked mainly thereafter as gagman or bit part actor, a ravaged version of the angelic Pierrot he had been: he worked on the stories of *The Jones Family in Hollywood* (39, St. Clair) and *The Jones Family in Quick Millions* (39, St. Clair); contributed gags for Red Skelton to *Bathing Beauty* (44, George Sidney), *Neptune's Daughter* (49, Edward Buzzell), and *A Southern Yankee* (49, Sedgwick); and appeared in *San Diego I Love You* (44, Reginald Le Borg); *That Night With You* (45, William A. Seiter); to Mexico for *El Moderno Barba Azul* (46, Jaime Salvador); *You're My Everything* (49, Walter Lang); *In the Good Old Summertime* (49, Robert Z. Leonard); *The Lovable Cheat* (49, Richard Oswald); playing bridge (a game he loved) in *Sunset Boulevard* (50, Billy Wilder); *Limelight* (52, Chaplin); *Around the World in 80 Days* (56, Michael Anderson); *It's a Mad, Mad, Mad, Mad World* (63, Stanley Kramer); *The Railrodder* (65, Gerald Potterton), a Canadian short in homage to his 1920s character; *Film* (65, Alan Schneider), a turgid exercise derived from Samuel Beckett; and *A Funny Thing Happened on the Way to the Forum* (66, Richard Lester).

Diane Keaton (Diane Hall),
b. Los Angeles, 1946
1987: *Heaven* (d). 1990: "Fever," an episode of
China Beach (TV); *The Girl with the Crazy
Brother* (s). 1991: "Slaves and Masters," an episode
of *Twin Peaks; Wildflower.* 1995: *Unstrung Heroes.*
1999: *Mother's Helper.* 2000: *Hanging Up.* 2001:
Pasadena (TV).

Diane Keaton won her Oscar in *Annie Hall* (77,
Woody Allen) doing . . . so little, if you come to
think about it, that the award must have been
tribute to her likability and to the amiable, cool
tolerance exhibited by her character. "Annie
Hall" was nearly an -ism in the late seventies, a
way of dressing, reacting, and feeling. When people fall in love with an idea, they don't bother to
check how much substance it has. Being Woody
Allen's best girl then seemed a very hip role; and
Keaton was so deadpan cute in her basic attitudes, no matter that her way of talking became
as jittery as Woody's. Even that had an edge of
parody to it. She had been with Allen in *Play It
Again, Sam* (72, Herbert Ross), *Sleeper* (73,
Allen), and *Love and Death* (75, Allen), but in
Annie Hall it was as if her real self had emerged.
Everyone felt good about her.

   Yet, elsewhere, in a very different mood, she
had shown herself a real actress in both parts of
The Godfather, so good that it was distressing to
hear her conventional complaint that the men in
it had all the big scenes. Her Kay is crucial to
Coppola's overall vision, and good enough to stir
one with thoughts of how the romantic despair
that watches the Corleones' murderous conservatism could have been pierced with a positive
alternative. Keaton's Kay is a grim, hurt face forever being shut out of family conclaves. She
comes to realize that she has been hired for
breeding, and she goes through with separation
from her children to maintain her sense of values.
The movie might have abandoned Puzo's original
and given her the dignity of action: taking her
own children and daring the ultimate revenge
from her self-pitying fascist husband. But that
would have needed the Rossellini who made so
much of Ingrid Bergman's spirit in *Europa '51.*

   That the possibility lay there waiting was due to
Keaton's humble gravity. If you want to talk about
acting, look again at that early scene when
Michael tells her about the way in which Johnny
Fontane got his freedom from the bandleader
who had him under contract. The gangster gloss
of "an offer he couldn't refuse," and the heartless
cynicism pleased with its own deadpan in "your
signature or your brains on the contract," are
shattered by the naïve bewilderment and loving
distress in Keaton's face. That scene is the touchstone of her performance, which contains all the
mature, humane moments allowed into the dark
fortress of *The Godfather.*

She tried hard to be a serious, brave actress in
Looking for Mr. Goodbar (77, Richard Brooks),
but she lacked the force of need or the recklessness that role called for. There are a few silly
marking-time movies on her list: *Lovers and
Other Strangers* (70, Cy Howard); *Harry and
Walter Go to New York* (76, Mark Rydell); and *I
Will, I Will, For Now* (76, Norman Panama). She
followed Allen meekly into the starched anguish
of *Interiors* (78), and she did a good character
study in *Manhattan* (79). But it was time for
another male influence.

   She gave her finest performance as Louise
Bryant in *Reds* (81, Beatty). It was a bizarre decision, when the best actress Oscar went instead to
Katharine Hepburn in *On Golden Pond*—worthy,
but hardly a match for the complex portrait of
lover, heroine, feminist, and weary companion to
a celebrity that Keaton (and Beatty) made of
Bryant. She was touching as the wife in *Shoot the
Moon* (82, Alan Parker), but she did not really
grasp the actress-terrorist-lover called for in *The
Little Drummer Girl* (84, George Roy Hill).
Mrs. Soffel (84, Gillian Armstrong) was a great
improvement: her own sense of mischief helped
bring the prison governor's wife into erotic flowering, and she seemed to impress Mel Gibson.

   Since then, there has been a gradual decline:
Crimes of the Heart (87, Bruce Beresford); lovely
but all too brief singing "You'd Be So Nice to
Come Home To" in *Radio Days* (87, Allen). She
directed a whimsical documentary, *Heaven* (87),
which hardly had the muscle required for a full-
length film, as well as an episode of *Twin Peaks*
and a cable movie, *Wildflower* (91). *Baby Boom*
(87, Charles Shyer) was very soft stuff, with
Keaton as a businesswoman who inherits a baby,
and gets everything in the end: rural life, success, happiness, and Sam Shepard. In *The Good
Mother* (88, Leonard Nimoy), she found belated
sexual fulfillment, too. Then she did *The Lemon
Sisters* (90, Joyce Chopra); returned one more
time—and without much reward—as Kay in *The
Godfather Part III* (90, Coppola); *Father of the
Bride* (91, Shyer), in which she had very little to
do; *Running Mates* (92, Michael Lindsay-Hogg);
replacing Mia Farrow and very funny in *Manhattan Murder Mystery* (93, Allen); and for TV as
Amelia Earhart (94, Yves Simoneau).

   She did more work as a director in the nineties,
and *Wildflower* and *Unstrung Heroes* showed real
progress and warmth, though *Mother's Helper*
was hardly released. As an actress, she was in
Father of the Bride Part II (95, Shyer); *The First
Wives Club* (96, Hugh Wilson); *Marvin's Room*
(96, Jerry Zaks); *The Only Thrill* (97, Peter Masterson); *The Other Sister* (99, Garry Marshall); in
her own *Hanging Up* (00); strictly for nostalgia in
Town & Country (01, Peter Chelsom); *Sister
Mary Explains It All* (01, Marshall Brickman);

Plan B (01, Niki Vraast-Thomas and Greg Yaitanes); a short; *Crossed Over* (02, Bobby Roth).

Michael Keaton (Douglas),
b. Coraopolis, Pennsylvania, 1951

Michael Keaton is a star: he has played Batman; he is on magazine covers; he does unexpected cameos in big pictures. Even his real name is a star's name. Yet who is he? What is he really like? Do we care? Of all the Batmen he was the most recessive, and he seemed to have come by it honestly. Am I alone in remembering above all his nasty, manic roles, as if they caught his interest most fully? There's a dark, comic urge in there—it could be quite dangerous; it might have been Ripley, even—but somehow neither he nor the business has quite trusted it yet.

He dropped out of Kent State and did a lot of odd jobs, including comedy, before he took on acting: in a big debut in *Night Shift* (82, Ron Howard); another hit with *Mr. Mom* (83, Stan Dragoti); *Johnny Dangerously* (84, Amy Heckerling); *Gung Ho* (86, Howard); *Touch and Go* (86, Robert Mandel); as a con man in *The Squeeze* (87, Roger Young); very energetic in *Beetlejuice* (88, Tim Burton); his best acting as the addict in *Clean and Sober* (88, Glenn Gordon Caron); *Batman* (89, Burton)—masked, no matter whether he's wearing a mask or not.

As a crazy on the loose in *Dream Team* (89, Howard Zieff); nearly revealed as the madman in *Pacific Heights* (90, John Schlesinger); *One Good Cop* (91, Heywood Gould); *Batman Returns* (92, Burton), where he is upstaged by Michelle Pfeiffer; *Much Ado About Nothing* (93, Kenneth Branagh), where his Dogberry is out of control; the dying man in *My Life* (93, Bruce Joel Rubin); *The Paper* (94, Howard); with Geena Davis in *Speechless* (94, Ron Underwood); cloned in *Multiplicity* (96, Harold Ramis); narrator on *Inventing the Abbotts* (97, Pat O'Connor); *Jackie Brown* (97, Quentin Tarantino); the convict in *Desperate Measures* (98, Barbet Schroeder); an unbilled cameo in *Out of Sight* (98, Steven Soderbergh); back from the dead as a snowman in *Jack Frost* (98, Troy Miller); *A Shot at Glory* (00, Michael Corrente); *Quicksand* (01, John Mackenzie); *Live from Baghdad* (02, Mick Jackson).

Ruby Keeler (1909–93), b. Halifax, Canada

Considering that she made only eleven films, it is odd that Ruby Keeler is so widely remembered as the pert, dancing sweetheart of Warners musicals of the 1930s. By the standards of Charisse, Rogers, Eleanor Powell, Vera-Ellen, Ann Miller, and Debbie Reynolds, she was an ordinary girl. (Indeed, talent was never her thing.) But her naïveté did slot into Dick Powell's lewdness and express the quick innuendo of the period. A chorus girl/dancer, in 1928 she married Al Jolson.

After starring for Ziegfeld she got the part of the girl who substitutes for the injured Bebe Daniels in the backstage musical *42nd Street* (33, Lloyd Bacon). The same slightly bemused parts were provided by *Gold Diggers of 1933* (33, Mervyn Le Roy) in which Powell takes a can opener to her metal costume; *Footlight Parade* (33, Bacon); *Dames* (34, Ray Enright); *Flirtation Walk* (34, Frank Borzage); *Go Into Your Dance* (35, Archie Mayo)—the only film she made with Jolson; *Shipmates Forever* (35, Borzage); *Colleen* (36, Alfred E. Green); and *Ready, Willing and Able* (37, Enright). When Jolson quit Warners, she went with him and floundered: *Mother Carey's Chickens* (38, Rowland V. Lee) was an RKO disaster. In 1941, after divorce, she made *Sweetheart of the Campus* (Edward Dmytryk) and then retired.

In 1971 she reclaimed her dancing shoes and appeared on Broadway in a very successful revival of *No, No, Nanette*.

William Keighley (1893–1984),
b. Philadelphia, Pennsylvania

1932: *The Match King* (codirected with Howard Bretherton); 1933: *Ladies They Talk About* (codirected with Bretherton); *Easy to Love*. 1934: *Journal of a Crime; Dr. Monica; Big-Hearted Herbert; The Kansas City Princess; Babbitt*. 1935: *The Right to Live; G Men; Mary Jane's Pa; Special Agent; Stars Over Broadway*. 1936: *The Singing Kid; The Green Pastures* (codirected with Marc Connelly); *Bullets or Ballots; God's Country and the Woman*. 1937: *The Prince and the Pauper; Varsity Show*. 1938: *The Adventures of Robin Hood* (codirected with Michael Curtiz); *Valley of the Giants; The Secrets of an Actress; Brother Rat*. 1939: *Yes, My Darling Daughter; Each Dawn I Die*. 1940: *The Fighting 69th; Torrid Zone; No Time for Comedy*. 1941: *Four Brothers; The Bride Came C.O.D.* 1942: *The Man Who Came to Dinner; George Washington Slept Here*. 1947: *Honeymoon*. 1948: *The Street With No Name*. 1950: *Rocky Mountain*. 1951: *Close to My Heart*. 1953: *The Master of Ballantrae*.

Keighley was never more than one of Warners' second-string directors. There is not much doubt about who is responsible for the flair of *Robin Hood;* Keighley's handling of Errol Flynn in, say, *The Prince and the Pauper, Rocky Mountain,* or *The Master of Ballantrae* is very pedestrian compared with Curtiz's panache. The one genre in which he matched the studio's standards was the thriller adventure. *Torrid Zone* is a good pairing of Cagney and Ann Sheridan in a banana republic, while *Each Dawn I Die* moves at great speed and even brings George Raft to life in the prison sequence. *Bullets or Ballots* is another racy piece of urban slaughter and conniving, without depth but sure of its pace. He was less happy with comedy and made a dull Bette Davis picture—*The*

Bride Came C.O.D.—although *George Washington Slept Here* was one of Jack Benny's better pictures and *The Man Who Came to Dinner* is an amusing transposition of Monty Woolley's great stage success (with Davis, again, lost in a dowdy role).

Keighley came to the movies late. He was an actor and director in the theatre before he worked as assistant director to William Dieterle on *Jewel Robbery* (32) and *Scarlet Dawn* (32), and to Curtiz on *The Cabin in the Cotton* (32). He stayed with Warners until *Honeymoon*—with a subadult Shirley Temple at RKO—and *The Street With No Name*, at Fox. But he returned to Warners and made three more pictures before retiring.

Harvey Keitel, b. Brooklyn, New York, 1939

There are few American actors whose careers are so intriguing—or so touching. Imagine a film about Harvey Keitel, the actor so good, so persistent, yet so regularly denied at the highest table; ceaseless in his fury, his bitterness, forever hurtling forward in that cold, determined aura that is a mix of menace and resentment. What a role! And probably De Niro would get it.

When Keitel began in pictures, he was Martin Scorsese's "made man." He was out of the Actors' Studio, he was brilliant, New York, and he was Jewish. Yet he had the lead in *Who's That Knocking at My Door* (68, Scorsese) and he was the central figure, Charlie, in *Mean Streets* (73, Scorsese)—Italian, Catholic—who faces the moral dilemma of whether to carry or abandon the out-of-control Johnny Boy (De Niro). Keitel was magnificent, but even then there were moments when he had nothing to do but survey, in grief or bewilderment, the mercurial leaps and departures of De Niro's character. As befitted *Mean Streets*, Keitel's face became sadder and older. And Keitel had recommended De Niro.

He was very frightening as the faithless Ben in *Alice Doesn't Live Here Anymore* (74, Scorsese); he played Bugsy Siegel on TV in *The Virginia Hill Story* (74, Joel Schumacher); *That's the Way of the World* (75, Sig Shore); as a helpless follower of the show business in *Buffalo Bill and the Indians* (76, Robert Altman); and *Mother, Jugs & Speed* (76, Peter Yates).

In *Taxi Driver* (76, Scorsese), Keitel was unforgettable, long-haired, and lyrical in his foul wooing of the child prostitute. His Sport was a brilliant conception, unerringly played. People would have raved about it, but for De Niro's Travis Bickle, a role that once Keitel could (would) have had, and that surely he has never believed was less than he deserved. De Niro was better—but maybe he wouldn't have been better without Keitel. For Harvey provoked Bobby, punched him, the way LaMotta helped define Ray Robinson's greatness. De Niro had to be quicker, wilder, deeper, more

vulnerable—yet they share the handicap of being instinctively enclosed or cut off.

Keitel could see that he faced De Niro for the rest of his life—there might be dreams of murder in our imaginary movie. Consciously, or subconsciously, he became a touch more willful, lonely, and dangerous. He could have gone into solitary. But he got better. Within two years of *Taxi Driver*, Keitel had delivered what may have been his two greatest performances.

Despite all the picture postcarding for the Dordogne, I can watch *The Duellists* (77, Ridley Scott) any time, just for Keitel. He had a look that was superbly of the period, going from a Lermontov-like flourish to a Napoleon on St. Helena. His grim soldier was driven through all the desponds of life by one absurd, magnificent duty. When Keitel faces the woeful Carradine after years of failure, it is a joy to see age, failure, and disappointment fall away as he recognizes that he's "on" again.

Next year, he was the concert pianist/debt collector in *Fingers* (78, James Toback), as understanding of New York street idiom as he was of Toback's psychosexual nightmare. His character shook with music, as if it were a fever. He zoomed in on women and danger with an unhindered, ecstatic self-destructiveness. *Fingers* is a great film, fearful and cleansing, and I don't think even De Niro could have played it from the hunched, fatalistic viewpoint of Keitel.

Those were lead parts in films that did poor or no business. Keitel's way ahead was that of a supporting actor, and we should note his willingness to go far beyond the mainstream in his choice of parts. This is a wild, eccentric list: *Welcome to L.A.* (77, Alan Rudolph); *Blue Collar* (78, Paul Schrader); *Eagle's Wing* (79, Anthony Harvey); *Deathwatch* (80, Bertrand Tavernier); *Bad Timing* (80, Nicolas Roeg); *Saturn 3* (80, Stanley Donen); *The Border* (82, Tony Richardson); as Tom Paine in *La Nuit de Varennes* (82, Ettore Scola); as the terrorist in *Exposed* (83, Toback); as a sidekick to De Niro again in *Falling in Love* (84, Ulu Grosbard); to Italy for *Un Complicato Intrigo di Donne, Vicoli e Delitti* (85, Lina Wertmuller); *Off Beat* (86, Michael Dinner); *The Men's Club* (86, Peter Medak); *Wise Guys* (86, Brian De Palma); *The Pick-Up Artist* (87, Toback); *The January Man* (89, Pat O'Connor); as Judas in *The Last Temptation of Christ* (88, Scorsese), a role that could not be denied him; *Two Evil Eyes* (90, George Romero and Dario Argento); in what had once been the Robert Evans role in *The Two Jakes* (90, Jack Nicholson).

Then, step by step, he made it back into the American limelight: as very similar, decent cops in *Mortal Thoughts* (91, Alan Rudolph) and *Thelma and Louise* (91, Scott); nominated for supporting actor as at least one authentic Jewish gangster,

Mickey Cohen, in *Bugsy* (91, Barry Levinson); naked, crucified, constantly at the end of his tether as *Bad Lieutenant* (92, Abel Ferrara); *Sister Act* (92, Emile Ardolino); *Reservoir Dogs* (92, Quentin Tarantino); *Point of No Return* (93, John Badham); *Rising Sun* (93, Philip Kaufman); intuitive, half-tender, half-primitive, and naked again in *The Piano* (93, Jane Campion); *Dangerous Game* (93, Ferrara); and *The Young Americans* (93, Danny Cannon).

In recent years, Keitel's rage has diminished a little—or is it that we are wearying of him? There's no doubting his zeal or risk-taking instincts, but charm and naturalness are still not his: *Point of No Return* (93, John Badham); *Somebody to Love* (94, Alexandre Rockwell); as Winston Wolf in *Pulp Fiction* (94, Tarantino); *Imaginary Crimes* (94, Anthony Drazan); *Monkey Trouble* (94, Franco Amurri); *Smoke* (95, Wayne Wang); *Ulysses' Gaze* (95, Theo Angelopoulos); *Clockers* (95, Spike Lee); *Blue in the Face* (95, Wang); *Get Shorty* (95, Barry Sonnenfeld); *From Dusk Till Dawn* (96, Robert Rodriguez); *Head Above Water* (96, Jim Wilson); *City of Industry* (97, John Irvin); *Cop Land* (97, James Mangold); as Houdini in *Fairy Tale* (97, Charles Sturridge); *Shadrach* (98, Susanna Styron); *Lulu on the Bridge* (98, Paul Auster); *Finding Graceland* (98, David Winkler); *Il Mio West* (98, Giovanni Veronesi); *Three Seasons* (99, Tony Bui); *Holy Smoke* (99, Campion); *Presence of Mind* (99, Antonio Aloy); *An Interesting State* (99, Wertmuller); *Fail Safe* (00, Stephen Frears); *U-571* (00, Jonathan Mostow); *Prince of Central Park* (00, John Leekley); *Little Nicky* (00, Steve Brill); *Ginostra* (00, Manuel Pradal); *Nailed* (01, Joel Silverman); *Taking Sides* (01, István Szabó); *The Grey Zone* (01, Tim Blake Nelson).

And now he returned to films hardly heard of: *Vipera* (01, Sergio Citti); *Dreaming of Julia* (01, Juan Gerard); *Nowhere* (02, Luis Sepulveda); *Red Dragon* (02, Brett Ratner); *Beeper* (02, Jack Sholder); *Wanted* (03, Brad Mirman).

Gene Kelly (Eugene Curran Kelly) (1912–96), b. Pittsburgh, Pennsylvania

Educated at Pennsylvania State University, Kelly had a variety of jobs before work as a dance instructor led him to the stage. He appeared in the New York productions of *Leave It to Me* and *Pal Joey* and entered films only when he was thirty.

His work in the cinema can be broken down into categories:

1. As a leading man in MGM musicals, dancing and singing with that pleasant note of strained voice: Busby Berkeley's *For Me and My Gal* (42); *Thousands Cheer* (43), *Anchors Aweigh* (45), and *The Three Musketeers* (48)—all for George Sidney; *Du Barry Was a Lady* (43, Roy del Ruth); Charles Vidor's *Cover Girl* (44)—at Columbia; *Living in a Big Way* (47, Gregory La Cava); *Summer Stock* (50, Charles Walters); and *Les Girls* (57, George Cukor).

2. As a straight actor: without success, in *The Cross of Lorraine* (43, Tay Garnett); *Pilot No. 5* (43, George Sidney); *Christmas Holiday* (44, Robert Siodmak); *Black Hand* (50, Richard Thorpe); *Marjorie Morningstar* (58, Irving Rapper); *Inherit the Wind* (60, Stanley Kramer); and *40 Carats* (73, Milton Katselas).

3. As a director: Kelly was credited as codirector on most of his films with Stanley Donen, although he seems only to have choreographed them. But he has established a career as an independent director—first on *Invitation to the Dance* (56) and *The Happy Road* (56), but subsequently on a variety of comedies, musicals, and even a Western: *The Tunnel of Love* (58); *Gigot* (63); *A Guide for the Married Man* (67); *Hello, Dolly!* (69); and *The Cheyenne Social Club* (70).

4. As a dancer and dance director: this is easily his most important and individual contribution. As a dancer, he is not the equal of Astaire. Kelly is balletic, Romantic, and sometimes mannered, a dancer who thinks and feels, whereas Astaire is a man who dances before he thinks. That said, Kelly has danced superbly on the screen: in the ballet from *The Pirate* (47, Vincente Minnelli); with Vera-Ellen doing "Slaughter on Tenth Avenue" in *Words and Music* (48, Norman Taurog); in *On the Town* (49, Donen); in Donen's *Singin' in the Rain* (52); most ambitious in the extensive ballet dream in Minnelli's *An American in Paris* (51); once more athletic and exuberant for Minnelli in *Brigadoon* (54); and Donen's *It's Always Fair Weather* (55).

As a dancer, he was seen very briefly as one of the three teachers in Cukor's *Let's Make Love* (60), and most touchingly in Jacques Demy's *The Young Girls of Rochefort* (67), a little like the ghost of his dancing past, now nervous of stretching his legs.

In 1951, Kelly was awarded a special Oscar for his contribution to dance in films and he is a major innovator in the history of the musical. More artistically adventurous than Astaire, it is proper that Kelly should be remembered for magnificent set pieces of choreography—enormously complex as in *An American in Paris,* and perfectly simple on Donen's raining street set. (But Astaire's *lack* of adventure is another aspect of his *natural* genius.)

Kelly's personality seems to me cold and aggressive. Whereas Astaire's basic reticence makes an intriguing contrast with his virtuosity as a dancer, the recurring portentousness in Kelly the dancer—that corny slow turn he loved—seems stamped with the harsh, calculating cheerfulness that exults in ringing up the curtain in *Singin' in the Rain* to expose Jean Hagen's Bronx accent. Too often, Kelly's teeth glared out at us, as the filling for a smile, and *The Pirate* is a nice, malicious portrait of brittle phoniness.

In later years, he appeared in *Xanadu* (80, Robert Greenwald) and *Reporters* (81, Raymond Depardon), and he introduced *That's Dancing* (85, Jack Haley Jr.).

Grace Kelly (1928–82), b. Philadelphia

Grace Kelly was enough to make Hollywood believe in itself. From a wealthy family and the American Academy of Dramatic Arts, she was in and out of Hollywood in six years: beautiful, articulate, graceful, and deserving. Not that she was unduly striking in Hathaway's *Fourteen Hours* (51), or as the Quaker wife in *High Noon* (52, Fred Zinnemann). And Ava Gardner made short work of her demureness in *Mogambo* (53, John Ford).

Who should play fairy godmother but Alfred Hitchcock? First he put her in a nightie and subjected her to Ray Milland's smiling trap in *Dial M for Murder* (54); next he used her to tease a James Stewart encased in plaster in *Rear Window* (54); finally he gave her Cary Grant to play with on the prince's very doorstep in *To Catch a Thief* (55). In all three, she was suggestive of high class (for Hitchcock is always a snob) and her regal claiming of Grant for a goodnight kiss in a Monte Carlo hotel, or her asking him to choose between breast or leg, are indelible. No wonder her future husband did what he could to keep the finished film under wraps. (There were plenty of rumors that the classy Kelly loved sex.)

Hollywood was enchanted, and pushed an Oscar on her for the drab *Country Girl* (54, George Seaton). For the rest, she was tearful in *The Bridges at Toko-Ri* (55, Mark Robson), less bright than emeralds in *Green Fire* (55, Andrew Marton), and coyly schooled for higher things in Charles Vidor's *The Swan* (56) and Charles Walters's *High Society* (56), in which she sang sweetly in Crosby's arms and gave an amateur impersonation of Katharine Hepburn.

After that she married Prince Rainier (in 1956) and confined herself to being the most plausible princess in the world, to distributing the prizes at the Monaco Grand Prix, and to hostessing charity concerts. The nearest to a comeback seems to have been an initial interest in playing *Marnie*.

She was killed in a car accident, driving on roads very close to those used in *To Catch a Thief*—where she had once driven so fast.

Kay Kendall (Kay Justine Kendall McCarthy) (1926–59), b. Withernsea, England

For some ten years, Kay Kendall flitted around the British cinema trying not to look too tall or too obviously a *Vogue* cover girl. It was *Genevieve* (53, Henry Cornelius) that revealed her as a comedienne bemused by her own lofty handsomeness.

She flourished briefly, married actor Rex Harrison, and made two good films in Hollywood before dying of leukemia. The British were suitably affected but still indifferent to their long neglect of her.

The daughter of dancers, and granddaughter of Marie Kendall, she played in variety before making her debut in *Fiddlers Three* (44, Harry Watt). Thereafter, she was in *Champagne Charlie* (44, Alberto Cavalcanti); *Dreaming* (44, John Baxter); *Waltz Time* (45, Paul L. Stein); and *London Town* (46, Wesley Ruggles). Unwelcomed, she worked in the theatre and TV before a second attempt: *Dance Hall* (50, Charles Crichton); *Happy Go Lovely* (51, Bruce Humberstone); *Lady Godiva Rides Again* (51, Frank Launder); *Wings of Danger* (52, Terence Fisher); *It Started in Paradise* (52, Compton Bennett); *Street of Shadows* (53, Richard Vernon); and *The Square Ring* (53, Basil Dearden and Michael Relph). After her eccentric, trumpet-playing girlfriend in *Genevieve*, she was rewarded with *Doctor in the House* (54, Ralph Thomas), *Simon and Laura* (55, Muriel Box), and *The Constant Husband* (55, Sidney Gilliat) in which she played opposite Harrison. She then went into American films: *The Adventures of Quentin Durward* (55, Richard Thorpe); *Abdullah's Harem* (56, Gregory Ratoff); *Les Girls* (57, George Cukor)—her best film; *The Reluctant Debutante* (58, Vincente Minnelli), with Harrison again; and *Once More With Feeling* (59, Stanley Donen), which has a very funny harp-playing sequence—she was an actress who made unexpected music.

Arthur Kennedy (1914–90),
b. Worcester, Massachusetts

Kennedy was educated at the Carnegie Institute of Technology. Originally on the stage, he was one of the subtlest American supporting actors, never more so than when revealing the malice or weakness in an ostensibly friendly man. He made his screen debut in Litvak's *City for Conquest* (40) and served his time as a bystander or pal in three Raoul Walsh films—*High Sierra* (41), *They Died With Their Boots On* (41), and *Desperate Journey* (43)—as well as being a member of Hawks's idyllic *Air Force* (43), before graduating to larger parts: *Cheyenne* (47, Walsh); the father in Ted Tetzlaff's *The Window* (49); the suspect in Kazan's *Boomerang* (47); the brother in Irving Rapper's *The Glass Menagerie* (50); *The Red Mountain* (51, William Dieterle); the blinded soldier in *Bright Victory* (52, Mark Robson).

As with many others, Kennedy's best work was done in a comparatively brief spell: the vengeful hero in Fritz Lang's *Rancho Notorious* (52); the treacherous ally in *Bend of the River* (52, Anthony Mann); the headstrong husband in Nicholas Ray's *The Lusty Men* (52); the gunrunning foreman for

Mann again in *The Man from Laramie* (55); the hypocritical brother in *Some Came Running* (58, Vincente Minnelli); perhaps his best but least-known part, as the central figure in Edgar G. Ulmer's *The Naked Dawn* (54). In these few years, without ever becoming a star, Kennedy's was one of the most interesting and ambivalent faces on the screen.

He worked hard later, but never with the same impact. In fact, his most consistent role was that of a skeptical outsider, observing but hardly participating in events: *Elmer Gantry* (60, Richard Brooks); *Barabbas* (62, Richard Fleischer); *Lawrence of Arabia* (62, David Lean); *Cheyenne Autumn* (64, John Ford); and *Nevada Smith* (66, Henry Hathaway). His best later parts are in *Monday's Child* (66, Leopoldo Torre Nilsson), as the drunk in *Shark* (68, Samuel Fuller), the father in David Miller's *Hail, Hero!* (69), in *My Old Man's Place* (71, Edwin Sherin), and as a Mafia boss in *Baciamo le Mani* (72, Vittorio Schiraldi). He was a bishop in *The Antichrist* (74, Alberto de Martino) and a priest in *The Sentinel* (76, Michael Winner).

He made some films in Italy and then appeared in *Signs of Life* (89, John David Coles) as a Maine boat-builder.

He had been nominated once as best actor—*Bright Victory*—and four times for supporting actor: *Champion* (49, Robson); *Trial* (55, Robson); *Peyton Place* (57, Robson); and *Some Came Running*. He never won. Yet he could easily have had victory with *The Lusty Men*, *The Man from Laramie*, or *The Naked Dawn*. And he made the most of the promising situation in *Impulse* (55, Cy Endfield), before the script went wild.

Deborah Kerr (Deborah Jane Kerr-Trimmer), b. Helensburgh, Scotland, 1921

The story goes that the turning point of Deborah Kerr's career came when she was cast, against all expectation, and after Joan Crawford had been fussy, as the lusting wife in *From Here to Eternity* (53, Fred Zinnemann). This meant an energetic roll on the beach with Burt Lancaster, but it still left a rather more restrained woman than James Jones had intended. She also suggested that the American army in Honolulu was incongruously comforted by memsahibs. Deborah Kerr was then, has always been, and still is true blue.

Educated at Bristol and then a debutante on the London stage, her first film was Michael Powell's *Contraband* (40). She worked in England throughout the war, as an ingenue, a heroine, a chip off the old block, and finally in devotional parts: *Major Barbara* (41, Gabriel Pascal); *Love on the Dole* (41, John Baxter); *Penn of Pennsylvania* (41) and *Hatter's Castle* (41) for Lance Comfort; *The Day Will Come* (42, Harold French); very good as the recurring redhead in *The Life and Death of Colonel Blimp* (43, for Powell and

Emeric Pressburger); with Robert Donat in *Perfect Strangers* (45, Alexander Korda); Frank Launder's *I See a Dark Stranger* (46); a nun in Powell's *Black Narcissus* (46).

She was then invited to America by MGM where she appeared in Jack Conway's *The Hucksters* (47) (MGM's campaign: "Deborah Kerr. It rhymes with star.") and Victor Saville's *If Winter Comes* (47). She was resolutely ladylike, and from Cukor's *Edward, My Son* (49) she drifted into ever less interesting parts: the female object in *King Solomon's Mines* (50, Compton Bennett and Andrew Marton); a glowing Christian in *Quo Vadis?* (51, Mervyn Le Roy); in Charles Vidor's *Thunder in the East* (52); as Princess Flavia in *The Prisoner of Zenda* (52, Richard Thorpe). It was a sign of trouble that she so seldom worked with American actors, as if her gentility had frozen real company.

After *Dream Wife* (52, Sidney Sheldon) she spoke up well as Portia in Mankiewicz's *Julius Caesar* (53). Then came *From Here to Eternity* (53), which revived her career, even if it only gave her more need to be pleasant in the future. She was in George Sidney's *Young Bess* (53), as support for Jean Simmons; and once more self-sacrificing in Dmytryk's *The End of the Affair* (55). She became a fixture when she whistled a happy tune as the governess in Walter Lang's *The King and I* (56). Regality survived a sordid encounter with William Holden in *The Proud and the Profane* (56, George Seaton); the considerate offering of herself to John Kerr along with *Tea and Sympathy* (56, Vincente Minnelli)—she had starred in the stage version; and a return to nun's habit, alone on a desert island with Robert Mitchum, in *Heaven Knows, Mr. Allison* (57, John Huston).

She was a little more credible in McCarey's *An Affair to Remember* (57); gauche being gauche in *Separate Tables* (58, Delbert Mann); but very good in Preminger's *Bonjour Tristesse* (58), in which her niceness is actually probed and disturbed; and in Zinnemann's *The Sundowners* (60). After that, she failed in the demanding parts of *The Innocents* (61, Jack Clayton) and *The Arrangement* (69, Elia Kazan), and continued to make soothing noises in King's *Beloved Infidel* (59), *The Chalk Garden* (63, Ronald Neame), Huston's *Night of the Iguana* (64), and Frankenheimer's *The Gypsy Moths* (69).

There was a period of retirement, after which she made *A Song at Twilight* (81, Cedric Messina); in the old Elsa Lanchester role, with Ralph Richardson in a TV *Witness for the Prosecution* (82, Alan Gibson); very good in *The Assam Garden* (85, Mary McMurray); with Robert Mitchum again in *Reunion at Fairborough* (85, Herbert Wise); and *Hold the Dream* (86, Don Sharp).

In 1994, she was the most touching part of the

Oscars evening, receiving an honorary award to make up for six unrewarded nominations: *Edward, My Son; From Here to Eternity; The King and I; Heaven Knows, Mr. Allison; Separate Tables;* and *The Sundowners.*

Irvin Kershner (Irvin Kerschner),
b. Philadelphia, Pennsylvania, 1923

1958: *Stake Out on Dope Street.* 1959: *The Young Captives.* 1961: *The Hoodlum Priest.* 1963: *A Face in the Rain.* 1964: *The Luck of Ginger Coffey.* 1966: *A Fine Madness.* 1967: *The Flim Flam Man/One Born Every Minute.* 1970: *Loving.* 1972: *Up the Sandbox.* 1974: *S°P°Y°S.* 1976: *Raid on Entebbe; The Return of a Man Called Horse.* 1978: *Eyes of Laura Mars.* 1980: *The Empire Strikes Back.* 1983: *Never Say Never Again.* 1990: *Robocop 2.* 1993: *SeaQuest DSV* (TV) (codirected with Jonathan Brandis).

Kershner has never settled, or secured a position from which he might dominate a film. In 1958, *Stake Out on Dope Street* was an early offshoot of Roger Corman's mezzanine empire, a second feature with a brash urban rawness. But sixteen years later, Kershner was still servant to the casual spontaneity of Donald Sutherland and Elliott Gould—so much so that the original title, *Wet Stuff*, was amended to remind us of the actors' earlier success in *M°A°S°H.*

In between, Kershner has had an inconsequential career. *The Hoodlum Priest* was his first large project, though centered on Don Murray's do-gooding intentions. *The Luck of Ginger Coffey* was a clumsy movie, made in Canada from a Brian Moore novel. *A Fine Madness* is a moderate comedy, and *The Flim Flam Man* contrives to waste George C. Scott. But *Loving* is a world apart, an anguished, tender, and disrupting movie with fine performances from George Segal, Eva Marie Saint, and Sterling Hayden—it has the sort of unconventional but lifelike approach to hurt feelings that Bob Rafelson has taken to exploring.

And there's the rub, for Rafelson is some twenty years older than Kershner, a man who studied film at the University of Southern California in the late 1940s and who spent the 1950s as an apprentice in documentary.

Kershner had his best opportunity ever with *The Empire Strikes Back* (under the care and control of the Lucas empire), but he was less successful in the Sean Connery comeback as James Bond or in the sequel to *Robocop.*

He has not worked much as a director lately. But he acts occasionally—as Zebedee in *The Last Temptation of Christ* (88, Martin Scorsese); *On Deadly Ground* (94, Steven Seagal); *Angus* (95, Patrick Read Johnson)—and he produced a small thriller, *American Perfekt* (97, Paul Chart).

Abbas Kiarostami, b. Teheran, Iran, 1940
1970: *Nan va Koutcheh/Bread and Alley* (s). 1972: *Zang-ze Tafrih/Breaktime* (s). 1973: *Tadjrebeh/The Experience.* 1974: *Mossafer/The Traveller.* 1975: *Dow Rahehal Baraye yek Massaleh/Two Solutions for One Problem* (s); *Man ham Mitoumam/So Can I* (s). 1976: *Rangha/The Colors* (s); *Lebassi Baraye Arossi/The Wedding Suit.* 1977: *Gozaresh/The Report; Bozorgdasht-e mo'Allem/Tribute to the Teachers* (s). 1978: *Solution* (s); *Jahan Nama Palace* (s). 1979: *Ghazieh-e Shekl-e Aval, Ghazieh-e Shekl-e Dou Wom/Case No 1, Case No 2.* 1980: *Behdash-e Dandan/Toothache* (s). 1981: *Be Tartib ya Bedoun-e Tartib/Regularly or Irregularly* (s). 1982: *Hamsarayan/The Chorus* (s). 1983: *Hamshahri/Fellow Citizen.* 1984: *Avaliha/First Graders.* 1987: *Khane-ye Doust Kodjast?/Where is the Friend's House?* 1989: *Mashgh-e Shab/Homework.* 1990: *Nema-ye Nazdik/Close-Up.* 1992: *Zendegi Edame Darad/And Life Goes On.* 1994: *Zire Darakhatan Zeyton/Through the Olive Trees.* 1997: *Ta'm e Guilass/Taste of Cherry.* 1999: *Bad ma ra Khahaad Bord/The Wind Will Carry Us; Beed-o Baad/Willow and Wind.* 2002: *Ten.*

Very large things have been said on behalf of Abbas Kiarostami. Laura Mulvey has likened the breakthrough of *Taste of Cherry* winning the Palme d'Or at Cannes in 1997 to the appearance of *Rashomon* at Venice in 1951. Quite early on, Godfrey Cheshire saw the masterly humanism of Kiarostami and called it "a cinema of questioning." Phillip Lopate has said that "we are living in the Age of Kiarostami, as once we did in the Age of Godard."

Well, I take all of that seriously, just as I can see, without question, that there are creative stirrings in Iran that deserve the most sensitive reception, if only to break out of the straitjacket in which so many Westerners are taught to think of Iran and all its neighbors. At the same time, we may note that *Taste of Cherry* played at Cannes (not without doubts, for it deals with suicide) before it played in Iran. And when Kiarostami accepted a congratulatory but formal kiss from Catherine Deneuve, along with the Palme d'Or, there were serious repercussions in Iran.

Consider *Taste of Cherry*, which is generally rated among his best, if not the best, by Kiarostami's adherents. It is about a man who drives around the hilly, twisty roads on the outskirts of Teheran (I think), searching for someone who will assist in his suicide. Much of the film is shot as from the man's Land Rover, with the sound of its engine. There is no music, for Kiarostami is as suspicious of that as he is of conventional storytelling. The film has the feel of Italian neo-realism: the sound and the picture are a little rough; the acting is nonprofessional; and we never discover why the man wants to kill himself—that may be too much "narrative," though equally it may impose on the actor a slightly doomy portentousness that I find monotonous. But maybe Kiarostami intends that; maybe he wants us to feel the mundane level of being urged to kill yourself.

The neo-realist look, however, is subtly undercut by a much more formal eye for beauty—especially in the long-distance twists and vanishings of the dirt road. In those passages, you feel Kiarostami's shaping eye and you can believe that he was first trained as a painter and graphic artist, and that he still takes very beautiful (if arty) photographs of landscape.

The man picks up several passengers, and they decline his request for help. There is a developing suspense—what will happen? Do we care? And gradually the arguments against death begin to resemble a testament to life. This is culminated in the last passenger, an older man, who will help but who speaks movingly of the small epiphanies in life, like the taste of mulberry. But a pact is made, the old man will help.

We then see our central character going out to his appointed grave, at night. There is thunder about. He composes himself. Fade to video footage, which quite quickly reveals the man as his actor, with a film crew (Kiarostami included) looking on. Soldiers in the distance, who were marching to make up a shot, are told to relax. There is the sound of jazz.

The ending is exhilarating and wondrous. We feel that life has won just as the bare "story" to which we have been exposed is revealed as a game, a routine. I do see and appreciate the putting together of something like a documentary style with the sudden revelation that it has all been a film all along. I feel that modernism, the intellectual surprise, the sense of some need to step back from and admit the archaic quality of self-contained stories in such an age of film.

But humbly, I suggest that Godard and many others did it, in another age, with more humor, intellect, beauty, and terror. Abbas Kiarostami is a fascinating figure. He represents a country that may be regaining its imagination. We need to attend. But if this is modern movie mastery, then our medium is gone and this is funerary art.

Nicole Kidman, b. Honolulu, Hawaii, 1967

Though she was taller than he was, Nicole Kidman and Tom Cruise clicked when they met on the set of *Days of Thunder* (90, Tony Scott). That meeting worked better than the on-screen collision of race-car driver and fond neurologist. What's more, the couple didn't sway the public in their next together, *Far and Away* (92, Ron Howard), in which she was a landowner's daughter to his poor farmer. But they became a very married pair: one smile slipped across their page, like a zipper, or like Scientology's positive attitude

(they were coreligionists) and the major-league ambition they shared. Maybe they needed comedy if they were going to work together on screen—and Kidman's great achievement in *To Die For* (95, Gus Van Sant), her personal breakthrough, was a kind of wide-eyed satire, as if Carole Lombard were doing Judy Holliday.

She was raised in Australia, where she made several films while still in her teens. The hit among these, *Dead Calm* (89, Phillip Noyce), brought her to America, where she has worked steadily: very smart in *Billy Bathgate* (91, Robert Benton); *Malice* (93, Harold Becker); *My Life* (93, Bruce Joel Rubin); commanding the camera with new authority in *Batman Forever* (95, Joel Schumacher). Her Isabel Archer in *The Portrait of a Lady* (96, Jane Campion) erred in casting (her voice was essentially wrong) and temperament (she was too confident, too modern), but she worked very hard against those obstacles. *The Peacemaker* (97, Mimi Leder) and *Practical Magic* (98, Griffin Dunne) were minor films. But she was a sensation on stage (in London especially) in *The Blue Room*, written by David Hare after Arthur Schnitzler, and directed by Sam Mendes. It was an event that signaled her sexual arrival—and thus a premature crack in the marriage.

If only Hare and Mendes had done *Eyes Wide Shut* (99, Stanley Kubrick). If only someone had had the wit to let her play all the female roles—so that Tom Cruise can't help seeing her everywhere. As it was, Kidman's character was away from the screen too long, and as the best thing about that forlorn venture she seemed the most wasted.

As that very big creative venture failed, so the marriage came apart. In the professional, or artistic, sense, Kidman has been the beneficiary, and even a freed star. Above all, that was the mood of *Moulin Rouge* (01, Baz Luhrmann), where she seemed in love with the movie itself. In a very different way, she was equally striking as a frigid nanny in *The Others* (01, Alejandro Amenábar) and as a Russian slut in *Birthday Girl* (02, Jez Butterworth). Next stop: *The Hours*, from Michael Cunningham's novel (02, Stephen Daldry)—a startling Virginia Woolf, and an Oscar..

There may be some limits to her talent, still, but in ambition and emotional energy—and in her sheer lust for the camera—she is a true star and a liberated force.

It speaks to her status, her on-going skill at choosing, and the amount she gets offered, that her immediate future looks like this: *Dogville* (03, Lars von Trier); *The Human Stain* (03, Robert Benton), from the Philip Roth novel; *Cold Mountain* (03, Anthony Minghella); *Birth* (04, Jonathan Glazer), about a woman who thinks her 10-year-old son may be her husband reincarnated; *The Stepford Wives* (04, Frank Oz); *Mr and Mrs Smith*

(Doug Liman); and *Alexander the Great* (05, Luhrman), in which she'll be some kind of goddess. Why not Alexander?

Krzysztof Kieślowski (1941–96),
b. Warsaw, Poland
1969: *From the City of Lodz* (d). 1975: *Personel* (d). 1976: *Spokoj* (d). 1979: *Amator/Camera Buff*. 1981: *Dlugi Dzien Pracy; Przypadek/Blind Chance*. 1984: *Bez Konca*. 1988: *Dekalog 1: I Am the Lord Thy God; Dekalog 2: Thou Shalt Not Take the Name of the Lord Thy God in Vain; Dekalog 3: Honor the Sabbath Day; Dekalog 4: Honor Thy Father and Thy Mother; Dekalog 5: Thou Shalt Not Kill/A Short Film About Killing; Dekalog 6: Thou Shalt Not Commit Adultery/A Short Film About Love; Dekalog 7: Thou Shalt Not Steal; Dekalog 8: Thou Shalt Not Bear False Witness; Dekalog 9: Thou Shalt Not Covet Thy Neighbor's Wife; Dekalog 10: Thou Shalt Not Covet Thy Neighbor's Goods*. 1990: *City Life*. 1991: *The Double Life of Veronique*. 1993: *Trois Couleurs: Bleu/Blue*. 1994: *Trois Couleurs: Blanc/White; Trois Couleurs: Rouge/Red*.

I suppose television is today's version of tablets of stone, and so in 1988, Kieślowski undertook to deliver a modern accounting of the great truths by way of Polish television as ten hour-long fictions. Of course, it would be truer to today for the tablets to come on a more interactive form of TV, so that we could purchase or rank our top ten. Not that there is any arguing with Kieślowski. He has a masterly, but austere, manner. There is no doubting his feeling for things seen and heard; there is no question but that he is a filmmaker, and one following in the steps of Bresson.

But, for me, Kieślowski frequently runs the risk of being precious, mannered, and so cold as to forbid touching. I have seen only two of the *Dekalogs*, the short films about love and killing (the rest have only been shown at film festivals in America). While admiring the plan to see all the rules demonstrated in the mundane lives in a Warsaw housing complex, I did find the two spoiled by a rather sanctimonious tidiness. Life doesn't quite breathe in those films. The superb style is so anxious for rules.

Consider, further, the hugely accomplished and beautiful *Blue*. Kieślowski has said it is a film about liberty: "If one loves, one stops being free. You become dependent on the person you love. When you love someone, you live your life and see your values differently, through the eyes of the person you love."

That is an interesting basis for a film, yet I cannot find it at work in *Blue*. Rather, Kieślowski— with the very passive beauty of Juliette Binoche— seems to be glorying in the spoiled stasis of grief, as if loss brought one closer to resignation and

a waiting emptiness. Do we really know this woman, or do we only feel her extraordinarily sensitive hesitation? Why is there so little about the child? The sensibility is very Catholic, yet the movie is nearly crushing in its pride and humorlessness.

I am a little uneasy saying this, for Kieślowski was clearly so good a filmmaker. In addition, I very much enjoy the notion, explored in *Blue* and *Veronique*, of all our lives receding into an infinity of other lives—a distance that alters meaning. But to see a Kieślowski film for me requires a steeling, as if I were going into torture or church. Those films seem to think they're perfect, and I want to scream.

Henry King (1888–1982),
b. Christianburg, Virginia
1916: *Who Pays*. 1917: *Southern Pride; A Game of Wits; The Mate of the Sally Ann*. 1918: *Beauty and the Rogue; Powers That Pray; Hearts or Diamonds; The Locked Heart; When a Man Rides Alone; Hobbs in a Hurry; All the World to Nothing*. 1919: *Brass Buttons; Some Liar; Where the West Begins; Sporting Chance; This Hero Stuff; Six Feet Four; 23½ Hours Leave; A Fugitive from Matrimony; Haunting Shadows*. 1920: *The White Dove; Uncharted Channels; One Hour Before Dawn; Help Wanted—Male; Dice of Destiny*. 1921: *When We Were 21; Mistress of Shenstone; Salvage; The Sting of the Lash; Tol'able David*. 1922: *The Seventh Day; Sonny; The Bond Boy*. 1923: *Fury; The White Sister*. 1924: *Romola*. 1925: *Sackcloth and Scarlet; Any Woman; Stella Dallas*. 1926: *Partners Again; The Winning of Barbara Worth*. 1927: *The Magic Flame*. 1928: *The Woman Disputed* (codirected with Sam Taylor). 1929: *She Goes to War; Hell's Harbor*. 1930: *Lightnin'; The Eyes of the World*. 1931: *Merely Mary Ann; Over the Hill*. 1932: *The Woman in Room 13*. 1933: *State Fair; I Loved You Wednesday* (codirected with William Cameron Menzies). 1934: *Carolina; Marie Galante*. 1935: *One More Spring; Way Down East*. 1936: *The Country Doctor; Lloyds of London; Ramona*. 1937: *Seventh Heaven*. 1938: *In Old Chicago; Alexander's Ragtime Band*. 1939: *Jesse James; Stanley and Livingstone*. 1940: *Little Old New York; Maryland; Chad Hanna*. 1941: *A Yank in the RAF; Remember the Day*. 1942: *The Black Swan*. 1943: *The Song of Bernadette*. 1944: *Wilson*. 1945: *A Bell for Adano*. 1946: *Margie*. 1947: *Captain from Castile*. 1948: *Deep Waters*. 1949: *Twelve O 'Clock High; Prince of Foxes*. 1950: *The Gunfighter*. 1951: *I'd Climb the Highest Mountain; David and Bathsheba*. 1952: *Wait Till the Sun Shines, Nellie; The Snows of Kilimanjaro; "The Gift of the Magi," episode from O. Henry's Full House*. 1953: *King of the Khyber Rifles*. 1954: *Untamed*. 1955: *Love Is a Many-Splendored Thing*. 1956: *Carousel*. 1957: *The Sun Also Rises*.

1958: *The Bravados.* 1959: *This Earth Is Mine; Beloved Infidel.* 1962: *Tender Is the Night.*

Having begun as an actor in local stock, King became a stage director in Chicago before the First World War. He went into films originally as an actor but by 1916 he was directing for Pathé. Thomas Ince hired him to make *23½ Hours Leave* and King became a prominent director of the silent era. In 1921, with Richard Barthelmess and Charles Duell, he formed the Inspiration Company to make *Tol'able David* and many others. That tone of rural virtuousness was picked up later in *Chad Hanna* and *I'd Climb the Highest Mountain.* It shows how far his own taste was for simplicity. King was also responsible for lavish emotional films such as *The White Sister, Romola,* and *Stella Dallas,* but in the sound era he was always an artisan unable to infuse narrative with life or any recognizable style.

His long period at Fox suffered from all the defects of that studio: routine material based on mediocre players, with an emphasis on detail in settings that never escaped the neat hand of the art department. Despite a fatal slowness and no real ability with action, King regularly made adventure pictures—some, like *Captain from Castile,* a severe test on one's patience. He is happier with more intimate, period subjects like *Margie,* and with solid biopics, such as *Stanley and Livingstone* and *Wilson.* The former has Tracy and Cedric Hardwicke; the latter profits from Alexander Knox's resemblance to Woodrow Wilson and from Leon Shamroy's creation of Washington interiors.

King seldom seemed to notice theme or to be sympathetic to actors. He labored time and again with Tyrone Power, but made two startlingly good films with Gregory Peck—*Twelve O'Clock High* and *The Gunfighter.* His retirement came at least ten years late and his dealings with Hemingway and Scott Fitzgerald are disastrous. Only *Love Is a Many Splendored Thing* has any romantic consistency. (He was one of the few directors Jennifer Jones trusted.)

Ben Kingsley, b. Scarborough, Yorkshire, England, 1943

Though raised in the north of England, Kingsley's roots are Indian and Russian Jewish—hence the genetic credentials for Gandhi and Meyer Lansky, the epitome of versatility. Despite the Oscar for *Gandhi* (82, Richard Attenborough), his is a career without fluency or character. Indeed, he seems bound to settle for being an available exotic: *Fear Is the Key* (72, Michael Tuchman); *Betrayal* (83, David Jones); *Harem* (85, Arthur Joffe), as an Arab prince; *Turtle Diary* (85, John Irvin); *Sleeps Six* (86, James Cellan Jones), playing a movie producer, as written by Frederic Raphael;

Maurice (87, James Ivory); as Shostakovich in *Testimony* (87, Tony Palmer); Turkish in *Pascali's Island* (88, James Dearden); as Dr. Watson in *Without a Clue* (88, Thom Eberhardt); *Slipstream* (89, Steven M. Lisberger); *The Children* (90, Palmer); *Bugsy* (91, Barry Levinson); *Sneakers* (92, Phil Alden Robinson); *Dave* (93, Ivan Reitman); and in *Schindler's List* (93, Steven Spielberg), where he is actually the center of the film.

In his fifties, Kingsley took wing: the teacher in *Searching for Bobby Fischer* (93, Steven Zaillian); *Death and the Maiden* (94, Roman Polanski); *Species* (95, Roger Donaldson); *The Lost Portrait* (95, Chris Grandlund); Potiphar in *Joseph* (95, Roger Young); as *Moses* (96, Young); as Feste in *Twelfth Night* (96, Trevor Nunn); as a Ted Turner figure in *Weapons of Mass Distraction* (97, Steve Surjik); *The Assignment* (97, Christian Duguay); *Photographing Fairies* (97, Nick Willing); *War Symphonies—Sjostakovitsj* (97, Larry Weinstein); as the barber in *The Tale of Sweeney Todd* (97, John Schlesinger); as Porfiry in *Crime and Punishment* (98, Joseph Sargent); *Parting Shots* (98, Michael Winner); *The Confession* (99, David Hugh Jones); the Caterpillar in *Alice in Wonderland* (99, Willing); *Spooky House* (99, William Sachs); *What Planet Are You From?* (00, Mike Nichols); *Rules of Engagement* (00, William Friedkin); brilliant in the talk of *Sexy Beast* (00, Jonathan Glazer); the father in *Anne Frank* (01, Robert Dornhelm); the narrator in *A.I.* (01, Spielberg); *The Triumph of Love* (02, Clare Peploe); *Tuck Everlasting* (02, Jay Russell).

What is an actor? He is Gandhi, Meyer Lansky, Moses, a Sexy Beast, Sweeney Todd, and a Caterpillar.

Keisuke Kinoshita (1912–98), b. Hamamatsu, Japan

1943: *Hana Saku Minato/The Blossoming Port; Ikite Iru Magoroku/The Living Magoroku.* 1944: *Kanko no Machi/Jubilation Street; Rikugun/Army.* 1946: *Osone-ke no Asa/Morning for the Osone Family; Waga Koi Seshi Otome/The Girl I Loved.* 1947: *Kekkon/Marriage; Fushicho/Phoenix.* 1948: *Onna/Woman; Shozo/Portrait; Hakai/Apostasy.* 1949: *Ojosan Kampai/A Toast to the Young Miss; Yotsuya Kaidan/The Yotsuya Ghost Story; Yaburedaiko/Broken Drum.* 1950: *Konyaku Yubiwa/Engagement Ring.* 1951: *Zemma/The Good Fairy; Karumen Kokyo ni Kaeru/Carmen Comes Home; Shonenki/A Record of Youth; Umi no Hanabi/Fireworks over the Sea.* 1952: *Karumen Junjosu/Carmen's Pure Love.* 1953: *Nihon no Higeki/A Japanese Tragedy.* 1954: *Onna no Sono/The Garden of Women; Nijushi no Hitomi/Twenty-four Eyes.* 1955: *Toi Kumo/Distant Clouds; Nogiku no Gotoki Kimi Nariki/You Were Like a Wild Chrysanthemum.* 1956: *Yuyake-gumo/Clouds at Twilight; Taiyo to Bara/The Rose on His Arm.*

1957: *Yorokobi mo Kanashimi mo Ikutoshitsuki/ The Lighthouse; Fuzen no Tomoshibi/A Candle in the Wind.* 1958: *Narayamabushi-ko/The Ballad of Narayama; Kono Ten no Niji/The Eternal Rainbow.* 1959: *Kazabana/Snow Flurry; Sekishun-cho/The Bird of Springs Past; Kyo mo Mata Kakute Ari Nan/Thus Another Day.* 1960: *Haru no Yume/Spring Dreams; Fuefukigawa/The River Fuefuki.* 1961: *Ein no Hito/The Bitter Spirit.* 1962: *Kotoshi no Koi/This Year's Love; Futari de Aruita Iku Shunju/The Seasons We Walked Together.* 1963: *Utae Wakodo-tachi/Sing, Young People!; Shito no Densetsu/Legend of a Duel to the Death.* 1964: *Koge/The Scent of Incense.* 1967: *Natsukashiki Fue ya Taiko/Lovely Flute and Drum.* 1976: *Sri Lanka no Ai to Wakare/Love and Separation in Sri Lanka.* 1984: *Kono Ko Wo Nokoshite.* 1986: *Shin Yorokobimo; Kanahimimo Ikutoshitsuki.*

Kinoshita—as far as I can trace—has never had a film open commercially in America or Britain. Thus, the opportunities to see his work are confined to festivals, museum screenings, and the invaluable presentations of the Japan Society. Whereas most readers of this book will "know" Kurosawa, and will likely have seen some of this films, Kinoshita will be a stranger. Yet again, we have been misled. Despite the flourish and fame of Kurosawa, the core of Japanese film is to be found in family stories, wistful romances, and in attention paid to women as much as to men. The great tradition in Japan is Ozu, Mizoguchi, Naruse (almost certainly), and Kinoshita.

He ran away from home as a teenager when his family resisted his desire to enter the movie industry. That led to formal training at the Oriental School of Photography and a first job at the Shochiku laboratories. By 1935, he was working as a camera assistant and he soon began to work for director Yasujiro Shimazu, for whom he wrote *Gonin no Kyodai* (39). For most of his career, Kinoshita has been his own screenwriter.

He worked in many different moods—the romantic, the satirically comic, and the sentimental—and, time and again, he made valiant, good-humored women his central characters. But *A Japanese Tragedy* uses the travails of a war widow to reflect upon modern Japanese history and rises to a level of unquestioned tragedy.

Elsewhere, Kinoshita won outstanding performances from Kinuyo Tanaka as the old woman in *The Ballad of Narayama* and the mother in *Army.* But probably his most original use of an actress—and Japan's first film in color—was *Carmen Comes Home,* which found an unexpected comic presence in Hideko Takamine's stripper. The same actress was as impressive, though far more conventional, as the teacher in *Twenty-four Eyes.*

Three of Kinoshita's films—*Morning for the Osone Family; Twenty-four Eyes;* and *The Ballad of Narayama*—won the critics' best picture award, but much of his work, however beautifully created, seems to Western eyes somewhat sentimental and politically naïve.

Klaus Kinski (Nikolaus Gunther Nakszynski) (1926–91), b. Zoppot, Poland

Film Dope's entry on Kinski lists some 125 films, as well as another thirty or so that have appeared in some filmographies but that cannot be verified. These are films made all over the world, leaving no stone of cunning coproduction unturned. And in many of them, Kinski had small roles, single scenes, a few days of work in the headlong scramble of his life, which also included a good deal of theatre—often one-man shows, as if no one could work with him, or he refused to share. Kinski loved to play madmen on screen; they fulfilled a dream he had of himself. In person, he was unreliable about his own work—he did not remember accurately, he lied, or he did not care: he did not honor the clerical rules of filmography.

He sounds like a fictional being—a nomadic actor taken from Rimbaud and Céline, so driven that he gave up on such bourgeois concepts as destination or direction. *Film Dope* chuckled to itself about the contrary perceptions of Kinski: "Either he is among the cinema's great tragic actors or among its great inadvertently comic ones." It was clear they leaned toward the latter view, and they gently chided me for some rather breathless things I had said about Kinski. But I had met him a few times. I had spent hours only a few feet away from one of life's more amazing faces. And *Film Dope* did not care to consider the possibility of something else I had written about Kinski: that he was both extremes at the same time—great actor *and* absurd figure. Yes, he could overact, just as he could be humorlessly intense in life. But neither fault was calculated, and Kinski was waiting for someone like Werner Herzog, a director whose taste was for faults in nature and monstrous paradoxes. Herzog found his own creative self in Kinski—and the actor found a frame that contained his unique frenzy.

One other thing: few actors trying to be great would deny their secret knowledge that the art, the profession, whatever, is demented and deranging. Kinski's originality was in living that secret to the full. The list that follows is far from complete. It is still chaotic and lurid enough to help one appreciate the moments when Kinski was simply a face that had seen hell sharing the shock with us: *Morituri* (48, Eugen York); *Decision Before Dawn* (51, Anatole Litvak); *Ludwig II* (54, Helmut Kautner); *Kinder, Mutter und ein General* (54, Laslo Benedek); *Sarajevo* (55, Fritz Kortner); *Hanussen* (55, O. W. Fischer); *A Time to Love and a Time to Die* (57, Douglas Sirk); *Der*

Racher (60, Karl Anton); *Die Toten Augen von London* (61, Alfred Vohrer); *Bankraub in der Rue Latour* (61, Curd Jürgens); *The Counterfeit Traitor* (61, George Seaton); *Kali-Yug, la Dea della Vendetta* (63, Mario Camerini); *Traitor's Gate* (65, Freddie Francis); *The Pleasure Girls* (65, Gerry O'Hara); *The Dirty Game* (65, Terence Young); *Doctor Zhivago* (65, David Lean); *For a Few Dollars More* (65, Sergio Leone); *Quien Sabe?* (66, Damiano Damiani); *Circus of Fear* (66, John Moxey); *Carmen, Baby* (67, Radley Metzger); *Sumuru* (67, Lindsay Shonteff); *Coplan Sauve sa Peau* (67, Yves Boisset); *I Bastardi* (68, Duccio Tessari); *Il Grande Silenzia* (68, Sergio Corbucci); *Marquis de Sade: Justine* (68, Jess Franco); *La Peau de Torpedo* (69, Jean Delannoy); *E Dio Disse a Caino* (69, Anthony M. Dawson); *El Conde Dracula* (70, Franco); *Aguirre, the Wrath of God* (72, Herzog); *L'Important c'est d'Aimer* (74, Andrzej Zulawski); *Lifespan* (74, Alexander Whitelaw); *Jack the Ripper* (76, Franco); *Madame Claude* (76, Just Jaeckin); *Entebbe: Operation Thunderbolt* (77, Menahem Golan); *Mort d'un Pourri* (77, Georges Lautner); *Nosferatu* (78, Herzog); *Zoo Zero* (78, Alain Fleischer); *Woyzeck* (79, Herzog); *Love and Money* (80, James Toback); *Les Fruits de la Passion* (81, Shuji Terayama); *Buddy Buddy* (81, Billy Wilder); *Venom* (81, Piers Haggard); *Fitzcarraldo* (82, Herzog); *The Soldier* (82, James Glickenhaus); *Android* (83, Aaron Lipstadt); *The Secret Diary of Sigmund Freud* (84, Danford B. Greene); *Titan Find* (84, William Malone); *The Little Drummer Girl* (84, George Roy Hill); *Codename Wildgeese* (86, Dawson); *Crawlspace* (86, David Schmoeller); *Cobra Verde* (88, Herzog); *Nosferatu a Venezia* (88, Augusto Caminito); and *Paganini* (89), which he also directed, a labor of romantic devotion and close to unwatchable.

Nastassja Kinski, b. Berlin, 1960

There was a moment, in the early eighties, when Kinski was the rage, a sensation . . . the most beautiful girl in the world. Her greatest interest may be in pioneering the new brevity of such rages.

In May 1982, she was on the cover of *Rolling Stone*, in one of several Avedon photographs that showed her naked and tousled in bed. John Simon's text began: "I ask myself what makes Nastassia [remember that?] Kinski, at twenty-one, the biggest sex symbol of 1982, and perhaps of many years to come . . ." The piece went on—as if Simon had been in that bed with Kinski—"The breasts are perfect, though some might think them a bit small, pubescent; over the youthfully querying eyes, the brows are adult and ripely female. Or consider the voice: high and trilling one instant, then, suddenly, overcast, sensually clouded, as if a dark velvet hood descended protectively over some precious crystal object. The

walk is emphatic: a very feminine presence approaching with masculine directness . . ."

But the rage wasn't just John Simon and *Rolling Stone*. Avedon photographed Kinski with a python—the reptile and the lady in just their shining skins. Paul Schrader, in love with Kinski, said she was like the young Ingrid Bergman. *Time* put her on its cover: the profile writer, Richard Corliss, called her "Nasty." Director James Toback told the press that Norman Mailer had told him she had a quality like Monroe's.

I met Ms. Kinski, and she was lovely, uncertain, tricky, and helplessly seductive: it was evident that she looked to every new movie director as potential lover. Yet she was somehow frozen, too, as if waiting to be memorialized in still photographs, conscious of the huge effect she was having. She had vague plans for more training, for theatre, and for a career. But it seemed plain that she was the victim of the speed with which her life was moving, the eroticism of allowing oneself to be looked at, and the sheer perishability of such intensity.

What can one say after the sensation? That she was like thousands of other young women? That she had an extraordinarily alert, waiting gaze, enough to rivet other people and sway the camera?

She was also Klaus Kinski's daughter. The family lived together for some eight years before divorce. What did that do to the child? There was a time when she did not speak to her father—yet talking to Klaus Kinski was never enough.

She was silent in *Wrong Movement* (75, Wim Wenders); *To the Devil—A Daughter* (76, Peter Sykes); *Reifenzeugnis* (76, Wolfgang Petersen); *Boarding School* (78, Andre Farwagi); *Stay As You Are* (78, Alberto Lattuada); very accomplished and touching as *Tess* (79, Roman Polanski); the circus girl in *One From the Heart* (82, Francis Ford Coppola); daringly sensual and often naked as the released sexual urge in *Cat People* (82, Schrader); as Clara Wieck in *Spring Symphony* (83, Peter Schamoni); *The Moon in the Gutter* (83, Jean-Jacques Beneix); her body played by violinist Rudolph Nureyev's bow in *Exposed* (83, Toback); the old Linda Darnell role in *Unfaithfully Yours* (84, Howard Zieff), her childishness awoken by Dudley Moore; at her best in *Paris, Texas* (84, Wenders); *The Hotel New Hampshire* (84, Tony Richardson); *Maria's Lovers* (84, Andrei Konchalovsky); *Revolution* (85, Hugh Hudson); and *Harem* (85, Arthur Joffe).

She married and had children. Later on, she moved in with musician Quincy Jones and had another child. There have been more films, made in Europe, but only a few are notable: *Intervista* (87, Federico Fellini); *Torrents of Spring* (88, Jerzy Skolimowski); *Night Sun* (90, Paolo and Vittorio Taviani); and *Faraway, So Close* (93, Wenders).

Her moment has passed, but she is better looking than ever—for she was only forty in 2000! She makes so many films, some for TV, some that never get a proper release, some because she will do nudity, some that give her a real part, some that are first-time directors looking for a name, and some that mean costarring with Charlie Sheen—thus *Terminal Velocity* (94, Deran Sarafian); *Crackerjack* (94, Michael Mazo); *Somebody Is Waiting* (96, Martin Donovan); *The Ring* (96, Eddy Marshall); *Fathers' Day* (97, Ivan Reitman); *One Night Stand* (97, Mike Figgis); *Bella Mafia* (97, David Greene); *Little Boy Blue* (97, Antonio Tibaldi); *Savior* (98, Predrag Antonijevic); good in *Your Friends & Neighbors* (98, Neil LaBute); *Susan's Plan* (98, John Landis); *Playing by Heart* (98, Willard Carroll); *Ciro Norte* (98, Ivan Cardoso); *The Lost Son* (99, Chris Menges); *The Intruder* (99, David Bailey); *Quarantine* (99, Chuck Bowman); *A Storm in Summer* (00, Robert Wise); *The Magic of Marciano* (00, Tony Barbieri); *Red Letters* (00, Bradley Battersby); *Time Share* (00, Sharon von Wietersheim); excellent in *The Claim* (01, Michael Winterbottom); *Cold Heart* (01, Dennis Rimster); *Blind Terror* (01, Giles Walker); *Town & Country* (01, Peter Chelsom); *An American Rhapsody* (01, Eva Gardos); *A Woman in Love* (01, Giorgio Serafini); *Say Nothing* (01, Allan Moyle).

She was in *Diary of a Sex Addict* (01, Joseph Brutsman); *The Day the World Ended* (01, Terence Gross); *All Around the Town* (02, Paolo Barzman); as Gauguin's wife in *Paradise Found* (02, Mario Andreacchio); *Beyond the City Limits* (02, Gigi Gaston); as Mme de Tourvel (still innocent?) in *Les Liaisons Dangereuses* (03, Josee Dayan).

Teinosuke Kinugasa (1896–1982),
b. Mie, Japan

1922: *Niwa no Kotori; Hibana*. 1923: *Hanasake J'ijii; Jinsei o Mitsumete; Onnayo Ayamaru Nakare; Konjiki Yasha; Ma no Ike*. 1924: *Choraku no Kanata; Kanojo to Unmei; Kiri no Ame; Kishin Yuri Keiji; Kyoren no Buto; Mirsu; Shohin; Jashumon no Onna; Tsuma no Himitsu; Koi; Sabishiki Mura; Koi to Wa Narinu*. 1925: *Koi to Bushi; Shinju Yoimachigusa; Tsukigata Hanpeita; Wakaki hi no Chuji; Nichirin*. 1926: *Tenichibo to Iganosuke; Kurutta Ippeiji/A Page of Madness; Kirinji; Teru Hi Kumoru Hi; Hikuidori; Ojo Kichiza; Oni Azami; Kinno Jidai*. 1927: *Meoto Boshi; Goyosen; Dochu Sugoruku Bune; Dochu Sugoruku Kago; Akatsuki no Yushi; Gekka no Kyojin*. 1928: *Jujiro/Crossways; Benten Kozo; Keiraku Hichu; Kaikokuki; Chokon Yasha*. 1931: *Tojin Okichi; Reimei Izen*. 1932: *Ikonokotta Shinsengumi; Chushingura*. 1933: *Tenichibo to Iganosuke; Futatsu Doro; Koina no Ginpei*. 1934: *Kutsukate Tokijiro; Fuyaki Shinju; Ippon Gatana*

Dohyoiri; Nagurareta Kochiyama. 1935: *Kurayami no Ushimatsu; Yukinojo Henge* (parts 1 and 2). 1936: *Yukinojo Henge* (part 3). 1937: *Osaka Natsu no Jin*. 1938: *Kuroda Seichuroku*. 1940: *Hebihimesama*. 1941: *Kawanakajima Kasen*. 1943: *Susume Dokuritsuki*. 1945: *Umi no Bara*. 1946: *Aru Yo no Tonosama*. 1947: *Joyu*; episode from *Yottsu no Koi no Monogatari*. 1949: *Kobanzame; Koga Yashiki*. 1950: *Satsujinsha no Kao*. 1951: *Beni Komori; Tsuki no Wataridori; Meigatsu Somato*. 1952: *Shurajo Hibun* (two parts); *Daibutsu Kaigen*. 1953: *Jigokumon/Gate of Hell*. 1954: *Yuki no Yo no Ketto; Hana no Nagadosu; Tekka Bugyo*. 1955: *Kawa no Aru Shitamachi no Hanshi; Bara Ikutabi; Yushima no Shiraume*. 1956: *Yoshinaka o Meguru Sannin no Onna; Hibana; Tsukigata Hanpeita* (two parts). 1957: *Ukifune; Naruto Hicho*. 1958: *Haru Koro no Hana no En; Osaka no Onna*. 1959: *Shirasagi; Joen; Kagero Ezu*. 1960: *Uta Andon*. 1961: *Midare-gami; Okoto to Sasuke*. 1963: *Yoso; Uso*. 1967: *Chiisana Tobosha* (codirected with Nkandrovich).

Kinugasa began directing in the year that the Japanese cinema forsook male actors in female parts. He had been a female impersonator himself, and when the retaliatory strike failed, he chose to become a director. Similarly, when sound was introduced, he went on a two-year excursion to Russia to study under Eisenstein. His enormous output, especially in the silent era, is inaccessible to Western audiences. Only *Gate of Hell, Crossways,* and the rediscovered *Page of Madness* are at all well known. They suggest a distinct talent, a master of shadow and low key, with a special interest in disturbed psychology. It seems likely that a thorough investigation of all those years would prove rewarding.

Kevin Kline, b. St. Louis, Missouri, 1947
No one quite knows why Kevin Kline hasn't made it bigger in movies. He's very versatile—he has terrific, wild comic energy and a rare ability to be alarming, as well as the basic good looks and intelligence. He has a high stage reputation based on years with John Houseman's company, *On the Twentieth Century, The Pirates of Penzance,* and a notable *Hamlet*. He got the supporting actor Oscar for *A Fish Called Wanda* (88, Charles Crichton), where he held his own with professional comics. But somehow he remains a marginal figure, never dominant, never truly displayed by a film. Is he too smart to relax with the camera?

His film debut was both brilliant and disturbing, in *Sophie's Choice* (82, Alan J. Pakula). He followed that with the movie of *The Pirates of Penzance* (83, Wilford Leach); *The Big Chill* (83, Lawrence Kasdan); *Silverado* (85, Kasdan); *Violets Are Blue . . .* (86, Jack Fisk); as newspaper editor Donald Woods in *Cry Freedom* (87, Richard Attenborough); *The January Man* (89, Pat O'Connor), just the sort of film not to get into; *I Love You to Death* (90, Kasdan), one too many films with the same director; *Soapdish* (91, Michael Hoffman); *Grand Canyon* (91, Kasdan), two too many; *Consenting Adults* (92, Pakula); fine as Doug Fairbanks in *Chaplin* (92, Attenborough), but again—why?; in one of his best opportunities, *Dave* (93, Ivan Reitman); with his wife, Phoebe Cates, in *Princess Caraboo* (94, Michael Austin); finding chemistry with Meg Ryan in *French Kiss* (95, Kasdan)—but Meg Ryan does chemistry with everyone; *Fierce Creatures* (97, Robert Young), the troubled sequel to *Wanda*; very good in *The Ice Storm* (97, Ang Lee); very funny in *In & Out* (97, Frank Oz); fine as Bottom in *A Midsummer Night's Dream* (99, Hoffman); *Wild Wild West* (99, Barry Sonnenfeld); good in *The Anniversary Party* (01, Alan Cumming and Jennifer Jason Leigh); but nearly drowned in the tears of *Life as a House* (01, Irwin Winkler); *Orange County* (02, Jake Kasdan). He did the voice of Phoebus in *The Hunchback of Notre Dame* (02, Bradley Raymond); *The Emperor's Club* (02, Michael Hoffman); and he will be Cole Porter in *Just One of Those Things* (03, Irwin Winkler).

Alexander Kluge,
b. Halberstadt, Germany, 1932

1960: *Brutalität in Stein* (codirected with Peter Schamoni) (s). 1961: *Thema Amore* (s); *Rennen* (codirected with Paul Kruntorad) (s); *Rennfahrer* (s). 1963: *Lehrer im Wandel* (s). 1965: *Portrait einer Bewahrung* (s). 1966: *Abschied von Gestern/ Yesterday Girl*. 1967: *Frau Blackburn wird Gefilmt* (s). 1968: *Die Artisten in der Zirkuskuppel: Ratlos/Artists at the Top of the Big Top; Disorientated*. 1969: *Ein Arzt aus Halberstadt; Die Unbezahmbare Leni Pelckert*. 1970: *Feuerloscher E. A. Winterstein* (s). 1971: *Der Grosse Verhrau; Das Krankheitsbild des Schlachtener-Problem Unteroffiziers in der Endsehlacht* (codirected with O. Mai and E. Zemann). 1972: *Willy Tobler und der Untergang der 6 Flotte*. 1974: *Gelegenheitsarbeit einer Sklavin/Occasional Work of a Female Slave*. 1975: *In Gefahr und Grösster not Bringt der Mittelweg den Tod*. 1976: *Der Starke Ferdinand/ Strong-Man Ferdinand*. 1978: episode from *Deutschland im Herbst*. 1979: *Die Patriotin* (d). 1980: *Der Kandidat* (d). 1982: *Krieg und Frieden*. 1983: *Die Macht der Gefühle/The Power of Emotions*. 1985: *Der Angriff der Gaegenwart auf die Ubrige Zeit/The Blind Director*. 1986: *Vermischte Nachrichten*.

Alexander Kluge's first participation in cinema was as assistant to Fritz Lang when the veteran was making his two Indian films, *Der Tiger von Eschnapur* (59) and *Das Indische Grabmal* (59),

themselves throwbacks to German cinema of 1919–20. Until his enforced departure from Germany in 1933, Lang had reflected the tumult of disillusioned insecurity through allegories of criminal organizations threatening to subvert the appointed authorities. His pictures were piercing indictments of political hysteria. Kluge's, by contrast, are fixed on the essential muddle of young reactions to the lurid history that Lang survived. Kluge's first two features, *Yesterday Girl* and *Artists at the Top of the Big Top*, are among the most interestingly German films from the young German cinema, but they are pondering work in which wit, personality, and incident only just keep their heads above conscientious dismay. *Yesterday Girl* was Godardian, but minus Godard's formal inventiveness and cut off from his sense of cinematic tradition. The political past, and Germany's inexplicable escape from it, hang over Kluge's world, and he resorted to cinema only after having begun as a novelist.

Since the late eighties Kluge has given his time to producing cultural programs for small cable TV channels in Germany.

Masaki Kobayashi (1916–96),
b. Otaru, Japan

1952: *Musuko no Seishun*. 1953: *Magokoro; Kabe Atsuki Heya*. 1954: *Mittsu no Ai; Kono Hiroi Sora no Dokokani*. 1955: *Uruwashiki Saigetsu*. 1956: *Anata Kaimasu; Izumi*. 1957: *Kuroi Kawa; Ningen no Joken*, part 1. 1960: *Ningen no Joken*, part 2. 1961: *Ningen no Joken*, part 3. 1962: *Karami-ai*. 1963: *Seppuku/Hara-Kiri*. 1964: *Kwaidan*. 1967: *Joi-uchi/Rebellion*. 1968: *Nippon no Seishun*. 1971: *Inochi Bonifuro*. 1974: *Kaseki*. 1978: *Moeru Aki*. 1983: *Tokyo Saiban/Tokyo Trial* (d). 1985: *Shokutaka no nai ie/ The Empty Table*.

A philosophy student, Kobayashi was taken prisoner by the Chinese during the war. On his return, he worked as assistant and scriptwriter to Keisake Kinoshita before himself directing. Those of his films that have been released in the West suggest an accomplished but unadventurous talent. Kobayashi shows a familiar concern with the conflict between emotional impulse and ritualistic pattern, but the concern seems somehow obligatory whereas in Mizoguchi, Ozu, and Oshima it is profound and original. One has the feeling that Kobayashi keeps an eye on the art-house market outside Japan and that native themes have thus become diluted. *Seppuku* and *Rebellion* treat the infringement of society on the individual but, in the first, indulge in an orgy of disembowelling and, in the second, permit coproducer Toshiru Mifune a samurai extravaganza. The idea of *Rebellion*—of a samurai who rebels against the cynical manipulation of the elders in making and then breaking a marriage involving his son—is intriguing, but the resolution is conventionally exciting, bloodthirsty, and never poignant. One has only to recall that brief arc of suicidal blood in *The Ceremony* to feel Oshima's greater gravity. Similarly, in *Kwaidan*, Kobayashi has resorted to three Lafcadio Hearn ghost stories as much in search of the exotic as to arouse the poetic and lyrical resignation that concludes *Ugetsu*.

Kobayashi's major work is *Ningen no Joken—The Human Condition*—an immense humane account of a Manchurian factory owner who is victimized for aiding Chinese workers and then suffers terribly in the war with Russia. The complete work is over nine hours long, gruelling, conventional, and a little portentous, but inescapably moving.

Tokyo Trial was a four-and-a-half-hour documentary on the Japanese war-criminal trials. It uses a great deal of newsreel, from many different sources, yet the film functions as a narrative.

Sir Alexander Korda (1893–1956),

b. Turkeye, Hungary

1916: *Egy Tiszti Kardbojt; Feher Ejszakak; Vergodo Szivek; Nagymama; Mesek az Ivogeprol; Egymillio Fontos Banko.* 1917: *Magnas Miska; A Ketszivu Ferfi; Szent Pter Esernyoje; A Golyakalifa; Magia; Faun, Harrison es Harrison; A Ketlelku Asszony.* 1918: *Az Aranyembr; Mary Ann; Se Ki Se Be.* 1919: *Ave Caesar; Feher Rosza; A 111-es; Yamata.* 1920: *Seine Majestat das Bettlekind.* 1922: *Herrin der Meere; Eine Versunkene Welt; Samson und Dalila.* 1923: *Das Unbekannte Morgen.* 1924: *Tragodie in Hause Hapsburg; Jedermanns Frau.* 1925: *Der Tanzer Meine Frau.* 1926: *Eine Dubarry von Heute; Madame Wunscht Keine Kinder.* 1927: *The Stolen Bride; The Private Life of Helen of Troy.* 1928: *The Yellow Lily; The Night Watch.* 1929: *Love and the Devil; The Squall; Her Private Life.* 1930: *Women Everywhere; Lilies of the Field; The Princess and the Plumber.* 1931: *Rive Gauche; Marius.* 1932: *Service for Ladies; Wedding Rehearsal.* 1933: *The Private Life of Henry VIII; The Girl from Maxim's.* 1934: *The Private Life of Don Juan.* 1936: *Rembrandt.* 1941: *That Hamilton Woman/ Lady Hamilton.* 1945: *Perfect Strangers.* 1948: *An Ideal Husband.*

Korda was the self-ordained khan of the British film industry. Having worked as a director in his native Hungary, Germany, America, and France, he went to England in 1931 and remained there the rest of his life, receiving the accolade as a solace when he had lost most of his money. No doubt the knighthood moved him, for he responded fulsomely to service and patriotism and would have absorbed all of England's heritage if he could. His films had already done more for English history than the rest of the industry put together. Should England, then, be grateful? Or is it possible that, in introducing the vain thought that England could rival Hollywood, Korda distracted England from a modest, secure native industry, working to small budgets on indigenous subjects with something like the stylistic innovation achieved in France in the 1930s? Of course, there is ample evidence of commercial wrongheadedness and limited talent apart from Korda, but still he dragged England in a fruitless direction, the ponderous aftermath being J. Arthur Rank's attempt at postwar imitation.

That said, it is ungenerous not to respond to the Hungarian's sense of "pomp, magic, and madness," nor to admire the shameless gaiety of the goulash he made out of England. He grasped one point—years later a credo of BBC TV—that the English had a limitless appetite for their own cozy history, that they loved its pretext for flashy acting, rich costumes, and class distinction. As for authenticity, Korda had that sinuous charm that can make the truth sound unreliable—not that he wasted much time on the truth. In America, he had tested the commercial viability of the "private life" of some household name from history. And with Henry VIII—the safest of all such figures—he successfully produced an international film that made a lot of money in America, never seemed threadbare, and found a major screen personality in Charles Laughton.

It was unfortunate that success came so early, for it urged Korda into grand plans. None of his later films had the same success, even if *Rembrandt* is a better movie. He founded London Films, Alexander Korda Film Productions, borrowed from the Prudential to build Denham studios, and surrounded himself with a coterie of talents—his brothers, Zoltan and art director Vincent, many indifferent Hungarians, and some technicians of great talent, like Georges Périnal.

The labor of organization drained his own zest for direction, so that his last film, from Oscar Wilde, with sets by Cecil Beaton, photographed by Périnal, and with Paulette Goddard as Mrs. Cheveley, is a listless mess. In America, he had directed for First National, often from Hungarian stories, and with Billie Dove or his first wife, Maria Corda. After a brief interlude in France, where his *Marius* fitted into Pagnol's trilogy, he came to England and married again to Merle Oberon, who appeared in *Henry VIII* and *Don Juan* and whose car accident mercifully interrupted *Claudius*, already riven by the impossible egotism of himself, Laughton, and von Sternberg.

Even so, in *Fun in a Chinese Laundry* Sternberg speaks with rare and unaffected warmth of Korda's ability to survive in a sea of deceits and debts. Sternberg paints a pretty picture of himself seeing an almost penniless Korda off from Hollywood. Truth to tell, they were made for each other. And if Sternberg was too prickly a talent for the fragile mock-Babylon at Denham, still he was a character from Korda's world. Either one might have immortalized the other with more luck. As it is, the footage of *Claudius* is exquisite and perverted.

After 1939, Korda devoted himself to the war effort, and in peace he smiled his way through decline. From 1949 onward he took up a rather vague role as executive producer. The result, as always, was a string of oddities, a sort of Xanadu necklace, each piece glittering but flawed. The British cinema is inconceivable without Korda, and yet perhaps he gave it illusory standards. Look at a selection of the pictures he produced: not a dull one among them, not one that does not sparkle with silliness (if nothing else): *Catherine the Great* (34, Paul Czinner), the Bergner version, made to tease Sternberg, perhaps; *The Scarlet Pimpernel* (34, Harold Young); *Sanders of the River* (35, Zoltan Korda); *The Ghost Goes West* (35, René Clair); *Things to Come* (36, William Cameron Menzies); *Elephant Boy* (36, Z. Korda and Robert Flaherty); *Knight Without Armour* (37, Jacques Feyder); *The Drum* (38, Z. Korda); *The Four Feathers* (39, Z. Korda); *The Thief of Bagdad* (40, Tim Whelan, Ludwig Berger, and Michael Powell)—perhaps the best, and the most influential; *The Jungle Book* (42, Z. Korda); *Anna Karenina* (48, Julien Duvivier); *The Fallen Idol* (48, Carol Reed); *The Small Back Room* (48, Powell); *The Third Man* (49, Reed); *Gone to Earth* (50, Powell); *Seven Days to Noon* (50, John Boulting); *The Tales of Hoffmann* (51, Powell); *Cry, the Beloved Country* (52, Z. Korda); *The Sound Barrier* (52, David Lean); *Hobson's Choice* (53, Lean); *The Deep Blue Sea* (55, Anatole Litvak); and *Richard III* (55, Laurence Olivier).

Anna Karenina is a dud, but consider that run from *The Fallen Idol* to *The Tales of Hoffmann*— six films, no two alike, all full of enterprise and showmanship, and all as moving as on the day they were shot. *The Third Man* was all the more of an achievement in that Korda had to ward off the heavy breathing of a fellow-monster, Selznick. Not that Selznick could ever have delivered the tough, bitter romance of *The Third Man*.

Zoltan Korda (1895–1961),

b. Turkeye, Hungary

1927: *Die Ey Teufel.* 1933: *Cash.* 1935: *Sanders of the River; Conquest of the Air.* 1936: *Elephant Boy* (codirected with Robert Flaherty); *Forget Me Not.* 1937: *Revolt in the Jungle.* 1938: *The Drum.* 1939: *The Four Feathers.* 1942: *The Jungle Book.* 1943: *Sahara.* 1945: *Counter-Attack.* 1947: *The Macomber Affair.* 1948: *A Woman's Vengeance.* 1952: *Cry, the Beloved Country.* 1955: *Storm Over the Nile* (codirected with Terence Young).

The younger brother of Alexander Korda, Zoltan fought throughout the First World War for Austria-Hungary. He entered films in Germany in the 1920s as an editor and cameraman. After making his first feature in Germany, he went to America and wrote the script for *Women Everywhere* (30, A. Korda). For the next ten years he worked in Britain as one of his brother's cohort of Magyars.

Zoltan played an enthusiastic part in that incongruous sympathy of one lost empire for another fast dying. *Sanders of the River* was so smugly jingoistic that Paul Robeson, who played the African chief, preferred to disown it. In retrospect, however, the imperial offensiveness seems peripheral to an engaging taste for adventurous nonsense. It was the feeling for romance that inspired the Korda empire, and it was only proper that they should need to establish themselves as refugees. Robeson may have been angered, but Sabu was exactly the Little Black Sambo they needed. He was featured in *Elephant Boy,* with an impact on Flaherty (used to indigenous peoples) that can only be imagined, in *The Drum* and *The Jungle Book.*

By then, Zoltan had gone back to Hollywood. *Sahara* is a foolish League of Nations war movie set in the Libyan desert. But in his next films, Zoltan unwrapped ambitions not encouraged by his brother. *The Macomber Affair,* from Hemingway's short story, is respectable and benefits from Joan Bennett; while *A Woman's Vengeance* is a version of Aldous Huxley's *The Gioconda Smile.* As if to make amends for *Sanders of the River,* Zoltan filmed Alan Paton's *Cry, the Beloved Country,* an early, if conventional, cinematic rehabilitation of the black experience. He came back to England to lend his experience to *Storm Over the Nile,* a remake of *The Four Feathers.*

Harmony Korine, b. Bolinas, California, 1974

1997: *Gummo.* 1999: *Julien Donkey-Boy.*

There's no wonder at the appeal of minimalism in an age of budgets over $100 million, of astonishing special effects and a widening gap between the harsh realities in which most people exist and the daft fantasies they are supposed to aspire to. But minimalism can grow out of political anger, a critique of capitalism, stylistic austerity, or a kind of numb, pretentious helplessness that sees the irony in a copy of *Vogue* floating on the toxic surface of a full latrine. A genuine political dismay would be best advised to get into politics, to change things that way. But then the aesthetic response—the urge, say, to make Dogme-like films, or simply to record the passing of unending human disaster— can seem cold and exploitative. In the end, what is the point of minimalism if it only works in the dark?

That said, minimalism can be a desperate attempt to hold on to real place, real time, and nature in the broadest sense against the infernal electronic possibilities for change. There is a great need for movies, or for film, that simply record real life and asks us to attend.

There are astonishing beauties in distance and duration, as Renoir, Mizoguchi, Dreyer, and so many great masters believed.

Harmony Korine had his first credit doing the script for *Kids* (95, Larry Clark). Some asked whether that drab, comatose scrutiny of grim life had or needed a script. But a script is not just a collection of pages. It can be an attitude to life, an element in casting, and an influence on the way of filming. Thus, *Gummo* came as no surprise (no matter how shocking or disturbing you might find it). It grew directly out of *Kids. Julien Donkey-Boy* is a very different kind of film—it has a plot and a looming psychic drama behind it. But it is made in a similar way, and it shows Korine developing.

Sight and Sound noted a dilemma: Bertolucci had called *Gummo* the one revolutionary film of the late twentieth century, whereas Janet Maslin of the *New York Times* had said it might be the worst ever made. *Sight and Sound* was seeking resolution, but it seems to me truer to Korine and the real cause of minimalism that a film might be both—for what we're on the edge of here is an explosive end to cinema, as a way of remaking its society.

Henry Koster (Hermann Kosterlitz) (1905–88), b. Berlin

1932: *Das Abenteuer der Thea Roland*. 1933: *Das Hässliche Mädchen; Peter*. 1934: *Kleine Mutti*. 1936: *Marie Bashkirtzeff; Three Smart Girls*. 1937: *One Hundred Men and a Girl*. 1938: *The Rage of Paris*. 1939: *Three Smart Girls Grow Up; First Love*. 1940: *Spring Parade*. 1941: *It Started with Eve*. 1942: *Between Us Girls*. 1944: *Music for Millions*. 1946: *Two Sisters from Boston*. 1947: *The Unfinished Dance; The Bishop's Wife*. 1949: *The Inspector General; Come to the Stable*. 1950: *Harvey; Wabash Avenue; My Blue Heaven*. 1951: *Mr. Belvedere Rings the Bell; No Highway;* "The Cop and the Anthem," episode from *O. Henry's Full House*. 1952: *Stars and Stripes Forever; My Cousin Rachel*. 1953: *The Robe*. 1954: *Desirée*. 1955: *Good Morning, Miss Dove; A Man Called Peter; The Virgin Queen*. 1956: *D-Day the Sixth of June; The Power and the Prize*. 1957: *My Man Godfrey; Fraulein*. 1959: *The Naked Maja*. 1960: *The Story of Ruth*. 1961: *Flower Drum Song*. 1962: *Mr. Hobbs Takes a Vacation*. 1963: *Take Her, She's Mine*. 1965: *Dear Brigitte; The Singing Nun*.

In 1926, Kosterlitz was making publicity films. Next year, he joined UFA as a writer, later working at Universal and Terra. His output was prolific but undistinguished, including several scripts filmed by Kurt Bernhardt—*Die Waise von Lowood* (26); *Kinderseelen Klagen an* (26); *Die Letzte Kom-*

panie (30); *Die Mann der den Mord Beging* (31). He began directing at Universal and in 1936 he left for America.

At Universal, he was chosen by Joe Pasternak (who had produced *Kleine Mutti*) to handle the studio's new property, Deanna Durbin. Koster was equal to that task, directing her six times: *Three Smart Girls; One Hundred Men and a Girl*, which pairs Durbin with Leopold Stokowski; *Three Smart Girls Grow Up; First Love; Spring Parade;* and *It Started with Eve*, which costars Charles Laughton. After two films with June Allyson, and a dull Cary Grant movie—*The Bishop's Wife*—Koster made the awful *Inspector General* (all Danny Kaye and no Gogol) and the charming *Harvey* and *No Highway*, which rely on James Stewart's facile absentmindedness. Now at Fox, he was once more trusted: this time with CinemaScope. *The Robe*, however, is a cautious innovation, and it inaugurated a solemn decline. *Desirée* is inept; *The Virgin Queen* a throwback; *Good Morning, Miss Dove* treacle; *My Man Godfrey* an ill-advised remake with David Niven and Allyson falling far short of Powell and Lombard; and *The Naked Maja* sedately overdressed.

Grigori Kozintsev (1905–73), b. Kiev, Russia

1924: *Pokhozhdeniya Oktyabriny/The Adventures of Oktyabrina*. 1925: *Mishki protiv Yudenicha/ Mishka against Yudenich*. 1926: *Chortovo Koleso/ The Devil's Wheel; Shinel/The Cloak*. 1927: *Bratishka; SVD/The Club of the Big Deed*. 1929: *Novyi Vavilon/The New Babylon*. 1931: *Odna/ Alone*. 1935: *Yunost Maksima/The Youth of Maxim*. 1937: *Vozvrashchenie Maksima/The Return of Maxim*. 1939: *Vyborgskaya Storona/The Vyborg Side*. 1945: *Prostye Lyudi/Plain People* (all these films codirected with Leonid Trauberg). 1947: *Pirogov*. 1953: *Bielinsky*. 1957: *Don Quixote*. 1964: *Hamlet*. 1971: *King Lear*.

With Leonid Trauberg and Sergei Yutkevich, Kozintsev was a founding member of the Factory of Eccentric Actors. After that, he became the regular collaborator of Leonid Trauberg in directing films. That partnership is best known for *The New Babylon*, a satire set in Paris during the 1871 Commune, and the Maxim films that trace the development of a party worker in the years 1913–20. They made the first postwar feature at Leninfilm, *Plain People*, but its release was held up for eleven years by the authorities. From that point, Kozintsev worked independently on a series of prestigious, literary transpositions. They are meticulous, literal films, inclined to make crude extensions of the original works toward Communist ideology. The acting is old-fashioned and Kozintsev labored to capture a visual equivalent of the density of Shakespeare's verse. His *Lear*, especially, is pedestrian, but *Hamlet* is graced by the performance of Innokennty Smoktunovsky, while the overemphatic *Don Quixote* allows every indulgence to Nikolai Cherkassov. Unfortunately, he never escaped the Russian taste for academic beauty—the one solacing proof of art for creators controlled by bureaucrats. Thus, the lamentable prettiness of so much Soviet composition, obscuring the lack of purposeful structure.

Stanley Kramer (1913–2001), b. New York
1955: *Not as a Stranger.* 1957: *The Pride and the Passion.* 1958: *The Defiant Ones.* 1959: *On the Beach.* 1960: *Inherit the Wind.* 1961: *Judgement at Nuremberg.* 1963: *It's a Mad, Mad, Mad, Mad World.* 1965: *Ship of Fools.* 1967: *Guess Who's Coming to Dinner?.* 1969: *The Secret of Santa Vittoria.* 1970: *R.P.M.* 1971: *Bless the Beasts and Children.* 1973: *Oklahoma Crude.* 1977: *The Domino Principle/The Domino Killings.* 1979: *The Runner Stumbles.*

In some quarters Kramer was a hero of the 1950s: an enterprising producer, cutting costs on "daring" or "topical" subjects, ultimately coming into his own as a director. But the test of direction revealed all the limitations of his entrepreneurial liberalism. His own films are middlebrow and overemphatic; at worst, they are among the most tedious and dispiriting productions the American cinema has to offer. Commercialism, of the most crass and confusing kind, has devitalized all his projects, just as his deliberate enlightenment seems to have wearied notable actors. He would answer that he makes films for the ordinary viewer and that *The Defiant Ones, Inherit the Wind,* and *Guess Who's Coming to Dinner?* might be subtle moderators of prejudice. Not a jot of evidence supports that hope. Very little encourages the thought that even vastly superior films could serve that purpose. Kramer is a hollow, pretentious man, too dull for art, too cautious for politics. There are few films as deeply depressing as *On the Beach* and *Judgement at Nuremberg,* because their visions of apocalypse are as numbstruck as a rabbit in headlights.

He was educated at New York University, and in 1933 he joined the research department at MGM, working subsequently as an editor and casting director. His first job as a producer was on Albert Lewin's *The Moon and Sixpence* (42) and it was only in the late 1940s that he set up as an independent producer with Sam Katz, Carl Foreman, and George Glass as partners. After *So This Is New York* (48, Richard Fleischer), he made his name with a series of economy productions, by turns prestigious and socially realistic: *Home of the Brave* (49, Mark Robson); *Champion* (49, Robson); *The Men* (50, Fred Zinnemann); *Cyrano de Bergerac* (50, Michael Gordon); and *High Noon* (52, Zinnemann). The latter was later claimed to be an allegory about McCarthyism—

which is a lot of allegory. The others have all dated badly, showing up the meretricious artistic conception.

To this point, Kramer had been commercially successful: that and his liberal respectability attracted Columbia, who signed him to produce thirty films in five years, all with low budgets and high profits. It was a disastrous contract in which Kramer claimed to be hindered by the studio's meanness, but still launched some unlikely ventures. There is not a good film in the lot: *Death of a Salesman* (51, Laslo Benedek); *The Happy Time* (52, Fleischer); *The Sniper* (52, Edward Dmytryk); *My Six Convicts* (52, Hugo Fregonese); *The Four Poster* (52, Irving Reis); *Eight Iron Men* (52, Dmytryk); *The 5,000 Fingers of Dr. T* (52, Roy Rowland); *The Wild One* (53, Benedek); *Member of the Wedding* (53, Zinnemann); and *The Juggler* (53, Dmytryk). The heavy losses incurred by most of these were covered by the one success, *The Caine Mutiny* (54, Dmytryk), but Columbia had had enough and bought up the contract.

Thus Kramer launched himself as producer/director. Suffice it to say that *Not as a Stranger* is his best film, *The Pride and the Passion* the silliest. After that, ordeal sets in and shows no sign of faltering. The greatest oddity is that his reputation has survived such critical pasting and so many box-office failures. When he died he was on the front page of the *New York Times,* plus a full page inside—more than twice the space given to Bresson.

Norman Krasna (1909–84),
b. Queens, New York
1943: *Princess O'Rourke.* 1950: *The Big Hangover.* 1956: *The Ambassador's Daughter.*

Krasna did a little bit of everything; never with distinction, but rarely without a feeling for comedy. Two of his own films—*Princess O'Rourke* and *The Ambassador's Daughter*—are pleasant settings for Olivia de Havilland; while *The Big Hangover* was a routine Metro romance with the young Elizabeth Taylor.

From Columbia University, Krasna became a New York drama critic, and then attached himself to the publicity department at Warners—the way in pioneered by Hal Wallis (who produced *Princess O'Rourke*). From 1932, Krasna worked as a writer, on either originals or his own stage plays: the story of *Meet the Baron* (33, Walter Lang), with Herman Mankiewicz; *The Richest Girl in the World* (34, William A. Seiter); the uncharacteristic *Fury* (36, Fritz Lang), for which he provided the story outline; *The Big City* (37, Frank Borzage), a Spencer Tracy–Luise Rainer film that Krasna wrote the story for and produced; the story for *You and Me* (38, Lang); the very funny script for *Bachelor Mother* (39, Garson Kanin); story and script for Hitchcock's underrated *Mr. and Mrs. Smith* (41); producer and writer of *The Devil and Miss Jones* (41, Sam Wood); the stories of *It Started with Eve* (41, Henry Koster) and *The Flame of New Orleans* (41, René Clair).

He concentrated on the theatre for most of the 1940s, though his play, *Dear Ruth* (47, William D. Russell), was filmed, and he returned to cinema with script work on *White Christmas* (54, Michael Curtiz); *Bundle of Joy* (57, Norman Taurog); *Indiscreet* (58, Stanley Donen), which he wrote from his own play; *Who Was That Lady?* (60, George Sidney), which he wrote and produced; the story for *Let's Make Love* (60, George Cukor); the story for *My Geisha* (62, Jack Cardiff); and the script for *Sunday in New York* (65, Peter Tewkesbury). In addition, in 1950, Krasna formed a production company with Jerry Wald that lasted long enough to produce *The Lusty Men* (52, Nicholas Ray), *Clash by Night* (52, Lang), and *The Blue Veil* (52, Curtis Bernhardt).

Werner Krauss (1884–1959),
b. Gestungshausen, Germany

Das Kabinett des Dr. Caligari (19, Robert Wiene) is a rough-and-ready piece of celluloid, no matter how complex the ideas it yields. But it has one of the first deeply frightening shots in cinema, in which the arousal of fear depends upon the manner of a performance and the way it is recorded:

> The top-hatted figure of Dr. Caligari appears walking up the flight of steps in the center of the fairground setting; he is clutching at the banister-rail. When he reaches the top of the steps, he turns towards the camera. His black cloak is tightly wrapped around him; he peers quizzically, irascibly, around him through large round spectacles, then hobbles painfully forward, leaning heavily on his stick with one hand and carrying a book in the other. He is wearing white gloves, on the back of which are painted three broad black stripes, extensions of the spaces between his fingers. Hobbling forward, he looks a sinister, menacing cripple, capable of the utmost evil. His lips are tightly pursed and he glares wildly ahead; his white hair straggles out from beneath the brim of his hat. Iris out on Caligari's face, leaning back slightly as if sniffing the atmosphere.

That is from a script transcribed and published in 1972, so that "a sinister, menacing cripple, capable of the utmost evil" is written with benefit of Kracauer's *From Caligari to Hitler.* But the images of Werner Krauss's Caligari are filled with dread. That threatening stare into the camera shows how far Caligari is the dominant presence in the film. In camera terms, it foreshadows the chilling denouement in which Caligari is found to be in charge of the asylum where the story of the

film is being told by an inmate. As far as Krauss is concerned, we can only admit the sense of concentrated, shabby rancor that the actor conveys, and suggest that his later work in central parts in Nazi films is life's banal attempt at coincidence.

Krauss was a stage-trained actor, suited to the Expressionist gesture: *Hoffmanns Erzahlungen* (16, Richard Oswald); *Nacht des Grauens* (16, Arthur Robison); *Zirkusblut* (16, Oswald); *Die Rache der Toten* (17, Oswald); *Die Seeschlacht* (17, Oswald); *Es Werde Licht* (18, Oswald); *Das Tagebuch einer Verlorenen* (18, Oswald); *Opium* (18, Robert Reinert); *Die Frau mit den Orchideen* (19, Otto Rippert); *Rose Bernd* (19, Alfred Halm); *Die Bruder Karamazoff* (20, Dmitri Buchowetzki and Carl Froelich); *Der Bucklige und die Tanzerin* (20, F. W. Murnau); *Johannes Goth* (20, Karl Gerhardt); *Das Lachende Grauen* (20, Lupu Pick); *Christian Wahnschaffe* (21, Urban Gad); *Danton* (21, Buchowetzki); *Grausige Nacht* (21, Pick); *Der Roman der Christine von Herre* (21, Ludwig Berger); *Scherben* (21, Pick); *Sappho* (21, Buchowetzki); *Der Brennende Acker* (22, Murnau); *Josef und Seine Bruder* (22, Froelich); *Luise Millerin* (22, Froelich); *Lady Hamilton* (22, Oswald); *Die Nacht der Medici* (22, Karl Grune); as Iago in *Othello* (22, Buchowetzki); *Tragikomodie* (22, Wiene); *Das Alte Gesetz* (23, E. A. Dupont); *Fridericus Rex* (23, Arsen von Cserepy); *I.N.R.I.* (23, Wiene); *Der Schatz* (23, G. W. Pabst); *Das Unbekannte Morgen* (23, Alexander Korda); *Zwischen Abend und Morgen* (23, Robison); *Dekameron-Nachte* (24, Herbert Wilcox); *Waxworks* (24, Paul Leni); as the butcher in *Die Freudlose Gasse* (25, Pabst); *Das Haus der Luge* (25, Pick); as Orgon in *Tartuff* (25, Murnau); *Geheimnisse einer Seele* (26, Pabst); *Man Spielt Nicht mit der Liebe* (26, Pabst); as Comte Muffat in *Nana* (26, Jean Renoir); as the devil in *Der Student von Prag* (26, Henrik Galeen); *Funkzauber* (27, Oswald); *Laster der Menschheit* (27, Rudolf Meinert); *Looping the Loop* (28, Robison); *Napoleon auf St. Helena* (29, Pick); *Yorck* (31, Gustav Ucicky); *Mensch Ohne Namen* (32, Ucicky); *Burgtheater* (36, Willi Forst); *Robert Koch, der Bekampfer des Todes* (39, Hans Steinhoff); several "Jewish" roles in *Jud Süss* (40, Veit Harlan); *Annelie* (41, Josef von Bady); *Die Entlassung* (42, Wolfgang Liebeneiner); *Zwischen Himmel und Erde* (42, Harald Braun); *Paracelsus* (43, Pabst); *Pramien auf den Tod* (50, Curd Jürgens); *Der Fallende Stern* (50, Braun); and *Sohn Ohne Heimat* (55, Hans Deppe).

Kris Kristofferson,
b. Brownsville, Texas, 1936

You can't take Kristofferson too solemnly as an actor, because you can hear his good-natured growl that he was always about so many other things—singing and writing songs, having every good time he could find, and just growing older gracefully, or whatever. At the same time, he has at least one great film (*Pat Garrett*), several fascinating curiosities, and a few genuine monstrosities to his credit. Plus there is the fact that his outer shell seems so thoroughly lived in that he may be at his best now, in his sixties.

From Pomona College, he became a Rhodes scholar, an army officer, a teacher, and only then a singer. It was as the latter that he began to be cast in pictures: acting in and doing the music for *The Last Movie* (71, Dennis Hopper); doing both on *Cisco Pike* (72, B. W. L. Norton); not doing the music but so puppy-fat fresh, lazy, and carnal as the Kid in *Pat Garrett and Billy the Kid* (73, Sam Peckinpah); *The Gospel Road* (73, Robert Elfstrom); pretty good in a plain role in *Blume in Love* (73, Paul Mazursky); a small role in *Bring Me the Head of Alfredo Garcia* (74, Peckinpah); *Alice Doesn't Live Here Anymore* (74, Martin Scorsese); a very romantic image in *The Sailor Who Fell from Grace with the Sea* (76, Lewis John Carlino); *Vigilante Force* (76, George Armitage).

He was self-parody in *A Star Is Born* (76, Frank Pierson); a football player in *Semi-Tough* (77, Michael Ritchie); *Convoy* (78, Peckinpah); looking superb as a Western gentleman in *Heaven's Gate* (80, Michael Cimino); in high finance with Jane Fonda in *Rollover* (81, Alan J. Pakula); *Flashpoint* (84, William Tannen); *Songwriter* (84, Alan Rudolph); *Trouble in Mind* (85, Rudolph); *Big Top Pee-Wee* (88, Randal Kleiser); *Millennium* (89, Michael Anderson); back from Cambodia in *Welcome Home* (89, Franklin J. Schaffner); *Night of the Cyclone* (90, David Irving); *Cheatin' Hearts* (93, Rod McCall); seeming older and impressive in *Lone Star* (96, John Sayles); *Fire Down Below* (97, Félix Enríquez Alcalá); very good as a James Jones figure in *A Soldier's Daughter Never Cries* (98, James Ivory); *Limbo* (99, Sayles); *The Joyriders* (00, Bradley Battersby); *Planet of the Apes* (01, Tim Burton); *Wooly Boys* (01, Leszek Burzynski); *D-Tox* (01, Jim Gillespie).

Stanley Kubrick (1928–99),
b. Bronx, New York
1953: *Fear and Desire*. 1955: *Killer's Kiss*. 1956: *The Killing*. 1957: *Paths of Glory*. 1960: *Spartacus*. 1962: *Lolita*. 1963: *Dr. Strangelove, or How I Learned to Stop Worrying and Love the Bomb*. 1968: *2001: A Space Odyssey*. 1971: *A Clockwork Orange*. 1975: *Barry Lyndon*. 1980: *The Shining*. 1987: *Full Metal Jacket*. 1999: *Eyes Wide Shut*.

Long before *The Shining*, Stanley Kubrick had retreated to his Overlook Hotel. It was not just an estate in Buckinghamshire, nor simply England—as opposed to America. His real aerie was withdrawal to the higher, more spiritual places, an abode of paranoia, kingdom, and the cunning suggestion of being grander than others could dream

of. His retreat was like the opening bars in a Wagner overture. Warner Brothers apparently abided by his view of himself (they funded films *after Barry Lyndon*), announcing themselves in advance as privileged to fund whatever he settled on. It cannot have been a profitable faith, which is enormous proof of Kubrick's cold, humorless authority.

Now that film-going has broken free of habit, we have an audience that is supposedly more discriminating. All that that seems to mean, in practice, is that whereas people once went to the pictures in the way they did to the baker's, they now make specific decisions to see films that have been made to match up to their supposedly loftier expectations. Clearly, the present system allows audiences to make wrong choices, as well as right ones, whereas once they never thought of choice. It also encourages certain directors into a garishly intelligent "evening out" package like *A Clockwork Orange*. Kubrick signaled his own gravity with years of preparation, endless painstaking in shooting, the courting of serious topics, and pandering to the audience's appetite for sensation and vulgarity in the guise of importance.

After 1961, Kubrick was based in England, with some of the precious decorousness of the writer in *A Clockwork Orange* who is broken in on by Alex and the Droogs. Five films were passed out to the world from that retreat, which took an increasingly sententious and nihilistic view of our social and moral ethics, but which are as devoid of artistic personality as the worlds that Kubrick elegantly extrapolates.

The laboriousness of this process needs to be stressed because it directly affects the seldom admitted tedium of the pictures. Preparation and shooting for Kubrick are extended operations, with special emphasis on art direction and the engineering of lenses, but with cursory attention to character or narrative. The point is crucial: cinematic inventiveness must grow out of an attitude to people, and in the form of a preoccupation with the medium. Grant that Hitchcock was a chilling man; his style fitted him perfectly. Kubrick's style, however, is meretricious, fussy, and detachable.

The ridiculous labor of *2001*, the cavernous sets, and the special lenses, ride upon a half-baked notion of the origins and purpose of life that a first-year student ought to have been ashamed of. But this message in a bottle lasts over three hours, and the movie has long sequences of directorial self-indulgence. One marvels at the trite sensibilities tickled by the use of the two Strausses—as silly as the effects of some instant TV program—amid so much ultimate philosophizing and so many interminable shots of notional machines.

Kubrick treats computers in the way Sternberg did Dietrich. The comparison that comprehensively diminishes 2001 is with *Metropolis*. *2001* is immeasurably more educated, not just in terms of the secret of existence, but because *Metropolis* is a childlike film. But all the inventiveness of *Metropolis*—as outstanding in its day as the budget of *2001*—is subordinated to the human aspect of the film. *Metropolis* is about society and it still resounds with the clash of anger at authority and hope for the future. Beside it, *2001* looks like an elaborate, academic toy, made slow to seem important and to divert attention from its vacuity.

2001 also made clear Kubrick's defects as a storyteller. This was a real loss, the result of narrative instinct submitting to intellectual pretensions. Initially, in *Killer's Kiss* and *The Killing*, Kubrick had been able to tell stories well enough, even if full of melodramatic punch and slick connections. But *Lolita* and *Dr. Strangelove* illustrated the gradual disparagement of narrative in an effort to achieve the blend of visual gaudiness and thematic load to which Kubrick aspires. *2001* is all implications and no story, whereas Kubrick's *Lolita* had been all story and not a trace of style, mood, or flavor. That love story to America was ruinously shot in England.

But the most striking evidence of Kubrick's faltering narrative is *A Clockwork Orange*. Despite its set-piece outrages, that film is uncertain how to develop narrative and pusillanimous in its attitude to violence. Anthony Burgess's novel is far more barbed because it avoids Kubrick's digression into the inane task of inventing the future with wide-angle lenses and art direction. Whereas *Alphaville* is based soundly on the way the world is already the future in the mind of a visionary, Kubrick thumps home his fearsomely clever sets and his shamelessly borrowed wide-angle views. Indeed, he has always been eclectic, especially given to imitation of Welles. But whereas *Kane*'s wide angles are the distortions of a man's soul, in *Clockwork Orange* they assist the obscene prettiness of set after set. The vulgar baroque of Kubrick's mind lies in his reluctance to let a plain or simple shot pass under his name. The consequences of an art director's cinema are rampant in *A Clockwork Orange*, as witness the condescension in the design of Alex's parents' home.

As for the philosophy of *A Clockwork Orange*, it is journalistic and tacked on. Its halfhearted suggestion that there is a relationship between watching violence in films and coming to terms with it is derisory beside Hitchcock's forty-year analysis of voyeurism. And it should be noted that *A Clockwork Orange* is a portrait of the future infused with reactionary fear, cowardly about thug violence or a serious analysis of its causes, and schizophrenically able to prettify it as a means of wishful condemnation. (Evidently, Kubrick has mixed feelings about *Clockwork Orange*. In

Britain, where he controls the movie, he has forbidden screenings after what seemed like a copy-cat killing.)

The Shining, for me, is Kubrick's one great film, so rich and comic that it offsets his several large failures. The elements of horror story have been turned into a study of isolation, space, and the susceptible imagination of a man who lacks the skills to be a writer. *The Shining* is about intuitive intimations, good or bad, and it has an intriguingly detached view of its story's apparent moral situation. Perhaps Jack Torrance is a monster, a dad run amok; perhaps family is the suffocation that anyone should dread. The film is very funny (especially as Nicholson goes over his edge), serenely frightening, and endlessly interesting. For the Overlook Hotel is not just a great set but a museum of movies, waiting for ghostly inhabitants.

Full Metal Jacket, however, was an abomination, obsessively disciplined, and striving to make a Vietnam in English locations. It is the sort of film Mr. Torrance might have made.

Kubrick died with *Eyes Wide Shut* finished but not yet open, so he was spared dire reviews, public dismay, and even the pained feelings of Cruise and Kidman. To my mind the film is a travesty, but Kubrick was always a "master" who knew too much about film and too little about life—and it shows.

Lev Kuleshov (1899–1970),
b. Tambov, Russia

1918: *Proekt Inzhenera Praita/Engineer Prite's Project*. 1919: *Pesn Lyubvi Nedopetaya* (codirected with Vitold Polonsky). 1920: *Na Krasnom Frontye/On the Red Front*. 1924: *Neobychainye Priklucheniya Mistera Vesta v Stranye Bolshevikov/The Extraordinary Adventures of Mr. West in the Land of the Bolsheviks*. 1925: *Luch Smerti/The Death Ray*. 1926: *Po Zakonu/By the Law*. 1927: *Vasha Znakomaya; Parovoz No. B 100*. 1929: *Veselaya Kanareika; Dva-Buldi-Dva* (codirected with Nina Agadzhanova-Shutko). 1931: *Sorok Serdets*. 1933: *Gortzont/Horizon; Velikii Uteshitel/The Great Consoler*. 1940: *Sibiryaki*. 1941: *Sluchai v Vulkanye*. 1942: *Klyatva Timura*. 1944: *My s Urala*.

Somewhere in a work of reference, the author should own up to a sheltered life: I have seen not one of Lev Kuleshov's films. Not all of Kuleshov's work can have survived in any form; from the mid-1930s onward he was out of favor in Russia, condemned by his own obligatory confession; several of his films, made on secondhand or inferior Russian stock, may now be scarcely visible. Yet Kuleshov has a place both as theoretician and as director. Much of his life was spent in film education, and our haphazard gatherings from his books, his films, his influence on other Russian directors, and the story of his life suggest a brave, unpredictable man, and a Russian director of rare originality.

In his youth, he studied painting at the School of Painting, Architecture and Sculpture and it was only by chance that he took a job as a set designer for Evgeni Bauer. That whetted his appetite for direction: his first film, *Engineer Prite's Project,* was made in the first months of the Revolution. In this period of analytical, creative fervor, Kuleshov turned into a film didact. Above all, he was struck by the implications of montage. On *Engineer Prite* he had noticed that a shot of a man looking, followed by a shot of another person, a place, or a building, suggested that the man was looking at that person or place.

By 1919, Kuleshov was teaching at the State Film School and conducting his famous experiments to extend the theory of montage. These included the shot of Mosjukhin intercut with shots of objects of quite different emotional values. He concluded, fairly enough, that the fickle face lent itself to those different objects with equal ease. In fact, Mosjukhin's face had been expressionless, but Kuleshov soon saw that montage was often more powerful than human expressiveness, and that audiences interpreted facial expressions as if they were codified. This relates Kuleshov to the cinema of, among others, Godard, where it is admitted that film helps us to see how far we always interpret expressions and gestures.

Kuleshov also liked experiments that cut together shots of people in far-flung locations. He stated that, if the grammar or dynamics of cutting was fluent, then the celluloid spatial relationship—he called it "artificial landscape" or "creative geography"—was more important than real space. His stress on that seems to me wrongheaded, but it is clearly a useful theory when dealing with Hitchcock and Fritz Lang, directors who often relate people by means of editing. Indeed, Hitchcock's obtrusive back projections cry out for the label "creative geography."

Kuleshov's own films—or those made in the period 1924–34—sound worth seeing. Originally, it was the cross-cutting of Griffith and Sennett comedy that had aroused him. And his own films show an interest in American subjects and some indifference to revolutionary conventions. *Mr. West in the Land of the Bolsheviks* was a comedy in the American style, as well as a view of Russia to correct American misunderstandings. *The Death Ray* is like a Mabuse story, with rival gangs and a much more violent melodrama than is usual in Russian cinema. *By the Law* is from a Jack London story set in the Yukon, in which a couple of prospectors attempt to execute a criminal they have tried. A simple evocation of landscape, community, and the moral melodrama of a lonely pio-

neer taking the law into his own hands, it also concentrated on a few characters drawn in depth—one of them played by Kuleshov's wife, Alexandra Khokhlova.

Theorizing had led Kuleshov to draw up a comprehensive but rigid code of "signs" to be conveyed by actors. This is something like an alphabet of responses, a system that any viewer might often conclude was implicit in cinema, but that has awful dangers as a method taught to actors. Kuleshov's teaching was all the more important because in the early 1920s Russia was so short of film stock that he acted out stories, as if they were being filmed, rather than expose film. Add to that his belief that, in montage, actors needed to know the scheme of editing and to emote almost by number, and it is easy to see the evolution of a stylized method that was exposed by the naturalism of sound.

Kuleshov never seems to have come to terms with this. But his later films still sound fascinating. *Horizon* is a Mr. West in reverse: the story of a Russian Jew who emigrates to America, is disappointed by what he finds, and returns to a Russia now Sovietized. *The Great Consoler,* however, is by far his most ambitious work. It deals with the period in which W. S. Porter (O. Henry) was in prison, and blends his life with the material of some of his stories. Of necessity, it does this to teach Porter the need for commitment, but in its mixture of fact and fiction it may prove worthy of greater attention.

That is effectively the end of Kuleshov's output. In 1935 he was denounced by Stalinist forces and obliged to recant. His only other films were for children. But in 1944, and on Eisenstein's recommendations, he was made head of the Moscow Film Institute, a teaching position he retained to the end of his life.

Akira Kurosawa (1910–98), b. Tokyo
1943: *Sugata Sanshiro* (in two parts). 1944: *Ichiban Utsukushiku.* 1945: *Zoku Sugata Sanshiro; Tora No-o/They Who Tread on the Tiger's Tail.* 1946: *Asu o Tsukuru Hitobito* (codirected with Kajiro Yamamoto and Hideo Segikawa); *Waga Seishun ni Kuinashi.* 1947: *Subarashiki Nichiyobi.* 1948: *Yoidore Tenshi/Drunken Angel.* 1949: *Shizukanaru Ketto; Nora Inu.* 1950: *Shuban; Rashomon.* 1951: *Hakuchi/The Idiot.* 1952: *Ikiru/Living.* 1954: *Shichinin no Samurai/Seven Samurai.* 1955: *Ikimono no Kiroku.* 1957: *Kumonosu jo/Throne of Blood; Donzoko/The Lower Depths.* 1958: *Kakushi Toride no San-Akunin/The Hidden Fortress.* 1960: *Warui Yatsu Hodo Yoku Nemuru/The Bad Sleep Well.* 1961: *Yojimbo.* 1962: *Tsubaki Sanjuro/Sanjuro.* 1963: *Tengoku to Jigoku/High and Low.* 1965: *Akahige/Red Beard.* 1970: *Dodeskaden.* 1975: *Dersu Uzala.* 1980: *Kagemusha.* 1985: *Ran.* 1990: *Akira Kurosawa's Dreams.* 1991:

Hachigatsu no Kyohshikyoku/Rhapsody in August.
1993: *Madadayo.*

The current awareness of Japanese cinema in the
West began with Kurosawa, even if he has now
been surpassed. The success of *Rashomon* at
Venice in 1951 ushered in Mizoguchi and Ozu,
directors who had been working some twenty
years before Kurosawa's debut. On the art-house
circuit, *Living, Seven Samurai,* and *Throne of
Blood* had enormous appeal. Such variety—a
deeply humane study of a bureaucrat dying in
modern Japan, a stirring samurai epic, an ingenious fusion of Noh and *Macbeth*—could hardly
be argued against. It is possible that *Rashomon*
was shrewdly aimed at Western audiences; time
has revealed Kurosawa as the director most alert
to Western art and American cinema in particular.
Despite his appetite for disparate subjects in the
1950s, his period films look insubstantial against
Mizoguchi's, just as *Rashomon*'s debate on truth is
trite beside *Ugetsu.* As to the contemporary
Japanese experience, Kurosawa now trails behind
a new generation.

But Kurosawa's legend is still very potent in the
West. Pictures he made as tributes to American
genres were slavishly remade in this country. In
1989, two of his great fans, Steven Spielberg and
George Lucas, presented him with an honorary
Oscar for "accomplishments that have inspired,
delighted, enriched and entertained audiences
and influenced filmmakers throughout the world."
He got a best director nomination for *Ran,* which,
like *Kagemusha,* played to large, respectful audiences in the West, unable to see that Kurosawa's
former dynamism had turned toward pageantry
and procession. Few in the West knew, or cared,
that his films were not popular in Japan.

Significantly, he trained to be a painter at a
Western art school; similarly, Shinobu Hashimoto,
the scriptwriter of *Rashomon* and *Seven Samurai,*
has confessed that *Stagecoach* is his favorite film.
It is not surprising that *Seven Samurai* was
remade by Hollywood because it was already close
to the Western in its use of an elite body of brave
warriors, a slow preparation for violent action, and
the generally pusillanimous civilian population—
like the townspeople in *High Noon. Seven Samurai* is as exciting as a good Western: its leading
characters are distinct and appealing; the situation
is contrived but compelling; the action is shot with
virtuoso skill. But it is almost twice as long as a
good Western, and its social theme—that the
samurai are disapproved of by the village they
protect—is made monotonously.

It is this unexpected knowingness that was
most startling about Kurosawa and that most limits him. *Rashomon* is a simpleminded proof of an
idea that informs many films. At that period of
his career, Kurosawa was visually inventive, but

Rashomon is as obvious as it sounds in synopsis.
Whereas, *Ugetsu* simply incorporates the principle that people see events differently—as, incidentally, do *Strangers on a Train, Exodus, Citizen
Kane,* and many other films less struck by the
mock-parable idea of variable truths. *The Idiot* is
intriguing in that it is Dostoyevsky, transposed
with pointless ingenuity to Japan. In the same
way, *Throne of Blood* is doggedly echoing of *Macbeth,* as Oriental as a travel agent's window;
Welles's *Macbeth,* ramshackle and cheapscape, is
a more tragic film.

Kurosawa's eminence led in the late 1950s to
his forming his own production company. *The Bad
Sleep Well,* his first independent venture, was
based on Ed McBain and it was enjoyable for the
way Warner Brothers of the 1940s was turned into
Tokyo 1960. But the contrivance was weird and
unsettling. Kurosawa's suicide attempt in 1971
speaks for an anguish that might be deduced from
a survey of his career, but which has only rarely
been expressed in the films, as in *Drunken Angel.
Living,* his best film, seems as much in debt to de
Sica and Zavattini as his samurai films are to Ford,
but there for once a troubled personality spoke
out.

The late Kurosawa films—*Kagemusha* and
Ran, especially—have enshrined the director in
many Western eyes. Of course, they are elegant
and spectacular films; there is no doubt about
who made them. Yet if an American director
proved so content to film nothing but battles and
their context, there would be eyebrows raised.
Kurosawa is a superb handler of action, and especially of crowds in action. He has a taste for
moody place and heroic character like that of the
illustrator N. C. Wyeth. I was tough on him once.
But I was tough only to ask viewers to see that
Ozu and Mizoguchi were his masters. And they
still are.

Emir Kusturica, b. Sarajevo, Yugoslavia, 1955
1981: *Sjecas li se, Dolly Bell/Do You Remember
Dolly Bell?.* 1985: *Onc Na Sluzbenom Putu/When
Father Was Away on Business.* 1988: *Dom Za
Vesanje/Time of the Gypsies.* 1993: *Arizona
Dream.* 1995: *Underground.* 1998: *Crna Macka,
Beli Macor/Black Cat, White Cat.* 2001: *Super 8
Stories* (d).

The Kusturica of *Underground* and *Black Cat,
White Cat* is hard to take, for an exceptional talent
seems to be whipping itself out of control. But
that may only be the response of relative cultural
stability beholding the many recent ordeals of the
Balkans. To put it another way: in his first two
movies—about coming of age and then, in *When
Father . . . ,* a child's dazed view of bureaucracy
and worse—Kusturica appeared to possess the
shapely irony and battered humanism that make

life comfortable for the customers of art-house cinemas in those countries that are not being bombed or cleansed. Or not so as you'd notice, or feel the hurt.

When Father Was Away on Business won the Palme d'Or at Cannes, and it got an Oscar nomination for best foreign film. All because of ways in which it was digestible, and not alien. But that Kusturica has blown himself up. Has he broken down, or gone crazy? Or has he simply found the assurance or horror to act out the fearful energies and real chaos for which irony is no medicine?

Time of the Gypsies may have been the turning point in that it was a willful departure—Kusturica is not Gypsy; he hardly grasped the language of his own film; and the style—whether magic realism or indulgent fantasy—lunged towards confusion. Or was it *Arizona Dream,* the bizarre encounter with Americana, well acted (by Faye Dunaway, Johnny Depp, and Jerry Lewis) but increasingly private, and so far from Arizona's understanding?

Underground and *Black Cat, White Cat* are very spectacular: indeed, there is the feeling of having all of film's possible or far-fetched elements thrown at one. Such dynamics have their admirers. But the essence grows thinner as the maelstrom becomes more contrived and angry. It's as if Kusturica now takes madness and the intolerable burden of the artist for granted. Yet such things are usually more affecting if they appear as surprises.

More recently, Kusturica acted—with power— as the man who is to be hanged in *The Widow of St. Pierre* (00, Patrice Leconte).

Machiko Kyo, b. Osaka, Japan, 1924
Knowledgeable moviegoers in the West were always aware of serious "foreign" film. They knew the Odessa steps, the frenzy of *Metropolis,* the baker's wife, and the bicycle thief. But although a very few movies were imported from Japan during the thirties, the great twenty-five-year tradition of Japanese film was unknown until it sprang, fully grown, from the head of Akira Kurosawa with his 1950 *Rashomon,* which won the Grand Prize at Venice in 1951. It also introduced a new actress to the West—Machiko Kyo, who played the wife. In 1953, two movies built on *Rashomon*'s success— *Ugetsu* (53, Kenji Mizoguchi) and *Gate of Hell* (53, Teinosuke Kinugasa)—and both featured Kyo. In *Ugetsu,* especially, as the ghost princess, she had a sensual languor that was both magical and sinister.

So Western introductions to Japanese film were automatically linked to our view of Kyo—always in period costume, always seductive, mysterious, and gently easing away that Western prejudice: that Asian women could not be erotic or attractive. Ironically, Kyo was probably more publicized than valued in Japan during this period—she had

begun as a dancer and in 1949 was given the full starlet treatment, the first Japanese actress to go the route of cheesecake and sex appeal.

This all led to her appearance with Marlon Brando in *The Teahouse of the August Moon* (56, Daniel Mann)—if only it could have been in *Sayonara!.* But her career was revitalized in Japan because of Western respect—it *had* begun to fade. Now there was no stopping her, and in all she has made over ninety films—as *Yang Kwei Fei* (55, Mizoguchi); out of period clothes as a defiant young prostitute in Mizoguchi's last film, *Street of Shame* (56); erotic, ambiguous, and deadly in Ichikawa's *Odd Obsession* (59), based on Junichiro Tanizaki's novel *The Key,* and one of four films for Ichikawa; effective as the leading lady of the theatre company in *Floating Weeds* (59)—the only film she made for Ozu. She worked once for Naruse, in *Older Brother, Younger Sister* (53); and more frequently for other leading directors— Kozaburo Yoshimura, Daisuke Ito, and, notably, Shiro Toyoda, in *Sweet Sweat* (64).

Though her range extended, she never lost her compelling sexual glamour—the seductive walk, the heavily lidded eyes, the inviting lips. But always in our mind's eye there is the secret, provocative expression of that sensual face, framed in the cascade of black hair, which riveted us in *Rashomon.* How far did that breakthrough owe its success to Kyo's resemblance to our femmes fatales and to *Rashomon*'s very persuasive evidence that women were not to be trusted? That paranoia is vital to world cinema.

L

Neil LaBute, b. Detroit, Michigan, 1963
1997: *In the Company of Men.* 1998: *Your Friends & Neighbors.* 2000: *Nurse Betty; Bash: Latterday Plays* (TV). 2002: *Possession.*

The titles of Neil LaBute's first two films were sometimes assaulted as cunning, or poker-faced, tricks to lure innocent viewers into his uniquely chilling way of observing a group. As if there were innocent viewers any longer! Some shrank from LaBute (it was pointed out with horror that he was a graduate of Brigham Young University and therefore . . . a Mormon?). A few others observed that the misanthropy went with a very cool directorial hand, observant writing, and fine playing. It made one wonder what Fritz Lang might have done with *Friends.*

LaBute is first of all a writer: he absorbs talk (like someone released from deafness) and the helpless ways it betrays us. He also seems to see everyone as a helpless, unpaid actor. His pose as a director is what is special: the detachment; the unwillingness to scold malice, wickedness, or unkindness; and the subsequent, quite casual suggestion that we sort it out. There is also a steady development in his work—after all, who could have guessed that the "nasty" setup in *In the Company of Men* would lead to the good-natured panorama of *Nurse Betty*?

Your Friends and Neighbors rose to nearly intolerable heights (in the Jason Patric performance—which was bravura but actually rather blunter than LaBute usually permits). I think there is a big future here, and I find it startling and exciting that he is now doing A. S. Byatt's novel *Possession*. Not suitable? Maybe. But suppose that LaBute is learning who he is slowly, at a pace he recommends to us?

Gregory La Cava (1892–1952),
b. Towanda, Pennsylvania

1921: *His Nibs.* 1924: *The New School Teacher; Restless Wives.* 1925: *Womanhandled.* 1926: *Let's Get Married; Say It Again; So's Your Old Man.* 1927: *The Gay Defender; Paradise for Two; Running Wild; Tell It to Sweeney.* 1928: *Feel My Pulse; Half a Bride.* 1929: *Big News; Saturday's Children.* 1930: *His First Command.* 1931: *Laugh and Get Rich; Smart Woman.* 1932: *Symphony of Six Million; The Age of Consent; The Half-Naked Truth.* 1933: *Gabriel Over the White House; Bed of Roses; Gallant Lady.* 1934: *The Affairs of Cellini; What Every Woman Knows.* 1935: *Private Worlds; She Married Her Boss.* 1936: *My Man Godfrey.* 1937: *Stage Door.* 1939: *Fifth Avenue Girl.* 1940: *Primrose Path.* 1941: *Unfinished Business.* 1942: *Lady in a Jam.* 1947: *Living in a Big Way.*

Trained as a political cartoonist, La Cava wrote scripts for comedy shorts before being given the chance to direct. Most of his silent pictures were made at Paramount, including five Richard Dix films and two W. C. Fields pictures—*So's Your Old Man* and *Running Wild* (Fields and La Cava were drinking buddies).

Some said La Cava drank on the set, and that he was a rebel. He didn't like studio authority, and he could easily turn indignant over social conditions in the 1930s. Yet he loathed Roosevelt and liberal solutions. Actors loved working with him, and he had a manner that could let careful preparation seem spontaneous. He is a terrific comedy director, but—as James Harvey has pointed out—with an edge of disquiet, or anger, even. That edge is very important to *My Man Godfrey*, one of the greatest of comedies, but with many shivery insights, social and personal, and a true sense of a daft paradise ready to topple over the brink. Its theme plainly fascinated La Cava, for *Fifth Avenue Girl* (a lesser film) is the same story, with a woman (Ginger Rogers) in the Godfrey role.

Equally, despite Selznick's heavy and sweet hand, *Symphony of Six Million* is moved by a city of painful contrasts, and *Gabriel Over the White House*—with Walter Huston as a crooked president who sees the light—plays with dangerous elements.

Stage Door and *The Half-Naked Truth* are wonderful entertainments (Morrie Ryskind was a writer on *Stage Door,* and he was on *Godfrey,* too). *The Primrose Path* has Ginger Rogers as a girl from the wrong side of the tracks in love with the decent Joel McCrea. *What Every Woman Knows* (from J. M. Barrie) has Helen Hayes sorting out her dim husband's political career. In general, La Cava delighted in struggles of moral intelligence between men and women. *She Married Her Boss* is a model title and attitude for La Cava films, and it was written by Sidney Buchman, but it is rather dull.

It's ironic, in view of his critical eye on America, that he lost his way when war came. He was invariably good with actors, and I would guess that the answer to his ups and downs lies in his relations with actors. Allan Scott (who was on *Fifth Avenue Girl* and *Primrose Path*) has said that La Cava mulled over many versions of a scene before giving actors their pages an hour before the camera rolled.

La Cava is still underrated. *My Man Godfrey* gets smarter as we revive its age of contrasts.

Alan Ladd (1913–64),
b. Hot Springs, Arkansas

As a child, he moved to California and excelled at athletics and diving. Even so, he grew no higher than five feet six inches and remained blond, blue-eyed, and more serene than other leading men. It was more than Universal, his first Hollywood employer, could stomach, and Ladd stayed on the fringes of "The Day of the Locust" world from 1932 onward. He appeared in *The Goldwyn Follies*, worked on radio, was credited in *Once in a Lifetime* (32, Russell Mack); *Pigskin Parade* (36, David Butler); *Souls at Sea* (37, Henry Hathaway); *Come On, Leathernecks* (38, James Cruze); *Rulers of the Sea* (39, Frank Lloyd); and he is a shadowy presence at the end of *Citizen Kane,* one of the several reporters packing up, pipe in mouth, hands in pockets, who says: "Or Rosebud." The stance and the voice are inimitably Ladd, so that one can imagine him simply waiting for Gregg Toland's low key to lift like the morning mist.

In fact, he was rescued by Sue Carol, an actress turned agent whom he later married, and in 1942 he had a first success in *Joan of Paris* (Robert Stevenson). Then, in a touch of Hollywood's haphazard genius, Paramount cast him opposite Veronica Lake as the hired killer in *This Gun for Hire* (42, Frank Tuttle) and as Hammett's man who walks alone in *The Glass Key* (42, Stuart

Heisler). Although in life they did not get on, in films their miniature blond(e) embraces seemed to define visual harmony. Once Ladd had acquired an unsmiling hardness, he was transformed from an extra to a phenomenon. These films are still exciting, and Ladd's calm slender ferocity make it clear that he was the first American actor to show the killer as a cold angel. He had a great voice, too, deeper than one expected.

For some ten years, Ladd was a prolific middle-rank star. His partnership with Lake was continued in *The Blue Dahlia* (46, George Marshall) and *Saigon* (48, Lesley Fenton). As well as making several films for John Farrow—*China* (43); *Two Years Before the Mast* (46); *Calcutta* (47); and *Beyond Glory* (48)—he made *Lucky Jordan* (42, Tuttle); *And Now Tomorrow* (44, Irving Pichel); *Salty O'Rourke* (45, Raoul Walsh); *OSS* (46, Pichel); *Wild Harvest* (47, Tay Garnett); and *Captain Carey USA* (50, Mitchell Leisen).

But by the end of the 1940s Ladd was slipping: he was not happy in *The Great Gatsby* (49, Elliott Nugent), and his action films were no longer major attractions: *Whispering Smith* (48, Fenton); *Chicago Deadline* (49, Lewis Allen); *Branded* (50, Rudolph Maté); and *Red Mountain* (51, William Dieterle). His single most successful part—as *Shane* (53, George Stevens)—came when Paramount had already lost interest in him, and was a nostalgic reference to his violent past. *Shane* has endured, no matter the mystery of the slender Ladd beating bigger men. It is both his gentlest film, and the one in which his lethal grace is most paternal. He seems like a ghost in the picture.

He remained a leading man in less important adventure films at Warners and Universal: *The Iron Mistress* (52, Gordon Douglas); *Botany Bay* (53, Farrow); *The Black Knight* (54, Garnett); *Saskatchewan* (54, Walsh); *Hell on Frisco Bay* (55, Tuttle); *The Big Land* (57, Douglas); *The Proud Rebel* (58, Michael Curtiz); and *The Badlanders* (58, Delmer Daves).

But he missed better parts and refused Stevens's offer of the James Dean role in *Giant*. As he grew older, his face puffed up, there were frequent stories about him having to stand on a box during love scenes—which once would have been irrelevant—and he developed an alcohol problem. In 1962, he tried to kill himself and after a last memorable performance—as the cowboy movie star in *The Carpetbaggers* (64, Edward Dmytryk)—he died as a result of alcohol and sedative poisoning.

His son from a first marriage—Alan Ladd Jr.—would come to be a leading executive at many studios.

Carl Laemmle (1867–1939),
b. Laupheim, Germany
As I write about Laemmle I have lit a cigar. My mouth is clamped around it in a theatrical sneer that signals a robust mogul's scorn of nicety. Laemmle is the authentic Cuddles Sakall mobster, a founding father of this great art, and a sweet mixture of idiot, rogue, and lucky. If you sometimes retreat in amazement and exhaustion from Michael Snow and Christian Metz, think of Uncle Carl. For it was in his outfit that one scrambling huckster noted that the movie business "takes less brains than anything else in the world." Big puff on fat cigar: the uncomplicated smoke of commercial mayhem may yet make rings round theoretical arguments.

Laemmle was born before every other American movie mogul. He was nearly forty before he thought of the picture business, yet he was the quickest dealer you could ask for. At this distance, it is hard to believe that he didn't regard the movies as a lot of fun. To this day, his studio, Universal, maintains a no-nonsense line in entertaining goods.

Carl was Jewish, the son of a poor property agent. He came to America when he was seventeen and settled in the Chicago area, working as a store clerk and in the stockyards. His prospects brightened when he joined a clothing store, married the owner's niece in 1898, and was promoted to manager. Eight years later, he got restless and took a notion to open a nickelodeon in Chicago. That was 1906, and the site was the Whitefront Theatre.

He expanded rapidly and started his own film service to provide for the Midwest chain that grew up around him. Thus he came into conflict with the Motion Picture Patents Company, and became one of the leading and most enterprising "independents" in the struggle against their monopoly. That crusade was a blithe alliance of outraged ethics and provoked envy: the pursuit of happiness is a race for the strongest. Laemmle never felt shy of using Justice as a business weapon.

There were hundreds of legal actions, protection and assault, scurrilous press campaigns, operations in, through, and under the law. Amid all the row, Laemmle started producing his own pictures. In 1909, he formed the Independent Motion Picture Company and that soon built up an empire as great as the Patents Company's. In 1912, the IMP itself split, and as Harry Aitken went his way so Laemmle defied retrenchment by naming himself Universal. Laemmle won the battle against monopoly, which was a key stage in the development of the industry. But in winning, he appropriated the gravy, the coarseness, and the methods fashioned by monopoly for the powers that would become the Hollywood majors. Laemmle himself moved to the Los Angeles area and in 1915 Universal City was opened as the first substantial picture factory in California.

Laemmle was a businessman at a stage of movie history when some of the most creative acts were commercial. He was a little man in a fancy suit, lovable and a buffoon when he chose, a little Caesar when he had to be. One story alleges that Lewis Selznick simply infiltrated Laemmle's intrigue-filled office, set up an executive desk with his name on it, and got to be general manager before anyone realized he'd never been hired. Which makes Laemmle out to be a classic bumbler. But it was the same Laemmle who, in 1909, stole "The Biograph Girl" away from Biograph, billed her as Florence Lawrence, and crystallized the phenomenon of identifiable stars. He won over Mary Pickford with the same insight. And, more significantly, he gave a kid called Irving Thalberg a job as a secretary and then put him in charge of the studio when he went to Germany on war-relief expeditions.

Laemmle's later years were only half spent at the studio that would cast him adrift in 1936. He was distressed at Germany's plight after the war, and just as moved by the thought that his charity might get a Nobel Peace Prize. Universal was often left to Thalberg and Laemmle's own son. Nevertheless, it is the studio that launched von Stroheim, Lon Chaney, the American horror film, and the woman's picture—as opposed to the lady's picture offered by MGM. Universal was often on the cheap side: horror is a spectacle in which darkness saves money and creates menace. It was neither pretentious nor pompous. It was a place where mavericks like James Whale could work, and it was in Carl Laemmle's day that the studio made *Blind Husbands* (19, von Stroheim); *Foolish Wives* (21, von Stroheim); *White Tiger* (23, Tod Browning); *The Hunchback of Notre Dame* (23, Wallace Worsley); *The Phantom of the Opera* (25, Rupert Julian); *The Goose Woman* (25, Clarence Brown); *The Cat and the Canary* (27, Paul Leni); *The Man Who Laughs* (28, Leni); *All Quiet on the Western Front* (30, Lewis Milestone); *Frankenstein* (31, James Whale); *Dracula* (31, Browning); *The Mummy* (32, Karl Freund); *Back Street* (32, John M. Stahl); *The Old Dark House* (32, Whale); *Imitation of Life* (34, Stahl); *Bride of Frankenstein* (35, Whale); *The Good Fairy* (35, William Wyler); and *My Man Godfrey* (36, Gregory La Cava).

Veronica Lake (Constance Frances Marie Ockelman) (1919–73), b. Brooklyn, New York
Lake was the daughter of a German-Danish seaman. After beauty contests and drama school, she was taken on by RKO—as Constance Keane—made her debut in John Farrow's *Sorority House* (39), and struggled against mass femininity in *All Women Have Secrets* (39, Kurt Neumann) and *Forty Little Mothers* (40, Busby Berkeley). Her

name changed, she was put under contract by Paramount after Mitchell Leisen's *I Wanted Wings* (41), and then established herself in four striking films: *Sullivan's Travels* (41, Preston Sturges); *This Gun for Hire* (42, Frank Tuttle) and *The Glass Key* (42, Stuart Heisler), both opposite Alan Ladd; and *I Married a Witch* (42, René Clair).

Petite, silky, and lurking behind the half curtain of her own blonde hair, she was a face in the dreams of American soldiers. But her hairstyle was so imitated by their girlfriends bending over factory machines that the government asked for her hair to be pulled back for the part of a military nurse in Mark Sandrich's *So Proudly We Hail* (43). She next played a Nazi spy in *The Hour Before the Dawn* (44, Tuttle)—a hint perhaps that her star was waning, made explicit when Paramount put her opposite the declining Eddie Bracken in three movies.

She made more films with Ladd—*Duffy's Tavern* (45, Hal Walker), *The Blue Dahlia* (46, George Marshall), and *Saigon* (48, Lesley Fenton)—but her fame did not really survive the war and the prohibition on her looks. She made *Miss Susie Slagle's* (46, John Berry) and two films for her second husband, André de Toth—*Ramrod* (47) and *Slattery's Hurricane* (49)—but after *Stronghold* (51, Steve Sekely) she filed for bankruptcy. She went first into the theatre and was rediscovered by the press as a waitress in Manhattan. Her comebacks never took, least of all two more movies, *Footsteps in the Snow* (66, Martin Green) and *Flesh Feast* (70, B. F. Grinter), partly because she was hardly recognizable as the dry, satin, delectable moll on Ladd's arm—two tiny people in their own world.

Hedy Lamarr (Hedwig Eva Maria Kiesler) (1913–2000), b. Vienna
She deserted school for the stage and the film studios and made her debut in *Stürm in Wasserglas* (31, Georg Jacoby). After *Die Koffer des Herrn O.F.* (31, Alexis Granowsky) and *Man Braucht Kein Geld* (31, Carl Boese), she won notoriety by appearing nude in a woodland idyll in the Czech film *Extase* (32) directed by Gustav Machaty.

The fleeting, dappled nakedness of that film sustained her misleading reputation, just as her euphonious new name, on Bob Hope's lips, say, was enough to get a laugh. *Extase* won her a millionaire husband, Fritz Mandl, who supported Hitler, and made enough munitions to become an Honorary Aryan. He also tried to buy up or ban all prints of *Extase*. Hedwig left him and went to London, where she met Louis B. Mayer. He signed her up, but warned her she could make only decent films in America. And so she came west, perhaps as beautiful as any woman ever filmed, but nearly stunned by all the things being said about her, and by her extensive limits as an actress. It became her lot to be cast as exotic, sultry women—and she did her best; but conscientiousness is not quite what we expect in our femmes fatales. Too often, she had a worried look.

Her American debut was on loan to Walter Wanger in John Cromwell's *Algiers* (38). Mayer tried to exploit this initial success by putting her in *Lady of the Tropics* (39, Jack Conway) and *I Take This Woman* (40, W. S. Van Dyke), and Lamarr had a short period of stardom, aping Garbo in *Comrade X* (40, King Vidor), seducing Gable in Conway's *Boom Town* (40), in *Ziegfeld Girl* (41, Robert Z. Leonard) where, incredibly, she saves herself for her husband, and very good in *H. M. Pulham Esq.* (41, Vidor). Her career declined into lightweight seductress roles: *Tortilla Flat* (42, Victor Fleming); *Crossroads* (42, Conway); *White Cargo* (42, Richard Thorpe); *The Heavenly Body* (43, Walter Reisch); *Experiment Perilous* (44, Jacques Tourneur)—which is very like *Gaslight* in story, and makes great play on her enchanting eyes; and *Her Highness and the Bellboy* (45, Thorpe).

Difficult to please, she rejected the Bergman parts in *Casablanca* and *Gaslight* and, at the end of the war, her contract with MGM lapsed. She rehashed sultriness in Edgar G. Ulmer's *The Strange Woman* (46) and *Dishonored Lady* (47, Robert Stevenson) and was close to neglect when in 1949 De Mille cast her as Delilah to Victor Mature's Samson. The result was nonsense redeemed by sheer conviction and the only evidence that Lamarr could convey the promise of sex on the screen. There are glimpses of sentimental wantonness and silly depravity in that film far more entertaining than publicity, or even the subsequent insistence on it in her autobiography, *Ecstasy and Me* (66).

Samson and Delilah barely slowed her decline. After John Farrow's *Copper Canyon* (50), *A Lady Without Passport* (50, Joseph H. Lewis), and an uneasy partnership with Bob Hope in *My Favorite Spy* (51, Norman Z. McLeod), she went to Italy and played Helen of Troy in *L'Amante di Paridi* (54, Marc Allégret). She returned to America for *The Female Animal* (57, Harry Keller), but then sank back on hard times. A few years later she was broke, with more divorces than funds. Her autobiography was a deliberate attempt to revive her own notoriety, in such bad taste that she later sued her own ghostwriters for the imaginative sum of $21 million. But the temple stayed intact.

Dorothy Lamour (Mary Leta Dorothy Kaumeyer) (1914–96), b. New Orleans
In the years when Pacific beaches were the scorched sites of hand-to-hand fighting between Japanese and Americans, Paramount concocted its

own South Sea island on which only a sarong separated Dorothy Lamour from the imaginings of any G.I. And as the filling, Lamour was good value—whether the smooth contents of decent undress or the amused goody squabbled over by Hope and Crosby in the *Road* films. She was a Gauguin girl taught to use lipstick and eye shadow and raised to ride on the subway. In that pose she is recalled with affection, and it was a gross misunderstanding of public taste when the ill-advised *The Road to Hong Kong* (62, Norman Panama) chose to have Joan Collins, instead of Lamour, as its female lead. The proper rebuke was her relaxed, good-natured appearance in *Donovan's Reef* (63, John Ford), still queen in the land of barroom Crusoes.

She began as a singer in nightclubs and on radio before Paramount put her in a sarong as *The Jungle Princess* (36, William Thiele). She played in *College Holiday* (36, Frank Tuttle), *Swing High, Swing Low* (37, Mitchell Leisen), and *High, Wide and Handsome* (37, Rouben Mamoulian) before another island part in *The Hurricane* (37, Ford). She worked steadily in musicals, the *Road* pictures, and Pacific pinups: *Her Jungle Love* (38, George Archainbaud); *Tropic Holiday* (38, Theodore Reed); *Spawn of the North* (38, Henry Hathaway); *St. Louis Blues* (39, Raoul Walsh); *Man About Town* (39, Mark Sandrich); *Disputed Passage* (39, Frank Borzage); *Johnny Apollo* (40, Hathaway); *Road to Singapore* (40, Victor Schertzinger); *Typhoon* (40, Louis King); *Moon Over Burma* (40, King); *Chad Hanna* (40, Henry King); *Road to Zanzibar* (41, Schertzinger); *Caught in the Draft* (41, David Butler); *Aloma of the South Seas* (41, Alfred Santell); *The Fleet's In* (42, Schertzinger); *Beyond the Blue Horizon* (42, Santell); *Road to Morocco* (42, Butler); *They Got Me Covered* (42, Butler); *Dixie* (43, Edward Sutherland); *Riding High* (43, George Marshall); *And the Angels Sing* (44, Marshall); *Rainbow Island* (44, Ralph Murphy); *Road to Utopia* (45, Hal Walker); and *A Medal for Benny* (45, Irving Pichel).

Such a fanciful legend could hardly be sustained in peace, and in the late 1940s her position declined: *Masquerade in Mexico* (45, Leisen); *My Favorite Brunette* (47, Elliott Nugent); *Variety Girl* (47, Marshall); *Wild Harvest* (47, Tay Garnett); *Road to Rio* (47, Norman Z. McLeod); *Lulu Belle* (48, Lesley Fenton); and *Slightly French* (49, Douglas Sirk). She was out of work for some years, returned for *The Greatest Show on Earth* (52, Cecil B. De Mille) and *Road to Bali* (52, Walker), and then retired until the two films of the early 1960s. Since then she has appeared in *Pajama Party* (64, Don Weis) and *Creepshow 2* (87, Michael Gornick).

Burt Lancaster (1913–94), b. New York
Lancaster was educated at New York University.

Well into his sixties, he was still a strapping athlete, his smile piercing, his hand outstretched, but with the hint that his grip could crush or galvanize. His vitality was more than cheerfulness or strength; he seemed charged with power. This accounts for his threatening, polite calm as a villain and coincides with Norman Mailer's comment that he never looked into eyes as chilling as Lancaster's. He seemed softly spoken and attentive, until one noticed the intensity of the gaze. The Oscar for *Elmer Gantry* (60, Richard Brooks) recognized his aptitude for the self-inflaming hype merchant, but *Gantry* is lightweight next to the monstrous J. J. Hunsecker in *Sweet Smell of Success* (57, Alexander Mackendrick), the first heartless titan of corrupt organization in American films, a foreshadowing of Watergate.

Lancaster was a circus acrobat and then on special military service in North Africa and Italy. He was chosen by Mark Hellinger for his debut in *The Killers* (46, Robert Siodmak) and quickly established himself in underworld movies: *I Walk Alone* (47, Byron Haskin); *Brute Force* (47, Jules Dassin); and *Criss Cross* (48, Siodmak). The first sign of his menace came in *Sorry, Wrong Num-ber* (48, Anatole Litvak). He made a few dull movies—*All My Sons* (48, Irving Reis); *Kiss the Blood Off My Hands* (48, Norman Foster); *Rope of Sand* (49, William Dieterle); and *Mister 880* (50, Edmund Goulding)—but circus habits asserted themselves. When Jacques Tourneur's fabulous *The Flame and the Arrow* (50) was released, competitions were organized to guess whether and how Lancaster did his own turret-top stunts.

There was the same Fairbanksian zest in Siodmak's *The Crimson Pirate* (52), and Lancaster never entirely lost his pleasure in physical spectacle: thus, his first direction, *The Kentuckian* (55); *Trapeze* (56, Carol Reed); *The Train* (64, John Frankenheimer); *The Professionals* (66, Brooks); and crawling through suburbia in the bizarre *The Swimmer* (67, Frank Perry). Perhaps because he leaped and tumbled so naturally, it was scarcely noticed that all Lancaster's movements were beautiful.

The key film in his career may have been *Come Back, Little Sheba* (53, Daniel Mann), in which he made himself a middle-aged, perilously reformed alcoholic with such suppressed tension that he eclipsed all Shirley Booth's fluttering as his wife. Now taken seriously, Lancaster played Sergeant Warden in *From Here to Eternity* (53, Fred Zinnemann). But his own production company allowed him to revert to horseplay in *Vera Cruz* (54) and one of his best performances as the renegade Indian in *Apache* (54)—both these films for Robert Aldrich.

At about this time, his screen character began to fluctuate, attempts at honest heroes mingling with sober acting: *The Rainmaker* (56, Joseph Anthony), effortlessly refreshing Katharine Hepburn; a staid Wyatt Earp in *Gunfight at the O.K. Corral* (57, John Sturges); far from his home territory in the Bournemouth of *Separate Tables* (58, Delbert Mann); trying to swashbuckle Shaw in *The Devil's Disciple* (59, Guy Hamilton); *The Unforgiven* (60, John Huston); *The Young Savages* (61, Frankenheimer); *Judgement at Nuremberg* (61, Stanley Kramer); aging cleverly and suggesting the austere obsession of *Birdman of Alcatraz* (62, Frankenheimer); *A Child Is Waiting* (62, John Cassavetes); turning very gracious for *The Leopard* (63, Luchino Visconti), and eerily anticipating godfathers to come; dreaming of a coup in *Seven Days In May* (64, Frankenheimer); *The Hallelujah Trail* (65, Sturges); *The Scalphunters* (68, Sydney Pollack); and *The Gypsy Moths* (69, Frankenheimer).

He seems to have oppressed Frankenheimer's insecure talent, but held together as a major star until a run of shabby pictures: *Airport* (70, George Seaton); *Lawman* (71, Michael Winner); *Valdez Is Coming* (71, Edwin Sherin); and *Scorpio* (72, Winner). However, he came back to form, with Aldrich again, on *Ulzana's Raid* (72), as a brindle-haired scout tracking down just such an Apache as he had himself played eighteen years before; and as a son of Hunsecker in *Executive Action* (73, David Miller).

In 1974, he acted in, produced, and codirected *The Midnight Man*, and then played another major role for Visconti in *Conversation Piece* (74). He also took the lead role in a TV series, *Moses* (75, Gianfranco de Bosio). His Ned Buntline was a fatalistic observer in *Buffalo Bill and the Indians* (76, Robert Altman). He was Shimon Peres in *Victory at Entebbe* (76, Marvin J. Chomsky); *The Cassandra Crossing* (76, George Pan Cosmatos); the rogue General in *Twilight's Last Gleaming* (77, Aldrich); *The Island of Dr. Moreau* (77, Don Taylor); and *Go Tell the Spartans* (78, Ted Post).

He played a British colonel in *Zulu Dawn* (79, Douglas Hickox); *Cattle Annie and Little Britches* (80, Lamont Johnson); and then, one of his greatest roles, Lou Pasco in *Atlantic City* (80, Louis Malle)—suave dandy, chronic beggar, persistent romantic, and gentle old man; *La Pelle* (81, Liliana Cavani); helping *Local Hero* (83, Bill Forsyth) get made; *The Osterman Weekend* (83, Sam Peckinpah); the hapless *Little Treasure* (85, Alan Sharp, who had written *Ulzana's Raid*); as a wicked publisher in *Scandal Sheet* (85, David Lowell Rich) for TV; with Kirk Douglas again in *Tough Guys* (86, Jeff Kanew); as the general rescuing Ross Perot's men in Iran in *On Wings of Eagles* (86, Andrew V. McLaglen); as a German industrialist in *Sins of the Fathers* (86, Bernhard Sinkel); *Control* (87, Giuliano Montaldo); *Rocket Gibraltar* (88, Daniel Petrie); simply legendary in *Field of Dreams* (89, Phil Alden Robinson); as father to *The Phantom of the Opera* (90, Tony Richardson) for TV; *Voyage of Terror—The Achille Lauro Affair* (90, Alberto Negrin); and *Separate But Equal* (91, George Stevens Jr.).

Brave, vigorous, handsome, and an actor of great range, Lancaster never yielded in his immaculate splendor, proud to be a movie actor. He was one of the great stars. Perhaps the last.

Elsa Lanchester (Elizabeth Sullivan)
(1902–86), b. Lewisham, England

She was the daughter of vegetarian pacifist Socialists, and she would be married to one of the great sacred monsters of acting, a neurotic, a homosexual, yet a child who required her steady care and affection. So Elsa Lanchester was, a lot of the time, "Mrs. Charles Laughton," attending to him, on and off screen. Sometimes it was reckoned that she came as part of the Laughton package, worth her weight and her fee because she could handle him when he was otherwise outrageous. Her own inner romantic life may have been diverted by such self-sacrifice, or stopped because of Laughton's innate homosexuality. Not that she disapproved, or really thought of leaving him. But there was something so large and daring in her, something that deserved her own help. Even if it emerged just once, as the hissing, feral, totally sexual *Bride of Frankenstein* (35, James Whale), there was an actress with greatness in her.

As a girl, she studied with Isadora Duncan in Paris, and then opened her own dancing school in London. She attended the Margaret Morris School and started a nightclub, the Cave of Harmony, on Charlotte Street. In short, she was one of the most idiosyncratic and diversely talented performers in London—with spiky red hair, popping eyes, a musical voice, and great intellectual daring. From the start, she was a match for Laughton: they were married in 1927.

Her film debut was in *One of the Best* (27, T. Hayes Hunter); *The Constant Nymph* (28, Adrian Brunel); *Comets* (30, Sasha Geneen); *The Love Habit* (30, Harry Lachman); *The Stronger Sex* (31, Gareth Gundrey); *Potiphar's Wife* (31, Maurice Elvey); *The Officers' Mess* (31, H. Manning Haynes); Anne of Cleves in *The Private Life of Henry VIII* (33, Alexander Korda), her first film with Laughton, though they played on stage in *Mr. Prohack*, in *The Tempest* (she was Ariel to his Prospero), and in *Peter Pan* (he was Hook, she was apparently a rather Hitlerian Peter!).

They then went to Hollywood together, and she played Clickett in *David Copperfield* (35, George Cukor); *Naughty Marietta* (35, W. S. Van Dyke II); and the title role in *Bride of Frankenstein*. She went back to England briefly for *The Ghost Goes West* (36, René Clair); *Rembrandt* (36, Korda); the missionary in *The Beachcomber* (38, Erich Pommer).

Thereafter, the couple were based in the United States, and she appeared in *Ladies in Retirement* (41, Charles Vidor); *Son of Fury* (42, John Cromwell); *Tales of Manhattan* (42, Julian Duvivier), and *Forever and a Day* (43, many directors), both with Laughton; *Lassie Come Home* (43, Fred M. Wilcox); trying to beat Hitler in *Passport to Destiny* (44, Ray McCarey); *The Spiral Staircase* (46, Robert Siodmak); very good in *The Razor's Edge* (46, Edmund Goulding); *Northwest Outpost* (47, Allan Dwan); *The Bishop's Wife* (47, Henry Koster); a comic eccentric artist in *The Big Clock* (48, John Farrow).

She is the maid in *The Secret Garden* (49, Wilcox); she was nominated as supporting actress in *Come to the Stable* (49, Koster); *The Inspector General* (49, Koster); *Buccaneer's Girl* (50, Frederick de Cordova); brilliant as a nosy landlady in *Mystery Street* (50, John Sturges); a gem in *The Petty Girl* (50, Henry Levin); *Frenchie* (50, Louis King); *Dreamboat* (52, Claude Binyon); *Les Misérables* (52, Lewis Milestone); *Androcles and the Lion* (52, Chester Erskine); *The Girls of Pleasure Island* (53, F. Hugh Herbert); *Hell's Half Acre* (54, John H. Auer); *Three Ring Circus* (54, Joseph Pevney); *The Glass Slipper* (55, Charles Walters).

She got a second supporting actress nomination as Miss Plimsoll, with Laughton, in *Witness for the Prosecution* (57, Billy Wilder); funny in *Bell Book and Candle* (58, Richard Quine). Laughton grew ill, and died in 1962, so there was an enforced layoff in Lanchester's career before she returned with *Honeymoon Hotel* (64, Levin); *Mary Poppins* (64, Robert Stevenson); *Pajama Party* (64, Don Weis); *That Darn Cat!* (65, Stevenson); with Elvis in *Easy Come, Easy Go* (67, John Rich); *Blackbeard's Ghost* (68, Stevenson); *Rascal* (69, Norman Tokar); *Me, Natalie* (69, Fred Coe); *Willard* (71, Daniel Mann); *Terror in the Wax Museum* (73, Georg Fenady); *Arnold* (73, Fenady); *Murder by Death* (76, Robert Moore); *Die Laughing* (80, Jeff Werner).

Martin Landau, b. Brooklyn, New York, 1928

Three times, between 1988 and 1994, the dankly enduring Martin Landau was nominated as best supporting actor: for *Tucker* (88, Francis Coppola); as the odious adulterer in *Crimes and Misdemeanors* (89, Woody Allen); and (his winner) as Bela Lugosi in *Ed Wood* (94, Tim Burton). His Lugosi was, beyond dispute, a daunting recreation thrust into the midst of an eccentric movie. It was, as such, rather more assertion than acting. But Landau's Bela did have the side advantage of making one forget the sheer unlikability of Mr. Landau. Perhaps a similar peace descended on the actor himself.

Landau, as he admits, has been around a long time—and not just on TV in *Mission: Impossible*

(1966–69), in which he played with his wife, Barbara Bain. He had been a newspaper cartoonist before becoming an actor, and he is a longtime member of the Actors Studio.

Yes, that is him, as one of the sadistic heavies, "Leonard," in *North by Northwest* (59, Alfred Hitchcock). He has also done *Pork Chop Hill* (59, Lewis Milestone); *The Gazebo* (60, George Marshall); *Stagecoach to Dancer's Rock* (62, Earl Bellamy); *Cleopatra* (63, Joseph L. Mankiewicz); *The Greatest Story Ever Told* (65, George Stevens); *The Hallelujah Trail* (65, John Sturges); *Nevada Smith* (66, Henry Hathaway); *They Call Me Mister Tibbs* (70, Gordon Douglas); *A Town Called Hell* (71, Robert Parrish); *Black Gunn* (72, Robert Hartford-Davis); *Strange Shadows in an Empty Room* (77, Martin Herbert); *Meteor* (79, Ronald Neame); *Without Warning* (80, Greydon Clark); *Alone in the Dark* (82, Jack Sholder); *The Being* (83, Jackie Kong); *Cyclone* (87, Fred Olen Ray); *Sweet Revenge* (87, Martin Sobel); and so to *Tucker.*

Paragraph break to mark a film you've heard of—and some reason for appreciating Landau's teary gratitude for a nomination after all that dross. Then: *Trust Me* (89, Bobby Houston); *Paint It Black* (89, Tim Hunter)—not exactly released; good in *Mistress* (91, Barry Primus); *Sliver* (93, Phillip Noyce); *Intersection* (94, Mark Rydell); *City Hall* (96, Harold Becker); *B.A.P.S* (97, Robert Townsend); *Rounders* (98, John Dahl); *The X-Files* (98, Rob Bowman); *Ed TV* (99, Ron Howard); the old man in *Bonanno: A Godfather's Story* (99, Michael Poulette); Geppetto in *The New Adventures of Pinocchio* (99, Michael Anderson); *Sleepy Hollow* (99, Burton); *Ready to Rumble* (00, Brian Robbins); *Very Mean Men* (00, Tony Vitale); Abraham on TV in *In the Beginning* (00, Kevin Connor); *The Majestic* (01, Frank Darabont).

Diane Lane, b. New York, 1965

Diane Lane is past thirty-five now, and for beautiful actresses who have not quite made it yet, or kept their power, being thirty-five-plus leaves you in hopes of getting a movie like *A Walk on the Moon* (99, Tony Goldwyn), a project too small to afford a major star. So Diane Lane got the chance of the vacationing mother who falls in love with "the blouse man." It was her best role—so much fuller than the "big" parts she got in the 1980s, and it showed how much the actress had learned. And don't forget the beauty, even if it turns out to be the last good movie she gets.

Her parents divorced only days after she was born. But Lane coped and was into pictures as a teenager: famously on a *Time* cover in *A Little Romance* (79, George Roy Hill), with Laurence Olivier; *To Elvis, with Love* (80, Gus Trikonis); with Amanda Plummer in *Cattle Annie and Little*

Britches (80, Lamont Johnson); *National Lampoon Goes to the Movies* (81, Henry Jaglom and Bob Giraldi); *Six Pack* (82, Daniel Petrie); *Ladies and Gentlemen, The Fabulous Stains* (82, Lou Adler); *The Outsiders* (83, Francis Coppola); *Rumble Fish* (83, Coppola); *Streets of Fire* (84, Walter Hill); *The Cotton Club* (84, Coppola).

Then a three-year break before *The Big Town* (87, Ben Bolt); *Lady Beware* (87, Karen Arthur); *Priceless Beauty* (88, Charles Finch), with Christopher Lambert, her husband; *Vital Signs* (90, Marisa Silver); *My New Gun* (92, Stacy Cochran); *Indian Summer* (93, Mike Binder); *Knight Moves* (93, Carl Schenkel); *Judge Dredd* (96, Danny Cannon); *Wild Bill* (95, Hill); *Mad Dog Time* (96, Larry Bishop); *Murder at 1600* (97, Dwight Little); *The Only Thrill* (97, Peter Masterson); *Grace and Glorie* (98, Arthur Allan Seidelman); *The Setting Sun* (99, Tomono Ro); *My Dog Skip* (00, Jay Russell); on TV in *The Virginian* (00, Bill Pullman); *The Perfect Storm* (00, Wolfgang Petersen), grieving from shore; *Hardball* (01, Brian Robbins); *The Glass House* (01, Daniel Sackheim); *Just Like Mona* (01, Joe Pantoliano); still gorgeous in *Unfaithful* (02, Adrian Lyne).

Fritz Lang (1890–1976), b. Vienna
1919: *Halbblut; Der Herr der Liebe; Die Spinnen, part 1: Der Goldene See; Hara-Kiri.* 1920: *Die Spinnen, part 2: Das Brillanten Schiff; Das Wandernde Bild; Vier um die Frau.* 1921: *Der Müde Tod/Destiny.* 1922: *Dr. Mabuse der Spieler, parts 1 and 2.* 1924: *Die Nibelungen, part 1: Siegfried; part 2: Kriemhilds Rache.* 1927: *Metropolis.* 1928: *Spione.* 1929: *Frau im Mond.* 1931: *M.* 1932: *Das Testament des Dr. Mabuse/The Last Will of Dr. Mabuse.* 1933: *Liliom.* 1936: *Fury.* 1937: *You Only Live Once.* 1938: *You and Me.* 1940: *The Return of Frank James.* 1941: *Western Union; Man Hunt.* 1943: *Hangmen Also Die!.* 1944: *The Woman in the Window; The Ministry of Fear.* 1945: *Scarlet Street.* 1946: *Cloak and Dagger.* 1948: *Secret Beyond the Door.* 1950: *House by the River; American Guerrilla in the Philippines/I Shall Return.* 1952: *Rancho Notorious; Clash by Night.* 1953: *The Blue Gardenia; The Big Heat.* 1954: *Human Desire.* 1955: *Moonfleet.* 1956: *While the City Sleeps; Beyond a Reasonable Doubt.* 1959: *Der Tiger von Eschnapur; Das Indische Grabmal.* 1961: *Die Tausend Augen des Dr. Mabuse/The Thousand Eyes of Dr. Mabuse.*

Whether in the futuristic cities constructed at UFA in the 1920s, the uncompromising urban grids made at various American studios in the 1940s and 1950s, or in the mythic fusion of a real and cardboard India, Lang's films all seem to have been made in a time of emergency. No other director so convinces us that melodramatic threat of extinction in the crime movie is the metaphor of a much greater danger. His sound-stage world is a necessary distillation of realism, a sort of concrete martial law imposed upon troubled constitutions. The tension that justifies this imposition is constantly maintained in Lang's relentless narrative pace and in the undeflected observation of fear, anger, joy, and action eating into nerves and morality.

Granted that Lang was trained in an idiom that liked to take three hours over a complex thriller, then it was artistically beneficial that in America he was compelled to cut that length in half. Few other directors gained so much from the commercial concentration of plot length. Lang's determination to film action and reaction allows us to see him simultaneously as a man who might have invented cinema—asking elementary questions about the minimum essential information for an audience, and evolving a taut equation of images to carry it out—and as a great modernist, uncovering the abstract forces of law, conspiracy, violence, revenge, and sacrifice beneath tortuous plots.

Lang's feeling for narrative function goes straight to the heart of our criminal corporate states. *Mabuse* is a fictional character in advance of historical examples. Lang's cities were oppressive before actual metropolises frightened us. And it was Lang who described how far society was estranging its nobler heroes, forcing them into crime, vengeful violence, and conspiracies like those of corrupt governments. Look past the melodrama and simplicity of Lang's films and he is the most stringent of political filmmakers. His analysis of society is structural, architectural, and narrative. But his unblinking commentary on the confusion of moral values and standards of sanity in the world is like that of a philosopher who poses simple examples because he is able to see them leading to profundity.

The son of an architect, Lang was first interested in being a painter and exhibited in Paris in 1914. He was badly wounded in the First World War and began writing scripts in convalescence. His first scenarios were made by Joe May, for example, *Hilde Warren und der Tod* (17), in which Lang played Death. The postwar German pessimism clearly affected Lang, but it is notable that the various ordeals of his own life reinforced his rigorous unsentimentality. Lang foresaw the German trauma of the 1930s, and was nearly overtaken by the way its thugs incarnated the assassins in his thrillers. Instead, he went on to America and began to film the future, a period to which his classical style always aspired.

His German films are long and rococo, but without an ounce of fat. *Die Spinnen* and *Dr. Mabuse der Spieler* are feverishly inventive stories, kept in order by Lang's selection of visual essentials. Throughout his career there was this same creative tension between teeming events

and the minimal necessary account of them. That is why Lang's films begin in top gear and then advance into higher ratios unknown to other directors. The acceleration is a matter of logic, analysis, and intense stylistic refinement. Behind it lies the assurance that comes from a world built entirely on sound stages and from his ability to make the emotional and moral resonance of interiors so clear.

It was this precise, cinematic care that enabled Lang to avoid the dead ends of Expressionism. It is why, despite the Utopian melodrama of *Metropolis* and the geometrical neatness of *M,* both films came into new life more than forty years after they were made. Invariably in cinema, narrative directness lasts longer than density.

The social argument of *Metropolis* is simpleminded, but the dynamic images of crowd behavior amid an urban labyrinth are still frightening. And it is the organized detachment of *M* that chills, the feeling that a sane man can no longer confidently take sides in the confrontation of society between organized law and outlawry, that Peter Lorre's murderer is already a protagonist of perverted sensitivity. It was the insight into malign purpose of *Das Testament des Dr. Mabuse*—a more cheerful thriller, but with a blatant portrayal of Nazi manners—that compelled Lang to leave Germany and to go first to France and then to America.

Of all the continental refugees, Lang adapted most naturally to America. The films he made there match his greatest because he found a studio system better organized and more adept at narrative genres. Between *Fury* and *Beyond a Reasonable Doubt* there is an achievement still not appreciated in English-speaking circles. The study of the relations between man, society, law, and crime moves toward increasingly uncompromising answers. It is astonishing that *Fury*, made at MGM under the bland Mankiewicz, should contain such an indictment of the mob and so uncomfortable a view of the way violence degrades Spencer Tracy. The moment in *Fury* when Tracy reappears in the doorway cauterized into hostility—"I'm dead . . . I could smell myself burning"—is the first evidence that the American Lang is to be an advance upon the German. *You Only Live Once* is now recognized as an origin of *Bonnie and Clyde* and *Pierrot le Fou* in its icy view of a vital young couple turned toward crime by a callous, obtuse society.

But the finest Lang films are *The Woman in the Window, The Ministry of Fear, Scarlet Street, Cloak and Dagger, Rancho Notorious,* and *The Big Heat. Woman in the Window* and *Scarlet Street* gain from the fact that their hero—Edward G. Robinson—is depicted in a very homely, bourgeois form so that the turmoil that overtakes him has to be all the more skillfully contrived. In *The*

Ministry of Fear and *The Big Heat* heroes have to vindicate themselves in nightmare worlds of conspiracy. They are interior films in which doorways frame and darkness threatens human beings. In *Cloak and Dagger,* espionage seems to coincide with the fallibility of appearance, whereby an apple can explode. *Rancho Notorious* shows Lang's ability to take the Western genre and strip it of sham atmosphere, landscape, and horses. It is a portrait of a man warped by his own need for vengeance, the theme that Lang pursued so fruitfully for forty years and which was the natural concern of an artist driven from his own country by tyranny.

The later work does not relax. *Beyond a Reasonable Doubt* is the proof of a savage theorem, despite a low budget. The Indian films are an enjoyable return to the world of *Die Spinnen.* They are children's stories, but made with an authority that could not be bettered as a model for students. If you wish to see how demanding and how simple filmmaking is, then study Lang. But be warned: he is an austere pessimist and only the glory of images put together to such damning effect can counter the implications of that effect. Lang's adult stories are too concentrated for today's standards.

Walter Lang (1898–1972),
b. Memphis, Tennessee

1925: *Red Kimono.* 1926: *The Earth Woman; The Golden Web; Money to Burn.* 1927: *By Whose Hand?; The College Hero; The Ladybird; Sally in Our Alley; The Satin Woman.* 1928: *The Desert Bride; The Night Flyer.* 1929: *The Spirit of Youth.* 1930: *The Big Fight; Brothers; Cock o' the Walk* (codirected with R. William Neill); *The Costello Case; Hello Sister.* 1931: *Hellbound; The Command Performance; Women Go On For Ever.* 1932: *No More Orchids.* 1933: *The Warrior's Husband; Meet the Baron.* 1934: *The Mighty Barnum; Whom the Gods Destroy.* 1935: *Carnival; Hooray for Love.* 1936: *Love Before Breakfast.* 1937: *Wife, Doctor and Nurse; Second Honeymoon.* 1938: *The Baroness and the Butler; I'll Give a Million.* 1939: *The Little Princess.* 1940: *The Blue Bird; Star Dust; Tin Pan Alley; The Great Profile.* 1941: *Moon Over Miami; Weekend in Havana.* 1942: *Song of the Islands; The Magnificent Dope.* 1943: *Coney Island.* 1944: *Greenwich Village.* 1945: *State Fair.* 1946: *Sentimental Journey; Claudia and David.* 1947: *Mother Wore Tights.* 1948: *Sitting Pretty; When My Baby Smiles at Me.* 1949: *You're My Everything.* 1950: *Cheaper by the Dozen; The Jackpot.* 1951: *On the Riviera.* 1952: *With a Song in My Heart.* 1953: *Call Me Madam.* 1954: *There's No Business Like Show Business.* 1956: *The King and I.* 1957: *The Desk Set.* 1959: *But Not for Me.* 1960: *Can-Can; The Marriage-Go-Round.* 1961: *Snow White and the Three Stooges.*

Lang served in France during the First World War and then graduated from the University of Tennessee. He was given his chance to direct by Mrs. Wallace Reid, who subsequently appeared in *The Satin Woman.* Lang worked for Columbia and James Cruze, but by the mid-1930s he found his proper place at Fox, where he stayed for the rest of his career. As well as making a few comedies and romances, including a John Barrymore spoof, *The Great Profile,* and two Shirley Temple pictures—*The Little Princess* and *The Blue Bird*—Lang worked largely on musicals, whipping up the enthusiasm of Alice Faye, Betty Grable, Don Ameche, Carmen Miranda, and Dan Dailey. It need only be emphasized that the Fox product pales beside the MGM musicals.

In the 1950s, survival ensured that Lang was put in charge of a few major Fox musicals. *The King and I* was a great popular success, and *With a Song in My Heart* encouraged the full-blooded emotion of Susan Hayward. But the films as a whole are crude, listless, and ugly. Nikita Khrushchev frowned upon the vulgarity of *Can-Can.* Cold War observers feared deeper motives behind this disapproval—perhaps the Russian only knew his Renoir.

Harry Langdon (1884–1944),
b. Council Bluffs, Iowa

The Picturegoer's Who's Who for 1933 had no entry for Langdon, so complete had been his downfall. Nothing that he could do in his last eleven years restored him to his former glory. But the fact that he lived on so haplessly has by now become part of the Langdon legend, the glum postscript to yet another career blighted by Hollywood's callousness.

However, people should be given credit for bad films and mistakes as much as for their successes. Langdon handled his affairs unwisely and, more important, he had an insecure grasp of why he was funny. Whether we think of comedians as instinctive, good-natured clowns or as disenchanted men who make us laugh to stop themselves from crying, neither interpretation fits well with the comedian himself as a professional technician. There seems to be, intrinsically, a gulf between actorly intelligence and the screen's image of guileless innocence at the center of comic disaster. Audiences tend to be less inquisitive about the manufacture of comedy than about the resources of drama. And the men who have run the industry have sometimes treated comedians with such brutality that they might be acting on the assumption that no comedian was really in charge of his or her career. The dramatic reversal in Harry Langdon's fortunes may even stem from his attempt to step outside the baby-faced, baggy-trousered simpleton that he played so well if in so few films. But if in so few, was the creation Langdon's or a light that fell briefly on him, but in which he never saw himself?

Langdon had knocked around so much before he got into movies that it was a wonder he still seemed vulnerable. He was part of a Kickapoo Indian Medicine Show, a juggler, a circus clown, and a newspaper cartoonist before he entered vaudeville. He stayed there some twenty years without getting anywhere near the top. In 1923, Mack Sennett recruited him, probably on the advice of gagman Frank Capra. Langdon's moony daydreamer was evolved in a series of two-reelers, and guided by director Harry Edwards and gagmen, Capra and Arthur Ripley. Langdon had a small part in the Colleen Moore *Ella Cinders* (26, Alfred E. Green), but left Sennett for Warners and formed the Harry Langdon Corporation for his first feature, *Tramp, Tramp, Tramp* (26, Edwards), with six credited gagmen, including Capra. Sennett then released an earlier feature, *His First Flame*, also directed by Edwards, and with the assistance of Capra and Ripley.

There is no question about the success of the team: in *Tramp . . .* and the next few films, Langdon is a most beguiling dope. Yet it could be that this is only a very skillful manipulation of Langdon's dullness. There are moments when he seems casual or indifferent, as if not fully aware of what is going on around him—imagine Laurel without Hardy, imagine Laurel preoccupied with the loss, and you are surprisingly close to Harry Langdon, not just in looks but in the self-absorbed dismay.

Nevertheless, Langdon was now immensely popular. His next film was his best, *The Strong Man* (26, Frank Capra). Why Capra took over is not clear, nor can the extra sharpness be proved as coming from him. But the group was splitting. *Long Pants* (27, Capra) was made with Capra, Ripley, and Langdon quarreling, and when it was finished, Capra was fired. Capra reacted fiercely in a letter to the press that charged Langdon with vain and harmful interference. Talented people often fight, but how much of this is the disparity between the real Langdon and the figure Capra had helped invent? The Langdon Corporation persevered and Langdon himself directed his next three films: *Three's a Crowd* (27), which has a new and unwelcome gravity; *The Chaser* (28); and *Heart Trouble* (28). They are inferior films and their returns fell away.

Warners let him go and he was out of work. Then Hal Roach made a series of shorts with him, and in 1930 Universal teamed him with Slim Summerville in *See America Thirst* (30, William James Craft). He went back to Warners for *A Soldier's Plaything* (30, Michael Curtiz), but next year he was bankrupt.

Thus, two years later, the removal from reference books. Sound only underlined the lack of personality. On and off during the 1930s, he made more comedy shorts and appeared in a few features. They were, generally, minor works and nothing Langdon did suggested he was worthier of better things: *Hallelujah, I'm a Bum* (33, Lewis Milestone); *My Weakness* (33, David Butler); *There Goes My Heart* (38, Norman Z. McLeod); with Oliver Hardy in *Zenobia* (39, Gordon Douglas); *All-American Co-Ed* (41, LeRoy Prinz); *Spotlight Scandals* (43, William Beaudine); *Block Busters* (44, Wallace Fox); and *Swingin' on a Rainbow* (45, Beaudine). He also helped to write the Laurel and Hardy picture, *A Chump at Oxford* (40, Alfred Goulding).

Jessica Lange, b. Cloquet, Minnesota, 1949

In the early 1980s, it was easy to make a case for Jessica Lange as the most exciting and dangerous young actress in America. (Debra Winger was her closest rival, which may be a way of seeing how harsh America is on threatening young women.) In one year, Lange won the best supporting actress Oscar for *Tootsie* (82, Sydney Pollack) and a best actress nomination for *Frances* (82, Graeme Clifford). Moreover, having had a child by Mikhail Baryshnikov, Lange was in the process of winning away Sam Shepard from wife and family. There was such ability and authority, yet still she had the wild-eyed, untidy manner of a young hitchhiker in Arkansas or Oklahoma. It was possible to believe in her unusual upbringing: intense devotion to the northern Midwest; time in Paris as a musician and dancer, before modeling in New York, and then the stunning aplomb that pulled off *King Kong* (76, John Guillermin) and supplied the comedy of that unfairly berated remake.

She had gone on to be the angel of death in *All That Jazz* (79, Bob Fosse) and part of the team in *How to Beat the High Cost of Living* (80, Robert Scheerer). Her breakthrough had come as a Cora worthy of James M. Cain in *The Postman Always Rings Twice* (81, Bob Rafelson), where she easily handled the neediness, the spite, and the lunging desperation of a woman who deserved more than roadside kitchens. This is still, arguably, her most complete and disturbing performance.

Her work in *Tootsie* was clever, gracious, and appealing—no more than a dozen others could have managed. *Frances* was an untidy film, filled with bravura set pieces, but never enough to persuade us that Frances Farmer had been less than ill or a pain in the neck. Moreover, for all her own loveliness, Lange just lacked that wide-browed, bright-eyed élan of the real Farmer.

Since then, in child-bearing partnership with Sam Shepard, she has grown older and less arresting. *Country* (84, Richard Pearce) was a decent, sensitive examination of rural life and the farming community, yet it felt like marking time and seemed to slight the actress's urge to identify herself with a simpler, if not Simple, Life. She was good, on TV, as Maggie in *Cat on a Hot Tin Roof* (84, Jack Y. Hofsiss), but somehow the danger of the original was gone. She made a convincing Patsy Cline in *Sweet Dreams* (85, Karel Reisz), yet the film had no sense of necessity. *Crimes of the Heart* (86, Bruce Beresford) was equally lacking in urgency. *Everybody's All-American* (88, Taylor Hackford) was her first unequivocal stooge female lead part, and *Far North* (88, Shepard) was too much *Country* revisited.

In *Music Box* (89, Costa-Gavras), she had a large part in a Big, Stanley Kramerish picture. She carried it off superbly and gave the predictable plot a chance of seeming like life. But there was something middle-aged about the film. *Men Don't Leave* (90, Paul Brickman), a delicate, small romance, secure in its family reality, showed how alert she could be still. But in the unpleasant *Cape Fear* (91, Martin Scorsese), she was a stock figure from melodrama, letting the cruel action have its way with her.

In 1992, in a Broadway revival, she played Blanche in *A Streetcar Named Desire*. That big event never quite came to life and reviewers observed Lange's lack of stage presence. She was much improved, on TV again, in a version of Willa Cather's *O Pioneers!* (91, Glenn Jordan), which Lange herself produced. But she was just "the woman" in *Night and the City* (92, Irwin Winkler).

She then won her Oscar as the forlorn, disorderly wife in *Blue Sky* (94, Tony Richardson); she was horribly abused in *Rob Roy* (95, Michael Caton-Jones); *Losing Isaiah* (95, Stephen Gyllenhaal); as Blanche for the screen (95, Glenn Jordan); very sly in *Cousin Bette* (97, Des McAnuff); *A Thousand Acres* (97, Jocelyn Moorhouse); *Hush* (98, Jonathan Darby); horribly abusive in *Titus* (99, Julie Taymor). It's odd that she seems less impressed by movies than, say, Michelle Pfeiffer, yet far more powerful on screen.

She is in the much delayed *Prozac Nation* (03, Erik Skjoldbjaerg); *Normal* (03, Jane Anderson); *Masked & Anonymous* (03, Larry Charles): *Big Fish* (03, Tim Burton).

Henri Langlois (1914–77), b. Smyrna, Turkey

Towards the end of his life, there were young, trained archivists who said that, well, of course, Henri Langlois was all very well, but he was chronically untidy, unsystematic, and so passionate that he was not above or beyond sometimes losing or inadvertently destroying some of the very things he treasured. People consumed with passion are not reliable, are they? Henri Langlois, they said, was his own worst enemy, and helplessly old-fashioned. In 1968, the famous attempt to remove Langlois from what was his Cinémathèque owed a great deal to clerical and bureaucratic squeamishness at his methods, and to the matter-of-fact observation that, after all, the Cinémathèque belonged to the nation.

Very well; there is some truth in the argument. But, just to take ownership as an issue, it is the case that one day in 1945 Langlois called upon Pierre Braunberger, a fine man and a good producer, Renoir's producer sometimes in the thirties, but Jewish and hounded during the war, and gave Braunberger a thing he thought was lost forever—the negative of Renoir's *Partie de Campagne*. One way or another, during German occupation, Langlois had saved those cans—and kept that film alive. He handed it over and asked for nothing in return (except a print for the Cinémathèque, perhaps).

And how many times could that story be multiplied?

Langlois was born in Smyrna because his father was a journalist posted there, as well as someone involved in a variety of export-import deals. His mother was of Italian descent, but from a family that had gone to America in the middle of the nineteenth century and then returned. It was only in 1922 that Henri was taken by his family to France, and to Paris.

He was in his early teens when sound transformed the medium he loved already, and emotionally he seems to have been especially saddened by the way in which a whole range of films, and often their stars, effectively disappeared with the new rage for sound. He wanted to hold on to them. He frequented the few Parisian cinemas that kept an allegiance to silent pictures. And he began to develop the notion that anyone's pleasure in the dark depended on cans of "stuff," awkward, unmanageable snakes of it, all on the dangerous and unstable nitrate stock, and all of it so easily junked for the prospect of reclaiming the silver that made film alive.

Langlois never passed his baccalaureate examination. It is said that he got a zero on a paper where instead of writing about Molière, he tried to argue that Chaplin was superior. So he passed into the world unqualified. He went to work at a printing shop, and that's how he met Georges Franju. Together, the two young men formed a Cercle du Cinéma, a club for enthusiasts, a place for showing rare movies. From that group there grew the idea of a Cinémathèque—an organization formed to collect, preserve, and show the great films of history. It was always Langlois's sense that they must preserve everything. He had his own strong tastes, but he was curiously open to a contrary idea—that at any given moment you couldn't be sure what would seem great later.

The Cinémathèque was founded in 1935, by Langlois and Franju, on a donation of 10,000 francs from Paul-Auguste Harle, publisher of a

French film trade weekly. The first prints they bought were *The Fall of the House of Usher* (28, Jean Epstein) and *The Birth of a Nation* (15, D. W. Griffith). They soon persuaded Alexandre Kamenka, a producer of avant-garde films, to deposit his collection with their Cinémathèque. And so they needed somewhere to put the stuff. Franju was friendly with Georges Méliès, the pioneer, who was living in a retirement home. Close to that establishment was a building for rent. They leased it, and Méliès became the first caretaker of a collection that included many of his own films.

It was not Langlois's choice to specialize, yet at the same time he was very ready to identify masters—often people in neglect, like Louis Feuillade, von Stroheim, Stiller, Sjöström, and Americans, too—Langlois was one of the first to see and crave more of the genius of Howard Hawks.

He also made moves to internationalize the archive movement by making friendships with Olwen Vaughan, at the British Film Institute in London, and with Iris Barry from the Museum of Modern Art in New York. Indeed, he cultivated a circle of women in love with film, and in Paris he employed Lotte Eisner (a refugee from Nazism), Mary Meerson (widow of the great art director Lazare Meerson), and Marie Epstein, sister to Jean.

War was the test, and the great victory, in Langlois's approach. For he maintained what he had—sometimes lodging films with friends in the country; moving them around; keeping track, without written records—and also added to it. Richard Roud's fine book on Langlois, *A Passion for Films,* adds this extra (something surely worthy of a movie): that Langlois found a fellow enthusiast on the German staff in Paris, Major Frank Hensel, who was secretly drawn into aiding and protecting the Cinémathèque. Shortly after the liberation of Paris, Langlois mounted a season of American films, most of which had been barred for the Nazi years: *Modern Times* (36, Chaplin); *Gone With the Wind* (39, Victor Fleming); *Goin' to Town* (35, Alexander Hall); *Each Dawn I Die* (39, William Keighley); *Abe Lincoln in Illinois* (40, John Cromwell); *Our Town* (40, Sam Wood); and *Young Mr. Lincoln* (39, John Ford).

After the war, on the Avenue de Messine, Langlois began his unique programmed shows—three screenings in an evening, with the films made to compare and contrast, sometimes to follow a career. And it was there that, by around 1950, Langlois had attracted the greatest film society we have ever known (though maybe some of the Hollywood screening rooms of the golden age could rival it): André Bazin, Alexandre Astruc, Roger Leenhardt, Truffaut, Godard, Rohmer, Chabrol, Rivette, Chris Marker . . . and so on.

Cahiers du Cinéma was not the publication of the Cinémathèque, but it was the yellow-covered clarion of that generation. To this day, there has never been a band of opinion makers who were so often right. It is the moment at which the history of film as a whole begins to be felt and described, and it would not have been possible without Langlois.

Thus, in 1968, when André Malraux, the minister of culture, attempted to oust Langlois and make his administration more modern, that generation rallied to the assistance of the great man. The French government caved in—which did not mean that Langlois by then was other than an autocrat, a muddle, and a man who could hardly recall where he had put everything. But he was an international figure, and he was involved in plans for an American Cinémathèque. In 1973, he received an honorary Oscar.

Of course, he died on the eve of video and before computerization had taken over so many archival processes. But we knew how much of the heritage of movies had been lost already, and we had the French example to inspire a generation of passionate archivists all over the world (it has embraced Enno Patalas, Bob Gitt, and David Meeker as well as Tom Luddy, William K. Everson, and David Packard—in short, anyone crazy about film and taking care of it).

Not that Langlois ever believed that films should be kept and not shown. He believed that the film stock needed to be exercised—to be run. No matter the hours and years he spent over cans, repairing sprocket holes, wiping off nitrate "sweat," he knew that the real life was on the screen, in the act of projection, with audiences. He loved everything film had done, which included silents, nitrate stock, Technicolor, and real manual projection. He would have seen the drabness and the usefulness in video, the loss of life, and I suspect he would have decried the loss of light in so much modern filmmaking.

But, of course, today, without any credentials, he would never be employed. The only chance he ever had of getting in on the archive game was by inventing it—and by treating it as a matter of life and death.

And so, the rest of us face this riddle: in all he did to preserve and show, was he forward-looking, or reactionary? In other words, is Henri Langlois's medium, the cinema, alive still, or is it to be found only in the archives he inspired—projected in perfect prints, with carbon-arc light, seen and felt as what one of his customers, Jean-Paul Sartre, once called "the frenzy on the wall"? However you answer, remember the great, shabby, untidy figure of Langlois, who might be walking around with *Eldorado* in his deep pockets—the Marcel L'Herbier version, from 1922, in one pocket, the later Hawks version in the other.

Angela Lansbury, b. London, 1925

Actress Angela Lansbury is the granddaughter of George Lansbury, onetime leader of the British Labour Party, and daughter of the mayor of Poplar. In fact, entertainment ran more strongly in her family than politics, and early in the war she was evacuated to Los Angeles, there to continue drama training. In 1944, after a screen test, she made her debut as the sly maid in George Cukor's *Gaslight*.

It was the start of a career as a supporting actress in which, pouting at the thought that she was not pretty enough to be a lead, she stole film after film from their advertised stars. Malicious, witty, fractious, bitchy, and highly attractive, she is a constant delight, and it is a sadness that Cukor or Minnelli never made more of her. She was very hardworking, and this list can only note some favorite moments: as the singer in Albert Lewin's *The Picture of Dorian Gray* (45); in George Sidney's *The Harvey Girls* (45); singing "How'd You Like to Spoon With Me?" in *Till the Clouds Roll By* (46, Richard Whorf); in Capra's *State of the Union* (48); as an extravagant princess in *The Three Musketeers* (48, Sidney); *The Red Danube* (49, Sidney); as a Philistine in *Samson and Delilah* (49, Cecil B. De Mille); contemplating Danny Kaye in *The Court Jester* (55, Melvin Frank and Norman Panama); with Tony Curtis in *The Purple Mask* (55, Bruce Humberstone); with Randolph Scott in *A Lawless Street* (55, Joseph H. Lewis); regaling Orson Welles in *The Long Hot Summer* (58, Martin Ritt); as an aristocratic Mama in *The Reluctant Debutante* (58, Minnelli); Australian for *Summer of the 17th Doll* (59, Leslie Norman); in Delbert Mann's *The Dark at the Top of the Stairs* (60); in *All Fall Down* (61, John Frankenheimer); impervious, chilling, and in heat for her son as Mrs. Iselin in *The Manchurian Candidate* (62, Frankenheimer)—only three years older than her "son" Laurence Harvey, but looking more interested in life; enjoying herself in *The World of Henry Orient* (64, George Roy Hill); the selfish mother in *Harlow* (65, Gordon Douglas); acid and peremptory in *Something for Everyone* (70, Hal Prince); and scarcely able to believe the magic of *Bedknobs and Broomsticks* (71, Robert Stevenson).

In the sixties, she had a great personal success on stage in *Mame*, but the movies could find no way of using her beyond *Death on the Nile* (78, John Guillermin) and Miss Froy in *The Lady Vanishes* (79, Anthony Page).

For Lansbury, the eighties meant Jessica Fletcher in *Murder, She Wrote*, a hit series since its launch in 1984, a way station for semiretired players, and—let it be said—a waste of Miss Lansbury. She does comfortable sugar as decently as anyone, but she is a real actress who is more interesting with a touch of lemon juice, or acid. I would trade all the Jessica Fletchers for her wife in

Stephen Sondheim's *Sweeney Todd*.

She has made a few more films, mostly for TV: *The Mirror Crack'd* (80, Guy Hamilton); excellent again as Gertrude Vanderbilt Whitney in *Little Gloria—Happy at Last* (82, Waris Hussein); *The Pirates of Penzance* (82, Wilford Leach); *The Gift of Love: A Christmas Story* (83, Delbert Mann); *Lace* (84, Billy Hall); *The Company of Wolves* (85, Neil Jordan); as an Italian in *Rage of Angels: The Story Continues* (86, Paul Wendkos); *Shootdown* (88, Michael Pressman); *The Shell Seekers* (89, Hussein); and *The Love She Sought* (90, Joseph Sargent).

Then she won a new generation of fans by being the sweet singing voice of the housekeeper teapot in *Beauty and the Beast* (91, Garry Trousdale and Kirk Wise). In 1999, for TV, she was *The Unexpected Mrs. Pollifax* (Anthony Pullen Shaw).

Mario Lanza (Alfred Arnold Cocozza)
(1921–1959), b. Philadelphia

Maybe it was all a dream. Did a corpulent Mamma's boy from Philadelphia named Alfred grow up to be a remarkable tenor, to perform with Koussevitsky at the Tanglewood Festival, to break into the movies at the age of twenty-eight and make eight films in ten years, to sell tens of millions of records, to die at the age of thirty-eight, and to go on being famous and adored, or famous and derided (or famous and loathed—he had a bizarre habit of urinating in public, on the set, in plain view of Kathryn Grayson) decades after his death?

First was *That Midnight Kiss* (49, Norman Taurog), in which Mario as a singing truck driver gives us "Celeste Aida," Kathryn Grayson gives us "Caro Nome," and J. Carroll Naish gives us "Santa Lucia." Next, in *The Toast of New Orleans* (50, Taurog) he's a singing *fisherman* and what he catches is Grayson, and a two-million seller, "Be My Love." Then, the climax of his career and a tremendous hit, *The Great Caruso* (51, Richard Thorpe), with twenty-two songs, Ann Blyth, and a number-one album that convinced some of his doting fans that he was greater than Caruso.

Because You're Mine (52, Alexander Hall) featured the title song and Doretta Morrow; *The Student Prince* (54, Thorpe) ended up with Mario's face on the cutting-room floor (actually, he was never filmed; after contractual and overweight problems, he was replaced onscreen by Edmund Purdom) but with his voice as strong as ever on the soundtrack; a tame version of James M. Cain's *Serenade* in 1956, with Joan Fontaine, and purportedly directed by Anthony Mann, but surely that's a dream, too. A "comeback" in 1958 with *The Seven Hills of Rome* (58, Roy Rowland), in which he impersonates various other singers, including (won't somebody wake me up?) Louis Armstrong. And, finally, *For the First Time* (59, Rudolph Maté), in which he's an opera singer in love with a deaf girl. He died that year, in Italy, under somewhat mysterious circumstances, though clearly in terrible health from his extravagant living. But he remains a larger-than-life figure—a weird mixture of Nelson Eddy, John Travolta, and John Gotti, a man with a big musical gift but no taste, restraint, or discipline; a pampered little boy pretending to be a ladies' man; a truck driver pretending to be an opera star.

In the winter of 1994, the great Spanish tenor José Carreras gave a Mario Lanza Memorial Concert at Radio City Music Hall. The dream goes on.

Jesse L. Lasky (1880–1958),
b. San Francisco

In the American Film Institute catalog of feature films for the years 1921–30, Jesse Lasky fills five columns and is credited with over 350 pictures. But his role as "presenter" stops at the end of 1928, after which most Paramount films carry the name of Adolph Zukor on the title credit. It is a puzzle that such authority could cease so suddenly, and it raises the question as to whether studio executives exercised creative power or merely tied their names to more products than any man could comprehend. There can be little doubt that in the early 1920s any observer would have listed Lasky among the handful of most powerful men in Hollywood. But after 1932, when his association with Paramount ended, he revealed himself as a man of no particular character or impact.

Moguls, emperors, and pharaohs leave only their names or portraits of themselves. Look as long as you like—Tutankhamen, Louis XIV, or Jesse Lasky—and you will never get the measure of a man. But an artist, a poet, or a director leaves us with the imprint of his mind. Perhaps moguls are led into exaggerated arbitrariness because they foresee that oblivion.

Lasky was of German descent. As a young man, he was a cornet player, assistant at a medicine show, and hopeful participant in the Yukon gold rush. The cornet took him into vaudeville, while his sister, Blanche, lips puckered from the same instrument, married Samuel Goldfish. In 1913, Lasky, Goldfish, and Cecil B. De Mille founded Lasky Feature Plays. In 1916, they merged with Adolph Zukor's Famous Players, thus providing the basis for the future Paramount. De Mille was always more intent on making films, but Lasky, Goldfish, and Zukor engaged in an immediate struggle for power. Goldfish resented for many years the way his brother-in-law Lasky had taken Zukor's side, and stalked off into independence.

Famous Players Lasky settled with Zukor as president, and Lasky as vice-president in charge of production. Zukor, of course, is the weird survivor of the movie world. Born in Ricse, Hungary, in 1873, he celebrated his one hundredth birth-

day, still "chairman emeritus" of Paramount, itself a subsidiary of Gulf and Western. Such longevity may owe itself to Zukor's apparent indifference to the product. He was essentially an East Coast man who took little part in production after the partnership with Lasky, but raised money on Wall Street and enlarged the distribution and exhibition arms of Paramount.

In theory, at least, Lasky was in charge of production—in Hollywood and New York—from 1916 to 1932. By then, Paramount was in dire trouble, the result of the Depression and Zukor's mistakes. The Paramount product was more consistent and as satisfying as any other company's. It is the period in which Paramount recruited Valentino from Metro; made *The Covered Wagon* and the early Schoedsack-Cooper films; hired Lubitsch, von Sternberg, Dietrich, and Gary Cooper; handled most of De Mille's movies; enlisted the Marx Brothers, W. C. Fields, Mary Pickford, Claudette Colbert, and Maurice Chevalier. But precise evidence of Lasky's role is scarce. From 1923 onward, he had to share the "presented by" tag with Zukor and that may indicate growing New York interference. Von Sternberg speaks of his own arrival at Paramount, meeting Lasky and exchanging pleasantries, whereupon Lasky said, "Don't forget, I said it first," as if anxious to be associated with success.

The slump hit Lasky hard and wiped out the larger part of his stock holding. He joined Fox and produced there for a few years: *Berkeley Square* (33, Frank Lloyd); *I Am Suzanne* (34, Rowland V. Lee); *Springtime for Henry* (34, Frank Tuttle); *Helldorado* (35, James Cruze); *Redheads on Parade* (35, Norman Z. McLeod); and *The Gay Deception* (35, William Wyler). A modest list. In 1935, Fox merged with Twentieth Century and Darryl Zanuck was the natural executive in charge of production for the new major. Lasky moved on to a brief partnership with Mary Pickford at United Artists: *One Rainy Afternoon* (36, Lee) and *The Gay Desperado* (36, Rouben Mamoulian). Then on to RKO, for a year, after which he worked for radio and was once again nearly broke.

But in 1941, Howard Hawks and Gary Cooper came to Lasky's aid by taking up his *Sergeant York* project and selling it to Warners. According to Hawks, again, he did all the work and let Lasky count the profit. But *Sergeant York* is not the most Hawksian of films; its patriotism and sentimentality suggest Lasky's hand. He stayed on at Warners and produced a few more films: *The Adventures of Mark Twain* (44, Irving Rapper) and *Rhapsody in Blue* (45, Rapper). Then he moved back to RKO for *Without Reservations* (46, Mervyn Le Roy) and *The Miracle of the Bells* (48, Irving Pichel). It was a sad procession of posts, completed by his moving to MGM in 1950, and back to Paramount in 1957. By then he owed the tax man so much that he was attempting to set up another project.

Alberto Lattuada, b. Milan, Italy, 1914

1942: *Giacomo l'Idealista.* 1944: *La Freccia nel Fianco; La Nostra Guerra.* 1946: *Il Bandito.* 1947: *Il Delitto di Giovanni Episcopo.* 1948: *Senza Pieta.* 1949: *Il Mulino del Po.* 1950: *Luci del Varieta/Lights of Variety* (codirected with Federico Fellini). 1951: *Anna.* 1952: *Il Cappotto.* 1953: *La Lupa;* "Gli Italiani si Voltano," episode from *Amore in Citta.* 1954: *La Spiaggia.* 1955: *Scuola Elementare.* 1957: *Guendalina; La Tempesta/Tempest.* 1960: *I Dolci Inganni; Lettere di una Novizia.* 1961: *L'Imprevisto.* 1962: *La Steppa; Il Mafioso.* 1965: *La Mandragola.* 1966: *Matchless.* 1967: *Don Giovanni in Sicilia.* 1968: *Fraulein Doktor.* 1969: *L'Amica.* 1970: *Venga a Prendero il Caffe da Noi.* 1973: *Sono State Io!.* 1975: *Le Faro Da Padre.* 1976: *Oh, Serafina!; Cosi Come Sei.* 1980: *La Cicala.* 1981: *Nudo di Donna.* 1985: *Una Spina nel Cuore.* 1988: *Fratelli* (TV). 1998: "Genoa", episode from *12 Registi per 12 Citta.*

The son of the Italian composer Felice Lattuada, Alberto was a writer and qualified architect before the war swept him into cinema. It was while writing for the review, *Corrente,* in 1940, that Lattuada, Luigi Comencini, and Mario Ferrari set up the beginnings of an Italian Archive and organized film shows of an anti-Fascist nature. After that, Lattuada began to work as a writer and assistant director: *Piccolo Mondo Antico* (40, Mario Soldati).

That film established Lattuada's early style: period atmosphere, good acting, and care with sets and costumes. Used amid harsh political realities, it was a style that sometimes seemed as innocuously pretty as the Carné of *Les Visiteurs du Soir.* In any event, Lattuada has revealed the versatility of a director with no pressing character of his own. But he has remained highly proficient and successful. *Il Bandito* was in the neo-realist strain, about a prisoner of war who returns to find his life so changed that he takes to crime. It starred Amedeo Nazzari and Anna Magnani.

But Lattuada was more comfortable in adapting novels with a firm narrative basis that lent themselves to romantic "literary" shape. *Giacomo l'Idealista* is from a novel by Emilio de Marchi about an affair between a chambermaid and a young man of higher class. *Il Delitto di Giovanni Episcopo* was adapted from a novel by Gabriele d'Annunzio. Lattuada's richest period came as neo-realism was declining. *Senza Pieta* is a melodrama about an American Negro soldier and a prostitute, coscripted by Fellini, and starring Giulietta Masina. It neatly combines the qualities of realism and theatricality that were to obsess Fellini, as does *Luci del Varieta*, Fellini's debut as a director. Not only its gallery of shabby traveling players, but the melancholy conclusion seem to derive more from Fellini than from Lattuada, who followed with *Anna,* a big box-office success, made for Dino de Laurentiis and starring Silvana Mangano. His next film is his best: *Il Cappotto,* an adaptation of Gogol's *The Overcoat,* with Renato Rascel as the bureaucrat. Since then, Lattuada has become a conventional figure, following whatever fashion held at the time, as witness the empty spectacle of *La Tempesta.*

Charles Laughton (1899–1962),
b. Scarborough, England

Laughton's is one of the most interesting and troubled careers in the cinema. Possessed by unbridled rhetorical vitality, he was responsible for some of the most recklessly flamboyant characterizations the screen has seen. At other times, his doubts crippled him. Recognized in the 1930s as the screen's principal creator of larger-than-life characters, his career declined into inconsequential movies. All too easily, he mocked the parts he was playing, thus acquiring a reputation for being unmanageable.

He was an artist with deep, volatile feelings who only occasionally found work in which he could believe. Thus there is an almost brutal contrast in his films between careful invention and unchallenged ham. Like so many large, ugly actors, he was sometimes incapable of escaping the grossly malicious man he often played. Though happily married to Elsa Lanchester (they were good company), he was a homosexual, tortured by the need to be secret and truly guilt-ridden because of it. So he came to see his own looks as a merited rebuke: he was his own hunchback.

Many of his "great performances" have dated badly, but one achievement grows richer with every viewing: his only direction, *The Night of the Hunter* (55), is one of the masterpieces of American cinema. It is proper to give some credit for it to James Agee, Stanley Cortez, and Robert Mitchum, but the Hans Andersen–like clarity of the conception, the extraordinary mythic precision, and the ease with which the film moves from nightmare to lyric—those great virtues come from Laughton. Better still, the movie brings to life a chill, dewy innocence enough to dissolve the rabid grasp of hatred.

Laughton, a Catholic and the son of hoteliers, went to Stonyhurst and had to battle against family opposition to go on the stage. He was led to film acting by his theatre work and by his marriage to Elsa Lanchester, who was making two-reelers. He made a few films in England, including E. A. Dupont's *Piccadilly* (28), *Comets* (30, Sasha Geneen), and Herbert Wilcox's *Wolves* (30), before taking the play, *Payment Deferred,* to Broadway. Although hesitant, Laughton eventually accepted an offer from Paramount. Inevitably, his looks meant that Hollywood employed him in grotesque roles. His first film in America was James Whale's *The Old Dark House* (32), made for Universal while Paramount searched out parts for him. In fact, the studio never came to terms with Laughton. He made *The Devil and the Deep* (32, Marion Gering); *White Woman* (33, Stuart Walker); lampooned De Mille's *The Sign of the Cross* (32); was memorable in his episode of *If I Had a Million* (32, Ernst Lubitsch); and luridly fearsome in Erle C. Kenton's adaptation of H. G. Wells's *Island of Lost Souls* (33). Otherwise, he was loaned to MGM for the unsuccessful movie version of *Payment Deferred* (32, Lothar Mendes).

It was in England, for Alexander Korda, that he achieved stardom, and an Oscar, in *The Private Life of Henry VIII* (34). He returned to Hollywood, to a personal friendship with Irving Thalberg and four of his most famous roles: the father in *The Barretts of Wimpole Street* (34, Sidney Franklin); *Ruggles of Red Gap* (35, Leo McCarey); Javert in Richard Boleslavsky's *Les Misérables* (35); and Bligh in *Mutiny on the Bounty* (35, Frank Lloyd). *Ruggles* now looks the best survivor of this period, if only because the character is more lowly and more truly observed. In masterful parts, Laughton snarls and leers like a show-off who despises movies—or himself for working in them.

And, indeed, Laughton disliked Hollywood; Thalberg's death was only one reason for his second departure. Back in England he played *Rembrandt* (36) for Korda and began the ill-fated *I Claudius* for Josef von Sternberg. The material that survives from that venture shows how far Laughton reached out for a nonrealistic type of acting—a hint that he may have been frustrated by the limits Hollywood set upon his exaggeration. He now joined forces with Erich Pommer to act in and produce *Vessel of Wrath* (37) and *St. Martin's Lane* (38, Tim Whelan). But after acting in and producing *Jamaica Inn* (39, Alfred Hitchcock), he returned to Hollywood and worked intensively throughout the war: brilliant as Quasimodo in Dieterle's *The Hunchback of Notre Dame* (39); in Garson Kanin's *They Knew What They Wanted* (40); *It Started with Eve* (41, Henry Koster); *The Tuttles of Tahiti* (42, Charles Vidor); an episode in Duvivier's *Tales of Manhattan* (42); *Stand by for Action* (42, Robert Z. Leonard); *Forever and a Day* (43, Lloyd); Renoir's *This Land Is Mine* (43)—another of his simple, decent, rather shy men. After *The Canterville Ghost* (44, Jules Dassin) and a very subtle, conscience-stricken man in *The Suspect* (45, Robert Siodmak), he returned to colorful ogres: *Captain Kidd* (45, Rowland V. Lee); laying his hand on Ann Todd in *The Paradine Case* (47, Hitchcock); and *The Big Clock* (48, John Farrow).

Laughton's decline dates from this period and seems to reflect a growing realization that few films could contain him: *Arch of Triumph* (48, Lewis Milestone); *The Girl from Manhattan* (48, Alfred E. Green); *The Bribe* (49, Leonard); *The Man on the Eiffel Tower* (50, Burgess Meredith); *The Blue Veil* (51, Curtis Bernhardt); *Abbott and Costello Meet Captain Kidd* (52, Charles Lamont); Herod in Dieterle's *Salome* (53); and Henry VIII in George Sidney's *Young Bess* (53).

Working more in the theatre again, he made only five further films: tedious in *Hobson's Choice* (54, David Lean); overdone, but Oscar-nominated for *Witness for the Prosecution* (57, Billy Wilder); a good Gracchus in *Spartacus* (60, Stanley Kubrick); *Under Ten Flags* (60, Diulio Coletti); finally, with charm and distinction, as Senator Seab Cooley in Preminger's *Advise and Consent* (62).

Stan Laurel (Arthur Stanley Jefferson) (1890–1965), b. Ulverston, England; and
Oliver Hardy (1892–1957),
b. Harlem, Georgia

Turn to Hardy in any alphabetical order and you find: "See Stan Laurel." In reference books, therefore, the fat and the thin have been reversed.

Critical estimates usually comply with that rating, just as accounts of their working relations make clear the greater creative contribution of Laurel. Here, for instance, is Leo McCarey, the most creative director involved in any of their films: "[Laurel] was one of the rare comics intelligent enough to invent his own gags. Laurel was remarkably talented, while Hardy wasn't. This is the key to the Laurel-Hardy association. Throughout their lives (I was one of their intimates), Laurel insisted on earning twice as much as Hardy. He said that he was twice as good and twice as important, that he wrote the film and participated in its creation, while Hardy was really incapable of creating anything at all—it was astonishing that he could even find his way to the studio."

That says a lot about their on-screen chemistry if only because it is invariably the gormless Laurel who spoils the dainty and painstaking plans of Ollie. There is not much doubt that, on a day-to-day basis, Hardy was content to turn up and fall in the whitewash. Whereas Laurel conceived gags, planned stories, and consulted in the direction. In which case, Laurel must take some of the blame for the dull gags, ruminating stories, and characterless direction—all of which run through their movies. Equally, let us give credit to Stan for the sudden strokes of invention, like the moment in *Swiss Miss* when Stan despairs of getting brandy from a truculent St. Bernard, consoles himself by plucking chickens, only for the dog to think the shower of feathers is snowflakes and disgorge his brandy.

But the critical relegation of Hardy is mistaken: he brought such variety to the humiliation of the fat man of ideas by the slender simpleton. Perhaps the invention was McCarey's or Laurel's, but Hardy had a marvelous babylike dignity in suffering, as witness this account by McCarey: "[Hardy] was playing the part of a maître d' who was coming in with a cake to be served. As he steps through a doorway, he falls and finds himself on the floor, his head buried in the cake. I shouted to him, 'Don't move! Above all, don't move! Stay like that, the cake should burn your face!' And, for a minute and a half, the public couldn't stop laughing. Hardy remained immobile, his head in the cake!"

So much for the argument that Hardy created nothing. In submitting endlessly to disaster, he took upon himself the mantle of suffering that has always earned more laughs than haplessness. The belly laughs of Laurel and Hardy movies usually greet Hardy, or more precisely, his being confounded by Laurel's simpleton destructiveness. Presence is sometimes as creative as ideas. Laurel and Hardy should be together in reference books, because they needed each other; it was the pairing that made them funny. That is a rarer achievement than is often recognized. Together, the Marx Brothers were a little uneasy, apart from the grindingly worked-out patter scenes between Groucho and Chico. Abbott and Costello proved how much extra Laurel and Hardy added to the thin man/fat man scheme. Chaplin, Keaton, Lloyd, and Langdon are essentially loners. The only human pairing to equal Laurel and Hardy is Hope and Crosby in the *Road* films, except that they had the lovely Lamour to bicker over. (The inhuman couple—unrivaled for anarchic comedy—is Tom and Jerry.)

Cat and mouse live in a world of their own, occasionally intruded on by the lower legs of a domestic, by a bulldog, or a pretty lady puss. But those are rare interruptions to a sufficient, inescapable antagonism between the two characters. The same applies to Laurel and Hardy. Girls seldom find a place in their world. The boys live together in lodgings; they attend constantly to one another, oblivious of outsiders. I do not mean to be fanciful or to spoil the fun with an unwelcome smear. But the mutual incompatibility and physical confrontation suggests the homosexual implication of Laurel and Hardy. Their need for each other, and the insistent grating of one personality on another, are images of an imprisoning marriage. (In *Their First Mistake* [32, George Marshall], they even "have" a child.) Neither of them is exactly manly; Laurel shuffles and minces like a clown; while Hardy is as overblown as a eunuch. The point need not be pressed. But their modestly funny films have lasted as well as they have because of the emotional undercurrent in their being together.

Laurel was a music-hall comedian in England who went to America in 1910 with Fred Karno. In vaudeville, he often copied Chaplin and made his first short in 1918: *Nuts in May.* He worked in movies from then on, for Universal, Bronco Billy Anderson, and Hal Roach, but without establishing himself in the competitive field of screen comedy. Hardy went into films after having been a cinema owner—thus the pained bourgeois respectability he clung to in every crisis. He worked with Larry Semon in the early 1920s and then joined Hal Roach. Being in the same company, a day arose when Laurel stepped in for Hardy on a film when the fat man was ill or failed to find the studio. They played together in *Slipping Wives* and Roach decided to team them: *Putting Pants on Philip* (27, Leo McCarey) was the first of "their" films. This was the period when McCarey directed most of their shorts—films such as *The Battle of the Century* (27); *Leave 'em Laughing* (28); *From Soup to Nuts* (28); *Early to Bed* (28); *Two Tars* (28); *Liberty* (29); *Double Whoopee* (29); *Bacon Grabbers* (29); *The Perfect Day* (29); *Night Owls* (30); *The Laurel and Hardy Murder Case* (30); *Another Fine Mess* (30); *Beau Chumps* (31); and *Helpmates* (31).

In 1931, they made their first full-length feature, *Pardon Us* (James Parrott). Gradually, their shorts stopped. McCarey had left them, and it is possible that Laurel's ambitions exceeded their abilities. The shorts are less flawed by tedium and plotlessness. One short made in 1932, *The Music Box* (Parrott), is arguably their best. Their full-length pictures were *Pack Up Your Troubles* (32, Marshall and Raymond McCarey); *Fra Diavolo* (33, Roach and Charles Rogers); *Sons of the Desert* (33, William A. Seiter); and *Babes in Toyland* (34, Gus Meins and Rogers). After 1935, they made no more shorts, and concentrated on features: *Bonnie Scotland* (35, James Horne) and *The Bohemian Girl* (36, Horne and Rogers). There was bad feeling now between Laurel, Hardy, and Roach, with frequent talk of breakup. But they stayed together for *Our Relations* (36, Harry Lachman), which Laurel produced; *Way Out West* (37, Horne); *Swiss Miss* (38, John G. Blystone); and *Blockheads* (38, Blystone). At this point, they severed their connection with MGM–Hal Roach; after *Flying Deuces* (39, Edward A. Sutherland); *A Chump at Oxford* (40, Alfred Goulding), the story of which came from Harry Langdon; and *Saps at Sea* (40, Gordon Douglas), they parted company with Roach.

The "boys" stuck together and formed a production company of their own, but were forced to seek aid from Fox and MGM: *Great Guns* (41, Monty Banks); *A Haunting We Will Go* (42, Alfred Werker); *Air Raid Wardens* (43, Edward Sedgwick); *Jitterbugs* (43, Malcolm St. Clair); *The Dancing Masters* (43, St. Clair); *The Big Noise*

(44, St. Clair); *Nothing but Trouble* (44, Sam Taylor); and *The Bullfighters* (45, St. Clair).

That really was the end, twenty years before Laurel died. They made one more film, in France, *Robinson Crusoeland* (51, Léo Joannon), and Hardy appeared, alone, in *The Fighting Kentuckian* (49, George Waggner).

Piper Laurie (Rosetta Jacobs),
b. Detroit, Michigan, 1932

Somewhere deep down in the Hollywood papers (all the reports, all the stories), there may be an explanation of how the name "Piper Laurie" came to be, and even a joyful self-tribute from the person who came up with the fabrication. What does it say? Cute, tomboyish, melodious, Scots perhaps? And what warning signs were there, in the late forties, in an actress named "Rosetta Jacobs"? The young woman from Michigan may have hated the name, eventually, yet she never changed it. Few Hollywood veterans have taken her leaves of absence—and few can point to a role that did as much to change the dramatic place of women in pictures as that of Sarah Packard, beautiful, wounded, limping, and expecting the worst in *The Hustler* (61, Robert Rossen). Laurie was nominated for an Oscar for Sarah (she lost to Sophia Loren in *Two Women*). But Sarah still seems like a woman any man touches at his peril. She is so strong that her eventual fate is a matter of bleak tragedy. If only someone had remembered her in *The Color of Money*.

Ms. Jacobs was screen-tested while still at school, and with her new name she became a Universal kid in *Louisa* (50, Alexander Hall). Thereafter, she was with Donald O'Connor in *The Milkman* (50, Charles T. Barton); with Tony Curtis in *The Prince Who Was a Thief* (51, Rudolph Maté); *Francis Goes to the Races* (51, Arthur Lubin); with Curtis in *No Room for the Groom* (52, Douglas Sirk); with Rock Hudson in *Has Anybody Seen My Gal?* (52, Sirk); with Curtis again in the classic *Son of Ali Baba* (52, Kurt Neumann); with Tyrone Power in *Mississippi Gambler* (53, Maté); *The Golden Blade* (53, Nathan Juran); *Dangerous Mission* (54, Louis King); *Johnny Dark* (54, George Sherman); *Dawn at Socorro* (54, Sherman); *Smoke Signal* (55, Jerry Hopper); *Ain't Misbehavin'* (55, Edward Buzzell); *Kelly and Me* (57, Robert Z. Leonard).

Until They Sail (57, Robert Wise), with Paul Newman, was actually her first grown-up film. But then she retired for four years before *The Hustler* came along. It should have brought her so many better offers, but in the event she married the critic Joseph Morgenstern and then retired seriously for fifteen years.

Her comeback was as the mother in *Carrie* (76, Brian De Palma), an overwrought performance that won a supporting nomination—she lost to Beatrice Straight in *Network*. Since that, Laurie has worked fairly steadily, often for television: *Ruby* (77, Curtis Harrington); *The Boss's Son* (78, Bobby Roth); in love with Mel Gibson in *Tim* (79, Michael Pate); *Skag* (80, Frank Perry); as Magda Goebbels, nominated for an Emmy in *The Bunker* (81, George Schaefer); *The Thorn Birds* (82, Daryl Duke); as Aunt Em in *Return to Oz* (85, Walter Murch); another Oscar nomination in *Children of a Lesser God* (86, Randa Haines)—she lost to Dianne Wiest in *Hannah and Her Sisters; Appointment with Death* (88, Michael Winner); *Tiger Warsaw* (88, Amin Q. Chaudhri); *Dream a Little Dream* (89, Marc Rocco); spectacular on TV in David Lynch's *Twin Peaks* (90); *Other People's Money* (91, Norman Jewison); *Storyville* (92, Mark Frost); *Trauma* (93, Dario Argento); *Wrestling Ernest Hemingway* (93, Haines); *The Crossing Guard* (95, Sean Penn); *The Grass Harp* (96, Charles Matthau); *The Faculty* (98, Robert Rodriguez); on TV in *Inherit the Wind* (99, Daniel Petrie); *The Mao Game* (99, Joshua John Miller); *Possessed* (00, Steven E. de Souza); *Midwives* (01, Glenn Jordan); *The Last Brickmaker in America* (01, Gregg Champion); *Eulogy* (03, Michael Clancy)..

(David) Jude Law, b. London, 1972

No, not Jude the Obscure, Hardy's melancholy hero, but "Hey, Jude," the Beatles' song from 1968. But how could anyone expect obscurity from this intensely on-fire actor? In just a few years, the southeast Londoner has proved himself one of the few modern actors with a confident grasp of old-fashioned charisma. He has a way of seizing films that reminds one of Blackbeard with treasure. There is a zeal for attention in his eyes reminiscent of Tyrone Power, yet Law is so much more up-to-date in his attitudes and prickly smarts. There has as yet been no one film that opts for his power, nerve, and witty stare. But they will come. Meanwhile, he has the slightly awkward ability to unbalance movies that try to keep him on a leash.

The child of teachers, he entered the National Youth Music Theatre in London, and in 1990 he got a role in the British TV soap *Families*. He went on stage and did *Indiscretions* in London and New York. His movie career began with *Shopping* (94, Paul Anderson III); *I Love You, I Love You Not* (96, Billy Hopkins), where he played opposite Claire Danes; outstanding, lovely, and dangerous, as Lord Alfred Douglas in *Wilde* (97, Brian Gilbert); *Gattaca* (97, Andrew Niccol), the first film in which his steel gaze was used as something more than human; a smaller role in *Bent* (97, Sean Mathias); the best thing in *Midnight in the Garden of Good and Evil* (97, Clint Eastwood); *Music from Another Room* (98, Charlie Peters); a vampire in *The Wisdom of Crocodiles* (98, Po-Chih Leong); *eXistenZ* (99, David Cronenberg), with another venture beyond ordinary limits.

His breakthrough came as Dickie Greenleaf in *The Talented Mr. Ripley* (99, Anthony Minghella). Much as I admire that film (and Matt Damon in it), it's hard to escape the feeling that the picture loses some drive and fascination when Dickie dies. It's a measure of how seldom we see raw human vitality on screen these days. He then did *Love, Honor and Obey* (99, Dominic Anciano and Ray Burdis); the marksman in *Enemy at the Gates* (01, Jean-Jacques Annaud); a dazzling Gigolo Joe in *A.I.: Artificial Intelligence* (01, Steven Spielberg), where his role is unnecessary to the plot but vital to any hope of pleasure.

He was nearly exotic as Weegee crossed with Widmark in *Road to Perdition* (02, Sam Mendes), and he clearly faces a great test in the lead role in *Cold Mountain* (03, Minghella).

Richard Leacock, b. London, 1921

Richard is the younger brother of Philip Leacock, a director of humdrum feature movies that have seldom exceeded the limits of entertainment cinema. Nothing in his own work reveals Richard as a more distinct or talented director. And yet he is vastly more important. Indeed, in the long-term survey of man's use of film, it may be that Leacock's part in the cinema verité movement will be seen as highly influential. If only because he is marginally the senior, and because the approach of cinema verité amounts to a blurring of the talents or personalities of the filmmakers, it is legitimate to include within an entry on Leacock his chief collaborators in the fusion of cinema and journalism: Robert Drew, Greg Shuker, the Maysles brothers, and D. A. Pennebaker. (In addition, as head of film at M.I.T., he produced far too many young men and women who carried a camera in nearly every life situation.)

Richard is first and foremost a cinematographer of documentary projects. Having come to America in his teens, he became photographer to Willard Van Dyke, for several wartime films made by the army, and in 1948, on Robert Flaherty's *Louisiana Story*, the last gesture of pioneering documentary, intent on going to the corners of the earth to bring back pictorial celebrations of the simple life that existed there. Leacock was capable of the beauty of the swamp scenery and the "symphonic" treatment of the oil rig. But Flaherty was enchanted by the idea of the noble savage so that his films are curiously out of touch with political and economic realities. *Louisiana Story* is nominally about oil drilling, but it has little sense of time and place, let alone political direction or human involvement. Even so, it was set up on much the same basis as the classic 1930s films by Pare Lorentz—*The River* and *The Plow That Broke the Plains*. In other words, it was made on institutional or corporation money, to propound some notion about how the world ought to be run, or rerun.

Documentaries of that sort may still be made: *Nuit et Brouillard*, for instance, was filmed by Alain Resnais for the Museum of the Second World War. But since 1948 a new, journalistic appetite for documentary or reportage had come into being: TV. *Louisiana Story*, and films like it, might have taken six to nine months to make, being composed with care and artistry before being released to rather select audiences, numbered in the thousands. But TV is geared quite differently. In any one evening it is likely to show seventy-seven minutes (the length of *Louisiana Story*) of newsreel or documentary footage—shot and processed with the emphasis on speed—to an audience measured in the millions. And the next night, and the next . . . Most of such footage comes to us because a cameraman was sent in time to . . . Vietnam, the Middle East, or wherever. We hardly know who "directed" or "was responsible for" the miles of film from Vietnam, but nevertheless we were moved to tears, anger, and dismay by it. Someone pressed the button, and we did the rest. It may be odious to "compose" a close-up of a child whose face has been stripped by napalm.

Cinema verité is based on the thought that film ought, as swiftly and directly as possible, to connect that child with our sensibilities. It is able to rest its case on the objectivity of its method and on the usefulness of filming important people at close quarters, without unsettling them, and then conveying those images to audiences. Leacock and Robert Drew began by making films for *Time-Life*, for TV showing, with novel cameras and tape recorders that allowed two men, as unobtrusively as possible, to cover such newsworthy events as the 1960 primary in Wisconsin between senators Kennedy and Humphrey (*Primary*); a motor race (*Eddie Sachs at Indianapolis*); the ordeal of a man sentenced to death (*The Chair*); and the rehearsal of a play and the effects on its actress (*Jane*). Drew and Leacock experimented with the famous and the unknown. But they found the recurring need for a subject that had wide appeal and where there was an extra dramatic interest in seeming to catch people under stress reacting spontaneously. Cinema verité has tended to founder on the everyday and mundane. Secretly, it has the journalist's uneasy lust for disaster or breakdown, for the moment when the subject "cracks."

Leacock and his colleagues argued that they did not believe that their remorseless coverage disturbed the people they were filming. Reasonably, they argued that a senator working for his life soon forgot one discreet camera that was always in his presence—after all, men forget their wives in that way. It might be different with a show-off like

Joseph Levine (*Showman*), and there were arguments that Jane Fonda's creative energy could have been sapped by the cameras that filmed her rehearsals. In part, that is journalism demanding the right to be everywhere and then being amazed by charges of intrusiveness. In fact, politicians hire TV coaches and makeup artists, and know as much as Dietrich about how they photograph best. Later cinema verité films have been more concerned about what effect filming has on reality. Godard asked runic questions and made films about the helpless answers to them. *Gimme Shelter*, made by the Maysles brothers in 1971, on the Rolling Stones concert at Altamont, edged up to the dilemma of how far the cameraman might have a duty to intervene. On the "American Family" series, made for TV, there came a moment when an affair between the unhappy wife and the sympathetic director seemed imminent.

The "artistic" importance of cinema verité is that it has asked these questions. We now look at real events as if they were also performances. The "American Family" situation only reproduced a common bond in fiction film production. That is no disgrace. For who believes that people have not always performed or played themselves, that they have not always had to present themselves in everyday life? Cinema verité has made us reappraise sincerity and see the qualities shared by fiction and documentary. When Sam Ervin at Watergate reacted to criticism by conceding that he was only a country lawyer, he was James Stewart in *Anatomy of a Murder* blunting the sharpness of George C. Scott. And when Orson Welles lumbered on set to be interviewed by Dick Cavett, he was only one more surrogate Kane ready to say, "They asked the questions quicker in my day."

Sir David Lean (1908–91),

b. Croydon, England

1942: *In Which We Serve* (codirected with Noel Coward). 1944: *This Happy Breed.* 1945: *Blithe Spirit; Brief Encounter.* 1946: *Great Expectations.* 1948: *Oliver Twist.* 1949: *The Passionate Friends; Madeleine.* 1952: *The Sound Barrier.* 1954: *Hobson's Choice.* 1955: *Summer Madness.* 1957: *The Bridge on the River Kwai.* 1962: *Lawrence of Arabia.* 1965: *Dr. Zhivago.* 1970: *Ryan's Daughter.* 1984: *A Passage to India.*

Lean's death was nearly a state occasion for many in British film. His reputation stayed very high, despite inactivity, despite even the sad disorder of *A Passage to India*, a film markedly less assured than the work of James Ivory (which is not to praise Ivory). I am more than ever of the opinion that Lean became lost in the sense of his own pictorial grandeur. *The Passionate Friends* and *Madeleine*, for instance, stand up so much better

than those battleship pictures that came later. Not even the rerelease of *Lawrence*—beautiful, and with some lost material restored—could furnish any sense of ideas behind it.

Lean was a Quaker by upbringing, not allowed to visit the cinema as a boy. After a spell in accountancy, he joined the film industry and rose from tea boy, to clapper/loader, to cutting room assistant, to assistant director, to editor on Movietone News. In 1934 he became an editor and worked on *Escape Me Never* (35, Paul Czinner); *Pygmalion* (38, Anthony Asquith and Leslie Howard); *Major Barbara* (41, Gabriel Pascal); *49th Parallel* (41, Michael Powell); and *One of Our Aircraft Is Missing* (42, Powell). His chance to direct arose in 1942 when he handled the action sequences of *In Which We Serve*.

What happened then with David Lean? By the time of his death, he was a knight and a famous master. It was taken as tragic that obscure circumstances had prevented Lean from doing his versions of the Bounty story and of Conrad's *Nostromo*. He had made a sad hash of E. M. Forster's *A Passage to India*, yet somehow people persuaded themselves that he could have handled Conrad's more difficult book. It is worth stressing that Lean was a charming egotist, endlessly handsome, and in pursuit of women, and achingly hopeful when he spoke. He was a spellbinder, and so it was easier for enthusiasts to miss his frequent discomfort with dialogue scenes. Lean was most striking when he could hark back to the pure narrative of silent films.

Whatever happened began in the 1950s. *The Sound Barrier* was an interesting subject, but a dull, inconclusive film; *Hobson's Choice* was woefully slow and unfunny, yet seemingly bewitched by its own period recreation. Then came *Bridge on the River Kwai*, a strange mixture of conventional British heroics and antiwar message lit up with the flash of Burmese jungles, schoolboy irony, and those little gods for best picture, best director, and actor. Lean was a romantic about himself, and those rewards may have persuaded him that he was too grand for small things. It was the Selznick syndrome.

The pictures that followed—*Lawrence, Zhivago,* and *Ryan's Daughter*—seem to me examples of size and "the visual" eclipsing sense. No matter the version, it is so hard to discern what *Lawrence* is about—it seems afflicted with very English intimations that the desert is a place for miracles; *Zhivago* is a syrupy romance, without poetry or plausibility; and *Ryan's Daughter* may be as bad a film as any "great" director ever made.

From 1952 to 1991, he made eight films—and in only one of them, I suggest—*Lawrence*—is the spectacle sufficient to mask the hollow rhetoric of the scripts. But the Lean before 1952 made eight films in ten years that are lively, stirring, and an inspiration—they make you want to go out and make movies, they are so in love with the screen's power and the combustion in editing. *Brief Encounter* is slight and cozy, a bit of an exercise, but it works on screen—Trevor Howard and Celia Johnson are lovers to shame the posing of *Dr. Zhivago*. *Oliver Twist* is ravishing still: magnificent in its period recreation, its rank city, and its evil; it is greedily edited and beautifully designed (with a lot of Russian influence showing), and shot in sooty shadow and imperiled light, with great performances from Guinness, Robert Newton, Kay Walsh, and John Howard Davies (all supporting parts, as it were—Lean was never as relaxed with lead roles). *Great Expectations* is not as good, but it's still worthwhile. *The Passionate Friends* is the film most deserving recovery—an intricate triangle story, with Howard, Claude Rains, and Ann Todd (who was Lean's wife then—she followed Kay Walsh). Todd is also the Scottish poisoner in the excellent *Madeleine*.

Those early films have pace, flourish, and a modesty of scale (even if *Oliver Twist* feels big). And then, slowly, Lean became the prisoner of big pictures, a great eye striving to show off a large mind. I challenge anyone to see *Oliver Twist* and *Dr. Zhivago* and not admit the loss. It will take a very good biography to explain that process.

Jean-Pierre Léaud, b. Paris, 1944

Léaud stared out of the frozen ending of *The 400 Blows* (59, François Truffaut), a crew-cut, round-faced adolescent, as torn between inhibition and cheeky humor as Truffaut himself. The spontaneity of that film, and its moving nostalgia for a nearly brutalized childhood, hung in large part on the complicity between Truffaut and Léaud. But was Truffaut well advised to persist with the emotional, autobiographical link? Was Léaud capable of sustaining a film?

He grew up a lean, furtive young man; his hair flopped lankly over a sharp fox's nose. No question that Léaud was alert and compelling, but he looked sly, living off events in films, not actually touched by them. His Antoine Doinel was too indifferent to the gentle daydream of *Stolen Kisses* (68, Truffaut), especially the wondrous pact that Delphine Seyrig makes with him. It seemed a case of Truffaut rationalizing his choice, rather than feeling it. He was too sure a judge of actors to accept Léaud's meanness of spirit, but Léaud was an emblem he felt unable to discard. The potential for a tender account of sentimental education in *Stolen Kisses* foundered on Léaud's frosty privacy. *Bed and Board* (70, Truffaut), with Doinel married, was Truffaut's poorest film, in which his offhand lyricism veered into irrelevant knockabout. Léaud was a good deal more integral to *Anne and Muriel* (71, Truffaut), but hardly

attuned to the literary resonance of the film and its emotional subtleties. We could barely accept him as a novelist, even if the ending, with his sudden recognition of himself as a wintry solitary, was suited to Léaud's hurrying selfishness.

The adult Léaud is a darting, paranoid personality, fit for the jagged political-strip cartooning of late Godard. When Godard violently abandoned tenderness in *Pierrot le Fou*, he made Léaud his central character in *Masculin-Feminin* (66), where the actor's tendency to abrupt denials of solitariness are countered by his self-nagging hunched stance. In keeping with his capacities, Léaud was the bellboy in Godard's sketch from *Le Plus Vieux Métier du Monde* (67); "Donald Siegel" in *Made in USA* (66, Godard); in *La Chinoise* (67, Godard); the figure of Saint-Just, breaking down to become another tripper in *Week-End* (67, Godard); the great-grandson of Rousseau in *Le Gai Savoir* (68, Godard).

Elsewhere, he appeared in *Le Testament d'Orphée* (60, Jean Cocteau); in Truffaut's episode, as Doinel again, from *L'Amour à Vingt Ans* (62); essaying his brusque charm in *Le Père Noel a les Yeux Bleus* (65, Jean Eustache); actually engaging in *Le Départ* (67, Jerzy Skolimowski); in an episode from *Dialog* (68, Skolimowski); in *Porcile* (69, Pier Paolo Pasolini); *Os Herdeiros* (69, Carlos Diegues); *Le Lion à Sept Têtes* (70, Glauber Rocha); *Une Aventure de Billy le Kid* (70, Luc Moullet); playing up as the filmmaker in *Last Tango in Paris* (72, Bernardo Bertolucci); as the central figure in *La Maman et la Putain* (73, Eustache), gradually dismantled by the more mature anguish of the women; as the blindly vain actor in *Day for Night* (73, Truffaut) who makes audiences gasp with distaste when he phones Jacqueline Bisset's husband.

The one film that fully employs Léaud's manic solitariness is *Out One: Spectre* (73, Jacques Rivette) in which he is the most obsessed victim of the idea of the "13."

In 1979, he was back again as Doinel in *Love on the Run*, thirty-five still going on seventeen, but shamed as an actor by the vitality and candor he had had in *The 400 Blows*.

Since then, one hears that he has had personal difficulties. But he works on, doggedly, the face increasingly haunted: *On a Pas Fini d'en Parler* (79, Bernard Dubois); *Parano* (81, Dubois); *Aiutami a Sognare* (81, Pupi Avati); *La Cassure* (83, Ramon Munoz); *Rebelote* (83, Jacques Richard); in the Rue Fontaine episode of *Paris Vu Par . . . 20 Ans Après* (84, Philippe Garel); *L'Herbe Rouge* (84, Pierre Kast); *Csak egy Mozi* (84, Pal Sandor); *L'Ile au Tresor* (85, Raul Ruiz); *Detective* (85, Godard); *Grandeur et Decadence d'un Petit Commerce de Cinema* (86, Godard); *36 Filette* (88, Catherine Breillat); *La Femme de Paille* (88, Suzanne Schiffman); *Jane B. par Agnes*

V. (88, Agnes Varda); *Les Ministères de l'Art* (88, André Téchiné); *I Hired a Contract Killer* (90, Aki Kaurismaki); *La Vie de Bohème* (90, Kaurismaki); and *J'Embrasse Pas* (91, Téchiné).

As he comes up on sixty, he works as hard, and as if he were an actor. Yet for many of us he seems like a startled being caught in the haunted house and never able to find the exit: *Paris s'Eveille* (91, Olivier Assayas); *Missä on Musette?* (92, Veikko Nieminen and Jarmo Vesteri); *La Naissance de l'Amour* (93, Garrel); *Personne ne M'Aime* (94, Marion Vernoux); *Mon Homme* (96, Bertrand Blier); *Le Journal du Séducteur* (96, Daniele Dubroux); *Irma Vep* (96, Assayas); *Pour Rire!* (97, Lucas Belvaux); uncredited in *Elizabeth* (98, Shakhar Kapur); *Innocent* (98, Costa Natsis); *Une Affaire de Goût* (99, Bernard Rapp); the lead in *L'Affaire Marcorelle* (00, Serge Le Peron); *Ni Neibian Jidian/What Time Is It Over There?* (01, Tsai Ming-liang); *Le Pornographe* (01, Bertrand Bonello); *La Guerre à Paris* (02, Yolande Zauberman).

Patrice Leconte, b. Paris, 1947

1968: *Autoportrait* (s). 1969: *L'Espace Vital* (s). 1970: *Tout a la Plume ou au Pinceau* (s). 1971: *Le Laboratoire de l'Angoisse* (s). 1972: *La Famille Heureuse* (s). 1975: *Les Vécés étaient Fermés de l'Interieur.* 1978: *Les Bronzés/French Fried Vacation.* 1979: *Les Bronzés Font du Ski.* 1980: *Viens Chez Moi, J'Habite Chez une Copine.* 1981: *Ma Femme S'Appelle Reviens.* 1982: *Circulez, Y'A Rien a Voir.* 1984: *Les Spécialistes.* 1986: *Tandem.* 1988: *Monsieur Hire.* 1990: *Le Mari de la Coiffeuse/The Hairdresser's Husband.* 1992: *Tango.* 1993: *Le Parfum d'Yvonne.* 1995: *Les Grands Ducs.* 1996: *Ridicule.* 1998: *Une Chance sur Deux.* 1999: *La Fille sur le Pont/The Girl on the Bridge.* 2001: *La Veuve de Saint-Pierre/The Widow of St. Pierre.* 2001: *Felix et Lola; Rue des Plaisirs.* 2002: *L'Homme du Train/Man on the Train.* 2003: *Confidences Trop Intimes.*

In France, Patrice Leconte now rates very highly as a winner of Césars and as a maker of provocative films. His *Ridicule* (the only one of his features on which he was not involved as a writer, too) was a modest international success, and a picture that drew attention to wit, language, and the whole art of teasing. But then, as his next venture, in *Une Chance sur Deux,* Leconte was acute enough to reunite Delon and Belmondo—but incapable of making a picture that got American release. You can propose that Leconte might do anything next—from rare period fable to fairy story to boulevard comedy. But to these eyes, that versatility begins to look like uncertainty.

He was a film-mad kid (a teenager during the New Wave), who went to IDHEC, and began making shorts as he worked as a cartoonist. He showed an early taste for comedy, but his outstanding work is *Monsieur Hire.* Taken from a Simenon novel, this is a film of great suspense in which the way of watching is crucial to the drama. It also has exceptional performances from Michel Blanc (normally a comic) and Sandrine Bonnaire. Next to *Hire, The Girl on the Bridge* seems a very fanciful construct, clever, promising, and done in beautiful black-and-white, but nowhere near as compelling as the earlier film about voyeurism. But *The Widow of St. Pierre* (with Juliette Binoche and Daniel Auteuil) was back to his best level.

Ang Lee, b. Taiwan, 1954

1983: *Dim Lake* (s). 1985: *Fine Line* (s). 1991: *Pushing Hands.* 1993: *The Wedding Banquet.* 1994: *Eat Drink Man Woman.* 1995; *Sense and Sensibility.* 1997: *The Ice Storm.* 1998: *Ride with the Devil.* 2000: *Crouching Tiger, Hidden Dragon.* 2003: *The Hulk.*

Yes, Ang Lee is at least as good as "everyone" says. More than that, he is capable of quietly giving the slip to his large, adoring following, and getting back to the vein of what I take for his best work, those two "failures" in his illustrious list, *The Ice Storm* and *Ride with the Devil.*

He came to America only when he was in his early twenties, and did theatre at the University of Illinois and then film at New York University, where he met James Schamus, who has been his producer and/or cowriter on all his projects.

The first thing to be remarked on is the most obvious—how a Taiwanese has moved from family stories in the world he grew up in to the atmospheres of Jane Austen, the swinging society of suburbia in the seventies, the borderlands in the American Civil War, and the coded legend of Asian swordplay films. Nothing now would surprise, whether he pursues the musical, science fiction, or something else entirely. For he seems to possess the ability to translate all periods and styles into fluent movie forms. *The Wedding Banquet* and *Eat Drink Man Woman* are a little like Ozu, but with more energy and spontaneity. They are filled with a respect for older people, and for anyone caught in a trap, that actually meshed perfectly with the worlds of Austen and Rick Moody (who wrote *The Ice Storm*).

No one would deny the plastic lyricism of *Crouching Tiger, Hidden Dragon,* or underestimate the special stress it places on women. It is also amused and intelligent enough to amount to a catalogue, not just of Asian films, but of film as a whole. Still, it was fanciful, crowd-pleasing, and spectacular in ways that could lead many people astray—especially granted its great success.

So it would be very sad if Ang Lee forgot the extraordinary complexity of *The Ice Storm* and

Ride with the Devil, their historical concern, their Renoir-like reluctance to take sides in tricky situations, and their sense of so many somber destinies tangled together. *The Ice Storm* won some critical praise, but was also widely deemed depressing. *Ride with the Devil* was barely noticed. Let those ironies feed the fertility of Ang Lee's mind, and let him remain someone happy to startle and put off public congratulation. His greatest work is likely to be his biggest "disaster." Alas, *The Hulk* is a little arty, and very dull.

Bruce Lee (Lee Yuen Kam) (1940–73),
b. San Francisco

In a way, it's hardly worth including Bruce Lee unless one can speak about him with passion. So, because I can't find that warmth, I'll quote Kenneth Turan, who wrote, "He is refreshing, youthful, invigorating, with an ingratiating grin and a totally unexpected, totally winning boyish personality. It is this pixie quality, coupled with his boggling, deadly physical abilities, that makes him, despite the amiable dross of low-grade exploitation films, irresistible."

It was an extraordinary life. Born in California, he actually spent much of his childhood in Hong Kong, where he made his first film—*The Birth of Mankind*—at the age of six. He studied philosophy at the University of Washington, and then in his mid-twenties he did some American television—in episodes of *Batman,* and playing Kato in *The Green Hornet* (66–67).

Neither of those shows gave a real hint of what was to come: for physical perfection turned into martial arts, and the pixie became, by many accounts, a rather tyrannical figure, the very self-aware manager of his own cult. And just as with James Dean, Lee's rise was cut off almost as soon as it had begun. The supposed perfect specimen collapsed suddenly with some kind of brain seizure, leaving behind a few pictures—the famous "chop sockies," mostly made by the Shaw Brothers in Hong Kong, in which Lee the tiny, coiled street fighter took on all comers, and dispatched them (sometimes with grisly violence, sometimes with balletic aplomb): *Marlowe* (69, Paul Bogart), where his impact is comic; *Fists of Fury* (71, Lo Wei); *The Chinese Connection* (72, Lo Wei); *Enter the Dragon* (73, Robert Clouse); *Return of the Dragon* (73, Lee).

Millions loved him, and clearly he is the pioneer figure in the West's adoption of Jackie Chan and John Woo as "masters." Moreover, Lee was a purist in that he preferred not to use movie tricks, or extra boosts in his leaping attacks. He did the stunts himself. He had unquestioned charisma. I suppose what troubles me is his lack of character or mind, set in contrast with his delirious physical excellence. He seems to me to celebrate a spur of cinema that separates violence from life, and rev-

els in it. To join with a Bruce Lee film is to forget such things as damage and pain—and I have always felt that that was a dead end for the movies and their society.

Of course, by today, the human image of Bruce Lee (and I can understand claims for its beauty) has turned into not just generations of imitators (including his son, Brandon), but the flickering pixel in video games. I happen to be writing this only a few days after September 11, 2001. I don't need to blame that on Lee, and I don't wish to be solemn. I will just say that, having failed to muster the interest to write this entry for months, I do now feel prompted.

Christopher Lee, b. London, 1922

My paperback copy of Carlos Clarens's *Horror Movies* has lasted very well over thirty years, but the last time I picked it up I noticed that one of my children had fondly touched up the frontispiece photograph of Lee—in *Dracula* (58, Terence Fisher)—with a scarlet daub on an eyetooth. I will need columns to describe Lee, but maybe that one adornment says it better.

Lee was like a taller, darker Dennis Price, which is to say he could have expected gentleman roles—romancer or bounder. And he was ten years in pictures, to no great effect, before someone realized that the Count fitted both sides better than any other part. Once infected, Lee could never get out of horror, and so he chose to invest the genre with dignity and feeling. If it possessed him, then it was worthy of proper attention and heartfelt acting.

On the way to Transylvania (and Hammer), he did *Corridor of Mirrors* (48, Terence Young); *Hamlet* (48, Laurence Olivier); *One Night with You* (48, Young); *Penny and the Pownall Case* (48, Slim Hand); *Scott of the Antarctic* (48, Charles Frend); *A Song for Tomorrow* (48, Fisher); *Saraband for Dead Lovers* (48, Basil Dearden); *My Brother's Keeper* (48, Alfred Roome); *Trottie True* (49, Brian Desmond Hurst); *They Were Not Divided* (49, Young); *Prelude to Fame* (50, Fergus McDonnell).

He was in *Captain Horatio Hornblower* (51, Raoul Walsh); *Valley of the Eagles* (51, Young); *Paul Temple Returns* (52, Maclean Rogers); *The Crimson Pirate* (52, Robert Siodmak); *Innocents in Paris* (53, Gordon Parry); *Moulin Rouge* (53, John Huston); *That Lady* (54, Young); *The Dark Avenger* (54, Henry Levin); *Storm over the Nile* (55, Zoltan Korda); *The Cockleshell Heroes* (55, José Ferrer); *Private's Progress* (55, John and Roy Boulting); *Port Afrique* (56, Rudolph Maté); *Alias John Preston* (56, David MacDonald); *Beyond Mombasa* (56, George Marshall); *Battle of the River Plate* (56, Michael Powell); *Moby Dick* (56, Huston); *Ill Met By Moonlight* (57, Powell); *Fortune Is a Woman* (57, Sidney Gilliat); *The Traitor*

(57, Michael McCarthy); *The Truth About Women* (57, Muriel Box); *Bitter Victory* (57, Nicholas Ray); St. Evremonde in *A Tale of Two Cities* (58, Ralph Thomas).

But in 1957 he was cast as the Monster in *The Curse of Frankenstein* (Fisher). Next year he was a sexy Dracula, and his future was set. There have been very few diversions allowed in a litany of films that is like a poem to the horror genre: *The Hound of the Baskervilles* (59, Fisher); *The Man Who Could Cheat Death* (59, Fisher); as *The Mummy* (59, Fisher); *The Two Faces of Dr. Jekyll* (60, Fisher); *Beat Girl* (60, Edmond T. Gréville); *Horror Hotel* (60, John Moxey); *Too Hot to Handle* (60, Young); *The Hands of Orlac* (61, Gréville); *Taste of Fear* (61, Seth Holt); *The Terror of the Tongs* (61, Anthony Bushell); *The Pirates of Blood River* (62, John Gilling); *Corridor of Blood* (62, Robert Day)—filmed several years earlier, and costarring Boris Karloff.

He was in *The Longest Day* (62, Ken Annakin and others); and he began to make many films in Europe. But he was back at Hammer for *The Gorgon* (64, Fisher); *Dr. Terror's House of Horrors* (65, Freddie Francis); *She* (65, Day); *The Skull* (65, Francis); *The Face of Fu Manchu* (65, Don Sharp); very good in *Rasputin: The Mad Monk* (66, Sharp); *The Brides of Fu Manchu* (66, Sharp); *Circus of Fear* (67, Moxey); *Blood Fiend* (67, Samuel Gallu); *Dracula Has Risen from the Grave* (68, Francis); *The Crimson Cult* (68, Vernon Sewell), with Karloff and Barbara Steele.

He played with Vincent Price in *The Oblong Box* (69, Gordon Hessler); he was a guest Dracula in *The Magic Christian* (69, Joseph McGrath); *Scream and Scream Again* (70, Hessler)—every title has been used, first as a verb and then as a noun; *Taste the Blood of Dracula* (70, Peter Sasdy); *Scars of Dracula* (70, Roy Ward Baker); as Artimedorus in *Julius Caesar* (70, Stuart Burge); as Mycroft in *The Private Life of Sherlock Holmes* (70, Billy Wilder); *The House That Dripped Blood* (70, Peter Duffell).

There is more, much more, but really you could invent the titles yourself. When Lee wrote his autobiography in 1977, what was it called? *Tall, Dark and Gruesome*. He played Rochefort in Dick Lester's two Musketeer films. He was James Bond's villain in *The Man with the Golden Gun* (74, Guy Hamilton)—face it, he could just as easily have been Bond. And he has been seen recently in *Police Academy VII—Mission to Moscow* (94, Alan Metter); as Rameses in the TV *Moses* (96, Roger Young); as Tiresias in *The Odyssey* (97, Andrei Konchalovsky); as *Jinnah* (98, Jamil Dehlavi); in *Sleepy Hollow* (99, Tim Burton); *Gormenghast* (00, Andy Wilson); outstanding as Saruman in *Lord of the Rings: The Fellowship of the Ring* (01, Peter Jackson); and very cool as Count Dooku in *Star Wars: Episode II,*

Attack of the Clones (02, George Lucas); *Lord of the Rings: The Two Towers* (02, Jackson).

Spike Lee (Shelton Jackson Lee), b. Atlanta, Georgia, 1956
1982: *Joe's Bed-Stuy Barbershop: We Cut Heads* (s). 1986: *She's Gotta Have It*. 1988: *School Daze*. 1989: *Do the Right Thing*. 1990: *Mo' Better Blues*. 1991: *Jungle Fever*. 1992: *Malcolm X*. 1994: *Crooklyn*. 1995: *Clockers*. 1996: *Girl 6*; *Get on the Bus*. 1997: *4 Little Girls* (d). 1998: *He Got Game*; *Freak* (TV). 1999: *Summer of Sam*. 2000: *The Original Kings of Comedy* (d); *Bamboozled*. 2001: *A Huey P. Newton Story* (TV). 2001: *Come Rain or Come Shine* (d); *Jim Brown All American* (d). 2002: "We Wuz Robbed", episode from *Ten Minutes Older: The Trumpet*; *25th Hour*.

I didn't approach *Malcolm X* with high hopes. Ten minutes before it began, I had just gotten out of *A Few Good Men*, a rousingly meretricious picture, empty of ideas or purpose, but a lot of fun. I knew how long *Malcolm X* was going to be. The theatre was unheated, which surely indicated the steep decline in the movie's audience after its "event" opening. More than all of that, I was not a Spike Lee fan. His unsmiling entrepreneur pose and his inclination to have no one not black write about *Malcolm X* were allied in my mind with his limits as a director. The early films by Lee seem to me opportunistic, stylistically uncertain, naïve yet reckless (*Do the Right Thing*). *Jungle Fever*, I felt, failed to deal with the real human story and the mixed motives of interracial love or sex. I could see how tough it was to be a black movie director, without having to assume the profile of Black Movie Director. But I didn't always admire Lee's responses to the difficulty, or his unblinking insistence that a white had no right to say that, or believe it. It was so cold in the theater, and *Malcolm X* reached so far into the evening.

It is a movie that needs its three-plus hours, because it concerns change and needs to feel gradual. *Malcolm X* is also the work of a man Lee had hitherto lacked the confidence to reveal. It is measured, careful, a little distant even; it has largely set aside fireworks; and it is almost as if, in studying Malcolm, Lee has himself developed. There was an attempt in *Do the Right Thing* to show that everyone had his or her reasons, but it was thwarted by the agitprop scenario. In *Malcolm X*, however, the enlargement of Malcolm's own perspectives becomes the structure of the film—without any need to treat him as Helen Keller or Rocky Balboa. The melodrama was gone.

It is no small thing for an American movie to lead its audiences into an unfamiliar religion, and then out of it, without ever lapsing into zealotry or scorn. Yet *Malcolm X* is a movie about the need for religion, or moral steadfastness; and as its central character complicates his thinking, so he distills his behavior, and the flashy "Red"-ism of the first half settles into Denzel Washington's extraordinary, meditative performance.

One might argue that Lee's prior films were his "Red" period, with one eye on art, another on "rep," and a third on how to make the next film. That is one eye too many already, yet it puts Lee in the context of every other moviemaker—what do I do next? how do I get to do it? and how do I make it at least 50 percent mine?

Lee's Malcolm battles through many kinds of fierceness to a kind of liberal humanism. If Lee has himself made that journey—and in the movie it does feel achieved—then he might want to try *Jungle Fever* again, or do a movie, or two or three, with white material, or stories that do not depend upon just one color. In which case, his continued interest in style, his verve with actors, his ear and his eye could be the basis for an extraordinary career. *Malcolm X* makes serious demands on its audiences—but graver ones still on Lee.

The great thing about Lee is that he has not tired or faltered. The question mark still hangs over the degree of his talent. So he has been a growing presence, producing such films as *Tales from the Hood* (95, Rusty Cundieff); *New Jersey Drive* (95, Nick Gomez); *The Best Man* (99, Malcolm D. Lee); *Love & Basketball* (00, Gina Prince) and *3 A.M.* (01, Lee Davis). But, in truth, none of those films is remarkable, or as daring and accomplished, as *Do the Right Thing*.

As a director, too, Lee has not matched his own best work. *Clockers* is a good picture of the drugs in the city, but more dogged than brilliant. *Bamboozled*—an attempt at satire—fell rather flat. Best of all was *Summer of Sam,* a great film in the making, but one that gave away its own control to lots of raw talk, improvs for their own sake, a settling for urban atmosphere, and a tough treatment of women. But Lee is doing so much, and he is still only in his mid-forties. He is capable, I think, of a great film about New York—and it might be better if he saw that as his subject and let the responsibility of being the best black director around look after itself.

Ernest Lehman, b. New York, 1920

Around the age of sixty, Ernest Lehman seemed to have stopped doing scripts—and that's our loss. Of course, he may have been writing away (like Billy Wilder) on screenplays that are smart, funny, and beautifully constructed, only to be told that no one has the patience for movies like that any more and, anyway, what does he know about what kids want? So the kids are deprived, too, and everyone misses Lehman's subtle way of getting us to grow up.

He went to City College in New York, and then he worked for a while for a show business publicity agency. That's where he saw and heard the world of *Sweet Smell of Success* (57, Alexander Mackendrick), which began life as a novella by Lehman and grew eventually into a screenplay where he shared credit with Clifford Odets. The novella and other short stories won offers from Hollywood—one story sold in the late forties and became *The Inside Story* (48, Allan Dwan).

Lehman was in Hollywood by the early fifties, where John Houseman found him "prickly but stimulating," loved his work, and hired him for *Executive Suite* (54, Robert Wise). Next, he had a baptism of fire-by-collaboration, working with Billy Wilder on *Sabrina* (54). For *The King and I* (56, Walter Lang), he displayed a very different talent, that of taking a war-horse from one medium and making it work in another. The script for *Somebody Up There Likes Me* (56, Wise) is Lehman's favorite, because he felt he had got at things left unsaid in boxer Rocky Graziano's autobiography.

As years pass, nothing dates in *Sweet Smell of Success:* the vision of ordinary corruption is still as fresh as a warm corpse. The only thing blurry in the film—the bond between Hunsecker and his kid sister—was always blurry. It is a terrific and important movie, with fabulous dialogue.

Lehman then did *North by Northwest* (59, Alfred Hitchcock), his only original script. No one ever found Hitchcock an easy master, but Lehman handled him very well, no matter how frustrated he felt. The end product is a sublime mix of farce, chase, and layered character—the sense of Grant's advertising man as a kid who has to find maturity in a hurry is marvelously embedded in the headlong action. Only movies could make such gossamer seem as solid as American distance.

From the Terrace (60, Mark Robson) was strictly routine; and *West Side Story* (61, Wise and Jerome Robbins) was a test case for not getting in the way. *The Prize* (63, Robson) is a very entertaining, very silly movie. *The Sound of Music* (65, Wise) is . . . well, you don't need me to tell you that.

At this point, Lehman negotiated his hot record into the job of writer-producer and he deserves great credit for turning a potential menagerie into the very effective *Who's Afraid of Virginia Woolf?* (66, Mike Nichols). He then wrote and produced the successful but hardly interesting *Hello, Dolly!* (69, Gene Kelly). Failure came in large and loud with *Portnoy's Complaint* (72), which he also directed personally. In hindsight, Lehman admitted that he had missed the quality of Philip Roth's book by selecting only a part of it for film. But how could that novel ever be filmed?

His only other credits are *Family Plot* (76, Hitchcock), a fascinating idea that doesn't click; and *Black Sunday* (77, John Frankenheimer), a knockout setup that didn't win an audience.

Since then, Lehman has worked as a novelist and was a columnist for *American Film* magazine in the late seventies. He was given an honorary Oscar in 2001.

Janet Leigh (Jeanette Helen Morrison), b. Merced, California, 1927

Despite looking like a studio-manufactured, circumspect blonde broad, she found herself in some adventurous films. After owing her discovery to Norma Shearer, she made her debut, in 1947, as the mountain girl in Roy Rowland's *The Romance of Rosy Ridge* and was a full-bosomed ingenue for MGM in Zinnemann's *Act of Violence* (48); as Meg in *Little Women* (49, Mervyn Le Roy); in *That Forsyte Woman* (49, Compton Bennett); *The Red Danube* (49, George Sidney); *Strictly Dishonorable* (51, Melvin Frank); *Angels in the Outfield* (51, Clarence Brown); *Scaramouche* (52, Sidney); *Walking My Baby Back Home* (53, Lloyd Bacon); and *My Sister Eileen* (55, Richard Quine).

Throughout the 1950s she was the barely characterized love interest in a series of costume and adventure pictures: *Prince Valiant* (54, Henry Hathaway) and, with her then husband, Tony Curtis, in *Houdini* (53, George Marshall), *The Black Shield of Falworth* (54, Rudolph Maté), and *The Vikings* (58, Richard Fleischer)—in which Tony helpfully ripped open her Saxon princess's dress so that she could row more freely; *The Perfect Furlough* (58, Blake Edwards); and *Who Was That Lady?* (60, Sidney). She appeared unobtrusively in a disappointing assortment of films: *Bye Bye Birdie* (63, Sidney); *Wives and Lovers* (63, John Rich); *Harper* (66, Jack Smight); and *Three on a Couch* (66, Jerry Lewis). Only *An American Dream* (66, Robert Gist) really caught the eye.

It might be a routine career but for her incredulous presence in von Sternberg's *Jet Pilot* (51); as a crop-haired girl among men in Anthony Mann's *The Naked Spur* (53); as the menaced wife in Orson Welles's *Touch of Evil* (58), throughout most of which she kept a coat draped over a broken arm; as the girl met by chance on a train who saves Frank Sinatra's sanity in *The Manchurian Candidate* (62, John Frankenheimer); and—imperishably—as Marion Crane in *Psycho* (60), a frustrated, hard-up secretary, stroked, hounded, and finally cut to pieces by Hitchcock's attention in a shower cubicle, cabin 1, at a bypassed motel.

She retired effectively in 1980, having made a few films in the preceding years, mostly for television: *Murder at the World Series* (77, Andrew V. McLaglen); *Telethon* (77, David Lowell Rich); *Boardwalk* (79, Stephen Verona); *Mirror, Mirror* (79, Joanna Lee)—about plastic surgery; and *The Fog* (80, John Carpenter), where she played with Jamie Lee Curtis, her daughter by Tony Curtis. Then, later, she did *In My Sister's Shadow* (97,

Sandra Stein); *Halloween H20* (98, Steve Miner); *A Fate Totally Worse Than Death* (00, John T. Kretchmer).

Jennifer Jason Leigh, b. Los Angeles, 1958

She is the daughter of actor Vic Morrow (1932–82), from *Blackboard Jungle* (55, Richard Brooks) and *Men in War* (57, Anthony Mann), and of actress-writer Barbara Turner, who acted in Robert Altman's *Nightmare in Chicago* (64) and wrote *Petulia* (68, Richard Lester) for Altman. Patrick McGilligan's biography of Altman, *Jumping Off the Cliff*, suggests that the relationship between Altman and Turner hastened the end of her marriage to Morrow. And then, nearly thirty years later, Leigh appears, brilliant (if a little too close to an audition set piece), as the dour phone-sex provider in *Short Cuts* (93, Altman).

It's natural to think that Leigh's grim pout comes from Vic Morrow, one of the most steadily blocked Method actors. But to judge from photographs, she resembles her mother, too. Hers has been a tough career, working in many poor films, sometimes close to exploitation. As if from necessity, she has a long-suffering, wistful air that comes close to depravity or saintliness. She was a blind-mute in *Eyes of a Stranger* (81, Ken Wiederhorn); catching the eye in *Fast Times at Ridgemont High* (82, Amy Heckerling); *Wrong Is Right* (82, Richard Brooks); *Easy Money* (83, James Signorelli); *Grandview, U.S.A.* (84, Randal Kleiser); *Flesh + Blood* (85, Paul Verhoeven); *The Hitcher* (86, Robert Harmon); a dead-eyed call girl in *The Men's Club* (86, Peter Medak); *Sister, Sister* (87, Bill Condon); *Under Cover* (87, John Stockwell); and *Heart of Midnight* (88, Matthew Chapman).

She was very funny in *The Big Picture* (89, Christopher Guest); wan, working-class, and endlessly raped as Tralala in *Last Exit to Brooklyn* (89, Uli Edel); authentically dumb in *Miami Blues* (90, George Armitage); credibly a junkie in *Rush* (91, Lili Fini Zanuck); beguiling and creepy in *Single White Female* (92, Barbet Schroeder) in which her very quietness was sinister; tense, mannered, and even amateurish in *The Hudsucker Proxy* (94, Joel Coen); and Dorothy in *Mrs. Parker and the Vicious Circle* (94, Alan Rudolph).

As she approached forty, it was plain that she was too frowningly independent to notice that hurdle. She may not be ingratiating; she may come off stranger than some films require, but she is full of damaged history and shy ideas: *Dolores Claiborne* (95, Taylor Hackford); *Georgia* (95, Ulu Grosbard), written by her mother; *Bastard out of Carolina* (96, Anjelica Huston); *Washington Square* (97, Agniezska Holland); *A Thousand Acres* (97, Jocelyn Moorhouse); *eXistenZ* (99, David Cronenberg). Then, in 2001, with actor Alan Cumming, she codirected a very nice, sour inside-Hollywood picture, *The*

Anniversary Party, a further, welcome sign of Altman's touch.

She was in *The Quickie* (01, Sergei Bodrov); *Crossed Over* (02, Bobby Roth); completely wasted in *Road to Perdition* (02, Sam Mendes); *In the Cut* (03, Jane Campion).

Mike Leigh, b. Salford, England, 1943
1972: *Bleak Moments.* 1975: *Nuts in May* (TV). 1977: *Abigail's Party* (TV). 1980: *Grown Ups* (TV). 1981: *Home Sweet Home* (TV). 1983: *Meantime* (TV). 1984: *Four Days in July* (TV). 1987: *The Short and Curlies* (s). 1988: *High Hopes.* 1991: *Life Is Sweet.* 1993: *Naked.* 1996: *Secrets & Lies.* 1997: *Career Girls.* 1999: *Topsy-Turvy.* 2002: *All or Nothing.*

Leigh was a doctor's son, raised in a working-class area of Manchester. His special territory is the underclass, of undereducated, often unemployed people. Yet, just as he is a sharp observer of a real society, Leigh is also a play-maker, addicted to actorly recreations of the underclass. He is sometimes described as a social realist, yet I'm not sure that he isn't just as much a rapt observer of the process of acting. And it is in the ornate, very funny details of masquerade that Leigh may come dangerously close to a patronizing attitude to the people in his films.

Leigh went to the Royal Academy of Dramatic Art, the most celebrated acting school in Britain. He found there an undue emphasis on technique at the expense of reality. He moved away, to art school and the London Film School, with his chief goal being to make films about ordinary existence in which the quality of the acting was so given over to the characters (rather than the actors' reputations) that the results seemed documentary.

He worked in theatre first, and in 1970 he turned a play, *Bleak Moments,* into his feature film debut. Since then he has worked in television and theatre, on plays that he devises and directs, which emerge from a process of improvisation and search by Leigh and his actors. He selects actors for his group out of an instinct that sees ability, a sense of reality, objectivity, and a distinct lack of movie glamour. Leigh then sits down with each actor alone. He asks him or her to compile a list of people the actor knows. They sort through the list and find a few about whom Leigh begins to question the actor, until a kind of gradual natural "casting," or suggestion, has been achieved.

He then brings the group of actors (or people) together, and asks, what happens if these people meet? Thereafter, in group work (inadequately called rehearsal), they move toward a play.

If that sounds too free or disordered, see the films. As a camera director, Leigh maintains a detached, medical watchfulness that is more caring and demanding than it seems at first, and that

has reasonably been compared to the sensibility of Ozu. More than that, "scripts" arrived at by means of group interaction close to the flux of life still possess flights of talk that are hilarious, poignant, and so wordy that, at one moment in *Grown Ups,* a character says "A handbag!" and we suddenly see how close this inspired spontaneity has come to Oscar Wilde, Harold Pinter, and Joe Orton.

Leigh has an obsessive ear for the rhythms of small talk, and he is very good at getting a certain kind of monotone English humor, of deprecation masked as irony. But he loves the strange lilt of it so much, he is sometimes carried away, or carried beyond the strict realism of character. His films are full of delicious performances—his wife, Alison Steadman, Lesley Manville, Philip Davis, Timothy Spaull, Tim Roth, Jim Broadbent, Jane Horrocks. And some of the films are superbly satisfying, comic, and touching: *Meantime* and *High Hopes,* most notably. But the line between the grimly real and the elegantly farcical is fine and perilous, and sometimes we feel we are seeing not so much life as "something by Mike Leigh." There's nothing wrong with that, and much that is good. But there's also a hint of false pretenses, and a danger of the underclass being condescended to.

Naked was a big advance: it is the film in which real pain breaks through, along with Leigh's political anger. Suddenly it was easier to see how far the high comedy of low manners had been masking Leigh's distress with modern England.

Secrets & Lies was classic Leigh, and his biggest hit yet. *Career Girls* relied on exceptional performances from Katrin Cartlidge and Lynda Steadman. But *Topsy-Turvy* was a big departure—into fond period reconstruction and the world of Gilbert and Sullivan. For me, the film was too slow, but no one could deny the courage of so much fresh thinking, and it leaves one wondering what next? Will Leigh pick up the tradition of James Ivory, or is he about to open up English history?

Vivien Leigh (Vivian Mary Hartley)
(1913–1967), b. Darjeeling, India
It was a Saturday evening, December 10, 1938, the first day of shooting on *Gone With the Wind.* On the forty-acre backlot behind the Selznick Studio in Culver City, the burning of Atlanta was to be staged. To that end, old sets—some as old as *King Kong* and *King of Kings*—were dressed up with Atlanta, 1864, facades. When all the burning was done, the real sets for *Gone With the Wind* could be built on the cleared ground, so that proper shooting might begin in the last week of January. Selznick as yet had no actress to play Scarlett O'Hara: the stand-ins for the escape from the fire were told to keep their faces averted so that they could match with any chosen star—most likely Paulette Goddard at that stage.

As the fire passed its peak, three visitors came to the backlot: Selznick's brother, Myron, the top agent in town; one of Myron's clients, Laurence Olivier, who was in Hollywood doing *Wuthering Heights;* and Olivier's mistress, an English actress named Vivien Leigh. Myron called out to David, "Hey, genius, meet your Scarlett O'Hara!" It was likely a line he had used often over the last two years—that's how long Selznick had been looking.

He saw Vivien Leigh's face in the firelight: she was always a Technicolor hunch for a movie that would do reds and oranges better than they had ever been done on the screen. And wasn't she the girl named after the color? That very evening, Leigh read a few scenes for George Cukor who laughed at her English accent, then saw the beauty, the fire, and the need. For this English beginner had read the book when it first came out, and read it many times since. She knew she could do it. She had wangled a contact with the Myron Selznick Agency. She had come to America out of her own will. To see Larry? That's what Olivier thought. But that evening, in the firelight, the newcomer began to lay hands on a size and importance in pictures that the great actor could never match.

By Christmas, Leigh had the part. She worked harder on the picture, and with more purpose, than anyone. Cukor was fired. His replacement, Victor Fleming, fell ill. Selznick was in agonies of exhaustion and indecision. But the gambler was rewarded: he had dreamed of a Scarlett, and waited, and one had stepped forward out of the darkness. She was Southern enough; she was beautiful, ambitious, bitchy, unforgivable, inescapable. She made the film work. The magic of casting was never on better behavior. Leigh won the Oscar. She was on the cover of *Time.* And then, more or less, she went home to be with Olivier. For she believed then that her greatest casting coup was being with him.

Before *Gone With the Wind,* she had been educated in Europe and briefly at RADA. As well as modest stage work (including an Ophelia to Olivier's Hamlet), she married and had a daughter. She made a screen debut in *Things Are Looking Up* (34, Albert de Courville), and then played in *The Village Squire* (35, Reginald Denham); *Gentleman's Agreement* (35, George Pearson); *Look Up and Laugh* (35, Basil Dean); attracting more attention, with Olivier, in *Fire Over England* (37, William K. Howard); *Dark Journey* (37, Victor Saville); *21 Days* (37, Dean); *Storm in a Teacup* (37, Saville); very fetching with Charles Laughton in *St. Martin's Lane* (38, Tim Whelan); and personally demoted by Louis B. Mayer, from star part to supporting role, for *A Yank at Oxford* (38, Jack Conway).

As *Wind* was shooting, she tried hard for *Rebecca*—to play with Olivier. Instead, Selznick loaned her out to Metro for *Waterloo Bridge* (40,

Mervyn Le Roy), a very successful romance that helped establish her. Then, after Emma to Olivier's Nelson in *That Hamilton Woman* (41, Alexander Korda, with whom she had another contract and a brief affair), the married couple went back to an England at war. *That Hamilton Woman*—though shot in Hollywood—was meant as a flag for British morale.

Selznick went to court in efforts to get her to do more films. But she preferred to stay in England, to learn her craft as a stage actress, and to be Olivier's consort. In the process, she had a miscarriage, she contracted tuberculosis, and she began to discover that she could not match Olivier: she was not in his class as an actor; and he was too competitive. She made two big films that never quite worked—with Claude Rains, vixenish and Sloane Square–ish, in *Caesar and Cleopatra* (45, Gabriel Pascal); but rather too placid and with a tame Vronsky in *Anna Karenina* (48, Julien Duvivier).

By then, her mental health was unstable. But she had played Blanche Du Bois on the London *Streetcar* (under Olivier's direction), and so she beat out Jessica Tandy (and others) for the movie of *A Streetcar Named Desire* (51, Elia Kazan). She won a second Oscar for a second Southern lady. She is often touching—but very stagy; she does not seem to be in Brando's film, and she may have felt innate resistance to Kazan's approach.

There was a melodramatic affair with Peter Finch, and she had to abandon *Elephant Walk* from sheer madness. The marriage was on the rocks, and she was every bit as poignant a figure as Blanche—some said that role had allowed her own madness to get a surer grip. Olivier left her, for a younger woman, the actress Joan Plowright. Leigh would make only three more films: *The Deep Blue Sea* (55, Anatole Litvak); often intriguing with Warren Beatty in *The Roman Spring of Mrs. Stone* (61, Jose Quintero), yet no match for his controlling skills; and ghastly in *Ship of Fools* (65, Stanley Kramer).

Look at all the evidence and it is clear how restricted she was as an actress, and how easily she could seem fake or ladylike if she didn't feel a Scarlett excitement. But she was the center of one of show business's great events, and of one of its most fascinating, if tragic, marriages. Either one of those would ensure her fame.

Mitchell Leisen (1897–1972),
b. Menominee, Michigan
1933: *Cradle Song.* 1934: *Death Takes a Holiday; Murder at the Vanities.* 1935: *Behold My Wife; Four Hours to Kill; Hands Across the Table.* 1936: *Thirteen Hours by Air; The Big Broadcast of 1937.* 1937: *Swing High, Swing Low; Easy Living.* 1938: *The Big Broadcast of 1938; Artists and Models Abroad.* 1939: *Midnight.* 1940: *Remember the*

Night; Arise, My Love. 1941: *I Wanted Wings; Hold Back the Dawn.* 1942: *The Lady Is Willing; Take a Letter, Darling.* 1943: *No Time for Love.* 1944: *Lady in the Dark; Frenchman's Creek; Practically Yours.* 1945: *Masquerade in Mexico; Kitty.* 1946: *To Each His Own.* 1947: *Suddenly It's Spring; Golden Earrings; Dream Girl.* 1949: *Bride of Vengeance; Song of Surrender.* 1950: *No Man of Her Own; Captain Carey, U.S.A./After Midnight.* 1951: *The Mating Season; Darling, How Could You?.* 1952: *Young Man With Ideas.* 1953: *Tonight We Sing.* 1955: *Bedevilled.* 1957: *The Girl Most Likely.* 1963: *Here's Las Vegas.* 1967: *Spree!.*

Leisen was trained as an architect and he worked on interior design before entering movies. His first credits came for the costumes on *Male and Female* (19, Cecil B. De Mille) and two Douglas Fairbanks swashbucklers: *Robin Hood* (22, Allan Dwan) and *The Thief of Bagdad* (24, Raoul Walsh). He then joined De Mille as art director and worked on *The Road to Yesterday* (25), *The Volga Boatman* (26), *Chicago* (27, Frank Urson), *Dress Parade* (27, Donald Crisp), *King of Kings* (27), *Dynamite* (29), *The Godless Girl* (29), *Madame Satan* (30), *The Sign of the Cross* (32), and *This Day and Age* (33). After being assistant director on *Tonight Is Ours* (33, Stuart Walker) and *The Eagle and the Hawk* (33, Walker), he became a director.

If Lubitsch has too generous a reputation as the mastermind of Paramount in the 1930s, then Leisen is surely a neglected figure, and a minor master. From the early thirties to the early forties, Leisen was an expert at witty romantic comedies, too reliant on feeling to be screwball, too pleased with glamour to be satires—and thus less likely to attract critical attention. Leisen was temperamentally more generous than Lubitsch, or Wilder. He loved sets and clothes; he was especially good with actors like Fred MacMurray and Ray Milland, who often grew bored in other films, being told to stand there and look good; and Leisen was as good with actresses, as kind and tender, as George Cukor—like Cukor, he was homosexual (or bisexual).

Take *Swing High, Swing Low,* the enchanting, bittersweet story of a feckless trumpet-player (MacMurray) and his love for Carole Lombard. When it is funny and happy, it is as light as play; in love it nearly swoons; but when it turns somber it is a love story noir in 1937! *Murder at the Vanities* is a raunchy variety show—Leisen was always good at musical numbers, and at integrating them in a story. In *Hands Across the Table,* Lombard is a manicurist going after MacMurray—those two players, both a little shy, both at ease in quick comedy with deep feelings, never had a more supportive director than Leisen.

Easy Living, from a Preston Sturges script, is a

delicious comedy about a fur coat in a hypocritical society, and one of Jean Arthur's best films. *Midnight* is the closest Leisen came to screwball, an elaborate web of deception and flirtation, beautifully played by Claudette Colbert, Mary Astor, John Barrymore, and Don Ameche—it is also one of the gentlest comedies ever written by Billy Wilder and Charles Brackett (which is to guess that Leisen warmed them up). *Remember the Night* is a prosecutor (MacMurray) in love with a shoplifter (Barbara Stanwyck); it is close to a great film, and arguably the most human love story Preston Sturges ever wrote. *Hold Back the Dawn* (another Wilder-Brackett script) has Charles Boyer marrying Olivia de Havilland to get into America.

The case has been made—not least by some of the writers—that Leisen depended upon good scripts. Perhaps. But delighting in good material is no crime, and there are seven or eight Leisen films from this period (with many different writers) that have a distinct refusal to go stale or dry. *Swing High, Swing Low,* one of the best, was written by . . . Virginia Van Upp and Oscar Hammerstein II.

In the forties, Leisen came to grief trying bigger pictures. *Lady in the Dark,* from the Moss Hart play, is terribly uneven, consistently pretentious, and no vehicle for Ginger Rogers—it needed Margaret Sullavan or even Judy Garland. *Frenchman's Creek* is rubbish and endless. *Kitty* is a case of costume smothering interest and proof that the pretty, funny Paulette Goddard could not carry a film. *Golden Earrings* seems bizarre . . . until you see *Bride of Vengeance,* which is absurd.

However, two other films stand out. *To Each His Own* is a super weepie, with Olivia de Havilland playing young and old, and John Lund as the father and son to whom she is devoted. De Havilland won the Oscar for herself, but the film as a whole has that rueful romance that Leisen understood so well. *No Man of Her Own* (adapted from Cornell Woolrich) has Stanwyck masquerading her way into a wealthy family and being blackmailed by Lyle Bettger. This is a richer noir than many more famous works, lovingly composed from coincidence, menace, and calm, and Stanwyck's equal skill at being tough and wounded.

His last years were spent as a night-club proprietor and an occasional director for TV. The falling off should not conceal Leisen's proper position as a leading American director, or the need for proper revaluation of his lyrical treatment of romantic luxury.

Claude Lelouch, b. Paris, 1937

1956: *U.S.A. en Vrac* (d); *Une Ville pas comme les Autres* (d). 1957: *Quand le Rideau se Lève* (d). 1960: *Le Propre de l'Homme.* 1963: *L'Amour avec des si.* 1964: *24 Heures d'Amants* (d); *Une Fille et des Fusils; La Femme Spectacle.* 1965: *Pour un Maillot Jaune* (d); *Les Grands Moments.* 1966: *Un Homme et une Femme/A Man and a Woman.* 1967: *Vivre pour Vivre; Loin du Vietnam* (codirected with Jean-Luc Godard, Joris Ivens, William Klein, and Alain Resnais) (d). 1968: *Treize Jours en France* (codirected with François Reichenbach). 1969: *La Vie, l'Amour et la Mort; Un Homme qui me Plaît.* 1970: *Le Voyou.* 1971: *Iran; Smic, Smac, Smoc.* 1973: "The Losers," episode from *Visions of Eight* (d); *La Bonne Année.* 1974: *Toute une Vie/And Now My Love.* 1975: *Le Chat et la Souris/Cat and Mouse.* 1976: *Si C'était à Refaire/Second Chance.* 1977: *Un Autre Homme, Une Autre Chance/Another Man, Another Chance.* 1978: *Robert et Robert.* 1979: *A Nous Deux/An Adventure for Two.* 1981: *Les Uns et les Autres/Bolero.* 1983: *Edith et Marcel; Vive la Vie!.* 1984: *Partir Revenir.* 1986: *Un Homme et une Femme: Vingt Ans Déjà/A Man and a Woman: Twenty Years Later.* 1987: *Attention Bandits.* 1988: *L'Itineraire d'un Enfant Gâté.* 1990: *Il y a des Jours . . . et des Lunes.* 1993: *Tout Ça . . . Pour Ça!.* 1995: *Les Misérables.* 1996: *Hommes, Femmes, Mode d'Emploi.* 1998: *Hasards ou Coïncidences.* 1999: *Une pour Toutes.* 2002: *And Now . . . Ladies and Gentlemen.*

Conceivably, more people were introduced to French cinema in the sixties and seventies by Lelouch than by any other director. *Un Homme et une Femme* was a lavishly admired movie, and it is never a pleasant task to deflate enjoyment. But Lelouch is a sapping director, slick, meretricious, yet high-minded. French cinema and innocent audiences alike need to be defended against him. His work is as clammy, strident, and wearying as color Sunday supplements and, like them, it manages to be profitable by smothering the prickly realities of people and by insinuating the style of advertising into fiction. His two early features— *Un Homme et une Femme* and *Vivre pour Vivre*— were extended commercials for the hope that pain is absorbed by prettiness. His characters are emotional stewpots always on the go in some heady, ultra-modern kitchen. They are beautiful people in glamorous jobs, able to travel at will. Their petty affairs and the entirely mechanical obstacles that are inserted and then withdrawn from their world are passed off as being typical of the emotional and intellectual demands of life.

But the reality is, as always, spelled out in the director's style. Lelouch works like a still photographer for a glossy magazine. His effects are decorative, trite, and invariably the trick of a lens rather than an observed interaction of people. Lelouch persistently films in telephoto: this leads to soulful close-ups of people cut off from their environment. The background is unnaturally flat, foreground detail is out of focus. There is an accu-

mulating, claustrophobic sterility in his films because the characters have no three-dimensional existence. They live only in the mind's maudlin telephoto, forever gazing sadly at their self-pity.

Just as fashion photographs try to make us want clothes, Lelouch's telephoto intimacy is intended to play on our most vicarious emotional responses. His world has already been taken over by the forces of devitalization: the sickly theme songs swan on; nothing detracts from the glamour of rational packaging; no piece of human behavior overthrows romantic cliché. And all the while, there is the ghostly intimation of greater significance so that, in *Vivre pour Vivre*, Yves Montand's private life is supposedly paralleled by his involvement as a reporter in the world's troublespots. Lelouch announces his concern for suffering with the offensive tact of a politician.

Lelouch works on, though he has not found the right mix of romance and advertising style to repeat the success of *A Man and a Woman*. His version of *Les Misérables* starred Jean-Paul Belmondo as Valjean and helped to revive that actor's career. *And Now Ladies and Gentleman* promises to be something rather more adventurous, with Jeremy Irons at its center.

Jack Lemmon (John Uhler Lemmon III) (1925–2001), b. Boston, Massachusetts
Wasn't it Julia Child who advised that a little lemon goes a long way? I have to confess that sometimes one squeeze of Lemmon is enough to set my teeth on edge. A whole wedge might turn Shirley Temple into Margaret Wycherly. There's no doubt but that, as a younger actor, Lemmon could be very funny. He is hugely skilled, meticulous, and yet—it seems to me—an abject, ingratiating parody of himself. Long ago, worry set in, the detail of his work turned fussy, nagging, and anal; his mannerisms are now like a miser's coins. There have been a few films—like *Glengarry Glen Ross* (92, James Foley)—that used this demented worryguts as necessary material. And Lemmon is very good in that film. But far too often, he stops his own roles and starts preaching anxiety, leading everything away from life and into the jitters. Thus the roles become Lemmons—or lemons: something that ought to be recalled or scrapped. Harsh words—I can picture Lemmon's friction and anguish—but I can't bear to see or hear that mannered regret any more.

Educated at Harvard, he worked on radio, in stock, and TV before his film debut in George Cukor's *It Should Happen to You* (54). He won a supporting Oscar as Ensign Pulver in *Mister Roberts* (55, Mervyn Le Roy and John Ford), but even there the character was edging toward shtick and fast burn anxiety. He tried adventure and the West, in *Fire Down Below* (57, Robert Parrish) and *Cowboy* (58, Delmer Daves), but he was ill at ease in anything except a slightly ill-fitting city suit.

He preferred to work in supporting parts in generally East Coast–oriented comedies: *Three for the Show* (53, H. C. Potter); *Phffft* (54, Mark Robson); Richard Quine's *My Sister Eileen* (55); and Dick Powell's *You Can't Run Away From It* (56). Preferring a few select directors, Lemmon enhanced his reputation in three more Quine movies: the hilarious *Operation Madball* (57); as a warlock in *Bell, Book and Candle* (58); with Doris Day in the more ponderous *It Happened to Jane* (59). At this stage, Lemmon was a rather fierce comic juvenile, ravenous for wit and intrigue. The part that changed him was in Billy Wilder's *Some Like It Hot* (59), an adventure in drag that seems to have opened up the seas of neuroses to Lemmon. Lemmon, above all, recognized how the 1920s setting, and the ostensible playfulness of the story, had introduced a more contemporary character: the socialized homosexual.

He became increasingly preoccupied by mannerism, worry, and effeminacy and agonized by the sort of moral compromise undergone by C. C. Baxter in Wilder's *The Apartment* (60). That character was central to American cinema of the 1960s and to a sort of honesty that quickly turned into solemnity and sentimentality when handled with less than rage or humor. Lemmon was the house actor now for such smart Broadway-based comedies, the world of dramatist Neil Simon, of the Nichols/May duologues overheard on a psychiatrist's couch. That he saw himself in this role was evident in the way he kept himself for certain directors: for Quine—*The Notorious Landlady* (62) and *How to Murder Your Wife* (65); for Blake Edwards—*Days of Wine and Roses* (63), in which he is deeply harrowing, and *The Great Race* (65); for Wilder—*Irma La Douce* (63), *The Fortune Cookie* (66), *Avanti!* (72), and *The Front Page* (74); and for David Swift—*Under the Yum Yum Tree* (64) and *Good Neighbor Sam* (64).

Nothing detracts from the self-lacerating irony and precision of most of these performances except the feeling that, despite repeated attempts, no blood flows. Lemmon did permit himself new directors but at the same time he took on lesser material in which the sameness of his work grew more obvious. Thus, although he was as good as ever in Gene Saks's *The Odd Couple* (68); *Luv* (67, Clive Donner); *The April Fools* (69, Stuart Rosenberg); *The Out-of-Towners* (70, Arthur Hiller); *The War Between Men and Women* (72, Melville Shavelson); and won the best actor Oscar in *Save the Tiger* (72, John G. Avildsen); they are heavy with the tramp of marking time. It seemed a natural development that Lemmon should become a director, and his first film, *Kotch* (71), though sharing his actor's neurosis and dependent on the very technical acting of Walter Matthau, was an interesting debut.

The Prisoner of Second Avenue (75, Melvin Frank) was one more step in the same direction—from Neil Simon again, about a middle-aged man, made redundant, unhappy, and insecure. No one could do it as well as Lemmon; but who else could have endured the monotony of doing it so often? He seemed increasingly at a loss with *Alex & the Gypsy* (76, John Korty) and the pilot in *Airport '77* (77, Jerry Jameson). But he had a hit in *China Syndrome* (79, James Bridges), no matter that its contrived melodrama did no more than put his nervous twitching in a novel setting.

For television, in 1975, he had played Archie Rice in *The Entertainer* (Lemmon says this was at the urging of Laurence Olivier—which may just show Olivier's cunning). Lemmon did *Tribute* (80, Bob Clark); *Buddy Buddy* (81, Wilder); *Missing* (82, Costa-Gavras); *Mass Appeal* (84, Glenn Jordan); *Macaroni* (85, Ettore Scola); and *That's Life!* (86, Edwards).

He was slipping, and who could bear to see Lemmon's anxiety in decline? But he rallied: he was a respectable Tyrone in *Long Day's Journey Into Night* (87, Jonathan Miller) on TV; and good again as Governor John Staton in TV's The *Murder of Mary Phagan* (88, Billy Hale); *Dad* (89, Gary David Goldberg); one of the better turns in *JFK* (91, Oliver Stone); briefly in *The Player* (92, Robert Altman); *Glengarry Glen Ross* (92, James Foley); the man who insists on delivering his own horror story in *Short Cuts* (93, Altman); and *Grumpy Old Men* (93, Donald Petrie).

There was no slackening in Lemmon's last years: *The Grass Harp* (95, Charles Matthau); *Grumpier Old Men* (95, Howard Deutch); awful as a Nazi war criminal in *Getting Away with Murder* (96, Harvey Miller); *A Weekend in the Country* (96, Martin Bergman); *My Fellow Americans* (96, Peter Segal); Marcellus in *Hamlet* (96, Kenneth Branagh); with Matthau again in *Out to Sea* (97, Martha Coolidge); the TV *12 Angry Men* (97, William Friedkin); *Puppies for Sale* (97, Ron Krauss); *The Long Way Home* (98, Glenn Jordan); *The Odd Couple II* (98, Deutch); on TV in *Inherit the Wind* (99, Daniel Petrie); *Tuesdays with Morrie* (99, Mick Jackson), which is either very moving or very unbearable, depending on your nature; *The Legend of Bagger Vance* (00, Robert Redford).

Paul Leni (1885–1929),

b. Stuttgart, Germany

1917: *Das Ratsel von Bangalor* (codirected with Alexander Antalffy). 1918: *Dornroschen*. 1919: *Die Platonische Ehe; Prinz Kuckuck*. 1920: *Fiesko; Patience; Die Verschworung zu Genua*. 1921: *Das Gespensterschiff; Die Hintertreppe* (codirected with Leopold Jessner); *Komodie der Leidenschaften; Das Tagebuch des Dr. Hartl*. 1924: *Das Wachsfigurenkabinett/Waxworks*. 1927: *The Cat* and the Canary; The Chinese Parrot; The Man Who Laughs. 1929: The Last Warning.

Leni was a painter, a set designer, and an art director before and after he became a director: Das Panzergewolbe (14, Joe May); Die Geierwally (21, E. A. Dupont); Kinder der Finsternis (21, Dupont); Tragodie der Liebe (23, May); and Der Tanzer meiner Frau (25, Alexander Korda). While his contribution to Expressionism is based chiefly on his visual sense, it is likely that his early death from blood poisoning lost us a first-class director. Waxworks and The Cat and the Canary are major items in the history of the horror film.

He had worked with both Max Reinhardt and Leopold Jessner in the theatre and he was art director on Hintertreppe—Lotte Eisner argues that the film might have profited if Leni had had greater control of the direction. Certainly, Waxworks is an advance, employing an overall pattern of design—in sets, grouping, and costume that is as effective an evocation of nightmare as Caligari. One of the three figures in that film was Ivan the Terrible (played by Conrad Veidt), and its influence on Eisenstein is clear.

Leni was a theorist, and in 1924 he wrote of using sets to transcend photographic reality. "For my film Waxworks I have tried to create sets so stylized that they evince no ideas of reality. . . . It is not extreme reality that the camera perceives, but the reality of the inner event, which is more profound, effective and moving than what we see through everyday eyes."

It is remarkable that so lucid and self-conscious a director should have moved so easily to Carl Laemmle's Universal studios. But The Cat and the Canary was a classic haunted house movie in which Leni's overall visual design seemed just as complete and in which he had acquired new narrative urgency. In The Man Who Laughs he was reunited with Conrad Veidt, who played the man whose face has been set in a ghastly permanent smile. The Last Warning was another skillful manufacture of fear in a semi-Gothic interior—this time a theatre where a murder was once committed. It reaffirmed Leni's preference for the atmosphere of menace, rather than the actual manifestation of horror.

Robert Z. Leonard (1889–1968),
b. Chicago

1916: The Plow Girl. 1917: A Mormon Maid; Princess Virtue; Face Value. 1918: Her Body in Bond; The Bride's Awakening; Danger, Go Slow; Modern Love. 1919: The Delicious Little Devil; The Big Little Person; The Scarlet Shadow; What Am I Bid?; The Way of a Woman; April Folly; The Miracle of Love. 1920: The Restless Sex. 1921: The Gilded Lily; Heedless Moths. 1922: Fascination; Peacock Alley; Broadway Rose. 1923: The French Doll; Jazzmania; Fashion Row. 1924: Love's Wilderness; Circe the Enchantress; Mademoiselle Midnight. 1925: Cheaper to Marry; Bright Lights; Time, the Comedian. 1926: Dance Madness; The Waning Sex; Mademoiselle Modiste. 1927: The Demi-Bride; A Little Journey; Adam and Evil; Tea for Three. 1928: Baby Mine; The Cardboard Lover; A Lady of Chance. 1929: Marianne. 1930: In Gay Madrid; The Divorcee; Let Us Be Gay. 1931: The Bachelor Father; It's a Wise Child; Five and Ten; Susan Lenox. 1932: Lovers Courageous; Strange Interlude. 1933: Peg o' My Heart; Dancing Lady. 1934: Outcast Lady. 1935: After Office Hours; Escapade. 1936: The Great Ziegfeld; Piccadilly Jim. 1937: Maytime; The Firefly. 1938: The Girl of the Golden West. 1939: Broadway Serenade. 1940: New Moon; Pride and Prejudice; Third Finger, Left Hand. 1941: Ziegfeld Girl; When Ladies Meet. 1942: We Were Dancing; Stand by for Action. 1943: The Man from Down Under. 1944: Marriage Is a Private Affair. 1945: Weekend at the Waldorf. 1946: The Secret Heart. 1947: Cynthia. 1948: BF's Daughter. 1949: The Bribe; In the Good Old Summertime. 1950: Nancy Goes to Rio; Duchess of Idaho; Grounds for Marriage. 1951: Too Young to Kiss. 1952: Everything I Have Is Yours. 1953: The Clown; The Great Diamond Robbery. 1954: Her Twelve Men. 1955: The King's Thief; La Donna piu Bella del Mondo/Beautiful but Dangerous. 1956: Kelly and Me.

Originally an actor, Leonard worked at Universal, Paramount, and for his own company, Tiffany, before joining MGM in 1925. He was married first to Mae Murray, who played in Jazzmania, Fashion Row, Circe the Enchantress, and Mademoiselle Midnight. For most of his career he was an efficient exponent of Metro's line in effulgent glamour; five times Irving Thalberg entrusted Norma Shearer to him—The Demi-Bride, Lady of Chance, The Divorcee, Let Us Be Gay, and the ill-advised O'Neill adaptation, Strange Interlude. In fact, near the end of her working life, in 1942, Shearer was reunited with him for We Were Dancing. In addition, he directed Marion Davies in The Cardboard Lover, Marianne, and Peg o' My Heart; and Jeanette MacDonald in Maytime, The Firefly, The Girl of the Golden West, Broadway Serenade, and New Moon—enough to make him master of that MGM high key in which blonde hair seems to have caught fire. Without ever exceeding romantic splendor, Leonard was capable of bringing a fond light to high-class cheesecake. He also directed Garbo and Gable in Susan Lenox, a subject worthy of von Sternberg; Dancing Lady was a Joan Crawford musical, squired by Gable and Astaire; The Great Ziegfeld, a good biopic with William Powell, Myrna Loy, and Luise Rainer; a garden party Pride and Prejudice; and

Ziegfeld Girl, with Judy Garland, Hedy Lamarr, and Lana Turner.

Sergio Leone (1921–89), b. Rome

1960: *Il Colosso di Rodi.* 1964: *Per un Pugno di Dollari/A Fistful of Dollars.* 1965: *Per Qualche Dollaro in Piu/For a Few Dollars More.* 1966: *Il Buono, Il Brutto, Il Caltivo/The Good, the Bad and the Ugly.* 1968: *C'Era una Volta il West/Once Upon a Time in the West.* 1971: *Giu' la Testa/A Fistful of Dynamite.* 1984: *Once Upon a Time in America/C'era una Volte in America.*

Leone has been tossed back and forth as camp amusement and spacey visionary. This enigma was enhanced by the gaps between films—reason enough for those who scorned him to be confirmed in the opinion that he was an opportunist who simply yoked samurai gestures to Western iconography and was helped alike by the deco solitariness of Clint Eastwood in a poncho and the inability of that actor to understand what the director was saying. The "dollars" trilogy are less silent films than studies of face masks looming up, gross and hysterical with detail, in sunblanched CinemaScope frames and drugged revenge plots. Leone also had the eerie fatalism of Ennio Morricone's music menace dropped in a deep well and echoing back. The films made Eastwood: they gave him box-office authority and an excuse for minimal acting. Impassivity went with the poncho, and cheroots kept the face still. But Leone himself came to America without conquering.

Once Upon a Time in the West is his best film: a mess of double-crossing stars, manic close-ups, and Rothko-like masses of color and space. I think Leone really despised the Western, and let the smart mockery exploit his remarkable eye. Despite Monument Valley and the stars, we never feel we're *in* America or with people who think in American. He makes fun of the very mythology and obsession that underlie film art, and he knows too much about his tricks to be persuasive. Leone's films force you back from the screen with hieratic compositions and sly contempt for "il West." Those who honor Leone should study Anthony Mann's *Man of the West,* but those who cherish CinemaScope will always luxuriate in Leone's inscrutable spaces.

Once Upon a Time in America was so long, and so obscure, that it had to be released first in a short version. But not even the restored cut made everything clear. Its would-be Jewish gangsters seemed very Italian; the attitude to women was horrendous—the two rape scenes are among the screen's nastiest. The leading actors do not seem at ease. But there are wonderful sequences, especially those involving the gangsters as kids in New York.

Irving Lerner (1909–76), b. New York

1948: *Muscle Beach* (codirected with Joseph Strick) (s). 1949: *C-Man.* 1953: *Man Crazy.* 1958: *Edge of Fury* (codirected with Robert Gurney Jr.); *Murder by Contract.* 1959: *City of Fear.* 1960: *Studs Lonigan.* 1963: *To Be a Man.* 1968: *The Royal Hunt of the Sun.*

Lerner's involvement with cinema remained that of a disapproving outsider, waiting for the medium to come round to his way of thinking, but bowing to its crazy rules occasionally and finding that he rather enjoyed them. Although Lerner is most associated with fringe activities—whether arty, educational, or technical—in 1958–59, he made two films on seven-day schedules that proved engrossing, interesting thrillers: *Murder by Contract* and *City of Fear.* Both photographed with distinction by Lucien Ballard, they showed the potential of the genre quickie when made by accomplished technicians. Lerner may have concluded that cheapness was viable, whereas the real lesson is that genre is intrinsic and can make elaborate screenplays redundant. But Lerner sought to apply the same working economy to a different type of subject, the period novel *Studs Lonigan,* which proved a tasteful failure.

Lerner was originally an academic, making films for the anthropology department of Columbia University years before Jean Rouch. He hovered around the industry as editor and second-unit director: *One Third of a Nation* (39, Dudley Murphy); *Valley Town* (40, Willard Van Dyke); and *The Children Must Learn* (40, Van Dyke). During the war, he produced two Office of War Information documentaries: *Toscanini: Hymn of the Nations* (44) and *A Place to Live* (44). After that, he was head of the Educational Film Institute at New York University, before teaming up with Joseph Strick to make the artfully edited *Muscle Beach. C-Man* and *Man Crazy* were second features, apparently now lost. Lerner was technical advisor on *The Savage Eye* (59, Strick, Ben Maddow, and Sidney Meyers) and editor and second-unit director on *Spartacus* (60, Stanley Kubrick).

To Be a Man was a minor war picture, *Royal Hunt of the Sun* a disastrously serious epic. He also produced and did second-unit work on *Custer of the West* (68, Robert Siodmak), produced and edited *Captain Apache* (71, Alexander Singer), and edited *Executive Action* (73, David Miller) and *New York, New York* (77, Martin Scorsese), which is dedicated to his memory.

Mervyn Le Roy (1900–87),
b. San Francisco

1927: *No Place to Go.* 1928: *Flying Romeos; Oh, Kay!; Harold Teen.* 1929: *Naughty Baby; Hot Stuff; Little Johnny Jones; Broadway Babies; Playing Around.* 1930: *Showgirl in Hollywood; Num-*

bered Men; Broken Dishes; Top Speed; Little Cae-sar. 1931: *A Gentleman's Fate; Tonight or Never; Five Star Final; Broad Minded; Local Boy Makes Good.* 1932: *High Pressure; Heart of New York; Big City Blues; Three on a Match; Hard to Han-dle; I Am a Fugitive from a Chain Gang; Two Sec-onds.* 1933: *Elmer the Great; The World Changes; Gold Diggers of 1933; Tugboat Annie.* 1934: *Heat Lightning; Hi, Nellie!; Happiness Ahead.* 1935: *Sweet Adeline; Oil for the Lamps of China; I Found Stella Parrish; Page Miss Glory.* 1936: *Anthony Adverse; Three Men on a Horse.* 1937: *The King and the Chorus Girl; They Won't Forget.* 1938: *Fools for Scandal.* 1940: *Waterloo Bridge; Escape.* 1941: *Blossoms in the Dust; Unholy Part-ners; Johnny Eager; Random Harvest.* 1943: *Madame Curie.* 1944: *Thirty Seconds Over Tokyo.* 1945: *The House I Live In* (d). 1946: *Without Reservations.* 1948: *Homecoming.* 1949: *Little Women; Any Number Can Play; East Side, West Side.* 1951: *Quo Vadis?.* 1952: *Lovely to Look At; Million Dollar Mermaid.* 1953: *Latin Lovers.* 1954: *Rose Marie.* 1955: *Mister Roberts* (codi-rected with John Ford); *Strange Lady in Town.* 1956: *The Bad Seed; Toward the Unknown.* 1958: *No Time for Sergeants; Home Before Dark.* 1959: *The FBI Story.* 1960: *Wake Me When It's Over.* 1961: *The Devil at Four O'Clock; A Majority of One.* 1962: *Gypsy.* 1963: *Mary, Mary.* 1965: *Moment to Moment.*

Le Roy was in vaudeville from his early teens (like Gypsy) and his first film work was as wardrobe assistant and actor: *The Call of the Canyon* (23, Victor Fleming); *Going Up* (23, Lloyd Ingraham); *Little Johnny Jones* (23, Arthur Rosson and Johnny Hines), which Le Roy later remade; *Broadway After Dark* (24, Monta Bell); and *The Chorus Lady* (24, Ralph Ince). From 1925–27, he was engaged as writer and gagman for Colleen Moore on seven of her pictures: *Sally* (25, Alfred E. Green); *We Moderns* (25, John Francis Dillon); *Ella Cinders* (26, Green); *Irene* (26, Green); *It Must Be Love* (26, Green); *Twinkletoes* (26, Charles Brabin); and *Orchids and Ermine* (27, Alfred Santell).

That led to a contract as director with Warners, and he stayed at the studio until 1939 when he joined MGM, returning to Warners in 1955. It is an indication of his professional neutrality that Le Roy served such different masters without appar-ent difficulty. Thus, he dealt equally happily with the social foreboding of *I Am a Fugitive* and the floral daydream of *Random Harvest.* Of course, the "realism" of Warners in the 1930s was a care-fully contrived style, but Le Roy drew punchy performances from Paul Muni (the *Fugitive*), Edward G. Robinson (in *Little Caesar* and *Five Star Final*), and Cagney (in *Hard to Handle*). Le

Roy also revealed a taste for musicals and com-edy: indeed, *Gold Diggers of 1933*, *Tugboat Annie*, and *Sweet Adeline* all show a predilection for glamour, as evident in the rosy treatment of such "uglies" as Wallace Beery and Marie Dressler as in that of Irene Dunne in *Sweet Ade-line.* But *Chain Gang* still throbs with anger, and the melodramatic present tense of the title is sus-tained by the film's fatalistic ending. While *Hard to Handle* is a scathing satire on money-grubbing, with Cagney as a glittering con-man who says, "The public is like a cow bellowing to be milked." The same pessimism colors *They Won't Forget*, a story of lynching in a Southern town, and further proof of how suddenly Le Roy could uncover a serious side.

But at MGM he abandoned any pretence to realism or brutality, and in Greer Garson he found the perfect leading lady for wartime romances. *Blossoms in the Dust* and *Random Harvest* are as dazzling as table decorations made out of sugar; *Escape* is smooth sentiment; while *Madame Curie* is a biopic such as Le Roy never had the chance to make at Warners. *Johnny Eager* is a fatuous gangster movie, with Robert Taylor looking like a male model after memories of Cagney and Robinson. After the war, Le Roy went into a decline, making some horribly insipid musicals at MGM as well as a tame *Little Women*. But Warners revived him: *Home Before Dark* is an unusually somber women's picture, with a good performance from Jean Simmons; and *Gypsy* was a robust musical that handled Ros-alind Russell with some tact and reaffirmed Le Roy's faith in razzmatazz and roses.

Le Roy produced a number of his own films, and when he first joined MGM in 1939 he worked as a producer—on *The Wizard of Oz* (Fleming) and *The Marx Brothers at the Circus* (Edward Buzzell). That suggests how prominent a figure he was during the 1930s; famous enough to be intro-duced as a visiting celebrity to the dance contest in Horace McCoy's *They Shoot Horses, Don't They?*

The House I Live In was a documentary short that won an Oscar—it featured Frank Sinatra, preaching tolerance to kids. Thirty years later, in 1975, Le Roy won the Thalberg award. So Holly-wood liked him. It never hurt that he had been married to Doris, Harry Warner's daughter.

Richard Lester,
b. Philadelphia, 1932
1959: *The Running, Jumping and Standing Still Film* (s). 1962: *It's Trad, Dad!.* 1963: *The Mouse on the Moon.* 1964: *A Hard Day's Night.* 1965: *The Knack; Help!.* 1966: *A Funny Thing Hap-pened on the Way to the Forum.* 1967: *How I Won the War.* 1968: *Petulia.* 1969: *The Bed-Sitting*

Room. 1973: *The Three Musketeers (The Queen's Diamonds)*. 1974: *Juggernaut*. 1975: *The Four Musketeers; Royal Flash*. 1976: *Robin and Marian; The Ritz*. 1979: *Butch and Sundance: The Early Days; Cuba*. 1980: *Superman II*. 1983: *Superman III*. 1984: *Finders Keepers*. 1989: *The Return of the Musketeers*. 1991: *Get Back* (d).

The uncomfortable mixture of nostalgia for silent comedy and high-pressure cutting never abated in Lester's supposedly humorous films. Not only history makes one suspicious of American filmmakers who come to Britain; Lester's example is a horrid warning, especially since *Petulia*, his one American and most viewable movie, suggests that there may be a real person within the demented dull gimmickry of his English films. It would serve Lester right if he is tied down by the swinging London image he cultivated. He failed to see how sentimental and donnish Goon humor was, and remained attached to that undisciplined prophet of pathetic revelation, Spike Milligan, in 1969, ten years after the *Running, Jumping and Standing Still Film* had exposed a joke that only cheered English complacency. Between those two films, Lester managed to make the Beatles at the time of their randy, aggressive best seem antiseptic and fey: the miles of newsreel and interviews of the Beatles are infinitely more funny and surreal than their two movies, while the TV show *Ready, Steady, Go* always did their songs better. Lester worked a good deal on TV commercials, and the modish, close-packed frenzy of that visual style marked him forever.

Even so, *Three Musketeers* is a merry, sunlit romance, still uncertain at storytelling, but based on very rich clothes, the palaces of Madrid, and a quirky, droll period authenticity. *Robin and Marian* was another revisiting of legend, done with humor and a wistful feeling of having grown older—the calmest film Lester ever made.

Lester went out of fashion with a bang. His *Superman* pictures were awful, and by 1991 he had been reduced to filming a Paul McCartney concert.

Oscar Levant (1906–72), b. Pittsburgh

Oscar Levant is one of the great sour saving graces in the blinding panorama of happiness and success offered by American film. And there is a moment, I feel, when Oscar became irretrievably Levant. In 1944, Warner Bros. decided that it was high time to make a biopic of George Gershwin, the unstoppable genius of American music who had died, suddenly, in 1937 of a brain tumor. They would call it *Rhapsody in Blue*. Ira Gershwin, George's brother, was quite content to have the film's scenario "entirely fictional as is the love story." The only things that would come from fact

were the names, the basic family setup, the music (of course), "and an occasional character like Oscar Levant."

The son of a watch mender, Oscar Levant was a virtuoso piano player whose dream of being a concert artist was diverted by Broadway and Hollywood. From the late 1920s onwards, Levant was a Hollywood figure, writing songs and scores for films, and sometimes appearing on screen in small parts. His songs were not remarkable, but he had a steady enough career: *My Man* (28, Archie Mayo); *Side Street* (29, Malcolm St. Clair); *Tanned Legs* (29, Marshall Neilan); *Love Comes Along* (30, Allan Dwan); *Leathernecking* (30, Edward Cline); *Crime Without Passion* (34, Ben Hecht and Charles MacArthur); the title song for *Steamboat 'Round the Bend* (35, John Ford); *Music Is Magic* (35, George Marshall); *In Person* (35, William Seiter); *Charlie Chan at the Opera* (36, H. Bruce Humberstone); the score for *Nothing Sacred* (37, William Wellman); *Made for Each Other* (39, John Cromwell).

It was in those years that he became not just the friend and admirer of George Gershwin, but the leading exponent of his work—in concert, on the radio, and on records. More than that, Levant appeared regularly on the radio show *Information, Please!*, starting in 1939, and then carried further in a series of one-reel movies. This show required unusual knowledge, as well as a radio personality—Levant was caustic, very funny, aggressively depressive, and a famous wit.

So it was natural enough that he should "ground" *Rhapsody in Blue* (45, Irving Rapper) in "reality." As is made clear in Sam Kashner and Nancy Schoenberger's excellent Levant biography, *A Talent for Genius*, the making of *Rhapsody in Blue* was not just farcical but a special humiliation to Levant. Initially, Clifford Odets had been assigned to do the script: his 800-page draft startled all readers in that it seemed to be the life of a fierce, radical artist (with music)—in short, the life of Clifford Odets. Other writers faltered. Gershwin's life had had no drama, no failure, no downs to help shape an arc. "Use my life instead," wailed Levant.

Not that Hollywood knew defeat in 1944–45. Levant was hired to be himself, for $25,000, in a film that was otherwise a dawdling travesty. He advised on decor, costumes, and facts—all ignored—and he volunteered sarcastic dialogue (mostly cut). "It got to be very Pirandelloish," said Levant, as he was filmed in the audience, standing and applauding, as actor Robert Alda (as George) went through the motions of playing the Concerto in F (actually played by Levant on the soundtrack).

But there's the rub: the true Hollywood person sees that plight as show business; he dines out on the joke; and his own career surges. Of course, that guy—handsome, smiling, charming—might have been asked to play Gershwin in the first place. But Levant had a face like a squeezed lemon, and he could hardly read a line without making it sour, snarly, or self-destructive. So he thought of Pirandello.

In life, Levant sank into melancholy, hypochondria, real illness, paranoia, and any other problem he could find in the textbooks. He became a sad joke—and thus in *An American in Paris* (51, Vincente Minnelli), where he has a real part as Gene Kelly's chum, he does the Concerto in F, and he is not just himself and the conductor but everyone in the audience.

Never mind, he is a figure for connoisseurs: he is hilarious as the piano player and universal deprecator in *Humoresque* (46, Jean Negulesco); *You Were Meant for Me* (48, Lloyd Bacon); seeing if he can turn the cream of Doris Day sour in *Romance on the High Seas* (48, Michael Curtiz); playing Tchaikovsky and Khatchaturian in *The Barkleys of Broadway* (48, Charles Walters); a kidnapper with Fred Allen in the "Ransom of Red Chief" episode from *Full House* (52, Howard Hawks); *The I Don't Care Girl* (53, Bacon); *The Band Wagon* (53, Minnelli); and as a psychiatric patient in *The Cobweb* (56, Minnelli).

Anyone liking Levant should search out his unique books of memoirs—*A Smattering of Ignorance* (1940), *The Memoir of an Amnesiac* (1965), *The Unimportance of Being Oscar* (1968). Just consider the wit and gloom of a man holding that title back for twenty-eight years! Then dream of a Levant biopic—with Steve Buscemi.

Barry Levinson,

b. Baltimore, Maryland, 1942

1982: *Diner.* 1984: *The Natural.* 1985: *Young Sherlock Holmes.* 1987: *Good Morning, Vietnam.* 1987: *Tin Men.* 1988: *Rain Man.* 1990: *Avalon.* 1991: *Bugsy.* 1992: *Toys.* 1994: *Jimmy Hollywood; Disclosure.* 1996: *Sleepers.* 1997: *Wag the Dog.* 1998: *Sphere.* 1999: *Liberty Heights.* 2000: *An Everlasting Piece.* 2001: *Bandits.* 2003: *Envy.*

Not many American moviemakers have a significant relationship with the place where they were born and raised. To be in pictures, very often, involves living on location or in hotels. Los Angeles can be viewed as a place for glorified hotel-living: the houses are like theme bungalows on the grounds, and in no other American city can so full a range of services be called in. More than that, the difficulties of getting work urge new directors to that vague, plastic setting for stories that often end up as L.A., or southern California. But three of Levinson's films—arguably the best—depend upon the dowdy glories of Baltimore and the atmosphere of great provincial cities.

He attended American University in Washing-ton, D.C., and became a writer for television. But after some time working for Carol Burnett, he went into screenwriting, often in partnership with his then-wife, Valerie Curtin: *The Internecine Project* (74, Ken Hughes); *Silent Movie* (76, Mel Brooks); *High Anxiety* (77, Brooks), in which he also has a funny cameo performance as a bellhop; *And Justice For All* (79, Norman Jewison); *Inside Moves* (80, Richard Donner); *History of the World, Part I* (81, Brooks); *Best Friends* (82, Jewison); and *Unfaithfully Yours* (84, Howard Zieff).

None of those pictures was much to boast about, and Levinson was forty already in the year that his first directing job opened. But *Diner* was in a different category, a slice of life, naturalistic but piquant, and full of characters. It only showed how meekly serviceable Levinson had been as a writer. Moreover, in its discovery and use of Mickey Rourke, Kevin Bacon, Daniel Stern, Steve Guttenberg, and Ellen Barkin, *Diner* gave us a director with a true fondness for players. Amid all its virtues, it was less evident that *Diner* lacked a pressing reason for being. It was about life, passing time, and plain, friendly places—none of which gets overdone in Hollywood—but it was short of drama.

The Natural was poor baseball and worse Malamud, and its very romantic look was at war with the humdrum setting, just as the movie ducked the novel's somber conclusion. Its acting was starry in the worst sense: the casting seemed to have settled all other approaches. And Levinson was uneasy with the sweeping epic reach of the fable. He seemed like a lifelong Orioles fan, used to dull games, having to gape at baseball according to the field of dreams.

Young Sherlock Holmes was written by Chris Columbus and it had Steven Spielberg as executive producer. It had charm, but Levinson seemed under the influence of others. Equally, *Good Morning, Vietnam* was not just a vehicle for Robin Williams, it was a road made for the occasion that had no purpose except his grinding drive. But *Tin Men* was Baltimore, with the smell of hard-earned experience and a gritty, unsentimental attitude. It was funny and tough. Yet curiously, the writer Levinson seemed happier watching life pass by than shaping it into story.

Rain Man was a test of managerial skills. The project had had previous writers and directors, and it had Dustin Hoffman in a self-induced creative coma of autism. It was a hit and Levinson got the Oscar for best director. His reputation soared in the business, for insiders knew that *Rain Man* could have been a calamity. So Levinson was allowed to make *Avalon*, a gentle, wry portrait of an immigrant family's early life, and softer than *Diner*'s guys could have tolerated.

Bugsy was one more occasion for Levinson to serve powerful personalities who had been arguing about a picture long before he came along: Warren Beatty and writer James Toback. In any event, they might have been wise to hire him earlier and let him urge some greater grounding in the showy, fake story. Still, Levinson discovered the sweet chump in Beatty, and he seemed intrigued by the neon dream of Las Vegas—the kind of risky escape that has long appealed to hard-earned money in Baltimore.

Barry Levinson is sixty now, and it's clear that he has a young man's urge to try anything (which includes his affectionate involvement with the TV series *Homicide*). But the movies accumulate without really adding up. For example, the aside, *Wag the Dog*, was so much better than the major effort, *Sphere*. *Liberty Heights* was a delight, while *Disclosure* was heavy-handed. Levinson has rare skills and ease, and he's in a position now to do whatever he wants (near enough). Yet the question remains—what does he want? Where is the creative nervous system? Where is the film that might break, or reveal, his heart?

Albert Lewin (1894–1968),
b. Newark, New Jersey

1942: *The Moon and Sixpence*. 1945: *The Picture of Dorian Gray*. 1947: *The Private Affairs of Bel Ami*. 1951: *Pandora and the Flying Dutchman*. 1953: *Saadia*. 1957: *The Living Idol*.

A graduate of New York University and Harvard (where he got his master's degree), Lewin joined MGM in 1924 as a writer: *Bread* (24, Victor Schertzinger); *The Fate of a Flirt* (25, Frank Strayer); *Blarney* (26, Marcel De Sano); *Ladies of Leisure* (26, Thomas Buckingham); *Tin Hats* (26, Edward Sedgwick); *A Little Journey* (27, Robert Z. Leonard); *Quality Street* (27, Sidney Franklin); *Spring Fever* (27, Sedgwick); and *The Actress* (28, Franklin), in which Norma Shearer played Rose Trelawney.

Lewin was a close associate of Irving Thalberg, who made him head of the story department and then the producer of most of his important projects. At MGM, and latterly at Paramount after Thalberg's death, he produced *The Kiss* (29, Jacques Feyder); *Cuban Love Song* (31, W. S. Van Dyke); *The Guardsman* (31, Franklin); *Red-Headed Woman* (32, Jack Conway); *What Every Woman Knows* (34, Gregory La Cava); *China Seas* (35, Tay Garnett); *Mutiny on the Bounty* (35, Frank Lloyd); *The Good Earth* (37, Franklin et al.); *True Confession* (37, Wesley Ruggles); *Spawn of the North* (38, Henry Hathaway); *Zaza* (39, George Cukor); and *So Ends Our Night* (41, John Cromwell).

His own films lack exactly those assets a Thalberg henchman might have been expected to command—narrative directness and box-office accuracy (he was dropped from *Madame Curie*). On the contrary, arty aspiration showed like a

teenage slip. His own scenarist, he cultivated a garish sophistication—in subject, setting, style, and actors—and sometimes achieved real vulgarity. But his first four films are all worth seeing: the first for George Sanders; the second, his best, for Hurd Hatfield and an absorbing contrast of soft, burnished close-ups and huge, interior perspectives; the third for its inane pleasure in literariness; and the fourth because it is gaudily ridiculous, impressive in a romantic, thundery way. In such moments as Ava Gardner in her nightie on the edge of a cliff, romantic sensation comes inadvertently near the vision of Delvaux and Ernst.

Jerry Lewis (Joseph Levitch),
b. Newark, New Jersey, 1926

1960: *The Bellboy*. 1961: *The Ladies' Man; The Errand Boy*. 1963: *The Nutty Professor*. 1964: *The Patsy*. 1965: *The Family Jewels*. 1966: *Three on a Couch*. 1967: *The Big Mouth*. 1969: *One More Time*. 1970: *Which Way to the Front?/Ja, Ja, Mein General! But Which Way to the Front?*. 1981: *Hardly Working*. 1983: *Cracking Up/Smorgasbord*.

The first six films directed by Lewis deserve a place in any study of American comedy—even if *The Nutty Professor* is also the most disturbing version of the Jekyll and Hyde story. It shows the somber side of Lewis's imagination usually obscured by sentimentality. It seems to reflect on Lewis's own appearance and the pain of all those disparaging asides in his partnership with Dean Martin.

Lewis maintained the American comic preoccupation with the little man beset by an incomprehensible, heartless, or intractable world. Keaton responds with disdain, Harry Langdon daydreams, Stan Laurel muddles through, while Chaplin practices all the guile and simpering of a waiter who plans to whip away the fat man's chair. Jerry Lewis's response is as novel as it is alarming: he becomes demented. In part, this is a clever exaggeration of a disposition toward cross-eyed goofiness, a tongue tied in knots, and a shambling walk. But no other performer went so far in suggesting a man animated by machinery or by the processing of human instincts implicit in advertising.

Lewis's period with Frank Tashlin was instrumental in drawing out this gibbering, spastic automaton. It also seems to have inspired Lewis to direct himself, and to see his character as not just the pathetic jerk patronized by Dean Martin, but as a Stan Laurel hero discomposed by every convenience of modern life. Just as Tashlin's movies are cartoon distortions of a world twisting to see itself in deceiving mirrors, so Lewis is adman's man, a robot degenerate overprogrammed by the conflicting gods of Americana, made schizoid by the clash of material luxuries and abstract ideals. *The Nutty Professor* deals with transformation and the side-by-side images of the loony scientist, timid, inept, sentimental, but inventive, and Buddy Love, the caricature of the Dean Martin "Dino" figure, a blasé stud, relaxed, insolent, and decadent. Lewis had nursed *The Nutty Professor* for ten years—from the period of his partnership with Martin—and it shows the troubled, naïve vein of seriousness on which his comedy is based.

In 1946, Lewis and Martin formed a night-club act that Hal Wallis later transferred to the movies. Their films together were broken affairs if only because the two men were at such odds: Lewis seemed hurt by Martin's callousness, just as Martin was offended by the proximity of a slob. That they prospered was due to Paramount's plugging, hard work, and the support of a largely juvenile audience: *My Friend Irma* (49, George Marshall); *My Friend Irma Goes West* (50, Hal Walker); *At War With the Army* (51, Walker); *That's My Boy* (51, Walker); *Sailor Beware* (52, Walker); *Jumping Jacks* (52, Norman Taurog); *The Stooge* (53, Taurog); *Scared Stiff* (53, Marshall); *The Caddy* (53, Taurog); *Money from Home* (53, Marshall); *Living It Up* (54, Taurog); *Three Ring Circus* (54, Joseph Pevney); *You're Never Too Young* (55, Taurog); *Artists and Models* (55, Tashlin); *Pardners* (56, Taurog); and *Hollywood or Bust* (56, Tashlin).

Lewis's range grew as the series went on, and *Hollywood or Bust* was an advance in Tashlin's matching of the idiot with the idiotic American dream—with Jerry's glasses knocked askew by Anita Ekberg's boobs. When the partnership ended, Lewis was able to carry on solo. His films with Tashlin enlarged his skill as much as his ambition: *The Delicate Delinquent* (57, Don McGuire); *The Sad Sack* (57, Marshall); *Rock-a-Bye Baby* (58, Tashlin); *The Geisha Boy* (58, Tashlin); *Don't Give Up the Ship* (59, Taurog); and *Visit to a Small Planet* (60, Taurog).

Once he was directing himself, Lewis mixed his own projects with appearances in other people's films: *Cinderfella* (60, Tashlin), where his rabid pathos eliminated much of Tashlin's original satire; *It's Only Money* (62, Tashlin); *Who's Minding the Store?* (63, Tashlin); *The Disorderly Orderly* (64, Tashlin); *Boeing Boeing* (65, John Rich); *Way . . . Way Out* (66, Gordon Douglas); *Don't Raise the Bridge, Lower the River* (68, Jerry Paris); and *Hook, Line and Sinker* (69, Marshall).

But by 1967, Lewis's momentum faltered. *Three on a Couch* had marked his departure from Paramount. Is it possible that an insecurity in Lewis needed a solid base? Was he also growing too old to carry off his late-teenage image of gauche destructiveness? Indeed, *One More Time* was made without his presence as an actor, but with the savorless Salt and Pepper—Sammy Davis and Peter Lawford.

Lewis is still a household name in America—loved or loathed—because of his annual Labor Day telethon on behalf of children with muscular dystrophy. Few other occasions say so much about America, and surely the event would have lapsed but for Lewis's commitment to it. It is an orgy of money and sentimentality on the one hand; and on the other, a ponderous, tasteless reflection of a country of huge wealth and boundless idealism. Lewis puts a year of energy into its twenty-four hours, and the event catches all his contrary moods—inspired clowning, trained imbecility, the breakdown of language as fatigue grows, and the heavy, maudlin boasting about feeling. The pressure of solemnity on a fragile intellect may be just as evident in Lewis's unreleased movie, *The Day the Clown Cried*. It was shot in 1974 and finished a year later, but legal problems or someone's reticence kept it back. It is not a comedy; it is about a circus clown employed by the Nazis to assist in the killing of children in concentration camps.

To live in America is to experience the native incredulity at Lewis being taken seriously. Few things are held against the whole of France more fiercely than French love of Lewis. He is hardly a filmmaker now. The telethon has been Lewis's annual movie, his life, and his show—and there in twenty-four hours one can still see the monster of his own sentimentality and the genius of timing—to say nothing of Buddy Love. In other words, Jerry Lewis has become not just an institution but a site, as lovely and/or depraved as Las Vegas, where the telethon has been done.

Surely Martin Scorsese was moved by this phenomenon in using Lewis in *The King of Comedy*—yet Lewis felt constrained in that film. He was a trussed-up straight man to De Niro and Sandra Bernhard. He has also acted in *Slapstick of Another Kind* (84, Steven Paul); *Fight for Life* (87, Elliot Silverstein); and *Cookie* (89, Susan Seidelman). For TV, he was very good for a season as Eli Sternberg, a veteran in the garment business, in *Wiseguy* (88–89).

In recent years, he has been seen in *Arizona Dream* (93, Emir Kusturica) and *Funny Bones* (95, Peter Chelsom).

Joseph H. Lewis (1907–2000), b. New York
1937: *Navy Spy* (codirected with Crane Wilbur); *Courage of the West; The Singing Outlaw.* 1938: *The Spy Ring; Border Wolves; The Last Stand.* 1939: *Two-Fisted Rangers.* 1940: *Blazing Six Shooters; Texas Stagecoach; The Man from Tumbleweeds; Boys of the City; The Return of Wild Bill; That Gang of Mine.* 1941: *The Invisible Ghost; Pride of the Bowery; Criminals Within.* 1942: *Arizona Cyclone; Bombs over Burma; The Silver Bullet; Secrets of a Co-Ed; The Boss of Hangtown Mesa; The Mad Doctor of Market Street.* 1944: *The Minstrel Man.* 1945: *My Name Is Julia Ross.* 1946:

So Dark the Night; The Jolson Story (codirected with Alfred E. Green). 1947: *The Swordsman.* 1948: *The Return of October.* 1949: *Undercover Man; Deadly Is the Female/Gun Crazy.* 1950: *A Lady Without Passport.* 1952: *Retreat—Hell!; Desperate Search.* 1953: *Cry of the Hunted.* 1954: *The Big Combo.* 1955: *A Lawless Street.* 1956: *7th Cavalry.* 1957: *The Halliday Brand.* 1958: *Terror in a Texas Town.*

Joseph Lewis is one of the pleasures of watching abbreviated movies on late-night television, interrupted by commercials so that scrappy plots sometimes begin to separate like reproducing amoebae. His films are mostly disreputable second features, bought for television in job lots. In no proper sense did Lewis ever make it. But *My Name Is Julia Ross, Undercover Man, Gun Crazy, The Big Combo, A Lawless Street, The Halliday Brand,* and *Terror in a Texas Town* are better than you will expect, adept at catching character in action, skillfully conveying underlying mood and violence while dispensing cliché plot lines.

There is no point in overpraising Lewis. The limitations of the B picture lean on all his films. But the plunder he came away with is astonishing and—here is the rub—more durable than the output of many better-known directors. *Julia Ross* with Dame May Whitty blithely tolerating her maniac son, George Macready, is not much less disturbing than *Strangers on a Train. Gun Crazy* is as odd as pairing John Dall and Peggy Cummings, and *The Big Combo* is as beautiful or noir as John Alton ever shot. Joseph Lewis never had the chance to discover whether he was an "artist," but—like Edgar Ulmer and Budd Boetticher—he has made better films than Fred Zinnemann, John Frankenheimer, or John Schlesinger.

Juliette Lewis, b. Los Angeles, 1973

Juliette Lewis's is an actual, if extreme career, and I can give you its outline facts. But I can't help regarding her as something beyond the real—as some mythic or warning enterprise. For she is—it seems to me (and this is all in the eye of the beholder)—a fidgety, pouting, perfect example of what appeals to voyeurism. She is an image animated by the wicked thrill of being seen, looked at, and her own thrill is generated by some intuitive measuring of our guilty pleasure. She is of age now, but she was established first as a kind of Lolita, with a knowingness that was not permissible, and as a breed of illicit spectacle. What child has ever had darker or blunter eyes, or a mouth more filled and sated with intimations of our desire?

I know, it is not common or proper to talk about real people—professionals!—like this, much less in an apparent work of reference. But this is a book about response, and I cannot escape my own feeling of awe and dismay at seeing Lewis. For it carries not just the certainty that she is inspired,

or magical, or understanding, but the anticipation of a Humbert Humbert and the father of daughters. Watching her, I feel like the George C. Scott character in *Hard Core,* or like the cineaste who has at last reached the back of the cave where ghosts grow on the wall like the slime of geology.

She is the child of the supporting actor Geoffrey Lewis. Her parents divorced and Lewis was apparently allowed to live on her own while still in her early teens. God knows whether she was "educated," or whether many of us could live with the knowledge she has picked up. For she has worked steadily, and almost willfully on the borders of derangement and abandon: at twelve, it is said, in a TV movie, *Home Fires;* a bit in *My Stepmother Is an Alien* (88, Richard Benjamin); *National Lampoon's Christmas Vacation* (89, Jeremiah S. Chechik); *A Family for Joe* (90, Jeffrey Melman); outstanding as the fifteen-year-old who ends up on Death Row in *Too Young to Die?* (90, Robert Markowitz); *Crooked Hearts* (91, Michael Bortman); getting a supporting actress nomination and being the complicit dancer to some of De Niro's most Satanic weavings in *Cape Fear* (91, Martin Scorsese); *That Night* (92, Craig Bolotin); excellent in *Husbands and Wives* (92, Woody Allen); close to human tenderness in *What's Eating Gilbert Grape* (93, Lasse Hallström); a wanton psychopath, with Brad Pitt, her companion in life then, in *Kalifornia* (93, Dominic Sena); eyebait for slaughter in *Romeo Is Bleeding* (94, Peter Medak); one of the *Natural Born Killers* (94, Oliver Stone); *Mixed Nuts* (94, Nora Ephron); as poisoned purity in *Strange Days* (95, Kathryn Bigelow); *From Dusk Till Dawn* (96, Robert Rodriguez).

She was away for a while, in recovery and rehabilitation, and she returned for *Some Girl* (98, Rory Kelly); *The Other Sister* (99, Garry Marshall); *The 4th Floor* (99, John Klausner); strenuously pregnant in *The Way of the Gun* (00, Christopher McQuarrie); *Room to Rent* (00, Khalid Al-Haggar); *Gaudi Afternoon* (00, Susan Seidelman); *My Louisiana Sky* (01, Adam Arkin) for TV; *Picture Claire* (01, Bruce McDonald); *Enough* (02, Michael Apted); *Hysterical Blindness* (02, Mira Nair); *Old School* (03, Todd Phillips); on TV in *Free for All* (03); *Cold Creek Manor* (03, Mike Figgis).

Val Lewton (Vladimir Ivan Leventon) (1904–51), b. Yalta, Russia

There was a time when James Agee, speaking to MGM executive Dore Schary, called Val Lewton one of the three most creative men in American films. That may have been too fanciful a claim to make Schary reappraise Lewton's place at the studio. Equally, it would be a disservice to Lewton's achievement to regard him as more than a maverick producer, eccentric if only because he was involved personally in several movies that restored the psychological basis of the horror genre. Just as it seems likely that he brought many ideas and a general theme of withheld horror to his films, it is unlikely that he possessed the concentrated artistic ambition or the studio stamina to direct or produce more penetrating films.

The good things in Lewton productions were unexpected and against the grain of B pictures. Their visual originality lay in the oppressive use of shadow to disguise cheap sets—a device that RKO may have learned from *Citizen Kane*. The brooding fascination with morbid subjects—which seems to have been Lewton's own contribution—is beautifully realized by that concealing cloak, but it remains B-picture philosophy, justified by the more-or-less inventive handling of action devised by Jacques Tourneur, Mark Robson, and Robert Wise.

Lewton's mother brought him to America in 1909, and he was brought up by her and his aunt, Alla Nazimova. He was a fertile writer, if slapdash. During the 1930s he published several novels, wrote news articles, and radio scripts. One of these novels, *No Bed of Her Own*, became the film *No Man of Her Own* (33, Wesley Ruggles). He worked for the MGM publicity department and from 1933–42 he was on David Selznick's staff. That involved a variety of tasks: writing, directing some crowd scenes for *A Tale of Two Cities* with Tourneur, recommending Ingrid Bergman and *Intermezzo* to his boss, and dissuading Victor Fleming from shooting a dinner table sequence of *Gone With the Wind* with two grapefruit in line with Vivien Leigh's breasts.

He left Selznick to join RKO as a producer and from 1942–46 he fortified the studio, the horror movie, and the reputation of the B picture. It is clear, too, that he filmed no script unless he had reworked it to his own satisfaction: *Cat People* (42, Tourneur), with Simone Simon amid a screen dark with feline images; the masterly sixty-eight-minute *I Walked With a Zombie* (43, Tourneur); *The Leopard Man* (43, Tourneur), so overtly violent that producer and director apologized for its crudeness; marvelous amends made with *The Seventh Victim* (43, Mark Robson) about a devil cult, with Jean Brooks balefully beautiful as the member who kills herself; *The Ghost Ship* (43, Robson); *The Curse of the Cat People* (44, Robert Wise and Gunther von Fritsch)—a lovely rendering of child psychology; *Youth Runs Wild* (44, Robson), an adventurous departure in subject, about teenage reaction to the war; a Maupassant translation, *Mademoiselle Fifi* (44, Wise); *Isle of the Dead* (45, Robson), with Boris Karloff; *The Body Snatcher* (45, Wise), from Robert Louis Stevenson, with Karloff as Cabman Gray; and *Bedlam* (46, Robson) based on Hogarth's Rake in the asylum. Most of these films were shot in four weeks with variable acting. They still intrigue and

frighten, because of Lewton's originality, directorial skill, and those RKO craftsmen: photographer Nicholas Musuraca, art director Albert D'Agostino, and set decorator Darrell Silvera.

Lewton went to Paramount for one bad movie—*My Own True Love* (48, Compton Bennett)—and to MGM for another, *Please Believe Me* (50, Norman Taurog). But at Universal he was responsible for one cheap, worthwhile Western, *Apache Drums* (51, Hugo Fregonese). He died on the point of taking up a job as associate producer with Stanley Kramer.

Marcel L'Herbier (1890–1979), b. Paris
1917: *Phantasmes*. 1918: *Rose France*. 1919: *Le Bercail; Le Carnaval des Vérités*. 1920: *L'Homme du Large*. 1921: *Prométhée Banquier; Eldorado; Villa Destin*. 1922: *Don Juan et Faust*. 1924: *L'Inhumaine* (s). 1925: *Feu Mathias Pascal*. 1927: *Le Vertige; Le Diable au Coeur*. 1928: *L'Argent*. 1930: *Nuits de Prince*. 1931: *L'Enfant d'Amour; Le Mystère de la Chambre Jaune; Le Parfum de la Dame en Noir*. 1933: *L'Epervier*. 1934: *L'Aventurier; Le Bonheur*. 1935: *Veillées d'Armes; La Route Impériale; Children's Corner*. 1936: *Le Scandale; Les Hommes Nouveaux; La Porte du Large; Nuits de Feu*. 1937: *La Citadelle du Silence; Forfaiture*. 1938: *La Tragédie Imperiale; Adrienne Lecouvreur; Terre de Feu; Entente Cordiale*. 1939: *La Brigade Sauvage; La Mode Revée*. 1940: *La Comédie du Bonheur*. 1941: *Histoire de Rire; La Vie de Bohème*. 1942: *La Nuit Fantastique; L'Honorable Cathérine*. 1945: *Au Petit Bonheur*. 1946: *L'Affaire du Collier de la Reine*. 1947: *La Revoltée*. 1948: *Les Derniers Jours de Pompeii*. 1953: *Le Père de Mademoiselle* (codirected with Robert Paul Dagan).

L'Herbier was a Parisian intellectual and literary critic who served in the army film unit during the First World War and emerged convinced of the new art form. Thus, in the early 1920s he assembled a number of outstanding supporting talents and made some aggressively expressionist films: *Eldorado*, with its distorted images suggesting subjectivity; *L'Inhumaine*, involving architect Mallet Stevens, painter Fernand Léger, designer Alberto Cavalcanti, and composer Darius Milhaud; and *Feu Mathias Pascal*, from a Pirandello novel. Alain Resnais has talked about how far the ambition of these films now seems more valuable than their actual achievement. Within a few years, L'Herbier began making much more conventional films, and diverting his conviction about cinema's importance into institutional channels. As well as writing several books—including *Intelligence du Cinématographe*—in 1932 he became advisor to the Comité Internationale du Cinéma d'Enseignement et de la Culture. During the Second World War, he founded IDHEC and served as president of the Cinémathèque Française. As soon as TV was active in France, he made a series of programs proclaiming and explaining cinema.

Max Linder (Gabriel-Maximilien Leuvielle) (1883–1925), b. Caverne, France

Despite the reissue, in 1958, of a Max Linder anthology, only a fraction of this early comedian's work is now known. What little evidence we have is muddled by assertions that Chaplin was influenced by Linder. Although Linder went to America and was reasonably successful there, he was the epitome of a French comedian. A Bordelais, he came to Paris when he was twenty-one and, after a year in theatre, he began acting in films. From 1905–07 he made some four hundred films for Pathé while starring in the Paris music hall. But after 1907, he took over from André Deed as the leading comedian at Pathé, at a steady rate of a film a week.

By 1911, he was writing and directing his own films, and the character of "Max" had emerged: remarkably restrained and adult; a diffident, handsome dandy; accident-prone but whimsical. He might have stepped out of a Feuillade serial, in evening dress, cloak, top hat, and moustache. Eschewing slapstick, his humor relied on gesture and facial reaction, and there was little of the sentimentality that American comedians resorted to. Linder was the rake, softened by a dreamy vagueness and by a fatalistic, bemused view of the frantic action around him.

In the years immediately before the First World War he was very successful in France. His output was sadly reduced during the war, when illness prevented him from enlisting. Many of his films at this period were patriotic propaganda efforts. But in 1916 he went to America to replace Chaplin at Essanay and made *Max Comes Across* (17), followed by *Max Wants a Divorce* (17), and *Max in a Taxi* (17). He returned to France and did live theatre shows for troops. But after two more films— *Le Petit Café* (19, Raymond Bernard) and *Le Feu Sacré* (20, Henri Diamant-Berger)—he went back to Hollywood and made three features: *Seven Years Bad Luck* (21), *Be My Wife* (21), and *The Three Must-Get-Theres* (22), a parody of the Douglas Fairbanks films with Linder playing "Dart-in-Again."

But Goldwyn had declined to handle his work in America and Linder went back to France, sick and depressed. His last years were increasingly melancholy. He played in *Au Secours!* (23, Abel Gance) and in 1925 he went to Austria to make *Roi de Cirque*. That same year, he and his wife killed themselves. It is clear that Linder's career was blocked by American interests, and this may have aggravated his nervous illness. But "Max" had always been an abstracted character, one who could never fully adapt to the world.

Anatole Litvak (1902–74), b. Kiev, Russia

1924: *Tatiana*. 1930: *Dolly Macht Karriere*. 1931: *Nie Wieder Liebe*. 1932: *Coeur des Lilas; Das Lied einer Nacht*. 1933: *Sleeping Car; Cette Vieille Canaille*. 1935: *L'Equipage*. 1936: *Mayerling*. 1937: *The Woman I Love; Tovarich*. 1938: *The Amazing Dr. Clitterhouse; The Sisters*. 1939: *Confessions of a Nazi Spy*. 1940: *Castle on the Hudson; City for Conquest; All This and Heaven Too*. 1941: *Out of the Fog; Blues in the Night*. 1942: *This Above All; The Nazis Strike* (codirected with Frank Capra) (d); *Divide and Conquer* (codirected with Capra) (d). 1943: *The Battle of Russia* (d). 1944: *The Battle of China* (codirected with Capra) (d). 1945: *War Comes to America* (d). 1947: *The Long Night*. 1948: *Sorry, Wrong Number; The Snake Pit*. 1951: *Decision Before Dawn*. 1953: *Act of Love*. 1955: *The Deep Blue Sea*. 1956: *Anastasia*. 1957: *Mayerling*. 1958: *The Journey*. 1961: *Goodbye Again*. 1962: *Five Miles to Midnight*. 1967: *The Night of the Generals*. 1969: *La Dame dans l'Auto avec des Lunettes et un Fusil/The Lady in the Car with Glasses and a Gun*.

At either end of Litvak's career there is a nomadic flurry, but in the center, from 1937–51, he looks like a Hollywood pro and a patriot. A philosophy student at St. Petersburg, he made *Tatiana* in Russia and then went to Germany, where he was called Lutwak and worked on the editing of *Die Freudlose Gasse* (25, G. W. Pabst), was an assistant director and then director. *Sleeping Car* was made in England for Gaumont British with Ivor Novello and Madeleine Carroll, after which he made three films in France before going to Hollywood to remake *L'Equipage* as *The Woman I Love* with Miriam Hopkins, his wife from 1937–39.

In America, he adopted a curious mixture of anti-Nazi, thriller, and women's pic material. During the war he was active in the *Why We Fight* series and worked on many propaganda films. But, with peace, he subsided into Broadway melodramas that grew more clotted with the years. *The Long Night* was an attempted remake of *Le Jour se Lève; Sorry, Wrong Number* is a classic sheetchewer, with Barbara Stanwyck cracking into fragments; while *The Snake Pit* is a dull central love story alongside some startlingly good footage of life in an asylum—there, in one film, the documentarist and the tearjerker rattled against one another.

The documentarist was abandoned and his films became increasingly turgid. *The Deep Blue Sea, Anastasia, The Journey,* and *Goodbye Again* are toppling on the edge of parody, but Litvak solemnly put his actresses through the motions of ordeal. The growing staidness in Ingrid Bergman owes a lot to Litvak's direction.

The plodding films give no hint of Litvak the

man—he was a great womanizer, a Hollywood socialite, and a dashing figure.

Frank Lloyd (1889–1960),
b. Glasgow, Scotland
1916: *The Code of Marcia Gray; Sins of Her Parent.* 1917: *The Price of Silence; A Tale of Two Cities; American Methods; When a Man Sees Red; The Heart of a Lion; The Kingdom of Love.* 1918: *Les Miserables; Blindness of Divorce; True Blue; For Freedom; The Rainbow Trail; The Riders of the Purple Sage.* 1919: *The Man Hunter; Pitfalls of a Big City; The Loves of Letty.* 1920: *The Silver Horde; The Woman in Room 13; Madame X; The Great Lover; The World and Its Woman.* 1921: *Roads of Destiny; A Tale of Two Worlds; The Invisible Power; A Voice in the Dark; The Man from Lost River; The Grim Comedian.* 1922: *The Eternal Flame; Oliver Twist; The Sin Flood.* 1923: *Within the Law; Ashes of Vengeance; The Voice from the Minaret.* 1924: *Black Oxen; The Silent Watcher; The Sea Hawk.* 1925: *Winds of Chance; Her Husband's Secret; The Splendid Road.* 1926: *The Wise Guy; The Eagle of the Sea.* 1927: *Children of Divorce.* 1928: *Adoration.* 1929: *The Divine Lady; Weary River; Drag; Dark Streets; Young Nowheres.* 1930: *Son of the Gods; The Way of All Men; The Lash.* 1931: *Right of Way; The Age for Love; East Lynne.* 1932: *A Passport to Hell.* 1933: *Cavalcade; Berkeley Square; Hoop-La.* 1934: *Servant's Entrance.* 1935: *Mutiny on the Bounty.* 1936: *Under Two Flags.* 1937: *Maid of Salem; Wells Fargo.* 1938: *If I Were King.* 1939: *Rulers of the Sea.* 1940: *The Howards of Virginia.* 1941: *The Lady from Cheyenne; This Woman Is Mine.* 1943: *Forever and a Day* (codirected). 1945: *Blood on the Sun.* 1954: *The Shanghai Story.* 1955: *The Last Command.*

"Normally an effective director of commercial films," was Josef von Sternberg's deadpan verdict on Frank Lloyd when B. P. Schulberg asked him to "salvage" *Children of Divorce,* a "sad affair," starring Gary Cooper and Clara Bow, that Lloyd had just completed. And yet, two years later, Lloyd won the best director Oscar for *The Divine Lady,* while in 1933 he received the direction Oscar for the prestigious *Cavalcade* (it got best picture, too). It is an odd contrast, as inexplicable as the way Lloyd declined in the 1940s, went into an early retirement, and made two last pictures at Republic.

He came to America in 1910, as an actor. By the early 1920s he was a leading director. *The Eternal Flame* was made for Natalie Talmadge's own company with Talmadge as Balzac's Duchesse de Langeais; while *Oliver Twist,* made for Jackie Coogan Productions, paired Lon Chaney's Fagin with Coogan's urchin. He set up his own production company for a version of Sabatini's *The Sea*

Hawk and for *Her Husband's Secret.* For the next few years his films were made for First National, notably *Divine Lady* with Corinne Griffith as Nelson's Emma. But from 1931, he worked for Fox: *East Lynne,* with Clive Brook, who also appeared in the adaptation of Noel Coward's *Cavalcade.* In 1935, he was loaned to MGM for *Mutiny,* a slow, stagy film in which Laughton and Gable both seem cramped. It is intrinsically dull, carried by its own publicity, the idea of history, and some second-unit exotica, but it won best picture and another director nomination for Lloyd. After *Under Two Flags,* Lloyd went over to Paramount and was given a string of swashbucklers.

Why did he fall away when still only middle-aged? Geraldine Farrar referred cryptically to his having had "better luck with ships than with people," as though studio spectacle was his only forte. But, in truth, his work is short of character and excitement, as flatulent as this definition of the role of a director from Lloyd quoted in *The Parade's Gone By:* "The director is essentially an interpreter. To him is given the task of making logical and understandable, pictorially, what the author and the continuity writer have set down."

Now, why can't every director behave like that?

Harold Lloyd (1893–1971),
b. Burchard, Nebraska
Although Lloyd is generally ranked alongside Chaplin and Keaton as masters of silent comedy, he is a more conventional personality. It is less Lloyd himself who is funny than the succession of gags in his films. When we see Chaplin, Keaton, Fields, or Groucho, laughter is inspired by character. It is their response to chaos or hostility that is amusing. But Lloyd's world is sunny, orderly, and tractable; it is rearranged to fit the maneuvers of his often very complex jokes. And Lloyd himself is not just the "college boy"—fresh-faced, neat, bespectacled—but the budding executive of Comedy Inc.

That famous skyscraper climb was forced upon Lloyd only when his stuntman broke a leg. In the same way, the rest of his films are like comedies made when the clown was ill and when bustling, eager Lloyd stood in for him. His strength was organizational. He took comedy very practically, controlling his own work whenever possible, inaugurating the circle of contributing gagmen, and actually directing most of his own films. It has been pointed out by Andrew Sarris that Lloyd survived, intact despite all the risks he took, very rich, and even in old age clinging to a rather vacant grin. Keaton was marooned, Fields a drunk, Chaplin an exile, and Groucho neutered by TV. Whereas Lloyd sat in his beautiful Californian home, rationing out the rerelease of his old films and "very active in civic organizations."

Lloyd was a traveling actor who, in 1912,

worked for Edison as an extra. He met Hal Roach and the two men set up a company with Lloyd playing "Willie Work." The pair joined Pathé and evolved "Lonesome Luke," a copy of Chaplin. By 1919, Lloyd had made over a hundred one- and two-reel comedies. He abandoned Luke because he was too derivative, and adopted ordinariness, spectacles, and "comedies where people would see themselves and their neighbors." Early clowns are all outsiders, men incapable of, or uninterested in, society's scale of merit. Chaplin admits that scale but criticizes it. Langdon never notices it, Keaton is bewildered by it, the Marx Brothers know it is a lie, Laurel and Hardy believe it will never come their way. But Lloyd became the least deviant of comedians, a man who never dreamed of being out of the ordinary.

Pathé liked the new image, and *Bumping Into Broadway* (19) and *Captain Kidd's Kidds*—both with Bebe Daniels—established him. Daniels went on her way and was replaced by Mildred Davis, whom Lloyd married. But after *From Hand to Mouth* (19) and *His Royal Slyness* (19), he was seriously injured while making *Haunted Spooks* (20). He recovered, and by 1921 was making three-reelers: *Now or Never, Never Weaken,* and *Among Those Present.* From those he moved into feature-length films: *A Sailor-Made Man* (21, Fred Newmeyer); *Grandma's Boy* (22, Newmeyer); *Dr. Jack* (22, Newmeyer); and *Safety Last* (23, Newmeyer and Sam Taylor).

The directorial presence of Roach on the early shorts and of Newmeyer and Taylor on the features was nominal: "I never took credit for direction, although I practically directed all my own pictures. The directors were entirely dependent on me. I had these boys there because I felt they knew comedy, they knew what I wanted, they knew me and they could handle the details." After *Why Worry?* (23, Newmeyer and Taylor), he formed his own company, still working for Pathé: *Girl Shy* (24), *Hot Water* (24), and *The Freshman* (25), all with Newmeyer and Taylor. He then moved over to Paramount: *For Heaven's Sake* (26, Taylor), *The Kid Brother* (27, Ted Wilde), and *Speedy* (28, Wilde). He made *Welcome Stranger* (29, Clyde Bruckman) with a few sound sequences, but *Feet First* (30, Bruckman) was a flop.

Thereafter he worked more slowly: *Movie Crazy* (32, Bruckman); *The Cat's Paw* (34, Taylor) for Fox; and, back at Paramount, *The Milky Way* (36, Leo McCarey). After *Professor Beware* (38, Elliott Nugent), he retired as an actor, but produced *A Girl, A Guy and A Gob* (41, Richard Wallace), with George Murphy and Lucille Ball, and *My Favorite Spy* (42, Tay Garnett). He was called out of retirement by Howard Hughes to appear in *The Sin of Harold Diddlebock* (46, Preston Sturges), spoiled, according to Lloyd, by

Sturges's inflexibility. In his last twenty years, Lloyd reissued some of his best silent work in two compilations: *Harold Lloyd's World of Comedy* (62) and *Harold Lloyd's Funny Side of Life* (64).

Ken Loach, b. Nuneaton, England, 1936
1965: *Up the Junction* (TV). 1966: *Cathy Come Home* (TV). 1967: *Poor Cow.* 1969: *Kes.* 1971: *Family Life.* 1979: *Black Jack.* 1980: *The Gamekeeper.* 1981: *Looks and Smiles.* 1986: *Fatherland/Singing the Blues in Red.* 1990: *Hidden Agenda.* 1992: *Riff-Raff.* 1993: *Raining Stones.* 1994: *Ladybird, Ladybird.* 1995: *Land and Freedom.* 1996: *Carla's Song.* 1997: *The Flickering Flame* (d). 1998: *My Name Is Joe.* 2000: *Bread and Roses.* 2001: *The Navigators.* 2002: *Sweet Sixteen.*

Born the son of an electrician in the English Midlands, Loach has remained steadfastly attentive to working-class experience—to such an extent that some of his films have had (or needed) "English" subtitles when released in America. He read law at Oxford and was active in experimental theatre at the same time. He did a little acting, before he joined the BBC and learned his craft on the excellent series *Z-Cars,* about police in the northwest of England. From there, he began to make docudramas, often with unknown actors and an air of improvisation, but just as often dependent on published source material.

Up the Junction may have seemed like a raw slice of south London life, but it came from a book by Nell Dunn. *Cathy Come Home* was a good deal tougher and better organized, and it caused great controversy in Britain as to whether or not the BBC should have revealed such harsh social conditions. *Poor Cow* was an attempt to carry the TV method over into a feature film, but it was less effective (perhaps because it used such excellent but conventional young actors as Terence Stamp and Malcolm McDowell).

In those early days, Loach worked in partnership with the producer Tony Garnett: *Kes* was their major film, about a working-class kid who tries to raise a falcon—it is probably still Loach's best-known film. *Family Life* was a very bleak work, written by David Mercer, about a nineteen-year-old woman whose failure in life leads to her being institutionalized and actually going crazy. The movie seemed as gloomy about mental health care as about the maddening pressures of the family—true to life, perhaps, but without redemption.

For the next few years, Loach had a hard time finding films. *The Gamekeeper* was a more conventional narrative, about the barriers of the class system. But Loach seemed less himself in traditional narrative. Gradually in the eighties, with varying degrees of success (perhaps because of his comfort with different writers), he worked his way back to tough, exploratory pictures about a more-or-less beleaguered working class. *Hidden Agenda*—set and filmed in Northern Ireland—is the most accessible of these, though its structure is awkward and the film requires a good deal of background knowledge in the viewer.

But Loach has persevered, and in *Riff-Raff* and *Raining Stones* he did his best work yet. These are still unforced, naturalistic movies, studies in banal and "hopeless" poverty, but well acted and with growing humor. For me, it is easier to respect Loach than enjoy him: he seldom has the bite of Alan Clarke, for instance. But in his dedication and seriousness, he is an exemplary figure.

Even in the insane prosperity of the nineties, Loach pursued his destiny, and he grew gentler, subtler, and funnier. It was one of the most impressive developments in a filmmaker. Who else—with *Bread and Roses*—would get to make a film about the Los Angeles janitors' strike that was a serious contender for prizes at Cannes? *Land and Freedom* was a remarkable recreation of the Spanish Civil War (with violence, boredom, and the interminable political arguments)—spoiled by a trite, didactic framework. *Carla's Song* brought together a Scotsman and a woman from Nicaragua—Loach has a nice, shy taste for Latin women. And best of all, *My Name Is Joe* followed a romance between a drunk (Peter Mullan) and a social worker. I still don't find myself getting excited with Loach—but I begin to see more clearly, and sadly, how that is my loss or shortcoming.

Margaret Lockwood (Day) (1916–90),
b. Karachi, India

Here's a little game: which English actress, born in India, with dark hair and flashing eyes, sauce and humor, got a huge chance in 1939? Yes, of course, it was Vivien Leigh, born in Darjeeling, three years earlier than Margaret Day. But just suppose: Lockwood looked a lot like Leigh; she looked as much like Joan Bennett (who was also in the running); she would have been twenty-two when Scarlett was cast—and she might have been pretty good, to judge by her several performances for Carol Reed in the late thirties and early forties, or to judge simply by Hitchcock's *The Lady Vanishes* (38), a better calling card than anything Vivien Leigh could muster. Of course, Leigh had Olivier and Myron Selznick—she got herself there in the firelight of Atlanta. But Margaret Lockwood was plainly a favorite of Carol Reed—maybe just not in the right way, or maybe Reed was a bit stuffy about Hollywood?

Still, it's an intriguing call, and enough to remind us that Margaret Lockwood had her moment as a woman of spirit, pride, and even danger. She had worked on stage first, but the camera clearly loved her: *Some Day* (35, Michael Powell); *Midshipman Easy* (35, Reed); *Man of the Moment* (35, Monty Banks); Annie Ridd in *Lorna Doone* (35, Basil Dean); *Honours Easy* (35, Herbert Brenon); *The Case of Gabriel Perry* (35, Albert de Courville); *The Amateur Gentleman* (36, Thornton Freeland); *The Beloved Vagabond* (36, Curt Bernhardt); *Jury's Evidence* (36, Ralph Ince); *Irish for Luck* (36, Arthur Wood); with George Arliss in *Doctor Syn* (37, Roy William Neill); *Who's Your Lady Friend?* (37, Reed); *The Street Singer* (37, Jean de Marguerat); *Melody and Romance* (37, Maurice Elvey); *Owd Bob* (38, Robert Stevens); *Bank Holiday* (38, Reed).

What's more, she did go to Hollywood. At the very moment in question, she was invited west for two pictures: *Rulers of the Sea* (39, Frank Lloyd), with Doug Fairbanks Jr., and *Susannah of the Mounties* (39, William A. Seiter), with Shirley Temple. Yet there's no evidence that Selznick knew of her.

She came back to Britain and did her best work in the war years: *The Stars Look Down* (39, Reed); *A Girl Must Live* (39, Reed); *Night Train to Munich* (40, Reed); *Quiet Wedding* (40, Anthony Asquith); *Alibi* (42, Brian Desmond Hurst); *The Man in Grey* (43, Leslie Arliss), with James Mason; *Give Us the Moon* (43, Val Guest); *Dear Octopus* (43, Harold French); *A Place of One's Own* (44, Bernard Knowles); *Love Story* (44, Arliss); and her big hit, with Mason, as highwaymen, *The Wicked Lady* (45, Arliss)—a very Scarlett role.

She was only thirty, but after the war she failed to attach herself to Rank or Ealing and her career suffered: *I'll Be Your Sweetheart* (45, Guest); *Bedelia* (46, Lance Comfort); *Hungry Hill* (47, Hurst); *The White Unicorn* (47, Knowles); *Jassy* (47, Knowles); a TV version of *Pygmalion* in 1948; *Look Before You Love* (48, Harold Huth); as Nell Gwynn in *Cardboard Cavalier* (49, Walter Forde); *Madness of the Heart* (49, Charles Bennett); *Highly Dangerous* (50, Roy Baker); and then three pictures for Herbert Wilcox—*Trent's Last Case* (52), *Trouble in the Glen* (53), and *Laughing Anne* (53).

She was doing stage again, and had a last movie fling in *Cast a Dark Shadow* (57, Lewis Gilbert), playing with Dirk Bogarde. Thereafter, it was just TV series—sometimes with her daughter, Julia—and the stepmother in *The Slipper and the Rose* (76, Bryan Forbes).

Barbara Loden (1932–80),
b. Marion, North Carolina
1970: *Wanda*.

Barbara Loden was Mrs. Elia Kazan, and the director of one film with a feeling for wayward, unordered lives, for the haphazard detracting from drama, and for an off-center, unsentimental pathos that are characteristics missing from her husband's work. *Wanda* did not go without praise, but sadly there were no more films from Ms. Loden. *Wanda* is a bank robbery picture, and never ashamed of that. It is by adhering to its narrative form that it is most eloquent about the benighted feminine character. A more strident director, with less respect for the medium, might have made a revolutionary tract out of *Wanda*. As it is, it shows a listless, none-too-bright woman on the point of a divorce who becomes the accomplice of a tetchy hold-up man. This is no pact of misbegotten romantics; *Wanda* is bolder than Kazan's movies in granting that people do not control their own destinies. Wanda interrupts one robbery and helplessly tags along, infuriating and bewildering the man and his headaches; and then muddles a larger job when she gets lost in traffic.

This action is no more underlined than the squalid small towns, bars, and motels; the impermanent life on the road; and the touching failure of the characters to conceive of any satisfactory role for themselves. Shot originally in 16mm Kodachrome, *Wanda* is full of unexpected moments and raw atmosphere, never settling for cliché in situation or character. It often has an air of improvisation—Loden admitted the influence of Warhol—but it is quite prepared for slow, simple effects, such as Wanda in white, in long shot, trudging through a coal yard. Above all, *Wanda* sees no need to stoke up the dignity or worth of its female victim. No woman director has given a fuller, less biased portrait of a man. *Wanda*—the title is a gentle pun as well as the woman's name—observes the unrealized desperation of millions of lives.

Otherwise, Barbara Loden acted in two of her husband's films—as the sour secretary in *Wild River* (60) and the rampaging sister in *Splendor in the Grass* (61). She worked more consistently in the theatre, playing the "Marilyn Monroe" part in the original production of Arthur Miller's *After the Fall*, but her sharp face was made for films.

Joshua Logan (1908–88),
b. Texarkana, Texas
1938: *I Met My Love Again* (codirected with Arthur Ripley). 1956: *Picnic; Bus Stop*. 1957: *Sayonara*. 1958: *South Pacific*. 1960: *Tall Story*. 1961: *Fanny*. 1964: *Ensign Pulver*. 1967: *Camelot*. 1969: *Paint Your Wagon*.

Logan was a man of the theatre. President of the drama group at Princeton, he formed a university company of actors that included Henry Fonda, James Stewart, and Margaret Sullavan. In the 1930s he visited Stanislavsky in Moscow, produced in London, and began a Broadway career as producer that included *Annie Get Your Gun*, *Happy Birthday*, *John Loves Mary*, *Mister Roberts*, *Charley's Aunt*, *South Pacific*, and

Fanny. In fact, he was coauthor of *Mister Roberts*, *South Pacific*, and *Fanny*.

His involvement in movies was principally as the conveyor of reliable theatrical packages to the screen, although *Camelot* did not keep up its stage success as a movie. Until *Picnic*, he had only dabbled in films, working on the dialogue for two Charles Boyer movies, *The Garden of Allah* (36, Richard Boleslavsky) and *History Is Made at Night* (37, Frank Borzage). *Picnic* was therefore something of a shock: a stage play (by William Inge) given cinematic life and authentic rural atmosphere, with a sense of color and design, a better-than-average William Holden, and a quartet of exceptional female performances—Rosalind Russell, Betty Field, Susan Strasberg, and Kim Novak looking like confectioner's custard.

There is no sham about *Picnic*: it wears well, especially the slumberous nocturnal dancing sequence, which is better than most of Logan's musical set pieces. Apart from that, he did a good comedy, *Tall Story*, early indication of Jane Fonda's vitality. And in *Bus Stop* (also from Inge) he coaxed the very best out of Marilyn Monroe, played fair by the provincial charm of the story, and helped Marilyn to make the "Black Magic" routine both excruciating and endearing. Did Monroe ever come closer to living with her limitations?

All too often, however, Logan was overwhelmed by theatrical originals. The films of *South Pacific* and *Paint Your Wagon* are dismal, inert versions of great shows. They are so depressing that they offer an oblique reminder that Logan was, for most of his life, a famous depressive.

Gina Lollobrigida (Luigina Lollobrigida), b.
Subiaco, Italy, 1927
Gina Lollobrigida: knickerbocker glory—not quite an anagram, but an indication of fruit and cream, unnourishing sweetness, and sheen. She was very beautiful, but it was the name that endeared her to non-Italian audiences and conveyed an erotic flavor. The full name is redolent of curvaceous softness on a firm framework—like Boucher's Miss O'Murphy sprawled on a sofa; but the abbreviation, "La Lollo," melted hearts and minds and confirmed foreign opinions of Italian frivolity.

She went to art school, but was apparently kept from her own easel by demands from her fellows that she pose. Under the name of Diana Loris— Anna Doloris?—she modeled for magazine picture stories. In the years after the war she had her first parts in films: *Aquila Nera* (46, Riccardo Freda); *Il Delitto di Giovanni Episcopo* (47, Alberto Lattuada); and *Campane a Martello* (49, Luigi Zampa). She soon became a continental star: *Achtung, Banditti!* (51, Carlo Lizzani); *Fan-*

fan la Tulipe (51, Christian-Jaque); *Altri Tempi* (51, Alessandro Blasetti); *Night Beauties* (52, René Clair); *The Wayward Wife* (52, Mario Soldati); *Le Infedeli* (52, Stefano Vanzina Steno and Mario Monicelli); *Pane Amore e Fantasia* (53, Luigi Comencini); *Le Grand Jeu* (53, Robert Siodmak); *Pane, Amore e Gelosia* (54, Comencini); and *La Bella di Roma* (54, Comencini).

It was *Woman of Rome* (54, Luigi Zampa) that made her famous beyond Italy. John Huston put her in *Beat the Devil* (54) and, after *La Donna piu Bella del Mondo* (55, Robert Z. Leonard), she was in *Trapeze* (56, Carol Reed). She now appeared in several "international" movies and had a few years in America: *The Hunchback of Notre Dame* (56, Jean Delannoy); *Anna di Brooklyn* (58, Reginald Denham); *La Loi* (58, Jules Dassin); *Solomon and Sheba* (59, King Vidor); *Never So Few* (59, John Sturges); *Go Naked in the World* (61, Ranald MacDougall); and *Come September* (61, Robert Mulligan).

Since then, she has slipped from eminence: *Venus Imperiale* (61, Delannoy); *Mare Matto* (62, Delannoy); *Woman of Straw* (63, Basil Dearden); *Strange Bedfellows* (64, Melvin Frank); with Akim Tamiroff in the "Monsignor Cupido" episode from *Le Bambole* (64, Mauro Bolognini); *Les Sultans* (65, Delannoy); *Hotel Paradiso* (66, Peter Glenville); *Cervantes* (67, Vincent Sherman); *La Morte la Fatto L'Uovo* (67, Giulio Questi); *Un Bellissimo Novembre* (68, Bolognini); *Buona Sera, Mrs. Campbell* (68, Frank); *Bad Man's River* (71, Eugenio Martin); and *King, Queen, Knave* (72, Jerzy Skolimowski).

In 1985, she did a TV movie, *Deceptions* (Robert Chenault and Melville Shavelson), and she appeared in the series *Falcon Crest*. In 1997, she was in *XXL* (97, Ariel Zeitoun).

Herbert Lom (Herbert Kuchacevich ze Schluderpacheru), b. Prague, 1917

Several earlier editions of this book "passed" on the magnificent longevity, the real menace, and the lugubrious comedy of Herbert Lom. I can only apologize for being so slow, so late. He would likely be the first to concede the quantity of honest and less honest junk that bears his name. Let us therefore pick out the exceptional things from this actor who arrived in Britain in 1939, and remained despite that country's urge to cast him as all manner of foreign (and criminal) rogues and idiots: *My Crimes* (40, Norman Lee); as Napoleon in *The Young Mr. Pitt* (42, Carol Reed); *The Seventh Veil* (45, Compton Bennett); *Good Time Girl* (48, David MacDonald); *The Girl in the Painting* (48, Terence Fisher); *Night and the City* (50, Jules Dassin); *The Black Rose* (50, Henry Hathaway); *State Secret* (50, Sidney Gilliat); *The Golden Salamander* (50, Ronald Neame); *Cage of Gold* (50, Basil Dearden); *The Man Who Watched* *the Trains Go By* (53, Harold French); *The Ladykillers* (55, Alexander Mackendrick); Napoleon again in *War and Peace* (56, King Vidor); *Fire Down Below* (57, Robert Parrish); *I Accuse!* (58, José Ferrer); *The Roots of Heaven* (58, John Huston); *Intent to Kill* (58, Jack Cardiff); *The Big Fisherman* (59, Frank Borzage); *I Aim at the Stars* (60, J. Lee Thompson); *Spartacus* (60, Stanley Kubrick); as the fascistic leader of the Moors in *El Cid* (61, Anthony Mann); *The Phantom of the Opera* (62, Fisher); *A Shot in the Dark* (64, Blake Edwards); *Gambit* (66, Neame); *Villa Rides!* (68, Buzz Kulik); *Assignment to Kill* (68, Sheldon Reynolds); *The Secret of Dorian Gray* (70, Massimo Dallamano); *Count Dracula* (70, Jess Franco); *Murders in the Rue Morgue* (71, Gordon Hessler); *The Return of the Pink Panther* (75, Edwards); *The Pink Panther Strikes Again* (78, Edwards); *The Dead Zone* (83, David Cronenberg); *The Pope Must Die* (91, Peter Richardson); *Son of the Pink Panther* (93, Edwards).

Carole Lombard (Jane Alice Peters) (1908–42), b. Fort Wayne, Indiana

Lombard didn't give a fuck, and she was famous for saying so. Although she died when only thirty-four, she had made forty-two talking pictures, four of which are among the best comedies America has produced: *Twentieth Century* (34, Howard Hawks); *My Man Godfrey* (36, Gregory La Cava); *Nothing Sacred* (37, William Wellman); and *To Be or Not to Be* (42, Ernst Lubitsch). In these, and many other films, she is still as enchanting and witty as any Hollywood actress. That brusque blonde superiority, the offhand hints of sexuality, and the exposure of feelings beneath screwball comedy made Lombard something of a legend in her own time. The tragically early death, and the way it interrupted a happy marriage to Clark Gable, ensured her reputation as someone slightly more than human. But, in truth, her range was narrow; she was far better just being herself than trying to act.

Her film debut was in 1921 when Allan Dwan spotted her playing baseball in the street and gave her a tomboy part in *A Perfect Crime*. By 1925 Fox had her under contract and she made *Marriage in Transit* (25, R. William Neill) and *Hearts and Spurs* (25, W. S. Van Dyke) before a motor accident caused the cancellation of the contract. In 1927, she joined Mack Sennett and made several two-reelers for him. Small parts in *The Perfect Crime* (28, Bert Glennon) and Raoul Walsh's *Me, Gangster* (28) led to a contract with Pathé which involved *High Voltage* (28, Howard Higgin), her first all-talking picture; *Racketeer* (29, Higgin), and Gregory La Cava's *Big News* (29).

After *Safety in Numbers* (30, Victor Schertzinger), and *The Arizona Kid* (30, Alfred Santell), she was put under seven-year contract by Paramount where she established herself as a romantic comedienne: *Fast and Loose* (30, Fred New-meyer); *It Pays to Advertise* (31, Frank Tuttle); *Man of the World* (31, Richard Wallace)—the lat-ter with William Powell, whom she married. She felt, with some justice, that Paramount did not fully appreciate her, and she made several films as little more than glamorous decoration: *Up Pops the Devil* (31, Edward Sutherland); *I Take This Woman* (31, Marion Gering); and *No One Man* (32, Lloyd Corrigan). She was loaned out on sev-eral occasions to Columbia, but was good at her own studio, opposite Clark Gable, in *No Man of Her Own* (32, Wesley Ruggles) and with Charles Laughton in *White Woman* (33, Stuart Walker). Having played opposite George Raft in *Bolero* (34, Ruggles), she really proved herself, grappling with John Barrymore in Hawks's *Twentieth Cen-tury* (34)—one of the comic masterpieces of the American cinema and the first of Hawks's double-edged sexual battles.

After *We're Not Dressing* (34, Norman Taurog) and Hathaway's *Now and Forever* (34), she was again loaned to Columbia and to MGM: *Lady by Choice* (34, David Burton) and *The Gay Bride* (34, Jack Conway). After *Rumba* (35, Gering), another Raft vehicle, she embarked on the most fruitful period of her career: *Hands Across the Table* (35, Mitchell Leisen); *Love Before Break-fast* (36, Walter Lang); *My Man Godfrey* (36, La Cava); *The Princess Comes Across* (36, William K. Howard); *Swing High, Swing Low* (37, Leisen), her most flawlessly romantic picture; and *Nothing Sacred* (37, Wellman), this made for Selznick, and her most gloriously cynical.

After *Fools for Scandal* (38, Mervyn Le Roy) for Warners, she made *Made for Each Other* (39, John Cromwell) and *In Name Only* (39, Cromwell), the first for Selznick, and both emphasizing emotional strain rather than com-edy. George Stevens's *Vigil in the Night* (40) and Garson Kanin's *They Knew What They Wanted* (40) made greater demands on her as a serious actress than she could match.

In 1941, she made *Mr. and Mrs. Smith,* for Hitchcock, an underrated film, and a hint of how well she and Hitch might have worked together. Her last film was arguably her best, Lubitsch's *To Be or Not to Be* (42), a black com-edy about ham actors defrauding Nazi enquiry. The audacity of that film owes a lot to Carole Lombard's nerve, just as its sense of real danger, feeling, and romance grows out of her personal-ity. Wit, glamour, and emotion came together in her adroit reply to a Gestapo invitation: "I'd like to present the Polish case in a more suitable dress." In 1939, she had married Clark Gable, and her death in a plane crash in 1942, while on a war bond tour, was an emotional shock for mil-lions. We live now with blunt, indolent actresses who would be shamed by a retrospective of Car-ole Lombard movies.

Anita Loos (1891–1981), b. Sisson, California
"There was a time a number of years ago," wrote Anita Loos in the introduction to *Gentlemen Pre-fer Blondes* (1925), when she and a number of Hollywood cronies were on the Santa Fe, headed west. They had just had a holiday in New York, "for we belonged to the elite of the cinema which has never been fond of Hollywood." There's the first sign that this inside voice has it in her to tell you something fresh about the movies—the truth. There was a girl with them, Doug Fairbanks's new costar, and everyone was waiting for her to drop something—handkerchiefs, handbags, or g's—and she was blond. The "situation"—the way gentle-men preferred blondes—"was palpably unfair," but it is the beginning of smart social commentary on movies. After all, "Gentlemen Prefer Blondes" is a phrase that warns us how education, civiliza-tion, and justice are all at an end.

Ms. Loos had a case. She was gamin, but very pretty and delicately smart, and years later she had to find out that her husband—silent director John Emerson, who had lived off her—was him-self inclined to pursue witless blondes. So it was all the more generous that Anita Loos the writer did not kill blondes—she celebrated them, she showed the poor lambs their way home, and then she helped teach Jean Harlow how to be a bomb-shell and gave Marilyn Monroe one of her few serene roles. Nevertheless, Ms. Loos has let us all know, for the foreseeable future, that we are idiots over a pretty girl—to such an extent that that girl can come out of Little Somewhere, with-out an education, and wait for the rocks to find her.

Her parents were in the theatrical business, and Anita was clearly pretty enough to think of an act-ing career. But writing appealed to her more. She began with plays, but found success when she started offering photoplays to the new movie busi-ness. An early success was *The New York Hat* (12, D. W. Griffith), which starred Mary Pickford and Lionel Barrymore. In time she wrote hundreds of scripts for silent movies—for Griffith and then for Douglas Fairbanks and various Talmadges. She did some of the titles on *Intolerance* (16, Grif-fith)—not really a testament to wit—and she wrote, among others, *Wild and Wooly* (17, Emer-son), with Fairbanks; *Come On In* (18, Emerson); *The Virtuous Vamp* (19, David Kirkland), with Constance Talmadge; *The Branded Woman* (20, Albert Parker), with Norma Talmadge; *Woman's Place* (21, Victor Fleming); *Polly of the Follies* (22, Emerson).

It was in 1923 that Emerson—a bit of a Willy to her Colette—told her to try plays: *The Whole Town's Talking* was a debut hit. Next year, at his orders again, she used coast-to-coast train journeys to write *Gentlemen Prefer Blondes*. It sold out overnight, and it became a stage hit (with June Walker) and then a movie, scripted by Loos (28, Malcolm St. Clair), with Ruth Taylor (Buck Henry's mother).

It was around this time that she discovered Emerson's philandering and elected not to take his advice on retirement. Instead, she took up a Metro offer to write for $1,000 a week, and found herself fashioning the screen image of Jean Harlow: *Red-Headed Woman* (32, Jack Conway); *Hold Your Man* (33, Sam Wood); and *Riffraff* (35, J. Walter Ruben).

She kept working with *San Francisco* (36, W. S. Van Dyke); *Mama Steps Out* (37, George Seitz); *Saratoga* (37, Conway); *The Women* (39, George Cukor); *Susan and God* (40, Cukor); *Blossoms in the Dust* (41, Mervyn LeRoy); *They Met in Bombay* (41, Clarence Brown); *When Ladies Meet* (41, Robert Z. Leonard); *I Married an Angel* (42, Van Dyke).

She moved to New York in 1947 and she would have Broadway hits with *Happy Birthday*, the musical of *Blondes* (it starred Carol Channing), and a version of *Gigi* (with Audrey Hepburn). She also wrote two books of memoirs, *A Girl Like I* and *Kiss Hollywood Good-by*.

Jennifer Lopez,
b. Bronx, New York, 1970

"J-Lo," as she is now widely referred to, is the first Hispanic actress to be taken for granted in Hollywood. You can regard that as a welcome innovation, or an absurdly belated recognition of how far the social order in Los Angeles depends on the employment of people from south of the border to do the menial work. That trend will only increase in California, and in other parts of America, but it remains to be seen how far some key elements in the Latin American imagination—music, religion, fantasy, family, and pleasure—can help rescue American pictures from the remorseless grind and anhedonia of box office.

Don't put all that load on the amused and amusing Lopez, who has worked hard and risen to every serious challenge offered her. The child of Puerto Rican parents, she was raised at Catholic schools, and broke into TV as a teenager, notably as a Fly Girl on the show *In Living Color*. More TV work led to her breakthrough role, as the young Maria Sanchez in *My Family* (95, Gregory Nava). She followed that with *Jack* (96, Francis Coppola); *Blood and Wine* (97, Bob Rafelson), in which she was clearly a new beauty; and then, full of energy as the murdered Tejano singer in *Selena* (97, Nava); *Anaconda* (97, Luis Llosa); *U-Turn* (97, Oliver Stone); very funny and sexy with George Clooney in *Out of Sight* (98, Steven Soderbergh—they were an item for a while); a

voice in *Antz* (98, Eric Darnell and Tim Johnson); as the psychologist in *The Cell* (00, Tarsem Singh); *The Wedding Planner* (01, Adam Shankman); *Angel Eyes* (01, Luis Mandoki); *Enough* (02, Michael Apted).

Her film career must now compete with her singing and her established place as one of the world's most photographed women. She struggled to find chemistry with Ralph Fiennes in *Maid in Manhattan* (02, Wayne Wang); probably found it much easier with Ben Affleck (her beau) in *Gigli* (03, Martin Brest); *Jersey Girl* (03, Kevin Smith).

Sophia Loren (Sofia Scicolone),
b. Rome, 1934

One of the modern cinema's great beauties, humorous, sympathetic, and an especially good listener, Sophia Loren has been badly wasted. Too often, lumpish high spirits have been encouraged instead of her relish for mischief. It might be said that her persistent association with obviousness—whether in comedy, romance, epic, or Italianateness—itself shows some preference. But *Heller in Pink Tights* (60, George Cukor) caught an out-of-breath, exuberant tenderness there for the right director. Even *That Kind of Woman* (59, Sidney Lumet) promised a mixture of glamour and meditation. Her marriage to Carlo Ponti only emphasized her flouncing as an "international" star and nudged her toward becoming an Italian momma. Statuesque and floridly handsome, she was a star from an earlier era needing the services of great cameramen, the imperious love of a Sternberg, or the warming sympathy of a Cukor.

But there is no question about her courage and determination, or her shrewdness. As a young woman, she overcame dark rumors about her past—she had known great poverty as a kid. Then, later on, Cary Grant was for a while head over heels in love with her (something had to come out of *The Pride and the Passion*). Yet she reasoned with herself and married Ponti instead.

She had bit parts in *Quo Vadis?* (51, Mervyn Le Roy) and *Il Sogno di Zorro* (51, Mario Soldati) and became a leading actress within a few years: *Aida* (53, Clemente Fracassi); *Tempi Nostri* (53, Alessandro Blasetti); *Carosello Napolitano* (54, Ettore Giannini); *Gold of Naples* (54, Vittorio de Sica); *Peccato Che Sia Una Caraglia* (54, Blasetti); *La Bella Mugnaia* (55, Mario Camerini); *Pane, Amore e . . .* (55, Dino Risi); and *La Fortuna di Essere Donna* (56, Blasetti).

Hollywood now took her up, but in a sequence of wretched films: *The Pride and the Passion* (57, Stanley Kramer); *Boy on a Dolphin* (57, Jean Negulesco); *Legend of the Lost* (57, Henry Hathaway); *Desire Under the Elms* (58, Delbert Mann); *Houseboat* (58, Melville Shavelson); *Black Orchid* (58, Martin Ritt); *The Key* (58, Carol Reed); *A Breath of Scandal* (60, Michael Curtiz); *It Started in Naples* (60, Shavelson); and *The Millionairess* (60, Anthony Asquith).

She was looking her best now—amusing in the latter and a resplendent heroine in *El Cid* (61, Anthony Mann). After an Oscar for a strenuous, if earnest, piece of ham in *Two Women* (61, de Sica), she began to work in both America and Europe: *Madame Sans-Gêne* (61, Christian-Jaque); in an episode from *Boccaccio '70* (62, de Sica); *Five Miles to Midnight* (62, Anatole Litvak); *The Condemned of Altona* (62, de Sica); *Yesterday, Today and Tomorrow* (64, de Sica); *The Fall of the Roman Empire* (64, A. Mann); *Lady L* (65, Peter Ustinov); *Operation Crossbow* (64, Michael Anderson); *Judith* (65, Daniel Mann); *Arabesque* (66, Stanley Donen); *A Countess from Hong Kong* (67, Charles Chaplin); *Cinderella, Italian Style* (67, Francesco Rosi); *Sunflower* (69, de Sica); *La Moglie del Prete* (70, Risi); *La Mortadella* (71, Mario Monicelli); *The Journey* (74, de Sica); *Verdict* (74, André Cayatte); *The Cassandra Crossing* (76, George Pan Cosmatos); *A Special Day* (77, Ettore Scola); *Brass Target* (78, John Hough); *Firepower* (79, Michael Winner); and *Revenge* (79, Lina Wertmuller).

For television, she played herself and her own mother in *Sophia Loren: Her Own Story* (80, Mel Stuart), and she has also appeared in *Aurora* (84, Maurizio Ponzi); *Courage* (86, Jeremy Kagan); *The Fortunate Pilgrim* (88, Stuart Cooper); and *Sobato, Domenica e Lunedi* (90, Wertmuller).

Nowadays, she appears rarely, but her beauty is unabated: *Ready to Wear* (94, Robert Altman); *Grumpier Old Men* (95, Howard Deutch); *Soleil* (97, Roger Hanin); *Destinazione Verna* (00, Michelangelo Antonioni); *Francesca e Nunziata* (01, Wertmuller).

Peter Lorre (Laszlo Loewenstein) (1904–64), b. Rosenberg, Hungary

He was the squat, wild-eyed spirit of ruined Europe, shyly prowling in and out of Warner Brothers shadows, muttering fiercely to himself, his disbelief forever mislaid.

Having run away from home, he was a traveling actor in Breslau, Zurich, and Vienna, and eventually so successful in *Fruhlings Erwachen* (29, Richard Oswald) and *Die Koffer des Herrn O.F.* (31, Alexis Granowsky) that Fritz Lang cast him as the Dusseldorf child-murderer in *M* (31), the soft, vulnerable human shape in an enclosing square of impersonal forces, a killer but a startlingly plausible victim of split personality.

After several more Austrian-German films— *Bomben auf Monte Carlo* (31, Hanns Schwarz); *F.P.1 Antwortet Nicht* (32, Karl Hartl); *Schuss im Morgengrauen* (32, Alfred Zeisler); *Fünf von der Jazzband* (32, Erich Engel); *Der Weisse Damon* (32, Kurt Gerron); *Was Frauen Traumen* (33, Geza von Bolvary); and *Unsichtbare Gegner* (33,

Rudolf Katscher)—he was persuaded to travel by Nazism.

He went first to France where he appeared in *De Haut en Bas* (33) for another exile, G. W. Pabst. Thence to England, where he managed to be more chilling even than Hitchcock in *The Man Who Knew Too Much* (34) and *The Secret Agent* (36). By then he was already adrift in Hollywood with his appearance as Dr. Gogol in Karl Freund's *Mad Love* (35), and as Raskolnikov in von Sternberg's *Crime and Punishment* (35). After *Crack-Up* (36, Malcolm St. Clair) and *The Lancer Spy* (37, Gregory Ratoff), Lorre created and stayed in the part of Mr. Moto—Japanese judo-expert private eye—in some eight films, five directed by Norman Foster.

But it was war in Europe that really identified Lorre as the inescapable refugee/spy/madman/murderer. He looked every lunatic part in the eye and transformed them into portraits of delicate, deranged kindness, pushed to the point of frantic malice: *Strange Cargo* (40, Frank Borzage); *Stranger on the Third Floor* (40, Boris Ingster); *I Was an Adventuress* (40, Ratoff); *They Met in Bombay* (41, Clarence Brown); as Joel Cairo in Huston's *The Maltese Falcon* (41); *All Through the Night* (41, Vincent Sherman); *The Face Behind the Mask* (41, Robert Florey); *Casablanca* (43, Michael Curtiz); *The Cross of Lorraine* (43, Tay Garnett); *Background to Danger* (43, Raoul Walsh); *Passage to Marseilles* (44, Curtiz); *The Mask of Dimitrios* (44) and *The Conspirators* (44) for Negulesco; *Arsenic and Old Lace* (44) for Capra; *Hotel Berlin* (45, Peter Godfrey); *Three Strangers* (46, Negulesco); *The Chase* (46, Arthur Ripley); *The Verdict* (46, Don Siegel); pursued by *The Beast with Five Fingers* (47, Florey); *Casbah* (48, John Berry); *Rope of Sand* (49, William Dieterle); and *Quicksand* (50, Irving Pichel).

A professional life so given up to sham, and a private life of continual breakdown, made for an ever-greater frustration. The turning point that failed to turn was his one direction, in Germany, of *Die Verlorene* (51), a worthy film that lacked his poetic eccentricity as a supporting actor. Growing fatter, he became more resigned and was an increasingly amiable distinction in generally unworthy films. Only *Beat the Devil* (54, Huston); *Silk Stockings* (57, Rouben Mamoulian); his belated meeting with Roger Corman in *Tales of Terror* (61); *The Raven* (62); and then *A Comedy of Terrors* (63, Jacques Tourneur) showed what comedy there was in his gentle madness. Otherwise he seemed content to be playing: including Fleischer's *20,000 Leagues Under the Sea* (54); *Congo Crossing* (56) for Pevney; with Jerry Lewis in *The Sad Sack* (57, George Marshall); a clown in Joseph Newman's *The Big Circus* (59); as a stooge to Jerry Lewis in *The Patsy* (64).

Lorre is one of the great screen personalities,

no matter that he had so few leading roles. Perhaps he was a genius frustrated by the various sanities and insanities of the world. But perhaps he came very close to the nature of film with his extraordinary combination of impact and nonsense. He hardly seems dead, just as it is difficult to believe he was ever clinically alive. He was Peter Lorre, and that was something no one else was capable of being. It was often enough to encourage directors and other actors to be more imaginative than they had ever thought likely. Indeed, it was hardly possible to make an unwatchable film with Lorre in it. His scenes in those films, no matter how arbitrary they may have seemed at the time, now run together with amazing consistency. He must be somewhere still, pattering around Sydney Greenstreet and doing what he can to dodge Bogart's laughter.

Joseph Losey (1909–84),
b. La Crosse, Wisconsin

1948: *The Boy with Green Hair.* 1949: *The Lawless.* 1951: *The Prowler; M; The Big Night.* 1952: *Stranger on the Prowl.* 1954: *The Sleeping Tiger* (made under the name of Victor Hanbury). 1955: *A Man on the Beach* (s). 1956: *The Intimate Stranger* (made under the name of Joseph Walton). 1957: *Time Without Pity; The Gypsy and the Gentleman.* 1959: *Blind Date.* 1960: *The Criminal.* 1962: *The Damned; Eve.* 1963: *The Servant.* 1964: *King and Country.* 1966: *Modesty Blaise.* 1967: *Accident.* 1968: *Boom; Secret Ceremony.* 1970: *Figures in a Landscape.* 1971: *The Go-Between.* 1972: *The Assassination of Trotsky.* 1973: *A Doll's House.* 1974: *Galileo.* 1975: *The Romantic Englishwoman.* 1976: *Mr. Klein.* 1978: *Les Routes du Sud/Roads to the South.* 1979: *Don Giovanni.* 1982: *La Truite/The Trout.* 1985: *Steaming.*

The hardening of Losey's arteries seems to date from 1964. He had just made *The Servant,* a highly wrought study of self-destruction and sexual sociology, subjects the fluctuating *Eve* hits and misses. Like all his best work, *The Servant* uses interior setting as an extension of character and finds a unique suggestibility in the spaces and shapes within a house. Its complex camera movements are meticulous and emphatic, but it is given vitality by the pain and surprise in the acting, and by the grim logic that breaks down people into fleshly hulks and contradictory impulses. Losey's heavy misanthropy shows through in the cheerless ending: one remembers the remark of Freya in *The Damned* of the Macdonald Carey character (an American in England): "I like him because he doesn't like the world. It's a good beginning."

More than that, *The Servant* marked Losey's coming of age among the artistic elite. Compelled to leave America at the time of Senator McCarthy, he had had to digest the mores of a new environ-

ment and struggle to obtain work. Times had changed, however; the man who had made *The Prowler* and *M* as gripping, low-budget thrillers was now working in a world ready to acclaim his seriousness. Thus, some critics praised the subtlety and ignored the hysteria in *The Servant.* That was a disservice to Losey, whose strength had always been a fusion of the two. From *The Criminal* onward, the attention that Losey had long enjoyed in France was growing in Britain. *The Servant* could not have completed the trick better: it indulged the facile guilt of the English intelligentsia; it was a collaboration with the playwright Harold Pinter; and it offered unexpected depth to an English favorite, Dirk Bogarde.

In retrospect, its success may have lured into the open Losey's yearning for significance. *The Boy with Green Hair* was a blatant allegory, unlike anything else in the American cinema; while in *M,* Losey was hoping to comment on American society as directly as Lang had on Germany. His *M* is a marvelous, frightening film, years ahead of its time and typical of his American virtues: narrative economy; sustained camera setups based on dynamic composition; the ability to make characters reveal themselves quickly and naturally; and the power to get good performances from actors. The policeman in *The Prowler* and the murderer in *M* are flawed men, driven to their own destruction by an unwholesome society that they inadequately comprehend. In that sense, *The Criminal* is an American picture; it sees the opposed hierarchies of law and crime squeezing together on the innate solitariness of the Stanley Baker character, and gives the criminal a politically tinged importance. In all these films, Losey used the thriller genre for larger purposes so that the melodrama expanded to support the metaphor.

But by the early 1960s, Losey was conforming to the English ideal of the director irked by commercial limits. Increasingly free, his work seemed to show how far it had thrived under restriction. But a man who could make *The Servant* must deserve better things—including the attention of *Sight and Sound,* who had barely noticed the confused achievement of *Blind Date* and the outright triumph of *The Criminal. King and Country* was a decent little film, except that it had no reason for being made; how could so open-and-shut a case really engage Losey? Its subject was so one-sided that anyone other than a Fritz Lang was bound to make it monotonous and brutal. It was the first plain film Losey had made. *Modesty Blaise* was amusing, but again unnecessary, a break in Losey's seriousness, without indicating any sense of humor. That led to the pastoral slowness and pretension of *Accident,* another Pinter script with echoes of E. M. Forster and the uncanny feeling that Losey was trying to make a film F. R. Leavis might teach. *Accident* was highly praised, whereas

it should have been taken to pieces for its ingrowing artiness, its self-conscious beauty, and its opting for restraint rather than urgency. It was
difficult not to conclude that Losey had fallen into
thinking of himself as an intellectual; whereas his
best films showed a passionate melodramatist,
torn between ideas and feelings.

Secret Ceremony was interesting, a true penetration of obsession, sadly spoiled by cuts. *Boom*
was high folly, *Figures in a Landscape* arid exercise, and *The Go-Between* exactly the sort of prettified, literary pomp that passes for intelligent
cinema in Britain. It is not equal to a paragraph of
Hartley's novel, nor a reel of so painful a film as
The Damned. The deterioration was one of the
saddest spectacles in modern cinema.

The significance of Losey's story is to show up
the deadly stupidity of too much criticism and the
uneasy public role of the director as an artist.
Nothing is more suspicious than the hollow stylistic smoothness of *The Go-Between*—broken only
by the ridiculous flashes forward. Losey is a director of violence: originally it was externalized—in
The Prowler, M, The Criminal, and *The Damned.*
In *Eve and The Servant* it went inward. Now it
was gone, and Losey was perched on calendar
photographs and the pinnacle dialogue of Harold
Pinter. Whereas, in 1960, he felt compelled to dig
into England and find the many layers of Wey-
mouth in *The Damned* and the mournful snowscapes of *The Criminal,* the *Trotsky* film looked
like Festival fodder, and *A Doll's House* was a gesture toward feminism. That last was especially odd
since Losey had seldom handled women well. The
exception—Jeanne Moreau's *Eve*—was achieved
only by turning the prostitute into an acid bath for
rotting social structures and the man's masochism.

But in 1976, Losey regained distinction with
Mr. Klein, the Borgesian study of a conniving art
dealer in occupied Paris haunted by the possibility
of a Jewish double. It is a very controlled film,
with more stress on decadent high society than
the approaching Gestapo. But the trap it poses is
gripping and intelligent, and there is even a trace
of sardonic humor watching the magnificent alienation of Alain Delon. *Mr. Klein* was among the
best of Losey's films, and one wondered if its
urgency came in part from the discovery of a new
environment—Paris.

In his last few films, Losey seemed neither
American nor British—he was an international
art-house man. Yet, in hindsight, it seems clear
that he was a director who needed to respond to
the exactness of place and social situation. It is a
career that demonstrates the difficulty in being
both itinerant and concentrated.

David Caute's careful biography showed
Losey's creativity growing out of a cheerless vanity
that kept few friends. He seemed determined to
give others no chance of liking him.

Myrna Loy (Myrna Williams) (1905–93),
b. Radersburg, Montana

Although her career spans a much greater period,
it was during the 1930s (when she made no less
than fifty-eight pictures) that Myrna Loy was at
her peak as a sophisticated, glamorous comedienne, perfectly cast as Nora Charles opposite
William Powell's Nick in the *Thin Man* series.
That movie marriage, always securely based emotionally but playing with hostility, flirtation, and
raillery, served in its time as the epitome of an
adult, liberated partnership. Equally, it was part of
Myrna Loy's appeal that she was so often the
hero's wife, suggesting sexual liberation without
actually exploiting it. Thus, while appearing one of
the cinema's most risqué stars, she was joining in
one of its subtlest dreams of conformity.

In her restrained, or withheld, smartness and
her consistent underplaying, for years Myrna Loy
seemed very modern and alluringly cool. But she
would not—could not?—dominate a film. Did the
idea seem indecent to her? She was only really
stirred if she liked the idea of a screen partnership. The attitude is allied to her own modesty and
the feeling that stardom just happened to her.

She was a dancer at Grauman's Chinese Theater, who made her debut in *Pretty Ladies* (25,
Monta Bell) and worked very hard for the next
few years under contract at Warners as native
girls, maids, spies, dancers, and molls, only occa-
sionally playing lead parts: *Across the Pacific* (26,
Roy del Ruth); *The Caveman* (26, Lewis Mile-
stone); *Don Juan* (26, Alan Crosland); *The Exquis-
ite Sinner* (26, Josef von Sternberg and Phil
Rosen); *So This Is Paris* (26, Ernst Lubitsch); *Bit-
ter Apples* (27, Harry Hoyt); *The Climbers* (27,
Paul L. Stein); *Girl from Chicago* (27, Ray
Enright); *The Jazz Singer* (27, Crosland); *If I Were
Single* (27, del Ruth); *State Street Sadie* (28,
Archie Mayo); *The Midnight Taxi* (28, John
Adolfi); and *Noah's Ark* (28, Michael Curtiz).

Sound only improved her as an actress, but she
was slow to become established and still found
herself cast in slinky, exotic roles: *The Desert Song*
(29, del Ruth); *The Black Watch* (29, John Ford);
The Squall (29, Alexander Korda); *The Show of
Shows* (29, Adolfi); *Under a Texas Moon* (30, Curtiz); *Cock o' the Walk* (30, R. William Neill and
Walter Lang); *Cameo Kirby* (30, Irving Cummings); *The Truth About Youth* (30, William A.
Seiter); *Renegades* (30, Victor Fleming); *Body and
Soul* (31, Alfred Santell); *A Connecticut Yankee*
(31, David Butler); *The Naughty Flirt* (31,
Edward Cline); *Transatlantic* (31, William K.
Howard); *The Devil to Pay* (31, George Fitzmau-
rice); and *Arrowsmith* (31, Ford).

Warners had not renewed her contract and she
now worked largely at Fox, but in 1932 Irving
Thalberg called her to MGM, a studio much more
likely to recognize her smart good humor. Even

so, Thalberg gave her modest work and loaned her out: *Emma* (32, Clarence Brown); *The Wet Parade* (32, Fleming); a poor version of *Vanity Fair* (32, Chester Franklin); *The Woman in Room 13* (32, Henry King); *Love Me Tonight* (32, Rouben Mamoulian); *The Mask of Fu Manchu* (32, Charles Vidor and Charles Brabin); very good as a manipulative "new" woman in *The Animal Kingdom* (32, Edward H. Griffith); *Topaze* (33, Harry d'Arrast); *Night Flight* (33, Brown); and *The Barbarian* (33, Sam Wood).

If any individual altered the shape of her career, it was director W. S. Van Dyke. Having used her in *Penthouse* (33) and *The Prizefighter and the Lady* (33), he persuaded MGM to put her opposite William Powell in *Manhattan Melodrama* (34). Next came the first of the screen portraits of Dashiell Hammett's private eye and wife: *The Thin Man* (34, Van Dyke), which made her a big star.

For the next seven years she hardly faltered: *Stamboul Quest* (34, Wood); *Evelyn Prentice* (34, Howard); *Broadway Bill* (34, Frank Capra); *Wings in the Dark* (35, James Flood); *Wife vs. Secretary* (36, Brown); *The Great Ziegfeld* (36, Robert Z. Leonard); *To Mary—With Love* (36, John Cromwell); *Libeled Lady* (36, Jack Conway); *After the Thin Man* (36, Van Dyke); as Kitty O'Shea in *Parnell* (37, John M. Stahl); *Double Wedding* (37, Richard Thorpe); *Test Pilot* (38, Fleming); *Too Hot to Handle* (38, Conway); *The Rains Came* (39, Brown); *Another Thin Man* (39, Van Dyke); *I Love You Again* (40, Van Dyke); *Love Crazy* (41, Conway); and *Shadow of the Thin Man* (41, Van Dyke).

During the war, she worked for the Red Cross and made only one film: *The Thin Man Goes Home* (44, Thorpe). She no longer had as strong an interest in movies, but she was very good as the wife in Wyler's *The Best Years of Our Lives* (46).

She was too competent ever to seem less than in charge, but her material now was seldom stimulating. Very few of all her films are outstanding, but in the 1930s she was close to the mainstream and thus flourished. After the war, she never regained that position and mixed government work with movies: *The Bachelor and the Bobby Soxer* (47, Irving Reis); *Song of the Thin Man* (47, Edward Buzzell); *Mr. Blandings Builds his Dream House* (48, H. C. Potter); *The Red Pony* (49, Milestone); *That Dangerous Age* (50, Gregory Ratoff); *Cheaper by the Dozen* (50, Walter Lang); *Belles On Their Toes* (52, Henry Levin); *The Ambassador's Daughter* (56, Norman Krasna); *Lonelyhearts* (58, Vincent Donehue); *From the Terrace* (60, Mark Robson); *Midnight Lace* (60, David Miller); Stuart Rosenberg's *The April Fools* (69); *Airport 1975* (74, Jack Smight); *The End* (78, Burt Reynolds); as the secretary in *Just Tell Me What You Want* (80, Sidney Lumet); and with Henry Fonda in *Summer Solstice* (83, Ralph Rosenbloom).

Ernst Lubitsch (1892–1947), b. Berlin
1914: *Blinde Kuh; Fraulein Seifenschaum; Meyer als Soldat*. 1915: *Auf Eis Geführt; Zucker und Zimt*. 1916: *Als Ich Tot War; Der Gemischte Frauenchor; Der Erst Patient; Der G.M.B.H. Tenor; Leutnant auf Befehl; Schuhpalast Pinkus; Der Schwarze Moritz; Wo Ist Mein Schatz?*. 1917: *Der Blusenkönig; Ein Fideles Gefängnis; Der Kraftmeyer; Ossis Tagebuch; Prinz Sami; Der Letzte Anzug; Wenn Vier Dasselbe Tun*. 1918: *Die Augen der Mumie Ma; Carmen; Der Fall Rosentopf; Fuhrmann Henschel; Das Madel vom Ballet; Meine Frau, die Filmschauspielerin; Der Rodelkavalier*. 1919: *Die Austernprinzessin; Ich Nochte Kein Mann Sein; Der Lustige Ehemann; Madame Dubarry; Meyer aus Berlin; Die Puppe; Rausch; Schwabenmadle*. 1920: *Anna Boleyn; Kohlhiesels Tochter; Medea; Romeo und Julia im Schnee; Sumurun; Die Tolle Rikscha*. 1921: *Die Bergkatze; Vendetta; Das Weib des Pharao*. 1922: *Die Flamme*. 1923: *Rosita*. 1924: *The Marriage Circle; Three Women; Forbidden Paradise*. 1925: *Kiss Me Again; Lady Windermere's Fan*. 1926: *So This Is Paris*. 1927: *The Student Prince in Old Heidelberg*. 1928: *The Patriot; Eternal Love*. 1929: *The Love Parade*. 1930: an episode from *Paramount on Parade; Monte Carlo*. 1931: *The Smiling Lieutenant*. 1932: *The Man I Killed; One Hour With You* (credited to and planned by Lubitsch, but directed by George Cukor); *Trouble in Paradise;* "The Clerk," episode from *If I Had a Million*. 1933: *Design for Living*. 1934: *The Merry Widow*. 1937: *Angel*. 1938: *Bluebeard's Eighth Wife*. 1939: *Ninotchka*. 1940: *The Shop Around the Corner*. 1941: *That Uncertain Feeling*. 1942: *To Be or Not to Be*. 1943: *Heaven Can Wait*. 1946: *Cluny Brown*. 1948: *That Lady in Ermine* (completed after Lubitsch's death by Otto Preminger).

As Hollywood recedes, Lubitsch's role as a creative entrepreneur and as the germ of European sophistication becomes more fascinating. Considering the way he was rebuffed by Mary Pickford on his first American film, *Rosita*, and so wittily mocked for his Teutonic stubbornness, it is remarkable that he achieved such eminence in Hollywood and that his reputation rested on the supposed delicacy of "touch."

It seems to me still questionable whether that touch was a matter of cinematic fluency. Or did Lubitsch possess a fine sense of a special kind of performing wit, the daring with which one character in a stage farce briefly shares his ironic superiority with the audience? Lotte Eisner has described the Lubitsch of the German period as the epitome of the servant to whom no man is a hero. And there is something of a droll Figaro who abets his master's adultery, hurrying on his trousers to avoid exposure, boldly winking at the audience as he does so. The effect is enchanting and flattering, for it makes the audience feel worldly. But the trick has a clear artistic limit: it puts the servant in a smug position from which he is never likely to be caught out himself. In other words, is Lubitsch's touch restricted to the cynical commentary on a comedy of manners? The tragic feeling that Ophuls or Renoir bring to the same form rarely darkens Lubitsch's consciousness.

Of course, Lubitsch had himself been an actor. From 1911 to 1918, he was a member of Max Reinhardt's company, and from 1913 onward he acted in films, usually playing comic old men. Until 1917 he acted in many of his own films, but after the war he developed the German historical romance with great success. He had a vivid if theatrical sense of composition and grouping, an equal mastery of large crowds and star players, and a clever if rather obvious way of inventing mundane, intimate business for noble characters—again, this is the servant's knowledge that a Casanova has piles. As humor it was more sly than penetrating, but even in his German films Lubitsch had a way of understating his ploys so that they flattered perception. His most notable historical pictures were *Madame Dubarry* (*Passion* in America), *Anna Boleyn*, and *Sumurun*, in which he played the part of a dwarf—a typically grotesque and inventive performance. Pola Negri and Emil Jannings added to their fame with appearances in Lubitsch's films.

He went to America in 1923, when the country and Hollywood were still hostile to foreign talent. As Lotte Eisner has said, in America Lubitsch's style refined itself, abandoning slapstick for "nonchalance." He worked for Warners, and in *The Marriage Circle* he made a model of sophisticated comedy for the silent era. He then went to Paramount for *Forbidden Paradise*, from a play by Lajos Biro. Starring Pola Negri and Adolphe Menjou, it transposed a continental and aristocratic setting to the American studios and introduced the idea of the comic underpinnings to pompous dignity. He stayed at Warners for *Lady Windermere's Fan* and directed Myrna Loy in *So This Is Paris*. By now his success was overcoming xenophobia. *The Student Prince*, made at MGM with Ramon Novarro and Norma Shearer, was a huge box-office hit. Apart from *Eternal Love*, made for United Artists, he was at Paramount from *The Patriot* to *Bluebeard's Eighth Wife*.

In time, he became director of production at that studio, with results that von Sternberg described and suffered from: "[he] held himself responsible for the work of other directors. This, of course, helps to impair a man's eyesight." In Sternberg's case, Lubitsch harried him the more for alleged extravagance in making *The Scarlet Empress;* in fact, Sternberg had only used spare footage from *The Patriot,* so evidently shot at silent speed it is incredible that Lubitsch did not realize what had happened. But there was something of a feud between the two men, perhaps because Sternberg had exactly the gravity beneath bitterness that Lubitsch scared off the more resolutely he tried to lay hands on it. As Sternberg said, "When Lubitsch was serious, not trying to indulge in little drolleries, he could make something unbelievably bad, like *The Man I Killed.*" And terrible that film is, just as *Ninotchka* and *Heaven Can Wait* are a good deal less funny than reputation would have us believe.

Lubitsch's sound comedies vary enormously. *The Love Parade, Monte Carlo, The Smiling Lieutenant,* and *The Merry Widow* are smart, gay, and urbane, but is it possible for a great comedy to star Maurice Chevalier and Jeanette MacDonald? *Design for Living* and *Bluebeard's Eighth Wife* are stagy, ill-cast, and formal, but wonderfully inventive for all that. The best films Lubitsch made in America are the truly amoral *Trouble in Paradise,* in which the cynicism is so indulged that it becomes energetic and liberating; *Angel,* which could be Lubitsch's tribute to Sternberg and Dietrich; *The Shop Around the Corner,* which recreates Budapest in America and inhabits it with James Stewart and Margaret Sullavan in a beguiling romantic comedy of pretence and cross purposes; and a film unto itself, *To Be or Not to Be.*

That film, made during the war, transcends cynicism and, for the only time, allowed Lubitsch to see the actor as a representative of humanity. "Touch" really means something here because we are made to laugh while in sight of outrageous situations. Tact is central to the style and is the tangible proof of a sane mind observing the dangerous farce. It is his funniest film because it is the most serious. American cinema has still hardly digested such startlingly brutal comedy; the model for that style is Buñuel, which reflects on the caution in so much of Lubitsch's work as in the films of Billy Wilder, Lubitsch's heir.

Only persistent viewing can test the theory that Lubitsch does not have too strong a visual imagination. His talent was always theatrical, literary, and to do with performance. Cukor has told how far Lubitsch worked out everything in advance, and the rigidity that came from that. And if the achievement is more modest than some claim, it may be because the quality of measured performance stemmed so much from Lubitsch and from the reputation he had in his own lifetime.

That sort of sophistication cannot be copied; it is either shared with actors or it seems contrived. Carole Lombard and Jack Benny seem in charge of *To Be or Not to Be,* while in, say, *Design for Living,* Gary Cooper, Fredric March, and Miriam Hopkins look awed by some monstrous ham behind the camera. Just as Chaplin has sometimes frozen good players with his unmanageable exhibitionism, so, according to Clarence Brown, "[Lubitsch] used to show them how to do everything, right down to the minutest detail. He would take a cape, and show the star how to put it on. He supplied all the little movements. He was magnificent because he knew his art better than anybody. But his actors followed his performance. They had no chance to give one of their own."

The Shop Around the Corner may be as sweet and light as an Esterhazy honey ball—whatever that is—but it is also among the greatest of films. Nor do its actors feel dominated or made to imitate anything. This is a love story about a couple too much in love with love to fall tidily into each other's arms. Though it all works out finally, a mystery is left, plus the fear of how easily good people can miss their chances. Beautifully written (by Lubitsch's favorite writer, Samson Raphaelson), *Shop Around the Corner* is a treasury of hopes and anxieties based in the desperate faces of Stewart and Sullavan. It is a comedy so good it frightens us for them. The café conversation may be the best meeting in American film. The shot of Sullavan's gloved hand, and then her ruined face, searching an empty mail box for a letter is one of the most fragile moments in film. For an instant, the ravishing Sullavan looks old and ill, touched by loss.

George Lucas, b. Modesto, California, 1944

1971: *THX 1138*. 1973: *American Graffiti*. 1977: *Star Wars*. 1999: *Star Wars: Episode I, The Phantom Menace*. 2002: *Episode II, Attack of the Clones*.

Star Wars was the beginning of one of the great American movie empires. From up in Marin County, George Lucas has presided over a series of films derived from *Star Wars* as well as the Indiana Jones pictures. He has made a vast fortune, yet he remains one of the saddest of moguls. He stopped directing; his marriage to editor Marcia Lucas broke up; and not even Lucas seems entirely confident about what he has wrought. For there can be no doubt that he was the example to a generation of filmmakers who worked with creatures, comic books, machines, and special effects. At this time, it is rumored that Lucas's research into effects could yet produce computer-generated imagery permitting new movies from the collected work of dead actors. And maybe one day the computers will make the films in a sterile atmosphere, unsullied by human intrusion. All too often his actors seem dead.

Lucas has been producer or executive producer on the following, and no mere figurehead. He has been involved at every step. No one should question his sense of storytelling, writing, casting, design, and editing. In opting not to direct, Lucas does not signal withdrawal or superiority. Rather, he testifies to the principle that American pictures are produced, not directed.

The pictures are: *More American Graffiti* (79, B. W. L. Norton); *The Empire Strikes Back* (80, Irvin Kershner); *Kagemusha* (80, Akira Kurosawa)—which Lucas backed, out of admiration for Kurosawa; *Raiders of the Lost Ark* (81, Steven Spielberg); *Return of the Jedi* (83, Richard Marquand); *Twice Upon a Time* (83, John Korty and Charles Swenson); *Indiana Jones and the Temple of Doom* (84, Spielberg); *The Ewok Adventure* (84, Korty); *Mishima: A Life in Four Chapters* (85, Paul Schrader); *Latino* (85, Haskell Wexler); *Ewoks: the Battle for Endor* (85, Jim and Ken Wheat); *Howard the Duck* (86, Willard Huyck), his first unmitigated failure; *Labyrinth* (86, Jim Henson); *The Land Before Time* (88, Don Bluth); *Powaqqatsi* (88, Godfrey Reggio); *Tucker: The Man and His Dream* (88, Francis Ford Coppola); *Willow* (88, Ron Howard); and *Indiana Jones and the Last Crusade* (89, Spielberg).

Lucas was a home-movie maker while in junior college in Modesto. From the start, he was interested in special effects and camera tricks. He was encouraged by Haskell Wexler, the photographer, and he went on to the University of Southern California film department. While there, he made a science-fiction short, *THX 1138: 4EB*, which won a prize at the National Student Film Festival.

He was the friend and protégé of Francis Ford Coppola, who allowed Lucas to attend the shooting of *Finian's Rainbow*. Lucas made promotional shorts on the filming of Coppola's *The Rain People* and J. Lee Thompson's *Mackenna's Gold*. Then Coppola's sponsorship enabled him to turn his student movie into a feature debut. *THX 1138* is Lucas's only flop: its Orwellian allegory is very cursory, but its imagery is more distinctive than anything in the later films. On screen, the future world of white interiors and shaved-head creatures in white uniforms is beautiful and disturbing. Nothing else Lucas has done has such an intriguing fusion of cleanliness and death.

Coppola stayed in Lucas's corner, and helped him set up *American Graffiti* at Universal. Very cheaply made, it is itself one of cinema's largest grossers, the source of many TV spin-offs, an easygoing endorsement of youthful complacencies, and the debut of many good young players. But *Graffiti* is very wholesome, very careful to skirt problems in its subject matter—a smooth amalgam of social observation and sweet marketing. Its solemn endnotes about the destiny of the four young men are superficial and pompous, and filled with the wish to keep pain at arm's length. No human situation is ever probed beyond its stereotypes; the mood is drunk on Coke. For all the teenage bounce, the music, and its screen omission of parents, there is nothing to alarm the middle-aged. It reflects Lucas's bland ideology that so many TV series sprang from the film with relatively little dilution. It is a movie full of the prospect of Muzak cinema, a light show where the music never stops, a diversion without delight or distress. Boredom and malice have been subtly erased, along with misery and ecstasy—all the real, untidy ingredients of adolescent experience.

Star Wars, too, overlaps with TV. Its acceptance marks the first occasion on which a movie reminded viewers of cozy modes and icons learned on the small screen. It is *Star Trek* with richer tricks, and a thinner dramatic or intellectual thread than the TV show generally offered. The film does not risk disapproval or recognize adults. Rebukes about its pretty mindlessness can seem grumpy or heavy-handed. But its excitement is never rooted in character or moral ordeal. There is no danger to the people on film, and no challenge to those watching. Its people are raised on junk food; they are pink, puffy, and anonymous. Good and evil are reduced to the level of opposing sides in electronic Ping-Pong. The film is sterile from lack of atmosphere or sensuality, and chilly with its own brittle humor. Above all, *Star Wars* and the Lucas empire raise the worry that brilliant film students know too little about life, and are then protected from learning more by their outlandish success.

He produced an intriguing series, *Young Indiana Jones,* for TV, and in 1991 he won the Thalberg award. Lucas remains in Marin, master of a magnificent facility, devoted to sound, special effects, and research. The future belongs to his work, but will he aid it or direct it?

Well, he returned as a director (after an interval of more than twenty years) with a retrospective first episode of *Star Wars—The Phantom Menace.* The special effects were delirious—the actors (from Liam Neeson to Ewan McGregor) were glum. The film was another massive hit, but there was a new mood—people hadn't enjoyed this picture. Those always averse to the *Star Wars* legend began to feel vindicated. *Episode II* was Lucas again, with a love story—but there was more passion felt for the clones and the computer. One day, for sure, all six episodes will exist—and maybe robots will watch them.

Tom Luddy, b. New York, 1943

I have been lucky with friends, and ever since moving to San Francisco (in 1981) Tom Luddy has been an essential companion and connection. I wonder how many more people in this book, or in the large world of film, would say the same. From that one easily reaches this conclusion: that while Tom is every film lover's ally (he is truly the friend of film as an idea and a practice), still it is his knack to make every one of us feel individually blessed with his advice, his recommendations, and the dinners where he may introduce you to . . . Chris

Marker, Manny Farber, Pierre Rissient, and so on, and so on.

I met him first in New York at Nick Ray's birthday party (his last, I think). Tom had done so much by then, including the attempt to look after the ailing Nick in the Bay Area, to put up with his scandals, excesses, and tantrums, trying to nurse him toward some project. Tom had come west originally to attend the University of California at Berkeley. While there he shifted his major from physics to English (and found golf as the marriage of the two), and attached himself to the Pacific Film Archive in Berkeley as viewer, helper, and eventual director (1972–79). In addition, he fell in with Alice Waters, lived with her, and helped her found the restaurant Chez Panisse (named after Pagnol's character, and a favorite place for the film community).

One service Tom did at the PFA was to offer and show movie classics to Francis Ford Coppola as his career bloomed—this was the late sixties and the seventies. It's fair to say that Zoetrope's great interest in foreign directors (from Gance to Kurosawa, from Syberberg to Godard) owed a lot to Tom's urgings. So it was natural that when Tom left the PFA (officially) in 1979, he became director for special projects at Zoetrope. Those ventures included the restoration and showing of Gance's *Napoléon* and Syberberg's *Our Hitler.*

Over the following years, therefore, Tom served as a producer on a number of exceptional ventures: he assisted on *Sans Soleil* (82, Chris Marker); he produced *Mishima* (85, Paul Schrader); *Tough Guys Don't Dance* (87, Norman Mailer); *Barfly* (87, Barbet Schroeder); *Wait Until Spring, Bandini* (90, Dominique Deruddere); *Wind* (92, Carroll Ballard); *The Secret Garden* (93, Agnieszka Holland); *My Family, Mi Familia* (95, Gregory Nava)—and had a helping hand in many other productions. I'm sure there are more to come.

Beyond that, in 1974 (with Bill Pence and James Card) Tom founded the Telluride Film Festival, a unique event, still led by Tom and Bill. It is a film festival that occurs over the Labor Day weekend in a small town in Colorado; it is intimate, it regularly mixes retrospectives and early viewings of important new works. It has a claim to be the most rarified and exhilarating film festival in the world.

Of course, it takes place at nine thousand feet, with thirteen-thousand-foot peaks looming overhead. This is not incidental. In 1982, Tom took me and my wife to Telluride on a drive that took in Nevada and southern Utah—Goosenecks, Bryce, Zion, Monument Valley. As it turned out, the landscape meant as much or more to me than the films—but Tom has always regarded that slight divergence on my part with fond amusement. We like most of the same films, and we have both driven the Burr Trail.

I cannot omit his ability to remember all telephone numbers; his wife, Monique, a brilliant, intuitive reader of films; his haunting appearance in *Invasion of the Body Snatchers* (78, Phil Kaufman); the fact that on my first Telluride trip he was also introducing Athol Fugard—not exactly a movie man, but Tom's sense of the movies is as large as the great deserts we crossed; the chance that even now there is a carrier bag on my doorstep containing one or two unexpected tapes, a copy of the latest piece by Christopher Hitchens and . . . well, I'd better go and find out for myself.

In the last edition I worried that one friend—Kieran Hickey—could never be replaced. Well, it's true: great friends are beyond replacement. But Tom has redefined friendship, and he has simply done wonders to help me without looking for thanks, reward, or credit. I daresay a hundred people in this book could say the same. Let me speak for the rest—thank you, Tom.

Bela Lugosi (Bela Blasko) (1882–1956),
b. Lugos, Hungary

While everyone knew that the Boris Karloff who played Frankenstein's monster was an upright Englishman, amused by the genre, Lugosi was a captive of horror. Small, dark, and severe in features, his acting was so florid and yet so macabre that only some fanciful notion of Hungarian mythology could explain it. He could be frightening in a way that other actors in horror never achieved: because he appeared to believe in the literal meaning of the films, and because it was possible to be persuaded that he was himself possessed. "I am Dracula"—his first words, were less introduction than assertion. While later in *Dracula* there is a moment when Lugosi's daringly slow delivery admits to his philosophy: "To die, to be really dead, that might be glorious."

There is the man tortured by half-life. His Dracula was an original that the cinema never attempted to match: after Lugosi, the Count became tall and handsome, as likely to kiss as bite. Yet Lugosi's pinched lips and his skullcap of hair were as black as congealed blood and his pallor was that of imminent extinction. Just as Peter Lorre, another Hungarian, became trapped by Hollywood in squalid spoofs of his earliest successes, so Lugosi lived on, tormented by the Ritz brothers, Abbott and Costello, and Old Mother Riley. The dross never affected his place in the history of cinema: for when the bell tolls and the door creaks, Lugosi is the one to be feared. So dire an actor smacks of authenticity in the horror game.

As Arisztid Olt, he made a few films in Hungary and a small part in *Der Januskopf* (20, F. W. Murnau). He came to America in 1921 with a touring theatrical company. By 1923 he had made a movie debut in *The Silent Command* (23, J. Gordon Edwards); *The Rejected Woman* (24, Albert Parker); and *The Midnight Girl* (25, Wilfred Noy). In 1927 he played Dracula in a Broadway adaptation of Bram Stoker's novel. After *Prisoners* (29, William A. Seiter), *The Thirteenth Chair* (29, Tod Browning), *Such Men Are Dangerous* (30, Kenneth Hawks), *Renegades* (30, Victor Fleming), and *Wild Company* (30, Leo McCarey), Lugosi took the part intended originally for Lon Chaney in *Dracula* (31, Tod Browning).

He made very few "straight" films after that: *Broad Minded* (31, Mervyn Le Roy); *Women of All Nations* (31, Raoul Walsh), and later, *Ninotchka* (39, Ernst Lubitsch). For the rest of his career he was, with Karloff, the touchstone of frightening intentions: as Dr. Mirakle, scientist kidnapper, in *Murders in the Rue Morgue* (32, Robert Florey); as *Chandu the Magician* (32, William Cameron Menzies and Marcel Varnel); as Murder Legendre in *White Zombie* (32, Victor Halperin); *The Death Kiss* (32, Edwin L. Marin); as a mutant in *Island of Lost Souls* (33, Erle C. Kenton); *Night of Terror* (33, Benjamin Stoloff); Dr. Vitus Verdegast, skinning Karloff alive in *The Black Cat* (34, Edgar G. Ulmer); *Gift of Gab* (34, Karl Freund); as the vampire in *The Mark of the Vampire* (35, Browning); *The Raven* (35, Lew Landers); *The Invisible Ray* (36, Lambert Hillyer); *Dracula's Daughter* (36, Hillyer); as Ygor, charming the monster with a mournful pipe tune, in *The Son of Frankenstein* (39, Rowland V. Lee); *Dark Eyes of London* (39, Walter Summers); *The Gorilla* (39, Allan Dwan); the remade *The Black Cat* (41, Albert S. Rogell); *The Wolf Man* (41, George Waggner); *The Ghost of Frankenstein* (42, Kenton); *Return of the Vampire* (43, Landers); *Frankenstein Meets the Wolf Man* (43, Roy William Neill); *The Body Snatcher* (45, Robert Wise); *Zombies on Broadway* (45, Gordon Douglas); *Devil Bat's Daughter* (46, Frank Wisbar); *Abbott and Costello Meet Frankenstein* (48, Charles Barton); *Mother Riley Meets the Vampire* (52); and *The Black Sleep* (56, Reginald le Borg). Death may have come mercifully, for Lugosi died a year after having been admitted to a hospital for drug addiction.

He died as he was filming *Plan 9 From Outer Space* (59, Edward D. Wood, Jr.), the perfect memorial for the undead.

Baz (Bazmark Anthony) Luhrmann,
b. New South Wales, Australia, 1962

1992: *Kids of the Cross* (TV); *Strictly Ballroom*. 1996: *Romeo + Juliet*. 2001: *Moulin Rouge*.

Opening the Cannes Film Festival in 2001, and unable to escape the publicity attendant on Nicole Kidman's first picture since the split with Tom Cruise, *Moulin Rouge* got very mixed reviews. Yet can anyone deny that it was far and away the most imaginative mainstream film of the summer season that followed? The charges were monotonous: that the camerawork was so busy as to make one giddy; that the gay camp attitude was crushing; and even, hadn't we seen it all before? Not me. I think it's the most exhilarating movie musical since *Les Parapluies de Cherbourg,* and just as important in showing a way ahead for that nearly abandoned genre. Moreover, who could miss the fond wave to Renoir's *French Cancan,* with all that meant in terms of seeing the show as an allegory of life?

What's more, who could fail to see the steady enrichment of Luhrmann's talent and ambition? *Strictly Ballroom* was a pleasant film, but undisguisedly coy and cute. *Romeo + Juliet* was a very effective trick. That's why *Moulin Rouge* (filmed in Australia with sets that reminded some people of Michael Powell) deserved credit for its complete theatrical world, for the bravura sweep that carries one song into another, and the wonderfully silhouetted treatment of all the players—not least Ms. Kidman herself, who seemed happier and less impeded than she had ever managed before.

It's as hard to think where Luhrmann goes as it was to predict Terence Davies's future after *The Long Day Closes.* But then look how well Davies turned out—except that most people missed the virtues of *The House of Mirth.* Luhrmann will direct *La Bohème* on Broadway—why not Brisbane?

Paul Lukas (1895–1971),
b. Budapest, Hungary

Lukas was a student at the Actors' Academy of Hungary and a leading player of the Hungarian stage and cinema when, in 1923, Max Reinhardt invited him to Vienna. As well as working in the theatre there, he made *Samson und Dalila* (23, Michael Curtiz) at UFA. He went back to the Budapest theatre and was spotted by Adolph Zukor, who gave him a contract with Paramount.

Ironically, having come to attention because of the enduring loyalties of Hungarians, Lukas was asked for most of his career to play stereotyped Hollywood foreigners, everything from caddish seducers to hissing Nazis. He began at Paramount with *Three Sinners* (28, Rowland V. Lee) and worked steadily without establishing himself as more than support: *The Woman from Moscow* (28, Ludwig Berger); *Two Lovers* (28, Fred Niblo); *Hot News* (28, Clarence Badger); *The Night Watch* (28, Alexander Korda); *Manhattan Cocktail* (28, Dorothy Arzner); and *The Shopworn Angel* (29, Richard Wallace). The studio's efforts to promote Lukas as a romantic hero were not helped by his obstinate accent, and he gradually slipped into character roles: *Halfway to Heaven* (29, George Abbott); *The Wolf of Wall Street* (29, Lee); *Behind the Make-Up* (30, Robert Milton);

Slightly Scarlet (30, Louis Gasnier and Edwin H. Knopf); and *Grumpy* (30, George Cukor and Cyril Gardner).

He briefly revived his leading status opposite Ruth Chatterton in *Anybody's Woman* (30, Arzner), *The Right to Love* (31, Wallace), and *Unfaithful* (31, John Cromwell), but his most distinctive American role was as the gang boss in *City Streets* (31, Rouben Mamoulian). After *The Vice Squad* (31, Cromwell), *Strictly Dishonorable* (31, John M. Stahl), *Tomorrow and Tomorrow* (32, Wallace), and *Thunder Below* (32, Wallace), he left Paramount and free-lanced: *A Passport to Hell* (32, Frank Lloyd); *Rockabye* (32, Cukor); *Grand Slam* (33, William Dieterle); and *The Kiss Before the Mirror* (33, James Whale). He now signed with Universal and, after *Captured!* (33, Roy del Ruth) and Professor Bhaer (at RKO) in *Little Women* (33, Cukor), settled into playing lead parts in relatively cheap pictures at that studio: *By Candlelight* (33, Whale); *The Countess of Monte Cristo* (34, Karl Freund); *Glamour* (34, William Wyler); and, at RKO, *The Fountain* (34, Cromwell). He free-lanced for the next few years: *The Casino Murder Case* (35, Lesley Fenton); *I Found Stella Parrish* (35, Mervyn Le Roy); *Dodsworth* (36, Wyler); *Ladies in Love* (36, Edward H. Griffith); and *Espionage* (37, Kurt Neumann), before leaving for England.

His work there was no more consistent, but he had the good fortune to play the villain in Hitchcock's *The Lady Vanishes* (38), and this set him up as a suitable actor for the espionage movies Hollywood would shortly adopt: thus *Confessions of a Nazi Spy* (39, Anatole Litvak); *Strange Cargo* (40, Frank Borzage); *They Dare Not Love* (41, Whale); and most successfully, *Watch on the Rhine* (43, Vincent Sherman and Herman Shumlin). The anti-Nazi agent of Lillian Hellman's play was a part Lukas had created on Broadway, and when the film was made he won the supporting actor Oscar; he was good in the film but it was an award worn on Hollywood's war-conscious sleeve, which did little to improve Lukas's prospects. He was now typecast as an anti-Nazi: *Hostages* (43, Frank Tuttle); *Uncertain Glory* (44, Raoul Walsh); and *Address Unknown* (44, William Cameron Menzies).

After the war, he slipped into smaller films: the wicked husband/brother in *Experiment Perilous* (44, Jacques Tourneur); *Deadline at Dawn* (46, Harold Clurman); *Temptation* (46, Irving Pichel); *Whispering City* (47, Fedor Ozep); and *Berlin Express* (48, Tourneur). Semiretirement dated from about this period and he subsequently limited himself to supporting or cameo parts in larger films: *Kim* (50, Victor Saville); *20,000 Leagues Under the Sea* (54, Richard Fleischer); *The Four Horsemen of the Apocalypse* (61, Vincente Minnelli); *Tender Is the Night* (62, Henry King); 55

Days at Peking (63, Nicholas Ray); and *Lord Jim* (65, Richard Brooks).

Sidney Lumet,

b. Philadelphia, 1924

1957: *Twelve Angry Men.* 1958: *Stage Struck.* 1959: *That Kind of Woman; The Fugitive Kind.* 1961: *A View From the Bridge.* 1962: *Long Day's Journey into Night.* 1963: *Fail-Safe.* 1965: *The Pawnbroker; The Hill.* 1966: *The Group.* 1967: *The Deadly Affair.* 1968: *Bye Bye, Braverman; The Seagull.* 1969: *The Appointment; Blood Kin.* 1971: *The Anderson Tapes.* 1972: *The Offence; Child's Play.* 1973: *Serpico; Lovin' Molly.* 1974: *Murder on the Orient Express.* 1975: *Dog Day Afternoon.* 1976: *Network.* 1977: *Equus.* 1978: *The Wiz.* 1980: *Just Tell Me What You Want.* 1981: *Prince of the City.* 1982: *Death Trap; The Verdict.* 1983: *Daniel.* 1984: *Garbo Talks.* 1986: *Power; The Morning After.* 1988: *Running on Empty.* 1989: *Family Business.* 1990: *Q & A.* 1992: *A Stranger Among Us.* 1993: *Guilty as Sin.* 1997: *Night Falls on Manhattan; Critical Care.* 1999: *Gloria.*

On the one hand, Lumet has made forty-three films. He has been nominated as best director four times. He has steady themes: the fragility of justice and the police and their corruption. He can deliver powerhouse performances from lead actors, and fine work from character actors. He is one of the stalwart figures of New York moviemaking. He abides by good scripts, when he gets them. Yet there is also the Lumet of such follies as *The Wiz, Power, Family Business, A Stranger Among Us,* and *Guilty as Sin*—all of which are 1978 and later. It is in his ostensible maturity that Lumet has been most wayward and inexplicable.

He was a child actor on the stage and in *One Third of a Nation* (39, Dudley Murphy). After an education at Columbia and the Actors Studio, he had his training in live TV drama. His debut, *Twelve Angry Men,* was an acclaimed picture in its day: it was a model for liberal reason and fellowship in the Eisenhower era; or maybe it was an alarming example of how easily any jury could be swayed. Perhaps, finally, it was just an exercise for group acting.

Lumet quickly became esteemed, even if he was out of his element with the romanticism of *Stage Struck* and *That Kind of Woman.* He did well by quality literary adaptations and gave due scope to Hepburn, Richardson, Robards, and Stockwell in what is a superb *Long Day's Journey.* Though not well known today, *The Fugitive Kind* was faithful to Tennessee Williams, it kept Brando and Magnani in intriguing balance and used Boris Kaufman's black and white poetically.

Solemnity set in where there had never been much humor. Lumet got a habit for big issues—*Fail-Safe, The Pawnbroker, The Hill*—and seemed torn between dullness and pathos. Still, in the seventies he made several good procedural thrillers—*The Anderson Tapes* (he was an early believer in an un-Bonded Sean Connery) and *Serpico*—and he was able to catch the wild, emotional panache of Pacino and John Cazale in the tragi-comic *Dog Day Afternoon. Network* plainly belonged to Paddy Chayefsky, but Lumet understood that and did nothing to impede the film. It was the closest he had come to a successful comedy. He was that rarity of the 1970s, a director happy to serve his material—yet seemingly not touched or changed by it.

Equus was a bad film, but maybe it's a bad play that reveals its flaws in close-up. *Prince of the City* is a very dogged, labyrinthine study of police corruption—and one that has twice defied wakefulness in this viewer. Was Lumet wary of humor because it needed energy? Whatever the answer, there's a gloom in *Prince of the City* that feels dutiful or depressed. *The Verdict* looked and felt like an Oscar vehicle for Paul Newman. As with *Twelve Angry Men,* its supposed criticism of how justice works was only the mechanics for suspense.

Daniel and *Running on Empty* are touching and stricken films, with good performances from such young actors as Amanda Plummer, River Phoenix, and Martha Plimpton. Time and again over the years (he has helped eighteen acting nominations), Lumet has shown us more than we expected in actors. That was true of Jane Fonda and Jeff Bridges in *The Morning After.* But the films seemed set, sad, and one-paced. *Q & A* is one of Lumet's best, with an extraordinary performance from Nick Nolte. But *A Stranger Among Us* (Melanie Griffith as an undercover cop in a Hasidic community) is as dotty a choice as any A-list director has ever made.

Lumet was seventy in 1994. How odd to think of him as a veteran, for he seems unformed still, and likely to do anything. It's a distinguished career, I suppose, but it doesn't begin to tell us who Sidney Lumet is.

Of his recent films, only *Night Falls on Manhattan* was compelling—that old instinct for corruption in law and order. But Lumet had another recent credit: in 1995, he published *Making Movies,* a genuinely instructive and thoroughly planned book about managing a picture into being. But it was so clear, so logical, so sensible, it left one at a loss as to how Lumet had made so many pictures that are travesties, and a few—like *The Verdict*—that never lose their harsh taste. If only making movies was as straightforward as he makes it seem—if only the book was wilder, angrier, and more in love. Then a few more films might be great.

The Lumière Brothers:
Louis (1864–1948), b. Besançon France;
Auguste (1862–1954), b. Besançon, France

This book does not include people simply because of their part in the invention of cinematography: there is no Muybridge or Marey. But although the Lumières are credited with the patent and the first film shows that defined the theatrical potential of a whole series of inventions, they are discussed here because their first films are still moving. The rapid sequence of still images so that an effect of lifelike animation is achieved was only the means to the movement of feelings and ideas. The Lumières themselves were largely unaware of the effects they had produced, but those short films touch on many of the subtlest mysteries of the movies. Whether they would have liked it or not, they are the antecedents of the mainstream of French and American cinema, the first men to discover—albeit unwittingly—the fictional content of documentary, and the men who established that films reached out toward audiences and were in turn altered in the process of being watched.

Their father, Antoine, had a photographic firm that moved in 1871 from Besançon to Lyons, and which they joined when they were old enough. Louis was a trained physicist, while Auguste managed the business. During the 1880s and early 1890s, Louis had a hand in several refinements of the still photographic process, but it was only in 1893, on the retirement of Antoine, that the brothers set themselves to produce moving film. Their most important patents concerned the engineering by which the film strip could be made to pass through the camera and projector. History recognizes their original use of sprocket holes in the film strip with a mechanical claw to pull the film through the gate. They used a single machine as camera and projector and called it the cinématographe. During 1895 they demonstrated this machine to scientific societies and then, on December 28, in the Grand Café, Boulevard des Capucines, they showed films to the public on a screen and charged for admission.

In 1896, the exhibition went on a tour that included London and New York. There was no question about the impact: although some spectators ran fearfully away from *L'Arrivée d'un Train*, they came back for more, hustled out of bourgeois complacency into a half-panicked, half-tickled inspection of themselves. Used to the frozen mirror of stills, people began to see for the first time how they walked, smiled, and gestured, how they looked from the back, and how other people watched them. Introspection and exhibitionism were thus simultaneously stimulated by the cinématographe.

But the scientific preoccupation of Louis and the questionable acumen of Auguste were not distracted by success. There is a story that Georges Méliès, dazzled by what those modest beginnings might lead to, begged to be allowed to buy the invention. Witless innovators, the Lumières insisted on saving him from his own recklessness and assured him that the cinématographe had no commercial future. That decision meant that the Lumières were out of cinema history as soon as they had inaugurated it. But the crassness is remembered affectionately, partly because we adhere to landmarks, but also because the Lumière movies have not dated. When, in *Contempt*, Jean-Luc Godard has a sequence in a screening room, he prints Lumière's finality beneath the screen—"The cinema is an invention without any future"—but fondly and in the knowledge that images sometimes speak more eloquently than words.

The Lumières used their camera in the way domestic customers employed still cameras: to keep a reference to the life around them. They did little more than record those fragments of the everyday that were too much for a still: workers coming out of a factory; a train entering the station; a baby being fed by its parents. Many of those fragments last only seconds and consist of single fixed shots. But the Lumières' films now lead to crucial insights: that train is frightening because it comes toward the camera, thereby involving it in the action; the sunlight that they needed is not physically warm but emotionally mellow; the people being filmed are already recognizing the need to address themselves to the camera, to organize themselves so that they may be more plausible and convincing—they sense the need to act themselves; and the camera is far enough away to cover all the action. Too often, the history books have seen that as a limitation, compared with D. W. Griffith's introduction of different shots from varying angles to produce a narrative. In fact, the meal table in *Le Déjeuner de Bébé* needs to be embraced in a single shot to convey the community of the family and the charm of the occasion. The violent meals of *The Miracle Worker* conform to the same principle.

But the Lumières went a little further. In *L'Arroseur Arrosé*, a single setup recorded a naïve prank involving a garden hose. That incident looks forward to comedy—slapstick and sophisticated—not just in the visual fun, but because the audience is made to anticipate the moment when the joker falls victim to his own trick and is soaked. That brief, flickering, sunny game of *L'Arroseur Arrosé* involves us in a process that leads directly to the way in which for over thirty minutes *The Godfather* schools us for Michael Corleone killing two men as they eat in an Italian restaurant. Anticipation was born, and we were accomplices in the action.

Ida Lupino (1918–95), b. Brixton, London
1950: *Outrage; Never Fear.* 1951: *Hard, Fast and*

Beautiful. 1953: *The Bigamist; The Hitchhiker.* 1966: *The Trouble with Angels.*

Ida Lupino had not worked in fifteen years. Nor did she seem inclined to come out for tributes. Surely she had been invited. For she was a woman director of real personality; her pictures are as tough and quick as those of Samuel Fuller. She was a pioneer for women, especially because she carved out her own territory instead of just waiting to be asked. But her own movies should not obscure Ida Lupino the actress. She knew how to play routine roles and play them well. But there are a few occasions when she had an out-of-the-ordinary part, and then she was riveting.

For instance, when her character turns nasty and crazy in *They Drive By Night* (40, Raoul Walsh), there is nothing to do but sit back and watch an astonishing emotional explosion. In *The Hard Way* (42, Vincent Sherman), as the strong sister driving Joan Leslie into show business, she senses a movie unknown to the other players. She is a demon, so forceful we have to realize how often in her career she kept the brakes on. In the first few scenes of *Road House* (48, Jean Negulesco), we could be meeting a woman from Jim Thompson—burned, dangerous, impatient, and pitiless. But then she sees that she has only a dud script and plain guys to work with. She decides to behave and the film goes downhill. "If only," you say so often with Ida Lupino. If only she and Gloria Grahame could have played wicked sisters—they looked alike, and they were both too odd for placid movies.

The daughter of comedian Stanley Lupino, she added to her family's vaudeville heritage a formal training at RADA. She was on the fringe of the British film industry when the visiting Allan Dwan gave her a small part in *Her First Affaire* (33). She made several more films and Paramount signed her up (she was still only fifteen) with the idea of her playing Alice in Wonderland. That fell through, but she appeared in *Come On, Marines!* (34, Henry Hathaway); *Paris in Spring* (35, Lewis Milestone); *Smart Girl* (35, Aubrey Scottio); *Peter Ibbetson* (35, Hathaway); and *Anything Goes* (36, Milestone). Her career faltered, picked up with *The Gay Desperado* (36, Rouben Mamoulian), but lapsed again with *Sea Devils* (37, Ben Stoloff) and *Artists and Models* (37, Walsh). She was even out of work for some time, but returned with *The Lone Wolf Spy Hunt* (39, Peter Godfrey), *The Adventures of Sherlock Holmes* (39, Alfred Werker), and *The Light that Failed* (39, William Wellman).

Warners then signed her as the mollish interest for gangster films and she flourished in *They Drive by Night* and *High Sierra* (41, Walsh) as well as the Jack London–based *The Sea Wolf* (41, Michael Curtiz). A variety of good, tough parts followed in which she seemed more worldly-wise

than her age might have suggested: *Out of the Fog* (41, Anatole Litvak); *Ladies in Retirement* (41, Charles Vidor); *Moontide* (42, Archie Mayo); *The Hard Way; Forever and a Day* (43, Frank Lloyd et al.); *In Our Time* (44, Sherman); *Devotion* (46, Curtis Bernhardt), playing Emily Brontë; *The Man I Love* (46, Walsh), with its great opening, and then the sentimental camp of *Deep Valley* (47, Negulesco); *Escape Me Never* (47, Peter Godfrey); and *Road House,* in which she credibly stills the assembly with a husky performance of several songs. Her delivery was randy and bossy, and in Hemingway's *Across the River and Into the Trees* his Italian heroine had copied Lupino's way of talking.

Finished with Warners, and with her first husband, actor Louis Hayward, she married the Columbia executive Collier Young, and turned to writing, directing, and producing. She produced *Not Wanted* (49, Elmer Clifton), and directed *Never Fear* and *Outrage,* two minor but interesting films. She played the blind woman in Nicholas Ray's *On Dangerous Ground* (51) and reportedly did some directing while Ray was ill. As an actress, she worked in *Woman in Hiding* (49, Michael Gordon); *Beware, My Lovely* (52, Harry Horner); *Private Hell 36* (54, Don Siegel); *The Big Knife* (55, Robert Aldrich); *Women's Prison* (55, Lewis Seiler); *While the City Sleeps* (56, Fritz Lang); and *Strange Intruder* (56, Irving Rapper).

She proved herself a competent director of second features, and an early discoverer of feminist themes. Thus *The Bigamist* is not just melodrama, but a critique of woman's vulnerability. Married again, this time to actor Howard Duff, she turned to TV but directed again, in 1966, *The Trouble with Angels*—which gathered together Rosalind Russell, Hayley Mills, and Gypsy Rose Lee in a convent, showing that idiosyncrasy was not dead yet. She directed for TV, and was outstanding as a man's woman fed up with the man in *Junior Bonner* (72, Sam Peckinpah). She also appeared in *The Devil's Rain* (75, Robert Fuest); *The Food of the Gods* (76, Bert I. Gordon); and *My Boys Are Good Boys* (78, Bethel Buckalew).

David Lynch, b. Missoula, Montana, 1946
1970: *The Grandmother* (s). 1977: *Eraserhead.* 1980: *The Elephant Man.* 1984: *Dune.* 1986: *Blue Velvet.* 1990–91: *Twin Peaks* (TV). 1990: *Wild at Heart; Industrial Symphony #1* (TV). 1992: *Twin Peaks: Fire Walk With Me.* 1993: *Hotel Room* (TV). 1997: *Lost Highway.* 1999: *The Straight Story.* 2001: *Mulholland Dr.*

It was in 1986, as film critic for *California* magazine, that I saw *Blue Velvet,* alone, in the theatre of what was then Dino de Laurentiis's D.E.G. building on Wilshire Boulevard in Los Angeles. The occasion stood as the last moment of transcendence I had felt at the movies—until *The Piano*. What I mean by that is a kind of passionate involvement with both the story and the making of a film, so that I was simultaneously moved by the enactment on screen and by discovering that a new director had made the medium alive and dangerous again. I was the more captivated in that I had not much liked David Lynch's earlier work.

My passion is the more mysterious now because Lynch's later work seemed horribly disappointing and jaded. Thus, for the moment, at least, *Blue Velvet* represents the precarious difficulty in making—or seeing (in the sense of recognizing)—great films. Had I blundered into comprehension, or had Lynch drifted into clarity? Did I need a great movie experience in 1986 as much as Lynch, or more? Having made *Blue Velvet*, did he need to turn his back on the challenging prospect of fusing art and box office? I ask that because the career of David Lynch seems so intertwined with his foxy sense of himself. At least, it does if one assumes that Lynch understood what he was doing in *Blue Velvet*. In conversation, he makes every effort to be nonchalant or dismissive of that burden. Why not? It would be as hard to advance on *Blue Velvet* as it must have been to work after *Citizen Kane*.

Lynch was the son of a research scientist with the U.S. Department of Agriculture: the family traveled a good deal and that fostered Lynch's love of middle America. By high school, however, they were in Alexandria, Virginia, so Lynch took art classes at Washington's Corcoran School of Art. He then studied painting at the Boston Museum of Fine Arts and at the Pennsylvania Academy of Fine Arts in Philadelphia in the late sixties. He even won a three-year scholarship to Europe, which he quit after fifteen days.

He made a one-minute animated film for a contest while in Philadelphia, and that led him to the American Film Institute, where he made *The Grandmother* and began *Eraserhead*. He continues to do some work as a painter, just as, since *Blue Velvet*, he has had a TV partnership with Mark Frost for the *Twin Peaks* venture and for the Fox show *American Chronicles*. In 1992, another series, *On the Air*, had a limited network run; and in 1993 Lynch was involved on *Hotel Room*, a series for HBO. In addition, he has made some television commercials, notably a series for Calvin Klein's Obsession.

It remains natural, I think, to wonder what Lynch wants. *Eraserhead* was not just a student film, but as private as any solitary art, like writing or painting. It seemed to indicate someone who saw his future in experimental cinema. Yet *The Elephant Man* and *Dune* were attempts at mainstream movies, no matter how personal or obscure they ended up. *The Elephant Man* was a prestigious stage play; it had Mel Brooks as a father figure, as well as a solid cast and properly focused

pathos. John Hurt's hero was exactly that, whereas nothing in *Eraserhead* acknowledges the function of heroism. *Dune* was a de Laurentiis sci-fi epic, taken from Frank Herbert. It cost, and lost, a lot of money. It is often brilliant, but frequently ponderous and unintelligible. Some observers marveled that Dino had let it happen.

But then the Italian producer let Lynch make *Blue Velvet*, which kept surrealism, hallucination, and "experiment" in perfect balance with Americana, a simple compelling storyline, and the huge, gravitational force of a voyeuristic setup. I believe *Blue Velvet* is also an allegory on sexual awakening, about innocence and peril, family ties and adulthood, such as no American film has achieved. The movie works: at the art-house level, it was a big hit. The performances are extraordinary: Dennis Hopper was savage yet lucid; Kyle McLachlan and Laura Dern were like Hansel and Gretel; Dean Stockwell was uncanny; and Isabella Rossellini seemed at last like a naked, forked actress. (She and Lynch were companions for years, and they acted together in *Zelly and Me* [88, Tina Rathbone].)

Was *Twin Peaks* a cynical move, or as "authentic" as *Blue Velvet*? Was Lynch seeking to cash in, to bring Magritte to the masses? Was he satirizing the mass audience, or rebelling against the critical celebration of *Blue Velvet*? I have a hunch he is not quite sure himself. There were beautiful passages to be found in *Twin Peaks* (notably those directed by Lynch), but the whole thing seemed a dead end reaching as far as the longest northwestern view. The subsequent movie—*Fire Walk With Me*—is the worst thing Lynch has done—and, I trust, the least necessary or sincere.

What will happen to Lynch? Where will he go? Such questions may have more to say about the institution of the movies and the nature of the audience. But whatever happens, I believe *Blue Velvet* will grow larger over the years, along with films like *Vertigo, The Night of the Hunter*, and *Citizen Kane*. There is a genius in Lynch that may have been lucky to get its one moment.

That was written in 1994, when there was still *Lost Highway* to come. That film has its devout fans, but I am not one of them. Indeed, I felt the director was still striving for the natural air of dream—and Lynch seems pretentious when he is straining. Equally, while touched by *The Straight Story*, I was suspicious of its straight-faced dedication to simple, honest feelings. It's not a film I want to see again—whereas *Blue Velvet* I review regularly. But *Mulholland Dr.* I want to see all the time. This seemed to me, emphatically, a second masterpiece, and the first film in which Lynch's style was so sweet, so serene, that one went with the drive or the dream of the movie without ever feeling those old panicky questions—Where are we going? What is it about? It's about itself and the dual process of dreaming and driving—it's also one of the greatest films ever made about the cultural devastation caused by Hollywood.

Adrian Lyne,

b. Peterborough, England, 1941

1980: *Foxes*. 1983: *Flashdance*. 1986: *9½ Weeks*. 1987: *Fatal Attraction*. 1990: *Jacob's Ladder*. 1993: *Indecent Proposal*. 1997: *Lolita*. 2002: *Unfaithful*.

In the 1980s, there came into being a kind of movie that was, at the same time, sensational and dead. These films had a self-induced hysteria in look, feel, and tempo—they never let go of us. They did not dare to, for their content was so attitudinizing, so removed from experience or life. These were movies founded in, and inspired by, the atmosphere of advertising. Some were more compelling than others: *Fatal Attraction* has suspense, some character, and a believable starting situation. Yet the movie aspires only to be what a friend of mine called it—"Every man's nightmare." In other words, it is nothing but concept or setup; it is a hook, and we are the fish. Others are ridiculous—*Flashdance*, *9½ Weeks* (the most indebted to advertising imagery), and *Indecent Proposal* (which takes a clever concept and makes nearly every imaginable mistake with it).

Adrian Lyne has made these films. He was once, in Britain, a director of commercials. Every article written on Lyne observes that he graduated from the short form to feature length. But the process was not exactly that. In fact, he dragged the full-length film down to the tense gestures of a commercial—and then allowed length to ruin the trick. Try this test: look at the trailers for Lyne films—they are unfailingly superior to the eventual product. He is still making commercials—and we are the fish.

Lolita will probably sit in solitary splendor—the only film Lyne made in ten years. Of course, it was dreadfully handled commercially, and so held up that it was almost bound to disappoint, whereas it was made with a care, taste, and elegance that Lyne had never shown before—so it might have worked, if Vladimir Nabokov's *Lolita* had been so fixed on care, taste, and elegance (as opposed to self-destruction, passion, and words). Nevertheless, Lyne's cover as a slick vulgarian has been blown for ever—that was no more than a winning pose.

M

Jeanette MacDonald (1901–65),

b. Philadelphia

It is possible that, without so accomplished a soprano voice, Jeanette MacDonald would now be more highly regarded as a comedienne. Without a song, she would not have had to keep company with the egregious Nelson Eddy. But millions gazed fondly on that team no matter that it made MacDonald's instinct for playfulness seem flighty and shrill. With less imperious male partners—Gable, or even Chevalier—MacDonald had looked like a lady used to greater politeness, but tickled by the glint of a lewd smile. "Your right eye says yes, and your left eye says no," Chevalier tells her in *The Merry Widow*. Perhaps she always condescended (she *was* known as The Iron Butterfly), but she seemed to enjoy raciness and to be encouraged by it. In *Love Me Tonight* (32, Rouben Mamoulian), for instance, she seems well aware of the frivolity in rhymed trills and to be in no doubt about Chevalier's saucy tailor. Especially in her Lubitsch period, she carried melodies lightly, rather like a duchess preferring to go incognito. But by the late 1930s, MGM had done so well with her and Eddy in strenuous, sentimental operetta that there was no alternative.

She sang and danced on stage during the 1920s and had been turned down once by Paramount before Lubitsch cast her with Chevalier in *The Love Parade* (29). She stayed there for *The Vagabond King* (30, Ludwig Berger), *Monte Carlo* (30, Lubitsch), and *Let's Go Native* (30, Leo McCarey). But Lubitsch was her sole advocate at Paramount and the studio let her go elsewhere for some dull films: *The Lottery Bride* (30, Paul L. Stein); *Oh for a Man!* (30, Hamilton MacFadden); *Don't Bet on Women* (31, William K. Howard); and *Annabelle's Affairs* (31, Alfred Werker). Lubitsch called her back for *One Hour With You* (32, Lubitsch and George Cukor) and *Love Me Tonight*, but she then went to Britain at Herbert Wilcox's invitation, only to be replaced by Anna Neagle.

On her return, she was signed up by MGM for *The Cat and the Fiddle* (34, Howard) and *The Merry Widow* (34), made with two more Paramount exiles, Lubitsch and Chevalier. MGM took her to their heart (Louis B. Mayer tried to go further), and found Nelson Eddy to sing with her in a series of films shared between Robert Z. Leonard and W. S. Van Dyke: *Naughty Marietta* (35, Van Dyke); *Rose-Marie* (36, Van Dyke); *San Francisco* (36, Van Dyke), with Gable and Spencer Tracy, herself singing with all the zeal of a social worker intent on rebuilding the spread-eagled city; *Maytime* (37, Leonard); *The Firefly* (37, Leonard); *The Girl of the Golden West* (38, Leonard); *Sweethearts* (38, Van Dyke); *Broadway Serenade* (39, Leonard); *New Moon* (40, Leonard); and *Bitter Sweet* (40, Van Dyke).

These films often involved MacDonald singing through the tears to recollect a lost Eddy: scenes undercut by the difficulty of knowing whether Eddy was dead or playing dead. (In *Bitter Sweet* he dies in a scrambled duel, but his emotions are so sluggish that the fatal thrust is not shown and he expires merely by closing his eyes.) *Smilin' Through* (41, Frank Borzage) is a crazy variation on that backward look, with Gene Raymond—MacDonald's husband—instead of Eddy. Her last film with Eddy was *I Married an Angel* (42, Van Dyke), and after *Cairo* (42, Van Dyke) she broke with MGM, reportedly over the dubbing of her voice in foreign language versions of her films. Subsequently, she tried opera, musicals, and cabaret, and made three more films at MGM in smaller roles: *Follow the Boys!* (44, Edward Sutherland); *Three Daring Daughters* (48, Fred M. Wilcox); and *The Sun Comes Up* (49, Richard Thorpe).

Gustav Machaty (1901–63),
b. Prague, Czechoslovakia
1919: *Teddy by Kouril/Teddy'd Like a Smoke.*
1926: *Kreutzerova Sonáta/The Kreutzer Sonata.*
1927: *Svejk v Civilu/The Good Soldier Schweik in Civilian Life.* 1929: *Erotikon.* 1931: *Naceradec, Král Kibicu/Naceradec, King of the Kibitzers; Ze Soboty na Nedeli/From Saturday to Sunday.* 1933: *Ecstasy.* 1934: *Nocturno.* 1936: *Ballerine.* 1937: *The Good Earth* (uncredited codirector). 1938: *The Wrong Way Out* (s). 1939: *Within the Law.* 1945: *Jealousy.* 1956: *Suchkind 312.*

Machaty's is a career that resembles the nomadic life forced on Hungarian Paul Fejos. For Machaty left Czechoslovakia and went by way of Austria and Italy to Hollywood, where he is supposed to have worked on *The Good Earth*, among other things. He stayed there during the war, and *Jealousy* is a seventy-one-minute noir that stars John Loder, Nils Asther, and Jane Randolph. If only, in America, Machaty could have been reunited with his discovery Hedwig Kiesler—who had become Hedy Lamarr at MGM. Their film, *Ecstasy*, is actually worth all the hype attached to it. The story of a young woman married to an old man who finds a young lover lacks subtlety, but the nude bathing scenes are gorgeous and the orgasm that "Eva" experiences is still startling and touching.

But just as Fejos has his *Lonesome*, so Machaty should be known for *From Saturday to Sunday*, a romance that says a lot about urban life and isolation and does so with a camera style that ignores the limitations of early sound. It's clear that Machaty was a man of real talent, and it is to be hoped that more of his films become available.

Alexander Mackendrick (1912–93),
b. Boston, Massachusetts
1949: *Whisky Galore/Tight Little Island.* 1951: *The Man in the White Suit.* 1952: *Mandy.* 1954: *The Maggie/High and Dry.* 1955: *The Ladykillers.* 1957: *Sweet Smell of Success.* 1963: *Sammy Going South.* 1965: *A High Wind in Jamaica.* 1967: *Don't Make Waves.*

Mackendrick was brought up in Scotland, and after a period in advertising he entered the British industry and worked in documentary. During the war, he was in Rome in charge of the film unit of the Psychological Warfare Branch. In peacetime he returned to the industry as a scriptwriter: *Saraband for Dead Lovers* (48, Basil Dearden and Michael Relph); *The Blue Lamp* (49, Dearden); and *Dance Hall* (50, Charles Crichton). As a director, Mackendrick's work flattered to deceive. After showing a sense of mordant fantasy quite beyond his beginnings in Ealing comedy, his work became more conventional and impersonal. After 1967, it stopped altogether.

There are recurring themes in his films: his interest in child psychology (*Mandy, Sammy,* and Richard Hughes's *High Wind in Jamaica*); the unconscious betrayals of life; plus an instinct for the straight-faced account of pain and cruelty. But his major characteristic is unexpectedness. His comedies are funny, but *The Man in the White Suit* is touched by Kafka and *The Ladykillers* is rooted in George Orwell's "English murder" and the Chamber of Horrors. Even *The Maggie*—a crucial film for an American Scot—has a sense of frustration that is genuinely tortured. The way in which native feyness conspires to sap the blustering Paul Douglas amounts to more than comedy. The ordeal is piled on until pain itself is dominant.

In other words, the creeping hysteria and acid disenchantment of *Sweet Smell of Success* have more background in his British films than seemed the case at the time. No other American director has come as close to the scathing clarity of Nathanael West or, at that time, had looked so straight at corruption. The accurate observer in Mackendrick was evident in the way both Burt Lancaster and Tony Curtis were admitted to previously locked parts of themselves.

Of his three last films only *High Wind in Jamaica* seemed to belong to him and that was somehow choked off, as if Mackendrick could no longer face its meaning. He is a great loss, but he set up and directed an exceptional film program at the California Institute of the Arts from 1969 to 1978.

Shirley MacLaine (Shirley Mclean Beaty),
b. Richmond, Virginia, 1934
Over the years, the making of this book has brought me so much pleasure. Perhaps a lifetime of misspent youth has amounted to something. Going back over the movies, there are so many memories. In attempting to see shape in the history of motion pictures there is a steady battle between scholarship and partiality, enough to suggest that learning is often more warped than it realizes, while daft enthusiasms do lead to quantities of obscure knowledge. There have

been moments of revelation, comedy, excitement, and the grim accumulation of experience, of all those frames gone by. We have faced them at the Granada, Tooting, and at screening rooms in the Thalberg Building. The author may begin to regard himself solemnly. But then, as come-uppance, without undue incredulity, malice, or frenzy, a grown man is required to sit down and compose a thousand or so words on Shirley MacLaine. Yes, that career has really happened; that energy has flowed.

She is the older sister of Warren Beatty, a relationship that seems to have been powerful and stimulating when they were young, and a source of friction and perplexity later. MacLaine the beginner was very impressive: she had smart bounce, a sense of humor, and a wicked streak that made her short red hair seem tomboyish. She was a dancer, who replaced Carol Haney in the Broadway production of *The Pajama Game* in 1954.

Hal Wallis signed her up and she made her debut, as auburn as the New England fall, in *The Trouble with Harry* (55, Alfred Hitchcock). She danced a little in *Artists and Models* (55, Frank Tashlin) and scooped the female lead in *Around the World in 80 Days* (56, Michael Anderson). After *Hot Spell* (57, Daniel Mann) and *The Matchmaker* (58, Joseph Anthony), she was as good as she has ever been as the tart in *Some Came Running* (58, Vincente Minnelli) and in *Ask Any Girl* (59, Charles Walters)—the first a small-town drama that is badly underrated, the second a pleasant comedy.

Neither *Career* (59, Anthony) nor *Can-Can* (60, Walter Lang) did much for her, but *The Apartment* (60, Billy Wilder) was a turning point: she was funny and touching to be sure, but there were signs of self-indulgence in her playing of the exploited elevator-girl, Fran Kubelik, subtly abetting Wilder's distaste for women. None of Wilder's tacked on happy endings seems as craven or unconvincing as MacLaine's headlong, back-projected run into the arms of Lemmon's Baxter. The self-destructive sentiment of Fran is too strong for the trite compromise, and Wilder's vision hardly comprehends a love that has no solid commercial motive.

In the 1960s, her choice of parts, not to mention her playing, seemed increasingly casual and mistaken: *Two Loves* (61, Walters); as the L—n in *The Children's Hour* (62, William Wyler); *My Geisha* (62, Jack Cardiff), produced by her husband, Steve Parker, and indulging her interest in Japan; self-consciously pathetic in *Two for the Seesaw* (63, Robert Wise); and *Irma la Douce* (63, Wilder).

By then, her kooky girl was becoming excessive, predictable, and a barrier to her former impishness. She needed more ambitious parts and more implacable directors than were generally available. For many years the earnestness of her screen character was borne out in life by her work for the Democratic party. She wrote an amusing book and did a TV series, *Shirley's World*, to divert her from some lame movies: *What a Way to Go* (64, J. Lee Thompson); *John Goldfarb, Please Come Home* (64, Thompson); *Gambit* (66, Ronald Neame); *Woman Times Seven* (67, Vittorio de Sica); *Sweet Charity* (68, Bob Fosse), based on Fellini's *Cabiria; The Bliss of Mrs. Blossom* (68, Joseph McGrath); *Two Mules for Sister Sara* (69, Don Siegel); and *Desperate Characters* (70, Frank D. Gilroy).

She was a middle-aged woman overtaken by the occult in *The Possession of Joel Delaney* (71, Waris Hussein). Then, after a long interval during which she did everything on the documentary *The Other Half of the Sky: A China Memoir* (74), she seemed overimpressed with the superficial earnestness of *The Turning Point* (77, Herbert Ross), in which she pandered to any woman who had ever given up a career too demanding for middle-class attitudes.

She was in *Being There* (79, Hal Ashby); *Loving Couples* (80, Jack Smight); *A Change of Seasons* (80, Richard Lang)—before a lively comeback as Aurora Greenaway in *Terms of Endearment* (83, James L. Brooks), for which she won the best actress Oscar. At the same time, she was running a second career as the author of several books that were variously autobiographical and inspirational. She was frank about her own life (her accounts of dealing with her parents and her brother are well done) and hopeful about the further horizons of re- and preincarnation. The more daft this image, the more serious she became. It took that to go without flinching into playing herself for television in the risible *Out on a Limb* (87, Robert Butler).

Since then, she played *Madame Sousatzka* (88, John Schlesinger); *Steel Magnolias* (89, Ross); in *Waiting for the Light* (90, Christopher Monger); as the mother in *Postcards from the Edge* (90, Mike Nichols), a role based in fact on Debbie Reynolds; doing a cameo in *Defending Your Life* (91, Albert Brooks); *Used People* (92, Beeban Kidron); *Wrestling Ernest Hemingway* (93, Randa Haines); and *Guarding Tess* (94, Hugh Wilson).

It is said that she has been trying to mount a film in which she would play Louise Brooks in the last decade or so of her life. As her character cried out, long ago, in *Some Came Running:* "You gotta remember, I'm human." And more.

The closest she has come to Brooks has been narrating the documentary *Looking for Lulu* (98, Barry Paris)—but there is time enough still. Meanwhile, she has also made *The West Side Waltz* (95, Ernest Thompson); *Mrs. Winterbourne* (96, Richard Benjamin); as Aurora again in *The*

Evening Star (96, Robert Harling); *A Smile Like Yours* (97, Keith Samples); *Joan of Arc* (99, Christian Duguay); *Bruno* (00, which she directed herself); *These Old Broads* (01, Matthew Diamond); as Rebecca Nurse in *Salem Witch Trials* (01, Joseph Sargent); *Carolina* (02, Marleen Gorris).

Fred MacMurray (1908–91),
b. Kankakee, Illinois

The ingredients of the MacMurray man are paradoxical but consistent: brittle cheerfulness; an anxious smile that subsides into slyness; a voice that tries to be jocular and easygoing but comes out fraudulent; the semblance of a masculine carriage that turns insubstantial and shifty. In other words, MacMurray is a romantic lead built on quicksand, a hero compelled to betray, a lover likely to desert.

In Hollywood this has been a rare character and MacMurray let the tawdry con-man grin through the all-American wholesomeness with a rare conjurer's swiftness so that the ear and eye suspected a dud despite every protestation of the script. For, sadly, Hollywood allowed him very few truly flawed characters: the insurance agent in *Double Indemnity* (44, Billy Wilder) urged into danger by the brazen Barbara Stanwyck; as Keefer, cowardly mischief maker in *The Caine Mutiny* (54, Edward Dmytryk); as a crooked cop entranced by Kim Novak in *Pushover* (54, Richard Quine); and as Sheldrake, the chronic exploiter, in *The Apartment* (60, Billy Wilder). Here are four memorable versions of a counterfeit nice guy in which the crispness of a new bank note turns sodden and limp once it is put down in spilt gin.

Against that, one has to set a lifetime of hollow good cheer. MacMurray began as a musician, crooner, and bit-part player before Paramount signed him up in 1934, originally as a male lead for Claudette Colbert in *The Gilded Lily* (35, Wesley Ruggles). He came on fast in *Alice Adams* (35, George Stevens) and *Hands Across the Table* (35, Mitchell Leisen, for whom he worked nine times). Paramount tried to vary his modern-dress smartness in *The Trail of the Lonesome Pine* (36, Henry Hathaway), *The Texas Rangers* (36, King Vidor), and *Maid of Salem* (37, Frank Lloyd), but the penthouse belt was his natural milieu: *Thirteen Hours by Air* (36, Leisen); *The Princess Comes Across* (36, William K. Howard); *Champagne Waltz* (37, Edward Sutherland); and brilliantly weak in *Swing High, Swing Low* (37, Leisen). He was with Ray Milland (an exact contemporary at Paramount) in *Men With Wings* (38, William Wellman) and carried on in *Sing You Sinners* (38, Ruggles); *Café Society* (39, Edward H. Griffith); *Invitation to Happiness* (39, Ruggles); *Honeymoon in Bali* (39, Griffith); *Remember the Night* (40, Leisen); and *Little Old New York* (40, Henry King).

He worked throughout the war, at home and on loan, without ever becoming a major star: *Virginia* (41, Griffith); *New York Town* (41, Charles Vidor); *Dive Bomber* (41, Michael Curtiz); *The Lady Is Willing* (42, Leisen); the male secretary in *Take a Letter, Darling* (42, Leisen); *The Forest Rangers* (42, George Marshall); *Above Suspicion* (43, Richard Thorpe); *No Time for Love* (43, Leisen); *Standing Room Only* (44, Sidney Lanfield); *And the Angels Sing* (44, Marshall); *Practically Yours* (44, Leisen); *Murder He Says* (45, Marshall); and *Captain Eddie* (45, Lloyd Bacon).

Briefly, in 1945, MacMurray had joined Fox, but after *Smoky* (46, Louis King) he went back to Paramount for *Suddenly It's Spring* (47, Leisen). Restlessness indicated a decline in his drawing power and he was forced to take work where he could: *The Egg and I* (47, Chester Erskine)—a big hit; *Singapore* (47, John Brahm); *The Miracle of the Bells* (48, Irving Pichel); and *An Innocent Affair* (48, Bacon).

After 1949, he found himself in inane comedies, routine adventure films, or tired women's pictures: apart from *The Caine Mutiny* and *Pushover,* he made *Woman's World* (54) and *Rains of Ranchipur* (55)—both for Jean Negulesco; *The Far Horizons* (55, Rudolph Maté); *There's Always Tomorrow* (56, Douglas Sirk); and then a string of cheap Westerns of which *Gun for a Coward* (57, Abner Biberman) and *Face of a Fugitive* (59, Paul Wendkos) are above average.

Two things rescued MacMurray's decline: a TV series, *My Three Sons,* which installed him as a consumer father such as the real MacMurray could have sold door-to-door; and, in the cinema, the favor of Walt Disney, who chose him as the older man kids would love to trust. It says something for stamina that MacMurray's smile stayed straight through *The Absent-Minded Professor* (61, Robert Stevenson); *Bon Voyage!* (62, James Neilson); *Son of Flubber* (63, Stevenson); *Follow Me, Boys* (66, Norman Tokar); *The Happiest Millionaire* (67, Tokar); *Charley and the Angel* (73, Vincent McEveety); *The Chadwick Family* (74, David Lowell Rich); *Beyond the Bermuda Triangle* (75, William A. Graham); and in *The Swarm* (78, Irwin Allen).

William H. (Hall) Macy,
b. Miami, Florida, 1950

There's not a lot William H. Macy can't do—except relax, or seem at ease: he has been a frequent voice in television commercials; he is a reliable supporting actor who rises easily to the chance of lead parts; and he is a good writer. He is something of a disciple of David Mamet (he was Mamet's student at Goddard College, and he later formed a theatre company with him), but he is just as available for the Coen Brothers, Paul Thomas Anderson, and any film prepared to let a parch-faced actor explore insecurity and plain American worrying.

As well as films and stage (notably Teach in *American Buffalo*), he has done a lot of television, with an ongoing role on *ER*. He made his movie debut in *Somewhere in Time* (80, Jeannot Szwarc), and then did *Without a Trace* (83, Stanley R. Jaffe); a voice in *Radio Days* (87, Woody Allen); *House of Games* (87, Mamet); on television in *The Murder of Mary Phagan* (88, Billy Hale); *Things Change* (88, Mamet); *Homicide* (91, Mamet); *Shadows and Fog* (92, Allen); *Benny & Joon* (93, Jeremiah Chechik); *Twenty Bucks* (93, Keva Rosenfeld); *Searching for Bobby Fischer* (93, Steven Zaillian); *Being Human* (93, Bill Forsyth).

He had the male lead in the film of *Oleanna* (94, Mamet); *The Client* (94, Joel Schumacher); *Murder in the First* (95, Marc Rocco); *Mr. Holland's Opus* (95, Stephen Herek); *Down Periscope* (96, David S. Ward); hideously frustrated in *Fargo* (96, Joel Coen); *Ghosts of Mississippi* (96, Rob Reiner); on TV for *Andersonville* (96, John Frankenheimer); *Air Force One* (97, Wolfgang Petersen); superb and suicidal in *Boogie Nights* (97, Anderson); *Wag the Dog* (97, Barry Levinson); *Pleasantville* (98, Gary Ross).

He was Arbogast in the remake of *Psycho* (98, Gus Van Sant); *A Civil Action* (98, Zaillian); *Happy, Texas* (99, Mark Illsley); *A Slight Case of Murder* (99, Steven Schachter), a very amusing inside-movies story which Macy wrote, and which also starred his wife, Felicity Huffman; the aged and wretched Quiz Kid in *Magnolia* (99, Anderson); the lead, and good, in *Panic* (00, Henry Bromell); *State and Main* (00, Mamet); *Jurassic Park III* (01, Joe Johnston); *Focus* (01, Neal Slavin).

He was in *Welcome to Collinwood* (02, Anthony and Joe Russo); actor and co-writer on *Door to Door* (02, Schachter); *The Cooler* (03, Wayne Kramer); *Stealing Sinatra* (03, Ron Underwood); on TV in *Out of Order* (03, Bromell and Wayne Powers); *Seabiscuit* (03, Ross).

Madonna (Madonna Louise Ciccone),
b. Detroit, Michigan, 1959

Imagine that you are watching something that especially moves you—your two-year-old child eating profiteroles; Joe Montana moving down the field; dawn at the Canyon de Chelly; or the close of *Ugetsu Monogatari*, whatever. Your communion with this spectacle is suddenly ruptured by what we will call a commercial break. This is all the more disturbing in that you did not know that what you were watching (the medium) was subject to such intrusions. You did not know the technology was yet available to come between you and the entire air and sky at Canyon de Chelly. But "they" have managed it, and the ad zips up every

horizon. In that disaster, the ad—I suggest—should be the insolent, in-your-face "attitude" of Ms. Ciccone. There is no need for a product. There is nothing in Madonna to be advertised, except for her ironic, deflecting contempt. She is an ad for advertising; she is the famousness of celebrity; and a fit vehicle for an unusual kind of serial-killing movie—one in which photography poisons the world.

You know the argument: guns, for example, are helpless things that only serve those who use them—guns may dispose of would-be rapists and murderers; guns permit the animals that provide meat to be killed swiftly; guns allow the exercise and pleasure of hunting; and armaments manufacturers build schools and hospitals.

Similarly, moving images have been a field for the dreams of Ozu, Hawks, Ophuls, etc. Photography has brought into being Lartigue, Ansel Adams, etc. But in addition, movie and photography are advertising, fashion spreads, and Madonna and *Truth or Dare* (91, Alek Keshishian).

There is no going back, and no way of not wondering whether somewhere along the way wrong paths have been taken. I am reminded of the image of Warren Beatty in *Truth or Dare,* in dark glasses, trying to edge away, trying to defy the camera with nothingness, and eventually marveling that anyone could suppose this Madonna has any life "off" camera. It is one of the great tragic images in modern film, not least because Mr. Beatty has evidently recognized the horrendous question, what is *he* doing there? And what are we doing watching?

Perhaps a case can be made for Madonna as singer and dancer. But as an actress, she is the person who got out of the empty car—I speak as someone who saw her on stage in David Mamet's *Speed-the-Plow* (where it was possible to lose sight and thought of her even as she walked across stage). But she hardly needs talent, so great is her "artistic integrity," and there are those ready to call her satire and her indifference the most audacious strokes of Dada. She has her defenders, and I suspect she loathes them even more than she scorns her enemies. She is disappointed about something, and hugely driven by resentment.

She appeared in *A Certain Sacrifice* (85, Stephen John Lewicki); *Desperately Seeking Susan* (85, Susan Seidelman); and *Vision Quest* (85, Howard Brookner). She did a song for *At Close Range* (86, James Foley), and she appeared in *Shanghai Surprise* (86, Jim Goddard)—both of which involved Sean Penn, to whom, briefly, she was married. She appeared in *Who's That Girl?* (87, Foley); *Bloodhounds of Broadway* (89, Brookner); *Dick Tracy* (90, Beatty); *Shadows and Fog* (91, Woody Allen); and—seemingly furious that Sharon Stone has so effortlessly mocked and surpassed her in *Basic Instinct*—in *Body of Evi-*

dence (93, Uli Edel); as an actress in *Dangerous Game* (93, Abel Ferrara).

The burden did not lighten: she made appearances in *Blue in the Face* (95, Wayne Wang); *Four Rooms* (95, Allison Anders); *Girl 6* (96, Spike Lee); and then all the ads said she was *Evita* (96, Alan Parker)—no matter that she managed hardly any emotional involvement, and again seemed incapable of understanding the nature of acting. Still, nothing before had been as fatuous as *The Next Best Thing* (00, John Schlesinger). Since then—as you may have heard—she has had a child with her new husband, the English director Guy Ritchie. Cross your fingers for the babe and ignore her siblings—*Star* (01, Ritchie) and *Love, Sex, Drugs & Money* (02, Ritchie).

Anna Magnani (1908–73), b. Rome

Her face was so ecstatically wounded, so sure of men's frailty, yet so driven to try again, it was hard to believe that Magnani had ever been young or demure. (She was nearly forty already in the films she is famous for.) Yet there are photographs of her from the 1930s, striving to look like a young Joan Crawford and with that striking sauce of Latin and Arabic looks. (She had had an Italian mother and an Egyptian father, and she lived part of her childhood in Alexandria.)

She attended the Eleanora Duse Royal Academy of Dramatic Art and was an outstanding theatre actress, in *Anna Christie* and *The Petrified Forest,* and had a big career in variety as well. Indeed, her husband, film director Goffredo Alessandrini (they were married in 1934) told her to stick to the stage. But she did a lot of films in the thirties in small roles: *La Cieca di Sorrento* (34, Nunzio Malasomma); *Tempo Massimo* (34, Mario Mattoli); a singer in *Cavalleria* (36, Alessandrini); *Trenta Secondi d'Amore* (36, Mario Bonnard); *La Principessa Tarakanova* (38, Fedor Ozep and Mario Soldati); *Una Lampada alla Finestra* (40, Gino Talamo); *La Fuggitiva* (41, Piero Ballerini); and her first good part, as a singer again, in *Teresa Venerdi* (41, Vittorio De Sica); *Finalmente Soli* (42, Giacomo Gentilomo); *La Fortuna Viene del Cielo* (42, Akos Rathonyi); *L'Avventura di Annabella* (43, Leo Menardi); *La Vita e Bella* (43, Carlo Ludovico Bragaglia); playing lower class with Aldo Fabrizi in *Campo de' Fiori* (43, Bonnard) and *L'Ultima Carrozzella* (43, Mattoli); *Il Fiore Sotto Gli Occhi* (44, Guido Brignone); and *Quartetto Pazzo* (45, Giulio Salvini).

So many of those films exploited her as singer and as a rather broad variety favorite. Everything changed with her small but riveting performance in *Rome, Open City* (45, Roberto Rossellini), the passionate death scene, and the film's reception overseas. She was given a new range of parts, and at her age she was too wise and insecure to take them with less than a wolf's appetite. In addition,

she and Rossellini were famous lovers.

She did *Abbaso la Miseria!* (46, Gennaro Righelli); *Un Uomo Ritorna* (46, Max Neufeld); *Il Banditto* (46, Alberto Lattuada); in a modern *Tosca,* with Tito Gobbi, *Davanti a lui Tremava tutta Roma* (46, Carmine Gallone); *Abbasso la Ricchezza!* (47, Righelli); *L'Onorevole Angelina* (47, Luigi Zampa); *Lo Sconosciuto di San Marino* (48, Michael Waszinsky); with Eduardo De Filippo in *Assunta Spina* (48, Mattoli).

Rossellini then showcased her in the two parts of *L'Amore* (48), first as the woman on the telephone to her lover in Cocteau's *La Voix Humaine,* and then as the shepherdess, seduced by a vagrant (Federico Fellini), whom she takes for a saint. This is acting in the grand manner, half-realism, half-opera—neither role has a hint of the humor that was so strong in Magnani. But, still, she was extraordinary in *L'Amore.*

As Rossellini exchanged her for Ingrid Bergman, Magnani was a figure in a real melodrama, her woundedness vindicated. She made *Molti Sogni per la Strada* (48, Mario Camerini) and *Vulcano* (50, William Dieterle), a blatant response to *Stromboli,* and a disaster. She was way over the top in *Bellissima* (51, Luchino Visconti), playing a woman trying to get her daughter into pictures. Then, after *Camicie Rosse* (52, Alessandrini), as Garibaldi's mistress, but trying to rehabilitate her former husband, she made her greatest picture, and one of the finest studies of acting—*The Golden Coach* (52, Jean Renoir). She also played herself in the episodic *Siamo Donne* (53, Visconti).

The Rose Tattoo had been written for Magnani by Tennessee Williams—he adored her and her courage in living beyond convention. The movie (55, Daniel Mann), for which she won the Oscar, feels like a set piece, and Magnani is not as tenderly supported by the production as she was by *The Golden Coach.* So we feel the force of the acting too much. In American films, Magnani could never find an ordinary context.

She was a nun in *Suor Latizia* (56, Camerini); with Anthony Quinn and so many sheep it feels as if someone is trying to get to sleep in *Wild Is the Wind* (58, George Cukor); *Nella Città l'Inferno* (58, Renato Castellani), in prison with Giulietta Masina; in her best American film, opposite Brando, *The Fugitive Kind* (60, Sidney Lumet); *Risate di Gioia* (60, Mario Monicelli); *Mamma Roma* (62, Pier Paolo Pasolini); *Le Magot de Josefa* (64, Claude Autant-Lara); *Made in Italy* (65, Nanni Loy); with Quinn again in *The Secret of Santa Vittoria* (69 Stanley Kramer); and then a series for Italian TV, directed by Alfredo Giannetti—*1943: Un Incontro* (71); *L'Automobile* (71); *La Sciantosa* (71); . . .*Correra l'Anno di Grazia* (72)—before a brief final appearance in *Roma* (72, Fellini).

Dusan Makavejev,
b. Belgrade, Yugoslavia, 1932
1966: *Covek Nije Tijka/Man Is Not a Bird.* 1967: *Ljubavni Slucaj, Tragedlja Sluzbenice P. T. T./The Switchboard Operator.* 1968: *Nevinost bez Zastite/Innocence Unprotected.* 1971: *WR-Misterije Organizma/WR-Mysteries of the Organism.* 1974: *Sweet Movie; Wet Dreams.* 1981: *Montenegro.* 1985: *The Coca-Cola Kid.* 1988: *Manifesto.* 1993: *Gorilla Bathes at Noon.* 1994: *Rupa u Dusi/A Hole in the Soul* (d). 1996: an episode from *Danske Piger Viser Alt/Danish Girls Show Everything.*

Part of the impact of *WR* lies in the way Makavejev was able to compare American and Eastern European experience without seeming fanciful. It is easy to relate Makavejev to Godard or Norman Mailer, on the grounds of his leaping associative technique that goes from the human particular to the social and political pattern, and that also sees political behavior as a response to psychological and sexual frustration. But the enterprising width of Makavejev's essayist cinema reminds me also of Chris Marker, partly because he works with the same nimbleness and not with the stalking obsessiveness of those romantic dictators, Godard and Mailer.

To see a Makavejev film is as close to a stimulating educational process as the cinema has come. The "stories" of his films are models, pulled this way and that until the flexibility of shape itself becomes the center of attention. The scenes in *WR* of background copulation are both casual and lyrical, experiments to alter our heavy preconceptions about such a spectacle. Only a very tender scientist could have filmed the plaster-cast-penis scene with so little emotional prurience and such human curiosity.

The persistent implication of Makavejev's work is that man is still a wild, anxious species, all too ready to rest his instinctive energies in such misleading causes as hero worship, the shouting of slogans, and the repressive support of authoritarianism. The relationship between sexual despair and gross political complacency—in both capitalist and Communist countries—is made strikingly clear. But *WR* also contrasts two heroes and their cohorts: Stalin and Wilhelm Reich. It seems to conclude that only the outcast hero is reliable, only the solitary prophet is the poet of the body, and that popular acceptance is the most serious threat of devitalization.

That is why Makavejev offends much doctrinaire commitment. Politics, his films reveal, is a behavior pattern that can be played into various forms and manners. The amusement that goes along with this realization—rather than anger or sadness—is his great virtue as an artist. Despite the bristling armory of his style and the violence of his contrasts, the gaze is always equable and tolerant.

Makavejev was a psychology graduate at Belgrade University who went on to study film. He made experimental films and a series of documentaries before getting into features. However, that term is inadequate as a description of the way he has worked. *The Switchboard Operator* is a love story, but also a description of how society reduces love to sexual pathology. While *Innocence Unprotected* is a reflection upon a classic Yugoslav film through the various personalities of the man who starred in it. In both cases, as in *WR*, Makavejev rejects anecdote and insists on the significance of the processes that produce anecdote.

It has proved difficult for Makavejev to make films—and he shows no readiness to compromise with material, or story forms, that are not his. Indeed, I doubt if he comprehends any way of proceeding except from his own dangerous, fertile mind. In *Montenegro*, Susan Anspach plays a wife who finds sexual liberation in the company of some Yugoslavian workers; in *Coca-Cola Kid*, Eric Roberts plays a salesman sent to Australia who finds among other things the unmitigated erotic image of Greta Scacchi; and *Manifesto* is a crazy comedy set in the Balkans. *Gorilla Bathes at Noon* is a lively return to form, about a Russian officer stranded in Berlin after Soviet withdrawal. It is artfully naïve, surreal, and it employs footage from the 1949 Russian epic, *The Fall of Berlin*. It is typical of Makavejev that his view of Berlin, history, and helpless refugees is so fresh and unexpected. In its climactic scene—the dismantling of a vast concrete statue of Lenin—Makavejev is as good as ever, averse to tyranny yet ready to see the beauty in concrete and to be respectful of Lenin.

Karl Malden (Karl Malden Sekulovich),
b. Chicago, 1914
Of Serbian descent, and an established Broadway character actor—in *Golden Boy, Key Largo, Truckline Cafe, All My Sons,* and Mitch in *A Streetcar Named Desire*—Malden made his movie debut in *They Knew What They Wanted* (40, Garson Kanin). His film appearances remained isolated, in Cukor's *Winged Victory* (44); Kazan's *Boomerang* (47); Hathaway's *13 rue Madeleine* (47) and *Kiss of Death* (47); Henry King's *The Gunfighter* (50); Preminger's *Where the Sidewalk Ends* (50); and Milestone's *Halls of Montezuma* (51), until in 1951 he won the supporting actor Oscar repeating the part he had played on the stage in Kazan's *Streetcar.*

He became increasingly indispensable as a good-natured but ugly support: *Decision Before Dawn* (51, Anatole Litvak); *Diplomatic Courier* (52, Henry Hathaway); the policeman in *I Confess* (52, Alfred Hitchcock); the kindly NCO in Brooks's *Take the High Ground* (53); the priest in *On the Waterfront* (54, Kazan). But, already, in

Vidor's *Ruby Gentry* (52), he had taken a leading part, and in 1956 Kazan cast him in his best movie part, Archie Lee Meighan in *Baby Doll,* a cuckold whose horns grew like pimples in front of the camera. He was also excellent as the domineering father in Mulligan's *Fear Strikes Out* (57) and in the same year he directed his only film, *Time Limit* (57), with Richard Widmark—a taut, reasonable movie. He was also in *Phantom of the Rue Morgue* (54, Roy del Ruth); *No Sleep Till Dawn* (57, Gordon Douglas); *The Great Imposter* (60, Robert Mulligan); *Parrish* (61, Delmer Daves); *Birdman of Alcatraz* (62, John Frankenheimer); and *All Fall Down* (62, Frankenheimer).

Gradually he found himself cast in villainy—in Daves's *The Hanging Tree* (59); a little bemused by Brando's *One-Eyed Jacks* (61); and outrageous in Ford's *Cheyenne Autumn* (64). His parts became either overfamiliar or hopelessly exaggerated, as if his care for realism no longer had a usefulness: thus the dealer in *The Cincinnati Kid* (65, Norman Jewison); *Murderer's Row* (66, Henry Levin); *Nevada Smith* (66, Hathaway); *Hotel* (67, Richard Quine); *Billion Dollar Brain* (67, Ken Russell); *Blue* (68, Silvio Narizzano); and *Wild Rovers* (71, Blake Edwards). Two performances stand out from this: as the agent/hustler in *Gypsy* (62, Mervyn Le Roy), cannily absorbing all Rosalind's Russell, and as Omar Bradley in *Patton* (69, Franklin Schaffner), again mopping up another's energy.

Otherwise, Malden's 1970s were dominated by the success of his TV series, *The Streets of San Francisco* (1972–77), in which his widower detective looked after the character played by Michael Douglas.

It was 1980 before Malden returned to movies, often for television: very good as a steelworker in *Skag* (80, Frank Perry); *Meteor* (80, Ronald Neame); as a newspaperman in *Word of Honor* (81, Mel Damski); *Miracle on Ice* (81, Steven Hilliard Stern); to Yugoslavia for *Twilight Time* (82, Goran Paskaljevic); *The Sting II* (83, Jeremy Paul Kagan); *With Intent to Kill* (84, Mike Robe); as the father in *Fatal Vision* (84, David Greene); *Billy Galvin* (86, John Gray); *Nuts* (87, Martin Ritt); *My Father, My Son* (88, Jeff Bleckner); as Klinghoffer in *The Hijacking of the Achille Lauro* (89, Robert Collins); *Call Me Anna* (90, Gilbert Cates); and *Absolute Strangers* (91, Cates), a study of the abortion debate. In working with Cates, Malden was extending a partnership, for Cates often directed the Academy Awards show for television—and Malden had become president of the Academy.

Terrence Malick, b. Waco, Texas, 1943

1973: *Badlands.* 1978: *Days of Heaven.* 1998: *The Thin Red Line.*

Badlands may be the most assured first film by an American since *Citizen Kane.* It does not have the persisting tragedy of another debut, *They Live by Night,* but it has the virtue of an oblique approach to a familiar genre and iconography that makes an easy transition from circumstantial detail to epic perspective. As a study of misbegotten energy run wild, it is as American as *Kane.* It was a modest film, though, whereas *Kane* set out to demolish and remake the temple of narrative film. Yet both films have a serene, willful disdain for the surrounding industry. In Welles's case, that attitude was a challenge to the picture business. But for Malick it seems increasingly like the lofty indifference of deliberate art. Whatever his failings, Welles had a zest for show business; he liked to chew on audiences. Malick's second film, *Days of Heaven,* underlined the European archness of the first, and it was as blithe and self-sufficient as a painting labored over in an attic. Whether we see Malick as leisurely or elitist in his approach, two such mannered films in twenty years bespeak an exquisite and uncompeting talent.

Malick was the son of an oil man, sent to Harvard and then awarded a Rhodes scholarship. He read philosophy and alternated between journalism and teaching at MIT, before he tried Greystone, the AFI academy in California. He thrived there and started writing scripts. He has a credit on *Pocket Money* (72, Stuart Rosenberg), a study of lugubrious male companionship that inaugurates the listless surrealism of dim people as conceived by a fine mind in the narration of Malick's two feature films. It is unique and eloquent; but it comes close to being patronizing.

Badlands is derived from a real incident, but its tone is the half-understood legend of fame pursued by boys watching James Dean and girls steeped in romantic magazines. Its beauty is never obtrusive or patronizing toward the uncultivated characters. The story moves on with an energetic fatalism, worthy of *You Only Live Once,* another of its sources. The narration was poignant rather than portentous, and the playing by Martin Sheen and Sissy Spacek was far more gripping than the numb gestures of *Days of Heaven.* Above all, *Badlands* balanced the externals of landscape and violence with their imaginative resonance. It was legitimate for the film to avoid explanation because the action was so dense and eloquent, the myth so solid and matter-of-fact.

Days of Heaven was a very disappointing follow-up. The imagery had become thunderous and stately, as if Malick and Nestor Almendros were so greedy for prestige that they couldn't release a frame unless it had that sentimental, decorous spaciousness beloved by Andrew Wyeth. And as the image had grown in vanity, so the action subsided into a vague biblical allegory. Monologue was used again, with such helpless repetition that one was forced to question Malick's inventiveness.

His obsession seemed defensive and wilting, even if it was unique. The young outlaws now appeared to be shadowy symbols becalmed by significance.

After that, Malick became not just an absentee but a recluse. It was said that he did an early script for what became *Great Balls of Fire* (89, Jim McBride). Occasionally, magazine journalists attempted to discover where he was and what he might have been doing.

There was enormous anticipation for *The Thin Red Line*. I can think of few recent American movies in which so many critics and viewers hoped to find glory and excellence. What happened? I have read a script (by Malick) very different from, and far more challenging than, the picture released. Yes, *The Thin Red Line* is "beautiful," but that sort of beauty had always been Malick's greatest jeopardy. It is also flagrantly incoherent and terribly arty. Too many of the dazzling cast are wasted, or embarrassed. One longs to hear the full story of how that film went astray.

John Malkovich, b. Benton, Illinois, 1953
There are people who rank Malkovich among the handful of top American actors of the moment—though they probably think of stage as much as screen. Yet is there more than a handful (at the level of audience) that wants to see him—let alone in leading romantic roles? There is no hiding his strangeness—gangling frame, thick legs, receding hair, buttony eyes, blank look, hallucinated voice . . . to all of which Malkovich brings a deliberate, nearly insolent, affectlessness. He does not seem quite normal or wholesome—he can easily take on the aura of disturbance or unqualified nastiness. So it is all the more remarkable that, by the age of fifty, he does stay within reach of being a lead actor.

From the University of Illinois, he joined the Steppenwolf theatre company in Chicago. It was there that he made his initial impact, and to this day he declares a greater allegiance to theatre work—"I don't like seeing this scene taken and put here when it was specifically constructed to be put there. Who the fuck says they [directors] can do that? I wouldn't *dream* of doing that to a *writer's* work."

He was seen first on the small screen: *Word of Honor* (81, Mel Damski); *American Dream* (81, Damski); as the older brother in Sam Shepard's *True West* (82, Gary Sinise and Alan Goldstein), a Steppenwolf production, transferred to American Playhouse. He played the blind man and won a supporting actor nomination in *Places in the Heart* (84, Robert Benton); *The Killing Fields* (84, Roland Joffe); *Eleni* (85, Peter Yates); as Biff to Dustin Hoffman's Loman in *Death of a Salesman* on Broadway and then as a TV movie (85, Volker Schlondorff); *Making Mr. Right* (87, Susan Seidelman); *The Glass Menagerie* (87, Paul New-

man); excellent as the survivor rat in *Empire of the Sun* (87, Steven Spielberg); and *Miles from Home* (88, Sinise).

He bought the rights to Anne Tyler's *The Accidental Tourist*, but then let William Hurt play the lead in the movie (88, Lawrence Kasdan); a box-office success, as Valmont in *Dangerous Liaisons* (88, Stephen Frears); on British TV, with Kate Nelligan and Miranda Richardson, in Harold Pinter's *Old Times* (90, Simon Curtis); brilliantly, innocently self-destructive in *The Sheltering Sky* (90, Bernardo Bertolucci); very droll in *The Object of Beauty* (91, Michael Lindsay-Hogg); *Queens Logic* (91, Steve Rash); *Shadows and Fog* (92, Woody Allen); a very gentle giant in *Of Mice and Men* (92, Sinise); and *Jennifer 8* (92, Bruce Robinson).

His intelligence and mischief were put to very cunning ends playing the assassin in *In the Line of Fire* (93, Wolfgang Petersen). With sheer deft detail of reaction and stealthy malice he made his killer essential to the movie's game. We love our movie monsters so much, and *In the Line of Fire* may have sealed Malkovich's future in villainy. For TV, he was Kurtz, up the river and as high as old cheese, in *Heart of Darkness* (94, Nicolas Roeg).

In the years since, Malkovich has made himself an institution—not just a fine and versatile actor but one who seems to divine the ease with which modern cinema ranges between garbage (*Con Air*) and ventures of exceptional integrity (*The Portrait of a Lady, Shadow of the Vampire*). In a single gesture or drawled word, Malkovich can go from high camp to rare delicacy. It leaves him as maybe the most mannered and riveting of modern players. As for his attitude—his mix of humor and adventure—one has only to realize the immense support he gave to *Being John Malkovich*—as if secure that no one else could do it.

Just think of the range, the risk, and the fun in this recent list: *Beyond the Clouds* (95, Wim Wenders and Michelangelo Antonioni); *The Convent* (95, Manuel de Oliveira); Jekyll and Hyde in *Mary Reilly* (96, Stephen Frears); the test site director in *Mulholland Falls* (96, Lee Tamahori); *Der Unhold* (96, Volker Schlondorff); Osmond in *The Portrait of a Lady* (96, Jane Campion); Cyrus the Virus in *Con Air* (97, Simon West); Athos in *The Man in the Iron Mask* (98, Randall Wallace); *Rounders* (98, John Dahl); as Charlus in *Time Regained* (99, Raul Ruiz); *Being John Malkovich* (99, Spike Jonze); the Dauphin in *Messenger: The Story of Joan of Arc* (99, Luc Besson); Herman Mankiewicz in *RKO 281* (99, Benjamin Ross); Murnau in *Shadow of the Vampire* (00, Elias Merhige); Javert in *Les Misérables* (00, Josee Dayan); *Les Ames Fortes* (01, Ruiz).

Does anyone so particular work harder: *Hotel* (01, Mike Figgis); *Je Rentre à la Maison* (01, de Oliveira); as Talleyrand on TV in *Napoleon* (02,

Yves Simoneau); and, at last, sublime casting, Ripley in *Ripley's Game* (02, Liliana Cavani). He also acted in *Johnny English* (03, Peter Howitt), and then directed a first film—*The Dancer Upstairs* (03)—altogether too calm and plain.

Louis Malle (1932–95),
b. Thumeries, France
1956: *Le Monde du Silence* (codirected with J. Y. Cousteau) (d). 1957: *Ascenseur pour L'Échafaud/ Lift to the Scaffold; Les Amants*. 1960: *Zazie dans le Métro*. 1962: *Vie Privée*. 1963: *Le Feu Follet/ Will of the Wisp*. 1965: *Viva Maria!*. 1967: *Le Voleur*. 1968: "William Wilson," an episode in *Histoires Extraordinaires*. 1969: *Inde 68* (d); *Calcutta* (d). 1971: *Le Souffle au Coeur/Dearest Love*. 1973: *Lacombe Lucien*. 1975: *Black Moon*. 1978: *Pretty Baby*. 1980: *Atlantic City*. 1981: *My Dinner with Andre*. 1984: *Crackers*. 1985: *Alamo Bay; God's Country* (d). 1987: *Au Revoir les Enfants*. 1990: *Milou en Mai/May Fools*. 1992: *Damage*. 1994: *Vanya on 42nd Street*.

A student at IDHEC, Malle participated on Cousteau's voyages for several years and was then assistant to Robert Bresson on *Un Condamné à Mort s'est Échappé* (56). Although he began to work at the same time as the New Wave directors, he was a speculative, conventional talent: sophisticated and polished, but moving rather aimlessly from one subject to another, only rarely discovering more than entertainment in his films. Too often, his choice of material was overambitious or fashionable, and his working out of human situations melodramatic. At worst, he had a taste for glossy, commercial packages that masquerade as artiness, and it seemed reasonable to regard him as the successor to such proficient but shallow directors as Autant-Lara and Duvivier.

Ascenseur pour L'Échafaud was a good thriller, though without the moral undertones in Chabrol's films, that wore its Miles Davis score rather modishly. *Les Amants* was a claustrophobic exercise in passion disrupting the bourgeoisie, foolishly proclaimed in its time for sexual candor but as cold as plastic flowers and with a fatal, world-weary slowness. It was also one of Jeanne Moreau's few heartless pictures. It may have been the eye for polite taste that suggested *Les Amants;* it was certainly a search for intellectual respectability that prompted *Zazie*, a crushingly unfunny film. *Vie Privée*, made with American money, was an opportunist decoration on Brigitte Bardot's own life, helpless with the limits of the woman and driven to an awful mock-operatic ending.

Even so, Malle captured huge audiences with his idiotic pairing of Bardot and Moreau in *Viva Maria!*, a silly extravaganza that was exactly the sort of "modern film" required by audiences frightened of Godard and Rohmer. His Indian documentaries, including a series of films shot for television, showed his visual elegance but offended many Indians with their superficial criticism of the country. The most glaring crack in Malle's output is the meretricious *Le Souffle au Coeur*, a sub-Truffaut study of youth in the 1950s, full of accurate detail and not without charm or humor, but ruined by its dependence on an unconvincing and rosily conveyed moment of incest.

Only two films stand out from this persistent cheating. *Le Feu Follet*, based on a novel by Drieu la Rochelle, penetrates a man's advance on suicide. This mood of pessimism is more compelling still in *Le Voleur*, Malle's best French film, a study of chronic theft as a response to social decay. It thrives on the abrupt laconicism of Belmondo and ends with one character saying, "Life seems so cold . . . We are surrounded by madness . . . It is so wearying." It is the most revealing moment in Malle's work, even if the other films might suggest it was only glib fatalism.

Pretty Baby was Malle's American debut, rich with the promise of a piquant subject, Sven Nykvist as photographer, and the eerie poise of Brooke Shields. It probably trapped itself in that it had to be timid to protect the child actress from charges of pornography and exploitation. The interior atmosphere of the brothel from the child's point of view was managed very well, but caution and taste smothered the city of New Orleans, the jazz, and the trade of sex. Worse, the beguiling topic of a photographer who can only make love with a lens was thrown away.

In his last years, Malle won a reputation as a smart, shrewd, but discerning "international" director. *Atlantic City* is a droll, noirish picture, and *My Dinner with Andre* was deemed a model of piquant originality in its day. But does anyone want to see it again? In recollection, it seems a meal to avoid, the meeting of two fabricated creatures, caught in a conversation enough to take away one's appetite. Even *Atlantic City* suffers a little from the cutes—and benefits from its writer, John Guare, from the raffish, aging heroics of Burt Lancaster, and the lemony fragrance of Susan Sarandon (who was Malle's squeeze at the time).

Elsewhere? *Crackers* and *Alamo Bay* are mistakes, without touch or understanding. *Au Revoir les Enfants* is Malle at his best in its story of children, Jewishness, loyalty, and betrayal during the war. *May Fools* is a sidebar, and *Damage* is a meretricious horror novel dressed up as something momentous. There is something subservient in Malle's devotion to its very nasty, rigged plot and to its hollow people. As so often, Malle seemed like a minor figure with pretensions to mastery. His eminence spoke to grave shortages of competition.

Dorothy Malone (Dorothy Eloise Maloney),
b. Chicago, 1925

She came into the movies during the war in small roles in *Falcon and the Co-Eds* (43, William Clemens), *One Mysterious Night* (44, Budd Boetticher), *Show Business* (44, Edwin L. Marin), and *Hollywood Canteen* (45, Delmer Daves), but her first impact was in Hawks's *The Big Sleep* (46), letting down her hair, removing her glasses, and shutting up shop while she entertained Bogart one thundery afternoon. She was always a bonus, never a star, and seldom used to the full, but quickly looking more mature than her age, soulful and lived in, a great lady of the B picture.

She soon outgrew ingenues: Curtiz's *Night and Day* (46); *Two Guys from Texas* (48, David Butler); Walsh's *One Sunday Afternoon* (49) and *Colorado Territory* (49); Daves's *To the Victor* (48); *South of St. Louis* (49, Ray Enright); *The Nevadan* (50, Gordon Douglas); Quine's *Pushover* (54); Siegel's *Private Hell 36* (54); *Young at Heart* (55, Douglas); *Battle Cry* (55, Walsh), with one splendid erotic moment when she undresses in an armchair; Corman's *Five Guns West* (55); especially brazen for Douglas Sirk as the headstrong sister in *Written on the Wind* (56), for which she won a supporting actress Oscar; and *The Tarnished Angels* (57) as a parachutist, wife, mother, and lover. Sirk's films demand self-belief in players, and Malone steered her wanton women past absurdity by sheer languorous conviction. She was also in *Pillars of the Sky* (56, George Marshall); *Tension at Table Rock* (56, Charles Marquis Warren); *Man of a Thousand Faces* (57, Joseph Pevney); *Tip on a Dead Jockey* (57, Richard Thorpe); as Diana Barrymore in *Too Much, Too Soon* (58, Art Napoleon); *Warlock* (59, Edward Dmytryk); horribly trapped throughout *The Last Voyage* (60, Andrew L. Stone); and *The Last Sunset* (61, Robert Aldrich). She then went into TV for *Peyton Place*, but has been seen in *Gli Insaziabili* (69, Alberto de Martino); *Abduction* (75, Joseph Zito); *The November Plan* (76, Don Medford); *Golden Rendezvous* (77, Ashley Lazarus); *Winter Kills* (79, William Richert); *The Day Time Ended* (80, John Cardos); *Good Luck, Miss Wyckoff* (79, Marvin J. Chomsky); *Condominium* (80, Sidney Hyers); *The Being* (83, Jackie Kong); *He's Not Your Son* (84, Don Taylor); *Peyton Place: The Next Generation* (85, Larry Elikann); and *Rest in Peace* (86, Joseph Braunstein).

Then, after a few years away, she returned briefly as a sad-eyed but polite veteran of murder in *Basic Instinct* (92, Paul Verhoeven), one of the few understated things in that picture, and thus all the more tempting—if only the movie could have gone off with her.

David Mamet, b. Chicago, 1947
1987: *House of Games.* 1988: *Things Change.* 1991: *Homicide.* 1994: *Oleanna.* 1997: *The Spanish Prisoner.* 1999: *The Winslow Boy.* 2000: *State and Main; Catastrophe* (s). 2001: *Heist.*

Prolific, hooked on the Ping-Pong of idiomatic dialogue that sometimes rules entire plays, Mamet has not established a character in movies as more than a cold, skilled mechanic. The films he has directed are games, or intrigues, but neither playful nor absorbing: the flamboyantly shallow Joe Mantegna seems like Mamet's ideal actor, grabbing attention but warding off scrutiny. Mamet's work has more power in the theatre—*American Buffalo*, especially—where he seems more comfortable trapped in time and space. *Speed-the-Plow* was overpraised as a play, for it does little more than run with the grisly riffs of two Hollywood men. But Mamet is altogether too beguiled by the staccato boasting of show-off guys. *Speed-the-Plow* had some satirical cutes, but it had nothing to wound the objects of the satire. Indeed, they loved it.

Mamet has done screenplays for *The Postman Always Rings Twice* (81, Bob Rafelson); *The Verdict* (82, Sidney Lumet); *The Untouchables* (87, Brian De Palma); *Lip Service* (88, W. H. Macy—for TV); *We're No Angels* (89, Neil Jordan); and *Glengarry Glen Ross* (92, James Foley), from his own Pulitzer Prize–winning play. But only *The Untouchables* caught the rattling tone of his plays, and only *The Verdict* (from a Barry Reed novel) had the smell of reality and place or the ruined lives and comical subterfuge of his plays.

One of the best things about *The Verdict* is the playing of Lindsay Crouse, Mamet's wife from 1977 to 1989. She is also the central figure in *House of Games*, so grimly controlling that the film closes around her enigma. Women are not quite Mamet's subject—as witness the nonevent of Madonna in *Speed-the-Plow*.

It seems to me that movie exposes the limits of a Mamet, just as it teaches us the self-satisfied tricks in a Pinter. To see Foley's *Glengarry Glen Ross* and the TV movie of Pinter's *Old Times* (90, Simon Curtis) was to discover the time-killing aridness in brilliant situations, crackling talk, and magnificent acting. How could such great actors be such wretched salesmen? It's a question that slowly collapses the movie as it proceeds, and leaves one aware of Mamet's imprisoned cruelty, the sadism that dots every "i."

In the nineties, Mamet has concentrated increasingly on movies—at the expense of playwriting. In hindsight, his very creative script for *Hoffa* (92, Danny DeVito) looks a vital step in that progress, and a welcome sign of human and social character. On the whole, however, the enclosed aridity remains—even with Mamet's new wife, Rebecca Pidgeon, in it, *The Winslow Boy* seemed a very odd choice, and the movie of *Oleanna* rang more false than the stage show. But *The Spanish Prisoner* was an intriguing puzzle, and *State and Main* even had hints of relaxation.

Mamet has been very active as a screenwriter,

though I can't say that the films made by others are any worse than, or distinct from, those he has done himself: *A Life in the Theater* (93, Gregory Mosher); *Vanya on 42nd Street* (94, Louis Malle); *Texan* (94, Treat Williams); *American Buffalo* (96, Michael Corrente); *The Edge* (97, Lee Tamahori); *Wag the Dog* (97, Barry Levinson); *Ronin* (98, John Frankenheimer); *Lansky* (99, John McNaughton); *Hannibal* (01, Ridley Scott), written with Steven Zaillian; *Whistle* (03, Lumet).

Rouben Mamoulian (1897–1987),
b. Tiflis, Russia

1929: *Applause*. 1931: *City Streets*. 1932: *Dr. Jekyll and Mr. Hyde; Love Me Tonight*. 1933: *Song of Songs*. 1934: *Queen Christina; We Live Again*. 1935: *Becky Sharp*. 1936: *The Gay Desperado*. 1937: *High, Wide and Handsome*. 1939: *Golden Boy*. 1940: *The Mark of Zorro*. 1941: *Blood and Sand*. 1942: *Rings on Her Fingers*. 1947: *Summer Holiday*. 1952: *The Wild Heart* (U.S. version of Michael Powell's *Gone to Earth*, with extensive fresh material by Mamoulian). 1957: *Silk Stockings*.

Mamoulian's is a fascinating career—like one of his own movies, a garland of pretty blooms held together without obvious support. Few other directors of his facility worked so spasmodically in movies, or made such disparate material unmistakably their own. What seems at first sight a disordered involvement in cinema is based on the most profound and fruitful integrity: Mamoulian, despite a distinguished career in the theatre, recognized that films were a matter of light and sound gracefully rendered on celluloid. At times, his ingenuity led him into preciousness, but much more often he succeeded on his own terms—the wish to blend movement, dancing, action, music, singing, decor, and lighting into one seething entity. His films rustle with sound and shimmer with the movement of light on faces, color, and decoration. More than any other director—more than Lubitsch, even—he should be known for his touch.

Educated at the universities of Moscow and London, Mamoulian also studied at the Moscow Arts Theatre. He first directed for the stage in London in 1922 and the next year joined the American Opera Company. That began a career as a stage director that ran concurrently with his work in the cinema. His first five films were made at Paramount and are notable for their exploration of sound and for their ranging between emotional intensity and satire on forced feelings. *Applause* is one of the best early sound films, with fascinating location work in New York. In *Applause* and *City Streets,* based on a story by Dashiell Hammett, Mamoulian evolved a highly wrought imagery, with shadow effects and camera movements, that comes to a climax in the magnificent *Jekyll and Hyde.* Just as Mamoulian had brought out the tragedy in a musical (*Applause*) and comedy in a gangster film (*City Streets*), so his *Jekyll and Hyde* is a horror film that barely seems frightening because of its emotional basis and because of the conviction Mamoulian brings to his Paramount London and to the idea of transformation. Given the swashbuckling *Mark of Zorro,* he managed to convey the impression of Tyrone Power and Basil Rathbone dancing to an unheard score.

Love Me Tonight is an hour of originality, a little too unrelenting to be appealing: a weirdly clever opening montage of street sound effects; rhyming dialogue; immense tracking shots; a parody of *Congress Dances;* suspended dissolves; and Chevalier doing the Apache song with his own shadow huge on the wall behind him. Each detail is fetching, but it is Mamoulian's failing that they do not add up and that the invention is glitteringly ostentatious. This stylistic precociousness did not improve Mamoulian's relations with the studios and few of his films were commercial successes. He is known, too, for the first Technicolor movie, *Becky Sharp,* even though the color is bitter and its use far too schematic, despite the miracle of pique flushing Miriam Hopkins's avid face.

Mamoulian's best films are often the least known or admired. *Queen Christina* is not as good as its famous set pieces, the bedroom scene, and the last close-up for which Mamoulian instructed Garbo: "I want your face to be a blank sheet of paper. I want the writing to be done by every member of the audience." Much better are *High, Wide and Handsome, Summer Holiday,* and *Silk Stockings,* three musicals outside the general pattern of the form and all critically neglected. The first is a period musical, with Jerome Kern songs and extraordinary set pieces; the second is an adaptation of Eugene O'Neill's *Ah, Wilderness!* with enchanting small-town atmosphere and open-air routines (Mamoulian later did *Oklahoma!* on stage); the last, a remake of *Ninotchka,* with Astaire and Cyd Charisse, has some of the best intimate dances in the history of the musical, subduing the expanses of CinemaScope screen and, in its amused but insistent preference for American glamour to Soviet rationality, reminding us that Mamoulian was an exile.

There is an interesting sidelight to Mamoulian's career of credits narrowly won and lost. He directed *Becky Sharp* only when the original director, Lowell Sherman, died. Against that, he worked on the script and rehearsed *Laura* before being replaced by Otto Preminger. As if that was not loss enough, he was intended to direct *Porgy and Bess*—he had directed the original stage production—but once again Preminger intervened. Last, Mamoulian began *Cleopatra* before the journeymen hacks, Mankiewicz and Darryl F. Zanuck, squandered its potential.

Silvana Mangano (1930–89), b. Rome
The gap between Italian neo-realism and the striving after international markets that dominated Cinecitta in the 1950s is straddled by the magnificent thighs of the teenage Silvana Mangano in *Bitter Rice* (49, Giuseppe de Santis). The social comment of that film was swamped by its popular elements, chief of which was Mangano, her skirts tucked up, standing in the rice fields. She had been trained as a dancer and performed with a rough, erotic energy in that film. Already, she had made two films—*Il Delitto di Giovanni Episcopo* (47, Alberto Lattuada) and *L'Elisir d'Amore* (48, Mario Costa)—but *Bitter Rice* was a vast hit, and in 1949 she married its producer Dino de Laurentiis.

That was enough to assure her of a place as a leading Italian actress, but for some fifteen years she was overshadowed—by Lollobrigida and Loren, her reluctance to go to America, and the nagging thought that the boss's wife need be no great actress. However, after 1966, she became a leading actress for Pier Paolo Pasolini and proved more beautiful in middle age than ever she was in that paddy field: *Black Magic* (49, Gregory Ratoff); *Il Brigante Musolino* (50, Mario Camerini); *Anna* (51, Lattuada); *Mambo* (54, Robert Rossen); *Gold of Naples* (54, Vittorio de Sica); as Penelope in *Ulysses* (55, Camerini); *Uomini e Lupi* (56, de Santis); *Tempest* (57, Lattuada); *The Sea Wall* (58, René Clément); *Five Branded Women* (60, Martin Ritt); *La Grande Guerra* (60, Mario Monicelli); *Crimen* (60, Camerini); *Una Vita Difficile* (61, Dino Risi); *Il Giudizio Universale* (61, de Sica); *Barabbas* (62, Richard Fleischer); *Il Processo di Verona* (62, Carlo Lizzani); in two episodes, directed by Mauro Bolognini and Luigi Comencini, from *La Mia Signora* (64); *Il Disco Volante* (65, Tinto Brass); in *Le Streghe* (66, Luchino Visconti, Bolognini, Pasolini, and de Sica); *Oedipus Rex* (67, Pasolini); *Theorem* (68, Pasolini); *Medea* (69, Pasolini); *Death in Venice* (71, Visconti); *The Decameron* (71, Pasolini); *Conversation Piece* (75, Visconti); *Dune* (84, David Lynch); and *Dark Eyes* (87, Nikita Mikhalkov).

Joseph L. (Leo) **Mankiewicz** (1909–93), b. Wilkes-Barre, Pennsylvania
1946: *Dragonwyck*. 1947: *The Late George Apley; The Ghost and Mrs. Muir; Somewhere in the Night*. 1948: *Escape*. 1949: *A Letter to Three Wives; House of Strangers*. 1950: *No Way Out; All About Eve*. 1951: *People Will Talk*. 1952: *Five Fingers*. 1953: *Julius Caesar*. 1954: *The Barefoot Contessa*. 1955: *Guys and Dolls*. 1958: *The Quiet American*. 1959: *Suddenly Last Summer*. 1963: *Cleopatra*. 1967: *The Honey Pot*. 1970: *There Was a Crooked Man*. 1972: *Sleuth*.

Mankiewicz's first job was for *The Chicago Tribune* in Berlin in 1928. While there, he also worked for UFA on subtitles, and in 1929 he went back to America to join his older brother Herman in Hollywood. There he worked on dialogue, titling, and story adaptation: *River of Romance* (29, Richard Wallace); *Thunderbolt* (29, Josef von Sternberg); *Fast Company* (29, Edward Sutherland); and *The Saturday Night Kid* (29, Sutherland). Within a few years, he had become a leading writer at Paramount: *Slightly Scarlet* (30, Louis Gasnier); *The Social Lion* (30, Sutherland); *Skippy* (32, Norman Taurog); *Million Dollar Legs* (32, Edward Cline); *This Reckless Age* (32, Frank Tuttle); and *Alice in Wonderland* (33, Norman Z. McLeod). He then moved to MGM and scripted three W. S. Van Dyke pictures: *Manhattan Melodrama* (34); *Forsaking All Others* (34); and *I Live My Life* (35).

By 1936 he was promoted to producer and made an auspicious if uncharacteristic debut with *Fury* (36, Fritz Lang). After that, his credits included: *Three Godfathers* (36, Richard Boleslavsky); *The Bride Wore Red* (37, Dorothy Arzner); *Mannequin* (38, Frank Borzage); *The Shopworn Angel* (38, H. C. Potter); *Three Comrades* (38, Borzage), the film on which he rejected Scott Fitzgerald's subtleties and provoked the cry "Can't a producer be wrong?"; *The Shining Hour* (38, Borzage); *The Adventures of Huckleberry Finn* (39, Richard Thorpe); *Strange Cargo* (40, Borzage); *The Philadelphia Story* (40, George Cukor); and *Woman of the Year* (42, George Stevens). In 1943 he moved to Fox to write and produce *The Keys of the Kingdom* (44, John M. Stahl) and, after the war, he remained at that studio to become a director.

Although still only thirty-five, it was remarkable how long Mankiewicz had chosen, or been made, to wait before directing. He is the classic instance of the efficient writer-producer who directs almost because there is no one else around to do it; in fact, his debut, the silly but florid *Dragonwyck*, arose with the last illness of Ernst Lubitsch. It took him his first five films to discard the worst defects of a training in dialogue and construction. *George Apley*, for instance, is an absurdly prolix, mannerly picture. But Mankiewicz's virtues were always literary: he could handle complicated stories involving flashbacks, interior monologues, half a dozen characters, and intricate plots—*A Letter to Three Wives; All About Eve; Five Fingers; The Barefoot Contessa;* he wrote intelligent, sarcastic dialogue, usually based on an ironic central figure, able to comment on the life he was observing: George Sanders in *Eve*, James Mason in *Five Fingers,* and Bogart in *The Barefoot Contessa.*

Above all, he created the atmosphere of a proscenium arch, a little Shavian in the way he arranged action for an audience. It was often enough that pungent situations, witty dialogue, and smart playing concealed his indifference to what a film looked like or his inability to reveal the emotional depths beneath dialogue. Tidiness, his great asset in the eyes of Hollywood, was his gravest handicap artistically. It limits *Eve* and *Five Fingers* to smart entertainments and leaves him helpless with the greater demands of *The Quiet American* and *Suddenly Last Summer.* There is something sad but final about the way so seasoned a professional was called in to salvage *Cleopatra,* and by emphasizing the talk just made the visual opulence seem more pointless. One has only to think of what Mamoulian—*Cleopatra's* original director—might have made with so much money, to realize Mankiewicz's deficiencies. *Guys and Dolls* is a pleasant film with songs, but defiantly without mood; *The Barefoot Contessa* is somewhat overrated; *People Will Talk,* a superb vehicle for Cary Grant, shows all Mankiewicz's skill and moderation. But *Sleuth* is a grotesque throwback to theatricality, indicative of Mankiewicz's readiness to be fooled by cleverness.

That said, for the early 1950s, Mankiewicz was the epitome of smart entertainment. He got the best director and best screenplay Oscars two years in a row, with *A Letter to Three Wives* and *All About Eve,* and the latter won best picture. In addition, Mankiewicz was a droll talker, full of great anecdotes and magnificent indiscretion, not always reliable but usually biting. He could explain everything except the lack of a pressing theme in his own work.

Anthony Mann (Emil Anton Bundsmann) (1906–67), b. San Diego, California
1942: *Dr. Broadway; Moonlight in Havana.* 1943: *Nobody's Darling.* 1944: *My Best Gal; Strangers in the Night.* 1945: *The Great Flamarion; Two O'Clock Courage; Sing Your Way Home.* 1946: *Strange Impersonation; The Bamboo Blonde.* 1947: *Desperate; Railroaded; T-Men.* 1948: *Raw Deal.* 1949: *Reign of Terror; Border Incident; Side Street.* 1950: *Devil's Doorway; Winchester 73; The Furies.* 1951: *The Tall Target.* 1952: *Bend of the River/Where the River Bends.* 1953: *The Naked Spur; Thunder Bay.* 1954: *The Glenn Miller Story; The Far Country.* 1955: *Strategic Air Command; The Man from Laramie.* 1956: *The Last Frontier; Serenade.* 1957: *Men in War; The Tin Star.* 1958: *God's Little Acre; Man of the West.* 1960: *Cimarron.* 1961: *El Cid.* 1964: *The Fall of the Roman Empire.* 1965: *The Heroes of Telemark.* 1968: *A Dandy in Aspic* (completed by Laurence Harvey after the death of Mann).

In Mann's great days as a director—in the forties and fifties—he had few intelligent admirers in America. Nowadays, he is taken for granted as someone from "that golden age." But, in truth, Mann's value arose in that age of transition after the gold: his heroes face more testing problems than gold allowed. So acceptance doesn't necessarily entail understanding, or the ability to look at what's happening on the screen—much less how it's happening. That's how Mann was neglected in his heyday, and that's why many people still regard movies as versions of theatre or literature. (It was good form to think well of Mankiewicz, Wyler, Zinnemann, and Kramer in the fifties.) Anthony Mann is one of those directors who has to be witnessed—on a big screen—before understanding can begin.

Even so, he owed a good deal to collaborators—to John C. Higgins, who wrote *Railroaded, T-Men, Raw Deal,* and *Border Incident;* to photographer John Alton, who shot *T-Men, Raw Deal, Reign of Terror, Border Incident,* and *Devil's Doorway;* to James Stewart, of course; to Borden Chase, who wrote *Winchester 73, Bend of the River,* and *The Far Country;* and to Philip Yordan, who wrote *Reign of Terror, The Man from Laramie, The Last Frontier, Men in War, God's Little Acre, El Cid,* and *The Fall of the Roman Empire.*

It's worth stressing those collaborators because—despite my admiration—I'm not sure that Mann was always master of his films. There's no doubting the savage economy of the B pictures from the forties, their dash of cruelty, and the panache of the lighting. But Mann was not, I think, by nature claustrophobic or quite as neurotic as those noirs suggest. It's no disparagement if he simply directed the earlier films, seeing what they were good for and getting the most out of them. It may be wishful thinking to reckon that anyone in Hollywood could have dreamed of imposing himself on a series of B pictures.

But in the fifties, with better budgets and more liberty, there's no question about emergent personality. Mann's Westerns are psychological, and his best heroes are beset by self-doubt. But it's too big a stretch to call those films neurotic when they revel in the beauty of daylight, space, and distance. Rather, I would suggest that Mann discovered his own Western sensibility, which was to see human stories as small, and even aberrant, in the vastness of terrain. Thus, *Winchester 73* is a round, a circle, that needs huge horizons; while in *El Cid,* the real beach at Valencia reaches into legend. No one has ever matched that feeling for heroic openness.

Whenever he went too far away from the Western, Mann looked a very conventional director, which is to say that *Men in War* and *El Cid* are disguised Westerns, working toward an ordeal by combat that defines honor. But *Serenade* is intolerable, or so Mann makes it seem despite the presence of his wife, Sarita Montiel; *Strategic Air Command* is boringly filled with giant aircraft; *The*

Glenn Miller Story is overwhelming nostalgia, but too obedient to fond memories of the bandleader to give the screen characters an existence of their own; *Thunder Bay*—even with James Stewart—is indifferent; *The Fall of the Roman Empire* and *The Heroes of Telemark* are without urgency; and *God's Little Acre* is a restrained attempt at the cheerful bawdiness of Erskine Caldwell.

The most intriguing failure is *The Tin Star*, a Western in which bounty hunter Henry Fonda educates raw sheriff Anthony Perkins and is himself domesticated. The set pieces in that film are VistaVision crisp, and the camera movements like proofs of theorems, for no other director could so elucidate violence. But most of the film is set in a town and its message is simplistically in favor of civic order and domestic calm—ideas that are remote from Mann's best work, apart from the matriarchal *Cimarron*. *The Tin Star* illustrates Mann's tendency to be clinical or academic, and both Fonda and Perkins look like business executives dressed up in cowboy togs.

Even his best Westerns—*Winchester 73, The Naked Spur, Bend of the River, The Far Country, The Man from Laramie*, and *The Last Frontier*—seem in retrospect rather too neatly self-contained. The parable starkness of the stories and the flawless command of the landscape photography tend to sidestep the actual issues of honor, betrayal, violence, and death that the films claim to deal with. What motivates so many of them is the presence of James Stewart and his suppressed neuroses as the adventurer hero. The concept of responsibility in *The Far Country* and of vengeance in *The Man from Laramie* turn on Stewart's involvement.

As a rule, though, Mann does not touch his actors very much. If they are not well cast he is prepared to ignore them and withdraw his camera to observe some of the most articulated moments of combat in the cinema: the implacable pursuit in *Bend of the River;* the scene at the salt flats in *The Man from Laramie;* the death of Walter Brennan in *The Far Country;* the entire, traveling engagement in *Men in War,* so abstract that the enemy is barely seen, so physical that one could draw a contour map of the terrain. The achievement of this topographical photography is unique in the history of the Western, and at its best it is inseparable from the feeling of peril in the conflict. At times one marvels at the combined visual elegance and emotional exhaustion in a film. *The Man from Laramie*, especially, is filled with pain, and it benefits from the fullest exposition of the friendly treachery in Arthur Kennedy. While *The Last Frontier* has an unusual hero, an Indian scout, and contains, from Anne Bancroft, one of the very few good performances from an actress in all of Mann's work.

Brilliant as these Westerns are, they remain a trifle neat and complacent. Mann might not deserve his high place on their strength alone. But *Men in War, Man of the West*, and *El Cid* substantially enlarged his commitment to the action he observes so faithfully. In all three, he managed to invest a legendary situation with an extra significance. No one could have doubted that *Men in War* would have a visual exactness beyond criticism, but its argument—that violence must be total if it is to succeed, and that its success is destructive of the man who resorts to it—is applied without any slackening, so that the last scenes of the film are resigned and foreboding.

In *Man of the West,* Mann has a dying Gary Cooper as his hero, an ex-outlaw robbed by former comrades. Whereas some of the Stewart films seem like exercises out of doors, there is no escaping the tragedy of *Man of the West* or the way it affects the Cooper character. Not as clean-looking as his earlier Westerns, it is more cruel and penetrating.

El Cid was an astonishing departure and a total success. Its treatment of the Spanish hero is based on Mann's abiding interest in the strains put upon the man of honor and the way that he vindicates himself through trial of arms. The simplicity of the conception does not seem artificial; instead it relates to the cinema's earliest portraits of the virtuous hero and to the medium's power to combine physical and moral tension. Austerely devoid of medievalism, *El Cid's* epic format contains vicious hand-to-hand battles that are made pivotal to the hero's integrity. Perhaps Mann was the last director able to see a Manichaean struggle within battle and to convey that significance without demur. Real battles are messy—like Fuller's—but Mann's are artistically ordered by heroic optimism, the very quality we feel being extinguished in *Men in War* and *Man of the West.*

Daniel Mann (1912–91),

b. Brooklyn, New York

1953: *Come Back, Little Sheba.* 1954: *About Mrs. Leslie.* 1955: *The Rose Tattoo; I'll Cry Tomorrow.* 1956: *The Teahouse of the August Moon.* 1958: *Hot Spell.* 1959: *The Last Angry Man; The Mountain Road.* 1960: *Butterfield 8.* 1961: *Ada.* 1962: *Five Finger Exercise; Who's Got the Action?* 1963: *Who's Been Sleeping in My Bed?.* 1965: *Our Man Flint; Judith.* 1968: *For Love of Ivy.* 1969: *A Dream of Kings.* 1970: *Willard.* 1971: *The Revengers.* 1978: *Matilda.* 1980: *The Incredible Mr. Chadwick; Playing for Time* (TV). 1981: *The Day the Loving Stopped.* 1987: *The Man Who Broke 1,000 Chains* (TV).

An actor and a musician, in 1939 he worked in Canada. After the war he directed on Broadway and worked with Elia Kazan. His films were bound by theatrical conventions and an allegiance to overblown female performances. His debut, *Come Back, Little Sheba,* was intended to display Shirley Booth, but although she won the Oscar, her performance was fussy and unfelt beside the anguished restraint of Burt Lancaster. To dispel the idea that Mann might have a good relationship with Lancaster, *The Rose Tattoo* encouraged his worst gloating and viewed Anna Magnani's feverish emotions rather clinically. Even so, *I'll Cry Tomorrow* allows Susan Hayward to suffer to her heart's content and *Teahouse* was one of Brando's oddest distractions. Mann helped earn a best actress Oscar for Elizabeth Taylor in *Butterfield 8,* one of her splendid, posturing performances. In eight years, Mann led three actresses to Oscar—Booth, Magnani in *Rose Tattoo,* and Liz Taylor. Seen at this distance, that trio stands for the strange fantasies of the fifties.

In the 1960s, Mann's work hardly moved from a rut of boredom—only James Coburn's *Flint* lightened the gloom. To judge by *For Love of Ivy* and *Willard,* he was trying desperately to discover novelty.

The wonder was that Mann continued to enjoy respectable projects in an era when Gerd Oswald was driven to TV, and Edgar Ulmer turned into a nomad of the backstreet quickie.

But Mann was very successful, for TV, directing Arthur Miller's script of *Playing for Time,* and he deserves credit for obtaining (and controlling) such performances from Vanessa Redgrave, Jane Alexander, Shirley Knight, and Viveca Lindfors (among others). It is unthinkable that Mann could have found such an opportunity by working only in theatrical movies.

Delbert Mann, b. Lawrence, Kansas, 1920
1955: *Marty.* 1957: *The Bachelor Party.* 1958: *Desire Under the Elms; Separate Tables.* 1959: *Middle of the Night.* 1960: *The Dark at the Top of the Stairs.* 1961: *Lover Come Back; The Outsider.* 1962: *That Touch of Mink.* 1963: *A Gathering of Eagles.* 1964: *Dear Heart; Quick, Before It Melts.* 1965: *Mister Buddwing.* 1967: *Fitzwilly.* 1968: *The Pink Jungle.* 1970: *David Copperfield.* 1971: *Jane Eyre; Kidnapped.* 1975: *Birch Interval.* 1977: *Tell Me My Name.* 1978: *Love's Dark Ride* (TV); *Home to Stay* (TV); *Breaking Up* (TV); *Thou Shalt Not Commit Adultery* (TV). 1979: *All Quiet on the Western Front* (TV); *Torn Between Two Lovers* (TV). 1980: *To Find My Son* (TV). 1981: *Night Crossing.* 1983: *Bronte; The Gift of Love: A Christmas Story* (TV). 1984: *Love Leads the Way* (TV). 1986: *Death in California* (TV); *The Last Days of Patton* (TV). 1986: *The Ted Kennedy Story* (TV). 1988: *April Morning* (TV). 1991: *Ironclads* (TV). 1992: *Against Her Will: An Incident in Baltimore* (TV). 1994: *Incident in a Small Town* (TV); *Lily in Winter* (TV).

Mann was educated at Vanderbilt and Yale universities, and after war service in the air force he worked in stock as a director. In 1949 he joined NBC and became a director on Philco Playhouse and many other series, handling the original productions of *Marty* and *The Bachelor Party.*

It is a long way from the TV originality of Paddy Chayefsky's *Marty* and *Bachelor Party* to Mann's hollow adaptations of nineteenth-century classics. Delbert Mann was among the most welcomed of directors who broke into movies from TV in the mid-1950s. *Marty* was a modest artistic achievement, but a popular novelty, given Oscars as tokens of Hollywood's good intentions. *Marty* was already flawed by the sentimentality that has increased in Mann's work—not least in the casting of Ernest Borgnine, a stock heavy only able to work through pathos. But *The Bachelor Party* was a far better film, beautifully acted and with an accurate sense of American middle-class anxieties, such as only John Cassavetes has since explored.

Perhaps Mann was warned off such mundane subjects. For he switched disastrously to stage adaptations, the first hopelessly inadequate, the second shamelessly ticking off every cliché in Rattigan's original—the well-made film. *Middle of the Night* was Chayefsky again with touching performances from Fredric March and Kim Novak. But Burl Ives and Sophia Loren *Under the Elms* were hopelessly shaded by the looming poetry of O'Neill's language.

In the 1960s, Mann lost interest and submitted to facile romances. Only *Dear Heart* and *Mister Buddwing* are watchable—for the sake of Glenn Ford and Geraldine Page in the first and Jean Simmons in the latter. Mann has since turned to devour himself. Once the prophet of TV realism, he makes bland TV versions of Great Novels. His *David Copperfield* is drab beside Cukor's, and *Jane Eyre,* despite George C. Scott and Susannah York, is not as enjoyable as the Orson Welles–Joan Fontaine haunted house version.

Mann became a stalwart of TV movies, versatile but anonymous, known for his proficiency. He did a version of *All Quiet on the Western Front* that used Richard Thomas and Ernest Borgnine; *Bronte* was Julie Harris doing her one-woman show on Charlotte Brontë; *The Gift of Love* was schmaltz; *The Last Days of Patton* lured George C. Scott back to his best-known role.

Michael Mann, b. Chicago, 1943
1979: *The Jericho Mile* (TV). 1981: *Thief.* 1983: *The Keep.* 1986: *Manhunter.* 1992: *The Last of the Mohicans.* 1995: *Heat.* 1999: *The Insider.* 2001: *Ali.*

No one has done more to uphold, extend, and enrich the film noir genre in recent years than Michael Mann. He is a director and producer, an organizer of TV series, a visionary of modern style who somehow integrates the fluency of Max Ophuls with the iconic poise of the most hip TV commercials. His theatrical movies come years apart, but his work for television has filled the time and been just as vital and creative a part of what he does. For Mann, *The Last of the Mohicans* was a conscious breaking of new ground, and instinctively he found not just an atmosphere and a sound but a style to fit the primeval forest and man's struggle to survive with dignity. As for civilization, in Michael Mann's eyes that has always been a tenuous extra.

He was educated at the University of Wisconsin and the London Film School, and he went on to write for the TV series *Police Story* and *Starsky and Hutch*. He was cowriter, as well as director, on *The Jericho Mile*, which had Peter Strauss as a Folsom Prison inmate who tries to make the Olympic team. Within the bounds of a TV movie, Mann brought out both the ferocity and the absurdity of the attempt to find redemption in hell.

Thief is, in many ways, another version of that same theme, with James Caan as an increasingly hopeless criminal whose grasp on integrity is canceled as the story unfolds. *The Keep* does not work nearly as well, but it has a group of German soldiers who stick to a benighted mission. Nothing matters in Mann's world so much as that ultimate resolution. It is the most interesting, quietist form of male dedication in our movie landscape crowded with macho posturing.

Manhunter is an unfairly neglected picture, largely because its Hannibal Lecter is less spectacular than that of Anthony Hopkins and Jonathan Demme. But *Manhunter* knows the dread with which the questing mind of the cop comes close to occupying that of the serial killer. Its puzzle is engrossing, and Mann's use of vivid supporting players can scarcely be rivaled today.

Nevertheless, it is Mann's TV work that looms largest. He has been the creator, and steady controller, of two series: *Miami Vice* (1984–89) and *Crime Story* (1986–88). The first is by far the better known. It recognized the potency of Miami (was Mann inspired by De Palma's *Scarface*?); it employed the drive of pop music and the patina of modern design; it was a racial melting pot, very sexy and violent; and it recovered the career of Don Johnson, while making a bizarre Hispanic cult out of Edward James Olmos. *Miami Vice* is pulp, but full of ideas, often gorgeous, rarely dull, and hugely influential—not only Miami aped it; TV ads picked up on Miami's electric colors.

Crime Story is several degrees greater. Indeed, the many hours of this unsuccessful series amount to a true American epic. It was a series and serial: the struggle between cop Mike Torello (Dennis Farina) and hood Ray Luca (Anthony Dennison) spanned years and reached from a Midwest city to the Nevada deserts, all propelled by Del Shannon's "Runaway." Watching it, week after week, was one of the joys of the mid-eighties, with meaty performances not just from the leads but from John Santucci, Stephen Lang, Jon Polito, Ted Levine, Joseph Wiseman, and Darlanne Fluegel and Patricia Charbonneau, who join Tuesday Weld, Madele'ue Stowe, Ashley Judd, and Amy Brenneman in Mann's corps of resolute dames in tight corners.

By the late nineties, Mann had clearly moved further ahead. *Heat,* it seems to me, was one of the best-made films of the decade, by which I mean that the need to look and listen closely was constantly rewarded. But even that richness of texture could not overcome the thematic triteness—the jungle prowled by cops and crooks alike. What more did it need? Less attitude, less deep-seated respect for these loner men, and a more intricate tracing of how money works. Something like the same could be said for *The Insider*—it was riveting and very well acted (though Al Pacino was allowed to be lazy in both films), but its view of different kinds of compromise was too pat. I think Mann the director needs better writing than he has been getting. But no one does film with better touch.

Ali, I fear, is his least interesting film, smothered in impersonation and evasion, an irrelevant footnote to all the newsreel and documentary.

Jayne Mansfield (Vera Jayne Palmer) (1934–67), b. Bryn Mawr, Pennsylvania
Jayne Mansfield is the swan song of prenude sexuality in films. For thirty years, since the coming of the Hays Code, Hollywood eroticism depended on the invitation to sex beneath whatever provocative clothing could be made to stay in place. There is an engineering of sexual fashion, whereby uplift is obtained without visible means of support, that is a matter of some technical ingenuity and of which Jayne Mansfield is the masterpiece. When she leans forward in Frank Tashlin's *The Girl Can't Help It* there is an extreme equation of tit exposed and fantasy induced. What the lady looked like in the raw might still be beyond public tolerance. Our cinema nudes are lean ladies, confined to some perfect diet and faintly adolescent. Because Jayne Mansfield was widely laughed at, it is now assumed that she was happy to deride her own comic-book glory. There is no evidence for or against that wishful thinking, but some to suggest that there was an actress trying to escape.

She made her debut in *Underwater* (54, John Sturges), and was in *Prehistoric Women* (55, Gregg Tallon), *The Female Jungle* (55, Bruno Ve Sota), *Illegal* (55, Lewis Allen), the excellent *The Burglar* (55, Paul Wendkos), and *Pete Kelly's Blues* (55, Jack Webb), before Tashlin used her in *The Girl Can't Help It* (56) and *Will Success Spoil*

Rock Hunter? (57), the latter a part she had created on the stage. Her real fame was short-lived: *The Wayward Bus* (57, Victor Vicas); *Kiss Them for Me* (57, Stanley Donen); and *The Sheriff of Fractured Jaw* (58, Raoul Walsh). She was soon forced farther afield to work and a number of European films were mixed with nightclub work: *Too Hot to Handle* (60, Terence Young); *The George Raft Story* (61, Joseph Newman); *It Happened in Athens* (62, Andrew Marton); *L'Amore Primitivo* (64, Luigi Scattini); *Single Room Furnished* (66, Matt Cimber, her third husband); and *Spree!* (67, Mitchell Leisen).

Jean Marais (Jean Villain-Marais) (1913–98), b. Cherbourg, France

The magnificent but rather fatuous blond figurehead of Jean Cocteau's world, Marais has been more icon than actor. He was absurdly Apollonian, even if he has since grown heavy and grumpy—as witness his lecherous king in *Peau d'Âne* (70, Jacques Demy). Indeed, Marais in other people's films tended to define the way Cocteau gave life to visually splendid but statuesque elements. Thus he lights up under Cocteau's fancy, especially in *Orphée* (50, Cocteau), where he was the numbed protagonist of the provincial mythology.

The beautiful young Tristan of *L'Eternal Retour* (43, Jean Delannoy, from a Cocteau script) became a thirty-five-year-old straining to look more youthful in *L'Aigle à Deux Têtes* (47, Cocteau) and *Les Parents Terribles* (48, Cocteau). And if, in reality, he was something of a dullard, then *Beauty and the Beast* (45, Cocteau and René Clément) gave him an opportunity to embody monstrousness. The makeup in that film had only to be worn, but that had always been Cocteau's method—beauty or ugliness in his films are emblematic. Marais said that Cocteau never directed speech or gesture but that he bathed entire crews in his own creative gaze—"he radiates a strength my pen cannot render, but of which my friendship and admiration are intensely aware."

He had been a stage actor for some ten years before he got into films, and had played in *Les Parents Terribles* in the theatre. But his movie record shows how far he was a star chiefly in Cocteau's firmament: *Le Pavillon Brûle* (41, Jacques de Baroncelli); *Le Lit à Colonne* (42, Roland Tual); *Voyage sans Espoir* (44, Christian-Jaque); *Les Chouans* (46, Henri Calef); *Ruy Blas* (47, Pierre Billon); *Le Secret de Mayerling* (49, Delannoy); *Le Château de Verre* (50, Clément); *La Voce del Silenzio* (52, G. W. Pabst); *Napoléon* (55, Sacha Guitry); the fire-eating general in *Eléna et les Hommes* (56, Jean Renoir); *SOS Noronha* (56, Georges Rouquier); *Typhon sur Nagasaki* (56, Yves Ciampi); *White Nights* (57, Luchino Visconti); *Un Amour de Poche* (57,

Pierre Kast); *Le Testament d'Orphée* (60, Cocteau); *Austerlitz* (60, Abel Gance and Roger Richebé); *La Princesse de Clèves* (60, Delannoy); *Ponzio Pilato* (61, Irving Rapper); *Fantômas* (64, André Hunebelle); *Patate* (64, Robert Thomas); *Fantômas se Déchaîne* (65, Hunebelle); *Le Paria* (68, Claude Carliez). He was in *Le Jouet Criminel* (70, Thomas); he did a version of *Les Parents Terribles* (80, Yves André Hubert) for television; *Ombre et Secrets* (82, Philippe Delabre); *Lieu de Parente* (85, Willy Rameau); and *Parking* (85, Demy).

Fredric March (Fredric Ernest McIntyre Bickel) (1897–1975), b. Racine, Wisconsin

March is a good instance of the durable leading man, much relied upon by major studios, but never a star who dominated audiences. The bulk of his work is nonassertive: he was content to give thoughtful, sensitive performances in support of either a real star or the plot of the film. Working often with his wife, Florence Eldridge, he moved between Broadway and Hollywood and thus acquired a reputation for seriousness that sometimes looked a little stodgy on film. But he had moments that are hard to forget: his Norman Maine in *A Star Is Born* (37, William Wellman) seems now to give that supposedly positive product a dark, cold after-feeling—he is so good as a drunk, so stricken by self-loathing and lost confidence. It is a performance of great daring, a gathering of horror stories about Hollywood crack-ups. And somehow it is the most glamorous thing March ever did. For in giving up the ghost, he found allure. Whereas striving to be appealing, he could be a little too classy sometimes.

He played a few small film parts in the early 1920s, but it was only with the coming of sound and after several years' work in the theatre that March prospered. He had the looks and voice to carry off the romantic comedies that Paramount specialized in, and he was contracted by that studio for *The Dummy* (29, Robert Milton). He was loaned out for *Paris Bound* (29, Edward H. Griffith) and *Jealousy* (29, Jean de Limur), opposite Jeanne Eagels; while at Paramount he was in *Sarah and Son* (30, Dorothy Arzner); *Ladies Love Brutes* (30, Rowland V. Lee); *Manslaughter* (30, George Abbott); *Laughter* (30, Harry d'Arrast); *The Royal Family of Broadway* (30, George Cukor and Cyril Gardner), in which he took the John Barrymore part; *Honor Among Lovers* (30, Arzner); *The Night Angel* (31, Edmund Goulding); and *My Sin* (31, Abbott).

In most of these, March was subordinate to his female costar, but he established himself, and won the best actor Oscar, in the tour de force of Mamoulian's *Dr. Jekyll and Mr. Hyde* (32). As in all Mamoulian's films, the performance was only the jewel in an elaborate setting (in this case the trick of transformation), and although the film added to March's prestige it did not deepen his screen character. But for the next few years he worked hard as one of the most desirable leading men: *Merrily We Go to Hell* (32, Arzner); Sidney Franklin's *Smilin' Through* (32); in De Mille's *The Sign of the Cross* (33); *The Eagle and the Hawk* (33, Stuart Walker); Lubitsch's *Design for Living* (33); and the figure of Death in Mitchell Leisen's *Death Takes a Holiday* (34).

At this stage, March refused to re-sign with Paramount and began free-lancing. Inevitably, he was caught up in the costume films that were in vogue: *The Affairs of Cellini* (34, Gregory La Cava); as Browning opposite Norma Shearer in Franklin's *The Barretts of Wimpole Street* (34); in Mamoulian's *We Live Again* (34), a version of Tolstoy's *Resurrection;* in *Les Miserables* (35, Richard Boleslavsky); Vronsky to Garbo's *Anna Karenina* (35, Clarence Brown); Bothwell to Katharine Hepburn's *Mary of Scotland* (36, John Ford); and *Anthony Adverse* (36, Mervyn Le Roy). He then made three films in a row that mark his best work: Hawks's *The Road to Glory* (36), and *A Star Is Born* (37) and *Nothing Sacred* (37), both for William Wellman. Next, he was in De Mille's *The Buccaneer* (38) and after a return to the theatre he made *Susan and God* (40, Cukor) and *Victory* (40) and *So Ends Our Night* (41), both for John Cromwell.

During the war, apart from René Clair's *I Married a Witch* (42) and *The Adventures of Mark Twain* (44, Irving Rapper), his material became more sentimental, and in 1946 he won his second Oscar for Wyler's *The Best Years of Our Lives.* The part's Oscar appeal was very obvious, but March found the real, awkward man.

He still did theatre—notably *A Bell for Adano* and *Long Day's Journey Into Night*—but his movies lacked stature: *Another Part of the Forest* (48, Michael Gordon); *An Act of Murder* (48, Gordon); as *Christopher Columbus* (49, David MacDonald); Willy Loman in *Death of a Salesman* (51, Laslo Benedek); *Man on a Tightrope* (53, Elia Kazan); *Executive Suite* (54, Robert Wise); *The Bridges at Toko-Ri* (55, Mark Robson); the father in *The Desperate Hours* (55, William Wyler); an interesting tycoon, half-Paley, half-Selznick, in *The Man in the Gray Flannel Suit* (55, Nunnally Johnson); Philip of Macedon in *Alexander the Great* (56, Robert Rossen); and very good as an older man infatuated with Kim Novak in *Middle of the Night* (59, Delbert Mann).

But he had seldom been worse than as William Jennings Bryan in *Inherit the Wind* (60, Stanley Kramer) and after that he made only four ill-assorted films: *The Young Doctors* (61, Phil Karlson); *Seven Days in May* (64, John Frankenheimer); a rare scoundrel in *Hombre* (67, Martin Ritt); and *Tick . . . Tick . . . Tick* (69, Ralph Nelson).

Chris Marker (Christian François Bouche-Villeneuve), b. Ulan Bator, Mongolia, 1921 (The previous edition and other reference books give Belleville, France, as his place of birth—but Marker told me himself that Mongolia is correct.) All films are documentaries, except for *La Jetée:* 1952: *Olympia '52.* 1953: *Les Statues Meurent Aussi* (codirected with Alain Resnais). 1955: *Dimanche à Pékin.* 1957: *Le Mystère de l'Atelier 15* (codirected with Resnais). 1958: *Lettre de Sibérie.* 1959: *Les Astronautes* (codirected with Walerian Borowczyk). 1960: *Description d'un Combat.* 1961: *Cuba Si!.* 1963: *Le Joli Mai; La Jetée.* 1965: *Le Mystère Koumiko.* 1966: *Si C'Etait Quatre Dromadaires.* 1968: *La Sixième Face du Pentagon.* 1969: *A Bientôt, J'Espère.* 1970: *La Bataille des Dix Millions* (codirected with Valerie Mayoux); *Les Mots Ont un Sens.* 1971: *Le Train en Marche.* 1977: *Le Fond de l'Air est Rouge.* 1981: *Junkopia* (s). 1982: *Sans Soleil.* 1984: *2084* (s). 1985: *A.K.* 1986: *Hommage à Simone Signoret.* 1988: *L'Heritage de la Chouette* (TV—thirteen-part series). 1993: *Le Dernier Bolchevik/The Last Bolshevik.* 1997: *Level Five.* 2000: *Une Journée d'Andrei Arzenevitch.* 2002: *Le Souvenir d'un Avenir.*

Jean Queval once called Marker "our unknown cosmonaut." It was a striking idea that, while Americans trod the ashy moon in cumbersome suits, so Marker with camera over his shoulder—like Dziga Vertov's hero—had proved himself a more penetrating traveler.

But Chris Marker is not just a promise of a world to come. Perhaps his physical existence in the era of Hitler, Hiroshima, Castro, and the new Israel is simply a nexus of ideas that reach back and forward in time. Marker is here, with us, but perhaps he is a man of the twenty-second and of the eighteenth centuries. Of course, it is easier to look for men who resemble Marker in our past than estimate where he stands in the future. It is quite possible that he is an ordinary enough fellow in the twenty-second century, for he does not carry himself with the self-importance expected of filmmakers in our present age. His films see nothing exceptional in an inquisitive traveler sending back films about the lands he has seen and the thoughts he has had while there.

For anyone who has not seen a Marker film, their varied effects may be compared with that obtained in reading the journal of some eighteenth-century traveler: Johnson in the Hebrides, Rousseau's promenade through his own sensibility, or Goethe's visit to Rome. The work makes no attempt to be cinematic or literary; it is based, instead, on the assumption that a cultivated man should express himself in words or in film. Add to that the engaging fusion of seriousness and humor; a precise eye for strange places and a quizzical response to unfamiliar people; an easy ability to move from the very small to the large and to see no slick simile or impossible gulf between the activity of an individual and the nature of a country. Beneath all this, there is the unaffected independence of a man who sees that all people are travelers, lonely or self-sufficient—depending on the cast of mind—whether they lap the Earth or stay at home.

Of course, we do not yet send letters to our friends that are sixty-minute films as informative, entertaining, and personal as Marker's. But we will, otherwise we must leave reports of foreign lands and strange ideas to the strident opinions of documentary TV, which invariably forsakes experience, research, and soul. Marker has visited several of the most newsworthy locales of modern times—Peking, provincial Russia, Tokyo, Israel, and Cuba—and returned with a report (or description) that bypasses the fixed problems that are supposed to beset our view of those places.

The variety of what he sees can only be hinted at here, just as the style of his films takes advantage of most of the unexpected freedoms of conversation. In *Lettre de Sibérie,* there is a delightful passage—about road-making in Iakoutsk—that incorporates the mutual incomprehension of Soviet and American propaganda films, without taking sides or forgetting that both stereotypes are parts of the total truth. For Marker knows how far men decide what is truth and untruth, how reality is colored by opinion. The babel of opinion delights him as much as the odd juxtaposition of modernity and antiquity. And perhaps it is because he is French that he has the sense to see life imitating art. Thus, this commentary on an Israeli girl in *Description d'un Combat* over our undirected view of the girl in a camera style that subverts the camera's neutrality as little as possible:

On the other side of fear, children are born.
They come to you and say "Tsalemoti"—Photograph me.
They are good-looking. Legend has them as tall and blond. But sometimes Oriental grace has corrected this European model, and among the Rubens there are Chagalls.
They multiply. You photograph this boy drawing. When you come back to film there are already two of them.
How many will there be next year? Who will they be? Who will she be, this little Jewess who will never be Anne Frank?

One might detect in that Marker's own leftist views. He was in the French Resistance during the war and he played an important organizing part in the final editing of *Loin du Vietnam* (67). *Les Statues Meurent Aussi* is hostile to imperialism, though less on doctrinaire grounds than out of a sense of betrayed ethnic nature. And if *Cuba Si!* is enthusiastic, its basis is not so much Marxist as the vitality of ordinary Cubans. Marker makes a

habit of catching us unawares. In *Lettre de Sibérie* there is a moment when he notices a resemblance between a Siberian and André Gide—it is an ephemeral point, but it weighs more strongly on the side of human experience than would a manifesto. And in *Si C'Etait Quatres Dromadaires* (or is it *Mystère Koumiko?*—as in correspondence, the individual dispatches run together) there is a moment in which Marker discovers, some ten years later, a survivor from the massacre of the secret police in Budapest in 1956. Politically, that survivor is anathema to Marker, but the peculiarity of his story and the way Marker recalls it through the famous photographs taken by John Sadovy in 1956 dispels animosity.

The man, and Marker's recognition of him, become events in the placid absorption of its experience by the world. Although he believes in the written word, Marker loves the photograph and its importance in the evolution of memory and conscience. He sees that all people live through the exchange of signs—outward facts that become transmuted into private fancies. His friendship with Resnais is signaled in this sense of the unreliability of memory, as if Diderot doubted the Encyclopedie. Here in *L'Amérique Rêve*—a commentary to an imaginary film, or to a film somewhat spoiled by François Reichenbach—Marker sees an entire people in solitariness: "So, America dreams. The prisoner in his prison, the traveller in his photographs, the black in his carnival, the young girl in her plans, the man in his memories."

L'Amérique Rêve stresses Marker's interest in his writings, an interest that makes his *Commentaries*—scripts illustrated by frames—works of art and not just the record of films. Marker began as a writer: he is the author of a novel and a study of Giraudoux, and was an editor with Editions du Seuil. His first film, on the Helsinki Olympiad, was strictly amateur, but Marker has not allowed himself to become rigidly professional. His originality has not made it easy for his films to be seen. It was only in the early 1960s that he became fashionable enough for showings outside France. Perhaps interested in his own success, he made two films of general appeal: *Le Joli Mai* was set in Paris, with a Rouch-like cinema verité study of a specific mood and moment. Even so, it manages to bear the flavor of a stranger's view. *La Jetée* is a marvelous thirty-minute science-fiction film that reclaims the filmed still photograph from rarefied prettiness and specious historicity.

But at the time of *Loin du Vietnam*, Marker forsook his accustomed solitariness: not just in the collaborative direction of that film, but with the founding in 1966 of SLON (*Société de Lancement des Oeuvres Nouvelles*). By 1968, Marker reactivated SLON and set in motion a group enterprise in filmmaking, especially to record the new workers' impulse to observe themselves on film. A

Bientôt deals with a factory in Lyons and *La Bataille des Dix Millions* is a commentary on a speech by Fidel Castro. SLON also made contact with the Russian documentarist, Medvedkin, revived his film *Happiness* (35), and made a film of their own, *The Train That Never Stops*, about the ciné-trains on which Medvedkin and his unit traveled and recorded the new Bolshevik state.

Sans Soleil is Marker's greatest work of the last decade or so, a documentary format that leads into a revery on Japan, technology, and the conjunction of different times and peoples in the world. It shows how rich the potential is for filmmaking, like the writing of essays and the keeping of journals. It is a tragedy that the collected work of Marker (and there are films not listed in my filmography, not even released or finished) is so hard to find. But he is innately elusive, just as much as he is a master of discovery.

The Last Bolshevik is a series of letters to Alexander Medvedkin, supported by interviews, footage from Soviet films, and newsreels and one of the most trenchant commentaries Marker has ever allowed himself. Indeed, it voices much anger at the failure of Communism.

Mae Marsh (Mary Wayne Marsh) (1895–1968), b. Madrid, New Mexico

The story is told in Robert Henderson's study of Griffith at Biograph how the director once had a shotgun fired off behind Mae Marsh to get the necessary alarm on her face. The effect apparently lasted several years.

In *The Birth of a Nation* (15, D. W. Griffith), she is the sister perpetually fearful of a fate worse than death, on the point of taking flight with so much fluttering agitation and the breathy intake of apprehension. Sadly, though, when pursued to the top of a cliff and most in need of wings, she plunges to her death, virginal, but like a sandbag.

She joined Griffith's company from school in 1912 and became one of his leading young ladies: *The Old Actor; A Siren of Impulse; The Lesser Evil; Lena and the Geese; The New York Hat;* accepting the grass skirt and bare feet declined by Mary Pickford for *Man's Genesis; The Sands of Dee; Brutality; The Telephone Girl and the Lady; An Adventure in the Autumn Woods* (all 12); *Fate; Love in an Apartment Hotel; The Perfidy of Mary; The Little Tease; The Wanderer; His Mother's Son; The Reformers; In Prehistoric Days; The Battle of Elderberry Gulch; Judith of Bethulia* (all 13); *The Escape; Home Sweet Home; The Avenging Conscience* (all 14).

Then, after her self-sacrifice in *The Birth of a Nation*, she was desperate again as the woman in the modern episode of *Intolerance* (16)—hers made the famous close-up of hands wrung together in anguish. She left Griffith for Goldwyn and starred in *Polly of the Circus* (17), *Spotlight*

Sadie (18), and *The Little 'Fraid Lady* (20). But in the 1920s she made only a few films before retiring in 1926: *Nobody's Kid* (21, Howard Hickman); to Britain for *Flames of Passion* (22, Graham Cutts); reunited with Griffith and starring with Ivor Novello in *The White Rose* (23); *Daddies* (24, William A. Seiter); and *Tides of Passion* (26, J. Stuart Blackton).

She made a comeback in the 1930s, but in much smaller parts: *Over the Hill* (31, Henry King); *Little Man, What Now?* (34, Frank Borzage); *The Grapes of Wrath* (40, John Ford); still frantic as Rochester's wife in *Jane Eyre* (44, Robert Stevenson); *A Tree Grows in Brooklyn* (45, Elia Kazan); *The Snake Pit* (48, Anatole Litvak); as Mrs. Purley Sweet in *Three Godfathers* (48, Ford); *The Gunfighter* (50, King); *The Robe* (53, Henry Koster); *The Sun Shines Bright* (53, Ford); *Blueprint for Murder* (53, Andrew Stone); *The Prince of Players* (55, Philip Dunne); *While the City Sleeps* (56, Fritz Lang); *The Searchers* (56, Ford); *Julie* (56, Stone); *The Wings of Eagles* (57, Ford); *Sergeant Rutledge* (60, Ford); and *Donovan's Reef* (63, Ford).

Garry Marshall (Marscharelli), b. New York, 1934

1982: *Young Doctors in Love.* 1984: *The Flamingo Kid.* 1986: *Nothing in Common.* 1987: *Overboard.* 1989: *Beaches.* 1990: *Pretty Woman.* 1991: *Frankie and Johnny.* 1994: *Exit to Eden.* 1996: *Dear God.* 1999: *The Other Sister; Runaway Bride.* 2001: *The Princess Diaries.*

Marshall is a very uneven director: *Exit to Eden* is a mess; *Nothing in Common* didn't work as it might have done; *Frankie and Johnny* was crushed by its star casting. On the other hand, *The Flamingo Kid* is an enjoyable comedy, with skilled performances from Matt Dillon and the richly fraudulent Richard Crenna. Then there's *Pretty Woman.* Few films took a worse critical battering, and surely it is wide open to charges of lunatic fantasizing. But without lunatic fantasy where would the movies be? I think *Pretty Woman* is so cunning and so well done that its white lies become creamy and intriguing. And its plain mean-spirited not to see that Julia Roberts is wonderful in it—nearly as good as Hector Elizondo.

So Marshall is a worthwhile figure, simply as a director. Of course, there's far more to it. For he has been a giant figure in the production of TV comedy. Having worked as a writer on *The Lucy Show* and *The Dick Van Dyke Show,* he went on to be a producer on *Hey Landlord* (66–67), *The Odd Couple* (70–75), *Happy Days* (74–84), *Laverne and Shirley* (76–83, which costarred his sister, Penny), and *Mork & Mindy* (78–82). From that alone, we are likely talking about one of the highest earners in the business.

More than that, he is a capable comic actor, very funny in *Lost in America* (85, Albert Brooks) and also in *Psych-Out* (68, Richard Rush); *Soapdish* (91, Michael Hoffman); *A League of Their Own* (92, Penny Marshall); and *Hocus Pocus* (93, Kenny Ortega).

He then made the ultra-naïve *The Princess Diaries*. In 2001. Not 1901.

George Marshall (1891–1975), b. Chicago

1919: *The Adventures of Ruth*. 1920: *Prairie Trails*. 1921: *After Your Own Heart; Hands Off; The Jolt; The Lady from Longacre; A Ridin' Romeo; Why Trust Your Husband?*. 1922: *Smiles Are Trumps*. 1923: *Don Quickshot of the Rio Grande; Men in the Raw; Where Is the West?*. 1926: *A Trip to Chinatown*. 1927: *The Gay Retreat*. 1932: *Pack Up Your Troubles* (codirected with Raymond McCarey); *Their First Mistake* (s). 1934: *Ever Since Eve; Wild Gold; She Learned About Sailors; He Learned About Women; 365 Nights in Hollywood*. 1935: *Life Begins at Forty; Ten Dollar Raise; In Old Kentucky; Show Them No Mercy; Music Is Magic*. 1936: *A Message to Garcia; Crime of Dr. Forbes; Can This Be Dixie?*. 1937: *Nancy Steele Is Missing; Love Under Fire*. 1938: *The Goldwyn Follies; Battle of Broadway; Hold That Co-Ed*. 1939: *You Can't Cheat an Honest Man; Destry Rides Again*. 1940: *The Ghost Breakers; When the Daltons Rode*. 1941: *Pot o' Gold; Texas*. 1942: *Valley of the Sun; The Forest Rangers; Star-Spangled Rhythm*. 1943: *True to Life; Riding High*. 1944: *And the Angels Sing*. 1945: *Murder He Says; Incendiary Blonde; Hold That Blonde*. 1946: *The Blue Dahlia; Monsieur Beaucaire*. 1947: *The Perils of Pauline; Variety Girl*. 1948: *Hazard; Tap Roots*. 1949: *My Friend Irma*. 1950: *Fancy Pants; Never a Dull Moment*. 1951: *A Millionaire for Christy*. 1952: *The Savage*. 1953: *Off Limits/Military Policeman; Scared Stiff; Houdini; Money from Home*. 1954: *Red Garters; Duel in the Jungle; Destry*. 1955: *The Second Greatest Sex*. 1956: *Pillars of the Sky*. 1957: *Guns of Fort Petticoat; Beyond Mombasa; The Sad Sack*. 1958: *The Sheepman; Imitation General*. 1959: *The Mating Game; It Started With a Kiss; The Gazebo*. 1960: *Cry for Happy*. 1962: *The Happy Thieves; How the West Was Won* (codirected); *Papa's Delicate Condition*. 1964: *Dark Purpose* (codirected with Vittorio Sala); *Advance to the Rear/Company of Cowards*. 1966: *Boy, Did I Get a Wrong Number!*. 1967: *Eight on the Lam*. 1969: *Hook, Line and Sinker*.

Marshall had few equals for labor and survival. In 1912 he was an extra, and by 1914 he was acting in Universal shorts and serials. He was a director by 1917, on Ruth Roland serials, Harry Carey Westerns, and even Bobby Jones golf shorts. His output of silent features was, in fact, considerably larger than his list of sound films. Only in the six-

ties did the pace begin to tell. Marshall seemed to have consented to retirement, and his last three movies were disappointing. But until the early 1960s he was an able director of most forms of comedy. Indeed, he had directed not only Laurel and Hardy, W. C. Fields (*You Can't Cheat an Honest Man*), Bob Hope (in *Fancy Pants* and *Monsieur Beaucaire,* as well as the two duds in 1967), Martin and Lewis (in their first film *My Friend Irma* and in *Scared Stiff*), but the droll Western, *The Sheepman*. That film, coaxing out the gentle humor of Glenn Ford, is one of his most engaging and characteristic pictures.

Longevity persuaded some commentators into the belief that Marshall had worked in all possible genres. This is not true: he disliked real violence, and hardly touched the crime film, the horror film, or the serious war picture, though *Advance to the Rear* relates to that genre as *The Sheepman* does to the Western. His happiest forte was mild, satirical comedy—*The Sheepman* is in much the same vein as *Destry Rides Again*, that inspired pairing of Dietrich and James Stewart. He had made straight Westerns, but with less success. Equally, *The Ghost Breakers* (remade as *Scared Stiff*) is a comic approach to horror. Among musicals, the stylized *Red Garters* was years ahead of its time (Marshall replaced Mitchell Leisen on that film). *The Blue Dahlia* is an excellent Alan Ladd/Veronica Lake romantic thriller. Marshall had also shown a taste for glamorous, scarcely accurate biopics and *Incendiary Blonde* (Betty Hutton as Texas Guinan), *The Perils of Pauline* (Hutton as Pearl White), and *Houdini* (Tony Curtis) are enjoyable hokum.

Herbert Marshall (1890–1966), b. London

Marshall was forty before becoming seriously involved with the cinema. By then, he had twenty years' stage experience in England and America, lost a leg in the First World War, but never quite shed the sobriety of early years spent apprenticed to a chartered accountant. Paramount planned to make him a great lover, but Marshall needed to move carefully in case his limp showed, and his good manners eventually reduced him to character parts. He was always thoughtful, able enough for the most intelligent comedy, and seldom out of place: it is tempting in retrospect to think of him as Paramount house servant in tales of overheated emotion—discreet and detached. With age, his work became exaggerated, but he could still rise to worthwhile material.

Mumsie (27, Herbert Wilcox) was his debut, in England, but he came to the fore opposite Jeanne Eagels in America in *The Letter* (29, Jean de Limur). However, for the next few years he divided his time between Hollywood and England, where his then-wife Edna Best worked. In 1930 he made his first talking picture, Hitchcock's *Murder*, and in 1931 he made *Michael and Mary* (Victor Saville) and went back to America to be opposite Claudette Colbert in *Secrets of a Secretary* (George Abbott). He followed this success with *Blonde Venus* (32, Josef von Sternberg) and, one of his best, immaculate but amoral in *Trouble in Paradise* (32, Ernst Lubitsch). Back in England, he made *The Solitaire Man* (33, Jack Conway) and *I Was a Spy* (33, Saville), but when his marriage ended he concentrated on American films: *Four Frightened People* (34, Cecil B. De Mille); *Riptide* (34, Edmund Goulding); *Outcast Lady* (34, Robert Z. Leonard); *The Painted Veil* (34, Richard Boleslavsky); *The Good Fairy* (35, William Wyler); *The Flame Within* (35, Goulding); and *The Dark Angel* (35, Sidney Franklin).

Marshall was slipping into character parts, but he was excellent in *The Lady Consents* (36, Stephen Roberts) and *Forgotten Faces* (36, E. A. Dupont), and as the deceived husband in *Angel* (37, Lubitsch). He had to engage in many dull films, where his expression sometimes suggested that his other leg had gone numb, but he usually made the most of good parts: *Zaza* (39, George Cukor); the husband in *The Letter* (40, Wyler); a suave paternal villain in *Foreign Correspondent* (40, Hitchcock); opposite Bette Davis in *The Little Foxes* (41, Wyler); in *When Ladies Meet* (41, Leonard); as the Maugham narrator in *The Moon and Sixpence* (42, Albert Lewin); in Jules Dassin's *Young Ideas* (43); *The Enchanted Cottage* (45, John Cromwell); Maugham again in *The Razor's Edge* (46, Goulding); the father in *Duel in the Sun* (46, King Vidor). He kept working, if a little less earnestly, until his death: *Ivy* (47, Sam Wood); *The High Wall* (48, Curtis Bernhardt); *The Secret Garden* (49, Fred M. Wilcox); *The Underworld Story* (50, Cy Endfield); *Anne of the Indies* (51, Jacques Tourneur); *Something to Live For* (52, George Stevens); the weak father in *Angel Face* (52, Otto Preminger); *The Black Shield of Falworth* (54, Rudolph Maté); *The Virgin Queen* (55, Henry Koster); *Stage Struck* (58, Sidney Lumet); *Midnight Lace* (60, David Miller); and *The Third Day* (65, Jack Smight).

Penny Marshall, b. Bronx, New York, 1942
1986: *Jumpin' Jack Flash*. 1988: *Big*. 1990: *Awakenings*. 1992: *A League of Their Own*. 1994: *Renaissance Man*. 1996: *The Preacher's Wife*. 2001: *Riding in Cars with Boys*.

The sister of Garry Marshall (who wrote for *The Dick Van Dyke Show* and produced *Happy Days*) and the ex-wife of Rob Reiner (of *All in the Family*), Penny Marshall would seem a child of TV even without her years as Laverne (1976–83), with Cindy Williams, in *Laverne and Shirley* (also produced by Garry). But she directed several episodes of that hit series, and by the middle 1980s she made her debut on the big screen. She is com-

petent and impersonal—like a TV director—and as such could become a workhorse director for mainstream movies. *Awakenings* was Hollywood's idea of a prestige production: there is nothing so respectable as the pathos of the handicapped, or as slick as the way clever tour-de-force acting gets away with being called truthful realism.

Dean Martin (Dino Paul Crocetti) (1917–95), b. Steubenville, Ohio
Nick Tosches's *Dino: Living High in the Dirty Business of Dreams* is one of the great showbiz biographies. Its research is not just thorough, but lunatic and perverse—for, plainly, Dean Martin has led a life indifferent or averse to recollection, accuracy, or fact. *Dino* is brilliant on the Lewis-Martin association, and inspired in its evocation of the drift, the haze, and at last, the numbing futility of being Dino, or being alive.

It was in 1946 that, as a straight-man singer, Dean Martin joined Jerry Lewis. They flourished in night clubs before a film debut in *My Friend Irma* (49, George Marshall). Together, they made sixteen films (mainly with Norman Taurog), in which Martin had only to sing the songs, kiss the female leads, and generally edge away from Lewis, as if next to an idiot in a line: *At War With the Army* (51); *That's My Boy* (52); *The Caddy* (52); *Scared Stiff* (53); *Living It Up* (54); *Artists and Models* (55); *Pardners* (56); and *Hollywood or Bust* (56).

When they parted, Martin was torn between being a singer—*Ten Thousand Bedrooms* (57, Richard Thorpe)—and a serious actor—*The Young Lions* (58, Edward Dmytryk). In fact, he was both, as his Dude in Hawks's *Rio Bravo* (59) demonstrated. His reforming drunk in that movie, perfectly adept at all the cross-currents of dialogue, should be borne in mind whenever he assumes the haze of stupor. He was also good as the gambler in Minnelli's *Some Came Running* (59), and in the same director's musical, *Bells Are Ringing* (60).

But having met Sinatra, he was drafted into the Clan and gave himself up to their spoofs: *Ocean's 11* (60, Lewis Milestone), *Sergeants Three* (62, John Sturges), *Four for Texas* (63, Robert Aldrich), and *Robin and the Seven Hoods* (64, Gordon Douglas); to routine Westerns: *The Sons of Katie Elder* (65, Henry Hathaway), *Texas Across the River* (66, Michael Gordon), *Rough Night in Jericho* (67, Arnold Laven), and *Five Card Stud* (68, Henry Hathaway); to sex comedies: *Who Was That Lady?* (60, George Sidney), *Who's Got the Action?* (62, Daniel Mann), and *Who's Been Sleeping in My Bed?* (63, Mann); and to the adventures of Matt Helm: *The Silencers* (66, Phil Karlson), *Murderers' Row* (66, Henry Levin), *The Ambushers* (67, Levin), and *The Wrecking Crew* (68, Karlson).

Whenever asked to act he turns silly—as in *Career* (59, Joseph Anthony); *Ada* (61, Mann); *Toys in the Attic* (63, George Roy Hill); and *Airport* (70, George Seaton). But that brief outburst of excellence, 1958–60, has been renewed once—in Wilder's *Kiss Me, Stupid* (64)—notable for the way it acidulously exploited his own picture of himself.

Some kind of ennui or disbelief took him out of show business, but he could be seen briefly in two silly movies—*The Cannonball Run* (81, Hal Needham) and *The Cannonball Run II* (83, Needham). The rest is silence, inertia, or some higher state between coma and vanishing—the secret must be pursued in Nick Tosches's magnificent book, a study of such shining nullity that it alone would justify the travail of being Dean Martin.

Steve Martin, b. Waco, Texas, 1945

There are comics who have to work very hard to be stand up, to get out there, to dominate a live audience, to get laughs—in short, to do comedy, which *is* hard. Alas, the hardness may enter into them, preventing the tenderness (or the pretense of tenderness) that is essential to acting. To this writer's mind, the team of comics who excelled on *Saturday Night Live* have been especially prey to this condition. I find it hard to get enthusiastic enough to want to write about Dan Aykroyd, John Belushi, Chevy Chase—all of whom have had substantial movie careers. I feel they are all as imprisoned in their comic armor as, say, Woody Allen. And while Steve Martin has the largest movie career of all the *SNL* people, he too—it seems to me—is fundamentally averse to acting. "Fake" bells go off in my head when he says lines. That is not to say he is unfunny—in *All of Me* and *Roxanne,* say—simply that this viewer feels a barrier, a tenseness in Martin, that cannot yield to pretending. Evidently, I am in a minority.

Thus, the list: *Sgt. Pepper's Lonely Hearts Club Band* (78, Michael Schultz); *The Jerk* (79, Carl Reiner), which he wrote; *Pennies from Heaven* (81, Herbert Ross), a test case for my theory, to be run side-by-side with the British TV version; *Dead Men Don't Wear Plaid* (82, Reiner), a clever idea, and one that Martin helped write; *The Man with Two Brains* (83, Reiner), which again he wrote; *All of Me* (84, Reiner); *The Lonely Guy* (84, Arthur Hiller); *Little Shop of Horrors* (86, Frank Oz); executive producer and screenwriter on *Three Amigos!* (86, John Landis); with John Candy in *Planes, Trains & Automobiles* (87, John Hughes); screenwriter and executive producer again on *Roxanne* (87, Fred Schepisi)—it is a special sensibility that opts to give the Cyrano story a happy ending, maybe one indifferent to story; a straight sets loser to Michael Caine in *Dirty Rotten Scoundrels* (88, Oz); *Parenthood* (89, Ron Howard), which showed a new, nonironic reaching for the mainstream; *My Blue Heaven* (90,

Ross); *L.A. Story* (91, Mick Jackson), the most interesting of the projects he has written and produced, albeit burdened by a soft, whimsical undertone; *Housesitter* (91, Oz); *Grand Canyon* (91, Lawrence Kasdan), where he stood out like a sore thumb; *Father of the Bride* (91, Charles Shyer); and *Leap of Faith* (92, Richard Pearce), which would have had a chance of interest with an actor, as opposed to a stand-up presence.

Martin has become a far more enterprising figure in the nineties. The onetime philosophy student and art collector has made telling ventures as a playwright and a novelist. It is as if he feels the limits of comic acting. There have been a few throwback movies, and a few that broke no ground. It will be a surprise if he does not soon turn to directing: *And the Band Played On* (93, Roger Spottiswoode); *Mixed Nuts* (94, Nora Ephron); *A Simple Twist of Fate* (94, Gillies MacKinnon); *Father of the Bride II* (95, Shyer); *Sgt. Bilko* (96, Jonathan Lynn); *The Spanish Prisoner* (97, David Mamet); the voice of Hotep in *The Prince of Egypt* (98, Brenda Chapman and Steve Hickner); *The Out-of-Towners* (99, Sam Weisman); the funny *Bowfinger* (99, Oz); *The Venice Project* (99, Robert Dornhelm); *Joe Gould's Secret* (00, Stanley Tucci); *Novocaine* (01, David Atkins).

Lee Marvin (1924–87), b. New York

"The profound unease we feel in identifying with an evil character in a movie is the recognition that we may be capable of such evil," wrote John Boorman, thinking about Lee Marvin. "Lee knew from his war experiences the depth of our capacity for cruelty and evil. He had committed such deeds, had plumbed the depths and was prepared to recount what he had seen down there." And so Marvin made the uncommon journey from flagrant, sadistic heavy in supporting parts to a central, necessary, inescapable man of violence—hero? avenger? professional? searcher? The answer was always enigmatic in his best films, and like a sleepwalker Marvin stared into the dream, trying to see an answer. He had such a way of looking—gazing, even—when blank hostility faded into hopeless desire: it's a look that Boorman discovered in *Point Blank*. Marvin was so strong, he leaves alleged rocks like Wayne or Schwarzenegger looking artificial. But he made so much junk; it took a rare director to explore the significance of so apparently brutal a character.

He led a sheltered childhood as a member of one of the earliest English families in America. Unhappy at school he joined the marines and fought in the South Pacific, being invalided home in 1944. After various jobs, he became an amateur actor, playing small parts off-Broadway before going to Hollywood in 1950.

His debut was below decks in Hathaway's *You're in the Navy Now* (51). He became a supporting actor and one of America's most authentic heavies: favored with close-ups in *Duel at Silver Creek* (52, Don Siegel); *Hangman's Knot* (52, Roy Huggins); *Diplomatic Courier* (52, Henry Hathaway); *Eight Iron Men* (52, Edward Dmytryk); *Down Among the Sheltering Palms* (52, Edmund Goulding); *Seminole* (53, Budd Boetticher); *The Stranger Wore a Gun* (53, André de Toth); *The Wild One* (53, Laslo Benedek); *Gun Fury* (53, Raoul Walsh); and *The Raid* (54, Hugo Fregonese). Above all, he is remembered as the hoodlum who throws scalding coffee in Gloria Grahame's face in *The Big Heat* (53, Fritz Lang) and as one of Spencer Tracy's opponents in *Bad Day at Black Rock* (54, John Sturges).

At this stage, he was thick-lipped, psychopathic, or degenerate. But he progressed to a quieter, more reflective and cynical hostility—in Fleischer's *Violent Saturday* (55); in *I Died a Thousand Times* (55, Stuart Heisler); as the lecherous heavy in *Seven Men from Now* (56, Boetticher); and as the scheming officer in Aldrich's *Attack!* (56). Already more impressive than many stars, Marvin turned to sour comedy—in *Raintree County* (57, Dmytryk) and Jerry Hopper's *The Missouri Traveller* (58)—before going into TV as a means to stardom. He was enormously successful in over a hundred episodes of *M Squad* and returned to films as a credible challenge to John Wayne in *The Comancheros* (61, Michael Curtiz), John Ford's *The Man Who Shot Liberty Valance* (62) and *Donovan's Reef* (63).

Marvin's owlish punch-pulling in these films led directly to his Oscar in *Cat Ballou* (65, Elliot Silverstein). Far more important artistically was his methodical, gray-haired, businessman-assassin in Don Siegel's *The Killers* (64). By the late 1960s he was at last a major star, walking on automatic through Brooks's *The Professionals* (66); *The Dirty Dozen* (67, Aldrich); and creating one of the most influential violent heroes as the destroyer of the "organization" in John Boorman's *Point Blank* (67). After a fascinating picture of a Robinson Crusoe marine in extremis confronting Toshiro Mifune in Boorman's *Hell on the Pacific* (68), there were signs of Marvin's mellowing. Thus in *Paint Your Wagon* (69, Joshua Logan) he hammed enjoyably and groaned "I Was Born Under a Wandering Star."

Marvin's career is central to the role of violence in the American cinema. It might be said that he moved from the irrational, unprincipled killer to the outsider figure in *Point Blank* who is as lethal as the criminal structure of society compels him to be. As a personality, Marvin dropped insensate cruelty for stoical self-defense. At his best, he was without sentimentality, mannerism, or exaggeration, frightening in his very clarity. But he did relax, like a fighter who had grafted his way to the title and then counts on some easier paydays: *Monte Walsh* (70, William Fraker); *Prime Cut* (72, Michael Ritchie); *Pocket Money* (72, Stuart Rosenberg); *The Emperor of the North Pole* (73, Aldrich); *The Spikes Gang* (74, Fleischer); *The Klansman* (74, Terence Young); *Shout at the Devil* (76, Peter Hunt); *The Great Scout and Cathouse Thursday* (76, Don Taylor); and *Avalanche Express* (78, Mark Robson).

His acting career then took second place to the court hearings to decide whether Michelle Triola deserved half of his earnings from the years they had lived together.

In his last years, he was perfectly employed as the sergeant to a young infantry platoon in *The Big Red One* (80, Samuel Fuller); *Death Hunt* (81, Hunt); *Gorky Park* (83, Michael Apted); *Dog Day* (84, Yves Boisset); *The Dirty Dozen: The Next Mission* (85, Andrew V. McLaglen); and *The Delta Force* (86, Menahem Golan).

When he died, it became suddenly apparent that the movies would not have anyone to follow him in hardness or in that secret wealth of spirit and impassive irony that makes the hardness fascinating. No young actor now could be so fixed without edging into camp. Lee Marvin was the last of the great wintry heroes.

The Marx Brothers:
Chico (Leonard) (1887–1961), b. New York;
Harpo (Adolph Arthur) (1888–1964),
b. New York;
Groucho (Julius Henry) (1890–1977),
b. New York;
Zeppo (Herbert) (1900–79), b. New York

These deliberately ill-fitting brothers are the first demonstration in movies of private, protesting anarchy within the rational state. Long before our tentative reaching out for the madman hero, the Marx Brothers made it clear that madness was not heroic or noble, not even a martyrdom, but a helpless, self-destructive liberty. Their anarchy is useless, withering, and sad; they dominate events only by exaggerating their own privacy until it becomes manic, antisocial, and ridiculous.

There have been attempts to argue that the brothers stand up for the little man, for eccentricity, and against pomp, formality, and respectability. On the contrary, I think they relentlessly estrange themselves from audiences. Of course, they make us laugh, like the professional comedians they always were. But they are not interested in us. Chaplin hypnotizes us, Keaton calls to us through his utter deadpan, but the Marx Brothers are as fiercely preoccupied as the inmates of psychiatric wards spinning nonexistent webs.

Except for Groucho. He is the most human, the one who serves as an unreliable go-between for us and the mad duo, Harpo and Chico, and the one who knows he is trapped and that we are watching him. He alone admits, with lacerating scorn, to emotions. Women and money move him, but so hopelessly that he has been compelled to make a comic persona out of lechery and money-grubbing: here is the American boy—intact in the work of Griffith—so ashamed of the mockery that greets his aspirations to romance and prosperity that he has had to distort them. It is no accident that Groucho's confessional confidence trickster bestrides the Wall Street crash, nor that his frigid lecher looks in retrospect like the brother of Gaston Modot in Buñuel's *L'Age d'Or,* an idealist warped by the system.

Groucho is visibly stranded by the complete insanity of Chico and Harpo. Chico wears a pixie hat and talks ice-cream Italian. He is an inert character, content with his stupor, and unable to deal with people on any other terms. As monotonous and stupid as his own virtuosity on the piano, he is able to interpret for Harpo, the most luridly dressed, most evidently infantile brother. Harpo is not dumb but refuses to speak, not human but able to give a protruding-tongue impersonation of idiocy, asexual but eager to scoop up women, as icy as his dreadful harp solos. These two operate on a single level, refusing to participate on any other.

But Groucho knows how alien his brothers are and concedes that his own greasepaint moustache and collapsible walk have not fully admitted him to their company. He still wears a straight suit and, like all confidence tricksters, he is neurotically attached to the emblems of bourgeois success. In every film, he carried the weight of the senseless plot, which does not distinguish him but humiliates him even further. His only weapon in defense, his tongue, also hacks away at himself. When he opens his mouth barbs fly out. But what damage have they done already to his own interior? As if to stand up for classical culture, he insists on making verbal, even donnish jokes. Sacrificing anything for a sharp answer, he has cut himself to pieces. He announces his lust because he is impotent, and his rascally concentration on money because he is a failure.

Look to the text for instances. In *Monkey Business,* Groucho crosses swords with the captain of the ship on which he has stowed away:

GROUCHO: I want to register a complaint.
CAPTAIN: Why, what's the matter?
GROUCHO: Matter enough. Do you know who sneaked into my stateroom at three o'clock this morning?
CAPTAIN: Who did that?
GROUCHO: Nobody, and that's my complaint. I'm young, I want gaiety, laughter, ha-cha-cha. I want to dance. I want to dance till the cows come home.

Standard Groucho. That harrowed gaze had come from a lifelong struggle to generate conversations that would prompt lines to set off his fire-cracker answers. There is also the admission of romantic frustration and the Perelman-like ogling of cliché that bespeaks a mind yearning after innocence. But how does Groucho fare with women when they materialize? In *Duck Soup,* he falls in with a hot little number, evidently willing, but his sexual urge is throttled by literary cross-reference:

GROUCHO: I could dance with you till the cows come home. On second thoughts I'd rather dance with the cows till you come home.

At moments of opportunity, Groucho's prick backs off, piercing himself. In *Monkey Business,* he emerges from Thelma Todd's closet to find that she wants life, laughter, and gaiety, and needs no wooing. Too much for Groucho. He retreats into surrealist anonymity:

GROUCHO: Madam, before I get through with you, you will have a clear case for divorce, and so will my wife. Now the first thing to do is to arrange for a settlement. You take the children, your husband takes the house, Junior burns down the house, you take the insurance, and I take you.
LUCILLE: But I haven't any children.
GROUCHO: That's just the trouble with this country. You haven't any children, and as for me, I'm going back in the closet where men are empty overcoats.

The ripe young women always frighten Groucho away or, as with Eve Arden in *At the Circus,* totally rout him. That is why Margaret Dumont is so necessary, as an absorbent victim for his insult and innuendo who does not offer a real threat of denouement. Her imperturbability is based on the placid knowledge that she is stronger than Groucho, that all his insult is childish prattle, so desperate is he that serious subjects may arise if he lets silence reign for a moment:

MRS. TEASDALE: As chairwoman of the reception committee, I welcome you with open arms.
RUFUS T. FIREFLY: Is that so? How late do you stay open?
MRS. TEASDALE: I've sponsored your appointment because I feel you are the most able statesman in all Fredonia.
FIREFLY: Well, that covers a lot of ground. Say, you cover a lot of ground yourself. You better beat it. I hear they're going to tear you down and put up an office building where you're standing. You can leave in a taxi. If you can't get a taxi you can leave in a huff. You know you haven't stopped talking since I came here? You must have been vaccinated with a phonograph needle.

The more Groucho talked, the more he exposed his own vulnerability. One grotesque line, from *Monkey Business*, caught his tragedy: "Love flies out the door when money comes innuendo."

If I have concentrated on Groucho it is because time has had that effect. Chico and Harpo look like hardworking vaudeville comics put into movies. They are valuable only for highlighting Groucho's poignant situation.

The history of the brothers is a commentary on their act. Their anarchical power within films was helpless: awesome to direct, they were putty in a producer's hands. First, their mother dragooned them into a stage act that led to Broadway successes in *The Cocoanuts* and *Animal Crackers*. Paramount signed them up and, with the nondescript Zeppo, they made: *The Cocoanuts* (29, Robert Florey and Joseph Santley); *Animal Crackers* (30, Victor Heerman); *Monkey Business* (31, Norman Z. McLeod); *Horse Feathers* (32, McLeod); and *Duck Soup* (33, Leo McCarey). The Paramount pictures are their most unbridled, but *Duck Soup* alone suggests a director: its humor is better organized, and its satire on war more serious, for all that McCarey felt abashed by the ruthlessly uncooperative brothers.

In fact, *Duck Soup* flopped and hurried them on to MGM where Irving Thalberg wrapped them up in romantic subplots and songs. He has been criticized for that, and it is true that the MGM films slacken, but the writing became ordinary and the brothers grew bored in the way that children are listless without order in their lives. It is irrelevant to praise or lament structure in their films. At MGM they made *A Night at the Opera* (35, Sam Wood) and *A Day at the Races* (37, Wood). There was an excursion to RKO for *Room Service* (38, William A. Seiter). Then back to MGM, increasingly unhappy with that studio, for *At the Circus* (39, Edward Buzzell), *Go West* (40, Buzzell), and *The Big Store* (41, Charles Reisner). After the war, they worked for United Artists in *A Night in Casablanca* (46, Archie L. Mayo) and *Love Happy* (50, David Miller) and appeared together in *The Story of Mankind* (57, Irwin Allen) and in a TV film, *The Great Jewel Robbery* (60), directed by Mitchell Leisen.

Groucho alone had an independent career of substance. In addition to a TV quiz show that he regularly reduced to chaos, *You Bet Your Life*, and the publication of *The Groucho Letters*, he appeared in several films: *Copacabana* (47, Alfred W. Green); *Mr. Music* (51, Richard Haydn); *Double Dynamite* (51, Irving Cummings); *A Girl in Every Port* (52, Chester Erskine); *Will Success Spoil Rock Hunter?* (57, Frank Tashlin); and *Skidoo* (68, Otto Preminger). But time has not altered that baleful, unreleased pool of ardor in his eyes. What a film it would have been: Groucho meets *Belle de Jour*.

James Mason (1909–84), b. Huddersfield, England

Talent, intelligence, versatility, independence, and enterprise made Mason's career remarkable. Trained as an architect, he had a few years on the stage before becoming the most stylish leading man in British films. He made his debut in *Late Extra* (35, Albert Parker) and played in *Twice Branded* (36, Maclean Rogers); *Troubled Waters* (36, Parker); *Prison Breaker* (36, Adrian Brunel); *Secret of Stamboul* (36, Andrew Marton); *The Mill on the Floss* (37, Tim Whelan); *Fire Over England* (37, William K. Howard); *The High Command* (37, Thorold Dickinson); *Catch as Catch Can* (37, Roy Kellino, brother of Pamela, Mason's wife, 1941–64); and *I Met a Murderer* (39, Kellino), which Mason also wrote and produced.

But he really came to the fore during the war years in a run of films where he brought a unique sensuality to polite arrogance. The blend of Yorkshire and trans-Atlantic drawl was very musical, and arguably there has never been a sexier Englishman in British films, especially when opposite Margaret Lockwood: *Hatter's Castle* (41, Lance Comfort); *The Night Has Eyes* (42, Leslie Arliss); *The Man in Grey* (43, Arliss); *Fanny by Gaslight* (44, Anthony Asquith); *The Wicked Lady* (45, Arliss); treating Ann Todd with hostile relish in Compton Bennett's *The Seventh Veil* (45).

His best performance, however, was in Carol Reed's *Odd Man Out* (47), and it was no surprise when Mason decided he deserved better things and left for Hollywood. He claimed that he never became a star in America, and it is true that few films prospered on his appeal alone. But his contribution was many-sided. He was always an attractive villain, whether in kids' stuff, as Rupert of Hentzau in *The Prisoner of Zenda* (52, Richard Thorpe), *Prince Valiant* (54, Henry Hathaway), and Captain Nemo in *20,000 Leagues Under the Sea* (54, Richard Fleischer), or at the more sophisticated level of Hitchcock's *North by Northwest* (59) in which he harks back to the chauvinism of the Leslie Arliss films.

He played Rommel in two dull movies: *Desert Fox* (51, Hathaway) and *The Desert Rats* (53, Robert Wise). He was Flaubert in Minnelli's *Madame Bovary* (49) and Brutus in Mankiewicz's *Julius Caesar* (53), if a little too suave in both cases. But he was masterly as the butler spy in Mankiewicz's *Five Fingers* (52), the best support Judy Garland ever had in *A Star Is Born* (54, George Cukor), and outstanding on the edge of a crack-up in *Bigger Than Life* (56, Nicholas Ray), a film Mason also produced.

Indeed, he was always ready to encourage and boost films that might not have been made, or been as successful, without him. Soon after he arrived in Hollywood, he befriended Max Ophuls and played in *Caught* (48) and *The Reckless*

Moment (49), magnificent films that also showed the generosity and the weakness he could deliver as an actor. In 1951, he went along with the high camp of Albert Lewin's *Pandora and the Flying Dutchman;* in 1953 he appeared in Carol Reed's *The Man Between;* he lent class to Andrew Stone's *Cry Terror* (58) and *The Decks Ran Red* (58), to Henry Levin's *Journey to the Center of the Earth* (59) while he committed himself to such worthwhile ventures as Leslie Stevens's *Hero's Island* (62) and Michael Powell's *Age of Consent* (69).

His Humbert in Kubrick's *Lolita* (62) was worthy of that idealist: it caught the sweet, tricky voice of the book. He pursued character parts, often with great success—*The Trials of Oscar Wilde* (60, Ken Hughes); *The Fall of the Roman Empire* (64, Anthony Mann); *The Pumpkin Eater* (64, Jack Clayton); *Lord Jim* (65, Richard Brooks)—but sometimes less happily: infatuated with Lynn Redgrave in *Georgy Girl* (65, Silvio Narizzano); as a supercilious Hun in *The Blue Max* (66, John Guillermin); *The Deadly Affair* (67, Sidney Lumet); *Duffy* (68, Robert Parrish); *Spring and Port Wine* (69, Peter Hammond); *Mayerling* (69, Terence Young); *Kill* (71, Romain Gary); *Child's Play* (72, Sidney Lumet); *The Mackintosh Man* (73, John Huston); *Frankenstein: The True Story* (73, Jack Smight); *The Marseilles Contract* (74, Parrish); *The Autobiography of a Princess* (75, James Ivory); a Southern gentleman in *Mandingo* (75, Richard Fleischer); *Inside Out* (75, Peter Duffell); Magwich in *Great Expectations* (75, Joseph Hardy); *Voyage of the Damned* (76, Stuart Rosenberg); a disenchanted commander in *Cross of Iron* (77, Sam Peckinpah); Mr. Jordan in *Heaven Can Wait* (78, Buck Henry and Warren Beatty). He was a smooth Nazi in *The Boys from Brazil* (78, Franklin Schaffner); Dr. Watson in *Murder by Decree* (78, Robert Clarke); *The Passage* (78, J. Lee Thompson); and *The Water Babies* (79, Lionel Jeffries).

Beyond the age of seventy, Mason was at the mercy of the business—yet until the end he was capable of lovely things, especially if they called for a silken faintly malign intelligence: *Bloodline* (79, Young); the antique dealer in *Salem's Lot* (79, Tobe Hooper); *ffolkes* (80, Andrew V. McLaglen); *A Dangerous Summer* (81, Quentin Masters); *Evil Under the Sun* (82, Guy Hamilton); as Isaac of York on TV in *Ivanhoe* (82, Douglas Camfield); as the master lawyer in *The Verdict* (82, Lumet); as *Dr. Fischer of Geneva* (83, Michael Lindsay-Hogg); *Yellowbeard* (83, Mel Damski); *The Shooting Party* (84, Alan Bridges); *A.D.* (84, Stuart Cooper); and *The Assisi Underground* (85, Alexander Ramati).

Raymond Massey (1896–1983),
b. Toronto, Canada
Originally on the English stage, Massey's film debut was as Sherlock Holmes in *The Speckled Band* (31, Jack Raymond). Although he made efforts to remain a theatre actor, his sinister leanness, staring eyes, and creaking voice made him a natural for films. His career was very varied: as well as such staple heroes as *Abe Lincoln in Illinois* (39, John Cromwell) and Dr. Gillespie to Richard Chamberlain's Kildare on TV in the early 1960s, he was a notable villain. But he was best as an ambiguous figure, a smiling threat or a calm tyrant: *The Woman in the Window* (44, Fritz Lang); *The Fountainhead* (49, King Vidor); *East of Eden* (55, Elia Kazan); and *The Naked and the Dead* (58, Raoul Walsh).

Those may be his most striking performances, but there is a long list of good supporting work, with the occasional lead: *The Face at the Window* (32, Leslie Hiscott); *The Old Dark House* (32, James Whale); Chauvelin in *The Scarlet Pimpernel* (34, Harold Young); *Things to Come* (36, William Cameron Menzies); *Fire Over England* (37, William K. Howard); as Michael in *The Prisoner of Zenda* (37, Cromwell); *Dreaming Lips* (37, Paul Czinner); *Under the Red Robe* (37, Victor Sjostrom); *The Hurricane* (37, John Ford); *Black Limelight* (38, Paul L. Stein); *The Drum* (38, Zoltan Korda); as John Brown in *Santa Fe Trail* (40, Michael Curtiz); *49th Parallel* (41, Michael Powell); *Dangerously They Live* (41, Robert Florey); *Desperate Journey* (42, Raoul Walsh); *Reap the Wild Wind* (42, Cecil B. De Mille); *Action in the North Atlantic* (43, Lloyd Bacon); *Arsenic and Old Lace* (44, Frank Capra); *God Is My Co-Pilot* (45, Florey); *Hotel Berlin* (45, Peter Godfrey); *A Matter of Life and Death* (46, Powell); *Possessed* (47, Curtis Bernhardt); *Mourning Becomes Electra* (47, Dudley Nichols); *Roseanna McCoy* (49, Irving Reis); *Chain Lightning* (50, Stuart Heisler); *Dallas* (50, Heisler); *Come Fill the Cup* (51, Gordon Douglas); *Carson City* (52, André de Toth); *The Desert Song* (52, Bruce Humberstone); *Prince of Players* (55, Philip Dunne); *Battle Cry* (55, Walsh); as John Brown again in *Seven Angry Men* (55, Charles Marquis Warren); *Omar Khayyam* (57, William Dieterle); *The Great Imposter* (60, Robert Mulligan); *The Queen's Guards* (61, Powell); *The Fiercest Heart* (61, George Sherman); and *MacKenna's Gold* (69, J. Lee Thompson).

Marcello Mastroianni (1923–96),
b. Fontana Liri, Italy
Melancholy and postcoital disenchantment shine in Mastroianni's eyes. Alexander Walker has analyzed his mixture of advertised sex appeal and actual apathy verging on impotence. Whether at the hands of Sophia Loren in the Italian sex comedies, disparaged by Jeanne Moreau in *La Notte* (61, Michelangelo Antonioni), or dismissed by Ursula Andress in *The Tenth Victim* (65, Elio Petri), Mastroianni cannot credit sexual satisfac-

tion. Is it possible, then, that he appeals to women because he is partly gelded by satiation? Or is his inertia a goad to women, to provoke their amorousness?

Whatever the answer, Mastroianni is clearly appreciative of a world of sexuality so permissive that it has begun to invent psychic contortions: in his case, the limp male—"What makes up for his deficiency," writes Walker, "is the wishful thinking of his mass public, in the main female and romantic, which is attracted by the sight of him as a suitable case for their care and at the same time aroused by the thought of him with all his powers restored." Mastroianni has certainly had an international appeal, but he has seldom ventured outside Italy to work. Perhaps he fits best in the matriarchal, Catholic conception of male sexuality.

Nor, in fact, was he an immediate star. During a distinguished stage career, he entered films in 1947—*I Miserabili* (Riccardo Freda)—and worked steadily through the 1950s: *Domenica d'Agosto* (50, Luciano Emmer); *Parigi e Sempre Parigi* (51, Emmer); *Le Ragazze di Piazza di Spagna* (52, Emmer); *Tempi Nostri* (54, Alessandro Blasetti); *Peccato che Sia una Canaglia* (54, Blasetti); *Cronache di Poveri Amanti* (54, Carlo Lizzani); *Giorni d'Amore* (54, Giuseppe de Santis); *Il Bigamo* (56, Emmer); *Padre e Figli* (57, Mario Monicelli); as the wistful suitor in *White Nights* (57, Luchino Visconti); *La Loi* (58, Jules Dassin); *I Soliti Ignoti* (58, Monicelli); and *Racconti d'Estate* (58, Gianni Francolini).

His reputation was enlarged when Fellini cast him as the center that does not hold amid the dissoluteness of *La Dolce Vita* (59), unsatisfied with and not satisfying fiancée, mistress, the fountain statue Anita Ekberg, or his own vapid conscience. In the 1960s, Mastroianni was in high demand, and his passivity should not disguise the variety and humor of his playing: as the near impotent husband in *Il Bell'-Antonio* (60, Mauro Bolognini); *Adua e le Compagne* (60, Antonio Pietrangeli); in *La Notte* scuffling with his wife in a bunker as another unpromising dawn leaks from the night; as the harassed suspect in *L'Assassino* (61, Petri); as an effete Sicilian in *Divorce, Italian Style* (61, Pietro Germi); the perplexed support to Bardot in *Vie Privée* (62, Louis Malle); *Cronaca Familiare* (62, Valerio Zurlini); as the bemused director in *8½* (63, Federico Fellini); as the professor in *I Compagni* (63, Monicelli); endlessly stuffing his wife with babies in *Yesterday, Today and Tomorrow* (63, Vittorio de Sica); reluctant to marry Loren in *Marriage, Italian Style* (63, de Sica); making a fetish of dangerous romance in *Casanova 70* (65, Monicelli); as the Camus outsider in *Lo Straniero* (67, Visconti); opposite Faye Dunaway in *A Place for Lovers* (69, de Sica); *Sunflower* (69, de Sica); *Dramma della Gelosia* (70, Ettore Scola); the benign but ineffectual rich man

in *Leo the Last* (70, John Boorman); *La Moglie del Prete* (71, Dino Risi); *What?* (72, Roman Polanski); *Mordi e Fuggi* (72, Risi); *Blow-Out* (73, Marco Ferreri); *Salut l'Artiste* (73, Yves Robert); *Rappresaglia* (73, George Pan Cosmatos); *The Slightly Pregnant Man* (73, Jacques Demy); *Allonsanfan* (74, Paolo and Vittorio Taviani); *Per le Antiche Scale* (76, Bolognini); as the homosexual in *A Special Day* (77, Ettore Scola); *Bye Bye Monkey* (78, Ferreri); *Cosi Come Sei* (78, Alberto Lattuada); and *Revenge* (79, Lina Wertmuller).

In his last twenty years, he became increasingly prone to comedy (even in serious roles), and so relaxed that he trusted his battered, wry face and his faithful presence to testify to the trials of modern man. Sometimes he trusted too much—for Mastroianni had an indolence that did not always disguise his own boredom: *L'Ingorgo* (79, Luigi Comencini); *City of Women* (79, Fellini); *La Terrazza* (79, Scola); *Giallo Napoleano* (79, Corbucci); *Fantasma d'Amore* (80, Risi); *La Pelle* (80, Liliana Cavani); as Casanova in *La Nuit de Varennes* (81, Scola); *Oltre la Porta* (82, Cavani); *Gabriela* (83, Bruno Barreto); *Enrico IV* (83, Marco Bellocchio); *Storia di Piera* (83, Ferreri); *Il Generale dell' Armata Morta* (83, Luciano Tovoli); *Macaroni* (85, Scola); *Ginger and Fred* (85, Fellini); *The Beekeeper* (86, Theo Angelopoulos); *Intervista* (87, Fellini); very touching in the Chekhovian *Dark Eyes* (87, Nikita Mikhalkov); *Splendor* (89, Scola); *Verso Sera* (90, Francesca Archibugi); *Stanno Tutti Bene* (90, Giuseppe Tornatore); *The Suspended Step of the Stork* (91, Angelopoulos); *Used People* (92, Beeban Kidron); and *Do Eso No Se Habla* (93, Maria Luisa Bemberg).

Finally, he tended to smile benignly at all the fuss: *Ready to Wear* (94, Robert Altman); *Al di là Delle Nuvole* (95, Antonioni and Wim Wenders); *A Che Punto è la Notte* (95, Nanni Loy); *Afirma Pereira* (96, Roberto Faenza); *Trois Vies & une Seule Mort* (96, Raul Ruiz); *Viagem ao Princípio do Mundo* (97, Manoel de Oliveira).

Rudolph Maté (Rudolf Matheh) (1898–1964), b. Cracow, Poland

1947: *It Had to Be You* (codirected with Don Hartman). 1949: *The Dark Past; D.O.A..* 1950: *No Sad Songs for Me; Union Station; Branded.* 1951: *The Prince Who Was a Thief; When Worlds Collide.* 1952: *The Green Glove; Paula; Sally and St. Anne.* 1953: *The Mississippi Gambler; Second Chance; Forbidden.* 1954: *The Siege at Red River; The Black Shield of Falworth.* 1955: *The Violent Men; The Far Horizons.* 1956: *The Rawhide Years; Miracle in the Rain; Port Afrique.* 1957: *Three Violent People.* 1958: *The Deep Six.* 1959: *For the First Time.* 1960: *The Immaculate Road; Revak the Rebel.* 1962: *The 300 Spartans.* 1963: *Seven Seas to Calais; Aliki.*

Educated in Vienna and Budapest, and a soldier in the First World War, Maté became an assistant to Alexander Korda in 1921, in Hungary. Next he went to Germany, first as an assistant to Karl Freund, then as director of photography on *Der Kaufmann von Venedig* (23, Peter Paul Felner); *Pietro der Korsar* (24, Arthur Robison); *Mitgiftjager* (26, Gaston Ravel); *Die Hochstaplerin* (26, Martin Berger); and *Unter Ausschluss der Oeffentlichkeit* (27, Conrad Wiene). He had also assisted on Carl Dreyer's *Mikael* (24), and in 1928 he went to France to be Dreyer's cameraman on *La Passion de Jeanne d'Arc* and *Vampyr* (32), where he experimented to obtain a ghostly image. He also photographed *Le Petit Babouin* (32, Jean Gremillon), *Die Abenteuer des Konigs Pausole* (33, Alexis Granowsky), *Liliom* (33, Fritz Lang), and *Le Dernier Milliardaire* (34, René Clair).

In 1935, he went to America and worked for twelve years as a lighting cameraman: *Metropolitan* (35, Richard Boleslavsky); *Navy Wife* (35, Allan Dwan); *Dante's Inferno* (35, Harry Lachman); *Professional Soldier* (35, Tay Garnett); *Dodsworth* (36, William Wyler); *Come and Get It* (36, Wyler and Howard Hawks); *Our Relations* (36, Lachman); *A Message to Garcia* (36, George Marshall); *Stella Dallas* (37, King Vidor); *Outcast* (37, Robert Florey); *Blockade* (38, William Dieterle); *Trade Winds* (38, Garnett); *Love Affair* (39, Leo McCarey); *Foreign Correspondent* (40, Alfred Hitchcock); *The Flame of New Orleans* (40, Clair); *My Favorite Wife* (40, Garson Kanin); *To Be Or Not To Be* (42, Ernst Lubitsch); *The Pride of the Yankees* (42, Sam Wood); *Sahara* (43, Zoltan Korda); *Cover Girl* (44, Charles Vidor); *Tonight and Every Night* (45, Victor Saville); *Gilda* (46, Vidor); *Down to Earth* (47, Alexander Hall); and *The Return of October* (48, Joseph H. Lewis).

As a director, Maté is a minor but distinct entertainer, working in a variety of genres with a sure sense of narrative and great visual clarity. He did good thrillers—*The Dark Past, Union Station,* and *Second Chance* (Mitchum, Darnell, and Palance)—but he had the humor necessary for *The Black Shield of Falworth* and reveled in the primeval forest explored by Lewis and Clark (or Fred MacMurray and Charlton Heston) in *The Far Horizons. The Violent Men* is a brutal range war, including Barbara Stanwyck's denial of crutches to a crippled Edward G. Robinson as his ranch burns around him.

His best film was *D.O.A.*, a waking nightmare, wickedly clever in its plot (by Russell Rouse and Clarence Greene), and with several assets that testify to the director's eye—the rise of Edmond O'Brien's panic, the jazz club, the headlong run down Market Street, Neville Brand's leer, and that supreme noir shot where poison glows in the dark. Action, landscape, and atmosphere always appealed to Maté more than content or character,

but he was a reliable source of pictorial adventure throughout the 1950s, unhappy in anything more or less than swift action. Nonetheless, he remains a proficient director and an outstanding photographer, witness to the gulf between the two roles. Nothing in his own films is as gorgeous as Rita Hayworth's dance in *Gilda,* as foreboding as the images of *Foreign Correspondent,* or as creative as the veiled grayness of *Vampyr* and the devotional close-ups of *Jeanne d'Arc.* But *D.O.A.* is a picture Dreyer would have liked.

Walter Matthau (1920–2000), b. New York
Matthau was the son of a Russian Orthodox priest who came to America. Deserted by the father, while his mother worked, Matthau was brought up by the Daughters of Israel Day Nursery and must have absorbed timing with his vitamin C. He served in the air force during the war and afterwards studied at the New School for Social Research Dramatic Workshop. He made his Broadway debut in 1948 and has been a leading comedy actor ever since, favoring the theatre and clearly liking "East Coast" projects.

He made his film debut in *The Kentuckian* (55, Burt Lancaster), and for a few years he was cast as a villain or a pipe-smoking friend (in *Strangers When We Meet,* the one turned into the other): *The Indian Fighter* (55, André de Toth); *Slaughter on Tenth Avenue* (57, Arnold Laven); *A Face in the Crowd* (57, Elia Kazan); *King Creole* (58, Michael Curtiz); *Strangers When We Meet* (60, Richard Quine); *Lonely Are the Brave* (62, David Miller); *Charade* (63, Stanley Donen); *Fail-Safe* (63, Sidney Lumet); and *Mirage* (65, Edward Dmytryk). He was always watchable, but there was no doubt that he was being wasted.

It was a great Broadway success in Neil Simon's *The Odd Couple* that pushed him into major film parts. As a preliminary, he was excellent as a Korda-type mogul in *Goodbye Charlie* (64, Vincente Minnelli). But his most characteristic work is in *The Odd Couple* (67, Gene Saks); *The Fortune Cookie* (66, Billy Wilder); *The Secret Life of an American Wife* (68, George Axelrod); *Cactus Flower* (69, Saks); *Plaza Suite* (70, Arthur Hiller); *A New Leaf* (70, Elaine May); *Kotch* (71, Jack Lemmon); *Pete 'n' Tillie* (72, Martin Ritt); *The Laughing Policeman* (73, Stuart Rosenberg); *The Front Page* (74, Wilder); and *The Taking of Pelham 123* (74, Joseph Sargent).

He is a great technician, in terms of movement, response, wisecrack, and exaggerated alarm, even though his sourness usually derides phoniness and self-deception. As a result, it is not easy to gauge Matthau's own nature, for he is fixed in the idiom of smart self-derision and always offers the brilliant spectacle of disguise mocking the need for disguise. The skill of his playing sometimes tends to dispel his assumed misanthropy. And if none of his films is without flaw, that may be because of a final reluctance on Matthau's part to reveal himself. So schooled to the wisecrack, he may be unable to talk straight. His immense facility, like that of Jack Lemmon, too often seems mannered and wearisome. And when the two are together the film is a hothouse of cold-blooded comic neurosis. His humor seemed closer to character when drafted into the thriller genre of *Charley Varrick* (73, Don Siegel), but in 1974, he mugged dreadfully under the name "Matuschanskayasky" as a drunk in *Earthquake* (Mark Robson).

In 1961, he acted in and directed *Gangster Story* but seems never to have been tempted that way again.

He played with George Burns in *The Sunshine Boys* (75, Herbert Ross); with Tatum O'Neal in *The Bad News Bears* (76, Michael Ritchie); with horses in *Casey's Shadow* (78, Martin Ritt); with Glenda Jackson in *House Calls* (78, Howard Zieff); with Elaine May in *California Suite* (78, Ross).

There's something sad in that Matthau's occasional appearances on talk shows—poker-faced, piss-eloquent, a collection of anecdotes and disguises—were invariably more interesting than his pictures: *Hopscotch* (80, Ronald Neame); *Little Miss Marker* (80, Walter Bernstein); *Buddy Buddy* (81, Wilder); *First Monday in October* (81, Neame)—as a Supreme Court justice; *I Ought to Be in Pictures* (82, Ross); *The Survivors* (83, Ritchie); *Movers and Shakers* (85, William Asher); *Pirates* (86, Roman Polanski), in a role once meant for Jack Nicholson; *The Couch Trip* (88, Ritchie); making his TV movie debut as a lawyer in *The Incident* (90, Joseph Sargent) who defends a German prisoner of war on a murder charge; as Senator Russell Long in *JFK* (91, Oliver Stone); and *Grumpy Old Men* (93, Daniel Petrie).

In his final years, Matthau was pretty shameless, and very broad, with the grumpy old guy: *Dennis the Menace* (93, Nick Castle); *Incident in a Small Town* (94, Delbert Mann); as Einstein in *I.Q.* (94, Fred Schepisi); *The Grass Harp* (95, Charles Matthau—his son); *Grumpier Old Men* (95, Howard Deutch); *I'm Not Rappaport* (96, Herb Gardner); *Out to Sea* (97, Martha Coolidge); *The Odd Couple II* (98, Deutch); *The Marriage Fool* (98, Matthau); and father to the girls in *Hanging Up* (00, Diane Keaton).

Victor Mature (1913–99),
b. Louisville, Kentucky

Mature is an uninhibited creature of the naïve. Simple, crude, and heady—like ketchup or treacle—he is a diet scorned by the knowing, but obsessive if succumbed to in error. It is too easy to dismiss Mature, for he surpasses badness. He is a strong man in a land of hundred-pound weaklings, an incredible concoction of beefsteak, husky

voice, and brilliantine—a barely concealed sexual advertisement for soiled goods. Remarkably, he is as much himself in the cheerfully meretricious and the pretentiously serious. Such a career has no more pattern than a large ham; it slices consistently forever. The more lurid or distasteful the part, the better Mature comes across.

He made his debut in *The Housekeeper's Daughter* (39, Hal Roach) and is treasured for his Tarzan-like progenitor in *One Million B.C.* (40, Roach, and wintrily surveyed by D. W. Griffith); with Anna Neagle in *No, No, Nanette* (40, Herbert Wilcox); a reptilian womanizer in *The Shanghai Gesture* (41, Josef von Sternberg); *My Gal Sal* (42, Irving Cummings); *Hot Spot* (42, Bruce Humberstone); a consumptive Doc Holliday hidden under a huge white handkerchief in *My Darling Clementine* (46, John Ford); *Moss Rose* (47, Gregory Ratoff); haunted by Widmark's giggle in *Kiss of Death* (47, Henry Hathaway); *Cry of the City* (48, Robert Siodmak); *Easy Living* (49, Jacques Tourneur); *Red Hot and Blue* (49, John Farrow); hairy and grandiloquent in *Samson and Delilah* (49, Cecil B. De Mille); *Wabash Avenue* (50, Henry Koster); *Gambling House* (51, Ted Tetzlaff); *Million Dollar Mermaid* (52, Mervyn Le Roy); *Affair with a Stranger* (53, Roy Rowland); *Veils of Bagdad* (53, George Sherman); *The Robe* (53, Koster); *Demetrius and the Gladiators* (54, Delmer Daves); *The Egyptian* (54, Michael Curtiz); *Violent Saturday* (55, Richard Fleischer); as *Chief Crazy Horse* (55, Sherman); as the scout in *The Last Frontier* (56, Anthony Mann); a lunatic period with Warwick and Terence Young—*Safari* (56, Young), *Zarak* (56, Young), *Interpol* (56, John Gilling), *No Time to Die* (58, Young), and *The Bandit of Zhobe* (58, Gilling); *China Doll* (58, Frank Borzage); *Timbuktu* (58, Tourneur); *The Big Circus* (58, Joseph H. Newman); *Hannibal* (59, Edgar G. Ulmer and Carlo Ludovico Bragaglia); *After the Fox* (66, Vittorio de Sica); wickedly well used in *Head* (68, Bob Rafelson); *Every Little Crook and Nanny* (72, Cy Howard); *Won Ton Ton, the Dog Who Saved Hollywood* (76, Michael Winner); *Firepower* (79, Winner); and playing Samson's father in a TV *Samson and Delilah* (84, Lee Philips).

Elaine May (Berlin), b. Philadelphia, 1932
1971: *A New Leaf*. 1972: *The Heartbreak Kid*. 1976: *Mikey and Nicky*. 1987: *Ishtar*.

Four films qualify anyone as a director, and one of those four, *Mikey and Nicky*, has a vital cult following, while *Ishtar* is nearly proverbial for disappointment. Me, I think *The Heartbreak Kid*—about a marriage that sees collapse and a fresh mate during the honeymoon—is the best, as well as the clearest indication of a startling satiric vision. Whereas *Mikey and Nicky* is a very different kind of film, far less coherent or shapely, but dedicated to a Cassavetes-like untidiness of personality. It's a remarkable film, full of pain, yet I'm not sure it's the sort of thing Elaine May was cut out to do.

Say that, however, and you have to concede that she has never been more comfortable than she was in her dialogues with Mike Nichols—live in clubs, on record, and on Broadway. That partnership ended in 1961, but it has influenced so much of American comedy, not least the self-deprecating humor of the modern woman. It's not clear why they broke up, or even what they meant to each other personally. But whereas Nichols went on to a very successful (and organized) career as a director on stage and screen, May didn't.

She has acted—in *Luv* (67, Clive Donner); *Enter Laughing* (67, Carl Reiner); *A New Leaf; California Suite* (78, Herbert Ross); *In the Spirit* (90, Sandra Seacat), where she does a double act with Marlo Thomas. (Note: May's father was a Yiddish actor and comic, Jack Berlin, and the air of Jewish fatalism is always there in her work, tugging at the surreal flights—and holding them down?)

She has also worked as a screenwriter, probably on more films than we know, for she has seemed to enjoy the anonymity of being a script doctor: *Such Good Friends* (71, Otto Preminger), under the name "Esther Dale"; *Heaven Can Wait* (78, Warren Beatty), cowritten with Beatty; as a writer on *Tootsie* (83, Sydney Pollack) and rewriter for *The Birdcage* (96, Nichols)—by far the most obvious things she has done; and on *Primary Colors* (98, Nichols).

What conclusions are there? That all the external problems in filmmaking may pale beside indecisions that no one else in life can fathom. All stories of Elaine May describe a brilliant woman and artist, yet her record is that of someone who can hardly see in her own dark. She is seventy now, and it is unlikely that time will clarify or resolve her puzzle. Her role in *Small Time Crooks* (00, Woody Allen) only revived the old questions. What one would give for a good book on what it has meant trying to be Elaine May.

Joe May (Julius Otto Mandl) (1880–1954), b. Vienna

1912: *In der Tiefe des Schachtes; Vorgluten des Balkanbrandes.* 1913: *Ein Ausgestossener; Heimat und Fremde; Verschleierte Bild von Gross Kleindorf; Die Unheilbringende Perle; Entsagungen.* 1914: *Die Geheimnisse Villa; Der Mann im Keller; Die Pagode; Der Spuk im Hause des Professors; Das Panzergewolbe.* 1915: *Das Gesetz der Mine; Charly, der Wunderaffe; Sein Schwierigster Fall; Der Geheimskretar.* 1916: *Die Gespensteruhr; Die Sunde der Helga Arndt; Nebel und Sonne; Ein Blatt Papier; Die Tat der Grafin Worms* (codirected with Karl Gerhardt); *Wie Ich Detektiv*

Wurde; Das Ratselhafte Inserat (codirected with Gerhardt). 1917: *Das Geheimnis der Leeren Wasserflasche; Des Vaters Letzer Wille; Die Silhouette des Teufels; Der Onyxknopf; Hilde Warren und der Tod; Der Schwarze Chauffeur; Krahen Fliegen um den Turm; Die Hochzeit im Excentric-club; Die Liebe der Hetty Raymond; Ein Lichstrahl im Dunkel; Das Klima von Vancourt.* 1918: *Sein Bester Freund; Wogen des Schicksals; Opfer; Die Kaukasierin* (codirected with Jens W. Krafft); *Die Bettelgrafin* (codirected with Bruno Ziener); *Ihr Grosses Geheimnis.* 1919: *Veritas Vincit; Fraulein Zahnarzt; Die Herrin der Welt.* 1920: *Die Schuld der Lavinia Morland; Legende von der Heiligen Simplicia.* 1921: *Das Indische Grabmal.* 1923: *Tragodie der Liebe.* 1925: *Der Farmer aus Texas.* 1926: *Dagfin.* 1928: *Heimkehr.* 1929: *Asphalt.* 1931: *Ihre Majestat, die Liebe; Und Das ist die Hauptsache; Paris-Mediterranée.* 1932: *Le Chemin de Bonheur.* 1933: *Voyages de Noces; Tout pour l'Amour; Le Dactylo se Marie; Ein Lied fur Dich.* 1934: *Music in the Air.* 1937: *Confession.* 1939: *Society Smugglers; The House of Fear.* 1940: *The Invisible Man Returns; The House of the Seven Gables; You're Not so Tough.* 1941: *Hit the Road.* 1944: *Johnny Doesn't Live Here Any More.*

Although a major figure of the German industry some years before Fritz Lang entered it, May looks like Lang's dull brother. One of the originators of the German adventure serial, May was outclassed by Lang's *Die Spinnen* and Mabuse films. And while May worked in Germany, France, and America—exactly Lang's pattern—he only illustrated the way Lang regularly exceeded German limits. And yet Lang was May's scriptwriter on *Die Hochzeit im Excentric-club* and *Das Indische Grabmal,* at a time when May had his own production company and was married to a leading actress, Mia May. May's first American film, *Music in the Air,* was a Gloria Swanson picture at Fox, while *Confession* was made for Warners. He settled down at Universal on second features, of which *The Invisible Man Returns,* with Cedric Hardwicke, is the most interesting. His last film, for Monogram, paired Simone Simon and the young Robert Mitchum.

Carl Mayer (1894–1944), b. Graz, Austria

"He was a careful, patient worker," wrote Paul Rotha. "He would take days over a few shots, a year or more over a script. He would wrestle and fight with his problems all day and all night. He would go long, lonely walks with them. He would never deliver a script until he was wholly satisfied that the problems were solved. He would rather cancel his contract and return the money than be forced to finish a script in the wrong way. He had iron principles arising from the film medium itself, and never once departed from them. His instinct and love for film dominated his way of living. Film mattered most and he gave everything, including his health, to it."

The tone of that eulogy may say as much about Rotha's sense of an unwholesome industry as about Carl Mayer. But it does suggest a man of exceptional integrity and a writer interested only in writing with film. Mayer is a central figure in silent German cinema, an author who hardly wrote for any other medium than film, and a man closely involved with the development of the most purely cinematic branch of German filmmaking, the work of F. W. Murnau. His role in the history of *kammerspielfilm* cannot be contested. Mayer was responsible for scripts that abandoned titles, that endeavored to represent psychological atmosphere, and that led directly to Murnau's expressive camera movements.

When Mayer was sixteen, his father committed suicide, having failed to break the bank at Monte Carlo with a system. That Dostoyevskyan background forced Mayer to fend for the family. He did any job involved with the theatre, painting, or drawing. During the war, he seems to have been on the verge of mental illness. That experience may have conspired in his association with Hans Janowitz on the screenplay of *Das Kabinett des Dr. Caligari* (19, Robert Wiene). I have argued elsewhere that the potency of that film may be curiously anonymous in that its novelty came about by accident. *Caligari* was unlike the body of Mayer's work, but it undoubtedly fixed his ambitions on the cinema.

In the next few years, Mayer became the most significant writer in German films. Rotha claimed that he often influenced the direction and supervised the editing of films. That is always a difficult claim to assess, but it seems clear that Mayer's importance in affecting the *kammerspielfilm* was nonliterary: *Brandherd* (20, Hans Kobe); *Der Bucklige und die Tanzerin* (20, Murnau); *Der Gang in die Nacht* (20, Murnau); *Genuine* (20, Wiene); *Johannes Goth* (20, Karl Gerhardt); *Das Lachende Grauen* (20, Lupu Pick); *Grausige Nachte* (21, Pick); *Die Hintertreppe* (21, Leopold Jessner and Paul Leni); *Scherben* (21, Pick); *Schloss Vogelod* (21, Murnau); *Phantom* (22, Murnau); *Tragikomodie* (22, Wiene); *Vanina oder die Galgenhochzeit* (22, Arthur von Gerlach); *Erdgeist* (23, Jessner); *Der Puppenmacher von Kiang-Ning* (23, Wiene); the original story for *Die Strasse* (23, Karl Grune); *Sylvester* (23, Pick); *The Last Laugh* (24, Murnau); *Tartuff* (25, Murnau); the idea for *Berlin, die Symphonie der Grosstadt* (27, Walter Ruttmann).

When Murnau was bidden to America by Fox, it was Mayer—still in Germany—who wrote the screenplay for *Sunrise* (27, Murnau), a remarkable instance of German material being made into an American subject (it came from a Hermann

Sudermann novel). Mayer also supplied the script for Murnau's next American film, *Four Devils* (28).

What was it that made Mayer falter? Murnau's death, the Nazis, or the arrival of sound? He went to Paris and wrote the scripts for two Paul Czinner–Elizabeth Bergner films: *Ariane* (31) and *Der Traumende Mund* (32). In 1932, he went to England and never had another screen credit. He was not entirely inactive. Among other films, he worked on *Pygmalion* (38, Anthony Asquith and Leslie Howard), *Major Barbara* (41, Gabriel Pascal), and *World of Plenty* (43, Rotha). He was advisor to Two Cities and a friend of Rotha and Gabriel Pascal, but the idleness must have made him despair, or dream of some evil genius who had invented a scheme for scooping the pool at the nearest casino.

Louis B. Mayer (Lazar Meir) (1885–1957), b. Dymer, Russia

Legend has accumulated an anthology on the barbarous wit and wisdom of Louis B. Mayer. In hindsight, there is a pleasing contradiction in the way he was once the highest paid man in movies yet always a trite, bigoted vulgarian. But it becomes much easier to call a man silly when he is dead and gone. While Mayer lived, people who worked for him feared his whim and prejudice: not only the power of employment that he exercised, the will to favor or victimize a film or a star; not simply the prospect of facing the squat, capricious man in his cream-colored office, uncertain when his maudlin acting out of films made and unmade would turn to attack; but the sense of irrationality in the way so many movie careers and projects—some built on talent, imagination, logic, and determination—could come to a final decision at the hands of a man who had a paranoid Monopoly-player's attitude toward his own product.

Mayer did not intervene that much on films. There is little to suggest that movies—sitting in the dark with the dream—interested him. But power drove him, and what Metro put on the screen was the treasure that came from L.B.'s power. He ran the West Coast operation. He organized the factory. He picked many future stars from nowhere. And he never relaxed in the attempt to feed America bright, wholesome dreams. That there is so seldom that much going on beneath the surface of Metro films is a measure of Mayer's insistence on surface values.

While L.B. was still a child, the Mayer family went from Russia to Canada, prompted by who knows what pogroms and dreams of gold. The child was soon helping in his father's Nova Scotia scrap business, and in 1904 he moved to Boston to set up on his own. It speaks for the pioneering years of the cinema that a junk merchant began to buy up nickelodeon arcades—his first, the Gem, in Haverhill, Massachusetts. He thrived and extended, largely because he exploited the northeast seaboard distribution rights of *The Birth of a Nation*. Griffith in the 1930s, out of work and out of date, may have smiled sadly to think that the largest studio and the most powerful mogul had picked his fruit.

Mayer began to produce films of a sort through the Alco Company, which soon became Metro. But he broke away in 1917, formed the Mayer Company, and built a studio in Brooklyn, before moving to Los Angeles. His company was not prolific, and there is little evidence of Mayer's participating personally in the production of films. But he did have an early association with John M. Stahl and specialized in leading actresses in romantic melodrama: he presented Anita Stewart in *The Child Thou Gavest Me* (21, Stahl), *Her Mad Bargain* (21, Edwin Carewe), *The Invisible Fear* (21, Carewe), *Playthings of Destiny* (21, Carewe), *Sowing the Wind* (21, Stahl); then produced for his own company *The Dangerous Age* (22, Stahl); *One Clear Call* (22, Stahl); *The Song of Life* (22, Stahl); Renée Adorée in *The Eternal Struggle* (23, Reginald Barker); *The Famous Mrs. Fair* (23, Fred Niblo); Anna Q. Nilsson in *Hearts Aflame* (23, Barker); a young Norma Shearer in *Pleasure Mad* (23, Barker); *Strangers of the Night* (23, Niblo); and *The Wanters* (23, Stahl).

It was in 1923 that Mayer hired Irving Thalberg from Universal as his production chief. When, next year, Mayer amalgamated with Loew's Metro and the Goldwyn companies to form Metro-Goldwyn-Mayer, Mayer was put in charge of the West Coast operation and Thalberg became the supervisor of film production. By 1926, Mayer abandoned all further "presented by" or "produced by" credits.

He liked to boast that Thalberg never proceeded with a film that Mayer himself did not approve; it is likely, too, that Thalberg kept the threat of Mayer for any project that got out of hand. Perhaps they operated like two interrogating policemen, one abrasive and one amiable. And as Thalberg worked very long hours to keep control of the MGM product and to maintain rather hollow production standards, Mayer took charge of the promotion of the studio as the supreme force in film production. It was he who kept in touch with William Randolph Hearst so that the Hearst papers promoted the studio as long as MGM made films with Marion Davies. It was Mayer, too, who sent *Ben-Hur* home from Italy, and then went on through Europe, picking up Garbo and Mauritz Stiller on the way.

There are only two ways of measuring the industrialist in Mayer: the balance sheet or office gossip. By the first test, Mayer triumphs: he had so great a salary because throughout the years of depression MGM alone continued to be profitable. Much of that must derive from the comprehensive safeness of the business operation, reflected in the comfortable propriety and caution of the films. MGM did have a reputation above those of other studios, it was well promoted, and it used its resources sensibly. More than that, Mayer plied the lowest common denominator of the audience, ruthlessly loaned out or abandoned stars he could not use himself, and permitted Thalberg to create a rather specious sophistication. Do not forget that he chose Thalberg, another man whose product is bland, prestigious, and indistinct. Mayer's own son-in-law David Selznick never worked too long at MGM, perhaps because of his imaginative lust for pictures and his innate rivalry with L.B.

As to the gossip, no doubt Mayer enjoyed playing the ogre. But there was no sham about his power. Marshall Neilan captured the practicing filmmaker's contempt for Mayer—"An empty taxicab drove up and Louis B. Mayer got out"—but Neilan's career suffered lastingly for that spurt of wit. Mayer adored and hated: he fostered Joan Crawford, but he stuck the knife in John Gilbert. Without doubt he had the will to assert himself, and the instinct for knowing when to strike. Clarence Brown called him "the greatest brains in the picture business." Von Sternberg said, "He was, outwardly at least, a charming, simple, and sincere person, who could use his eyes, brimming over with tears, to convince an elephant that it was a kangaroo." Katharine Hepburn adored him. Most of his human properties regarded him as arbitrary, vindictive, reactionary, and as powerful as the tide. In this respect, his reputation does him justice, for just as Mayer is one of the most notorious of business executives, so he acted sometimes out of a calculating attempt simply to express irrational power.

Whenever he stopped calculating and acted spontaneously, he was sentimental, cruel, and anxious. MGM may have been the most successful studio in the great days of cinema, but it is also the dullest. It never risked the sophistication of Paramount, the harshness of Warners, or the range of Columbia and RKO. If you wish to catch American moods of the 1920s, 1930s, or 1940s, you seldom need to go to MGM.

And when Thalberg died, Mayer's failings were more exposed. His identification with right-wing philosophies and platitudinous family virtues led to Andy Hardy, the film creature that struck most surely at Mayer's trite heart. The MGM product of the 1940s is especially regrettable, save for George Cukor and the Arthur Freed musical. Consider the growing darkness and humor at RKO, Columbia, and Warners, and then look at the glazed sunniness of MGM. *The Big Sleep* or *Johnny Eager? To Be or Not to Be* or *Mrs. Miniver? They Live By Night* or *The Yearling? The Woman in the Window* or *Pride and Prejudice? A Star Is Born* or *Strike Up the Band? The Outlaw* or *Billy the Kid?*

By the late 1940s, MGM was remarkable for its lack of new stars and directors—the great finds, Judy Garland and Mickey Rooney, had been tragically mishandled by Mayer or proved beyond his control. He defied TV and rejected new attitudes to material and treatment. When public taste changed and competition bit deep, he was helpless. Nothing shows that as clearly as the way he hired Dore Schary as a would-be Thalberg. Briefly at RKO, Schary had produced intelligent, cheap pictures. But Mayer remembered him as the man who had once written *Boys Town,* and at MGM Schary was the lever that removed Mayer.

In June 1951, Mayer left MGM, forced out by East Coast pressure. He issued a statement that included this blithe confession of ignorance and cozy optimism: "I am going to be more active than at any time during the last fifteen years. It will be at a studio and under conditions where I shall have the right to make the right kind of pictures—decent, wholesome pictures for Americans and for people throughout the world who want and need this type of entertainment." But the studio, the conditions, the decent, wholesome pictures, and even the decent, wholesome Americans were gone for good or sitting at home with the TV. Movies had been taken out of Mayer's hands by the small, discerning, and aspiringly "indecent" element of the public, and by people who loved film for its own sake.

He died six years later, having made not another film during his efforts to attack and undermine the board of Loew's.

Archie L. Mayo (1891–1968), b. New York

1926: *Money Talks; Unknown Treasures; Christine of the Big Tops.* 1927: *Johnny, Get Your Hair Cut* (codirected with B. Reaves Eason); *Quarantined Rivals; Dearie; Slightly Used; The College Widow.* 1928: *Beware of Married Men; Crimson City; State Street Sadie; On Trial; My Man.* 1929: *Sonny Boy; The Sap; Is Everybody Happy?; The Sacred Flame.* 1930: *Vengeance; Wide Open; Courage; Oh! Sailor, Behave!; The Doorway to Hell.* 1931: *Illicit; Svengali; Bought.* 1932: *Under 18; The Expert; Two Against the World; Night After Night.* 1933: *The Life of Jimmy Dolan; Mayor of Hell; Ever in My Heart; Convention City.* 1934: *Gambling Lady; Desirable; The Man With Two Faces.* 1935: *Go Into Your Dance; Border Town; The Case of Lucky Legs.* 1936: *The Petrified Forest; I Married a Doctor; Give Me Your Heart; Black Legion.* 1937: *Call It a Day; It's Love I'm After.* 1938: *The Adventures of Marco Polo; Youth Takes a Fling.* 1939: *They Shall Have Music.* 1940: *The House Across the Bay; Four Sons.* 1941: *The Great American Broadcast; Charley's Aunt; Confirm or Deny.* 1942: *Moontide; Orchestra*

Wives. 1943: *Crash Dive.* 1944: *Sweet and Low Down.* 1946: *A Night in Casablanca; Angel on My Shoulder.*

Although a Warners contract director from sound until 1937, Mayo's record there is not striking. *Black Legion,* about the Ku Klux Klan, is a trenchant social melodrama, visually much darker than its tacked-on optimism. But *The Petrified Forest* is far worse than its reputation. A schematic stage play is never escaped, and Bogart, Leslie Howard, and Bette Davis remain separate trees in an unlikely forest. Later, Mayo made a good Walter Wanger thriller, *House Across the Bay,* and took over from Fritz Lang on *Confirm or Deny* and *Moontide.* It shows his flexibility that, in the same year, he could make *Orchestra Wives,* which has some nice catty bickering. And it was Mayo who directed the scene in *Night in Casablanca* in which Harpo is found leaning against a building. What are you doing? he is asked. Holding it up? So he removes himself and the building collapses.

Virginia Mayo (Virginia Jones),
b. St. Louis, Missouri, 1920

With all the well-fed carnality of wartime blondes, Mayo made her debut in 1943 in bit parts: *Sweet Rosie O'Grady* (43, Irving Cummings) and *Pin-Up Girl* (43, Bruce Humberstone). She came to greater attention in *The Princess and the Pirate* (44, David Butler), as romantic interest for Danny Kaye in *Up in Arms* (44, Elliott Nugent), *Wonder Man* (45, Humberstone), *The Kid from Brooklyn* (46, Norman Z. McLeod), *The Secret Life of Walter Mitty* (47, McLeod), and *A Song Is Born* (48, Howard Hawks). By then, she mixed musicals and adventure films, usually at Warners: very good in a rare, modern-dress drama, *The Best Years of Our Lives* (46, William Wyler); *Colorado Territory* (49, Raoul Walsh); *Always Leave Them Laughing* (49, Roy del Ruth); roughed up by Cagney in *White Heat* (49, Walsh); *The Flame and the Arrow* (50, Jacques Tourneur); *Along the Great Divide* (51, Walsh); as Lady Barbara in *Captain Horatio Hornblower* (51, Walsh); *Painting the Clouds with Sunshine* (51, David Butler); *She's Working Her Way Through College* (52, Humberstone); *The Iron Mistress* (52, Gordon Douglas); *She's Back on Broadway* (53, Douglas); *Pearl of the South Pacific* (55, Allan Dwan); *Great Day in the Morning* (56, Tourneur); *Congo Crossing* (56, Joseph Pevney); *The Big Land* (57, Douglas); *Fort Dobbs* (58, Douglas); and *Westbound* (59, Budd Boetticher).

She was limited but not unaware of the fact, and not without a cosmetic splendor in the hands of Tourneur and Walsh. Retired for the next seven years, she reappeared, ill-advisedly, in *Fort Utah* (66, Lesley Selander) and *Castle of Evil* (66, Francis D. Lyon). And then in *French Quarter* (78, Dennis Kane).

Paul Mazursky (Irwin Mazursky),
b. Brooklyn, New York, 1930
1969: *Bob & Carol & Ted & Alice*. 1971: *Alex in Wonderland*. 1973: *Blume in Love*. 1974: *Harry and Tonto*. 1975: *Next Stop, Greenwich Village*. 1977: *An Unmarried Woman*. 1980: *Willie & Phil*. 1982: *Tempest*. 1984: *Moscow on the Hudson*. 1986: *Down and Out in Beverly Hills*. 1988: *Moon Over Parador*. 1989: *Enemies, a Love Story*. 1991: *Scenes from a Mall*. 1993: *The Pickle*. 1996: *Faithful*. 1998: *Winchell* (TV).

Mazursky began with a juicy box-office success, an amiable satire on the new permissiveness and its fashion for encounter-group philosophy. But the wide appeal of his first film soured some critics, so that they thought the picture opportunist, lightweight, and cynical. It begins at an encounter-group session in which Robert Culp and Natalie Wood discover their freedom, independence, and responsibility amid the embraces of a body-contact group. Far from being sly or superior, Mazursky managed to show that what might seem a comic, undignified performance was actually capable of a domestic revolution. As Culp and Wood preach their new doctrine, to themselves and to friends Elliott Gould and Dyan Cannon, Mazursky never loses control of searching comedy of manners, real vulnerable feelings, and the way his characters are torn between idealism and prejudice. At its heart there lay the intriguing notion that sexuality and marriage might be too important to people to require liberation: some of us need some prisons. With excellent performances—especially from a revived Natalie Wood—and a fluent style, *Bob & Carol . . .* awaits the remorse of some critics. Now that its first gloss has passed, it should be easier to see that it is a serious comedy where we laugh on behalf of the characters.

Mazursky showed his mettle by taking as his second project his own situation—a young director with one hit, wondering what to do next. *Alex in Wonderland* is a deliberately indulgent film that can have had little doubt about being a flop. It suffers from the shadow of 8½, but lacks the nerve to satirize Fellini. Its dream sequences are a mess. But those scenes involving the director and his family are observant, fresh, and touching, and make excellent use of Donald Sutherland, Ellen Burstyn, and Mazursky's own daughter. In addition, Mazursky contributes a witty cameo as a movie mogul that reveals sharp timing and taste for unmalicious caricature.

Alex in Wonderland may have been made to restore his own equilibrium. It was worth it if it assisted the clear advance in maturity of *Blume in Love*, the story of a man trying to regain his divorced wife. As in his debut, Mazursky reexamines the institution of marriage (and divorce) and reasserts the strength of affection and tenderness. More than in *Bob & Carol . . .* , pain intrudes in *Blume in Love* and excludes any note of flippancy or modishness. George Segal and Susan Anspach are always alert to its fragile tone and underlying character.

Greenwich Village was a very underrated study of a bohemian group, but *An Unmarried Woman* was a good movie right on target with public taste. Its ending is soft, but it was still two-thirds honest on divorce.

Mazursky has remained congenial, good-natured, and capable of rising to fine material. Thus *Beverly Hills* and *Parador* are coarse-grained, unashamed entertainments—and both very funny. Yet *Enemies* is worthy of Renoir, a comedy of lies and consequences, beautifully acted, not least by the slippery Ron Silver who embodies Mazursky's fondness for dishonest heroes. In hindsight, it's hard to know why *Willie & Phil* did so poorly, or *Moscow on the Hudson* so well. But Mazursky is seldom less than good value (*Scenes from a Mall* is the one film that failed to take—but Allen is a long way from Mazursky's rowdy, generous nature).

In most cases, Mazursky helps write his own pictures, and he has an irrepressible urge to pop up here and there as an actor, notably as a weary judge in *Carlito's Way* (93, Brian De Palma).

Mercedes McCambridge,
b. Joliet, Illinois, 1918
I don't know whether it is a matter of good luck, or bad luck, but there are people one sometimes meets in real life who have a smell of danger about them. Sometimes they are self-destructive, but that is not necessarily an answer to the matter. Are there really people who have been picked out by God, or fate, as the recipients of special, remarkable, hideous burdens of misfortune? Or is it in some way their fault, or in their nature—a response to a kind of recklessness that keeps them off balance? Or is all of this just one aghast way of trying to rationalize misfortune?

Of the people in this book that I have met, Nicholas Ray had something of that quality. Among the others, who can fail to be moved by (yet terrified of) the bare facts of being Mercedes McCambridge?

First, let us say that she is a great, uncommon actress who never possessed a trace of conventional loveliness. Of course, in certain dark moods she could seem beautiful—but beauty is another matter next to that serene, alluring, unthreatening look that was essential when McCambridge was a young woman. Add to that her major bout with alcoholism in the 1960s and her foundation of the Livengrin organization as a means of help for drunks. But then, in the late eighties, her son (by second husband Fletcher Markle) shot his wife, their two daughters, and then himself.

Of course, these disasters came after the small body of her film work. Which leaves us helpless with that retrospective understanding—the way of seeing hints of future agony in her fierce, twisted, desperate face.

She had worked in theatre and radio before she made her debut—flat-out brilliant—as the political manager in *All the King's Men* (49, Robert Rossen), for which she won the supporting actress Oscar. Thereafter, she did *Inside Straight* (51, Gerald Mayer); *Lightning Strikes Twice* (51, King Vidor); *The Scarf* (51, E. A. Dupont); riveting in *Johnny Guitar* (54, Ray); nominated again and by far the most Texan figure in *Giant* (56, George Stevens); the hospital matron in *A Farewell to Arms* (57, Charles Vidor); in black leather, so scary we're still catching up with the fear, in *Touch of Evil* (58, Orson Welles—one of her greatest admirers); *Suddenly Last Summer* (59, Joseph L. Mankiewicz); *Cimarron* (60, Anthony Mann); magnificent in *Angel Baby* (61, Paul Wendkos); in the women's-prison picture *99 Women* (69, Jess Franco); the uncredited voice of Satan coming up out of Regan in *The Exorcist* (73, William Friedkin); *Like a Crow on a June Bug* (72, Lawrence Dobkin); *Thieves* (77, John Berry); a Russian gymnastics coach in *Concorde: Airport '79* (79, David Lowell Rich); *Echoes* (83, Arthur Allan Seidelman).

Leo McCarey (1898–1969), b. Los Angeles
1921: *Society Secrets*. 1929: *The Sophomore; Red Hot Rhythm*. 1930: *Let's Go Native; Wild Company; Part-Time Wife*. 1931: *Indiscreet*. 1933: *The Kid from Spain; Duck Soup*. 1934: *Six of a Kind; Belle of the Nineties*. 1935: *Ruggles of Red Gap*. 1936: *The Milky Way*. 1937: *The Awful Truth; Make Way for Tomorrow*. 1939: *Love Affair*. 1942: *Once Upon a Honeymoon*. 1944: *Going My Way*. 1945: *The Bells of St. Mary's*. 1948: *Good Sam*. 1952: *My Son John*. 1957: *An Affair to Remember*. 1958: *Rally Round the Flag, Boys!*. 1962: *Satan Never Sleeps*.

Society Secrets, an Eva Novak picture made for Universal, is now only an item in the reference books. McCarey claims to have begun as a "script girl," so enthusiastic that he accepted work usually passed off on women. He dogged the steps of directors, learning whatever he could, and became assistant to Tod Browning: *The Virgin of Stamboul* (20) and *Outside the Law* (21). In the mid-1920s, he made several comedy shorts with Charlie Chase and, in 1926, as production executive for Hal Roach, he was responsible for pairing the innocent Stan Laurel with the worldly Oliver Hardy. He made some of their finest shorts—

including *From Soup to Nuts* and *Putting Pants on Philip*—developed one of the classic comedy teams (with all its undertones of scrawny mysticism and fat stupidity in mutually dependent disharmony), and discovered his own talent as a purveyor of visual gags.

One could easily list most early Laurel and Hardy films under McCarey's name in that he effectively supervised everything they did from 1926 to 1929. Supervision, at that time and place, meant: "writing the story, cutting it, stringing the gags together, coordinating everything, screening the rushes, working on the editing, sending out the prints, working on the second editing when the preview reactions weren't good enough and even, from time to time, shooting sequences over again." Thus McCarey is a useful warning that in early American films we often need to look beyond published credits to discover actual authorship.

Laurel and Hardy refined McCarey's intuition of comedy in disaster, and his use of the "slow burn," which runs all through his best work, even the much more sophisticated *The Awful Truth*. That film was made at Columbia as proof that the studio could manage without Frank Capra. It is an exuberant, tender comedy of feelings thrusting aside the proprieties of an imminent divorce. In Cary Grant and Irene Dunne, McCarey found the right balance of warmth and comedy technique. And as always with McCarey, it is our ability to see the joke coming and then watch the small improvement on expectation that constitutes the real impact. The "slow burn" is the deliciously delayed reaction to disaster on the part of a clown. It works because the audience responds to this superb intellectual disdain of the quantity of custard hanging from the comic's face. McCarey is best with the audience in the palm of his hand, encouraged to improvise by that confidence, but never betraying the characters in his story. His warmth consists of liking virtually everyone in his films, often against expectations. Even *Rally Round the Flag, Boys!*—an uneven movie—has moments of absolute glee, and it is typical of McCarey that he should make Paul Newman the straight man and Joan Collins so tipsily funny.

Beneath that, however, there was too wide and coarse a vein of sentiment that produced movies such as the Grant character in *The Awful Truth* might have flinched at. That bizarre wartime interlude with Crosby and Barry Fitzgerald as a Roman Catholic double act was carried off with skill, but they remain appalling projects. *Good Sam* and *My Son John*, equally, hardly seem the work of the man who established Laurel and Hardy. As with Capra, another gagman, there were ominous signs of solemnly pondered balderdash. *My Son John*, made at the time of McCarthy, is an obnoxious endorsement of patriotic and familial loyalty—the blunt doctrine of those playful priests.

The closer one looks at McCarey's career, and his own memories of it, the more contradictions appear. For instance, McCarey reported that he was overwhelmed by the Marx Brothers on *Duck Soup,* and that he was a little sorry to have to fall back on Groucho's verbal jokes. Whereas *Duck Soup* is the most audacious of Marx Brothers films, with a war sequence that shows how deeply their surrealism could penetrate the real world. And although Groucho was a dispenser of verbal jokes, it is lopsided to see him as nothing else. On the other hand, in *Ruggles of Red Gap* McCarey drew out the comedian in Charles Laughton more subtly than anyone else. Even in the potentially crazy plot of *Satan Never Sleeps,* he manages to find the comedy—and find it in the tight anxiety of William Holden. Against that, he was clearly devoted to the adroit romantic comedy of *Love Affair*—remade as *An Affair to Remember*—and faintly regretted that Grant's irony in the remake had offset the "beauty" of the original. *Make Way for Tomorrow* is his most serious and touching work, an uncommonly fond look at old age.

Joel McCrea (1905–90),
b. Pasadena, California

McCrea was a sweet, modest man, not in the least starry. The one flaw in *Sullivan's Travels* may be that McCrea's movie director is, from the outset, someone you might trust and go to a ball game with. But just because he seemed so grateful for a long career in which he felt lucky at all the good roles, good directors, and actresses he had known, it was easy to miss how much McCrea himself offered. He was not comic, like a Cary Grant. And he seemed rather shy about his own sierralike handsomeness. But he had a rare gentleness, a great way of listening to women (like an umbrella he was sharing with them), and a knack of underplaying key moments. Consider *The More the Merrier:* all through that film, he has an absent-minded gruffness or stillness, as if amid the romantic overcrowding he's heard what the war will be like. It becomes more intriguing as the film lasts, an audacious offhandedness—maybe he was just doing director George Stevens. Still, it is proof that McCrea repays close attention.

After being the only boy at the Hollywood School for Girls, he was educated at Pomona University, worked on the stage, and had a bit part in *A Self-Made Failure* (24, William Beaudine) several years before his proper debut in *The Jazz Age* (29, Lynn Shores). After a spell at MGM, where he made *The Single Standard* (29, John S. Robertson), De Mille cast him in *Dynamite* (29), and he went to Fox for the Will Rogers movie *Lightnin'* (30, Henry King). But he settled at RKO for *The*

Silver Horde (30, George Archainbaud) and *Kept Husbands* (31, Lloyd Bacon). He made several romances with Constance Bennett and, on loan to Paramount, *Girls About Town* (31, George Cukor). He then earned his pay as a robust, athletic adventurer in *The Lost Squadron* (32, Archainbaud); pursuing Dolores del Rio in *Bird of Paradise* (32, King Vidor); pursued by Leslie Banks in *The Most Dangerous Game* (32, Irving Pichel and Ernest Schoedsack).

Although McCrea was genially unpretentious and generally ignored by critics, he accumulated a highly creditable list of films, and a surprising variety of parts: *Business and Pleasure* (32, David Butler); *Rockabye* (32, Cukor); *The Silver Cord* (33, John Cromwell); *Bed of Roses* (33, Gregory La Cava); *Chance at Heaven* (33, William A. Seiter); *Gambling Lady* (34, Archie Mayo); and *Private Worlds* (35, La Cava). Most of these were romances, but Goldwyn saw McCrea as a fit hero for rougher work: thus Howard Hawks's *Barbary Coast* (35), as well as the conventional *Splendor* (35, Elliott Nugent) and *These Three* (36, William Wyler). This mixture of parts continued, although McCrea seemed to thrive best out-of-doors: slapping his wife, Frances Dee, in *Come and Get It* (36, Hawks and Wyler); *Banjo On My Knee* (36, Cromwell); *Dead End* (37, Wyler); *Wells Fargo* (37, Frank Lloyd); with Barbara Stanwyck in *Union Pacific* (39, De Mille). He then made *Espionage Agent* (39, Bacon); *He Married His Wife* (40, Roy del Ruth); *Primrose Path* (40, La Cava); rather "too easygoing," as Hitchcock thought, in *Foreign Correspondent* (40); *Reaching for the Sun* (41, William Wellman); as the movie director in *Sullivan's Travels* (41, Preston Sturges); *The Great Man's Lady* (42, Wellman); the pursuing husband in *The Palm Beach Story* (42, Sturges); *The More the Merrier* (43, George Stevens); as *Buffalo Bill* (44, Wellman); and as the Boston dentist in *The Great Moment* (44, Sturges)—a consistently enjoyable body of work.

After the war, McCrea settled into conventional Westerns and he worked steadily for the next fifteen years, weathering well and never losing his relaxed sense of the genre. The most notable of these autumnal movies are: *Ramrod* (47, André de Toth); *South of St. Louis* (49, Ray Enright); *Colorado Territory* (49, Raoul Walsh); *Saddle Tramp* (50, Hugo Fregonese); *Frenchie* (50, Louis King); very good, with Dean Stockwell, in *Stars in My Crown* (50, Jacques Tourneur); *Stranger on Horseback* (55, Tourneur); as Wyatt Earp in *Wichita* (55, Tourneur); as Sam Houston in *The First Texan* (56, Byron Haskin); *Fort Massacre* (58, Joseph Newman); and *The Gunfight at Dodge City* (59, Newman).

It was appropriate that McCrea should bow out in Sam Peckinpah's nostalgic tribute to the ortho-

dox Western: in respectful but lethal rivalry with
Randolph Scott in *Ride the High Country* (62).

Hattie McDaniel (1895–1952),
b. Wichita, Kansas

Hattie McDaniel was the first black person to win
an Oscar—as supporting actress in *Gone With the
Wind* (39, Victor Fleming). Is it a good performance? Is it better than Olivia de Havilland's
Melanie from the same film, or Geraldine Fitzgerald in *Wuthering Heights*, or Edna May Oliver in
Drums Along the Mohawk, or Maria Ouspenskaya
in *Love Affair*? How does one begin to make such
measurements, or extricate McDaniel's performance from all the preconceptions in the minds
of Margaret Mitchell, David Selznick, or Ms.
McDaniel herself? When she accepted the Oscar,
her speech of thanks—written by the Selznick
organization—hoped she had been a credit to her
race. She said that line—she was an actress, used
to reading the scripts put in front of her.

Her Mammy is a record of the great difficulty
America was having in dealing with blacks. Here
are others: when *Gone With the Wind* was set
to premiere in Atlanta, the city authorities let
Selznick know that it would be preferable if Hattie
McDaniel did not make the journey. Selznick was
angry, but he consented. At the Academy dinner to
mark the Oscars, Hattie McDaniel was invited—
but not to the big Selznick table. She sat in a corner with her partner at a small table for two.

That said, she is of great historical importance
(along with her colleague Butterfly McQueen),
and she is one of the stalwarts at playing domestic
help in the thirties and forties. A singer first, she
went into radio and played the lead in the popular
series *Beulah*. Her major movies are as follows:
The Golden West (32, David Howard); *Blonde
Venus* (32, Josef von Sternberg); *I'm No Angel* (33,
Wesley Ruggles); *Babbitt* (34, William Keighley);
Imitation of Life (34, John M. Stahl); *Judge Priest*
(34, John Ford); *The Little Colonel* (35, David
Butler); *China Seas* (35, Tay Garnett); *Alice
Adams* (35, George Stevens); *Libeled Lady* (36,
Jack Conway); *Show Boat* (36, James Whale);
Valiant Is the Word for Carrie (36, Ruggles);
Reunion (36, Norman Taurog); *Saratoga* (37,
Conway); *Nothing Sacred* (37, William Wellman);
The Shopworn Angel (38, H. C. Potter); *Carefree*
(38, Mark Sandrich); *Maryland* (40, Henry King);
The Great Lie (41, Edmund Goulding); *The Male
Animal* (42, Elliott Nugent); *In This Our Life* (42,
John Huston); *Johnny Come Lately* (43, William
K. Howard); *Since You Went Away* (44, John
Cromwell); *Margie* (46, King); *Never Say Good-
bye* (46, James V. Kern); *Song of the South* (46,
Harve Foster); *The Flame* (47, John H. Auer);
Mickey (48, Ralph Murphy); *Family Honeymoon*
(48, Claude Binyon).

In 1950, when ABC began *Beulah* as a TV

series, McDaniel was set to replace Ethel Waters
but fell ill and was replaced by Louise Beavers.

Frances McDormand, b. Illinois, 1957

With pancake vowels and a look that gazed on
malefactors as if to ask, "Who's got a poopy diaper,
then?" Frances McDormand entered folklore as
Marge, the conscientious cop of the northern
prairie. And when she had to throw up, that natural gesture was equally a tribute to her life force
and her poker-faced shock at the kinds of wicked
things people do. *Fargo* (96, Joel Coen) may not
be as profound as its reputation, but in its lead
actress it had a chance to be better than anyone
else in the film seemed to know. The sad eyes of
Ms. McDormand may be as humane a measure of
inquiry at the end of the century as any other. And
while she stays narrowly loyal to husband and
brother-in-law, someone ought at least to raise the
question: do they make the best of her?

A preacher's daughter, she attended the Yale
School of Drama and had a success in New York
playing Stella in a revival of *A Streetcar Named
Desire*. She began with the Coen brothers in 1984,
as they began, and she has since married Joel:
Blood Simple (84, Coen); *Raising Arizona* (87,
Coen); nominated for an Oscar in *Mississippi
Burning* (88, Alan Parker); *Chattahoochee* (90,
Mick Jackson); to Northern Ireland for *Hidden
Agenda* (90, Ken Loach), which caught her
implacable seriousness; just walking across an
office floor so as to show all her humor in *Miller's
Crossing* (90, Coen); *Darkman* (90, Sam Raimi);
The Butcher's Wife (91, Terry Hughes); *Crazy in
Love* (92, Martha Coolidge); *Passed Away* (92,
Charlie Peters); *Short Cuts* (93, Robert Altman);
wasted in *Beyond Rangoon* (95, John Boorman);
the Oscar for *Fargo*; *Palookaville* (96, Alan Tay-
lor); the psychiatrist in *Primal Fear* (96, Gregory
Hoblit); as a German doctor in *Paradise Road* (97,
Bruce Beresford); as Miss Clavel in *Madeline* (98,
Daisy von Scherler Mayer); *Talk of Angels* (98,
Nick Hamm); *Wonder Boys* (00, Curtis Hanson);
lovely as the mother in *Almost Famous* (00,
Cameron Crowe); neglected in *The Man Who
Wasn't There* (01, Coen); narrating *State of Grace*
on TV (01, Melanie Mayron); *Laurel Canyon* (02,
Lisa Cholodenko).

Roddy (Roderick Andrew Anthony Jude) McDowall (1928–99), b. London, England

Roddy McDowall made many films as child and
adult. He had several notable performances to his
credit. But that is not quite the point. To try to say
what is, let me offer a few words of criticism.
McDowall published several photographic books,
pictures of the stars (his friends). These were not
the most penetrating pictures. They had an overall
aura of fondness, of stargazing respect, enough to
suggest that there was always a fan and a teenager

in McDowall. But what went with that was an absolute trust: he was self-effacing, a great listener, a loyal friend, and that rare thing, a person Hollywood people could open their hearts to without any fear of betrayal. A more sharply intelligent or adult man might have lacked his patience with so many self-centered neurotics. McDowall knew a lot and never breathed an unfair or improper word. Which is not to say that he was anything less than immensely helpful to biographers or researchers who wanted to do honest work on Hollywood people. "What Roddy knew," if it had ever become a title, would have sold millions and blown the city apart. But what he knew died with him. You could make a plausible argument that his death marked official closure on old Hollywood.

He began in English movies: *Scruffy* (38, Randall Faye); *Murder in the Family* (38, Albert Parker); *Hey! Hey! USA* (38, Marcel Varnel); *Poison Pen* (39, Paul L. Stein); *The Outsider* (39, Stein); *Dead Man's Shoes* (39, Thomas Bentley); *Just William* (39, Graham Cutts); *Saloon Bar* (40, Walter Forde); *This England* (41, David MacDonald).

It was in 1940, because of the Blitz, that he was evacuated to America and a great run of films as boy and teenager: *Man Hunt* (41, Fritz Lang); hugely appealing in *How Green Was My Valley* (41, John Ford); *Confirm or Deny* (41, Archie Mayo); *Son of Fury* (42, John Cromwell); *The Pied Piper* (42, Irving Pichel); with a horse in *My Friend Flicka* (43, Harold Schuster); with dog, and Elizabeth Taylor—a close friend—in *Lassie Come Home* (43, Fred M. Wilcox); *The White Cliffs of Dover* (44, Clarence Brown); as the young Gregory Peck in *The Keys of the Kingdom* (44, John M. Stahl); *Thunderhead, Son of Flicka* (45, Louis King); *Molly and Me* (45, Lewis Seiler); *Holiday in Mexico* (46, George Sidney); good as Malcolm in *Macbeth* (48, Orson Welles); as David Balfour in *Kidnapped* (48, William Beaudine); *Tuna Clipper* (49, Beaudine), which he helped produce; *Black Midnight* (49, Budd Boetticher); *Killer Shark* (50, Boetticher); *The Steel Fist* (52, Wesley Barry).

Those last few films were adventure stories in which McDowall looked a little frail. So he went into theatre and television for several years and came back to film only with *The Subterraneans* (60, Ranald MacDougall); *Midnight Lace* (60, David Miller); *The Longest Day* (62, Ken Annakin); as Octavian in *Cleopatra* (63, Joseph L. Mankiewicz); as a murderer in *Shock Treatment* (64, Denis Sanders); Matthew in *The Greatest Story Ever Told* (65, George Stevens); *The Loved One* (65, Tony Richardson); *That Darn Cat!* (65, Robert Stevenson); *Inside Daisy Clover* (66, Robert Mulligan); *Lord Love a Duck* (66, George Axelrod); *The Defector* (66, Raoul Levy); as the

butler in *The Adventures of Bullwhip Griffin* (67, James Neilson); *The Cool Ones* (67, Gene Nelson); *It!* (67, Herbert J. Leder).

He then had the strange luck to fall into a kind of simian franchise: *Planet of the Apes* (68, Franklin J. Schaffner); *Escape from the Planet of . . .* (71, Don Taylor); *Conquest of the Planet of . . .* (72, J. Lee Thompson), and *Battle for the Planet of . . .* (73, Thompson).

Without the makeup, he did *5 Card Stud* (68, Henry Hathaway); *Hello Down There* (69, Jack Arnold); *Midas Run* (69, Alf Kjellin); *Angel, Angel, Down We Go* (69, Robert Thom). He then directed *Tam Lin* (71), an uneasy balance of horror and positivism that starred Ava Gardner and came from a Robert Burns poem.

He continued to act: *Pretty Maids All in a Row* (71, Roger Vadim); *Bedknobs and Broomsticks* (71, Stevenson); *The Poseidon Adventure* (72, Ronald Neame); *The Life and Times of Judge Roy Bean* (72, John Huston); *The Legend of Hell House* (73, John Hough); *Arnold* (73, Greg Fenady); *Dirty Mary Crazy Larry* (74, Hough); *Funny Lady* (75, Herbert Ross); *Mean Johnny Barrows* (76, Fred Williamson); *Embryo* (76, Ralph Nelson); *Laserblast* (78, Mitchell Raye); *The Cat from Outer Space* (78, Norman Tokar); *Circle of Iron* (79, Robert Moore); *Scavenger Hunt* (79, Michael Schultz); *Charlie Chan and the Curse of the Dragon Queen* (81, Clive Donner); *Evil Under the Sun* (82, Guy Hamilton); *Class of 1984* (82, Mark L. Lester); *Fright Night* (85, Tom Holland); *Dead of Winter* (87, Arthur Penn); *Overboard* (87, Garry Marshall), on which he was also executive producer; *Fright Night: Part 2* (89, Tommy Lee Wallace); *Last Summer in the Hamptons* (95, Henry Jaglom); *The Grass Harp* (96, Charles Matthau); *It's My Party* (96, Randal Kleiser); *Rudyard Kipling's Second Jungle Book: Mowgli & Baloo* (97, Duncan McLachlan); a voice in *A Bug's Life* (98, John Lasseter and Andrew Stanton).

Malcolm McDowell (Taylor), b. Leeds, England, 1943

This is a strange, thwarted career if one recollects McDowell's emotionally greedy look in the late sixties, to say nothing of his being one of the classic images of film history—the elaborately made-up eyes gazing up at the camera with all the loaded essence of charm, insolence, and trickery. I'm talking about Alex in *A Clockwork Orange* (71, Stanley Kubrick), the credit and the look that mark McDowell, and many of us, forever. He seemed then less an actor than a life force, but someone who could have made twins of Ariel and Caliban. The potential was enormous. But it has led in so many forlorn directions.

He worked in British theatre for a while and he had a scene cut from *Poor Cow* (67, Ken Loach) before he got the role of the rebel schoolboy in *If . . .* (68, Lindsay Anderson). He was in *Figures in a Landscape* (70, Joseph Losey); as a paraplegic in love (with Nanette Newman) in *The Raging Moon* (70, Bryan Forbes). Then, after *Clockwork Orange,* he was reunited with Lindsay Anderson for *O Lucky Man!* (73).

He was the lead in the swashbuckling *Royal Flash* (75, Richard Lester); *Voyage of the Damned* (76, Stuart Rosenberg); *Aces High* (76, Jack Gold); very overdone as a Nazi in *The Passage* (79, J. Lee Thompson); as H. G. Wells in *Time After Time* (79, Nicholas Meyer), playing with Mary Steenburgen, who would be his second wife (1980–90); the title role in *Caligula* (80, Tinto Brass); the feral brother in *Cat People* (82, Paul Schrader); *Britannia Hospital* (82, Anderson); *Cross Creek* (83, Martin Ritt), playing Max Perkins to Steenburgen's Marjorie Kinnan Rawlings; Mick Jagger-ish in *Get Crazy* (83, Allan Arkush).

That's when things seemed to fall apart: for TV in *Gulag* (85, Roger Young); *Sunset* (88, Blake Edwards); *Buy & Cell* (89, Robert Boris); *The Caller* (89, Arthur Allan Seidelman); *Class of 1999* (90, Mark L. Lester); the lead in *Schweitzer* (90, Gray Hofmeyr); very funny in *Disturbed* (91, Henry Winkler); *Moon 44* (91, Roland Emmerich); a rather humiliating cameo in *The Player* (91, Robert Altman); the awful *Chain of Desire* (92, Temístocles López); *Bopha!* (93, Morgan Freeman); *Milk Money* (94, Richard Benjamin); *Star Trek: Generations* (94, David Carson); *Tank Girl* (95, Rachel Talalay); *Hugo Pool* (97, Robert Downey Sr.); *The First 9½ Weeks* (98, Alex Wright); *My Life So Far* (99, Hugh Hudson); on TV as Jack Cassidy in *The David Cassidy Story* (00, Jack Bender); the spirit of underworld malice in *Gangster No. 1* (00, Paul McGuigan).

Ewan McGregor, b. Crieff, Scotland, 1971

There's an interesting rupture in the career of Ewan McGregor. Having grown up on films made by writer John Hodge and director Danny Boyle—*Shallow Grave* (94), *Trainspotting* (96), and *A Life Less Ordinary* (97)—McGregor is said to have severed ties with his old pals when they elected to make the lousy but lucrative *The Beach* with Leonardo DiCaprio as their hero. This after McGregor's eerie commitment to the drug vision of *Trainspotting* and his embodiment of the new, bare-forked Scotsman. *The Beach,* a sellout, was its own reward, but one trembles to think that it was in retaliation that McGregor traded himself away to fit into the plasticized games of *Star Wars: Episode I—The Phantom Menace* (99, George Lucas), a project that could add as many zeroes to an actor's life as to his bank balance.

Still, confidence and good cheer returned with his exuberant singing lead, Christian, in *Moulin Rouge* (01, Baz Luhrmann). Maybe being close to Nicole Kidman helped, but it's hard to think of an actor having such a good time since the early days of Jack Nicholson. Perhaps that goes too far—McGregor's strength is in being young, an obstacle Nicholson overcame with characteristic panache. And the Boyle breach may show how far the actor likes to feel himself in the company of like minds and dedicated spirits. Whereas one could see perplexity and boredom settling on him as the young Obi-Wan Kenobi. A middle-aged Obi-Wan would be a disaster.

So far, after a terrific launch, as the lead on TV in Dennis Potter's *Lipstick on Your Collar* (93, Renny Rye), he has put together a jazzy record: *Being Human* (93, Bill Forsyth); Julian Sorel in a TV version of Stendhal, *Scarlet & Black* (93, Ben Bolt); *The Pillow Book* (96, Peter Greenaway); *Emma* (96, Douglas McGrath); a small bit in *Karaoke* (96, Renny Rye); *Brassed Off* (96, Mark Herman); *The Serpent's Kiss* (97, Philippe Rousselot); *Nightwatch* (98, Ole Bornedal); *The Eye of the Beholder* (98, Stephan Elliott); *Velvet Goldmine* (98, Todd Haynes); *Little Voice* (98, Herman); as Nick Leeson in *Rogue Trader* (99, James Dearden); very good as James Joyce in *Nora* (00, Pat Murphy), on which he was also a coproducer; *Black Hawk Down* (01, Ridley Scott). He returned in *Star Wars II: Attack of the Clones* (02, Lucas); he then played in *Solid Geometry* (02, Dennis Lawson); *Down With Love* (03, Peyton Reed), where he was cute and funny; *Young Adam* (03, David Mackenzie).

Dorothy McGuire (1918–2001),
b. Omaha, Nebraska

So tolerant and sweet-faced, Dorothy McGuire was somehow secretly designed to play Disney mothers. Not even devoutness could take it amiss that she was cast as the Virgin Mary in *The Greatest Story Ever Told* (65, George Stevens), not after Linda Darnell had taken the part in *Song of Bernadette.* But in the middle 1940s, at Twentieth Century and RKO, she had been very winning as a wide-eyed romantic heroine, predisposed to smile against sadness. Her slightly staring humility was best used as the deaf-mute horribly menaced in *The Spiral Staircase* (45, Robert Siodmak).

She came to the movies from the theatre, and *Claudia* (43, Edmund Goulding), her debut, was a repeat of her own Broadway success. Thereafter, she was best in soft focus, dreamy and benign, having to work against Fox's grainy black and white: *A Tree Grows in Brooklyn* (45, Elia Kazan); with Robert Young (costar in *Claudia*) in *The Enchanted Cottage* (45, John Cromwell); *Claudia and David* (46, Walter Lang); outstanding in a halting, understated love scene with Guy Madison in *Till the End of Time* (46, Edward Dmytryk); rather stuffy in *Gentleman's Agreement* (47,

Kazan); *Mister 880* (50, Goulding); *Mother Didn't Tell Me* (50, Claude Binyon); *I Want You* (51, Mark Robson); *Callaway Went Thataway* (51, Melvin Frank and Norman Panama); *Invitation* (52, Gottfried Reinhardt); *Make Haste to Live* (53, William A. Seiter); *Three Coins in the Fountain* (54, Jean Negulesco); *Trial* (55, Robson); the Quaker Mom in *Friendly Persuasion* (56, William Wyler); *Old Yeller* (57, Robert Stevenson); *This Earth Is Mine* (59, Henry King); *The Remarkable Mr. Pennypacker* (59, Henry Levin); *A Summer Place* (60, Delmer Daves); *The Dark at the Top of the Stairs* (60, Delbert Mann); *Swiss Family Robinson* (60, Ken Annakin); *Susan Slade* (61, Daves); *Summer Magic* (62, James Neilson); and *Flight of the Doves* (71, Ralph Nelson).

She was a voice in *Jonathan Livingston Seagull* (73, Hal Bartlett); and she has played on TV in *The Incredible Journey of Doctor Meg Laurel* (79, Guy Green); *Ghost Dancing* (83, David Greene); *Amos* (85, Michael Tuchner); *American Geisha* (86, Lee Philips); and *Caroline?* (90, Joseph Sargent).

Sir Ian McKellen, b. Burnley, England, 1939

It's been a delight to see the growing confidence and aplomb with which this great stage actor has been taking to the movies in his late fifties and early sixties. Arguably, the role of James Whale in *Gods and Monsters* (98, Bill Condon) was one that any well-trained English actor could have impressed in. But never doubt McKellen's evident pleasure as he discovered the intricacies of the camera and learned to trust presence (as opposed to fidgeting) in the excellent example of Brendan Fraser. McKellen has much to offer, and we should hope that the picture business finds proper ways of challenging him.

On stage, since the early sixties, McKellen has had so many triumphs: early on with *Hamlet;* Salieri in *Amadeus;* a stunning, hungry *Macbeth*, with Judi Dench (filmed and now available on cassette—Trevor Nunn, 1976); *Richard III; Uncle Vanya;* and his Shakespearean one-man show. In public life, however, McKellen has become a very sensible, dedicated spokesman for gay rights—he may even be the first British actor to come out of the closet. It seems likely that this emotional candor assisted in his more appreciative grasp of movies. He was knighted in 1991.

He made his screen debut in *Thank You All Very Much* (69, Waris Hussein) and in *Alfred the Great* (69, Clive Donner). Then he worked fitfully: *The Promise* (69, Michael Hayes); as D. H. Lawrence, with Janet Suzman as Frieda, in *Priest of Love* (81, Christopher Miles); *The Keep* (83, Michael Mann); brilliant and heartrending for British television in *Walter* (82) and *Walter and June* (83), both directed by Stephen Frears; remarkable as a cameo in *Plenty* (85, Fred Sche-

pisi); *Zina* (85, Ken McMullen); as John Profumo in *Scandal* (89, Michael Caton-Jones); in the Western *The Ballad of Little Jo* (93, Maggie Greenwald); *And the Band Played On* (93, Roger Spottiswoode); *Last Action Hero* (93, John McTiernan); *Six Degrees of Separation* (93, Schepisi); *I'll Do Anything* (94, James L. Brooks)—proof of his new approach; *The Shadow* (94, Russell Mulcahy); the preacher in *Cold Comfort Farm* (95, John Schlesinger); *Jack & Sarah* (95, Tim Sullivan); *Restoration* (95, Michael Hoffman); as a 1930s fascist *Richard III* (95, Richard Loncraine), very nasty but still too stagy; as the Tsar in *Rasputin* (96, Uli Edel); *Bent* (97, Sean Mathias); as the Nazi in *Apt Pupil* (98, Bryan Singer); *Swept from the Sea* (98, Beeban Kidron).

He was Mr. Creakle in *David Copperfield* (99, Simon Curtis); Magneto in *X-Men* (00, Singer); and a magisterial, amused Gandalf in *Lord of the Rings: The Fellowship of the Ring* (01, Peter Jackson). He then did a double repeat: *Lord of the Rings: The Two Towers* (02, Jackson) and *X2* (03, Singer).

Victor McLaglen (1886–1959),
b. Tunbridge Wells, England

Of all the screen's tough guys, McLaglen could have claimed the most authentic grounding in personal experience. Fatherly care kept the teenager out of the Boer War, but nothing stopped McLaglen from becoming a notable boxer, a vaudeville performer, a gold miner in Australia, and a soldier in the First World War. The instinct to fight never deserted him or his great bulk. Even so, muscle and a rather whining heartiness made him a swaggeringly implausible actor forever doing his "turn." Self-pity and barroom Irish bravado were the keys to his work, and the fact that so much of it was done for John Ford only exposes the maudlin bullying in Ford's poetic vision.

McLaglen was taken from the boxing ring to the movies in England in 1920 and he was a successful roughneck for several years: *The Call of the Road* (20, A. E. Coleby); *Carnival* (21, Harley Knoles); *Corinthian Jack* (21, Walter Rowden); *The Sport of Kings* (21, Arthur Rooke); *The Glorious Adventure* (22, J. Stuart Blackton); *A Romance of Old Bagdad* (22, Kenelm Foss); *The Romany* (23, F. Martin Thornton); *M'Lord of the White Road* (23, Rooke); and *The Gay Corinthian* (25, Rooke).

He escaped a slump in British films by going to America for *The Beloved Brute* (25, Blackton) and soon became established: *Winds of Chance* (25, Frank Lloyd); *The Fighting Heart* (25, John Ford); *Beau Geste* (26, Herbert Brenon); *What Price Glory?* (26, Raoul Walsh); opposite Dolores del Rio in *The Loves of Carmen* (27, Walsh); *Mother Machree* (28, Ford); with Louise Brooks in *A Girl in Every Port* (28, Howard Hawks);

Hangman's House (28, Ford); *Strong Boy* (29, Ford); and *The Black Watch* (29, Ford and Lumsden Hare). Then he repeated the part of Captain Flagg (opposite Edmund Lowe's Sergeant Quirk) from *What Price Glory?* in Raoul Walsh's *The Cock-Eyed World* (29), and later in *Women of All Nations* (31, Walsh).

At this time, McLaglen was a top star at Fox, and he appeared in *Hot for Paris* (29, Walsh); *A Devil With Women* (30, Irving Cummings); surprisingly at ease in *Dishonored* (31, Josef von Sternberg); *Annabelle's Affairs* (31, Alfred Werker); *Wicked* (31, Allan Dwan); and *While Paris Sleeps* (32, Dwan). But Fox dropped him, and he was forced back to England to make *Dick Turpin* (33, W. Victor Hanbury).

Ford restored him to American stardom in *The Lost Patrol* (34), and after *The Wharf Angel* (34, William Cameron Menzies and George Somnes), *Murder at the Vanities* (34, Mitchell Leisen), *The Captain Hates the Sea* (34, Lewis Milestone), and *Under Pressure* (35, Walsh), McLaglen won the best actor Oscar as Gypo in *The Informer* (35, Ford). It is a hard film to endure, and symptomatic of Ford's Irish willingness to see brutality inflated into religion and patriotism by drink. This performance was so far outside American traditions of economy, the Academy persuaded themselves that it was noble acting.

He followed this with *Professional Soldier* (35, Tay Garnett); *Klondike Annie* (36, Walsh), with Mae West; *Under Two Flags* (36, Frank Lloyd); *The Magnificent Brute* (36, John Blystone); *Sea Devils* (37, Ben Stoloff); *Nancy Steele Is Missing* (37, George Marshall); with Shirley Temple in *Wee Willie Winkie* (37, Ford), and both in skirts, since McLaglen played a kilted NCO.

He then went trundling downhill: *Let Freedom Ring* (39, Jack Conway); *Gunga Din* (39, George Stevens); *Full Confession* (39, John Farrow); *Captain Fury* (39, Hal Roach); *Rio* (39, John Brahm); *The Big Guy* (40, Arthur Lubin); *China Girl* (42, Henry Hathaway); *The Princess and the Pirate* (44, David Butler); *Roger Touhy, Gangster* (44, Robert Florey); *Calendar Girl* (47, Dwan); and *The Foxes of Harrow* (47, John M. Stahl).

He was saved from extinction by Sergeants Mulcahy and Quincannon in Ford's cavalry trilogy: *Fort Apache* (48); *She Wore a Yellow Ribbon* (49); and *Rio Grande* (50), a punch-drunk clown, bursting out of his uniform and calling everyone "darlin'." Ford then pursued his private world to the point of burlesque—and made one of his most entertaining films, *The Quiet Man* (52), which involved McLaglen in windmill fisticuffs with John Wayne and so actually travestied violence that fighting reverted to slapstick. The draught of so many punches unsteadied him, and in his last years he tottered from one silliness to another: *Fair Wind to Java* (53, Joseph Kane); *Prince*

Valiant (54, Hathaway); *Trouble in the Glen* (54, Herbert Wilcox); *Lady Godiva* (55, Lubin); *Bengazi* (55, Brahm); *The Abductors* (57, Andrew V. McLaglen, his son); and *Sea Fury* (58, Cy Endfield).

Norman Z. McLeod (1898–1964),
b. Grayling, Michigan
1928: *Taking a Chance.* 1930: *Along Came Youth* (codirected with Lloyd Corrigan). 1931: *Monkey Business; Finn and Hattie* (codirected with Norman Taurog); *Touchdown.* 1932: *The Miracle Man; Horse Feathers;* "The Forger," episode from *If I Had a Million.* 1933: *Mama Loves Papa; Alice in Wonderland; A Lady's Profession.* 1934: *Many Happy Returns; A Melody in Spring.* 1935: *Here Comes Cookie; Redheads on Parade.* 1936: *Pennies from Heaven; Early to Bed; Mind Your Own Business.* 1937: *Topper.* 1938: *Merrily We Live; There Goes My Heart.* 1939: *Topper Takes a Trip; Remember?.* 1940: *Little Men.* 1941: *The Trial of Mary Dugan; Lady Be Good; Jackass Mail.* 1942: *Panama Hattie; The Powers Girl.* 1943: *Swing Shift Maisie.* 1946: *The Kid from Brooklyn.* 1947: *The Secret Life of Walter Mitty; Road to Rio.* 1948: *The Paleface; Isn't It Romantic?.* 1950: *Let's Dance.* 1951: *My Favorite Spy.* 1953: *Never Wave at a WAC.* 1954: *Casanova's Big Night.* 1957: *Public Pigeon No. 1.* 1959: *Alias Jesse James.*

With his name on several perennial comedies, McLeod is better known than his record deserves. Between the Marx Brothers, Danny Kaye, and Bob Hope there are doldrums enough to convince us that McLeod merely conducted these comics to the screen. The Marx Brothers were beyond the control of more decisive directors; Danny Kaye was a self-indulgent sentimentalist, so indulged by Goldwyn that no director could restrain him. *The Paleface* is probably the film in which McLeod was most successful, though dependent on Frank Tashlin's inventive script. McLeod studied as a gagwriter and animator during the 1920s, but it was his First World War service as a fighter pilot that allowed him to script *The Air Circus* (28, Howard Hawks and Lewis Seiler) and work as assistant director on *Wings* (29, William Wellman). That led him into work as a director at Paramount, but generally earthbound. He roamed around—from MGM, to Hal Roach, Goldwyn, and back to Paramount—but seldom set his character on a film. Still, he brought *Topper* to the screen with exactly the right touch.

Steve McQueen (Terrence Steven McQueen) (1930–80), b. Beech Grove, Indiana
McQueen did too much routine work in which his famed, if not dogmatic, impassivity grew monotonous. Even in his years of stardom—and he was

immensely popular, with men and women, in the late sixties and early seventies—he was inclined to be more interested in machines, or a boyish, incommunicable honor, than in other people. But as time passes, his remorseless honesty becomes more affecting. He may be brutal, or brutish, at times—but when is he fake? He made too few good films, and his range was severely limited. But as he grew older, sadder—and sicker?—something like grace arose in his battered, tense face.

He was a difficult child, but he had less than ideal parents. Raised in Slater, Missouri, by a grandmother, he did two years in a school for wayward boys, and three years in the marines—he had a drilled look, and an unquestioning commitment. Then he went to New York for drama training. He replaced Ben Gazzara in the lead for *A Hatful of Rain* in 1956, and from 1958 to 1961 he was in the TV series, *Wanted: Dead or Alive*. He had small parts in *Somebody Up There Likes Me* (56, Robert Wise) and *Never Love a Stranger* (58, Robert Stevens). He won more attention in *The Blob* (58, Irvin S. Yeaworth); *The Great St. Louis Bank Robbery* (58, Charles Guggenheim and John Stix); and *Never So Few* (59, John Sturges). Then Sturges gave him a key role in *The Magnificent Seven* (60), which established him as a laconic loner in action.

After the dismal *The Honeymoon Machine* (61, Richard Thorpe), he was very good as the psychopathic soldier in *Hell Is for Heroes* (62, Don Siegel)—the first hint of a death wish in McQueen. He worked hard in *The War Lover* (62, Philip Leacock), and he exulted in his duet with motorbike in *The Great Escape* (63, Sturges).

Then four films in a row took him indoors, and into emotional difficulties with women. He was valiant every time, even if some of these seemed to call for more conscience than he had, or was willing to show: *Love With the Proper Stranger* (63, Robert Mulligan); *Soldier in the Rain* (63, Ralph Nelson); *Baby, the Rain Must Fall* (65, Mulligan); and *The Cincinnati Kid* (65, Norman Jewison), where his poker-faced lack of animation suffers beside Edward G. Robinson, Tuesday Weld, and Joan Blondell. Nor was *Nevada Smith* (66, Henry Hathaway) or *The Sand Pebbles* (66, Wise) an advance.

But in 1968, he delivered two quite different but very successful pictures: as the suave mastermind in *The Thomas Crown Affair* (Jewison), and as the rough, surly cop (preferably in a car) in *Bullitt* (68, Peter Yates), a San Franciscan rebel, and a pioneer for Dirty Harry—McQueen's style helped shape Eastwood. He ventured into Faulkner country for *The Reivers* (69, Mark Rydell) and then used his new power for the dire *Le Mans* (71, Lee H. Katzin), fatal proof that he preferred playing with cars to making movies.

He next fell in with Sam Peckinpah and showed a puzzled calf's charm as the feckless rodeo cowboy, *Junior Bonner* (72). He brought a kind of exhausted presence to *The Getaway* (72), but his violent inwardness was enough to woo costar Ali McGraw, who became his second wife. *Papillon* (73, Franklin J. Schaffner) is not that good a film, but McQueen is very touching as the man who defies solitary confinement, madness, and aging and becomes a wistful genius of survival. In the last hour of that film, he has moments of inspired, heroic craziness—and he makes Dustin Hoffman look like an artful actor.

In *The Towering Inferno* (74, John Guillermin), he presided over a worthless all-star project. Then years passed and he was unrecognizable in a version of Ibsen's *An Enemy of the People* (78, George Schaefer). He was trying to beat cancer; he married again; and he made two last films—patient unto death as *Tom Horn* (80, William Wiard), and going through the motions for *The Hunter* (80, Buzz Kulik).

Since his death, several books (one by his first wife, Neile Adams, and another by Penina Spiegel) have addressed McQueen's darker side and his abusive ways with women. But he has become something of a hero, as witness Kevin Costner's crew-cut tribute in *The Bodyguard* (92, Mick Jackson), a project that might have burned more dangerously with McQueen's grimly suppressed sexuality.

Georges Méliès (1861–1938), b. Paris

Firmly but kindly, Méliès needs to be restored to his true role of stage conjuror who designed so many of the illusions available to the filmmaker—no longer regarded as the father figure of cinema of the imagination.

I say "kindly" because of a plausible cult grown up around Méliès that confuses the homeliness of his primitivism and ingenuity with serious imaginative insight. That owes something to the melancholy of Méliès's virtual disappearance after the First World War, the subsequent sale and dispersal of most of his movies, and his rehabilitation in 1930–31. We readily respond to the spectacle of a cinematic innovator who ends his life neglected or disappointed. Méliès is the first of a line that includes Griffith, von Stroheim, von Sternberg, and Orson Welles.

That wistful old age was tenderly caught in Georges Franju's documentary tribute, *Le Grand Méliès*, made in 1952. Franju and many others tried to resurrect Méliès as the first surrealist in cinema and as the harbinger of the medium's appeal to fantasy. Méliès clearly felt that power, but only as a conjuror. The poetic, visual, or imaginative content of his films seems to me theatrical, crude, and monotonous. Which is only to say that he was an inventor and not an artist. Cinema has always been too ready to read art into technical mastery or novelty. It is useful to recall the words of Georges Sadoul, the foremost authority on Méliès: "But, with Méliès, the gimmick is always trying to startle us: it is the end, and not a means of expression. Méliès invents the syllables of a future language, but still prefers 'abracadabras' to words. He illustrates the gap between magic formulae and the use of language." Arguably, there is more lasting mystery in the mundane images of the Lumière brothers; as for art, that had to wait until Louis Feuillade.

Méliès came from a background of successful Parisian trade. The father owned a shoe factory in an age of city pavements. The son had artistic leanings that the father discouraged. Thus he worked in the factory for several years, and any higher thoughts were diverted into amateur magic. Sleight of hand and the sighs of bourgeois wonder preoccupied Méliès. When the father retired, Georges asked his brother Gaston to look after the shoes while he took over the Theatre Robert-Houdin. From 1888, the pointed beard and beady eyes compelled audiences to be caught in his illusions. In addition, Méliès wrote, produced, designed, engineered, and acted in a succession of theatrical performances that emphasized magical change. Magic lantern shows and his stature as a showman ensured his presence at the Lumières' first show in December 1895, and his acumen suffered their famous rebuff: that cinema had no future.

Méliès had no doubt about the prospects for film and rapidly identified himself with it. From England, he bought a camera and film, and set to work. But this pioneer could at first only imitate the Lumière films, until one day in 1897 the film jammed in his camera. In Sadoul's words, "This ghostly accident did not stop the Paris traffic." The jammed and multiexposed frame showed seething metamorphoses that liberated Méliès's engineering spirit. He built a studio at Montreuil and began to manufacture trick movies, stimulated by Albert Hopkins's book, *Magic*.

He worked until 1913 at Montreuil, helplessly dominated by technique. He made over a thousand films, the bulk of them before 1905, with a new burst of activity in 1908. The failure of Méliès was in relating his often childish delight in trickery to any greater purpose. There is something wearying in all his tricks, isolated as they are from meaning: superimposition, multiexposure, models and live action together, stop motion, slow and quick action, etc. But all these devices were kept within a proscenium arch. The Méliès films are photographed very flatly, partly because a conjuror likes the spectator directly in front of him, but also because Méliès failed to see that audiences might be more interested in people than in magic. More damaging, he set these homemade wonders in

methodical, melodramatic stories. It is difficult to grant Méliès insight as a magician, when his structures were so pedestrian. For instance, in one of his last films, *À la Conquête du Pole*, made in 1912, and no real advance on films made twelve years before, he is still putting on one trick after another, failing to see that the wonder or terror of the journey could be more profound if the audience identified with any of the voyagers. A year later, in America, Griffith's *Judith of Bethulia* had close-ups that brought human individuality to the director's Victorian biblical sensibility.

Of course, Méliès was immensely successful in the years around 1900. But he began to bore even his own audiences. The rigid filming techniques proved more influential than the skillful deceptions of the eye. And Méliès made hardly anything longer than twenty minutes, always seeing film as a rival to variety "acts" in the theatre. It was Griffith who had the ponderous daring to insist on length. That was rewarded by the faith of audiences in the perilously preserved honor of his young ladies.

There are magical moments in Méliès that have more than historical interest. But I cannot see a coherent sense of cinema language or a challenging notion of the audience. Behind all his stage-bound pantomime transformations, there lurked a solid factory owner and the vague apprehension of authorship:

> The composition of a scene, an episode, a drama, a fairy story, a comedy or an artistic tableau naturally requires a scenario taken from the imagination. Then there is a search for ways of affecting the audience: drawings and models for costumes and scenery; the settling on a chief attraction, without which there is no chance of success. And as for tales of illusion or fairy stories, the tricks and processes must be studied with particular care. The rendering on film must be prepared in advance, just as much as the groupings and movements of the players. It is exactly like preparing a stage play. The only difference is that the author must know how to do everything himself and, consequently, be author, director, designer and, sometimes, actor, if everything is to be as he wishes it. The author of a scene must direct it himself, because it is absolutely impossible if two people meddle in it.

Such independence made Méliès no easy collaborator and may have blinded him to the changes in the film industry. His American distribution suffered from the Edison monopoly; in France, he became subordinate to Pathé. Longer films and the real imaginative departure from theatricality eluded Méliès. Nineteen-thirteen was the turning point, when his brother and wife died.

War disrupted his world and turned him back into a conjuror entertaining troops. His studio was converted into a theatre and he made no more films. In 1923, the Robert-Houdin was torn down and Méliès sold his negatives. When cinéastes rediscovered him he was living in poverty. Happily, his last years were more comfortable, and in 1931 he was awarded the cross of the Legion d'Honneur. Doubtless he spent his last years turning it into bouquets and white rabbits.

Jean-Pierre Melville (Jean-Pierre Grumbach) (1917–73), b. Paris

1946: *Vingt-Quatre Heures de la Vie d'un Clown* (s). 1947: *Le Silence de la Mer.* 1949: *Les Enfants Terribles.* 1952: *Quand Tu Liras Cette Lettre.* 1955: *Bob le Flambeur.* 1958: *Deux Hommes à Manhattan.* 1961: *Léon Morin, Prêtre.* 1962: *Le Doulos.* 1963: *L'Aîné des Ferchaux/Magnet of Doom.* 1966: *Le Deuxième Souffle/The Second Breath.* 1967: *Le Samourai.* 1969: *L'Armée des Ombres/Shadow Army.* 1970: *Le Cercle Rouge.* 1972: *Un Flic/Dirty Money.*

As acknowledged by his appearance in *Breathless* (59, Jean-Luc Godard), Melville was an ancestor of the New Wave. *Le Silence de la Mer* was an heroic instance of the outsider making a film and renovating the medium as he did so. *Bob le Flambeur* was immensely influential in the way it recreated the ambiance of the American thriller and yet encouraged spontaneous, location shooting. No one who had named himself after the author of *Moby Dick,* who had Melville's affection for American cinema of the 1930s, and yet who insisted on prickly French truths, could fail to appeal to the new generation. Good enough, but Melville exists in his own right.

Bob was a turning point for Melville himself, inaugurating a Hustonian dream of tough, self-sufficient men in trench coats, fickle girls, and a maelstrom of treachery and heroic gestures. The romance was made astringent by the casual humor, the remarkable eye for honor, friendship, and double-cross, and the pleasure at a world Melville made his own, even to the extent of having his own studio. There is a haphazard grace in his pictures that stems from the deliberate offhandedness with which they were made: "I'm incapable of doing anything but rough drafts. Each time I see one of my films again, then and only then can I see what I should have done. But I only see things this clearly once the finished print is being shown on the screen everywhere and it's too late to do anything about it."

He had a built-in breathlessness, in fact, an adopted resignation to transience and mutability that is partly an eccentric individualism and partly what Melville inherited from American mobility and obsolescence. It gives his gangster films a true supercharge—"en quatrième vitesse"—and he transformed Belmondo and Delon into beautiful destructive angels of the dark street. But this gain was at some cost. For Melville's later films were more youthful than his earlier ones.

Melville was in the Resistance and in Britain during the war. Afterwards, he reverted to an amateur interest in moviemaking and, in 1947, he made his first feature from the story by Vercors about a German officer billeted in rural France who falls in love with a French girl. It was a more concentrated, sensitive, and interior film than the later movies would suggest. Sadly, it is little known today. If memories are accurate, it is a major film, important to the development of Bresson, Astruc, Resnais, and possibly Rohmer. In 1949, Melville played a small part in Cocteau's *Orphée* and then directed an adaptation of Cocteau's *Les Enfants Terribles,* this at the author's request. At a time when Cocteau the filmmaker was at his peak, the personality of *Les Enfants Terribles* is still Melville's. Cocteau collaborated on the script and haunted the set, and the film is faithful to the novel; but its sense of complicity and betrayal, of disorder and luminous death, are all part of Melville's persistent vision.

But the dream world of *Les Enfants* was over a decade in crystallizing. *Quand Tu Liras Cette Lettre* is a pedestrian melodrama. *Bob le Flambeur,* although a turning point, was a sort of lyrical documentary thriller. *Deux Hommes à Manhattan,* in which Melville played a leading role, was filmed in America and meant as a love letter to New York. In fact, its intentions are stronger than its effects. *Léon Morin* was nearly a return to the delicate unpicking of emotion in *Silence de la Mer,* and an odd reappearance of Melville's interest in the spirit and the Occupation.

Le Doulos was the first of the new thrillers and the beginning of Melville's development of a world filled with doors through which bullets may come at any moment. These films are virtually interchangeable; for the environment and legend are important above everything else. It was an independent path, very entertaining, but not as demanding of Melville himself as his first films, as evident in the late return to France during the war—*L'Armée des Ombres*—which subtly turns the underworld into the Resistance.

Still, it was in this last period that Melville made a masterpiece of French noir—*Le Samourai*—with Alain Delon as a fatalistic icon moving toward certain closure. Done on the wide screen, with mysteries in every corner, the film is quick, deadly, and so tough that its impassive romanticism is not just fascinating, but nearly comic.

Sam (Samuel) Mendes,
b. Reading, England, 1965
1999: *American Beauty.* 2002: *Road to Perdition.*

When *American Beauty* won the Oscar for best

picture, and Sam Mendes pocketed another for best director, there was sniffiness in some circles— that *American Beauty* wasn't really very good or new, and that it was a sign of unhappy times when a British stage director could win everything on his first shot. There was another line that said, just notice how closely and fondly Mendes is working with veteran cameraman Conrad Hall—see how eager he is to learn, and how excited by the new toys. It was worth adding that *American Beauty* was an uncommonly tart, melancholy view of Americana that looks all the more prescient and striking in the Bushy empire of Crawford, Texas, as we wait for *Road to Perdition*.

In other words, I think Sam Mendes is going to do very well indeed in an age when so many talents raised in British theatre do seem able to grasp sufficient rudiments of American film in a quick, greedy look: I'm thinking of David Hare, Anthony Minghella, Stephen Daldry, Richard Eyre, and Nicholas Hytner. Let me go one step further: in an age of excessive concentration on "filmic effects" it is absolutely refreshing to feel some sense of the large world and life experience, some real knowledge of dramaturgy, acting, and rehearsal in people coming into movie directing. The lessons and experience of good theatre still have enormous value for filmmaking.

American Beauty was a film that helped crystallize the uncertain mood of self-criticism in America. It was a fine movie, and I don't see Sam Mendes as anything but someone who means to get better.

Adolphe Menjou (1890–1963),
b. Pittsburgh, Pennsylvania

Menjou was Paramount's glittering mannequin, sleek, dapper, hair smoothed back, the face slit by a smile and the suggestion of a sharp triangle of moustache. Menjou was famous as a dandy. Even without *The Ace of Cads* (26, Luther Reed) among his credits, it would be hard to remember him as anything other than the meticulous exploiter of the screen's ladies. But he is the dignified victim of Dietrich in *Morocco* (30, Josef von Sternberg), the first example of the amused, fatalistic man observing the sex goddess in Sternberg's work—and, like John Lodge, in *Scarlet Empress*, bearing an odd resemblance to Sternberg himself. *Morocco* shows the finesse Menjou was capable of, like a man taking stock of a snooker.

But he was typecast for suggestive deference over some twenty years; no wonder he became a stylized little man. As Louise Brooks remembered: "Look at Adolphe Menjou. He never felt anything. He used to say, 'Now I do Lubitsch number one.' 'Now I do Lubitsch number two.' And that's exactly what he did. You felt nothing, working with him, and yet see him on the screen—and he was a great actor."

Menjou was on the stage before coming to the movies: *The Amazons* (17, Joseph Kaufman); *Courage* (21, Sidney Franklin); as Louis XIII in *The Three Musketeers* (21, Fred Niblo); *The Eternal Flame* (22, Frank Lloyd); *Is Matrimony a Failure?* (22, James Cruze); *Bella Donna* (23, George Fitzmaurice); *The Spanish Dancer* (23, Herbert Brenon); *A Woman of Paris* (23, Charles Chaplin); *The World's Applause* (23, William C. De Mille); *Broadway After Dark* (24, Monta Bell); *For Sale* (24, George Archainbaud); *The Marriage Circle* (24, Ernst Lubitsch); *Forbidden Paradise* (24, Lubitsch); *Open All Night* (24, Paul Bern); *Are Parents People?* (25, Malcolm St. Clair); *The King on the Main Street* (25, Bell); *A Kiss in the Dark* (25, Frank Tuttle); *Lost—a Wife* (25, W. C. De Mille); *The Swan* (25, Dmitri Buchowetzki); *The Grand Duchess and the Waiter* (26, St. Clair); *A Social Celebrity* (26, St. Clair); as the Devil figure in *The Sorrows of Satan* (26, D. W. Griffith); *A Gentleman of Paris* (27, Harry d'Arrast); *Service for Ladies* (27, d'Arrast); *His Private Life* (28, Tuttle); *A Night of Mystery* (28, Lothar Mendes); *New Moon* (30, Jack Conway); *The Easiest Way* (31, Conway); as the editor in *The Front Page* (31, Lewis Milestone); *Prestige* (32, Tay Garnett); *Forbidden* (32, Frank Capra); as the impresario in *Morning Glory* (32, Lowell Sherman); as Rinaldi in *A Farewell to Arms* (33, Frank Borzage); *Easy to Love* (33, William Keighley); *Convention City* (33, Archie Mayo); *Journal of a Crime* (34, Keighley); *The Mighty Barnum* (34, Walter Lang); *Gold Diggers of 1935* (35, Busby Berkeley); *Broadway Gondolier* (35, Lloyd Bacon); *The Milky Way* (36, Leo McCarey); *Wives Never Know* (36, Elliott Nugent); *One Hundred Men and a Girl* (37, Henry Koster); *Stage Door* (37, Gregory La Cava); the producer in *A Star Is Born* (37, William Wellman); *The Goldwyn Follies* (38, George Marshall); and *Letter of Introduction* (38, John M. Stahl).

That was his last romantic role, after which he slipped into supporting parts or as the nonsinger in musicals: *Golden Boy* (39, Rouben Mamoulian); *The Housekeeper's Daughter* (39, Hal Roach); *A Bill of Divorcement* (40, John Farrow); *Road Show* (41, Gordon Douglas); *You Were Never Lovelier* (42, William A. Seiter); *Roxie Hart* (42, Wellman); *Syncopation* (42, William Dieterle); *Hi, Diddle Diddle* (43, Andrew L. Stone); *Step Lively* (44, Tim Whelan); *Heartbeat* (46, Sam Wood); *The Hucksters* (47, Conway); *State of the Union* (48, Capra); *To Please a Lady* (50, Clarence Brown); *The Tall Target* (51, Anthony Mann); *Across the Wide Missouri* (51, Wellman); *The Sniper* (52, Edward Dmytryk); *Man on a Tightrope* (53, Elia Kazan); *The Ambassador's Daughter* (56, Norman Krasna); as the corrupt general in *Paths of Glory* (57, Stanley Kubrick); and *Pollyanna* (60, David Swift).

William Cameron Menzies (1896–1957),
b. New Haven, Connecticut
1931: *The Spider* (codirected with Kenneth
McKenna); *Always Goodbye* (codirected with
McKenna). 1932: *Chandu the Magician* (co-
directed with Marcel Varnel). 1933: *I Loved You
Wednesday* (codirected with Henry King). 1934:
The Wharf Angel (codirected with George
Somnes). 1936: *Things to Come*. 1940: *The Green
Cockatoo*. 1944: *Address Unknown*. 1951: *Drums
in the Deep South; The Whip Hand*. 1953:
Invaders from Mars; The Maze.

Menzies's most famous film, *Things to Come*, is
known for the futuristic splendor of its sets. In the
1920s he built up a reputation for lavish art direc-
tion: *Serenade* (21, Raoul Walsh); *Kindred of the
Dust* (22, Walsh); *Rosita* (23, Ernst Lubitsch); *The
Thief of Bagdad* (24, Walsh); *Cobra* (25, Joseph
Henabery); *The Eagle* (25, Clarence Brown); *Her
Sister from Paris* (25, Sidney Franklin); *The Bat*
(26, Roland West); *The Son of the Sheik* (26,
George Fitzmaurice); *The Beloved Rogue* (27,
Alan Crosland); *The Dove* (27, West); *Two Ara-
bian Knights* (27, Lewis Milestone); *The Awaken-
ing* (28, Victor Fleming); *Drums of Love* (28,
D. W. Griffith); *The Garden of Eden* (28, Mile-
stone); *Sadie Thompson* (28, Walsh); *Tempest* (28,
Sam Taylor); *Alibi* (29, West); *Condemned* (29,
Wesley Ruggles); *Lady of the Pavements* (29, Grif-
fith); *The Taming of the Shrew* (29, Taylor); *Abra-
ham Lincoln* (30, Griffith); *Du Barry, Woman of
Passion* (30, Taylor); and *The Lottery Bride* (30,
Paul L. Stein).

In the 1930s he diversified. *Chandu the Magician* was a Bela Lugosi film. In 1933, he helped to
write the script for *Alice in Wonderland* (Norman
Z. McLeod), and in 1936 he was invited to
England by Alexander Korda to design and direct
Things to Come. With an H. G. Wells script, music
written in advance by Arthur Bliss and photogra-
phy by Périnal, the film was top-heavy with
Korda's lusting after prestige. It is underdirected
but the sets are very beautiful. As well as directing, Menzies was involved in the production of
The Thief of Bagdad (40, Michael Powell, Tim
Whelan, and Ludwig Berger); *Ivy* (47, Sam
Wood); *Raw Deal* (48, Anthony Mann); *Reign of
Terror* (49, Mann); and *Around the World in 80
Days* (56, Michael Anderson). But he was most
successful as an art director: *Gone With the Wind*
(39, Victor Fleming), on which Selznick admitted
that Menzies "spent perhaps a year of his life in
laying out camera angles, lighting effects and
other important directorial contributions"; *Our
Town* (40, Wood); *Foreign Correspondent* (40,
Alfred Hitchcock)—remember that Dutch wind-
mill?; *So Ends Our Night* (41, John Cromwell);
For Whom the Bell Tolls (43, Wood); and *Arch of
Triumph* (48, Milestone).

Burgess Meredith (1909–97),
b. Cleveland, Ohio
Educated at Amherst, Meredith went into the
theatre and played in *Winterset* with great success
after Maxwell Anderson had written the play for
him. He made his movie debut in the adaptation
of that play (36, Alfred Santell) and also appeared
in *Idiot's Delight* (39, Clarence Brown). At that
time he played Hal to Orson Welles's Falstaff with
the Mercury Theater—John Houseman rated his
Hal the best he had ever seen.

Meredith was an occasional and outstanding
character actor in movies, excellent as George in
Of Mice and Men (39, Lewis Milestone), and also
in *Castle on the Hudson* (40, Anatole Litvak), *That
Uncertain Feeling* (41, Ernst Lubitsch), with
Paulette Goddard and Astaire in *Second Chorus*
(41, H. C. Potter), and Ginger Rogers in *Tom,
Dick and Harry* (41, Garson Kanin).

He served in the Army Air Corps and returned
to films as war correspondent Ernie Pyle in *The
Story of G.I. Joe* (45, William Wellman). Married
now to Paulette Goddard, he played with her in
and produced *The Diary of a Chambermaid* (46,
Jean Renoir). That film is unique in American cinema for its tone of macabre surrealism; it is also
Renoir's best American film. Meredith's own performance—as the infantile Captain—is as swift
and inquisitive as a sparrow. He was in *Magnificent Doll* (46, Frank Borzage), the psychiatrist in
the excellent *Mine Own Executioner* (47, Anthony
Kimmins), and an episode of *On Our Merry Way*
(48), which he also coproduced.

Thereafter, he seems to have lost his roots:
in 1949 he went to France to direct Charles
Laughton and Franchot Tone in *The Man on the
Eiffel Tower*, and was away from the United States
for some years, possibly for political reasons,
although in 1955 he was in *Joe Butterfly* (Jesse
Hibbs), and in 1956 he produced a documentary,
Alexander Calder. He returned in the 1960s as a
small-part player of unusual distinction, especially
for Otto Preminger: first as the informing witness
in *Advise and Consent* (62), a weak-willed man
trying to live up to the one truth he has to tell, and
also in *The Cardinal* (63), *In Harm's Way* (65),
Hurry Sundown (67), *Skidoo* (68), and *Such Good
Friends* (71).

In addition, he appeared in *Madame X* (65,
David Lowell Rich); *A Big Hand for the Little
Lady* (66, Fielder Cook); *The Torture Garden* (67,
Freddie Francis); *Stay Away, Joe* (68, Peter
Tewkesbury); *MacKenna's Gold* (69, J. Lee
Thompson); *There Was a Crooked Man* (70,
Joseph L. Mankiewicz); and *The Day of the
Locust* (75, John Schlesinger). He has also
directed one more film, *The Ying and the Yang*,
made in Hong Kong.

It is a wayward, independent but personal
career, as eye-catching as his TV appearances as

the Penguin in *Batman* (66–68) and as an enthusiastic editor hunched over the video, patching data and action, in *Search* (72–73). He was in *B. Must Die* (73, Jose Luis Borau); *The Hindenburg* (75, Robert Wise); *The Sentinel* (76, Michael Winner); the bird on the rhinoceros's back, trainer to Stallone, in *Rocky* (76, John G. Avildsen); *Burnt Offerings* (76, Dan Curtis); *Golden Rendezvous* (77, Ashley Lazarus); *The Manitou* (78, William Girdler); *Magic* (78, Richard Attenborough); *Foul Play* (78, Colin Higgins); and *Rocky II* (79, Sylvester Stallone).

He was in *When Time Ran Out* (80, James Goldstone); *Final Assignment* (80, Paul Almond); *Clash of the Titans* (81, Desmond Davis); very good as a stubborn priest in *True Confessions* (81, Ulu Grosbard); *The Last Chase* (81, Martyn Burke); *Rocky III* (82, Stallone); narrating *Twilight Zone—The Movie* (83, John Landis); *Wet Gold* (84, Dick Lowry); *Santa Claus* (85, Jeannot Szwarc); *Outrage!* (86, Walter Grauman); *King Lear* (87, Jean-Luc Godard); *Mr. North* (88, Danny Huston); *Full Moon in Blue Water* (88, Peter Masterson); *State of Grace* (90, Phil Joanou); *Rocky V* (90, John G. Avildsen)—he had missed *Rocky IV*; *Grumpy Old Men* (93, Donald Petrie); *Ripper* (96, Phil Parmet).

Bette Midler, b. Honolulu, Hawaii, 1945

The Rose (79, Mark Rydell) is not a great film. It offended some people because it was not completely Janis Joplin, because the music was not always "authentic," and because the atmosphere at the concerts was "wrong." No matter. Bette Midler—who was nominated for best actress Oscar in what was really her debut—was remarkable: without ever being conventionally beautiful as movies measure that myth, she was pretty, appealing, sexy, needy, disturbing, and repellent. There was a commitment to the performance and the singing that legitimately carried the film. To be so good so far out on a limb is a way of indicating how "uncastable" a player may be. Ms. Midler ran into very difficult times from which she has only emerged as a comic, camp gorgon—often very funny, and usually defiantly likeable. But there is a hurt in her cocky grin, as if to say we have let the rose wither.

She had a small role in *Hawaii* (65, George Roy Hill), years before *The Rose*. After that, she worked as singer and comedienne before the great challenge of the Joplin biopic. Thereafter, she did a concert film, *Divine Madness* (80, Michael Ritchie), and got into much publicized disputes during and after the making of *Jinxed!* (82, Don Siegel).

For several years she did no film work, and then made a happy return in *Down and Out in Beverly Hills* (86, Paul Mazursky). This was the start of a run of films in which she was encouraged to overdo everything: *Ruthless People* (86, Jim Abrahams, David Zucker, and Jerry Zucker); *Outrageous Fortune* (87, Arthur Hiller); *Beaches* (88, Garry Marshall); *Big Business* (88, Abrahams); *Stella* (90, John Erman); and patently ill-matched with Woody Allen in *Scenes from a Mall* (91, Mazursky). She then took another big role, as the entertainer in *F r the Boys* (91, Rydell), a call resolutely resisted by audiences. After *Hocus Pocus* (93, Kenny Ortega), she had a personal success on TV as Rose in *Gypsy* (93, Emile Ardolino).

Her uneasy relationship with the movies has not altered: she had an uncredited bit in *Get Shorty* (95, Barry Sonnenfeld); she excelled in *The First Wives Club* (96, Hugh Wilson) and *That Old Feeling* (97, Carl Reiner); but *Drowning Mona* (00, Nick Gomez) did nothing, and with *Isn't She Great* (00, Andrew Bergman), where she played Jacqueline Susann, it was as if the audience had forgotten the woman from history.

In 2001, she did the TV series, *Bette* (Andrew D. Weyman).

Toshiro Mifune (1920–97),
b. Tsingtao, China

If any hundred customers at the New York or London film festivals were asked to make a list of Japanese actors and actresses, I doubt if anyone would get more than ten votes—except for Toshiro Mifune, who might get ninety. It is also likely that he would be the *only* name appearing—with no mention of Kinuyo Tanaka, Machiko Kyo, Hideko Takamine, Setsuko Hara, or even Takashi Shimura, who is magnificent as the man who is dying in *Ikiru/Living* (52, Akira Kurosawa), as the leader of the *Seven Samurai* (54, Kurosawa), and in *The Life of Oharu* (52, Kenji Mizoguchi).

I have nothing against Toshiro Mifune (or nothing much—I *am* averse to actors who huff and puff that much). The greater problem is the degree to which he is revered in the West for endorsing so many Western fallacies about the virtues of valor, swordplay, and rigor mortis in the upper lip (or upper head). Japanese film may be innately feminine—its actresses are more glorious than its actors—but Japanese acting (as witness Shimura) is so rich in restraint, detail, and inner life. While Mifune was, patently, an actor made for such barbarous things as *Grand Prix* (66, John Frankenheimer); the animalistic confrontation with Lee Marvin in *Hell in the Pacific* (68, John Boorman); *Red Sun* (71, Terence Young); *Paper Tiger* (75, Ken Annakin); his Admiral Yamamoto in *Midway* (76, Jack Smight); *1941* (79, Steven Spielberg); *Winter Kills* (79, William Richert); on TV in *Shogun* (80, Jerry London); *The Bushido Blade* (81, Tom Kotani); *The Challenge* (82, Frankenheimer); and *Inchon* (82, Young).

Of course, there is more to Mifune than that drab list. In Japan, he was an heroic actor, furiously energetic when young, yet laconic in middle age. Surely he copied John Wayne, and surely others (like Eastwood) have copied him. He functioned as a producer on several samurai films. Yet note that he was never used by Ozu or Naruse—just as Mifune needs to be put in his decent place, so there is greater need to understand Akira Kurosawa's secure hold on the second rank.

Though born in China, he had Japanese parents. After service in the army during the war, he made *Snow Trail* (47, Senkichi Taniguchi); *Drunken Angel* (48, Kurosawa); the bandit in *Rashomon* (50, Kurosawa); *The Life of Oharu; Miyamoto Murashi* (54, Hiroshi Inagaki); a little mature for the young showoff in *Seven Samurai; Throne of Blood* (57, Kurosawa); *The Rickshaw Man* (58, Inagaki); *The Bad Sleep Well* (60, Kurosawa); *The Important Man* (61, Ismael Rodriguez); *Yojimbo* (61, Kurosawa); *Legacy of the 500,000* (62), which he directed himself; *Red Beard* (65, Kurosawa); *Rebellion* (67, Masaki Kobayashi); *Akage* (69, Kihachi Okamoto), and many others.

This is not to say that Mifune is other than remarkable—in the battle scenes of *Seven Samurai* he seems as powerful and as elemental as the great rain. But consider—in how many films does Mifune play a man who has a family relationship such as you know from your own life? In other words, he is America's Japanese. If Ozu had made *Hell in the Pacific,* or half of it, Lee Marvin might have faced tougher competition—a shy, wordy man, with family stories to tell, habits to observe, and butterflies to follow on the island. *Talk in the Pacific* perhaps? Hell comes so early in the American imagination but is often so crude an ordeal.

Sarah Miles, b. Ingatestone, England, 1941
Called up straight from RADA to seduce Olivier in *Term of Trial* (62, Peter Glenville), Sarah Miles was originally typed as slut material—a husky, wide-eyed nymphet. But in *The Servant* (63, Joseph Losey), as Vera from Manchester, she shattered the stereotype and thrust sexual appetite into British films. She managed the sultry authority of the waif on the kitchen table who pats her stomach as she complains of the heat and the wretched misery of the outcast who tumbles in out of the rain in a garish wig. Her performance, like that of Bogarde, was part of a sexual ballet, swooping in and out of seduction and dictatorship. It also smelled of a provincial scrubber up in the smoke—remember her excitement as she is driven away from the railway station.

Perhaps Sarah Miles's unexpected willfulness had something to do with Vera being one of the few whole women in Losey's work. It certainly affected her subsequent career. For she moved hesitantly away from the slut, to the short *The Six-Sided Triangle* (63, Christopher Miles, her

brother) and *The Ceremony* (63, Laurence Harvey). She was a poppet in boater and scarf in *Those Magnificent Men in Their Flying Machines* (65, Ken Annakin) and then an Irish innocent in *I Was Happy Here* (65, Desmond Davis). She seemed bewildered and disenchanted by her peripheral part in *Blow-Up* (66, Michelangelo Antonioni) and dropped out of films.

She was brought back by Robert Bolt, whom she married: as another Irish girl, *Ryan's Daughter* (70, David Lean), and a jittery rag doll *Lady Caroline Lamb* (72, Bolt). Neither was especially rewarding; whereas she might have saved *The Go-Between* from complacency if she had been coaxed into bringing the spite, selfishness, and sensuality to the part that Julie Christie ignored or if Alan Bridges had directed that film as sharply as he did *The Hireling* (73), with Miles in another L. P. Hartley story. She was incongruous in *The Man Who Loved Cat Dancing* (73, Richard C. Sarafian); Estella in *Great Expectations* (75, Joseph Hardy); at the soft center of some silly sex scenes in *The Sailor Who Fell from Grace with the Sea* (76, Lewis John Carlino); vainly trying to be a pre-Raphaelite Lauren Bacall in *The Big Sleep* (78, Michael Winner).

She was in *Priest of Love* (80, Miles) as a film star; *Venom* (81, Piers Haggard); *Walter and June* (82, Stephen Frears); *Ordeal by Innocence* (84, Desmond Davis); *Steaming* (85, Losey); *Hope and Glory* (87, John Boorman); *White Mischief* (87, Michael Radford); *A Ghost in Monte Carlo* (90, John Hough); *Dotkniecie Reki* (92, Krzysztof Zanussi); *The Accidental Detective* (00, Vanna Paoli); *Days of Grace* (01, Claver Salizzato); *Jurij* (01, Stefano Gabrini).

Vera Miles (Vera Ralston),
b. Boise City, Oklahoma, 1929
There is a moment in *The Wrong Man* (57, Alfred Hitchcock) when the audience's agony for Henry Fonda is expressed on screen by the first sign of mental breakdown in his wife, Vera Miles. Immediately, the film becomes more profound, a marvelous touch of the coldness and sympathy that go hand in hand with Hitchcock. Vera Miles breaks up in a way that shows how seldom one has seen untheatrical distress. She turns plain and inept. No wonder Hitchcock put such ability under contract. But, in truth, she has never been used as searchingly again. Pregnant by her first husband, Tarzan Gordon Scott, she had to miss the part in *Vertigo* that Hitchcock had groomed her for, and that lifted Kim Novak into immortality.

She had had to change her name to avoid confusion with the less interesting first lady of Republic, Vera Hruba Ralston. She worked on TV and made her debut in *For Men Only* (52, Paul Henreid). Thereafter she was the woman in Westerns: *The Charge at Feather River* (53, Gordon Douglas); *Wichita* (55, Jacques Tourneur); excellent in *The Searchers* (56, John Ford). She was second fiddle to Joan Crawford in *Autumn Leaves* (56, Robert Aldrich); *23 Paces to Baker Street* (56, Henry Hathaway); *Beau James* (57, Melville Shavelson); *The FBI Story* (59, Mervyn Le Roy); *Beyond This Place* (59, Jack Cardiff); *Five Branded Women* (60, Martin Ritt); and *A Touch of Larceny* (59, Guy Hamilton).

Hitchcock recalled her for the ordeal of seeking out Mrs. Bates at the end of *Psycho* (60), but left her character underdeveloped. Since then, she has worked in less significant roles: *Back Street* (61, David Miller); *The Man Who Shot Liberty Valance* (62, Ford); *The Hanged Man* (64, Don Siegel); *The Spirit Is Willing* (67, William Castle); *Gentle Giant* (67, James Neilson); *Sergeant Ryker* (67, Buzz Kulik); *One of Our Spies Is Missing* (67, E. Darrel Hallenbeck); *Kona Coast* (68, Lamont Johnson); *Hellfighters* (68, Andrew V. McLaglen); *Mission Batangas* (68, Keith Larsen, her second husband); *The Wild Country* (71, Robert Totten); *Baffled!* (71, Philip Leacock); *One Little Indian* (73, Bernard McEveety); *Runaway* (73, David Lowell Rich); and *The Castaway Cowboy* (74, Vincent McEveety).

She was in *Run for the Roses* (79, Henry Levin); *Roughnecks* (80, Bernard McEveety); *Our Family Business* (81, Robert Collins); *Travis McGee* (82, McLaglen); *Brainwaves* (82, Uli Lommel); *Mazes and Monsters* (82, Steven H. Stern); *Psycho II* (83, Richard Franklin); *Helen Keller: The Miracle Continues* (84, Alan Gibson); *The Invitation* (84, Larry Stewart); *International Airport* (85, Charles S. Dubin and Don Chaffey); *Into the Night* (85, John Landis); *The Hijacking of the Achille Lauro* (89, Collins); *Separate Lives* (95, David Madden).

Lewis Milestone (Lewis Milstein), (1895–1980), b. Chisinaw, Ukraine
1925: *Seven Sinners*. 1926: *The Caveman; The New Klondike*. 1927: *Two Arabian Knights*. 1928: *The Garden of Eden; The Racket*. 1929: *Betrayal; New York Nights*. 1930: *All Quiet on the Western Front*. 1931: *The Front Page*. 1932: *Rain*. 1933: *Hallelujah, I'm a Bum*. 1934: *The Captain Hates the Sea*. 1935: *Paris in Spring*. 1936: *Anything Goes; The General Died at Dawn*. 1939: *Of Mice and Men*. 1940: *The Night of Nights; Lucky Partners*. 1941: *Our Russian Front* (codirected with Joris Ivens) (d); *My Life with Caroline*. 1943: *Edge of Darkness; The North Star*. 1944: *The Purple Heart*. 1945: *A Walk in the Sun*. 1946: *The Strange Love of Martha Ivers*. 1948: *Arch of Triumph; No Minor Vices*. 1949: *The Red Pony*. 1951: *Halls of Montezuma*. 1952: *Kangaroo; Les Miserables*. 1953: *Melba*. 1954: *They Who Dare*. 1955: *The Widow*. 1959: *Pork Chop Hill*. 1960: *Ocean's 11*. 1962: *Mutiny on the Bounty*.

Milestone came to the United States in 1917 and served in the First World War. In 1920 he went to Hollywood and worked as assistant editor and writer with, among others, William A. Seiter. It was the film version of Erich Maria Remarque's novel, *All Quiet on the Western Front,* that established Milestone as a leading director, partly because the warning of the film was reinforced by sound, and partly because the battle scenes, contrary to the theme of the movie, were undeniably spectacular.

At this period, Milestone had an inventive, flashy technique that passed for style and a knack of picking or being picked for interesting properties. *The Front Page* was one of the best early talking comedies, although the talk belonged to Ben Hecht and Charles MacArthur and was to be used rather better by Hawks in *His Girl Friday*. *Rain* was a failure; it was a controversial subject, cannily cast: Joan Crawford as Sadie Thompson and Walter Huston as Rev. Atkinson. *Hallelujah, I'm a Bum* was an eccentric Depression piece, pairing Jolson and Harry Langdon. *The Captain Hates the Sea* was John Gilbert's last movie.

Throughout the 1930s, Milestone worked in the theatre as well as the movies and this added to the idea that he chose his films carefully. In fact, his selection seemed based on variety for its own sake: *Anything Goes* was an Ethel Merman/Bing Crosby musical; *The General Died at Dawn* an excellent Gary Cooper adventure set in China; *Of Mice and Men* an honorable version of Steinbeck, helped by a sensitive performance from Burgess Meredith. Nothing suggested that Milestone was more than a competent director. War showed that he could be a good deal less.

Although his initial reputation rested on a monument against war, his Second World War projects settled for the glamour of battle and the standard group portrait of unambiguous soldiers: *The North Star, The Purple Heart, A Walk in the Sun,* and later, *Halls of Montezuma*. After the war, the surface excitement flickered out. *The Strange Love of Martha Ivers* was a rich, neurotic thriller, but *Arch of Triumph*—again from a Remarque novel—was an overlong commercial failure (it is also the one really disturbing film he made). He had an inexplicable interest in Australian subjects (*Kangaroo* and *Melba*) and did a very dull remake of Victor Hugo. *Pork Chop Hill* was the Korean war, dutifully disenchanted, but still stirring whenever his tracking shots began traversing the battlefield. *Ocean's 11* needed a Gordon Douglas, while *Mutiny on the Bounty* ran aground on a loathing between Brando and Richard Harris that obscured the original antagonism between Bligh and Fletcher Christian.

John Milius, b. St Louis, Missouri, 1944
1973: *Dillinger*. 1975: *The Wind and the Lion*. 1978: *Big Wednesday*. 1982: *Conan the Barbar-*

ian. 1984: *Red Dawn*. 1989: *Farewell to the King*. 1991: *Flight of the Intruder*. 1994: *Motorcycle Gang* (TV). 1997: *Rough Riders* (TV).

Milius's father was a shoe manufacturer. When the family moved to California, the child devoted himself to surfing, kendo, Hemingway, Patton, MacArthur, and Teddy Roosevelt. In later years, the study and firing of guns was added to the pantheon. Milius studied film at the University of Southern California and started writing scripts furiously. Many were shelved, but he got a credit on *The Devil's 8* (69, Burt Topper), and thereupon used his knowledge of the Vietnam war and his sympathy for tyrant-heroes to write the first version of *Apocalypse Now* for Coppola. The dynamic Kilgore sequences in the finished film seem closest to Milius.

In the next few years, Milius rewrote *Dirty Harry* (71, Don Siegel) and undoubtedly contributed the vigilante fervor that overflowed Siegel's customary cynicism; he also worked on *Evel Knievel* (71, Marvin Chomsky), another movie that might have benefited from more of Milius's enthusiasm for its subject. He wrote *Jeremiah Johnson* (72, Sydney Pollack); *The Life and Times of Judge Roy Bean* (72, John Huston); *Magnum Force* (73, Ted Post), written with Michael Cimino; and *Melvin Purvis—G Man* (74, Dan Curtis). Those are four problem pictures: *Jeremiah Johnson* required more extravagance than Redford or Pollack could muster. Instead of ecological treatise, it should have been a wilderness legend, Jack London verging on King Ubu. *Roy Bean* sacrificed madness to whimsicality. *Magnum Force* was too much a Clint Eastwood vehicle, too little a study of fascism wearing a badge. And *Melvin Purvis* was a TV afterthought to Milius's first feature.

Of the films he has directed, *Dillinger* is the best: shot with raffish elegance and humor, imaginatively cast, and made with the same sardonic bravura that characterized *Scarface*. The rivalry of Ben Johnson and Warren Oates is always comic, but never taken too far. *The Wind and the Lion* is cheerfully fabricated Rooseveltiana, with Sean Connery as a Berber. It's a boys' book of heroes kind of film, a foolish but consistent throwback to forties cinema and earlier imperialist confidence. The flair for youthful adventure was just as strong in *Big Wednesday*, a hymn to surfing, and Milius's least focused narrative.

Over the years, Milius had earned and even provoked the press reputation of a strident, magnum-brandishing reactionary. But he is more than that. He is an anarchist, he is articulate, and he has an unshakable faith in human grandeur that might work very well with a more humdrum topic than he has yet taken on. Film may be too small or ephemeral a passion for him. But he has

one great scene already: he helped write the speech Robert Shaw's Quint pronounces on the sinking of the *Indianapolis* in *Jaws* (75, Steven Spielberg).

He was also an executive producer on *1941* (79, Spielberg), which he helped write; on *Hardcore* (79, Paul Schrader); and on *Used Cars* (80, Robert Zemeckis). A little later, he coproduced *Uncommon Valor* (83, Ted Kotcheff) and *Fatal Beauty* (87, Tom Holland), and contributed the story to *Extreme Prejudice* (87, Walter Hill).

But as a director, Milius has wandered and strayed. His own great confidence and the lyricism of his heroism have seemed forced. *Conan* gave a boost to the career of Arnold Schwarzenegger; *Flight of the Intruder* and *Red Dawn* were abject and stupid. *Farewell to the King* is the one interesting project, though it falls far short of its Melville-like potential.

In 1993, Milius could do no more than the script for *Geronimo* (Walter Hill). A year later, he wrote *Clear and Present Danger* (94, Phillip Noyce). His two TV movies repeated earlier, and younger, interests. But they were shown—which is more than happened with *Lion's Share*.

Ray Milland (Reginald Alfred Truscott-Jones) (1905–86), b. Neath, Wales

Milland had little trouble playing American as a young man. He wore clothes like an officer, and he was good-looking in a glossy way. He smiled to order, and partnered a lot of actresses with aplomb. But there was something else in the man, something more autocratic or less good-natured, and it was promise of the saturnine figure from *Dial M for Murder* and the man who, at fifty, would make films of his own that were stark and forbidding.

He had begun in Britain. After King's College, London, and service in the Guards, he drifted into movies apparently while visiting a girlfriend actress at the studios. As Spike Milland, he had a small part in *The Plaything* (29, Castleton Knight). Smoothed out into Raymond Milland, he made several more British pictures, including *The Flying Scotsman* (29, Knight) and *Lady from the Sea* (29, Knight), before going to Hollywood to appear at Metro, opposite Marion Davies, in *The Bachelor Father* (31, Robert Z. Leonard). He stayed a year in America, in several films, the best of which was *Payment Deferred* (32, Lothar Mendes).

Returning to Britain, he was in *Orders Is Orders* (33, Walter Forde) before going back to Paramount, to small parts in *Bolero* (34, Wesley Ruggles) and *We're Not Dressing* (34, Norman Taurog), and thence to a contract. For the next ten years, Milland worked hard in a variety of supporting roles and romantic leads at Paramount and on loan: *Many Happy Returns* (34, Norman

Z. McLeod); *Four Hours to Kill* (35, Mitchell Leisen); *The Glass Key* (35, Frank Tuttle); *The Gilded Lily* (35, Ruggles) with Claudette Colbert and Fred MacMurray; at Universal with Deanna Durbin in *Three Smart Girls* (36, Henry Koster); in Mitchell Leisen's *Easy Living* (37), *Arise My Love* (40), *I Wanted Wings* (41), and *Lady in the Dark* (44); for Wellman in *Men With Wings* (38) and *Beau Geste* (39); *Hotel Imperial* (39, Robert Florey); a great success back in Britain in Asquith's *French Without Tears* (39); in De Mille's *Reap the Wild Wind* (42), and otherwise the model squire to Paulette Goddard, Loretta Young, and Dorothy Lamour. Then in 1942 he played with Ginger Rogers in Billy Wilder's first film, *The Major and the Minor.*

After his first hint of vulnerability as the man freed from an asylum and plunged into intrigue in Fritz Lang's *The Ministry of Fear* (44), *Till We Meet Again* (44, Frank Borzage), and *The Uninvited* (44, Lewis Allen), Wilder cast Milland as the drunk in *The Lost Weekend* (45). That Oscar-winning performance is far too self-destructive, too dreamily trapped in the dire romance of booze, to be saved by the happy ending appended to the film. Milland suddenly revealed himself as an actor capable of showing all the flaws in attractiveness. But that promise was not taken up by his employer, largely because the bleakness of *Lost Weekend* was so far ahead of its time.

Milland was able to exploit the decline in his romantic appeal by pursuing more interesting parts in less successful films: thus *Kitty* (45) and *Golden Earrings* (47) for Leisen were throwbacks; but *California* (46), *The Big Clock* (48), *Alias Nick Beal* (49), and *Copper Canyon* (50), all for John Farrow, extended his range. In 1948, he returned to Britain to act in *So Evil, My Love* (Allen), and again in 1951 when he acted in and produced Jacques Tourneur's dismal *Circle of Danger.* In America, his contract with Paramount was running out. After *A Life of Her Own* (50, George Cukor), he made two more films that tried to renew the theme of alcoholism: *Night into Morning* (51, Fletcher Markle) and George Stevens's *Something to Live For* (52), with Joan Fontaine, before making *Jamaica Run* (53, Lewis R. Foster), his last Paramount contract film.

He now embarked on a series of offbeat films. In 1952, he had appeared in Russell Rouse's *The Thief*, an interesting thriller with very little dialogue. In 1954, he played a charming conspirer toward Grace Kelly's death in *Dial M for Murder*, scathingly attuned to Hitchcock's black comedy; he also directed his own Western, *A Man Alone.* The next year he had the right rich man's languor as Stanford White in Fleischer's *The Girl in the Red Velvet Swing.* After that, he directed *Lisbon* (56), the brilliant *The Safecracker* (58), *Panic in Year Zero* (62), and less notably *Hostile Witness*

(68). He also acted in *Three Brave Men* (57, Philip Dunne), *The River's Edge* (57, Allan Dwan), and in two Roger Corman films: *The Premature Burial* (61) and *The Man with the X-Ray Eyes* (63).

It was sad that this low-budget excellence should pass unnoticed and that the world should rediscover him as the father in the sickly *Love Story* (70, Arthur Hiller). However, he seemed conscious of that inadequate offering for new audiences and once more demonstrated his range and enterprise: acting in *Company of Killers* (70, Jerry Thorpe); *Embassy* (72, Gordon Hessler); renewing his taste for science fiction, in the remarkable *Frogs* (72, George McCowan); with Frankie Howerd in *The House in Nightmare Park* (73, Peter Sykes); *Terror in the Wax Museum* (73, George Fenady); *Gold* (74, Peter Hunt); *The Swiss Conspiracy* (75, Jack Arnold); *Aces High* (76, Jack Gold); *The Last Tycoon* (76, Elia Kazan); *Mayday at 40,000 Feet!* (76, Robert Butler); and *Oliver's Story* (78, John L. Korty).

In his last years, he was to be seen in many different kinds of rubbish, his aplomb still plummy: *Battlestar Galactica* (79, Richard A. Colla); *The Darker Side of Terror* (79, Gus Trikonis); *Game for Vultures* (79, James Fargo); *The Attic* (79, George Edwards); *The Dream Merchants* (80, Vincent Sherman); *Survival Run* (80, Larry Spiegel); *Our Family Business* (81, Robert Collins), playing a Mafia boss; *The Royal Romance of Charles and Diana* (82, Peter Levin); *Starflight: The Plane That Couldn't Land* (83, Jerry Jameson); *Cave-in!* (83, Fenady); *Sherlock Holmes and the Masks of Death* (84, Roy Ward Baker); and *The Sea Serpent* (86, Gregory Greens).

David Miller (1909–92),
b. Paterson, New Jersey

1941: *Billy the Kid.* 1942: *Sunday Punch; Flying Tigers.* 1949: *Top o' the Morning.* 1950: *Love Happy; Our Very Own.* 1951: *Saturday's Hero.* 1952: *Sudden Fear.* 1954: *The Beautiful Stranger/Twist of Fate.* 1955: *Diane.* 1956: *The Opposite Sex.* 1957: *The Story of Esther Costello.* 1959: *Happy Anniversary.* 1960: *Midnight Lace.* 1961: *Back Street.* 1962: *Lonely Are the Brave; Captain Newman M.D.* 1968: *Hammerhead.* 1969: *Hail, Hero!.* 1973: *Executive Action.* 1979: *The Best Place to Be* (TV); *Love for Rent* (TV); *Goldie and the Boxer* (TV). 1981: *Goldie and the Boxer Go to Hollywood* (TV).

Miller began as an editor with Columbia in 1940 and moved on to MGM where he made a number of shorts. His work as a director was very inconsistent: thus an initial, stolid Western that neglects every opportunity evident to a director like Arthur Penn and that was made by MGM to thwart Howard Hughes's *The Outlaw;* a second, *Lonely Are the Brave,* that is one of the most original accounts of the modernization of the West. Nor is it easy to equate the benevolence of *Captain Newman M.D.* with the romance of *Back Street,* the rampant melodrama of *Esther Costello,* much less the Republic period *Flying Tigers,* which has John Wayne aiding Chiang Kai-shek against the Japanese, or *Love Happy,* the last of the true Marx Brothers movies, with Groucho homing in on Marilyn Monroe.

But Miller has two very effective suspense films to his credit—*Sudden Fear* and *Midnight Lace.* Both involve a woman increasingly aware of her peril, with a sure sense of shadowy interiors and editing, an ability to build tension, and better-than-average threatened performances from Joan Crawford and Doris Day. Miller was a lightweight, but he had enough good moments to excuse *The Opposite Sex,* a declawed remake of Cukor's *The Women.*

George Miller, b. Brisbane, Australia, 1945
1979: *Mad Max.* 1981: *The Road Warrior.* 1983: an episode from *Twilight Zone—The Movie.* 1985: *Mad Max Beyond Thunderdome.* 1987: *The Witches of Eastwick.* 1992: *Lorenzo's Oil.* 1995: *Babe.* 1998: *Babe: Pig in the City.*

It's a great stretch to go from the very stylish, utterly cheerful mayhem of *Mad Max* to the harrowingly small world of *Lorenzo's Oil.* Has there ever been another qualified M.D. who became a movie director? And then recall the beautiful, playful, and very idiosyncratic view of New England, Updike, and modern sexuality in *The Witches of Eastwick.* The range is so great that no one may have an adequate sense of Miller yet from his work. But this is spectacular versatility with a true eye for action, whether on the large or very small scale. Added to which, Miller did the best episode from *Twilight Zone,* with John Lithgow as a desperate passenger on a plane.

The vision of a bizarre, postapocalyptic art and heroism in the outback had the smack of comic books. But in *The Witches of Eastwick,* Miller's dynamic camera style went from comedy to horror with such ease that it was easy to miss the affectionate gaze on the women and a Satanic Nicholson who never stopped being dead attractive or lethally funny. *Lorenzo's Oil* revealed the doctor, as well as an unshakable dedication to the detailed facts of its story.

Then, out of the blue, he made two films about a sweet pig—one warm, and a hit; the next darker and alarming.

Sir John Mills (Lewis Ernest Watts Mills),
b. North Elmham, England, 1908
The Mills family has so crowded us out with insipid, tennis-club talent it is easy to forget that Mills is a reasonable actor. He has made more trite or bad films than good ones, and suffered

from the way British cinema has used him as officer material under stress. Nevertheless, his long career is sprinkled with worthwhile things, and if the supporting actor Oscar for his village idiot in *Ryan's Daughter* (70, David Lean) was more a tribute to the makeup artist and to English admiration of impersonation, he might have had the same award for his peasant caught up in the retreat from Moscow in *War and Peace* (56, King Vidor). For Mills is a small man, with an East Anglian complexion and a sense of the ordinary that suits him better to the ranks than to the mess. He was trained in song-and-dance, and one suspects he should have been encouraged in comedy.

But Britain forced responsibility on him: *In Which We Serve* (42, David Lean and Noel Coward); *We Dive at Dawn* (43, Anthony Asquith); *This Happy Breed* (44, Lean); *Scott of the Antarctic* (48, Charles Frend); *Morning Departure* (50, Roy Baker); *The Colditz Story* (54, Guy Hamilton); *Above Us the Waves* (54, Ralph Thomas); *Ice Cold in Alex* (58, J. Lee Thompson); and *I Was Monty's Double* (58, John Guillermin). He was a private soldier in *Dunkirk* (58, Leslie Norman), but the strain of so many stiff upper lips was finally released in the crack-up of *Tunes of Glory* (60, Ronald Neame).

Mills had been in British films since the early 1930s: *The Midshipmaid* (32, Albert de Courville); *Those Were the Days* (34, Thomas Bentley); *Britannia of Billingsgate* (35, Sinclair Hill); *Forever England* (35, Walter Forde), a version of C. S. Forester's *Brown on Resolution; Tudor Rose* (36, Robert Stevenson); *O.H.M.S.* (37, Raoul Walsh); *Goodbye, Mr. Chips* (39, Sam Wood); *The Green Cockatoo* (40, William Cameron Menzies); *Old Bill and Son* (40, Ian Dalrymple); *Cottage to Let* (41, Asquith); *The Black Sheep of Whitehall* (42, Basil Dean and Will Hay); *The Big Blockade* (42, Frend); and *The Young Mr. Pitt* (42, Carol Reed).

Invalided out of the forces, Mills was inevitably drawn into the celluloid war effort, but in 1946 he was excellent (if too old) as Pip in *Great Expectations* (46, Lean). And as the years went by he took the few serious opportunities that came his way amid pompous or jolly nonsense: *The October Man* (47, Baker); *So Well Remembered* (47, Edward Dmytryk); *The History of Mr. Polly* (49, Anthony Pelissier); *The Rocking Horse Winner* (49, Pelissier); *Mr. Denning Drives North* (51, Anthony Kimmins); *The Long Memory* (52, Robert Hamer); *The Gentle Gunman* (52, Basil Dearden); *Hobson's Choice* (54, Lean); *The End of the Affair* (54, Dmytryk); *Escapade* (55, Philip Leacock); *It's Great to Be Young* (56, Cyril Frankel); *The Baby and the Battleship* (56, Jay Lewis); and *Town on Trial* (57, Guillermin).

In 1959, for the first time on screen, he appeared, tactfully upstaged, with daughter Hayley in *Tiger Bay* (Thompson). That signaled a decline and some direly cheerful adventures: *Summer of the 17th Doll* (59, Norman); *Swiss Family Robinson* (60, Ken Annakin); *The Singer Not the Song* (61, Baker); *Flame in the Streets* (61, Baker); *Tiara Tahiti* (62, William T. Kotcheff); *The Chalk Garden* (64, Neame); *The Truth About Spring* (65, Richard Thorpe); *Operation Crossbow* (64, Michael Anderson); *King Rat* (66, Bryan Forbes); *Sky West and Crooked* (66, which he directed himself); *The Wrong Box* (66, Forbes); *The Family Way* (66, Roy Boulting); *Africa, Texas Style* (67, Andrew Marton); *Chuka* (67, Gordon Douglas); *Lady Hamilton* (68, Christian-Jaque); *Oh! What a Lovely War* (69, Richard Attenborough); *Run Wild, Run Free* (69, Richard C. Sarafian); *Adam's Woman* (70, Leacock); *Lady Caroline Lamb* (72, Robert Bolt); *Oklahoma Crude* (73, Stanley Kramer); *The "Human" Factor* (75, Edward Dmytryk); *A Choice of Weapons* (76, Kevin Conner); *The Devil's Advocate* (78, Guy Green); *The Big Sleep* (78, Michael Winner); and *The Thirty-Nine Steps* (78, Don Sharp).

He was in *Young at Heart* (80, Stuart Allen); *The Umbrella Man* (80, Claude Whatham); *Operation Safecrack* (81, Alan Gibson); as the Viceroy in *Gandhi* (82, Attenborough); *Sahara* (83, Andrew V. McLaglen); *A Woman of Substance* (84, Sharp); as Dr. Watson in *Sherlock Holmes and the Masks of Death* (84, Roy Ward Baker); *Edge of the Wind* (85, Kenneth Ives); *Murder with Mirrors* (85, Dick Lowry); *Hold That Dream* (86, Sharp); *The True Story of Spit MacPhee* (88, Marcus Cole); *A Tale of Two Cities* (89, Philippe Monnier); *The Lady and the Highwayman* (89, John Hough); *Around the World in 80 Days* (89, Buzz Kulik); and *Ending Up* (89, Peter Sasdy).

Not always well, at or around ninety, Mills has persisted in work: *Night of the Fox* (90, Charles Jarrott); *Harnessing Peacocks* (92, James Cellan Jones); *Frankenstein* (93, David Wickes); as Jack the Ripper in *Deadly Advice* (93, Mandie Fletcher); *The Big Freeze* (93, Eric Sykes); as Mr. Chuffey in *Martin Chuzzlewit* (94, Pedr James); *The Grotesque* (95, John-Paul Davidson); as Old Norway in *Hamlet* (96, Kenneth Branagh); *Bean* (97, Mel Smith); *Cats* (98, David Mallet); *The Gentleman Thief* (01, Justin Hardy); *Bright Young Things* (03, Stephen Fry).

Anthony Minghella,

b. Ryde, Isle of Wight, England, 1954
1991: *Truly, Madly, Deeply*. 1993: *Mr. Wonderful*. 1996: *The English Patient*. 1999: *The Talented Mr. Ripley*. 2000: *Play*. 2003: *Cold Mountain*.

Something quite odd has happened with the career of Anthony Minghella. In 1996, he was lavishly rewarded—first by the critics and then by the Academy—for a brilliant screen translation of

a novel by Michael Ondaatje that seemed one of the least likely movies in waiting. I admired the film very much—not just for its screenplay, for Minghella's rapt collaboration on editing and sound with Walter Murch, but for the sustaining of so many disparate moods and stories. Yet it was possible, even in '96, to feel that the movie had been overpraised—and wonderfully promoted by Miramax.

Rebuke set in three years later with *The Talented Mr. Ripley*, a considerably better film and—as I suspect—a much more personal work. It was not exactly, or simply, Patricia Highsmith, and that offended some people and helped them to ignore the deeply felt study of a personality so insecure that it wants to be someone else. What made *Ripley* so remarkable was not just the feeling for jazz, Italy, young people, and class in the 1950s, but using all those things to explore an existential topic—being and acting—that had come to mean so much more by the nineties.

Minghella rose by way of the University of Hull (where he studied and taught) to be a playwright and then a writer and director with Jim Henson. I have seen one of his Henson works, a fairy story that is filled with a sense of death and magic—something that leads directly into his very striking and touching debut feature, *Truly, Madly, Deeply*, one of the funniest and yet most serious films about death and mourning.

My guess is that Minghella, for all his great skills, is a slow and even a shy developer. I doubt we have yet seen the best or even the darkest from him. But it is so rare nowadays to look at a filmmaker approaching fifty and feel that much confidence or anticipation.

Liza Minnelli, b. Los Angeles, 1946

Genetically, it must have been possible that Judy Garland and Vincente Minnelli would produce a child made to be a plumber or a nurse. But not this one. It is difficult to exaggerate the problems that must have confronted Liza Minnelli. No matter that she coped with life with her mother, many others failed—notably Mother herself. Living in a variety of locations and being perpetually hauled up and down financial and emotional hillsides, Liza Minnelli grew up as a performer in the reckless area of emotional exposure that her mother had made famous. How could one expect a daughter looking so like the mother, and so naturally repeating Garland's breathless vocal mannerisms, not to pursue the mother?

The ordeal MGM imposed on their child actress was at least compensated for by a stream of films before she broke down. Today, the musical is desert territory, so that the same undeniable impulse that gripped mother and daughter is all the harder to channel through fruitful artistic forms. And how much one fears that Judy Garland's chaotic life may be replayed—out of inheritance, the shared need for audience love, and the unvoiced urging of the media in their search for the ghoulish echo. In Garland and Liza Minnelli, there is the same perilous confusion of talent and taste with exhibitionism and neurosis. And if Garland's childhood was more strained than any other, Minnelli has the burden of matching or departing from her mother. The latter might seem betrayal, but the former could lead to destruction. Just as there was a grotesque milking of maudlin sensibilities (as well as a quite brutal rivalry) when Garland and Minnelli appeared together at the London Palladium, so Minnelli has once reprised that occasion with a nightclub entertainer, a man who does an impersonation of Garland that epitomizes all the preying upon self-indulgence that dragged her down.

Liza Minnelli is a brash singer and a lumpish dancer, trading on nervous vitality. Both shortcomings were right for *Cabaret* (72, Bob Fosse) and the sprawling coarseness of 1930s Berlin. But the Oscar for that performance was proof of how ready the Academy was to be nostalgic. The film of *Cabaret* was built up to suit her, not just with added songs but in the way the Sally Bowles character was turned to fit our notion of Liza Minnelli's heritage, especially in "What good is sitting, alone in your room?" and "She was the loveliest corpse I've ever seen." How near that comes (and with that inimitable showbiz bad taste) to an endorsement of the way Garland "lived life to the full, rejecting caution." And on stage, Minnelli has her mother's need to talk to the audience, to fluff as a pretext for confiding until it becomes unclear whether the fluffs are accidental or endemic. The same strident, anxious self-advertisement once called a press conference to confess that she was in love with Peter Sellers.

To be harsh, when Liza Minnelli tries to be soulful as an actress—and that is her only vein, apart from the scatty commercials for her self—she looks half-baked, derivative, and untrained. That is as true in the dreadful emotional passages from *Cabaret* as in *Pookie* (69, Alan J. Pakula), a mannered celebration of kooky spontaneity, and *Tell Me That You Love Me, Junie Moon* (69, Otto Preminger). Only one film captures the sparrow's gaiety that her mother once had: her debut, *Charlie Bubbles* (67, Albert Finney). Otherwise, mother and daughter alike seem to insist that there is a virtue in fatal judgment.

Her reputation was battered by *Lucky Lady* (75, Stanley Donen) and its glum evidence that she could look bewildered and awkward—less vulnerable than numbed. *A Matter of Time* (76, Vincente Minnelli) devastated all hopes of family fruitfulness and was an outright disaster at the box office. From that low point, she came back as Francine Evans in *New York, New York* (77, Mar-

tin Scorsese). Her part there is overshadowed by De Niro's, but she sings well in the forties idiom, impersonates her mother only once, and best of all, channels the emotional distress of that film through her large, suffering eyes. She is subdued in that film—and so she seems to be a good singer as an incidental. She was filmed with great fondness, and her marriage—her second—to Jack Haley Jr. collapsed under pressure of her feelings for Scorsese. Her acting in *New York, New York* was the first sign of maturity, but her life clung to turbulence. Scorsese began to direct her in a stage show, *The Act,* but after disputes he was forced to accept the experienced assistance of Gower Champion.

By 1993, Liza Minnelli was reduced to lip-synching a disastrous song tribute to women at the Academy Awards show that ended up with a wave to Hillary Clinton. And still she comes on to sing the few, cast-iron songs that are hers, dancing less than ever, tactically costumed, and flashing that artillery grin, as if she had never been on a stage before. Her movies have been few: the romantic interest in *Arthur* (81, Steve Gordon); a cameo in *The Muppets Take Manhattan* (84, Frank Oz); she introduced *That's Dancing* (85, Jack Haley Jr.); good on TV as a mother with a son suffering from muscular dystrophy in *A Time to Live* (86, Rick Wallace); *Rent-a-Cop* (88, Jerry London); *Arthur 2: On the Rocks* (88, Bud Yorkin); *Stepping Out* (91, Lewis Gilbert); *Parallel Lives* (94, Linda Yellen); *The West Side Waltz* (95, Ernest Thompson).

Then the wedding—not quite a movie, but a production.

Vincente Minnelli (1910–86), b. Chicago

1943: *Cabin in the Sky; I Dood It.* 1944: *Meet Me in St. Louis.* 1945: *The Clock; Yolanda and the Thief.* 1946: *Ziegfeld Follies* (Minnelli directed ten out of thirteen episodes); *Undercurrent.* 1947: *The Pirate.* 1949: *Madame Bovary.* 1950: *Father of the Bride.* 1951: *An American in Paris; Father's Little Dividend.* 1952: *The Bad and the Beautiful.* 1953: "Mademoiselle," episode from *The Story of Three Loves; The Band Wagon.* 1954: *The Long, Long Trailer; Brigadoon.* 1955: *The Cobweb; Kismet.* 1956: *Lust for Life; Tea and Sympathy.* 1957: *Designing Woman; The Seventh Sin* (codirected with Ronald Neame, uncredited). 1958: *Gigi; The Reluctant Debutante; Some Came Running.* 1960: *Home from the Hill; Bells Are Ringing.* 1961: *The Four Horsemen of the Apocalypse.* 1962: *Two Weeks in Another Town.* 1963: *The Courtship of Eddie's Father.* 1964: *Goodbye Charlie.* 1965: *The Sandpiper.* 1970: *On a Clear Day You Can See Forever.* 1976: *A Matter of Time.*

In *Crazy Like a Fox,* S. J. Perelman included an appreciation of Vincente Minnelli that had the poker-faced disapproval of a particular type of showbiz friendship. It ended with one concession to sentiment: the recollection that Minnelli's work on the stage as a designer and director transcended alleged defects of character—"I owe him plenty," admitted Perelman. And no obsessive filmgoer of the 1940s and 1950s would not echo the cry. When credits seemed to a boy a protracted teasing of proper expectation, it dawned slowly that certain names went with certain pleasures. Those recurring names were the basis of an approach to art: George Cukor, Anthony Mann, Howard Hawks, and—the most flamboyant—Vincente Minnelli.

There was a memory of a shuddering Margaret O'Brien in the Halloween sequence of *Meet Me in St. Louis;* Fred Astaire and Lucille Bremer in Limehouse in *Ziegfeld Follies;* the crane camera swooping down on Astaire's nightmare dance in *Yolanda and the Thief;* the extraordinary profusion of the last part of *An American in Paris,* when plot stopped for extravaganza; the transformation in *Story of Three Loves* when Ricky Nelson looks into the mirror and sees Farley Granger; the puffball blondeness of Lana Turner goaded by Kirk Douglas in *The Bad and the Beautiful.*

But Minnelli's career presents great problems as soon as one looks beyond that initial fondness. Do the fragments come together? Do those melodious camera movements, the most inventive conception of background action, and such ceaseless use of color, costume, and sets make him a major director? Or is he a stylist, unconcerned with subject matter, for years content to film whatever material MGM assigned him? Certainly, the loyalty to one studio seems to have been borne without the agonies that beset, say, Nicholas Ray. And Minnelli was eager to move into new genres; from the musical, he went on to psychological drama, classic novel, domestic comedy, Hollywood melodrama, biopic, epic. Nor is it adequate to pass him off as a ringmaster of the frivolous. For his biopic is a heartrending identification with an artist, as moving as anything in the American cinema. And the artist concerned is not Firbank or Toulouse-Lautrec—but Van Gogh, a harsh, clumsy mystic. *Lust for Life* has everything that is often found absent from Minnelli's work: the use of color, setting, costume, and bravura emotional acting to define a tragic human situation. Yet it was made between the property-box colorfulness of *Kismet* and an uncertain, ladylike venture into "serious" theatre—*Tea and Sympathy.* Perhaps inconsistency is his chief characteristic.

Minnelli came to films with a great reputation in the New York theatre as a designer: at Radio City Music Hall; with the Ziegfeld Follies, and on *Very Warm for May,* a Jerome Kern musical. The talent was immense, but imprecise, and Hollywood was at first uncertain how to use him. Producer Arthur Freed had invited him to MGM, but Minnelli spent two years being generally helpful before he made the inevitable step into direction.

Working usually for Freed, he coincided with the MGM musical—but only coincided. *Cabin in the Sky* is all-black, dwelling gloriously on Lena Horne and Ethel Waters. *Meet Me in St. Louis* is a period piece, more intent on personality and nostalgia than musical routines—a sort of home theatricals musical in which "The Trolley Song" is beautifully integrated with the action. *Ziegfeld Follies* is a series of sketches. While *Yolanda and the Thief, The Pirate,* and *An American in Paris* are willfully stylized and fantastic, inclining toward a new form that might consist only of dance, song, and color. Stunning as these pictures are in moments, the open-air musicals of Donen seem more original. *The Pirate,* especially, looks like the work of a man more eager to decorate than design.

Then there is the odd history of Minnelli and Judy Garland. He was often gay; she was close to frenzy. He was a consummate professional; she was ready to break any rule she could discover. He was tender and considerate; he loved her talent, and he saw the chance of revealing an adult Judy. She always needed protectors. So Minnelli was brought in to replace Fred Zinnemann on *The Clock,* and he delivered a flawless, sweet romance. *Meet Me in St. Louis* was made in chaos but Judy was never more beautiful, and never placed in so stable a family setting. Minnelli's kindness lay in showing Garland looking after Margaret O'Brien, rising to the bittersweet "Have Yourself a Merry Little Christmas," which in her voice is as forlorn a song as "Over the Rainbow." Their marriage lasted from 1945 to 1951, technically, but by the time of *The Pirate* they were estranged. Yet they served each other, and they gave life (and the burden of their unlikely union) to Liza to sort out.

As Minnelli's musicals became less dramatically necessary—*The Band Wagon, Brigadoon, Kismet*—he made delightful comedies in which his rococo instinct in no way distracted one from the dry homespun of Spencer Tracy. *Undercurrent* was a contrived psychological movie, but often intriguing; *Madame Bovary* never worked as a whole, or as the dream of a bourgeois wife. But *The Bad and the Beautiful* was a breakthrough: it opened up a potential for sudden insights in brilliantly regulated melodrama that was one of Minnelli's most fascinating assets. It can be seen in *The Cobweb, Some Came Running, Two Weeks in Another Town,* and *The Courtship of Eddie's Father*—all underrated films, ostensibly lurid or soft subjects that he invested with such intense psychological detail that the narrative faults vanish. In those films, as in *Lust for Life,* the personal story and the visual story lock together. The use of the goldfish in *The Courtship of Eddie's Father*, and the emphasis on interior shape and decor in *The Cobweb*, may be symptomatic of Minnelli's most lasting achievements.

Regularly, his work plunged and rose again: *The Sandpiper* is a dreadful film; *Four Horsemen* a hopeless one, saved locally by the color and by Ingrid Thulin; *Goodbye Charlie* has fine moments but lacks coordination. It was his first film away from MGM and marked an unexplained drying up in his output. *On a Clear Day . . . ,* despite its mangled form on release, shows the same visual distinction and the same interest in imaginative exclusion of outside reality, so that three films in ten years is hard to understand.

On a Clear Day . . . also returned to Minnelli's persistent interest in dream experiences. There is a nice moment in *Yolanda and the Thief* when Frank Morgan wakes Fred Astaire from the dream sequence with the words, "When you have a nightmare you sure keep busy." True enough, and cut off from inner, imaginary feelings, Minnelli sometimes looks uninterested. *Yolanda* is a dull story, transformed in the dream sequences that suddenly call into being all of Minnelli's fantastic control of light, color, shape, and movement. *Meet Me in St. Louis* is a daydream, *An American in Paris* a pretext for a dream. And remember that Minnelli introduces a rather frightening nightmare into *Father of the Bride*. Not only do such enchanted visions recur, but Minnelli's stress on style is itself reaching out for dream: the fluid, self-sufficient sequences of fantastic imagery. That could explain the occasional feeling of indifference to narrative, just as it directs attention to his style.

Carmen Miranda (Maria do Carmo Miranda da Cunha) (1909–55),
b. Marco de Canvezes, Portugal

It was a short career, and in her bizarre fusion of the lacquered look of Punch's Judy with the fruity effulgence of her head she was hardly the most useful or coherent image of things "Latin." Today, anyone doing "Carmen Miranda" might be attacked as a stereotype, barely protected by camp. But in the early forties, she was a cheerful purveyor of the American notion that things south of the border were hot and absurd. Probably 90 percent of Americans believed she was Spanish, whereas she was a Portuguese who had gone to Brazil as a child and become a star in Rio on radio, records, and in movies. She made some films in Brazil, and in 1939 she was in the musical *Streets of Paris* on Broadway. She also did a show at the Waldorf-Astoria, the New York hotel most favored by Hollywood moguls.

Fox snapped her up, and she had her moment: singing "South American Way" in *Down Argentine Way* (40, Irving Cummings); "I-yi-yi-yi-yi like you very much" in *That Night in Rio* (41,

Cummings); *A Weekend in Havana* (41, Walter Lang); *Springtime in the Rockies* (42, Cummings); doing "The Lady in the Tutti-Frutti Hat" in *The Gang's All Here* (43, Busby Berkeley).

That was her peak, but she was in *Four Jills in a Jeep* (44, William A. Seiter); *Greenwich Village* (44, Lang); *Something for the Boys* (44, Lewis Seiler); *Doll Face* (45, Seiler); *If I'm Lucky* (46, Seiler); *Copacabana* (47, Alfred E. Green); *A Date with Judy* (48, Richard Thorpe); *Nancy Goes to Rio* (50, Robert Z. Leonard); with Martin and Lewis in *Scared Stiff* (53, George Marshall).

Isa Miranda (Ines Isabella Sampietro) (1909–82), b. Milan, Italy

Twice for Max Ophüls, Isa Miranda played the part that interested him most—the actress in search of herself: as a sketch among many in *La Ronde* (50) and wonderfully delicate and touching in *La Signora di Tutti* (34). It was that earlier film that decided her on a film career. In fact, she did not attain her Ophülsian tenderness with many other directors—but neither did Martine Carol.

Although most of her films were Italian, she also worked in France and America: *Il Caso Haller* (33, Alessandro Blasetti); *Comele Foglie* (34, Mario Camerini); *L'Homme de Nulle Part* (37, Pierre Chenal); *Scipione L'Africano* (37, Carmine Gallone); to Hollywood, to play opposite Ray Milland in *Hotel Imperial* (39, Robert Florey); *Malombra* (42, Mario Soldati); *Zaza* (43, Renato Castellani); *Lo Sbaglio di Essere Vivo* (45, Carlo Ludovico Bragaglia); *Audela des Grilles* (48, René Clément); her episode in *Siamo Donne* (53, Luigi Zampa); *Raspoutine* (53, Georges Combret); *Avant le Déluge* (54, André Cayatte); *Summer Madness* (55, David Lean); *Gli Sbandati* (55, Francesco Maselli); *Une Manche et la Belle* (57, Henri Verneuil); *La Noia* (63, Damiani Damiani); *The Yellow Rolls Royce* (64, Anthony Asquith); *Hell Is Empty* (66, Bernard Knowles and John Ainsworth); *Caroline Chérie* (67, Denys de la Patellière); *The Shoes of the Fisherman* (68, Michael Anderson); *L'Assoluto Naturale* (69, Mauro Bolognini); and *The Night Porter* (73, Liliana Cavani).

Helen Mirren (Ilyena Lydia Mironoff),
b. London, 1945

The movies only really caught up with Helen Mirren by the time she was thirty-five or so. Thus, despite the generous indications of Michael Powell when he cast her as the beach nymph in *Age of Consent* (69), Mirren's fiery youthful beauty was largely confined to the stage in Britain. She was outstanding in the sixties and early seventies as Miss Julie, Cressida, Ophelia, Lady Macbeth, Titania, Cleopatra, and the Duchess of Malfi. Her exceptional *Miss Julie* was done for British TV (72, John Gleniston and Robin Phillips).

On screen, she generally had small roles: in Peter Hall's film of *A Midsummer Night's Dream* (68); as suffragette and mistress in *Savage Messiah* (72, Ken Russell); *O Lucky Man!* (73, Lindsay Anderson); as Gertrude *and* Ophelia in the sixty-seven-minute *Hamlet* (76, Celestino Coronado); in *The Collection* (76, Michael Apted), from Pinter; as Caesonia in the *Penthouse Caligula* (79, Tinto Brass); as one of the adults playing children in Dennis Potter's *Blue Remembered Hills* (79, Brian Gibson); and *The Fiendish Plot of Dr. Fu Manchu* (80, Piers Haggard).

Then she was outstandingly sinister, centuries apart, as the mistress in *The Long Good Friday* (79, John Mackenzie) and Morgana in *Excalibur* (81, John Boorman). She was in *2010* (84, Peter Hyams); winning the best actress prize at Cannes for *Cal* (84, Pat O'Connor); Russian in *White Nights* (85, Taylor Hackford, her companion); *The Gospel According to Vic* (85, Charles Gormley); as the mother in *The Mosquito Coast* (86, Peter Weir); *Pascali's Island* (88, James Dearden); *The Cook, the Thief, His Wife and Her Lover* (89, Peter Greenaway); *When the Whales Came* (89, Clive Rees); *The Comfort of Strangers* (90, Paul Schrader); and *Where Angels Fear to Tread* (91, Charles Sturridge).

Still and all, she has never had a movie role as meaty as the lady cop in *Prime Suspect* on TV (91, Christopher Menaul). Nor have the movies had a fuller portrait of an attractive woman as soured by career. *Prime Suspect* is doggedly realistic and old-fashioned, despite its feminist slant, but it conjures up a Buñuel black comedy in which gigolos, aristocrats, and bishops are forever turning themselves in for interrogation. *Prime Suspect 2* (93, John Strickland) was not as good, but who could deny Ms. Mirren a franchise? *Prime Suspect 3* (93, David Drury) played on television in Britain in December 1993. She also appeared in *The Hawk* (93, David Hayman).

There have been two more *Prime Suspect* series (in 1995 and '96), and Jane Tennison has made it all the way to superintendent without turning into a serial killer herself. Elsewhere, she was the Gertrude figure in *Prince of Jutland* (94, Gabriel Axel); the queen in *The Madness of King George* (94, Nicholas Hytner); *Some Mother's Son* (96, Terry George), which she helped produce; *Losing Chase* (96, Kevin Bacon); *Critical Care* (97, Sidney Lumet); in the TV series *Painted Lady* (97, Julian Jarrold); the voice of the queen for *The Prince of Egypt* (98); showing just how far she can go in *The Passion of Ayn Rand* (99, Menaul); *Teaching Mrs. Tingle* (99, Kevin Williamson); *Greenfingers* (00, Joel Hershman); directing *Happy Birthday* (00); *The Pledge* (00, Sean Penn); *Last Orders* (01, Fred Schepisi); *Gosford Park* (01, Robert Altman); *No Such Thing* (01, Hal Hartley); *Door to Door* (01, Steven Schachter).

She took the old Vivien Leigh role in a TV version of *The Roman Spring of Mrs Stone* (02, Robert Allan Ackerman); she was on TV in *Georgetown* (02) and *Pride* (03, John Downey).

Thomas Mitchell (1892–1962),
b. Elizabeth, New Jersey

Nineteen-thirty-nine was a prodigious year for Thomas Mitchell and supporting parts: *The Hunchback of Notre Dame* (William Dieterle); as Kid Dabb, denying failing sight, in *Only Angels Have Wings* (Howard Hawks); as the alcoholic doctor in *Stagecoach* (John Ford), for which he won the supporting actor Oscar; *Mr. Smith Goes to Washington* (Frank Capra); and as Scarlett's father in *Gone With the Wind* (Victor Fleming). That sort of vivid enthusiasm has not dated, and it is typical of the sure sense of idiom that Hollywood bred in supporting players. *Stagecoach*, for instance, is a blueprint movie, in that any actor could have known exactly how to play it from one reading of the script: it is exactly centered on convention. *Only Angels . . .* is far more original in that its conventions are entirely Hawksian. Arguably, it is Mitchell's most testing part. The man he plays is, indeed, a kid, despite being in his forties. Mitchell very subtly suggested the undertone of homosexuality in such male camaraderie, just as he played on the same theme, more robustly, as Pat Garrett in *The Outlaw* (46, Howard Hughes).

Mitchell only went to Hollywood in 1935, after an all-round career in the theatre as actor and director. He was immediately drafted into good parts in big films: *Craig's Wife* (36, Dorothy Arzner); *Theodora Goes Wild* (36, Richard Boleslavsky); *Make Way for Tomorrow* (37, Leo McCarey); *Lost Horizon* (37, Capra); *The Hurricane* (38, Ford); *Trade Winds* (38, Tay Garnett); *The Long Voyage Home* (40, Ford); *Three Cheers for the Irish* (40, Lloyd Bacon); *Our Town* (40, Sam Wood); *Angels Over Broadway* (41, Lee Garmes and Ben Hecht); *Out of the Fog* (41, Anatole Litvak); *Joan of Paris* (42, Robert Stevenson); *Song of the Islands* (42, Walter Lang); *Moontide* (42, Archie Mayo); *This Above All* (42, Litvak); *Tales of Manhattan* (42, Julien Duvivier); *The Immortal Sergeant* (42, John M. Stahl); *The Black Swan* (42, Henry King); *Flesh and Fantasy* (43, Duvivier); *Bataan* (43, Garnett); *The Sullivans* (44, Bacon); *Wilson* (44, King); *Dark Waters* (44, André de Toth); *Buffalo Bill* (44, William Wellman); *The Keys of the Kingdom* (44, Stahl); *Captain Eddie* (45, Bacon); *Adventure* (45, Fleming); the forgetful Uncle Billy in *It's a Wonderful Life* (46, Capra); *The Dark Mirror* (46, Robert Siodmak); *The Romance of Rosy Ridge* (47, Roy Rowland); *High Barbaree* (47, Jack Conway); *Silver River* (48, Raoul Walsh); *Alias Nick Beal* (49, John Farrow); *Journey into Light* (51, Stuart Heisler);

High Noon (52, Fred Zinnemann); *Destry* (54, George Marshall); *Secret of the Incas* (54, Jerry Hopper); *While the City Sleeps* (56, Fritz Lang); *By Love Possessed* (61, John Sturges); and *A Pocketful of Miracles* (61, Capra).

Robert Mitchum (1917–97),
b. Bridgeport, Connecticut

Dialogue from Jacques Tourneur's *Out of the Past* (47), a taxi driver to private eye Mitchum:

> "You look like you're in trouble."
> "Why?"
> "Because you don't look like it."

This is the man mocked throughout his career for listlessness, inertia, hooded eyes, and lack of interest. It is a well-worked argument. Words like "beefcake," "tough," and "laconic" hang from it, as well as the 1948 jail sentence for possessing marijuana, a variety of publicized scuffles, and his candid unhappiness marooned on the Dingle peninsula with David Lean's lush and slow *Ryan's Daughter*.

How can I offer this hunk as one of the best actors in the movies? Start by referring back to that dialogue: it touches the intriguing ambiguity in Mitchum's work, the idea of a man thinking and feeling beneath a calm exterior that there is no need to put "acting" on the surface. And for a big man, he is immensely agile, capable of unsmiling humor, menace, stoicism, and above all, of watching other people as though he were waiting to make up his mind. Of course, Mitchum has been in bad films, when he slips into the weariness of someone who has read the script, but hopes it may be rewritten. But, since the war, no American actor has made more first-class films, in so many different moods.

Mitchum's father died when he was very young and he left home in his teens. After a variety of jobs, he entered the Long Beach Theater and began working as a writer, actor, and producer. He wrote for radio and then entered movies, first as an extra and then as a heavy in Hopalong Cassidy movies. It was with the end of the war, the appetite for new faces, and the onset of naturalism that Mitchum became a star. At first, he was a guy like all the others, in *The Human Comedy* (43, Clarence Brown); in Laurel and Hardy's *The Dancing Masters* (43, Malcolm St. Clair); *Corvette-K225* (43, Richard Rosson); Tay Garnett's *Bataan* (43); Ray Enright's *Gung Ho;* Le Roy's *Thirty Seconds Over Tokyo* (44); and getting special attention in Wellman's *The Story of G.I. Joe* (45).

But he had already been much more individual in William Castle's *When Strangers Marry* (44) and he was remarkably good in Minnelli's *Undercurrent* (46), John Brahm's *The Locket* (46), and Dmytryk's *Till the End of Time* (46). He was already acclaimed as a tough guy and was cast in a

series of excellent B films at RKO: the already noted *Out of the Past; The Big Steal* (49, Don Siegel); *My Forbidden Past* (50, Robert Stevenson); two excellent John Farrow movies, *Where Danger Lives* (50) and *His Kind of Woman* (51); von Sternberg's *Macao* (52); with Jack Palance and Linda Darnell in *Second Chance* (53, Rudolph Maté). Usually opposite Jane Russell and Jane Greer in these movies, Mitchum created the character of a fatalistic "underworld" man with a lightness not even Bogart could rival. Thought of as immediate audience fodder when they were made, these films now look much better than the vaunted "realist" thrillers made at Fox.

Mitchum was already broadening his range; no matter how casual he seemed, he figured in so many unconventional and adventurous films: thus in Raoul Walsh's *Pursued* (47); in *Crossfire* (47)—Dmytryk's best film; *Desire Me* (47, George Cukor and Jack Conway); Robert Wise's *Blood on the Moon* (48); *The Red Pony* (49, Lewis Milestone); Tay Garnett's *One Minute to Zero* (52); John Cromwell's *The Racket* (51); Preminger's marvelous *Angel Face* (52); Nicholas Ray's *The Lusty Men* (52); and Wellman's *Track of the Cat* (54). His performance in *The Lusty Men* as the veteran rodeo rider is a beautiful study in independence brought to a realization of loneliness without a trace of sentimentality, never far from humor and never separating manliness from intelligence. It was a character that Mitchum refined in Preminger's *River of No Return* (54); *Not as a Stranger* (55, Stanley Kramer); in Sheldon Reynolds's enjoyable *Foreign Intrigue* (56); in Richard Fleischer's *Bandido* (56); in two films for Robert Parrish, *Fire Down Below* (57) and *The Wonderful Country* (59); and in *The Angry Hills* (59, Robert Aldrich).

At about this time, Mitchum began to attract respectable attention—if for the wrong reasons. For Huston's *Heaven Knows, Mr. Allison* (57) and Zinneman's *The Sundowners* (60), for instance, rather than Minnelli's *Home from the Hill* (60), while his preacher in Charles Laughton's *The Night of the Hunter* (55) went largely unnoticed. In this unusually stylized film, for the only time in his career Mitchum acted outside himself, and his demented fraud is one of the most compelling studies of evil in American cinema.

In fact, the more praise Mitchum got the less interesting his films became: *The Grass Is Greener* (60, Stanley Donen); *Cape Fear* (61, J. Lee Thompson); *Rampage* (63, Phil Karlson); *Two for the Seesaw* (62, Robert Wise); and *Mister Moses* (65, Ronald Neame). In 1967 Mitchum made what was, sadly, his only Hawks film, *El Dorado*, and was excellent in it. But he seemed increasingly restless with films like *Ryan's Daughter* and barely exercised by pleasant but unenterprising Westerns like *Five Card Stud* (68, Henry

Hathaway), *Young Billy Young* (69, Burt Kennedy), and *The Good Guys and the Bad Guys* (69, Kennedy). Against this, he was excellent in Losey's *Secret Ceremony* (68) and seemed to need more demanding parts than *The Wrath of God* (72, Ralph Nelson), in which he played a supposedly fast-shooting defrocked priest, infinitely more coarse-grained than the rabid preacher from *The Night of the Hunter*.

His weary genius rose again as the luckless, small-time informant in *The Friends of Eddie Coyle* (73, Peter Yates), and he went back to violence in *The Yakuza* (75, Sydney Pollack). His Marlowe in *Farewell, My Lovely* (75, Dick Richards) was a loving portrait of aging honor among all the remembered traps of film noir.

He stayed busy, in movies wretchedly beneath his classical status: Admiral Halsey in *Midway* (76, Jack Smight); wasted as Brady in *The Last Tycoon* (76, Elia Kazan); *The Amsterdam Kill* (77, Robert Clouse); Marlowe again in the unspeakable *The Big Sleep* (78, Michael Winner); with a kangaroo in *Matilda* (78, Daniel Mann).

Just as Mitchum was once indifferent to the great work he was doing, so now he was impervious to the dross that awaits most loyal veterans. He was never more himself or less involved than in the hours and years as "Pug" Henry in *The Winds of War* and *War and Remembrance*, undying studies of mental fatigue in the human face. Elsewhere, Mitchum worked as if he had a fruit machine for an agent: *Breakthrough* (78, Andrew V. McLaglen); *Nightkill* (80, Ted Post); *Agency* (81, George Kaczender); *That Championship Season* (82, Jason Miller); *One Shoe Makes It Murder* (82, William Hale); *A Killer in the Family* (83, Richard T. Heffron); *Maria's Lovers* (84, Andrei Konchalovsky); *The Ambassador* (84, Thompson); with Deborah Kerr again in *Reunion at Fairborough* (85, Herbert Wise); as William Randolph Hearst in *The Hearst and Davies Affair* (85, David Lowell Rich); *Thompson's Last Run* (86, Jerrold Freedman); *Promises to Keep* (86, Noel Black), playing with his son, Chris; *Mr. North* (88, Danny Huston) on which he replaced John Huston; *Scrooged* (88, Richard Donner); *Brotherhood of the Rose* (89, Marvin J. Chomsky); *Jack Spanner, Private Eye* (89, Lee H. Katzin); *A Family for Joe* (90, Jeffrey Melman) as a homeless man who adopts some kids—it was a short-lived TV series; and in the remake of *Cape Fear* (91, Martin Scorsese). His voice could be heard on commercials, too—best of all in those for beef—"It's what's for dinner!" (the most excited he had sounded in years). He narrated *Tombstone* (93, George Pan Cosmatos) and bowed out with *Dead Man* (96, Jim Jarmusch).

Untouchable.

Tom (Thomas) **Mix** (1880–1940),
b. Mix Run, Pennsylvania

One of the biggest problems in making Westerns is getting the horses to act without fuss or delay. You need decent, amenable animals; you need actors who can ride and who can get the horses back to a start line quickly for a retake; you need men who can handle the horses between setups. They are called wranglers, and there is a tradition of people who got a movie career for no better reason than their skill with horses: Ben Johnson began that way; for years before his glorious performance in *The Grey Fox*, Richard Farnsworth had done stunt riding for pictures like *Red River* and *The Tin Star*. For decades, Yakima Canutt did the most daring stunts. But no one so surely rode into stardom as Tom Mix.

He was the son of a lumberman, a sergeant in the army who never saw action, and a rider of such skill that he went from the Texas Rangers to a Wild West show in 1906. He was hired first by the Selig studio to provide and look after horses. But when the movie crews saw how he could ride he was promoted to stunt work. Then they noticed his dark, lean looks, his way with clothes, and wondered why the guy taking the risks might not be the star.

Mix was making movies—one- or two-reelers—from 1910 onward. In 1917, he went over to Fox and took on a more dandyish look. He directed some of his own pictures, and he very carefully organized his image—along with his horse Tony. His movies were full of fast action and thrills, a clear advance on the grave claims for authenticity made by William S. Hart. Mix was happy to be a showman and he was king of the celluloid range in the 1920s, making five or six films a year.

Sound reduced him, though he returned for a few years in the early thirties. Today, Mix is a curiosity, seldom seen, vaguely performed by Bruce Willis in the film *Sunset*. But he was a knockout in his day, and he was a surviving star on radio and in comic books at least ten years after his death (in a car crash). Kids would not let him go. He stands for that posse of cowboy stars who made thousands of films, nearly all with the same plot, but with a great-looking guy on an adorable horse: William Boyd, Dustin Farnum, Broncho Billy Anderson, Roy Rogers . . . and Harry Carey, except that Carey went further, to be the vice-president in *Mr. Smith Goes to Washington* and the cattle dealer in *Red River*, a man who could talk and think without a horse under him.

Kenji Mizoguchi (1898–1956), b. Tokyo
1922: *Ai Ni Yomigaeru Hi; Furusato; Seishun no Yumeji; Joen no Chimata; Haizan no Uta wa Kanashi; Rupimono; Chi to Rei*. 1923: *Kiri no Minato; Yoru; Haikyo no Naka; Toge no Uta*. 1924: *Kanashiki Hakuchi; Gendai no Jowo; Josei wat Suyoshi; Shichimencho no Yukue; Samidare Soshi; Jin Kyo*. 1925: *Musen Fusen; Kanraku no*

Onna; Akatsuki no Shi; Kyokubadan no Jowo; Gakuso o Idete; Shiragiku wa Nageku; Daichi wa Hohoemu; Akai Yuhi Ni Terasarete; Furusato no Uta; Ningen; Gaijo no Sukechi; Shirayuri wa Nageku. 1926: Nogi Shogun to Kuma San; Dokao; Kami-ningyo Haru no Sassayaki; Shin Ono Ga Tsumi; Kyoren no Onna Shisho; Kane; Kaikoku Danji; Kin ou Kane. 1927: Ko-on; Jihi Shincho. 1928: Hito no Issho. 1929: Nihonbashi; Tokyo Koshin-Kyoku; Asahi Wa Kagayaku; Tokai Kokyogaku. 1930: Furusato; Tojin Okichi. 1931: Shikamo Karera wa Yuku. 1932: Toki no Ujigami; Manmo Kengoku no Reimei. 1933: Takino Shiraito; Gion Matsuri; Kamikaze Ren; Shimpu Ren. 1934: Aizo Toge; Orizuru Osen. 1935: Maria no Oyuki; Gubijinso. 1936: Naniwa Ereji; Gion no Shimai/Sisters of the Gion. 1937: Aien-Kyo. 1938: Ah Furusato; Roei no Uta. 1939: Zangiku Monogatari/The Story of the Last Chrysanthemum. 1940: Naniwa Onna; Geido Ichidai Otoko. 1942: Musashi Miyamoto; Genroku Chushingura/The Loyal 47 Ronin of the Genroku Era. 1944: Danjuro Sandei. 1945: Hissyo Ka; Meito Bijomaru. 1946: Josei no Shori; Utamaro o Meguru Gonin no Onna. 1947: Joyu Sumako no Koi. 1948: Yoru no Onna Tachi; Waga Koi wa Moenu. 1950: Yuki Fujin Ezu. 1951: Oyusama; Musashino Fujin/Madame Musashino. 1952: Saikaku Ichidai Onna/The Life of Oharu. 1953: Ugetsu Monogatari; Gion Bayashi. 1954: Sansho Dayu; Chikamatsu Monogatari; Uwasa no Onna/The Crucified Woman. 1955: Yôkihi/Princess Yang Kwei Fei; Shin Heike Monogatari. 1956: Akasen Chitai/Street of Shame. 1957: Osaka Monogatari (completed by Kimisiburo Yoshimura after Mizoguchi's death).

It is said that only about a third of Mizoguchi's work survives. Of those thirty or so films, very few ever opened in the West commercially, and few are available on videotape. Moreover, this is a place to say that, despite all its advantages for research and preservation, video is unkind to any movie and cruel to any great movie. Mizoguchi worked with scale, space, and movement, and movement on a TV set is like a fish moving across a tank, whereas movement on a real screen is that of a great fish passing us in the water. So the greatness of Mizoguchi is no easier to discover now than it was in 1975. And this is a greatness that could one day soon be lost. By 2010 will it be possible to see these films on the screen they deserve: Ugetsu, Princess Yang Kwei Fei, Shin Heike Monogatari, Chikamatsu Monogatari, Sansho Dayu, The Life of Oharu, Gion Music, Sisters of the Gion, Genroku Chushingura, etc.?

Mizoguchi was raised in poverty. He studied painting and worked in newspaper layout before entering the movies. He excelled at period films, but he was equally interested in modern stories.

He has no superior at the unfolding of narrative by way of camera movement, and he was a great director of actresses—notably Isuzu Yamada, Kinuyo Tanaka, and Machiko Kyo.

Ugetsu Monogatari is probably the Mizoguchi film seen by most cinema-goers—and it is enough to sustain his reputation.

Ugetsu is set at a time of uncomprehended war, perhaps an accurate representation of medieval Japan, but equally the sort of world that a Vietnamese peasant might have experienced in the 1960s. It picks out two potters, Genjuro and Tobei; incidentally, Eric Rhode went to the heart of Mizoguchi's placid view of human travail when he said that it is unclear whether these men are at the center or the periphery of the world. In other words, as in a fable, the human figures are picked out and universalized, without any note of contrived significance. War has made their ambitions feverish and obsessive: Tobei wants to be a samurai; Genjuro wishes to sell his pottery successfully. Their wives stress domesticity and urge the men to recognize the immediate dangers of leaving the home. Again, without undue emphasis, the women represent the life force, physical continuity, and endurance; while the men are discontented by their own dreams.

Against the warnings of the women, the families split. While Tobei buys amour, his wife is raped. And while Genjuro's wife is killed by beggars, he is lured to the house of Lady Wakasa. Photographed like any other character, save for the whiteness of her costume and the beauty of her face, Wakasa is a ghost. She asks Genjuro to marry her and they enjoy an enchanted idyll. But reality obtrudes. Tobei is now a samurai, having "proved" himself with the stolen head of a warlord who had committed suicide. His triumph takes him to a brothel and there he meets his degraded wife. Genjuro learns that Wakasa is not real and is reminded of his wife. He returns home at night, and finds his wife and child awaiting him. He drinks sake and goes to sleep. When he wakes, his wife is gone. She too was a ghost for one night. Tobei and his wife return and life continues.

Ugetsu ends with Mizoguchi's serene camera craning up from a shot of Genjuro's son at his mother's grave to a view of fields beyond being tilled. It is one of the most moving shots in all cinema: the rise of the camera expressing subdued hope and human transience: death and life in one image show the harmony of tragedy and happiness.

That sort of artistic effect obtains throughout the film. The camera is often detached from human action, looking down on it, moving in order to see it more clearly and to explain consequences and feelings. When Genjuro's wife is killed, it is in a single setup. The camera is high. The woman hurries into frame, her child strapped to her back. Beggars enter the frame. We look helplessly down on the petty, fatal meeting. There is no grand murder, but a scuffle in which the woman is stuck by a spear almost casually. She writhes on the ground, her gasps barely audible beneath the crying of the child. As she drags herself away, the camera draws back to show the beggars squabbling over the scraps of food they have stolen from her. How can such grimness be spared melodrama but by the consuming tolerance of a great director?

The idyll with Wakasa invites beauty more directly, perhaps. And certainly Mizoguchi has made it visually enchanting: Wakasa's stately dance; the vague dimensions of the haunted palace; the bathing scene, where the steaming water is an emblem of dream and a reminder of the misty lake on which the potters and their wives earlier made their way to town. Exquisite, too, is the diagonal, high-angled pan/dissolve that ends with a shot of their lakeside picnic, spread out on a silken square. But the most beautiful thing about the Wakasa sequences is the way that the ghost is made touching. Her need for a redeeming love prepares us for the later presence of Genjuro's wife as a ghost. And that last ghostly appearance is possibly the most stunning moment in the film. Genjuro enters his house. It is night and the interior is gloomy. There is a semicircular pan as he comes in, revealing emptiness. But then we pan slowly back to discover the wife sitting in the firelight where seconds before there was nothing. So magical is the shot that we never consider how actress and fire must have been hurried into place while the camera panned. Our immersion in the imaginative life of the film is total.

Other Mizoguchi films only confirm the conviction, based on *Ugetsu*, that he was a master. I cannot offer a proper survey of his work except to say that *Chikamatsu Monogatari*, *The Life of Oharu*, *Sansho Dayu*, *Princess Yang Kwei Fei*, and *Shin Heike Monogatari* are the films most likely to be available. Any one of them offers the eloquence of *Ugetsu*. The use of the camera to convey emotional ideas or intelligent feelings is the definition of cinema derived from Mizoguchi's films. He is supreme in the realization of internal states in external views. At a time when Japanese cinema is deservedly in fashion, it is necessary to repeat Jacques Rivette's claim that one cannot compare, say, Kurosawa and Mizoguchi: "You can compare only what is comparable and that which aims high enough. Mizoguchi, alone, imposes a feeling of a unique world and language, is answerable only to himself.

"If Mizoguchi captivates us, it is because he never sets out deliberately to do so and never takes sides with the spectator. He seems to be the only Japanese director who is completely Japanese and yet is also the only one that achieves a true universality, that of an individual."

Gustaf Molander (1888–1973),
b. Helsinki, Finland

1920: *Bodakungen.* 1921: *En Ungdomsaventry.* 1922: *Thomas Graals Myndling* (s); *Parlorna; Amatorfilmen.* 1923: *Malarpirater.* 1924: *33.333; Polis Paulus Paskasmall.* 1925: *Ingmarsarvet; Till Osterland.* 1926: *Hon, den Enda; Hans Engelska Fru.* 1927: *Forseglade Lappar; Parisiskor.* 1928: *Synd.* 1929: *Hjartats Triumf.* 1930: *Fridas Visor.* 1931: *Charlotte Lowenskold; Fran Yttersta Skaren; En Natt.* 1932: *Svarta Rosor; Karlek och Kassabrist; Vi som gar Koksvagen.* 1933: *Kara Slakten.* 1934: *En Stilla Flirt; Fasters Miljoner; Ungkarlspappan.* 1935: *Swedenhielms; Under Falsk Flagg; Brollopsresan.* 1936: *Pa Solsidan; Intermezzo; Familjens Hemlighet.* 1937: *Sara lar sig Folkvett; Der Kan man Kalla Karlek; Dollar.* 1938: *En Kvinnas Ansikte; En Enda Natt; Ombyte Fornojer.* 1939: *Emilie Hogqvist.* 1940: *En, Men ett ett Lejon; Den Ljusnande Framtid.* 1941: *I Natt eller Aldrig; Striden Gar Vidare.* 1942: *Jacobs Stege; Rid i Natt.* 1943: *Alskling, Jag ger Mig; Ordet; Det Brinner en Eld.* 1944: *Den Osynliga Muren.* 1945: *Kejsaren av Portugallien; Galgmannen.* 1946: *Det Ar min Modell.* 1947: *Kvinna utan Ansikte.* 1948: *Nu Borjar Livet; Eva.* 1949: *Karleken Segrar.* 1950: *Kvartetten som Sprangdes.* 1951: *Fastmo Uthyres; Franskild.* 1952: *Trots; Karlek.* 1953: *Glasberget.* 1954: *Herr Arnes Pengar.* 1955: *Enhorningen.* 1956: *Sangen om den Eldroda Blomman.* 1967: "Smycket," episode from *Stimulantia.*

Molander lasted longer than the two other founding figures of the Swedish industry, Stiller and Sjostrom. When nearly eighty, he returned to direct a Maupassant-based episode from *Stimulantia* starring Ingrid Bergman, his great discovery of the 1930s. He had directed the young Bergman in *Pa Solsidan, Intermezzo, En Enda Natt,* and *En Kvinnnas Ansikte.* When Bergman went to America, Selznick offered an invitation to Molander as well. But the Swede may have recollected the way Stiller was cut adrift so that Garbo should be made the studio's property, and he elected to remain in Sweden. Little of his work is well known, but *Ordet,* from a play by Kaj Munk, is a moving allegory about the raising from the dead of a young farm girl, starring Victor Sjöström. (A decade later, it was remade by Carl Dreyer.) However, it seems that the majority of Molander's work is far lighter than this, with an emphasis on romantic comedy. As well as launching Ingrid Bergman, he was married to the actress Karin Molander from 1910 to 1918, and was Garbo's first teacher at the Royal Dramatic Theatre, Stockholm.

Molander had himself acted in Finland and Sweden, and he entered films originally as a writer: *Millers Dokument* (16, Konrad Tallroth);

Terje Vigen (17, Sjostrom), from an Ibsen poem; *Thomas Graals Basta Film* (17, Stiller), with Karin Molander in the cast; and then a few years later, *Gunnar Hedes Saga* (23, Stiller).

Marilyn Monroe (Norma Jean Mortenson) (1926–62), b. Los Angeles

There have been so many extensive postmortems of Marilyn Monroe that we can do without one more. They all err in interpreting a life that was unordered. Norman Mailer's "novel" about her shows how far her untidiness has preyed upon America's sense of itself. If her own experience was hopelessly beyond her, it is best to try to collect some of the broken pieces that she was unable to sort into a recognizable shape:

1. Consider the huge social and intellectual journey of an orphan, married at sixteen to a small-town policeman; in her twenties to Joe DiMaggio, national baseball hero; and in her thirties to Arthur Miller, epitome of American radical intellect. Not that any marriage lasted, or that there were not other liaisons, some entered into with an attempt at the calculated opportunism of Lorelei Lee in *Gentlemen Prefer Blondes* (53, Howard Hawks), and others with the battered romanticism of Sugar in *Some Like It Hot* (59, Billy Wilder).

2. In the late 1940s and early 1950s she had small parts in some dozen undistinguished movies. The clothes of the time were lavish and fussy but could not conceal the alienation of such a body from so blank and pursed a face. No one could see *Ladies of the Chorus* (49, Phil Karlson); *A Ticket to Tomahawk* (50, Richard Sale); *The Fireball* (50, Tay Garnett); *Right Cross* (50, John Sturges); *As Young As You Feel* (51, Harmon Jones); *Love Nest* (51, Joseph M. Newman); *Let's Make It Legal* (51, Sale); or *We're Not Married* (52, Edmund Goulding) without recognizing her as the archetypal forlorn starlet.

3. But scattered through these early years there are cameos of unusual impact in which she plays versions of the sexual careerist protected by an older and wiser man, or at least illuminated by the attention of a worldly male. That is true of Groucho's lascivious hounding of her in *Love Happy* (50, David Miller) and of George Winslow's solicitousness for her predicament in a porthole in *Gentlemen Prefer Blondes*. But the most interesting instances occur in *The Asphalt Jungle* (50, John Huston) and *All About Eve* (50, Joseph L. Mankiewicz). In the first she is the callow mistress of gangster Louis Calhern, seen spread out on a sofa in the first truly erotic image of her career. She barely comprehends the world about her but, as he faces disgrace, Calhern wryly predicts "a lot of trips" lying ahead of her. In the second, she is the dummy amid all Mankiewicz's sophisticates, arriving at the party on George

Sanders's arm. The film and Sanders patronize her, seeing sexual connivance as her sole tool. Sanders introduces her as a graduate of the Copacabana School of Dramatic Art and says, "I can see your career rising in the East like the sun." She has to swallow the mockery—or act dumb.

4. These situations, as well as the attitude toward her of other actors, reflected the knowledge at the Fox studios that she was picked out for higher things. Gossip would not have been slow to provide the means by which she negotiated the executive office. Monroe herself, or her advisors, engineered a whole battery of publicity stunts, the most famous of which were the nude photographs, themselves redolent of a small-town girl's imprecise notions of sexual glory.

5. In 1952, she ventured outside her plastic personality to play the young, fishpacking wife in *Clash by Night* (52, Fritz Lang). Lang had trouble with her reliance on dialogue coaches and with her already fazed memory for lines and action. He saw a contradiction within her: "She was a very peculiar mixture of shyness and uncertainty and— I wouldn't say 'star allure'—but . . . she knew exactly her impact on men." Knowingness and uncertainty or, as Ginger Rogers and Cary Grant say of her in *Monkey Business* (52, Hawks), half child, but not the half that shows.

6. By 1952–53, Fox began to thrust her out at the public in salacious publicity and a mixed bag of films: *Don't Bother to Knock* (52, Roy Baker); *Niagara* (53, Henry Hathaway); *How to Marry a Millionaire* (53, Jean Negulesco); *River of No Return* (54, Otto Preminger); and *There's No Business Like Show Business* (54, Walter Lang). These were leading parts, and it must be said that she seldom escapes ordinariness and is often jittery. The long takes of a Preminger were more than she could survive. Badly dressed, as in *Show Business* and *Niagara*, she looked a mess. Called on to play an unbalanced girl in *Don't Bother to Knock,* her own immature personality disabled her. However, her looks did improve during this period: her hair abandoned curl for swathes; she was taught to widen her eyes, and her mouth slipped open—as it is in Andy Warhol's painting. To control shyness, she moved with a fanciful, comic lethargy. If she sometimes resembled a sleepwalker, perhaps that showed how many dreams impelled her.

7. As the contrast between her image of voluptuousness and the reality of near-breakdown became more extreme, so her films became wondering, and even sniggering, comments on the paradox. George Axelrod's play *The Seven Year Itch* (55, Billy Wilder) emphasized Monroe's ignorance of the effect she was making and used Tom Ewell as a surrogate dirty old man tormented by such stupid opportunity. *Bus Stop* (56,

Joshua Logan) was her most touching film and the nearest she came to recognizable character. But *The Prince and the Showgirl* (57, Laurence Olivier) was condescending to her, and *Some Like It Hot* (59, Wilder) had her as the yielding instrument of a funny but dirty joke, made to ply Tony Curtis with herself to restore his virility, but also coarsened by the two exquisite studies in drag. Crack-up was signaled portentously in *The Misfits* (60, Huston), from an Arthur Miller script, in which she postured vaguely as the spirit of kind nature.

8. If she rarely seemed at ease or comprehending in dialogue scenes, her musical numbers are delightful: "Diamonds Are a Girl's Best Friend" from *Blondes;* "That Old Black Magic" from *Bus Stop;* "One Silver Dollar" and "I Gotta File My Claim" in *River of No Return;* "I Want to Be Loved by You" in *Some Like It Hot,* and above all, "My Heart Belongs to Daddy" from *Let's Make Love* (60, George Cukor). Cukor was the director of her last project—*Something's Got to Give*, at Fox. She was fired from it for persistent lateness, and committed suicide shortly thereafter. But not before Fox had filmed tests in which she is radiant and calmer than she ever managed in a film. In addition, she did a nude scene beside a pool—hopelessly coy with her rawness, like a waitress who has seen a Rubens.

9. The viewer must decide when or whether she had talent, whether she was a comedienne or a voluptuous ideal laughed at by her films. It seems to me difficult to accept her as a tragic figure, because she was hardly able to grasp what was happening to her. But one substantial realization came out of her career: even if morbidly, the public was made aware of the special destruction that may attend a star.

10. The wisdom of hindsight. She is like the Kennedys. Mailer noticed how she edged into their look. Gossip has ensured that we can hardly now detach her life and death from the rumor of links to Jack and Bobby. As with the Kennedys, there is no fatigue in her legend. Her fame increases, and as it does so we see how far she depended on, and excelled in, photographs—not movies. She gave great still. She is funnier in stills, sexier, more mysterious, and protected against being. And still pictures may yet triumph over movies in the history of media. For stills are more available to the imagination.

Yves Montand (Ivo Livi) (1921–91),
b. Monsummano Alto, Italy

So the perfect Frenchman was Italian. How authentic, then, is that spirit of black-coffee worldliness that Montand seemed to generate so effortlessly? In a way, one feels guilty of mistrusting him. In two films for Costa-Gavras—*Z* (68) and *L'Aveu* (70)—he acted out the left-wing prin-

ciples that he was known for in his public life. And yet, I cannot forget how easily he slid into the odiously fake world of Claude Lelouch in *Vivre pour Vivre* (67). His face seemed made for the glib revelation of Lelouch's hurried emotional journalism, and the unprincipled mixture of cheap romantic melodrama and supposed commitment to the world's travails seemed to fit Montand's professional shrug to the inch. Although an actor who relied on mature appeal, he seemed always a little shifty. His face in repose was sulky and calculating, and the smile that appeared when he knew he was being observed could have been pulled open by strings.

He went to France while very young and lived in Marseilles. From music hall, he went into movies and had a striking postwar debut: *Etoile sans Lumière* (45, Marcel Blistène); *Les Portes de la Nuit* (46, Marcel Carné); *Souvenirs Perdus* (49, Christian-Jaque); the international success of *The Wages of Fear* (53, H.-G. Clouzot); *Napoleon* (55, Sacha Guitry); *Les Héros sont Fatigués* (55, Yves Ciampi); *Marguerite de la Nuit* (55, Claude Autant-Lara); *Uomini e Lupi* (56, Giuseppe de Santis); in an episode from *Die Vind Rose* (56, Yannik Bellon); *Les Sorcières de Salem* (57, Raymond Rouleau), the latter with his wife, Simone Signoret; and *La Grande Strada Azzurra* (57, Gillo Pontecorvo). After *La Loi* (58, Jules Dassin), he went to Hollywood, but failed as an "international" star; as the essentially unmalleable material in *Let's Make Love* (60, George Cukor), famously involved with Monroe; as a bowdlerized Popeye in *Sanctuary* (61, Tony Richardson); as the philanderer in *Goodbye Again* (61, Anatole Litvak); and in *My Geisha* (62, Jack Cardiff).

After that, he was based in Europe with occasional forays to America: *The Sleeping Car Murders* (65, Costa-Gavras); very good in *La Guerre est Finie* (66, Alain Resnais); *Grand Prix* (66, John Frankenheimer); *Mr. Freedom* (68, William Klein); *Un Soir . . . un Train* (69, André Delvaux); *Le Diable par la Queue* (69, Philippe de Broca); *On a Clear Day You Can See Forever* (70, Vincente Minnelli); *Le Cercle Rouge* (70, Jean-Pierre Melville); *La Folie des Grandeurs* (71, Gerard Oury); *Tout Va Bien* (72, Jean-Luc Godard and Jean-Pierre Gorin); *Etat de Siège* (73, Costa-Gavras); *Le Sauvage* (75, Jean-Paul Rappeneau); *Vincent, François, Paul et les Autres* (75, Claude Sautet); *Flashback* (77, Alain Corneau); *La Menace* (77, Corneau); and *The Roads to the South* (78, Joseph Losey).

In his final decade, Montand did maybe his best and most challenging work: *Clair de Femme* (79, Costa-Gavras); *I Comme Icare* (80, Henri Verneuil); as a veteran crook in *Le Choix des Armes* (81, Corneau), playing with Deneuve and Depardieu; *Tout Feu, Tout Flamme* (82, Jean-Paul

Rappenau); *Garçon!* (83, Sautet); superb in *Jean de Florette* (86, Claude Berri) and *Manon des Sources* (86, Berri); as an artful projection of himself in *Trois Places pour le 26* (88, Jacques Demy); and *IP5* (92, Jean-Jacques Beneix).

Robert Montgomery (Henry Montgomery Jr.) (1904–81), b. Fishkill Landing, New York

For more than a decade, Montgomery was an elegant leading man in romantic confections at MGM, rarely boosted, more often treated as an arm for the studio's star actresses. He had worked in the New York theatre before a debut in *So This Is College* (29, Sam Wood) and a contract with MGM. For the next seven or eight years, his work hardly altered: with Joan Crawford in *Untamed* (29, Jack Conway); better in *The Big House* (30, George Hill); with Norma Shearer in *The Divorcee* (30, Robert Z. Leonard); *Sins of the Children* (30, Wood); with Garbo in *Inspiration* (31, Clarence Brown); Constance Bennett in *The Easiest Way* (31, Conway); Shearer in *Private Lives* (31, Sidney Franklin); with Crawford in *Letty Lynton* (32, Brown); opposite Marion Davies in *Blondie of the Follies* (32, Edmund Goulding); *Night Flight* (33, Brown); with Shearer in *Riptide* (34, Goulding); in *Hide-Out* (34) and *Forsaking All Others* (34), both for W. S. Van Dyke; with Helen Hayes in *Vanessa* (35, William K. Howard); with Crawford in *No More Ladies* (35, Edward H. Griffith); *Piccadilly Jim* (36, Leonard); and with Crawford again in *The Last of Mrs. Cheyney* (37, Richard Boleslavsky).

Montgomery was not popular with the studio, and they may have given him the part of the killer in *Night Must Fall* (37, Richard Thorpe) to shatter his glossy image. In the event, he was well received, though still neglected by his employers: *Ever Since Eve* (37, Lloyd Bacon); *Three Loves Has Nancy* (38, Thorpe); and *The Earl of Chicago* (40, Thorpe). Despairing of good parts, he went elsewhere and in 1941 made *Mr. and Mrs. Smith* (Alfred Hitchcock) with Carole Lombard at RKO; the curious *Rage in Heaven* (Van Dyke) at MGM; an unexpected hit, *Here Comes Mr. Jordan* (Alexander Hall) at Columbia; and *Unfinished Business* (Gregory La Cava) at Universal.

At this point, he joined the navy and returned only in 1945 as the commander in John Ford's *They Were Expendable.* For his last MGM project, he acted in and directed a Raymond Chandler adaptation, *The Lady in the Lake* (46), helplessly slowed by a subjective camera and thus ponderously illustrating how he preferred directing to acting. His next direction, *Ride the Pink Horse* (47), though a failure, was much more interesting. In 1948 he acted in two more movies: *The Saxon Charm* (Claude Binyon) and *June Bride* (Bre-

taigne Windust); next year he directed again: *Once More My Darling* and, in Britain, *Eye Witness,* another interesting work. He then went into TV and served as Eisenhower's television consultant. In 1960, he directed a labor of love: his friend James Cagney as Admiral Halsey in *The Gallant Hours.*

Colleen Moore (Kathleen Morrison) (1900–87), b. Port Huron, Michigan

In his invaluable biography of Louise Brooks, Barry Paris goes into contortions of research trying to decide whether Brooks or Colleen Moore created the flapper look. The truth is that, at this moment—say, 1923–28—Moore was a phenomenon, while Brooks was a curiosity. Moore was a major American star, while Brooks was too smart, too difficult, too everything to be that. By 1927, Colleen Moore was the top box-office attraction in the country, and she was making $12,500 a week. Brooks earned $250 a week, and so she went off to Germany to do *Pandora's Box.* But Colleen Moore is not known today. Few readers of this book will have seen her in a film, or know what she looked like. Well, she looked like a less interesting version of Louise Brooks. A lot less interesting. But that took a while to sink in.

Moore said that she got into pictures because her uncle, Walter Howey, a Chicago press lord, was owed a favor by D. W. Griffith on account of having helped to get *Birth of a Nation* and *Intolerance* past the censor. So she got her new name, played with Tom Mix in several movies, established herself as a standard heroine, and was there, cuteness itself, ready to have her hair cut for the breakthrough flapper movie, *Flaming Youth* (23, John Francis Dillon).

Her glory years had her in *The Perfect Flapper* (24, Dillon); *Flirting With Love* (24, Dillon); *So Big* (25, Charles Brabin); *Sally* (25, Alfred E. Green); *We Moderns* (25, Dillon); *Irene* (26, Green); *Ella Cinders* (26, Green); *It Must Be Love* (26, Green); *Twinkletoes* (26, Brabin); *Her Wild Oat* (28, Marshall Neilan); *Lilac Time* (28, George Fitzmaurice); *Oh Kay!* (28, Mervyn Le Roy); *Why Be Good?* (29, William A. Seiter); and *Smiling Irish Eyes* (29, Seiter).

She took a few years off and then returned for *The Power and the Glory* (33, William K. Howard); *Social Register* (34, Neilan); and *Success at Any Price* (34, J. Walter Ruben). She then bowed out after a ludicrous failure as Hester Prynne in *The Scarlet Letter* (34, Robert G. Vignola).

Moore's later life was as rock-steady as Louise Brooks's was insecure. Ms. Moore had several businessmen husbands, one of whom, Homer Hargrave, was a vice-president at Merrill Lynch. She learned so well that she wrote a book, *How Women Can Make Money in the Stock Market.*

Demi Moore (Demi Guynes),
b. Roswell, New Mexico, 1962

In the January–February 1993 *Movieline,* asked to assess her "position in the business right this second," Demi Moore said, "That's tough. I'm probably in a better position than I've ever been thus far, okay? I think people in the business are certainly interested in doing business with me." Gone are the days of longing to be alone, of cute answers and wistful smiles. Today a hot young actress can sound as if she's in plastics (and Moore's voice is as harsh as unfinished polymer). And Demi Moore is a very keen purveyor of her own image. Despite some good movie work, it is likely that the public's most immediate sense of Demi Moore is still vested in two images—the covers she did for *Vanity Fair,* one nude and pregnant, the other nude and painted. Further, these covers were not simply Tina Brown's wit and wisdom. Demi Moore consented to them, and kept as much control as she could contrive.

After working on TV's *General Hospital,* she got into movies in the early 1980s, married Bruce Willis, had two children, and generally hustled herself to the forefront: *Choices* (81, Silvio Narizzano); *Parasite* (82, Charles Band); *Young Doctors in Love* (82, Garry Marshall); *Blame It On Rio* (84, Stanley Donen); as a singer in *No Small Affair* (84, Jerry Schatzberg); *St. Elmo's Fire* (85, Joel Schumacher); *About Last Night* (86, Edward Zwick); *One Crazy Summer* (86, Savage Steve Holland); *Wisdom* (86, Emilio Estevez); pregnant and threatened in *The Seventh Sign* (88, Carl Schultz); *We're No Angels* (89, Neil Jordan); riding the hit of *Ghost* (90, Jerry Zucker); excellent and touching in *Mortal Thoughts* (91, Alan Rudolph); blonde in *The Butcher's Wife* (91, Terry Hughes); *Nothing But Trouble* (91, Dan Akroyd); wasted in *A Few Good Men* (92, Rob Reiner).

She was the wife open to *Indecent Proposal* (93, Adrian Lyne), a movie that drew upon the ghost of a computer behind her fully sexed but tough stare. The film was so listless and underdone, at $1 million the actress seemed overpriced.

She was a far more flagrant sexual aggressor, ravishing Michael Douglas, in *Disclosure* (94, Barry Levinson). She helped produce *Now and Then* (95, Lesli Linka Glatter), and then went out for big acting in the risible *The Scarlet Letter* (95, Roland Joffe). She was at a perilous point. *The Juror* (96, Brian Gibson) was routine, but for *Striptease* (96, Andrew Bergman) she offered her all (for a record $12 million), and showed that the bod was still awesome. It was more than the public wanted, though, and *G.I. Jane* (97, Ridley Scott) was a more hysterical assertion of physical splendor. She was in *Deconstructing Harry* (97, Woody Allen). The marriage to Willis broke up. And she did *Passion of Mind* (00, Alain Berliner) as if to prove that she had her sixth, and seventh, senses, too. But no dramatic sense. At present it is not quite clear if she is active, resting, or just out of it.

Julianne Moore (Julie Smith),
b. Fayetteville, North Carolina, 1960

On half a dozen occasions at least, Julianne Moore has given ample demonstration of her ability and intelligence. Thus, she lent herself faithfully to the increasingly pale and withdrawn figure for Todd Haynes's *Safe* (1995), while staying in the memory as the half-naked, very talkative, and fiery red young woman for Robert Altman's *Short Cuts* (93). Then there was the porn queen for *Boogie Nights* (97, Paul Thomas Anderson), in which drugs and natural kindness had led to a rosy, shiny blur of warmth.

She was trained at the Boston Museum School of Fine Arts, she has worked on stage, and won an Emmy for *As the World Turns.* But she had the looks and attitude that led her more naturally to independent films (classic Hollywood complains at her freckles), until late 1999, when she found herself in two big lead roles—as the adulteress who turns away in *The End of the Affair* (99, Neil Jordan) and as the young wife in *Magnolia* (99, Anderson). The former was disappointing. But the latter was good—clearly, Moore had arrived as a major figure.

She made her debut in *Tales from the Darkside: The Movie* (90, John Harrison) and appeared in *The Gun in Betty Lou's Handbag* (92, Allan Moyle); *The Hand That Rocks the Cradle* (92, Curtis Hanson); *Benny & Joon* (93, Jeremiah Chechik); *Body of Evidence* (93, Uli Edel); *The Fugitive* (93, Andrew Davis); *Vanya on 42nd Street* (94, Louis Malle); *Assassins* (95, Richard Donner); *Nine Months* (95, Chris Columbus); *Roommates* (95, Peter Yates); *Surviving Picasso* (96, James Ivory); *The Lost World: Jurassic Park* (97, Steven Spielberg); *The Myth of Fingerprints* (97, Bart Freundlich, her companion); *The Big Lebowski* (98, Joel Coen); *Chicago Cab* (98, Mary Cybulski and John Tintori); in the Vera Miles part in *Psycho* (98, Gus Van Sant); *Cookie's Fortune* (99, Altman); *An Ideal Husband* (99, Oliver Parker); superb in *A Map of the World* (99, Scott Elliott).

She had little to do in *The Ladies Man* (00, Reginald Hudlin), but after the short *Not I* (00, Jordan), adapted from Beckett, she took over the role of Clarice Starling and helped make *Hannibal* (01, Ridley Scott) into a wistful romance. She was wasted in *Evolution* (01, Ivan Reitman) and in *World Traveler* (01, Freundlich); but she was good again in *The Shipping News* (01, Lasse Hallström); brilliant in *Far From Heaven* (02, Haynes); and fair in *The Hours* (02, Stephen Daldry).

Agnes Moorehead (1906–74),
b. Clinton, Massachusetts

What are the two most indelibly humane moments in the work of Orson Welles? There is a case for saying that Agnes Moorehead figures in both: in *Kane*, the scene with Kane's mother opening the window to call in her son from the snow so that he may advance on his destiny; and in *Ambersons*, where Aunt Fanny watches Georgie devouring her strawberry shortcake, pleased to be useful, daunted by his appetite but knowing that he does not need her, deeply aware that her vibrant romantic hopes are growing shrill with neglect.

It is hardly coincidence that these are moments of loss and frustration that stay with us long afterwards, just as the last close-up of Kane's mother, sinking down to the son's face, is the way in which Kane has recalled her all his life—as stylized and emotional as the sort of operas in which he imprisons Susan Alexander. Sadly, they predicted the course of Agnes Moorehead's career. She was one of several Mercury players brought to movies by Welles. Mrs. Danvers in *Rebecca* on radio showed her flair for melodrama and, in truth, she may have been best confined to brief passages where her intensity was limited. Her subsequent parade of shrews, rancorous mothers, bitches, and spinsters shows how quickly she overheated. But she was perfectly equipped for the controlled theatricality of Welles's debut.

After those two first performances, what is worth remembering? *The Big Street* (42, Irving Reis); *Journey into Fear* (43, Norman Foster); *Jane Eyre* (44, Robert Stevenson); *Mrs. Parkington* (44, Tay Garnett); *Since You Went Away* (44, John Cromwell); *Dragon Seed* (44, Jack Conway and Harold Bucquet); *The Seventh Cross* (44, Fred Zinnemann); *Our Vines Have Tender Grapes* (45, Roy Rowland); *Dark Passage* (47, Delmer Daves); *Summer Holiday* (47, Rouben Mamoulian); as the 105-year-old woman in *The Lost Moment* (48, Martin Gabel); *Johnny Belinda* (48, Jean Negulesco); *The Great Sinner* (49, Robert Siodmak); *Caged* (50, Cromwell); *Fourteen Hours* (51, Henry Hathaway); *Show Boat* (51, George Sidney); *The Blue Veil* (51, Curtis Bernhardt); *The Blazing Forest* (52, Edward Ludwig); *Those Redheads from Seattle* (53, Lewis R. Foster); *Main Street to Broadway* (53, Garnett); *Scandal at Scourie* (53, Negulesco); *Magnificent Obsession* (54, Douglas Sirk); *All That Heaven Allows* (55, Sirk); *The Conqueror* (55, Dick Powell); *The Swan* (56, Charles Vidor); *The Revolt of Mamie Stover* (56, Raoul Walsh); *Jeanne Eagels* (57, Sidney); *The True Story of Jesse James* (57, Nicholas Ray); *Raintree County* (57, Edward Dmytryk); *Tempest* (57, Alberto Lattuada); *The Bat* (59, Crane Wilbur); *Pollyanna* (60, David Swift); *Twenty Plus Two* (61, Joseph Newman); *Who's Minding the Store?* (63, Frank Tashlin); and *Hush . . . Hush, Sweet Charlotte* (64, Robert Aldrich). That stark face was latterly hidden

behind false eyelashes as she played the mother in the TV series *Bewitched,* a part that relates to Aunt Fanny in the same grisly way as sherry commercials recall the great sad mouth of Charles Foster Kane.

Jeanne Moreau, b. Paris, 1928

Moreau is one of the most challenging of screen actresses. Far from beautiful, she sometimes seems plain-faced, dumpy, and sullen. But when her personality is engaged, we have the feeling of an intelligent, intuitive woman wanting to commit herself to the inner rhythm of the movie. She flowers under sympathetic, intimate direction. At her best, she is riveting, capable of persuading us that she is beautiful, and able to vary her own appearance according to mood. Above all, and without any trace of rhetoric, she bares a vivid but vulnerable soul. Nothing expresses her so well as that instant in *Eve* (62, Joseph Losey) when she glares after the departing Stanley Baker and mutters "Bloody Welshman." Those words embody not just the sensual dominance of the woman, but a residual sadness that so brutal a sexual conflict should exist.

Moreau's eminence coincided with the cinema's new interest in feminism. Her blend of intelligence and feelings is common to all great actresses, but it had seldom been based on less glamorous looks. Like the Catherine in *Jules and Jim* (61, François Truffaut), Moreau asserted herself so that stories took shape from a woman encouraged to experiment in front of the camera. *Eve* may be her most extreme role, but it involves the greatest risks and the most extraordinary triumph. Losey is not renowned for his handling of women, but *Eve* glories in Moreau's emotional pragmatism and her instinctive, sour fun. That long sequence in which she takes over Baker's bathroom, and the moment when she deludes him with a pathetic farrago about her own childhood, are perfect expressions of the cruelty and playfulness in Eve. Only Moreau could have made her so flouncingly sexy, so devouringly commercial, without losing sight of her loneliness or the moments in which she resembles a little girl.

The daughter of a chorus girl, Moreau was a leading actress at the Théâtre Nationale Populaire before she made her name in movies. She had acted regularly in movies since 1948, but she was thirty before the New Wave found a proper use for her, or saw that she was deeply attractive and animated. After *Touchez Pas au Grisbi* (54, Jacques Becker), *La Salaire du Péché* (56, Denys de la Patellière), and *Le Dos au Mur* (57, Edouard Molinaro), she made two films for Louis Malle: *Lift to the Scaffold* (57) and *Les Amants* (57). The first showed a new "modern" woman, while the second was a notorious advance into sexual frankness—a dishonest vein more in keeping with bourgeois French cinema, and not central to Moreau's later work where she has usually suggested sexuality obliquely. In 1959, she went from *Le Dialogue des Carmélites* (Philippe Agostini) to Madame de Merteuil in Vadim's updated *Les Liaisons Dangereuses*. That was a part worthy of her, but cheated by Vadim's insistence on novelty at the expense of examination.

She was one of Martin Ritt's *Five Branded Women* (60), and then began the run of outstanding parts: *Moderato Cantabile* (60, Peter Brook), an opaque study of a Marguerite Duras wife and mother on the point of breakdown, wonderfully inhabited by Moreau; *La Notte* (61, Michelangelo Antonioni), another portrait of alienation that Moreau steered carefully away from the self-pity growing in the director's work—no one else could have sustained the long section in which she wanders through Milan, observing the harsh, uncoordinated fragments of life; *Jules and Jim,* a key character in Truffaut's work, barely plausible on paper, but in Moreau's image a moving, capricious self-destructive woman torn between being a happy and a sad fool; the nervy, blonde gambler in *La Baie des Anges* (62, Jacques Demy), harrowed by the dilatory wheel and blithely ridding herself of the winnings at the best hotel in town.

Those films made her one of the most desirable actresses in the world. In the event, she did not always choose parts well, but she was still more watchable in neutral than most others in top gear: *The Victors* (63, Carl Foreman); *Peau de Banane* (63, Marcel Ophuls); as Fraulein Becker in *The Trial* (63, Orson Welles), a brief flash of lewdness; *Will of the Wisp* (63, Malle); cool, matter-of-fact, and flexible in *Diary of a Chambermaid* (64, Buñuel).

Her insecurity was proved by her inability to dominate silly vehicles: thus *Mata-Hari, Agent H.21* (64, Jean-Louis Richard, who, briefly, had been her husband). She was dowdy in *The Train* (65, John Frankenheimer), a little strained with Bardot in *Viva Maria!* (65, Malle) and uncomfortable in *The Yellow Rolls-Royce* (64, Anthony Asquith). But she was a splendidly sordid Doll Tearsheet in *Chimes at Midnight* (66, Welles). Two Tony Richardson projects would have best been avoided, despite the nominal basis in Genet and Duras: *Mademoiselle* (66) and *The Sailor from Gibraltar* (67). The part of the avenging Julie Kohler in *The Bride Wore Black* (67, Truffaut) wavered in and out of life, but seemed as outside her ken as it was imposed on Truffaut by his admiration of Hitchcock.

In 1968, however, Welles cast her with characteristic tender mischief as the aging prostitute reclaimed by romance in the realization of Mr. Clay's *Immortal Story*. The most poetic thing in that film is the way Moreau does seem to become younger from the moment she blows out the candles in the magical chamber appointed for the enactment of the story. It suggested that she might yet lead Welles into a film that dealt profoundly with women.

She looked her age and roamed the film world rather uncertainly: *Le Corps de Diane* (68, Richard); *Great Catherine* (68, Gordon Flemyng); to Hollywood for *Monte Walsh* (70, William Fraker) and *Alex in Wonderland* (71, Paul Mazursky); *Compte à Rebours* (70, Roger Pigaut); *Mille Baisers de Florence* (71, Guy Gilles); singing "Quand l'Amour se Meurt" in *Le Petit Théâtre de Jean Renoir* (69); excelling once more for Marguerite Duras in *Nathalie Granger* (72); and *Chère Louise* (72, Philippe de Broca).

She yielded with ardent regret to middle age, married William Friedkin briefly, became a director herself—with *Lumière* (75)—and kept involved with enterprising pictures: to Brazil for *Joanna Francesca* (73, Carlo Diegues); *Souvenirs d'en France* (74, André Téchiné); *Making It* (74, Bertrand Blier); *Le Jardin qui Bascule* (75, Guy Gilles); *Mr. Klein* (76, Losey); a temperamental actress in *The Last Tycoon* (76, Elia Kazan). In 1979, she directed her second film *L'Adolescente*.

She was in *Night Fires* (79, Mary Stephen); *Your Ticket Is No Longer Valid* (81, George Kaczender); *Plein Sud* (81, Luc Beraud); *Mille Milliards de Dollars* (81, Henri Verneuil); as an icon of foreboding in *Querelle* (82, Rainer Werner Fassbinder); *The Trout* (82, Losey); *L'Arbre* (84, Jacques Doillon); *Vicious Circle* (84, Kenneth Ives); *Le Paltoquet* (86, Michel Deville); *Sauve-toi Lola* (86, Michel Drach); *La Miracule* (86, Jean-Pierre Mocky); *The Last Seance* (86, John Wyndham-Davies); *Hotel Terminus* (87, Marcel Ophuls); *La Nuit de l'Ocean* (88, Antoine Perset); *La Femme Nikita* (90, Luc Besson); *Alberto Express* (90, Arthur Joffé); *Until the End of Time* (91, Wim Wenders); *Map of the Human Heart* (93, Vincent Ward); and *The Summer House* (93, Warris Hussein).

Her voice spoke the words of Marguerite Duras looking back on the events of *The Lover* (92, Jean-Jacques Annaud)—as if too many Gauloises could have given Jane March a French accent. In addition, Moreau has contributed to documentaries on Fassbinder, Truffaut, Jean-Louis Barrault, and, not least, Lillian Gish—the latter of which she directed.

As she came to seventy, she was as commanding as ever: *L'Absence* (93, Peter Handke); *Je M'Appelle Victor* (93, Guy Jacques); *A Foreign Field* (93, Charles Sturridge); *Beyond the Clouds* (95, Wenders and Antonioni); narrating *Belle Epoque* (95, Gavin Millar); *Catherine the Great* (95, Marvin J. Chomsky and John Goldsmith); *I Love You, I Love You Not* (96, Billy Hopkins); *The Proprietor* (96, Ismail Merchant); *Amour et Confusions* (97, Patrick Braoudre); *Un Amour de Sorcière* (97,

Rene Manzor); *Ever After* (98, Andy Tennant); ferocious as the mother in *Balzac* (99, Josee Dayan); *Il Manoscritto de Principe* (00, Roberto Ando); *Les Misérables* (00, Dayan); *Zaïde* (01, Dayan); as Marguerite Duras in *Cet Amour-Là* (01, Dayan).

Antonio Moreno (1886–1967),
b. Madrid, Spain

Not many careers begin at Biograph in 1912 (*Voice of the Million*) and end with John Ford's 1956 *The Searchers*. But it was during the in-between period—the silents of the twenties—that Antonio Moreno made his name (and his best films). He came to America from Spain young and tried the stage, his strikingly handsome looks helping him to supporting roles in vehicles for Maude Adams, Julia Marlowe, and Mrs. Lesley Carter, but it was the silents that provided sanctuary for good-looking Europeans with strong accents. He worked hard at Biograph, appearing in bit parts in *The Musketeers of Pig Alley* (1912) and *Judith of Bethulia* (1914), then drifted into serials, before signing with Paramount in 1923.

At once he was a leading man, appearing in four or five movies a year, either opposite a major star (Swanson in the 1923 *My American Wife* and Negri the same year in *The Spanish Dancer*) or as the star himself (*The Trail of the Lonesome Pine*, also 1923, and the following year in things like *Tiger Love*). By this time, he was an official Latin Lover, just below Valentino and Novarro. Nineteen twenty-six was his miracle year, including his greatest role, the Captain in Rex Ingram's superb *Mare Nostrum*, revealing a gravity and depth that somehow hadn't manifested themselves in *Tiger Love*. There was also *Beverly of Graustark*, opposite Marion Davies, and *The Temptress*, opposite Garbo.

And 1927 wasn't far behind, given *It*, in which he's a department store heir who falls for Clara Bow (as who wouldn't). Elinor Glyn, the inventor of "It," proclaimed that the only ones in Hollywood who had it were Bow, Moreno, the Ambassador Hotel doorman, and Rex, the wild stallion. (Clara supposedly commented, "I was awfully confused about the horse, but if she thought he had 'it,' then I figured he must be quite an animal.") Only cynics would point out that she had previously pinned the "It" medal on Wallace Reid, John Gilbert, and Valentino. In 1927, Moreno also made *Venus of Venice* with Constance Talmadge and, in England, *Madame Pompadour* with Dorothy Gish. Then came sound, and he was back where he began: relegated to ethnic roles because of his accent. But he soldiered on for almost thirty years, with supporting roles in minor movies (*The Spanish Main, Mark of the Renegade, Creature from the Black Lagoon*) and major ones: not only *The Searchers* but *Captain from Castile*.

There had been shady moments in his own life—he was a close friend of the mysteriously murdered William Desmond Taylor, with whom he spent a good deal of time the week of Taylor's death. And his wife, the oil heiress Daisy Canfield Danziger, went over a Mulholland Drive cliff in a car, sparking all kinds of rumors about Moreno's possible complicity in her death as well as about his sexuality. Is this what Michael Powell, who was on the set during the filming of *Mare Nostrum,* is implying when he observes in his autobiography that "not a speck of sexual fire passed between honest Tony and statuesque Alice [Terry]. They were 'just good friends'"? We'll never know. A final claim to fame: apparently Mauritz Stiller was fired from *The Temptress* when he demanded that Moreno shave off his mustache, on the grounds that it made him look like an Italian waiter. The Latin Lover was not amused.

Frank Morgan (Francis Philip Wupperman) (1890–1949), b. New York City

There are stories that Frank Morgan turned up for work day after day, year after year, on the MGM lot, bringing a small black briefcase containing the modest alcoholic refreshment that he required. Everyone loved him, he did whatever he was told, and as a rule managed it with finesse and invention. His only passing irritability arose when the black case went astray. He followed his brother Ralph (1882–1956) onto the stage and began working in films as early as 1916, at Vitagraph. But it was at Metro, invariably seeming more than his real age, that he established himself as a lovable fusspot, not nearly as competent as he would have liked—and it was that persona that graced Professor Marvel and the Wizard himself in *The Wizard of Oz* (39, Victor Fleming), the movie that ensures Morgan's survival, just as *The Shop Around the Corner* (40, Ernst Lubitsch) and his Mr. Matuschek are proof of his greatness.

It's a longer list than this, so marvel at the loyalty as well as the patience: with Gloria Swanson in *Manhandled* (24, Alan Dwan); *Dangerous Nan McGrew* (30, Malcolm St. Clair); *Queen High* (30, Fred Newmayer); *Laughter* (30, Harry d'Abbadie d'Arrast); *Fast and Loose* (30, Newmayer); *Secrets of the French Police* (32, Edward Sutherland); *The Half-Naked Truth* (32, Gregory La Cava); *Hallelujah, I'm a Bum* (33, Lewis Milestone); *Reunion in Vienna* (33, Sidney Franklin), his MGM debut; *The Kiss Before the Mirror* (33, James Whale); *The Nuisance* (33, Jack Conway); *When Ladies Meet* (33, Harry Beaumont); *Bombshell* (33, Fleming); *The Cat and the Fiddle* (34, William K. Howard); *The Affairs of Cellini* (34, La Cava); *The Good Fairy* (35, William Wyler); *Enchanted April* (35, Beaumont); *Naughty Marietta* (35, W. S. Van Dyke); *Escapade* (35, Robert Z. Leonard); *I Live My Life* (35, Van Dyke); *The Great Ziegfeld* (36,

Leonard); *Trouble for Two* (36, J. Walter Ruben); *Piccadilly Jim* (36, Leonard); father to Shirley Temple in *Dimples* (36, William A. Seiter); *The Last of Mrs. Cheyney* (37, Richard Boleslavsky); *The Emperor's Candlesticks* (37, George Fitzmaurice); in Jean Harlow's last film, *Saratoga* (37, Conway); *Rosalie* (37, Van Dyke).

He was an American in Germany in *Paradise for Three* (38, Edward Buzzell); Panisse in an adaptation of Pagnol, *Port of Seven Seas* (38, Whale); Robert Taylor's father in *The Crowd Roars* (38, Richard Thorpe); the producer in *Sweethearts* (38, Van Dyke); *Broadway Serenade* (39, Leonard); *Balalaika* (39, Reinhold Schünzel); back from the dead in *The Ghost Comes Home* (40, William Thiele); *Broadway Melody of 1940* (40, Norman Taurog); *The Mortal Storm* (40, Frank Borzage); *Boom Town* (40, Conway); pretending to be *The Wild Man of Borneo* (41, Robert B. Sinclair); very good in *Honky Tonk* (41, Conway); a real local hero in *The Vanishing Virginian* (42, Borzage); with a dog in *Tortilla Flat* (42, Fleming), for which he got a supporting actor nomination; *White Cargo* (42, Thorpe); *The Human Comedy* (43, Clarence Brown); *Thousands Cheer* (43, George Sidney); *The White Cliffs of Dover* (44, Brown); *Casanova Brown* (44, Sam Wood); *Yolanda and the Thief* (45, Vincente Minnelli); *Courage of Lassie* (46, Fred M. Wilcox); back from the dead again in *The Cock-eyed Miracle* (46, S. Sylvan Simon); *Lady Luck* (46, Edwin L. Marin); *Green Dolphin Street* (47, Victor Saville); *Summer Holiday* (48, Rouben Mamoulian); the king in *The Three Musketeers* (48, Sidney); *The Stratton Story* (49, Wood); *The Great Sinner* (49, Robert Siodmak); *Key to the City* (50, Sidney).

Michèle Morgan (Simone Roussel),
b. Neuilly, France, 1920

Her most memorable appearance was at the age of eighteen in Marcel Carné's *Quai des Brumes* (38), in which she played the timid, slant-eyed ward of Michel Simon who falls in love with Jean Gabin. Her austere features were accentuated by beret and trench coat and her eyes seemed to foresee the pain and loss in the foggy, fatalistic world that Carné and Prévert created on the brink of war.

She had made her debut for Marc Allégret in 1937 in *Gribouille* and *Orage* (38), and after *Quai des Brumes* she made *La Loi du Nord* (39, Jacques Feyder), *Untel Père et Fils* (40, Julien Duvivier), and *Remorques* (41, Jean Grémillon) before leaving for America. While there, she was the resistance heroine in *Joan of Paris* (42, Robert Stevenson), played opposite Sinatra and sang in *Higher and Higher* (43, Tim Whelan), appeared in *Passage to Marseilles* (44, Michael Curtiz) and *The Chase* (46, Arthur Ripley).

After the war, she returned to France for *La Symphonie Pastorale* (46, Jean Delannoy) and then went to England to play in *The Fallen Idol* (48, Carol Reed). Since then, she has been a faltering but beautiful star of the French cinema, if rarely in good films: *Aux Yeux du Souvenir* (48, Delannoy); *Fabiola* (49, Alessandro Blasetti); *Le Château de Verre* (50, René Clément); *La Minute de Vérité* (52, Delannoy); *Les Orgueilleux* (53, Yves Allégret); *Napoléon* (55, Sacha Guitry); excellent in *Summer Manoeuvres* (55, René Clair); *Marguerite de la Nuit* (55, Claude Autant-Lara); *Si Paris Nous Était Conté* (56, Guitry); *The Vintage* (57, Jeffrey Hayden); *Le Miroir à Deux Faces* (58, André Cayatte); *Fortunat* (60, Alex Joffé); *Le Crime ne Paie pas* (61, Gérard Oury); *Landru* (62, Claude Chabrol); *Lost Command* (66, Mark Robson); *Benjamin* (67, Michel Deville); and *Cat and Mouse* (75, Claude Lelouch).

She played herself in *Robert et Robert* (78, Lelouch), and she has appeared in *Un Homme et une Femme: 20 Ans Déjà* (86, Lelouch) and *Stanno Tutti Bene* (90, Giuseppe Tornatore). Then she moved over to TV for *La Veuve de l'Architecte* (95, Philippe Monnier); *Des Gens si Bien Elevés* (97, Alain Nahum); *La Rivale* (98, Nahum).

Masayuki Mori (1911–73), b. Tokyo

It is appropriate that the two men in the triangle that is *Rashomon* (50) were Toshiro Mifune and Masayuki Mori—Mifune, the essential macho swaggerer, and Mori, the essential refined and sensitive aristocrat. They are the opposite masculine poles of fifties and sixties Japanese film.

Mori, the son of a novelist, attended Kyoto University and became a stage actor. Throughout his career, both onstage and on-screen, his personal elegance was matched by the careful intelligence of his acting. He worked for Naruse eight times, most notably as the uncaring lover in *Floating Clouds* (55) and in *When a Woman Ascends the Stairs* (60). He is the unhappy young brother in *The Ball at the House of Anjo* (Kozaburo Yoshimura, 47); the emperor in Mizoguchi's *Princess Yang Kwei Fei* (55); the leading character in *The Idiot* (51) for Kurosawa; and with Mifune again in *The Bad Sleep Well* (60). Most important of all, he is Genjuro, the enchanted potter, in Mizoguchi's *Ugetsu Monogatari* (53).

Robert Morley (1908–92), b. Semley, England

Robert Morley was a stage actor, an occasional playwright, as well as a radio and television personality blessed by impromptu wit and deep good nature. But for more than fifty years he was a supporting actor in films, and a routine lead, of enormous versatility—nearly always funny, often touching, indubitably English, despite the range of notions (and wretched pictures) he lent himself to: as Louis XVI with Norma Shearer in *Marie*

Antoinette (38, W. S. Van Dyke), for which he won a supporting actor nomination; *Return to Yesterday* (40, Robert Stevenson); as Andrew Undershaft in *Major Barbara* (41, Gabriel Pascal); *The Big Blockade* (41, Charles Frend); *The Foreman Went to France* (41, Frend); Charles James Fox in *The Young Mr. Pitt* (42, Carol Reed); *I Live in Grosvenor Square* (45, Herbert Wilcox); *The Small Back Room* (45, Michael Powell); at his best in *Outcast of the Islands* (51, Reed); as the brother in *The African Queen* (51, John Huston); the director in *Curtain Up* (52, Ralph Smart); *Melba* (53, Lewis Milestone); as Gilbert in *The Story of Gilbert and Sullivan* (53, Sidney Gilliat); superb in *Beat the Devil* (53, Huston); *The Good Die Young* (54, Lewis Gilbert); George III in *Beau Brummell* (54, Curtis Bernhardt); another French king in *Quentin Durwood* (55, Richard Thorpe); *Loser Takes All* (56, Ken Annakin); *Law and Disorder* (58, Charles Crichton); *The Sheriff of Fractured Jaw* (58, Raoul Walsh); *The Journey* (59, Anatole Litvak); *The Doctor's Dilemma* (59, Anthony Asquith); *Libel* (59, Asquith); *The Battle of the Sexes* (60, Crichton); the lead in *Oscar Wilde* (60, Gregory Ratoff), a role he had played onstage in the 1930s; *The Young Ones* (61, Sidney J. Furie); *The Road to Hong Kong* (62, Norman Panama); *Nine Hours to Rama* (63, Mark Robson); *Murder at the Gallop* (63, George Pollack); *The Old Dark House* (63, William Castle); *Take Her, She's Mine* (63, Henry Koster); *Topkapi* (64, Jules Dassin); *Of Human Bondage* (64, Ken Hughes); *Hot Enough for June* (64, Ralph Thomas); *Those Magnificent Men in Their Flying Machines* (65, Ken Annakin); *A Study in Terror* (65, James Hill); *Life at the Top* (65, Ted Kotcheff); *Genghis Khan* (65, Henry Levin); *The Loved One* (65, Tony Richardson); *The Alphabet Murders* (66, Frank Tashlin); *Hotel Paradiso* (66, Peter Glenville); *Tender Scoundrel* (66, Jean Becker); *Way . . . Way Out* (66, Gordon Douglas); *The Trygon Factor* (67, Cyril Frankel); *Hot Millions* (68, Eric Till); *Sinful Davey* (69, Huston); *Cromwell* (70, Ken Hughes); *Song of Norway* (70, Andrew L. Stone); *When Eight Bells Ring* (71, Etienne Perrier); *Theatre of Blood* (73, Douglas Hickox); *The Blue Bird* (76, George Cukor); *Who Is Killing the Great Chefs of Europe?* (78, Kotcheff), as a great gourmet; *The Human Factor* (79, Otto Preminger); *Loophole* (80, John Quested); *High Road to China* (83, Brian G. Hutton); *The Wind* (87, Nico Mastorikis); *Little Dorrit* (87, Christine Edzard); *Istanbul* (90, Mats Arehn).

Ennio Morricone, b. Rome, 1928

Well over seventy now, Morricone is supposed to have written more than three hundred movie scores. The majority of those have been for Italian films, and Morricone is always associated with Sergio Leone (in fact, the two were at school

together, though only Morricone remembered that useful fact). As such, Morricone has a real part in the history of music in the Western, especially with the extravagantly romantic (and derivative) frontier symphonics for *Once Upon a Time in the West* (68). In addition, with use of flutes, wind instruments, the voice, and bare rhythmic accompaniment, Morricone has a great skill at building tension. How much you like such things may depend on your response to Leone's work as a whole.

The list that follows is far from complete: *A Fistful of Dollars* (64, Leone); *Before the Revolution* (64, Bernardo Bertolucci); *Fists in His Pockets* (66, Marco Bellocchio); *The Good, the Bad and the Ugly* (66, Leone); *The Battle of Algiers* (66, Gillo Pontecorvo); *Guns for San Sebastian* (68, Henri Verneuil); *Teorema* (68, Pier Paolo Pasolini); *Burn!* (69, Pontecorvo); *Two Mules for Sister Sarah* (70, Don Siegel); *Investigation of a Citizen Above Suspicion* (70, Elio Petri); *Salo* (75, Pasolini); *1900* (76, Bertolucci); *Exorcist II: The Heretic* (77, John Boorman); *Days of Heaven* (78, Terrence Malick)—the foreign air of Americana being fed back into the real thing; *The Island* (80, Michael Ritchie); *The Tragedy of a Ridiculous Man* (81, Bertolucci); *White Dog* (82, Samuel Fuller); *The Night of the Shooting Stars* (82, the Taviani Brothers); *The Eyes, the Mouth* (82, Bellocchio); *Once Upon a Time in America* (84, Leone), which is like the score for *The Godfather* made even more romantic; *Ginger and Fred* (85, Federico Fellini); *The Mission* (86, Roland Joffé)—Oscar-nominated; *Good Morning, Babylon* (87, the Tavianis); *The Untouchables* (87, Brian De Palma), one of his best scores—again nominated for an Oscar; *Casualties of War* (89, De Palma); *Fat Man and Little Boy* (89, Joffé); *Cinema Paradiso* (89, Giuseppe Tornatore); *Hamlet* (90, Franco Zeffirelli); *Bugsy* (91, Barry Levinson)—another nomination; *Love Affair* (94, Glenn Gordon Caron); *Disclosure* (95, Levinson); *Lolita* (97, Adrian Lyne); *Bulworth* (98, Warren Beatty); *Malena* (00, Tornatore).

Errol Morris, b. Hewlett, New York, 1948
1978: *Gates of Heaven* (d). 1981: *Vernon, Florida* (d). 1988: *The Thin Blue Line* (d). 1992: *A Brief History of Time* (d). 1994: *The Dark Wind*. 1997: *Fast, Cheap & Out of Control* (d). 1999: *Mr. Death: The Rise and Fall of Fred A. Leuchter Jr.* (d). 2000: *First Person* (TV). 2003: *The Fog of War* (d).

Not uncommonly, Errol Morris is interested in people like himself—in obsessives, trying to negotiate the intractable difficulties of life and the widespread yet indifferent misunderstanding of others. In some ways, his world is a little like that of Hal Hartley, but Morris is so much more vividly intelligent, and his sense of inquiry does so much to animate the style and structure of his work. No, really, the best comparison is with Chris Marker—though Morris lacks, as yet, the great man's Borgesian serenity. Maybe that comes with time. And maybe when it does come it dispels the faintly aggressive air of intelligence for its own sake—the risk of smugness—that sometimes makes Morris seem an exploiter of his own raw material.

The child of a doctor and a musician, Morris attended the Putney School in Vermont before the University of Wisconsin (history) and the University of California at Berkeley (philosophy). It was while there that he drifted to the Pacific Film Archive, for which he wrote program notes and became an enthusiast of such things as film noir. But Morris is not a natural storyteller. The superb noir essay *The Thin Blue Line* seemed dramatic enough to bring him Hollywood offers. But *The Dark Wind* (for Robert Redford) was a very unhappy experience, from which Morris was fired, and the film hardly released. It was said that he could not communicate with actors, but I suspect that really refers to a clash of artistic visions.

So Morris has gone in search of eccentricity as subject matter, which is fine. But I have the feeling that his greatest challenge might be the real mainstream—not just people as bizarre as Fred Leuchter and Stephen Hawking, but lives as decent, "ordinary," and mainstream as that led by Mr. Morris. If he could curb his need for oddballs, he might find a level of universality that could prompt his best work. Maybe I'm looking for the minds of Ken Burns and Errol Morris to fuse—now we are close to the Marker.

Robert Mulligan,
b. Bronx, New York, 1925
1957: *Fear Strikes Out.* 1960: *The Rat Race; The Great Imposter.* 1961: *Come September.* 1962: *The Spiral Road.* 1963: *To Kill a Mockingbird; Love With the Proper Stranger.* 1965: *Baby, The Rain Must Fall.* 1966: *Inside Daisy Clover.* 1967: *Up the Down Staircase.* 1969: *The Stalking Moon.* 1970: *The Pursuit of Happiness.* 1971: *Summer of '42.* 1972: *The Other.* 1974: *The Nickel Ride.* 1978: *Blood Brothers; Same Time Next Year.* 1982: *Kiss Me Goodbye.* 1988: *Clara's Heart.* 1991: *The Man in the Moon.*

There is something wrong with a thirty-five-year career of twenty movies that is still indistinct and tentative. Mulligan appeared once to have the typical promise of the New Wave American director. After naval service, he graduated to TV where he won a reputation for prestige drama that soon admitted him to Hollywood. *Fear Strikes Out* was not only his debut but that of producer Alan J. Pakula, who was to collaborate with Mulligan on another six films. It has most of Mulligan's virtues—an unusual setting within which he observes a young person under emotional stress;

an effacing camera style that is pledged to intimate performances; and his besetting flaw—the preference for tastefulness rather than true rawness.

Just as he lacks artistic character, so his films do not live in the memory. Professional compromise seems always to round off initial promise. Although attempting to deal with anguish and loneliness, the films are irresolute, neat, and appealing—unwilling to probe their audience sufficiently. Thus, it is notable that *Klute*—made by the now independent Pakula—goes much deeper into its characters and emerges with more disturbing conclusions than Mulligan ever dared.

The four films made after Mulligan's debut were all uneasy, especially *The Great Imposter,* a marvelous vehicle for Tony Curtis that stated rather than realized the black comedy of imposture. With *To Kill a Mockingbird,* Mulligan was reunited with Pakula (they worked together until *The Stalking Moon*). *Mockingbird* was a big hit, an important event in liberalizing attitudes, and it is sound work. The films that followed all flattered to deceive: *Love With the Proper Stranger* is as coy as its title; *Inside Daisy Clover* cries out for Minnelli; *The Stalking Moon* is earnestly slow; while *Summer of '42* is a cunning piece of nostalgic romance, sadly minus the real period character of *The Last Picture Show.*

To make serious material easeful is Mulligan's greatest fault and it is now more likely that he will succumb to a solemn and respectable sentimentality than surpass it. He has the sophistication and sensibility of a producer rather than a director. His tact is too infectious.

Mulligan's career did not work out well: *Kiss Me Goodbye* was a remake of *Donna Flor and Her Two Husbands,* but it found no spark between Sally Field and James Caan; *Clara's Heart* had Whoopi Goldberg as a Jamaican servant to an upper-middle-class family. But then Mulligan came back to life with *The Man in the Moon,* a lovely small film about children growing up in a rural setting—it was *To Kill a Mockingbird* again, and it left the intervening years seeming all the stranger.

Paul Muni (Muni Weisenfreund) (1895–1967),
b. Lemberg, Austria
Muni believed he was a great actor. And in the mid-1930s, at least, he managed to persuade his employer, Warner Brothers, the Academy of Motion Pictures, and a large part of the cinema audience. In retrospect, he looks owlish in his overacting, ridiculous in his makeup, and insanely awful in his feelings. Thus, he is a crucial negative illustration in any argument as to what constitutes screen acting.

The child of actors, he came to America early in the 1900s and played in Yiddish stock for many years. Only in 1926 did he play a part in English. This novelty and the greater one of sound prompted Fox to hire him: in 1929 he made *The Valiant* (William K. Howard), for which he was nominated for an Oscar, and *Seven Faces* (29, Berthold Viertel), in which he and his makeup box played seven people—including Don Juan, Schubert, Napoleon, and boxer Joe Gans (it was a movie about a waxworks).

Despite, or because of, such a virtuoso debut, Fox were happy to let him go and it was only after his Broadway success in Elmer Rice's *Counsellor at Law* that Howard Hawks cast him as *Scarface* (32). It is remarkable that that film should have been considered a glorification of the gangster, since Muni's flagrant overplaying is so remote from the sort of man that interests Hawks. Muni then excelled in Mervyn Le Roy's *I Am a Fugitive from a Chain Gang* (32) and was contracted by Warners. He followed with two more Le Roy films—*The World Changes* (33) and *Hi Nellie!* (34)—with Bette Davis in *Border Town* (35, Archie Mayo), and in 1935 encountered a director worthy of him: William Dieterle, who indulged Muni in *Doctor Socrates* (35), *The Story of Louis Pasteur* (35), and an Oscar, *The Life of Emile Zola* (37) and *Juarez* (39). These films were born out of an attitude to Great Men of History—pious, unsubtle, and naïve—that is unlikely to be revived. What Muni brought to them was the unchecked confidence that a great actor was as noble as any other benefactor of mankind. He was also a self-conscious, well-cushioned radical who did much to push *Black Fury* (35, Michael Curtiz), a study of labor relations in mining that Hollywood muffled. Muni's impressiveness came from the shameless heroics of identifying himself with Great Causes and Heroes.

Oddly, all this flourished at Warners where, in five years, Bogart would drive such myths from the temple. Muni also played in Litvak's *The Woman I Love* (37), was a Chinaman in Sidney Franklin's *The Good Earth* (37), and in the underrated *We Are Not Alone* (39, Edmund Goulding). By the time war came, his fashion had already faded. He was a Frenchman in Pichel's *Hudson's Bay* (41) and then made only another six films before his death: *Commandos Strike at Dawn* (42, John Farrow); *Counter-Attack* (45, Zoltan Korda); grotesque as Chopin's teacher in Charles Vidor's *A Song to Remember* (45); *Angel on My Shoulder* (46, Mayo); in Losey's blighted *Stranger on the Prowl* (52); finally as the slum doctor in Daniel Mann's *The Last Angry Man* (59).

Andrzej Munk (1921–61),
b. Cracow, Poland

1949: *Sztuka Mlodych* (d). 1950: *Zaczelo sie w Hiszpanii* (d). 1951: *Nauka Blize; Zycia* (d); *Kierunek Nowa Huta* (d). 1952: *Poemat Sym-* *foniczny "Bajka" St. Moniuszki* (d); *Pamietniki Chlopow* (d). 1953: *Kolejarskie Slowo* (d). 1954: *Gwiazdy Musza Plonac* (codirected with Witold Lesiewicz) (d). 1955: *Niedzielny Poranek/One Sunday Morning* (d); *Blekitny Krzyz/Men of the Blue Cross* (d). 1956: *Czalowiek na Torze/Man on the Track*. 1957: *Eroica*. 1958: *Spacerek Staromtejski/A Walk in the Old City of Warsaw* (d). 1959: *Zezowate Szczescie/Bad Luck; Polska Kronika Filmowa, no. 52* (d). 1961: *Pasazerka/ Passenger* (completed by Lesiewicz after Munk's death).

Until the more dramatically absurd death of Zbigniew Cybulski in a railway accident, the loss of Munk in a car crash was the tragedy of sixties Polish cinema. No doubt that he had an ironic, antiheroic view that was unusual in Poland, and no question of the feeling and care in his work. Even so, the argument remains that the best Poles are the ones who left—Polanski and Skolimowski—and that Munk never fully shed the mantle of tasteful social consciousness that is in all but the best Polish cinema. Just as Wajda's *A Generation* seems like a marvelous student film, so the lessons of Lodz hang over Polish cinema—the sense of working according to doctrine. Even early Polanski looks like argued-out storyboards duly put on film. And in the famous Munk shot—of a deserting soldier drinking and the bottle mimicked by a tank's gun looming over a ridge behind him—there is something of a seminar's self-congratulatory rightness.

After studying at Lodz, Munk worked for six years in documentary; *Man on the Track* was his first feature; *Eroica* the clearest expression of his skeptical approach to Polish heroics. *Passenger* is by far his most interesting work, pregnant with the fact of Munk's death and the stills that were used to complete it, not to mention its concentration-camp setting.

Walter Murch, b. New York, 1943

In 1968–69, Francis Ford Coppola had taken to the road to make *The Rain People*. It was a unit on which many people were barely out of the two film schools in Los Angeles: Francis had been at UCLA, and George Lucas and Walter Murch had been to USC. As the shooting concluded, out of love with Hollywood and Los Angeles, Coppola, Lucas, and Murch elected to move their families up to northern California and the Bay Area, there to make a new version of American cinema. Lucas is now one of the richest men in the country, with his facilities in Marin; Coppola has been one of the most celebrated directors in the world—rich, poor, and rich again, living in his house and winery in Rutherford. And in a smaller house than his comrades, Walter Murch still lives in Bolinas, California, not rich, except in the range of his interests and the record of his achievements. Walter Murch is the scholar, gentleman, and superb craftsman of modern film. And like any master of sound, he is a quiet man.

He was the son of a good painter, Walter Murch, who had his family roots in the west country of England. As a boy, Walter fell in love with the tape recorder and the games it could play. He was also enormously affected by a father who painted at night because he had to keep a paying job in the day. Walter went to Johns Hopkins, where he started on oceanography and geology and let the tide of interest carry him over to Romance languages and art history. He then studied in Paris and Perugia before driving across the United States on a Matchless motorcycle with his new wife, Aggie, to study film at USC.

In time, his skills at filmmaking would extend to sound and editing, and in both areas he is now without a peer. But film is not his whole world: he has a lifelong hobby pursuing the proof of the Titius-Bode theory (on the spatial intervals between planets) and he translates Italian poetry. He has also directed one film—*Return to Oz* (85). It was not a success, yet I don't think he has given up hopes of directing again. But let us look at what he has done.

He did sound on *The Rain People; Gimme Shelter* (70, David and Albert Maysles); *THX 1138* (71, Lucas)—he also collaborated on its script; *American Graffiti* (73, Lucas). He did the sound and was vital to the editing of *The Conversation* (74, Coppola), a picture that brought sound into the forefront of our consciousness. He was in charge of sound on *The Godfather Part II* (74, Coppola). He edited *Julia* (77, Fred Zinnemann). He did the sound on *Apocalypse Now* (79, Coppola), for which he won an Oscar. He edited *The Unbearable Lightness of Being* (88, Philip Kaufman); *Ghost* (90, Jerry Zucker); *The Godfather Part III* (90, Coppola); *Romeo Is Bleeding* (93, Peter Medak). He edited *House of Cards* (93, Michael Lessac) and *First Knight* (95, Zucker).

On *The English Patient* (96, Anthony Minghella), one of the most densely textured of films, he did the editing and sound and won Oscars for both. He was responsible for the reconstruction of Orson Welles's *Touch of Evil*. He did editing and sound on *The Talented Mr. Ripley* (99, Minghella). And he did the detailed work on *Apocalypse Now Redux* (01, Coppola).

Friedrich Wilhelm Murnau

(F. W. Plumpe) (1888–1931),
b. Bielefeld, Westphalia

1919: *Der Knabe in Blau; Satanas.* 1920: *Sehnsucht; Der Januskopf; Abend . . . Nacht . . . Morgen; Der Gang in die Nacht; Der Bucklige und die Tänzerin.* 1921: *Marizza, Gennant die Schmuglermadonna; Schloss Vogelöd.* 1922: *Nosferatu,* *Eine Symphonie des Grauens; Der Brennende Acker; Phantom.* 1923: *Die Austreibung; Die Finanzen des Grossherzogs.* 1924: *Der Letzte Mann/The Last Laugh.* 1925: *Tartüff.* 1926: *Faust.* 1927: *Sunrise.* 1929: *Four Devils.* 1930: *Our Daily Bread/City Girl; Die Zwolfte Stunde* (sound version of *Nosferatu*). 1931: *Tabu* (codirected with Robert Flaherty).

It was in 1964 that Lotte Eisner's study of Murnau was published in France. Reviewing it, David Robinson argued that its timing was significant, presumably because it confronted English audiences with the issue of Murnau's greatness. But Lotte Eisner's obscure book remained untranslated until 1973 and Murnau was still far short of his proper recognition in Britain and America. Even today, with more of the early films available, and the America achievement clearer, Murnau is a neglected master.

But he does not lend himself easily to massive interpretation. *Nosferatu* can be shunted off into the horror genre, along with *Faust. The Last Laugh* can be seen as a contribution to German Expressionism. *Sunrise* is certainly a major example of the women's picture. *Tabu* does abandon the sort of literal authenticity that preoccupied Flaherty. There are no persistent thematic or literary bonds to tie Murnau's straggling work together. Our notion of the film director is of a grandiose self-publicist, partly because the movie industry has always lived by those inflated terms. But Murnau never adhered to that pattern. Tentativeness was one of the keys to his life and work, and it cuts right across the grain of the world in which he worked.

Expressionism, after all, is based on a near-clinical certainty about states of mind, taken to the point where they invade and distort external reality. Although it is often called a morbid and hysterical genre, it is still marked by dogmatic German self-confidence and a rigid sense of narrative structure and moral values. There is ambiguity in *Caligari*, but it is far from clear that it was intended. Even in Lang, the unease that arises from *Metropolis* or *The Testament of Dr. Mabuse* is part of a fixed imaginative anticipation of malign fate. It is only in America, in *Fury*, that Lang grasps the role of free will. In general, German films of the 1920s suffer from the thoroughness with which they are conceived and controlled. It is a composed and designed cinema, always concentrating on angles, objects, or faces, certain that a whole world can be based on them. Whatever the emotional or the intellectual undercurrents of German cinema, it is conclusive in its faith that images prove ideas and that messages can be easily digested from films.

Murnau, by contrast, is much less sure of the message. *The Last Laugh* is the least interesting of his better-known films because it is most affected by the German belief in narrative finality: the idea of a proud commissionaire reduced to a lavatory attendant has all the banal simplicity of a clever short story. The film would be maudlin and trite if that were its only subject. But the obviousness of the story, plus the potent sentimentality of Emil Jannings in the central part, are partially reduced by Murnau's cinematic creation of a world that is not only representational, but in which the real and the created are subtly merged. His films are about individual melodrama prompted by the pressure of the world. And Murnau's greatness lies in this realization—that it is possible to photograph the real world and yet invest it with a variety of poetic, imaginative, and subjective qualities. The camera itself allowed audiences to experience actuality and imagination simultaneously.

Of course, Murnau often used sets. *The Last Laugh* is a studio film, as is *Sunrise*. What distinguished Murnau from other Expressionists busy building their worlds on sets is that he made his camera move. It moves elsewhere, but implacably in Lang and decoratively in Dupont. As soon as a film builds sets, the camera movements become preconceived and measured. When a wall stops, so must a tracking shot: the shooting script envisages setting and movement simultaneously. But Murnau's camera moved to suggest spatial actuality and to implicate a world outside the frame. In Expressionism proper, the world stops at the frame, but Murnau's emphasis on physical movement meant that the unseen was constantly being implied. As Gilberto Perez Guillermo has said:

> Murnau's cinema . . . is primarily a cinema of empty space . . . space becomes the central object: the space traversed during the trolley ride in *Sunrise,* immeasurably more expressive than any of the individual objects passed; the space surrounding the lovers' hut in *Tabu,* charged with the menace of a hostile world. . . . Like Velazquez, Murnau looks past the foreground and into the background. Attention is not restricted to a sharply delimited object standing in the foreground, or even to a number of significant objects strategically placed within the frame. It is dispersed throughout the whole, throughout space; and space, fluid in nature and not likely to be contained within sharp limits, palpably extends all around the frame of the film. Murnau's compositions, his shots of details, have a certain imbalance, a deliberate incompleteness which relates them inextricably to the world around them.

That deliberate incompleteness is the source of the highest cinematic beauty: not the ornate compositional elegance of Eisenstein, Lang, or even Hitchcock, but the dynamic visual sense that Stro-

heim had and that runs through Sternberg, Renoir, Ophüls, Welles, and Mizoguchi. It is very close to Astruc's theory of *la caméra stylo,* and there is an eerie prediction of subsequent critical pronouncements in this quote from Murnau: "The camera is the director's pencil. It should have the greatest possible mobility in order to record the most fleeting harmony of atmosphere. It is important that the mechanical factor should not stand between the spectator and the film."

The "mechanical" was always likely to obtrude in Germany if only because the German view of cinema was schematic. I think it likely that Murnau never found a subject he liked in Germany. *The Last Laugh* is a film working against its own limits and finally made absurd by the tacked-on happy ending. Even the extraordinary naturalism of *Nosferatu* is impeded by having its origins in Bram Stoker's essentially unenterprising *Dracula.* It is poetic, subtle, and marvelously employs real locations to suggest the atmosphere of plague and menace. But Murnau's art transcends genre, and he is ultimately wasting himself on so direct a horror picture. In the same way, he was not able to overcome the picturesque elements of costume in *Tartüff* or the supernatural in *Faust.*

It was in America that he felt liberated. (Incidentally, Lotte Eisner has shown how far Murnau's homosexuality was inhibited by the German criminal code.) Much of *Sunrise* was shot in the studio, with whatever artifice was necessary. It was also a strange combination of American material and German talents. As well as scriptwriter Carl Mayer, Murnau had Rochus Gliese and Edgar Ulmer as art directors and Karl Struss assisting Charles Rosher with the photography. What freed him was the opportunity to use sunlit locations, the spontaneity of Janet Gaynor and George O'Brien, the American optimism of the story, and the American cinema's aptitude for casualness. For Murnau's own shyness and pessimism are made to illuminate the raw cheerfulness of America. *Sunrise* is a great film; a landmark in the use of a moving camera; and of crucial importance in showing how genre cinema may be complemented by the gravity of a true artist's feelings. *Sunrise* is a world of art made out of a novelette, as are *Shanghai Express, The Mortal Storm, The Shop Around the Corner, Letter From an Unknown Woman, Imitation of Life, A Star Is Born,* and *Daisy Kenyon.*

Murnau flopped with *Sunrise*—years ahead of its time—and with *Four Devils.* The last of his three films at Fox, *Our Daily Bread,* was begun on location in Oregon, but the studio lost its nerve and Murnau was replaced by hacks. In reaction, he and Flaherty went off to the South Seas to make *Tabu.* It is bad Flaherty in the sense that it barely bothers to deal with the natives anthropologically. But it is a great work of art that uses the natives as Everyman figures. What Grierson took for the fake glamour of Hollywood, turning indigenous peoples into stars, is really the beautiful depiction of a doomed love story. As in *Sunrise,* Murnau fused locations and the finest studio lighting to make a reinvention of reality. *Tabu* and *Sunrise* are masterworks. We are lucky that they both survive.

Murnau died in a car accident on the point of taking up a contract with Paramount. Lotte Eisner says that he picked chauffeurs for their looks rather than their driving abilities. If so, that whim deprived us of a great director at a time when he was going to the studio most likely to encourage him.

He was only forty-three when he died, and in *Sunrise* he had already married a German narrative fatalism to the naturalism of actors like Janet Gaynor, George O'Brien, and Margaret Livingstone, who is so poignant as the vamp. Above all, he had found a crucial American subject, the ordinary person's dream of something more than fate has allowed, and the dread that goes with the dream. For *Sunrise* is a key step toward film noir as well as the woman's picture. It is the city and the country, jazzy futures and the old frontier. Murnau might have done more for American film than Lang or Lubitsch.

Audie Murphy (1924–71), b. Kingston, Texas

It was all very well for Murphy to be America's most decorated soldier of the Second World War, the slayer of some 240 Germans, and the holder of the Congressional Medal of Honor, but on the screen his baby face seemed unconvincing in action and unhappy when called upon to speak. He was a sharecropper when he came out of the army and a clerk and garage attendant before his Hollywood debut in *Beyond Glory* (48, John Farrow).

John Huston made the first serious attempt to carry Murphy's real-life experiences over to the screen when he cast him as the Young Soldier in *The Red Badge of Courage* (51). It was one of Huston's whimsical insights to notice that this young veteran could look a novice amid the poetic battlescapes intended for that film. To judge by Lillian Ross's *Picture,* Murphy was bewildered by the project, but he does not let the film down and conveys the epic simplicity of Stephen Crane's novel.

Murphy was much closer to the glamorous infantryman playing himself in *To Hell and Back* (55, Jesse Hibbs). He never claimed to be an actor, and it is a mystery that he was called upon to play *The Quiet American* (58) by Joseph Mankiewicz. Apart from this, he made a herd of second-feature Westerns: *Sierra* (50, Alfred E. Green); *Kansas Raiders* (50, Ray Enright); *The Kid from Texas* (50, Kurt Neumann); *The Cimarron Kid* (51, Budd Boetticher); *Duel at Silver Creek* (52, Don Siegel); *Ride Clear of Diablo* (54, Hibbs); *Destry* (54, George Marshall); *Night Passage* (57, James Neilson); as the Harry Morgan figure in *The Gun Runners* (58, Siegel), a version of Hemingway's *To Have and Have Not;* and *No Name on the Bullet* (59, Jack Arnold). His only other big picture was *The Unforgiven* (60, Huston), an old horse whistled back from the meadow by a kind master.

In the late 1960s, fatter but still boyish, Murphy mixed Lyles Westerns and *A Time for Dying* (69, Boetticher) with acting as a private policeman against drug-runners and the Mafia. The onetime hero was acquitted on a charge of attempted murder after beating up a man. He died in a private plane crash in Virginia.

Eddie Murphy (Edward Regan Murphy), b. Bushwick, New York, 1961

However much one appreciates Spike Lee's *Malcolm X,* its steadfast length never quite conveys the turbulent, contradictory passions evident in one of Eddie Murphy's savage smiles. Should he entertain us, or kill us? Is there some compromise response more useful to him than taking our money? Here are two remarks that ride on Murphy's tense smiles:

The first is from Ned Tanen, production chief at Paramount in the years when Eddie Murphy was so important that he sometimes treated the studio the way gangsters loom over double-crossers: He has

a rebelliousness that affects people. An ability to say things that you wish you could say. He's someone who is in charge of his own life—and I'm talking about the portrayal, not the person. He doesn't need anything from anyone. He's a person who is really an off-center character, but very likeable, very identifiable.

And what's most amazing, he totally crosses all color lines and all ethnic lines internationally, not just American, which is unheard of. I'm always amazed by the international aspect of it because American black actors have never made it internationally, and so much of that appeal is based on verbalization, and yet it doesn't seem to make any difference. There is an attractiveness to him as a bad boy . . .

And this, from Murphy himself: "A very militant black woman said to me, 'How come no serious black actors get the same kind of deals you get or Richard Pryor gets? How come it's always a comic?' I said because America is still a racist society."

The idea of an essentially angry man who cannot resist being made into a lucrative clown, and whose anger becomes the more reckless, cynical, and self-destructive . . . this is a great subject for an Eddie Murphy film. Certainly, it is more promising than the increasingly feeble and/or nasty material that has been generated for him. "Generated" is most apposite, for as the case of *Coming to America* and the book *Fatal Subtraction* make evident, Eddie Murphy is a cow that gives rich cream.

Not that Murphy makes himself available for sympathy. His grasp on gross receipts is matched by an instinct for gross or raw behavior. Then he makes himself out to be a kind of hip outlaw, womanizer and misogynist, gay-basher, vulgarian . . . anything that may offend. He surely knows how far his act, his wealth, his power, and his offense have stirred up vengeance.

Whereas, his talent is at best immediate, spur of the moment, cheeky, and reactive. He is, among all the other things, a stand-up comic trying to find full-length films that don't seem like unsuitable garb.

From *Saturday Night Live* in the early 1980s, he has gone on through hits and abject pictures, by way of $8 million a shot, entourages, bodyguards, etc., absolutely confident in his exploitation of the system and of his fans' hopes that he is himself used, screwed, and abused. It is a vicious cycle that seems to offer no way out: *48 Hrs.* (82, Walter Hill); *Trading Places* (83, John Landis); *Best Defense* (84, Willard Huyck); at his best in *Beverly Hills Cop* (84, Martin Brest); *The Golden Child* (86, Michael Ritchie); *Beverly Hills Cop II* (87, Tony Scott), on which he also has a story credit; *Eddie Murphy Raw* (87, Robert Townsend), a concert film; *Coming to America* (88, Landis); *Harlem Nights* (89), which he directed himself; *Another 48 Hrs.* (90, Hill); *Boomerang* (92, Reginald Hudlin); *Distinguished Gentleman* (92, Jonathan Lynn); and *Beverly Hills Cop III* (94, Landis).

If anything, Eddie Murphy has become even more successful—and he is by now a black movie star who has retained his position for twenty years. What that means is that he has no peers. At the same time, I regret the directions he has taken in the last ten years or so, for he has concentrated on two franchises (full of brilliance—especially in their makeup, by Rick Baker and others) but also increasingly likely to leave America as a whole with the opinion that blacks are stupid, low, and dirty-minded. The old Eddie Murphy has sold out—not that we ever feel that the malice and sourness have gone. It's not a simple matter, for Murphy is very funny; but I fear the new ghetto of his commercial cashing-in. It seems a drab way for his energy to go: *Vampire in Brooklyn* (95, Wes Craven); *The Nutty Professor* (96, Tom Shadyac); *Metro* (97, Thomas Carr); *Dr. Dolittle* (98, Betty Thomas); *Holy Man* (98, Stephen Herek); *Life* (99, Ted Demme); *Bowfinger* (99, Frank Oz)—his best recent film; *The Nutty Professor II: The Klumps* (00, Peter Segal); a very funny voice in *Shrek* (01, Andrew Adamson and Vicki Jenson); *Dr. Dolittle 2* (01, Steve Carr); *Showtime* (02, Tom Dey); *The Adventures of Pluto Nash* (02, Ron Underwood); *I Spy* (02, Thomas); *Daddy Day Care* (03, Steve Carr).

Bill Murray, b. Wilmette, Illinois, 1950

Of all the people who made their reputation with *Saturday Night Live* in the late 1970s, Murray has worked hardest with a movie career, and seemed the most open to the challenge of acting. Not that he is unfunny: indeed, as so often in film, it is those who are merely inhabiting a difficult position (up a tree or at the dead end of argument) who have the best chance of being funny. Murray is ambitious and adventurous, and he seems set on perseverance with less and less stress on mannerism or mania.

He was a founding member of the Second City team in Chicago before he made it on *Saturday Night Live*. He did a voice on *Shame of the Jungle* (75, Picha and Boris Szulzinger) before he appeared in *Meatballs* (79, Ivan Reitman); *Caddyshack* (80, Harold Ramis); *Where the Buffalo Roam* (80, Art Linson); *Loose Shoes* (80, Ira Miller); in the army in *Stripes* (81, Reitman); *Nothing Lasts Forever* (82, Tom Schiller); very funny as the friend in *Tootsie* (82, Sydney Pollack); with a huge hit in *Ghostbusters* (84, Reitman); acting in and coscreenwriter on the listless *The Razor's Edge* (84, John Byrum)—a sudden revelation of disquiet; *Little Shop of Horrors* (86, Frank Oz); *Scrooged* (88, Richard Donner); *Ghostbusters II* (89, Reitman); *Quick Change* (90, Howard Franklin and Murray), a failure, yet a promising debut; *What About Bob?* (91, Oz); maybe his best work yet—*Groundhog Day* (93, Ramis); and standing up to De Niro as the gangster in *Mad Dog and Glory* (93, John McNaughton).

An intriguing pattern began to emerge—give him a big, obvious comedy, with himself in the lead, and it was likely to flop: *Larger Than Life* (96, Howard Franklin); *The Man Who Knew Too Little* (97, Jon Amiel)—but put him in a modest role, here or there, and invariably you wondered why no one really gives Bill Murray his head: *Ed Wood* (94, Tim Burton); *Kingpin* (96, Bobby and Peter Farrelly); *Wild Things* (98, McNaughton); *Rushmore* (98, Wes Anderson). Is there really something in the man that hates to be exposed? Will any big movie ever trap him? He gives chances: *With Friends Like These* (98, Philip F. Messina); *Cradle Will Rock* (99, Tim Robbins); *Scout's Honor* (99, Neil Leifer); Polonius in *Hamlet* (00, Michael Almereyda); *Charlie's Angels* (00, McG); *Osmosis Jones* (01, the Farrellys); *The Royal Tenenbaums* (01, Anderson); *Speaking of Sex* (01, John McNaughton); *Lost in Translation* (03, Sofia Coppola).

N

Mikio Naruse (1905–69), b. Tokyo, Japan

Naruse sounds wonderful. He is a favorite director of this book's editor—Bob Gottlieb—who has steadily urged the films on me. "If you love Ozu," he says, "you'll love Naruse." It is something I look forward to. Indeed, I anticipate at some stage in the future a Naruse season—it is said he made nearly ninety films—in fine 35mm prints, on a large screen. I will see them one day. But like all lifelong filmgoers, I know the allure of films unseen. Going to the movies has always been a matter of immediate expectation, which—on seeing the trailers—makes me suddenly wish it could be next week now. I may never maintain the highest love of Naruse without refusing to see the films. No, not refusing—declining, postponing, putting off, keeping that bounty for a rainy day.

But, really, I'm persuaded already that Naruse was a master, a teller of domestic dramas, small and sweeping, built around indomitable women. I have heard how impressive Hideko Takamine is in his films, not to mention Machiko Kyo and Masayuki Mori. And if there is only a time for a few films—and, as far as I know, no Naruse film ever had commercial release in the United States or Great Britain—then I have to see *Wife, Be Like a Rose!* (35), *Repast* (51), *Mother* (52), *Older Brother, Younger Sister* (53), *Sound of the Mountain* (54), *Floating Clouds* (55), *Flowing* (56), *When a Woman Ascends the Stairs* (60), and *Yearning* (64).

There is nothing like knowing that one has still to see a body of great work. And no gamble as interesting as pushing the desire to its limit.

Very well: the above was a ruse—I have seen Naruse films, and they are . . . ineffable. But I hold to the official stance of vital anticipation. Thus, so far, I have seen nothing made by Nicholas Thomson (but he is only thirteen).

Alla Nazimova (1879–1945), b. Yalta, Russia

Eugene O'Neill and Tennessee Williams had one experience in common—they had been transfixed by seeing Nazimova play Ibsen, so much so that they reckoned they had never quite confronted the *reality* of theatre before. So many critics and observers reported that Nazimova, on stage, brought a startling immediacy to every scene, so that people believed they were beholding real life. And so the legends of acting went—before movies lasted long enough to show that nearly every style of acting dates. Nazimova was a great figure of the early movies: her *War Brides* (16, Herbert Brenon) was a huge hit. But no copy survives, and so we can only heed the word of O'Neill and Williams and try to measure the melodramatic stills of *War Brides* against movies from her last years.

Of course, Nazimova is more than just that enigma. She is a link between cultures and ages. She had studied with Stanislavsky and known Chekhov. In America, she would earn $13,000 a week—this in 1915. She was a bisexual society hostess in Hollywood at her house, the Garden of Allah. She was a force behind the flimsy being of Valentino. She was aunt to Val Lewton. All of this, and much more, can be explored in Gavin Lambert's finely researched biography, published in 1997.

She left Russia for America in 1905, and for ten years she played Ibsen—*Hedda Gabler, The Master Builder, A Doll's House,* and Regina in *Ghosts* (later, she would move on to Mrs. Alving). She worked and lived with the actor/director Charles Bryant (though there was a husband alive still back in Russia) and she entered movies. She made *War Brides* for the Lewis Selznick Company and went on to Metro with *Revelation* (18, George D. Baker), in which she plays a prostitute who poses for a painter (Bryant) and who when asked to pose as the Madonna, becomes her! So much miracle—yet no film surviving: it's the pattern of Nazimova's early movies.

She played mother and daughter in *Toys of Fate* (18, Baker) and Hassouna, an Arab girl, in *Eye for Eye* (18, Albert Capellani). She played two women (one European, one Eurasian) in love with one man in *The Red Lantern* (19, Capellani) and a slum girl in *The Brat* (Herbert Blaché). I should add that for most of these lost films Lambert reckons that Nazimova was the actual director.

She did an Indian temple dance in *Stronger Than Death* (20, Blaché). In *Heart of a Child* (20, Ray C. Smallwood), she was a Cockney girl who marries a lord. She was a Russian princess in *Billions*, another mother and daughter in *Madame Peacock*. It was in her *Camille* (21, Smallwood) that Valentino played Armand. There was a movie of *A Doll's House* (22, Bryant)—yet another lost film. And then she played the teenaged *Salome* in her forties—"a Pantomime after the play by Oscar Wilde," she called it, with costumes by Natacha Rambova. After that came *Madonna of the Streets* (24, Edwin Carewe); *The Redeeming Sin* (25, J. Stuart Blackton); and *My Son* (25, Carewe)—in which Constance Bennett plays her romantic rival.

She retired from movies and did more theatre, everything from *Ghosts* again to *The Cherry Orchard* (she was Ranevskaya and Eva Le Gallienne was Varya) to *Mourning Becomes Electra* and O-Lan in *The Good Earth* (with Claude Rains). David Selznick offered her the role of Madame Defarge in *A Tale of Two Cities,* and she seems to have tested for Mrs. Danvers in *Rebecca.* She also yearned to play Pilar in *For Whom the Bell Tolls.* In fact, her final credits are less striking: *Escape* (40, Mervyn LeRoy); Tyrone

Power's mother in *Blood and Sand* (41, Rouben Mamoulian); Paul Henreid's mother in *In Our Time* (44, Vincent Sherman); the Marquesa in *The Bridge of San Luis Rey* (44, Rowland V. Lee); and as the Eastern European immigrant in Selznick's *Since You Went Away* (44, John Cromwell).

Dame Anna Neagle (Marjorie Robertson) (1904–86), b. London

I have a friend who was once struggling to use a London telephone box when out of the thresh of crossed wires a sweet voice boomed at him: "This is Anna Neagle speaking." He hurried away, head down against the crowd, unnerved by such melody emitting from the technological maelstrom. All this at a time when Miss Neagle was tripping her way through *Charlie Girl* on the London stage in order to pay off some of her husband's debts. It shows serene pluck that she was still prepared to pick up her own phone and announce herself with the cheerfulness of London calling the world at war.

I can recall being taken as a child to see *The Courtneys of Curzon Street* (47, Herbert Wilcox), *Spring in Park Lane* (48, Wilcox), and *Maytime in Mayfair* (49, Wilcox), enchanted by such tales of Samarkand on the other side of the river and thinking how long-suffering it was of my mother to go on living in south London. The Anna Neagle of those days brought out the urchin chimney sweep in me; perhaps we could never have lived so long with ration books and whale meat but for her innocuous impersonation of a lady nourished by romance.

She was a dancer originally and then one of Charles Cochran's young ladies. After small parts in *Should a Doctor Tell?* (30, H. Manning Haynes) and *The Chinese Bungalow* (31, J. B. Williams), Herbert Wilcox costarred her with Jack Buchanan in his film of *Goodnight Vienna* (32). He did not marry her until 1943, but he was in doting charge of her career thereafter and directed nearly all her films: *The Flag Lieutenant* (33, Harry Edwards); *The Little Damozel* (33); *Bitter Sweet* (33); *The Queen's Affair* (34); a great success as a very girlish *Nell Gwynn* (34); followed by *Peg of Old Drury* (35). It comes as something of a shock years later to realize that Miss Neagle is probably essaying Restoration and Hogarthian sex in those films, and that the other characters, chiefly Cedric Hardwicke, respond as if she was succeeding. Her next films were musicals: *Limelight* (36), *The Three Maxims* (36), and *London Melody* (37). At this point, Wilcox took advantage of the new freedom to present Queen Victoria and delivered a decorous one-two to the soft British belly of sentimental patriotism: *Victoria the Great* (37) and *Sixty Glorious Years* (38). (If Hitler saw those films it might explain his eager hustling toward the brink of war. Though in her next film, *Nurse Edith Cavell* [39], Miss Neagle gave warning of the severity of welfare services.)

Miss Neagle and Wilcox did go to Hollywood during the darkest days: *Irene* (40); *No, No Nanette* (40), with Victor Mature; *Sunny* (41); and an episode from *Forever and a Day* (43). She returned to London to play Amy Johnson in *They Flew Alone* (42) and *The Yellow Canary* (43). After the war she began to map out the arbors of chivalry that might exist in a blitzed, black market London: *I Live in Grosvenor Square* (45), *Piccadilly Incident* (46), and so on, by way of Curzon Street, Park Lane, and Mayfair—a purple patch in the Monopoly of love and idleness, with Michael Wilding as the male object. But after *Elizabeth of Ladymead* (49), she took on sterner things in the rather grisly *Odette* (50). Her healing vocation was recalled as Florence Nightingale in *The Lady with the Lamp* (51).

Her time was nearly up, but she carried on blithely in *Derby Day* (52); *Lilacs in the Spring* (54); *King's Rhapsody* (55)—the latter two in the unsuitable company of a declining Errol Flynn—*My Teenage Daughter* (56); *No Time for Tears* (57); *The Man Who Wouldn't Talk* (58); and *The Lady Is a Square* (59). That was her last film, and for it she "discovered" Frankie Vaughan, a cruel test of the affection of her admirers but one that she apparently weathered. *Charlie Girl* played to full houses for some five years, with Dame Anna's admirers being bused in from the Midlands by charabanc.

Patricia Neal, b. Packard, Kentucky, 1926

Educated at Northwestern University, she was a model before working in summer stock and making her Broadway debut in 1946 in *The Voice of the Turtle*. Her film debut was in *John Loves Mary* (49, David Butler) and she was outstanding in King Vidor's *The Fountainhead* (49), entering without hesitation into that unique film's study of elemental creative power and being effectively wooed by Gary Cooper and a pneumatic drill. She was a blonde, yet she had a dark look. Her voice was grownup, drawling, but a little harsh—all beyond her years. She had something new, and Gary Cooper was shaken by it. He and Neal had an intense affair that nearly unhinged his marriage.

But in the next few years she failed to establish herself as a major screen actress, perhaps by choice: *The Hasty Heart* (49, Vincent Sherman); *Bright Leaf* (50, Michael Curtiz); *Three Secrets* (50, Robert Wise); *The Breaking Point* (50, Curtiz); *The Day the Earth Stood Still* (51, Wise); *Weekend with Father* (51, Douglas Sirk); *Operation Pacific* (51, George Waggner); *Canyon Pass* (51, Edwin L. Marin); *Washington Story* (52, Robert Pirosh); *Diplomatic Courier* (52, Henry

Hathaway); *Something for the Birds* (52, Wise); *Immediate Disaster* (54, Burt Balaban), a 16mm production; and *Stranger from Venus* (54, Balaban).

Having married the writer Roald Dahl, she made only a few, carefully selected films: Kazan's *A Face in the Crowd* (57); Blake Edwards's *Breakfast at Tiffany's* (61); as the long-suffering housekeeper in Martin Ritt's *Hud* (63), for which she won the best actress Oscar. But after Alexander Singer's *Psyche 59* (64) and Preminger's *In Harm's Way* (65), she suffered a debilitating stroke. Her recovery from paralysis has been extraordinary and she has since made *The Subject Was Roses* (68, Ulu Grosbard); *Baxter!* (72, Lionel Jeffries); *Happy Mother's Day . . . Love George* (73, Darren McGavin); *B. Must Die* (73, Jose Luis Borau); *The Passage* (78, J. Lee Thompson); *All Quiet on the Western Front* (79, Delbert Mann); and *Ghost Story* (81, John Irvin).

In 1981, her recovery from the stroke was filmed as *The Patricia Neal Story* (Anthony Harvey and Anthony Page)—with Glenda Jackson playing her and Dirk Bogarde as Dahl. Since then, she has acted in *Shattered Vows* (84, Jack Bender); *Love Leads the Way* (84, Mann); *Caroline?* (90, Joseph Sargent); as Shelley Winters's sister in *An Unremarkable Life* (89, Amin Q. Chaudhri).

Since then she has been in *A Mother's Right: The Elizabeth Morgan Story* (92, Linda Otto); *Heidi* (93, Michael Ray Rhodes); *Cookie's Fortune* (99, Robert Altman); *For the Love of May* (00, Mary McDonough and Mary Beth McDonough).

Ronald Neame, b. London, 1911
1947: *Take My Life.* 1950: *The Golden Salamander.* 1952: *The Card.* 1953: *The Million Pound Note.* 1956: *The Man Who Never Was.* 1957: *The Seventh Sin* (partly directed by Vincente Minnelli). 1958: *Windom's Way.* 1959: *The Horse's Mouth.* 1960: *Tunes of Glory.* 1961: *Escape from Zahrain.* 1962: *I Could Go On Singing.* 1963: *The Chalk Garden.* 1964: *Mister Moses.* 1966: *A Man Could Get Killed* (codirected with Cliff Owen); *Gambit.* 1968: *The Prime of Miss Jean Brodie.* 1970: *Scrooge.* 1972: *The Poseidon Adventure.* 1974: *The Odessa File.* 1979: *Meteor.* 1980: *Hopscotch.* 1981: *First Monday in October.* 1987: *Foreign Body.* 1990: *The Magic Balloon.*

The son of photographer Elwin Neame and actress Ivy Close, Neame entered British films as a camera assistant and went on to photograph *Drake of England* (35, Arthur Woods); *The Ware Case* (38, Robert Stevenson); *Pygmalion* (38, Anthony Asquith and Leslie Howard); *Come on, George* (39, Anthony Kimmins); *Major Barbara* (41, Gabriel Pascal); *In Which We Serve* (42, Noel Coward and David Lean); and *Blithe Spirit* (45, David Lean). His association with Lean expanded

when Neame became producer of *Brief Encounter* (45), *Great Expectations* (46), *Oliver Twist* (48), and *The Passionate Friends* (49). He also produced the Festival of Britain film, *The Magic Box* (51, John Boulting).

Neame's work has fluctuated, but it remains above the dismal average of British cinema. *The Seventh Sin* i· an intriguing guessing game, but Neame deserves some credit for its picture of feminine hysteria, if only because two other films show a special taste for romantic feverishness: *I Could Go On Singing* and *The Prime of Miss Jean Brodie*. *The Seventh Sin* looks a good deal better than the two later films, but Neame did manage to draw on the same sort of nervous animation in Eleanor Parker, Judy Garland, and Maggie Smith. Something of that bursting shrillness could be seen in John Mills's performance in *Tunes of Glory* and in *The Chalk Garden's* assembly of tremulous women. In addition, *The Horse's Mouth* is a worthy attempt at Joyce Cary's novel, with Alec Guinness exhilarating as the luminous scoundrel painter, Gulley Jimson. At the very least, Neame has a filmmaker's eye and the ability to produce attractive entertainments. Too often, however, he has been caught up in tame adventure films. *Scrooge* is an ugly and turgid picture, while *Mister Moses, Escape from Zahrain*, and *The Poseidon Adventure* are far beyond his proper territory.

Hopscotch was an effective comedy pairing of Glenda Jackson and Walter Matthau—but in *First Monday in October* Matthau seemed tied down by judicial robes. Neame was also the executive producer on the engaging *Bellman and True* (87, Richard Loncraine).

Liam Neeson,
b. Ballymena, Northern Ireland, 1952
There's something not quite "right" about Liam Neeson—and it's his most intriguing quality. He is an authentically big man—over six feet three—and we can credit that he was once a bit of a boxer and a brewery worker. Yet, at the same time, he has a soft look and a softer voice. When he was chosen to narrate the TNT tribute to Clark Gable, *Tall, Dark and Handsome* (96), it was so evident that Neeson was taller by far, yet problematic and mysterious. Of course that indecision is at the heart of his performance in *Schindler's List* (93, Steven Spielberg), so uncanny a mining of large unsoundness, of producer's flair and actor's unease, that one wonders sometimes how fully Neeson grasped his own work. But who else could have done Schindler so well? Or left intact the question whether Schindler was a saint or an opportunist?

He was doing theatre in Belfast when John Boorman discovered him for the role of Gawain in *Excalibur* (81). He has worked steadily ever since, and he has become an American actor, even if he seldom dominates a picture: *Krull* (83, Peter Yates); *The Bounty* (84, Roger Donaldson); in the Irish film *Lamb* (85, Colin Gregg); *The Innocent* (85, John Mackenzie); *Arthur the King* (85, Clive Donner), for TV; *Duet for One* (86, Andrei Konchalovsky); as the mute accused in *Suspect* (87, Yates); *A Prayer for the Dying* (87, Mike Hodges); *Satisfaction* (88, Joan Freeman); *The Dead Pool* (88, Buddy Van Horn); with Diane Keaton in *The Good Mother* (88, Leonard Nimoy); *High Spirits* (88, Neil Jordan); *Next of Kin* (89, John Irvin); as the vengeful, disfigured scientist in *Darkman* (90, Sam Raimi); *Crossing the Line* (91, David Leland); *Shining Through* (91, David Seltzer); *Under Suspicion* (92, Simon Moore).

He was in *Husbands and Wives* (92, Woody Allen); *Leap of Faith* (92, Richard Pearce); *Deception* (93, Graeme Clifford); and *Ethan Frome* (93, John Madden). He played on Broadway in *Anna Christie* with Natasha Richardson and married her (he had romanced several actresses in the past). They played together without much spark in *Nell* (94, Jodie Foster), and he was then an odd sort of Ballymena Highland hero in *Rob Roy* (95, Michael Caton-Jones). He was the father in *Before and After* (96, Barbet Schroeder).

It is an unresolved career, and one that may lead to serious casting difficulties. Misfits as rich as Oskar Schindler are not common Hollywood material. He did his best as *Michael Collins* (96, Neil Jordan) and as Valjean in yet another *Les Misérables* (98, Bille August), but by 1999 he was plainly bored out of his mind in the empty *Star Wars: Episode I—The Phantom Menace* (99, George Lucas) and unable to prevent the inanity of *The Haunting* (99, Jan de Bont).

He has narrated a number of documentaries—notably *The Endurance* (00, George Butler); and he acted in *Gun Shy* (00, Eric Blakeney); *K-19: The Widowmaker* (02, Kathryn Bigelow); *Gangs of New York* (02, Martin Scorsese); *Love Actually* (03, Richard Curtis).

Pola Negri (Barbara Appolonia Chalupiec) (1894–1987), b. Janowa, Poland
Negri was the first European actress to be wooed by Hollywood: in response, she scorned the shoddiness of American, as compared with German, films, gradually lost the popularity earned by American versions of those films, was the gloomy heavy in a stoked-up rivalry at Paramount with Gloria Swanson, and, cruellest twist of all, was offered to Mauritz Stiller as compensation for the Garbo he had brought to America but whom MGM preferred to keep to themselves.

The dark, soulful concentration of Negri, as well as her deliberate cultivation of an aura of mystery, now make her seem a very dated figure. Rodney Ackland's verdict places her as the archetypal "great actress": "She had a blind and uncritical admiration of her own genius in the blaze of which her sense of humor evaporated like a dewdrop on a million-watt arc lamp." Most memorably, she is the star described in Dos Passos's portrait of Valentino, swooning at the actor's funeral "after she had shown the reporters a message allegedly written by one of the doctors alleging that Rudolph Valentino had spoken of her at the end as his bride to be." The press mocked her for that, just as many people in movies laughed at her extravagant immersion in her own emotions. The irony was that she launched the career of Ernst Lubitsch, but was sadly untouched by his restraint.

She had trained as a dancer in St. Petersburg and, during the First World War, she made a number of films in Poland with Aleksander Hertz. But in 1917, Max Reinhardt brought her to Berlin to play in the stage version of *Sumurun*. She quickly became a star in the German cinema and, after several pictures for Curt Matull, she asked for the young Lubitsch to direct her in *Die Augen der Mumie Ma* (18). She worked for other directors—Georg Jacoby, Paul Ludwig Stein, and Dmitri Buchowetzki (*Sappho*, 20)—but she was outstanding in Lubitsch's costume films to which she brought not only beauty and expressiveness, but unusual depth of character, so that, as Lotte Eisner wrote, she showed up stage actors for their artifice: *Carmen* (18); *Madame Dubarry* (19); *Medea* (20); *Sumurun* (20); *Die Bergkatze* (21); and *Die Flamme* (22).

Madame Dubarry, retitled *Passion*, had been shown with enormous success in America, and in 1922 Paramount invited her to America. Her first films there were far short of her German work: *Bella Donna* (23, George Fitzmaurice); *The Cheat* (23, Fitzmaurice); *The Spanish Dancer* (23, Herbert Brenon); and *Shadows of Paris* (24, Brenon). In an effort to revivify her, she was paired with one of her directors in Germany, Buchowetzki, for *Men* (24) and *Lily of the Dust* (24). But it was only with Lubitsch, in *Forbidden Paradise* (24), that she matched her former glory.

She worked in Hollywood for another four years until sound and her accent forced her to abandon America: *East of Suez* (25, Raoul Walsh); *The Charmer* (25, Sidney Olcott); *Flower of Night* (25, Paul Bern); *A Woman of the World* (25, Malcolm St. Clair); *The Crown of Lies* (26, Buchowetzki); *Good and Naughty* (26, St. Clair); *Hotel Imperial* (26, Stiller); *Barbed Wire* (27, Rowland V. Lee); *The Woman on Trial* (27, Lee); *Three Sinners* (28, Lee); *The Secret House* (28, Lee); as Rachel in *Loves of an Actress* (28, Lee); and *The Woman from Moscow* (28, Ludwig Berger). She went to England to make *The Woman He Scorned* (29, Paul Czinner) and after one more film in America, *A Woman Commands* (32, Paul L.

Stein), and *Fanatisme* (34, Gaston Ravel), in France, she returned to Germany.

She had a great popular success in *Mazurka* (35, Willi Forst) and played in *Moskau-Shanghai* (36, Paul Wegener); as *Madame Bovary* (37, Gerhard Lamprecht); *Tango Notturno* (37, Fritz Kirchhoff); *Die Fromme Luge* (38, Nunzio Malasomma); and *Die Nacht der Entscheidung* (38, Malasomma). In the first years of the war she was in France, but in 1943 she went to America and made *Hi, Diddle Diddle* (43, Andrew L. Stone). She retired and reappeared in only one cameo in *The Moonspinners* (64, James Neilson).

Jean Negulesco (1903–93),
b. Craiova, Rumania

1941: *Singapore Woman*. 1944: *The Mask of Dimitrios; The Conspirators*. 1946: *Nobody Lives Forever; Three Strangers*. 1947: *Humoresque; Deep Valley*. 1948: *Johnny Belinda; Road House*. 1949: *Britannia Mews/The Forbidden Street*. 1950: *The Mudlark; Under My Skin; Three Came Home*. 1951: *Take Care of My Little Girl*. 1952: *Phone Call From a Stranger; Lydia Bailey; Lure of the Wilderness*; "The Last Leaf," episode from *O. Henry's Full House*. 1953: *Scandal at Scourie; Titanic; How to Marry a Millionaire*. 1954: *Three Coins in the Fountain; Woman's World*. 1955: *Daddy Long Legs; The Rains of Ranchipur*. 1957: *Boy on a Dolphin*. 1958: *The Gift of Love; A Certain Smile*. 1959: *Count Your Blessings; The Best of Everything*. 1962: *Jessica*. 1965: *The Pleasure Seekers*. 1969: *The Heroes*. 1970: *Hello-Goodbye; The Invincible Six*.

Anyone coming upon Negulesco in the early 1950s could be forgiven for associating him with trashy, sentimental novelettes. By the end of that decade, even the titles of his movies screeched out a warning of bogus romantic comfort foisted on enervated melodramatic plots: *The Gift of Love, A Certain Smile, Count Your Blessings, The Best of Everything*. That era represents the worst of cinema, when production schedules had not shrunk to the new, smaller audience or begun to aspire to its higher standards. For a few years, major studios still churned out a pale version of their blithe past. Nowhere was the pallor more gruesome than at Twentieth Century–Fox.

Andrew Sarris has argued that the watershed in Negulesco's career was CinemaScope, Fox's ploy to defeat TV. Certainly those late women's pics are the less intimate for being stretched out over a wider frame. But the real turning point for Negulesco seems to me a matter of where he was employed. For in 1948, he moved from Warners to Fox, and thus lost the chance to continue the romantic treatment of "hard" people, and gave himself up to the sentimental view of coziness. Different studios perpetrated different attitudes to the world. Warners learned from the success of *Casablanca*, in 1943, which emphasizes narrative pace and density—an old hallmark of the gangster pictures—low-key black-and-white photography, and the glamour of cynical, worldly people exchanging offhand, knowing dialogue—Bogart hunched up in the dark, urging Sam to play it again. Negulesco bloomed in that Indian summer: *The Mask of Dimitrios*, from the Eric Ambler thriller, is Sydney Greenstreet and Peter Lorre; *The Conspirators* is Hedy Lamarr, Paul Henreid, and Greenstreet; *Nobody Lives Forever* is John Garfield; *Three Strangers* is Lorre, Greenstreet, and Geraldine Fitzgerald; *Humoresque* is a fine Jerry Wald women's picture, with Joan Crawford and Garfield; *Deep Valley* is Ida Lupino. In most of them, there is an entrancing, velvety quality of dream world brought to life. The timing, mood, and nuance are as precise as in *Casablanca*, and Negulesco seems as assured a director as Michael Curtiz.

There is an exception to this, just as his first Fox film was untypical of that studio. *Johnny Belinda* (at Warners) and *Road House* (at Fox) are in curiously opposite corners. The first is Jane Wyman as a deaf and mute girl, raped but loved. Its characters are rural, one-dimensional, and blatant, quite unlike the eccentric, independent sophistication of the Warners films, or of *Road House*, which has Widmark and Lupino again, as a sultry chanteuse stilling a provincial audience with her laconic delivery of moody songs. It speaks of the aplomb of the lady, and the harking back to dark cabarets, that she made Widmark seem young.

But Fox soon dragged Negulesco down, more through the intrinsic sentimentality of the story department than the devitalizing elements of wide screen and De Luxe Color, surely the least happy process for a world of supposedly intense daydream. *How to Marry a Millionaire* is good Monroe, with a nice airplane meeting with David Wayne, and *Three Coins in the Fountain* was very big at the box office. Otherwise, Negulesco illustrates the power of the studios over minor talents.

Marshall Neilan (1891–1958),
b. San Bernardino, California

1916: *The Cycle of Fate; The Prince Chap; The Country that God Forgot*. 1917: *Those Without Sin; The Bottle Imp; The Tides of Barnegat; The Girl at Home; The Silent Partner; Freckles; The Jaguar's Claws; Rebecca of Sunnybrook Farm; The Little Princess*. 1918: *Stella Maris; Amarilly of Clothes-Line Alley; M'liss; Hit-the-Trail Holliday; Heart of the Wilds*. 1919: *Three Men and a Girl; Daddy Long Legs*. 1920: *In Old Kentucky; Her Kingdom of Dreams; Go and Get It* (codirected with Henry Symonds); *Don't Ever Marry* (codirected with Victor Heerman); *Dinty* (codirected with John MacDermott). 1921: *Bits of Life; Bob Hampton of Placer; The Lotus Eater*. 1922: *Fools*

First; Minnie (codirected with Frank Urson); *Penrod; The Stranger's Banquet.* 1923: *The Eternal Three* (codirected with Urson); *The Rendezvous.* 1924: *Dorothy Vernon of Haddon Hall; Tess of the D'Urbervilles.* 1925: *The Great Love; The Sporting Venus.* 1926: *Diplomacy; Everybody's Acting; Mike; The Skyrocket; Wild Oats Lane.* 1927: *Her Wild Oat; Venus of Venice.* 1928: *His Last Haul; Take Me Home; Taxi 13; Three-Ring Marriage.* 1929: *The Awful Truth; Tanned Legs; The Vagabond Lover.* 1930: *Sweethearts on Parade.* 1931: *Black Waters; Catch as Catch Can.* 1934: *Chloe, Love Is Calling You; Social Register; The Lemon Drop Kid.* 1935: *This Is the Life.* 1937: *Sing While You're Able; Swing It, Professor.*

American directors illustrate the sustaining powers of hard work and regular habits. Very few sank from eminence as dramatically as Neilan or with such vague legends of drunken promise. Some say he loathed sound, because of its initial restriction of camera mobility; some that he was outspoken enough to give lasting offense to Louis B. Mayer. But Allan Dwan, who provided Neilan's first chance, believed that his promise sank with the level in the bottle: "Well, he ruined himself with liquor and indifference and bitterness. He became a humorous cynic. But liquor did it."

Dwan also acknowledged Neilan's Irish ancestry—he was usually known as "Mickey"—which may have contributed to his boasting fondness for casual methods on set. Inclined to make things up as he went along—or to extend that widespread approach into the era of producers and accountancy—he was also a famous womanizer, and not always punctual. There is a story of Mary Pickford being forced to direct one of her own films because of his absence and of Neilan arriving during the day, as one of the watching crowd, to see how she was doing. Years later, however, in 1933, Pickford fired Neilan from *Secrets* when he was too drunk to work.

Neilan began his movie career as an actor. He was in *Judith of Bethulia* (13, D. W. Griffith) and a number of Dwan's early pictures before Dwan gave him a chance to direct. Neilan went to the Selig company and by 1920 he was directing for his own production company. He was among the most perceptive of Mary Pickford's directors, showing a sense of comedy as well as the necessary melodramatic flourish on *Rebecca of Sunnybrook Farm, The Little Princess, Stella Maris*—in which Pickford played two parts, rich girl and waif—*Amarilly of Clothes-Line Alley, M'Liss, Daddy Long Legs,* and *Dorothy Vernon of Haddon Hall.* Otherwise, Neilan moved from Goldwyn, to MGM, to First National, and then to the nomadic career of someone famed for being unreliable and frowned upon by Louis B. Mayer. *The Lotus Eater* was John Barrymore and Colleen

Moore; *Tess of the D'Urbervilles* starred Conrad Nagel and Blanche Sweet, Neilan's wife; Peggy Hopkins Joyce made one of her appearances in *The Skyrocket;* Bebe Daniels was in *Take Me Home;* Ina Claire in *The Awful Truth.* Neilan was in decline from 1930 onward, although he had a writer's credit that year on *Hell's Angels* (Howard Hughes). Impoverished during the 1940s, his last appearance was in 1957 in a small role in *A Face in the Crowd* (Elia Kazan).

Sam (Nigel) **Neill**,
b. Omagh, Northern Ireland, 1947

There's a Sam Neill who seems always there in large films, watching Meryl Streep or the dinosaur with the basic common sense that knows all stars are alike. That actor has been a patient, loyal servant to great ladies, even having his bodily fluids (well, one of them) conjured up by Sigourney Weaver in *Snow White* (97, Michael Cohn). Then look again, and see what a wry, watchful actor he is. If you doubt his considerable intelligence, then track down *Cinema of Unease,* the documentary he wrote and directed (with Judy Ryner) on the history of movies (and himself) in New Zealand.

His family emigrated across the ocean when he was a small boy (with mumps). He attended the University of Christchurch and was thinking of being a filmmaker before being encouraged to act. For he had a handsome, English look—worthy of that original "Nigel"—and one should recall his dashing BBC-TV series, *Reilly: Ace of Spies,* as well as the fact that he was considered for James Bond before Pierce Brosnan got the part. But Neill, apparently, knew he was too interesting to be a 007.

His earliest big picture was *Sleeping Dogs* (77, Roger Donaldson), followed by his first work with Judy Davis in *My Brilliant Career* (79, Gillian Armstrong). After *Attack Force Z* (81, Tim Burstall), he appeared with Isabelle Adjani in *Possession* (81, Andrzej Zulawski); in the third "Omen" film, *The Final Conflict* (81; Graham Baker); a Russian in *Enigma* (82, Jeannot Szwarc); a Norman in *Ivanhoe* (82, Douglas Camfield); on French TV in *The Blood of Others* (84, Claude Chabrol); as the Australian outlaw, Captain Starlight, in *Robbery Under Arms* (85, Ken Hannam); as the resistance fighter who makes love to Meryl Streep in *Plenty* (85, Fred Schepisi).

By now, he could be found working in Australasia, Europe, or America: *For Love Alone* (86, Stephen Wallace), from the Christina Stead novel; *The Good Wife* (86, Ken Cameron); as Streep's husband in *A Cry in the Dark* (88, Schepisi); *Dead Calm* (89, Phillip Noyce); a Russian officer in *The Hunt for Red October* (90, John McTiernan); with Judy Davis again in *One Against the Wind* (91, Larry Elikann); *Until the End of the World* (91, Wim Wenders); *Hostage* (92, Robert Young);

Memoirs of an Invisible Man (92, John Carpenter); *Family Pictures* (93, Philip Saville), with Anjelica Huston.

He was the voice of informed reason in *Jurassic Park* (93, Steven Spielberg); happily back in New Zealand for *The Piano* (93, Jane Campion); *Rainbow Warrior* (94, Michael Tuchner); as the artist Norman Lindsay—the figure James Mason played in *Age of Consent*—in *Sirens* (94, John Duigan); *Rudyard Kipling's The Jungle Book* (94, Stephen Sommers); outstanding in *In the Mouth of Madness* (95, Carpenter); doing Chekhov in *Country Life* (95, Michael Blakemore); as Charles II in *Restoration* (95, Michael Hoffman); with Judy Davis once more in *Children of the Revolution* (96, Peter Duncan); *Event Horizon* (97, Paul Anderson); on TV as *Merlin* (98, Steve Barron); the husband at home in *The Horse Whisperer* (98, Robert Redford); *The Revengers' Comedies/Sweet Revenge* (98, Malcolm Mowbray); *Molokai: The Story of Father Damien* (99, Paul Cox); *Bicentennial Man* (99, Chris Columbus).

On TV, he was Jefferson in *Sally Hemings: An American Scandal* (00, Charles Haid); *The Dish* (00, Rob Sitch); on TV in *Submerged* (01, James Keach); *Jurassic Park III* (01, Joe Johnston); *The Zookeeper* (01, Ralph Ziman); *Framed* (01, Daniel Petrie Jr.); *Dirty Deeds* (02, David Caesar); and as Victor in a TV *Doctor Zhivago* (03, Giacomo Campbell).

Ralph Nelson (1916–87), b. New York

1962: *Requiem for a Heavyweight.* 1963: *Lilies of the Field; Soldier in the Rain.* 1964: *Fate Is the Hunter; Father Goose.* 1965: *Once a Thief.* 1966: *Duel at Diablo.* 1967: *Counterpoint.* 1968: *Charly.* 1969: *Tick . . . Tick . . . Tick; Soldier Blue.* 1971: *Flight of the Doves.* 1972: *The Wrath of God.* 1974: *The Wilby Conspiracy.* 1976: *Embryo.* 1978: *A Hero Ain't Nothin' But a Sandwich.*

Although well into middle age before he directed a movie, Nelson must presumably be dealt with as typical of the new type of commercial director, desperate for novelty and managing to string a few successful films together. He was prepared to compromise with sentimentality or savagery and, seemingly, there are those not disturbed by the lack of moral or intelligent focus in his films. Thus, although his pictures are all overemphatic—whether in the oozing self-pity of Anthony Quinn in *Requiem for a Heavyweight;* the prettiness of Sidney Poitier won over by a chorus of German nuns; the slick irony with which idiot becomes genius in *Charly;* or the gratuitous violence in *Soldier Blue*—the human content seems always reduced or bowdlerized. That such a director should thrive, let alone work, is one of those ghastly cracks in the ground that the world has to school itself to step over. His only passable movie, *Soldier in the Rain,* owes its

merit to the script by Blake Edwards and to Tuesday Weld.

Nelson had a career of thirty years as a stage actor, a dramatist and theatrical producer, and a TV director—all with some success. His first film came after he had won an Emmy for the TV production of Rod Serling's play, *Requiem for a Heavyweight.* Twice—for Sidney Poitier, and for Cliff Robertson in *Charly*—Nelson's special vulgarization led to Oscars. And in *Duel at Diablo* and *Soldier Blue* he has an unenviable place in the continuing history of gruesome, picturesque bloodletting, at the cost of emotional or dramatic significance. *The Wrath of God* is an odious use of Robert Mitchum as a gun-toting bogus priest, as disrespectful to the memory of *Night of the Hunter* as to Nelson's cozy gathering of nuns in *Lilies of the Field.*

Mike Newell, b. St. Albans, England, 1942

1976: *The Man in the Iron Mask.* 1980: *The Awakening.* 1981: *Bad Blood.* 1984: *Dance with a Stranger.* 1986: *The Good Father.* 1987: *Amazing Grace and Chuck.* 1988: *Soursweet.* 1991: *Enchanted April.* 1992: *Into the West.* 1993: *Four Weddings and a Funeral.* 1995: *An Awfully Big Adventure.* 1997: *Donnie Brasco.* 1999: *Pushing Tin.* 2002: *How to Lose a Guy in 10 Days.*

Mike Newell is solidly professional, and represents that generation that learned its craft in British television doing just about anything, and sees no reason why it shouldn't be able to grasp both England in the 1950s and Mafia lowlife in the 1990s. "One reason I don't claim to perceive any particular shape in the overall work," he says, "is that I think people go wrong through self-importance and pomposity." You don't have to add much to that modesty to see why *Four Weddings and a Funeral* had true charm, yearning romance, and a canny head-fake on the real world—while *Notting Hill* doesn't. In other words, to learn craft can be another way of thinking about life and plausibility—as well as what plays.

Newell worked very hard for Granada and the BBC for some fifteen years before he did features: along the way, he worked on *Coronation Street* and *Budgie,* a lot of serials, and a ton of plays. In this respect, he is both a contemporary of and a rival to Michael Apted, with whom he shared duties on *Big Breadwinner Hogg.*

Four Weddings and a Funeral is his big hit—though *Enchanted April* did very well, too, and helped fashion the modern Italian travel movie. But his best work was on *Dance with a Stranger,* which is very good on class, casual cruelty, and the suppressed emotional energies of Britain (and has a superb performance from Miranda Richardson), and *Donnie Brasco,* which gets the mob talk and idleness to perfection, and made better use of Al Pacino than anyone had managed in years.

There are also failures—*Amazing Grace and Chuck*—and fascinating adventures—*Into the West*. But Newell has a clear respect for material and scripts (his screenwriters range from Clive Exton and Shelagh Delaney to Ian McEwan, Charles Wood, Richard Curtis, and Paul Attanasio). If there was anything like a reasonable movie industry, pledged to reliable entertainments without excuses or pretense, Newell would be a much better known name. As it is, he has all the right qualifications (and the experience) now to make a great picture if the script and the players come along. Whether he has the ability, or even the nature, to seek and find those things is another matter.

Paul Newman, b. Cleveland, Ohio, 1925

Since so many people all over the world have found Newman so appealing, it matters very little that I am skeptical of such blue-eyed likability. He seems to me an uneasy, self-regarding personality, as if handsomeness had left him guilty. As a result, he was more mannered than Brando when young, while his smirking good humor always seemed more appropriate to glossy advertisements than to good movies. The crucial film in his career was *The Hustler* (61, Robert Rossen), in which George C. Scott surveys and dismisses him as a born loser, a flashy athlete without stamina or character. Repeated viewings of *The Hustler* only show up the "sensitive" muscularity of Newman's part. Scott's intended heavy grows in interest and appeal, and I find myself rejecting Rossen's sentimental drama, barricaded as it is by billiard balls, and itching for Scott's insight to be vindicated. Hawks, surely, would have stood *The Hustler* on end and rubbed Newman's nose in the chalk.

That said, Newman was very good impersonating Rocky Graziano in *Somebody Up There Likes Me* (56, Robert Wise), a fair comedian in McCarey's *Rally Round the Flag, Boys!* (58), perfectly if unknowingly used in *The Hustler,* and best of all, reduced to animal high spirits by Arthur Penn in *The Left-Handed Gun* (58), even if his Billy the Kid was very much the intellectual's noble savage, a character that had badly betrayed Newman's earnestness in other parts. His millions of fans would point to his string of prestigious box-office successes—for Richard Brooks playing Tennessee Williams's heroes in *Cat on a Hot Tin Roof* (58) and *Sweet Bird of Youth* (62); as *Hud* (63) for Martin Ritt; as the hero in Preminger's *Exodus* (60); as *Harper* (66, Jack Smight) and suspended forever on the brink of middle age in *Butch Cassidy and the Sundance Kid* (69, George Roy Hill). I would answer that he, and those films, cheat the real picture of insecurity and opportunism that Tennessee Williams offers; that his Hud is genuinely heartless; that his contempt for *Exodus* shows his poor understanding of the cinema, that

in *Harper* he is like a teenager aping Bogart, and that *Butch Cassidy* is a castrated Western.

To revert to beginnings, Newman studied at the Yale School of Drama and at the Actors' Studio, appearing on Broadway in *Picnic*—in which he met his second wife, Joanne Woodward—*The Desperate Hours,* and subsequently, *Sweet Bird of Youth.* He made his debut in Victor Saville's nonsensical *The Silver Chalice* (55) and in *The Rack* (56, Arnold Laven) before taking the part intended for James Dean in *Somebody Up There Likes Me* and building up his smoother, romantic appeal in *Until They Sail* (57, Wise), *The Helen Morgan Story* (57, Michael Curtiz), *The Young Philadelphians* (59, Vincent Sherman), and *From the Terrace* (60, Mark Robson).

A major star by the early 1960s, Newman worked hard to be something more than the vehicle for other people's fantasies. In 1968, he directed his wife in *Rachel, Rachel,* a very creditable movie albeit made solemnly and ostentatiously to provide her with a decent part. After that, Newman also codirected *Sometimes a Great Notion* (71) with Richard Colla, and directed his wife again in *The Effect of Gamma Rays on Man-in-the-Moon Marigolds* (72). As a director, he is full of good intentions, thematic gravity, and the wish to foster sensitive acting. But not much more; not enough, certainly, to prevent the feeling of a diligent, intelligent, reformed hustler trying to work for the good of the community.

That may seem an unkind characterization. But there were early and unmistakable signs of a young middle-aged man wondering what could replace prettiness. Just as his habitation of rugged "wild ones" was never totally convincing—*The Long Hot Summer* (58, Ritt); as the punch-drunk boxer in Hemingway's *Adventures of a Young Man* (62, Ritt); *Hud; The Outrage* (64, Ritt); *Hombre* (67, Ritt); *Cool Hand Luke* (67, Stuart Rosenberg); *Pocket Money* (72, Rosenberg); *The Life and Times of Judge Roy Bean* (72, John Huston)—so, too, his "straight" parts seem neutered and derivative: *Torn Curtain* (66, Alfred Hitchcock); *Winning* (69, James Goldstone); *WUSA* (70, Rosenberg); *The Mackintosh Man* (73, Huston); a pickled schoolboy pretending to be a confidence man in *The Sting* (73, Hill); and *The Towering Inferno* (74, John Guillermin). Could it be that Newman was always uncomfortable with his natural assets—such handsomeness—and never convinced by them? That would account for the uneasy mixture of porous cockiness and mumbling naturalism, just as it fits with his urge to prove himself as a serious citizen.

He was with his wife once more in *The Drowning Pool* (75, Rosenberg); he was fascinating amid the failure of *Buffalo Bill and the Indians* (76, Robert Altman), more surely identified than ever before in the long-haired fraud, and finding pathos in the living legend's fuddle—the performance needed more support from the film and its director. The urge to disabuse doting and middle-aged fans was evident again in *Slap Shot* (77, Hill), where he played a raucous, battered, and unscrupulous hockey coach—a good ol' boy making use of Newman's delayed adolescence. He was still slick and sly, but sleaziness fit that face so much more interestingly than nobility. *Slap Shot's* shallow tour de force may have been a first reminder to the Academy that Newman had not yet collected his Oscar.

But *Quintet* (79, Altman) gave one the feeling that age was shaving away all the early charm and making any award less likely.

Newman did get his Oscar, at last, as the character from *The Hustler* twenty-five years older in *The Color of Money* (86, Martin Scorsese). It was not Newman's fault, but *The Hustler* is so superior a film that the Academy's mercy seemed like a model for the decline of movies. Newman had been more deserving as the alcoholic lawyer in *The Verdict* (82, Sidney Lumet), a film in which the action and Boston's winter light got through his mask and into a raw soul—but Newman lost that year to Ben Kingsley as *Gandhi. The Verdict* is a tormenting picture for it shows what Newman is capable of once his aversion to intimacy can be broken down. He could be an actor for great parts now—for the cockiness is gone—but somehow he seems bitter and granitic about his own art.

He has also appeared in *When Time Ran Out* (80, James Goldstone); *Fort Apache, The Bronx* (81, Daniel Petrie); *Absence of Malice* (81, Sydney Pollack); as General Groves in *Fat Man and Little Boy* (89, Roland Joffe); and grimly inhibited in *Blaze* (89, Ron Shelton)—he is not the actor for sexual delight, let alone abandon. He was well cast as the enclosed husband in *Mr. and Mrs. Bridge* (90, James Ivory); and as the tycoon in *The Hudsucker Proxy* (94, Joel Coen).

At the same time, he has continued to direct: the very moving *The Shadow Box* (80), for TV, which starred his wife; *Harry and Son* (84), in which he acted with Robby Benson and Joanne Woodward; and a worthy but overcontrolled *The Glass Menagerie* (87), starring Woodward, John Malkovich, Karen Allen, and James Naughton.

Since then, he has done four portraits in gruff old age—more relaxed, grumpier, and truly likeable: the excellent *Nobody's Fool* (94, Robert Benton), showing sweet awe for Melanie Griffith's breasts, and for which he picked up an eighth Oscar nomination; *Twilight* (98, Benton); *Message in a Bottle* (99, Luis Mandoki); *Where the Money Is* (00, Manek Kanievska); *Road to Perdition* (02, Sam Mendes).

Robert Newton (1905–56),
b. Shaftesbury, England

The British comedian Tony Hancock used to do an excellent impersonation of Robert Newton's Long John Silver, but Newton had done it before him, a character actor leaving a lasting memory of a man used to the company of a parrot. The eye-rolling exaggeration of villainy would have delighted Stevenson as much as it did children, but Newton had once been a frightening villain, possessed of a grinding, slow voice. With time (and alcohol), the voice slurred and the characters he played became inflated. Some sense of an abandoned, malicious intensity comes from Hitchcock's admission that he would have preferred Newton to Louis Jourdan in *The Paradine Case,* a Newton "With horny hands, like the devil!"

He was a stage actor who, after a debut in *Reunion* (32, Ivar Campbell), settled for movies in 1937, largely at the instigation of the American director, William K. Howard: *Fire Over England* (37, Howard); *Farewell Again* (37, Tim Whelan); *The Squeaker* (37, Howard); *21 Days* (37, Basil Dean); *Dark Journey* (37, Victor Saville); as a centurion in the unfinished *Claudius* (37, Josef von Sternberg); *Vessel of Wrath* (38, Erich Pommer); *Yellow Sands* (38, Herbert Brenon); *Jamaica Inn* (39, Hitchcock); *Dead Men Are Dangerous* (39, Harold French); *Poison Pen* (39, Paul L. Stein); *Hell's Cargo* (39, Harold Huth); *Bulldog Sees It Through* (40, Huth); *Busman's Honeymoon* (40, Arthur Woods); *The Green Cockatoo* (40, William Cameron Menzies); in the short, *Channel Incident* (40, Anthony Asquith); *Gaslight* (40, Thorold Dickinson); *Major Barbara* (41, Gabriel Pascal); *Hatter's Castle* (42, Lance Comfort); *They Flew Alone* (42, Herbert Wilcox); *This Happy Breed* (44, David Lean); as Pistol in *Henry V* (45, Laurence Olivier); *Night Boat to Dublin* (46, Lawrence Huntington); the painter in *Odd Man Out* (47, Carol Reed); *Temptation Harbour* (47, Comfort); *Snowbound* (48, David MacDonald); a brutal Bill Sikes in *Oliver Twist* (48, Lean); hounding Burt Lancaster in *Kiss the Blood Off My Hands* (48, Norman Foster); *Obsession* (50, Edward Dmytryk); *Treasure Island* (50, Byron Haskin); *Waterfront* (50, Michael Anderson); *Soldiers Three* (51, Tay Garnett); as Dr. Arnold in *Tom Brown's Schooldays* (51, Gordon Parry); as Javert in *Les Miserables* (52, Lewis Milestone); *Blackbeard the Pirate* (52, Raoul Walsh); *Androcles and the Lion* (53, Chester Erskine); *The Desert Rats* (53, Robert Wise); *The Beachcomber* (54, Muriel Box); *The High and the Mighty* (54, William Wellman); *Long John Silver* (55, Haskin); and *Around the World in 80 Days* (56, Anderson).

Fred Niblo (Frederico Nobile) (1874–1948),
b. York, Nebraska
1918: *The Marriage Ring; Fuss and Feathers; Happy Though Married; When Do We Eat?.*
1919: *The Haunted Bedroom; The Law of Men;*

Partners Three; The Virtuous Thief; Dangerous Hours; What Every Woman Learns; Stepping Out. 1920: *Sex; The Woman in the Suitcase; The False Road; Hairpins; Her Husband's Friend; Silk Hosiery; The Mark of Zorro.* 1921: *The Three Musketeers; Mother o' Mine; Greater than Love.* 1922: *The Woman He Married; Rose o' the Sea; Blood and Sand.* 1923: *The Famous Mrs. Fair; Strangers of the Night.* 1924: *Thy Name Is Woman; The Red Lily.* 1926: *The Temptress* (codirected with Mauritz Stiller). 1927: *Ben-Hur; Camille; The Devil Dancer* (codirected with Alfred Raboch and Lynn Shores). 1928: *The Enemy; Two Lovers; The Mysterious Lady; Dream of Love.* 1930: *Redemption; Way Out West.* 1931: *Young Donovan's Kid; The Big Gamble.* 1932: *Diamond, Cut Diamond* (codirected with Maurice Elvey); *Two White Arms.* 1941: *Three Sons o' Guns.*

Until 1917, Niblo had had a varied career as an actor, first in vaudeville, then touring, and finally on Broadway. But in that year he married the actress Enid Bennett, who worked for Thomas Ince. Within a year Niblo himself was directing for Ince. He continued to act, on and off, and appeared in two films in 1922 with his wife, both directed by Victor Schertzinger—*The Bootlegger's Daughter* and *Scandalous Tongues*—and as late as 1932, played in *Two White Arms.* Niblo's first films, made for Ince, were not distinguished, but he was hired by Douglas Fairbanks to direct *The Mark of Zorro* and *The Three Musketeers.* He directed Valentino in *Blood and Sand* for Famous Players and then went to work for Louis B. Mayer on romantic melodramas: *Thy Name Is Woman,* starring Ramon Novarro and Barbara La Marr.

Mayer carried Niblo with him on the merger that made MGM, and Niblo directed his wife and Novarro in *The Red Lily.* By then, *Ben-Hur* seemed likely to prove the first and last great disaster of the new company. When the idea to replace George Walsh with Novarro was accepted, it was a short step to drop the original director, Charles Brabin, and hope that Niblo might recollect Nobile. So it was that Niblo was the director of Hollywood's greatest epic. But he was the choice of Thalberg and Mayer and, as with Joseph Mankiewicz years later on *Cleopatra,* Niblo's task was contradictory: to spend money to save money. *Ben-Hur* is a film of many talents and trades, spectacular but inflated, needing the dynamic eye of a King Vidor.

While *Ben-Hur* was being edited, Niblo took over from Stiller on the Garbo project, *The Temptress,* and then directed Norma Talmadge as *Camille.* He remained a leading director for only a short time, despite the initial praise for *Ben-Hur.* Sound appears to have probed the cavities in his style.

Thus, he made some key silent films after sound had become a possibility. He directed Lillian Gish in *The Enemy,* Ronald Colman and Vilma Banky in *Two Lovers,* and Garbo again in *The Mysterious Lady.* But by 1930 he left MGM, made a few films at RKO, and went to Britain for two pictures before retiring. A few years before his death he took up acting again.

Dudley Nichols (1895–1960),
b. Wapakoneta, Ohio
1943: *Government Girl.* 1946: *Sister Kenny.* 1947: *Mourning Becomes Electra.*

The three films directed by Dudley Nichols are garishly ill-assorted, unlikely, and pretentious—a sign, perhaps, of the strain of writing dutiful scenarios for most of his Hollywood career. *Government Girl,* which he wrote, produced, and directed at RKO, was Olivia de Havilland and Sonny Tufts; *Sister Kenny,* written with Mary McCarthy, was an admiring biopic with Rosalind Russell as an Australian nurse; while *Mourning Becomes Electra* is a hams' free-for-all, with Russell, Michael Redgrave, Katina Paxinou, and Kirk Douglas rolling their eyes at one another. Clearly, someone suggested that Nichols abandon directing and return to his regular output of safe scripts for major films.

Nichols is what passed in Hollywood for a durable, talented writer. Yet he was a sausage machine for Ford's sentimentality, cardboard characters, and predictable situations. His screenplay for *For Whom the Bell Tolls* (43, Sam Wood), for instance, is defeated by the sententious grandeur of the novel and Hollywood's appetite for Spanish cliché; whereas, in the same year, *Air Force* (43, Howard Hawks) proved snappy, with colloquial talk and a suggestion of how often scripts were refashioned in the shooting.

Nichols was a top journalist who moved into films with the coming of sound: *Born Reckless* (30, John Ford and Andrew Bennison); *A Devil with Women* (30, Irving Cummings); *Men Without Women* (30, Ford); *On the Level* (30, Cummings); *Seas Beneath* (31, Ford); *The Lost Patrol* (34, Ford); *Judge Priest* (34, Ford); *Steamboat Round the Bend* (35, Ford); an Oscar for the script of *The Informer* (35, Ford); *The Crusades* (35, Cecil B. De Mille); *Mary of Scotland* (36, Ford); *The Plough and the Stars* (37, Ford); *The Hurricane* (38, Ford); an exceptional comedy, *Bringing Up Baby* (38, Hawks), which hardly seems to belong to the scribe of the Ford saga; *Stagecoach* (39, Ford); *The Long Voyage Home* (40, Ford); *Swamp Water* (41, Jean Renoir); *Man Hunt* (41, Fritz Lang), turned down by Ford, made into a gem by Lang, thus showing the vulnerability of writers to a director's authorship. According to Lang, Nichols himself admitted: "A script is only a blueprint—the director is the one who makes the picture." It follows that Ford might have ruined *Air Force* and Hawks transformed *For Whom the Bell Tolls*, just as there can be no doubt how much extra backchat Hawks would have added to *Stagecoach*. Nichols worked on *This Land Is Mine* (43, Renoir), which he coproduced; *It Happened Tomorrow* (44, René Clair); *And Then There Were None* (45, Clair); *Scarlet Street* (45, Lang), which treats people with a depth and sharpness missing in the Ford films; *The Bells of St. Mary's* (45, Leo McCarey); *The Fugitive* (47, Ford); *Pinky* (49, Elia Kazan); *Rawhide* (51, Henry Hathaway); *Return of the Texan* (52, Delmer Daves); *The Big Sky* (52, Hawks); *Prince Valiant* (54, Hathaway); *Run for the Sun* (56, Roy Boulting); *The Tin Star* (57, Anthony Mann); *The Hanging Tree* (59, Daves); and *Heller in Pink Tights* (60, George Cukor).

Mike Nichols (Michael Igor Peschkowsky), b. Berlin, 1931
1966: *Who's Afraid of Virginia Woolf?*. 1967: *The Graduate*. 1970: *Catch-22*. 1971: *Carnal Knowledge*. 1973: *The Day of the Dolphin*. 1975: *The Fortune*. 1980: *Gilda Live* (d). 1983: *Silkwood*. 1986: *Heartburn*. 1988: *Biloxi Blues; Working Girl*. 1990: *Postcards from the Edge*. 1991: *Regarding Henry*. 1994: *Wolf*. 1996: *The Birdcage*. 1998: *Primary Colors*. 2000: *What Planet Are You From?*. 2001: *Wit* (TV). 2003: *Angels in America* (TV).

Mike Nichols is an unquestioned figure in our culture, a smart man, a funny man, a proven success in cabaret, on records, as a stage director, and as a deliverer of talking-point movies—movies that are smart, funny, "adult," "on the pulse," and "of their moment." Yet I find it hard to grasp a him in there, a movie director: after a dozen or so films, is there anything there more substantial than a high reputation and a producer's instinct for what smart people might want to see? Is there soul, intelligence, theme, or character holding these films together in series? Or, if Nichols is essentially a producer, a packager of things, then we have to note how well he fits the law of averages for producers. He is hit and miss. *Virginia Woolf, The Graduate*, and *Working Girl* were all nominated for best picture, and Nichols won the directing Oscar for *The Graduate*. *The Fortune, Heartburn*, and *Regarding Henry*, on the other hand, are movies that send audiences out into the night with the lament, "Why did they ever think of making that?"

Actually, you can see why. Warren Beatty and Jack Nicholson competing to have or kill an heiress is a neat idea. Everyone smart thought that movie would make a bundle. *Heartburn* was a story about real infidelities in the smart set: there must have been ten thousand bold-type names from the columns who were wild to see that one. And *Regarding Henry* is the sort of 1950s plot idea—smart husband goes back to zero because of brain damage—that usually guarantees Oscars (so long as you don't cast Harrison Ford). Those are magazine stories; any one of them could have made a good segment on *60 Minutes* as handled by Mike Nichols's lovely and smart wife, Diane Sawyer.

Nichols makes movies from really neat, cute, smart ideas that can be grasped in twenty minutes. Sometimes they do go off the deep end—*Carnal Knowledge* and *Silkwood*, for instance, don't leave too much room for the comfortable feeling that just thinking smart will sort things out. In that respect, *Working Girl* was a knockout, smart picture: terrific entertainment, topical issue, Melanie Griffith in her underwear, and very positive, smart ending: working women rule, okay? With a Carly Simon song.

The Graduate was the cutest package (oddly, it is a film that derides the plastics-packaging urge in America), in which a numb rebel (very intriguing concept) becomes a happy conformist, with terrific sideshows along the way, like Mrs. Robinson as a zipless fuck and great songs. Nichols never neglects the songs. Yes, Mike Nichols gives me a pain. With *Postcards from the Edge*, say, I can only see the taming of a tough, wry book and the remorseless, smart casting that went for MacLaine and Streep instead of Debbie Reynolds and Carrie Fisher. Maybe it was smarter to have smart people just know who the characters were. And maybe someone thought MacLaine and Streep were better box office—which only shows the tangle being smart can get into.

The child Nichols came to America as a refugee at the age of seven. When the father died, the family had difficult times, but Nichols worked his way through the University of Chicago, and studied to be an actor. Then he formed a comedy group with Alan Arkin, Barbara Harris, Paul Sills, and Elaine May, which led to the Nichols and May double act in the late fifties and early sixties—on stage, in clubs, on records. They were a brilliant team, and their dialogues had as big an effect on screenplays and how smart people talked and thought as Jules Feiffer cartoons.

It says something about the team that Nichols has been so much more successful and organized than Elaine May. More recently, it says a great deal about his producer's acumen that he allowed *The Remains of the Day* to be a Merchant-Ivory film (though Nichols retains a credit from his early ownership of the book's screen rights). Did he know in advance that he couldn't deliver the closed heart in that intriguing project?

He had a fairly obvious commercial success with *The Birdcage*, and made a good sharp comedy from *Primary Colors*. But, to my mind, *Wit*, done for HBO, with the maximum severity, made so many of his recent movies look fussy and decorative. *Wit* trusted the aching iron of its subject and the steel of its players. I think it is the best work he has ever done.

Jack Nicholson,
b. Neptune, New Jersey, 1937

In 1975 and 1980, I wrote:

There was once a reference book that claimed Nicholson as the son of James H. Nicholson, chief executive of American International Pictures. Further research discloses that he was the son of a small-town alcoholic of Irish descent. It is a proof of Nicholson's suggestive flexibility that both seem plausible; indeed, they both might be admissions—half drawling, half whining—from a sleepy, deadpan tease. The source of Nicholson's charm lies in his sweet evasiveness. There goes with it a subtle mastery of his own appearance, so that he is never quite the same in looks, from one film to the next, if always the same droll, bleakly cheerful, enigmatic Nicholson. Remember the truculent wavy hair of *Five Easy Pieces*, the middle-aged thinning of *The King of Marvin Gardens,* the navy crewcut of *The Last Detail*, and the central parting of *Chinatown* where he looks like a sleek, more prosperous Elisha Cook, his eyes slitted by some narcotic fatalism.

It is an attractive, humorous but skeptical face, pleased to make people laugh, but ready for those cold mornings when he will ditch his pregnant girl at a filling station and hitch, helplessly, to Alaska. In *Five Easy Pieces* (70, Bob Rafelson), an engrossing film made around Nicholson's living in two worlds, there are marvelous moments that express his contradictoriness: caught in a Texas traffic jam, he gets out of his car, jumps on a truck, and plays the piano tethered there—the vehicle glides off the freeway with Nicholson lost in his crazy concerto. But when the oil-rigger goes north to his family, embedded in music, he churlishly rebukes praise for his playing of Chopin and warns off the most promising relationship of his life. The persistent call of the road is a characteristic of immaturity—for Nicholson's character, Robert Eroica (or Bobby) Dupea, will desert those who need him—but it is also an expression of an implacable American dissatisfaction with present things and a yearning for something more convincing: Huckleberry Finn has it, so do Jay Gatsby (surely the part that needed Nicholson), Dos Passos's Vag and Mailer's heroes. In cinematic terms, Nicholson is the most intriguing contemporary development of the Bogart of *High Sierra* and *Casablanca,* but a man who does not conceal middle age, increasing baldness, or the hurtful intractability of his failings.

His career is itself a demonstration of noncon-

formity, unwilling to settle into pattern, quixotic and disenchanted at the same time, but always returning to the classical mystery of sensibility and instinct—the solitary trying to be one of the group, the detective with a broken puzzle in his hands. He also looks like the ebony around which oddball talents have clustered, a gentle entrepreneur who has already worked as actor, writer, and director.

At first he played in low-budget quickies and ambitious B pictures: *Cry-Baby Killer* (57, Jus Addis); *Too Soon to Love* (60, Richard Rush); *The Little Shop of Horrors* (60, Roger Corman); *Studs Lonigan* (60, Irving Lerner); *The Raven* (62, Corman); *The Terror* (62, Corman); and *The Broken Land* (62, John Bushelman). In 1963 he wrote the script for *Thunder Island* (63, Jack Leewood); and then in 1964 he acted in Monte Hellman's *Back Door to Hell* and *Flight to Fury*. The two men had previously written a script that they were unable to place. Their association led to the momentous expedition to the Utah desert in 1965 to make, simultaneously, *The Shooting* (Hellman) and *Ride the Whirlwind* (Hellman). Nicholson was closest to Hellman in that uneasy but productive foray. He scripted and acted in *Ride the Whirlwind* and played the gunman, Billy Spear, in *The Shooting*. After that, he wrote the scripts for *The Trip* (67, Corman) and *Head* (68, Rafelson).

But as an actor he became increasingly popular, so that he was drawn into the edges of stardom: *Hell's Angels on Wheels* (67, Rush); *Psych-Out* (68, Rush); then as the lawyer who takes to the road in *Easy Rider* (69, Dennis Hopper); *Five Easy Pieces;* largely cut from *On a Clear Day You Can See Forever* (70, Vincente Minnelli); *Carnal Knowledge* (71, Mike Nichols); *A Safe Place* (71, Henry Jaglom); as the reserved, staid brother who only expands into fantasy on his late-night radio show in *The King of Marvin Gardens* (72, Rafelson); *The Last Detail* (74, Hal Ashby); *Chinatown* (74, Roman Polanski); and *The Passenger* (75, Michelangelo Antonioni).

He has also directed his first film—*Drive, He Said* (70)—a flawed, but personal study of escapees from the rigid environment of an athlete-oriented college. It is part of Nicholson's wry charm that he could as easily have admired the only boxer at Yale.

The canonization of Nicholson's *homme moyen sensuel* occurred with *One Flew Over the Cuckoo's Nest* (75, Milos Forman), one of those rare but happy occasions of serious, agonized meaning, superb entertainment, and money and glory for all involved. Without Nicholson the film might not have been made. His glamour did ease a difficult subject, and his willingness to act in an ensemble accounts for the startling "institutional" atmosphere. But it lies in Nicholson's dangerous libertarianism that the film goes from comedy to tragedy, and it is to his credit that millions felt the dignity of MacMurphy's slapdash, subversive vitality. With an indisputable Oscar to his name, he was a proper rival for, but a little awed by, Brando in *The Missouri Breaks* (76, Arthur Penn); then he filled out the sketch of Brimmer in *The Last Tycoon* (76, Elia Kazan).

His near two-year absence from the screen was explained by the problems of mounting a movie that he wanted to direct himself, a picaresque Western titled *Goin' South* (78).

The story goes on: around the time the last edition of this book appeared, it was revealed that the woman Nicholson had grown up thinking of as his sister was actually his mother. To this day, the full truth remains unclear. But Nicholson is the Hollywood celebrity who is most like a character in some ongoing novel of our times. He is also the most beloved of stars—not even his huge wealth, his reckless aging, and the public disasters of his private life can detract from this. Nicholson actually appeared on the cover of *Vanity Fair* holding two babies—purportedly his. Yet inside, the small print admitted these babies were models! Actors! And he lost not a prosciutto slice of public affection. When it was time for the presentation of best picture at the 1993 Oscars, Billy Crystal had only to say, "Jack," and everyone knew who was coming. It must be a huge strain being "Jack," and there are signs of dismay, indirection, and doubt, as well as age. His acting fluctuates, as if he was bored sometimes, or simply wanted to see what he could get away with. The huge impact of *Batman* makes it easier to see the ways in which Nicholson is becoming more like a cartoon.

The Shining (80, Stanley Kubrick) was one of his great films—the wicked naughty boy, the thwarted genius, the monster of his own loneliness. No one else could have been so daring and yet so delicate. In *The Postman Always Rings Twice* (81, Rafelson), he was less tested, but he had a look of the 1930s and a chronic deadbeat while never losing touch with the common beast whose eyes might widen at thoughts of money, murder, and great sex.

He was nominated for the supporting actor Oscar for his remote but romantic Eugene O'Neill in *Reds* (81, Warren Beatty). He slouched and muttered his way back and forth across *The Border* (82, Tony Richardson). Effortlessly he won the supporting actor Oscar in *Terms of Endearment* (83, James L. Brooks). He was suitably heavy, dogged, and humorless as the respectable killer in *Prizzi's Honor* (85, John Huston), yet there's reason to think he didn't quite get the tone or drift of that odd, slow comedy. *Heartburn* (86, Nichols) was a misfire.

In *The Witches of Eastwick* (87, George Miller), he was self-indulgent as his own horny little devil, but very funny and richly entertaining. In hindsight, it seems like a significant excursion into fantasy. He appeared briefly in *Broadcast News* (87, Brooks) and could not help looking overfed as the street bum in *Ironweed* (87, Hector Babenco). He acted very well in the film, but he was miscast.

As for *Batman* (89, Tim Burton), one can only say that his flashy Joker pulled down at least $50 million in pay, profits, and merchandising deals. Jack Torrance would have howled at the moon.

In 1985, he had been about to reprise Jake Gittes for writer-director Robert Towne in *The Two Jakes*, the long-awaited *Chinatown* sequel. The venture collapsed. Then in 1990, it was really made, with Nicholson directing. The picture was a disaster; the old friendship with Towne seemed over. Decades of hope were disappointed.

Man Trouble (91) reunited Nicholson with Rafelson and screenwriter Carole Eastman (who had done *Five Easy Pieces*). But it was a witless, draggy film that seemed to show how time had passed on, leaving some people stranded. This was a low point, coupled with Nicholson's regular and hardly flattering appearances in gossip columns.

But he bounced back. His marine colonel in *A Few Good Men* (92, Rob Reiner) was hardly plausible—indeed, he was rigged to explode for the purposes of melodrama—but Nicholson blazed and roared, and looked in great shape. He even got a supporting actor nomination. Far better was the terribly neglected *Hoffa* (92, Danny DeVito), one of his best things—snarly, dumb, smart, noble, rascally—all the parts of "Jack."

In 1994, he appeared in *Wolf* (Nichols) and acted beautifully until asked to grow hair and fangs.

As time went on, Nicholson worked for old friends, or people he trusted. The results were mixed, and Nicholson has expressed his dismay at the state of modern film. Also, his own innate fun has rather clouded over. He seems sadder with life, and that hurts us all, I think. For he is still a touchstone, someone we value for the way he helps us see ourselves: *The Crossing Guard* (95, Sean Penn); *Blood and Wine* (97, Rafelson); *Mars Attacks!* (96, Burton); briefly in *The Evening Star* (96, Robert Harling); winning another Oscar, his third, in *As Good As It Gets* (97, Brooks); *The Pledge* (00, Penn); *About Schmidt* (02, Alexander Payne); with Adam Sandler in *Anger Management* (03, Peter Segal).

Asta Nielsen (1883–1972),

b. Vesterbro, Denmark

The first great actress of the German cinema, and arguably the most animated and beautiful, Asta Nielsen retired with sound, and made only one further film. But far from a casualty of technology, she was already middle-aged. Although she was a leading actress throughout the 1920s, her greatest impact had been in the decade before that when she arrived in Germany with a spontaneity exceeding any native talent. Had she been born ten years later, she would have lasted well into the sound period. As it is, her work is not well known—not much has survived, and her reputation is clouded with factual errors, such as the suggestion (noted in *The Times'* obituary) that she played in Pabst's *Die Buchse der Pandora*. In fact, she played Lulu in an earlier version, directed in 1922 by Arsen von Czerepy. Lotte Eisner has said that "People nowadays cannot understand what that pale mask, with its immense blazing eyes, meant for the nineteen-tens and twenties. . . . A hypercultivated, unstable, sophisticated period had found its ideal, an intellectual of great refinement. . . . Asta Nielsen was more than what a generation cultivating the linear and the arabesque was in search of. It was impossible to put a label on this great actress: she was neither 'modernistic' nor 'Expressionistic.' Her warm humanity, full of the breath of life and presence, refuted both abstraction and the abruptness of Expressionist art." The few films available, and a range of stills, suggest that by the standards of her time—which are those of Theda Bara—she was exceptionally unmannered. The variety of her work indicates a full-blooded artistic ambition.

She was discovered on the Danish stage by August Blom who directed her in *Ved Faengslets Port* (10), *Livets Storme* (11), and *Ballet Danserinden* (11). Then she married the director Urban Gad who directed her in *Afgrunden* (10). He took her to Germany and directed her next thirty films, until 1914: *Der Fremde Vogel* (11); *Der Schwarze Traum* (11); *Die Arme Jenny* (12); *Das Madchen ohne Vaterland* (12); *Der Totentanz* (12); *Engelein* (13); *Die Filmprimadonna* (13); *Die Suffragetten* (13); *Der Tod in Sevilla* (13); *Elena Fontana* (14); *Die Ewige Nacht* (14); *Das Feuer* (14); *Die Tochter der Landstrasse* (14); and *Zapatas Bande* (14).

That remarkable continuity could only be broken by divorce. From 1916 onward, she worked with a much wider range of directors: *Das Liebes-ABC* (16, Magnus Shifter); *Das Eskimo-Baby* (17, Walter Schmidthassler); *Die Rose der Wildnis* (17, Schmidthassler); *Der Fackeltrager* (18, Holger Madsen); *Das Ende vom Lied* (19, Willy Grundwald); and *Rausch* (19, Ernst Lubitsch). With her second husband, Danish director Svend Gade, she formed a company specially to film *Hamlet* (20), playing the prince herself. Then *Kurfurstendamm* (20, Richard Oswald); *Der Reigen* (20, Oswald); *Die Spielerin* (20, Oswald); *Die Geliebte Roswolskys* (21, Felix Basch); *Irrende Seelen* (21, Carl Froelich); as Mata Hari in *Die Spionin* (21, Paul Ludwig Wolff); as Strindberg's *Fraulein Julie* (22, Basch); *Vanina oder die Galgenhochzeit* (22,

Arthur von Gerlach); *Erdgeist* (23, Leopold Jessner); *I.N.R.I.* (23, Robert Wiene); *Die Frau im Feuer* (24, Carl Boese); *Hedda Gabler* (24, Fritz Eckstein); *Lebende Buddhas* (24, Paul Wegener); *Die Freudlose Gasse* (25, G. W. Pabst); *Dirnentragodie* (27, Rahn); *Gehetzte Frauen* (27, Oswald); *Kleinstadtsunden* (27, Rahn); *Laster der Menscheit* (27, Rudolph Meinert); only one sound film, *Unmogliche Liebe* (32, Erich Waschnech).

David Niven (1910–83),
b. Kirriemuir, Scotland

Remember all those robust actors hauling themselves up the cliff in *The Guns of Navarone* (61, J. Lee Thompson)? All pulling their weight except for David Niven, who looked too spruce for such effort. Yet Niven had served as a young man in the Highland Light Infantry and, during the Second World War, he was a major in the Commandos. It was an ingredient of his self-deprecating flavor of pink gins that he should seem implausible as a man of action, more suitably cast as the bogus major in *Separate Tables* (58, Delbert Mann), caught committing an indecent offense in a Bournemouth cinema. In fact, neither Niven's actual vigor nor literary wit—he wrote a novel, as well as two funny autobiographies—properly carried across the screen. He preferred to seem brittle, unreliable, a man whose banter and charm occasionally crumbled to reveal inadequacy: that is the vein abused, if rewarded with an Oscar, in *Separate Tables*, and best displayed in the superb *Bonjour Tristesse* (58, Otto Preminger).

From the army, Niven went into lumberjacking and thence into cheap Westerns as an extra. Without any preliminaries in British cinema, in 1935, he was signed up by Goldwyn in what was a long and abrasive relationship. It was several years before he began to get proper parts: *Splendor* (35, Elliott Nugent); *Barbary Coast* (35, Howard Hawks); *Feather in Her Hat* (35, Alfred Santell); *Dodsworth* (36, William Wyler); *The Charge of the Light Brigade* (36, Michael Curtiz); as Fritz in *The Prisoner of Zenda* (37, John Cromwell); *Dinner at the Ritz* (37, Harold Schuster); *Beloved Enemy* (37, H. C. Potter); Scotty in *The Dawn Patrol* (38, Edmund Goulding); *Four Men and a Prayer* (38, John Ford); *Bluebeard's Eighth Wife* (38, Ernst Lubitsch); as Edgar in *Wuthering Heights* (39), loathing Wyler's endless retakes; *Bachelor Mother* (39, Garson Kanin); *The Real Glory* (39, Henry Hathaway); *Eternally Yours* (39, Tay Garnett); and *Raffles* (40, Sam Wood).

Niven returned to Britain for the war and made two pictures—*The First of the Few* (42, Leslie Howard) and *The Way Ahead* (44, Carol Reed)—between active service.

After the war, Niven was not quite as welcome in America and Goldwyn often loaned him away to Korda: *Magnificent Doll* (46, Frank Borzage);

The Perfect Marriage (46, Lewis Allen); the pilot whose fate is judged in *A Matter of Life and Death* (46, Michael Powell); *The Other Love* (47, André de Toth); *The Bishop's Wife* (47, Henry Koster); *Bonnie Prince Charlie* (48, Anthony Kimmins); *Enchantment* (48, Irving Reis); *A Kiss in the Dark* (48, Delmer Daves); *The Elusive Pimpernel* (50, Powell); *A Kiss for Corliss* (50, Richard Wallace); *Happy Go Lovely* (51, Bruce Humberstone); *Soldiers Three* (51, Garnett); *The Moon Is Blue* (53, Preminger); *Happy Ever After* (54, Mario Zampi); *Love Lottery* (54, Charles Crichton); *The King's Thief* (55, Robert Z. Leonard); *Carrington V.C.* (56, Anthony Asquith); as Phileas Fogg, in a hurry but unflappable, in *Around the World in 80 Days* (56, Michael Anderson); *The Birds and the Bees* (56, Norman Taurog); *The Little Hut* (57, Mark Robson); *Oh Men! Oh Women!* (57, Nunnally Johnson); *My Man Godfrey* (57, Koster); *The Silken Affair* (57, Roy Kellino); *Ask Any Girl* (59, Charles Walters); *Happy Anniversary* (59, David Miller); *Please Don't Eat the Daisies* (60, Walters); *Guns of Darkness* (62, Asquith); *The Best of Enemies* (62, Guy Hamilton); unusually observant as the British ambassador in *55 Days at Peking* (63, Nicholas Ray); *The Pink Panther* (64, Blake Edwards); *Bedtime Story* (64, Ralph Levy); and *Lady L* (65, Peter Ustinov).

He was consistent, cheery, good value, funny yet polite—an Englishman abroad, too well mannered to insist on being Scottish.

By then, he was made to resort to such nonsense that even his smile looked aghast: *Casino Royale* (67, John Huston); *The Impossible Years* (68, Michael Gordon); *Before Winter Comes* (68, Thompson); *The Extraordinary Seaman* (69, John Frankenheimer); and *Prudence and the Pill* (69, Fielder Cook). But he was close to Nabokov's sense of elegant humiliation in *King, Queen, Knave* (72, Jerzy Skolimowski), and a charming Dracula in *Vampira* (74, Clive Donner). His real smile was based on the foresight he showed in 1953 by joining in the Four Star TV Theatre, a project that allowed him his greatest asset, calm.

His image as a laid-back elitist was strained by TV commercials for instant coffee—not so much deadpan as dead pot. Then he ventured out as a grandad for Disney in *No Deposit, No Return* (76, Norman Tokar), the title a comment on his involvement; a smoothie in *Murder by Death* (76, Robert Moore); an English butler for Disney in *Candleshoe* (77, Tokar).

His health was suffering, but he was in *Death on the Nile* (78, John Guillermin); *A Nightingale Sang in Berkeley Square* (79, Ralph Thomas); *Escape to Athena* (79, George Pan Cosmatos); *The Sea Wolves* (80, Andrew V. McLaglen); *Rough Cut* (80, Don Siegel); *Better Late Than Never* (82, Bryan Forbes); *Trail of the Pink Panther* (82, Edwards), and *Curse of the Pink Panther* (83,

Edwards), for which his voice had to be dubbed by another actor.

Philippe Noiret, b. Lille, France, 1930

For over forty years, Noiret has averaged three films a year. They are not all good, or explicable. He has had his fling in English-language films and done well enough. But he looks to American eyes like a character actor, damned by his own casual unobtrusiveness. He is akin to Robert Mitchum in that, after decades of professional assignment, very little fuss, and no large claim on grandeur, he emerges as one of the medium's treasures, a man whose enormous versatility is managed almost without a trace and certainly without strain. One may list a few "greatest" performances—for Tavernier, Ferreri, or even in *Cinema Paradiso*—but really it is the body of work that is powerful. Past sixty now, Noiret can only mean more as he comes to his generation of "old man parts."

The list cannot be complete, but it includes the major works, the films one would most like to see and those that deserve to be seen over and over: *Gigi* (48, Jacqueline Audry); *Olivia* (50, Audry); *Agence Matrimoniale* (53, Jean-Paul Le Chanois); *La Pointe Courte* (55, Agnes Varda); the transvestite uncle in *Zazie* (60, Louis Malle); *Le Rendezvous* (61, Jean Delannoy); *Tout l'Or du Monde* (61, René Clair); the husband in *Thérèse Desqueyroux* (62, George Franju); Louis XIII in *Cyrano et d'Artagnan* (64, Abel Gance); *Lady L* (65, Peter Ustinov); *La Vie de Chateau* (66, Jean-Paul Rappeneau); *Qui Etes-Vous, Polly Magoo* (66, William Klein); *Tendre Voyou* (66, Jean Becker); *Les Sultans* (67, Delannoy); *The Night of the Generals* (67, Anatole Litvak); *L'Une et l'Autre* (67, René Allio); *Woman Times Seven* (67, Vittorio De Sica); *Alexandre le Bienheureux* (68, Yves Robert); *The Assassination Bureau* (69, Basil Dearden); *Mister Freedom* (69, Klein); *Justine* (69, George Cukor); and *Clérambard* (69, Robert).

Ambiguity was now so ingrained in his nature, it is to be regretted that he worked only once for Hitchcock in the flawed *Topaz* (70). Then he did *Les Caprices de Marie* (70, Philippe de Broca); *A Time for Loving* (71, Christopher Miles); *Les Aveux les Plus Doux* (71, Edouard Molinaro); *Murphy's War* (71, Peter Yates); *La Mandarine* (72, Molinaro); as the TV producer in *L'Attempt* (72, Yves Boisset); *Le Serpent* (73, Henri Verneuil); *La Grande Bouffe* (73, Marco Ferreri); *Touche Pas la Femme Blanche* (74, Ferreri); hunched and quiet as the father in *The Watchmaker* (74, Bertrand Tavernier); *Le Secret* (74, Robert Enrico); *Le Jeu avec le Feu* (75, Alain Robbe-Grillet); as Philippe of Orleans, extrovert and upstanding in *Let Joy Reign Supreme* (75, Tavernier); as the man who seeks vengeance against the Nazis in *Le Vieux Fusil* (75, Enrico);

Amici Mei (76, Mario Monicelli); the judge in *The Judge and the Assassin* (76, Tavernier); *Coup de Foudre* (76, Enrico); *Tendre Poulet* (78, de Broca); *Le Témoin* (78, Jean-Pierre Mocky); *Who Is Killing the Great Chefs of Europe?* (78, Ted Kotcheff); *Un Taxi Mauve* (78, Boisset); *A Leap into the Void* (79, Marco Bellocchio); and *Deathwatch* (79, Tavernier).

On a Volé la Cuisse de Jupiter (80, de Broca); *A Week's Vacation* (80, Tavernier); *Pile ou Face* (80, Enrico); *Three Brothers* (81, Francesco Rosi); as the Jim Thompson sheriff from *Pop. 1280* transferred to French West Africa in *Coup de Torchon* (81, Tavernier); *Fort Saganne* (84, Alain Corneau); *Le Cop* (84, Claude Zidi); *L'Été Prochain* (85, Nadine Trintignant); *Speriamo Che Sia Femmina* (85, Monicelli); *Masques* (87, Claude Chabrol); as a homosexual in *Gli Occhiali Ora* (87, Giuliano Montaldo); *La Famiglia* (87, Ettore Scola); *Young Toscanini* (88, Franco Zeffirelli); *Cinema Paradiso* (89, Giuseppe Tornatore); outstanding as the major who clerks for the dead in *Life and Nothing But* (89, Tavernier); *Faux et Usage de Faux* (89, Laurent Heynemann); *Ripoux Contre Ripoux: Le Cop 2* (89, Zidi); *Di Menticare Palermo* (90, Rosi); *Uranus* (90, Claude Berri); *J'Embrasse Pas* (91, André Téchiné); *Max et Jeremie* (92, Claire Devers); and *Tango* (93, Patrice Leconte).

He played himself in *Grosse Fatigue* (94, Michel Blanc); D'Artagnan in *La Fille d'Artagnan* (94, Tavernier); a huge international hit with *Il Postino* (94, Michael Radford); *Les Milles* (94, Sebastien Grall); *Le Roi de Paris* (95, Dominique Maillet); *Facciamo Paradiso* (95, Monicelli); *Les Grands Ducs* (96, Leconte); *Fantôme avec Chauffeur* (96, Gerard Oury); *La Veilleur de Nuit* (96, de Broca); *Marianna Ucrìa* (96, Roberto Faenza); *Les Palmes de M. Schutz* (97, Claude Pinoteau); *Soleil* (97, Roger Hanin); as Philippe d'Orléans in *Le Bossu* (97, de Broca); *Le Pique-nique de Lulu Kreutz* (00, Didier Martiny); *Un Honnête Commerçant* (02, Philippe Blasbard); *On Guard* (02, de Broca).

Nick Nolte, b. Omaha, Nebraska, 1941

The life of Nick Nolte is a good deal more interesting than many of his roles. Yet it deepens our appreciation of someone who has grown to be America's most elemental actor, the only person around who challenges the immersion in work of Marlon Brando. Nolte is said to be the smallest full-grown male his family has known. He learned to read only as an adult. In 1962 he received a suspended jail sentence of forty-five years for selling draft cards. He bummed around from college to college in the Southwest simply in order to play football. And he was truly raised in Iowa and Nebraska—Brando country. He was also thirty-five (looking a dozen years younger) before he got his break in the TV miniseries *Rich Man, Poor Man* (76, David Greene and Boris Sagal).

For years thereafter, Nolte was somewhere between rugged, dumb, or brutal on screen. And it is only in the last few years that the rather bewildered, forceful presence has begun to reveal complicated talents. Consider, in *Rich Man, Poor Man,* Nolte was already several years older than Tom Cruise is now. When we favor kid actors we risk getting immature stories. But if actors are to find courage and wisdom, they need years of work and the chance to outlive our prejudices. In that sense, Nolte is to be compared with Robert Mitchum.

After his TV success, he was a hunk in *The Deep* (77, Peter Yates); Ray Hicks in *Who'll Stop the Rain* (78, Karel Reisz)—very good, but far too subtle then for public recognition; a footballer in *North Dallas Forty* (79, Ted Kotcheff); and Neal Cassady in the very arty *Heartbeat* (80, John Byrum).

He made a commercial impact with Eddie Murphy in *48 Hrs.* (82, Walter Hill), and then he was a very nice, shambling "Doc" in *Cannery Row* (82, David S. Ward). Despite their on-screen rapport, his costar in that film, Debra Winger, has said she never knew whether Nolte's personality was courageous or just stupid.

He was slipping with *Under Fire* (83, Roger Spottiswoode), *Teachers* (84, Arthur Hiller), and *The Ultimate Solution of Grace Quigley* (85, Anthony Harvey). Recovery appeared in the form of his Boudu reincarnation in *Down and Out in Beverly Hills* (86, Paul Mazursky), his first chance to play comedy. He suffered through poor films, and macho attitudes: *Extreme Prejudice* (87, Hill); *Weeds* (87, John Hancock); *Three Fugitives* (89, Francis Veber); *Farewell to the King* (89, John Milius); and *Everybody Wins* (90, Reisz).

Then he was cast as the painter in *New York Stories* (89, Martin Scorsese), and in half an hour he showed us a talented man confused by love and romance, by work and growing old. Better still was his cop in *Q & A* (90, Sidney Lumet), one of the great modern performances in American film, a kind of latter-day Hank Quinlan, a muddle of insight and bigotry. All of a sudden one had to see the growth that had occurred.

Another 48 Hrs. (90, Hill) was honestly titled. But in 1991, Nolte delivered two extraordinarily skillful and touching performances—as the central figure in *The Prince of Tides* (91, Barbra Streisand) and as the trim, soulless lawyer in *Cape Fear* (91, Martin Scorsese). The latter was the real redeeming feature of a disappointing picture: some spectators may have been dazzled by De Niro's creation of lurid evil, but Nolte was all the while delivering a small masterpiece about ordinary compromise. In *Lorenzo's Oil* (92, George Miller), he was as evidently Italian as Brando had been twenty years earlier.

Nolte is a subject for rejoicing and great hope. For we face the next decades with at least one actor capable of playing large, mature, but deeply troubled men. This actor carries his wounds, his talent, his past mistakes, and his urgent promise like a man trying to tidy up—there is something of Norman Mailer about him. But he deserves better than *I'll Do Anything* (94, James L. Brooks), *Blue Chips* (94, William Friedkin), or *I Love Trouble* (94, Charles Shyer).

But he moved, profitably, towards drama and more adventurous choices: a fascinating *Jefferson in Paris* (95, James Ivory); very good as the lead cop in *Mulholland Falls* (96, Lee Tamahori); doing Kurt Vonnegut in the ambitious *Mother Night* (96, Keith Gordon); romantic in *Afterglow* (97, Alan Rudolph); *U Turn* (97, Oliver Stone); excellent and nominated for *Affliction* (97, Paul Schrader); *Nightwatch* (98, Ole Bornedal); one of the few emerging with credit from *The Thin Red Line* (98, Terrence Malick); Vonnegut again in *Breakfast of Champions* (99, Rudolph); *Simpatico* (99, Matthew Warchus); Adam Verver in *The Golden Bowl* (00, Ivory); *Trixie* (00, Rudolph): *Investigating Sex* (01, Rudolph); *The Good Thief* (02, Neil Jordan); *Northfork* (03, Michael Polish); *The Hulk* (03, Ang Lee).

Mabel Normand (1894–1930),
b. Boston, Massachusetts

"Mabel" was the sweet young thing at the Keystone studio, the pretty, dark girl with lively eyes who loved diving into pools and who thrilled the hearts of Chaplin and Fatty Arbuckle in the early years of the First World War. A contemporary of Mary Pickford and the Gish sisters, she was one of the first proofs that a good-looking girl with charm and a sense of fun could succeed in the movies without any special pretense to acting. The Keystone setup helped to make her seem the more charming—as Chaplin put it, beauty among the beasts.

She was a model before joining Griffith at Biograph in 1911. Still only sixteen, she acted several times for him, most notably in *The Squaw's Love* (11), in which she did a back flip into a river first take. But it was Mack Sennett who used her most at Biograph, as the female attraction in comedy shorts. When Sennett left Biograph to form Keystone in 1912, Mabel went with him to even greater prominence. She remained with Sennett until 1917; she depended on his advice, and she was his girl. As well as appearing in over a hundred shorts directed by him, she had gone as far as directing herself by 1914, when still only twenty: *Mabel's Stormy Love Affair; Mabel's Bare Escape; Mabel's Nerve; Mabel's New Job; Mabel's Latest Prank; Mabel's Blunder;* and *Mabel at the Wheel*. It was on this last that she and Chaplin fell out, in a way that suggests a lot about work at Keystone,

as well as their different attitudes to film. This account of it, by Chaplin, also suggests that he knew his Lumière:

> Now I was anxious to write and direct my own comedies, so I talked to Sennett about it. But he would not hear of it; instead he assigned me to Mabel Normand who had just started directing her own pictures. This nettled me, for, charming as Mabel was, I doubted her competence as a director; so the first day there came the inevitable blow-up. We were on location in the suburbs of Los Angeles and in one scene Mabel wanted me to stand with a hose and water down the road so that the villain's car would skid over it. I suggested standing on the hose so that the water can't come out, and when I look down the nozzle I unconsciously step off the hose and the water squirts in my face. But she shut me up quickly: "We have no time! We have no time! Do what you're told."
>
> That was enough, I could not take it—and from such a pretty girl. "I'm sorry, Miss Normand, I will not do what I'm told. I don't think you are competent to tell me about what to do."

Mabel seems to have held no grudge. Before Chaplin moved on, they worked together several times—*Mabel's Strange Predicament* (14, Sennett and Henry Lehrmann); *Mabel's Busy Day* (14); *Mabel's Married Life* (14); *The Fatal Mallet* (14); *Caught in a Cabaret* (14); *Her Friend the Bandit* (14); *Gentlemen of Nerve* (14); *His Trysting Place* (14); *Getting Acquainted* (14); and *Tillie's Punctured Romance* (14, Sennett). Her new partner was Fatty Arbuckle and she worked with him for most of 1915: *Mabel and Fatty's Wash Day; Fatty and Mabel's Simple Life; Fatty and Mabel at the San Diego Exposition; Mabel, Fatty and the Law*—foreboding title; *Mabel and Fatty's Married Life; That Little Band of Gold; Fatty's Tintype Tangle*—all directed by Arbuckle; and *Mabel's Wilful Way* and *Mabel Lost and Won*, both directed by Mabel herself.

She stayed with Sennett two more years, but was anxious for a feature debut and got it, in 1918 at Paramount, in *Mickey* (Richard Jones). She then worked for Goldwyn for the next few years: *Sis Hopkins* (19, Clarence Badger); *The Pest* (19, Christy Cabanne); *When Doctors Disagree* (19, Victor Schertzinger); *Pinto* (19, Schertzinger); *Jinx* (19, Schertzinger); *The Slim Princess* (20, Schertzinger); *What Happened to Rosa?* (21, Schertzinger).

Disaster struck in 1922. Already on drugs, Mabel was implicated in the murder of director William Desmond Taylor and badly damaged by the scandal. Sennett took her back and tried to retrieve her fortunes with *Suzanna* (23, Jones) and *The Extra Girl* (23, Jones). But to no avail.

Her last pictures were a few shorts for Hal Roach in 1926: *Raggedy Rose, One Hour Married,* and *The Nickel Hopper.*

Edward Norton,
b. Boston, Massachusetts, 1969
2000: *Keeping the Faith*

The story goes that the people producing *Primal Fear* (96, Gregory Hoblit) had just about given up. Lots of young actors appreciated the split personality they were trying for—the stuttering, exploited wreck and the swaggering mastermind—but they simply couldn't go from one to the other in the middle of a sentence. Then Edward Norton—from Yale and the theatre—came along and did it. He did it so that Frances McDormand blinked, Richard Gere giggled, and even the camera wanted to do a double-take. It was brilliant—but was it human? Was it life, or acting? By which I mean to say that since very few (if any) of us have actually encountered that kind of hard-edged schizoid, to see *Primal Fear* was to appreciate the acting above all. And so we will have to wait and see whether Edward Norton is just an uncanny actor or someone who might also move us.

His other work is all interesting, yet unresolved so far: *Everyone Says I Love You* (96, Woody Allen); the lawyer in *The People vs. Larry Flynt* (96, Milos Forman); an Oscar nomination for *American History X* (98, Tony Kaye); *Rounders* (98, John Dahl); *Fight Club* (99, David Fincher); his first dud performance, in *The Score* (01, Frank Oz); *Death to Smoochy* (02, Danny DeVito); as Nelson Rockefeller in *Frida* (02, Julie Taymor); *Red Dragon* (02, Brett Ratner); very good in *25th Hour* (02, Spike Lee); in another foolish caper film, *The Italian Job* (03, F. Gary Gray); *Fear Itself* (03, John Polson).

Kim Novak (Marilyn Pauline Novak),
b. Chicago, 1933

Novak was a big, shy blonde, diffident about her beautiful body and forever trying to speak up and project. Many critics saw this tense endeavor and concluded that she was not an actress. But film sometimes flinches at the expertise of actresses, and the sympathetic viewer may come to realize that there was a mute honesty in Novak: she did not conceal the fact that she had been drawn into a world capable of exploiting her. Filming seemed an ordeal for her; it was as if the camera hurt her. But while many hostile to the movies rose in defense of the devastation of Marilyn Monroe—whether or not she was a sentient victim—Novak was stoical, obdurate, or sullen. She allowed very few barriers between that raw self and the audience and now looks dignified, reflective, and responsive to feeling where Monroe appears haphazard and oblivious. Novak is the epitome of

every small-town waitress or beauty contest winner who thought of being in the movies. Despite a thorough attempt by Columbia to glamorize her, she never lost the desperate attentiveness of someone out of her depth but refusing to give in. Her performances improve with time so that ordinary films come to center on her; even *Vertigo* (58), Hitchcock's masterpiece, owes some of its power to Novak's harrowing suspension between tranquillity and anxiety.

She was Miss Deepfreeze—beauty queen of unthawed flesh—when Columbia recruited her. After a tiny part in *The French Line* (53, Lloyd Bacon), Harry Cohn "organized" her as Columbia's backyard goddess. In a curious allusion to Hitchcock, she was the equivocal girl in *Pushover* (54, Richard Quine), and then in *Phffft!* (54, Mark Robson) and *Five Against the House* (55, Phil Karlson). The studio loaned her out for *The Man with the Golden Arm* (56, Otto Preminger), and she returned to Columbia for four films that slowly brought her into bloom. In *Picnic* (56, Joshua Logan), she was the insecure country belle; she was an agonized *Jeanne Eagels* (57, George Sidney) and a bashful chorine in *Pal Joey* (57, Sidney) making a marvelous, solemn lament out of "My Funny Valentine." But it was *Bell, Book and Candle* (57, Quine) that first caught her special ambiguity: the witch yearning to be mortal; the beautiful woman who cries again and thereby abandons her magical powers. Quine was clearly in sympathy with her and Jame Wong Howe made her a beauty of the late 1950s. Hitchcock then drew her into *Vertigo* as a substitute for pregnant Vera Miles. Less a performance than a helpless confession of herself, Novak's contribution to that film is one of the major female performances in the cinema. Among its many themes, *Vertigo* is about a rough young woman who gives a superb performance as a kind of Grace Kelly blind to being watched, and then finds herself trapped. The "Judy" in *Vertigo* loves Scotty, but it is her tragedy that she can only meet his desire for her by returning to the dream woman, "Madeleine." *Vertigo* contains a very subtle analysis of the ordeal and the self-obliteration in acting, and it works all the better because Novak was so direct, unschooled, and slavelike. There are actresses whose intelligence always shows—like Katharine Hepburn, Louise Brooks in *Pandora's Box,* or Dietrich in the Sternberg films. Then there are actresses who seem stripped of any chance of control. They are simply there, caught in the lights by the camera and the movie—like Brooks in *Pandora's Box,* Karina in *Pierrot le Fou,* and Novak in *Vertigo.*

Novak was gloomily touching in *Middle of the Night* (59, Delbert Mann); so good in *Strangers When We Meet* (60, Quine) that a novelettish subject acquired the sadness of Ophuls. In the 1960s she declined: the system that created stars was fading, Novak was putting on weight and was the victim of an automobile accident. *The Notorious Landlady* (62, Quine) was a silly film; *Boys' Night Out* (62, Michael Gordon) a stag comedy; *Of Human Bondage* (64, Ken Hughes and Henry Hathaway) beyond her histrionic capacity; *Kiss Me, Stupid* (64, Billy Wilder), her last classic part—Polly the Pistol, wistful for domesticity and forgetting the routine of seduction; *The Amorous Adventures of Moll Flanders* (65, Terence Young), a project that required a Cukor; *The Legend of Lylah Clare* (68, Robert Aldrich), in which she struggles to play a Dietrich-like actress; *The Great Bank Robbery* (69, Hy Averback); *The White Buffalo* (77, J. Lee Thompson), and *Just a Gigolo* (79, David Hemmings).

She appeared in *The Mirror Crack'd* (80, Guy Hamilton); on TV in *Malibu* (83, E. W. Swackhamer); in *The Children* (90, Tony Palmer); and still beautiful as a dying woman in *Liebestraum* (91, Mike Figgis).

Ramon Novarro (Ramon Samaniegos) (1899–1968), b. Durango, Mexico

As a youth, Samaniegos and his family fled from revolution to Los Angeles. The young man had a variety of jobs before working as an extra in movies. His first real part was dancing in *A Small Town Idol* (21, Erle C. Kenton) and he had a supporting part in *Mr. Barnes of New York* (22, Victor Schertzinger). He was then signed up by Rex Ingram, who had already launched Valentino. Ingram persuaded the change of name and strenuously promoted Novarro as a Latin lover. After playing Rupert of Hentzau in Ingram's *The Prisoner of Zenda* (22), Novarro was in Ingram's next four movies: *Trifling Women* (22); *Scaramouche* (23); *Where the Pavement Ends* (23); and *The Arab* (24).

Novarro was by now a leading star with MGM and he made *Thy Name Is Woman* (24, Fred Niblo), *The Red Lily* (24, Niblo), and *The Midshipman* (25, Christy Cabanne). Then, after its initial disaster, Niblo and Novarro were chosen by the MGM hierarchy to replace Charles Brabin and George Walsh on *Ben-Hur* (27). Novarro was as successful as that film, but he lacked the special faunlike beauty of Valentino. His face tended to a rather flabby reproach, and he was clearly not as personally caught up in the idea of himself as romantic hero as was Valentino. He remained at MGM and was successful until the full arrival of sound: *Lovers?* (27, John M. Stahl); *The Road to Romance* (27, John S. Robertson); *The Student Prince in Old Heidelberg* (27, Ernst Lubitsch); *Across to Singapore* (28, William Nigh); *Forbidden Hours* (28, Harry Beaumont); *The Flying Fleet* (29, George Hill); *The Pagan* (29, W. S. Van Dyke), in which he sang "Pagan Love Song"; and *Devil-May-*

Care (29, Sidney Franklin). Thereafter, his appeal declined and his acting seemed increasingly dull: *In Gay Madrid* (30, Robert Z. Leonard); *Call of the Flesh* (30, Brabin); *Son of India* (31, Jacques Feyder); *Daybreak* (31, Feyder); opposite Garbo in *Mata-Hari* (32, George Fitzmaurice).

His last years at MGM were a search for former glory: *The Son-Daughter* (32, Clarence Brown); *The Barbarian* (33, Sam Wood); *Laughing Boy* (34, Van Dyke); and *The Cat and the Fiddle* (34, William K. Howard), opposite Jeanette MacDonald. After *The Night Is Young* (35, Dudley Murphy), he left the studio, went to Spain and directed *Contra la Corriente* (36). He was back in Hollywood for *The Sheik Steps Out* (37, Irving Pichel) and *A Desperate Adventurer* (38, John Auer) and went to France to act in *La Comédie du Bonheur* (40, Marcel L'Herbier). During the war he lived in Mexico and afterwards he returned to Hollywood for only small parts: *We Were Strangers* (49, John Huston); *The Big Steal* (49, Don Siegel); *Crisis* (50, Richard Brooks); and *Heller in Pink Tights* (60, George Cukor). Novarro's retirement was brutally ended in 1968 by a homosexual murder.

Phillip Noyce, b. Griffith, Australia, 1950

1975: *God Knows Why, But It Works* (d). 1977: *Backroads.* 1978: *Newsfront.* 1982: *Heatwave.* 1987: *Echoes of Paradise.* 1989: *Dead Calm; Blind Fury.* 1992: *Patriot Games.* 1993: *Sliver.* 1994: *Clear and Present Danger.* 1997: *The Saint.* 1999: *The Bone Collector; Blast Off.* 2001: *The Rabbit-Proof Fence.* 2002: *The Quiet American.*

By now, Australia must regard Phillip Noyce as someone who always reckoned to find his place in Hollywood. His American pictures are conventional fantasies of heroism, masquerading behind the ostensible realism of the Cold War, Harrison Ford, and New York crime. But *The Bone Collector* shows just how far violence, the decay of flesh, and the horrors of a subterranean world are just material for a very deft fantasy about Denzel Washington and Angelina Jolie getting it on. Whereas in Australia, Noyce made tough pictures about race, the newspaper world, and the small evil of murder. He was a truly promising director who has acted out the ease of transition from real material to movie bombast. Equally, he shows how easily the prize-winning student can become the warning figure held up to future generations.

The Quiet American will be decisive in revealing whether Noyce has real character or survival instincts.

Elliott Nugent (1900–80), b. Dover, Ohio

1932: *The Mouthpiece* (codirected with James Flood); *Life Begins* (codirected with Flood). 1933: *Whistling in the Dark; Three-Cornered Moon; If I*

Were Free. 1934: *She Loves Me Not; Strictly Dynamite; Two Alone.* 1935: *Love in Bloom; Enter the Madam; College Scandal; Splendor.* 1936: *And So They Were Married; Wives Never Know.* 1937: *It's All Yours.* 1938: *Professor Beware; Give Me a Sailor.* 1939: *Never Say Die; The Cat and the Canary.* 1941: *Nothing But the Truth.* 1942: *The Male Animal.* 1943: *The Crystal Ball.* 1944: *Up in Arms.* 1947: *My Favorite Brunette; Welcome Stranger.* 1948: *My Girl Tisa.* 1949: *Mr. Belvedere Goes to College; The Great Gatsby.* 1950: *The Skipper Surprised His Wife.* 1951: *My Outlaw Brother.* 1952: *Just for You.*

Like his father, the actor J. C. Nugent, Elliott Nugent was first and last a man of the theatre, equally polished as writer, actor, and director. A Broadway actor in the early 1920s, he wrote plays with his father and made his movie acting debut in *Headlines* (25, Edward H. Griffith). The emphasis on words that came with sound made Nugent exactly the sort of stage talent required in Hollywood. In 1929, he went west, as an actor, a writer, and eventually, a director. He played the lead in *So This Is College* (29, Sam Wood); *For the Love o' Lil* (30, James Tinling); *Not So Dumb* (30, King Vidor); and *Romance* (30, Clarence Brown). He acted in and wrote dialogue for *Wise Girls* (29, E. Mason Hopper); *Sins of the Children* (30, Wood); and *The Unholy Three* (30, Jack Conway).

When he graduated to directing, from 1934 onward he worked for Paramount, specializing in romantic comedy—thus *Three-Cornered Moon,* starring Claudette Colbert and Mary Boland, a clever gilding of a Depression subject. His style seemed more sophisticated than low-down, but after *Professor Beware*—one of Harold Lloyd's last films—Nugent played an important part in Bob Hope's career. He worked five times with Hope: in *Give Me a Sailor, Never Say Die, Nothing But the Truth, My Favorite Brunette,* and best of all, *The Cat and the Canary,* a comedy horror that is always a little too frightening for comfort and very good-looking. He directed Danny Kaye in *Up in Arms,* but still retained a feeling for wit in *The Male Animal,* an adaptation of a stage play he had written with James Thurber, and starring Henry Fonda and Olivia de Havilland. He went back to the stage in 1952 after two less successful but more ambitious excursions—*My Girl Tisa* and *The Great Gatsby*—and the domestic comedy, *Mr. Belvedere Goes to College.*

O

Warren Oates (1928–82), b. Depoy, Kentucky
In 1981, without having met the man, or knowing much about him, I wrote of Oates in *Film Comment:*

Oates seems at first sight grubby, balding, and unshaven. You can smell whiskey and sweat on him, along with that mixture of bad beds and fallen women. He's toothy, he's small, he's 53 this year, and he has a face like prison bread, with eyes that have known too much solitary confinement. But the eyes bulge and shrink in a sweet game of fear and courage. . . . Sublimest thing with Oates is when he does nothing. Only Mitchum could do nothing so well, until you think a hole is opening up in the middle of the picture and everything is gonna fall down it. Then you see Oates starting that shy grin of his, and you shake yourself because he could've been dead. The greatest trick to writing about Oates is to catch the spirit of obituary.

The trick got easier, for Oates was dead within the year. Since then it has been pleasing to feel the swell of appreciation for Oates the actor. There is a cult, maybe, much helped by Tom Thurman's resourceful documentary film on Oates. It owes something also to the notion that the Oates world—the Southwest, Mexico, the borderlands—has passed on with Sam Peckinpah's death and our new squeamishness about rough men or films that celebrate them. Oates was narrow in range, until you got into those narrows, and then you felt depths of humor, ferocity, foolishness, and honor. Let Oates have a word. In an interview, he said this of Peckinpah, and it could be applied to himself: "I don't think he's a horrible maniac; it's just that he injures your innocence, and you get pissed off about it."

Carrying a modest fee, and being intrigued by the experimentalism of Monte Hellman, Oates took leading parts in two films outside the scope of his "industrial work": as Gashade and Coigne (twin brothers, the slowly converging faces of the existential coin) in *The Shooting* (66, Hellman); and as G.T.O., the fantasizing little man behind a large engine, solitary but craving sociability in *Two-Lane Blacktop* (70, Hellman). Both parts abandoned mannerism and showed that a plain, balding man with a toothy grin could carry a movie.

Oates had been a steady TV actor, and he accumulated a long list of films: *Up Periscope* (58, Gordon Douglas); *Yellowstone Kelly* (59, Douglas); the brother in *The Rise and Fall of Legs Diamond* (60, Budd Boetticher); *Private Property* (60, Leslie Stevens); *Ride the High Country* (62, Sam Peckinpah); *Hero's Island* (62, Stevens); *Mail Order Bride* (63, Burt Kennedy); *The Rounders* (65, Kennedy); *Major Dundee* (65, Peckinpah); *Return of the Seven* (66, Kennedy); *Welcome to Hard Times* (67, Kennedy); *In the Heat of the Night* (67, Norman Jewison); *The Split* (68, Gordon Flemyng); *Crooks and Coronets* (69, James O'Connolly); magnificently stupid in *The Wild Bunch* (69, Peckinpah); *Smith* (69, Michael

O'Herlihy); *Barquero* (70, Douglas); *There Was a Crooked Man* (70, Joseph L. Mankiewicz); *The Hired Hand* (71, Peter Fonda); *The Thief Who Came to Dinner* (73, Bud Yorkin); *Tom Sawyer* (73, Don Taylor); *Kid Blue* (73, James Frawley); very good as a subtler *Dillinger* (74, John Milius) than the cinema has ever shown before; as another of Monte Hellman's dour obsessives in *Cockfighter* (74); *Badlands* (74, Terrence Malick); effortlessly raising a scruffy little adventurer to the legend of *Bring Me the Head of Alfredo Garcia* (74, Peckinpah) and coming close to a portrait of Peckinpah; *The White Dawn* (74, Philip Kaufman); *Race with the Devil* (75, Jack Starrett); *92 in the Shade* (75, Thomas McGuane); *Drum* (76, Steve Carver); *Dixie Dynamite* (76, Lee Frost); and *China 9, Liberty 37* (78, Hellman). He was superb as a style-mad thief in *The Brink's Job* (78, William Friedkin), and he went to New Zealand to make *Sleeping Dogs* (78, Roger Donaldson).

He did *My Old Man* (79, John Erman), for TV; *1941* (79, Steven Spielberg); a flat-out comedy role in *Stripes* (81, Ivan Reitman); *The Border* (82, Tony Richardson); *Tough Enough* (83, Richard Fleischer); and *Blue Thunder* (83, John Badham).

Merle Oberon (Estelle Merle O'Brien Thompson) (1911–79), b. Tasmania, Australia

Oberon was a renowned beauty with a graven face and the legend of mixed blood. There is footage that survives from the unfinished *Claudius* (37, Josef von Sternberg) in which she looks as delectable as any woman ever filmed in Britain. Alas, she was often a dull actress. Perhaps only her marriage to Alexander Korda (1939–45) contributed the sense of regal allure that her acting lacked.

When she first came to Britain, as a dancer, she was using the working name of Queenie O'Brien, more barmaid than enchantress. She worked as an extra in *Alf's Button* (30, Will P. Kellino), *Never Trouble* (31, Lupino Lane), and *Fascination* (31, Miles Mander) before Korda noticed her. In 1932, she made *Service for Ladies* and *Wedding Rehearsal* for him, and also appeared in *For the Love of Mike* (32, Monty Banks); *Ebb Tide* (32, Arthur Rosson); and *Aren't We All* (32, Harry Lachman). The next year, she starred in *Men of Tomorrow* (Leotine Sagan) and played Anne Boleyn in *The Private Life of Henry VIII* (Korda). In 1934 she was opposite Douglas Fairbanks in Korda's *The Private Life of Don Juan* and played the female lead in *The Scarlet Pimpernel* (Harold Young).

Korda then sold a share of her to Samuel Goldwyn and she went to America to make *Folies Bergere* (35, Roy del Ruth); *The Dark Angel* (35, Sidney Franklin); *These Three* (36, William Wyler); and *Beloved Enemy* (36, H. C. Potter).

Back in England, it was her taxi accident that terminated *Claudius*. By 1938, she was again with Goldwyn for *The Cowboy and the Lady* (Potter) and in 1939 she was cast, optimistically, as Cathy in Wyler's *Wuthering Heights*. Married now to Korda, she made *The Lion Has Wings* (39, Michael Powell, Brian Desmond-Hurst, and Adrian Brunel) in England and returned to Hollywood for *Till We Meet Again* (40, Edmund Goulding); *Affectionately Yours* (41, Lloyd Bacon); *That Uncertain Feeling* (41, Ernst Lubitsch); *Lydia* (41, Julien Duvivier); *Forever and a Day* (43, Frank Lloyd, et al.); *First Comes Courage* (43, Dorothy Arzner); *The Lodger* (44, John Brahm); *Dark Waters* (44, André de Toth); as George Sand in *A Song to Remember* (44, Charles Vidor); *This Love of Ours* (45, William Dieterle); *A Night in Paradise* (46, Arthur Lubin); *Temptation* (46, Irving Pichel); *Night Song* (47, John Cromwell); and *Berlin Express* (48, Jacques Tourneur).

Her career took some odd turns—*24 Hours of a Woman's Life* (52, Victor Saville); *Todo es Possible en Granada* (54); as Josephine in *Desirée* (54, Henry Koster); *Deep in My Heart* (54, Stanley Donen); *The Price of Fear* (56, Abner Biberman); *The Oscar* (65, Russell Rouse); and *Hotel* (67, Richard Quine).

She spent her later years as a grand hostess eventually to be novelized by her husband's nephew, Michael Korda, in *Queenie*.

Edmond O'Brien (1915–85), b. New York

Actors do not sweat: an interesting essay could be researched on the methods they employ to prevent it. For sweat is not glamorous—no matter that, photographically, it is just a shining. Edmond O'Brien sweated—not always, yet often enough for him to seem, in memory's eye, always disheveled, out of breath, and aglow. There was never a truer role for this actor than *D.O.A.* (49, Rudolph Maté), in which an insurance salesman goes to San Francisco for the cool air and some fun, only to get fatally overheated. He is desperately energetic in *D.O.A.*, living his circumscribed life to the full, terrified of stopping, and past caring that sweat shows.

Twice in his career, he ventured into direction: *Shield for Murder* (54, codirected with Howard W. Koch) and *Mantrap* (61), emphatic, tabloid movies, with actors chased by boom shadows.

A stage actor, he had played with the Mercury Theater before his debut in *The Hunchback of Notre Dame* (39, William Dieterle). He made a few more films and then went into the service. But on emerging he soon became a regular character actor: *Winged Victory* (44, George Cukor); the investigator in *The Killers* (46, Robert Siodmak); *The Web* (47, Michael Gordon); *A Double Life* (47, Cukor); *Another Part of the Forest* (48, Gordon); *Fighter Squadron* (48, Raoul Walsh); *An Act of Murder* (48, Gordon); the plant in *White Heat* (49, Walsh); *711 Ocean Drive* (50, Joseph M. Newman); *Between Midnight and Dawn* (50, Gordon Douglas); *Warpath* (51, Byron Haskin); *Silver City* (51, Haskin); *Two of a Kind* (51, Henry Levin); *Denver & Rio Grande* (52, Haskin); *The Turning Point* (52, Dieterle); as Casca in *Julius Caesar* (53, Joseph L. Mankiewicz); *The Hitchhiker* (53, Ida Lupino); *The Bigamist* (53, Lupino); *Broken Lance* (54, Edward Dmytryk); winning the supporting actor Oscar as the press agent in *The Barefoot Contessa* (54, Mankiewicz); *Pete Kelly's Blues* (55, Jack Webb); as Winston Smith in *1984* (56, Michael Anderson); *A Cry in the Night* (56, Frank Tuttle); *The Girl Can't Help It* (56, Frank Tashlin); *The Big Land* (57, Douglas); *The Third Voice* (59, Hubert Cornfield); *Up Periscope* (59, Douglas); *The Last Voyage* (60, Andrew Stone); *The Great Imposter* (60, Robert Mulligan); *The Man Who Shot Liberty Valance* (62, John Ford); *Birdman of Alcatraz* (62, John Frankenheimer); *Seven Days in May* (64, Frankenheimer); *Rio Conchos* (64, Douglas); *The Hanged Man* (64, Don Siegel); *Sylvia* (65, Douglas); *Synanon* (65, Richard Quine); *Peau d'Espion* (66, Edouard Molinaro); *Fantastic Voyage* (66, Richard Fleischer); an elderly survivor in *The Wild Bunch* (69, Sam Peckinpah); *Lucky Luciano* (73, Francisco Rosi); and *99 44/100% Dead* (74, Frankenheimer).

Margaret O'Brien, b. Los Angeles, 1937

Downstairs at the Smith house in a suburb of St Louis, circa 1904, there is a teenage party. The two younger children of the house creep out of bed and watch from the stairs. But they are noticed and called down by their tolerant elders. No party was ever more fruitfully interrupted. For one of those children, "Tootie," was played by Margaret O'Brien, and with her sister, Esther, played by Judy Garland, she performs a gorgeous front-parlor cakewalk to the tune "Under the Bamboo Tree." We need not be too surprised that a seven-year-old could carry that off without disrupting the marvelous grace of Vincente Minnelli's camera in *Meet Me in St. Louis* (44). More subtle is the discretion and intimacy of the number, for *Meet Me in St. Louis* is a family story that happens to be illustrated by songs. The cakewalk sequence never loses sight of Tootie's moment of glory nor the light of nostalgia that warms the entire film. The spectacle is allowed to rest with character and plausibility. Add to that her full-blooded conviction in the Halloween sequence and you can see what an extraordinary young actress Margaret O'Brien was. The droll overplaying in, for instance, *Our Vines Have Tender Grapes* (45, Roy Rowland) is a great comic

achievement, so that one regrets the number of times she was restricted to the sentimental stereotype of children.

She made her debut at the age of four and had ten good years at MGM: *Babes on Broadway* (41, Busby Berkeley); *Journey for Margaret* (42, W. S. Van Dyke); *Dr. Gillespie's Criminal Case* (43, Willis Goldbeck); singing "In a Little Spanish Town" in *Thousands Cheer* (43, George Sidney); *Lost Angel* (43, Rowland); *Madame Curie* (43, Mervyn Le Roy); *Jane Eyre* (44, Robert Stevenson); *The Canterville Ghost* (44, Jules Dassin); *Music for Millions* (44, Henry Koster); *The Unfinished Dance* (47, Koster); *Tenth Avenue Angel* (48, Rowland); *Big City* (48, Norman Taurog); as Beth in *Little Women* (49, Le Roy); *The Secret Garden* (49, Fred M. Wilcox), her finest performance, a study in the rigid dignity of an orphan quelling panic; and *Her First Romance* (51, Seymour Friedman).

She made only two films as a young adult: the horsy *Glory* (55, David Butler) and *Heller in Pink Tights* (60, George Cukor) when, as the inept daughter, her talent for comedy still seemed real. But perhaps she had been formed by an earlier age and style. When she auditioned for the Natalie Wood part in *Rebel Without a Cause* she lost the role because "she answered all the questions by professing love for parents and teachers." The mood and pace of a cakewalk can last a lifetime.

She was seen in *Amy* (81, Vincent McEveety).

Pat O'Brien (1899–1983),
b. Milwaukee, Wisconsin

When Warner Brothers were industriously covering the wrong side of the tracks in the 1930s, Pat O'Brien was their resident apologist for the social order, either as cop or priest. Always retaining a hint of his Irish origins, O'Brien brought a welcome astringency to several parts that could have been horribly pious. His partnership with James Cagney—like Guinness and bootleg hootch—was especially successful.

It had been thought that O'Brien's movie debut was as Hildy Johnson, the reporter—a part he had played on the stage—in *The Front Page* (31, Lewis Milestone). But there is a Pat O'Brien who played in three earlier, and very cheap films: *Shadows of the West* (21, Paul Hurst); *The Freckled Rascal* (29, Louis King); and *Fury of the Wild* (29, Leon d'Usseau).

After *The Front Page*, he was an established player: *Air Mail* (32, John Ford); *Virtue* (32, Edward Buzzell); *American Madness* (32, Frank Capra); *Laughter in Hell* (33, Edward L. Cahn); *Destination Unknown* (33, Tay Garnett); *Bombshell* (33, Victor Fleming); *Oil for the Lamps of China* (33, Mervyn Le Roy); *Flirtation Walk* (34, Frank Borzage); *Twenty Million Sweethearts* (34,

Ray Enright); with Cagney in *Here Comes the Navy* (34, Lloyd Bacon); *Stars Over Broadway* (35, William Keighley); *Devil Dogs of the Air* (35, Bacon); *In Caliente* (35, Bacon); with Cagney again in *The Irish in Us* (35, Bacon) and *Ceiling Zero* (36, Howard Hawks); as *The Great O'Malley* (37, William Dieterle); as the priest watching over Cagney in *Angels With Dirty Faces* (38, Michael Curtiz); *Boy Meets Girl* (38, Bacon); *Till We Meet Again* (40, Edmund Goulding); *Knute Rockne: All-American* (40, Bacon); *The Fighting 69th* (40, Keighley); *Escape to Glory* (41, John Brahm); *Broadway* (42, William A. Seiter); *His Butler's Sister* (43, Borzage); *Having Wonderful Crime* (45, Edward Sutherland); *Man Alive* (45, Enright); *Crack-Up* (46, Irving Reis); *Riff Raff* (47, Ted Tetzlaff); *Fighting Father Dunne* (48, Tetzlaff); as Gramps in *The Boy with Green Hair* (48, Joseph Losey); *Johnny One-Eye* (50, Robert Florey); *The People Against O'Hara* (51, John Sturges); *Ring of Fear* (54, James Edward Grant); *Inside Detroit* (56, Fred F. Sears); *The Last Hurrah* (58, Ford); effortlessly knowing when raiding the speakeasy in *Some Like It Hot* (59, Billy Wilder); *Town Tamer* (65, Lesley Selander); *The End* (78, Burt Reynolds); *Scout's Honor* (80, Henry Levin); and *Ragtime* (81, Milos Forman).

Willis H. O'Brien (1886–1962),
b. Oakland, California

"O'Brien was a genius," said Merian C. Cooper, "*Kong* is as much his picture as it is mine. There was never anybody in his class as far as special effects went, there never was and there probably never will be." Well, special effects have undergone another revolution since Cooper spoke—that of computer assistance. But O'Brien's place is still unquestioned, just as his role in that great testament to collaboration, serendipity, and blind chance—the making of *King Kong*—has been made clear by the film's several scholars. And there is more still to O'Brien's story.

As a boy, he was a clever drawer and an experimenter with models. That led to work as a sculptor and as a cartoonist for the *San Francisco Daily News*. To that end he made a series of toy dinosaurs and then experimented with stop motion—frame-by-frame advancing of the action—on a movie camera. Two months' work led to a five-minute film, *The Dinosaur and the Missing Link* (14). Edison purchased it and advanced O'Brien the money to make ten more films. That in turn led to *The Ghost of Slumber Mountain* (19), which was a great hit.

O'Brien was developing all his processes toward greater sophistication, as shown in *The Lost World* (25, Harry Hoyt). That was the picture that intrigued Merian Cooper and Ernest B. Schoedsack in the halting development of *King Kong*. By then, O'Brien had gone over to rubber models,

and he had found several different versions of matte work and miniature projection that could marry the model work and the live action.

Pedantic schoolchildren are sometimes heard to complain that you can see (and feel) the flickering trickery in *King Kong*. Well, yes, you can; it's the trembling poetry of the magic. For myself, I think *Kong* is still one of the most compelling special effects movies, in large part because it is not perfect, and because the seams that show (so to speak) are the friction of one reality against another.

The story of *King Kong's* production is of struggle and battles (with Cooper generally having the clearest sense of where they were going), but O'Brien—or Obie—was the boffin who answered all the impossible problems. He worked just as hard on *Son of Kong* (33, Schoedsack), and just before that film opened his estranged wife murdered their two sons.

He was deeply dismayed, and he put aside or forgot many favorite projects. But there were other credits: *The Last Days of Pompeii* (35, Schoedsack); *Mighty Joe Young* (49, Schoedsack)—after which O'Brien was awarded an honorary Oscar. The story for *The Beast of Hollow Mountain* (56, Edward Nassour and Ismael Rodríguez); *The Animal World* (56, Irwin Allen), with Ray Harryhausen as his assistant; *The Black Scorpion* (57, Edward Ludwig); *The Giant Behemoth* (59, Eugène Lourié); *The Lost World* (60, Allen); *It's a Mad Mad Mad Mad World* (63, Stanley Kramer).

Clifford Odets (1906–63), b. Philadelphia
Well, yes, you're right, Clifford Odets was a playwright, and the great, radical hope of the 1930s. He was intensely associated with the Group Theatre and with leftist themes—as witness *Waiting for Lefty, Awake and Sing!,* and *Paradise Lost.* Elia Kazan observed how Odets became "the most sought-after celebrity in town": "Everyone wanted to meet him, look him over, ask him questions, listen to what he had to say—and fuck him."

And now we come close to why Odets is in this book, for the fuckability of the writer, or the artist, is close to the mysterious heart of Hollywood. Odets was never a beauty, but everyone who met him was entranced: he was magnetic, a great talker, funny, with burning eyes, and that forlorn attractiveness of a natural actor (he had acted professionally) who had never got big parts. But along the way, and among others, he had Frances Farmer as a mistress, Luise Rainer as a wife, and then Betty Grayson, another actress. What can we say of guys who fuck only actresses? Not just that they're obsessed with the art and the business, but that they are committed to self-dramatization (still the essential wellness for getting on in Hollywood).

Then we come to the way in which being in reach of celebrated women, and large fees for rewriting bad screenplays, got in the way of Odets as the white hope of the theatre. For he moved—physically and temperamentally—to Los Angeles, and he began devoting himself to causes that could not compare with the satisfaction of plays. This is a model of selling out, which Odets did with fiery humor, comic self-deprecation, and actorly panache. But it meant that in the rest of his life his plays were "only" *Golden Boy* (1937), a treatise on selling out; *Rocket to the Moon* (1938); *Night Music* (1940); *Clash by Night* (1941)—which would become a Fritz Lang film; *The Big Knife* (1941)—a scabrous account of Hollywood and selling out; the fascinating *The Country Girl* (1950), on how a woman can sap a creative man's juices; and *The Flowering Peach* (1954).

Some of those plays worked very well—and would do so on screen—but they became increasingly melodramatic. Meanwhile, as part of his Hollywood dues, Odets wrote a screenplay for *The General Died at Dawn* (36, Lewis Milestone). Out of his friendship with Cary Grant, he wrote and directed *None but the Lonely Heart*, a seriously underrated picture. And he built up an 800-page screenplay on the life of George Gershwin as the first step in the process that led to *Rhapsody in Blue* (45, Irving Rapper). Oscar Levant read that script and reckoned that Odets had told his own story—with songs. That script was dumped, but a few years later Odets resurrected some of it for *Humoresque* (46, Jean Negulesco), in which the ethos of *Golden Boy*, John Garfield (and Oscar Levant) meets the world and romance of Joan Crawford.

For other credits, Odets did *Deadline at Dawn* (46, Harold Clurman—an old colleague from the Group Theatre). He also had a hand in *Sweet Smell of Success* (57, Alexander Mackendrick), working on the streets at night from Ernest Lehman's original script. He directed *The Story on Page One* (59), and he wrote the Elvis Presley film *Wild in the Country* (61).

More than that, "stranded" in Hollywood, Odets became one of the first script doctors (an attached name so big it has to be hush-hush) and the entertaining model of self-betrayal. Again, Kazan saw how it worked:

Cliff spent the last dozen years of his life writing films to pay bills that were too large for a man who hoped to continue working in the theatre. He made his home in a Beverly Hills "Spanish mansion." He drove a Lincoln Continental and had what he claimed to be the outstanding collection of Paul Klees in the country. He worked frequently and was well paid by New York theatre standards. But he was always broke or near it. . . .

His rewriting jobs were the trail of his friendships—and he was close to Nicholas Ray, so that he advised on *Rebel Without a Cause* and actually took to the typewriter on *Bigger Than Life* . . . until the James Mason character reminded some people of Clifford Odets.

Maureen O'Hara (Maureen Fitzsimmons), b. Dublin, Ireland, 1920

A gorgeous red-haired, green-eyed heroine, the perfect test material for color processes, but short of inner significance. She was a woman in a man's world, inclined to thrust her hands on her hips, speak her mind, and be told, "You're pretty when you're angry." She is remembered now, with affection, as a very ardent, true (and rather limited) woman in several Ford pictures.

From the theatre, she went into British films: *My Irish Molly* (38, Alex Bryce); *Kicking the Moon Around* (38, Walter Forde); and *Jamaica Inn* (39, Alfred Hitchcock). She moved to Hollywood and was quickly employed to adorn color spectaculars, and to inhabit John Ford's curious, reinvented Ireland: *The Hunchback of Notre Dame* (39, William Dieterle); *A Bill of Divorcement* (40, John Farrow); *Dance, Girl, Dance* (40, Dorothy Arzner); "Ireland" in Wales in *How Green Was My Valley* (41, Ford); *The Black Swan* (42, Henry King); *The Immortal Sergeant* (42, John M. Stahl); *The Fallen Sparrow* (43, Richard Wallace); *This Land Is Mine* (43, Jean Renoir); *Buffalo Bill* (44, William Wellman); *The Spanish Main* (45, Frank Borzage); *Sentimental Journey* (46, Walter Lang); *The Foxes of Harrow* (47, Stahl); *Miracle on 34th Street* (47, George Seaton); *Sitting Pretty* (48, Lang); *Britannia Mews* (49, Jean Negulesco); *A Woman's Secret* (49, Nicholas Ray); "Ireland" in Texas in *Rio Grande* (50, Ford); "Ireland" actually in Ireland in *The Quiet Man* (52, Ford); *Against All Flags* (52, George Sherman); *Kangaroo* (52, Lewis Milestone); *Flame of Araby* (52, Charles Lamont); *The Redhead from Wyoming* (53, Lee Sholem); *Malaga* (54, Richard Sale); "Ireland" at West Point in *The Long Gray Line* (55, Ford); letting down her glorious hair for *Lady Godiva* (56, Arthur Lubin); *The Magnificent Matador* (55, Budd Boetticher); *Lisbon* (56, Ray Milland); *The Wings of Eagles* (57, Ford), in which Wayne calls her "my Teetian-haired darling"; *Our Man in Havana* (60, Carol Reed); *The Deadly Companions* (61, Sam Peckinpah); *The Parent Trap* (61, David Swift); *Mr. Hobbs Takes a Vacation* (62, Henry Koster); *Spencer's Mountain* (63, Delmer Daves); still making a tempestuous romantic partnership with John Wayne in *McClintock!* (63, Andrew V. McLaglen); *The Battle of the Villa Fiorita* (65, Daves); *The Rare Breed* (66, McLaglen); *How Do I Love Thee?* (70, Michael Gordon); *Big Jake* (71, George Sherman); and *The Red Pony* (73, L. Robert Totten).

She made a lovely comeback in *Only the Lonely*

(91, Chris Columbus), playing John Candy's mother.

Gary Oldman,

b. New Cross, London, 1958

After a dozen or so films, did the public have a better idea of Gary Oldman's own personality than before he began? That is not ingratitude, merely a way of observing that Oldman seems like a blank, anonymous passerby (like someone in Dallas on November 22, 1963, running interference for a real Lee Harvey Oswald), who waits to be occupied by demons. He is a suit hanging in a closet, waiting to be possessed, which means that he brings an uncommon, self-effacing service to his roles. Part of that attitude is his complete and easy readiness not to be liked. So he is both vacant and uningratiating: it will be intriguing to see how long such a career can last.

He had done a good deal of theatre in England, and a few modest movies—*Remembrance* (82, Colin Gregg), *Meantime* (83, Mike Leigh), and *Honest, Decent and True* (85, Les Blair)—before he turned in a performance of unnerving, aggressive immersion as Sid Vicious in *Sid and Nancy* (85, Alex Cox). The switch to Joe Orton in *Prick Up Your Ears* (87, Stephen Frears) was dazzling proof of a genius for impersonation.

Since then, Oldman has had to put up with a lot of poor roles and bad films. Yet his reticence, mixed with his great facility, makes it unlikely that he will ever be more than the victim of whimsical, or desperate, casting calls: *Track 29* (88, Nicolas Roeg); *We Think the World of You* (88, Gregg); *Criminal Law* (89, Martin Campbell); brilliant on TV in *The Firm* (89, Alan Clarke); *Chattahoochee* (89, Mick Jackson); *State of Grace* (90, Phil Joanou); with Tim Roth in *Rosencrantz and Guildenstern Are Dead* (90, Tom Stoppard); on British TV in *Heading Home* (90, David Hare); as Lee Harvey Oswald in *JFK* (91, Oliver Stone).

Then, for Francis Ford Coppola, he played the archetypically pale, enervated prowler after other lives, in *Bram Stoker's Dracula* (92). He had many looks in that film, but none meant more than the self-intoxicated spectacle of the direction. He was a drug dealer, theatrically black, in *True Romance* (93, Tony Scott); and a crooked cop in *Romeo Is Bleeding* (94, Peter Medak).

Oldman has become an international actor, I suppose, but time and again his talent goes to waste. He has directed one film—the remarkable, abrasive *Nil by Mouth* (97), a fair measure of his very tough London. But what is that man doing as Beethoven in the fatuous *Immortal Beloved* (94, Bernard Rose)—and when does a modern actor realize that you don't play Christ, Beethoven, or Francis of Assisi? This is a record of skills perverted and of Oldman's blankness turning increasingly toxic—his own loathing of where he is rises off his movies like mustard gas: *Léon* (94, Luc Besson); *Murder in the First* (95, Marco Rosso); Dimmesdale in the pathetic *Scarlet Letter* (95, Roland Joffe); *Basquiat* (96, Julian Schnabel); *The Fifth Element* (97, Besson); the hijacker in *Air Force One* (97, Wolfgang Petersen); *Lost in Space* (98, Stephen Hopkins); a voice in *Quest for Camelot* (98, Frederik DuChau); Pilate in *Jesus* (99, Roger Young); *The Contender* (00, Rod Lurie); Mason Verger in *Hannibal* (01, Ridley Scott); *Nobody's Baby* (01, David Seltzer); *Interstate 60* (02, Bob Gale); as Satan, with James Brown, in *The Hire* (02, Tony Scott); *Tiptoes* (03, Matthew Bright); *Sin* (03, Michael Stevens).

Lena Olin, b. Stockholm, Sweden, 1956

She is the daughter of the Swedish actor Stig Olin, who was in several Ingmar Bergman films—*Crisis* (45); *To Joy* (49); *This Can't Happen Here* (50)—and directed a few of his own. It was Bergman who promoted the young Lena at the Stockholm Royal Dramatic Theatre and then cast her in his own work: she has a small role as a saleswoman in *Face to Face* (75); she is a nursemaid in *Fanny and Alexander* (82); and she is the young actress (pregnant—as in life) in *After the Rehearsal* (84).

Granted those credentials, and her own beauty and ability, it would seem natural for Olin to become a star in English-language pictures. And she has worked in America for over a decade, often with great impact, without establishing herself: astounding as the sophisticate in *The Unbearable Lightness of Being* (88, Philip Kaufman); nominated as supporting actress for *Enemies: A Love Story* (89, Paul Mazursky); she was the (Ingrid) Bergmanesque lead in *Havana* (90, Sydney Pollack), and that film's failure seems to have affected her prospects badly; *Mr. Jones* (93, Mike Figgis); *Romeo Is Bleeding* (93, Peter Medak); *Night Falls on Manhattan* (97, Sidney Lumet); *Polish Wedding* (98, Theresa Connelly); *Hamilton* (98, Harald Zwart); *Mystery Men* (99, Kinka Usher); *The Ninth Gate* (99, Roman Polanski); *Chocolat* (00, Lasse Hallström—her husband); *Ignition* (01, Yves Simoneau); *Darkness* (01, Jaume Balagueró); *Queen of the Damned* (02, Michael Rymer); in *Alias* on TV; *The United States of Leland* (03, Matthew Ryan Hoge); *Hollywood Homicide* (03, Ron Shelton).

Lord Laurence Olivier (1907–89),

b. Dorking, England

It's easier, in hindsight, to appreciate the brave energy of Olivier. He loved to be a public figure in Britain, and if that reputation relied on his being the great actor, still he became both leader and emblem of the National Theatre. He was devoted to theatre, to Shakespeare, to the church of acting;

and it surely underlined his patriotism that, when he was young, Hollywood never quite took to him, and never crowned him as the new Ronald Colman, an ambition that had preoccupied him. Then, he was the husband to Vivien Leigh who went from novice to Scarlett O'Hara in the brief span of their love affair. She was a greater star and a lesser actor, and a rival in his need for prime attention. In his last years, when he had been retired by the National Theatre, and when large stage parts were too much for him, he told himself he had poverty to avoid, and a legend to protect. All of these pressures played their part in Olivier's curiously fluctuating interest in film.

He was a movie director once: *Henry V* (45), *Hamlet* (48), and *Richard III* (55), famous models that schools hire for students reading the plays. But the first two are more than educational tools. *Richard III* was not much more than the recording of a famous performance: the film settles for melodrama (Olivier had a taste for it—he loved fights, falls, and alarums), and Olivier's rather lurid way with crippled villainy does not carry much weight now (perhaps he was too set on copying Jed Harris). Whereas, *Hamlet,* if slow, is a film noir—a 1948 movie in black and white, full of shadows and brooding, a very clever director's vision in which Olivier's prince is one of the few shortcomings. He's a little too pretty, or smug, for the concept.

Then there is *Henry V,* a film I like more and more as time goes by. It was a project that Olivier only took on when William Wyler and Carol Reed proved unavailable—yet if it resembles anyone, it should be a film by the Archers, Powell, and Pressburger. For it has such magic, gaiety, and flights of fancy: the re-creation of the Globe; the actor clearing his throat to be the king; the fluent shift from staginess to rolling Irish verdure; William Walton's music and the rush of arrows in the air; the look of the very rich hours of the Duc de Berri mixed with the flourish and pride of an England winning its war. And Technicolor. How could the man who made that film show so little interest in returning to cinematic adventure? How could he let *The Prince and the Showgirl* (57) come out so dull and plodding? Was it just because he could not see or credit Marilyn Monroe's crazed potential, because his professionalism was offended, because he liked to keep his pretending as a trick? Or was it that Olivier could never get that excited about women, once the thrill of the young Vivien had gone from his life? He was not happy—don't we feel that?—and he rather cultivated a magnificent solitude.

After that Olivier treated the movies either doubtfully or cynically. Most of his performances were lavishly paid cameos. The National Theatre preoccupied him, and the movies were a way of relaxation and reward. He directed only once

more: *The Three Sisters* (70), which was made with the same careless rush as ruined the film of his *Othello* (65, Stuart Burge). Incidentally, that praised stage performance looks on film like a curry-colored show-off. The only other movie performance that seems to have engaged Olivier was his Archie Rice in *The Entertainer* (60, Tony Richardson). That, too, is embarrassing for its misjudged intimacy and because of the way the actor's schemes can almost be seen and heard. Otherwise, he was aristocratic and sinister in *Spartacus* (60, Stanley Kubrick), flashy but vacuous as the Mahdi in *Khartoum* (66, Basil Dearden), and seemingly bored by *Bunny Lake Is Missing* (65, Otto Preminger).

It is not always realized that Olivier made his film debut in 1930 in the English version of a Lillian Harvey movie, *The Temporary Widow* (Gustav Ucicky). In those days, he was unmistakably a romantic lead, much less squeamish about the threadbare material offered by movies. By 1931, he was in Hollywood under contract to RKO: *Friends and Lovers* (31, Victor Schertzinger), with Ann Harding in *Westward Passage* (32, Robert Milton); and, on loan to Fox, *The Yellow Ticket* (31, Raoul Walsh). But he was not happy in America and came back to London to make *Perfect Understanding* (33, Cyril Gardner) with Gloria Swanson. Garbo politely rejected him for *Queen Christina* and Olivier stayed in England as Orlando to Elizabeth Bergner's Rosalind in *As You Like It* (36, Paul Czinner) and *Fire Over England* (37, William K. Howard).

He made *21 Days* (37, Basil Dean), *The Divorce of Lady X* (38, Tim Whelan), and *Q-Planes* (39, Whelan and Arthur Woods) before accepting Goldwyn's invitation to return to America to play Heathcliff in *Wuthering Heights* (39, Wyler). It was a good part for him, and it raised his standing, but he knew the film was a folly. He stayed on as Darcy in *Pride and Prejudice* (40, Robert Z. Leonard) and Maxim de Winter in *Rebecca* (40, Alfred Hitchcock)—the latter by far the best film he had been involved with and Hitchcock's first portrait of the attractive man unable to digest his "secret" past. In America, he made *That Hamilton Woman* (41, Alexander Korda) as Nelson opposite his then-wife, Vivien Leigh; as Frenchie in *49th Parallel* (41, Michael Powell); and *The Demi-Paradise* (43, Anthony Asquith). Only a few more performances need to be mentioned: in *Carrie* (52, Wyler)—his Hurstwood is a masterpiece of crushed hope; as Macheath in *The Beggar's Opera* (53, Peter Brook); an urbane Burgoyne in *The Devil's Disciple* (59, Guy Hamilton); *Term of Trial* (62, Peter Glenville); and *Sleuth* (72, Joseph L. Mankiewicz). So much diversity, but with a mixture of self-effacement and time-serving. If only Olivier could have blended his middle-aged underplaying with his zest for the medium and glamour in the 1930s. As it is, his underplaying hogs the screen in *Lady Caroline Lamb* (72, Robert Bolt), but is abandoned in *Sleuth,* where it might have redeemed the cross-plot of identity from such a wearying wealth of high Shaftesbury cleverness.

Converted into a Lord and beset by ill-health and the prolonged gestation of the British National Theatre, his movies were either ways of getting away from demanding work or means to provide for his children: a fearful but remote villain in *Marathon Man* (76, John Schlesinger); *A Bridge Too Far* (77, Richard Attenborough); as a founding father of the Detroit auto industry in *The Betsy* (78, Daniel Petrie), in which visible distress owed itself to grave illness, the struggle to master the American accent, having to screw every woman in the picture, and the realization that with just a little less taste the picture could have been one of the most memorable pieces of high schlock. Looking frailer than ever, he contrived to swamp dignity and pain with mannerism in *The Boys from Brazil* (78, Franklin Schaffner), stole screen time from the pleasant kids in *A Little Romance* (79, George Roy Hill), and appeared in *Dracula* (79, John Badham).

In his last decade, he was either very sick, or working desperately to provide for his little ones—in all manner of rogue films. Another interpretation is that he could not stop acting, and that even illness had become a performance. In fact, his late interviews are often better value than the films. Long before death, Olivier realized he had an immortality that could sustain any whim or oddity in his work. He was not simply a great actor; he was the human being as actor.

The last films are *The Jazz Singer* (80, Richard Fleischer); *Clash of the Titans* (81, Desmond Davis); the blind father in *A Voyage Round My Father* (81, Alvin Rakoff); Lord Marchmain in *Brideshead Revisited* (81, Charles Sturridge and Michael Lindsay-Hogg); *King Lear* (82, Michael Elliott) for television; Douglas MacArthur in *Inchon!* (82, Terence Young); *Wagner* (83, Tony Palmer); *A Talent for Murder* (83, Rakoff); *The Jigsaw Man* (84, Young); *The Bounty* (84, Roger Donaldson); *The Last Days of Pompeii* (84, Peter Hunt); *Wild Geese II* (85, Hunt); *Peter the Great* (86, Marvin J. Chomsky and Lawrence Schiller); and *War Requiem* (88, Derek Jarman).

Ermanno Olmi, b. Bergamo, Italy, 1931
1959: *Il Tempo si è Fermato/Time Stood Still.* 1961: *Il Posto.* 1962: *I Fidanzati/The Engagement.* 1964: *E Venne un Uomo/A Man Named John.* 1968: *Un Certo Giorno/One Fine Day.* 1969: *Il Recuperanti/The Scavengers.* 1971: *Durante l'Estate/During the Summer.* 1974: *La Circostanza/The Circumstance.* 1978: *L'Albero degli Zoccoli/The Tree of the Wooden Clogs; Cam-*

mina Cammina/Keep Walking. 1987: *Lunga Vita alla Signora/Long Live the Lady.* 1988: *La Leggenda del Santo Bevitore/The Legend of the Holy Drinker.* 1993: *Il Segreto del Bosco Vecchio/The Secret of the Old Wood.* 1994: *Genesi: La Creazione e il Diluvio.* 1999: *Il Denaro non Esiste* (codirected with Alberto Rondalli). 2000: *Il Mestiere delle Armi.* 2002: *Cantando dietro I Pararenti.*

The uneventful life of a clerk—like that of the young man in *Il Posto*—led Olmi into more creative work. Having worked as an actor and producer in the theatre, he made industrial documentaries in the late 1950s before his first feature, a study of a veteran and a younger man living together in isolation because of their work on a dam project.

Olmi is a director in a reticent, elliptical, and detached vein that is not characteristically Italian. Equally, it is not easy to fix him in neo-realism, despite his preference for real settings, ordinary people, and slight plots. Although he has professed a debt to de Sica, his near-mystical tenderness for people is more impressive than de Sica's sentiment, and the most intriguing element in his films seems closer to the abstracting eye of an Antonioni.

In *Time Stood Still,* the elements of human kindliness and documentary observation of work rested on a gradual distillation of the relations between the two men. At his best—in *I Fidanzati*—Olmi achieves a subtle mastery of apparent visual simplicity to suggest complex emotions. The subject of the film is very plain—the separation of a couple because of the job the man must take. But the filming of it wonderfully suggests the feeling of separation and melancholy through the concentration on ordinary street scenes and interiors and the use of natural silence. Olmi's true subject is the state of mind made manifest in a way of seeing undramatic reality. *I Fidanzati* is an ostensibly neutral account that, we suddenly realize, is so subjective as to be nearly hallucinatory.

The quality has been present, too, in *Il Posto* (which is generally closer to neo-realistic sentiment) and *Durante l'Estate*—the first, promising sign of comedy in Olmi with a note of Chaplinesque social criticism and a defense of eccentrics that veers toward whimsicality.

E Venne un Uomo is too dutiful and vague a life story of Pope John XXIII, while the other films were made for Italian television. *I Recuperanti* repeated the relationship of *Time Stood Still.* This time the two men recover ironmongery from battlefields. As well as the evolving relationship between them, Olmi is commenting on the way a war's wounds heal. The observation is clear, sympathetic, and amusing, but Olmi still seems passive, too deeply rooted in a laudable but commonplace humanism: "I am interested in 'producing' ideas. In order to distribute these ideas, it seems to me that the cinema is the most useful medium of our times. So I make films because I desire to talk about the reality of the times in which I live, in other words I desire to express ideas and propose them to the largest number of people. The only unit of measure for me, the only point of reference, the only common denominator is Man."

There is a hint of the evangelical bureaucrat about that, a conventional sensitivity belied by the subtlety of Olmi's style. Visually, he is not far short of being austere; yet that suggests an intensity that he seems shy of. A question mark hangs over Olmi, as if he needed some gust of passion or surrealism to free him from the aspirations of realism.

His masterpiece is *The Tree of the Wooden Clogs,* a peasant epic set in Lombardy at the end of the nineteenth century, yet made with innate fondness for the commonplace and for humble attitudes. The daily routine blends effortlessly into a spiritual perspective so that the three-hour movie is like a religious panorama, a mix of Breughel and neo-realism. Since then, Olmi has worked less frequently. But he is his own man, a devout Catholic, cameraman and editor as well as director, determined on an unstressed view of life.

His version of Genesis is a kind of revery, with a narrative read by Paul Scofield, while his latest film would seem to be a story about the innovative impact of artillery.

Marcel Ophüls,

b. Frankfurt, Germany, 1927

1962: Munich episode from *L'Amour à Vingt Ans.* 1963: *Peaux de Bananes.* 1965: *Feu à Volonté.* 1967: *München* (d). 1969: *Le Chagrin et la Pitié/The Sorrow and the Pity* (d). 1972: *A Sense of Loss* (d). 1975: *The Memory of Justice* (d). 1980: *Kortner Geschichte* (d). 1988: *Hotel Terminus: Klaus Barbie, His Life and Times* (d). 1992: *November Days* (d). 1994: *Veillées d'Armes* (d).

The itinerant life Marcel Ophüls led as a child has surely affected the political and philosophical discrimination of most of his documentaries. Their chief target is nationalist confidence, and the crimes done in its name. Their obvious, but decent and hard-earned, message is for individual responsibility that will resist the surge of righteousness, especially when it calls itself manifest destiny. No personal ideological allegiance shows in Ophüls's work. His pictures have the dogged tone and density of a lawyer's self-examination. Stylistic flourishes and rhetorical ploys never occur to the dry conscience that produces them. Yet it is to Marcel's credit that he reveres his father (Max) and aspires one day to make movies like *Madame de . . .* and *Lola Montès.* Father and son do not seem close as artists, but they both know how headstrong people can be and they

both present the implacable touchstones of time, death, and the records. Marcel is the more honorable documentarist because of his commitment to observe impartially but with sympathy; he is not that far from the master of ceremonies's helpless amusement in *La Ronde.*

Still, Marcel's own comedies—*Peaux de Bananes* and *Feu à Volonté*—do not challenge the supremacy of his father's art. The son's wish to be lighter may only be the conscientious guarding against gravity. He says that his inquiries into some of the wounds of modern history were merely assignments. I think that is ingenuous when the pictures make such demands on audiences and have brought so many problems to their maker. Let Marcel follow his own path and admit a sense of duty; there are ample subjects along the way deserving his attention.

He went with his father to France in 1933, and then to America in 1941, as the survival of Jews became more threatened. And just as he commands several languages and understands many national insecurities, so Ophüls is happy in English and attracted to American culture. He attended Hollywood High School and he served from 1945 to 1947 in the Far East in the American army. He dropped out of the Sorbonne when it denied his proposed doctoral thesis—on the links between fashion and philosophy—and, in the seventies, a brief service at CBS ended when the network wanted him to make a conventional program on McCarthyism, rather than an essay entitled "Fred Astaire and the Protestant Work Ethic."

As an adolescent, he appeared in Frank Capra's *Prelude to War* (42), and in the fifties he was an assistant to John Huston, on *Moulin Rouge* (53), and to his father, on *Lola Montès* (55). He worked for a German TV station and came into movies on the tail end of the New Wave. His French features are not notable, and in 1967 he joined ORTF and made a thirty-two-hour documentary on the 1938 Munich crisis, using newsreel and interviews with participants. That has always been his method, with the aim of creating an intricate web of contrary or unresolved opinions that slowly turn into historical argument and pleas for rational, judicial compromise. The visual sense is neither strong nor cultivated: TV's influence shows there. Time and again, one needs to listen to views and test statements rather than appreciate an exposed person. That may show a lack of flair, a prohibition of melodrama, or thorough investigative caution. It also pertains to the thought that it is safer to like people than to trust them—an implicit conclusion of Max's films and a cautionary enough attitude for any filmmaker to dissolve boundaries of fact and fiction. It serves to make the length of Marcel's films a considerable obstacle—proof of worthiness or necessary fullness? One conclusion from his best films is that the topics he has chosen demand book treatment, and that it is risky to give any hint in film's decisiveness that a solution is possible.

The Sorrow and the Pity deals with the German occupation of France, and the variety of moral reactions offered by the French; *A Sense of Loss,* with the Irish problem; and *The Memory of Justice,* with the practice and philosophy of war crimes and retribution. The first is far and away the best because it is so intriguing a picture of everyday hypocrisy and compromise—superb subjects for film, since the straight face cannot quite hide its duplicity. *A Sense of Loss* seems the least sure of all its historical facts, and much more vulnerable to the shrill pleading of its interested parties. To the extent that it is the most partial of his films, it is the weakest and the most open to challenge. *The Memory of Justice* is an elaborate, worthy essay that stumbles in the attempt to find a coherent pattern in different war crimes—chiefly, the German and the Japanese from 1939 to 1945, and the American in Vietnam. Earnestness easily seems didactic, and Ophüls is well aware of how readily film can distort ideas and load facts. He may be the victim of the size and intractability of the subject, and of the scant human ground it refers to. The local flavor of *The Sorrow and the Pity* is its greatest asset, just as the film is more touching because it does not leave an impossible question for the viewer to answer. The French film makes us realize how we might have behaved from day to day, but *The Memory of Justice* confronts us with so great a dilemma that it is easier to fall asleep. Film records surfaces and moments too avidly for it to be much help in forming the wisdom that can settle issues. You go along with film or bend to its suggestion; you do not assume the certainty of a judge.

Hotel Terminus was better than anything that had gone before—rich, complex, humane, mysterious, and determinedly calm. It was also France, again, a country whose lies and truth Ophüls finds especially intriguing. In Ophüls's documentaries, film has shown an ability to contribute to the large cause of history that leaves in question even the best fictional war films—as well as the daily grind of TV news.

His most recent film is a study of the journalistic process in Sarajevo and Yugoslavia, not as searching as his best work, but more filled with immediate pain.

Max Ophüls (Max Oppenheimer) (1902–57), b. Sarrebruck, Germany
1930: *Dann Schon Lieber Lebertran.* 1931: *Die Verliebte Firma.* 1932: *Die Verkaufte Braut; Die Lachenden Erben; Liebelei.* 1933: *Une Histoire d'Amour* (a remake of *Liebelei*). 1934: *On a Volé un Homme; La Signora di Tutti.* 1935: *Divine.* 1936: *Valse Brillante de Chopin* (s); *Ave Maria de Schubert* (s); *Komedie om Geld; La Tendre Ennemie.* 1937: *Yoshiwara.* 1938: *Werther; Sans Lendemain.* 1940: *De Mayerling à Sarajevo; L'École des Femmes* (uncompleted). 1947: *The Exile.* 1948: *Letter From an Unknown Woman.* 1949: *Caught; The Reckless Moment.* 1950: *Vendetta* (Ophüls directed part of this film, as did Preston Sturges, Stuart Heisler, its producer Howard Hughes, and Mel Ferrer, to whom it was finally credited); *La Ronde.* 1952: *Le Plaisir.* 1953: *Madame de . . .* 1955: *Lola Montès.*

In June 1960, in the third part of a season of French films, the London National Film Theatre showed the best version available of *Lola Montès.* The season itself, organized by Richard Roud, is one for which I will always be grateful. Above all, it had placed Renoir in his rightful eminence. But it had introduced me to several other major figures and, because it coincided with the incoming tide of the New Wave, it served to stress the abiding themes and vitality of French cinema. I was at film school then and I recognized Renoir as a cinematic ideal to which the young spectator or filmmaker could best aspire. Roud's presence at the NFT also meant a reassessment of American cinema: that third part of the French season, for instance, was followed by an Orson Welles retrospective. But I had never seen a Max Ophüls film and, since *Lola Montès* came at the end of the season, I went to it a little dutifully, complacently full with new lessons learned.

In that mood, I might have missed the point of *Lola Montès* but for the company of a Belgian friend who insisted in advance on the extraordinary experience I was about to have, nudged me throughout the film to let me know that I was not dreaming, and—against the contented sighs that used to greet the end of any film in those days—badgered me into joining in applause, so fierce and isolated that it reawakened the curiosity of the audience. However, once they had satisfied themselves that it was not a fight breaking out, only two young men noisily clapping—and since, evidently, we could only be responding to the film—they smiled good-naturedly and shuffled out.

Too aware of the journey in appreciation I had already made, and of the way my response was being prompted, I doubt if I felt deeply about *Lola Montès* at the time. It took further viewings, of that and other films, to discover the justice of my reaction. To talk of Ophüls then was to meet ignorance or bland assertions that he was a frivolous, romantic director, concerned with decoration rather than content, a stylist for style's sake, a chronic camera fidget.

Well, as Richard Roud and my Belgian friend knew then, and I know now, Max Ophüls is one of the greatest of film directors. He is frivolous only if it is frivolous to be obsessed by the gap between the ideal and the reality of love.

"Obsessed" is the crucial word. There are many authorities who describe Ophüls as adhering to "the cynical sentimentalism of an older Europe." Penelope Houston wrote that in a passage that quoted approvingly from Peter Ustinov's obituary on Ophüls: "like a watchmaker intent on making the smallest watch in the world and then, with a sudden flash of perversity, putting it up on a cathedral." Ophüls might have smiled to read such withering inappropriateness from the man who played his alter ego in *Lola Montès*. Of course, the epitaph is affectionate and admiring, but it is condescending. What gives it away is the unwitting use of an image so close to Ophüls's art, so uncannily reflective of his greatness.

The cinema offers very few easy careers, and Ophüls's was insecure and peripatetic—characteristics of his films—and yet he pursued certain themes with undeterred ardor. First, consider the idea of circularity. Cinematically, that was embodied in full 360-degree pans or by breathtaking tracks round the circumference of some emotional arena. In *Lola Montès*, when Lola arrives in the circus ring to reenact scenes from her life, she is enthroned on a turntable. As it revolves in one direction so the camera tracks around her in the reverse direction: is that merely and frivolously beautiful? Or is it only beautiful because of the way it expresses the contrariness of her life in which past and present, hopes and reality, move in sight of one another, but never in unison?

Lola's turntable is the last revolving machine in Ophüls's work. *Le Plaisir*, taken from three Maupassant stories, includes *La Modèle*, a story about a painter in the habit of making mistresses of his models. But one girl is less easily discarded when the time comes for a replacement. Instead, she tries suicide, but succeeds only in crippling herself so that the softhearted exploiter is compelled to marry her. That wing of a triptych is worth recounting for it shows that women were not always victims in Ophüls's work, just as men could seem lechers, lovers, or philosophers from moment to moment; indeed, he saw everyone as the victim of his or her own shifting emotions. And although the original story offers no basis for it, Ophüls has the painter painting the girl as a figure astride a horse on a carousel. The movement in Ophüls is enchanting but foreboding: the poignant manifestation of exhilaration that will fade. *La Ronde*, of course, is the mechanism of an entire film, the means by which human beings encounter transitory happiness as they demonstrate their own fickleness and mortality.

The fairground toy gives *La Ronde* a structure adored by Ophüls. It allows a consequential chain of meetings to come full circle: you may call that a piece of Viennese playfulness, but it is also a resigned viewing of the passing of the sperm. In *Madame de . . .* Ophüls uses a pair of earrings, working their way from person to person, to illuminate the small domestic tragedy.

It is the essence of such circularity, and of the carousel's motion, that people stay in their posture, but that time changes, dramatically altering their circumstances. In many of his films, Ophüls takes in a great span of time, or makes a briefer period seem enormous, by the interchange of episodes, or the rhythm of flashback and present. In *Lola Montès*, the circus performance allows Lola to revive crucial fragments of her life. More than twenty years before, Isa Miranda's actress had the same structure of experience in *La Signora di Tutti*. *La Tendre Ennemie* is set at a party attended by ghosts, whose flashbacks endorse their present efforts to prevent a loveless marriage. *Liebelei* allows death to reflect back on life. *Caught* puts a felt love in conflict with notional romance.

It is principally in the sense of remembrance making up for unhappiness, or fixing tragedy forever, and of time advancing as exquisitely as his tracking camera that Ophüls is a tragic artist. If film is essentially the capacity to show a moment of drama or change as it happens, then Ophüls's films are uniquely attuned to such transience. Changing time is the central consciousness, and the subtle ways in which it changes the subjective experience of what happened at any moment is his most poignant realization. Admit time's ceaseless, calm advance, and you fall in love as a means to falling out of love—as Renoir quotes from Beaumarchais at the beginning of *La Règle du Jeu*, "Why has Cupid wings, if not to fly away again?" But this transitory creature, man, has consuming romantic passions. Far from cynical, Ophüls concedes that a sense of transience makes love seem no less affecting when it comes. The ability to rationalize one's feelings leads to this self-deception. What better illustration than the bedroom scene in *La Ronde* between Daniel Gélin and Danielle Darrieux? Their assignation has faltered. Darrieux has come to him to become his mistress, but time is pressing. "What time is it?" she asks persistently, for she cannot stay long. But Gélin cannot deal with her either swiftly or slowly enough to stop that distracting question. They go to bed, but then he is briefly impotent. Her worry is replaced by tenderness (again the awareness of feminine power) and when she asks what time it is, that is a ruse to stretch her bare arm in front of him to his coat on a chair beside the bed. The arm restores his amorousness and the sequence ends in fulfillment as the camera observes the coat that contains his watch—one other roundabout.

The watch, therefore, is huge, whatever Ustinov may have fancied. It is as large as *La Ronde*, as far-reaching as the flashback, and as spacious as the circus ring in *Lola Montès*—where Ustinov himself stood, whip in hand, conducting proceedings, but as much in love with Lola as every other man in her life. Those contrary circles are like wheels within a watch. Ophüls's is the cinema of movement because time and the heart die when they stand still. His films are not decorated by movement, they consist of it. Thus, in *Caught,* the slow track across the dance floor becomes James Mason's decision to propose to Barbara Bel Geddes.

That, in itself, is a vindication of cinema, which asserts that the moment never stays to be studied, it can only be participated in. There is nothing petty or shameful in responding to the crane and tracking shots of Max Ophüls, they are the mainstream of cinema. Just as time never stands still, so feelings never stay certain, and Ophüls's camera must move on because it conforms to the nature of the celluloid strip where still pictures become alive only so long as they keep pace with time.

And look—I haven't even mentioned *Letter From an Unknown Woman,* which is only a perfect film, and only less obvious because it is a rehearsal for the greater tragedy of *Madame de. . . .* But *Letter* makes Joan Fontaine a youth, a romantic young woman, and then a victim; it employs the solemn handsomeness and self-regard of Louis Jourdan to wonderful effect; it makes a quite credible Vienna and Linz; and in its melodic variations on staircases, carriages, rooms, glances, and meetings, it is a film about forgetfulness and the inescapable rhyming of separate times. No one had more sympathy for love than Ophüls, but no one knew so well how lovers remained unknown, strangers.

Julia Ormond, b. Epsom, England, 1965

I say it without glee or joy, but Julia Ormond probably shouldn't be here. For her early stardom was a mystery, as well as easy evidence that so many acting careers perish very quickly. (On the other hand, Jeanne Tripplehorn was cast in lead roles over a full seven years, so there's no reasoning.)

Ms. Ormond was seen on television in *Traffik* (89, Alastair Reid), *Young Catherine* (91, Michael Anderson), and *Stalin* (92, Ivan Passer), and that led to the year in which she had three lead parts: Guinevere in *First Knight* (95, Jerry Zucker); *Legends of the Fall* (95, Edward Zwick); and *Sabrina* (95, Sydney Pollack). Isn't that enough in the way of opportunity or exposure, even if Ormond showed promise in *The Baby of Macon* (93, Peter Greenaway); as the dentist who falls for prisoner Tim Roth in *Captives* (95, Angela Pope); *Nostradamus* (94, Roger Christian)?

However, once the curtains had started to close—as it were—Ms. Ormond showed a tougher and much more interesting persona in at least the first half of *Smilla's Sense of Snow* (97, Bille

August). If she'd done that first and avoided the black hole of *Sabrina,* who knows what might have happened? She was also in *The Barber of Siberia* (98, Nikita Mikhalkov) and did a voice in the TV *Animal Farm* (99, John Stephenson). Of late, she has done notably little: *The Prime Gig* (00, Gregory Mosher); *Varian's War* (00, Lionel Chetwynd) for TV; *Resistance* (02, Todd Komarnicki).

Nagisa Oshima, b. Kyoto, Japan, 1932

1959: *Ai to Kibo no Machi/A Town of Love and Hope.* 1960: *Seishun Zankoku Monogatari/Naked Youth, a Story of Cruelty; Taiyo no Hakaba/The Sun's Burial; Nihon no Yoru to Kirz/Night and Fog in Japan.* 1961: *Shiiku/The Catch.* 1962: *Amukusa Shiro Tokisada/The Rebel.* 1965: *Etsuraku/The Pleasures of the Flesh; Yunbogi no Nikki/The Diary of Yunbogi.* 1966: *Hakuchu no Torima/Violence at Noon.* 1967: *Ninja Bugeicho/Band of Ninja; Nihon Shunka-ko/A Treatise on Japanese Bawdy Song.* 1968: *Daitoa enso/The Pacific War; Koshikei/Death by Hanging; Kaeyyekita Yopparai/Three Resurrected Drunkards; Shinjuku Dorobo Nikki/Diary of a Shinjuku Thief.* 1969: *Shonen/Boy; Mo Taku-To to Bunkadaikatumei/Mao Tse-tung and the Cultural Revolution.* 1971: *Tokyo; Senso Sengo Hiwa/He Died After the War; Gishiki/The Ceremony.* 1972: *Natsu no Imoto/Dear Summer Sister.* 1976: *Ai no Corrida/In the Realm of the Senses.* 1978: *Ai no Borei/Empire of Passion.* 1982: *Merry Christmas, Mr. Lawrence.* 1987: *Max Mon Amour.* 1991: *Kyoto, My Mother's Place* (d). 1994: *100 Years of Japanese Cinema* (d). 1999: *Gohatto/Taboo.*

Japanese cinema in the 1960s produced a battery of young talent, but none as serious, precise, or versatile as Oshima. Arguably, he was the first Japanese director who seemed to be functioning within a totally modern world. He had rejected the period film and grappled with the agonizing forces compelling Japan to choose between its traditions and modernity. Much of his early work is still unknown in the West, but his subject matter indicates the new postwar consciousness: *The Sun's Burial* is a picture of a seething slum community; *The Catch* deals with a Negro soldier taken prisoner during the war.

But it was in 1968 that Oshima made his decisive impact with *Death by Hanging* and *Diary of a Shinjuku Thief.* The first is the story of the execution of a young Korean who had raped and killed two Japanese girls. It has the icy clarity of composition, scraped clean of direct emotional associations, and with the first evidence of Oshima's almost surrealist eye for the ritual workings of Japanese society. As for *Shinjuku Thief,* it is not fanciful to compare it with the Buñuel of *L'Age d'Or,* for it sees animal self-expression as being in brutal confrontation with social mores and the codes of Japanese living. Like Buñuel, Oshima is effortlessly shocking but always chaste, watching the vivid sexual performance of his characters as if they were insects.

Oshima has shown a taste for dramatic human stories that are metaphors of the recent history of Japan. *Boy,* an extraordinary account of a wandering family that fake road accidents for insurance settlements, as well as having great narrative interest, is a portrait of the moral confrontations forced upon the new Japan.

But his masterpiece is *The Ceremony,* a bleak but luminous picture of how domestic ritual destroys or perverts the life force in a family. Once again, the stinging touch of a Buñuel is evident in the scenes like that in which the young mistress is discovered bound to a tree dead and, as the camera circles, the sword is drawn out of her body and an arc of blood jumps out behind it.

In the Realm of the Senses and *Empire of Passion* were erotic events of the 1970s, provoking censorship and controversy, and treating the body with a new graphic directness seldom free from sadomasochism. These films made Oshima famous, but they seemed calculated sensations compared with his earlier films. There was worse to come. *Merry Christmas, Mr. Lawrence* was a story about British and Australians in a Japanese prisoner-of-war camp, but it was also smitten with the aura of David Bowie—in short, it came out bizarre, confused, and with little bearing on reality. In trying for an international picture, Oshima had lost his roots. *Max Mon Amour* attempted to describe the love between a woman and a gorilla—and it made *King Kong* seem ever better than one had thought. Oshima must be regarded now as a major example of fatal hesitation or misdirection.

Oshima was then hampered by illness for many years. In response, he turned to documentary and work for television. But in 1999, he returned with the remarkable *Gohatto*—a triumph of style and wit, dazzlingly beautiful, and full of poetic innuendo about gender and role-playing. It was so complete a return that Oshima was automatically reacclaimed as a master.

Haley Joel Osment, b. Los Angeles, 1988
Young Mr. Osment has been good (at least) on screen too many times now for anyone to have doubts. He is a brilliantly skilled and intuitive actor who carries the natural, and ordinary, charm of childhood without ever milking it. It's not possible, or useful, to wonder what he might be like grown up. But it is instructive to consider how far modern filmmakers now like to employ child characters to reach their audience, but also to mine the more timeless and universal aura of the child's experience. So it's notable how often Osment has been used as the emblem of some greater, or purer,

knowledge of life that may exist in a child. To that extent, of course, his growing up is not only beside the point; it may be counterproductive.

He is the son of a teacher and an actor (Eugene Osment), and he appeared in his first TV commercial when he was only four. He then got a role in the TV series *Thunder Alley* (94) and the role of Tom Hanks's son in *Forrest Gump* (94, Robert Zemeckis). Still, he had those normal, dues-paying years before his big breakthrough in *The Sixth Sense: Mixed Nuts* (94, Nora Ephron); a lead role, a woeful orphan, in *Bogus* (96, Norman Jewison); *Last Stand at Saber River* (97, Dick Lowry); redoing the George Winslow role for TV in *The Ransom of Red Chief* (98, Bob Clark).

The Sixth Sense (99, M. Night Shyamalan) was an exceptional film, a very canny merger of horror and those few movies that deal in a child's perception of the immense world. He gave a fine performance, much aided by Bruce Willis and his director, both of whom could truly claim that it would have been impossible without the kid. In turn, *Pay It Forward* (00, Mimi Leder) was a horrible exploitation in which the boy's grace barely survived. Far more intriguing was *A.I.: Artificial Intelligence* (01, Steven Spielberg), in which Osment was uncannily good as the robot/puppet coming to life, but ultimately betrayed by the inability of his director to keep control of the very ambitious material.

His voice is used in *The Country Bears* (02, Peter Hastings). He did other voice jobs and then reappeared as a teenager in *Secondhand Lions* (03, Tim McCanlies).

Gerd Oswald (1916–89), b. Berlin
1956: *A Kiss Before Dying; The Brass Legend.* 1957: *Fury at Sundown; Valerie; Crime of Passion.* 1958: *Paris Holiday; Screaming Mimi.* 1959: *Am Tag als der Regen Kam.* 1960: *Three Moves to Freedom/Schachnovelle.* 1961: *Brainwashed.* 1963: *Tempestà su Ceylon.* 1965: *Agent for H.A.R.M.* 1969: *80 Steps to Jonah.* 1970: *Bunny O'Hare.*

The son of German director Richard Oswald (1880–1963), Gerd worked all over Europe as an assistant director in the late 1930s, and in 1940 he went to America. He was assistant to Litvak, Kazan, Mankiewicz, Hathaway, King, Wilder, and Stevens and on his father's *The Loveable Cheat* (49). He was producer of *Man on a Tightrope* (53, Kazan), *Oasis* (54, Yves Allégret), and *Night People* (54, Nunnally Johnson) before becoming a director.

In the space of five years, when the film industry was revealing little enterprise and few fresh talents, Oswald showed some skill with the low-budget quickie. In fact, his first film, based on an Ira Levin novel, was a large project, and proved a tense, ingenious thriller, with an exciting climax at an industrial plant and with excellent performances from Robert Wagner and Joanne Woodward. *Fury at Sundown* and *Valerie* were enjoyable Westerns, the latter being that paradox, a complex film involving Anita Ekberg; *Crime of Passion* was an outstanding thriller with Barbara Stanwyck and Sterling Hayden. *Paris Holiday* was a canceling out of Bob Hope and Fernandel, but *Three Moves to Freedom,* about a man in prison obsessed by chess, was as good as anything he had done. After that, Oswald found TV more receptive than movies. His work there was prolific but far less interesting.

Peter O'Toole,

b. Connemara, Ireland, 1933

The 1960s was a period of foundering for commercial cinema, and rather than true stars it produced quasars—quasi-stellar personalities. One of those, it seems to me, is Peter O'Toole, a striking but unnerving figure. His blue eyes were pale and staring, and drama exaggerated the strain in his face.

After national service in the navy, O'Toole went into the theatre and had a big success in *The Long and the Short and the Tall.* He made a promising film debut in *Kidnapped* (60, Robert Stevenson) and, uncredited, as the Mountie rescued by Anthony Quinn in *The Savage Innocents* (60, Nicholas Ray). After *The Day They Robbed the Bank of England* (60, John Guillermin), he played *Lawrence of Arabia* (62, David Lean) with a desperate intensity as unrevealing as it was uncharacteristic of the director. While Lean was content for a placid historical epic, with a curt nod toward the Lawrence enigma, O'Toole seemed to be searching in a smaller, more neurotically based film.

Becket (64, Peter Glenville) was what passes for a film of ideas: but concentration on literary meaning only made O'Toole sound like the Player King. *Lord Jim* (65, Richard Brooks) was a box-office flop that might have ended his career, but he was given another chance: hysterical and implausible as the object of so much female interest in *What's New, Pussycat?* (65, Clive Donner); *How to Steal a Million* (66, William Wyler); *The Bible* (66, John Huston); *The Night of the Generals* (67, Anatole Litvak); *The Lion in Winter* (68, Anthony Harvey); *Great Catherine* (68, Gordon Flemyng); *Goodbye, Mr. Chips* (69, Herbert Ross); *Murphy's War* (71, Peter Yates); *Country Dance* (71, J. Lee Thompson); *Under Milk Wood* (72, Andrew Sinclair); *The Ruling Class* (72, Peter Medak); *Man of La Mancha* (72, Arthur Hiller); *Rosebud* (75, Otto Preminger); *Man Friday* (75, Jack Gold); *Coup d'Etat* (78, Martyn Burke); *The Stunt Man* (78, Richard Rush); and *Zulu Dawn* (79, Douglas Hickox).

He was nominated as best actor for *The Stunt*

Man, a picture that drew upon O'Toole's magnificent, if end-of-his-tether, charm. As he grew older, and battled alcoholism, he could look and behave like his own ghost. He could overact; he could be ridiculous. But he was never dull, and often riveting: as the Roman in *Masada* (80, Boris Sagal) on TV; in *Caligula* (80, Tinto Brass); nominated again for best actor and elegantly hilarious in *My Favorite Year* (82, Richard Benjamin); with Jodie Foster on TV as *Svengali* (83, Harvey). Also on British television, he played Sherlock Holmes a few times with perfect authority. He was in *Supergirl* (84, Jeannot Szwarc); as an Indian in *Kim* (84, John Davies); *Creator* (85, Ivan Passer); *Club Paradise* (86, Harold Ramis); magnificently starchy as the English tutor in *The Last Emperor* (87, Bernardo Bertolucci); *High Spirits* (88, Neil Jordan); *Crossing to Freedom* (90, Norman Stone); *Wings of Fame* (90, Otakar Votocek); *King Ralph* (91, David S. Ward); *Rebecca's Daughters* (91, Karl Francis); and *The Seventh Coin* (92, Dror Soref).

His later years have been distinguished by his haunting gauntness, his record of seven unrewarded Oscar nominations, his autobiography—beginning with *Loitering with Intent* (1992)—his stage success in *Jeffrey Bernard Is Unwell,* his ragbag of parts on television and his sheer survival: *Civvies* (92, Francis); *Heavy Weather* (95, Jack Gold), a TV series; the Emperor of Lilliput in *Gulliver's Travels* (96, Charles Sturridge); as Conan Doyle in *FairyTale* (97, Sturridge); *Phantoms* (98, Joe Chappelle); *Coming Home* (98, Giles Foster); *The Manor* (99, Ken Berris); *Molokai: The Story of Father Damien* (99, Paul Cox); as Cauchon in *Joan of Arc* (99, Christian Duguay); *Jeffrey Bernard Is Unwell* (99, Tom Kinniment and O'Toole); *The Final Curtain* (01, Patrick Harkins); *Global Heresy* (01, Sidney J. Furie).

Maria Ouspenskaya (1876–1949),

b. Tula, Russia

If there had been no Maria Ouspenskaya, Hollywood would have had to invent one. For half a dozen years she was indispensable to any big-budget movie that required a shriveled old lady with an autocratic air and a strong accent. To the industry she was the goods, given her background with Stanislavsky and her successes on Broadway after she turned up in America, in 1923, on a Moscow Art Theatre tour, and stayed. Her first Hollywood movie was Wyler's wonderful *Dodsworth* (1936), in which she is an Austrian baroness, laying down the law to poor aging Ruth Chatterton. (It was a role she had done on stage.) As further proof of her nobility, she was a countess in the Garbo-Boyer *Conquest* (37, Clarence Brown) and a maharani in *The Rains Came* (39, Brown), even a queen (though only an Amazon queen) in *Tarzan and the Amazons* (45, Kurt Neumann). But mostly she was a madame: Madame Olga Kirowa (her best role, Vivien Leigh's stern ballet mistress) in the 1940 *Waterloo Bridge* (Mervyn LeRoy); Madame Lydia Basilova in *Dance, Girl, Dance* (40, Dorothy Arzner); Madame Tanya in *Beyond Tomorrow* (40, A. Edward Sutherland); Madame Cecile Roget in *The Mystery of Marie Roget* (42, Phil Rosen); Madame von Eln in *King's Row* (42, Sam Wood); Madame Goronoff in *I've Always Loved You* (46, Frank Borzage); Madame Karina in her last film, *A Kiss in the Dark* (49, Delmer Daves).

To be fair, she had a democratic streak: she was Boyer's non-noble French grandmother in McCarey's *Love Affair* (39); an Austrian peasant—Jimmy Stewart's mother!—in *The Mortal Storm* (40, Borzage); a grandmother here, a frau there, even an amah (in the 1941 *Shanghai Gesture*, von Sternberg). But rank, nationality, costume, made no difference to her art: that inexorable Russian accent wiped out all distinctions. Nor did she vary her emotional pitch: "I luff you" has exactly the same weight and intonation as "I hate you." And why not? Did Hollywood really know or care what a maharani or an amah (or an Austrian peasant) sounded like? Ouspenskaya had authority. Not even in what has turned out to be her most famous role—Maleva, the old Gypsy woman, in *The Wolf Man* (41, George Waggner) and *Frankenstein Meets the Wolf Man* (43, Roy William Neill)—does she modify her performance by a whit. There are the famous trademarks—the immobile face; the completely flat, unnuanced intonation; the total lack of emotional register. No wonder everyone was terrified of her.

God knows what she taught generations of acting hopefuls in her highly respected and well-attended acting classes! (Lee Strasberg was one of her students.) In his biography of Alla Nazimova—a rival for many roles—Gavin Lambert tells us that Ouspenskaya "was a formidable presence who entered the classroom wearing a monocle and carrying a pitcher of what looked like water but was in fact gin. Her opening line to the class, delivered without a smile, became famous: 'Make for me friendly atmosphere, please.' One student reported that she would tell us to imagine we were blades of grass on the oceanbed. And everyone swayed."

Michael Ovitz, b. Encino, California, 1947

He was born and raised in the San Fernando Valley, whence he attended high school and U.C.L.A. He married his college sweetheart in 1969. They lived in a decent house in Brentwood with two children. On graduating, he took a job with the William Morris Agency in Beverly Hills, and there learned the business—or more especially the art of packaging television—with special debt to the agent Howard West. He left Morris to go to law school, but that was never finished and he found himself back at the agency. He moved ahead very rapidly for simple reasons: he was smart, he worked all hours, he was determined. There isn't really any more mystery to being a good agent. As for being a great agent, two things should be said: (1) a great agent may be a contradiction in terms, because (2) what does he really want? In other words, to be a terrific agent is to be self-effacing, even anonymous.

Michael Ovitz has the style of the first, but it has not led to obscurity. He was once the best-known person in the business, simply because most people in show business would have voted for him as the most powerful person around. He makes films? No, not really. There are some movies that are famous for his role as packager and kingmaker—for example, *Legal Eagles, Rain Man, Bugsy*, and *Ghostbusters*. But no one suggests he interfered with them, or proposed creative involvement. He made the deal: agents exist as 10 percent of the deal. And in an age of pay-or-play, it is not strictly necessary for the pictures to be made. Ovitz is a great deal-maker.

In 1975, he formed a dissident group within William Morris with Ron Meyer, William Haber, Michael Rosenfeld, and Rowland Perkins. They believed Morris was archaic, complacent, and too set at the top. Young lions could not get ahead. Ovitz and Meyer were fired, and they set up CAA on a very small budget. They undercut Morris on TV deals, and they found rapid success.

CAA had about one hundred agents, an annual gross of at least $100 million, a spiffy I. M. Pei–designed building at the junction of Wilshire and Santa Monica. And clients—for example, Steven Spielberg, Barbra Streisand, Madonna, Michael Jackson, Magic Johnson, Kevin Costner, Dustin Hoffman, Sean Connery, Barry Levinson, Warren Beatty, Michael Douglas, Tom Cruise, and Robin Williams.

The agency had rivals: William Morris, still, and ICM. But CAA enjoyed several years of preeminence, reliant on revenue and talent, and on Ovitz's superb insinuation of his mysterious self in the higher politics of show business. He was feared, envied, and disapproved of in some quarters. It is said that he had inflated the salaries of top talent; that he had reduced the studios to functionaries desperate to get enough big projects; that he saw the vital alliance of independent stars and the lawyerlike protection of their interests.

All of this is true, natural, and inevitable. Ovitz is only the man who crystallized the new state of power once the studio system collapsed. Every talent became his or her own studio. But talent is generally insecure, and Ovitz saw how far agencies could shelter, promote, and boost the stars. He did his job, and it was not really his job to worry about the movies except to the extent that they affect career prospects and bargaining positions.

There is more to Ovitz. He played very important but discreet roles in the deals whereby Matsushita purchased MCA (for $6.6 billion) and Sony purchased Columbia ($3.4 billion). He involved CAA in consulting deals with Coca-Cola and Credit Lyonnais (the effective owner of MGM). He made the strategy that took David Letterman to CBS. These developments seem natural in a young man who may be bored just putting movies together. In other words, the logic of Ovitz's career must carry him higher, and the higher he goes the more dangerous life gets, because then he is doing so much more than make deals. He is involved in policy, dreams, and strategies—all of which know the way to hell.

That was 1994. A year later, of his own volition, but with the feeling that there is no stability, Ovitz left his own agency. He wanted the top job at Universal, but was disappointed—the first sign of enemies ready to see him humbled. Instead, Michael Eisner hired him as number two at Disney, an assignment that lasted a little over a year and ended in a severance deal of around $100 million. Thereafter, Ovitz was involved in several ventures—Livent, getting an NFL franchise to Los Angeles—without success. And so he went back to what he thought he had known, agenting, but with an industry arranged against him, and with the role of the agent more suspect. He formed a new company, Artists Television Group. However, by the summer of 2001, he was laying off many employees with rumors of losses in the region of $70 million. Mercy came in May 2002 as his company changed hands. At fifty-five, the Ovitz arc was complete. Or was it? Would he accept this story or not? Of course, his legacy is intact: he had presided over the most massive increase in prices there had ever been.

François Ozon, b. Paris, 1967

1988: *Photo de Famille* (s); *Les Doigts dans le Ventre* (s); 1991: *Une Goutte de Sang* (s); *Le Trou Madame* (s); *Peau Contre Peau* (s); *Deux Plus Un* (s); 1992: *Thomas Reconstitué* (s); 1993: *Victor* (s); 1994: *Action Vérité* (s). 1995: *La Petite Mort* (s); *Jospin S'Éclaire* (s); 1996: *Une Robe d'Été* (s); 1997: *Regarde la Mer/See the Sea; Scènes de Lit* (s). 1998: *Sitcom; X 2000* (s). 1999: *Les Amants Criminels/Criminal Lovers; Gouttes d'Eau sur Pierres Brûlantes/Water Drops on Burning Rocks.* 2000: *Sous le Sable/Under the Sand.* 2002: *8 Femmes/8 Women.* 2003: *Swimming Pool.*

8 Femmes is an all-star murder mystery, fondly old-fashioned, and likely to repeat its French success all over the world. But it would be a mistake to identify Ozon with its nostalgic style or attitude. He is a film-school kid who made movies on

Super 8 as a teenager and naturally carried on in a series of short films, many of which are funny, pretty (in the best sense), and so piquant as narratives as to make one ask yet again—what happened to the short?

But there is a darker or graver Ozon, most evident so far in *See the Sea,* which builds from calm and friendship to a troubling climax; a murder story in *Criminal Lovers;* and—best of all—*Under the Sand,* in which Charlotte Rampling is a woman who "loses" her husband and has to go through mourning to whatever else may be beyond. With the eloquent image of Rampling, *Under the Sand* was a little reminiscent of Antonioni with Monica Vitti. It makes me hope that there are great films—far better than *8 Women*—to come from Ozon.

Yasujiro Ozu (1903–63), b. Tokyo

1927: *Zange no Yaiba/The Sword of Penitence.* 1928: *Wakado no Yume/The Dreams of Youth; Nyobo Funshitsu/Wife Lost; Kabocha/Pumpkin; Hikkoshi Fufu/A Couple on the Move; Nikutai Bi/Body Beautiful.* 1929: *Takara no Yama/Treasure Mountain; Wakaki Hi/Days of Youth; Wasei Kenka Tomodachi/Fighting Friends, Japanese Style; Daigaku wa Deta Keredo/I Graduated, But . . . ; Kaisha-in Seikatsu/The Life of an Office Worker; Tokkan Kozo/A Straightforward Boy.* 1930: *Kekkongaku Nyomon/An Introduction to Marriage; Hogaraka ni Ayume/Walk Cheerfully; Rakudai wa Shita Keredo/I Flunked, But . . . ; Sono Yo no Tsuma/That Night's Wife; Erogami no Onryo/The Revengeful Spirit of Eros; Ashi ni Sawatta Koun/Lost Luck; Ojosan/Young Miss.* 1931: *Shukujoto Hige/The Lady and the Beard; Bijin Aishu/Beauty's Sorrow; Tokyo no Gassho/Tokyo's Chorus.* 1932: *Haru wa Gofujin Kara/Spring Comes from the Ladies; Umarete wa Mita Keredo/I Was Born, But . . . ; Seishun no Yume Ima Izuko/Where Now Are the Dreams of Youth?; Mata Au Hi Made/Until the Day We Meet Again.* 1933: *Tokyo no Onna/A Tokyo Woman; Hijosen no Onna/Dragnet Girl; Dekigokoro/Passing Fancy.* 1934: *Haha o Kowazu-Ya/A Mother Should Be Loved; Ukigusa Monogatari/A Story of Floating Weeds.* 1935: *Hakoiri Musume/An Innocent Maid; Tokyo no Tado/An Inn in Tokyo.* 1936: *Daigaku Yoi Toko/College Is a Nice Place; Hitori Musuko/The Only Son.* 1937: *Shukujo wa Nani o Wasuretaka/What Did Her Lady Forget?* 1941: *Toda-ke no Kyodai/The Brothers and Sisters of the Toda Family.* 1942: *Chichi Ariki/There Was a Father.* 1947: *Nagaya no Shinshi Roku/The Record of a Tenement Gentleman.* 1948: *Kaze no Naka no Mendori/A Hen in the Wind.* 1949: *Banshun/Late Spring.* 1950: *Munekata Shimai/The Munekata Sisters.* 1951: *Bakushu/Early Summer.* 1952: *Ochazuke no Aji/The Flavor of Green Tea Over Rice.* 1953: *Tokyo Monogatari/Tokyo Story.*

1956: *Soshun/Early Spring.* 1957: *Tokyo Boshoku/Twilight in Tokyo.* 1958: *Higanbana/ Equinox Flower.* 1959: *Ohayo/Good Morning; Ukigusa/Floating Weeds.* 1960: *Akibiyori/Late Autumn.* 1961: *Kohayagawa-ke no Aki/The End of Summer.* 1962: *Samma no Aji/An Autumn Afternoon.*

When Roger Manvell's *Film and the Public* was published in 1955, it had not one mention of Ozu, and would not have been attacked for the omission. Penelope Houston's *Contemporary Cinema*, published in the year of Ozu's death, had no doubt about his significance, but still employed Ozu as an example of filmmaking too austere, slow, or quietist for large audiences.

The West caught up with Ozu only a few years before his death, when his greatest movies urged their way into European film festivals. The story is not so different from the late appreciation of Mizoguchi. But Mizoguchi's films—especially the "monogatari"—are more eventful, more passionate, and more "moving" than Ozu's contemplation of the seasons. There is an easy joke that no one can tell one Ozu film from another: but is that a failing or a virtue? After all, we notice a similar consistency in Hawks, Godard, Bergman, or Buñuel.

Ozu's most important characteristic is his way of watching the world. While that attitude is modest and unassertive, it is also the source of great tenderness for people. It is as if Ozu's one personal admission was the faith that the basis of decency and sympathy can only be sustained by the semi-religious effort to observe the world in his style; in other words, contemplation calms anxious activity. As with Mizoguchi, one comes away from Ozu heartened by his humane intelligence and by the gravity we have learned.

The intensive viewing of Ozu—and such stylistic rigor encourages nothing less—makes questions of Japaneseness irrelevant. There have been attempts to explain Ozu by reference to his native culture, and it is easy to pin his mysticism to facile notions of the East. Even Ozu himself believed that his subject matter was too provincial to travel outside Japan. Some critics have tried to illuminate his films by reference to Buddhism, Japanese pottery, domestic ritual, and haiku.

All of those are worth considering. But the most useful point to make is that Ozu uses a minimal but concentrated camera style: static, a little lower than waist height, with few camera movements, dissolves, or fades. The intentness of the image, and its emotional resonance, is not only as relevant to the West as to Japan; it is a return to fundamental cinema, such as we can see in Dreyer, Bresson, Lang, and even Warhol, whose characters sit as habitually as Ozu's. Nor is there anything limitingly Oriental in Ozu's ability to create deep anguish or joy in the cross-cutting of faces.

There are similar moments in Hitchcock or Lang, when we are made to apprehend the unverbalized feelings that rush between people, and which are only defined by the constructive power of editing.

This Ozu is less difficult than demanding. When you watch him, think more of the camera than of what little we know of Japanese culture. The seeming repetition of his work—of middle-class domestic interiors, marital stories, the same actors, and abiding camera setups—is a proof of his constancy. The family relationships he describes are by no means un-Western. Ozu has a sense of pathos that travels easily, while only Mizoguchi can treat overwhelming feelings with such restraint. Ozu is worthy of attention by the highest claims of an international art; demurring from rhetorical outburst, expressive camera angles, and the turmoil of melodrama, he insists on the photographic substance in faces, interiors, and the spaces between people.

Not enough of Ozu is available; little can be seen easily, or in ideal circumstances. But these are key films to look for: *I Was Born, But . . .* (32), a picture of the world as seen through children's eyes, aware of pain, but boisterous, funny, and earthy; *A Story of Floating Weeds* (34), about traveling players in the countryside, a movie filled with the chanciness of weather; *Late Spring* (49), a very delicate study of a father and a daughter both wondering about marriage, but anxious not to offend the other; *Tokyo Story* (53), the film that established Ozu in the West; and the late masterpieces, still lifes with intense movements of hope and yearning passing across the fame of the family—*Late Autumn* (60); *The End of Summer* (61); and *An Autumn Afternoon* (62).

It may be that Ozu's greatness depends on stories about the family, and so often parents and grown-up children. But something should be said about his versatility. In his rich silent period, he was often very funny—never so much as when dealing with children: *I Was Born, But . . .* finds enormous comic spirit in the kids. *Dragnet Girl*, from 1933, is a kind of film noir, about a gangster and his woman; equally, *That Night's Wife* was a tribute to von Sternberg's underworld films. Then again, in the 1930s, Ozu did several movies—like *An Inn in Tokyo*—that prefigure Italian neorealism. During the war, he made movies about stability and family dramas that ignore the state of war.

There is one crucial way in which Ozu is, if not purely Japanese, a challenge to American movie habits. The Western moviegoer will hardly be able to resist Ozu (he *is* a treasury), but there is some truth in the claim that he is resigned or conservative. The world, the family, and ordinary persistence hold firm in his pictures. For example, in *A Hen in the Wind*, a soldier returns from the war to discover that his wife has turned to prostitution in his absence. Disruption threatens. But the couple find compromise, reconciliation, and the necessary sadness of going on. In so many family pictures, the suffocation of a relationship is not escaped. Kindness may free the young to marry (as in *Late Spring* and its companion, *Late Autumn*), but marriage is only another room in the same small house. The use of the seasons in so many titles suggests the circular and impregnable round of life. Ozu *is* conservative: he does not believe in escape, and so he arranges his tales in moods of acceptance and quietism.

That disturbs some American viewers because so many American films are pledged to the energy that "breaks out." Our stories promote the hope of escape, of beginning again, of beneficial disruptions. One can see that energy—hopeful, and often damaging, but always romantic—in films as diverse as *The Searchers, Citizen Kane, Mr. Smith Goes to Washington, Run of the Arrow, Rebel Without a Cause, Vertigo, Bonnie and Clyde, Greed,* and *The Fountainhead.* No matter how such stories end, explosive energy is endorsed.

Those explosions are a metaphor for the light of movies and for the emphasis on indulged fantasy in American pictures. Our films are spirals of wish fulfillment, pleas for envy, the hustle to get on with the pursuit of happiness. By contrast, Ozu's films seem to be modeled on novels or plays—Tolstoy or Chekhov—certain that there is no escape, no getting away, and no proper place for fantasy in living. Which is not to say that Ozu's people lack energy or the habit of dreaming. But that urge is contained within the sense of fatality and certain outcome—as it is, say, in *The Earrings of Madame de . . . , The Shop Around the Corner, The Magnificent Ambersons, French Can Can.* So Ozu is a vital lesson to American film, and provocation to us to be wise, calm, and more demanding in what we want of our films.

P

Georg Wilhelm Pabst (1885–1967),
b. Raudnitz, Czechoslovakia

1923: *Der Schatz.* 1924: *Gräfin Donelli.* 1925: *Die Freudlose Gasse.* 1926: *Geheimnisse einer Seele; Man Spielt Nicht mit der Liebe.* 1927: *Die Liebe der Jeanne Ney.* 1928: *Abwege/Begierde; Die Büchse der Pandora/Pandora's Box.* 1929: *Die Weisse Hölle von Piz-Palü* (codirected with Arnold Fanck); *Das Tagebuch einer Verlorenen.* 1930: *Westfront 1918; Skandal um Eva.* 1931: *Die Dreigroschenoper/The Threepenny Opera; Kameradschaft.* 1932: *Die Herrin von Atlantis/L'Atlantide.* 1933: *Don Quichotte; Du Haut en Bas.* 1934: *A Modern Hero.* 1936: *Mademoiselle Docteur.* 1938: *Le Drame de Shanghai.* 1939:

Jeunes Filles en Détresse. 1940: *Feuertaufe* (d). 1941: *Komodianten.* 1943: *Paracelsus.* 1944: *Der Fall Molander.* 1947: *Der Prozess.* 1949: *Geheimnisvolle Tiefen.* 1952: *La Voce del Silenzio.* 1953: *Cose da Pazzi.* 1954: *Das Bekenntnis der Ina Kahr.* 1955: *Der Letzte Akt; Es Geschah am 20 Juli.* 1956: *Rosen für Bettina; Durch die Walder, Durch die Auen.*

By vague consent, Pabst is one of those directors we have a duty to remember, even if there is only a single film still compulsory viewing. With the years, *Pandora's Box* has grown into one of the most compelling studies of sensual self-destruction, whereas the once respected humanitarianism of *Kameradschaft* seems facile; and *Westfront 1918* is no more or less profound an antiwar film than Milestone's *All Quiet on the Western Front.*

There is no doubt that around 1930 Pabst was enormously accomplished, as a realist and in his psychological exploration—what was then called his "X-ray eye camera." But it is the skill that impresses more than personal conviction. In retrospect, we may notice that *Pandora's Box* and *Kameradschaft* endorse diametrically opposite attitudes to people. Was Pabst an opportunist then, a drifting director waiting for a breeze? *Kameradschaft,* for instance, is a compromise between locations in a real mining town and clever studio reconstruction of the mine tunnels.

It has even been discovered that Pabst shot two endings to that film—one hopeful, one despairing.

It seems appropriate to the conflicting method that he could not settle for one attitude or the other. *Die Freudlose Gasse,* despite its attack on inflation and urban misery, revels in its melodramatic consequences, especially the threat of the brothel awaiting Greta Garbo. And as for Pabst's undeniable coup with Louise Brooks, the originality of *Pandora* comes from Brooks's fearless sense of an intelligent woman unable to resist her own sensuality. Pabst's contribution is that of entrepreneur, selecting Brooks to enact the erotic spiral of Wedekind's original.

The filming is proficient and expressive, but Pabst is content to create a heavy, fogbound Victorian atmosphere, such as he used in *Die Dreigroschenoper,* to smother the dramatic starkness that Brecht had intended. Such background detail is common to much of Pabst's work and it is secondhand compared with the worlds invented by Lang for *Metropolis, Frau im Mond, M,* or the Mabuse films. Pabst excelled in the selection of detail—objects, expressions, and quick effects of light. Certainly, with Brooks this alertness was fully stimulated; her darting spontaneity as Lulu adds to the meaning because it runs counter to the massive premeditation of the German actors. Lulu still thrills us because of Louise Brooks's effect of vulnerable emotional vitality. *Pandora's Box* seems the one occasion when Pabst trusted a player to carry a film, rather than the theory that the camera could penetrate psychological reality.

With *Geheimnisse einer Seele* this approach added to a schematic and tendentious dramatization of Freudian theories, but with *Pandora's Box* and *Das Tagebuch einer Verlorenen* the discovery is startling and moving. Is Pabst or Brooks the true creative personality in those films? The tentativeness in all Pabst's work, and the dullness of most of his later films, support Lotte Eisner's feeling that Brooks had "succeeded in stimulating an otherwise unequal director's talent to the extreme."

Like many other German filmmakers, in 1933 Pabst moved to France. While there he made a picturesque version of *Don Quixote* starring Chaliapin as the Don (and with George Robey as Sancho in the English version). His one Hollywood venture, *A Modern Hero*, at Warners, starring Richard Barthelmess, was a flop and Pabst returned to France, and then to Austria. Lotte Eisner reported that he had tried to justify the return with a string of family circumstances, so plausible that they seemed more suspicious. Whatever the real motives, the decision weighed on him. *Feuertaufe* was a documentary on the conquest of Poland, and by 1943 he was forced back on the life of *Paracelsus* as a way of keeping in work.

His postwar films included two made in Italy, as well as *Der Letzte Akt,* based on Erich Maria Remarque's account of the last days of Hitler, and a film about the July 1944 plot. But Pabst was never rehabilitated, chiefly because that surface brilliance had gone from his films, revealing only a plodding sentimental pursuit of psychological orthodoxy.

Al Pacino (Alberto Pacino),
b. New York, 1940

He is "big Al" now, to public and actors alike, no matter that he is a small man. Only outrageous inner size—wicked will—could have gotten away with *Scent of a Woman*. Somehow he conveys the charm and the neediness of a perilously recovered invalid. With rare, sweet stealth, he has insinuated himself as one of our great actors. He is so much more accessible and beguiling than De Niro or Hoffman. He has learned to be seductive. But he cannot rid himself of that faint edge of the sinister. I'm not sure he tries. Did playing Michael Corleone seep that far into his system? For Michael is the great role of modern American movies, and it lives with Pacino still.

When American television remixed both parts of *The Godfather* in 1977 and poured them out again in chronological order, a striking error emerged. Whereas Brando and De Niro had won

Oscars in the films—for distinguished performances—Al Pacino went unrewarded. Yet he dominates the work. As the story advances, Pacino's Michael betrays values and gentleness with creeping isolation, and turns the social spectacle of immigrant glory into a bitter chamberwork. But he made the poison of vengeance and paranoia absolutely persuasive. Coppola may have hoped for critical detachment in the film, but his lethal hero commands the tone with the self-pity that must order such executions. He is the natural armchair tyrant for a medium that makes us sitting accomplices in every witnessed death.

Pacino came to *The Godfather* (72, Francis Ford Coppola) as nearly a newcomer. He had made only *Me, Natalie* (69, Fred Coe) and *Panic in Needle Park* (71, Jerry Schatzberg), quirky films deemed worthy of an enterprising Off-Broadway actor. He looked a lot less than thirty in the first hour of *The Godfather.* He is a hero home from the war, nearly as green as Robert Walker in *The Clock.* Brothers and mafiosi tease him good-naturedly; he is shy of telling Diane Keaton he loves her over the phone in front of a kitchen full of gangsters. His hair flops over his brow, and his wide eyes seem too vacant to have faced combat.

But there is already a warning coldness that relishes the shock to Keaton when he explains the offer his father once made to the bandleader who owned Johnny Fontane. At that point, Michael has seemingly rejected his family's ways, but the deadpan account of brains or signature on the contract is filled with military instinct. When he draws the protesting Kay into the family photograph, it is less a gesture of romantic warmth than his plan for dynasty.

Michael discovers himself through family allegiance, and it is notable in the first two parts of the film how little affection he displays for either of his wives. He is touched by father and sons only; brothers he first surveys, then humbles and eliminates. They are too nearly rivals to his succession. When Don Vito is shot, it is Michael who happens to visit the hospital and recognizes a plot to finish off his father. With another chance visitor, the timid Enzio, he holds off the assassins with a daring masquerade. The two small men mount guard on the hospital steps and the hoodlums' car creeps away in frustration. Enzio's nerves are in tatters, and he can hardly feed himself a cigarette. But Michael notices how steady his own hand is as he supplies a light. He never mentions this control to anyone else in the film, but Pacino pounces on the instant and gives it a cold-blooded intellectual satisfaction.

When Sterling Hayden's rogue cop arrives, Michael exults in his own physical punishment. Pacino can radiate spiritual morbidity, and he martyrs himself passionately. The effect on his delicate face is awesome. Swelling and bruising stay there well into his Sicilian exile. It shows brutal maturity and suffering, but it is also a premonition of malignance in Michael. The bruising turns into the various hollows of compromise, lying, and manipulation. It also prepares us for the sonata close-ups of *Part II* when Michael's face lurks in half-darkness. He needs no one and rejects honest dealing: so the man hides behind the obelisk stare of a demoralized god. If acting for movies is allowing the camera to look within or through the surface, then Pacino achieves something remarkable, for he leads *The Godfather* from a study of the world of action to the immobile reverie of a lonely tyrant.

His other work showed the vagaries of the movie scene, and the bankable asset of moody romanticism in Pacino's screen persona. *Scarecrow* (73) was another windy allegory from Jerry Schatzberg, an attempt at poetic hoboism that ends in depressed silence. In *Serpico* (73, Sidney Lumet), too, another character says of Pacino's, "either you're exploding or you're lying around like a catatonic." The explosions are not convincing or moving, but Serpico is a fascinating instance of overt New York realism succumbing to the introspection of the actor. Lumet may have wanted a lively drama of cops on the take and big city cover-ups. But Pacino diverted it into the ballad of a sad, aloof hippie. It is his cutest film, a self-righteous pose.

Dog Day Afternoon (75, Lumet) was his least restrained film, yet his untidy prettiness did help explain the jittery excitement of the ardent bank robber. More challenging was *Bobby Deerfield* (77, Sydney Pollack), in which he caught the austere, nearly frigid insecurity of the racing driver who has A+ on his suit. Deerfield is in hiding from pain and complication; he longs for a circuit free from error in which he merges with his machine. He will use anything as a cover or defense: cars, his helmet, dark glasses, and indifference. Yet again, his pallor seems scarcely able to subdue a dark inner lining, sometimes only anxiety or perplexity, but sometimes equivalent to decay. Pacino often guards his face with his hands, as if afraid of loss, wounding, or being seen. His identity is acutely vulnerable there and, as well as the battering he endures in *The Godfather,* in *Serpico* he is shot in the face. That reprisal leaves his speech affected, and he has a variety of lisps and tricks of the voice that suggest subterfuge. Bobby Deerfield is from Newark, and the devices to disguise a New Jersey whine are very cunningly introduced. He never quite sounds adult.

Best of all in that film, however, is the moment when Marthe Keller challenges him to risk his precious celebrity—as hard and encumbered as a turtle—by walking down a Florentine street without his shades. The way in which Pacino bears the indignity of not being recognized is funny and touching. It is a heartwarming scene in an unexpectedly mordant film. It showed how winsome Pacino might be if he let his charm loose, and how much he needed the internal conflict of guarding against his loveliness and trying to make it baleful.

In the eighties, Pacino sometimes seemed like a man in a dark room, who feared monsters in the corners and holes in the floor—perhaps, secretly, he had set himself on playing a blind man. He was away from the screen for lengthy periods; he undertook daring theatrical ventures; some of his films were major failures; and yet . . . the Pacino cult grew. When he "returned" to the screen as the world-weary cop in *Sea of Love* (89, Harold Becker), he could not help seeming a disenchanted actor wondering whether the far-fetched melodrama would hold. But in theatres it was easy to feel audience relief and pleasure that he was back. The sad, wry look on Pacino's face now inspired love.

He had been a rabble-rousing lawyer in . . . *And Justice for All* (79, Norman Jewison); a writer with problems of love and marriage in the disappointing *Author! Author!* (82, Arthur Hiller); and the subject of gay protests when he played a cop in *Cruising* (80, William Friedkin). Collectively, those films were at best a marking time. But in *Scarface* (83, Brian De Palma), Pacino left no doubts: he was Cuban now, mouthing the accent as if it were one hot strawberry after another; he was outgoing, randy, a show-off. Tony Montana was gripping from start to finish—monstrous, operatic, overdone, yet filled with detail and an unforgettable love of life.

Alas, the next picture—*Revolution* (85, Hugh Hudson)—was a dreadful mistake, a silly story, a lousy accent, and the object of much abuse. Thus, Pacino waited four years before the modest *Sea of Love*, where he was sustained by Richard Price's rattling dialogue and Ellen Barkin's sour-lemon sexpot—Pacino has always done talk brilliantly, but now he had an appetite for sex.

He had a flashy cameo in *Dick Tracy* (90, Warren Beatty), the best performance in the film. Then he returned as an older, contrite Michael Corleone in *The Godfather Part III* (90, Coppola). The concept of this third film was that Michael had changed—and that may do fatal damage to what made Michael so compelling once. But the version of *III* released theatrically was so rushed that Pacino's performance suffered—he is a lot more touching in the later video release.

Pacino then did two films in which he was miscast, but in which he defied the "error" and willed us into liking the result: *Frankie and Johnny* (91, Garry Marshall) and *Scent of a Woman* (92, Martin Brest). The notion of Pacino and Michelle Pfeiffer as drab folks who work in a diner and seem unsuited to romance must stand among Hollywood's wildest self-delusions: Pacino and

Pfeiffer are Wagnerian in their capacity for grand passion.

In *Scent of a Woman,* Pacino was asked to play a blinded, military martinet, close to suicide but taken out of himself by a weekend spent on the town with a young preppie. The film is absurd. No self-respecting army would entertain Pacino as a spy let alone an officer. The film ran two and a half hours on a very slight story! And Pacino made it a hit, brought the tango back into fashion, and got an Oscar—his first, after seven nominations.

One other thing should be said about the Pacino cult: he owns and seemingly carries with him a short fiction film, *The Local Stigmatic,* from a play by Heathcote Williams, in which he plays a power-mad, petty, English gangster. This film is Pacino's passion. He shows it to small groups personally. He believes in it in ways that are hard to explain: it is a study in evil, and its secondary theme is putting on an act. I have seen it, and I think it's awful in many ways—yet it's fascinating, and vitally important to the man who is our greatest actor now.

He was one of the salesmen in *Glengarry Glen Ross* (92, James Foley). In 1993, Pacino was reunited with De Palma for *Carlito's Way,* but the result only helped illustrate the decline of De Palma and Pacino's weakness for old allies.

With his Oscar at last, did Pacino relax, take on airs, or reckon to have fun? Whatever the answer, his work has been very mixed: sentimental as the grandfather in *Two Bits* (95, Foley); too macho and swaggery in *Heat* (95, Michael Mann), where De Niro treats him the way Robinson used to handle La Motta; less than credible in *City Hall* (96, Becker); superb in *Donnie Brasco* (97, Mike Newell); too broad, yet fun, in *The Devil's Advocate* (97, Taylor Hackford); again, too much attitude in *The Insider* (99, Mann); not plausible as a football coach, but very enjoyable in *Any Given Sunday* (99, De Palma).

He also directed the odd Shakespearean mishmash, *Looking for Richard* (96), and made one more "private" movie, *Chinese Coffee* (00).

Faults and all, he is still unmissable, and if I grieve over the way he took *Heat* off course, I can't stop watching the film. He was good again in *Insomnia* (02, Christopher Nolan); *Simone* (02, Andrew Niccol); *People I Know* (02, Daniel Algrant); *The Recruit* (03, Roger Donaldson); *Gigli* (03, Brest); as Roy Cohn in *Angels in America* (03, Mike Nichols).

Geraldine Page (1924–87),

b. Kirksville, Missouri

A florid theatrical character actress, who seemed to resort to movies as a relaxation from the stage, Geraldine Page was nominated for the best actress Oscar three times. Yet she seldom treated the movies to more than a rather mannered

Southern bloom—an orchid or a camellia, with a strong sweet scent, just beginning to harden at the edges, but with a bee in its heart.

She trained at the Chicago Academy of Fine Arts and was working in the theatre from the early 1940s, especially in Tennessee Williams plays and in *The Immoralist,* where she appeared with the young James Dean. She had two movie roles in the 1950s: *Taxi* (53, Gregory Ratoff), and as the widow giving as good as she got to John Wayne in the moody *Hondo* (53, John Farrow).

It was 1961 before she began to work steadily in films: repeating stage successes in *Summer and Smoke* (61, Peter Glenville), and as Alexandra del Largo in *Sweet Bird of Youth* (62, Richard Brooks); *Toys in the Attic* (63, George Roy Hill); a desperate wooer of Glenn Ford in *Dear Heart* (64, Delbert Mann); *The Happiest Millionaire* (66, Norman Tokar); *Monday's Child* (66, Leopoldo Torre Nilsson); *You're a Big Boy Now* (67, Francis Ford Coppola); *Truman Capote's Trilogy* (69, Frank Perry), made for TV; *Whatever Happened to Aunt Alice?* (69, Lee H. Katzin); teaching young ladies how to be discreetly randy and serve up questionable mushrooms in *The Beguiled* (71, Don Siegel); as Cliff Robertson's mother in *J. W. Coop* (71, Robertson); and *Pete 'n' Tillie* (72, Martin Ritt).

She contributed a performance of exquisite enclosed self-pity to a movie that required exactly and only that, *Interiors* (78, Woody Allen).

She was then in *Harry's War* (81, Keith Merrill); *Honky Tonk Freeway* (81, John Schlesinger); *I'm Dancing as Fast as I Can* (82, Jack Hofsiss); *The Dollmaker* (84, Daniel Petrie); *The Pope of Greenwich Village* (84, Stuart Rosenberg); *The Adventures of Huckleberry Finn* (85, Peter H. Hunt); winning the Oscar as the widow making *The Trip to Bountiful* (85, Peter Masterson); *The Bride* (85, Franc Roddam); *White Nights* (85, Taylor Hackford); *Walls of Glass* (85, Scott Goldstein); *My Little Girl* (86, Connie Kaiserman); *Native Son* (86, Jerrold Freedman); as a camp survivor in *Nazi Hunter: The Beate Klarsfeld Story* (86, Michael Lindsay-Hogg).

Marcel Pagnol (1895–1974),

b. Aubagne, France

1934: *Angèle; Le Gendre de Monsieur Poirier; Jofroi.* 1935: *César; Cigalon; Merlusse.* 1937: *Regain/Harvest.* 1938: *Le Schpountz; La Femme du Boulanger/The Baker's Wife.* 1940: *La Fille du Puisatier/The Welldigger's Daughter.* 1948: *La Belle Meunière.* 1950: *Topaze.* 1952: *Manon des Sources.* 1954: *Les Lettres de Mon Moulin.*

It's impressive to see how well the influence of Pagnol has lasted. In the middle eighties, Claude Berri enjoyed international success with *Jean de Florette* and *Manon des Sources,* both taken from a Pagnol story (and filmed by him in 1952). But it was black and white then; thirty years later, the very good Berri films had color in the flowers, and Montand, Depardieu, Daniel Auteuil, and Emmanuelle Béart. The aura of these new movies mingled with the fragrant allure of our culture's travel section and the supplement on cuisine. This is not to belittle the films, or Pagnol's virtues, but he has been taken up. One of the most celebrated French restaurants outside France is Alice Waters's Chez Panisse, in Berkeley, California, its name and sensibility inspired by Pagnol films shown by Tom Luddy just a few blocks away at the Pacific Film Archive. So Pagnol is a flavor in our food now, and a name to drop in tourist brochures.

Pagnol was a very popular playwright who used the Midi area and Marseilles as his settings. After working as a teacher, he turned to writing plays. He founded a film magazine and in 1931 wrote the script for the film of his own play *Marius* (Alexander Korda), and in 1932 for *Fanny* (Marc Allégret). The experience was enough to persuade him to set up his own studio in Marseilles and to continue through the 1930s with sentimental, well-written plays about young lovers and their lovable elders. It was an achievement based on charm, an unerring sense of popular taste, and the naturalistic acting of people like Raimu. *Marius, Fanny,* and *César* are frequently revived, their charm intact, their world forever warm. Once upon a time, *The Baker's Wife* was a model French film.

But as cinema, it fell short of *Toni,* the film Renoir made out of Pagnol's studio and that knifed through the mythology of rural life, preferring locations to studio-built country scenes. Pagnol always treated Marseilles as a vivacious backdrop, no matter that he knew and loved it. Renoir, however, saw quickly how to make the Midi as everyday as it is for its inhabitants. *Toni,* I think, has not one interior that was not real and lived in. The sunshine in *Toni* burns and tires, whereas in Pagnol it bathes everything in mellow, comfortable warmth. In *Toni,* the quarry cracks open and subsides, just as the little domestic drama rises and falls. Whereas Pagnol was beguiled by the notion of a comforting bond between his characters and their balmy studio Marseilles. In the 1940s and 1950s, Pagnol's attention returned to the theatre, but his private Midi could not be re-created.

Alan J. Pakula (1928–98), b. New York

1969: *The Sterile Cuckoo/Pookie.* 1971: *Klute.* 1972: *Love and Pain and the Whole Damn Thing.* 1974: *The Parallax View.* 1976: *All the President's Men.* 1978: *Comes a Horseman.* 1979: *Starting Over.* 1981: *Rollover.* 1982: *Sophie's Choice.* 1986: *Dream Lover.* 1987: *Orphans.* 1989: *See You in the Morning.* 1990: *Presumed Innocent.* 1993: *The Pelican Brief.* 1997: *The Devil's Own.*

Pakula and his colleague of the 1960s, Robert Mulligan, worked in the dilute vein of intelligent, cautiously bold entertainment still congratulating itself in American movies. Thus Pakula spoke of his own approach: "I am oblique, I think that has to do with my own nature. I like trying to do things which work on many levels, because I think it is terribly important to give an audience a lot of things they may not get as well as those they will, so that finally the film does take on a texture and is not just simplistic communication."

But that earnestness, and the "texture" of his films, are too bland and calculated. Pakula is a little simpler than he hopes, and *Klute* and *The Parallax View* (though very gripping) show the dangers of falling between brilliantly acted crime melodrama and intellectual coat trailing. It is too easy to say that *Klute* reveals brooding urban paranoia, confused sexual identity, and a type of morbid voyeurism. No one could miss those themes or allow them to disguise Jane Fonda's clutching of the film to herself so that the potentially disturbing Klute is left a blank character and the audience is as preoccupied with the actress's studied feelings as are Bree Daniels's clients.

Perhaps that balance of the commercial and the perilous is in the character of an ex-producer, a confessed admirer of actors, and someone who once thought of being a psychoanalyst (the surrogate and passive director in *Klute*). From Yale, where he majored in drama, he went to the cartoons department of Warner Brothers and then into producing. In retrospect, it seems likely that his taste for out-of-the-way people and situations, plus an instinct for respectable, well-planned pathos, were guiding elements in the partnership with Robert Mulligan that made *Fear Strikes Out* (57), *To Kill a Mockingbird* (63), *Love With the Proper Stranger* (63), *Baby, The Rain Must Fall* (65), *Inside Daisy Clover* (66), *Up the Down Staircase* (67), and *The Stalking Moon* (69).

Pakula's debut, and his third film, were attempts at unsentimental portraits of emotional grotesques: Liza Minnelli as a gauche college girl, and Maggie Smith trembling with terminal illness. Both films suffer from the somewhat distasteful way in which they "work" so well. In other words, the grotesques are the result of neat scripting and very cute acting. Their essential vulgarity should be remembered against the welcome touch and subtlety of the thrillers. *Klute* is much better, but still a meek vehicle for a grave actress encouraged into mannerism. The best thing about it is the deliberate visual claustrophobia.

Pakula was exactly the director for the Watergate thriller in that he allowed film noir to obscure the chance of a more searching study of American compromise. The film is deft, thrilling, and cheerful; whereas the events it trades on were clumsy, tedious, and very depressing. Hollywood is not dead or defunct when it turns that story into the heroics of crusading journalism as embodied in two star actors. Pakula has such mastery with the melodramatics of Deep Throat and the sinister climate of a spooked Washington that one could believe in Mabuse again. The disregard of interpretation or political understanding in the movie (and the book) bear witness to the way the media have made justice a theme for entertainment. It follows from this that anxiety and conspiracy theory—neurotic preoccupations of Pakula—are never treated, only preyed upon. *All the President's Men* proved that the sense of fiction was so rampant in America that you could go from fact to legend in three years without passing understanding.

Just as Pakula seemed very close to the jittery pulse of America in the seventies, so in the eighties a gap opened up. Good as he had been at conveying paranoia, he seemed less interested in other moods. *Sophie's Choice* was his only success, and that had literary prestige, a fine cast, and Meryl Streep at her most virtuoso moment. Still, Pakula didn't quite make that queasy story work or flow; rather he left us reminded of its implausibilities and of things a screen cannot show without prompting revulsion.

So many of his other films have been strained in tone and less than compelling. He tried to regain commercial momentum with the old-fashioned legalese melodrama of *Presumed Innocent* and *The Pelican Brief,* and it worked well enough. But *The Devil's Own* was a mess over which Harrison Ford and Brad Pitt had fought. It was a sad decline, capped by Pakula's death in a freak accident. In his absence now, it's easier to see how good *Klute* is and how well Pakula felt a moment in American history.

Jack Palance (Vladimir Palanuik—proceed with caution, since there are a handful of versions of his true name),
b. Lattimer, Pennsylvania, 1919
The son of Russian immigrants. He studied journalism at the universities of North Carolina and Stanford, was a boxer, and then a member of the U.S. air corps. On active service, his face was badly burned, so plastic surgery added to the taut strain of his features.

Writing for radio led him to stage acting, including work on Broadway with Elia Kazan, who cast him as the plague-carrying criminal in *Panic in the Streets* (50) (in which he was credited as Walter Jack Palance). After Milestone's *Halls of Montezuma* (50), he made his best-known appearance, as Stark Wilson, the hired gun, in *Shane* (53, George Stevens). His Slav looks always pointed Palance at exotic or sinister parts—*Sudden Fear* (52, David Miller) and *Sign of the Pagan* (54, Douglas Sirk)—but Robert Aldrich saw that the

same face might appear sensitive and nerve-racked: thus he played the movie star in *The Big Knife* (55), the doomed officer in *Attack!* (56), and in *Ten Seconds to Hell* (59).

His work usually carried a unique note of repressed hysteria: *Second Chance* (53, Rudolph Maté); as Jack the Ripper in *Man in the Attic* (53, Hugo Fregonese); *Kiss of Fire* (55, Joseph M. Newman); *I Died a Thousand Times* (55, Stuart Heisler), a remake of *High Sierra;* as twin brothers, changing places in Sing Sing in *House of Numbers* (57, Russell Rouse); as the father in *The Lonely Man* (57, Henry Levin).

But Palance was too unsettling to last as a star, and from about 1960 he worked as much in Europe as in America, giving several distinctive performances, happiest when most free to indulge in flamboyant menace: *The Mongols* (61, André de Toth and Riccardo Freda); *Barabbas* (62, Richard Fleischer); in manic charge of a little red book and a snarling red Maserati as the producer in Godard's *Contempt* (63); the Mexican in Brooks's *The Professionals* (66); as a crazy Edgar Allan Poe enthusiast in *The Torture Garden* (67, Freddie Francis); as Castro in Fleischer's *Che!* (69); as a lawman in *They Came to Rob Las Vegas* (69, Antonio Isasi); as the father in Frankenheimer's *The Horsemen* (70); and as the sidekick in *Monte Walsh* (70, William Fraker).

A word is in order for his TV *Dr. Jekyll and Mr. Hyde* (72, Charles Jarrott), without obvious makeup effects, but the two personae frighteningly alike. That proved again how disturbing Palance can be when under restraint. In the movies he increasingly gave himself up to satanic laughter and teeth-baring: *Justine: Le Disavventure della Virtu* (68, Jess Franco); *The Desperadoes* (69, Levin); *Vamos a Matar, Companeros!* (70, Sergio Corbucci); *Si Puo Fare . . . Amigo* (71, Maurizio Lucidi); *Chato's Land* (71, Michael Winner); *Oklahoma Crude* (73, Stanley Kramer); *Te Deum* (73, Enzo G. Castellani); *Craze* (73, Francis); *Dracula* (73, Dan Curtis); and *The Cop in Blue Jeans* (76, Bruno Corbucci).

Since then, he has been all over the place: *Portrait of a Hitman* (77, Allan J. Buckhantz); *One-Man Jury* (78, Charles Martin); *Angels' Brigade* (79, Greydon Clark); *The Shape of Things to Come* (79, George McCowan); *Cocaine Cowboys* (79, Ulli Lommel); *The Last Ride of the Dalton Gang* (79, Dan Curtis); *The Ivory Ape* (80, Tom Kotani); *Hawk the Slayer* (80, Terry Marcel); *Without Warning* (80, Clark); *Alone in the Dark* (82, Jack Sholder)—in which he costars with Donald Pleasence—some films are like rainbows, best seen from a great distance; a cameo in *Gor* (88, Fritz Kiersch); suddenly reclaimed by class for *Bagdad Cafe* (88, Percy Adlon); *Young Guns* (88, Christopher Cain); the wicked priest amid the swords and sorcery of *Outlaw of Gor* (89, John

Cardos); *Batman* (89, Tim Burton); and *Tango and Cash* (89, Andrei Konchalovsky).

He won the supporting actor Oscar in *City Slickers* (91, Ron Underwood), though he was more entertaining receiving the award than in the film. Then he was in *Radio Flyer* (92, Richard Donner); *Salmonberries* (92, Adlon); *Cops & Robbersons* (94, Michael Ritchie); *City Slickers II* (94, Paul Weiland); and a whole bunch of television stuff.

Lilli Palmer (Lillie Marie Peiser) (1914–86), b. Posen, Germany

The daughter of an actress and a surgeon, she studied acting in Berlin and began work in stock and cabaret. In 1933, she left for France and in 1934 she came to England under contract to Alexander Korda. He changed his mind about her but she stayed on and made a film debut in *Crime Unlimited* (35, Ralph Ince). In the next year she had several small parts, including *First Offence* (36, Herbert Mason) and *The Secret Agent* (36, Alfred Hitchcock), and by 1937 she starred in *Sunset in Vienna* (Norman Walker), *Command Performance* (Sinclair Hill), and *Crackerjack* (Albert de Courville). She was a leading actress throughout the war: *Blind Folly* (39, Reginald Denham); *A Girl Must Live* (39, Carol Reed); *Thunder Rock* (42, Roy Boulting); *The Gentle Sex* (43, Maurice Elvey and Leslie Howard); *English Without Tears* (44, Harold French); with her husband, Rex Harrison, in *The Rake's Progress* (45, Sidney Gilliat); and *Beware of Pity* (46, Elvey).

When Harrison went on contract to America, she accompanied him as a free-lancer. In Britain, she had looked pretty, but "European." In Hollywood she was turned into an intriguing beauty in four movies: *Cloak and Dagger* (46, Fritz Lang); *Body and Soul* (47, Robert Rossen); *My Girl Tisa* (48, Elliott Nugent); and *No Minor Vices* (48, Lewis Milestone). She jumped on *Cloak and Dagger* like a refugee offered a passport. Her quick change of the two Ginas—an Italian girl, and a woman hardened by war—is very touching. She played Shaw's Cleopatra on Broadway, went to France for *Hans le Marin* (49), and played in *The Long Dark Hall* (50, Anthony Bushell) in England. With Harrison, she appeared on Broadway in *Bell, Book and Candle*, and they then made *The Four Poster* (52, Irving Reis).

During the London run of *BB and C*, the marriage broke up and Lilli Palmer commenced a nomadic career, working in France, Germany, Britain, America, Italy, or Spain, with all the insouciance of the mysterious, continental woman she was usually asked to play. It is a story of drudgery, haphazardly illuminated by parts worthy of her, chiefly *Montparnasse 19* (57, Jacques Becker) and *Le Rendez-vous de Minuit* (62, Roger Leenhardt). Otherwise, even a sample list sounds wayward and

forlorn: *Feuerwerk* (54, Kurt Hoffmann); *Anastasia die Letzte Zarentochter* (56, Falk Harnack); *Madchen in Uniform* (58, Geza von Radvanyi); *But Not For Me* (59, Walter Lang); *Conspiracy of Hearts* (60, Ralph Thomas); *Frau Warren's Gewerbe* (60, Akos von Rathony); *The Pleasure of His Company* (61) and *The Counterfeit Traitor* (61), both by George Seaton; *Leviathan* (61, Leonard Keigel); *Finche Dura la Tempesta* (62, Charles Frend); *The Flight of the White Stallions* (63, Arthur Hiller); *Le Grain de Sable* (64, Pierre Kast); *Operation Crossbow* (64, Michael Anderson); *The Amorous Adventures of Moll Flanders* (65, Terence Young); *Le Tonnerre de Dieu* (65, Denys de la Patellière); *Kongress amusiert sich* (66, von Radvanyi); *Sebastian* (67, David Greene); *Paarungen* (67, Michael Verhoeven); *Nobody Runs Forever* (68, Thomas); *Oedipus the King* (68, Philip Saville); *Hard Contract* (69, S. Lee Pogostin); *De Sade* (69, Cy Endfield and Roger Corman); *La Peau de Torpedo* (69, Jean Delannoy); *La Residencia* (70, Narciso Ibanez Serrador); *Night Hair Child* (71, James Kelly); then regular performances, still beautiful but bereft of chance, in the TV series, *The Zoo Gang; Lotte in Weimar* (75, Egon Gunther); *The Boys from Brazil* (78, Franklin Schaffner); and *The Holcroft Covenant* (85, John Frankenheimer).

Gwyneth Paltrow, b. Los Angeles, 1972

There have been too many Gwyneth Paltrow jokes by far—ranging from the play on words with "paltry" to the evident rapture felt for her by the boss of Miramax, Harvey Weinstein. But honest adoration in a mogul can be a fine and warming thing, and all his obsession has done is give her a host of silly films in which she can learn her craft. More useful by far to recollect that she is the child of director Bruce Paltrow and actress Blythe Danner—one of the more strangely overlooked great actresses in America. So Paltrow may have been pushed in odd directions—into a leather bikini in *Talk* magazine; in the general direction of being "our" Grace Kelly. But she can act, and she seems to have a strong character that will cause little harm even if she doesn't last as long as Katharine Hepburn or Bette Davis. An Oscar for *Shakespeare in Love* (98, John Madden) was too generous—though she carried that role off without a fluff or a hesitation—but there have always been actresses (like Audrey Hepburn) who inspire daft generosity.

She began in *Hook* (91, Steven Spielberg) and *Shout* (91, Jeff Hornaday), so she had early lessons in the need to get better. But then she attracted real attention being slinky in *Malice* (93, Harold Becker) and *Flesh and Bone* (93, Steve Kloves), where she stole the show. Next she was in *Mrs. Parker and the Vicious Circle* (94, Alan Rudolph); *Jefferson in Paris* (95, James Ivory); *Moonlight and Valentino* (95, David Anspaugh); *Se7en* (95, David Fincher), where she is very touching; *Hard Eight* (96, Paul Thomas Anderson), another of her tougher performances; *The Pallbearer* (96, Matt Reeves), with David Schwimmer.

Emma (96, Douglas McGrath) was her break-through, and a deserved success, followed by a run of poor pictures—*Great Expectations* (98, Alfonso Cuarón); *Hush* (98, Jonathan Darby); *Sliding Doors* (98, Peter Howitt); *A Perfect Murder* (98, Andrew Davis)—before the high demands of *The Talented Mr. Ripley* (99, Anthony Minghella).

It was about 1999, I'd guess, that the public began to feel they'd seen too much of her, that maybe they didn't really like her. She stays working, but as if in panic: *Duets* (00, Bruce Paltrow, Daddy); *Bounce* (00, Don Roos); funny and sharp in *The Anniversary Party* (01, Alan Cumming and Jennifer Jason Leigh); *The Royal Tenenbaums* (01, Wes Anderson); *Shallow Hal* (01, Bobby and Peter Farrelly); *Possession* (02, Neil LaBute); *View from the Top* (03, Bruno Barreto); and as Sylvia Plath in *Ted and Sylvia* (03, Christine Jeffs).

Sergei Paradjanov (Sarkis Paradjanian) (1924–90), b. Tiflis, USSR
1951: *Moldovskaya Skazka/Moldavian Fairy Tale* (s). 1954: *Andriesh* (codirected with Y. Bzelian). 1958: *Pervyi Paren/The First Lad.* 1961: *Ukrainskaya Rapsodiya/Ukrainian Rhapsody.* 1963: *Tsvetok na Kamne/The Stone Flower.* 1964: *Dumka/The Ballad.* 1965: *Tini Zabutykh Predkiv/Shadows of Our Forgotten Ancestors.* 1972: *Sayat Nova/The Color of Pomegranates.* 1978: *Return to Life* (s). 1985: *Ambavi Suramis Tsikhitsa/The Legend of the Suram Fortress* (codirected with Dodo Abashidze). 1986: *Arabeskebi Pirosmanis Temaze/Arabesque on Themes from Pirsomani.* 1988: *Ashik Kerib.*

There are lives in film that make the commercial travails (and the domestic turmoil) of some Hollywood neurotics seem scarcely mentionable. An Armenian, Paradjanov was talented at music and painting as well as film, and in his least inhibited work one can feel the natural confluence of all three urges. To say nothing of the visionary originality.

He abandoned the idea of becoming a singer to study film, with Kuleshov as one of his teachers (in Moscow). After a few years of obedience to official attitudes, he announced himself with *Shadows of Our Forgotten Ancestors*, a dazzlingly beautiful evocation of village life in the nineteenth century. Though very well received overseas, the film was attacked by Soviet authorities for its decadence and excessive visual expression. Thereafter, Paradjanov was subject to mounting persecution. He was exiled to Armenia, he was prevented from working for several years, but still came through

with the magnificent *Color of Pomegranates*, a celebration of color, form, and vitality as well as its central character, the rebel poet Arutiun Sayadian.

Paradjanov was now outlawed, and hounded, and in 1974 he was imprisoned for four years. Even when released, he was desperately poor and unable to work until the coming of *glasnost*. He died of cancer before he could complete *Confession*, his autobiographical film. But the 1991 documentary *Bobo* is a tribute to his life and work. *Swan Lake—The Zone* was another Paradjanov project, completed by his cameraman, Yuri Ilienko.

The contrast between Paradjanov's abused life and the radiance of his vision is incomparable and exemplary. The stress on beauty in the nature of things is not exactly Western, or European—and Paradjanov heralded a kind of glorying in imagery that may speak for Georgia, Armenia, and the countries of what we call the Middle East. More even than Tarkovsky (who has a more Western eye), Paradjanov stands for the link between film and religious renewal and exultation over the fact of light and its harvest. When watching his work, we often feel an association with cultures that existed long before the coming of photography and movies. So it is an even greater shock to be reminded of the terrible difficulties under which this transcendent artist continued to affirm the miracles of light and appearance. In every film, there is dark first to remind us of so many calamitous possibilities. And then . . .

Sir Alan Parker, b. Islington, London, 1944
1973: *Our Cissy* (s); *Footsteps* (s). 1974: *No Hard Feelings* (TV). 1975: *The Evacuees* (TV). 1976: *Bugsy Malone.* 1978: *Midnight Express.* 1980: *Fame.* 1982: *Shoot the Moon; The Wall/Pink Floyd—The Wall.* 1984: *Birdy.* 1986: *A Turnip Head's Guide to the British Cinema* (TV). 1987: *Angel Heart.* 1989: *Mississippi Burning.* 1990: *Come See the Paradise.* 1991: *The Commitments.* 1994: *The Road to Wellville.* 1996: *Evita.* 1998: *Angela's Ashes.* 2003: *The Life of David Gale.*

Parker's choice of material is invariably interesting and bold—yet very few of his pictures stand up to repeated viewing. He grabs attention, but he has no sustained grip. And sometimes, as with grabbers, there is an undue stress on suspense and intimidation. Nevertheless, Parker is an intriguing case, a working-class Londoner—and proud of it—who has successfully sought international audiences. It is not that he is without craft or skill: he has an eye (trained in years of making TV commercials), and he rarely permits slack performances. Still, he seems in many ways like a good producer, full of new ideas, but too impatient or defensive to trust himself to depth.

There's something in Parker's face that seems

interesting—not that a director's appearance is generally relevant, even in an art attentive to external expression. Parker looks angry and wary, beaten down by the pain of the world. Time and again he films ordeals of a kind, yet isn't there a sense of fatigue in his unquestioned melodramatic energy? No director has felt driven to spend more time fighting attacks against himself on the chance that he is being slighted. This leaves a feeling of hunched, guarded shoulders in Parker, a pressure that may prevent him from looking out, or in, in peace.

In the early seventies, with Alan Marshall, Parker had a very successful company that produced major TV commercials at the rate of one a week. Was that another inducement to the grab that lacks longer-term aims?

Bugsy Malone was a frank attempt to do something so different it *would* get made as a feature film. *Midnight Express* was Parker's greatest hit, so suspenseful that matters of race and morality slipped by. *Fame* seemed even at the time an idea for a TV series, accessible to incident, charm, musical numbers, and guest stars. It was as extreme a study of education as *The Wall* (a project made with cartoonist Gerald Scarfe—Parker is also a talented caricaturist).

Shoot the Moon is well acted, and deeply anguished—but its final bout of violence seems just a way of ending the show. *Birdy*, from William Wharton, is precious. *Angel Heart* is cheerfully macabre, but too lip-smacking to believe in evil. *Mississippi Burning* is a well-made, very old-fashioned political melodrama that seems unable to grasp the implications of its own dilemma. *Come See the Paradise* concerned Japanese-American internees in America during World War II, and was one of Parker's least viable pictures. But *The Commitments*—a rare return to the United Kingdom (or Dublin)—showed an unusual fondness for people, place, and music. It was as close as Parker has come to optimism.

He remains the determined handler of big projects—*Evita*, a broad-stroke musical, allegedly concerned with politics; *Angela's Ashes*, a best-selling book, supposedly about poverty. I still find those atmospheres capitalized and vulgarized, and thus the one film hardly sniffs out the real corruption of Argentinian politics, while the other never pauses to think that its own story might be a little on the tall side. But the legend of poverty and the cult of personality are two appealing shams that go beyond Parker's plain thinking.

Eleanor Parker, b. Cedarville, Ohio, 1922

Parker was an actress most celebrated for her wound-red hair and the ability to bring a rueful, shrewish feeling to "the other woman." She grew bitter and harsh as the prisoner in *Caged* (50, John Cromwell); ravishing and resentful in *Scara-*

mouche (52, George Sidney); beautiful but hateful as the wheelchair wife in *The Man with the Golden Arm* (56, Otto Preminger); quite crazy in *Interrupted Melody* (55, Curtis Bernhardt); and was the hostile wife killed at the outset of *An American Dream* (66, Robert Gist).

She made her debut in *They Died With Their Boots On* (41, Raoul Walsh) and was put under contract by Warners. After supporting parts in *Mission to Moscow* (43, Michael Curtiz), *The Very Thought of You* (44, Delmer Daves), and *Pride of the Marines* (45, Daves), she came to the fore in *Never Say Goodbye* (46, James V. Kern) and as Mildred in *Of Human Bondage* (46, Edmund Goulding) and played in *The Voice of the Turtle* (47, Irving Rapper); *Escape Me Never* (47, Peter Godfrey); *The Woman in White* (48, Godfrey); *Chain Lightning* (50, Stuart Heisler); *Three Secrets* (50, Robert Wise); and *Valentino* (50, Lewis Allen).

She was good in *Detective Story* (51, William Wyler), but usually remained an adventurer's lady: *Above and Beyond* (52, Melvin Frank and Norman Panama); *Escape from Fort Bravo* (53, John Sturges); *The Naked Jungle* (54, Byron Haskin); *Many Rivers to Cross* (55, Roy Rowland); and *The King and Four Queens* (56, Walsh). After *Lizzie* (57, Hugo Haas), she appeared as the adulterous wife in *The Seventh Sin* (57, Ronald Neame and Vincente Minnelli); *A Hole in the Head* (59, Frank Capra); and *Home from the Hill* (60, Minnelli). After that, her career declined, despite her part in *The Sound of Music* (65, Robert Wise); *Warning Shot* (66, Buzz Kulik); *Il Tigre* (67, Dino Risi); *How to Steal the World* (68, Sutton Roley); *Eye of the Cat* (69, David Lowell Rich); *She's Dressed to Kill* (79, Gus Trikonis); *Sunburn* (79, Richard C. Sarafian); *Once Upon a Spy* (80, Ivan Nagy); *Madame X* (80, Robert Ellis Miller); *Dead on the Money* (91, Mark Cullingham).

Gordon Parks, b. Fort Scott, Kansas, 1912

1969: *The Learning Tree*. 1971: *Shaft*. 1972: *Shaft's Big Score*. 1974: *The Super Cops*. 1976: *Leadbelly*. 1985: *Solomon Northrup's Odyssey* (TV).

Gordon Parks has been so many things: the youngest in a poor black farm family; piano player in a brothel; basketball player; a composer of music; the author of autobiographical books, including *The Learning Tree;* a master still photographer; a very urbane gentleman who has lived much of his adult life in Paris—*and* the confident director of the slick integration of black cool, movie violence, seventies music, and attitude in the two *Shaft* films. Sure, they they owe a lot to writer Ernest Tidyman and actor Richard Roundtree, but they are very well made, without a trace of superior irony or disdain. Nor do they show the overly classical composition of Parks's still photography and the heartfelt mood of *The*

Learning Tree. It's easy to place Parks as just the first black director of mainstream films. But this is to miss the wit of *Shaft* and the passion in *Leadbelly*, as well as the great diversity of Parks's life and culture. The achievement may not be as great, but he is an Ellingtonian figure, a renaissance person in whom we never forget the importance of charm, intelligence, and grace.

Robert Parrish (1916–95),
b. Columbus, Georgia
1951: *The Mob; Cry Danger*. 1952: *The San Francisco Story; Assignment Paris; My Pal Gus*. 1953: *Rough Shoot*. 1954: *The Purple Plain*. 1955: *Lucy Gallant*. 1957: *Fire Down Below*. 1958: *Saddle the Wind*. 1959: *The Wonderful Country*. 1963: *In the French Style*. 1965: *Up from the Beach*. 1967: *The Bobo*. 1968: *Duffy*. 1969: *Doppelganger*. 1971: *A Town Called Bastard*. 1974: *The Marseille Contract*. 1984: *Mississippi Blues* (d) (codirected with Bertrand Tavernier).

This is a sad story: once vigorous, Parrish never passed the point of wondering where his next film would come from. As the movie world grew more unreliable as an employer, so his projects became intractable. His reflective, anecdotal books became more worthwhile than his films.

Parrish was a teenage actor: *Four Sons* (28, John Ford); *Mother Machree* (28, Ford); *The Iron Mask* (29, Allan Dwan); *Men Without Women* (30, Ford); *The Right to Love* (30, Richard Wallace); *Up the River* (30, Ford); *All Quiet on the Western Front* (30, Lewis Milestone); *City Lights* (31, Charles Chaplin); and *The Informer* (35, Ford). He was with Ford as assistant editor in the late thirties and assistant director on *Gunga Din* (39, George Stevens). He was Ford's editor during the war on *The Battle of Midway* and *December 7th*, and after the war on *Body and Soul* (47, Robert Rossen); *A Double Life* (48, George Cukor); *No Minor Vices* (48, Milestone); *Caught* (49, Max Ophuls); *All the King's Men* (49, Rossen); and *Of Men and Music* (50, Irving Reis). He also directed some of *The Lusty Men* (52) during Nicholas Ray's absence through illness.

His first thrillers benefited from being economical and direct: *Cry Danger* is especially exciting. Parrish appeared to expand with better material and actors. *My Pal Gus* is an engaging comedy, *The Purple Plain* a startlingly vivid account of Gregory Peck in extremis, *Lucy Gallant* a domestic Western with character, *Fire Down Below* amusing nonsense, and *The Wonderful Country* a Western of real distinction. *In the French Style* was unconvincing, but *Up from the Beach* was a good war picture.

After that, however, Parrish produced either the pretentious—*Duffy* (the remains of a Donald Cammell script)—or the messy—*The Bobo and*

Doppelganger. But after ten years' absence, he reappeared as codirector of an American documentary, a labor of love, but a slow, uninvolving film.

Louella Parsons (Oettinger) (1881–1972),
b. Freeport, Illinois; and
Hedda Hopper (Elda Furry) (1885–1966),
b. Hollidaysburg, Pennsylvania
People once regarded Hedda and Louella as a great rivalry—like Robinson and La Motta for five or six years, vital to the circulation war among Los Angeles newspapers. Yet, truly, in hindsight, they work best the way we refer to them: as a team, as two old, overdressed biddies (a bit like dahlias battered by rain) who needed each other. In fact, Hedda studied Louella and then set up the contest with her. But if you were to tell their story today, you would need a complicit Louella mistress-minding the whole furor.

Louella led the way (she was the older of two women who practiced lying with their own ages), but she was the less smart of the two—as if that had much to do with it, or as if their writings are recommended for wit or insight. But Louella attended high school in Dixon, Illinois (something a native of the town, Ronald Reagan, later cultivated), and she was a teenage reporter on the local paper before marrying John Parsons (in 1905) and having a daughter, Harriet, who would become her assistant and substitute.

There was a quick divorce, and it was as a single mother that Mrs. Parsons tried screenwriting at Chicago's Essanay Studios and then joined the *Chicago Record-Herald*. She had one bright idea: as celebrities training across the country made the two-hour stopover in Chicago, she would interview them. In 1918, she joined the *New York Morning Telegraph*, married again (to Jack McCaffrey), and had a passionate affair with labor leader Peter Brady.

What changed everything was her joining William Randolph Hearst's *New York American* in 1923, for $250 a week, to be its entertainment writer. Legend, and Peter Bogdanovich's entertaining film *The Cat's Meow* (in which Jennifer Tilly does a good job as Louella), offer the story that Louella was on the Hearst yacht when Thomas Ince died (in 1924), that she had the inside dope on the scandal, and that's how she secured her position with the Hearst papers.

It may have helped. But Louella's contract was earlier, and Louella had paid her dues by sucking up to Marion Davies. It is true that in 1925 Louella fell sick with TB and that Hearst paid for her recuperation. A year later, he insisted that she come out to Los Angeles (in other words, she was actually still posted in New York in 1924). And so began her empire: seven columns a week for the *L.A. Herald Examiner*, plus a radio show, with a syndication deal that went to over 370 papers at its peak.

It was the early thirties before Hedda Hopper came into Louella's life. In 1913, Hedda had married DeWolf Hopper: she was a Broadway dancer, he was a matinee idol. Together, in 1915, they went to Hollywood: he joined Triangle and she began a career as an actress that easily outlasted the marriage (over in 1922). For a few years, she was a lead, but then she happily accepted supporting roles and went on doggedly until the late thirties. If I skip titles, it's because she wouldn't be in this book as an actress.

But she was no fool, and she had sense enough to know that in Hollywood then information had a currency. She became one of Louella's sources, and she was able to observe and learn from the older woman's routine. In 1936, she started a radio talk show, and in 1938 she promoted herself into a job at the *L.A. Times* that rapidly made her Louella's match, or rival.

What did the two of them do? Essentially, they played ball with the studios. They recognized that they could become important and wealthy parts of the promotional machine, running star interviews, profiles, and "secrets" from their private lives. The legend goes that they often angered stars with their indiscretion, yet I think it's closer to the truth that (as journalists) they were remarkable for the stories they buried, for ugly truths they were prepared to ignore. For, more or less, their power coincided with the contract system, a part of which was the "morals clause"—a blanket warning that any unruly or improper behavior could end a career.

What they and people like MGM head of publicity Howard Strickling knew is another matter—that is the lost history of Hollywood. But Louella and Hedda were writers who left a legacy in which little printed in the L.A. press and the fan magazines in those days can be trusted. They were partners with the publicity machine in spreading a picture that suited the studios. They hardly ever dealt with real business, or money, and they never offended the real powers. If they picked on a star, it was a sign that that star's number was up. In other words, they helped erect the barrier that has always protected Hollywood from our scrutiny.

Gossip press today is far rougher. (These were both ladies raised in the Victorian age.) But there is no contract system, and so every star needs to hire an agency—like PMK—to run publicity or protection. That manipulation of truth or impression—we call it "spin"—is a true American art, much neglected, and it is arguable that it began in show business before it set in in politics.

But these days the public has acquired a greater taste for trashiness or even criminal behavior in stars. Hedda and Louella took it for granted that the movies were good for business and for America, and they stirred the pot.

Hedda is semifamous for her appearance in the waxworks bridge game in *Sunset Boulevard* (50, Billy Wilder) and even made a final appearance in *The Oscar* (66, Russell Rouse). She had a son, William Hopper (he played Paul Drake on *Perry Mason* and Natalie Wood's father in *Rebel Without a Cause*), who was said to be his mother's spy. She died without having to see *Bonnie and Clyde, Easy Rider,* or worse intrusions on wholesome entertainment. Louella faltered in 1962 when the *Herald Examiner* folded. She spent her last years, silent, in a Santa Monica rest home, paid for by Hearst money.

No one reads them now. No one, much, would go to their files for reliable material. Louella, famously, led the charge against *Citizen Kane,* and that has only been the most admired film for fifty years. As to wounds, I suspect that Pauline Kael did more hurt to Hollywood feelings, and she never used a hatpin—she didn't even wear hats.

Pier Paolo Pasolini (1922–75),
b. Bologna, Italy

1961: *Accattone.* 1962: *Mamma Roma;* "La Ricotta," episode from *RoGoPaG.* 1963: *La Rabbia* (part 1; film never released because of difficulties over part 2, directed by Giovanni Guareschi); *Sopraluoghi in Palestina per "Il Vangelo Secondo Matteo"* (d). 1964: *Comizi d'Amore; Il Vangelo Secondo Matteo/The Gospel According to St. Matthew.* 1966: *Uccellacci e Uccellini/The Hawks and the Sparrows;* "La Terra Vista dalla Luna," episode from *Le Streghe;* "Che Cosa Sona le Nuvole?" episode from *Capriccio all'Italiana.* 1967: *Edipo Re/Oedipus Rex;* "La Fiore di Campo," episode from *Amore e Rabbia.* 1968: *Teorema/Theorem.* 1969: *Il Porcile/Pigsty.* 1969: *Medea.* 1971: *Il Decamerone/The Decameron; I Muri di Sana.* 1972: *I Racconti di Canterbury/The Canterbury Tales.* 1974: *The Arabian Nights.* 1975: *Salo o le Centoventi Giornate di Sodoma/ Salo, or the 120 Days of Sodom.*

Pasolini was never merely a movie director. He was a Marxist, a poet, and a novelist, an intellectual prophet, and committed to the homosexual life. He was a figure in the Italian cultural landscape, and it may be that his violent death (murdered by a teenage hustler) is best understood in terms of the many controversies he had stirred up. For, finally, he was a dramatic corpse, as if that was the ultimate way of declaring his truth. In his films, too, there are many creative forces at war with his flux of gravity and emotionalism. Though not a believer, he was preoccupied with belief; he recognized the need to address contemporary issues; yet he also loved the epic, scholarly and homoerotic re-creation of earlier literary worlds—

he was thrilled by decor, light, and the great beauty of battered faces and heroic bodies. He was very articulate, very determined—yet he frequently went off in opposed directions.

Like Buñuel, Pasolini despised the establishment's imaginative life for being decadent and threadbare compared with that of the vigorous outsider—whether the legendary man who figures in *Theorem*, the slum kid in *Accattone*, or even the artisan Christ of the Matthew Gospel.

He persistently offended Italian authority—Church and State—and the absurd suspended sentence after *La Ricotta* was only the most notorious brush he had (and courted). Just as his films often pointed accusingly at his own society, so he retained a creative interest in other arts. Originally a poet, essayist, and novelist, his writing was a vital part of his work. Indeed, his paper, "Il Cinema di Poesia," read at the 1965 Pesaro Festival, is one of the most worthwhile contributions to cinema theory. An esoterically argued and barbarously worded essay, it marked a deepening poetic content in Pasolini's own films.

Despite admiration for Pasolini as theorist, I cannot like his films too much. He often inflicted a portentous mystery on his images, and was not the most graceful of visual realizers. His strident compositions were clumsy and monotonous, and his appetite for faces often overrode the ability to edit shots together fluently. The style was top-heavy, just as the meanings of his films were too literary, too immediate, and too inconsistent. Very close in mood to Buñuel, *Pigsty* and *Theorem*—his best films—have a showy and gratuitous cruelty and an unresolved desire to brandish fantasy within the everyday.

The Decameron was an odd departure, hardly sustained by the simplistic pretext that the Middle Ages were like our own, or by the interest of Pasolini himself playing Giotto in search of good faces to adorn the stories. But to extend that choice to *The Canterbury Tales* was eccentric, and it meant the elimination of Chaucer's May mood for the bawdy anecdote. *The Arabian Nights* was the dullest of the sequence, and *Salo* was gratuitously disgusting—as if something had shaped or clarified in its director's mind. Intellect and artiness were gone, and a kind of gay pornography was revealed.

Before he began directing, Pasolini had written several novels dealing with lowlife in Rome and had moved on from Friulian dialect poetry to be an important Italian poet. During the 1950s, he worked as a writer on many films, including *La Donna del Fiume* (54, Mario Soldati); *Nights of Cabiria* (56, Federico Fellini); as a dialogue man on Selznick's *A Farewell to Arms* (57, Charles Vidor); *Marisa la Civetta* (57, Mauro Bolognini); *Giovani Mariti* (58, Bolognini); *La Notte Brava* (59, Bolognini); *Morte di un Amico* (60, Franco

Rossi); *I Bell'Antonio* (60, Bolognini); *La Lunga Notte del '43* (60, Florestano Vancini); *La Ragazza in Vetrina* (61, Luciano Emmer); and *La Commare Secca* (62, Bernardo Bertolucci).

Bill Paxton, b. Fort Worth, Texas, 1955

Bill Paxton can vary his action hero by several degrees one way or another—towards introspection or loudmouthed enthusiasm. *One False Move* (92, Carl Franklin) is easily his best film, but not that many directors are as interested in ambivalent heroes. So it may be to the point that Paxton is getting older in a genre that has scant patience with middle age (unless it is a source of wickedness). So it's worth noting that Paxton is now trying out as a director, on a picture intriguingly titled *Frailty* (02).

He got a job dressing sets on *Big Bad Mama* (74, Steve Carver), but there was a gap of several years before he began acting: *Stripes* (81, Ivan Reitman); *The Lords of Discipline* (83, Franc Roddam); *Streets of Fire* (84, Walter Hill); *Impulse* (84, Graham Baker); *The Terminator* (84, James Cameron); *Weird Science* (85, John Hughes); *Aliens* (86, Cameron); *Near Dark* (87, Kathryn Bigelow); *Next of Kin* (89, John Irvin); *Navy SEALS* (90, Lewis Teague); *Predator 2* (90, Stephen Hopkins); *The Vagrant* (92, Chris Walas); *Trespass* (92, Hill); *Monolith* (94, John Eyres); *Boxing Helena* (93, Jennifer Chambers); *Indian Summer* (93, Mike Binder); *Tombstone* (94, George Pan Cosmatos); *True Lies* (94, Cameron); *Apollo 13* (95, Ron Howard); *The Last Supper* (96, Stacy Title); *Twister* (96, Jan de Bont); *Evening Star* (96, Robert Harling); *Traveller* (97, Jack N. Green), which he coproduced; *Titanic* (97, Cameron); *A Bright Shining Lie* (98, Terry George); *A Simple Plan* (98, Sam Raimi); *Mighty Joe Young* (98, Ron Underwood); *U-571* (00, Jonathan Mostow); *Vertical Limit* (00, Martin Campbell).

Gregory Peck (1916–2003)

b. La Jolla, California

Peck's one failing as an actor—that he wants to be respectable—is excused because it confirms the aura of responsibility and commitment to proper causes that surrounds him. It was a sign of blocked feelings among politicians that the Nixon White House should have rated Peck one of its most serious enemies. For Peck's modest radicalism clearly preferred stability.

From his debut, Peck was always a star and rarely less than a major box-office success. The image of a sound protagonist, of an escort who will not exploit a lady, of a lawyer who will diligently pursue just cases, still comes through, despite a few interesting attempts to escape it.

But, first to deal with Peck the noble, Gregory the champion of uncomplicated emotions: his debut in the enterprising *Days of Glory* (44, Jacques Tourneur), where he plays a Russian partisan and looks faintly Slav; as the Roman Catholic priest, turning away all wrath, and with flour in his hair recalling each of his young good deeds in *The Keys of the Kingdom* (44, John M. Stahl); as the father in *The Yearling* (46, Clarence Brown), as pristine as the heroes from Inspiration pictures of 1920; as the reporter uncovering anti-Semitism in *Gentleman's Agreement* (47, Elia Kazan); resisting all Richard Widmark's threats in *Yellow Sky* (48, William Wellman); implacably resourceful beneath a tricorn hat in *Captain Horatio Hornblower* (51, Raoul Walsh); making a Bering Straits seal pirate into an instrument of American mercantilism in *The World in His Arms* (52, Walsh); squiring the young Audrey Hepburn in *Roman Holiday* (53, William Wyler); stoically enduring that moment in *Designing Woman* (57, Vincente Minnelli) when Lauren Bacall tips a plate of spaghetti in his lap; never fighting rough in an immense fist bout with Charlton Heston in *The Big Country* (58, Wyler); as the conscience-laden platoon commander in Korea in *Pork Chop Hill* (59, Lewis Milestone); the submarine commander sailing into the nuclear haze in *On the Beach* (59, Stanley Kramer); the center that holds firm in *The Guns of Navarone* (61, J. Lee Thompson), the idea of a moral officer who might protect a nation against the excesses of its own brutal soldiers; the wronged father in *Cape Fear* (61, Lee Thompson), battling Robert Mitchum's depravity; winning an Oscar for his liberal country lawyer and kindly, widower father in *To Kill a Mockingbird* (63, Robert Mulligan); as a hard-working psychiatrist in *Captain Newman, M.D.* (63, David Miller); leader of the expedition again in *MacKenna's Gold* (69, Lee Thompson); and as the Mission Controller in *Marooned* (69, John Sturges).

He is a protagonist for middle American aspiration, pathfinder of the straight and narrow, and able to suggest a false ease and gloss that go with probity. This Peck never succumbs to the awful doubts that drag down Gary Cooper. He is Kennedy-like, preferring to act in crisis, and always cosmetically vindicated. It is a cardboard character, but carried off with a heavy sense of care and usually the figurehead of major productions. This is the actor turned producer as proud of *The Trial of the Catonsville Nine* (72, Gordon Davidson) as of *The Dove* (74, Charles Jarrott).

It is a good deal harder to remember Peck's relaxations. Some of these were offered at the time as follies, but some reach down to a real man who might find it a strain looking so Lincolnian: originally, as the fake head of a clinic, himself haunted by ski trails beneath the smooth surface in *Spellbound* (45, Alfred Hitchcock); bringing a sardonic pleasure to Lewt in *Duel in the Sun* (46, King

Vidor), riding into the bloody sunset, singing "I've been working on the railroad," and engaged in a constant knife fight of sensuality with Jennifer Jones; in *The Macomber Affair* (47, Zoltan Korda); as the lawyer fatally in love with his client in *The Paradine Case* (47, Hitchcock); staidly dissolute as the Dostoyevsky figure in *The Great Sinner* (49, Robert Siodmak); quite riveting as the colonel with a breakdown in *Twelve O'Clock High* (49, Henry King), and again for King, with a drooping moustache, weary of killing as *The Gunfighter* (50); if that pair suggested a special rapport with King, they then made the stuffy *David and Bathsheba* (51) to dispel such hopes; as Hemingway's wounded husband in *The Snows of Kilimanjaro* (52, King), although as prettied up as the changed ending, and spared that gangrenous smell; in *Night People* (54, Nunnally Johnson); excellent, isolated in the jungle, in *The Purple Plain* (55, Robert Parrish); socializing wartime adultery in *The Man in the Gray Flannel Suit* (56, Johnson); not half as bad an Ahab in *Moby Dick* (56, John Huston) as some alleged, and actually suggesting the ingrained, heroic misanthropy; stern and vengeful in *The Bravados* (58, King); helplessly adrift as Scott Fitzgerald in *Beloved Infidel* (59, King); led astray by Tuesday Weld in *I Walk the Line* (70, John Frankenheimer); chewing on an oaty Scottish accent in *Billy Two Hats* (73, Ted Kotcheff).

The older man out of control of his life in *I Walk the Line* came as a startling admission after the 1960s had been filled by comedy thrillers such as *Mirage* (65, Edward Dmytryk) and *Arabesque* (66, Stanley Donen). Peck still looked less than his real age, still too complacent for great suffering, too bland to rule in an age of Watergate.

His dignity and solidity were used well as the impossibly harassed ambassador in *The Omen* (76, Richard Donner), and he was intelligent and proud as *MacArthur* (77, Joseph Sargent), even if he could not quite expose himself to overweening arrogance or sublime wrongheadedness. Reserve has always been Peck's charm, and his liability. He was too genteel and restrained for the Nazi in *The Boys from Brazil* (78, Franklin Schaffner), so he wasted the part's evil in overacting.

Since then, he has been in *The Sea Wolves* (80, Andrew V. McLaglen); *The Scarlet and the Black* (83, Jerry London) on TV; *Amazing Grace and Chuck* (87, Mike Newell); as Ambrose Bierce in *Old Gringo* (89, Luis Puenzo)—touching but never catching fire; *Other People's Money* (91, Norman Jewison); as a shady lawyer helping an old nemesis in *Cape Fear* (91, Martin Scorsese)—another hint (to him) to lay off the honor thing; on TV in *The Portrait* (93, Arthur Penn); and as Father Mapple in another *Moby Dick* (98, Franc Roddam).

Peck is probably today's most distinguished veteran. Young people even conclude that he is of the golden age—though he only came to films in the forties. He does state occasions very well—he did the tribute to Audrey Hepburn at the 1993 Oscars with evident feeling.

But the old man is very staid, and it comes as a shock now to see how lethally handsome he was in, say, *Spellbound* or *Duel in the Sun*.

Sam Peckinpah (1925–84),
b. Fresno, California

1961: *The Deadly Companions*. 1962: *Ride the High Country/Guns in the Afternoon*. 1965: *Major Dundee*. 1969: *The Wild Bunch*. 1970: *The Ballad of Cable Hogue*. 1971: *Straw Dogs*. 1972: *Junior Bonner; The Getaway*. 1973: *Pat Garrett and Billy the Kid*. 1974: *Bring Me the Head of Alfredo Garcia*. 1975: *The Killer Elite*. 1977: *Cross of Iron*. 1978: *Convoy*. 1983: *The Osterman Weekend*.

In the years since Peckinpah's death, the "rogue" in him has taken on a clear but absurdly distant glow—like Monument Valley at magic hour seen in the rearview mirror. In other words, it seems farfetched that Peckinpah existed, let alone that we witnessed and wrestled with his films as they appeared. He could be just a warning or a hope painted on the sky: the director who got out of line. Not that this indicates stumbling or mistake. No, he got out of line from sheer, willful resolve, as if certain that self-destruction would be his only peace. Was there really a movie director that rueful, that passionate, that dangerous? That beautiful? Surely "they" would have disappeared him.

Peckinpah was born into a ranching family, and military school and service with the marines hardened his deliberate masculinity. He studied drama at the University of Southern California and worked in the theatre as an actor and director. After small jobs on TV he entered movies as a dialogue director and, eventually, as a writer. He had a small acting part in Don Siegel's *Invasion of the Body Snatchers* (56), on which he also worked as a writer, before making a reputation in TV Westerns—creating *The Rifleman* and *The Westerner*. After the freshness of his first two Westerns, Peckinpah was fired from *The Cincinnati Kid* and then quarreled badly with producer Martin Ransohoff so that *Major Dundee* emerged a broken thing, with intriguing moments jostling together. For several years he was unemployed as a director. He scripted *The Glory Guys* (65, Arnold Laven) and *Villa Rides!* (68, Buzz Kulik) and only after more TV work—including a notable direction of Katherine Anne Porter's *Noon Wine*—did he make a comeback with *The Wild Bunch*, a significant advance into "authentic" violence, and the basis for his "commercial" career.

Throughout Peckinpah's work there is the theme of violently talented men hired for a job that is loaded with compromise, corruption, and double-cross. They strive to perform with honor, before recognizing the inevitable logic of self-destruction. The theme was invariably dressed up as a Western—classical and modern: the air was sultry with analogy, yet Peckinpah also pioneered the fruitful history of 1881 to about 1918. *The Wild Bunch* trade guns to Mapache as a prelude to stunning slaughter. Pat Garrett contracts to eliminate an old friend, knowing in his bones that he and the Kid have lived too late on the business-ready frontier. Deke Thornton must track down the old bunch to save his life. The hero of *Alfredo Garcia* must deliver that head, and wonder how he can keep his soul. Those contracts are jobs, yet they are also arrangements with death—ways of getting there, ways of breaking out. They are also metaphors for the eating of shit required in making a picture. Peckinpah was a romantic—and most of all when thinking about himself. Thus, these Westerns are parables about life in Hollywood.

I said "wrestled" earlier, and I meant it. There's hardly a better director I find so problematic. That gloomy self-romance is so humorless. People laugh at fate in Peckinpah films, yet they have a dogged, drunken humorlessness by which you have to worship Peckinpah's fatalism—or quit. The celebration of bloodletting is monotonous as well as beautiful; it became its own code and cliché, and the slow-mo gaze it summoned up was only proof of an addiction to booze, drugs, brutality, and arrogance. The style was cripplingly self-important. But it is beautiful, for Peckinpah knew more about composition, editing, and sound than anyone that narrow had a right to. And there are times—in *Pat Garrett* above all—where the beauty redeems the boorish attitudes and, like a flooding river, breaks their banks. Moreover, it was in looking that Peckinpah seemed most open or uncertain; he looked to see—whereas Ford looked to discover what he knew already.

That is why *Pat Garrett* is one of the great American films, entrancing, perplexing, and—may I add—growing: only recently, a letterboxed videotape came my way with a long, bitter scene between Garrett and his wife that changes my sense of the film (yet again). For there are versions of *Pat Garrett*, and there is a Peckinpah cult that delivers Sam's real or deepest wishes long after his death. Why not? So many of his films were butchered, adding confusion to plot lines that are often cryptic and episodic.

Then there is the matter of women. Peckinpah on screen was a merciless misogynist. His women are bitches, whores, whore-saints, sluts, betrayers, native madonnas—they are also riveting, for Peckinpah's eye extended to women, and sometimes he must have charmed actresses into the indignities they suffered. But these women are so silent, so passive, so fit for male paranoia. Only one is central—in *Straw Dogs*—a revolting film of grinding menace, stilted, and very uneasy in England. Again, the hatred he disclosed was finally a proof of how enclosed and protected the alleged adventurer was. Time and again, Peckinpah is loathsome.

The final films deteriorate terribly, leaving us to suppose the wreck Peckinpah had become, the victim of his addictions, unable to find fresh subjects. Nevertheless, we are left with a handful of films that have not gone stale—*The Wild Bunch, Cable Hogue, Pat Garrett,* and *Alfredo Garcia.* I omit the two Steve McQueen pictures, though they both work. McQueen was not quite a Peckinpah actor—the director preferred, and did wonders with, ensembles. McQueen was too impregnable, and not quite open to delusion: that may be why Peckinpah's *The Getaway* stops well short of the terror in Jim Thompson's novel.

So we have four films, all in the haze of Mexico and the Southwest, tales of self-extinction worthy of Borges, yet true to the history of the American West, and crammed with the best stock company ever put on American film: Holden, Borgnine, Ryan, Strother Martin, L. Q. Jones, Warren Oates, Ben Johnson, James Coburn, Kris Kristofferson, Harry Dean Stanton, Richard Bright, Slim Pickens . . . the list goes on (and ignores women).

The more that emerges on Peckinpah the man, the clearer it is that he was in brazen pursuit of his own fantasies—and expecting others to pay for it. A very dangerous man, because he could be so damn good. *Pat Garrett and Billy the Kid* makes Clint Eastwood look like a carpetbagger.

Arthur Penn,

b. Philadelphia, 1922

1958: *The Left-Handed Gun.* 1962: *The Miracle Worker.* 1965: *Mickey One.* 1966: *The Chase.* 1967: *Bonnie and Clyde.* 1969: *Alice's Restaurant.* 1970: *Little Big Man.* 1973: "The Highest," episode from *Visions of Eight* (d). 1975: *Night Moves.* 1976: *The Missouri Breaks.* 1981: *Four Friends.* 1985: *Target.* 1987: *Dead of Winter.* 1989: *Penn and Teller Get Killed.* 1993: *The Portrait* (TV). 1996: *Inside* (TV).

What has happened with Arthur Penn? In the last twenty years, he has been nearly a nonentity. In the fifteen years before that, he was one of the best directors in America, and the filmmaker with the most acute sense of what the audience dreamed and feared. Can talent and instinct like that fade? Does a filmmaker weary of his own ordeal? Was Penn always more reliant on collaboration than I had allowed?

In the late seventies I said there was a cultivated perfection in his work that smacked of limits. Cinema is restricted by emphatic, exclusive meanings, and always encouraged by divergent, suggestive styles. It is contradictory that a director so committed to spontaneity and physical immediacy should seem to be striving for a solitary rightness. In Penn, meticulousness is sometimes alien to vitality. The best films by Nicholas Ray show how violence can be intrinsic, not illustrated by form but embodied in it, so that the whole shape and imagery of *In a Lonely Place* or *Rebel Without a Cause* seem vibrant with danger. In Penn's case, it is the premeditated, beautiful significance of violence, and the thorough schematic approach to it, that sometimes jar.

The Left-Handed Gun, The Chase, Bonnie and Clyde, and *Little Big Man* are commentaries on the conflict between law and violence in America and on the disillusion with corrupt government, racial disharmony, and the military machine. It is still not fully appreciated how the attractiveness of *Bonnie and Clyde* led the viewer toward political and social nihilism. Just as Penn presents Billy the Kid and Helen Keller as dynamic life forces unable to deal with the treacherous or crass world, so the link in *Bonnie and Clyde* between sexual satisfaction and outlawry is explicit. The death roll of the central characters is their final passion, a giving up of all hope of social order or justice. The world around Bonnie and Clyde is unremittingly hostile, and Penn depicts it with reciprocal animosity. The same foreboding haunts *The Chase,* where a small town proves unworthy of a noble sheriff and is seen as the breeding ground of the spasm violence in which Jack Ruby shot Lee Oswald in a police station. That comparison, like the orgasmic use of slow motion at the end of *Bonnie and Clyde,* is as calculated as the way in *Little Big Man* the Indians are called the "human beings" and the massacre of Jack Crabbe's family resembles My Lai.

On paper, such devices only seem to prove the schematic bones of Penn's style. What usually transcends such objections is the way he fixes on people and the way they speak, move, listen, and breathe. In terms of camerawork, Penn's films are measured. The impression of sensual experience comes principally from the sympathy he has with actors and the charge he gives them. Rather in the manner of Kazan, Penn redeems his own emphatic attitudes by taking flight with his actors.

It is therefore relevant that he came to films from TV and the theatre. After war service, he studied at the Actors' Studio and with Michael Chekhov in Los Angeles. By 1951 he was in TV as a floor manager and playwright. He wrote three plays before turning to direction. His TV work includes *The Miracle Worker,* which he later produced on Broadway, with Anne Bancroft and Patty Duke. His stage productions have also included *Two for the See-Saw, Toys in the Attic, All the Way Home,* and *Wait Until Dark.*

His first film, made at Warners rather against

the grain of studio orthodoxy, was from a play by Gore Vidal, scripted by Leslie Stevens. Its substitution of a modern American youth for the mythical Billy the Kid is largely due to Paul Newman's ambitious performance and the clear-cut psychological case history in the script. Like many Penn films, it is clinical allegory dressed up in period clothes. It also thrives on the restrictions Penn felt at Warners. It is so visually inventive that the deliberation hardly shows. There is a capturing of the psychology in the imagery—Billy planning a kill on a steamy window—a very moving tragic progression and specific moments of great tension.

The delay before *The Miracle Worker* may have reflected the trouble *Left-Handed Gun* had with large audiences and Penn's decision to wait until a proper film could be made of a subject that he had made his own. All the more credit then that the film often seems nearly improvised. Using very long takes, Penn achieved an audience involvement in the confrontation of emotional teacher and wild child that is physically and morally draining. The sentimentality that lies in wait is avoided with the insistence that Annie and Helen are stubborn, private creatures, the one with a message of civilization, the other a savage. And it is crucial to Penn's development that Helen's education is not just deeply moving when it succeeds, but also aware of a natural solitariness that has been lost. Education is vindicated, but not whitewashed, because we see how far Annie teaches to soothe her own emotional wounds. Like the outsiders trapped in the car dump in *The Chase*, Annie and Helen are joined by their flaws. Penn's romanticism is clear in his treatment of Helen as a noble savage restrained by culture. At a secondary level, *The Miracle Worker* is also a study of a suffocating Southern family. The two levels are connected in the conclusion to the dining-room battle—"the room's a wreck, but her napkin's folded."

Mickey One was a determined excursion into European existentialism, but still an intriguing commentary on an America beset by conspiracy. It was made after Penn had been fired from *The Train* by Burt Lancaster, and its Kafka treatment of Warren Beatty paranoid about "the organization" shows Penn's brooding dismay at modern America, fearful of menace and waiting in vain for a word from the Lord. Thus it leads into *The Chase* more readily than might be expected. Once the sheriff of that film has abdicated, then the arena is left to outlaws and depraved citizens.

Some critics have remarked on the way scriptwriters David Newman and Robert Benton turned to Penn only after Truffaut and Godard had been unable to make *Bonnie and Clyde*, as if to underline the tragi-comedy of the script. It is more important that Warren Beatty took up the subject and asked Penn to direct it. As with Paul Newman, Duke, and Bancroft, Penn ignited Beatty and Faye Dunaway. The idea of their nobility would be untenable but for their cinematic vividness: Clyde's shy limp, Bonnie's glistening skin. In photographing the quick and the dead in people, Penn has few equals. Time and again he has coaxed more out of a player than is usual: not only with Beatty and Dunaway, but John Dehner, Hurd Hatfield, Victor Jory, Janice Rule, the unwholesome gallery from *The Chase*, Gene Hackman, Gene Wilder, and Michael J. Pollard.

Alice's Restaurant is the most casual and perhaps the most fruitful of his films for his own future. Its ballad form is a once and only thing, and its direct use of fact and fiction is alien to Penn's taste for allegory. But because it is open to improvisation, and in the shadow of the droll Arlo Guthrie, Penn's formal intelligence stands back. *Little Big Man* concludes his great work; it goes past destruction, to resignation, and can hardly be advanced upon. Its perfection is that of an important theme thoroughly rendered. What will activate Penn now? Some ten years earlier, Preminger took on a run of major subjects, and was a tamer man thereafter. Penn is over seventy now. If he means to make more films, his need for precision and literal effects may seem handicaps. *Alice's Restaurant* offers a way out of the dilemma in the successful use of informality. In addition, it suggests a theme touched on in *Mickey One,* of the entertainer "talking" to the world.

Night Moves was made in the untrusting aftermath of assassinations and Watergate, and it tries to show personal failure at the heart of a larger national malaise. But it ends up a perplexing film noir, more unclear than disturbing, its allegory tangled with its anecdote. *The Missouri Breaks* is far more achieved and mature: using a conventional Western outline, Penn invests it with quirky history and a gang of originals. It is his most relaxed, digressive movie, with time for *Tristram Shandy*, urgent set pieces, an idiosyncratic girl, a running debate between order and freedom, and a Marlon Brando who manages to make every odd tangent believable and personal.

I would not back off on a word of the above. But then I must add that Penn's last six films are as if made by someone else (apart from that moment in *Four Friends* when James Leo Herlihy goes crazy). What happened? Times changed. Penn may have lost touch with vital friends and audience tastes. The lesson is clear: auteurship is no protection—great directors can go cold.

Sean Penn, b. Santa Monica, California, 1960

1991: *The Indian Runner.* 1995: *The Crossing Guard.* 2001: *The Pledge.*

Sean Penn is clearly a figure in the Hollywood landscape. In his friendship and association with

Dennis Hopper, he harks back to the era of Dean and Brando. And he is maybe the only actor now who, in interviews, can summon up the tortured introspection of early Method actors without irony or shame. He is also an icon for a group of actors who are more or less his age—for Tim Roth, Brad Pitt, and so on. More than that, because of his pronounced hostility towards the press—culminating in a six-month jail sentence for assault in 1987—he has acquired the hangdog glamour of a rebel. Don't let such things obscure his talent as an actor, or his limits as a director. He threatens to give up the former for the latter, which may be one of the misguided ambitions in American film now.

He is the son of a TV and movie director Leo Penn and the actress Eileen Ryan (who appears in *The Indian Runner*). He abandoned college to join the Group Repertory Theatre of Los Angeles. As well as a little TV work, he made a striking movie debut in *Taps* (81, Harold Becker) as a commanding kid. He was equally impressive in *Fast Times at Ridgemont High* (82, Amy Heckerling); in prison in *Bad Boys* (83, Rick Rosenthal); *Crackers* (84, Louis Malle); *Racing with the Moon* (84, Richard Benjamin); quite brilliant, going to pieces on drugs, in *The Falcon and the Snowman* (85, John Schlesinger).

In 1985, he married Madonna—an odd move for anyone so shy of attention—and they made the wretched *Shanghai Surprise* (86, Jim Goddard) together, a venture so grisly that it added to one's reverence for the deranged power of love. But then Penn was remarkable again, and very moving, especially with Christopher Walken, in *At Close Range* (86, James Foley). He played a cop in *Colors* (88, Hopper) and he took a small role in his father's *Judgment in Berlin* (88). Then he was the rogue sergeant in *Casualties of War* (89, Brian De Palma), riveting, yet with the first suspicion of mannerism.

The marriage to Madonna ended, and shortly thereafter Penn married another actress, Robin Wright. Comedy escaped him in *We're No Angels* (89, Neil Jordan), but he was back on form in *State of Grace* (90, Phil Joanou), a movie that felt like an actors' class.

Since then, he has been the jittery lawyer in *Carlito's Way* (93, De Palma) and the condemned man in *Dead Man Walking* (95, Tim Robbins), perfect demonstrations of his range and immersion, even if they were both so arresting that one could not quite forget the skill and authority of the acting. Still, Penn got a best actor nomination for *Dead Man Walking* and moved wonderfully from the sexual insolence of the man to the terror.

As a director, he is awkward, not gifted with narrative, pretentious, but very good with actors. In *The Crossing Guard*, for instance, the performances were so strong that one longed to liberate

the film from his rather repressive artiness. *The Pledge* (from Dürrenmatt) is dark, obscure, and, finally, not as complex as it seems.

He was good again (with Wright) in *She's So Lovely* (97, Nick Cassavetes), a film that was a tribute to John Cassavetes and to Penn's earnest love of untidiness. He followed with the brother in *The Game* (97, David Fincher); *U Turn* (97, Oliver Stone); the indulgent *Hugo Pool* (97, Robert Downey); one of the larger roles in *The Thin Red Line* (98, Terrence Malick); a full-throttle coke addict in *Hurlyburly* (98, Anthony Drazan); a performance of great charm as the guitarist in *Sweet and Lowdown* (99, Woody Allen); romantic in *Up at the Villa* (00, Philip Haas); *Before Night Falls* (00, Julian Schnabel); *The Weight of Water* (00, Kathryn Bigelow); spectacularly retarded, and nominated for an Oscar, in *I Am Sam* (01, Jessie Nelson); *It's All About Love* (03, Thomas Vinterburg); *Mystic River* (03, Clint Eastwood); *21 Grams* (03, Alejandro Gonzalez Inarritu).

Anthony Perkins (1932–92), b. New York
Perkins was the son of character actor Osgood Perkins. Educated at Rollins College in Florida and Columbia University, he seemed caricatured in his first movies by lonely sincerity. This adolescent archetype was very fashionable at the time, and it was hammered home by his Broadway performance as Eugene in the play taken from Thomas Wolfe's *Look Homeward, Angel*. Thus in his film debut, *The Actress* (53, George Cukor), he was a gawky boyfriend; in *Friendly Persuasion* (56, William Wyler) a troubled Quaker; a petulant son in *The Lonely Man* (57, Henry Levin); in *Fear Strikes Out* (57, Robert Mulligan) a baseball player with a nervous breakdown; an inexperienced sheriff in Anthony Mann's *The Tin Star* (57); and then anxiously clutching Sophia Loren in *Desire Under the Elms* (58, Delbert Mann). Joseph Anthony's *The Matchmaker* (58) and especially Joshua Logan's *Tall Story* (60) revealed a sense of fun in Perkins, and the first allowed him to experiment with drag.

In fact, long skirts suited his tall frame. It was Alfred Hitchcock who showed how closely that fun could be related to mental disturbance. His Norman Bates in *Psycho* (60) is not only one of the best performances in a Hitchcock film, but very influential in the way that it mixed the horrors and sly attractiveness. Robert Walker had done some groundwork in *Strangers on a Train* (51), but Perkins's Norman is more refined, more truly feminine, and more confusing of comedy and melodrama. The details of sidling walk, incipient stammer, chewing jaws, and snake-quick smile are marvelously organized. Above all, in that cold-supper sequence with Janet Leigh, Perkins showed us that Norman Bates is a sensitive, humane man in a world that has brutalized those virtues.

Perkins's career never lived up to *Psycho:* perhaps it could not, for some films leave no room for development, while imprisoning the actor in a narrow image. He left Hollywood and settled in Europe. This involved him in two disastrous films: *Goodbye Again* (61, Anatole Litvak) and *Phaedra* (62, Jules Dassin); in *Une Ravissante Idiote* (63, Edouard Molinaro) and *Quelqu'un Derrière la Porte* (71, Nicolas Gessner); but a happy association with Claude Chabrol—in *The Champagne Murders* (66) and *Ten Days' Wonder* (71); and in offbeat returns to America—for Noel Black's *Pretty Poison* (68); as Major Major in *Catch-22* (70, Mike Nichols); as the priest in *WUSA* (70, Stuart Rosenberg); as the preacher in *The Life and Times of Judge Roy Bean* (72, John Huston); writing the script of *The Last of Sheila* (73, Herbert Ross); *Murder on the Orient Express* (74, Sidney Lumet); *Mahogany* (75, Berry Gordy); *Remember My Name* (78, Alan Rudolph); and *Winter Kills* (79, William Richert).

One other part needs to be stressed: as Joseph K. in Welles's *The Trial* (63). Again, his weird playfulness and spinsterly charm captured very serious human uncertainties and fears. Perkins always carried a hint of anxiety that was unique and alarming. An inconsistent worker and far from a star, he was a major screen personality, a gentle man.

He was doomed to be Norman Bates and other spectral frighteners no matter that he had a far wider range, and a capacity for gentleness. He was very good on TV as Javert in *Les Miserables* (78, Glenn Jordan), but no one seemed to notice, or respond; *The Black Hole* (79, Gary Nelson); *Double Negative* (80, George Bloomfield); *ffolkes* (80, Andrew V. McLaglen); *Twee Frouwen* (80, George Sluizer); *Psycho II* (83, Richard Franklin); *The Sins of Dorian Gray* (83, Tony Maylam); *Crimes of Passion* (84, Ken Russell); *Psycho III* (86, which he directed himself); *Lucky Stiff* (88, another directorial job); *Edge of Sanity* (89, Gerard Kikoine); *Psycho IV: The Beginning* (90, Mick Garris); and *I'm Dangerous Tonight* (90, Tobe Hooper). He died of AIDS.

Frank Perry (1930–95), b. New York
1962: *David and Lisa*. 1963: *Ladybug, Ladybug*. 1968: *The Swimmer* (some sequences directed by Sydney Pollack). 1969: *Truman Capote's Trilogy; Last Summer*. 1970: *Diary of a Mad Housewife*. 1971: *Doc*. 1972: *Play It As It Lays*. 1973: *Man on a Swing*. 1975: *Rancho Deluxe*. 1980: *Skag* (TV). 1981: *Mommie Dearest*. 1982: *Monsignor*. 1985: *Compromising Positions*. 1987: *Hello Again*. 1992: *On the Bridge* (d).

Frank Perry has battered away with strenuous seriousness and left a trail of broken, confused, but intriguing films. His background is theatre,

where he worked as a director. His first wife, Eleanor, was scriptwriter on most of his films. His approach is to probe a human relationship until realism gives way to Freudian melodrama. This results in good character studies, humor, and a way with actors that degenerates into symbolism, allegory, and actors subdued by the portentousness of what they are doing.

David and Lisa and *Last Summer* begin as sensitive portraits of young people, but gradually harden into crude psychiatric landscapes. *The Swimmer* is a splendidly silly parable, taken from a John Cheever story, about Burt Lancaster swimming across suburbia. Although Perry was taken out of the film so that Sydney Pollack could shoot a tidier ending, and while the film is pretentious, its view of suburban atrophy is based on a stunning metaphor, and the film stays in the memory. *Diary of a Mad Housewife* is beautifully acted, but rather overawed by its unmitigated black view of marital destructiveness. It speaks with a literary pessimism that may be more appropriate to the novel. However, the film of *Play It As It Lays* is a disaster among literary adaptations, a disgrace to Joan Didion and Tuesday Weld. *Doc* is another solemn elevation of a well-known myth, too deliberate to please.

Mommie Dearest was his biggest picture, yet it had its brakes on, somehow—as if tact had been preferred to the deadpan abandon of an Andy Warhol. *Compromising Positions* (from a Susan Isaacs novel) is a nice, tart comedy. *Monsignor,* however, is one of those pictures made only for the purpose of later parody. Which is not enough reason for making it.

Joe Pesci, b. Newark, New Jersey, 1943
Just as Walter Brennan used to have two ways of acting—with teeth or without—so Joe Pesci has fallen into two approaches: street rough; or in-your-face gruesome appealing. It's a close call whether he is more frightening, or disturbing, as the unpredictable hood in *Goodfellas* (90, Martin Scorsese), which he dominated and for which he won the supporting actor Oscar, or as the sleazebag-you-love-to-hate in any kind of *Lethal Weapon Home Alone*. Still, as Joe Pesci has become a popular "character," one has to worry that he is the less as an actor.

He tried to stay in honest work for twenty years before he established himself as the long-suffering brother in *Raging Bull* (80, Scorsese). Thereafter, he played in *I'm Dancing As Fast As I Can* (82, Jack Hofsiss); *Dear Mr. Wonderful* (82, Peter Lilienthal); *Easy Money* (83, James Signorelli); *Eureka* (83, Nicolas Roeg); *Once Upon a Time in America* (84, Sergio Leone); *Man on Fire* (87, Elie Chouraqui); in Michael Jackson's "Moonwalker" video (88); *Lethal Weapon 2* (89, Richard Donner); *Backtrack* (90, Dennis Hopper); *Betsy's*

Wedding (90, Alan Alda); *Home Alone* (90, Chris Columbus); *The Super* (91, Rod Daniel); brilliant as David Ferrie in *JFK* (91, Oliver Stone); *My Cousin Vinny* (92, Jonathan Lynn); *Lethal Weapon 3* (92, Donner); as a Weegee-like photographer in *The Public Eye* (92, Howard Franklin); *Home Alone 2: Lost in New York* (92, Columbus); and *Jimmy Hollywood* (94, Barry Levinson).

His output declined in the nineties, but not before *Casino* (95, Martin Scorsese), which is in many ways a helpless tribute to the energy, anarchy, and life force of his disruptive character. As with *Goodfellas,* the principle was proved yet again that Pesci could be uniquely fearsome and dangerous. More than that, one has the feeling that Scorsese is fascinated by his actor's loss of control, and yearns to sail away with it. By comparison, Pesci was dull in *8 Heads in a Duffel Bag* (97, Tom Schulman); *Gone Fishin'* (97, Christopher Cain); *Lethal Weapon 4* (98, Richard Donner).

Wolfgang Petersen,

b. Emden, Germany, 1941
1973: *Einer von uns Beiden.* 1976: *Vier Gegen die Bank; Reiferzeugnis.* 1977: *Die Konsequenz/The Consequence.* 1978: *Schwarz und Weiss wie Tage und Nächte/Black and White Like Day and Night.* 1981: *Das Boot/The Boat.* 1984: *The NeverEnding Story.* 1985: *Enemy Mine.* 1991: *Shattered.* 1993: *In the Line of Fire.* 1995: *Outbreak.* 1997: *Air Force One.* 2000: *The Perfect Storm.*

The popular wisdom is that the suspenseful submarine picture *Das Boot* changed the direction of Petersen's career and carried him from small, psychological pictures to Hollywood. In fact, *Das Boot* was originally a German TV miniseries that went all the way to dubbed American theatrical release. But I think *In the Line of Fire* was really the turning point in that it proved Petersen's ability to operate suspense on the small and the grand scale at the same time, and to catch a snappy American idiom. It is a very cute film that sets up two intriguing relationships for the often impenetrable Clint Eastwood—with a rich, eccentric villain, John Malkovich, and a warm woman, Rene Russo. Since then, Petersen has cornered the market in upscale disaster films that have vestiges of human character. *Air Force One*—simultaneously bland and hysterical—is very close to an ideal modern movie. And Petersen seems able to balance the frenzy and the emptiness without a qualm. He also helped produce the equally desperate and banal *Red Corner* (97, Jon Avnet).

The Perfect Storm was a perfect marketing operation, predictable in every detail and line, but undeniably impressive in its great storm.

Elio Petri (1929–82), b. Rome
1961: *L'Assassino/The Assassin.* 1962: *I Giorni*

Contati. 1963: *Il Maestro di Vigevano.* 1964: "Peccato nel Pomeriggio," episode from *Alta Infedelta.* 1965: *La Decima Vittima/The Tenth Victim.* 1966: *A Ciascuno il Suo.* 1968: *Un Tranquillo Posto di Campagna/A Quiet Place in the Country.* 1970: *Indagine su un Cittadino al di Sopra di Ogni Sospetto/Investigation of a Citizen Above Suspicion.* 1972: *La Classe Operaia va in Paradiso.* 1973: *La Proprieta non e piu un Furto.* 1976: *Todo Modo.* 1979: *Buone Notizie.* 1981: *Chi Illumina la Grande Notte?*

Although his manner of filming increasingly tended toward flashiness, Petri's films are often made from very intriguing subjects. His use of glamorous players, pretty colors, and a frantic visual style served to make some films modish and too deliberately mystifying. Part of the difficulty may lie in his inability to achieve the truly neutral, futurist world, a Kafka environment, that his situations demand. Arguably, Welles's *The Trial* also reproduced Kafka's distilled reality through a mixture of wide-angled close-ups and distracting camera movements. Petri's real shortcoming may be that his attitude toward a world of lost identities and invented purpose is only sardonic, that black comedy is his natural vein rather than the philosophical thriller.

Even so, at least three of his films make compelling viewing. *L'Assassino* has Marcello Mastroianni as an indolent, wealthy dilettante, charged with a crime that conforms with all his secret knowledge of his own culpability. *The Tenth Victim* is genuine futurism, with Mastroianni hunted by the lethal Ursula Andress. Both films were lip-smacking dissections of the effete Italian bourgeoisie. But *Investigation of a Citizen . . .* is his most ambitious work, about a fascist policeman who kills his mistress and then taunts the law with clues to see how long it is before his own authority is discredited. The man is a grotesque, strutting tyrant, a puppet trying to strangle himself in his own strings. The meaning is patent, but built around startling revelations of plot, a fascinating performance from Gian Maria Volonte, and arrangements of individual and group that may have affected *The Conformist.* Few films so reveal our macabre need to be found out and accused. Thus its reference to Kafka seems merited.

Michelle Pfeiffer,

b. Santa Ana, California, 1957
As a regular Hollywood performer, Michelle Pfeiffer is a mystery. For a few years (around 1990), she was beautiful, mysterious, and potent. People guessed she could do anything—but then anything turned into so many forlorn choices. She still carries the rather stunned, obedient air of an ex–checkout girl at the El Toro Vons supermarket,

as well as the luster of an Orange County beauty pageant winner. Someone as successful, and as popular, from Manhattan or Cleveland, might have earned a higher reputation as trouble. Moreover, to judge by her appearance on the Barbara Walters show, Pfeiffer is not all honey and buttermilk. Indeed, she seemed odd, hidden, and rather ungiving in spirit. Yet she has been (and given up on being) the young American actress most in demand and most trusted to find something fresh in routine or underwritten roles. She has great skill and inventiveness, a genuine glamour, and an appealing vulnerability, even when she is as tough as she was in *Scarface* (83, De Palma).

Before that she had done whatever came her way—*Charlie Chan and the Curse of the Dragon Queen* (81, Clive Donner) and *Grease II* (82, Patricia Birch), from which she was the only newcomer to survive. But it was as Elvira, in *Scarface*, dangerously thin and pale, coming down in a glass elevator, wearing an aqua sheath and an air of recrimination, her eyes ruined already, that she made her real entry. Her junkie was the only source of moral intelligence within that film, a nymph turning into a witch before our eyes.

She has not looked back: in *Ladyhawke* (85, Richard Donner) she was a fair maiden; in *Into the Night* (85, John Landis) she did countless variations on charm without ever being grating; she was sweet and smart in *Sweet Liberty* (86, Alan Alda); and in *The Witches of Eastwick* (87, George Miller) she seemed to understand the helpless rapture of having the devil as a lover, as well as conveying the stunned summeriness of New England women late in the afternoon. Her face seemed to know the effect of humidity.

In the next few years, she made film after film that took her, and our expectations, further. *Tequila Sunrise* (88, Robert Towne) was the least of these films, and it had moments when her half-teary, half-bloodshot eyes swam in the soft focus. But she lifted *Married to the Mob* (88, Jonathan Demme) with her timing and her humor. In *Dangerous Liaisons* (88, Stephen Frears), she brought life to the least interesting role. Then in *The Fabulous Baker Boys* (89, Steve Kloves), she was a slinky sensation, singing her own songs, dominating the film, and deserving of huge success. Next, she was very close to Bergman and effortlessly European in *The Russia House* (90, Fred Schepisi). *Frankie and Johnny* (91, Garry Marshall) was a rather strained reunion with Al Pacino, for she was no longer credible as a dumb waitress.

Her Catwoman in *Batman Returns* (92, Tim Burton) was a real portrait of neurosis that seemed more than Burton was interested in noticing. But she was astounding as the Texas girl hooked on Jackie Kennedy in *Love Field* (92, Jonathan Kaplan). That movie was long delayed, and then little seen, but it contained her best work

yet. In *The Age of Innocence* (93, Martin Scorsese), she seemed the only one of the three leading players who understood the rhythms and layers of the piece. Opposite Nicholson in *Wolf* (94, Mike Nichols), she brought grave intelligence to a modest role.

But then, despite marriage to the powerful TV mogul David E. Kelley, she fell into a pattern of edgeless or worse material (as if she were Loretta Young, instead of Bette Davis): *Dangerous Minds* (95, John N. Smith); *Up Close & Personal* (96, Jon Avnet); *One Fine Day* (96, Mark Hoffman); *To Gillian on Her 37th Birthday* (96, Michael Pressman), coproduced by Kelley; *A Thousand Acres* (97, Jocelyn Moorhouse); Titania in *A Midsummer Night's Dream* (99, Hoffman); *The Story of Us* (99, Rob Reiner); *What Lies Beneath* (00, Robert Zemeckis); *I Am Sam* (01, Jessie Nelson).

With *White Oleander* (02, Peter Kosminsky), the truth was inescapable—Pfeiffer had not made a decent movie for ten years.

Gérard Philipe (Gérard Philip) (1922–59), b. Cannes, France

There is a type of romantic actor who imprints himself the more deeply by dying early: Valentino, James Dean, and Gérard Philipe. Philipe was younger than Yves Montand and only three years older than Michel Piccoli. He died as the regeneration of French cinema was beginning, and it is tantalizing to imagine him in the films of Demy, Chabrol, or Rohmer. In fact, from the end of the war until his death, Philipe had foreshadowed the precarious shift of comedy and tragedy in the New Wave. Although he often exploited his reputation of matinée idol, Philipe never hammed. Like most great stars, he smiled when sad and never forgot melancholy in moments of gaiety.

At either end of his career he played men preoccupied with sex: as the urgent but flawed adolescent in love with Micheline Presle in *Le Diable au Corps* (47, Claude Autant-Lara) and as the amused, meditative orgiast, Valmont, bringing some of Laclos's calm to Roger Vadim's *Les Liaisons Dangereuses* (59). He was well suited to the self-observation of Stendhal's young men. Although neither *La Chartreuse de Parme* (47, Christian-Jaque) nor *Le Rouge et le Noir* (54, Autant-Lara) is as true to Stendhal as Max Ophuls might have ensured, in both cases Philipe's central performances—as Fabrizio and Sorel—caught the simultaneous involvement and detachment of Stendhal's heroes.

Originally a stage actor, Philipe never abandoned the theatre. His first film was *Les Petites du Quai aux Fleurs* (43, Marc Allégret), but it was only after the war that his air of blighted hope made its impact, notably in *Le Diable au Corps* and as a wistful Mishkin in *L'Idiot* (46, Georges Lampin). His ability to bring a creative tension to modest films was emphasized in Yves Allégret's *Une Si Jolie Petite Plage* (48). Not many films derive such poignant pessimism from the face that gazes out of its screen across that desolate wintry beach. After that, he was in *Souvenirs Perdus* (49, Christian-Jaque); as Faust in *La Beauté du Diable* (50, René Clair); as the Count in *La Ronde* (50, Ophuls) who regretfully assures Isa Miranda that happiness does not exist; *Avec André Gide* (51, M. Allégret); as the dreaming prisoner in *Juliette ou la Clé des Songes* (51, Marcel Carné); *Fanfan la Tulipe* (51, Christian-Jaque); once more as a romantic dreamer in *Night Beauties* (52, Clair); *Les Orgueilleux* (53, Y. Allégret); captivating as the Frenchman in London in pursuit of English roses, in *Knave of Hearts* (54, René Clément); *Si Versailles M'Etait Conté* (53, Sacha Guitry); the provincial garrison Don Juan, in *Summer Manoeuvres* (55, Clair); *La Meilleure Part* (55, Y. Allégret); in 1956 he acted in and directed *Les Aventures de Till l'Espiegle*; *Pot-Bouille* (57, Julien Duvivier); as Modigliani in *Montparnasse 19* (57, Jacques Becker); *La Vie à Deux* (58, Clement Duhour); in a version of Dostoyevsky's long short story, *Le Joeur* (58, Autant-Lara). His last part, when he was seriously ill with cancer, was as the doomed South American administrator in *La Fièvre Monte à El Pao* (59, Luis Buñuel).

River Phoenix (1970–93), b. Madras, Oregon

From his classic beginnings as the child of hippies who had moved from a cult, the Children of God, to getting on in Hollywood, to his abrupt death on the sidewalk outside the Viper Room in Los Angeles, River Phoenix is easier to accept as a character (in a TV movie of the week) than as an actual person. Yet at all stages of his short life, rumor and PR get in the way of the real facts. For anyone that famous that early, there is so little point in turning to reality as a point of saving reference.

He was a rock musician as well as an actor, and even before death he had become an icon to a generation. Was he promising, or good? Yes. But put his work next to Dean's three films, and you can feel the difference between the loss of a myth and celebrity accident.

He made his debut in *Explorers* (85, Joe Dante); *Stand By Me* (86, Rob Reiner); *The Mosquito Coast* (86, Peter Weir); *A Night in the Life of Jimmy Reardon* (88, William Richert); *Little Nikita* (88, Richard Benjamin); getting a supporting actor nomination as the son of runaway radicals in *Running on Empty* (88, Sidney Lumet); as young Indy in *Indiana Jones and the Last Crusade* (89, Steven Spielberg); *I Love You to Death* (90, Lawrence Kasdan); *Dogfight* (91, Nancy Savoca); narcoleptic and available in *My Own Private Idaho* (91, Gus Van Sant), the major source of his cult still; *Sneakers* (92, Phil Alden Robinson);

singing in *The Thing Called Love* (93, Peter Bogdanovich); *Silent Tongue* (94, Sam Shepard).

It was a large family, and his younger brother, Joaquin, promises to be better still.

Maurice Pialat (1925–2003)
b. Cunlhat, France
1960: *L'Amour Existe* (s). 1964: *La Fleur de l'Age, ou les Adolescentes*. 1969: *L'Enfance Nue/Naked Childhood/Me*. 1971: *La Maison des Bois* (TV). 1972: *Nous ne Veillirons pas Ensemble/We Will Not Grow Old Together*. 1974: *La Gueule Ouverte/The Mouth Agape*. 1979: *Passe Ton Bac d'Abord*. 1980: *Loulou*. 1983: *A Nos Amours*. 1985: *Police*. 1987: *Sous le Soleil de Satan/Under Satan's Sun*. 1991: *Van Gogh*. 1995: *Le Garçu*. 1997: *Les Auto-Stoppeuses*.

The French critic Jean Narboni once wrote of Pialat's performance—as the policeman—in *Que La Bête Meure* (69, Claude Chabrol), that it was: "Massive, abrupt and incredibly gentle." The description applies to Pialat's work as a director just as it seems to fit the very controversial filmmaker in person. He can be confrontational and arrogant; he is renowned as a difficult, demanding director; yet there is a delicacy and a compassion to his work that evokes the French naturalist tradition of Renoir.

He was over forty before he directed his first feature, *L'Enfance Nue*. He had studied art at the École des Arts Décoratifs and the École des Beaux Arts in Paris, and he worked for some years as a painter (his films sometimes refer to Bonnard—and, obviously, Van Gogh). It was in doing some work as an actor that he was led into film, and initially TV, and he came to his feature debut somewhat shyly. This should be stressed, for Pialat is now famous as a tyrant. There need be no contradiction, only the psychological truth of modesty and anger being neighbors.

His essential subjects are childhood and family, stability and the urge toward risk and adventure. He has often worked with nonprofessional actors, and he can show us a rougher, more naked texture in established actors we believe we know. He was himself a brooding presence as actor, notably in *Que La Bête Meure, Mes Petites Amoureuses* (74, Jean Eustache), and as the father in *A Nos Amours*. But, in addition, he has given us—and perhaps given herself—Sandrine Bonnaire, Gérard Depardieu in a couple of his major roles, and Jacques Dutronc as Van Gogh. Those are pieces of acting that seem like direct being, scarcely mediated or trained. In working and being with actors, Pialat seems to discover what he feels about life.

L'Enfance Nue concerns an unwanted boy; *We Will Not Grow Old Together* describes the tortured end to an affair (the actors are Jean Yanne and Marlène Jobert); *The Mouth Agape* shows the way a mother's imminent death from cancer affects her husband and children; *Passe Ton Bac* shows kids settling into an arid adult life; *Loulou* is a study in sexual affinity between a "beast" (Depardieu) and a more refined woman (Isabelle Huppert); *A Nos Amours* is one of the great movies about wild adolescence, granted that the older people in the movie know the dead ends wildness leads to; *Police* is the story of a cop (Depardieu) and a girl on the wrong side of the law; *Under Satan's Sun* is a priest facing temptation (Depardieu and Bonnaire); and *Van Gogh* is that rare thing, a biopic in which the great man is in some ways less fascinating than the other characters.

Pialat's is an actor's cinema; yet that could make one forget the remarkable tenderness of his filming and editing. He is like Renoir and Truffaut in that he has a mastery of both very long scenes and fragments, and a way of putting them together that only film can manage. But, finally, he is a wounded, battered humanist, one of the few links we have now to the heritage of Ozu, Mizoguchi, and Renoir.

Michel Piccoli, b. Paris, 1925

There is a marvelous note of the gloomy connoisseur in Piccoli. It is a quality that adjusts to films of very different mood, but that never seems to depart from the original. Apparently calm and even detached, Piccoli has the consistency that distinguishes important screen actors and that enables him to find something of himself in every part without striving. Such a personality is admirably suited to filling out parts only sketched in a scenario: thus he is excellent as the uneasy, self-reflective writer in *Contempt* (63, Jean-Luc Godard); as the sardonic lecher, complaining of the cold in *Belle de Jour* (67, Luis Buñuel); or as the man meditating on violence and escape in *Dillinger e' Morto* (69, Marco Ferreri).

Piccoli is of Italian origins, as his lean dark looks as well as his name might suggest. He was on the stage for ten years, during which time he made only one film, *Le Point du Jour* (49, Louis Dacquin). But from 1955 he entered seriously into movies, soon to gather a string of parts as notable as those of any other French actor of his time: *French Can Can* (55, Jean Renoir); *Les Mauvaises Rencontres* (55, Alexandre Astruc); *Evil Eden* (56, Buñuel); *Les Sorcières de Salem* (57, Raymond Rouleau); *Le Doulos* (62, Jean-Pierre Melville); *Le Jour et l'Heure* (62, René Clément); *Climats* (62, Stellio Lorenzi); *De l'Amour* (64, Jean Aurel); the master of the house in *Diary of a Chambermaid* (64, Buñuel); *Masquerade* (64, Basil Dearden); *Le Coup de Grâce* (65, Jean Cayrol); *The Sleeping Car Murders* (65, Costa-Gavras); *Lady L* (65, Peter Ustinov); *Is*

Paris Burning? (66, Clément); *La Guerre est Finie* (66, Alain Resnais); *Les Créatures* (66, Agnes Varda); *Un Homme de Trop* (66, Costa-Gavras); *La Voleuse* (66, Jean Chapot); *La Curée* (66, Roger Vadim); as Monsieur Dame (Guillotine in the English version) in *The Young Girls of Rochefort* (67, Jacques Demy); *Mon Amour, Mon Amour* (67, Nadine Trintignant); *Benjamin* (67, Michel Deville); *Diabolik* (67, Mario Bava); *La Chamade* (68, Alain Cavalier); *La Prisonnière* (68, Henri-Georges Clouzot); *La Voie Lactée* (68, Buñuel); *Topaz* (69, Alfred Hitchcock); *L'Invitata* (69, Vittorio de Seta); *Les Choses de la Vie* (70, Claude Sautet); *Max et les Ferrailleurs* (70, Sautet); *L'Invasion* (70, Yves Allégret); *La Poudre d'Escampette* (71, Philippe de Broca); *Ten Days' Wonder* (71, Claude Chabrol); as the modern caveman *Themroc* (72, Claude Faraldo); *Red Wedding* (73, Chabrol); *Blow-Out* (73, Ferreri); *Le Trio Infernal* (74, Francis Girod); *The Phantom of Liberté* (74, Buñuel); *Vincent, François, Paul et les Autres* (75, Sautet); *Couleur Clair* (77, François Weyergans); *Le Part du Feu* (77, Etienne Perrier); *Mado* (77, Sautet); *Des Enfants Gâtés* (77, Bertrand Tavernier); *L'Imprécateur* (77, Jean-Louis Bertuccelli); *La Petite Fille en Velours Bleu* (78, Alan Bridges); and *Le Sucre* (78, Jacques Rouffio).

He was in *Giallo Napoletano* (79, Sergio Corbucci); *Leap Into the Void* (80, Marco Bellocchio); *La Fille Prodigue* (80, Jacques Doillon); *Atlantic City* (81, Louis Malle); *Passion* (82, Godard); *Une Chambre en Ville* (82, Demy); *Le Prix du Danger* (82, Yves Boisset); Louis XVI in *La Nuit de Varennes* (83, Ettore Scola); *The Eyes, the Mouth* (83, Bellocchio); *Viva la Vie* (83, Claude Lelouch); *Adieu Bonaparte* (84, Youssef Chahine); *Dangerous Moves* (84, Richard Dembo); *Peril en la Demeure* (85, Deville); *Success Is the Best Revenge* (85, Jerzy Skolimowski); *Mauvais Sang* (86, Leos Carax); *Paltoquet* (87, Deville); *May Fools* (90, Malle); *Martha und Ich* (90, Jiri Weiss); at his best as the sculptor in *La Belle Noiseuse* (91, Jacques Rivette); as Jean Genet in *L'Equilibriste* (91, Nico Papatakis).

As a veteran, he has apparently felt able to do anything. In fact, there are fewer good films, but that is hardly his fault: *Das Schicksal des Freiherrn von Leisenbohg* (91, Edouard Molinaro); *Le Bateau de Lu* (91, Christine Citti); *Le Bal des Casse-Pieds* (92, Yves Robert); as Jules Verne in *From Time to Time* (92, Jeff Blyth); *Le Souper* (92, Molinaro); *La Vie Crevée* (92, Guillaume Nicloux); *Archipel* (92, Pierre Granier-Deferre); *La Cavale des Fous* (93, Marco Pico); *Rupture(s)* (93, Citti); *L'Ange Noir* (94, Jean-Claude Brisseau); a short, *Train de Nuit* (94, which he wrote and directed himself; *al-Mohager* (94, Chahine); *Bête de Scène* (94, Bernard Nissille); *Tödliches Geld* (95, Detlef Ronfeldt); *L'Insolent Beaumar-*

chais (96, Molinaro); *Party* (96, Manoel de Oliveira); *Tykho Moon* (96, Enki Bilal); *Compagna di Viaggio* (96, Peter Del Monte); *Généalogies d'un Crime* (97, Raul Ruiz); *Passion in the Desert* (97, Lavinia Currier); *Rien sur Robert* (99, Pascal Bonitzer); *Libero Burro* (99, Sergio Castellitto); *París Tombuctú* (99, Luis García Berlanga); *Tout Va Bien, On s'en Va* (00, Claude Mourieras); *Je Rentre à la Maison* (01, Oliveira); *Yadon Ilaheyya* (01, Elia Suleiman)—just a voice: *La Petite Lili* (03, Clause Miller), adapted from *The Seagull; Un Homme, Un Vrai* (03, Arnaud and Jean-Marie Larrieu).

Mary Pickford (Gladys Marie Smith)
(1893–1979), b. Toronto, Canada

In 1923, when she was thirty, Mary Pickford appealed through the pages of *Photoplay* for suggestions about parts she might play. Back came the answers: Cinderella, Heidi, Alice, Anne of Green Gables. Alexander Walker has suggested that those answers disappointed Mary's search for a pretext to become a more mature woman on the screen. And there are hints throughout her ingenue roles of vigor, realism, and a no-nonsense understanding of sex. As Molly Haskell put it, "She was a little girl with gumption and self-reliance who could get herself out of trouble as easily as into it."

But it may be misleading to regard Pickford simply as an actress, retarded by the public's preference for her in juvenile roles. Any frustration was greatly alleviated by her astonishing financial rewards, and her artistic aspirations seem to have taken second place to an uncompromising emphasis on her career. She was an expert businesswoman, prepared to take great pains to hone herself down to a desired product. Indeed, she was the business brains in United Artists, and her historical importance is as the silent era star who controlled her directors and held production companies to ransom.

She was also the first vestige of Hollywood royalty, with Doug Fairbanks. She was loved, but her status was just as popular, for she ordained the power of movies.

The contrast between the curly-haired, dewy-eyed "Little Mary" and the imperious organizer of her own affairs is obviously central, but there should be no doubt about the pragmatic equanimity with which she conducted herself. She knew when to retire and she assessed herself with the simple pride of an industrial titan: "I left the screen because I didn't want what happened to Chaplin to happen to me. . . . The little girl made me. I wasn't waiting for the little girl to kill me. I'd already been pigeonholed. I know I'm an artist, and that's not being arrogant, because talent comes from God. . . . My career was planned, there was never anything accidental about it. It was planned, it was painful, it was purposeful. I'm not exactly satisfied, but I'm grateful."

Her father was killed in an accident when little Gladys was five, and when the widowed mother let rooms to actors it introduced the child to the stage. Alexander Walker has argued that these family circumstances, and the child's love of her lost father, figure strongly in the psychology of her films. But "Little Mary" is not morbid. Her strength was comedy and high spirits, and it is doubtful that she was conscious of any underground meanings to her long-lived childhood on celluloid.

In her teens, she was acting in the theatre for David Belasco, but in 1909 she was engaged by D. W. Griffith at Biograph. She stayed with him until 1912, appearing in seventy-five of his two-reelers and becoming one of his leading players. But after the last of these, *The New York Hat*, she was stung by Griffith's lordly introduction of Mae Marsh and so returned to Belasco. Of all his actresses, Pickford was coolest about Griffith: although she admired him, she was irked by the legend fostered by the Gish sisters.

Her departure was also a means to an end. In 1910 she had briefly left Griffith for Independent and had thereby boosted her salary. In 1913, she was back in movies with Zukor's Famous Players at $500 a week; by 1916, it was up to $10,000 a week. She bid her price higher and higher as her films helped to establish Zukor and to enshrine the sentimental heroine that Griffith had first called "Little Mary": *A Good Little Devil* (13, J. Searle Dawley); *Hearts Adrift* (13, Edwin S. Porter); *Tess of the Storm Country* (14, Porter); *Cinderella* (14, James Kirkwood); *Dawn of Tomorrow* (15, Kirkwood); *A Girl of Yesterday* (15, Allan Dwan); *The Foundling* (15, Dwan); *Poor Little Peppina* (16, Sidney Olcott); *Madame Butterfly* (16, Olcott). Zukor even named a studio after her as her earnings went over $500,000 a year.

As Zukor and Jesse Lasky joined forces, they tried to reduce her power—but to no avail. In fact she often directed her films and had no equal as a judge of her own material. In the last years of the war, she reached a peak, touring the country to sell bonds and making *The Pride of the Clan* (17, Maurice Tourneur); *The Poor Little Rich Girl* (17, Tourneur); *Romance of the Redwoods* (17, Cecil B. De Mille); *The Little American* (17, De Mille); *Rebecca of Sunnybrook Farm* (17, Marshall Neilan); *The Little Princess* (17, Neilan); *Stella Maris* (18, Neilan), in which she played two parts, one a crippled serving girl who shocked Mary's fond admirers; and *Captain Kidd Junior* (19, William Desmond Taylor).

Nineteen-nineteen was the turning point. She left Zukor for First National. With Chaplin, Griffith, and Douglas Fairbanks she formed United Artists, intended to distribute their work. And, after the breakdown of her first marriage to actor

Owen Moore, she married Fairbanks. Although nearing thirty, this is the period of her best films and the most complete exploitation of America's Sweetheart: *Daddy Long Legs* (19, Neilan); *The Hoodlum* (19, Sidney Franklin); and *Heart o' the Hills* (19, Franklin). She then formed the Mary Pickford Corporation and released through United Artists: *Pollyanna* (20, Paul Powell); *Suds* (20, Jack Dillon); *The Love Light* (21, Frances Marion); as mother and son in *Little Lord Fauntleroy* (21, Alfred E. Green and Jack Pickford); a remake of *Tess of the Storm Country* (22, John S. Robertson). She chose directors and had the sense to cultivate Charles Rosher as her cameraman—the effort to show her as still adolescent led to significant advances in the art of lighting. In 1923, she brought Lubitsch over from Germany. It was a matching of opposites; *The Parade's Gone By* has an amusing account of German innuendo and chilly American response. She made *Rosita* (23, Lubitsch), but loathed the experience and reverted to more amenable, indigenous directors: *Dorothy Vernon of Haddon Hall* (24, Neilan); *Little Annie Rooney* (25, William Beaudine); *Sparrows* (26, Beaudine); and *My Best Girl* (27, Sam Taylor).

The decline in quality in her work may indicate reduced enthusiasm, the difficulties of her marriage, and an inability, artistically or commercially, to transcend the teenage character. But she tried sound and made *Coquette* (29, Taylor)—winning an Oscar—and her only film with Fairbanks, *The Taming of the Shrew* (29, Taylor). She made only two more films: *Kiki* (31, Taylor) and *Secrets* (33, Frank Borzage), the last with Leslie Howard. Like so many who flourished in the period 1915–25, she had been coarsened by the exaggeration that passed for mime. She was too set in her ways to learn, and there was no obvious character she could adopt to bridge Pollyanna and a world peopled by Garbo, Bette Davis, and Katharine Hepburn.

When her marriage to Fairbanks ended, she married actor Charles "Buddy" Rogers. Her retirement allowed her to develop as an executive and she produced *One Rainy Afternoon* (36, Rowland V. Lee), *The Gay Desperado* (36, Rouben Mamoulian), and years later, *Sleep, My Love* (48, Douglas Sirk). She and Chaplin sold up their share of United Artists only in 1953—though, according to Chaplin, an earlier and better opportunity was lost when Pickford was upset at having to wait two years for $7,000,000.

Walter Pidgeon (1897–1984),
b. East St. John, Canada

With or without a moustache, Pidgeon was unfailingly handsome and attentive. But he never established himself as a player capable of sustaining films. How shrewd of Preminger to cast so loyal and industrious a support as the Senate majority leader in *Advise and Consent* (62), competent and experienced, but self-effacing, deferring to the idea of democracy. That is one of his few good films. For his long career was depressingly filled with unworthy pictures.

He was a stage actor, invited to Hollywood by Joseph Schenck to play opposite Constance Talmadge. By the time he arrived, Schenck had had second thoughts, and Pidgeon drifted from one studio to another: *Mannequin* (26, James Cruze); *The Outsider* (26, Rowland V. Lee); *Old Loves and New* (26, Maurice Tourneur); and *Marriage License?* (26, Frank Borzage). As a bland male model, he fronted films without ever dominating them, even if his gentle, deep voice responded to sound: *The Heart of Salome* (27, Victor Schertzinger); *The Gorilla* (27, Alfred Santell); *The Thirteenth Juror* (27, Edward Laemmle); *The Girl from Rio* (27, Tom Terriss); *The Gateway of the Moon* (28, John Griffith Wray); *Turn Back the Hours* (28, Howard Bretherton); *Her Private Life* (29, Alexander Korda); *A Most Immoral Lady* (29, Wray); *Bride of the Regiment* (30, John Francis Dillon); *Sweet Kitty Bellairs* (30, Alfred E. Green); *Renegades* (30, Victor Fleming); *Viennese Nights* (30, Alan Crosland); and *Going Wild* (30, William A. Seiter).

In these last films, Pidgeon had already sunk to supporting parts. Illness now conspired to reduce him further so that after twenty-two films in five years, he made only seven films from 1931 to 1936, usually in nonlead roles: *The Hot Heiress* (31, Clarence Badger); a remake of *The Gorilla* (31, Bryan Foy); *Rockabye* (32, George Cukor); *The Kiss Before the Mirror* (33, James Whale); *Journal of a Crime* (34, William Keighley); *Big Brown Eyes* (36, Raoul Walsh); and *Fatal Lady* (36, Edward Ludwig).

In 1937, he was put under contract by MGM when his career was at its lowest point. At first the studio used him as a support: *Saratoga* (37, Jack Conway); *My Dear Miss Aldrich* (37, George Seitz); *Manproof* (38, Richard Thorpe); *The Girl of the Golden West* (38, Robert Z. Leonard); *The Shopworn Angel* (38, H. C. Potter); and *Too Hot to Handle* (38, Conway). He played leads in several B pictures, including *Nick Carter—Master Detective* (39, Jacques Tourneur), and was then loaned out for better opportunities: *It's a Date* (40, Seiter); *Dark Command* (40, Walsh); *The House Across the Bay* (40, Archie Mayo); as the hero in *Man Hunt* (41, Fritz Lang); and *How Green Was My Valley* (41, John Ford).

Meanwhile, at MGM, he made *Phantom Raiders* (40, Tourneur); *Flight Command* (40, Borzage); was teamed for the first time with Greer Garson in *Blossoms in the Dust* (41, Mervyn Le Roy); and *White Cargo* (42, Thorpe). The mature, conservative romance with Garson was astonishingly elevated by war in *Mrs. Miniver* (42, William Wyler); *Madame Curie* (43, Le Roy), and *Mrs. Parkington* (44, Tay Garnett). The titles indicate Pidgeon's escort status, but it was evident that he enjoyed feeding Garson.

After the war, he slipped back into duller pictures: *Weekend at the Waldorf* (45, Leonard); *Holiday in Mexico* (46, Sidney); *The Secret Heart* (46, Leonard); *If Winter Comes* (47, Victor Saville); *Command Decision* (49, Sam Wood); *Julia Misbehaves* (48, Conway), with Greer Garson again; *The Red Danube* (49, Sidney); as Jolyon in *That Forsyte Woman* (49, Compton Bennett) to Garson's Irene; and, unwisely reprised, in *The Miniver Story* (50, Potter). Once more, he found himself a supporting actor: *Soldiers Three* (51, Garnett); *Million Dollar Mermaid* (52, Le Roy); *The Bad and the Beautiful* (52, Vincente Minnelli); *Scandal at Scourie* (53, Jean Negulesco); *Executive Suite* (54, Robert Wise); *The Last Time I Saw Paris* (54, Richard Brooks); *Deep in My Heart* (54, Stanley Donen); *Hit the Deck* (55, Roy Rowland); as the Prospero figure in *Forbidden Planet* (56, Fred M. Wilcox); and *The Rack* (56, Arnold Laven).

He left MGM and returned to the theatre. After that, *Advise and Consent* was a happy exception to some very ordinary films: *Big Red* (62, Norman Tokar); *Warning Shot* (67, Buzz Kulik); *Funny Girl* (68, Wyler); *Skyjacked* (72, John Guillermin); *The Neptune Factor* (73, Daniel Petrie); *Harry in Your Pocket* (73, Bruce Geller); *Live Again, Die Again* (74, Richard A. Colla); *The Girl on the Late, Late Show* (74, Gary Nelson); *Murder on Flight 502* (75, George McCowan); *The Lindbergh Kidnapping Case* (76, Kulik); *Two-Minute Warning* (76, Larry Peerce); and *Sextette* (78, Ken Hughes).

Frank Pierson,
b. Chappaqua, New York, 1925
1970: *The Looking Glass War.* 1976: *A Star Is Born.* 1978: *King of the Gypsies.* 1990: *Somebody Has to Shoot the Picture.* 1992: *Citizen Cohn* (TV). 1995: *Truman* (TV). 2000: *Dirty Pictures* (TV); *Conspiracy* (TV).

Frank Pierson was raised (after Harvard and journalism) as a writer-producer in television, where he worked on the *Have Gun Will Travel* show, in which Richard Boone introduced the urbane, educated gunfighter Paladin. From that he went into screenwriting for movies and three nominations in a decade: *Cat Ballou* (65, Elliott Silverstein); *Cool Hand Luke* (67, Stuart Rosenberg); and *Dog Day Afternoon* (75, Sidney Lumet), for which he won an Oscar. He also did scripts for *The Happening* (67, Silverstein); *The Anderson Tapes* (71, Lumet); *In Country* (89, Norman Jewison); and *Presumed Innocent* (90, Alan J. Pakula).

As a director, he developed much more slowly: *The Looking Glass War* was le Carré, but it's very

stiff. He was clearly no match for his stars or their heady sense of show business in *A Star Is Born*, and rather shy of the full-blooded melodrama in *King of the Gypsies*. But, more recently, for television, he has shown much better results. His *Truman*, with Gary Sinise, was an exemplary biopic, his *Cohn* was riveting, and *Conspiracy*—written by Loring Mandel and based on the Wannsee Conference of 1943—proved to be a revelatory study of Nazi clerical in-fighting, and one of the best pictures of 2001.

Harold Pinter, b. Hackney, London, 1930
There are writers who would have had a large influence upon screenwriting even if they had never attempted a screenplay. I am thinking of Hemingway, Graham Greene, and Simenon (at least), novelists who seem formed by the ways films can tell stories. They may describe some elements of scenery and appearance, yet more than that their narratives provoke us into visualizing, or imagining. Landscapes, action, and "beautiful" people evidently benefit from this. Yet the most visually creative of novelists may be those who have a character deliver a line of dialogue so that we *see* the pause, *feel* the hesitation, and *guess* what has been left unsaid. And that is where Harold Pinter would deserve a place in this book, even if he had never met Joseph Losey, or looked at Marcel Proust.

Paul Schrader observed this when he directed Pinter's script of Ian McEwan's *The Comfort of Strangers* (90): "Pinter's characters are always saying one thing and meaning something slightly different. There are layers of nuance and innuendo and seemingly inexplicable actions and events which are in fact very explicable in a non-prosaic fashion. I'm very attracted to the idea of a psychological life running just under the surface of normal life and motivating the normal life in subtle ways: it goes back to why does Travis [Bickle] take the girl to the porno movie? It seemingly doesn't make sense, but of course it does make sense."

Now, some might say—in praise or attack—that for years Pinter had been writing stage plays that were really movie scripts needing to be recited. In other words, he was not actually concerned about "the psychological life running just under the surface." Indeed, he was enchanted by the surface, by the patter of talk, the rhythm of silences. Thus, his plays have usually translated to film or TV very fluently—even if the tension feels greater in theatres. His stage structures were cinematic and his TV plays were already gripping little movies—I think, especially, of the version for TV of *The Lover*, which paired the uncanny Alan Badel with Pinter's then wife, Vivien Merchant.

Sooner or later, Pinter was going to become a target for the movies. His first script was actually a version of his own play, *The Caretaker* (64, Clive

Donner). But that appeared after *The Servant* (63, Losey), an adaptation of the Robin Maugham novel that had been originally commissioned by Michael Anderson.

The matching of Losey and Pinter blessed both men. Losey was a real filmmaker, and an egoist determined that Pinter should serve him. Thus, the films were pitched more ambitiously. For Losey, Pinter was someone who knew English class hypocrisies like an eavesdropping butler (Pinter was definitely lower middle class, and Jewish). And Pinter wrote dialogue for nervy, minimalist actors, leaving the look of things available for Losey. As Losey saw it, he liked Pinter because of: "Observations of characters, a very acute awareness of class dynamics and contradictions. He does superbly evoke the visual for me, but I don't think he has any visual sense at all."

That's an intriguing notion—for Pinter did begin in, and has always played well on, radio. Moreover, if Pinter is a great screenwriter, as some say (particularly those besotted with his never-yet-filmed adaptation of *À la Recherche du Temps Perdu*), then we have to wonder about the overall quality of his contribution to films.

I would guess that Pinter and Losey got so entangled in talk and a battle of wills that their films benefited: *The Servant* broke so much new ground—and was so reliant on its trashy novel for a basis; Nicholas Mosley's *Accident* (67, Losey) is a better novel, but less of a film; L. P. Hartley's *The Go-Between* (71, Losey) is close to a great novel—and the least worthy or striking as a movie.

Elsewhere, Pinter's films have ranged from the plain to the pretentious, by way of the inept. However good the Proust screenplay may be, let us recall how abysmal *The Last Tycoon* (76, Elia Kazan) turned out. Why? Was Pinter overpowered by Kazan and Sam Spiegel? Was he content to be paid? Was the film miscast? Is the novel tedious or incomplete as drama? There are times when a writer can make no impression.

The other Pinter scripts are: *The Pumpkin Eater* (64, Jack Clayton); *The Quiller Memorandum* (66, Anderson); *The Homecoming* (73, Peter Hall); *The French Lieutenant's Woman* (81, Karel Reisz)—which is a foolish idea for making the romance novelette "relevant"; *Betrayal* (83, David Jones), which is worse than foolish; *Turtle Diary* (85, John Irvin), which could have been written by Pinter's second wife, Lady Antonia Fraser; and three pieces of thin-blooded and mean-spirited artiness—*The Handmaid's Tale* (90, Volker Schlondorff); *The Comfort of Strangers* (91, Paul Schrader); and *Reunion* (91, Jerry Schatzberg). *Old Times* (90, Simon Curtis) felt like a claustrophobic parody of the Pinteresque, a ten-minute piece extruded to ninety minutes. *The Trial* (93, Jones) felt like something one had already seen.

Pinter has directed a few times for TV—Simon Gray's *Butley* (74), content to let Alan Bates have a good time, and three of his own works: *Rear Column* (79), *The Hothouse* (82), and *Party Time* (92).

In recent years, he has concentrated more on the stage. He has done only one film script—*Bez Pogorova* (99, Slobodan Z. Jovanovic)—but he has indulged himself more as an actor: *Breaking the Code* (96, Herbert Wise); *Mojo* (97, Jez Butterworth); *Mansfield Park* (99, Patricia Rozema); *Catastrophe* (00, David Mamet); *Wit* (01, Mike Nichols); *The Tailor of Panama* (01, John Boorman).

Brad (William Bradley) Pitt,
b. Shawnee, Oklahoma, 1963

There have been enough moments when Brad Pitt seemed ready to pick up the smoldering torch of James Dean to remind ourselves that Dean died at the age of twenty-four—at which point in life, Pitt had shot not a foot of film. That's not to dispute Pitt's farmboy charm in certain movies, or what Michael Angeli called "a smile that could set feminism back twenty-five years." For when he had his slinky, shiftless bit in *Thelma & Louise* (91, Ridley Scott)—replacing William Baldwin, who had elected to do *Backdraft* instead—he did more than give the Geena Davis character her first, revelatory orgasm. He left the public wanting more. He was lean, shy, and authentically cowboyish; he was also droll, wicked, and very sexy. That actor could have been Cal in *East of Eden*, or Huck Finn, or Gary Gilmore. But has Pitt yet really gone beyond his own early promise—when he was protected by being on screen for only fifteen or twenty minutes?

He was raised in Springfield, Missouri, and he nearly graduated with a journalism degree from the University of Missouri. But he went out to Los Angeles and, having knocked around for a few years, began to get work: *Cutting Class* (89, Rospo Pallenberg); *Happy Together* (89, Mel Damski); on TV in *Glory Days* (90); and with Juliette Lewis in *Too Young to Die?* (90, Robert Markowitz).

He was the track star in *Across the Tracks* (91, Sandy Tung), and then he took on the stylish adventure of *Johnny Suede* (91, Tom DiCillo) and *Cool World* (92, Ralph Bakshi). He gave his best performance yet as the self-destructive, at-one-with-nature wild kid in *A River Runs Through It* (92, Robert Redford), a film that used his coltish air very kindly (as if Redford envied it). His "Early Grayce" in *Kalifornia* (93, Dominic Sena) was not just villainy, but elaborate Method grunge, and Juliette Lewis was his partner now both on screen and off. He also contributed a smart cameo to *True Romance* (93, Tony Scott).

He was itching to expand, but *Interview with the Vampire* (94, Neil Jordan) was far less convincing than *Legends of the Fall* (94, Edward

Zwick), another shot at noble, prairie wildness. But he was effective and touching as the rebel cop in *Se7en* (95, David Fincher), understandably impressed and helped by Morgan Freeman and Gwyneth Paltrow (his new love). But then his maniac in *12 Monkeys* (95, Terry Gilliam) only showed how easy it is for young, barely trained actors these days to show off—and be praised for it. It was a terrible performance, and it left one guessing that Pitt could only deal adequately with characters that were versions of his own idea, or ideal, of self. That worked once, for people like Gable and Cooper, but do audiences now tolerate that sort of acting? Meanwhile, Pitt approaches forty in a world crowded with moody young actors who can do the attitude of a lonesome puppy at the drop of a hat.

His most recent work has seemed less exciting or excited, as if the labor of being a movie star and the vagaries of popular taste are beginning to depress him: *Sleepers* (96, Barry Levinson); the bizarre *Seven Years in Tibet* (97, Jean-Jacques Annaud); *The Devil's Own* (97, Alan J. Pakula), which he said he despised, even if he had done much to unsettle it; the misguided *The Dark Side of the Sun* (97, Bozidar Nikolic), shot many years earlier; the huge failure of *Meet Joe Black* (98, Martin Brest); the buffed outlaw in *Fight Club* (99, Fincher), where the actor's commitment deserved more directorial intelligence.

The rut deepened with *Snatch* (00, Guy Ritchie); *The Mexican* (01, Gore Verbinski); *Spy Game* (01, Tony Scott); and *Ocean's 11* (01, Steven Soderbergh), where the suspicion dawned that he might be another Mickey Rourke. This was only supported by *Full Frontal* (02, Soderbergh); a voice-over for *Sinbad* (03, Tim Johnson); and the promise of his Achilles in *Troy* (04, Wolfgang Petersen).

Zasu Pitts (1898–1963), b. Parsons, Kansas
One day in 1919, King Vidor was riding on a Hollywood trolley car: "A strange angular young girl sat opposite me watching anxiously for her destination. Each time she turned she managed by weird gesticulation to strike the passenger on either side of her. When the conductor announced that hers was the next stop, she showed her delight and appreciation with a good backhand slap on his stomach. . . . I just couldn't sit there and let this interesting creature go out of my life for ever. I bounded out of the car and caught up with her as she reached the corner of Hollywood and Gower.

" 'What is your name, please?'

" 'Zasu. Last of Eliza, first of Susie.' "

It might be a scene from a von Stroheim film, with the wide-eyed, eccentric ingenue engaged in "weird gesticulation." Vidor snapped her up and wrote a script for her in which she played "Nancy Scroogs," a girl in a boarding school who pretends to receive love letters from a famous baseball player. That film, *Better Times* (19), caught the forlorn romantic hopes of a girl who foresees spinsterhood.

Her pale face was nearly ghoulish with large, staring eyes—no wonder she transfixed a trolley car. By popular standards she was not pretty, and in her later films she was a comic little old lady. But Stroheim's poetic melodrama recognized her passionate daydream of married bliss in the ordinary girl and cast her as Trina in *Greed* (25). She shows how Stroheim's "realism" is a mixture of full-blooded melodrama and psychological insight. She made over 120 films, many of poor quality, but in *Greed* she gives one of the most compelling performances in silent cinema, with the bursting frenzy of a trapped bird.

Vidor claimed to have discovered Pitts, but she had already been in films for two years before *Better Times*. His instinct about her proved correct, except that this "strange angular" girl usually played cameos and supporting parts: *The Little Princess* (17, Marshall Neilan); *How Could You, Jean?* (18, William Desmond Taylor); *The Other Half* (19, Vidor); *Poor Relations* (19, Vidor); *Patsy* (21, John McDermott); *A Daughter of Luxury* (22, Paul Powell); *Is Matrimony a Failure?* (22, James Cruze); *Youth to Youth* (22, Emile Chautard); *Poor Men's Wives* (23, Louis J. Gasnier); *Tea With a Kick* (23, Erle C. Kenton); *Three Wise Fools* (23, Vidor); *Daughters of Today* (24, Rollin Sturgeon); *The Fast Set* (24, William De Mille); *The Goldfish* (24, Jerome Storm); *Triumph* (24, Cecil B. De Mille); *The Great Divide* (25, Reginald Barker); *The Great Love* (25, Neilan); *Lazybones* (25, Frank Borzage); *Pretty Ladies* (25, Monta Bell); *The Re-creation of Brian Kent* (25, Sam Wood); *Thunder Mountain* (25, Victor Schertzinger); *Wages for Wives* (25, Borzage); *Early to Wed* (26, Borzage); *Mannequin* (26, Cruze); *Monte Carlo* (26, Christy Cabanne); *Sunny Side Up* (26, Donald Crisp); *Casey at the Bat* (27, Monte Brice); *Sins of the Fathers* (28, Ludwig Berger); *The Wedding March* (28, von Stroheim); *Her Private Life* (29, Alexander Korda); *The Locked Door* (29, George Fitzmaurice); *Oh Yeah!* (29, Garnett); *Paris* (29, Clarence Badger); *The Squall* (29, Korda); *This Thing Called Love* (29, Paul L. Stein); *Twin Beds* (29, Alfred Santell); she played the mother in *All Quiet on the Western Front* (30, Lewis Milestone), but her scenes were refilmed for sound with Beryl Mercer in the part; *The Devil's Holiday* (30, Edmund Goulding); *Honey* (30, Wesley Ruggles); *The Lottery Bride* (30, Stein); *No, No, Nanette* (30, Badger); *Monte Carlo* (30, Ernst Lubitsch); *River's End* (30, Michael Curtiz); *Seed* (31, John M. Stahl); *Finn and Hattie* (31, Norman Taurog); *The Guardsman* (31, Sidney Franklin); *The Big Gamble* (31, Fred Niblo); *Blondie of the Follies* (32,

Goulding); *Back Street* (32, Stahl); *The Roar of the Dragon* (32, Ruggles); *The Man I Killed* (32, Lubitsch); also in 1932, she was cast—as a girl called Zasu, half in love with death—in Stroheim's *Walking Down Broadway*. But that film foundered on production quarrels, was largely reshot and released as *Hello Sister* (33).

At about this time, she combined with Thelma Todd in a series of comedy shorts and went in for more character parts: *Mr. Skitch* (33, Cruze); *Her First Mate* (33, William Wyler); *Aggie Appleby, Maker of Men* (33, Mark Sandrich); *The Gay Bride* (34, Jack Conway); *Their Big Moment* (34, Cruze); *Dames* (34, Ray Enright); *Mrs. Wiggs of the Cabbage Patch* (34, Taurog); *Ruggles of Red Gap* (35, Leo McCarey); *Going Highbrow* (35, Robert Florey); *Sing Me a Love Song* (36, Enright); *Mad Holiday* (36, George Seitz); *Naughty But Nice* (39, Enright); *Nurse Edith Cavell* (39, Herbert Wilcox); *Eternally Yours* (39, Garnett); *No, No, Nanette* (40, Wilcox); *Broadway Limited* (41, Gordon Douglas); *Weekend for Three* (41, Irving Reis); *The Bashful Bachelor* (41, Malcolm St. Clair); *Let's Face It* (43, Sidney Lanfield); *Life With Father* (47, Curtiz); *Francis* (50, Arthur Lubin); *Denver & Rio Grande* (52, Byron Haskin); *This Could Be the Night* (57, Robert Wise); *The Gazebo* (59, George Marshall); *The Thrill of It All* (63, Norman Jewison); and *It's a Mad, Mad, Mad, Mad World* (63, Stanley Kramer).

Christopher Plummer,
b. Toronto, Canada, 1927

One of the first men who noticed Christopher Plummer's promise was David O. Selznick, who nearly cast the Canadian actor as Dick Diver in the 1962 film of *Tender Is the Night*. So it's nice to be able to say that Plummer did the narration for TNT's documentary *The Making of a Legend: Gone With the Wind* (89, David Hinton). Along the way, Plummer has been, variously, a star in big pictures, a fine supporting actor, and—quite simply, as Mike Wallace in *The Insider* (99, Michael Mann)—a great movie actor. Of course, he has always stayed loyal to the stage as well—in recent years he has done a John Barrymore one-man show in triumph. He has one other contribution to the film arts (not his least) in that he is father (as Tammy Grimes was mother) to the remarkable Amanda Plummer.

He was the young playwright in *Stage Struck* (58, Sidney Lumet); the Audubon man in *Wind Across the Everglades* (58, Nicholas Ray); a fine, chilling Commodus in *The Fall of the Roman Empire* (63, Anthony Mann); seeming very uncomfortable or unmelted as Baron von Trapp in *The Sound of Music* (65, Robert Wise); *Inside Daisy Clover* (66, Robert Mulligan); safecracker-spy in *Triple Cross* (66, Terence Young); Rommel in *Night of the Generals* (67, Anatole Litvak);

Oedipus the King (68, Philip Saville); *The High Commissioner* (68, Ralph Thomas); Atahualpa in *The Royal Hunt of the Sun* (69, Irving Lerner); *Battle of Britain* (69, Guy Hamilton); *Lock Up Your Daughters* (69, Peter Coe); as Wellington in *Waterloo* (71, Sergei Bondarchuk); *The Pyx* (73, Harvey Hart); *The Return of the Pink Panther* (75, Blake Edwards); *Conduct Unbecoming* (75, Michael Anderson); excellent as Kipling in *The Man Who Would Be King* (75, John Huston); *Aces High* (76, Jack Gold); the Archduke Ferdinand in *The Day That Shook the World* (77, Veljko Bulajic); *The Assignment* (77, Mats Aréhn); *The Disappearance* (77, Stuart Cooper); as Sherlock Holmes in *Murder by Decree* (79, Bob Clark); very good in *The Silent Partner* (79, Daryl Duke); *Hanover Street* (79, Peter Hyams); *Somewhere in Time* (80, Jeannot Szwarc); *Eyewitness* (81, Peter Yates); *Dreamscape* (84, Joseph Ruben); with Maggie Smith in *Lily in Love* (85, Károly Makk); *Ordeal by Innocence* (85, Desmond Davis); *The Boss' Wife* (86, Ziggy Steinberg); *Dragnet* (87, Tom Mankiewicz); *Mindfield* (90, Jean-Claude Lord); *Where the Heart Is* (90, John Boorman); *Wolf* (94, Mike Nichols); *12 Monkeys* (95, Terry Gilliam); *Dolores Claiborne* (95, Taylor Hackford); *Skeletons* (96, David DeCoteau); *Hidden Agenda* (98, Iain Patterson); *The Clown at Midnight* (98, Jean Pellerin); *Blackheart* (98, Dominic Shiach); Sir David Maxwell-Fyfe in the TV *Nuremberg* (00, Yves Simoneau); F. Lee Bailey in *American Tragedy* (00, Lawrence Schiller); Van Helsing in *Dracula 2000* (00, Patrick Lussier); the old Henry Fonda part in *On Golden Pond* (01, Ernest Thompson) for TV; a doctor in *A Beautiful Mind* (01, Ron Howard).

He was in *Full Disclosure* (01, John Bradshaw); *Night Flight* (02, Nicholas Renton); *Ararat* (02, Atom Egoyan); *Agent of Influence* (02, Michel Poulette); as Ralph in *Nicholas Nickleby* (02, Douglas McGrath); *Blizzard* (02, LeVar Burton); *Cold Creek Manor* (03, Mike Figgis).

Sidney Poitier, b. Miami, Florida, 1924
1971: *Buck and the Preacher*. 1972: *A Warm December*. 1974: *Uptown Saturday Night*. 1975: *Let's Do It Again*. 1977: *A Piece of the Action*. 1980: *Stir Crazy*. 1982: *Hanky Panky*. 1985: *Fast Forward*. 1990: *Ghost Dad*.

It's not easy in the age of Spike Lee, Michael Jordan, and Eddie Murphy to realize how important Sidney Poitier was in the late fifties and early sixties. He played lead roles in self-consciously liberal films, and he was liked and accepted by large parts of the American population. When Poitier was nominated for the best actor Oscar for *The Defiant Ones* (Tony Curtis was nominated, too—they stayed chained together), no black actor had ever been nominated before. For black actors were more threatening than black actresses.

Was Poitier a threat? Seen again, pictures like *The Defiant Ones* seem polite and careful, and Poitier is so decent, so well spoken, so handsome, so reasonable, that he looks rather like a white black. (It's relevant to note that he was raised in the Bahamas, where his family came from. He did not share totally in the black American experience. He had a confidence and a smile not often found in American blacks.) At any event, when Poitier received the American Film Institute's Life Achievement Award in 1992, Morgan Freeman noted how vital a lead Poitier had given succeeding generations.

He made his debut in Joseph Mankiewicz's *No Way Out* (50) and was in *Cry the Beloved Country* (52, Zoltan Korda), *Red Ball Express* (52, Budd Boetticher), and *Go Man, Go* (53, James Wong Howe), before two excellent performances: in Richard Brooks's *Blackboard Jungle* (55) and Martin Ritt's *Edge of the City* (57). Thereafter, however, his films became more directly conscious of race—in tune with American public feeling: *Something of Value* (57, Brooks) and Stanley Kramer's ponderous *The Defiant Ones* (58) are the first of the self-conscious films in which Poitier carried the wearying banner of racial harmony: Daniel Petrie's *A Raisin in the Sun* (60); Ralph Nelson's *Lilies of the Field* (63), an unctuous study of Poitier and a band of German nuns charming each other to pieces, leading to a best actor Oscar for Poitier; Guy Green's *A Patch of Blue* (66); James Clavell's *To Sir With Love* (67); Kramer's *Guess Who's Coming to Dinner?* (67); *The Lost Man* (69, Robert Alan Aurthur)—a black reworking of *Odd Man Out*; *Brother John* (70, James Goldstone); a woeful attempt to be a South African freedom fighter in *The Wilby Conspiracy* (74, Nelson).

Clearly Poitier saw the danger in such soul-destroying movies, and he made efforts to escape into parts that might be judged purely as entertainment: thus Raoul Walsh's *Band of Angels* (57); *The Long Ships* (64, Jack Cardiff); *The Bedford Incident* (65, James B. Harris); *The Slender Thread* (65, Sydney Pollack); and *Duel at Diablo* (66, Nelson).

Naturally, he played Porgy for Preminger in 1959, but confined to his knees and only miming the songs, he illustrated the dilemma of a black actor in movies. Richard Roundtree's *Shaft* seemed freer and much more enjoyable than anything the resolutely polite Poitier tried. Perhaps his most conventional work is best, namely the trilogy of Virgil Tibbs, which began with *In the Heat of the Night* (67, Norman Jewison) as a crude black-white confrontation, but which he developed into a run-of-the-mill black detective in *They Call Me MISTER Tibbs* (70, Gordon Douglas) and *The Organization* (71, Don Medford).

Poitier also branched into direction with three foolishly conceived and miserably handled projects: *Buck and the Preacher* (71), *A Warm December* (72), and *Uptown Saturday Night* (74) in all of which he also acted.

In the seventies, Poitier turned to acting-directing movies largely inhabited by blacks. If they were determinedly righteous films for blacks, it was only for those not used to the stalest clichés of white movies. *Let's Do It Again* was the best, thanks to Bill Cosby. But Poitier looked increasingly tenuous claiming a middle ground between *Roots*, the Richard Pryor comedies, and the austere cult hardness of black art made and shown in the no-go areas of large cities.

What drives Poitier now? He is handsome, articulate. He could be a commanding figure. Yet his career has trailed away in irrelevant comedies: *Stir Crazy* is Gene Wilder and Richard Pryor; *Hanky Panky* is Wilder and Gilda Radner (replacing Pryor); *Fast Forward* is teenagers; and *Ghost Dad* is Bill Cosby. There's little else to be said for the lot of them.

For ten years or so Poitier did not act. Then he returned as a cop in the fanciful *Shoot to Kill* (88, Roger Spottiswoode); *Little Nikita* (88, Richard Benjamin); playing Thurgood Marshall on TV in *Separate But Equal* (91, George Stevens Jr); and *Sneakers* (92, Phil Alden Robinson).

Poitier seems semiretired, now. But he *is* mythic—as witness the legend that inspires *Six Degrees of Separation* (93, Fred Schepisi). He made a comeback in *The Jackal* (97, Michael Caton-Jones) and *Mandela and de Klerk* (97, Joseph Sargent). In the Oscars for 2002, his honorary Oscar could have been scripted to grace the awards to Denzel Washington and Halle Berry. Close to eighty, Poitier looked noble—and unthreatening.

Roman Polanski, b. Paris, 1933

1957: *Rower* (unfinished); *Morbectwo* (s); *Rozbigimi Zabawe* (s). 1958: *Ewag Ludzie z Szasa/Two Men and a Wardrobe* (s). 1959: *Anioly Spadaja* (s). 1962: *Noz w Wodzie/Knife in the Water*; *Ssaki/Mammals* (s). 1963: *Le Gros et le Maigre* (s); "La Riviere de Diamants," episode from *Les Plus Belles Escroqueries du Mond*. 1965: *Repulsion*. 1966: *Cul-de-Sac*. 1967: *Dance of the Vampires*. 1968: *Rosemary's Baby*. 1971: *Macbeth*. 1972: *Che?/What?*. 1974: *Chinatown*. 1976: *Le Locataire/The Tenant*. 1979: *Tess of the d'Urbervilles*. 1986: *Pirates*. 1988: *Frantic*. 1992: *Bitter Moon*. 1995: *Death and the Maiden*. 1999: *The Ninth Gate*. 2002: *The Pianist*.

Who would have thought in 1978, when Polanski jumped bail, left America, and fled from the charge of having seduced a fourteen-year-old girl, that the subsequent exile would become his way of life? Don't such problems get worked out? Isn't that what Hollywood lawyers do? Until that moment (and he was still only forty-five) Polanski was famous as a survivor. His mother had perished in Auschwitz; his father had been at another camp. His childhood had been so haunted and hunted it was said to have inspired Jerzy Kosinski's *The Painted Bird*.

Still, the tiny, rather ugly man had asserted himself. He had been a brilliant student, and a subversive guest in Britain. Then he had gone on to America and made two huge hits, both highly influential: *Rosemary's Baby* (high-class horror) and *Chinatown* (political noir). That triumph had been won in defiance of the slaughter of his pregnant wife, Sharon Tate, one of the victims of the Manson gang in their raid on Cielo Drive. His was a story of tragedy and obstacle overcome. *Chinatown* had many talents, but most people reckoned it was the decisive Polanski who had made it work. He seemed acutely American in being on the nose.

And then . . . ? Idleness and the oddity of *The Tenant*, which seemed like an unexpected admission of his own distress. Did success crack Polanski, or make him relax? Based ever since his "incident" in Paris, he has made films that do not seem his. *Tess* is stately and pretty. *Frantic* is a silliness, perfectly titled. And *Bitter Moon* was a big flop that struggled to get released in America. Polanski has done some acting; he wrote an autobiography; he has married Emmanuelle Seigner, the beautiful but glassy actress from *Frantic* and *Bitter Moon*. It seems less and less likely that he will leave Paris—or that anyone would care if he did.

The violence in Polanski's films is not especially prominent; it has seldom erupted with the force achieved by Peckinpah, Arthur Penn, Fuller, or Losey. Much more characteristic is the underlying alienation and hostility: the feeling that people are cut off, unsupported by any shared view of life and society. From this solitariness, the move toward acts of violence is stealthy, remorseless, and even comic. Thus *Cul-de-Sac* is a mixture of Beckett and English social satire, uneasily concealing a situation fraught with menacing implications. The couple living in the bizarre house on bleak Holy Island are married, but as incompatible as Donald Pleasence and Françoise Dorléac. They might be together simply to savage one another. While Lionel Stander, who intrudes helplessly upon them, is a refugee from thrillers of the 1940s. The black fun of the film never eases the threat. It was her psychotic sense of decay that led to an overwhelming mental pressure on Catherine Deneuve in a South Kensington flat in *Repulsion*, and that justified her feeling that the world was so demented she needed to begin to destroy it.

Cul-de-Sac offered the sort of remote locale that shows how far Polanski puts people at their own extremes. Similarly, the shapes and decor of the Kensington flat are the outward signs of Deneuve's madness: the fragile blonde driven to fearful slaughter by her distorted sensibility.

By the time he was three, the Polanskis lived in Cracow. Both parents were sent to concentration camps; the mother died at Auschwitz. After the war, he went to art school and in 1955 to the Lodz Film School. *Two Men and a Wardrobe*, made as a school project, attracted considerable international attention for its stripped-down view of absurdity. He put up the script of *Knife in the Water*, but it was rejected. He went to France and returned only in 1962 to make his first feature, an academic study of sexual tension and of fiercely contrasting personalities. It showed what Kenneth Tynan called Polanski's interest in people who can "impose" themselves on others. *Le Gros et le Maigre* is a servant-master relationship, a little like *End Game,* but clearly of Polanski's own vision. In *Repulsion,* Catherine Deneuve is so imposed upon that she can only reassert herself through murder. *Cul-de-Sac* is a dead end jostling with subtle but crazy power play. *Rosemary's Baby*, the film Polanski made in New York for Paramount, is about the resonance of evil. *Macbeth,* too, is a story of a man imposed upon by the supernatural, by the outward voicing of his own hopes, and by his wife.

Put in these terms, Polanski's world sounds narrow and repetitive. What enlarges it is his sense of humor, the lack of self-pity, and the curiosity that he retains for human behavior. Despite every ordeal, his films have a cheerful interest in oddity and a cinematic willingness to give it full play. He uses long, simple takes to encourage the actors and to involve them so totally as to achieve extraordinary moments. There is no better test of the approach than the beach scene in *Cul-de-Sac,* all in one take, with Pleasence and Stander engaged in lugubrious mutual confession, neither one understanding the other, while the pale naked figure of Dorléac goes swimming in the distance and an inexplicable aircraft drones overhead.

That *Chinatown* feels so expert on Los Angeles (and America) owes a lot to Robert Towne. The script was his, and it was enriched by a life in Southern California and by unusual research. Moreover, the project had been conceived for Jack Nicholson as Jake Gittes, and for Robert Evans as producer. Polanski came to the table later. He warred with Faye Dunaway, and he challenged what he took for softness in Towne's conclusion. It was Polanski's experience and his storytelling expertness that insisted on affirming Noah Cross's power and on having Evelyn Mulwray killed, with Gittes left powerless. Surely that decision was vital, and maybe it required Polanski's level appreciation of what wickedness could do.

That's what makes *Chinatown* a great film, as well as a great show. Polanski is everywhere in the film, greedy for detail, jabbing at Nicholson's nose, urging John Huston's Cross to be heroic and expansive, harassing Evelyn and getting the look and the feel just right. Years later, the dire sequel, *The Two Jakes,* celebrated Polanski through his absence. By then, he was fatally Parisian.

The Tenant contains the best and worst of Polanski. It begins with a situation pregnant with discomfort: a precise, enclosed place and a nervous hero longing to be victimized. Polanski plays the part himself and shows us how far the shy wolf face is an image of guilt that knows its destiny will be dreadful. But the promise explodes in exaggeration, and the set turns into a cabinet of grand guignol. In the end it is ridiculous, and evidence that Polanski gets out of hand whenever he loses that stealthy pace of comic fear.

Once upon a time, it would have seemed impossible for Polanski to stagnate. Yet it has happened. *Death and the Maiden* and *The Ninth Gate* did not seem to belong to him, whereas, once, he had put his stamp on anything and everything. This liberty has not enriched him. There has been no talk of a return to America; and no hint of that music not having to be faced. In Paris, Polanski seems disconsolate, a thumb-twiddler. And while time passes, the mood for his best films is nearly forgotten.

The Pianist was a triumphant return. The winner at Cannes, it was deemed old-fashioned. But at the Oscars, it seemed classical and unusually personal. The best director award was a surprise—but it didn't persuade Polanski to appear.

Sydney Pollack, b. Lafayette, Indiana, 1934
1965: *The Slender Thread.* 1966: *This Property Is Condemned.* 1968: *The Scalphunters; Castle Keep; The Swimmer* (credited to Frank Perry, with sequences by Pollack). 1969: *They Shoot Horses, Don't They?.* 1972: *Jeremiah Johnson.* 1973: *The Way We Were.* 1975: *The Yakuza; Three Days of the Condor.* 1977: *Bobby Deerfield.* 1979: *The Electric Horseman.* 1981: *Absence of Malice.* 1982: *Tootsie.* 1985: *Out of Africa.* 1990: *Havana.* 1993: *The Firm.* 1995: *Sabrina.* 1999: *Random Hearts.*

Originally an actor, and then a director on TV, Pollack has always shown an interest in enterprising material, persistently let down by his middlebrow approach. Yet he has become one of the leading producer-directors in America.

This Property Is Condemned, from a promising Tennessee Williams playlet, is packed with atmosphere and has one of Robert Redford's more committed performances. But it follows meekly in the line of Williams adaptations, endorsing the Kazan/Brooks clash of theatrical style and predictable images. *Castle Keep* handles William Eastlake's inventive novel straight, but only to simplify it. Above all, *They Shoot Horses, Don't They?* glamorizes Horace McCoy's pungent novella. Dif-

ficult to make a dull film of a marathon dance contest, and all credit to the conventional excellence of Jane Fonda, Gig Young, and Susannah York, but McCoy is apocalyptic and contemptuous of society, whereas the film is a shallow account of pointless energy. The brutal flash-forwards of McCoy's original should chop in and out like a butcher's axe. In the film th·y are made studied and mournful with pretty photography.

Similarly, *Jeremiah Johnson* is a meticulous landscape picture that fails to convey the mythic nature of its subject and reveals how complacent an actor Redford had become. *The Way We Were* never overcomes the implausibility of Streisand and Redford loving each other, but it had a strange chemistry that made for a big hit. *Three Days of the Condor* is a tortuous spy film, heavy with stars but unnecessary and unconvinced, despite a script that proposed unexpected aspects of Robert Redford and Faye Dunaway—in the first instance, so unexpected that the part might have been entrusted to someone else. *Bobby Deerfield* came as a genuine surprise, a film about death that never lets motor racing or pretty European scenery soften its point. It uses Al Pacino and Marthe Keller remarkably well to illustrate different degrees of intensity—the one ingrowing and the other flamboyant and generous—and it achieved a depth that had hitherto eluded Pollack.

Tootsie and *Out of Africa* were big pictures, heavy with praise and awards—*Out of Africa* won best picture. Yet they were both the work of a good producer rather than a director with character.

With *Havana,* not even the producer's touch remained. But Pollack seems aware of his own inclination, and he has become an active impresario for other people's films: *Honeysuckle Rose* (80, Jerry Schatzberg); *Bright Lights, Big City* (88, James Bridges); the excellent *The Fabulous Baker Boys* (89, Steve Kloves); *Presumed Innocent* (90, Alan J. Pakula); and *White Palace* (90, Luis Mandoki).

He is also a nice, comic actor, as witness his agent in *Tootsie, Death Becomes Her* (92, Robert Zemeckis), his splendidly fluent self-deceiver in *Husbands and Wives* (93, Woody Allen), and his attempt to make sense of *Eyes Wide Shut* (99, Stanley Kubrick).

The Firm was long, unduly elaborate, and—in the end—heavy with a feeling of so what? But it worked on screen as one watched, and if one gives Pollack general credit for making that happen, it is a way of noting how few others have that knack today. His sheer professionalism is endearing, but *Sabrina* and *Random Hearts* were so awful their polish seemed absurd.

He turns more and more to production, through his company, Mirage: *The Talented Mr Ripley* (99, Anthony Minghella); *Birthday Girl* (01, Jez Butterworth); *Iris* (01, Richard Eyre);

Heaven (02, Tom Tykwer); *The Quiet American* (02, Phillip Noyce); *Cold Mountain* (03, Minghella).

Abraham Polonsky (1910–99),
b. New York
1948: *Force of Evil.* 1969: *Tell Them Willie Boy Is Here.* 1971: *Romance of a Horse Thief.*

Twenty-one years between first and second films is longer than any director should have to wait. The case of Polonsky is one of the most dismal hangovers from the McCarthy period. Long after Carl Foreman and Losey had been rehabilitated, Polonsky stayed out in the cold, working under assumed names so that the actual list of his writing credits is unclear. Polonsky was possibly the most creative personality in Enterprise Films. He scripted *Body and Soul* (47, Robert Rossen) and may have had as much influence on it as the director. The following year he made *Force of Evil* for MGM, a B thriller, starring John Garfield, that employs crisp, blank-verse dialogue without preciosity and lifts the urban thriller to a magnificent allegory of corrupt ambition. He scripted *Golden Earrings* (47, Mitchell Leisen) and *I Can Get It for You Wholesale* (51, Michael Gordon) and was then blacklisted.

His first new credit, under his own name, was as scriptwriter on *Madigan* (68, Don Siegel). In the same year, he directed *Willie Boy,* the story of a rogue Indian tracked down by a callous society, too painfully applicable to Polonsky's own history, and as visually rusty as one might expect from a man so long out of action. Polonsky's third film is a story set on the Polish border in the year 1904, and goes back to the director's ethnic roots.

He said that it was part of his life—both as European refugee, and as young immigrant in New York devouring fiction: "In this strange way *Romance of a Horse Thief* is attached closely to the films of my childhood long before I had heard of fine art. For me, movies are irrevocably and richly rooted in kitsch, in childhood, in storytelling, in the rubbish of paperbacks and sitting under the streetlights while off in the zoo across the lots flowering with burdock, lions roared out their fantasy of freedom. . . . It was a great pleasure to make a movie again. Nothing is better; perhaps revolution, but there you have to succeed and be right, dangers which never attach themselves to making movies, and dreaming."

Many of the simple facts of his life are obscure. But it seems that, among other occupations, he had been a teacher at City College, New York, in the 1930s, a soldier, a writer for radio, and the author of at least three novels—*The Discoverers, The World Above,* and *The Season of Fear.* There are greater tragedies in the world, but if you ever feel comfortable, search out *Force of Evil* and recollect how thoroughly its director was excluded

from filmmaking.

More recently, he wrote the screenplay for *Avalanche Express* (78, Mark Robson). He also wrote the early drafts of the script that became *Guilty By Suspicion* (91, Irwin Winkler)—a project that had Bertrand Tavernier as its director when Polonsky was involved.

Gillo Pontecorvo (Gilberto Pontecorvo),
b. Pisa, Italy, 1919
1956: "Giovanna," episode from *Die Vind Rose.* 1957: *La Grande Strada Azzurra.* 1959: *Kapo.* 1965: *La Battaglia di Algeri/The Battle of Algiers.* 1968: *Queimada!.* 1979: *Operazione Ogro.* 1984: *L'Addio a Enrico Berlinguer* (d). 1997: "Nostalgia di Protezione," an episode from *I Corti Italiani.*

In *The Meaning of Treason,* Rebecca West claims that it was the revelation that Bruno Pontecorvo's younger brother, Gilberto, had been a Communist since 1939 that first brought the Harwell physicist under suspicion. As she dryly pointed out, it was a substantial connection for five screenings to miss, since Gillo Pontecorvo was an active journalist for the party. Whether Gillo subverted or illuminated his brother, the notorious influence may have been too difficult to live down.

But Gillo's films contradict the idea of a proselytizing, doctrinaire man. After the war, he spent several years as assistant to Yves Allégret and Mario Monicelli, and in the early 1960s he made a number of unsung documentaries. His feature debut was in East Germany, on an episode of the women's rights movie presided over by Joris Ivens and Cavalcanti. Something of Ivens's flexible decency seems to have touched Pontecorvo. His first features were clumsy infusions of large subjects and melodrama, especially *Kapo,* a concentration camp story. But six years later, still lacking facility, Pontecorvo made a fascinating commentary upon documentary, *The Battle of Algiers,* shot in actual locations and with actors and real-life participants. The French government impeded the release of the film, but it is far less hostile to them than it might have been. Pontecorvo makes many French soldiers and colonists credible and sympathetic figures, caught up in a larger, politico-economic pattern of exploitation. In short, it is the more politically convincing because it does not manipulate its people. *Queimada!* is a more generalized picture, about slavery and sugar in the Caribbean. But it too insists on seeing the imperialists as victims of their own system, and it is enormously helped by Marlon Brando's performance as the disillusioned English adventurer.

Dennis Potter (1935–94),
b. Berry Hill, England
Potter deserves to be viewed as a major figure in film history. And Potter is TV.

In the great age of film studies (early 1960s to 1980s), television was in fact the dominant cultural medium that nostalgists cherished the movies for having been.

All but a few movie fanatics have seen more moving imagery on a television screen than "at the movies." It is likely that the regular, the reviewer who sees maybe six or seven movies a week, still submits to TV for several hours a day. It is on—like the light. The ordinary viewer, the average citizen, would delight the movie business if he or she saw one movie every six weeks. But he, she, we, the moblike broken family, goes back and forth, like leopards in our cage, while TV is "on," six or seven hours a day. The world works by way of TV: that is where marketing occurs; that is how politicians play at running the country; and that is where news is defined and focused. It is lamentable, if you want to take that view. Though I suspect a greater damage to our culture and our ideas came earlier, in permitting photography. That was the first great drug, and it trained us for the others.

Television has shaped us—you can blame it for "abbreviated attention span" and a failure to believe in realities; or you can notice how it promotes a low-level passive surrealism in expectations, and an uncatalogued memory bank for our minds. We may be more like crazed movie editors trying to splice our lives together because of TV. There is a resistance it has bred, as well as a chaos: you can't have one without the other. And in the end, there is no point in being gloomy or cheerful about it. It's there, here, without moratorium or chance of reversal.

Intensive film study and film scholarship now work by way of the TV screen. It is seldom possible to review the great movies "at the movies." Suppose I wanted to see *Sunrise, Duel in the Sun,* and *Ugetsu Monogatari* on big screens—where would I go? The difficulties I would face, of prints, screens, access, and so on, are only going to grow greater. Yet I might be able to summon them up on video, where I could see them as often as I liked, with "pause" to access the full beauty of the frame. Everyone is doing it, no matter that the color is forlorn (the United States has the worst TV color in the world), the image format is different, the sound is tinny . . . and the passion is not there. That passion is made by the dark, the brightness, the very large screen, the company of strangers, and the knowledge that you cannot stop the process, or even get out. That is being at the movies, and it is becoming a museum experience. How can one tell one's students or one's children what it was like seeing *Vertigo* (in empty theatres—for no one liked it once) or *The Red Shoes* from the dark. We watch television with the lights on! Out of some bizarre superstition that it protects our eyes. How so tender for one part of us, and so indifferent to the rest?

In Hollywood, or in the movie community, television has been disdained. Nothing may be so telling a secret sign of the stars' horror of the public; and nothing so surely accounts for the decline of movies as *the* American entertainment. This superiority should come to terms not just with the public and its viewing habits. It should face the potency of careers like those of Lucille Ball, Johnny Carson, and Michael Mann, as well as the difficulty of dealing with so many problematic realities on the big screen. For movie fantasy has moved away from us, like a rogue moon, drawn off by some greater source of gravity. Once, movie dreams were dangerously and tormentingly close to our lives: it made the medium irresistible. But now, television has us in its grip. Week after week, TV deals with the experience of such things as AIDS, drugs, hopeless ordinary existence, undramatic madness, in a way that shames movies. One reason why television is watched is the plain state of recognition.

Even so, television in America is ruthlessly controlled by commercial structures. It is a horror of American life that no one has ever made the full case for public broadcasting. And it is too late now, for Britain is surely killing off its own BBC. So there will be no chance left of an example. But for close to twenty years in Britain, amid expanses of gentility, banality, and severe boredom such as no American could tolerate, television stirred the nation. From the early sixties on, there was an accepted forum for strong talk, subversive comedy, and risky drama. This was the time and the studio that gave careers to Stephen Frears, John Cleese, Alan Bennett, and Dennis Potter.

Potter evidently told all questioners that he was born in the Forest of Dean. Britain is not an extensive country, and the Forest is a small part of it. Still, he must have been born somewhere in the forest, and I don't know where. So he emerges as some kind of sprite or devil, from out of the woods, and I suspect this suggestion was intended, for Potter is intent on getting us back into his woods. (Did Stephen Sondheim ever know the Forest of Dean?)

He was the son of a coal miner. The family was large and poor. But when he was twelve (this would be in the terrible winter of 1947, a cold occasion in British folklore), the Potters went to live in London. The father was unhappy and he took the others home again, but Dennis stayed on with relatives. He went to St. Clement Dane's grammar school and that led to a scholarship to Oxford. There he was president of the Labour Club and editor of *Isis*. The country sprite became an angry young man.

A career in journalism (writing for the *Daily*

Herald, one of the few Labour papers) led him toward writing plays for television. These "plays" were usually made as films, but they were advertised as plays of the week, or whatever, and they were meant to have a sense of rational immediacy. Or rather, if that was not meant, Potter and several others helped supply it.

Potter began as a realist with two plays about a young man coming alive in the sixties and attempting a career in politics (Potter, too, ran as a Labour candidate in 1964): *Stand Up, Nigel Barton* (65, Gareth Davies) and *Vote, Vote, Vote for Nigel Barton* (65, Davies).

Once established, Potter moved irrevocably toward novel forms, often tinged by autobiography, but imaginatively daring and fueled with the power of fantasy. He was as much affected by popular songs and silly old movies as by his own childhood and the Britain of the war, the welfare state, Suez, Macmillan, and Swinging London. In all that followed, he was the writer who came to exert a moral force (not to say bullying) on directors and actors so that they were grateful for the chance to serve him. Authority is natural, and authorship follows it. I have not space to list every work, but here are highlights:

Alice (65, Davies) concerns a boy being told Carroll-like stories. In *Where the Buffalo Roam* (66, Davies), a youth in drab Swansea believed he was Shane. A *Beast With Two Backs* (68, Lionel Harris) is a Forest of Dean legend about the guilt of the people and a relieving ritual: it was an early sign of Potter's entirely agnostic sense of moral retribution. *Moonlight on the Highway* (69, James MacTaggart) had Ian Holm as a man devoted to the 1930s English singer Al Bowlly. *Son of Man* (69, Davies) was a source of controversy: it offered a Jesus for the working class, played by Colin Blakely. (Notice how Potter drew on superb players.)

Lay Down Your Arms (70, Christopher Morahan) concerned a bored clerk who imagines he is a great goalkeeper. *Traitor* (71, Alan Bridges) had John Le Mesurier, a fine character actor, as a Philby-like figure in Moscow. *Casanova* (71, John Glenister, Mark Cullingham) was a series, over six hours in all, with Frank Finlay as the great lover. The period detail was exact, yet this Casanova was an intellectual lecher—sensuality for Potter has always been a play on the mind.

Follow the Yellow Brick Road (72, Alan Bridges) had a bad actor who would sooner make TV commercials than fierce Potter-like plays—for Potter has always been suspicious over the "failure" of escapism and the "importance" of serious work. He trusts any imagination and the way it twists, for only there are we free from lies. *Schmoedipus* (74, Barry Davis) is the story that would grow into *Track 29* (88, Nicolas Roeg). *Where Adam Stood* (76, Brian Gibson) is about a

child whose fundamentalist father is trying to deny the meaning of evolution. (The child is frequently vital in Potter stories—even if it is the child remembered, the child absent, or just the hope in adults to regain childishness.)

Brimstone and Treacle (76, Davis) caused another scandal with its unsentimental vision of ordinariness invaded, exploited, and invalid innocence raped. The original *Pennies from Heaven* (78, Piers Haggard) was another series, four and a half hours, with Bob Hoskins as the wretched sheet-music salesman. The novelty of songs interacting with the drama was something Potter had been advancing on for years. *Blue Remembered Hills* (79, Gibson) is a masterpiece, a play about childhood in a forest tangled in games, passions, friendships, and war, and all played by adults.

Then for London Weekend Television, he did a trio of films—*Blade on the Feather* (80, Richard Loncraine), *Rain on the Roof* (80, Bridges), and *Cream in My Coffee* (80, Gavin Millar), which played in successive weeks—the output has been prodigious, for I should add that Potter also did TV dramatizations of *The Mayor of Casterbridge* and *Tender Is the Night.*

The movies claimed him after *Pennies from Heaven.* He did the screenplay for Hollywood's grotesquely overblown remake (81, Herbert Ross), which only shows how misguided some admiration can be. He did *Brimstone and Treacle* (82, Loncraine) for theatres—the BBC had banned it from the small screen. He did the scripts for *Gorky Park* (83, Michael Apted) and *Dreamchild* (85, Millar)—the first pedestrian and the second inventive, but a minor work by Potter's standards. A few years later, *Track 29* proved a travesty of *Schmoedipus.*

It was in 1986 that Potter wrote the six-part *The Singing Detective* (Jon Amiel), his greatest work, and the amalgamation of all his themes and loves—not least that of chronic illness. Potter was the victim of psoriasis and arthritis, and of their attending drugs. The topic is too large to be explained here. Suffice it to say that Potter called illness both his friend and his enemy. It seems to me to have sharpened his life and his work: it defined his authority with others; it condensed his anger; and it enraged his passion. For Potter found difficulty and turmoil in his own flesh.

He did another TV series in 1993, *Lipstick On My Collar* (Renny Rye), set in the fifties. It had Potterian elements: song, the glamour of murder, the clash of classes, and a special lyrical pathology. But by the standards of *Singing Detective, Lipstick* was a minor work.

Along the way, with wife and children, Potter had taken on much other work. He did a stage play in 1983, *Sufficient Carbohydrate.* He had written novels—*Ticket to Ride* and *Blackeyes;* and he had directed pictures of *Blackeyes* (1989) and

Secret Friends (1991), which is based on *Ticket to Ride*. The latter is the only example of his work that I have found less than riveting.

He died in June 1994 after the sudden onset of cancer. He had done a valiant farewell interview—and finished two last plays for TV: *Karaoke* (96, Rye) and *Cold Lazarus* (96, Rye). He was always on a deadline.

Dick Powell (1904–63),
b. Mountain View, Arkansas

Powell had his origins in the heyday of abandon—Warner Brothers musicals of the 1930s—from where he hauled himself home to citizen respectability. By the time he died, he was known internationally as the host of TV's *Dick Powell Show,* an agreeable, pipe-smoking dullard who talked to the audience with Nixonian solemnity. He had come through to be one of the pioneers of TV drama; he acted rarely and, in the 1950s, indulged himself as a director five times. But the most lasting image of Powell is still the wide-eyed hoofer, face alight with lewdness tunneling through the splayed legs of Busby Berkeley's chorines in *42nd Street* (33, Lloyd Bacon) and boasting that he was "Young and Healthy."

From 1932, Powell fretted through a seven-year contract at Warners, despairing of the musicals he adorned as a singer and dancer, often with Joan Blondell. These are only the highlights: *Blessed Event* (32, Roy del Ruth); *Gold Diggers of 1933* (33, Mervyn Le Roy); *Footlight Parade* (33, Bacon); *Dames* (34, Ray Enright); *Happiness Ahead* (34, Le Roy); *Flirtation Walk* (34, Frank Borzage); *Gold Diggers of 1935* (35, Busby Berkeley); *Page Miss Glory* (35, Le Roy); *Thanks a Million* (35, del Ruth); as Napoleon's brother in *Hearts Divided* (36, Borzage); *Stage Struck* (36, Berkeley); *Gold Diggers of 1937* (36, Bacon); *On the Avenue* (37, del Ruth); *Varsity Show* (37, William Keighley); *Hollywood Hotel* (37, Berkeley); and *Naughty But Nice* (39, Enright).

He then went to Paramount and appeared as the man who mistakenly believes he's a big winner in *Christmas in July* (40, Preston Sturges) before slipping back into more musicals: *Model Wife* (41, Leigh Jason); *Happy Go Lucky* (43, Curtis Bernhardt); and *Riding High* (43, George Marshall). René Clair gave him the lead in *It Happened Tomorrow* (44), but the part that really changed Powell's image was that of Philip Marlowe in *Murder My Sweet* (45, Edward Dmytryk). At last he seemed to have won the dramatic, tuneless work he had set his heart on.

For six years he was a straight actor, even if his movies varied greatly in quality: *Cornered* (45, Dmytryk); *Johnny O'Clock* (47, Robert Rossen); *To the Ends of the Earth* (48, Robert Stevenson); *Stations West* (48, Sidney Lanfield); *Pitfall* (48, André de Toth); with June Allyson, his second

wife (Joan Blondell had been first), in *The Reformer and the Redhead* (50, Melvin Frank and Norman Panama) and *Right Cross* (50, John Sturges); *The Tall Target* (51, Anthony Mann); *Cry Danger* (51, Robert Parrish); probably his best work as the writer (with pipe) in *The Bad and the Beautiful* (52, Vincente Minnelli); and in *Susan Slept Here* (54, Frank Tashlin).

As a director he made these consistently anonymous movies: *Split Second* (52); *The Conqueror* (55)—with John Wayne as Genghis Khan; *You Can't Run Away from It* (56); *The Enemy Below* (57); and *The Hunters* (58).

Eleanor Powell (1912–82),
b. Springfield, Massachusetts

You are in solitary confinement for the rest of your life. There is a screen built into the cell wall, and it is a condition of your sentence that you may have just one sequence from a movie to play on that screen. This is my choice: black and white and a hard reflective floor, a set that recedes into darkness. Fred in all white with a black bowtie. Eleanor Powell wears three-quarter heels and a dress that stops just below the knees. She wears short sleeves and puff shoulders; the skirt is magnificently light and fluid, moving to the sway of the profound, yet casual, tap masterpiece, "Begin the Beguine," from *Broadway Melody of 1940* (40, Norman Taurog). Much of the dance is in exact unison, but there are fleeting solos and imitation repeats, as well as exquisite arm movements, especially from Powell. I know of nothing as exhilarating or unfailingly cheerful, and maybe the loveliest moment in films is the last second or so, as the dancers finish, and Powell's alive frock has another half-turn, like a spirit embracing the person. Give credit to Taurog, to dance director Bobby Connolly, to Astaire as always, but still this is a rare Astaire dance in that the lady actually holds the eye. Powell was not much of an actress, she was a modest singer, and she was single-mindedly a tap dancer. But this is a rapture.

She danced on Broadway, in the Follies, and came to movies in 1935: *George White's Scandals* (35, George White, Thornton Freeland, and Harry Lachman); *Broadway Melody of 1936* (35, Roy Del Ruth); *Born to Dance* (36, Del Ruth); *Broadway Melody of 1938* (37, Del Ruth); *Rosalie* (37, W. S. Van Dyke), with Nelson Eddy; *Honolulu* (39, Edward Buzzell); *Lady Be Good* (41, Norman Z. McLeod); *Ship Ahoy* (42, Buzzell); *Thousands Cheer* (43, George Sidney); *I Dood It* (43, Vincente Minnelli); and *Sensations of 1945* (44, Andrew L. Stone) where she dances inside a pinball machine.

She married actor Glenn Ford in 1943 and then retired. After that, she made only one more film, *Duchess of Idaho* (50, Robert Z. Leonard). She and Ford were divorced in 1959, and she made a short-lived return as a nightclub performer.

Michael Powell (1905–90),
b. Canterbury, England

1931: *Two Crowded Hours; My Friend the King; Rynox; The Rasp; The Star Reporter.* 1932: *Hotel Splendide; Born Lucky; C.O.D.; His Lordship.* 1933: *The Fire Kaisers.* 1934: *The Night of the Party; Red Ensign; Something Always Happens; The Girl in the Crowd.* 1935: *Some Day; Lazybones; Her Last Affaire; The Love Test; The Price of a Song; The Phantom Light.* 1936: *The Brown Wallet; Crown v. Stevens; The Man Behind the Mask.* 1937: *The Edge of the World.* 1939: *The Spy in Black* (codirected with Emeric Pressburger—EP); *The Lion Has Wings* (codirected with Brian Desmond Hurst and Adrian Brunel). 1940: *The Thief of Bagdad* (codirected with Ludwig Berger and Tim Whelan); *Contraband.* 1941: *An Airman's Letter to His Mother* (d); *49th Parallel* (EP). 1942: *One of Our Aircraft Is Missing* (EP). 1943: *The Volunteer* (s); *The Life and Death of Colonel Blimp* (EP). 1944: *A Canterbury Tale* (EP). 1945: *I Know Where I'm Going* (EP). 1946: *A Matter of Life and Death* (EP). 1947: *Black Narcissus* (EP). 1948: *The Red Shoes* (EP); *The Small Back Room* (EP). 1950: *Gone to Earth/The Wild Heart* (EP); *The Elusive Pimpernel* (EP). 1951: *The Tales of Hoffman* (EP). 1955: *Oh, Rosalinda!!* (EP). 1956: *The Battle of the River Plate* (EP); *Ill Met by Moonlight.* 1959: *Honeymoon.* 1960: *Peeping Tom.* 1961: *The Queen's Guards.* 1964: *Bluebeard's Castle.* 1966: *They're a Weird Mob.* 1969: *Age of Consent.* 1972: *The Boy Who Turned Yellow* (s).

There is not a British director with as many worthwhile films to his credit as Michael Powell. Yet in the age of Richardson and Schlesinger, in the sixties and seventies, Powell had hardly any adequate critical appreciation. The sadness was that he was written off as an eccentric decorator of fantasies. Against persistent British attempts to dignify realism, Powell must have seemed gaudy, distasteful, and effete. All three ingredients contribute to his vision, but so do an imaginative evocation of the erotic and the supernatural; a pioneering enthusiasm for visual autonomy always likely to break out in passages of stunning delight; the adherence to what Raymond Durgnat once called "High Tory" values; a wicked sense of humor and private jokes; and most distinctive—like Colonel Blimp's dreams—an unsettling mixture of emotional reticence and splurging fantasy. Thus, as late as 1969, *Age of Consent*, a mild beachcombing anecdote, is lit up by baroque passages of Helen Mirren, naked and underwater.

It is revealing that *Peeping Tom* was dismissed in Britain as wayward nastiness. Worst of all, Powell may have been inhibited by the feeling that his imagination was un-British. Powell stayed English despite the merry excursion to Australia when he cried out for the geography of light and shade that von Sternberg illuminated on the Paramount sound stages. Even when Britain rediscovered horror in the late 1950s, as O. O. Green has remarked, Powell was ignored. Green compared Powell and King Vidor, whose *Duel in the Sun* Jennifer Jones was reduced to *Country Life* fretfulness by Powell in *Gone to Earth:* "Vidor, intellectually, perhaps, less sophisticated, or at least less cautious, than Powell, has retained just that Wagnerian authenticity of emotional excess which gives his films that genuine mysticism, a Nietzschean pantheism. But Powell lived in a class and a country which suspects, undermines, is embarrassed by, emotion; his diversity of qualities rarely find their holding context."

As if in early accord with that verdict, Powell left Dulwich College for the studio Rex Ingram had set up in Nice. He assisted the ex-Dubliner, ex–Hollywood director, on *Mare Nostrum* (26), *The Magician* (26), and *The Garden of Allah* (27). Undoubtedly that experience encouraged his interest in the expressionist treatment of the supernatural; Ingram's splendid isolation may also have confirmed a young man's belief in "artistic" cinema. It was several years before Powell's own films showed such strange fruit. He slogged away for some time in England as cameraman, writer, and director; only in the late 1930s do his films seem his own.

Thereafter, in vital partnership with the writer Emeric Pressburger, they struggle with great, clashing virtues—with marvelous visual imagination and uneasy, intellectual substance: *I Know Where I'm Going* is a genuinely superstitious picture; *49th Parallel* is a strange war odyssey, with escaping Germans wandering across Canada—naïve, very violent, at times unwittingly comic, but possessed by a primitive feeling for endangered civilization; an interesting sequel is *One of Our Aircraft Is Missing*—English fliers getting out of Holland; *A Matter of Life and Death* is pretentious in its way, yet very funny and absolutely secure in its dainty stepping from one world to another. But the two Conrad Veidt movies—*The Spy in Black* and *Contraband*—are exciting and atmospheric studies in Langian intrigue; *The Thief of Bagdad* is delightful; *The Life and Death of Colonel Blimp* a beautiful salute to Englishness. After the war, Powell expanded, attempting to fuse the talents of painters, designers, and dancers. In fact, *The Red Shoes, Tales of Hoffman,* and *Oh, Rosalinda!!* underline the search for respectability in his work. But *The Red Shoes knows* that creative dreams easily surpass reality. It raised people to dance, but it is also a lovely tribute to creative collaboration. And Anton Walbrook's Lermontov—so hot, so cold—is a portrait of Powell himself. With a very personal mixture of wisdom and naïveté, Powell treated the artist or wizard as the last potent pagan deity. *Black Narcissus* is that rare thing, an erotic English film about the fantasies of nuns, startling whenever Kathleen Byron is involved. *The Small Back Room* profits from the use of unexpected expressionism on an ostensibly realistic subject and quivers with nervous tension. Equally, *The Elusive Pimpernel* has gorgeous moments despite a routine swashbuckling story.

After about 1950, dejection seemed to set in, only to be dispelled by *Peeping Tom*, Powell's most completely realized and intellectually somber film. Full of dark jokes, including his own presence as the cruel father, it also shows Powell's sense of the cinema's own contribution to frenzy. The central character is a moving portrait of the imaginative young man who is unsociable with real people but familiar with the stars of movies. He is a shy focus puller who takes film of girls using a tripod that contains a swordstick. The stuck victims goggle horribly at the picture they make in the reflector above the camera; and so reaction stimulates the spectacle even further. The film was reasonably criticized as an exercise in de Sade's principles, and it is the one work in which Powell discarded all inhibitions.

I was fortunate to know Michael Powell in the last decade of his life. He was in America a good deal at that time: teaching for a term at Dartmouth; as director emeritus with Coppola's American Zoetrope; as treasured Merlin at the court of Scorsese; and in his marriage to the editor, Thelma Schoonmaker. I had the chance to watch many of his films with him, discussing them and learning the passion of his vision. It is all the more agreeable now to see Michael's influence spreading: the ardent antirealist has inspired so many people; the man in love with color, gesture, and cinema helped to educate viewers as well as filmmakers—not least in the two volumes of his autobiography, *A Life in Movies*. The work looks better and better, simpler yet more ambiguous. The great Powell and Pressburger films do not go stale; they never relinquish their wicked fun or that jaunty air of being poised on the brink. To put an arrow in our eye—to leave a nurturing wound—that was Michael's eternal thrill. I do not invoke the figure of Merlin lightly: Powell was English but Celtic, sublime yet devious, magical in the resolute certainty that imagination rules.

William Powell (1892–1984),
b. Pittsburgh, Pennsylvania

Here is Josef von Sternberg describing his dealings with Powell: "As the actor who was to portray the cruel and supercilious film director [in *The Last Command*, 28] I chose William Powell, who

with that performance, which, to use his own words, was forced on him, was lifted from the ranks of minor players to become a star in his own right. He acknowledged his debt to me by specifying in the new contract that was offered that he was never to be assigned to one of my films again."

The biter bit, perhaps, and typical of the amused sophistication that Powell projected. He retired in 1955, having made ninety-four films, in danger of being forgotten. His glossy comedies of adultery and deception, even the *Thin Man* series, were then strangely out of fashion. Powell expresses 1930s American cinema rather better than some of the larger names of the era. While other stars have been undermined by time, Powell remains as alive and sour as a cocktail put down momentarily for a telephone assignation, or an Abdullah still burning while its destroyer engages in a condescending kiss. (William Powell could be the patron saint of those politically incorrect, but very cinematic, habits—smoking and drinking.)

Powell began on the stage and had worked a few years in small parts when he made his movie debut in *Sherlock Holmes* (22, Albert Parker). In the silent cinema, he was villainous, treacherous, and sneering, and never more than a supporting player: among others, *The Bright Shawl* (23, John S. Robertson); *Under the Red Robe* (23, Alan Crosland); *Romola* (25, Henry King); *Too Many Kisses* (25, Paul Sloane); *Faint Perfume* (25, Louis Gasnier); *Aloma of the South Seas* (26, Maurice Tourneur); as Wilson in *The Great Gatsby* (26, Herbert Brenon); *Sea Horses* (26, Allan Dwan); *Beau Geste* (26, Brenon); *Love's Greatest Mistake* (27, Edward Sutherland); *Paid to Love* (27, Howard Hawks); an Arab lusting after Bebe Daniels in *She's a Sheik* (27, Clarence Badger).

The Last Command was a big step forward—in fact, Powell worked for Sternberg once more, in *The Dragnet* (28)—but it was sound that really established him. It is a commentary on the artistic consequences of the technical innovation that, without altering his screen character, articulacy made Powell more appealing—the lofty, well-mannered cad. He was in Paramount's first all-talkie, *Interference* (29, Lothar Mendes and Roy Pomeroy), and was then cast as Philo Vance, a detective, in *The Canary Murder Case* (29, Malcolm St. Clair). After *The Four Feathers* (29, Merian Cooper, Ernest Schoedsack, and Mendes), *Charming Sinners* (29, Robert Milton), and another Vance role in *The Greene Murder Case* (29, Frank Tuttle), Paramount starred Powell in *Pointed Heels* (29, Edward Sutherland). He now made a team with Kay Francis in *Behind the Make-Up* (30, Milton), *Street of Chance* (30, John Cromwell), and *For the Defense* (30, Cromwell). With his wife-to-be, Carole Lombard, he added to his comic range with *Man of the World* (31, Richard Wallace) and *Ladies' Man* (31, Mendes).

Powell was then traded to Warners, along with Kay Francis and Ruth Chatterton—significantly, he was the only one of the three to disprove Paramount's long-term judgment. At Warners he made *High Pressure* (32, Mervyn Le Roy); with Kay Francis in *Jewel Robbery* (32, William Dieterle) and *One Way Passage* (32, Tay Garnett), a quintessential weeper: he's headed for the chair, she's dying; *Lawyer Man* (32, Dieterle); and at RKO, *Double Harness* (33, Cromwell). He was Philo Vance again at the new studio in *The Kennel Murder Case* (33, Michael Curtiz) and for the same director in *The Key* (34).

But Warners found him too expensive and he was on the point of going to Columbia when Selznick and W. S. Van Dyke called him to MGM to make *Manhattan Melodrama* (34) opposite Myrna Loy. The match was perfect: two slender sophisticates, smiling haughtily at each other through a mist of wisecracks. They were not the Nick and Nora Charles that Dashiell Hammett had in mind, but that did not prevent them from making one of the most enjoyed screen marriages in *The Thin Man* (34, Van Dyke). The studio kept them together in *Evelyn Prentice* (34, William K. Howard) and then Powell came into his own: *Star of Midnight* (35, Stephen Roberts); *Reckless* (35, Victor Fleming); *Escapade* (35, Robert Z. Leonard); *Rendezvous* (35, Howard); the title role in *The Great Ziegfeld* (36, Leonard); *The Ex-Mrs. Bradford* (36, Roberts); with Carole Lombard again in *My Man Godfrey* (36, La Cava), where his intelligence was nearly Shavian; with Loy, Harlow, and Tracy in *Libeled Lady* (36, Jack Conway); and *After the Thin Man* (36, Van Dyke).

He continued with Joan Crawford in *The Last of Mrs. Cheyney* (37, Richard Boleslavsky), *The Emperor's Candlesticks* (37, George Fitzmaurice), and with Loy in *Double Wedding* (37, Richard Thorpe). Illness meant that he never worked as hard again: *Another Thin Man* (39, Van Dyke); a double role—as con-man and pillar of society—in *I Love You Again* (40, Van Dyke); *Love Crazy* (41, Conway); *Shadow of the Thin Man* (41, Van Dyke); *Crossroads* (42, Conway); *The Heavenly Body* (44, Alexander Hall); *The Thin Man Goes Home* (44, Thorpe); as Ziegfeld in heaven introducing the celebrity acts in *Ziegfeld Follies* (46, Vincente Minnelli); *The Hoodlum Saint* (46, Norman Taurog); and *Song of the Thin Man* (47, Edward Buzzell).

He then went to Warners and to Michael Curtiz for *Life With Father* (47), a delicious comic performance. Sadly, his career suffered some relaxation. He worked for Universal International: *The Senator Was Indiscreet* (47, George F. Kaufman); *Mr. Peabody and the Mermaid* (48, Irving Pichel); *Take One False Step* (47, Chester Erskine); *The Treasure of Lost Canyon* (51, Ted Tetzlaff); with Elizabeth Taylor in *The Girl Who Had Everything*

(53, Thorpe); and ended with two respectful farewells—in *How to Marry a Millionaire* (53, Jean Negulesco), and as the doctor in *Mister Roberts* (55, Mervyn Le Roy and John Ford).

Tyrone Power (1913–58),
b. Cincinnati, Ohio

The son of Tyrone Power, a theatre matinee idol, there was never any doubt about the career he should follow. With resplendent looks and parentage, he went years before anyone thought to ask whether Power Jr. was more than a handsome, unexceptional man. After early work on stage and radio, he followed his father to Hollywood. When Power Sr. died while filming, the son was given a bit part debut in *Tom Brown of Culver* (32, William Wyler). He returned to the stage, understudying Burgess Meredith in *The Flowers of the Forest* and playing a small part in *St. Joan*.

A Fox scout saw him and by 1936 Power was under contract to the studio that diligently boosted him throughout most of his career. (He was especially the protégé of Zanuck.) He had energy, humor, and an honest faith in adventure and romance. At first he was a romantic lead opposite Loretta Young in *Ladies in Love* (36, Edward H. Griffith); *Love Is News* (37, Tay Garnett); *Café Metropole* (37, Griffith); *Second Honeymoon* (37, Walter Lang); opposite Sonja Henie in *Thin Ice* (37, Sidney Lanfield) and *Second Fiddle* (39, Lanfield); and a rather staid companion for Alice Faye in *In Old Chicago* (38) and *Alexander's Ragtime Band* (38)—both for Henry King— as well as Gregory Ratoff's *Rose of Washington Square* (39).

He was already best displayed in romantic costume films. In 1936, Henry King—who remained loyal to Power for twenty years—had used him in *Lloyds of London*, and he was then loaned to Metro to appear in the Norma Shearer *Marie Antoinette* (38, W. S. Van Dyke). Back at Fox, he played de Lesseps (with Loretta Young and his first wife, Annabella) in Allan Dwan's *Suez* (38); *Jesse James* for King; and most successfully the Indian Prince in Clarence Brown's *The Rains Came* (39). This was his classic period when athletic ardor and his persistent smile were enough: two films for Henry Hathaway, *Johnny Apollo* (40) and *Brigham Young* (40); two for Mamoulian that show him at his iconographic best, *The Mark of Zorro* (40) and as a bullfighter in *Blood and Sand* (41); opposite Joan Fontaine in Litvak's *This Above All* (42); as a pirate in *The Black Swan* (42), a Sabatini novel by way of Henry King; and in a submarine in *Crash Dive* (43, Archie Mayo).

Power then entered the marines, and after the war his vein of romance was never as undiluted. Fox assembled labored costume vehicles for him: *Captain from Castile* (47) and *Prince of Foxes* (49), both for King, and *The Black Rose* (50) for

Hathaway. But other films attempted, without much success, to create a more troubled Power: Somerset Maugham's mystical dropout in *The Razor's Edge* (46) and as the geek in *Nightmare Alley* (47)—both for Edmund Goulding. He made two comedies, *The Luck of the Irish* (48, Henry Koster) and *That Wonderful Urge* (48, Robert B. Sinclair), but returned to adventure films, no longer as dashing or devastating as he had been. After the minor *American Guerrilla in the Philippines* (50) for Fritz Lang, and *Rawhide* (51) and *Diplomatic Courier* (52) for Hathaway, Power's stay at Fox ended. He made *The Mississippi Gambler* (53) for Rudolph Maté at Universal and thereafter freelanced.

In his last years he tried to work again in the theatre, he was a solid pillar of West Point for John Ford in *The Long Gray Line* (55); smiled his way across the ivories of *The Eddy Duchin Story* (56, George Sidney); starred in and produced *Seven Waves Away* (56, Richard Sale) in England; was reunited with Henry King as a thoroughly lacking Jake Barnes in *The Sun Also Rises* (57); and proved an implausible murderer in Billy Wilder's *Witness for the Prosecution* (57). He died while filming (like his father): the last project was a hopeful return to the films that had made him famous—King Vidor's *Solomon and Sheba*, in which he was replaced by Yul Brynner.

Otto Preminger (1906–86), b. Vienna

1931: *Die Grosse Liebe*. 1936: *Under Your Spell*. 1937: *Danger, Love at Work*. 1943: *Margin for Error*. 1944: *In the Meantime, Darling; Laura*. 1945: *A Royal Scandal/Czarina; Fallen Angel*. 1946: *Centennial Summer*. 1947: *Forever Amber; Daisy Kenyon*. 1948: *That Lady in Ermine* (begun by and credited to Ernst Lubitsch, but completed by Preminger after Lubitsch's death). 1949: *The Fan/Lady Windermere's Fan; Whirlpool*. 1950: *Where the Sidewalk Ends*. 1951: *The 13th Letter*. 1952: *Angel Face*. 1953: *The Moon Is Blue*. 1954: *River of No Return; Carmen Jones*. 1955: *The Court Martial of Billy Mitchell/One Man Mutiny*. 1956: *The Man with the Golden Arm*. 1957: *Saint Joan*. 1958: *Bonjour Tristesse*. 1959: *Porgy and Bess; Anatomy of a Murder*. 1960: *Exodus*. 1962: *Advise and Consent*. 1963: *The Cardinal*. 1964: *In Harm's Way*. 1965: *Bunny Lake Is Missing*. 1967: *Hurry Sundown*. 1968: *Skidoo; Tell Me That You Love Me, Junie Moon*. 1971: *Such Good Friends*. 1975: *Rosebud*. 1979: *The Human Factor*.

Preminger was never bashful about presenting himself as a commercial moviemaker. From the mid-1950s onward—from the piquant novelty of *The Moon Is Blue* and *Carmen Jones*—he chose a mixture of prestigious and popular literary projects, balancing action/excitement and "food for thought," taking pains to preserve authenticity of locale and drawing together superb casts. Thus, *Bonjour Tristesse, Anatomy of a Murder, Exodus, Advise and Consent,* and *The Cardinal* were in the best Hollywood tradition of intelligent entertainment. But the question of whether they were substantially more was one of the great critical issues of the early 1960s. Preminger's enthusiasts were not helped by the startling decline in his work from 1965 onward. Of all the Hollywood veterans, none lost his way as completely as Preminger.

But, even at the time, it was difficult to imagine where he could go after having treated justice (*Anatomy of a Murder*), nationalism (*Exodus*), democracy (*Advise and Consent*), and religion (*The Cardinal*).

Although *Laura*—the first film to which Preminger liked to own up—is clothed in the sumptuous, dream atmosphere of Joseph La Shelle's photography and the famous theme tune, it excels in the matter-of-fact observation of characters. The lingering feeling of the supernatural in the film may reflect Mamoulian's preparation of the project. Preminger is much more interested in the flawed ordinariness of Dana Andrews and Gene Tierney: the fact that Laura proves slightly commonplace and the detective insecure and immature.

Preminger turned the postwar Fox thriller away from urban neo-realism to an interest in people under pressure and a series of fascinating character studies: in *Whirlpool, Where the Sidewalk Ends,* and *The 13th Letter,* our predisposition to take sides is undercut by the all-round picture of people. *Whirlpool* is interesting not as a picture of a hypnotist mastermind, but in the way that the Gene Tierney character harbors all the feelings of unreliability imposed on her by Jose Ferrer.

Just as the thrillers defy expectations, so his two women's pictures—*Fallen Angel* and *Daisy Kenyon*—treat melodrama with an extraordinary lack of hysteria. Alone among Hollywood directors, Preminger triumphs in that genre by deflecting it. Rather than inducing the passion that underlies it—in the way of Frank Borzage, Stahl, or Sirk—he eases it in the direction of documentary. The camera style is implacably objective, observant of such detail that in *Daisy Kenyon,* even Joan Crawford is made touching. For all his Viennese origins, Preminger's cool is never spiked on Wilder's cynicism or warmed by Ophulsian tenderness. He is essentially lucid, as convinced as Renoir of everyone having their reasons and enriching his films with doubt. The process is unique, and if it is best used in the later films, it was present from the beginning.

The four lengthy disquisitions on the pillars of civilization are all entertaining films, packed with incident and remarkable characters. But, notably, they all end unexpectedly: *Exodus* in suspension; *The Cardinal* in doubt; *Advise and Consent* with the process of carrying on regardless; and *Anatomy of a Murder* on the sharpest probe into our complacency that Preminger has ever launched. The film has concerned the efforts of attorney James Stewart to defend Ben Gazzara against a charge of having murdered a man who may have raped his wife, Lee Remick. The personalities of the actors are crucial. Stewart has always commanded the naïve, gangling, provincial hero: in no other film has that command been so revealed as mechanism. Thus the traditionally devoted defense attorney—the idiotic Perry Mason—is shown as a true professional, himself an actor in a play before the court, trying to convince himself that his client is innocent. That client is Gazzara at his most calculatingly insolent, barely troubling to conceal his own violence. Lee Remick as the wife makes no effort to disguise her provocative sensuality.

In other words, we are put in the position of the jury: the workings of the film become the due process of law. Gazzara is acquitted on the esoteric defense of "irresistible impulse." When Stewart calls for his fee, Gazzara has left a note on his wife's tarty shoe—he had an irresistible impulse to get out of town. Irony does not actually detract from the nobility of the law as an instrument reluctant to make up its mind about people. Preminger's enquiring camera—always tracking with characters, rarely separating people engaged with one another—is the manifestation of intelligent reticence, and it produced half a dozen great movies.

It must be admitted that Preminger on several occasions foundered with unsuitable material— *Forever Amber, Lady Windermere's Fan, Porgy and Bess,* and all the movies from 1968 onward— as if he only needed to relax to become the buffoon director one might expect from his camp commandant in *Stalag 17* (53, Wilder).

It should also be said that this brief account of his central achievement has neglected the brilliance of *Angel Face* and *Bonjour Tristesse,* movies that both deal with scheming malice in a young girl—the first as melodrama, the second as a considerable deepening of Françoise Sagan's novel. Incidentally, they contain probably the best screen performances from Jean Simmons and Jean Seberg. It is a tribute to Preminger's objectivity that Seberg's girl in *Bonjour Tristesse* and her *Saint Joan* are treated with the same interested caution.

Elvis Presley (1935–77),
b. Tupelo, Mississippi

There is a tradition of singers who made a string of movies because of their proven following. But is there a greater contrast between energy and routine than that between Elvis Presley the phenomenon, live and on record, and Presley the automaton on film? His movies still play on televi-

sion. But Presley now is in a kind of retreat, and I can believe that in another ten years the movies will be reclaimed with camp glee for their specious, monotonous "youthfulness"—so wholesome, so bouncy, and so riotously clean when set against what we know of the real Presley. There are exceptions: he gives a genuine performance in *Flaming Star* (60, Don Siegel); the Clifford Odets script for *Wild in the Country* (61, Philip Dunne) works well, and Tuesday Weld and John Ireland get under the flaccid dude's skin; there are numbers with Ann-Margret in *Viva Las Vegas* (64, George Sidney)—notably "What'd I Say?"—that expose the soporific air of most Presley films.

So it is a list of titles more suggestive than the movies: *Love Me Tender* (56, Robert D. Webb); *Loving You* (57, Hal Kanter); *Jailhouse Rock* (57, Richard Thorpe); *King Creole* (58, Michael Curtiz), *G.I. Blues* (60, Norman Taurog); *Wild in the Country; Blue Hawaii* (62, Taurog); *Follow That Dream* (62, Gordon Douglas); *Kid Galahad* (62, Phil Karlson); *Fun in Acapulco* (63, Thorpe); *It Happened at the World's Fair* (63, Taurog); *Viva Las Vegas; Roustabout* (64, John Rich); *Tickle Me* (65, Taurog); *Girl Happy* (65, Boris Sagal); *Frankie and Johnnie* (66, Frederick de Cordova); *Paradise Hawaiian Style* (66, Michael Moore); *Double Trouble* (67, Taurog); *Speedway* (68, Taurog); and *Stay Away Joe* (68, Peter Tewkesbury). He had a straight role in *Charro!* (69, Charles Marquis Warren), and his best recording of live performance in *Elvis—That's the Way It Is* (70, Denis Sanders).

Edward R. Pressman,
b. New York, 1946

Ed Pressman is the son of a New York toy manufacturer. He was supposed to follow along in that business, but as he went off to Stanford and the London School of Economics, so he began to get a taste for film. It was in meeting Paul Williams that he found his own role as enabler or producer for adventurous material. Ed is quiet, patient, tenacious, careful with money; but he is open to all manner of imaginative ideas and unlikely ventures. As such, he is an essential figure in American independent cinema, a good friend to many (me included), and someone to whom nearly every out-of-the-mainstream filmmaker has turned at some time or other. Are all his films good? Of course not. But are any of them dull? Let the list speak for itself.

Out of It (69, Williams); *The Revolutionary* (70, Williams); *Dealing* (72, Williams); *Badlands* (73, Terrence Malick); *Sisters* (73, Brian De Palma); *Phantom of the Paradise* (74, De Palma); *Despair* (78, Rainer Werner Fassbinder); *Paradise Alley* (78, Sylvester Stallone); *Old Boyfriends* (79, Joan Tewkesbury); *Heart Beat* (80, John Byrum); *Victoria* (80, Bo Widerberg); *The Hand* (81, Oliver Stone); *Conan the Barbar-*

ian (82, John Milius); *Das Boot* (82, Wolfgang Petersen); *The Pirates of Penzance* (83, Wilford Leach); *Plenty* (85, Fred Schepisi); *Crimewave* (86, Sam Raimi); *Half Moon Street* (86, Bob Swaim); *True Stories* (86, David Byrne); *Cherry 2000* (87, Steve De Jarnatt); *Good Morning, Babylon* (87, Paolo and Vittorio Taviani); *Masters of the Universe* (87, Gary Goddard); *Walker* (87, Alex Cox); *Wall Street* (87, Stone); *Talk Radio* (88, Stone); *Paris by Night* (89, David Hare); *Blue Steel* (90, Kathryn Bigelow); *Martians Go Home* (90, David Odell); *Waiting for the Light* (90, Chris Monger); *To Sleep with Anger* (90, Charles Burnett); *Reversal of Fortune* (90, Barbet Schroeder); *Iron Maze* (91, Hiro Yoshida); *Homicide* (91, David Mamet); *Year of the Gun* (91, John Frankenheimer); *Storyville* (92, Mark Frost); *Bad Lieutenant* (92, Abel Ferrara); *Hoffa* (92, Danny DeVito); *Dream Lover* (94, Nicholas Kazan); *The Crow* (94, Alex Proyas); *Street Fighter* (94, Steven de Souza); *Judge Dredd* (95, Danny Cannon); *City Hall* (95, Harold Becker); *The Island of Dr. Moreau* (96, Frankenheimer); *The Crow: City of Angels* (96, Tim Pope); *The Winter Guest* (97, Alan Rickman); *Black Out* (97, Ferrara); *Two Girls and a Guy* (98, James Toback); *New Rose Hotel* (98, Ferrara); *Legionnaire* (99, Peter MacDonald); *Endurance* (99, Leslie Woodhead); *Black and White* (00, Toback); *The Crow: Salvation* (00, Bharat Nalluri); *American Psycho* (00, Mary Harron); *Harvard Man* (01, Toback); *The Endurance* (01, George Butler); *The 10th Victim* (02, Josef Rusnak); *The Cooler* (03, Wayne Kramer); *Owning Mahowny* (03, Richard Kwietniowski); *Love Object* (03, Robert Parigi).

Vincent Price (1911–93),
b. St. Louis, Missouri

To the head of the house of Price, himself ruler of the National Candy Company, was born a son, Vincent—a tall youth, of striking nobility, a boy brought up to be obeyed and respected, but mysteriously flawed by the family's sweet tooth. As a young man he made exceptional progress as a student of art history. All things beautiful he loved and the knowledge of them that Yale, the Courtauld Institute, and the University of Vienna provided. Alas, fatal sweetness beckoned. Rather than follow Michelangelo or Bernard Berenson, because he chewed gum so stylishly he was cast on the London stage as a gangster.

From this he was raised to play Albert in *Victoria Regina*, a success in London and on Broadway. He was for a time a compatriot of a darkly influential young man of magic power, Orson Welles, and appeared for his Mercury Theater in *The Shoemaker's Holiday* and *Heartbreak House*. Then, in 1938, the good Vincent was lured westwards to the land of haunted romance where the sun shines

so fraudulently bright. The desperate moguls at the house of Fox chewed on their cold cigars, immediately discerned all the hollows behind his actorly handsomeness, and picked out decayed teeth like dentists.

Thus he was required to be effete, caddish, insolent, malicious, or weak: *Service de Luxe* (38, Rowland V. Lee); as Raleigh in *The Private Lives of Elizabeth and Essex* (39, Michael Curtiz); *Green Hell* (40, James Whale); *Tower of London* (40, Lee); as Joseph Smith in *Brigham Young* (40, Henry Hathaway); *The Song of Bernadette* (43, Henry King); as a worldly prelate in *The Keys of the Kingdom* (44, John M. Stahl); *Buffalo Bill* (44, William Wellman); *The Eve of St. Mark* (44, Stahl); *Wilson* (44, King); as the spineless fiancé to *Laura* (44, Otto Preminger); *A Royal Scandal* (45, Preminger); *Leave Her to Heaven* (46, Stahl); anticipating Poe in *Dragonwyck* (46, Joseph L. Mankiewicz); and *The Long Night* (47, Anatole Litvak).

"He's not mean enough," said the desperate men. "He doesn't mean to be mean." For they had seen that Vincent was a good-natured man; a fruit drop melted slowly in his mouth. Thus his career became listless for several years and slighter films: as Richelieu in *The Three Musketeers* (48, George Sidney); *The Bribe* (49, Robert Z. Leonard); *Champagne for Caesar* (49, Richard Whorf); *The Baron of Arizona* (50, Samuel Fuller); as a ham movie actor, Mark Cardigan, in *His Kind of Woman* (51, John Farrow); *Las Vegas Story* (52, Robert Stevenson); *Casanova's Big Night* (54, Norman Z. McLeod); and *Son of Sinbad* (55, Ted Tetzlaff).

Disenchantment and sweetness together made Vincent incredulous at his own nightmare and so he found himself as the hideously scarred owner of *House of Wax* (53, André de Toth). He surveyed the horror genre as if it were a tray of eclairs. Nothing then distracted him from the feast, no matter that the delicacies never satisfied him. It is a paradox that he should be the king of that genre, for he knew that no one was really frightened by such an old humbug—the softie who was also art advisor for Sears Roebuck and the author of several cookbooks. He always smiled happily on ovens and butchers' tools: *The Mad Magician* (54, John Brahm); *The Ten Commandments* (56, Cecil B. De Mille); *While the City Sleeps* (56, Fritz Lang); *The Fly* (58, Kurt Neumann); *The House on Haunted Hill* (58, William Castle); *The Return of the Fly* (59, Edward L. Bernds); *The Tingler* (59, Castle); *Confessions of an Opium Eater* (62, Albert Zugsmith); and *Diary of a Madman* (65, Reginald le Borg).

But it was Roger Corman, American International Pictures, and cheapskate adaptations of Edgar Allan Poe that fully displayed Price's dilettante menace: this was a brotherhood of camp terror, a veritable Theleme of heightened apprehension, all in lollipop colors: *The House of Usher* (60); *The Pit and the Pendulum* (61); *Tales of Terror* (61); *The Raven* (62); *A Comedy of Terrors* (63, Jacques Tourneur); *The Masque of the Red Death* (64); and *The Tomb of Ligeia* (64).

Alas, Roger departed for more serious fields and Vincent was left, an aging but still charming frightener. Working largely in England, he found himself involved in some vulgar confections—*Dr. Goldfoot and the Bikini Machine* (65, Norman Taurog); *The Oblong Box* (69, Gordon Hessler); *Scream and Scream Again* (69, Hessler); some more acid than he had reckoned with—*Witchfinder General* (68, Michael Reeves); and a character who promised the same sort of implausible and demented longevity that Vincent had shown: *The Abominable Dr. Phibes* (71, Robert Fuest) and *Dr. Phibes Rises Again* (72, Fuest). Most richly extravagant was his Edward Lionheart in *Theatre of Blood* (73, Douglas Hickox), a Shakespearean actor who murders harsh drama critics by reprising some gruesome deaths from the work of the bard. (The cast also included Price's wife, Coral Browne.)

He was in *Madhouse* (74, Jim Clark); *Percy's Progress* (74, Ralph Thomas); *Journey Into Fear* (75, Daniel Mann); *Scavenger Hunt* (79, Michael Schultz); *The Monster Club* (80, Roy Ward Baker); *House of the Long Shadows* (83, Pete Walker); *Escapes* (85, David Steensland); *The Offspring* (86, Jeff Burr); *The Whales of August* (87, Lindsay Anderson); *Dead Heat* (88, Mark Goldblatt); *Backtrack* (89, Dennis Hopper); *Edward Scissorhands* (90, Tim Burton). And for several years he was host of the PBS series *Mystery*.

Jonathan Pryce, b. Holywell, Wales, 1947
Past fifty now, Jonathan Pryce strikes most observers as a better actor than he has had the chance to demonstrate. He is familiar, yet versatile, prepared to do modest roles in promising pictures. On the other hand, he may be best known for a very stylish series of Lexus commercials that played off his cool authority. Not long after that, he acquitted himself just as ably as a James Bond villain—further evidence of his stature and of how often he is wasted. Whereas his superb Lytton Strachey in the little-seen *Carrington* (95, Christopher Hampton) is unmistakably the work of a great actor.

After studying at RADA, he began stage work—notably in Trevor Griffith's *Comedians*. He has never given up the stage, and he earned unusual attention for his Eurasian pimp in *Miss Saigon* and for the way his presence prompted union opposition when that show transferred from London to New York.

He began on screen in *Voyage of the Damned*

(76, Stuart Rosenberg); playing the saxophone in *Breaking Glass* (80, Brian Gibson); *Loophole* (80, John Quested); *Something Wicked This Way Comes* (83, Jack Clayton); the lead in *The Ploughman's Lunch* (83, Richard Eyre); the central clerk in *Brazil* (85, Terry Gilliam); *The Doctor and the Devils* (85, Freddie Francis); *Haunted Honeymoon* (86, Gene Wilder); *Jumpin' Jack Flash* (86, Penny Marshall); in the very strange *Man on Fire* (87, Elie Chouraqui); *Consuming Passions* (88, Giles Foster); *The Adventures of Baron Munchausen* (89, Gilliam); *The Rachel Papers* (89, Damian Harris), from a Martin Amis novel; as the Indian in *Glengarry Glen Ross* (92, James Foley); *The Age of Innocence* (93, Martin Scorsese); *Shades of Fear* (93, Beeban Kidron); Juan Perón in *Evita* (96, Alan Parker); *Behind the Lines* (97, Gillies MacKinnon); *Tomorrow Never Dies* (97, Roger Spottiswoode); *Ronin* (98, John Frankenheimer); *Stigmata* (99, Rupert Wainwright); *The Testimony of Taliesin Jones* (00, Martin Duffy); *The Suicide Club* (00, Rachel Samuels); *Il Gioco* (01, Claudia Florio); *Very Annie Mary* (01, Sara Sugarman); Mahler in *Bride of the Wind* (01, Bruce Beresford); King Leopold in *Victoria & Albert* (01, John Erman); *The Affair of the Necklace* (01, Charles Shyer).

He was in *Confessions of an Ugly Stepsister* (02, Gavin Millar); *Unconditional Love* (02, P. J. Hogan); *What a Girl Wants* (03, Dennie Gordon); *Pirates of the Caribbean: The Curse of the Black Pearl* (03, Gore Verbinski).

Richard Pryor, b. Peoria, Illinois, 1940
It's easy to imagine the harrowed face of Richard Pryor gazing out at us through his own wreckage. This life seems far more his "work" or "art" than all the individual films or comedy routines. Grant that Pryor is a victim of racism, of family troubles, of drugs, fame, and illness, still he impresses as someone who might have found a way of liberating self-destructiveness even if his circumstances had stayed tidy and nurturing. There is a raw wildness in Pryor that is close to genius, more in his live, improvisational work than in any "set" movie. Once upon a time, Pryor talked of playing Charlie Parker. That he did not is our loss, for he has that strung-out frenzy for dangerous lines of invention that is vital to Parker. Pryor is the jazziest of comics.

From club work and performances on TV, Pryor made his way into movies: *The Busy Body* (67, William Castle); *Wild in the Streets* (68, Barry Shear); *The Phynx* (70, Lee H. Katzin); *You've Got to Walk It Like You Talk It or You'll Lose That Beat* (71, Peter Locke); *Dynamite Chicken* (71, Ernie Pintoff); in a straight role in *Lady Sings the Blues* (72, Sidney J. Furie); *Wattstax* (73, Mel Stuart); *Hit!* (73, Furie); *The Mack* (73, Michael Campus); and *Some Call It Loving* (73, James B. Harris).

So much of these films had been black exploitation as made by white men. But slowly Pryor got into the American mainstream: he helped write *Blazing Saddles* (74, Mel Brooks); and he acted in *Adios Amigo* (75, Fred Williamson), *The Bingo Long Traveling All-Stars and Motor Kings* (76, John Badham), and the very lively *Car Wash* (76, Michael Schultz). In *Silver Streak* (76, Arthur Hiller), he started an on-screen partnership with Gene Wilder. He played race-car driver Wendell Scott in *Greased Lightning* (77, Schultz), and *Which Way Is Up?* (77, Schultz) was an attempt to redo Lina Wertmuller for black America.

Blue Collar (78, Paul Schrader) was his best role as an actor. He played with Bill Cosby in *California Suite* (78, Herbert Ross), and he was the title role in *The Wiz* (78, Sidney Lumet). *Richard Pryor—Live in Concert* (79, Jeff Margolis) was the first of four concert films, and the best (others were *Back Live in Concert, Live on Sunset Strip,* and *Here and Now*). He was God in *In God We Trust* (80, Marty Feldman), and with Wilder again in *Stir Crazy* (80, Sidney Poitier).

After *Wholly Moses* (80, Gary Weis), he produced and wrote *Bustin' Loose* (81, Oz Scott). Then he was in *Some Kind of Hero* (82, Michael Pressman); *The Toy* (82, Richard Donner); *Superman III* (83, Richard Lester); and *Brewster's Millions* (85, Walter Hill). He then wrote, produced, directed, and acted in the autobiographical *Jo Jo Dancer Your Life Is Calling* (86). Since then, he has appeared in *Critical Condition* (87, Michael Apted); *Moving* (88, Alan Metter); *Harlem Nights* (89, Eddie Murphy), as Murphy's father; with Gene Wilder again in *See No Evil, Hear No Evil* (89, Hiller); *Another You* (91, Maurice Phillips); and in *Lost Highway* (96, David Lynch).

Vsevolod Illareonovitch Pudovkin

(1893–1953), b. Penza, Russia
1921: *Golod . . . Golod . . . Golod* (codirected with Vladimir Gardin) (d). 1925: *Shakhmatnaya Goryachka/Chess Fever* (codirected with Nikolai Shpikovsky) (s). 1926: *Mekhanika Golovnovo Mozga* (d); *Mat/Mother.* 1927: *Konets Sankt/The End of St. Petersburg* (codirected with Mikhail Doller). 1928: *Potomok Chingis Khan/Storm Over Asia/The Heir to Genghis Khan.* 1932: *Prostoi Sluchai* (codirected with Doller). 1933: *Desertir.* 1938: *Pobeda* (codirected with Doller). 1939: *Minin i Pozharskii* (codirected with Doller). 1940: *Kino za Dvadtsat Let/Twenty Years of Soviet Cinema* (codirected with Esther Shub) (d). 1941: *Suvurov* (codirected with Doller); *Pir v Zhirmunka* (codirected with Doller). 1942: *Ubiitsy Vykhodyat na Dorogu* (codirected with Yuri Tarich). 1943: *Vo Imya Rodiny* (codirected with Dmitri Vasiliev). 1946: *Admiral Nakhimov* (codi-

rected with Vasiliev). 1948: *Tri Vstrechi* (codirected with Sergei Yutkevich and Alexander Ptushko). 1950: *Zhukovsky* (codirected with Vasiliev). 1953: *Vozvrashchienle Vasilya Bortnikova.*

Having studied physics and chemistry at Moscow University, Pudovkin was wounded in the war and spent three years in a German prison camp. Soon after his release, he went to the State Film School and became a pupil of Vladimir Gardin and Lev Kuleshov. He assisted both men and also acted for them. In addition, his training under Kuleshov led to the material for his two books on cinematic theory: *Film Technique* and *Film Acting.*

It was Pudovkin who made famous the experiments in which Kuleshov intercut shots of Mosjukhin with shots of a bowl of soup, a coffin, and a child to produce quite different emotional meanings. Pudovkin was especially intrigued by the way in which narratives could be altered by a simple change of shot order. But it followed that he thought of each shot as a static, fixed quality. Indeed, he first used algebraic terms to suggest the effects of montage.

By the time he made *The End of St. Petersburg,* Pudovkin had achieved a very rapid cutting style, but the shots themselves remain rigid, rattling together like trucks in a freight train. Attributions of "poetic" or "emotional" qualities in Pudovkin now seem very fanciful. His films are more the work of a blackboard theoretician who arranges events into neat equations: in *Mother,* the cross-cutting of the revolutionary march and the breaking up of the ice floe; and in *The End of St. Petersburg* between Russian losses in the war and frantic speculation on the stock exchange at home. The former is mere rabble-rousing, showing the propagandist excesses of the Kuleshov experiment and suffering from the grandiose vagueness of Russian cinema. The latter, too, is a tendentious, literary comparison; one has only to think of the stock exchange sequence in Antonioni's *The Eclipse* to see how much more complex the same location can be.

That comparison is not remote. It shows that cinema has a duty to location above and beyond the adherence to any theory of montage. It matters little in *The End of St. Petersburg* that Pudovkin has insisted on actors whose experience is like that of his characters. That sort of authenticity is a sop to insecure dogma; amateurs can overact as much as professionals, while all actors are misled by fallacies in conception and method.

As with most of the Russian theories on editing, the case is confounded by academic, lifeless films, by the special pleading of political bias, and by the reminder that elsewhere far greater films were being made without such shaky justification. Whether or not *Mother* conforms to classic montage is an arid question beside the astonishing and subtle language of *The General, Underworld,* or *Sunrise,* made at much the same time. Unlike Eisenstein, Dziga Vertov, or Dovzhenko, Pudovkin used images in an invariably dull way—the photographed storyboard, relying on the clinching significance of a + b, and very slow for all that the cutting is often so fast.

There is one saving, if accidental, virtue in Pudovkin's writing. From his theory of montage he deduced that the movie actor could be passive. His animation was irrelevant compared with the spark obtained in a cut. That argument led to advice to the actor that finds itself, by chance, on the bull's-eye. For this, and much else in the same vein, Pudovkin may still be read, so long as one looks not to his films but to Bresson, Hitchcock, or Sternberg for the demonstration:

> Extremely interesting are those passages in Stanislavsky's memoirs where he speaks of the necessity for "gestureless" movements of immobility on the part of the actor, to concentrate on his feelings all the attention of the spectator.
>
> Stanislavsky felt that an actor striving towards truth should be able to avoid the element of portraying his feelings to the audience, and should be able to transmit to it the whole fullness of the content of the acted image in some moment of half-mystic communion. Of course he came up against a brick wall in his endeavors to find a solution to this problem in the theatre.
>
> It is amazing that solution of this very problem is not only not impracticable in the cinema, but extreme paucity of gesture, often literal immobility, is absolutely indispensable in it.

That literal immobility that Pudovkin desired in an actor was something he assumed in his audience. Although Soviet cinema is learnedly propagandist, it is based on naïve attitudes about how audiences relate to film. The sort of quiescence in actors that true cinema exploits derives from the realization that films and actors belong to the fantasies of audiences. It sees film as near to dream: whereas in Russia it was hoped that it was like a broadsheet.

Bill Pullman, b. Hornell, New York, 1953

Bill Pullman has charm and intelligence to spare, as well as a real comic edge, but I'm not sure that it isn't his strategy to stay cool, good-looking, and hidden (or blank) in the knowledge that those limitations can these days set up a fair career as a leading man. He has done a serious number of films, but seems reluctant to reveal himself, as if that kind of excess or vanity could take him out of the mainstream category of OK, safe guys. In which case, his amiable survival may reflect our own lack of concern or involvement: never better

or funnier than in his debut, *Ruthless People* (86, Jim Abrahams, David Zucker, and Jerry Zucker); *Spaceballs* (87, Mel Brooks); *The Serpent and the Rainbow* (88, Wes Craven); *Rocket Gilbraltar* (88, Daniel Petrie); the publisher in *The Accidental Tourist* (88, Lawrence Kasdan)—note, Pullman is the cool star now just as William Hurt is the difficult, less-used actor; *Cold Feet* (89, Robert Dornhelm); *Sibling Rivalry* (90, Carl Reiner); *Bright Angel* (91, Michael Fields); *Liebestraum* (91, Mike Figgis); *A League of Their Own* (92, Penny Marshall); *Singles* (92, Cameron Crowe); *Newsies* (92, Kenny Ortega); *Sommersby* (93, Jon Amiel); *Malice* (93, Howard Becker); the dull boyfriend in *Sleepless in Seattle* (93, Nora Ephron); *The Favor* (94, Donald Petrie); *Wyatt Earp* (94, Kasdan); very funny as the stooge husband in *The Last Seduction* (94, John Dahl); the dad in *Casper* (95, Brad Silberling); *Mr. Wrong* (96, Nick Castle); with Sandra Bullock in *While You Were Sleeping* (95, Jon Turteltaub); the President in *Independence Day* (96, Roland Emmerich); staying very cool until *Lost Highway* (97, David Lynch) ended; *The End of Violence* (97, Wim Wenders); *Mistrial* (97, Heywood Gould); on TV, as George in a clever redoing of *It's a Wonderful Life* called *Merry Christmas, George Bailey* (97, Matthew Diamond); *The Zero Effect* (98, Jake Kasdan); *Lake Placid* (99, Steve Miner); *Brokedown Palace* (99, Jonathan Kaplan); *The Virginian* (00, himself) on TV; *The Guilty* (00, Anthony Waller); *Lucky Numbers* (00, Nora Ephron); *Ignition* (01, Yves Simoneau); *29 Palms* (01, Leonardo Ricagni).

Lord David Puttnam, b. London, 1941

For about ten years—from 1975 to 1985—Puttnam was one of the more adventurous producers in the world. Three times he earned best picture nominations: for *Midnight Express* (78, Alan Parker), *The Killing Fields* (84, Roland Joffe), and *Chariots of Fire* (81, Hugh Hudson), which won the Oscar. These were only the highlights of a record that also included *Melody* (71, Waris Hussein); *The Pied Piper* (72, Jacques Demy); *The Final Programme* (73, Robert Fuest); *Mahler* (73, Ken Russell); *That'll Be the Day* (74, Claude Whatham); the clever, engaging documentary, *Brother, Can You Spare a Dime?* (75, Philippe Mora); *Stardust* (75, Michael Apted); *James Dean, the First American Teenager* (75, Ray Connolly); *Lisztomania* (75, Russell); *Bugsy Malone* (76, Parker); *The Duellists* (77, Ridley Scott); *Foxes* (80, Adrian Lyne); *Experience Preferred But Not Essential* (82, Peter Duffell); *Kipperbang* (82, Apted); *Local Hero* (83, Bill Forsyth); *Cal* (84, Pat O'Connor); *Defence of the Realm* (85, David Drury); *Mr. Love* (85, Roy Battersby); and *The Mission* (86, Joffe).

Only a few of these films seem to me indispensable—*The Duellists* and *Local Hero,* say. But producing successfully in Britain is very tough, and Puttnam won big prizes, did well enough at the box office, and encouraged some valuable talents. Still, his strengths were English, and Puttnam was cheerfully disapproving of many things American.

However, in 1986, Coca-Cola invited him to be production head at Columbia. Puttnam handled himself like an outsider. He announced lower budgets, lower salaries, braver pictures, and a lot of opportunities for European directors. Did he ever plan on staying long? Or did he prefer to be a gambler and a challenge? Was it too laborious, or too American, to apply his several worthwhile ideas slowly, with cunning, duplicity, and all the other American methods? He lasted less than two years, and it's arguable that his rhetoric and his provocation did more damage than good. It's unlikely that anyone else will ever get such a chance again.

Puttnam was paid off, lavishly. He went back to Britain and taught for a time. Then gradually he slipped back into production and made *Memphis Belle* (90, Michael Caton-Jones); *Being Human* (94, Bill Forsyth); *War of the Buttons* (94, John Roberts); *My Life So Far* (99, Hudson).

Q

Dennis Quaid, b. Houston, Texas, 1954

In an age of heavy-duty stars, whose presence is hardly possible without at least $10 million above the line, there comes into being a second string of known quantities, good-looking guys, reliable and fairly trouble-free performers, as the project slips a notch or two. These fellows don't do badly, but they lack the crust of vanity or certainty that can lead bigger stars into unmitigated disasters. Thus, by and large, the bench players have an edge and a need that I find more attractive than the hard gloss of stardom. Dennis Quaid is such a figure. He's been around so long now he isn't going to surprise many people. Or so you think, until you see his magnificent Doc Holliday in the otherwise languid *Wyatt Earp* (94, Lawrence Kasdan). This is the best Holliday in pictures—a physical and attitudinal transformation—and enough to make Kevin Costner turn to stone (if he hadn't been there already).

Dennis is the younger brother of Randy Quaid, whom he followed into pictures. Married once to P. J. Soles, he was married to Meg Ryan for ten years—a further proof of his high amiability. He had a small part in *Crazy Mama* (75, Jonathan Demme); *I Never Promised You a Rose Garden* (77, Anthony Page); and then came *September 30, 1955* (78, James Bridges); *The Seniors* (78, Rod Amateau); *Our Winning Season* (78, Joseph Ruben), with Soles; *Breaking Away* (79, Peter Yates); *G.O.R.P.* (80, Ruben); Ed Miller in *The*

Long Riders (80, Walter Hill); *All Night Long* (81, Jean-Claude Tramont); *Caveman* (84, Carl Gottlieb); with Kristy McNichol as brother-sister country singers in *The Night the Lights Went Out in Georgia* (81, Ronald F. Maxwell); *Johnny Belinda* (82, Page); a singer/boxer in *Tough Enough* (83, Richard Fleischer); *Jaws 3-D* (83, Joe Alves).

That was a pretty tough education, but Quaid got a great boost of energy with his swaggering "Gordo" Cooper in *The Right Stuff* (83, Philip Kaufman); *Dreamscape* (84, Ruben); *Enemy Mine* (85, Wolfgang Petersen); and then a real hit as the New Orleans detective with Ellen Barkin in *The Big Easy* (87, Jim McBride), another picture that caught his jazzy rhythms and his sexy recklessness; *Innerspace* (87, Joe Dante), the film on which he met Meg Ryan (they were married in 1991).

Since then, too few films have inspired or required his daring: the juror in *Suspect* (87, Yates); wasted in *D.O.A.* (88, Rocky Morton and Annabel Jankel); *Everybody's All-American* (88, Taylor Hackford); a little over the top as Jerry Lee Lewis in *Great Balls of Fire!* (89, McBride); *Postcards from the Edge* (90, Mike Nichols); *Come See the Paradise* (90, Alan Parker); *Undercover Blues* (93, Herbert Ross), a flop, and then another—*Wilder Napalm* (93, Glenn Gordon Caron); with Ryan again in *Flesh and Bone* (93, Steve Kloves); trying to loosen Julia Roberts up in *Something to Talk About* (95, Lasse Hallström); *Dragonheart* (96, Rob Cohen); *Switchback* (97, Jeb Stuart); *Gang Related* (97, Jim Kouf); the unduly neglected *The Savior* (98, Predrag Antonijevic); then rather ominously in *The Parent Trap* (98, Nancy Myers); *Playing by Heart* (98, Willard Carroll).

In 1998, he directed *Everything That Rises*—a warm, family Western. He was the injured quarterback in *Any Given Sunday* (99, Oliver Stone), and then he had a kind of hit in the ludicrous *Frequency* (00, Gregory Hoblit); *Traffic* (00, Steven Soderbergh); *Dinner with Friends* (01, Norman Jewison); *The Rookie* (02, John Lee Hancock). But the marriage with Ryan broke up.

He showed further proof of acting ambition as the guilty gay husband in *Far from Heaven* (02, Todd Haynes); and he will be seen in *Cold Creek Manor* (03, Mike Figgis).

Richard Quine (1920–89),

b. Detroit, Michigan

1948: *Leather Gloves* (codirected with William Asher). 1951: *The Sunny Side of the Street; Purple Heart Diary.* 1952: *Sound Off; Rainbow Round My Shoulder.* 1953: *All Ashore; Siren of Bagdad; Cruisin' Down the River.* 1954: *Drive a Crooked Road; Pushover; So This Is Paris.* 1955: *My Sister Eileen.* 1956: *The Solid Gold Cadillac.* 1957: *Full of Life; Operation Madball.* 1958: *Bell, Book and*

Candle. 1959: *That Jane from Maine/It Happened to Jane.* 1960: *Strangers When We Meet; The World of Suzie Wong.* 1962: *The Notorious Landlady.* 1963: *Paris When It Sizzles.* 1964: *Sex and the Single Girl.* 1965: *How to Murder Your Wife; Synanon.* 1967: *Oh Dad, Poor Dad, Mamma's Hung You in the Closet and I'm Feelin' So Sad; Hotel.* 1970: *The Moonshine War.* 1974: *W.* 1979: *The Prisoner of Zenda.*

Quine was a child actor, first in the Broadway production of *Counsellor at Law* in 1931 and then in movies: *The World Moves On* (34, John Ford); *Counsellor at Law* (33, William Wyler); *Dames* (34, Ray Enright); and *A Dog of Flanders* (35, Edward Sloman). After a few years on the stage and radio he returned to the movies as an adult and dancer: *Babes on Broadway* (41, Busby Berkeley); *For Me and My Gal* (42, Berkeley); *My Sister Eileen* (42, Alexander Hall); *Stand By for Action* (42, Robert Z. Leonard); and *We've Never Been Licked* (43, John Rawlins). After war service, he coproduced and codirected *Leather Gloves,* and acted again in *Words and Music* (48, Norman Taurog); *Command Decision* (49, Sam Wood); *The Clay Pigeon* (49, Richard Fleischer); and *No Sad Songs for Me* (50, Rudolph Maté). Having directed a few comedy shorts, he graduated to features.

It was predictable that Quine should begin with musicals, and *So This Is Paris* and *My Sister Eileen* are engaging works. But by the mid 1950s Quine's ambitions grew, as did his instinct for imitation. *Drive a Crooked Road* and *Pushover* are excellent minor thrillers, but the latter was a rehash of *Double Indemnity* and *Rear Window.* In the same way, Quine's two Judy Holliday pictures—*The Solid Gold Cadillac* and *Full of Life*—were sub-Cukor.

But at this stage, Quine briefly flourished. *Operation Madball* was an unusually zany comedy, owing much to Mickey Rooney; *Bell, Book and Candle* had a thorough cast and James Wong Howe's photography of Kim Novak at her most beautiful. Quine's best and most personal picture again involves Novak: *Strangers When We Meet,* a wistful study of suburban adultery that melted Novak's reserve better than most of her films.

But as soon as he had seemed on the point of finding a character, Quine's career wasted away into fainthearted comedies in which sexual sophistication was regularly missed and in which even his skill with actors seemed jaded. Gone the onetime dancer's lightness and his interest in beautiful women, he was barely tolerable in the advocacy of *Synanon,* the bizarre rural muddle of *The Moonshine War,* and the espousal of Twiggy.

He committed suicide, after a period of depression. He had not worked in ten years, and very few recalled the special frenzy of *Operation Madball* or the melancholy of *Strangers When We Meet.*

Anthony Quinn (1915–2001),
b. Chihuahua, Mexico

Quinn had an Irish father and a Mexican mother. Before he established himself as a star, he had worked twenty years as Hollywood exotic—Redskin, dago, wop, greaser: his mixed origins swallowed every variation. He grunted, leered, had bad table manners, made suggestive remarks to the ladies, and generally cultivated the uncouth. But this roughness already had the phony swagger of a professional wrestler.

Before movies, Quinn had been boxer and painter, and while he dutifully let every Paramount white man slug him, he married Katherine De Mille, the adopted daughter of Cecil B. After a debut in *Parole* (36, Louis Friedlander), he played a Sioux in De Mille's *The Plainsman* (37), and generally hammed up the background in *Swing High, Swing Low* (37, Mitchell Leisen); *Daughter of Shanghai* (37, Robert Florey); *The Buccaneer* (38, De Mille); *Dangerous to Know* (38, Florey); *King of Alcatraz* (38, Florey); *Union Pacific* (39, De Mille); *Television Spy* (39, Edward Dmytryk); *Emergency Squad* (40, Dmytryk); *Road to Singapore* (40, Victor Schertzinger); *Parole Fixer* (40, Florey); *City for Conquest* (40, Anatole Litvak); *Blood and Sand* (41, Rouben Mamoulian); *The Ghost Breakers* (40, George Marshall); *The Black Swan* (42, Henry King); *Larceny Inc.* (42, Lloyd Bacon); *Road to Morocco* (42, David Butler); *The Ox-Bow Incident* (43, William Wellman); *Buffalo Bill* (44, Wellman); *Roger Touhy, Gangster* (44, Florey); *Guadalcanal Diary* (44, Lewis Seiler); *China Sky* (45, Ray Enright); *Back to Bataan* (45, Dmytryk); *Black Gold* (47, Phil Karlson); *California* (47, John Farrow); *Tycoon* (48, Richard Wallace).

He then had three years in the theatre. After his return, he remained in second features, but began to play the first of his shaggy romantics in whom boisterousness turned to a humorless apprehension of the life force. The adventures were *Mask of the Avenger* (51, Karlson); *Against All Flags* (52, George Sherman); *The World in His Arms* (52, Raoul Walsh); *Ride, Vaquero!* (53, Farrow); *Blowing Wild* (53, Hugo Fregonese); and four Budd Boetticher movies: *City Beneath the Sea* (53); *Seminole* (53); *East of Sumatra* (53); and *The Magnificent Matador* (55). That last, a film à clef for Boetticher, undoubtedly stirred Quinn's cojones.

The specious nobility of the bullfighter, plus the Mexican references, had already lured the ponderous, heroic Quinn into the open in *The Brave Bulls* (51, Robert Rossen). In 1952, the would-be Mexican peasant won a supporting actor Oscar in *Viva Zapata!* (Elia Kazan). Since that was a characterization that had passed unremarked in countless smaller films, no wonder Quinn began to suppose he might be a neglected actor, in touch with the wellspring of primitiveness.

The matter was clinched when, after *The Long Wait* (54, Victor Saville), Quinn went to Italy and played in Fellini's *La Strada* (54), as something alarmingly like a life force. Sincerity, anguish, and significance were Quinn's to command: this was great acting, or a daft spaniel doing its tricks, depending on your point of view. Wrapping up frivolity, he played *Attila* (54, Pietro Francisci); in *Ulysses* (55, Mario Camerini); *Man from Del Rio* (56, Harry Horner); and *The River's Edge* (57, Allan Dwan). But then he set himself at fame with a piratical Gauguin, straight out of la vie bohème, in *Lust for Life* (56, Vincente Minnelli). It is hard to be angry with a dog so pleased with itself, but a second supporting Oscar for Quinn and widespread abuse for Kirk Douglas's Van Gogh were hard to digest.

Having played Quasimodo in *The Hunchback of Notre Dame* (57, Jean Delannoy), Quinn shed his moustache, put on weight, and let his hair go gray. He threw in his lot with vulgar emotional dramas: *Hot Spell* (58, Daniel Mann), *Black Orchid* (58, Martin Ritt), and, most comically, with Anna Magnani and a flock of sheep in George Cukor's very silly *Wild Is the Wind* (57). Then in 1958, Quinn directed De Mille's remake of *The Buccaneer*, an uneasy case of pirate turned patrolman. Dull in two Westerns, *Last Train from Gun Hill* (58, John Sturges) and *Warlock* (59, Dmytryk), he was beautifully restrained by Cukor in *Heller in Pink Tights* (60) and by Nicholas Ray in *The Savage Innocents* (60). Of all his noble savages, only Ray's Eskimo possesses a simplicity that seems honest and interesting.

By the 1960s, however, Quinn was an earth-father, settling ever deeper into the ground: *The Guns of Navarone* (61, J. Lee Thompson); *Barabbas* (62, Richard Fleischer); *Requiem for a Heavyweight* (62, Ralph Nelson); *Lawrence of Arabia* (62, David Lean); *Behold a Pale Horse* (64, Fred Zinnemann); *Zorba the Greek* (65, Michael Cacoyannis); *A High Wind in Jamaica* (65, Alexander Mackendrick); *The Happening* (67, Elliot Silverstein); *The Shoes of the Fisherman* (68, Michael Anderson); *The Secret of Santa Vittoria* (69, Stanley Kramer); *A Walk in the Spring Rain* (69, Guy Green); *The Last Warrior* (70, Carol Reed); *R.P.M.* (70, Kramer); *Across 110th Street* (72, Barry Shear); *Los Amigos* (73, Paolo Cavara); *The Don Is Dead* (73, Fleischer); and *The Marseille Contract* (74, Robert Parrish).

Even at sixty, esteemed for his longevity and heavy-sighing philosophy, Quinn was treated like the all-purpose actor for diverse exotics: an Arab in *The Message* or *Mohammad Messenger of God* (76, Moostapha Akkad), the title depending upon terrorist pressure; and offering the Aristotelian

grin in *The Greek Tycoon* (78, J. Lee Thompson). A sort of esperanto now enfolded him, and he became as vague and as implausible as the United Nations: a Mexican in *The Children of Sanchez* (78, Hall Bartlett), another Arab in *Caravans* (78, James Fargo), a Basque in *The Passage* (78, Thompson).

He played the Libyan guerrilla Omar Mukhtar who opposed Mussolini in *Lion of the Desert* (81, Akkad); *High Risk* (81, Stewart Raffill); he was executive producer of *Circle of Power* (81, Bobby Roth); *The Salamander* (81, Peter Zinner); *The Last Days of Pompeii* (84, Peter Hunt); as the tycoon's father in *Onassis: The Richest Man in the World* (88, Waris Hussein); not as the sea in a TV *The Old Man and the Sea* (90, Jud Taylor); *Ghosts Can't Do It* (90, John Derek); *Revenge* (90, Tony Scott); *Only the Lonely* (91, Chris Columbus); *Jungle Fever* (91, Spike Lee); and *Mobsters* (91, Michael Karbeinikoff).

In the midnineties he played Zeus in a TV series devoted to the adventures of Hercules. He was also in *A Star for Two* (91, Jim Kaufman); *Last Action Hero* (93, John McTiernan); *This Can't Be Love* (94, Anthony Harvey); *Somebody to Love* (94, Alexandre Rockwell); *A Walk in the Clouds* (95, Alfonso Arau); *Seven Servants* (96, Daryush Shokof); *Gotti* (96, Robert Harmon); *Il Sindaco* (96, Ugo Fabrizio Giordani); *Carmino de Santiago* (99, Robert Young); *Avenging Angelo* (01, Martyn Burke).

R

Bob Rafelson, b. New York, 1933
1968: *Head*. 1970: *Five Easy Pieces*. 1972: *The King of Marvin Gardens*. 1976: *Stay Hungry*. 1981: *The Postman Always Rings Twice*. 1987: *Black Widow*. 1990: *Mountains of the Moon*. 1992: *Man Trouble*. 1994: *Wet* (s). 1996: *Blood and Wine*. 1998: *Poodle Springs* (TV). 2002: *Erotic Tales*; *The House on Turk Street*.

From Dartmouth College, Rafelson went into the service and, while stationed in Japan, he worked as a radio disc jockey and a consultant to Shochiku, a film company exporting to America. Back in America, he was a story editor for TV. He hovered around the edge of the film industry without finding a role that satisfied his urge for independence. In recompense, in partnership with Bert Schneider, he indulged his love of plastic trash culture by forming the Monkees pop group, promoting, directing, and designing them, and being finally both fascinated and alarmed by his role as puppet master. *Head* is a wild, fragmented fantasy about the life and death of such a group, and it was written by Rafelson and a close friend, Jack Nicholson.

Five Easy Pieces and *The King of Marvin Gardens* come from the same partnership. They share a rapt attention to intimate, family stories, to people who are fresh and lifelike, and to parts of America that seldom reach the screen. In both, Nicholson plays a vaguely artistic outcast member of a family, disturbed by his failure to be convinced by domesticity or to feel the relationships that attract him. Rafelson was still a little concealed by the hesitant but very appealing presence of Nicholson, and by his own restraint. However, certain characteristics could be picked out: he was a storyteller—much of his personality lay in the unexpected turns of his narratives, the awareness of point of view, and the tender treatment of quirky individuality.

Like the central character in *Marvin Gardens,* Rafelson was a raconteur of vivid, touching events, himself looking on from the dark. And the narration is deeply convincing. Indeed, the sense of actuality is so great that, at this stage, Rafelson seemed like a novelist not much affected by cinematic genres, but quietly intent on describing lives and places he had known. (This is rare in American cinema, where films invariably realize ideas and images imagined by directors. The people in such films, and often the places, are idealized: e.g., the West, the city, the hero, the tart.) His visual style was functional. The sense of caring for people and places was a result of an undemonstrative, watchful camera that only occasionally allowed itself an evidently "beautiful" shot—such as the moment in *Marvin Gardens* when the camera cuts to a high angle to show the herringbone boardwalk promenade of Atlantic City.

The continuity of the two films is very intriguing. *Five Easy Pieces* begins in Texas with Nicholson as an oil-rigger, living with Rayette, a local girl. It is the raw vulgarity of Rayette that makes us realize how out of his element Nicholson is. Not that Rayette is disparaged or patronized. She is treated with exactly the weary compassion and intermittent affection that makes Nicholson endure her. She is pregnant, and Nicholson begins to escape her by going to visit his sick father. This is a characteristic Rafelson enlargement of a situation. For the family is elitist, tucked away in the rural north, intent on its own classical music-making. As we move from sunny plains to gloomy, wooded country, we discover that Nicholson was once a good pianist who fled from the narrow intensity of his family. The father has had a stroke and is inert, and Nicholson has an affair with his brother's fiancée, a "perfect" creature, rarefied but passionate, before Rayette too comes noisily north. Thus, again, Nicholson flees, on the spur of the moment but chronically, to Alaska, leaving Rayette in a filling station lavatory. The irresponsible behavior does not exclude a clear feeling that Nicholson is touched and perplexed by people.

In *Marvin Gardens,* Nicholson is a radio storyteller—a quiet man who expands over the mike—called away to Atlantic City by his raffish younger brother, a buffoon crook whose work for "Lewis" seems to have brought him within reach of the gambling concession on a Hawaiian island. The brother lives with a wife and his wife's stepdaughter. The wife is an aging Kewpie doll, more sophisticated than Rayette, but essentially like her; while the stepdaughter is of the same Pre-Raphaelite beauty as the fiancée in *Five Easy Pieces.* Although beautifully drawn and played, this "young wanton" character is perilously contrived—the most rooted in movies, in fact, and there is a weakness (by his own terms) in the way Rafelson succumbs to the charm of such a hippie princess.

That said, *Marvin Gardens* goes further than *Easy Pieces,* into tragedy. The Hawaiian plan is moonshine, an impossible venture that no one can explain away. The brother ditches wife for stepdaughter, and in a superb scene of cross-purpose, the wife is driven in anguish and rebuffed love to kill the brother. Few screen killings have so equated melodrama with the everyday and traced the spasm release of domestic intractability that makes people murderers. Once more, the family has been disproved. Nicholson goes back to Philadelphia with a coffin to the house where he lives with his grandfather, who is watching old home movies of the brothers as kids playing on the shore of Atlantic City where most of the action has taken place.

Marvin Gardens and *Five Easy Pieces* can easily be seen as metaphors for the creative impulse in America—wanting to speak, yet unconvinced by speech, and torn between art and commerce. The brothers in *Marvin Gardens* are versions of the writer/director and the producer/showman: and the two cancel each other out, as if Rafelson saw family struggle as the root of an eventual, exhausted silence.

The decline in Rafelson may be dated from *The Postman Always Rings Twice:* despite its qualities of mood, loneliness, and sexual desperation, and no matter the force of Nicholson and Lange, there did not seem an overpowering reason for remaking that story. And Rafelson needs to be doing something urgent and even dangerous. *Black Widow* was more plainly, and more disastrously, an attempt at a routine, genre piece. But the plot was confused and a test of our credulity; Theresa Russell was not inventive enough for the killer, and Debra Winger is not a natural heroine. *Mountains of the Moon* is the one film that indulges Rafelson's own taste for adventurous travel, but its central story collapses because of sketchy writing and awkward playing. *Man Trouble* and *Blood and Wine* were, sadly, the poorest films Rafelson has made.

George Raft (George Ranft) (1903–80),
b. New York

Raft spent his last decades nomadically, often pursued by American tax authorities and turned away by foreign immigration officials. In the early 1960s, Britain refused him entry when he had been set to host a Berkeley Square nightclub. It was said that he had Mafia connections—this in the days before we learned to wonder whose hands pulled all our strings. Hollywood even made *The George Raft Story* (61), a vacuous biopic working so hard to look away from iniquity let alone a rosebud.

It is still hard to decide whether Raft is an honest notoriety or a tame curiosity. Rumors have always suggested that he knew more about the real-life underworld than other Hollywood actors. If so, why could he not portray gangsters with animation? And if he was really an honored friend to Bugsy Siegel, why should he have spent so many years embroiled in such dismal movies? The saddest and most scathing picture of Raft is in Billy Wilder's *Some Like It Hot* (59) where, as the starch-faced Spats Colombo, he has to watch his own coin-tossing tricks being paraded before him and then suffer an assassin jumping out of a premature birthday cake.

Raft was a bad actor, and worse, an apprehensive one—if he might have been a real gangster, perhaps he held just as insecure a place in the underworld. What a movie it might make: a diffident guy employed in the movies because the studios think he knows Mr. Big, and tolerated by Big so long as he remains a companion of stars. It is a droller story than a bed and a horse's head.

The legend goes that while providing young muscle in the protection racket Raft was given the small role of "Gigolo" in a Texas Guinan movie, *Queen of the Night Clubs* (29, Bryan Foy), and then another in Rowland Brown's *Quick Millions* (31). A clutch of gangster parts followed, the best of which were in Roy del Ruth's *Taxi* (32) and Howard Hawks's *Scarface* (32). After *Night Court* (32, W. S. Van Dyke) and *Love Is a Racket* (32, William Wellman), Raft was signed up by Paramount and gradually gelded from a hood to a Latinate leading man: thus he was in Mae West's first film, *Night After Night* (32, Archie Mayo), and opposite Sylvia Sidney in *Pick-Up* (33, Marion Gering). He made *The Bowery* (33, Raoul Walsh) on loan to the new Twentieth Century and was then launched by Paramount as a tango-salon lizard: *Bolero* (34, Wesley Ruggles) and *Rumba* (35, Gering). He was tried as a bullfighter and then as a Chinaman in Alexander Hall's *Limehouse Blues* (35), but his only appeal was in crime pictures: *Every Night at Eight* (35, Walsh) and *The Glass Key* (35, Frank Tuttle). Unhappy at Paramount, he was loaned out for *She Couldn't Take It* (35, Tay Garnett) and *It Had to Happen*

(36, Del Ruth), and he finished out his contract with *Souls at Sea* (37, Henry Hathaway); *You and Me* (38, Fritz Lang); *Spawn of the North* (38, Hathaway); and *The Lady's from Kentucky* (38, Hall).

In retrospect, it seems remarkable that Warners then snapped him up. While there, he made *Each Dawn I Die* (39, William Keighley); *Invisible Stripes* (39, Lloyd Bacon); *They Drive by Night* (40, Walsh); *Manpower* (41, Walsh); *Background to Danger* (43, Walsh); as well as *The House Across the Bay* (40, Mayo) for Walter Wanger. But he refused *Casablanca*, *The Maltese Falcon*, and *High Sierra*—which suggests a more troubled personality than his films gave evidence of, or a more persuasive patronage of Bogart. Warners loaned him out for *Broadway* (42, William A. Seiter) and slipped him in 1943.

Thereafter, Raft appeared increasingly anxious in ever-stranger movies: after a few character parts—a lackluster Tony Angelo in *Nob Hill* (45, Hathaway)—he was asked only to imitate his former criminal self in cheap, spurious films. His legal problems also forced him further afield: *Nocturne* (46, Edwin L. Marin); *Johnny Allegro* (49, Ted Tetzlaff); *A Dangerous Profession* (49, Tetzlaff); *Red Light* (49, Del Ruth); *Nous Irons à Paris* (49); *Lucky Nick Cain* (51, Joseph Newman, who made *The George Raft Story*); *The Man from Cairo* (53, Ray Enright); *Black Widow* (54, Nunnally Johnson); and *A Bullet for Joey* (55, Lewis Allen)—these are the best of a bad bunch.

After 1955, however, he had bit parts—for Wilder, for Jerry Lewis, and in films that emerged from some of the most devious passages of the industry. As if Wilder's demolition were not brutal enough, Raft was asked to play himself in *The Ladies' Man* (61), only for Jerry to assure him that he couldn't be George Raft and then lead him into the darkness in an elegant tango. It is a telling doubt, for the actor who went under the name always seemed a stooge compared with the figure talked about in the newspapers.

At the end of his life, he played a small part in *Sextette* (78, Ken Hughes), Mae West's final film, and he was in *The Man with Bogart's Face* (80, Robert Day).

Sam Raimi, b. Detroit, Michigan, 1960
1983: *The Evil Dead*. 1985: *Crimewave/Broken Hearts and Noses*. 1987: *Evil Dead 2: Dead by Dawn*. 1990: *Darkman*. 1993: *Army of Darkness*. 1995: *The Quick and the Dead*. 1998: *A Simple Plan*. 1999: *For Love of the Game*. 2000: *The Gift*. 2002: *Spider-Man*.

More than fifteen years before *The Blair Witch Project*, the very young Sam Raimi had promoted the idea of a cabin in the woods where evil forces made killers of ordinary people. And *The Evil*

Dead was a low-budget picture that played at Cannes. There was far more style than funds, and this all led to *Darkman*, a full-scale studio horror movie. But Raimi was not content to be labeled a horror kid. *The Quick and the Dead* was a bizarre, camp Western that attracted a lot of name actors. Then all of a sudden *A Simple Plan* was a real picture about rural folks, paranoia, and what the snow can cover. Of course, *A Simple Plan* could have been played for horror, yet it suggested that Raimi had higher ambitions. Who would have thought those would have shifted to Kevin Costner's dotty daydream, and thence to a major franchise, *Spider-Man*?

Raimu (Jules Muraire) (1883–1946),
b. Toulon, France

Perhaps because we are all actors now (I mean, too well aware of trying to be convincing), we have become anxious about the intelligence (or otherwise) of professional actors. No matter that "acting" (as opposed to being) ourselves might be regarded as stupid, futile, vain, and neurotic, we are highly concerned to vouch for the intelligence—the intellect, even—in actors. Whereas once upon a time, people were content to observe great brilliance in actors riding along without a parsable thought for anything else in the world— as if actors were great sportsmen, kings or queens, or immense lovers.

For example, Raimu—that glorious, unrestrained performer, of whom the solicitous Jean Renoir once said, "Although Raimu was perhaps the greatest French actor of the century, he was completely ignorant of some things. All he knew about the cinema was that a close-up showed the details of a face. During shooting he would constantly say to the cameraman, 'Make me big.' " It is a primitive approach, Boudu-esque—except that Michel Simon himself was a refined and articulate man. Another great admirer of Raimu's instinctive approach was Orson Welles, surely a fine example of the actor too chronically clever for his own good, so that he was compelled to take up the consequent air of fraud in his persona. As for Raimu—nothing deterred or deflected him.

He was a star of music hall, the Folies-Bergère, and the stage long before he got into film. Once established on camera, he revealed his fondness for naturalness and a select body of directors with whom he felt comfortable. Of course, he is treasured above all for his César in the Pagnol trilogy, but there are many other fine films in the list, and Raimu is central to that French faith in the grand, "ugly" actor—something that helps explain the great success of Depardieu, and which testifies to the ongoing nineteenth-century romance in French acting.

Raimu probably did a few silent films, but the established list of credits begins with *Le Blanc et le Noir* (31, Robert Florey); *Marius* (31, Pagnol and Alexander Korda); *Mam'zelle Nitouche* (31, Marc Allégret); *Fanny* (32, Allégret); *La Petite Chocolatière* (32, Allégret); *Les Gaietés de l'Escadron* (32, Maurice Tourneur); *Théodore et Cie* (33, Pierre Colombier); *Charlemagne* (33, Colombier); *Ces Messieurs de la Santé* (33, Colombier); *L'Ecole des Cocottes* (34, Colombier); *Tartarin de Tarascon* (34, Raymond Bernard); *Minuit Place Pigalle* (34, Roger Richebé); *J'Ai une Idée* (34, Richebé); *Gaspard de Besse* (35, André Hugon); *César* (36, Pagnol).

The three César films had made him immensely popular, and he was now a star who had vehicles, or roles, conceived for him: *Le Secret de Polichinelle* (36, André Berthomieu); *Le Roi* (36, Colombier); *Les Jumeaux de Brighton* (36, Claude Heymann); *Les Perles de la Couronne* (37, Christian-Jaque and Sacha Guitry); *Gribouille* (37, Allégret); *L'Etrange Monsieur Victor* (37, Jean Gremillon); *Vous N'Avez Rien à Déclarer?* (37, Léo Joannon); *Carnet de Ball* (37, Duvivier); *Les Rois du Sport* (37, Colombier); *Le Fauteuil 47* (37, Fernand Rivers); *Faisons un Rêve* (37, Guitry); *La Chaste Suzanne* (37, Berthomieu); and then a huge hit in *La Femme du Boulanger* (38, Pagnol)—which was one of the last French films to play in Britain and America at the start of the war, and which romanticized French rural life with its stress on eating. (In time, that taste would turn into Alice Waters's restaurant, Chez Panisse, in Berkeley, California, which was inspired by the Pagnol films and has always been a favored place for filmmakers.)

For Raimu to have left France (because of war) would have been unthinkable: *Les Nouveaux Riches* (38, Berthomieu); *Noix de Coco* (39, Jean Boyer); *Le Héros de la Marne* (39, Hugon); *Monsieur Brotonneau* (39, Alexandre Esway); *Dernière Jeunesse* (39, Jeff Musso); *Le Duel* (39, Pierre Fresnay); *L'Homme Qui Cherche la Verité* (40, Esway); *La Fille du Puisatier* (40, Pagnol); *Parade en Sept Nuits* (41, Allégret); *Les Inconnus dans la Maison* (42, Henri Decoin); *Monsieur La Souris* (42, Georges Lacombe); *Le Bienfaiteur* (42, Decoin); *Les Petits Riens* (42, Raymond Leboursier); *Le Colonel Chabert* (43, René Le Hénaff); *Untel Père et Fils* (43, Duvivier); *Les Gueux au Paradis* (45, Le Hénaff); *L'Homme au Chapeau Rond* (46, Pierre Billon).

Luise Rainer, b. Vienna, 1912

How are the Oscars awarded? That question intrigues public and nominees alike. It is easy now to charge that the statuettes have become devalued as the movie industry has lost confidence. The gauche gestures of the Academy to great stars who unaccountably slipped through their net—Cary Grant and, too late, Edward G. Robinson—have added to the impression that Oscars were always political rewards, shared out among major studios and stars. But close scrutiny of the list of winners reveals a charming eccentricity. Go to the heyday of the industry—mid-1930s, for instance—and in consecutive years a lady named Luise Rainer won the best actress Oscar. The Academy quickly flinched from its generosity, and the actress herself was overawed by the twin household gods. Her career crumbled so completely afterwards that they might have been voodoo idols.

Rainer was a distinguished Berlin stage actress, a member of Max Reinhardt's company, invited to Hollywood by MGM in 1935. She had made a few films in Germany—*Sehnsucht 202* (32, Max Neufeld); *Heute Kommt's Drauf An* (33, Kurt Gerron)—but nothing to suggest unusual promise. Her American debut came about only when Myrna Loy abandoned *Escapade* (35, Robert Z. Leonard). That proved simply that Rainer photographed well and that she was monotonously expressive in the manner of silent screen humility. MGM then cast her as the first, long-suffering wife of *The Great Ziegfeld* (36, Leonard), and she won her first Oscar (because of a long, tear-filled telephone scene). The second came with her Chinese peasant in Thalberg's last production, *The Good Earth* (37, Sidney Franklin, et al.), another wife who has to endure a husband's mistress. All this at the studio that had Garbo, Norma Shearer, and Joan Crawford as its leading ladies.

It was an astonishing beginning, but it was effectively the end. Rainer was a limited, mostly appealing screen personality, quite unable to survive the reaction against two in a row. Her marriage to Clifford Odets was foundering and her remaining films at Metro were forlorn ventures: *The Emperor's Candlesticks* (37, George Fitzmaurice); *Big City* (37, Frank Borzage); *The Toy Wife* (38, Richard Thorpe); *The Great Waltz* (38, Julien Duvivier); and *Dramatic School* (38, Robert Sinclair). The studio then dropped her and her retirement from the screen was interrupted only once, in 1943, with *Hostages* (Frank Tuttle).

There was nothing more until Rainer appeared in 1991 as perhaps the best witness in TNT's history of MGM—beautiful, intelligent, and mesmerizing.

Ella Raines (Raubes) (1921–88),
b. Snoqualmie Falls, Washington
Ella Raines had that look on her face—saucy, knowing, and eager. Elisha Cook's mad drummer could see it in *Phantom Lady* (44, Robert Siodmak), and it's likely that Ms. Raines knew it herself. After the University of Washington, she got herself noticed by David Selznick, then by Howard Hawks. They had an affair, and then she was passed on to Hawks's partner, Charlie Feldman, ending his marriage to Jean Howard. Hawks

only used her in his production of *Corvette K-225* (43, Richard Rossen), but it's said he shot some of her scenes himself. Thereafter, she was picked up—professionally—by Siodmak, who used her four times: *Cry Havoc* (43, Richard Thorpe); *Hail the Conquering Hero* (44, Preston Sturges); with John Wayne in *Tall in the Saddle* (44, Edwin L. Marin); *Enter Arsene Lupin* (44, Ford Becker); as the love of Charles Laughton's imagination in *The Suspect* (44, Siodmak); very touching with George Sanders in *The Strange Affair of Uncle Harry* (45, Siodmak); *The Runaround* (46, Charles Lamont); *White Tie and Tails* (46, Charles Barton); *Time Out of Mind* (47, Siodmak); *The Web* (47, Michael Gordon); *Brute Force* (47, Jules Dassin); with William Powell in *The Senator Was Indiscreet* (47, George S. Kaufman); in a Western, *The Walking Hills* (49, John Sturges); *Impact* (49, Arthur Lubin); *A Dangerous Profession* (49, Ted Tetzlaff); with Vaughn Monroe in *Singing Guns* (50, R. G. Springsteen); having plastic surgery in *The Second Face* (50, Jean Bernhard); *The Fighting Coast Guard* (51, Joseph Kane); *Ride the Man Down* (52, Kane); and then to England for her last film, *Man in the Road* (56, Lance Comfort).

Claude Rains (1889–1967), b. London
For consistent enterprise in supporting parts, Rains had few equals. Technically, he often filled roles that were leads, but he treated them as character parts. Slight, elegant, and detached, he was middle-aged before he came to Hollywood and he specialized in lawyers, politicians, doctors, and as a discreet support for Bette Davis. But he also gave unusual individuality to a number of villains, and even the occasional florid madman. It says something for Hollywood's coming of age during the war that Rains was a corrupt, obnoxious politician for Capra in 1939, and yet, four years later, in *Casablanca*, a most engaging cynic, surviving with amusement amid so much compromise.

Rains was a noted actor before 1914, and a respected teacher at RADA (Charles Laughton was one of his students). He was well into his forties before being cast by James Whale in *The Invisible Man* (33), a remarkable debut for so responsive a face, since Rains played in bandages throughout. He was only revealed to the world in Ben Hecht and Charles MacArthur's *Crime Without Passion* (34). After a few more films, including *The Mystery of Edwin Drood* (35, Stuart Walker), in which he is a pinch-faced drug addict, and back to Britain for *The Clairvoyant* (35, Maurice Elvey), Rains was put under contract by Warners: *Anthony Adverse* (36, Mervyn Le Roy); Napoleon in *Hearts Divided* (36, Frank Borzage); *Stolen Holiday* (36, Michael Curtiz)—about the Stavisky affair; *They Won't Forget* (37, Le Roy)—an indictment of lynch law, with Rains as a conniving district attorney; *The Prince and the Pauper* (37,

William Keighley); *Gold Is Where You Find It* (38, Curtiz); as an amused, giggly Prince John in *The Adventures of Robin Hood* (38, Curtiz and Keighley); *White Banners* (38, Edmund Goulding); *Four Daughters* (38, Curtiz); the detective pursuing John Garfield in Busby Berkeley's *They Made Me a Criminal* (39); Napoleon III in *Juarez* (39, William Dieterle); magnificent as Senator Payne in Frank Capra's *Mr. Smith Goes to Washington* (39, made for Columbia)—note his complex reaction as he is being introduced: he is the most interesting person in the film; *Four Wives* (39, Curtiz); a classic picture, *The Sea Hawk* (40, Curtiz); playwright David Belasco in *The Lady With Red Hair* (40, Curtis Bernhardt); *Here Comes Mr. Jordan* (41, Alexander Hall); *The Wolf Man* (41, George Waggner); *King's Row* (42, Sam Wood); *Moontide* (42, Archie Mayo); the psychiatrist in *Now, Voyager* (42, Irving Rapper); the police chief in *Casablanca* (43, Curtiz); *The Phantom of the Opera* (43, Arthur Lubin); *Passage to Marseilles* (44, Curtiz); grace under pressure as the Jew in *Mr. Skeffington* (44, Vincent Sherman).

George Bernard Shaw then chose Rains to play in *Caesar and Cleopatra* (45, Gabriel Pascal) and, back in America, he was in Dieterle's *This Love of Ours* (45) and Hitchcock's *Notorious* (46), the latter one of his finest performances, as a pro-Nazi spy subtly redeemed by his love for Ingrid Bergman. Rains completed his Warners contract with *Angel on My Shoulder* (46, Mayo); over the top in *Deception* (46, Rapper) and *The Unsuspected* (47, his tenth film with Michael Curtiz).

As a free-lancer, he appeared in several offbeat pictures: *Strange Holiday* (47, Arch Oboler); *The Passionate Friends* (48, David Lean); *Rope of Sand* (49, Dieterle); *Song of Surrender* (49, Mitchell Leisen); *The White Tower* (50, Ted Tetzlaff); caught between Mitchum and Faith Domergue in *Where Danger Lives* (50, John Farrow); *Sealed Cargo* (51, Alfred Werker); *The Man Who Watched Trains Go By* (53, Harold French); and *Lisbon* (56, Ray Milland).

At this point, Rains gave up the screen for the stage and played in a version of Koestler's *Darkness at Noon* and in Eliot's *The Confidential Clerk*. But he returned, still authoritative, for *This Earth Is Mine* (59, Henry King); in a claptrap version of *The Lost World* (60, Irwin Allen); as Dryden in *Lawrence of Arabia* (62, Lean); *Twilight of Honor* (63, Boris Sagal); and as Herod in *The Greatest Story Ever Told* (65, George Stevens).

He had been nominated four times as best supporting actor—*Mr. Smith Goes to Washington, Casablanca, Mr. Skeffington,* and *Notorious.* No wins. Yet as time goes by, is there anyone more watchable, more delicate or acidic? He was also much married—five or six times: sources quarrel. It is amazing that this mix of decorum and wildness has not yet inspired a biography.

Charlotte Rampling,
b. Sturmer, England, 1946

Though she looks and sounds English enough to play the Thatcherite politician in David Hare's *Paris by Night* (1988), Charlotte Rampling has worked all over the place, and in several different languages. She has not just a chilly edge but the capacity to make us suspect a cold heart. So, she has her share of narrow-faced villains, not always more than baleful gargoyles. Yet, once at least, in Woody Allen's *Stardust Memories* (80), she gave a heartbreaking account of breakdown.

She made her debut in *The Knack, and How to Get It* (65, Richard Lester) and she was impressive as the catty friend in *Georgy Girl* (66, Silvio Narizzano). Then came *The Long Duel* (67, Ken Annakin); *The Damned* (69, Luchino Visconti); *Target: Harry* (69, Henry Neill), a TV reworking of *The Maltese Falcon; The Ski Bum* (71, Bruce Clark); *Vanishing Point* (71, Richard C. Sarafian)—though her role was cut after previews; a psychopath in *Asylum* (72, Roy Ward Baker); *Corky* (72, Leonard Horn); *Caravan to Vaccares* (74, Geoffrey Reeve); passive, wounded, and half-naked, a sadist's wet dream in *The Night Porter* (74, Liliana Cavani)—and thoroughly disturbing; one of the Eternals in *Zardoz* (74, John Boorman); *Farewell, My Lovely* (75, Dick Richards); *Foxtrot* (76, Arturo Ripstein); *Orca . . . Killer Whale* (77, Michael Anderson); treachery is woman in *The Verdict* (82, Sidney Lumet); *Viva la Vie* (84, Claude Lelouch); in love with a monkey in *Max, Mon Amour* (86, Nagisa Oshima); *Angel Heart* (87, Alan Parker); *Mascara* (87, Patrick Conrad); *D.O.A.* (88, Rocky Morton and Annabel Jankel); and *Hammers Over the Anvil* (93, Ann Turner).

Her work in the nineties, most of it in Europe, has become increasingly varied and impressive. Her looks have become more intriguing, and one feels a rebirth of her own interest in acting. *Time Is Money* (94, Paola Barzman); *Murder In Mind* (94, Robert Bierman); *Radetzky March* (94, Axel Corti and Gernot Roll); *Samson le Magnifique* (95, Etienne Perier); *Asphalt Tango* (96, Nae Caranfil); *Invasion of Privacy* (96, Anthony Hickox); *La Dernière Fête* (96, Pierre Granier-Deferre); *The Wings of the Dove* (97, Iain Softley); Miss Havisham in *Great Expectations* (99, Alfonso Cuaron); Madame Ranyevskaya in *Varya* (99, Michael Cacoyannis); *Signs & Wonders* (00, Jonathan Nossiter); *Aberdeen* (00, Hans Petter Moland); excellent in *Under the Sand* (00, Francois Ozon); *Clouds: Letters to My Son* (00, Marion Hansel); *The Fourth Angel* (01, John Irvin); *Superstition* (01, Kenneth Hope).

She was in *Spy Game* (01, Tony Scott); *Embrassez Qui Vous Voudrez* (02, Michel Blanc); once more outstanding in *Swimming Pool* (03, Ozon); *Jerusalem* (03, Jakov Sedlar); as Livia in *Augustus* (03, Roger Young).

Irving Rapper (1898–1999), b. London
1941: *Shining Victory; One Foot in Heaven*. 1942:
The Gay Sisters; Now, Voyager. 1944: *The Adventures of Mark Twain*. 1945: *The Corn Is Green;
Rhapsody in Blue*. 1946: *Deception*. 1947: *The
Voice of the Turtle*. 1949: *Anna Lucasta*. 1950:
The Glass Menagerie. 1952: *Another Man's
Poison*. 1953: *Forever Female; Bad for Each
Other*. 1956: *Strange Intruder; The Brave One*.
1958: *Marjorie Morningstar*. 1959: *The Miracle*.
1960: *Giuseppe Venduto dai Fratelli/Joseph
and His Brethren/Sold into Egypt* (codirected
with Luciano Ricci). 1961: *Ponzio Pilato/Pontius
Pilate*. 1970: *The Christine Jorgensen Story*. 1978:
Born Again.

Rapper went from the theatre to be an assistant
director at Warners: *The Story of Louis Pasteur*
(35, William Dieterle); *The Walking Dead* (36,
Michael Curtiz); *Kid Galahad* (37, Curtiz); *The
Life of Emile Zola* (37, Dieterle); *The Sisters* (38,
Anatole Litvak); *Juarez* (39, Dieterle); *The Story
of Dr. Ehrlich's Magic Bullet* (40, Dieterle); and
All This and Heaven Too (40, Litvak).

The mark of Curtiz, Dieterle, and Litvak shows
in his own films—if nothing else, Rapper learned
a gilded craft. But his bio-pics suffer from casting:
Robert Alda as Gershwin in *Rhapsody in Blue,*
where the music is smothered by extravagant
camera movements. *Now, Voyager* is rather better
Litvak than Anatole could have managed: a gorgeous, wallowing film, admirably played by Bette
Davis and Claude Rains.

After the war, Rapper seems to have lost touch
with genre—*Anna Lucasta* was always a forlorn
project; *The Glass Menagerie* is very dull stage
talk, apart from Arthur Kennedy's brittle frailty as
the brother; *The Brave One* is appealing, and won
a writer's Oscar for Dalton Trumbo under a false
name; *Marjorie Morningstar* wasted Natalie
Wood; while *The Miracle* was uncalled for. *The
Christine Jorgensen Story* is possibly the most
bizarre departure by any director once in steady
work; it grotesquely echoes the nature of his earlier films, for the emotionalism of Bette Davis's
Charlotte Vale in *Now, Voyager* is an underground intimation of sexual transference. The
women's picture appeals so often to butch ladies
and softy studs.

Basil Rathbone (1892–1967),
b. Johannesburg, South Africa
"Some men play with handkerchiefs," says Rathbone's Esteban in *The Mark of Zorro* (40, Rouben
Mamoulian), "but I like to keep a rapier in my
hand." Thus the racing allegro duel with Tyrone
Power at the end of that film is the natural culmination of the restlessness that is always picking
at other people's noses with a swordtip. Even
unarmed, Rathbone was sharp and dangerous, a

cruel dandy. The inverted arrow face, the razor
nose, and a mustache that was really two fine
shears stuck to his lip. Ladies looked fearfully at
him, knowing that one embrace could cut them to
ribbons. And if Mamoulian's flickering, swashbuckling play of light and shadow uses Rathbone
most wittily, he managed invariably to be both
imaginatively nasty and yet amused by himself.

He was educated in England at Repton and
went on the stage. After a Military Cross in the
war, he starred at Stratford and made his movie
debut in Britain: *The Fruitful Vine* (21, Maurice
Elvey); *Innocent* (21, Elvey); and as Joseph Surface in *The School for Scandal* (23, Bertram
Phillips). Stage work took him to America, and in
1924 he went to Hollywood: *Pity the Chorus Girl*
(24, T. Hayes Hunter); *The Masked Bride* (25,
Christy Cabanne); and *The Great Deception* (26,
Howard Higgin).

But it was sound that made him a distinguished
and articulate villain: *The Last of Mrs. Cheyney*
(29, Sidney Franklin); *This Mad World* (29,
William De Mille); *A Notorious Affair* (30, Lloyd
Bacon); *Sin Takes a Holiday* (30, Paul L. Stein); *A
Lady Surrenders* (30, John M. Stahl); *The Lady of
Scandal* (30, Franklin); and *A Woman Commands*
(31, Stein). He did himself no good by returning
to Britain for *One Precious Year* (32, Henry
Edwards); *Loyalties* (33, Basil Dean); and *Just
Smith* (33, Tom Walls); but 1934 saw him back in
America with some deep-etched scoundrels: as
Murdstone in *David Copperfield* (34, George
Cukor); in *Captain Blood* (35, Michael Curtiz); as
Karenin to Garbo's *Anna Karenina* (35, Clarence
Brown); as Pilate in *The Last Days of Pompeii* (35,
Ernest Schoedsack); as St. Evremonde in *A Tale of
Two Cities* (35, Jack Conway); and *Kind Lady* (35,
George B. Seitz).

He was assured now of good supporting roles:
Tybalt in *Romeo and Juliet* (36, Cukor); *The Garden of Allah* (36, Richard Boleslavsky); *Private
Number* (36, Roy del Ruth); *Tovarich* (37, Anatole
Litvak); *Love from a Stranger* (37, Rowland V.
Lee); *Confession* (37, Joe May); Sir Guy of Gisbourne in *The Adventures of Robin Hood* (38,
Curtiz and William Keighley); *The Adventures of
Marco Polo* (38, Archie Mayo); *If I Were King* (38,
Frank Lloyd); *The Dawn Patrol* (38, Edmund
Goulding); as Baron Frankenstein in *The Son of
Frankenstein* (39, Lee); as Richard III in *Tower of
London* (39, Lee); *The Sun Never Sets* (39, Lee);
and *Rio* (39, John Brahm).

Then Fox called on him to play Sherlock
Holmes in *The Hound of the Baskervilles* (39, Sidney Lanfield) and *The Adventures of Sherlock
Holmes* (39, Alfred Werker). He was limited by
the screen conception of Holmes—sardonic, playful, and elitist—and never suggested the man who
took drugs against boredom. Nevertheless, he is
the best screen Holmes, and he played the part

another twelve times, from 1942 to 1946, all for Universal, directed usually by Roy William Neill.

That sure meal ticket led to his decline. Too familiar as the maestro detective, he was cut off from the Moriarties he was made for. But he worked on: *Rhythm on the River* (40, Victor Schertzinger); *The Mad Doctor* (41, Tim Whelan); *The Black Cat* (41, Albert S. Rogell); *Fingers at the Window* (42, Charles Lederer); *Crossroads* (42, Jack Conway); *Above Suspicion* (43, Richard Thorpe); *Frenchman's Creek* (44, Mitchell Leisen); *Bathing Beauty* (44, George Sidney); and *Heartbeat* (46, Sam Wood). Then an interval while he returned to the New York stage for, among others, Sloper in *The Heiress*. His final period of film work begins in 1954 with *Casanova's Big Night* (Norman Z. McLeod); then *We're No Angels* (55, Curtiz); *The Black Sleep* (56, Reginald Le Borg); *The Court Jester* (56, Norman Panama and Melvin Frank); *The Last Hurrah* (58, John Ford); *Ponzio Pilato* (61, Irving Rapper); *Tales of Terror* (61, Roger Corman); *The Comedy of Terrors* (63, Jacques Tourneur); and *Queen of Blood* (66, Curtis Harrington).

Gregory Ratoff (1897–1960),
b. St. Petersburg, Russia

1936: *Sins of Man* (codirected with Otto Brower). 1937: *Lancer Spy*. 1939: *Wife, Husband and Friend; Barricade; Rose of Washington Square; Hotel for Women; Day-Time Wife; Intermezzo.* 1940: *I Was an Adventuress; Public Deb No. 1.* 1941: *Adam Had Four Sons; The Men in Her Life; The Corsican Brothers.* 1942: *Two Yanks in Trinidad; Footlight Serenade.* 1943: *The Heat's On; Something to Shout About.* 1944: *Song of Russia; Irish Eyes Are Smiling.* 1945: *Where Do We Go From Here?; Paris Underground.* 1946: *Do You Love Me?.* 1947: *Carnival in Costa Rica; Moss Rose.* 1949: *Black Magic.* 1950: *That Dangerous Age.* 1951: *Operation X.* 1953: *Taxi.* 1956: *Abdullah's Harem.* 1960: *Oscar Wilde.*

Trained in the Russian theatre and in the Russian army in the First World War, Ratoff soon shed any trace of diligent schooling or harsh experience. He was an endearing, flamboyant ham, physically reminiscent of Emil Jannings in *The Last Command*. Before he took to directing, his acting work included the father in *Symphony of Six Million* (32, Gregory La Cava); the producer in *What Price Hollywood?* (32, George Cukor); *Under Two Flags* (36, Frank Lloyd); *The Road to Glory* (36, Howard Hawks); and *Sing, Baby, Sing* (36, Sidney Lanfield).

His own films are confections: the earlier ones moderately prestigious, the latter sadly shady. *Lancer Spy* was a nice matching of George Sanders, Dolores del Rio, and Peter Lorre, while *I Was an Adventuress* had Lorre and Erich von Stroheim together. That sort of larger-than-life performance was Ratoff's forte, so that the striving for sincerity by Leslie Howard and Ingrid Bergman in *Intermezzo* was rather swamped by the director's schmaltz. (In fact, Ratoff was "director" on that to pay off a gambling debt; Leslie Howard handled the actors.)

Similarly, *The Corsican Brothers*, with two Douglas Fairbanks Jrs., Akim Tamiroff, and Ratoff himself, is a gay farrago; *The Heat's On* was a poor Mae West picture; *Song of Russia* was patriotic rubbish, about as ethnically authentic as *Irish Eyes Are Smiling*. But *Black Magic*, with Welles as Cagliostro, is great fun, and proof of the charm with which Welles adopts the lowdown. After the war, Ratoff spent more time acting, notably in *All About Eve* (50, Joseph L. Mankiewicz); *The Sun Also Rises* (57, Henry King); and *Once More With Feeling* (59, Stanley Donen). Hopelessly crossbred by then, in 1960 he brought tears to his own eyes as a Jewish refugee in *Exodus* (Otto Preminger), and made a hopeless mess directing the Robert Morley *Oscar Wilde.*

Aldo Ray (Aldo DaRe) (1926–91),
b. Pen Argyl, Pennsylvania

For every insistence on the vitality of American cinema, it must be said that Hollywood has made a bland, genteel picture of redneck America. The prejudice, barroom stink, and narrow-minded expansiveness of America has not often been portrayed honestly. From John Ford onward, provincialism has been gilded by sentiment and nostalgia. All credit then to Aldo Ray for some intriguing views of the American ordinary ranker. Ray was lured into films from California politics—he was sheriff of the California town Crockett—by director David Miller. He never lost the arrogant strut and insecure grasp of *lex* in a crossroads settlement law-enforcement agent.

Miller put him in *Saturday's Hero* (51) and Ray was then briefly drafted into the much more sophisticated world of George Cukor: *The Marrying Kind* (52) and *Pat and Mike* (52). But his bullnecked coarseness assured him a string of soldier parts: *Miss Sadie Thompson* (53, Curtis Bernhardt); as a convict in *We're No Angels* (55, Michael Curtiz); *Three Stripes in the Sun* (55, Richard Murphy); breaking into tears in *Battle Cry* (55, Raoul Walsh).

This development reached a splendid climax in three films: as the sergeant who takes over the war from Robert Ryan's officer in *Men in War* (57, Anthony Mann); lusting after Tina Louise in Mann's re-creation of Erskine Caldwell's country, *God's Little Acre* (58, Mann); and as Norman Mailer's Sergeant Croft in *The Naked and the Dead* (58, Walsh). The two military pictures caught the raucous, neo-fascist spirit of the American army eerily well. Ray was a match for Mailer's

Croft and it was no surprise that, ten years later, he was back in combat in John Wayne's *The Green Berets* (68).

Ray may have been too strong a flavor for America. By the late 1950s he was a wandering actor in less and less worthy films: *Nightfall* (56, Jacques Tourneur); *The Siege of Pinchgut* (58, Harry Watt); *The Day They Robbed the Bank of England* (60, John Guillermin); *Johnny Nobody* (61, Nigel Patrick); *I Moschettieri del Mare* (62, Stefano Vanzina Steno); *Nightmare in the Sun* (64, Marc Lawrence); *Sylvia* (65, Gordon Douglas); *What Did You Do in the War, Daddy?* (66, Blake Edwards); *Dead Heat on a Merry-Go-Round* (66, Bernard Girard); *Welcome to Hard Times* (67, Burt Kennedy); *Kill a Dragon* (67, Michael Moore); *Riot on Sunset Strip* (67, Arthur Dreifuss); *The Power* (67, Byron Haskin and George Pal); *The Violent Ones* (67, Fernando Lamas); *Angel Unchained* (70, Lee Madden); *Seven Alone* (74, Earl Bellamy); *Inside Out* (75, Peter Duffell); as Stubby Stebbins in *Won Ton Ton, the Dog Who Saved Hollywood* (75, Michael Winner). Thereafter, he was reported as a star of porno movies and low-budget action pictures. But he also played in *The Executioner Part II* (84, James Bryant) and *The Sicilian* (87, Michael Cimino).

Nicholas Ray (Raymond Nicholas Kienzle)
(1911–79), b. Galesville, Wisconsin

1948: *They Live By Night.* 1949: *A Woman's Secret; Knock on Any Door.* 1950: *In a Lonely Place; Born to Be Bad.* 1951: *On Dangerous Ground; Flying Leathernecks.* 1952: *The Lusty Men.* 1954: *Johnny Guitar.* 1955: *Run for Cover; Rebel Without a Cause.* 1956: *Hot Blood; Bigger Than Life.* 1957: *The True Story of Jesse James.* 1958: *Bitter Victory; Wind Across the Everglades; Party Girl.* 1960: *The Savage Innocents.* 1961: *King of Kings.* 1963: *55 Days at Peking.* 1973: *We Can't Go Home Again.* 1974: "The Janitor," an episode from *Dreams of Thirteen/Wet Dreams.* 1980: *Lightning Over Water* (d) (codirected with Wim Wenders).

When *Sight and Sound* was obliged to respond to the French endorsement of American cinema, it seized on Nicholas Ray as the best demonstration of misplaced enthusiasm. "Ray or Ray?" one article began—Nicholas or Satyajit?—suggesting that whereas the Indian made films of his own choosing, inspired by humanitarian sensitivity, the American made whatever entertainment movies he was allowed to. There is no need to disparage the maker of the Apu films, or their restrained insight, to justify the intense visual emotion in the best of Nicholas Ray's work.

Ray is famous for the remark, "If it were all in the script, why make the film?," and it is as the source of a profusion of cinematic epiphanies that

I recall him: Mitchum walking across an empty rodeo arena at evening in *The Lusty Men,* the wind blowing rubbish around him; that last plate settling slowly and noisily in *55 Days at Peking;* the livid-coated hunting pack in the Trucolor *Johnny Guitar;* the lethal, trembling night operation in *Bitter Victory;* the CinemaScope frame suddenly ablaze with yellow cabs in *Bigger Than Life.* He remains a test case of the way such gathered moments exceed the hackneyed idioms of commercial cinema: with the piercing enactment of human solitariness through gesture, color, and space, and because—as with any film director—one comes away from his work moved by the spectacle of human nature that he has revealed.

Ray studied architecture with Frank Lloyd Wright, and then worked as an actor and a traveling researcher into American folklore. Those interests remained alive. Few other directors had such a sense of the effect of locations and interiors on people's lives, or the visual or emotional relationship between indoors and outdoors, upstairs and downstairs. His characters contract or expand according to the emotional tone of the place in which they find themselves. For example, consider the transient caravan world of *The Lusty Men* that Susan Hayward tries to domesticate; the courtyard that joins but separates Bogart and Gloria Grahame in *In a Lonely Place;* the saloon in *Johnny Guitar;* the police station, the Stark house, the planetarium, and the deserted mansion in *Rebel Without a Cause;* and the staircase in *Bigger Than Life.* There is not a director who films or frames interior shots with Ray's dynamic, fraught grace and who thereby so explodes the rigid limits of "script" material. No one made CinemaScope so glorious a shape as Ray, because it seemed to set an extra challenge to his interior sensibility.

It is not unusual in America to find directors with an innate skill at handling actors. But in Ray's case, this ability often jolted placid material and dull players into a life they never showed elsewhere. Ray's special, perilous humanism gained performances that seem to have been penetrated and hurt by reality. It is not only a matter of using good actors: Mitchum in *The Lusty Men;* Bogart in *In a Lonely Place;* Robert Ryan in *On Dangerous Ground;* James Mason in *Bigger Than Life;* and the wonderfully touching trio in *Rebel:* James Dean, Natalie Wood, and Sal Mineo. In *Lusty Men,* Mitchum was playing subtly against his screen character, as a reflective, increasingly perplexed man. Equally, only *In a Lonely Place* came to grips with the malevolence in Bogart, or so effectively saw through the knowingness of his 1940s films.

That air of superiority in Bogart was contrary to Ray's sense of vulnerability: in *Bigger Than Life* it is the suave James Mason who is cracking up. As for *Rebel,* it now looks like the first film to catch the revolutionary unease of the young generation. Dean is less a rebel in it than a dreamer, plainly engaged by his director's nervous vitality.

Who else has made Farley Granger seem as appealingly vulnerable as he is in *They Live By Night,* and who else so joined battle with Joan Crawford's manly fierceness? How well the domineering Susan Hayward is used in *The Lusty Men.* And how inventive it is to probe Charlton Heston's heroism in *55 Days at Peking* with the most demanding, intimate, and exposing scene that he has ever played, where he stumbles over telling the Chinese girl that her father is dead.

Ray's personality emerged in his handling of people and their environments. But he would not be a major figure if he did not also have a fundamental conception of American legend and society. This is not just a matter of the balladlike *True Story of Jesse James,* but the recognition that self-sufficiency and free-for-all in American life have made for alienation and violence. All Ray's visual inventiveness and all his sympathy for people under stress come down to his brooding and romantic vision of a hero forced in on himself, touching and meeting other people but never understanding or being understood. At times, this action is bleak and primitive: thus the inability of Mitchum to settle in *The Lusty Men* and the way he is killed by a proud gesture to assert his independence; the realization of the Bogart character in *In a Lonely Place* that frustration has bred in him a homicidal violence; the loss of Sal Mineo at the end of *Rebel;* the implacable hopelessness of the desert expedition in *Bitter Victory* and Richard Burton's helpless killing of the living and saving of the dead. There is never more than modest hope at the end of his films: in *Wind Across the Everglades* that the birds might be saved, although Burl Ives is dead; in *Rebel* that the friendship of Dean and Wood might last; that Mason's recovery in *Bigger Than Life* might save his family life. More often, friendship and love break down; death severs the odd bond between young and old; the world is regenerated only through destruction.

Ray's own chaos in the last two decades of his life—the wandering, the gambling, the lack of work, the excess of existential gesture—made him a self-conscious poet of American disenchantment. *Bigger Than Life* had all the ingrowing sickness of the good life. *Savage Innocents* is the last prairie, already corrupted by the trading post jukebox that howls over the snow.

Ray always seemed under pressure. There is a constant nervous tension in his films to be seen in the restless camera movement, the turbulent, hurt editing, the immediacy of action and discord in the colors, the intensity of the acting. His career as a whole was uneasy. More than *Sight and Sound* ever realized, his films transcended the Holly-

wood genres. It is not only that so many of his endings were not happy or that they blazed with lucid pessimism. He was an insecure figure, often ill— or averse to work—so that *On Dangerous Ground* was aided by Ida Lupino, *The Lusty Men* by Robert Parrish, *55 Days at Peking* by Andrew Marton. Although his films were as rigorously spectacular as any made during the 1950s, he was not happiest with the Bronston epics. His best work is done with a few characters, where external action expresses their uncontainable dilemmas. This is true of all his best films: *They Live By Night, On Dangerous Ground, In a Lonely Place, The Lusty Men, Rebel Without a Cause, Bigger Than Life,* and *Bitter Victory.*

He stopped working in the decade that an American idealist would have found least endurable. He returned as the instigator of film studies at New York State University. *We Can't Go Home Again* was made there—a plethora of images meant to be projected in unison about . . . alienated America, Ray, and cinema itself. Jonathan Rosenbaum called it "cinema at the end of its tether." But Ray had always set himself as near the brink as possible.

In poor health in the seventies, Ray appeared with great aplomb and concealed courage in *The American Friend* (77, Wim Wenders) as an artist believed dead, but "forging" his own works—and in *Hair* (79, Milos Forman), as the General.

Nick Ray was a hero to many, and he loved the admiration of the young. He was also indulgent, irresponsible, wanton, sentimental, self-destructive. In other words, there are warnings in his life for the hero-worship of movie directors. Bernard Eisenchitz's careful biography lays the groundwork for that confusion, but still celebrates Ray. I take the view now that Ray was—as well as everything else—a would-be actor and a fantasist. Those traits are not uncommon in Hollywood. But recognition of them helps us understand the beautiful, dangerous dreaminess of his films. Ray is the American director in whom greatness is inseparable from the refusal to grow up. It leaves him even worthier of study.

Satyajit Ray (1921–92), b. Calcutta, India
1955: *Pather Panchali.* 1957: *Aparajito.* 1958: *Paras Pathar/The Philosopher's Stone; Jalsaghar/The Music Room.* 1959: *Apu Sansar/The World of Apu.* 1960: *Devi/The Goddess.* 1961: *Rabindranath Tagore* (d); *Teen Kanya/Three Daughters.* 1962: *Kanchenjunga; Abhijan/Expedition.* 1963: *Mahanagar/The Big City.* 1964: *Charulata/The Lonely Wife.* 1965: *Aranyer Din Ratri/Days and Nights in the Forest.* 1971: *Kapurush-O-Mahapurush/The Coward and the Holy Man.* 1966: *Nayak/The Hero.* 1967: *Chiriakhane/The Menagerie.* 1968: *Goupi Gyne, Bagha Byne/The Adventures of Goopy and Bagha.* 1970: *Pratidwandi/*

Siddhartha and the City/The Adversary. 1972: *Seemabadha/Company Limited.* 1973: *Distant Thunder.* 1975: *Jana-Aranya/The Middleman.* 1977: *Shatranj Ke Khilari/The Chess Players.* 1978: *Joi Baba Felunath/The Elephant God.* 1980: *Hirok Rajar Deshe/The Kingdom of Diamonds.* 1981: *Pikoo* (s); *Sadgati/Deliverance* (TV). 1984: *Ghare-Baire/The Home and the World.* 1989: *Ganashatru/An Enemy of the People.* 1990: *Shaka Proshakha/Branches of the Tree.* 1991: *Agantuk/ The Stranger.*

Satyajit Ray tended to produce superbly accomplished and humane studies of human failure or misunderstanding in which there is no immediate conflict between the miniaturist grace of the strokes and the cracks in the lives of people that they describe. I say "no immediate conflict," but recollect that François Truffaut walked out of *Pather Panchali*, wearied by such precise care. That incident strikes oddly, for both Truffaut and Ray are thought of as disciples of Renoir, and directors with unusual tenderness for their own characters. And Ray has had many admirers, especially in the West, where he is celebrated as a central figure of humanist cinema, a Chekhovian artist of great refinement, and a director worthy of E. M. Forster's *A Passage to India*. Perhaps the reference to Forster gives the game away, for it relies upon an essentially patronizing British view of India and on Forster's tragic confrontation of English tolerance and Indian mysticism. In fact, *A Passage to India* is a book about passion, unfathomable mystery, and hysteria beneath the Bloomsbury delicacy. I suspect that its wildness would have been as elusive for Ray as it was for David Lean.

For Ray was an aristocratic Indian, an admirer of European literature and music, and a filmmaker deliberately aimed at the art houses of the West by the Indian government. He was born into a distinguished Bengali family, the son of a writer, painter, and photographer. After reading economics at Calcutta University, he spent two years with Rabindranath Tagore studying painting. This was the period when he found himself creatively; the influences of Tagore and of traditional fine art have been abiding. Thus, the warmth of his literary conception is as undeniable as a remorselessly tasteful sense of composition. The camera is all too easily the tool of pictorialism and Ray had an inbred reluctance to broach that persistent calm. He worked in advertising as a visualizer and did some illustrations for an edition of the novel of *Pather Panchali*. Advertising took him to London where he was bowled over by *Bicycle Thieves*. That vindicated his interest in realism, in everyday stories, and in nonprofessional actors. On his return to India, he was further encouraged by meeting Renoir and searching locations for *The River*. But Ray did not work on that film and, while admiring it, thought it not typically Indian.

But what is an Indian film? Was Ray the West's notion of the worthy Indian artist? How did he relate to the vast, seething, naïve but censorious cinema for the Indian masses? How far did Ray seem to be working within one of the most agonized and contradictory countries in the world? It is not fair to blame Ray for smallness of subject, when Chekhov wrote country-house plays in the years before the Revolution. But Chekhov seems to feel external breezes, while Ray's world too often closed in on itself. A Bengali, he confessed to the impracticability of his pursuing neo-realism in modern Calcutta. Thus, while there is genuine and very moving individual pain in his work, there was not a great sense of India's turmoil.

For all the acclaim that greeted the Apu trilogy, his best early work seems to me to focus on women—*Devi, Charulata, Three Daughters, Mahanagar.* Invariably, the personal factor in his films is beyond reproach. He devises richly credible people, surveys them with true charity, and encourages his actors into unaffected revelation. His own interest in music and painting adds to the feeling that sheer taste is eliminating flavor. The question remains as to whether he really advanced in thirty years' work, or was the wonderful, beguiling skill and tenderness of, say, *Days and Nights in the Forest* simply a refinement of the first films?

Perhaps Ray was the victim of his origins; certainly that is often the predicament of his characters. For instance, *Jalsaghar*—a film about an aristocrat's inability to shed his heritage—relates the man's estrangement from reality to the obsession with art in a way that is more intriguing than the Apu trilogy. At various times—*Devi, The Philosopher's Stone*, and *The Adventures of Goopy and Bagha*—Ray resorted to Indian mythology. It is possible that that was truer material for what may be a visual sense torn between Western refinement and the profuseness of Indian art.

Ray once spoke of the Indian stress on detail, the pearl of dew that contains the world, and of the mystical references of that meticulousness, to be seen in the way extreme close-ups of cell life seem to describe passages from the Upanishads.

But can India's myriad stories still be referred to such models? The most encouraging aspect of Ray's later career was his troubled attempt to discover a modern Indian subject. *Company Limited* was about ambitious and successful young people in Calcutta; its human observation was sterner than Ray had usually managed, and there was a fresh sense of political background. *Distant Thunder* went further still. Set in 1942, it showed the effects of famine on Bengal. For the first time, Ray made a connection between the individual and the national plight.

The Middleman was a further exploration of the

muddle, corruption, and forgotten traditions of contemporary Calcutta, about a young man trying to make his way as an obliging assistant in the business jungle. But *The Chess Players* was a step backwards—into the safer, academic prettiness of the past. Taken from a Munshi Premchand story, it was Ray's first film with Hindi and English dialogue; it also had color, and the starry participation of Saeed Jaffrey and Richard Attenborough. It had two stories that reflected upon each other a little too obviously for the rather cozy sense of irony.

In the eighties, he was hindered by poor health, and left exposed by the variety of Indian cinema. Still, his stature was established, and there he was, on video and on his deathbed, the recipient of a special Oscar in 1991 for "rare mastery of the art of motion pictures and for his profound humanitarian outlook." The rhetoric had been earned, but Ray seemed more clearly than ever the projection of "our" India—not quite India's India.

Stephen Rea,

b. Belfast, Northern Ireland, 1949
There's something long-suffering, or self-denying, in Stephen Rea's presence that may have made him easy casting as the husband in *The End of the Affair* (99, Neil Jordan). Yet I wonder: could that film have been any less depressing or empty if Rea and Ralph Fiennes (the lover) had exchanged roles? Are there smothered feelings behind Rea's starched face, or just that creased, constipated look?

Trained for the stage, Rea came into pictures (after years in TV) at the behest of Neil Jordan in *Angel* (82). Thereafter, he did *Loose Connections* (83, Richard Eyre); *The Company of Wolves* (84, Jordan); *The Doctor and the Devils* (85, Freddie Francis); *Life Is Sweet* (91, Mike Leigh); earning an Oscar nomination as the IRA man in *The Crying Game* (91, Jordan); very good with Sinéad Cusack in *Bad Behaviour* (93, Les Blair); as Lovborg in a TV version of *Hedda Gabler* (93, Deborah Warner); *Angie* (94, Martha Coolidge); *Princess Caraboo* (94, Michael Austin); *Ready to Wear* (94, Robert Altman); *Interview with the Vampire* (94, Jordan); as the Russian cop in *Citizen X* (95, Chris Gerolmo); on TV in *Shadow of a Gunman* (95).

He had perhaps his best role, for TV, as Bruno Hauptmann in *Crime of the Century* (96, Mark Rydell); as the traitor in *Michael Collins* (96, Jordan); *Trojan Eddie* (96, Gillies Mackinnon); *The Van* (96, Stephen Frears); *The Last of the High Kings* (96, David Keating); *The Butcher Boy* (97, Jordan); *Fever Pitch* (97, David Evans); *Still Crazy* (98, Brian Gibson); as a terrorist in *The Break* (98, Robert Dornhelm), which began as his idea; *In Dreams* (99, Jordan); very good in *Guinevere* (99, Audrey Wells); *This Is My Father* (99,

Paul Quinn); as Cardinal Richelieu in *The Musketeer* (01, Peter Hyams); *Armadillo* (01, Howard Davies).

Ronald Reagan, b. Tampico, Illinois, 1911

It was the greatest career move in the history of entertainment—simple, audacious, revolutionary. Washed up as a movie actor, spun desert dry over the years on television, he had secured a West Coast daytime talk show, *Ask the Governor,* from 1966 to 1974. But he was vigorous and amiable still, and advertisers could imagine a bigger audience. He could learn lines overnight; even when he forgot them, he spoke naturally in movie-ese. Only occasionally did he confuse camera right and camera left, and his double-take recovery was an unfailing delight. His walk across the White House lawn, his cupping of a deaf ear to catch questions, his humble "Well . . ."—these strokes became epic. Babies had them down flat. And so, he made it as a nationwide series in which, for eight years, he played *Mr. President?—That's Me!*, amassing more camera time than anyone else in the Actors' Guild and deftly feeding the lines and situations of Warner Brothers in the 1940s back into world affairs.

He was a hugely successful and evasive president, as blind to disaster, iniquity, and humiliation as he was to the Constitution. And he was as lucky as he had been a loser in pictures. Thus, in the years 1981–88, America made a gentle transition—from nation to show—that disturbed no one's fun. Especially not the president's. If he ever woke in the night, or the day, and murmured "Why me?" to the nanny, he knew the answer—he'd have seen it in *Network:* "Because you're on television, dummy."

As a younger man, at Eureka College, he was as noted as an athlete as for his acting. He became "Dutch" Reagan, a sports commentator on local radio, and then worked for NBC. In 1937, Warners signed him up, and he had some ten years in B pictures first, then as a reliable support and a hero's stolid pal: *Love Is On the Air* (37, Nick Grinde); *Boy Meets Girl* (38, Lloyd Bacon); with his wife-to-be, Jane Wyman, in *Brother Rat* (38, William Keighley); *Cowboy from Brooklyn* (38, Lloyd); *Swing Your Lady* (38, Ray Enright); an insurance-claims adjuster in *Accidents Will Happen* (39, William Clemens); *Angels Wash Their Faces* (39, Enright); *Dark Victory* (39, Edmund Goulding); *Hell's Kitchen* (39, Lewis Seiler and E. A. Dupont); *Naughty But Nice* (39, Enright); *An Angel from Texas* (40, Enright); *Brother Rat and a Baby* (40, Enright); as footballer George Gipp, urging on the team as he fades away, "Just win one for the Gipper," in *Knute Rockne, All American* (40, Bacon); *Murder in the Air* (40, Seiler); as Custer in *The Santa Fe Trail* (40, Michael Curtiz).

In 1940, he and Jane Wyman were married (divorce was final in 1948, after her career had surged ahead of his and she was heard to lament his dullness). He was with Wyman in *Tugboat Annie Sails Again* (40, Seiler); *The Bad Man* (41, Richard Thorpe); a crack airman in *International Squadron* (41, Lothar Mendes); a piano player in *Million Dollar Baby* (41, Curtis Bernhardt); a newspaperman in *Nine Lives Are Not Enough* (41, Edward Sutherland); *Desperate Journey* (42, Raoul Walsh); a fruit picker in *Juke Girl* (42, Bernhardt); winning note and a catchphrase in *King's Row* (42, Sam Wood), playing a man whose legs are amputated and who comes round after the operation to ask, "Where's the rest of me?"

He entered the air force, but was prevented from combat mayhem by his short sight: he had very narrowed eyes from an early age, an attribute that could have cast him in villainy if there had been a spark of mischief. After the war, as his Rooseveltian attitudes hardened, he became president of the Screen Actors' Guild from 1947 to 1952. As such, he was a bureaucrat of McCarthyism, and a shortsighted searcher after redness. His acting career was foreshortened by office work (at least, that's the story): a vet in *Stallion Road* (47, James V. Kern); *The Voice of the Turtle* (47, Irving Rapper); *The Girl from Jones Beach* (49, Peter Godfrey); *The Hasty Heart* (49, Vincent Sherman); with Patricia Neal in *John Loves Mary* (49, David Butler); and *Night Unto Night* (49, Don Siegel).

He left Warners to free-lance: *Louisa* (50, Alexander Hall); with a chimpanzee in *Bedtime for Bonzo* (51, Frederick de Cordova); *Hong Kong* (51, Lewis R. Foster); *The Last Outpost* (51, Foster); the D.A. in *Storm Warning* (51, Stuart Heisler).

In 1952, he married the actress Nancy Davis—Madame Fulcrum—and appeared in *She's Working Her Way Through College* (52, H. Bruce Humberstone); as pitcher Grover Cleveland Alexander in *The Winning Team* (52, Seiler); *Law and Order* (53, Nathan Juran); *Tropic Zone* (53, Foster); *Cattle Queen of Montana* (54, Allan Dwan); *Prisoner of War* (54, Andrew Marton); *Tennessee's Partner* (55, Dwan); with Nancy Davis in *Hellcats of the Navy* (57, Juran).

This faltering career was helped out by his work as host on TV's *G.E. Theater* (54–61), and then *Death Valley Days* (65–66). (As president of SAG, he had assisted deals with MCA and others that made TV series more lucrative for producers.) His last movie role was as the villain in *The Killers* (64, Siegel), in which he slaps Angie Dickinson around—the manifest petulance of someone giving up the ghost.

But America and story were at hand. Rescue was managed. The rest would be history—and he did seem rested. To paraphrase Gore Vidal, the

wisdom and integrity of someone told where to stand and what to say for twenty years were made manifest. The fraudulence of the presidency was revealed so that the office could never quite be honored again.

Robert Redford,
b. Santa Monica, California, 1937
1980: *Ordinary People*. 1988: *The Milagro Beanfield War*. 1992: *A River Runs Through It*. 1994: *Quiz Show*. 1998: *The Horse Whisperer*. 2000: *The Legend of Bagger Vance*.

He went to the University of Colorado on a baseball scholarship and tried to become a painter before acting tempted him. Eventually he entered the AADA and made a stage debut in *Tall Story* in 1959 (as a baseball player). He then worked in TV and, apart from a small part in *War Hunt* (62, Denis Sanders), did not go into movies until *Situation Hopeless, But Not Serious* (65, Gottfried Reinhardt). His first important parts came in 1966 with *This Property Is Condemned* (Sydney Pollack), *Inside Daisy Clover* (Robert Mulligan), and as the hunted Bubber Reeves in *The Chase* (Arthur Penn). He seemed both decent and detached, sympathetic but disillusioned.

That promise has never been fully realized. There is some restraint in Redford that resists exploration of humor or anger, or even sex—all of which seem on his cards. After *Barefoot in the Park* (67, Gene Saks), which he had played on Broadway, he refused *Blue* and appeared in *Butch Cassidy and the Sundance Kid* (69, George Roy Hill). An immense success, that film offered a debilitating, modish glamour instead of real character. *Downhill Racer* (69, Michael Ritchie), about an obsessive skier, was so close to Redford's heart that he produced it himself, and *Tell Them Willie Boy Is Here* (69, Abraham Polonsky) used his natural reserve well.

But did he have the personality or interest to impress himself upon films as more than a handsome athlete? *Little Fauss and Big Halsy* (70, Sidney J. Furie) and *The Hot Rock* (72, Peter Yates) suggest not. And while looking every bit the Kennedyesque venturer into politics for *The Candidate* (72, Ritchie), he seemed overawed by the legendary resonance of *Jeremiah Johnson* (72, Pollack). His lonely trapper should have become elderly, solitary, and eccentric, but Redford retreated behind a bushier beard and makeup scars.

By the mid-seventies, cinemas were clotted with his effacing handsomeness. The enervated neatness of *The Way We Were* (73, Pollack) wasted an intriguing subject, while his fending off of reality helped to take any venom out of *The Sting* (73, Hill). It was a perfect fit of periods that he should inhabit the hollow shell of *The Great*

Gatsby (73, Jack Clayton). Fitzgerald's fascinating lacuna turned into an archetypal hollow man, so that the movie seemed a dilatory commercial for hair dressing, lawn fertilizers, and those absorbent tissues that take away difficulty. That we liked him so much was an unnerving sign of our need for tranquilizing actors. His third film for George Roy Hill was *The Great Waldo Pepper* (75).

It was not easy to swallow him as a minor operative in an obscure part of the CIA in *Three Days of the Condor* (75, Pollack), and that film's sinister intrigue never threatened Redford's anxious but lovely eminence. Playing Gatsby, his greatest failure had been his helpless gestures toward the social transformation the character had undergone. He seemed muscle-bound by gloss and charisma, unwilling or unable to tease his own godlike image—he was much less keen on risk or extravagance than Barbra Streisand.

How could he be a lowly reporter making good in *All the President's Men* (76, Alan J. Pakula)? Instead, he was one of nature's Galahads coming sweetly and inevitably to the surface to still the ugly disturbance of American politics. All credit to Redford for producing that movie, and for appreciating its commercial chance so early on. But melodramatic simplifications cruelly exposed the limits of his disquiet. Political paranoia can be a very naïve emotion in the mind of a great star. In the next two years, Redford delivered a bare half-hour of screen time, as a gallant officer in *A Bridge Too Far* (77, Richard Attenborough), for which, allegedly, he was paid $2 million.

He played in *The Electric Horseman* (79, Pollack) and *Brubaker* (80, Stuart Rosenberg). He then won the Oscar for best direction for *Ordinary People* (80), a decent, concerned, pained story told with grim restraint bordering on numbness.

Few observers dared notice the lack of character in *Ordinary People,* and Redford's status as icon was enhanced when he founded the Sundance Institute in 1981, a forum for independent filmmaking, a retreat and a resort, a way of thinking well of oneself, and eventually, a gift catalogue. Sundance has had its successes, and it embodies a view of the arts and nature that is sweetly Utopian. But Sundance is the kind of institution that seeks to sanctify the necessary rough edges and raw meat of American moviemaking. Its true destiny may be to provide the locus for a great satire.

Redford was a deeply mature baseball phenom in *The Natural* (84, Barry Levinson), one of the most unreal sports films ever made, not to mention its damage to Bernard Malamud—if Redford had done similar wrong to a bald eagle in public he would probably have had to shave his head in contrition. (What would he look like bald?) He was a very dapper "English" hunter in *Out of*

Africa (85, Pollack), this time carrying the ethos of the Banana Republic catalogue. *Legal Eagles* (86, Ivan Reitman) was a famous disaster and further proof of his paper-thin range as an actor.

Since then, he has been executive producer on *Promised Land* (88, Michael Hoffman) and *Some Girls* (89, Hoffman), projects that had grown out of Sundance. He directed *The Milagro Beanfield War* (88), a looser and more intriguing work than *Ordinary People.* He could do nothing to avert the commercial disaster of *Havana* (90, Pollack), and he did begin to look as if he'd spent an undue part of his more than fifty years out in the sun. He had his most interesting part for years in *Indecent Proposal* (93, Adrian Lyne), but the script was so undeveloped, and the sex so absent, we were left with time to see how far Redford resembled used wrapping paper.

In 1992 he also directed again—*A River Runs Through It*—a spectacular tribute to nature, running water, and fly-fishing, but also a movie of subtlety and force, with Brad Pitt giving a fine performance as just the kind of wild, dangerous kid Redford has never let himself play. As a director, Redford has improved, but as an actor he is as hidden as ever. If only he would play a scoundrel, an enemy to eagles—something more challenging than *Sneakers* (93, Phil Alden Robinson).

Instead, he was close to fatuous in *Up Close & Personal* (96, Jon Avnet) and followed everywhere by a nimbus of gold back-lighting in his own *The Horse Whisperer.* What was it that appealed in those aging male-dream roles? What permitted the sentimentalizing of his own appearance? After all, that would never have been tolerated in *Quiz Show*, the best and sharpest film he has directed, the last proof that he is awake and thinking, as opposed to dozing in his own dream. *The Legend of Bagger Vance* was one more dud, but then he seemed to regain an appetite for acting with two weird throwbacks: *The Last Castle* (01, Rod Lurie); *Spy Game* (01, Tony Scott).

Lynn Redgrave, b. London, 1943

When Lynn Redgrave won a supporting actress nomination for her fusspot Hungarian housekeeper to James Whale in *Gods and Monsters* (98, Bill Condon), she showed a kind of expertise that suggested she could have rivaled Thelma Ritter in nominations. But, in truth, it's a strange career, which includes several shows on American TV—*Not for Women Only, House Calls, Teachers Only,* and *Chicken Soup*—as well as commercials for weight reduction plans.

She is the younger sister of Vanessa and Corin Redgrave and the daughter of Rachel Kempson and Sir Michael. She has had a varied stage career, which includes playing Ophelia to Peter O'Toole's *Hamlet, Much Ado About Nothing, Hay Fever, Black Comedy, The Three Sisters, Mrs. Warren's*

Profession, and her one-woman show, *Shakespeare for My Father.*

In movies, she began with supporting roles in *Tom Jones* (63, Tony Richardson) and *The Girl with Green Eyes* (64, Desmond Davis) before her breakthrough in *Georgy Girl* (66, Silvio Narizzaro), taken from the Margaret Forster novel. It's a strange film, all the stranger in that there was a real romance between Redgrave and her male lead, James Mason.

Films followed, but there was no strong pattern: *The Deadly Affair* (67, Sidney Lumet); with Rita Tushingham in *Smashing Time* (67, Davis); *The Virgin Soldiers* (69, John Dexter); *Last of the Mobile Hot-Shots* (70, Lumet); *Every Little Crook and Nanny* (72, Cy Howard); *Everything You Always Wanted to Know About Sex (but Were Afraid to Ask)* (72, Woody Allen); *Don't Turn the Other Cheek* (73, Duccio Tessari), a comic spaghetti Western; *The National Health* (73, Jack Gold); as Xaviera Hollander in *The Happy Hooker* (75, Nicholas Sgarro); *The Big Bus* (76, James Frawley); *Sunday Lovers* (80, Bryan Forbes); *Morgan Stewart's Coming Home* (87, Alan Smithee, Paul Aaron); *Getting It Right* (89, Randal Kleiser); *Midnight* (89, Norman Thaddeus Vane); with her sister, Vanessa, in a TV remake of *What Ever Happened to Baby Jane?* (91, David Greene); as the wife to David Helfgott in *Shine* (96, Scott Hicks).

She has also been a regular in the TV series *Rude Awakening*, as the drunken mother. Her résumé is absurdly crowded still with minor work.

Sir Michael Redgrave (1908–85),
b. Bristol, England

As a young man, Redgrave seemed interested in and respectful of the cinema. His debut was the prancing musicologist in Hitchcock's *The Lady Vanishes* (38), a lively study of the ingenious idiot hero, too seldom investigated by Hitchcock. Apart from an interval during the war, he worked steadily in the British cinema in more than usually interesting parts. As well as three films for Carol Reed—*Climbing High* (39), *The Stars Look Down* (39), and *Kipps* (41)—he was the lighthouse keeper in *Thunder Rock* (42, Roy Boulting). He was in *The Way to the Stars* (45, Anthony Asquith) and *The Captive Heart* (46, Basil Dearden), and all aquiver as the ventriloquist whose dummy comes to life in *Dead of Night* (45, Cavalcanti).

After *The Man Within* (47, Bernard Knowles) and *Fame Is the Spur* (47, the Boultings), he went to America for the portentous *Mourning Becomes Electra* (47, Dudley Nichols), but stayed on for *Secret Beyond the Door* (48, Fritz Lang). In England he gave two excellent contrasted character studies: as the repressed teacher in *The Browning Version* (51, Asquith) and as the inane Worthing in *The Importance of Being Earnest* (52, Asquith).

But the British cinema smothered Redgrave's interest: apart from playing Barnes Wallis better than *The Dambusters* (54, Michael Anderson) deserved, bringing the necessary chill to Big Brother in *1984* (56, Anderson), and quavering deliciously in *Confidential Report* (55, Orson Welles), his alcoholic father in Losey's *Time Without Pity* (57) was his last worthwhile movie part.

He then drifted aimlessly from one guest spot to another, as if he lacked the stamina or concentration for a full-scale role. *The Quiet American* (58, Joseph L. Mankiewicz) was a failure, if not his fault. Otherwise he seemed oblivious of a film's nature or objectives: *The Sea Shall Not Have Them* (54, Lewis Gilbert); *Oh, Rosalinda!!* (55, Michael Powell); *Shake Hands with the Devil* (59, Anderson); *The Innocents* (61, Jack Clayton); *The Loneliness of the Long Distance Runner* (62, Tony Richardson); never better than in the film of the National Theatre's *Uncle Vanya* (63, Stuart Burge); as Yeats in *Young Cassidy* (65, Jack Cardiff and John Ford); *The Hill* (65, Sidney Lumet); *The Heroes of Telemark* (65, Anthony Mann); *Oh! What a Lovely War* (69, Richard Attenborough); *The Battle of Britain* (69, Guy Hamilton); and *David Copperfield* (70, Delbert Mann). His growing discomfort was put to some use as L. P. Hartley's little boy, still numb with shock at sixty, in *The Go-Between* (71, Losey).

Vanessa Redgrave, b. London, 1937

Vanessa Redgrave is over sixty now and a famous mother; she has outlasted the controversies she provoked—in the seventies especially, when she was an ardent supporter of the Palestinian cause. She has put on natural weight, and she seems a woman of mature years, if still vulnerable to young hopes and ideas. That mixture is rare. Jane Fonda—Redgrave's contemporary—has retired, still very trim, "young"-looking, but not as open. No one would claim that Fonda is Redgrave's equal as an actress. Redgrave is romantic, wayward, and—to judge by her autobiography—swept along by forgetfulness or wishful thinking. She has made mistakes, but there is a case for her as the best actress alive, ready for further challenge.

She was the daughter of Michael Redgrave and Rachel Kempson; she graduated from the Central School of Speech and Drama with a glowing reputation; she was tall, beautiful, and commanding. And she was devoted to the theatre. That helped keep her out of movies after a disastrous debut in *Behind the Mask* (58, Brian Desmond Hurst).

Eight years later, she reappeared, lovely yet not much more than emblematic as the wife in *Morgan* (66, Karel Reisz), and a brilliant human exclamation mark in *Blow-Up* (66, Michelangelo Antonioni), where she is no more than a photograph—yet angry, alarmed, with her arms rigorously folded over her breasts. She may have disliked Antonioni's indifference to character, but he saw how electric she could be.

She was Anne Boleyn in *A Man for All Seasons* (66, Fred Zinnemann), and gorgeous in *Camelot* (67, Joshua Logan), having an affair with Franco Nero that produced a child. She also had children (Natasha and Joely) by her marriage to director Tony Richardson for whom she made *The Sailor from Gibraltar* (67), where she was secondary to Richardson's new amour, Jeanne Moreau, and *The Charge of the Light Brigade* (68).

Isadora (68, Reisz) was meant as her breakthrough. She was Oscar-nominated for it, but she could not convey the élan of the dancer—Redgrave danced, seminude sometimes, but she seemed more sensual than aesthetic, and she stressed the elements of feminine liberation in the role. In the next ten years, she worked regularly but in unpredictable material, not a star, yet not quite a character actress: *The Seagull* (68, Sidney Lumet); *A Quiet Place in the Country* (68, Elio Petri); *The Devils* (71, Ken Russell); *Mary, Queen of Scots* (71, Charles Jarrott)—and another nomination; *The Trojan Women* (71, Michael Cacoyannis); and *Murder on the Orient Express* (74, Lumet).

She played Katherine Mansfield for British TV. She was in *Out of Season* (75, Alan Bridges); Lola Devereaux in *The Seven-Per-Cent Solution* (76, Herbert Ross); winning the best supporting actress Oscar as *Julia* (77, Zinnemann), in which she seems more radiant as she becomes crippled and hunted. When she received that Oscar, she spoke out against "Zionist hoodlums" and stirred up protest that is still not altogether gone. She also produced and appeared in a documentary, *The Palestinians* (77, Roy Battersby), and she was famous, and mocked, for being a member of the Workers' Revolutionary Party. Yet she did not give up on mainstream work—*Agatha* (79, Michael Apted) and *Yanks* (79, John Schlesinger).

She was unresolved as an actress and evidently far enough into her forties to be beyond romantic lead parts. Her politics ensured her many enemies, and her outspokenness was easily built into a proof of her being difficult. All the more reason therefore to stress that she quietly went about her business of being astonishingly skilled and versatile: *Bear Island* (80, Don Sharp); winning an Emmy as Fania Fenelon on TV in *Playing for Time* (80, Daniel Mann); *My Body, My Child* (82, Marvin J. Chomsky) for TV, about abortion; *Wagner* (83, Tony Palmer); *The Bostonians* (84, James Ivory); *Steaming* (85, Joseph Losey); outstanding as the troubled teacher whose calm is destroyed in *Wetherby* (85, David Hare); *Three Sovereigns for Sarah* (85, Philip Leacock), about the Salem witch trials; as the literary agent in *Prick Up Your Ears* (86, Stephen Frears); *Comrades* (86, Bill

Douglas); as Renee Richards in *Second Serve* (86, Anthony Page), handling the tennis and the sex change with tact and insight; *Consuming Passions* (88, Giles Foster); in the old Wendy Hiller role in *A Man for All Seasons* (88, Charlton Heston); making *Orpheus Descending* (90, Peter Hall) work by sheer force of imagination; with her sister Lynn in a TV remake of *Whatever Happened to Baby Jane?* (91, David Greene); *Young Catherine* (91, Michael Anderson); close to stumped in *The Ballad of the Sad Cafe* (91, Simon Callow); superb and fading as fine wisteria in *Howards End* (92, Ivory); and *A Wall of Silence* (93, Lita Stantic).

As a great lady of film, she has become vulnerable to casting and the strange notions of what a middle-aged woman is, or wants. But nothing has taken away her instincts: *The House of the Spirits* (93, Bille August), showing how bad the results can be; *They* (93, John Korty); *Storia di una Capinera* (93, Franco Zeffirelli); *Mother's Boys* (93, Yves Simoneau); *Great Moments in Aviation* (93, Beeban Kidron); *Little Odessa* (94, James Gray); *A Month by the Lake* (95, John Irvin); *Down Came a Blackbird* (95, Jonathan Sanger); *Mission: Impossible* (96, Brian De Palma); *Looking for Richard* (96, Al Pacino); the narrator to *The Wind in the Willows* (96, Terry Jones); *Two Mothers for Zachary* (96, Peter Werner); *Smilla's Sense of Snow* (97, August).

She was outstanding as the mother in *Wilde* (97, Brian Gilbert) and as *Mrs. Dalloway* (97, Marleen Gorris); *Déjà Vu* (97, Henry Jaglom); *Bella Mafia* (97, David Greene); *Deep Impact* (98, Mimi Leder); *Lulu on the Bridge* (98, Paul Auster); *Cradle Will Rock* (99, Tim Robbins); *Uninvited* (99, Carlo Gabriel Nero); *Girl, Interrupted* (99, James Mangold); *Toscano* (99, Dan Gordon); *Mirka* (99, Rachid Benhadj); *An Interesting State* (99, Lina Wertmuller); *If These Walls Could Talk 2* (00, Jane Anderson); *A Rumor of Angels* (00, Peter O'Fallon); as Raskolnikov's mother in *Crime and Punishment* (00, Golan Menahem); *The Pledge* (01, Sean Penn); the matriarch in *Jack and the Beanstalk: The Real Story* (01, Brian Hanson); *The Assumption of the Virgin* (02, Walter Salles).

Sir Carol Reed (1906–76), b. London

1935: *Midshipman Easy; It Happened in Paris* (codirected with Robert Wyler). 1936: *Laburnam Grove; Talk of the Devil.* 1937: *Who's Your Lady Friend?; No Parking.* 1938: *Bank Holiday; Penny Paradise.* 1939: *Climbing High; A Girl Must Live; The Stars Look Down.* 1940: *Night Train to Munich; The Girl in the News.* 1941: *Kipps; A Letter From Home.* 1942: *The Young Mr. Pitt.* 1943: *The New Lot* (d). 1944: *The Way Ahead.* 1945: *The True Glory* (codirected with Garson Kanin). 1947: *Odd Man Out.* 1948: *The Fallen Idol.* 1949:

The Third Man. 1951: *Outcast of the Islands.* 1953: *The Man Between.* 1955: *A Kid for Two Farthings.* 1956: *Trapeze.* 1958: *The Key.* 1960: *Our Man in Havana.* 1963: *The Running Man.* 1965: *The Agony and the Ecstasy.* 1968: *Oliver!.* 1970: *Flap/The Last Warrior.* 1971: *Follow Me.*

Reed began as an actor and then worked as stage manager for Edgar Wallace. At Ealing, he was an assistant to Basil Dean before moving on to his own pictures. In the late thirties and early forties, he made a number of modest films full of craft and good performances—*The Stars Look Down* (about Welsh miners), *Night Train to Munich* (nearly a sequel to Hitchcock's *The Lady Vanishes*), and *Kipps* (which starred his first wife, Diana Wynyard)—but subservient to conventions and English expectations of tidy realism. *The Way Ahead* was an inspirational piece of wartime propaganda and togetherness—totally at odds with the mood of *The Third Man*, which was just a few years ahead.

It was in the first few years after the war that Reed revealed himself: *Odd Man Out, The Fallen Idol,* and *The Third Man* were three winners in a row—with directing nominations for the latter two, and a knighthood in 1952. *Odd Man Out* was from a novel by F. L. Green, about an Irish rebel on the run. The movie begins with a sense of the real Belfast—harsh, Dickensian, and beautifully photographed by Robert Krasker—but as James Mason's wounded hero grows weaker and more delirious, so fantasy and expressionism take over. It is one of the greatest Irish films ever made, and as well as Mason's heartrending performance it has fine work from Robert Newton, Cyril Cusack, Kathleen Ryan, Robert Beatty, F. J. McCormick, and Denis O'Dea.

The Fallen Idol comes from a Graham Greene short story, made for Korda, a tragedy of how friendship between a boy and the butler in a large house destroys the butler's life. The house is alive with intriguing, perilous spaces (Georges Périnal was the cameraman); the narrative traps are excruciating; and Ralph Richardson is noble yet doomed as the butler. The tone may be straight Greene—that drip of mortification, of agony vindicated—but Reed served it with understanding.

Then there is *The Third Man,* a tour de force on postwar Vienna, once again from Greene, and for Korda (for Selznick, too, though he was always the potential spoiler to be kept at a distance). Reed acknowledged that Orson Welles had a lot to do with his own scenes, and Welles may have influenced the saturnine look of the film (Krasker again). But Welles was not the best casting (Noel Coward had been thought of): he gives Harry Lime more charm than Greene intended. There is a struggle between Greene's bleak attitude (poisoned penicillin for children) and the film's urge

to give people a lift (not just Welles, but the comedy and the zither).

Still, for decades *The Third Man* has worked as a mystery: you can smell the sewers, the fear, and the mistrust in Vienna. A time and a place were captured; scenario and locale were stirred, like cream going into dark coffee. Joseph Cotten and Holly Martin are from a writer's forgotten drawer. But Trevor Howard, Valli, and the wolfish Viennese faces tell the truth. *The Third Man* has one of the most intense atmospheres the screen has ever delivered—seeing it again always brings back the scent of the grandmother who took me to see it.

But then Reed ran out of steam, or need. *Outcast of the Islands* is a Conrad story, with Trevor Howard and Ralph Richardson, and it's effective. But *A Kid for Two Farthings* was insipid whimsy passed off as urban folklore; *Trapeze* was a tame rehearsal of the duel between Lancaster and Curtis actually achieved by Alexander Mackendrick; *The Key* is heavy with Carl Foreman's pretension. *Oliver!* was a hit (it won best picture and best direction), but it's awful and unrecognizable as the work of the man who made *Odd Man Out. Our Man in Havana* was even poor Greene. *The Agony and the Ecstasy* was a picturesque hoot.

If Reed had died in, say, 1950, then he would probably be treasured now as a great director. As it is, we can only puzzle over the complex of collaborators, timing, inspiration, and chance that made those three films in a row—perhaps the swan song of black-and-white's grandeur. The illegitimate son of actor Sir Herbert Beerbohm Tree, Reed had access to inner circles. Yet he was as diffident as a rich boy used to the company of servants.

Donna Reed (Donna Mullenger) (1921–86), b. Denison, Iowa

I have a soft spot for this lovely lady, since she it was who first impressed upon me the trade of whoring. Not that *From Here to Eternity* (53, Fred Zinnemann) ever refers to her part as anything other than a nice girl who sits on a sofa and talks to soldiers. In the 1930s, there would have been less shyness, and more skillful suggestions of the sexuality in James Jones's novel. But in the 1950s, Hollywood was suppressed sexually. As if conscious of a breakthrough to come, and nervous of the huge forces of reaction, sexy ladies in movies were often overdressed, tight-lipped, and genteel. A proof of this was the fact that Donna Reed should ever have been playing a whore. She was so plainly decent, wholesome, and romantic that Harry Cohn's personal casting of her in what was a major production bespeaks the system's inhibition (she was also married to one of his executives). So perhaps Donna Reed was only a twelve-year-old's whore, but I remember still the wondering way she stroked Montgomery Clift. Hollywood seemingly was affected by this hint of wantonness in so nice a girl and gave her the supporting actress Oscar.

It was years later that I discovered her Mary Bailey in *It's a Wonderful Life* (46, Frank Capra), the epitome of wholesomeness, loyalty, and the patient, small-town sweetheart. Donna Reed had the sure look of a first love that lasts forever. Yet she was pretty enough to be the classy whore in a Honolulu brothel. And she was the ideal embodiment of sensuality within the proper niceness that appealed to a twelve-year-old male imagination— for so long the gold in the hills of the movie business. There is a dream in American movies that the girl who looks like mother may be a sexual paradise—and that a slut is really a good girl: it's there not just in *From Here to Eternity,* but in such recent hits as *Risky Business* and *Pretty Woman.* Compare that abiding fantasy with the nearly savage psychological insights of Jean Eustache's *The Mother and the Whore,* and you begin to measure the odd way that Hollywood arouses and tranquilizes us at the same time.

She won a beauty contest and was taken up by MGM: *Babes on Broadway* (41, Busby Berkeley); *The Getaway* (41, Edward Buzzell); *Shadow of the Thin Man* (41, W. S. Van Dyke); *Eyes in the Night* (42, Zinnemann); *Calling Dr. Gillespie* (42, Harold S. Bucquet); *Apache Trail* (42, Richard Thorpe); *The Courtship of Andy Hardy* (42, George Seitz); *The Human Comedy* (43, Clarence Brown); *The Man from Down Under* (43, Robert Z. Leonard); *See Here, Private Hargrove* (44, Wesley Ruggles); *Gentle Annie* (44, Andrew Marton); overshadowed by Hurd Hatfield in *The Picture of Dorian Gray* (45, Albert Lewin); the nurse in *They Were Expendable* (45, John Ford); *Green Dolphin Street* (47, Victor Saville); *Beyond Glory* (48, John Farrow); *Chicago Deadline* (49, Lewis Allen); *Saturday's Hero* (51, David Miller); *Scandal Sheet* (52, Phil Karlson), and probably her best film; *The Caddy* (53, Norman Taurog); fetchingly disturbed in her bath by Phil Carey in *Gun Fury* (53, Raoul Walsh); *Trouble Along the Way* (53, Michael Curtiz); *They Rode West* (54, Karlson); *This Is My Love* (54, Stuart Heisler); as Liz Taylor's frosty sister in *The Last Time I Saw Paris* (55, Richard Brooks); as an Indian girl in *The Far Horizons* (55, Rudolph Maté); the wife in *The Benny Goodman Story* (55, Valentine Davies); *Three Hours to Kill* (55, Alfred Werker); *Ransom!* (56, Alex Segal); halfway aggressive in the interesting *Backlash* (56, John Sturges); *Beyond Mombasa* (57, George Marshall); and *The Whole Truth* (58, John Guillermin).

She did a great deal of television—notably *The Donna Reed Show* (1958–66), a commercial for niceness, and a brief life as Miss Ellie on *Dallas* (1984–85)—and she was in two TV movies: *The*

Best Place to Be (79, David Miller) and *Deadly Lessons* (83, William Wiard).

Christopher Reeve, b. New York City, 1952

On Saturday, May 27, 1995, in Virginia, riding the cross-country section of a three-day event, Christopher Reeve was thrown at the third fence. He landed on his head. He was unconscious for four days. His first and second cervical vertebrae were fractured. He was paralyzed, and seven years later the damage remains extensive. Since then, he has worked a little—as actor and director—and he has campaigned for further research into spinal injuries. In the SuperBowl telecast of January 2000, there was even an advertisement in which he stood and walked. But such superiority is the norm in those little movies.

Christopher Reeve was never a great or indelible actor, but his likability shone through, and that and his physique were all that Clark Kent and Superman needed. So Reeve became the star in a franchise where the dream of flying is the most important special effect. He got into other movies, but he was always regarded as a curiosity. Then fate, and irony, turned him into a real hero—and he made his most famous movies seem even more specious.

He worked in the theatre and on the soap opera *Love of Life* before movies—and he was effectively an "unknown" at the time of *Superman: Gray Lady Down* (78, David Greene); *Superman* (78, Richard Donner); *Superman II* (80, Richard Lester); *Somewhere in Time* (80, Jeannot Szwarc); *Deathtrap* (82, Sidney Lumet); out of his depth in *Monsignor* (82, Frank Perry); *Superman III* (83, Lester); *The Bostonians* (84, James Ivory); *The Aviator* (85, George Miller); as Vronsky, with Jacqueline Bisset, in a TV version of *Anna Karenina* (85, Simon Langton); *Street Smart* (87, Jerry Schatzberg)—his best film; *Superman IV: The Quest for Peace* (87, Sidney J. Furie), on which he helped write the story and did some second-unit directing; *Switching Channels* (88, Ted Kotcheff); *Noises Off* (92, Peter Bogdanovich); *The Remains of the Day* (93, Ivory); *Speechless* (94, Ron Underwood); *Village of the Damned* (95, John Carpenter); *Above Suspicion* (95, Steven Schachter).

Since his accident, for TV, he has directed *In the Gloaming;* played the old Jimmy Stewart role in a remake of *Rear Window* (99, Jeff Bleckner); and done *A Step Toward Tomorrow* (96, Deborah Reinisch).

Keanu Reeves, b. Beirut, Lebanon, 1965

Keanu Reeves has come through all the routine questions that seem to face a young, on-the-margins American movie actor. Questions like "What does that hair style mean?" "What sort of name is that?" "Where are you really from?" and "Are you for real?" By the time he was thirty,

Reeves had made around twenty films—some were forgettable, a few were very big hits, a few seemed beyond him; yet Reeves kept coming, the energy undaunted, his watchful face unclouded. As yet, maybe, he shows not too much of what it is like to be in your thirties—being thirty now for actors is akin to the difficulty of being forty for actresses. But Reeves has been good often enough to have earned respect.

He is the son of an English mother and a father of mixed Chinese and Hawaiian extraction. There are even rumors that "Kee-ah-noo" means "cool breeze over the mountains." He lived for a while in Australia, but was mostly raised in Canada, in Toronto, where he had his start in local TV and had a role in a picture called *The Prodigal* (84).

His progress was rapid: *Flying* (86, Paul Lynch); *Youngblood* (86, Peter Markle); outstanding as the kid who goes to the cops in *River's Edge* (87, Tim Hunter); *The Night Before* (88, Thom Eberhardt); as the hero's friend in *Permanent Record* (88, Marisa Silver); very good in *The Prince of Pennsylvania* (88, Ron Nyswaner); rather uneasy with costume and poised dialogue in *Dangerous Liaisons* (88, Stephen Frears); generating big money and funny in *Bill & Ted's Excellent Adventure* (89, Stephen Herek); *Parenthood* (89, Ron Howard); an assassin, with William Hurt, in *I Love You to Death* (90, Lawrence Kasdan), hovering between comedy and gravity; good again in *Tune in Tomorrow . . .* (90, Jon Amiel), adapted from Mario Vargas Llosa.

He was the undercover FBI man in *Point Break* (91, Kathryn Bigelow); reunited with Alex Winter for *Bill & Ted's Bogus Journey* (91, Peter Hewitt); rather in the shadow of River Phoenix (a close friend) in *My Own Private Idaho* (91, Gus Van Sant); as Harker, wide-eyed and helpless, in *Bram Stoker's Dracula* (92, Francis Coppola); laboring in *Much Ado About Nothing* (93, Kenneth Branagh); *Even Cowgirls Get the Blues* (93, Van Sant).

Then, in 1994, he went from Siddhartha in *Little Buddha* (Bernardo Bertolucci) to *Speed* (Jan de Bont). After the former, he needed the latter the way Harker needed blood transfusions. But at last he seemed grown up, not much short of tough, and potentially sexy. *Speed* is a vehicle, of course, but it required warmth and deftness in its playing, and Reeves kept the bus on a human and funny course.

Johnny Mnemonic (95, Robert Longo) was a misstep, but in the full-blooded *A Walk in the Clouds* (95, Alfonso Arau), he developed his romantic capacity and looked like the Indiana Jones in between River Phoenix and Harrison Ford. One could feel something like an old-fashioned heartthrob might be carried on his cool breeze.

He was in *Chain Reaction* (96, Andrew Davis); *Feeling Minnesota* (96, Steven Baigelman); *The Last Time I Committed Suicide* (97, Stephen T. Kay); game for everything in *The Devil's Advocate* (97, Taylor Hackford); and as Neo, one of the great millennial images, Valentino in black leather, in *The Matrix* (99, Andy and Larry Wachowski).

He has been downright serene since then (waiting for a *Matrix* sequel): *The Replacements* (00, Howard Deutch); *The Watcher* (00, Joe Charbanic); *The Gift* (00, Sam Raimi); *Sweet November* (01, Pat O'Connor); *Hardball* (01, Brian Robbins).

Serge Reggiani,
b. Reggio Emilia, Italy, 1922

Having come to France as a child, Reggiani went into films in his late teens. For half a dozen years after the war, in the mood of romantic pessimism, he was a handsome lead, especially good as the doomed man in *Casque d'Or* (52, Jacques Becker). He has worked on, but never again with the success he enjoyed in those years: *Nuit de Décembre* (39, Curtis Bernhardt); *Le Voyageur de la Toussaint* (42, Louis Daquin); *Le Carrefour des Enfants Perdus* (43, Leo Joannon); *Étoile sans Lumière* (45, Marcel Blistène); as the brother who commits suicide in *Les Portes de la Nuit* (46, Marcel Carné); and in Carné's unfinished *La Fleur de l'Age* (47); *Le Dessous des Cartes* (47, André Cayatte); *Manon* (48, H. G. Clouzot); as the Romeo figure in *Les Amants de Vérone* (48, Cayatte); *Au Royaume des Cieux* (49, Julien Duvivier); *Le Parfum de la Dame en Noir* (49, Daquin); as the soldier in *La Ronde* (50, Max Ophuls); *Secret People* (52, Thorold Dickinson); *Act of Love* (53, Anatole Litvak); *Napoléon* (55, Sacha Guitry); *Les Salauds vont en Enfer* (55, Robert Hossein); *Echec au Porteur* (57, Gilles Grangier); *Les Misérables* (57, Jean-Paul le Chanois); *Marie-Octobre* (58, Duvivier); *Tutti a Casa* (60, Luigi Comencini); *Paris Blues* (61, Martin Ritt); *Le Doulos* (62, Jean-Pierre Melville); *The Leopard* (63, Luchino Visconti); *Compartiment Tueurs* (64, Costa-Gavras); *Marie-Chantal Contre le Docteur Kha* (65, Claude Chabrol); *Les Aventuriers* (67, Robert Enrico); *La Vingt-Cinquième Heure* (67, Henri Verneuil); *Il Giorno della Civetta* (68, Damiano Damiani); *L'Armée des Ombres* (69, Melville); *Comptes à Rebours* (70, Roger Pigaut); *Les Caids* (72, Enrico); *Cat and Mouse* (75, Claude Lelouch); *Vincent, François, Paul et les Autres* (75, Claude Sautet); *Une Fille Consue de Fil Blanc* (77, Michel Lang); *Violette et François* (77, Jacques Rouffio); *Fantastica* (80, Gilles Carles); *The Beekeeper* (86, Theo Angelopoulos); *Mauvais Sang* (87, Leos Carax); and *I Hired a Contract Killer* (90, Aki Kaurismaki).

He appeared in *Plein Fer* (90, Josee Dayan), and then in *De Force avec d'Autres* (93), directed by his son, Simon Reggiani. He has also made *Rosenemil* (93, Radu Gabrea); *Le Petit Garçon* (94, Pierre Granier-Deferre); *Héroïnes* (97, Gerard Krawczyk); *La Clef des Champs* (98, Charles Nemes); *El Pianista* (98, Mario Gas).

Wallace Reid (1891–1923), b. St. Louis

There's no top Hollywood star we know less about today than Wallace Reid, because there's no single movie that defines him for us—and no single image. But he's a central figure in the story of American film, as well as the protagonist of one of the greatest tragedy/scandals ever to hit Hollywood. Think back to the great silent male stars: the comics, swashbuckling Fairbanks, sheik Valentino, passionate lover Gilbert, freak Chaney. Where's the great-looking all-American guy, the prototype of Gable, of Robert Redford, of Tom Cruise? It's Wallace Reid.

He was the son of a successful playwright, and grew up in the world of theatre, but he wasn't just a kid actor: he was a star athlete, a musician, a writer. And amazingly handsome. He seems to have appeared in at least 100 two- and three-reelers before he caught Griffith's eye and was given the small but highly visible part of the blacksmith in the 1915 *Birth of a Nation*—stripped to the waist. That did it. Immediately he became a leading man, then a star, summoned to Famous Players–Lasky (later Paramount) and trusted to play five times opposite their great catch from opera, Geraldine Farrar: in her *Carmen* (15, as Don Jose); *Maria Rosa* (16, Spanish again); *The Woman God Forgot* (17; Farrar is Tecsa, daughter of Montezuma, and Reid is the conquistador who loves her); *The Devil Stone* (17, nonsense about an emerald); the love interest (!) in *Joan the Woman* (17). De Mille was crazy about him, casting him as well in *The Golden Chance* (15), and the very different *Affairs of Anatol* (21), in which he's newly married to swanky Gloria Swanson but swarmed over by Bebe Daniels, Agnes Ayres, and Wanda Hawley. This was Schnitzler—dinner jackets rather than bare chests or the racing outfits he wore in a wildly successful series of car-racing dramas. (He was a superb driver in real life.) But he carried it off easily.

Few of his non–De Mille movies are very good, but he dominates them with his virile looks, energetic acting, and sunny, dependable nature that conceals an inner toughness. Maybe it's Gary Cooper he most resembles. (Apparently, the influential Elinor Glyn saw him on a set and announced, "My dear boy, you're really very wonderful to look at. And, besides, you know you have—It." This was long before she anointed Clara Bow and Antonio Moreno.) In 1923, the year of his death, a poll was taken of 37,000 high-school students across the country. The boys voted Fairbanks their favorite male star, the girls picked Valentino.

But Wallace Reid was number two with both sexes, a stunning demonstration of his mass appeal. Years later, Conrad Nagel tried to explain his unique popularity: "Wallace was the number-one box-office star, the King. And he was one of the most charming, most lovable, wonderful guys I've ever known. There wasn't the slightest bit of conceit in him. He never took himself seriously. No ego there at all." For half a dozen years he was the reigning male star, like the later King, Clark Gable, and like Gable he even affected fashion. In 1922, when men were all wearing detachable starched collars, Reid appeared in a soft white shirt. The Errol Collar people went to the Motion Pictures Producers' Association, crying, "Can't you do something about this? The collar manufacturers are being put out of business. Can't you get Wally Reid to wear a starched collar?" That's stardom!

In 1913 he had married costar Dorothy Davenport, a famously happy marriage, and had two children. He was generous, easygoing, unaffected by his fame. (He also liked a drink or two, and may have been more susceptible than the fan mags acknowledged to the countless women who pursued him.) Then he was in a train accident, was given morphine for the pain, and slowly became an addict. Finally, making a heroic effort, he went cold turkey, but the damage had been done and he slipped into a coma and died. This wasn't a seamy scandal, like Fatty Arbuckle's in 1921, or a sinister, unsolved crime, like the William Desmond Taylor murder of 1922. It was the drug death of Mr. Straight Arrow, and, wrote De Mille decades later, "the terrible shock of his death shattered the public's image of him and almost shattered Hollywood." Apparently, Reid had said to De Mille just before entering the sanitarium where he died, "I'll either come out cured or I won't come out."

After his death, his wife dedicated herself to publicizing the terrible story of his narcotics addiction in an attempt to warn others of the dangers of dope. His mother, Bertha Westbrook Reid, wrote a memorial book: *Wallace Reid: His Life Story*. She quotes many of the condolence letters she received, of which one will suffice:

> Naïve, playful, the soul of a boy in the body of a giant. Irresponsible, carefree, gentle-hearted, forgiving. With malice toward none, and limitless charity for all—Wallace Reid. The world is a fairer, lovelier place for us all to live in and the path to the Garden of God, plainer and the distance to everlasting joy and peace many weary miles less because God lent us your gifted, gladsome, loving lad for just a little while.
>
> —A Mother

That famous sob sister/scriptwriter/Hollywood know-all Adela Rogers St. Johns was perhaps the Reids' closest friend—he called her his mother confessor. In her memoirs, she speaks of him with passionate affection, and with fury at De Mille, whom she accuses of having exposed the naïve young man to every kind of temptation (though not directly to drugs). "What he did was constantly flaunt his philosophy of hedonism, of virtue begging pardon of vice, of wickedness as the *most fun* of anything. De Mille made Wally feel that his natural loving kindness and tenderness, his desire for true love, was ridiculous and immature and, again that horrid word that can somehow tempt and mortify people—unsophisticated." St. Johns and Dorothy Reid collaborated on a movie, *Human Wreckage,* that somewhat fictionalized the story of Wally's destruction, and they barnstormed it across the country, arousing women to band together to halt the drug wave. They didn't succeed, and they didn't succeed, either, in keeping the name of Wallace Reid prominent in film history. But that's where it belongs.

Rob Reiner (Robert Reiner),
b. Bronx, New York, 1947
1984: *This Is Spinal Tap.* 1985: *The Sure Thing.* 1986: *Stand By Me.* 1987: *The Princess Bride.* 1989: *When Harry Met Sally.* 1990: *Misery.* 1992: *A Few Good Men.* 1994: *North.* 1995: *The American President.* 1996: *Ghosts of Mississippi.* 1997: *I Am Your Child* (d) (TV). 1999: *The Story of Us.*

The son of comic actor and writer Carl Reiner, Rob moved with his family to Los Angeles in 1960. The son followed in the father's footsteps, doing stand-up comedy, writing for TV, and forming an improvisational group, The Session. He appeared in a few movies: *Enter Laughing* (67, Carl Reiner); *Halls of Anger* (70, Paul Bogart); *Where's Poppa?* (70, Reiner); and *Summertree* (71, Anthony Newley), which he helped write.

But he became a household figure as Michael Stivic, "Meathead," that steady liberal stooge and dogged straight man to Archie Bunker in *All in the Family.* That lasted from 1971 to 1978 and won him two Emmys. He worked outside that hot show, too: acting in *Thursday's Game* (74, Robert Moore) and *Fire Sale* (77, Alan Arkin); writing and beginning to produce—he launched the series *More Than Friends* in 1978, which starred his then wife, Penny Marshall.

As a director, Reiner is not unlike Michael Stivic: decent, self-effacing, reliable, and entertaining. Crushing praise? Not in these times. *Spinal Tap* was a novel debut. *Stand By Me* is sentimental but touching. *The Princess Bride* was unexpected. *When Harry Met Sally* was a sweet comedy about two cute people. *Misery* was much less than it might have been, because it settled for the basic character setup rather than a film about two tyrants, competing for authorship. There was a black comedy present in *Misery* that could have surpassed all of Reiner's easy laughs.

A Few Good Men was preposterous and rigged—why should that Marine colonel crack open so conveniently?—but it took a grim audience to resist having a good time. Reiner has that old, unbeatable sense of silly things that work. But he may be at that point where he needs to deliver something more lasting, and more rooted in life.

He acted again in *Sleepless in Seattle* (93, Nora Ephron). And kept up that work over the decade: *Bullets Over Broadway* (94, Woody Allen); *Mixed Nuts* (94, Nora Ephron); *Bye Bye, Love* (95, Sam Weisman); *The First Wives Club* (96, Hugh Wilson); *Mad Dog Time* (96, Larry Bishop); *For Better or Worse* (96, Jason Alexander); *Primary Colors* (98, Mike Nichols); *Ed TV* (99, Ron Howard); *The Muse* (99, Albert Brooks).

As a director, he seemed more struck (or poleaxed) by the notion that niceness could save the world. It is a pretty thought, but one that stifles so many human and social realities. And so his work turns to pie in the sky with "good" and "bad" all too clearly labeled. He's carried along by a fundamental decency and a sense of scenes that play. But his films are predictable from their first moments, and they begin to establish a weird, dumb orthodoxy—that if we're good to our kids everything will be okay. This is not true. Life is more interesting.

Karel Reisz (1926–2002)
b. Ostrava, Czechoslovakia
1958: *We Are the Lambeth Boys* (d). 1960: *Saturday Night and Sunday Morning.* 1964: *Night Must Fall.* 1966: *Morgan: A Suitable Case for Treatment.* 1968: *Isadora.* 1974: *The Gambler.* 1978: *Who'll Stop the Rain?/Dog Soldiers.* 1981: *The French Lieutenant's Woman.* 1985: *Sweet Dreams.* 1990: *Everybody Wins.* 2000: *Act Without Words 1* (s) (TV).

If ever there was thought to be a northwest passage to moviemaking in Britain, Reisz was its pathfinder. Having arrived in Britain shortly before the war, he served in the Czech squadron of the RAF and then read chemistry at Cambridge. He was a member of the *Sequence* group, the first critical attempt in Britain to look for moral earnestness in cinema; in 1953, he published *The Technique of Film Editing,* a curiously unenthusiastic, if helpful, book; he was, briefly, programs officer of the National Film Theatre, and by the mid-1950s he was a leading figure in the Free Cinema movement. It is difficult now to decide what that movement stood for. The aim of showing and celebrating everyday life is one that TV was already wolfing down whole. Realism, by 1956, was an archaic mode, and yet for a few years in Britain it became a proof of social and political seriousness. In attaching itself to the "angry" movement and to the Campaign for Nuclear Disarmament, it constituted one of the most irrelevant of artistic breakthroughs that England has suffered.

Of the three directors involved in the movement, Lindsay Anderson was the most talented, Tony Richardson the most dispensable, and Reisz the most unresolved. He directed, with Richardson, *Momma Don't Allow* (55), produced Anderson's *Every Day Except Christmas* (57), and made *We Are the Lambeth Boys*, arguably one of the most dated "innovations" in all cinema. He did seem impressed by the obscure glory of Vanessa Redgrave in *Morgan*, where she was meant to be a trivial person beside the looming self-pretension disguised as pathetic Idiot of the David Mercer/David Warner/Morgan. *Isadora* is a clumsy failure, confused in chronology, hampered by a gangling actress playing a natural mover, and uncertain how seriously to deal with the earnest vulgarity of its heroine. His other films are woefully ideological: *Saturday Night and Sunday Morning* could now pass for parody; *Night Must Fall* helped set back the career of Albert Finney by several years.

It was at least enterprising of Reisz to make a move to America. On *The Gambler*, Reisz neither caught nor tamed the pretentious but authentic existentialism of James Toback's script, and finished with a strangely inert movie. *Who'll Stop the Rain?* proved his most interesting film, reasonably true to Robert Stone's novel and digging fine performances out of Nick Nolte and Tuesday Weld. *Who'll Stop the Rain?* was a failure in its time, but it has survived very well, and it has an uncommonly truthful eye for compromised lives and sudden danger.

Back in England, Reisz could not conceal the strangeness of *French Lieutenant's Woman* (a work torn between being genteel and crazy), and he could not make useful sense of the modern, mirroring part of the story. Startling once, it is unwatchable now. *Sweet Dreams* was a decent, small picture, reliant on Jessica Lange. *Everybody Wins*, however, needed patience in (or restraints for) its very sparse audiences if it was to complete a single showing. The film has credentials—Arthur Miller's script; Nick Nolte trying to ignore the chaos; Debra Winger hoping to change identities as she changes clothes. It is so dire it may have a life as a midnight movie in ages yet to come.

Lee Remick (1935–91),

b. Quincy, Massachusetts

Lee Remick had a fine entry in movies: as tit-bouncing Southern drum majorette advancing on a low-angle camera in *A Face in the Crowd* (57, Elia Kazan). And despite a Bostonian upbringing, she was for several years a Hollywood Southerner, forever fretting at the heat. It was interesting to

see how far she excelled in parts of modest literary origin, but seemed vapid as Faulkner's women. She could do nothing to overcome the addled conception of *The Long Hot Summer* (58, Martin Ritt), in which she played Eula Varner, or the monstrous waste of *Sanctuary* (61, Tony Richardson), where she took on Temple Drake.

However, she gave a deeply suggestive performance as the (raped?) wife in *Anatomy of a Murder* (59, Otto Preminger). That has a wonderful moment in court when she shakes down her hair and takes off her spectacles at which the jury audience wavers like chaff in the sensual breeze. The next year, she was very touching as the anxious Tennessee girl warmed back to life by Montgomery Clift in *Wild River* (60, Kazan). That admirably exploited the rather tense expression on her face whenever it was not smiling hard.

Such promise was never properly gathered together. Too many dull films allowed her to slip toward obscurity: rather monotonous in *Experiment in Terror* (62, Blake Edwards); again deeply pathetic as the alcoholic in *The Days of Wine and Roses* (63, Edwards); *The Running Man* (63, Carol Reed); *The Wheeler Dealers* (63, Arthur Hiller); good in *Baby, The Rain Must Fall* (65, Robert Mulligan); *The Hallelujah Trail* (65, John Sturges). Then, after she had played the blind girl in Arthur Penn's Broadway production of *Wait Until Dark* in 1966, *No Way to Treat a Lady* (68, Jack Smight), and *Hard Contract* (69, S. Lee Pogostin). She went to Britain, but was uncomfortable in the demanding worlds of Iris Murdoch and Joe Orton: *A Severed Head* (70, Dick Clement) and *Loot* (70, Silvio Narizzano). After that, she played in *Sometimes a Great Notion* (71, Paul Newman); *The Blue Knight* (73, Robert Butler); and *A Delicate Balance* (74, Tony Richardson).

She had a popular success as Jennie Jerome/Churchill for TV, a graceful enough bearer of costume to sustain the small screen's old-fashioned reverence for "real" people in hackneyed fiction. Again for TV, she was a rather too attractive Maria Gostrey opposite Paul Scofield in *The Ambassadors*. In the cinema, she was not more than a bystander in *Hennessy* (75, Don Sharp), the register of horror in *The Omen* (76, Richard Donner), helpless in both *Telefon* (77, Don Siegel) and *The Medusa Touch* (78, Jack Gold). She passed honorably for English, opposite Robert Duvall, in the TV drama *Ike* (78, Melville Shavelson) and appeared in *The Europeans* (79, James Ivory).

She was in *Tribute* (80, Bob Clark); she made a very good shot at being Margaret Sullavan in *Haywire* (80, Michael Tuchner); *The Competition* (80, Joel Oliansky); *The Women's Room* (80, Glenn Jordan); in the Bette Davis role for TV in *The Letter* (82, John Erman); *The Gift of Love: A Christmas Story* (83, Delbert Mann); *A Good Sport* (84,

Lou Antonio); *Rearview Mirror* (84, Antonio); *Toughlove* (85, Jordan); *Of Pure Blood* (86, Joseph Sargent); *The Vision* (87, Norman Stone); *Jessie* (88, Jordan); *Bridge to Silence* (89, Karen Arthur); and *Dark Holiday* (89, Antonio).

Jean Renoir (1894–1979), b. Paris

1925: *La Fille de l'Eau.* 1926: *Nana.* 1927: *Charleston; Marquitta.* 1928: *La Petite Marchande d'Allumettes* (codirected with Jean Tedesco); *Tire-au-Flanc.* 1929: *Le Tournoi dans la Cité; Le Bled.* 1931: *On Purge Bébé; La Chienne.* 1932: *La Nuit de Carrefour; Boudu Sauvé des Eaux.* 1933: *Chotard et Compagnie.* 1934: *Madame Bovary; Toni.* 1935: *Le Crime de Monsieur Lange; La Vie est à Nous* (codirected with Jean-Paul le Chanois, Jacques Becker, Andre Zwoboda, Pierre Unik, and Henri Cartier-Bresson). 1936: *Une Partie de Campagne* (s); *Les Bas-Fonds.* 1937: *La Grande Illusion.* 1938: *La Marseillaise; La Bête Humaine.* 1939: *La Règle du Jeu.* 1940: *La Tosca* (begun by Renoir, but completed by and credited to Karl Koch). 1941: *Swamp Water.* 1943: *This Land Is Mine.* 1944: *Salut à la France* (codirected with Garson Kanin) (d). 1945: *The Southerner.* 1946: *The Diary of a Chambermaid.* 1947: *The Woman on the Beach.* 1951: *The River.* 1952: *La Carrozza d'Oro/The Golden Coach.* 1955: *French Can Can.* 1956: *Eléna et les Hommes.* 1959: *Le Déjeuner sur l'Herbe.* 1961: *Le Testament du Dr. Cordelier.* 1962: *Le Caporal Épingle.* 1971: *Le Petit Théâtre de Jean Renoir.*

It is easy to take a sentimental view of Jean Renoir, to settle for the conclusion that he was an admirable man, despite the implication of his films that good men are as inconsistent as bad. We are readily charmed by his Octave in *La Règle du Jeu*, as glad to be urged this way and that as the household guests who respond to his boisterous direction by participation. But Octave is as much a muddler as any of the other characters, and we do the film an injustice if we miss Octave's heartbreak or his inadvertent instigation of the fatal accident.

The extraordinary interweaving of laughter and tears is not so much warming as a warning to tread warily in life. Recollect the title, and it becomes clearer that Renoir is reproducing the fraught indecisiveness of the game. *La Règle* is thus the first great realization that the openness of cinema lends itself to the chaos of experience. The "rule" is that there are no rules. That may be why the film alarmed the French bourgeoisie as war drew nearer.

Again, his jolly country restaurateur in *Partie de Campagne* easily seems like a sign of Renoir's fatherly care of a film crew in the country. In fact, *Partie* was dogged by miserable weather and bitter quarrels among its makers. I make these points not to suggest that Renoir is anything but the greatest of directors, only to free his greatness from the cloak of charm that could settle on it as fatally as Octave's coat fell on André Jurieu's back in the frenzy of garment changing at the end of *La Règle.*

Of course, Renoir was a humanist, but how could an audience, or the artist himself, relax in that knowledge? Self-conscious humanism is inflationary—it is the ersatz integrity of John Ford, Stanley Kramer, and Capra—and we should insist that Renoir is an intelligent, feeling man. Only that hard fact properly establishes the artistic achievement of charity and tolerance in his films. Renoir would be a trite director if the beauty of his films did not grow naturally out of sadness, anger, disappointment, and failure. Now that he is dead, it is increasingly necessary to describe his dark side, to remember his hesitations, and to be clear about the creative dangers in his way of making films. For Renoir's greatness lies in his repeated desire to take risks, to make new sorts of film, to be experimental.

We know how Renoir grew up in the midst of a creative household. There are enough portraits, shining with affection, of the child Jean by the father Auguste for us to think of Jean as an extraordinary fruit of French culture, carrying the rich Romantic impetus on to the new form of popular theatre. Auguste painted his son like a peach, and we can sense from those portraits the large curve of maturation, ripeness, and decline that comprises Jean's tender acknowledgment of time rupturing stability. And the essentially nonintellectual character of the Renoir family, with its emphasis on manual crafts, self-made entertainment, the pleasures of the table, *la campagne* as opposed to Paris, has a lot to do with Renoir's happy acceptance of the *conte* as his basis for films. Thus, he liked simple incidents and their fusion with popular theatre and never chose to go beyond elementary narrative forms. The depth in his films is all a matter of the exact way of looking at people. There was never, for instance, the supposedly "original" narrative flavor of a Carné in Renoir's films, and that is why for so many years Renoir was neglected.

But it is important to note the ways in which Jean departed from Auguste, and to allow for the strains that may have existed in their relationship, and that are to be felt beneath the surface of *Renoir, My Father,* the biography Jean wrote in 1958, at about the time his own career as a director ended. That coincidence is instructive, for *Renoir, My Father* is about an aging artist and father. Auguste was fifty-three when Jean was born, and it was Jean who attended him during his last years when the father was crippled by arthritis. Auguste was not a saint, and we should try to imagine the sharp-faced old man of photographs in old age, rather than some vague, benevolent soul. Auguste painted beauty, despite his own pain. But he is not a great artist because the suffering is not felt in his work. Moreover, Jean must have seen the antagonism between his father's art and life. Not only his father's habitual disrobing of the family servants to act as models—but the early sense that he was himself both a real child in a real family, and an imaginary figure in the art of a painter. When we note the interplay of life and theatre in Renoir's later films, it should be referred back to that experience of being an artist's son (and model).

As if inextricably affected by that upbringing, Jean married his father's last model, Catherine Hessling, and was then led to cinema by his desire to photograph her. And out of Auguste's history of subtly organizing his household so that it was forever prompting him to paint, so Jean's films are often logical and uncomplicated pretexts for filming people and places that he knew. Perhaps his greatest innovation as a director was in the way of naturalism: building up a little story around, say, Michel Simon, prepared always to bend the plot material to the impulse of actors, the exigencies of situation and mood.

La Chienne, Boudu, and *Toni* are all insignificant little melodramas, given an unexpected vigor and depth by a sense of momentary occasion in the filming, influenced in part by Abel Gance (as witness the window scenes in *La Roue* and *Partie de Campagne*). The congealing melodramatic cliché of American and German cinema was broken by Renoir's saying to himself: Boudu throws himself into *this* river on this day and is seen by Lestingois on the other side of *that* street. To embrace the crucial moment, Renoir withdrew his camera from the expressive close-ups of melodrama and showed the events. By doing so, he discarded all the rigidities of genre and allowed his characters to seem like figures in a theatre of life.

Theatricality always fascinated Renoir: he accepted very obvious plots and encouraged flamboyant acting, especially performances of the whole body. What produced the glorious tension of his films was the naturalism of the cinematography, so that during the 1930s there is not an adventure in natural light, camera movement, depth of focus, real location, or the blending of interior and exterior that Renoir did not make.

The Renoir retrospective at London's National Film Theatre in 1962 amounted to the clearest revelation of the nature of cinema that I have ever had. Again, joy for the medium should not hide Renoir's melancholy. Nor should we be swayed by his attempt to immerse himself in the populist spirit: *Lange, La Vie est à Nous,* and *La Marseillaise* (especially) have great things, but the collab-

orative message is not as convincing as the clear gulfs between friends that are reasserted in *La Grande Illusion* and *La Règle du Jeu.* The heartbreaking spatial relationship between Fresnay and von Stroheim in which duty has to destroy friendship, and the demented fusion of farce and tragedy in *La Règle,* are unrivaled commentaries on the irresolvable confusion of life.

Nor should we underrate Renoir's own presence in *La Règle* as another victim of that Cupid who has wings so that he may fly away again. *La Règle* is still the most dynamic juxtaposition of moods and feelings that cinema has achieved. Thus the shoot is a slaughter in which we do not lose sympathy for the killers. All of the leading characters are felt from moment to moment as being possessed of nobility and foolishness, wisdom and meanness. And as the château is filmed in such depth, with so many briefly revealed perspectives, we see how helplessly people try to hold on to their own nature, almost urging on tragedy as a way of imposing a solution from outside. Renoir is a master at suggesting the frightening flux in a man's mind as he has to decide between one course or another, and at showing how action is sometimes taken haphazardly simply to evade that abyss.

La Règle is a comedy of manners, a romantic melodrama, an invasion of life by theatre, but also a nod backwards toward *L'Age d'Or,* Buñuel's scathing view of society made nine years before. The links are sly but provocative. There is Gaston Modot in both, as a man obsessed by a woman; in *La Règle* he is a gamekeeper, the casual assassin of *L'Age d'Or;* there is a social gathering crazily interrupted, and Renoir's Octave remembers a conductor, perhaps the one in *L'Age d'Or* who was unbearably moved by Wagner and staggered away through the garden?

Renoir in America is still misunderstood. In one sense, he was clearly lost, bewildered by American production and shy of urban America. But that led to two masterpieces. *The Southerner* is his first excursion into gentle epic, the first poetic generalization of people, the first unflawed resort to a philosophy of endurance. Incidentally, it shows up the dishonesty of so much American "rural" cinema and suggests that Renoir might have been the man to film Faulkner. *The Diary of a Chambermaid,* however, is his darkest film, a harrowing miniature of evil that manages still to be airy, gay, and to be lifted by the prettiness of Paulette Goddard. It returns to the rather whimsical notion of a world that might be shared one day, but it is darkened by Francis Lederer's villain. Too easy to say that all Renoir's people have their own reasons, when Lederer stands as a reasonable but utterly malign figure.

Renoir was not a rationalist but an emotionalist. Better to say that all his characters have their own feelings, and it is that shared experience that brings them physically together but that keeps them apart—what *La Règle du Jeu* refers to as "the exchange of two fantasies and the coming together of two epidermises." That is the true severity of Renoir, the recognition of physical need and emotional incompatibility. Here too, Renoir has helped to define cinema, preeminently the form that shows the confrontation of human exteriors but that leaves the interiors to our imagination.

The reason to rejoice in his work is in the way Renoir came to terms with that truth. After the war, he seems to have faltered and it was five years before he filmed again. *The River* is seldom seen and still referred to critically with great reservations. As if modest actors could sap a film that took so warm a view of people. The river is a potent image for Renoir—remember *Boudu* and *Partie de Campagne*—but, in India, Renoir learned its value as a mystical symbol, of continuity in the face of all local, human tragedy. *The River* is not too interested in people as individuals—which is to show how far Renoir had come from the 1930s—but in their relationship with time and the regenerating creativity of nature. From that eminence, Renoir went on to two films that show life and love as theatrical performances. Again, only distance allows the pain to be observed calmly. *French Can Can* never conceals the hurt that Danglars brings to women, but never doubts the pleasures that his work offers the world. Chronic self-expression is its subject, as it is for Anna Magnani in *The Golden Coach*, and as it has always shown in Renoir's sympathy for actors, whether Michel Simon's Boudu or Barrault's extraordinary Opal/Cordelier. Renoir's cinema, too, is infectious, and a dictionary should note its supreme influence, most notably on Truffaut and Godard, but still active for anyone who wishes to see.

Renoir asks us to see the variety and muddle of life without settling for one interpretation. He is the greatest of directors; he justifies cinema. But he shrugs off the weight of "masterpieces" or "definitive statements." The impossibility of grasping final solutions or perfect works is his "rule." In *Renoir, My Father*, and in his own autobiography, *My Life and My Films*, Jean clearly adopts his father's wish to float on life like a cork. That same stream carries Boudu away to freedom, wrinkles with pain at the end of *Partie de Campagne*, overflows and endangers precarious existence in *The Southerner*, and is meaning itself in *The River:*

The river runs, the round world spins
Dawn and lamplight, midnight, noon.
Sun follows day, night stars and moon.
The day ends, the end begins.

Alain Resnais, b. Vannes, France, 1922

1948: *Van Gogh* (d). 1950: *Gauguin* (d); *Guernica* (d). 1953: *Les Statues Meurent Aussi* (codirected with Chris Marker) (d). 1955: *Nuit et Brouillard* (d). 1956: *Toute la Mémoire du Monde* (d). 1957: *Le Mystère de l'Atelier Quinze* (codirected with Marker) (s); *Le Chant du Styrène* (d). 1959: *Hiroshima, Mon Amour*. 1961: *L'Année Dernière à Marienbad/Last Year at Marienbad*. 1963: *Muriel*. 1966: *La Guerre est Finie*. 1967: *Loin du Vietnam* (codirected with Jean-Luc Godard, Joris Ivens, William Klein, and Claude Lelouch). 1968: *Je t'Aime, Je t'Aime*. 1974: *Stavisky*. 1977: *Providence*. 1980: *Mon Oncle d'Amérique*. 1983: *La Vie est un Roman*. 1984: *L'Amour à Mort*. 1986: *Mèlo*. 1989: *Je Veux Rentre à la Maison*. 1993: *Smoking; No Smoking*. 1997: *On Connaît la Chanson/Same Old Song*.

Resnais has made fifteen feature films in forty years, and has confessed sometimes to wondering where a next picture might come from. Is this sparseness the result of an uncompromisingly difficult artistic personality, or does Resnais pursue complexity at the expense of self-expression? It is all very well to claim that Resnais is dedicated to the immense subjects of time and memory, and then adopt his rather pusillanimous defenses of his own films. Those same topics loom very large in, say, *Citizen Kane, Lola Montès*, and *Vertigo*, all of which are rather more humanly engaging than *Muriel*. And when asking whether screen events are real or imaginary, I prefer the erotic wit of *Belle de Jour* to the enervating High Vogue solemnity of *Marienbad*. In short, I have the feeling that Resnais's seriousness is more elevated than his use of film, and that he has shown himself unable to make a communicative contact with audiences.

That failure is hard to reconcile with his origins, but I would still point to it as one of the several contradictions in his career. Resnais is sometimes presented as a movie-mad child. In his early teens he is reported to have made two 8mm films, one a schoolboy version of *Fantomas*. And in a fascinating interview with Richard Roud he referred to the primitive longing for moving images:

> I never dreamed of being a film director when I was young, but when I saw the first Ginger Rogers/Fred Astaire dance numbers (or maybe it was even before, with Dick Powell and Ruby Keeler), I suddenly had a strong, even violent, desire to make films. Those dance numbers had a kind of sensual movement which really took hold of me, and I remember thinking I would like to make films which had the same effect upon people, that I wondered if I could find the equivalent of that exhilaration.

Roud gamely asserted that Resnais's films did partake of that exhilaration, but one has only to think of the swooping camera of Demy to feel the weight of consideration on Resnais's traveling shots and to recall his stress on talk.

Resnais originally wanted to be an actor, and he joined IDHEC as a would-be editor, partly to retain contact with the world of actors. He left IDHEC without completing a course and for the first few years after the war made films privately. That suggests independent means and an isolationist mentality. The private works include two fiction films, one of which—*Schema d'une Identification* (45)—had Gérard Philipe in its cast. But the bulk of these films were "visits to" painters, made, Resnais admits, to meet them: thus there are documentaries on Hans Hartung, Max Ernst, Felix Labisse, Lucien Coutard, and others.

These studies of painting pushed him into professional work with a study of Van Gogh, followed by documentaries on Gauguin and Picasso's *Guernica*. All of these seem to me conventional celebrations of painting. But in the 1950s, Resnais began to produce some intriguing documentaries, most of which were derived from vigorous, literary scripts. The best of these are *Nuit et Brouillard* and *Toute la Mémoire du Monde*, which, I would argue, are among his most compelling films. Their impersonality seems truly a reflection of Resnais and something required by the material. It might be difficult to make a dull film of Auschwitz, but much harder to produce one as judicious as *Nuit et Brouillard*.

Time, clearly, is the structure of that film, while in *Toute la Mémoire*—a film about the Bibliothèque Nationale—Resnais grasped the surrealist futility of archives and made the library a Borges-like image of our obsession with memory. It is worth noting that his grand camera style was inaugurated in these films, and that it worked more happily with landscapes, rows of huts, and bookshelves than in the features where people are all too often posed semblances of human personality, alienated by the awesome puzzles of time and space.

Herein may lie the real direction of Resnais's intelligence. He has always professed a liking for science fiction, and the cool, methodical enquiry of those two documentaries does have a futuristic quality, like that of a machine unable to respond to narrative or character but immensely intelligent. *Je t'Aime* is his most uncompromising piece of science fiction, enough to make *Marienbad* look equally futuristic, and to remind us that science fiction is often borne on curiously sparse artistic sensibilities: thus Jules Verne is imaginative, but a characterless writer. I would suggest that Resnais's features have not overcome that sort of imbalance and that his efforts to produce warmth and anecdote have usually pushed him into an oddly cold fever reminiscent of women's-picture material. All of his features treat romance with a surprising

banality, while the most romantic—*La Guerre est Finie*—looks like an attempt to escape his own nature.

The contradictions are troubling. *Nuit et Brouillard* was based on the imperative not to forget, yet in 1961 Resnais's growing emphasis on emotional forgetfulness produced this odd statement: "If one does not forget, one can neither live nor function. The problem arose for me when I made *Nuit et Brouillard*. It was not a question of making yet another war memorial, but of thinking of the present and the future. Forgetting ought to be constructive." That seems to lead to an interest in time more philosophical than dramatic, more a matter of sophistry than of personal response. His first three features seem to me avid, overwrought melodramas imposed upon by a heavy but speculative interest in temporality. Again, there is a contradiction in the way, after *Hiroshima*, Resnais spoke like a stranger of the possible direction the characters might take after the last frame. That sort of objectivity—offered again with *Marienbad*—and the erroneous faith in real life detract from the artist's paramount concern with what happens within the film. It is also flatly challenged by this statement from Marguerite Duras, scenarist of *Hiroshima*:

> Before shooting his film, Resnais wanted to know everything about the story he would tell, and about the story he would not tell. As to the characters we were dealing with, he wanted to know everything about them: their youth; their lives before the film and, up to a point, their future after the film ends. Therefore I did biographies of my characters. And Resnais translated those biographies into images, as though he was conveying a film that already existed from the previous lives of those characters.

The discrepancy between such preliminary thoroughness and the subsequent open-mindedness is a sign of Resnais's dependence upon writers—Duras, Alain Robbe-Grillet, Jean Cayrol, Jorge Semprun, and Jacques Sternberg—and of the doubts that arise as a philosophical attitude rather than as an artistic statement. It is a confusion to think of movie characters having actual lives. Just as cinema exploits real people—actors and actresses—so its characters are kidnapped by the fantasies of the audience. The variation in Resnais's style—from the elaborate tracking shots of *Marienbad* to the static, fragmented *Muriel*—is deliberate and schematic and not something that arises naturally from the subject. The anguish in Resnais films, and the women who suffer it, are too often held back from us by the deadly intelligence of the approach. It is something that afflicts Virginia Woolf and sometimes drains experience out of the work, as if it were vulgar. The emotional relationships in Resnais's work are invariably denied the present tense—but strongest when recollected, or invented. The love scenes in *La Guerre est Finie* are the exception to that: lush, sensual, and trying to compensate for the cerebral emphasis elsewhere.

The resort to English-speaking actors in *Providence* seemed no problem for Resnais; he may have had more difficulty with David Mercer as a scenarist. Mercer likes to wear away at his characters with their guilts and fears; Resnais generally regards such things as elements of a pattern. *Providence* is a fascinating project, sumptuously realized: a dying novelist in a dark house where the phantoms of family memory and a new novel mingle together. But it took the cruel amusement of John Gielgud's best-ever film acting to make the pattern gripping. Elsewhere, it seems an intellectual construction, lacking the humor required and, as ever, willing to treat its women as mannequins in the cold avenues of memory.

Over eighty now, and still working, Resnais is in need of serious reappraisal. Several of the earlier films are hard to track down now—*Muriel*, especially. Also, much of the recent work has seemed caught between intellectual theory and conventional melodrama. Yet *Mèlo* seems to me the best of his recent films by far, the one in which formal intricacy is most devoted to character and feeling. It may yet emerge as a pattern that Resnais has been constantly torn between artistic aspirations and a deeper sense of old-fashioned dramatic impact. But should the struggle be closer to being settled? Still, *Providence* grows as time passes. Once upon a time, Emmanuelle Riva in *Hiroshima* was the emblem of Resnais's work. But now I think of Gielgud's novelist, torn between bodily pain and the rapture of invention.

Fernando Rey (Fernando Casado Arambillet Vega) (1917–94), b. La Coruña, Spain

Is there a tastier piece of internal rhyming in the history of cinema than the way, in the early seventies, the serene insouciance of Fernando Rey served as both the archetypal bourgeois gentleman for Luis Buñuel, wondering if dinner would ever be served, and the ungraspable Frog One, Alain Charnier, ready to serve everyone, in *The French Connection*? What's more, the politeness, the discretion, he exhibited for Buñuel was so very close to the modest wave of the hand that teased Gene Hackman for being on the wrong side of the subway window.

Manners maketh the man, whether he is a bishop, a pillar of respectability, or the blackest scoundrel ever photographed—for the movies note surfaces first. In that sense, Fernando Rey is unrivaled as an ambiguous front, a bystander waiting to be charged, or canonized. And as the bearer of one of the screen's great mustaches with the pubic triangle of beard, he is always poised on the brink of being exposed as fraud or lecher. Until then, of course, he is to be trusted with valuables, daughters, and intimate confessions. He would have made a very fine Clare Quilty—and a perfect Humbert. Imagine a Buñuel film where Rey takes both roles, with a different Lo in every shot. After all, the mystery of *That Obscure Object of Desire* is held in place, lovely yet unanswerable, by Fernando's pious and steadfast inability to see the switch that keeps occurring.

Now, the IMDb lists well over two hundred works, film and television, in which Rey worked, or let the light slip off his surface. There's a way in which he might have been in every film ever made, and simply assigned his ghosts—like George Sanders, Marcel Dalio, Adolphe Menjou, Dennis Price, et cetera—to those beyond his reach. So we must be stringent with our selection. Suffice it to say that before 1940 Rey studied architecture at the University of Madrid, fought for the Republican Army in the Civil War, and made a few movie appearances, but then really settled in (as a beautiful young man) after 1945.

He was in *La Pródiga* (46, Rafael Gil); *La Princesa de los Ursinos* (47, Luis Lucia); with Maria Félix in *Mare Nostrum* (48, Gil); *Locura de Amor* (48, Juan de Orduna); *Aventuras de Juan Lucas* (49, Gil); *Cielo Negro* (51, Manuel Mur Oti); *La Señora de Fátima* (51, Gil); *La Laguna Negra* (52, Arturo Ruiz Castillo); *Cómicos* (54, Juan Antonio Bardem); *Billete par Tánger* (54, Ted Leversuch); *El Amor de Don Juan* (56, John Berry); *El Cantor de México* (56, Richard Pottier); *El Andén* (57, Eduardo Manzanos Brochero); *La Venganza* (57, Bardem); *Heaven Fell That Night* (57, Roger Vadim).

Fluent in French and English, he was well suited to "international" production: *The Last Days of Pompeii* (59, Mario Bonnard); *Sonatas* (59, Bardem); with Lex Barker in *Mission in Morocco* (59, Anthony Squire); *Culpables* (60, Castillo); *Teresa* (60, Alfredo B. Crevenna); in the Rhonda Fleming epic, *Revolt of the Slaves* (61, Nunzio Malasomma); and then Don Jaime in *Viridiana* (61, Luis Bunuel).

He was Bokan, the Usurper in *Goliath Against the Giants* (62, Guido Malatesta); *The Running Man* (63, Carol Reed); *The Ceremony* (63, Laurence Harvey); *Échappement Libre* (64, Jean Becker); *La Nueva Cenicienta* (64, George Sherman); *Son of a Gunfighter* (65, Paul Landres); Worcester in *Chimes at Midnight* (65, Orson Welles); Goldginger himself (this is not made up) in *Due Mafiosi contro Goldginger* (65, Giorgio Simonelli)—big G was an evil genius who sought to turn all government employees into drones; on TV in support in *Don Quijote* (66, Jacques Bourdon and Louis Grospierre); in an Eddie Constantine picture, *Attack of the Robots* (66, Jesus Franco); *Return of the Seven* (66, Burt Kennedy); with Burt Reynolds in *Navajo Joe* (66, Sergio Corbucci); as the king in *El Greco* (66, Luciano Salce); and the king again in *Cervantes* (66, Vincent Sherman).

Enough kings and you get a castle: *Run Like a Thief* (67, Bernard Glasser and Harry Spalding): *The Immortal Story* (68, Welles); *Land Raiders* (69, Nathan Juran); *Un Sudario a la Medida* (69, José María Elorrieta); *The Adventurers* (70, Lewis Gilbert); and then, sublime in the chaos— *Tristana* (70, Buñuel), with Catherine Deneuve; *Il Prezzo del Potere* (70, Tonino Valerii); *Aoom* (70, Conzala Suarez); *Trinity Sees Red* (71, Mario Camus); *A Town Called Hell* (71, Robert Parrish), as Old Blind Man; and *The French Connection* (71, William Friedkin), where he is suave and suaver.

After *The Light at the Edge of the World* (71, Kevin Billington), he did *La Duda* (72, Gil); *Zanna Bianca* (72, Lucio Fulci); *The Discreet Charm of the Bourgeoisie* (72, Buñuel); *Un Camino* (72, Jorge Darnell); Lepidus in *Antony and Cleopatra* (73, Charlton Heston); *Tarots* (73, José María Forqué); *Pena de Muerte* (73, Jorge Grau); *Challenge to White Fang* (74, Fulci); with Deneuve in *La Femme aux Bottes Rouges* (74, Juan Luis Buñuel); *Alle Origini della Mafia* (74, Enzo Muzii); *French Connection II* (75, John Frankenheimer); *Illustrious Corpses* (76, Francesco Rosi); *A Matter of Time* (76, Vincente Minnelli); *Striptease* (76, Germán Lorente); *El Segundo Poder* (76, Forqué); *Seven Beauties* (76, Lina Wertmuller).

He won awards for *Elisa, Vida Mía* (77, Carlos Saura); and eternity for *That Obscure Object of Desire* (77, Buñuel); *Le Dernier Amant Romantique* (78, Just Jaeckin); *Rebeldía* (78, Andrés Velasco); *Quintet* (79, Robert Altman); *Memorias de Leticia Valle* (79, Miguel Angel Rivas); *Caboblanco* (80, J. Lee Thompson); *El Crimen de Cuenca* (80, Pilar Miro); *La Dame aux Camélias* (81, Mauro Bolognini); *Monsignor* (82, Frank Perry); *Cercasi Gesù* (82, Luigi Comencini); as the dry policeman in *The Hit* (84, Stephen Frears); *Un Amour Interdit* (84, Jean-Pierre Dougnac); *Saving Grace* (85, Robert M. Young); *Rustlers' Rhapsody* (85, Hugh Wilson); *Padre Nuestro* (85, Francisco Regueiro); *Hôtel du Paradis* (86, Jana Bokova); *Commando Mengele* (86, Andrea Bianchi); *L'Été 36* (87, Yves Robert), *El Túnel* (87, Antonio Drove); *Captain James Cook* (87, Peter Yeldham).

Closing in on seventy, he still labored: *Moon Over Parador* (88, Paul Mazursky); *Diario de Invierno* (88, Regueiro); *La Bahía Esmeralda* (89, Franco); *Naked Tango* (90, Leonard Schrader); *Diceria dell' Untore* (90, Beppe Cino); on TV as the Don in *El Quijote de Miguel de Cervantes*

(91, Manuel Gutiérrez Aragón); *Después del Sueño* (92, Camus); *1492: Conquest of Paradise* (92, Ridley Scott); *La Marrana* (92, José Luis Cuerda); *Madregilda* (93, Regueiro).

Burt Reynolds (Burton Leon Reynolds Jr.), b. Waycross, Georgia, 1936

In the years from 1973 to 1980, Burt Reynolds was always in the top ten box-office attractions. In 1978, he was the most popular actor in America. Yet he worried: he wanted more respect, better material; he wanted to be like Cary Grant. His films came nowhere near Cary Grant, and Burt without his mustache (but with his rug) could look grim and shifty. Nevertheless, in his ongoing interview (and he is a great, helpless talker), he showed that he was smarter and funnier than his films led anyone to expect. It was an intriguing dilemma. But people who worry over respect seldom get it; those who own it do not notice it.

Reynolds was unable to find the strength to do without the sexual admiration he despised. He was a footballer when young; he retained a disciplined physique; and his grin made him the natural heir to Clark Gable, swaggering authority. His love life was sung in the gossip papers, and once Burt posed nude for a *Cosmopolitan* centerfold— with sweet, demure taste. He says now that that was a mistake, but he says it so often that he doesn't help us forget it. I have seen him on a TV talk show, in front of a daytime devotion of women, struggling to define his earnest intentions. Opportunity faces him with the question, "How important to you is directing?" His face is taut: "Oh, it's the best . . ." Then the knowing smirk slips in. "Well, the second-best sensation I've ever known." Howls of glee from the ladies, and another chance is squandered. What the ladies don't know, and even Burt may have forgotten, is that that afterthought was scripted: it comes from *Deliverance* where Burt's character says exactly the same thing about shooting rapids.

Reynolds was quarterback for Florida State University, and he might have played for the Baltimore Colts but for an accident. Still, he tried being a stuntman and that took him into movies and TV. His small-screen personality was based in shows like *Riverboat, Hawk,* and *Dan August;* it carried on in talk shows and regular appearances on the *Tonight* show.

His movie career developed slowly, and it is notable that he was most comfortable in unprestigious pictures where he was able to explore the possibilities of a shrewder-than-average good ol' boy, without much competition: *Angel Baby* (61, Paul Wendkos); *Operation C.I.A.* (65, Christian Nyby); *Sam Whiskey* (68, Arnold Laven); *Impasse* (68, Richard Benedict); *Caine* (68, Samuel Fuller); *100 Rifles* (69, Tom Gries); *Skullduggery* (69, Gordon Douglas); *Deliverance* (72, John

Boorman); *Fuzz* (72, Richard A. Colla); *Shamus* (72, Buzz Kulik); *White Lightning* (73, Joseph Sargent), the debut of Gator McKlusky; *The Man Who Loved Cat Dancing* (73, Richard C. Sarafian); as a football-playing convict in *The Longest Yard* (74, Robert Aldrich); very good in *Hustle* (75, Aldrich) as a cop made edgy by Catherine Deneuve as the whore he loves; *W.W. and the Dixie Dancekings* (75, John G. Avildsen); *Lucky Lady* (75, Stanley Donen); *At Long Last Love* (75, Peter Bogdanovich), in which he nearly carried off clumsy song-and-dance amateurishness; *Gator* (76), which he directed himself as an unequivocal adolescent daydream; *Nickelodeon* (76, Bogdanovich); *Smokey and the Bandit* (77, Hal Needham), a drive-in recordbreaker; *Semi-Tough* (77, Michael Ritchie); *The End* (78), a well-intentioned but spasmodic attempt at a taboo subject; *Hooper* (78, Needham), in which he plays a stuntman; and *Starting Over* (79, Alan J. Pakula).

By 1980, Burt Reynolds was slipping away from being a major box-office figure. He made many forgettable pictures, and he had a prolonged illness. But he seemed more relaxed, not least in his marriage to Loni Anderson, and he began to acquire the comic technique he had often talked about. In short, he improved—a remarkable claim in American film nowadays—as is evident most of all in the TV series, *Evening Shade,* where he could be a delight. The films are: *Smokey and the Bandit II* (80, Needham); *Rough Cut* (80, Don Siegel); *The Cannonball Run* (81, Needham); *Sharky's Machine* (81), which he directed; *Paternity* (81, David Steinberg); *The Best Little Whorehouse in Texas* (82, Colin Higgins); *Best Friends* (82, Norman Jewison); *The Man Who Loved Women* (83, Blake Edwards); *Stroker Ace* (83, Needham); *Smokey and the Bandit III* (83, Dick Lowry); *Cannonball Run II* (84, Needham); *City Heat* (84, Richard Benjamin), with Clint Eastwood; *Stick* (85), which he directed, from Elmore Leonard's novel, and which is quite funny; *Heat* (87, R. M. Richards); *Malone* (87, Harley Cokliss); *Rent-a-Cop* (88, Jerry London); *Switching Channels* (88, Ted Kotcheff); *The Dancer's Touch* (88, William A. Fraker); *Physical Evidence* (89, Michael Crichton); *Breaking In* (89, Bill Forsyth), in which he is as good as he has ever been; *Modern Love* (90, Robby Benson); and *Cop-and-a-Half* (93, Henry Winkler).

When the time came for breakup with Loni Anderson, there was still an edginess in Reynolds that made for a tabloid mess of rare proportions.

Reynolds is now sixty-five after the busiest time of his life—he had eight credits in 1999 alone. Not that the story is cheerful. He has had his first Oscar nomination, for *Boogie Nights* (97, Paul Thomas Anderson). He has become white-haired. Yet, for the most part, he is caught in a pattern of

banal action films, few of which are properly opened or reviewed. There's not much doubt that he could be better. He is, by now, a more accomplished performer than many people who still have leads. But he is actually the grim personification of a kind of bottom-of-the-barrel work that is made chillingly appealing in *Boogie Nights.* He has directed a few more times—*The Man from Left Field* (93), *Hard Time* (98), *The Last Producer* (00)—and I'm sure he knows more than most of his directors. But even a select record makes sad reading: *The Maddening* (95, Danny Huston); *Striptease* (96, Andrew Bergman); *Citizen Ruth* (96, Alexander Payne); *Mad Dog Time* (96, Larry Bishop); *The Cherokee Kid* (96, Paris Barclay); *Meet Wally Sparks* (97, Peter Baldwin); *Bean* (97, Mel Smith); *Crazy Six* (98, Albert Pyun); the director of the CIA in *Universal Soldier II* (98, Jeff Woolnough); *Stringer* (99, Klaus Biedermann); *Mystery, Alaska* (99, Jay Roach); *Big City Blues* (99, Clive Fleury); *The Crew* (00, Michael Dinner); *Driven* (01, Renny Harlin); *The Hollywood Sign* (01, Sonke Wortmann); *Hotel* (01, Mike Figgis); *The Hermit of Amsterdam* (01, Rudolf van den Berg).

Debbie Reynolds (Mary Frances Reynolds), b. El Paso, Texas, 1932

Educated in Burbank, Debbie Reynolds was a French-horn and bassoon player in the Burbank Youth Symphony Orchestra and Miss Burbank of 1948. She has few rivals for cheerfulness and bounce. François Truffaut has already eulogized the moment in *Singin' in the Rain* (52, Stanley Donen and Gene Kelly) when, at the end of a vigorous dance routine, she has the presence of mind to restrain her disordered skirt so that her knickers will not show.

She was always a competent dancer and singer in a succession of musicals: *The Daughter of Rosie O'Grady* (50, David Butler); playing but being dubbed by Helen Kane in *Three Little Words* (50, Richard Thorpe); *Singin' in the Rain* and *Give a Girl a Break* (53) for Donen; *I Love Melvin* (53) and *The Affairs of Dobie Gillis* (53) for Don Weis; *Susan Slept Here* (54) and *Say One for Me* (59) for Frank Tashlin; *Hit the Deck* (55, Roy Rowland); Charles Walters's *The Tender Trap* (55) and *The Unsinkable Molly Brown* (64); and Gower Champion's *My Six Loves* (63).

Toward the end of the 1950s, she became bogged down in sentimentality in *Tammy and the Bachelor* (57, Joseph Pevney); *It Started with a Kiss* (59, George Marshall); and *The Mating Game* (59, Marshall). But she is a versatile comedienne and her acting built up over the years with Richard Brooks's *The Catered Affair* (56); Blake Edwards's *This Happy Feeling* (58); *The Rat Race* (60, Robert Mulligan); excellent in Minnelli's *Goodbye Charlie* (64); in Curtis Harrington's

What's the Matter with Helen? (71); as well as in her own engaging television show (1969–70).

She was in *Sadie and Son* (87, John Llewellyn Moxey) and *Perry Mason: The Case of the Musical Murder* (89, Christian I. Nyby II); and she took a small role in *Heaven and Earth* (93, Oliver Stone).

Bounce hit the skids in the 1990s. In 1997, Debbie and her small neighborhood casino in Las Vegas had to file for bankruptcy; it had been her hope to mount a Hollywood museum there. She was pretty good in *Mother* (96, Albert Brooks), but after that she was working to survive, playing herself on *Hollywood Squares* and doing a voice on *Rugrats*. There was *In & Out* (97, Frank Oz); a voice in *Fear and Loathing in Las Vegas* (98, Terry Gilliam); *Zack and Reba* (98, Nicole Bettauer); *Halloweentown* (98, Duwayne Dunham); *The Christmas Wish* (98, Ian Barry); *A Gift of Love: The Daniel Huffman Story* (99, John Korty); *Virtual Mom* (00, Laurie Lynd); and then—the coup de grace—playing "Piper Grayson" in a would-be TV sit-com called *These Old Broads,* in which her costars were Elizabeth Taylor, Joan Collins, and Shirley MacLaine.

Ving (Irving) **Rhames**, b. New York, 1959

On a few occasions—like *Pulp Fiction* and the Don King biopic—Ving Rhames has soared into areas of humor and fantasy that were unexpected, but emphatically right. If, much more of the time, he has been simply a stalwart—as a sidekick, a cop, or a heavy—that testifies to the limits set upon all actors, black or otherwise. But there is some magic in Rhames, some impulse (as witness the way he passed his Golden Globe to Jack Lemmon) that begs to be used.

He studied at the State University of New York, Purchase, and at Juilliard, and it was in those days that friend Stanley Tucci gave him the name "Ving." He made his debut in *Go Tell It on the Mountain* (84, Stan Latham) and carried on with *Native Son* (86, Jerrold Freedman); *Patty Hearst* (88, Paul Schrader); *Casualties of War* (89, Brian De Palma); *The Long Walk Home* (90, Richard Pearce); *Jacob's Ladder* (90, Adrian Lyne); *Flight of the Intruder* (90, John Milius); *Homicide* (91, David Mamet); *The People Under the Stairs* (92, Wes Craven); *Stop! Or My Mom Will Shoot* (92, Roger Spottiswoode); *Bound by Honor* (93, Taylor Hackford); *Dave* (93, Ivan Reitman); *The Saint of Fort Washington* (93, Tim Hunter).

He was Marsellus Wallace in *Pulp Fiction* (94, Quentin Tarantino); *Drop Squad* (94, Clark Johnson); *Kiss of Death* (95, Barbet Schroeder); *Mission: Impossible* (96, De Palma); *Striptease* (96, Andrew Bergman); *Dangerous Ground* (97, Darrell James Roodt); *Rosewood* (97, John Singleton); winning that Golden Globe as Don King in *Only in America* (97, John Herzfeld); *Body Count* (98, Robert Patton-Spruill); *Out of Sight* (98, Steven

Soderbergh); *Entrapment* (99, Jon Amiel); *Bringing Out the Dead* (99, Martin Scorsese); *Mission: Impossible II* (00, John Woo); as Johnnie Cochran on TV in *American Tragedy* (00, Lawrence Schiller); *Holiday Heart* (00, Robert Townsend); *Baby Boy* (01, Singleton); *Sins of the Father* (02, Robert Dornhelm); *Little John* (02, Dick Lowry); *Undisputed* (02, Walter Hill); *RFK* (02, Dornhelm); *Dark Blue* (02, Ron Shelton).

Christina Ricci,
b. Santa Monica, California, 1980

For years now, it seems, with or without effects makeup, Christina Ricci has been like our Shirley Temple on leaving the asylum where Frances Farmer was ruined. Except that, at the age of twenty-two, this flat-stare actress continues to show astonishing skill, the drive to make over thirty films, and the urge to be her own producer. The next few years will be crucial in determining whether she has the ideas and the range for a big career, or whether she was "just" a teen phenomenon (and one of the most accurate portraits of that mindset ever dared by American movies). Whatever the case, there are young women who hold to Christina Ricci as an attitudinal model.

How she got a proper education is hard to say, she was working so much. Let's just say that wisdom (seeking shelter) clung to her. She made her debut in *Mermaids* (90, Richard Benjamin) and followed it with *The Hard Way* (91, John Badham) and really established herself as the chilly Wednesday in *The Addams Family* (91, Barry Sonnenfeld) and *Addams Family Values* (93, Sonnenfeld); *The Cemetery Club* (92, Bill Duke); helpless to rescue *Casper* (95, Brad Silberling); *Now and Then* (95, Lesli Linka Glatter); *Gold Diggers: The Secret of Bear Mountain* (95, Kevin James Dobson); *Bastard Out of Carolina* (96, Anjelica Huston—her mother twice!); *Last of the High Kings* (96, David Keating); *That Darn Cat* (97, Bob Spiers); superb in *The Ice Storm* (97, Ang Lee); disturbingly grown up in *Buffalo 66* (98, Vincent Gallo); *Fear and Loathing in Las Vegas* (98, Terry Gilliam); another breakthrough in *The Opposite of Sex* (98, Don Roos); *Desert Blue* (99, Morgan J. Freeman); *I Woke Up Early the Day I Died* (98, Aris Iliopulos); *Pecker* (98, John Waters); *200 Cigarettes* (99, Risa Bramon Garcia); with Johnny Depp in *Sleepy Hollow* (99, Tim Burton); *Bless the Child* (00, Chuck Russell); *The Man Who Cried* (00, Sally Potter); *The Laramie Project* (02, Moises Kaufman); *Pumpkin* (02, Anthony Abrams and Adam Larson Broder); *Miranda* (02, Marc Munden); *The Gathering* (02, Brian Gilbert); *Anything Else* (03, Woody Allen); and in a project she had nursed through serious delays—*Prozac Nation* (03, Erik Skjoldbjaerg).

Miranda Richardson,

b. Southport, England, 1958

Is it because of her innate, nearly shifty, capacity to alter herself and to become anyone, that Miranda Richardson is not yet as famous as she deserves? There are actresses with far more obvious claims to a place in this book—Ashley Judd, Barbara Hershey, and Ellen Barkin, I suppose—yet the declared principles of opinion and particularity (not to say eccentricity) opt for Ms. Richardson instead. Why? She is brilliant, wayward, unpresumptuous, and uncanny. If that verdict seems an exaggeration, I suspect that any American observer would be taken further aback still to see all of her British TV work—to say nothing of her performances in radio drama, the medium she prefers and finds most challenging.

Her debut in film remains her best-known work: as white as bone china, wounded in lipstick, flighty, cold, desperate, and bitter as Ruth Ellis in *Dance With a Stranger* (85, Mike Newell). Since then, she has done *The Innocent* (85, John Mackenzie); she was wildly funny, sexy, and disturbing in *After Pilkington* (86, Christopher Morahan); *The Death of the Heart* (86, Peter Hammond); *Underworld* (86, George Pavlou); *Eat the Rich* (87, Peter Richardson); riveting in *Empire of the Sun* (87, Steven Spielberg), playing an upper-class woman whose façade of respectability breaks down; *Ball Trap on the Cote Sauvage* (89, Jack Gold); *The Bachelor* (90, Roberto Faenza); *The Fool* (90, Christine Edzard); as the crippled agent in *Twisted Obsession* (90, Fernando Trueba); wonderfully composed, yet seething, in *Old Times* (90, Simon Curtis); *Enchanted April* (91, Newell); two faces of terrorism in *The Crying Game* (92, Neil Jordan); the wife in *Damage* (92, Louis Malle)—the best character in the film, yet the most disruptive, for she reminded us of emotional reality. Her confrontation scene with Jeremy Irons blows away the entire flimsy and vicious proceedings. She was also in *Century* (93, Stephen Poliakoff); and the maddened wife in *Tom and Viv* (94, Brian Gilbert), which won her an Oscar nomination.

The nomination seemed to act as an advertisement in America—so her range widened: *Fatherland* (94, Christopher Menaul); *The Night and the Moment* (94, Anna Maria Tato); as the kidnapped woman in *Kansas City* (96, Robert Altman); *The Evening Star* (96, Robert Harling); the writer in *Swann* (96, Anna Benson Gyles); *Saint-Ex* (97, Anand Tucker); *The Designated Mourner* (97, David Hare); Pamela Flitton in *A Dance to the Music of Time* (97, Christopher Morahan and Alvin Rakoff); mysteriously cast but a delight in *The Apostle* (98, Robert Duvall); *Merlin* (98, David Winning); *St. Ives* (99, Harry Hook); *Jacob Two Two Meets the Hooded Fang* (99, George Bloomfield); *The Big Brass Ring* (99, George Hickenlooper); the voice of Mrs. Tweedy in *Chicken Run* (00, Peter Lord and Nick Park); *Get Carter* (00, Stephen Kay); the queen in *Snow White* (01, Caroline Thompson); Vanessa Bell in *The Hours* (02, Stephen Daldry).

She gave a stunning tripartite performance in *Spider* (02, David Cronenberg); as Princess Mary in *The Last Prince* (03, Steven Poliakoff); *The Actors* (03, Conor McPherson); *The Rage on Placid Lake* (03, Tony McNamara).

Natasha Richardson, b. London, 1963

As the daughter of Vanessa Redgrave and Tony Richardson, and an heir to all the other Redgraves, Natasha Richardson is loaded with credentials. To which one must add marriage to Liam Neeson (who appeared with her on the New York stage in *Anna Christie*). Her stage career has been widely celebrated, and it therefore seemed natural that she should make movies. But in truth, she has not made much more than a wounded, pained impact, playing several notable but not very appealing victims. Above all, she lacks her mother's extraordinary sense of need for air, light, and pretending.

She made her debut in *Ellis Island* (84, Jerry London); as Mary Shelley in *Gothic* (86, Ken Russell); *A Month in the Country* (87, Pat O'Connor); as *Patty Hearst* (88, Paul Schrader)—it should have been a tour-de-force, but never escaped ordeal; touching as Oppenheimer's mistress in *Fat Man and Little Boy* (89, Roland Joffe); *The Handmaid's Tale* (90, Volker Schlöndorff); *The Favor, the Watch and the Very Big Fish* (91, Ben Lewis); *The Comfort of Strangers* (91, Schrader); *Past Midnight* (91, Robin B. Armstrong); in the Elizabeth Taylor role in a TV remake of *Suddenly, Last Summer* (92, Richard Eyre); *Zelda* (93, O'Connor) for TV; *Nell* (94, Michael Apted); *Widow's Peak* (94, John Irvin); unaccountably, in *The Parent Trap* (98, Nancy Myers); *Haven* (01, John Gray) for TV; *Blow Dry* (01, Paddy Breathnach); *Waking Up in Reno* (02, Jordan Brady).

And then a hit on Broadway in *Cabaret; Maid in Manhattan* (02, Wayne Wang).

Sir Ralph Richardson (1902–83),

b. Cheltenham, England

Richardson was like a character from an H. G. Wells novel: a young insurance clerk in Brighton, who on receiving a legacy decided to study first art, and then acting. His career was distinguished, but his abstracted charm lacked worldliness, and led him into the most inconsequential work without apparently noticing. The career looks dreamy and disorganized, just as, in interviews, he often seemed to forget who or where he was. It is a puzzle sometimes whether he was really a dolt, intermittently powered by grace, or a very wise man gently turning aside praise and curiosity. But of all the noble English actors he was the most mysterious, the one in whom character and performance were most intriguingly confused. As the years go by, only genius and pity can explain his work in *The Fallen Idol, The Heiress,* and *Long Day's Journey Into Night.*

The pattern of his film work is haphazard, showing how little he considered it. There are several periods of absence, too many awful pictures, and only a few that did him justice: *The Ghoul* (33, T. Hayes Hunter); *Friday the 13th* (33, Victor Saville); *The Return of Bulldog Drummond* (33, Walter Summers); *Java Head* (33, J. Walter Reuben); *The King of Paris* (33, Jack Raymond); *Bulldog Jack* (35, Walter Forde); *Things to Come* (36, William Cameron Menzies); *The Man Who Could Work Miracles* (36, Lothar Mendes); *Thunder in the City* (37, Marion Gering); *South Riding* (38, Saville); *The Divorce of Lady X* (38, Tim Whelan); *The Citadel* (38, King Vidor); *Q Planes* (39, Whelan); *The Four Feathers* (39, Zoltan Korda); *The Lion Has Wings* (39, Adrian Brunel, Brian Desmond Hurst, and Michael Powell); *On the Night of the Fire* (39, Hurst); *The Day Will Dawn* (42, Harold French); *The Silver Fleet* (42, Vernon Sewell); *The Volunteer* (43, Powell), about the Fleet Air Arm, in which he himself served; *School for Secrets* (46, Peter Ustinov); as Karenin opposite Vivien Leigh in *Anna Karenina* (48, Julien Duvivier); magnificent as the gentle butler in *The Fallen Idol* (48, Carol Reed); to America excelling as Dr. Sloper in *The Heiress* (49, William Wyler) and nominated for the supporting actor Oscar; *Outcast of the Islands* (51, Reed); *Home at Seven* (51), which he directed personally, though without trace; as the De Havilland figure in *The Sound Barrier* (52, David Lean); *The Holly and the Ivy* (52, George More O'Ferrall); as Buckingham in *Richard III* (55, Laurence Olivier); *Smiley* (56, Anthony Kimmins); *Our Man in Havana* (59, Reed); as Sir Edward Carson in *Oscar Wilde* (60, Gregory Ratoff); as an inane British military administrator in *Exodus* (60, Otto Preminger); very touching as Tyrone in *Long Day's Journey Into Night* (62, Sidney Lumet); *The 300 Spartans* (62, Rudolph Maté); *Woman of Straw* (63, Basil Dearden); *Dr. Zhivago* (65, Lean); *The Wrong Box* (66, Bryan Forbes); as Gladstone in *Khartoum* (66, Dearden); *The Midas Run* (69, Alf Kjellin); *The Bed-Sitting Room* (69, Dick Lester); *The Looking Glass War* (69, Frank R. Pierson); *Oh! What a Lovely War* (69, Richard Attenborough); *The Battle of Britain* (69, Guy Hamilton); *David Copperfield* (70, Delbert Mann), as Micawber; *Eagle in a Cage* (70, Fielder Cook); *Who Slew Auntie Roo?* (71, Curtis Harrington); as George IV in *Lady Caroline Lamb* (72, Robert Bolt); and *Rollerball* (75, Norman Jewison).

He was a voice in the animated picture *Watership Down* (78, Martin Rosen); *Charlie Muffin* (79, Jack Gold); *Time Bandits* (81, Terry Gilliam);

Dragonslayer (81, Matthew Robbins); doing Charles Laughton in *Witness for the Prosecution* (82, Alan Gibson); *Wagner* (83, Tony Palmer); *Invitation to the Wedding* (83, Joseph Brooks); *Give My Regards to Broad Street* (84, Peter Webb); and, finally, sublime as the aristocratic grandfather ready for monkey business in *Greystoke* (84, Hugh Hudson), including sliding downstairs on a silver tray.

Tony Richardson (Cecil Antonio Richardson) (1928–91), b. Shipley, England
1959: *Look Back in Anger.* 1960: *The Entertainer.* 1961: *Sanctuary.* 1962: *A Taste of Honey; The Loneliness of the Long Distance Runner.* 1963: *Tom Jones.* 1965: *The Loved One.* 1966: *Mademoiselle.* 1967: *The Sailor from Gibraltar.* 1968: *The Charge of the Light Brigade; Red and Blue* (s). 1969: *Laughter in the Dark; Hamlet.* 1970: *Ned Kelly.* 1973: *Dead Cert.* 1974: *A Delicate Balance.* 1976: *Joseph Andrews.* 1978: *A Death in Canaan* (TV). 1981: *The Border.* 1984: *The Hotel New Hampshire.* 1986: *Penalty Phase* (TV). 1988: *Shadow on the Sun* (TV). 1990: *The Phantom of the Opera* (TV); *Blue Sky* (unreleased); "Hills Like White Elephants," an episode in *Women and Men: Stories of Seduction* (TV).

Richardson died relatively young, from AIDS, to exceptional and eloquent regret among those who loved him. It is also clear from the two volumes of John Osborne's autobiography that Richardson was a rare character—a wit, a very good stage director (he was at the Royal Court in London in its great years), a provocateur, a man of parties and affairs, an enthusiast, and a tennis maniac. I look forward to a brilliant biography (Richardson's autobiography is disappointing), so that I can more easily digest the travesty he made of John Irving's *Hotel New Hampshire.* The last years do not persuade me to moderate my opinion—that he was a wretched film director. But I should add that he was the father (by marriage to Vanessa Redgrave) of two good actresses—Natasha and Joely Richardson.

The supposed "free" cinema of *Momma Don't Allow* was soon channeled into an extraordinary nailing down of unlikely literary sources. The films are all abject, but I still feel provoked by the mistreatment of some of the original authors. As far as Osborne, Shelagh Delaney, and Alan Sillitoe were concerned, Richardson tacked a literal-minded realism on to their rhetoric. But the inconsequential *Sanctuary* had to be seen to be believed; *Tom Jones* was a tricksy evasion of one of the best constructed of English novels, shaming the audience who thought it original and replacing Fielding's robust humor with flashy knowingness; *The Loved One* was very dilute acid; *Mademoiselle* was ludicrous, made worse by the fact that Franju had been deprived of the chance of filming Genet's original with Anouk Aimée; *The Sailor from Gibraltar* was one of the wettest films of all time, though Richardson always protested that there should have been a great film in the Marguerite Duras novel. *Hamlet* can look after itself, but Nabokov's *Laughter in the Dark* is a novel that even a competent director would have to go out of his way not to make stunning—Richardson strenuously hacked out such a path. The fact that he squandered Anna Karina in it was in character; already he had misused Claire Bloom, Lee Remick, Susannah York, Jeanne Moreau, not to mention Vanessa Redgrave, and Mick Jagger in *Ned Kelly.*

It is such a pitiful record that I should add a word for the intermittent period verisimilitude of *The Charge of the Light Brigade.*

Leni Riefenstahl, b. Berlin, 1902

1932: *Das Blaue Licht/The Blue Light.* 1933: *Sieg des Glaubens* (d). 1935: *Tag der Freiheit—Unsere Wehrmacht* (d). 1936: *Triumph des Willens/Triumph of the Will* (d). 1938: *Olympiad: Fest der Schonheit* (d); *Olympiad: Fest der Volker* (d). 1945: *Tiefland.* 1956: *Schwarze Fracht* (uncompleted).

If succeeding generations find it harder to understand the mood that carried Nazism across Europe in the period 1933–45, then *Triumph of the Will* may be the most succinct proof of that hysterical confidence. The film is not simply a record of a fascist event, it is an event in itself. And now that all the leaders have been tracked down, the camps made into museums, and memories fuddled by guilt, remorse and self-righteousness, *Triumph of the Will* may be the most honest and compelling fruit of fascist temperament. I have watched it in small viewing theatres, with a handful of people, and been stirred by its confusion of power and regeneration. That experience helps to explain how so many Germans responded to National Socialism. For *Triumph of the Will* is such a monument to warped beauty that it serves to make us cautious of beauty itself.

Its maker, Leni Riefenstahl, has never escaped the ambiguous pall of her film. Since the end of the war, she has been in turn prisoner, wanderer, and litigant, a director without work; arguably the most talented woman ever to make a film, she is still neglected in an age of feminist militancy. In 1964, she could look back on her career and see it as the work of destiny:

> I was thinking of this: in *The Blue Light,* I played the role of a child of nature who, on the nights of the full moon, climbed to this blue light, the image of an ideal, an aspiration dreamed of, a thing to which each being, above all when young, ardently desires to attain. Well, when her

dream is destroyed Yunta dies. I spoke of that as my destiny. For that is what was accomplished, much later, in me, after the war when everything collapsed on us, when I was deprived of all possibility of creating. For art, creation—this is my life, and I was deprived of it. My life became a tissue of rumours and accusations through which I had to beat a path; they all were revealed to be false, but for twenty years they deprived me of my creation. I tried to write, but what I wanted to do was to make films.

> I tried to make films, but I couldn't. Everything was reduced to nothingness. Only my vocation was left. Yes, at that moment, I was dead.

Leni Riefenstahl was a haughty, handsome girl, absorbed in painting and dance. It would be hard to find features nearer the ideal of purposeful, Aryan health, or a body so caught up in the fulsome postures of vitality. She studied fine art at the Berlin Academy and was a ballet student with Mary Wigman and Max Reinhardt before an injury turned her toward movie acting.

She was the spirit of the mountains, an intense naïf, aspiring to the dramatic purity of mountains and the towering sharpness of peaks. There was a whole school of German mountain films, vaguely pantheistic, fumbling toward some great force that could capture idealism—the hills were alive with the echo of the future: *Der Heilige Berg* (26, Arnold Fanck, her mentor); *Der Grosse Sprung* (27, Fanck); *Die Weisse Holle von Piz Palu* (29, Fanck and G. W. Pabst); *Sturme über den Mont Blanc* (30, Fanck); and *Die Weisse Rausch* (31, Fanck). She also appeared in *SOS Eisberg* (33, Fanck and Tay Garnett).

But by then she had formed her own production company and made *The Blue Light,* the preeminent work of mountain mysticism, from a screenplay by Bela Balasz. What followed is open to some debate, but Hitler himself admired her work and wanted her to make a film of the 1934 Nazi Party rallies at Nuremberg. That she was never a party member seems true, but that she meekly recorded those rallies is a nonsense. Her resources were extensive, and the rally itself was conceived and organized with filming in mind.

One must go further. It is a question of seeing this, on the one hand, from Leni Riefenstahl:

> A commission was proposed to me. Good, I accepted. Good. I agreed, like so many others, to make a film that so many others, with or without talent, could have made. Well it is to this film that I am obliged for spending several years, after my arrest by the French, in different camps and prisons. But if you see this film again today you ascertain that it doesn't contain a single reconstructed scene. Everything in it is true. And it contains no tendentious commen-

tary at all. It is history. A pure historical film . . . it is film-vérité. It reflects the truth that was then, in 1934, history. It is therefore a documentary. Not a propaganda film. Oh! I know very well what propaganda is. That consists of recreating certain events in order to illustrate a thesis or, in the face of certain events, to let one thing go in order to accentuate another. I found myself, me, at the heart of an event which was the reality of a certain time and a certain place. My film is composed of what stemmed from that.

Yet *Triumph of the Will* is entirely lacking in doubt, accident, or uncomposed shots; that is why its beauty becomes relentless, oppressive, and demented. The camera is a party to the staging of events. It characterizes them in the way it frames and shoots them. The pace of the film shatters real time, the tedium of waiting crowds, and moves with the destined gravity of editing. The film shrieks with camera aptitude, integrated design, sense of composition, the flush of light, a feeling for martial resolve, for the shapes of crowds, for the splendor of the lone individual, the resonance of banners and trumpets and of torchlight seen through the languorous folds of a flag stirred on a summer night. Few films so illustrate the effects of camera angles, of moving shots, of editing. The whole is based on a dynamic tension between monolithic close-ups of uneasy, unwholesome demagogues and surging traveling shots of burnished masses—a fatal mixture of immense destiny and fake heroism.

The skill is not only subordinated to fascist conviction. It has a sense of beauty that is trite, vulgar, and stupid. The beauty of *Triumph of the Will* is predesigned and underlined; it never risks any threat to visual order; it smothers the momentary and mistrusts the viewer's ability to perceive. Thus, it defines the simpleminded craving for respectability that leads to dogma in fascism. But it is still terrifying to watch, for it shows how far we all nurture that urge to be conclusive and sure.

The films of the 1936 Olympic Games are far less of an achievement: prolix, arty, and pretentious. The Games were so much more diffuse an event that the film has none of the total mise-en-scène of *Triumph of the Will*. It is notable for foolish, heady excesses—the Isadora Duncan–like scenes in Greece, the emphasis on shape at the expense of competition, the slightly prurient relish of glistening muscle, and the editing delirium over high-diving.

Since then, Leni Riefenstahl has been in camps, trying to rehabilitate herself and, for many years, in Africa, doubtless trying to recapture the remote, ardent conviction of the mountain films. Her own life is sad, troubled, and intriguing. But her greatest work is triumphant, certain, and dreadful.

Her astonishing longevity shows a health that would not die. She did books of photographs, and at last she did an autobiography—a fascinating, dotty, and unreliable book. Along with the remarkable documentary film made about her—*The Wonderful Horrible Life of Leni Riefenstahl* (93, Ray Muller)—she has remained an issue in the age of *Schindler's List*.

Molly Ringwald,
b. Sacramento, California, 1968

Molly Ringwald was on the cover of *Time* once, as part of a celebration of herself and the John Hughes films that embodied a rather sweet, nostalgic view of teenagers. A few years later, it was unclear whether she wanted, or could sustain, an "adult" career. She was pretty, cool, with haughty, deadpan eyes. She could say a line; she was a magnet of appeal and likability—she was, maybe, an advertising icon for the high concept of Teen U.S.A. or Teenagers 'r' Us. I do not underestimate her: she kept powerful company, and kept it at bay. That very guarded look of hers masked a considerable intelligence.

She was the daughter of jazz musician Bob Ringwald, with whose band she sang as a child. *Tempest* (82, Paul Mazursky), her debut, cast her as a modern-day Miranda, but she quickly settled in midtown America, an apparently independent teenager, the suburban dream child for anxious parents: *P.K. and the Kid* (82, Lou Lombardo); *Spacehunter: Adventures in the Forbidden Zone* (83, Lamont Johnson); *Sixteen Candles* (84, John Hughes); *The Breakfast Club* (85, Hughes); *Pretty in Pink* (86, Howard Deutsch); as a kind of Cordelia for *King Lear* (87, Jean-Luc Godard); venturing into a lurid, adult world in *The Pick-up Artist* (87, James Toback), a film silently produced by her advisor, Warren Beatty; *For Keeps* (88, John Avildsen); not too comfortable playing a slut in *Fresh Horses* (88, David Anspaugh); *Strike It Rich* (90, James Scott); *Betsey's Wedding* (90, Alan Alda); *Women & Men: Stories of Seduction* (90, Ken Russell), doing Dorothy Parker's "Dusk Before Fireworks."

But if you hoped in those teen years that Ms. Ringwald was getting an education, and making proper plans for the future, then it's a letdown to find how hard she is working in pictures and TV projects you've not heard of. She is still only thirty-three, and her titles often shriek with unintended irony: *Something to Live For: The Alison Gertz Story* (92, Tom McLoughlin); *Some Folks Call It a Sling Blade* (93, George Hickenlooper); *Face the Music* (93, Carol Wiseman); *The Stand* (94, Mick Garris); to France for *Tous les Jours Dimanche* (95, Jean Charles Tacchella) and *Enfants de Salaud* (96, Tonie Marshall); *Malicious* (95, Ian Corsen); *Baja* (95, Kurt Voss); *Townies* (96, Pamela Fryman); *Office Killer* (97, Cindy

Sherman); *Since You've Been Gone* (98, David Schwimmer); *Twice Upon a Time* (98, Thom Eberhardt); *Teaching Mrs. Tingle* (99, Kevin Williamson); *Kimberly* (99, Frederic Golehan); *Requiem for Murder* (99, Douglas Jackson); *The Giving Tree* (99, Cameron Thor); *Cut* (00, Kimble Rendall); *In the Weeds* (00, Michael Rauch); *The Translator* (00, Leslie Anne Smith).

Rin Tin Tin (1916–32), b. Germany

Deanna Durbin supposedly saved Universal, Mae West may well have saved Paramount, but the actor who saved Warners—he was known as "the mortgage lifter"—was the great and unique Rin Tin Tin. At the height of his career, Jeanine Basinger tells us in *The Silent Stars*, he received up to 12,000 fan letters a week, earned $6,000 a month, was insured for $100,000, and had his own valet, chef, limo, and driver. When he was discovered, there were other dog stars, most prominently Strongheart, but Rinty quickly eliminated him as competition. It may sound far-fetched or campy, but when you watch his movies, everything becomes clear. First of all, they're well made—full of action and feeling; but more important, Rinty is really talented. This was a dog who not only obeyed orders perfectly, performing amazing feats without a stumble (according to witnesses, he was a far quicker study than most biped actors), but who seemed to grasp the emotion of scenes and actions and then convey them. (He didn't even look embarrassed when saddled with a mate, the charming Nanette.) And what other dog star could nimbly disguise himself with a beard or put on little boots? If you doubt all this, take a look at *Night Cry* (26) or *Jaws of Steel* (27).

Rin Tin Tin was a German shepherd discovered by an American soldier, Lee Duncan, in a German trench at the end of World War I and brought home to California. Quickly it became apparent just how biddable he was, and how photogenic. Duncan trained him, Warners snapped him up, and soon he was a huge moneymaker for them—and for Duncan, who controlled the career and the movies. He starred in feature after feature through ten years, even surviving the coming of sound (Rinty barks!), before succumbing at the age of sixteen. He was playing with Duncan outside his elaborate home when he fell to the ground. Jack Warner, with his exquisite sensibility, was to write: "Rinty's heart was tired and old, the strength had long since ebbed from the massive shoulders and legs. He was barely able to crawl to his master's side, and Duncan knew at once that no power on earth could help. He phoned across the street to his neighbor, the lovely shimmering Jean Harlow, and she came running. And she cradled the great furry head in her lap, and there he died." Could Jack have been projecting?

Rinty, we can see in hindsight, was a kind of canine Shirley Temple—a failure-proof specialty act—and as Fox did for her, Warners provided him with strong production values and good actors in supporting roles, among them Louise Fazenda, Leila Hyams, Charles Farrell, Georgia Hale, and, in his last film, the serial *Lightning Warrior* (31), George Brent. Among his directors were Ray Enright and Malcolm St. Clair. After his death, there was a string of faux Rin Tin Tins in both movies and TV, but none of them was in his league.

By contrast, Lassie was a role (played by a pack of nervy collies). But Rinty was a star—and no other Shepherd could match him.

Michael Ritchie (1939–2001), b. Waukesha, Wisconsin

1969: *Downhill Racer.* 1972: *Prime Cut; The Candidate.* 1975: *Smile.* 1976: *The Bad News Bears.* 1977: *Semi-Tough.* 1979: *An Almost Perfect Affair.* 1980: *Divine Madness* (d); *The Island.* 1983: *The Survivors.* 1985: *Fletch.* 1986: *The Golden Child; Wildcats.* 1988: *The Couch Trip.* 1989: *Fletch Lives.* 1993: *Diggstown; The Positively True Adventures of the Alleged Texas Cheerleader-Murdering Mom* (TV). 1994: *Cops & Robbersons; The Scout.* 1995: *The Fantasticks* (not released until 2000, recut by others). 1997: *A Simple Wish; Comfort, Texas* (TV).

The son of a Berkeley professor, Ritchie went to Harvard and then into TV, where he worked on *Omnibus, Profiles in Courage, Dr. Kildare, The Big Valley,* and *The Man from U.N.C.L.E.,* among other shows. Ritchie did a two-hour pilot for *The Outsider,* on the strength of which Robert Redford hired him to do *Downhill Racer.* It says as much about vanity and fulfillment in competition as the rest of his films put together, and as a debut it was the more striking for its view of implacability in Redford. *Prime Cut* is a failure, but a situation that a Fuller or even an Aldrich might have relished. It made Ritchie seem too genteel, too far from the flagrant identification with things larger than life called for by the subject. *The Candidate* has an undeserved reputation for political shrewdness; actually it is chaste with its half-baked homilies of disapproval. Its liberalism would prefer to do without politics—as if politics were any more corrupt or less essential than other parts of American life.

Smile is sometimes called a satirical masterpiece. It seems to me only a series of sketches, the product of narrative reticence, cheap shots, and careless technique—few films have more obtruding mikes. The attitude toward characters is patronizing and fragmentary, and the superiority of the picture's tone treats everyone as some kind of rascal or jerk. Only great affection for people could have redeemed its imagery, but Ritchie's method is off the cuff and unfeeling. It is a journalistic film, skimming a story and ignoring the deeper possibilities. And like journalism, it settles for mockery as it pursues the facile path of recording foolishness.

The Bad News Bears and *Semi-Tough* show a further coarsening, as showbiz formulae cloud over truth. The first is woefully short of parents, and it ends up as a movie pandering to kids. The latter rejects an unusual novel, submits to its own brutish male stars and their delusions of sophistication, and casually derides women, football, and alternative lifestyles without ever finding the grace or intelligence that makes disparaging comedy cleansing and useful. It is a symptom of Ritchie's evasiveness that so few of his films fit clearly into American genres. That could be a way of praising him—with Altman, it is—but in Ritchie's case there is no fresh territory claimed or explored, because no real risk has been taken.

Of Ritchie's work in the 1980s, nothing need or should be said. There are passages that can only be observed in silence. But in the nineties, he bounced back: *Diggstown* was decent, while *The Positively True . . .* was his best work, a raging satire such as only TV attempts now. Indeed, Ritchie was moving towards cable TV: he actually did a documentary on Einstein for French TV and in 1999 he directed an episode of the series *Beggars and Choosers*. But *The Scout* (about baseball, with Albert Brooks) and *A Simple Wish* (with Martin Short) both did poorly. Ritchie was one of those many directors who deserved better things.

Martin Ritt (1914–90), b. New York
1956: *Edge of the City/A Man Is Ten Feet Tall.* 1957: *No Down Payment.* 1958: *The Long Hot Summer; Black Orchid.* 1959: *The Sound and the Fury.* 1960: *Jovanka e l'Altri/Five Branded Women.* 1961: *Paris Blues.* 1962: *Hemingway's Adventures of a Young Man.* 1963: *Hud.* 1964: *The Outrage.* 1965: *The Spy Who Came In from the Cold.* 1967: *Hombre.* 1968: *The Brotherhood.* 1969: *The Molly Maguires.* 1970: *The Great White Hope.* 1972: *Sounder.* 1973: *Pete 'n' Tillie.* 1974: *Conrack.* 1976: *The Front.* 1978: *Casey's Shadow.* 1979: *Norma Rae.* 1981: *Back Roads.* 1983: *Cross Creek.* 1985: *Murphy's Romance.* 1987: *Nuts.* 1990: *Stanley and Iris.*

Ritt was himself an actor, playing in *Golden Boy* on Broadway and in *Winged Victory* (44, George Cukor). After the war, he taught at the Actors' Studio and worked in TV as an actor and director. His debut was one of several mid-1950s graduations from small to large screen and, on the strength of his work with John Cassavetes and Sidney Poitier, it seemed to show some ability with naturalistic acting.

But the promise was illusory. Far from a realist, Ritt chose heavily literary originals, most of which got the better of him. His versions of Faulkner are shamefully dull, no matter how much Fox flinched away from the density of Yoknapatawpha County. He lurched from one bizarre subject to another: missing the essence of Hemingway and Le Carré; aping *Rashomon* in *The Outrage*, but only laboring with the variety of truths; skirting around the potential of *The Molly Maguires;* and making one of the silliest boxing movies. *Hombre* is a dull Western with a flashy script; *The Brotherhood* is a modest Mafia story that, one suspects, Mario Puzo never forgot.

Only *Hud* has touched on the early sense of raw lives uncovered. That is also a film full of good acting, even from Paul Newman, once Ritt's pupil, whose decline owes a good deal to the way Ritt's movies have indulged and wasted him. *Sounder* and *Conrack* revived the inane view of Ritt as a conscientious liberal. But the day when every young black is as delectable as Cicely Tyson is still far off; in his very first film, Ritt had done no more and no less to glamorize Sidney Poitier.

By his final years, it was hard to avoid the truth that Ritt made dull, amiable films (at his best). *Norma Rae* was his strongest picture, preaching to the converted and making the most of the drab cuteness of Sally Field, but an effectively righteous picture. *Cross Creek* had a pleasant rural mood, and a good performance from Alfre Woodard. *Murphy's Romance* knew nothing but the adorability of James Garner and Sally Field. But *Nuts* was a misbegotten venture—with Barbra Streisand in the film it is likely that only her direction could have controlled the script. *Stanley and Iris* had pathos coming out of its ears.

Thelma Ritter (1905–69),
b. Brooklyn, New York
Thelma Ritter always seemed worn out. In a flower-print dress and flat shoes, her hair screwed up in a home perm, and her face like a used newspaper, she might have had a full day washing and cooking before she came to the studio, and a few hours' office cleaning ahead of her as soon as she finished. It is a tribute to her sour inventiveness that such deep-grained tiredness never seemed boring, nor did her Brooklyn accent grate.

Quite the contrary, she is a treasured supporting player, immortalized in one brilliant scene from Samuel Fuller's *Pickup on South Street* (53). In that film she plays a necktie saleswoman, wearying unto death of trudging round New York with her ties and patter. One night she returns to her cramped room and retreats to her bed. Fuller shows this in one steady shot that aches with the exhaustion of her long day and yet does not show, in the darkness beside her bed, a man waiting to kill her if she will not betray Richard Widmark. She does not appear to notice him, but Ritter has seen (or sensed) the man, guessed his purpose, and foreseen its conclusions. Thus, the shot gains enormously in pathos as she sees her tiredness drawing to a close. That shot says more about city life, and more poetically, than whole movies that assault the subject directly.

She had been an actress on stage and radio before her friend George Seaton asked her to play in his *Miracle on 34th Street* (47). Thereafter she became a fixture: *Call Northside 777* (48, Henry Hathaway); *A Letter to Three Wives* (49, Joseph L. Mankiewicz); *Father Was a Fullback* (49, John M. Stahl); Bette Davis's dresser in *All About Eve* (50, Mankiewicz); *Perfect Strangers* (50, Bretaigne Windust); *The Mating Season* (51, Mitchell Leisen); *As Young as You Feel* (51, Harmon Jones); *The Model and the Marriage Broker* (51, George Cukor); *With a Song in My Heart* (52, Walter Lang); *Titanic* (53, Jean Negulesco); *The Farmer Takes a Wife* (53, Henry Levin); as the lady who comes in to scratch James Stewart's back in *Rear Window* (54, Alfred Hitchcock); *Lucy Gallant* (55, Robert Parrish); *Daddy Long Legs* (55, Negulesco); *The Proud and the Profane* (56, Seaton); *Pillow Talk* (59, Michael Gordon); *A Hole in the Head* (59, Frank Capra); *The Misfits* (60, John Huston); *The Second Time Around* (61, Vincent Sherman); *Birdman of Alcatraz* (62, John Frankenheimer); *For Love or Money* (63, Gordon); *A New Kind of Love* (63, Melville Shavelson); *Move Over, Darling* (63, Gordon); and *Boeing Boeing* (65, John Rich).

She was nominated six times for supporting actress—but never won: *All About Eve, The Mating Season, With a Song in My Heart, Pickup on South Street* (that was four years in a row), and then for *Pillow Talk* and for the unlikable mother in *Birdman of Alcatraz*.

Jacques Rivette, b. Rouen, France, 1928
1960: *Paris Nous Appartient/Paris Belongs to Us.* 1965: *Suzanne Simonin, La Religieuse de Diderot.* 1968: *L'Amour Fou.* 1971: *Out One* (unreleased). 1973: *Out One: Spectre* (abridged version). 1974: *Céline et Julie Vont en Bateau/Céline and Julie Go Boating.* 1975: *Duelle/Twhylight.* 1976: *Noroit/Nor'west.* 1981: *La Pont du Nord.* 1983: *Merry Go Round.* 1984: *L'Amour par Terre/Love on the Ground.* 1986: *Hurlevent.* 1989: *La Bande des Quatre/The Gang of Four.* 1991: *La Belle Noiseuse.* 1994: *Jeanne la Pucelle.* 1995: *Haut Bas Fragile/Up, Down, Fragile.* 1998: *Secret Défense.* 2000: *Va Savoir.*

The informed filmgoer might not leap to support the contention that Rivette is the most important filmmaker of the last thirty-five years. After all, Rivette has made films blatantly outside the con-

ventional scheme. Even *La Religieuse*—which was made according to industrial traditions—was once banned in France. Eventually it shrugged off the disapproval of authorities, and it may be the Rivette film that most people have seen, but it is the least interesting and characteristic because it conforms to so many normal procedures. It is based on a script and a celebrated work of literature. It dutifully reinvents Diderot through costume, furnishings, and proper locations. Actors and actresses are cast in set parts and given dialogue to learn and speak. The film is professionally appealing, no matter the human ugliness of its subject. Indeed, *La Religieuse* was made for the arthouse audience it shocked in France and rather bored elsewhere. All of which has little to do with Rivette's significance.

That importance rests in the uncompromising way that he has identified the future of film as something other than the two-hour work shown to paying audiences in special buildings, and telling tidy stories. There is a scene in *Paris Nous Appartient* where a group of young people at a party watch the Tower of Babel sequence from Fritz Lang's *Metropolis*. Apart from its place within the film, the scene captures that all-embracing atmosphere of the New Wave that exists, probably, among any band of people intent on film.

In addition, Rivette used people in darkness examining some bright display as an example of the way we must judge life in terms of its performance. Film for Rivette is less art form or entertainment than the unstable coinage of communication and experience. Thus, he has regularly deprofessionalized it. That party sequence has film being shown informally, in the way one might put on a record or pick up a book. And the use of an extract without context hints at the greater power of the audience at private shows: power to show a film in any order, to show one reel over and over again, to deconstruct a work as a reader may a book.

Films could be of any length. The excerpt from *Metropolis* runs perhaps three minutes; another film might last three days. Rivette's films have tended toward the latter. The regular production system would protest at such expense. But film stock is the cheapest item in any production. It is the skilled labor to make it glamorous, exact, or "professional" that multiplies the costs. Like Warhol, Rivette can make a long film on a cost-scale and with a sort of collaboration that defies commercial cinema.

The intuition of that capacity coincided with the way TV ate up cinema's audience, and with a critical reappraisal of the nature of film. Rivette was a member of the *Cahiers du Cinéma* group of writers anxious to turn into filmmakers; he alone among them continues to make films as an "amateur" that take their personality from intense but unresolved artistic aspiration.

He worked as assistant to Jacques Becker and Renoir and led up to *Paris Nous Appartient* with four shorts: *Aux Quatre Coins* (50); *Quadrille* (50); *Le Divertissement* (52); and *Le Coup de Berger* (56). As a writer, he proclaimed American cinema and the comprehensive mise-en-scène of Stroheim, Rossellini, Murnau, and Lang. His articles remain essential reading whenever he was dealing with a director who fully engaged him. As well as having a fine response to film as language, Rivette was conscious of the "retirement" around 1958–60 of Fritz Lang and of the bold venture into documentary of Rossellini.

History may show that the feature form was exhausted by 1960, waiting to be transformed by diversity and experiment. Rivette had praised the luminous portrait of betrayal in *Beyond a Reasonable Doubt* and the juxtaposition of spontaneity, documentary, and theatricality in *Viaggio in Italia*. Predictably, his own work went in pursuit of stylistic plainness and thematic obsession. For Rivette had reached the conclusion that it is the medium that is fantastic; that imagery on a screen—what Sartre called "the frenzies of a wall"—is so potent that the style need not be assertive or florid.

His first feature was made piecemeal, from 1958 to 1960, with borrowed equipment and as funds accumulated. Naturally, its scenario changed during that period, but as the surface details fluctuated so its preoccupation deepened. *Paris Nous Appartient* has been attacked for its pretentiousness, its slackness, and its willful mystification. All those charges have substance, but they are side effects of Rivette's attitude to meaning and his willingness to be open to chance in the way that the camera is open to whatever transpires in front of it. His films reproduce life's pressure to decide about people on the evidence available.

Paris is a beautiful expression of the amateur passion for film. Its long time in the making became an aspect of its subject; its vicissitudes were subtly mirrored in the "story" of the movie. For in his debut, Rivette began to define a bond between fiction and a modern myth: the uneasiness that we are victims of a great conspiracy. At one level, the film is as sensitive an account of Paris as Franju's documentaries; it is also a picture of a restless creative group—the filming is reflected in the situation of the film, an abortive production of Shakespeare's *Pericles*. The immediate themes ride above a pervasive mood of disorganization to the point of breakdown. For this Paris is the universal metropolis; it looks forward to *Alphaville*, just as it quotes from Lang—in which our sense of meaning is undermined and justified by an infinite but imprecise conspiracy.

That owed something to Mabuse and the fear of nuclear disaster. But it also anticipated the paranoia that rippled outward from Kennedy's assassination, irrational urban violence with a vague political background, the Pentagon papers, the Howard Hughes fraud, and the raveling together of Watergate. The haphazard conditions under which the film was made, and the frequent gap between intellectual aspiration and professional appearance, only added to its menace. Years before Godard, Rivette seemed to be saying, "Art is no guarantee of integrity or meaning.... Any film is victim of interpretation.... It is not mine and cannot comfort me."

Indeed, one could not attribute the film to Rivette alone, in the way that film critics dignify cinema by treating it as the work of an author. The *Cahiers* group had played a large part in persuading the world that directors were instrumental. But Rivette saw how far that was already an archaic notion, about to be superseded by improvisation that allowed some authorship to actors and some to limbo. *Paris Nous Appartient* was 140 minutes and often of a professionally unacceptable visual quality: it looked like snapshots, and thus its poetry arose casually and furtively.

L'Amour Fou was 256 minutes, with 35mm sequences and rougher 16mm material cut together. Its topic was the relationship between a man and wife (producer and actress) rehearsing Racine's *Andromache*. Simultaneously, they are being filmed for a TV cinema verité documentary. This strain (like that on Jane Fonda in the Drew-Leacock movie) forces the actress out of the play, to be replaced by the husband's former mistress. Again, the setting is Paris and the focus is a dramatic production; again the real subject is the evanescence of human contact. *L'Amour Fou* pursues the dying relationship more closely than Rivette usually examines specific characters, and is oddly anticipatory of *Last Tango in Paris*. But its chief actor was in fact a stage producer preparing *Andromache*, and there was indeed a TV film being made of the proceedings. Clearly, now, Rivette's preoccupation was the interplay of fact and fiction.

L'Amour Fou had trouble in distribution. A two-hour version was insisted on by producers and given a wider showing than the original. This only encouraged Rivette's extremism. For TV, or even for the coming cassette audience, he made *Out One*, running twelve hours and forty minutes, and never shown properly without technical breakdown.

Two years later, Rivette cut out of it (or from its cloth) *Out One: Spectre*, which runs for four hours and twenty minutes. The prodigality of length must not obscure its enormous achievement. *Spectre* is an enquiry into the ceremonies we make of order and disorder, and it is largely free of the looming melodramatic menace in *Paris*. It concerns the inept efforts of two eccentric outsiders—Jean-Pierre Léaud and Juliet Berto—to fathom the extent and purpose of an apparently dormant cabal of thirteen. Melodrama seeps away as the film grows longer. The rationale of such length is to hint at the vast entropic vagueness of reality. And the motif of the film is the obsessive, hopeless, comic, and possibly tragic human duty to detect significance in that wildness. Its effect is to reveal a constant, undiscriminating coincidence or doubling going on in the world, regardless of the pretty little affinities that artists and madmen concoct to give form to their works. It is as if Rivette felt an implicit tendency to simile or synchronicity in events that was like a virus.

Once more the film grows out of theatre groups: two rival concerns, preparing but never producing *Prometheus* and *Seven Against Thebes.* The documentarylike account of rehearsal merges intriguingly with the fictional undertones in the improvised scenes between the "real" people. The method is minimal: long takes, a sense of unchosen camera positions, an unadorned image. Only the assembly of scenes admits to shape, and here there is a most complex design of groups, characters, movie, and stills that is the more absorbing because of the way it aspires to a wider disorder.

Out One: Spectre defies final judgment, but redefines our expectation of cinema. Of course, it is a folly, an absurd, self-indulgent monster. But it is a film that declares the readiness of cinema to replace rather than represent life. And it had to be made before Rivette could make *Céline and Julie Go Boating,* which I take to be the most innovative film since *Citizen Kane.*

It deals with two girls—Juliet Berto and Dominique Labourier—who exist only to the extent that they conspire in each other's effort to make the world fictional. Through their own imaginative conviction, they visit a haunted house where a solemn melodrama is forever being played. This is also like a movie palace where one film runs forever, and the melodrama is like an RKO women's pic of circa 1949. Céline and Julie double as the maid in this little story. After every visit to the house, they come away stunned and possessed, but with a sweet in their mouths that enables them to relive the story.

Eventually, they go to the house together and try to avert the conclusion of the tale—the killing of a child. This involves breathtaking sequences of themselves—like people from a Rouch movie—in the same images as the very composed and made-up creatures of, say, *Slightly Scarlet.* They take the child away into what had seemed reality but is now revealed as only one more closet of the imaginary.

I make great claims for *Céline and Julie.* It is a comedy, and that is liberty after the ominousness of Rivette's earlier work. Its length is a balance between the cinema movie and the *Out One* infinity of length. It is a commentary on the history of cinema. It is a generous reconciliation with literature through fiction, and whereas *Kane* was the first picture to suggest that the world of the imagination was as powerful as reality, *Céline and Julie* is the first film in which everything is invented.

Repeated viewings of *Céline and Julie* have only cemented my claims for it: in terms of a summation of classical narrative cinema that has itself amounted to a mythology ready to be reworked by actors, directors, and writers, and in a form that dissolves every notion of duration in cinema. Above all, *Céline and Julie* asserts fiction as a freedom, not just a kind of remedial service or pleasure. It pursues humor, idiosyncrasy, and exhilaration and provides a way of seeing how old-fashioned such concepts as comedy and melodrama have become.

However, I must confess that Rivette's subsequent work—often with the same people, and embarking from the same enchanted ground—is chic, gloomy, and insubstantial. The exhilaration has been replaced by a mystical patterning that is too subject to the occult and all the old melodrama. *Duelle* is so claustrophobic and so pat that one is reduced to admiring pictorial grace. I remain hopeful that such decorative games could become tempting sports with more vigor, and a more dynamic group assault on the possibilities of a picture. That is how Rivette's scrupulous survey of Paris uncovered a magic realm: the magic in cinema lies within reality, and should not be imposed on it.

Rivette's work has not traveled much outside France—a measure of its lack of commercial success, and of his tranquil pursuit of his own themes, often at great length. In *Love on the Ground,* two actresses (Geraldine Chaplin and Jane Birkin) are hired to enact and even finish a play, or a ritual. When it played in America, it found little understanding, but it needed to be read in the full context of Rivette's work. However, *La Belle Noiseuse* stood on its own, no matter that it was rooted in the earlier films, with its astonishing variations on the theme of artist and model, life and imagination. This masterpiece, coming close to twenty years after *Céline and Julie,* confirmed Rivette as one of the great directors.

Then he took on a classic—Joan of Arc—in a six-hour movie, with the best actress available, Sandrine Bonnaire. It has been a while since a major director delivered masterpieces past the age of sixty. But Rivette has that promise. Without ever really establishing a commercial reputation, Rivette continues to follow his obsessions. *Va Savoir*—an elegant, if slightly studied, romantic comedy—opened the New York Film Festival of 2001 and found an audience in theatres. To my mind, it was less interesting than *Fragile* and a good deal less compelling than *Secret Defénse* (a well-plotted noir with Sandrine Bonnaire). But at last the feeling began to stir—that Rivette is one of the masters. A time will come when proper ret-rospective will prove his greatness, but at the cost of so many younger and flashier reputations. No one has done more to experiment with narrative and duration than Rivette.

Hal Roach (1892–1992),
b. Elmira, New York

In 1983 (when he was ninety-one), the Academy gave Hal Roach a special Oscar for his "unparal-leled record of distinguished contributions to the motion picture art form." A full nine years later, as Roach attended the awards ceremony once again, the host Billy Crystal referred to his one hun-dredth birthday. The assembly rose in applause. Roach stood and gave a speech—unheard by the masses, because there was no mike for him. Whereupon, Crystal observed, with quick grace, that the glitch was fitting—"Because Mr. Roach started his career in silent movies."

What else was an enterprising twenty-two-year-old to do? He couldn't wait forever, and he had put in those obligatory years as a gold-miner in Alaska, as a mule-skinner, and as a cowboy stunt-man. So he went into production and became the generous, accommodating boss to Harold Lloyd, Our Gang, Charley Chase, Laurel and Hardy, to say nothing of Leo McCarey, George Marshall, and George Stevens when they were young.

In his early days, Roach did some directing, but he seems to have been happy to rise above that chore. He is credited with story and script for Lloyd's *Safety Last* (23, Fred Newmeyer), and it is clear that Roach's easygoing attitude helped put together the team that made Lloyd films work. While Roach was not especially assertive or color-ful, he understood the efficacy of a friendly studio. Walter Kerr is one commentator who gives Roach special credit for this creative, family background. Nevertheless, Roach was slow to see how well Laurel and Hardy worked together. But genius in Hollywood should never overlook the good luck that rides out its blindness and its errors.

Of course, Roach was not just a silent-film maker. Laurel and Hardy made the transition to sound very well. In addition, in the thirties the Roach studio produced *Topper* (37, Nor-man Z. McLeod); *Captain Fury* (39, directed by Roach himself); *The Housekeeper's Daughter* (39, Roach)—the debut of Victor Mature; *Of Mice and Men* (39, Lewis Milestone); and *One Million B.C.* (39), an everyday caveman story, with Mature and Carole Landis, directed by Roach, his son, and—so it is said—D. W. Griffith.

In truth, after the early forties, Roach turned a lot of the business over to his son, tried a televi-sion company (without success), and became a landmark. There is never anything like a new busi-ness for encouraging enterprise. Today, to run a movie company is to follow in the steps of tradi-tion, to be hounded by dreams and traditions of success. Whereas, Roach picked up a new ball and just began to throw it.

Jason Robards Jr. (1922–2000),
b. Chicago

The son of an actor, Jason Robards Sr. (1896–1963), and himself closely associated with stage revivals of Eugene O'Neill, Robards must be seen as a surviving exponent of the grand manner. He is romantic, crusty, weather-beaten, and easily carried away on his own soulfulness; his earnest commitment as an actor does not prevent his blood from being filled with that sublime idealiza-tion of self that furnishes ham. He seemed to be searching for a part where he had only to stand around gloomily, growl, chuckle, and do his gnarled thing.

His divorced father settled in Hollywood and, from living there, the son formed an early aver-sion to acting that always fueled his grumbling pipe dream that it is a foolish thing he does—instead of the very thing he was made for. He served in the navy during the Second World War, and only then took up acting. In 1946 he entered the American Academy of Dramatic Arts. Ten years later, he made a name as Hickey in O'Neill's *The Iceman Cometh*. He also played the elder son in *Long Day's Journey Into Night*, and Manley Halliday (based on Scott Fitzgerald) in the stage version of Budd Schulberg's *The Disenchanted*. In 1959, for TV, he played Robert Jordan in *For Whom the Bell Tolls*—early on, he had a list of prestigious parts.

His movie debut was as a Hungarian freedom fighter in *The Journey* (59, Anatole Litvak). After that he was in *By Love Possessed* (61, John Sturges); Dick Diver in *Tender Is the Night* (61, Henry King); the son again in *Long Day's Journey Into Night* (62, Sidney Lumet); *A Big Hand for the Little Lady* (66, Fielder Cook); *A Thousand Clowns* (66, Fred Coe); *Any Wednesday* (66, Robert Miller); *Divorce American Style* (67, Bud Yorkin); Old Man Clanton in *Hour of the Gun* (67, Sturges); Al Capone in *The St. Valentine's Day Massacre* (67, Roger Corman); *The Night They Raided Minsky's* (68, William Friedkin); Singer in *Isadora* (68, Karel Reisz); *Once Upon a Time in the West* (69, Sergio Leone); *Tora! Tora! Tora!* (70, Richard Fleischer); Brutus in *Julius Caesar* (70, Stuart Burge); *Fools* (70, Tom Gries); astounding in *The Ballad of Cable Hogue* (70, Sam Peckinpah); *Murders in the Rue Morgue* (71, Gor-don Hessler); the father in *Johnny Got His Gun* (71, Dalton Trumbo); *The War Between Men and Women* (72, Melville Shavelson); *The Execution* (72, Reza S. Badiyi); Lew Wallace in *Pat Garrett and Billy the Kid* (73, Peckinpah); Ben Bradlee in *All the President's Men* (76, Alan J. Pakula); Dashiell Hammett in *Julia* (77, Fred Zinnemann);

Comes a Horseman (78, Pakula); and in *Hurricane* (79, Jan Troell).

He won supporting actor Oscars for *All the President's Men* and *Julia*—tributes to the real people he played and to his easy histrionic stylization of them.

Robards played yet more "real" figures, covering them with his extending crust, like an alien force taking over natural life: a legendary Howard Hughes found in the desert in *Melvin and Howard* (80, Jonathan Demme); Leland Hayward for *Haywire* (80, Michael Tuchner); *F.D.R. The Last Year* (80, Anthony Page); *Sakharov* (84, Jack Gold); Clarence Darrow in *Inherit the Wind* (88, David Greene); and then there was the voice—if some voices lead us to say they have a weary, rasping, "lived in" quality, then Robards had a voice to accommodate all the streets and tenements of Brooklyn—which we are used to in everything from commercials to his portrayal of Ulysses S. Grant in *The Civil War* (89, Ken Burns).

But Robards played fictional beings, too, and few worked harder: *Raise the Titanic!* (80, Jerry Jameson); *Caboblanco* (80, J. Lee Thompson); *The Legend of the Lone Ranger* (81, William A. Fraker); *Max Dugan Returns* (83, Herbert Ross); *Something Wicked This Way Comes* (83, Jack Clayton); *The Day After* (83, Nicholas Meyer); *The Atlanta Child Murders* (85, John Erman); in the old Orson Welles role in *The Long Hot Summer* (85, Stuart Cooper); *Johnny Bull* (86, Claudia Weill); to Australia for *The Last Frontier* (86, Simon Wincer); *Square Dance* (87, Daniel Petrie); with Julie Harris in *The Christmas Wife* (88, David Jones); *Bright Lights, Big City* (88, James Bridges); *The Good Mother* (88, Leonard Nimoy); *Dream a Little Dream* (88, Marc Rocco); *Parenthood* (89, Ron Howard); with Rosanna Arquette as a clairvoyant team in *Black Rainbow* (89, Mike Hodges); *Reunion* (90, Jerry Schatzberg); *Quick Change* (90, Howard Franklin and Bill Murray); *The Perfect Tribute* (91, Jack Bender); *Chernobyl: The Final Warning* (91, Page); *An Inconvenient Woman* (91, Larry Elikann); and *Philadelphia* (93, Demme).

There were parts and films by then hardly worth trying without Robards. Yet he could move from agreeable hamminess to greatness with such ease. It was natural that so many actors should love him: as the King in *The Adventures of Huck Finn* (93, Stephen Sommers); *The Enemy Within* (94, Jonathan Darby); *The Paper* (94, Howard); *Little Big League* (94, Andrew Scheinman); *Crimson Tide* (95, Tony Scott); *My Antonia* (95, Joseph Sargent); *Journey* (95, Tom McLoughlin); as a Lear figure in *A Thousand Acres* (97, Jocelyn Moorhouse); *Heartwood* (98, Lanny Cotler); *The Real Macaw* (98, Mario Andreacchio); *Beloved* (98, Demme); *Enemy of the State* (98, Scott); remarkable on his deathbed in *Magnolia* (99,

Paul Thomas Anderson); *Going Home* (00, Ian Barry).

Tim Robbins,
b. West Covina, California, 1958
1992: *Bob Roberts*. 1995: *Dead Man Walking*. 1999: *Cradle Will Rock*.

Robbins has a little boy's face, and a wicked grin to go with it. He can easily seem like a dope, but watch out—he's as agile and dangerous as Griffin Mill in *The Player* (92, Robert Altman). That serpentine narrative owed a good deal to our sense of Mill's witty Machiavellian streak, and Robbins kept the comedy under expert control (thus, his Mill flattered Hollywood executives). He has real promise—if he can avoid disasters like *The Hudsucker Proxy* (94, Joel Coen).

He helped form the Actors' Gang, a theatre group, in Los Angeles, and made his debut in *No Small Affair* (84, Jerry Schatzberg); *Fraternity Vacation* (85, James Frawley); *The Sure Thing* (85, Rob Reiner); *Howard the Duck* (86, Willard Huyck); *Top Gun* (86, Tony Scott); and *Five Corners* (88, Tony Bill).

But he won attention as the wild pitcher in *Bull Durham* (88, Ron Shelton), a project that led to his relationship with Susan Sarandon—they have had two children. He wandered a good deal as an actor: *Tapeheads* (88, Bill Fishman); *Erik the Viking* (89, Terry Jones); *Miss Firecracker* (89, Thomas Schlamme); *Cadillac Man* (90, Roger Donaldson); and *Jacob's Ladder* (90, Adrian Lyne).

The Player set him up, and in the following year he delivered a very funny, womanizing cop in *Short Cuts* (93, Altman), and also made his directorial debut—*Bob Roberts*, a remarkably consistent black comedy about American politics. It's evident by now that Robbins stands up for liberal sentiments—which makes the balance and human depth of *Dead Man Walking* all the more admirable. For this is a fairly complex treatment of the matter, in which the parents are very carefully examined. By comparison, *Cradle Will Rock* is an enthusiastic tribute to famous heroes—but not much more.

As an actor, Robbins stays out of the mainstream, willing to help tough projects: *The Shawshank Redemption* (94, Frank Darabont); *Ready to Wear* (94, Altman); *I.Q.* (94, Fred Schepisi); *Nothing to Lose* (97, Steve Oedekerk); very frightening in *Arlington Road* (99, Mark Pellington); *Mission to Mars* (00, Brian De Palma); *High Fidelity* (00, Stephen Frears); *AntiTrust* (01, Peter Howitt); *Human Nature* (01, Michel Gondry); *The Truth About Charlie* (02, Jonathan Demme).

Julia Roberts, b. Smyrna, Georgia, 1967
The first thing to say about Julia is that she is a star of the highest force, and I'm not sure she has a female rival.

She is the sister of Eric Roberts (younger by a decade)—their parents ran an actors' workshop in Atlanta. Brother and sister played together in her first film, *Blood Red* (89, Peter Masterson), which had actually been shot in 1986, and shelved. Thus she first attracted attention in *Mystic Pizza* (88, Donald Petrie) and in *Satisfaction* (88, Joan Freeman). She got a supporting actress nomination for *Steel Magnolias* (89, Herbert Ross), but it was *Pretty Woman* (90, Garry Marshall) that made her a phenomenon. She played the kind of adorable whore whom a respectable man could take to the opera and put through college; she was an Audrey Hepburn who'd give head. The actress was helplessly available for what remains one of the most insidious and comprehensive lifestyle commercials masquerading as a movie. For a year, her nervy laugh—jittery but innocent—and her look (beautiful yet hinting at illness or depravity) were preeminent.

The moment passed; in *Flatliners* (90, Joel Schumacher) she was dull, and in *Sleeping With the Enemy* (91, Joseph Ruben) her haunted eyes were used to conventional effect. *Dying Young* (91, Schumacher) was a flop: even a phenomenon could not carry a title so foreboding to the youth audience. Then, dogged by publicity about romances and difficulty, she played Tinkerbell for no evident reason in *Hook* (91, Steven Spielberg), and in the movie within the movie in *The Player* (92, Robert Altman).

She retreated for a time. Romances with Kiefer Sutherland and Jason Patric preceded marriage to Lyle Lovett. Then she returned as the threatened law student in *The Pelican Brief* (93, Alan J. Pakula), and in *I Love Trouble* (94, Charles Shyer).

At that point, there were those who felt Roberts had shot her bolt, that the messy publicity would crush our interest. That was enforced by *Ready to Wear* (94, Altman) and two more failures—*Something to Talk About* (95, Lasse Hallström) and *Mary Reilly* (96, Stephen Frears). On the other hand, her Reilly was a very brave piece of acting in a film that is far better than its reputation. It's the moment I became interested in Roberts.

Not that *Michael Collins* (96, Neil Jordan) was an early dividend—she looked pretty, but no more than window dressing. But then she began a run of pictures that understood her screen persona and the way we wanted to like her: *Everyone Says I Love You* (96, Woody Allen); *My Best Friend's Wedding* (97, Richard Donner) was a misstep. But she was securely back on message with the daft *Notting Hill* (99, Roger Michell), where she is close to brilliant; *Runaway Bride* (99, Marshall), where Gere really looked like her father and behaved like her agent; and *Erin Brockovich* (00, Steven Soderbergh), the hittable fast ball she had been practicing for. It's a nice movie and a knock-out performance, and she was an automatic Oscar-winner.

What next? Well, anything she does for a while will sell. But if she's going to remain a big star in her forties, then the material will have to be better than *The Mexican* (01, Gore Verbinski), *America's Sweethearts* (01, Joe Roth), or *Ocean's 11* (01, Soderbergh). She has also made *Full Frontal* (02, Soderbergh) and *Confessions of a Dangerous Mind* (02, George Clooney).

Cliff Robertson,

b. La Jolla, California, 1925

The son of a wealthy rancher, Robertson was in the navy during the Second World War. While at college, he worked in local radio and after graduating he attended the Actors' Studio. From 1948–50 he played in *Mister Roberts* (directed on stage by Joshua Logan), and in the early 1950s he was regularly on Broadway. He was given his screen debut by Logan in *Picnic* (56).

Columbia signed him up and he was a match for Joan Crawford in *Autumn Leaves* (56, Robert Aldrich). But after *The Girl Most Likely* (57, Mitchell Leisen) and *The Naked and the Dead* (58, Raoul Walsh), he slipped into poorer pictures, supplemented with regular TV work. He made *Gidget* (59) and *Battle of the Coral Sea* (59) with Paul Wendkos, and was then outstanding as Fuller's hoodlum-turned-crusader in *Underworld USA* (61). His Tolly Devlin in that film has few equals for the accuracy of its self-pitying brutality. He came back to respectability in *The Interns* (62, David Swift), as John Kennedy in *PT-109* (63, Leslie H. Martinson), in *Sunday in New York* (63, Peter Tewkesbury), and as the tamely ruthless candidate in *The Best Man* (64, Franklin Schaffner).

His career has varied wildly: dull action pictures mixed with much more demanding parts—*633 Squadron* (64, Walter Grauman); *Love Has Many Faces* (65, Alexander Singer); *Masquerade* (64, Basil Dearden); *Up from the Beach* (65, Robert Parrish); *The Honey Pot* (67, Joseph L. Mankiewicz); *The Devil's Brigade* (68, Andrew V. McLaglen); *Charly* (68, Ralph Nelson), for which he won the best actor Oscar as a retarded man who becomes a genius; *Too Late the Hero* (70, Aldrich); and *The Great Northfield Minnesota Raid* (72, Philip Kaufman).

He acted in and directed an appealing but unadventurous rodeo movie, *J. W. Coop* (71), and acted in *Man on a Swing* (73, Frank Perry). He was in *Out of Season* (75, Alan Bridges); *Three Days of the Condor* (75, Sydney Pollack); too stolid for *Obsession* (76, Brian De Palma); and *Midway* (76, Jack Smight). An increasingly unobtrusive screen presence, Robertson raised his greatest stir for years when he sounded the alarm on David Begelman's checking practices with Columbia.

It is said that this civic-mindedness was regarded in Hollywood as less than team spirit. Equally, Robertson was by then of an age and a dogged calm that did not provoke the imagination. He acted in and directed *The Pilot* (79), about a flyer in trouble with booze. He was also in *Brainstorm* (81, Douglas Trumbull); *Two of a Kind* (82, Roger Young); *Class* (83, Lewis John Carlino); far too decent and cozy for Hugh Hefner in *Star 80* (83, Bob Fosse); *Shaker Run* (85, Bruce Morrison); *Dreams of Gold: The Mel Fisher Story* (85, Mel Goldstone), about a treasure hunter; *Malone* (87, Harley Cokliss); *Dead Reckoning* (90, Robert Lewis); *Wild Hearts Can't Be Broken* (91, Steve Miner); and *Wind* (92, Carroll Ballard).

His marriage to actress Dina Merrill (begun in 1966) had ended after twenty years. In terms of career, Robertson could easily have thought that the fix was in—or did he realize he had always been on the dull side? He was in *Renaissance Man* (94, Penny Marshall); *Pakten* (95, Leidulv Risan); *Dazzle* (95, Richard A. Colla); the president in *Escape from L.A.* (96, John Carpenter); *Melting Pot* (97, Tom Musca); *Assignment Berlin* (98, Tony Randel); *Family Tree* (99, Duane Clark); *Mach 2* (00, Fred Olen Ray); *The 13th Child, Legend of the Jersey Devil* (01, Steven Stockage); *Spider-Man* (02, Sam Raimi).

Paul Robeson (1898–1976),
b. Princeton, New Jersey

Even in an age that has many fine black actors in America, it's an awkward question as to who could play Paul Robeson in a biopic—if anyone mustered the courage for such a thing. For Robeson was made on a scale—inside and out—that leaves most actors seeming fragile. It's no discredit to Sidney Poitier to say that that vital actor of the 1950s might have played Robeson at eighteen—but how far beyond that? It's too easy, and quite useless now, to romanticize Robeson, but he had so many talents he made acting seem narrow (or a marginal concern). He was an athlete. He was academically distinguished. He was singer, actor, and public speaker. He was compelled then to be a public figure. And he was so early in America's leisurely liberalization that he drew down upon himself all the anger and hostility kept for the "uppity."

He was drawn, in the 1930s especially, to what he took for the example of the Soviet Union. In that, he was not alone; but he was virtually the only black person attacked for that sympathy, because he was the most prominent black of his time. He was terribly hurt by the attacks, and it is arguable that he began to betray himself (or his potential) with the withdrawal that followed. But it is so cruel to test anyone always against his "potential" instead of his reality. Robeson could sing the works of the masters; he could play

O'Neill and Shakespeare; but, in the end, he had no natural repertoire of movie roles, because there were no "ordinary" black parts save for servants or "boys." It was hard enough trying to be Paul Robeson—and testament enough that hardly anyone now would dare to fill his part.

As in most areas, his movie record is fragmented, bizarre, and shaming to the alleged picture business. A great deal of what he did depended on offers from Britain: *Body and Soul* (25, Oscar Micheaux); *The Emperor Jones* (35, Dudley Murphy)—a poor film; *Sanders of the River* (35, Zoltan Korda); singing "Ol' Man River" in *Show Boat* (36, James Whale); as a London docker who is actually an African prince in *Song of Freedom* (36, J. Elder Wills), playing with Elisabeth Welch, who is also in *Big Fella* (37, Wills), taken from a Claude McKay novel; as Umbopa in *King Solomon's Mines* (37, Robert Stevenson); as a soldier who flees to Africa and lives like a king in *Jericho* (37, Thornton Freeland); to Wales for the mining story *Proud Valley* (40, Pen Tennyson)—"the one film I could be proud of having played in"; *Tales of Manhattan* (42, Julien Duvivier); the narration on *Native Land* (42, Leo Hurwitz and Paul Strand); singing in the East German film *Das Lied der Strome* (54).

Edward G. Robinson (Emmanuel Goldenberg) (1893–1973),
b. Bucharest, Romania

His family came to America in 1902, and it was at Columbia University and the American Academy of Dramatic Arts that Goldenberg changed his name (the *G* was simply an initial). He appeared on the New York stage in 1913, and after war service his fame increased and he made his first film as an old man in *The Bright Shawl* (23, John S. Robertson). But it was an isolated debut and he remained in the theatre until the coming of sound when Paramount invited him to play a gangster in Robert Florey's *The Hole in the Wall* (29).

Within a year, Robinson was installed as Hollywood's most Latinate gangster. He had an enormous success as Little Rico in Mervyn Le Roy's *Little Caesar* (30) and played the Cobra in *Outside the Law* (30, Tod Browning). Short and stocky, with a curiously swollen, pale face and a voice that could snarl or whine, Robinson was able to alternate palpable sadism and cowardice. He was a tough editor in *Five Star Final* (31) and a condemned killer in *Two Seconds* (32), both for Le Roy.

But Robinson soon saw the danger in so many hissing psychopaths and it is probably a reflection of his own good humor (and his longing for respect) that he turned to retired gangsters, to decent men mistaken for gangsters, or to rather sentimental immigrants. In 1930, he played an Italian in Victor Sjöström's *A Lady to Love,* and in

1932 he brought a special zest to the fisherman in Howard Hawks's *Tiger Shark*. He played more respectable figures—a senator in *Silver Dollar* (33, Alfred E. Green) and a tycoon in *I Loved a Woman* (33, Green). In Roy del Ruth's *The Little Giant* (33) he was a retired gangster, and in Ford's *The Whole Town's Talking* (35) he was both a gangster and a placid bank clerk mistaken for the hoodlum.

He still had a ration of killing and crooks: in Archie Mayo's *The Man With Two Faces* (34), in Hawks's *Barbary Coast* (35), and in *The Last Gangster* (38, Edward Ludwig). But in 1936 he was working against the outlaw for the first time in William Keighley's *Bullets or Ballots*, and in Curtiz's *Kid Galahad* (37) he was a fight manager. Lloyd Bacon's *A Slight Case of Murder* (38) was another gangster comedy and in 1939, for Anatole Litvak, Robinson made one of the earliest anti-Nazi movies, *Confessions of a Nazi Spy*.

The next year he played the title part in Dieterle's *The Story of Dr. Ehrlich's Magic Bullet*, about the German Jew who discovered a cure for syphilis. Robinson was now free of the hard gangster image, and in Bacon's *Brother Orchid* (40) he was a hood who takes refuge in a monastery and grows to like the life. In 1940 he played the founder of the news agency in Dieterle's *A Dispatch from Reuter's;* in Le Roy's *Unholy Partners;* in Curtiz's *The Sea Wolf* (41); and in Raoul Walsh's *Manpower* (41), in which his wife, Marlene Dietrich, is implausibly seduced by the best man, George Raft. Perhaps this signified true middle age, for in 1942 Robinson made *Larceny Inc.* for Bacon, his last film under contract to Warners.

He now spent most of his time doing propaganda broadcasts (he spoke eight languages) to occupied Europe and had time only for the best episodes in Duvivier's *Tales of Manhattan* (42) and *Flesh and Fantasy* (43). His newfound sobriety was put to excellent use as the cigar-smoking insurance investigator in *Double Indemnity* (44, Billy Wilder) and then in probably his best two films, both for Fritz Lang, *The Woman in the Window* (44) and *Scarlet Street* (45), in which he is a gentle bourgeois sucked into sordid murders. Lang made Robinson's stature seem vulnerable and his face tragic where before he had been presented as a scowling killer. Few films make so engrossing an ordeal out of the ordinary man's alarm at being trapped in situations more appropriate to cinema.

In 1945, in Britain, he played a flying instructor in John Boulting's *Journey Together,* a propaganda movie, and in 1946 he excelled as another dogged investigator in Orson Welles's *The Stranger.* It was a surprise when the next year he put on the frighteners again, and very convincingly, in Delmer Daves's *The Red House,* which Robinson himself

produced. He was in *The Night Has a Thousand Eyes* (48, John Farrow), a father figure in *All My Sons* (48, Irving Reis), and in Mankiewicz's *House of Strangers* (49), and gave a brief reprise of Little Rico, whispering obscenely in Lauren Bacall's ear in Huston's *Key Largo* (48).

At about that time, Robinson's career suffered, despite being subsequently cleared, when he was called before the House Committee on Un-American Activities. He made *Actors and Sin* (52, Ben Hecht and Lee Garmes) and dropped into a run of lesser films in which he was forced to be a gangster again: *The Glass Web* (53, Jack Arnold); Aldrich's *The Big Leaguer* (53); Fregonese's excellent *Black Tuesday* (54); *Tight Spot* (55) for Phil Karlson; *A Bullet for Joey* (55) and *Illegal* (56) for Lewis Allen; and *The Violent Men* (56, Rudolph Maté).

Then, after appearing in De Mille's *The Ten Commandments* (56), Robinson retired to look at his paintings and to work in the theatre again. He played in Arthur Koestler's *Darkness at Noon* in 1951 and created the leading role in Chayefsky's *Middle of the Night* in 1956. He returned to Hollywood as one of its most revered veterans, not entirely well and involved in several unworthy films but appearing with credit in Capra's *A Hole in the Head* (59); in Hathaway's *Seven Thieves* (60); in Mackendrick's *Sammy Going South* (63); devious and exaggerated as the movie mogul in Minnelli's *Two Weeks in Another Town* (62); as the secretary of the interior in Ford's *Cheyenne Autumn* (64); in a double role in *The Prize* (64, Mark Robson); and by far the most assured poker player in *The Cincinnati Kid* (65, Norman Jewison). Toward the end, he was in sillier films—*The Biggest Bundle of Them All* (68, Ken Annakin); *MacKenna's Gold* (69, J. Lee Thompson); *Song of Norway* (70, Andrew L. Stone); and *Soylent Green* (72, Richard Fleischer). He died a few months before he could receive the overall Oscar belatedly awarded to him by the Academy.

Mark Robson (1913–78),

b. Montreal, Canada
1943: *The Seventh Victim; The Ghost Ship.* 1944: *Youth Runs Wild.* 1945: *Isle of the Dead.* 1946: *Bedlam.* 1949: *Home of the Brave; Champion; Roughshod; My Foolish Heart.* 1950: *Edge of Doom.* 1951: *Bright Victory; I Want You.* 1953: *Return to Paradise.* 1954: *Hell Below Zero; Phffft.* 1955: *The Bridges at Toko-Ri; A Prize of Gold; Trial.* 1956: *The Harder They Fall.* 1957: *The Little Hut; Peyton Place.* 1958: *The Inn of the Sixth Happiness.* 1960: *From the Terrace.* 1962: *Nine Hours to Rama.* 1963: *The Prize.* 1965: *Von Ryan's Express; Lost Command.* 1967: *Valley of the Dolls.* 1969: *Daddy's Gone A-Hunting.* 1971: *Happy Birthday, Wanda June.* 1974: *Earthquake.* 1978: *Avalanche Express.*

Robson is perhaps the most superficial talent to emerge from the Orson Welles circle. After studying at the Pacific Coast University he joined RKO as an editor and worked on both *Citizen Kane* and *The Magnificent Ambersons*, though without credit, and as fully fledged editor on *Journey Into Fear* (43). Like his marginally more talented colleague, Robert Wise, Robson graduated to directing through Val Lewton's small-budget horror pictures. His first five films were for Lewton, and the fact that he has never equaled the atmospheric inventiveness of *The Seventh Victim, The Ghost Ship,* and *Youth Runs Wild* is a reflection of Lewton's authorship and of Robson's neutrality. Brought up under one genius and one petit-maître, Robson oscillated between styles and genres. He indulged in a spurious, Kramerian realism—in *Home of the Brave, Champion,* and later with *Trial* and *The Harder They Fall*—but without missing a step he abandoned that for the most calculating sentimentality—*The Inn of the Sixth Happiness, The Bridges at Toko-Ri,* and *Nine Hours to Rama*—or a special taste for bestseller vulgarity: *Peyton Place* and *Valley of the Dolls.* But the business trusted him with big projects—as witness *Earthquake.* To see *The Seventh Victim* again, so strange, morbid, and poetic, is enough to let the auteur theory slip through a crack in *Earthquake's* silly ground.

Nicolas Roeg, b. London, 1928

1968: *Performance* (codirected with Donald Cammell). 1971: *Walkabout.* 1973: *Don't Look Now.* 1976: *The Man Who Fell to Earth.* 1980: *Bad Timing.* 1982: *Eureka.* 1985: *Insignificance.* 1986: *Castaway;* an episode from *Aria.* 1988: *Track 29.* 1989: *The Witches; Sweet Bird of Youth* (TV). 1992: *Cold Heaven.* 1994: *Heart of Darkness* (TV). 1995: *Two Deaths; Full Body Massage* (TV); *Hotel Paradise* (s). 1996: *Samson and Delilah* (TV). 2000: *The Sound of Claudia Schiffer* (s).

Need a man be praised for taking interesting pictures of Mick Jagger, the Australian desert, or Venice? Or would any novice find it difficult to make those subjects unspectacular?

It is the old question of the margin between exposure and revelation. Nicolas Roeg is often reckoned as one of the best photographers to move on to be a director. But the films he photographed are as variable as the directors who made them; it is impossible to discern Roeg beneath the deliberate gaudiness of *The Masque of the Red Death* (64, Roger Corman), the pastoral dullness of *Far from the Madding Crowd* (67, John Schlesinger), or the uneasy science-fiction abstraction of *Fahrenheit 451* (66, François Truffaut). A cameraman rarely hinders an inspired director or resolves the confusion of a mediocre one. *Fahrenheit 451* is visually stranded between offhand realism and fire-engine red schematics because Truffaut failed to discover his necessary intimacy in England.

Yet Roeg's reputation led him into direction and to that intriguing puzzle, *Performance* (68). When Warner Brothers delayed over releasing that film, and finally hacked it about, there were several cries in defense of mutilated art. But the film suggests that Warners only added to existing confusion. *Performance* looks like a film self-consciously attempting to use the gangster genre as the basis for existentialist riddle.

Donald Cammell seemed intent on drawing in every possible comment on the mysteries of identity, shuffling the spurious in with the portentous and the eclectic. The film howls with ideas, like the Babel of *Paris Nous Appartient,* and the reluctance to order wide reading into something more lasting than an arrogant catalogue of the holy underground. Jagger was an extraordinarily magnetic androgyne, apparently unwilling to relate himself to material or themes. While Roeg looked like a very skilled photographer full of superficial originality.

Roeg went on to direct, alone, *Walkabout* (71), a pretty piece of middlebrow anthropology about civilization and savagery confronting each other in the Australian outback. There was more reason to hope that Donald Cammell might one day make a film in which his Borgesian preoccupations were worked out temperately than that Roeg might direct a film in which the photography was only a means to an end.

But in 1973, he directed his third film, *Don't Look Now,* a Venice-bound occult thriller. Its widespread praise neglected the gulf between busy cinematic skill and the specious melodrama of the situation. From a Daphne du Maurier story, *Don't Look Now* makes a fascinating contrast with *The Birds:* whereas Hitchcock uses the bird invasion as a symptom of psychological unease, Roeg never relates the manifestation to his characters. While Hitch teases us with the idea of birds, Roeg jolts us into realizing that we doubt the occult.

The Man Who Fell to Earth is a dazzling idea, with the added prospect of the gauntly beautiful David Bowie as the fallen angel. Needless to say, it is a wonderful-looking film. But the aggressive imagination in the visuals is even further from narrative coherence. Roeg seemed ready to sacrifice sense to visual pretension, and long before the end this bleak parable has become nonsensical and precious. It was the thematic vanity that is most disconcerting.

Roeg has had a long career in films, working his way up by the hallowed but rarely trod ladder of clapper boy, assistant operator, operator, lighting cameraman, and director. He was assistant operator on, among others, *Bhowani Junction* (56, George Cukor) and operator on *The Trials* of *Oscar Wilde* (60, Ken Hughes). As director of photography he also worked on the second unit of *Lawrence of Arabia* (62, David Lean) and was in charge of *The Caretaker* (63, Clive Donner); *Nothing But the Best* (64, Donner); cameraman and second-unit director on *Judith* (65, Daniel Mann); *A Funny Thing Happened on the Way to the Forum* (66, Dick Lester); and *Petulia* (68, Lester).

In his age of Theresa Russell (Mrs. Roeg), Roeg became ever more wayward and unpredictable. *Bad Timing* (on which they met and Russell played the blank-eyed temptress) is an authentically disturbing sexual picture, as well as Roeg's most pessimistic work. *Eureka* is incoherent, but pretentious; *Insignificance* is fatuous; *Castaway* is a subject for Buñuel or Strindberg; *Track 29* is unintentionally comic; *The Witches* is a nearly perfect horror movie for wise children on their second breakdown, with a superb use of naïve effects; *Sweet Bird of Youth* was as windy as Miami waiting for a hurricane; *Cold Heaven* is a fine story lost in cloudbanks of mysticism. *Heart of Darkness* left one wondering—again—why anyone ever wanted to film that story. Conrad's horror is so elusive, while movie's has to be there. Life is actually not quite as strange as Roeg believes.

Since then, Roeg has had a very odd career—as if age or his reputation for lofty incoherence had caught up with him. But once upon a time he would have run riot with *Samson and Delilah*, and caused a storm with Claudia Schiffer (even silent). It's not a kind world for visionaries.

Ginger Rogers (Virginia Katherine McMath) (1911–95), b. Independence, Missouri

Ginger was not the most sophisticated lady in films, and yet she had an enormously popular partnership with Fred Astaire, that sublime mannequin and rare distillation of masculine aplomb. Astaire was never the easiest man to partner: not only because as a dancer he was meticulously exacting, but because his screen character was almost abstract—especially in the RKO 1930s musicals, in which slicked-down hair and perfect costume add to the effect of some spirit of the dance floor and cocktail lounge. Very difficult for a woman to be so rarefied without seeming vapid; all too easy to frighten the faun away with cheerfulness or to expose oneself as brash.

On her own, Ginger could be brash—as many post-Astaire movies proved; and she had a rather nasty edge. But she contrived to complement Astaire rather than alarm him. In rehearsal, their relations were sometimes strained by Astaire's perfectionism (though Ginger was a fast, sure dancer). On the screen, her robustness rubbed off on his remoteness so that he seemed warmed by her, just as she gained cool in his draft. As a result, they became one of the clearest expressions of 1930s style in the way they blended two contrary archetypes: the man about town and the girl next door.

But before her first film with Astaire, Ginger had made nineteen pictures. Her mother was always immensely ambitious for her, and young Virginia was in Hollywood at the age of six. In her teens she toured in vaudeville, and by the late 1920s was working in New York as a singer. (In 1930 she was the original ingenue in Gershwin's *Girl Crazy*, Ethel Merman's first show.) Paramount hired her, and in the early thirties she was a blonde with a disbelieving face and a fast line in smart dialogue: she steals many scenes in *42nd Street* (33, Lloyd Bacon) on that basis, and her apprenticeship also included *The Young Man of Manhattan* (30, Monta Bell); *The Sap from Syracuse* (30, Edward Sutherland); *Follow the Leader* (30, Norman Taurog); *Honor Among Lovers* (31, Dorothy Arzner); *The Tenderfoot* (32, Ray Enright); *Hat Check Girl* (32, Sidney Lanfield); *You Said a Mouthful* (32, Bacon); *Gold Diggers of 1933* (33, Mervyn Le Roy); *Professional Sweetheart* (33, William A. Seiter); and *Sitting Pretty* (33, Harry Joe Brown).

This last was made at RKO, who put her under contract and later in 1933 introduced her and Astaire as second leads in *Flying Down to Rio* (Thornton Freeland). Their success was such that after *Chance at Heaven* and *Rafter Romance* (both 33, Seiter) and two at Warners—*Twenty Million Sweethearts* (34, Ray Enright) and *Upperworld* (34, Roy del Ruth)—the partnership was resumed in earnest: *The Gay Divorcee* (34, Mark Sandrich); *Roberta* (35, Seiter); *Top Hat* (35, Sandrich); *Follow the Fleet* (36, Sandrich); *Swing Time* (36, George Stevens); *Shall We Dance?* (37, Sandrich); *Carefree* (38, Sandrich); and *The Story of Vernon and Irene Castle* (39, H. C. Potter).

This is the peak of the 1930s black-and-white musical. The stress on plastic glamour, lighthearted stories, and cosmopolitan high life was unashamed and insignificant. It is trite to say that the films were cheerful, anti-Depressive, and insubstantial. Like Marx Brothers movies, they run together, so casual was the story line and so subservient the direction. But the films are very strong in character: they glisten with glass, polished floors, satin dresses, celluloid costume flowers, and Astaire's hairstyle. They also enjoyed some of the greatest songs by Jerome Kern, Irving Berlin, Cole Porter, and the Gershwins. The look of the films, and the way it conspired toward the rapid-fire choreography, is a self-sufficient personality: in short, the film in which dance comes first, such as Gene Kelly strove for in the 1950s.

Not that anyone thought of that at RKO in the 1930s, least of all Astaire. But he was like an anonymous Gothic decorator, so intent on making every dance step right that he did not see the astonishing entirety. Only Astaire's subsequent difficulty in finding partners shows how important a contribution Ginger made—she was always princess for the moment in this rapt genius's arms, and that contrived to make him seem prince charming rather than the puppet who had to dance. There were even moments when Ginger had a few jokes at Fred, as in *Roberta* where she says of him, "A piccolo player! How *charmante!*"

Their run ended with the Castles biopic: there had been tensions and Ginger was eager to prove herself as an actress. In 1937 she had had her best part to date in *Stage Door* (Gregory La Cava), and in 1938 George Stevens made the best of her youthful flexibility in a comedy, *Vivacious Lady*. For the next five years, she managed to be a leading actress, usually in comedy. She worked hard and the effort showed a little too much for easy viewing, especially when she was doing one of her child impersonations. She was in *Bachelor Mother* (39, Garson Kanin); *Fifth Avenue Girl* (39, La Cava); *Primrose Path* (40, La Cava); *Lucky Partners* (40, Lewis Milestone); *Kitty Foyle* (40, Sam Wood), a women's pic for which she won the best actress Oscar; *Tom, Dick and Harry* (41, Kanin); *Roxie Hart* (42, William Wellman); *The Major and the Minor* (42, Billy Wilder); *Once Upon a Honeymoon* (42, Leo McCarey); *Tender Comrade* (43, Edward Dmytryk); *Lady in the Dark* (44, Mitchell Leisen); and *I'll Be Seeing You* (44, William Dieterle).

After the war her star waned. She made *Weekend at the Waldorf* (45, Robert Z. Leonard), *Magnificent Doll* (46, Frank Borzage), and *It Had to Be You* (47, Rudolph Maté and Don Hartman). Then came a two-year gap before a reunion with Astaire in *The Barkleys of Broadway* (49, Charles Walters). By then, however, she was mixing comedies and souped-up dramas, for which she was not really suited. Only *Monkey Business* (52, Howard Hawks) is memorable among her late films. Otherwise, she was seldom at ease: *Perfect Strangers* (50, Bretaigne Windust); *Storm Warning* (50, Stuart Heisler); *Dreamboat* (52, Claude Binyon); *Forever Female* (53, Irving Rapper); *The Beautiful Stranger* (54, David Miller); *Black Widow* (54, Nunnally Johnson); *Tight Spot* (55, Phil Karlson); *Teenage Rebel* (56, Edmund Goulding); *Oh, Men! Oh, Women!* (57, Johnson); and *The First Traveling Saleslady* (56, Arthur Lubin). Since then, she has made only two oddities: *Quick, Let's Get Married* (65, William Dieterle) and *Harlow* (65, Alex Segal).

Will Rogers (1879–1935),
b. Cologah, Oklahoma

Although his films are seldom revived these days, and many younger filmgoers will never have seen him, Will Rogers was one of the most reflective and influential of American film stars. He was a superbly skillful presentation of guileless good sense. Every American instinct that there ought to be an earthy, unsophisticated wisdom residing on the range and on the verandas of small towns, and that this untutored, natural empathy with order should at the same time be utterly winning, charming, and accomplished, was vindicated in Will Rogers. He is the marketable noble savage, the casual raconteur who steps neatly between cracker-barrel and fascism, and who leaves us puzzling out whether his diffident ramble was spontaneous or cunningly scripted.

Rogers's philosophy was reactionary, dispiriting, and provincial, despite every affectation of bonhomie and tolerance. It scorned ideas and people who held them, it relied on vague evolution rather than direct action, its fixed smile concealed rigidity of opinion that middle America need not be disturbed from its own prejudices and limitations. But the style was beguiling. Rogers had so digested the role of cowboy philosopher that it is dangerous to make charges of conscious deception, such as mar the portrait of Lonesome Rhodes in Kazan's *A Face in the Crowd*.

The essence of the style is that it convinces the performer: as with Rogers, so with every notable American public figure since the 1930s, Kane or H. Ross Perot. The bowdlerization of democracy, the professionalism of delivery, and the assumption of homeliness were the ingredients of the threadbare benevolence of Richard Nixon as well as the slapdash gestures toward compassion in the films of John Ford. Indeed, in cinematic terms, Rogers's persona played a part in Ford's development, and his pious, sly presentation of mediocrity as humanity is the most persistent vice of American cinema. You have only to discover the old men in Faulkner to realize what charlatans Ford's veterans are.

Rogers had been cowboy and merchant seaman before Wild West Shows led him into vaudeville. Beyond lariat tricks, his method was to "pause a while" and speak up for the droll intuition of cowboys everywhere. This gauche demagoguery found many listeners toward the end of the First World War. Samuel Goldwyn, unable to discern in Rogers's success the necessity of speech, signed him up for a string of films that proved how plain Rogers was without time to yarn: *Laughing Bill Hyde* (18, Hobart Henley); *Jubilo* (19); *Jes' Call Me Jim* (20); *Cupid the Cowpuncher* (20); *Honest Hutch* (20); *Guile of Woman* (21, Clarence Badger)—it was part of the Rogers America that women were essentially tricky and dishonest, whereas male deceptions were only playful: *Boys Will Be Boys* (21, Badger); *An Unwilling Hero* (21, Badger); and *Doubling for Romeo* (21, Badger).

Goldwyn eventually saw his error and dropped Rogers. The lonesome cowboy made two more films—*One Glorious Day* (22, James Cruze) and *The Headless Horseman* (22, Edward Venturini)—before he went, disastrously, into production himself. He returned to the stage, apart from some shorts he made for Hal Roach. Meanwhile, his legend grew. He published a monstrous collection of homilies that chimed neatly with widespread aversion to 1920s permissiveness: *Rogers-isms: The Cowboy Philosopher on the Peace Conference*. He worked as a wry surveyor of the European scene for the *Saturday Evening Post* and, while in England, made *Tiptoes* (27, Herbert Wilcox). Back in America, he played a rancher who goes to straighten out Washington in *A Texas Steer* (27, Richard Wallace).

It was sound that capitalized on his style and Fox who seized him for themselves. He died in a plane crash in 1935, but for six years he had been a huge American hero, a counseling voice during the Depression, a reassurance to the bewildered, and a considerable asset in the 1932 election campaign of Franklin Roosevelt. The films are period pieces, but to deny their impact would be to conceal the basic hostility to enlightenment in America: *They Had to See Paris* (29, Frank Borzage); *So This Is London* (30, John Blystone); *Lightnin'* (30, Henry King); *A Connecticut Yankee* (31, David Butler); *Young As You Feel* (31, Borzage); *Business and Pleasure* (32, Butler); *Down to Earth* (32, Butler); *State Fair* (33, King); *Doctor Bull* (33, John Ford); *Mr. Skitch* (33, Cruze); *David Harum* (34, Cruze); *Handy Andy* (34, Butler); *Judge Priest* (34, Ford), the character revived by Ford, incredibly, in *The Sun Shines Bright* (53); *Life Begins at Forty* (35, George Marshall); *Doubting Thomas* (35, Butler); *Steamboat Round the Bend* (35, Ford); and *In Old Kentucky* (35, Marshall).

There is a fascinating memento of Rogers's influence in the early 1930s in Peter Bogdanovich's *Paper Moon*, where *Steamboat Round the Bend* is playing in some dusty prairie town to narrow-minded farmers and hopeful confidence tricksters.

Eric Rohmer (Jean-Marie Maurice Scherer), b. Nancy, France, 1920

1950: *Journal d'un Scélérat* (s). 1952: *Les Petites Filles Modèles* (codirected with P. Guilband, uncompleted); *Presentation* (s). 1954: *Bérénice* (s). 1956: *La Sonate à Kreutzer* (s). 1958: *Véronique et Son Cancre* (s). 1959: *Le Signe du Lion*. 1962: *La Boulangère de Monceau* (s). 1963: *La Carrière de Suzanne*. 1964: *Nadja à Paris* (s); "Place de l'Etoile," episode from *Paris Vu Par. . . .* 1966: *Une Étudiante d'Aujourd'hui* (s); *La Collectionneuse*. 1968: *Fermière à Montfauçon* (s); *Ma Nuit Chez Maud/My Night at Maud's*. 1970: *Le Genou de Claire/Claire's Knee*. 1972: *L'Amour, L'Après-Midi/Chloe in the Afternoon*. 1976: *Die Marquise von O*. 1978: *Perceval le Gallois*. 1980: *La Femme de l'Aviateur/The Aviator's Wife*. 1981: *Le Beau Mariage*. 1982: *Pauline à la Plage/Pauline*

at the Beach. 1984: an episode in *Paris Vu Par . . . 20 Ans Après; Les Nuits de la Pleine Lune/Full Moon in Paris*. 1986: *Le Rayon Vert/Summer*. 1987: *L'Ami de Mon Amie/My Girlfriend's Boyfriend; 4 Aventures de Reinette et Mirabelle*. 1990: *Conte de Printemps/A Tale of Springtime*. 1991: *Conte d'Hiver/A Tale of Winter*. 1993: *L'Arbre, le Maire et la Médiathèque*. 1995: *Les Rendez-vous de Paris*. 1996: *Conte d'Eté*. 1998: *Conte d'Automne*. 2001: *L'Anglaise et le Duc/The Lady and the Duke*.

Without wishing to prejudice the prospects of cinema as intelligent as Eric Rohmer's, it is remarkable that *Maud, Claire, L'Amour, L'Après-Midi*, and so on have been so successful. It would not be difficult to advertise these films in a way calculated to alarm prospective spectators; it is only honest to describe them as semiformal, literary inquiries into the sensibilities and thoughts of a group of people gathered round some modest action—so modest, indeed, that an outsider might not notice it. There are real dangers in such a method: of prettiness, or an archly natural debate in adolescent psychology, and of a rather passive opting for discussion instead of behavior. Rohmer can be criticized, to some extent, on all those grounds. But he has not been challenged, as it happens, and I am perplexed as to whether that speaks for a rare homing in of a select audience on worthy material, for a genuine raising of standards, or for the serious, if scarcely evident, flaw of complacency in Rohmer's work.

His success may even have surprised Rohmer, in exactly the way that spontaneity sometimes disarms the poised young men in his *contes moraux*. Rohmer has confessed the strategy that made him announce these six contes in advance: *La Boulangère de Monceau; La Carrière de Suzanne; Ma Nuit Chez Maud* (number 3 was made after number 4); *La Collectionneuse; Le Genou de Claire;* and *L'Amour, L'Après-Midi:*

> I thought audiences and producers would be more likely to accept my idea in this form than in another. Instead of asking myself what subjects were most likely to appeal to audiences, I persuaded myself that the best thing would be to treat the same subject six times over. In the hope that by the sixth time the audience would come to me! . . . I was determined to be inflexible and intractable, because if you persist in an idea it seems to me that in the end you do secure a following. Even with a distributor . . . it's much more difficult for him to put up arguments and criticisms about a scenario which is part of a group of six than about an isolated script.

There speaks the young outsider of the 1950s

plotting his way into an unsympathetic industry, the friend and companion critic of Rivette, Godard, and Chabrol. It is easy to forget, because of the direction their work has taken, that Rohmer was not just coauthor with Chabrol (in 1957) of the first study of Hitchcock, but author of the bulk of it. *Le Signe du Lion* speaks much more directly of Rohmer the Parisian scraping money together to buy film stock. It has a stark view of penury and urban unfriendliness that was put aside with the *contes moraux.*

Today, one would not readily guess that Rohmer had done so much to explain Hitchcock, despite his own interest in psychological ploys, and in knowing why people act. In fact, his hindsight confession of strategy is very close to the way some of his characters dissect their predicaments and then select a course of action to which they must conform. For instance, the two young men "bargaining" over Haydée in *La Collectionneuse,* Trintignant in *Maud* determining to marry the blonde girl on the bicycle, and Brialy seeing the world in a hand's brief delay on a knee.

The films have a subtle and absorbing tension between the intellectual inflexibility (or resolve) of the characters and the evanescence of the situations in which they act. Thus Rohmer often presents surrogate artists—an antique dealer, a painter, a philosopher, an engineer, a novelist—with emotional scenarios that break down their elegant detachment, educate them in the interwoven complex of feelings and thoughts, and leave them doubtful at the realization that life is as shifting and indefinite as water in the sun. Very often, Rohmer so clearly outlines the range of action open to his central characters that the clarity takes precedence. There are several occasions on which characters draw back from daring or possibly harmful actions.

Indeed, there is the underlying hint in Rohmer's work that freedom is a dangerous state from which most men flee—into demanding jobs, marriage, and a framework of intellectual self-justification. But few directors have given us as many self-possessed, articulate women as Rohmer. Still, Rohmer has just as much interest in instinctive and unknowable women: Haydée in *La Collectionneuse,* Claire, and Chloe in *L'Amour, L'Après-Midi* are such figures, while the men are always as rational and lucid as Rohmer himself.

The director's own definition of the *contes moraux* is worth quoting, because as criticism it could not be improved, and because it might be a speech from one of his films—a seventh *conte* in which the man is a filmmaker:

What I call a *conte moral* is not a tale with a moral, but a story which deals less with what people do than with what is going on in their minds while they are doing it. . . . The peo-

ple in my films are not expressing abstract ideas—there is no "ideology" in them, or very little—but revealing what they think about relationships between men and women, about friendship, love, desire, their conception of life, happiness . . . boredom, work, leisure. . . . Things which have of course been spoken about previously i the cinema, but usually indirectly, in the context of a dramatic plot. Whereas in the *contes moraux* this just doesn't exist, and in particular there's no clear-cut line of tragedy or comedy. You can say that my work is closer to the novel—to a certain classic style of novel which the cinema is now taking over—than to other forms of entertainment, like the theatre.

Literary influences and strands do abound: not simply the willingness to have characters talk seriously at length, but the frequent use of narration and, especially in *Claire,* the fluctuating attempt to make a novel of the action. Partly because of the presence of Aurora Cornu, a novelist, playing a novelist, partly because of the deliberate filming of pages of a journal, *Claire* has an extra ingenuity and resonance in the way it moves between events and a fictional account of them.

All the literary content is peripheral to Rohmer's eye. It is in the quality of his imagery that we feel the intellectual appeal of experience. The camera style is classically simple, but Rohmer adores the effects of natural light, whether the reflections from snow in *Maud,* the rainy day in *Claire,* or the Côte d'Azur interiors in *La Collectionneuse.* The breathtaking coda to *Maud,* for instance, owes a lot to the sudden resort to a warmer light. The effect of time passing and feelings altering has seldom been conveyed so well. Again, Rohmer chooses and films his setting with great imaginative care: the lakeside house in *Claire* and the snowscapes of Clermont Ferrand in *Maud* are integral to the effect of the film, as is the choice of precise locations for key moments.

But it is the way he films people that is most characteristic, and most reflective of his sense of the limits to intelligence. Beauty, its nature, and contrary opinions of it are recurring themes. And Rohmer gives us time to consider whether and how people are beautiful. In one of the prologues to *La Collectionneuse,* the camera takes semiabstract but very sensual pictures of the indifferent Haydée Politoff. And in the next prologue several characters argue about beauty: is it, as one claims, an effect of appearance that reflects moral nature? Do people look as they are? Cinema has always nagged at that question, few directors more enchantingly than Rohmer with his gallery of women: Politoff, Françoise Fabian, Marie-Christine Barrault, Aurora Cornu, Beatrice Romand, Lawrence de Monaghan, Zouzou, and Françoise Verley.

L'Amour, L'Après-Midi brings that entire gallery to life and ends with the married man eschewing adultery when he sees himself in a mirror before the act.

With the *contes moraux* complete, Rohmer turned to the eighteenth century and a novella by Kleist. Its visual elegance and its ambiguity as to what has happened were a shade too prolonged and pious. The setting, for the first time in Rohmer, was classical and cold, and the woman in this case, Edith Clever, lacked the animation of his other heroines.

Sometimes I wonder if, after the destruction of the rest of the world, Rohmer might not still be making his fourth six-part series, on love at different times of day, with holograms of yet more slender, lovely girls, torrents of witty dialogue, and contrivances of misunderstanding. This seems ungrateful: Rohmer's exquisite industry is genuine; his intelligence is beyond dispute. It is only his seemingly isolated momentum that I find incredible and . . . inhuman. A few years after any film, it has been folded into the mix of the others, like an extra egg going into batter. The later series are not as compelling as the *contes moraux*. But Rohmer is so steadily active he may lull us into feeling that everything has become habitual.

At eighty, having completed his seasonal *contes*, Rohmer delivered *L'Anglaise et le Duc*, a ravishing period re-creation, and a lovely, small film. I remain with my reservations (or maybe it is just diminished patience), but how can one admire a painter like Chardin and not see that Rohmer is a similar kind of artist, serenely attached to ideals of spiritual and historical permanence? Indeed, it is as if—in fact—he was a moviemaker from the eighteenth century come to visit.

George A. Romero, b. New York, 1940
1968: *Night of the Living Dead.* 1972: *There's Always Vanilla/The Affair.* 1973: *The Crazies/ Code Name Trixie; Hungry Wives.* 1978: *Martin.* 1979: *Dawn of the Dead.* 1981: *Knightriders.* 1982: *Creepshow.* 1985: *Day of the Dead.* 1988: *Monkey Shines.* 1990: "The Truth About the Valdemar Case," an episode from *Two Evil Eyes.* 1993: *The Dark Half.* 2000: *Bruiser.*

I am far from an enthusiast of horror—ordinary life is alarming enough. But I often prefer the cheap brand to the expensive, and the homemade and obsessive to the realm of special effects. Thus my soft spot for George Romero, and the matter-of-fact nightmares that he has delivered from Pittsburgh. His concept of the living dead was brilliant and poetic (as well as recognizably lifelike). It was heaven for nonprofessionals. And it brought a real beauty to horror, a slightly slow-mo, lyrical desperation. *Night of the Living Dead* and *Dawn of the Dead* (the one set in a shopping mall) are unforgettable and seminal works of modern America. They are also correctives to the terrible hollowness of the *Scream* movies. Romero has a deep, tender belief in crippled, blighted states, and there is a haunting ambiguity in his best passages—for, just as we yearn to obliterate these living dead, so we long for their triumph and their banquet.

Mikhail Romm (1901–71), b. Irkutsk, Russia
1934: *Pushka/Boule de Suif.* 1937: *Trinadtsat; Lenin v Oktyabre* (codirected with Dimitri Vasiliev). 1939: *Lenin v 1918 Godu.* 1943: *Mechta.* 1945: *Chelovek 217.* 1948: *Russkii Vopros; Vladimir Ilyich Lenin* (codirected with V. Belyaev); *Zhivoi Lenin* (codirected with Marcia Slavinskaya) (d). 1950: *Sekretnaya Missiya.* 1953: *Admiral Ushakov; Korabli Shturmuyut Bastiony.* 1956: *Ubiistvo na Ulitsye Dante/Murder on Dante Street.* 1961: *Devyat dni Odnovo Goda/Nine Days of One Year.* 1965: *Obyknovennie Fashizm/Ordinary Fascism* (d).

Romm worked with decent tact and skill in several types of film, well enough to come through without suffering any substantial authoritarian disapproval. He entered films rather late and was assistant on *Dela i Lyudi* (32, Alexander Macheret) before directing himself. *Boule de Suif* was of some historical importance: though still a silent picture, it was the first film made on entirely Russian stock. Ironically, its basis in Maupassant was artfully turned into a faithful work of French nineteenth-century realism, a worthy film but vastly inferior to *Partie de Campagne, Le Plaisir,* or *Une Vie.* When Stalin ordered a tribute to Lenin in 1937, it was Romm who hurried the epic through and went on to a sequel, both with Boris Shchukin as the Bolshevik hero. He returned to the same subject in 1948, and at the deep-freeze moment of the Cold War made a somber study of the possible effects of radiation, *Nine Days of One Year.*

Mickey Rooney (Joe Yule Jr.),
b. Brooklyn, New York, 1920
Do we laugh or cry for Rooney? Is it possible within a brief entry to convey the dementia of his life and career, and yet suggest his spasmodic ability to transcend vulgarity and make it into an astonishing portrait of the all-American boy-hero in which the motor is accelerating by some geometric progression? Mickey Rooney is important, and yet he is ridiculous; it is in the pitch of his absurdity that he is significant. One feels like a coroner presented with a cadaver shot through the head, poisoned, thrown off a cliff, and with a bad heart. Rooney could have died long ago from sheer disbelief; he lives on. It is all very well for Yeats to say "the center cannot hold" and believe

that such a verdict is sufficient. Rooney has been an exploding galaxy all his life, endlessly fragmenting, but against all laws he still holds together. Let us try to pick out some of the principles of survival.

1. In at least three films, Rooney is not just an actor of genius, but an artist able to maintain a stylized commentary on the demon impulse of the small, belligerent man. His Puck in *A Midsummer Night's Dream* (35, Max Reinhardt and William Dieterle) is a masterpiece amid that weirdly isolated evocation of the fairy spirit. Rooney seems inhuman, he moves like mist or water, his body is burnished by the extraordinary light, and his gurgling laugh is ghostly and enchanting.

Could such a performance have been directed? Could the brash kid he has always insisted on being have made such an imaginative leap? Or is there some primal instinct in Rooney that draws his vitality from psychic identification with fantasy? Such a man might live on make-believe, and Rooney's Puck is truly inhuman, one of cinema's most arresting pieces of magic.

The second sensation is his toughie in *Boys Town* (38, Norman Taurog), seeming ten rather than sixteen years old, who struts and bullies like something out of a nightmare and then comes clean in a grotesque but utterly frank outburst of sentimentality in which he aspires to the boy community. Easy to mock the hysteria of *Boys Town*, but look only a little beyond such bad taste and it becomes a vivid study of American simplemindedness, with Rooney expressing all the impossible, brutal simplicity of American ideals.

The third is what might happen to that same toughie if *Boys Town* had expelled him: *Baby Face Nelson* (57, Don Siegel), the manic, destructive response of the runt against a pig society. The little man with a tommy gun as big as himself, his innocence diverted into slaughter. *Nelson* is a classic gangster movie, made by a master of the form, but achieving a fearful poetry because of Rooney's seizure of part of his own appalling destiny.

2. By 1935, when MGM put him under proper contract, Rooney had made twenty films, dozens of shorts and serials. From the age of seven onward, he had never been out of work, originally under the name of Mickey McGuire.

3. At MGM, he endeared himself to Louis B. Mayer, who saw in Rooney the embodiment of the amiable American boy who stands for family, humbug, and sentiment. Such wholesome and homely virtues were celebrated on screen through a sweatshop labor system that left permanent wounds on Rooney and his costar, Judy Garland. Yet, on screen, has there ever been so exhilarating a portrait of such garishly innocent teenage energy? Garland's crack-up was public, maudlin, and tragic. Rooney's has been none the less, but it has never been pathetic. There is an American

way, between the tragic and the certifiably insane, a constant raising of gear to no effect, that Rooney has road-tested.

4. The basis of that all-American dream and private nightmare was Andy Hardy, begun in 1937 with *A Family Affair*. Andy became Rooney: cheeky, naughty, improvisational, immensely talented as mime, dancer, comic, singer, and ham. But he lacked all the roots that Mayer tried to cultivate. He was not the true native product, but a Madison Avenue cuckoo dropped into the nest, able to refer only to a set of consumer rules whereby family feelings and youthful ideals were all part of a package description.

5. From 1938 to 1944, Rooney was one of the most popular stars in the world. He acted, he sang, he danced, and still he seemed impatient. He excelled not just in thirteen Andy Hardy films, but in musicals, sentimental comedies, and those subtle apologias for American coarseness in which he made fun of the priggish Freddie Bartholomew. This was the period in which, aged fifteen to twenty-five, Rooney made forty-three pictures, the best part of $10 million, won a special Oscar, and was married to and divorced by Ava Gardner. The films, or a selection from them: *Reckless* (35, Victor Fleming); *Ah, Wilderness!* (35, Clarence Brown); *Little Lord Fauntleroy* (36, John Cromwell); *The Devil Is a Sissy* (36, W. S. Van Dyke); *Captains Courageous* (37, Fleming); *Slave Ship* (37, Tay Garnett); *Thoroughbreds Don't Cry* (37, Alfred E. Green); *The Adventures of Huckleberry Finn* (39, Richard Thorpe); *Babes in Arms* (39, Busby Berkeley); *Young Tom Edison* (40, Taurog); *Strike Up the Band* (40, Berkeley); *Babes on Broadway* (41, Berkeley); *A Yank at Eton* (42, Taurog); *The Human Comedy* (43, Brown); *Girl Crazy* (43, Taurog); *Thousands Cheer* (43, George Sidney); and *National Velvet* (44, Brown).

6. In 1944, Andy Rooney went to war. When he returned, the skids were put under him. Of course, they had always been built in to the career MGM made for him. Part of Rooney's great appeal was the way fame had come to someone unequipped to deal with it. He had been made the center of a huge fantasy. But now his time was up. In four years after the war he made five films at MGM—including one more Andy Hardy, *Killer McCoy* (47, Roy Rowland), *Summer Holiday* (47, Rouben Mamoulian), and *Words and Music* (48, Taurog), in which he played Lorenz Hart.

7. By 1949 he was freelance. Aged twenty-nine, he looked like an eighteen-year-old rejuvenation of someone fifty-five years old. He had been used to vast salaries, great praise, and constant humoring of his crazy whims. All were withdrawn.

The glib consequence is easy to script. But Rooney scorned it. He had made many bouncy, energetic good pictures. He would now make almost as many tawdry, bad pictures. There have been exceptions, like *Baby Face Nelson,* although that was a disaster in project, rescued against odds by the concurrence of Siegel and Rooney and some inspired supporting playing. So Rooney became a dreadful joke, the chronic accumulation of divorces and more dreadful credits than any other actor.

In his early fifties, he looked like a teenager trying to play the part of middle age. His energy remained; his sentimentality was violent; his vulgarity as emotional as ever. He cried out for inventive casting—such as his 1970 Broadway playing of W. C. Fields. A sudden magnificence would add a characteristic incongruity to his list of B pictures and broken-backed first features: *The Fireball* (50, Garnett); *My Outlaw Brother* (51, Elliott Nugent); *Sound Off* (52, Richard Quine); *All Ashore* (53, Quine); excellent in *Drive a Crooked Road* (54, Quine); *A Slight Case of Larceny* (53, Don Weis); *The Atomic Kid* (54, Leslie H. Martinson); *The Bridges at Toko-Ri* (55, Mark Robson); *The Bold and the Brave* (56, Lewis R. Foster); the driving force for the teeming comedy of *Operation Madball* (57, Quine); brilliant on TV's *Playhouse 90* in Rod Serling's *The Comedian* (57, John Frankenheimer); *Andy Hardy Comes Home* (58, Howard W. Koch); *The Last Mile* (59, Koch); *Platinum High School* (59, Albert Zugsmith); *The Private Life of Adam and Eve* (60, Zugsmith); *King of the Roaring Twenties* (61, Joseph M. Newman); grotesque as the Japanese in *Breakfast at Tiffany's* (61, Blake Edwards); *Requiem for a Heavyweight* (62, Ralph Nelson); *It's a Mad, Mad, Mad, Mad World* (63, Stanley Kramer); *The Secret Invasion* (63, Roger Corman); *The Extraordinary Seaman* (68, Frankenheimer); *Skidoo* (68, Otto Preminger); *80 Steps to Jonah* (69, Gerd Oswald); and *Pulp* (72, Mike Hodges).

8. A suggestion: Fool to Orson Welles's Lear in a version adapted so that the two are revealed to be long-lost twins. No, no one has ever seen that movie—but there are other Welles projects as farfetched and as hard to discover. I believe in this film; I can see it.

9. Rooney had a Broadway success in the late seventies in *Sugar Babies.* He was not just good as the trainer in *The Black Stallion* (79, Carroll Ballard), he was the engine for the second half of that film—nominated as supporting actor, but Melvyn Douglas won in *Being There.* Thereafter, Rooney has done *Arabian Adventures* (79, Kevin Connor); *My Kidnapper, My Love* (80, Sam Wanamaker); *Leave 'em Laughing* (80, Jackie Cooper); winning an Emmy as a retarded man in *Bill* (81, Anthony Page); *Bill: On His Own* (83, Page); *It Came Upon a Midnight Clear* (84, Peter H. Hunt); *Lightning, the White Stallion* (86, William A. Levey); as an agent in *The Return of Mickey Spillane's Mike*

Hammer (86, Ray Danton); *Bluegrass* (88, Simon Wincer); *Erik the Viking* (89, Terry Jones); and *My Heroes Have Always Been Cowboys* (91, Stuart Rosenberg).

10. There are, allegedly, homes for retired actors, as well as Guild pension schemes. At the same time, Rooney is now past eighty—and he may well earn no residuals on his famous pictures; after all, they were done before actors came in for profit participation. So the chances are he is close to broke, and on the edge—where he has always been—which may account for the following: *La Vida Láctea* (92, Juan Estelrich Jr.); *Sweet Justice* (92, Allen Plone); *Silent Night, Deadly Night 5* (92, Martin Kitrosser); *Maximum Force* (92, Joseph Merhi); *The Legend of Wolf Mountain* (92, Craig Clyde); *Revenge of the Red Baron* (94, Robert Gordon); *Making Waves* (94, George Saunders); *Killing Midnight* (97, Alexander J. Dorsey); *Boys Will Be Boys* (97, Dom De Luise); *Animals* (97, Michael Di Jiacomo); *Michael Kael Contra le World News Company* (98, Christophe Smith). . . . The list goes on. Are we meant to believe it? Or is this list an encrypted guide to the end of the world? . . . *Phantom of the Megaplex* (00, Blair Treu).

Francesco Rosi, b. Naples, Italy, 1922

1952: *Camicie Rosse* (completed by Rosi after the work of Goffredo Alessandrini and Franco Rossi). 1957: *Kean* (codirected with Vittorio Gassmann). 1958: *La Sfida.* 1959: *I Magliari.* 1960: *Sicilia 43/60* (d). 1962: *Salvatore Giuliano.* 1963: *Le Mani Sulla Citta.* 1965: *I Momento della Verita.* 1967: *C'Era una Volta/Cinderella, Italian Style.* 1970: *Uomini Contro.* 1972: *Il Caso Mattei.* 1973: *Lucky Luciano; Cadaveri Eccellenti/Illustrious Corpses.* 1979: *Cristo si e Fermato a Eboli/Christ Stopped at Eboli.* 1981: *Tre Fratelli/Three Brothers.* 1984: *Bizet's Carmen.* 1987: *Cronaca di una Morte Annunciata/Chronicle of a Death Foretold.* 1990: *Di Menticare Palermo.* 1992: *Diario Napoletano.* 1996: *La Tregua/The Truce.*

Rosi's career illustrates the difficulty an Italian director has in pursuing native material rather than opting for the various international styles of Antonioni, Fellini, or de Sica. His early promise seemed fully justified with *Salvatore Giuliano,* a film that rejected the easy heroic spectacle and insisted on a Rossellini-like exploration of environment and objectivity. The "story" of the film emerges only grudgingly from a documentary account of the peasantry. It is an austere, committed model that makes most mafiosi movies seem very superficial. It carried on the careful sense of place and social context of *La Sfida* and *I Magliari* and spoke for the young man who had assisted Visconti on *La Terra Trema* (48) and *Bellissima* (51) and Antonioni on *I Vinti* (53). After *Giuliano,*

Rosi took on an ambitious study of urban corruption, but with the frail insurance of Rod Steiger in the lead role. After that, he could not escape cliché in his Spanish bullfighting movie, and then abandoned his own character for Carlo Ponti's frothy Cinderella story. *Il Caso Mattei* is a good version of an Italian cause célèbre, but *Lucky Luciano* is the more marketable aspect of *Giuliano*.

The Truce is a remarkable picture, based on Primo Levi's autobiography covering the years after his release from Auschwitz. John Turturro plays the lead, and the film was one more measure of both the humanism and the complex political sensibility in Rosi. There are not many masters as little known outside their own countries.

Herbert Ross (1927–2001), b. New York
1969: *Goodbye, Mr. Chips.* 1970: *The Owl and the Pussycat.* 1971: *T. R. Baskin.* 1972: *Play It Again, Sam.* 1973: *The Last of Sheila.* 1975: *Funny Lady; The Sunshine Boys.* 1976: *The Seven Per Cent Solution.* 1977: *The Goodbye Girl; The Turning Point.* 1978: *California Suite.* 1980: *Nijinsky.* 1981: *I Ought to Be in Pictures; Pennies from Heaven.* 1982: *Max Dugan Returns.* 1984: *Footloose; Protocol.* 1987: *Dancers; The Secret of My Success.* 1989: *Steel Magnolias.* 1990: *My Blue Heaven.* 1991: *True Colors.* 1993: *Undercover Blues.* 1995: *Boys on the Side.*

One way of trying to pin down the elusive, if not phantom, Ross is to track his recurring working ties: with producer Ray Stark—*The Owl and the Pussycat, Funny Lady, The Sunshine Boys, The Goodbye Girl, California Suite,* and *Steel Magnolias;* with writer Neil Simon—*The Sunshine Boys, The Goodbye Girl, California Suite, I Ought to Be in Pictures,* and *Max Dugan Returns;* and with Nora Kaye, the dancer and choreographer, as well as wife and ally until her death in 1987. Kaye's influence and her life story were especially strongly felt on *The Turning Point,* which was Oscar nominated for best picture and best direction.

Now, *The Turning Point* always struck me as dire and unintentionally comic. Nor do I admire Ross's *Pennies from Heaven* as much as some critics—it seemed to me cumbersome and hollow next to Dennis Potter's original. But, still, Ross has had hits with *Steel Magnolias, The Secret of My Success, Footloose, California Suite, The Goodbye Girl,* and Woody Allen's *Play It Again, Sam.*

He was a dancer and choreographer who came into movies as dance director on *Carmen Jones* (54, Otto Preminger); *Doctor Dolittle* (67, Richard Fleischer); and *Funny Girl* (68, William Wyler). His own more serious studies of dance— like *The Turning Point, Nijinsky,* and *Dancers*— are somehow less energetic or pleasing than the

absurd but appealing *Footloose.* Without dance, Ross has an airy comic touch and a way with theatrical performance that often conceals the shallow, sexless quality of his people.

He married again, in 1988, to Lee Radziwill, and his pictures since then only serve to indicate the good judgment of Nora Kaye. But Ross is a curiosity and a throwback to the heyday of, say, George Cukor, when overall proficiency made up for lack of substance. But Ross had so little of Cukor's generosity—and so little sense of missing it.

Isabella Rossellini, b. Rome, 1952
Isabella Rossellini has been one of the most broadcast beauties of her time—thanks to Lancôme. She is clearly intelligent, creative, and a social creature, as befits the child of Roberto Rossellini and Ingrid Bergman. She is also a very sympathetic actress—as witness her wife to Bruno Hauptmann in the TV *Crime of the Century* (96, Mark Rydell)—who can rise to a performance of great courage and psychic insight, such as her Dorothy in *Blue Velvet* (86, David Lynch). In addition, she has been the wife of Martin Scorsese and the lover of David Lynch and Gary Oldman. Yet she is independent and practical—a dedicated mother and a capable businesswoman. Still, her screen career is spasmodic and incoherent, as if she had never been entirely sure that it was her destiny—her first aim was to be a journalist: as a young nun in *A Matter of Time* (76, Vincente Minnelli); *The Meadow* (79, the Taviani brothers); *White Nights* (85, Taylor Hackford); *Tough Guys Don't Dance* (87, Norman Mailer); *Siesta* (87, Mary Lambert); acting with Lynch in *Zelly and Me* (88, Tina Rathbone); *Cousins* (89, Joel Schumacher); *Wild at Heart* (90, Lynch); *Death Becomes Her* (92, Robert Zemeckis), as some guru of cosmetics; *Fearless* (93, Peter Weir); *The Innocent* (93, John Schlesinger); *The Pickle* (93, Paul Mazursky); *Immortal Beloved* (94, Bernard Rose); Big Nosed Kate in *Wyatt Earp* (94, Lawrence Kasdan); *Big Night* (96, Stanley Tucci); *The Funeral* (96, Abel Ferrara); Athene in the TV *Odyssey* (97, Andrei Konchalovsky); *Left Luggage* (98, Jeroen Krabbé); *The Imposters* (98, Tucci); the Duchess in *Don Quixote* (00, Peter Yates) for TV; *Il Cielo Cade* (00, Andrea and Antonio Frazzi); *Empire* (01, Franc Reyes); Josephine in the TV miniseries *Napoleon* (02, Yves Simoneau).

Roberto Rossellini (1906–77), b. Rome
1936: *Daphne* (s). 1938: *Prelude à l'Après-Midi d'un Faune* (s); *Luciano Serra Pilota* (codirected with Goffredo Alessandrini). 1939: *Fantasia Sottomarina* (s); *Il Tacchino Prepotente* (s); *La Vispa Teresa* (s). 1941: *Il Ruscello di Ripasottile* (s); *La Nave Bianca.* 1942: *Un Pilota Ritorna.* 1943: *L'Uomo della Croce; Desiderio* (codirected with Marcello Pagliero). 1945: *Roma, Città Aperta/*

Rome, Open City. 1946: *Paisàn.* 1947: *Germania, Anno Zero/Germany, Year Zero.* 1948: *L'Amore* (containing "Una Voce Umana" and "Il Mira-colo"); *La Macchina Ammazzacattivi.* 1949: *Stromboli, Terra di Dio.* 1950: *Francesco, Giullare di Dio.* 1952: "L'Invidia," episode from *Les Sept Péchés Capitaux; Europa '51.* 1953: *Dov'è la Libertà?; Viaggio in Italia;* "Ingrid Bergman," episode from *Siamo Donne.* 1954: "Napoli '43," episode from *Amori di Mezzo Secolo; Giovanna d'Arco al Rogo; La Paura/Die Angst.* 1958: *L'India Vista da Rossellini* (d); *India* (d). 1959: *Il Generale della Rovere.* 1960: *Era Notte a Roma; Viva l'Italia.* 1961: *Vanina Vanini/The Betrayer; Torino Nei Centi'anni* (d). 1962: *Anima Nera;* "Illi-batezza," episode from *Rogopag.* 1964: *L'Eta del Ferro* (d). 1966: *La Prise de Pouvoir par Louis XIV.* 1967: *Idea di un'Isola* (d). 1968: *Atti degli Apostoli.* 1970: *Socrate.* 1972: *Agostino di Ippona.* 1974: *Anno Uno/Italy: Year One.* 1975: *Il Mes-sia/The Messiah.* 1976: *The Age of the Medici.*

Rossellini was less a filmmaker than someone who observed the world through film. He had worked his way toward the idea that any situation could be made intelligible and moving by film and that "human stories" were natural illustrations of his-tory and politics. Rossellini thought that "The real creative artist in the cinema is someone who can get the most out of everything he sees—even if he sometimes does this by accident." The novel implication of this was that the spectator needed to be as active as the director in the experience of cinema.

That was not just a hopeful assertion of solidar-ity, but part of the demanding critical basis of his films. He encouraged the spectator into testing his or her own emotional and intellectual responses. He tried less to entertain than to synthesize the performer and the spectator: for the viewer is a participant, while a part of the performer is always watching to see what effect he or she has.

In 1958, the year of his divorce from Ingrid Bergman, and the point at which documentary film began to dominate his work, he spoke of the need "to hold people up to people" and of the realization that "it is in the images themselves (as opposed to montage) that the creative artist can really bring his own observation to bear, his own moral view, his particular vision."

Viaggio in Italia is not so much his masterpiece as the film that manifests most of his investigative methods. Its enigmatic title leads into a wealth of inner meanings. An English couple named Joyce—Ingrid Bergman and George Sanders—are going to Naples to supervise the sale of their house. Their marriage is breaking up. But the con-fusing experience of Italy is enough, temporarily at least, to reconcile them.

The situation is not extended by plot, apart from Sanders's passing interest in two other women and Bergman's reminiscence of a young poet she once knew. The action of the film consists largely of the two characters observing Italy and its effect on them. While Sanders deals with the business, Bergman explores the sights of Naples, including Pompeii.

Time and again, the simplicity of the narrative forces the viewer to participate in the actual lan-guage of the camera: the cramped, static shots of the couple, like flies, in their car, and the libera-tion of the tracking shots on the sunroof of their home when people and place are rapturously united. Bergman's wandering through Naples has meaning not just in the impression made on her by antiquity, by so many pregnant women, and by the unearthing of a Pompeiian couple arrested by lava, but in the dynamics of camera movements and the constant "documentary" shooting of per-son (or actress) in location.

Much rests in the disharmony between Bergman and Sanders. She is not easily diverted from anxiety, while he shrinks from emotion. Rossellini's tact in adapting such characteristics is all the more comprehensive in that Bergman was then his wife. The mingling of fictional and actual marriages is reflected at the end of the film when, at the moment of reconciliation, the shadow of the camera crane falls across the scene. This comes quickly and with as little emphasis as Rossellini's style ever allows. It needs to seem accidental or careless. But it crystallizes the feeling that grows throughout of *Viaggio* being an investigation of marriage, in which the characters come together again, not finally, but as speculatively as an audi-ence responding to the signs in life that support lasting human feelings. The "voyage" or "journey" is, finally, into the spectator's consciousness.

The collision of Rossellini and Ingrid Bergman was as spontaneous as desire, and so chancy it was enough to make one believe in gambling. But, very quickly, their "affair" and their art became a drama (and a melodrama): the scandal exempli-fied the world's mixed feelings about movie peo-ple; this was Hollywood meeting a new way of doing things; it was north and south; and for both parties, it was a half-comic, half-tragic, and always miraculous mix of hope and terror. She wanted reality; he wanted a star. She was an icon of ideal-ism and a woman at the mercy of her feelings; he was a genius and a rascal—a gambler, a woman-izer, a user of people. It may be they never quite understood what was happening. Yet their films are engrossing. They were changed—to be better, sadder, and wiser. We have their films, and their story to learn from.

After the making of *Stromboli*, Rossellini described his cinematic aspiration, directly relat-ing the tremulous existence of a person to the stare of the camera:

I need a depth which perhaps only the cinema can provide, both the ability to see characters and objects from any angle and the opportunity to adapt and omit, to make use of dissolves and internal monologue (not, I might add, Joyce's stream of consciousness, but rather that of Dos Passos), to take or leave, putting in what is inherent in the action and what is perhaps its distant origin. I will combine my talent with the camera to haunt and pursue the character: the pain of our times will emerge just through the inability to escape the unblinking eye of the lens.

Rossellini's work begins in the pain and disruption of war and works toward the essayist calm of a philosopher. Where the other neo-realists fumbled with a new fad, he produced three films that conveyed specific fictional incident and historical survey. In *Paisan,* for instance, there is an accumulation of fragments: human moments, all rendered with astonishing clarity, all capable of sustaining an entire feature, but packed together to suggest the total experience of Italy. The achievement is a lesson in how to watch and see: not just as street-scene observers, but as beholders of history in the making. *Paisan* is the truest Second World War movie, preparation for the endless newsreel from Vietnam or for the matter-of-fact hostilities of *Les Carabiniers* (made from a play adapted by Rossellini and meant by Godard as a homage to the Italian). With *Roma, Città Aperta,* and *Germania, Anno Zero,* he expressed Italy's contemporary experience and, without sentimentality, observed the social origins of evil in postwar Berlin.

From 1948 he moved into more personal stories, beginning with *L'Amore,* the film dedicated to Anna Magnani (his lover at the time). Again, it is important to stress how creative the very organization of the film is. *Paisan* is less episodic than symphonic. And *L'Amore* has two parts, apparently very different: the first is a version of Cocteau's *The Human Voice,* a virtuoso piece for an actress in which a woman desperately tries to hold on to a bored lover over the phone; the second, "Il Miracolo," tells how a simple peasant woman is seduced by a man she believes to be St. Joseph, and how she believes that she is pregnant with the Son of God. The contrast is of sophisticated theatre and peasant drama, and Magnani clearly links the two—a "grand actress" known for her portraits of peasants. Both stories are artificial, but both concentrate on the near-delusion of a woman's subjective experience. The physical isolation in the Cocteau piece is reflected in the social ostracism of the woman in "Il Miracolo." Both cling to their "truth." It is in putting them side by side that *L'Amore* becomes universal rather than the sum of a facile stage play and a rather patronizing peasant story (by Fellini).

After *L'Amore,* Ingrid Bergman approached Rossellini with a frankness that was the least reserved reward the honesty of his films ever met. They married in 1950 and together made *Stromboli; Europa '51; Viaggio;* the Ingrid Bergman episode from *Siamo Donne; Giovanna d'Arco al Rogo;* and *La Paura.* Bergman was, artistically, a great challenge to Rossellini. In truth to his art, he could not film her without introducing autobiography, and yet I am not sure she grasped his artistic intelligence. That disparity may have contributed to their eventual separation, for most of their films together are as harrowing as an actual marriage. Only briefly, in *Stromboli,* did the movie marriage of Bergman and Rossellini lead to passionate or erotic cinema. For him, she was a strange planet—an experiment.

Rossellini showed two things that a husband could teach the movie world about Bergman: that she was a plain actress left to herself, but that there was a very touching quality in her stolidity. He dramatized her Scandinavian presence in Italy very simply but very skillfully: thus in *Stromboli* she is a Lithuanian refugee who marries a fisherman on the volcanic island; in *Viaggio* she is an Englishwoman holidaying in Italy; in *La Paura* she is an unhappy, adulterous wife to a German, who ultimately leaves her husband; while in *Europa '51* she is a mother whose child commits suicide, who in remorse tends the sick and deprived and who is confined in an asylum by her husband. It is clear that such roles suit Bergman's instinctive agonizing; less clear, but likely, that they reflect the strain of what was a notorious liaison between Latin and Nordic temperaments. Bergman and Rossellini together seem now as unlikely, yet rewarding, as the pairing of Bergman and Sanders in *Viaggio.*

After the divorce, he settled for documentary—despite such exceptions as *Il Generale della Rovere,* with de Sica playing a wartime swindler—and for historical reconstruction. Thus, after *India,* he concentrated on the history of Italy in *Viva l'Italia* and *Vanina Vanini.* These films employed his own invention, Pancinor, a sophisticated zoom that frees the camera for even more elaborate setups. They also took great pains to be authentic and to reduce the obvious sources of drama. *Viva l'Italia* follows Garibaldi's unification of Italy, inspired by a feeling for landscape filled by skirmishes and the precise ebb and flow of struggle. Increasingly, Rossellini chose historical subjects to be filmed for television. As early as 1950, in the film about St. Francis, he had worked out a form that tried to reconstruct history.

"History," he said, "through teaching visually, can evolve on its own ground rather than evaporate into dates and names. Abandoning the usual litany of battle, it can surrender to its social, economic and political determinants. It can build, not on fantasy, but on historical knowledge, situations, costumes, atmospheres, and men who had historical significance and helped the social developments by which we live today. Some characters then, considered from a psychological viewpoint can, through their human qualities, become the embodiment of action."

That has the optimism of an encyclopedist in an age when film studies await their enlightenment. Rossellini—with his studies of iron, Louis XIV, Socrates, and St. Augustine (not to mention the earlier periods of his work)—will appear one day as the Diderot of the cinema.

Robert Rossen (1908–66), b. New York
1947: *Johnny O'Clock; Body and Soul.* 1949: *All the King's Men.* 1951: *The Brave Bulls.* 1954: *Mambo.* 1955: *Alexander the Great.* 1957: *Island in the Sun.* 1959: *They Came to Cordura.* 1961: *The Hustler.* 1963: *Lilith.*

As a young man, just out of New York University, Rossen wrote and produced for the theatre. It was his own play, *The Body Beautiful,* that took him to Hollywood as a scriptwriter. He worked at Warners, and was formed by the socially conscious thriller: *Marked Woman* (37, Lloyd Bacon); *They Won't Forget* (37, Mervyn Le Roy); *Racket Busters* (38, Bacon); *Dust Be My Destiny* (39, Lewis Seiler); *The Roaring Twenties* (39, Raoul Walsh); *A Child Is Born* (39, Bacon); *The Sea Wolf* (41, Michael Curtiz); *Out of the Fog* (41, Anatole Litvak); *Blues in the Night* (41, Litvak); *Edge of Darkness* (43, Lewis Milestone); *A Walk in the Sun* (45, Milestone); *The Strange Love of Martha Ivers* (46, Milestone); *Desert Fury* (47, Lewis Allen); uncredited on *The Treasure of the Sierra Madre* (47, John Huston).

Like Huston, Rossen developed as a director in those years after the war. His association with actor John Garfield and writer Abraham Polonsky (in Enterprise Productions), and his subsequent fate at the hands of the House Committee on Un-American Activities, lends a pinkish glow to his films that the unprepared viewer would have difficulty in seeing. Rossen favored intelligent psychological stories in realistic settings, but that is a long way from political preoccupation, and shows how tentative the "Marxist" element in American cinema has always been. *They Won't Forget* is a more blatant criticism of American society than any of Rossen's own films. *Body and Soul,* written by Polonsky and starring Garfield, is an honest boxing story, but its view of corruption was itself conventional and comfortable. Even *All the King's Men,* based on Robert Penn Warren's novel about a Southern demagogue, contents itself with melodrama, unfamiliar, real locations, and a bravura

performance from Broderick Crawford. Indeed, as all through his career, these early films profit from good acting and scripts. Rossen was his own scenarist and he always retained an ability for drawing more than usual out of his players. Those two early films have fine performances from Lilli Palmer and Mercedes McCambridge.

The Brave Bulls, made in Mexico, heralded Rossen's enforced exile from America. His wandering films are without any consistent theme and are deprived of Rossen's feeling for American locations and characters. He returned to America for the interesting failure *They Came to Cordura,* a study of courage and cowardice. But Rossen regained his early form with *The Hustler,* a poolroom story about winners and losers, crammed with atmosphere and cleverly cast. It is a gripping movie but a superficial one, unconscious of the way George C. Scott emerges as a more interesting character than Paul Newman's hero. It showed Rossen's virtues and limitations. Given an intense man's world, he had a flair for the details of timing, talk, and rivalry. But the meanings of his films are commonplace and signaled in advance. Nevertheless, *The Hustler* was a deserved success as entertainment, if only because the pool scenes had a unique place in the filming of sports and games.

Rossen was in poor health, and the idea of illness and weakness figured a lot in *The Hustler.* It dominated *Lilith,* a very ambitious reworking of legend, set in a mental institution and built around beautiful performances from Jean Seberg and Warren Beatty. Rossen did not seem to have the stylistic depth that the film strived after; many of its supposedly lyrical moments are ill judged. But it is an oddity, the only one of his films that seems passionate, mysterious, and truly personal. The other films will look increasingly dated and self-contained, but *Lilith* may grow.

Tim Roth, b. London, 1961
Tim Roth had his face right at the beginning—a nasty, lean, mean attitude, street stink, and an embedded air of grievance. See him as the juvenile delinquent in *Made in Britain* (83, Alan Clarke) and the whole act is there, its strutting dance, its lust for danger, and the total authority of the hopeless outsider who refuses to give a fuck. Since then, Roth has repeated himself, on both sides of the Atlantic, he has made adventures into period and biopic, he has even played Charlie Starkweather for TV in *Murder in the Heartland* (93, Robert Markowitz). But he is and always will be a terrific piece of South London, rancid yet fresh, treacherous yet driven by his own punk integrity.

He was snapped up by Mike Leigh for *Meantime* (83) and Stephen Frears for *The Hit* (84), where he is very good as John Hurt's sidekick. Since then, he has done *A World Apart* (88, Chris Menges); *To Kill a Priest* (88, Agnieszka Holland);

The Cook, the Thief, His Wife, and Her Lover (89, Peter Greenaway); with Gary Oldman in *Rosencrantz and Guildenstern Are Dead* (90, Tom Stoppard); as van Gogh in *Vincent and Theo* (90, Robert Altman); *Jumpin' at the Boneyard* (92, Jeff Stanzler); undercover and soaked in blood for *Reservoir Dogs* (92, Quentin Tarantino); *Bodies, Rest & Motion* (93, Michael Steinberg); with Amanda Plummer as his pumpkin in *Pulp Fiction* (94, Tarantino); with Julia Ormond in *Captives* (94, Angela Pope); as Marlow in the TV *Heart of Darkness* (94, Nicolas Roeg); a little beyond his class in *Rob Roy* (95, Michael Caton-Jones), though it got him a supporting actor nomination; *Little Odessa* (95, James Gray); and as the unfortunate bellboy who had to be in all the episodes of *Four Rooms* (96, Tarantino, Allison Anders, Alexandre Rockwell, Robert Rodriguez).

His brave choices have led to several unreleased pictures, as well as his unruly intrusion in *Everyone Says I Love You* (96, Woody Allen); *Gridlock'd* (97, Vondie Curtis-Hall); Dutch Schultz in *Hoodlum* (97, Bill Duke); and *La Leggenda del Pianista sull'Oceano* (98, Giuseppe Tornatore). But nothing prepared us for the stark beauty and restraint of *The War Zone* (99), the first film he directed. There was a clear debt to Alan Clarke and a steadfast respect for horrifying material. The film alarmed many critics, but in its imagery, its pacing, and its use of professional and novice actors it is one of the great debuts of the nineties.

Somehow he convinces as an international star, but surely that stretch for versatility misses his point: *Vatel* (00, Roland Joffé); *Lucky Numbers* (00, Nora Ephron); the heavy in *Planet of the Apes* (01, Tim Burton); very awkward in *Invincible* (01, Werner Herzog); *The Musketeer* (01, Peter Hyams); *Emmett's Mark* (02, Keith Snyder); in a short, *Whatever We Do* (03, Kevin Connolly); and as Cromwell in *To Kill a King* (03, Mike Barker).

Jean Rouch, b. Paris, 1917

All films are documentaries, except (f). 1947: *Au Pays des Mages Noirs* (codirected with Jean Sauvy and Pierre Ponty). 1948: *Initiation à la Danse des Possédés*. 1949: *Les Magiciens Noirs* (codirected with Marcel Griaule); *La Circoncision*. 1951: *Bataille sur le Grand Fleuve; Les Cimetières dans la Falaise; Les Hommes qui Font la Pluie; Les Gens du Mil*. 1952: *Alger—Le Cap; Les Fils de l'Eau* (anthology of previous films). 1955: *Les Maîtres Fous; Mamy Water*. 1957: *Moro Naba*. 1958: *Moi, un Noir*. 1959: *La Pyramide Humaine*. 1960: *Hampi; Chronique d'un Été* (codirected with Edgar Morin). 1962: *Monsieur Albert Prophète; Urbanisme Africain; Abidjan, Port de Pêche; Le Miel; Pêcheurs du Niger; La Punition*. 1963: *Les Cocotiers; Le Palmier à Huile; Rose et Landry*. 1964: "La Gare du Nord," episode from

Paris Vu Par; "Marie-France et Veronique," episode from *La Fleur de l'Age ou les Adolescentes; Les Veuves de Quinze Ans; Le Tambour des Dogons*. 1965: *La Chasse au Lion à l'Arc*. 1966: *La Goumbe des Jeunes Noceurs*. 1967: *Jaguar*. 1968: *La Signe* (codirected with Germaine Dieterlen). 1969: *Petit à Petit* (f). 1976: *Babatou/Babuta, les Trois Conseils*. 1979: *Cocorico! Monsieur Poulet; Funérailles à Bongo: Le Vieux Anai*. 1981: *Ambara Dama*. 1984: "Dionysos," an episode from *Paris Vu Par... 20 Ans Après*. 1987: *Brise-Glace; Enigma*. 1988: *Boulevards d'Afrique; Folie Ordinaire d'une Fille de Cham*. 1990: *Cantate pour Deux Généraux*. 1993: *Madame L'Eau*. 1997: *Faire-part: Musée Henri Langloss; Moi Fatigué Debout, Moi Couché*.

It is a tribute to the intellectual and academic acceptance of cinema in France that Jean Rouch had such an influence on film theory and feature movies during the 1960s. Rouch came to "cinema" by a roundabout way. He was a literature graduate turned civil engineer who went into ethnology and anthropology in the early 1940s. It was during the war that he first visited West Africa. Repeated trips, especially to Nigeria, Senegal, and the Gold Coast, became equipped with a secondhand 16mm camera that Rouch used to record tribal rituals. He was convinced that the camera would inevitably replace verbal reports in describing fieldwork. But it was in the gradual application of this method to European peoples that Rouch's work became widely interesting. *Moi, un Noir* was a more conventional documentary on the life of a black stevedore in Abidjan on the Ivory Coast. The film was silent and Rouch fell upon the innovation of having the stevedore himself improvise a commentary as he watched the film. That proved a creative extension of amateur or underground filmmaking. It meant that the subject of a film might digest the draft, comment on it, expand the finished film, and learn something about himself. The practice has by now left its mark on journalistic film, on cinema verité, and on Godard and Warhol. *La Pyramide Humaine* was made with students at Abidjan and worked toward a spontaneous group psychodrama. The same approach, allied to Edgar Morin's sociology-based interviewing, was applied to Paris in *Chronique d'un Été*, a film that carefully uncovers the layers of fiction in real life.

As a feature-length director, Rouch knows his limitations. *Petit à Petit* is a slight but charming account of a Niger businessman's perplexity in Paris. But in *La Chasse au Lion à l'Arc*, especially, he went back to African anthropology, and produced a brilliant study of a tribe's need to make a legend to sustain its own primitive existence. That film, *Chronique d'un Été, Moi, un Noir*, and *La Pyramide Humaine* ensure Rouch a key place in the history of documentary, and particularly the discovery that it was an unexpectedly complex form.

Mickey (Philip André) **Rourke**,

b. Schenectady, New York, 1956

It's a fond touch in Francis Coppola's *The Rainmaker* (97) that Mickey Rourke should play the master lawyer, the boss on the lam, reached by phone, but living in splendid ease on some tropic island. For Mickey Rourke has rather "gone away," leaving us to marvel over what happened to this glorious, rebellious kid actor, so tempted by silly sexual show-off, by the idea of becoming a boxer, and just being difficult, out of reach. He could come again. The guy one sees in *The Rainmaker* could still be waiting for his right moment, the big role, the unequivocal revelation that he has always been in charge.

He is the kind of guy who has tried nearly every oddball occupation you can think of, and that fringe feeling has frequently showed in his knowing, amused eyes. He carries knowledge with him, and he has a panache, a wintry humor, that is not common in actors of his generation. He made his debut in *1941* (79, Steven Spielberg); *Fade to Black* (80, Vernon Zimmerman); as a character named Nick Ray in *Heaven's Gate* (80, Michael Cimino); the arson expert in *Body Heat* (81, Lawrence Kasdan); as Boogie in *Diner* (82, Barry Levinson); *Eureka* (83, Nicolas Roeg); brilliant in *Rumblefish* (83, Coppola); *The Pope of Greenwich Village* (84, Stuart Rosenberg); *Year of the Dragon* (85, Cimino); and then, in his greatest hit, the movie that made him a cult object in some countries and an undying idiot in other people's eyes, *9½ Weeks* (86, Adrian Lyne).

He was the private eye in *Angel Heart* (87, Alan Parker); Irish in *A Prayer for the Dying* (87, Mike Hodges); Charles Bukowski in *Barfly* (87, Barbet Schroeder); an ex-fighter in *Homeboy* (88, Michael Seresin); to Italy, as Assisi's saint, in the ridiculous *Francesco* (89, Liliana Cavani); *Johnny Handsome* (89, Walter Hill); getting back to chic sex in *Wild Orchid* (90, Zalman King); in the old Bogart role in *Desperate Hours* (90, Cimino); *Harley Davidson & the Marlboro Man* (91, Simon Wincer); *White Sands* (92, Roger Donaldson); opposing Jean-Claude Van Damme and Dennis Rodman in *Double Team* (97, Tsui Hark).

It was not encouraging that he had to do *Love in Paris* (97, Anne Goursaud), a kind of child of *9½ Weeks; Point Blank* (97, Matt Earl Beesley); *Buffalo '66* (98, Vincent Gallo); a priest in *Thicker Than Blood* (98, Richard Pearce); *Thursday* (98, Skip Woods); *Shades* (99, Erik Van Looy). By the time of *Shergar* (99, Dennis C. Lewiston), a daft piece of Irishness about a great horse, it looked as if he had had plastic surgery—or the IRS had caught up with him. Whatever, he seems less

given to smirking or frowning: *Animal Factory* (00, Steve Buscemi); *Get Carter* (00, Stephen Kay); *The Pledge* (01, Sean Penn); *The Follow* (s) (01, Wong Kar-Wai); *Picture Claire* (01, Bruce McDonald); *They Crawl* (01, John Allardice); *Spun* (02, Jonas Akerlund); *Masked & Anonymous* (03, Larry Charles); *Once Upon a Time in Mexico* (03, Robert Rodriguez).

Russell Rouse (1916–87), b. New York

1951: *The Well* (codirected with Leo Popkin). 1952: *The Thief*. 1954: *Wicked Woman*. 1955: *New York Confidential*. 1956: *The Fastest Gun Alive*. 1957: *House of Numbers*. 1959: *Thunder in the Sun*. 1964: *A House Is Not a Home*. 1965: *The Oscar*. 1966: *The Caper of the Golden Bulls*.

Rouse was a mysterious privateer, whose handful of films are all trembling with some crazy ingenuity: in *The Well*, the girl who can save a black from being lynched is—guess where? *The Thief* has no speech. Why?—to show that it can be done. *House of Numbers* has Jack Palance playing twins, one inside San Quentin, the other outside, although the plot has them back and forth like a tennis rally. *Thunder in the Sun* is about a wagon train of gypsies. While *The Caper of the Golden Bulls* is a robbery story that reaches its climax in the running of the bulls in Pamplona. This blatant originality is surely due to Rouse, who wrote most of his scripts with Clarence Greene. Their partnership also wrote films for others to direct, and they were the authors of the inspired story and script for *D.O.A.* (50, Rudolph Maté), recycled for the far less gripping *Color Me Dead* (69, Eddie Davis).

Gena (Virginia Cathryn) **Rowlands**,

b. Madison, Wisconsin, 1930

She was of Welsh descent, the daughter of a man who would be a state assemblyman and a state senator, and of a serious amateur painter. But, compelled by some mysterious emotional crisis in the family, she dropped out of the University of Wisconsin and went to New York, to the American Academy of Dramatic Art (she would drop out of that, too). But it was there, in the early 1950s, that she met John Cassavetes. He would later say: "She and I have friction in terms of lifestyle and taste. We agree in taste on absolutely nothing. She thinks so totally opposite to anything I could ever conceive!"

The perfect recipe? They were married in 1954, and they were married still at his death in 1989. She was his actress; he was her director. And in the intense atmosphere of the extended Cassavetes family, those assignments were not always too closely examined in terms of wisdom. They were essential, and Gena Rowlands was wife, mother, and general provider for the cast and crew on their films. That doesn't mean that they necessarily found too many ways to agree. In life as much as in matters of taste, Cassavetes was a wishful liberal who actually imposed a kind of tyranny on his followers. It was the only way, and surely American film needed their contrary example.

Still, the thought persists that Gena Rowlands was not just the greatest talent in the group, but one that might have gone other ways. I daresay she is now the only one who might admit that story—but to speak it out loud would be to defy so many sacrifices and so much of their family tradition.

But she was a young beauty, who rather modeled herself on Dietrich, and who was very serious about the theatre. She had had an understudy role in *The Seven Year Itch* on Broadway, and when Eva Marie Saint proved unavailable (because of new motherhood), Joshua Logan cast Rowlands opposite Edward G. Robinson in Paddy Chayefsky's *Middle of the Night* (54). She gave a stunning performance, but even then she advanced slowly, in part because of her family duties. But she did get some Hollywood work: *The High Cost of Loving* (58, José Ferrer); *Lonely Are the Brave* (62, David Miller); *The Spiral Road* (62, Robert Mulligan). She attracted a lot of attention with her role as the deaf-mute Teddy Carella in the TV series *87th Precinct* (61–62). She also had a supporting part in her husband's career disaster, *A Child Is Waiting* (63, Cassavetes), and roles in *Tony Rome* (67, Gordon Douglas) and *Machine Gun McCain* (68, Giuliano Montaldo), with Cassavetes.

And so it was 1968—when she was thirty-eight—that she appeared in *Faces* (Cassavetes). Her performance in that film, and in several that followed, were widely hailed. She would get two Academy Award nominations for her husband, which surely helped his films at the box office. But notice how seldom, in fact, she worked, as he struggled to put pictures together: *Minnie and Moskowitz* (71); Mabel Longhetti, with Peter Falk, in *A Woman Under the Influence* (74); *Opening Night* (77); *Gloria* (80); *Love Streams* (84), by which time she was fifty-four.

Gradually, over the years, she did a few other things, but often within the extended family: an episode of *Columbo* (75); *Two Minute Warning* (76, Larry Peerce), with Cassavetes; *The Brink's Job* (78, William Friedkin); and a few TV movies. They did *Tempest* (82, Paul Mazursky) together, and she was with Ben Gazzara in the pioneering TV movie about AIDS, *An Early Frost* (85, John Erman). She had the title role in *The Betty Ford Story* (87, David Greene); she was the mother in *Light of Day* (87, Paul Schrader); and she did *Another Woman* (88, Woody Allen). But by the time Cassavetes died, she was sixty.

She has worked much harder since, often on TV, and she is regarded with universal fondness. But it is hard for that actress to get great parts:

Once Around (91, Lasse Hallström); *Night on Earth* (91, Jim Jarmusch); *Ted & Venus* (91, Bud Cort); *Silent Cries* (93, Anthony Page); *Something to Talk About* (95, Hallström); *The Neon Bible* (95, Terence Davies); *Unhook the Stars* (96, Nick Cassavetes, her son); *She's So Lovely* (97, N. Cassavetes); *Paulie* (98, John Roberts); *Hope Floats* (98, Forest Whitaker); *The Mighty* (98, Peter Chelsom); *Playing by Heart* (98, Willard Carroll); *The Weekend* (99, Brian Skeet); *The Color of Love: Jacey's Story* (00, Sheldon Larry); *Wild Iris* (01, Daniel Petrie); *Charms for the Easy Life* (01, Joan Micklin Silver); *The Incredible Mrs Ritchie* (03, Paul Johansson).

Alan Rudolph, b. Los Angeles, 1943
1977: *Welcome to L.A.* 1979: *Remember My Name.* 1980: *Roadie.* 1982: *Endangered Species.* 1983: *Return Engagement* (d). 1984: *Choose Me; Songwriter.* 1985: *Trouble in Mind.* 1987: *Made in Heaven.* 1988: *The Moderns.* 1990: *Love at Large.* 1991: *Mortal Thoughts.* 1993: *Equinox.* 1994: *Mrs. Parker and the Vicious Circle.* 1997: *Afterglow.* 1999: *Breakfast of Champions.* 2000: *Trixie.* 2001: *Investigating Sex.* 2002: *The Secret Lives of Dentists.*

Old-school auteurists could go crazy with Rudolph—it would be a good graduate-school film-studies exam question to require a paper that vindicates every Rudolph film and fits it into the scheme of l'oeuvre. Escaped auteurists can just say with glee (and relief) that the man is constitutionally unpredictable.

Let us suppose, in addition, that Rudolph is affected by the company he keeps. *Remember My Name* had Robert Altman as its producer—but Rudolph did the script. It had a great score by Alberta Hunter, and it was an early example of Rudolph's taste for unexpected casting calls: Geraldine Chaplin, Anthony Perkins, Alfre Woodard, Jeff Goldblum, and Berry Berenson. The result is a picture securely, if not sanely, placed within the deranged vision of its heroine. It is also a movie that reminds one of the marvel of the late seventies: acerbic, lyrical, independent, yet faithful to a southern California that Hollywood now tries to ignore.

The Moderns is Rudolph at his most literary and artificial; there are moments when one can believe the film was made by Nabokov and Charlie Parker after seeing *F for Fake*. In fact, Rudolph had Jon Bradshaw as his writer, and yet another amazing cast: Keith Carradine did seem capable of the paintings; Linda Fiorentino and John Lone made flesh out of notional roles; Chaplin and Geneviève Bujold were very funny; and Kevin O'Connor was the screen's best-ever Hemingway. Even Wallace Shawn was tolerable. Along the way, *The Moderns* was a glorious joke about creative reputation, a vivid pastiche of period bohemianism, and so alive a film it trembled with views, hints, glances, and possibilities.

In addition, Rudolph has made some of the most unwatchable films to be signed by a first-class director: *Songwriter, Trouble in Mind, Made in Heaven,* and *Love at Large. Choose Me* is that rarity for the director, a film with good and bad. But *Mortal Thoughts* seemed to mark a step forward. At last, Rudolph seemed to understand mainstream entertainment. The structure was intricate and perhaps overly indicative of the ending. But the movie gave us working-class life, and it had exceptional performances from Glenn Headley and Demi Moore.

Rudolph is the son of director Oscar Rudolph. He was in the Director's Guild training program, and he grew up artistically with Robert Altman as an assistant director on *California Split* and *Nashville,* and as cowriter on *Buffalo Bill and the Indians* (76). Thus, in a strange way, this child of Los Angeles has always been at cross-purposes with Hollywood's sense of the city and its task. Rudolph could do anything, but it is surely reasonable to hope for another one or two off-the-wall triumphs.

I liked *Mrs. Parker,* though I'm not sure I could have found a circle of admiration for it. *Afterglow* was clearly fond of its cast—but, if so, why not offer them a better script? *Breakfast of Champions* and *Trixie* were among the poorest things Rudolph had done.

Raúl Ruiz, b. Puerto Montt, Chile, 1941
If this book were as honest as its claims for itself, as reliable and as dull, it would already have started this entry with an immense list of films. Aged sixty as I write (my own age), Ruiz has made close to one hundred films, he says—some short, some unfinished, some never shown, some not much more than gestures towards films, or acts of defiance against what Hollywood, say (not that he flat-out loathes American film), likes to regard as a movie. But the list is obsessive, ridiculous, a diversion, so this time I'll set it aside. You can find the list in other places, and have as little reason to trust or comprehend it as if I had printed it here.

Better to realize that one Ruiz is thrilled by sheer quantity (earlier in life he set out to write one hundred plays by the age of twenty), while another revels in the suggestion that some, or many, of his films are not very good. As if that mattered when, for Ruiz, virtually every experience or encounter in life is like the challenge to make a film. Or write a story (granted his own special definition of what constitutes story).

I was criticized a few years ago, very reasonably, by Jonathan Rosenbaum for important maverick and foreign figures left out of this book. But I refuse to include them all, and I am always happi-

est to find a new way of sizing up a person—let alone one as torrential as Raúl Ruiz. For the last edition, I felt daunted by having seen so few of his scores of films. I have only seen a few more now, but I feel more comfortable facing him—because we are the same age, maybe, and because, I think, we are as torn between film and literature. And I have always known that for me, this book was in part a way of staying loyal to writing in face of the nearly total seduction the movies had made of me. I feel stronger about that struggle now, and more than ever certain that this thing, in your hands, is and must be a book. And in part that's because of the beautiful depiction of Proust in what may be Ruiz's first (and only) great film—*Time Regained* (99), a work that leaves the much vaunted Pinter script looking schoolboyish. (And surely in Pinter there has always been a Flashman of silences.)

Not the least thing about *Time Regained* is the grudging admission by Ruiz that if trapped into a corner, with enough money offered, he can put together a film as sumptuous as Visconti (actually far more elegant) and as epic and commonplace as Proust, with stunning performances from such as John Malkovich (as Charlus), Catherine Deneuve, Emmanuelle Béart, and so on. It is a little like Picasso drawing as well as Ingres and Rembrandt, once in his life. Which, of course, only guides us gently into reexamining all the various experiments with form, line, and story that Ruiz has attempted over the years.

His cover for this was obvious and sound: it is, more or less, that film should by now have got beyond the novel. It should be the journal, the daybook, the confessional of the mind that is always looking, and always tempted by that astonishing insolence with which appearance vulgarizes essence. After all, isn't that the crushing vulgarity (launched with photography) that has ended literature, language, humanism, et cetera? And isn't it the constant self-torture of the enlightened man of modern times—am I thinking movie because the vulgarity got me, or is it that I have no talent as a writer? (You see, I take it as a given that virtually every person in this book who is a filmmaker wanted to be a writer first and found it too hard.)

Ruiz is brilliantly educated, irresistibly drawn to the confusion of languages and the exigencies of being an émigré. So, Chilean once, he could no more resist the role of exile than the rapturous tracking shots he loves. Thus driven, film or the attempt at film became his notebook. But he abhorred that chestnut about story depending on conflict, and he shied away from every orthodoxy about how to film things, faces, and action. He actually sees action as a kind of mathematical principle—an x that happens to other people and which permits, from time to time, the illusion of story. Except that in life (as in Musil and Joyce and

Proust and Borges) the storyness of it all is really far more telling for us impatient souls than any long-winded narrative.

So Ruiz was for years a natural (in that he could make a film on nothing) at festivals: he was funny, he could be magical realist or grade-B noirish. He resembled Guillermo Cabrera Infante in his obsessiveness and his straight-faced comedy. He seemed incapable of pausing, reflecting, or ever making a whole or finished or normal film. That said, you could have a terrific time with, at least, *The Hypothesis of the Stolen Painting* (78), *On Top of the Whale* (81), *Three Crowns of the Sailor* (82), and *City of Pirates* (83).

There were also insufferable or impossible Ruiz films, and that imbalance was the intimidating thing: it made you feel you needed to see the whole oeuvre. You don't. You can pass by on the other side of the street. But, especially if you're American, Ruiz is one of those figures you owe it to yourself to sample, to become obsessed with, for all the wonderful non-American ways he knows of holding the screen and turning your passing involvement into a critical model of what it is to be you.

You see, no country but America would have achieved such an hegemony in film and then starved the medium so.

Start with *Time Regained* (whether or not you know Proust). Absorb the fluent mix of tracking shots (as beguiling as Ophüls) with all the clever ways the people and the scenery are slid in and out of view (which is like Godard or Syberberg or Fritz Lang showing his own workings). Then dwell in the magical conclusion in which we have two or three ages of Proust mingling with his own characters, like Welles taking you on a conducted tour of the Xanadu junk collection before he strikes the match.

Geoffrey Rush,

b. Toowoomba, Australia, 1951

It was only at the age of forty-five—as David Helfgott in the very bizarre *Shine* (96, Scott Hicks)—that Geoffrey Rush broke through as a movie actor. Prior to that, after studying at the University of Queensland and being part of the Queensland Theatre Company, he had worked on stage and in television in Australia. His Helfgott was a bravura piece of impersonation, including the mastery of neurotic speech patterns and extreme emotional instability. It was a performance that won the best actor Oscar, and drew enormous attention, but it left some people cold as being no more than eccentric behavior in a dead end. So Rush's second best actor nomination, as Sade in *Quills* (00, Philip Kaufman), was actually far more impressive, because it offered an extremist whose every action reflected on the common realities of love, desire, and lust. The brilliance was no less, but it

was serving a purpose and helping us see that Rush might be one of those actors who reach nearly any extreme. He played Sir Andrew Aguecheek, yet who could say that Falstaff was not within his reach?

He had played in *Children of the Revolution* (96, Peter Duncan) before *Shine*. Since then, he has been the narrator on *Oscar and Lucinda* (97, Gillian Armstrong); *A Little Bit of Soul* (98, Duncan); Javert in *Les Misérables* (98, Bille August); Walsingham in *Elizabeth* (98, Shekhar Kapur); Henslowe in *Shakespeare in Love* (98, John Madden); *Mystery Men* (99, Kinka Usher); *House on Haunted Hill* (99, William Malone); *The Tailor of Panama* (01, John Boorman); *Lantana* (01, Ray Lawrence).

He was Trotsky in *Frida* (02, Julie Taymor); not very convincing in *The Banger Sisters* (02, Bob Dolman); *Swimming Upstream* (03, Russell Mulcahy); as the cop after *Ned Kelly* (03, Gregor Jordan); *Pirates of the Caribbean: The Curse of the Black Pearl* (03, Gore Verbinski); *Intolerable Cruelty* (03, Joel Coen); and in a great challenge, as the lead, in *The Life and Death of Peter Sellers* (04, Stephen Hopkins).

David O. (Owen) Russell, b. New York, 1958

1990: *Hairway to the Stars*. 1994: *Spanking the Monkey*. 1996: *Flirting with Disaster*. 1999: *Three Kings*.

Three Kings is exactly the kind of movie that the American system is supposedly incapable of producing: personal but far-ranging; stylistically innovative—if only by virtue of the toxic color photography that manages to be new and beautiful as well as a poetic warning of peril; the screwball regard for that hallowed military component the unit; and a thriving satirical attitude towards American foreign policy as well as the wit and wisdom that turns pratfall into the historical record. And all this—no matter the decisive support of George Clooney—came from a young writer-director whose earlier films could easily be mistaken as witty festival fodder. By which I mean to say that they are funny, novel, but not quite disturbing. Whereas it felt as if someone new, or more confident, had sprung up to do *Three Kings*. So it's a little unsettling that Russell seems to have paused for a moment—as if success had made his edginess more questionable. Of course, since *Three Kings* our foreign affairs have taken a turn that would probably have prevented the film from being made if it had reached us five years earlier. So we wait to see.

Jane Russell, b. Bemidji, Minnesota, 1921

Of all the screen's sex goddesses, Jane Russell seemed most amused by the performance. Not that she was undeserving. She was a chiropodist's assistant when a photograph of her was sent to Howard Hughes. That rare blend of artist, engineer, and businessman designed a bra that would do her justice and then abandoned his invention in the most delightful scenes of his own film *The Outlaw*. That film, made in 1940 and released in 1946, is generally mocked. But it is very funny, quite sexy, and as much Howard Hawks as Hughes. Russell is the primal female object in it and the raison d'être of a long, drawn-out publicity campaign to launch the movie. When at last Hughes let it out, the poster had a drawing of Russell, holding a pistol, lolling in the hay, with the caption: "Mean . . . Moody . . . Magnificent."

Russell was no actress, but she was dryly skeptical and physically glorious. Such droll eroticism is rare in Hollywood, and we are lucky that she was allowed to decorate so many adventure movies: *The Young Widow* (47, Edwin L. Marin); very good with Bob Hope in *The Paleface* (48, Norman Z. McLeod); *Double Dynamite* (50, Irving Cummings); *His Kind of Woman* (51, John Farrow); *Macao* (52, Josef von Sternberg); *Montana Belle* (52, Allan Dwan); *Son of Paleface* (52, Frank Tashlin); *The Las Vegas Story* (52, Robert Stevenson); generous to Monroe in *Gentlemen Prefer Blondes* (53, Hawks); *The French Line* (53, Lloyd Bacon), a dull, garish film, but with two startlingly direct songs; *Underwater* (55, John Sturges); *Gentlemen Marry Brunettes* (55, Richard Sale); *Foxfire* (55, Joseph Pevney); *The Tall Men* (55, Raoul Walsh); *Hot Blood* (56, Nicholas Ray); *The Revolt of Mamie Stover* (56, Walsh); and *The Fuzzy Pink Nightgown* (57, Norman Taurog).

Her retirement was broken by occasional guest appearances—in *Johnny Reno* (65, R. G. Springsteen) and *Waco* (66, Springsteen)—and prominence on TV—in bra commercials where she brought "great news for us full-figure gals," a message from Arcadia to Levittown.

Ken Russell,

b. Southampton, England, 1927

1962: *Elgar* (d). 1963: *French Dressing*. 1964: *A House in Bayswater* (d). 1965: *Debussy* (d); *Douanier Rousseau* (d). 1966: *Isadora Duncan* (d). 1967: *Dante's Inferno* (d); *Billion Dollar Brain*. 1968: *Song of Summer* (d). 1969: *Women in Love*. 1970: *Dance of the Seven Veils* (d). 1971: *The Music Lovers; The Devils; The Boy Friend*. 1972: *Savage Messiah*. 1974: *Mahler*. 1975: *Tommy; Lisztomania*. 1977: *Valentino*. 1978: *Clouds of Glory* (TV). 1980: *Altered States; Crimes of Passion*. 1986: *Gothic*; an episode from *Aria*. 1988: *Salome's Last Dance; Lair of the White Worm*. 1989: *The Rainbow*. 1990: "Dusk Before Fireworks," episode from *Women & Men: Stories of Seduction*. 1991: *Whore; Prisoner of Honor* (TV). 1992: *The Mystery of Dr. Martinu* (TV). 1993: *Lady Chatterley* (TV); *The Insatiable*

Mrs. Kirsch (s). 1995: *Mindbender; Classic Widows* (d) (TV); *Alice in Russialand*. 1997: *Ken Russell "In Search of the English Folk Song"* (d). 1998: *Dogboys* (TV). 2000: *Lion's Mouth*.

No other British director advanced with such effect from TV to movies, or demonstrated the perilous cultivation of heartless prettiness by TV that on a larger screen looks like an odiously picturesque self-loathing. Just as a Lang, a Buñuel, or a Renoir always conceals style and eliminates the distractions of "beauty," so Russell hurls it at us with a remorseless facility. That he is oblivious of his own vulgarity and the triteness of his morbid misanthropy serves as a contrast to illuminate the vigorous pessimism of Buñuel.

A training in still photography nurtured meretricious accomplishment. Russell was a photographer on *Picture Post* who made several prizewinning amateur films—notably *Amelia and the Angel* (57)—as a way into TV. There, he became the prize enfant terrible of the BBC arts section. It is worth recalling that his *Elgar* appealed shamelessly to the stuffed Malvern pride of English conservatives whom most of the more recent films have outraged. Hardly a frame of *Elgar* went by that did not evince approving sighs from those as pious about music as they were insensitive to cinema.

The BBC's pursuit of the dead artist led Russell into increasingly eccentric or—as he thought—decadent subjects. *Debussy* was allowed to hide the music beneath one of the key works in Swinging London's narcissistic reveling in its own listlessness. Only *Song of Summer*—about Delius, and evidently restrained by the presence of the composer's amanuensis, Eric Fenby—stilled itself long enough to be accurate and touching. But *Dance of the Seven Veils* was a travesty of the historical details of Richard Strauss's life and a gratuitous gathering together of Russell's unbridled sense of pictorial madness and decay. It is the overweening grasp of perfection in such images that contradicts their intentions, and only a spirit as complacent and conventional as Russell's would so insist on being shocked. The overall need to sensationalize artists and to reduce them to comic-book Freud and TV commercial glamour is justified by Russell as a means to making them more popular.

His cinema films began by being pedestrian, although *French Dressing* had moments of surrealism as Russell's imagination prodded at the forlorn English seaside. But *Women in Love* was drawn largely to the melodrama and callow primitivism in D. H. Lawrence. *The Music Lovers* and *The Devils* seem to me the work of self-induced mania, where visual grotesqueness has swamped intellect or feelings. There is no intrinsic objection to a vision of teeming corruption. But it demands the passion of a Bosch. Russell's is hysterical and hollow. Thus, in the same year, he could move from the melting of martyrs in *The Devils* to entirely wax-dummy people in *The Boy Friend*. Just as he fell far short of Dreyer's or Bergman's examinations of religious mania, so he was incapable of carrying off the amateur charm of Sandy Wilson's musical.

Russell will try anything, go anywhere, secure in the knowledge that the results would never be attributed to anyone else. His spiritual home may be that England that runs from, say, William Beckford to D. H. Lawrence, and as late as 1993 he was back to the Lawrentian novel, though less happily than before. *Altered States*, on the other hand, was sci-fi as seen by Paddy Chayefsky—at least, before the writer saw the end product. *Crimes of Passion* was a bold idea, but Russell was too excited by it for it to remain an idea. *Whore* is Theresa Russell in-your-face with an X rating.

Passing seventy, Russell showed no signs of moderation or being reasonable. *Mindbender* was a dramatized life of Uri Geller. The *Insatiable Mrs. Kirsch* was a strange piece of aural erotica. *Classic Widows* was a tribute to the wives left behind by great composers. His energy and his rather simpleminded trust in creativity could keep him going for decades yet.

Kurt Russell,
b. Springfield, Massachusetts, 1951

Though it's fairly clear that Kurt Russell would rather have had a pro career as a baseball player, he's given good value in movies as a tough guy, a blue collar guy, and, above all, as Snake Plisskin, his frowning dude in the *Escape* films. As a Hollywood personality, he is liked for his long-running relationship with Goldie Hawn (they have never been married—but they're busy).

He was the son of Bing Russell, a baseball player who became a small-part actor, and he had a rich career as a child actor in the 1960s, including the lead in the TV series *The Travels of Jaimie McPheeters* (63–64). On the big screen, he was in *The Absent-Minded Professor* (61, Robert Stevenson); *It Happened at the World's Fair* (63, Norman Taurog)—an Elvis Presley picture; *Follow Me, Boys!* (66, Norman Tokar); *The One and Only Genuine, Original Family Band* (68, Michael O'Herlihy), with a kid credited as Goldie Jeanne—Hawn to be; *The Horse in the Gray Flannel Suit* (68, Tokar); *The Computer Wore Tennis Shoes* (70, Robert Butler).

He was grown for *The Barefoot Executive*, but with a monkey for a costar; *Fool's Parade* (71, Andrew V. McLaglen); *Now You See Him, Now You Don't* (72, Butler); *Charley and the Angel* (73, Vincent McEveety); *Superdad* (74, McEveety); *The Strongest Man in the World* (75, McEveety).

He was then absent for a few years of serious baseball, before returning for what is still his best

performance: on TV in *Elvis* (79, John Carpenter), in which he actually makes a lot of the real guy seem second-rate. That film also starred Russell's wife, Season Hubley. He followed that with *Used Cars* (80, Robert Zemeckis); the splendid *Escape From New York* (81, Carpenter); *The Thing* (82, Carpenter); *Silkwood* (83, Mike Nichols); with Goldie Hawn in *Swing Shift* (84, Jonathan Demme); *The Mean Season* (85, Phillip Borsos); *The Best of Times* (86, Roger Spottiswoode); *Big Trouble in Little China* (86, Carpenter); with Goldie again in *Overboard* (87, Garry Marshall); the cop in *Tequila Sunrise* (88, Robert Towne); *Winter People* (89, Ted Kotcheff); *Tango & Cash* (89, Andrei Konchalovsky); a tough firefighter in *Backdraft* (91, Ron Howard); *Unlawful Entry* (92, Jonathan Kaplan); *Captain Ron* (92, Thom Eberhardt); as Wyatt Earp in *Tombstone* (93, George Pan Cosmatos); *Stargate* (94, Roland Emmerich); *Escape From L.A.* (96, Carpenter), which he coproduced; *Executive Decision* (96, Stuart Baird); the very successful *Breakdown* (97, Jonathan Mostow); *Soldier* (98, Paul Anderson).

He returned to Elvis-ness in the daft *3000 Miles to Graceland* (01, Demian Lichtenstein), and then—for some reason—agreed to be the shrink in *Vanilla Sky* (01, Cameron Crowe), a performance of great, if unintended, comic value; *Interstate 60* (02, Bob Gale); *Dark Blue* (02, Ron Shelton).

Rosalind Russell (1911–76),
b. Waterbury, Connecticut

You only realize how good a film Howard Hawks's *His Girl Friday* (40) is when you remember that Rosalind Russell is in it. Top-speed comedy and the floating aggression of Cary Grant actually managed to control the bossiness and overemphasis that spoiled so many of her films.

Trained at AADA, performances on Broadway led to an invitation from Hollywood. Not that the film world ever properly took her on. Although under contract at MGM, she was often loaned out and remained conscious of being second choice to the studio's other leading ladies. She made her debut in William K. Howard's *Evelyn Prentice* (34) and was in Wellman's *The President Vanishes* (34); W. S. Van Dyke's *Forsaking All Others* (34); Victor Fleming's *Reckless* (35); and Tay Garnett's *China Seas* (35) before getting a lead part, intended originally for Myrna Loy, in Howard's *Rendezvous* (35). There followed *It Had to Happen* (36, Roy del Ruth); *Under Two Flags* (36, Frank Lloyd); *Craig's Wife* (37, Dorothy Arzner)—her first big personal success; *Manproof* (37, Richard Thorpe); *Night Must Fall* (38, Thorpe); *The Citadel* (38, King Vidor); and in a series of daft hats as the group gossip in Cukor's *The Women* (39).

She was now typed as a career woman in comedies that veered from the hard-boiled to the sentimental: *No Time for Comedy* (40, William Keighley); *The Feminine Touch* (41, Van Dyke); *They Met in Bombay* (41, Clarence Brown); pretty good as the boss in *Take a Letter, Darling* (42, Mitchell Leisen); *My Sister Eileen* (42, Alexander Hall); and *Roughly Speaking* (45, Michael Curtiz).

After the war, she embarked on heavy "acting" in two films for Dudley Nichols—*Sister Kenny* (46) and *Mourning Becomes Electra* (47)—and after *The Guilt of Janet Ames* (47, Henry Levin), *The Velvet Touch* (48, John Gage), and *Tell It to the Judge* (49, Norman Foster) she went back to the theatre and to a big success in *Wonderful Town*. After that, she concentrated on her unique form of overacting—shrill in the otherwise excellent *Picnic* (56, Joshua Logan); incredible in *Auntie Mame* (57, Morton da Costa), a role she had played on Broadway; terrible in Daniel Mann's *Five Finger Exercise* (62); and well cast as Rose in Mervyn Le Roy's film of *Gypsy* (62). It would barely have been accepted, as an invention, that her last work in movies included playing a Mother Superior to Hayley Mills, as directed by Ida Lupino, in *The Trouble with Angels* (66). The record books claim that there was even a sequel to this, *Where Angels Go . . . Trouble Follows* (67, James Neilson).

Theresa Russell (Theresa Paup),
b. San Diego, California, 1957

If ever a proper history is written of directors obsessed with, married to, or simply enslaved by actresses, then the case of Theresa Russell and her husband Nicolas Roeg will be especially important. It is not that Russell has given up working for other filmmakers, nor that she is less than a grave presence in her husband's work, stunning in a Ingres-like way, yet stunned, too, like someone offering a first reading of a strange role. There has always been a sensual quality to Ms. Russell, a blunt staring in at the inquisitive, lewd process of film, as well as an untrained, even uncouth, unactorly air. She sometimes seems like a woman encountered at a Greyhound station and inveigled before the camera—unready, ungiving, suspicious, yet definitely there; more than an actress. She works in an uncommon terrain, between startling directness and our notion that perhaps she lacks a wealth of technique. Does Roeg love her for this charming flirtation with bad acting? Does he lead her down its path? Does he notice it?

She trained at the Lee Strasberg Institute and was well cast by Elia Kazan as Cecelia Brady in *The Last Tycoon* (76). But it was as Dustin Hoffman's rather forlorn, even Faulknerian, girlfriend in *Straight Time* (78, Ulu Grosbard) that she really caught the eye. Indeed, this may be her most accomplished work yet, along with her exquisite,

deadpan Mo Dean in TV's *Blind Ambition* (79, George Schaefer).

Her first working encounter with Roeg was in his *Bad Timing* (80) where she was an authentic icon of passive sexuality, somewhere between Klimt and the drabbest porn parlor. Was she acting, or was she being observed? The question surely added to the discomfort of the film. Since then, for Roeg, she was the daughter in *Eureka* (82), Marilyn Monroe in *Insignificance* (85), out of her depth in *Track 29* (87), in *Aria* (87), and as the wife/lover in *Cold Heaven* (91).

She has also played, with Bill Murray, doing the Gene Tierney role in *The Razor's Edge* (84, John Byrum); as the serial killer in *Black Widow* (87, Bob Rafelson)—one can't help feeling that that awkward thriller would have had a better chance with the female roles reversed; as a lawyer in *Physical Evidence* (89, Michael Crichton); good as a narc under strain in *Impulse* (90, Sondra Locke); variably sensational and miscalculated, head on, in the title role of *Whore* (91, Ken Russell); as a victim in *Kafka* (92, Steven Soderbergh).

As Roeg has worked less, so Russell seems to have been busier: on TV in *A Woman's Guide to Adultery* (93, David Hayman); *Thicker Than Water* (93, Marc Evans); the narrator in *Being Human* (93, Bill Forsyth); *The Flight of the Dove* (94, Steve Railsback); *The Grotesque* (95, John-Paul Davidson); as Morgan Le Fay in *A Young Connecticut Yankee in King Arthur's Court* (95, Ralph Thomas); *Trade Off* (95, Andrew Lane); *Hotel Paradise* (95, Roeg); as Ma Barker in *Public Enemies* (96, Mark Lester); *Once You Meet a Stranger* (96, Tommy Lee Wallace); *The Proposition* (97, Strathford Hamilton); *Wild Things* (98, John McNaughton); *Running Woman* (98, Rachel Samuels); *Luckytown Blues* (00, Paul Nicholas); *The Believer* (01, Henry Bean); *Earth vs. the Spider* (01, Scott Ziehl); *Now & Forever* (01, Bob Clark); *The House Next Door* (01, Joey Travolta); *Passionada* (02, Dan Ireland); *Destiny* (02, James Fargo); *Love Comes Softly* (03, Michael Landon Jr); *Save It for Later* (03, Charles Brigham); *The Box* (03, Peter Bauer).

Walter Ruttmann (1887–1941),
b. Frankfurt, Germany

All films documentaries, except those marked (s) and (f).

1921: *Opus I* (s); *Opus II* (s). 1923: *Der Seiger* (s); *Das Verlorene Paradies* (s); *Kantorowitz* (s); *Gesolei* (s). 1925: *Opus III* (s); *Opus IV* (s). 1927: *Berlin, Die Symphonie der Grosstadt/Berlin, Symphony of a City*. 1928: *Wochenende* (s); *Tonende Welle* (s); *Deutscher Rundfunk*. 1929: *Die Melodie der Welt* (s). 1931: *In der Nacht* (s); *Feind im Blut* (s). 1932: *Acciaio* (f). 1933: *Arbeit macht Glucklich* (f). 1934: *Altgermanische Bauernkultur; Metall des Himmels*. 1935: *Stadt der*

Verheissung; Cannstatter Volksfest; Stuttgart.
1936: *Dusseldorf; Schiff in Not.* 1937: *Mannes-mann.* 1938: *Henkel; Weltstrasse See; Im Dienste
der Menschheit; Im Zeichen des Vertrauens.* 1939:
Hinter den Zahlen. 1940: *Aberglaube; Deutsche
Panzer; Volkskrankheit Krebs.*

Within twenty years, Ruttmann moved from being
the proponent of absolute, abstract cinema to a
leading propagandist, fatally wounded while plan-ning another cinematic celebration of the German
army. The "purity" of Ruttmann's cinema was
always sterile and formalistic, waiting to be
exploited by a totalitarian message. It is hardly
thorough to remember Leni Riefenstahl as an
active Nazi, but still to associate Ruttmann with
the experimental documentary of the 1920s. His
method was always meretricious and dangerous,
as John Grierson saw:

> The symphonists have found a way of building
> such matters of common reality into very pleas-ant sequences. By uses of tempo and rhythm,
> and by the large-scale integration of single
> effects, they capture the eye and impress the
> mind in the same way as a tattoo or a military
> parade might do. But by their concentration on
> mass and movement . . . they tend to avoid the
> larger creative job. What more attractive (for a
> man of visual taste) than to swing wheels and
> pistons about in a ding-dong description of a
> machine, when he has little to say about the
> man who tends it, and still less to say about the
> tin-pan product it spills? And what more com-fortable if, in one's heart, there is avoidance of
> the issue of underpaid labour and meaningless
> production? For this reason I hold the sym-phony tradition of cinema for a danger and
> *Berlin* for the most dangerous of all film models
> to follow.

This is a sound objection, even if it is one that
self-conscious British documentary did not always
avoid. *Berlin* is artful decoration. *Metropolis,* by
comparison, is obvious, but it loathes automation,
foresees what it inflicts on people, and has a poetic
and precise view of the way a city lends itself to
intrigue and oppression. Ruttmann is an example
of the beguiled cinema intellectual, so intent on
cutting and composition that the artist vanished
under artiness.

Originally a painter, he fought in the First
World War and then devoted himself to abstract
cinema. The Opus movies are archetypal experi-ments; even in the early 1920s Ruttmann foresaw
the role of sound and tried to create a cinema in
which the visuals were subordinate to the sound
track. Such deliberate pioneering won him some
fame: he "created" the "Falkentraum" sequence
for *Siegfried* (24, Fritz Lang); he directed some

special sequences for *Lebende Buddhas* (24, Paul
Wegener); collaborated with Lotte Reiniger on
Die Abenteuer des Prinzen Achmed (26). His own
major urban documentaries began in 1927 with
Berlin. Acciaio was made in Italy from a Piran-dello script. He assisted on the editing of
Olympiad (36, Riefenstahl), the telling demon-stration of the "ding-dong" applied, gloriously but
fallaciously, to the human figure.

Meg Ryan (Margaret Mary Emily Anne Hyra),
b. Fairfield, Connecticut, 1961
Unerringly the girl next door—with resem-blances to Doris Day and Goldie Hawn—Meg
Ryan has been a steady, "cute" romantic lead for
several years, best suited to playing rather con-ventional women who are tested by the circum-stances of a love story. As such, she might easily
have come and gone—and she has made her
share of poor pictures, or ones in which she
defers to the men. But she improves. She carried
the flimsy *French Kiss* (95, Lawrence Kasdan),
gave it charm and depth, outplayed the inventive
Kevin Kline, and sometimes seemed as eager for
more as an adventurous executive producer. It's
possible that she could be better still—even in
the tradition of Jean Arthur and Stanwyck—given
better material.

The daughter of a casting agent (her mother),
she was Candice Bergen's daughter in *Rich and
Famous* (81, George Cukor). She had a small role
in *Amityville 3-D* (83, Richard Fleischer), a cou-ple of TV seasons on *As the World Turns,* and then
an eye-catching turn in *Top Gun* (86, Tony Scott).
She was in *Armed and Dangerous* (86, Mark L.
Lester), and in *Innerspace* (87, Joe Dante), where
she met her future husband, Dennis Quaid.

She was striking as a tough girl in *Promised
Land* (88, Michael Hoffman)—the feeling often
lurks that she is both smarter and stronger than
Hollywood wants her to be. But she was no more
than a stooge to Quaid in *D.O.A.* (88, Rocky Nor-ton and Annabel Jankel), and Sean Connery's
headstrong daughter in *The Presidio* (88, Peter
Hyams).

Her breakthrough came in *When Harry Met
Sally . . .* (89, Rob Reiner), not only for the cele-brated fake orgasm in the delicatessen, but
because the gimmick got at the real tension
between primness and wildness in her character.
She was the best thing—as three women—in *Joe
Versus the Volcano* (90, John Patrick Shanley), but
she could not help being a forlorn, teary onlooker
in *The Doors* (91, Oliver Stone).

But then she found her level—as the confident
lead in a series of romances and dramas: with Alec
Baldwin in *Prelude to a Kiss* (92, Norman René);
torn between two men—the real and the heard—in the cunning smash hit *Sleepless in Seattle* (93,
Nora Ephron, who had written *When Harry Met*

Sally . . .); with Quaid once more in *Flesh and Bone* (93, Steve Kloves); impressively and affectingly alcoholic in *When a Man Loves a Woman* (94, Luis Mandoki); as Einstein's niece in *I.Q.* (94, Fred Schepisi). And then as the neurotic who blooms in France in *French Kiss*. It was harder to understand why she was in, or what she was doing in, *Restoration* (95, Hoffman). But her military officer in *Courage Under Fire* (96, Edward Zwick) was the most intriguing thing she had done.

Can she go further? Are there films in America with better parts? In recent years, she began to be the victim of a meek, repetitive system: *Addicted to Love* (97, Griffin Dunne); as the voice of *Anastasia* (97, Don Bluth); knocked about in *Hurlyburly* (98, Anthony Drazan); *City of Angels* (98, Brad Silberling); *You've Got Mail* (98, Ephron)—which seemed too calculating a reprise of her chemistry with Tom Hanks; *Hanging Up* (00, Diane Keaton)—one of the girls again, yet nearly forty.

So she made *Proof of Life* (00, Taylor Hackford), an interesting, if rather old-fashioned, love story, and got so involved with costar Russell Crowe that her marriage to Quaid ended. Was the public really hurt? Or was it all a midlife crisis? *Kate & Leopold* (01, James Mangold) seemed more whimsy than an answer.

She tried acting tough in *Against the Ropes* (03, Charles Dutton)—a lot will depend on *In the Cut* (03, Jane Campion).

Robert Ryan (1909–73), b. Chicago

Some while before his final struggle with cancer, Robert Ryan's career seemed in retreat. He was going on sixty; he did not command starring roles; and he had never established much screen rapport in romance—put him with a woman and he was likely to become a threat. So it was sad sometimes to see him in passive, or even humiliated support—in *The Professionals* (66, Richard Brooks), say, or as the ridiculed officer in *The Dirty Dozen* (67, Robert Aldrich). He seemed old and weary, hanging on. Yet he had been one of the most particular and remarkable of American actors, a truly frightening man, not so much because of external menace but because of what he was thinking. If some people grind their teeth, Ryan was an eye-grinder.

John Houseman called him "a disturbing mixture of anger and tenderness who had reached stardom by playing mostly brutal, neurotic roles that were at complete variance with his true nature." That's a strange remark, hard to read, for isn't it the mix of anger and tenderness that comprises the neurosis of Ryan's character in, say, *On Dangerous Ground* (51, Nicholas Ray, and produced by Houseman)?

He's a Los Angeles cop in *On Dangerous Ground*, a man fit for the era of Chief Daryl Gates. The character, Jim Wilson, lives alone in a drab apartment. On the sideboard we see a crucifix and a statuette, a prize for boxing. Nick Ray was not one to ignore the real lives of his actors, and these two objects are very pointed: Ryan had attended a Jesuit high school before going on to Dartmouth where he was a champion boxer.

Wilson is not a corrupt cop so much as someone warped by the job. Ryan's taut, unsmiling face, his slightly naggy voice, one degree whinier than you expect for such a figure, his stooped, almost ashamed tallness, and those harsh eyes are the clues to Wilson's imminent crack-up—and no one was as attentive to such confused images of strength and weakness as Ray. Wilson nearly attacks the wrong man as he goes after a suspect. When a pretty girl in a drugstore smiles at him, he flinches. "What's with you?" she asks, and when he tells her, "Nothing's with me," it is the spirit of nihilism speaking. Wilson looks the perfect cop, but a partner says he's tougher to work with all the time. And you notice Ryan's way of standing, his coat like a shroud, his body tipped forward at the neck—the tall man always having to look down, but as if some burden weighed on his spine.

Pursuing a lead, Wilson goes to question Myrna, a noir slut. She shows him a bruise on her arm, and she says, "You'll make me talk, you'll squeeze it out of me with those big, strong arms, won't you?" In a moment, Ray has built a suffocating sadomasochistic atmosphere, which is intensified when the image fades out.

Wilson is a sadist who feels self-pity about his weakness. A few scenes later, he prepares to beat up a suspect, with fearful lamentation: "I always make you punks talk! Why do you make me do it?" These are scenes that many lead actors today would not play; they'd know they should never let themselves look so far from good.

In the late forties and early fifties, Ryan had cornered such roles. Just think of Montgomery in *Crossfire* (47, Edward Dmytryk), a cop turned soldier, a stickler for order who wants to call people "sir," yet a bully searching for weakness. There's a low-angle shot of Ryan's Monty near the end of *Crossfire*, as he judges the proposal meant to set him up, where his jaw fidgets in doubt and worry and then sets in the jut of superiority. You can call that great acting. But you can't separate the filmmaking from the cold clay of Ryan's face.

Crossfire and *On Dangerous Ground* may have the most ambiguous glimpses of this Ryan. But the same man is there, shell-shocked, in Renoir's *The Woman on the Beach* (47); magnificently menacing, a justified scourge and terror, as the limping victim of Van Heflin's cowardice in *Act of Violence* (49)—the best film Fred Zinnemann ever made; so brilliantly adept at paranoia and aggrandizement as Smith Ohlrig in *Caught* (49)— whether or not he was being Howard Hughes, whether or not the sardonic Hughes coached him—that you want more of Ohlrig in that film, no matter that you and Max Ophüls will fall in love with James Mason's gentle Dr. Quinada; loathsome and cynical as Earl, the seducer, in *Clash By Night* (52, Fritz Lang), a jerk who thinks he's dying of loneliness; and flat-out terrifying as the handyman who comes to Ida Lupino's house in *Beware, My Lovely* (52, Harry Horner).

For the actor, these opportunities were mixed blessings. Only two of the films mentioned—*On Dangerous Ground* and *Clash By Night*—had love stories: in the latter, Ryan is seen as unwholesome and sick; while *On Dangerous Ground* places love against a snowy landscape, a metaphor for Wilson's breakdown and for the Ida Lupino character's blindness. So the only real love story Ryan had was one in which he had a strange psychic shelter: the woman could not see him. There was more at RKO—Ray's *Born to Be Bad* (50); the kindly psychiatrist in *The Boy with Green Hair* (48, Joseph Losey), and maybe his most celebrated early role, the forlorn boxer in Robert Wise's *The Set-Up* (49). He is good in that film, yet oddly remote, too, as if he knew he was a noble stereotype in a dead end. Playing a simply good, tragic victim, Ryan seemed a touch shallow—did he need to make Stoker Thompson more vicious, closer to a raging bull?

Ryan was a contemporary of Burt Lancaster, Kirk Douglas, and William Holden, and only six months younger than Errol Flynn. That pinpoints his failure to establish himself as a star or a romantic lead. No matter his uniqueness as an actor, Ryan did not easily convey normal emotional neediness on screen. Yet he was rarely cast as mere villains, and it is likely that he would have been disturbed to find himself so confined.

Even in *Bad Day at Black Rock* (54, John Sturges), with Borgnine and Marvin as unequivocal henchmen, Ryan's boss of the Nevada whistlestop is more complex than the film has time for. *Black Rock*, despite color and Scope, is a kind of RKO remake. Elsewhere in the fifties, Ryan tried to be a chuckling scoundrel in *The Naked Spur* (53, Anthony Mann); he did wonders as the rich man left to die in the desert of *Inferno* (53, Roy Baker)—that is a modest venture, handicapped by 3D, but Ryan was in his element alone, struggling with the elements and talking to himself—in which the isolation is revealing; he was the leader of the gang in Fuller's *House of Bamboo* (55), a mastermind of rare, nearly homosexual leanings for the men in his outfit; he could not really stand up to the warmth and easy energy of Gable in *The Tall Men* (55, Raoul Walsh). Maybe the best film Ryan ever made was Anthony Mann's *Men in War* (57), yet as the hapless, unwarlike officer, he had not a great deal to do except oppose the uninhibited commitment of Aldo Ray's sergeant. Still, by the time of *Men in War*, Ryan looked his forty-

eight; the young hardness had gone from his face, to be replaced by fatigue and sadness.

Ryan's darkness had at least two more moments, etched blacker by age. In Robert Wise's *Odds Against Tomorrow* (59), he was a rancid, self-pitying racist again—Montgomery ten years older. Now he had a scene with Gloria Grahame, the clincher in the uncovering of Ryan's sexy unsuitability for romance. There are not many meetings that so quickly catch the force of violence in sexual association. In so many films, Ryan scorned or sneered at women—that's how he treats his wife, Myrna Loy, in *Lonelyhearts* (58, Vincent J. Donehue). Was that the character or the actor's own misogyny?

Billy Budd (62) is a parable for which Peter Ustinov chose Ryan to play Claggart, the master-at-arms so affronted by the grace and fineness of Budd that he drives Budd to murder him. There is a terrifying instant in which Billy's good nature nearly softens Claggart, and Ryan turns on him—"You would charm me, too. Get away!"—in which Melville's story gains a note of homosexual dread. *Billy Budd* may need to be sung; is it too elemental for photography? But Ryan's Claggart is indelible. Who else could have played the part without insinuating some sinister charm or humor?

He was past his peak, with smaller parts in big pictures—like John the Baptist in *King of Kings* (61, Ray), and the deserter in *Custer of the West* (68, Robert Siodmak and Irving Lemar). His role as the martinet in *The Dirty Dozen* was even a humiliation: a fusspot, not one of the guys, the object of ridicule. He stood up to the mockery honorably; again, some actors of his rank would have declined the part. Then he was the loneliest figure in *The Wild Bunch* (69, Sam Peckinpah), Deke Thornton, the betrayer, the man who hates his new associates as he tries to destroy his old friends. Ryan was perfect, yet it seemed cruel to cast him.

From the outset, Ryan plays a watcher who is doomed to be a survivor. Was it Peckinpah's respect for the actor, or did the director discover a sadness that helped enrich the role of Thornton? In the last part of the movie, Ryan's character loses his hat. With brindle hair and melancholy mustache Thornton seems as dry and gray as chaparral.

He was not well. He had his own cancer, as well as the one that killed his wife. But he was resolute and skeptical enough, in 1973, to lend himself to *Executive Action* (David Miller), the first film about the Kennedy assassination. He plays the powerful, conservative leader of the plot, and he brought a pitiless, sepulchral grandeur to Dalton Trumbo's best lines on death and insignificance.

Finally, for the American Film Theatre and John Frankenheimer, Ryan played Larry Slade in Eugene O'Neill's *The Iceman Cometh* (73). He looked haggard and never more human: it was an uncanny farewell and the whole movie deserves revival. Ryan was dead before it played. In *Newsweek,* Paul Zimmerman wrote, "It is Robert Ryan, his face a wreck of smashed dreams, who provides the tragic dimension that makes this *Iceman* a moving, unforgettable experience. Ryan played his part in the shadow of his own death. He died this year, leaving behind a lifetime of roles too small for his talent."

Mark Rydell, b. New York, 1934

1967: *The Fox.* 1969: *The Reivers.* 1971: *The Cowboys.* 1973: *Cinderella Liberty.* 1976: *Harry and Walter Go to New York.* 1979: *The Rose.* 1981: *On Golden Pond.* 1984: *The River.* 1991: *For the Boys.* 1994: *Intersection.* 1996: *Crime of the Century* (TV). 2001: *James Dean* (TV).

It is not really any more incongruous that the man who played Marty Augustine should have made *On Golden Pond,* than that Augustine should introduce the Coke bottle to his girlfriend's face in *The Long Goodbye* (73, Robert Altman). After all, Augustine's raison d'être is to be unpredictable— to be an actor, to be amazing. Rydell is so good in the small part (it *is* one of the most frightening scenes in film) that one wishes he had acted more. Instead, he has put together a career in the spirit of the hare in a cunning game of hare-and-hounds—leaving a trail but refusing to be identified.

He has made two more films for television in recent years: *Crime of the Century,* about the kidnapping of the Lindbergh baby; and a James Dean biopic that revolved around the remarkable performance by James Franco. In the same film, Rydell gave a good performance as Jack Warner— just as he had played Meyer Lansky in *Havana* (90, Sydney Pollack)—but tame stuff next to Augustine. He was good again as the agent in *Hollywood Ending* (02, Woody Allen).

Winona Ryder (Winona Laura Horowitz),

b. Winona, Minnesota, 1971

In 1994, pressed for space and surrounded by young actresses, I backed a hunch that Winona Ryder would outlast Nicole Kidman and some others. Well, Ryder holds her place, but Kidman has clearly outstripped her in both daring and accomplishment. And Ryder is now thirty, and pretty in a way more suited to twenty. She has developed as an actress, for sure, but she does not intimidate her own pictures into seeing her as a demon or a goddess. Nothing else lasts as well.

She was trained at A.C.T. in San Francisco, and she lived some of her childhood in a northern California commune (she was very active in the search for the kidnapped Polly Klaas in Petaluma in 1993). She made her debut in *Lucas* (86, David Seltzer), and then appeared in *Square Dance* (87,

Daniel Petrie); *1969* (88, Ernest Thompson); *Beetlejuice* (88, Tim Burton); as the teen wife to Jerry Lee Lewis in *Great Balls of Fire* (89, Jim McBride)—a touching, adroit performance; wonderful in *Heathers* (89, Michael Lehmann), a very testing, comic role; *Edward Scissorhands* (90, Burton); *Mermaids* (90, Richard Benjamin); *Welcome Home, Roxy Carmichael* (90, Jim Abraham); and *Night on Earth* (91, Jim Jarmusch).

Exhaustion meant she had to drop out of the role of the daughter in *The Godfather, Part III.* But she maintained her promise with two very challenging roles in flawed films: passionate in *Bram Stoker's Dracula* (92, Francis Ford Coppola); sweetly cunning in *The Age of Innocence* (93, Martin Scorsese); and in *Reality Bites* (94, Ben Stiller). She may have lacked some of the technique required for period.

She was an ideal family member in *Little Women* (94, Gillian Armstrong); *How to Make an American Quilt* (95, Jocelyn Moorhouse); *Boys* (96, Stacy Cochran); *Looking for Richard* (96, Al Pacino); overshadowed by Sigourney Weaver in *Alien Resurrection* (97, Jean-Pierre Jeunet); *Celebrity* (98, Woody Allen); out-diva'd by Angelina Jolie in *Girl, Interrupted* (99, James Mangold); *Autumn in New York* (00, Joan Chen); *Lost Souls* (00, Janusz Kaminski); *Zoolander* (01, Stiller); and doing the Stanwyck role in *Mr. Deeds* (02, Steven Brill).

And then—shopping trouble!

S

Sabu (Sabu Dastagir) (1924–63),

b. Karapur, India

Sabu was just twelve, working in the stables of a rich man (some say the Maharajah of Mysore), when he was spotted by Robert Flaherty and signed to play the central role in the muchadmired semidocumentary *Elephant Boy* (37). This film was produced by Alexander Korda, who brought the boy to England and three major movies: *The Drum* (38, Zoltan Korda); as Abu, the Douglas Fairbanks role, in the great fantasyspectacle *The Thief of Bagdad* (40, Michael Powell, Ludwig Berger, Tim Whelan, Zoltan Korda, William Cameron Menzies, Alexander Korda); and as Mowgli in *The Jungle Book* (42, Zoltan Korda), actually filmed in Hollywood. Everyone was enchanted with the appealing little guy— Michael Powell called him "a wonderful, graceful, frank, intelligent child." Somewhere in there he joined the American Army, but soon he was at Universal, back to being a cute lad, in a series of nonsensical exotic Technicolor romps.

First came *Arabian Nights* (42, John Rawlins) with Maria Montez (the Dancing Girl) and Jon Hall (the Caliph); they would also be his costars in

White Savage (43, Arthur Lubin) and that camp classic *Cobra Woman* (44, Robert Siodmak), in which Montez gets to play twin high priestesses—one good, one evil—and there's a volcano and a curse, and a different kind of curse: Lon Chaney Jr. as the high priest. Sabu is his shining self, loincloth and all. Although he's now twenty, he looks thirteen, and therefore exempt from the lure of la Montez. (If he weren't so obviously innocent you could take him for hunky Jon Hall's playmate.) Montez is along for the ride in *Tangier* (46, George Waggner), but Hall is somewhere else. Even so, Sabu doesn't get the girl (Robert Preston does), but he does sing "She'll Be Coming Round the Mountain."

Then comes Sabu's last major film: the Michael Powell/Emeric Pressburger *Black Narcissus* (47), about a group of nuns in the Himalayas. He plays a rich young general—at last, at twenty-three, he's postadolescent. He's then in a minor Powell/Pressburger movie, *End of the River* (47), and from there on in there's nothing worth talking about: *Man-Eater of Kumaon* (48, Byron Haskin); *Song of India* (49, Albert S. Rogell); *Savage Drums* (51, William Berke—Sabu confronts the Commies). After these flops, he was in an Italian-financed fiasco called *Buongiorno, Elefante!* (1952, Gianni Franciolini). It had been produced by, and starred, Vittorio de Sica, but alas, it wasn't directed by him.

Baghdad was Indian (52, Nanabhai Bhatt); *Il Tesoro del Bengala* was Italian (54, Gianni Vernuccio). There was *Jaguar* (56, George Blair), *Jungle Hell* (56, Norman A. Cerf—Sabu meets flying saucers); *The Black Panther* (56, Ron Ormond); *Sabu and the Magic Ring* (57, Blair—put together from a failed TV series); *Herrin der Welt, Teil I* (60, William Dieterle); *Rampage* (63, Phil Karlson). Finally, *A Tiger Walks* (64, Norman Taurog) for Disney.

When things went wrong in Hollywood, Sabu took up custom-furniture making, working with his brother—who was killed in a store robbery. But he had just made his Disney movie when he died of a heart attack, at thirty-nine, so maybe things were looking up. He was survived by his wife and two children, one of whom—Jasmine—has recently written a sequel to *The Thief of Baghdad* and has seen it filmed.

Eva Marie Saint,

b. Newark, New Jersey, 1924

Educated at Bowling Green State University, she had done a little work on radio, TV, and Broadway before being cast by Elia Kazan in *On the Waterfront* (54), for which she won the supporting actress Oscar.

Wanly beautiful, she was one of the more discreet and sensitive American actresses of the late fifties. But her intelligence was seldom used properly. Twice, she exposed Elizabeth Taylor, simply by looking at her in a pained and wondering way: *Raintree County* (57, Edward Dmytryk) and Minnelli's appalling *The Sandpiper* (65), which, deep down, contains a fine twenty-minute movie about Saint. She was funny in *That Certain Feeling* (56, Melvin Frank and Norman Panama) and *Cancel My Reservation* (72, Paul Bogart) with Bob Hope, and in *The Russians Are Coming . . .* (66, Norman Jewison); more moving than *A Hatful of Rain* (57, Fred Zinnemann) or *36 Hours* (64, George Seaton) deserves; and a tolerant spectator of her own neglect in *Grand Prix* (66, John Frankenheimer) and *The Stalking Moon* (69, Robert Mulligan).

She worked comparatively rarely, and it was no credit to Hollywood that only a few films were worthy of her: in Frankenheimer's *All Fall Down* (62); as the mysterious Eve Kendall in *North by Northwest* (59, Alfred Hitchcock), where as seductress, betrayer, and sacrificial victim, she is the pale blonde sign of seriousness beneath the initial comedy; ideal as the central observant sensibility in Preminger's *Exodus* (60); forlornly stranded as the wife in Irvin Kershner's *Loving* (70). She was older than she looked, but we are content with the restrained eroticism of the auction scene in *North by Northwest* where she sits mute in red brocade between the inflamed politeness of Grant and Mason; and later, in an alarmed orange dress, as she dangles from the stone lip of George Washington.

She was the wife of a POW in *When Hell Was in Session* (79, Paul Krasny); a mother in TV's *Splendor in the Grass* (81, Richard Sarafian); the mother to Jennifer Jason Leigh's anorexia in *The Best Little Girl in the World* (81, Sam O'Steen); *Jane Doe* (83, Ivan Nagy); *Love Leads the Way* (84, Delbert Mann); *Fatal Vision* (84, David Greene); *The Last Days of Patton* (86, Mann); *Nothing in Common* (86, Garry Marshall); *Norman Rockwell's Breaking Home Ties* (87, John Wilder); *I'll Be Home for Christmas* (88, Marvin J. Chomsky); and *Voyage of Terror: The Achille Lauro Affair* (89, Alberto Negrin). She also played Cybill Shepherd's mother for a season in *Moonlighting.*

George Sanders (1906–72),

b. St. Petersburg, Russia

The son of a rope manufacturer and a British horticulturalist—it could be the start of a Nabokov novel. And Sanders's own cultivated offensiveness, his ostentatious and articulate disdain, and his grammatical malice are all the display of an amused, intelligent, and playful Nabokov narrator. No one but Sanders by this reckoning would have derived so much rueful pleasure from the grotesque disarray of his movies; no one would have been more aghast at the intensity of his own labor over thirty years; and no one would be more dismissive of that handful of roles that properly exercised him.

His best part was the critic/narrator, Addison de Witt, in Joseph Mankiewicz's *All About Eve* (50), a demonstration of soft-spoken, tranquil caddishness. And how would de Witt have described Sanders's career? "Sanders had early gauged that there was a profitable, supporting life to be had in Hollywood as a gracious scoundrel: he noticed that his English drawl, provokingly good manners, and high sartorial standards were vouchsafes of insolence and bad intentions. He so practiced the sneer that eventually he required no words. He imagined his mouth drawn down by some astringent spirit that he was on the point of swallowing—hemlock perhaps—and gazed skeptically at earnest heroes and condescendingly at ripe bosoms afforded by his height and so many costume films."

When the Depression obliged him to abandon tobacco farming, Sanders took up acting and made a few films in England: *Find the Lady* (36, Ronald Gillette); *Strange Cargo* (36, Lawrence Huntington); *The Man Who Could Work Miracles* (36, Lothar Mendes); and *Dishonour Bright* (36, Tom Walls). But it was clear that his hollow loftiness was worthy of bolder nonsense: he went to Hollywood to play in *Lloyds of London* (36, Henry King) and stayed. Fox put him under contract and, when war came, employed his polish as Hun, spy, or Gestapo in several films. In addition, they loaned him to the more perceptive RKO where he was the lounge-suit hero in two B-picture series, featuring the Saint and then the Falcon. These are in advance of Ian Fleming's James Bond, the depraved gentleman, supposedly acting in the name of honor and probity, but visibly unconvinced by such causes: *The Saint Strikes Back* (39, John Farrow); *The Saint in London* (39, John Paddy Carstairs); *The Gay Falcon* (41, Irving Reis); *A Date with the Falcon* (41, Reis); and *The Falcon Takes Over* (42, Reis).

Apart from those enjoyable excursions, Sanders was a hard-worked support: *Slave Ship* (37, Tay Garnett); *Love Is News* (37, Garnett); *Lancer Spy* (37, Gregory Ratoff, another old St. Petersburg ham); *Four Men and a Prayer* (38, John Ford); *Confessions of a Nazi Spy* (39, Anatole Litvak); grilling Anna Neagle in *Nurse Edith Cavell* (39, Herbert Wilcox); *Green Hell* (40, James Whale); *Bitter Sweet* (40, W. S. Van Dyke); *Son of Monte Cristo* (40, Rowland V. Lee); roguishly stepping through the window in *Rebecca* (40, Alfred Hitchcock); *The House of the Seven Gables* (40, Joe May); *Foreign Correspondent* (40, Hitchcock); *Man Hunt* (41, Fritz Lang); *Rage in Heaven* (41, Van Dyke); *Sundown* (41, Henry Hathaway); *Son of Fury* (42, John Cromwell); *Her Cardboard Lover* (42, George Cukor); the painter in *The Moon and Sixpence* (42, Albert

Lewin); *They Came to Blow Up America* (43, Edward Ludwig); *This Land Is Mine* (43, Jean Renoir); *The Lodger* (44, John Brahm); harking back to Russia in the Chekhov-based *Summer Storm* (44, Douglas Sirk); brilliant in *Uncle Harry* (45, Robert Siodmak); *The Picture of Dorian Gray* (45, Lewin); *Hangover Square* (45, Brahm); *A Scandal in Paris* (46, Sirk); *The Strange Woman* (46, Edgar G. Ulmer); *The Ghost and Mrs. Muir* (47, Mankiewicz); as Charles II in *Forever Amber* (47, Otto Preminger); *The Private Affairs of Bel Ami* (47, Lewin, and his third film for that idiosyncrat); *Lured* (47, Sirk); *Lady Windermere's Fan* (49, Preminger); and *Samson and Delilah* (49, Cecil B. De Mille).

How could any actually uninterested actor have appeared in so many fetching films? Plainly, languor was a disguise for stamina. But once Hollywood had given him a supporting actor Oscar for *All About Eve*, it set about discouraging him. He was asked to dress up in armor and ride horses, engage in sword fights and other arduous contests. He went into a decline that was remarkable for lasting so long without reaching extinction: *I Can Get It For You Wholesale* (51, Michael Gordon); *The Light Touch* (51, Richard Brooks); *Ivanhoe* (52, Richard Thorpe); *Assignment Paris* (52, Robert Parrish); *Call Me Madam* (53, Walter Lang); *Witness to Murder* (54, Roy Rowland); *King Richard and the Crusaders* (54, David Butler); *The Scarlet Coat* (55, John Sturges); and *The King's Thief* (55, Robert Z. Leonard).

But the next ten years were far worse; good dialogue became scarcer, and Sanders was forced to roam Europe for cheap movies. Only a diligent biographer would recall such stray mercies as *Moonfleet* (55, Lang); *While the City Sleeps* (56, Lang); *The Seventh Sin* (57, Ronald Neame and Vincente Minnelli); *Solomon and Sheba* (59, King Vidor); *That Kind of Woman* (59, Sidney Lumet); *Bluebeard's Ten Honeymoons* (60, W. Lee Wilder); *A Shot in the Dark* (64, Blake Edwards); and although Sanders derived no pleasure from it, *Viaggio in Italia* (53, Roberto Rossellini). In fact, Rossellini boldly cut through irritability to the shy observer of life who hid behind Sanders's barbs. The actor was visibly unsettled by this and by the heat and spontaneity of Naples, and thus he more profoundly resembled an inhibited English snob at a loss with his marriage.

In his last years he worked on films of such dreadfulness that one longs to know his comments on them. He was in drag in *The Kremlin Letter* (70, John Huston) and the voice of Shere Khan in *The Jungle Book* (67, Wolfgang Reitherman). He was found dead in a Barcelona hotel room, having left a plangent suicide note that complained of boredom. It is Nabokov pinned helpless in Locustland.

There was also the undergrowth of his marriages—four in all, yet since two of the wives were Gabor sisters (Zsa Zsa and Magda), the number must have seemed greater. The movie business feels so flat nowadays without figures like George Sanders.

Mark Sandrich (1900–45), b. New York
1928: *Runaway Girls*. 1930: *The Talk of Hollywood*. 1933: *Melody Cruise; Aggie Appleby, Maker of Men*. 1934: *Hips, Hips, Hooray!; Cockeyed Cavaliers; The Gay Divorcee*. 1935: *Top Hat*. 1936: *Follow the Fleet; A Woman Rebels*. 1937: *Shall We Dance?*. 1938: *Carefree*. 1939: *Man About Town*. 1940: *Buck Benny Rides Again; Love Thy Neighbour*. 1941: *Skylark*. 1942: *Holiday Inn*. 1943: *So Proudly We Hail*. 1944: *Here Come the Waves; I Love a Soldier*.

Without ever suggesting that he had the orgiastic eye of Busby Berkeley, the wit of Stanley Donen, or Minnelli's sense of character and fantasy, Mark Sandrich still has a place in the history of the musical. He it was who maintained that sprightly, asexual elegance and the black hat/white tie contrast of *The Gay Divorcee, Top Hat, Follow the Fleet, Shall We Dance?*, and *Carefree*, the main body of the Astaire/Rogers musicals at RKO. Perhaps Sandrich was no more than an able recorder of Astaire's designs, but those movies have a genuine gaiety and a happy feeling for decent luxury and polite exuberance that is a part of our view of the 1930s. Sandrich expired on a wave of patriotic movies that have dated less well, but *Holiday Inn*—a Paramount pairing of Astaire and Crosby—has the bright confidence of the RKO films and an easy coverage of dance that was innovatory in its intimacy. Sandrich and Astaire showed that dance in films could be like conversation; at Warners, it had been magnificent, but always a set piece.

Susan Sarandon (Susan Tomalin),
b. New York, 1946
In what must be called her middle age, Susan Sarandon moved from the status of reliable trouper to American favorite. She works hard, she has had children with the younger actor Tim Robbins (without seeming inclined to marry him), and if she seems just a touch too world-weary to commit too deeply to anything, still she has Bette Davis eyes and enough knockout punch to command romantic roles. She has made enough bad or routine films to know that making a movie may be just a matter of luck and fortitude. If ever one hoped that, past fifty, she would become more dangerous, the reality was sadder. She seems to be looking for dignity now—and sooner or later dignity means plastic surgery.

She studied drama at Catholic University in Washington, D.C. She was then a model and, as she got into pictures, she took her name from her marriage to actor Chris Sarandon. She appeared in *Joe* (70, John G. Avildsen); *Lady Liberty* (72, Mario Monicelli); playing the woman in "The Last of the Belles" for TV in *F. Scott Fitzgerald and the Last of the Belles* (74, Anthony Page); *Lovin' Molly* (74, Sidney Lumet); enshrined in late-night cult as Janet in *The Rocky Horror Picture Show* (75, Jim Sharman); eyes popping from the danger of wing-walking in *The Great Waldo Pepper* (75, George Roy Hill); *One Summer Love* (76, Gilbert Cates); in a thousand-mile off-road car-race picture with Joe Don Baker in *Checkered Flag or Crash* (77, Alan Gibson)—that look of disbelief has been earned; and *The Other Side of Midnight* (77, Charles Jarrott), facing more silken idiocies.

She coproduced a documentary, *The Last of the Cowboys* (77, John Leone), and was a stunning, milk-breasted mother in *Pretty Baby* (78, Louis Malle). She felt the hysteria of *King of the Gypsies* (78, Frank Pierson). After *Something Short of Paradise* (79, David Helpern Jr.) and *Loving Couples* (80, Jack Smight), she found her best part as the would-be croupier in *Atlantic City* (80, Malle), a woman helplessly romantic and cunning at the same time. She rose wonderfully to the John Guare script, and had her first great on-screen love affair, with Burt Lancaster.

Still, Sarandon was not quite a lead actress. If that hurt, she never showed it. Instead, she has gone greedily after a range of parts that stars might have disdained: *Tempest* (82, Paul Mazursky); with Christopher Walken in *Who Am I This Time?* (82, Jonathan Demme) for TV; *The Hunger* (83, Tony Scott); *The Buddy System* (84, Glenn Jordan); as the dictator's daughter in *Mussolini: The Decline and Fall of Il Duce* (85, Alberto Negrin), with Bob Hoskins as Dad and Anthony Hopkins as her husband, Count Ciano, 192 minutes of it for cable; *Compromising Positions* (85, Frank Perry); as a leader of P.O.W. women in the Philippines in *Women of Valor* (86, Buzz Kulik) for TV.

Then she hit the run of parts that allowed her to be a forty-year-old standing up for herself, getting many of the best lines and ready to use a gun: *The Witches of Eastwick* (87, George Miller); *Bull Durham* (88, Ron Shelton), with Tim Robbins and Kevin Costner; *Sweet Hearts Dance* (88, Robert Greenwald); *The January Man* (89, Pat O'Connor); *A Dry White Season* (89, Euzhan Palcy); with James Spader in *White Palace* (90, Luis Mandoki); managing to make a very literary character seem like a small-town waitress in *Thelma and Louise* (91, Ridley Scott); and making the most of the hints in the script of *Light Sleeper* (92, Paul Schrader). She had cameos in *The Player* (92, Robert Altman) and *Bob Roberts* (92, Robbins), and she was nominated for best actress for her mother in *Lorenzo's Oil* (92, George Miller), a woman to alarm Corleones; *The Client* (94, Joel Schumacher).

The next year, Sarandon won the Oscar as Sister Helen Prejean in *Dead Man Walking* (95, Robbins). It was a fine performance, and a deserved victory, but it seems to have persuaded her that she was an institution. She narrates high-minded documentaries, she lends her voice to animated films, but she hasn't done anything very interesting since Oscar: the Spider in *James and the Giant Peach* (96, Henry Selick); *Twilight* (98, Robert Benton); *Illuminata* (98, John Turturro); dying gracefully in *Stepmom* (98, Chris Columbus); *Earthly Possessions* (99, James Lapine); *Cradle Will Rock* (99, Robbins); *Anywhere but Here* (99, Wayne Wang); *Joe Gould's Secret* (00, Stanley Tucci); Coco LaBouche in *Rugrats in Paris* (00, Stig Bergqvist and Paul Demeyer); *Time of Our Lives* (00, Mary Agnes Donoghue); Ivy in *Cats & Dogs* (01, Lawrence Guterman).

She remains reliable and enterprising: *Igby Goes Down* (02, Burr Steers); with Goldie Hawn in *The Banger Sisters* (02, Bob Dolman); *Moonlight Mile* (02, Brad Silberling); *Children of Dune* (03, Greg Yaitanes); *Ice Bound* (03, Roger Spottiswoode).

Carlos Saura, b. Huesca, Spain, 1932

1957: *La Tarde del Domingo* (s). 1958: *Cuenca* (d). 1960: *Los Golfos*. 1964: *Llanto por un Bandido*. 1966: *La Caza/The Hunt*. 1967: *Peppermint Frappé*. 1968: *Stress es Tres, Tres*. 1969: *La Madriguera*. 1970: *El Jardín de las Delicias/The Garden of Delights*. 1973: *Ana y los Lobos*. 1974: *La Prima Angélica/Cousin Angelica*. 1976: *Cría Cuervos*. 1977: *Elisa, Vida Mía*. 1978: *Los Ojos Vendados*. 1979: *Mama Cumple 100 Anos*. 1980: *Deprisa, Deprisa*. 1981: *Bodas de Sangre/Blood Wedding*. 1982: *Antonieta; Dulces Horas*. 1983: *Carmen*. 1984: *Los Zancos*. 1986: *El Amor Brujo*. 1988: *El Dorado*. 1989: *La Noche Oscura*. 1990: *Ay, Carmela*. 1992: *Sevillanas; El Sur*. 1993: *¡Dispara!*. 1995: *Flamenco*. 1996: *Taxi*. 1998: *Pajarico; Tango; ¡Esa Luz!*. 1999: *Goya*. 2001: *Buñuel y la Mesa del Rey Salomón*.

There was a moment in the career of Carlos Saura when he seemed like a great director. Nor do I want to back off in my admiration for the pictures he made during and just after the last days of Franco. From *The Hunt* in 1966 to *Elisa, Vida Mía* in 1977, Saura was fermenting under the pressure of a dictatorship that was beginning to weaken from age and weariness. Nevertheless, Saura was having to combat censorship, and having to lead his films into allegory, dreams, and symbol. The deviousness was very fruitful—and it may have encouraged his creative personality far more than liberty ever could. For his sense of family and national history is meditative, Freudian, and secretive.

He was a child of the Civil War and its after-math—and the child's view of warped authority is crucial to Saura's hushed tone. Already a talented still photographer, he entered film school in Madrid. His first feature film, *Los Golfos*, was a study of street kids, far more affected by De Sica than by Buñuel. Indeed, Saura had not seen Buñuel films, and he only met the Spanish exile at Cannes when *Los Golfos* was shown there. But Buñuel of the sixties and early seventies was a considerable influence on Saura—for that is the era when Buñuel's surrealism gained a greater enjoyment of movie style (as well as Carrière's clever scripts).

Carefully, cautiously—for Saura is shy and oblique—his films became portraits of Spain in a dark mirror. The producer Elias Querejeta became a supporter. Saura formed a loyal crew, and by *Peppermint Frappé* he had met Geraldine Chaplin. They lived together for several years, and had a child, and Chaplin became the exquisite face in the shadows in so many Saura films. It was a great partnership for both of them, and it reached a peak with *Cría Cuervos* and *Elisa, Vida Mía*. In the first, Chaplin was playing with the little girl, Ana Torrent; and in the second she was the daughter to Fernando Rey. They are masterly films, dense, luminous, and very moving in their sense of a society and families trying to escape from the lies and deformities of the past. Yet the films also seem to believe in the chronic ways in which people cling to emotional imprisonment. In the end, Franco may have been only a way for Saura to discover depths of guilt and servitude that excited him more than freedom.

He has done fine films since then—*Dulces Horas,* a lovely mingling of fact, dreams, and hope, and *Antonieta*, which starred Isabelle Adjani. But Saura moved in an unexpected direction, to films about dance. With the dancer and choreographer Antonio Gades he made *Blood Wedding, Carmen,* and *El Amor Brujo,* which are feature-length dance dramas. They are exciting . . . and monotonous. The macho stare of Gades and the hammering of heels seem to me a poor exchange for the murmuring disquiet of earlier films and the harrowed smile of Geraldine Chaplin. It is as if, in the new Spain, Saura has felt compelled to give up dark worries for tourist movies.

Saura has gone a good deal further along this road. *Tango* is the record of a performance, reflections on Argentinian history, and the story of a love affair—which is a lot to sustain, even with Vittorio Storaro on camera. I see how these ideas might dawn, yet I long for the feeling of *Cría Cuervos*. *Goya* is a biopic of the painter's last years, with Francisco Rabal, and without any story within its story, but terribly old-fashioned. Still, I look forward to the Buñuel project, a fantasy in which both Buñuel and Dalí are promised as characters.

Victor Saville (1897–1979),
b. Birmingham, England
1927: *The Arcadians; The Glad Eye* (codirected
with Maurice Elvey); *Tesha*. 1929: *Kitty; Woman
to Woman; Me and the Boys*. 1930: *The W Plan; A
Warm Corner; The Sport of Kings*. 1931: *Sunshine
Susie; Michael and Mary*. 1932: *Hindle Wakes;
The Faithful Heart; Love on Wheels*. 1933: *The
Good Companions; I Was a Spy; Friday the 13th*.
1934: *Evergreen; Evensong; The Iron Duke*. 1935:
Me and Marlborough; The Dictator. 1936: *First a
Girl; It's Love Again*. 1937: *Storm in a Teacup;
Dark Journey*. 1938: *South Riding*. 1943: *Forever
and a Day* (codirected). 1945: *Tonight and Every
Night*. 1946: *The Green Years*. 1947: *Green Dol-
phin Street; If Winter Comes*. 1949: *Conspirator*.
1950: *Kim*. 1951: *Calling Bulldog Drummond*.
1952: *24 Hours of a Woman's Life*. 1954: *The Long
Wait*. 1955: *The Silver Chalice*.

The most interesting point about Saville's career is
paradoxical: in the 1930s, in England, he showed
versatility, gaiety, and humor, but once he had
gone to Hollywood, in 1939, he singularly lapsed
as a director. He makes a sharp contrast with
Alfred Hitchcock, who graduated to America at
about the same time and became a more profound
artist in the process.

Several of Saville's English movies—*The Good
Companions, I Was a Spy, Evergreen, South Riding,* and *Hindle Wakes*—are still worthwhile, even
if they show more craft and decorum than personality. In general, his British films escape national
failings of tattiness and technical caution. His
musicals and costume pieces often wear their
glamour and theatricality with a naturalness that
seems to aspire to Hollywood. Saville had been
associated with MGM in Britain and he went to
America as producer and director. But the films
he made there himself are sadly enervating, suggesting that his British period may have been fla-
vored by a certain sense of superiority to the
medium and its genres that was exposed in America. The intensity of popular romance, adventure,
and violence are all missed in, say, *If Winter
Comes, Kim,* and *The Long Wait,* the latter a
Spillane adaptation that never dreams of Aldrich's
creative criticism of Mike Hammer, and settles for
maudlin cruelty. (However, we owe *Kiss Me
Deadly* to Saville. He bought up the film rights to
several Spillane books, and he has a credit as executive producer on the Aldrich film.) And although,
in Britain, he had brought out the light prettiness
of Jessie Matthews, that seems irrelevant compared with the way *Tonight and Every Night*—
made between *Cover Girl* and *Gilda*—reflects
Rita Hayworth's surgent luster.

In other words, Saville is a man with more sense
of production than eye for an image. His record as
producer is creditable, especially in America. He
had gone into pictures on the production side and

formed an early partnership with Michael Balcon.
He produced briefly before he began directing
and then, most fruitfully, in the period 1937–43:
Hindle Wakes (27, Maurice Elvey); *Roses of
Picardy* (27, Elvey); *Action for Slander* (37, Tim
Whelan); *The Citadel* (38, King Vidor); *Goodbye,
Mr. Chips* (39, Sam Wood); *The Earl of Chicago*
(40, Richard Thorpe); *Bitter Sweet* (40, W. S. Van
Dyke); *The Mortal Storm* (40, Frank Borzage);
Smilin' Through (41, Borzage); *A Woman's Face*
(41, Cukor); *White Cargo* (42, Thorpe); *Keeper of
the Flame* (42, Cukor); *Above Suspicion* (43,
Thorpe); years later, *The Greengage Summer* (61,
Lewis Gilbert). Of those, it seems that he took an
important part on *The Mortal Storm* and *A
Woman's Face,* while *The Citadel* resembles his
own provincial films. But *Smilin' Through* smacks
of a silly producer impeding the director. Whatever Saville's contribution, *The Mortal Storm* and
Keeper of the Flame are radically better than his
own films and immutably the work of Borzage and
Cukor.

Nancy Savoca, b. New York, 1960
1989: *True Love*. 1991: *Dogfight*. 1993: *Household
Saints*. 1999: *The 24 Hour Woman*.

A graduate of the film program at NYU, Nancy
Savoca made three startlingly raw and authentic
films in five years. But the interest following the
third left me with high hopes not fulfilled by the
schematic treatment of career and motherhood in
The 24 Hour Woman. *True Love* (with Annabella
Sciorra) is about an Italian wedding in the Bronx.
Dogfight has some Marines off to Vietnam, with
one of them (River Phoenix) forced to bring a
plain girl (Lili Taylor) to a party. *Household Saints*
traces the lives of three Italian-American women
(Judith Molina, Tracey Ullman, Lili Taylor again).
Savoca usually works with her husband, screenwriter Richard Guay. Her world, so far, is narrow,
but there's no question about her knowledge of it,
or the force with which she depicts it.

John Sayles, b. Schenectady, New York, 1950
1979: *The Return of the Secaucus Seven*. 1982:
Lianna. 1983: *Baby, It's You*. 1984: *The Brother
from Another Planet*. 1987: *Matewan*. 1988: *Eight
Men Out*. 1991: *City of Hope*. 1993: *Passion Fish*.
1994: *The Secret of Roan Inish*. 1996: *Lone Star*.
1997: *Men with Guns*. 1999: *Limbo*. 2002: *Sunshine State*.

As befits a connoisseur of extended groups and
variegated perspectives, John Sayles is himself a
mass of men—not just the director of essentially
independent films rooted in good talk, character
study, and social reflection, but the writer of take-
the-money-and-run screenplays; an odd, droll
actor; a writer of fiction; a MacArthur Foundation
fellow; and an altogether earnest, likeable, hardworking example to other independents. Indeed,

for all his variety, there is an emphatic integrity to Sayles—it may be his greatest limit as an artist, as if he lacked the imagination for betrayal.

He has a degree in psychology from Williams College, and he had published two novels before he turned to film—*Pride of the Bimbos* (1975) and *Union Dues* (1977). Since then he has published a collection of stories, *The Anarchist's Convention* (1979), and another novel, *Los Gusanos* (1991).

His first movie involvement was with Hollywood at its most raw. He wrote scripts for Roger Corman: *Piranha* (78, Joe Dante); *The Lady in Red* (79, Lewis Teague); *Alligator* (80, Dante); *The Howling* (81, Dante); and *The Challenge* (82, John Frankenheimer).

Famously, *The Return of the Secaucus Seven* was made for just $40,000—and well made. The actual moviemaking was less restricted than unconcerned. There was a face-saving basketball sequence to show willing craft. But Sayles at this stage was frankly unimpressed with cinema. He liked people, real truth, and actors—those virtues won an audience delighted at seeing themselves on screen.

Sayles never seemed to waver under the great attention that came with success. But it was less certain that he knew what to do with it. *Lianna*, a story about a lesbian affair, was stilted and pedestrian, and *Brother from Another Planet* was painfully awkward. But *Baby, It's You* was full of old-fashioned charm and very cute acting from Rosanna Arquette and Vincent Spano.

Meanwhile, Sayles continued to write and act for others. He worked on the screenplay for *Enormous Changes at the Last Minute* (83, Mirra Bank) from Grace Paley, and *The Clan of the Cave Bear* (86, Michael Chapman) from Jean Auel. As an actor, he was striking in *Hard Choices* (86, Rick King) and *Something Wild* (86, Jonathan Demme).

His most recent films show a developing assurance and a greater interest in filmmaking. They are all group stories. Though a fine discoverer of actors, and a devotee of large casts (male on the whole), Sayles abhors starriness. *Matewan* concerned a West Virginia miners' strike in the 1920s, while *Eight Men Out* described the 1919 baseball scandal of the Chicago White Sox. The feeling for period and place was intense in both. The narrative handling of many characters was adroit—and a Sayles stock company was emerging in which David Strathairn was a notable figure. Still, both pictures left this viewer with a slight feeling of "so what?" Their targets were so predictable that the drama seemed overdetermined. There was a lack of surprise or passion, and some threat of the films seeming like executed scripts.

Can Sayles overcome this? Does he feel the need to? His films have improved, and he seems to be an eager learner. *City of Hope* was another crowded canvas, but with a contemporary setting, a mass of anecdote, a mix of races, and a genuine attempt to confront modern urban America. The talk was as good as ever, even if there remained some sense of Sayles as the impresario for a very good TV series (like *Shannon's Deal*) rather than the shaper of great drama.

Lone Star found many fans, and I admired the reaching out for historical and racial context. But I was stupefied by the succession of conversations between pairs of people, filmed in the same dull way. Made in Spanish, *Men with Guns* was more valiant than coherent. But *Limbo* was a film with the richness of a novel, and a genuine feeling for untidy people. Still, I can't help feeling that the novel is Sayles's true calling.

Franklin J. Schaffner (1920–89), b. Tokyo

1963: *The Stripper/Woman of Summer.* 1964: *The Best Man.* 1965: *The War Lord.* 1967: *The Double Man; Planet of the Apes.* 1969: *Patton/Patton: Lust for Glory.* 1971: *Nicholas and Alexandra.* 1973: *Papillon.* 1976: *Islands in the Stream.* 1978: *The Boys from Brazil.* 1980: *Sphinx.* 1982: *Yes, Giorgio.* 1987: *Lionheart.* 1989: *Welcome Home.*

Once upon a time, Gore Vidal was discombobulated to see a theatre marquee with the proud come-on: "Franklin Schaffner's *The Best Man.*" This was the auteur theory up in lights, and it was nonsense (years later, *Gore Vidal's Billy the Kid*, on TV, may have been a little more authorship than anyone wanted). The movie of *The Best Man* is as acerbic and as limited as Vidal's play. It is full of good, insider talk; it has an eager love of power—despite Vidal's steady, bitchy disavowal of that force; and it is an overly neat, schematic narrative. Schaffner served Vidal, and it would have been interesting for Vidal to have been given the job of directing. He might have learned how to write a better play.

But Schaffner was blessed by a moment. Having spent much of his childhood in Japan (as the son of missionaries), he served in the navy and then joined *March of Time*. From there he went to CBS and moved from news to directing drama: *Twelve Angry Men* (54) and *The Caine Mutiny Court Martial* (55), for instance, both of which won him directing Emmys—he got another, a few years later, for handling Jacqueline Kennedy's tour of the White House.

His movie debut was highly praised, but it is an adolescent melodrama in which Joanne Woodward and Richard Beymer seem staid. It does not convey the claustrophobic small-town tumescence in William Inge's original play, *A Loss of Roses*. Schaffner's style was cold, neutral, and classy, and so he demonstrated only aimless versatility in his best years, ranging from the Dark Ages epic of *The War Lord* to the TV-like *Planet of the Apes*.

But *Planet of the Apes* was a very influential hit on which Schaffner's numbness got out of the way of the Pierre Boule novel and Rod Serling's script. *Patton* was another hit, but a strange product. Francis Ford Coppola did a lot of the script. George C. Scott commandeered the project (he said he believed it needed Henry Hathaway's boldness). But maybe George Patton made the picture, along with the very arresting opening and the way, in 1969, that the topic cut against the liberal age.

Thereafter, Schaffner was booked in for big pictures—long, slow, and allegedly "major." *Nicholas and Alexandra* is only long and slow. *Papillon* is very slow, but it has a fine performance from Steve McQueen. *Islands in the Stream* was Schaffner's most intriguing film, for it came close to an intimate rendering of Hemingway's disorganized confessional. With Scott again, it is moody and wistful. *Boys from Brazil* was too stark for Schaffner: it came out as mere political melodrama—the horror and absurdity took second place to Gregory Peck's tortured act as Mengele.

His final pictures ranged from Egyptology to the movie debut of Pavarotti to a story of children searching for Richard I to a story about a returned veteran who finds his wife has remarried. And so the onetime maker of big pictures was reduced to inconsequence.

Dore Schary (1905–80),

b. Newark, New Jersey

"How to be head of the studio and not very important"—that might be the Schary story. It amounts to the hypothesis that, the higher an executive position in movies, the less creative influence it exercised, and the more its holder was exposed as a would-be seer trying to handle prickly talents and preempt public fickleness.

Schary figures prominently in *Picture*, Lillian Ross's account of the making of *The Red Badge of Courage*. The idea for the film had been proposed to MGM by John Huston and Gottfried Reinhardt, a producer. Huston takes up the story, as recorded by Lillian Ross: "'Dore loved the idea,' Huston said. 'And Dore said he would read the novel.' A couple of weeks later, Schary had asked Huston to write a screen treatment—a rough outline for the detailed script. 'I did my treatment in four days,' Huston said . . . Schary approved the treatment, and the cost of making the picture was estimated at a million and a half dollars.' Huston wrote the screenplay in five weeks, and Schary approved it. 'Then the strangest things began to happen,' Huston said. 'Dore is called vice-president in charge of production. L. B. [Mayer] is called vice-president in charge of the studio. Nobody knows which is boss.'"

It was a classic contrast between two men equally insecure—in 1950—about their ability to make consistently successful, prestigious pictures, such as MGM prided itself on. Although forty-five years old at the time of *Red Badge*, Schary was thought of as "young," if only because of the looming seniority of Mayer, sixty-five years old and one of the founding fathers of the industry. Mayer had flourished in the days when movies had no rival, and when returns proved the merit of aiming at the lowest common denominator of the audience. If MGM had risen above Andy Hardy it was because of men like Irving Thalberg and Arthur Freed. But Mayer had survived, in power, and apparently vindicated by longevity.

Some in the studio may have recognized the searching test put on movies by TV, and Schary's appointment in 1948 was on the basis of his brief success at RKO with enterprising, low-budget movies made from more intelligent scripts than Hollywood was used to. In the mid-1940s, Selznick hired Schary despite MGM warnings that he "was more interested in trying to sell his causes than in making pictures." But Schary's whole record signaled a lightweight, whereas Mayer was plainly a godfather reluctant to hand over office. What most characterizes the fumbling ineptness of Hollywood moguls is not the way that they allegedly ruined a potentially great film: in the outline and tattered remains, *Red Badge* looks like Huston in his lofty, "art" mood. The real giveaway is that no one at MGM had the confidence of their misgivings. Mayer was flatly hostile, but Schary hedged around with a pusillanimous cheerfulness caught naked in Ross's recollection: "There was resistance, great resistance, to making *The Red Badge of Courage*. In terms of cost and in other terms. This picture has no single incident. This is a period picture. The story—well there's no story in this picture. It's just the story of a boy. It's the story of a coward. Well, it's the story of a hero."

The picture went ahead, with cheerfulness turning colder every day. The intrinsic bias of the studio executive was to curse a project with gloom, to fulfill that bias by withholding promotion, and then to incorporate the failure into some glib paternal philosophy. The most odious moment at the end of *Picture* comes when Nicholas Schenck, chairman of the board, says that he knew the picture would flop but that Schary had to be taught a lesson. But the most likely reasons for proceeding with a forlorn venture were scuttling insecurity and the secret design to oust Mayer. For in 1951, Mayer resigned from MGM (with compensation of $2,600,000) and Schary became the nervous occupant of Mayer's seat. Perhaps he trembled at such an exposed eminence. He lasted only five years, and in 1956 was abandoned to roam listlessly about the theatre and independent production.

In retrospect, the wonder is that he ever got so

far. An actor in stock and small Broadway parts, he began writing plays, and in 1932 was briefly hired by Walter Wanger at Columbia. He was an itinerant screenwriter through the 1930s who had his successes at MGM in pictures close to Mayer's rabble-rousing ideals: *Big City* (37, Frank Borzage); *Boy's Town* (38, Norman Taurog); *Young Tom Edison* (40, Taurog); and *Edison, the Man* (40, Clarence Brown). In 1942, MGM promoted him and he produced *Joe Smith, American* (42, Richard Thorpe); *Journey for Margaret* (42, W. S. Van Dyke); and *Lassie Come Home* (43, Fred M. Wilcox).

He then went to Selznick and worked for his Vanguard company on *I'll Be Seeing You* (44, William Dieterle). Next he packaged a few things that Selznick traded away to RKO: *The Spiral Staircase* (45, Robert Siodmak); *The Farmer's Daughter* (47, H. C. Potter); and *The Bachelor and the Bobby Soxer* (47, Irving Reis). That led to his appointment in charge of production at RKO: *Till the End of Time* (46, Edward Dmytryk); *Crossfire* (47, Dmytryk); *Mr. Blandings Builds His Dream House* (48, Potter), this for Selznick through RKO; executive producer on *The Boy with Green Hair* (48, Joseph Losey) and *They Live By Night* (48, Nicholas Ray); and *Walk Softly, Stranger* (50, Robert Stevenson).

He went to MGM in charge of production in 1948, but was never responsible for anything as exciting as the Losey and Ray debuts. His time was largely spent in company politics and in supervising all the films on the floor. But he did have a more personal hand in the production of: *Battleground* (49, William Wellman); *The Next Voice You Hear* (50, Wellman); *Westward the Women* (51, Wellman); *Plymouth Adventure* (52, Brown); *Take the High Ground* (53, Richard Brooks); *Bad Day at Black Rock* (54, John Sturges); *Trial* (55, Mark Robson); *The Last Hunt* (56, Brooks); *The Swan* (56, Charles Vidor); and *Designing Woman* (57, Vincente Minnelli). In the main, these are orthodox, old-fashioned films, with *Black Rock* the most pungent and the greatest success.

After that, he produced two pretentious and dull films: *Lonelyhearts* (58, Vincent J. Donehue), which he scripted from the Nathanael West novella; *Sunrise at Campobello* (60, Donehue), from his very successful play about Franklin Roosevelt. He also directed a film version of Moss Hart's autobiography *Act One* (63), but it was barely released.

Roy Scheider, b. Orange, New Jersey, 1932

With a narrow face, broken nose, and furtive eyes, it was always most likely that Roy Scheider would be a supporting actor. So it has worked out—and there must be disappointment after several leading roles in large and successful ventures, most notably the police chief in *Jaws* (75, Steven Spielberg), and an Oscar nomination playing the Bob Fosse figure in *All That Jazz* (79, Fosse). Since then, a real decline has set in, leading to a rather half-hearted monster of medical insurance in *The Rainmaker* (97, Francis Coppola).

He was educated at Rutgers and Franklin & Marshall, and he had several years on stage before he got into movies. His debut was as Roy R. Sheider in *The Curse of the Living Corpse* (64, Del Tenney); but then he did *Stiletto* (69, Bernard Kowalski); *Loving* (70, Irvin Kershner); *Puzzle of a Downfall Child* (70, Jerry Schatzberg); memorable and sly as a pimp in *Klute* (71, Alan J. Pakula); winning a supporting actor nomination as the sidekick cop to Gene Hackman in *The French Connection* (71, William Friedkin); *The Outside Man* (73, Jacques Deray); *The French Conspiracy* (73, Yves Boisset); *The Seven-Ups* (73, Philip D'Antoni); *Sheila Levine Is Dead and Living in New York* (75, Sidney J. Furie); *Marathon Man* (76, John Schlesinger); *Sorcerer* (77, Friedkin); *Jaws 2* (78, Jeannot Szwarc); *The Last Embrace* (79, Jonathan Demme); *Still of the Night* (82, Robert Benton); *Blue Thunder* (83, John Badham); *2010* (84, Peter Hyams); *The Men's Club* (86, Peter Medak); *52 Pick-Up* (86, John Frankenheimer); *Cohen and Tate* (89, Eric Red); *Listen to Me* (89, Douglas Day Stewart); *Night Game* (89, Peter Masterson); *The Fourth War* (90, Frankenheimer); *The Russia House* (90, Fred Schepisi); *Naked Lunch* (91, David Cronenberg); *Romeo Is Bleeding* (94, Medak); *The Myth of Fingerprints* (97, Bart Freundlich); as RKO boss George Schaefer in *RKO 281* (99, Benjamin Ross).

Maria Schell, b. Vienna, 1926

She is the older sister of Maximilian Schell. It is a curiosity that Maria Schell's narrow talent should twice have been employed to perfect effect, and twice so ludicrously as to undermine films entirely. As the long-suffering wife in *Une Vie* (58, Alexandre Astruc) and the girl in *White Nights* (57, Luchino Visconti) her shortcomings were turned to advantage. That fretful cheerfulness and the distraught smile that might curdle milk were very touching in Astruc's portrait of a naïve girl gradually made aware that her husband is cheating her. *Une Vie* contains marvelous images of her rising panic and apprehensive romanticism, and it says a lot that she is made a figure of tragic dignity. In *White Nights*, however, Visconti channeled all her wide-eyed feyness into Dostoyevsky's dream story of a girl whose faith in a mysterious lover is finally vindicated. On the debit side, her giggly Grushenka in *The Brothers Karamazov* (57, Richard Brooks) is one of MGM's more risible casting coups. That film was always a forlorn project, but her presence in *Cimarron* (60, Anthony

Mann) is a serious obstacle to what could have been a fascinating story of pioneers being domesticated.

As these four films would suggest, she was a cosmopolitan actress, moving from one country to another for some fifteen years. In addition to that ill-balanced quartet: *Steibruch* (42, Sigfrit Steiner); *Maturareise* (43, Steiner); *Der Engel Mit der Posaune* (48, Karl Harth); *Maresi* (48, Hans Thimig); *Die Letzte Nacht* (49, Eugen York); *Es Kommt ein Tag* (50, Rudolf Jugert); *The Magic Box* (51, John Boulting); *So Little Time* (52, Compton Bennett); wretched in adultery with Trevor Howard in *The Heart of the Matter* (52, George More O'Ferrall); *Der Träumende Mund* (53, Josef von Baky); *Tagebuch einer Verliebten* (53, von Baky); *Die Letzte Brücke* (54, Helmut Kautner); *Gervaise* (55, René Clément), the picture that introduced her to America; *Die Ratten* (55, Robert Siodmak); *Rose Bernd* (57, Wolfgang Staudte); *Die Schinderhannes* (58, Kautner); *The Hanging Tree* (59, Delmer Daves); *Das Riesenrad* (61, Geza von Radvanyi); *The Mark* (61, Guy Green); *Ich bin auch nur eine Frau* (62, Alfred Weidenmann); and *Zwei Whisky und ein Sofa* (63, Gunter Grawert).

Her apparent retirement has been interrupted by *Le Diable par le Queue* (68, Philippe de Broca); *99 Women* (69, Jess Franco), in which she and a butch Mercedes McCambridge vie for control of a women's prison; *The Odessa File* (74, Ronald Neame); as the mother of Katharine Ross in *Voyage of the Damned* (76, Stuart Rosenberg); and in *Superman* (78, Richard Donner). She was also in *Just a Gigolo* (78, David Hemmings); *Christmas Lilies of the Field* (79, Ralph Nelson); as a onetime patient of Freud in *Nineteen Nineteen* (84, Hugh Brody); *Samson and Delilah* (84, Lee Philips); *Die Glückliche Familie* (87, Nikolai Mullerschon); *Le Dernier Mot* (91, Gilles Behat); *Maria des Eaux-Vives* (92, Robert Mazoyer); *Der Clan der Anna Voss* (95, Herbert Ballmann); *Tatort—Heilig Blut* (96, Hartmut Griesmayr); and in her brother's documentary, *Meine Schwester Maria* (02).

Maximilian Schell, b. Vienna, 1930
1970: *Erste Liebe/First Love*. 1974: *Der Füssganger/The Pedestrian*. 1975: *Der Richter und Sein Henker*. 1978: *Geschichten aus dem Wienerwald/Tales from the Vienna Woods*. 1984: *Marlene* (d). 1993: *Candles in the Dark* (TV). 2002: *Meine Schwester Maria* (d).

Viennese cinema is a neglected field: at its best, it embodies literature, psychology, theatre, and music, while pouring them all into the new elixir. Without Vienna, we would not have Preminger, Fritz Lang, Wilder, Axel Corti, or even Max Ophüls. Maximilian Schell may not have a place at quite that level; nevertheless, his wandering career testifies to the cultural wealth of Vienna.

The younger brother of Maria Schell, he is the son of actress Margaretha Noe and writer Ferdinand Hermann Schell. He was educated at the universities of Zurich and Munich, and went on to careers as actor, stage director, screenwriter, movie director . . . and man of the world. *First Love* (from a Turgenev story) starred Dominique Sanda and John Moulder Brown; *The Pedestrian* was a story about war crimes and historical guilt; *Tales from the Vienna Woods* was an Odon von Horvath play, previously directed by Schell for London's National Theatre. *Marlene* was a droll, feature-length tribute to Dietrich in which the old lady is heard but not seen.

Schell has often acted in his own films, as well as in: *Die Letzte Brucke* (54, Helmut Kautner); *Kinder, Mutter und ein General* (55, Lazlo Benedek); to Hollywood for *The Young Lions* (58, Edward Dmytryk); winning the best actor Oscar as the defense lawyer in *Judgment at Nuremberg* (61, Stanley Kramer); *Five Finger Exercise* (62, Daniel Mann); St. Joseph of Cupertino in *The Reluctant Saint* (62, Dmytryk); *The Condemned of Altona* (63, Vittorio De Sica); *Topkapi* (64, Jules Dassin); *Return from the Ashes* (65, J. Lee Thompson); a Nazi general in *Counterpoint* (67, Ralph Nelson); the arch betrayer in *The Deadly Affair* (67, Sidney Lumet).

He produced, as well as acted in, a version of Kafka's *The Castle* (68, Rudolf Noelte). His own movies were now balanced off by increasingly meretricious acting jobs: *Krakatoa, East of Java* (69, Bernard Kowalski); *Simon Bolivar* (69, Alessandro Blasetti); and *Pope Joan* (72, Michael Anderson). He was nominated for best actor Oscar in *The Man in the Glass Booth* (74, Arthur Hiller), then came *The Odessa File* (74, Ronald Neame); *St. Ives* (76, Thompson); *A Bridge Too Far* (77, Richard Attenborough); *Cross of Iron* (77, Sam Peckinpah); nominated for the supporting actor Oscar as a resistance liaison in *Julia* (77, Fred Zinnemann); *Avalanche Express* (79, Mark Robson); *The Black Hole* (79, Gary Nelson); *Players* (79, Anthony Harvey); *The Diary of Anne Frank* (80, Boris Sagal); *The Chosen* (81, Jeremy Paul Kagan); *The Phantom of the Opera* (83, Robert Markowitz); *The Assisi Underground* (84, Alexander Rameti); *The Rose Garden* (89, Fons Rademakers), as a man who attacks ex-Nazis; *The Freshman* (90, Andrew Bergman); Lenin in *Stalin* (92, Ivan Passer); *Miss Rose White* (92, Joseph Sargent); and *A Far Off Place* (93, Mikael Salomon).

Past sixty, Schell makes a grand villain and a learned authority figure, hovering between cardinals and devils: *Justiz* (93, Hans W. Geissendorfer); Pharaoh in *Abraham* (94, Sargent); *Little Odessa* (94, James Gray); *The Thorn Birds: The Missing Years* (96, Kevin James Dobson); *Telling Lies in America* (97, Guy Ferland); *The Eigh-*

teenth Angel (97, William Bindley); *Left Luggage* (98, Jeroen Krabbe); *Vampires* (98, John Carpenter); *Deep Impact* (98, Mimi Leder); *Wer Liebt, dem Wachsen Flügel* (99, Gabriel Barylli); *Joan of Arc* (99, Christian Duguay); *I Love You, Baby* (00, Nick Lyon); *Fisimatenten* (00, Jochen Kuhn); *The Song of the Lark* (00, Karen Arthur); *Festival in Cannes* (02, Henry Jaglom); *Bestseller* (02, Jörg Grünler).

Joseph M. Schenck (1876–1961),
b. Rybinsk, Russia; and
Nicholas Schenck (1880–1969),
b. Rybinsk, Russia

You pronounced the name "Skenk," as in "skunk," and maybe that's all one needs to say. Except that very few brothers were so unalike: I don't think it's entirely safe to exclude the possibility that they just said they were brothers, in the hope that that outrageous assertion would make them more noticeable, or sympathetic. But it's easier to be funny about them now than it was in the days when the Schenck boys had real power. Today, the general public has forgotten them, but between them they once ran pictures. I'm inventing the possibility that they weren't brothers, but it grows more plausible the longer you look at them. And it's enough to give their story charm and menace.

Joe was a big slob, nearly bald, rather Slavic looking; an actress he once chased round the office (when he should have been past those things) said he had a nose like a large boiled potato. He was effusive, sentimental, affectionate, and grabby. Anita Loos thought he was the ugliest man she'd ever seen on first meeting. Then, "five minutes later I thought he was one of the most attractive."

There was no five-minute makeover with Nick. He was cold, watchful, controlled, with silver hair and glaring spectacles; a natural frightener, and the one man who had an emotional edge on Louis B. Mayer. Irene Mayer said that Nick always asked polite questions about you, but never listened to the answer.

As collaborators, if not brothers, Nick and Joe went into the pharmacy business soon after they came to America. From that, they jumped over into amusement arcades, with majority interests first in Paradise Park and then Palisades Park. It was at the latter that they featured the entertainment where customers sat in rail cars and watched the passing footage of back-projected scenery. That enterprise brought them into contact with Marcus Loew, so that by 1910 they were inside the Loew organization—with Joe actually running the theatres while Nick was the company secretary.

Joe branched off in 1917, the year in which he married Norma Talmadge. As such, he became the producer of her pictures, then of those of her sisters, Natalie and Constance, and then of those

of Natalie's husband, Buster Keaton. He made a fortune (largely on Connie), and in 1924, he accepted the position as president of United Artists.

Meanwhile, Nick waited and positioned himself at Loew's, and when Marcus died, in 1927, Nicholas Schenck became president of Loew's Inc., a position he held until 1955. As such, going under the nickname of "the General," he was the most powerful person in the MGM outfit on the East Coast, and so powerful on the West that he stimulated and fueled the antagonism between Mayer and Thalberg. He was also, of course, the president of the most successful operation the business has ever known. And he was the man who, one day in 1951, told L.B. it was all over (or had Dore Schary tell him).

Long before then, Joe Schenck had helped found 20th Century (with Darryl Zanuck) and then merged it with Fox two years later. From 1935 until 1941, he was president of Fox. But then he had to take a break, in prison, for tax offenses and perjury. His U.S. citizenship was even withdrawn, but he cleared his slate by informing on those gangsters and union bosses (notably George E. Browne and Willie Bioff) who had been taking protection money from the studios. President Truman himself helped clear Joe's name. He got his citizenship back, and in 1952 he won a special Oscar "for long and distinguished service." He was also restored to Fox, and is said to have played his part in comforting Marilyn Monroe. In hindsight, of course, it's fascinating to think that there was this guy, born in Russia!, sent to prison, and with a record in the amusement parks that didn't bear looking into—and the club he had helped form came to his aid, restored and rewarded him. If he'd been a screenwriter, he might have been thrown out of the country. And Nick would have been buying beer for the throwers.

Fred Schepisi, b. Melbourne, Australia, 1939
1971: *The Priest.* 1973: *Libido* (codirector). 1975: *The Devil's Playground.* 1978: *The Chant of Jimmie Blacksmith.* 1982: *Barbarosa.* 1984: *Iceman.* 1985: *Plenty.* 1987: *Roxanne.* 1988: *A Cry in the Dark.* 1990: *The Russia House.* 1992: *Mr. Baseball.* 1993: *Six Degrees of Separation.* 1994: *I.Q.* 1997: *Fierce Creatures.* 2001: *Last Orders.* 2003: *It Runs in the Family.*

Though he was the sole screenwriter on the startling *Chant of Jimmie Blacksmith*, Schepisi is a director of uncommon yearning and thematic complexity who seems hard pressed to find or settle on his own vein of material. *Jimmie Blacksmith* came from a Thomas Keneally novel; *Plenty* is from David Hare's play; *Roxanne* is one of the staler renderings of the Rostand play, a star vehicle uneasily set in Colorado; *A Cry in the Dark* was from life; *The Russia House* is from John Le Carré by way of Tom Stoppard's script; while *Six Degrees of Separation* was scripted by John Guare from his own play.

Throw in the attempt at a Western (*Barbarosa*) and science fiction (*Iceman*), as well as the trip to Japan for *Mr. Baseball*, and one can view Schepisi's journey as adventurous or wayward, in search of something, working with American money but never yet coming to ground in Hollywood. The coziness of *Roxanne* seems the more out of place once one grasps Schepisi's interest in misplaced people driven to violence or irrationality by confusion. *Jimmie Blacksmith* was not just a film about race and sex, but a study of Australia's muddle. *A Cry in the Dark* had the same impact and the same inner concern: it was about disintegration, and the woeful attempt to impose plastic order on unheeded or denied savagery.

Most intriguing of all, *Plenty* is a kind of aghast celebration of a woman who will not settle for popular answers about what she wants or what it is to be English. With Hare's text, and Meryl Streep's very brave performance, Schepisi showed us a woman helplessly drawn to terrible, dangerous gestures. Perhaps one needs to have been—or to have wanted to be—English to feel the movie's pain. *Plenty* seemed to me at first a failure, too tied to self-pity and too blurred in writing and casting. But I cannot get the film out of my head, and I'm still not sure how much of that comes from Hare, Streep, or Schepisi. My only answer so far is that there are three profound, unstable talents, drawn toward difficulty and discomfort.

Sean Connery's Barley in *The Russia House* could have been—should have been?—as much of a disaster as Susan Traherne in *Plenty*. That the film winds slowly toward a happy ending seems finally a little unworthy of Schepisi. But along the way we see so many unexpected things—there is something effortlessly wandering in Schepisi. He is like an absentminded surgeon. *The Russia House* is a fine Cold War thriller, and one of the gravest recent love stories.

Wandering became a very intricate dance in the exhilarating *Six Degrees of Separation*, a small story that explodes in range and implication, and that showed Schepisi's unexpected capacity for comedy.

By now, though, one has to see that Schepisi has never really made a successful American film. *I.Q.* was a strange piece of whimsy coming from him, while on *Fierce Creatures* he was brought in late as a rescue act—and how rarely that works. But then he took Graham Swift's novel, *Last Orders*, and made a superb, very touching picture of it with an assurance that suggested (yet again) that Schepisi has to feel comfortable with the social setting he is examining. Which British director has made three films that get Englishness better than *Plenty, The Russia House*, and *Last Orders*?

John Schlesinger, b. London, 1926

1962: *A Kind of Loving.* 1963: *Billy Liar.* 1965: *Darling.* 1967: *Far from the Madding Crowd.* 1969: *Midnight Cowboy.* 1971: *Sunday, Bloody Sunday.* 1973: "The Longest," episode from *Visions of Eight* (d). 1975: *The Day of the Locust.* 1976: *Marathon Man.* 1979: *Yanks.* 1981: *Honky Tonk Freeway.* 1983: *An Englishman Abroad* (TV). 1984: *The Falcon and the Snowman; Separate Tables* (TV). 1987: *The Believers.* 1988: *Madame Sousatzka.* 1990: *Pacific Heights.* 1991: *A Question of Attribution* (TV). 1994: *The Innocent.* 1995: *Cold Comfort Farm* (TV). 1996: *Eye for an Eye.* 1998: *The Tale of Sweeney Todd.* 2000: *The Next Best Thing.*

Schlesinger has been acclaimed as one of the world's leading directors, on the strength of two equivocal studies of sexual undertone. Yet I feel bound to stand against the tide and list my reservations.

He uses anecdotes that are shy of thematic coherence or human roots. This may be because he is reluctant to contradict the self-pity of his characters. Thus there is a wasteful pain in his work whereby feelings are worked up only to be wiped away by the resolution of the story. The pessimism is not searching but decorative, and he does not observe people so much as gossip about them.

Because he believes in "story" above all, his pictures seem opportunist, and employ superficial, gimmicky stylistic imitations. This is not uncommon in the cinema, and would be tolerable if his films were not so plain-looking. In other words, he has a dull eye, he is often unsure as to where to put the camera, and he edits uneasily. *Billy Liar, Darling,* and *Sunday, Bloody Sunday* contain more lapses in mise-en-scène than most other directors could offer: cuts that do not match, setups that miss the action that needs to be shown, shots that take the easy way out.

He indulges actors. This has two consequences: talented players like Dirk Bogarde, Peter Finch, and Dustin Hoffman are allowed to pose or impersonate, while someone as uneasy as Julie Christie is displayed. *Darling* deserves a place in every archive to show how rapidly modishness withers. Beauty is central to the cinema and Schlesinger seems an unreliable judge of it, overrating Christie and rarely getting close enough to the action to make a fruitful stylistic bond with it.

Midnight Cowboy, it must be said, is free from most of his defects; it does seem taken with the taut vitality of New York; it prospers to the extent that it has no women in main parts. But that only makes it a sly transposition of a women's picture, with Hoffman a grotesque Joan Crawford sacrificing himself for a blond stud.

His return to America produced two dreadful

clangers in a row, evidence of unease with period, genre, and actors. *Marathon Man* was never going to be more than routine suspense, but it at least needed a director capable of delivering that. *Day of the Locust,* though, is an original dear to most movie lovers, and there is no forgiving Schlesinger's shrill, hysterical ruining of its stark vision.

I have found no greater pleasure in Schlesinger's subsequent theatrical work—apart from a druggy edginess in the acting in *The Falcon and the Snow-man.* But the director is something like the Lubitsch of English espionage in two delicious films made for television and taken from Alan Bennett scripts. In the first, *An Englishman Abroad,* the actress Coral Browne, doing Shakespeare in Moscow, meets the exiled Guy Burgess (Alan Bates); and in the second, *A Question of Attribution,* Sir Anthony Blunt (James Fox) meets the Queen (Prunella Scales). The two pieces *are* very alike in structure, in veiled cross talk and in their worried fidgeting over matters of loyalty and taste. They may be just set pieces of writing and clever playing (to say nothing of the poised comedy of embarrassment). But I think they are better than that—crucial English comedies—and I am happy to acclaim Schlesinger for his expert realization.

Cold Comfort Farm was very funny—though I can't believe many outside Britain (or a certain age range) got the joke. But it showed Schlesinger's sense of class and it was one of the first pictures to see the prospects in Kate Beckinsale. The rest is grim: *Eye for an Eye* was a hideous melodrama; *The Next Best Thing* was a contender for the worst film ever made. And what can one say about a version of *Sweeney Todd* made in this age if it isn't Stephen Sondheim's version?

Volker Schlöndorff,

b. Wiesbaden, Germany, 1939
1960: *Wenn Kummert's* (s). 1966: *Der Junge Törless/Young Torless.* 1967: *Mord und Totschlag.* 1969: *Michael Kohlhass Der Rebell.* 1970: *Baal.* 1971: *Der Plötzliche Reichtum der Armen Leute von Kombach/The Sudden Fortune of the Poor People of Kombach.* 1972: *Die Ehegattin; The Moral of Ruth Halbfass; Summer Lightning.* 1974: *Übernachtung in Tirol.* 1975: *Die Verlorene Ehre der Katharina Blum/The Lost Honor of Katharina Blum* (codirected with Margarethe von Trotta). 1976: *Der Fangschuss/Coup de Grâce.* 1978: *Deutschland im Herbst* (codirected). 1979: *The Tin Drum; Kaleidoskop: Valeska Gert, Nur zum Spass-nur zum Spiel* (d). 1980: *Der Kandidat* (d). 1981: *Die Falschung/Circle of Deceit; Krieg und Frieden* (d). 1984: *Un Amour de Swann/Swann in Love.* 1985: *Death of a Salesman* (TV). 1986: *Vermischte Nachrichten.* 1987: *A Gathering of Old Men* (TV). 1990: *The Handmaid's Tale.* 1991: *Voyager.* 1992: *Interview with Billy Wilder* (TV).

1996: *Der Unhold.* 1998: *Palmetto.* 1999: *Die Stille Nach dem Schuss/Legend of Rita.*

Schlöndorff's training was largely in France, an indication of the aridity of German cinema in the late 1950s. He studied at IDHEC and worked for Louis Malle and Alain Resnais as an assistant. But he had an especially close relationship with Jean-Pierre Melville, and may have inherited some of that director's flexible movement from entertainments to more personal works. He was an assistant director on Melville's *Léon Morin, Prêtre* (61) and *Le Doulos* (62), and was also involved on the preparation of *L'Aîné des Ferchaux* (63).

His own work began with TV reportage in Algeria and Vietnam—French colonial situations— and his first short film was about French people living in Frankfurt. But with the resurgence in experimental, committed filmmaking in Germany, Schlöndorff found himself in his own country, more particularly as one of the Munich-based directors. *Young Torless* was a thorough, psychologically detailed version of Robert Musil's novel. At the time, it seemed a conventional if accomplished period piece. But in the light of Schlöndorff's later work, it seems the beginning of an historical analysis of German irrationality. It is not just a study of the defects of pre-Nazi militarism, but a sign of the way individual conscience is smothered and suppressed.

Schlöndorff made several films for TV and had to play off traditional features—*Michael Kohlhass* and *The Moral of Ruth Halbfass*—with more searching works. *The Sudden Fortune of the Poor People of Kombach* is his most original film, telling how, in 1821, a group of peasants rob the local tax cart and are pursued, interrogated, and tried by the harsh authorities. Its style is deliberately plain and analytic, stressing the inevitable failure of the robbery, and the extent to which the peasants' revolutionary action is neutralized by their own conformity to rules and by their inability to comprehend their condition. As a film about the daydreaming conservatism of the poor it is exact, poignant, and subtly pointed at later worlds.

Summer Lightning is his most intimate film, about a divorced woman in contemporary Germany attempting to live and work on her own in a society centered on men. The leading part is played by Schlöndorff's wife, Margarethe von Trotta, who also collaborated on the script.

Schlöndorff has turned himself into an international director. *The Tin Drum* was an international art-house event, and it is a hardworking picture, as distressing as anyone could expect. Yet his bigger projects are often less satisfying than the smaller ones: *Swann in Love* is a feeble, prettified pass at the huge novel; *The Handmaid's Tale* is grimly didactic; and his TV version of *Death of a Salesman* is given over to the chronic neediness of

Dustin Hoffman. But *Circle of Deceit* is a fine story of loyalty and betrayal actually filmed in war-torn Beirut, and *Voyager* is a chilling study of inadvertent incest, adapted from Max Frisch, and all the more remarkable in that it coaxes genuine acting from the hitherto intractable Sam Shepard.

In addition, Schlöndorff has done a fascinating three-part conversation with Billy Wilder, which Wilder, for no good reason, refuses to have shown.

Nothing lately has been anywhere near the class of *Voyager*. By contrast, *Palmetto* seemed like a very silly film noir. But *Die Stille Nach* concerns a former West German terrorist living quietly in East Germany, and then exposed after reunification, and that sounds much more promising.

Bert Schneider, b. New York, 1934

No one interested in this elusive, wealthy, radical producer can afford to miss Bo Burlingham's fine essay "Politics Under the Palms." And no one concerned with American cinema should underestimate the part Bert Schneider played from about 1968 to 1975. Those were years of dismay for America, and Schneider's films deal more honestly with human failure than Hollywood can normally stomach.

Where and whether he is now are in some question. Did his will and his energy lapse, or was his creative policy defined by Vietnam, the contested crusade of drugs, and an America reluctant to face dangerous futures? Schneider may have had too many interests and too much money to be a dedicated, career producer. Perhaps he's hanging out somewhere, regathering and trying to overcome yesterday's urgency and its sad aftermath.

His father, Abraham, was a top executive at Columbia. According to Burlingham, "Bert remembers himself as a rebellious youth, the black sheep, hanging out with the caddies on the golf course and the help in the kitchen." He was thrown out of Columbia University, and the army refused him because of his radical connections. So he worked for Columbia's Screen Gems until 1965 when he formed a company with his friend, Bob Rafelson. With the addition of Steve Blauner, they became BBS Productions.

Schneider and Rafelson invented the Monkees, perhaps his most effectively Dada political action, and made *Head* (68, Rafelson). That got Schneider into movies as a producer, and BBS hit a hot streak with *Easy Rider* (69, Dennis Hopper)—protest and counterculture costing $350,000 and making $35 million; *Five Easy Pieces* (70, Rafelson); *The Last Picture Show* (71, Peter Bogdanovich); *A Safe Place* (71, Henry Jaglom); *Drive, He Said* (71, Jack Nicholson); *The King of Marvin Gardens* (72, Rafelson); and *Goin' South* (78, Nicholson).

It is an impressive list, and the generous launching of several careers. *Marvin Gardens* is a masterpiece, and none of the others less than unique, personal, and a foray into fresh ground for movies. Schneider was apparently a very tolerant producer: he let the boys do what they liked, and for a few years it worked until box-office failure led to inhibition. He may have protected some of his talent from real commercial pressures: Rafelson is an intermittent director, and Bogdanovich has not fared well in recent years. Schneider may have presided over the making of his films while concentrating on deeper interests—Cuba, Black militancy, drugs, Candice Bergen, and an eventual Oscar for the Vietnam documentary *Hearts and Minds* (75, Paul Williams). Give him credit for being a focus for some remarkable people and for letting his own mixed background out on film. In many of the BBS films there is a conflict of artistic yearning, business flair, and the painful texture of ordinary life that reflects parts of Schneider's own history and predicament: a creative man used to commerce, an idealist fighting compromise. *Marvin Gardens*, especially, is a picture that wonders if business is not the great American art.

Schneider's next production—*Days of Heaven* (78, Terrence Malick)—was another example of that conflict, and a victim of the fallacy that astonishing beauty necessarily yields inner truth.

Romy Schneider (Rosemarie Albach-Retty) (1938–82), b. Vienna

The daughter of actress Magda Schneider and actor Wolf Albach-Retty, Romy Schneider broke into films as a German teenager in a run of plump, plain, sentimental movies: *Wenn der Weisse Flieder Wieder Bluht* (53, Hans Deppe); *Feuerwerk* (54, Kurt Hoffmann); *Madchenjahre einer Konigin* (54, Ernst Marischka); *Die Deutschmeister* (55, Marischka); *Der Letzte Mann* (55, Harald Braun); *Sissi* (55, Marischka); *Kitty und die Grosse Welt* (56, Alfred Weidenmann); *Sissi, die Junge Kaiserin* (56, Marischka); *Robinson Soll Nicht Sterben* (57, Josef von Baky); *Monpti* (57, Helmut Kautner); *Sissi, Schicksalsjahre einer Kaiserin* (57, Marischka); *Scampolo* (58, Weidenmann); *Madchen in Uniform* (58, Geza von Radvanyi); *Die Halbzart* (59, Rolf Thiele); *Ein Engel auf Erden* (59, von Radvanyi); and *Die Schone Lugnerin* (59, Fritz Kortner).

It was a hard grind and depressing work to judge by her retirement in 1960. But she came back and, after *Die Sendung der Lysistrata* (61, Kortner), she escaped to play the wife in the "Il Lavoro" episode from *Boccaccio '70* (62, Luchino Visconti). Immediately, she looked prettier, sharper, and wittier. In 1963, Orson Welles touched her with the morbid inquisitiveness of Kafka's work when she played Leni, the advocate's depraved ward, in *The Trial*. Her scenes with Anthony Perkins in that film had a nightmarish seductiveness that culminated in her childish pride at showing her webbed hand.

After that, she was an international actress, invariably interesting if never quite as funny as when guesting on TV's *Laugh-In*: excellent in *The Cardinal* (63, Otto Preminger); *The Victors* (63, Carl Foreman); *Good Neighbor Sam* (64, David Swift); *What's New, Pussycat?* (65, Clive Donner); *Schornstein No. 4* (66, Jean Chapot); *10:30 p.m. Summer* (66, Jules Dassin); *Triple Cross* (66, Terence Young); *La Piscine* (68, Jacques Deray); *My Lover, My Son* (69, John Newland); *Qui?* (70, Léonard Keigel); *Les Choses de la Vie* (70, Claude Sautet); *Bloomfield* (71, Richard Harris); *Max et les Ferrailleurs* (71, Sautet); *The Assassination of Trotsky* (71, Joseph Losey); *Ludwig II* (72, Visconti); *César et Rosalie* (72, Sautet); *Le Trio Infernal* (74, Francis Girod); *Le Mouton Enragé* (74, Michel Deville); *L'Importance c'est d'Aimer* (75, Andrzej Zulawski); *Le Vieux Fusil* (75, Robert Enrico); *Une Histoire Simple* (78, Sautet); *Bloodline* (79, Terence Young); *La Banquiere* (80, Girod); *Deathwatch* (80, Bertrand Tavernier); *Fantasma d'Amore* (80, Dino Risi); *The Inquisitor* (81, Claude Miller); and *La Passante de Sans-Souci* (82, Jacques Rouffio).

Ernest B. Schoedsack (1893–1979),
b. Council Bluffs, Iowa

1926: *Grass* (codirected with Merian C. Cooper and Marguerite Harrison) (d). 1927: *Chang* (codirected with Cooper) (d). 1929: *The Four Feathers* (codirected with Cooper and Lothar Mendes). 1931: *Rango*. 1932: *The Most Dangerous Game/The Hounds of Zaroff* (codirected with Irving Pichel). 1933: *King Kong* (codirected with Cooper); *Son of Kong; Blind Adventure*. 1934: *Long Lost Father*. 1935: *The Last Days of Pompeii*. 1937: *Trouble in Morocco; Outlaws of the Orient*. 1940: *Dr. Cyclops*. 1949: *Mighty Joe Young*. 1953: *This Is Cinerama* (codirected with Ruth Rose).

The standard photograph of Schoedsack might have been submitted for casting Allan Quatermain: a lean-faced man with long jaw and direct gaze, open-necked shirt, pipe in mouth, and pith helmet on his head. He is an engagingly wayward figure in the American cinema, attracted equally to authenticity and hokum—like the producer who goes in search of Kong. His work is so much a matter of collaboration that it is difficult to assess his talent. But his long partnership with Merian C. Cooper never lost its faith in thrills, never forsook a schoolboy's rapture with spectacle.

When the First World War broke out, Schoedsack was a cameraman at Keystone. He joined the U.S. Signal Corps and filmed battle scenes. After the war he went into journalism and it was in 1926 that he met Cooper. Paramount hired them first to visit Abyssinia to film Haile Selassie, then to make documentaries: *Grass* (about the Bakhtiari tribes in Iran) and *Chang* (in Thailand). The two men filmed locations in the Sudan for *The Four Feathers* while producer David Selznick hired Lothar Mendes for the studio story scenes. Schoedsack then went to Sumatra on his own to make *Rango*.

When he returned, he shared *The Most Dangerous Game* with Irving Pichel at RKO. A disturbingly sadistic suspense film, produced by Cooper, its studio-made Malaya clearly owes something to Schoedsack. Selznick was now at RKO, and he backed Cooper and Schoedsack to make *King Kong* from the Edgar Wallace story. Still a very exciting film, it owes a lot to the sexual undertones—perhaps provided by scriptwriter Ruth Rose, Schoedsack's wife—and to the superbly animated models by Willis O'Brien. *King Kong* is the original wild monster film, and its images of Kong striding between skyscrapers seem more potent as our cities grow increasingly insecure.

Thereafter, Schoedsack's career waned. *Son of Kong* was a dismal failure: perhaps significantly, it had O'Brien still, but no Cooper. *Long Lost Father* was a film John Barrymore made on the slide. Cooper produced *Last Days of Pompeii* and, in the same year, Schoedsack went to India to shoot location footage for *The Lives of a Bengal Lancer*. The film stock deteriorated so Henry Hathaway reshot it in California, a sign of Hollywood's retreat from expensive documentary material for adventure features. From 1937, he was making second features at Columbia, but *Dr. Cyclops* was a good color horror film at Paramount. *Mighty Joe Young*, made with Cooper, Ruth Rose, and O'Brien, was an attempt to revive the Kong potency, but to no avail. Cinerama came as a new toy for this perpetually enthusiastic outsider.

Paul Schrader,
b. Grand Rapids, Michigan, 1946

1977: *Blue Collar*. 1978: *Hardcore*. 1979: *American Gigolo*. 1981: *Cat People*. 1985: *Mishima*. 1987: *Light of Day*. 1988: *Patty Hearst*. 1991: *The Comfort of Strangers*. 1992: *Light Sleeper*. 1994: *Witch Hunt* (TV). 1997: *Touch; Affliction*. 1999: *Forever Mine*. 2002: *Auto Focus*. 2003: *Exorcist: The Beginning*.

In his gruff, giggly way, battling with, but owning up to, his obsession, Schrader is one of the most likeable of film directors. He is also among the best talkers, capable of mixing high-flown theory with nuts-and-bolts Hollywood anecdotes. He has so many roots: Dutch Calvinism in provincial Michigan; discipleship to Pauline Kael, and then Pauline's chilling rebuke; he is the author of a fine book on Ozu, Bresson, and Dreyer; he is addicted to rock and roll; he is aesthete and sensualist; he could probably do anything or anyone, if addicted. I went to interview him as *Cat People* was opening, and on his desk he had a book of French film criticism, the trades, and a Bible. Of course, he does decor as well as he talks, and he is a chronic scene-maker. I'm not sure the addict can do much without thinking about it, and that may be why he doesn't much like himself.

At UCLA, around 1970, Schrader wrote for the *Los Angeles Free Press*, and he edited a magazine, *Cinema*. His writing was like his talk—packed, allusive, and looking for fresh thoughts. He was as sensitive to Peckinpah and film noir as he was to Bresson—and no one studying his films should overlook the wealth and slyness of his quotes and references. There is a scholar in Schrader, a true devotee who probably worries over his creativity and knows how often he runs the risk of being pretentious.

As a screenwriter, he and his brother Leonard drew on knowledge of Japan for *The Yakuza* (74, Sydney Pollack), which had a Robert Towne rewrite. Far more important was the script for *Taxi Driver* (76, Martin Scorsese), which grew out of Schrader's own urban depression and feelings about violence and suicide. It is characteristic of Schrader, I think, that that script is so structured and rational in dealing with someone out of control. His work has the organizational stress of a paranoid. However, *Taxi Driver* was not just a collaboration with Scorsese and De Niro. It was a picture that helped those two identify their talents.

In other scripting jobs, Schrader was less organically involved: *Obsession* (76, Brian De Palma); he worked uncredited on *Close Encounters of the Third Kind* (77, Steven Spielberg); *Rolling Thunder* (77, John Flynn); *Old Boyfriends* (78, Joan Tewkesbury); *Raging Bull* (80, Scorsese), where other writers did later work, without hiding Schrader's typically schematic vision of a brute; *The Mosquito Coast* (86, Peter Weir); and *The Last Temptation of Christ* (88, Scorsese), where the dialogue was often at odds with the period re-creation.

As a director, Schrader has placed himself on the edge of the mainstream. He understands commerce very well: he could explain how to make hits. But some perverse, rugged integrity has left his work increasingly hermetic and narrow in its range. Indeed, there are times when he does not seem to be simply an American director. Yet *Blue Collar* and *Hardcore* are both valuable for their view of the underside of American life. The first was an unusual portrait of racial mix, and George Scott's agonized puritan in the latter was a fair measure of Schrader's own tensions as he compared pure and profane.

American Gigolo was his one hit. Yet it is Bressonian, as austerely aesthetic as the Ferdinando

Scarfiotti design, and it had the very cool Richard Gere as the lead—John Travolta dropped out late in the day. It is a deeply ambiguous film, inhuman in some ways, nearly gay in others. It is like a New Wave film shot in L.A. on an American budget. Perhaps its success came from the title (brilliant) and the pounding music—Schrader composes his films to music.

Cat People is his most flagrantly sensational work, beautifully vulgar, as energetic as Val Lewton, and a love letter to Nastassja Kinski (even if eventually she tried to return it to sender). The film is not highly regarded—it is truly disturbing in the nakedness of its confession and its unbridled fantasy. But I believe it is Schrader's most dynamic work.

Thereafter, he went to Japan, to lower budgets, to England, and to Natasha Richardson as a lead actress. He was fighting to keep in work, but he seemed less and less persuaded by the hope of a large audience. I have not enjoyed the later films too much, but I do not expect Schrader to start making dull or routine movies. He is married to the actress Mary Beth Hurt, and he has children. Perhaps, closing in on sixty, he is becoming settled, or more wary. Or perhaps he is waiting for America to come round to small, dangerous pictures.

In recent years, Schrader has found it harder to make movies for theatres. Two films have been for television, and he has gone back to working on screenplays for others—*City Hall* (96, Harold Becker) and *Bringing Out the Dead* (99, Scorsese). Ironically, the film that got most attention (with a nomination for Nick Nolte and an Oscar for James Coburn) was *Affliction*, which had had to wait two years before it found release. But the most movielike work is surely *Forever Mine*, an ecstatic romantic fantasy, beautifully made, which might have been even better but for some casting problems.

Barbet Schroeder, b. Teheran, Iran, 1941
1968: *More*. 1971: *Sing-Sing* (d). 1972: *La Vallée/The Valley Obscured by Clouds*. 1974: *Idi Amin Dada* (d). 1976: *Maîtresse*. 1978: *Koko, A Talking Gorilla* (d). 1983: *Les Tricheurs*. 1984: *The Charles Bukowski Tapes* (d). 1987: *Barfly*. 1990: *Reversal of Fortune*. 1992: *Single White Female*. 1995: *Kiss of Death*. 1996: *Before and After*. 1998: *Desperate Measures*. 2000: *La Virgen de los Sicarios/Our Lady of the Assassins*. 2002: *Murder by Numbers*.

From Teheran to Telluride, Schroeder has the air of a stranger who is always at ease. He is a man of many worlds, an entrepreneur as well as a director, and for anyone who knows his hilarious, spectral performance in *Céline and Julie Go Boating* (73, Jacques Rivette), it is tempting to think that Schroeder could himself have played Claus Von Bülow in *Reversal of Fortune*.

In fact, Schroeder is essentially Parisian: he took a degree in philosophy at the Sorbonne; he organized jazz concerts; and he was a journalist. It was there, in 1964, that he formed Les Films du Losange, a company that gave immense support to Rivette and, especially, to Eric Rohmer. Thus, Schroeder was involved on most of Rohmer's *contes moraux* and on *Céline and Julie* and *Out One: Spectre*.

As a director, he began as a documentarian. *La Vallée* was a weird mix of Paul Bowles and hippie pretension, as Bulle Ogier tried to be a diplomat's wife being drawn deeper into the exotic wilds of New Guinea (with music by Pink Floyd). The attempt to add story to documentary riches was a disaster. But *Maîtresse* was, for its time, a startling examination of sexual power games, full of eros and role playing, with Gérard Depardieu and Bulle Ogier (a close friend to Schroeder for years) in the title role. Still, he could not develop a feature film career. *Les Tricheurs* was overlooked: it is a good, nervy movie about gambling.

A European-made TV series of interviews with the writer Charles Bukowski led to *Barfly*, a succès d'estime, even if to these eyes it is a rare kind of mess and posturing with several unbelievable performances. *Reversal of Fortune* has many problems of construction, and far too many loose ends. But Schroeder's connections (he has had private money) were close to the world depicted, and he has a connoisseur's eye for decadence. Of course, he could not have matched Jeremy Irons, but he may have helped Irons grasp the air of blithe comedy that made the grisly tale a small success. With *Single White Female*, and the fearsome performance by Jennifer Jason Leigh, Schroeder seemed to be, at last, an American director. But he stopped short of the real emotional vampirism possible in that film.

Still, *Barfly, Reversal of Fortune,* and *Single White Female* made three pretty good pictures in a row. Payback time followed: *Kiss of Death, Before and After,* and *Desperate Measures* were so much less original or lively. But then Schroeder revealed his enterprise and courage by going to Colombia and returning with the very impressive *Our Lady of the Assassins*. In truth, he is too interesting to be confined in America.

Joel Schumacher, b. New York, 1939

1974: *The Virginia Hill Story* (TV). 1979: *Amateur Night at the Dixie Bar and Grill* (TV). 1981: *The Incredible Shrinking Woman*. 1983: *D.C. Cab.* 1985: *St. Elmo's Fire.* 1987: *The Lost Boys.* 1989: *Cousins.* 1990: *Flatliners.* 1991: *Dying Young.* 1993: *Falling Down.* 1994: *The Client.* 1995: *Batman Forever.* 1996: *A Time to Kill.* 1997: *Batman & Robin.* 1999: *8MM; Flawless.* 2000: *Tigerland.* 2002: *Bad Company.* 2003: *Phone Booth; Veronica Guerin.*

While at art school, at Parsons School of Design in New York, Schumacher got a job as window designer at Henri Bendel's. A few years later, he opened a store of his own, and he later worked for Revlon and Halston. From that, he slipped into costume design and art direction, and he worked on—among others—*Play It As It Lays* (72, Frank Perry); *The Last of Sheila* (73, Herbert Ross); *Sleeper* (73, Woody Allen); and *Interiors* (78, Allen).

In the meantime, he was writing scripts and doing some directing for TV: his *Virginia Hill Story* is a decent job, with Dyan Cannon in the lead and Harvey Keitel as her Bugsy Siegel. He was a screenwriter on *Car Wash* (76, Michael Schultz), *Sparkle* (76, Sam O'Steen), and *The Wiz* (78, Sidney Lumet), before, in 1981, he got his first theatrical movie to direct, the Lily Tomlin *Shrinking Woman* project.

This is rare training and versatility for a director, so it would be nice to report that Schumacher is thriving. He has had hits (*St. Elmo's Fire* and *Flatliners*), and *The Lost Boys* and *Falling Down,* at least, are interesting projects. But it's hard to find character or much more than industrial competence. Nor does Schumacher seem comfortable making waves. His films with kids are blandly flattering to the young. And *Falling Down* had the makings of a troubling, subversive portrait of Los Angeles, until it opted for keeping the Michael Douglas character deranged and supplying us with a harmless, amiable cop to like. It could have been so much more challenging if Douglas had been the movie, and if he had had no greater handicap than ordinary desperation.

In the next few, especially with two very campy Batman pictures, Schumacher hauled himself into the category of top directors. But just as the Batman movies were very detached, so *A Time to Kill* was ponderously earnest. Not that Schumacher seemed prepared to linger at the top—*8MM, Flawless,* and *Tigerland* were a very effective ladder directed downwards. So he's a maverick, talented, good with actors and raw young people, but maybe a touch too amused by it all to be fully involved.

Arnold Schwarzenegger,
b. Graz, Austria, 1947

I remember how a friend came back from a visit to the set of *Stay Hungry* (76, Bob Rafelson) with reports that the not unobservant Rafelson was saying that this hulk with the impossible name was the smartest person on the picture, and that he was going somewhere. Fifteen years later, we think we know where. But consider: Arnold may have more dreams yet behind that rippling grin.

There has never been a major American star with a name people were fearful of pronouncing, let alone spelling. There has never been an

"Arnold" big in pictures. The closest movies had come in the past to a body-builder as an actor was Johnny Weissmuller, Steve Reeves, or Victor Mature—which is as much to say, too far already. By comparison, Arnold is a new man, a new body, a true pumper of iron where the great Mature would have seldom raised anything weightier than a glass or a lissome babe, for purposes of sardonic inspection. Arnold is beyond reality, beyond bodies even—and he knows it. How beautifully he coincides with and climaxes the movies' passion for mechanical men, or robot insurgents.

If you doubt this genetic inclination, recollect the barbells of abuse and mockery he has had to carry away cheerfully to some dump of the soul, without apparent guilt, wrath, or dismay. He has grinned the more and become a self-mocking monolith prince, a pal of the Bushes, and a Kennedy by marriage (to Maria Shriver). He *can* walk through walls. Suppose Ross Perot picked him as Secretary for Drills and Exercise? And wonder if, for all the bonhomie, there isn't yet a seed of revenge—a seed as revolutionary as those Jack got for his cow.

Legend has it that he was a frail child—or you can believe that he was found fully formed (with agent) in a mountain cave in the Alps. All you have to do is believe something. Nights in the gym led him to contests and titles: he was Junior Mr. Europe, Mr. World, a five-time Mr. Universe, and seven-time Mr. Olympia. That phase of his life is amusingly revealed in the documentary *Pumping Iron* (77, George Butler and Robert Fiore), derived from the book by Butler and novelist Charles Gaines. It was Gaines, screenwriter on *Stay Hungry*, who helped get Arnold into real pictures. Before then, he had appeared (as Arnold Strong) in *Hercules in New York* (70, Arthur Allan Seidelman), and he was a bodyguard for Mark Rydell in *The Long Goodbye* (73, Robert Altman).

He played *The Villain* (79, Hal Needham), and on TV he was Mickey Hargitay for Loni Anderson in *The Jayne Mansfield Story* (80, Dick Lowry). His breakthrough was the fatuous but violent and very successful *Conan the Barbarian* (82, John Milius), followed by the atrocious *Conan the Destroyer* (84, Richard Fleischer). Then, for the first time, he played a character not born of woman: *The Terminator* (84, James Cameron). With Cameron's help, he found the humor and even a certain pathos in robotics, and he was a large part of the film's originality.

There were several ill-considered castings in his new status: *Commando* (85, Mark L. Lester); *Red Sonja* (85, Fleischer); *Raw Deal* (86, John Irvin); *The Running Man* (87, Paul Michael Glaser); *Predator* (87, John McTiernan); and *Red Heat* (88, Walter Hill).

Twins (88, Ivan Reitman) was another advance, a comedy pairing with Danny DeVito: they played twins who came out wrong in an experiment—again, his birth was beyond the normal. *Total Recall* (90, Paul Verhoeven) also cast him as a being interfered with by science: the picture was expensive, but it was a smash and Arnold got $10 million and 15 percent of the gross.

Kindergarten Cop (90, Reitman) was over-cute—he was teamed with precocious kids—but kids loved it, and the picture found a gentle clumsiness in Arnold. This vanished in time for *Terminator 2* (91, Cameron), bigger than anything yet. But *The Last Action Hero* (93, McTiernan) was a large, mortifying failure that put many other projects from the same studio on hold.

He has begun to direct, rather in the way of a giant picking up a baby, with great caution and potential for charm: he did an episode for *Tales from the Crypt* (91) and *Christmas in Connecticut* (92) for TNT. But he has been such a learner in the past. What will the world do if, on learning the explanation that anyone born in Graz, Austria, cannot be president, Arnold says, "Why, baby?" Paul Verhoeven once said that this man could be as big as Charlton Heston—which may be Verhoeven's one recorded instance of naïveté.

In 1994 he made *True Lies* (Cameron) and *Junior* (94, Reitman), a measure of his intriguing wish to be cuddly and tough at the same time—with that dash of something beyond human. Indeed, in an age of more and more androids in movies, Arnold seemed to have a God-given (or Austrian) advantage. He played the kid market again in *Jingle All the Way* (96, Brian Levant) and he was quite funny as Mr. Freeze in *Batman & Robin* (97, Joel Schumacher). But then he faltered: he had a heart condition—alas, it proved he had a heart. He worked much less, and on the strength of *End of Days* (99, Peter Hyams) and *The 6th Day* (00, Roger Spottiswoode), might have done less still.

But the word is that he has recovered, and he has something called *Collateral Damage* (02, Andrew Davis) as well as *Terminator 3* (03, Jonathan Mostow) in the offing. This is fine, so long as Arnold isn't suddenly exposed as a fifty-five-year-old going carefully, and so long as his violence isn't too close to contemporary experience.

Paul Scofield,

b. Hurstpierpoint, England, 1922

He is perhaps the best example of a truly great stage actor who has never seemed interested in conquering film. Yet he has an Oscar to his credit—for Thomas More in *A Man for All Seasons* (66, Fred Zinnemann)—as well as a fine *King Lear* (71, Peter Brook), and several telling supporting performances. Nevertheless, this book would trade the lot for his two dry, elegant, dreary narrations in two films by Patrick Keiller—*London* (94) and *Robinson in Space* (97). It's not just that Scofield catches the rhythm of eighteenth-century prose. Just as important, he has the authority and the casual charm for a kind of movie voice that really has no equal. Why, after all, aren't all movies like Keiller's, and why shouldn't the urbane but essentially disinterested Scofield narrate everything, as right and habit?

On the other hand, Scofield has a face that was never quite young or sociable, and a strange bunch of film roles that might have been picked at random: Philip II in *That Lady* (55, Terence Young); with Virginia McKenna in *Carve Her Name with Pride* (58, Lewis Gilbert); *The Train* (64, John Frankenheimer); *Tell Me Lies* (68, Brook); the boss in *Bartleby* (72, Anthony Friedman); *Scorpio* (73, Michael Winner—alas, that one); doing Edward Albee in *A Delicate Balance* (73, Tony Richardson); a onetime patient of Freud's in *1919* (85, Hugh Brody); the King of France in *Henry V* (89, Kenneth Branagh); as a deaf birdwatcher in *When the Whales Came* (89, Clive Rees); the Ghost in *Hamlet* (90, Franco Zeffirelli); *Utz* (92, George Sluzier); superb and characteristically elusive as Mark Van Doren in *Quiz Show* (94, Robert Redford); the judge in *The Crucible* (96, Nicholas Hytner).

Martin Scorsese, b. New York, 1942
1964: *It's Not Just You, Murray* (s). 1968: *I Call First/Who's That Knocking at My Door?*. 1972: *Boxcar Bertha*. 1973: *Mean Streets*. 1974: *Alice Doesn't Live Here Anymore; Italian-American* (d). 1976: *Taxi Driver*. 1977: *New York, New York*. 1978: *The Last Waltz* (d); *American Boy* (d). 1980: *Raging Bull*. 1983: *The King of Comedy*. 1985: *After Hours*. 1986: *The Color of Money*. 1988: *The Last Temptation of Christ*. 1989: an episode from *New York Stories*. 1990: *Goodfellas*. 1991: *Cape Fear*. 1993: *The Age of Innocence*. 1995: *Casino; A Personal Journey with Martin Scorsese Through American Movies* (d). 1997: *Kundun*. 1999: *Il Mio Viaggio in Italia/My Voyage to Italy* (d); *Bringing Out the Dead*. 2002: *Gangs of New York*.

For years now, those who cherish the tradition and the prospect of American filmmaking have talked of Scorsese as "our best." He is a self-declared movie fanatic, a collector, a man devoted to film preservation and to celebrating careers like that of Michael Powell. He likes to play small parts in films, so great is his appetite, and he has been a friendly enabler or executive producer lately for a number of films—notably *The Grifters* (90, Stephen Frears).

Yet all is not well. One might as well start with *Raging Bull*, which is often hailed as his best film, and one of the greatest ever made. It is beautiful in ways that make beauty the first thing one notices—by that I mean not just its loyalty to black and white, but its insistence on form and emotional design being more important than the facts of boxing. I don't think Scorsese knows or cares much about boxing. That means that he is using its ritual for some personal journeying into the heart of savagery. And I am not sure he really knows that savagery either, except as a literary or cinematic context. In other words, amid the spectacle and power of *Raging Bull* I felt artistic will rising far above experience. Much the same thing can be said of *Taxi Driver*. This leaves me suspicious of what the film is about. *Raging Bull* is full of subtexts—not least, fear of women and a fascination with homosexuality. There cannot be space here to examine such things thoroughly. But Scorsese does not get enough proper scrutiny for his ideas. And if he is our best, then his films need ideas and themes more lasting and useful than the romantic fantasies that may have been acquired in a lifetime of watching movies.

The King of Comedy does have ideas—more than it has digested. Yet I think it showed a Scorsese trying to move in new directions. But the attempt wilted. *After Hours* was a disappointment. *The Color of Money* is slick, opportunistic, and nowhere near as tough-minded as *The Hustler*. *The Last Temptation of Christ* seemed to me dutiful—as if Scorsese had become trapped in a venture he told everyone he *had* to make. *Goodfellas* had passages of extraordinary danger and fear, and it surely came closer to the mob than most Mafia films. But still Scorsese yearned for these made men, and still it was hard to know why he was making the picture except for the thrill of all those gangster riffs and lines. *Cape Fear* was horrible, unnecessary, and adolescent, no matter that Scorsese was close to fifty. It was Brian De Palma on a good day, yet De Palma without the humor of *Scarface*. And that is not good enough for our best.

Scorsese is the adult version of a delicate, hypersensitive kid who grew up in a rough neighborhood and ever afterwards felt bound to pretend that he was hit man as well as a violinist. He wants it both ways—like all fantasists—even if it does jar a little when his cameo would-be killer in *Taxi Driver* speaks profane poetry, as a way of putting off real revenge. He's a back-seat director who manages to suggest that the guy up-front (De Niro) is his own surrogate. His end-of-my-tether nervous vitality is dangerously studied and superficial. Scorsese would be more demanding and durable if he wasn't so chronically aware that his films are part of the sex-and-violence hang-ups of erring Catholics, or that *New York, New York* grew somber as his own marriage broke up. That is the *pathétique des auteurs*.

That sounds snide, but I only hope to see Scorsese recognizing a funnier, theatrical vein in himself. It ill-becomes any movie director to cry the wild song of the streets, much less anyone as successful that young as Scorsese. He is a devotee of intelligence, visual beauty, and verbal style; there is hardly a grain of committed naturalism in him. When he uses the St. Gennaro festival, he is intoxicated with its Sternbergian decor. Language, color, and design are self-sufficient riches in his films. The killings in *Taxi Driver* are a soaring cadenza of space, composition, and editing in which the camera rises finally to a brilliant vantage above a set and its concoction. When Travis shoots Sport it is to topple the house of cards set up by their jive talk. The taxi is yellow not because New York cabs are, not even to add fire and brimstone, but to harmonize with the gasps of white steam and the carbon slick of mean streets.

Taxi Driver may be hysterical and holocaustic, but it is still a movie in the tradition of Vincente Minnelli, the acknowledged stylist behind *New York, New York*. That influence shows in many ways: the virtuosity of the camera, the bravura of color, the resort to movement, music, and decor as the imprint of feelings, plus a hero as tortured as Van Gogh in *Lust for Life*. But the strongest link with Minnelli is in the reliance on dream. *Taxi Driver* is not an indictment of New York City, no matter how faithfully it was filmed there, no matter how devoutly Scorsese recalls growing up in Little Italy, struggling for air and opportunity. *Taxi Driver* is the work of a man happy with the fervent claustrophobia of film noir, and perhaps inexperienced from spending so many hours at the movies.

It is a paranoid film: Travis Bickle believes all the metropolis is turned in against him. He is as furtive as someone who suspects he may be in a movie instead of life. "Are you talking to me? You must be, 'cause I'm the only one here." It is also the paranoia of a slender man who looks like a Renaissance saint, alarmed at the unkind streets, and carried away by feverish imagination. *Taxi Driver* goes further than that: it invests its own killer with all the damaged sensitivity of the paranoid author, so that the film turns into a warped projection of his triumph overpowering defunct codes of censorship, common sense, and the initial basis of redeemable mankind. Film and dream have no more ominous or transcendent moment than that in *Taxi Driver* when Travis survives his pitched battle, returns as a hero, but still presents a haunted face to his own rearview mirror. Scorsese cherishes his hero and the dream too much to have either perish: the man in the front seat has to live on with his dreadful anxiety. Otherwise, all the occupants of the vehicle might have to reassess the hell they're filling their heads with.

Growing up may offend Scorsese; he may prefer to die young, frenzied but "immaculate." In which case, *Mean Streets, Taxi Driver,* and *New York, New York* amount to an extraordinary, youthful tribute to Hollywood modes of the 1940s. No student or teacher of film at New York University, or anywhere else, has been more eloquent in extolling his love. In that sense, though, the films are academic and self-indulgent, abrasive with mannerisms and a Godardian assumption of worldliness. They reexplore the hallucination of film noir, they reclaim the threatened sensibility of Nicholas Ray, and they are comprehensive proof that a film is never all in the script. Scorsese aspires toward the delirium and heat of fever. He might become a deeper artist if he could see the artificiality of this and tease the ponderous weight of torment he has been determined not to lose. He is as dedicated a designer as Minnelli, but he lacks the humility still that lets design run free. The dream alone can ease the terror of sleep and make it graceful.

Scorsese's pact with Robert De Niro has been vital; it may be that the director was in greater need of it than the actor. Yet, evidently, Scorsese hero-worships De Niro and allows the actor to obscure the nature of the characters he plays. He needs to work with other people, especially with actresses in situations that resist heavy male gloom. *Alice . . .* was not such a film, and Liza Minnelli was thoroughly upstaged in *New York, New York*—albeit willingly.

The Age of Innocence had many admirers, but it seemed to me like a story muffled in decor and prestige. Scorsese is not good being respectable, or literary. The attempt showed far more than achievement. His search for new subjects is absorbing and important—for Scorsese still has it in him to be a great director. But he seems weary of not getting large public success and uneasy. Just because he is "the best," his career dramatizes the question of how an American director develops once youth is past.

Scorsese's case became increasingly delicate. *Casino* was brilliant, ravishing to the eye; there was no one else who could have made it—or would have thought to do so. And if one had never seen his clannish male groupings before, it would have been riveting. But what was most striking now was Scorsese's need to repeat those motions once more, without seeming to grasp them. Nothing now could shake the sense that he was hypnotized by the tumultuous talk and attitude of De Niro and Pesci. The best to be said about the film was the real ambiguity as to whether this Las Vegas was heaven or hell. But that's a question America (as well as Scorsese) needs to explore.

Kundun seemed to me a desperate attempt to believe in something, and it rang hollow. And nearly everyone seemed to agree that *Bringing Out the Dead* was a minor work, or a misstep, or a marking of time. In which case, that puts more pressure than ever on *Gangs of New York,* which has apparently faced some difficulties in its editing. The documentaries he has made lately are both scholarly and passionate, model contributions from our greatest director. But, again, greatness in America is a cruel privilege that can turn on its recipient and ruin him. Scorsese's may be the greatest biography in American film since that of Welles. And the most painful.

George C. (Campbell) Scott (1927–99), b. Wise, Virginia

There was a moment when Scott seemed like the great threat in American acting—he had such drive and bite, such timing and authority. In two films, cast in important supporting parts, he seemed like a marauder, seizing the pictures away from stars. His prosecuting attorney from Lansing in *Anatomy of a Murder* (59, Otto Preminger) was a player in a game, but his manager in *The Hustler* (61, Robert Rossen) was a wicked destroyer of people, a watcher who made Paul Newman seem tender and edible—a loser. This was fearsome promise; maybe other actors began to avoid him, in the way champions do not want to get in the ring with hungry challengers.

He had been educated at the University of Missouri, and he served in the Marines. His movie debut was as the villain in *The Hanging Tree* (59, Delmer Daves). But despite the impact of his first few films, the choices he made (or had to make) were not always clear: *The Power and the Glory* (61, Marc Daniels); *The Brazen Bell* (62, James Sheldon); the detective in *The List of Adrian Messenger* (63, John Huston); in the TV series, *East Side/West Side* (63–64); as Abraham in *The Bible* (66, Huston); *Not With My Wife, You Don't* (66, Norman Panama); *The Flim Flam Man* (67, Irvin Kershner); very good as a man in confusion in *Petulia* (68, Richard Lester)—his vulnerability seemed like his strength.

Patton (69, Franklin Schaffner) was a part on a plate—whatever Scott thought of the film. He impersonated the General, and let his instinct for megalomania rip. When he won the Oscar, he refused to accept it. Next year, when he won an Emmy for Arthur Miller's *The Price,* he refused that, too.

He was said to be difficult, hard to cast. He was Rochester in *Jane Eyre* (70, Delbert Mann) and played in *The Last Run* (71, Richard Fleischer). That last was as perfunctory a movie as *Oklahoma Crude* (73, Stanley Kramer) and *The New Centurions* (72, Fleischer). But there, Scott has one magnificent scene, where his retiring cop commits suicide, that completely exceeds Fleischer's half-hearted approach. The scene comes unexpectedly, in a ramshackle apartment on a hot afternoon as traffic drones along a freeway outside. It is easier to believe that Scott was in charge of the sequence,

so totally is it a matter of the way he reveals the desperation of a man retired from a relentless job.

The flavor of that sequence, and a similar enigma of where authorship lies, is sustained throughout *The Hospital* (72, Arthur Hiller) in which Scott plays the near-demented senior doctor in a hospital that is in administrative and ethical chaos. No one could attribute the savage humor of the film to Hiller, and although Paddy Chayefsky must deserve great credit, the film has its heart in Scott's shaggy, fatigued modern hero, worn out by disbelief, unable to escape his own staggering momentum. Only Scott's intelligence could make *The Hospital* simultaneously so bleak and heroic a film, so funny and touching. Furthermore, Scott's ultimate rationality constitutes the tragedy of the film, for the hospital and its benevolence are symbols of intelligent charity overwhelmed by babel and breakdown. Scott moves and breathes with the growing pain of ruined hopes, and his sudden launching himself at Diana Rigg is a most beautiful moment of terrible frustration momentarily allayed.

One should also mention that box-office disaster, *They Might Be Giants* (71, Anthony Harvey), in which Scott plays a widower lawyer who believes he is Sherlock Holmes; *The Day of the Dolphin* (73, Mike Nichols); and *Bank Shot* (74, Gower Champion). The failure of *Giants* is a mystery, if only because of the compassion and skill with which it portrays a modern archetype, the decent man driven into delusion. For Scott, this character is directly in line with *The Hospital* and, while neither film smacks of a director, they both glow with his own personality.

Scott's attitude to life may have been softened by marriage to Trish Van Devere (he had been married to Colleen Dewhurst). Still, his approach to film has seemed hardened and disenchanted by the failure of two films he chose to direct himself: *Rage* (74) and *The Savage Is Loose* (75). It was easy to believe that his deepest allegiance was to the theatre. He was very touching in *Islands in the Stream* (76, Schaffner), catching the sense of loss and the need for honor in a way that bypassed the limits of the picture's conception. He had fun with two parts in *Movie Movie* (78, Stanley Donen), but he needed no more than technique and panache. Worst of all, in the fine and demanding part of *Hardcore* (79, Paul Schrader), he seemed desolate and uninterested.

Past fifty, Scott should have been in his prime. But too much of his work was on TV, and nothing shook his reputation for being difficult and his admitted weakness for drink: *The Changeling* (79, Peter Medak); *The Formula* (80, John G. Avildsen); *Taps* (81, Harold Becker); Fagin in a TV *Oliver Twist* (82, Clive Donner); *China Rose* (83, Robert Day); *Firestarter* (84, Mark L. Lester); Scrooge in *A Christmas Carol* (84, Donner); for

TV, *Mussolini: The Untold Story* (85, Hal Polaire) and *The Last Days of Patton* (86, Delbert Mann); *Murders in the Rue Morgue* (86, Jeannot Szwarc); *Pals* (87, Lou Antonio); *The Ryan White Story* (89, John Herzfeld); *Descending Angel* (90, Jeremy Kagan); and *The Exorcist III* (90, William Peter Blatty).

He worked on, despite uncertain health: *Finding the Way Home* (91, Rod Holcomb); *Malice* (93, Harold Becker); *Curacao* (93, Carl Schultz); *The Whipping Boy* (94, Sydney Macartney); as Cus D'Amato in *Tyson* (95, Ulrich Edel); *Angus* (95, Patrick Read Johnson); the captain in a TV *Titanic* (96, Robert Lieberman); *12 Angry Men* (97, William Friedkin); *Country Justice* (97, Graeme Campbell); *Gloria* (99, Sidney Lumet); and with Jack Lemmon in the TV *Inherit the Wind* (99, Daniel Petrie).

When he died, the obituaries knew that a great actor had passed. He was two years younger than Brando—yet think of Scott's extraordinary record onstage, his great films, and his determination to keep working. Which would you have as the actor of their age?

Randolph Scott (Randolph Crane) (1903–87), b. Orange, Virginia

For twenty years, Scott was a reliable, uninspired actor. Having begun as a romantic lead, he moved into action films and increasingly noir Westerns. It might have been expected that he would slip into oblivion during the 1950s. Instead, he seemed to realize that, at fifty, he looked a more convincing cowboy than anyone else around. He formed his own production company, Ranown, with Harry Joe Brown and, largely through Budd Boetticher, he produced a series of second-feature Westerns built around his own harsh sense of morality and an absolute concentration on a man alone against great odds.

Scott attended the University of North Carolina and then went on the stage before a screen debut in *The Far Call* (29, Allan Dwan). He had small parts in *Women Men Marry* (31, Charles Hutchison); *The Lone Cowboy* (31, Paul Sloane); *Sky Bride* (31, Stephen Roberts); *Wild Horse Mesa* (32, Henry Hathaway); *Island of Lost Souls* (32, Erle C. Kenton); *Supernatural* (33, Victor Halperin); *Heritage of the Desert* (33, Hathaway); and *To the Last Man* (33, Hathaway) before coming to larger parts, often as the nonsinging guy in musicals: *Roberta* (35, William A. Seiter) where his innate, husky appeal is summed up by Ginger Rogers—"you big beautiful American"; *She* (35, Irving Pichel and Lansing C. Holden); *So Red the Rose* (35, King Vidor); *A Village Tale* (35, John Cromwell); *Follow the Fleet* (36, Mark Sandrich); *Go West, Young Man* (36, Hathaway); *Last of the Mohicans* (36, George Seitz); *High, Wide and Handsome* (37, Rouben Mamoulian); with Shirley Temple in *Rebecca of Sunnybrook Farm* (38, Dwan) and *Susannah of the Mounties* (39, Seiter); Wyatt Earp in *Frontier Marshall* (39, Dwan); *Jesse James* (39, Henry King); and second fiddle to Cary Grant in *My Favorite Wife* (40, Garson Kanin)—they were once famous pals.

In the 1940s, he abandoned romance for war films and then exclusively Westerns: *Virginia City* (40, Michael Curtiz); *When the Daltons Rode* (40, George Marshall); *Belle Starr* (41, Irving Cummings); *Paris Calling* (41, Edwin L. Marin); *Western Union* (41, Fritz Lang); *To the Shores of Tripoli* (42, Bruce Humberstone); *The Spoilers* (42, Ray Enright); *Corvette K-225* (43, Richard Rossen); *Gung Ho!* (43, Enright); *The Desperadoes* (43, Charles Vidor); *Belle of the Yukon* (44, Seiter); *Captain Kidd* (45, Rowland V. Lee); *China Sky* (45, Enright); *Abilene Town* (46, Marin); *Badman's Territory* (46, Tim Whelan); *Albuquerque* (47, Enright); *Trail Street* (47, Enright); *Coroner Creek* (48, Enright); *Return of the Bad Men* (48, Enright); *Colt 45* (50, Marin); and *Santa Fe* (51, Pichel).

By the late 1940s, Scott was making a great many quickie Westerns. How did he rediscover the dignity of the form? In the first instance, he made six films for André de Toth that related violence and betrayal to moral dilemma: *Man in the Saddle* (51); *Carson City* (52); *Thunder Over the Plains* (53); *The Stranger Wore a Gun* (53); *Riding Shotgun* (54); and *The Bounty Hunter* (54). *Hangman's Knot* (53, Roy Huggins), *Lawless Street* (55, Joseph H. Lewis), and *Ten Wanted Men* (55, Humberstone) were also above average, but it was the seven films Scott made with Boetticher that etched out his place in the history of the Western: *Seven Men from Now* (56); *The Tall T* (57); *Decision at Sundown* (57); *Buchanan Rides Alone* (58); *Ride Lonesome* (59); *Westbound* (59); and *Comanche Station* (60). Throughout this series, one feels that Scott's middle-aged Westerner is as unsentimental and self-sufficient as the cinema has achieved. The man's integrity never looks less than hard-earned and desperately sustained. Perhaps he sensed the value of these films, for he made only one more, *Ride the High Country* (62, Sam Peckinpah), which was itself a valediction.

Ridley Scott, b. South Shields, England, 1939

1977: *The Duellists*. 1979: *Alien*. 1982: *Blade Runner*. 1986: *Legend*. 1987: *Someone to Watch Over Me*. 1989: *Black Rain*. 1991: *Thelma and Louise*. 1992: *1492: Conquest of Paradise*. 1996: *White Squall*. 1997: *G.I. Jane*. 2000: *Gladiator*. 2001: *Hannibal; Black Hawk Down*. 2003: *Matchstick Men*.

After being an art student and then a film student at London's Royal College of Art, Ridley Scott directed some episodic television before ten years as a director of commercials—many of them prizewinners, and all of them forged at that eclectic place where high art is now channeled into pop idioms. Scott is a decorator, a borrower, and a synthesist; like a great machine he contains all striking images and can deliver and fuse them, so long as the product is impersonal. Even during his movie career, he has continued to do star ads (e.g., the Apple spot shown during the 1984 Super Bowl—Orwell's vision turned into a glossy, hip joke). He and his brother, Tony, still have a company that produces commercials. I am bound to add that Tony has also directed feature films—but I feel no need to say more.

How easy it is to point to Ridley Scott as an example of the look and sensibility of advertising corrupting moviemaking. With *The Duellists,* he seemed to be composing endless endorsements for Napoleon brandy, Périgord truffle-burgers, and vacations in Sarlat. Yet those products had been replaced with the outline of a Conrad novella and what may still be the movies' finest use of that unappeasable demon, Harvey Keitel. More than a decade later, it was hard to watch *Thelma and Louise* without remembering that Monument Valley has become the romantic testing ground of every automobile ad. (That abused location has gone from the clichés of one Ford to the homilies of another in forty years.)

Still, I find it hard to be disapproving. The movies would be duller without Scott's chronic eye for flash, sheen, and instant spectacle. He has no character: it is as difficult now after fifteen years and eight films to guess the kind of person he is as it was before he started. He is a decorator who often grows awkward or vague over story line. Little heed is paid to plausibility or linkage in a Scott film (Park Avenue socialites do fall for Brooklyn cops; Susan Sarandon does kill the would-be rapist; and no one pauses for second thoughts—no one notices how long it takes the police to catch up with the outlaws; that would take a spoilsport).

For all that, he is as blithe and versatile as Michael Curtiz, who always made hokum look as good as quality. Scott can find his imagery in 1800 or 1492, in the Dark Ages or the darker future of twenty-first century L.A. His two pieces of advance looking—*Alien* and *Blade Runner*—have been highly influential of high-tech design and future shock. Of course, they have also fed back into TV advertising. Both films illustrate the role of collaborators for Scott: they are vital, even if they come away weary of being misused. On *Alien,* screenwriter Dan O'Bannon and designers H. R. Giger and Michael Seymour were plainly important: Walter Hill was also one of the producers. *Blade Runner* had a clever script by Hampton Fancher and David Peoples, to say nothing of the Philip K. Dick novel. Its team of designers

included Lawrence Paull and Syd Mead—to say nothing of Kubrick's outtakes from *The Shining* for the end.

Someone to Watch Over Me is far richer than reputation suggests: the luxurious Manhattan apartment becomes a character in the story, a hideaway for love as well as a threatened nest, a place where objects and decor resonate as much as feeling. Yet Scott was as happy, inventive, and hollowed-out in Tokyo (for *Black Rain*) and in the wide-open spaces of *Thelma and Louise.*

Finally, from the bevy of luscious bystanding women in *The Duellists,* Scott has gone on to be a generous director of actresses. He saw the wan passion of Sean Young ahead of others; he made Daryl Hannah eerie and startling; he drew a rough strength from Lorraine Bracco that prevented *Someone* from toppling into the glossy pages of *Vogue* and *House and Garden.* And he freed Geena Davis so that we felt the character and the actress expanding in unison.

What was then most remarkable about Scott was the way he made himself into a top-line commercial director—this after several failures, like *White Squall,* which is an impressive picture, and the daft modishness of *G.I. Jane* (which would have made Michael Curtiz blush). But then Scott delivered three big hits in a row—*Gladiator, Hannibal,* and *Black Hawk Down.* I don't think *Gladiator* is more than fun and effects, though I can see that Scott and Russell Crowe play the schoolboy stuff very straight. But *Hannibal* is something else: a satire on Lecterism, a love story, a tribute to recondite learning and swish manners—it was Scott's first true comedy, and very welcome. Anyone capable of the ironies in *The Duellists* and *Hannibal* must have great determination and dedication in making conventional entertainments. But with six or seven pictures I'd happily see any night, Scott is that modern rarity—a natural crowd-pleaser.

Tony Scott,
b. Stockton-on-Tees, England, 1944
1983: *The Hunger.* 1986: *Top Gun.* 1987: *Beverly Hills Cop II.* 1990: *Revenge; Days of Thunder.* 1991: *The Last Boy Scout.* 1993: *True Romance.* 1995: *Crimson Tide.* 1996: *The Fan.* 1998: *Enemy of the State.* 2001: *Spy Game.* 2002: "Beat the Devil", episode from *The Hire.*

Tony is the younger brother of Ridley Scott, and by the most inane tests that now prevail the more successful of the two. There are those who find *True Romance* (based on a Quentin Tarantino script) a refreshing departure from Scott's flashy implausibility. They have the advantage of me. Tony Scott has the visual sensibility of a maker of commercials, and an attitude to material and narrative that is absurd without ever taking off into the fanciful. He likely believes in the overheated nastiness of *The Hunger, Revenge,* and *The Fan,* just as he can believe in the presentation of women in his two Tom Cruise pictures (one film really—different forms of propulsion). *Crimson Tide*, with the high-class professionalism of Denzel Washington and Gene Hackman, is his most watchable film, but even there nothing sustains belief except the confinement of the submarine.

Kristin Scott Thomas,
b. Redruth, England, 1960

Kristin Scott Thomas has the graven look of a fashion model from the 1950s—plus an education in London and Paris (she has done a good deal of work for French TV, too). From this point of view, she seemed ideally cast as the heartless Brenda Last in *A Handful of Dust* (88, Charles Sturridge), and then artfully enlarged as the wistful friend and onlooker in *Four Weddings and a Funeral* (94, Mike Newell). But granted the larger, yet vaguer, chances of a great love affair in *The English Patient* (97, Anthony Minghella), she seemed a little mummified before the script had actually reached that point. Still, the travesty of her Tina Brown–ish editor in *The Horse Whisperer* (98, Robert Redford) showed only that a graven face has little humor (or judgment). She has also appeared in *Under the Cherry Moon* (86, Prince); *The Tenth Man* (88, Jack Gold); *Bitter Moon* (92, Roman Polanski); *An Unforgettable Summer* (94, Lucien Pintile); *Angels and Insects* (95, Philip Haas); *Richard III* (95, Richard Loncraine); *Le Confessionale* (95, Robert Lepage); *Mission: Impossible* (97, Brian De Palma), in which her unflappable face was perfectly suited for ignoring the elephantine and nonsensical plot; *Up at the Villa* (99, Haas); unable to stir or be stirred by Harrison Ford in the woeful *Random Hearts* (99, Sydney Pollack). By now, she seems to be slipping away into a kind of gaunt, ladylike pose: *Play* (00, Minghella), adapted from Samuel Beckett; *Life as a House* (01, Irwin Winkler); *Gosford Park* (01, Robert Altman).

George Seaton (1911–79),
b. South Bend, Indiana

1945: *Billy Rose's Diamond Horseshoe; Junior Miss.* 1946: *The Shocking Miss Pilgrim.* 1947: *Miracle on 34th Street.* 1948: *Apartment for Peggy.* 1949: *Chicken Every Sunday.* 1950: *The Big Lift; For Heaven's Sake.* 1952: *Anything Can Happen.* 1953: *Little Boy Lost.* 1954: *The Country Girl.* 1956: *The Proud and the Profane.* 1958: *Teacher's Pet.* 1961: *The Pleasure of His Company; The Counterfeit Traitor.* 1962: *The Hook.* 1964: *36 Hours.* 1968: *What's So Bad About Feeling Good?.* 1970: *Airport.* 1972: *Showdown.*

Once a radio and stage actor, Seaton entered movies as a writer and worked in that capacity for some twelve years: *A Day at the Races* (37, Sam Wood); *Coney Island* (43, Walter Lang); *The Song*

of *Bernadette* (43, Henry King); and *The Eve of St. Mark* (44, John M. Stahl). *Coney Island* and *Bernadette* were both produced by William Perlberg, with whom Seaton formed a partnership in 1952. They functioned together until *36 Hours* and also produced *The Bridges at Toko-Ri* (55, Mark Robson); *The Tin Star* (57, Anthony Mann); and *The Rat Race* (60, Robert Mulligan). The latter two are a good deal more serious than any of Seaton's own films. He is a run-of-the-mill artisan sentimentalist, who discerned talent in the very young Natalie Wood and marshaled the tears well enough in *The Country Girl* to win Oscars for Grace Kelly and for his own screenplay. Essentially predictable in his writing and direction, Seaton was not up to the promising situation of *36 Hours*—a subject that Hitchcock or Lang might have reveled in—of a Nazi attempt to set up a fake Allied hospital so that James Garner, coming out of a coma, may spill the beans. But he had big hits with *Teacher's Pet* and *Airport*.

Jean Seberg (1938–79),
b. Marshalltown, Iowa

There was an endearing small-town common sense about Jean Seberg that stood up to the powerful attentions of several discoverers and that, on occasion, brought a deliberate naturalism to good films. Although at the time she was treated contemptuously by the critics, her *Saint Joan* (57, Otto Preminger) is a shrewd and touching fusion of provincial America, rural France, and Shaw's notion of a fustian saint picking logic with kings and bishops. She was chosen for that film, by Preminger, after an exhaustive search; even cropped and in armor she looked pretty and robust, and managed through her very disavowal of spirituality to bring odd conviction to the claims that she had heard voices.

Preminger persisted, despite critics, and won a marvelous performance from her as the spoilt adolescent in *Bonjour Tristesse* (58). It was apparent by now that unlike most discoveries who had previously only done local stock, she was self-possessed and mature. Beauty, the conventional asset of the newcomer, had been restricted by the hairstyles of her first two films. Perhaps it was in reaction against the bad reviews, and as an emotional gesture toward American cinema, that—after *The Mouse That Roared* (59, Jack Arnold) and *Let No Man Write My Epitaph* (59, Philip Leacock)—Jean-Luc Godard got her to play Patricia, the American girl in Paris in *Breathless* (59).

At first, she rather rebelled against his conception of a treacherous escapee from some film noir, but in the end was credibly *degeulgasse*, the more so for not knowing what the word meant. She then became the first notable American actress to work in France. Learning the language quickly, she was given a wig for *Infidelity* (61, Philippe de Broca) and matched Micheline Presle for sexiness. Here again, the Iowa girl proved surprisingly worldly. She married Frenchman François Moreuil and he directed her rather limply in *Playtime* (62). She divorced him and married novelist Romain Gary, and then played in *In the French Style* (63, Robert Parrish) and the "Grand Escroc" episode from *Les Plus Belles Escroqueries du Monde* (63, Godard), a Patricia Leacock blithely subjecting all around her to cinema verité.

In 1963, despite the fact that Yvette Mimieux had recommended *Lilith* to him, Robert Rossen chose Seberg for that part. As with Joan, she brought an earthiness to a mythological character. The film is ambitious beyond its director's talent, but her playing throughout has a proper rapture and it is Seberg's most evident proof of poetic imagination.

After that she worked in France and America, but never in really testing parts: *Un Milliard dans un Billiard* (65, Nicholas Gessner); *Moment to Moment* (65, Mervyn Le Roy); *A Fine Madness* (66, Irvin Kershner); *La Ligne de Démarcation* (66, Claude Chabrol); *Estouffade à la Caraibe* (66, Jacques Besnard); *Les Oiseaux Vont Mourir au Pérou* (68, Gary)—wildly pretentious and arty; *Pendulum* (68, George Schaefer); *Paint Your Wagon* (69, Joshua Logan); *Airport* (70, George Seaton); *Macho Callahan* (70, Bernard Kowalski); *Kill* (71, Gary); *L'Attentat* (72, Yves Boisset); *La Corrupcion de Chris Miller* (72, Juan Antonio Bardem); and *Cat and Mouse* (74, Daniel Petrie).

She married Dennis Berry, son of John Berry, and appeared in his *Le Grand Délire* (75). She directed a short film, *Ballad of the Kid* (74), and acted in *Die Wildente* (76, Hans Geissendorfer).

On September 8, 1979, two policemen looked into a white Renault that had been parked ten days on a quiet street in Paris. They found the decomposing body of Jean Seberg, with a bottle of barbiturates. She had been involved with black activists. The FBI had hounded and harassed her. A child of hers had died. The hideous story is well told in David Richards's *Played Out,* but Seberg's tragedy has been attempted on stage, and it lingers.

Peter Sellers (1925–80), b. Southsea, England
When commercial cinema was breaking down in the late fifties, it adopted many novelties in a frenzied search for security. One of them was Peter Sellers. He was, beyond argument, a brilliant radio comedian, capable of inventing vivid fantasy characters with his great flair as a mimic. But cinema flinches from mimicry and peels away bogusness. Moreover, as Sellers became world famous, so strains of vanity and neurosis arose, so close to madness that his real heart disease seemed incidental.

He became an international figure without ever apparently considering the nature of acting. Darting in and out of comic personae could seem slippery or chronic on screen. He was often funny—though on film he was broader than he had been on radio—but he was too evidently a virtuoso, and little else. His comedy never helped him find a character—as happened with Fields, Groucho, and so many others. There was no attitude there in Sellers: his deftness was ghostly; yet he could be very dull when some serious fancy took him. His health was poor, but his ego was very strong. He was not easy to work with, and he was very self-indulgent as Inspector Clouseau.

After many years on radio in *Ray's a Laugh* and *The Goon Show* (which revolved around him), he played supporting parts in British films: *The Ladykillers* (55, Alexander Mackendrick); *The Smallest Show on Earth* (57, Basil Dearden); and *The Naked Truth* (57, Mario Zampi). He rose to leading parts, but seldom appeared without some disguise: *Carlton-Browne of the F.O.* (59, Roy Boulting); *The Mouse That Roared* (59, Jack Arnold); *I'm All Right, Jack* (59, R. Boulting); *Battle of the Sexes* (59, Charles Crichton); *Two-Way Stretch* (60, Robert Day); as a gangster in *Never Let Go* (60, John Guillermin); as his caricature Indian in *The Millionairess* (60, Anthony Asquith); in his one direction of himself, *Mr. Topaze* (61); and *Only Two Can Play* (61, Sidney Gilliat).

His elevation to major stardom began with the part of Quilty in *Lolita* (62, Stanley Kubrick) and *Waltz of the Toreadors* (62, Guillermin). Then came the three parts—British flier, U.S. president, and evil genius—in *Dr. Strangelove* (63, Kubrick), in which his own pretensions vied with those of the director.

The "international comedian" label was now pinned on him: as Inspector Clouseau in *The Pink Panther* (64, Blake Edwards) and *A Shot in the Dark* (64, Edwards); and *The World of Henry Orient* (64, George Roy Hill). He had a heart attack before *Kiss Me, Stupid* could get under way, and soulfully declared his regeneration. But there was no firmer grip on a character for himself, and the films got worse: *What's New, Pussycat?* (65, Clive Donner); *The Wrong Box* (66, Bryan Forbes); *After the Fox* (66, Vittorio de Sica); *The Bobo* (67, Robert Parrish); *Woman Times Seven* (67, de Sica); *I Love You, Alice B. Toklas* (68, Hy Averback); *The Party* (68, Edwards); *The Magic Christian* (69, Joseph McGrath); *Hoffman* (69, Alvin Rakoff); *There's a Girl in My Soup* (70, R. Boulting); *Soft Beds, Hard Battles* (73, R. Boulting); *The Optimists of Nine Elms* (73, Anthony Simmons); as Queen Victoria in *The Great McGonagall* (74, McGrath). He stayed loyal to Clouseau, but came close to being surpassed by Herbert Lom's Dreyfuss in *The Return of the Pink Panther* (74), *The Pink Panther Strikes Again* (76), and *The*

Revenge of the Pink Panther (78)—all by Blake Edwards. He was another comic policeman in *Murder by Death* (76, Robert Moore), and the traditional double-act in *The Prisoner of Zenda* (79, Richard Quine).

He was wonderfully well used as the empty vessel who rises to command in *Being There* (80, Hal Ashby)—it's hard to think of another actor who could have played the vital yet elusive role so well, and perhaps he was all the better in it because illness kept him quiet, still, and impassive. His last film was *The Fiendish Plot of Fu-Manchu* (80, Piers Haggard), but *Trail of the Pink Panther* (82, Edwards) used old footage from Clouseaus of the past.

David O. Selznick (1902–65),
b. Pittsburgh, Pennsylvania

The *O* was added later in his youth by Selznick himself for euphony and to keep up with other moguls. Having elected *O*, he called himself Oliver.

He was the son of Lewis J. Selznick. Educated briefly at Columbia University, he began working in his teens for his father's film company. He edited the company magazine and was in charge of newsreels and short subjects. After his father's bankruptcy in 1923, David embarked on independent newsreels—on the boxer Luis Firpo and a beauty contest judged by Rudolph Valentino. In 1924, he produced his first feature, *Roulette* (S. E. V. Taylor), and in 1926 he left New York for Hollywood. His name barred him from good jobs and he worked for MGM as assistant story editor. He reformed the writers' department and became chief assistant to Harry Rapf on cheap quickies. While there, with W. S. Van Dyke directing, he made two Tim McCoy vehicles simultaneously at great savings, fought with Louis B. Mayer, and was fired after an argument with Hunt Stromberg.

He joined Paramount and there produced or supervised *Forgotten Faces* (28, Victor Schertzinger); *Chinatown Nights* (29, William Wellman); *The Dance of Life* (29, John Cromwell and Edward Sutherland); *The Four Feathers* (29, Merian Cooper, Ernest Schoedsack, and Lothar Mendes); *The Man I Love* (29, Wellman); *Street of Chance* (30, Cromwell); *Sarah and Son* (30, Dorothy Arzner); *Honey* (30, Wesley Ruggles); *The Texan* (30, Cromwell); *For the Defense* (30, Cromwell); and *Manslaughter* (30, George Abbott).

In 1930, he married Irene Mayer, the daughter of Louis B. He resigned from Paramount in 1931 and was hired as studio boss of the new RKO. It was there that he first showed his special talent by hiring George Cukor, Merian Cooper, and Katharine Hepburn. His productions at RKO included *Symphony of Six Million* (32, Gregory La Cava); *What Price Hollywood?* (32, Cukor); *A Bill of Divorcement* (32, Cukor); *Bird of Paradise* (32, King Vidor); *The Age of Consent* (32, La Cava); *Topaze* (33, Harry d'Arrast); *Little Women* (33, Cukor); *Our Betters* (33, Cukor); and *King Kong* (33, Schoedsack and Cooper).

In 1933 he returned to MGM with his own production unit and made *Dinner at Eight* (33, Cukor); *Night Flight* (33, Clarence Brown); *Dancing Lady* (33, Robert Z. Leonard), and Astaire's first film; *Viva Villa!* (34, Jack Conway and Howard Hawks); *Manhattan Melodrama* (34, W. S. Van Dyke); *David Copperfield* (34, Cukor); *Reckless* (35, Victor Fleming); *Anna Karenina* (35, Brown); and *A Tale of Two Cities* (35, Conway).

In 1935 he left to form Selznick International Pictures with John Hay Whitney as his chief partner. There he produced *Little Lord Fauntleroy* (Cromwell); *The Garden of Allah* (36, Richard Boleslavsky); *A Star Is Born* (37, Wellman); *Nothing Sacred* (37, Wellman); *The Prisoner of Zenda* (37, Cromwell); *The Adventures of Tom Sawyer* (38, Norman Taurog); *Made for Each Other* (39, Cromwell); and *Intermezzo* (39, Gregory Ratoff), before *Gone With the Wind*, a triumph with which he never came to terms.

Margaret Mitchell's novel was published in 1936, the year in which Selznick went independent. It took him three years to prepare and shoot, and he spared nothing—to buy the novel or shoot the movie. Any number of writers worked on the script, but Selznick always outwrote them with variant scenarios or prolix midnight memos. Three directors had a hand in the shooting, Cukor, Sam Wood, and Victor Fleming. Just as Cukor probably did most for Vivien Leigh, so Fleming was in Gable's corner. *Gone With the Wind* is, not surprisingly, void of creative personality. But it has vast entrepreneurial aplomb, for Selznick loved the glamour of movies and of the independent empire. He cared for every facet of making a film and had a greater sense of how to photograph individuals, how to use sets and music, and how to construct a picture than many directors. His memos, laughed at by many, radiate an intuitive, loving preoccupation with detail in what has to be a painstaking form. He inaugurated epic, even if with a twopence colored novelette. Wonderful to relate, the glory swamped the rewards, for Selznick had mortgaged much of the profits away to MGM.

Ever afterwards, he was in search of a greater project, increasingly interfering. Only Hitchcock on *Rebecca* (40) absorbed his energy, his memos, and his mixture of insight, shrewdness, and wild dreaming. In the 1940s Selznick appeared to have lost interest in production and he largely functioned through loaning out the stars he had made (Ingrid Bergman, Gregory Peck, Joseph Cotten, and Joan Fontaine), by selling already packaged projects, like *Notorious* (46), to other companies, and by taking a 25 percent interest in United Artists.

He made *I'll Be Seeing You* (44, William Dieterle); his own experience of psychoanalysis resulted in *Spellbound* (45, Hitchcock); while his adoration of Jennifer Jones shaped the rest of his life. He starred her in his own productions of *Since You Went Away* (44, Cromwell) and *Duel in the Sun* (46, Vidor), the latter his most serious attempt to match *Gone With the Wind*. He contributed enormously to the film, not least in the way he brought fire to Jennifer Jones, but his reluctance to settle on a limit to the film finally forced King Vidor to quit. Fortunately for the cinema, but confusingly for analysis, Vidor was the sort of director Selznick aspired to be. At any event, *Duel in the Sun* was another great success.

He formed Selznick Releasing Organization to distribute it and then kept the offshoot supplied with expensive failures—*The Paradine Case* (47, Hitchcock) and *Portrait of Jennie* (49, Dieterle). The latter is a good example of Selznick's way of breathing his own conviction into romance, and of cinema's way of making the novelette an eerie and touching genre.

By 1948 he was divorced, he was $12 million in debt, and his companies closed down. In 1949 he married Jennifer Jones and, while living in Europe, was involved with her in *Gone to Earth* (50, Michael Powell) and *Indiscretion of an American Wife* (53, Vittorio de Sica). His chief interest now was his wife's career, and he exchanged his rights in *A Star Is Born* for the chance to put her in *A Farewell to Arms* (57, Charles Vidor). When that was a severe failure, he made no more films and died in 1965 of heart attacks.

Selznick never forgot his father's fall or his advice to be lavish in everything. A chronic gambler, he had seething energy and care for detail as well as a youthful faith in literary values that hindered as much as it helped. Nearly all his films are adaptations of successful books and plays. But he had remarkable skill with people—launching Cukor and Hepburn, harnessing Cooper and Schoedsack, choosing Fields for *David Copperfield*, recognizing Ingrid Bergman and Alfred Hitchcock. Finally, he was proved right in his insistence on Jennifer Jones. *Gone With the Wind* is film history and *Duel in the Sun* is a masterpiece of the primitive. *David Copperfield* and *Rebecca* are masterpieces without qualification. At least a dozen more of his films survive as brilliant entertainments. For all Scott Fitzgerald's comparison of Thalberg with Monroe Stahr, is Selznick really not the more heroic and talented figure?

Myron Selznick (1898–1944),
b. Pittsburgh, Pennsylvania

So much of old Hollywood history depends on the traps and coils of family. There were three Selznick boys—Howard (1897–1980), Myron, and David (1902–65). Howard was born with some kind of brain damage or retardation: the family variously ignored or finessed the problem so that it is impossible to be sure about it medically. David was the apple of his father's eye, and his own favorite genius. He was inept in many ways, indecisive, neurotic, yet he had charm, need, energy, and a daft kind of radiance. The good and the bad all came together in *Gone With the Wind* and that crusade called Jennifer Jones. Myron was the smart one: brilliant, shrewd, decisive, and an enormous influence on the picture business—he invented agenting.

Myron Selznick also died at the age of forty-five (looking sixty-five), divorced from his wife, a hopeless alcoholic, his great agency in ruins. Myron had some fearful demons that kept him from being the potentate of his Hollywood. If he had had one ounce of need or belief to go with his efficiency, he might have taken the town. He might have been Mike Ovitz, early. But he was twisted: he had to look after Howard the stooge; he had to protect David the romantic chump. And he was not his father's favorite. He never believed in anything except the booze.

He had a magnificent office on Wilshire Boulevard; he had a team of agents; he worked the telephone; he was abrasive, arrogant, and surreal in his demands. He was also an extraordinary, collusive aid to his brother, as David Selznick set up independently. Myron Selznick also invented the conflict of interests. He was usually drunk; he was belligerent; he was famous for his ski lodge in the mountains, Hillhaven, for his Japanese butler, Ishii, and for Myron Selznick stories. And it all rolled off his back like Johnnie Walker going down his throat.

What did he do? He made and represented, for much of the thirties, people such as William Powell, Myrna Loy, Carole Lombard, Constance Bennett, Fredric March, Lewis Milestone, William Wellman, Loretta Young, Paulette Goddard, Charles Laughton, W. C. Fields, George Cukor, Miriam Hopkins, Rouben Mamoulian, Kay Francis, Laurence Olivier, Vivien Leigh, and Alfred Hitchcock. It was Myron who had the idea, in the late thirties, of getting star names to produce their own films: he nearly began with Lubitsch on a thing called *Shop Around the Corner*, but the studios ganged up against him. It was Myron who owned, and kept, a piece of *Gone With the Wind*, and left it to his daughter—the last Selznick to have profit participation in the great movie.

And Myron pioneered something else in agentry, maybe the most comical thing: self-hatred. He couldn't finish himself off quickly enough.

Ousmane Sembene,
b. Ziguenchor, Senegal, 1923

1963: *Barom Sarrett* (d). 1965: *La Noire de . . . / Black Girl*. 1968: *Mandabi/The Money Order*.

1971: *Taaw* (d); *Emitai*. 1974: *Xala*. 1977: *Ceddo*. 1988: *Camp de Thiaroye/The Camp at Thiaroye* (codirected with Thierno Faty Sow). 1992: *Guelwaar*. 2000: *Faat Kiné*.

Sembene was a manual laborer in his late teens who then joined the Free French army in 1942. He worked on the railways in Senegal after the war, and then for ten years he lived in France, working at a Citroën factory and as a docker in Marseilles. While there, he began to write novels—in French—notably, *Le Docker Noir*, published in 1957. He turned to moviemaking as a way of reaching the large African audience. To that end, he went to study in Russia in the early sixties and was a student of Mark Donskoi.

He began in shorts and documentaries, but made an impact at film festivals with *La Noire de . . .*, about an African woman who works for a family in France. *Mandabi* was a comedy about the bureaucratic difficulties in cashing a foreign money order. *Emitai* recounts the confrontations between a Senegalese tribe and French soldiers. *Xala* was a sophisticated comedy about a successful Dakar businessman who takes a new wife and finds himself impotent. *Ceddo* was Sembene's most ambitious film, set in no fixed place, but an exploration of all the influences that have worked on tribal Africa.

It is often said that Sembene is the father figure of African cinema. Yet that kind of comment shows how far Africa is like another planet. Sembene is a fine director, with his own European ties. But Africa has so many other sources, languages, and visions, most of which we never see.

Mack Sennett (Mikall Sinnott) (1880–1960), b. Danville, Canada

The name Sennett is nearly an adjective. If he had named the studio after himself, instead of Keystone, then "Sennett comedy" would stand for all that frantic, innocent knockabout that signifies a moment in history. For, supposedly, Sennett invented screen comedy. In 1937, his special Oscar cited "his lasting contribution to the comedy technique of the screen the basic principles of which are as important today as when they were first put into practice."

What were those principles? Charlie Chaplin got this instruction from the boss: "We have no scenario—we get an idea then follow the natural sequence of events until it leads up to a chase, which is the essence of our comedy." Charlie wanted more: it was for Sennett that he discovered the look and the attitude of the Tramp; and it was Sennett, a year later, who couldn't bring himself to pay the clever limey $1,000 a week.

Sennett was not really a performer. He had acted for Griffith, but then Griffith assigned Sennett to supervise the production of comedies. Sennett was a good laugher; he was energetic and enthusiastic. Chaplin and others used him as a sample audience: Mack knew what was funny. And then he got that joke done and he punched it out at the audience. The most important thing Sennett pioneered was being a producer.

When only in his teens, the family friend Marie Dressler introduced Sennett to the theatrical impresario, David Belasco. So Sennett went into vaudeville as a minor performer, and in 1908 he went to Biograph looking for work. Griffith hired him and used him a lot in the years from 1908 to 1911. He wrote some scripts, and he did some directing, and at Griffith's suggestion he began to study the mechanics of comedy—not Griffith's forte.

In 1912, Sennett left Biograph and with a couple of bookmakers for backing he formed Keystone. He brought along Ford Sterling and Mabel Normand from Biograph and he laid down the pattern of slapstick humor—with gorgeous girls, owlish idiots, noble simpletons, antlike armies of cops, and the riot of pursuit. He loved tricks, but he also had an unconscious feeling for light and space, and his great movies give fascinating glimpses of early Los Angeles.

No one ever accused Sennett of planning this, but he filmed disorder, or order reappraised—collisions, accidents, chaos, the mechanization of the chase, the pixillation of life. Run his movies, forward *and* backward, and you may see how little difference there is. He was pouring action from one vessel to another. He had discovered a kind of surrealism in which people played pinball rather than lived life. It is vital to the nature of movies, and it is as terrifying as it may be liberating. For it is not quite human.

Theodore Dreiser, for one, saw this as it happened. He interviewed Sennett and said of him: "The trains or streetcars or automobiles . . . collided with one another and by sheer impact transfer whole groups of passengers to new routes and new directions! Are not these nonsensicalities illustrations of the age-old formula that underlies humor? Isn't this an inordinate inflation of fantasy to heights where reason can only laughingly accept the mingling of the normal with the abnormal?"

Sennett ran a factory, and he became a supervising editor as well as a very good picker of talents. He admired Mabel Normand, and she would likely have married him but for his fling with Mae Busch. He backed Fatty Arbuckle, Mack Swain, Chaplin, Slim Summerville, and later, Gloria Swanson and Harry Langdon.

By 1915, Keystone had become a part of Triangle: Sennett, Griffith, and Thomas Ince were the three great figures of that moment. When Triangle broke up, Sennett went back to his own unit, releasing through Paramount and then Pathé.

Most of his pictures were one- or two-reelers, but over the years there were a few features: *Tille's Punctured Romance* (15), which he directed himself, and *Mickey* (18, Richard Jones), a vehicle for Mabel Normand.

By the early twenties he was in decline, or passed by. As he admitted, he was not that receptive to story, character, or attitude. And his energy now looked raw and naïve. Of course, it was both, but looking back it is easier to see the dynamism of the age and its new technology. Keystone comedy has become a version of Dada where we see the specter of great terrors. The most alarming thing of all is that the pictures were played for laughter.

Delphine Seyrig (1932–90),
b. Beirut, Lebanon

How beautiful was Delphine Seyrig? What did she look like? Was it she, unheard, seen at some distance, in 1967, in *Accident*? Why did so entrancing an actress so restrict her work in cinema? Because she knew memory thrived best on fragments?

Her diffident, disjointed career—cameos here, extraordinary, innovatory intensity there—is part of the abstracted calm that hung over her. She was able to invest small gestures with an enormous imaginary train. As she said herself:

> I have to create an entire past history for her/me (a character). If one isn't provided, I create it for myself. I invent it. I can't work any other way. The act of moving, say, a cigarette lighter doesn't interest me in itself; what interests me is how to move it as the character would. I think the real reason why one loves acting lies in this conception of the gesture bound by personality. I think that even actors who don't admit it actually play much more than the text and the necessary movements. They act because they are inventing a character. And when one invents a character, one doesn't invent her at thirty-five or seventy years old; one makes her arrive there. One creates a past for her.

While working in New York, she had appeared as Larry Rivers's wife in *Pull My Daisy* (58, Robert Frank). But her first large part was as the woman in *Last Year at Marienbad* (61, Alain Resnais), the instrument of feeling through whom the idea of the past is brought to bear on the present. That deadly film is sustained by the grace of her movements and the emotional alertness of her expressions: a more hackneyed or less resourceful actress could never have carried the constant, but nonspecific attention. *Muriel* (63, Resnais) went beyond exercise and allowed Seyrig to create one of the most anguished and tender of screen women. As Jean Cayrol's notes for the script make

clear, the part of Hélène was an embodiment of past, present, and future, a crucible of experience. Seyrig astonishingly altered herself to fit these requirements:

> Hélène's figure is still young, but her face must be very mobile. In fact, she could pass for a slightly used 20-year-old or a 45-year-old on whom worry and fatigue have left their marks. She has kept her hair natural and untinted. And the wind can play in her hair continually, which will give it a life of its own, like the changes in her face.
>
> Her expression is direct. It can be very fixed, as if she looked through the people in front of her at something else; but at the same time her gaze can be uneasy. One has the impression that her eyes become like those of someone who is mad.

Nothing she did after *Muriel* was as comprehensive, but much of the earlier creation has spread usefully into *La Musica* (66, Marguerite Duras and Paul Seban); *Accident* (67, Joseph Losey), where her brief liaison with Dirk Bogarde, without direct sound, is—contrary to Losey's intention—more intriguing than anything else in the film; *Mr. Freedom* (68, William Klein); *Stolen Kisses* (68, François Truffaut), where her breathless playing of the seduction scene was aided by the practical measure of running up two flights of stairs immediately beforehand; *La Voie Lactée* (68, Luis Buñuel); a lady Dracula in *Daughters of Darkness* (70, Harry Kumel); *The Magic Donkey* (70, Jacques Demy), as a sophisticated fairy godmother; as the airy, felicitous, ultimately groomed lady at thwarted dinner parties in *The Discreet Charm of the Bourgeoisie* (72, Buñuel), who restrains her lover's advances because of "her scars"; as Kristine Linde in *A Doll's House* (73, Losey); *The Day of the Jackal* (73, Fred Zinnemann); and *The Black Windmill* (74, Don Siegel).

Her sheer presence, at the same time declaratory and mysterious, and her rapport with Marguerite Duras, sustained the levels of *nouveau roman* and fashion show in *India Song* (75). But she was more real and resourceful in the very demanding *Jeanne Dielman, 23 Quai du Commerce—1080 Bruxelles* (75, Chantal Akerman). Her range remained as extraordinary as it was because of an abiding reticence: *Aloise* (75, Liliane de Kermadec); *Le Jardin qui Bascule* (75, Guy Gilles).

She directed one film, *Sois Belle et Tais-Toi* (77), and she appeared in *Vera Baxter* (77, Duras); *Le Chemin Perdu* (80, Patricia Moraz); *Chere Inconnue* (80, Moshe Mizrahi); *Dorian Gray im Spiegel der Boulevard Presse* (84, Ulrike Ottinger); *Golden Eighties* (86, Akerman); *Letters Home* (86, Akerman); and *Joan of Arc of Mongolia* (89, Ottinger).

Omar Sharif (Michael Shalhoub),
b. Alexandria, Egypt, 1932
Of Syrian-Lebanese descent, Sharif was given an essentially European education, as well as a solid grounding in American films. It was his ambition to be an international movie star, and he became the sex symbol of the Egyptian cinema toward that end. He attracted a certain amount of art-house attention in Jacques Baratier's *Goha* (59), but his star rose when David Lean ventured eastwards and cast Sharif as the fierce, tribesman ally of *Lawrence of Arabia* (62). Such brigandlike handsomeness and the playful conjuring up of a latter-day Valentino left no doubt about Sharif's international appeal.

He worked hard throughout the 1960s in a variety of blockbusters: thus *The Fall of the Roman Empire* (64, Anthony Mann); *Behold a Pale Horse* (64, Fred Zinnemann); *The Fabulous Adventures of Marco Polo* (64, Christian-Jaque); *Genghis Khan* (65, Henry Levin); very subdued as *Dr. Zhivago* (65, Lean); *The Night of the Generals* (67, Anatole Litvak); *Cinderella Italian Style* (67, Francesco Rosi); *Funny Girl* (68, William Wyler); *Mayerling* (68, Terence Young); *MacKenna's Gold* (69, J. Lee Thompson); *The Appointment* (69, Sidney Lumet); *Che!* (69, Richard Fleischer); *The Last Valley* (70, James Clavell); *The Horsemen* (71, John Frankenheimer); *Le Casse* (71, Henri Verneuil); *L'Isola Misteriosa e il Capitano Nemo* (73, Juan Antonio Bardem); *The Tamarind Seed* (74, Blake Edwards); *Juggernaut* (74, Richard Lester); and *Funny Lady* (75, Herbert Ross). Which is an awful lot of dull film, and much less interesting than the real picture of a cosmopolitan, bridge-playing Sharif, deprecating his own success and sophistication.

He was in *Crime and Passion* (76, Ivan Passer); *Ashanti* (79, Fleischer); *Bloodline* (79, Young); *Oh Heavenly Dog!* (80, Joe Camp); *Pleasure Palace* (80, Walter Grauman); *The Baltimore Bullet* (80, Robert Ellis Miller); *Green Ice* (81, Ernest Day); *Top Secret!* (84, Jim Abrahams, David Zucker, and Jerry Zucker); *Anastasia: The Mystery of Anna* (86, Marvin J. Chomsky); *Harem* (86, Billy Hale); *Peter the Great* (86, Chomsky and Lawrence Schiller); *The Possessed* (86, Andrzej Wajda); *Grand Larceny* (88, Jeannot Szwarc); and *Memories of Midnight* (91, Gary Nelson).

He is still a star in Egypt, a handsome figure at the tables, and likely to turn up anywhere as some kind of sheik: *Al-Aragoz* (91, Hany Lasheen); as an Armenian escaping Nazis in *Mayrig* (91, Verneuil), *588 Rue Paradis* (92, Verneuil); *Beyond Justice* (92, Duccio Tessari); a TV *Mayrig* (93, Verneuil); *Lie Down with Lions* (94, Jim Goddard); *Catherine the Great* (95, Chomsky and John Goldsmith); the sorcerer in *Gulliver's Travels* (96, Charles Sturridge); Kahlil Gibran in *Heaven Before I Die* (97, Izadore K. Musallam);

The 13th Warrior (99, John McTiernan); *The Parole Officer* (01, John Duigan); *Return of the Thief of Baghdad* (02, Dutchen Gersh).

Robert Shaw (1927–78),
b. West Houghton, England
Swashbuckling encounters with trash and meal-ticket movies do not dull the thought that Robert Shaw could have been one of the most frightening people in pictures. It would be easy to dismiss him as a hopeless ham, an actor drunk on power (and drink), and either laughable or disconcerting as a result of his reckless exaggeration. But he was a profound man, very talented, often troubled, and well aware of the compromises he was making. Movies sometimes seem too small for him—as they did for Charles Laughton. He heard strange voices and might do uncanny things if a project held his attention and stilled his arrogance. He put himself into his children (ten of them from three wives—one of whom was actress Mary Ure) and his novels. Perhaps he scorned movies. But he gave us moments of a child's passion in a fierce man's body, of gaiety suddenly consumed by a thundercloud.

His movie record is an odd one. For nearly twenty years he played supporting parts, seldom forgettable, but a flop whenever he starred. It was only in 1973, as a comic rogue, Doyle Lonnegan, exactly suited to the comic-strip adventure of *The Sting* (73, George Roy Hill), that he became an established star. He was nearly twenty years waiting for that: *The Dam Busters* (55, Michael Anderson); *Sea Fury* (58, Cy Endfield); *The Valiant* (62, Roy Baker); *Tomorrow at Ten* (62, Lance Comfort); a startling blond Russian in *From Russia with Love* (63, Terence Young); *The Caretaker* (63, Clive Donner); *The Luck of Ginger Coffey* (64, Irvin Kershner); shrill cheerfulness only signaling violent temper as Henry VIII in *A Man for All Seasons* (67, Fred Zinnemann); mangling an American accent in *Custer of the West* (67, Robert Siodmak); *The Royal Hunt of the Sun* (68, Irving Lerner); *The Battle of Britain* (69, Guy Hamilton); *Figures in a Landscape* (70, Joseph Losey); *A Reflection of Fear* (71, William Fraker); very good as Lord Randolph Churchill in *Young Winston* (72, Richard Attenborough); *The Hireling* (73, Alan Bridges); *The Taking of Pelham 1,2,3* (74, Joseph Sargent); as Quint in *Jaws* (75, Steven Spielberg); identical twins in *Diamonds* (75, Menahem Golan); the Sheriff of Nottingham in *Robin and Marian* (76, Richard Lester); *End of the Game* (76, Maximilian Schell); *Swashbuckler* (76, James Goldstone); the Israeli in *Black Sunday* (77, John Frankenheimer); another barnacle-encrusted sea-dog in *The Deep* (77, Peter Yates); and *Avalanche Express* (79, Mark Robson).

Norma Shearer (Edith Norma Shearer)
(1904–93), b. Montreal, Canada

It is only reasonable that the wife of an enigma should be difficult to account for. Undoubtedly, her highest fame owed itself to the determination of her husband, Irving Thalberg, that she should be "the first lady of Hollywood." But it would be facile to allege simply that she happened to marry the right man. If not a star, she was at least a moderate success before the marriage, while it seems clear that she and Thalberg were deeply in love. Perhaps this was because they had so much in common. Like her husband, Norma Shearer was very hardworking, utterly practical, and seemingly fully conscious of the way packaging and publicity could enhance performance. Equally, Thalberg's promotion of her bypassed the fact—evident to anyone who cares to look at her films—that she was fluttery, chilly, and more nearly vacant than any other goddess. Lillian Hellman talks of Shearer's "face unclouded by thought." (Even her fans have to decide whether or not she had a squint.)

She was the daughter of the president of a construction company, and she studied at the Canadian Royal Academy of Music. After working briefly in a music store, she was taken to New York by an ambitious mother to be placed in movies. But she seldom got beyond extra and bit parts, reputedly in D. W. Griffith's *Way Down East* (20) and *The Flapper* (20, Alan Crosland), at Trans-Atlantic and Biograph. She went back to Montreal and worked as a model (she was Miss Lotta Miles for tire ads) before renewing her attack through several small production companies: *The Bootleggers* (22, Roy Sheldon); *Channing of the Northwest* (22, Ralph Ince); *The Man Who Paid* (22, Oscar Apfel); and *A Clouded Name* (23, Austin O. Huhn).

She was then signed up by Louis B. Mayer, who tested her worth in John M. Stahl's *The Wanters* (23), handled by First National, and loaned her to Fox for *The Wolf Man* (24, Edmund Mortimer) with John Gilbert and to Paramount for *Empty Hands* (24, Victor Fleming). MGM repossessed her with *Pleasure Mad* (23, Reginald Barker) and *Broken Barriers* (24, Barker), and she had a great success in a Lon Chaney film, *He Who Gets Slapped* (24, Victor Sjöström). By now, she was under Thalberg's control and he cast her with John Gilbert in *The Snob* (24, Monta Bell), and built her up as a sophisticated woman in comedies and romances: *Lady of the Night* (25, Bell); *Excuse Me* (25, Alf Goulding); *His Secretary* (25, Hobart Henley); *Pretty Ladies* (25, Bell); with Chaney again in *The Tower of Lies* (25, Sjöström); *A Slave of Fashion* (25, Henley); Benjamin Christensen's *The Devil's Circus* (26); and *Upstage* (26, Bell).

Even so, her impact remained modest, and if Thalberg had not married her in 1927 it is possible that Mayer would have dropped her—though not her brother, Douglas, who led the studio's sound department. Shearer was quickly elevated into one of MGM's leading ladies in Lubitsch's *The Student Prince in Old Heidelberg* (27); *The Demi-Bride* (27, Robert Z. Leonard); *The Latest from Paris* (28, Sam Wood); *The Actress* (28, Sidney Franklin); *A Lady of Chance* (29, Leonard); *The Trial of Mary Dugan* (29, Bayard Veiller)—hers and MGM's first all-talking drama; Franklin's *The Last of Mrs. Cheyney* (29); *Their Own Desire* (30, E. Mason Hopper); *Let Us Be Gay* (30, Leonard); and *The Divorcee* (30, Leonard), for which she won the best actress Oscar.

Having reached this peak, she was gradually withdrawn from circulation, first by having a child, then with Thalberg's death, but throughout as an assertion of her special, rarefied quality. Would that the films supported this attitude: *Strangers May Kiss* (31, George Fitzmaurice); Clarence Brown's *A Free Soul* (31); Franklin's *Private Lives* (31); Leonard's *Strange Interlude* (32), in which the gulf between her and the O'Neill material is comic; Franklin's *Smilin' Through* (32); Edmund Goulding's *Riptide* (34); and, notoriously, as Elizabeth Barrett Browning in Franklin's *The Barretts of Wimpole Street* (34). Then, despite a disastrous preliminary attempt in *The Hollywood Revue of 1929*, she persuaded Thalberg to mount *Romeo and Juliet* (36) for her, directed by George Cukor.

With Thalberg's death, in 1936, Shearer was something of an embarrassment to MGM, chiefly because she was a large stockholder. In 1938, she played *Marie Antoinette* (W. S. Van Dyke) amid rumors that the studio wanted to be free of her. In fact, it is one of her better performances; much sillier was Clarence Brown's *Idiot's Delight* (39) in which she wore a blonde wig. In the same year, she was the central figure in Cukor's *The Women*, the best film in which she appeared and arguably the only good one. She worked out her contract with Mervyn Le Roy's *Escape* (40), a fanciful war story; *We Were Dancing* (42, Leonard); and, finally, Cukor's *Her Cardboard Lover* (42). She then retired and refused several offers to return.

She married again, to Marti Arrougé, and then she went into a decline marked by loss of sight, failing memory, depression, and what she believed was a version of the mental illness that had beset her sister, Athole. Her looks had gone and she had long white hair. One of her last visitors was detained by Shearer's unreachable anxiety. She held the man's hand: "Are you Irving? Were we married?" she asked.

Ally (Alexandra Elizabeth) **Sheedy**,
b. New York, 1962

A lot of people were delighted to see the performance given by Ally Sheedy as the reclusive, neu-rotic photographer, Lucy Berliner, in *High Art* (98, Lisa Cholodenko). It wasn't just the evidence of a real, mature actress that worked—somehow the actress and her director managed to convey the sense that Lucy was a genuine artist who had photographed the film. But that was already sev-eral years ago, and Sheedy (who has come back from drug problems, to say nothing of a very pre-cocious youth) now faces the ordinary difficulties that confront forty-year-old actresses.

She is the daughter of an advertising executive and of the literary agent Charlotte Sheedy. As such, she had an excellent education and unusual opportunities. She attended the Bank Street School and was a child dancer with the American Ballet Theatre. Then she began writing: her chil-dren's book, *She Was Nice to Mice,* was published in 1974, and she sometimes served as a teenage movie reviewer for the *Village Voice.* As an actress, she began in 1981 on TV in *I Think I'm Having a Baby,* and was soon a regular as a teenager in movies—often with Molly Ringwald (the Charlotte to Sheedy's Emily Brontë?).

There has been a lot of TV, and probably too much of everything, but these are the highlights: her movie debut, as Sean Penn's girlfriend in *Bad Boys* (83, Rick Rosenthal); with Matthew Broder-ick in *WarGames* (83, John Badham); with Rob Lowe in *Oxford Blues* (84, Robert Boris); *The Breakfast Club* (85, John Hughes); *St. Elmo's Fire* (85, Joel Schumacher); as Gene Hackman's daughter in *Twice in a Lifetime* (85, Bud Yorkin); *Blue City* (86, Michelle Manning); *Short Circuit* (86, Badham), with a robot; *Maid to Order* (87, Amy Jones); *She's Having a Baby* (88, Hughes); *Heart of Dixie* (89, Martin Davidson); *Fear* (90, Rockne S. O'Bannon).

She was still second banana in *Betsy's Wedding* (90, Alan Alda); *Only the Lonely* (91, Chris Columbus); *Home Alone 2: Lost in New York* (92, Columbus); on TV in *Chantilly Lace* (93, Linda Yellen); *The Pickle* (93, Paul Mazursky); with a dog in *Man's Best Friend* (93, John Lafia); and more and more dismal TV until *High Art.*

Sad to say, that fine film led nowhere. But Sheedy is married now, with a child of her own. An autobiography would not lack for material.

Martin Sheen (Ramon Estevez),
b. Dayton, Ohio, 1940

Sheen is known for his productivity—for the quantity of his own work, for the great variety of liberal causes he serves, and for a family of actors that includes his two sons, Emilio Estevez and Charlie Sheen. Rather in the spirit of a union leader who will talk at any gathering, Sheen has done many forgettable films. Sometimes, it seems, he has lost his youthful and ironic edge under the weight of jobs. But there have been enough

instances of outstanding work for us to stay alert. He runs the risk of being typecast in rectitude and social responsibility (such a curse!), but there are demons in Sheen, as witness the indolent, casual humor of his Charles Starkweather in *Badlands* (73, Terrence Malick) and his unyielding commit-ment to *Apocalypse Now* (79, Francis Ford Cop-pola), especially in the early scene in the hotel room.

He had worked on the stage before getting into movies: *The Incident* (67, Larry Peerce); *The Sub-ject Was Roses* (68, Ulu Grosbard), which he had done on the stage; *Catch-22* (70, Mike Nichols); a conscientious objector in *No Drums, No Bugles* (71, Clyde Ware); *Pickup on 101* (72, John Flo-rea); *Rage* (72, George C. Scott); for TV in *The Execution of Private Slovik* (74, Lamont Johnson); *The Cassandra Crossing* (77, George Pan Cos-matos); *The Little Girl Who Lives Down the Lane* (77, Nicolas Gessner); *Eagle's Wing* (79, Anthony Harvey); *The Final Countdown* (80, Don Taylor); *Loophole* (80, John Quested); *Enigma* (82, Jean-not Szwarc); the journalist in *Gandhi* (82, Richard Attenborough); as Judge Samuel Salus II in *In the King of Prussia* (82, Emile de Antonio); *Man, Woman and Child* (82, Dick Richards); *That Championship Season* (82, Jason Miller); *The Dead Zone* (83, David Cronenberg); and *Firestarter* (84, Mark L. Lester).

He narrated *Broken Rainbow* (85, Maria Flo-res), an Oscar-winning documentary about the Navajo; he acted in a melodrama about Santeria, *The Believers* (87, John Schlesinger); and then helped narrate the letters-from-Vietnam docu-mentary, *Dear America* (87, Bill Couturie). After *Siesta* (87, Mary Lambert), he played a union offi-cial to his son Charlie Sheen's financier in *Wall Street* (87, Oliver Stone) and then son to Barnard Hughes in *Da* (88, Matt Clark), on which he was also executive producer.

He also acted in and helped produce *Judgment in Berlin* (88, Leo Penn); *Beverly Hills Brats* (89, Dimitri Sotirakis); *Cadence* (91), which he wrote and directed and in which he acted with his two sons; and *Hear No Evil* (93, Robert Greenwald).

Between *Hear No Evil* and now, the Interna-tional Movie Database lists more than seventy act-ing jobs for Martin Sheen. And it's being modest, for just one of those is *The West Wing,* in which, for three seasons now, Sheen has been our most appealing current president (and maybe the hard-est working). He does many narrating jobs, which might be handled in a day. But he also seems ready to consider any project offered, especially those with a liberal pull to them. But how strange that an actor should make so many minor films and be the cherished lead in a hit TV series at the same time: *The Killing Box* (93, George Hicken-looper); as Robert E. Lee in *Gettysburg* (93, Ronald Maxwell); *Fortunes of War* (93, Thierry

Nitz); *Roswell* (94, Jeremy Paul Kagan); an assistant to Michael Douglas in *The American President* (95, Rob Reiner); Dillinger in *Dillinger and Capone* (95, Jon Purdy); *Captain Nuke and the Bomber Boys* (95, Charles Gale); *The War at Home* (96, Emilio Estevez); *Truth or Consequences, N.M.* (97, Kiefer Sutherland); *Free Money* (98, Yves Simoneau); *A Letter from Death Row* (98, Marvin Baker and Bret Michaels); *Voyage of Terror* (98, Brian Trenchard-Smith); *Stranger in the Kingdom* (98, Jay Craven); a President in *Family Attraction* (98, Brian Hecker); *Lost & Found* (99, Jeff Pollack); *O* (01, Tim Blake Nelson).

Ron Shelton, b. Whittier, California, 1945
1988: *Bull Durham*. 1989: *Blaze*. 1992: *White Men Can't Jump*. 1994: *Cobb*. 1996: *Tin Cup*. 2000: *Play It to the Bone*. 2002: *Dark Blue*. 2003: *Hollywood Homicide*.

One can hear Ron Shelton asking, "But isn't everyone interested in sports?" Well, no, actually, plenty of men aren't, and most women regard it as one of the ways of diverting their child-men. More to the point, for the men who are crazy about sports, there is television's real-life ongoing documentary account—filmed with the care and the cameras usually reserved for Spielberg and Hitchcock. What is left, therefore? Well, there are some decent, and forgivable, sports movies, and *Bull Durham* is one of them. *Tin Cup* is fun. But the question remains how the likable Ron Shelton has the patience and the narrowness to persist. (We also have to add to the above list *Blue Chips*, 1994, a basketball movie, with Nick Nolte and Shaquille O'Neal, actually directed by William Friedkin, but written and coproduced by Shelton.)

Shelton was a college star at basketball and baseball, and he was a few years in the Baltimore Orioles system before deciding he wasn't good enough. A wide variety of jobs led to screenwriting and second-unit work: *The Pursuit of D. B. Cooper* (81, Roger Spottiswoode); *Under Fire* (83, Spottiswoode); *The Best of Times* (86, Spottiswoode), about high-school football and its aftermath.

Of course, Shelton has hit into the rough: *Blaze* is about politics, and *White Men* is a passable comedy on race. *Cobb*, however, concerns bigotry, malice, and the media as well as indulging Tommy Lee Jones. But I have to say that despite the fact that I watch too much sports live on TV, few directors depress me more.

Sam Shepard (Samuel Shepard Rogers),
b. Fort Sheridan, Illinois, 1943
After thirty-five years in the performing arts, and at least half that time hanging around moviemak-

ing, Sam Shepard remains an enigma—and America does not really have much patience with unsolved mysteries. He is a frequent actor these days—he was even nominated for best supporting actor for his Chuck Yeager in *The Right Stuff* (83, Philip Kaufman). Yet he seems impeded by the notion that it is not quite manly to pretend in public. As Yeager, he did just about serve in Kaufman's idealization of a lanky, laconic Gary Cooper figure. But Shepard seemed impervious to depth or nakedness, and his Mach 1 cowboy was not as rich or intriguing as the far more sprightly, energetic, and commercially compromised Yeager—a grinning imp who looks over Shepard's shoulder at one moment in the film.

Then again, when Shepard's play *Fool for Love* had its world premiere at the Magic Theater in San Francisco in 1984, with Ed Harris and Kathy Baker, Shepard's direction was so visual and dynamic it seemed to signal his desire to make movies. After all, as a writer he had created a vision of poor, rural, and familial violence that smacked of film and surely influenced many filmmakers, even if few of his plays have reached the screen. But in 1985, Shepard did the script and contributed a glum, helpless appearance to Robert Altman's wretched film of *Fool for Love*, so that memories of the evening at the Magic were eclipsed. When Shepard did direct a film at last—*Far North* (88), which he also wrote—it seemed that much of his own excitement had drained away.

Not the least part of the mystery is Shepard's relationship with Jessica Lange. They have lived together, often in Virginia, with children and horses. *Vanity Fair* ran a photo spread of the couple glamorous enough to inspire imitation, scenario, and advertising. But the relationship has remained private: whenever they have worked together, there has been an air of convalescence, or going gently, as if one of them were ill and the other working as a nurse—*Frances* (82, Graeme Clifford), where Shepard is a loyal prop; *Country* (84, Richard Pearce), in which rural life is so much cleaner than in, say, *Buried Child* or *Crime of the Starving Class; Crimes of the Heart* (86, Bruce Beresford); and *Far North*. Am I alone in hoping for one great bloody fight between the two of them on screen—for something like *Fool for Love* even?

There are other things to mention: Shepard helped write *Me and My Brother* (68, Robert Frank) and *Zabriskie Point* (70, Michelangelo Antonioni); he acted in *Renaldo and Clara* (78, Bob Dylan), after he had been on Dylan's Rolling Thunder Revue. He was the rich man in *Days of Heaven* (78, Terrence Malick), the first film that saw his iconic value, and which never asked for more. He was also in *Resurrection* (80, Daniel Petrie); *Raggedy Man* (81, Jack Fisk); *Baby Boom*

(87, Charles Shyer)—either selling out his harsh, intractable heritage or testifying to the charm of Diane Keaton; *Steel Magnolias* (89, Herbert Ross); *Defenseless* (91, Martin Campbell); *Bright Angel* (90, Michael Fields); and *The Pelican Brief* (93, Alan J. Pakula). He directed *Silent Tongue* (92).

I have three other things to say: (1) his script for *Paris, Texas* (84, Wim Wenders) may have been embroidered, improved upon, and improvised upon, but it is his contribution to film that comes closest to the poetic sundering of family in his best plays; (2) he really acts in *Voyager* (91, Volker Schlöndorff), that remarkable parable of coincidence and incest, about family being put back together; and (3) his book of sketches, views, and moods from the road, *Motel Chronicles*, is one of those books movie people seem to have read. Its influence on the urge to road pictures, loneliness, and a fateful wildness is very large.

I think it's to be regretted that Shepard has acted so often lately (without anyone noticing how little he brings to the party). For he seems to have been distracted from theatre. Even when writing a play—*The Late Henry Moss*—his mind seemed to be wandering. But there is, in view, another collaboration with Wim Wenders—*In America* (02). Meanwhile, he is a rather gloomy presence in *The Pelican Brief* (93, Alan J. Pakula); *Safe Passage* (94, Robert Allan Ackerman); *The Good Old Boys* (95, Tommy Lee Jones); as Pea-Eye Parker in *Streets of Laredo* (95, Joseph Sargent); *Lily Dale* (96, Peter Masterson); *The Only Thrill* (97, Masterson); *Purgatory* (99, Uli Edel); with Judy Davis in *Dash and Lily* (99, Kathy Bates); *Curtain Call* (99, Peter Yates); *Snow Falling on Cedars* (99, Scott Hicks); the Ghost in *Hamlet* (00, Michael Almereyda); *All the Pretty Horses* (00, Billy Bob Thornton); *The Pledge* (01, Sean Penn); *After the Harvest* (01, Jeremy Podeswa); *Swordfish* (01, Dominic Sena); *Shot in the Heart* (01, Agnieszka Holland); the increasingly dismayed commander in *Black Hawk Down* (01, Ridley Scott).

Larissa Shepitko (1939–79),
b. Armtervosk, USSR
1961: *Slepoj Kukhar/The Blind Cook* (s). 1962: *Zhivaya Voda/Living Water* (s). 1963: *Znoj/Heat.* 1966: *Krylya/Wings.* 1968: *The Homeland of Electricity* (not released until 1987). 1972: *Ty i Ya/You and I.* 1977: *Voskhozhdeniye/The Ascent.*

Larissa Shepitko could hardly help being a romantic figure—for she was as close to beautiful as film directors can hope to come. In addition, she had been a young student of Dovzhenko and had helped his widow, Yulia Solntseva, complete *Poem of the Sea* (58). She was also a spokesperson for new moods and hopes in Soviet life, a harbinger of thaw. Then, finally, she and several members of her crew were killed in a car crash near Moscow,

so that her husband, Elem Klimov, was left to complete her last project—*Farewell* (81).

In her best work, *You and I* and *The Ascent,* Shepitko tackled modern morality issues with vigor and boldness. *The Ascent,* set during the Second World War, won the Golden Bear at Berlin, and it is likely that Shepitko would have left for America. How would that have worked out? Why would a real artist have wanted to escape (or miss) what has happened in the old Soviet Union in the last ten years? Sooner or later, a terrifying new Russian cinema will be revealed.

Ann Sheridan (Clara Lou Sheridan)
(1915–67), b. Denton, Texas
Called the "Oomph Girl" by Warners, Ann Sheridan always appeared too intelligent to be merely a glamour queen. Far more versatile than Hollywood ever allowed, she had an unusually broad face, a wide, full-lipped mouth, and eyes set far apart. Asked to be sultry, she invariably appeared to be making fun of her admirers.

Trained as a teacher, she won a beauty contest, the prize of which was a test at Paramount, where she made her debut in *Search for Beauty* (34, Erle C. Kenton). She remained with Paramount for two years, generally wasted on bit parts, but with larger roles in *Behold My Wife* (35, Mitchell Leisen), *The Glass Key* (35, Frank Tuttle), and *Mississippi* (35), an Edward Sutherland musical. In 1936, she was put under contract by Warners, originally for musicals—Ray Enright's *Sing Me a Love Song* (36)—but most successfully as the romantic interest in gangster films. She appeared in Mayo's *Black Legion* (36), Dieterle's *The Great O'Malley* (37), and Lloyd Bacon's *San Quentin* (37) in small parts, and was then worked up in B-picture leads, including three directed by John Farrow: *She Loved a Fireman* (38); *Little Miss Thoroughbred* (38); and *Broadway Musketeers* (38), another musical.

She was loaned to Universal for *Letter of Introduction* (38, John M. Stahl) and returned to thrillers as the good girl opposite Cagney in Curtiz's *Angels with Dirty Faces* (38), then with John Garfield in *They Made Me a Criminal* (39, Busby Berkeley). After another musical, *Naughty But Nice* (39, Enright) and playing a floozy in *Dodge City* (39, Curtiz), she was publicized by Warners as a wartime sex symbol: *Castle on the Hudson* (40, Anatole Litvak); Lewis Seiler's *It All Came True* (40); William Keighley's *Torrid Zone* (40), where she sings like Lauren Bacall's elder sister, throws sandwiches at Cagney, and generally lolls about; Raoul Walsh's *They Drive by Night* (40); and Litvak's *City for Conquest* (40). Her extra knowingness worked well in these hard-boiled films, but she was quickly switched to more conventional, dramatic films: at first excellent in Keighley's *The Man Who Came to Dinner* (42) and Sam Wood's

King's Row (42), but wasted in Milestone's *Edge of Darkness* (43) and back to musicals in David Butler's *Shine On, Harvest Moon* (44).

After the war, she was never again as successful, and after two women's pictures—*Nora Prentiss* (47, Vincent Sherman) and *The Unfaithful* (47, Sherman)—and Raoul Walsh's Western, *Silver River* (48), Warners did not renew her contract. She reacted by making *Good Sam* (48, Leo McCarey) and then one of America's most sophisticated comedies, Howard Hawks's *I Was a Male War Bride* (49). No question of whether she understands the joke of that film. But as a freelancer, her career declined and she made a few musicals and romances at Universal: *Woman on the Run* (50, Norman Foster); Pevney's *Just Across the Street* (52); excellent as the woman with a past in *Take Me to Town* (53, Douglas Sirk), a musical. She was as good as ever in Tourneur's *Appointment in Honduras* (53) and better than either film deserved in *Come Next Spring* (55, R. G. Springsteen) and *The Opposite Sex* (56, David Miller). She made one more film, *Woman and the Hunter* (57, George Breakston), in Britain, and was a regular on the TV soap, *Another World,* before her death from cancer.

She married three actors, one of whom was George Brent.

Jim Sheridan, b. Dublin, Ireland, 1949

1989: *My Left Foot.* 1990: *The Field.* 1993: *In the Name of the Father.* 1997: *The Boxer.* 2002: *In America.*

There are so many reasons to hope for a lively film business in Ireland. The country has all the creative stimulus of being "on the edge" of Europe. For most of the history of the movies it has known the ferment of battles with England for independence, and with Northern Ireland over union. That struggle has served to mask the deeper confrontation between modernism, free thinking, Europe, and enlightenment and a repressive social system, the Catholic Church, determined existence on the fringe, illiteracy, poverty, and a strange, willful brutality. Then again, Ireland is a land of actors, writers, and storytellers. One way or another, it has given to the movies through the careers of Rex Ingram, John Ford, John Huston, Orson Welles, Barry Fitzgerald, Brian Donlevy, Greer Garson, Maureen O'Hara, Cyril Cusack, Richard Harris, Peter O'Toole, John Boorman, and Neil Jordan—to say nothing of Scarlett O'Hara.

Still, for decades, it proved very hard for the Irish to make *their* films. Neil Jordan has managed it, though most of his Irish pictures are small stories that might have happened elsewhere. And Jordan has made repeated moves to get away. Jim Sheridan's career as a director is thumpingly Irish, and so successful that it has woken the whole

world up to the possibility, the necessity even, of Irish material.

Sheridan was educated at University College, Dublin, and he studied film at NYU. He has worked in the theatre as director and playwright, and he has been involved in the writing of his three pictures. His pictures take very different tacks on Ireland—*My Left Foot* is about that eternal Irish hero, a dangerous, warped genius who would not be ignored; *The Field* is a pastoral epic, strongly influenced by the plays of Synge and O'Casey; and the third, *Father,* is the greedy gobbling up of *the* subject, "the problem."

The Field is the one failure, as if Sheridan was himself too modern, too urban, to inhabit the theme of the dispossessed peasant patriarch. (The difficulty may have something to do with Richard Harris being a coarser actor than Daniel Day-Lewis.) Evidently, Lewis made *My Left Foot* not just because of his assured impersonation of so many handicaps but because of his insistence on the emotional danger—the sexiness—within all the physical problems.

As for *In the Name of the Father,* it is made with a bludgeon. But why not? What else would suit the story better? The case of the Guildford Four (in truth, several more than four) is such a disgrace to the English police and legal system, and so brimming with natural drama, it *had* to be made. And it is one of those films that might help alter our politics. It is, along the way, crude, evasive, manipulative—none of which matters too much. There is an air of "J'Accuse" to the film that dominates and surpasses failings.

Sheridan the director is still rather hidden. Can he do "quiet" subjects? What would he do in a peaceful Ireland? Perhaps then he would turn to the pressing subtext of all three films—the suffocating warmth of the Irish family. When you add to Sheridan's credits as a director-writer the fact that he also wrote *Into the West* (93, Mike Newell) and helped write and produce *Some Mother's Son* (96, Terry George), it's clear how far he has cornered the market in modern troubled Irish stories. What would become of him if ever Ireland settled its differences? Some chance! His characters inhabit an Anglo-Irish antagonism that transcends immediate problems or disadvantages. So Sheridan is a kind of poet of grievance. That said, the handicap faced by the hero in *My Left Foot* felt more passionate than that of anyone suffering wrongful imprisonment. Sheridan's work is hardly conceivable without Daniel Day-Lewis, though he has a terrific ear and eye for urban speech and the tight warren of Irish cities and English prisons. But the luck of urgency and excellence has declined: *My Left Foot* is his best film; *In the Name of the Father* feels a little too tricky to be trusted—and it seeks little else; and *The Boxer* is the most conventional. But recently, he has served as producer on several Irish projects: *Agnes Browne* (99, Anjelica Huston); *Borstal Boy* (00, Peter Sheridan); *On the Edge* (00, John Carney); *Bloody Sunday* (01, Paul Greengrass).

Lowell Sherman (1885–1934),

b. San Francisco

1930: *Lawful Larceny; The Pay-Off.* 1931: *Bachelor Apartment; The Royal Bed; High Stakes.* 1932: *The Greeks Had a Word for Them; Ladies of the Jury; False Faces.* 1933: *She Done Him Wrong; Morning Glory; Broadway Thru a Keyhole.* 1934: *Born to Be Bad.* 1935: *Night Life of the Gods.*

An urbane and romantic actor, Lowell Sherman's brief career as a director showed real promise: *Morning Glory* is a crucial film in Katharine Hepburn's early career; Mae West was seldom as lewd as in *She Done Him Wrong;* and *Born to Be Bad* was a stylish women's picture with Cary Grant and Loretta Young. It was a modest talent, but Sherman was scheduled to direct *Becky Sharp—* the first full color film—when he died, and might have been an established figure in a few more years.

He had gone over to directing after a successful career as an actor during the 1920s: *Way Down East* (20, D. W. Griffith); *The Gilded Lily* (21, Robert Z. Leonard); *The Face in the Fog* (22, Alan Crosland); *Monsieur Beaucaire* (24, Sidney Olcott); *Lost at Sea* (26, Louis J. Gasnier); *You Never Know Women* (26, William Wellman); with Garbo in *The Divine Woman* (28, Victor Sjöström); *The Garden of Eden* (28, Lewis Milestone); *A Lady of Chance* (28, Leonard); *The Whip* (28, Charles J. Brabin); *General Crack* (29, Crosland); with Barbara Stanwyck in *Ladies of Leisure* (30, Frank Capra); *Mammy* (30, Michael Curtiz); *Midnight Mystery* (30, George B. Seitz); *Oh! Sailor, Behave!* (30, Archie Mayo); as the alcoholic movie director in *What Price Hollywood?* (32, George Cukor).

That last role was typecasting, for Sherman was famous as a laconic drunk, the kind of man who declined to hide his perplexity at being a success in anything as silly as movies. Cukor thought he was brilliant just because of his "slightly odious quality." Those were the days.

Elisabeth Shue,

b. South Orange, New Jersey, 1963

How tempting it is in Hollywood to see turning points. Yet how hard it can be, even with the energy of transformation, to be in charge of one's own career. Elisabeth Shue had been around for over ten years. She was blonde, pretty, and apparently one of that large gang. Nothing she had done had really suggested unusual depth or force. Then she got the role of Sera, the hooker, in *Leaving*

Las Vegas (95, Mike Figgis), and delivered one of the great performances in modern American film, one so rounded that the reawakened passion and honesty in her role left room for us to see all the weakness and dishonesty that have got Sera where she is. She was nominated as best actress, and though she lost—to Susan Sarandon in *Dead Man Walking*—there was the hope that she moved at a different level now.

Alas, not so. The only change was that she was regarded as sexier now, and soiled. She could not assert herself enough to change direction or organize a career. And so the films before *Las Vegas* and the films after it are sadly consistent: *The Karate Kid* (84, John G. Avildsen); with Terence Stamp and a lot of monkeys in *Link* (86, Richard Franklin); *Adventures in Babysitting* (87, Chris Columbus), a modest hit; Tom Cruise's girlfriend in *Cocktail* (88, Roger Donaldson); *Back to the Future, Part II* (89, Robert Zemeckis); *Back to the Future, Part III* (90, Zemeckis); dumped for Kim Basinger in *The Marrying Man* (91, Jerry Rees); *Soapdish* (91, Michael Hoffman); *Twenty Bucks* (93, Keva Rosenfeld); *Heart and Souls* (93, Ron Underwood); *The Underneath* (94, Steven Soderbergh); *The Trigger Effect* (96, David Koepp); *Deconstructing Harry* (97, Woody Allen); *The Saint* (97, Phillip Noyce); *Cousin Bette* (98, Des McAnuff); *Palmetto* (98, Volker Schlöndorff); *Molly* (99, John Duigan); *Hollow Man* (00, Paul Verhoeven); *Amy & Isabelle* (01, Lloyd Kramer) on TV; *Leo* (02, Mehdi Norowzian); *Tuck Everlasting* (02, Jay Russell).

M. Night (Manoj Nelliyattu) Shyamalan,

b. Pondicherry, India, 1970

1992: *Praying with Anger.* 1998: *Wide Awake.* 1999: *The Sixth Sense.* 2000: *Unbreakable.* 2002: *Signs.*

A few years ago, it would not have seemed possible that a young Indian (under thirty) might go to the citadel and get $10 million as a fee for directing a film like *Unbreakable.* Of course, there was a reason for this: *The Sixth Sense,* written and directed by M. Night Shyamalan, was a box-office sensation, the second biggest grosser of its year. It was also one of the most touching and surprising ghost stories ever put on screen, a tender portrait of a child's pained imagination (and thus the start of Haley Joel Osment), and a very welcome sign that there might yet be a way of reclaiming soul or spirit in the defiled horror genre.

Now, *Unbreakable* (it seemed to me) was awful, obscure, and as private as *Sixth Sense* had been expansive. But *The Sixth Sense* repays further viewings; it is very well acted (not least by Bruce Willis); and it remains one of those pictures that give one hope for Hollywood.

That said, Shyamalan is still very young. He

came to the United States as a child, the son of two successful doctors. So he was raised in comfort (in the Philadelphia area—still his beat), and educated at Episcopal Academy in Lower Merion and New York University's Tisch School of the Arts. He had a Super-8 camera as a child. He churned out homemade movies, and he set his goal as being the next, unexpected Steven Spielberg. There are resemblances: the genuine interest in imagination and children—he also scripted *Stuart Little* (99, Rob Minkoff). *Praying with Anger* describes a trip back to India, while *Wide Awake* is a good picture about a boy coming to terms with the death of his grandfather.

There are obvious threats ahead, wrapped up in dollars: Shyamalan could yield to sentiment and horror (he took on the name Night himself). On the other hand, he could be a director of unique stature and force. *Signs* will be a big picture from Disney, and the first step towards an answer.

George Sidney (1916–2002), b. New York
1941: *Free and Easy.* 1942: *Pacific Rendezvous.* 1943: *Pilot No. 5; Thousands Cheer.* 1944: *Bathing Beauty.* 1945: *Anchors Aweigh; The Harvey Girls.* 1946: *Holiday in Mexico.* 1947: *Cass Timberlane.* 1948: *The Three Musketeers.* 1949: *The Red Danube.* 1950: *Annie Get Your Gun; Key to the City.* 1951: *Show Boat.* 1952: *Scaramouche.* 1953: *Kiss Me, Kate; Young Bess.* 1955: *Jupiter's Darling.* 1956: *The Eddie Duchin Story.* 1957: *Jeanne Eagels; Pal Joey.* 1960: *Who Was That Lady?; Pepe.* 1963: *Bye Bye Birdie; A Ticklish Affair.* 1964: *Viva Las Vegas.* 1966: *The Swinger.* 1967: *Half a Sixpence.*

Sidney's work was seldom distracted from fond portraits of showbiz glamour. As well as biopics, he liked backstage stories, as witness the traveling theatricals of *Scaramouche* and *Show Boat*, the nightclub of *Pal Joey*, the show within the show of *Kiss Me, Kate.* There is no depth to his movies, but a variable surface dazzle and vivid coloring.

The child of actors, he played small film parts as a child, and in 1932 joined MGM as a second-unit director. He made shorts for most of the 1930s and was promoted to major musicals during the war, often starring Gene Kelly. His most important projects—*Annie Get Your Gun, Show Boat,* and *Kiss Me, Kate*—are not the most enjoyable. Much better are *The Harvey Girls, The Three Musketeers,* and especially, *Scaramouche, Jeanne Eagels, Pal Joey,* and *Who Was That Lady?* If he has a special characteristic, it is his skill at deriving an extra, animated voluptuousness from such as Lana Turner, Esther Williams, Kim Novak, and Ann-Margret. *Half a Sixpence,* his last film, was as competent as his best work.

But consider the real pleasures of "My Funny Valentine" in *Pal Joey,* Elvis and Ann-Margret

shaking together in *Viva Las Vegas,* and the "On the Atcheson, Topeka, and Santa Fe" number in *The Harvey Girls.*

Sylvia Sidney (Sophia Kosow) (1910–99),
b. Bronx, New York
The daughter of a Romanian father and a Russian mother, Sylvia Sidney studied at the Theater Guild School and made her stage debut in 1926. She flourished and Fox gave her a part in *Thru Different Eyes* (29, John Blystone). But it was Paramount that really took her up, originally as a replacement for Clara Bow in Mamoulian's *City Streets* (31). She followed this with the pregnant girl in the rowing boat in Von Sternberg's *An American Tragedy* (31) and Goldwyn borrowed her for a similarly anguished role in King Vidor's *Street Scene* (31). She was also in three pictures for Marion Gering: *Ladies of the Big House* (32), *Pick-Up* (33), and a second Dreiser dramatization, *Jennie Gerhardt* (33).

Although one of Paramount's most prized properties, she was unhappy with the number of "victim" parts she was given: for example, in the remake of *The Miracle Man* (32, Norman Z. McLeod). The fact remains that she is most memorable in such films, partly because her eyes so readily pictured dismay and shed glowing tears. Her lighter films are less striking: Dorothy Arzner's *Merrily We Go to Hell* (32); two more Gering films, *Madame Butterfly* (33) and *Thirty Day Princess* (34); Mitchell Leisen's *Behold My Wife* (35); and Wesley Ruggles's *Accent on Youth* (35).

Both the studio's faith in her and her departure from Paramount in 1935 owed something to the fact that B. P. Schulberg, one of the studio executives, fell in love with her at the cost of his own marriage. She was put under contract by Walter Wanger, she was married very briefly to Bennett Cerf, and then made a series of outstanding movies in which she seldom escaped ordeal, disaster, and travail: William K. Howard's *Mary Burns, Fugitive* (35); Henry Hathaway's *The Trail of the Lonesome Pine* (36); as Mrs. Verloc in Hitchcock's *Sabotage* (36), compelled by dynamic editing to stick Oscar Homolka with the carving knife; an especially unhappy experience in Wyler's *Dead End* (37); and the female lead in Fritz Lang's first three American films: *Fury* (36), *You Only Live Once* (37), and *You and Me* (38). In all of these, she caught exactly the fragile happiness allowed in Lang's world and played with a restraint that perfectly matched the fatal simplicity of the plots. There are close-ups in *Fury* of Sidney watching Spencer Tracy in a burning jail that are as harrowed as Lillian Gish close-ups.

She was married now to actor Luther Adler. After Dudley Murphy's *One Third of a Nation* (39), and *The Wagons Roll at Night* (41, Ray

Enright), she exchanged movies for the theatre, making a brief return at the end of the war, in Frank Lloyd's *Blood on the Sun* (45); *Mr. Ace* (45, Edwin L. Marin); Dieterle's *The Searching Wind* (46); and *Love from a Stranger* (47, Richard Whorf). She was away for a while, and then appeared in Milestone's *Les Miserables* (52); Fleischer's *Violent Saturday* (55); and *Behind the High Wall* (56, Abner Biberman).

She made a comeback in *Summer Wishes, Winter Dreams* (73, Gilbert Cates); Dora Bloch in *Raid on Entebbe* (76, Irvin Kershner); *I Never Promised You a Rose Garden* (77, Anthony Page); *Damien—Omen II* (78, Don Taylor); *Siege* (78, Richard Pearce); *The Gossip Columnist* (79, James Sheldon); *The Shadow Box* (80, Paul Newman); *A Small Killing* (81, Steven Hilliard Stern); *F.D.R.: The Last Year* (80, Anthony Page); *Having It All* (82, Edward Zwick); *Hammett* (83, Wim Wenders); *Order of Death* (83, Roberto Faenza); *Finnegan Begin Again* (85, Joan Micklin Silver); *An Early Frost* (86, John Erman); *Pals* (87, Lou Antonio); *Beetlejuice* (88, Tim Burton); *Andre's Mother* (91, Deborah Reinisch); *Used People* (93, Beeban Kidron); and, finally, in *Mars Attacks!* (96, Burton).

Don Siegel (1912–91), b. Chicago

1946: *The Verdict*. 1947: *Night Unto Night*. 1949: *The Big Steal*. 1952: *No Time for Flowers; Duel at Silver Creek*. 1953: *Count the Hours; China Venture*. 1954: *Riot in Cell Block 11; Private Hell 36*. 1955: *An Annapolis Story/The Blue and the Gold*. 1956: *Invasion of the Body Snatchers; Crime in the Streets*. 1957: *Spanish Affair; Baby Face Nelson*. 1958: *The Gun Runners; The Line-Up*. 1959: *Edge of Eternity; Hound Dog Man*. 1960: *Flaming Star*. 1962: *Hell Is for Heroes*. 1964: *The Killers; The Hanged Man*. 1967: *Stranger on the Run*. 1968: *Madigan; Coogan's Bluff*. 1969: *Death of a Gunfighter* (codirected with Robert Totten); *Two Mules for Sister Sara*. 1970: *The Beguiled*. 1971: *Dirty Harry*. 1972: *Charley Varrick*. 1974: *The Black Windmill*. 1976: *The Shootist*. 1977: *Telefon*. 1979: *Escape from Alcatraz*. 1980: *Rough Cut*. 1982: *Jinxed!*.

There were postwar American directors who seemed more occupied by keeping in work than by pursuing their talent, but Siegel was one of the most admirable survivors. Never quite a leading director, he vindicated modesty of scale; deliberately viewing himself as something of a misfit, he looked like the last upholder of orthodoxy. He made few films that are not personal, inventive, and interesting. Some are exceptional works that transcend limitations of budget, time, and script. Almost alone, Siegel usefully extended the conception of the Hawksian hero, observed action without brutality, treachery without dismay, and romance without glamour. If anything, his films became more terse, more drily amused, and more economically exciting. He is a test case of the intelligent, unpretentious entertainer.

Siegel was educated at Jesus College, Cambridge, and graduated with a B.A. In America, Hal Wallis got him a job in the film library at Warners. From cutting in stock shots, he rose to be head of the Montage Department, an editor, and an occasional second-unit director. The training at Warners was what Siegel made of it, shooting montage sequences in the style of the studio's directors. His montages were outstanding: especially good ones are to be seen in Curtiz's *Yankee Doodle Dandy* and *Casablanca*.

In 1945, he directed two shorts for Warners, *A Star in the Night* and *Hitler Lives?*, both of which won Oscars. Then his career as a features director was launched with *The Verdict*, a Victorian thriller starring Sydney Greenstreet and Peter Lorre. Its fogbound London makes a sophisticated contrast with the incisive leads. That and *The Big Steal*, a delicious RKO comedy thriller with Mitchum and Jane Greer, are his best early films. Others are less happy: *Duel at Silver Creek* is a weirdly naïve narrated Western.

It was with *Riot in Cell Block 11*, produced by Walter Wanger, that Siegel began to develop his own theme of an outsider figure gazing balefully at society. *Private Hell 36* showed the sort of inconsistency that was still spoiling all his films, but *Invasion of the Body Snatchers* was a simple, ingenious conception carried out at least three-quarters adequately. It had a sure sense of rural atmosphere, a talent for filling in character quickly, and a reluctance to allow melodrama to smother wit. *Body Snatchers* is exemplary science fiction because it needs no visual tricks and knows that zombies and vital people look alike.

The next years could not avoid the vagaries of the job market, but whenever good material came his way, Siegel exploited it with the sureness of a professional sportsman. *Crime in the Streets* was one of his first treatments of the modern city; *Baby Face Nelson* was a minor gangster masterpiece, turning the bizarre figure of Mickey Rooney to exceptional advantage; *The Line-Up* was a very influential study of two hired killers increasingly lost in a strange city.

By the 1960s, Siegel had earned himself a reputation for expertise so great that he was called upon to do several TV pilots. In the cinema, he salvaged *Hound Dog Man* against vast odds and ensured that *Flaming Star* was the best of Elvis Presley's films. Then came two more substantial successes—*Hell Is for Heroes* and *The Killers*, the first a lucid study of war psychopathy, the second a reworking of the Hemingway double-cross story that had an intriguingly flawed romantic relationship between John Cassavetes and Angie Dickinson. *The Hanged Man* and *Stranger on the Run* were eighty-minute TV movies way above average, while *Madigan* was the first in a sequence of films that dealt with an aggressive cop-hero who pragmatically straddled the law. Steve McQueen in *Hell Is for Heroes,* Lee Marvin in *The Killers,* and Richard Widmark in *Madigan* had all been additions to Siegel's gallery of tough, solitary heroes.

That figure was then taken over by Clint Eastwood in an unusually fertile actor-director relationship. *The Beguiled* is an amusing excursion into the Southern backwoods during the Civil War, with the lying, lusting Eastwood destroyed by vigorous lady neurotics; *Two Mules for Sister Sara* was too slow; but *Coogan's Bluff* and *Dirty Harry* are among Siegel's best films. Eastwood was a strong, commercial personality who could have overwhelmed Siegel. But Siegel was as adept at maneuver and as effortlessly to the point as Marvin's character in *The Killers.* With at least half a dozen movies to count in the records of postwar American cinema he begins to emerge as one of Jesus College's most unexpectedly notable alumni.

Although briefly married to actress Viveca Lindfors (whom he directed in *Night Unto Night* and *No Time for Flowers*), Siegel's cinema has scant time for women, apart from the hothouse of *The Beguiled.*

Dirty Harry, for instance, has women only as the killer's victims, as Harry's briefly mentioned dead wife, and as strippers lurid in night-town. The lone cop in that film is emotionally shriven, preoccupied by the impossible demands society makes of him and by his unarticulated independent code of honor. *Dirty Harry* is clearly a character near to Siegel's view of himself: a battered survivor who lives in a criminal, psychopathic jungle and who eventually throws away his badge, frustrated by the compromises of the law and politics.

The end of *Dirty Harry* is more painful than all the film's physical violence, for it is a picture of rough decency despairing of intractability. Few films suggested so subtly how a cop might turn into an outlaw. Ironically, Siegel had difficulty in persuading Eastwood to go through with the scene (in the way that directors sometimes have to wheedle actresses out of their clothes). Perhaps that speaks for the probing seriousness Siegel had reached beneath a crime picture's hard surface.

In his last years, Siegel faltered. *The Shootist* is a solid, respectful vehicle, and *Charley Varrick* is an outstanding example of Siegel's irony. His influence on Eastwood has proved lasting, and touching. After Siegel's death, Eastwood said, "If there is one thing I learned from Don Siegel, it's to know what you want to shoot and to know what you're seeing when you see it." A very American credo.

Simone Signoret (Simone Kaminker) (1921–85), b. Wiesbaden, Germany

Gallantry cannot conceal the thought that few women, so dazzling at thirty, faded so much by fifty. As the tart in *La Ronde* (50, Max Ophuls), the Renoir-like blonde in *Casque d'Or* (52, Jacques Becker), and the adulteress in *Thérèse Raquin* (53, Marcel Carné), she was moody, sensual, and glowing like a greengage. But those features became lost in overweight, and her brooding face went sour with dismay. It was a great loss, and it was interpreted as part of her indifference to glamour and her commitment to serious, political issues. Perhaps so, but she made no film as serious as *La Ronde,* and lost beauty is a more cinematic tragedy than some famous causes.

She made her debut toward the end of the war: *La Boîte aux Rêves* (43, Yves Allégret, her first husband); *Les Démons de l'Aube* (45, Allégret); *Macadam* (46, Marcel Blistène); *Dedée d'Anvers* (48, Allégret); to England for *Against the Wind* (48, Charles Crichton); *Manèges* (49, Allégret); and *Le Traqué* (50, Frank Tuttle). By the mid-1950s, her reputation began to spread beyond France: as one of the plotters in *Diabolique* (55, H. G. Clouzot); *Evil Eden* (56, Luis Buñuel); in an episode from *Die Vind Rose* (56, Yannik Bellon); *Les Sorcières de Salem* (57, Raymond Rouleau); very good as the older woman in *Room at the Top* (58, Jack Clayton), a relic of the British view of French sophistication and winner of the best actress Oscar; *Les Mauvais Coups* (60, François Leterrier); *Adua e le Compagne* (60, Antonio Pietrangeli); *Le Jour et l'Heure* (62, René Clément); opposite Olivier in *Term of Trial* (62, Peter Glenville); *Dragées au Poivre* (63, Jacques Baratier); *Ship of Fools* (65, Stanley Kramer); *The Sleeping Car Murders* (65, Costa-Gavras); *Is Paris Burning?* (66, Clément); *The Deadly Affair* (67, Sidney Lumet); *Games* (67, Curtis Harrington); as Arkadina in *The Seagull* (68, Lumet); *L'Armée des Ombres* (69, Jean-Pierre Melville); *L'Aveu* (70, Costa-Gavras), with Yves Montand, her husband since 1951; *Comptes à Rebours* (70, Roger Pigaut); *L'Américain* (70, Marcel Bozzuffi); and *Rude Journée pour la Reine* (73, René Allio).

She had an immense personal triumph as *Madame Rosa* (77, Moise Mizrahi), offering her decline into ruggedness as part of a very sentimental philosophy, and carrying the film to a best foreign-language picture Oscar. She also played in *Judith Therpauve* (78, Patrice Chereau) and *L'Adolescente* (79, Jeanne Moreau); *Chère Inconnue* (81, Mizrahi); and *L'Etoile du Nord* (82, Pierre Granier Deferre).

Jean Simmons, b. London, 1929

English actresses have often complained of inadequate opportunity in their own industry. Jean Simmons struck out for America in that spirit, and surely had the makings of a vivacious, flirty comedienne.

She was educated at the Aida Foster School and went into British films in her teens: *Give Us the Moon* (44, Val Guest); *Kiss the Bride Goodbye* (44, Paul L. Stein); *Meet Sexton Blake* (44, John Harlow); *Mr. Emmanuel* (44, Harold French); *Caesar and Cleopatra* (45, Gabriel Pascal); *The Way to the Stars* (45, Anthony Asquith); as Estella in *Great Expectations* (46, David Lean); *Hungry Hill* (46, Brian Desmond Hurst); as a Gauguin dancing girl in *Black Narcissus* (47, Michael Powell); *Uncle Silas* (47, Charles Frank); *The Woman in the Hall* (47, Jack Lee); as a blonde Ophelia in *Hamlet* (48, Laurence Olivier).

It was to follow her husband-to-be, Stewart Granger, and to escape the creeping gentility of *The Blue Lagoon* (48, Frank Launder); *Adam and Evelyne* (49, French), with Granger; *Trio* (50, French); *Cage of Gold* (50, Basil Dearden); *The Clouded Yellow* (50, Ralph Thomas); and *So Long at the Fair* (50, Terence Fisher and Anthony Darnborough) that she left for America in 1950. Her first two years there were spent under contract to Howard Hughes; it was an indecisive period, shadowed by his desire to control her, terminated in 1952, but responsible for the "Bride Comes to Yellow Sky" an episode from *Face to Face* (52, Bretaigne Windust), *Affair with a Stranger* (53, Roy Rowland), *She Couldn't Say No* (54, Lloyd Bacon), and far more important, her wide-eyed murderess in *Angel Face* (52), one of Otto Preminger's most refined studies of obsession and possibly a sign of Hughes's admiration for his unhappy actress.

Englishness then put her in dull costume films: very effective in *Young Bess* (53, George Sidney); but only a stooge in *Androcles and the Lion* (52, Chester Erskine); *The Robe* (53, Henry Koster); and *The Egyptian* (54, Michael Curtiz). She was much better as the young hopeful in *The Actress* (53, George Cukor); appeared to enjoy herself opposite Brando in *Désirée* (54, Koster); as Sister Sarah, singing like a sweet bell in *Guys and Dolls* (55, Joseph L. Mankiewicz); and in *A Bullet Is Waiting* (54, John Farrow) as a tomboy. But plain films set in: *Footsteps in the Fog* (55, Arthur Lubin), made back in England with Granger; earnestly notorious as *Hilda Crane* (56, Philip Dunne); *This Could Be the Night* (57, Robert Wise); *Until They Sail* (57, Wise); *The Big Country* (58, William Wyler); *This Earth Is Mine* (59, Henry King); especially *Spartacus* (60, Stanley Kubrick), in which she could not quite suppress the giggles. But she was remarkably good as the disturbed wife in *Home Before Dark* (58, Mervyn Le Roy) and, married now to Richard Brooks, she played the Aimee Semple McPherson evangelist in his *Elmer Gantry* (60), a large and worthwhile part, if one that neglected her sense of mischief;

seen briefly, in fur coat and underwear, in *The Grass Is Greener* (60, Stanley Donen). She has worked sparingly since then, and with discouraging results: *All the Way Home* (63, Alex Segal); as Mrs. Lampton in *Life at the Top* (65, Ted Kotcheff); *Mister Buddwing* (65, Delbert Mann); *Divorce American Style* (67, Bud Yorkin); *Rough Night in Jericho* (67, Arnold Laven); *The Happy Ending* (69, Brooks); the deplorable *Say Hello to Yesterday* (71, Alvin Rakoff). She played in *Mr. Sycamore* (74, Pancho Kohner); *Dominique* (78, Michael Anderson); *Beggarman, Thief* (79, Lawrence Doheny); *Golden Gate* (81, Paul Wendkos); *Jacqueline Susann's Valley of the Dolls* (81, Walter Grauman); *A Small Killing* (81, Steven Hilliard Stern); *Midas Valley* (85, Gus Trikonis); *Going Undercover* (88, James Kenelm Clarke); *The Dawning* (88, Robert Knights); *Inherit the Wind* (88, David Greene); and, for British TV, she played Miss Havisham in *Great Expectations* (89, Kevin Connor).

In recent years, she has worked for TV: *Laker Girls* (90, Bruce Seth Green); *People Like Us* (90, William Hale); *Sensibility and Sense* (90, David Hugh Jones); *Dark Shadows* (91, Rob Bowman and Dan Curtis); *One More Mountain* (94, Dick Lowry); *How to Make an American Quilt* (95, Jocelyn Moorhouse); *Daisies in December* (95, Mark Haber); *Her Own Rules* (98, Bobby Roth).

Michel Simon (François Simon) (1895–1975), b. Geneva, Switzerland

When people see *Boudu Sauvé des Eaux* (32, Jean Renoir) or *L'Atalante* (34, Jean Vigo) for the first time, they sometimes ask, "Was Michel Simon really like that?" It is a revealing question, that shows the trace of threatened bourgeois in all of us at Simon's sprawling, unclean satyr, and points at the special mingling of self and character that is so necessary (and dangerous) in screen acting.

The answer to the question perhaps is, "No, yet that is as he wanted to be and was afraid of becoming." Renoir has admitted that his own pursuit of improvisation with actors began with Simon, and these studies in unrestrained behavior influenced the most creative strain of French cinema—both actors and directors. Thus Belmondo's excellent impersonation of Simon in *Pierrot le Fou* is not only a tribute to an actor, but an acknowledgment that Boudu's aimless purity is one of the ideals that haunts Ferdinand/Pierrot/Belmondo.

Few actors have had so rich and lasting an impact as Simon sitting braced in doorways, swimming on a tabletop, spitting in books, cleaning his shoes with a bedspread, or taking to the Seine as naturally as a seal bored with land. It is said that *Boudu* is a minor Renoir film, and that may be so, but for Simon it was the part of a lifetime. His Jules in *L'Atalante* is a dark extension of Boudu, an ugly, secretive man who has been all over the world, keeps severed hands in a jar, and is tattooed like an aboriginal. Again, notably, he is a river creature, too rank, overwhelmingly private, and innately alien for polite society.

Simon was a boxer, a photographer, and an acrobat before he went into the theatre in Geneva in 1920. His film career had a Boudu-like wandering, as if he could not tolerate organization, or directors were cautious about such primal energy. He was still an actor who might carry away a film. *La Vocation d'André Carrel* (25, Jean Choux); *Feu Mathias Pascal* (25, Marcel L'Herbier); seen briefly in *La Passion de Jeanne d'Arc* (28, Carl Theodor Dreyer); *Tire-au-Flanc* (28, Renoir); *L'Enfant de l'Amour* (31, L'Herbier); *Jean de la Lune* (31, credited to Choux, but largely directed by Simon himself); *On Purge Bébé* (31, Renoir); as the deceived bourgeois who perhaps wanders away to be a tramp in *La Chienne* (31, Renoir); *De Haut en Bas* (33, G. W. Pabst); *Le Lac-aux-Dames* (34, Marc Allégret); *Le Bonheur* (34, L'Herbier); *Sous les Yeux d'Occident* (36, Allégret); *Faisons un Rêve* (36, Sacha Guitry); *Drôle de Drame* (37, Marcel Carné); *Les Disparus de Saint-Agil* (38, Christian-Jaque); as Michele Morgan's odious guardian in *Quai des Brumes* (38, Carné); *La Belle Etoile* (38, Jacques de Baroncelli); *La Fin du Jour* (39, Julien Duvivier); *Fric-Frac* (39, Claude Autant-Lara); *La Comédie du Bonheur* (40, L'Herbier); as Scarpia in *La Tosca* (40, begun by Renoir, but directed by Karl Koch); *Au Bonheur des Dames* (43, André Cayatte); *Panique* (46, Duvivier); as the Devil in *La Beauté du Diable* (49, René Clair); *La Poison* (51, Guitry); *La Vie d'un Honnête Homme* (52, Guitry); as Shylock in *Il Mercante di Venezia* (52, Pierre Billon); *Saadia* (53, Albert Lewin); *Les Trois Font la Paire* (57, Clément Duhour); *Austerlitz* (60, Abel Gance and Roger Richebé); *Candide* (60, Norbert Carbonnaux); *Cyrano et d'Artagnan* (63, Gance); *The Train* (65, John Frankenheimer); *Le Vieil Homme et l'Enfant* (66, Claude Berri); *Contestazione Generale* (70, Luigi Zampa); *La Maison* (70, Gerard Brach); unerringly medieval in *Blanche* (71, Walerian Borowczyk); *La Più Bella Serata della Mia Vita* (72, Ettore Scola); and *L'Ibis Rouge* (75, Jean-Pierre Mocky).

Simone Simon, b. Bethune, France, 1910

It was a small, pretty face, a little pinched round the nose and slanted in the eyes. Her first appearance in *La Bête Humaine*, in 1938, has her caressing a silken cat. But it was five years before the cinema realized that Simone Simon had a feline cast to her features. The connection was made with stunning effect in *Cat People* (43, Jacques Tourneur), Val Lewton's first horror film, about a frigid girl who comes to believe that she descends from a race of Balkan cat-worshippers. The idea ripens on that pensive face, without violently dra-

matic eruptions of whiskers or teeth, but with every nuance of a personality being overpowered. Simon was restored to screen life in the sequel, *The Curse of the Cat People* (44, Robert Wise and Gunther von Fritsch), as the dead wife reinvented as a playmate for the little girl. It was part of Lewton's plan and Tourneur's skill that so beguiling a face should become menacing without any distortion except for the impinging background darkness. In the first film, especially, her unease with English supports the sense of occult, while her buttoned-up prettiness is a poignant sign of sexual inhibition.

Simon had been in French films since 1931, but without leaving a special imprint: *Le Chanteur Inconnu* (31); *Mam'zelle Nitouche* (31, Marc Allégret); *La Petite Chocolatière* (32, Allégret); *Le Roi des Palaces* (32, Carmine Gallone); *Un Fils d'Amérique* (32, Gallone); *Le Lac-aux-Dames* (34, Allégret); and *Les Beaux Jours* (35, Allégret). In 1936 she went to America, returning only for the restless wife in *La Bête Humaine* (38, Jean Renoir). Renoir offered her the part of Christine in *La Règle du Jeu,* but she asked for an American-scale salary and was abandoned.

As well as the two "cat" films, her American period includes *Girls' Dormitory* (36, Irving Cummings); *Seventh Heaven* (37, Henry King); *Josette* (38, Allan Dwan); *All That Money Can Buy* (41, William Dieterle); *Tahiti Honey* (43, John Auer); excellent as the laundress in *Mademoiselle Fifi* (44, Wise); and *Johnny Doesn't Live Here Any More* (44, Joe May). After the war, she returned to France and worked in Britain and Italy: *Pétrus* (46, Allégret); *Temptation Harbor* (47, Lance Comfort); *Donna Senza Norme* (49); as the chambermaid in *La Ronde* (50, Max Ophüls); as the girl in the "La Modèle" episode from *Le Plaisir* (52, Ophüls); *The Extra Day* (56, William Fairchild); and *La Femme en Bleu* (72, Michel Deville). Since then she has worked only in the theatre.

Don (Donald) **Simpson** (1945–96),
b. Seattle, Washington

Don Simpson behaved like someone who half hoped, half believed he was already in a movie, and one of his strategies with filmmakers was to seem more melodramatic, more dangerous and sensational than anything they could bring to him. So it's worth noting that he often pushed himself in front of the camera, while in James Toback's *The Big Bang* (89), he presents a good portrait of the black-garbed, happy, self-destructive adventurer.

The psychological case history that lay behind this, and hustled him to his early death (as a victim of drugs, booze, mounting crisis, and willful lack of control), is not settled in Charles Fleming's book, *High Concept: Don Simpson and the Hollywood Culture of Excess*, because Fleming is too easily seduced by Simpson's own glee. Does it matter whether or not there was something challenging, or interesting, in Simpson's tortured progress?

He could be intensely cynical in his pronouncements—"We have no obligation to make history. We have no obligation to make art. We have no obligation to make a statement. Our obligation is to make money." Well, of course, he did that, but the anti-statement just quoted is so deeply hewn in movie rock you can't escape his desperate, adolescent dream of significance. He was a Sammy Glick who would have hired Budd Schulberg to write that book, and in his lurid, kid's way he had a true sense of how a certain kind of movie was abomination in the eyes of academia—and perfect Don Simpson. He had had an intense religious upbringing—of a sort he scorned and rejected—but in truth he was a little like Norman Mailer's Marion Faye, cut with . . . with, Norman, why not, a furious ball of energy waiting and hoping to explode, determined to take as many with him as possible. He deserved some big crash, but it was God's gentle rebuke to off him quietly, while sitting on the toilet, reading about Oliver Stone.

He had spent much of his youth in Anchorage, Alaska, before entering the University of Oregon. On graduating, he went into movie publicity, thence to the Paramount of Barry Diller and Michael Eisner, where he rose to be president of production by 1981; one of his biggest coups at Paramount was *An Officer and a Gentleman* (82, Taylor Hackford)—he had an odd taste for militaristic codes. By 1983, he was off on his own in partnership with Jerry Bruckheimer, and they together developed a special kind of physically destructive movie that is almost entirely without resonance.

His great works as producer or executive producer are *Flashdance* (83, Adrian Lyne); *Beverly Hills Cop* (84, Martin Brest); *Thief of Hearts* (84, Douglas Day Stewart); *Top Gun* (96, Tony Scott); *Beverly Hills Cop II* (87, Scott); *Days of Thunder* (90, Scott); *The Ref* (94, Ted Demme), his most worthwhile film; *Bad Boys* (95, Michael Bay); *Crimson Tide* (95, Scott); *Dangerous Minds* (95, John N. Smith); *The Rock* (96, Bay).

What else can one say about a self-declared Genghis Khan of the popular imagination than that Tony Scott and Michael Bay were his favored instruments?

Frank Sinatra (1915–98),
b. Hoboken, New Jersey
Although a regular screen performer for twenty-five years, during which he had two distinct triumphs as a popular singer—one as a band crooner, the other as the first great exponent of the long-playing record—Sinatra's film work has only a few successes amid many indifferent and ill-chosen projects. The surly charm of the runt's ugliness

made him too broody, too lazy, or too bored to pick films carefully or to attend to them with due seriousness. The extraordinary flair for dramatic ballads and the complete assurance with a live audience have all too seldom shown themselves on the screen. Perhaps the "master" always preferred immediate reassurance.

There are three phases to Sinatra's film career. He began as a singer with the Tommy Dorsey band in *Las Vegas Nights* (41, Ralph Murphy) and *Ship Ahoy* (42, Edward Buzzell). His great following led to a contract with MGM, where he appeared singing, occasionally dancing, and projecting a scrawny soulfulness in *Higher and Higher* (43, Tim Whelan); *Step Lively* (44, Whelan); *Anchors Aweigh* (45, George Sidney); *It Happened in Brooklyn* (46, Richard Whorf); singing "Ol' Man River" in a white suit in *Till the Clouds Roll By* (46, Whorf); *The Kissing Bandit* (48, Laslo Benedek); *The Miracle of the Bells* (48, Irving Pichel); *Take Me Out to the Ball Game* (49, Busby Berkeley); and *On the Town* (49, Stanley Donen and Gene Kelly). In none of these did he make a lasting personal contribution to the history of the musical.

By then, his whole career was in decline. He left MGM and made *Meet Danny Wilson* (51, Joseph Pevney) at Universal. He lost a recording contract and his marriage to Ava Gardner foundered. At last, he seemed as vulnerable as he had looked. The total crisis in his life was overcome with his portrayal of Maggio in *From Here to Eternity* (53, Fred Zinnemann). Although it won the supporting Oscar, the performance is superficial. But it changed the public image of Sinatra and allowed him to mix musicals and acting. Thereafter he had the earned wryness of a lowlife victim.

Having signed with Capitol and met arranger Nelson Riddle, his records found a new popularity, and he was confident enough to spend the next five years active in Hollywood. More than that, he experimented. Most successfully, in comedy with songs he perfected the character of a moody, soft-hearted womanizer: *Young at Heart* (54, Gordon Douglas), which is in the line of those films in which John Garfield is the grit in a household of fond women; *The Tender Trap* (55, Charles Walters); as Nathan Detroit in *Guys and Dolls* (55, Joseph L. Mankiewicz); *High Society* (56, Walters); and *Pal Joey* (57, George Sidney). These are the films that made the largest screen contribution to Sinatra's image of offhand glamour.

But in the same period he set up two rather adventurous movies: *Suddenly* (54, Lewis Allen), in which he is a would-be presidential assassin, indulging tough-guy fantasies and very credibly malicious; and a coward in *Johnny Concho* (55, Don McGuire). They are ambitious but strained films, better than the grandiose silliness of *Not as a Stranger* (55, Stanley Kramer) and *The Pride and the Passion* (57, Kramer). Best of all, Sinatra played a drug addict with startling pain in *The Man with the Golden Arm* (56, Otto Preminger), and was most at ease in *The Joker Is Wild* (57, Charles Vidor), a vague biopic of comedian Joe E. Lewis (about an entertainer who falls foul of the mob), and *Some Came Running* (58, Vincente Minnelli), one of the few movies in which he permitted himself to appear vulnerable—and unusually moving for that.

At this stage, his interest in movies was consumed in the thought that the Pack should appear together in films. If those movies adequately reflect the society of that group, no wonder Sinatra looked more disgruntled with the years. After a bad comedy—*A Hole in the Head* (59, Frank Capra)—and a terrible musical—*Can-Can* (60, Walter Lang)—he appeared with entourage in *Ocean's 11* (60, Lewis Milestone); *Sergeants Three* (62, John Sturges); *Four for Texas* (63, Robert Aldrich); and *Robin and the Seven Hoods* (64, Gordon Douglas). Worse than these, his judgment seemed to have deserted him, for he took on one lame project after another: *The Devil at Four O'Clock* (61, Mervyn Le Roy); *Come Blow Your Horn* (63, Bud Yorkin); *None But the Brave* (65, directed by Sinatra); *Marriage on the Rocks* (65, Jack Donohue); *Von Ryan's Express* (65, Mark Robson); *Assault on a Queen* (66, Donohue); and *The Naked Runner* (67, Sidney J. Furie).

Only *The Manchurian Candidate* (62, John Frankenheimer) used his real abilities until 1967 when he played *Tony Rome* (67, Douglas). That film was deeply nostalgic of Chandler and Bogart, but it did contain the marvelous image of a soured Sinatra watching chloroform poured on a rag for himself and saying "when." He stayed with Douglas for the deeper disenchantment of *The Detective* (68) and for a Tony Rome sequel, *Lady in Cement* (68). Only one other film—*Dirty Dingus Magee* (70, Burt Kennedy)—appeared before his retirement in 1971. He had given up movies long before.

He returned once more to movies, or to television, as a cop against the Mob in *Contract on Cherry Street* (77, William A. Graham); and then he played a cop whose wife is dying in the dark-etched *The First Deadly Sin* (80, Brian G. Hutton). He took a cameo role in *Cannonball Run II* (84, Hal Needham).

What all of this misses, I think, is Sinatra's pervasive influence on American acting: he glamorized the fatalistic outsider; he made his own anger intriguing; and in the late fifties, especially, he was one of our darkest male icons. It helps illustrate the interaction of singing and acting. Sinatra is a noir sound, like saxophones, foghorns, gunfire, and the quiet weeping of women in the background.

Bryan Singer, b. New York, 1965
1993: *Public Access*. 1995: *The Usual Suspects*. 1998: *Apt Pupil*. 2000: *X-Men*. 2003: *X2*

The Usual Suspects won an Oscar for its screenwriter, Christopher McQuarrie, and he may yet prove the most interesting person behind *Suspects*. As it is, McQuarrie's first directing job, *The Way of the Gun*, is rather better than *Apt Pupil* or *X-Men*—and Singer is supposedly at work on *X-Men 2*.

Singer is a graduate of the USC film school, where he made the unreleased *Lion's Den*. He then wrote *Public Access*, about a man who develops a cable TV talk show for sinister reasons. *The Usual Suspects* was an enormous advance on that, a film buff's homage, but a very witty exploration of the noir mood, beautifully acted. It's sad to think that that sensibility is already caught up in *X-Men*, and enough to suggest that the interest in noir legend was more technical than human. *Apt Pupil* (from a Stephen King story) is another portrait of a smart kid getting lost in the real world—and maybe a warning sign. So we come back to the first question: where did the intelligence in *The Usual Suspects* come from?

Robert Siodmak (1900–73),
b. Memphis, Tennessee
1929: *Menschen am Sonntag* (codirected with Edgar G. Ulmer). 1930: *Abschied*. 1931: *Der Mann, der Seinen Morder Sucht; Voruntersuchung*. 1932: *Sturme der Leidenschaft; Le Sexe Faible; Quick*. 1933: *Brennendes Geheimnis*. 1934: *La Crise est Finie*. 1935: *La Vie Parisienne; Mister Flow*. 1937: *Cargaisons Blanches*. 1938: *Mollenard; Ultimatum* (codirected with Robert Wiene). 1939: *Pièges*. 1941: *West Point Widow*. 1942: *Fly-by-Night; My Heart Belongs to Daddy; The Night Before the Divorce*. 1943: *Someone to Remember; Son of Dracula*. 1944: *Phantom Lady; Cobra Woman; Christmas Holiday*. 1945: *The Suspect; The Strange Affair of Uncle Harry/Uncle Harry; The Spiral Staircase*. 1946: *The Killers; The Dark Mirror*. 1947: *Time Out of Mind*. 1948: *Cry of the City; Criss Cross*. 1949: *The Great Sinner; The File on Thelma Jordon*. 1950: *Deported*. 1951: *The Whistle at Eaton Falls*. 1952: *The Crimson Pirate*. 1953: *Le Grand Jeu*. 1955: *Die Ratten*. 1956: *Mein Vater, der Schauspieler*. 1957: *Nachts, Wenn der Teufel Kam*. 1959: *Dorothea Angermann; The Rough and the Smooth; Bitter Sweet*. 1960: *Der Schulfreund*. 1961: *L'Affaire Nina B*. 1962: *Escape from East Berlin*. 1964: *Der Schut; Der Schatz der Azteken*. 1965: *Die Pyramide der Sonnengottes*. 1968: *Custer of the West* (codirected with Irving Lerner). 1969: *Der Kampf um Rom*.

When he was only a year old, Siodmak's parents moved to Leipzig. As a young man he worked as a stage director, and in the 1920s he made and lost a fortune in banking. By 1925, he was assisting Kurt Bernhardt as an editor and scenarist, and in 1929, with Edgar Ulmer, Billy Wilder, Fred Zinnemann, and Eugene Schuftan, he made *Menschen am Sonntag*, a casual, free portrait of young people more French in feeling than German and, arguably, more in key with Ulmer's later work than Siodmak's. Nevertheless, *Abschied* and *Vorunter-suchung* showed a special skill with sound and a sensitivity that made him unusual in German cinema. With Nazism, he left Germany for Paris and did not really settle until he reached Hollywood in 1940.

Like many Germans, Siodmak thrived in America, quickly learning to blend the melodrama of German cinema, its visual expressionism, and the technical facilities of the big studios. He was never more than an assignment director, but he never lost a mordant sense of humor, narrative economy, a relish for actors and actresses, a special care for interiors, and a readiness to extract the best from the system. His American films are made with a proper awareness of the limits and potential of each project. Thus *The Great Sinner* is meant as silly vibrato where many lesser men might have labored hopelessly after the real Dostoyevsky; *Son of Dracula* is all in the spirit of lugubriousness with which a coffin arrives at a lonely railway station bearing the inscription ALUCARD; *Phantom Lady* is an excellent thriller, using Franchot Tone and Ella Raines very well; *Cobra Woman* is Maria Montez (as twins) in full idiotic splendor—at one point the good lady describes some subplot as "a wild dream of her decaying brain"; *The Spiral Staircase* is truly frightening, and extracts every ounce of tension from Dorothy McGuire as a deaf-mute; *Uncle Harry* is one of the few films to abandon George Sanders the cad and discover a meek, put-upon man bullied by sisters; *The Suspect* is enlivened by Charles Laughton's presence and by the unusual rapport that Siodmak obtained with him. *The Killers* is a thriller that exploits the postwar fashion for realism more creatively than was usual and has a clumsy spontaneity in the actual robbery; *The File on Thelma Jordon* knows what a mistress of the medium Barbara Stanwyck is; and *The Crimson Pirate* is boys' knockabout as bright and snappy as Christmas crackers. Time and again, humdrum material proves more entertaining than one would have suspected.

Siodmak's return to Germany was accompanied by a general slackening, and *The Rough and the Smooth*, made in England, and *Custer of the West* (though commonplace) are rather better than the German pictures.

That's what I wrote about Siodmak in 1975. All I want to add is that it's not enough. Siodmak was more than just an entertainer. Looking closely at *Criss Cross* is what opened my eyes. Yes, it's a noir

thriller, seemingly, with a cleverly constructed script by Daniel Fuchs. But Lancaster's doomed hero in *Criss Cross*—a sweet, tough sucker, a very subtle character—helps explain the fatalism of *The Killers*. And there are links to the irony and humor in *The Suspect* and *Uncle Harry*, rare studies of plain decency driven to break the law. Siodmak had not just a great eye but a way of seeing life. He was an artist, and he deserves fuller retrospectives.

Douglas Sirk (Claus Detlev Sierck) (1900–87), b. Hamburg, Germany
1935: *'Twas een April; April, April; Das Madchen vom Moorhof; Stutzen der Gesellschaft.* 1936: *Schlussakkord; Das Hofkonzert; La Chanson du Souvenir.* 1937: *Zu Neuen Ufern; La Habañera.* 1939: *Accord Final; Boefje.* 1943: *Hitler's Madman.* 1944: *Summer Storm.* 1946: *A Scandal in Paris.* 1947: *Lured.* 1948: *Sleep, My Love.* 1949: *Slightly French; Shockproof.* 1950: *Mystery Submarine.* 1951: *The First Legion; Thunder on the Hill; The Lady Pays Off; Weekend with Father.* 1952: *Has Anybody Seen My Gal?; No Room for the Groom; Meet Me at the Fair.* 1953: *Take Me to Town; All I Desire.* 1954: *Taza, Son of Cochise; Magnificent Obsession; Sign of the Pagan.* 1955: *Captain Lightfoot; All That Heaven Allows.* 1956: *There's Always Tomorrow; Written on the Wind.* 1957: *Battle Hymn; Interlude; The Tarnished Angels.* 1958: *A Time to Love and a Time to Die.* 1959: *Imitation of Life.* 1975: *Sprich mit mir wie der Regen* (s). 1977: *Sylvesternacht* (s). 1978: *Bourbon Street Blues* (s).

Chairs and professorships in cinema studies, proliferating college courses on the art of film, institutes, archives, doctoral dissertations—all have hauled the movies into the academic world. But teachers of film to Americans, for instance—and nowhere is the lust for worth more pronounced—should still be wary of choosing raw American cinema for their material. If they do, then be sure that the directors are such as Orson Welles, John Ford, Hitchcock, John Huston, or Martin Scorsese. If they want to risk an academic dean reappraising their program, or students doubting their own loyalty, begin with the roots of cinema—melodrama—and base a course on Griffith, Lon Chaney, John Stahl, Val Lewton, Frank Borzage, Joan Crawford, and Douglas Sirk.

Cinema—as an entertainment, an art form, an academic topic, or an institution—is addicted to melodrama. What greater contrast of chiaroscuro is there than that between burning screen and darkened audience? Take any photograph of an intent audience, and it is an image from Fuseli: of pale faces staring out of the night. What medium is so dependent on sensation, with the screen so much larger than life and the constant threat that in a fraction of a second the image we are watching can change unimaginably? And what are the abiding themes of cinema but glamour, sexuality, fear, horror, danger, violence, suspense, averted disaster, true love, self-sacrifice, happy endings, and the wholesale realization of those hopes and anxieties that we are too shy to talk about in the daylight? Why is it dark in cinemas? So that the compulsive force of our involvement may be hidden.

Long live melodrama, and let us stress the quality of Douglas Sirk. The son of Danish parents, Sirk spent his early life in Skagen, but was a student in Munich immediately after the First World War, and then at Hamburg. His subsequent work in the theatre, as playwright and director, is given extra dignity by such biographical morsels as translation of Shakespeare sonnets and attendance at some of Einstein's lectures. Hardly a worthwhile theatrical classic is omitted from the list of Sirk's productions, at Bremen from 1923–29 and at Leipzig from 1929–36. As Nazi hostility constrained work in the theatre, Sirk moved into the German cinema (as Detlev Sierck, still) and worked at UFA.

Allowing for Sirk's inexperience and Germany's deliberate advance on the horrors, it would be understandable if those first films were uneasy or muffled. In fact, they immediately fell into the graphic fluency that distinguishes his later work. They also showed a rapid and uninhibited grasp of the principles of the melodramatic movie. In one sense they are studio concoctions: costume films, made with loving care for sets and clothes; studies of bourgeois society that employ ponderous love stories to illuminate the lifelessness and hypocrisy within that class. Their abiding cinematic themes are music, sumptuous interiors that are always "drawn" by the camera rather than "shown," and anxious beautiful women. The meaning of the films is a subdued attack on society; they know that social decorum smothers love and lovers. This is the secret hope of most audiences in that it would explain and excuse their sense of failure and disappointment. Melodrama is timeless, and the films of Sirk, Stahl, and Leisen are much closer to the Buñuel of *L'Age d'Or* than we are supposed to believe. For melodrama soothes away the romantic wound that bleeds in Buñuel. *Zu Neuen Ufern* is his best German film, and intriguingly like Hitchcock's *Under Capricorn*. The beautiful Zarah Leander (also in *La Habañera*) is a singer (how often music and musicians figure in Sirk) imprisoned in Australia for a crime committed by her lover. But whereas in *Under Capricorn*, the love between Ingrid Bergman and Joseph Cotten is saved, in *Zu Neuen Ufern* Leander is betrayed by her fluctuating lover.

A gap follows in Sirk's career. Moving westwards, he paused in Switzerland and Holland, and then went to America, first for Warners, but even-

tually to Columbia. His early years there were not happy, even if they led to several striking films. Columbia at first gave him no work, but let him free-lance: *Hitler's Madman*, made for Seymour Nebenzal and taken up by MGM, a version of the Heydrich assassination, overshadowed by Fritz Lang's *Hangmen Also Die*; another Nebenzal project, *Summer Storm*, a poignant dramatization of Chekhov's *The Shooting Party* with George Sanders as one of Sirk's finest "weak, interesting" men; *A Scandal in Paris*, with Sanders as the Parisian detective Vidocq; and *Lured*, a superbly atmospheric nineteenth-century thriller.

These films, all made quickly and cheaply, proved Sirk as a great stylist, reason enough for his neglect in an era of "forceful, sincere" directors, such as Zinnemann, Kazan, Wise, et al. I mean by "stylist" that Sirk is always thinking through lighting, camera movements, flexible composition, the values in settings, interiors, and costumes. There are no ugly or gross shots in Sirk. But, answer his critics, the material is trite. To which the proper reply is that the material is the style. Cinema lends itself to melodrama and Sirk's grace eases into appearance the furtive emotional life that we decline to admit.

Columbia only belatedly recognized Sirk, and in 1949 he returned to Germany. But by 1950 he was back in America, with Universal International. His work there is one of the isolated triumphs of the dying 1950s. In outlook, Universal was resolutely lowbrow. It does not diminish Sirk the artist to claim that such an attitude was suited to his talent. He seems to have had moderately good relations with producers Ross Hunter and Albert Zugsmith, he relished the presence there of photographer Russell Metty, and excelled in the handling of generally abused players—Rock Hudson, Jane Wyman, Robert Stack, and Dorothy Malone. Furthermore, he kept a last contact between movie melodrama and large audiences. *Magnificent Obsession, All That Heaven Allows, Written on the Wind, The Tarnished Angels,* and *Imitation of Life* are the swansong of compelling tears. Visually, they are made with a fluidity and density that are still barely acknowledged.

Supporters of Sirk's films point to their social criticism, and to the signs of seriousness coming through as he prospered. I think this is a disservice to the real Sirk, and a fallacy. *Written on the Wind* may be seen, in hindsight, as a study of insecurity in wealthy America. The same could be said of *Bigger Than Life*. But that is retrospective criticism. I do not believe that either Sirk or Ray could have spelled out that analysis as they made the films. *Written on the Wind* is as good as it is because of Sirk's conviction with the form of visual narrative, and because of the quality of overwrought performance he has gained from Stack and Malone.

Equally, *The Tarnished Angels* is not Sirk seizing on respectability and filming a long-cherished project, Faulkner's *Pylon;* but the happy coincidence of a somber, pretentious novel and the very director to fasten it down to the particulars of cinematic life. *Pylon* is a thundery book. But on screen, Sirk has the threatened romantic self-belief of Stack and Malone, the growing intelligence of Hudson, the constant pessimistic darkness of the interiors, and the sublime images of the flying sequences. That is, for me, Sirk's finest film, partly because he has resolved the novel's tension between poetry and hokum.

The more turgid seriousness of Remarque's novel makes *A Time to Love and a Time to Die* rather less of a film. The literary approach is dogged and uniform and, though the film is wonderful to look at, Sirk is daunted by the war background, and by the lusterless central playing. Melodrama on film is often a world in which a few people live amid shadow: the image sustains the thought that romantic dreams are the pivot of life. In *A Time to Love,* the CinemaScope frame bravely takes on the whole German context but cannot help but be diluted by it. So much of the film is authentic, whereas Sirk's basis is the "imitation of life" that flourishes in immature self-obsession.

Sirk shows cinema's great capacity for uncovering the lives of ordinary people. The sensibility is musical but lowbrow. What other medium can pick out the seriousness in vulgarity without condescension?

The last three works listed in the filmography are short fiction films made at the Munich film school. They are adaptations of Tennessee Williams and Arthur Schnitzler, and they are said to be remarkable.

Alf Sjöberg (1903–80),
b. Stockholm, Sweden
1929: *Den Starkaste* (codirected with Axel Lindblom). 1940: *Med livet som insats; Den Blomstertid.* 1941: *Hem fran Babylon.* 1942: *Himlaspelet/ The Road to Heaven.* 1944: *Kungajakt; Hets/ Frenzy.* 1945: *Resan bort.* 1946: *Iris och Lojtnantshjarta.* 1949: *Bara en Mor.* 1951: *Froken Julie/Miss Julie.* 1953: *Barabbas.* 1954: *Karin Mansdotter.* 1955: *Vildfaglar.* 1956: *Sista Paret ut.* 1960: *Domaren.* 1966: *On.* 1969: *Fadern/The Father.*

Sjöberg deteriorated, almost as if abashed by the eminence of his former scenarist, Ingmar Bergman. Perhaps it was a hard thing—at fifty-five or so—to become the number two in Sweden. But this interpretation obscures the fact that Sjöberg was once a major talent, with a handful of very inventive films.

He trained at the Royal Dramatic Theatre in Stockholm and went on the stage in 1927. His first film is an oddity, an utterly realistic story set in Lapland. During the 1930s he was the foremost stage director in Sweden. He became a director during the difficult war years and made two films that showed an astonishing range and sharpness considering Sweden's neutrality: *The Road to Heaven* is a b autiful fairy tale in which a young man sets out for heaven to ask for the life of his girl to be returned after she has died. Its easy creation of a spirit world amid idyllic countryside is entirely natural. *Frenzy,* however, is a claustrophobic study of sexual insecurity related to guilt and sadism that makes a very striking comment on fascism.

That film was scripted by Bergman and introduced the young Mai Zetterling. Sjöberg used her again in *Iris och Lojtnantshjarta,* about a maid left pregnant by a young officer of good family. Atmospheric, psychological, and melancholy, it shows Sjöberg's increasing camera mobility. *Bara en Mor* concerns a young woman who scandalizes society by bathing naked and is thus forced into a life of lonely drudgery; it is virtually a vehicle for the vibrant Eva Dahlbeck.

But Sjöberg's finest period is in the early 1950s. *Miss Julie,* played by Anita Bjork, is a remarkable version of Strindberg that avoids flashbacks by having past and present on screen at the same time. As so often with Sjöberg, such ingenuity seems uncontrived in the very fluid realization. Indeed, Sjöberg has a more flexible camera style, and employs movement and perspective more than is usual in Sweden. This is best demonstrated in *Barabbas,* a very complex film involving flashbacks, great use of shadow, and a marvelous period reconstruction. *Karin Mansdotter,* another period piece, is a version of Strindberg's play, *Erik XIV,* and a compelling study of increasing madness growing out of the corruption of the court.

There is no clear consistency in Sjöberg, and his last four films were ordinary, but there seems every reason to reappraise those ten years after the war.

Victor Sjöström/Seastrom (1879–1960),
b. Silbodal, Sweden
1912: *Tradgardsmastaren; Ett Hemligt Giftermal; En Sommarsaga.* 1913: *Aktenskapsbyran; Lojen och Tarar; Blodets Rost; Lady Marions Sommarflirt; Ingeborg Holm; Prasten; Lirets Konflikter.* 1914: *Karlek Starkare an Hat; Harlblod; Miraklet; Domen Icke; Bra Flicka Reder Sig Sjalv; Gatans Barn; Hogfjallets Dotter; Hjartan som Motas.* 1915: *Strejken; En av de Manga; Sonad Skuld; Skomakare bliv vid Bin Last; Judaspengar; Landshovdingens Dottrar; Havsgamarna; Det Var i Maj.* 1916: *I Provningens Stund; Skepp som Motas; Hon Segrade; Therese.* 1917: *Dodskyssen; Terje Vigen; Tosen fran Stormyrtorpet.* 1918:

Berg-Ejvind och hans Hustru/The Outlaw and His Wife. 1919: *Ingmarssonerna, pts 1 and 2; Hans nads Testamente.* 1920: *Klostret i Sendomir; Karin Ingmarsdotter; Masterman.* 1921: *Korkarlen/The Phantom Carriage.* 1922: *Vem Domer?; Eld Ombord; Det Omringade Huset.* 1924: *He Who Gets Slapped; Name the Man.* 1925: *Confessions of a Queen; The Tower of Lies.* 1926: *The Scarlet Letter.* 1928: *The Divine Woman; The Masks of the Devil; The Wind.* 1930: *A Lady to Love; Markurells i Wadkoping.* 1937: *Under the Red Robe.*

Sjöström is the father figure of Swedish cinema, a man who produced major films around 1920, went on to a varied and striking period in Hollywood, and—unlike his contemporary, Stiller—returned to influence succeeding generations. But that epitaph too easily obscures the worth of his Hollywood films and the fact that he is the author of a body of early fiction films that gives him more than a national role in cinema history. Sjöström before 1924, no matter how isolated Sweden was, is of importance in the blending of popular melodrama and intense naturalism. Thus to have founded Swedish cinema is the more significant because of Sweden's special acumen for moralizing allied to nature. All the potential of joy and anguish in sun and rain had been signaled in Sjöström's films, and with an intensity that often wears better than Griffith.

He spent much of his childhood in New York and made his Swedish debut as an actor in 1896. In 1912, he joined Svenska Bio and worked as a director and actor. He played in several of Mauritz Stiller's films: *De Svarta Maskerna* (12); *Vampyren* (13); *Nar Karleken Dodar* (13); *Thomas Graals Basta Film* (17); and *Thomas Graals Basta Barn* (18)—in the two latter he played the author/filmmaker of the title.

But Sjöström's own films were very different from Stiller's comedy of manners and identity. It accounts in part for his success in America that Sjöström had a profound feeling for narrative melodrama and for the relationship between characters and landscape. He preferred subjects that dealt with fishermen or peasants and he managed to mix social consciousness, a taste for the morbid, and a mystical view of wild scenery. *Ingeborg Holm* was a social tract about a widow who is driven mad when she has to sell her children. *Terje Vigen* is a story of the Napoleonic wars in which a fisherman becomes a recluse when his family starves while he runs the English blockade. Sjöström himself played the leading part and the theme of physical isolation expressing emotional loss is repeated in *The Outlaw and His Wife,* Sjöström's masterpiece. In it, he plays a man charged with sheep-stealing who flees to the mountains with the woman landowner who loves

him. They live there for years in solitary happiness before they are compelled to retreat farther and farther into the wilderness. Eventually they commit suicide. The great passion in the exteriors, the brooding fatalism, and the elegy that precedes it are all main themes in Swedish cinema—not least in *Elvira Madigan* and the earlier films of Bergman.

Sjöström went to America, for Goldwyn in the first instance. However, all but one of his films were made at MGM, under the name Seastrom. He adapted easily to American emotional drama, even if he introduced a fresh emphasis on real locations and naturalistic acting once he became established. *He Who Gets Slapped* is a stirring melodrama, with Lon Chaney as a wronged man who takes to the circus and meets Norma Shearer. *Confessions of a Queen* is from Daudet with Alice Terry and Lewis Stone. But gradually Sjöström flexed his muscles. *Name the Man* is one of cinema's few movies set on the Isle of Man; while *The Tower of Lies* (with Chaney and Shearer again) is from Selma Lagerlof and set in Sweden. *The Divine Woman* was conventional studio romance, but it allowed him to pair Garbo with Lars Hanson, whom Sjöström had called over from Sweden.

Hanson also appeared with Lillian Gish in Sjöström's two finest American pictures: *The Scarlet Letter* and *The Wind.* The first is from the Hawthorne novel, predictably relating American puritanism and Swedish attitudes toward guilt. It is hard to think of another MGM director of that time who could have conveyed its passion with such restraint. *The Wind* is far better, a prairie story of a girl who marries another man because her real love is already married, and is eventually driven to kill another man to save her virtue. The melodrama is subdued by the conviction of Gish's performance and by the way Sjöström rediscovers primitive nature in the Midwest emptiness. Louise Brooks said: "They were meant for each other—Seastrom and Gish—like the perfume and the rose"—and yet she had never heard of *The Wind* until 1956, so little did MGM promote it. It remains one of the greatest silent films—and one of our great movies.

Sjöström returned to Sweden in 1930, but—apart from *Under the Red Robe,* made in England for Korda—he mysteriously abandoned direction for acting. He played in *Walborgsmassoafton* (35, Gustaf Edgren); *Gubben Kommer* (39, Per Lindberg); *Striden gar Vidare* (41, Gustaf Molander); *Ordet* (43, Molander); and *Det Brinner en Eld* (43, Molander). From 1943–49—the period of *Frenzy* and Bergman's first films—Sjöström was artistic director at Svensk Filmindustri. Even in his last years, he remained busy as an actor; *To Joy* (49, Bergman); *Kvartetten som Sprangdes* (50, Molander); *Hard Klang* (52, Arne Mattson); *Mannen i Morker* (55, Mattson); and unforgettably, as

Professor Borg, the man on the brink of death, in *Wild Strawberries* (57, Bergman).

That part was not only an advance in Bergman's pursuit of the intellectual passions but a tribute to Sjöström's vital presence in Swedish cinema. More than that, the ending of *Wild Strawberries* is the most tranquil scene in all Bergman's work. It is a fascinating comparison of the two men to note Bergman's words recording the filming of that moment: "[Sjöström's] face shone with secretive light, as if reflected from another reality. His features became suddenly mild, almost effete. His look was open, smiling, tender. It was like a miracle. . . . Yet it was all nothing more than a piece of acting in a dirty studio. . . . This exceedingly shy human being would never have shown us lookers-on this deeply buried treasure of sensitive purity, if it had not been in a piece of acting. . . ." That may help to explain the sense in much of Sjöström's work of wild feelings bursting through moral and social inhibition.

Stellan Skarsgård,

b. Gothenburg, Sweden, 1951

By the age of fifty, Stellan Skarsgård had over seventy film or television credits as an actor. No one would claim that every one of them is glowing or even fit to be reviewed now. But actors are—above and beyond geniuses—craftsmen and professionals who develop their craft slowly, and who need nothing so much as work. So, if Stellan Skarsgård has by now, unobtrusively, pressed himself upon us as a rare, versatile, and humane actor, don't forget the advantage of steady work and ordinary payment.

The list that follows is far from complete, and it passes over the fact that, from 1972–88, Skarsgård was a working member of the Royal Dramatic Theatre in Stockholm. Skarsgård made a name first as the lead in the Swedish TV miniseries about teenagers, *Bombi Bitt och Jag* (68). These are some major events that followed: *Firmafesten* (72, Jan Halldoff); *Tabu* (77, Vilgot Sjöman); a breakthrough performance of extraordinary pathos in *The Simple-Minded Murderer* (82, Hans Alfredson); he played Hamlet on Swedish TV in 1984, and then Strindberg in 1985; *Hip Hip Hurrah!* (87, Kjell Grede); his first English-language role, in *The Unbearable Lightness of Being* (88, Philip Kaufman); *Kvinnorna på Taket* (89, Carl-Gustaf Nykvist); *The Hunt for Red October* (90, John McTiernan).

In 1990, he played the Swedish diplomat in *God Afton, Herr Wallenberg* (Grede); *The Ox* (91, Sven Nykvist); *Wind* (92, Carroll Ballard); *Breaking the Waves* (96, Lars von Trier); *Insomnia* (97, Erik Skjoldbjærg); *My Son the Fanatic* (97, Udayan Prasad); *Amistad* (97, Steven Spielberg); *Good Will Hunting* (97, Gus Van Sant); *Ronin* (98, John Frankenheimer); *Deep Blue Sea* (99, Renny

Harlin); *Passion of Mind* (00, Alain Berliner); *Timecode* (00, Mike Figgis); *Dancer in the Dark* (00, von Trier); *Aberdeen* (00, Hans Petter Moland); *The Glass House* (01, Daniel Sackheim).

He played Wilhelm Furtwangler in *Taking Sides* (01, Istvan Szabo); *D-dag* (01, Soren Kragh-Jacobsen); *The House on Turk Street* (01, Bob Rafelson); *City of Ghosts* (02, Matt Dillon); Theseus in *Helen of Troy* (03, John Kent Harrison); *Dogville* (03, von Trier); young Father Merrin in *Exorcist: The Beginning* (03, Paul Schrader).

Jerzy Skolimowski,

b. Warsaw, Poland, 1938

1964: *Rysopis/Identification Marks: None*. 1965: *Walkover*. 1966: *Bariera/Barrier*. 1967: *Le Départ; Rece do Gory/Hands Up!*. 1968: an episode from *Dialog*. 1970: *The Adventures of Gerard; Deep End*. 1972: *King, Queen, Knave*. 1978: *The Shout*. 1981: *Hands Up!* (revised). 1982: *Moonlighting*. 1984: *Success Is the Best Revenge*. 1985: *The Lightship*. 1989: *Torrents of Spring*. 1993: *30 Door Key*.

Skolimowski is a director who stalks us like a fighter, with stunning blows in either hand. But there remains something incomplete, or reticent, in the performance. Skolimowski moves with arbitrary agility, a flurry of spectacular effects culminating in the cinematic equivalent of a knockout—a momentary glimpse of the sublime whereby we lose our senses long enough to be counted out. And all the while Skolimowski hunches up within that rather contrived pose of threatening hostility in which a boxer enwraps himself in shadow boxing. But the classic knockout is precisely timed: in fifteen seconds we are on our feet, in a minute ourselves again, and soon bewildered that something so slight as the flick of a fist won the contest.

That said, knockouts are rare. *Deep End*, for instance, is a positive barrage of delicious punches in our sensibility: the realization of a shabby suburban swimming bath; Diana Dors working herself into a goalmouth mêlée; the adolescent view of a neon city; the amazing London shrewishness of Jane Asher; the whore with a broken leg; the hot-dog salesman; the blue movie intercut with such innocent overtures in the cinema itself; the diamond in the snow; and the final seduction in the empty swimming bath when sexuality is swept away in the rush of blood and water. *Deep End* is another of those British films made by a foreigner—even if much of it was shot in Munich—that ought to shame the British cinema. It is funny, touching, sexy, surreal, and tragic—all at the same time and all with the sting of a punch in the nose.

Skolimowski has told rather proudly how he took the entrance exam for the Lodz film school on impulse and on the advice of Andrzej Wajda. He had studied ethnography at Warsaw University and already published some poetry and short stories. While at Lodz—where he did poorly—he collaborated on the scripts of *Innocent Sorcerers* (60, Wajda), and *Knife in the Water* (62, Roman Polanski), acted a little, filmed a documentary on boxing (he had himself been a boxer), and made *Rysopis* for himself.

His early Polish films were antiheroic and aggressively personal: they concern idiosyncratic outsiders played by himself. In *Rysopis* he is a student who suddenly decides to enlist in the army, and in *Walkover* a seasoned boxer who enters contests for novices. There is an odd mixture here of national anguish, wistful optimism about sex, and self-indulgent stylistic devices. But the films bristle with invention and Skolimowski's own bitter romanticism. *Barrier* was the most directly contrary to the 1950s view of Poland's recent history, and the most assured in the way it turned Warsaw into a mysterious, alien city.

But Skolimowski was plainly near to breaking the local rules. His films were both pungent and formally indulgent. *Hands Up!* was banned and *Le Départ* was filmed in Brussels from a story Godard might have had no time to make. With Jean-Pierre Léaud and Catherine Duport it was a dazzling comedy, but without roots and a sign of how quickly Skolimowski's art and thrust might seem mannered. After that, *The Adventures of Gerard* was a funny and accomplished lampoon of Napoleonic glory, *Deep End* his most intense venture into fantasy, and *King, Queen, Knave,* the best film of a Nabokov original. The odd circumstances of his later work may indicate the problem Skolimowski faces in finding an environment in which he can work fruitfully.

Living in London and Los Angeles much of the time, Skolimowski has not had an easy ride, despite the considerable success of *Moonlighting,* a droll, sad comedy about Polish building workers in London. *Success* is a parable of the eighties, very little seen, and *The Lightship* is a tense power struggle between Klaus Maria Brandauer and an inspired Robert Duvall. *Torrents of Spring* is Turgenev, shot in Europe, with Timothy Hutton and Nastassja Kinski.

Skolimowski has also acted in a few films, and done it well: *Circle of Deceit* (81, Volker Schlöndorff); *White Nights* (85, Taylor Hackford); *Big Shots* (87, Robert Mandel); *Torrents of Spring* (89, Skolimowski); *Mars Attacks!* (96, Tim Burton); *L.A. Without a Map* (98, Mika Kaurismäki); *Before Night Falls* (00, Julian Schnabel).

Christian Slater (Hawkins),
b. New York, 1969

Christian Slater has worked very hard for fifteen years. He has been in some successful pictures.

He has had to get used to being told that he could be a young Jack Nicholson. Trouble is, Jack Nicholson did that once, and did it better. Slater has a face that may resist growing older. He has done too much that is ordinary. He has to wonder whether he has had his run.

The son of an actor and a casting director (Mary Jo Slater), he was in the TV soap opera *One Life to Live* as a child before movies: *The Legend of Billie Jean* (85, Matthew Robbins); *The Name of the Rose* (86, Jean-Jacques Annaud); *Tucker* (88, Francis Coppola); a skateboarder in *Gleaming the Cube* (89, Graeme Clifford); at his best with Winona Ryder in *Heathers* (89, Michael Lehmann); *The Wizard* (89, Todd Holland); *Tales from the Darkside: The Movie* (90, John Harrison); *Young Guns II* (90, Geoff Murphy); *Pump Up the Volume* (90, Allan Moyle), the best tribute to his ability to carry a picture; *Robin Hood: Prince of Thieves* (91, Kevin Reynolds); *Mobsters* (91, Michael Karbelnikoff); *Star Trek VI: The Undiscovered Country* (91, Nicholas Meyer); *Kuffs* (92, Bruce Evans); a voice-over in *FernGully: The Last Rainforest* (92, Bill Kroyer); uncredited in *Where the Day Takes You* (92, Marc Rocco); *Untamed Heart* (93, Tony Bill); *True Romance* (93, Tony Scott); *Interview with the Vampire* (94, Neil Jordan); with Joe Pesci in *Jimmy Hollywood* (94, Barry Levinson); the defense lawyer in *Murder in the First* (95, Rocco); *Bed of Roses* (96, Michael Goldenberg); jousting with John Travolta in *Broken Arrow* (96, John Woo); *Hard Rain* (98, Mikael Saloman); *Very Bad Things* (98, Peter Berg); *The Contender* (00, Rod Lurie); *3000 Miles to Graceland* (01, Demian Lichtenstein); *Who Is Cletis Tout?* (01, Chris Ver Wiel); *Hard Cash/Run for the Money* (01, Predrag Antonijevic); and a good role again in *Windtalkers* (02, Woo); *Masked and Anonymous* (03, Larry Charles).

Everett Sloane (1909–65), b. New York

The more times you see *Citizen Kane,* the more strands it has. One such mode is old age: of course, Kane and all his associates grow old; the entire film might be the recollection of Kane on hearing chimes at midnight. But, more than that, its sense of time past, of a life withered away, is the grave looking forward of a young man. Dressing up as the elderly Kane, Welles was inventing an old age that he would inevitably come to fill. Falstaff and Clay in *The Immortal Story* are men obsessed with the contrast of physical decline and imaginative vibrancy. Even Hank Quinlan, in *Touch of Evil,* is the wreck of a younger man who might once have been Marlene Dietrich's lover.

What does that mean for Everett Sloane? Simply, that within that strand of old age, Sloane seems to be central to the film. He is the brash, vulgar manager: the man who arrives in a clatter of junky furniture; who joins in the yelling repartee with his master at the party; and who stands, moved and naïve, without a trace of cynicism, over the two headlines on election night; he is the man who could never pronounce the name of the opera in which Susan Alexander Kane wails so desperately. It is hard to believe that there was not as much of Sloane in Bernstein as there was of Welles and Cotten in Kane and Leland. The trio in charge of the *Inquirer* so beautifully reflect the volatile companionship of the Mercury Theater. But Sloane has one immense scene as an old man, all in one very simple take, that is curiously relaxed in a film where most scenes are rigorously tied in to brilliant organization. Like an old man, Bernstein meanders. Sitting in a large office, reflected in the tabletop, chairman of the board and redundant. He tells a story—the first story within stories in Welles's work—about a day in 1896 on the ferry over to Jersey when he saw a girl carrying a white parasol, a girl he has never forgotten: that clinging moment is a clue to Rosebud, and a gorgeous, affectionate flourish from Welles, embracing Sloane's perky sentimentality, and going to the heart of experience. The incident imprints itself just as that girl did on Bernstein: like Welles/Kane, we are persuaded of momentary epiphanies. The world is changed as we are offered a way of experiencing it: "A fellow will remember a lot of things you wouldn't think he'd remember."

Sloane did more than that. He enjoyed himself in *Journey Into Fear* (43, Norman Foster) and was brilliant as the crippled lawyer in *The Lady from Shanghai* (48, Welles). Who can forget him lurching through the courtroom, the reptile stare at Rita Hayworth, and the way his arm goes up involuntarily—part to ward off the image, part a gesture of languor—when Welles tells the story of the sharks devouring one another? What else? *Prince of Foxes* (49, Henry King); *The Men* (50, Fred Zinnemann); *The Enforcer* (51, Raoul Walsh and Bretaigne Windust); *Bird of Paradise* (51, Delmer Daves); *Sirocco* (51, Curtis Bernhardt); *Rommel, Desert Fox* (51, Henry Hathaway); *Way of a Gaucho* (52, Jacques Tourneur); *The Big Knife* (55, Robert Aldrich); *Lust for Life* (56, Vincente Minnelli); *Somebody Up There Likes Me* (56, Robert Wise); *Patterns* (57, Fielder Cook); *Marjorie Morningstar* (57, Irving Rapper); *The Gun Runners* (58, Don Siegel); *Home from the Hill* (60, Minnelli); *The Patsy* (64, Jerry Lewis); and *The Disorderly Orderly* (65, Frank Tashlin).

Dame Maggie Smith,
b. Ilford, England, 1934
One of the great stage comediennes of recent years, Maggie Smith still looks unsure of how to behave in the movies. One cause of irresolution may be that she was never the most beautiful woman in the world. Has she been tempted to hide rather sharp, sensible features beneath various disguises? Certainly, her central part in *Travels With My Aunt* (72, George Cukor) is a fussy, insecure piece of impersonation that tends to play to the audience rather than to the camera.

Her dilemma is understandable. On the stage, in *Much Ado About Nothing, The Country Wife, Private Lives,* and many substantial plays, she has achieved an enormously happy rapport with audiences and taught them to laugh in time with her heartfelt tricks. She *is* tricky. Her timing is so wicked, one can forget the play. It is not easy to know who she is, or to believe she trusts mere feelings. On screen, a succession of inconsequential cameos led suddenly to the best actress Oscar for *The Prime of Miss Jean Brodie* (68, Ronald Neame). The elitist Edinburgh schoolteacher, talking of the life force but actually frigid and authoritarian, is a meal of a part based on the theatrical division of unhappy woman and actress relishing flamboyance. In fact, the part is more touching than she made it; sheer comic technique made Smith's Brodie seem a calculating phony, whereas she could be a true, hysterical virgin.

Maggie Smith is a very mannered actress, but no more so than the young Katharine Hepburn. As with Hepburn, the mannerism is not coy but an audacious sign of spirit and personality. The difference is that Hepburn committed herself to films, and had the confidence to take risks. As it is, Maggie Smith's beginnings have taught her to feel that she looked plain and uninteresting in movies. Thus the resort to exaggeration and the rattle of staginess. The early films are *Nowhere to Go* (58, Seth Holt); *The V.I.P.s* (63, Anthony Asquith); *The Pumpkin Eater* (64, Jack Clayton); *Young Cassidy* (66, Jack Cardiff and John Ford); *Othello* (66, Stuart Burge); *The Honey Pot* (67, Joseph L. Mankiewicz); *Hot Millions* (68, Eric Till); by turns genteel and depraved as the music-hall singer offering to make a man of you in *Oh! What a Lovely War* (69, Richard Attenborough).

Graham Greene's aunt, guided home by Cukor, seemed in prospect another natural. But Katharine Hepburn was denied the role she wanted by the studio. Perhaps there was an impossible balance in the novel between age and vitality, an idea rather than a woman who could be made real. Nevertheless, it exposed Maggie Smith's failings as did the many discordant moods in *Love and Pain (and the Whole Damn Thing)* (72, Alan J. Pakula). Her film career dematerialized as quickly as it began, and she was lost in the crowd in *Murder by Death* (76, Robert Moore). But she treated *California Suite* (78, Herbert Ross) to a funny but slick cameo and—to her evident surprise—picked up the supporting actress Oscar.

Her movie career remains blithely indifferent

to reason or line. She does a little bit of anything, so consistently over the top in lighter material that no one notices. But she has more recently offered some harrowing portraits of loss, loneliness, and incipient madness: *Clash of the Titans* (81, Desmond Davis); *Quartet* (81, James Ivory); *Evil Under the Sun* (82, Guy Hamilton); *Better Late Than Never* (82, Bryan Forbes); *The Missionary* (82, James Loncraine); *Double Play* (84, Karoly Maak); *A Private Function* (84, Malcolm Mowbray); *A Room With a View* (85, Ivory); *The Lonely Passion of Judith Hearne* (87, Jack Clayton); brilliant in the extended monologue of *Bed Among the Lentils* (88, Alan Bennett); *Memento Mori* (91, Clayton); *Hook* (91, Steven Spielberg); *Sister Act* (92, Emile Ardolino); the housekeeper in *The Secret Garden* (93, Agnieszka Holland); and *Sister Act II* (93, Bill Duke).

It's a sign of timidity, I suppose, that she is regarded as unsexy or too old for lead roles: *Richard III* (95, Richard Loncraine); *The First Wives Club* (96, Hugh Wilson); *Washington Square* (97, Holland); *Tea with Mussolini* (99, Franco Zeffirelli); *The Last September* (99, Deborah Warner); *Curtain Call* (99, Peter Yates); Queen Alexandra in *All the King's Men* (99, Julian Jarrold); Betsey Trotwood in *David Copperfield* (99, Simon Curtis); *Harry Potter and the Sorcerer's Stone* (01, Chris Columbus); *Gosford Park* (01, Robert Altman); *Divine Secrets of the Ya-Ya Sisterhood* (02, Callie Khouri); *Harry Potter and the Chamber of Secrets* (02, Chris Columbus); *My House in Umbria* (03, Richard Loncraine).

Will Smith (Willard Christopher Smith Jr.),
b. Philadelphia, 1968

Will Smith is the first black actor to capitalize on the widespread white realization that you don't have to act to be in pictures. Far more fundamentally, just be in them and let it show that you're not overly impressed or intimidated. In addition, Smith has applied the same easygoing indifference to hit records and being cool. It's a policy that could easily sweep the heights of business and the pinnacles of politics. For what Smith really embodies is the other side of the coin named in *Network* ("Because you're on television, dummy"), which is, approximately, "Hey, dude, I'm on TV."

Indeed, it's TV that really defines Smith: he thrives on a live audience, multi-cameras, and a sort of twelve-minute segmenting. So he made his name and his groove in TV's *The Fresh Prince of Bel-Air.* That led to what was then his most demanding part, the serene interloper who might be Sidney Poitier's son in *Six Degrees of Separation* (93, Fred Schepisi). He also had roles in *Where the Day Takes You* (92, Mark Rocco) and *Made in America* (93, Richard Benjamin). Stardom—or celebrity appearance—followed with

Bad Boys (95, Michael Bay); *Independence Day* (96, Roland Emmerich); *Men in Black* (97, Barry Sonnenfeld); *Enemy of the State* (98, Tony Scott); *Wild Wild West* (99, Sonnenfeld); *Men in Black: Alien Attack* (00, David C. Cobb and Lymal Coleman), a short; *The Legend of Bagger Vance* (00, Robert Redford).

Then he did *Ali* (01, Michael Mann). In the ring, he was perfect. To listen to, uncanny. Yet the film foundered on its failure to explain the multitudes of Ali, or to match our memories from so much newsreel coverage. An honorable failure in a film that needed a more searching script. So back to *MIIB* (02, Sonnenfeld) and *Bad Boys II* (03, Michael Bay).

Steven Soderbergh,
b. Atlanta, Georgia, 1963
1989: *sex, lies and videotape.* 1991: *Kafka.* 1993: *King of the Hill.* 1995: *The Underneath.* 1996: *Gray's Anatomy; Schizopolis.* 1998: *Out of Sight.* 1999: *The Limey.* 2000: *Erin Brockovich; Traffic.* 2001: *Ocean's Eleven.* 2002: *Full Frontal; Solaris.*

The published screenplay of *sex, lies and videotape* includes a diary of the production that is an excellent portrait of young, independent filmmaking scarcely able to credit how close it has come to the big time. The diary makes Soderbergh seem a good deal younger and less searching than his finished film. There are also unwitting ironies: at one point, looking ahead, Soderbergh says that Lem Dobbs's script for *Kafka* is so good it will probably never be made.

Soderbergh was a film student at Louisiana State University, the maker of several short films, who then went to Los Angeles and got some work as an editor while he wrote scripts. Thus, he wrote and contrived to make *sex, lies and videotape* at approximately the age at which Welles made *Kane.* There *are* differences: *sex, lies* was a hit; it won several prizes at Cannes; and it has a deeper knowledge of human vagary than Welles ever permitted himself. But both films possessed precocious authority. *sex, lies and videotape* is novelistic in its development and is unusually interested in out-of-the-way traits of character emerging as something like triumph. Beneath its intrigue of marriage and adultery, it also posed a remarkable view of the potency of video as an alternative to experience. The film did not moralize, or even push through with its conclusion, but not many recent movies have given the exuberant and closed community of movie maniacs so much ground for unease.

sex, lies is many other things: a delicate blend of drama and comedy; a model in picture-making economics; and a display of wonderful acting—Andie MacDowell has never been so touching; James Spader showed how intelligent and profound diffidence could be; Peter Gallagher and Laura San Giacomo were excellent.

With the world at his feet, Soderbergh did make *Kafka,* thereby helplessly endorsing the theories of sophomore disaster and freeing the enemies always earned by early success. More interestingly, the strained attempt of *Kafka* stands beside the mature ease of *sex, lies* so that we had to wonder who Steve Soderbergh might become.

But *King of the Hill* returned to form. Adapted from A. E. Hotchner's book about a troubled childhood, it was assured and very well acted—as if to show that careful realism is Soderbergh's strength.

It's interesting seven years later to look back on the Soderbergh of 1996—*The Underneath* was his worst film yet (it still is), while *Gray's Anatomy* (it was Spaulding Gray) and *Schizopolis* seemed to signal a shift to independence, or even privacy. Then something happened, and Soderbergh apparently woke up to the notion that he might be a hit. *Out of Sight* and *The Limey* were both good thrillers in which we liked the leads. They weren't actually that good, but they were learning processes. *Erin Brockovich* was the hit he needed—a perfect star vehicle, allied to a moderately liberal story. But it worked because Soderbergh played the game the system's way, and maybe told himself he was doing it all for Julia Roberts.

Traffic (for which he actually won the directing Oscar—having been nominated twice in one year) seems to me a little too showy for its own good. The British TV series, *Traffik,* is superior and far more compellingly coherent. But lots of people thought it was a masterpiece. Personally, I don't think Soderbergh has yet come within reach of such a film. But he might easily turn into our best mainstream director. In which case, we must all agree to forget the wretched *Ocean's Eleven.*

Aleksandr Sokurov,
b. Podorvikha, Russia, 1951

1980: *Razzhalovannyi.* 1987: *Zhertva Vechernyaya; Terpenie, Trud; Skorbnoye Beschuvstivye; Odinokij Golos Cheloveka; Moskovskaya Elegiya; I Nichego Bolshe.* 1988: *Mariya; Dni Zatmeniya; Altovaya Sonata: Dmitri Shostakovich.* 1989: *Spasi i Sokhrani; Sovetskaya Elegiya; Sonata dlya Gitlera; Peterburgskaya Elegiya.* 1990: *Krug Vtoroj; Prostaya Elegiya; Leningradskaya Retrospektiva.* 1992: *Kamen'.* 1993: *Tikhiye Stranitsy/Whispering Pages.* 1995: *Dukhovnye Golosa/Spiritual Voices.* 1996: *Vostochnaya Elegiya; Robert Schlastlivaya Zhizn.* 1997: *Mat i Syn/Mother and Son.* 1999: *Molokh; The Knot.* 2000: *Dolce.* 2002: *Russian Ark.*

Sokurov was born in Siberia, and he attended the University of Gorky, where he read history, and then the Moscow Film Academy. He made many documentaries (especially films about cities) and ran into trouble with the old Soviet authorities. "I was always driven by visual aesthetics, aesthetics which connected to the spirituality of man, and set certain morals. The fact that I was involved in the visual side of art made the government suspicious. The nature of my films was different from others. They didn't actually know what to punish me for—and that confusion caused them huge irritation."

On the other hand, the feeling for nature and relationship is so intense in *Mother and Son* (the only film I've seen) that I can understand Paul Schrader's belief that Sokurov is a master worthy of a place in the transcendental tradition. He was a friend to Tarkovsky, but he regards Chekhov as his forming influence. *Mother and Son* is, on the one hand, minimalist: a 73-minute rhapsody on a mother's last day of life. On the other, it is a film with that classically large Russian embrace of all of being, something we know from Dovzhenko and Tolstoy.

Todd Solondz, b. Newark, New Jersey, 1960
1998: *Fear, Anxiety and Depression.* 1995: *Welcome to the Dollhouse.* 1998: *Happiness.* 2001: *Storytelling.*

A lot of people didn't even want to talk about *Happiness.* It was precisely what they didn't go to the movies for. Its deadpan title was like the ultimate poisoned stiletto slipped between the ribs of comfort and sentimentality. Not every charge against the film need be dismissed. The gruesomeness was a little posed or polished; and such perversions are not really found so often in a dumb slice of life. Still, there's room in America for movies as well made as *Happiness,* and for anything that finds a poker-faced way of offering that title for inspection sitting over so many misfits and outcasts. Somehow the feel-good rhetoric we inflict on ourselves has to be frightened away. And Solondz might be an exemplary figure in a group of "nasty" filmmakers. (For, honestly, there's nothing more contrived in finding fault, decay, and abscesses than in saying everyone is A-OK.)

I've never seen the first film—but I suspect its title plays fair. The second film had an audience, in that it had a resolute, nerd heroine who was plucky in the face of everyday horror. That America is out there, many layers thick, and it is high time our popular culture faced it. In people like Solondz, LaBute, and Terry Zwigoff we have a generation (more or less) that simply won't swallow the white lies anymore. It's up to us, and the system, whether we subvert it by calling it black humor.

Barry Sonnenfeld, b. New York, 1953
1991: *The Addams Family*. 1993: *For Love or Money; Addams Family Values*. 1995: *Get Shorty*. 1997: *Men in Black*. 1999: *The Wild Wild West*. 2002: *MIIB*.

Sonnenfeld makes hits, with all the new Hollywood's easygoing disowning of substance, character, or drama. *For Love or Money* is the one project that hasn't turned up trumps for everyone concerned. He established a pretty, poisonous lust for the Addams Family, and he kept kids happy with the Will Smith Picture. But *Get Shorty* is the only picture with real wit—and most of that comes from Elmore Leonard. If only Sonnenfeld could show some hints of the best pictures he photographed before turning to directing—*Miller's Crossing* (90, Joel Coen), say, or *When Harry Met Sally . . .* (89, Rob Reiner). He was at NYU film school with Joel and Ethan Coen, and it was their patronage that got him his first work as a director of photography: *Blood Simple* (84, Joel Coen); *Compromising Positions* (85, Frank Perry); *Raising Arizona* (87, Coen); *Three O'Clock High* (87, Phil Joanou); *Throw Momma from the Train* (87, Danny DeVito); *Big* (88, Penny Marshall); *Misery* (90, Reiner).

Ann Sothern (Harriette Lake) (1909–2001), b. Valley City, North Dakota
Several months after the release of Tay Garnett's *Trade Winds* (1939), he tells us in his memoirs,

> I was working at my desk when a blonde blur burst through the open door, body-surfed across my desk, and landed in my lap, wiping out the two of us onto the floor. I had my arms full of glorious girl, but she was giggling, which unnerved me. "What the hell goes on?" I managed to say. Kiss on the forehead. Kiss on the cheek. Kiss on the chin. "Oh, Tay! You'll never guess! You've done it this time—you've really done it. MGM has stolen your Jeanie character right out of *Trade Winds* and they're going to build a series around her for ME. They're going to call her Maizie," chortled Miss Sothern.

When you watch *Trade Winds* today, you can see why. The main point of the movie seems to be the endless process shots, all made by Garnett and friends as they wandered around the Far East in his boat, the *Athene*. This cuckoo movie starts as film noir, swerves into romantic drama, flirts with screwball. Fredric March is pallid and irritating as the hero, Joan Bennett has a defining moment when exigencies of the crackpot plot demand that her hair be changed from its lifetime blonde to black—the look that carried her into her great noir period; Ralph Bellamy as a Klutzy Kop is unbearable—and Sothern, as March's secretary,

steals the show, strutting up and down, gnawing gum, cracking wise, and letting her heart of gold twinkle through her tough exterior. No wonder MGM grabbed her.

There were to be ten Maisie (not Maizie) films, including *Maisie* itself (39), *Congo Maisie* and *Gold Rush Maisie* (40), *Maisie Was a Lady* and *Ringside Maisie* (41), *Maisie Gets Her Man* (42), *Swing Shift Maisie* (43), *Maisie Goes to Reno* (44), *Up Goes Maisie* (46)—its tag line was "It's Maisie flying . . . fighting . . . falling—for a guy. You'll have a helicopter of a time!"—and closure at last with *Undercover Maisie* (47). Sothern as Maisie had nine different leading men (George Murphy was volunteered twice), including Robert Young in the original, Lew Ayres, Lee Bowman (poor Maisie), and Red Skelton. The Maisies were probably, after the Andy Hardys, the most successful B-picture series of their day, so they were certainly a triumph for Ann Sothern. But they were a burden, too: she *was* Maisie, so how could she be anything else?

Sothern had worked her way up along the Betty Grable/Lucille Ball route—chorus girls and bit parts in early-thirties musicals—until in 1934 she was the first-cast girl, ahead of Ethel Merman, in *Kid Millions* (Roy del Ruth), one of Eddie Cantor's Goldwyn vehicles. But she was only a conventional thirties romantic comedienne, trapped in a romance with George Murphy (it was his first movie) and, in one musical number, in a hoop skirt larger than Australia. For the next few years, she was a second-string Joan Blondell—the same adorable oval face, the same sassy charm, just not as individual. (When Blondell was asked by John Kobal, years later, what had brought her back to the screen, she grinned and said, "My friends told me Ann Sothern had forgotten how to do me.") Sothern was queen of the B's and programmers; if you need proof, she was given Gene Raymond half a dozen times as her costar—and she didn't even like him. Then came *Trade Winds*.

Finally, she got some classier material: the musical *Lady Be Good* (41, Norman Z. McLeod), in which she upstages Eleanor Powell; *Panama Hattie* (42, McLeod); a nurse on Bataan in *Cry Havoc* (43, Richard Thorpe)—ironically, cast above Blondell though below Margaret Sullavan; best of all, *Letter to Three Wives* (49), Joe Mankiewicz's Oscar winner, where she more than holds her own against Linda Darnell and Jeanne Crain. It went downhill from there, despite interesting roles in *Blue Gardenia* (53, Fritz Lang) and *The Best Man* (Franklin J. Schaffner) and *Lady in a Cage* (Walter Grauman), both 1964. A few scattered appearances ending in 1980, a gap of more than half a dozen years, and then an amazing comeback: nominated for best supporting actress to Bette Davis and Lillian Gish in the 1987 *Whales of August* (Lindsay Anderson). What a grand finale—and in what company—for *Congo Maisie!*

Sissy (Mary Elizabeth) **Spacek**,
b. Quitman, Texas, 1949
I cannot begin to explain why Sissy Spacek has not been in this book before. She should never have slipped through any rudimentary clerical search— after all, she is an Oscar-winner (*Coal Miner's Daughter*) as well as the recipient of five other nominations. Add to that the fact that she was not nominated for her greatest performance—that in *Badlands* (73, Terrence Malick)—and clearly we are faced with a major actress, with an authentic sense of rural life and uneducated ways. For years, she had a genius for roles much younger than her real age and a sense of that rare challenge, beyond so many actors: that of playing a simpler, more naïve or limited person than the actor may be in life. Just as important, at the age of fifty, she gave a startling and beautiful performance as the afflicted daughter in *The Straight Story* (99, David Lynch)—it deserved another nomination. But she merits her place for *Badlands* alone, for her flat-voiced narration, her artless dancing in the headlights, and her complete absorption in the life of escape (and the escape from life).

She studied at the Actors Studio and made her screen debut in *Prime Cut* (72, Michael Ritchie) and followed it with *Ginger in the Morning* (73, Gordon Willis), in which she played a hitchhiker. *Badlands* came next, and then her tour de force of menstrual hysteria and psychic dynamism in *Carrie* (76, Brian De Palma)—surely a very difficult part to carry off without seeming comic. She then did *Welcome to L.A.* (76, Alan Rudolph); the end-lessly mysterious *Three Women* (76, Robert Altman), which could easily have won another nomination; *Heartbeat* (80, John Byrum), where she was Carolyn Cassady; as Loretta Lynn in *Coal Miner's Daughter* (80, Michael Apted); *Raggedy Man* (81, Jack Fisk, her husband); *Missing* (82, Costa-Gavras); *The River* (84, Mark Rydell); *Marie* (85, Roger Donaldson); *Violets Are Blue* (86, Fisk); *'Night, Mother* (86, Tom Moore), with Anne Bancroft; *Crimes of the Heart* (86, Robert Benton).

She took a few years off then and came back as someone happy to play supporting parts: as the Southern woman who is taught reality by her housekeeper in *The Long Walk Home* (90, Richard Pearce); *Hard Promises* (92, Martin Davidson); doing her best as Mrs. Garrison in *JFK* (91, Oliver Stone); *Trading Mom* (94, Tia Brelis); *The Good Old Boys* (95, Tommy Lee Jones); *Beyond the Call* (96, Tony Bill); *The Grass Harp* (96, Charles Matthau); *If These Walls Could Talk* (96, Nancy Savoca); *Affliction* (97, Paul Schrader); *Blast from the Past* (99, Hugh Wilson).

She was in the TV movie *Songs in Ordinary Time* (00, Rod Holcomb); delivering another out-standing and quiet performance in *In the Bedroom* (01, Todd Field); and *Midwives* (01, Glen Jordan) for TV. She also appeared as Zelda Fitzgerald with Jeremy Irons in *Last Call* (02, Henry Bromell); *Tuck Everlasting* (02, Jay Russell); *A Home at the End of the World* (03, Michael Mayer).

Kevin Spacey (Fowler),
b. South Orange, New Jersey, 1959
In interviews nowadays, and on camera at the awards shows he gets invited to, Kevin Spacey is slowly accumulating his most intriguing performance. It is of a man forty years old who has a twenty-year-old's gravity. He is a disciple of acting, the theatre, and good work. He cannot abandon his terrific smarts, but he is patient (as if that could pass for slow and sincere), and he is unerr-ingly of the mainstream. This could easily turn him into Our Greatest Actor, and it is self-sufficiently delicious. But do not be fooled: Kevin Fowler is and always was a chronic pretender, a naughty boy, a wicked mimic, and a scathing mind. Keyser Soze indeed! He can be our best actor, but only if we accept that acting is a bag of tricks that leaves scant room for being a real and considerate human being. So you can see his Lester Burnham in *American Beauty* (99, Sam Mendes), if you like, as the salt of the earth gone sour, a Mr. America saddened to death. Me, I think he's just one of Kevin's nasty jokers. But it won him the Oscar.

He attended Juilliard and had notable stage successes in *Henry IV, Part I; Ghosts; Long Day's Journey Into Night;* and *Lost in Yonkers*. In addi-tion to that, he had a great hit, in London and then New York, in 1998–99, as Hickey in O'Neill's *The Iceman Cometh*.

His movie debut was in *Heartburn* (86, Mike Nichols); *Rocket Gibraltar* (88, Daniel Petrie); *Working Girl* (88, Nichols); his remarkable, and neurotic, Mel Profitt in the TV series *Wiseguy* (88)—the first unmistakable evidence of genius; *Dad* (89, Gary David Goldberg); *See No Evil, Hear No Evil* (89, Arthur Hiller); *Henry & June* (90, Philip Kaufman); *A Show of Force* (90, Bruno Barreto); *Glengarry Glen Ross* (92, James Foley); the murderer in *Consenting Adults* (92, Alan J. Pakula); *The Ref* (94, Ted Demme); *Outbreak* (95, Wolfgang Petersen); as the brilliant, scholarly killer in *Se7en* (95, David Fincher).

There was hilarious nastiness in his Hollywood executive in *Swimming with Sharks* (94, George Huang), which he also coproduced. Then he won a supporting actor Oscar as Verbal Kint in *The Usual Suspects* (95, Bryan Singer). He was the prosecuting attorney in *A Time to Kill* (96, Joel Schumacher); Buckingham in *Looking for*

Richard (96, Al Pacino); and he then directed his first film, *Albino Alligator* (97).

He was very adroit as the TV cop in *L.A. Confidential* (97, Curtis Hanson), since when he has been swanning through the nonsense of *Midnight in the Garden of Good and Evil* (97, Clint Eastwood); as *The Negotiator* (98, F. Gary Gray); *Hurlyburly* (98, Anthony Drazan). He did the bad-guy voice in *A Bug's Life* (98, John Lasseter and Andrew Stanton); and he was in *The Big Kahuna* (99, John Swanbeck); *Ordinary Decent Criminal* (00, Thaddeus O'Sullivan); *Pay It Forward* (00, Mimi Leder); *K-PAX* (01, Iain Softley); *The Shipping News* (01, Lasse Hallström).

His resolve to be mainstream, a nice guy or a romantic lead is by now as obstinate as it is fatuous. It's like asking Lassie to be treacherous, and it may lead to films worse even than *The Life of David Gale* (03, Alan Parker). The sooner he delivers as Bobby Darin in *Beyond the Sea* the better—and not one hint of redemption, please! But he is set to direct that project, and that could lead to solemnity.

Sam Spiegel (1904–85), b. Jaroslau, Austria

Spiegel's films won more Oscars than there have been films. Enough to stock a bowling alley with skittles and the rewards for slow preparation, the tarting up of ostensibly solemn subjects with melodrama, soporific production values, and a personality that comes on radical but is always cautious. Oscars in such profusion show how far a man has fulfilled Hollywood's view of itself. His films were assembled with the tedious care that went into those weapons that once trundled across Red Square on May Day. They take as long to go past and they are greeted with dutiful applause.

In David Lean, Spiegel found his ideal director: a man who could spend several million dollars without revealing an inch of himself or without unsettling an audience. *Lawrence of Arabia* is moronic history based on a tidy conception of character analysis that horribly glamorizes a legend; *The Bridge on the River Kwai* is portentous with a capsule message of futile war—as if war were not a useful, profitable, and enjoyable occupation for many; while *On the Waterfront* is a shameless piece of Stanislavskyan barnstorming in which Spiegel and Kazan glossed over union racketeering and the subtleties in informing.

It is the sham gravity that offends. If only Spiegel showed a trace of humor, frivolity, or awareness of his own ponderous earnestness. As it is, the one truly penetrating film he produced in later years, *The Chase* (66, Arthur Penn), he chose to take from Penn in an attempt at doctoring. Still, the violence in *The Chase* hurts, while that in Spiegel's other films is artificial. *The Chase* will last; *Lawrence* and *Kwai* only prove the misplaced faith of respectable taste. Yet Spiegel probably

expected the opposite and went on in this drab spirit: "They may cost a lot. But none of the money is wasted. All my pictures can be reissued again and again. They stand up pretty well, and they retain their residual values, both financial and prestige-wise."

From the University of Vienna, Spiegel went to America selling Palestinian cotton. While there, he lectured on drama and was briefly hired by MGM to advise on foreign-language versions. He was fired and went to Universal. In 1929, they sent him to Berlin to work on German productions for them. There is little record of what he did then or until he reappeared in America early in the war, so shy of his name that he called himself S. P. Eagle. He produced *Tales of Manhattan* (42, Julien Duvivier), but did not surface again until after the war when he produced *The Stranger* (46, Orson Welles) for RKO. John Huston was involved on that film in an uncredited writing capacity. He and Eagle formed Horizon Pictures, which produced three films: the risible *We Were Strangers* (49, Huston); the excellent *The Prowler* (51, Joseph Losey); the hammy *The African Queen* (51, Huston).

After that Eagle/Spiegel produced independently, usually for release through Columbia: *Melba* (53, Lewis Milestone); *On the Waterfront* (54, Elia Kazan); *End as a Man* (57, Jack Garfein); *The Bridge on the River Kwai* (57, David Lean); *Suddenly Last Summer* (59, Joseph L. Mankiewicz); *Lawrence of Arabia* (62, Lean); *The Night of the Generals* (67, Anatole Litvak); *The Happening* (67, Elliot Silverstein); *Nicholas and Alexandra* (71, Franklin Schaffner); and, with ravishing cast, distinguished scenarist and director, yet leaden effect, *The Last Tycoon* (76, Elia Kazan), suspiciously like the vain hope of a big dealer to justify his business with a tasteful mix of art and philosophy—and brutally silly as a result.

Steven Spielberg,
b. Cincinnati, Ohio, 1947

1971: *Duel.* 1974: *The Sugarland Express.* 1975: *Jaws.* 1977: *Close Encounters of the Third Kind.* 1979: *1941.* 1981: *Raiders of the Lost Ark.* 1982: *E.T., the Extra-Terrestrial.* 1983: an episode from *Twilight Zone—the Movie.* 1984: *Indiana Jones and the Temple of Doom.* 1985: *The Color Purple.* 1987: *Empire of the Sun.* 1989: *Always; Indiana Jones and the Last Crusade.* 1991: *Hook.* 1993: *Jurassic Park; Schindler's List.* 1997: *The Lost World: Jurassic Park; Amistad.* 1998: *Saving Private Ryan.* 2001: *A.I.* 2002: *Minority Report; Catch Me If You Can.*

Schindler makes pots and pans; he then buys the lives of Jews who would otherwise die in camps. The numbers are precise—as in any serious business. And so, in one year, 1993, Steven Spielberg delivered to the screen *Jurassic Park* and *Schindler's List*, enamelware and human flesh, if you like. *Jurassic Park*, it seemed to me, was shoddy, foolish in plot and characters, and nearly immediately forgettable. It was also, for a while, the biggest grossing film of all time; the numbers are precise, if growing still. *Jurassic Park* is a superb producer's coup according to the principle "Show them something they've never seen." And in its comprehensive revelation of a lifelike, or movielike, fluency for unreal, unborn things it may prove more influential than any film since *The Jazz Singer.*

Schindler's List is the most moving film I have ever seen. That does not mean it is faultless. To take just one point: the reddening of one little girl's coat in a black-and-white film strikes me as a mistake, and a sign of how calculating a director Spielberg is. For the calculating reveal themselves in those few errors that escape. I don't really believe in Spielberg as an artist: I don't believe that much soul or doubt is there, or that much heartfelt trust in the organic meaning of style. But *Schindler's List* is like an earthquake in a culture of gardens. And it helps persuade this viewer that cinema—or American film—is not a place for artists. It is a world for producers, for showmen, and Schindlers. The closest *Schindler's List* comes to art may be in aiding Steven Spielberg to back into the upheld coat of his own mysterious, brilliant, actorly nature. The film works so well because he is Schindler, and 1993 has been his 1944.

From the mid-1970s, there was an accepted wisdom that Spielberg was the junior mechanic as movie director. It grew out of the interest in cars and trucks in his first two films; a motorized shark in the third; and some of the most elaborate special effects ever organized in *Close Encounters.* Even Spielberg himself acknowledged the prominence of smooth-working parts in his films, and looked forward to smaller, more intimate, and by implication, more humane pictures. He had nothing to be ashamed of, even if he uttered the regrettable industry homily of appreciating "movie ideas that you can hold in your hand"—as opposed to those that dwell in your mind.

The rivalry of car and truck in *Duel* is a vivid allegory of the common man facing an enigmatic threat of terror and destruction. The motorcades of *Sugarland Express* never obscure the frantic emotions of a redneck mother blind to all but the need to retain her child. The mechanical shark in Spielberg's hands was a wittier version of the truck in *Duel,* and the means to an authentic pop art *Moby Dick.* And *Close Encounters* had a flawless wonder, such that it might be the first film ever made. Its laboratory effects and its models are all harnessed to an unusual plot structure, a view of personal stories that is remarkably detached for American pictures but never cold, and a kind of inquisitive awe for the unknown that transcends the paranoia and melodrama so widespread in science fiction. *Close Encounters* is a tribute to the richness of the ordinary human imagination. The inevitable comparison of *Star Wars* and *Close Encounters* reveals Lucas as a toymaker, and Spielberg as an explorer of the mind's power.

The son of an electrical engineer and computer expert, Spielberg began making 8mm films in high school with his father's camera. At that time he lived in Phoenix, Arizona, and he learned from and commandeered his father's hobby. *Firelight* was a twenty-one-hour epic, according to its maker, anticipating some of the themes and images brought to fruition in *Close Encounters.* He took a degree in English at California State College, Long Beach, but was always working on movies. *Amblin'* was a short that won prizes and earned a release with *Love Story*—early evidence of Spielberg's ability at drawing together good luck and commercial acumen.

He moved into TV and quickly won a reputation as an efficient director—the height of TV's needs. He worked on the pilot for *Night Gallery* and contributed episodes to *Columbo, Marcus Welby, The Name of the Game, The Psychiatrist,* and *Owen Marshall.* On that basis, he did *Duel* as a movie-of-the-week for ABC. Its impact was such that it got a theatrical release outside America. Deservedly so, for it stands up as one of the medium's most compelling spirals of suspense. The ordinariness of the Dennis Weaver character and the monstrous malignance of the truck confront one another with a narrative assurance that never needs to remind us of the element of fable. The ending is unsatisfactory, partly because the rest of the film is so momentous, but also because sheer skill needed more philosophy for a fitting resolution.

Sugarland Express is another epic of the road— raucous, feverish, and based on an actual incident. What makes its quest and journey so touching is the treatment of the central characters. They are not self-aware, enlightened, or stereotyped, and the movie never patronizes them. Goldie Hawn's wife is an untidy, vibrant woman, a robust departure from the social gentility that usually encloses Hollywood women. She is genuinely vulgar, but is never mocked because of it.

Jaws is Spielberg's most old-fashioned film, and the occasion on which he was under most commercial pressure. But, like Coppola on *The God-father,* Spielberg asserted his own role and deftly organized the elements of a roller coaster entertainment without sacrificing inner meanings. The suspense of the picture came from meticulous technique and good humor about its own surgical cutting. You have only to submit to the travesty of *Jaws* 2 to realize how much more engagingly Spielberg saw the ocean, the perils, and the sinister beauty of the shark, and the vitality of its human opponents. The terror of his films is healthy and cathartic because his faith in the unknown is so generous and sensible and his trust in the plain man's ingenuity and pluck so precise.

Close Encounters is as close to a mystical experience as a major film has come, but it is the mysticism of common sense. I don't think Spielberg believes in UFOs or specific answers in the universe. But he believes in man's vision and the determination that trusts its own experience more than official versions of the truth. The Dreyfuss character is no fanatic; he is another ordinary man whose life is disrupted by what he believes in. The way his domestic life is violated by increasing obsessiveness gives the film the flavor of surrealism. But the characters are smaller than the happenings that inspire them. Smallness never diminishes them. There is no violence to oppress them, only an invitation to the highest flights of fancy. The movie could have been naïve and sentimental—it was inspired by Disney—but Spielberg never relinquishes his practicality and his eye for everyday detail. It is extraordinary that so big and popular a film should have such a slender dramatic thread, and that the central marriage should be permitted to break up without apology, adultery, or the promise of reunion. It is the essence of Spielberg's attitude that when Dreyfuss and Melinda Dillon embrace, it is not as lovers brought together by plot, but as fellow believers.

At first sight, the Spielberg of the eighties may seem more an impresario—or a studio, even—than a director. Yet he directed seven films in the decade, including the Indiana Jones trilogy, the phenomenon of *E.T.*, and *Empire of the Sun* (a fine work, rather "explained" by *Schindler's List*), an adaptation of J. G. Ballard's book about childhood in Shanghai after the Japanese invasion. *Empire of the Sun* was among Spielberg's box-office failures, and there are signs that he writes failure out of history. Yet it combines the life of a child with the momentous world of adults in a way scarcely attempted in his other films. So busy, so enterprising, Spielberg had time for three flat-out bad films—*The Color Purple, Always,* and *Hook* (warning enough to any critic who seems ready to categorize Spielberg as a master of control and market forces).

At the same time, he became a producer, a tireless master of many ceremonies, and many of them simultaneous. Even *E.T.* feels calculated—to these eyes, it is not as inspired or involuntary as the wondrous *Poltergeist* (82, Tobe Hooper), on which Spielberg was producer, author of the story, and reshooter. Some argue that *Hook* was personal; I found it maudlin, fussy, and misjudged. Could it be that Spielberg's judgment smothers the vestiges of personal expression he can muster? Or is it that he is truly most himself when satisfying the enormous audience? He is a tycoon such as few can compre-

hend. He has done astonishing things; he has become vital to the business. And like Schindler, he has made us all think deeply about the nature of business. As a director, he took a rest after 1993— and then came back with a new, improved *Jurassic Park, Amistad,* and *Saving Private Ryan,* all in the space of a couple of years. *Ryan* changed war films: combat, shock, wounds, and fear had never been so graphically presented; and yet there was also a true sense of what duties and ideas had felt like in 1944. I disliked the framing device. I would have admired a director who trusted us to get it without that. Never mind—*Ryan* is a magnificent film. Which is very much more than I could say for *A.I.,* which seemed to me far too self-conscious in its thinking. Indeed, I suspect that, for all his power with futuristic technology, Spielberg's mind was made in the forties and fifties. There were worse times to be raised.

At any event, the filmography would be incomplete without the list of works that he has produced: *I Wanna Hold Your Hand* (78, Robert Zemeckis); *Used Cars* (80, Zemeckis); *Continental Divide* (81, Michael Apted); *Poltergeist; Gremlins* (84, Joe Dante); *Back to the Future* (85, Zemeckis); *The Goonies* (85, Richard Donner); *Young Sherlock Holmes* (85, Barry Levinson); *The Money Pit* (86, Richard Benjamin); the animated film, *An American Tail* (86, Don Bluth); . . . *batteries not included* (87, Matthew Robbins); *Innerspace* (87, Dante); *Who Framed Roger Rabbit?* (88, Zemeckis); *Back to the Future II* (89, Zemeckis); *Dad* (89, Gary David Goldberg); *Joe Versus the Volcano* (90, John Patrick Shanley); *Arachnophobia* (90, Frank Marshall); *Gremlins 2: The New Batch* (90, Dante); *Back to the Future III* (90, Zemeckis); and *An American Tail: Fievel Goes West* (91, Phil Nibbelink and Simon Wells).

On *The Flintstones* (94, Brian Levant) he was credited as Steven Spielrock; *Twister* (96, Jan De Bont); *Men in Black* (97, Barry Sonnenfeld); *Deep Impact* (98, Mimi Leder); *The Mask of Zorro* (98, Martin Campbell); *Shrek* (01, Andrew Adamson and Vicky Jenson); *Jurassic Park III* (01); and the HBO miniseries *Band of Brothers* (01), which he and Tom Hanks had spun off from *Saving Private Ryan.*

In fact, his producing hat had grown larger still with the formation of DreamWorks in 1995. With that enterprise (formed with Jeffrey Katzenberg and David Geffen), Spielberg was part of a new studio, involved in decisions on whether to build studio space as well as every individual project they took on. So it is one more measure of the inhuman—or of a level of performance beyond common humanity—that Steven Spielberg is also still a writer and a director. Moreover, he has maintained his own level of excellence for close to twenty-five years. He has never had significant or prolonged failure.

Robert Stack (1919–2003), b. Los Angeles

The American cinema of action has always depended upon the ability of certain actors to express moral energy—conscience and intelligence—in motion, without the elaborate benefit of character study or dialogue. It has persistently seen intellectual and spiritual personality in violent activity: force of arms equals moral integrity. James Stewart in the films of Anthony Mann is a fine example. But America has had a clutch of actors with this power. Although he has never been identified with evidently important parts, Stack's drawn face brings urgency and tension to his films. Part of his presence is the capacity for persuading us that a film can turn on a brief, intense physical demonstration. Watch his bleak blue eyes closely and you may begin to understand the depth of American cinema.

He made only a few films before service in the navy: giving Deanna Durbin her first screen kiss in *First Love* (39, Henry Koster); *The Mortal Storm* (40, Frank Borzage); *A Little Bit of Heaven* (40, Andrew Marton); *Badlands of Dakota* (41, Alfred E. Green); *Men of Texas* (42, Ray Enright); *To Be or Not to Be* (42, Ernst Lubitsch) as the Polish flier "able to drop three tons of dynamite in two minutes"; and *Eagle Squadron* (42, Arthur Lubin). After the war, he had ten years as a leading actor, though rarely in big films: *A Date with Judy* (48, Richard Thorpe); *Miss Tatlock's Millions* (48, Richard Haydn); *Fighter Squadron* (48, Raoul Walsh); *Mr. Music* (50, Haydn); *My Outlaw Brother* (51, Elliott Nugent); *The Bullfighter and the Lady* (51, Budd Boetticher); *Sabre Jet* (53, Louis King); *Bwana Devil* (53, Arch Oboler); *Conquest of Cochise* (53, William Castle); *The Iron Glove* (54, Castle); *The High and the Mighty* (54, William Wellman); marvelously shabby as the masquerading agent in *House of Bamboo* (55, Samuel Fuller); *Good Morning, Miss Dove* (55, Koster); and *Great Day in the Morning* (55, Jacques Tourneur).

Then came two Douglas Sirk films—*Written on the Wind* (56) and *The Tarnished Angels* (57). All of Stack's incisiveness was confounded by Sirk's use of the actor as a man desperate to stave off insecurity. In the first, he is a wealthy oil man who fears his own impotence, and in the second, the flier who risks death for the woman he shamed by winning at dice and for the son who may not be his own. Sirk's critical portrait of the American hero would not have been as penetrating without so monolithic a figure as Stack—a hard jaw getting the jitters. He was never so firm again in movies: *The Gift of Love* (58, Jean Negulesco); as *John Paul Jones* (59, John Farrow); and as Eliot Ness, the Chicago detective, in *The Scarface Mob* (59, Phil Karlson). That last film was a pilot for the TV series *The Untouchables*, on which for many years Stack blasted or arrested the guest stars. With that

meal ticket, he made fewer movies: excellent as the distraught father in *The Last Voyage* (60, Andrew Stone); *The Caretakers* (63, Hall Bartlett); *Is Paris Burning?* (66, René Clément); *The Peking Medallion* (67, James Hill); *Le Soleil des Voyous* (67, Jean Delannoy); *Storia di una Donna* (69, Leonardo Bercovici); and *Un Second Souffle* (78, Gerard Blain).

He was in *1941* (79, Steven Spielberg); *Airplane!* (80, Jim Abrahams, David Zucker, and Jerry Zucker); *Uncommon Valor* (83, Ted Kotcheff); *Big Trouble* (84, John Cassavetes); *Midas Valley* (85, Gus Trikonis); *Dangerous Curves* (88, David Lewis); *Caddyshack II* (88, Allan Arkush); *Plain Clothes* (88, Martha Coolidge); and *Joe Versus the Volcano* (90, John Patrick Shanley).

In recent years, he had been the enthusiastic host of TV's *Unsolved Mysteries*.

John M. Stahl (1886–1950), b. New York

1918: *Wives of Men*. 1919: *Her Code of Honor; Suspicion; A Woman Under Oath*. 1920: *Women Men Forget; The Woman in His House*. 1921: *The Child Thou Gavest Me; Sowing the Wind*. 1922: *The Song of Life; One Clear Call; Suspicious Wives*. 1923: *The Wanters; The Dangerous Age*. 1924: *Husbands and Lovers; Why Men Leave Home*. 1925: *Fine Clothes*. 1926: *Memory Lane; The Gay Deceiver*. 1927: *Lovers?; In Old Kentucky*. 1930: *A Lady Surrenders*. 1931: *Seed; Strictly Dishonorable*. 1932: *Back Street*. 1933: *Only Yesterday*. 1934: *Imitation of Life*. 1935: *Magnificent Obsession*. 1937: *Parnell*. 1938: *Letter of Introduction*. 1939: *When Tomorrow Comes*. 1941: *Our Wife*. 1942: *The Immortal Sergeant*. 1943: *Holy Matrimony*. 1944: *The Eve of St. Mark; The Keys of the Kingdom*. 1946: *Leave Her to Heaven*. 1947: *The Foxes of Harrow*. 1948: *The Walls of Jericho*. 1949: *Father Was a Fullback; Oh, You Beautiful Doll*.

Among those Hollywood careers that still need to be appraised is John Stahl's. I came to his films in reverse order. *Walls of Jericho, Foxes of Harrow,* and *Keys of the Kingdom* are tedious films, helped only by Linda Darnell in the first and the luminous glow of every detail in those crowded period interiors beloved of Fox. But, despite the stolidity of Gregory Peck, *Keys of the Kingdom* has moments of dreamlike if absurd beauty that point to the man Stahl once was.

The revelation came with *Leave Her to Heaven*, a film seemingly made in a trance and best seen in a state of fever. It concerns a woman of monstrous selfishness, referred to by the plot as an ogress but celebrated by Stahl's attentions as the imperious goddess in some never-never land of tyrannical emotions. When it is said that the part is played by the sweet Gene Tierney, the effect of Medusa, Cousin Bette, and the devouring female presence of von Sternberg's films may be recognized as an astonishing invention. The scenes in which Tierney allows her child brother-in-law to drown and coldly throws herself downstairs to abort her baby, and the moment when, on horseback, she scatters her father's ashes, reveal Stahl as a thrilling artist in the cause of self-destructive Technicolor emotionalism.

He was always associated with the women's picture, throughout the 1920s with Louis Mayer and MGM. Of that period, *The Wanters, Memory Lane,* and *Lovers?,* with Ramon Novarro and Alice Terry, are outstanding. At a time when he might have looked forward to directing Garbo, Crawford, and Shearer at MGM, he went to Universal to lay down the foundation works of the genre: *Back Street* (with John Boles and Irene Dunne); *Only Yesterday* (with Boles and Margaret Sullavan); *Imitation of Life* (with Claudette Colbert); *Magnificent Obsession* (with Dunne and Robert Taylor); *Letter of Introduction* (with Andrea Leeds and Adolphe Menjou); and *When Tomorrow Comes* (with Dunne and Charles Boyer). In its day, *Parnell* was thought a great failure, but today, its reprise and a chance to see *The Immortal Sergeant* might redeem Stahl from oblivion. He seems the forerunner and at best the equal of Douglas Sirk.

Sylvester Stallone (Michael Sylvester Stallone), b. New York, 1946

Stallone may be the most self-conscious noble savage since Mussolini. His weird monument, *Rocky* (76, John G. Avildsen), is a fairy tale that fakes everything down to its own naïveté. A large, domineering presence, Stallone is not casually nicknamed Sly. He is as nimble and cunning as a much smaller know-it-all. His script for *Rocky* and his way of selling its package were concocted with the same chutzpah; his version of an innocent oaf is shot through with poker-faced calculation. Those lavish spaniel eyes are worked on like a muscle. The appeal to little men is as much arrogant demagoguery as was Chaplin's. And, since Chaplin, who has offered tramps with such velvety romantic eyes? Such men know they are really princes in disguise, and scorn ordinariness.

He had a Sicilian father and a French mother, the one a hairdresser and the other a dancer. After some time at a private school for children with learning or behavior problems, he attended an American college in Switzerland. He studied drama at the University of Miami, and worked Off-Broadway. The alleged obscurity out of which *Rocky* emerged was actually filled with quite memorable bit parts and one major supporting role: *Bananas* (71, Woody Allen); *The Lords of Flatbush* (74, Stephen Verona and Martin Davidson); *Death Race 2000* (75, Paul Bartel); very good as the nemesis of *Capone* (75, Steve Carver); *The Prisoner of Second Avenue* (75, Melvin Frank); and *Farewell, My Lovely* (75, Dick Richards).

His script for *Rocky*, he claims, was written over a long weekend. Instead of taking $265,000 for it from Robert Chartoff and Irwin Winkler, he held out for $75,000, a percentage, and the lead part. I think it's true that no one else could have so disguised the sentimentality of the concept, or counted on an actor's craving for success fitting the boxer's corny shell.

Stallone also worked on the script of his follow-up, *F.I.S.T.* (78, Norman Jewison), an interesting treatment of American labor unions that would have been more absorbing if the hero had been more thoroughly infected by Stallone's own second-nature manipulativeness. He wrote, directed, and starred in *Paradise Alley* (78), a benign, Runyon-esque view of Bronx lowlife in 1946 that caught everybody off-guard. But *Rocky II* (79) was so brutally obvious a package that it only made one suspicious of Stallone's sympathy for little men.

Within the space of a few years, Stallone converted himself from a raw naïve to a sad-eyed stale smoothie. Rocky picked up Rambo as a friend, and Stallone became the unmistakable comforter to rednecks. His more recent work has sought fresh directions and more humor, but he lacks the will or the wit to change: *Nighthawks* (81, Bruce Malmuth); *Victory* (81, John Huston); *First Blood* (82, Ted Kotcheff); *Rocky III* (82, Stallone); *Staying Alive* (83, Stallone), a sequel to *Saturday Night Fever* for John Travolta; *Rhinestone* (84, Bob Clark), with Dolly Parton; *Rambo: First Blood Part II* (85, George P. Cosmatos); *Rocky IV* (85, Stallone); *Cobra* (86, Cosmatos); arm-wrestling in *Over the Top* (87, Menahem Golan); *Rambo III* (88, Peter Macdonald); *Lock Up* (89, John Flynn); *Tango and Cash* (89, Andrei Konchalovsky); *Rocky V* (90, Avildsen); *Oscar* (91, John Landis); *Stop! Or My Mom Will Shoot* (92, Roger Spottiswoode); *Cliffhanger* (93, Renny Harlin), his most entertaining film in years; and *Demolition Man* (93, Marco Brambilla).

In recent years, Stallone seems to have taken more punishment from his own films than ever Rocky endured. He looks miserable and picture-drunk. In America, his popularity has diminished, but it is said that he is still "very big, foreign." Maybe, but then one must conclude that that condition is not healthy. *The Specialist* (94, Luis Llosa); *Judge Dredd* (95, Danny Cannon); *Assassins* (95, Richard Donner); *Daylight* (96, Rob Cohen); *Cop Land* (97, James Mangold), where he tried to be ordinary; the voice of the Weaver on *Antz* (98, Eric Darnell and Tim Johnson); *Get Carter* (00, Stephen T. Kay); *Driven* (01, Harlin), which he wrote and produced; *Avenging Angelo* (02, Martyn Burke); *D-Tox* (02, Jim Gillespie).

Terence Stamp, b. Stepney, London, 1939

What on earth was Terence Stamp doing in *Star Wars: Episode 1—The Phantom Menace* (99, George Lucas)—and why was he looking so angry? Because he'd had no direction and couldn't follow the script? Because the rubbishy movie was a poor sixtieth birthday present for one of the most beautiful actors on film? Because he'd been this thankless route before—with an equally inane General Zod in the absurd but pompous *Superman* (78, Richard Donner)? Because he guessed that he wouldn't even figure in the abbreviated cast list for *Phantom Menace* in the *New York Times* review? Or was it just that he'd been left out of the first three editions of this book?

Well, I wronged Mr. Stamp. Yet I feel that he feels I am not alone. Is he chilly, difficult, a loner—or does he just give haughty imitations of those qualities? Whatever, it is remarkable that he hasn't been more important: for he is a good actor, very striking looking, and seldom far from magic at his best. Even now, is it possible that some great venture could take the fatalism out of his eyes—or make it one of the most alarming things we've ever seen?

He was a real cockney and working-class before Peter Ustinov put him in the lead role in *Billy Budd* (62), where he effortlessly suggested Melville's intimation of a seaman Christ. He seemed like a new star, but within a few years his career choices were those of a determined lone wolf—and so he has remained: *Term of Trial* (62, Peter Glenville); as the young man after butterflies in *The Collector* (65, William Wyler)—for which he won the best actor prize at Cannes; sidekick to *Modesty Blaise* (66, Joseph Losey); as the soldier in *Far from the Madding Crowd* (67, John Schlesinger); *Poor Cow* (67, Kenneth Loach); *Blue* (68, Silvio Narizzano); in Fellini's episode of *Spirits of the Dead* (68); as the mysterious stranger who masters everyone in *Teorema* (68, Pier Paolo Pasolini); as the man who emerges from a cave in *The Moods of Mr. Sommer* (70, Alan Cooke).

Then for several years he traveled and made only a few foreign films before his strictly supporting parts in a TV *Thief of Baghdad* (78, Clive Donner) and *Superman*. He seemed fully committed to the quest for the mystery of existence in *Meetings with Remarkable Men* (78, Peter Brook) and the bizarre sex intrigues of *I Love You, I Love You Not* (79, Americo Balducci).

If he had become disenchanted with film, his work now only explained that malaise: *Monster Island* (80, Juan Piquer Simón); *Superman II* (80, Donner); *Death in the Vatican* (81, Marcello Aliprandi). But then he gave maybe his greatest performance as the betrayer being brought home to death in *The Hit* (84, Stephen Frears), in which he worked wonderfully with John Hurt and Tim Roth and made clear that he was one of England's best actors. In which case how could one explain *Link* (84, Richard Franklin) or his stooge role in *Legal Eagles* (86, Ivan Reitman)?

Since then, he has made *The Sicilian* (87, Michael Cimino); *Wall Street* (87, Oliver Stone); *Young Guns* (88, Christopher Cain); *Alien Nation* (88, Graham Baker); *Stranger in the House* (91), which he directed; *The Real McCoy* (93, Russell Mulcahy); *The Adventures of Priscilla, Queen of the Desert* (94, Stephen Elliott), in which he was faultless as the transsexual; *Mindbender* (95, Ken Russell); the sex guru of all time in *Bliss* (97, Lance Young); *Kiss the Sky* (98, Roger Young); *Love Walked In* (98, Juan José Campanella).

In 1999, reviving footage from *Poor Cow*, he had a great personal success in *The Limey* (99, Steven Soderbergh)—it was the same territory as *The Hit*, but neither as sharp nor as cerebral. Still, the world was ready to acclaim him at last. He was also in *Bowfinger* (99, Frank Oz); *Red Planet* (00, Antony Hoffman); *Ma Femme Est une Actrice* (01, Yvan Attal); *Revelation* (01, Stuart Urban).

Harry Dean Stanton,
b. West Irvine, Kentucky, 1926

When Harry Dean arrived at last at his first great and surely last romantic leading part—in *Paris, Texas* (84, Wim Wenders)—he was fifty-eight, while his bride (Nastassja Kinski) was twenty-four. Yet Harry had looked gaunt and timeless for years, and he scarcely looks older now as he goes past seventy. Everyone rejoiced at *Paris, Texas*—whatever they thought of the film—to see Stanton rewarded. And it was only proper that his Travis in that film was just another of Harry Dean's wolf-faced loners writ large. He is among the last of the great supporting actors, as unfailing and visually eloquent as Anthony Mann's trees or "Mexico" in a Peckinpah film. Long ago, a French enthusiast said that Charlton Heston was "axiomatic." He might want that *pensée* back now. But Stanton is at least emblematic of sad films of action and travel. His face is like the road in the West.

He saw navy service in the Second World War, and then attended the University of Kentucky at Lexington and the Pasadena Playhouse. There is nothing to add, except the list (knowing that it leaves out a lot, to say nothing of TV work in Westerns): *Revolt at Fort Laramie* (57, Lesley Selander); *Tomahawk Trail* (57, Robert Parry); *The Proud Rebel* (58, Michael Curtiz); *Pork Chop Hill* (59, Lewis Milestone); *The Adventures of Huckleberry Finn* (60, Curtiz); *Hero's Island* (62, Leslie Stevens); *The Man from the Diner's Club* (63, Frank Tashlin); *Ride in the Whirlwind* (66, Monte Hellman); *Cool Hand Luke* (67, Stuart Rosenberg); *A Time for Killing* (67, Phil Karlson); *Day of the Evil Gun* (68, Jerry Thorpe); *The Miniskirt Mob* (68, Maury Dexter); *Cisco Pike* (71,

B. W. L. Norton); and *Two-Lane Blacktop* (71, Hellman).

He was Homer Van Meter in *Dillinger* (73, John Milius); a sidekick in a silly hat in *Pat Garrett and Billy the Kid* (73, Peckinpah); *Where the Lillies Bloom* (74, William A. Graham); *Cockfighter* (74, Hellman) with fellow-Kentuckian, Warren Oates; an FBI man guarding Frankie Pentangeli in *The Godfather, Part II* (74, Francis Ford Coppola); *Rancho Deluxe* (74, Frank Perry); *Zandy's Bride* (74, Jan Troell); *92 in the Shade* (75, Thomas McGuane); and *Farewell, My Lovely* (75, Dick Richman).

He had a lovely twilight talk with Jack Nicholson in *The Missouri Breaks* (76, Arthur Penn); *Renaldo & Clara* (77, Bob Dylan); *Straight Time* (78, Ulu Grosbard); *Alien* (79, Ridley Scott); *The Black Marble* (80, Harold Becker); *Deathwatch* (80, Bertrand Tavernier), as a villainous mastermind; briefly superb in *The Rose* (79, Mark Rydell); seriously brilliant in *Wise Blood* (79, John Huston); *Private Benjamin* (80, Howard Zieff); *UFOria* (80, John Binder); *Escape from New York* (81, John Carpenter); funny, casual, and quietly disintegrating in *One from the Heart* (82, Coppola); *Young Doctors in Love* (82, Garry Marshall); *Christine* (83, Carpenter); and *The Bear* (84, Richard Sarafian).

In *Paris, Texas,* he was as good walking, stiff-legged, across the desert as he was talking to his son and his wife—so many films should really have supporting actors as their central characters. He was in *Red Dawn* (84, Milius); he won a youthful cult following in *Repo Man* (84, Alex Cox); he seemed lost in *Fool for Love* (85, Robert Altman); he was a guardian angel with a satanic countenance in *One Magic Christmas* (85, Philip Borsos); *Pretty in Pink* (86, Howard Deutsch); *Slam Dance* (87, Wayne Wang); *The Last Temptation of Christ* (88, Martin Scorsese); *Mr. North* (88, Danny Huston); *Stars and Bars* (88, Pat O'Connor); *Dream a Little Dream* (89, Marc Rocco); *Twister* (89, Michael Almereyda); *The Fourth War* (90, John Frankenheimer); *Wild at Heart* (90, David Lynch); *Man Trouble* (92, Bob Rafelson); *Twin Peaks: Fire Walk with Me* (92, Lynch); and *Hostages* (93, David Wheatley).

In his seventies, he played smaller parts, often in minor films: *Blue Tiger* (94, Norberto Babu); *Never Talk to Strangers* (95, Peter Hall); *Playback* (95, Oley Sassone); *Midnight Blue* (96, Skott Snider); *She's So Lovely* (97, Nick Cassavetes); a judge in *Fear and Loathing in Las Vegas* (98, Terry Gilliam); still striking and iconic as the brother in *The Straight Story* (99, Lynch); *The Green Mile* (99, Frank Darabont); *The Man Who Cried* (00, Sally Potter); *Cadillac Tramps* (00, Thomas Sjolund); *The Pledge* (01, Sean Penn).

Barbara Stanwyck (Ruby Stevens) (1907–90), b. Brooklyn, New York

So much of her character lay in the distance between the real and the professional names. If "Barbara Stanwyck" was the woman of the world, sophisticated, ruthless, and a fierce careerist, the lady generally smothering the moll in herself, then "Ruby Stevens" was the girl from the wrong side of the tracks, hard outside and soft inside, generous but ambitious: the girl in burlesque who can masquerade as a lady when the chance offers. Time and again, her best work fell within this range, displaying her on sliding emotional, social, and moral scales.

Stanwyck was more intelligent, warmer, and a good deal tougher than Joan Crawford, whose work showed certain similarities to hers, and she was always more interesting and entertaining to watch. The manner of her survival, no matter if often undercutting melodramatic and romantic material, was a vindication of the personality and attitude she accumulated in her films. There is not a more credible portrait in the cinema of a worldly, attractive, and independent woman in a man's world than Stanwyck's career revealed. In middle and old age, her looks distilled into narrowed eyes and silver hair; thus it is worth insisting that in the 1930s and 1940s she was delectable, a stirring mixture of toughness and sentiment, a truly and creatively two-faced woman.

Orphaned when young, Ruby was brought up by an older sister who was a dancer. She had a tough life. Inevitably, she began working in the same world, in speakeasies and eventually on Broadway in *The Noose* and as the star of *Burlesque* in 1926. She was a dancer in her first movie, *Broadway Nights* (27, Joseph C. Boyle) for First National, and in 1929 she played in George Fitzmaurice's *The Locked Door.* Stanwyck's own talent, her husky speaking voice, and the managerial efforts of her husband, comedian Frank Fay, soon made her a star of the early sound cinema. She managed, with varying success, to play Warners and Columbia off against each other and was never tied exclusively to one studio: *Mexicali Rose* (30, Erle C. Kenton); *Ten Cents a Dance* (31, Lionel Barrymore); and *The Secret Bride* (34, William Dieterle).

Two directors stand out in her early work: Frank Capra and William Wellman. With Capra, at Columbia, she made *Ladies of Leisure* (30), *The Miracle Woman* (31), *Forbidden* (32), and *The Bitter Tea of General Yen* (32)—the latter including a vivid erotic shimmer as Stanwyck dreams of being ravished by Nils Asther. While for Wellman, she was menaced by Gable in *Night Nurse* (31), aging in *So Big* (32), and in *The Purchase Price* (32).

Her image of the hard-boiled girl of easy virtue

was kept up in William Keighley's *Ladies They Talk About* (33) and in *Baby Face* (33, Alfred E. Green), in which she maneuvers her way up the length of the business ladder—by every seductive means at her command. It would be difficult to think of an actress so expressive of the early 1930s girl on the make—as intimate, shiny, and flimsy as a discarded slip, but with eyes ever sly and alert. So often with great movie actresses, we have a first thought of skin tone: with Stanwyck it is of tacky paint, too warm for glossy hardness.

Archie Mayo's *Gambling Lady* (34) and Robert Florey's *The Woman in Red* (35) ended her contracts with Warners and Columbia. She then came to an agreement with RKO, which allowed her to free-lance, and made *Annie Oakley* (35, George Stevens), *A Message to Garcia* (36, George Marshall), and *His Brother's Wife* (36, W. S. Van Dyke). (It was in this film that she first worked with Robert Taylor, her second husband, 1939–52.) Stanwyck now mixed comedies with two uncompromisingly serious movies: John Cromwell's *Banjo On My Knee* (36) and John Ford's *The Plough and the Stars* (37). Immediately, she made one of her classic movies: as the mother in *Stella Dallas* (37) for Goldwyn and King Vidor, more emotional than most of her work, and enforced by Vidor's full-blooded indignation at social barriers to raw nature.

After *The Mad Miss Manton* (38, Leigh Jason), she was a De Mille tomboy heroine in *Union Pacific* (39); in Mamoulian's *Golden Boy* (39); superb as a shoplifter in Mitchell Leisen's *Remember the Night* (40); giving one of the best American comedy performances in Preston Sturges's *The Lady Eve* (41); reunited with Capra for *Meet John Doe* (41); *You Belong to Me* (41, Wesley Ruggles); teaching criminal slang to Gary Cooper in Hawks's *Ball of Fire* (41); two more films with Wellman: *The Great Man's Lady* (42) and *Lady of Burlesque* (43), the latter as a wisecracking stripper.

If the unscrupulousness in her character had been under wraps for some years, it was unveiled again in Billy Wilder's *Double Indemnity* (44). As the double-crossing, blonde wife she is marvelously sinuous and insulting, the perfect exploiter of Fred MacMurray's lazy moral inertia. She is a presence openly inviting touching; so many handholds—ringlets, block-heeled shoes, flounced dresses, anklets, padded shoulders, and barbed remarks—that snap shut on idly philandering hands. It is part of the American dream, a comfort to weary salesmen, that such glittering Medusas are waiting behind doors in every other home.

As she grew older and with the postwar reaction to many established stars, Stanwyck found herself in several poor comedies and as a single woman, harassed by a man. This was a role that Joan Crawford made her own, but Stanwyck had three notable attempts at it: *Cry Wolf* (47, Peter Godfrey), *The Two Mrs. Carrolls* (47, Godfrey), and best of all, menaced by Burt Lancaster, in Litvak's *Sorry, Wrong Number* (48). Stanwyck had always been a man's woman and it was sad to see her drifting into women's melodramas: *The Strange Love of Martha Ivers* (46, Lewis Milestone); *The Other Love* (47, André de Toth); and *East Side, West Side* (49, Mervyn Le Roy). She was much better in *California* (46, John Farrow), in Anthony Mann's *The Furies* (50), and outstanding again as the woman with a past yearning for a secure marriage in Fritz Lang's *Clash By Night* (52); this is her most humane and touching performance.

Undeniably, her career now began to decline in terms of prestige and worthwhile parts. Nevertheless, even in weepies or as domineering women she made several excellent films: Siodmak's *The File on Thelma Jordon* (49), in which she sighs, "Maybe I'm just a dame and didn't know it," when Wendell Corey first kisses her; very touching in Mitchell Leisen's *No Man of Her Own* (50); *All I Desire* (53, Douglas Sirk); the excellent *Blowing Wild* (53, Hugo Fregonese), which replenished her as a sexy woman; two Allan Dwan adventures, *Escape to Burma* (55) and *Cattle Queen of Montana* (54). A modern businesswoman in Robert Wise's *Executive Suite* (54), she was happier in full-blooded adventure: loathing her crippled husband, Edward G. Robinson, in *The Violent Men* (55, Rudolph Maté); *The Maverick Queen* (56, Joseph Kane); Gerd Oswald's *Crime of Passion* (57); and Samuel Fuller's *Forty Guns* (57). *There's Always Tomorrow* (56, Sirk) was an attempt to reunite her with Fred MacMurray, but she then went into reluctant retirement.

She reemerged to dominate the nonsense of *Walk on the Wild Side* (62, Edward Dmytryk), to join Elvis Presley in *Roustabout* (64, John Rich), and to play with Robert Taylor in the miserable *The Night Walker* (65, William Castle). She made no more movies, but her TV series, *The Big Valley*, was a personal success (65–69) and she played the matriarch in *The Thorn Birds* (83).

While she was alive, she did not seem one of the great stars. But at her death, it was clear how widely she was loved. She was honest, sharp, gutsy, and smart. Terrific.

Rod Steiger (Rodney Stephen Steiger) (1925–2002), b. Westhampton, New York
The child of a song-and-dance team divorced when he was a baby, he acted at school. At sixteen he lied about his age and served four years in the navy as a torpedoman. After the war, he studied at the Actors Studio, and in 1951 made his Broadway debut in *Night Music*. In the same year, he appeared in Fred Zinnemann's *Teresa*, but as yet his major work was on TV where he played Chayefsky's *Marty* in the original production, as

well as Rudolf Hess in the series *You Were There*.

His first substantial film part was as Brando's brother in *On the Waterfront* (54, Elia Kazan). This began a sequence of heavies, some alarmingly mannered and overblown, some loathsome, but all compellingly personal: *The Big Knife* (55, Robert Aldrich) as the movie producer; *The Court Martial of Billy Mitchell* (55, Otto Preminger); *Jubal* (56, Delmer Daves); *The Harder They Fall* (56, Mark Robson); a disturbing Judd Fry in *Oklahoma!* (55, Zinnemann); and *Back from Eternity* (56, John Farrow). Although Steiger now dislikes the film, none of these performances has survived as well as his Irish-Confederate-Comanche in Fuller's *Run of the Arrow* (57), or the tommygun-in-cheek *Al Capone* (58, Richard Wilson).

But Steiger insisted on taking himself seriously: *The Mark* (61, Guy Green); *Le Mani Sulla Citta* (63, Francesco Rosi); *A Man Named John* (64, Ermanno Olmi); *The Pawnbroker* (65, Sidney Lumet); *Dr. Zhivago* (65, David Lean); *The Sergeant* (68, John Flynn), which are generally fraught with an oppressive sincerity and a very clammy technique. He is much better in the old-fashioned setting of *Seven Thieves* (60, Henry Hathaway); *In the Heat of the Night* (67, Norman Jewison)—for which he won the Oscar; and the comedy of *No Way to Treat a Lady* (68, Jack Smight).

His marriage to Claire Bloom led to their joint Broadway appearance in 1959 in *Rashomon*, and two interesting failures: *The Illustrated Man* (69, Smight) and *Three Into Two Won't Go* (69, Peter Hall).

Steiger was ambitious eventually of writing, directing, and acting in his own films. But he had to content himself with playing broken tyrants: a bloodshot Napoleon in *Waterloo* (70, Sergei Bondarchuk); the Hemingway figure in *Happy Birthday, Wanda June* (71, Mark Robson); as the force of brutal nature bandit in *A Fistful of Dynamite* (71, Sergio Leone); as a hillbilly patriarch in *The Lolly-Madonna War* (73, Richard C. Sarafian); in *Lucky Luciano* (73, Rosi).

He was the crumbling Duce in *Mussolini Ultimo Alto* (74, Carlo Lizzani); a vengeful IRA explosives man in *Hennessy* (75, Don Sharp); the husband in *Innocents with Dirty Hands* (75, Claude Chabrol); trying to imitate a man who was too shifty or haphazard to pin down in *W. C. Fields and Me* (76, Arthur Hiller), but never showing how that great humbug was funny; an investigating senator in *F.I.S.T.* (78, Jewison); *Love and Bullets* (78, Stuart Rosenberg); and *Breakthrough* (79, Andrew V. McLaglen).

He was in *The Amityville Horror* (79, Rosenberg); *Cattle Annie and Little Britches* (80, Lamont Johnson); *Klondike Fever* (80, Peter Carter); *The Lucky Star* (80, Max Fischer); as Mussolini again in *Lion of the Desert* (81,

Moustapha Akkad); *The Chosen* (81, Jeremy Paul Kagan); *Der Zauberberg* (82, Hans W. Geissendorfer); as Peary in *Cook and Peary: The Race to the Pole* (83, Robert Day); *The Naked Face* (84, Bryan Forbes); *Feel the Heat* (86, Joel Silberg); *Sword of Gideon* (86, Michael Anderson); *The Kindred* (87, Stephen Carpenter); *American Gothic* (87, John Hough); *Desperado: Avalanche at Devil's Ridge* (88, Richard Compton); *The January Man* (88, Pat O'Connor); *Passion and Paradise* (89, Harvey Hart); *That Summer of White Roses* (89, Rajko Grlic); *Men of Respect* (90, William Kelly); *The Ballad of the Sad Cafe* (91, Simon Callow); *Time to Kill: In the Line of Duty* (91, Dick Lowry); for British TV, in *Tales of the City* (93, Alastair Reid).

He stayed busy, having overcome illness: *The Specialist* (94, Luis Llosa); *Tous les Jours Dimanche* (95, Jean Charles Tacchella); *In Pursuit of Honor* (95, Ken Olin); *Captain Nuke and the Bomber Boys* (95, Charles Gale); *Dalva* (96, Ken Cameron); *Mars Attacks!* (96, Tim Burton); *Truth or Consequences, N.M.* (97, Kiefer Sutherland); *Modern Vampires* (98, Richard Elfman); *Legacy* (98, T. J. Scott); *Body and Soul* (98, Sam Henry Kass); *Crazy in Alabama* (99, Antonio Banderas); as the judge who frees the *Hurricane* (99, Jewison); *End of Days* (99, Peter Hyams); *The Last Producer* (00, Burt Reynolds); *The Flying Dutchman* (00, Robin P. Murray).

James Stephenson (1889–1941),
b. Selby, Yorkshire, England

Bette Davis never mentions James Stephenson in her book *The Lonely Life*, which is odd. After all, Davis was a very perceptive actress, well aware that *The Letter* (40, William Wyler) was among the best, and least impeded, things she would ever do. She had been in love with Wyler during the film's making, and she surely saw and felt how far Stephenson was used in that film as a man torn between love and loathing for Leslie Crosbie . . . or Bette Davis.

Stephenson lacks a body of work that insists on being dealt with here. Yet I welcome him into the book, because his Howard Joyce in *The Letter* is one of the great performances in film history. And that was noted at the time: after a string of minor roles, Stephenson was nominated as best supporting actor in the film (he lost to Walter Brennan in *The Westerner*—a comic reversal of justice). Except that Stephenson is hardly a supporting actor in the film. He is actually credited as a star, and I'm sure he's on screen more than Herbert Marshall as the husband. Indeed, I think of *The Letter* as a series of terrible examinations in which Stephenson gradually exposes Davis's guilt, and his own distress.

He was an English stage actor (as far as I can tell) who arrived in Hollywood (at Warners) only in the mid-1930s. He worked hard for the next few years, but so many of his parts were far smaller than his capacity: *King of the Underworld* (37, Lewis Seiler); *The Cowboy from Brooklyn* (38, Lloyd Bacon); *Boy Meets Girl* (38, Bacon); *Nancy Drew, Detective* (38, William Clemens); *Devil's Island* (39, Clemens), with Boris Karloff; *Torchy Blane in Chinatown* (39, William Beaudine); *Secret Service of the Air* (39, Noel Smith), a Ronald Reagan picture; *Confessions of a Nazi Spy* (39, Anatole Litvak); *The Old Maid* (39, Edmund Goulding), with Bette Davis; as Major de Beaujolais in *Beau Geste* (39, William Wellman); as Egerton in *The Private Lives of Elizabeth and Essex* (39, Michael Curtiz); *We Are Not Alone* (39, Goulding); the lead in *Calling Philo Vance* (40, Clemens); *The Sea Hawk* (40, Curtiz); *Murder in the Air* (40, Seiler); *A Dispatch from Reuters* (40, William Dieterle); as a shrink who hardly realizes Geraldine Fitzgerald loves him in *Shining Victory* (41, Irving Rapper); teaching Reagan in *International Squadron* (41, Lothar Mendes); *Flight from Destiny* (41, Vincent Sherman).

He died, of a heart attack, in Los Angeles in 1941. Of course, he didn't look well in *The Letter,* but one reads that as the impact of Leslie Crosbie.

George Stevens (1904–75),

b. Oakland, California

1933: *Cohens and Kellys in Trouble.* 1934: *Bachelor Bait; Kentucky Kernels.* 1935: *Alice Adams; Laddie; The Nitwits; Annie Oakley.* 1936: *Swing Time.* 1937: *Quality Street; A Damsel in Distress.* 1938: *Vivacious Lady.* 1939: *Gunga Din.* 1940: *Vigil in the Night.* 1941: *Penny Serenade.* 1942: *Woman of the Year; The Talk of the Town.* 1943: *The More the Merrier.* 1948: *I Remember Mama.* 1951: *A Place in the Sun.* 1952: *Something to Live For.* 1953: *Shane.* 1956: *Giant.* 1959: *The Diary of Anne Frank.* 1965: *The Greatest Story Ever Told.* 1969: *The Only Game in Town.*

There is a George Stevens film not in the filmography, seldom seen, and not even shaped into a "movie." It is the 16mm color footage he shot himself in Europe as head of the Signal Corps Special Motion Picture Unit. It includes scenes of death and ruin, as well as coverage of Dachau taken shortly after its liberation. I mention this because it is often said that the war changed Stevens, and made it less easy for him to believe in entertainment. Was he a Sullivan who went too far to be comfortable again in Hollywood? There is no biography as yet, so the question is hard to answer. But something seems to have afflicted Stevens. He was never a great director. But in the thirties he had a feeling for fun, grace, and story. Thereafter, he was always somber—and sometimes heavier than that.

This falling off is all the sadder in view of Stevens's origins. Hal Roach hired him as gagman and, eventually, director for Laurel and Hardy. Once established, he made a string of pleasant pictures, usually with a comic emphasis and allowing special opportunities to actors. *Alice Adams* is still a major Katharine Hepburn film; *Swing Time* is classic Astaire and Rogers with Astaire's virtuoso "Bojangles" dance and one of the most mercurial of the intimate dance routines with Ginger, "Pick Yourself Up"; *Quality Street, Vivacious Lady, Gunga Din, Penny Serenade, Woman of the Year, The Talk of the Town,* and *The More the Merrier* all seem scarcely to belong to the laborious director of later years, dulled by overcraft. *Woman of the Year,* especially, is an excellent emotional comedy that introduced Spencer Tracy and Katharine Hepburn and never lost the charge of feeling between them, even if it settles for a male chauvinist attitude. *Talk of the Town* has unresolved echoes of Capra and *Fury,* too much piety toward the Supreme Court, and too great a willingness to keep Cary Grant in hiding while Jean Arthur and Ronald Colman talk.

The theory outlined above doesn't quite hold. *I Remember Mama* is decent and very fond of the Bay Area, and *A Place in the Sun* is a beautifully pessimistic love story, nearly rapturous in its treatment of Clift and Elizabeth Taylor and in its observation of their feelings for each other. Indeed, there is a gravitational pull toward death in the love scenes that is unashamed and subversive.

Of the rest, *Shane* works because of a simple fable, the jeweled grandeur of the landscape, and the rapport between Alan Ladd and Brandon de Wilde. *Giant* is bloated, seldom plausible, with actors who never settle into the story or the idea of Texas. The three films after that are strenuous disasters. Maybe Stevens was miscast as a maker of big pictures, and rather exposed when he had to take up the load of theme or ideas.

After all, in the thirties, he directed scripts, stories, projects, and stars that had built-in virtues. There have always been directors who were most generously used if asked to do no more. But maybe war and its horrors compelled Stevens into authorship and philosophy, things beyond his craft.

Mark (Richard) Stevens (1915–94),

b. Cleveland, Ohio

1954: *Cry Vengeance.* 1956: *Timetable.* 1965: *Sunscorched.*

Mark Stevens was an actor principally, but in the mid-fifties he turned out two deft thrillers that are worth pursuing. In *Cry Vengeance* he is a man trying to find those who sent him to prison; in *Timetable,* he is an insurance investigator on the track of a robbery he has organized himself. *Sun-*

scorched I've never seen, or really heard of—it also goes by the title *Tierra del Fuego*.

Before that, Stevens went from radio to the movies in the early forties: *Passage to Marseille* (44, Michael Curtiz); *Objective Burma* (45, Raoul Walsh); *Within These Walls* (45, Bruce Humberstone); *Pride of the Marines* (45, Delmer Daves); *I Wonder Who's Kissing Her Now* (47, Lloyd Bacon); *The Street with No Name* (48, William Keighley); *The Snake Pit* (48, Anatole Litvak); *Sand* (49, Louis King); *Oh, You Beautiful Doll* (49, John M. Stahl); *Dancing in the Dark* (49, Irving Reis); *Reunion in Reno* (51, Kurt Neumann); *Little Egypt* (51, Frederick de Cordova); *Mutiny* (52, Edward Dmytryk); *Torpedo Alley* (53, Lew Landers); *Jack Slade* (53, Harold Schuster); *Gunsmoke in Tucson* (58, Thomas Carr); *September Storm* (60, Byron Haskin); *Fate Is the Hunter* (64, Ralph Nelson).

From 1954–56, he was producer, director, and star of the TV series *Big Town*, in which he was a newspaper editor.

James Stewart (1908–97),
b. Indiana, Pennsylvania

Stewart is one of the most trusted and beloved of American actors, an icon arousing great public affection chiefly because of his comedies, *It's a Wonderful Life*, and his artful portrait of simplicity. His body of mature films, made during the 1950s for Hitchcock and Anthony Mann, while generally presenting him as a troubled, querulous, or lonely personality, clearly play on the immense reputation for charm that his early films had won. Thus Stewart is one of the most intriguing examples of a star cast increasingly against his accepted character. The emotional subtlety of films like *The Naked Spur*, *Rear Window*, *The Far Country*, *The Man from Laramie*, and *Vertigo* derives from the way in which we are intrigued by the contradictions in Stewart himself, between hardness and vulnerability. Who can forget his nightmare in *The Naked Spur*, or his cries of distress?

Yet in the years before the war, Stewart was preeminently a diffident, wide-eyed, drawling innocent, a country boy who had wandered into a crazily sophisticated world. After a brief foray as a heavy—in *Rose Marie* (36, W. S. Van Dyke) and *After the Thin Man* (36, Van Dyke)—he settled down as a romantic lead and an honest crusader, thriving on grassroots virtues of honor and simplicity long forgotten by Hollywood's lounge lizards.

Stewart had studied architecture at Princeton before he joined a theatrical company led by Joshua Logan and also including Henry Fonda. He worked steadily in the theatre until 1935 when he made his debut in *The Murder Man* (Tim Whelan) on an MGM contract. He was loaned to Universal for *Next Time We Love* (36, Edward H.

Griffith), opposite Margaret Sullavan, and his own studio gave him supporting parts: *Wife vs. Secretary* (36, Clarence Brown); *Small Town Girl* (36, William Wellman); and *The Gorgeous Hussy* (36, Clarence Brown). He had the lead opposite Eleanor Powell and sang (with very thin voice) in *Born to Dance* (36, Roy del Ruth) and then played with Simone Simon in *Seventh Heaven* (37, Henry King). He had more support work in *The Last Gangster* (37, Edward Ludwig), *Navy Blue and Gold* (37, Sam Wood), and *Of Human Hearts* (38, Brown), before finding his place in romantic comedies: *Vivacious Lady* (38, George Stevens); as the Texan soldier who meets Margaret Sullavan in New York in *The Shopworn Angel* (38, H. C. Potter); and Frank Capra's *You Can't Take It With You* (38).

He followed these with *Made for Each Other* (39, John Cromwell); *It's a Wonderful World* (39, Van Dyke); the classic early Stewart role, Jefferson Smith, in Capra's *Mr. Smith Goes to Washington* (39); the taciturn cowboy taming Dietrich in *Destry Rides Again* (39, George Marshall); two more clever pairings with Margaret Sullavan—a wise Lubitsch comedy, *The Shop Around the Corner* (40) and Frank Borzage's *The Mortal Storm* (40)—one of cinema's best two-shots is Sullavan reclining and inspecting the shining diffidence of a young Stewart; a rather generous best actor Oscar in *The Philadelphia Story* (40, George Cukor).

His popularity was undoubtedly enhanced by a distinguished war record in the air force—a record later invoked in Anthony Mann's *Strategic Air Command* (55). After the war, Stewart left MGM and free-lanced for several years: one of his favorite roles, George Bailey, in Capra's *It's a Wonderful Life* (46), a picture that caught the first hint of frenzy and gloom; Wellman's *Magic Town* (47); the reporter in *Call Northside 777* (48, Henry Hathaway); and his first Hitchcock movie, the relentlessly interior *Rope* (48), playing a rather monotonous seeker-out of truth.

Briefly, his career faltered, but in 1950 he went to Universal to make *Winchester 73* (Anthony Mann) and to Fox for *Broken Arrow* (Delmer Daves). He then made two movies for Henry Koster that successfully reworked his shy charm: *Harvey* (50) and *No Highway* (51). But the Western—especially the unexpected intensity he had revealed in *Winchester 73*—now claimed him. After playing the clown in De Mille's *The Greatest Show on Earth* (52), Stewart struck an innovatory contract with Universal whereby he took a percentage of his films' profits.

It was this deal that allowed Stewart and Anthony Mann to make *Bend of the River* (52); *Thunder Bay* (53); *The Glenn Miller Story* (54); and *The Far Country* (54). Curiously, *The Naked Spur*, made with Mann in 1953, and looking like a

Universal Western, is an MGM picture. These Westerns redefined Stewart's character: he was now revealed as a tougher, more pained and selfish man, who was often made to suffer and put to a brutal test of courage and wounding. It was the more of an achievement since, as Glenn Miller, Stewart was as homely, sentimental, and appealing as ever.

In 1954, Hitchcock pounced on this new Stewart and put him in a wheelchair as the voyeur photographer in *Rear Window* (54), while in 1955, at Columbia, Mann and Stewart made another Western, *The Man from Laramie*, which dealt especially well with the effect of violence on Stewart. The scene in which Alex Nicol maims Stewart's hand, and Stewart's swooning reaction, introduce a new frankness about violence in American films. Hitchcock used him in the much simpler central role in *The Man Who Knew Too Much* (55) and Billy Wilder made an inexplicable failure with Stewart playing Lindbergh in *The Spirit of St. Louis* (57).

Despite every hint of the darker side of Stewart, Hitchcock's *Vertigo* (58) was still a surprise. A masterpiece by any terms, Stewart's portrayal of the detective who loses his nerve and then becomes entranced by the two forms of a mythic Kim Novak is frightening in its intensity: a far cry from a man who talked to rabbits.

But as if to assert versatility, Stewart then returned (with Novak) to middle-aged comedy in Richard Quine's *Bell, Book and Candle* (58). Perhaps his last major role, and one played with comfortable fraudulence, was the country lawyer in Preminger's *Anatomy of a Murder* (59). Thereafter, mannerism, laziness, and indifference set in, perhaps encouraged by John Ford, who tolerated a growing self-indulgence in *Two Rode Together* (61); *The Man Who Shot Liberty Valance* (62); as Wyatt Earp in *Cheyenne Autumn* (64). Otherwise, Stewart tried to revive his 1930 comedy character in some very dull movies and surrendered to knockabout Westerns that are sad indeed when one recalls the cold, laconic hero of Mann's films: *How the West Was Won* (62, Hathaway); *Shenandoah* (65, Andrew V. McLaglen); *Firecreek* (67, Vincent McEveety); *Bandolero!* (68, McLaglen); *The Cheyenne Social Club* (70, Gene Kelly); and *Dynamite Man from Glory Jail* (71, McLaglen). Only Aldrich's *The Flight of the Phoenix* (65) used Stewart honestly—as a harassed, elderly, and oldfashioned pilot in a crisis. All too briefly, he was compelled to tell John Wayne his negative prognosis in *The Shootist* (76, Don Siegel): a case of the doctor looking less hearty than the patient. Stewart was a very frail General Sternwood in the awful remake of *The Big Sleep* (78, Michael Winner), giving up the ghost in a film not worthy of him. But he looked fitter in *The Magic of Lassie* (78, Don Chaffey).

After that he made *Afurika Monogatari* (81, Susumu Hani) and *Right of Way* (83, George Schaefer), with Bette Davis; and he gave his quavery voice to Sheriff Wylie Burp in *American Tail: Fievel Goes West* (91, Phil Nibbelink). When he died, *Time* and Richard Corliss called him "A Wonderful Fella." It was the world's thought. And in time to come, the young Stewart may stand for the great America of the thirties and forties, when few doubted life's prospect.

Mauritz Stiller (1883–1928),
b. Helsinki, Finland
1912: *Mor och Dotter; De Svarta Maskerna; Den Tyranniske Fastmannen*. 1913: *Vampyren; Nar Karleken Dodar; Barnet; Nar Larmklockan Ljuder; Den Moderna Suffragetten; Pa Livets Odesvagar; Den Okanda; Mannekangen; Livets Konflikter*. 1914: *Broderna; Nar svarmor regerar; Gransfolken; For sin karleks skull; Kammarjunkaren; Stormfageln; Skottet; Det Roda Tornet*. 1915: *Nar konstnarer alska; Lekkamraterna; Hans Hustrus forflutna; Dolken; Mastertjuven; Madame de Thebes*. 1916: *Hamnaren; Minlotsen; Hans Brollopsnatt; Lyckonalen; Karlek och Journalistik; Vingarna; Kampen om hans hjarta; Balettprimadonnan*. 1917: *Thomas Graals Basta Film; Alexander den store*. 1918: *Thomas Graals Basta Barn*. 1919: *Sangen om dem eldroda blomman; Herr Arne's Pengar/Sir Arne's Treasure*. 1920: *Fiskebyn; Erotikon*. 1921: *Johan; De Landsflyktige*. 1923: *Gunnar Hedes Saga*. 1924: *Gosta Berlings Saga/The Atonement of Gosta Berling*. 1926: *Hotel Imperial; The Temptress* (begun by Stiller, but completed by Fred Niblo). 1927: *The Woman on Trial*. 1928: *The Street of Sin*.

Stiller has been overshadowed by his own discovery, Greta Garbo. He chose her for her first big part in *The Atonement of Gosta Berling*, a film seen by Louis B. Mayer in 1925. It is not clear on exactly what terms Mayer invited its actress and director to Europe. MGM were not averse to Swedish talent: they were having some success with Victor Sjöström. Josef von Sternberg let it be known that he urged Stiller on Mayer and suggested that Garbo be brought along "in the luggage." But the briefest survey of Mayer's career emphasizes that he would have been more susceptible to Garbo's talents than to Stiller's. Events make it fairly clear that Stiller was the passenger. MGM never really employed him, and Mayer jealously guarded Garbo against her former Svengali. Garbo's American debut, *The Torrent*, was assigned to Monta Bell, and Stiller pointedly neglected. *Hotel Imperial, The Woman on Trial*, and *The Street of Sin* were all made at Paramount, while *The Temptress*—Garbo's second film—was quickly removed from Stiller's hands. He returned to Sweden in rage and died within a year.

All of which makes it difficult to assess his contribution as a director. He was widely held to be one of the leading Swedish directors, matched only by Sjöström. Stiller worked in a variety of genres, and *Sir Arne's Treasure* is a magnificent spectacle concerning Scottish mercenaries in a wintry, sixteenth-century Sweden. But his most characteristic vein was comedy—unusually sophisticated and often dealing with an artist figure. Thus the two Thomas Graal films are instances of the fusion of art and life, such as has preoccupied Bergman. While *Erotikon,* a story about the love life of a sculptor, has the sort of sexual interchange of *Smiles of a Summer Night* and *Now, About These Women.*

Dean Stockwell,
b. North Hollywood, California, 1936

With the TV series *Quantum Leap* and with his regular work as a supporting actor in movies, Dean Stockwell may never have been better known. Yet he has experienced so many stages and changes already—the piercing child; the beautiful yet not quite penetrating young lead; the wanderer, hippie, and biker; the realtor in New Mexico; and now, for a decade at least, the versatile, reliable, yet never quite predictable character actor who seems blessed to play men brushed by the wing of uncommon experience—as if they might once have had green hair. The child who was once the center of films has become a man content to be an outcast or an eccentric.

He is the son of actor Harry Stockwell, and the older brother of Guy Stockwell, and he was a steady movie child at Metro by the age of nine: *Anchors Aweigh* (45, George Sidney); *The Valley of Decision* (45, Tay Garnett); *The Green Years* (46, Victor Saville); *Home Sweet Homicide* (46, Lloyd Bacon); *The Mighty McGurk* (46, John Waters), with Wallace Beery; *The Arnelo Affair* (47, Arch Oboler); *Gentleman's Agreement* (47, Elia Kazan); *The Romance of Rosy Ridge* (47, Roy Rowland); *Song of the Thin Man* (47, Edward Buzzell); rising to the great challenge of *The Boy with Green Hair* (48, Joseph Losey); *Deep Waters* (48, Henry King); *Down to the Sea in Ships* (49, Henry Hathaway); precociously aware of invalid psychology in *The Secret Garden* (49, Fred M. Wilcox), that masterpiece of child acting; *The Happy Years* (50, William Wellman); with Errol Flynn in *Kim* (50, Saville); very moving with Joel McCrea in *Stars in My Crown* (50, Jacques Tourneur) and *Cattle Drive* (51, Kurt Neumann).

He was away from the screen for several years and came back as a twenty-year-old: *Gun for a Coward* (56, Abner Biberman); *The Careless Years* (57, Arthur Hiller); with Bradford Dillman as Leopold and Loeb in *Compulsion* (59, Richard Fleischer); as the young D. H. Lawrence in *Sons and Lovers* (60, Jack Cardiff); and worthy of the exceptional cast as Eugene O'Neill's alter ego in *Long Day's Journey into Night* (62, Sidney Lumet).

Again, he stopped, and within a few years he was an available actor for a strange assortment of sixties dreams and delusions: *Rapture* (65, John Guillermin); *Psych-Out* (68, Richard Rush); as a warlock in *The Dunwich Horror* (70, Daniel Haller); *The Last Movie* (71, Dennis Hopper); *Paper Man* (71, Walter Grauman) for TV; *The Loners* (72, Sutton Roley); *Werewolf of Washington* (73, Milton Ginsberg); narrating *Eadweard Muybridge, Zoopraxographer* (74, Thom Anderson); *Win, Place or Steal* (75, Richard Bailey); *Won Ton Ton, the Dog Who Saved Hollywood* (75, Michael Winner); *Tracks* (76, Henry Jaglom); and *The Killing Affair* (77, Richard C. Sarafian).

Then, after another absence, he did *Born to Be Sold* (81, Burt Brinckerhoff) for TV; *Wrong Is Right* (82, Richard Brooks); he codirected *Human Highway* (82) with Neil Young; and he went to Nicaragua to make *Alsino y El Condor* (83, Miguel Littin). Then in 1984, he had a real part in the forlorn *Dune* (David Lynch) and unexpected attention as the decent, steady brother in *Paris, Texas* (84, Wim Wenders). That picture did well enough in America to begin to ease away his freaky reputation. He was back to the mainstream.

He was in *The Legend of Billie Jean* (85, Matthew Robbins); *To Live and Die in L.A.* (85, William Friedkin); uncanny, terrifying, and wonderful in the best scenes from *Blue Velvet* (86, David Lynch); *Gardens of Stone* (87, Francis Ford Coppola); *Beverly Hills Cop 2* (87, Tony Scott); *Buying Time* (88, Mitchell Gabourie); delicious as Howard Hughes in *Tucker* (88, Coppola); broad and funny as a camp don in *Married to the Mob* (88, Jonathan Demme)—he was nominated for the supporting actor Oscar; *The Blue Iguana* (88, John Lafia); *Limit Up* (89, Richard Martini); *Backtrack* (90, Hopper); *Sandino* (90, Littin); *Son of the Morning Star* (91, Mike Robe); and making the most of morsels in *The Player* (92, Robert Altman).

In recent years, he has done a lot of TV as well as *Friends and Enemies* (92, Andrew Frank); *Chasers* (94, Hopper); the father in *Madonna: Innocence Lost* (94, Bradford May); *Naked Souls* (95, Lyndon Chubbuck); *Mr. Wrong* (96, Nick Castle); *Unabomber: The True Story* (96, Jon Purdy); *Midnight Blue* (96, Skott Snider); *The Last Resort* (97, Lyman Dayton); *Air Force One* (97, Wolfgang Petersen); *The Rainmaker* (97, Coppola); *The Shadow Men* (97, Timothy Bond); *Restraining Order* (99, Lee H. Katzin); *The Venice Project* (99, Robert Dornhelm); *Water Damage* (99, Murray Battle); *Rites of Passage* (99, Victor Salva); *In Pursuit* (00, Peter Pistor); *The Quickie* (01, Sergei Bodrov); *Buffalo Soldiers* (01, Gregor Jordan); *Inferno* (01, Dusty Nelson).

Andrew L. Stone (1902–99),
b. Oakland, California

1927: *The Elegy*. 1928: *Dreary House; Lieben-straum*. 1930: *Sombras de Gloria*. 1932: *Hell's Headquarters*. 1937: *The Girl Said No*. 1938: *Stolen Heaven; Say It in French; There's Magic in Music*. 1939: *The Great Victor Herbert*. 1941: *The Hard-Boiled Canary*. 1943: *Stormy Weather; Hi, Diddle Diddle*. 1944: *Sensations of 1945*. 1945: *Bedside Manner*. 1946: *The Bachelor's Daughter*. 1947: *Fun on a Weekend*. 1950: *Highway 301*. 1952: *Confidence Girl; The Steel Trap*. 1953: *A Blueprint for Murder*. 1955: *The Night Holds Terror*. 1956: *Julie*. 1958: *Cry Terror; The Decks Ran Red*. 1960: *The Last Voyage*. 1961: *Ring of Fire*. 1962: *The Password Is Courage*. 1963: *Never Put It in Writing*. 1965: *The Secret of My Success*. 1970: *Song of Norway*. 1972: *The Great Waltz*.

One wet Saturday afternoon in the early seventies, when rain had disappointed the author and his three children of the Wimbledon finals, TV offered as a substitute *The Last Voyage*. Initial enthusiasm could not have been lower. And yet within fifteen minutes the assembly were chewing furniture in anxiety, quite as concentrated as we were to be next day by Stan Smith and Nastase.

Stone's best movies are devoid of thematic interest; they are unashamed manipulations of tension. And on that basis, everything from *The Steel Trap* to *The Last Voyage* is totally compelling. Stone underlined the authenticity of his films by shooting on location whenever possible, by exposing actors and crew to real dangers, and by buying old trains, boats, and planes to blow up or sink for finales. In fact, this effort is peripheral to the ruthless exclusion of all but plot from his films: the lip-smacking, traditional cross-cutting of his wife-editor, Virginia; a vivid eye for cliff-hanging imagery—e.g., an attempted rescue (in *The Last Voyage*) by Robert Stack of his daughter from a shattered cabin.

Invariably, he liked to present "ordinary" people with a sudden, shattering emergency that involves a race against time. Thus *Julie* has Doris Day piloting a plane for the first time in her life, and in *Cry Terror* James Mason is forced to serve the interests of a gang comprising Rod Steiger, Neville Brand, and Angie Dickinson. The comparison with Hitchcock is instructive. For, despite Hitchcock's reputation for suspense, the Stone films are often technically purer. However, they are infinitely inferior because they are interested in that technique alone. The lesson by implication is that, whatever his claims, Hitch is concerned with much more than the mechanics of excitement.

Stone joined Universal in 1918 and he learned his craft, not surprisingly, on serials at Paramount. He formed Andrew Stone Productions in 1943,

and it is to be emphasized that his early films were musicals, *Stormy Weather* being one of the first "Negro" films and offering Lena Horne with the title song. That earlier taste revived in *Song of Norway* and *The Great Waltz*. The explanation of such a contrast in material is simply that Stone is not an artist and possibly that Virginia was the brains behind the cliffhangers (they separated, it seems, between *Song of Norway* and *The Great Waltz*). But that still leaves the engaging comedy of *The Password Is Courage* as an aside from so much urgency, and a film that blithely uses English villages as occupied Germany and encourages flagrant German stereotypes.

Stone invented "disaster" pictures before the world was complacent. Andrew Sarris has the last word: "One sobering deduction: If the Stones had made *On the Beach*, none of us would be around now to review it."

Oliver Stone, b. New York, 1946

1974: *Seizure*. 1981: *The Hand*. 1986: *Salvador; Platoon*. 1987: *Wall Street*. 1988: *Talk Radio*. 1989: *Born on the Fourth of July*. 1991: *The Doors; JFK*. 1993: *Heaven and Earth*. 1994: *Natural Born Killers*. 1995: *Nixon*. 1997: *U Turn*. 1999: *Any Given Sunday*. 2003: *Comandante* (d).

The child of a Jewish stockbroker and a French Catholic woman, Stone carries himself in the rather breathless, tireless way of someone who believes he contains multitudes. It is easy to scorn him, for he can be very bad and very foolish. Still, he is an example of the confidence that believes it can turn complex ideas and problems into crowd-pleasing movies. There is little point in having a popular American film business without that attempt. Of course, Otto Preminger did it all thirty years ago with more taste and intelligence. But Stone's faults are part of his energy, and in *Salvador* and *Platoon* that force achieves searing popular drama.

Even then, Stone has severe limits. He has no sense of humor and startlingly little use for women: just think of Daryl Hannah in *Wall Street*, Meg Foster in *Born on the Fourth of July*, and Sissy Spacek in *JFK*. Indeed, he follows the dangerous fallacy that the important, controversial issues of the day are made for serious men alone. It is some consolation that he has drawn, or punched, such very good work from James Woods, Tom Berenger, Willem Dafoe, Charlie Sheen, Michael Douglas, and Tom Cruise. One cannot add Kevin Costner to that list, though one of the few interesting parts of *JFK* was its glimpse of a lurid gay underworld, fleshed out by Joe Pesci, Tommy Lee Jones, and Kevin Bacon.

Stone went to good boarding schools and then dropped out of Yale. He taught school in Saigon, worked as a merchant seaman, and then volunteered for the 25th Infantry Division in Vietnam, where he got a bronze star and a purple heart. He then entered New York University and took film classes—with Scorsese as one of his teachers. (He became a taxi driver who was also writing screenplays.)

His script for *Midnight Express* (78, Alan Parker) won an Oscar, and he went on to write, or cowrite, *Conan the Barbarian* (82, John Milius); *Scarface* (83, Brian De Palma); *Year of the Dragon* (85, Michael Cimino); and *Eight Million Ways to Die* (86, Hal Ashby).

In that work, he displayed a rare facility for unbridled male arrogance and situations of intense fear. Even before *Platoon*, he was fascinated by male loyalty, honor, and betrayal, and he is a victim of the attractive fallacy that authoritarian villains can be glamorous.

As a director, he is a ringmaster of spectacle, editing, performance, and pungent dialogue—even in the travesty of *JFK*, the screen was often alive with his craft. *Salvador* seemed very novel when it came out, and *Platoon* fully deserved its reputation as the proper American admission of pain over Vietnam. Moreover, it had a command that reminded one of the Norman Mailer of *The Naked and the Dead*.

Nothing since has been as good. *Wall Street* is a showcase for Michael Douglas, but it never makes financial dealing clear and so it turns into comic book. *Talk Radio* was utterly misanthropic, and it seemed as if Stone had lost interest and drive before the end. *Born on the Fourth of July* was vivid and moving, but Stone now seemed not just immersed but lost in the trauma of the 1960s.

The Doors was wretched, despite a brave performance from Val Kilmer. *JFK*, in this writer's view, is loony irresponsibility of a kind that ill-equips its maker to defend the claims of history. I do not approve the Warren Commission or have a settled mind about what happened in Dallas that day in November 1963. But I fear the kind of movie power in the service of a reckless paranoia that can never be eased or satisfied. Yes, the film surely "affected public opinion" and helped liberate all the files. But Congress, please—insist that Oliver Stone be the one to read them all and make a decent report. Better that task than more abominations like *Heaven and Earth*.

By the mid-nineties, there were signs that Stone's energy was turning sour and dark. Was he ill, depressed, or under some influence? Had paranoia taken him over? *Nixon* was a haunting picture, hideously exaggerated (who needs to exaggerate Nixon?), but full of a compassion for madness, and severely impeded by Anthony Hopkins's helpless competition with all the miles of Nixon on film. *U Turn* was like a fever dream. But then *Any Given Sunday* was silly, old-fashioned, macho, yet suffused with a love of what movies

can do. Stone is down now, and he may have dug his own hole. But he is capable of a great comeback.

Sharon Stone, *see* Frances Farmer

Tom Stoppard (Tomas Straussler),
b. Zlín, Czechoslovakia, 1937

It happens that I wrote this piece immediately after doing the entry on Clifford Odets. Never mind any comparison between the two as dramatists. Odets seems to me a man and writer who was obsessed with movies and acting out the part of himself; Stoppard, no matter his Oscar for screenwriting—for *Shakespeare in Love* (98, John Madden)—his having directed one film, *Rosencrantz and Guildenstern Are Dead* (90), and his several screenplays, seems to me essentially distant from the film business. He is deeply concerned with language, levels of reality, and theatrical enactment. He is far from charmless himself, yet he seems to have no vested interest in being "Tom Stoppard."

Of course, things could change. His work on *Shakespeare in Love* was likely vital to that film's success, and it did seem as if the wordsmith had at last become intrigued with the medium. On the other hand, Stoppard is now older than Odets was when he died. And whereas much of Odets's later voice was given over to lamentations over what he had missed, Stoppard is the steady author of his own plays.

As a screenwriter, he has also worked on *The Romantic Englishwoman* (75, Joseph Losey); from Nabokov, *Despair* (78, Rainer Werner Fassbinder); from Graham Greene, *The Human Factor* (79, Otto Preminger); *Brazil* (85, Terry Gilliam); from J. G. Ballard, *Empire of the Sun* (87, Steven Spielberg), his most interesting film; *The Russia House* (90, Fred Schepisi); *Billy Bathgate* (91, Robert Benton); for TV, *Poodle Springs* (98, Bob Rafelson); *Vatel* (00, Roland Joffé); *Enigma* (01, Michael Apted).

Madeleine Stowe,
b. Eagle Rock, California, 1959

I was going to begin by saying: Of course, all the young actresses are beautiful. Though not even that is true anymore. There are new actresses who seem inclined toward some abrasive or sluttish oddity—as if no one could endure the cult of flawless looks any longer. In that sense, Ms. Stowe is a throwback: one reason for her impact in *The Last of the Mohicans* (92, Michael Mann)—the first time she was properly *noticed*—was the way Mann's inarticulate but very sensual attention to presence helped us recognize a silent screen rapture in period costume. Maybe the movie helped the actress gain confidence, for she has seemed stronger in the years since and now seems capable of real stardom—if the right parts come her way; or if she determines that they are hers.

Her mother is Costa Rican and her father from Oregon. She was a student at USC, and she went on to do a little theatre and TV. But she made her debut as the likely victim in *Stakeout* (87, John Badham). *Tropical Snow* (86, Ciro Duran)—in which she played a Colombian—had been filmed earlier, but it was not released until much later, on video. She was not much more than romantic spectacle in *Worth Winning* (89, Will Mackenzie) and *Revenge* (90, Tony Scott), where she had to suffer a great deal. But she had a comic seduction scene with Nicholson in *The Two Jakes* (90, Jack Nicholson); and there was ample show of enterprise in *Closet Land* (91, Radha Bharadwaj).

In *Mohicans,* she was genuinely brave, and persuasively moved by her Hawkeye. Mann's camera homed in on her bold, frontal stare, her nostrils twitching like a fine mare's. *Unlawful Entry* (92, Jonathan Kaplan) was more conventional, but she was one of many admirable women in *Short Cuts* (93, Robert Altman)—tough, wry, shrewd, and credibly trapped in a tricky life. In *Blink* (94, Michael Apted), she was a rugged Irish violin-player who was blind; in truth, she was more interesting that way than with her sight restored. But she made a slight premise intriguing. She has also done *China Moon* (94, John Bailey); and *Bad Girls* (94, Kaplan).

She has tended to be a hanger-on in her more recent pictures: *Twelve Monkeys* (95, Terry Gilliam); *The Proposition* (98, Lesli Linka Glatter); *Playing by Heart* (98, Willard Carroll); *The General's Daughter* (99, Simon West); *Impostor* (02, Gary Fleder); *Avenging Angelo* (02, Martyn Burke); as Isabelle in the TV *The Magnificent Ambersons* (02, Alfonso Arau); *We Were Soldiers* (02, Randall Wallace); *Avenging Angelo* (02, Martyn Burke); *Octane* (03, Marcus Adams).

Lee Strasberg (Israel Strasberg) (1901–82), b. Budzanow, Austria

Was there ever a more adroit or enchanting casting coup than to have Lee Strasberg play Hyman Roth in *The Godfather Part II* (74, Francis Ford Coppola)? Roth is in poor health from the moment we see him. He plays so many of his scenes sitting, or on his back. He rests in the shade in a small Miami home, with lunch on his lap, and football on television. He sighs, he defers, he does not reckon to have long to go. Yet in Strasberg's being, Roth is a monster of soft-voiced control, a serene monotone dictator. We know that Roth has never contemplated a way of life in which he does not have his own way.

Strasberg's Roth flattered the real-life model, Meyer Lansky (movies usually flatter such brutal heroes of our time). But Coppola's Roth surely caught Strasberg, the teacher of actors who failed

to find much success himself as an actor, or director, but who quietly appropriated the Method and led the Actors Studio in its most influential years. Strasberg's colleague, Elia Kazan, was so much more successful, dynamic, and charismatic. But Strasberg persisted with the Studio until it became his family and he became its godfather. He exerted a steely authority such that many of his best students slipped into a state of dependence. If you doubt the thoroughness with which this personal history assisted Roth in *The Godfather Part II* (and Al Pacino was Strasberg's star pupil), then you are missing some of the subtlest intricacies of casting.

Lee Strasberg came to America when he was nine. He trained at the American Laboratory Theater, under Richard Boleslavsky and Maria Ouspenskaya. He was a cofounder of the Group Theater, artistic director of the Actors Studio from 1948 onward, and, after 1969, head of the Lee Strasberg Institute of the Theater. His influence on movie acting was enormous, and it surely fostered the sense of malady and victimization in people. We should not lose sight of how far Strasberg's teaching made for a depressive yet sentimentalized monster like Michael Corleone.

After his nomination for Hyman Roth, Strasberg acted a good deal in his last years and gradually revealed a fussy ham: *The Cassandra Crossing* (77, George Pan Cosmatos); on TV in *The Last Tenant* (78, Jud Taylor); *Boardwalk* (79, Stephen Verona); with Pacino again in . . . *And Justice for All* (79, Norman Jewison); as one of a trio of old men in *Going in Style* (79, Martin Brest); on TV again in *Skokie* (81, Herbert Wise).

A word should be added for the women in his life: Paula, his first wife, a feared figure on many sets; Susan, his daughter, who had great moments as an actress; Marilyn Monroe, his disciple; and the many actresses he inspired, intimidated, and quietly lusted after.

David Strathairn, b. San Francisco, 1949

By now, no one can have any prospect of David Strathairn ever giving a poor performance. Maybe the only question that remains is whether the actor is capable of taking on a large part, and carrying a picture—in the way that Kevin Spacey, say, carried the stage revival of *The Iceman Cometh.* As it is, Strathairn has earned a reputation for reliability, care, self-effacement, and detail in a world that seems decreasingly impressed by those things.

He was a student at Williams College and the Ringling Brothers School for Clowns—there could be a richer comic side than we have ever seen. One of his contemporaries at Williams was John Sayles, and so Strathairn made his debut in *Return of the Secaucus Seven* (79) and became a part of the Sayles group: *Enormous Changes at the Last Minute* (83, Mirra Bank and Ellen Hovde); *Lovesick* (83, Marshall Brickman); *Silkwood* (83, Mike Nichols); *The Brother from Another Planet* (84, Sayles); *Iceman* (84, Fred Schepisi); *At Close Range* (86, James Foley); *Matewan* (87, Sayles); *Call Me* (88, Sollace Mitchell); *Dominick and Eugene* (88, Robert M. Young); *Eight Men Out* (88, Sayles); *Stars and Bars* (88, Pat O'Connor); *The Feud* (89, Bill D'Elia); *Memphis Belle* (90, Michael Caton-Jones); *City of Hope* (91, Sayles); *Big Girls Don't Cry . . . They Get Even* (92, Joan Micklin Silver); *Bob Roberts* (92, Tim Robbins); blind in *Sneakers* (92, Phil Alden Robinson); *Passion Fish* (92, Sayles); *Shadows and Fog* (92, Woody Allen); *A League of Their Own* (92, Penny Marshall); *Lost in Yonkers* (93, Martha Coolidge); *The Firm* (93, Sydney Pollack); *A Dangerous Woman* (93, Stephen Gyllenhaal); plainly second billing as husband to Meryl Streep in *The River Wild* (94, Curtis Hanson); nasty in *Dolores Claiborne* (95, Taylor Hackford); equally subordinate to Jessica Lange in *Losing Isaiah* (95, Gyllenhaal); *Mother Night* (96, Keith Gordon); *L.A. Confidential* (97, Hanson); *Limbo* (99, Sayles); *A Midsummer Night's Dream* (99, Michael Hoffman); excellent in *A Map of the World* (99, Scott Elliott); *Freedom Song* (00, Phil Alden Robinson) for TV; *Harrison's Flowers* (00, Elie Chouraqui); the father in *The Miracle Worker* (00, Nadia Tass) on TV; *The Victim* (02, Doug Magee); *Blue Car* (02, Karen Moncrieff); *Lathe of Heaven* (02, Philip Haas); *Master Spy: The Robert Hanssen Story* (02, Lawrence Schiller); *Speakeasy* (02, Brendan Murphy); *The Blackout Murders* (03, Philip Kaufman).

Jean-Marie Straub, b. Metz, France, 1933
1963: *Machorka-Muff* (s). 1965: *Nicht Versohnt/Unreconciled* (s). 1967: *Chronik der Anna Magdalena Bach.* 1968: *Der Bräutigam, die Komödiantin und der Zuhälter/The Bridegroom, the Actress and the Pimp* (s). 1970: *Les Yeux ne Veulent pas en Tout Temps se Fermer/Peut-être qu'un jour Rome se permettra de choisir a son tour/Othon.* 1972: *Leçons d'Histoire.* 1975: *Moses and Aaron.* 1976: *Fortini/Cani.* 1979: *Della Nube alla Resistenza/From the Cloud to the Resistance.* 1982: *Trop Tot Trop Tard* (d). 1983: *En Rachachant* (d). 1984: *Klassenverhaltnisse/Class Relations.* 1986: *Tod des Empedokles/The Death of Empedokles; Schwarze Sunde.* 1989: *Cézanne.* 1992: *Antigone.* 1994: *Lothringen!* (s). 1997: *Von Heute auf Morgen.* 1999: *Sicilia!*

Straub is an extreme, austere exponent of minimalist cinema. His work is an attempt to clarify the nature of his medium, and no task is as likely to unsettle or offend people who consider themselves familiar with the medium. Cinema has always adhered to its own reputation as a form of popular narrative entertainment for general audiences. But within that approach there have often been apparent inconsistencies: for instance, audiences actually respond as much to particular, recurring photographs of, say, Garbo, Gable, darkness, and skin, as to the stories in which they figured. What we think of as the story is invariably the effect of a chosen way of filming. The medium is intensely decision based, and thus there has always been an abiding formal element to it.

In that light, film is a succession of still images that seem to move, and it is more appropriate to call a film sequential than narrative. Every frame has its own shapes and forms. Those forms may alter during the sequence of frames in a shot. There is a further, inevitable kind of order in the sequence of shots within a film. And although Straub's work has alarmed audiences and been enjoyed by relatively few, it is built upon the assertion that in cinema we respond to those sequences; that composition, light, movement, and sound play upon our thoughts and feelings.

What emerges in Straub's hands are films that are composed out of bare necessity, with an eye-level, unprejudiced camera looking diagonally at unarranged events and stripped-down settings, with people who are not actorly or charming, non-professionals who speak their lines without intonation or personality. He reasserts reality and hopes only to record it. Thus his insistence on actual sound and unassisted appearance.

There is a paradox in Straub's work in that, from a political point of view, he is humorlessly intent on making films for a total audience in order radically to improve their attitudes to their own lives. Yet, the formal care—which is stringent, demanding, and admirable—has undoubtedly carried his films toward that very select band supporting modern music, painting, and literature. The stirring potential of cinema, as I see it, is the size of an audience, the way that it illuminates without solving the confusion of reality and fantasy, and the way it may contribute toward a society of observant, critical spectators. While admiring Straub, I cannot convince myself that his uncompromising pursuit of independence is not self-indulgent. Nevertheless, he is an intense purist and a stark eminence.

He studied literature at Strasbourg and Nancy and ran a film society at Metz, where he made the crucial discovery of the abstraction of Bresson's *Les Dames du Bois de Boulogne.* Already marked by French and German influences, he went to Paris in the mid-1950s and worked as an assistant on *La Tour de Nesle* (54, Abel Gance); *French Can Can* (55, Jean Renoir); *Eléna et les Hommes* (56, Renoir); *Le Coup de Berger* (56, Jacques Rivette); *Un Condamné à Mort s'est Echappé* (56, Bresson); and *Une Vie* (58, Alexandre Astruc). He married Danièle Huillet, his subsequent collaborator, and left France to avoid military service in Algeria.

Since then, he has become the single-minded follower of his own path, and, in the event, an inspiration to the new German cinema. His formal preoccupations make any short account of his films comic and useless. There is a good, enthusiastic book by Richard Roud. But Straub's films need to be seen and heard, time and again, for their full complexity and their possible limits to become clear.

His first two films are derived from works by the German novelist Heinrich Böll. The Bach film was ten years in preparation and achievement, a meticulous study in period authenticity and actual sound, an intriguing celebration of Bach open to the diversity of random suggestion that occurs while watching the film. Like few films, it brings the viewer back to him- or herself. *The Bridegroom, the Actress and the Pimp* emerged from an invitation to Straub to direct a play that he proceeded to cut from two hours to under ten minutes. Since then, he has filmed plays by Corneille and Brecht, in costume, but in unashamedly modern settings. He then made a long-nurtured record of Schoenberg's opera, *Moses and Aaron,* which emphasizes the struggle between word and image.

His austerity may leave gaps in his output, and the films themselves will usually be hard to find. But no one seriously interested in film should neglect them or the theoretical issues that attend them.

Meryl Streep (Mary Louise Streep),
b. Summit, New Jersey, 1949

Meryl Streep is a model actress in American pictures—but in a way that makes acting seem overly solemn or calculated. At forty, she was not simply regarded as the most talented woman in pictures, but the most distinguished. Distinction is not common praise in movies, nor is it often well intended. The distinguished are sometimes those the public does not love: the term lay heavily on the heads of Olivier, Katharine Hepburn, and even Al Pacino, at times. But at the very end of the eighties, Streep had been brilliant, properly enclosed, and unquestionably Australian in *A Cry in the Dark* (88, Fred Schepisi). Very few people went to see that picture—its subject and setting were not appealing—but some reckoned that Streep's presence was by then sufficient warning to wary audiences. She would be superb, rather cold, in a movie that had little vulgar magic. Even critics who admired her had grown weary of the complaint that in her highest flights of skill one felt the strenuous breathing of a mistress technician. She had been nominated six times for best actress in ten years, and twice as supporting actress. She had a win in both categories. But did anyone care?

Something like panic seemed to set in. She *was* forty; she had never been universally acclaimed as a beauty; and she was generally associated with serious, if not tragic, material. So she made a plunge into comedy little short of disastrous: as the romantic novelist in *She-Devil* (89, Susan Seidelman); as Carrie Fisher's alter ego in *Postcards from the Edge* (90, Mike Nichols); *Defending Your Life* (91, Albert Brooks); and with Goldie Hawn in the horribly miscalculated *Death Becomes Her* (92, Robert Zemeckis).

In trying to be funny, Streep became harder to like. A haughty edge showed, no matter that she was bravely urging herself into strange territory. She was nominated again for *Postcards from the Edge,* and she was as clever as ever in the picture, not to say funny with many of its throwaway lines. But the movie (let alone its audience) hardly knew how to handle Streep in the role of a failure, a woman dominated by her mother, not that good at her work, and humiliated by her own weaknesses. *Postcards* cried out for a lead actress of less stature—it was so obvious that it deserved Carrie Fisher (just as she deserved it). Streep is not easily small, abject, or a discard—she should have played the mother. Indeed, given the assignment, she may magnify failure until it becomes magnificent and operatic—for example, *Ironweed* (87, Hector Babenco). She has such problems now with seeming natural.

Streep's parents were well-to-do (the father an executive in pharmaceuticals, the mother a commercial artist). She was raised in Bernardsville, New Jersey, and she went on to Vassar and to the Yale Drama School—she graduated from there in 1975. By then, she was famous already as an arresting stage actress of uncommon range and intensity. She appeared at the Public Theater in a musical, *Alice in Concert*—she was trained as a singer as well as an actress. Among her other stage roles, she was in a Shakespeare in the Park *Measure for Measure* (as Isabella), where she met and fell in love with the actor John Cazale. She nursed him in his final illness, up to his death in March 1978. Later, she married a sculptor, Don Gummer, and they have had children together.

She made her screen debut, on television, in *The Deadliest Season* (77, Robert Markowitz), and in a black wig as a bitchy friend in *Julia* (77, Fred Zinnemann)—Jane Fonda is said to have predicted a great career. But Streep made a bigger impact, and won an Emmy, in the TV miniseries *Holocaust* (78, Marvin J. Chomsky).

The Deer Hunter (78, Michael Cimino) was her first big movie, though her part was very little developed in the script. But Streep brought a remarkable presence to her scenes and a quality of uncertainty that enriched the entire film. She was vivid and hostile in *Manhattan* (79, Woody Allen), and doing her best against two woeful child-guys in *Kramer vs. Kramer* (79, Robert Benton).

In two films, she worked very hard to be gorgeous and sexy, yet something failed to click—was it inner restraint, or some fierce certainty that actresses should not sell themselves: *The Seduction of Joe Tynan* (79, Jerry Schatzberg) and *Still of the Night* (82, Benton)?

It hardly seemed to matter, for now she was a reigning figure, capable of any accent or period—a labeled great actress: *The French Lieutenant's Woman* (81, Karel Reisz); luminous, touching, yet oddly remote in *Sophie's Choice* (82, Alan J. Pakula)—as if her very genius led us to see how fake that story is. She was at her best, wilder, more dangerous, and less respectable in *Silkwood* (83, Nichols). *Falling in Love* (84, Ulu Grosbard) was a novelette love story, with De Niro.

She was astounding again in *Plenty* (85, Schepisi), though it was ominously clear by then that her taste was for women no one else could endure. *Out of Africa* (85, Sydney Pollack) was a sensation for a moment, but I can hardly recall her in the film. *Heartburn* (86, Nichols) was a folly of a special kind of celebrity. *Ironweed* might have worked on stage—on film it felt dead and studied. And *A Cry in the Dark* is a film that any young actress should examine.

Is this Streep's fate—is she just an academic model? I think her depth is too great to accept failure now. But she has shown no instinct for organizing her own career, and she cannot expect to have new Sophies presented to her on Dresden china. She is going to have to take her future into her own hands. She might do worse than return to the stage for a few years. Better that than travesties like *House of the Spirits* (93, Bille August) or the determined athleticism of *The River Wild* (94, Curtis Hanson).

She made a fabulous character out of *The Bridges of Madison County* (95, Clint Eastwood)—and got another nomination. She did *Before and After* (96, Barbet Schroeder); *Marvin's Room* (96, Jerry Zaks); the mother of an epileptic on TV in *. . . First Do No Harm* (97, Jim Abrahams); *Dancing at Lughnasa* (98, Pat O'Connor); then back to her very best as the dying mother—not so smart, but full of understanding—in *One True Thing* (98, Carl Franklin); *Music of the Heart* (99, Wes Craven).

She was the voice of the Blue fairy in *A.I.* (01, Steven Spielberg); she was Susan Orlean in *Adaptation* (02, Spike Jonze); *The Hours* (02, Stephen Daldry); *Angels in America* (03, Nichols).

Barbra Streisand,
b. Brooklyn, New York, 1942

Only in her early sixties, Streisand seems like an institution now, a creation of the ages, as volatile and brooding as the San Andreas fault, even if we cannot always take her as seriously as she would wish. She has the grand manner in the way some people are ill—in other words, it is her constant handicap, the joke about her, an instant means of identification. If her eye falls upon something—a cause, a president, a tennis player, or a line of art deco—the world thrills and giggles. There is no ordinary reality left for Barbra Streisand. If she ever wanted it.

She is, or was, a great singer. She was never a beautiful woman, and so the drama of her singing sometimes seemed a battle with her looks. After all, opera singers are not required to be gorgeous—but those who sing love ballads have to face the test of sexiness. Streisand won that fight through huge will and self-belief. Maybe they turned to armor.

The victory had come on records, on TV, and on stage in *I Can Get It For You Wholesale* and *Funny Girl*. When the film of the latter (68, William Wyler) flourished, and won her the Oscar, she became an untouchable in show business. She could do anything. Her own horizons expanded.

In fact, she was far from infallible. Her next three films had very mixed fortunes: *Hello, Dolly!* (69, Gene Kelly); *On a Clear Day You Can See Forever* (70, Vincente Minnelli); and *The Owl and the Pussycat* (71, Herbert Ross), the first sign that perhaps she was interested in being an actress. But singers stand up alone, with just a mike to control the crowd: it is as hard for them to relax as it was for silent actresses to be quiet.

A startling advance was clear in *What's Up, Doc?* (72, Peter Bogdanovich). She lacked the finesse of Hepburn, one could not be sure that she knew what a screwball comedy was, but she was growing more beautiful—in floppy cap and red shirt she dominated attention; she ably carried off Bogdanovich's addition to screwball scheme by knowing as much as the professor about rocks; she is glorious discovered on a piano in a mauve sweater, prepared to break into "As Time Goes By," and she asks "What's up, Doc?" as if she really loves the man. As Larrabee says in *Doc*, she's a gem.

If only she could have done more screwball, instead of such ordinary material as *Up the Sandbox* (72, Irvin Kershner), the radical chick to sleepy Redford in *The Way We Were* (73, Sydney Pollack), or *For Pete's Sake* (74, Peter Yates). What a swan song she could have made for Cukor, or he might have made out of *Funny Lady* (75, Ross), a sequel to Streisand's first success with Fanny Brice.

She was one of the few uninhibited stars, yet she would hardly risk her status in ordinary projects. A touch of madness was necessary. It came to her with Jon Peters, a hairdresser-impresario who got her into *A Star Is Born* (76, Frank Pierson). It is as if Bernhardt had met Judy Garland.

The movie was a kind of home movie in which mother knew best. Barbra was executive producer and Jon was producer. Jon directed for a time, keeping the seat warm between Jerry Schatzberg and Pierson. Barbra wrote some of her songs, wore her own clothes, and doubtless rewrote the script. The film is lunatic, but eventually hard to resist—as proved by its huge success. Barbra said she was playing a rock singer, but anyone with any sense knew she was just having a whale of a time.

She acted with Ryan O'Neal in *The Main Event* (79, Howard Zieff) and with Gene Hackman in *All Night Long* (81, Jean-Claude Tramont). Was she running out of steam, or desire? Far from it: in 1983 she directed and played the lead in *Yentl*, a musical adaptation of a story by Isaac Bashevis Singer. She made herself unpopular; she may be egotist and tyrant beyond compare. Never mind—*Yentl* is one of the great American debuts, an authentic musical film such as no one dreams of now, with gorgeous songs that exactly dramatize a rich, clever story.

She acted in *Nuts* (87, Martin Ritt), and effectively revealed her limits as an actress—she has a fierceness of her own that does not easily give way to other characters now. *The Prince of Tides* (91) was her second direction, from the Pat Conroy novel—it was less original or beguiling than *Yentl*, but it was a decent domestic melodrama with one of Nick Nolte's finest performances.

Over New Year's in 1993/4, she took Las Vegas (and America) by storm for a two-night stand. She arranged a grand sale of her deco collection, and embarked on a high-ticket world tour—all in the echo chamber of publicity.

She rations herself these days, and so—apart from the occasional concert extravaganza—she has restricted herself to directing and starring in *The Mirror Has Two Faces* (96). Not that "restricted" seems the proper word, when unbridled self-dramatization made that one of the most inadvertently comic pictures of the century. I know: I've been warned all along that this was the real Streisand—and how could I like *Yentl* so much? Well, I still like *Yentl*, and I still think she's a great singer. But *The Mirror Has Two Faces* (and its dreadful abuse of Jeff Bridges) doesn't need to go to trial.

Joseph Strick,

b. Pittsburgh, Pennsylvania, 1923

1948: *Muscle Beach* (codirected with Irving Lerner) (s). 1953: *The Big Break*. 1959: *The Savage Eye* (codirected with Ben Maddow and Sidney Meyers) (d). 1963: *The Balcony*. 1967: *Ulysses*. 1969: *Tropic of Cancer*. 1970: *Interviews with My Lai Veterans* (d). 1973: *Janice*. 1977: *A Portrait of the Artist as a Young Man*. 1996: *Criminals* (d).

It is a weird dividend of Strick's immersion in modern confusion that his My Lai film was set up on profits from his production of *Ring of Bright Water* (69, Jack Couffer), that inquiry into whether Bill Travers/Virginia McKenna is/are more cuddly/dumb than various otters. Strick is a schizoid, looking to make commercial underground movies, to turn a blind eye to the sexational reputation of classics of the literary avant-garde. His *Ulysses*, for instance, could only distress devotees of Joyce; it would hardly prompt anyone to read the book; its Irishness, its sex, its mythology, its Bloom are all desperately cautious creations. Its Dublin is a pasteboard suburb.

Strick impresses as a wintry, disenchanted personality, much more suited to the cynicism of *The Savage Eye* and the brutal pragmatism of *Tropic of Cancer* than to the lyrical exuberance of a Joyce, Genet, or even Lawrence Durrell—Strick originally began *Justine*, before the mangled subject was dumped on George Cukor. Strick has fought strident battles over freedom from censorship, freedom to bring art to the people, freedom of speech; but his work is tight-lipped, grindingly unfluent, and unable to shed the approach to life's variety of the tabloid press. Far too simple to call him a phony, he genuinely stands for disintegrating purpose, striving for significance and the life force, but coming across with the implausible and dispiriting frankness of a barker outside a strip show.

John Sturges (1910–92),

b. Oak Park, Illinois

1946: *The Man Who Dared; Shadowed*. 1947: *Alias Mr. Twilight; For the Love of Rusty; Keeper of the Bees*. 1948: *The Best Man Wins; The Sign of the Ram*. 1949: *The Walking Hills*. 1950: *Mystery Street; The Capture; The Magnificent Yankee; Right Cross*. 1951: *Kind Lady; The People Against O'Hara; It's a Big Country* (codirected). 1952: *The Girl in White*. 1953: *Jeopardy; Fast Company; Escape from Fort Bravo*. 1954: *Underwater!; Bad Day at Black Rock*. 1955: *The Scarlet Coat*. 1956: *Backlash*. 1957: *Gunfight at the OK Corral*. 1958: *The Old Man and the Sea* (codirected with Fred Zinnemann); *The Law and Jake Wade*. 1958: *Last Train from Gun Hill*. 1959: *Never So Few*. 1960: *The Magnificent Seven*. 1961: *By Love Possessed*. 1962: *Sergeants Three*. 1963: *The Great Escape; A Girl Named Tamiko*. 1965: *The Satan Bug; The Hallelujah Trail*. 1967: *Hour of the Gun*. 1968: *Ice Station Zebra*. 1969: *Marooned*. 1972: *Joe Kidd*. 1973: *Valdez il Mezzosangue/Valdez, the Halfbreed*. 1974: *McQ*. 1976: *The Eagle Has Landed*.

The fact that Sturges was born in the same suburb of Chicago as Hemingway prompts the thought that there is action that expresses human beings and action that merely exercises them. Sturges was an athlete director, obsessed by inane feats of skill and strength—like Steve McQueen's teaching his motor bike to jump barbed-wire fences in a film that tastefully avoids the massive reprisals taken after *The Great Escape*. Equally, *The Magnificent Seven*—a transplantation of Kurosawa that began the wholesale internationalization of the Western—prefers to dwell on the feats of lethal dexterity rather than invest the story with any social irony.

Sturges joined the RKO art department in 1932 and went on to be an assistant editor. Selznick then hired him as an assistant producer and editor. During his war service, Sturges directed an instructional film, *Thunderbolt*, with William Wyler. After the war, he joined Columbia where he quickly became a director. The period around 1960 saw the elevation of Sturges as the maker of successful spectacles: *The Magnificent Seven; The Great Escape; The Hallelujah Trail; Marooned*. But the size of these films only emphasized his lack of substance. In the 1950s, when films were more modest and compressed, he made some pictures in which the action was less pretentious, more compressed, and more enjoyable. Thus *Escape from Fort Bravo, Bad Day at Black Rock*, and *The Law and Jake Wade* were effective adventure stories, and *Backlash* seemed not too far from the intense concept of honor in Anthony Mann's Westerns. Later, *Joe Kidd* was a well-paced handling of Clint Eastwood's grudging explosiveness.

It should be said that whenever Sturges forsook the Western or the West he was inclined to be clumsy: *The Old Man and the Sea, By Love Possessed*, and *A Girl Named Tamiko* are all inept—the first so bad that Sturges may never have been told about Oak Park's other famous son.

Preston Sturges (Edmond Preston Biden) (1898–1959), b. Chicago

1940: *The Great McGinty; Christmas in July*. 1941: *The Lady Eve; Sullivan's Travels; The Palm Beach Story*. 1944: *The Miracle of Morgan's Creek; Hail the Conquering Hero; The Great Moment*. 1946: *The Sin of Harold Diddlebock/Mad Wednesday*. 1948: *Unfaithfully Yours*. 1949: *The Beautiful Blonde from Bashful Bend*. 1956: *The Diary of Major Thompson/Les Carnets du Major Thompson/The French They Are a Funny Race*.

It is tempting to see Preston Sturges as a character from a novel that Scott Fitzgerald never actually wrote: a versatile, humorous, charming man, an artist by fits and starts, yet lacking the stamina, graft, or authority to keep his own works intact. His best movies came in a rush, from 1940 to 1944, and were notably out of key with the musi-

cals, war heroics, and sultry dream world of *Casablanca* that Hollywood opted for. But when would Sturges's mixture of affectionate satire and eccentric originality have been close to traditions? It was his apartness from Hollywood modes, as well as the exposure of the movie kingdom in *Sullivan's Travels*, that endeared him to people fundamentally hostile to American cinema. By birth and upbringing, Sturges was an outsider: rich, cosmopolitan, artistic, worldly. Yet Sturges was deeply rooted in a merry, corrupt but absurd America, as wayward and frequently misled as an inventor, but at his best the organizer of a convincingly cheerful comedy of the ridiculous, which is rare in American cinema.

Sturges's own life was a comedy—or that's how he chose to play it. His parents led largely separate lives, and Sturges was enthralled by his mother, Mary Desti. "My mother was in no sense a liar, nor even intentionally unacquainted with the truth . . . as she knew it. She was, however, endowed with such a rich and powerful imagination that anything she had said three times, she believed fervently. Often, twice was enough."

The mother took the boy to Europe where they were part of the untidy court of Isadora Duncan (if only Sturges could have directed *Isadora*). Then Mary Desti took a fresh husband, a Chicago broker named Sturges, who was well disposed to the boy. In time, the son ran the mother's cosmetics business and invented a kiss-proof lipstick. Stated once, it does seem unlikely. He fought in the war and only then started work writing plays, several of which were hits on Broadway. He married Barbara Hutton's cousin.

In the 1930s, he gravitated toward Hollywood where he worked as a scriptwriter: *The Big Pond* (30, Hobart Henley); *Fast and Loose* (30, Fred Newmeyer); *The Power and the Glory* (33, William K. Howard), a supposed forerunner of *Citizen Kane; We Live Again* (34, Rouben Mamoulian); *The Good Fairy* (35, William Wyler); *Easy Living* (37, Mitchell Leisen), a Wall Street satire, including the nucleus of Sturges's later company of supporting actors; *Port of Seven Seas* (38, James Whale); and *Remember the Night* (40, Leisen).

Sturges was the first of modern writer-directors, but his films are undisciplined in their scenarios. The novelty of his central situation—for instance, the film director at large in *Sullivan's Travels*, the uncomfortable good fortune in *Christmas in July*, the comic misunderstanding of *Miracle of Morgan's Creek*, or the bold use of contradictory subjectivity in *Unfaithfully Yours;* the pungent wit, above all, in *Lady Eve;* and the sense of supporting characters piling in pell-mell, as in *Palm Beach Story*, together make for confusion; a unique, American whipping up of local chaos, without that rigorous artistic order that underlies *La Règle du Jeu* and *Eléna et les Hommes*, two films that

Sturges would surely have admired. Thus *Sullivan's Travels*, it seems to me, falls flat when it tries to move from comedy to pathos—though Andrew Sarris sees the change working as well as the altering of mood in *The Winter's Tale*.

If *The Lady Eve* is his best film, it is also the most conventional—the story is Hawksian in the pugnacity of its sexual conflict—and the one least troubled by background characters, delightful but foolish coincidence, and those sudden lurches in a new direction that suggest a magician losing control of his assistants. The "Ale and Quail" club is symptomatic of Sturges's dilemma; initially appealing, they soon drag *Palm Beach Story* away from the very fruitful central plot of Joel McCrea, Claudette Colbert, and Rudy Vallee.

In the same way, Sturges's fatal fondness for novel casting and eccentric behavior led him on from the excellence of Brian Donlevy and Akim Tamiroff in *The Great McGinty* and McCrea and Veronica Lake in *Sullivan's Travels* to a disappointing interest in Betty Hutton, Eddie Bracken, Betty Grable, and Rex Harrison. And yet even *The Beautiful Blonde from Bashful Bend* has an elegant structure, witty dialogue, and inventive slapstick. By then, Sturges had frankly lost his own comedic purpose—much clearer in *Lady Eve* and *Palm Beach Story*—but the conclusion must stand that he was too busy, too carried away by the moment to give his films a true calm and order.

In the end, it seems that Sturges could never stand far enough back from his comedy to see the human perspective. As G. W. Stonier wrote:

The curious thing about this caricaturist . . . with his packed, active screen, is that he should have quite a streak of sentiment. It isn't sentimentality. It leaks out not only in parodies, which cherish some of the feelings they mock, but in efforts to express or at least unearth a love of humanity. That Sturges scarcely succeeded in this does not in itself fatally reduce him: indeed it is the fate and inspiration of most comedians. What *is* damaging is that, so yearning, he shouldn't have been able to go on splashing satire and discovering fun. The giddy whirl declines into raucousness; he tries being serious and can't square it with side-splitting.

The strain grew, and showed itself in fewer films. *Beautiful Blonde* is the excess of action over subject, while *Unfaithfully Yours* is an insane and, at times, disturbing picture of marital hostility. *Major Thompson* was a disastrous attempt to turn his exile in France to advantage. Long before that he was worn out. A year before his death, he played a small part in *Paris Holiday* (58, Gerd Oswald). The death itself occurred at the Algonquin Hotel—and only once.

Margaret Sullavan (1911–60),
b. Norfolk, Virginia

Sullavan was an elusive woman, enchanting before the cameras but uneasy with life and something of a tyrant. Louise Brooks admired her above others: "That wonderful voice of hers—strange, fey, mysterious—like a voice singing in the snow." Sullavan seemed to listen to what was being said in a film, and to be changed by what happened. She was slight and deceptively conventional in looks. One realized that she was beautiful when her face lit up in response to the events of a film. Above all, she seemed vulnerable, harboring her strength and the chance of happiness. Her voice and bearing were haughty, frail, and bold, like that of a perilously recovered invalid, or a girl in a summer dress on a winter day.

She made four films with Frank Borzage, the director who coaxed out the shy intelligence to make romance mature, and she suffers to the extent that he is neglected. Equally, in *Next Time We Love, The Shopworn Angel, The Shop Around the Corner*, and *The Mortal Storm*, she was ideally cast with James Stewart, a little awed by his gangling sincerity. Perhaps her heart was never in a movie career, but in the late 1930s, as war cast its shadow on young people, she was exceptionally poignant and delicate.

She was originally a stage actress, seen by John Stahl and chosen to play in *Only Yesterday* (33). Universal signed her up, but only on terms so liberal as to suggest an actress anxious to protect herself against the system. She then made *Little Man, What Now?* (34, Borzage), *The Good Fairy* (35, William Wyler, and her second husband), and *So Red the Rose* (35, King Vidor). Her material was often tear-soaked: *Next Time We Love* (36, Edward H. Griffith); *The Moon's Our Home* (36, William A. Seiter), a comedy, opposite Henry Fonda, her first husband; as the tubercular wife in *Three Comrades* (38, Borzage); *The Shopworn Angel* (38, H. C. Potter); *The Shining Hour* (38, Borzage).

A return to the stage and illness restricted her appearances, but her third husband, agent Leland Hayward, won her a good contract at MGM. With the onset of war, her skill with sentiment and some European settings reestablished her as a star: magnificent—no, better—in *The Shop Around the Corner* (40, Ernst Lubitsch); *The Mortal Storm* (40, Borzage); *So Ends Our Night* (41, John Cromwell); *Back Street* (41, Robert Stevenson); and *Appointment With Love* (41, Seiter).

After that flurry, she made *Cry Havoc* (43, Richard Thorpe) and went back to the theatre. She had a great success in *The Voice of the Turtle*, came back for a last movie, dying of cancer in *No Sad Songs for Me* (50, Rudolph Maté), and took to the stage again. During her last ten years she was further beset by the deafness that had meant she could often not hear what actors were saying in front of the cameras, and eventually she committed suicide.

Anyone intrigued by her story is urged to read her daughter Brooke Hayward's *Haywire,* one of the best books about family life in show business.

Donald Sutherland,
b. New Brunswick, Canada, 1934

From the University of Toronto, he went into acting and a period in England at RADA. He knocked around for several years in small parts: *Il Castello dei Morti Vivi* (64, Herbert Wise); *Dr. Terror's House of Horrors* (64, Freddie Francis); *Fanatic* (65, Silvio Narizzano); *The Bedford Incident* (65, James B. Harris); and *Promise Her Anything* (66, Arthur Hiller). His part as a reprieved psychopath in *The Dirty Dozen* (67, Robert Aldrich) showed how securely an earlier generation and idiom identified him as a nasty. But after *Billion Dollar Brain* (67, Ken Russell); *Interlude* (68, Kevin Billington); *Oedipus the King* (68, Philip Saville); *Joanna* (68, Mike Sarne); *The Split* (68, Gordon Flemyng); he played two parts in *Start the Revolution Without Me* (70, Bud Yorkin) and, with Elliott Gould, comprised the shambling, esoteric sanity amid carnage in *M*°*A*°*S*°*H* (70, Robert Altman). That revealed him as a shy clown, but *M*°*A*°*S*°*H* holds all its characters at a distance and says more about corporate acting than about Sutherland's real nature. It is in favor of private backchat affronting the outsider world, and it lends a glowing romance to these casual heroes.

Since then, Sutherland has had much larger parts: *Kelly's Heroes* (70, Brian G. Hutton); as the movie director in *Alex in Wonderland* (70, Paul Mazursky); *Act of the Heart* (70, Paul Almond); as Christ in *Johnny Got His Gun* (71, Dalton Trumbo); with Gould in *Little Murders* (71, Alan Arkin); outstanding as the detective who is less than well or steady in *Klute* (71, Alan J. Pakula); with Jane Fonda again in *Steelyard Blues* (72, Alan Myerson); *Lady Ice* (73, Tom Gries); *Don't Look Now* (73, Nicolas Roeg); and once more with Gould in *S.P.Y.S.* (74, Irvin Kershner). There are several flops there and not one picture that Sutherland carried alone. He seemed more useful in films for his gaunt, disturbing, and disturbed appearance: the wretched Homer in *The Day of the Locust* (75, John Schlesinger); the bestial fascist in *1900* (75, Bernardo Bertolucci); an Irish rogue in *The Eagle Has Landed* (76, John Sturges); the cadaverous cock, without delight or direction, in Fellini's *Casanova* (76); and *National Lampoon's Animal House* (78, John Landis). He also made two pictures in his native Canada: *Blood Relatives* (78, Claude Chabrol) and *The Disappearance* (78, Stuart Cooper). Working at a gallop, he was in *Murder by Decree* (78, Bob Clark); a suitably nervy, paranoid victim in *Inva-*

sion of the Body Snatchers (78, Philip Kaufman); a robber in *The Great Train Robbery* (79, Michael Crichton); and in *A Very Big Withdrawal* (79, Noel Black).

The older Sutherland has become not just versatile or unpredictable in his choices; he is nearly eccentric: *Bear Island* (79, Don Sharp); the best performance, as the father, in *Ordinary People* (80, Robert Redford); *Gas* (81, Les Rose); as the German agent in *Eye of the Needle* (81, Richard Marquand); *Threshold* (81, Richard Pearce); *Max Dugan Returns* (83, Herbert Ross); the Steinbeck adaptation *The Winter of Our Discontent* (83, Waris Hussein); *Crackers* (84, Louis Malle); *Ordeal by Innocence* (85, Desmond Davis); *Heaven Help Us* (85, Michael Dinner); *Revolution* (85, Hugh Hudson); as Gauguin in *The Wolf at the Door* (87, Henning Carlsen); *The Rosary Murders* (87, Fred Walton); *The Trouble with Spies* (87, Burt Kennedy); *Apprentice to Murder* (88, R. L. Thomas); a psychiatrist in *Lost Angels* (89, Hudson); the sadistic warden in *Lock Up* (89, John Flynn); *A Dry White Season* (89, Euzhan Palcy); *Eminent Domain* (90, John Irvin); *Bethune: The Making of a Hero* (90, Phillip Borsas); *Scream of Stone* (91, Werner Herzog); as a mad firebug, the best thing in *Backdraft* (91, Ron Howard); in *JFK* (91, Oliver Stone), loony and so omniscient he must be the scriptwriter; and *Six Degrees of Separation* (93, Fred Schepisi).

He remains an actor hovering between lead and supporting roles: *The Puppet Masters* (94, Stuart Orme); *Disclosure* (94, Barry Levinson); *Outbreak* (95, Wolfgang Petersen); *Hollow Point* (95, Sidney J. Furie); *A Time to Kill* (96, Joel Schumacher); *Shadow Conspiracy* (97, George P. Cosmatos); *The Assignment* (97, Christian Duguay); *Fallen* (98, Gregory Hoblit); coach Bill Bowerman in *Without Limits* (98, Robert Towne); *Free Money* (98, Yves Simoneau); *Virus* (99, John Bruno); *Instinct* (99, Jon Turteltaub); as General Beauregard in *The Hunley* (99, John Gray); *Toscano* (99, Dan Gordon); *Panic* (00, Henry Bromell); *Space Cowboys* (00, Clint Eastwood); *The Art of War* (00, Duguay); *Big Shot's Funeral* (02, Xiaogang Feng); as Clark Clifford in *Path to War* (02, John Frankenheimer); *The Italian Job* (03, F. Gary Gray); *Baltic Storm* (03, Reuben Leader); *Cold Mountain* (03, Anthony Minghella); *Hating Her* (03, Thomas Bezuche).

Edward Sutherland (1895–1974),
b. London

1925: *Wild, Wild Susan; Coming Through; A Regular Fellow.* 1926: *It's the Old Army Game; Behind the Front; We're in the Navy Now.* 1927: *Love's Greatest Mistake; Fireman, Save My Child; Figures Don't Lie.* 1928: *Tillie's Punctured Romance; The Baby Cyclone.* 1929: *Close Harmony* (codirected with John Cromwell); *What a*

Night!; The Dance of Life (codirected with Cromwell); *Fast Company; The Saturday Night Kid; Pointed Heels.* 1930: *Burning Up; Paramount on Parade* (an episode); *The Social Lion; The Sap from Syracuse.* 1931: *Gang Buster; June Moon; Up Pops the Devil; Palmy Days.* 1932: *Sky Devils; Mr. Robinson Crusoe; Secrets of the French Police.* 1933: *Murders in the Zoo; International House; Too Much Harmony.* 1935: *Mississippi; Diamond Jim.* 1936: *Poppy.* 1937: *Champagne Waltz; Every Day's a Holiday.* 1939: *Flying Deuces.* 1940: *The Boys from Syracuse; Beyond Tomorrow; One Night in the Tropics.* 1941: *The Invisible Woman; Nine Lives Are Not Enough; Steel Against the Sky.* 1942: *Sing Your Worries Away; Army Surgeon; The Navy Comes Through.* 1943: *Dixie.* 1944: *Follow the Boys; Secret Command.* 1945: *Having Wonderful Crime.* 1946: *Abie's Irish Rose.* 1956: *Bermuda Affair.*

Sutherland was in America by the time he was twenty, as a stuntman and actor. His rise left him with several versions of the same name: Edward Sutherland, A. Edward Sutherland, and Eddie Sutherland. Perhaps that confusion showed a deeper insecurity. Louise Brooks, his wife from 1926–28, has said that Sutherland's hopeful emulation of Chaplin was only skin-deep: "What they [Sutherland and Malcolm St. Clair] didn't know was that when they were out drinking and playing around and dancing all night, Chaplin and Sennett were thinking about tomorrow." In 1923, Sutherland had taken an ostentatious pay cut to be Chaplin's assistant on *A Woman of Paris,* and by the late 1920s he was sometimes thought of as a leading director of comedy. But he cannot escape the slur that, despite being married to her, he allowed other directors to find the best in Louise Brooks. If Sutherland had been more talented, Brooks might have become a major star of the 1930s.

But it was an eventful career, with some pleasant moments. At Paramount as a young director, he worked with Raymond Griffith in *A Regular Fellow,* with Wallace Beery and Raymond Hatton in *Behind the Front* and *We're in the Navy Now.* In 1926 he directed the first important W. C. Fields movie, *It's the Old Army Game,* which also starred Brooks. Sutherland and Fields worked often together—*Tillie's Punctured Romance; International House; Mississippi; Poppy,* when Fields was very ill from drink; and *Follow the Boys,* one of the best wartime all-star anthologies, in which Orson Welles saws Marlene Dietrich in half.

By then, Sutherland was on the slide. With Paramount through the early 1930s—apart from *Mr. Robinson Crusoe* with Douglas Fairbanks for United Artists—he had moved on to Laurel and Hardy in *Flying Deuces,* and then to Abbott and Costello in *One Night in the Tropics. The Invisible Woman,* made at Universal, has Maria Montez and John Barrymore together. After the war, he went into TV.

Gloria Swanson (1897–1983), b. Chicago
It would be interesting to see a diary kept by Gloria Swanson while considering whether to play Norma Desm nd in Billy Wilder's *Sunset Boulevard* (50). Some twenty-five years before, she had been the most successful and highly paid actress of the silent screen. Venturing into independent production, she had foundered on Erich von Stroheim's extravagance in making *Queen Kelly* (28). After that, she made only seven more films before her retirement in 1934. Her first comeback had been in 1941 with the inept *Father Takes a Wife* (Jack Hiveley). Now she was offered the part of a deluded star of the silent screen, living like a witch in a decayed mansion, attended only by her ex-husband, ex-director butler.

When did Wilder tell her that von Stroheim was to play that part? Undoubtedly, *Sunset Boulevard* is the film by which Swanson will be remembered. Inevitably, audiences tend to link the failure of Norma Desmond—to survive sound, and to retain a sense of reality after the fantasy life of early success—with that of Swanson herself. However much that film exploited and distorted her, she gained one undeserved credit from it. Out of nostalgia or novelty, her performance was highly acclaimed whereas her conception is attitudinizing and vague and the playing itself emphatic and feverish.

Much of that may be due to Wilder's characteristic betrayal of the characters in his own films, but something too seems to come from Swanson herself. Her staring imperiousness is chronic and unconscious, and when she rebukes an indifferent Hollywood—"I'm still big, it's the pictures that got small"—it is difficult not to feel that this obscurantism is the exact reflection of Swanson's thunderous acting style. *Sunset Boulevard* provides a telling study in the way mime had so trained actors and actresses that when sound arrived they could not stop shouting. In truth, Swanson is not the woman to write diaries so much as the preposterous scenarios that Norma Desmond composes for her impossible comeback.

Swanson's father was a civilian attached to the army so that as a child Gloria followed the troops. She entered movies when only seventeen: a visit to the Essanay studio in Chicago turning into a job. In 1915, small parts in several Wallace Beery films led to marriage to the actor and their joint departure for Hollywood. Swanson joined Mack Sennett and adorned a number of two-reel comedies, but her ambitions were for grand drama and by 1918 she moved on to Triangle where, among others, she made *Her Decision* and *You Can't Believe Everything,* both directed by Jack Conway.

Her great fame began in 1919, when she signed with Cecil B. De Mille. She made six films for him, hypocritical and calculated offerings of postwar sexual adventure under the guise of moralizing. Invariably, Swanson was the newly married woman persuaded to treat marriage as a sexual obstacle course. Although only in her early twenties, she was made to appear sophisticated and older: *Don't Change Your Husband* (19); *For Better For Worse* (19); *Male and Female* (19), a version of *The Admirable Crichton; Why Change Your Wife?* (20); *Something to Think About* (20); and *The Affairs of Anatol* (21). This character is the mass-market version of the society female described in Scott Fitzgerald's early work, and it seems odd that Swanson retained a dutiful, daughterly affection for De Mille—yet another aspect of her own life treated in *Sunset Boulevard*.

Swanson stayed at Paramount as one of their major stars, survived her supposed rival Pola Negri, and eventually persuaded the studio to let her work in New York. Her parts were generally dramatic, affected by her image in the De Mille pictures, concentrating on a rather severe, black-eyed, prune-lipped woman of affairs, incredibly clothed, made up as if for war and brazenly flouting the camera. Ten times she worked for Sam Wood: *The Great Moment* (21); *Under the Lash* (21); *Don't Tell Everything* (21); *Her Husband's Trademark* (22); *Beyond the Rocks* (22); *Her Gilded Cage* (22); *The Impossible Mrs. Bellew* (22); *My American Wife* (22); *Prodigal Daughters* (23); and *Bluebeard's Eighth Wife* (23).

Even at this stage, she was attempting to gain fuller control of her films and she insisted on playing *Zaza* (23), directed by Allan Dwan, the third and most interesting director to work with her at length. After *The Humming Bird* (24, Sidney Olcott), she worked with Dwan on more comic material: *A Society Scandal* (24); *Manhandled* (24); *Her Love Story* (24); and *Wages of Virtue* (24). Dwan loved working with her, admired her professionalism, and had no doubts about her ability as a comedienne. She went to France to make *Madame Sans-Gêne* (25, Leonce Perret), and there married her third husband, the Marquis de la Falaise. Back in America she made *The Coast of Folly* (25) and *Stage Struck* (25) with Dwan, followed by *The Untamed Lady* (26, Frank Tuttle) and *Fine Manners* (26, Richard Rossen).

Her contract was up for renewal and, despite offers of $17,500 a week, she chose to form her own production company to release through United Artists. Swanson Producing Corporation starred her in *The Love of Sunya* (27, Albert Parker), and then in 1928 she went into partnership with her lover, Joseph Kennedy, to make *Queen Kelly*. Again, a diary would be priceless. The original script had Swanson as a girl beloved by a prince and traced her progress from orphan-

age to convent to brothel to palace. Even the remaining footage shows it as Stroheim's most unbridled conjuring up of baroque sexual imagery. In any event, the extraordinary footage of sadomasochistic harshness may have been beyond Swanson. But she understood the bills, fired the director, and attempted to edit a shorter, marketable film. *Queen Kelly* was never released in America, and Swanson claimed that her debts were only finally paid off after *Sunset Boulevard*.

The same year, Gloria Swanson Productions made *Sadie Thompson* (28, Raoul Walsh) with Walsh playing a soldier and Lionel Barrymore as Atkinson. In 1929, Gloria Productions starred the boss in *The Trespasser* (Edmund Goulding) and *What a Widow!* (Dwan). All three were successful, and yet within a few years she went into grudging retirement. Was it because Hollywood disapproved of her independence, because she was too emphatic in style for the taste of the early 1930s, or because, as Dwan alleged, she "was surrounded by sycophants"? That retirement came after *Indiscreet* (31, Leo McCarey); *Tonight or Never* (31, Mervyn Le Roy); *Perfect Understanding* (33, Cyril Gardner), made in England; and *Music in the Air* (34, Joe May), the last after MGM had signed and neglected her.

Her first comeback did not take, and after *Sunset Boulevard* she made two humiliatingly bad pictures: *Three for Bedroom C* (52, Milton H. Bren) and *Nero's Weekend* (56, Stefano Vanzina Steno). Her final comeback was as herself in *Airport 1975* (74, Jack Smight). But she was a commanding figure at the end of her life and the author of a very good autobiography.

Blanche Sweet (1895–1986), b. Chicago

Mary Pickford, Lillian Gish, Norma Talmadge, Gloria Swanson, Pola Negri—the greatest women stars of the silents were immediately identifiable; however talented they were, they registered first as extreme personalities. Blanche Sweet was different: she was so various an actress that it's sometimes hard even to recognize her. You can't really spot the spunky young heroine of *The Lonedale Operator* (Griffith, 11) in the majestic heroine of *Judith of Bethulia* (Griffith, 14). She was yet another Griffith discovery, joining Biograph when she was fourteen after a long career as a child actress on the stage. Because she looked so mature, she was often cast as a real grown-up woman, unlike Pickford and Gish, and although she claimed that all was sweetness and light among the young Griffith protégées, Gish snatched the role of Elsie Stoneman in *Birth of a Nation* out from under her. (To add insult to injury, Gish was known to refer to her as "Miss Sweet and Sour.") No wonder that, like Pickford, she left Griffith early on, first for the Famous Players–Lasky company, where she made seven movies, including two for Cecil B. De Mille (*The Warrens of Virginia* and *The Captive*, both in 1915), and met her first-husband-to-be, director Marshall Neilan. After two years, she formed her own company, Blanche Sweet Productions, and eventually moved on to other major studios.

She looked large on the screen for a star of that period, and she was consistently confident and capable. But her natural wholesomeness was easily discarded when the script called for it. You can believe her masquerading first as a tough boy, then as an Indian maid, then turning into a romantic heroine in *That Girl Montana* (21, Robert Thornby). She was a notable *Tess of the D'Urbervilles* (24) for Neilan (they had to fight to retain the unhappy ending) and widely applauded for the first film version of *Anna Christie* (23, John Griffith Wray), which she says O'Neill preferred to all other film versions of his plays. She's strong in it, but let's face it—she wasn't Garbo; she still depends too much on the Griffith gestural approach to acting.

Sweet was a major film presence for a dozen or more years, a real leading lady. But there had been extended absences from the screen, caused by emotional and/or physical problems. By the time of *Diplomacy* (26, Neilan), she was losing her edge and her judgment: this conventional high-society melodrama wasn't her meat, but she insisted on doing it, and she petered out after a few undistinguished sound films. Then it was back to the theatre, and successes like *The Petrified Forest* with Leslie Howard. Her film career was in many ways exemplary, if erratic, and at a major retrospective at MOMA in New York in the nineties, she made a tremendous impression. If she had lived just a little longer, she could have enjoyed it—she was over ninety when she died, in 1986.

Tilda (Katherine Matilda) Swinton,
b. London, England, 1960

Margaret Hall in *The Deep End* (01, Scott McGehee and David Siegel) is a kind of single mother. Her husband is far away in the Navy, so she is left in Tahoe City to look after three children and an ailing father-in-law. It's a movie about the ways in which that kind of woman can lose or abandon her own emotional life—until it is reawoken by a strange blackmailer, the very person who has split her crammed routine, of driving kids to this or that, with the absurd demand for $50,000. As I watched the film, I wondered what Margaret might have been like as a young or younger woman—so tall, so milk-white in complexion, so red-headed, so romantic a figure. And I recalled something from Derek Jarman's diary, *Modern Nature*, something from 1989, when he was filming *The Garden* (90) and Tilda was his Madonna—"Tilda glitters in the grass-green sari holding on to the wobbly Van Eyck crown."

Quite a journey—and not over yet: how the daughter of a military commander, raised in grand homes, schooled with the future Princess Diana, went from being a fascinating icon in the imagination of Derek Jarman to an actress who could play an American housewife.

Moreover, I'll be surprised if the later Ms. Swinton ever abandons her loyalty to experimental projects done for the love of the thing.

So, once upon a time, Tilda Swinton was a part of that extended group around Jarman, capable of stepping from the role of cook or foot masseuse to become one of his figureheads. She was in *Caravaggio* (86), *The Last of England* (87), *Aria* (87), a nurse in *War Requiem* (89), Queen Isabella in *Edward II* (91), Lady Ottoline Morrell in *Wittgenstein* (93), and one of the voices on *Blue* (93).

Her most important work away from Jarman was the title role in *Orlando* (92, Sally Potter), a work that let itself be overly infatuated with her striking appearance. But then, after Jarman's death (1994), she moved on to the solemn and pretentious *Female Perversions* (96, Susan Streitfield); Ada Augusta Byron King in *Conceiving Ada* (97, Lynn Hershman); Muriel Belcher, the legendary Soho figure, in *Love Is the Devil* (98, John Maybury); Mum in *The War Zone* (99, Tim Roth); *The Beach* (00, Danny Boyle); *Teknolust* (01, Hershman); *Vanilla Sky* (01, Cameron Crowe); *Adaptation* (02, Spike Jonze).

Hans-Jürgen Syberberg,
b. Nossendorf, Germany, 1935

1968: *Skarabea/How Many Earths Does a Man Need?*. 1972: *Ludwig II—Requiem für einen Jung Fräulichen König/Ludwig Requiem for a Virgin King*. 1973: *Theodor Hierneis oder Wie Man ein Ehemaliger Hofkoch Wird/Ludwig's Cook*. 1974: *Karl May*. 1975: *Winifred Wagner und die Geschichte des Hauses Wahnfried 1914–1975/The Confessions of Winifred Wagner*. 1977: *Hitler—a Film from Germany*. 1982: *Parsifal*. 1984: *Die Nacht*. 1990: *Ein Traum, Was Sonst*.

Syberberg is among the most absent and absorbing modern directors. Even as you list his films, it is a riddle as to whether they are fiction, documentary, or a patchwork of epic theatre on film that exceeds labels. No German director has so conscientiously assaulted his country's recent past, and no one apart from Rossellini has so explored the cinema's disciple relationship with history. Syberberg's Hitler film is not just a way of making us aware of Hitlerism as a universal instinct, not just a profusely inventive and original puppet show on modern history, but a movie made in the awed spirit that appreciates Hitler as a monstrous Selznick who hoped to leave the world a mixture of Wagner and film noir. Syberberg is a theatrical genius too rich for the stage, and a brilliant analyst of the way media have become our messages. It is Brecht meeting McLuhan on one track; but it is Wagner going *Cabaret* on another. And those are just two tracks of the cinema's ringmaster of quadrophonic ideas. The films are still little seen, and they are works that need to be experienced before it is profitable to read about them.

As a youth, he was a keen photographer lucky enough to get in to see Berliner Ensemble rehearsals and to record them on an 8mm movie camera. Twenty years after that adventure, the material was blown up and released as *Last Time I Moved* (73), a vital document on Brecht's methodology. Syberberg grasped two things from the experience: that film added an impenetrable glaze or mystique to theatre—like legend rather than practice; and that Brecht's energetic mixture of drama, parable, farce, and lesson offered a way for other artists to work in different media: it is relevant to Godard and Warhol, as well, two of Syberberg's acknowledged influences.

After university, he went into German TV, where he made many documentaries on theatrical subjects—including one on Fritz Kortner rehearsing scenes from Schiller. This period taught him the value of research and original documents, as well as the way media imagery transformed their findings into slogans, games, and icons, a language of intimate cliché known to nearly everyone. It was with this background that Syberberg launched himself at the last century in Germany and a line of tainted hero figures—perfect source material for tracing the media's knack of turning ideals into ogres and plastic toys.

"I thought I would make [*Ludwig*] like Warhol's *Lonesome Cowboys*. . . . I imagined Ludwig on a motorcycle, Wagner in a little car, people with long hair, drugs. I thought that Ludwig should be some kind of hermaphrodite, a homosexual, that he should sell Bavaria to the Prussians. I invented all these things, and then, when I read the books, I learned that I was right!" *Ludwig* was cheaply made, but it is a baroque fusion of periods, fragmented forms, and projected backgrounds. Narrative is overwhelmed by the collage of points of view; history becomes a shooting gallery of grotesque interpretations, as much of a circus as Ophüls created in *Lola Montès*. His theatrical re-creation of history serves as satire, but Syberberg also cherishes Wagner's romanticism and frequently fills the movie with unabashed heroic grandeur. His analytical approach to German history is achieved through a balance of detachment and immersion, and never carries any note of sanctimonious hindsight.

Ludwig's Cook has an actor playing the cook and leading us on a tour of Ludwig's palaces. It is history reconstructed from the kitchen's vantage:

domestic, irreverent, but demented in that the cook himself is a tyrant who monopolizes the camera and shuffles his roles as actor and character as if he were masturbating. *Karl May* is a kind of primitive biopic, peopled with actors from the thirties and forties, about the writer of inspirational adventures, the link between Ludwig and Hitler at that hysterical level of blood-and-thunder patriotism. *Winifred Wagner* was another innovation: a five-hour interview with the composer's daughter-in-law. There is a two-hour version in general circulation, and it is a compelling portrait of a person involved in history's making, revealing part of that mentality and yet still unaware of all its implications.

These projects were leading to the gargantuan *Hitler* film: twenty-two chapters in four parts and seven hours, it is the sum total of images, ghosts, and interpretations of Hitler. Most akin to *Ludwig*, it is theatrical and fairground-like, but always a jungle made into an argument by the calm scrutiny of the camera. Its freedom with levels of artifice and reality makes it a study of the ways we have tried to assimilate, forget, or reform ourselves after the ghastliest event of our time. Like Lang, though, Syberberg employs the didactic stance produced by offsetting the world's disorder with the camera's superb authority.

This marked as great a turning point for Syberberg as the conclusion of the moral tales did for Rohmer. He may need history's text as much as Rossellini did, but he is not unappreciative of the narrative illusion of cinema: "My [*Hitler*] film shows how the war ended in Europe with a whole culture, a whole continent destroyed. If, in his black way, Hitler had succeeded in establishing his concept of a heroic Europe (and he was very near to doing so), it would have been the tragic end of mankind as we had known it before. At the beginning of the film I show a little corner of the hell; at the end, I show, not only hell, but also how the reality of Hitler is turned into a part of the entertainment industry."

Since *Parsifal*, Syberberg has largely withdrawn from any conventional pattern of work. Instead, he has collaborated intensely with the actress Edith Clever in a series of dramatic monologues to be staged in theatres and then filmed. *Die Nacht*—six hours long—was the first of these, and the series culminated in 1990 with *Ein Traum, Was Sonst,* in which Clever plays the widowed daughter-in-law of Bismarck, recounting the events of her life and the passage of Germany.

This work has scarcely been seen outside Germany, and it has not found proper funding. Moreover, Syberberg has elected not to distribute the films he has finished. A fatal magnificence has set in: "People must come to my films on their own."

In addition, he has written three books, notably *On the Misfortune and Fortune of Art in Germany*

Since the Last War—which have earned a great deal of criticism and charges of anti-Semitism.

Recluse or tyrant, Syberberg is a self-conscious, self-confessed genius, and it is hard to believe that such isolation is good for his work, or that it will diminish his passion for history. He is supposed to be writing his autobiography, and it can hardly be less than epic. Syberberg gives us this advice, tablets sent down from the mountain: "People have to trust the development and make the transformation with me."

István Szabó, b. Budapest, Hungary, 1938
1964: *Almodozasok Kora/Age of Illusions*. 1966: *Apa/Father*. 1970: *Szerelmesfilm/Love Film*. 1974: *Tuzolto Utca 25/25 Firemen's Street*. 1977: *Budapest Tales*. 1979: *Bizalon/Confidence*. 1981: *Mephisto*. 1985: *Redl Ezredes/Colonel Redl*. 1988: *Hanussen*. 1991: *Meeting Venus*. 1992: *Edes Emma, Drága Böbe—Vázlatok Aktok*. 1996: *Offenbach Titkai*. 1999: *Sunshine*. 2002: *Taking Sides*. 2003: *Being Julia*.

A graduate of the Academy for Theater and Film Art in Budapest, Szabó deepened his own craft steadily in the sixties and seventies. His focus was Hungary, and his essential approach was realistic, but he had an intricate way with symbols and the interaction of past and present. *Father* was very touching, and *25 Firemen's Street* was like an anthology of hopes, fears, and dreams in an apartment building about to be demolished.

But in the eighties, Szabó made an international trilogy of films all dealing with flawed heroes, ambition and power, egotism and betrayal. Szabó has usually been his own writer, and in the trilogy he discovered the perfect actor for his theme, Klaus-Maria Brandauer, uncertain whether to love or loathe himself. All three stories—*Mephisto, Colonel Redl,* and *Hanussen*—had a basis in fact, and they seemed to describe European politics in this century. (In his use of symbols, Szabó has often made allusions to the relations between Hungary and its neighbors.)

Mephisto is a startling film. It moved forward rather lurchingly, half-wounded, but half-driven. Its women were vivid, and Brandauer was a marvel as the actor who will do anything for career. In turn, *Colonel Redl* and *Hanussen* seemed slighter, and even a little repetitive—and Brandauer's persistence only drew attention to this problem.

Meeting Venus was a departure: much lighter and more romantic, it told of the love between a conductor and a singer—Glenn Close was excellent in this role, though whenever she sang Kiri Te Kanawa did the work.

Sunshine was another epic film on Europe in the twentieth century. It dealt with three generations of a Jewish Hungarian family, and had excellent performances from Ralph Fiennes and William Hurt. It proved yet again that Szabó is at

his best when dealing with moral courage and compromise.

T

Hideko Takamine, b. Hakodate, Japan, 1924
Takamine must be the only actress in movie history to have three distinct careers. She began at the age of five, quickly becoming the most adored child star in Japan—appearing in over a hundred movies as a cute, perky tot, male or female depending on the exigencies of plot, her adorable smile plastered on posters and toothpaste ads across the country in her stepparents' determination to squeeze money out of their meal ticket. She was called the Japanese Shirley Temple, but she says she was more natural—more like Margaret O'Brien.

Then came her teenage period, which lasted through the war (she was a pinup girl for the boys overseas). She had an immense success in 1938 with *Composition Class* (Kajiro Yamamoto), about a poor young schoolgirl who wins a composition contest with an essay about raising rabbits. Then in 1941 she triumphed in *Horse* (Yamamoto), a semi-documentary that took four years to make, about a seventeen-year-old girl who raises a horse she loves and eventually sacrifices it to the need of the army. This movie, much of it shot in primitive locations, involved her with Akira Kurosawa, who was a young man in charge of the location shooting. Their tentative romance was ruthlessly ended by her family and the studio authorities, and she never worked with him again.

Finally, after a spell as a popular club singer during the Occupation, came her mature period, during which she was one of the most popular and highly paid actresses, playing strong, energized women.

She worked for many directors after the war. With Ozu in *The Munekata Sisters* (50), though her rebellious and rather lower-class demeanor was less suited to Ozu's drama of resignation (and innately conservative attitudes?) than was Setsuko Hara's more well-bred presence. They had appeared together in *The Opium War* (43, Masahiro Makino), a strange adaptation of Griffith's *Orphans of the Storm* (22), in which Takamine took the Dorothy Gish role of the blind girl while Hara replaced Lillian. Hara was the refined ideal; Takamine, with her nasal voice and direct manner, was the woman next door. She worked for Gosho in *Where the Chimneys Are Seen* (53), in which she almost drives her suitor out of his mind with nagging; with Shiro Toyoda in a period film, *The Mistress/Wild Geese* (53), in which she is forced to become the concubine of an elderly merchant; and several times for her husband, Yasuzo Masamura, a screenwriter who turned to directing.

But for twenty years her most important work was divided between Naruse and Kinoshita. She made seventeen movies with Naruse, the most important of which demonstrate her capacity for struggle and endurance. In *Floating Clouds* (55), set in the impoverished postwar period, she suffers everything a woman can at the hands of a worthless lover—she is beaten, abandoned, betrayed; she is arrested, forced to have an abortion, stricken with tuberculosis—and then she dies, still hoping for his love. But she is equally noted for her resistance to adversity in Naruse's *Lightning* (52), *Flowing* (56), *When a Woman Ascends the Stairs* (60), and *Yearning* (64).

Floating Clouds won the critics' award for Naruse as best picture for 1955. The year before, another Takamine vehicle had won the prize for Kinoshita: *Twenty-Four Eyes,* a sentimental epic about a noble schoolteacher on a remote island who lives through the quarter century that saw the rise of militarism, the war, and defeat. All Japan wept at Takamine's resolute teacher and the fate of her twelve pupils (twenty-four eyes). For Kinoshita she also made the hilarious comedy *Carmen Comes Home* (51), in which she is a not very bright stripper who returns to her native village for a brief but eventful visit. This was Japan's first color film, and another huge success. She made almost a dozen films for Kinoshita, and it was he who coaxed her out of retirement, in 1979, for her last appearance on the screen, *Oh My Son!*

More or less self-educated, angry at her family who exploited her, suspicious of the studios, resentful about acting, still Takamine had a triumphant career. Today, she and her husband happily divide their time between Japan and Hawaii; and she has written a number of books, ranging from her two-volume, very frank autobiography, *My Professional Diary* (76), to a travel book and a cookbook. Like so many of her beset heroines, she has survived.

Constance Talmadge (1898–1973),
Brooklyn, New York
Constance Talmadge had three great advantages. She had her mother, Peg, the most implacable of the famous Hollywood mothers, known throughout the industry as Ma Talmadge. (Having steered Constance and Norma into stardom, she failed to do the same for her third daughter, Natalie, and married her off to poor Buster Keaton.) From Ma, Connie went on to a kind of Pa—her sister Norma's much older mogul husband, Joseph M. Schenck, who took over her affairs in 1917 and steered her through more than a decade of almost uninterrupted success. Finally, she had a hoydenish charm, a happy nature, and a piquant Irish prettiness. Everybody loved this madcap girl, most famously Irving Thalberg, who pursued her to no

avail before settling for the more placid Norma Shearer. It was just as well: given his fragile health, Connie's wild streak might have speeded up his already premature death.

Big sister Norma was the tragedienne, all glamour and suffering. Connie—known to her pals as Dutch—was the comedienne. (They were like a rerun of the Gishes.) She shot to national attention as the Mountain Girl in Griffith's *Intolerance* (16), where her tomboy high spirits and good humor provided what lightness there is to that monumental epic. Soon she was starring in vehicles handmade for her, almost all of them sophisticated romantic comedies in which she dresses up in glorious gowns, furs, and the odd tiara, and gets her man. In every one of her films that I've been able to see she's utterly appealing. Typical Constance Talmadge titles: *Wedding Bells* (21); *The Primitive Lover* (22); *Her Night of Romance* (24); *The Goldfish* (24); *Her Sister from Paris* (25); *The Duchess of Buffalo* (26); *Venus of Venice* (27); *Breakfast at Sunrise* (28). Among her leading men: Conway Tearle, Ronald Colman, and Antonio Moreno, twice each. But leading men weren't the point: a film with Constance Talmadge was a Constance Talmadge film.

Her great pal Anita Loos and Loos's husband, John Emerson, wrote half a dozen of her films. Everything about them was super-deluxe, even when the heroine pretended to be slumming, but Dutch herself was sensible, down-to-earth, and fun. She walked away from movies when sound came in and never looked back. In a telegram to Norma, who was making a stab at the talkies, she wrote, "Quit pressing your luck, baby. The critics can't knock those trust funds Mama set up for us."

Norma Talmadge (1897–1957),
b. Niagara Falls, New York
There may have been Hollywood veterans who winced at the blithe malice with which, at the end of *Singin' in the Rain,* Gene Kelly hauls up the curtain to show Debbie Reynolds singing the words that had seemed to be emerging from Jean Hagen's mouth. For Hagen's grinding Bronx accent and the eighteenth-century French setting of the film within *Singin' in the Rain* have a cruel relevance to the sudden retirement from movies of Norma Talmadge. She was the oldest of the three Talmadge sisters (the others were Natalie and Constance) and the most successful; but sound proved the incongruity of salon prettiness and tenement voice and made *Du Barry, Woman of Paris* (30, Sam Taylor) her last film. Only thirty-three years old, she had been in the movies since 1911 and was one of the most popular of silent screen actresses. Not without merit. She was as animated as all the sisters, able to play romance and comedy. Clarence Brown thought her "the

greatest pantomimist that ever drew breath. She was a natural-born comic; you could turn on a scene with her and she'd go on for five minutes without stopping or repeating herself."

In fact, her specialty was to be "a brave, tragic, and sacrificing heroine," as well as a clotheshorse. Adela Rogers St. Johns called her "our one and only great actress."

By her late teens she was already an experienced actress with Vitagraph and had been in over a hundred shorts: a one-reel *A Tale of Two Cities* (11, William Humphrey); *Under the Daisies* (13, Van Dyke Brooke); *Goodbye Summer* (14, Brooke); *The Criminal* (15, Brooke). It was in 1917 that she, Allan Dwan, and Joseph Schenck formed a company to make *Panthea*. At that stage, Norma was under contract to Lewis Selznick. During the filming, however, Talmadge and Schenck were married and Dwan complained of having to direct against "pillow talk" interpretations. The Norma Talmadge Production Company was formed with Schenck personally supervising the majority of her films: *The Forbidden City* (18, Sidney Franklin); *Probation Wife* (19, Franklin); *The Branded Woman* (20, Albert Parker); *Love's Redemption* (21, Parker); *The Passion Flower* (21, Herbert Brenon); *The Sign on the Door* (21, Brenon); *The Wonderful Thing* (21, Brenon); as the Duchesse de Langeais in *The Eternal Flame* (22, Frank Lloyd); *Smilin' Through* (22, Franklin); *Ashes of Vengeance* (23, Lloyd); *The Song of Love* (23, Chester Franklin and Frances Marion); *The Voice from the Minaret* (23, Lloyd); *Within the Law* (23, Lloyd); *The Only Woman* (24, Sidney Olcott); *Secrets* (24, Frank Borzage); *Graustark* (25, Dmitri Buchowetzki); *The Lady* (25, Borzage); *Kiki* (26, Brown); *Camille* (27, Fred Niblo); *The Dove* (27, Roland West); *The Woman Disputed* (28, Henry King and Sam Taylor); and *New York Nights* (29, Lewis Milestone).

Norma called Schenck "Daddy." He controlled her in alliance with "Ma" Talmadge and, in the early 1920s, used Norma's box-office power to buy himself into United Artists. The Schencks parted in 1930, the year of *Du Barry*. As if to show how far movies were now a matter of harmony between sound and image, Norma took her maligned voice into radio and later married George Jessel, but she never made another film. In 1934, in *Tender Is the Night*, Scott Fitzgerald referred to her as the epitome of late 1920s glamour who "must be a fine, noble woman beyond her loveliness."

Lee Tamahori,
b. Wellington, New Zealand, 1950
1989: *Thunderbox*. 1994: *Once Were Warriors*. 1996: *Mulholland Falls*. 1997: *The Edge*. 2001: *Along Came a Spider*. 2002: *Die Another Day*.

If only Lee Tamahori's films were getting better.

For just consider: *Once Were Warriors* is a blazing look at a strange world—Maori life in New Zealand—with unforgettable scenes of love, boozing, and domestic violence. It's always credible, often frightening, and very moving, and the main performances—by Rena Owen and Temuera Morrison—are painfully real. After that? Well, *Mulholland Falls* is a very entertaining film on a subject that might have made a masterpiece, but Tamahori was content to go along with too much 1940s nostalgia. As for *The Edge* and *Along Came a Spider*, they show a very smart talent going in ever more artificial circles.

Tamahori was a boom operator and then an assistant director for years, notably on *Merry Christmas, Mr. Lawrence* (83, Nagisa Oshima); *Utu* (83, Geoff Murphy); *The Quiet Earth* (85, Murphy): *Bridge to Nowhere* (86, Ian Mune). So, it's a long journey to Hollywood, and England—where he is scheduled to make the next Bond film (that pinhead circle, with inane wonders flying round it).

Akim Tamiroff (1899–1972), b. Baku, Russia
Tamiroff was a squat, scuttling rogue, ready to sell you a fake icon or a filthy picture; his face slipped as readily into a gloating smile or a contemptuous sneer; he could never escape a hint of sweat and bad breath or the idea of some shabby lodgings from which he emerged every day with implausible spruceness. And yet he managed to be one of the most beguiling men in movies, a connoisseur of the crazy paving life of the supporting actor.

He was called to the devious art of acting at a time when earnestness was the new Russian vogue. In 1920, he joined the Moscow Arts Theatre, then led by Stanislavsky. He waited until the Theatre took Chekhov and Gorky to America in 1923, and got dropped off somewhere along the way, opting for the character of the perpetual refugee. It was ten years before he entered movies: time to learn English, and then decorate it with that accent that moved within a word from whine to growl.

The 1930s was an age for supporting players: they worked on several films at a time, an Anatolian hashish merchant at Paramount this week; next week, at Warners, a slippery middleman in the white slave trade. Directors relied on men like Tamiroff to invent their own characters, and he was allowed great freedom for as long as he was content with lurid and monotonous villainy. But the Hollywood system never took villains seriously; it seldom allowed them to be brave, intelligent, witty, tender, or imaginative—all those qualities that make real-life villains so interesting. Tamiroff recognized that handicap and created a unique cowardly villain, so inefficient a liar and cheat that raw helplessness shone through: a dumpy little man with an insecure scowl and an anxious snarl, alarmed by anything other than immediate submission from his victims.

Tamiroff's films come round now after respectable people have gone to bed. There is barely a dull one among them, or one that does not come to life for the twenty minutes in which he flourishes: *Okay America* (32, Tay Garnett); *Gabriel Over the White House* (33, Gregory La Cava); *Storm at Daybreak* (33, Richard Boleslavsky); *Queen Christina* (33, Rouben Mamoulian); *Sadie McKee* (34, Clarence Brown); *The Merry Widow* (34, Ernst Lubitsch); *The Captain Hates the Sea* (34, Lewis Milestone, fellow Russian exile who used Tamiroff six times); *Lives of a Bengal Lancer* (35, Henry Hathaway); *China Seas* (35, Garnett); *The Story of Louis Pasteur* (35, William Dieterle); *Anthony Adverse* (36, Mervyn Le Roy); *The General Died at Dawn* (36, Milestone), as a Chinese; *Desire* (36, Frank Borzage); *King of Gamblers* (37, Robert Florey); *The Great Gambini* (37, Charles Vidor); *High, Wide and Handsome* (37, Mamoulian); *Dangerous to Know* (38, Florey); *The Buccaneer* (38, Cecil B. De Mille); *Spawn of the North* (38, Hathaway); playing two roles—banana republic president and masquerader—in *The Magnificent Fraud* (39, Florey); *King of Chinatown* (39, Nick Grinde); *Union Pacific* (39, De Mille); *Disputed Passage* (39, Borzage); *North West Mounted Police* (40, De Mille); *The Great McGinty* (40, Preston Sturges); *The Corsican Brothers* (41, Gregory Ratoff); *Tortilla Flat* (42, Victor Fleming); *Five Graves to Cairo* (43, Billy Wilder); *For Whom the Bell Tolls* (43, Sam Wood); *His Butler's Sister* (43, Borzage); *The Bridge of San Luis Rey* (44, Rowland V. Lee); *Dragon Seed* (44, Jack Conway); as stooge to George Sanders's Vidocq in *A Scandal in Paris* (46, Douglas Sirk); *Fiesta* (47, Richard Thorpe); *My Girl Tisa* (48, Elliott Nugent); *Outpost in Morocco* (49, Florey); *Black Magic* (49, Ratoff), his first film with Orson Welles; *Desert Legion* (53, Joseph Pevney); *They Who Dare* (54, Milestone); *The Widow* (55, Milestone); *Anastasia* (56, Anatole Litvak); *The Black Sleep* (56, Reginald Le Borg); as a Chinese officer in *Yangtse Incident* (57, Michael Anderson); *Me and the Colonel* (58, Peter Glenville); *Ocean's 11* (60, Milestone); *Romanoff and Juliet* (61, Peter Ustinov); *Il Giudizio Universale* (61, Vittorio de Sica); as "Monsignor Cupido," with Gina Lollobrigida—like a beetle on her switchback curves—in *Le Bambole* (64, Mauro Bolognini); *Topkapi* (64, Jules Dassin); *Lord Jim* (65, Richard Brooks); *Marie-Chantal Contre le Docteur Kha* (65, Claude Chabrol); *After the Fox* (66, de Sica); *Great Catherine* (68, Gordon Flemyng); and *Then Came Bronson* (70, William A. Graham).

His dainty servility and guile were made for the mountainous self-glorification of Welles. In three films together, they presented the same spectacle of doubled-up Akim hiding fearfully beneath the Sultan's great belly. In *Confidential Report* (55), Tamiroff was Jakob Zouk, a companion-in-crime eliminated by Welles. In *Touch of Evil* (58), he breathed garlic anxiety into Uncle Joe Grandi, the petulant border-town crook so flustered and jumpy that when he moved too quickly his wig slipped. Once again, he was murdered, throttled by Welles's corrupt police chief. And in *The Trial* (63), he was Bloch, the hopeless client to Welles's indifferent advocate, humiliated but still dependent. By then, Kafka must have seemed to him almost a documentary writer.

The Trial was made all over Europe, as money and opportunity coincided; in much the same way, since 1957 Tamiroff had been playing Sancho Panza in Welles's movie of *Don Quixote*. But once supporting-part movies drained away, Tamiroff wandered from one bizarre venture to another. One film caught the plight of the outcast exactly: Jean-Luc Godard's *Alphaville* (65), in which he played Henri Dickson, a worn-out private eye, dying in a squalid hotel in some wintry suburb of the computer city. His end comes in that film as he attempts to revive passion in the cold arms of a "second-class seductress." He recalls a lofty past, not too far from that of a Moscow Arts actor who preferred the draughty and impermanent sound stages of the world: "Thank you, Madame Pompadour . . . Ah, Madame Bovary . . . Marie Antoinette . . . that's love . . . l'amour . . . and I know it in Russian too . . . ah, darling."

Kinuyo Tanaka (1909–77),
b. Shimonoseki, Japan

Garbo and Dietrich were central to the movies for a dozen or so years; Crawford and Davis for perhaps twenty-five; Gish and Pickford for fifteen. Kinuyo Tanaka—their equal or superior as an actress—was a major force in Japanese film for most of her fifty-year career (Katharine Hepburn, I suppose, is her only peer). She appeared in nearly 250 films, many of them very successful, very fine, or both.

Tanaka wasn't an obvious beauty—she wasn't really a beauty at all—but one comes to treasure her face: slightly plump, small piercing eyes, and thin lips that can express anything with the slightest tightening or the merest smile. In the fifty or so films that have been shown in the West, we have seen her play shy innocents, tough working girls, crooks, tragic victims, romantic heroines, man-eaters, suffering mothers, cruel stepmothers, aristocrats, peasants, formidable actresses, dying crones. She makes even Stanwyck's range seem narrow.

She was born poor in a remote part of Japan, joined a music troupe at eleven, and slid quickly into the emerging Japanese film industry. Among her early films were seven silents for Ozu, the most interesting of which is *Dragnet Girl* (33), in which she is a bad girl who goes good, reforming her boyfriend along the way. Well before that she had starred in Japan's first talkie, *The Neighbor's Wife and Mine* (31, Heinosuke Gosho). During the thirties she acted for Naruse, Gosho, Yasujiro Shimazu, Hiroshi Shimizu (her husband for a while), and Hiromasa Nomura, whose *Yearning Laurel* (38) was probably her most popular film at a time when she was Japan's most popular star. *Yearning Laurel* is a quintessential Japanese weepie—Tanaka plays a young, sacrificing mother whose true love only runs smooth when she enters a song contest and wins both contest and man. (She's also a dedicated nurse.)

Despite her early success, her greatest period came in the early fifties at the height of her association with Mizoguchi. They had worked together on seven films in the forties, including *Utamaro and His Five Women* (46) and *Women of the Night* (48), a blistering attack on prostitution; but *The Life of Oharu* (52), *Ugetsu* (53), and *Sansho the Bailiff* (54) would alone guarantee her screen immortality. Her performance as the potter's wife in *Ugetsu*, and her reappearance in the last dream, are among the finest things in world film.

In the same period, she appeared in Naruse's *Mother* (52) and Gosho's powerful *Where Chimneys Are Seen* (53) in which a poor working couple take in an abandoned child. In 1953, she also directed the first of her own six movies, *Love Letters*, with a script by the director Keisuke Kinoshita, and with herself playing a small role. A further tribute to her came from Ozu, who chose to collaborate on the script of her second film, *The Moon Has Risen* (55), a very appealing love story, with Tanaka in another supporting part.

Her films grew more adventurous: *The Eternal Breasts* (55), about a poet dying of cancer; *The Wandering Empress* (60); *Girls of the Night* (61), her own protest against prostitution; and *Love Under the Crucifix* (62), about a woman's struggle to fulfill herself. Her directing career was the first of any significance for a Japanese woman, and it displayed the same intelligence, taste, and intensity as her acting.

In the postwar period she worked with Ozu three times: *A Hen in the Wind* (48); *The Munekata Sisters* (50); and *Equinox Flower* (58). There were fourteen films in all with Mizoguchi between 1940 and 1954, and five with Naruse, including *Ginza Cosmetics* (51) and *Flowing* (56), in which she is a maid in a declining geisha house, with three other very famous actresses—Hideko Takamine, Isuzu Yamada, and Haruko Sugimura. She acted for Ichikawa in *Her Brother* (60) and *An Actor's Revenge* (63); for Kobayashi in *Sincerity* (53); and for Kurosawa in *Red Beard* (65). But,

apart from Mizoguchi, her most consistent collaborator was Kinoshita, with whom she worked nine times from 1944–64. The most famous of these films is *The Ballad of Narayama* (58), in which she plays an old woman doomed by custom to be abandoned on a mountaintop to die. She was forty-nine then, and seems eighty—she had several teeth pulled to make her face ancient enough.

This is worthy of Gish, whom Tanaka somewhat resembles. Yet Tanaka flourished so much longer, and was more completely fulfilled. A lasting image—reminiscent of Gish—comes from Kinoshita's *Army* (44). Tanaka is again a mother, whose son is going off to war. At first, she refuses to accept what's happening. Then, away in the distance, she hears the new recruits parading and she starts running through the empty streets until she reaches the avenue where they're marching. Rushing frantically through the crowd, she dodges and pushes her way until she finds her son. The emotion builds in a long tracking shot, and (because film stock was so scarce by then) it had to be done in one take. That was all Tanaka needed.

Jessica Tandy (1909–94), b. London
Here is a strange career. Jessica Tandy began in the movies in the 1940s, in small and supporting parts. She then played Blanche Du Bois in the first production of Tennessee Williams's *A Streetcar Named Desire* (47)—and won the Tony award. But when the movie of that play was made, the role of Blanche was recast. Vivien Leigh was deemed sexier and surer box office. Leigh won her second Oscar, and Tandy did very little film work. For anyone able to see, Tandy's mother in *The Birds* (63, Alfred Hitchcock) left it clear how much was being missed. Still, decades more elapsed before Tandy was hailed as a grand old lady, Oscar-worthy, an institution.

Tandy was married first to Jack Hawkins, and then, lastingly, to Hume Cronyn. Her strange record goes as follows: *Murder in the Family* (38, Albert Parker); *The Seventh Cross* (44, Fred Zinnemann); *The Valley of Decision* (45, Tay Garnett); *Dragonwyck* (46, Joseph L. Mankiewicz); *The Green Years* (46, Victor Saville), playing Hume Cronyn's daughter; *Forever Amber* (47, Otto Preminger); *A Woman's Vengeance* (47, Zoltan Korda); as Rommel's wife in *The Desert Fox* (51, Henry Hathaway); *September Affair* (50, William Dieterle); *The Light in the Forest* (58, Herschel Daugherty); *Hemingway's Adventures of a Young Man* (62, Martin Ritt); *Butley* (74, Harold Pinter); *Honky Tonk Freeway* (81, John Schlesinger); *Best Friends* (82, Norman Jewison); *Still of the Night* (82, Robert Benton); *The World According to Garp* (82, George Roy Hill); *The Bostonians* (84, James Ivory); *Cocoon* (85, Ron Howard); *Batteries Not Included* (87, Matthew Robbins); *Foxfire* (87, Jud Taylor); *Cocoon: The*

Return (88, Daniel Petrie); *The House on Carroll Street* (88, Peter Yates); a best actress Oscar in *Driving Miss Daisy* (89, Bruce Beresford); *Fried Green Tomatoes* (91, Jon Avnet); *The Story Lady* (91, Larry Elikann); *Used People* (91, Beeban Kidron); *Camilla* (94, Deepa Mehta); *Nobody's Fool* (94, Robert Benton).

Alain Tanner, b. Geneva, Switzerland, 1929
1957: *Nice Time* (d) (codirected with Claude Goretta). 1964: *Les Apprentis* (d). 1966: *La Vie à Chardigash* (d). 1969: *Charles: Mort ou Vif.* 1971: *La Salamandre/The Salamander.* 1972: *Le Rétour d'Afrique.* 1974: *Le Milieu du Monde.* 1976: *Jonas, Qui Aura 25 Ans en L'An 2000/Jonah, Who Will Be 25 in the Year 2000.* 1978: *Messidor.* 1981: *L'Années Lumières/Light Years Away.* 1982: *Dans la Ville Blanche/In the White City.* 1985: *No Man's Land.* 1987: *Une Flamme dans Mon Coeur/A Flame in My Heart; La Vallée Fantôme.* 1989: *La Femme de Rose Hill.* 1991: *The Man Who Lost His Shadow.* 1993: *The Diary of Lady M.* 1995: *Les Hommes du Port* (d). 1996: *Fourbi.* 1998: *Requiem.* 1999: *Jonas et Lila, à Demain.* 2002: *Fleurs de Sang* (co-directed with Myriam Mezieres).

In *La Vallée Fantôme,* a movie about the dilemma of making movies, a central character says he cares only about cinema, women, and history. The Godardian remark is made by a man of advanced middle age (played by Jean-Louis Trintignant, at fifty-five-plus), and there is some sense of history being the least reliable consolation as movies and women work their way toward betrayal or disillusionment. Tanner has been around, and lived through many stages of development. They have all been vital and personal, and there is much to commend. But Tanner cannot resist a brooding disquiet, a weary sensualism that says, alas, that in the end, all is history.

He was the son of an actress and a writer-painter, and he was educated in economics at Calvin College in Geneva. In the fifties he went to London and was on the edges of the Free Cinema documentary movement—that was how he and Goretta made *Nice Time* together. Then Tanner worked in television documentary in Europe.

In the seventies, he made three films in collaboration with John Berger—*The Salamander, Le Milieu du Monde,* and *Jonas.* Berger was and is novelist, writer of polemical nonfiction, and art critic. But he is also one of those people whose passing comments on film and photography are filled with insight and passion. The collaboration was very fruitful. Berger brought a sense of play and community to Tanner that kept his own inner melancholy at bay. They also managed to convey the nature and the problem of being Swiss in telling ways. *The Salamander* is a young woman (Bulle Ogier) who refuses to succumb to the views

of her held by two suitors. *Jonas* is a rumination on how Europe will develop, but it is also one of those films in which a group of individuals build a portrait of a society—anyone familiar with Berger's nonfiction can see how important he was to the film.

As Tanner moved on, without Berger, he delved more deeply into personal and then sexual dismay. *Messidor* shows the relationship between two women breaking up. *Light Years Away* picks up the *Jonas* character, in Ireland, and it has fine performances from Trevor Howard and Mick Ford. The *White City* is Lisbon, with Bruno Ganz living alone, infatuated with a waitress, drawn to violence and the history of the city, yet half lost in tracking shots that explore the city. The mood becomes sadder, but *In the White City* may be the archetypical Tanner film in its depiction of a man working his way toward solitude.

Tanner made another collaboration with the actress-writer Myriam Mézières: she acts in *No Man's Land* and both wrote and acted in *A Flame in My Heart,* a study of a woman's sexual self-determination, and a truly erotic movie. This mood was repeated in *La Femme de Rose Hill.* But Tanner's most recent films have not prospered, or been seen widely. One might guess that without the presence of another galvanizing collaborator, he is increasingly a poet of isolation, trying to insist on a gloomy eroticism as he grows older—the sadness of older eyes gazing at ever youthful pictures.

Tanner would seem to have found fresh collaborators in writer Bernard Comment, and his daughter, actress Cécile Tanner. His recent films have not been seen much outside the festival circuit, but *Requiem* has a high reputation as an Alt-manesque mingling of overlapping stories. This is a director who deserves retrospective seasons.

Quentin Tarantino,
b. Knoxville, Tennessee, 1963
1992: *Reservoir Dogs.* 1994: *Pulp Fiction.* 1995: "The Man from Hollywood," an episode from *Four Rooms.* 1997: *Jackie Brown.* 2003: *Kill Bill.*

It's easy to be distracted by the fuss and hype over Tarantino, not least by his own interviews (no one else can so swiftly bring "incessant" and "insufferable" to mind). There are already more biographies of Tarantino than pictures to his credit; too many youthful, brutal, but perversely talking pictures funded in hopes of repeating the *Pulp Fiction* bonanza; and too many hysterically manic young geniuses doing "a Tarantino" and behaving as if they knew every B picture ever made but nothing else about life. In so many ways, he is the epitome of that brilliant, remorseless, empty-life student that every film teacher has tried to avoid.

And yet, he is a real, weird writer, a conduit for

swinging, hardboiled talk which, if it is gang-
sterese for the moment, might one day end in
inspired comedy. For all the much-copied riffs
and routines, sometimes Tarantino's characters
are eloquent and human in their talk—especially
in *Jackie Brown*. In addition, he seems to know his
own crippling immaturity for what it is: for
instance, he declined Kit Carson's script for
Walker Percy's *The Moviegoer* because he felt it
was too grown-up for him. Of course, how a raging
success in Hollywood, with time to act in *From
Dusk to Dawn* (96, Robert Rodriguez) and pre-
side over the travesty of *Four Rooms,* actually gets
to grow up is another matter. As yet, Tarantino is
an uneasy mix of sage and sensationalist, doing the
rewrites on *Crimson Tide* and using the money to
finance debauch.

Still, in his years in the dark and as a clerk at
video stores, Tarantino learned to love Hawks and
Godard—you can do worse. And in *Pulp Fiction*,
one can see Godard's love of structure and
Hawks's delight in comic vagary just as much as
the violence and the overall swagger of kid noir.
Pulp Fiction has rare energy, exuberant panache,
and comedy—it is a self-sufficient arabesque, not
so far from *The Big Sleep*. Anyone as blessed with
a sense of movie shape might get away with knowing nothing else. Was Hawks a paragon of human
behavior, or an artist who worshipped a certain
notion of cool elegance?

But then there is the Tarantino of violence: not
just the maker of *Reservoir Dogs*—which seems to
me gloatingly cruel and mechanical—but the
screenwriter of *True Romance* (93, Tony Scott)
and the supplier of story and first script for *Natural Born Killers* (94, Oliver Stone). Tarantino has
said he regards the violence in his films as
comic—even the grisly sequence of torture in
Reservoir Dogs? Perhaps it is more the result of
constant sugar highs generated by the collective
movie violence of the ages.

Everything, I suspect, comes down to this
barbed idea of humor. When, towards the end of
Pulp Fiction, the curve of the story bends back to
meet itself, there is something deeply, musically
satisfying—a formal magic that is also very moving.
Let us put all our chips on that number, and hope.
Then, even if nothing else comes our way—and
that could happen—*Pulp Fiction* may stand as the
macabre farewell to classic American movie grace.

Tarantino responded to arrival by doing—not
very much. Perhaps he is giving himself time to
live and grow up. Certainly, *Jackie Brown* caught
his hard-core fans off guard. I like it a lot, and I
see it as the best evidence that Tarantino could
become a maker of great comedies.

Andrei Tarkovsky (1932–1986),
b. Laovrazhe, USSR
1959: *There Will Be No Leave Today* (s). 1960:
The Steamroller and the Violin (s). 1962: *Ivanovo
Detstvo/Ivan's Childhood*. 1966: *Andrei Roublev*.
1972: *Solaris*. 1975: *The Mirror*. 1979: *Stalker*.
1983: *Nostalghia*. 1985: *The Sacrifice*.

Tarkovsky sounded out of Russia like the triumphant bell cast at the end of *Andrei Roublev*—
according to Nigel Andrews "the one indisputable
Russian masterpiece of the last decade." It is a
very striking film, as spectacular and confident as
any epic, but to call it a masterpiece may only
reflect upon the conditions of Russian art in the
sixties.

Tarkovsky studied at the Soviet State Film
School under Mikhail Romm and graduated in
1961 with his friend Andrei Konchalovsky. His
first feature seems to me his most conventional,
his most Sovietized, and his most successful. It
concerns the activities of a boy working for the
Russian army to bring back information from
behind the German lines. The unambiguously
heroic situation, the patriotic conviction, and the
sensitive but sentimental view of the boy make it a
familiar Russian report from the war. But
Tarkovsky's eye was not commonplace, and the
sentiment was given a poetic quality by the way he
made the winter landscapes eerie and foreboding,
and by the magical aura that hovered over the boy.
Ivan is lost on a mission, and the film hurries forward to Berlin at the end of the war and the discovery of a file that describes his capture and
death. That ending explains the film's tone of awe:
for this is a child touched by the cold hand of
fate—his childhood sacrificed to war, his innocence turned into an unnatural skill and nobility.
The child is presented to us through the eyes of
reverent adults, as if he were a legend for the
army.

Andrei Roublev was not released in Russia until
five years after its making, though more on
account of its length, violence, and arbitrary structure than because it threatened to disturb the anxious order. Originally, it ran over three hours; it is
in CinemaScope, with a concluding sequence in
rich color. Its central figure is another legend—
the most famous of Russian icon-painters. So little
is known about the real Roublev that Tarkovsky
was able to use him as a basis for a sketchy celebration of the creative process. Roublev moves
with increasing horror and revulsion through
scenes of medieval horror—slaughter, rapine, and
destruction—until he resolves to give up art. His
mind changes only when he finds a youth—played
by Kolya Burlyayev, the boy in *Ivan*—who is
attempting to cast a bell. As the moment of truth
comes, the youth admits to Roublev that he has no
knowledge of casting, that he simply yearned to
try. The bell proves sound and the movie ends
with a gorgeous sequence of the icons that,
Tarkovsky supposes, Roublev went on to paint.

The simple-minded schematics of this may be illustrated by a comparison with *Lust for Life*, Vincente Minnelli's biopic of Van Gogh. That film, too, ends with a series of Van Gogh's greatest paintings, but Minnelli and Kirk Douglas managed to make "the artist" an unmistakable, tragic individual. The torment of Van Gogh is much more local than that faced by Roublev: it is personal, unique, and neurotic. But we share it, see how it fosters and hinders Van Gogh, and feel purged of tragedy by the way the paintings redeem the cornfield suicide. We never have such a knowledge of Roublev that we comprehend the thwarted passion in his art. He is too much "the artist" and his world as teeming a hell on earth as a Breughel—and quite as vivid and authentic. Most depressing is the way that Tarkovsky fell in with the Soviet notion of the artist as an archetype, rather than as a lonely individual. The length, bloodletting, and period detail of *Andrei Roublev* are extravagant because the film's point was preconceived and not earned. *Andrei Roublev* suffers from the rhetoric and depersonalization that have always hung over Russian cinema, and that make as modest a writer as Solzhenitsyn a brave victim and exile while Nabokov was a master in another country.

Solaris is on as grand a scale as *Roublev*. A science-fiction movie, from a novel by Stanislaw Lem, it is 165 minutes long, and again in Scope and color. Its central scientist, Kris Kelvin, is posted to the planet Solaris where a crew has been all but wiped out. The "enemy" on Solaris is the way the planet can generate the people that its inhabitants are thinking about. I do not mean to be snide when I say that an episode of *Star Trek* explored this theme with more wit and ingenuity, less sentimentality, and at a third the length. Kelvin is confronted by a wife who committed suicide, which is a long way to go for a story about a failed marriage and enough of a gimmick to evade any adequate study of how love failed. The visualization of *Solaris* is as senselessly elaborate as in *2001*, and the philosophy as mediocre.

After *The Mirror* and *Stalker*, Tarkovsky became an exile—*Nostalghia* was made in Italy, and *The Sacrifice* in Sweden (with many people who had worked for Ingmar Bergman). He was inclined to deliver mighty, earnest harangues at film festivals on the devastation of world culture. I was at the Telluride Film Festival when Tarkovsky's lengthy and humorless speech was followed the next night by a wry, yet just as earnest Richard Widmark who opted for less self-laceration and more honest entertainment. But Tarkovsky was distraught at being an exile, and he was suffering from lung cancer. Those things added to his foreboding, and enhanced the mountingly baroque pessimism of his films.

Nostalghia is lustrous, deliquescent almost (it dwells in water and rain), brimming with pain—yet close to parody. *The Sacrifice* is a parable, about nuclear holocaust being averted by some great personal sacrifice. It has some of the most glorious extended shots in film history. The mise-en-scène is relentless. The perfection has something monstrous about it, as if trouble had made Tarkovsky into a magnificent island gradually receding from the rest of the world. For this viewer, there is something tyrannical about it that spurs irreverent thoughts of resistance.

Frank Tashlin (1913–72),
b. Weehawken, New Jersey

1951: *The Lemon Drop Kid* (uncredited, but codirected with Sidney Lanfield). 1952: *The First Time; Son of Paleface*. 1953: *Marry Me Again*. 1954: *Susan Slept Here*. 1955: *Artists and Models*. 1956: *The Lieutenant Wore Skirts; Hollywood or Bust; The Girl Can't Help It*. 1957: *Will Success Spoil Rock Hunter?*. 1958: *Rock-a-Bye Baby; The Geisha Boy*. 1959: *Say One for Me*. 1960: *Cinderfella*. 1962: *Bachelor Flat; It's Only Money*. 1963: *The Man from the Diner's Club; Who's Minding the Store?*. 1965: *The Disorderly Orderly*. 1966: *The Glass-Bottom Boat; The Alphabet Murders*. 1967: *Caprice*. 1968: *The Private Navy of Sergeant O'Farrell*.

Frank Tashlin was absorbed in the most unrestrained products of Americana; yet he never resolved his conflicting feelings about throwaway culture. He filmed a caricature America, but never found an equivalent of the distancing permitted by cartoon. His failure becomes clearer when one sees *The Nutty Professor*, made by his onetime pupil, Jerry Lewis. That resorts to myth as a way of commenting on modern America, and a myth that cleverly exploits the idea of metamorphosis inherent in animation. The way in which cartoon creatures are nearly obliterated and then made whole again was something Tashlin's features never matched. As a result, his satire is an unsatisfying tirade against hollow, helpless characters.

He began in the studio of Max Fleischer in 1928 and worked almost twenty years as cartoonist, animator, and writer. Among other jobs, he was a gagman for Hal Roach, a magazine cartoonist ("Tish-Tash"), story director for Disney, and director on *Merrie Melodies, Looney Tunes,* and *Bugs Bunny*. He worked on the scenario for *Delightfully Dangerous* (44, Arthur Lubin), invented gags for Harpo Marx in *A Night in Casablanca* (46, Archie Mayo)—including the house that collapses—and, in 1946, joined Paramount. He had writing credits on *Variety Girl* (47, George Marshall); *The Paleface* (48, Norman Z. McLeod); *The Fuller Brush Man* (48, S. Sylvan Simon); *One Touch of Venus* (48, William A.

Seiter); *Miss Grant Takes Richmond* (49, Lloyd Bacon); *Love Happy* (50, David Miller); *A Woman of Distinction* (50, Edward Buzzell); *Kill the Umpire* (50, Bacon); *The Good Humor Man* (50, Bacon); and *The Fuller Brush Girl* (50, Bacon).

Tashlin's films are intermittently and inorganically funny; the humor comes in splashes and quickly dries up. Sometimes his gags are actually destructive of visual continuity and can only be ended with a fade-out and a fresh start. Without animation's capacity for remaking its image, Tashlin was always in danger of disrupting human reality or of stopping his jokes short of their distorting logic. This tension is reflected in his unresolved love-hate at the excessiveness of such things as advertising, packaging, rock and roll, TV, Jayne Mansfield's breasts, and the general pixilation of rat-racing. The tone of his satire is momentarily much more mordant than the sentimental form of the finished films allows. Why should Jerry Lewis live happily ever after when Tashlin sees him as a demented creature, driven by pathos in one direction and the American success motor in the other?

As an example, one of Tashlin's luckiest coups was in finding Jayne Mansfield, perhaps the nearest to a "drawn" woman ever to have appeared in films. In *The Girl Can't Help It* there is much ogling mockery of her shape and breasts. One sequence begins with shots of her walking along a street in which her own shape is already hallucinatory: the cartoon arabesque of waist and hourglass bulges that Jayne and corsets actually managed. Tashlin then has a succession of jokes about the way people react to her: an ice-lorry driver grabs an ice block and it melts; a milkman stands in awe and milk bottles in his hands boil over; another man gawks and his glasses shatter. This is the chronic gag-maker unable to choose one joke from several, and unable to see that the milk bottles are infinitely funnier and more suggestive in that they reflect back, nightmarishly, on the maternal function of Jayne's boobs. The sequence is overextended, but also grotesque because it is based on a fallacy. Jayne was never sexy, but monstrous and pathetic; eventually, her own willingness to walk through so many cruel jokes makes her pitiable. Tashlin seems oblivious of the fact that we at last see a human being, visually and emotionally deformed by the treatment. Tashlin's manic despair is unable to declare itself or to engage us with people. Tom and Jerry manage the lunatic American conflict of energy and sentiment far better. Logically Jerry Lewis ought to go into catatonia, Jayne become a milk-bar for teeny-boppers. But Tashlin remained the safe, cold-blooded side of bad taste, never came to terms with the full-length form or the live-action image, but never sensed the pungent onslaught in

cartoon that, say, Gillray or Ralph Bakshi have achieved.

Jacques Tati (Jacques Tatischeff) (1908–82), b. Le Pecq, France

1947: *L'Ecole des Facteurs* (s). 1949: *Jour de Fête*. 1953: *Les Vacances de M. Hulot/M. Hulot's Holiday*. 1958: *Mon Oncle*. 1967: *Playtime*. 1970: *Trafic/Traffic*. 1974: *Parade*.

Tati was a deliberate exponent of austere charm who insisted on subjects of considerable public significance. His elaborate talent for refined visual comedy was expressed with the consistency and neatness of a great miniaturist. But the delicacy of line and mime was always vulgarized by a humorless preoccupation with such issues as the aridity of modern urban life. Tati's theme was that personality is being warped by the unfeeling organization of our times. But his art so relied on detached, graceful views of mime that he omitted individuality. Hulot is, in outline, very close to Buster Keaton—a romantic bewildered by the vagaries of the world—but whereas Buster has a passive human strength, Tati made Hulot a remote creature, a shape in the landscape. The comedy seemed increasingly an inconsequential attempt at avoiding the harshness that Tati recognized in the world. Just as he never let a shot go by that was not formally balanced and tasteful, so he evaded the real nature of the destructiveness he loathed. It is not enough for comedy to be socially moralizing; it must deal with personal anguish and still make us laugh.

Tati came from a Russian family. As a young man he played rugby, and when he went into music hall and cabaret as a mime comedian he specialized in studies of sporting activity. This led to his first film, as writer and actor, *Oscar, Champion de Tennis* (32). During the 1930s, he appeared in several other shorts: *On Demande une Brute* (34, Charles Barrois); *Gai Dimanche* (35, Jacques Berr); *Soigne ton Gauche* (36, René Clément); and *Retour à la Terre* (38). After the war he had small parts in *Sylvie et le Fantôme* (45, Claude Autant-Lara) and *Le Diable au Corps* (47, Autant-Lara). But thereafter, he began his angular and rather haughty independence as writer, director, and actor on his own projects. *L'Ecole des Facteurs* became a tryout for his first feature, a rough-and-ready rural story centering on the village postman. It allowed Tati several virtuoso set pieces, the balletic meticulousness of which made an unsettling contrast with the technical shortcomings of the photography. The lovingly recreated rural setting was very much in keeping with the ideals of Tati's absentminded hero, but the presence of the postman permitted him to contrast the rural operator and the obtusely progressive methods of the urban service, as shown in a documentary projected in the village.

His next film introduced the character of M. Hulot in a provincial seaside resort. The bourgeois on the beach was well suited to Tati's gentle but penetrating eye for our absurdities. Once more, he stresses visual comedy in preference to sound, and organizes several long, complex, but delicious constructed gags. If only because the balance of personality and style was best preserved in this first presentation of Hulot, *Les Vacances* deserved its great international success.

After that, however, Hulot moved into the city so that his mournful feyness could show up the brutality of progress. The point was well made, but tritely thought out and endlessly reiterated. The comedy was more quietist and sometimes lost within the dense texture of Tati's habitual long shot. *Mon Oncle* opposed two ways of living in a city with a simplistic monotony; *Playtime* was a study of the excesses of modern tourism, and *Trafic* was devoted to the undemanding proposition that the motor car is a convenience that is inconvenient. *Trafic* was pretty and empty, not worth the car chase sequence in Bogdanovich's *What's Up, Doc?* American farce, from Keaton and Groucho to *Bringing Up Baby* and *Doc?*, has always let social significance look after itself and concentrated instead on plausible character studies and inescapable narrative spirals. But the Tati man moves with the tendentious vagueness of a monk, garbed in salvation but not visibly human.

Bertrand Tavernier, b. Lyon, France, 1941
1963: an episode from *Les Baisers* (s). 1973: *L'Horloger de St. Paul/The Watchmaker*. 1975: *Que la Fête Commence/Let Joy Reign Supreme.* 1976: *Le Juge et l'Assassin/The Judge and the Assassin*. 1977: *Des Enfants Gâtés/Spoiled Children*. 1979: *La Mort en Direct/Deathwatch*. 1980: *Une Semaine de Vacances/A Week's Holiday*. 1981: *Coup de Torchon/Clean Slate*. 1983: *Mississippi Blues* (d) (codirected with Robert Parrish). 1984: *Un Dimanche à la Compagne/Sunday in the Country*. 1986: *'Round Midnight; La Passion Béatrice/Beatrice*. 1989: *La Vie et Rien d'Autre/Life and Nothing But; Lyon, Regard Intérieur* (d). 1990: *Daddy Nostalgie*. 1992: *La Guerre sans Nom* (d); *L627*. 1994: *La Fille de d'Artagnan*. 1995: *L'Appât/Fresh Bait*. 1996: *Capitaine Conan*. 1997: *La Lettre* (TV). 1998: *De l'Autre Côté du Périph* (d) (TV). 1999: *Ça Commence Aujourd'hui*. 2000: *Laissez-passer; Les Enfants de Thiès* (TV).

The author of any would-be meticulous yet helplessly emotional work of cinema reference must give a special salute to Bertrand Tavernier. When we last met—on the streets of Telluride in 1990 (he was there with *Daddy Nostalgie*)—greetings quickly turned to his overpowering need to have an answer, "Tell me, if you can, exactly what is the year of birth for Robert Towne?" Such are the great enigmas of the compiler's life.

Tavernier was engaged on *50 Ans de Cinéma Americain,* the work that he and Jean-Pierre Coursodon published in 1991—a much enlarged sequel to their 1970 book, *30 Ans de Ciné Americain*. Of course—as with Cole Porter observing Rodgers and Hart—one may marvel that it took two of them to do it. Nevertheless, and although only in French still, *50 Ans* is a work of love and scholarship worthy of two eighty-year-olds, yet written with the *essential* arrogance that peaks in the years seventeen to twenty-three. Bertrand is one of those non-Americans whose cherishing of the byways of Hollywood cinema shocks most Americans. They would be more shocked still if they could ever grasp that this very important filmmaker has a faith in knowing the history of the medium that feeds naturally into his own work.

As a youth, he founded a cinema club. He went on to be not just a ceaseless gatherer of facts and anecdotes but a critic and then a publicist in the French film business. He wrote for *Cahiers du Cinéma* and *Positif*, and as a publicist he worked for Melville, Kazan, Losey, Ford, and Walsh. When a publicist can retain his hero-worship without shame or sigh, then that man is possessed of mighty love, or need.

That career, and Tavernier's lifelong vocation as a chronicler, have left time for him to be a director. After two decades, the most important thing to say about Tavernier is how versatile he is, how prepared for change. Further, while his films do benefit from American virtues (of a past age, admittedly)—intricate but rapid narratives, fluent mise-en-scène, fine acting—he has never aped American styles. He is an entirely French director, close to the generation of the New Wave, yet less concerned with formal innovation and more anxious to re-create the moral ambiguities of, say, Renoir, Jacques Becker, Melville, and Grémillon.

The Watchmaker was a Simenon adaptation, set in Lyon, and using Philippe Noiret, who would come to embody the complexities of a leading male role for Tavernier. *Let Joy Reign Supreme* is costume history, set in 1719, yet as urgent and real as Rossellini, and it has a superb passage where the mood of fete turns dark and foreboding. It remains a dazzling work of re-creation, and a sign of the historian in Tavernier.

The Judge and the Assassin was, once more, provincial and period, and it had a note of Hitchcock or Preminger in its probing of power and ethics. *Spoiled Children* is about a movie director thrown off course by an unexpected love affair. It established Tavernier's great sense of sex driving human situations, and in Christine Pascal it demonstrated his skill with actresses.

Deathwatch is science fiction, and for this writer something of a mess—perhaps because Tavernier had American actors to work with. *Coup de Torchon* took Jim Thompson's pulp novel *Pop. 1280* and transferred it to French colonial Africa. It was not quite Thompson, but it gave Noiret a fine chance to be the ambiguous monster. *A Week's Vacation* had Nathalie Baye as a woman who begins to reappraise the nature of her own family. *Mississippi Blues* was a fond, if somewhat undisciplined, documentary.

Sunday in the Country is a masterpiece, his greatest film. It is period again, about an elderly painter and the ways in which his family regard him. The influence of Renoir was obvious, but the film was Tavernier's in its study of elaborate relations and hallowed interiors, in its use of just one day for all the action, and in glorious performances from Louis Ducreux and Sabine Azema.

'Round Midnight was a sentimental favorite, a misty biography, and an overly romantic view of a hero, perhaps. But it was redeemed by the sheer idiosyncrasy of Dexter Gordon and the beguiled coverage of the music. For two hours, Dexter was at peace.

Beatrice seemed to me a second failure: it is a brilliant remaking of the Dark Ages, but its severity of mood is so misanthropic as to seem forced. *Life and Nothing But* is a second masterpiece, however, and a clear signal of Tavernier's urge to become more and more the historian. He appeared as an interviewer in Marcel Ophüls's *Hotel Terminus*, and that seems to have prompted him to make *La Guerre sans Nom*, an Ophülsian study of the Algerian war.

In the nineties, Tavernier films no longer opened regularly in America or England. *La Fille* was a swashbuckler with Sophie Marceau. *L'Appât* was a tough-minded film about young people living rough. *Capitaine Conan* concerned a rogue warrior in World War I. *La Lettre* was Somerset Maugham, with Sandrine Bonnaire in the old Bette Davis part. *Ça Commence* is the story of a teacher who faces impoverished children and a tangle of bureaucratic relations. They all sound interesting, and Tavernier ought to be in his prime.

Paolo Taviani, b. San Miniato, Italy, 1931; and
Vittorio Taviani, b. San Miniato, Italy, 1929
1954: *San Miniato, Luglio '44/San Miniato, July 1944* (s). 1962: *Un Uomo da Bruciare/A Man for Burning* (codirected with Valentino Orsini). 1963: *I Fuorilegge del Matrimonio* (codirected with Orsini). 1968: *Sovversivi*. 1969: *Sotto il Segno dello Scorpione/Under the Sign of Scorpio*. 1972: *San Michele Aveva un Gallo*. 1974: *Allonsanfan*. 1977: *Padre Padrone*. 1979: *Il Prato/The Meadow*. 1982: *La Notte di San Lorenzo/The Night of the Shooting Stars*. 1984: *Kaos*. 1987:

Good Morning, Babylon. 1990: *Il Sole Anche di Notte/The Sun Also Shines at Night*. 1994: *Fiorile/Wild Flower*.

The Tavianis encourage everyone to regard their work as that of one being—for they collaborate intimately at every stage, taking turns in actually directing scenes. That kind of compassionate tolerance, the lack of ego or pride, is vital to the glorious fusion of neo-realism and spiritual grace in their best work. Occasionally (as in *The Meadow*) their work has yielded to sentimentality. But more generally—in *Padre Padrone*, *The Night of the Shooting Stars*, and *Kaos*—the kindness is set in a rugged, even tough view of human survival and social realities. They are country people, most at ease with peasants, but declining to ennoble them. They are also folklorists enthralled by the way story begins to alter or elevate factual incidents. *Kaos*—based on Pirandello stories—is their most complex and absorbing picture. *Good Morning, Babylon* nearly works. It is the story of two stonemason brothers who build sets for D. W. Griffith (Charles Dance) and *Intolerance*. But it is a touch too whimsical—as if romanticism had covered up their ignorance of early Hollywood. It feels like a shot at the big time, whereas at their best the Tavianis exist in a sublime harmony with an intricate eternity.

It's clear in hindsight that the Tavianis are the fruitful inheritors of Rossellini's approach. They did assist him in the 1950s. And their achievement, like his, is part of that neglected topic—the way in which films have helped build the folk culture of societies for whom reading is still a challenging process. In that sense, the Tavianis' films should also be related back to popular Italian music and theatre. And even their Griffith movie shows how far early cinema helped link drastically opposed ages of man.

Elizabeth Taylor, b. London, 1932
It is years now since Elizabeth Taylor made a proper movie. Yet we know she's there, still: her face blooms for perfume promotions, and she's always likely to be standing up for AIDS victims or Michael Jackson. Are we meant to think she has the same sincerity for all three? Or is she resting? That would be sad—for at one time, she seemed uncommonly engaged, in movies and scandal alike.

Though her love life and the soap opera of her health seem to have been with us as long as the H-bomb, Liz was younger than, say, Audrey Hepburn or Rock Hudson. When they made *Giant* (56, George Stevens), she was actually a year younger than James Dean. Brought up at a time when sexuality on the screen was still creatively suppressed by censorship, her private life was paraded by the press as that of a love goddess. That now looks like the last flare of classic star charisma, the last time the public could read any imagined voluptuousness into a decorous, sulky princess of *House & Garden*. Image and reality clashed like cymbals in *Cleopatra* (63, Joseph L. Mankiewicz). But though the chaos of that film's making included Liz dangerously ill and Liz exchanging a fourth husband (Eddie Fisher) for a fifth (Richard Burton), her Queen of the Nile emerged a plump, complacent clotheshorse.

She may have been apprehensive about the lurid extreme of public attention; intrigued by the label of "acting" that trailed from Burton; and she was surely perplexed by the way fashion accelerated away from the sexual mode of 1958–62. In *Cat on a Hot Tin Roof* (58, Richard Brooks), as Maggie the Cat, she seemed aggressively candid about sex. But by 1970, she was a throwback to elaborate hairdos, fussy clothes, and earnest emoting. She had not matured, but regressed into that vague eligible debutante—or her mother—that she once infused with indolent wantonness, half asleep from being stared at. Even her good films were prominently signaled as "serious acting," whereas there was once a poignant osmosis of young Hollywood doll and the parts she played. It is the difference between her two Oscar films—*Who's Afraid of Virginia Woolf?* (66, Mike Nichols) and *Butterfield 8* (60, Daniel Mann)—the first based on a clever stage play, the second on a hack novel. Martha in the first is a "character," far deeper and more demanding. You can hear Taylor thinking out all her complexities as she plays. In *Butterfield 8*, however, she serenely inhabits the melodrama in exactly the way that cinema encourages audiences to live through its stars. Like the audience, Liz had a superstitious preoccupation with glamour.

The marriage to Burton may have unsettled her, showing her how simple her own dramatic taste was. Once a presence, she became an actress. Not a bad actress, but one unable to regain the shallow clarity of *Butterfield 8*. In the event, she reduced the brittle respectability in Burton to her level—that of boasting of diamonds. Martha in *Virginia Woolf* was an "ugly" woman, something the Taylor of the 1950s would never have been allowed to take on, and a part fundamentally offensive to her view of herself. Later, she tried to look like her former self, as witness the neurotic wealth of costume in *Divorce His, Divorce Hers* (73, Waris Hussein), the TV film released ghoulishly as she and Burton broke up.

She was evacuated to America during the war and made her debut in *There's One Born Every Minute* (42, Harold Young) before finding her place at MGM as a rapturous face in a collie's mane: *Lassie Come Home* (43, Fred M. Wilcox). In her next film, *Jane Eyre* (44, Robert Stevenson), she was like a young Lizzie Siddall as the child who dies. She was a child still in *The White*

Cliffs of Dover (44, Clarence Brown), a big hit in *National Velvet* (44, Brown), and *Life with Father* (47, Michael Curtiz). Her teenage period was happily brief: *A Date with Judy* (48, Richard Thorpe); *Julia Misbehaves* (48, Jack Conway); *Little Women* (49, Mervyn Le Roy); *Conspirator* (49, Victor Saville); and *The Big Hangover* (50, Norman Krasna).

It was Vincente Minnelli and the parental guidance of Spencer Tracy and Joan Bennett that ushered in her maturity in *Father of the Bride* (50) and *Father's Little Dividend* (51). But her first really striking part was away from MGM as the rich girl in love with Montgomery Clift in *A Place in the Sun* (51, Stevens). That film not only established her own black-haired beauty, but set a popular standard for a decade. In the fifty years since, has any movie actress been so blatant about extraordinary beauty? Julia Roberts in *Pretty Woman* is the only case that I can think of.

It also showed how unlucky she was to be the property of MGM, still dealing in Thalberg's innocuous glamour. In the next few years she was wasted on insubstantial romances and genteel adventure pictures: indeed, her Rebecca in *Ivanhoe* (52, Thorpe) had something of the splendor of the silent screen. Otherwise she tended to sigh and dilate her violet eyes: *Love Is Better Than Ever* (51, Stanley Donen); *The Girl Who Had Everything* (53, Thorpe); *Rhapsody* (54, Charles Vidor); replacing Vivien Leigh in *Elephant Walk* (54, William Dieterle); *Beau Brummel* (54, Curtis Bernhardt); and *The Last Time I Saw Paris* (54, Brooks). But *Giant* was an improvement and signaled a special responsiveness to the naturalistic care of George Stevens. As if to prove her aptitude for saga romance, she was as atmospheric as a fading camellia in *Raintree County* (57, Edward Dmytryk), as a Southern girl who goes mad with love. These were her best years, leading to the Oscar for *Butterfield 8* and the brimming explicitness of her beach bait for young men in *Suddenly, Last Summer* (59, Mankiewicz).

After *Cleopatra*, she clung to Burton to prove fidelity and professionalism: *The VIPs* (63, Anthony Asquith); the risible *The Sandpiper* (65, Minnelli); *The Taming of the Shrew* (67, Franco Zeffirelli); as Helen of Troy in *Doctor Faustus* (67, Neville Coghill and Burton); *The Comedians* (67, Peter Glenville); *Boom!* (68, Joseph Losey); and *Hammersmith Is Out* (72, Peter Ustinov). She was much more deeply stirred in *Secret Ceremony* (68, Losey), where she seems to catch the sense of sexual instability, and in *Reflections in a Golden Eye* (67, John Huston). But she was restored to former melodrama in *The Only Game in Town* (69, Stevens), *Zee & Co* (71, Brian G. Hutton), *Night Watch* (73, Hutton), and *Ash Wednesday* (73, Larry Peerce), shameless movies, but enough to reprise her brooding self-belief. She rediscovered dignity in *A Little Night Music* (78, Harold Prince).

Fifteen years later, the update could list the continuing marital career—but no one cares now. It should mention *The Mirror Crack'd* (80, Guy Hamilton) and *Young Toscanini* (88, Zeffirelli) in theatres, as well as several TV movies: *Between Friends* (83, Lou Antonio); a juicy Louella Parsons in *Malice in Wonderland* (85, Gus Trikonis); as a star who comes out of a mental hospital to make a comeback in *There Must Be a Pony* (86, Joseph Sargent); running a Western brothel in *Poker Alice* (87, Arthur Allan Seidelman); and with Mark Harmon in *Sweet Bird of Youth* (89, Nicolas Roeg).

Yet the work of which she is probably most proud is her feisty, eloquent, and quite implacable resolve to have people talk and know about AIDS. It is somehow fitting that her astonishing strength and durability should now be given so generously to the vulnerable, and in 1993 she received the Jean Hersholt Humanitarian Award for this service.

Over the years, there have been jokes about Elizabeth Taylor—more than that, she was for a decade or so a roaring comedy of disaster. Yet at the tender age of seventy, she is one of those stars whose mere look or voice brings back so many memories. Her worthless movies of the seventies and eighties are not really held against her. It is to be hoped that she may yet give us a few sensational old ladies—something better than her role in *The Flintstones* (94, Brian Levant).

Nothing yet, except for *These Old Broads* (01, Matthew Diamond).

Robert Taylor (Spangler Arlington Brugh) (1911–69), b. Filley, Nebraska
There can be no argument that Taylor was at best a journeyman player, and yet in the late 1930s he was immensely popular. Despite the publicity endorsement of the ideal romantic man, MGM actually emasculated all of its male stars except Gable and Tracy. Taylor was the handsome, inoffensive young smiler that an exceptionally solicitous studio could allow to take its daughters to the dance. Taylor's history is like that of Tyrone Power: of hollow, gorgeous youth dwindling into anxiety. But in Taylor's case, there is something touching in the decline. For he became not plainer, but harsher: churlish, peeved, disagreeable—no more than that, never enough to make him an absorbing villain. Perhaps it was the slow inroad of the cancer that eventually killed him. Perhaps the petulant residue of a man who never quite recovered from being called Spangler Arlington Brugh.

He studied as a cellist, and then went to drama school. Goldwyn gave him a screen test but MGM contracted him—and kept him for twenty-five years, long after he had outlived his usefulness. The studio loaned him out first, to Fox for *Handy Andy* (34, David Butler), but then cast him in George B. Seitz's *Buried Loot* (34). After a few small parts and B-picture leads—*Society Doctor* (35, Seitz) and *Times Square Lady* (35, Seitz)—Taylor made his name dancing with Eleanor Powell in *Broadway Melody of 1936* (35, Roy del Ruth) and at Universal opposite Irene Dunne in John Stahl's classic weepie, *Magnificent Obsession* (35).

He was very popular as a romantic lead and played in *Small Town Girl* (36, William Wellman) and *The Gorgeous Hussy* (36, Clarence Brown), opposite Joan Crawford, and in *His Brother's Wife* (36, W. S. Van Dyke), opposite Barbara Stanwyck, before throbbing at Garbo's cough in *Camille* (36, George Cukor) and gazing with inappropriate fondness at Jean Harlow in *Personal Property* (37, Van Dyke). Now at his peak, he appeared again opposite his wife-to-be, Stanwyck, in *This Is My Affair* (37, William A. Seiter) and went to Britain to make *A Yank at Oxford* (38, Jack Conway). He was in Frank Borzage's *Three Comrades* (38); *Lady of the Tropics* (39, Conway); *Remember?* (39, Norman Z. McLeod); *Lucky Night* (39, Norman Taurog); and made his first Western, *Stand Up and Fight* (39, Van Dyke).

He was working hard to establish a tougher image and after playing a boxer in *The Crowd Roars* (38, Richard Thorpe), a mustachioed serviceman in *Waterloo Bridge* (40, Mervyn Le Roy), and escorting MGM's dowager duchess, Norma Shearer, in *Escape* (40, Le Roy), he played *Billy the Kid* (41, David Miller)—the most innocuous attempt on that subject. Before navy service he made *When Ladies Meet* (41, Robert Z. Leonard); *Johnny Eager* (41, Le Roy); *Her Cardboard Lover* (42, Cukor), again with Norma Shearer; *Stand by for Action* (42, Leonard); and *Bataan* (43, Tay Garnett). During the war, Taylor began to slide and he was cast as the mentally disturbed villain—without much insight—in Minnelli's *Undercurrent* (46). Compared with his former blandness, Taylor was now playing flawed and even corrupt men: he was a neurotic in Curtis Bernhardt's *The High Wall* (48); remarkably successful as the doomed Indian in Anthony Mann's *Devil's Doorway* (50)—probably the best and most adventurous use of him throughout his career; the Hiroshima pilot in *Above and Beyond* (53, Melvin Frank and Norman Panama); as a *Rogue Cop* (54, Roy Rowland); the morose killer in Brooks's *The Last Hunt* (56); a crooked lawyer, with a limp, in *Party Girl* (58, Nicholas Ray); and *The Hangman* (59, Michael Curtiz). Even in Westerns, he tended to nurse a past, to be ill-tempered or querulous—thus *Ambush* (49, Sam Wood), *Westward the Women* (51, Wellman), and *The Law and Jake Wade* (58, John Sturges). In terms of popularity, his last years at MGM were justified by schoolboy heroics: *Quo Vadis?* (51, Le Roy); and *Ivanhoe* (52), *Knights of the Round Table* (54), and *The Adventures of Quentin Durward* (56), all for Richard Thorpe. Only two other MGM films were worthwhile: Farrow's *Ride, Vaquero!* (53) and Parrish's *Saddle the Wind* (58). Taylor left MGM in 1959 and passed quickly into cheap Westerns and films made in England and Spain: *Killers of Kilimanjaro* (60, Thorpe); Tay Garnett's *Cattle King* (63); *The Night Walker* (65, William Castle); Paul Wendkos's *Johnny Tiger* (66); Hugo Fregonese's *Savage Pampas* (66); and *Where Angels Go . . . Trouble Follows* (68, James Neilson).

André Téchiné,

b. Valence d'Agen, France, 1943

1969: *Paulina S'en Va.* 1975: *Souvenirs d'en France/French Provincial.* 1977: *Barocco.* 1979: *Les Soeurs Brontë/The Brontë Sisters.* 1981: *Hôtel des Amériques.* 1983: *La Matiouette, ou L'Arrière-Pays.* 1985: *Rendez-vous.* 1986: *Le Lieu du Crime/Scene of the Crime.* 1987: *Les Innocents.* 1991: *J'Embrasse Pas.* 1993: *Ma Saison Préférée/My Favorite Season.* 1994: *Les Roseaux Sauvages/Wild Reeds.* 1996: *Les Voleurs/Thieves.* 1999: *Alice et Martin.* 2001: *Loin/Far Away.* 2003: *Les Egares/Strayed.*

Téchiné has all the credentials: *Cahiers du Cinéma* and IDHEC; over thirty years as a director; an easy rapport with leading players (especially actresses); and a nice, economical way with small, complex stories, provincial settings, awkward young people, and rather solitary, eccentric leading characters. As such, he is a fairly reliable source of intelligent entertainment. But is he also, now, France's leading director? Pretty close to it, I suppose. In which case, this record is not enough—and hardly promises radical departures, even if *Loin* concerns a long-distance trucker and the world of Tangier.

He made his name with *French Provincial*, a Jeanne Moreau vehicle, and the considerable ambition of *The Brontë Sisters*, starring Adjani, Huppert, and Pisier. But the latter showed too much taste and restraint, things Téchiné has never shrugged off—not even in the sultry and very stylish sex noir of *Rendez-vous* and *Wild Reeds* (maybe his best study of youth). *Les Voleurs* is a good example of his limits—a clever story, good actors, such as Melville and even Chabrol might have broken your heart with. But the film is unduly academic—as if Téchiné had never seen how easy it is to photograph the mature Catherine Deneuve and still have her inner turmoil take over a picture.

Shirley Temple,

b. Santa Monica, California, 1928

It is a sidelong proof of how far Depression had inroaded confidence in the 1930s that it took Shirley Temple to reassure so many. She was not only the top box-office attraction from 1935–38, but the solace and inspiration for an essentially adult audience. *Heidi* (37, Allan Dwan), set nominally in the cockpit of Europe, offered family bliss as an example of reconciliation to a war-ready world.

For the characteristic Temple situation is not just of a child leading her life under adult shadows, but of a Lilliputian moralist in ringlets, tap-dancing into your heart and then delivering the sententious message that sorts out confusion. Of course, she had her skeptics. Anyone who thought that the difficulties of the time had more to do with economics and politics was offended by Shirley's masquerade as the Statue of Liberty. Graham Greene, recently returned from Mexico, alleged that she was an adult impersonating a child—in *Wee Willie Winkie* (37, John Ford)— and the magazine that carried his article was bankrupted by the subsequent litigation.

But Greene's opinion was penetrating, even if inaccurate. Shirley Temple was a supreme technical actress unequaled for the amount of sentiment she could dispense without disturbing gullibility. In *Wee Willie Winkie*, for instance, Victor McLaglen seems clumsy and maudlin, but Shirley Temple acts to the inch. The fact that in their big scene he is in bed and she sits beside him like a mother shows eerily the relationship that Shirley achieved with adults. It was not that a child spoke her lines, danced, mugged, and listened so shrewdly, but that she unnerved or outclassed the adults in her films so that they seem uneasy, shambling monsters beside her. Only Bill "Bojangles" Robinson could stand up to her. But no matter the costars, or whether her directors were journeymen (Irving Cummings and David Butler) or craftsmen (Ford and Allan Dwan)—she shapes and colors them.

Despite all the contrivance of her films, the evasions accomplished by so much sugar, she was a phenomenon who had only to be observed for an audience to be held. That is why so many of her big scenes—both musical numbers and emotional set pieces—are done in single setups. There was an elfin perfection about her. Once she grew older, it was replaced by an unremarkable teenager. The public was bewildered at the loss and rejected her. She returned as a cheerful, wholesome mother, first on TV, then in the political arena. If she failed to win enough votes for the Senate, perhaps it was because the public knew she was an irretrievably retired fairy godmother, too large now to handle the wand that had cast her spells. Nevertheless, in the week that one American ambassador was killed in Cyprus, she was asked to be ambassador in Ghana.

The driving force in her career was her mother, and at the age of three Shirley was working for

Educational Films. She had small parts in *The Red-Haired Alibi* (32, Christy Cabanne) and *To the Last Man* (33, Henry Hathaway) before Jay Gorney recommended her to Fox for a featured spot in *Stand Up and Cheer* (34, Hamilton Mac-Fadden). Fox put her under contract and after *Carolina* (34, Henry King) and *Change of Heart* (34, John Blystone), they starred her in *Little Miss Marker* (34, Alexander Hall). She rapidly achieved stardom: *Now and Forever* (34, Henry Hathaway) was a Paramount film that cast her with Gary Cooper and Carole Lombard, but Fox soon established a vehicle form for her—*Bright Eyes* (34, Butler); *The Little Colonel* (35, Butler); *Curly Top* (35, Cummings); *The Littlest Rebel* (35, Butler); *Captain January* (36, Butler); *Poor Little Rich Girl* (36, Cummings); *Dimples* (36, William Seiter); and *Stowaway* (36, Seiter).

Her apogee came in 1937–38 with *Wee Willie Winkie, Heidi, Rebecca of Sunnybrook Farm* (38, Dwan), *Little Miss Broadway* (38, Cummings), and *Just Around the Corner* (38, Cummings). But after *The Little Princess* (39, Walter Lang), *Susannah of the Mounties* (39, Seiter), *The Blue Bird* (40, Lang), and *Young People* (40, Dwan), Fox and Miss Temple quarreled. Her rating was already declining, puberty beckoned, and war demanded the more knowing comforts of Grable and Veronica Lake.

In the event, MGM took Shirley on and kept her idle, save for *Kathleen* (41, Harold S. Bucquet). She made *Miss Annie Rooney* (42, Edwin L. Marin) and then passed her adolescence as a Selznick actress: awed by Claudette Colbert and Jennifer Jones in *Since You Went Away* (44, John Cromwell) and downright gauche in *I'll Be Seeing You* (44, William Dieterle). Selznick noted, perhaps grudgingly, that Temple still drew more fan mail than his other three ladies—Jennifer Jones, Ingrid Bergman, and Joan Fontaine. Even so, she did not mature, and remained in movies another four, mistaken years: *Kiss and Tell* (45, Richard Wallace); *Honeymoon* (47, William Keighley); *The Bachelor and the Bobby Soxer* (47, Irving Reis); *Fort Apache* (48, Ford); *Mr. Belvedere Goes to College* (49, Elliott Nugent); *Adventures in Baltimore* (49, Wallace); and *A Kiss for Corliss* (49, Wallace).

In 1989, George Bush appointed her to be ambassador to Czechoslovakia.

Ted Tetzlaff (1903–95), b. Los Angeles
1941: *World Premiere*. 1947: *Riff Raff*. 1948: *Fighting Father Dunne*. 1949: *The Window; Johnny Allegro; A Dangerous Profession*. 1950: *The White Tower; Under the Gun*. 1951: *Gambling House; The Treasure of Lost Canyon*. 1953: *Terror on a Train/Time Bomb*. 1955: *Son of Sinbad*. 1956: *Seven Wonders of the World* (codirected). 1957: *The Young Land*.

Ted, or Teddy as he was known circa 1930, had a long apprenticeship in photography and camerawork at Fox. From 1926–50 he was an active lighting cameraman, not in the first rank but an accomplished exponent of low-key black and white with a feeling for intrigue. That culminated in the lustrous, shadowy interiors of *Notorious* (46, Alfred Hitchcock), even if the subtlest visual effects in that movie may have come from Hitch, thus prompting Tetzlaff's "Getting a bit technical, aren't you, Pop?" A telling remark, since Hitchcock's genius rested more in his technique than a technician—already beginning to direct—could see. Tetzlaff's twenty-five years with the camera included *The Power of the Press* (28, Frank Capra); *The Donovan Affair* (29, Capra); *The Younger Generation* (29, Capra); *Mexicali Rose* (29, Erle C. Kenton); *Tol'able David* (30, John G. Blystone); *Fugitive Lovers* (34, Richard Boleslavsky); *Paris in Spring* (35, Lewis Milestone); *My Man Godfrey* (36, Gregory La Cava); *Easy Living* (37, Mitchell Leisen); *Fools for Scandal* (38, Le Roy); *Remember the Night* (40, Leisen); *I Married a Witch* (42, René Clair); and *The Enchanted Cottage* (45, John Cromwell).

World Premiere, at Paramount, was John Barrymore's penultimate film, an undoubted trial for a new director up from the ranks. Tetzlaff seems to have been much happier at RKO after the war, where he was hired by Dore Schary to work as director and photographer. His films there are B pictures, mostly thrillers, with such stars as George Raft and Pat O'Brien. But *The White Tower* is six people climbing an Alpine peak—including Valli, Claude Rains, Glenn Ford, and Cedric Hardwicke. And *The Window* is a genuinely original film, about an overimaginative child not believed when he sees a murder. At a modest scale, it is a Hitchcockian subject, and the maker of *Rear Window* may have liked it enough to remember the idea. (Both came from stories by Cornell Woolrich.) Bobby Driscoll is pop-eyed with fright as the boy, but Tetzlaff deserves special credit for his use of Paul Stewart as the villain, the yes-and-no sentimental butler from *Kane*, and a face of sly malice.

Irving G. (Grant) **Thalberg** (1899–1936), b. New York
Thalberg was the son of a German immigrant lace importer. A blue baby, Thalberg never enjoyed good health, was always pale and slender, and only grew to five feet six inches. At the age of seventeen he had rheumatic fever, but was educated while ill by his ambitious mother. He began working as a clerk for his grandfather's department store and did a business course by night at New York University, as well as studying typing and Spanish. In 1918, he met Carl Laemmle, the head of Universal, and so impressed him that he

became Laemmle's private secretary in New York. A year later, he went to California with Laemmle and, while still twenty, Thalberg was appointed studio manager at Universal City, effectively in charge when Laemmle was in New York.

It was an appointment that owed nothing to nepotism, private wealth, or experience in the film industry. Add to that Thalberg's youth, modest education, and frail appearance and it is clear that he had the charm, insight, and ability, or the appearance of it, to captivate the film world. He is the most difficult of all the moguls to appraise: in part his life is inextricably confused with Scott Fitzgerald's Monroe Stahr in *The Last Tycoon;* no other production chief earned so much admiration from colleagues and rivals for his immediate skill with a script or a cut; and yet it is difficult to point to any one film as bearing Thalberg's personality. It was part of his carefully maintained search for sophistication and gentlemanly prestige that he did not credit himself on the screen. Theoretically, everything that came out of MGM from 1924–33 passed under his eye. But it is easier to attribute the overall preeminence and high production standards at MGM to Thalberg than any film, director, or—apart from Norma Shearer— star. Thalberg was an exponent of accountancy propriety. The mogul with a passion for film, glory, and an actress is David Selznick.

At Universal, the young Thalberg first crossed swords with von Stroheim, especially when the Austrian insisted on a replica of Monte Carlo being built on the Monterey peninsula for *Foolish Wives.* Thalberg urged Stroheim to begin editing his vast accumulation of material and remained suspicious even when *Foolish Wives* proved successful. When Stroheim's extravagance was resumed on his next film, *Merry-Go-Round,* Thalberg replaced him—an action entirely in his power, and one that most Hollywood executives would have taken earlier, but that added to Thalberg's growing reputation for rationalization and firmness. Against this case of ruction, it was while at Universal that Thalberg sponsored Lon Chaney in *The Hunchback of Notre Dame* (23, Wallace Worsley), and deliberately enlarged the movie to ensure that the New York office promoted it.

Thalberg's beneficial effects on the profits of Universal were noticed less by Laemmle than by Louis B. Mayer, and in 1923 Thalberg was persuaded to become vice-president of the Mayer Company with special responsibilities for production. A year later, Mayer had merged with Metro and Goldwyn, and Thalberg was appointed production supervisor. Von Stroheim's *Greed* was by then a ten-hour monster and Thalberg duly ordered it to be reduced to a practical length.

One of his earliest challenges in the uniquely powerful post at MGM produced a characteristic response. The Goldwyn Company had been labor-ing with *Ben-Hur:* the rights had been expensive and so was the location shooting in Italy. Mayer reappraised the film. He replaced star George Walsh with Ramon Novarro and director Charles Brabin with Fred Niblo. Eventually, he brought the unit home to film the Colosseum sequences in California and then devoted himself to supervising the shooting and editing. The strain was so great that Thalberg had to watch the rushes from a hospital bed. *Ben-Hur* was not profitable (it had cost too much), but it drew huge audiences and great prestige for the new studio.

What gave Thalberg such a reputation? In part, of course, he was lucky to head a studio of great financial and creative resources at a time of boom economy. At the same time, alone among the major studios, MGM stayed out of the red during the Depression. Thalberg was lucky in having a remarkably sympathetic Louis Mayer to fight the grueling administrative battles for him and to draw off the inescapable antagonism toward the Company of its creative staff. Mayer's truculence and crass commercialism enabled Thalberg to enjoy an unusual rapport with directors, writers, and actors without really proving that he had a special understanding of them. He appears to have earned respect by clear-eyed editorial instinct, the ability to appreciate and improve a script or rushes in a rapid, decisive, and yet tactful way. In addition, he worked dangerously hard on the premises without often sacrificing his good manners. Perhaps this was the real distinction in that the MGM enterprise flourished less through traditional brutality and deceit than with the effect of a sensitive and brilliant young man in charge. In that sense, he and Mayer were opposites using each other to maintain the balance of the Company. But Thalberg did initiate that blunt instrument—the producer. He gave MGM the enervating administrative ingredient of producers responsible to him and his office for every film. Thus the diminished influence of directors at the studio during the thirties, something that may have made accountants smile, but that now leaves the standard MGM film bland and characterless.

Ironically, the decisions that can be pinned down to Thalberg with confidence are often negative: for instance, the unavoidable interference in Stroheim's *Greed,* the enthusiasm for *Grand Hotel,* the rescue of the Marx Brothers that entailed filling out their films with romantic subplots and songs, and last but least credible, the elevation of Norma Shearer to one of the studio's first ladies. In fact, Thalberg married Shearer in 1927 after romances with Isabelle Laemmle, Peggy Hopkins Joyce, and Constance Talmadge.

On the credit side, Thalberg persisted with Stroheim on *The Merry Widow;* helped his friend King Vidor to make, among others, *The Big Parade* and *The Crowd;* led MGM into sound with

The Broadway Melody (although he did not immediately see its importance); carefully promoted Garbo's American career; insisted that MGM make *Freaks* (32, Tod Browning); and helped win Oscars for Norma Shearer in *The Divorcee* (30, Robert Z. Leonard), Lionel Barrymore in *A Free Soul* (31, Clarence Brown), Marie Dressler in *Min and Bill* (30, George Hill), and Helen Hayes in *The Sin of Madelon Claudet* (31, Edward Selwyn).

By late 1932 Thalberg's relations with MGM had deteriorated. He had largely lost the support of Mayer through a series of claims for larger salary and a greater share of the profits. He was also shocked by the suicide of Paul Bern (friend and producer) and distressed by the decline in production standards during the Depression. He asked to be freed for a year so that he could travel. Nick Schenk and Mayer tried to dissuade him, but also hired David Selznick as a possible replacement. Thalberg left for Europe and while still away, in 1933, was relieved of his duties in charge of production.

On his return, he was given an autonomous unit. Never again as powerful, Thalberg nevertheless spent his last three years producing entertainment films of glossy smartness, if little real sparkle: *Riptide* (34, Edmund Goulding); *The Barretts of Wimpole Street* (34, Sidney Franklin); *The Merry Widow* (34, Ernst Lubitsch); the robust *China Seas* (35, Tay Garnett); *Mutiny on the Bounty* (35, Frank Lloyd); *Romeo and Juliet* (36, George Cukor); *The Good Earth* (37, Franklin, et al.), and *Camille* (36, Cukor), one of Garbo's finest pictures.

He died in 1936, from pneumonia, to immense obituary tributes, a dedication on *The Good Earth,* and the foundation of the Irving G. Thalberg Memorial Award for high production achievement. It is the final irony in this mysterious career that he should be remembered largely through the disputed portrait in *The Last Tycoon.* It is hard now to credit the idea of a great producer. Easier to see how he graciously guided every department at MGM toward smoothness. But most plausible of all to see him as the untypical figure idealized by the inhabitants of a dream world craving dignity and seriousness. Thus, the strange adulation of this fictional portrait from Fitzgerald, a writer never happy at MGM: "He had flown up very high to see, on strong wings, when he was young. And while he was up there he had looked on all the kingdoms, with the kind of eyes that can stare straight at the sun. Beating his wings tenaciously—finally frantically—and keeping on beating them, he had stayed up there longer than most of us, and then, remembering all he had seen from his great height of how things were, he settled gradually to earth."

That Fitzgerald could write with such romantic grandiloquence speaks not only of Thalberg's personal impact but of the self-induced thralldom in which he could be King Arthur. A contrary view comes from Lillian Hellman, who thought that Fitzgerald had "got sticky moon-candy about a man who was only a bright young movie producer."

David Thewlis, b. Blackpool, England, 1963

Trained at the Guildhall School of Music and Drama in London, David Thewlis was both a rock guitarist and an actor at first. He won attention as a villain in *Prime Suspect 3* (93, David Drury). He had joined Mike Leigh's unofficial company and showed his great sense of humor, in shorts and full-length works. Since then, Thewlis's rare dedication has turned him into an international figure and one of the more esteemed actors in film. But his status is still uncertain—much of his work unworthy: *Little Dorrit* (88, Christine Edzard); *Life Is Sweet* (91, Leigh); *Afraid of the Dark* (91, Mark Peploe); *Damage* (92, Louis Malle); alarmingly good as the spellbinding drifter in *Naked* (93, Leigh); *The Trial* (93, David Hugh Jones); *Black Beauty* (94, Caroline Thompson); *Restoration* (95, Michael Hoffman); as Verlaine in *Total Eclipse* (95, Agnieszka Holland); *Dragonheart* (96, Rob Cohen); a voice in *James and the Giant Peach* (96, Henry Selick); *The Island of Dr. Moreau* (96, John Frankenheimer); *Seven Years in Tibet* (97, Jean-Jacques Annaud); *The Big Lebowski* (98, Joel Coen); excellent again in *Besieged* (99, Bernardo Bertolucci); *Whatever Happened to Harold Smith?* (99, Peter Hewitt); the voice of Judas in the TV *The Miracle Maker* (00, Derek W. Hayes and Stanislav Sokolev); *Gangster No. 1* (00, Paul McGuigan); *Endgame* (00, Conor McPherson) for TV; *Goodbye Charlie Bright* (01, Nick Love).

Emma Thompson, b. London, 1959

By the spring of 1993, Emma Thompson seemed like a guaranteed summer. She had her Oscar, playing Margaret Schlegel in *Howards End* (92, James Ivory); she was about to open as Beatrice in the Tuscan sunniness of her husband Kenneth Branagh's *Much Ado About Nothing* (93). Ahead lay the promise of the movie of *Remains of the Day* (93, Ivory), in which she was cast once more with Anthony Hopkins. She was on magazine covers everywhere, yet she remained modest, funny, ironic, a protestant in the High Church of Celebrity. One remembered her shamelessly camp performance of surprise—and the garish frock—when she heard that she had won the Oscar. It was the response not just of a natural, but of a chronic, subversive comedienne. Let us hope she finds the chance to stay that unruly.

She is the daughter of actors—of Phyllida Law and Eric Thompson, who also created a lovely BBC television show for young children, *The*

Magic Roundabout. She was well educated at Camden School for Girls and Newnham College, Cambridge. From Footlights shows at Cambridge she took to the stage, to television, and eventually to film. Her role in Kenneth Branagh's Renaissance Theatre Company led to their marriage in 1989. She did some song-and-dance on the London stage in *Me and My Girl;* she did a lot of writing for her TV comedy series, *Thompson* (88); she played the Fool to Branagh's *Lear* on stage, and Alison to his Jimmy Porter in *Look Back in Anger.* Moreover, by now, she and Branagh can hardly breathe in Britain without being told how much they resemble that fabled, "golden" couple—Laurence Olivier and Vivien Leigh. Let us hope that today's goldens have a proper sense of the awkwardness of that first partnership. Vivien Leigh was a helpless rival to Olivier, and a well-cast victim for his jealousy and cunning. Emma Thompson may yet discover the need to look after herself.

To these eyes, she has never been as good as she was in the TV adaptation of Olivia Manning's Balkan novels: *Fortunes of War* (87, James Cellan Jones). In addition, she was very funny in two minor films—*The Tall Guy* (89, Mel Smith) and *Impromptu* (91, James Lapine). Then she was the dutiful female presence, variously stranded or neglected, in several of Branagh's projects: the films of *Look Back in Anger* (89, David Jones and Judi Dench), where she looks merely wan and weary; as the French princess in *Henry V* (89, Branagh); and in the dire and fatuous *Dead Again* (91, Branagh) and *Peter's Friends* (93, Branagh)—ventures that might yet arouse something more than loyalty in a wife. Summers in Britain can turn into horrid disappointments.

Her housekeeper in *Remains of the Day* was faultless, yet not very interesting: the woman in question is so fixed in her own place, and so much the innocent bow to Hopkins's stealthy fiddle. She needed a bit more Mrs. Danvers—but then she wouldn't have been hired, in that home, or in that film.

She was very good as the lawyer in *In the Name of the Father* (93, Jim Sheridan), even if the role was unduly fabricated.

Her marriage to Branagh concluded, but that may have been a release. Her recent work has been very mixed—often trying comedy—yet also seizing on drama such as only Meryl Streep could handle: with Schwarzenegger in *Junior* (94, Ivan Reitman); uncredited in *My Father the Hero* (94, Steve Miner); *The Blue Boy* (94, Paul Murton); brilliant and tragic as *Carrington* (95, Christopher Hampton), a badly neglected film; doing the script and pulling *Sense and Sensibility* (95, Ang Lee) together; *Hospital!* (97, John Henderson); with her mother in *The Winter Guest* (97, Alan Rickman); very funny as the president's wife in *Primary Colors* (98, Mike Nichols); *Judas Kiss* (98,

Sebastian Gutiérrez); *Maybe Baby* (00, Ben Elton); and magnificent as the dying woman in *Wit* (01, Nichols).

J. (John) **Lee Thompson** (1914–2002),
b. Bristol, England
1950: *Murder Without Crime*. 1952: *The Yellow Balloon*. 1953: *The Weak and the Wicked*. 1954: *For Better For Worse*. 1955: *As Long As They're Happy; An Alligator Named Daisy*. 1956: *Yield to the Night; The Good Companions*. 1957: *Woman in a Dressing Gown*. 1958: *Ice Cold in Alex; No Trees in the Street*. 1959: *Tiger Bay; North-West Frontier.* 1960: *I Aim at the Stars*. 1961: *The Guns of Navarone; Cape Fear.* 1962: *Taras Bulba*. 1963: *Kings of the Sun*. 1964: *What a Way to Go; John Goldfarb, Please Come Home*. 1965: *Return from the Ashes*. 1966: *Eye of the Devil*. 1968: *Before Winter Comes*. 1969: *The Most Dangerous Man in the World; MacKenna's Gold*. 1971: *Country Dance*. 1972: *Conquest of the Planet of the Apes*. 1973: *Battle for the Planet of the Apes*. 1974: *Huckleberry Finn; The Reincarnation of Peter Proud*. 1976: *St. Ives*. 1977: *The White Buffalo*. 1978: *The Greek Tycoon; The Passage*. 1980: *Caboblanco*. 1981: *Happy Birthday to Me*. 1983: *The Evil That Men Do; Ten to Midnight*. 1984: *The Ambassador*. 1985: *King Solomon's Mines*. 1986: *Murphy's Law; Firewalker*. 1987: *Death Wish 4: The Crackdown*. 1988: *Messenger of Death*. 1989: *Kinjite: Forbidden Subjects*.

An actor and playwright, Lee Thompson wrote for the screen in the late 1930s—*The Price of Folly* (37, Walter Summers); *Glamorous Night* (37, Brian Desmond Hurst); *The Middle Watch* (40, Thomas Bentley); *East of Piccadilly* (41, Harold Huth)—and began directing with his own play, *Murder Without Crime*.

Not that he has subsequently impressed one as a director looking for good material. On the contrary, he has lunged about in wayward maneuvers, dabbling in British comedy, sham realism, lip-smacking psychological tension, epics, and such lunacy as *Eye of the Devil* and *Country Dance*. The enormous box-office success of *The Guns of Navarone* and *MacKenna's Gold* appears almost accidental and owes more to Carl Foreman's single-minded production than to Lee Thompson. He has tended over the years to choose sensational subjects: *The Yellow Balloon* and *Yield to the Night* were both thought outspoken in their time, and *Cape Fear* is still downright nasty. Perhaps the last word on Lee Thompson is that nothing from him would come as a surprise, much less a revelation.

Billy Bob Thornton,
b. Hot Springs, Arkansas, 1955
1996: *Sling Blade*. 2000: *All the Pretty Horses*.

2002: *Daddy and Them.*

When Billy Bob Thornton leaped into prominence with *Sling Blade* (96) as a remarkable triple threat (writer, actor, and director), there was retaliatory talk that he might be a one-film wonder. Clearly, some people hadn't seen *One False Move* (92, Carl Franklin), where Thornton was coauthor of a very original script, and a brilliant actor in a vein so removed from his retard in *Sling Blade.* Then we had Thornton's fine performance in *A Simple Plan* (98, Sam Raimi) to demonstrate authentic range.

How will he settle? It's as writer-director, I suspect, that the real future rests. He was in *South of Reno* (87, Mark Rezyka); *For the Boys* (91, Mark Rydell); *Bound by Honor* (93, Taylor Hackford); *Indecent Proposal* (93, Adrian Lyne); as the saloon bully in *Tombstone* (93, George P. Cosmatos); *On Deadly Ground* (94, Steven Seagal); *Floundering* (94, Peter McCarthy); *The Stars Fell on Henrietta* (95, James Keach); winning the adapted screenplay Oscar and being nominated as supporting actor in *Sling Blade; Dead Man* (96, Jim Jarmusch); *A Family Thing* (96, Richard Pearce), which he cowrote; *The Apostle* (97, Robert Duvall); *U-Turn* (97, Oliver Stone); *The Winner* (97, Alex Cox); *Armageddon* (98, Michael Bay); *Home Grown* (98, Stephen Gyllenhaal); *Primary Colors* (98, Mike Nichols); *A Gun, a Car, a Blonde* (98, Stefani Ames); *Pushing Tin* (99, Mike Newell).

Then in 2000, he entered into what was his third or fourth marriage—with Angelina Jolie (from *Pushing Tin*)—enough to deserve a break. But he works hard. He experiments with his looks—and with doing very little, as in *The Man Who Wasn't There* (01, Joel Coen) and *Bandits* (01, Barry Levinson). Nothing is clear yet, beyond his range, talent, and poker-faced humor—plus his real skill in *Monster's Ball* (01, Marc Forster), deserving Halle Berry's thanks.

That marriage foundered in a fluster of tattoos and tabloid stories, and Thornton quietly increased his ragbag collection of outsiders, hippies and people not quite there: *The Badge* (02, Robby Henson); *Waking Up in Reno* (02, Jordan Brady); *Levity* (03, Ed Solomon); *Intolerable Cruelty* (03, Coen); *Bad Santa* (03, Terry Zwigoff); and as Davy Crockett in *The Alamo* (04, John Lee Hancock).

Ingrid Thulin, b. Solleftea, Sweden, 1929
Ingrid Thulin's marriage to Harry Schein, head of the Swedish Film Institute, may account for her early wish to move into international films. But her films for Ingmar Bergman were crucial in showing the harrowing trauma that waits on a beautiful woman. That expressive face has doleful eyes unable to forget pain and a wide mouth that can convey passionate suffering and fraught plea-

sure. It is a tragic face, the unforgettable image of the anxiety that surrounds Bergman's world.

She studied ballet and then trained at the Royal Dramatic Theatre in Stockholm. She began acting in films in the late 1940s: *Dit Vindarna Bar* (48, Ake Ohberg); *Havets Son* (49, Rolf Husberg); *Karleken Segrar* (49, Gustaf Molander); *Hjarter Knekt* (50, Hasse Ekman); *Nar Karleken kom till Byn* (50, Arne Mattsson); *Leva pa 'Hoppet'* (51, Goran Gentele); *Mote med Livet* (52, Gosta Werner); *Kalle Karlsson fran Jularbo* (52, Ivar Johansson); *En Skargardsnatt* (53, Bengt Logardt); *Goinge-hovdingen* (53, Ohberg); *Tva Skona Juveler* (54, Husberg); *I Rok och Dans* (54, Yngve Gamlin and Bengt Blomgren); *Hoppsan!* (55, Stig Olin); and *Danssalongen* (55, Borje Larsson).

But it was as the youthful, fresh-air heroine in *Foreign Intrigue* (56, Sheldon Reynolds) that she first attracted attention outside Sweden. Next year, she played the daughter-in-law in *Wild Strawberries* and soon became one of Bergman's favorite actresses: the woman who has had a miscarriage in *So Close to Life* (58); visually stunning as Vogel's wife, masquerading as a youth, in *The Face/The Magician* (58); the mistress in *Winter Light* (63); the lesbian nymphomaniac in *The Silence* (63); the dead mistress in *Hour of the Wolf* (68); the wife/mistress in *The Rite* (69); and with Liv Ullmann and Harriet Andersson in Bergman's immense study of Three Swedish Sisters, *Cries and Whispers* (72).

In Sweden, she has also appeared in *Donnaren* (60, Alf Sjoberg); *Night Games* (66, Mai Zetterling); and *Badarna* (68, Gamlin); as well as directing a short, *Hangivelse* (65).

Elsewhere, in 1962, Vincente Minnelli proved alert to her beauty in *The Four Horsemen of the Apocalypse,* and the autumn sequence at Versailles is one of the most sensuous in all his work. She was wasted in *Return from the Ashes* (65, J. Lee Thompson), but silently loving in *La Guerre est Finie* (66, Alain Resnais). *The Damned* (69, Luchino Visconti) is gaseous opera compared to Bergman's taut chamber music, but it owes much to Thulin's archetypal proneness to tragedy. She has also appeared in *Agostino* (62, Mauro Bolognini); *Adelaide* (68, Jean-Daniel Simon); *N.P. Il Segreto* (72, Silvano Agosti); as Miriam in *Moses* (75, Gianfranco de Bosio); *The Cassandra Crossing* (76, George Pan Cosmatos); and as the brothel madam in *Salon Kitty* (76, Giovanni Tinto Brass). In 1978, she acted in and directed *One and One* with Erland Josephson and Sven Nykvist.

She directed another film, *Brusten Himmsel* (82), and she acted in *After the Rehearsal* (83, Bergman); *Control* (87, Guiliano Montaldo); and *La Casa del Sorriso* (90, Marco Ferreri).

Uma (Karunna) **Thurman**, b. Boston, 1970
Well, of course, Uma Thurman is beautiful—who

ever said she wasn't? There she was, slender, pale, blond, on the half-shell as Venus in *The Adventures of Baron Munchausen* (89, Terry Gilliam), but not much more. And the question remains, is she an actress, or just a wan nymph with her own brief morning?

She is the child of a university professor in comparative literature, and as such she grew up on the campus of Amherst. But she put off higher education for herself to work as a model. That led to *Kiss Daddy Goodnight* (87, Peter Ily Huemer) and *Johnny Be Good* (88, Bud Smith). She was the seduced virgin in *Dangerous Liaisons* (88, Stephen Frears) and she then played in *Where the Heart Is* (90, John Boorman). Her best acting to date, by far, occurred in *Henry & June* (90, Phil Kaufman), where she gives a good account of uneducated toughness caught in a net of poseurs.

Since then, she has been a pouty Maid Marian in *Robin Hood* (91, John Irvin); *Final Analysis* (92, Phil Joanou); blind in *Jennifer Eight* (92, Bruce Robinson); the "present" in *Mad Dog and Glory* (93, John McNaughton). She won a supporting actress nomination for her gangster's wife in *Pulp Fiction* (94, Quentin Tarantino), when she contributed not much more than a baleful look, a cool attitude, black hair, and some Egyptian fresco moves on the dance floor. She was barely competent in *A Month by the Lake* (95, Irvin), and then appeared in *Beautiful Girls* (96, Ted Demme); *The Truth About Cats & Dogs* (96, Michael Lehmann); *Gattaca* (97, Andrew Niccol); as Poison Ivy in *Batman and Robin* (97, Joel Schumacher); *Les Misérables* (98, Bille August); Emma Peel in the dreadful *The Avengers* (98, Jeremiah S. Chechik); *Sweet and Lowdown* (99, Woody Allen); *Vatel* (00, Roland Joffé); *The Golden Bowl* (00, James Ivory); *Tape* (01, Richard Linklater); *Chelsea Walls* (02, Ethan Hawke, her husband); *Hysterical Blindness* (03, Mira Nair); *Kill Bill* (03, Tarantino).

Gene Tierney (1920–91),
b. Brooklyn, New York
An effulgent, heart-shaped face made her one of the beauties of 1940s cinema. She is treasured especially for her appearances in Preminger's *Laura* (44) and *Whirlpool* (49). In the first, her portrait was enough to cast a spell over Dana Andrews, long before she appeared. But Laura proves a conventionally pretty, rather commonplace girl—a sign of Preminger's interest in the gulf between reputation and personality. In *Whirlpool,* Tierney moved with a childlike dreaming calm as the unhappy wife hypnotized by a demon José Ferrer. The long speeches in that film proved rather too demanding for her and she seldom got past her own gorgeousness. But in *Leave Her to Heaven* (46), she was ignited by John M. Stahl's commitment to melodrama and by Techni-

color. Her selfish girl in that film is frighteningly credible and she fully grasped the intensity of the astonishing staircase scene.

The daughter of a New York socialite family, she made her debut in 1940 in Fritz Lang's *The Return of Frank James.* She worked steadily for Fox: as a breathtaking, doelike Ellie May in *Tobacco Road* (41, John Ford); *Hudson's Bay* (41, Irving Pichel); *Sundown* (41, Henry Hathaway); *The Shanghai Gesture* (41, Josef von Sternberg); *Son of Fury* (41, John Cromwell); *Rings on Her Fingers* (42, Rouben Mamoulian); *Belle Starr* (42, Irving Cummings); *Thunder Birds* (42, William Wellman); *China Girl* (43, Hathaway); *Heaven Can Wait* (43, Ernst Lubitsch); blonde in *A Bell for Adano* (45, Henry King); *The Razor's Edge* (46, Edmund Goulding); *Dragonwyck* (46, Joseph L. Mankiewicz); *The Iron Curtain* (48, Wellman); *Where the Sidewalk Ends* (50, Preminger); *Night and the City* (50, Jules Dassin); *The Mating Season* (51, Mitchell Leisen); *On the Riviera* (51, Walter Lang); *The Secret of Convict Lake* (51, Michael Gordon); *Close to My Heart* (51, William Keighley); *Way of a Gaucho* (52, Jacques Tourneur); *Plymouth Adventure* (52, Clarence Brown); *Never Let Me Go* (53, Delmer Daves); *The Egyptian* (54, Michael Curtiz); and *The Left Hand of God* (55, Edward Dmytryk).

She was seldom a happy woman. Her marriage to Oleg Cassini, the designer, produced a daughter, but Tierney had German measles during the pregnancy. The child was retarded, and later institutionalized. A nervous breakdown kept her out of action for several years, until 1962, when she returned in Preminger's *Advise and Consent* as Walter Pidgeon's urbane and just as beautiful "front-elevator romance"; less happily, she stayed on for *Toys in the Attic* (63, George Roy Hill) and *The Pleasure Seekers* (65, Jean Negulesco).

James Toback, b. New York, 1944
1978: *Fingers.* 1982: *Love and Money.* 1983: *Exposed.* 1987: *The Pick-up Artist.* 1989: *The Big Bang.* 1997: *Two Girls and a Guy.* 1999: *Black and White.* 2001: *Harvard Man.*

Dear Jim,
You may not know it, but you are the best friend I feel obliged to include in this book. That may be a wretched position, for both of us. You are also one of the friends I most value in life. Our friendship is the odder in that so many others I know marvel that we get on. They have read so many lurid stories about you. They must see in me so much duller, and more domestic, a person than you are. (I could go senile trying to remember your new phone numbers.) In short, we are very different in outward ways. Yet we may have one thing in common: we are both torn between watching, making, and analyzing films—and

behaving as if we were *in* one. Maybe I should stop there, just adding that you have been the writer on *The Gambler* (74, Karel Reisz) and *Bugsy* (91, Barry Levinson). For the rest, I will repeat what I wrote about *Fingers* before friendship had begun, with the coda that I think it remains your best work yet:

"James Toback's *Fingers* is the best first film by an American director since *Badlands*. Even that is inadequate praise, for whereas Terry Malick's debut was an inventive ballad about innocent energy run amuck, *Fingers* is ingrowing and wounding. It does not belong to any familiar genre: it is more like a psychological allegory or ordeal. The outward signs of a New York crime movie are only its vehicle—like the body that houses the shivers of a dream. *Fingers* is that genuine oddity: an American feature movie that treats plot as merely the imprint for compulsive passions of terrible but dynamic force."

I can't run the whole review—there isn't a *Real Paper* in Boston now, so where would I go to get permission? And the review may be breathless—like the movie. But I agree with myself: I think it's a great picture, and I'm happy to see that the belated fame of Harvey Keitel is helping to bring it back.

"Jimmy (Harvey Keitel) is an aspiring concert pianist and the best debt collector in New York. The juxtaposition is as implausible as his polarized parents: a father out of a Mafia film, wondering whether to marry a nineteen-year-old redhead; and a fearfully troubled mother, who lives in an asylum. Jimmy is preparing for a Carnegie Hall audition, but his father calls on him now and then to collect debts from sulky restaurateurs and imposing members of the mob. The young man is full of nervous intensity that he can channel in either direction: his mastery of Bach sonatas extends to pistol whipping defaulters or screwing their mistresses in the ladies' room.

"But Jimmy is haunted by his lack of wholeness. He finishes a piece by Bach, looks out of his window and sees a lovely, wan woman (Tisa Farrow) who has stopped to listen to his passionate, disciplined spilling of notes. He falls for her as rapidly as a child, but she is aloof and nearly stoned by her allegiance to some sexual current far greater than Jimmy can muster. That sardonic life force proves to be Jim Brown, a secret shit-brown id glowing with a mastery that lashes out in moments of magnificent, authoritative punishment. He is power and magic, radiant with a lack of anxiety. The pale woman yields her body once to Jimmy's petulant demands, but it is a flawed coupling. Brilliant in lonely rehearsal, Jimmy disintegrates at his audition: his deft fingers stick in the cracks between notes. Even as a collector he fails: one gangster outwits him, and Jimmy has to cringe under the loudmouth abuse of his father and the ravaged

contempt of his mother. He is a naughty little boy being told off."

And so on. . . . Anyway, our friendship began a few days after the review ran, and it lasts. I hope. Have you known, or guessed, that I've never liked anything of yours quite as much—or nearly as much—since? Have we betrayed each other? Is it possible for a moviemaker and a critic to be friends?

That's really my point in this essay. In no small measure, it was you who introduced me to the society of moviemakers. And I know now that those writers on film who reject such offers cannot really understand American movies—they cannot know the swamp of compromise that produces them, or the determination. I value that education: I believe the world needs to know how the dreams are done. But in knowing you—and others—am I cut off from critical objectivity? Or is objectivity a kind of ignorance? I don't know, except that I know your friendship is too much to lose.

Gregg Toland (1904–48),
b. Charleston, Illinois

Toland was forty-four when he died of a heart attack. He was, by general consent, the outstanding cameraman in Hollywood, yet his longtime employer, Samuel Goldwyn, deplored the fact that no stars attended Toland's funeral. Men like Toland didn't get the respect they deserved. Much of the time, they didn't even get worthy pictures. Immediately before his death, Toland had shot three unremarkable pictures for Goldwyn: *The Bishop's Wife* (47, Henry Koster); *Enchantment* (48, Irving Reis); and *A Song Is Born* (48, Howard Hawks). Had he lived, it is most likely that Toland's filmography would have continued as it had been for twenty years—a cross section of industrial output, with here and there outbursts of something extraordinary.

Toland was vital at a key moment in film history. I think it is clear that *Citizen Kane* (41, Orson Welles) could not have had its look or its élan without him. He was excited to work with the outrageous newcomer; and Welles was so innocent of photography that he did not feel threatened by Toland's advice. That shared credit of theirs at the end of the film is testament to Welles's sentimental feeling for friendship—which is to say that while Orson wanted to be friends he was not always able to make the meeting. But for once the scorpion held hands with another kind of creature. And so all of Toland's private experiments with lenses, coatings, lights, and new film stock bore fruit. He photographed a great film—his only one, I think—and he was essential to its greatness. Yet not one of his other films took that bulging new "realism" in photography and turned it into the passionate, hallucinatory, and slightly warped view from inside monomania's head. Like Méliès seeing the Lumières' invention, Welles understood what Toland had found.

As a kid, Toland had studied electrical engineering. He was a teenager still when he went to Hollywood, found work as an office boy, and then became apprentice to George Barnes (1893–1953), the man who shot King Vidor's *Alice Adams* (23); *The Eagle* (25, Clarence Brown), with Valentino; and Raoul Walsh's *Sadie Thompson* (28).

Toland was promoted when very young, and he signed up with Goldwyn, who would allow him unusual liberties in choice of subject, as well as his own camera crew. Such things were not possible without a clear strain of eminence and authority in Toland himself: he did contrive the trade to RKO for *Kane,* on which the package was him, his crew, his equipment, and the lenses he had refined. Yet he hardly ever sought to shape a project or to be more than vision's servant. He did remark that *Kane* was a joy because of the extensive preproduction time, but in that time Toland tried only to meet Welles's needs and aims. Toland had the cameraman's curse: he had no subject.

You can see this in the very mixed list of pictures that the most discriminating cameraman shot: *Bulldog Drummond* (29, P. Richard Jones), which he and Barnes shot together; *One Heavenly Night* (30, George Fitzmaurice), again with Barnes; Eddie Cantor's *Whoopee!* (30, Thornton Freeland), done in two-strip Technicolor; *Palmy Days* (31, Edward Sutherland); *The Unholy Garden* (31, Fitzmaurice); *The Kid from Spain* (32, Leo McCarey); *The Masquerader* (33, Richard Wallace); *Roman Scandals* (33, Frank Tuttle); loaned out to MGM for *Tugboat Annie* (33, Mervyn Le Roy).

To this point, opportunity for Toland had been largely a question of furnishing the very different atmospheres of Ronald Colman or Eddie Cantor. But gradually, his range widened—he got Anna Sten pictures, too: *Forsaking All Others* (34, W. S. Van Dyke), at Metro again; *Nana* (34, Dorothy Arzner); *We Live Again* (34, Rouben Mamoulian); *The Dark Angel* (35, Sidney Franklin); *Mad Love* (35, Karl Freund), on loan to Metro again, and maybe the first film in which people have identified *Kane*-like images; *Les Miserables* (35, Richard Boleslavsky), for which he got an Oscar nomination; *Splendor* (35, Elliott Nugent); *The Wedding Night* (35, King Vidor); *Come and Get It* (36, Hawks and William Wyler); *The Road to Glory* (36, Hawks); *These Three* (36, Wyler); another nomination for the stagy *Dead End* (37, Wyler); *History Is Made at Night* (37, Frank Borzage); *The Cowboy and the Lady* (38, H. C. Potter); *The Goldwyn Follies* (38, George Marshall); and *Kidnapped* (38, Alfred L. Werker).

To this point, Toland's black and white was often moody, but it showed no great command of, or yearning for, the deep focus that was to come. Surely developments in lenses and new film stock, and the decision to film black and white under Technicolor arcs, had a lot to do with the deepening of the images. And, sometimes, the reaching out was very uneasy: *Intermezzo* (39, Gregory Ratoff), for Selznick; the Jascha Heifetz vehicle *They Shall Have Music* (39, Archie Mayo). Then came *Wuthering Heights* (39, Wyler), for which Toland won the Oscar. That film is often noirlike, and it has moments of striking depth—but it never gets the feeling of Yorkshire or Emily Brontë. *The Grapes of Wrath* (40, John Ford) is very Walker Evans and Dorothea Lange, but very sharply framed—Toland was now getting a more precise, jeweled image than anyone else.

The Long Voyage Home (40, Ford) seems to me an example of terrible, arty photography—but it has depth, like echoes, and it got another nomination. *The Westerner* (40, Wyler) is routine, and *Ball of Fire* (41, Hawks) was rather claustrophobic. And then Toland shot *Kane,* which is the supreme merger of art and journalism in cinematography, and uniquely rooted in dramatic need.

For Wyler again, Toland shot *The Little Foxes* (41), which uses deep focus like a teaching textbook. Toland then joined John Ford's military unit, where he shot and codirected the documentary, *December 7th* (43).

Toland never worked for Welles again—why, I wonder? Was he more comfortable with Wyler? Was he seeking to soften the very startling look of *Kane* and *The Long Voyage Home* to be more acceptable? He shot some of *The Outlaw* (43, Howard Hughes)—the single display of erotics in his credits. Then he shot *The Best Years of Our Lives* (46, Wyler), a display of deep focus that established the reliability of the world—whereas, in *Kane,* the depth was a mark of delusion. Then came *The Kid from Brooklyn* (46, Norman Z. McLeod), the live-action sequences from *Song of the South* (46, Harve Foster), and the final films listed above.

Franchot Tone (1905–68),
b. Niagara Falls, New York

Tone perhaps was all Franchot had—that and Joan Crawford. She liked his pedigree and his Group Theatre reputation. The son of a wealthy industrialist, educated privately and at Cornell, he was an ingenue from New York's radical theatre who was used in movies as romance fodder: the best friend, a feeble cad, or the sticky end of eternal triangles. He made his debut in Paramount's *The Wiser Sex* (32) but was signed up by MGM for *Gabriel Over the White House* (33, Gregory La Cava) and Howard Hawks's *Today We Live* (33) on which he met Joan Crawford, whom he married in 1935. Inevitably, this attachment sustained his presence in so many of the studio's romantic comedies: *Stranger's Return* (33, King Vidor); *Bombshell* (33, Victor Fleming), with Jean Harlow; *Sadie McKee* (34, Clarence Brown), with Crawford; *The Girl from Missouri* (34, Jack Conway), with Harlow; *Dancing Lady* (35, Robert Z. Leonard), with Crawford.

He generally found better parts on loan: in John Ford's *The World Moves On* (34) at Fox; in *Gentlemen Are Born* (34, Alfred E. Green) and *Dangerous* (35, Green) at Warners; and in Henry Hathaway's *The Lives of a Bengal Lancer* (35) at Paramount. But he could not exceed handsomeness as the midshipman in *Mutiny on the Bounty* (35, Frank Lloyd); *One New York Night* (35, Conway); *Reckless* (35, Fleming); *No More Ladies* (35, Edward H. Griffith); *The King Steps Out* (36, Josef von Sternberg); *Suzy* (36, George Fitzmaurice); and *The Gorgeous Hussy* (36, Brown).

Despite so many hollow parts, Tone was never to be as busy again. He was in *Quality Street* (37, George Stevens) and unusually cast as a gangster in *They Gave Him a Gun* (37, W. S. Van Dyke). His marriage broke up and his MGM contract ended acrimoniously with *The Bride Wore Red* (37, Dorothy Arzner), with Crawford; *Manproof* (38, Richard Thorpe); *Three Comrades* (38, Frank Borzage); and *Fast and Furious* (39, Busby Berkeley).

Tone stayed in Hollywood for another ten years, free-lancing and finding more varied parts; but his stock steadily declined: *Trail of the Vigilantes* (40, Allan Dwan); *She Knew All the Answers* (41, Richard Wallace); *The Wife Takes a Flyer* (42, Wallace); *Pilot No. 5* (43, George Sidney); *Five Graves to Cairo* (43, Billy Wilder); *His Butler's Sister* (43, Borzage); *True to Life* (43, George Marshall); *The Hour Before the Dawn* (44, Frank Tuttle); *Phantom Lady* (44, Robert Siodmak); *Dark Waters* (44, André de Toth); *Because of Him* (46, Wallace); *Honeymoon* (47, William Keighley); *Every Girl Should Be Married* (48, Don Hartman); *Jigsaw* (49, Val Guest, in England); *Without Honor* (49, Irving Pichel); *The Man on the Eiffel Tower* (49, Burgess Meredith), which he produced; and *Here Comes the Groom* (51, Frank Capra).

His second marriage, to actress Jean Wallace, ended in divorce and the short-lived third, to starlet Barbara Payton, was embroidered by nightclub brawls. Tone went back to the theatre where he played in *Uncle Vanya* and O'Neill's *A Moon for the Misbegotten*. In 1958, he acted in, produced, and directed with John Goetz a disastrous film version of *Uncle Vanya*; in 1959, his fourth marriage broke up. A visibly sadder man, Tone was recalled to play the dying president in Preminger's *Advise and Consent* (62)—a striking cameo as good as anything he had ever done. And

after *La Bonne Soupe* (63, Robert Thomas), he made two more, brief but memorable appearances: in Preminger's *In Harm's Way* (65) and as Ruby Lapp in Arthur Penn's *Mickey One* (65), magnificently foreboding as he tells Mickey of the way "they" will want him to pay for every little pleasure in life.

Rip (Elmer Rual) **Torn**, b. Temple, Texas, 1931

Those of us who have delighted in Rip Torn's performances on *The Larry Sanders Show* could easily be forgiven for forgetting, or not knowing, that Rip Torn was once touched by danger and violence. As an actor, he was famous for going his own way, and for bringing a real darkness to the screen. Hadn't he turned on his director and fellow actor, Norman Mailer, on camera, during the making of *Maidstone* (71)? By now, Torn is a figure of fun, an overplayer or a rather thick-coated villain. But the younger man could be alarming, uncouth and full of life. It would be no surprise if Torn resents the ways in which his passion has been tamed. But, of course, that name was always verging on self-parody.

He had been set on ranching as a career, but he hitchhiked to Hollywood and was led astray by offers: a small part in *Baby Doll* (56, Elia Kazan); *Time Limit* (57, Karl Malden); *A Face in the Crowd* (57, Kazan); *Pork Chop Hill* (59, Lewis Milestone); Judas in *King of Kings* (61, Nicholas Ray); very nasty in *Sweet Bird of Youth* (62, Richard Brooks); *Critic's Choice* (63, Don Weis); an early drawling Southerner in *The Cincinnati Kid* (65, Norman Jewison); *One Spy Too Many* (66, Joseph Sargent); *You're a Big Boy Now* (66, Francis Coppola); *Beach Red* (67, Cornel Wilde); *Sol Madrid* (68, Brian G. Hutton); *Coming Apart* (69, Milton Moses Ginsberg); as Henry Miller in *Tropic of Cancer* (70, Joseph Strick); *Slaughter* (72, Jack Starrett); as a country singer in *Payday* (73, Daryl Duke); *Crazy Joe* (74, Carlo Lizzani); *The Man Who Fell to Earth* (76, Nicolas Roeg); *Birch Interval* (77, Delbert Mann); *Nasty Habits* (77, Michael Lindsay-Hogg); *The Private Files of J. Edgar Hoover* (77, Larry Cohen); *Coma* (78, Michael Crichton); *The Seduction of Joe Tynan* (79, Jerry Schatzberg); *One-Trick Pony* (80, Robert M. Young); *The First Family* (80, Buck Henry); unusually restrained in *Heartland* (80, Richard Pearce); *Jinxed!* (82, Don Siegel); *The Beastmaster* (89, Don Cascarelli); a psycho in *A Stranger Is Watching* (82, Sean Cunningham); *Cross Creek* (83, Martin Ritt); *City Heat* (84, Richard Benjamin); *Songwriter* (84, Alan Rudolph); *Misunderstood* (84, Jerry Schatzberg); *Summer Rental* (85, Carl Reiner); *Nadine* (87, Robert Benton); *Extreme Prejudice* (87, Walter Hill); *The Hit List* (89, William Lustig).

In 1988, for reasons that are not clear, he directed the disastrous *The Telephone*, which its star, Whoopi Goldberg, tried to ban. He acted again in *Cold Feet* (89, Robert Dornhelm); as Walt Whitman in *Beautiful Dreamers* (90, John Kent Harrison); the defense attorney in *Defending Your Life* (91, Albert Brooks); uncredited in *Hard Promises* (92, Martin Davidson); *RoboCop 3* (93, Fred Dekker); *Canadian Bacon* (95, Michael Moore); *How to Make an American Quilt* (95, Jocelyn Moorhouse); *Down Periscope* (96, David S. Ward); *Trial and Error* (97, Jonathan Lynn); *Men in Black* (97, Barry Sonnenfeld); *Senseless* (98, Penelope Spheeris); *The Insider* (99, Michael Mann).

Leopoldo Torre Nilsson (1924–78),
b. Buenos Aires, Argentina
1947: *El Muro* (s). 1950: *El Crimen de Oribe* (codirected with Leopoldo Torres Rios). 1953: *El Hijo del Crack* (codirected with Torres Rios). 1954: *Días de Odio; La Tigra.* 1955: *Para Vestir Santos.* 1956: *Graciela; El Protegido.* 1957: *Precursores de la Pintura Argentina* (d); *Los Árboles de Buenos-Aires* (d); *La Casa del Angel.* 1958: *El Secuestrador.* 1959: *La Caída/The Fall.* 1960: *Fin de Fiesta; Un Guapo del '900.* 1961: *La Mano en la Trampa/Hand in the Trap; Piel de Verano/Summer Skin.* 1962: *Setenta Veces Siete; Homenaje a la Hora de la Siesta/Homage at Siesta Time.* 1963: *La Terraza/The Roof Garden.* 1964: *El Ojo de la Cerradura.* 1966: *Cavar un Foso; Monday's Child.* 1967: *Los Traidores de San Angel.* 1968: *Martin Fierro.* 1970: *El Santo de la Espada.* 1971: *Guernes.* 1972: *Mafia.* 1974: *Boquitas Pintadas/Painted Lips.* 1975: *El Pibe Cabeza.* 1976: *Piedra Libre/Free for All; Diario de la Guerra del Cerdlo.*

In the late 1950s and early 1960s, as film festivals grew in size and self-importance, Torre Nilsson was everyone's South American entry. Thus we had to sit through his judicious melodramas to convince ourselves that we were seeing, say, *Tirez sur le Pianiste* or *L'Avventura* in a proper perspective. He was the son of Leopoldo Torres Rios, another director, and of a Swedish mother. While reading philosophy and writing poetry, he helped his father and eventually became his country's most prestigious director. Who knows whether he is representative? In 1960, Argentina was producing some thirty movies a year; only Mexico took the medium more seriously in Latin America. Nilsson's movies aspire toward Europe; they say little about the pampas or about a country where a raw actress named Eva Peron could become a goddess. Nilsson was the writer on many of his early films, but he also collaborated on scripts with his wife, novelist Beatriz Guido. He seems to me less interesting, or more solemn, than Hugo Fregonese, an Argentine-born wanderer, with something of the way of a gaucho. Yet, *Días de Odio* is taken from the Borges story,

"Emma Zunz"; and *Boquitas Pintadas* is a fierce piece of social criticism, taken from a novel by Manuel Puig.

Jacques Tourneur (1904–77), b. Paris
1931: *Tous ça ne Vaut pas l'Amour.* 1933: *Pour Être Aimé; Toto.* 1934: *Les Filles de la Concierge.* 1939: *They All Come Out; Nick Carter—Master Detective.* 1940: *Phantom Raiders.* 1941: *Doctors Don't Tell.* 1943: *Cat People; I Walked With a Zombie; The Leopard Man.* 1944: *Days of Glory; Experiment Perilous.* 1946: *Canyon Passage.* 1947: *Out of the Past.* 1948: *Berlin Express.* 1949: *Easy Living.* 1950: *Stars in My Crown; The Flame and the Arrow.* 1951: *Circle of Danger; Anne of the Indies.* 1952: *Way of a Gaucho.* 1953: *Appointment in Honduras.* 1955: *Stranger on Horseback; Wichita.* 1956: *Great Day in the Morning; Nightfall.* 1957: *Night of the Demon/Curse of the Demon.* 1958: *The Fearmakers; Timbuktu;* an episode from *Fury River.* 1959: *Frontier Rangers;* an episode from *Mission of Danger; La Battaglia di Maratona/The Giant of Marathon.* 1963: *The Comedy of Terrors.* 1965: *City Under the Sea.*

The son of director Maurice Tourneur, Jacques emigrated to America in 1913 with his father. He functioned as script clerk on many of his father's films and acted small parts in *Scaramouche* (23, Rex Ingram); *The Fair Co-Ed* (27, Sam Wood); *Love* (27, Edmund Goulding); and *The Trail of '98* (29, Clarence Brown). His slow apprenticeship was tied to his father's return to Paris in 1929. Jacques went back too and was assistant and editor to Maurice until 1933. He made a few films of his own in France but then broke away and committed himself to America. He was second-unit director on *The Winning Ticket* (34, Charles Reisner) and on *A Tale of Two Cities* (35, Jack Conway), where he met Val Lewton.

From 1936–39 he directed some twenty shorts, principally for MGM. The delay in breaking into serious American direction is the odder in that Tourneur quickly proved himself an adroit director of action pictures with an exceptional visual sense. He remained basically a B-picture director, assigned to a series of projects and rarely asserting any creative personality, let alone consistency.

His reputation still refers initially to the sense of unrevealed horror within the everyday that he showed in the films made for Val Lewton—*Cat People, I Walked With a Zombie,* and *The Leopard Man.* But the same talent is evident in the British *Night of the Demon,* taken from an M. R. James story. Time and again in these films, it is the imaginative use of light, decor, space, and movement that makes the impact of the movie. There is nothing finer in Lewton's work than the zoo sequences or the swimming-pool nightmare in *Cat People,* supreme vindications of the menacing nature of shadow, composition, and pace. Short of ideas, Tourneur is a classic instance of cinematic fluency, invaluable as a contrast to such opinionated drabs as Zinnemann, Kramer, or latter-day Stevens.

In addition to his horror pictures, *Experiment Perilous* is a first-class period thriller; *Out of the Past* a classic B picture and a major Robert Mitchum film; *Berlin Express* is a good "train" film; *Stars in My Crown* is a gentle Western about the relationship between Joel McCrea and Dean Stockwell; *The Flame and the Arrow* a cheerful attempt to make Burt Lancaster a Tuscan Robin Hood; *Way of the Gaucho* a very successful opening up of strange territory; and *Great Day in the Morning* another Western with unusual attention to atmosphere. There are duds, including *Circle of Danger* and most of the more recent films, which are lazy TV originals or tongue-in-cheek horror pictures. The director of B pictures always needed a prosperous industry: today, in TV, he has been rationalized into the ground. But from 1942 to 1955, for Lewton or RKO, Tourneur made modest, cheap, quick films that still radiate narrative imagination and visual invention.

I like Tourneur as much as I did in 1975. But something now makes me flinch from propositions that he was a genius with a unique vision. Tourneur, rather, was a functionary blessed with rare plastic . . . skills? No, skills is not enough. He had talent, grace even—there is so little in his work that comes close to being clumsy or awkward. But is it more? Could—or can—directors handling assignments be more?

Consider *Out of the Past*. That noir is a lasting joy—because of story structure, dialogue, the imagery, the playing. But isn't it actually nonsensical as an idea, the old genre given one more wicked twist? And isn't there a profound clash between Tourneur's grace (which always aspires to intelligence and taste) and the cynical dead-endedness of the project? So many of the allegedly great auteurs prompt this question. *Out of the Past* is terrific—and not good enough: it is like a brilliant palace made of matchsticks, by a prisoner on a life sentence.

Maurice Tourneur (Maurice Tourneur Thomas) (1876–1961), b. Paris

1912: *Rouletabille*. 1913: *Le Dernier Pardon; Soeurette*. 1914: *Mother; The Man of the Hour; The Wishing Ring; The Pit*. 1915: *Alias Jimmy Valentine; The Cub; Trilby; The Ivory Snuff Box; A Butterfly on the Wheel*. 1916: *The Pawn of Fate; The Hand of Peril; The Closed Road; The Rail Rider; The Velvet Paw*. 1917: *A Girl's Folly; The Whip; The Pride of the Clan; The Poor Little Rich Girl; The Undying Flame; The Law of the Land; Exile; Barbary Sheep; The Rise of Jennie Cushing*. 1918: *Rose of the World; A Doll's House; The Blue Bird; Prunella; Sporting Life; Woman*. 1919: *Victory; The White Heather; The Broken Butterfly; The Life Line*. 1920: *My Lady's Garter; Treasure Island; The Great Redeemer; The White Circle; Deep Waters; The Last of the Mohicans* (completed by Clarence Brown after Tourneur was injured). 1921: *The Bait; The Foolish Matrons* (codirected with Brown). 1922: *Lorna Doone*. 1923: *While Paris Sleeps* (filmed in 1920, but not released until 1923); *The Brass Bottle; The Christian; The Isle of Lost Ships; Jealous Husbands*. 1924: *Torment; The White Moth*. 1925: *Never the Twain Shall Meet; Clothes Make the Pirate; Sporting Life*. 1926: *Aloma of the South Seas; Old Loves and New*. 1927: *L'Equipage*. 1929: *The Mysterious Island* (codirected with Benjamin Christensen and Lucien Hubbard); *Das Schiff der Verlorenen Menschen*. 1930: *Accusée, Levez-Vous*. 1931: *Maison de Danses; Partir!*. 1932: *Au Nom de la Loi; Les Gaîtés de l'Escadron*. 1933: *Les Deux Orphelines; Obsession*. 1934: *Le Voleur*. 1935: *Justin de Marseille; Konigsmark*. 1936: *Samson; Avec le Sourire*. 1938: *Le Patriote; Katia*. 1940: *Volpone*. 1941: *Péchés de Jeunesse; Mam'zelle Bonaparte*. 1942: *La Main du Diable*. 1943: *La Val d'Enfer; Cécile est Morte*. 1947: *Après l'Amour*. 1948: *L'Impasse des Deux Anges*.

Tourneur is one of the barely known pioneers of silent cinema. His reputation for pictorial invention, often touching on the fantastic, tends to be accepted, if only because he is the father of Jacques Tourneur, a proven adept at visual excitement. But this account given by Clarence Brown, Tourneur's devoted assistant, has more than a hint of artiness: "He was a great believer in dark foregrounds. No matter where he set his camera up, he would always have a foreground. On exteriors, we used to carry branches and twigs around with us. If it was an interior, he always had a piece of the set cutting into the corner of the picture, in halftone, to give him depth. Whenever we saw a painting with an interesting lighting effect we'd copy it." It should be added that in 1918—a year before *Caligari*—for *The Blue Bird*, Tourneur had used impressionistic painted backdrops. It is doubtful if even the archives could settle the question of his talent, but likely that he was an exponent of the sort of profuse prettiness to be seen in Victorian book illustrations.

He was a painter and an actor with André Antoine before he began directing for Eclair. In 1914, he went to America and eventually set up Maurice Tourneur Productions. An individualist, he quit Hollywood when MGM insisted that he have and pay heed to a producer on *The Mysterious Island* (27, later completed by and credited to Lucien Hubbard, 29). Thus he stands as an example of early, individualist cinema, in the age before Thalberg regularized production.

Back in Paris (with his son as assistant), he

directed some of Harry Baur's films—*Samson, Le Patriote,* and *Volpone.*

Robert Towne (Robert Schwartz),
b. Los Angeles, 1934

1982: *Personal Best.* 1988: *Tequila Sunrise.* 1998: *Without Limits.*

Three years in a row, in the 1970s, Towne was nominated for the best screenplay Oscar—for *The Last Detail* (83, Hal Ashby), *Chinatown* (74, Roman Polanski), for which he won, and *Shampoo* (75, Ashby). And those were just the movies he had his name on! Towne's extraordinary prestige rested on the legend of how many other important movies he had helped silently, or doctored. Of course, people have written, rewritten, polished, and roughed up scripts without credit since the movies began. The practice was far more common—if not automatic—in the 1930s and 1940s. But Towne was the first man who made a reputation out of it (since Ben Hecht). On *Bonnie and Clyde* (67, Arthur Penn), he had had a "Special Consultant" credit, but his vital contribution to *The Godfather* (72, Francis Ford Coppola) was left to trust and rumor.

Towne is one of the picture business's great talkers and wisest seers—yet, let it be said, he understands the business rather in the way of a hypochondriac who believes he is ahead of his own doctors. He is a fascinating contradiction: in many ways idealistic, sentimental, and very talented; in others, a devout compromiser, a delayer, so insecure that he can sometimes seem devious. The novelist John Fante, who hoped for years that Towne would write and make Fante's novel *The Brotherhood of the Grape,* once called Towne "as tender as a kitten, and as crafty as a fox."

Thus, he has two careers, above and below the credit line. It is safe to assume that Towne has been available to be talked to about most of the films of his circle—Warren Beatty, Jack Nicholson, Roman Polanski, at least. This doesn't mean he has doctored everything; that he wants to own up to every choice; or that he does not cannily leave some doubt. There is also the point that talkative writers do not always know just when or how they've had an influence. Sometimes, Towne has been in the air, like the scent of eucalyptus, or fluorine in the water. And, generally, he's been as sweet and beneficial.

The official Towne worked on *The Last Woman on Earth* (61, Roger Corman) and *The Creature from the Haunted Sea* (61, Corman). He also acted in those films under the name Edward Wain. He helped write *The Tomb of Ligeia* (65, Corman); *Villa Rides* (68, Buzz Kulik); and *Drive, He Said* (72, Jack Nicholson), in which he also acted.

In addition, he did doctoring work on *A Time for Killing* (67, Phil Karlson), *Cisco Pike* (72, B. W. L. Norton), and *The New Centurions* (72, Richard Fleischer).

His three breakthrough scripts were all done for friends, and for two actors, Beatty and Nicholson. They show a deft command of narrative structure and natural dialogue in the service of a warm, untidy humanism and a special love of southern California. *Chinatown* was especially close to his heart, not just as a tribute to private-eye fiction, but as a magnificent portrait of Los Angeles as it came of age and as maybe the last of the great complicated story lines that movies dared. Even in the 1970s, Towne dreamed of carrying his hero, Jake Gittes, into the 1940s and 1950s as L.A.'s water problems turned into the story of gasoline and automobiles. We should add, however, that Polanski toughened up the ending of *Chinatown.* Towne meant for Evelyn Mulwray to get away with her daughter. Polanski guessed that the picture had to end badly for the paranoid mood of the seventies to be fulfilled.

Over the next few years, Towne was a largely uncredited writer: *The Yakuza* (75, Sydney Pollack), where he was credited; *Marathon Man* (76, John Schlesinger); *The Missouri Breaks* (76, Penn); *Orca . . . Killer Whale* (77, Michael Anderson); *Heaven Can Wait* (78, Beatty and Buck Henry); and *Reds* (81, Beatty).

He had worked years on the script of what became *Greystoke: The Legend of Tarzan, Lord of the Apes* (84, Hugh Hudson), researching Africa and the apes with fanatical care. The picture was finally taken from him and Towne took his credit as P. H. Vazak (the name of his dog). He had gotten himself in the predicament of needing to trade it away because of the way *Personal Best* had exceeded budget and schedule and led to a bitter conflict with producer David Geffen. Towne's first film was odd and original, and it had a pioneering eye for athletic erotics. But it was softer and more clichéd than anything Towne had written for others.

It was in 1985 that he began, and then lost, his sequel to *Chinatown, The Two Jakes.* The script for that film was very promising—more comic, more human, more Renoir-like than *Chinatown.* The cast were aces, except for Towne's choice of Robert Evans to play opposite Jack Nicholson. Shooting began, but Evans was ill-prepared, Nicholson was less than fully supportive, and there were wider anxieties about Towne's authority. This was his second great loss, in no way redeemed by the eventual film (90), directed by Jack Nicholson, whose friendship with Towne had been sundered.

The reputation Towne had once enjoyed for mysterious power was now sadly altered. He seemed more like a loser, someone who could not quite take charge in a crisis. *Tequila Sunrise* was a very disappointing follow-up, and Towne's more recent writing has lacked character as often as credit: *Swing Shift* (84, Jonathan Demme), where he was called in by Goldie Hawn; *8 Million Ways to Die* (86, Ashby); *The Bedroom Window* (87, Curtis Hanson), on which he was executive producer; *Frantic* (88, Polanski); *The Pick-up Artist* (89, James Toback), in which he also acted; and the lamentable *Days of Thunder* (90, Tony Scott). He was cowriter on *The Firm* (93, Pollack). For Beatty, he wrote the script of *Love Affair* (94, Glenn Gordon Caron)—which was then discreetly doctored by others. Paranoids are always right.

And so, one way and another, Towne had lost friendships with Nicholson and Beatty, who were the twin engines of his work. But *Days of Thunder* and *The Firm* showed a new motor—alliance with Tom Cruise. Thus, Towne came to be the screenwriter on two massive hits, *Mission: Impossible* (96, Brian De Palma) and *Mission: Impossible II* (00, John Woo). At the same time, Cruise produced Towne's second athletics film—and the second film on the runner Steve Prefontaine—*Without Limits*. This was a real achievement, for a sports film, but Towne's recent "success" is a sad measure of where talent has gone in Hollywood. One somehow longs to hear Jake Gittes's candid opinion on the *Mission* pictures, and on films with colons in the title.

Spencer Tracy (1900–67),
b. Milwaukee, Wisconsin

Educated at the Northwestern Military Academy, at Ripon College, and AADA, Tracy made his New York stage debut in 1922 as a robot in Karel Capek's *R.U.R.* He worked in the theatre throughout the 1920s, often for George M. Cohan, and it was his 1930 performance as a killer in jail in *The Last Mile* that made his name and earned him several movie tests. He made two shorts for Vitaphone before John Ford cast him in *Up the River* (30), whereupon Fox put him under contract. But he was not happy with the parts Fox provided: *Quick Millions* (31, Rowland Brown); *She Wanted a Millionaire* (32, John Blystone); *Young America* (32, Frank Borzage); and *Me and My Gal* (32, Raoul Walsh).

In any event, Tracy was to earn himself the role of a robust, decent American; a gruff, unpretentious man, capable of temper or horseplay, embarrassed by women, and led by sincerity either to self-sacrifice or to brooding concentration. In comedy or drama, he was very near the roots of American ideals: not handsome but rugged; not intelligent but shrewd; not imaginative but sympathetic. Long before his death he had been raised above the generality of actors; even professionals claimed that his inability to be anything other than himself was a mark of special intuition and application. He has also had the best P.R.—Katharine

Hepburn. A clear eye may decide that he became homespun, inclined to sentimentality and best as the object of affectionate ridicule in comedy or as a man transformed by rage. Age made him crusty and it must be stressed that his most original work came in the 1930s.

In 1933 Warners borrowed him for Curtiz's *20,000 Years in Sing Sing* and for the next two years Tracy seemed intent on freeing himself from Fox and finding a more amenable studio. Even so, Fox put him in one interesting movie: *The Power and the Glory* (33, William K. Howard)—but he was more often on loan: *Man's Castle* (33, Frank Borzage); *Looking for Trouble* (34, William Wellman) and, at MGM, *The Show-Off* (34, Charles Reisner). After making *Dante's Inferno* (35, Harry Lachman) and *It's a Small World* (35, Irving Cummings), a drunken Tracy landed briefly in jail and later that year Fox fired him and MGM hired him. (Booze and womanizing were fuel for Tracy's errors—and he was a Catholic, too, haunted by his own failings.)

Tracy was a subtle expression of the hero in the Depression: a proud man who had suppressed his frustrations to stand still in welfare lines; a romantic already hardened by the realization that fortune is capricious and callous; a man whose patience was always being tested. Both *Man's Castle* and *The Power and the Glory* use Tracy's sense of the fickleness of success and failure. Never glamorous, he was the idealized screen version of every American who could make or lose a million. But amid such free enterprise, Tracy showed how far the system isolated the American. No wonder, in 1944, that King Vidor wanted him for *An American Romance*, for Tracy was able to play the industrialist and the laborer: he proved that the one could be the other, encouraged ambition but never lost the haunting shadow of recession and the humbled tycoon.

It was several years before Tracy properly established himself at MGM, but he collected on the way a number of his best and best-known performances: as Fritz Lang's wronged hero himself driven to malice in *Fury* (36)—a beautiful use of Tracy's truculence, especially when he returns from the grave, stands silhouetted in the doorway, and tells his brothers, "I could smell myself burning"; as the priest in *San Francisco* (36, W. S. Van Dyke); in *Libeled Lady* (36, Jack Conway); winning an Oscar as the Portuguese fisherman in *Captains Courageous* (37, Victor Fleming); *They Gave Him a Gun* (37, Van Dyke); *Big City* (37, Borzage), as a cab driver who stands up to organized crime, a beautiful portrait of rugged individualism; uneasily opposite Joan Crawford—beer and sweet martini—in *Mannequin* (38, Borzage); *Test Pilot* (38, Victor Fleming); and a second Oscar as Father Flanagan in Norman Taurog's *Boy's Town* (38)—an unbridled masterpiece of boys' sentiment, very well suited to Tracy's clipped emotionalism. For the next few years, he was the obvious candidate for major parts: *Stanley and Livingstone* (39, Henry King); with Hedy Lamarr in *I Take This Woman* (40, Van Dyke)—beer and crème de menthe; in King Vidor's *Northwest Passage* (40), challenging nature itself; as *Edison, The Man* (40, Clarence Brown); very enjoyable sparring with Gable in *Boom Town* (40, Conway); as Flanagan again in *Men of Boy's Town* (41, Taurog); uneasy with masquerade but very menacing in the Victor Fleming *Dr. Jekyll and Mr. Hyde* (41).

It was at this point that he met Katharine Hepburn—beer and salty crackers. Their relationship was special, if easy to sentimentalize. Tracy's marriage, though never dissolved, was not a success and he was on close terms with Hepburn to his death. More to the point, she teased him without making him feel insecure. It put up his hackles and made for one of the most emotionally natural of comedy pairings: *Woman of the Year* (42, George Stevens); outstanding as the reporter deflating the career of a dead great man in *Keeper of the Flame* (42, George Cukor); *State of the Union* (48, Frank Capra); delicious as married lawyers in *Adam's Rib* (49, Cukor); *Pat and Mike* (52, Cukor); *The Desk Set* (57, Walter Lang); and finally, visibly reduced, in Stanley Kramer's awful *Guess Who's Coming to Dinner?* (67)—a gross banality of which the supposedly hokum-dispelling Tracy seemed unaware.

He made not many other satisfactory films after 1942—as though by soothing his hurts, Hepburn left him more unmanageable for others. After two more for Victor Fleming, *Tortilla Flat* (42) and *A Guy Named Joe* (43), he was in two war pictures: *The Seventh Cross* (44, Fred Zinnemann) and *Thirty Seconds Over Tokyo* (44, Mervyn Le Roy). After the war, he was awkward with Hepburn in *The Sea of Grass* (46, Elia Kazan); *Cass Timberlane* (47, George Sidney); *Edward, My Son* (48, Cukor); before he found himself again with Vincente Minnelli and Joan Bennett (a partner from the 1930s) in *Father of the Bride* (50) and *Father's Little Dividend* (51), delightful portraits of an ineffectually gruff father.

Thereafter, judgment seemed largely to have deserted him—apart from *The Actress* (53, Cukor), the one-armed investigator in *Bad Day at Black Rock* (54, John Sturges), and in one of his best films, as the lovably conniving politician in John Ford's *The Last Hurrah* (58). Against these must be set *Plymouth Adventure* (52, Clarence Brown); *Broken Lance* (54, Edward Dmytryk); *The Mountain* (56, Dmytryk); the very unhappy *Old Man and the Sea* (58, Sturges and Fred Zinnemann)—an elderly beer drinker, belching sourly at back projections of sea; and the last surrender to Stanley Kramer—*Inherit the Wind* (60);

Judgment at Nuremberg (61); *It's a Mad, Mad, Mad, Mad World* (63); and *Guess Who's Coming to Dinner?* (67).

John Travolta,

b. Englewood, New Jersey, 1954

Travolta is a remarkable example of the kiddie hipster, thirty-minute demonstration of the screen's magical transmission of animated presence, but sad evidence of the picture business's betrayal of adulthood. In 1978, he had two films in circulation that dominated the year commercially. They were pictures that could persuade the industry of its own vitality and universal audience only because so many juveniles went to see them more than once. *Saturday Night Fever* (77, John Badham) had raunchy sex action and a fatal accident, but children ignored its rating and its sordid suburban context. That film only existed when Travolta danced, or when he made his camp *paso doble* assertion: "Here, *this* is dancing, not that Fred Astaire thing—I just move and strut, and *that's dancing!*"

The kid carried the crowd. His will enlarged (or narrowed) dance and made for a hothouse enchantment as he hit his protective but mannered poses and the floor changed color. It was homemade, but it was exotic too. Disco-movie: smooth, unending, thoughtless, and a total rendering of personality into style. No self-respecting adolescent, I hope, could believe in it. But the ten- to fifteen-year-old age group was captivated. It was like the early Beatles' cheeky swagger turned into Pop Art. The story was trite, but no one was listening to it: you could go out for popcorn and hot dogs, knowing that the beat would bring you back in time. And Travolta had all the anodyne sexual thrust of virginal horniness. It's a mother's boy's face, a gaunt, narcissistic horse's head flabby with self-regard and butterfly lips. Vinnie Barbarino, the sweathog he played in *Welcome Back, Kotter*, was his emotional touchstone: a street dandy so dedicated to impressing people that he has bypassed self-knowledge. It's the face of heavy, swollen passion brought on by mirror-gazing. Travolta was an odalisque of sorrowful self; his dynamic was inward and stroking.

He never dominated *Kotter*; he looked like nothing in *The Devil's Rain* (75, Robert Fuest), and only flashy in *Carrie* (76, Brian De Palma). Though *Grease* (78, Randal Kleiser) was another huge success, it was far less of a vehicle. It had its own pastiche of the fifties, plenty of songs, and a lively cast. Travolta sang like someone whose voice hadn't broken yet, and again it was the solemn, infant fierceness of his movements that won attention.

Moment by Moment (78, Jane Wagner) was the end of the dream. If only that film had had the wit or nerve to run with its suggestive undertone—

that Travolta and Lily Tomlin were incestuous mother and son—instead of attempting a forlorn mixed-generations romance.

No rescue arrived. He was rather upstaged by Debra Winger and Scott Glenn in *Urban Cowboy* (80, James Bridges); *Blow Out* (81, De Palma); as the *Saturday Night Fever* character—later—in *Staying Alive* (83, Sylvester Stallone); in the dreadful *Two of a Kind* (83, John Herzfeld); and the helplessly camp *Perfect* (85, Bridges). After a few years away, he made *The Experts* (89, Dave Thomas), which was barely released. Despite *The Dumb Waiter* (89, Robert Altman) and *Shout* (91, Jeffrey Hornaday), he regained the mainstream in *Look Who's Talking* (89, Amy Heckerling); *Look Who's Talking Too* (90, Heckerling); *Look Who's Talking Now* (93, Heckerling); and *Pulp Fiction* (94, Quentin Tarantino).

Pulp Fiction brought Travolta back, and it seemed for a while as if he and the public were both touched by the reunion. But enough time has passed for us to relearn something we always knew: that he's a limited actor with the kind of confidence that burns off before lunch. *Eyes of an Angel* (91, Robert Harmon), a wretched shelf-jailed film freed by *Pulp Fiction; Get Shorty* (95, Barry Sonnenfeld), at his relaxed best; *White Man's Burden* (95, Desmond Nakano); as a fancy villain in *Broken Arrow* (96, John Woo); *Phenomenon* (96, Jon Turteltaub); not sharp enough in *Michael* (96, Nora Ephron); with Nicolas Cage in *Face/Off* (97, Woo); *She's So Lovely* (97, Nick Cassavetes).

Seven films in three years was the opportunism of someone who knew how fickle success could be. He was rich again, but plumper and older, and it began to show: *Mad City* (97, Costa-Gavras); as the president in *Primary Colors* (98, Mike Nichols); *A Civil Action* (98, Steven Zaillian); *The Thin Red Line* (98, Terrence Malick); *The General's Daughter* (99, Simon West); *Battlefield Earth* (00, Roger Christian), a piece of rubbish derived from Travolta's own wise man, L. Ron Hubbard; *Domestic Disturbance* (01, Harold Becker); *Swordfish* (01, Dominic Sena); *Basic* (03, John McTiernan); *Ladder 49* (03, Jay Russell).

Claire Trevor (Claire Wemlinger)
(1909–2000), b. New York

After AADA, she went into stock and then to Warners where she appeared in some of the early Vitaphone shorts. She returned to the theatre and was signed by Fox in 1932. Her career is a classic case of an actress perpetually in support, rarely working in major movies, and taking on the whole range of blowsy molls and blasé dolls. What stamina it must have required to stay fresh. She made her debut in 1933 in *Life in the Raw* (Louis King) and worked steadily until the late 1950s. Her career lacks shape—but it is as inconsequential

and arresting as chatter: *Jimmy and Sally* (33, James Tinling); *Hold That Girl* (34, Hamilton McFadden); *Wild Gold* (34, George Marshall); *Spring Tonic* (35, Clyde Bruckman); *Black Sheep* (35, Allan Dwan); *Navy Wife* (35, Dwan); opposite Spencer Tracy in *Dante's Inferno* (35, Harry Lachman); *Song and Dance Man* (36, Dwan); *Human Cargo* (36, Dwan); *15 Maiden Lane* (36, Dwan); *One Mile from Heaven* (37, Dwan); a tart in *Dead End* (37, William Wyler); *King of Gamblers* (37, Robert Florey); a gangster's girl in *The Amazing Dr. Clitterhouse* (38, Anatole Litvak); a saloon girl in *Valley of the Giants* (38, William Keighley); her best remembered part, as the prostitute hustled by small-town censoriousness onto the *Stagecoach* (39, John Ford); *I Stole a Million* (39, Frank Tuttle); *The Dark Command* (40, Raoul Walsh); *Texas* (41, Marshall); *Honky Tonk* (41, Jack Conway); *Crossroads* (42, Conway); *The Desperadoes* (43, Charles Vidor); *Good Luck, Mr. Yates* (43, Ray Enright); excellent in *Murder, My Sweet* (45, Edward Dmytryk); *Crack-Up* (46, Irving Reis); sharp and nasty in *Born to Kill* (47, Robert Wise); *Raw Deal* (48, Anthony Mann); Edward G. Robinson's mistress, in *Key Largo* (48, John Huston), for which she won the supporting actress Oscar; *The Babe Ruth Story* (48, Roy del Ruth); *The Velvet Touch* (48, John Gage); *Hard, Fast and Beautiful* (51, Ida Lupino); *My Man and I* (52, William Wellman); *Stop, You're Killing Me* (52, Roy del Ruth); *The Stranger Wore a Gun* (53, André de Toth); *The High and the Mighty* (54, Wellman); *Man Without a Star* (55, King Vidor); *Lucy Gallant* (55, Robert Parrish); and *Marjorie Morningstar* (58, Irving Rapper).

After that, her work on film grew limited: as Edward G. Robinson's "lawful wedded nightmare" in *Two Weeks in Another Town* (62, Vincente Minnelli); as Richard Beymer's mother in *The Stripper* (63, Franklin Schaffner); in *How to Murder Your Wife* (65, Richard Quine); and an oddity—in the Thelma Ritter part in *The Cape Town Affair* (67, Robert D. Webb), a dull remake of Fuller's *Pickup on South Street*. Years later, she appeared in *Kiss Me Goodbye* (82, Robert Mulligan) and *Norman Rockwell's Breaking Home Ties* (87, John Wilder).

Jean-Louis Trintignant,
b. Port-St.-Esprit, France, 1930

It often takes a major director to identify the latent personality of an actor who has been around many years without finding himself. Raoul Walsh did this for Humphrey Bogart in *High Sierra;* while Catherine Deneuve was explained—and her other films illuminated—by *Belle de Jour.* Jean-Louis Trintignant had been working hard in European films for fifteen years, his face frozen by so many supposedly romantic leads. From the mid-1960s, he found his diffidence leading him into increasingly detached, voyeuristic characters. This trend culminated in his magnificent scuttling assassin in *The Conformist* (70, Bernardo Bertolucci).

Bertolucci was himself aware of the discovery: "I think Trintignant is that person, that this is his first film in which he is himself. . . . I chose Trintignant because when I think of him two adjectives immediately come to mind: moving and sinister. And these are qualities of the character. The point of departure is reality, then the actor transcends it. Because there is a camera which moves and which is itself an actor, an actor who makes the others react. The camera is a character like Trintignant, a living presence, not a recording machine."

Indeed, Trintignant reacts to the camera as if it were his conscience; he hunches up, retreats behind his own basilisk stare, and regards the other people in the film with a long-distance curiosity such as audiences lavish on films. His personality in *The Conformist* is the weakness of the obsessive fantasist, his face closed to guard his own private image of the world. How intriguing that the first plan for *Last Tango in Paris* was based on Trintignant; how revealing of the way films change with alterations of casting.

After *The Conformist* it is easy to see that sense of separateness growing through Trintignant's work. He came to the movies from the theatre: *Si Tous les Gars du Monde* (55, Christian-Jaque); *And God Created Woman* (56, Roger Vadim); *Estate Violenta* (59, Valerio Zurlini); *Les Liaisons Dangereuses* (59, Vadim); *Austerlitz* (60, Abel Gance and Roger Richebé); *Le Coeur Battant* (60, Jacques Doniol-Valcroze); *Pleins Feux sur l'Assassin* (61, Georges Franju); *Le Combat dans l'Île* (61, Alain Cavalier); *Le Jeu de la Vérité* (61, Robert Hossein); in the luxury episode from *Les Sept Péchés Capitaux* (62, Jacques Demy); *Il Sorpasso* (62, Dino Risi); *Château en Suède* (63, Vadim); *Mata-Hari, Agent H21* (64, Jean-Louis Richard); *The Sleeping Car Murders* (65, Costa-Gavras); *Le Dix-Septième Ciel* (66, Serge Korber); *La Longue Marche* (66, Alexandre Astruc); *Is Paris Burning?* (66, René Clément); *A Man and a Woman* (66, Claude Lelouch); *Col Cuore in Gola* (67, Tinto Brass); *Trans-Europ Express* (67, Alain Robbe-Grillet); *Mon Amour, Mon Amour* (67, Nadine Trintignant, his wife); *La Morte La Fatto l'Uovo* (67, Giulio Questi); *La Matriarca* (68, Pasquale Festa Campanile); *L'Homme qui Ment* (68, Robbe-Grillet); as the pusillanimous male object in *Les Biches* (68, Claude Chabrol); *Z* (68, Costa-Gavras); *Le Voleur de Crimes* (69, Trintignant); *Metti una Sera a Cena* (69, Giuseppe Patroni Griffi); as the man hesitating over *My Night at Maud's* (68, Eric Rohmer); *L'Américain* (70, Marcel Bozzuffi); *Le Voyou* (70, Lelouch); *L'Homme au Cerveau Greffé* (71, Doniol-Valcroze); as the treacherous journalist in *L'Attentat* (72, Yves Boisset); *Les Violons du Bal* (74, Michel Drach); and *Le Secret* (74, Robert Enrico). Trintignant had also directed his first film, *Une Journée bien Remplie* (72). He also appeared in *Le Mouton Enragé* (74, Michel Deville); *Voyages de Noces* (75, N. Trintignant); *Les Passagers* (76, Serge Leroy); *Repérages* (78, Michel Soutter); and *L'Argent des Autres* (78, Christian de Chalonge).

As he grew older, Trintignant stepped aside with ease to become a character actor, underplaying but commanding: *La Banquiere* (80, Francis Girod); *Malevil* (81, Chalonge); *Passione d'Amore* (81, Ettore Scola); *Eaux Profondes* (81, Deville); *Colpa al Cuore* (82, Gianni Amelio); *Le Bon Plaisir* (83, Girod); *Under Fire* (83, Roger Spottiswoode); *La Nuit de Varennes* (83, Scola); *Confidentially Yours* (83, Francois Truffaut); *Viva la Vie* (84, Lelouch); *Partir, Revenir* (84, Lelouch); *L'Eté Prochaine* (85, N. Trintignant); the director in *Rendezvous* (86, André Téchiné); *La Vallée Fantôme* (86, Alain Tanner); *Un Homme et une Femme: 20 Ans Déjà* (87, Lelouch); *Le Moustachu* (87, Dominique Chaussois); *Bunker Palace Hotel* (89, Enki Bilal); *Merci la Vie* (91, Bertrand Blier); and *Rouge* (94, Krzysztof Kieślowski).

He does smaller things now, but he has a distinct and distinguished presence: a voice in *The City of Lost Children* (95, Marc Caro and Jean-Pierre Jeunet); *C'est Jamais Loin* (96, Alain Centonze); *L'Insoumise* (96, Charlotte Silvera); *Tykho Moon* (96, Bilal); *Un Héros Très Discret* (96, Jacques Audiard); *Un Homme Est Tombé dans la Rue* (96, Dominique Roulet); *Ceux Qui M'aiment Prendront le Train* (98, Patrice Chereau).

François Truffaut (1932–84), b. Paris
1957: *Les Mistons* (s). 1958: *Une Histoire d'Eau* (codirected with Jean-Luc Godard) (s). 1959: *Les Quatre Cents Coups/The 400 Blows*. 1960: *Tirez sur le Pianiste/Shoot the Piano Player*. 1961: *Jules et Jim*. 1962: "Antoine et Colette," episode in *L'Amour à Vingt Ans*. 1964: *La Peau Douce/Soft Skin*. 1966: *Fahrenheit 451*. 1967: *La Mariée était en Noir/The Bride Wore Black*. 1968: *Baisers Volés/Stolen Kisses*. 1969: *La Sirène du Mississippi/Mississippi Mermaid; L'Enfant Sauvage*. 1970: *Domicile Conjugale/Bed and Board*. 1971: *Les Deux Anglaises et le Continent/Anne and Muriel*. 1972: *Une Belle Fille Comme Moi/A Gorgeous Bird Like Me*. 1973: *La Nuit Américaine/Day for Night*. 1975: *L'Histoire d'Adèle H./The Story of Adèle H.* 1976: *L'Argent du Poche/Small Change*. 1977: *L'Homme qui Aimait les Femmes/The Man Who Loved Women*. 1978: *La Chambre Verte/The Green Room*. 1979: *L'Amour en Fuite/Love on the Run*. 1981: *Le Dernier Mètro/The Last Mètro; La Femme d'à Côté/The Woman Next Door*. 1982: *Vivement Dimanche/Confidentially Yours*.

Truffaut made only a few films that are not flawed, several that have serious weaknesses in conception and realization, one or two content to treat the surface of a subject, but none without a youthful enthusiasm for movies. He treated material speculatively, in the way of an idealized Hollywood director in the days of constant production, priding himself on an ability to make any assignment beautiful and entertaining. Even in 1973, his own appearance as the director in *Day for Night* showed the unabashed attempt to think himself into Warner Brothers, *circa* 1943. One cannot deny the infectious charm of that attempt. But Truffaut was self-consciously enthusiastic, and that has dangers as well as virtues. Of course, he was very alert to the moods of young people, and especially of children; but his work is curiously short of people over the age of forty. Overall, I think his continued leaning on American cinema misled him or kept him from a more interesting personality.

Youthfulness made all his films like debuts. Truffaut might have adopted the policy of making some films as throwaways. That frank diary on the making of *Fahrenheit 451* so eagerly hunts through his own feelings about cinema that it could easily have included some such rationalization of the disaster on which he was engaged. Like Charlie in *Shoot the Piano Player*, and the Jean-Pierre Léaud character, Truffaut talked to himself as he lived, daring himself to take action, gambling on the consequences.

He was a key figure in the New Wave: for his vigorous articles in *Arts* and *Cahiers du Cinéma;* for *The 400 Blows*, an autobiographical movie that securely tied the new films to Renoir, Vigo, and the French tradition of location shooting, flowing camera, and offhand lyricism; but also because of his role as instigator of new projects. Truffaut was the source of the idea for *Breathless* (59, Jean-Luc Godard); the coproducer of *Paris Nous Appartient* (60, Jacques Rivette); and writer and producer of the remake of Renoir's *Tire au Flanc* (62, Claude de Givray). That spearhead activity was accentuated by *The 400 Blows*'s prize at Cannes and by the popular success of *Jules et Jim.*

But that should not disguise the theme of privacy in his films. Truffaut had an instinct for timidity and shyness, especially in characters who harbor overwhelming feelings. His most fruitful way of making films was to show the tragi-comic consequences of restrained, smothered, or diverted impulses; and his most serious insight—coming in *Deux Anglaises* and *Jules et Jim*—is that emotion is expressed more openly in art than in life. Time and again, he dealt with people unable to express themselves: the reticence of Charlie in *Shoot the Piano Player;* the delinquent isolation of the boy in *The 400 Blows* (Truffaut was himself

only kept from an institution by the good offices of André Bazin); the unexpected charm of Cyril Cusack's reserved captain in *Fahrenheit 451;* the way in *La Sirène* that Belmondo conceals his knowledge so as not to disturb his fatal relationship with Deneuve; the intractability of the boy in *L'Enfant Sauvage;* the way that *La Mariée* is undermined by our being drawn to see the depths within the ostensibly odious Michel Bouquet character; the somber aloofness and gusts of silent tenderness in Muriel in *Deux Anglaises;* Catherine in *Jules et Jim* taking Jim away into a world she commands, that of death.

In his first three films, Truffaut showed a vital ability to disclose offhand intimacy, to mingle laughter and tears, and to make the shape of his films flexible. *Shoot the Piano Player* was the sort of film Laurence Sterne might have made, and generally Truffaut neglected his skill at stretching the form of a movie—though structural surprise is wonderfully employed in *Les Deux Anglaises.* The speed of farce chasing pathos was very influential, not least on the writers of *Bonnie and Clyde.* In *Jules et Jim,* Truffaut formed his most fruitful collaboration, with the novelist Henri-Pierre Roché, author of *Les Deux Anglaises* and of a situation dear to Truffaut—the passionate triangle in which three people are trapped, all in love with all, all reluctant to hurt the others.

With such an inheritance from Renoir, Truffaut dragged himself toward Hitchcock. It was a sign of his intellectual earnestness that he worked so hard to admire a man far from his own feelings. *Le Cinéma selon Alfred Hitchcock* is not a successful book simply because the two men so seldom occupy common ground. The interviewer's attempts to make Hitch confess to his greatness and Hitch's whimsical reluctance are very funny and the sort of scene Truffaut might have invented. There is the same self-exposure in the diary on *Fahrenheit 451,* a film that splits apart on the director's inadequate English, on his bewilderment at the way in which former companion Oskar Werner turned into a self-interested actor, but chiefly because the abstraction of science fiction was alien to Truffaut's commitment to behavior. That is his worst film. But *Soft Skin* is as muddled and not helped by clumsy resort to melodrama. *La Mariée était en Noir* is another misguided effort at revealing Hitchcock, a film based on a concept of vengeance that Truffaut is too kind to share.

There was therefore a serious and prolonged lapse in his work. *Baisers Volés* and *Domicile Conjugale* are minor films, reprising the boy from *400 Blows* but without firsthand reflections from Truffaut's own life. They are vehicles for Léaud, and the worse for that. But with Delphine Seyrig in the first he at least rediscovered his contact with actresses, an ability he has always cherished and that sustains a film like *Une Belle Fille Comme Moi.*

But Truffaut also made three films that considerably enlarged his talent. *Mississippi Mermaid* actually masters Hitchcockian themes and turns into a rhapsody on a fatal obsession, largely because of the way it defines solitariness in the Belmondo character; *L'Enfant Sauvage* is a limpid account of wildness being schooled, based on fact and with Truffaut himself playing the teacher. Best of all, however, is *Les Deux Anglaises et le Continent*, a story of "Proust and the Brontë Sisters," sure of period and place, so beautifully acted by Kika Markham and Stacey Tendeter that Léaud's coldness is not a handicap. Because its central character is a writer, Truffaut was able to use interior monologue and to measure the gulf between art and reality. In *La Mariée était en Noir*, someone speaks of "happy fools and unhappy fools," being the generality of human beings. That wistfulness is the real Truffaut, and *Les Deux Anglaises* goes a step further—to present the intelligent fool and the passionate fool. Death comes very often in Truffaut as the only resolution to misunderstanding. It always leaves one character looking back, indelibly marked by the loss, the recollection of missed chances and the perspective that shows people passing in the dark. By implication, or in fact, that character is an artist.

It may seem churlish to carp at so enjoyable a film as *Day for Night*. But it was the work of a man in his forties, and it did precede an announced, short retirement from films. No question of the facility of *Day for Night*, the pleasure with all cinema's tricks and the way that it makes them clear to a lay audience. But it is best on first viewing. The characters in the film lie very near the surface. The mood seems playful after *Contempt*.

It seemed likely, and necessary, that the confessional summary of *Day for Night*, (like a young conjurer revealing his apparatus), and his self-imposed two-year withdrawal from movies, would mark a change and a maturing in Truffaut. In the event, one can see loss of fluency and verve and a withering onset of doubt and melancholy. To grow old is inescapable; yet perhaps Truffaut's artistic sensibility was a matter of deliberate youthful enthusiasm—something appreciated by Steven Spielberg when he cast him as the wide-eyed master of ceremonies in the great light show of *Close Encounters of the Third Kind* (77).

Truffaut's own films became less compelling. *Adèle H.* is a begging subject about demented and unwarranted obsession; Isabelle Adjani possesses the bursting emotional energy for it. But Truffaut's earlier studies in obsession had been from the stance of a shy, rational observer who admired the overthrow of common sense but could not partake of it. *Adèle H.* needed complicity from its director. Without it, the girl's *amour fou* seemed

merely silly, a folly disapproved of by the chilly, tense style. It needed the compassionate severity of Bresson or the adoration of a Borzage; it needed mad humor and self-sufficient lyricism; the girl should become a demon, whereas Truffaut couldn't quite justify her as a victim. He fumbled dialogue, the contrasting locations, and even one of his earlier strengths: the lonely writing to the dark outside world.

Small Change was horribly cute, and seemed like an attempt to revive box-office memories of his former success with kids. It is a facile collage about the vitality and preciousness of childhood, but spoiled by its creeping sense of adult nostalgia and sentimentality. Still, nothing prepared one for the sheer nastiness of *The Man Who Loved Women*. Unaccountably in Truffaut, the movie disdained women and refrained from crushing the reptilian self-regard of its hero, a heartless womanizer on his way to writing a book.

He died young, of a brain tumor, after the great box-office success of *The Last Mètro,* and two last, minor films that starred Fanny Ardant, with whom he had a child in the last year of his life. Since his death, a collection of his letters has been published to remind us of his intelligence as writer. Whether or how well his films will last remains to be seen. Whatever the answer to that question, for many people who love film Truffaut will always seem like the most accessible and engaging crest to the New Wave.

Stanley Tucci, b. Katonah, New York, 1960
1996: *Big Night* (codirected with Campbell Scott).
1998: *The Impostors*. 2000: *Joe Gould's Secret.*

Joe Gould's Secret did no business, and that may bring down the shutters on Tucci's career as a director—no matter that it was a far more intriguing picture than the feel-good, eat-good *Big Night*. If the bonhomie of the first film seemed superficial, the chill in the third was authentic and disturbing. Indeed, it was one of the better films about writing as a way of life, a good glancing portrait of the smug club called *The New Yorker,* as well as a fond yet fearful picture of the incipient madness in Gould. There was a tenderness and respect, akin to one actor's awe for the remarkable performance from Ian Holm as Gould. One should add that *The Impostors* was a well-handled farce, enough to suggest that the modest Tucci possesses a skill that might seem dazzling today— if he chose to work in any of the brutal genres so popular with the young.

Of course, Tucci is an actor, too, deft enough a lot of the time to let us forget he is Italian (in an age when all Italians get their Equity card at birth, it seems). He has been seen, to increasing effect, in *Prizzi's Honor* (85, John Huston); *Monkey Shines* (88, George Romero); *Billy Bathgate* (91, Robert Benton); *Men of Respect* (91, William

Reilly); *Beethoven* (92, Brian Levant); *In the Soup* (92, Alexander Rockwell); *Prelude to a Kiss* (92, Norman René); *The Public Eye* (92, Howard Franklin); *The Pelican Brief* (93, Alan J. Pakula); very funny in *Undercover Blues* (93, Herbert Ross); *It Could Happen to You* (94, Andrew Bergman); *Somebody to Love* (95, Rockwell); *The Daytrippers* (96, Greg Mottola); *Deconstructing Harry* (97, Woody Allen); *A Life Less Ordinary* (97, Danny Boyle); *The Alarmist* (98, Evan Dunsky); as the lead for TV in *Winchell* (98, Paul Mazursky); as Eichmann for TV in *Conspiracy* (01, Frank Pierson); *America's Sweethearts* (01, Joe Roth); Frank Nitti in *Road to Perdition* (02, Sam Mendes); *Maid in Manhattan* (03, Wayne Wang); *The Core* (03, Jon Amiel).

Kathleen Turner,

b. Springfield, Missouri, 1954

Miss Turner has angry eyes. I thought so when she first appeared, in *Body Heat* (81, Lawrence Kasdan). No matter how obliging, overwarm, and available her Matty made herself in that film, didn't the eyes warn us of danger and intrigue too heady for Ned Racine? She could not keep the warning light of Femme Fatale out of her eyes. It was still there, at the end, when Matty is tanning in her listless paradise. She should have stayed home and fed on weak men forever.

It was a remarkable debut, a begging part in a clever, funny celebration of male disaster. Along with her eyes was a voice that had an unaccountable harshness—did it come from the years spent in Latin America as her diplomat father got posted around? There was a strength in the woman that seemed likely to break out. It was not entirely comfortable, and the career has been hard to track.

She was aloof, adulterous, and headachy in *The Man With Two Brains* (83, Carl Reiner), and she did her best with the designer by day and hooker by night in *Crimes of Passion* (84, Ken Russell) and the awful *A Breed Apart* (84, Philippe Mora). Then came the big-contract role of the romance novelist in *Romancing the Stone* (84, Robert Zemeckis) and *The Jewel of the Nile* (85, Lewis Teague), where she entered into the robust physical comedy adventure with a will, and consequently had less time to smolder.

In *Prizzi's Honor* (85, John Huston) she seemed rather more natural killing or lying than making love—but it was a tough task to make that gimmicky character credible, and anyone would have had a hard time stopping our hope that Mae Rose was going to get some more scenes. In *Peggy Sue Got Married* (86, Francis Ford Coppola) there was the real burden of having to be nice and sweet, without too much irony, for a director who has a poor record with women on screen. She was also a late replacement for Debra Winger.

She went to Italy to make *Giulio and Giulia* (87, Peter Del Monte), she tried to redo Rosalind Russell in *Switching Channels* (88, Ted Kotcheff), and she had the unappealing role of the wife in *The Accidental Tourist* (88, Kasdan). Neither of these was as fun, or as wicked, as the donation of her voice to Jessica Rabbit in *Who Framed Roger Rabbit?* (88, Robert Zemeckis)—the kind of sexpot ball-breaker she was made for. She seemed to spring to her full potential in *The War of the Roses* (89, Danny DeVito), a mess of a picture but an uncommon view of marital recrimination. All of a sudden it was possible to think of Turner playing Strindberg or Ibsen. She has acquired the reputation of being difficult—but was it difficult or adventurous to hope to play the nun in a film of Robert Stone's *A Flag for Sunrise*? She has a power, a capacity for outrage, that is not likely to be indulged in America. *V. I. Warshawski* (91, Jeff Kanew) is no answer to what she might do: playing a slob, "a female dick," only dulls Turner's rare harshness. She is so much more startling as a lady whose fire flares up. That anger could yet leave her a figure of little but empty fun. Where do strong American actresses go at forty, when there are so many soft twenty-year olds coming along?

She played the mother in *House of Cards* (93, Michael Lessac) and was in *Undercover Blues* (93, Herbert Ross). Neither made an impact, but Turner was in her gutsy element—wicked and demure—giving cartoony muscle to the feeble plot of *Serial Mom* (94, John Waters).

And now the anger seemed explained. For, in her forties, Turner was pushed into television more often, and eased down the cast list. There were some bad films, and some that no one ever saw. But the belligerence and the daring never backed off. What we were seeing was age—not an unnatural thing: *Naked in New York* (94, Dan Algrant); *Leslie's Folly* (94), a TV movie about a very unhappy woman—Anne Archer—directed by Turner herself; *Moonlight and Valentino* (95, David Anspaugh); *A Simple Wish* (97, Michael Ritchie); *Legalese* (98, Glenn Jordan); the Snow Queen in *Stories from My Childhood* (98); a mad psychologist breeding *Baby Geniuses* (99, Bob Clark); *The Virgin Suicides* (99, Sofia Coppola); *Cinderella* (00, Beeban Kidron); *Prince of Central Park* (00, John Leekley): *Delilah* (00, Radha Bharadway).

In addition there was an overtrumpeted nude scene on the stage as Mrs. Robinson in *The Graduate,* and her pièce de résistance—Chandler's father in *Friends.*

Lana Turner (Julia Jean Mildred Frances Turner) (1920–95), b. Wallace, Idaho

What executive aberration was it that, for the best years of her career, put Lana Turner under contract to MGM? That studio revered ladies, while

Turner had the unanimated, sluggish carnality of a thick broad on the make. No actress, always inclined to veil her nature in the posturing of melodrama, she was close to the spirit of small-town waitresses ready to be picked up by a tooth-brush salesman with a cousin in casting. Her private life only proved that a dull face could have a tempestuous romantic passage. Had she been at Warners, like Ann Sheridan—they looked very alike, though Turner lacked Sheridan's fun—she might have been much more impressive as a moll waiting for a light. At MGM, the studio usually seemed reluctant to lay hands on her. To add to that impression she was often dressed in burning white.

Ironically, she was discovered working in a Los Angeles drugstore and put under contract at Warners: *They Won't Forget* (37, Mervyn Le Roy); *The Great Garrick* (37, James Whale); and *Four's a Crowd* (38, Michael Curtiz). She moved to MGM and was idling in minor films—*Love Finds Andy Hardy* (38, George Seitz); *Dramatic School* (38, Robert B. Sinclair)—when the studio began to promote her as the "Sweater Girl." The blanc-mange in the sweater, her exhausted sultriness and floppy hair let her seep into public conscious-ness: killed off as the trouper prepared to sell her-self in *Ziegfeld Girl* (41, Robert Z. Leonard); marooned as the English ingenue when Ingrid Bergman swapped her for the floozy in *Dr. Jekyll and Mr. Hyde* (41, Victor Fleming); attempting to imitate Jean Harlow opposite Gable in *Honky Tonk* (41, Jack Conway); *Johnny Eager* (41, Le Roy); *Somewhere I'll Find You* (42, Wesley Rug-gles); *Slightly Dangerous* (43, Ruggles); *Marriage Is a Private Affair* (44, Leonard); *Keep Your Pow-der Dry* (44, Edward Buzzell); *Weekend at the Waldorf* (45, Leonard); most notably as the mur-derous adulteress in *The Postman Always Rings Twice* (46, Tay Garnett), a film that showed how clearly Turner might appeal to the feckless, frus-trated wives of redneck America. Imagine a girl like Turner seeing a film like that . . . almost casu-ally, hack culture could be deeply revealing.

After the war, her fortunes declined with *Cass Timberlane* (47, George Sidney); *Green Dolphin Street* (47, Victor Saville); *Homecoming* (48, Le Roy); *The Three Musketeers* (48, Sidney); and *A Life of Her Own* (50, George Cukor). By now, she was something of a problem for MGM and, apart from being admirably used as a film star in *The Bad and the Beautiful* (52, Vincente Minnelli), she was displayed in trite costume films: *The Merry Widow* (52, Curtis Bernhardt); *Latin Lovers* (53, Le Roy); *The Flame and the Flesh* (54, Richard Brooks); *The Prodigal* (55, Richard Thorpe); and *Diane* (55, David Miller). At Warners, she was excess baggage on *The Sea Chase* (55, John Far-row).

She moved on to Fox where she played in *The Rains of Ranchipur* (55, Jean Negulesco) and as the mother with an illegitimate daughter in *Pey-ton Place* (57, Mark Robson). She was exactly right in that mixture of social anxiety and sexual gossip, and in 1958 her own life mimicked Grace Metal-ious. Her daughter, Cheryl Crane, killed Johnny Stompanato, a small-time gangster and Turner's lover.

There was public alarm, but Ross Hunter at Universal smelled the lust for sensation and cast her as a movie actress confronted by troublesome children in *Imitation of Life* (59, Douglas Sirk). She is as blatant and mediocre in that as ever; but that exactly suits Sirk's adaptation of melodrama to social comment. As with *The Postman Always Rings Twice,* it is hard to believe that a more accomplished actress could have expressed so much about the uneasy pursuit of respectability.

Imitation of Life was a big success, but it was her swan song. Subsequent films only showed how quickly her looks went puffy: *Portrait in Black* (60, Michael Gordon); *By Love Possessed* (61, John Sturges); *Bachelor in Paradise* (61, Jack Arnold); *Who's Got the Action?* (62, Daniel Mann); *Love Has Many Faces* (64, Alexander Singer); *Madame X* (65, David Lowell Rich); *The Big Cube* (69, Tito Davison); and *Persecution* (74, Don Chaffey).

She has acted in *Bittersweet Love* (76, Miller) and *Witches' Brew* (80, Richard Shorr). But nei-ther of these offers a fraction the value of Cheryl Crane's book, *Detour*, published in 1988.

John Turturro,
b. Brooklyn, New York, 1957

Turturro has demonstrated enough quirky bril-liance for us to hunt down his performances as once we did those of Peter Lorre or Warren Oates. He lacks the looks or bearing likely to be cast in American leading roles, but that only reminds us of how great character actors are time and again the way to more adventurous movies. With enough real people around, stars, hams, bal-loons, and mirrors sometimes have to shape up.

Turturro is an East Coast actor, to such an extent that it sometimes seems as if he is as essen-tial as the Teamsters and Danny Aiello to films coming out of New York: allegedly in *Raging Bull* (80, Martin Scorsese); *Exterminator II* (84, Mark Buntzman); *The Flamingo Kid* (84, Garry Mar-shall); *Desperately Seeking Susan* (85, Susan Sei-delman); *To Live and Die in L.A.* (85, William Friedkin); as a pool player in *The Color of Money* (86, Scorsese); *Gung Ho* (86, Ron Howard); *Han-nah and Her Sisters* (86, Woody Allen); *Off Beat* (86, Michael Dinner); *The Sicilian* (87, Michael Cimino); as the threat in *Five Corners* (88, Tony Bill); *Do the Right Thing* (89, Spike Lee); *Back-track* (90, Dennis Hopper); *Men of Respect* (90, William Reilly); magnificent as the betrayer in *Miller's Crossing* (90, Joel and Ethan Coen); *Mo'*

Better Blues (90, Lee); State of Grace (90, Phil Joanou); Jungle Fever (91, Lee); a cross between George S. Kaufman and Eraserhead in Barton Fink (91, Coens); Brain Donors (91, Dennis Dugan); Fearless (93, Peter Weir); and Being Human (94, Bill Forsyth).

He has already directed a film, Mac (92), in which he also acts. Then a few years later he made the adventurous Illuminata (98)—about turn-of-the-century theatre.

Still, it is his acting, and his range, that are most admirable. Time and again he makes interesting choices: very good as Herbie Stempel in Quiz Show (94, Robert Redford); Search and Destroy (95, David Salle); Unstrung Heroes (95, Diane Keaton); Clockers (96, Lee); as Sam Giancana in Sugartime (95, John N. Smith); Girl 6 (96, Lee); The Search for One-Eye Jimmy (96, Sam Henry Kass); Box of Moon Light (96, Tom DiCillo); Grace of My Heart (96, Allison Anders); as Primo Levi in The Truce (96, Francesco Rosi); Lesser Prophets (97, William DeVizia); Animals (97, Michael DiJiacomo); The Big Lebowski (98, Coen); O.K. Garage (98, Brandon Cole); He Got Game (98, Lee); Rounders (98, John Dahl); as Allen Ginsberg in The Source (99, Chuck Workman); Cradle Will Rock (99, Tim Robbins); O Brother, Where Art Thou? (00, Coen); Two Thousand and None (00, Arto Paragamian); The Luzhin Defence (00, Marleen Gorris); The Man Who Cried (00, Sally Potter); 13 Conversations About One Thing (01, Jill Sprecher); as Howard Cosell in Monday Night Mayhem (01, Ernest R. Dickerson).

Frank Tuttle (1892–1963), b. New York
1922: The Cradle Buster. 1923: Puritan Passions; Second Fiddle; Youthful Cheaters. 1924: Grit; Dangerous Money. 1925: A Kiss in the Dark; Miss Bluebeard; Lucky Devil; The Manicure Girl; Lovers in Quarantine. 1926: The American Venus; Kid Boots; Love 'Em and Leave 'Em; The Untamed Lady. 1927: Blind Alleys; One Woman to Another; The Spotlight; Time to Love. 1928: Easy Come, Easy Go; His Private Life; Love and Learn; Something Always Happens; Varsity. 1929: The Greene Murder Case; The Studio Murder Mystery; Sweetie. 1930: The Benson Murder Case; Her Wedding Night; Love Among the Millionaires; Men Are Like That; Only the Brave; Paramount on Parade (codirected); True to the Navy. 1931: No Limit; It Pays to Advertise. 1932: This Reckless Age; The Big Broadcast; This Is the Night. 1933: All the King's Horses; Roman Scandals. 1934: Springtime for Henry; Here Is My Heart. 1935: Two for Tonight; The Glass Key. 1936: College Holiday. 1937: Waikiki Wedding. 1938: Dr. Rhythm. 1939: Paris Honeymoon; I Stole a Million; Charlie McCarthy, Detective. 1942: This Gun for Hire; Lucky Jordan. 1943: Hostages. 1944: The Hour Before the Dawn. 1945:

The Great John L.; Don Juan Quilligan. 1946: Suspense; Swell Guy. 1950: Le Traqué. 1951: The Magic Face. 1955: Hell on Frisco Bay. 1956: A Cry in the Night. 1958: Island of Lost Women.

Tuttle is a sign of the quality of Paramount in the 1920s. There is no reason to build him up as an important director: he was subservient to fashion; none of his films has survived as more than a typical studio product; he was not entrusted with Paramount's most prestigious ventures. That is not to say that careful re-viewing would not disclose a brisk, sophisticated eye for glamour. Louise Brooks has remarked that Tuttle played comedy straight—this in the 1920s when so many emotions were underlined.

He came from Yale and Vanity Fair into the movies in the early 1920s and worked his way into Paramount as a writer: The Conquest of Canaan (21, Roy William Neill); and then on his two outstanding Allan Dwan/Gloria Swanson comedies, redolent of the vivacious shopgirl as an ingenious fighter in her own romantic cause—Manhandled (24) and Her Love Story (24). Tuttle's own films celebrated that Paramount heroine: four films with Bebe Daniels, including The Manicure Girl and Miss Bluebeard; Evelyn Brent in Love 'Em and Leave 'Em; Swanson in The Untamed Lady; several with Nancy Carroll, Florence Vidor, Louise Brooks, and Esther Ralston; and six with Clara Bow—Grit; Kid Boots (Eddie Cantor's first film); Her Wedding Night; Love Among the Millionaires; True to the Navy; and No Limit.

In the 1930s, Tuttle was inexplicably switched from these shining ladies to male-oriented pictures, chiefly Bing Crosby musicals, of which he directed five. In addition, he went to Goldwyn to put Cantor through Roman Scandals; and at Paramount he directed Jack Benny in College Holiday and made the first film of Hammett's The Glass Key, with George Raft. That glossy thriller harked back to two William Powell/Philo Vance films and looked forward to his most striking movie, made shortly before he left Paramount, This Gun for Hire, the first vision of the blond sheen of Ladd and Lake. Also worthwhile as a curiosity is The Magic Face, where Luther Adler plays a man who impersonates Hitler.

U

Liv Ullmann, b. Tokyo, 1939
1992: Sofie. 1995: Kristin Lavransdatter. 1996: Enskilda Samtal. 2000: Trolösa/Faithless.

There are circles and circles. I never saw more than a glimpse in a trailer of Liv Ullmann leading a band of children across the hillsides of Shangri-La in Lost Horizon (72, Charles Jarrott) singing

"The World Is a Circle." But I never went back for more. This was far from the idea of circularity and interchangeability in *Persona* (66, Ingmar Bergman). In that film, Ullmann plays Elizabeth Vogler, an actress made speechless on stage, who is taken to recuperate on an island by Nurse Alma, played by Bibi Andersson. Vogler/Ullmann makes barely a sound in the film. Though passive, she is dominating; her silence prompts Alma into a talkative breakdown. Silence became Bergman's last retort to life and the tragic dilemma of playing yourself. Ullmann's poignant face, staring often straight into the camera, carried the burden of the artist who feels unable to participate in life. Ullmann persuaded us that acting has left Elizabeth not a person but the changing effects of appearance. Thus the final dissolves of the two faces, showing the blending of activity and reflection. *Persona* is a magnificent recognition of meaninglessness, an artist/actress admitting that all her effort has been misled, that life is only a pretext for art. The clarity of this bleak message shows in the tragic sensibility of Ullmann's face, isolated from the other action. There is no suggestion of her acting in *Persona*, only the extraordinary, indefinite emotions of a photographed face—one of the greatest images in world cinema.

Ullmann is Norwegian, brought up in Canada during the war. She began as an actress in Stavanger and Oslo. Her first films were made in Norway, but her first non-Scandinavian films were ill-chosen, and she was too deeply touched by Bergman's attitudes (she had been his mistress), too prone to Elizabeth Vogler's lacunae, to tolerate Shangri-Las: *Fjols til Fjells* (57, Edith Kalmar); *Tonny* (62, Nils R. Muller); *Kort ar Sommaren* (62, Bjarne Henning-Jonsen); *De Kalte ham Skarven* (64, Erik Folke Gustavson); *Ung Flukt* (66, Kalmar); *Hour of the Wolf* (68, Bergman); *The Shame* (68, Bergman)—outstanding as the active wife, dismayed by her husband's lazy spite, a wonderful balance of feeling, remorse, and despair; *Passion* (70, Bergman); *An-Magritt* (69, Arne Skouen); as the anxious Swedish wife going to America in *Utvandrarna* (70, Jan Troell) and *Invandrarna* (70, Troell). After working on Fred Zinnemann's aborted *Man's Fate,* she made *Cold Sweat* (70, Terence Young); *Pope Joan* (72, Michael Anderson); *Cries and Whispers* (72, Bergman) and *Scenes from a Marriage* (73), Bergman's work for TV, in which she confirmed her international reputation; *Nybyggarna* (73, Troell); *40 Carats* (73, Milton Katselas); and pursuing Garbo as Queen Christina in *The Abdication* (74, Anthony Harvey).

She was an international figure now, thanks to appearances on the American stage and publication of a blithe rumination on being a great actress, *Changing*. On screen, she was the psychiatrist in *Face to Face* (75, Bergman), the figure of

civilian charity and regret in *A Bridge Too Far* (76, Richard Attenborough), and a cabaret artiste in *The Serpent's Egg* (77, Bergman). She was in *Couleur Clair* (77, François Weyergans), and the willing figure of dowdy self-effacement and grievance in *Autumn Sonata* (78, Bergman).

She had a cameo in *Players* (79, Harvey) and then played the widow seduced by her husband's lover in *Richard's Things* (80, Harvey); *Jacobo Timerman: Prisoner Without a Name, Cell Without a Number* (83, Linda Yellen); *The Wild Duck* (83, Henri Safran); *The Bay Boy* (84, Daniel Petrie); *Dangerous Moves* (84, Richard Dembo); *Let's Hope It's a Girl* (85, Mario Monicelli); *Gaby—A True Story* (87, Luis Mondoki); *La Amiga* (88, Jeanine Meerapfel); *The Rose Garden* (89, Fons Rademakers), as the attorney who defends Maximilian Schell on charges of having been a Nazi; and *Mindwalk* (90, Bernt Capra).

She acts less now—*The Ox* (91, Sven Nykvist); *The Long Shadow* (92, Vilmos Zsigmond); *Drømspel* (94, Unni Straume); *Zorn* (94, Gunnar Hellstrom)—but she directs more. *Faithless* is far and away the best of what she has done. It was scripted by Bergman, but he left Ullmann to direct it. One can only say that she delivered something that was a vital extension to Bergman's work, and a magnificent picture in its own right.

Edgar G. Ulmer (1900–72), b. Vienna
1929: *Menschen am Sonntag* (codirected with Robert Siodmak). 1933: *Damaged Lives.* 1934: *The Black Cat; House of Doom.* 1936: *Green Fields* (codirected with Jacob Ben-Ami). 1938: *The Singing Blacksmith.* 1939: *Moon Over Harlem.* 1942: *Tomorrow We Live.* 1943: *My Son, the Hero; Girls in Chains; Isle of Forgotten Sins; Jive Junction.* 1944: *Bluebeard.* 1945: *Out of the Night/Strange Illusion.* 1946: *Club Havana; Detour; The Wife of Monte Cristo; Her Sister's Secret; The Strange Woman.* 1947: *Carnegie Hall.* 1948: *Ruthless.* 1949: *I Pirati di Capri.* 1951: *St. Benny the Dip; The Man from Planet X.* 1952: *Babes in Bagdad.* 1954: *The Naked Dawn; Murder Is My Beat.* 1957: *Daughter of Dr. Jekyll.* 1959: *Hannibal* (codirected with Carlo Ludovico Bragaglia). 1960: *The Amazing Transparent Man; Beyond the Time Barrier.* 1961: *Antinea l'amante della Citta/Atlantis/The Lost Kingdom.* 1964: *Sette Contro la Morte/The Cavern.*

This list may include no more than a quarter of the output of one of the most fascinating talents in the worldwide labyrinth of sub-B pictures. Andrew Sarris once wrote that most of Ulmer's films "are of interest only to unthinking audiences or specialists in *mise en scène*." The contrast is at its most extraordinary in *The Naked Dawn,* a wretched Western plot made in a few days, but transformed by Ulmer's camera style. His sense of movement, of changing composition in elaborately long takes, and his ability to record confined action with utter clarity, all show a debt to Murnau. But the talent is quite personal and, on the strength of that film alone, one must think of Ulmer as a rich talent who became hopelessly tangled in the depths of the movie industry. Douglas Sirk pointed out that Ulmer illustrated Hollywood's cautious glee in confining any success to the form in which he was successful: thus, once Ulmer had made the most of quickies and cut-rate B pictures, he was confined forever.

He studied architecture at the Academy of Arts and Sciences in Vienna and was originally a stage designer for Arthur Nikisch and Max Reinhardt. By 1920 he had moved into films in Berlin and he also worked in Vienna with Alexander Korda. But his most important early work was as designer and assistant director for F. W. Murnau: *The Last Laugh* (24); *Tartuff* (25); and *Faust* (26). He accompanied Murnau to America and worked with him on *Sunrise* (27), *Four Devils* (28), *City Girl* (30), and *Tabu* (31). Meanwhile, in 1929 he had collaborated with Robert Siodmak on *Menschen am Sonntag.*

He remained in the United States after Murnau's death, working as a set designer in opera and with MGM. In 1933, he directed his first film and thus began a career with generally small, short-lived companies. In later years, he was forced overseas to find work and he directed in Mexico, Spain, Germany, and Italy. As a result, it is difficult to see even a fraction of his films, while it is likely that many have not survived. But, as well as *Naked Dawn,* these are remarkable: *The Black Cat,* a Universal adaptation of Poe with Karloff and Lugosi; *Isle of Forgotten Sins; The Strange Woman,* a Hedy Lamarr vehicle; *Ruthless,* with Zachary Scott carving his way to success; *The Man from Planet X,* an ingenious science-fiction exercise; and the consumptive look of John Carradine as *Bluebeard.*

Detour is beyond remarkable. Shot in six days, on the road and in wretched, cramped rooms, its attempt at a love story never stands a chance. The Tom Neal character is waiting for a nemesis, Ann Savage—were these actors, hoping for careers, or derelicts resolved to treat the idea of a movie with contempt? Six-day B pictures may be horribly limited, but they were wide open, too—if an Ulmer could make a film that fast it might emerge dripping with disgust.

Sir Peter Ustinov, b. London, 1921

1946: *School for Secrets.* 1947: *Vice Versa.* 1949: *Private Angelo* (codirected with Michael Anderson). 1961: *Romanoff and Juliet.* 1962: *Billy Budd.* 1965: *Lady L.* 1972: *Hammersmith Is Out.* 1983: *Memed My Hawk.*

There is an ostentatious, dilettante laziness in the way Ustinov handles his varied talents. In a casual setting—such as a television conversation—he can appear charming, witty, and immensely entertaining. But on film, his variety has tended to lead to shallowness and waste. As a director, he seems diffident; as an actor, a show-off. In the first, he is eclectic and basically sentimental—that blurs the stark potential of *Billy Budd,* just as much as it clogs in *Romanoff and Juliet. Billy Budd* is sincere and unambiguous, but thrown off balance by the intensity of Robert Ryan's conception of Claggart. How often in films does the subtle portrayal of evil alter the meaning of a work. The camera becomes entranced by Ryan, whereas Melville's sublime prose watches everything as if from the foretop. Small but striking evidence of this is the way Ustinov adds to Melville by having Ryan's Claggart smile with satisfaction the instant before he dies from Billy's outraged blow. That small addition turns Claggart into an evil genius. The addition is striking, but a diminution of Melville.

Ustinov's comedy is only decoration, not a true response to life. As a player, he is basically a comic mimic. At dinner he might be captivating; in front of the camera he is an owl. It says a lot about the supporting actor Oscar that he won it twice: for *Spartacus* (60, Stanley Kubrick) and *Topkapi* (64, Jules Dassin). The difficulty lies in reminding oneself that it is really Ustinov as the ringmaster in *Lola Montès* (55, Max Ophüls). For once there, he appeared as a fat, sly, austere man totally controlled by Ophüls's marvelous design.

As an actor, he has also played in *Hullo Fame* (40, Andrew Buchanan); *Mein Kampf, My Crimes* (40, Norman Lee); *The Goose Steps Out* (42, Basil Dearden and Will Hay); the priest in *One of Our Aircraft Is Missing* (42, Michael Powell); *The Way Ahead* (44, Carol Reed), for which he wrote the script; *Odette* (50, Herbert Wilcox); as Nero in *Quo Vadis?* (51, Mervyn Le Roy); *Hotel Sahara* (51, Ken Annakin); as Prinny in *Beau Brummel* (54, Curtis Bernhardt); *The Egyptian* (54, Michael Curtiz); *I Girovaghi* (56, Hugo Fregonese); *Les Espions* (57, Henri-Georges Clouzot); *The Sundowners* (60, Fred Zinnemann); *The Comedians* (67, Peter Glenville); *Hot Millions* (68, Eric Till); and *Blackbeard's Ghost* (68, Robert Stevenson). He worked for Disney again in *One of Our Dinosaurs Is Missing* (75, Stevenson) and *Treasure of Matecumbe* (76, Vincent McEveety). He was a mock villain in *The Last Remake of Beau Geste* (77, Marty Feldman) and a detective in *Death on the Nile* (78, John Guillermin). He played in *Doppio Delitto* (78, Steno) and *Ashanti* (79, Richard Fleischer).

He was in *Players* (79, Anthony Harvey); *The Great Muppet Caper* (81, Jim Henson); *Charlie Chan and the Curse of the Dragon Queen* (81, Clive Donner); as Hercule Poirot in *Evil Under* the Sun (82, Guy Hamilton); *Dead Man's Folly* (85, Donner); *Thirteen at Dinner* (85, Lou Antonio); and *Appointment With Death* (88, Michael Winner), both as Poirot again; *La Revolution Française* (89, Robert Enrico and Richard T. Heffner); and a rather stuffy expert in *Lorenzo's Oil* (92, George Miller).

He was Grandfather in *The Old Curiosity Shop* (94, Kevin Connor); *The Phoenix and the Magic Carpet* (95, Zoran Perisic); *Stiff Upper Lips* (98, Gary Sinyor); the Walrus in *Alice in Wonderland* (99, Nick Willing); the voice of Old Major in *Animal Farm* (99, John Stephenson); *The Bachelor* (99, Sinyor); William IV in *Victoria & Albert* (01, John Erman); *Salem Witch Trials* (01, Joseph Sargent).

V

Roger Vadim (Roger Vadim Plemiannikov) (1928–2000), b. Paris
1956: *Et Dieu Créa la Femme/And God Created Woman*. 1957: *Sait-on Jamais?/When the Devil Drives; Les Bijoutiers du Clair de Lune/Heaven Fell That Night*. 1959: *Les Liaisons Dangereuses*. 1960: *Et Mourir de Plaisir/Blood and Roses*. 1961: *Le Bride sur le Cou;* "*L'Orgeuil*," an episode from *Les Sept Péchés Capitaux*. 1962: *Le Vice et la Vertu/Vice and Virtue; Le Repos de Guerrier/Warrior's Rest*. 1963: *Château en Suède*. 1964: *La Ronde*. 1966: *La Curée/The Game Is Over*. 1968: "*Metzengerstein*," an episode from *Histoires Extraordinaires; Barbarella*. 1971: *Pretty Maids All in a Row; Hellé*. 1973: *Don Juan 1973 ou Si Don Juan Etait une Femme/Don Juan or If Don Juan Were a Woman*. 1974: *La Jeune Fille Assassinée/Charlotte*. 1976: *Une Femme Infidèle*. 1980: *Night Games*. 1982: *Hot Touch*. 1983: *Surprise Party*. 1987: *And God Created Woman*. 1988: an episode from *Deadly Nightmares*. 1994: *Amour Fou/Mad Love*.

It takes an empty-headed intellectual debauchee to enjoy so many pretty maids in the flesh and on celluloid, to watch them pass by him one after another, and yet persist with films that have all the suspended animation of a masturbatory dream. There was an idiot splendor once as Vadim turned cinema into his own seraglio, absurd enough to leave us stranded between envy and reproach.

The reality of sex (if such a thing still obtains) ought to be an interior exchanged emotion (these are the claims made by its makers), ridiculously glamorized and trivialized by naked, Cinema-Scopic eroticism. Sex in prospect, or healing retrospect; sex as a consumer product; as a magical idea—these are Vadim's preoccupations. Scolds claimed that he disrobed so many of his own conquests to taunt us, and to make his prowess notorious. But perhaps he made so many sumptuous

images to enable him to live in ideas. Human realities do not obtrude on his world, and there are depressing signs of an actual hostility to women as people, rather than the sex object that is possessed in the moment of being seen. This is what makes Vadim's *La Ronde* mechanical and uninhabited, a toy in wraps, and Ophüls's a perilous vehicle that carries fragile, uninsured people.

But even if you decide that Vadim's voyeurism is sad, sordid, and lifeless, it is also a universal corruption of humanity (so universal that it becomes normal), and deep in the heart of cinema. If it is possible that the majority of sexual activity in the world is notional and private—that is to say, not mutual, but enjoyed behind closed eyes—then Vadim is worthy of study. Perhaps he is the smudged meeting place of art cinema and the sort of uninhibited catering to erotic taste that darkness has always encouraged and that the cinema may yet discover as its commercial destiny. When the streets are painful and dangerous, who is to deny the use of cinemas for lonely self-expression, where the flickering image gives a brief substance to dreams that lift intolerable pressures?

Is there an unalloyed warning to be made? *Pretty Maids All in a Row* is, sociologically, a film of disturbing insights in that its central character—an amused Rock Hudson (once all that Universal allowed to the lovelorn)—does not separate his fucking of campus nymphets from his murder of them. Too unreal to know in bed, these chicks are plastic enough to be disposed of. The sexual idea in *Pretty Maids* has become psychotic, acting out the dismissal of human reality that has always been implied in the method. And yet the film is tritely playful and the succession of postpubic children are gilded by the loving photography of that veteran, Charles Rosher, who once caught the rapture of Janet Gaynor in *Sunrise*. *Pretty Maids* could only be excused by lacerating satire, but Vadim was always humorless, unable to discard his obsession with glamour. Attractiveness wastes away character, and leaves the horrifying insecurity of a world of appearances. Vadim's cinema bespeaks the isolation of the viewer.

There lies his interest: the sense of useless power stoked up in the spectator. Vadim created the Bardot legend. He began in movies as an assistant to Marc Allégret: *Blanche Fury* (47). And it was through Allégret, on *Futures Vedettes* (55), that he met Bardot. No doubt, he was sufficiently alert to tumescent fashion to see the coming relevance of such dumb glory. He made a blank, magnificent body aware that it was being watched and tolerant of the spectacle. In pinups, the girl knows that the man may be jacking-off (within touch however far away), and still she smiles, lips moist, with a maternal inability to be angry. Despite the farce of his Jane Fonda period, it is likely that *Klute* would not have been as frank had Vadim not taught her first to admire herself (*Barbarella*) and then to loathe that nihilist insight. Fonda brought Vadim his one moment of humor, making Barbarella a simpleton in the pleasure machine. But in *Klute,* as the call girl who looks at the time as she impersonates bliss in a salesman's arms, she might be sticking out her tongue at Vadim.

By all literary standards Vadim purveys rubbish. But on film, that leads one to ask, "Are widescreen displays of naked women rubbish, or am I the rubbish watching them?" Visually, his films are as adolescent and as imaginative—for what age is more imaginative?—as advertisements for body lotions and lingerie. Where he is of unavoidable importance for the horny humanist is in the emphasis on titillation of himself and his audience. He suggests that eroticism is superior to sex. We claim that it ought not to be. But if we have righteousness on our side, then perhaps he has accuracy. The sexiest woman in his work is Françoise Arnoul in *Sait-on Jamais?,* who hardly drops a garment. The resplendent nakedness of Bardot and Fonda—in *Et Dieu Créa la Femme, Bijoutiers du Clair de Lune, Le Repos de Guerrier, La Curée,* and *Barbarella*—is purely iconographic. He is instinctively a decadent, subordinating plot, people, and meaning to visual harmony. But in *Sait-on Jamais?,* at least, the hero who slips into Venetian intrigue from a Gerald McBoing-Boing film is a forerunner of Belmondo in *Breathless.* Otherwise, that film employs Venice and the Modern Jazz Quartet as modishly as he later resorted to Laclos, Sheridan le Fanu, and so many ladies, stripped bare but undiscovered. Most distressing is the publicity-conscious nastiness. Instinctively, Vadim always had a feeling for depraved taste: thus the pairing of Peter and Jane Fonda in *Histoires Extraordinaires* and the return to Bardot helplessly aged—for *Don Juan 73,* in bed with Jane Birkin in an effort to revive his jaded fantasies.

So many sexual revolutions (and catastrophes) left Vadim looking more of an anachronism. Thus, in 1987, when he was nudging sixty, his camera caressed Rebecca De Mornay in a forlorn remake of the Bardot movie that needed so much of 1956's innocence to seem daring.

Rudolph Valentino (Rodolpho Guglielmi di Valentina d'Antonguolla) (1895–1926), b. Castellaneta, Italy

In the summer of 1926, Valentino collapsed in New York. Doctors cut open that dreamed-of, sleek body and found peritonitis. It was an inoperable case, but when Valentino came round, according to Dos Passos in *U.S.A.,* he asked anxiously, "Well, did I behave like a pink powder puff?" That question still hangs in the air, even if Valentino himself is beyond comfort. For he had an extraordinary career, sufficient to bring out

huge crowds for his funeral, to persuade many women that he spoke to them from the grave, and to unsettle a rather dull, uninspired boy from the Italian countryside. There were at least three ways of interpreting Valentino.

1. He was the screen's great lover, who in five years and a dozen films carnalized the idea of the hero as a sexual weapon. Although he had his first great success in *The Four Horsemen of the Apocalypse* (21, Rex Ingram) and starred in *Uncharted Seas* (21, Wesley Ruggles), with Nazimova in *Camille* (21, Ray C. Smallwood), and in *The Conquering Power* (21, Ingram), this image was based principally on *The Sheik* (21, George Melford). In that he played an Arab who captures "a proud and spirited English girl." Rape is imminent for much of the film, and only gradually domesticated when the Sheik is wounded, nursed by the girl, and brought to see the desirability of marriage.

The banality is easy to mock, but it was the guileless credulity of so many feminine imaginations that explained Valentino's passionate following. *The Sheik* embodied the ambivalence of the cinema: offering to ravish callow minds with dreams of taboo glamour but eventually settling for social stability. It is worth recalling that the "English" girl in *The Sheik* is captured when masquerading as an Arab slave girl. Slavery, capture, peril, nurse, beloved, and wife—there is the nightly gamut of the middle-class Mrs., a safe, easeful journey, renewing hopes of excitement and restoring the lady's estimate of her own attractiveness. For Valentino, it meant a split personality: initially, the wild man, his body oiled, his eyes as hard as his penis; but finally, the wounded thruster, humbled, brought back to a calmer, subservient health and marriage.

2. Since, clearly, he was no actor, those immune to the dream reviled him. They chose first to regard him as a gigolo. Such interpretation emphasized his shady beginnings in America, from 1914 onward, as a café dancer, an extra in movies, a petty thief, and a flexible sexual opportunist. In time, they grasped the fact that the rapist was very insecure. His first marriage, to dancer Jean Acker, had reputedly never been consummated. After that, two women vied for control of him: Natacha Rambova, his second wife, and June Mathis, an executive at Metro. Mathis had been the brains behind *Four Horsemen* and she had insisted that Valentino play in it. Rambova was the art director on *Camille.* She increasingly dominated the Italian and, with Mathis, persuaded him to abandon Metro for Paramount, where *The Sheik* was made. After that, he played in *Moran of the Lady Letty* (22, Melford), with Gloria Swanson in *Beyond the Rocks* (22, Sam Wood), and as the bullfighter in *Blood and Sand* (22, Fred Niblo).

But then the two ladies urged him to insist on

greater freedom. First Mathis wrote *The Young Rajah* (22, Philip Rosen) for him and then Rambova persuaded him to set up as an independent with J. D. Williams, releasing through Paramount. She wrote and designed him into a more effeminate character in *Monsieur Beaucaire* (24, Sidney Olcott), *A Sainted Devil* (24, Joseph Henabery), and *Cobra* (25, Henabery). It transpired that Rambova had lesbian traits, but she only drew out qualities of homosexuality that had always been latent in Valentino. The agreement with Williams broke up, and Valentino moved to United Artists for two final, improved films: *The Eagle* (25, Clarence Brown) and *The Son of the Sheik* (25, George Fitzmaurice). But by then, male hostility had fastened on him. The faun stripling, author of silly poetry and tool of domineering women, was called "The Pink Powder Puff" in the press. Death rescued him from sordid scandal, thrust him instead into mythology, and, incidentally, saved him from the exposure that sound would have threatened. (Note that Jeanine Basinger reckons he might have turned into George Raft.)

3. The third view is Valentino's. For it seems likely that he was bewildered by his fame and the wealth of characters it opened up for him. His screen personality and his reputation are both inaccessible now because they depended upon the fashion of the moment. Men have always had an insecure hold on the camera, and male sex appeal vanished much quicker than the sway exerted by actresses. But Valentino was the original in an important line of screen heroes: the sexual androgyne, an icon for lovelorn ladies and for homosexuals alike. He is the first in a small but striking band of brilliantined exquisites that has included Presley, Mick Jagger, and the athletes from the Warhol stable.

Alida Valli (Alida Maria Altenburger), b. Pola, Italy, 1921

Without ever being compelling, Valli—as she was once known—has been in a number of fascinating, flawed movies. She had a promising debut in the Italian cinema with *Manon Lescaut* (39, Carmine Gallone); *Piccolo Mondo Antico* (40, Mario Soldati); *Luce nelle Tenebre* (40, Mario Mattoli); *Catene Invisibili* (41, Mattoli); and *Noi Vivi* (42, Goffredo Alessandrini), but went into hiding from the Fascists once she had refused further films.

In peace, she made *La Vita Ricomincia* (45, Mattoli) and *Eugenia Grandet* (46, Soldati) before David Selznick called her to America as an emblem of dark, continental fatalism. In fact, she was more brooding and reproachful than a femme fatale. Hitchcock muttered that Garbo would have been better for *The Paradine Case* (47), but Valli still managed to suggest baleful self-destructiveness and looked like a Latin Mrs. Danvers. After *The Miracle of the Bells* (48,

Irving Pichel), she gave a good portrait of vulnerable mixed origins as the Limestruck actress in *The Third Man* (49, Carol Reed). In close-up, she photographs very soulfully in that film and it was not her fault that Reed made her walk straight at the camera, rather than past it, obliquely, in the last shot.

Since then, she has worked nomadically: *Walk Softly, Stranger* (50, Robert Stevenson); *Les Miracles n'ont lieu q'une Fois* (50, Yves Allégret); *The White Tower* (50, Ted Tetzlaff); *Les Amants de Tolède* (52, Henri Verneuil); in an episode from *Siamo Donne* (53, Gianni Francolini); doing her best as the supposedly wanton countess in Visconti's *Senso* (54), but more eloquent as the woman humiliated by a fickle Farley Granger; deserted and harshly resentful in *Il Grido* (57, Michelangelo Antonioni); dourly inspecting Bardot's young body in *Heaven Fell That Night* (57, Vadim); *La Grande Strada Azzurra* (57, Gillo Pontecorvo); *The Sea Wall* (58, René Clément); *Le Dialogue des Carmélites* (59, Philippe Agostini); the procuress in *Eyes Without a Face* (59, Georges Franju); *Ophélia* (62, Claude Chabrol); *Une Aussi Longue Absence* (62, Henri Colpi); *Homenaje a la Hora de la Siesta* (62, Leopoldo Torre Nilsson); *The Happy Thieves* (62, George Marshall); *Il Disordine* (62, Franco Brusati); *Oedipus Rex* (67, Pier Paolo Pasolini); *The Spider's Strategy* (70, Bernardo Bertolucci); *The Antichrist* (74, Alberto De Martino); *The House of Exorcism* (75, Mario Bava); *1900* (75, Bernardo Bertolucci); *The Cassandra Crossing* (76, George Pan Cosmatos); *Suspiria* (76, Dario Argento); *Zoo Zero* (78, Alain Fleischer); and *La Luna* (79, Bertolucci).

She has also appeared in *Inferno* (80, Argento); *Aspern* (81, Eduardo de Gregorio); *Sezona Mira u Parizu* (81, Predrag Golubivic); *La Caduta degli Angeli Ribelli* (81, Mario Tullio Giordano); *Segreti, Segreti* (85, Giuseppe Bertolucci); *Jupon Rouge* (87, Genevieve Lefebvre); *Il Lungo Silenzio* (93, Margarethe von Trotta); *A Month by the Lake* (95, John Irvin); *Fatal Frames* (96, Al Festa); *Il Dolce Rumore della Vita* (99, G. Bertolucci); *Vino Santo* (00, Xaver Schwarzenberger); *L'Amore Probabilmente* (01, G. Bertolucci); *Semana Santa* (02, Pepe Danquart).

W. S. (Woodridge Strong) **Van Dyke** (1889–1943), b. San Diego, California

1918: *The Land of Long Shadows; Open Spaces; Men of the Desert; Gift o' the Gab.* 1919: *Lady of the Dugout.* 1920: *Our Little Nell.* 1922: *According to Hoyle; The Boss of Camp 4; Forget-Me-Not.* 1923: *The Destroying Angel; The Little Girl Next Door; The Miracle Makers.* 1924: *The Battling Fool; The Beautiful Sinner; Loving Lies; Gold Heels; Half-a-Dollar Bill; Winner Take All.* 1925: *Barriers Burned Away; The Desert's Price; Hearts* and Spurs; Ranger of the Big Pines; Timber Wolf; The Trail Rider. 1926: War Paint; The Gentle Cyclone. 1927: California; Eyes of the Totem; Foreign Devils; The Heart of the Yukon; Spoilers of the West; Winners of the Wilderness. 1928: Wyoming; Under the Black Eagle; White Shadows in the South Seas (begun by Robert Flaherty). 1929: The Pagan. 1931: Trader Horn; Never the Twain Shall Meet; Guilty Hands; Cuban Love Song. 1932: Tarzan, the Ape Man; Night Court. 1933: Penthouse; Eskimo; The Prizefighter and the Lady. 1934: Laughing Boy; Manhattan Melodrama; The Thin Man; Hide-Out; Forsaking All Others. 1935: Naughty Marietta; I Live My Life. 1936: Rose-Marie; San Francisco; His Brother's Wife; The Devil Is a Sissy; Love on the Run; After the Thin Man. 1937: Personal Property; They Gave Him a Gun; Rosalie. 1938: Marie Antoinette; Sweethearts. 1939: Stand Up and Fight; It's a Wonderful World; Andy Hardy Gets Spring Fever; Another Thin Man. 1940: I Take This Woman; I Love You Again; Bitter Sweet. 1941: Rage in Heaven; The Feminine Touch; Shadow of the Thin Man; Dr. Kildare's Victory. 1942: I Married an Angel; Cairo; Journey for Margaret.

"Woody" Van Dyke's was a prolific and eventful career, with rather more than three films a year for twenty-five years. He was held in some awe for the speed at which he worked and for his ability to complete a film against odds. In the early days of sound he had returned from Africa, after a great physical ordeal, with Trader Horn. And in 1938, when Norma Shearer was the dowager duchess at MGM, her cherished Marie Antoinette was given not to that tortoise, Sidney Franklin, but to the sprinting Van Dyke. Some even alleged that he was on a bonus for every day he finished under schedule. He was a trusted servant of MGM, able to turn his hand to most of the studio's idioms and to invent one of the most beguiling.

In his first days as a director—after serving as an actor and assistant to Griffith—he handled melodramas, Buck Jones and Tim McCoy Westerns, and when Flaherty resigned, his first Pacific adventure, White Shadows in the South Seas. Spoilers of the West and Wyoming were made simultaneously, at Selznick's behest. (They so satisfied the young producer that ten years later he hired Van Dyke to touch up the fencing scenes in The Prisoner of Zenda.)

After White Shadows and The Pagan, Van Dyke was the obvious choice for Trader Horn, and for the first Johnny Weissmuller Tarzan movie, which has a florid pleasure in well-lit muscle and plastic jungle. But in the 1930s, he was just as happy with cocktail-lounge romances: Myrna Loy in Penthouse; Loy and Max Baer in The Prizefighter and the Lady; Loy, William Powell, and Gable in Manhattan Melodrama (another Selznick film); Joan

Crawford in Forsaking All Others, I Live My Life, and Love on the Run. When Nelson Eddy and Jeanette MacDonald were teamed by Metro, he handled many of their musicals, indulging that airy warbling but gently spoofing it at the same time: Naughty Marietta; Rose-Marie; Sweethearts; Bitter Sweet; and I Married an Angel.

Add to that the assured balance of Gable, Tracy, MacDonald, and the near-Soviet montage of the earthquake in San Francisco, an Andy Hardy, a Kildare, the barmy Rage in Heaven; Mickey Rooney, Jackie Cooper, and Freddie Bartholomew together in The Devil Is a Sissy; the somber They Gave Him a Gun, starring Tracy and Franchot Tone—and still one has not reached his shrewdest moment. On Manhattan Melodrama, he had noticed that Loy and Powell worked together better than most other couples. He persuaded the studio to cast them as Nick and Nora Charles in The Thin Man, thus inaugurating one of the most entertaining of series, and one so successful that it went on after Van Dyke himself was dead. Van Dyke may have been only a fast worker, but the flippant exchanges of The Thin Man are long-lasting and the relationship in that film is both artificial and plausible, a very pleasing image of a happy marriage on the rocks.

Gus Van Sant, b. Louisville, Kentucky, 1953
1985: Mala Noche. 1987: Five Ways to Kill Yourself (s); Ken Death Gets Out of Jail (s); My New Friends (s). 1988: Junior (s). 1989: Drugstore Cowboy. 1991: My Own Private Idaho. 1994: Even Cowgirls Get the Blues. 1995: To Die For. 1997: Good Will Hunting. 1998: Psycho. 2000: Finding Forrester. 2002: Gerry. 2003: The Best of Bowie (co-directed); Elephant.

Van Sant's father was a traveling salesman, and so the boy had an itinerant upbringing, ranging through the Midwest into Colorado and California, and living in Connecticut, before settling in Portland, Oregon. He studied painting at the Rhode Island School of Design, but switched the emphasis of his studies to film. With a degree, he tried Los Angeles, where he did some commercials. But he decided to make Portland his base, and his Paris: there is something sublimely casual and confident in the way My Own Private Idaho moves from Portland to an empty road in Idaho to "Rome." Whatever else, Van Sant has established a view, a place, and an axis as his own.

Great claims have been made for Van Sant already: Donald Lyons has called Idaho the best American film of the nineties, daring anything else to top it. Moreover, Van Sant gives every sign of believing in the security of his independence as much as he cleaves to the sad, rain-swamped epic extent of the northwest. He has used "Hollywood" actors, but he keeps them shabby, quiet, and unglamorous—and he helps them be better than any system has allowed: Matt Dillon in *Drugstore Cowboy* and River Phoenix in *Idaho*. Van Sant is gay, gritty, and arty all at the same time. There is no trace of camp or swishiness: he is determined on heartfelt feelings and commonplace tragedy. He has a great eye, and an even better sense of adjacency—not quite cutting, but a feeling for cut-up simultaneity.

He has not yet made a film I find fully satisfying—or entirely without some lapse of judgment. But the characters and the potential are unquestioned. Whenever *Idaho* is dealing with the River Phoenix story, it has stirrings of greatness. Phoenix is superb (and there are moments when one gives him more credit than Van Sant), but the idea of his character—a troubled, gay hustler, searching for his mother, vulnerable to narcoleptic attacks, yet slow, patient, and decent—is Faulknerian. Why, I wonder, did Van Sant feel the need to crowd this character with the Keanu Reeves friend, altogether slicker and less substantial? And why did he persist with the whim of dragging the Falstaff story into this subplot? It's as if, half-drunk one night, Van Sant had seen *Chimes at Midnight* and resolved to pay tribute.

The two parts of the movie do not quite work or match, despite the bold flights of interaction and cross-cutting. The mannered attempt compromises the riveting authenticity of everything Phoenix does. Everything vital about the Reeves character could have survived the omission of Van Sant's northwest Falstaff, Bob, no matter how good a job William Richert does in the role.

This is a big disclaimer, but still *Idaho* has fine passages: the easy movement from neo-realism to dream to joke to flashback; the wondrous poetry of a blow-job orgasm that cuts to a whole house landing on the prairie (with all the resonance of *The Wizard of Oz*); the sense of gaudy and brash colors against the somber beauties of nature; the endless readiness for waywardness and the kindliness that gathers so many things in; and, of course, the acting.

But it hasn't worked out very well. *To Die For* is his best picture, very funny, rather sinister, with a wicked eye on suburbia, beautifully acted, and one of the first films in which Nicole Kidman was given her (and anyone else's) head. *Good Will Hunting* was Van Sant's biggest hit, but it shows a horrible lurch towards the sentimentality of saving lives and is one of the grossest examples of Robin Williams-ism. *Psycho* was bereft, insane and glaring evidence of someone uncertain where to go. And *Finding Forrester* was just another version of *Good Will Hunting*. In summary: it's very hard to know who Van Sant is, or what he wants to do.

Agnès Varda, b. Brussels, Belgium, 1928

1955: *La Pointe Courte*. 1957: *O Saisons, O Châteaux* (d). 1958: *L'Opéra-Mouffe* (s); *Du Côté de la Côté* (d). 1959: *La Cocotte d'Azur* (d). 1962: *Cléo de 5 à 7/Cleo from 5 to 7*. 1963: *Salut les Cubains* (d). 1965: *Le Bonheur*. 1966: *Les Créatures*. 1967: *Loin du Vietnam* (codirector) (d); *Elsa* (d). 1968: *Black Panthers* (d). 1969: *Lions Love*. 1975: *Daguerreotypes* (d). 1977: *L'Une Chante, l'Autre Pas/One Sings, the Other Doesn't; Réponses des Femmes* (TV). 1981: *Murs Murs* (d); *Documenteur: An Emotion Picture* (d). 1983: *Ulysse* (d). 1984: *Les Dites Caryatides* (d). 1985: *Sans Toit ni Loi/Vagabond*. 1988: *Jane B par Agnès V* (d); *Kung Fu Master*. 1991: *Jacquot de Nantes* (d). 1993: *Les Demoiselles Ont eu 25 Ans* (d). 1995: *The Universe of Jacques Demy* (d). 2000: *Les Glaneurs et la Glaneuse/The Gleaners and I* (d).

Before turning to movies, Agnès Varda was a successful and widely traveled photo-journalist. Her first feature, made when she was confessedly ignorant of movies, *La Pointe Courte*, was supposedly inspired by the parallel narratives of Faulkner's *The Wild Palms*. Because of that pointless imitation, and because Alain Resnais edited it, *La Pointe Courte*'s dullness has been obscured by its putative place as a forerunner of *nouveau roman* cinema.

But the photographer of *Marie-France* asserted herself in the glossy imagery and superficially sardonic commentary of *O Saisons, O Châteaux* and *Du Côté de la Côté*. The mordantly pregnant consciousness of *Opéra-Mouffe* was much more personal: scenes of the Mouffetard area of Paris through an expectant mother's eyes, but glibly intercut with an arty nude ballet. Varda was herself pregnant when the film was made, and its abrupt movement from disturbing slum reality to a chilly dreamlike romanticism proved typical of her work.

Opéra-Mouffe is also broken into sections, like the parts of a photographer's published oeuvre. It is all too easy to give such work the benefit of shape, to accept speculativeness as originality. *Cléo* certainly had a continuous shape, although it too is more photographs of two hours in a woman's life than an organic structure. It also balances uneasily a morbid and a sentimental view of the world and uses Cléo herself as another anxious but depersonalized lens, not pregnant but waiting for a medical verdict. *Salut les Cubains* was still photographs put to music. *Le Bonheur* was a startling piece of romantic wish-fulfillment put to Mozart. It is colorful, sweet, and cold—like dessert fresh out of the deep freeze. Admittedly its abandonment of social morality is novel, but it is still hard to see the movie as anything other than a shamelessly pretty intellectual shocker—not dealing with real people. Such beauty is hollow because it is won against no opposition. The eye that arranges those relentless harmonies and skin tones is irresponsible and facile. This failure looks especially odd beside the genuine rapture of the films made by her husband, Jacques Demy.

After *Le Bonheur*, Varda made *Les Créatures*, another elegant fantasy with the same lack of human perspective. *One Sings, the Other Doesn't* was a real step forward. Its feminist ardor was still led astray by prettification, but there was a new simplicity, a useful distance from the story and the dry narrative of the director herself that brought fiction and essay together.

Varda has stayed loyal to documentary, given the flavor of essay or even the charm of story-telling—as in *Jacquot de Nantes*, her tribute to the dying Jacques Demy. But easily her most powerful film of recent years—and probably her best ever—is *Vagabond*, the tracking of a fierce, willful outcast, set more surely on a path to death than Cléo ever contemplated. *Vagabond* burns in the memory, lucid and unsentimental, like the challenging gaze of Sandrine Bonnaire.

Conrad Veidt (Conrad Weidt) (1893–1943), b. Potsdam, Germany

Veidt was the most highly strung and romantically handsome of German expressionist actors. He was a creature from Poe's nightmares—tall, gaunt, glowing with a mixture of illness and ecstatic anxiety. Amid so many overweight actors, Veidt was an attenuated, hypersensitive figure, the aesthete or artist tormented by dark forces and driven to violence. His movements were deliberately slowed and prolonged, and the somnambulist Cesare in *Das Kabinett des Dr Caligari* (19, Robert Wiene) is one of the most influential performances in the history of fantasy and horror film. Veidt was supremely able to suggest the noble hero possessed by some torturing spirit. Thus the riveting first close-up of Cesare, a pale face and harrowed eyes, awakened from sleep; the rhythmic, boldly diagonal way he creeps along a wall to kidnap Lil Dagover; and the sense of emotional exhaustion in his collapse at the end of the chase. These are dancer's movements. Lotte Eisner speaks of the way in *Orlacs Hande* (24, Wiene) Veidt "dances a kind of Expressionist ballet, bending and twisting extravagantly, simultaneously drawn and repelled by the murderous dagger held by hands which do not seem to belong to him."

Veidt studied under Max Reinhardt and played on the Berlin stage before Richard Oswald encouraged him into films: *Das Ratsel von Banga-lor* (17, Paul Leni and Alexander Antalffy); *Die Seeschlacht* (17, Oswald); *Dida Ibsens Geschichte* (18, Oswald); *Das Tagebuch einer Verlorenen* (18, Oswald); *Es Werde Licht* (18, Oswald); *Prostitu-tion* (19, Oswald); *Satanas* (19, F. W. Murnau); before making *Caligari*. He worked in the full range of German cinema: in *Prinz Kuckuck* (19,

Leni); *Unheimliche Geschichten* (19, Oswald); the lead in Murnau's Jekyll and Hyde movie, *Der Januskopf* (20); in *Das Indische Grabmal* (21, Joe May); in the historic films—*Danton* (22, Dmitri Buchowetzki); *Lady Hamilton* (22), *Carlos und Elizabeth* (22), and *Lukrezia Borgia* (22), all by Richard Oswald; as Ivan the Terrible in *Waxworks* (24, Leni); in two Paul Czinner films, *Nju* (24) and *Der Geiger von Florenz* (26); in *Die Bruder Schel-lenberg* (26, Karl Grune); and an enormous success in *Der Student von Prag* (26, Henrik Galeen). In addition, he directed one film himself, *Lord Byron* (22).

He worked briefly in Italy—*Enrico I* (27); in Sweden—*Jerusalem* (27, Ernst Mattson); and in France—*Les Maudits* (27); before he took up an offer to play Louis XI to John Barrymore's François Villon in *The Beloved Rogue* (27, Alan Crosland). Veidt stayed in Hollywood for *The Man Who Laughs* (27, Leni), *A Man's Past* (27, George Melford), and *The Last Performance* (27, Paul Fejos). Back in Germany, he made an English-language version of *The Last Company* (30, Kurt Bernhardt), *Der Mann der den Mord Beging* (31, Bernhardt), and the German version of *Cape For-lorn* (30, E. A. Dupont). After *Rasputin* (30, Adolf Trotz), he played Metternich in *Der Kongress Tanzt* (31, Erich Charell) and then moved to England for *Rome Express* (32, Walter Forde) and *I Was a Spy* (33, Victor Saville). Back in Germany he was in *F.P.1 Antwortet Nicht* (32, Karl Hartl), *Der Schwarze Huzar* (32, Gerhard Lamprecht), *Ich und die Kaiserin* (33, Frederick Hollander), and *Wilhelm Tell* (34, Heinz Paul).

In England he made *The Wandering Jew* (33, Maurice Elvey) and *Bella Donna* (34, Robert Mil-ton) and while visiting Germany he was briefly detained—he had a Jewish wife and was about to make *Jew Süss* (34, Lothar Mendes). Thereafter he stayed in Britain for *The Passing of the Third Floor Back* (35, Berthold Viertel); *King of the Damned* (35, Forde); *Under the Red Robe* (37, Victor Sjöström); *Dark Journey* (37, Saville); went to Paris for *Tempête sur l'Asie* (38, Oswald) and *Jouer d'Echecs* (38); and returned to Britain for two films with Michael Powell and Emeric Press-burger, *The Spy in Black* (39) and *Contraband* (40). When war came, the Kordas shipped Veidt to the United States to play the vizier in *The Thief of Bagdad* (40, Powell, Tim Whelan, and Ludwig Berger), and he spent his last years playing Ger-mans in Hollywood films: *Escape* (40, Mervyn Le Roy); *A Woman's Face* (41, George Cukor); *The Men in Her Life* (41, Gregory Ratoff); *Whistling in the Dark* (41, S. Sylvan Simon); *All Through the Night* (41, Vincent Sherman); *Nazi Agent* (42, Jules Dassin); shot down on the phone in *Casablanca* (43, Michael Curtiz); and *Above Sus-picion* (43, Richard Thorpe).

Paul Verhoeven,

b. Amsterdam, Holland, 1938

1971: *Business Is Business* (TV). 1973: *Turks Fruit/Turkish Delight*. 1975: *Keetje Tippel*. 1977: *Soldier of Orange*. 1980: *Spetters*. 1984: *The Fourth Man*. 1985: *Flesh + Blood*. 1987: *Robocop*. 1990: *Total Recall*. 1992: *Basic Instinct*. 1995: *Showgirls*. 1997: *Starship Troopers*. 2000: *Hollow Man*.

Verhoeven was well into his forties before he came to work in America. But he has redefined himself, and in the space of a few years he has placed himself in the company of James Cameron and Tim Burton (nearly twenty years younger) as masters of modern sensation. Indeed, a case can be made that no immigrant has as fully embraced the New World since the days of Lang and Hitchcock.

He took a degree in math and physics at the University of Leiden and began to make short films for the Dutch Navy, and then for television. *Turkish Delight* got an Oscar nomination for best foreign film: it has Verhoeven's chief actor in Holland, Rutger Hauer, as a sculptor in a variety of erotic situations. Even then, there were some who saw a pornographer in Verhoeven. *Soldier of Orange* was a story about the Dutch resistance, with Hauer as a handsome hero. But in *Spetters*— a teenage story—sex was once more at the center, and Renee Soutendijk was the available beauty. She was the lead in *The Fourth Man,* a picture about a hairdresser who may be murdering her men—a film that Catharine Trammell might have researched.

Flesh + Blood was set in the sixteenth century; it was the director's first work in the English language; and it paired Hauer and Jennifer Jason Leigh. It promised very little. Since then, Verhoeven has made three authentic smash hits, all three violent, nasty, and flirting with the inhuman. Just as the two male protagonists in *Robocop* and *Total Recall* are more and less than men, so Sharon Stone's Catharine in *Basic Instinct* is most interesting as a blonde machine testing how far the absence of pity, morality, or consequence can take her. Verhoeven may not be all to blame for the incoherence of the picture, but does he notice such a problem when he has ice picks, orgasms, and what looks like a nearly bald pussy to stare at? The basic instinct toward which he may be working is that of lustrous impersonality.

That was 1994, and not bad as a prediction of *Showgirls* and *Starship Troopers*, which are twin versions of human nature being reappraised as plastic toys.

Dziga Vertov (Denis Arkadievitch

Kaufman) (1896–1954), b. Bialystock, Poland

All films are documentary: 1918–19: *Kino Nedelya/Cine Weekly* (forty-three editions). 1919: *Godovshchina Revolyutsii/Anniversary of the Revolution* (twelve episodes); *Boi pod Tsaritsynom*. 1920: *Vskrytie Moshchei Sergiya Radonezhskovo; Vserossiiskii Starosta Kalinin; Protsess Mironova*. 1921: *Agitpoezhd Vtsika/Train of the Central Executive*. 1922: *Istoriya Grazhdanskoi Voiny; Univermag; Protsess Eserov*. 1922–25: *Kino Pravda/Cinema Truth* (twenty-three editions). 1923: *Pyat let Borby i Pobedy*. 1923–25: *Goskino Kalendar* (fifty-five editions). 1924: *Kino Glaz/Camera Eye* (six episodes); *Dayesh Vozdukh; Segodnya; Sovetskie Igrushki; Grimaci Parizhi; Zhumoreski*. 1926: *Shagai, Soviet!/Stride, Soviet!; Shestaya Chast Mira/A Sixth of the World* (six episodes). 1928: *Odinnadtstyi/The Eleventh* (five episodes). 1929: *Chelovek s Kinoapparatom/Man with a Movie Camera*. 1930: *Entuziazm/Symphony of the Don Basin*. 1934: *Tri Pesni o Leninye/Three Songs of Lenin*. 1937: *Kolybelnaya/Lullaby; Pamyati Sergo Ordzhonikidzye*. 1938: *Slava Sovetskim Geroinyam; Tri Geroini*. 1941: *V Raionye Vysoty A; Krov za Krov, Smert za Smert; Na Linii Ognya-Operatory Kino-Khroniki/In the Line of Fire*. 1943: *Tebye Front*. 1944: *Klyatva Molodykh*. 1947–54: *Novosti Dnya/Daily News* (fifty-five editions).

There are Russian films that we will never see, and nobody made (or supervised) as many of them as Dziga Vertov. For that reason alone, we should be cautious about defining him. Nevertheless, he seems not only the director most engaged with the Constructivist enthusiasm to make a new art for a newly conscious people, but also the most appealing. *The Man with a Movie Camera* is more touching, more historically informative and comic than any Russian film of the period. Who can say what its influence has been? Godard fastened the Dziga Vertov flag to his mast, but in the spirit that the *Potemkin* ran up the red flag—as an emotional gesture of honorable intentions. Chris Marker tried to re-create the mobile film units that Vertov and Alexander Medvedkin organized. But Marker had always been a traveler. It is more likely that Godard had seen in Dziga Vertov the first apprehension of the documentary dilemma. For, like Godard, Dziga Vertov had an instinctive love of cinema and a relentless need to intellectualize and politicize that enthusiasm:

> We rise against the collusion between the "director-enchanter" and the public which is submitted to the enchantment . . .
>
> We need conscious people, not an unconscious mass, ready to yield to any suggestion.
>
> Long live the consciousness of the pure who can see and hear!
>
> Down with the scented veil of kisses, mur-

ders, doves and conjuring tricks!
Long live the class vision!
Long live Kino-Eye!

Trained as a musician and neurologist, Vertov was also a poet and journalist who had served in the Red Army. By 1918 he was involved on the Committee of Cinematography and, with Lev Kuleshov's encouragement, he took over *Cine Weekly* and formed the Kino-Eye group to launch a massive campaign of newsreel coverage of Russia. The result was one of the most exciting manifestations of the Revolution: an attempt to break down the social barriers by showing the life of Russians to other Russians. Dziga Vertov was part of the first flush of Constructivism and a disciple of Mayakovsky, but he blended education, propaganda, and artistic thrill better than any other Russian artist.

His group included his brother, Mikhail Kaufman, as cameraman, and Yelizaveta Svilova, his editor and wife. There was originally a dynamic tension between the two forces—photography and editing. Vertov loathed the theatre, staged events, and fiction in film. In part, he was rejecting a bourgeois mode, but Vertov had a genuine sense of observing life. He used a candid camera, filming undercover or from a distance, and he proudly went into the streets, the factories, and roamed across the interior of the Soviet Union. The tricks of the camera fascinated him: *Man with a Movie Camera* has split screen, dissolves, superimposition, slow motion, crude animation, and freeze frames. But it also contains some very beautiful and uncontrived footage of citizens caught unawares. That liveliness is still undiminished. It goes with Vertov's friendly eye for life, his irrepressible sense of humor, and the endearing insistence on the cameraman as a proletarian hero, a worker like any other, simultaneously recording and activating the Revolution.

Vertov also loved machines, without any hint of it being an enthusiasm recommended by the need for production. He seems devoted to the tramcars, shuttle looms, hydraulic power, traffic signals, slimming apparatus . . . the whole range of urban engines. In *Man with a Movie Camera* there is a sequence of a factory girl folding cigarette packets. Today, that drab task might epitomize industrial alienation of the worker. But Vertov sees the job lyrically. He speeds up the process—for the sake of cinematic fun, and to comment playfully on the need for more production, and the girl only smiles the more. Was Vertov ingenuous or insensitive? Both, perhaps, but there is no suggestion that he lied. He did love machines and he did see hope in them: his footage still celebrates them, no matter how much we are culturally suspicious of the message. And, in that sense, montage was another engine. Vertov's mon-

tage, like his photography, is both suppler and more energetic than any other Russian examples. The close of *Man with a Movie Camera* is deliriously cheerful, and as heartening as Norman McLaren's movies.

But the seeds of conflict are there already: as Vertov pressed on, the clash between his righteous emphasis on cinema verité and his naïve pleasure at orchestrating the natural became greater. But by 1930, the bases of his attitude had all been removed. Constructivism, Lenin, and Bolshevik idealism had been replaced by realist cliché, Stalin, and bureaucracy. The ideological complexity of cinema verité was more than Russia in the 1930s could have tolerated. By the mid-1930s, Vertov was no longer favored by the regime. *Three Songs of Lenin* was delayed in its release, allegedly because it neglected Stalin. Thus Vertov was denied the chance to make films of his own. However, by 1989, in the supposedly liberating air of perestroika, Vertov was labeled as an exponent of totalitarian cinema, on a par with Leni Riefenstahl, as someone who did not stand up sufficiently against the cruel and inhuman system. You can't win.

Lullabye was his last full-length film, the prelude to semiretirement. His roving reportage was carried on in name only during the Second World War. Much of the work was done by his wife, and his personal contributions to *Daily News* were few and far between.

Charles Vidor (1900–1959),
b. Budapest, Hungary

1929: *The Bridge* (s). 1932: *The Mask of Fu Manchu* (codirected with Charles Brabin). 1933: *Sensation Hunters*. 1934: *The Double Door*. 1935: *Strangers All; The Arizonian; His Family Tree*. 1936: *Muss 'em Up*. 1937: *A Doctor's Diary; The Great Gambini; She's No Lady*. 1939: *Blind Alley; Romance of the Redwoods; Those High Gray Walls*. 1940: *My Son, My Son!; The Lady in Question*. 1941: *New York Town; Ladies in Retirement*. 1942: *The Tuttles of Tahiti*. 1943: *The Desperadoes*. 1944: *Cover Girl; Together Again*. 1945: *A Song to Remember; Over 21*. 1946: *Gilda*. 1948: *The Loves of Carmen*. 1951: *It's a Big Country* (codirected). 1952: *Thunder in the East; Hans Christian Andersen*. 1954: *Rhapsody*. 1955: *Love Me or Leave Me*. 1956: *The Swan*. 1957: *The Joker Is Wild; A Farewell to Arms*. 1960: *Song Without End* (completed by George Cukor on the death of Vidor).

After service in the First World War, Vidor joined UFA and became an assistant director. He came to America in the late 1920s, financed the short *The Bridge* himself, and made second features at MGM, Paramount, and RKO before joining Columbia in 1939. There he became a leading director, especially of musicals and romances. But in 1946 he was involved in comic, angry litigation with Harry Cohn, the head of Columbia, over Cohn's profane language. He lost the case and was obliged to return to Columbia in humiliation. It was an impossible situation, and in 1948 Vidor bought out his contract for $75,000.

It is difficult to become enthusiastic about Vidor as a director. His only talent was for glamour: he made two good Rita Hayworth films—*Cover Girl* and *Gilda,* the latter deserving a place in the history of screen erotica and perverse psychology. Some credit should go to the actress, photographer Rudolph Maté, and writer Virginia Van Upp, but the fact remains that very few men managed to make Hayworth relax as much as she does in *Gilda.* Elsewhere, Vidor was no more than pretty and insubstantial. The *Joker Is Wild* gave Sinatra one of his better parts as comedian Joe E. Lewis and repeats the pleasing bittersweet view of showbiz menaced by gangsters first established in *Love Me or Leave Me* (Doris Day as Ruth Etting, with Cagney as her lover). Under the eye of Selznick, Vidor managed to make a weepie out of *A Farewell to Arms.* Finally, he had Dirk Bogarde as Liszt in *Song Without End,* a piece of posh hokum, made as if there was only a pause between movements separating it from 1945 and *A Song to Remember,* which is Cornel Wilde as Chopin—a world in which composers retreat to the piano to avoid clinging women. In all, it is hard to credit that Vidor had sufficient squeamishness to be disturbed by bad language.

King Vidor (1894–1982), b. Galveston, Texas
1919: *The Turn in the Road; Better Times; The Other Half; Poor Relations.* 1920: *The Jack-Knife Man; The Family Honor.* 1921: *The Sky Pilot; Love Never Dies.* 1922: *Conquering the Woman; Woman, Wake Up; The Real Adventure; Dusk to Dawn.* 1923: *Peg o' My Heart; The Woman of Bronze; Three Wise Fools.* 1924: *Wild Oranges; Happiness; Wine of Youth; His Hour; Wife of the Centaur.* 1925: *Proud Flesh; The Big Parade.* 1926: *La Bohème; Bardelys the Magnificent.* 1928: *The Crowd; The Patsy; Show People.* 1929: *Hallelujah.* 1930: *Not So Dumb; Billy the Kid.* 1931: *Street Scene; The Champ.* 1932: *Bird of Paradise; Cynara.* 1933: *Stranger's Return.* 1934: *Our Daily Bread.* 1935: *Wedding Night; So Red the Rose.* 1936: *The Texas Rangers.* 1937: *Stella Dallas.* 1938: *The Citadel.* 1940: *Northwest Passage; Comrade X.* 1941: *H. M. Pulham Esq.* 1944: *An American Romance.* 1946: *Duel in the Sun.* 1948: *A Miracle Can Happen/On Our Merry Way* (codirected with Leslie Fenton). 1949: *The Fountainhead; Beyond the Forest.* 1951: *Lightning Strikes Twice.* 1952: *Japanese War Bride; Ruby Gentry.* 1955: *Man Without a Star.* 1956: *War and Peace.* 1959: *Solomon and Sheba.*

In his 1954 autobiography, *A Tree Is a Tree,* Vidor recounted a meeting with Irving Thalberg:

> "Well, what are you going to try next?" asked Thalberg. "It's going to be hard to top The Big Parade. . . ."
> I really hadn't an idea ready, but one came to me in the emergency. "Well, I suppose the average fellow walks through life and sees quite a lot of drama taking place around him. Objectively life is like a battle isn't it?"
> "Why didn't you mention this before?" he asked.
> "Never thought of it before," I confessed.
> "Have you got a title?"
> "Perhaps One of the Mob."
> Thalberg showed immediate enthusiasm. "That's a wonderful title . . . How long will it take you to write it?"
> "Two or three days."

It is hard to believe that Thalberg's empire functioned with such sunny casualness, but it's unlikely that Vidor deliberately misrepresented his recollections. There is an unconscious simplicity and naïve straightforwardness in that passage characteristic of Vidor's best films, just as the conception he offered Thalberg is the one that obsessed him for forty years. His hero was the ordinary man, whether the doughboy of *The Big Parade,* the urban archetype of *The Crowd* or *Our Daily Bread,* the immigrant in *American Romance,* the ambitious architect in *The Fountainhead,* or Pierre in *War and Peace.* It is typical of Vidor that he should want the simplicity of Gary Cooper for the Frank Lloyd Wright figure in *The Fountainhead* and John Ford's prairie philosopher Henry Fonda for Tolstoy's observer.

The battle Vidor describes is not only between men, but between man and the land, man and the physical world, man and the elements. In *The Fountainhead,* as in *The Crowd,* there is a constant stress on the visual tension of man and concrete filmed with a simplicity that would be audacious if it were studied. Vidor's eye for composition is unendingly based on the emotional content of man's struggle. It takes many forms: the human chain that crosses a torrent in *Northwest Passage;* Robert Donat blowing up the tainted water system in *The Citadel;* Brian Donlevy learning to operate the huge excavator in *American Romance;* Gary Cooper drilling in the stone quarry in *The Fountainhead;* the sudden glare of sun on shields in the climactic battle of *Solomon and Sheba;* the sequence in *War and Peace* when the retreating French are caught crossing the river; the delirious close of *Duel in the Sun* when Peck and Jennifer Jones crawl toward each other over the cruel rocks.

Nothing demonstrates Vidor's vitality more than the way his natural sense of the primitive concentrated with the years. Many of his silent films are lost—though *The Jack Knife Man* is full of emotional energy and is a glowing tribute to Griffith. *The Big Parade* is often slack and clumsy, while *The Crowd* is too deliberate a social comment for Vidor's inventiveness to be unfettered. In addition, he is not at his best with oppressed characters, preferring achievement, survival, and victory. For most of the 1920s he was at MGM, indulged with *The Crowd* and *Hallelujah*, and employed to bring visual distinction to such films as the Lillian Gish *La Bohème* and the John Gilbert *Bardelys the Magnificent*.

His three Marion Davies comedies—*The Patsy, Show People*, and *Not So Dumb*—leave one marveling that he never tried comedy again.

But in the 1930s he free-lanced, directing *Bird of Paradise* for Selznick and setting up *Our Daily Bread* himself. Until about 1935, Vidor had dealt only in generalized characters, but with *So Red the Rose* (starring Margaret Sullavan) and Barbara Stanwyck in *Stella Dallas*, a new theme appeared: the emotional life of a woman, the power of it when properly directed and the hysteria when thwarted. Thus, years before *Duel in the Sun, Beyond the Forest*, and *Ruby Gentry*, Vidor had tapped this raw feminine strength, and seen it as a driving commodity in America, as much as wheat, rock, and steel, his other favorite subjects. Not that he gave up the epic: *Northwest Passage* is an immensely vigorous film about the great woods, and *An American Romance* is a homespun legend on an immigrant's rise from miner to tycoon.

But epic and feminine psychology were deliriously combined (or melted) in *Duel in the Sun*, his second film for David Selznick. The operatic use of inflamed color, the balladlike simplicity, the unremitting obsessiveness of the two central characters, the ferocity of Jennifer Jones, and—above all—the ability to see a woman's pic story in terms of battle make it arguably the greatest—and last—primitive film in the American cinema. Selznick's contribution cannot be denied, but there is no reason to attribute the power of the image to anyone other than Vidor. If proof is wanted, the vastly cheaper *Ruby Gentry* has the same Jennifer Jones, a similar story, and at least 70 percent the power of Pearl Chavez (albeit in black and white).

It is a tragedy that Vidor did not work after *Solomon and Sheba* and that he is not more widely recognized. *The Fountainhead* is one of the most beautiful and mysterious of films; *An American Romance* has no equal as a rags-to-riches epic; *Duel in the Sun* has a ketchup prairie bathed in *l'amour fou*; and who else in America would have had the confidence to make *War and Peace* so simple a film?

In his last years, Vidor lectured and taught; he made two short films—*Truth and Illusion: An Introduction to Metaphysics* (64) and *Metaphor*

(80); he researched the murder of William Desmond Taylor; and he gave a lovely performance as the irascible grandfather in *Love and Money* (82, James Toback).

No other American director of his time is more engaging or less easy to pin down. Vidor could be radical and conservative (*Our Daily Bread* and *The Fountainhead*). He could handle so many genres while retaining such a vibrant sense of the oddity of people. For example, in the very melodramatic setup of *Duel in the Sun*, notice how the characters grow in complexity as the film advances. Moreover, Vidor could be shocking—there's a kind of spiritual violence in, say, *Beyond the Forest, The Fountainhead*, or *Stella Dallas* that is still engrossing. Was he optimist or pessimist?

Jean Vigo (1905–34), b. Paris

1929: *À propos de Nice* (d). 1931: *Taris* (d). 1933: *Zéro de Conduite* (s). 1934: *L'Atalante/Le Chaland qui Passe*.

The polling of critics to arrive at the "ten best films ever made" that *Sight and Sound* conducts every ten years has shown some surprising changes of taste. Not least, the apparently declining reputation of Jean Vigo. It does not necessarily mean that if asked, "How good is Vigo?" most critics would not reply "more than good." But whereas in 1962 *Zéro de Conduite* and *L'Atalante* collected twenty-four votes, and *L'Atalante* was "tenth best film," in 1972 they had only six votes between them. The decline continued in 1982, but by 1992 *L'Atalante* was back where it belonged—in the top ten. I have known students retreat wearily from a poor 16mm copy of *L'Atalante*, but I have seen children entranced by an excellent TV print of the same film. The 1992 recovery had much to do with the fully restored *L'Atalante*. That may suggest that much of Vigo's impact is in the sensuousness of the image.

But it is still mysterious that the poignancy of Vigo's career has been treated lightly. He is the first young martyr to "cinema," and it is not clear why his fame should have suffered when his self-consuming devotion to film has become increasingly current among young people. There is a prize named after him in France, and there could equally be film schools pledged to his example. Vigo needed film, and died in its pursuit.

Biography, therefore, is worth spelling out, and we are lucky to have the thorough life by P. E. Salles Gomes. Vigo was the son of the French anarchist known as "Miguel Almereyda." That led him into politics and the first potent sense of outrage when Almereyda died in mysterious circumstances in Fresnes prison in 1917, and Vigo was taken south to be educated. He returned to Paris at age nineteen, to study at the Sorbonne, but soon succumbed to illness that was to hinder him for the rest of his life. It was while in a tubercular clinic that he met his future wife, "Lydou," Elisabeth Lozinska. He had already been encouraged by Autant-Lara and worked as assistant to the photographer Léonce-Henry Burel. But in 1929, his father-in-law loaned or gave him money with which he bought a camera and made *À propos de Nice*, with the aid of photographer Boris Kaufman, younger brother of Dziga Vertov.

Vigo now had four years to live, and he spent them in beleaguered communion with Lydou, Kaufman, and his camera. He and his wife had bouts of illness: he was forced to sell the camera for money to live on; none of his films prospered. Germaine Dulac helped him to set up the documentary on the French swimmer, Jean Taris. Jacques-Louis Nounez financed *Zéro de Conduite*, which caused such a controversy that it was banned. Finally, Vigo made his only feature, *L'Atalante*, again with Nounez's support and Gaumont's backing. But the distributor took fright at its intensity and released a "popularized" version. Vigo was too ill to contest the matter actively and within months he was dead.

The sequence of Vigo's work is of anger being replaced by tenderness, and of his poetic surrealism moving from social survey to the realization of states of mind. *À propos de Nice* was undoubtedly influenced by Dziga Vertov's newsreel eulogies of Bolshevik Russia. But whereas Vertov's lyricism is based in the hoped-for harmony between the movie man and a rejuvenated society, Vigo's love of the visual is turned toward a satire of the Côte d'Azur playground. *À propos de Nice* is startlingly modern: as with all important satire, the object of attack is enduring. The neurotic sunning of themselves of the rich and would-be rich beside a stagnant Mediterranean was already noticed in Vigo's inquisitive documentary. There is an admirable, hostile irony in the way his dissolves strip down an idle young woman as she sits cross-legged at a table in the sun. Above all, the camerawork is strolling, intimate, and liberated.

There was ample reason in Vigo's life for such antipathy toward the pleasure-seeking bourgeois. *Taris* was something of a diversion, an exercise in camera effects on an isolated subject, which nevertheless allowed Vigo to discover one of his most pregnant images, the underwater swimmer. All of his own wretched schooling was avenged in *Zéro de Conduite*, forty-four minutes of sustained, if roughly shot, anarchist crescendo. The attempt by society to regiment raw childhood, and the failure of the attempt, are conveyed by the very tender high-angle photography. What still impresses about *Zéro* is the vivid characterization of midget, straw-doll, or macabre authorities, and the engaging spontaneity of the children, very truthful to their private language, their casual fierceness, and the unflawed love that can exist between them.

That new warmth is at the heart of *L'Atalante*, a very simple story assigned to Vigo by Gaumont: a young skipper takes a wife and installs her on the roaming barge he works with an older man, Jules; the marriage falters and, in Paris, the wife runs away; but separation weighs on them and they are reunited. The distributor coarsened the love story, but in recent years the film has been restored. In addition, *L'Atalante* is a piece of working-class cinema: the harsh Seine towns and the barge life are shown without flinching and with a human directness that deflates such films as Ruttmann's *Berlin* and is an advance on Dziga Vertov.

At the same time, Vigo gave *L'Atalante* an imaginary, dreamlike setting: the river is the flow of life; the barge a human island; and Paris the universal city. Godard's delight in making Paris an imaginary city was felt years before by Vigo. But, most important, *L'Atalante* is about a more profound attitude to love than Gaumont understood. It is love without spoken explanation, unaffected by sentimental songs; but love as a mysterious, passionate affinity between inarticulate human animals. A fairy tale about plain, even ugly people, its intensity is always to be found in its images: of Michel Simon, an exotic tattooed figure in the cramped cabin; of the bride leaning uncertainly against the tiller of the barge; and of Jean Daste swimming underwater in search of his lost love.

The achievement was already enormous; but his nature was too prone to pain and disaster to survive. He was too deliberately an extremist to find a safe place in the French film industry, much less one advancing on war. Vigo's vulnerable sensibility emphasizes Buñuel's greater calm and robustness. But Vigo has been a primary influence on French cinema, especially on Truffaut; and *If* is a conscious tribute to *Zéro de Conduite*. Every film student scraping together money for a hopelessly unsalable project is following a hard path that Vigo pioneered.

Luchino Visconti (Duke of Modrone)
(1906–76), b. Milan, Italy

1942: *Ossessione*. 1948: *La Terra Trema*. 1951: *Bellissima*. 1953: "Anna Magnani," episode from *Siamo Donne*. 1954: *Senso*. 1957: *Le Notti Bianche/White Nights*. 1960: *Rocco e i Suoi Fratelli/Rocco and His Brothers*. 1962: "Il Lavoro," episode from *Boccaccio '70*. 1963: *Il Gattopardo/The Leopard*. 1964: *Vaghe Stelle dell'Orsa/Of a Thousand Delights/Sandra*. 1966: "La Stregha Bruciata Viva," episode from *Le Streghe*. 1967: *Lo Straniero/The Stranger*. 1969: *La Caduta degli Dei/The Damned*. 1970: *Mortea Venezia/Death in Venice*. 1972: *Ludwig II*. 1974: *Gruppo di Famiglia in un Interno/Conversation Piece*. 1976: *L'Innocente/The Innocent*.

As with Antonioni, there is an unresolved conflict in Visconti's work between socio-political awareness and the pursuit of more self-sufficient, aesthetic values. Antonioni sometimes toppled into his suave gravity; while Visconti's solemnity only revealed him as a flagrant middlebrow.

Visconti is less penetrative than Antonioni, and more vulgar. The fortuitous association with neo-realism, the increasing resort to heavy emotional drama—not to mention Visconti's casually maintained sense of aristocracy—enabled him to appear, always politely, as a "great artist," what Geoffrey Nowell-Smith called one of "a select company of major directors whose international reputation was established early in their careers and has been maintained, on the basis of a relatively small output, ever since."

It is certainly true that on the international art-house circuit Visconti's flamboyant treatment of a few prestigious ventures passed for respectability. If there was a Nobel prize for cinema, Visconti would have had it long ago; he was as deserving as a Steinbeck, and he was very social. But he does not begin to rate at the highest level: his work is trivial, ornate, and unconvinced. Dressed up so solemnly, the result is not without humor. Visconti never lost that shameless but calculated illustration of significance, what Nabokov once celebrated as *poshlust*. Remember that he is a minor director, a sedate melodramatist, and he can be entertaining. Thus, think of *Rocco* not as translated Dostoyevsky but as a coy challenge to King Vidor, Douglas Sirk, and John Stahl, directors more deeply respectful of melodrama than Visconti.

The secret lies in Visconti's shockingness, which genteel ladies can clasp to their bosoms as if it were a fur coat. Visconti may have known that he never quite owned up to his own melodrama. Despising his own instinctive garishness, he went for ever more dignified projects, until *Death in Venice*, a disguised tearjerker, its surface a sticky crust, covering nothing. His style was depressingly literal, full of theatrical gesture, ignoring the quality of the image. The rape and final killing in *Rocco* are such as the bourgeoisie think necessary for "the point of the film": the momentous way in which Annie Girardot lifts up her arms to the crucifixion pose satisfies the plainest sensibility because of its predictability.

Visconti was a wealthy aristocrat whose chief interest was horses before his attention turned to cinema. He went to France and assisted Jean Renoir on *Une Partie de Campagne* (36) and *Les Bas-Fonds* (36), designed sets in Italy, and assisted Carl Koch when Renoir abandoned *La Tosca* (40). In 1942, he made his first film, *Ossessione,* based on James M. Cain's novel *The Postman Always Rings Twice*. Against the zabaglione lightness of Italian cinema, *Ossessione* was like a meat sauce. It was adopted as the herald of neo-realism simply because Visconti had used real locations, emphasized grossness in his players and sets, and under-

lined greed, malice, and selfishness as human motives. In fact, *Ossessione* is realistic only in the totally organized way that Balzac's pessimism passes for naturalism. *La Terra Trema,* two hours forty minutes of Sicilian fisherfolk, was called a proof of Marxist attitudes. In fact, it is a film made in the spirit of Greek tragedy, sure of its own composed splendor and attitudinizing universality. Here is Visconti's romantic description of how his supposedly realistic film came into being: "The peasant episode came to me in the center of Sicily. This is a region of the latifundia, the immense domain left uncultivated by their rich owners. These huge plateaus are like the most spectacular landscapes in Mexico. Suddenly there came the sound of galloping horses. Hundreds of peasants galloped up from over the horizon. The sound came closer, the land trembled (whence the title of my film)."

Visconti soon abandoned the trappings of realism. *Bellissima* is a woman's pic vehicle for Anna Magnani; *Senso* is genteel melodrama, modeled on Italian painting where, say, *Viva l'Italia* is based on an entirely open-air reality. But with *Notti Bianche,* Visconti's taste for high-minded literary thunder grew apace. *Rocco, Il Gattopardo,* and *Death in Venice* are splendid art-circuit packages, with dazzling production values, meticulous if unsurprising acting and well-signposted significance. *The Damned, Lo Straniero,* and *Vaghe Stelle dell'Orsa* show that even amid so much photogenic obviousness Visconti's control could desert him. Those three are silly movies, ornamental studies of corruption and decay. No wonder he offered to film Proust, or that he shared his time between cinema, theatre, and opera.

Toward the end of his life, as social attitudes advanced, so Visconti felt more able to let his homosexual aesthetic show. But somehow he made it resemble consumption in nineteenth-century melodramas. Visconti had a gloomy premonition of something like AIDS (especially in *Death in Venice*) years before the virus was recognized. There is always the feeling in those last films that Visconti is composing (or arranging) his own requiem opera, full of morbid art direction, fateful pauses, and the wistful glances of stricken beauties.

Monica Vitti (Maria Luisa Ceciarelli), b. Rome, 1933

Vitti is inextricably bound up with Antonioni's sentimental pessimism, a forlorn figure of sensibility in a world of lost feelings and alienated beauty. In other men's films, she tended to look coarser than Antonioni ever permitted. He made her face graven and her blondeness a sign of spirituality. She is a numb disapproving observer of emotional mortality, a bleak Mrs. Dalloway in the *Metropolis*. There was a halfhearted nod toward such a figure in *Modesty Blaise* (66, Joseph Losey), but it only showed her up as an ungainly comedienne.

Antonioni's declared method: "The film actor ought not to understand, he ought to be. One might argue that in order to be, he needs to understand. This is not true. If it were true, the most intelligent actor would be the best actor. . . . It is not possible to have true collaboration between actor and director. They work on two quite different levels." This was most fully demonstrated in his treatment of Vitti. It would be trespassing to say how far he made her a character in his autobiography; but from the films alone it is impossible to ignore the weight he put upon her by subjecting her to the tragic ordeal of his mise en scène. She is the imaginative consciousness on which the films turn; and as they resort to comprehensive neurosis, the wound works on her.

She first worked for Antonioni dubbing Dorian Gray in *Il Grido* (57). Thereafter, she was the girl-friend drawn into replacing the vanished Lea Masari in *L'Avventura* (60); the brittle society girl who sees the impossibility of loving Mastroianni in *La Notte* (61); the girl subtly brutalized by Alain Delon in *The Eclipse* (62); and the demented wife in *The Red Desert* (64). That is her most anguished film, less through acting than because the actress is struggling to grasp the unexplained psychosis of the part. Against that, we can remember the lifted sky at certain moments in *The Eclipse*: the airfield scene, and the brief abandon of the African dance. It is a series of films that will always be of importance in the history of director-actress relations—not least because of her relative ordinariness in other directors' hands.

Away from Antonioni, Monica Vitti has often seemed thick-lipped, husky, and stolid, no more or less than the young Silvana Mangano: an episode from *Les Quatres Vérités* (62, Luis Garcia Berlanga); *Château en Suède* (63, Roger Vadim); *Dragées au Poivre* (63, Jacques Baratier); in an episode from *Alta Infidelta* (64, Luciano Salce); "La Minestre," episode from *Le Bambole* (65, Franco Rossi); *Il Disco Volante* (65, Tinto Brass); *Fai in Fretta ad Uccidermi . . .* (65, Francesco Maselli); "Fata Sabina," episode from *Le Fate* (66, Salce); as a Sicilian girl hunting for her seducer in Britain in *La Ragazza con la Pistola* (67, Monicelli); *La Femme Ecarlate* (68, Jean Valére); *La Cintura di Castita* (69, Festa Campanile); *La Moglie del Prete* (69, Dino Risi); *Amore, Mio Aiutami* (69, Alberto Sordi); *Nini Tirabuscio la Donna che Invento la Mossa* (70, Marcello Fondato); *La Pacifista* (71, Miklos Jancsó); in two episodes from *Le Coppie* (71, Monicelli and Vittorio de Sica); *Teresa la Ladra* (72, Carlo di Palma); *Tosca* (73, Luigi Magni); *The Phantom of Liberty* (74, Luis Buñuel); *La Raison d'Etat* (78, André Cayatte); *An Almost Perfect Affair* (79, Michael Ritchie); *The Mystery of Oberwald* (80, Antonioni); *I Know*

That You Know I Know (82, Alberto Sordi); *Trenta Minuti d'Amore* (83, Marco Vicario); and *Scandolo Segreto* (89), which she also directed.

Jon Voight, b. Yonkers, New York, 1938
This is one of the least explicable of American careers. Nominated three times for the best actor Oscar, and winner once, Voight can easily be regarded as one of the best actors of his generation (which includes Nicholson, Hoffman, Beatty, Pacino, and Redford). For a while, he hardly worked, and when he did it was often in projects that perplex anyone who has heard Voight's earnest pleas that actors should do only responsible and meaningful work.

He was educated at Catholic University in Washington, D.C., and his first film was *Fearless Frank* (67, Philip Kaufman), which was actually made in 1964, and in which he plays a country boy who comes to Chicago. He had a small part as a baby-faced gunslinger against Wyatt Earp in *Hour of the Gun* (67, John Sturges), and was then cast in *Midnight Cowboy* (69, John Schlesinger), where he gave a fine performance as another naïve country kid trying to live up to the big city (and got his first nomination).

But he wasn't easy to cast, or to be persuaded into a film, and so disorder set in early: *Out of It* (69, Paul Williams); *Catch-22* (70, Mike Nichols); *The Revolutionary* (70, Williams); *Deliverance* (72, John Boorman); as a boxer in *The All-American Boy* (73, Charles Eastman); as the teacher in *Conrack* (74, Martin Ritt); tracking down Nazis in *The Odessa File* (74, Ronald Neame).

In Europe, he made *End of the Game* (76, Maximilian Schell); and then he won the Oscar as the paraplegic vet in *Coming Home* (78, Hal Ashby)—sincere and tender, but rather arranged in the scheme of the film. *The Champ* (79, Franco Zeffirelli) was a bizarre follow-up and an unconvincing film. Then came an interval before Voight scripted and produced as well as acted in the very poor *Lookin' to Get Out* (82, Ashby), about gambling.

He again produced and acted in the routine weepie *Table for Five* (83, Robert Lieberman). All his career, Voight had been boyish and gentle, but next he played the roaring demon in *Runaway Train* (85, Andrei Konchalovsky), his best performance, which got him a third nomination, but led nowhere.

After that, he played the alcoholic stepfather in *Desert Bloom* (86, Eugene Corr), and did several things for TV: as the surgeon helping victims of *Chernobyl: The Final Warning* (91, Anthony Page); as the anthropologist in *The Last of His Tribe* (92, Henry Hook); and in *Return to Lonesome Dove* (93, Mike Robe).

Then, in the early nineties some passion came back to him—perhaps it was the urge to impress his emerging daughter, Angelina Jolie. Perhaps he saw the fun to be had as a supporting actor: he was sly, edgy, and furtive as the fence in *Heat* (95, Michael Mann); another villain in *Mission: Impossible* (96, Brian De Palma); *Rosewood* (97, John Singleton); a hammy snake poacher in *Anaconda* (97, Luis Llosa); ostentatiously blind in *U Turn* (97, Oliver Stone); *Most Wanted* (97, Glenn Hogan); a lovely Southern lawyer in *The Rainmaker* (97, Francis Coppola); co-producer on *The Fixer* (98, Charles Robert Carner), for TV; a ruthless National Security chief in *Enemy of the State* (98, Tony Scott); very good as the Dublin cop in *The General* (98, Boorman); the coach in *Varsity Blues* (99, Brian Robbins); the captain in *Noah's Ark* (99, John Irvin); *A Dog of Flanders* (99, Kevin Brodie); *Second String* (00, Robert Lieberman); so good as FDR in *Pearl Harbor* (01, Michael Bay), you wanted more of him; with Angelina in *Lara Croft: Tomb Raider* (01, Simon West); *Zoolander* (01, Ben Stiller); as Howard Cosell in *Ali* (01, Mann); *Second String* (02, Lieberman); *Unleashed* (03, Bob Clark); *Jasper, Texas* (03, Jeff Byrd); *Holes* (03, Andrew Davis).

Josef von Sternberg (Josef Stern)

(1894–1969), b. Vienna

1925: *The Salvation Hunters.* 1926: *The Exquisite Sinner* (codirected with Phil Rosen); *A Woman of the Sea.* 1927: *Underworld; Children of Divorce* (codirected with Frank Lloyd). 1928: *The Last Command; The Dragnet; The Docks of New York.* 1929: *The Case of Lena Smith; Thunderbolt.* 1930: *The Blue Angel/Der Blaue Engel; Morocco.* 1931: *Dishonored; An American Tragedy.* 1932: *Shanghai Express; Blonde Venus.* 1934: *The Scarlet Empress.* 1935: *The Devil Is a Woman; Crime and Punishment.* 1936: *The King Steps Out.* 1937: *Claudius* (unfinished). 1939: *Sergeant Madden.* 1941: *The Shanghai Gesture.* 1943: *The Town* (d). 1951: *Jet Pilot* (codirected with Jules Furthman). 1952: *Macao* (codirected with Nicholas Ray). 1953: *The Saga of Anatahan.*

Von Sternberg made it easy for us to dislike him; his favored tone was one of disdain. He courted enemies just as he went out of his way to make himself unemployable with a serene arrogance. In *The Scarlet Empress*, the John Lodge character, in love with Dietrich but knowing she will humiliate him, is asked to admit a junior officer to the Empress's bedchamber. As he does so, he smiles sardonically, asks the officer to give Dietrich a message, and then says, no matter, she will understand. So it is that von Sternberg leaves us either to understand or to expose our stupidity. Complicity breathes out of his films, not just in the fatalistic adoration that the camera offers Dietrich and that she answers enigmatically, but in the admission, "Of course, this is a farrago. Utter nonsense.

Only the most enlightened can see the beauty within it." Sternberg cultivated his own elitism, astonishingly survived with it at Paramount for thirteen films, and then tolerated an increasingly bizarre exile.

His youth was divided between Vienna and New York, and in his work he balanced a sense of the Continental femme fatale and the laconic American hero more completely than anyone else: in *The Blue Angel* and *Morocco,* for instance, he bridged the worlds of German humiliation and Hawksian pride. By turns, he worked for the World Film Corporation and served in the American army. After the war, he made his debut as assistant director on *The Mystery of the Yellow Room* (19, Emile Chautard). He worked on *The Highest Bidder* (21, Wallace Worsley) and *By Divine Right* (24, Roy William Neill) on which a "von" was added to his name "without my knowledge."

The Salvation Hunters, made very cheaply and in novel locations, was seen as refreshing realism. But Sternberg quickly settled for a private world of light and shade, romance and violence, strong men and mysterious women. *Underworld* and *The Docks of New York* show his erotic imagery coming into being, and *The Last Command* is a rehearsal for the undermining of the inflated, self-pitying Emil Jannings achieved in *The Blue Angel.*

Although he was sparing with dialogue, sound was essential to Sternberg because of his taste for very intimate behavioral realism within a surrealist artifice of plot and setting. No less essential was Dietrich. With the best will in the world, his films without her lack that marvelous, scathing languor. He was not an easy man to be directed by. Many actors—notably Jannings and William Powell—reacted violently to him. Dietrich adored him, and trusted him. That is why their films together have an amazing privacy against which the sensible concerns of Paramount look irrelevant.

In retrospect, it seems ridiculous that Lubitsch should have been treasured at Paramount for sophistication, and Sternberg thought of as an unmanageable fantasist. He asserted on celluloid that many images of Dietrich's face, moving in and out of light and shade, were a better subject for film than any of Lubitsch's theatrical ploys. He invented art-direction countries for her—North Africa, China, Spain, and Russia—that were authentic only in emotional terms. He made woman the sexual arbiter, the serene observer of an absurd life that offered no other solace than the taking of pleasure. Thus *The Scarlet Empress* is the proof that the sexual image is more lasting and more serious than love, politics, and history. In its final, delirious vindication of Dietrich's open-mouthed depravity it is American cinema's triumph of *l'amour fou* and a surrealist masterpiece. Beside it, *Morocco* and *Shanghai Express* are only beautiful celebrations of romance, the insistence on sentimental attachment conquering reason. *Scarlet Empress* has that spirit made splendidly aggressive with Sternberg's own pessimistic wit. It seems so startling that no one today would dare to make it.

After Dietrich, Sternberg took assignments. *Claudius* broke down because of Merle Oberon's accident and Laughton's intransigence, but it is most characteristic of Sternberg as a blighted project. His later work is virtually defined by the obstacles and impediments he created for himself. Thus he had left Paramount under a cloud, fired by Lubitsch, apparently too proud to admit that the "extravagant" crowd scenes in *Scarlet Empress* came from a Lubitsch silent picture, *The Patriot*. *Shanghai Gesture, Jet Pilot*, and *Macao* are fragmentary films, clearly manhandled by their own production companies, but still offering glimpses of the play of light on a female smile that Sternberg had identified as fundamental cinema. *Macao*, especially, has glorious, hallucinatory images of the lattice of fake moonlight swimming over cardboard sets.

It needed the ridiculous impossibility of *Anatahan* to end his filmmaking career. A wild plot— about Japanese sailors and one woman marooned on an island not knowing the war is over—shot under the simplest conditions. The island was made out of paper, cellophane, and light. Sternberg himself photographed the film, reveling in such pure artificiality, regretting only that he had to use real water. Very rarely seen, *Anatahan* is a masterpiece, to rank with the Dietrich films. For total absorption in style, remorseless interest in sexual existence, subtle conviction of hopelessness and amorality, Sternberg now stands clear as one of the greatest directors and the first poet of underground cinema.

After *Anatahan*, he lectured on cinema and wrote his outrageous compendium of bitter joy and concealed confessions, *Fun in a Chinese Laundry*. The chapter there on Dietrich is a major contribution to film literature, and a great, mordant love story.

Erich von Stroheim (Erich Oswald Stroheim) (1885–1957), b. Vienna

1918: *Blind Husbands*. 1919: *The Devil's Passkey*. 1921: *Foolish Wives*. 1922: *Merry-Go-Round* (begun by Stroheim; he was replaced by Rupert Julian). 1925: *Greed; The Merry Widow*. 1928: *The Wedding March; Queen Kelly*. 1933: *Walking Down Broadway* (never released; reworked and released as *Hello Sister*).

Stroheim's is generally known as the most blighted of cinema careers, and yet it is hardly sensible to think of him as a victim. Much easier to see "the Von," the director of *Greed*, the greatest of all "lost" films, and "the man you love to hate," as the most fulfilling invention of Erich Oswald, the Viennese son of a German Jewish merchant and a mother who came from Prague.

In later years, it suited Stroheim to claim aristocratic origins and a notable military career. But his undoubted style and persuasiveness were more the product of artistic aspiration than of any great familiarity with Austro-Hungarian high life. After brief military service, he emigrated to the United States in 1906 and went through the dark years of obscurity before reappearing in 1914 as a Hollywood hustler. For the next few years, he strove to be indispensable in the Griffith–John Emerson empire, playing bit parts in *Birth of a Nation, Intolerance*, and *Hearts of the World*; assisting Griffith whenever he could; acting as military advisor on Emerson's *Old Heidelberg* (15); and getting his first credits as an art director. In 1917, in Wesley Ruggles's *Old France*, he established the role of the Prussian officer so central to his image.

Stroheim's ambition was to direct, and in 1918 he persuaded Carl Laemmle at Universal to let him make his own original screenplay, "The Pinnacle": the result was *Blind Husbands*, in which Stroheim himself played Lt. Erich von Steuben, the fastidious, ironic, and heartless military superman. This was followed by *The Devil's Passkey* (19) and *Foolish Wives* (21), both for Universal. The latter again starred Stroheim as an officer cad and swindler at large in a Continental playground. A prestigious success, it was a financial failure despite or because of Universal's insistence that it should be substantially cut. He was taken off his next film, *Merry-Go-Round* (22), largely because of the intervention of Irving Thalberg, then Laemmle's caretaker at Universal.

Stroheim moved to the Goldwyn Company and in 1923 shot *Greed* from Frank Norris's novel, *McTeague*. It was perhaps the most injudiciously ambitious film ever made: did Stroheim dream that his ten-hour version would be released? Or did he draw trouble upon himself? He could not have invented a more bitter stroke of fate than the way that, as he worked on *Greed*, the Goldwyn Company became Metro-Goldwyn-Mayer, with Thalberg as one of its heads. Successive cuts reduced *Greed* until a final release version, in 1925, of ten reels—perhaps a quarter of the original conception.

Stroheim retaliated with a great commercial success for MGM, *The Merry Widow*, starring John Gilbert and Mae Murray. But in 1926–28, he was in trouble again with Paramount over *The Wedding March*, a two-part project in which he also acted—as Prince Nicki von Wildliebe-Rauffenberg. Part One, "The Wedding March," was released much as intended. But Part Two, "The Honeymoon," was taken out of Stroheim's hands and given to several others, including von Sternberg, to edit down. It appeared only briefly in Europe as *Mariage de Prince*. In 1928, Stroheim joined in unlikely partnership with Gloria Swanson and Joseph Kennedy to make *Queen Kelly*. His partners' unhappiness with Stroheim's arrogance and extravagance took effect when sound interrupted the shooting. Yet again, the release version was a shrunken image of its director's plans.

Stroheim directed only once again: *Walking Down Broadway*. But producer Sol Wurtzel quarreled with executive Winfield Sheehan and eventually a reshot version appeared: *Hello Sister.*

The rest of Stroheim's career is as a traveling writer and actor. In America, he appeared in, among others, James Cruze's *The Great Gabbo* (29); with Garbo in *As You Desire Me* (32, George Fitzmaurice), and in *The Crime of Dr. Crespi* (35, John Auer). He also worked as military advisor or dialogue writer on Garbo's *Anna Karenina* (35, Clarence Brown), *San Francisco* (36, W. S. Van Dyke), and Tod Browning's *The Devil Doll* (36).

In 1936, he went to France and played Von Rauffenstein, the crippled airman, in Renoir's *La Grande Illusion* (37), as well as in *Marthe Richard* (37, Raymond Bernard) and two Christian-Jaque movies: *Les Pirates du Rail* (38) and *Les Disparus de Saint-Agil* (38). He had hoped to direct again, *La Dame Blanche*, with Renoir's collaboration, but war canceled the film and Stroheim returned to America.

He appeared on Broadway in 1941–43 in *Arsenic and Old Lace* and had several exotic film parts to catch the war spirit: *I Was an Adventuress* (40, Gregory Ratoff); in *So Ends Our Night* (41, John Cromwell); as Rommel in Billy Wilder's *Five Graves to Cairo* (43); in Milestone's *The North Star* (43); as *The Great Flamarion* (45, Anthony Mann); and in *The Mask of Dijon* (46, Lew Landers) opposite Denise Vernac, his future wife.

In 1946, he went back to France but made only one film, *La Danse de Mort* (47, Marcel Cravenne), based on the Strindberg play, of any interest. In 1950 he returned to Hollywood to play Max von Mayerling, the butler, ex-director, and ex-husband in Billy Wilder's *Sunset Boulevard*. That film is by turns a deliberate humiliation of Stroheim and one of Hollywood's most confused pieces of self-adulation. Complete with a clip from *Queen Kelly* and a care for sets atypical of Wilder, *Sunset Boulevard* is the acid ending to a cynic's vision as Stroheim directs the crazy Norma Desmond–Gloria Swanson for the press photographers. (But what an influence Stroheim had on Wilder as a warning against refusal to compromise.)

After that, Stroheim appeared in his only German film, *Alraune* (52, Arthur Maria Rabenalt)

and a few more French pictures before his death.

It is hard now to see even what the studios chose to make available of Stroheim's work. But once seen, *Greed, The Wedding March,* and *Queen Kelly*—no matter how palely they reflect originals—are never forgotten. They contain the essential contradictions in Stroheim's work: between melodrama and naturalism; romanticism and cynicism; psychological detail and epic perspectives. Like all the great silent directors he knew how necessary it was to abandon taste for obsession. His reckless enlargement of situations was a form of improvisation, even if it entailed crazy expense and delay. Left to himself, Stroheim might never have finished a film, so chronic was the fever for detail. For all that he explored realism of character and delighted in location work, nonetheless he was capable of sudden, exquisite insights—usually into perversion, lust, malice, or pride. His films amassed detail relentlessly, but never lost sight of character or structure. Thalberg's famous verdict—that Stroheim was a footage fetishist—was truer than the producer knew, for Stroheim was as precise as he was expansive. Despite all the hindrance, Stroheim made utterly personal films, apparently enduring insult, disappointment, and reverse with a stoicism that recognized how every betrayal enhanced the identity and reputation of the Von. The sad nobility that gazes out of *La Grande Illusion* and *Sunset Boulevard* was as much a part of his oeuvre as the Death Valley end game of *Greed*.

Max von Sydow (Carl Adolf von Sydow), b. Lund, Sweden, 1929

Von Sydow is best known for some of the leading male roles in the work of Ingmar Bergman, which is to admit that Bergman takes rather less trouble with men than with women in his films. Even the artist figure that von Sydow has played three times allows Bergman to view himself (or to have others view him) without the participatory anguish that he has shared with his actresses. Von Sydow is dissected and found to be a sham. But in *Persona*, Liv Ullmann's silent actress is a more profound portrait of Bergman's impossible artist. Beside Ullmann, von Sydow looks gloomy, sickly, and irritable—intensely real, but shorn of the compassion that Bergman's camera bestows on women and of the strength he sees in them.

Ever since his ascetic knight in *The Seventh Seal* (57), as stripped down and emblematic as a chess piece, von Sydow has been a passive dismembered representation of the male artistic personality. Suffering has found a home in that long face; but with his women—with Thulin, Andersson, Ullmann, and Lindblom—Bergman has gone painfully beneath that surface. Von Sydow was the magician Vogler in *The Face/The*

Magician (58); the father in *The Virgin Spring* (59); Borg, the painter, in *Hour of the Wolf* (68); and the musician in *Shame* (68). In addition, he has worked for Bergman on *Wild Strawberries* (57), in a small part; as a husband in *So Close to Life* (58); as the husband in *Through a Glass Darkly* (61); in *Winter Light* (63); *A Passion* (70); and *The Touch* (71).

Not only eleven films but his major part in the three island films show how far his gaunt presence was relevant to Bergman's view of modern man emaciated by the struggle between his appetite and guilt. He is especially striking in *Shame*, a film that subjects the artistic sensibility to the ordeal of a mysterious war, and shows that von Sydow's musician is a selfish, cowardly man. Bespectacled, with receding hair, too dispirited to shave, the small inroads of aging are clearly signs of moral failure, evident in the opening scene where his chief emotional contact with Liv Ullmann is to ask her to look into his mouth for a swollen wisdom tooth.

Von Sydow was at the Stockholm Royal Dramatic Theatre from 1948 to 1951. In addition to his work for Bergman he played in these Swedish films, without settling into that Gothic revery that Bergman encourages: *Bara en Mor* (49, Alf Sjöberg); *Miss Julie* (51, Sjöberg); *Ingen Mans Kvinna* (53, Lars-Eric Kjellgren); *Ratten att Alska* (56, Mimi Pollack); *Prasten i Uddarbo* (58, Kenne Fant); *Brollopsdagen* (60, Fant); *Alskarinnan* (62, Vilgot Sjöman); *Nils Holgerssons Underbara Resa* (62, Fant); in an episode from *4 × 4* (65, Jan Troell); *Made in Sweden* (68, Johan Bergenstrahle); *Svarta Palmkronor* (68, Lars Magnus Lindgren); as the husband in *Utvandrarna* (70, Troell); *Invandrarna* (70, Troell); and *Nybyggarna* (73, Troell).

Like most of the leading Swedes, he attracted American attention. It shows the inability of Hollywood to digest Bergman's players that his English-speaking parts have ranged from Christ in *The Greatest Story Ever Told* (65, George Stevens) to the knuckle-cracking Nazi in *The Quiller Memorandum* (66, Michael Anderson). In addition: *The Reward* (65, Serge Bourguignon); *Hawaii* (66, George Roy Hill); *The Kremlin Letter* (69, John Huston); *The Night Visitor* (71, Laslo Benedek); *Embassy* (72, Gordon Hessler); as *The Exorcist* (73, William Friedkin); as *Steppenwolf* (74, Fred Haines); a wintry assassin in *Three Days of the Condor* (75, Sydney Pollack); *The Ultimate Warrior* (75, Robert Clouse); *Illustrious Corpses* (75, Francesco Rosi); *Egg! Egg?—A Hardboiled Story* (75, Hans Alfredson); *Cuore di Cane* (76, Alberto Lattuada); *Voyage of the Damned* (76, Stuart Rosenberg); *The Exorcist Part II: The Heretic* (77, John Boorman); *March or Die* (77, Dick Richards); *Brass Target* (78, John Hough); and *Hurricane* (79, Troell).

In the last fifteen years, he has roamed all over the world, seemingly unlimited in range, and never quite losing his authority: *Flash Gordon* (80, Mike Hodges); *Deathwatch* (80, Bertrand Tavernier); *She Dances Alone* (80, Robert Dornhelm); *Victory* (81, Huston); *Conan the Barbarian* (82, John Milius); flying a balloon to the North Pole in *The Flight of the Eagle* (82, Troell); *Strange Brew* (83, Dave Thomas and Rick Moranis); in the James Bond film *Never Say Never Again* (83, Irvin Kershner); as a Spanish police chief in *Target Eagle* (84, Jose Antonio de la Loma); *Dreamscape* (84, Joseph Ruben); *Samson and Delilah* (84, Lee Philips); *Dune* (84, David Lynch); *Kojak: The Belarus File* (85, Robert Markowitz); *Code Name Emerald* (85, Jonathan Sanger); *Il Pentito* (85, Pasquale Squitieri); *Quo Vadis?* (85, Franco Rossi); *Hannah and Her Sisters* (86, Woody Allen); *The Second Victory* (86, Gerald Thomas); *Duet for One* (86, Andrei Konchalovsky); *The Wolf at the Door* (87, Henning Carlsen); superb in *Pelle the Conqueror* (88, Bille August); *Red King, White Knight* (89, Geoff Murphy); *Mio Caro Dottor Graesler* (90, Roberto Faenza); *Awakenings* (90, Penny Marshall); *A Kiss Before Dying* (91, James Dearden); *Until the End of the World* (91, Wim Wenders); the narrator in *Europa* (91, Lars Von Trier), and the best thing in that mannered film; *The Best Intentions* (92, August); the Devil in *Needful Things* (93, Fraser Heston).

He has also directed a film, *Katinka* (88), adapted from a favorite novel by Herman Bang.

Meanwhile, passing seventy, he paces towards some destiny—to work with every registered director?: *Time Is Money* (94, Paolo Barzman); *Onkel Vanja* (94, Bjorn Melander); *Radetzky March* (94, Axel Corti); *Citizen X* (95, Chris Gerolmo); *Judge Dredd* (95, Danny Cannon); *Hamsun* (96, Troell); *Jerusalem* (96, August); *Enskilda Samtal* (96, Liv Ullmann); *Truck Stop* (96, Michael Muschner); a Russian admiral in *Hostile Waters* (97, David Drury); *La Principessa e il Povero* (97, Lamberto Bava); as David in *Solomon* (97, Roger Young); *What Dreams May Come* (98, Vincent Ward); *Snow Falling on Cedars* (99, Scott Hicks); *Nuremberg* (00, Yves Simoneau); *Non Ho Sonno* (01, Dario Argento); *Vercingétorix* (01, Jacques Dorfmann); *Intacto* (01, Juan Carlos Fresnadillo); *Minority Report* (02, Steven Spielberg).

Lars von Trier,

b. Copenhagen, Denmark, 1956
1981: *Nocturne* (s). 1982: *Befrielsesbilder/Pictures of a Liberation* (s). 1984: *Forbrydelsens Element/ The Element of Crime*. 1987: *Epidemic*. 1988: *Medea*. 1991: *Europa/Zentropa*. 1994: *Riget/The Kingdom* (TV). 1996: *Breaking the Waves*. 1997: *Riget II/The Kingdom II* (TV). 1998: *Idioterne*.

2000: *D-dag—Lise* (TV); *D-dag* (TV); *Dancer in the Dark.* 2003: *Dogville.*

"There is only one excuse for having to go through, and force others to go through, the hell that is the creative process of film," wrote Lars von Trier in what, in 1991, was his third manifesto. "The carnal pleasure of that split second in the cinemas, when the projector and the loudspeakers, in unison, allow the illusion of sound and motion to burst forth, like an electron abandoning its orbit to generate light, and create the ultimate: a miraculous surge of life."

We could note several things from this—that one man's carnal ecstasy may be another's imagination; that sometimes there are no excuses; and that the language of self-inducing cinematic exultation is oddly akin to the rhetoric of fascism.

On the strength of *The Element of Crime* and *Zentropa,* I would have to say von Trier is brilliant in a way that gives that term a bad name. He knows no reality—only film. His movies refer only to the accumulated culture of all those split seconds. Thus, it is natural that, in *Zentropa,* back projection begins to take over from any vestige of social or spatial reality.

He has wanton skills, a greedy eye, and a taste for lush morbidity that is easily regarded as "the heritage of film noir" but that may have more to do with personal and private dysfunction. *Zentropa,* especially, has amazing scenes and transformations—collapsing sets, streaks and stains of bloody color in gravure black-and-white imagery, and an unashamed merger of Kafka, Welles, Fuller, and engine grease. It all goes on and on—profane, deft, drop-dead stunning . . . and a terrible lesson in how hollow aesthetic virtuosity can be. Von Trier is like a seven-year-old serial killer whose bombs and weapons have all gone into his eye.

If this sounds like the description of a shameless opportunist, then marvel that his next move was to attach himself to a movement, known as Dogme, full of high-minded preaching about its own austerity and purity. On the principle that any recommended system of how to make films is the height of fraud, then von Trier added bogusness to his vulgarity. Much of the Dogme approach was worked out in *Riget,* a TV soap opera for Denmark that was painfully derived from David Lynch. However, the gross faults of *Breaking the Waves* and *Dancer in the Dark* (including my urge—restrained, restrained—to break the necks of Emily Watson and Björk) should be laid at von Trier's feet alone. Whereupon, he would probably reinvent soccer.

W

Andrzej Wajda, b. Suwalki, Poland, 1927
1951: *Ceramika Ilzecka* (s). 1953: *Kiedy ty Spisz* (s). 1954: *Pokolenie/A Generation.* 1955: *Ide do Slonca* (s). 1956: *Kanal.* 1958: *Popiol i Diament/Ashes and Diamonds.* 1959: *Lotna.* 1960: *Niewinni Czarodzieje/Innocent Sorcerers.* 1961: *Samson.* 1962: *Sibirska Ledi Magbet/Siberian Lady Macbeth;* "Warsaw," episode from *L'Amour à Vingt Ans* (codirected with Andrej Zulawski). 1965: *Popioly/Ashes.* 1967: *Gates to Paradise.* 1968: *Wszystko na Sprzedaz/Everything for Sale; Roly-Poly.* 1969: *Polowanie na Muchy/Hunting Flies.* 1970: *Krajobraz po Bitwie/Landscape After Battle.* 1971: *The Birch Wood.* 1972: *Wesele/The Wedding.* 1974: *Ziemia Obiecana/Land of Promise.* 1976: *Czlowiek z Marmuru/A Man of Marble.* 1978: *Bez Znieczulenia/Without Anesthesia.* 1979: *Panny z Wilko/The Young Girls of Wilko.* 1980: *Cziowiek z Zelaza/Man of Iron; Dyrygent/The Conductor.* 1983: *Eine Liebe in Deutschland/A Love in Germany; Danton.* 1986: *Kronika Wypadkow Milosnych/Chronicle of a Love Affair.* 1987: *Les Possédés/The Possessed.* 1990: *Dr. Korczak.* 1993: *Pierscionek z Orlem w Koronie.* 1994: *Nastasja.* 1995: *Wielki Tydzien.* 1996: *Panna Nikt.* 1999: *Pan Tadeusz.* 2000: *Wyrok na Franciszka Klosa* (TV).

In the mid-eighties, in his book *Double Vision,* Andrzej Wajda regretted that "Films made in Eastern Europe seem of little or no interest to people in the West. The audience in Western countries find them as antediluvian as the battle for workers' rights in England in the time of Marx."

Wajda has remained committed to Poland, the country on whose behalf so much began in September 1939. His recent participation in the era of Solidarity should not eclipse the dramatic influence of his earlier "trilogy": films about Poland during and just after the Second World War. It was with *A Generation, Kanal,* and *Ashes and Diamonds* that Wajda secured his place in film history. Those films are brought to mind by the recent opening of Steven Spielberg's *Schindler's List*—a Polish subject? Much more, of course. But still, it is a story set largely in the Poland of Wajda's youth. It is also a picture enriched by the design of Allan Starski, someone trained by Wajda during the seventies and eighties. I deeply admire the Spielberg film; I recognize how hard it must have been to mount, even with the world's most bankable director. Yet isn't there an irony in Poland continuing to serve the imagination of other countries?

Immediately after the war, Wajda went from Cracow Academy of Fine Arts to the film school at

Lodz. Having assisted the distinguished veteran, Aleksander Ford, on *Five Boys from Barska Street* (53), Wajda thrust Polish cinema at the rest of the world and dramatized the tragedy of his generation, of teenagers who waited for Warsaw's fate to be decided.

His war trilogy remains an intense study of Polish nationality, Communist idealism, and a more basic youthful romanticism in one of this century's cruelest melting pots. *Kanal,* at least, conveys the horrors of Poland's wartime experience. But, more generally, Wajda seemed literary, intelligent, and speculative, uneasily attempting to balance Polish themes and the feeling for modern compulsiveness in Polanski and Skolimowski. Polanski may run dangerously close to modishness and exploitation, but there is no question of the pain in his films. Skolimowski is perhaps rootless, but he goes deeper into the origins of behavior. Wajda, by contrast, seems too comfortable.

There is a scene in *Ashes and Diamonds* in which Zbigniew Cybulski, playing a young resistance fighter stranded by a sellout peace, sets fire to glasses of spirit in requiem for lost comrades. It captured the curious fusion in that film of Wajda's honest account of Poland's ordeal in the Second World War, and of a new consciousness—contemporary with the making of the film—in which Cybulski reached out for the rhetoric and broodiness of an existential screen hero. Cybulski's manner seemed to mourn James Dean as much as the people in *Kanal.* Where *A Generation* had been a touching, naturalistic recollection of young people suddenly aged by the war, *Kanal* was a claustrophobic account of an historical action hardly separable from nightmare. Rather than extend that hallucinatory insight, *Ashes and Diamonds* was baroque, partly because it was made thirteen years after the last days of the war, partly because Cybulski's gloating animation hustled Wajda forward into a view of existential dilemmas, but also because of Wajda's taste for symbolism and allegory.

The burning alcohol was repeated in *Everything for Sale,* where it represented the loss of Cybulski himself. Indeed, the actor appeared to have shown Wajda directions and a sense of excitement only equaled by the war. The autobiographical enquiry in *Everything for Sale* was as centered on the nature of film as, say, *8½, Blow-Up,* or *Persona.* Wajda was not at that level as an artist, but the journey that that film had made toward introspection was hopeful, and *Everything for Sale* was his most interesting picture. His other work veered from further attempts to illuminate Poland's past—*Lotna* and *Ashes*—to less explicable historical films—*Siberian Lady Macbeth* and *Gates to Paradise*—to the deliberate and rather academic exploration of "aesthetic, psychological, introspective experiences": *Samson, Innocent Sorcerers* (coscripted by Skolimowski), and *Hunting Flies.*

With the flowering of Polanski and Skolimowski away from Poland, Wajda may have felt stranded. He came to Britain to make *Gates to Paradise,* but the film was never properly released. Indeed, his films of the late sixties and early seventies had only a very sparse showing outside Poland. Best known was *The Wedding,* from a famous Polish play, indulging his taste for allegory and advancing on mystification and complexity only as means to evasion.

Wajda rose to the challenge of Solidarity with a group of political chronicles, notably *Man of Marble* and *Man of Iron,* in which Krystyna Janda played a documentary filmmaker researching the life of a workers' hero. Wajda left Poland because of political repression and he made *Danton* as an international art-house film, and as an allegory on Poland. *A Love in Germany* examines, in flashback, the story of an affair between a German woman and a Polish prisoner of war.

Since then, Wajda has been elected to the Polish parliament. His most recent film, *Dr. Korczak,* is the story of a Jewish teacher who died in a concentration camp. *Nastasja* was taken from Dostoyevsky, and in general Wajda remains a craftsman, still determined to remind Poland of awkward home truths. In 2000, he received an honorary Oscar for the integrity of his career in changing times.

Anton Walbrook (Adolf Wohlbruck)
(1900–67), b. Vienna

A foggy evening or a haze of lights? A deserted street or a stage set? A dark man appears in a belted raincoat, the collar turned up. He speaks: "La Ronde? . . . And me, what am I in this little story? . . . The author? . . . The master of ceremonies? . . . A passer-by? . . . Let us say I am one of you. I am the incarnation of your desire . . . your desire to know everything." Thus spake Anton Walbrook, "le meneur de jeu," at the beginning of Max Ophüls's *La Ronde* (50).

It is possible for one role to earn an actor a permanent place in the history of moving images. For Walbrook, it was this tender and ironic strolling master of affairs in Ophuls's great film—a role filled less happily by Peter Ustinov in *Lola Montès* (55), in which Walbrook is the deaf Ludwig of Bavaria, an elderly man who rediscovers his feelings only to be trapped by duty into denying them. These two parts have all the sad grace of an actor who seemed never to recover from being driven out of Europe, and who changed his name because another man with a mustache had the same Christian name. Despite his succinct, dry talent, Walbrook's career drifted from England to America to France. He died ten years after his last film, possibly forgotten by cinema audiences.

He was born into a family of clowns, and may have always moved gingerly in case his dignity shattered. He trained at Max Reinhardt's school and went on the German stage. By the mid-1920s he was working in movie serials, and in *Mater Dolorosa* (22, Geza von Bolvary) and *Das Geheimnis auf Schloss Elmshoh* (25, Max Obal). But his fame grew with sound: *Der Stolz der 3. Kompagnie* (31, Fred Sauer); *Salto Mortale* (31, E. A. Dupont); *Cinq Gentilshommes Maudits;* (31, Julien Duvivier); *Baby* (32, Carl Lamac); *Melodie der Liebe* (32, Georg Jacoby); *Regine* (33, Erich Waschnech); *Keine Angst vor Liebe* (33, Hans Steinhoff); *Viktor und Viktoria* (33, Reinhold Schunzel); *Maskerade* (34, Willi Forst); *Die Englische Heirat* (34, Schunzel); *Zigeuner-baron* (35, Karl Harth); *Der Student von Prag* (35, Arthur Robison); *Ich War Jack Mortimer* (35, Carl Froelich); and *Allotria* (36, Forst). He then made two films in German, French, and English versions—*Michael Strogoff* (36, Richard Eichberg) and *Port Arthur* (36, Nikolaus Farkas)—and Herbert Wilcox hired him as consort to Anna Neagle in *Victoria the Great* (37) and *Sixty Glorious Years* (38).

He remained in England for *The Rat* (37, Jack Raymond); as the husband in *Gaslight* (40, Thorold Dickinson); *Dangerous Moonlight* (41, Brian Desmond Hurst); leader of the religious community in *49th Parallel* (41, Michael Powell/Emeric Pressburger); *The Life and Death of Colonel Blimp* (43, Powell/Pressburger); *The Man from Morocco* (44, Max Greene); and *The Red Shoes* (48, Powell/Pressburger). His Lermontov in that last film was variously austere and shrill, solitary but a master of collaboration. The strangely hot-and-chilly impresario is also a remarkable, thinly disguised portrait of Michael Powell—or of his dream of himself. Walbrook's playing leaves little doubt of his awareness of the connection. Lermontov is the actor's second great claim on posterity.

His most original performance in Britain was as a clean-shaven nerve-wracked Herman in *The Queen of Spades* (48, Dickinson), wonderfully suggesting the breakdown of a scheming opportunist persuaded to believe in both ghosts and luck at cards. His last years moved from the sublime to the ridiculous, as though he had something else on his mind: as well as the two Ophuls films, *Wiener Walzer* (51, Emile Edwin Reinert); *L'Affaire Maurizius* (54, Duvivier); *Oh, Rosalinda!!* (55, Powell/Pressburger); *König für eine Nacht* (56, Paul May); Cauchon in *Saint Joan* (57, Otto Preminger); and a sardonic Esterhazy in *I Accuse* (57, José Ferrer).

Jerry Wald (1911–62), b. New York

Wald had thirty busy years in cinema; when he died it seemed incredible that a fifty-year-old could have had a hand in so many films. Perhaps it was the hectic activity on humdrum ventures that earned Wald the reputation of being a model for Budd Schulberg's novel *What Makes Sammy Run?* Certainly he was a vulgarian in the Selznick mold, combining a brutal instinct for the lowest common denominator with earnest literary pretensions. Originally a writer himself, when he died he was flexing his muscles over *Ulysses,* having already taken on Hemingway and D. H. Lawrence. It made him the sort of producer that outsiders laughed at. But plenty of professionals—from Joan Crawford to Fritz Lang—attested to his enthusiasm for movies, and to the foolish good nature that swept him along.

The irony of a producer's role was often that he had immense power but childish insights. In many cases, it was the director who needed a producer's tact with people, to mollify and manipulate his own muddleheaded boss. Wald seems to fit that specter, just as his career shows the grim fate of inadequate men once they emerged from the shelter of smooth-running film factories and talented directors. In human terms, many producers may have been victims, highly paid and heavily armed, but out of their depth, unable to grasp the nature of a film, the logistics of a schedule, or the aspirations of a director. The producers who survive with any credit are those who maintained at least a love of movies. If only on that score, Wald is worth remembering.

He had worked on radio and as a journalist before he began writing for Warners: *Living on Velvet* (35, Frank Borzage); *Sing Me a Love Song* (36, Ray Enright); *Hollywood Hotel* (37, Busby Berkeley); *Hard to Get* (38, Enright); *Going Places* (38, Enright); *Naughty But Nice* (39, Enright); *The Roaring Twenties* (39, Raoul Walsh); and *They Drive by Night* (40, Walsh).

In 1942, Warners promoted him to the rank of producer. He stayed there eight years, either producing or supervising a variety of genres, supporting the career of Joan Crawford and striking a happy partnership with Michael Curtiz. In retrospect, there are signs that he turned Warners from crime to the women's picture. His output included films like *Mildred Pierce* (45, Curtiz) that seems the epitome of highly organized studio hokum. Did they need producing? Perhaps Wald sensed that *Mildred* had a lasting chemistry missing in the more mundane virtues of *Navy Blues* (41, Lloyd Bacon); *Across the Pacific* (42, John Huston); *Desperate Journey* (42, Walsh); *Destination Tokyo* (43, Delmer Daves); *Background to Danger* (43, Walsh); *The Very Thought of You* (44, Daves); *Objective Burma* (45, Walsh); *Pride of the Marines* (45, Daves); *Humoresque* (47, Jean Negulesco); *Possessed* (47, Curtis Bernhardt); *Dark Passage* (47, Daves); *To the Victor* (48, Daves); *Key Largo* (48, Huston); *Johnny Belinda* (48, Negulesco);

One Sunday Afternoon (49, Walsh); *Flamingo Road* (49, Curtiz); *Task Force* (49, Daves); *Young Man with a Horn* (50, Curtiz); *Caged* (50, John Cromwell); *The Glass Menagerie* (50, Irving Rapper); *The Damned Don't Cry* (50, Vincent Sherman); and *Storm Warning* (51, Stuart Heisler).

Wald left Warners, and he was hired by RKO where he would form a unit with Norman Krasna. Two films there were both highly original projects and great artistic successes: *Clash by Night* (52, Fritz Lang) and *The Lusty Men* (52, Nicholas Ray). Both films deal with a sort of life and middle-aged character seldom seen in American films. He also produced *The Blue Veil* (51, Bernhardt) for RKO. But if Wald was finding himself, he next became vice-president at Columbia, where he necessarily had to be wired to Harry Cohn's ass. He stayed at Columbia for four years as executive producer, involved (if only nominally, as a producer of producers) on *From Here to Eternity* (53, Fred Zinnemann); *The Big Heat* (53, Lang); *Gun Fury* (53, Walsh); *It Should Happen to You* (54, George Cukor); *Pushover* (54, Richard Quine); *Human Desire* (54, Lang); *The Long Gray Line* (55, John Ford); *The Last Frontier* (56, Anthony Mann); *Picnic* (56, Joshua Logan); *Jubal* (56, Daves); *The Eddy Duchin Story* (56, George Sidney); and *The Harder They Fall* (56, Mark Robson).

He then moved on to Fox as an independent producer. With more effective power than ever before, he blew most of his reputation on literary melodramas: *An Affair to Remember* (57, Leo McCarey); *No Down Payment* (57, Martin Ritt); *Kiss Them for Me* (57, Stanley Donen); *Peyton Place* (57, Robson); *The Long Hot Summer* (58, Ritt); *The Best of Everything* (59, Negulesco), with Joan Crawford; *The Sound and the Fury* (59, Ritt); *Hound Dog Man* (59, Don Siegel); *The Story on Page One* (59, Clifford Odets); *Sons and Lovers* (60, Jack Cardiff); *Let's Make Love* (60, Cukor), scripted by Krasna and reuniting Wald and Marilyn Monroe, whose calendar picture he had exploited for *Clash by Night; Return to Peyton Place* (61, José Ferrer); *Wild in the Country* (61, Philip Dunne); *Hemingway's Adventures of a Young Man* (62, Ritt); and *The Stripper* (63, Franklin Schaffner). The remarkable thing about those last films is how many of them are based on glaring mistakes—in casting, script, or approach—that a competent producer should have eliminated at an early stage.

Christopher (Ronny) Walken,

b. Queens, New York, 1943

There is something a touch too chilly, or alien, about Walken to make a lead actor. He calls it "a natural kind of foreignness—very hard for me to play a regular guy." So he has made himself a rarity: the supporting actor who changes his look, his

voice, and his demeanor at will. He can be frightening, and unexpectedly funny; he has been a credible cowboy, a dancer, a figure of evil, and, in *The Deer Hunter* (78, Michael Cimino), a remarkable portrait of disintegration and self-destruction.

He was educated at Hofstra University, but as a child actor he had done a lot of live television. His movie debut was *The Anderson Tapes* (71, Sidney Lumet), after which he did *The Happiness Cage* (72, Bernard Girard); the poet in *Next Stop, Greenwich Village* (75, Paul Mazursky); *Annie Hall* (77, Woody Allen); *Roseland* (77, James Ivory); winning the supporting actor Oscar in *The Deer Hunter; Last Embrace* (79, Jonathan Demme); *The Dogs of War* (80, John Irvin); as Nate Champion in *Heaven's Gate* (80, Cimino); a dazzling dancer in *Pennies from Heaven* (81, Herbert Ross); and *Brainstorm* (83, Douglas Trumbull), the last film of Natalie Wood's—Walken was on the boat when she died.

He was the actor in *Who Am I This Time?* (82, Demme) for TV; and the man who can see terrible futures in *The Dead Zone* (83, David Cronenberg); the villain in the James Bond film *A View to a Kill* (85, John Glen); Sean Penn's father in *At Close Range* (86, James Foley); the sergeant in *Biloxi Blues* (88, Mike Nichols); *Homeboy* (88, Michael Seresin); *The Milagro Beanfield War* (88, Robert Redford); as Whitley Strieber in *Communion* (89, Philippe Mora); as creepy as fog in *The Comfort of Strangers* (90, Paul Schrader); not quite hard enough as *King of New York* (90, Abel Ferrara); with Glenn Close in *Sarah, Plain and Tall* (91, Glenn Jordan), as the widowed farmer; *McBain* (91, James Glickenhaus); as Max Schreck in *Batman Returns* (92, Tim Burton); *Mistress* (92, Barry Primus), as a suicidal actor; *Skylark* (93, Joseph Sargent); *True Romance* (93, Tony Scott); and *Wayne's World 2* (93, Bill Duke).

Alas, Walken has become the ghost that haunts American film, hired so often to be spooky, pale, staring, eccentric, Satanic, and so on. And there's a lot of "so on" in modern American film. This has nearly buried the brilliant actor from *The Deer Hunter* or *At Close Range;* it has forgotten the dancer and the potential comic. And it seems to bore him as much as some of his fans. He is remarkable, but he has been turned into a "type": *A Business Affair* (94, Charlotte Brandstrom); excellent in *Pulp Fiction* (94, Quentin Tarantino); *Search and Destroy* (95, David Salle); *The Prophecy* (95, Gregory Widen); *The Addiction* (95, Ferrara); who else could be the lead in Donald Cammell's last, misbegotten film, *Wild Side* (95); *Nick of Time* (95, John Badham); grotesque in *Things to Do in Denver When You're Dead* (95, Gary Fleder); *Celluloide* (96, Carlo Lizzani); *Basquiat* (96, Julian Schnabel); excellent in *The Funeral* (96, Ferrara); *Last Man Standing* (96,

Walter Hill); *Touch* (97, Schrader); *Excess Baggage* (97, Marco Brambilla); *Suicide Kings* (97, Peter O'Fallon); *Mouse Hunt* (97, Gore Verbinski); *The Prophecy II* (98, Greg Spence); *Illuminata* (98, John Turturro); *Trance* (98, Michael Almereyda). He was terrific as the voice of Colonel Cutter in *Antz* (98, Eric Darnell and Tim Johnson); *New Rose Hotel* (98, Ferrara); *Blast from the Past* (99, Hugh Wilson); *Vendetta* (99, Nicholas Meyer); the Hessian Horseman in *Sleepy Hollow* (99, Burton); *Sarah, Plain and Tall: Winter's End* (99, Jordan); *Kiss Toledo Goodbye* (99, Lyndon Chubbuck); *The Prophecy 3* (00, Patrick Lussier); *The Opportunists* (00, Myles Connell); *Scotland, PA* (01, Billy Morrissette); *Joe Dirt* (01, Dennie Gordon); *America's Sweethearts* (01, Joe Roth); *The Affair of the Necklace* (01, Charles Shyer); *Poolhall Junkies* (01, Gregory Martin); *Inside Job* (01, Laszlo Papas); *Down and Under* (01, David McNally); *Plots with a View* (02, Nick Hurran); *The Country Bears* (02, Peter Hastings).

Robert Walker (1918–51),
b. Salt Lake City, Utah

Robert Walker had the kind of heartbreaking smile that tells an audience he is doomed. He was so thin, so earnest, so likeable, so brittle as Jennifer Jones's soldier boyfriend in *Since You Went Away* (44, John Cromwell), we know how short-lived their idyll must be, and we guess that the laws of melodrama will prove his courage too late to win a crusty grandfather's love and forgiveness. You want to reach out and warn Walker, or put an umbrella over his head. And that's without knowing that the love scenes in the picture were shot as the marriage between Walker and Jones came apart, and as Jones pursued her affair with the picture's producer, David Selznick.

Walker and the then–Phylis Isley were married in 1939: they had two sons (one of whom, Robert Jr., had an acting career and an uncanny resemblance to his father). But in 1941, Phylis met Selznick, and before long she was "Jennifer Jones." Walker had a few bit roles as early as 1939: he asks Ann Sheridan for a dance in *Winter Carnival* (39, Charles F. Riesner); *These Glamour Girls* (39, S. Sylvan Simon); and *Dancing Co-Ed* (39, Simon).

With a cultivated, clingingly sincere voice and very winning charm, Robert Walker could easily present himself as an appealing boy next door and an object of orthodox romantic interest. Most of his film work was in that vein, and he was particularly successful during the war as a young soldier at MGM: a debut in *Bataan* (43, Tay Garnett); and then in *Madame Curie* (43) and *Thirty Seconds Over Tokyo* (44), both for Mervyn Le Roy; in Wesley Ruggles's *See Here, Private Hargrove* (44); and above all, opposite Judy Garland in *The Clock* (45,

Vincente Minnelli), one of Hollywood's most endearing love stories.

After the war, Walker's career never quite fulfilled its promise, partly because of MGM's insistence on his eligibility for blithe heroines, partly because of his reaction to the failure of his marriage. He was in *Her Highness and the Bellboy* (45, Richard Thorpe); *What Next, Corporal Hargrove* (45, Thorpe)—a series foreclosed only by peace; *The Sea of Grass* (46, Elia Kazan); he played Jerome Kern in *Till the Clouds Roll By* (46, Richard Whorf); the young Brahms in *Song of Love* (47, Clarence Brown); *One Touch of Venus* (48, William A. Seiter); *Please Believe Me* (50, Norman Taurog); and *Vengeance Valley* (51, Thorpe).

Walker was by then in a bad way: divorced by Jennifer Jones, he had been convicted for drunken driving, spent a long period in the Menninger clinic, and had a second marriage, to John Ford's daughter, break up. The unease lurking behind faded boyishness was recognized by Alfred Hitchcock in *Strangers on a Train* (51). His Bruno Anthony in that film was not only his best performance but a landmark among villains—a man of piercing ideas transformed by crossed lines into a smiling psychopath. Walker manages to be very disturbing and yet never loses our sympathy. See how much he suggests in the first meeting: the inactive man who dominates the athlete Granger, the subtle notes of homosexuality, and that beautiful moment when he leans back, sighs, and tells how he "puts himself to sleep" scheming up plans. Bruno is one of Hitchcock's greatest creations and a sign of how seriously Walker was cramped by wholesomeness. He so monopolizes the film that he may even have led Hitchcock to appreciate its underground meanings. This demonic vitality is the key to the film and one of Hitchcock's cleverest confusions of our involvement. Touched and intrigued by his gestures—the boyish pleasure at the fairground, the mischievous bursting of the little boy's balloon, the evident superiority of his mind to that of Guy's brassy wife—we become accomplices to the murder he commits. Thus he hands the dead body down to us, distorted by the spectacles that have fallen from the victim's goggling head.

That great performance is bizarrely recalled elsewhere. Walker's last film, *My Son John* (52, Leo McCarey), another evident proof of his sense of madness, was not completed when Walker died; Hitchcock kindly gave McCarey one of the spare takes of the death scene from *Strangers*, and so Bruno dies twice, even if the character lives on.

Walker's own death was the final breath of bad luck. He was drinking; he was having psychiatric treatment; his moods were very volatile. Doctors came to his house one night to find him ranting and incoherent. He was given a sedative, sodium amytal; it mixed with the alcohol in his body and he died from respiratory failure. It was far more a case of medical incompetence than suicide, yet Walker had been self-destructively inclined for years.

Hal B. (Brent) Wallis (1898–1986), b. Chicago

By 1943, one production executive had won the Irving Thalberg Award twice. It wasn't Goldwyn, or Zanuck, or Selznick. It was Hal Wallis who has a fair claim to be the producer who worked at the top of the business for the longest time. In 1938 (for his first Thalberg Award) three of his movies were in contention for best picture—*The Adventures of Robin Hood, Four Daughters,* and *Jezebel.* In 1943, he won his second Thalberg along with best picture for *Casablanca* (as Aljean Harmetz's invaluable book on the making of that picture shows, Wallis was as detailed and determined as Selznick—and rather more efficient). He would have more best picture nominations down the road for *The Rose Tattoo, Becket,* and *Anne of the Thousand Days.*

Wallis was tough, smart, a tremendous manager, and a man of unshakable self-confidence. Studio boss Jack Warner literally beat Wallis to the stage to pick up the *Casablanca* Oscar, and Wallis was so angry and so firm that the incident led to his departure from Warners. It is arguable that neither he nor his old studio was ever quite as good again.

Wallis came into movies in the publicity department at Warners, which he headed from 1922 onward. In 1928, he was made head of Warners' First National subsidiary, and in 1930 he became a producer. As such, he had his name on several of the studio's most pungent crime pictures: *Little Caesar* (30, Mervyn Le Roy); *Five Star Final* (31, Le Roy); *I Am a Fugitive from a Chain Gang* (32, Le Roy); *The World Changes* (33, Le Roy); and *Gold Diggers of 1933* (33, Le Roy). It must be said that this is Le Roy's best period, and the panache of *Little Caesar* as well as the somber conviction of *Chain Gang* may owe something to Wallis's youthful force.

In 1933, Darryl Zanuck left Warners and Wallis was put in charge of production. Thereafter, he took overall responsibility for what is a more remarkable run of staple products than Thalberg's record at MGM: *Flirtation Walk* (34, Frank Borzage); *Captain Blood* (35, Michael Curtiz); *Sweet Adeline* (35, Le Roy); *A Midsummer Night's Dream* (35, William Dieterle and Max Reinhardt); *The Story of Louis Pasteur* (35, Dieterle); *G Men* (35, William Keighley); *The Charge of the Light Brigade* (36, Curtiz); *Stolen Holiday* (37, Curtiz); *Green Light* (37, Borzage); *Kid Galahad* (37, Curtiz); *The Life of Emile Zola* (37, Dieterle); *Confes-*

sion (37, Joe May); *Tovarich* (37, Anatole Litvak); *The Adventures of Robin Hood* (38, Curtiz and Keighley); *Four Daughters* (38, Curtiz); *Jezebel* (38, William Wyler); *The Dawn Patrol* (38, Edmund Goulding); *The Sisters* (38, Litvak); *They Made Me a Criminal* (39, Busby Berkeley); *Juarez* (39, Dieterle); *Daughters Courageous* (39, Curtiz); *The Roaring Twenties* (39, Raoul Walsh); *The Private Lives of Elizabeth and Essex* (39, Curtiz); *We Are Not Alone* (39, Goulding); *The Old Maid* (39, Goulding); *The Story of Dr. Ehrlich's Magic Bullet* (40, Dieterle); *All This and Heaven Too* (40, Litvak); *The Sea Hawk* (40, Curtiz); *They Drive by Night* (40, Walsh); *A Dispatch from Reuters* (40, Dieterle); *The Letter* (40, William Wyler); *The Great Lie* (41, Goulding); *The Sea Wolf* (41, Curtiz); *The Strawberry Blonde* (41, Walsh); *Manpower* (41, Walsh); *The Bride Came C.O.D.* (41, Keighley); *Sergeant York* (41, Howard Hawks); *The Maltese Falcon* (41, John Huston); *They Died With Their Boots On* (41, Walsh); *High Sierra* (41, Walsh); *King's Row* (42, Sam Wood); *The Male Animal* (42, Elliott Nugent); *Desperate Journey* (42, Walsh); *Yankee Doodle Dandy* (43, Curtiz); *Casablanca* (43, Curtiz); *Air Force* (43, Hawks); *Watch on the Rhine* (43, Herman Shumlin); and *Passage to Marseilles* (44, Curtiz).

In 1944, Wallis formed his own production company as a part of Warners, and in 1948 he moved it over to Paramount. He remained on that footing ever after, and, while his output there was not without interest, it is remarkable how suddenly it loses the halcyon swagger at Warners: *Love Letters* (45, Dieterle); *You Came Along* (45, John Farrow); *Saratoga Trunk* (46, Wood); *The Searching Wind* (46, Dieterle); *The Strange Love of Martha Ivers* (46, Lewis Milestone); *I Walk Alone* (47, Byron Haskin); *Sorry, Wrong Number* (48, Litvak); *The Accused* (49, Dieterle); *My Friend Irma* (49, George Marshall), the first Martin and Lewis picture; *Rope of Sand* (49, Dieterle); *The File on Thelma Jordon* (49, Robert Siodmak); *Paid in Full* (50, Dieterle); *The Furies* (50, Anthony Mann); *Dark City* (50, Dieterle); *September Affair* (51, Dieterle); *Peking Express* (51, Dieterle); *Red Mountain* (51, Dieterle); the forlorn introduction of Shirley Booth in *Come Back, Little Sheba* (53, Daniel Mann); *Scared Stiff* (53, Marshall); *About Mrs. Leslie* (54, Mann); *The Rose Tattoo* (55, Mann); *Artists and Models* (55, Frank Tashlin); *Hollywood or Bust* (56, Tashlin); *The Rainmaker* (56, Joseph Anthony); *Gunfight at the O.K. Corral* (57, John Sturges); Elvis Presley's second film, *Loving You* (57, Hal Kanter); *Last Train from Gun Hill* (58, Sturges); *G.I. Blues* (60, Norman Taurog); *Summer and Smoke* (61, Peter Glenville); *Boeing Boeing* (65, John Rich); *The Sons of Katie Elder* (65, Henry Hathaway); *Anne of the Thousand Days* (69, Charles Jarrott); *True Grit* (69, Hathaway); *Mary, Queen of Scots* (71,

Jarrott); *Bequest to the Nation* (73, James Cellan Jones); *The Don Is Dead* (73, Richard Fleischer); and *Rooster Cogburn* (75, Stuart Miller).

Wallis was not neurotic, or much of a show-off. He was married twice, to actresses Louise Fazenda and Martha Hyer, but without scandal. Men with less potent records and more garish manners became household names. Maybe efficiency was never part of Hollywood's dream.

Raoul Walsh (1887–1981), b. New York

1912: *The Life of General Villa* (codirected with Christy Cabanne). 1915: *The Regeneration; Carmen.* 1916: *Honor System; Blue Blood and Red; The Serpent.* 1917: *Betrayed; The Conqueror; The Pride of New York; The Innocent Sinner; Silent Lie.* 1918: *Woman and the Law; This Is the Life; The Prussian Cur; On the Jump; Every Mother's Son; I'll Say So.* 1919: *Evangeline; Should a Husband Forgive?.* 1920: *From Now On; The Deep Purple; The Strongest.* 1921: *The Oath; Serenade.* 1922: *Kindred of the Dust.* 1923: *Lost and Found on a South Sea Island.* 1924: *The Thief of Bagdad.* 1925: *East of Suez; The Spaniard.* 1926: *The Lady of the Harem; The Lucky Lady; The Wanderer; What Price Glory?.* 1927: *The Loves of Carmen; The Monkey Talks.* 1928: *Me, Gangster; The Red Dance; Sadie Thompson.* 1929: *The Cock-Eyed World; Hot for Paris; In Old Arizona* (codirected with Irving Cummings). 1930: *The Big Trail.* 1931: *The Man Who Came Back; Women of All Nations; The Yellow Ticket.* 1932: *Wild Girl; Me and My Gal.* 1933: *Bad Boy; Sailor's Luck; The Bowery; Going Hollywood.* 1935: *Under Pressure; Baby Face Harrington; Every Night at Eight.* 1936: *Klondike Annie; Big Brown Eyes; Spendthrift.* 1937: *O.H.M.S./You're in the Army Now; When Thief Meets Thief; Artists and Models; Hitting a New High.* 1938: *College Swing.* 1939: *St. Louis Blues; The Roaring Twenties.* 1940: *Dark Command; They Drive by Night.* 1941: *The Strawberry Blonde; Manpower; They Died With Their Boots On; High Sierra.* 1942: *Desperate Journey; Gentleman Jim.* 1943: *Background to Danger; Northern Pursuit.* 1944: *Uncertain Glory.* 1945: *The Horn Blows at Midnight; Salty O'Rourke; Objective Burma.* 1946: *San Antonio* (codirected with David Butler); *The Man I Love.* 1947: *Pursued; Cheyenne.* 1948: *Silver River; Fighter Squadron.* 1949: *One Sunday Afternoon; Colorado Territory; White Heat.* 1950: *Montana* (codirected with Ray Enright). 1951: *Along the Great Divide; Captain Horatio Hornblower; Distant Drums; The Enforcer/Murder Inc.* (codirected with Bretaigne Windust). 1952: *Glory Alley; The World in His Arms; The Lawless Breed; Blackbeard the Pirate.* 1953: *Sea Devils; A Lion Is in the Streets; Gun Fury.* 1954: *Saskatchewan.* 1955: *Battle Cry; The Tall Men.* 1956: *The Revolt of Mamie Stover; The King and Four Queens.*

1957: *Band of Angels.* 1958: *The Naked and the Dead; The Sheriff of Fractured Jaw.* 1959: *A Private's Affair.* 1960: *Esther and the King.* 1961: *Marines, Let's Go.* 1963: *A Distant Trumpet.*

On the one hand, Raoul Walsh simply made movies for a very long time. He spanned the medium from Griffith to Troy Donahue, and he probably had his name on a couple of hundred pictures. As long as most people could remember, Walsh had been a veteran, taken for granted. He was never nominated as best director, nor for best picture. Though he lived into the early eighties, when veteran achievement was generally honored by the Academy, he got no special Oscar. Was it just that he was so reliable, so direct and "simple" an entertainer? Or was it a matter of not making the proper "big" pictures? Still, you have to marvel that, in 1949, *Battleground* got a best picture nomination, while Richard Todd was nominated for *The Hasty Heart.* Nineteen forty-nine—the year of James Cagney in Raoul Walsh's *White Heat*, a picture that got no nod.

They see such things differently in France, and have another way of saying them. Walsh was a hero in France for decades, taken for granted as a pillar of action cinema. But as so much more. Here is Jean Douchet on Walsh: "A force of nature directs the forces of nature and, suddenly, the world lives on—whirlwind and passion. It is time to consider Walsh as rather more than a tough guy, a fellow who likes to laugh, a primitive with rough sentiments. This passionate Shakespearean is a physical film-maker only because he depicts a world of spiritual turmoil. His characters are projected on the world by their own energy and committed to a space that only exists for their actions, fury, spirit, craft, ambition and unbridled dreams."

The son of an Irish father and a Spanish mother, he went to Seton Hall, and then had a few vagrant years as a seaman and a cowboy. He was first employed in the theatre as someone who could ride a horse on a treadmill. That led to a job at Pathé, before he got a position (in the saddle) with Griffith. It was when Griffith went to California that Walsh really learned his craft: not just as actor, but as scenarist and director. *The Life of General Villa* was a Griffith assignment that sent Walsh (plus gold) south of the border to meet the general for documentary scenes, and then playing him in dramatized passages. He appeared as John Wilkes Booth in *Birth of a Nation* (15, Griffith), and he was married (from 1916 to 1927) to one of Griffith's stars, Miriam Cooper. He lost an eye during the shooting of *In Old Arizona*, and his last acting job was as the soldier opposite Gloria Swanson in his own *Sadie Thompson.*

He was always happy filming in wide open spaces. *The Big Trail* (though a flop) was a crucial early Western, with superb cattle-drive scenes and the newcomer John Wayne. *Pursued* and *Colorado Territory* are black-and-white Westerns with a great feeling for desolate canyon country. In addition, the one—from a Niven Busch script—is a pioneering fusion of Western and noir, full of dread, while *Colorado Territory* is a fatalistic reworking of Walsh's own *High Sierra*. But Walsh loved sunshine and optimism, too: *The Tall Men* and *The King and Four Queens* are blithely heroic.

He could do modern war—*Objective Burma, Battle Cry, The Naked and the Dead*—with such an eye for combat and such unforced sympathy for common soldiers under stress. (From the moment of *What Price Glory?* Walsh was a devotee of privates and sergeants.) He could do costume and swashbuckling adventure—*Captain Horatio Hornblower* (which crams three novels into one picture), *Blackbeard the Pirate*, and *The World in His Arms*. He was Errol Flynn's best director, and he was terrific with Cagney, Mitchum, McCrea, Aldo Ray, Gable, and Peck. Time and again, he got the best out of undervalued actresses like Virginia Mayo, Jane Russell, Ida Lupino, and Dorothy Malone.

When he came to Warners (from Fox) in 1939, he got into the habit of crime movies. But *High Sierra* has such a special sadness in its desperate need to "crash out," and *White Heat* is so tender and reflective a portrait of a psychopath. Such movies evade cut-and-dried genre labels. They are so willing to go with the instincts of their wayward loners. Walsh often likes to take doomed heroes or lively demons to extreme places.

There's a key to Walsh in those films. He was great at action, heroes, and combat—if that's all that was called for. But there were so many other things he noticed: the forlorn romantic attempt in *High Sierra;* the bond between Cagney and Edmond O'Brien in *White Heat,* and the vibrant strangeness of Margaret Wycherly's mother. He loved comedy and he had a rare fondness for ordinary people and quiet lives. More or less, those are the virtues of films that distinguish Walsh in his vision of heroes made humble by circumstances— *Me and My Gal* (with Tracy as a cop in love with Joan Bennett's waitress); *The Bowery,* an exhilarating black comedy with terrific fights and unstoppable energy; *They Drive by Night,* which has Raft and Bogart as trucker pals, with a scary Ida Lupino; *The Strawberry Blonde,* a quite remarkable study of ambition and its absence, with outstanding performances from Cagney, Olivia de Havilland, Rita Hayworth, and Jack Carson; *Manpower*—silly and nearly campy, but very well played by Edward G. Robinson and Dietrich; *Gentleman Jim,* maybe the most humane and romantic film about boxing ever made—a film with an unflawed nobility; and the moody nightclub opening to *The Man I Love,* with Lupino and Robert Alda.

This is just a short list of treasures, omitting so much. Just because Walsh made it look so natural is no reason for us to ignore him. Is it too late for that Oscar—or do we just put his rugged eyepatch face on a stamp and be done with it? Raoul Walsh—a natural.

Nobody now knows how to make movies his way.

Charles Walters (1911–82),
b. Pasadena, California

1947: *Good News.* 1948: *Easter Parade.* 1949: *The Barkleys of Broadway.* 1950: *Summer Stock/You Feel Like Singing.* 1951: *Three Guys Named Mike; Texas Carnival.* 1952: *The Belle of New York.* 1953: *Dangerous When Wet; Lili; Torch Song; Easy to Love.* 1955: *The Glass Slipper; The Tender Trap.* 1956: *High Society.* 1957: *Don't Go Near the Water.* 1959: *Ask Any Girl.* 1960: *Please Don't Eat the Daisies.* 1961: *Two Loves/Spinster.* 1962: *Billy Rose's Jumbo.* 1964: *The Unsinkable Molly Brown.* 1966: *Walk, Don't Run.*

Educated at the University of Southern California, Walters was himself a dancer before becoming a director of stage musicals: *Let's Face It* and *Banjo Eyes* in 1941. Next year, he joined MGM as a choreographer and worked on *Seven Days' Leave* (42, Tim Whelan); *Presenting Lily Mars* (43, Norman Taurog); *Du Barry Was a Lady* (43, Roy del Ruth) (in the stage version of which he had danced); *Girl Crazy* (43, Taurog); *Best Foot Forward* (43, Edward Buzzell); *Broadway Rhythm* (44, del Ruth); *Meet Me in St. Louis* (44, Vincente Minnelli); *The Harvey Girls* (45, George Sidney); *Ziegfeld Follies* (46, Minnelli); and *Summer Holiday* (47, Rouben Mamoulian), before making his debut as a director. His choreography credits stand up rather better than his own films. Whatever the overall view of the directors concerned, Walters deserves some credit for the cakewalk in *St. Louis,* the swirling movements of "The Atcheson, Topeka" in *Harvey Girls,* and the Fourth of July sequence in *Summer Holiday.*

Walters made tuneful, smart, and colorful movies, and if his musicals are essentially innocuous, that serves to underline the greater artistic character in Donen and Minnelli. *Easter Parade* is an uneasy alliance of Astaire and Garland, while *The Barkleys of Broadway* and *Summer Stock* are not always successful concealments of the age or anxiety of their leading players. In the 1950s, his range gradually widened. *Lili* was a curiously melancholy film with songs, while *Torch Song* was a key film in making Joan Crawford's camp fire manifest. Walters then developed his comic talent with *The Tender Trap; High Society; Don't Go Near the Water;* and *Ask Any Girl. Two Loves* was another unexpected venture into romantic drama;

Billy Rose's Jumbo was as exuberant as ever; and *Walk, Don't Run* a very funny last bow from Cary Grant.

Wayne Wang, b. Hong Kong, 1949

1975: *Man, a Woman and a Killer.* 1981: *Chan Is Missing.* 1985: *Dim Sum: A Little Bit of Heart.* 1987: *Slam Dance.* 1989: *Eat a Bowl of Tea; Life Is Cheap . . . But Toilet Paper Is Expensive.* 1993: *The Joy Luck Club.* 1995: *Smoke; Blue in the Face* (codirected with Paul Auster). 1997: *Chinese Box.* 1999: *Anywhere but Here.* 2001: *The Center of the World.* 2002: *Maid in Manhattan.*

At the end of 1993, no serious moviegoer could be in doubt about where new things were happening. It was Asia, and more particularly China and Hong Kong, countries that may enjoy a uniquely momentary relationship that could also form a vital hinge for our futures. Chen Kaige, Zhang Yimou, John Woo, and Hou Hsiao-hsien are in this book. And one of the best films I've seen in recent years is Stanley Kwan's *Actress.* Then there is Wayne Wang, a Mandarin Chinese named after John Wayne.

Wang was born in Hong Kong as his upper-middle-class parents fled by way of Tsingtao and Shanghai. He was raised in the British colony, and educated at Catholic schools. He came to America to go to college: Foothill College and the California College of Arts and Crafts. Once graduated, he went back to Hong Kong and was able to work as a director on the TV series, a soap opera, *Below the Lion Rock.*

He returned to San Francisco to make *Chan Is Missing* for $22,000, a whimsical mystery story set in Chinatown. Better by quite a bit was *Dim Sum* (still his best film), a tender, meditative story about family, once again set in San Francisco.

But Wang was already uncertain about where he belonged. (He has been married twice: to the American scenarist Terrel Seltzer and to Hong Kong TV actress Cora Miao.) Can he make films for Asians living in America? Can he make American pictures? *Slam Dance* was his most complete failure. How many times can he count on the providential availability of rich material like Amy Tan's *The Joy Luck Club*? Things have not worked out well. With a script by Paul Auster, *Smoke* was a modestly entertaining picture about a cross-section of life. But when the same team improvised *Blue in the Face,* afterwards, the results were dismal. Equally, *Chinese Box,* set in the last days of British Hong Kong, turned into a dreary and implausible romance with two uneasy leads—Jeremy Irons and Gong Li. *Anywhere but Here* then reduced the Mona Simpson novel to sweet pap. But nothing was as bad, as clumsy, or as naïve as the alleged eroticism of *The Center of the World.*

Walter Wanger (Walter Feuchtwanger) (1894–1968), b. San Francisco

Walter Wanger was the gent, known for class, diction, wardrobe, and education. He had graduated from Dartmouth College, and some said he was as keen on Ivy League honorary degrees as he was on Oscars. Hollywood was proud of him, and a little protective. Observing Wanger one day in 1932, Morris Safier (a small-time hustler) remarked: "Mr. Wanger is certainly a very fine gentleman and while I hope I am wrong for his sake, it is my opinion that he has too much class for this gang around here and I doubt very much whether they even understand his English."

A case can be made that Wanger only qualified for the men's club in 1951. That was when he shot Jennings Lang in or close to the groin. Lang was an agent, above all the agent to Wanger's wife, actress Joan Bennett, and the producer had some reason to think that affections were being alienated. The bullet put Wanger in prison for a spell, but it seems to have impressed Ms. Bennett. And prison moved the educated man: he came away inspired to make a picture advocating prison reform. Still, Wanger was one of the boys by then, a trusted con, a guy who could believe in making *Cleopatra* (not quite honorary degree material).

Cleopatra was a project Wanger had nursed for forty years and that, between 1958 and 1963, he brought laboriously to life. It was his dream; since seeing *A Place in the Sun,* he had imagined Elizabeth Taylor in the lead. Wanger published a hilarious account of *My Life with Cleopatra,* which shows Hollywood's confusion at the time. No one man could be held to blame for the monstrous swelling of the budget. It was as if, in its death throes, Hollywood wished to demonstrate how it had always been administered by incompetent men. Wanger's presence eventually proved sacrificial. He was at that time an independent producer who hired himself out to Fox to make the movie. He survived the resignation of director Rouben Mamoulian, the wholesale recasting and rewriting, Taylor's London illness, the miserable Pinewood weather, even the paparazzi-haunted romance between his Antony and Cleopatra. It was late in a very long day that Fox dismissed him and Darryl Zanuck arrived to cut off all loose ends. Although technically fired, Wanger could not be denied a credit, and thus his name fronts this monument to expensive dullness, a dream rendered null by misapplied resources. And even at the end of his career, the "thoughtful" Wanger seemed short of real cinematic judgment. The one man on *Cleopatra* who might have made it spectacular was Mamoulian. Mankiewicz, by contrast, was a forlorn resort to order and respectability. And yet here is Wanger's comment on the "difficulties" that Mamoulian posed to the smooth running of the Fox zoo:

"Rouben is an Armenian who is very set in his ways but he has great integrity. He cannot tolerate not knowing what is going on, he doesn't like interference, and he doesn't like to be 'pushed' as Rogell [one of many studio herd-riders] is 'pushing' him. He takes great pride in his artistry. Like many directors, he fancies himself an expert on the entire art of cinema. He considers himself a cameraman—and is not always tactful about speaking out."

Mamoulian's films amply justify such confidence, and it is proof of Wanger's limitations that he could not recognize that, even though *My Life with Cleopatra* is littered with references to his own vast experience and achievement. Wanger's record is good, but hit and miss; and the hits coincide with directors of exceptional talent. Time leaves producers as stranded as Ozymandias.

Wanger worked in the theatre, served in the First World War, and was on Woodrow Wilson's Peace Mission before, in 1921, he joined Paramount as a purchaser of material and talent. He claimed to have brought Valentino to the studio for *The Sheik,* to have bought the rights to *Beau Geste,* and to have insisted that the studio film Dreiser's *An American Tragedy* (no wonder he liked *A Place in the Sun*).

He took a holiday in the theatre, but returned to Paramount as manager in charge of production and was responsible for, among others, *Applause* (29, Mamoulian's first film). Between 1929 and 1934, he held executive positions at Columbia and MGM—where he produced a lofty political allegory, *Gabriel Over the White House* (33, Gregory La Cava), and Garbo in *Queen Christina* (34, Mamoulian)—and it was then, with a third period at Paramount, that he began to function consistently as a producer: *The President Vanishes* (35, William Wellman); *Every Night at Eight* (35, Raoul Walsh); *Private Worlds* (35, La Cava), which starred Joan Bennett; *Mary Burns, Fugitive* (35, William K. Howard); and *The Trail of the Lonesome Pine* (36, Henry Hathaway).

He left Paramount for United Artists and produced a string of interesting pictures: *You Only Live Once* (37, Fritz Lang); *History Is Made at Night* (37, Frank Borzage); *Stand-In* (37, Tay Garnett); *Blockade* (38, William Dieterle), a sententious parable about the Spanish Civil War; *Trade Winds* (38, Garnett); *Algiers* (38, John Cromwell), Hedy Lamarr's American debut; *Eternally Yours* (39, Garnett); *Stagecoach* (39, John Ford); *Foreign Correspondent* (40, Alfred Hitchcock); *The Long Voyage Home* (40, Ford), that strange rehearsal of deep-focus photography by Gregg Toland; and *Sundown* (41, Hathaway).

In 1941, Wanger and Joan Bennett married. He was president of the Academy of Motion Picture Arts and Sciences. Apparently at his peak, he moved to Universal and to smaller fry: *Squadron* (42, Arthur Lubin) and Maria Montez and Sabu in *Arabian Nights* (42, John Rawlins). With his wife and Fritz Lang he formed Diana Productions, who made *Scarlet Street* (45, Lang) and *Secret Beyond the Door* (48, Lang). But his other films at Universal were more conventional: *Gung Ho!* (43, Ray Enright); *Salome, Where She Danced* (45, Charles Lamont); the excellent *Canyon Passage* (46, Jacques Tourneur); *Smash-Up* (47, Stuart Heisler); *The Lost Moment* (47, Martin Gabel), a misguided and slow rendering of *The Aspern Papers;* and *Tap Roots* (48, George Marshall).

He left Universal in 1948 and free-lanced for small companies: the Ingrid Bergman *Joan of Arc* (48, Victor Fleming) for RKO; *Tulsa* (49, Heisler) for Eagle Lion; and *Reign of Terror* (49, Anthony Mann). He produced his wife in *The Reckless Moment* (49, Max Ophuls) for Columbia, and not long afterwards served some three months in prison. When he emerged, he made *Riot in Cell Block 11* (54, Don Siegel), out of social conscience, and *The Adventures of Hajji Baba* (54, Don Weis), out of cell daydreams perhaps. *Invasion of the Body Snatchers* (56, Siegel) was his last really interesting film. But in 1958 he had great success with *I Want to Live* (58, Robert Wise), which won an Oscar for Susan Hayward—star of *Canyon Passage, Smash-Up, The Lost Moment, Tap Roots,* and *Tulsa.*

After that, he made *Cleopatra,* final cost not much short of $40 million. *Cleopatra* had many handicaps, including Wanger's faith that immense vulgar spectacle could be harnessed to distinguished psychological case histories—that these gods could *talk.* Whereas, in smaller films—like *Scarlet Street* and *The Reckless Moment*—Wanger had seen the eloquence of fallen angels.

Andy Warhol (Andrew Warhola) (1928–87), b. Cleveland, Ohio

That blank, friendly inertia Warhol offered the world—somewhere between spiritual lassitude, behavioral acquiescence, curiosity about us, and willing edging toward automaton existence—does not fit the thousand-word introductions to significant moviemakers of our time. He would not see any difference between such essays and the brochures for motorcycles, the rapturous endorsements of cosmetics, or the interminable monologue of any person trying to hold back silence. But Warhol might respond to this book if it were described as the enormous, chronic, and purposeless expression of its author's obsession. It is the difference between calling the book "A Dictionary of Cinema" or "Ten Thousand Hours in the Dark."

Warhol's subject was looking itself, and for anyone reading this book alphabetically it is a happy chance that—near the end—Warhol insists on its theme more uncompromisingly than anyone else.

Because the medium is his interest, not his message, it is useful to call Warhol a conceptual filmmaker. Although we are taught to think of his previous, graphic art as "pop" art, that too was conceptual, exactly in the way Duchamp requalified a urinal by signing it, picking it out as the work of an artist, an artwork. Thus Warhol made an epic movie of the Empire State Building and turned several modestly talented associates into superstars by trusting so many long setups to their whim. Warhol's "museum" art was mundane, commercial, what McLuhan called "ditto devices," copies that deceived the eye, infinitely reproducible—mass produced, unauthored, glossy but impersonal. The soup cans were to make us redefine art, just as the variation portraits of Marilyn Monroe and Elizabeth Taylor were studies in the deforming power of different portraiture processes. The extreme thematic simplicity—if not insolence—of these works should not have obscured their philosophical subtlety.

Exactly the same thing struck me in Warhol's films. What are the ingredients of his film style? First, there is the meek, childlike pleasure in taking photographs. Warhol saw that the mass of people bought cameras that were foolproof, that exposed automatically, so that images could be recorded under all feasible conditions. The deliberate use of lights and a variable aperture struck him as archaic craftsmanship—like Dürer drawing every sinew in a leg infinitely and tediously—less important than the fact that the camera is a recording instrument, requiring neither skill nor technique, but still capable of making us say, "Yes, that's Suki, or me."

Thus, his images are grainy, flatly illumined, sometimes out of focus, and invariably uncomposed. Now, it is not possible to abandon composition by deciding to do without it. That abdication itself constitutes a policy and a style. Warhol and his actual director, Paul Morrissey, chose to be as radical as possible, setting the camera down in one corner and directing it at people in another corner—often crowded there so that the camera could be static. He might leave the camera unattended and eschew those small adjustments in framing that we take for granted and that signal the tidiness of artistry. But no matter how automatic the emphasis, Warhol's films have the sort of stylistic minimalism and dislike of expressiveness to be found in Ozu, Hawks, Bergman, Dreyer, Rossellini, Godard, and Renoir; the style, I would argue, that is most elevated in cinema. Those directors compose and frame, but only in the way that most novelists try to write lucidly. They shared Warhol's reluctance to urge meaning into the action through the ingenious placing of the camera. Like him, they tried to serve their actors.

With that, we come to Warhol's single overriding defense of his method: to let us see that "the people are beautiful." But as always with a conceptual artist, that statement needs to be considered at several levels:

1. His people contradict Hollywood's definition of beauty: they are unschooled—they often speak unclearly, and invariably without a script—their "talent" is not defined in terms of the story being told, but remains muddy, personal, and private; they are unkempt, sometimes unwashed, and occasionally visibly flawed and unhealthy. Even Viva, the most conventionally attractive, is scrawny, mannered, and prickly. While Joe, who is good-looking, is obdurately impassive and unable to animate his beauty. So abruptly stars, they have no need to be actors. Presence and the performance of self are enough, as they are, incidentally, with all true stars. Pimpled, inadequate, and inarticulate, they move with the ponderous shyness of gods at play. Warhol's "superstars" are thus a tacit illustration of the nature of screen presence. *Blue Movie*, an extensive study of love-making between Viva and Louis Waldron, is intimate, funny, reflective, and tender. It bridges the gap between performed and achieved sex and shows that mature people need be no more alarmed by that gap than trapeze artists by the absence of a net.

2. These everyday gods aspire to the notion of Hollywood, especially to the camp nostalgia for bygone glamour. They talk among themselves about beauty and attractiveness with an obsessiveness that may be a very accurate portrait of Hollywood private life, as well as a touching evocation of a world of fans trying to emulate cosmetic mythologies.

3. But their circumstances on screen are more sordid and plain than Hollywood has shown us. Warhol's world is one of total sexual exchange, in which heterosexual, monogamous relations have broken down into a crazy paving of alternatives, and where the element of power in sex has been reinforced by narcotics and idleness. Thus, in *Trash*, Joe has reached a forlorn state of being so filled with dope that he cannot get a hard-on. The film's effort to restore that vigor has nothing to do with affection, simply the need to live up to the pleasure principle. Warhol's scheme of life is bland, unthinking, and Utopian in that pleasure alone is its object; but hellish, since the pursuit of pleasure has been ruthless enough to forsake all material, bourgeois comforts. This is made clear in *Trash* by the squalor of Joe and Holly's home, despite the residual homemaking stolidity that haunts them, and the arid magazine luster of Jane's place, counterpointed by her neurotic, "straight" inability to confess that she is a nymphomaniac. In general, Warhol has regarded the physical decay of his world with the equanimity of a camera. But *Trash* actually moralizes and sees a Griffith-like romantic splendor in the battered but loyal Holly—"Joe, can I suck your cock"—even if

she is a man who must masturbate with a beer bottle because of Joe's limpness.

4. Like Holly, many of the characters are androgynous. Plastic people are like plastic dolls: they can go back to the maker for their sexual organs to be altered. Again, Warhol's predilection for homosexuals and bisexuals is utterly unsentimental or lip-smacking. He is not doctrinaire; he is so open to behavior that he has disposed of deviation. The sexual flux is experimental, just as we are made to speculate about the consistency of the people.

Because of that inability to judge people—again, a characteristic of the camera, quite unlike words that pick out meanings—it is easy for a humanist to be depressed by Warhol. He believes only in visible presence: that is why his early films were immense studies of the tiny diurnal changes in the Empire State Building or the static mutability of a man sleeping; and why his method has always relied on very long takes of spontaneous action. Or, to be more precise, continuing inaction and meandering conversations about action. Warhol's people usually sit and talk in corners. (The greater physical action of *Lonesome Cowboys* is influenced by the out-of-doors and recollections of the Western.)

Later Warhol films took on greater structure. It may be Paul Morrissey who made *Heat* a mock-up of *Sunset Boulevard,* and *Trash* a journey movie of Joe in search of a hard-on. But that seems to me an irrelevant (almost "decadent") shaping compared with Warhol's initiating clarity. The factory, or family, could not have existed without him. His distaste for the cult of authorship is another creative paradox within his conceptual art. Nothing establishes the austerity and disabused romanticism of Warhol's vision so much as the way he has taken to heart the influence of the camera on action, and the decision-making role of a spectator.

His films are simultaneously boring and hallucinatory—like the effect of certain narcotics. They make us ask ourselves whether we are watching actors or real people, actual sex or simulated sex. From that, it is a short step to wonder whether we are ourselves real or theatrical, performing impressions made on the minds of the people we meet; whether our sex is actual or simulated. That is Warhol's achievement: to so simplify filmmaking that we reappraise what happens when we watch other people. His method is so lunatically documentary that we learn to reassess candor. We can think of Warhol as a primitive, as an extreme modernist, as the satirist or apologist of old Hollywood, or as the anthropological moviemaker of our metropolis. He was all of these, yet pale and withdrawn; he told us that the camera is more powerful than any purpose handling it. That the camera cannot lie has dissolved the concept of discriminating truth.

Jack L. Warner (1892–1978),
b. London, Canada

It defies understanding that no one ever made a movie about the Warner boys. There were four of them, the sons of Ben, a cobbler from Kraznashiltz in Poland: Harry (1881–1958), actually born in Poland; Albert (1884–1967), born in Baltimore; Sam (1888–1927), also from Baltimore; and Jack, the kid. They did anything. By 1923, they could claim experience with shoes, butchery, general merchandise, ice cream, the fairground business, soap, bicycles, and even motion pictures. Jack had toured as a boy soprano. They ran a theatre in Newcastle, Pennsylvania; they had been in exhibition and exchanges; and Jack had dabbled in production. Warner Brothers was established in 1923: it sounds like the turning point, yet evidently it was just one more wriggle in a series.

They were not doing that much, with a studio over the hill in Burbank, Jack in charge of production, Albert the treasurer, Harry the businessman, and Sam playing with sound. They proved themselves in 1927 by pioneering talking pictures: in fact, they had been more interested in music than synchronized talk, and their system was one that used discs, not sound on film. But the sequence of *Don Juan* (26) and *The Jazz Singer* (27) changed the business. Sam died in the struggle to make sound work, but the three remaining brothers worked out a tough, lean economy, with Jack in Burbank and Harry and Albert in New York. For years, Warners made small pictures, with unusual edge and realism.

Jack was shrewd enough to hire two exceptional production executives: Darryl Zanuck (from 1929–33) and Hal Wallis (1933–44). Nevertheless, he deserves a lot of credit for the talents he hired, for the genres he helped promote, and for that string of movies. Call it the era of Zanuck or Wallis, if you will; still the "Warners" style is tough, routinely black and white, gangster pictures, hardboiled musicals, adventure, costume, and a political undertone. It is Cagney, Robinson, Bogart, Raft, Paul Muni, Errol Flynn, Bette Davis, and Olivia de Havilland. It is Michael Curtiz, Raoul Walsh, Howard Hawks, and Busby Berkeley. And it is *42nd Street, Gold Diggers of 1933, Captain Blood, The Life of Emile Zola, The Adventures of Robin Hood, Jezebel, The Roaring Twenties, The Private Lives of Elizabeth and Essex, Juarez, The Letter, Sergeant York, High Sierra, The Strawberry Blonde, The Maltese Falcon, Gentleman Jim, Yankee Doodle Dandy*, and *Casablanca.*

Warner allowed rivalry to end the relationship with Hal Wallis. And so, from 1945 to 1967, he was personally in charge of production, albeit with a string of assistants. These were difficult years for the business, yet Warners stayed lively. They rescued Joan Crawford with *Mildred Pierce;* they let Hawks make *To Have and Have Not* and *The Big*

Sleep; they developed the Doris Day musical; they maintained a reputation for swashbuckling (with *The Flame and the Arrow* and *Captain Horatio Hornblower*); they did *White Heat* and *The Fountainhead, A Star Is Born,* and *A Streetcar Named Desire;* they made the James Dean pictures and *Strangers on a Train, The Searchers, Rio Bravo, What Ever Happened to Baby Jane?,* and *Bonnie and Clyde.*

Jack Warner personally produced *My Fair Lady* in 1964, and he presided over the sale of the studio to Seven Arts in 1967. He won the Thalberg Award in 1958. He was a suntanned dandy, a loudmouth, a wisecracker; he was conservative, tough, arrogant, and often stupid. But he outlived the brothers and he is the Warner that everyone means when they allude to three or four terrific decades. If he'd been, or known, any better, he'd never have gone into pictures.

Denzel Washington,
b. Mount Vernon, New York, 1954

At the end of Spike Lee's *Malcolm X* (92), there is a montage of stills and newsreel of the real Malcolm. He was gaunter than Denzel Washington, maybe, and he had a hardened carapace—to life and the camera—that no actor could conceive of. Nevertheless, the montage reminds us of the journey Washington has taken in the three-plus hours of the film, and of the profound attempt he has made on the real life. We seem to see matters of bearing and thought in the real Malcolm that Washington has schooled us for. The coda is proof of a major performance, not just Lee's best work but a sign of nobility in the actor.

Washington was educated at Fordham and A.C.T. in San Francisco. He played Dr. Philip Chandler on TV in *St. Elsewhere,* and gradually developed a movie career: George Segal's seventeen-year-old bastard in *Carbon Copy* (81, Michael Schultz); *A Soldier's Story* (84, Norman Jewison); *Power* (86, Sidney Lumet); nominated for best supporting actor as Steven Biko in *Cry Freedom* (87, Richard Attenborough); to England for the excellent *For Queen and Country* (88, Martin Stellman); winning the best supporting actor Oscar in *Glory* (89, Edward Zwick); *The Mighty Quinn* (89, Carl Schenkel); laboring through *Heart Condition* (90, James D. Parriott); the trumpeter in *Mo' Better Blues* (90, Lee); *Mississippi Masala* (91, Mira Nair); *Ricochet* (91, Russell Mulcahy); as Don Pedro in *Much Ado About Nothing* (93, Kenneth Branagh); helping Julia Roberts in *The Pelican Brief* (93, Alan J. Pakula); helping Tom Hanks in *Philadelphia* (93, Jonathan Demme).

At that point, Washington was a lead actor. Now, seven years later, it is evident that he is a big star—second only to Sidney Poitier in the history of black acting, if you like; yet, truly, I think he is the first black whose stardom transcends race. I felt that in not his best picture, *The Bone Collector* (99, Phillip Noyce), where he was paralyzed and utterly dominating, even to the point of having Angelina Jolie itching for his finger (the one part where he had a little action).

With that extra confidence, he has become a major American presence. Sure, there have been silly films along the way, but the command is authentic: a crucial conflict with Gene Hackman in *Crimson Tide* (95, Tony Scott); *Virtuosity* (95, Brett Leonard); very good as Easy Rawlins in *Devil in a Blue Dress* (95, Carl Franklin); very subtle in *Courage Under Fire* (96, Edward Zwick); *The Preacher's Wife* (96, Penny Marshall), which was silly; *Fallen* (98, Gregory Hoblit), as was this; *He Got Game* (98, Lee); very sure of himself in *The Siege* (98, Zwick); so good in *Hurricane* (99, Norman Jewison) he made you forget the deceits in the film; *Remember the Titans* (00, Boaz Yakin), where he began to seem Wayne-like; *Training Day* (01, Antonio Fuqua), winning the Oscar; *John Q* (02, Nick Cassavetes).

He is also directing *Finding Fish* (02) and he has produced two thorough documentaries: *Hank Aaron: Chasing the Dream* (95, Michael Tollins) and *Half Past Autumn: The Life and Work of Gordon Parks* (00, Craig Rice). He acted in and directed *Antwone Fisher* (02).

John Waters, b. Baltimore, Maryland, 1946
1970: *Mondo Trasho.* 1971: *Multiple Maniacs.* 1972: *Pink Flamingos.* 1975: *Female Trouble.* 1977: *Desperate Living.* 1981: *Polyester.* 1988: *Hairspray.* 1990: *Cry-Baby.* 1994: *Serial Mom.* 1998: *Pecker.* 2001: *Cecil B. DeMented.*

John Waters is, in many ways, the classic modern homosexual movie director, with wit, courage, and mischief to spare, born a Catholic in middlebrow Baltimore and gradually encouraged to make mock of everything his mom cherished—while secretly longing to be Mom. He has achieved a great deal, becoming a recognizable cultural icon way beyond Baltimore, and being generally endearing. But it's notable that he has mellowed as he's grown older, which is another way of pointing to the variety of ploys the American mainstream has for muffling the outright offensive. Waters might, once upon a time, have been a candidate to be the American Buñuel, especially when he had the raw hatred of Divine at his command (notably in *Pink Flamingos, Female Trouble, Polyester,* and *Hairspray*). But when Divine died, in 1989, Waters was rather exposed for his innate kindness and moderation. His subsequent films are, if you will, "regular" satires—and Kathleen Turner carried *Serial Mom* way beyond Waters's normal cult following.

So we like John Waters, and regard him as dirty-naughty and middle-aged. Will he retaliate? Can he find it in himself to be monstrous or explosive? I doubt it. Indeed, if you ever contemplated the anarchist end of American filmmaking from the point of view of J. Edgar Hoover, or Jack Valenti, say, and wanted to invent an ostensibly dangerous but truly safe figure to occupy it, you couldn't do better than John Waters. Alas.

Emily Watson, b. London, England, 1967

I am not one of those who speak of Emily Watson as a luminous saint of truth. In fact, very often during *Breaking the Waves* (96, Lars von Trier), I wanted to get up on screen and wring her character's neck. I loathe and despise that film, its maudlin religiosity, its cruel, reckless mix of sensationalism and sentimentality, and its own sense of being very significant. This is much more the fault of von Trier than of Ms. Watson (it could be that I'm the outcast, I admit). But there have been other signs of the actress's readiness to be woeful and manipulative at the same time that leave me very guarded.

She spent time at the Shakespeare School of Acting, and did some theatre in Britain, but she won the role of Bess in *Breaking the Waves* when Helena Bonham Carter flinched at the sexual explicitness it called for. Watson was nominated for that performance, but she has had an odd career since then: *Metroland* (97, Philip Saville); *The Boxer* (97, Jim Sheridan); Maggie Tulliver in *The Mill on the Floss* (97, Graham Theakston) for British TV; as Jacqueline du Pré in *Hilary and Jackie* (98, Anand Tucker); as Olive Stanton in *Cradle Will Rock* (99, Tim Robbins); the mother in *Angela's Ashes* (99, Alan Parker); awful in the more-than-awful *Trixie* (00, Alan Rudolph); *The Luzhin Defense* (00, Marleen Gorris); as a maid in *Gosford Park* (01, Robert Altman); *Punch-Drunk Love* (02, Paul Thomas Anderson); *Red Dragon* (02, Brett Ratner); *Equilibrium* (02, Kurt Wimmer); *The Life and Death of Peter Sellers* (04, Stephen Hopkins).

John Wayne (Marion Michael Morrison) (1907–79), b. Winterset, Iowa

I once showed *Red River* in a course for American students and at the end—like Charles Foster Kane at the opera—I stood up alone to applaud. This was 1971. Later we argued about the film. Yes, they could see the relaxed epic storytelling. They admitted that Hawks brought a beautiful simplicity to the filming. Of course, the action scenes were breathtaking. They liked the way Walter Brennan was used as a narrator. They had been very impressed by the shots of cattle on the move. Grudgingly, they conceded that the theme of family relationship and conflicting stubbornness was well worked out. They had nothing against the special masculine romanticism. Clift was astonishing, was he really dead? And even Joanne Dru was pleasing. Pushed to the limit, they allowed that this film showed more aspects of John Wayne than most. But ultimately, *Red River* never had a chance because they would not stomach John Wayne.

The reasons for that are not obscure. One has only to remember the unctuous moment in *The Alamo* (60) when Crockett/Wayne, having cuddled "Angelina Dickinson," turns to Widmark and Laurence Harvey and with good nature bathing his features says: "Kind of a shame kids have to grow up to be people." My students were people who could not transport Wayne's heroics into adulthood. Nor would they have liked the uncompromising political bias of *The Alamo* when Wayne addressed the world: "Republic—I like the sound of the word . . . One of those words that makes me tight in the throat." Less still did they admire his remorseless weighing in on the American right and that heartfelt tribute to political obscurantism: *The Green Berets* (68), a film Wayne directed and profited from against every humane and tactful objection.

They are reasons enough for qualifying Wayne the man, but not for shutting *Red River* out of one's mind. At worst Wayne was unthinking, a boor, harsh, and arrogant—the character he plays in *Red River*. But just as reaction has misled the world into ignoring Leni Riefenstahl's worth as an artist, so Wayne's sincere wrongheadedness once obliterated the fact that he was a great screen actor.

As a child he moved West and, after a football scholarship at the University of Southern California, Tom Mix got him a job at Fox. There he met John Ford and worked as a set decorator on *Mother Machree* (28). Gradually he edged into acting, by the storybook means of being a bystander. His first big part was in *The Big Trail* (30, Raoul Walsh). Walsh had seen him carrying a big armchair above his head—carrying it with flair and flourish. Throughout the 1930s Wayne was a star of matinee Westerns, sometimes a singing cowboy, working his way round most of the smaller studios and making something like a hundred films. By 1939 he was with Republic when John Ford asked him to be the Ringo Kid in *Stagecoach*. The success of that film lifted Wayne from regular work to stardom. Republic pulled themselves together for a major vehicle for him—*Dark Command* (40, Walsh)—and Ford called on him again to play a seaman in *The Long Voyage Home* (40).

Even at that stage, Wayne had this virtue denied to Ford's "stock company": he did not ham. Universal put him opposite Dietrich in *Seven Sinners* (40, Tay Garnett) and Republic lowered its sights to more Westerns. For the next few years he made fodder at his home studio and more adventurous work outside, much of which only exposed his monotonous fierceness: *Reap the Wild Wind* (42, Cecil B. De Mille); *The Spoilers* (42, Ray Enright); *Flying Tigers* (42, David Miller); with Joan Crawford in Jules Dassin's crazy *Reunion in France* (42); and *The Fighting Seabees* (44, Edward Ludwig). In 1945, he was in *Back to Bataan* (Edward Dmytryk), *Flame of the Barbary Coast* (Joseph Kane), and overshadowed by Robert Montgomery in *They Were Expendable* (Ford). He was bizarrely paired with Claudette Colbert in a comedy, *Without Reservations* (46, Mervyn Le Roy), but Republic still pushed straight Westerns at him.

Then came two films that radically enlarged his image: *Fort Apache* (48, Ford), in which he played a cavalry captain, and *Red River* (48, Howard Hawks). Not least of his achievements as a guide to players is the way Hawks was the first to see the slit-eyed, obdurate side to Wayne's character. Tom Dunson is a fine character study: a man made hard by an early mistake and by the emphasis on achievement with which he tried to conceal that mistake. With Ford again, Wayne was one of *Three Godfathers* (48), a truly awful movie. But in 1949, he was Captain Nathan Brittles at the point of retirement in *She Wore a Yellow Ribbon* (Ford), and in 1950 the trilogy was completed with the leisurely *Rio Grande* (Ford). Asked to be older, a husband and a father, Wayne became human and touching.

All the while, Wayne had soldiered on at Republic: *The Wake of the Red Witch* (48, Edward Ludwig); *The Fighting Kentuckian* (49, George Waggner); and *Sands of Iwo Jima* (49, Allan Dwan). In 1951, Wayne made two oddities at RKO: *Flying Leathernecks* (Nicholas Ray) and *Jet Pilot* (Josef von Sternberg, but remade by Howard Hughes), and in 1952 he made his last, and best, film at Republic: as *The Quiet Man* (John Ford)— which reunited him with Maureen O'Hara (his costar from *Rio Grande*), one of the few actresses capable of addressing and interesting him.

Wayne was now a Warners actor—not that the films were much better: *Big Jim McLain* (52, Ludwig)—one of the first movies in which Wayne's rabid anti-Communism was made clear; *Trouble Along the Way* (53, Michael Curtiz); and *Island in the Sky* (53, William Wellman). But *Hondo* (53, John Farrow) was far better in the way it pursued the abrasive solitary man revealed in *Red River*. *The High and the Mighty* (54) and *Blood Alley* (55)—both by Wellman—were above average, but *The Sea Chase* (55, Farrow) was foolish and *The Conqueror* (55, Dick Powell) ludicrous with Wayne a sulky Genghis Khan. Next, however, came *The Searchers* (56, Ford), one of his finest films—once more a study of an unapproachable, stubborn man, finally excluded from the family reunion as a romantic but lonely figure facing the

landscape. He coasted with *The Wings of Eagles* (57, Ford), *Legend of the Lost* (57, Hathaway), and *The Barbarian and the Geisha* (58, John Huston), before making *Rio Bravo* (59, Hawks). Once more, Hawks enlarged Wayne by concentrating on an alcoholic Dean Martin and having Wayne watch him "like a friend." It worked—as did the application of Angie Dickinson's talkative emotional crises to Wayne's solidity—so that *Rio Bravo* is not just Wayne's most humane picture but the one that makes him most comic.

In the 1960s, Wayne became a monolith of survival. He subdued cancer, seemingly ignored age, and increasingly became an American public figure. His real veterans were less intriguing than the older men he played in *Red River* and the cavalry trilogy. Gradually he succumbed to lazy Westerns for Andrew V. McLaglen, but, against that, comedy adventure lightened the potential heaviness: *The Horse Soldiers* (59, Ford); *North to Alaska* (60, Hathaway); *The Comancheros* (61, Curtiz); *The Man Who Shot Liberty Valance* (61, Ford); *Hatari!* (62, Hawks); *Donovan's Reef* (62, Ford); still battling with Maureen O'Hara in *McLintock!* (63, McLaglen); *In Harm's Way* (65, Otto Preminger); *El Dorado* (67, Hawks); *The War Wagon* (67, Burt Kennedy); *Rio Lobo* (70, Hawks); *The Train Robbers* (73, Kennedy); *McQ* (74, John Sturges)—all these are worthy films for one old man.

It was disheartening that his unavoidable Oscar should have come for *True Grit* (69, Hathaway), and no one could argue but that he looked nearly seventy. In *The Cowboys* (71, Mark Rydell), the monolith even died, to be avenged with fantastic, cold blood-lust by the band of children he has employed as cattlehands. The cinema shook, my son wept, but Wayne was truly dead.

He knew no restraint: disappointed in Vietnam and loyal to Nixon, he attended Carter's inaugural gala; a survivor of cancer, he then appeared in TV ads for research funds, using that scene from *The Shootist* (76, Don Siegel), in which he is himself diagnosed. *The Shootist* is a modest picture, but Wayne had rarely disclosed such warmth or gentleness. Elsewhere, he was a Chicago cop in London in *Brannigan* (75, Douglas Hickox), and with Katharine Hepburn in *Rooster Cogburn* (75, Stuart Millar).

His death moved nearly everyone, as had his brave walk down the Academy staircase, two months before death, to give the best picture Oscar to ... *The Deer Hunter* (that'll be the day, indeed).

He made too many pictures, of course; but only because for so long he was a guarantee of profit. There were challenging genres that he never tried. So it is not right to regard him as a great actor. But what a star, what a presence, and what a wealth of reserve he brought to that bold presence. (So you wonder if he couldn't have played comedy.)

Nor has he dated. All one can say is that he filled the screen role of a necessarily difficult man as naturally as most actors wore clothes. There was an age when people could be stars without undue grandeur or self-mockery. Whether Wayne is looking at the land that may make a great ranch, or turning in a doorway to survey his true home, the desert, every gesture was authentic and a prized disclosure. He moved the way singers sing, with huge confidence and daring. You have to imagine how it all began in the way Raoul Walsh saw him carrying that armchair—as if it was a young girl in a red robe being lifted up in mercy and wonder.

Sigourney Weaver (Susan Weaver),
b. New York, 1949

Lofty, droll, ready for surprise, smart, attractive, and plainly desperate for comedy, Sigourney Weaver has a robust reasonableness worth bearing in mind when other actresses kill themselves, ascend the Olympus of vanity, or disgrace the human race. In *Alien* (79, Ridley Scott) and *Aliens* (86, James Cameron), she went by sheer willpower and assertiveness from the bimbo in bikini underwear to the driven crew leader who gave the second picture dramatic substance. By *Aliens³* (92, David Fancher), she was coproducer and proud about getting her piece of the action, yet in the rush of business she had let herself take on a victimized look and a tragic role. Didn't she know she was made to be heroic?

In one year, Weaver was nominated as best actress in *Gorillas in the Mist* (88, Michael Apted) and as supporting actress for the thankless role in *Working Girl* (88, Mike Nichols). At other extremes, she was insouciantly naked for much of *Half Moon Street* (86, Bob Swain), deliriously vampy in *Ghostbusters* (84, Ivan Reitman), and mysteriously along for *Ghostbusters II* (89, Reitman). She tried France in *One Man or Two* (86, Daniel Vigne), southeast Asia in *The Year of Living Dangerously* (83, Peter Weir), and conventional female support in *Eyewitness* (81, Peter Yates) and *Deal of the Century* (83, William Friedkin).

Susan Weaver was the daughter of NBC executive Pat Weaver and actress Elizabeth Inglis. She attended Stanford and the Yale Drama School, and she played on Broadway in David Rabe's *Hurlyburly,* earning a Tony nomination.

It is in her readiness to go to extremes—to be out of breath and control, unmade up, naked in a flop, or slumming in a silly hit—that Weaver is most herself. Who knows what the system can make of her at and beyond forty? At last, the creature in *Alien* got her—unless she comes back as a fatal carrier, a sweet-smiling destructress. She is

so intelligent, so well-spoken, she could end up in Merchant-Ivory films or on PBS. In which case, watch for her introduction of slapstick.

She played Queen Isabella in *1492: Conquest of Paradise* (92, Scott) and she returned to comedy in *Dave* (93, Reitman).

I've left my questions open from 1994, but the answers are richer than I imagined. Yes, Ripley did come back, in *Alien Resurrection* (97, Jean-Pierre Jeunet), and it's only fair to say that that mistake hinged on Ms. Weaver making a lot of money (like $12 million). The fourth part of the quartet was awful, but it has extraordinary hints of what might have been—not least a lithe, dangerous Weaver (closing in on fifty), who sees the monster as her true kin. It should have been better, but the quartet may stand up years from now as one of the most fascinating narratives of the late twentieth century. And it was clear, at the end, that for good and ill, she was Ripley.

Elsewhere, Weaver continues to take risks: anguished and passionate in *Death and the Maiden* (94, Roman Polanski), but let down by the material; *Jeffrey* (95, Christopher Ashley); as a dotty shrink in *Copycat* (95, Jon Amiel); excellent in *The Ice Storm* (97, Ang Lee); fascinating and hideous as the stepmother in *Snow White: A Tale of Terror* (97, Michael Cohn); wonderful in the badly overlooked *A Map of the World* (99, Scott Elliott); hilarious in the not-to-be-ignored *Galaxy Quest* (99, Dean Parisot); *Heartbreakers* (01, David Mirkin); and the woman with a hot stepson in the very low budget *Tadpole* (02, Gary Winick).

Clifton Webb (Webb Parmallee Hollenbeck)
(1891–1966), b. Indianapolis, Indiana

The legend goes that when Otto Preminger took over *Laura* (44) from Rouben Mamoulian, he introduced the Broadway actor Clifton Webb to play the bitchy columnist Waldo Lydecker, as thin and exquisite as a case clock. But Webb had made films before. He had been a dancing teacher and a star actor in musicals and reviews. In 1925, however, he had small parts in two films: *New Toys* (John S. Robertson) and *The Heart of a Siren* (Phil Rosen). Clearly, it was *Laura* that established Webb, even if he seldom caught the elderly, baleful homosexual so well again—or was allowed to. "I'm not kind, I'm vicious," says Lydecker. "It's the secret of my charm."

Webb's skill at nastiness was too often swaddled in sentimental comedy, chiefly the Mr. Belvedere part. He may have suffered from Preminger's introduction of him in that he remained a Fox player. That studio had a short supply of the dialogue Webb needed and few sophisticated directors. Instead, he was asked to coax out an acidulous smile as the sort of uncle who yearned secretly to knife a nephew: *The Dark Corner* (46, Henry Hathaway); very camp in *The Razor's Edge*

(46, Edmund Goulding); *Sitting Pretty* (48, Walter Lang); *Mr. Belvedere Goes to College* (49, Elliott Nugent); *Cheaper by the Dozen* (50, Lang); *For Heaven's Sake* (50, George Seaton); *Mr. Belvedere Rings the Bell* (51, Henry Koster); *Dreamboat* (52, Claude Binyon); as John Philip Sousa in *Stars and Stripes Forever* (52, Koster); *Titanic* (53, Jean Negulesco); *Three Coins in the Fountain* (54, Negulesco); *Woman's World* (54, Negulesco); *The Man Who Never Was* (56, Ronald Neame); *Boy on a Dolphin* (57, Negulesco); *The Remarkable Mr. Pennypacker* (59, Henry Levin); and *The Devil Never Sleeps* (62, Leo McCarey).

Harvey Weinstein,

b. Buffalo, New York, 1952

Actually most sources cite "circa 1952" for the birth—as if some legendary imprecision was there from the beginning (and don't forget brother Bob). In other matters—such as the number of pictures where Harvey is credited as producer or executive producer (so that he could be there, on stage, for a best picture award)—the number is precise (at well over one hundred by now, and growing). Still, if that seems like an impossible contradiction of philosophy, rest assured: there is something not just ancient, but nearly primordial, about Harvey Weinstein. After more than a hundred years of change and development, he is the living, bursting, sometimes perspiring proof that pictures is a business for those who love to act like moguls, khans, and tsars. Harvey is a throwback—if you could pick him up. But he is now and the future, too, and I don't rule out, sometime soon, the chance of a year in which he executive-produced every picture made.

What does an executive producer do? Whatever he wants to do, because Harvey is a self-made man and in love with his own work. He is also the man who has done more than anyone else to erase the potentially dangerous (or liberating) schism that was beginning to appear between mainstream American pictures and independents. How did he do that? By arguing deep into so many nights with every indie artist he could find to let them know that they deserved the limos, the best tables, the Gwyneths, the Oscars, the ads, the participation, the glory, and the Weinsteins. So they would be shouted at now and then, bullied, threatened with physical violence or overwhelming embrace. Live a little! How do you guys expect to be artists without you've lived a little?

And, of course they tell stories about Harvey Weinstein. Indeed, he is not just the kind of tentpole that maintains the lore of picture gossip. He is the kind of guy who can keep "they" in business. And as he will tell you himself (or get Bob to tell you), he is over the top because he loves pictures. Not for Harvey your dry business-school training,

your stress on the numbers. No, Harvey loves a show, he loves actors, he loves love. And so he stands steadfastly by that old standard, that you can do anything, screw anyone, so long as you insist that you love the business.

There was a time when Harvey and Bob were filmmakers. They made something called *Playing for Keeps* (Harvey wrote it, and they together directed it), so bad that nothing but love explains it. But they persevered, and in 1979 they founded their company, Miramax, dedicated to the making and distribution of independent pictures. They were good at what they did, and especially at identifying foreign-language pictures that would have an audience in America (e.g., *Pelle the Conqueror* and *Cinema Paradiso*).

They progressed on stepping stones called *Scandal; Sex, Lies and Videotape; The Crying Game;* and *Pulp Fiction.* Then in 1993, they took their decisive step, selling the company to Disney in return for more investment money. There were uneasy times: the Disney management did not exactly like or trust the boys; and Miramax went on a spree, buying up far more projects than they could handle properly. There are filmmakers still imprisoned on their shelves, but reluctant to upset Harvey (or Bob).

But they weathered their own storm and came back strong with *Emma; The English Patient; Scream; The Wings of the Dove; Good Will Hunting; Scream 2; Velvet Goldmine; Halloween H₂O; Shakespeare in Love; The Cider House Rules; Scream 3; Chocolat; Iris; The Shipping News; In the Bedroom.*

You know those films because they are among the best promoted in modern times. Miramax has virtually defined the art of Oscar advertising, and in *The English Patient* (which they picked up late in the day) and *Shakespeare in Love* they have two best pictures, and the unquestionable fact that the onetime indie, Miramax, is now a major studio.

Peter Weir, b. Sydney, Australia, 1944

1967: *Count Vim's Last Exercise* (s). 1968: *The Life and Times of The Reverend Buck Shotte* (s). 1970: "Michael," an episode from *Three to Go.* 1971: *Homesdale* (d). 1972: *Incredible Floridas* (d). 1973: *Whatever Happened to Green Valley?*. 1974: *The Cars That Ate Paris.* 1975: *Picnic at Hanging Rock.* 1977: *The Last Wave.* 1978: *The Plumber.* 1981: *Gallipoli.* 1983: *The Year of Living Dangerously.* 1985: *Witness.* 1986: *The Mosquito Coast.* 1989: *Dead Poets Society.* 1990: *Green Card.* 1993: *Fearless.* 1998: *The Truman Show.*

Weir has an uncommon and beguiling aptitude for atmosphere of menace and mystery, often linked to strange and desolate places. He loves that brink of the occult, when perfectly found in landscape. But how pedestrian he becomes when he tries to explain these pregnant moods. The first part of *Picnic at Hanging Rock* is exquisite; *The Last Wave* never stops being—or advances on—a great idea for a film; the Indonesia disclosed in *The Year of Living Dangerously* is fascinating; and the Amish community in *Witness* cries out to take over the picture.

But plots get preference, and the films become clumsy and conventional. Without those alluring riddles of place and wonderment, Weir has shown himself as middlebrow decent as *Gallipoli* and *Dead Poets Society*, worthy cause pictures. The great failure of his career is *Mosquito Coast*, seeming an ideal subject in that Paul Theroux had given him themes of disquiet and place as good structure. But Weir could not see that the project was beyond Harrison Ford, and he delivered a muted muddle instead of a chilling *Swiss Family Robinson*.

Fearless was a characteristic Weir project. Who else could have been so fascinated by the sensation of an air disaster and the dislocation of grief? The first half hour is dazzling, yet gradually the film succumbs to problems of script development and facile resolution.

So who was prepared for *The Truman Show*, which I rate as one of the great American movies, magically balanced between farce and dread, a unique exploration and prediction of America's nature and fantasies—and this in many respects a portrait of the movies. I give a lot of credit to Andrew Niccol (who wrote it), to Jim Carrey and Ed Harris who made tricky roles human. But for Weir, and all of us, it was like a man stepping aside from, and above, his whole career and his medium—as if to say, this has to be said.

Johnny Weissmuller (Peter John Weissmuller) (1904–84), b. Windber, Pennsylvania

He was six foot three, a little over two hundred pounds, and in the early 1930s he was the least dressed and most magnificent male body on the screen. Tarzan was the excuse, but Weissmuller was an extraordinary image—the high voice, the wide-spaced, stunned eyes, the very Aryan, carved head, with a sketch of loincloth glued to his body. He shaved his chest and his legs; he shone with body oil; and he did most of his own action, swimming and swinging through the trees. Lest anyone think he was taking it too seriously, he had a cry that was part Austrian yodel, part gorilla, and part testosterone. "Me Tarzan, You Jane," he grunted, and every woman from Maureen O'Sullivan onward got the message. No subsequent Tarzan ever matched him—the loincloth was retired.

Weissmuller's parents were Viennese (hasn't Arnold Schwarzenegger ever considered doing Johnny's story?). When they moved to Chicago, the boy learned swimming in public pools and in Lake Michigan. He became an unbeatable crawl swimmer, his very powerful arm movements dragging him to countless world records and five gold medals at the 1924 and 1928 Olympic Games.

He turned professional in 1929 and played himself in *Glorifying the American Girl* (29, Millard Webb and John Harkrider). Then Louis B. Mayer and Irving Thalberg chose him as the new Tarzan. He was a remarkable success in films that used sound well, often borrowed jungle footage from other productions, and that seldom forgot the erotic undertones of Johnny and O'Sullivan or her successor, Brenda Joyce: *Tarzan the Ape Man* (32, W. S. Van Dyke); *Tarzan and His Mate* (34, Cedric Gibbons); *Tarzan Escapes* (36, Richard Thorpe); *Tarzan Finds a Son* (39, Thorpe)—his "Boy," Johnny Sheffield; *Tarzan's Secret Weapon* (41, Thorpe); *Tarzan's New York Adventure* (42, Thorpe), the funniest of the series; *Tarzan Triumphs* (43, William Thiele), in which there is no Jane, but Frances Gifford plays a jungle princess; *Tarzan's Desert Mystery* (43, Thiele); *Tarzan and the Amazons* (45, Kurt Neumann), with Brenda Joyce as Jane and Maria Ouspenskaya as Queen of the Amazons; *Tarzan and the Leopard Woman* (46, Neumann); a foolish attempt to extend—*Swamp Fire* (46, William Pine); *Tarzan and the Hunters* (47, Neumann); and his last turn in the part, *Tarzan and the Mermaids* (48, Robert Florey).

Weissmuller was a little rotund and elderly, to be sure, and the stunts were proving demanding. But what a disastrous mistake it was to replace him with that slick gigolo, Lex Barker. Weissmuller was reappraised as a B-picture hero, fully dressed—*Jungle Jim* (48, William Berke), a role he played in another fifteen films up until *Devil Goddess* (55, Spencer Bennett), by which time, absentmindedly, everyone called the character "Johnny."

He was a famous swinger in real life, too: there were five wives (including Lupe Velez, a pro golfer, and a San Francisco socialite), and years of difficulty with the IRS. By the seventies, he was a host at Caesars Palace in Las Vegas, and by the late seventies, he was diminished by strokes and heart disease.

Tuesday Weld (Susan Ker Weld), b. New York, 1943

From *Rock, Rock, Rock* (56, Will Price) to *Falling Down* (93, Joel Schumacher), so little of Tuesday Weld has been ordinary or expected. Is there any richer subject for Hollywood biography, or autobiography—for she is plainly smart and articulate enough, and she has survived all the craziness of being a mass media nymphet in the age of Eisenhower, as well as a girl burdened by the name Tuesday, while still managing to show that she can be an extraordinary actress as well as a great beauty, who was somehow woeful and ravaged by the age of twenty-five.

To take just one out-of-the-way example: she has scenes as Zelda in the TV movie *F. Scott Fitzgerald in Hollywood* (76, Anthony Page) that are as good as any American actress has done on screen. Her best work is often that hidden, or that little proclaimed. Whereas, she seldom got the roles her talent and nerve cried out for—Lolita, say, or Bonnie in *Bonnie and Clyde*, a part she missed because of pregnancy. She has made many dismal pictures—and none more grisly than the "distinguished" *Falling Down*. It is hard to follow a line through her career. But I have never found a Weld performance not worth study. She never departs from her own tough standards of what is human and interesting.

She played Thalia Menninger in *The Many Loves of Dobie Gillis* (59–60) on TV; *Rally Round the Flag, Boys!* (58, Leo McCarey); *The Five Pennies* (59, Melville Shavelson); *Because They're Young* (60, Paul Wendkos); *High Time* (60, Blake Edwards); *Sex Kittens Go to College* (60, Albert Zugsmith); *The Private Lives of Adam and Eve* (60, Zugsmith); *Bachelor Flat* (61, Frank Tashlin); *Return to Peyton Place* (61, José Ferrer); with Elvis in *Wild in the Country* (61, Philip Dunne); *Soldier in the Rain* (63, Ralph Nelson); *I'll Take Sweden* (65, Frederick de Cordova); very good with Steve McQueen in *The Cincinnati Kid* (65, Norman Jewison); very funny in *Lord Love a Duck* (66, George Axelrod); brilliant, seductive, and lethal as the high-school Lulu in *Pretty Poison* (68, Noel Black), and very well matched with Anthony Perkins; rural, simple, and effortlessly treacherous in the love story with Gregory Peck in *I Walk the Line* (70, John Frankenheimer); *A Safe Place* (71, Henry Jaglom); as Joan Didion's wasted heroine, Maria Wyeth, in *Play It As It Lays* (72, Frank Perry); in a TV version of Clouzot's *Diaboliques—Reflections of Murder* (74, John Badham), her hair cropped, her demeanor agonized; epically stoned as Marge in *Who'll Stop the Rain* (78, Karel Reisz), in a tragic love scene with Nick Nolte; a divorcée accused of killing her own child in *A Question of Guilt* (78, Robert Butler) for TV; *Serial* (80, Bill Persky); on TV again in *Madame X* (80, Robert Ellis Miller) and *Mother and Daughter: The Loving War* (80, Burt Brinckerhoff); *Thief* (81, Michael Mann); *Author! Author!* (82, Arthur Hiller); as the off-screen voice in one of the movies' most ambiguous rape scenes in *Once Upon a Time in America* (83, Sergio Leone); *The Winter of Our Discontent* (83, Waris Hussein); *Scorned and Swindled* (84, Wendkos); *Circle of Violence: A Family Drama* (86, David Greene); as a woman in love with a younger man in *Something in Common* (86, Glenn Jordan); *Heartbreak Hotel* (88, Chris Columbus); and *Feeling Minnesota* (96, Steven Baigelman).

More recently, she had small roles in *Chelsea Walls* (01, Ethan Hawke) and *Investigating Sex* (01, Alan Rudolph).

If she had been "Susan Weld" she might now be known as one of our great actresses.

Orson Welles (1915–85),
b. Kenosha, Wisconsin

1941: *Citizen Kane*. 1942: *The Magnificent Ambersons*. 1943: *Journey Into Fear* (codirected with Norman Foster); *It's All True* (uncompleted). 1946: *The Stranger*. 1948: *The Lady from Shanghai; Macbeth*. 1952: *Othello*. 1955: *Confidential Report/Mr. Arkadin*. 1958: *Touch of Evil; The Fountain of Youth* (TV). 1959: *Don Quixote* (uncompleted). 1963: *The Trial/Le Proces*. 1966: *Chimes at Midnight/Campanadas a Medianoche*. 1968: *The Immortal Story/Histoire Immortelle*. 1973: *Vérités et Mensonges/F for Fake* (d). 1977: *Filming Othello* (d).

The delving into the circumstances under which *Citizen Kane* was conceived—by Pauline Kael in *The Citizen Kane Book*, and by Welles's colleague, John Houseman, in *Run-Through*—concentrated on literary authorship. Miss Kael's work, especially, amounted to an attempt to dull Welles's flashy reputation, to expose the charlatan, to reassert literary merit, and puncture performing flatus. Happily, it only played to Welles's glorification of ineluctable failure in his bogus mogul self.

No one can now deny Herman Mankiewicz credit for the germ, shape, and pointed language of the screenplay, but no one who has seen the film as often as it deserves to be seen would dream that Welles is not its only begetter. *The Citizen Kane Book* may persuade us to reassess Mankiewicz, but he never becomes more than a clever, aphoristic, self-loathing pen-pusher. His plan for *Kane* was ingenious, malicious, and provocative. All of those qualities Welles endorsed, and shared. But he added his own nobility, which is none the less for centering on himself. Through observing his own melancholy passage as falling star, Welles made a universal portrait of failure, decline, chimes at midnight, snuffed-out pipe dream, and of the foolish play-acting we devise to conceal those brutal truths. *Kane* is a lasting achievement because of Welles's capacity for folie de grandeur, and that may be seen in his theatricality, his storytelling, and his visual imagination, as much as in his dramatization of himself.

Kane is not simply a matter of a novice director's immediate creation of a visual style that is simultaneously baroque and precise, overwhelmingly emotional, and unerringly founded in reality. Deep-focus photography, ceilinged sets, and exaggerated low-key lighting—such tangible effects were not born with *Kane*. Anyone can see how much Welles's eye had learned from German expressionism and its influence on stage production in the 1930s. In France and America, elaborate, lifelike sets and comprehensive photography had been played with for ten years. Look at *The Long Voyage Home* and you can see Gregg Toland in possession of all the photographic measures of *Kane;* you may see, too, how little he or Ford knew what to do with them. The Ford film is senselessly pretty. The deep-focus, chiaroscuro image works in *Kane* ("works" is a tame word) because it dramatizes the inside of Kane's head, curving at the edges or fading into darkness with the diffuseness of egotism.

Nor is *Kane* just the visible energy of Welles badgering away from center-screen at his fellow-actors, most of whom were colleagues of some years, already bewildered by their own confused feelings of love and resentment for the boy genius. It is also the fact that, before or since, no one in Hollywood has carved out such freedom for himself, and then used it to initiate a chorus of damnation, mistrust, and rumor that would reliably hinder him from a lasting commercial career. As if Welles would ever knuckle under to stability! He handled RKO like a conjuror. Without their being able to prevent it, he charmed, bullied, and provoked Mankiewicz, Houseman, Toland, and Bernard Herrmann into their best work for the screen. That is a sort of authorship that consists of dictating the terms in which collaborators deal with him. It was only when he had brought Hollywood to its knees, that Welles—always a chronic victim of boredom, and an actor unconvinced by his own masquerade—spurned carte blanche so that he should himself be made a Falstaffian outcast.

Kane is less about William Randolph Hearst—a humorless, anxious man—than a portrait and prediction of Welles himself. Given his greatest opportunity, Mankiewicz could only invent a story that was increasingly colored by his mixed feelings about Welles and that, he knew, would be brought to life by Welles the overpowering actor, who could not resist the chance to dress up as the old man he might one day become, and who relished the young showoff Kane just as he loved to hector and amaze the Mercury Theater. As if Welles knew that *Kane* would hang over his own future, regularly being used to denigrate his later works, the film is shot through with his vast, melancholy nostalgia for self-destructive talent. Kane goes out of his way to destroy and isolate himself by calling Geddes's bluff. In the same way, Welles repaid astonishing freedom by gratuitously insulting William Randolph Hearst. And in *Confidential Report,* the scorpion still stings the frog, no matter that it will destroy them both, because it is his character. Kane is Welles, just as every apparent point of view in the film is warmed by Kane's own

memories, as if the entire film were his dream in the instant before death.

Beyond question, *Kane* is the film that influenced filmmakers in the years from about 1955 onward—until then it was neglected. The reasons for that are several. We feel now how far its study of the flawed tycoon embraces Gatsby, Howard Hughes, and the American recipe of public charm and actual demagoguery. This too is the age that sees Welles coming into the inheritance of Kane at Xanadu, the aging hulk, haplessly issuing uncompleted projects. More than that, Kane expresses the nature of cinema. Kane's enterprise is so evidently Welles's. His surrender to glory is equally the overwhelming of the performer by his own glamour. But visually, *Kane* is about the gulf between concrete things and their mysterious, emotional meanings. There is still not a film that so grows out of that discrepancy, that is so vividly material and so deeply imaginary, that advances ultimately on a forgotten sledge and reveals to us its significance, while denying it forever to the people in the film who are in search of it. Where else is there such intense complicity between the heart of a film and its audience? Rosebud is the greatest secret in cinema, and cinema the most secretive of public shows.

The bond between Welles and Charles Foster Kane compels us to see Welles's later work as offshoots of *Kane,* variations on its rich theme. Call the later films lesser works if you will, but consider whether everything else Welles did was not an extension and fulfillment of *Kane.* It is worth insisting that not one of his immediate followers has made a film to be compared with *Ambersons, Lady from Shanghai,* or *Touch of Evil.* Any of such lesser works would raise a director like Robert Wise from dubious variability. Charles Higham reports that Wise actually directed Major Amberson's death scene. Which only proves Welles's infectious power: Nothing in the rest of Wise's work is as powerful or serious. And when we remember the firelight on the faces of Falstaff and Shallow in *Chimes at Midnight,* it seems quite natural that Wise should have identified an image implicit in Welles's world. To be with Welles was to share his vision. Everything about the *Inquirer* is colored by Kane's greater skill at organizing other people's lives. It is equally a part of Welles's dominant but evasive imagination that he urged people to make his own vague purposes manifest. *Ambersons* was terribly curtailed by Welles's flight south for *It's All True. Lady from Shanghai* was left to Columbia professionals to tidy up. But both now seem his work, fragmentation adding to the Xanadu clutter. He inspired actors and technicians alike, and who can doubt that Welles's own zest for life came largely from daring or provoking people to excel themselves, to become creatures he can believe he invented. *Ambersons* deserted only focuses attention the more conclusively on Welles. That "garbled" thriller, *The Lady from Shanghai*, is unavoidably a commentary on Welles's marriage to Rita Hayworth and, incidentally, the clearest sign of his misogyny and his shyness of attractive, mature women.

Not only his own films but his work as an actor, as a part-time conjuror, as a guest on so many worthless TV shows, are continuing facets of *Kane*. Think how often his parts in other films are distorted portraits of grandeur: as Colonel Haki in *Journey Into Fear* (43, Norman Foster), the Mercury film where Welles first essayed his magician's ploy of directing through another man; as the barnstorming Rochester, reinhabiting RKO haunted houses in *Jane Eyre* (44, Robert Stevenson); as the "Great Orsino," sawing Dietrich in half—pretext for that mordant reunion in *Touch of Evil*—in *Follow the Boys* (44, Edward Sutherland); as the husband returned from the dead, only vaguely remembered by wife Claudette Colbert in *Tomorrow Is Forever* (45, Irving Pichel); as Harry Lime in *The Third Man* (49, Carol Reed), hypnotizing Reed into his own style and making a sophomoric speech about Switzerland a highlight of the film; as Cesare Borgia in *Prince of Foxes* (49, Henry King); as the illusionist Cagliostro in *Black Magic* (49, Gregory Ratoff); as a mighty war-making Khan (Kane) in *The Black Rose* (50, Henry Hathaway), expounding on the nature of war with the sentimental pessimism of Michael O'Hara describing the blood-lust of sharks, and borrowing the costumes for his own *Othello;* as Father Mapple, luridly overpaid for a sermon he could have done in one take, in *Moby Dick* (56, John Huston), using the money in his own mind to finance a dazzling stage production of Melville's novel; as Clarence Darrow in *Compulsion* (59, Richard Fleischer), declaiming the need for mercy with all the hollow promise of Kane making his "Declaration of Principles"; as a bloated film director in an episode from *RoGoPaG* (62, Pier Paolo Pasolini); as the outcast Wolsey in *A Man for All Seasons* (67, Fred Zinnemann); the Swedish consul playing fire-prevention officer in *Is Paris Burning?* (René Clément), and as moved by war-torn cities as Harry Lime; in *La Décade Prodigieuse* (71, Claude Chabrol); typically lending himself to the adventurousness of *A Safe Place* (71, Henry Jaglom), in which he plays a magician who makes things vanish; a Cuban industrialist in *Voyage of the Damned* (76, Stuart Rosenberg).

The later films have every defect alleged against them. They are flawed by cheapness, by reckless or capricious casting, by impulsiveness and self-indulgence in shooting, and by Welles's increasing reluctance to complete a project. On several occasions, he fled from the precise tedium of the cutting room, too bulky to be contained, too hopefully flighty to be pinned down to a fixed version of a work. Uncompleted films or films taken from him and spoiled by others allowed his thoughts of perfection to endure. Xanadu was such a venture, still sprawling, its smoke reaching up to the stars, never defined or finished. His failings conform to its imaginative ideal and enhance the mystification so dear to Welles, evident in conjuring and blatant melodrama. *Chimes at Midnight* was hideously postsynched, as were parts of *Macbeth;* but that blurring assists the dreamy ambiance of his Shakespeare. The weird locations and unlit darkness of *The Trial* and the anxiety of some of its acting are essential to Welles's Kafka. Self-assertion binds carelessness together: Hank Quinlan is tripped up by his own "cane," Mr. Clay in *Immortal Story* walks with a stick, while Falstaff clings to a gnarled walking cane.

Anything involving Welles takes on this dream of the self. A Shredded Wheat or a wine commercial sounds like "rosebud." Guest appearances on comedy shows gobble up the humiliating context. He made Dick Cavett and Merv Griffin into other Thompson figures. Welles was always proliferating the helpless self-idealism. That is another source of his relevance to our age; not as someone who stood back and saw himself but as simultaneous participant and commentator. Without his devoted film record of his own life as a director, there would have been no 8½, no *Persona*, no *Pierrot le Fou*. Such films might exist, but their confidence in the right to be personal while spending so much money comes from Welles. *Kane* is a source of cinema, of corrupted beauty and evanescent meanings, making most subsequent films items from Xanadu inventory. Like cinema itself, he drew together poetry and melodrama so that we no longer feel sure that one is reputable and the other suspect.

In his last years, Welles did more commercials, he narrated documentaries, he attempted to launch fresh projects and to complete old ones. He appeared in *It Happened One Christmas* (77, Donald Wrye), *The Muppet Movie* (79, James Frawley), and *Butterfly* (81, Matt Cimber). But none of those matched his provocative role as the wise man in the back row of the theatre in his friend Henry Jaglom's *Someone to Love* (87). In short, he presided over the special chaos of his life as it closed, apparently seeking help and friends, yet secretly sealed against trespass. His unfinished films are now seeing the light of day—even pieces of *It's All True*. But so little about the life and work of Welles is all or anywhere near true. He inhaled legend—and changed our air. It is the greatest career in film, the most tragic, and the one with most warnings for the rest of us.

William A. (Augustus) **Wellman**

(1896–1975), b. Brookline, Massachusetts

1923: *The Man Who Won; Second Hand Love; Big Dan; Cupid's Fireman.* 1924: *Not a Drum Was Heard; The Vagabond Trail; The Circus Cowboy.* 1925: *When Husbands Flirt.* 1926: *The Boob; The Cat's Pajamas; You Never Know Women.* 1928: *Legion of the Condemned; Ladies of the Mob; Beggars of Life.* 1929: *Chinatown Nights; The Man I Love; Woman Trap; Wings.* 1930: *Dangerous Paradise; Young Eagles; Maybe It's Love.* 1931: *Public Enemy; Other Men's Women; Star Witness; Night Nurse; Safe in Hell.* 1932: *Hatchet Man; So Big; Love Is a Racket; The Purchase Price; The Conquerors.* 1933: *Frisco Jenny; Central Airport; Lady of the Night; Lilly Turner; Heroes for Sale; Wild Boys of the Road; College Coach.* 1934: *Looking for Trouble; Stingaree.* 1935: *The President Vanishes; Call of the Wild.* 1936: *Small Town Girl; Robin Hood of El Dorado.* 1937: *A Star Is Born; Nothing Sacred.* 1938: *Men With Wings.* 1939: *Beau Geste; The Light that Failed.* 1941: *Reaching for the Sun.* 1942: *Roxie Hart; The Great Man's Lady; Thunder Birds.* 1943: *Lady of Burlesque; The Ox-Bow Incident.* 1944: *Buffalo Bill.* 1945: *This Man's Navy; The Story of G.I. Joe.* 1946: *Gallant Journey.* 1947: *Magic Town.* 1948: *The Iron Curtain; Yellow Sky.* 1949: *Battleground.* 1950: *The Happy Years; The Next Voice You Hear.* 1951: *Across the Wide Missouri; It's a Big Country* (codirected); *Westward the Women.* 1952: *My Man and I.* 1953: *Island in the Sky.* 1954: *The High and the Mighty; Track of the Cat.* 1955: *Blood Alley.* 1956: *Goodbye, My Lady.* 1957: *Lafayette Escadrille; Darby's Rangers.*

Louise Brooks, who worked with Wellman on *Beggars of Life,* called him an "intricate" man. She found that his pacing and his interest fluctuated; she was intrigued by his sadism toward women; and she wasn't quite sure how much to believe about the stories that he had flown with the Lafayette Escadrille unit—American pilots flying in the First World War under French colors. Yet much of "Wild Bill's" reputation derived from that fabled beginning, and it was the legend that got him so many flying pictures, most notably *Wings,* which is actually rather routine, even if it did get the first Oscar for best picture.

Wellman was, rather by self-advertisement, a man's man, brusque, laconic, and aggressive toward his players. But not enough of that "intricacy" comes across on screen. His long and honorable list of films has too few items that raise the pulse: so many of his aviation pictures are predictable—not just *Wings,* but *The High and the Mighty, Island in the Sky, Thunder Birds, Men With Wings,* and so on. Put the best things in those films together and you're still nowhere near the exact lyricism and the feeling for space in, say,

Only Angels Have Wings or *The Right Stuff.*

In addition, Wellman was often a meek servant to quite unexpected schemes: he directed Ruth Chatterton in *Frisco Jenny* and *Lilly Turner,* and then years later he made that garish prefeminist Western, *Westward the Women.* Yet no one could claim that he seemed to be interested in such projects. *Yellow Sky* is a disappointing Western; *Across the Wide Missouri* is ponderous; *Battleground* was Dore Schary's regimental liberalism—and it's not as interesting as *The Story of G.I. Joe.* *The Light That Failed,* from Kipling, is mannered and stilted, except when Ida Lupino is involved. And *The Oxbow Incident* is one of those solemn, acclaimed works that you really don't need to see. As for *Track of the Cat,* it is flat-out arty in its attempt at a black-and-white color movie, a notion that gets in the way of a nice ghost story set in the snowy wilds.

It's so untidy a career, as sentimental and hokey as *Buffalo Bill,* but then as rough and socially urgent as *Wild Boys of the Road. The Conquerors* is a routine epic of building up the West, but *Night Nurse* is edgy, frightening, and very tough. *Public Enemy* has a higher reputation than it deserves, yet the famous grapefruit scene is always unexpected and nasty. *Beau Geste* did well at foreign legion heroics, but it's an entirely foreseeable picture.

Still, it comes in the period of three movies that aren't on automatic, and which are Wellman's best—if they are his: *A Star Is Born, Nothing Sacred,* and *Roxie Hart,* romantic satires that pour on the acid in mounting glee. Wellman and Robert Carson got the Oscar for original story on *A Star Is Born,* and Wellman at different times admitted that it was all David Selznick's idea, really—but hell, no, *he* wrote the damn thing!

Wellman was always like that, show-off tough and . . . intricate. Anyway, *Nothing Sacred* is swift, funny, and very cynical, while *Roxie Hart* is a wicked satire, with Ginger Rogers giving a knockout brassy act in the lead. Nunnally Johnson wrote *Roxie Hart,* while Ben Hecht did *Nothing Sacred.* Yet at other times, hours could go by in a Wellman movie without so much as a smile.

Maybe he was called Wild Bill because he was just out of order?

Wim Wenders,

b. Dusseldorf, Germany, 1945

1967: *Schauplatze* (s); *Same Player Shoots Again* (s). 1968: *Silver City* (s); *Polizeifilm* (s). 1969: *Alabama* (s); *3 Amerikanische LPs* (s). 1970: *Summer in the City/Summer in the City: Dedicated to the Kinks.* 1971: *Die Angst des Tormanns beim Elfmeter/The Goalie's Anxiety at the Penalty Kick.* 1972: *Der Scharlachrote Buchstabe/The Scarlet Letter.* 1974: *Alice in den Stadten/Alice in the Cities; Aus der Familie der Panzereschen* (s).

1975: *Falsche Bewegung/Wrong Movement*. 1976: *Im Lauf der Zeit/Kings of the Road*. 1977: *Der Amerikanische Freund/The American Friend*. 1979: *Lightning Over Water/Nick's Movie* (codirected with Nicholas Ray). 1982: *Quand Je m'Eveille/Reverse Angle* (s); *The State of Things*. 1983: *Hammett*. 1984: *Chambre 666* (s); *Paris, Texas*. 1985: *Tokyo-Ga* (d). 1987: *Himmel uber Berlin/Wings of Desire*. 1989: *Auszeichnunger zu Kleidern und Stadten/Notebooks on Cities and Clothes* (d). 1991: *Bis ans Ende der Welt/Until the End of the World*. 1993: *Faraway, So Close!*. 1994: *Lisbon Story*. 1995: *Beyond the Clouds* (codirected with Michelangelo Antonioni); *Die Gebrüder Skladanowsky*. 1997: *The End of Violence*. 1998: *Willie Nelson at the Teatro* (d). 1999: *Buena Vista Social Club* (d). 2000: *The Million Dollar Hotel*. 2001: *In America*. 2002: *Viel Passiert—Der BAP-Film*.

Of all the new German directors of the 1970s, none had Wim Wenders's rhapsodic sense of America.

He was brought up on American Forces radio and the glut of Hollywood movies that occupied Germany after the war. The influence of the first is on nearly all his soundtracks, and in the tough urban blues that challenges fate. The second tradition rose to a peak with the affectionate use of Nicholas Ray and Samuel Fuller in *The American Friend*, that seminal film for determined outcasts that might just as well have for its title Ray's own tattered motto, "I'm a stranger here, myself."

Wenders studied medicine, philosophy, and painting, and it was while he was taking etching classes in Paris in 1965–66 that he discovered the Cinemathèque. He went back to Germany, to film school in Munich, and to work as a film critic. His early shorts were often built around pop music, and *Summer in the City* is a three-hour love letter to the Kinks.

Goalie's Anxiety got made because of the novel and script by Peter Handke. But it had an extraordinary visual capacity for revealing the alienation of the beaten goalie, and the violence that awaits him. Filmed in Robbie Muller's somber color, and filled with the realities of Vienna, it is still indebted to the dead ends of film noir. *Alice in the Cities* is a journey film for a lost child and a photographer bruised after an American assignment. It is fragmentary, meandering, and proof of Wenders's eye and ear for inconsequential scenes that build into a subtle mood. A little reminiscent of Truffaut, its mixture of humor and sadness manages to move from everyday reality to a grand, poetic allusion to John Ford.

Wrong Movement was another Handke script, based on Goethe's *Wilhelm Meister*. It is a journey again, in which physical enquiry resembles the movements of the mind and feelings. That method had its richest expression in *Kings of the Road*, a three-hour study of two men who are on the road, servicing the projectors in failing movie theatres. It is full of film references and the situation of a Hawksian bond tested against the newer threats of tedium and cultural deterioration in which Germany has become a satellite of Americana. The pace is leisurely, and the action is not emphatic, but *Kings of the Road* is one of the best films of the seventies. It seemed to predict Wenders's future: an increasingly existential concern underlying the unforced dealings between lonely people.

That certainly describes *American Friend*, the most vivid film Wenders had yet made, but as self-contained as a dream. The use of Highsmith/Hitchcock motifs, the antagonistic casting of Bruno Ganz and Dennis Hopper, the rogues' gallery of movie directors in small parts, the variety of bloody sunset reds, and the jaunty pleasure with set-piece murders shot through with New Wave spontaneity, all made for a film of high enjoyment. Still, the view of women was hostile, the comradeship went into an obscure spiral at the end and the entire picture relied on a piece of implausible motivation that Wenders was not good enough to hide.

Wenders is forever a wanderer, and seemingly set upon his own furious ups and downs. *Lightning Over Water* is a difficult film for anyone who loved Nicholas Ray (as director or man), for it seems exploitative of his illness and his desperate urge to make the film. *The State of Things* seemed to me naïve and pretentious, rather like a Kafka view of the world in which the Law has been replaced with the Movie Business. *Hammett* was a disastrous foray to the real America, long premeditated, supposedly a gift from Zoetrope, yet a clear proof of limits in Wenders. Yet *Paris, Texas* is the real thing: a gentle, slow unpeeling of the family onion, sublime in its use of desert, city, Harry Dean Stanton, and Nastassja Kinski, and one of the fondest and most ambivalent films about America that a European has ever made. There are many people who esteem *Wings of Desire* as much as I like *Paris, Texas*—I will not argue, I walked out. But I would defend the position that *Until the End of the World* is as awful a film as a good director has made.

Wenders remains romantically itinerant, in love with music, America, and the idea of the movies. But he is closing in on sixty, and nothing lately has been as big or as cogent as one would like to see. Not that one isn't appreciative: it was Wenders's tact and assistance that helped Antonioni to make another film—far from worthless and altogether cleaner than the earlier hero-worship of Nick Ray; *Buena Vista Social Club* is a delight—if a little monotonous. On the other hand, *The End of Violence* is pretentious and silly, and no feature film has really reminded us of the younger Wenders.

In America is a project involving Sam Shepard, and one can only say that they both need the best in each other.

Oskar Werner (Josef Bschliessmayer)
(1922–84), b. Vienna

Sad falling out of former comrades: 29 March 1966, François Truffaut's diary on the making of *Fahrenheit 451*:

> Oskar's performance isn't as "cool" as I would like. Clearly he doesn't want to appear less intelligent than Clarisse, although that is the situation. He always manages to sneak in a couple of unnecessary smiles. In his resistance to playing the part the way I want it, there is faulty reasoning in relation, for example, to theatrical dramatization which is therefore nobly meant, but there are also some more dubious reasons bound up with his new Hollywood aspirations. So many women went into ecstasies over his smile in *Ship of Fools* and his sticky kisses with La Signoret, that he seems determined now to play the "glamour game" to titillate elderly American ladies. When we were making *Jules et Jim* five years ago he was a long way from all that; he wasn't thinking about building up his part, thought even less about his make-up, his hair-style or his comfort. He did his work in an honest and dignified way.

The hurt in that is made all the more comic by the subsequent revelation that *Fahrenheit 451* never ignited, and by Truffaut's slightly petulant siding with the disconsolate Julie Christie.

Poor Oskar! He had been in and out of films for several years: *Eroica* (49, Walter Kolm-Veltee); *Decision Before Dawn* (51, Anatole Litvak); and *Der Letzte Akt* (55, G. W. Pabst). Never much of an actor, it seemed, but endearing himself as the student whose scarf brought him to the eye and caravan of *Lola Montès* (55, Max Ophüls), and who proved a most touching innocent in *Jules et Jim* (61, Truffaut). Images persist from that film, of Werner in the trenches writing letters, and of his blond waif escorting the ashes of Jim and Catherine to the grave. All Truffaut's lofty disapproval of the Hollywood Werner is borne out by the handful of films he made as an international actor: *Ship of Fools* (65, Stanley Kramer); *The Spy Who Came In From the Cold* (65, Martin Ritt); *Interlude* (68, Kevin Billington); *The Shoes of the Fisherman* (68, Michael Anderson); and *The Voyage of the Damned* (76, Stuart Rosenberg).

After that, he returned to the theatre. His face never lost its boyishness but turned sulky in middle age. Werner looked the eerie proof of Truffaut's principle that men are happy fools or unhappy fools.

He died two days after the death of Truffaut . . .

Lina Wertmuller (Arcangela Wertmuller von Elgg), b. Rome, 1928

1963: *I Basilischi/The Lizards*. 1965: *Questa Volta Parliamo di Uomini/Let's Talk About Men*. 1971: *Mimi Metallurgico Ferito nell 'Onore/The Seduction of Mimi*. 1972: *Film d'Amore e d'Anarchia/Love and Anarchy*. 1973: *Tutto a Posto e Niente in Ordine/All Screwed Up*. 1974: *Travolti da un Insolito Destino nell' Azzuro Mare d'Agosto/Swept Away by an Unusual Destiny in the Blue Sea of August*. 1975: *Pasqualino Settebellezze/Seven Beauties*. 1977: *The End of the World in Our Usual Bed in a Nightful of Rain*. 1979: *Fatto di Sangue fra Due Uomini per causa di una Vedova. Si Sospettano Moventi Politici/Blood Feud*. 1981: *E una Domenica sera di Novembre* (TV). 1983: *Scherzo del Destino in Agguato Dietro l'Angolo come un Brigante di Strada/A Joke of Destiny, Lying in Wait Around the Corner Like a Street Bandit*. 1984: *Sotto, Sotto*. 1986: *Notte d'Estate, con Profilo Greco, Occhi Amandorla e Odore di Basilico/Summer Night with a Greek Profile, Almond Colored Eyes and the Scent of Basil*. 1989: *In una Notte di Chiaro Luna; Decimo Clandestino*. 1990: *Saturday, Sunday, Monday*. 1993: *Io Speriamo Che Me La Cavo/Ciao, Professore!* 1996: *Ninfa Plebea; Metalmeccanico e Parrucchiera in un Turbine di Sesso e di Politica*. 1999: *Ferdinando e Carolina; An Interesting State*. 2001: *Francesca e Nunziata*.

When they come to be exported, Lina Wertmuller's films do usually shed their train-length titles. (Though, nowadays, they often fail to get a foreign release.) But if anyone watching them, and wondering what toffee it is he's trapped in, needs a clue, the original titles will confirm the pretensions toward facetious cuteness. Which is no small thing. Cuteness generally is perfunctory, and facetiousness normally a superficial response meant to evade demanding issues. But Wertmuller makes a liberal monument out of declamatory whimsy; it is a sugar monument, even when it marks concentration camps.

Her brief rage in America in the mid-seventies was probably inevitable in a country ravenous for a female purveyor of smart cultural artifacts. How sad: Stephanie Rothman, Chantal Ackerman, and Yvonne Rainer, say, could feast on the attention given erroneously to the Italian lady and her woeful *lumpen* lapdog, Giancarlo Giannini. She has sometimes been called a feminist and a socialist, a modern Aristophanes and a Chaplinesque defender of humble individuals. Jerzy Kosinski delivered an opposing rebuke when he called *Seven Beauties* a cartoon trying to be a tragedy. (There was a more complete protest from Bruno Bettelheim.)

Wertmuller's family was of Swiss origin, but she identifies herself with Rome. Her creative career began as a writer with traveling puppet shows, and there is still an undisciplined sprawl in her films that might serve in street theatre. She wrote plays and one of them, *Two and Two Are No Longer Four,* was a hit. She worked on musical and variety shows for radio and television, and in 1962 she was assistant to Fellini on 8½. Surely his flamboyant self-rapture influenced her fussy, picaresque allegories with so little grasp of style and so little love of people. Her films are top-heavy with captions, yet the cinematic form is often only a flashy skin stretched over them. The lyricism is garish, the pleas for tolerance are cold-blooded. There is neither pain nor joy, despite the insistence that those things count above all.

I will end unscrupulously with a pretense of balance. This is Lina Wertmuller's own credo: "I'm a socialist. I love anarchists very much, even though I know very well that anarchism is a total utopia, and that it can have horrendous faces. But in the utopian ideology of anarchism is the key to the human being, which means the desire of man to become a free and civilized being. The freedom of each of us must end where the other person's freedom begins. This is wonderful, even if anarchy is utopian." And this is Ellen Willis, in *Rolling Stone:* "Wertmuller's basic appeal is a clever double-dealing that allows high-minded people to indulge their lowest-minded prejudices. She is . . . a woman hater who pretends to be a feminist. She pities the benighted masses and calls it radicalism, evades responsibility for what she says and calls it comedy."

Mae West (1892–1980), b. Brooklyn, New York
It was never likely that a plump, forty-year-old from vaudeville could be a basis for movies. In fact, Mae West made very few films—nine in the thirties, a halfhearted comeback in 1943, and against every expectation, at age seventy-eight, the appalling *Myra Breckinridge* (70, Mike Sarne). Ironically, Gore Vidal's novel was the richest source material she ever had, a view of sexual extremism and moral confusion as witty as her own. But the film required a cross between Luis Buñuel and Russ Meyer, and was ruined by directorial ineptness and studio jitters.

Mae West still emerged intact. It had never mattered who directed her films. She looked a faintly blurred version of her former self, but the voice was unchanged—in the 1960s she made an album of modern pop, singing the Beatles' "Day Tripper" like a Billie Holiday who had come through. Most important, the return capitalized on a reputation that had been growing steadily with the revival of her old films. For Mae West is one of the most subtly influential and mysterious of superstars. Those who discern in Marilyn Monroe either the inclination or the ability to satirize her own sexuality can never have seen the great

Mae, or held an unpeeled grape and wondered.

Her films are about suggestiveness, private jokes that slide through every institutional defense of prudery to encourage randiness in a shy audience. No other major star knows such contentment and such libidinous Arcadia. Few sex goddesses have been as swathed in so many yards of gown; but no one else has spoken so tenderly of sexual pleasure and been so resplendent a monument to it. Mae West was low-down—some of her innuendo is limpidly provocative—but she was a lady. Sex itself remains private in her world, a thing to be known rather than described. The discussion of its satisfaction and, most important, the persistent faith that it can be seen and read into all things, shows how far she was a philosopher: the real conclusion of her work is that sex is an idea, an obsession for the human being, and one of the most reliable distractions from the equally potent idea that life is tragic. One of her great lines is, "It's not the man in my life, but the life in my man"—an epigram worthy of Oscar Wilde and underlining her sense of the 1890–1910 period. Such verbal dexterity, and the disposition toward inversion of accepted ideas, shows how far she meant to chide established attitudes to sex, disparaging sexual reputations but at the same time provoking them: "When I'm good I'm very good, but when I'm bad I'm better."

Extraordinary as this artistic personality is, and though it was based on the control of scripts and writing of her own dialogue, her originality and impact are as much visual as verbal. She was a cornucopia of rococo shapes—the sweep of a hat brim; the froth of curls; the undulating feather boa; the sequin swirls on her dress; and that body—a padded arabesque, a chaise-longue, a bed on which the Cheshire cat face seemed always nestling. She was physically a dreadnought, but emotionally dainty: as a result she moved very slowly. Films have a steady pace that imposes itself on all players. Hurry and you seem nervous; delay and the effect is ponderous. And yet, intrigue an audience, and then pause, and they are yours forever. Every great star acted according to that precept. But Mae West made languor virtually the plot line of her films. The stories were no more than contrived buildups for her eventual appearance; the camera drooled over her sailor's roll; dialogue scenes existed for her drawling boasts and for those moments of reflection in which the anticipation of sexual encounter to come merges with the recollection of encounters just concluded. She had such timing that one could see an entire way of life—and she was pleased with it. Censorship might trim her lines, but it could not alter the way she appraised a man. Lucky Cary Grant, that he played opposite her twice as a young man.

The career is as remarkable as the personality.

She went on the stage as a child and by the First World War was a leading vaudeville performer, with a special skill at impersonation. During the 1920s she rose to unique eminence: as singer, rather lazy dancer, and author of her own plays. The most notorious of these were *Sex, The Drag, Diamond Lil,* and *The Pleasure Man.* A succession of legal battles reflected the uncompromising sexual celebration in these shows. In 1932, she accepted an offer from Paramount and appeared with George Raft in *Night After Night* (Archie Mayo).

She was a sensational success and went on to make *She Done Him Wrong* (33, Lowell Sherman), based on *Diamond Lil,* and *I'm No Angel* (33, Wesley Ruggles). Her next film, *Belle of the Nineties* (34, Leo McCarey), suffered a little from censorship and heralded the attempts of the Motion Picture Production Code and the League of Decency to curtail suggestiveness. In the event, she was hobbled by restrictions and her subsequent films lack the sweltering intimation of an orgy that will be begun as soon as the camera stops. She was a serious casualty of the studios' decision to pursue mass wholesomeness, and the later films have moments of banality when she is made to mouth such bourgeois sentiments as, "Any time you take religion for a joke, the laugh's on you": *Going to Town* (35, Alexander Hall); *Klondike Annie* (36, Raoul Walsh); *Go West Young Man* (36, Henry Hathaway); *Every Day's a Holiday* (37, Edward Sutherland); the disappointing pairing with W. C. Fields in *My Little Chickadee* (39, Edward Cline).

She made one more film, *The Heat's On* (43, Gregory Ratoff), and then gave way to war, secure in the knowledge that every sailor in the drink would think of her no matter that he kept the underfed Betty Grable in his locker. Sex in the cinema is often related to audience anxiety. Warners' musicals of the 1930s offered dames to welfare lines and young soldiers kept blonde pinups. But the girls had to be modestly desirable, in case lusting GIs deserted. And the Depression of the 1930s could not tolerate the convincing way that Mae West spoke of satisfaction and paradise. That is a very private domain, only fully admitted in Andy Warhol's family movies. Sex in movies is withheld, no matter how much it is advertised. In that connection, one recalls the verdict of George Jean Nathan who saw a magazine picture of West as the Statue of Liberty and retitled it the Statue of Libido. Mae West gazes at us as if to say the two are one, liberty can be yours as easily as it can be the delight of a plump, middle-aged broad.

In 1978, she appeared once more after *Myra Breckinridge,* in *Sextette* (Ken Hughes).

James Whale (1896–1957),
b. Dudley, England

1930: *Journey's End.* 1931: *Waterloo Bridge; Frankenstein.* 1932: *The Impatient Maiden; The Old Dark House.* 1933: *The Kiss Before the Mirror; The Invisible Man; By Candlelight.* 1934: *One More River.* 1935: *The Bride of Frankenstein; Remember Last Night?.* 1936: *Show Boat.* 1937: *The Road Back; The Great Garrick.* 1938: *Sinners in Paradise; Wives Under Suspicion; Port of Seven Seas.* 1939: *The Man in the Iron Mask.* 1940: *Green Hell.* 1941: *They Dare Not Love.* 1949: *Hello Out There* (never released).

Whale is a notable figure in a limited but rich strain: of Englishmen who went to direct films in America. Despite his "respectable" theatrical background, he was involved in several of cinema's rawest genres. And very often, there is an absorbing tension between his wish to keep tongue in cheek and the ability to find unexpected depths in hokum. His films fluctuate wildly, and it is all too clear that some sequences engrossed him, while on others he didn't give a damn. One never knows with Whale when imagination will set in; he may not have been sure himself.

A magazine cartoonist, he was imprisoned by the Germans during the First World War and it was in captivity that he first acted. In peacetime he entered the theatre professionally, first as an actor and then as a producer. It was the successful production of R. C. Sherriff's *Journey's End,* in 1928, that took him to New York. He supplied dialogue for *Hell's Angels,* directed the film of *Journey's End,* and followed that with a version of Robert E. Sherwood's maudlin romance, *Waterloo Bridge,* starring Bette Davis. At that time, Universal were preparing to film *Frankenstein,* with Robert Florey directing Bela Lugosi. The actor turned down the part, and Whale was assigned to it. He offered the part of the monster to a friend, Boris Karloff.

Frankenstein is not the greatest horror film, but historically and artistically it was a landmark. It is most frightening when dealing with the "ordinary" people. When treating Karloff's monster it is surprising, lyrical, and gravely tolerant. His fear of fire is by far the most compelling "horror" in the movie; his yearning for the light its most spiritual image. In the scene of the monster and the little girl floating flowers on a pond, the balance of hope and menace is so exact that the scene still has the riveting effect of the best Hitchcock. Above all, Whale and Karloff had created a new hero, a helpless outcast so much nobler than the little man from Universal at the beginning of the film who prattles on about how frightened we will be.

The film was a vast success, and Whale became a studio hero. He was never entirely happy amid the sensationalism of horror so far from the clumsy earnestness of *Journey's End*—and it may be that his own mixed feelings added to the misanthropic flavor of his other horror films. At any event, he hired good writers and actors and generally extended the range of the form. *The Old Dark House* is a pastiche Gothic study of an English family in decline, starring Karloff, Ernest Thesiger, and Charles Laughton. *The Invisible Man* is a parade of trick photography, adorned by the voice of Claude Rains. But *The Bride of Frankenstein* is among the greatest of horror films. It contrived to overcome Universal's anxiety about a sequel by re-creating a Mary Shelley prepared to continue the story, and then by having the same actress—Elsa Lanchester—play both Mary and the bride monster. Once more, Whale's real concern is for the emotional life of his monsters. The sequences in which Karloff is "schooled" and domesticated are very funny and poignant, as though Whale only half-grasped the meaning he was conveying, of a noble savage living in a deformed society.

But Whale then abandoned horror for more theatrical pictures. He seldom recaptured the consistent inventiveness of those four films. *Show Boat* shirks none of the sentiment and there is every suggestion, in the last view of Ol' Man River, that the Mississippi consists of tears alone. But between those soggy moments, the "showbiz" scenes are very exciting and active. There is a fond sense of barnstorming in the show-boat scenes, especially when Charles Winninger explains an interrupted melodrama; sumptuous trembling close-ups of Helen Morgan as she sings "Bill"; moments reminiscent of *French Can Can* in the music hall sequences; and an inane but gorgeous track around Paul Robeson as he sings "Ol' Man River." Time and again, *Show Boat* surprises with its vivacity and the equal skill out-of-doors and in front of cardboard backdrops. It is never as bold or influential as the Frankenstein pictures, but it does suggest true versatility, plus the mixture of sophistication and unashamed sentiment.

His later work is very varied and not without interest: Tom Milne has written about the freshness of *Remember Last Night?* and Brian Aherne as Garrick; *Port of Seven Seas* is a reworking of *Fanny*, with Frank Morgan, John Beal, and Maureen O'Sullivan; Louis Hayward was *The Man in the Iron Mask; Green Hell* was an adventure melodrama that George Sanders and Vincent Price could scarcely play for laughing. In 1941, Whale retired, and became a painter, only to make a disastrous attempt at a comeback in 1949 with a forty-minute version of a Saroyan play shot on a set designed by Whale. He is an enigmatic figure, never at ease in Hollywood, who died eventually as if in a Universal scenario—"in his swimming pool, in mysterious circumstances." This story was well told in *Gods and Monsters* (98, Bill Condon), which is a surprisingly full portrait of Whale's odd, poignant life.

Forest Whitaker, b. Longview, Texas, 1961
1993: *Strapped* (TV). 1995: *Waiting to Exhale*. 1998: *Hope Floats*.

Forest Whitaker brings strange baggage to much of his work, and asks us to puzzle it out. He is large, yet he does not seem like the football player he was once. For he is gentle, a touch clumsy, and is it walleyed, or is that just something he does from time to time? There are no answers, and not many limits to what he's willing to try. You have to keep your wits about you nowadays when he appears—but time and again his presence encourages our trust (or attention).

His biggest film, of course, is *Bird* (88, Clint Eastwood). No one doubts how he worked at that. Still, the few bits of Charlie Parker on film don't make one think of Whitaker. Parker, I suspect, was harsher, tougher, and less tender to people—he was off on his own line and level, hearing things that made other people say he was crazy. Whereas Whitaker, naturally, gives off some of the sweet good nature of Louis Armstrong.

He made his debut in *Fast Times at Ridgemont High* (82, Amy Heckerling); *Vision Quest* (85, Harold Becker); very good as a passing hustler in *The Color of Money* (86, Martin Scorsese); *Platoon* (86, Oliver Stone); *Stakeout* (87, John Badham); *Good Morning, Vietnam* (87, Barry Levinson); *Bloodsport* (88, Newt Arnold); *Johnny Handsome* (89, Walter Hill); very good in *Downtown* (90, Richard Benjamin); *A Rage in Harlem* (91, Bill Duke), which he helped produce; *Article 99* (92, Howard Deutch).

At that point he was outstanding as a British soldier in *The Crying Game* (92, Neil Jordan); *Diary of a Hitman* (92, Roy London); *Consenting Adults* (92, Alan J. Pakula); the prison guard in *Last Light* (93, Kiefer Sutherland); *Body Snatchers* (94, Abel Ferrara); *Bank Robber* (94, Nick Mead); *Lush Life* (94, Michael Elias)—this deals with jazz, though it's not about Billy Strayhorn, but what a subject that might be for Whitaker; *Blown Away* (94, Stephen Hopkins); *Jason's Lyric* (94, Doug McHenry); *Ready to Wear* (94, Robert Altman); *Smoke* (95, Wayne Wang); *Species* (95, Roger Donaldson); *Phenomenon* (96, Jon Turteltaub); *Body Count* (98, Robert Patton-Spruill); *Ghost Dog: The Way of the Samurai* (99, Jim Jarmusch); one of the villains in *Panic Room* (02, David Fincher).

Bo Widerberg (1930–97),
b. Malmo, Sweden
1961: *Pojken och Draken* (codirected with Jan Troell) (s). 1963: *Barnvagnen/The Pram; Kvarteret Korpen/Raven's End*. 1965: *Karlek 65/Love 65*. 1966: *Heja Roland!/Thirty Times Your Money*. 1967: *Elvira Madigan*. 1968: *Den Vita Sporten/The White Game* (codirected) (d). 1969: *Adalen*

Riots/Adalen 31. 1970: *The Ballad of Joe Hill.* 1974: *Fimpen/Stubby.* 1976: *Mannen pa Taket/The Man on the Roof.* 1979: *Victoria.* 1983: *Grifesten.* 1984: *Mannen fran Mallorca/The Man from Majorca.* 1986: *Ormen's vag pa Halleberget/The Serpent's Way.* 1988: *En Far* (TV). 1989: *Vildanden* (TV). 1990: *Hebriana* (TV). 1992: *Efter Föreställningen* (TV). 1995: *Lost och Fägring Stor.*

The combination of the sententious and the meretricious in Bo Widerberg's work shows modern Sweden absorbing film into the crass neatness of its comprehensive social democracy. Life in Sweden may be cleaner, more rational, and more institutionalized against suffering than anywhere else. The artist then risks becoming another social engineer, unable to escape moral complacency and self-satisfied visual distinction. The Bergman of *The Seventh Seal* was in danger of producing inert parables to adorn regularized social democratic homes—dutiful, unfeeling messages of apocalypse. Once he surpassed that simplification, Bergman rediscovered the fruitfully Swedish ways of describing the solitary life people live with their emotions, consciences, and minds for company. Widerberg's characters are shriven of those loads, absolved by the director's gentility.

The success that Widerberg enjoyed in art houses all over the world was shaming, but his trite claims on commitment and the surreptitious resort to prettification were typical of a dreadful hollow that could easily come to occupy the center of "serious" cinema. He is not the only exponent of such soft options: Lelouch, Schlesinger, Kubrick, and Mike Nichols have all enjoyed some of the popular success of *Elvira Madigan* and been hailed in some quarters for novelty and insight.

In Widerberg's case, there has been a rapid softening in his work, in step with his success. He was a novelist originally, a film critic and author of an earnest book, *Vision in Swedish Film.* The first two features he made—*The Pram* and *Raven's End*—were modest, academic but promising. They both concerned young people from stifling, provincial backgrounds facing the need to break away. Their social accuracy may have owed itself to autobiographical content, even if *Raven's End* was set, with great care, in 1936. In subject and style, neither film exceeded the grinding Swedish flaw of tastefulness, but it was possible in *Raven's End* to see personal and political themes working together. *Love 65* was a Fellini-like account of a director having difficulty making a film. Despite such obvious derivation, it did not treat its subject too glibly.

Elvira Madigan, however, was a total plunge into intellectual sentimentality that mooned over the fatal tryst of an army officer and a tightrope dancer: remorselessly graceful telephoto composition, cosmetic color, blurred foreground foliage caressing the pristine, advertising meadow picnic, a Mozart piano concerto, and central players—Pia Degermark and Thommy Berggren—of enervating and gutless beauty. It is a film made without a trace of humor or awareness of how close it comes to a parody of specious high art. Compare it with Penn's *Bonnie and Clyde* and you may begin to see the vastly superior compassion in the American movie. Penn uses our identification with the central couple as a means of probing and disturbing our attitudes to glamour, violence, love, and social justice. We are made to feel the destructiveness of their world in two contradictory ways: they bleed and society falters. Liberty and order are locked in opposition. But in *Elvira Madigan* the discrepancy between the couple and the world is artificial and irrelevant.

As for *Adalen 31* and *Joe Hill,* the first was about a strike that occurred in Sweden in 1931, and the latter an American-made would-be ballad on the founding figure of International Workers of the World. Together, they address us with a flat, unappealing smugness about the self-righteousness of Swedish moral concern. Gavin Millar took *Adalen 31* to task with proper bite when he complained that Widerberg "is not speaking to us but shouting delicately." Thus, there is a clammy, painterly treatment of its tragic events, and the effect of the eye overpowering the mind. "In other words," said Millar, "at every real moment of dialectic, the thinness of the idea is disguised by an assault of charm." Widerberg makes Sweden look like a land taken over by body-snatchers or placidly content with the manufacture of Orson Welles's cuckoo clocks.

Richard Widmark,
b. Sunrise, Minnesota, 1915

Widmark came into movies a little later than most male stars, already in his early thirties. But that debut is still haunting, no matter that Widmark was later turned into an authentic hero, suntanned, laconic, and grudgingly aligning himself with proper causes.

Educated at Lake Forest College, he worked there as a teacher, and as a stage and radio actor, before being cast as Tommy Udo in *Kiss of Death* (47, Henry Hathaway). The sadism of that character, the fearful laugh, the skull showing through drawn skin, and the surely conscious evocation of a concentration camp degenerate established Widmark as the most frightening person on the screen. The glee in the performance may even have shocked Widmark himself. It made *Kiss of Death* untypical of Fox or Hathaway. The studio kept him on a leash, and mixed more conventional heavies with nerve-strained heroes, as if to imply that Tommy Udo was the result of overwork: as the spoiled-child owner of *Road House* (48, Jean

Negulesco); the gangster in *The Street With No Name* (48, William Keighley); menacing Gregory Peck in *Yellow Sky* (48, William Wellman); a boy's best friend in *Down to the Sea in Ships* (49, Hathaway); *Slattery's Hurricane* (49, André de Toth); as a whining coward hounded by the London underworld in *Night and the City* (50, Jules Dassin); as the doctor racing against time and bubonic plague in *Panic in the Streets* (50, Elia Kazan); as a hardnosed, bigoted cop in *No Way Out* (50, Joseph L. Mankiewicz).

But even as a hero, Widmark barely suppressed malice, anxiety, and violence; the straight voice readily broke into a sneer or a giggle; and the eyes once had an insolent way of staring a woman out. That was how he lifted microfilm from Jean Peters's handbag at the beginning of *Pickup on South Street* (53, Samuel Fuller). He was excellent as Fuller's sentimental hoodlum and brought a special relish to the brutal love scenes and to the situation of a guttersnipe able to crow to the police.

Not enough films reprised that spiteful urban knowingness. In the 1950s, Widmark found himself following the middle of the road: *Halls of Montezuma* (51, Lewis Milestone); *The Frogmen* (51, Lloyd Bacon); as a milder Udo in the "Clarion Call" episode from *O. Henry's Full House* (52, Hathaway); with Marilyn Monroe in *Don't Bother to Knock* (52, Roy Baker); *Red Skies of Montana* (52, Joseph Newman); in his first comedy *My Pal Gus* (52, Robert Parrish); as the martinet sergeant in *Take the High Ground* (53, Richard Brooks); *Destination Gobi* (53, Robert Wise); highly strung and aggressive in *Hell and High Water* (54, Fuller); as a gambler in *Garden of Evil* (54, Hathaway).

Having left Fox, he found rather more worthwhile parts: the analyst whose own life is breaking up in *The Cobweb* (55, Vincente Minnelli); in three enterprising Westerns (even if one is ostensibly set in modern-day Latin America)—*Backlash* (56, John Sturges), *Run for the Sun* (56, Roy Boulting), and *The Last Wagon* (56, Delmer Daves); outstanding as the shriveled, timid intelligence of the Dauphin in *Saint Joan* (57, Otto Preminger); as actor and coproducer on *Time Limit* (57, Karl Malden); an old-fashioned, sardonic heavy in *The Law and Jake Wade* (58, Sturges); with Doris Day in *The Tunnel of Love* (58, Gene Kelly); and *Warlock* (59, Edward Dmytryk). He was Jim Bowie in *The Alamo* (60, John Wayne) and then actor and producer on a violent espionage movie, *The Secret Ways* (61, Phil Karlson). His third venture into production, *The Bedford Incident* (65, James B. Harris), had him as an overwrought naval commander edging the world into nuclear holocaust. At one point in that film, Widmark turns on a critic and says, "It's a lot of work being a mean bastard," as if truly tired.

In addition, he made two pictures with John Ford—*Two Rode Together* (61) and *Cheyenne Autumn* (64)—and was the unsubtle prosecutor in *Judgement at Nuremberg* (61, Stanley Kramer).

Working rather less, he was refreshingly ruthless in *Alvarez Kelly* (66, Dmytryk); initiated Don Siegel's appraisal of the new brutal cop in *Madigan* (68); in *Death of a Gunfighter* (69, Siegel and Robert Totten); and made two offbeat studies of rural America: *The Moonshine War* (70, Richard Quine) and as an alcoholic has-been rodeo man in *When the Legends Die* (72, Stuart Millar). He was elderly and fussy as the man killed in *Murder on the Orient Express* (74, Sidney Lumet); *The Sellout* (75, Peter Collinson); *To the Devil a Daughter* (76, Peter Sykes); *Twilight's Last Gleaming* (77, Robert Aldrich); *Rollercoaster* (77, James Goldstone); *The Domino Principle* (77, Stanley Kramer); and *Coma* (78, Michael Crichton).

He was in *The Swarm* (78, Irwin Allen); *Mr. Horn* (79, Jack Starrett); *All God's Children* (80, Jerry Sharp); *Bear Island* (80, Don Sharp); *A Whale for the Killing* (81, Richard T. Heffron); *Hanky Panky* (82, Sidney Poitier); *Who Dares Wins* (82, Ian Sharpe); *Against All Odds* (84, Taylor Hackford); *Blackout* (85, Douglas Hickox); *A Gathering of Old Men* (87, Volker Schlöndorff); *Once Upon a Texas Train* (88, Burt Kennedy); *Cold Sassy Tree* (88, Joan Tewkesbury); and *True Colors* (91, Herbert Ross).

Robert Wiene (1881–1938), b. Sasku, Germany

1914: *Arme Eva* (codirected with A. Berger). 1915: *Er Rechts, Sie Links; Die Konservenbraut.* 1916: *Der Liebesbrief der Konigin; Der Mann im Spiegel; Die Rauberbraut; Der Sekretar der Konigin; Das Wandernde Licht.* 1919: *Ein Gefahrliches Spiel; Das Kabinett des Dr. Caligari/The Cabinet of Dr. Caligari; Der Umweg zur Ehe.* 1920: *Die Drei Tanze der Mary Wilford; Genuine; Die Nacht der Konigin Isabeau; Die Rache einer Frau.* 1921: *Hollische Nacht; Das Spiel mit dem Feuer* (codirected with Georg Kroll). 1922: *Salome; Tragikomodie.* 1923: *I.N.R.I.; Der Puppenmacher von Kiang-Ning; Raskolnikoff.* 1924: *Orlacs Hande.* 1925: *Pension Groonen.* 1926: *Der Gardeoffizier; Die Konigin vom Moulin-Rouge; Der Rosenkavalier.* 1927: *Die Beruhmte Frau; Die Geliebte.* 1928: *Die Frau auf der Folter; Die Grosse Abenteurerin; Leontines Ehemanner; Unfug der Liebe.* 1930: *Der Andere.* 1931: *Panik in Chikago; Der Liebesexpress.* 1934: *Polizeiakte 909; Eine Nacht in Venedig.* 1938: *Ultimatum* (codirected with Robert Siodmak).

There is no reason to dispute Lotte Eisner's proposal that Wiene was a second-rate director who capitalized on the vogue for Expressionism. But he is forever associated with one of the most intriguing of cinema landmarks—*Das Kabinett des Dr. Caligari*—and for that he deserves rather more personal credit than he is usually given. As to his other movies, very few are well known.

He was originally an actor and director in the Berlin theatre, but in 1914 he went into the cinema, principally to direct Emil Jannings pictures. *Caligari* had begun as a script by Carl Mayer and Hans Janowitz that dealt with what is now the central plot of the story: how Caligari, a fairground entertainer, keeps a somnambulist, Cesare, who murders by night; and of how Caligari is discovered to be the director of an asylum, himself a madman obsessed by sleepwalking; of how he is exposed and confined.

Kracauer calls it a "revolutionary" story: "reason overpowers unreasonable power, insane authority is symbolically abolished." Historically that may be so, but today it seems a conventional Hoffmanesque fate. Erich Pommer of Decla accepted the famous, neurotically distorted sets by Hermann Warm, Walter Reimann, and Walter Röhrig, and asked Fritz Lang to direct. When Lang was diverted by *Die Spinnen*, the project fell to Wiene. Lang, apparently, had suggested a framing to the story, which Wiene endorsed: now, the story was told by a man seen in a prologue sitting in a gloomy garden; in the epilogue, this setting is revealed as another asylum, all the figures in the story, including the narrator, are patients there, and Caligari is the doctor in charge.

At the time, Mayer and Janowitz fought bitterly against the framework, but today it seems the greatest coup in what is often a plain film, slowed by so many iris effects, rarely using its sets enterprisingly, and most vivid in Conrad Veidt's movements. The extra perspective makes the implication of madness far more chilling. For *Caligari* is one of the first films to exploit the resemblance between watching a film and dreaming. The framework implies a sense of spectators and projects the view of insanity upon an audience that has been identified with the storyteller. In other words, its impact bypasses any local German relevance. In fact, *Caligari* seems to represent German intellectual disillusion just as much as the images in *Metropolis* invalidate its own glib happy ending. *Caligari* asks, crudely, the basic question that confronts a movie audience: are we watching reality or fantasy? That is why the film has lasted and why Wiene should not be dismissed.

Dianne Wiest, b. Kansas City, Missouri, 1948
Dianne Wiest had won the best supporting actress Oscar twice by the age of fifty—in *Hannah and Her Sisters* and *Bullets Over Broadway*—and she's quite capable of winning more if someone has need of vivid, comic cameos rooted in human nature. For just as Wiest's eyes seem to narrow (is it short sight?), so her imaginative being can open up. She can make us believe that she is pretty or plain, a freak or the salt of the earth (well, the grease or the greasepaint).

She has worked frequently on stage, even as a director occasionally, but she had a steady run of film work once she had been discovered: *It's My Turn* (80, Claudia Weill); *I'm Dancing As Fast As I Can* (82, Jack Hofsiss); a battered wife in *Independence Day* (83, Robert Mandel); very touching as the wife in *Footloose* (84, Herbert Ross); *Falling in Love* (84, Ulu Grosbard); *The Purple Rose of Cairo* (85, Woody Allen); *Hannah and Her Sisters* (86, Allen); *The Lost Boys* (87, Joel Schumacher); the romantic aunt in *Radio Days* (87, Allen); *September* (87, Allen); *Bright Lights, Big City* (88, James Bridges); *Parenthood* (89, Ron Howard); as the mistress in *Cookie* (89, Susan Seidelman); *Edward Scissorhands* (90, Tim Burton); the school director in *Little Man Tate* (91, Jodie Foster); Helen Sinclair, the actress, in *Bullets Over Broadway* (94, Allen); *Cops and Robbersons* (94, Michael Ritchie); *The Scout* (94, Ritchie); *The Associate* (96, Daniel Petrie); *The Birdcage* (96, Mike Nichols); *Drunks* (96, Peter Cohn); uncommonly glum as a Montana housewife in *The Horse Whisperer* (98, Robert Redford); *Practical Magic* (98, Griffin Dunne); *The Simple Life of Noah Dearborn* (00, Gregg Champion); *I Am Sam* (01, Jessie Nelson); *Not Afraid, Not Afraid* (01, Annette Carducci); *Merci Docteur Rey* (02, Andrew Litvack).

Fred McLeod Wilcox (1908–64),

b. Tazewell, Virginia
1938: *Joaquin Murrieta* (s). 1943: *Lassie Come Home*. 1946: *Blue Sierra; The Courage of Lassie*. 1948: *Three Daring Daughters; Hills of Home/ Master of Lassie*. 1949: *The Secret Garden*. 1951: *Shadow in the Sky*. 1953: *Code Two*. 1954: *Tennessee Champ*. 1956: *Forbidden Planet*. 1960: *I Passed For White*.

Nothing in Wilcox's early career prepared one for *Forbidden Planet*. He knocked around for fifteen years—on publicity, as assistant to King Vidor, and directing tests—before he began directing Lassie and Elizabeth Taylor at MGM. *Lassie Come Home* is as pretty as a Victorian Christmas card with fine character studies and a surprising sense of Scotland. *The Secret Garden*, from the Frances Hodgson Burnett novel, is a most accomplished rendering of child psychology, brilliantly played by Margaret O'Brien, Dean Stockwell, and Brian Roper.

His last film for MGM was *Forbidden Planet*, one of the most delightful and inventive of science-fiction films. It is a free adaptation of *The Tempest*, with Ariel a computer and Caliban a destructive ray. Full of clever effects, it is a pretty and amusing fantasy, enchanting to children and an intriguing study of the more profound theme.

Cornel Wilde (1915–89), b. New York
1956: *Storm Fear.* 1957: *The Devil's Hairpin.*
1958: *Maracaibo.* 1963: *Lancelot and Guinevere.*
1965: *The Naked Prey.* 1967: *Beach Red.* 1970: *No Blade of Grass.* 1974: *Sharks' Treasure.*

When one considers how much the cinema has catered to childish audiences, it is remarkable that there are so few childlike directors. Primitives are to be found—although King Vidor is a lonely eminence—but the naïve picturing of the world is represented by Cornel Wilde, and by no one else. Was there a hint of such conviction in the unmitigated sincerity of his cheerfully flat acting? Wilde's own films deal with adventure situations that became increasingly parablelike with the years. It is easy to say that the thunderous message behind, say, *The Naked Prey* and *No Blade of Grass* is innocent—but so are the Dordogne cave paintings. In both cases, the images are self-sufficient and very moving. In *Naked Prey* and *Beach Red,* there are moments where one has the illusion of watching the first films ever made. Although she never seemed remotely prehistoric, Wilde's beautiful blonde wife, Jean Wallace, featured in most of his films, is one of the cinema's true Eves.

As an actor, he was forceful but blunt, like someone shouting "Hallo," or like the Olympic fencer he might have been in 1940 but for war: *The Lady with Red Hair* (40, Curtis Bernhardt); *High Sierra* (41, Raoul Walsh); *Life Begins at Eight Thirty* (42, Irving Pichel); *Wintertime* (43, John Brahm); *Guest in the House* (44, Brahm); as Chopin in *A Song to Remember* (46, Charles Vidor); bewildered by the astonishing Gene Tierney in *Leave Her to Heaven* (46, John M. Stahl); *The Bandit of Sherwood Forest* (46, George Sherman); *Centennial Summer* (46, Otto Preminger); *Forever Amber* (47, Preminger); *It Had to Be You* (47, Rudolph Maté and Don Hartman); *Road House* (48, Jean Negulesco); *Shockproof* (49, Douglas Sirk); *Two Flags West* (50, Robert Wise); *The Greatest Show on Earth* (52, Cecil B. De Mille); *Treasure of the Golden Condor* (53, Delmer Daves); *Saadia* (53, Albert Lewin); *Star of India* (53, Arthur Lubin); *Passion* (54, Allan Dwan); *The Big Combo* (54, Joseph H. Lewis); *Woman's World* (54, Negulesco); *The Scarlet Coat* (55, John Sturges); *Hot Blood* (56, Nicholas Ray); *Omar Khayyam* (57, William Dieterle); *Edge of Eternity* (59, Don Siegel); *The Norseman* (78, Charles Pierce); D'Artagnan in *The 4th Musketeer* (79, Ken Annakin).

Billy Wilder (1906–2002), b. Vienna
1934: *Mauvaise Graine* (codirected with Alexander Esnay). 1942: *The Major and the Minor.* 1943: *Five Graves to Cairo.* 1944: *Double Indemnity.* 1945: *The Lost Weekend.* 1948: *The Emperor Waltz; A Foreign Affair.* 1950: *Sunset Boulevard.* 1951: *Ace in the Hole.* 1953: *Stalag 17.* 1954: *Sabrina.* 1955: *The Seven Year Itch.* 1957: *The Spirit of St. Louis; Love in the Afternoon; Witness for the Prosecution.* 1959: *Some Like It Hot.* 1960: *The Apartment.* 1961: *One, Two, Three.* 1963: *Irma la Douce.* 1964: *Kiss Me, Stupid.* 1966: *The Fortune Cookie/Meet Whiplash Willie.* 1969: *The Private Life of Sherlock Holmes.* 1972: *Avanti!.* 1974: *The Front Page.* 1978: *Fedora.* 1981: *Buddy Buddy.*

Billy Wilder spent most of the 1980s in a state of eloquent, bitter indignation, because Hollywood would not hire him to make more films. They were too busy finding kids who could erase the tradition of the well-made film. Wilder spent more time with his magnificent art collection, fretting and fuming over unconsummated projects. Not even his anger depleted his exceptional vitality. Meanwhile, the witless world turned ever softer over him. He was not just a survivor, but *the* survivor, our last link with the merry, wicked talk of the golden age. By his very being, Wilder could make old Hollywood seem like a suburb of Vienna.

Then along came *Sunset Boulevard,* the Andrew Lloyd Webber musical from his film, tribute enough to its classic status (and tacit admission that the very tricky story had worked in 1950 only because of someone's rare magic). *Sunset Boulevard* never quite worked on stage: it was always too big, too unironic, and more adoring of show business than Wilder ever felt. For there is not really anyone in the original film whom Wilder would want to spend half an hour with—except for Max von Mayerling. (Wilder might have been Stroheim's son.)

Still, Wilder went along with the big show, coolly pouring on praise so that he wouldn't have to consult too much. And surely he was adroit enough to feel the comedy of his own "comeback" on Norma Desmond's tacky legend. Meanwhile, his *Sunset Boulevard* was safer than ever, not just a classic but a monument to ambiguity—and one of the earliest cultural admissions that we love these gods and goddesses we hate. When all was said and done, who beyond Louis B. Mayer had really been offended by *Sunset Boulevard?*

Wilder had his ups and downs critically. Andrew Sarris once saw "less than meets the eye," then thought again and drew the very barbed director back into the fold. I remain skeptical. Wilder was always a collaborator, a man who loved lines and stories more than pictures. He was a trimmer, who knew how to sweeten his own sour pills but who time and again slipped out of the ugly position of offering tough medicine. He could be ordinary to dull far too often (*The Major and the Minor, Foreign Affair, Stalag 17, Sabrina, Spirit of St. Louis, Love in the Afternoon, Witness for the Prosecu-*

tion, *Irma la Douce, Avanti!, The Front Page, Fedora, Buddy Buddy*—these are grim things on a dark night, and *Witness for the Prosecution* is among the crassest offenses ever given to innocent celluloid). And yet, there are a few films that have changed the way we measure our own duplicities: *Double Indemnity, Sunset Boulevard, The Lost Weekend,* and *Some Like It Hot.* Not one of these works does other than bite its own tail, furious that brilliance has been so tortured. But you cannot forget the vicious twist, whether it is grotesque or hilarious.

Any assessment of Wilder must begin and end with the stress he lays on writing, and on barbed lines that often outlive his persistent compromise. He began as a journalist and, after court reporting, he moved into the German film industry as a scriptwriter: he was a junior collaborator on *Menschen am Sonntag* (29, Robert Siodmak and Edgar G. Ulmer); thereafter, *Der Teufelsreporter* (29, Ernst Laemmle); *Seitensprunge* (30, Stefan Szekely); *Der Mann, der seinen Morder sucht* (31, Siodmak); *Emil und Detektive* (31, R. A. Stemmle); *Ein Blonder Traum* (32, Paul Martin); *Scampolo, ein Kind der Strasse* (32, Hans Steinhoff); *Das Blaue vom Himmel* (32, Victor Janson); and *Madame wunscht keine Kinder* (33, Steinhoff).

Wilder left Germany and went by way of France to America and to Paramount. There, he wrote, or helped to write, *Bluebeard's Eighth Wife* (38, Ernst Lubitsch); *Ninotchka* (39, Lubitsch); *Midnight* (39, Mitchell Leisen); *Arise, My Love* (40, Leisen); *Hold Back the Dawn* (41, Leisen); and *Ball of Fire* (41, Howard Hawks). He was already working with writer Charles Brackett, just as in later years he was to collaborate with I.A.L. Diamond.

In Germany and in Hollywood, Wilder had written smart romances. Nothing indicated the nagging account of weakness and delusion that preoccupied his own films. For Wilder embarked on a series of ostensibly daring, disenchanted movies, against the grain of American cheerfulness: *Double Indemnity* was a thriller based on the principle that crime springs from human greed and depravity; *The Lost Weekend* was the cinema's most graphic account of alcoholism; *A Foreign Affair* has shots of a ruined Berlin accompanied by the tune "Isn't It Romantic?"; *Sunset Boulevard* mocks the maddening glamour within Hollywood; *Ace in the Hole* exposes the unscrupulousness of the sensational press; *Stalag 17* is a prisoner-of-war film that undercuts camaraderie.

But every bitter pill had enough sugar somewhere for the public to be able to swallow it. The "realism," misanthropy, or balefulness never exceeded a melodramatic approach. The situations are set up, without benefit of characterization. Wilder is a heartless exploiter of public taste who manipulates situation in the name of satire. He prefers dialogue to character, sniping to structure. The ending of *The Lost Weekend* is a dispiriting compromise not just for the way it betrays the rest of the film, the strength of the book on which it is based, and the power of Ray Milland's performance, but because Wilder was so clumsy that he dealt with the subject in a way that could not avoid Hollywood's sense of a "happy ending." Comparison with Preminger shows how meekly Wilder relinquishes his own venom. *A Foreign Affair* soon forsakes its picture of postwar Germany for a sub-Lubitsch love story. *Sunset Boulevard* slyly confronts Swanson and von Stroheim with their past without ever really analyzing or attempting to understand them. *Stalag 17* cheats by having its outsider hero eventually join the gang. Although he believes in the worst of people, Wilder lacked the will to make misanthropy credible.

There is a moment in *Sunset Boulevard* where William Holden's interior monologue—so many of Wilder's films rely on narration—mentions the childlike handwriting of the Gloria Swanson character. We do not see that writing. It is a writer's ploy, astonishingly unadapted to the medium. That is typical of Wilder. He outlines characters on paper—in dialogue, setting, and situation—rather than in revealed behavior. Very often in his films, the actual images are incidental to the "facts" of narration and dialogue. It follows that the films are frequently bare or fussy: because in the first instance he has given too meager a brief to the art department, and in the second too much. The house in *Sunset Boulevard* bulges with detail that is all referred to in the script but that is never more than a gesture at plausible atmosphere. *The Apartment,* however, is as plain as Wilder's conception of Baxter.

As to his players, Wilder depends upon good readers of his mordant dialogue. Stanwyck, MacMurray, and Edward G. Robinson carry *Double Indemnity* very well and, if it is unusually complete amid Wilder's work, that may be because of Raymond Chandler's presence and the intrinsic tendency of the thriller form toward pessimism. *Some Like It Hot* is a dazzling verbal comedy, well played by Curtis and Lemmon. But compare it with the best screwball of the 1930s and see how necessary the stream of jokes is to conceal the indifference to character or meaning. It is ninety-odd minutes of jokes, based on one ingenious situation, without any attempt at dramatic progress or culmination. Yet, in hindsight, we can see how much that film did to unsettle gender confidence.

Time has only underlined Wilder's merits and failings. *One, Two, Three* is another exercise in comedy fast enough to manage on puns, wise-cracks, and double meanings alone. *Kiss Me, Stupid* is one more acid solution suddenly made alkaline. Jack Lemmon and Walter Matthau—in

The Fortune Cookie—are exactly the sort of virtuoso technician actors that suit Wilder. *The Apartment*, really penetrating and touching in situation, is the clearest proof of Wilder's lack of courage or persistence. It is as if on paper he could plan mayhem, but when presented with actors and sets his lack of human or cinematic coherence forces him into irresolution and the unforgivable asides that mock Swanson, Cooper in *Love in the Afternoon*, Monroe in *Some Like It Hot*, and Novak in *Kiss Me, Stupid*. There is a satiric instinct in Wilder, but one that he giggles over, nervous of its outrageousness. Thus in throwaways and background action we have his least watered-down admissions of human nastiness—as in *The Apartment* when Sheldrake talks of his son putting live flies in the nose cone of a toy rocket. Equally, Wilder's contempt for women is an undertone, seldom brought out into the open.

Look at the films repeatedly and only a few things emerge—the dislike of people, the flinching from women, the show of smart skills, the compromise and the superiority, and the flair for riveting, grisly moments. When you think about it, the characters Wilder did best were self-betrayers, and how he loved to have them talk out their own ruin. Along the way, in fifty years, Wilder had some great picture ideas, visions of men as pretty (and pretty-talking) reptiles, drunks, fantasists, and sexual wrecks. Of course, he was correct. But with that knowledge, if he'd had a pinch more courage and grace he could have been a great man—instead of just a scathing observer. As it is, too often I feel he's dead, or lost, to the life of his films, a grinning corpse floating on top, preserved by sardonic fluids and voice-over.

Esther Williams, b. Los Angeles, 1923

A freestyle swimming champion and attraction at the 1940 San Francisco World's Fair Aquacade, she made her debut at MGM, in 1942, in *Andy Hardy Steps Out*. Granted the success of former skater Sonja Henie, it was inevitable and just that Esther Williams should prosper. For she was a pretty girl, in or out of a bathing suit. The studio contrived a pool at all unlikely moments and otherwise kept her in musicals: *Andy Hardy's Double Life* (42, George B. Seitz); *A Guy Named Joe* (43, Victor Fleming); *Bathing Beauty* (44, George Sidney); *This Time for Keeps* (46, Richard Thorpe); grinning tight-teethed in the underwater ballet in *Ziegfeld Follies* (46, Vincente Minnelli); *Fiesta* (47, Thorpe); *Take Me Out to the Ball Game* (49, Busby Berkeley); *Neptune's Daughter* (49, Edward Buzzell); *Pagan Love Song* (50, Robert Alton); *Duchess of Idaho* (50, Robert Z. Leonard); *Texas Carnival* (51, Charles Walters); *Skirts Ahoy!* (52, Sidney Lanfield); *Million Dollar Mermaid* (52, Mervyn Le Roy); *Dangerous When Wet* (53, Walters)—which starred her future husband, Fer-

nando Lamas; and *Jupiter's Darling* (55, Sidney). Only when she left the studio did two films—*The Unguarded Moment* (56, Harry Keller) and *Raw Wind in Eden* (58, Richard Wilson)—show that she was worthy of drier things. But after *The Big Show* (61, James B. Clark), she retired.

Robin Williams, b. Chicago, 1952

There is a nervousness in Robin Williams that supplies the energy in his improvisations. One can see the ideas popping up behind his desperate eyes, and one may feel the overwhelming need for laughter, response, and being liked. He is an electric, brilliant talent, yet his own personality is couched in anxiety, if not guilt. As a result, he seldom has the confidence or patience to enter into a movie-long masquerade. Sometimes it seems that pretense offends or alarms him. Yet this is an uncannily intelligent face, if only something could still the man and ask him to . . . be a villain? I suggest that only because his nice guys are becoming dangerously sanctimonious and superficial. So, if the sincerity of being decent grates on him, try a little darkness.

He made his name as the extraterrestrial on the hit TV series, *Mork and Mindy* (1978–82), and he continues to perform on TV specials, at clubs, parties, on sound tracks and, surely, in the shower. His movie work is the epitome of unevenness: *Popeye* (80, Robert Altman); *The World According to Garp* (82, George Roy Hill); *The Survivors* (83, Michael Ritchie); Russian in *Moscow on the Hudson* (84, Paul Mazursky); as a high school football failure in *The Best of Times* (86, Roger Spottiswoode); *Club Paradise* (86, Harold Ramis); excruciating in the Saul Bellow adaptation, *Seize the Day* (86, Fielder Cook); *Good Morning, Vietnam* (87, Barry Levinson), for which he was nominated for best actor Oscar; *The Adventures of Baron Munchausen* (89, Terry Gilliam); nominated again for best actor in *Dead Poets Society* (89, Peter Weir); as Oliver Sacks in *Awakenings* (90, Penny Marshall); *Cadillac Man* (90, Roger Donaldson); *The Fisher King* (91, Gilliam); a Peter out of Willy Loman in *Hook* (91, Steven Spielberg); as the voice of the Genie in *Aladdin* (92, John Musker and Ron Clements); *Toys* (92, Levinson); dreadfully indulged in a vacuous hit, *Mrs. Doubtfire* (93, Chris Columbus); and *Being Human* (94, Bill Forsyth).

So it goes on, with Williams as the man-child of American film, hideously "likable," often enough in films for children, but invariably in works for those unwilling to grow up: *Nine Months* (95, Columbus); *Jumanji* (95, Joe Johnston); better in *The Birdcage* (96, Mike Nichols); *Jack* (96, Francis Ford Coppola); a villain in *The Secret Agent* (96, Christopher Hampton), and interesting; Osric in *Hamlet* (96, Kenneth Branagh); *Father's Day* (97, Ivan Reitman); *Deconstructing Harry*

(97, Woody Allen); *Flubber* (97, Les Mayfield); winning the supporting actor Oscar as the shrink in *Good Will Hunting* (97, Gus Van Sant); *What Dreams May Come* (98, Vincent Ward); simply dreadful in *Patch Adams* (98, Tom Shadyac); *Jakob the Liar* (99, Peter Kassovitz); *Bicentennial Man* (99, Columbus); a voice in *A.I.* (01, Spielberg).

Just as "the Robin Williams picture" had become a warning signal, he tried to shift into less ingratiating roles: *Death to Smoochy* (02, Danny DeVito); *Insomnia* (02, Christopher Nolan); *One Hour Photo* (02, Mark Romanek).

Bruce Willis (Walter Willison),
b. Idar-Oberstein, Germany, 1955

A time may come when Bruce Willis is treasured for his small parts, twenty lively minutes here or there, a flash, a wisecrack, a voice off, or even—simply—an implication: thus, I prefer his doomed gangster in *Billy Bathgate* (91, Robert Benton); the eminently murderable husband in *Mortal Thoughts* (91, Alan Rudolph); the nice parody within *The Player* (92, Robert Altman); the voices off, or within, in *Look Who's Talking* (89, Amy Heckerling) and *Look Who's Talking, Too* (90, Heckerling); and even his off-the-picture contribution to his wife Demi Moore's first Henry Moore–like *Vanity Fair* cover.

Still, there is a more extended Willis, launched in the TV series *Moonlighting* (85–89), which was actually at its best as bits and pieces but in which Willis struck up a pleasing brittle banter with Cybill Shepherd, and in which his cocksureness got enough comeuppance to be entertaining. He had had tiny parts in New York movies—he is said to be in Sidney Lumet's *Prince of the City* (81) and *The Verdict* (81)—but he made his starring debut in *Blind Date* (87, Blake Edwards). He played Tom Mix in *Sunset* (88, Edwards), before falling into *Die Hard* (88, John McTiernan) and *Die Hard 2* (90, Renny Harlin).

Their success beggared description or reasoning, and left Willis exposed to the just-as-lavish failure of *In Country* (89, Norman Jewison), *The Bonfire of the Vanities* (90, Brian De Palma), and *Hudson Hawk* (91, Michael Lehmann). Chances are that comedy is his most fruitful pursuit, yet he clings to adventure, as in *The Last Boy Scout* (92, Tony Scott). In *Death Becomes Her* (92, Robert Zemeckis), he was again not much more than a support to two actresses going through athletic motions. He was in *North* (94, Rob Reiner); and super in *Pulp Fiction* (94, Quentin Tarantino).

The mystery of Mr. Willis goes on. He makes quantities of commercial junk, where his raised eyebrows soar into the space left by his receding hairline as he offs so many minor players. And then he comes in with something that unmistakably reveals a tender, wise actor. I still have the hunch that he's going to walk off with an Oscar someday soon, for some piece of breathtaking humility. He came close with *The Sixth Sense* (99, M. Night Shyamalan), and he was brilliant in a supporting role in *Nobody's Fool* (94, Benton). Against that, there is *Die Hard: With a Vengeance* (95, McTiernan); *Twelve Monkeys* (95, Terry Gilliam); *Last Man Standing* (96, Walter Hill); *The Fifth Element* (97, Luc Besson); *The Jackal* (97, Michael Caton-Jones); *Mercury Rising* (98, Harold Becker); and *Armageddon* (98, Michael Bay).

He was a little better, or quieter, or more humorous, in *The Siege* (98, Edward Zwick); *Breakfast of Champions* (99, Alan Rudolph); *The Story of Us* (99, Rob Reiner); *The Whole Nine Yards* (00, Jonathan Lynn), and—just—*Unbreakable* (00, Shyamalan), which was as opaque as *Sixth Sense* was lucid. He has also been shameless in *The Kid* (00, Jon Turteltaub), *Bandits* (01, Barry Levinson), *Hart's War* (02, Gregory Hoblit) and *Tears of the Sun* (03, Antoine Fuqua).

Debra Winger, b. Cleveland, Ohio, 1955

I met Debra Winger in the early eighties, to write a profile for *California* magazine. She had so much going for her then: she was articulate, unruly, raucous, funny, but very smart; she had something of the young Stanwyck; and she was young enough for her evident insecurities to seem natural—she was not yet thirty. Though it was not her first film, in *Urban Cowboy* (80, James Bridges) she had stolen a big picture with her bravura tough prettiness, her through-and-through snappiness, and one sequence on a mechanical bull. In *An Officer and a Gentleman* (82, Taylor Hackford), she had delivered an authentic working-class woman, she had seemed hot, urgent, and gritty, and the film was another hit. Just ahead lay *Terms of Endearment* (83, James L. Brooks) in which her portrait of a young woman dying of cancer was free from sentimentality or easy pathos. That Debra Winger had projects of her own in mind—she wanted to play the singer Libby Holman and Mabel Normand—and she seemed capable of a large career.

Yet there were stories that she was difficult, argumentative, wild . . . one never knows what those reports mean. It can be a matter of disobedience or simply seeking more understanding; or of being too gritty, not quite beautiful, and too edgily Jewish.

Ten years later, Winger's looked like a falling career, made up of willful misjudgments, her eyes ever more desperate at the realization of not being accepted or loved by the public. By then, the real puzzle was that she had no grasp of why or how she was threatening.

She was raised in the San Fernando Valley, she was in Israel for a time, and she had a serious yet still rather mysterious accident while working at Magic Mountain. She was adventurous or reckless—take your pick. She played Lynda Carter's younger sister on TV in *Wonder Woman,* and she made an unremarkable movie debut in *Slumber Party '57* (77, William A. Levey), followed by *Special Olympics* (78, Lee Philips) for TV, *Thank God It's Friday* (78, Robert Klane), and *French Postcards* (79, Willard Huyck).

Urban Cowboy launched her heady years, during which she contributed at least something to the voice of *E.T.* (82, Steven Spielberg). *Cannery Row* (82, David S. Ward) was a complete flop, but Winger was robust, funny, and touching as the young whore, and she and Nick Nolte made an unusually attractive pair of wayward lovers. *Mike's Murder* (84, Bridges) was a star vehicle and a disaster, a film that went through agonies before it was released. Among other things, it showed Winger cast beyond her real range—actors need so much more work than they have a chance for today, and Winger had had little training.

Legal Eagles (86, Ivan Reitman) is famous only as a grotesque agency package: Winger was miscast and physically overshadowed by the far less talented Daryl Hannah. For *Black Widow* (86, Bob Rafelson), she was offered her choice of either of the two female roles. The plot is implausible, yet maybe the killer would have tested her better. She had an uncredited walk-on in *Made in Heaven* (87, Alan Rudolph), which starred her then-husband, Timothy Hutton. She could do nothing to bring a shred of credibility to the dreadful *Betrayal* (88, Costa-Gavras).

There are mixed feelings over *Everybody Wins* (90, Karel Reisz). Pauline Kael believed Winger was extraordinary in it, playing a schizophrenic, swooping from sexuality to coldness. I felt the picture was incoherent and foolish, and another sign of the actress's lack of technique. No player could be blamed for *Everybody Wins.* The script was the root of the problem. But why had she accepted the part? And how did she seem so undirected?

The Sheltering Sky (90, Bernardo Bertolucci) was her best work in years. She looked like Jane Bowles, and understood her jittery intelligence. The movie betrayed the actress in its last third, but until then, with John Malkovich, she had made a wonderful picture of a failed yet inescapable marriage. Still, no one went to see *The Sheltering Sky,* and, closing in on forty, Winger seemed a problem to the business and herself.

She was good, and a little removed from center stage, in *Leap of Faith* (92, Richard Pearce), a film that made little mention of her in its promotion. Her next film, *Wilder Napalm* (93, Glenn Gordon Caron), came and went as quickly as a fire. But as *A Dangerous Woman* (93, Stephen Gyllenhaal), she gave an uncanny performance as a disturbed woman. The film was a mess, and yet another failure, but it was hard to miss the sanity and danger in Winger. At last, she had a mainstream hit, in *Shadowlands* (93, Richard Attenborough).

Forget Paris (95, Billy Crystal) was nowhere near working. At that point, despite her three Oscar nominations—*An Officer and a Gentleman, Terms of Endearment,* and *Shadowlands*—Ms. Winger effectively retired. I'm not sure that she ever announced it, but there was no work and no real word, apart from news of her marriage to actor Arliss Howard (they had met on *Wilder Napalm*). Then, in 2001, he directed her in *Big Bad Love.*

Kate Winslet, b. Reading, England, 1975

Kate Winslet was the female lead, the figurehead and a very fetching cabin companion, in what is, so far, history's most successful film, *Titanic* (97, James Cameron). But, of course, Mark Hamill was the lead in the *Star Wars* trilogy. Winslet has more on her side: she gave a miraculous debut performance in *Heavenly Creatures* (94, Peter Jackson), where her command of the fragile line between blithe teenage friendship and murderous force was the heart of the film. Against that, it may be said that Winslet has seemed specially suited to period costume. Does she feel like a modern woman? Is she a little too inclined towards Edwardian fleshiness? For the moment, as she continues to attract major directors (like Jane Campion and Philip Kaufman), let's trust the talent: *A Kid in King Arthur's Court* (95, Michael Gottlieb); *Sense and Sensibility* (95, Ang Lee); as Ophelia in *Hamlet* (96, Kenneth Branagh); excellent again in *Jude* (96, Michael Winterbottom); *Hideous Kinky* (98, Gilles MacKinnon); *Holy Smoke* (99, Campion).

At this point, it was evident that Winslet had pushed herself less than, say, Cate Blanchett, Gwyneth Paltrow, or Helena Bonham Carter. But she may pass them all. Her performance as the maid in *Quills* (00, Kaufman) was not just brilliant; it was the center of the film that allowed Geoffrey Rush his eccentricity. She was the eager, bespectacled helper in *Enigma* (01, Michael Apted); and she was ravishing as the young author or siren in *Iris* (01, Richard Eyre). But *The Life of David Gale* (03, Alan Parker) was a blunder.

Michael Winterbottom,
b. Blackburn, England, 1961
1990: *Forget About Me* (TV). 1992: *Under the Sun* (TV); *Love Lies Bleeding* (TV). 1993: *Cracker: The Mad Woman in the Attic* (TV). 1994: *Family* (TV); *Butterfly Kiss.* 1995: *Go Now* (TV); *Jude.* 1996: *Welcome to Sarajevo.* 1997: *I Want You.* 1998: *With or Without You.* 1999: *Wonderland.* 2000: *The Claim.* 2002: *24 Hour Party People; In This World.*

In just a few years, Winterbottom has given us

several indelible locations: not just the uncertainties of Sarajevo, but the bleak English seaside resort in *I Want You* (maybe the gloomiest getaway since Yves Allégret's *Une Si Jolie Petite Plage*), the modern London of *Wonderland,* and the epic Sierra Nevada (by way of Hardy's Wessex) for *The Claim.* There are some who say that no one of those films is flawless, and that their diversity is so great it's not easy to know much about Winterbottom. I think those critics are being inventively difficult. All four films, it seems to me, are far more right than wrong—and emphatically successful emotionally. Winterbottom has come out of British television, full of ideas but blessed with practical need and an urge to tell different stories. Let the unity of character settle in as it may. But it seems to me, already, that Winterbottom does have a theme: that of lost souls who are putting on a busy and ingenious display of being safe and sound. He is working in the mainstream, and he may have no higher urge than to be versatile and entertaining. I will settle for that.

Shelley Winters (Shirley Schrift),
b. St. Louis, Missouri, 1922

Blowsy, effusive, brash, and maternal, either voluptuous or drab, Shelley Winters is at her best when driven to wonder, "How did a girl like me get into a high-class movie like this?"

In fact, she had a very respectable New York stage training before her debut in *What a Woman* (43, Irving Cummings), followed by *She's a Soldier, Too* (44, William Castle), *Nine Girls* (44, Leigh Jason), and *Tonight and Every Night* (45, Victor Saville). She may be seen, briefly, walking across screen in the wagon train dance sequence in *Red River* (48, Howard Hawks). But her first really worthy part was as the waitress in the Kanin/Cukor *A Double Life* (47) and she featured notably in *Cry of the City* (48, Robert Siodmak); *Take One False Step* (49, Chester Erskine); *The Great Gatsby* (49, Elliott Nugent); *Johnny Stool Pigeon* (49, Castle); *South Sea Sinner* (49, Bruce Humberstone); *Winchester 73* (50, Anthony Mann); and George Stevens's *A Place in the Sun* (51) in which she is last seen hunched up in a rowing boat before Montgomery Clift's uneasy resolve drowns her.

This same vulnerability characterized *Phone Call From a Stranger* (52, Jean Negulesco), *The Big Knife* (55, Robert Aldrich), *The Night of the Hunter* (55, Charles Laughton), in which she is discovered on the bottom of the lake, still sitting up in a car, hair flowing like weed, and *The Chapman Report* (62, Cukor). But she is equally adept, if hard to restrain, in more domineering parts: *Mambo* (54, Robert Rossen); *Executive Suite* (54, Robert Wise); *I Am a Camera* (55, Henry Cornelius); Stevens's *The Diary of Anne Frank* (59), for which she won the supporting Oscar; as Charlotte Haze in *Lolita* (62, Stanley Kubrick); *The*

Balcony (63, Joseph Strick); *A Patch of Blue* (65, Guy Green) and another supporting Oscar; *The Scalphunters* (68, Sydney Pollack); the delirious *Bloody Mama* (70, Roger Corman). Add to this Wellman's *My Man and I* (52); Fregonese's *Untamed Frontier* (52); Fred M. Wilcox's *Tennessee Champ* (54); Walsh's *Saskatchewan* (54); Heisler's *I Died a Thousand Times* (55); Wise's *Odds Against Tomorrow* (59); Frankenheimer's *The Young Savages* (61); Lewis Gilbert's *Alfie* (66); Barry Shear's *Wild in the Streets* (68); Curtis Harrington's *Whoever Slew Auntie Roo?* (71) and *What's the Matter with Helen?* (71); and Paul Mazursky's *Blume in Love* (73); and it looks a very versatile career that has never lost its sense of loudmouth fun. Not least in *The Poseidon Adventure* (72, Ronald Neame) in which she asks us to believe that, as New York underwater swimming champion, she once held her breath for two minutes forty-seven seconds.

She was garrulous still in *That Lucky Touch* (75, Christopher Miles); *Diamonds* (75, Menahem Golan); a casebook Jewish mother in *Next Stop, Greenwich Village* (75, Mazursky); the sleazy concierge in *The Tenant* (76, Roman Polanski); *Tentacles* (76, Oliver Hellman); *Pete's Dragon* (77, Don Chaffey); *The Magician of Lublin* (79, Golan); and *City on Fire* (79, Alvin Rakoff).

Since then she has published two lively volumes of autobiography and appeared in: *Elvis, the Movie* (79, John Carpenter); *S.O.B.* (81, Blake Edwards); *Fanny Hill* (83, Gerry O'Hara); *Over the Brooklyn Bridge* (83, Golan); *Ellie* (84, Peter Wittman); *Deja Vu* (85, Anthony Richmond); *The Delta Force* (86, Golan); *Very Close Quarters* (86, Vladimir Rif); *Purple People Eater* (88, Linda Shayne); *An Unremarkable Life* (89, Amin Q. Chaudhri); *Touch of a Stranger* (90, Brad Gilbert); and *Stepping Out* (91, Lewis Gilbert). And on TV, as the grandmother in *Roseanne.*

Now eighty, she has plugged on: *Weep No More, My Lady* (92, Michel Andrieu); *The Pickle* (93, Mazursky); *Il Silenzio del Prosciutti* (94, Ezio Greggio); *Backfire!* (95, A. Dean Bell); *Jury Duty* (95, John Fortenberry); *Mrs. Munck* (95, Diane Ladd); *Heavy* (95, James Mangold); *Raging Angels* (95, Alan Smithee); *The Portrait of a Lady* (96, Jane Campion), in which, on screen, she was married to John Gielgud—you see, the movies are better than life; *Gideon* (99, Claudia Hoover); *La Bomba* (99, Giulio Base).

Robert Wise, b. Winchester, Indiana, 1914
1944: *The Curse of the Cat People* (codirected with Gunther von Fritsch); *Mademoiselle Fifi.* 1945: *The Body Snatcher; A Game of Death.* 1946: *Criminal Court.* 1947: *Born to Kill.* 1948: *Mystery in Mexico; Blood on the Moon.* 1949: *The Set-Up.* 1950: *Two Flags West; Three Secrets.* 1951: *The House on Telegraph Hill; The Day the Earth Stood*

Still. 1952: *The Captive City; Something for the Birds.* 1953: *Destination Gobi; The Desert Rats; So Big.* 1954: *Executive Suite.* 1955: *Helen of Troy.* 1956: *Tribute to a Bad Man; Somebody Up There Likes Me.* 1957: *This Could Be the Night; Until They Sail.* 1958: *Run Silent, Run Deep; I Want to Live.* 1959: *Odds Against Tomorrow.* 1961: *West Side Story* (codirected with Jerome Robbins). 1962: *Two for the Seesaw.* 1963: *The Haunting.* 1965: *The Sound of Music.* 1966: *The Sand Pebbles.* 1968: *Star!.* 1971: *The Andromeda Strain.* 1975: *The Hindenburg.* 1977: *Audrey Rose.* 1979: *Star Trek: The Motion Picture.* 1989: *Rooftops.* 2000: *A Storm in Summer.*

There was a time when Wise was thought promising. But it is now clear that his better credits are only the haphazard products of artistic aimlessness given rare guidance. He has wandered as easily into mediocrity or worse, and it is a proof of the Hollywood bizarre that he should have edited and completed that masterpiece deserted by its maker, *The Magnificent Ambersons*, and also brought to the screen the appalling but grotesquely successful *The Sound of Music*.

Wise began as a journalist and then joined the sound department at RKO. From there, he rose to become an editor, working on *Fifth Avenue Girl* (39, Gregory La Cava); *The Story of Vernon and Irene Castle* (39, H. C. Potter); *The Hunchback of Notre Dame,* (39, William Dieterle); *Bachelor Mother* (39, Garson Kanin); *My Favorite Wife* (40, Kanin); *All That Money Can Buy* (41, Dieterle); *Seven Days' Leave* (42, Tim Whelan)—as well as *Citizen Kane* and *Ambersons.* Wise deserves no blame for the hurried change of tone that ends *Ambersons;* indeed, it is likely that his tact saved it from worse fates. But neither does he qualify for much credit. One has only to recall Welles's complaint about the hours spent with *Kane* on the moviola to identify the editing style of that film.

In 1944, Wise was promoted to take over direction of Val Lewton's *The Curse of the Cat People*—and thus he began auspiciously. Two more Lewton pictures, *Mademoiselle Fifi* and *The Body Snatcher,* are confirmation of the producer's overall conception. Thus Wise began with his most interesting pictures. Years later, he went back to the supernatural with *The Haunting,* and made an opulent-looking but muddled, tentative movie. The schematic, contrived, and overrated *The Set-Up* still hangs on Robert Ryan. A better boxing movie, *Somebody Up There Likes Me,* comes alive with Paul Newman's appetite for the big break. The prominent melodrama of *I Want to Live* is due to Susan Hayward. Against that, the failures can be attributed to Wise: *So Big,* a restrained women's picture; *Run Silent, Run Deep*—but not quite unobtrusive enough; the chocolate box travesty of *West Side Story;* the sorry waste of

Mitchum and MacLaine in *Two for the Seesaw.*

There is nothing to be said about *The Sound of Music* except that three years later Wise managed to make as big a flop with the same Julie Andrews in *Star!* He has tried for realism and romance with equal vagueness, and there is a restless, dispiriting search among subject areas—war, epic, musical, science fiction, horror, crime, Western—that has never caught up with interest.

Wise won best picture twice (with *West Side Story* and *The Sound of Music*). He won best director for the same movies, and he was nominated again for *I Want to Live.* Less known, but so much better, is 1947's *Born to Kill* at RKO, a harsh, unsettling thriller in which Claire Trevor and Lawrence Tierney display grown-up attitudes and ugly instincts enough to still the sound of music. Yet it was easier to do good work in 1947 than in the early sixties. *Born to Kill* could easily have been written by Jim Thompson.

Frederick Wiseman,
b. Boston, Massachusetts, 1930

1967: *Titicut Follies* (d). 1968: *High School* (d). 1969: *Law and Order* (d). 1970: *Hospital* (d). 1971: *Basic Training* (d). 1972: *Essene* (d). 1973: *Juvenile Court* (d). 1974: *Primate* (d). 1975: *Welfare* (d). 1976: *Meat* (d). 1977: *Canal Zone* (d). 1978: *Sinai Field Mission* (d). 1979: *Manoeuvre* (d). 1980: *Model* (d). 1982: *Seraphita's Diary.* 1983: *The Store* (d). 1985: *Racetrack* (d). 1987: *Blind* (d); *Deaf* (d); *Missile* (d). 1989: *Near Death* (d). 1990: *Central Park* (d). 1991: *Aspen* (d). 1993: *Zoo* (d). 1994: *High School II* (d). 1995: *Ballet* (d). 1996: *La Comédie-Française, ou L'Amour Joué.* 1997: *Public Housing.* 1999: *Belfast, Maine.* 2002: *The Final Letter; Domestic Violence.*

Fred Wiseman pledges himself to being straightforward, but his work has taught us how ambivalent an attitude that is. There are touchstones of conscientious austerity and simplicity throughout his films: hand-held eavesdropping records of actuality, black-and-white photography, the absence of any narrative or music. They add up to the sincere hope that "If the films do anything, they provide people with information which they may be in a position to use at some point along the line along with other kinds of information to influence the way they make a decision about something that's going on in society."

That sounds constructive and rational, very much what you would expect from a moderately radical and creative lawyer who became interested in films as "a form of natural history. I try to look at what is going on to discover what kind of power relationships exist and differences between ideology and the practice in terms of the way people are treated. The theme that unites the films is the relationship of people to authority."

That promises general understanding and a kind of sociological survey that sorts evidence on the way to principles. But Wiseman's films, like anyone else's, are helplessly particular: he can only select unique institutions, film certain moments, and compose them in one way. We are not seeing the generality, much less an objective view. But the patina of fairness excuses Wiseman from that most dangerous and necessary thing: the transition from data to opinion. We are seeing through Wiseman's eyes, so that it is perplexing and perverse of him to try to disown his own power of sight and the consequent effects on conscience. After all, it is ridiculous for Wiseman to have so obsessive a subject while denying frame of mind. Whoever said that movies offer "information"? They are about atmosphere—yet Wiseman proposes clean air.

His minimalism is decent, but puritanical and repressed. It does nothing to prohibit the power of atmosphere and experience in his films. His loyalty to bureaucracy is as great as Kafka's, but Wiseman has so purged himself of his own reactions that he sometimes makes what seem like unattended films, sustained by the listless momentum of the system and the demoralized complicity of all of us who are involved in it. Shy of ideological commitment and formal construct, and alarmed at the prospect of his own anger or dismay, Wiseman often seems as meek as the animals who engage his sensibility most strongly—in *Primate* and *Meat*.

His films are remarkable records of institutions, seemingly untroubled by the dilemma of how far ordinary people act when their monotony is filmed (and instantly glamorized). But why do so many institutions admit Wiseman's camera? Is it out of the vanity that likes to keep records of itself, or is it because bureaucrats feel kinship with the director's dispassionate method? Despite the obvious conclusion that Wiseman is accumulating an epic documentary panorama of American systems, it is oddly short of Americans and averse to the thought that policy is within Americans' control. The persistent implication is of a condition that is self-sufficient, unquestionable, and forlorn. One has to compare Wiseman's work with any of the great nineteenth-century social surveys to feel the lack of humor, cantankerousness, and energy. The camera's placid obedience to its own pressed button is the energy center in most Wiseman films. And that pardons the mind from protesting. It is instructive that his films have generally grown longer and more remote, as pungency and morals slipped out of reach. One longs for a shot of journalistic bias.

His admirers assert that Wiseman is always controversial, and thus provocative. Yet only *Titicut Follies*, his first film, really outraged anyone. *Primate* is his most personal film, mercifully rash and partial and an urgent essay, if absolutely conventional in its sentiments and thinking. Too many of the other films trail away into minutely observed inconsequentiality—as if film's own process had become a bureaucratic structure.

It's ironic that Wiseman himself is as conscious of his editing, even to the point of claiming, "The result is a sequence which is totally arbitrary in that it never existed in real life, but it works in film terms. All the material is manipulated so that the final film is totally fictional in form although it is based on real events." As a rule, he shoots quick and edits slow, hoping that implicit points will be made in the organization of the material. On the other hand, he likes everyone to make what they will of the movies. There is something pusillanimous in this restrained conflict of motives; and something bland and lulling in the neutrality. No wonder so much of his work has found its outlet on American Public Broadcasting, a comfortable and pious institution for sedate liberalism that runs parallel to, but seldom crosses, the huge force of demonic America. If only Wiseman were crazier, or less depressively guarded.

Googie (Georgette) **Withers**,
b. Karachi, India, 1917

Ms. Withers is included not just because her basic information contains a trick question—for Karachi is now in Pakistan—nor even as a reminder that someone calling herself "Googie Withers" once mounted a career. She is here because she is magnificent in two films by Robert Hamer: as the straight-faced poisoner in *Pink String and Sealing Wax* (45) and as the married woman given a glimpse of romantic escape in *It Always Rains on Sunday* (47). Those are major films, and they depend on the restrained emotion of Miss Withers. "Her beauty had an erotic quality," wrote Michael Powell, "strange and provocative." Powell also liked her laugh, and the way she refused to change her name to enhance her career.

She was the daughter of an Eighth Army officer and a Dutch woman, sent back to England to be educated. She appeared often on stage, and with her Australian husband, John McCallum (he is the former lover in *It Always Rains*). They returned to Australia together in the late fifties. Her work includes: *The Girl in the Crowd* (34, Michael Powell); *The Love Test* (34, Powell); *Windfall* (35, George King); *Her Last Affaire* (35, Powell); *All at Sea* (35, Anthony Kimmins); *Dark World* (35, Bernard Vorhaus); *Crown v. Stevens* (36, Powell); *King of Hearts* (36, John Mills); *She Knew What She Wanted* (36, Thomas Bentley); *Accused* (36, Thornton Freeland); *Crime over London* (36, Alfred Zeisler); *Pearls Bring Tears* (37, Manning Haynes); *Paradise for Two* (37, Freeland); *Paid in Error* (38, Maclean Rogers); *If I Were Boss* (38, Rogers); *Kate Plus Ten* (38, Reginald Denham); *Strange Boarders* (38, Herbert

Mason); *Convict 99* (38, Marcel Varnel); *The Lady Vanishes* (38, Alfred Hitchcock); *You're the Doctor* (38, Roy Lockwood).

Murder in Soho (39, Norman Lee); *Trouble Brewing* (39, Kimmins); *The Gang's All Here* (39, Freeland); *She Couldn't Say No* (39, Graham Cutts); *Bulldog Sees It Through* (40, Harold Huth); *Business Honeymoon* (40, Arthur Words); *Jeannie* (41, Harold French); *Back Room Boy* (41, Mason); as the Dutch woman in *One of Our Aircraft Is Missing* (42, Powell); *The Silvery Fleet* (42, Vernon Sewell); *On Approval* (44, Clive Brook); *They Came to a City* (44, Basil Dearden), *Dead of Night* (45, Alberto Cavalcanti and Charles Crichton).

The Loves of Joanne Godden (47, Charles Frend); *Miranda* (48, Ken Annakin); *Once Upon a Dream* (48, Ralph Thomas); *Traveller's Joy* (49, Thomas); *Night and the City* (50, Jules Dassin); *White Corridors* (51, Pat Jackson); *The Magic Box* (51, John and Roy Boulting); *Derby Day* (52, Herbert Wilcox); *Devil on Horseback* (54, Cyril Frankel); *Port of Escape* (56, Tony Young).

Years later, she made *The Nickel Queen* (70, John McCallum); the long-lost cousin in *Time After Time* (85, Bill Hays); superb as the maid in *Country Life* (95, Michael Blakemore); *Shine* (96, Scott Hicks).

(Laura Jean) **Reese Witherspoon**,
b. Nashville, Tennessee, 1976

Reese Witherspoon is a year younger than Angelina Jolie. She is not as transportingly sensual or hilarious as Jolie. But what she has on her side is a wicked and controlled comic drive so that, even when cast in a Jolie-like role—as the innocent disaster area in *Freeway* (96, Matthew Bright)—she leaves us in no doubt but that we are beholding a comic creation. There is something of Madeline Kahn, and maybe a memory of Tuesday Weld, but the result is all Ms. Witherspoon, with the ability to present, without patronizing, an old-fashioned, nerdily decent, but helplessly dangerous girl.

She was a child model who made her debut on TV in *Wildflower* (91, Diane Keaton). Since then, she has grown and prospered in *The Man in the Moon* (91, Robert Mulligan); in Africa in *A Far Off Place* (93, Mikael Salomon); *Jack the Bear* (93, Marshall Herskovitz); *S.F.W.* (95, Jefery Levy); *Fear* (96, James Foley); *Pleasantville* (98, Gary Ross); as the good girl in *Cruel Intentions* (99, Roger Kumble); in what is so far her tour de force, a performance of Katharine Hepburn range, in *Election* (99, Alexander Payne); in her first big hit, *Legally Blonde* (01, Robert Luketic); and Cecily Cardew in *The Importance of Being Earnest* (02, Oliver Parker).

Alarm bells sounded with *Sweet Home Alabama* (02, Andy Tennant)—for sweetness is not what Ms

Witherspoon needs to pursue. But sugar is box-office, and the tide of a talent had turned, tartness had turned pink in *Legally Blonde 2: Red, White and Blonde* (03, Charles Herman-Wurmfeld).

John Woo (Yusen Wu),
b. Guangzhou, China, 1946

1975: *Nu Zi Tai Quan Qun Ying Hui/The Dragon Tamers; Tie Han Rou Qing/The Young Dragons.* 1976: *Dinu Hua/Princess Chang Pin; Shao Lin Men/Countdown in Kung Fu.* 1977: *Fa Qian Han/The Pilferer's Progress.* 1978: *Da Sha Xing Yu Xiao Mei Tou/Follow the Star; Ha Luo, Ye Gui Ren/Hello, Late Homecomers.* 1979: *Hao Xia/Last Hurrah for Chivalry.* 1980: *Qian Zuo Guai/From Riches to Rags; Hua Ji Shi Dai/Laughing Times.* 1982: *Mo Deng Tian Shi/To Hell with the Devil; Ba Cai Lin Ya Zhen/Plain Jane to the Rescue; Xiao Jiang/The Time You Need a Friend.* 1985: *Liang Zhi Lao Hu/Run Tiger Run.* 1986: *Ying Xiang Ben Se/A Better Tomorrow; Ying Xiong Wei Lei/Heroes Shed No Tears.* 1987: *Ying Xiang Ben Se II/A Better Tomorrow II.* 1989: *Die Xue Shuang Xiong/The Killer; Yi Dan Qun Ying/Just Heroes.* 1990: *Die Xue Jie Tou/Bullet in the Head.* 1991: *Zong Sheng Si Hai/Once a Thief.* 1992: *Lashou Shentan/Hard-Boiled.* 1993: *Hard Target.* 1996: *Broken Arrow.* 1997: *Face/Off.* 2000: *Mission Impossible II.* 2002: *Windtalkers.*

Even before John Woo came to Hollywood, there were connoisseurs of his Hong Kong work who would seek out his action films at video stores. Equally, there are those who claim to find a kind of streamlined poetry in his American pictures—as opposed to the evidence of how a culture like that of Hong Kong had become degraded, long ago, by the attempt to live up to American models.

At the age of three, Woo was taken to Hong Kong, where he studied at Matteo Ricci College. He was a film fan as a kid and he entered Cathay Film in 1969 and worked his way up from script boy, studying with Chang Sen and Chang Cheh. Though enthusiastic about martial arts pictures, his Hong Kong work is actually quite varied—and much of it was very successful.

He came to America first for the Jean-Claude Van Damme picture *Hard Target.* He had a big success with *Broken Arrow,* one of those films that make hay with the idea of a nuclear explosion. *Face/Off* is his most interesting English-language picture, with a clever script and flamboyant performances from John Travolta and Nicolas Cage. As for *Mission: Impossible II,* what can one say except that it is—and isn't—the new version of "Chinatown"?

Edward D. Wood Jr. (1922–78),
b. Poughkeepsie, New York

1952: *Glen or Glenda?/I Changed My Sex.* 1953: *Bride of the Monster.* 1954: *Jail Bait.* 1959: *Plan 9*

from Outer Space. 1960: *Night of the Ghosts.* 1972: *Necromancy.*

We are used to the legend of the youth who becomes obsessed with making movies and who begins in the very amateur ways of childhood. Spielberg and Scorsese are such figures. Which means to say that we treasure the affinity between early inspiration and professional and artistic fulfillment. Tim Burton's movie *Ed Wood* (1994) is of special charm and corrective value in that it says, remember the obsessives who had no talent (or not enough, or not the right talent), but who had every tenderness towards the image, the actor, and the camera that we imagine in Carl Dreyer, say. And thank God there are some—millions, maybe—without inspiration. Otherwise, the available facility of movies might surround us with stupid talent. (You've never had that feeling, that fear? You're lucky.)

Edward D. Wood Jr.'s films are bad. Yet today it may be easier to think that some droll, camp masquerade made them deliberately bad, instead of the Burton line—that ardor, effort, soul, and talent's void labored over these pictures. Because, today, we are loaded up with guilty pleasures, the films we love to hate, bad movies we treasure and giggle over, and the merciful entertainment of all that money, vanity, and self-gravity falling flat on its face. Indeed, there are very important films—like *Schindler's List,* I fear, or *Casino*—where the importance and the vulgarity are as close as lovers (yet far more loyal—the one would never give the other away).

This can mean that decent, ordinary, consistent badness may be a rare or threatened thing. And Edward Wood (with Johnny Depp's eyes) comes awfully close to genius in disguise. But here's the rub: if we can no longer quite place rotten films, are we any more reliable with the good?

Natalie Wood (Natasha Gurdin) (1938–81), b. San Francisco

She was the youngest veteran in movies, with quite distinct periods to her career: divine child; edgy kid; beautiful young woman; slow sad fade. The daughter of a set decorator and a ballet dancer, she made her debut, at age five, in Irving Pichel's *Happy Land* (43). Unlike most child stars, she had no real break in her film work: *Tomorrow Is Forever* (45, Pichel); *The Bride Wore Boots* (46, Pichel); *The Ghost and Mrs. Muir* (47, Joseph L. Mankiewicz); *Miracle on 34th Street* (47, George Seaton); *Driftwood* (47, Allan Dwan); *Chicken Every Sunday* (49, Seaton); *No Sad Songs for Me* (50, Rudolph Maté); *The Jackpot* (50, Walter Lang); *Never a Dull Moment* (50, George Marshall); *The Blue Veil* (51, Curtis Bernhardt); Bing Crosby's daughter in *Just for You* (52, Elliott Nugent).

She then graduated to teenage parts: Stuart Heisler's *The Star* (53) and Nicholas Ray's *Rebel Without a Cause* (55), a masterpiece on unhappy youth that promoted her from child to adult. Although her work with Ray and Dean was outstanding, she was still too young for many good parts and, apart from the girl who has lived with the Indians in Ford's *The Searchers* (56), for a few years she marked time as an adolescent: *The Burning Hills* (56, Heisler); *The Girl He Left Behind* (56, David Butler); *Cry in the Night* (56, Frank Tuttle); Gordon Douglas's *No Sleep Till Dawn* (57); the syrupy *Marjorie Morningstar* (58, Irving Rapper); Daves's *Kings Go Forth* (58); Pevney's *Cash McCall* (60).

She was fully matured, however, in Kazan's *Splendor in the Grass* (61), which has a controlled use of sexual hysteria. In 1961, she was a star as Maria in *West Side Story* (Robert Wise and Jerome Robbins), and in 1962 she played an all-too-discreet stripper in Le Roy's *Gypsy*. She was harassed in Mulligan's *Love With the Proper Stranger* (63), and was at her best in his *Inside Daisy Clover* (66), but was generally happier with humor: from the pastiche of Blake Edwards's *The Great Race* (65) to the comedy of manners in Paul Mazursky's *Bob & Carol & Ted & Alice* (69). In that, she looked like a ripe plum, ready to be persuaded to try *Gypsy* again. But sadly, she came to seem a little weary of filming: *The Affair* (73, Gilbert Cates); *Peeper* (75, Peter Hyams); and *Meteor* (79, Ronald Neame).

She was married to Robert Wagner from 1957 to 1963, then to producer Richard Gregson, and then to Wagner again from 1972 onward. In 1976, they had played together as Maggie and Brick (with Olivier as Big Daddy) in a British television production of *Cat on a Hot Tin Roof* (Robert Moore). She played Karen Holmes (the Deborah Kerr role) in the TV mini-series *From Here to Eternity* (79); *The Cracker Factory* (79, Burt Brinckerhoff), about an alcoholic who goes to a mental hospital; *The Last Married Couple in America* (79, Cates); *The Memory of Eva Ryker* (80, Walter Grauman); and *Brainstorm* (83, Douglas Trumbull). It was during the shooting of this last film that she drowned off Catalina Island.

Sam Wood (1883–1949), b. Philadelphia

1919: *Double Speed.* 1920: *Excuse My Dust; The Dancin' Fool; What's Your Hurry?; Sick Abed.* 1921: *Don't Tell Everything; The Great Moment; Peck's Bad Boy; The Snob; Under the Lash.* 1922: *Beyond the Rocks; Her Gilded Cage; Her Husband's Trademark; The Impossible Mrs. Bellew; My American Wife.* 1923: *Bluebeard's Eighth Wife; His Children's Children; Prodigal Daughters.* 1924: *Bluff; The Female; The Mine with the Iron Door; The Next Corner.* 1925: *The Re-creation of Brian Kent.* 1926: *Fascinating Youth; One Minute to Play.* 1927: *The Fair Co-ed; A Racing Romeo; Rookies.* 1928: *The Latest from Paris; Telling the World.* 1929: *It's a Great Life; So This Is College.* 1930: *Paid; They Learned About Women* (codirected with Jack Conway); *Sins of the Children; The Girl Said No; Way for a Sailor.* 1931: *New Adventures of Get Rich Quick Wallingford; A Tailor Made Man; Man in Possession.* 1932: *Huddle; Prosperity.* 1933: *Hold Your Man; The Barbarian; The Late Christopher Bean.* 1934: *Stamboul Quest.* 1935: *A Night at the Opera; Whipsaw; Let 'em Have It.* 1936: *The Unguarded Hour.* 1937: *A Day at the Races; Navy Blue and Gold; Madame X.* 1938: *Lord Jeff; Stablemates.* 1939: *Goodbye, Mr. Chips; Gone With the Wind* (Wood directed some sequences when Victor Fleming was ill). 1940: *Rangers of Fortune; Raffles; Our Town; Kitty Foyle.* 1941: *The Devil and Miss Jones.* 1942: *King's Row; The Pride of the Yankees.* 1943: *For Whom the Bell Tolls.* 1944: *Casanova Brown.* 1945: *Guest Wife.* 1946: *Saratoga Trunk; Heartbeat.* 1947: *Ivy.* 1949: *The Stratton Story; Command Decision; Ambush.*

Perhaps the most staid director ever to be entrusted to the Marx Brothers, Wood interfered with their riot no more or less than other MGM directors. Even so, *The Groucho Letters* contains a new use of "knock on Wood" to commemorate the director's obstructiveness. He had begun as an assistant to De Mille, and thus he worked for Paramount before serving through the 1930s as an assignments man at MGM. His work there was without distinction, despite his guiding of Robert Donat to an Oscar in *Goodbye, Mr. Chips.* In the 1940s, as a free-lancer, he was involved in rather more prestigious movies—another Oscar, for Ginger Rogers as *Kitty Foyle;* the entertaining *Devil and Miss Jones;* the supposedly classy *King's Row;* and a quartet of Gary Cooper pictures that were among his last portraits of the hero unhindered by doubts—*Pride of the Yankees,* a baseball biopic; *For Whom the Bell Tolls,* a studio-bound and mock Spanish rendering of Hemingway; *Casanova Brown;* and *Saratoga Trunk,* the latter an interminable, fussy movie, the ending of which has twice been denied to me by sleep. After the war, only the genteel frenzy of Joan Fontaine in *Ivy* is memorable.

Alfre Woodard, b. Tulsa, Oklahoma, 1953

For over twenty years now, in movies and on TV, Alfre Woodard has been about as reliable as an actress can be. She can be very funny, deadpan, tragic, brave, tough, wise, street smart, or stupid. Yet she has never been trusted to carry a big picture, which is a way of complaining that such trust is often misplaced. At the age of almost fifty, Alfre

Woodard has shown more, more often, with more controlled craft than—let us say—Debra Winger or Anjelica Huston, actresses of about her age.

She attracted a lot of attention as the hotel manager in *H.E.A.L.T.H.* (79, Robert Altman) and as the supermarket checkout girl in *Remember My Name* (78, Alan Rudolph). She had as good a watchful look—wary and sexy—as anyone in pictures. She was in *The Ambush Murders* (82, Steven Hilliard Stern) on TV; and she did a season in the series, *Tucker's Witch* (82–83).

It was in 1983 that she really had a breakthrough: she got a supporting actress nomination in *Cross Creek* (Martin Ritt), but won a far larger audience in three episodes of *Hill Street Blues,* one of which—"Dani in Wonderland"—won her an Emmy. Also on TV, she began a two-year run (opposite Denzel Washington) as Dr. Roxanne Turner in *St. Elsewhere.* In 1986, she won a second Emmy for the pilot of *L.A. Law* (Gregory Hoblit).

There had been movies, too: *Go Tell It on the Mountain* (84, Stan Latham); *Extremities* (86, Robert M. Young); and then back to TV for *Unnatural Causes* (86, Lamont Johnson), written by John Sayles; *Mandela* (87, Philip Saville), as Winnie; and *The Child Saver* (88, Latham).

Since then, she has been in *Scrooged* (88, Richard Donner); *Miss Firecracker* (89, Thomas Schlamme); as basketball player Isiah Thomas's mother in *A Mother's Courage* (89, John Patterson); *Grand Canyon,* opposite Danny Glover (91, Lawrence Kasdan); as the nurse in *Passion Fish* (92, Sayles); *The Gun in Betty Lou's Handbag* (92, Allan Moyle); *Rich in Love* (93, Bruce Beresford); *Bopha!* (93, Morgan Freeman); *Blue Chips* (94, William Friedkin); and *Crooklyn* (94, Spike Lee).

Sadly, very few things in recent years have really challenged Ms. Woodard, or approached her abilities. The obstacle remains in America in 2001 that some people are reckoned actresses, and others black actresses; thus, some films only fire white bullets—their explosive force (their budget) demands it. So a lot of Alfre Woodard is to be found on television or in small parts. It's still worth the search: *The Piano Lesson* (95, Lloyd Richards); *How to Make an American Quilt* (95, Jocelyn Moorhouse); the Queen of Brobdingnag in *Gulliver's Travels* (96, Charles Sturridge); the judge in *Primal Fear* (96, Gregory Hoblit); *A Step Toward Tomorrow* (96, Deborah Reinisch); *Star Trek: First Contact* (96, Jonathan Frakes); the lead in *Miss Evers' Boys* (97, Joseph Sargent); *Follow Me Home* (97, Peter Bratt); *Secrets* (97, Sheryl Lee Ralph).

She was superb, with Anna Paquin, in a TV version of *The Member of the Wedding* (97, Fielder Cook); *Down in the Delta* (98, Maya Angelou); *Brown Sugar* (98, John Eyres); *Funny Valentines*

(99, Julie Dash); *Mumford* (99, Kasdan); *The Wishing Tree* (99, Ivan Passer); *What's Cooking?* (00, Gurinder Chadha); *Love & Basketball* (00, Gina Prince); *Holiday Heart* (00, Robert Townsend); *K-PAX* (01, Iain Softley); *Baby of the Family* (01, Jonee Ansa); *The Singing Detective* (03, Keith Gordon); *The Core* (03, Jon Amiel); *Radio* (03, Michael Tollin).

James Woods, b. Vernal, Utah, 1947

We all know—don't we?—that appearance is a matter of chance? We've all had *Beauty and the Beast* read to us so often we can recite the principle that sometimes great ugliness masks a rich and generous heart. We have learned that the best-looking people sometimes behave the worst. But the movies remain loyal to the code that good-looking equals good. It follows that the guys with faces as narrow as James Woods, with eyes so close together, play finks, villains, snakes, liars, hoods, cheats, and rats, and even Roy Cohn. We may gather or deduce that Mr. Woods likes himself, but how can a movie act upon the same faith?

He studied political science at M.I.T., and has been known to expound on his own great intelligence (is this rat behavior or what?). He made his debut in *The Visitors* (72, Elia Kazan) and soon found himself as an available nasty: *Hickey and Boggs* (72, Robert Culp); *The Way We Were* (73, Sydney Pollack)—as a radical; *The Gambler* (74, Karel Reisz); *Distance* (75, Anthony Lover); as the stuntman in *Night Moves* (75, Arthur Penn); *The Disappearance of Aimee* (76, Anthony Harvey); *Alex & the Gypsy* (76, John Korty); *The Choirboys* (77, Robert Aldrich); *Holocaust* (78, Marvin J. Chomsky); *The Black Marble* (79, Harold Becker); and *And Your Name Is Jonah* (79, Richard Michaels).

He was memorably loathsome in his breakthrough film, *The Onion Field* (79, Becker), and followed it with *Eyewitness* (81, Peter Yates); *Fast-Walking* (82, James B. Harris); *Split Image* (82, Ted Kotcheff); in the Kirk Douglas role in *Against All Odds* (83, Taylor Hackford); *Videodrome* (83, David Cronenberg); oddly subdued as the traitor in *Once Upon a Time in America* (84, Sergio Leone); *Joshua Then and Now* (85, Kotcheff); very good in *Salvador* (86, Oliver Stone) as journalist Richard Boyle (and nominated for best actor); *Best Seller* (87, John Flynn); *The Boost* (88, Becker); *Cop* (88, Harris); *Immediate Family* (89, Jonathan Kaplan)—trying to adopt a child!; *True Believer* (89, Joseph Ruben); *The Hard Way* (91, John Badham); *Diggstown* (92, Michael Ritchie); *Straight Talk* (92, Barnett Kellman); and a wicked lawyer in *Chaplin* (92, Richard Attenborough).

Strangely, he has had his best opportunities on television: winning Emmys as James Garner's schizophrenic brother in *Promise* (86, Glenn Jordan) and as the founder of Alcoholics Anonymous in *My Name is Bill W.* (89, Daniel Petrie); in a Hemingway short story, "Hills Like White Elephants" in *Women and Men: Stories of Seduction* (90, Tony Richardson); in the part from heaven, Roy C. in *Citizen Cohn* (92, Frank Pierson). For movies, he was the villain in *The Getaway* (94, Roger Donaldson).

Time and again in the dreary nineties, Woods's exuberance lit up the screen and established him as a founder member of that select club for nasties we love to hate (Christopher Walken and Steve Buscemi are other stalwarts): goosing Stallone in *The Specialist* (94, Luis Llosa); *Curse of the Starving Class* (95, J. Michael McClary); very good as the tireless defense lawyer in *Indictment: The McMartin Trial* (95, Mick Jackson); the perfect scumbag, Lester Diamond, in *Casino* (95, Martin Scorsese); so good as Haldeman in *Nixon* (96, Stone) that you could see a better film with Haldeman as the central figure; *The Summer of Ben Tyler* (96, Arthur Allan Seidelman); glittery and odious as Byron De La Beckwith in *Ghosts of Mississippi* (96, Rob Reiner); *Killer: A Journal of Murder* (96, Tim Metcalfe); *Kicked in the Head* (97, Matthew Harrison); *Contact* (97, Robert Zemeckis); *Vampires* (98, John Carpenter); *Another Day in Paradise* (98, Larry Clark); the editor in *True Crime* (99, Clint Eastwood); *The Virgin Suicides* (99, Sofia Coppola); *The General's Daughter* (99, Simon West); *Any Given Sunday* (99, Stone); the museum director defending Mapplethorpe in *Dirty Pictures* (00, Pierson); *Riding in Cars with Boys* (01, Penny Marshall).

He never stops: *Race to Space* (01, Sean McNamara); *Jon Q* (02, Nick Cassavetes); *Northfork* (03, Michael Polish); and one more in his gallery of real-life charismatics, *Rudy: The Rudy Giuliani Story* (03, Robert Dornhelm). With Roy Cohn, Haldeman and Giuliani already notched up, a nightmare looms in which James Woods is every demon in American history.

Joanne Woodward,
b. Thomasville, Georgia, 1930

Educated at Louisiana State University, she studied at the Neighborhood Playhouse Dramatic School and appeared on Broadway in *Picnic*. Hers is a career full of contradictions: one of Hollywood's most respected actresses, few films have actually explained her reputation. Known as a wife and mother and as an articulate participant in radical, third-party politics, she is most striking on the screen in slatternly roles that encourage her to exaggerate her Southern accent. Her marriage to Paul Newman has too often involved her in poor films: *The Long Hot Summer* (58, Martin Ritt); *From the Terrace* (59, Mark Robson); *Paris Blues*

(61, Ritt); *A New Kind of Love* (64, Melville Shavelson); *Winning* (69, James Goldstone); *WUSA* (70, Stuart Rosenberg), in which she is like a dutiful wife who goes along on the husband's fishing trips. His direction of her in the decent and touching *Rachel, Rachel* (68) and *The Effect of Gamma Rays on Man-in-the-Moon Marigolds* (72) went only some way to canceling this debt. Even in her best film with her husband, *Rally Round the Flag, Boys!* (58, Leo McCarey), her sense of humor is neglected.

On the credit side there is *Count Three and Pray* (55, George Sherman); the Oscar-rewarded tour de force in *The Three Faces of Eve* (57, Nunnally Johnson); an original and touching victim in Gerd Oswald's *A Kiss Before Dying* (56); a radiant, outcast heroine, opposite Brando, in Lumet's *The Fugitive Kind* (59); in Schaffner's *The Stripper* (62); a good comic performance in *A Fine Madness* (66, Irvin Kershner). But she is dreadfully suited to the worthy smothering of hysteria in *Summer Wishes, Winter Dreams* (73, Gilbert Cates). Sadly, she is more attractive and interesting in interviews than in films. And even her portraits of Southern helplessness seem sedate when put beside Barbara Loden's *Wanda*. She was a good Dr. Watson in *They Might Be Giants* (71, Anthony Harvey) and the ex-wife in *The End* (78, Burt Reynolds).

She was in *Streets of L.A.* (79, Jerrold Freedman); *Crisis at Central High* (80, Lamont Johnson); *The Shadow Box* (80, Newman)—all for TV. She was in *Harry & Son* (84, Newman) in theatres, but then returned to TV for *Passions* (84, Sandor Stern) and *Do You Remember Love?* (85, Jeff Bleckner), for which she won an Emmy. She played Amanda in *The Glass Menagerie* (87, Newman) and then costarred with her husband in *Mr. and Mrs. Bridge* (90, James Ivory).

She was the narrative voice for *The Age of Innocence* (93, Martin Scorsese), allegedly spreading style and wit over the glossy imagery, but actually sounding like the resort of a director unsure whether his story was working. She also played the mother in *Philadelphia* (93, Jonathan Demme). For TV, she was in *Foreign Affair* (93, Jim O'Brien) and *Breathing Lessons* (94, John Erman).

Fay Wray, b. Mountain View, Canada, 1907

It is 1933, and movies know enough about us and themselves to goose us. But is it Merian Cooper, David Selznick, or just Robert Armstrong's magnificent Carl Denham (so much more monstrous than Kong) who says, "This is how the dame will look and see and scream—and this is how we'll show it"? The dame is Fay Wray, on deck, in satiny décolletage, getting ready to open up a lovely mouth and *scream*. This is one of the great moments of screen irony, just as *King Kong* (33, Merian Cooper and Ernest Schoedsack) is an untouchable, the epitome of cute sensation that makes great movies. Fay Wray is forever the wisp of near-naked woman in the beast's paw. Seventy years later the image is as stirring and as surreal as ever.

In truth, Fay Wray made a lot of minor films, especially after about 1935. But everyone has always loved her for *Kong,* and for her exceptional good nature. She was a social figure in Hollywood, too, in part because of marriages to two screenwriters—John Monk Saunders (from 1927–40) and Robert Riskin (1942–55)—and her long romance with Clifford Odets.

She came to Los Angeles in 1920 and within a few years was working, rising to a position of near stardom at Paramount: *The Coast Patrol* (25, Bud Barsky); *Lazy Lightning* (26, William Wyler); *A One Man Game* (27, Ernest Laemmle); *The First Kiss* (28, Rowland V. Lee); *Legion of the Condemned* (28, William Wellman); *The Street of Sin* (28, Mauritz Stiller); *The Wedding March* (28, Erich von Stroheim); *The Four Feathers* (29, Schoedsack and Cooper); *Thunderbolt* (29, Josef von Sternberg); *The Texan* (30, John Cromwell); *Dirigible* (31, Frank Capra); *The Unholy Garden* (31, George Fitzmaurice); *Doctor X* (32, Michael Curtiz); *The Most Dangerous Game* (32, Schoedsack and Irving Pichel); *The Bowery* (33, Raoul Walsh); *Mystery of the Wax Museum* (33, Curtiz); *One Sunday Afternoon* (33, Stephen Roberts); and *The Affairs of Cellini* (34, Gregory La Cava).

Decline followed, with several films made in Britain: *The Countess of Monte Cristo* (34, Karl Freund); *Madame Spy* (34, Freund); *The Richest Girl in the World* (34, William A. Seiter); *Viva Villa!* (34, Jack Conway); *White Lies* (34, Leo Bulgakov); *Bulldog Jack* (35, Walter Forde); *The Clairvoyant* (35, Maurice Elvey); *They Met in a Taxi* (36, Alfred E. Green); *When Knights Were Bold* (36, Jack Raymond); *Smashing the Spy Ring* (39, Christy Cabanne); *Adam Had Four Sons* (41, Gregory Ratoff); *Not a Ladies Man* (42, Lew Landers); *Small Town Girl* (53, Leslie Kardos); *Treasure of the Golden Condor* (53, Delmer Daves); *The Cobweb* (55, Vincente Minnelli); *Queen Bee* (55, Ranald MacDougall); *Hell on Frisco Bay* (56, Frank Tuttle); *Crime of Passion* (57, Gerd Oswald); *Rock, Pretty Baby* (57, Richard Bartlett); *Tammy and the Bachelor* (57, Joseph Pevney); *Dragstrip Riot* (58, Basil Bradbury); and *Summer Love* (58, Charles Haas).

Teresa Wright, b. New York, 1918

For fifteen years, Teresa Wright was one of the more perceptive actresses in films, not glamorous enough to be a star, but too quickly pushed into motherly or plain roles. She had been on the stage for only a few years when Lillian Hellman recommended her for a movie debut in *The Little Foxes* (41, William Wyler). Next year, for Wyler again, she won the supporting actress Oscar in *Mrs. Miniver* and played opposite Gary Cooper in *The Pride of the Yankees* (Sam Wood). Hitchcock then borrowed her from Goldwyn to play the niece, Charlie, in *Shadow of a Doubt* (43). The screenplay for that film was by Thornton Wilder, in whose *Our Town* Wright had played on tour. In *Shadow of a Doubt,* she beautifully caught the small-town adolescent unable to comprehend the complicity she feels for her murdering uncle. It showed just how subtly Hitchcock could work up anguish in a relatively plain-faced actress.

She then played in *Casanova Brown* (44, Sam Wood); *The Best Years of Our Lives* (46, Wyler); *Imperfect Lady* (47, Lewis Allen); *Pursued* (47, Raoul Walsh), written by her then-husband, Niven Busch; *Enchantment* (48, Irving Reis); *The Capture* (50, John Sturges); *The Men* (50, Fred Zinnemann); *Something to Live For* (52, George Stevens); *The Steel Trap* (52, Andrew L. Stone); as the mother (although only thirty-four years old, when her "daughter," Jean Simmons, was twenty-four years old) in *The Actress* (53, George Cukor); *Count the Hours* (53, Don Siegel); *Track of the Cat* (54, William Wellman); *The Search for Bridie Murphy* (56, Noel Langley); and *The Wonderful Years* (58, Helmut Kautner). She went back to the stage and returned to films only for *Hail, Hero!* (69, David Miller); as Jean Simmons's mother again in *The Happy Ending* (69, Richard Brooks); *Flood* (76, Earl Bellamy); as a dancer with memories in *Roseland* (77, James Ivory); *Somewhere in the Night* (80, Jeannot Szwarc); *Bill—On His Own* (83, Anthony Page); *The Good Mother* (88, Leonard Nimoy); and *Perry Mason: The Case of the Desperate Deception* (90, Christian Nyby II).

She has not done too much lately, but she was in *Lethal Innocence* (91, Helene Whitney) and *Wonderworks: The Fig Tree* (91, Calvin Skaggs), and then a few years later she was good in a short film, *The Red Coat* (93, Robin Swicord), and a nice Miss Birdie in *The Rainmaker* (97, Francis Coppola).

William Wyler (1902–81),

b. Mulhouse, Germany

1926: *Lazy Lightning; Stolen Ranch.* 1927: *Blazing Days; Hard Fists; Straight Shootin'; The Border Cavalier; Desert Dust; Shooting Straight.* 1928: *Thunder Riders; Anybody Here Seen Kelly?.* 1929: *The Shakedown; The Love Trap.* 1930: *Hell's Heroes; The Storm.* 1931: *A House Divided.* 1932: *Tom Brown of Culver.* 1933: *Her First Mate; Counsellor at Law.* 1934: *Glamour.* 1935: *The Good Fairy; The Gay Deception.* 1936: *Come and Get It* (codirected with Howard Hawks); *Dodsworth; These Three.* 1937: *Dead End.* 1938: *Jezebel.* 1939: *Wuthering Heights.* 1940: *The Letter; The Westerner.* 1941: *The Little Foxes.* 1942: *Mrs. Miniver.* 1944: *The Memphis Belle; The Fighting Lady; Thunderbolt* (wartime documentaries, the latter codirected with John Sturges). 1946: *The Best Years of Our Lives.* 1949: *The Heiress.* 1951: *Detective Story.* 1952: *Carrie.* 1953: *Roman Holiday.* 1955: *The Desperate Hours.* 1956: *Friendly Persuasion.* 1958: *The Big Country.* 1959: *Ben-Hur.* 1962: *The Children's Hour/The Loudest Whisper.* 1965: *The Collector.* 1966: *How to Steal a Million.* 1968: *Funny Girl.* 1970: *The Liberation of L. B. Jones.*

In the years that followed the Second World War, Wyler was Hollywood's idea of a great director—respectable, diligent, tasteful, a servant of stars and box-office potential, a reliable master of big projects. He won the best director Oscar three times—for *Mrs. Miniver, The Best Years of Our Lives,* and *Ben-Hur*—but he was nominated for that award a full twelve times. I would concede that *Best Years* is decent and humane, piling on Gregg Toland's deep-focus photography for the sake of simple authenticity and extended context. *Best Years* is acutely observed, despite being so meticulous a package: it would have taken uncommon genius and daring at that time to sneak a view of an untidy or unresolved America past Goldwyn or the public. And the deep focus works like a proof, a sign of trust; whereas, for Welles, there was always a strain of madness in the deep focus. As for *Mrs. Miniver* and *Ben-Hur,* those box-office wonders have dated very badly: little remains but sturdy righteousness.

Wyler was educated at Lausanne and Paris (but does Europe ever show in him?), and he was twenty before he came to America to write publicity material at Universal. He went to Hollywood and got work as an assistant on such films as *The Hunchback of Notre Dame* (23, Wallace Worsley) and the original *Ben-Hur* (25, Fred Niblo).

When he began directing himself, he had several years on low-budget Westerns. He developed very slowly—caution was always Wyler's watchword, and it schooled him in getting as much coverage as possible, sometimes beyond the patience of his actors. For two years in the mid-thirties he was married to Margaret Sullavan, whom he directed in *The Good Fairy,* a bright romantic comedy written by Preston Sturges. (Wyler later married the actress Margaret Tallichet.)

By 1936, Wyler had signed on with Goldwyn: the two men fought a lot, but still it was a fruitful alliance in which Wyler surely delivered the goods the boss ordered. *Come and Get It* owes its liveliness to Hawks, and *These Three* was a censored treatment of Lillian Hellman's play *The Children's Hour.* But *Dodsworth* is a Wyler film: a sober, shrewd adaptation (by Sidney Howard out of Sinclair Lewis), level, fair, and very well acted.

Dead End is stagy, but it was very lofty and prestigious in its day. *Jezebel* is rather tame melodrama, though evidently Wyler understood Bette Davis's emotional energy early on. *Wuthering Heights,* to these eyes, is as bad as a careful adaptation can be when no one quite gets the original material but everyone feels obliged to deliver a quality production. But *The Letter* is stirring, content to be a small melodrama, secure in its sense of the depraved Bette Davis and of the strains she puts on decent men.

Wyler did very well later on with similar projects: for instance, he understands the decay in Olivier's character in *Carrie* and quietly produces a social realist tragedy worthy of Dreiser. But *Carrie* was one of the later Wyler's few failures. Instead, people congratulated themselves on the charm of *Roman Holiday* or *Friendly Persuasion,* as well as the spuriously "intelligent epic" of *Ben-Hur* or *The Big Country.* Steadily in the fifties, America rejoiced in the anodyne accomplishment of Wyler, Stevens, and Zinnemann, while rejecting or ignoring the real beauty in Nick Ray, Fuller, Anthony Mann, and Minnelli.

Whenever he could, Wyler did adaptations, from sensible scripts. But the results were mixed: nearly thirty years later, he fumbled again with *The Children's Hour.* But *The Little Foxes* is played for all its worth, and *The Heiress* is truly frightening because of Ralph Richardson's hushed, condescending tyrant. There are fine performances in Wyler films, not least Kirk Douglas in the grim and remorseless *Detective Story* (from the Sidney Kingsley play), Bette Davis always, and just about everyone in *Dodsworth, Carrie,* and *Best Years.*

Still, I can't get excited. Wyler was available for the social optimism of *Best Years* as well as the inherent disintegration of *Carrie* or *Detective Story.* It's as if in executing the scripts he never found the need to ponder them deeply. Was there ever really anything larger in Wyler than the ideal director for several miles of *Masterpiece Theatre?*

Jane Wyman (Sarah Jane Fulks),
b. St. Joseph, Missouri, 1914

Plucky girls with baby faces can take heart: Jane Wyman was in movies more than ten years before people began to cry over her. But she clutched on to ingenuous sincerity and the world came round, forgiving all the parts she had had in tame musicals and Westerns. *Johnny Belinda* (48, Jean Negulesco), the film for which she won an Oscar, is an evasive, slick sob story. The way in which, at age thirty-four, she played a girl supposedly half her age, ostensibly deaf-mute but looking as neat and wholesome as a Mabel Lucy Attwell cherub, is evidence of make-believe becoming more artificial as it lumbers toward a subject that is "authentic" and "daring." *Johnny Belinda* is uncut corn, but Wyman had a soulful, wide-eyed face (such as made handicap acceptable) and, under Negu-

lesco's gloating direction, it was no surprise that she won an Oscar. That film also established her as a stimulant to tears for another eight years.

She had begun in small parts in musicals at Warners: *The King of Burlesque* (35, Sidney Lanfield); a bit part at Universal in *My Man Godfrey* (36, Gregory La Cava); *Cain and Mabel* (36, Lloyd Bacon); *Gold Diggers of 1937* (36, Bacon); *Stage Struck* (36, Busby Berkeley); *The King and the Chorus Girl* (37, Mervyn Le Roy); *Ready, Willing and Able* (37, Ray Enright); *Slim* (37, Enright); and *The Singing Marine* (37, Enright). In 1938, she made *Brother Rat* (38, William Keighley), with Ronald Reagan, whom she married in 1940 (divorced in 1948). By then, Warners were loaning her out or putting her in minor Westerns: *The Spy Ring* (38, Joseph H. Lewis); *The Crowd Roars* (38, Richard Thorpe); *Fools for Scandal* (38, Le Roy); *Tail Spin* (39, Roy del Ruth); *An Angel from Texas* (40, Enright); *Brother Rat and a Baby* (40, Enright); *My Love Came Back* (40, Curtis Bernhardt); *Bad Men of Missouri* (41, Enright); and *Larceny Inc.* (42, Bacon). She made *My Favorite Spy* (42, Tay Garnett) at RKO and *Footlight Serenade* (42, Gregory Ratoff) at Fox. Back at Warners, she was in *Princess O'Rourke* (43, Norman Krasna), and then Billy Wilder gave her a thankless, suffering role of the girlfriend in *The Lost Weekend* (45).

Things looked up a little after that: *Night and Day* (46, Michael Curtiz); *The Yearling* (46, Clarence Brown); *Magic Town* (47, William Wellman); *Cheyenne* (47, Raoul Walsh); and *A Kiss in the Dark* (48, Delmer Daves). But it was *Johnny Belinda* that defined her place in women's pictures: *The Lady Takes a Sailor* (49, Curtiz); a cloying performance in one of Hitchcock's worst films, *Stage Fright* (50); bewildered in *The Glass Menagerie* (50, Irving Rapper); *Here Comes the Groom* (51, Frank Capra); *Three Guys Named Mike* (51, Charles Walters); *The Blue Veil* (51, Bernhardt); *Just For You* (52, Elliott Nugent); as the matriarch in Edna Ferber's *So Big* (53, Robert Wise); and then in two outstanding Douglas Sirk women's pix, her swan song: as the blind woman in *Magnificent Obsession* (54), which she persuaded Universal to make, and the sequel to success, *All That Heaven Allows* (55). That she is innocuous and the films so impressive speaks for Sirk's orchestration of players within his graceful images. After *Lucy Gallant* (55, Robert Parrish) and *Miracle in the Rain* (56, Rudolph Maté), she went into semiretirement, interrupted by *Pollyanna* (60, David Swift); *Bon Voyage!* (62, James Neilson); *How to Commit Marriage* (69, Norman Panama); *The Incredible Journey of Doctor Meg Laurel* (79, Guy Green); and the TV series *Falcon Crest* for most of the eighties.

Y

Isuzu Yamada b. Osaka, Japan, 1917

Unlike Japan's other most famous women stars, Isuzu Yamada has been as important a stage actress as a screen presence—partly from preference, partly because she had serious battles with the studios over political and labor issues, and was sporadically blacklisted. Even so, she was a central figure for over four decades—beginning at the age of fourteen, and in her twenties starring in Mizoguchi's two most important films of the 1930s, *Osaka Elegy* (36) and *Sisters of the Gion* (36). In the West, her best-known roles were for Kurosawa: the Lady Macbeth of *Throne of Blood* (57); the shrewish landlady of *The Lower Depths* (57); and the vicious brothel keeper of *Yojimbo* (61)—all highly theatrical performances. She was superb in Ozu's *Tokyo Twilight* (57), as a mother who abandoned her children; in Naruse's *Flowing* (56), as the madame of a seedy geisha house; and as the older woman in Shiro Toyoda's comedy *A Man, a Cat and Two Women* (56). She has also worked for Gosho, for Ichikawa, and for Teinosuke Kinugasa (one of her six husbands) in *Actress* (47), a film based on the life of Japan's first female stage star, whose rebellious story mirrors Yamada's own.

Peter Yates, b. Ewshotts, England, 1929

1962: *Summer Holiday.* 1964: *One Way Pendulum.* 1967: *Robbery.* 1968: *Bullitt.* 1969: *John and Mary.* 1971: *Murphy's War.* 1972: *The Hot Rock.* 1973: *The Friends of Eddie Coyle.* 1974: *For Pete's Sake.* 1976: *Mother, Jugs & Speed.* 1977: *The Deep.* 1979: *Breaking Away.* 1981: *Eyewitness.* 1983: *Krull; The Dresser.* 1985: *Eleni.* 1987: *Suspect; The House on Carroll Street.* 1989: *Hard Rain; An Innocent Man.* 1992: *Year of the Comet.* 1995: *Roommates; The Run of the Country.* 1999: *Curtain Call.* 2000: *Don Quixote* (TV). 2003: *A Separate Peace* (TV).

Bullitt is an odd coincidence of interests: of Steve McQueen's identification with automobiles and Peter Yates's earlier experience in motor racing. Yates was also a product of Charterhouse and the Royal Court Theatre but, apart from *One Way Pendulum*, these roots have still to show themselves in his work. There is a dependence on novelty that reveals Yates's lack of character. *Summer Holiday* was a "breakthrough" English musical, with Cliff Richard, suddenly upstaged by the arrival of the Beatles. *Robbery* was a version of the Great Train Robbery, too close to reality to feel free, too coy about that proximity to be penetrating. In America, Yates has done nothing more profound than send hubcaps careering round corners. *John and Mary* is as wet and still as a pud-

dle. *Murphy's War* is about another machine, a wrecked airplane rebuilt for war by Peter O'Toole. Just as the vehicles are better tended than the actors in *Bullitt*, so *Murphy's War* fails even to give a routine service to O'Toole. *The Hot Rock* is a watchable film with a welcome hint of comedy, and *The Friends of Eddie Coyle* contains the first impressive performance in Yates's work—from Robert Mitchum. Another gift to us all has been the startling prospect of Jacqueline Bisset's nipples in *The Deep*, a film of such silliness and massive box-office returns that even a conscientious critic is driven to consider the merits of soaked shirts.

Breaking Away was one of Yates's most original and amiable concepts, though it had a tried and trusted climax. Still, he is at ease in such diverse efforts as Albert Finney doing Donald Wolfit in *The Dresser* or Cher doing heavy legal thinking in *Suspect*. In addition, there are atmospheric moments in the creaky *House on Carroll Street* when a past but sunnier New York is nicely captured.

Roommates came from a Max Apple novel, and starred Peter Falk. The next two films showed a decline, but with *Don Quixote* (scripted by John Mortimer), Yates reaffirmed his storytelling and his likability, plus the ability to make the best of John Lithgow and Bob Hoskins as the Don and Sancho Panza.

Philip Yordan (1913–2003),

b. Chicago

Movie reference books have one essential level of data: the credits on pictures. Yet anyone who spends long contemplating the product, or listening to the stories told by men and women who have worked in film, knows that credits are not to be trusted. To take one example: yes, that *is* Ronald Colman, Douglas Fairbanks Jr., and Mary Astor in the Selznick *A Prisoner of Zenda*, a picture credited to director John Cromwell, and to writers John L. Balderston and Wells Root. Yet there is unquestioned documentation that George Cukor and Woody Van Dyke shot some scenes, and that Sidney Howard did some rewriting. Then there is the legend of chronic Selznickian interference, of writers in and out of the office, giving a line here or there.

A movie script is many things, or versions, along the way. In the end, it is the transcript of the finished film that may involve structures only perceived in the editing room, as well as lines looped over resistant lips. The script is always changing, and there are people who have had busy and well-paid lives assisting the changes with hardly a credit to show for it. Some writers are doctors; and nearly all writers feel sick sooner or later.

Philip Yordan is included here as a buoy to mark an area of whirlpool, crosscurrents, rocks, and wrecks. Yordan has his name all over the place—it *is* a very illustrious career. And no one has ever argued but that he was a superb entrepreneur, a deal-maker, a hustler, a money man. But did he write "his" scripts, or did he depend on anonymous blacklisted authors, willing kids, or even the comfort of strangers? Yordan *is* a real man, but he is far more than the collection of anecdotes and rumors. Some say he never wrote a word. Hardly a credit stands clear of dispute or doubt. He could have written nothing, or everything. The truth will never be known, and if Yordan is half the operator one suspects, then it is probably beyond remembering. The interested reader is referred to a long interview with Yordan, by Patrick McGilligan, in *Backstory 2*. It settles nothing, yet it gives a piercing account of what the underworld of filmmaking is like, and it makes an inadvertent explanation of why so many movies are about tough, solitary, depressive men who can't stop acting.

He wrote a play, *Anna Lucasta*, which is a gloss on O'Neill's *Anna Christie*. He got a law degree and, although he has denied it, some say he only hired a surrogate to attend classes for him. And then the good offices of William Dieterle got him to Hollywood. Yordan kept fascinating company: Dieterle was to be followed by the King Brothers (of Monogram), Sidney Harmon, Anthony Mann, Nicholas Ray, Samuel Bronston, and the actor Robert Shaw. The films he has a claim to are no less impressive—and it would not be hard to see a pattern of tough loners, dangerous situations, laconic women, and doomy finishes. In short, it sounds like movies:

All That Money Can Buy (41, Dieterle); *Syncopation* (42, Dieterle); *The Unknown Guest* (43, Kurt Neumann); *Johnny Doesn't Live Here Anymore* (44, Joe May); *When Strangers Marry* (44, William Castle); *Dillinger* (45, Max Nosseck), which got an Oscar nomination for original screenplay; *The Chase* (46, Arthur Ripley); *Whistle Stop* (46, Léonide Moguy); *Suspense* (46, Frank Tuttle); *Bad Men of Tombstone* (48, Neumann); *House of Strangers* (49, Joseph L. Mankiewicz)—on which Yordan wrote a story, Mankiewicz rewrote it as a script, and then dropped his name when the Writers' Guild insisted on Yordan's keeping some credit; *Anna Lucasta* (49, Irving Rapper); *Reign of Terror* (49, Mann); *Edge of Doom* (50, Mark Robson); *Detective Story* (51, William Wyler); *Drums in the Deep South* (51, William Cameron Menzies); *Mara Maru* (52, Gordon Douglas); *Mutiny* (52, Edward Dmytryk); *Houdini* (53, George Marshall); *Blowing Wild* (53, Hugo Fregonese); *Man Crazy* (53, Irving Lerner), which he also coproduced; *The Naked Jungle* (54, Byron Haskin); *Johnny Guitar* (54, Ray)—one of the most vexed credits; *Broken Lance* (54, Dmytryk)—which got the Oscar because it was a remake of *House of Strangers; Conquest of Space* (55, Haskin); *The*

Man from Laramie (55, Mann); *The Last Frontier* (55, Mann); *The Big Combo* (55, Joseph H. Lewis); *The Harder They Fall* (56, Mark Robson), which he also produced; *Joe MacBeth* (56, Ken Hughes); *Four Boys and a Gun* (57, William Berke); *Men in War* (57, Mann)—on which it seems clear that Ben Maddow had a hand; *No Down Payment* (57, Martin Ritt); *Street of Sinners* (57, Berke); *The Bravados* (58, Henry King); *God's Little Acre* (58, Mann); *Island Woman* (58, Berke); *The Fiend Who Walked the West* (58, Douglas); *Anna Lucasta* (58, Arnold Laven); *Day of the Outlaw* (59, André de Toth); *The Bramble Bush* (59, Daniel Petrie); *Studs Lonigan* (60, Lerner), which he produced; *King of Kings* (61, Ray); *El Cid* (61, Mann); *55 Days at Peking* (62, Ray); *The Day of the Triffids* (62, Steven Sekely); *The Fall of the Roman Empire* (64, Mann); *Battle of the Bulge* (64, Ken Annakin); *Circus World* (64, Henry Hathaway); *Custer of the West* (68, Robert Siodmak); *The Royal Hunt of the Sun* (69, Lerner); and *Captain Apache* (71, Alexander Singer).

After that, Yordan worked on religious pictures and made-for-video features. Thus, far from settling into distinguished retirement, he seemed to pursue the nether regions of film production.

Susannah York (Susannah Yolande Fletcher), b. London, 1941

Despite an inescapable British quota of misconceived and underrealized films, Susannah York is an English rose from a wilder garden than nurtured Madeleine Carroll or Virginia McKenna. There have always been hints of character and independence, as well as unusual literary ambition that few films have captured.

After a debut with Norman Wisdom in *There Was a Crooked Man* (60, Stuart Burge), she was clearly an atypical British ingenue as two tense teenagers, in *Tunes of Glory* (60, Ronald Neame) and *The Greengage Summer* (61, Lewis Gilbert). *Freud: The Secret Passion* (62, John Huston) was a great failure, but it was the first indication of her unusual enterprise. She was sadly left to herself as Sophie Western in *Tom Jones* (63, Tony Richardson), and in *The Seventh Dawn* (64, Gilbert), while two deliberate experiments only showed the stilted nature of such sports in England: *Scene Nun, Take One* (64, Maurice Hatton) and *Scruggs* (65, David Hart). She ventured forth demurely as a potential rape victim in *Sands of the Kalahari* (65, Cy Endfield), but was very funny in *Kaleidoscope* (66, Jack Smight). In *A Man for All Seasons* (67, Fred Zinnemann), as More's daughter, she was no worse or better than a score of young English ladies might have been. But *Sebastian* (68, David Greene) once more showed a sense of humor. *Duffy* (68, Robert Parrish) was a ruined film, *Lock Up Your Daughters* (69, Peter Coe) a lazy one, but *The Killing of Sister George* (68,

Robert Aldrich) alarmingly hysterical. Her professional uneasiness with the demands made on her by lesbian melodrama was touchingly candid, and the performance itself was the one human element in the film (if short of Eileen Atkins's stage performance—York may have been wasted, but Atkins has been criminally ignored).

She had a bit in *Oh! What a Lovely War* (69, Richard Attenborough) and a piece in *The Battle of Britain* (69, Guy Hamilton) peripheral enough to write her off, even. But in *They Shoot Horses, Don't They?* (69, Sydney Pollack) she was excellent as the English girl defiantly trying to break into sordid movies. There is a speculative flightiness about her in that film; especially in the breakdown scene in a shower cubicle, she seemed for the first time a human animal touched to the quick. Her *Jane Eyre* (71, Delbert Mann) was unadventurous, and other work shows a helpless attempt to be versatile: *Country Dance* (71, J. Lee Thompson); *Happy Birthday, Wanda June* (71, Mark Robson); *Zee & Co.* (72, Brian G. Hutton); *Gold* (74, Peter Hunt); *Images* (72, Robert Altman)—a failure, but one that only a worthwhile actress could have dreamed of.

Images is very much about Susannah York, and one regrets that it settled for mystification. It is based upon a children's book written by the actress, and perhaps on her own thoughts about obscure sexual identity. Wildly pretentious, it retains interest because of the actress's resolute seriousness.

Waste and misuse now seem her lot: *The Maids* (74, Christopher Miles); *That Lucky Touch* (75, Miles); *Conduct Unbecoming* (75, Michael Anderson); *Sky Riders* (76, Douglas Hickox); *The Shout* (78, Jerzy Skolimowski); *The Silent Partner* (78, Daryl Duke); and *Superman* (78, Richard Donner).

She was in *The Golden Gate Murders* (79, Walter Grauman); *The Awakening* (80, Mike Newell); *Alice* (80, Jerry Gruza and Jacek Bromski); *Loophole* (80, John Quested); *Superman II* (80, Richard Lester); *Falling in Love Again* (81, Steven Paul); *Yellowbeard* (83, Mel Damski); *A Christmas Carol* (84, Clive Donner); *Prettykill* (87, George Kaczender); *Just Ask for Diamond* (88, Stephen Bayly); *A Summer Story* (88, Piers Haggard); *American Roulette* (88, Maurice Hatton); and *Melancholia* (89, Andi Engel).

She still works, though rarely at her own best levels: *The Man from the PRU* (89, Rob Rohrer); *En Handfull Tid* (89, Martin Asphaug); *After the War* (89, John Glenister); *Fate* (90, Stuart Paul); *Trainer* (91, Tristan DeVere Cole); *Devices and Desires* (91, John Davies); *Illusions* (92, Michael Houldey); *Piccolo Grande Amore* (93, Carlo Vanzina); *The Higher Mortals* (93, Colin Finbow); *Romance and Rejection* (96, Kevin W. Smith); *Loop* (97, Allan Niblo); *Dark Blue Perfume* (97,

Sandy Johnson); *St. Patrick: The Irish Legend* (00, Robert Hughes); *Jean* (00, Anthony Fabian).

Gig Young (Byron Elsworth Barr) (1913–78), b. St. Cloud, Minnesota

"Gig Young" was the name of the character Byron Barr played in *The Gay Sisters* (42, Irving Rapper), and so much can be concluded from that transition. "Gig Young" is hyperbolically cute and immediate—yet imagine a Gig Young at forty, or fifty? Won't a giggle creep in among those watching? On the other hand, "Byron Barr" feels just as fabricated, but gentile romantic, raised to higher hopes than life ever comes close to making. "Byron Barr" could be the awful, mocking real name for the aghast MC in *They Shoot Horses, Don't They?* (69, Sydney Pollack), a man who knows the better deal horses get.

It worked out for a while. Gig Young was kept busy as a fresh-faced friend or brother to more troubled men—in *Young at Heart* (54, Gordon Douglas), say, where Frank Sinatra is supposed to know and feel so much more. He even had his chance at something more interesting—as witness his supporting actor nomination for *Come Fill the Cup* (51, Douglas), where he is a drunken playboy. But then imagine getting that *Young at Heart* duty after *Come Fill the Cup*—and for the same director! That's how hopelessness sets in.

He began in *Misbehaving Husbands* (40, William Beaudine); *Dive Bomber* (41, Michael Curtiz); *Sergeant York* (41, Howard Hawks); *The Male Animal* (42, Elliott Nugent); *Air Force* (43, Hawks), where he has a real part; *Old Acquaintance* (43, Vincent Sherman). Then, after service in the Coast Guard, he came back for *Escape Me Never* (47, Peter Godfrey); *The Woman in White* (48, Godfrey); *The Three Musketeers* (48, George Sidney); *Wake of the Red Witch* (49, Edward Ludwig); *Lust for Gold* (49, S. Sylvan Simon); *Hunt the Man Down* (49, George Archainbaud), where he is the lead; *Only the Valiant* (51, Douglas).

Come Fill the Cup was followed by another lead, in *Holiday for Sinners* (52, Gerald Mayer); the cop in *The City That Never Sleeps* (53, John H. Auer); a rodeo rider in *Arena* (53, Richard Fleischer); *Torch Song* (53, Charles Walters), with Joan Crawford, but second to Michael Wilding; the boyfriend in *The Desperate Hours* (55, William Wyler); second lead in *Desk Set* (57, Walter Lang).

It was at this time that he became a fixture (secondary) in allegedly sophisticated comedies: very good with Doris Day in *Teacher's Pet* (58, George Seaton), for which he got another supporting actor nomination; with Day and Richard Widmark in *The Tunnel of Love* (58, Gene Kelly); with David Niven and Shirley MacLaine in *Ask Any Girl* (59, Walters); *The Story on Page One* (59, Clifford Odets); *That Touch of Mink* (62, Delbert

Mann), with Day and Cary Grant; *Five Miles to Midnight* (62, Anatole Litvak); *A Ticklish Affair* (63, Sidney); *Strange Bedfellows* (65, Melvin Frank); *The Shuttered Room* (67, David Greene).

He was working less in film and more on TV (*The Rogues*), but then in 1969 he got the chance of a lifetime (and maybe the confirmation of despair) with the MC in *They Shoot Horses, Don't They?* On his third attempt, he won the supporting actor Oscar—defeating Jack Nicholson in *Easy Rider* among others.

After that, he made *Lovers and Other Strangers* (70, Cy Howard); *Bring Me the Head of Alfredo Garcia* (74, Sam Peckinpah); *The Killer Elite* (75, Peckinpah); *The Hindenberg* (75, Robert Wise); *Game of Death* (78, Robert Clouse).

Then, in 1978, he was found in a New York City apartment with his fifth wife—both shot dead.

Loretta Young (Gretchen Michaela Young) (1913–2000), b. Salt Lake City, Utah

In 1971, Loretta Young fought one of the most curious of legal actions: that her old films should not be shown on TV for fear of spoiling her current image. It was a nervy, defensive gesture from a woman who looked so lovely throughout the 1930s. Not that she was ever a profound screen personality, but Young was a genuine star, an elegant clotheshorse, and famously devout. Although she made ninety films, it is remarkable how consistently she kept company with moderate directors and costars. Her good films seem to have occurred by chance and owe their qualities to other people: thus *Platinum Blonde* (31, Frank Capra); *Taxi* (32, Roy del Ruth); *Zoo in Budapest* (33, Rowland V. Lee); *Man's Castle* (33, Frank Borzage); *Suez* (38, Allan Dwan); and *The Stranger* (46, Orson Welles). It is a rag-bag for someone so persistently ladylike and wholesome—somewhere between Joan Crawford and Greer Garson.

The sister of an actress, she had a convent education and was working as an extra when she got a bit part in *Naughty But Nice* (27, Millard Webb) by answering a phone call meant for someone else in the family. Over the next few years she worked at First National and Warners, often with Douglas Fairbanks Jr. in romances, but playing the girl adopted by Lon Chaney in *Laugh, Clown, Laugh* (28, Herbert Brenon) and in *The Magnificent Flirt* (28, Harry d'Abbadie d'Arrast). Her first sound film was *The Squall* (29, Alexander Korda), at about which time she married actor Grant Withers—they were divorced before she was twenty-one. She was in *The Forward Pass* (29, Eddie Cline); *Kismet* (30, John Francis Dillon); *Loose Ankles* (30, Ted Wilde); with Lionel Barrymore in *The Man from Blankley's* (30, Alfred E. Green); *The Truth About Youth* (30, William A. Seiter); and *Beau Ideal* (31, Brenon). Warners kept her hard at work in *The Hatchet Man* (32, William

Wellman); *Life Begins* (32, Elliott Nugent and James Flood); quite tough in *Employees' Entrance* (33, Del Ruth); *Heroes for Sale* (33, Wellman); to MGM for *Lady of the Night* (33, Wellman); and *She Had to Say Yes* (33, Busby Berkeley).

But in 1934 she joined Zanuck's new Twentieth Century and had a hit in *House of Rothschild* (Alfred Werker). She made *Born to Be Bad* (34, Lowell Sherman), *Clive of India* (35, Richard Boleslavsky), and went on location with Clark Gable for *Call of the Wild* (35, Wellman). (While there, camped in the cold, they became personally close, and in a recent book her adopted daughter states that she is actually Young's biological daughter by Gable.) Then she went to Paramount to play Berengaria in *The Crusades* (35, Cecil B. De Mille) and to MGM for *The Unguarded Hour* (36, Sam Wood). Back at Twentieth she made *Ramona* (36, Henry King); *Ladies in Love* (36, Edward Griffith); *Love Is News* (37, Tay Garnett); *Kentucky* (38, David Butler); *Four Men and a Prayer* (38, John Ford); *The Story of Alexander Graham Bell* (39, Irving Cummings); and *Wife, Husband and Friend* (39, Gregory Ratoff).

At this point, she broke with the studio—over parts and money—made *Eternally Yours* (39, Garnett) for Walter Wanger and was a year out of work before Columbia came to her rescue (with half-pay) with *The Doctor Takes a Wife* (40, Alexander Hall), *He Stayed for Breakfast* (40, S. Sylvan Simon), *The Men in Her Life* (41, Ratoff), and *A Night to Remember* (42, Richard Wallace). She was uneasy but still handsome opposite Alan Ladd in *China* (43, John Farrow) and *And Now Tomorrow* (44, Irving Pichel), and with Gary Cooper in *Along Came Jones* (45, Stuart Heisler). Unmarked by her encounter with Welles on *The Stranger*, she made *The Perfect Marriage* (46, Lewis Allen) and then, by surprise, took the best actress Oscar for her Swedish accent in *The Farmer's Daughter* (47, H. C. Potter).

The award hardly delayed her movie decline. After *The Bishop's Wife* (47, Henry Koster), *Rachel and the Stranger* (48, Norman Foster), *The Accused* (49, William Dieterle), *Mother Is a Freshman* (49, Lloyd Bacon), *Come to the Stable* (49, Koster), and *Key to the City* (50, George Sidney), she began her retreat. Her last films were *Cause for Alarm* (51, Garnett); *Because of You* (52, Joseph Pevney); *Paula* (52, Rudolph Maté); and *It Happens Every Thursday* (53, Pevney).

After that came the *Loretta Young Show* on TV for eight years and three Emmys. She came through a door in a fabulous gown to introduce the story. Years later, when she realized that old shows (and old gowns) were in syndication, she sued— and won $600,000! As for the uplift of the stories, that never dated.

She made a comeback, on TV, in *Christmas Eve* (86, Stuart Cooper).

Robert Young (1907–98), b. Chicago

Father Knows Best and *Marcus Welby, M.D.* are sufficient demonstration of Young's survival power—from 1954 to 1963 and then from 1969 to 1976. Young looked smart, sympathetic, and honest, the sort of man a girl can talk to without great risk. Of course, Young often won the girl in movies—eminently Dorothy McGuire—but never with such ardor as to threaten them, and seldom without the saving readiness to be disappointed. Over eighty films in romantic parts, more in B pictures or male leads than in starred roles, trained him as a stayer. So long on the slopes of the industry, he learned to take nothing too seriously, and that showed—as lightness, indifference, or amusement.

King Vidor once called him "a director's dream . . . Popular regard, which sets its idols aside in the awe-enthralling class, sometimes demands a quality of neuroticism which Bob healthily doesn't possess": *The Black Camel* (31, Hamilton Mac-Fadden); *The Sin of Madelon Claudet* (31, Edward Selwyn); *The Wet Parade* (32, Victor Fleming); *Strange Interlude* (32, Robert Z. Leonard); *The Kid from Spain* (32, Leo McCarey); *Today We Live* (33, Howard Hawks); *Hell Below* (33, Jack Conway); *Tugboat Annie* (33, Mervyn Le Roy); *The Right to Romance* (33, Alfred Santell); *Carolina* (34, Henry King); *Spitfire* (34, John Cromwell); *House of Rothschild* (34, Alfred Werker); *Lazy River* (34, George Seitz); *Whom the Gods Destroy* (34, Walter Lang); *Calm Yourself* (35, Seitz); *Remember Last Night?* (35, James Whale); to Britain for a surprise villain in *The Secret Agent* (36, Alfred Hitchcock) and *It's Love Again* (36, Victor Saville); *Three Wise Guys* (36, Seitz); *Dangerous Number* (37, Richard Thorpe); *I Met Him in Paris* (37, Wesley Ruggles); *The Emperor's Candlesticks* (37, George Fitzmaurice); *The Bride Wore Red* (37, Dorothy Arzner); *Navy Blue and Gold* (37, Sam Wood); *Josette* (38, Allan Dwan); *The Toy Wife* (38, Thorpe); *Three Comrades* (38, Frank Borzage); *The Shining Hour* (38, Borzage); *Bridal Suite* (39, William Thiele); *Miracles for Sale* (39, Tod Browning); *Northwest Passage* (40, King Vidor); *The Mortal Storm* (40, Borzage); *Western Union* (41, Fritz Lang); *The Trial of Mary Dugan* (41, Norman Z. McLeod); *Lady Be Good* (41, McLeod); very good at showing the decency of *H. M. Pulham Esq.* (41, Vidor); *Joe Smith, American* (42, Thorpe); *Cairo* (42, W. S. Van Dyke); *Journey for Margaret* (42, Van Dyke); *Slightly Dangerous* (43, Ruggles); *Claudia* (43, Edmund Goulding); *Sweet Rosie O'Grady* (43, Irving Cummings); *The Canterville Ghost* (44, Jules Dassin); *The Enchanted Cottage* (45, Cromwell); *The Searching Wind* (46, William Dieterle); *Claudia and David* (46, W. Lang); *They Won't Believe Me* (47, Irving Pichel); *Crossfire* (47, Edward Dmytryk); *Sitting Pretty* (48,

W. Lang); *Adventure in Baltimore* (49, Richard Wallace); *That Forsyte Woman* (49, Compton Bennett); *And Baby Makes Three* (49, Henry Levin); *Goodbye My Fancy* (51, Vincent Sherman); *The Half Breed* (52, Stuart Gilmore); and *Secret of the Incas* (54, Jerry Hopper).

After that, Young returned only for a few Marcus Welby movies for TV and for *Mercy or Murder* (86, Steven Gethers) and *Conspiracy of Love* (87, Noel Black).

Sergei Yutkevich (1904–85),
b. St. Petersburg, Russia

1924: an episode from *Give Us Radio!*. 1926: *Predatel/The Traitor* (codirected with Abraham Room). 1927: *Tretya Meshchanskaya* (codirected with Room). 1928: *Kruzheva*. 1929: *Chernyi Parus*. 1931: *Zlatye Gory*. 1932: *Vstrechnyi/Counterplan* (codirected with Friedrich Ermler). 1934: *Ankara, Serdtsye Turki* (codirected with Lev Arnshtam) (d); *Shakhtory*. 1938: *Chelovek s Ruzhom*. 1940: *Yakov Sverdlov*. 1943: *Novye Pokhozhdeniya Shveika/New Adventures of Schweik*. 1944: *Dmitri Donskoi* (d). 1946: *Ozvobozhdennaya Frantsya/France Liberated* (d); *Zdravstvui Moskva/Greetings, Moscow* (d); *Molodost Nashi Stranyi* (d). 1947: *Tvet Nad Rossiei* (unreleased) (d). 1948: *Tri Vstrechi/Three Encounters* (codirected with Vsevolod Pudovkin and Alexander Ptushko). 1951: *Przhevalskii*. 1954: *Velikii Voin Albanii Skanderbeg/The Great Warrior Skanderbeg*. 1956: *Otello/Othello*. 1957: *Yves Montand Sings* (codirected with M. Slutzky) (d). 1958: *Rasskazi o Leninye/Stories About Lenin*. 1960: *Rencontre avec la France* (d). 1962: *Banya/The Bath House* (codirected with Anatoli Karanovich). 1964: *Lenin v Polshe/Lenin in Poland*. 1969: *Siuzhet Dlya Nebolshovo Rasskaza*. 1975: *Mayakovsky Smejotsja* (codirected with Anatoly Karanovich). 1981: *Lenin v Paridzhe/Lenin in Paris*.

Not many came through the vicissitudes of Soviet cinema as unscathed as Sergei Yutkevich; or retained such enthusiastic memories of "astonishing and wonderful days . . . a period of tumultuous expansion for Soviet art" when theatre and cinema rushed forward uncertain of whether they were on the edge of chaos or revelation. In childhood, Yutkevich worked in puppet theatre, and went on to study painting and stage design. As a young man he was a founding member of the Factory of Eccentric Actors with Grigori Kozintsev and Leonid Trauberg. Its aims were to inspire actors with the spirit of circus and music hall; naturally enough, it enjoyed American slapstick comedy and Yutkevich wrote a book on the virtues of Max Linder. In addition, he had enormous enthusiasm for the Pearl White serials and for the work of Louis Feuillade. He worked in the theatre, with

Eisenstein and Meyerhold, and began to work in movies in the mid-1920s: "I experienced the feelings of a simple mortal who has liberated magic powers which are beyond his control, on the memorable, icy morning of the winter of 1924, when I found myself for the first time alone with a camera." That thrill is more winning than much of the work that Yutkevich did. Bolshevik art is so vibrant with liberation that it is often out of control. Time has led to a grim reassessment, just as the Revolution betrayed Victor Serge's lyrical account of its Year One.

It is difficult in retrospect to believe in the spirit of slapstick adding to Meyerhold's mechanical analysis of acting, and hard to see any personal development in Yutkevich's films beyond a cheerful feeling for people, warmer, more playful, and more naturalistic than the work of Eisenstein and Pudovkin. In fact, Yutkevich was part of the group that tended to rebel against Eisenstein in the early 1930s. Above all, Yutkevich wanted to reach the ordinary man, notably in *Vstrechnyi*, and the construction of a gas turbine. The documentary element, persistently adhered to by Yutkevich, does not prevent a deliberate sentimentalization of the workers or blatant underlining of an old message.

If Eisenstein felt that Yutkevich had surrendered once shared ideals, at least Yutkevich survived and continued to work: it is impossible to discuss the artistic achievement in isolation from the harsh political realities. Equally, it is barely possible to judge Yutkevich's talent or personality because of the contortions imposed on both by the state. In the 1930s, he directed a training program; even so, his own *Shakhtory* was reedited on official orders. During the war, he made both patriotic martial documentaries and a version of the Soldier Schweik story. After Stalin's death, he emerged as a director of sympathetic but archaic bio-pics of Russian heroes, supposedly freed from the personality cult but irretrievably marked by prudence. More questionably, he had the distinction of having directed the first feature film made in Albania, *The Great Warrior Skanderbeg*.

Z

Saul Zaentz, b. Passaic, New Jersey, 1911

Looking like Father Christmas may only enable Saul Zaentz to be a more lucid, and even ruthless, dealer. Equally, we may see in him what is now a rarity—the real idealism of the showman who yearns to bring good things to the masses going hand in hand with the rigorous practicality that determines to get the best in every deal. So I rejoice in Saul Zaentz's Thalberg Award—maybe the most deserving of modern recipients—but I would urge anyone to keep awake when making contracts with him. Above all, I would suggest, the

exactness and the ambition come out of the same genes. Saul Zaentz is the nearest we have to teach ourselves what the great age of Goldwyn, Mayer, Zanuck, and Selznick was like.

He achieved fame first as a producer of jazz and pop records—but he had been a professional gambler before that. It was only in 1975 that he joined forces with the much younger Michael Douglas to make *One Flew Over the Cuckoo's Nest* (75, Milos Forman)—and his first best picture. The second came for *Amadeus* (84, Forman) and the third for *The English Patient* (96, Anthony Minghella), only after—at the last minute—Zaentz had lost Paramount's participation and secured rescuing funds from Miramax. Those three pictures—literary adaptations—are also outstanding examples of challenging modern entertainments. And on every one of them, the filmmakers attested to the vital role of Zaentz's support, enthusiasm, and friendship.

Not everything has worked as well, but nothing else has been less than uncommon: the animated *The Lord of the Rings* (78, Ralph Bakshi); *The Mosquito Coast* (86, Peter Weir); *The Unbearable Lightness of Being* (88, Philip Kaufman); *At Play in the Fields of the Lord* (91, Hector Babenco).

Steven Zaillian, b. Fresno, California, 1953

1993: *Searching for Bobby Fischer*. 1998: *A Civil Action*.

The eminence of Steven Zaillian is comforting proof that a quiet, serious, humane intelligence can find a place in American pictures at the end of the twentieth century. That said, his laudable qualities hardly seem to compete with what gets directors hired today. The two films he directed are almost deliberately nonbrilliant accounts of real situations—one domestic, one a civic betrayal—done carefully, slowly, and in a way that television has nearly made its own territory. One wonders how many films such a director can expect.

Before that, Zaillian was—and promises to remain—a distinguished screenwriter, whose powers of adaptation, comprehension, and diligence are most evident in *Schindler's List* (93, Steven Spielberg), a film that surely owes some of its depth to the screenwriter. It's an unusual history in that Zaillian was an editor before he was a writer: he edited *Kingdom of the Spiders* (77, John Cardos); *Starhops* (78, Barbara Peeters); *Below the Belt* (80, Robert Fowler). But it was as a screenwriter that he established himself: on the very clever *The Falcon and the Snowman* (86, John Schlesinger); *Awakenings* (90, Penny Marshall), adapted from Oliver Sacks; *Jack the Bear* (93, Marshall Herskovitz); *Clear and Present Danger* (94, Phillip Noyce), which is more slow than careful; the excellent *Primal Fear* (96, Gregory Hoblit); and the overpoweringly decent *Amistad* (97, Spielberg).

Darryl F. Zanuck (1902–79),
b. Wahoo, Nebraska

Zanuck had a small, anxious mouth, but he used it to grip the giant cigar longer than any of his mogul rivals. He was one of the last production executives left alive. And of those, he was the only one to have founded and chaired one of the major companies. But it was a Pyrrhic victory when, in 1962, he returned from European exile to scoop up the wreckage of Twentieth Century–Fox and to give the last, rough push that launched the monstrous *Cleopatra*. By then, Zanuck's Hollywood was in grotesque disarray, less a Xanadu than the warehouses bulging with Kane's junk, ready for the furnaces. Hard to believe that Zanuck's cigar had burned for many years. It must have been shut off from air as the little man stared aghast at his empire regressed into witless fantasy. To match that new shift, in 1969 Twentieth Century–Fox amended its name to Twenty-First Century Fox. Then, and only then, they dispensed with Zanuck.

He had fought in France with the Nebraska National Guard and returned, still only in his teens, to a variety of ignominious jobs that seem an obligatory prelude to success only to those people who have not dreamed up stories while working in rivet factories or selling shirts door to door. He was intent on getting into movies and, to establish his status as a writer—for such reputation is only assertive—he persuaded a hair oil company to publish some of his stories. Warners scented the sly mixture of brilliantine and ambition and gave him Rin Tin Tin to compose for. In 1924, he became a Warners writer, and when he had walked the studio dog long enough, he got on to humans.

Perhaps he worked harder than other writers and felt it necessary to make his fecundity tactful with pseudonyms—Mark Canfield, Melville Crossman, or Gregory Rogers (a resounding trio). From 1924–29, he was story supplier, adaptor, or scenarist on at least forty pictures, including *The Lighthouse by the Sea* (24, Malcolm St. Clair); *Find Your Man* (24, St. Clair); *Red Hot Tires* (25, Erle C. Kenton); *Three Weeks in Paris* (25, Roy Del Ruth); *Seven Sinners* (25, Lewis Milestone); *Eve's Lover* (25, Del Ruth); *On Thin Ice* (25, St. Clair); *Footloose Widows* (26, Del Ruth); *The Better 'Ole* (26, Charles Reisner); *The Caveman* (26, Milestone); *Oh, What a Nurse!* (26, Reisner); *The Desired Woman* (27, Michael Curtiz); *Jaws of Steel* (27, Ray Enright); *Tracked by the Police* (27, Enright); *Irish Hearts* (27, Byron Haskin); *Slightly Used* (27, Archie Mayo); *Good Time Charley* (27, Curtiz); *Ham and Eggs at the Front* (27, Del Ruth); *Old San Francisco* (27, Alan Crosland); *Noah's Ark* (28, Curtiz); *My Man* (28, Mayo); *Tenderloin* (28, Curtiz); *State Street Sadie* (28, Mayo); *Pay as You Enter* (28, Lloyd Bacon);

The Madonna of Avenue A (29, Curtiz); *Maybe It's Love* (30, William Wellman).

Zanuck does not appear to have had a special part in Warners' saving venture into sound. Nor did his writing hint at a personal predilection for the thriller. But late in 1929 he became an executive at Warners and in 1931 he was put in charge of production. Zanuck's name disappeared from the screen in these years, the period in which Warners embraced the gangster. Much credit must go to him, even if Hal Wallis may have been directly responsible for those first crime films. But Zanuck and the Warner Brothers were not happy with one another, and in 1933 Zanuck took the crucial step of his career.

With Joseph Schenck, and a substantial loan from Nick Schenck, he formed Twentieth Century, releasing through United Artists. Two years later, they absorbed Fox, and Zanuck became vice-president in charge of Twentieth Century–Fox. That studio's output—in terms of individual quality and house style—is far short of Paramount, Warners, or RKO. But it survived and prospered and is the source of many famous films. Its keynotes are, too often, pretentious gravity (especially after 1945), spurious social responsibility (most evident in the John Ford pictures), listless biopics, middlebrow directors (like Henry King and Joseph Mankiewicz), and polite ladies (Grable, Loretta Young, Sonja Henie, Alice Faye, Jeanne Crain, Shirley Temple). Zanuck seems shy of unrestrained melodrama, of intelligence, sexuality, and violence—all cockeyed ingredients of Selznick's character.

Let it be noted that Zanuck's name is on none of the films Otto Preminger made at Twentieth after the war, arguably the pictures most worthy of their searchlights. Zanuck's known tastes were for Tyrone Power and a string of continental ladies who seldom flourished in America. The strident social seriousness of the postwar thrillers and of Kazan's "problem" pictures is the height of his ambition. Yet *Pinky* is as cozy as *Grapes of Wrath* had been a decade earlier. It is revealing that Zanuck himself wrote the humbug ending to *The Grapes of Wrath*—Ma Joad's "We are the people and we go on forever," a mixture of demagoguery and flattery of the helpless, ordinary man. Zanuck made dull, pious movies, but he made a lot of them: *The Bowery* (33, Raoul Walsh), Twentieth's first picture; *House of Rothschild* (34, Alfred Werker); *The Mighty Barnum* (34, Walter Lang); *Cardinal Richelieu* (35, Rowland V. Lee); *Clive of India* (35, Richard Boleslavsky); *Les Miserables* (35, Boleslavsky); *The Prisoner of Shark Island* (36, John Ford); *A Message to Garcia* (36, George Marshall); *Lloyds of London* (36, King); *Seventh Heaven* (37, King); *Heidi* (37, Allan Dwan); *In Old Chicago* (38, King); *Suez* (38, Dwan); *Kentucky* (38, David Butler); *Alexander's Ragtime Band*

(38, King); *The Story of Alexander Graham Bell* (39, Irving Cummings); *The Three Musketeers* (39, Dwan); *Jesse James* (39, King); *Stanley and Livingstone* (39, King); *The Rains Came* (39, Clarence Brown); *Young Mr. Lincoln* (39, Ford); *Drums Along the Mohawk* (39, Ford); *The Grapes of Wrath* (40, Ford); *The Return of Frank James* (40, Fritz Lang); *The Mark of Zorro* (40, Rouben Mamoulian); *Tobacco Road* (41, Ford); *Western Union* (41, Lang); *How Green Was My Valley* (41, Ford); and *Blood and Sand* (41, Mamoulian).

Zanuck worked for the army during the war years and only a few studio films carried his name: *Son of Fury* (42, John Cromwell), *Winged Victory* (44, George Cukor), *The Purple Heart* (44, Milestone), and the curiously devoted *Wilson* (44, King), epitome of the studio's period props. In peace, Zanuck endorsed realistic thrillers and himself produced *Anna and the King of Siam* (46, Cromwell); *The Razor's Edge* (46, Edmund Goulding); *Dragonwyck* (46, Joseph L. Mankiewicz); *Gentleman's Agreement* (47, Elia Kazan); *Twelve O'Clock High* (49, King); *Pinky* (49, Kazan); *No Way Out* (50, Mankiewicz); *All About Eve* (50, Mankiewicz)—that rarity, a Zanuck comedy; *David and Bathsheba* (51, King); *People Will Talk* (51, Mankiewicz); *The Snows of Kilimanjaro* (51, King); and *Viva Zapata!* (52, Kazan).

It was a long spell, and when Fox fell in love with Spyros Skouras and CinemaScope, Zanuck went to Europe, to be independent. The films he made there are all very poor despite the inspiring company he kept with Juliette Greco and the recurring presence in them of Orson Welles. It is further proof of the frailty of moguls alone with their cigar: *The Man in the Gray Flannel Suit* (56, Nunnally Johnson); *Island in the Sun* (57, Robert Rossen); *The Sun Also Rises* (57, King); and *The Roots of Heaven* (58, John Huston). All of these were based on "major novels," but Mark Canfield reemerged to write *Crack in the Mirror* (60, Richard Fleischer) with no more success. *The Big Gamble* (61, Fleischer) made six duds in a row. But Zanuck then carried out the last great executive assault on a project: *The Longest Day* (62), with the producer as a five-star general. The account of D-Day had directors—Andrew Marton, Ken Annakin, and Bernhard Wicki included—but its drive was that of a producer desperate to make a landing.

It was a huge success, just as the studio of which he had remained a large stockholder foundered with *Cleopatra*. Zanuck returned to replace Skouras, rationalize *Cleopatra,* and install his son Richard as head of production. In those hectic days he still found time to cut George Cukor's *The Chapman Report* (62) to shreds.

This account does not do justice to Zanuck's drive or efficiency. He was inadvertently comic (a life of Zanuck might call for, say, Bill Murray). He never compromised with the status of monster-in-his-own-time. But Twentieth Century films in his time know what they are after—that may restrict them, ultimately, but it makes a model of business intelligence that leaves so many lessons. Zanuck was a sportsman (he pioneered polo and croquet), and he believed in keeping your eye on the ball, and giving it a good crack.

Renée Zellweger, b. Katy, Texas, 1969

It's a long way from Katy, Texas (just outside Houston), to the London of *Bridget Jones's Diary* (01, Sharon Maguire), but Renée Zellweger made the transition without spilling a drop of her likability. She wasn't the most obvious casting, yet her success as Bridget—carrying the film at the box office—was proof of how much she had learned, and of that unshakable inner quality that the audience likes. A lot of young actresses these days don't bother to be pleasing; others try too hard. But there has always been a natural decency in some players—it was there in Jean Arthur and Carole Lombard—an innate honesty that the public trusts. Ms. Zellweger has it, along with great range. She is one of the few young actresses who could grow old fruitfully before our eyes.

She majored in English at the University of Texas, and benefited from the intriguing creative circles based in Austin. She did a little television and then had small roles in *My Boyfriend's Back* (93, Bob Balaban) and *Dazed and Confused* (93, Richard Linklater). Her first lead was in the white-trash outlaw picture, *Love and a .45* (94, C. M. Talkington), followed by *Reality Bites* (94, Ben Stiller); and the girl with glasses who survives *Texas Chainsaw Massacre: The Next Generation* (94, Kim Henkel).

She was in *The Low Life* (95, George Hickenlooper) and *Empire Records* (95, Allan Moyle). Her breakthrough came in two roles: as the teacher in love with pulp writer Robert E. Howard (Vincent D'Onofrio) in *The Whole Wide World* (96, Dan Ireland), her exceptional work got her the female lead in *Jerry Maguire* (96, Cameron Crowe).

Since then she has done *Deceiver* (98, Jonas and Joshua Pate); *A Price Above Rubies* (98, Boaz Yakin); excellent as the daughter in *One True Thing* (98, Carl Franklin); *The Bachelor* (99, Gary Sinyor); *Nurse Betty* (00, Neil LaBute); with Jim Carrey—her onetime companion—in *Me, Myself & Irene* (00, Bobby and Peter Farrelly); *Chicago* (02, Rob Marshall); *White Oleander* (02, Peter Kosminsky); *Down With Love* (03, Peyton Reed); *Cold Mountain* (03, Anthony Minghella).

Robert Zemeckis, b. Chicago, 1952

1978: *I Wanna Hold Your Hand.* 1980: *Used Cars.* 1984: *Romancing the Stone.* 1985: *Back to the Future.* 1988: *Who Framed Roger Rabbit?*. 1989:

Back to the Future II. 1990: *Back to the Future III.* 1992: *Death Becomes Her.* 1994: *Forrest Gump.* 1997: *Contact.* 2000: *What Lies Beneath; Cast Away.* 2004: *The Polar Express.*

No other contemporary director has used special effects to more dramatic and narrative purpose. Grant the lapse of *Back to the Future II* (a mere marking time) and the miscalculation of *Death Becomes Her,* and Zemeckis has done nothing that is not fresh, startling, difficult, and intriguing. In partnership with his cowriter, Robert Gale, he has taken movies into fascinating realms of what might be—the fusion of live action and cartoon, the overlay of past and future, and most recently the dynamic engineering of cosmetics. To know that a future project is the life and work of Houdini is to recapture a child's impatience for coming attractions.

Zemeckis met Gale at USC film school and together they made two inventive and human pictures that found no real audience. *I Wanna Hold Your Hand* is about American teenagers trying to get into the Beatles' appearance on the *Ed Sullivan Show*—a simple, lovely idea for a crazy group comedy. *Used Cars* had a similar sense of mounting riot. The team had a more serious failure with the script for *1941* (79, Steven Spielberg, who was their early patron).

It was Michael Douglas who backed Zemeckis for *Romancing the Stone,* and helped build it into a hit. The concept of *Back to the Future* may not be original (it does echo the previous year's *Terminator*), but Zemeckis turned it into an exuberant comedy that never forgot the real bonds of family and genetics. As writer and director, he has rarely allowed the show to lose sight of such human realities.

Who Framed Roger Rabbit? is a triumph of organization, a film that manages to make its laborious tricks seem airy and magical, *and* the true sequel to *Chinatown* with its portrait of Los Angeles mugged by the automobile.

Back to the Future III has no equal in the category of IIIs—this is not saying much, but that film's recovery of the Western genre showed how smart and enterprising Zemeckis is.

Death Becomes Her never found the right tone, so its tricks were startling and unpleasant. Moreover, Streep and Goldie Hawn hardly needed help in playing natural enemies. At forty, Zemeckis seemed too busy, too restless, and too natural a story magician to fail the promise. He was cowriter and co–executive producer on *Trespass* (92, Walter Hill). *Forrest Gump* was a very big hit, best picture, and one of those travesties that set back the American movie at a stroke.

In 1994, I wondered if Zemeckis might be a great director in the making. It was a lesson in curbing one's optimism. For in the years since, he has delivered three clunkers in a row—*Contact,*

which was nearly literally sweet potato pie in the sky; *What Lies Beneath,* a Hitchcock rip-off without any real point; and *Cast Away,* which took product placement (for Federal Express) to new, insane heights. These were big, splashy films that consistently dodged their most promising points. The magic had slipped away, and there was little talk of Houdini.

Catherine Zeta-Jones,
b. Swansea, Wales, 1969

Catherine Zeta-Jones has every reason to believe in the Church of Show Business, high or low. When she was only seventeen, she was in the chorus of a London revival of *42nd Street.* The star fell sick, and Jones was promoted to the lead—and never gave it up. Suppose we accept that this had no trace of publicity ploy; still we have to believe that she then met, fell in love with, and married that rather tarnished prince of Hollywood Michael Douglas, and made him aglow (and a father) again. What next?

The "Zeta" in her name (a shrewd move) does suggest some Latin blood that would match her extreme, ripe, dark good looks. But in truth, it was her grandmother's name—and if one knows Wales at all, there is a very Welsh look to Jones, a kind of Polly Garter flash, full of flirt, anger, and sauce. In the real valleys, it must be said, it is a prettiness that tends to fade early.

She made her movie debut as Scheherazade in *Les Mille et Une Nuits* (90, Philippe de Broca), and she did a run of shows for British TV that established her popularity: as Mariette in H. E. Bates's *The Darling Buds of May* (91, Rodney Bennett and David Giles); as Eustacia Vye in Hardy's *The Return of the Native* (94, Jack Gold); and the lead in *Catherine the Great* (95, Marvin J. Chomsky and John Goldsmith).

On the big screen, she was in *Christopher Columbus: The Discovery* (92, John Glen); *Splitting Heirs* (93, Robert Young); *The Phantom* (96, Simon Wincer); her breakthrough, having her clothes removed by rapier, in *The Mark of Zorro* (98, Martin Campbell); photographed like a pinup in *Entrapment* (99, Jon Amiel); *The Haunting* (99, Jan De Bont); *High Fidelity* (00, Stephen Frears); *Traffic* (00, Steven Soderbergh); *America's Sweethearts* (01, Garry Marshall). In hindsight, there is a third trace of magic—her having survived so many poor pictures. She then did *Chicago* (02, Rob Marshall), the first movie with two Z-initialed leading ladies.

Mai Zetterling (1925–94),
b. Vasteras, Sweden

1963: *The War Game* (d). 1964: *Alskande Par/Loving Couples.* 1966: *Nattlek/Night Games.* 1967: *Doktor Glas.* 1968: *Flickorna/The Girls.* 1972: *Vincent the Dutchman* (d). 1973: "The

Strongest," episode from *Visions of Eight* (d). 1981: *Love*. 1982: *Scrubbers*. 1986: *Amarosa*.

She was a teenage actress in Sweden, with the Royal Dramatic Theatre, and in films: *Lasse-Maja* (41, Gunnar Olsson); *Jag Drapte* (43, Olof Molander); *Frenzy* (44, Alf Sjöberg); *Prins Gustaf* (44, Schamyl Bauman); and *Iris och Lojtnantshjarta* (46, Sjöberg). In 1946, she went to Britain and the Rank empire, as it proved, never to be more than an exotic decoration: *Frieda* (47, Basil Dearden); *The Bad Lord Byron* (48, David MacDonald); and *Quartet* (48, Ralph Smart).

She worked over the next years in Britain, Sweden, and America, clearly with growing indifference to poor parts and with rising eagerness to direct herself: *Night Is My Future* (47, Ingmar Bergman); *Nu Borjar Livet* (48, Gustaf Molander); *The Lost People* (49, Bernard Knowles); *The Romantic Age* (49, Edmond Greville); *Blackmailed* (51, Marc Allégret); *Desperate Moment* (53, Compton Bennett); *Knock on Wood* (54, Melvin Frank/Norman Panama); *A Prize of Gold* (55, Mark Robson); *Seven Waves Away* (56, coproduced with Tyrone Power, directed by Richard Sale); *Giftas* (57, Anders Henrikson); *The Truth About Women* (58, Muriel Box), an especially trite work that may have preyed on her conscience; *Lek Pa Regnbagen* (58, Lars-Erik Kjellgren); *Jet Storm* (59, Cy Endfield); *Faces in the Dark* (59, David Eady); *Piccadilly Third Stop* (60, Wolf Rilla); *Offbeat* (60, Cliff Owen); *Only Two Can Play* (61, Sidney Gilliat); *The Main Attraction* (62, Daniel Petrie); *The Man Who Finally Died* (62, Quentin Laurence); *The Bay of St. Michel* (63, John Ainsworth); and *Lianbron* (65, Sven Nykvist).

Her own films are not free from unresolved anger and a jaundiced view of humanity. She grew into directing out of a series of BBC documentaries. Her study of Van Gogh is as sensuous and as severe as the painter's personality and—like all her films—made with awesome sincerity. At times, that led her into strident overemphasis: *The Girls* is almost a parody of feminist cinema. But *Loving Couples* and *Night Games* are trenchant, violent, and authentically Strindbergian visions of sexual hypocrisy. A sense of fun (often evident in her acting) shows itself in her view of the bulging concentration in Olympic weightlifters.

She also acted in *Hidden Agenda* (90, Ken Loach) and *The Witches* (90, Nicolas Roeg).

Zhang Yimou,
b. Shaanxi Province, China, 1951

1987: *Hong Gao Liang/Red Sorghum*. 1989: *Deihao Meizhoubao*. 1990: *Ju Dou*. 1992: *Da Hong Deng Long Gao Gao Gua/Raise the Red Lantern; Qui Ju Da Guan Si/The Story of Qiu Ju*. 1994: *Zuozhe/To Live*. 1995: *Yao a Yao Yao Dao Waipo Qiao/Shanghai Triad; Lumière et Compagnie.* 1997: *You Hua Hao Hao Shuo/Keep Cool*. 1999: *Yi Ge Dou Bu Neng Shao/Not One Less*. 2001: *Wo De Fun Qin Mu Qin/The Road Home*. 2002: *Xingfu Shignang/Happy Town; Ying Xiong*.

Zhang Yimou was trained in cinematography at the Beijing Film Academy, and he proved an outstanding cameraman in the 1980s: *Yellow Earth* (84, Chen Kaige) and *Lao Jing* (87, Wu Tianming). It is hard to think of a cameraman who has made the graduation to directing with such assurance. Indeed, in cinema at large, there are few directors whose next works are more eagerly anticipated. Above all, his four films show a progress that is very exciting. *Ju Dou*, for instance, has elements of James M. Cain and Jacobean tragedy, but in *Raise the Red Lantern* there was a new depth and compassion.

Zhang Yimou's strengths are many: he has a command of intricate, quick narratives all the more surprising in that he sometimes dwells on shots or scenes—but complexities mount up very rapidly (as in the development of the brutal son in *Ju Dou*); he is as great a director of interiors as Ozu or Mizoguchi—the dye works in *Ju Dou* and the household in *Raise the Red Lantern* become superb stages for the melodrama; and he has Gong Li as his actress. It has been a wonder to see her grow from *Red Sorghum* into the power-player of *Raise the Red Lantern* and the nagging negotiator of *Qiu Ju*. She is an actress with the same range of sensuality, insight, and force as Sandrine Bonnaire.

Gong Li starred again in *Shanghai Triad*, the most ambitious and ravishing of Zhang Yimou's films, and a fond nod to American gangster films. The late films are much less flamboyant—they deal with modern Chinese history, with problems in the education system, and even with a kind of nostalgia for calmer, pre-Mao days—and it is notable that they have won far less distribution in the West. It's not just that film is new in China (and daunted by the examples of Hong Kong and Taiwan); it's also that modern society is hardly yet of age. But America ought to remember the great role of film in any society finding itself, and trying to reconcile realities with heady dreams.

Fred Zinnemann (1907–97), b. Vienna
1942: *Kid Glove Killer; Eyes in the Night*. 1944: *The Seventh Cross*. 1946: *Little Mr. Jim; My Brother Talks to Horses*. 1948: *Act of Violence; The Search*. 1950: *The Men*. 1951: *Teresa; Benjy* (d). 1952: *High Noon*. 1953: *Member of the Wedding; From Here to Eternity*. 1955: *Oklahoma!*. 1957: *A Hatful of Rain*. 1959: *The Nun's Story*. 1960: *The Sundowners*. 1964: *Behold a Pale Horse*. 1967: *A Man for All Seasons*. 1973: *The Day of the Jackal*. 1977: *Julia*. 1983: *Five Days One Summer*.

Trained first as a violinist and lawyer, Zinnemann studied at the University of Vienna and, in 1929, was one of the several collaborators on *Menschen am Sonntag* (Robert Siodmak and Edgar Ulmer). He went to America and played a small part in *All Quiet On the Western Front* (30, Lewis Milestone). Having worked as an assistant to Berthold Viertel, Robert Flaherty, and Paul Strand, he went to Mexico and directed a documentary, *Redes* (34), with Strand. In 1937 he joined MGM to make shorts in the *Crime Doesn't Pay* series. One of these, *That Mothers Might Live* (38), won an Oscar, and during the war he was promoted to full direction, initially on second features.

Julia was sad proof of the grinding good taste that always inhibited Zinnemann. It settles for scenery, costumes, suspense, and the vague sisterly pact of Fonda and Redgrave. No wonder it pleased so many, for it made all its harsh subject smooth and digestible—terror was brought down to the level of discreet soap opera.

Zinnemann worked with the parsimony that he may have believed was appropriate to high principles and great talent. With those other middlebrows, George Stevens and William Wyler, he was reckoned a paragon of safe seriousness as the guts ran out of Hollywood. But it is a hapless, irrelevant fastidiousness that waits six years between Robert Bolt's play for complacent thinkers and Frederick Forsythe's thriller for readers as indifferent to politics as they are untouched by violence. And how is it that both films share the same glossy anonymity yet still tickle witless audiences?

It is not a pressing question, for Zinnemann always made films remotely. He had all the disposable qualities: diligence instead of imagination; more care than instinct; solemnity, but no wit. In the immediately postwar years he earned a reputation as a social realist with *Act of Violence, The Search*, and *The Men*. The first, I think, is the best film he ever made, the rest unexpected and shocking; but the latter two are mild-mannered and sentimental, intriguing only for the scope they give the young Montgomery Clift and Marlon Brando. Perhaps to redress the underground pretensions of Kramer and Foreman he stressed the minute-by-minute excitement of *High Noon*.

But then he plunged into major prestige literary or theatrical originals. *Member of the Wedding's* subtlety was beyond him, just as the robustness of James Jones's *From Here to Eternity* scared him off. After that, he took the exclamation mark away from *Oklahoma!* and drifted into mulch with *The Nun's Story. Behold a Pale Horse* was a gravely silly parable and *A Man for All Seasons* showed that if you make a movie around a fine, intelligent stage performance you can emerge with a rather vague film. Zinnemann over the years has suffered several curtailed projects, including *The Old Man*

and the *Sea, Hawaii,* and *Man's Fate.*

The Day of the Jackal is all the more depressing a work to see through; plot-heavy, without any of the honest character study that Zinnemann once knew how to manage, and with Frenchmen talking like zis and zat. No director could have made a flop out of *The Day of the Jackal,* but few could have taken its listless neglect of style so compliantly. *Act of Violence* is the one film that endures—a seemingly conventional piece of menace that uncovers depths of character, guilt, malice and small-town life. A real movie, but a line Zinnemann did not pursue.

Adolph Zukor (1873–1976),
b. Ricse, Hungary

Alphabetically nearly last, and historically nearly first, Adolph Zukor testifies to the business battleground as a basis for longevity. Imagine a supreme Paramount star—Gary Cooper, say—and check the dates: Zukor was twenty-eight when Cooper was born, and he lived another fifteen years after the death of the star who towered above him physically and in the public's knowledge of who counted in pictures. How did he do it? It looks as if he kept healthy so long by avoiding the ordeal of sitting in the dark watching films. The movies did not interest Adolph Zukor: he wanted just power, empire, and profit. Otherwise, fresh air and exercise were his ideals—no wonder Paramount took that splendid mountain as its logo. While some pioneers regretted the post-1945 decline of the picture business, no doubt Zukor was happy to become a part of a richer concern, Gulf & Western. A little younger when that merger took effect and he might have aimed at taking over the parent. Like all Hungarians of the Hapsburg era, he knew the tonic of aggrandizement.

And like all conservative progressives, while the Austro-Hungarian empire was in its death-throes, Zukor was carving out fresh domain. For some businessmen in New York, 1914–18 was significant as the birth of an industry when competitive intolerance fought for the hearts of the world. Zukor had come to America when he was sixteen, after an upbringing of great hardship in Hungary. He learned English selling furs, and in 1903 he went into the amusement arcade business—a tiny man in a fur-collared coat. He had one large failure, trying to promote Hales Tours, where the audience sat in a railway carriage and views floated past (a similar device figures in Max Ophüls's *Letter from an Unknown Woman*). In 1910, he merged some of his interests with a friend, Marcus Loew, but he kept several theatres for himself. Zukor never trusted anyone, and that prophetic caution is usually self-fulfilling.

He had not sold furs to the urban lower-class audiences who came to early movies. Zukor noticed that he was dealing with a different clientele, and he wondered how the middle classes might be enticed into the dark—allegedly a place of wasting disease, self-indulgent escapism, and bad habits, all anathema to respectable people. He knew that they would only venture in under the guise of worthy enlightenment. While the social fabric of Europe was torn apart by war and revolution, in America Zukor exploited the self-importance of class distinction and perhaps did more than Marx or Marcuse to sap American middle-class strength of will. He sold unreality to sensible people, and they have not yet been able to do without it. The trick was to make movies like theatre: prestigious, long, and dull. It worked, and it helped transform movies from a sensation to a narrative fantasy.

Before 1912, no film in America stretched the audience beyond thirty minutes' concentration, and most were shorter. Zukor left Loew and helped to finance the hour-long French film, *Queen Elizabeth*, starring Sarah Bernhardt, in return for U.S. distribution rights. He leased it on a states rights basis and found that middle-class audiences gathered to see the famous actress as if she were Niagara Falls brought to their town. In 1912, he formed Famous Players Film Company and hired Edwin Porter to make similar films of American stage stars: James Hackett in *The Prisoner of Zenda* and James O'Neill (Eugene's father) in *The Count of Monte Cristo*.

They were deadweight entertainments, but the marketing approach worked and within two years Griffith would galvanize the new potential for length. Theatres began to be built fit for this refined audience; there were cloakrooms where they could leave their coats, but no equivalent closet where hardworking earnestness was exchanged for flesh and fantasy. Zukor was a magician who never mentioned his most comprehensive trick.

In 1916, he merged with Jesse Lasky's Feature Plays, and for the next five years there was a bitter struggle for control of that incipient major. Zukor won through boldness and insight: he floated loans, he based himself in New York where the money was, he seldom interfered in picture-making. He guessed that the audience would watch anything. Only the structure of the industry was at issue. And it was Zukor who determined that the company making and distributing pictures should also own theatres. Paramount—as it was called eventually—set the pattern for such a monopoly. Zukor created a business strategy that lasted until the late forties and was only broken by federal intervention. He was president of Paramount until 1935, and thereafter chairman. That post remained his until long after the mountain had turned into a fake, conical form.

As a studio, Paramount was known for sophistication, wit, glamour, style, smartness—so many of its films were sleek as fur. It was the home for years of De Mille, Lubitsch, Leisen, von Sternberg, La Cava, Chevalier, March, Cooper, Mae West, the Marx Brothers, Fields, Hope and Crosby, Dietrich, Clara Bow, Gloria Swanson, Colbert and Lombard, Jerry Lewis, Ladd and Lake. It would be too generous to credit Zukor with all those hirings, but the studio was consistent, cultivated, and a world unto itself. *The Devil Is a Woman* angered Spain that such a decor-and-light charade might traduce the real thing, and Ernst Lubitsch once admitted that Paris, France was a tamer place than Paris, Paramount.

Edward Zwick, b. Winnetka, Illinois, 1952
1986: *About Last Night . . .* 1989: *Glory.* 1992: *Leaving Normal.* 1994: *Legends of the Fall.* 1996: *Courage Under Fire.* 1998: *The Siege.* 2003: *The Last Samurai.*

Edward Zwick makes solid, dramatic films that seem to be taken from the news magazines. He has also tried his hand at adapting such disparate authors as David Mamet (*About Last Night . . .* came from *Sexual Perversity in Chicago*) and Jim Harrison (*Legends of the Fall*). He is a writer-director, a former journalist, a regular figure behind the camera on the TV series *Family,* and the creator of another, *thirtysomething.* That may be the best work he has done, despite the obvious historical significance of *Glory* and the careful handling of its male cast. *Legends of the Fall* is his most ambitious film, and the most uncertain, despite a true sense of legend and icon in the handling of Brad Pitt. He has not yet made a movie that reveals Edward Zwick or stands out above the crowd, but *Courage Under Fire* is the most intriguing—because of its pursuit of a rare subject (women in combat), its fine casting, and its overall sense of doubt over what actually happened versus what the state wants to say happened. Zwick is fond of the military, he has worked very steadily with Denzel Washington, and he directs in a straightforward, if anonymous, manner. But we may not yet have seen his best, or most relaxed, work.

Terry Zwigoff, b. Appleton, Wisconsin, 1948
1985: *Louie Bluie* (d). 1994: *Crumb* (d). 2001: *Ghost World.* 2003: *Bad Santa.*

After the University of Wisconsin, Zwigoff went to live in San Francisco, where he did all manner of things—including the collecting of popular song recordings from the late twenties, and a dedication to adult comic books. He is reclusive, not much short of depressive, and possibly more self-deprecating than any other filmmaker this author has met. Yet he has to be considered as a rare, individual voice. *Ghost World* (taken from the comic book by Daniel Clowes) turned into a refreshingly wry picture about awkward, deadpan teenagers who simply refuse to fall for the commercialized lies of the consumer society. With excellent performances by Thora Birch, Steve Buscemi, and Scarlett Johansson, it was an intriguing fusion of adult point of view with the most rugged kind of anarchistic teenage culture.

In a fascinating way, it showed the fictionalized version of those remarkable Crumbs—the dysfunctional yet very talented and tender family celebrated in what is one of the most unusual of American documentaries. So far, *Crumb* is Zwigoff's most striking work, but—if he could sustain a run of movies—it seems possible that he could yet deliver some major satirical pictures.